WORLD HISTORY
HUMAN LEGACY
TEACHER'S EDITION

Authors

Susan Ramírez

Peter Stearns

Sam Wineburg

Senior Consulting Author

Steven A. Goldberg
New Rochelle High School, New York

HOLT, RINEHART AND WINSTON
A Harcourt Education Company
Orlando • **Austin** • New York • San Diego • London

Authors

Steve Goldberg

Steve Goldberg has taught world history at the high school and college levels for 35 years. Currently, he is the Social Studies Department Chair at New Rochelle High School in New Rochelle, New York. He earned his undergraduate degree from the University of Rochester. He has studied in Tokyo, holds a master's degree in East Asian Studies from Yale University, and in 1986 studied in the Netherlands on a Fulbright Fellowship. In addition to his teaching and administrative duties, Goldberg has been active in state and national professional organizations, serving as President of the New York Council for the Social Studies and on the Board of Directors for the National Council of the Social Studies.

WORLD ALMANAC® and **WORLD ALMANAC AND BOOK OF FACTS®** are trademarks of World Almanac Education Group, Inc., registered in the United States of America and other jurisdictions.

Printed in the United States of America

ISBN-13: 978-0-03-093843-6

ISBN 0-03-093843-0

1 2 3 4 5 6 7 8 9 048 12 11 10 09 08 07

Susan Ramírez

Susan Elizabeth Ramírez is the Penrose Chair of History and Latin American Studies at Texas Christian University. She received her Ph.D. in History from the University of Wisconsin, Madison, and taught for many years at DePaul University. A specialist in the history and culture of the Andean region, Professor Ramírez is the author of numerous articles and books, including *The World Upside Down: Cross-Cultural Contact and Conflict in Sixteenth Century Peru*. Her most recent book, *To Feed and Be Fed: The Cosmological Bases of Authority and Identity in the Andes*, offers a new interpretation of the rise and fall of the Inca Empire. She serves on the editorial boards of the *Hispanic American Historical Review* and *The Americas*.

Peter Stearns

Peter N. Stearns is Professor of History and Provost at George Mason University. Founder and longtime editor of the *Journal of Social History*, Stearns is also author and editor of numerous books, including the *Encyclopedia of World History* and the six-volume *Encyclopedia of European Social History from 1350 to 2000*. Professor Stearns received his Ph.D. from Harvard University and has taught for over 40 years. He is a member of the American Historical Society and the Social Science History Association, among other professional organizations. His current research topics include the history of gender, body image, and emotion. His most recent book is *Childhood in World History*.

Sam Wineburg

Sam Wineburg is Professor of Education and Professor of History (by courtesy) at Stanford University, where he directs the only Ph.D. program in History Education in the nation. Educated at Brown and Berkeley, he spent several years teaching history at the middle and high school levels before completing a doctorate in Psychological Studies in Education at Stanford. His book *Historical Thinking and Other Unnatural Acts: Charting the Future of Teaching the Past* won the Frederic W. Ness Award from the Association of American Colleges and Universities. His work on teacher community won the 2002 Exemplary Research on Teaching and Teacher Education Award from the American Educational Research Association. He was a member of the blue-ribbon commission of the National Research Council that wrote the widely circulated report, *How People Learn: Brain, Mind, Experience, and School*. He is also the Senior Consulting Author on Holt's *American Anthem*.

Consultants

Program Consultant

Kylene Beers, Ed.D.
Senior Reading Researcher
School Development Program
Yale University
New Haven, Connecticut

Academic Consultants

**Elizabeth Shanks
  Alexander, Ph.D.**
*Professor of Rabbinic Judaism and
  Talmudic Literature*
Department of Religious Studies
University of Virginia
Charlottesville, Virginia

Elizabeth A. Clark, Ph.D.
*John Carlisle Kilgo Professor
  of Religion*
Department of Religion
Duke University
Durham, North Carolina

Ahmet T. Karamustafa, Ph.D.
*Professor of History and
  Religious Studies*
Department of History
Washington University in
  St. Louis
St. Louis, Missouri

Christopher L. Salter, Ph.D.
*Professor of Geography and Chair
  Emeritus*
Department of Geography
University of Missouri-
  Columbia
Columbia, Missouri

Program Advisers

Academic Reviewers

Christian Appy, Ph.D.
Department of History
University of Massachusetts, Amherst
Amherst, Massachusetts

Jonathan Beecher, Ph.D.
Department of History
University of California, Santa Cruz
Santa Cruz, California

Stanley M. Burstein, Ph.D.
Professor Emeritus of Ancient History
Department of History
California State University,
    Los Angeles
Los Angeles, California

Prasenjit Duara, Ph.D.
Department of History
University of Chicago
Chicago, Illinois

Benjamin Ehlers, Ph.D.
Department of History
University of Georgia
Athens, Georgia

Lamont King, Ph.D.
Department of History
James Madison University
Harrisonburg, Virginia

Geoff Koziol, Ph.D.
Department of History
University of California
Berkeley, California

Robert J. Meier, Ph.D.
Department of Anthropology
Indiana University
Bloomington, Indiana

Vasudha Narayannan
Department of Religion
University of Florida
Gainesville, Florida

David L. Ransel, Ph.D.
Department of History
Indiana University
Bloomington, Indiana

Susan Schroeder, Ph.D.
Department of History
Tulane University
New Orleans, Louisiana

Helaine Silverman, Ph.D.
Department of Anthropology
University of Illinois
Urbana, Illinois

Paolo Squatriti, Ph.D.
Department of History
University of Michigan
Ann Arbor, Michigan

Marc Van De Mieroop, Ph.D.
Department of History
Columbia University
New York, New York

Teacher's Edition

Contents

New York State Learning Standards

Each chapter of *Holt World History: Human Legacy, New York Edition* covers one or two Key Ideas from the New York State Learning Standards. These Key Ideas are listed below.

KEY IDEA 1: The study of world history requires an understanding of world cultures and civilizations, including an analysis of important ideas, social and cultural values, beliefs, and traditions. This study also examines the human condition and the connections and interactions of people across time and space, and the ways different people view the same event or issue from a variety of perspectives.

KEY IDEA 2: Establishing time frames, exploring different periodizations, examining themes across time and within cultures, and focusing on important turning points in world history help organize the study of world cultures and civilizations.

KEY IDEA 3: Study of the major social, political, cultural, and religious developments in world history involves learning about the important roles and contributions of individuals and groups.

KEY IDEA 4: The skills of historical analysis include the ability to investigate differing and competing interpretations of the theories of history, hypothesize about why interpretations change over time, explain the importance of historical evidence, and understand the concepts of change and continuity over time.

New York State Learning Standards
Key Idea 1, Key Idea 2

History's Impact Video Series
Impact of Archaeology

New York State Learning Standards
Key Idea 2, Key Idea 3

History's Impact Video Series
Impact of Judaism throughout the World

UNIT 2

2100 BC–AD 1500

The Growth of Civilizations

UNIT 3
100–1500
Cultures in Contact 253

New York State Learning Standards
Key Idea 1, Key Idea 3

History's Impact Video Series
Impact of the Salt Trade

New York State Learning Standards
Key Idea 1, Key Idea 2

History's Impact Video Series
Impact of Chinese Culture on Japan

1200–1800
New Ideas, New Empires 433

UNIT 6

1500–1820

Changes in European Society 531

UNIT 7

1700–1920
Industrialization and Nationalism

UNIT 8

1914–1945
The World at War

Features

Focus on Themes

Explore a world history theme in two contexts—the past and the present.

Themes Through Time

Study historical themes through key dates and moments in world history.

HISTORY CLOSE-UP

Explore key developments and events in world history through in-depth and close-up illustrations and photo essays.

GEOGRAPHY Starting Points Maps

⋆Interactive *Start with a map that establishes the geographical setting of the chapter.*

COUNTERPOINTS

Examine some issues in world history through different viewpoints.

Maps

Interpret maps to see where important events happened and analyze how geography influenced world history.

✷ Interactive

Charts and Graphs

Charts, Graphs, and Time Lines

Analyze information presented visually to learn more about history.

To examine key facts and concepts, look for this special logo:

Primary Sources

Relive history through eyewitness accounts, literature, and documents.

Detailed correlation of
Holt World History: Human Legacy, New York Edition to the

New York State Core Curriculum:
Global History and Geography

Explanation of Correlation

The following document is a correlation of *Holt World History: Human Legacy* to the New York Core Curriculum: Global History and Geography. The format for this correlation follows the same basic format established by the Core Curriculum, modified to accommodate the addition of page references. The correlation provides a cross-reference between the skills in the Core Curriculum, and representative page numbers where those skills are taught or assessed. Those references marked with an asterisk represent pages which offer secondary support or where application of the required skill is implied.

The references contained in this correlation reflect Holt, Rinehart and Winston's interpretation of the Social Studies objectives outlined in the New York State curriculum.

KEY TO REFERENCE	
Prefix	**Explanation**
SE	*Student's Edition*

Page number references apply to both the student's edition and the teacher's edition.

I. Methodology of Global History and Geography

A. HISTORY

1. Skills of Historical Analysis

a. investigate differing and competing interpretations of historical events-multiple perspectives	SE	H9, H29, H33, 96, 152, 216–217, 320, 396–397, 576, 620–621, 679, 706–707, 766–767, 800–801, 831, 864–865, 930–931, 960–961, 974, 1011
b. hypothesize about why interpretations change over time	SE	H32, 9, 28–29, 75, 78–79, 95, 114–115, 117, 199, 216–217, 568–573, 617, 636, 669, 974
c. explain the importance of historical evidence	SE	H22–H25, H30–H31, 26–27, 35–36, 56–57, 59, 61, 63, 65, 69, 75, 78–79, 86–87, 114–115, 165, 190, 207, 239, 424–425, 451, 480, 560–567, 577, 597, 611, 636, 652–653, 709, 793, 841, 847, 879

2. Understand the concepts of change and continuity over time	SE	H24, 6–8, 11, 15–17, 29, 40–41, 44, 66–67, 70, 153, 418, 427, 570–571, 598–599, 662–663, 678–679, 694, 790–791, 820–822, 1022–1025, 1030–1035
3. The connections and interactions of people across time and space	SE	23–25, 44, 54, 71, 84, 156–157, 192–193, 231, 265, 318–319, 321, 352, 398–399, 461, 546, 580–583, 586–587, 638–639, 656–657, 686–687, 724–725, 737, 787–788, 854–855, 867
4. Time frames and periodization	SE	H7, H14, H24, 7, 11 13, 17, 89, 130, 187, 360, 381, 454, 811, 822, 842, 893, 959, 1002–1003, 1039

5. Roles and contributions of individuals and groups	**SE**	6, 11, 34–37, 44, 78–79, 143–144, 146–148, 154–155, 159, 180–182, 241, 271–274, 312–315, 318, 337, 375–376, 567, 588, 613, 637–639, 654, 660–664, 667–670, 705, 792, 840, 856, 889, 979
6. Oral histories	**SE**	283, 286, 287, 304, 305

B. GEOGRAPHY

1. Elements of geography		
a. Human geography	**SE**	4, 9, 12, 14–17, 23, 33–34, 40–41, 44, 62, 68, 106, 204, 225, 402, 412, 566, 632, 650, 658, 689, 702–703, 725, 982, 990, R30–R31
b. Physical geography	**SE**	14, 17, 24–25, 28–29, 32–34, 37, 62, 108–109, 198, 632, 665, 702, 1009, R30–R31
c. Political geography	**SE**	40–41, 48, 51,137, 140, 222, 242–243, 372, 390, 592, 612, 615, 618–619, 638, 684, 697, 704, 716, 721, 778, 781–782, 787, 798, 806, 837, 876, 878, 915, R19, R30–R31
d. Migration	**SE**	4, 8–9, 11, 216–217, 287, 380, 584, 673
e. Trade	**SE**	15, 17, 19, 21, 23, 43, 44, 68, 175–176, 230–231, 239, 268–269, 315, 330–331, 409–412, 444–445, 662, 816, 993–994, 1007–1029
f. Environment and society	**SE**	13–15, 24–25, 29, 64, 92, 62, 198, 202, 212–213, 289, 632, 650, 661, 853
g. The uses of geography	**SE***	H18, H19, 17
2. Critical thinking skills		
a. Asking and answering geographic questions	**SE**	H12–H13, H18–H19, 14, 17, 32, 37, 41, 43, 51, 54, 64, 68, 70, 137, 162, 204, 210, 225, 243, 330, 355, 409, 584, 612, 618–619, 632, 658, 806, 845, 982, 1009
b. Analyzing theories of geography	**SE**	8–9, 17, 62, 268–269, 632, 661, 1009
c. Acquiring, organizing, and analyzing geographic information	**SE**	H15–H19, 4, 8–9, 14, 23–25, 64, 156–157, 198, 225, 287, 355, 477, 481, 592, 612, 618–619, 632, 650, 658, 755, 806, 982
3. Identifying and defining world regions	**SE**	4, 24–25, 32, 34, 37, 62, 92, 198, 222, 242–243, 282, 308, 330, 404–405, 498, 566, 632, 650, 820, 960

C. ECONOMICS

1. Major economic concepts (scarcity, supply/demand, opportunity costs, production, resources)	**SE**	22, 294, 296, 410, 484, 486–487, 543, 577, 634–635, 645–647, 662, 813, 968, 975, 977, 992–993, 1026–1035, R48–R53
2. Economic decision making	**SE**	H20, 22, 89, 213–215, 543, 613, 815–817, 897, 968, 975, 982–983, 987
3. The interdependence of economics and economic systems throughout the world	**SE**	22, 409–410, 412, 484–487, 634–635, 646–647, 650–651, 798–799, 813–817, 831, 897, 927–929, 979–981, 1026–1035
4. Applying critical thinking skills in making informed and well-reasoned economic decisions	**SE**	H46, 22, 89, 296, 486, 634, 651, 975, 984–985, 1033–1035, R53

D. POLITICAL SCIENCE

I. The purposes of government	**SE**	20, 66, 71, 129, 165–166 388–389, 391, 440–441, 575, 576, 584–585, 649, 785, 814–816, 825–827
2. Political systems around the world	**SE**	34, 66, 71, 129–130, 165–166, 224, 244–245, 383–384, 584–585, 598–599, 648–649, 690, 792–793, 809–811, 823–824, 969–977, 982–983
3. Political concepts of power, authority, governance, and law	**SE**	36, 71, 135–136, 157, 165–166, 176, 213, 224, 244–245, 348–349, 383–384, 389, 393–394, 501, 575, 578–579, 584–585, 604–606, 613, 649, 690, 785, 790–792, 823–824, 831, 977, 979
4. Rights and responsibilities of citizenship across time and space	**SE**	36, 213, 215, 229–230, 239, 581, 585, 599, 607, 613, 644, 693, 785, 799, 979
5. Critical Thinking Skills		
a. Probing ideas and assumptions	**SE**	71, 165, 170, 195, 227, 399, 585, 587, 599, 606–607, 649, 793, 801, 803, 811, 924, 987, 1008, 1024–1025
b. Posing and answering analytical questions	**SE**	H10, 37, 57, 70–71, 195, 227, 389, 395, 575, 585, 587, 599, 606, 649, 793, 799, 803, 924, 945, 1008
c. Assuming a skeptical attitude toward questionable political statements	**SE**	644, 793, 847, 983, 987
d. Evaluating evidence and forming rational conclusions	**SE**	H27, 56–57, 76, 159, 165, 227, 389, 397, 550, 587, 599, 793, 803, 847, 983, 1024–1025
e. Developing participatory skills	**SE**	H36, H38–H39, 191, 333, 360, 391, 412, 579, 599, 613, 705, 717, 782, 803, 811, 842, 924, 983, 995

Unit One: Ancient World-Civilizations and Religion (4000 BC–500 AD)

A. EARLY PEOPLES

I. Human and physical geography	**SE**	4, 9, 11, 13, 14, 17
2. Hunters and gatherers-nomadic groups	**SE**	10, 13, 17, 23, R2
3. Relationship to the environment	**SE**	8–11, 13, 17, 22–25, 29
4. Migration of early human populations		
a. Out of Africa	**SE**	4, 8–9, 11, R2
b. Other theories	**SE**	8–9, 199
5. Early government		
a. Purposes	**SE**	20, 29, 34
b. Decision making	**SE**	19–20, 22, 29, 34
c Move toward more complex government systems	**SE**	19–20, 34

B. NEOLITHIC REVOLUTION AND EARLY RIVER CIVILIZATIONS

1. Compare and contrast (Mesopotamia, Egypt, the Indus Valley, and Yellow River civilizations)

a. Human and physical geography of early river civilizations **SE** 19, 24–25, 32–34, 40–41, 43, 48, 51, 54–55, 58, 64, 68, 92, 94, 97, 106, 109, 111, 117, R2, R3

b. Traditional economies **SE** 19, 22, 95

c. Political systems **SE** 20–21, 34–37, 42, 47–48, 51–53, 56–57, 64–68, 71, 96, 111, 113, 117

d. Social structures and urbanization **SE** 20–22, 34–37, 42, 47–49, 51, 66, 76–77, 95–97, 109, 117, R3

e. Contributions **SE** 36, 54–55, 66, 78

    1) Writing systems **SE** 21, 23, 35, 37, 42, 44, 58, 78, 93, 111

    2) Belief systems **SE** 20, 22–23, 34–35, 37, 45, 54, 66, 68–69, 71–75, 97, 99–102, 104, 107, 110, 113, 117

    3) Early technology—irrigation, tools, weapons **SE** 23–25, 34, 36–37, 39–40, 44, 58, 78, 113

    4) Architecture **SE** 33–34, 36, 42–43, 55, 60–61, 64–65, 72, 80, 95

    5) Legal systems-Code of Hammurabi **SE** 36, 37, 42, 47, 49, R3

2. Identify demographic patterns of early civilizations and movement of people-Bantu migration (500 B.C.–1500 A.D.)

a. Human and physical geography **SE** 287, 305

b. Causes of migration **SE** 287, 305

c. Impact on other areas of Africa **SE** 287, 305

C. CLASSICAL CIVILIZATIONS

1. Chinese civilization

a. Human and physical geography **SE** 111, 113, 222, 225, 230–231

b. Chinese contributions (engineering, tools, writing, silk, bronzes, government system) **SE** 112, 224, 226, 231–232, 247

c. Dynastic cycles **SE** 111, 113, 223–227, 246

d. Mandate of Heaven **SE** 111, 113, 225

2. Greek Civilization

a. Human and physical geography **SE** 126, 128–129, 137, 140, 151, 153, 156–157

b. the rise of city-states-Athens/Sparta **SE** 129–130, 133, 135, 159, R5

c. Contributions: art, architecture, philosophy, science-Plato, Socrates, Aristotle **SE** 131, 133, 143–149, R55, R56

d. Growth of democracy in Athens versus the Spartan political system **SE** 130, 135–136, 141, 159

e. Alexander the great and Hellenistic culture-cultural diffusion **SE** 151–153, 156–157, 159, R5

NEW YORK EDITION

E. THE EMERGENCE AND SPREAD OF BELIEF SYSTEMS

1. Place of origin and major beliefs

a. Animism—African	**SE**	286–287
b. Hinduism	**SE**	99–102, 117, 912
c. Buddhism	**SE**	103–107, R4
d. Chinese Philosophies (Confucianism, Taoism)	**SE**	113, 117, R4
e. Judaism	**SE**	45–49, R4
f. Christianity	**SE**	183–184, R5, R6
g. Islam	**SE**	258–259, 261, R6–R7
h. Legalism	**SE**	224, 244, 245
i. Shintoism	**SE**	323, 327
j. Jainism	**SE**	102, 117
2. Expansion of Christianity, Islam, Confucianism, and Buddhism	**SE**	107, 185–187, 195, 225–226, 229, 231–235, 263–266, 289–290, 311, 324, 346, 349–351, 358, 362–363, 365, 369

Unit Two: Expanding Zones of Exchange and Encounter (500–1200)

A. GUPTA EMPIRE (320–550 AD)

1. Human and physical geography	**SE**	235, 239
2. Artistic, scientific, and mathematical contributions	**SE**	240–241, 247
3. Ties to Hinduism	**SE**	236–237
4. Organizational Structure	**SE**	236–237, 247

B. TANG AND SONG DYNASTY (618–1126 AD)

1. Human and physical geography	**SE**	308, 311
2. Contributions	**SE**	312–315, 337
3. Chinese influence on Korea and Japan	**SE**	310, 324–325, 327, 337
4. Cultural flowering	**SE**	312–314
5. Growth of commerce and trade	**SE**	310, 315

C. BYZANTINE EMPIRE (330–1453 A.D.)

1. Human and physical geography	**SE**	346–347, 354–355
2. Achievements (law, Justinian Code, engineering, art, and commerce)	**SE**	348–349, 353, R6
3. The Orthodox Christian Church	**SE**	350–351
4. Political Structure and Justinian Code	**SE**	348–349
5. Role in preserving and transmitting Greek and Roman Cultures	**SE**	347, 349, 369, R6

NEW YORK EDITION

NEW YORK EDITION

4. Key individuals—Urban II, Saladin, and Richard the Lion-Hearted | **SE** | 403–407

Unit Three: Global Interactions (1200–1650)

A. EARLY JAPANESE HISTORY AND FEUDALISM

1. Human and physical geography | **SE** | 323–324, 498, 577

2. Early Traditions (Shintoism) | **SE** | 322–324, 327

3. Ties with China and Korea: cultural diffusion of Buddhism and Confucianism | **SE** | 324–325, 327, 337, 517

4. Tokugawa Shogunate | **SE** | 519–521, 525, R11

5. Social hierarchy and stratification | **SE** | 517, 519–521

6. Comparison to European feudalism | **SE** | 517, 521, 522–523, 529

7. Zen Buddhism | **SE** | 517, 519

B. RISE AND FALL OF THE MONGOLS AND THEIR IMPACT ON EURASIA

1. Human and physical geography | **SE** | 317, 319, 337

2. Origins—Central Asian nomadic tribes | **SE** | 317–318, 337, R8

3. The Yuan Dynasty: A foreign non-Chinese dynasty | **SE** | 318–319, 321

4. Extent of empire under Ghengis Khan and Kublai Khan | **SE** | 317–321

5. Impact on Central Asia, China, Korea, Europe, India, Southwest Asia | **SE** | 243, 267, 318–321, 332, 327, 358–359, 499, R8

6. Impact on the rise of Moscow | **SE** | 318, 321, 337

7. Interaction with the West and global trade, Pax Mongolia (e.g., Marco Polo) | **SE** | 318–321, 337

8. Causes of Decline | **SE** | 321, 337

C. GLOBAL TRADE AND INTERACTIONS

1. The Resurgence of Europe

    a. Hanseatic League and Italian city-states | **SE** | 409, 412, 438, 444–445, 465, R8

    b. Trade fairs and towns | **SE** | 410–412, 437, R8

    c. Medieval guilds | **SE** | 411–412

    d. Commercial revolution | **SE** | 409–410, 412

2. Major trading centers—Nanjing/Calicut/Mogadishu/Venice | **SE** | 291, 409, 436, 472, 510–511

3. Ibn Battuta | **SE** | 291, 303, R61

4. Expansion of the Portuguese spice trade to Southeast Asia and its impact on Asia and Europe | **SE** | 471–472

D. RISE AND FALL OF AFRICAN CIVILIZATIONS: GHANA, MALI, AXUM, AND SONGHAI EMPIRES

1. Human and physical geography | **SE** | 282, 284–285, 287, 289, 297, 305

2. Organizational structure | **SE** | 285, 289, 297, 299–300, 305

NEW YORK EDITION

3. The impact of China on East Asia and Southeast Asia	**SE**	511, 513
4. China's relationship with the West	**SE**	510–513
5. Contributions	**SE**	512–513
6. Expansion of trade (Zheng He, 1405–1433)	**SE**	511, 514–515

B. THE IMPACT OF THE OTTOMAN EMPIRE ON THE MIDDLE EAST AND EUROPE

1. Human and physical geography	**SE**	498, 500, 502, 525
2. Contributions	**SE**	499, 501–502
3. Suleiman I (the Magnificent, the Lawgiver)	**SE**	501–502
4. Disruption of established trade routes and European search for new ones	**SE**	471–473
5. Limits of Ottoman Europe	**SE**	500, 502

C. SPAIN AND PORTUGAL ON THE EVE OF THE ENCOUNTER

1. Human and physical Geography	**SE**	472–473, 475
2. Reconquista under Ferdinand and Isabella	**SE**	391, 399
3. Expulsion of Moors and Jews	**SE**	391, 458
4. Exploration and Overseas Expansion		
a. Columbus	**SE**	469, 474–475, 495
b. Magellan circumnavigates the globe	**SE**	473–475, 475, R9

D. THE RISE OF MESOAMERICAN EMPIRES: AZTEC AND INCAN EMPIRES BEFORE 1500

1. Human and physical Geography	**SE**	208–210, 212
2. Organizational Structure	**SE**	209, 215
3. Contributions	**SE**	210, 215, R9
4. Trade	**SE**	208–209, 213

E. THE ENCOUNTER BETWEEN EUROPEANS AND THE PEOPLES OF AFRICA, THE AMERICAS AND ASIA; CASE STUDY: THE COLUMBIAN EXCHANGE (FLORA, FAUNA, AND DISEASES)

1. Human and physical geography	**SE**	468, 472–473, 477, 479, 483–484
2. European competition for colonies in the Americas, Africa, East Asia, and Southeast Asia–The "old imperialism"	**SE**	477, 479, 481
3. Global demographic shifts; case study: The triangular trade and slavery	**SE**	488–491, 495
4. The extent of European expansionism	**SE**	477, 492, 494
5. European mercantilism	**SE**	484–485, 487, 495
6. Spanish colonialism and the introduction of the Encomienda system to Latin America	**SE**	477, 481, 493, R10
7. Dutch colonization in East Asia (Japan and Indonesia)	**SE**	480, 752
8. Exchange of food and disease (Columbian exchange)	**SE**	483–484, 487, 492, 493, 495

c. Case Studies: Simon Bolivar, Toussaint L'Overture, Jose de San Martin	**SE**	695–696, 698–700, 707

D. THE REACTION AGAINST REVOLUTIONARY IDEAS

1. Human and physical geography	**SE**	618–619, 623
2. Balance of power politics and the Congress of Vienna (Klemens von Metternich)	**SE**	618–619, 623, 712, 714, 724
3. Revolutions of 1848	**SE**	692–693, 735, 737, R13
4. Russian Absolutism: reforms and expansion		
a. Impact of the French Revolution and Napoleon	**SE**	615–616, 623
b. 19th Century Russian Serfdom	**SE**	729–730, 732, 737
c. Expansion of Russia into Siberia	**SE**	730

E. LATIN AMERICA: THE FAILURE OF DEMOCRACY AND THE SEARCH FOR STABILITY

1. Human and physical geography	**SE**	684, 697
2. Roles of social classes: land-holding elite, creoles, mestizos, native peoples, and slaves	**SE**	696, 700
3. Roles of the Church and military	**SE**	696–699, 762
4. Role of cash crop economies in a global market	**SE**	483–484
5. The Mexican Revolution (1910–1930)		
a. Cause and effect	**SE**	762–763, 765, 769
b. Roles of Porfiro Diaz, Francisco "Pancho" Villa, and Emiliano Zapata	**SE**	761–763, 765
c. Economic and social nationalism	**SE**	762–763

F. GLOBAL NATIONALISM

1. Human and physical geography	**SE**	712, 716, 721, 727
2. Role in political revolutions	**SE**	714–715, 720–721, 724–727, 737
3. Force for unity and self-determination		
a. Unification of Italy and Germany (Camillo Cavour, Otto von Bismarck)	**SE**	714–717, 719–722, 735, 737, R13–R14
b. Asian and Middle Eastern Nationalism		
1) India (Indian National Congress, Moslem League)	**SE**	744–745
2) Turkey—Young Turks	**SE**	727
4. Zionism	**SE**	694, 950
5. Force Leading to Conflicts		
a. Balkans before World War I	**SE**	726–727
b. Ottoman Empire as the pawn of European powers	**SE**	725–727, 798

NEW YORK EDITION

NEW YORK EDITION

c. African resistance—Zulu Empire	**SE**	758–760	
d. Boer War	**SE**	758, 769	
e. Cecil Rhodes	**SE**	757	
f. 19th century anti-slave trade legislation	**SE**	687, 709	
5. European spheres of influence in China			
a. Opium Wars (1839–1842 and 1858–1860) and the Treaty of Nanjing			
1) Unequal treaties	**SE**	747, 753	
2) Extraterritoriality	**SE**	747, 769	
b. Boxer Rebellion	**SE**	749, 753	
c. Sun Yat-sen (Sun Yixian) and the Chinese Revolution (1910–1911)	**SE**	749, 766–767	
6. Multiple perspectives toward imperialism			
a. immediate/long-term changes made under European rule	**SE**	744–745, 747–750, 752–753	
b. long-term effects in Europe and the rest of the world	**SE**	750, 753–755, 780	

I. JAPAN AND THE MEIJI RESTORATION

1. Human and physical geography	**SE**	747, 750–751	
2. The opening of Japan			
a. Commodore Matthew Perry	**SE**	750, 769, R14	
b. Impact upon Japan of Treaty of Kanagawa	**SE**	750–751, 753, R14	
3. Modernization, industrialization	**SE**	639, 750–751, 753	
4. Japan as an imperialist power			
a. First Sino-Japanese War (1894–1895)	**SE**	751–752	
b. Russo-Japanese War	**SE**	730, 752	
c. Annexation of Korea	**SE**	752	
d. Dependence on world market	**SE**	754–755	

Unit Six: A Half Century of Crisis and Achievement (1900–1945)

A. WORLD WAR I

1. Europe: the physical setting	**SE**	728, 781, 787	
2. Causes	**SE**	780–782, 803	
3. Impacts	**SE**	786–788, 794–795, 797–799	
4. Effects of scientific/technological advances	**SE**	783–785, 788	
5. Armenian Massacre	**SE**	788	
6. Collapse of the Ottoman Empire	**SE**	787, 798–799	
7. The war as reflected in literature, art, and propaganda	**SE**	796, 801, 803, R72	

NEW YORK EDITION

B. REVOLUTION AND CHANGE IN RUSSIA—CAUSES AND IMPACTS

1. Czar Nicholas II	**SE**	730, 789–791, 803
2. The Revolution of 1905	**SE**	730–732, 790
3. March Revolution and provisional government	**SE**	791–792
4. Bolshevik Revolution	**SE**	791–793, 803, R17
5. V.I. Lenin's rule in Russia	**SE**	792–793, 803
6. Stalin and the rise of a modern totalitarian state: industrialization, command economy, collectivization	**SE**	824–825, 827
7. Russification of ethnic republics	**SE**	824–825, 827
8. Forced famine in Ukraine	**SE**	825, 827
9. Reign of Terror	**SE**	825, 827

C. BETWEEN THE WARS

1. Human and physical geography	**SE**	797–798, 806, 808, 820
2. Treaty of Versailles and the League of Nations	**SE**	797, 799, 808
3. Modernization and westernization of a secular Turkey—Kemal Ataturk	**SE**	809, 1037, 1039
4. Women's suffrage movement	**SE**	686–689, 709
5. Great Depression—causes and impacts	**SE**	813–816, 830–831
6. Weimar Republic and the rise of fascism as an aftermath of World War I	**SE**	826–827, 829
7. Japanese militarism and expansion		
a. Manchuria, 1931	**SE**	820–822, 831
b. Second Sino-Japanese War (1937–1945)	**SE**	822, 831
8. Policy of appeasement—Munich Pact	**SE**	836, 842
9. Colonial Response to European Imperialism; Case studies: Mohandas Gandhi, Reza Khan, Jiang Jeshi (Chiang Kai–shek), Mao Zedong, Zionism, Arab nationalism, the Amritsar massacre–Indian nationalism, Salt March, civil disobedience	**SE**	808–811, 828–829, 831, R73
10. Arabic and Zionist nationalism	**SE**	810–811, 955–957

D. WORLD WAR II—CAUSES AND IMPACT

1. Human and physical geography	**SE**	834, 837, 839, 844–845, 849–850, 852–853, 857, 859, 862, 864
2. The Nazi and Japanese states	**SE**	819–822, 826–827, 831, 837, R15
3. Key individuals—Hitler, Mussolini, Stalin, Churchill, and Roosevelt	**SE**	823–824, 826–827, 831, 836–838, 840–841
4. Key events—Dunkirk, the Blitz, D-Day, Hitler's second front, the war in the Pacific	**SE**	839–840, 846, 848–850, 859–860, 863, 867
5. The Nazi Holocaust: the extermination of Jews, Poles, other Slavs, Gypsies, disabled, and others	**SE**	855–857, 864–865, 867, R15–R16, R75

6. Resistance	SE	838, 840, 845–846, 848
7. Japan's role—Nanjing, Bataan, Pearl Harbor	SE	821–822, 841–842, 848–849, 867, R15–R16
8. War in China—Long March	SE	807–808, 822, 831
9. Impacts of technology on total war	SE	840, 861, 863
10. Hiroshima and Nagasaki	SE	861, 863, 867, R15–R16
11. War crime trials	SE	878, 926
12. Global spatial arrangements—post-World War II world	SE	862–863, 867

Unit Seven: The 20th Century Since 1945

A. COLD WAR BALANCE OF POWER

1. Human and physical geography	SE	876, 878, 880–881, 885
2. The world in 1945: physical setting	SE	878–879, 890
3. United States occupation of Germany and Japan		
a. The adoption of democratic systems of government	SE	880, 926
b. Economic rebuilding of Germany and Japan	SE	879, 926–927
4. Emergence of the superpowers	SE	878–879, 882–883, 891
5. Political climate of the Cold War		
a. Marshall Plan	SE	879, 881, 890, R16
b. Truman Doctrine	SE	879, 881, R16
c. Berlin airlift and a divided Germany	SE	880–884
d. North Atlantic Treaty Organization (NATO)/Warsaw Pact—expanding membership and role of NATO	SE	880–881, 891, 893, R16
e. Hungarian Revolt	SE	891–892
f. Soviet invasion of Czechoslovakia	SE	891–892
g. Nuclear weapons and space	SE	882–885, 887, 900–901, 905
h. Surrogate superpower rivalries; Case studies: (Egypt, Congo, Angola, Chile, Iran, Iraq, Vietnam, Guatemala)	SE	879, 884–886, 905, 915–917, 919
i. Role of nonaligned nations	SE	886, 911
6. Korean War		
a. United States role in the division of Korea	SE	880–881
b. Comparison of Korea and Germany	SE	880–881
c. Conduct of the war	SE	881, R17

B. ROLE OF THE UNITED NATIONS

1. Peace keeping	SE	1041, 1043, R16
2. Social and economic programs	SE	1040–1044, R16
3. Contemporary social conditions	SE	997, 999, 1041–1044

NEW YORK EDITION

C. ECONOMIC ISSUES IN THE COLD WAR AND POST-COLD WAR ERA

1.	Human and physical geography	**SE**	890, 892
2.	A comparison of market v. command economies (Western Europe v. Soviet Union)	**SE**	891–892
3.	Economic recovery in Europe and Japan		
	a. Western Germany becomes a major economic power	**SE**	890–891, 893
	b. European Economic Community/Common Market/ European Union—steps toward European integration	**SE**	890–891, 893, 897
	c. Japan becomes an economic superpower	**SE**	927, 929, 933
4.	Organization of Petroleum Exporting Countries (OPEC): oil crisis in the 1970's	**SE**	954–955
5.	Pacific Rim economies/economic crisis	**SE**	927–929, 933
6.	North America Free Trade Agreement (NAFTA), 1997	**SE**	960, 984–985, 994

D. CHINESE COMMUNIST REVOLUTION

1.	Human and physical geography	**SE**	908, 922–923
2.	Communist rise to power (1936–1949); Jiang Jeshi (Chiang Kai-shek), Mao Zedong	**SE**	920–924, 933, R16–R17
3.	Communism under Mao Zedong		
	a. Great Leap Forward	**SE**	921, 924, 933
	b. The Cultural Revolution and the Red Guard	**SE**	922, 924, 930–931, 933
4.	Communism under Deng Xiaoping		
	a. Economic reforms—Four Modernizations	**SE**	923–924, R17
	1) Limited privatization	**SE**	923–924
	2) Dismantling of communes	**SE**	923–924
	3) Introduction of "responsibility system"	**SE**	923, 1031
	4) Foreign Investment	**SE**	924, 1031
	b. Fifth modernization—democracy		
	1) April/May 1989	**SE**	922–923
	2) Tiananmen Square	**SE**	922–924
5.	Return of Hong Kong–July 1, 1997	**SE***	929
6.	The social system in communist China versus dynastic China	**SE**	513, 921–922, 924

E. COLLAPSE OF EUROPEAN IMPERIALISM

1.	Human and physical geography	**SE**	908–910, 915–916, 936, 940, 1035
2.	India—independence and partition		
	a. Political system	**SE**	910–911, 913, 1032
	b. Muslim/Hindu Conflicts	**SE**	910–911, 913
	c. Status of the Caste System	**SE**	911, 913

d. Roles of Mohandas Gandhi and Jawaharlal Nehru	**SE**	910–911, 1032
e. Non-alignment	**SE**	886, 911
f. Kashmir and Punjab	**SE**	911, 913
3. African independence movements and Pan Africanism		
a. Changing political boundaries in Africa (Nigeria, Ghana, and Kenya)	**SE**	938–939
b. Roles of Jomo Kenyatta and Kwame Kkrumah	**SE**	937–939
c. Continuance of economic linkages with former colonial powers	**SE**	938–939, 945–947
d. Ethnic tensions versus nationalism: Nigeria and civil war	**SE**	945, 947
e. Apartheid—policy of racial separation and segregation		
1) Historical circumstances	**SE**	940–941, 944–945, 947, 963
2) African National Congress	**SE**	944–945
3) Leadership—Nelson Mandela, Desmond Tutu, F.W. de Klerk	**SE**	944–945, 963, R18, R77
f. Political and economic instability—Congo (Zaire) or any other examples	**SE**	945–947
g. Ethnic tensions: Rwanda—Hutu-Tutsi	**SE**	945, 996, 1004
4. Southeast Asia		
a. Vietnam/Ho Chi Minh	**SE**	915–917, 919, 933, R17
b. Cambodia/Pol Pot/Khmer Rouge	**SE**	919, 933
c. Aung San Suu Kyi—Myanmar	**SE**	919, R78
F. CONFLICTS AND CHANGE IN THE MIDDLE EAST		
1. Human and physical geography	**SE**	950–951, 955
2. The Creation of the State of Israel, Arab Palestinians, and Israel's Arab neighbors	**SE**	950–951, 955–956, 963
3. Roles of individuals–Golda Meir, Yasir Arafat, Anwar Sadat, King Hussein, Yitzhak Rabin, Palestine Liberation Organization (PLO)	**SE**	956–957
a. Arab-Israeli wars	**SE**	951, 956–957, 959, R16
b. Peace treaties	**SE**	956, 959, 1043
4. Role of terrorism	**SE**	899, 905, 1001–1004, 1013, R18
5. Turkey and Iraq—Kurds	**SE**	958, 1003
6. Migration of Jews from Europe, the United States, the Soviet Union, and Africa	**SE**	950–951, 956
7. The Iranian Revolution		
a. Causes and impact	**SE**	958–961
b. Ayatollah Ruhollah Khomeini versus Reza Pahlavi	**SE**	958–961
8. Persian Gulf War—Saddam Hussein	**SE**	898, 958–959, 1002

NEW YORK EDITION

b. Global migration; Suggested case studies: Turkish, Italian, and Russian immigration to Germany, North African immigration to France, Latin American and Asian immigration to the United States, and Hutu and Tutsis immigration	**SE**	981, 998–999, 1013

4. Modernization/tradition—finding a balance

a. Japan	**SE**	926–927, 929, 933, 991
b. Middle East (Saudi Arabia, Egypt, Afghanistan, and Algeria)	**SE**	950, 952–953, 956–957
c. Africa	**SE**	942–947
d. Latin America	**SE**	1027–1029

5. Scientific and technological advances

a. Treatment of infectious diseases	**SE**	946, 1008, 1013
b. Improved standard of living	**SE**	926–927, 1008, 1013, 1031–1035

6. Urbanization–use and distribution of scarce resources (Africa, India, Latin America) — **SE** 912, 1005, 1027–1029

7. Status of women and children

a. Economic issues, e.g., child labor	**SE**	912, 1036–1037
b. Social issues, e.g., abuse and access to education	**SE**	1034, 1038–1039
c. Political issues, e.g., participation in the political process	**SE**	911–913, 1037–1039

8. Ethnic and religious tensions: an analysis of multiple perspectives

a. Northern Ireland	**SE** **SE***	1001 1037*
b. Balkans: Serbs, Croats, and Muslims	**SE**	726–727, 896–897, 899, 905
c. Sikhs and Tamils	**SE**	912–913, 1001
d. Indonesian Christians	**SE**	918–919
e. China—Tibet	**SE***	106*
f. Indonesia—East Timor	**SE**	918–919

B. ECONOMIC ISSUES

1. North/South dichotomy: issues of development (post colonialism)

a. Africa	**SE**	944–947, 1005
b. Latin America	**SE**	1027–1029

2. Korea's economic miracle	**SE**	928–929
3. Economic interdependence	**SE**	897–899, 992, 1013, 1028–1029
4. World hunger	**SE**	921–922, 946, 968, 997, 999, 1010–1011

C. THE ENVIRONMENT AND SUSTAINABILITY

1. Pollution—air, water, toxic waste (Europe)	**SE**	1006–1007, 1013
2. Deforestation (Amazon Basin)	**SE**	1007–1008, 1013
3. Desertification (Sahel)	**SE**	946, 1007, 1013
4. Nuclear safety (Chernobyl)	**SE**	1007, 1013
5. Endangered species (Africa)	**SE**	1006, 1013

D. SCIENCE AND TECHNOLOGY

1. Information age/Computer Revolution/Internet	**SE** **SE***	898–899, 1007–1008 992
2. Impact of satellites	**SE**	1007–1008
3. Green Revolution	**SE**	1008, 1010–1011
4. Space exploration	**SE**	884, 901, 1007–1008
5. Literacy and education	**SE**	1007, 1034–1035, 1039
6. Medical breakthroughs—disease control/life expectancy/ genetics	**SE**	998, 1006, 1008
7. Epidemics–AIDS	**SE**	946–947, 998–999, 1013
8. Nuclear proliferation	**SE**	900–901, 1003, 1013

Detailed Correlation of
Holt World History: Human Legacy, New York Edition to the
New York Learning Standards
for Social Studies

Explanation of Correlation

The following document is a correlation of *Holt World History: Human Legacy* to the New York State Learning Standards for Social Studies. The format for this correlation follows the same basic format established by the Learning Standards, modified to accommodate the addition of page references. The correlation provides a cross-reference between the skills in the Learning Standards, and representative page numbers where those skills are taught or assessed. Those references marked with an asterisk represent pages which offer secondary support or where application of the required skill is implied.

The references contained in this correlation reflect Holt, Rinehart and Winston's interpretation of the Social Studies objectives outlined in the New York State curriculum.

KEY TO REFERENCE	
Prefix	**Explanation**
SE	*Student's Edition*

Page number references apply to both the student's edition and the teacher's edition.

Standard 2 – World History

> **KEY IDEA I** The study of world history requires an understanding of world cultures and civilizations, including an analysis of important ideas, social and cultural values, beliefs, and traditions. This study also examines the human condition and the connections and interactions of people across time and space and the ways different people view the same event or issue from a variety of perspectives.

I.I	Students will define culture and civilization, explaining how they developed and changed over time. Investigate the various components of cultures and civilizations including social customs, norms, values, and traditions; political systems; economic systems; religions and spiritual beliefs; and socialization or educational practices.	**SE** 6, 15, 17, 19–23, 28, 29, 34–44, 45–55, 64–85, 89, 93–113, 117, 127–155, 159, 163–169, 170, 175–182, 183–191, 195, 200–215, 219, 223–241, 247, 258–267, 271–279, 283–305, 309–337, 347–365, 367, 373–399, 410–412, 419, 420, 423, 427, 477–481, 809–811, 819, 823–827, 992–994
I.2	Students will understand the development and connectedness of Western civilization and other civilizations and cultures in many areas of the world and over time.	**SE** 43, 44, 46, 47, 59, 68, 106, 107, 131, 134, 135, 149, 153, 156, 157, 159, 170, 175, 176, 180–182, 187, 192, 193, 195, 199–202, 231, 232, 234–237, 241, 264, 265, 268, 269, 319–321, 353, 358, 360, 407, 427, 459, 461, 470–475, 476–485, 488–493, 511–513, 586–587, 619, 741–769, 815, 816, 968, 971, 974, 977
I.3	Students will analyze historic events from around the world by examining accounts written from different perspectives.	**SE** 57, 101, 105, 112, 114, 115, 152, 156, 157, 172, 190, 192, 193, 195, 216, 217, 244, 245, 256–257, 260, 320, 334–335, 359, 363, 367, 394, 397, 424, 425, 438, 462, 463, 485, 512, 523, 561, 576, 586–587, 620, 621, 678, 679, 766, 767, 800, 801, 828, 829, 851, 864–865, 902, 903, 917, 930–931, 960, 961, 984, 985, 1010, 1011, 1024–1025, 1029, 1033–1035, 1039, 1043–1044

| 1.4 | Students will understand the broad patterns, relationships, and interactions of cultures and civilizations during particular eras and across eras. | **SE** | 24–25, 44, 81–85, 106, 107, 131, 149, 153, 156, 157, 159, 168, 169, 170, 175, 176, 180–182, 186, 187, 190, 192, 193, 195, 200–202, 213–215, 231, 232, 241, 243, 250–251, 264, 265, 268–269, 296–301, 302–303, 319–321, 322–325, 331, 351, 358, 360, 404–407, 420–422, 427, 459, 461, 470–475, 476–481, 483–487, 488–493, 501, 507, 511–513, 522–523, 558–559, 580–585, 726, 741–769, 810, 815, 837, 846, 856, 862, 910, 911, 916, 968, 984–985, 1003–1004 |
| 1.5 | Students will analyze changing and competing interpretations of issues, events, and developments throughout world history. | **SE** | H9, H23, H24, 156, 157, 172, 190, 192, 193, 195, 216, 217, 244, 245, 320, 334, 335, 367, 394, 397, 424, 425, 462, 463, 485, 512, 576, 620, 621, 678, 679, 828, 829, 864, 865, 902, 903, 917, 960, 961, 984, 985, 1006–1009, 1010, 1011, 1025, 1039, 1044 |

KEY IDEA 2 Establishing timeframes, exploring different periodizations, examining themes across time and within cultures, and focusing on important turning points in world history help organize the study of world cultures and civilizations.

2.1	Students will distinguish between the past, present, and future by creating multiple-tier timelines that display important events and developments from world history across time and place.	**SE***	H7, H14, 49, 172, 187, 261, 360, 381, 447, 521, 613, 700, 793, 811, 822, 842, 857, 893, 953, 1002–1003, 1039
2.2	Students will evaluate the effectiveness of different models for the periodization of important historic events, identifying the reasons why a particular sequence for these events was chosen.	**SE***	H7, H14, H24, 109, 439
2.3	Students will analyze evidence critically and demonstrate an understanding of how circumstances of time and place influence perspective.	**SE**	H25–H33, H41, 56, 57, 86, 87, 89, 117, 156, 157, 216, 217, 245, 333-334, 363-367, 397, 424, 425, 512, 523, 561, 595–597, 620, 621, 652, 653, 679, 715, 734-735, 757, 766, 767, 797, 800, 801, 864, 865, 949, 950, 951, 961
2.4	Students will explain the importance of analyzing narratives drawn from different times and places to understand historical events.	**SE**	38, 57, 133, 152, 156, 157, 172, 190, 192, 193, 195, 216, 217, 244, 245, 328, 334, 335, 367, 377, 394, 397, 424, 425, 462, 463, 485, 512, 561, 576, 600, 620, 621, 678, 679, 733, 766, 767, 800, 801, 828, 829, 864, 865, 902, 903, 917, 948, 960, 961, 984, 985
2.5	Students will investigate key events and developments and major turning points in world history to identify the factors that brought about change and the long-term effects of these changes.	**SE**	8–11, 13, 14, 17, 35, 36, 104, 107, 135, 141, 153, 165, 172, 176, 184, 187, 190–193, 195, 224, 231, 258, 265, 298, 318, 320, 347, 352, 363–364, 374, 388, 389, 396–397, 404, 407, 422–425, 427, 439, 445, 450, 453, 473, 477, 483, 488, 528, 538, 539, 545–550, 568, 569, 574, 581, 585, 596, 602–606, 609, 619, 633–635, 638–639, 641–651, 660, 693, 702–705, 730, 743, 747–751, 754–755, 763–765, 767, 780, 788, 792, 838, 841, 846–850, 852–853, 855, 861, 879, 894, 899, 920, 938–941, 944, 950, 956–959, 998

NEW YORK EDITION

NEW YORK EDITION (vertical sidebar text)

KEY IDEA 3 Study of the major social, political, cultural, and religious developments in world history involves learning about the important roles and contributions of individuals and groups.

3.1 Students will analyze the roles and contributions of individuals and groups to social, political, economic, cultural, and religious practices and activities.

SE 36, 37, 40–44, 46, 48, 49, 69, 98–107, 113, 139, 143–147, 151, 173, 174, 176, 184–187, 195, 224, 226, 239–241, 258, 262–267, 271–274, 283, 286, 288, 290, 298, 317, 320, 347, 348, 359, 360, 364, 373, 380, 383–386, 388, 389, 392–395, 405, 406, 415–417, 420, 424–425, 427, 440–448, 450–456, 471, 473, 477, 501, 505–508, 509–513, 517–521, 537, 541, 546, 549, 554, 568–575, 602, 609–617, 637, 647–649, 660–664, 667–670, 676, 695–700, 706, 707, 714, 715, 719, 724–727, 757–760, 792, 797, 809, 814, 823–827, 836, 841, 889, 895, 899, 902–903, 910, 911, 915, 921, 930–931, 973–977, 1008

3.2 Students will explain the dynamics of cultural change and how interactions between and among cultures has affected various cultural groups throughout the world.

SE 51, 54–55, 106, 107, 131, 149, 153, 156, 157, 159, 168, 169, 170, 175, 176, 180–182, 186, 187, 190, 192, 193, 195, 231, 232, 241, 264, 265, 268, 269, 302–303, 319–321, 351, 354–355, 358, 360, 379–381, 404–407, 416–418, 420–422, 427, 459, 461, 470–475, 476–484, 487–495, 505–508, 514–515, 641–645, 685–690, 726, 741–765, 766–767, 889, 894, 895, 926, 927, 995, 1003–1004, 1038–1039

3.3 Students will examine the social, cultural, political, economic, and religious norms and values of Western and other world cultures.

SE 46–49, 53–55, 59, 99–107, 112, 113, 117, 134–136, 143, 144, 159, 165, 166, 169, 170, 175, 179, 182, 183–187, 192, 193, 195, 244– 245, 259–261, 279, 335, 349–352, 363–365, 410–412, 419, 420, 423, 427, 439, 440, 451, 452, 463, 487, 514–515, 522–523, 574–579, 582–589, 598, 620– 621, 646–651, 652–653, 688, 689, 765, 766–767, 879, 916, 919, 922, 925, 927, 978–983, 997, 1038–1039

KEY IDEA 4 The skills of historical analysis include the ability to investigate differing and competing interpretations of the theories of history, hypothesize about why interpretations change over time, explain the importance of historical evidence, and understand the concepts of change and continuity over time.

4.1 Students will identify historical problems, pose analytical questions or hypotheses, research analytical questions or test hypotheses, formulate conclusions or generalizations, raise new questions or issues for further investigation.

SE H11–H13, H24, H37, 89, 93, 96, 97, 157, 217, 305, 367, 399, 427, 460–463, 539, 561, 621, 653, 655, 667, 670, 707, 735, 780, 801, 803, 886, 900-901, 905, 963, 1013, 1029, 1044

4.2 Students will interpret and analyze documents and artifacts related to significant developments and events in world history.

SE 27, 35, 36, 38, 47, 56, 57, 59, 63, 69, 80, 82, 86, 87, 89, 101, 105, 133, 138, 145, 152, 156, 157, 159, 165, 172, 181, 182, 185, 195, 244, 245, 260, 275, 302, 303, 335, 349, 363, 366, 367, 396, 397, 440, 441, 445–448, 463, 551, 560, 561, 586, 587, 598, 677, 678, 679, 706–707, 733–735, 793, 796, 800, 801, 825, 828, 829, 886, 902–903, 942, 1024–1025, 1028–1029, 1033–1035, 1043–1044

4.3 Students will plan and organize historical research projects related to regional or global interdependence.

SE 492–493, 933, 1013, 1029, 1035, 1044
SE* H37

4.4 Students will analyze different interpretations of important events, issues, or developments in world history by studying the social, political, and economic context in which they were developed; by testing the data source for reliability and validity, credibility, authority, authenticity, and completeness; and by detecting bias, distortion of the facts, and propaganda by omission, suppression, or invention of facts. (Taken from National Standards for World History)

SE H23. H24, H29. H31, H32, H33, 86, 87, 114–115, 152, 156, 157, 172, 190, 192, 193, 195, 216, 217, 244, 245, 320, 334, 335, 367, 394, 397, 424, 425, 462, 463, 485, 512, 543, 560–561, 576, 620, 621, 678–679, 766, 767, 800–801, 821, 828, 829, 864, 865, 902, 903, 917, 960–961, 984, 985, 1010, 1011, 1025, 1039, 1044

HOLT WORLD HISTORY:
HUMAN LEGACY, NEW YORK EDITION
Pacing Guides

Explanation

The following pages offer quarterly and weekly pacing guides for teaching the chapters of *Holt World History: Human Legacy, New York Edition* over a two school-year period. The quarterly pacing guide offers an at-an-glance approach for keeping your class on track. The weekly pacing guide breaks units down by chapter and section, and suggests materials to be taught and assessed during an average 45-minute class period.

YEAR ONE **FIRST QUARTER**	**Progress Assessment**	Diagnostic Test
	Human Legacy	Chapters 1–4
	History and Geography Document-Based Investigations	Chapter 1 Chapters 1–4
	Themes and Global Connections	Unit 1
	Progress Assessment	Chapter Tests 1–4 Unit Test 1
YEAR ONE **SECOND QUARTER**	*Human Legacy*	Chapters 5–9
	Document-Based Investigations History and Geography	Chapters 5–9 Chapters 8, 9
	Themes and Global Connections	Unit 2
	Progress Assessment	Chapter Tests 5–9 Unit Test 2
YEAR ONE **THIRD QUARTER**	*Human Legacy*	Chapters 10–13
	Document-Based Investigations History and Geography	Chapters 10–13 Chapter 12
	Themes and Global Connections	Unit 3
	Progress Assessment	Chapter Tests 10–13 Unit Test 3
YEAR ONE **FOURTH QUARTER**	*Human Legacy*	Chapters 14–17
	Document-Based Investigations History and Geography	Chapters 14–17 Chapter 17
	Themes and Global Connections	Units 4–5
	Progress Assessment	Chapter Tests 14–17 Unit Tests 4–5

YEAR TWO FIRST QUARTER	*Human Legacy*	Chapters 18–21
	History and Geography	Chapter 18
	Document-Based Investigations	Chapters 18–21
	Themes and Global Connections	Unit 6
	Progress Assessment	Chapter Tests 18–21 Unit Test 6
YEAR TWO SECOND QUARTER	*Human Legacy*	Chapters 22–25
	Document-Based Investigations	Chapters 22–25
	History and Geography	Chapter 25
	Themes and Global Connections	Unit 7
	Progress Assessment	Chapter Tests 22–25 Unit Test 7
YEAR TWO THIRD QUARTER	*Human Legacy*	Chapters 26–29
	Document-Based Investigations	Chapters 26–29
	History and Geography	Chapters 28, 29
	Themes and Global Connections	Unit 8
	Progress Assessment	Chapter Tests 26–29 Unit Test 8
YEAR TWO FOURTH QUARTER	*Human Legacy*	Chapters 30–33 Case Studies
	Document-Based Investigations	Chapters 30–33 Case Studies
	Themes and Global Connections	Units 9–10
	Progress Assessment	Chapter Tests 30–33 Unit Test 9 End of Year Test

Unit 1: The Dawn of Civilization, Prehistory–AD 300

TIME	LESSON AND ACTIVITY (NUMBER OF 45-MINUTE CLASSES)
Week 1	**Diagnostic Assessment:** Diagnostic Test (1)

Weeks 1–2	*HUMAN LEGACY*
	Unit 1: The Dawn of Civilization, Prehistory–AD 300 *(38)*
	Chapter 1: The Beginnings of Civilization, Prehistory–1000 BC *(8)*
	  Section 1: The First People (2)
	  Section 2: The Beginning of Agriculture (2)
	  Section 3: Foundations of Civilization (2)
	Document-Based Investigation (1)
	Progress Assessment: Chapter 1 Test (1)

Weeks 3–4	**Chapter 2:** The Ancient Near East, 4000 BC–550 BC *(10)*
	  Section 1: Mesopotamia and Sumer (2)
	  Section 2: Fertile Crescent Empires (2)
	  Section 3: The Hebrews and Judaism (2)
	  Section 4: The Persian Empire (2)
	Document-Based Investigation (1)
	Progress Assessment: Chapter 2 Test (1)

Weeks 5–6	**Chapter 3:** Nile Civilizations, 5000 BC–AD 300 *(8)*
	  Section 1: The Kingdom of Egypt (2)
	  Section 2: Egyptian Culture (2)
	  Section 3: The Nubian Kingdoms (2)
	Document-Based Investigation (1)
	Progress Assessment: Chapter 3 Test (1)

Weeks 7–8	**Chapter 4:** Ancient India and China, 2500 BC–250 BC *(10)*
	  Section 1: Early India (2)
	  Section 2: Hinduism (2)
	  Section 3: Buddhism (2)
	  Section 4: China's First Dynasties (2)
	Document-Based Investigation (1)
	Progress Assessment: Chapter 4 Test (1)

Week 8	**Themes and Global Connections** *(1)* **Progress Assessment:** Unit 1 Test *(1)*

NEW YORK EDITION

Unit 2: The Growth of Civilizations, 2100 BC–AD 1500

TIME	LESSON AND ACTIVITY (NUMBER OF 45-MINUTE CLASSES)

Weeks 9–10	***HUMAN LEGACY***
	Unit 2: The Growth of Civilizations, 2100 BC–AD 1500 *(44)*
	Chapter 5: Classical Greece, 2100 BC–150 BC *(10)*
	  Section 1: Early Greece (2)
	  Section 2: The Classical Age (2)
	  Section 3: Greek Achievements (2)
	  Section 4: Alexander the Great and His Legacy (2)
	Document-Based Investigation (1)
	Progress Assessment: Chapter 5 Test (1)

Weeks 11–12	**Chapter 6:** Rome and Early Christianity, 750 BC–AD 500 *(13)*
	  Section 1: The Foundations of Rome (3)
	    • *Focus on Themes:* Government and Citizenship
	  Section 2: From Republic to Empire (2)
	  Section 3: Roman Society and Culture (2)
	  Section 4: The Rise of Christianity (2)
	  Section 5: The Fall of Rome (2)
	Document-Based Investigation (1)
	Progress Assessment: Chapter 6 Test (1)

Weeks 13–14	**Chapter 7:** The Americas, 1000 BC–AD 1500 *(8)*
	  Section 1: North America (2)
	  Section 2: Mesoamerica (2)
	  Section 3: South America (2)
	Document-Based Investigation (1)
	Progress Assessment: Chapter 7 Test (1)

Weeks 15–16	**Chapter 8:** Empires of China and India, 350 BC–AD 600 *(11)*
	  Section 1: The Growth of China (2)
	  Section 2: Chinese Society and Culture (2)
	  Section 3: Indian Dynasties (2)
	  Section 4: Indian Society and Culture (3)
	    • *History and Geography:* Nomads and Empires
	Document-Based Investigation (1)
	Progress Assessment: Chapter 8 Test (1)

Week 17	**Themes and Global Connections** *(1)* **Progress Assessment:** Unit 2 Test *(1)*

Unit 3: Cultures in Contact, 100–1500

TIME	LESSON AND ACTIVITY (NUMBER OF 45-MINUTE CLASSES)

Weeks 17–18	**HUMAN LEGACY**
	Unit 3: Cultures in Contact, 100–1500 (29)
	Chapter 9: Muslim Civilization, 550–1250 (9)
	  Section 1: The Origins of Islam (2)
	    • *World Religions (Sacred Texts):* The Qur'an
	  Section 2: The Spread of Islam (2)
	    • *History and Geography:* Diffusion of a Civilization
	  Section 3: Society and Culture (3)
	    • *The Arts Around the World:* Islamic Calligraphy
	Document-Based Investigation (1)
	Progress Assessment: Chapter 9 Test (1)

Weeks 19–20	**Chapter 10:** African Kingdoms, 100–1500 *(8)*
	  Section 1: Early Civilizations of Africa (2)
	  Section 2: Trading States of East Africa (2)
	    • *Focus on Themes:* Economic Systems
	  Section 3: Kingdoms of West Africa (2)
	    • *History and Economics:* Scarcity, Supply and Demand
	Document-Based Investigation (1)
	Progress Assessment: Chapter 10 Test (1)

Weeks 21–22	**Chapter 11:** Cultures of East Asia, 550–1400 *(10)*
	  Section 1: Chinese Empires (2)
	  Section 2: The Mongol Empire (2)
	    • *Faces of History:* Kublai Khan
	  Section 3: Japan and Korea (2)
	    • *World Literature:* The Tale of Genji
	  Section 4: Civilizations of Southeast Asia (2)
	Document-Based Investigation (1)
	Progress Assessment: Chapter 11 Test (1)

Week 23	**Themes and Global Connections** *(1)* **Progress Assessment:** Unit 3 Test *(1)*

NEW YORK EDITION

Unit 4: Medieval Europe, 300–1500

TIME	LESSON AND ACTIVITY (NUMBER OF 45-MINUTE CLASSES)

Weeks 23–24	***HUMAN LEGACY***
	Unit 4: Medieval Europe, 300–1500 *(32)*
	Chapter 12: Kingdoms and Christianity, 300–1250 *(8)*
	  Section 1: The Byzantine Empire (2)
	    • *History and Geography:* City Astride Two Continents
	  Section 2: The Rise of Russia (2)
	    • *Faces of History:* Alexander Nevsky
	  Section 3: Christianity in Western Europe (2)
	  Document-Based Investigation (1)
	  Progress Assessment: Chapter 12 Test (1)

Weeks 25–26	**Chapter 13:** The Early Middle Ages, 800–1215 *(12)*
	  Section 1: Charlemagne's Empire (2)
	  Section 2: New Invaders (2)
	  Section 3: The Feudal and Manorial Systems (3)
	  Section 4: The Growth of Monarchies (2)
	    • *Faces of History:* Eleanor of Aquitaine
	  Section 5: Power of the Church (2)
	    • *Counterpoints:* Two Sources on the Power of the Papacy
	  Document-Based Investigation (1)
	  Progress Assessment: Chapter 13 Test (1)

Weeks 27–28	**Chapter 14:** The High Middle Ages, 1000–1500 *(10)*
	  Section 1: The Crusades (2)
	  Section 2: Trade and Towns (2)
	  Section 3: Art and Culture of the Middle Ages (2)
	    • *Focus on Themes:* Arts and Ideas
	  Section 4: Challenges of the Late Middle Ages (2)
	  Document-Based Investigation (1)
	  Progress Assessment: Chapter 14 Test (1)

Week 29	**Themes and Global Connections** *(1)* **Progress Assessment:** Unit 4 Test *(1)*

NEW YORK EDITION

Unit 5: New Ideas, New Empires 1200–1800

TIME	LESSON AND ACTIVITY (NUMBER OF 45-MINUTE CLASSES)

Weeks 30–31	**HUMAN LEGACY**
	Unit 5: New Ideas, New Empires, 1200–1800 *(35)*
	Chapter 15: Renaissance and Reformation, 1300–1650 *(11)*
	  Section 1: The Italian Renaissance (3)
	  Section 2: The Northern Renaissance (2)
	    • *World Literature:* Sonnets of Petrarch and Shakespeare
	  Section 3: The Protestant Reformation (2)
	  Section 4: The Counter-Reformation (2)
	    • *Focus on Themes:* Migration and Diffusion
	Document-Based Investigation (1)
	Progress Assessment: Chapter 15 Test (1)

Weeks 32–33	**Chapter 16:** Exploration and Expansion, 1400–1700 *(11)*
	  Section 1: Voyages of Discovery (3)
	  Section 2: Conquest and Colonies (2)
	  Section 3: New Patterns of Trade (2)
	  Section 4: The Atlantic Slave Trade (2)
	Document-Based Investigation (1)
	Progress Assessment: Chapter 16 Test (1)

Weeks 34–35	**Chapter 17:** New Asian Empires, 1200–1800 *(11)*
	  Section 1: The Ottoman and Safavid Empires (2)
	  Section 2: The Mughal Empire (2)
	  Section 3: The Ming and Qing Dynasties (3)
	    • *History and Geography:* The Voyages of Zheng He
	  Section 4: Medieval Japan and Korea (2)
	Document-Based Investigation (1)
	Progress Assessment: Chapter 17 Test (1)

Week 36	**Themes and Global Connections** *(1)* **Progress Assessment:** Unit 5 Test *(1)*

Unit 6: Changes in European Society, 1500–1820

TIME	LESSON AND ACTIVITY (NUMBER OF 45-MINUTE CLASSES)

Weeks 37–38	**HUMAN LEGACY**
	Unit 6: Changes in European Society, 1500-1820 *(33)*
	Chapter 18: Monarchs of Europe, 1500–1800 *(11)*
	  Section 1: The Power of Spain (2)
	  Section 2: Absolute Monarchy and France (3)
	    • *History and Economics:* Making Economic Decisions
	  Section 3: Monarchy in England (2)
	    • *The Arts Around the World:* Classical Music
	  Section 4: Rulers of Russia and Central Europe (2)
	    • *History and Geography:* Imperial St. Petersburg
	Document-Based Investigation (1)
	Progress Assessment: Chapter 18 Test (1)

Weeks 39–40	**Chapter 19:** Enlightenment and Revolution, 1550–1800 *(10)*
	  Section 1: The Scientific Revolution (2)
	  Section 2: The Enlightenment (3)
	    • *Reading Like a Historian:* Voltaire's *Candide*
	  Section 3: The American Revolution (3)
	Document-Based Investigation (1)
	Progress Assessment: Chapter 19 Test (1)

Weeks 41–42	**Chapter 20:** The French Revolution and Napoleon, 1789–1815 *(10)*
	  Section 1: The Revolution Begins (2)
	    • *World Literature: A Tale of Two Cities*
	  Section 2: The Republic (2)
	    • *Focus on Themes:* Government and Citizenship
	  Section 3: Napoleon's Europe (2)
	    • *Faces of History:* Napoleon Bonaparte
	  Section 4: Napoleon's Fall and Europe's Reaction (2)
	Document-Based Investigation (1)
	Progress Assessment: Chapter 20 Test (1)

Week 43	**Themes and Global Connections** *(1)* **Progress Assessment:** Unit 6 Test *(1)*

NEW YORK EDITION

Unit 7: Industrialization and Nationalism, 1700–1920

TIME	LESSON AND ACTIVITY (NUMBER OF 45-MINUTE CLASSES)

Weeks 43–44	*HUMAN LEGACY*
	Unit 7: Industrialization and Nationalism, 1700–1920 *(50)*
	Chapter 21: The Industrial Revolution, 1700–1900 *(8)*
	   Section 1: A New Kind of Revolution (2)
	   Section 2: Factories and Workers (2)
	   Section 3: New Ideas in a New Society (2)
	Document-Based Investigation (1)
	Progress Assessment: Chapter 21 Test (1)

Weeks 45–46	**Chapter 22:** Life in the Industrial Age, 1800–1900 *(8)*
	   Section 1: Advances in Technology (2)
	   Section 2: Scientific and Medical Achievements (2)
	   Section 3: Daily Life in the Late 1800s (2)
	Document-Based Investigation (1)
	Progress Assessment: Chapter 22 Test (1)

Weeks 47–48	**Chapter 23:** Reforms, Revolutions, and War, 1800–1900 *(11)*
	   Section 1: Reforms in the British Empire (2)
	   Section 2: Revolution and Change in France (2)
	   Section 3: Independence in Latin America (2)
	   Section 4: Expansion and War in the United States (3)
	Document-Based Investigation (1)
	Progress Assessment: Chapter 23 Test (1)

Weeks 49–50	**Chapter 24:** Nationalism in Europe, 1800–1920 *(11)*
	   Section 1: Italian Unification (2)
	   Section 2: German Unification (2)
	   Section 3: Austria-Hungary and the Ottoman Empire (2)
	   Section 4: Unrest in Russia (3)
	Document-Based Investigation (1)
	Progress Assessment: Chapter 24 Test (1)

Weeks 51–52	**Chapter 25:** The Age of Imperialism, 1800–1920 *(10)*
	   Section 1: The British in India (2)
	   Section 2: East Asia and the West (2)
	   Section 3: The Scramble for Africa (2)
	   Section 4: Imperialism in Latin America (2)
	Document-Based Investigation (1)
	Progress Assessment: Chapter 25 Test (1)

Week 53	**Themes and Global Connections** *(1)* **Progress Assessment:** Unit 7 Test *(1)*

NEW YORK EDITION

Unit 8: The World at War, 1914–1945

TIME	LESSON AND ACTIVITY (NUMBER OF 45-MINUTE CLASSES)

Weeks 54–55	**HUMAN LEGACY**
	Unit 8: The World at War, 1914–1945 *(35)*
	Chapter 26: World War I, 1914–1918 *(11)*
	  Section 1: The Great War Begins (2)
	    • *Faces of History:* Kaiser Wilhelm II
	  Section 2: A New Kind of War (3)
	  Section 3: Revolution in Russia (2)
	    • *Faces of History:* Vladimir Lenin
	  Section 4: The War Ends (2)
	    • *Faces of History:* Woodrow Wilson
	Document-Based Investigation (1)
	Progress Assessment: Chapter 26 Test (1)

Weeks 56–57	**Chapter 27:** The Interwar Years, 1919–1939 *(10)*
	  Section 1: Unrest in Asia and Africa (2)
	    • *Faces of History:* Mohandas Gandhi
	  Section 2: The Great Depression (2)
	    • *Focus on Themes:* Society
	  Section 3: Japanese Imperialism (2)
	  Section 4: Dictators in Europe (2)
	    • *Faces of History:* Adolf Hitler
	Document-Based Investigation (1)
	Progress Assessment: Chapter 27 Test (1)

Weeks 58–59	**Chapter 28:** World War II, 1930–1945 *(11)*
	  Section 1: Axis Aggression (2)
	  Section 2: The Allied Response (2)
	    • *History and Geography:* The Battle of Stalingrad
	  Section 3: The Holocaust (3)
	    • *Faces of History:* Anne Frank
	  Section 4: The End of the War (2)
	Document-Based Investigation (1)
	Progress Assessment: Chapter 28 Test (1)

Week 60	**Themes and Global Connections** *(1)* **Progress Assessment:** Unit 8 Test *(1)*

Unit 9: The Contemporary World, 1945–Present

TIME	LESSON AND ACTIVITY (NUMBER OF 45-MINUTE CLASSES)

Weeks 61–62	**HUMAN LEGACY**
	Unit 9: The Contemporary World, 1945–Present *(55)*
	Chapter 29: Europe and North America, 1945–Present *(11)*
	   Section 1: Beginnings of the Cold War (2)
	   Section 2: Superpower Rivalries (3)
	   Section 3: Changing Societies (2)
	   Section 4: After the Cold War (2)
	Document-Based Investigation (1)
	Progress Assessment: Chapter 29 Test (1)

Weeks 63–64	**Chapter 30:** Asia, 1945–Present *(11)*
	   Section 1: South Asia after Empire (2)
	   Section 2: Independence Struggles in Southeast Asia (2)
	   Section 3: China Changes Course (3)
	   Section 4: The Rise of Pacific Rim Economies (2)
	Document-Based Investigation (1)
	Progress Assessment: Chapter 30 Test (1)

Weeks 65–66	**Chapter 31:** Africa and the Middle East, 1945–Present *(11)*
	   Section 1: African Independence Movements (2)
	   Section 2: Post-Colonial Africa (2)
	   Section 3: Nationalism in the Middle East and North Africa (2)
	   Section 4: Conflicts in the Middle East (3)
	Document-Based Investigation (1)
	Progress Assessment: Chapter 31 Test (1)

Weeks 67–68	**Chapter 32:** Latin America, 1945–Present *(8)*
	   Section 1: Revolution and Intervention (2)
	   Section 2: The Rise of Dictatorships (2)
	   Section 3: Democratic and Economic Reforms (2)
	Document-Based Investigation (1)
	Progress Assessment: Chapter 32 Test (1)

Weeks 69–70	**Chapter 33:** Today's World *(12)*
	   Section 1: Trade and Globalization (3)
	   Section 2: Social Challenges (2)
	   Section 3: Threats to World Security (3)
	   Section 4: Environment and Technology (2)
	Document-Based Investigation (1)
	Progress Assessment: Chapter 33 Test (1)

Week 71	**Themes and Global Connections** *(1)* **Progress Assessment:** Unit 9 Test *(1)*

Unit 10: CASE STUDIES: Issues in the Contemporary World

TIME	LESSON AND ACTIVITY (NUMBER OF 45-MINUTE CLASSES)

Weeks 71–72	**HUMAN LEGACY**
	Unit 10: Case Studies: Issues in the Contemporary World *(8)*
	   Case Study 1: Civic Participation: The United Kingdom and South Africa (2)
	   Case Study 2: Developing Societies: Brazil and Mexico (2)
	   Case Study 3: Building Economic Powerhouses: China and India (2)
	   Case Study 4: Women in Society: Ireland and Turkey (2)
	   Case Study 5: The Role of the United Nations (2)
	Unit 10 Review (1)

Week 72	**Themes and Global Connections** *(1)* **Progress Assessment:** End-of-Year Test *(1)*

NEW YORK EDITION

HOLT brings history to life with an **engaging narrative** and **instructional visuals**

THE INSIDE STORY

What drove a Paris mob to fury? In April 1789 a rumor was flying through the Paris workers' neighborhoods: Réveillon the wallpaper manufacturer was about to slash his employees' wages in half. Although the rumor was probably false, an angry crowd of unemployed workers from various industries gathered at Réveillon's home. The home was famous for its gorgeous furnishings. Such wealth was in sharp contrast to the miserable poverty of the thousands of Parisians assembled there. When the crowd pushed into the house, Réveillon's family fled. Seeing the home's splendor—evidence of wealth that workers could never even hope for—the crowd went on a rampage, breaking and burning everything in sight. This event was just the beginning. Poverty and inequality would drive French workers to violence again and again. ■

Causes of the Revolution

In the 1780s, long-standing resentments against the French monarchy fueled anger throughout France. The source of the French people's ill will could be found in the unequal structure of French government and society.

Inequalities in Society A social and political structure called the **Old Order**, or ancien régime (ahns-yan ray-ZHEEM), created inequalities in French society. Under the Old Order, the king was at the top, and three social groups called estates were under him.

A Wallpaper Maker's BAD LUCK

▼ Poor laborers riot in the streets of Paris

The Inside Story introduces each section with a "story behind the story" that looks at key events and crystallizes them in compelling human terms.

Geography Starting Points provides geographical orientation for what students are studying.

GEOGRAPHY Starting Points

▶ Interactive
EUROPE, 1789

France was a powerful European country at the start of the French Revolution.

SWEDEN
NORWAY
RUSSIAN EMPIRE
ATLANTIC OCEAN
North Sea
DENMARK
Baltic Sea
GREAT BRITAIN
NETHERLANDS
London
PRUSSIA
POLAND
HOLY ROMAN EMPIRE
Paris
FRANCE
SWITZERLAND
Vienna
CARPATHIAN MTS.
HUNGARY
PARMA
MODENA
LUCCA
PAPAL STATES
Black Sea
PORTUGAL
Lisbon
Madrid
GENOA
Rome
VENICE
OTTOMAN EMPIRE
Constantinople
SPAIN
KINGDOM OF SARDINIA
KINGDOM OF THE TWO SICILIES
Mediterranean Sea

FRENCH EMPIRE, 1812
The French Empire controlled much of Europe.
Paris
Vienna
Madrid
Rome

0   150   300 Miles
0   150   300 Kilometers
Azimuthal equal-area projection

— Holy Roman Empire
☐ Habsburg possessions

Starting Points In the late 1700s France was one of Europe's large and powerful kingdoms. At that time, Europe was made up of a few large kingdoms and empires as well as many smaller states and territories. Then in 1789, the French Revolution set off a chain of events that reshaped Europe's political map.

1. Analyze Compare France on the large map to the French Empire on the inset map. What might have happened to allow France to become an empire?

2. Predict How do you think leaders of other European countries might have reacted as France expanded into other parts of Europe?

🎧 **Listen to History**
Go online to listen to an explanation of the starting points for this chapter.

go.hrw.com
Keyword: SHL NAP

592 CHAPTER 20

History's Impact Video Program
Watch the video to understand the impact of the French Revolution.

History's Impact Video Program helps students make connections between the impact of historical events and the world students live in today.

History Close-up features put students into the context of the time period, bringing to life the people, places, and concepts that they will learn.

Listening to History Audio CD Program includes musical and oratory selections that stimulate student interest and help them understand the sounds of an era.

Dynamic Maps and Quick Facts Charts offer a way to engage students and help review key content.

HOLT integrates reading strategies and fosters strong comprehensive skill development

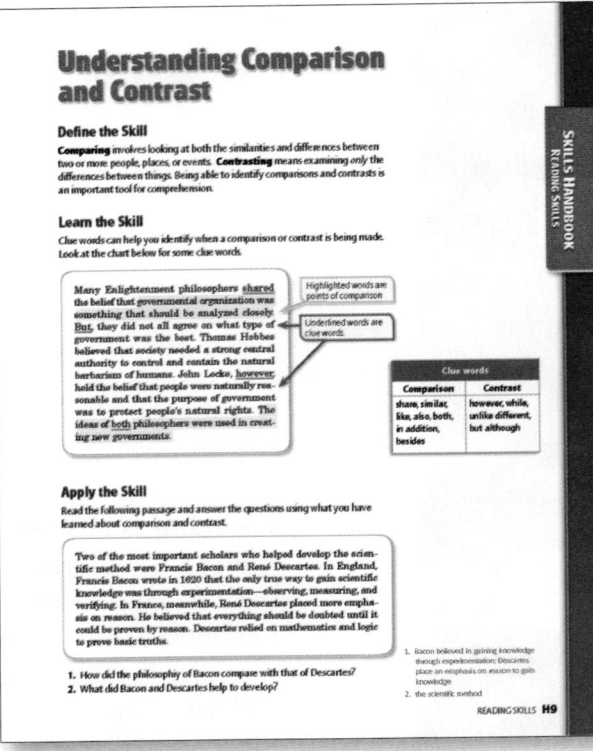

Reading Skills lessons focus on reading skills to help students learn how to access information that they will learn.

History and Geography features incorporate visual images and special-purpose map activities that help students see the connection geography has to history.

The **Interactive Reader and Study Guide** helps **all** students understand and master the content using
- visual summary and critical thinking questions to organize chapter content
- section-by-section interactive note-taking to master main ideas
- challenge activities to extend concept learning

Also available
Spanish/English Interactive
Reader and Study Guide

Focus on Themes

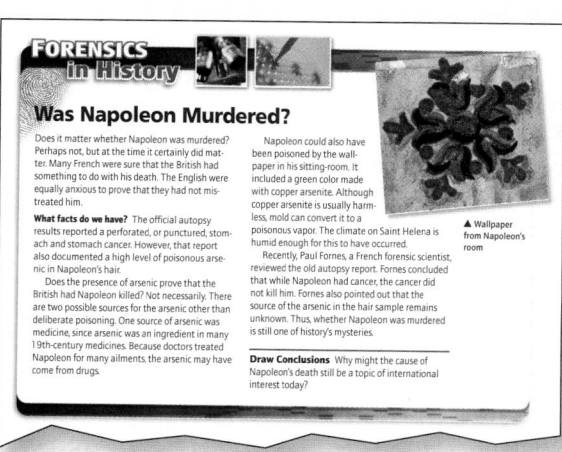

Forensics in History features uncover a mystery in history using the tools of modern science.

Focus on Themes and **Themes and Global Connections** encourage students to closely examine the content in context of a theme, developing their understanding of how historical events relate over time and to the present.

HOLT encourages the investigation of history and prepares students to succeed on tests through **document-based instruction**

Reading Like a Historian, integrated throughout the text, teaches students to analyze written and visual documents.

Reading like a Historian

Storming the Bastille

Analyzing Visuals One way we can learn about the past is by carefully analyzing works of art. The watercolor image on the right is Claude Cholat's *Storming the Bastille*. Even though Cholat was not a professional artist his painting interests historians because he was at the storming of the Bastille.

To interpret what this painting suggests about the French Revolution, think about

- the subject of the painting
- the title of the work
- the details in the painting

Skills Focus READING LIKE A HISTORIAN

1. **Subject and Title** Why do you think Cholat chose to paint the storming of the Bastille rather than some other event in the Revolution?
2. **Details** Why do you think Cholat included details of the entire day—from the initial attack on the Bastille to the flag of surrender—in this one image?
3. **Details** Why do you think Cholat put the scene in the courtyard in the foreground and the Bastille itself in the background?

See Skills Handbook, p. H26

Cholat compressed all the day's events into this single image.

A soldier atop the Bastille is waving a white flag to surrender. Other accounts of the day support this detail.

The men on the wall are cutting the chains that will lower the drawbridge leading to the Bastille.

Document-Based Investigation features have students analyze multiple documents, reach conclusions based on the investigation, answer critical thinking questions, and write DBQ essays.

CHAPTER 28 Document-Based Investigation

The Holocaust

Historical Context The documents below provide information about the Holocaust.

Task Examine the selections and answer the questions that follow. After you have studied the documents, you will be asked to write an essay about how an event like the Holocaust could have taken place. You will need to use evidence from these selections and from the chapter to support the position you take in your essay.

DOCUMENT 1

An American Soldier's Reaction

Leon Bass was an African American soldier who visited the Buchenwald camp in April 1945, shortly after it had been liberated by the Allies.

Then we saw the crematorium where the dead bodies were outside, stacked up like cordwood, and we went into the crematorium and you could see the residue in the ovens—the rib cages, the skulls. And it was so hard to believe—to understand why. What did these people do that merited this kind of treatment? And it boggles the mind when you think that it had gone on for almost ten years before we got into the war! Why wasn't it dealt with? Why did nobody scream and shout, 'Stop!' They never did.

DOCUMENT 2

A Gestapo Officer's Justification

Maximilian Grabner was the head of the Gestapo, or secret police, at the Auschwitz-Birkenau death camp. After the war's end, he tried to explain his actions.

To kill three million people is in my view the greatest crime of all. I only took part in this crime because there was nothing I could do to change anything. The blame for this crime lay with National Socialism [the Nazi Party]. I myself was never a National Socialist. Nevertheless, I still had to join the Party.

... I only took part in the murder of some three million people out of consideration for my family.

DOCUMENT 3

Nazi Camp Locations

Nazi prison camps spread throughout Europe as military victories brought more Jews under German control. Death camps were designed mainly to kill large numbers of Jews, while mobile killing units were Nazi police forces that traveled throughout Europe to execute Jews. Many of the Nazi camps were located near towns or cities in areas that had large Jewish populations.

NAZI CAMP LOCATIONS

DOCUMENT 4

A German Witness

Herman Graebe was a German engineer working in the Ukraine. On October 5, 1942, he accidentally discovered a Nazi mobile killing unit executing Ukrainian Jews. He later described what he saw.

I heard rifle shots in quick succession from behind one of the earth mounds . . . I walked around the mound and found myself confronted by a tremendous grave. People were closely wedged together and lying on top of each other so that only their heads were visible. Nearly all had blood running over their shoulders from their heads. Some of the people shot were still moving. Some were lifting their arms and turning their heads to show that they were still alive. The pit was nearly two-thirds full. I estimated that it already contained about a thousand people. I looked for the man who did the shooting. He was an SS [Nazi military police] man, who sat at the edge of the narrow end of the pit, his feet dangling into the pit. He had a tommy-gun on his knees and was smoking a cigarette.

DOCUMENT 5

An American Learns about Hitler's Plan

Howard Elting, Jr., was an American official stationed in Switzerland. The document below is from a letter he wrote to the U.S. secretary of state on August 10, 1942.

This morning Mr Gerhart M. RIEGNER, Secretary of the World Jewish Congress in Geneva, called in great agitation. He stated that he had just received a report from a German business man of considerable prominence, who is said to have excellent political and military connections in Germany and from whom reliable and important political information has been obtained on two previous occasions, to the effect that there has been and is being considered in Hitler's headquarters a plan to exterminate all Jews from Germany and German controlled areas in Europe after they have been concentrated in the east (presumably Poland). The number involved is said to be between three-and-a-half and four millions and the object is to permanently settle the Jewish question in Europe. The mass execution if decided upon would allegedly take place this fall.

Skills Focus READING LIKE A HISTORIAN

DOCUMENT 1
a. **Recall** What did Bass see at the camp?
b. **Infer** Do you think Bass believed that the Allies should have done more to stop the Holocaust? Why or why not?

DOCUMENT 2
a. **Explain** How does Grabner try to justify his actions?
b. **Analyze** What does Grabner mean by saying he took part in the murder "out of consideration for my family"?

DOCUMENT 3
a. **Identify** Which large cities were Nazi camps near?
b. **Draw Conclusions** Where were most Nazi camps and killing units located? Why?

DOCUMENT 4
a. **Recall** How many bodies does Graebe say were in the mass grave?

b. **Infer** What was the executioner's attitude toward the mass murder? How can you tell?

DOCUMENT 5
a. **Identify** What did Gerhart Riegner believe was going to happen to European Jews?
b. **Infer** Compare the date of Elting's letter to the date of the War Refugee Board's establishment. What do these dates suggest about the U.S. response to the Holocaust?

DOCUMENT-BASED ESSAY QUESTION

How could an event as large and as terrible as the Holocaust have taken place? Using the documents above and information from the chapter, form a thesis that explains your position. Then write a short essay to support it.

See Skills Handbook, p. H25

864 CHAPTER 28

WORLD WAR II **865**

Reading Like a Historian: World History Toolkit

encourages students to be history detectives through analysis of sources from a variety of perspectives on key historical topics. Includes:

- Professional essays
- Teaching strategies
- Primary and secondary sources
- Transparencies
- A classroom poster
- Online presentation resources

HOLT

Reading Like A Historian: World History Toolkit

- Encourage students to be history detectives
- Analyze sources from a variety of perspectives
- Investigate key historical topics

HOLT, RINEHART AND WINSTON

PRIMARY SOURCES

Hiroshima

Father John A. Siemes, a German priest, was in Hiroshima when the atomic bomb was dropped on August 6, 1945. He later described the explosion:

"Suddenly . . . the whole valley is filled by a garish light which resembles the magnesium light used in photography, and I am conscious of a wave of heat. I jump to the window to find out the cause of this remarkable phenomenon, but I see nothing more than that brilliant yellow light . . . I realize now that a bomb has burst . . .

"The bright day now reveals the frightful picture … Where the city stood everything, as far as the eye could reach, is a waste of ashes and ruin. Only several skeletons of buildings completely burned out in the interior remain. The banks of the river are covered with dead and wounded, and the rising waters have here and there covered some of the corpses . . .

"As a result of the explosion of the bomb … almost the entire city was destroyed at a single blow."

Skills FOCUS · READING LIKE A HISTORIAN

1. **Make Generalizations** What does this source tell you about the power of the atomic bomb?
2. **Analyze Primary Sources** How would you expect the Japanese government to respond to the bombing of Hiroshima?

See **Skills Handbook**, p. H25

Primary Sources help students analyze written and visual sources.

World Literature

CHARLES DICKENS (1812–1870)

About the Reading The French Revolution is the setting for *A Tale of Two Cities*, but the book was written many years later, in 1859. In both cities—London and Paris—the reader meets people who show the best and worst of human qualities. The passage below introduces one of the book's villains, here called Monsieur the Marquis, as he rides through Paris in his carriage. The scene takes place before the Revolution has truly begun.

AS YOU READ Think about why the poor people in the street react as they do.

Excerpt from

A Tale of Two Cities

by Charles Dickens

Driving his Mail Coach in Nice, by Alphonse de Toulouse-Lautrec-Monfa, 1881

With a wild rattle and clatter, and an inhuman abandonment of consideration not easy to be understood in these days, the carriage dashed through streets and swept round corners, with women screaming before it, and men clutching each other and clutching children out of its way. At last, swooping at a street corner by a fountain, one of its wheels came to a sickening little jolt, and there was a loud cry from a number of voices, and the horses reared and plunged.

But for the latter inconvenience, the carriage probably would not have stopped; carriages were often known to drive on, and leave their wounded behind, and why not? But the frightened valet had got down in a hurry . . .

"What has gone wrong?" said Monsieur, calmly looking out.

A tall man in a nightcap had caught up a bundle from among the feet of the horses, and had laid it on the basement of the fountain, and was down in the mud and wet, howling over it like a wild animal.

"Pardon, Monsieur the Marquis!" said a ragged and submissive man, "it is a child."

"Why does he make that abominable noise? Is it his child?"

"Excuse me, Monsieur the Marquis—it is a pity—yes." . . .

The people closed round, and looked at Monsieur the Marquis. . . [He] ran his eyes over them all, as if they had been mere rats come out of their holes.

He took out his purse.

"It is extraordinary to me," said he, "that you people cannot take care of yourselves and your children. One or the other of you is for ever in the way. How do I know what injury you have done my horses?"

Skills FOCUS · READING LIKE A HISTORIAN · World Literature Keyword: SHL WRLIT

1. **Explain** What was the Monsieur's main concern?
2. **Interpret Literature as a Source** What bias may show in Dickens's novel? What sources do you think Dickens used for information on the Revolution?

See **Skills Handbook**, p. H28

600 CHAPTER 20

World Literature features present students with the opportunity to analyze significant literature excerpts of the time period.

A World History Teacher's Guide to Analyzing Movies

HOLT

WORLD HISTORY

HUMAN LEGACY

HOLT, RINEHART AND WINSTON

A World History Teacher's Guide to Analyzing Movies provides full classroom support for critically viewing commercial movies with historical content and helps teachers use film as a source document.

HOLT ensures you can **differentiate instruction** for all students

Live Ink Online Reading Help is an online tool that displays the text of the *Holt Interactive Online Editions* in a way that improves comprehension and increases test scores.

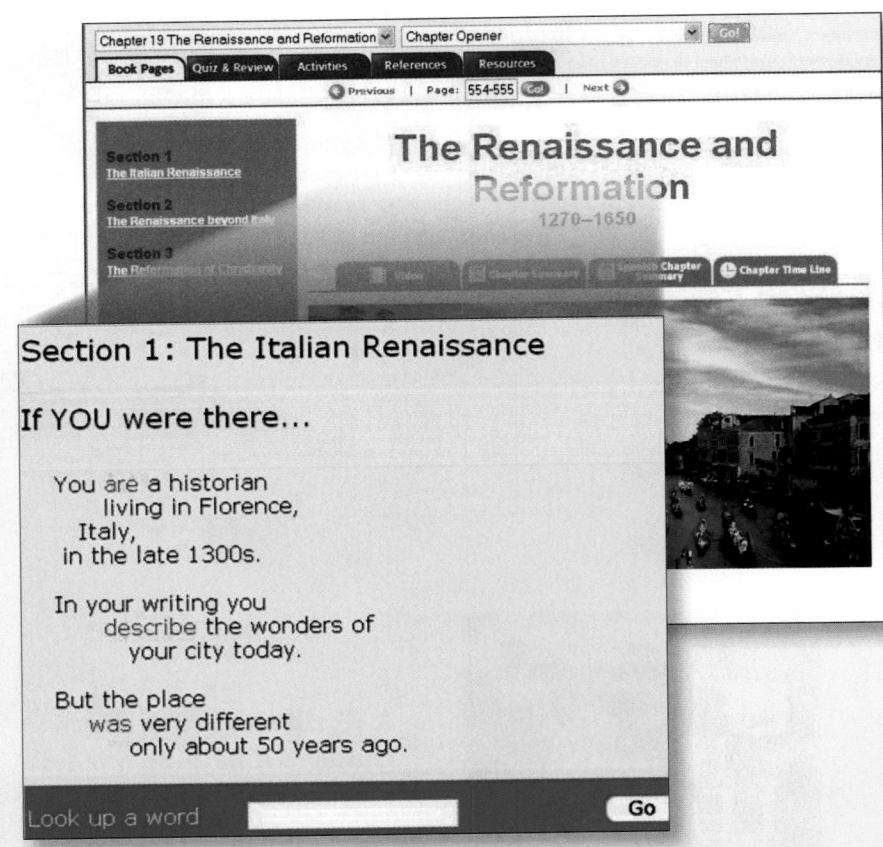

Differentiated Instruction Teacher Management System

HOLT

WORLD HISTORY

HUMAN LEGACY

INCLUDES:
- Benchmarking Guides
- Section Lesson Plans
- Lesson Plans for Differentiated Instruction
- Interactive Reader and Study Guide Teacher's Guide and Answer Key
- Test Preparation Workbook Answer Key

HOLT, RINEHART AND WINSTON

The **Differentiated Instruction Teacher Management System** provides Section Lesson Plans, Benchmarking guides, Lesson Plans for Differentiated Instruction, Teaching Guide, and Answer Keys.

Differentiated Instruction Modified Worksheets and Tests CD-ROM

HOLT

WORLD HISTORY

HUMAN LEGACY

The **Differentiated Instruction Modified Worksheets and Tests CD-ROM** provides all the key resources for the program modified to meet the specifications for students' Individualized Education Plans (IEPs.)

Interactive Skills Tutor CD-ROM

HOLT SOCIAL STUDIES

HOLT, RINEHART AND WINSTON

Interactive Skills Tutor CD-ROM helps students learn the Social Studies skills presented in the program. Each skill is introduced, practiced through interactive student activities, and then assessed for student mastery.

The **Progress Assessment Support System (PASS)** includes all the assessment for every chapter and unit to help you monitor students' progress.

PASS includes:
- Test-Taking Tips
- Diagnostic Test
- Section Quizzes
- Chapter Tests
- Unit Tests
- End-of-the-Year Test
- Answer Keys

The **ExamView® Version 5 Assessment Suite**, on the **Teacher's One-Stop Planner® CD-ROM**, makes it easy for you to reteach and offer more support to those students who need it.

Document-Based Activities for World History and the **Regents Test Prep Workbook** prepare students to succeed on high-stakes exams.

Quiz Game CD-ROM is an interactive multimedia game that assesses student understanding, makes learning fun, and tracks student performance.

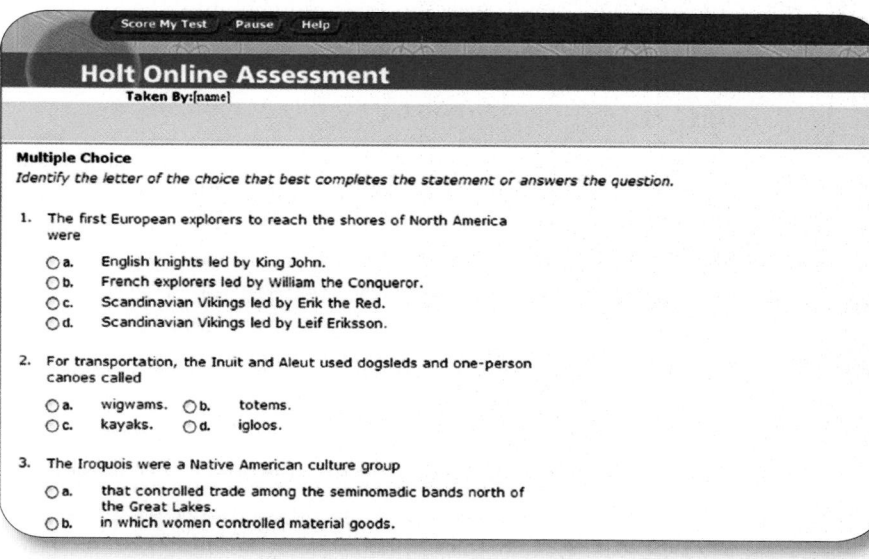

A new technology, **Holt Online Assessment** helps you assess students' mastery of the content.

◀ **Step 1**
Create a test

Step 2 ▶
Assign a test

Step 3 ▶
View Reports

EDUCATION GROUP

Teaching Readers About Our World Since 1868

#1 New York Times Bestseller

THE WORLD ALMANAC AND BOOK OF FACTS

80 MILLION COPIES SOLD

The World Almanac and Book of Facts has been delivering information about our world since the presidency of Johnson—Andrew Johnson! First published in 1868, *The World Almanac and Book of Facts* is America's all-time best-selling reference book, with more than 80 million copies sold.

Today, The World Almanac's experience and expertise at compiling, authenticating and distributing information extends throughout The World Almanac Education Group. We specialize in helping illuminate World History and the other social studies for students.

World Almanac **Key Events** in World History is a brief summary of important turning points in World History. It provides a capsule description of an event or movement, along with brief accounts of its significance. Use the section to review the content of Holt *World History Human Legacy*.

The World Almanac and Book of Facts itself devotes more than 200 pages to world history, providing quick answers about elections, world leaders, and events of the most recent year.

For information on all of these products, please contact
The World Almanac Education Group at
1-800-321-1147
or visit
www.worldalmanacbooks.com

World Almania
The game of fact-filled fun

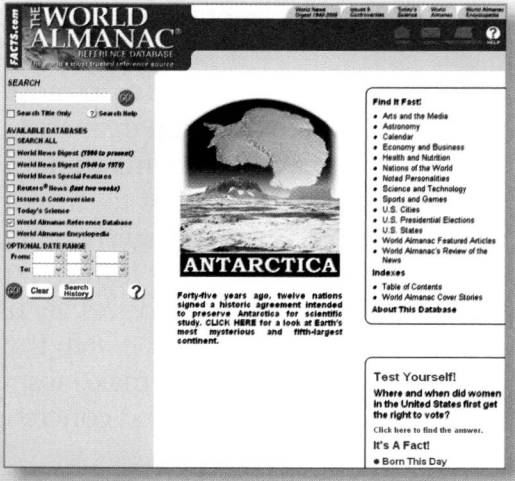

Social Studies Books, Kits and Databases for Your Classroom and Library

The World Almanac Education Group comprises *World Almanac Books, Facts On File News Services, World Almanac Education Library Services,* and *Gareth Stevens Inc.* These companies all offer valuable resources for world history and the other social studies. From engaging worksheet activities and supplemental classroom books that delve deeper into key curriculum areas to online database subscriptions, these materials can help you inspire your students to inquire about the world around them.

Social Studies Books

Gareth Stevens publishes acclaimed books series (with Teacher's Guides) in U.S. and World Geography, American and World History and American Government. Popular series include: *Great Cities of the World, Places in History,* and the *Great Rivers of the World.*

Teaching Kits

World Almanac Education Library Services offers skills kits that combine class sets of authoritative reference works with worksheets, videos, and posters to teach students valuable map and research skills. With a set of almanacs or atlases at hand, students quickly learn how to find and use information, while discovering the world around the corner and around the globe.

On-line Databases

Facts On File News Services delivers award-winning on-line subscription databases at **FACTS.com.** These easy-to-use, accessible-from-anywhere databases teach kids about current events, topical issues, and science news. For a free trial visit: **www.facts.com/legacy.** Teachers also love the *Issues & Controversies Yearbooks,* which give students a quick understanding of more than sixty of the year's most talked-about topics.

The World Almanac & World Almanac Book of Records

The World Almanac Education Group is founded on the reputation of *The World Almanac and Book of Facts,* the perennial number-one bestseller. Also look for the brand new *World Almanac Book of Records,* which includes fun and extensive coverage of World History.

Making Social Studies Accessible to English Learners

by Dr. Julie M.T. Chan

Dr. Julie M.T. Chan, Ed.D., is Director of Literacy Instruction in the Newport-Mesa Unified School District, located in Costa Mesa, California. She is a member of the California Reading and Literature Project, UCI/Orange County region, and serves on the state level CRLP Secondary Academic Language Tools development team. In addition, Dr. Chan teaches graduate courses on "The Sociocultural Contexts of Literacy and Learning" in the Masters of Reading program at California State University, Fullerton, and "Linguistics in Action in the Multicultural Classroom" at Concordia University in Irvine, California.

As increasing numbers of English-Language Learners (ELLs) enter the nation's secondary schools each year, it is incumbent upon all of us to help each student fully access the Social Studies curriculum.

Social Studies instruction relies heavily on language—oral language (listening/speaking) and written language (reading/writing). Because of their limited—but developing—proficiency in the English language, ELLs have a difficult time grasping the information presented orally by the teacher. In addition, they struggle when reading the printed text in Social Studies textbooks.

Chamot and O'Malley (1994) identified six areas where teachers can support ELLs: (1) Conceptual understanding, (2) Vocabulary, (3) Language functions and discourse, (4) Structures, (5) Academic language skills, and (6) Study skills and learning strategies. Here are some ways that teachers can make Social Studies accessible to English-Language Learners.

Conceptual Understanding While all students need to develop the concepts of time, chronology, distance, and differing ways of life, some ELLs may have never studied history or geography. Teachers could approach unfamiliar concepts and content by reading aloud trade books to build background knowledge and/or to provide a mental model at the beginning of a unit of study.

Vocabulary Students need to learn the content-specific, specialized terminology of Social Studies in order to discuss and report on the ideas studied. As students move up through the grades, the academic vocabulary of Social Studies becomes increasingly difficult because of the complexity of the concepts it represents. Thus, knowing which words to introduce and how and when to introduce them is critical.

Language Functions and Discourse In most school districts, students are expected to analyze, compare, contrast, and make judgments about Social Studies information. In contrast to the narrative discourse of texts designed for English language development, Social Studies materials feature expository patterns across various text structures. By using graphic organizers or mind maps that match the different text structures, teachers can make abstract ideas, concepts, and content visible and concrete for English Learners.

Differentiating Instruction

Below Level

English-Language Learners

1. Have students make a diagram of the power and social structure of feudal Japan. Students should write "Shogun" at the top edge of their papers. Have a volunteer name the next ruling class below the shogun. Have students add this to their papers.

2. Have students refer to the map and information in the section to make an approximate count of the daimyos. They can count the areas on the map and record an appropriate number next to the word (around 35).

3. Have volunteers name the working classes in descending order. Have students add the information to their own diagrams.

4. As a last step, have students work in mixed-ability pairs to add important details next to each class. **LS Verbal-Linguistic, Visual-Spatial**

Alternative Assessment Handbook, Rubric 1: Acquiring Information

Lessons designed to support instruction for English-Language Learners can be found throughout the Teacher's Edition.

Structures Oral and written language structures present special challenges to English-Language Learners. When teachers use research-based effective strategies to support oral and written language as well as published text structures, they can nudge their ELLs toward thinking, talking, reading, and writing like historians.

Academic Language Skills Students typically learn Social Studies through the receptive modes of listening and reading. In contrast, they "show what they know" through the productive modes of class discussions, oral presentations, and written products such as projects, reports, and expository/analytical essays. When the academic vocabulary of the content/concept to be studied is explicitly taught, ELLs can be more productive and therefore more successful at showing what they know.

Study Skills and Learning Strategies Chamot and O'Malley (1994) note that study skills, thinking skills, and social skills are also important components of the Social Studies curriculum. ELLs may not have, as yet, developed the learning strategies essential to these three skill areas. Thus teachers should help ELLs develop these skills so they can be better prepared to cope with the growing demands of new and abstract information found in grade-level Social Studies classrooms, textbooks, print materials, and primary source documents.

Teachers who are aware of the difficulties that ELLs encounter in their Social Studies classes will use this as an opportunity to explicitly teach those skills and strategies needed to be successful learners. Whether a teacher instructs regular Social Studies classes or a sheltered section, the result will be ELLs who have greater access to the Social Studies curriculum and who experience greater success as students moving toward the mainstream.

Billmeyer, Rachel (1996). *Teaching Reading in the Content Areas: If Not Me, Then Who?* Aurora, CO: McREL.

Buehl, Doug (2001). *Classroom Strategies for Interactive Learning.* Newark, DE: International Reading Association.

Chamot, Anna Uhl and J. Michael O'Malley (1994). *The CALLA Handbook: Implementing the Cognitive Academic Language Learning Approach.* Reading, MA: Addison-Wesley Publishing Company.

Roe, Betty, et al (1991). *Secondary School Reading Instruction: The Content Areas.* Boston, MA: Houghton Mifflin.

Tompkins, Gail E. (1997). *Literacy for the Twenty-First Century: A Balanced Approach.* Upper Saddle River, N.J.: Merrill.

ELL Instructional Support Services

- Use graphic organizers to teach abstract ideas.
- Teach specialized Social Studies vocabulary and usage.
- Promote development of study skills, thinking skills, and social skills.
- Read aloud content–related materials to help students build background knowledge.

Literacy and the Social Studies Teacher

by Carol Jago

Carol Jago teaches English at Santa Monica High School and directs the California Reading and Literature Project at UCLA. She is the author of *Cohesive Writing: Why Concept Is Not Enough* and *Papers, Papers, Papers: A Teacher's Survival Guide* (Heinemann 2005).

Q: Why should a Social Studies teacher have to teach reading and writing?

A: With a full curriculum of their own, many Social Studies teachers wonder why they should be expected to provide instruction in reading and writing? Isn't there enough to do just teaching history? There certainly is, but without strong literacy skills, students' ability to learn history is impaired. The idea is not that Social Studies teachers should become reading and writing teachers but rather that they should emphasize the classroom practices that are specific to learning history. For example, by helping students learn how to determine how to determine the gist of a textbook passage, Social Studies teachers reinforce what students need to know about distinguishing between important concepts and supporting details. By encouraging students to write like a historian, Social Studies teachers help students see how writing can be a powerful tool for thinking about controversial issues. By guiding students as they examine conflicting historical sources, Social Studies teachers help their students become critical readers with an eye for detail and point of view. The more students read and write, the more likely they are to retain what has been taught. Reading and writing help students learn history.

Q: What does research say about writing in Social Studies curriculum?

A: The National Commission on Writing in America's Schools and Colleges issued a report titled "The Neglected 'R'" calling for a writing revolution. NAEP research shows that only 50 percent of students meet "basic" levels of performance in writing and only one in five can be called "proficient." One student in five produces completely unsatisfactory prose. The 2003 report recommends that writing be incorporated into all state standards and that writing be required in every curriculum at all grade levels. "Very few things are more important to improving student achievement that restoring writing to its proper place in the classroom," said Commission Vice-Chair Arlene Ackerman, San Francisco superintendent of schools. "Writing is how we can teach students complex skills of synthesis, analysis, and problem solving." Given the controversial nature of so many topics in their curriculum, Social Studies teachers are uniquely positioned to help students develop these skills through persuasive writing.

Q: But how am I supposed to grade all those papers?

A: It isn't possible for teachers to work any harder. We need to work smarter. One method for assessing student writing effectively is to use rubrics. When the features of each numerical rubric score are laid out alongside a writing task, it is possible to assign a number to each student paper with confidence and, if not ease, efficiency.

Sample Scoring Rubric: Persuasive Essays

4 The Writing

- Clearly addresses all parts of the writing task
- Authoritatively defends a position with precise and relevant evidence
- Demonstrates a clear understanding of purpose and audience
- Maintains a consistent point of view, focus, and organizational structure, including the effective use of transitions
- Includes a clearly presented central idea with relevant facts, details, and/or explanations
- Includes a variety of sentence types
- Contains few, if any, errors in the conventions of the English language

2 The Writing

- Addresses only parts of the writing task
- Defends a position with little, if any, evidence and may address the reader's concerns, biases, and expectations
- Demonstrates little understanding of purpose and audience
- Maintains an inconsistent point of view, focus, and organizational structure, which may include ineffective or awkward transitions that do not unify important ideas
- Suggests a central idea with relevant facts, details, and/or explanations
- Includes little variety of sentence types
- Contains several errors in the conventions of the English language

3 The Writing

- Addresses all parts of the writing task
- Generally defends a position with relevant evidence and addresses the reader's concerns, biases, and expectations
- Demonstrates a general understanding of purpose and audience
- Maintains a mostly consistent point of view, focus, and organizational structure, including the effective use of some transitions
- Includes a central idea with relevant facts, details, and/or explanations
- Includes a variety of sentence types
- Contains some errors in the conventions of the English language

1 The Writing

- Addresses only one part of the writing task
- Fails to defend a position with any evidence and fails to address the reader's concerns, biases, and expectations
- Demonstrates no understanding of purpose and audience
- Lacks a point of view, focus, organizational structure, and transitions that unify important ideas
- Lacks a central idea but may contain marginally relevant facts, details, and/or explanations
- Includes no sentence variety
- Contains serious errors in the conventions of the English language

Scoring rubrics help Social Studies teachers assess student writing efficiently and effectively.

Social Studies teachers needn't feel that they must teach the mechanics of correctness. Language arts teachers recognize that this as their primary responsibility. By assigning writing, Social Studies teachers reinforce the lessons learned in English.

Q: With so much history to read, why are we asking students to read literature?

A: Literature helps bring history to life, animating historical events and allowing students to walk in the shoes of those who have lived long ago in places distant from their own experience. Good literature is also disturbing. It forces readers to examine the lives of others from the inside out, exposing young people to the complexity of the world they live in. Literature doesn't offer simple solutions. While reading fiction is not a vaccine for small-mindedness, it does make it difficult to think only of one's self. If one purpose of public education is to prepare students for the complex responsibilities of citizenship, I can think of no better preparation for these responsibilities than reading the work of Stephen Crane, Jack London, Frank Norris, Theodore Dreiser, and Upton Sinclair. Literature creates empathy and without empathy there can be little hope of a civilized society.

Standard English Learners
Language Acquisition as a Scaffold to Social Studies Curricula
by Dr. Noma LeMoine

Dr. Noma LeMoine, Ph.D., is a nationally recognized expert on issues of language variation and learning in African American and other students for whom Standard English is not native. She is Director of Academic English Mastery and Closing the Achievement Gap Branch for the Los Angeles Unified School District. She is a member of the National Citizen's Commission on African American Education, an arm of the Congressional Black Caucus Education Brain Trust. Dr. LeMoine is also the author of *English for Your Success: A Language Development Program for African American Students.*

Who are Standard English Learners?

Standard English Learners (SELs) are students for whom standard English is not native or whose home language—the language acquired between infancy and five years of age—structurally does not match the language of school. Standard English Learners include African American, Hawaiian American, Mexican American, and Native American students who have in common a linguistic history grounded in languages other than English. Prior to coming in contact with English their ancestors spoke African languages, Hawaiian languages, Latin American Spanish, or Native American languages. In each case these "involuntary minorities"—people who were enslaved, colonized, conquered, or otherwise subordinated in the context of America—combined English vocabulary with their native language and fashioned new ways of communicating in their new environments. These language forms, African American Language (often referred to as Black English); Hawaiian American Language (referred

Standard English Learners arrive at school in kindergarten as competent users of the language of their home but demonstrating limited proficiency in the language of school, that is, Standard American English. They are generally classified as English Only on school language surveys even though many of the rules that govern their home language are based in languages other than English. Because of their designation as English Only, these students' need for structured programs that support their acquisition of standard and academic English is often overlooked.

SEL Administrative Support Strategies

- Provide ongoing, comprehensive professional development for teachers and paraeducators including "literature circles" centered around the literature on the culturally and linguistically responsive instruction.

- Support the development of cooperative learning communities at the school site that engage teachers in review of the research, lesson study, peer coaching, and analysis of student work as a condition necessary for effectively educating SELs.

- Infuse information on the origin and historical development of standard and non-standard languages into the instructional curriculum.

to as Hawaiian Pidgin English); Mexican American Language (referred to as Chicano English); and Native American Language (sometimes referred to as Red English) incorporate English vocabulary, but differ in structure and form from standard American English.

Language Variation and Learning in SELs

In order for culturally and linguistically diverse Standard English Learners to succeed academically they must acquire the language, culture, and literacies of school. They must become literate in the forms of English that appear in newspapers, magazines, textbooks, voting materials, and consumer contracts. How best to facilitate this learning in Standard English Learners has proven elusive for most American public educational institutions and minimal emphasis has been placed on identifying instructional methodologies that scaffold SELs' access to core curricula. Learning is viewed as a social phenomenon and knowledge is recognized as a social construction that is influenced by the cultural and linguistic experiences, perspectives, and frames of references both students and teachers bring to the learning environment. For Standard English Learners this suggests that an instructional model, which validates and builds on prior knowledge experiences, language and culture while supporting the acquisition of school language through content learning is an appropriate pedagogy.

The Social Studies curriculum is perhaps the best vehicle for creating learning opportunities in both content and language acquisition areas. Opportunities to engage in critical thinking and participate in knowledge building abound in the Social Studies curriculum. As teachers help students develop skills as historians who re-create and share knowledge, students can also be provided opportunities to develop skills as speakers, readers, and writers.

SELs must be provided opportunities to add school language and literacy to their repertoire

SEL Instructional Support Strategies

- Incorporate contrastive analysis strategies (linguistic, contextual, situational, and elicited) into the daily instruction of SELs to facilitate mastery of academic language.

- Incorporate applicable SDAIE (Specially Designed Academic Instruction in English) strategies into instruction including utilization of visuals, manipulatives, graphic organizers, media and other tools to explain concepts.

- Provide continuous and varied opportunities for students to use language to interact with each other and the content through instructional conversations.

- Provide 30 to 45 minutes per day of Mainstream English Language Development (MELD) instruction that promotes the development of listening, speaking, reading, and writing skills in standard and academic English.

- Establish classroom libraries that include culturally relevant books and provide opportunities for SELs to be read to and to engage in free voluntary reading (FVR) on a daily basis.

- Encourage student/classroom development of a personal thesaurus of conceptually coded words to support the acquisition of academic vocabulary.

- Convey knowledge on ancient Africa, Mexico, Hawaii, and North America; their cultures and history.

- Convey knowledge of the impact of diverse cultures on the modern world with an emphasis on historical and contemporary achievers.

- Make connections to students' prior knowledge, experiences, and cultural funds of knowledge to support learning and retention of learned concepts.

of skills using instructional approaches that build on the culture and language they bring to the classroom. In order for SELs to experience greater success in accessing core curricula, teachers will need to construct learning environments that are authentic, culturally responsive, support language acquisition, and build upon the experiences, learning styles, and strengths of SELs.

Teaching Vocabulary and Comprehension

by Dr. Kylene Beers

Dr. Kylene Beers, Ed.D., is a Senior Reading Researcher in the School Development Program of the Child Study Center at Yale University. A former middle school teacher, Dr. Beers is a respected authority on struggling readers. She is the current editor of *Voices from the Middle,* the journal of the National Council of Teachers of English; co-editor of *Into Focus: Understanding and Creating Middle School Readers;* and the author of *When Kids Can't Read—What Teachers Can Do.* Dr. Beers was the 2001 recipient of the Richard W. Halle Award given by NCTE for outstanding contributions to middle school education.

Effective Vocabulary Instruction

"Preteaching vocabulary . . . requires that the words to be taught must be key words . . . be taught in semantically and topically related sets, . . . and that only a few words be taught per lesson."

—Tierney and Cunningham

The Right Words and the Right Number

The more vocabulary words we give students to learn weekly, the less chance students have of learning a word to the level needed to move it from short-term to long-term memory. Keeping the number between 5 and 10 means students have a better chance of retaining that word beyond the end of the week (Beers, 2002).

Consequently, choose wisely the words to be taught. Avid readers benefit by studying rare words—those highly unusual ones—because these students already have a solid vocabulary of the more common words. Struggling readers, however, benefit by focusing on high-utility words—those more common words that they are likely to see in other contexts. So, in the sentence, "The boys banked the canoe to the lee side of the rock," the inclination might be to teach the word *lee,* a rare word. However, if students don't know what *banked* means in this context or don't know the word *canoe,* it matters little what *lee* means. For struggling readers, a focus on high-utility words is more beneficial than a focus on rare words.

The Right Instructional Approach

Tierney and Cunningham (1984) explain that offering students a list of vocabulary words with their definitions is not as effective as placing each word within a semantic context. Students learn how to use words as they read or hear them used correctly. This textbook lists the key terms and people for each section at the beginning of that section. Defining these terms and using them in a sentence provides students with the semantic placement that most helps them learn words. Choosing the right number of the right words and presenting words in a semantic context helps students build their vocabulary and, as a consequence, improve their comprehension.

Improving Comprehension

"Comprehension is both a product and a process, something that requires purposeful, strategic effort on the reader's part as he or she predicts, visualizes, clarifies, questions, connects, summarizes, and infers."
—Kylene Beers

When the Text is Tough

"Comprehension is only tough when you can't do it," explained the eleventh-grader. I almost dismissed his words until I realized what truth they offered. We aren't aware of all the thinking we do to comprehend a text until faced with a difficult text. Then all too clearly, we're aware of what words we don't understand, what syntax seems convoluted, and what ideas are beyond our immediate grasp. As skilled readers, we know what to do—we slow our pace, reread, ask questions, connect whatever we do understand to what we don't understand, summarize what we've read thus far, and make inferences about what the author is saying. In short, we make that invisible act of comprehension visible as we consciously push our way through the difficult text. At those times, we realize that, indeed, comprehension is tough.

Reading Strategies for Struggling Readers

It's even tougher if you lack strategies that would help you through the difficult text. Many struggling readers believe they aren't successful readers because that's just the way things are (Beers, 2002). They believe successful readers know some secret that they haven't been told (Duffy, 2002). While we don't mean to keep comprehension a secret, at times that is what we do. For example, though we tell students to "reread," we haven't shown them how to alter their reading. We tell them to "make inferences," or "make predictions," but we haven't taught them how to do such things. In other words, we tell them what to do, but don't show them how to do it, in spite of several decades of research showing the benefit of direct instruction in reading strategies to struggling readers (Baumann, 1984; Pearson, P. D., 1984; Dole, et al., 1996; Beers, 2002).

Direct Instruction Direct instruction means telling students what you are going to teach them, modeling it for them, providing assistance as they practice it, then letting them practice it on their own. It's not saying, "visualize while you read," but, instead, explaining, "today, I'm going to read this part aloud to you. I'm going to focus on seeing some of the action in my mind as I read. I'm going to stop occasionally and tell you what I'm seeing and what in the text helped me see that." When we directly teach comprehension strategies to students by means of modeling and repeated practice, we show students that good readers don't just get it. They work hard to get it. Direct instruction takes the secret out of comprehension as it provides teachers the support they need to reach struggling readers.

Baumann, J. 1984.
"Effectiveness of a Direct Instruction Paradigm for Teaching Main Idea Comprehension." *Reading Research Quarterly,* 20: 93–108.

Beers, K. 2002.
When Kids Can't Read—What Teachers Can Do. Portsmouth: Heinemann.

Dole, J., Brown, K., and Trathen, W. 1996.
"The Effects of Strategy Instruction on the Comprehension Performance of At-Risk Students." *Reading Research Quarterly,* 31: 62–89.

Duffy, G. 2002.
"The Case for Direct Explanation of Strategies." *Comprehension Instruction: Research-Based Best Practices.* Eds. C. Block and M. Pressley. New York: Guilford Press. 28–41.

Pearson, P. D. 1984.
"Direct Explicit Teaching of Reading Comprehension." *Comprehension Instruction: Perspectives and Suggestions.* Eds. G. Duffy, L. Roehler, and J. Mason. New York: Longman. 222–233.

Tierney, R. J., and Cunningham, J. W. 1984.
"Research on Teaching Reading Comprehension." *Handbook of Reading Research.* Eds. P. D. Pearson, R. Barr, M. Kamil, P. Mosenthal. New York: Longman. 609–656.

Professional Resources and Bibliography

Professional References

This section provides information about resources that can enrich your Social Studies class. Included is information about guest speakers, museum visits, electronic field trips, nonprofit organizations, and many others. Since addresses change frequently, you may want to verify them before you send your requests. You may also want to refer to the HRW Web site at http://www.hrw.com for current information.

GUEST SPEAKERS

National Council for History Education
26915 Westwood Rd., Suite B-2
Westlake, Ohio 44145
440-835-1776
www.nche.net

K-12 Outreach for International and Area Studies
University of California, Berkeley
2223 Fulton Street Room 338 #2324
Berkeley, CA 94720-2324
510-643-0868
orias@berkeley.edu

MUSEUM VISITS

American Association of Museums
1575 Eye Street NW, Suite 400
Washington, DC 20005
202-289-1818
www.aam-us.org

ELECTRONIC FIELD TRIPS

Library of Congress/Congressional Server
www.loc.gov

E3 Electronic Field Trips
Teachers College (TC 1008)
Ball State University
Muncie IN 47306
866-279-8716
www.bsu.edu/eft

eFieldTrips.org
2960 W. Player Dr.
Snowflake, Arizona 85937
928-536-4954

NONPROFIT ORGANIZATIONS

The World History Association
Sakamaki Hall
A203, 2530 Dole St.
University of Hawai'i at Manoa
Honolulu Hawai'i 96822-2383
808-956-7688
www.thewha.org

PBS
www.pbs.org/history/history_world
html

National Council for the Social Studies
8555 Sixteenth Street, Suite 500
Silver Spring, MD 20910
301-588-1800
www.socialstudies.org

National Trust for Historic Preservation
1785 Massachusetts Ave. NW
Washington, DC 20036
202-588-6000
www.nationaltrust.org

National History Day
University of Maryland
at College Park
0119 Cecil Hall
College Park, MD 20742
301-314-9739
www.nationalhistoryday.org

GOVERNMENT RESOURCES

U.S. Department of Education
400 Maryland Ave., SW
Washington, D.C. 20202-0498
800-USA-LEARN
www.ed.gov

Smithsonian Institution
Smithsonian Information
P.O. Box 37012
SI Building, Room 153, MRC 010
Washington, DC 20013-7012
202-357-2700
www.si.edu

The Library of Congress
101 Independence Ave, SE
Washington, DC 20540
202-707-5000
www.loc.gov

National Register of Historic Places
National Park Service
1201 Eye Street, NW MS 2280
Washington, DC 20005
202-354-2213
www.cr.nps.gov/nr

SUBSCRIPTION SERVICES

Magazines.com Inc.
P.O. Box 682108
Franklin, TN 37068
800-929-2691
www.magazines.com

MISCELLANEOUS

Educational Resources Information Center (ERIC)
ERIC Project
c/o Computer Sciences Corporation
4483-A Forbes Blvd.
Lanham, MD 20705
800-538-3742
www.eric.ed.gov

The International Initiatives Program
American Council on Education
One Dupont Circle NW, Washington
DC 20036

Busy Teachers' WebSite K-12
http://www.ceismc.gatech.edu/busyt

A Bibliography for the Social Studies Teacher

This bibliography is a select compilation of resources available for professional enrichment.

SELECTED AND ANNOTATED LIST OF READINGS

Social Studies and Language Arts

Burke, Jim. *Writing Reminders: Tools, Tips, and Techniques*
Portsmouth, NH: Heinemann, 2003
Burke offers a collection of strategies for teaching writing, complete with the instructional tools for implementing the strategies.

Jago, Carol. *Cohesive Writing: Why Concept Is Not Enough*
Portsmouth, NH: Heinemann, 2002
This book provides a coherent roadmap for teaching students how to write in each of the writing types required for the STAR assessment: summary, narrative, response to literature, and persuasion.

Social Studies and Standard English Mastery

LeMoine, N. and Los Angeles Unified School District. *English for Your Success: A Language Development Program for African American Students. Handbook of Successful Strategies for Educators.*
New Jersey: The Peoples Publishing Group, 1999
English for Your Success provides lessons using proven strategies for facilitating language acquisition and learning in African American Standard English Learners.

Ornstein-Galicia, J. *Form and Function in Chicano English*
Malabar, FL: Krieger Publishing Co., 1988
This text address issues of language and learning in Mexican American Standard English Learners (SELs) who speak mainly Chicano English.

Social Studies and English Learners

Billmeyer, Rachel and Mary Lee Barton. *Teaching Reading in the Content Areas: If Not Me, Then Who?* Second Edition
Aurora, CO: Mid-Continent Regional Educational Laboratory (McREL), 1998
These 40 strategies help students of all ages expand their vocabularies, understand different types of texts, and discuss what they have read.

Buehl, Doug. *Classroom Strategies for Interactive Learning,* Second Edition
Newark, DE: International Reading Assoc., 2001
More than 40 literacy strategies for middle school and high school educators outside the reading field.

Readance, John, Thomas W. Bean and R. Scott Baldwin. *Content Area Literacy: An Integrated Approach.* Eighth Edition
Dubuque, IA: Kendall/Hunt Publishing Company, 2000
The authors provide strategies for helping students read, understand, and enjoy nonfiction. A CD accompanies this widely used text.

Themes of History

No two historical events or periods are exactly alike, but there are common themes that can be traced through all of human history. As you read *Human Legacy,* look for the eight themes described below. They appear again and again, not just in this textbook, but throughout history. These themes help you see ways all peoples and societies are alike and ways they are different.

ARTS AND IDEAS

Some of the noblest human aspirations and achievements have been enshrined in artworks and in ideas. The arts can inspire us, and ideas can move us to action.

- What ideas unite and motivate a society?
- How does a culture express itself through its arts and ideas?
- How do the arts of different societies express enduring human needs and beliefs?

BELIEF SYSTEMS

Beliefs can be powerful forces for societies as well as individuals. Religious beliefs, for instance, have inspired great works of devotion, sacrifice, and art. They can also serve to define and divide people.

- What do people believe about the nature of the universe?
- What do people believe about how society should be ordered and governed?
- How do beliefs motivate people?

ECONOMIC SYSTEMS

Because resources are scarce and people's needs and wants are many, every society needs an economic system by which to allocate available resources. Economic systems may change—from a simple barter system to today's complex global capitalism—but the need to order the exchange of goods, services, and resources remains a constant in human history.

- How are scarce resources allocated in a society?
- Why have some people or groups of people had more resources than others?
- How do economic systems affect political and social systems?
- How do different systems strive to ensure efficiency? fairness?

GEOGRAPHY AND ENVIRONMENT

Geography and environment influence the way societies develop. A desert society develops different economic and social practices than a sea faring one. People both modify their environment and adapt to it in order to best meet their needs.

- How do people change their environment and make changes to their environment?
- In what ways do geography and environment influence a society?

Economic Systems

NORTH POLE

Since 1979 more than 20% of the Polar Ice Cap has melted away.

ARCTIC SEA ICE BOUNDARY IN 1979

Geography and Environment

GOVERNMENT AND CITIZENSHIP

Today, most people believe that a government's power comes from the consent of the governed—that in government, citizens are the ultimate authority. But that belief is relatively new. Different societies—in the past and even today—adopt different forms of government.

- What is the proper form of government?
- Who should be a citizen? Why has that question had different answers at different times?
- What is the relationship between those who govern or rule and those who are governed or ruled?

MIGRATION AND DIFFUSION

From the days of the earliest humans in Africa, people have been on the move, hunting animals, looking for fresh fields to plant, and seeking new places for trade. The movement of peoples, goods, and ideas has the power to transform and even destroy empires and nations.

- What are the large patterns of movement that shape human history?
- How are new ideas, ways of doing things, and diseases spread?
- What motivates people to seek new lands?

SCIENCE AND TECHNOLOGY

Humans use science to try to understand their environment, and they use technology to try to shape and control it. The urge to understand the world and to invent new tools to shape it is a fundamental aspect of human nature.

- What are the different concepts that people have had about the world? How have they changed over time?
- How have the tools people used changed over time, often radically reshaping the limits of human possibility?
- How have technological advances given one society advantages over another?

SOCIETY

The complex pattern of relationships—political, economic, cultural—that bind people together make a society. In any historical period, these patterns may be loosely defined or they may be embodied in institutions such as governments and churches.

- What are the social classes that make up a society?
- How is political and economic power distributed?
- What are the customs and norms that unite a society?

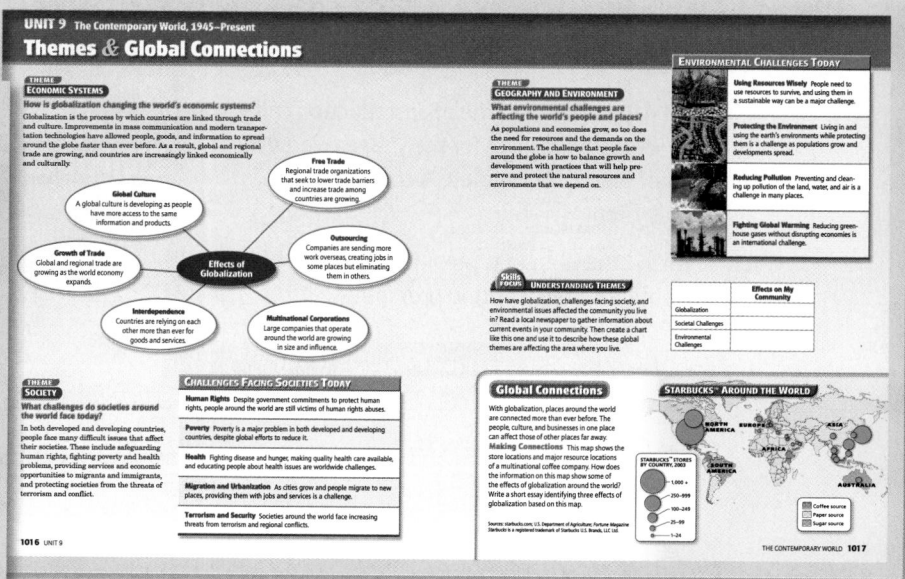

Human Legacy allows you to track important themes through history. Look for special themes of history features as you read.

How to Use Your Textbook

Holt World History: Human Legacy, New York Edition was created to make your study of world history an enjoyable, meaningful experience. Take a few minutes to become familiar with the book's easy-to-use organization and special features.

Unit

Unit Openers list the chapter titles and the years the chapters cover. Each unit opener identifies the main themes covered in the unit. A historic painting or photograph or painting illustrates the time period you are about to explore.

Themes and Global Connections features end each unit. Graphic organizers and tables show how each unit theme relates to the period of history covered in the unit. A Global Connections box helps you examine the global impact of key developments in history.

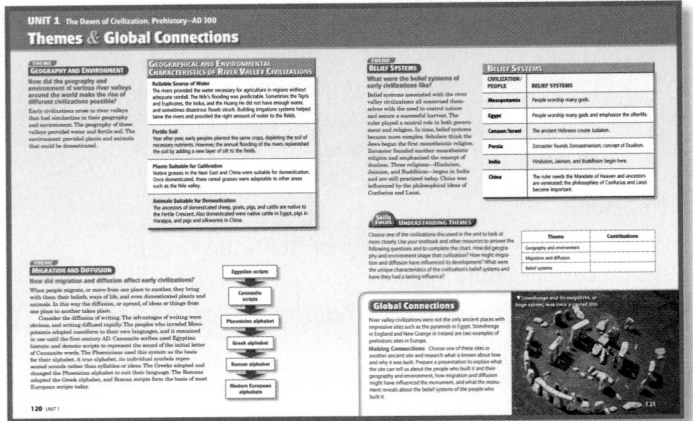

Chapter

Chapter Openers include an introduction called The Big Picture, a time line for the years covered in the chapter, and a photograph. A chapter theme is also highlighted.

Chapter Review pages provide a full array of assessments, including writing prompts.

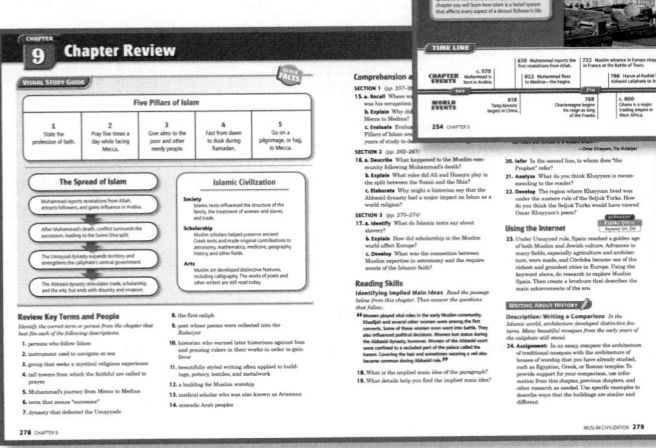

Section

Each section begins with a Main Idea statement, Focus Questions, and Key Terms and People. In addition, each section includes the following special features:

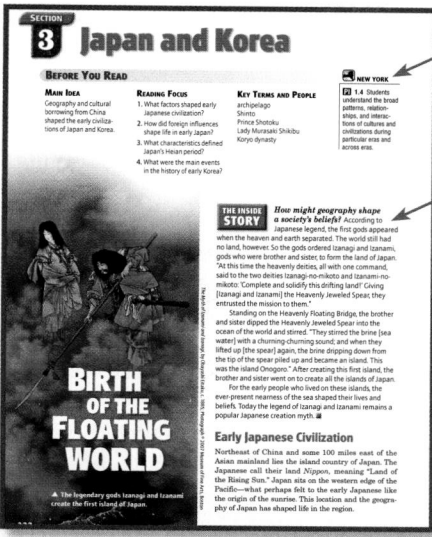

New York Learning Standards for Social Studies Performance Indicators appear at the beginning of each section.

The Inside Story begins the section with an on-the-scene story from history.

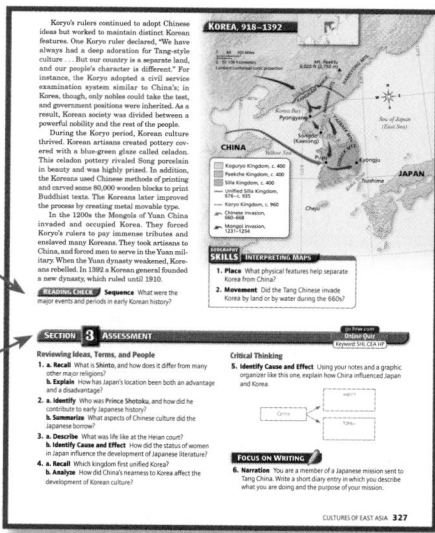

Reading Check questions provide frequent opportunities to review and assess your understanding.

Section Assessment questions help you check your understanding of a section's main ideas. There is also assessment practice online.

Regents Prep and Practice

Holt World History: Human Legacy, New York Edition provides many opportunities to help you prepare for the Regents Exam.

Document-Based Investigation features appear at the end of every chapter. They allow you to analyze and write about historical documents.

Regents Practice tests appear at the end of every unit. They follow a format like the kind used on the Regents Exam.

> **TIP** For extra practice in getting ready for the New York Regents Exam, go to the New York Department of Education website address below. There you will find an archive of Regents exams from years past.
>
> http://www.nysedregents.org/testing/hsregents.html

Scavenger Hunt

Holt World History: Human Legacy, New York Edition opens a window on the past. Before you begin your journey into the past, take a minute to familiarize yourself with this book and its contents.

On a separate piece of paper, write the answers to the Scavenger Hunt questions below. Enjoy your journey.

1 How many units and chapters are in the book? How do you know?

2 Where in *Human Legacy* do you find the atlas?

3 The Reading Like a Historian section in the front of the book offers students instruction in various skills, such as analyzing primary sources. Name two other places in *Human Legacy* where you find additional Reading Like a Historian skills practice.

4 Where and how do you find key terms and people for Chapter 7, Section 1?

5 Where in *Human Legacy* do you find case studies on issues in particular parts of the world?

6 *Human Legacy* was created to help you meet all of the New York social studies standards. Where do you find a description of these standards?

7 Where do you find review questions to help you study?

8 If you want help with test-taking strategies, where do you look?

9 Where do you look to find a list of all of the primary sources used?

10 Where can you find a map that gives you an introduction to Chapter 31?

xxxiv

Answers

1. *10 units and 33 chapters; by checking the table of contents;* **2.** *in the reference section in the back of the book;* **3.** *Students should list any two of the following features: Reading Like a Historian, Primary Sources, World Literature, and Document-Based Investigation.* **4.** *beneath the heading "Key Terms and People" at the top of page 671;* **5.** *in Unit 10: Case Studies: Issues in the Contemporary World;* **6.** *in the front of the book on pages NY2–NY9;* **7.** *the Reading Check questions throughout each section, the Section Assessment questions at the end of each section, and in the Chapter Reviews;* **8.** *in the Test-Taking Strategies section beginning on page H40;* **9.** *in the table of contents;* **10.** *in the Geography Starting Points feature on page 936*

Skills Handbook
with Test-Taking Strategies

Reading Skills

Social Studies Skills

Reading Like a Historian Skills

Writing and Speaking Skills

Test-Taking Strategies

New York Standards

Key Idea 4 The skills of historical analysis include the ability to investigate differing and competing interpretations of the theories of history, hypothesize about why interpretations change over time, explain the importance of historical evidence, and understand the concepts of change and continuity over time.

Becoming an Active Reader

by Dr. Kylene Beers

Do you read a letter or email from a friend the same way you read a newspaper article? What about a poem and the instructions to an exam? Or a novel and a textbook? Chances are the answer is no: you read differently depending on your purpose for reading. When you are reading for information, such as when you are reading a textbook, you have a different purpose than when you are reading just for fun.

A different purpose calls for a different way of reading. In a textbook, especially a history book, there are a lot of facts, concepts, and unfamiliar words and names. You can't expect to absorb all that if you just let the words slide by. You have to be an active reader—questioning what you read, anticipating, making connections, stopping to review.

Human Legacy is structured to help you be an active reader. Sections, for example, are organized in outline format, with main heads and subheads to help you navigate the material. There are frequent review questions to help you assess whether or not you are absorbing the main points. Take a moment to familiarize yourself with some of the ways that this textbook facilitates reading comprehension.

❶ Reading Focus and Reading Check The Reading Focus questions act as a type of outline for each section. The Reading Check questions offer opportunities to assess what you have learned as you go.

❷ Key Terms and People At the beginning of each section you will find a list of terms, people, places, and events that you will need to know. Watch for these words as you read.

❸ Reading Skills Good readers use a number of reading skills and strategies to make sure they understand what they are reading. In the margins, look for questions that reinforce the reading skills you will be learning in this handbook.

❹ Academic Vocabulary When we use a word that is important in all classes, not just in social studies, we define it in the margin under the heading Academic Vocabulary. You will see these words in other textbooks, so you should learn what they mean while reading this book.

SECTION 1

Revolution and Intervention

BEFORE YOU READ

MAIN IDEA
In reaction to economic and social conditions in Latin America after World War II, many Central American countries experienced conflicts that involved intervention by the United States.

READING FOCUS
1. What were some key economic and social trends in postwar Latin America?
2. How did the Cuban Revolution come about and what changes did it bring?
3. What other conflicts arose in Central America?

KEY TERMS AND PEOPLE
import-substitution led industrialization
Liberation Theology
Fidel Castro
Che Guevara
Sandinistas
junta
Contras

NEW YORK
11 1.2 Students understand the development and connectedness of Western civilization and other civilizations and cultures in many areas of the world over time.
11 1.4 Students understand the broad patterns, relationships, and interactions of cultures and civilizations during particular eras and across eras.

LAND FOR THE LANDLESS

◀ Members of Brazil's Landless Workers' Movement march to the capital.

THE INSIDE STORY *Who has a right to a country's land?* ...

LATIN AMERICA **967**

U.S. Involvement Cuba's move toward communism during the Cold War troubled U.S. leaders. They viewed Latin America as part of a U.S. sphere of influence and wanted to keep communism out of the region. Shortly after World War II, the United States helped set up the Organization of American States (OAS), an organization of countries in the Americas that promotes economic and military cooperation. The OAS was strongly anticommunist.

Repeated U.S. attempts to oust Cuba's communist leaders failed. In 1961 a U.S.-trained invasion force of Cuban exiles landed in the Bay of Pigs, along Cuba's southern coast. Their mission was designed to spark a nationwide uprising against Castro. But it was a disaster. Cuban troops easily defeated the invaders.

Still stinging from this defeat, U.S. president John F. Kennedy soon found himself in a far more serious crisis with Cuba and the Soviet Union. In 1962 the CIA learned that the Soviet Union was building nuclear missile sites in Cuba. Missiles from these sites would be able to easily hit targets in America. Kennedy ordered a naval blockade to intercept Soviet ships loaded with missiles for Cuba. This tense confrontation, known as the Cuban missile crisis, brought the world as close to nuclear war as it had ever been. In the end, however, a compromise was reached, and the Soviet Union removed the missile sites.

Results of the Revolution In the years since these Cold War conflicts, the Cuban Revolution has had mixed results. For example, Cubans have good access to health care and education. However, people's civil liberties are restricted under a one-party system. The government jails opponents and watches citizens through a network of neighborhood spies.

Economic effects have also been mixed. Castro's policies led many Cubans to leave the country. Most went to the United States, and Cuba's economy struggled as a result. Castro relied on the Soviet Union for economic support. But when the Soviet Union collapsed in 1991, Cuba's economy suffered. Cuba has also suffered for decades because of a U.S. economic embargo.

READING CHECK **Identify Cause and Effect** What were some of the causes and effects of the Cuban Revolution?

Other Conflicts
As in Cuba, economic inequality was a serious problem in other Central American countries. Yet economic conditions were not the only cause of conflicts. Political corruption and repression affected many places as well. In addition, U.S. support for anticommunist but corrupt governments stirred nationalist passions in Guatemala, El Salvador, and Nicaragua.

Guatemala In 1952 Guatemala's president, Jacobo Arbenz, used land reform to take over large landholdings and distribute the land to peasants. This policy hurt the United Fruit Company, an American company that owned huge amounts of mostly uncultivated land in Guatemala.

Pressure from the United Fruit Company, along with concerns that Arbenz was a leftist, or radical, persuaded the U.S. government that Guatemala's president must be removed from power. The CIA intervened in a coup that toppled Arbenz in 1954 and replaced him with a military dictator. The coup was the start of nearly a half century of repressive dictatorships in Guatemala.

The harshness of the government and the end of social reforms upset many peasants. Some joined rural guerrilla forces, and civil war raged from the 1970s to the 1990s between the guerrillas and government troops. Finally, in 1996, a peace accord brought an end to the fighting.

El Salvador Civil war also struck El Salvador, where military dictatorships kept power through unfair elections and repression. In 1980 government assassins gunned down Archbishop Oscar Romero, an outspoken government critic, as he was leading mass. Romero was one of many priests in Latin America who supported Liberation Theology.

Romero's murder sparked a bloody civil war between Communist-supported guerrilla groups and the army. Peasant villagers were often caught in the middle as government-sponsored "death squads" roamed the countryside killing civilians suspected of aiding the opposition. The Reagan administration supported the Salvadoran government and the army by providing money and military aid. Violence continued into the 1990s.

READING SKILLS
Understanding Causes and Effects What caused conflicts in Central America?

ACADEMIC VOCABULARY
intervene to enter into an event to affect its outcome

LATIN AMERICA **971**

Read Like a Skilled Reader

How can you become a more skilled reader? For starters, you first need to *think* about how to become a better reader. You also can use the following ideas and strategies.

Skilled readers . . .

- Preview what they are supposed to read before they begin reading. They look for titles of chapters and sections, listings of main ideas and focus questions, vocabulary words and key terms, information in the margin such as Academic Vocabulary, and visuals such as charts, graphs, maps, and photographs

- Construct tables or K-W-L charts into which they organize ideas from the reading. They write notes in the tables or charts as they read.

- Use clues from the text, such as the signal words shown below, to help determine or cement understanding.

  Sequencing words: *first, second, third, before, after, soon, later, next, then, following that, earlier, finally*

  Cause and effect words: *because, so, since, due to, as a result of, the reason for, therefore, brought about, led to, thus, consequently*

  Comparison and contrast words: *likewise, similarly, also, as well as, unlike, however, on the other hand*

Active Reading

*Successful readers are **active readers**. Active readers know that it is up to them to figure out what the text means. Here are some steps you can take to become an active and successful reader.*

Predict what will happen next on the basis of what already has happened in the text. When your predictions do not match what happens in the text, reread to clarify meaning.

Question what is happening as you read. Constantly ask yourself why events happen, what certain ideas mean, and what causes events to occur.

Summarize what you are reading frequently. Do not try to summarize an entire chapter! Instead, break a chapter into smaller parts. Read some of the text and summarize. Then move on.

Connect events in the text to what you already know or have read.

Clarify your understanding by pausing occasionally to ask questions and check for meaning. You may need to reread to clarify or read further to collect more information before you gain understanding.

Visualize people, places, and events in the text. Envision events or places by drawing maps, making charts, or taking notes about what you are reading.

Building Your Vocabulary

Holt Human Legacy helps you build your vocabulary by highlighting two types of vocabulary words. Key terms and people are listed at the beginning of every section. These are words you need to know to master the social studies content. You will encounter the definitions of the terms as you read the section. You can also turn to the Glossary for definitions. Academic vocabulary are words you need to know for other classes. They appear in the margins of sections. Below is a list of these academic vocabulary words, along with their definitions.

Academic Word/Definition

administer to manage or to run	**export** an item sent to other regions for trade
allocate to distribute for a particular purpose	**framework** the context or background for an action or event
amendment a written change to a legal document	**fundamental** basic
assessed evaluated or determined	**generation** group of people born and living about the same time
assume believe to be true	**hypothesis** assumption or theory
blockade to isolate an enemy by using troops or warships	**ideology** a system of ideas, often political
commerce trade or the exchange of goods	**immigrate** to move to another country to live
commission to order the creation of something such as a piece of art	**import** bring into a place or country
component part or element	**incorporated** combined or made into one body or unit
constraints limitations	**infrastructure** public works, such as buildings and roads, that are needed to support a population
currency money	**initiate** to begin
cycle to alternate among two or more things or events	**institute** to originate and establish
despite in spite of	**integrate** to blend or join together
deviate to turn away from a course or topic	**intermittent** happening from time to time, not constant
discrimination the act of treating a person differently because of race, gender, or national origin	**intervene** to enter into an event to affect its outcome
displace to cause a person, animal, or thing to move from its usual place	**invest** to commit money in order to make a financial return
distribution the spread of something among a group of people	**irrelevant** not appropriate or related to the subject
diverse made up of many elements, varied	**labor** work
domestic relating to the home or to household activities	**legislation** laws or rules passed by a governing body
entity having an independent or separate distinction	**legitimacy** the right to rule
ethnic common background or culture	**liberal** supporter of political and social reform
	maintain keep up or support

maximize	to increase to the greatest possible level
patriarch	father figure
perspective	personal point of view
phase	a period or stage within a longer process
portray	to show or depict something, such as a person or a scene
preclude	to prevent something or someone from doing something
predominant	most common or important
prejudiced	biased against a racial, religious, or national group
preliminary	coming before and usually forming a necessary introduction to something else
privileges	special rights granted to certain people because of their position in society
prohibition	an order or law that forbids
proportion	the size or amount of a thing in relation to another thing
prosperity	wealth or success
rational	having reason or understanding
regime	a specific and often harsh government
region	an area with one or more common features
regulation	a law designed to control or govern conduct

resolved	determined
revenue	money that a government uses to pay for public programs
sacraments	solemn Christian rites believed to have been instituted by Jesus Christ
scope	extent or degree
sector	a subdivision of society
security	freedom from danger or fear
stability	resistance to change or destruction
stance	an attitude, position, or view about someone or something
status	position or rank
subsequent	later; following in time
sufficient	enough of what is needed
synthesize	to combine several parts into a whole
technique	method, way of performing a task
theories	plausible general principles offered to explain what has been observed
utilize	to make use of
valid	correct or justified
violate	break or ignore
welfare	well-being

A Note about Chronological Terms

Historians like to fix exact dates on events, but that isn't as easy as it seems. Different cultures and different historical eras use different methods for dating events. The ancient Romans, for example, measured dates by the years in the reign of an emperor.

The system of dating used in the West began around AD 525, though it did not gain general acceptance in Europe until the 1200s. *Holt Human Legacy* follows this common usage. The table below shows some of the terms used in dating events and their meanings.

Chronological Terms

BC short for "Before Christ," it refers to dates before the birth of Jesus	**BCE** short for "Before the Common Era," it refers to dates before the birth of Jesus
AD short for Anno Domini, Latin for "in the Year of the Lord," it refers to dates after the birth of Jesus	**CE** short for "Common Era," it refers to dates after the birth of Jesus

Identifying Main Ideas and Details

SKILLS HANDBOOK
READING SKILLS

Define the Skill

The **main idea** is the central thought in a passage. It is a general statement that conveys the key concept the author wants the reader to know. The main idea can come at the beginning, middle, or end of a passage, although it is most often found at the beginning. The main idea can be one or two sentences and can be implied or directly stated.

Details are statements that support or explain the main idea. Details are specific and provide additional information to the reader, such as the *who, what, when, where, why,* and *how* of the main idea. Details include statements, statistics, examples, explanations, and descriptions.

Learn the Skill

Read the passage below and note how the details support the main idea.

> France continued to grow and change during the era of the Third Republic. Officials wrote a new constitution under which the government would have a two-house legislature and a president. Public education laws required free education for children between the ages of 6 and 13. Union membership became legal. All men now had the right to vote.

Main Idea
France continued to grow and change during the era of the Third Republic.

Details			
Detail 1	**Detail 2**	**Detail 3**	**Detail 4**
Officials wrote a new constitution that would have a two-house legislature and a president.	Public education laws required free education for children aged 6 to 13.	Union membership became legal.	All men had the right to vote.

Apply the Skill

Turn to Section 4 of the chapter titled Reforms, Revolutions, and War and locate the blue head titled "Effects on Native Americans." Use a graphic organizer like the one above to identify the main idea and details of the passage.

1. Identify the main idea in the passage. Restate it in your own words.
2. What details support the main idea?
3. Explain how the details add to the main idea.

1. By moving west, white settlers were often moving onto land that had been inhabited for thousands of years by Native Americans. Conflict between Native Americans and settlers was frequent.
2. Indian Removal Act, Trail of Tears
3. Answers will vary; possible answer: Supporting details give the results of the conflicts between settlers and Native Americans.

Sequencing

Define the Skill

Placing events in chronological order is called **sequencing**. By sequencing, you can gain a greater, more accurate understanding of the events that took place. Learning to sequence can also help you to understand relationships among events, including how a past event can influence present and future events.

Learn the Skill

Days, months, and years can help in determining sequence. Clue words, such as *before, after, then, by, first,* and *next,* can also help.

First Event World War I
Date 1914

By 1914 conditions in Russia were so bad that the arrival of World War I provided some relief for Nicholas and his top government officials. In late 1915 Czar Nicholas II decided to take personal command of the Russian forces. After the czar took command of the troops, things grew even worse for Russia. By the end of 1916, Russia was once again on the edge of a revolution. Change finally arrived in Russia on March 8, 1917 as unhappy citizens took to the streets of Petrograd, the Russian capital, to protest the lack of food.

Second Event Czar Nicholas II takes command of Russian forces.
Date 1915

Last Event Citizens take to the streets.
Date March 8, 1917

Third Event Things grew worse for Russia.
Clue Word *after*

Apply the Skill

Identify the three main events in the passage below and place them in correct chronological order. List the clue words or dates that signal the order of the events.

The year 1917 went badly for the Allies. A failed French offensive in the spring caused rebellion among some French troops. In July, the British launched an offensive near Ypres, in Belgium. Known as the Third Battle of Ypres, it was a disaster for the British. The Germans held the only bit of high ground in the very flat area, and they used it effectively to defend the region. In November, the British assault was finally called off.

1. In what year did the British launch the offensive near Ypres?
2. What happened in November 1917?
3. How long did the Battle of Ypres last?

1. 1917
2. the British assault was called off
3. 5 months

Identifying Causes and Effects

Define the Skill

By understanding **causes and effects** and seeing connections between them, you can determine why certain events occurred and whether events are related. A *cause* is something that makes something else happen. Often times a cause will be directly stated in the text. Occasionally, a cause will be implied—or stated indirectly. An *effect* is something that happens as the result of a cause. One cause may have more than one effect and, similarly, an effect may have several causes. Identifying causes and effects can help you better understand what you have read.

Learn the Skill

Identify the causes and effects in the passage. Start by identifying a cause and then look for one or more of the effects. Look for clue words such as *since, because, therefore,* and *however.*

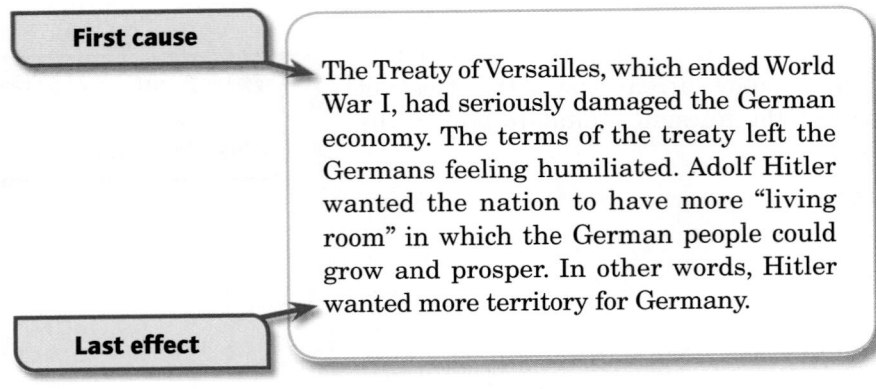

First cause

The Treaty of Versailles, which ended World War I, had seriously damaged the German economy. The terms of the treaty left the Germans feeling humiliated. Adolf Hitler wanted the nation to have more "living room" in which the German people could grow and prosper. In other words, Hitler wanted more territory for Germany.

Last effect

Cause
The Treaty of Versailles

↓

Effect
The German economy was damaged.

↓

Effect
Germans felt humiliated.

↓

Effect
Hitler wanted more territory for Germany.

Apply the Skill

Read the following sentences and answer the questions using what you have learned about identifying causes and effects.

At the end of the war, much of Europe and Asia lay in ruins. Tens of millions of people had died in the war, many of them civilians. In many areas the physical devastation was nearly complete. Entire cities, villages, and farms had been destroyed or damaged heavily, and national economies were near collapse.

1. What were the effects of the war on civilians?
2. What caused the collapse of national economies?
3. Identify one effect of the war on cities and villages.

1. millions of civilians died
2. the devastation of farms from the war
3. entire villages and cities were destroyed

Understanding Comparison and Contrast

Define the Skill

Comparing involves looking at both the similarities and differences between two or more people, places, or events. **Contrasting** means examining *only* the differences between things. Being able to identify comparisons and contrasts is an important tool for comprehension.

Learn the Skill

Clue words can help you identify when a comparison or contrast is being made. Look at the chart below for some clue words.

> Many Enlightenment philosophers <u>shared</u> the belief that governmental organization was something that should be analyzed closely. <u>But</u>, they did not all agree on what type of government was the best. Thomas Hobbes believed that society needed a strong central authority to control and contain the natural barbarism of humans. John Locke, <u>however</u>, held the belief that people were naturally reasonable and that the purpose of government was to protect people's natural rights. The ideas of <u>both</u> philosophers were used in creating new governments.

Highlighted words are points of comparison.

Underlined words are clue words.

Clue Words	
Comparison	**Contrast**
share, similar, like, also, both, in addition, besides	however, while, unlike, different, but, although

Apply the Skill

Read the following passage and answer the questions using what you have learned about comparison and contrast.

> Two of the most important scholars who helped develop the scientific method were Francis Bacon and René Descartes. In England, Francis Bacon wrote in 1620 that the only true way to gain scientific knowledge was through experimentation—observing, measuring, and verifying. In France, meanwhile, René Descartes placed more emphasis on reason. He believed that everything should be doubted until it could be proven by reason. Descartes relied on mathematics and logic to prove basic truths.

1. How did the philosophy of Bacon compare with that of Descartes?

2. What did Bacon and Descartes help to develop?

1. Bacon believed in gaining knowledge through experimentation; Descartes place an emphasis on reason to gain knowledge.

2. the scientific method

Making Inferences

Define the Skill

Sometimes reading effectively means understanding both what the writer tells you directly and what the writer implies. By filling in the gaps, you are **making inferences**, or educated guesses. Making inferences involves using clues in the text to connect implied ideas with ideas that are stated. You also draw on your own prior knowledge and use common sense to make inferences.

Learn the Skill

To make an inference, study what the passage says. Think about what else you know about the subject, and then make an educated guess about the implied meaning.

> Though he became prime minister through democratic means, Mussolini quickly became a dictator. Not satisfied with simply having political control, he sought to influence the thoughts, feelings and behaviors of the Italian people. This attempt to control all aspects of life is called totalitarianism.

1. What the passage says
Mussolini favored a totalitarian form of government.

2. What you know about the topic or can connect to your experience. In their drive for control, dictators violate the democratic rights of their citizens.

3. Make an inference. Totalitarianism threatened democracy in Italy.

Apply the Skill

Read the following passage and then use the three steps described above to make an inference about it.

> The worst day was October 29, known as Black Tuesday. On that single day, investors sold off 16 million shares. With few people wanting to buy the stocks that flooded the Market, stock prices collapsed completely. Many investors who had borrowed money to buy stocks were forced to sell at a loss to repay their loans.

1. On Black Tuesday, what economic crisis did the United States face?
2. Using the reading and your prior knowledge, explain the effects that a major economic crisis can have on a country's people.
3. What can you infer about the effects of the stock market crash?

1. the stock market collapse
2. possible answers: unemployment, loss of savings, homelessness
3. Answers will vary; possible answer: The collapse of the stock market led to such economic crises as unemployment and loss of life savings on a large scale.

Identifying Problems and Solutions

Define the Skill

Throughout history, people have faced problems and sought solutions to those problems. As a result, historians describing historical events often structure their writing by identifying a problem and then describing its actual or possible solutions. By **identifying problems and solutions**, you can better understand the challenges that people have faced over time and the means by which they have resolved such difficulties.

Learn the Skill

Look for problems that are identified in the reading and then determine what solutions were or are being pursued. Most problems have more than one solution.

In spite of international agreements, <u>people around the world continue to suffer human rights abuses.</u> Arbitrary arrest, torture, slavery, and even killing are daily occurrences in some countries. <u>The United Nations works to protect human rights</u> by monitoring areas of concern, investigating abuses, and working with national governments to improve conditions. Moreover, as <u>globalization advances, stronger economic conditions can help foster adherence to human rights standards.</u> Not only do opportunities increase, helping children to get an education and more women to find jobs, but businesses gain an incentive to follow practices that will help them avoid potentially ruinous publicity.

Problem
Human rights are being violated in the world.

Solution 1
The UN works to protect human rights.

Solution 2
Globalization improves economic situations in many countries.

Apply the Skill

Use a graphic organizer like the one above to identify the problems and solutions in the following passage.

During recent years, the number of worldwide terrorist attacks has increased, as has the violence of these attacks. After September 11, 2001, the United States government took many actions to prevent future terrorist attacks. It sought to strengthen its international and domestic intelligence services. It increased its focus on the security of the nation's borders and transportation networks. It sought to find and cut off the funding sources for terrorist networks.

1. What problem does the U.S. face from terrorism in recent years?

2. Identify two solutions that the U.S. used to address these problems after September 11.

1. the number of worldwide terrorist attacks have increased as well as the violence level of such attacks

2. strengthened its international and domestic intelligence service; increased its focus on the security of the nation's borders; found and cut off the funding sources for terrorist networks

Drawing Conclusions

Define the Skill

Historical writing provides you with facts and information. But often you have to determine the meaning of events on your own. You need to combine the facts and information, along with your prior knowledge, to draw conclusions about the reading. In **drawing conclusions**, you analyze the reading and form opinions about its meaning.

Learn the Skill

To draw conclusions, combine the information you find in the reading with what you already know. Look for a common link or theme. Then put it all together.

> Drawing on the work of Faraday and Swan, Thomas Edison developed the first usable and practical lightbulb in 1879. The new invention caused a sensation. Having created a demand for lightbulbs, Edison then needed to supply the electricity that powered them. So he built the world's first central electric power plant in New York City. The plant illuminated several city blocks. As a result of Edison's work, life during the Industrial Age became easier and more convenient.

Information gathered from the passage you are reading	+	What you already know about the topic	=	What all the information adds up to—your conclusion
Thomas Edison invented the lightbulb in 1879 and built the world's first central electric plant.		Electricity is a huge part of people's lives today and is used in many capacities in everyday life.		The invention of the lightbulb was one of the first steps towards the modernized world we know today.

Apply the Skill

Read the following sentences. Think about what you know about telephone usage today. Use the process above to draw conclusions about the passage.

> One day, Bell and his assistant Thomas Watson were working on a new device. Bell suddenly yelled, "Mr. Watson, come here, I need you!" Watson was pleased to hear Bell's voice not just from across the room, but through the device's receiver as well. The telephone was born.
>
> During the 1880s, demand for telephones increased, and telephone companies quickly laid thousands of miles of phone lines in every region of the United States. By 1900 almost 1.5 million telephones were in American homes and offices. The telephone was on its way to becoming the ubiquitous instrument it is today.

1. When did telephone usage become commonplace in the United States?
2. What information can you conclude about the importance of the telephone in creating modern communications?

1. 1900
2. Answers will vary; possible answer: Modern communications rely heavily on the use of the telephone and related products that have been made after its advent, like the cell phone.

Making Generalizations

Define the Skill

A generalization is a statement that applies to different examples or situations not just to one. When **making generalizations**, you collect different examples, identify what they have in common, and then make a statement that applies equally to all examples.

Learn the Skill

In the passage, identify examples that have something in common. Then try to make a generalization that applies to all the examples.

> For many years, right-wing military dictatorships ruled Argentina. They struggled with declining industry as well as rising unemployment, inflation, and foreign debt. Meanwhile, they cracked down on dissent by severely limiting personal freedoms.
>
> In Brazil, as opposition to their military dictatorship grew, the economy crashed. Oil prices rose in the 1970s and the economy fell into debt and hyperinflation, a very high level of inflation that grows rapidly in a short period of time. The inflation rate exceeded 2,500 percent by 1993.

Example 1:
Argentina's military dictatorships struggled with declining industry, inflation, and foreign debt.

+

Example 2:
In Brazil, the military dictatorships led the economy into debt and hyperinflation.

=

Generalization:
Many Latin American countries under military dictatorships had struggling economies.

Apply the Skill

Using the process described above, make a generalization about the struggles in Latin America.

> In El Salvador, a civil war broke out in which Communist-supported groups battled the army. Villagers were often caught in the middle as the government's army roamed the countryside killing civilians suspected of aiding the opposition.
>
> In Nicaragua, control was in the hands of the Somoza family who had ruled for four decades. The Somozas' anticommunist views kept them in favor with the United States, but their corruption and violent repressive tactics alarmed many Nicaraguans. An anti-Somoza movement gained strength.

1. What conflict took place in El Salvador?

2. What was a problem of the Somoza family in Nicaragua?

3. Make a generalization about Latin American political struggles.

1. a civil war

2. They were corrupt and violent.

3. Answers will vary; possible answer: Many Latin American countries are plagued with violence and war as a result of their governments.

Interpreting Time Lines

Define the Skill

A **time line** organizes events that occurred during a specific period of time into chronological order. It has a beginning date and an ending date. The *time span* is the years between the beginning date and the ending date. *Time intervals* mark shorter increments of time within the time span. They appear at regular intervals, for example, every 5 or 10 years. Two time lines can be used to list events that happened within a certain time span but at different places. These are called *parallel time lines*. There are parallel time lines at the beginning of each chapter in this book.

By organizing events chronologically, time lines can help you see how events are related. Seeing how events are related can help you find cause-and-effect relationships between the events. Time lines also allow you to compare, contrast, and draw conclusions about historical events.

Learn the Skill

Use the following strategies to read the time line.

1 Identify the time span of the time line.
Look at the beginning date and the ending date to determine the time period.

TIME LINE

Changes in France's Government

1830 King Charles fled France during the July Revolution and Louis Philippe was crowned king.

1848 After the Revolution of 1848, Louis Philippe abdicated and the Second Republic formed with Louis Napoleon as president.

1852 Louis Napoleon arrested members of the National Assembly and the French elected him emperor.

1871 A strong democratic government with a new constitution emerged during the Third Republic.

2 Determine the time intervals of the time line.
Check to see whether the years are evenly spaced. Determine whether the time is divided by decades, by centuries, or by another division.

3 Analyze the events on the time line.
Recognize the types of events that the time line describes and determine how they are related.

Apply the Skill

1. What is the time span of the time line?
2. What are the time intervals of the time line?
3. How are the events on the time line related?

1. 1830–1871
2. They vary: 18 years, 4 years, 19 years.
3. They all deal with changes in the French government in the mid-1800s.

Interpreting Line and Bar Graphs

Define the Skill

Graphs are diagrams that present statistical or numeric data. They can display amounts, trends, ratios, or changes over time. A **line graph** is a visual representation of data organized so that you can see a pattern of change over time. In most cases, the *vertical axis* of a line graph shows quantities while the *horizontal axis* shows time. A **bar graph** compares quantities. A single bar graph compares one set of data, while a double bar graph compares two sets of data. Knowing how to interpret line graphs and bar graphs can help you recognize historical trends.

Learn the Skill

Use the following strategies to interpret the line graph.

Use the following strategies to interpret the bar graph.

1 **Read the title of the graph.**
The title tells you the subject or purpose of the graph.

1 **Read the title of the graph.**
Read the title and the legend to determine the subject of the graph.

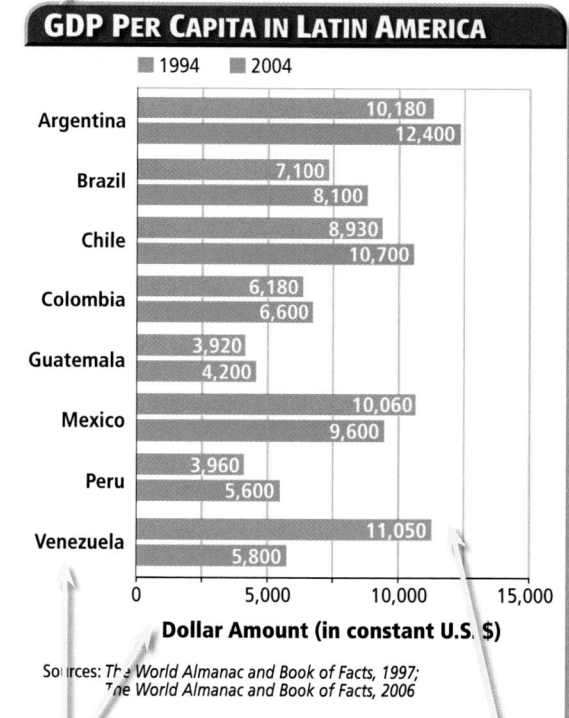

2 Read the horizontal and vertical axis labels.
The labels explain what the graph measures and gives the units of measurement.

3 Analyze the information on the graph.
Look at the slant of the line. The closer the line is to being parallel to the horizontal axis, the slower the change. The closer the line is to being perpendicular to the horizontal axis, the quicker the change.

2 Read the horizontal and vertical axis labels.
The labels tell what the bar graph measures and gives the units of measurement.

3 Analyze the information on the graph.
Compare the amounts shown on the bar graph.

Apply the Skill

1. What information does the line graph compare?
2. What information does the bar graph compare?
3. What conclusion can you draw from the data in the bar graph?

1. Brazil's foreign debt from the years 1965 to 1985
2. the GDP per capita for selected countries in Latin America in 1994 and 2004

3. possible answers: Venezuela had a greater GDP per capita in 1994 than in 2004; Argentina had a greater GDP per capita in 2004 than in 1994; Guatemala had the lowest GDP per capita in both years.

Interpreting Pie Graphs

Define the Skill

A **pie graph** is a circular chart that shows how individual parts relate to the whole. The circle of the pie symbolizes the whole amount. The slices of the pie represent the individual parts of the whole. Knowing how to interpret pie graphs will allow you to better understand and evaluate historical data as well as to recognize historical trends.

Learn the Skill

Use the following strategies to interpret the pie graph.

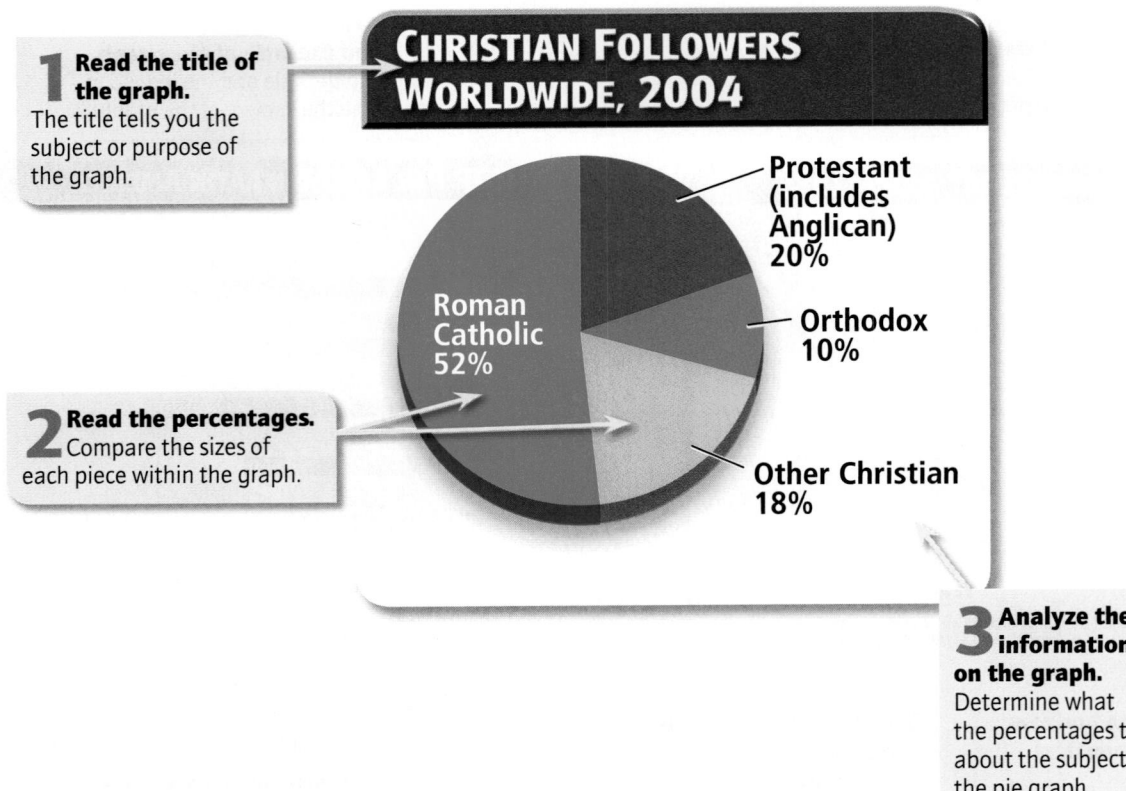

1 **Read the title of the graph.**
The title tells you the subject or purpose of the graph.

CHRISTIAN FOLLOWERS WORLDWIDE, 2004

Protestant (includes Anglican) 20%

Orthodox 10%

Roman Catholic 52%

Other Christian 18%

2 **Read the percentages.** Compare the sizes of each piece within the graph.

3 **Analyze the information on the graph.** Determine what the percentages tell about the subject of the pie graph.

Apply the Skill

1. What information does the pie graph compare?

2. Which religion has the fewest number of followers?

3. What percentage of the world follows other religions not listed in the graph?

1. the percentage of people who practice each religion
2. Orthodox
3. 55%

Interpreting Charts

Define the Skill

Charts are visual representations of information. Historians use charts to organize, condense, simplify, and summarize information in a convenient, easy-to-read format.

Simple charts combine or compare information. *Tables* classify information by groups. Numbers, percentages, dates, and other data can be classified in the columns and rows of a table for reference and comparison. *Diagrams* illustrate the steps involved in a process so that the information is easier to understand. Knowing how to read and use charts allows you to interpret, compare, analyze, and evaluate historical information.

Learn the Skill

Use the following strategies to interpret the chart.

1 Read the title of the chart. The title tells you the subject of the chart.

2 Look at the way the information is organized. Charts can be organized alphabetically, chronologically, or by topic.

3 Analyze the information found in the chart. Interpret, compare, and contrast the information in the chart to draw conclusions and make inferences or predictions.

MAJOR JAPANESE EVENTS 1929 TO 1940

QUICK FACTS

1929 The Great Depression hits Japan.

1931 Japan takes control of Manchuria, China.

1933 Japan withdraws from the League of Nations.

1934 Japan announces it will no longer submit to limits on its navy.

1936 Japan signs agreement with Germany.

1937 Japanese troops kill hundreds of thousands of civilians in Nanjing, China.

1940 Japan attempts to expand its power in Asia by proposing an economic alliance of Asian nations.

▼ Japanese troops in Shanghai, China

Apply the Skill

1. How is the information in the chart organized?
2. How many events are listed on the chart?
3. According to the chart, what major event occurred in Japan in 1931?

1. by date
2. 7
3. Japan took control of Manchuria, China.

Interpreting Movement Maps

Define the Skill

Different types of maps are used for different purposes. **Movement maps** show travel from one point to another. They can track sea voyages, explorations, or migrations. They can span a week, a few months, or thousands of years. Understanding how to read and interpret a movement map can help you learn more about historical events, their chronology, and the geographical locations they have affected.

Learn the Skill

Use the following strategies to interpret movement maps.

THE SLAVE TRADE

1 Read the title and legend. The title tells you the subject of the map. The legend explains what the symbols and the colors on the map mean.

2 Identify the patterns of movement shown on the map. Trace the path of movement from start to finish.

NORTH AMERICA

ATLANTIC OCEAN

40°N

BRITISH NORTH AMERICA 453,000

SPANISH EMPIRE 1,553,000

Tropic of Cancer
20°N

BRITISH WEST INDIES 1,665,000

AFRICA

St. Louis
James Island
Elmina   Accra
Assini   Whydah

PACIFIC OCEAN

FRENCH WEST INDIES 1,600,000

0° Equator

DUTCH WEST INDIES 528,000

SOUTH AMERICA

INDIAN OCEAN

BRAZIL 3,596,000

3 Analyze the information on the map. Draw conclusions based on the information provided in the map.

- British North America
- Spanish Empire
- British West Indies
- French West Indies
- Dutch West Indies
- Brazil
- ■ Slave fort
- ← Direction of slave trade

0   800   1,600 Miles
0   800   1,600 Kilometers
Miller projection

Apply the Skill

1. What was the path of the slave trade?
2. Which continents were directly involved in the slave trade?
3. To which continent were most enslaved people sent?

1. from Africa to South and North America
2. Africa, South America, and North America
3. North America

Interpreting Historical Maps

Define the Skill

Historical maps provide information about a place at a certain time in history. You can use historical maps to locate historical events, to learn how geography influences history, or to trace human interaction with the environment. Historical maps can show information such as population density, economic activity, political alliances, battles, and movement of people and goods. Historical maps can help you learn how places have changed over time.

Learn the Skill

Use the following strategies to interpret historical maps.

1 Read the title and legend.
The title will help you identify the subject and the purpose of the map. The legend explains the meaning of the symbols and the colors on the map.

Westward Expansion of the United States

1803

CANADA
Claimed by Great Britain until 1842
ROCKY MOUNTAINS
LOUISIANA PURCHASE 1803
Great Plains
UNITED STATES Before 1785
MEXICO

1845

Ceded by Great Britain, 1818
CANADA
OREGON COUNTRY 1818
ROCKY MOUNTAINS
Great Plains
UNITED STATES
TEXAS ANNEXATION 1845
MEXICO
Ceded by Spain, 1819
FLORIDA CESSION 1819

UNITED STATES, 1853

CANADA
ROCKY MOUNTAINS
Great Plains
MEXICAN CESSION 1848
UNITED STATES
GADSDEN PURCHASE 1853
MEXICO

2 Identify the areas that have changed.
Note which parts of the map changed as time passed.

3 Analyze how places have changed over time.
Compare and contrast the differing areas and think about the historical events that led to these changes.

— Present-day boundary

0   400   800 Miles
0   200   800 Kilometers
Albers equal-area projection

Apply the Skill

1. What is the purpose of these historical maps?
2. How did the United States change from 1803 to 1853?

1. to show how the United States gained more territory in the mid-1800s

2. The United States gained a third of the land that it already owned and stretched from the Atlantic Ocean to the Pacific.

Analyzing Costs and Benefits

Define the Skill

A **cost-benefit analysis** is a process that measures whether a project or a policy is worthwhile by calculating its benefits and comparing those benefits to its costs. Businesses large and small as well as government agencies all conduct cost-benefit analyses before deciding on a course of action.

Historians have the benefit of hindsight. They can look at events that have already happened and make cost-benefit analyses to determine whether a decision was the right one. The process is relatively straightforward when costs and benefits can be expressed in terms of money or basic economic indicators such as employment figures, gross domestic product, and inflation. Some costs and benefits, however, such as time or safety, are not easily measured by how much money is earned or lost. Also, people may disagree about the value of the costs and benefits.

Learn the Skill

Use the following strategies to analyze costs and benefits.

1 Identify the costs.
Determine the costs of this project.

2 Identify the benefits.
Determine the benefits of the proposed project.

BUILDING VERSAILLES

COSTS	BENEFITS
• Cost five percent of the country's annual revenue • Created resentment among the people • Palace uncomfortable and crowded	• Kept court safer from Paris crowds • Was clear symbol of king's power • Palace had many grand and beautiful features.

3 Analyze the costs and the benefits and draw conclusions.
Compare the costs with the benefits.

Apply the Skill

1. What was one cost of building Versailles?
2. What was one benefit of this project?
3. Based on the cost-benefit chart, do you think it was a good investment to build the palace? Explain.

1. five percent of country's annual revenue, resentment among the people, crowded and uncomfortable
2. court safe from Paris crowds, symbol of king's power, grand and beautiful features
3. Answers will vary.

Evaluating Information on the Internet

Define the Skill

The **Internet** is an international computer network that connects schools, businesses, government agencies, and individuals. Every Web site on the Internet has its own address called an *URL*. Each URL has a domain. The *domain* tells you the type of Web site you are visiting. Common domains in the United States are .com, .net, .org, .edu, and .gov. A Web site with the domain .edu means that it is sponsored by an educational institution. A Web site with the domain .gov means that it is sponsored by a government institution. The collection of Web sites throughout the world is called the *World Wide Web*.

The Internet can be a valuable research tool. Evaluating the content found on the Internet will help you determine the accuracy and reliability of the information.

Learn the Skill

Use the following strategies to evaluate information on the Internet.

1 Identify the Web site's domain.
Determine who sponsors the Web site. Web sites sponsored by reputable organizations, educational institutions, and government agencies usually provide accurate and reliable information.

2 Understand the purpose of the site.
Find out whether the purpose of the site is to inform, to persuade, or to entertain.

3 Identify the author and check for bias.
Not all sites provide you with an author. If the site does, try to determine the author's credentials. If the site does not, decide whether the Web site presents balanced information or is overly biased toward a certain point of view.

Apply the Skill

1. What is the domain of the Web site? Do you think the information on the Web site will be reliable? Why or why not?
2. What is the purpose of this Web site?
3. Do you think this Web site presents a balanced point of view or a biased point of view? Explain your response.

1. .edu. Yes, because it is sponsored by an educational institution.
2. to give information on modern history
3. Answers will vary.

Reading like a Historian

What does it mean to read like a historian? When I asked a group of 10th graders, they were stumped. "Maybe it's like having a mind that spins around like a computer, crammed with dates and facts and stuff," answered one. "Remembering everything you've ever read—you know, like a photographic memory," said another.

The truth is that historians are not computers and they have no better memories than the rest of us. While many historians know a lot about their areas of expertise, when you ask them questions about topics and eras they haven't studied, they seem pretty much like anyone else. So, if historians are not walking encyclopedias, what makes them distinctive?

How they read.

History as an Argument

When historians sit down to read a letter from a 16th century Spanish cleric, a novel from a 19th century Russian writer, or even a chapter from the textbook you are now holding, they approach it as an *argument*. Not in the sense of a brawl or street fight. But in the sense of someone making a claim, stating a position, trying to convince us that his or her description of events should be believed.

Historians rely on primary sources, such as nonfiction and literary works, to tell their stories—and to bolster their arguments.

When we read like a historian we notice things we've never seen before. Look at the name of the book you're holding, *Holt World History: Human Legacy*. Even the two little words "human legacy" form an argument—or the beginning of one.

World Literature

Leo Tolstoy (1828–1910)

NEW YORK STANDARDS

PI 2.4 Students explain the importance of analyzing narratives drawn from different times and places to understand historical events.

About the Reading Leo Tolstoy's novel *War and Peace*, published from 1865 to 1869, is considered one of the greatest novels of all time. It follows the lives of five Russian families in the early 1800s and presents a picture of Russian society during this time. In the passage below, two of the novel's characters, Pierre Bezukhov and Prince Andrew Bolkonsky, argue about whether or not people should live their lives to help others or to help themselves.

AS YOU READ Think about how Prince Andrew views Russia's serfs.

Excerpt from

War and Peace

by Leo Tolstoy

"Come on let's argue then," said Prince Andrew. "You talk of schools," he went on, crooking a finger, "education and so forth; that is you want to raise him" (pointing to a peasant who passed by them taking off his cap) "from his animal condition and awaken in him spiritual needs, while it seems to me that animal happiness is the only happiness possible, and that is just what you want to deprive him of. I envy him, but you want to make him what I am, without giving him my means. Then you say, 'lighten his toil.' But as I see it, physical labor is as essential to him, as much a condition of his existence, as mental activity is it to you or me. You can't help thinking. I go to bed after two in the morning, thoughts come and I can't sleep but toss about till dawn, because I think and can't help thinking, just as he can't help plowing and mowing; if he didn't, he would go to the drink shop or fall ill. Just as I could not stand his terrible physical labor but should die of it in a week, so he could not stand my physical idleness, but would grow fat and die. The third thing—what else was it you talked about?" and Prince Andrew crooked a third finger. "Ah, yes, hospitals, medicine. He has a fit, he is dying, and you come and bleed him and patch him up. He will drag about as a cripple, a burden to everybody, for another ten years. It would be far easier and simpler for him to die. Others are being born

This painting shows Russian serfs in the 1800s.

and there are plenty of them as it is. It would be different if you grudged losing a laborer—that's how I regard him—but you want to cure him from love of him. And he does not want that. And besides, what a notion that medicine ever cured anyone! Killed them, yes!" said he, frowning angrily and turning away from Pierre.

Skills Focus   READING LIKE A HISTORIAN

1. **Describe** How would you describe Prince Andrew's attitude toward Russia's serfs?
2. **Interpret Literature as a Source** Do you think this novel accurately portrays the views of some upper-class Russians toward serfs? Why or why not?

See Skills Handbook, p. H28

go.hrw.com
World Literature
Keyword: SHL WRLIT

PRIMARY SOURCES

The Treatment of Native Americans

Bartolomé de Las Casas was vocal in his protests of the treatment of Native Americans by Europeans. In his *Brief Account of the Destruction of the Indies*, Las Casas described the terrible ordeals that the Native Americans faced as forced laborers, despite orders from the king of Spain that they be protected and taught Christianity.

"The Indians were totally deprived of their freedom and were put in the harshest, fiercest, most horrible servitude and captivity which no one who has not seen it can understand. Even beasts enjoy more freedom when they are allowed to graze in the fields. When the Indians were allowed to go home, they often found it deserted and had no other recourse than to go out into the woods to find food and die. When they fell ill, which was very frequently because they are a delicate people unaccustomed to such work, the Spaniards did not believe them and pitilessly called them lazy dogs, and kicked and beat them; and when illness was apparent they sent them home as useless. I sometimes

came upon dead bodies on my way, and upon others who were gasping and moaning in their death agony, repeating "Hungry, hungry." And this was the freedom, the good treatment, and the Christianity that Indians received.

Is there a single nation which would not think that the world is full of just such evildoers as the Spaniards if their first experience with that outside world was with a people who entered territories by force, killed the people, and deprived them of their rights? Just because the Spaniards told them to obey the King of Castile [Spain], supposing they understood, what obligation did they have to obey since they already had their own kings?"

Skills Focus   READING LIKE A HISTORIAN

1. **Analyze** According to Las Casas, how have the Spanish mistreated Native Americans?
2. **Draw Conclusions** For what audience do you think Las Casas was writing? What makes you think so?

See Skills Handbook, p. H25

Think about it. Compare your book with those written 30 or 40 years ago, which had titles like *Rise of Western Civilization* or the *Triumph of the West* or the *Tradition of Western Society*. These older books taught students that what mattered most was what happened in the West, particularly in Europe. They drew a straight line from the Greeks and Romans to Medieval Europe to the Renaissance and the "discovery" of the New World. Now and then the four-fifths of the world's population who are not heirs to the Western tradition would make an appearance. But the message was clear. The West and its peoples were at the center. Everyone else was in the margins.

Holt World History: Human Legacy makes a different argument: the whole of human history, not just the West, is our *legacy*, our inheritance. Accordingly, for us to truly understand the world we need to look beyond our narrow slice of it. Ancient China is as much a part of who we are, and who we will become, as ancient Greece.

Your Role in the Argument

Once you understand history as an argument you have a crucial role to play in it. History can no longer be served on a silver platter for you to swallow whole. Once you see history as an argument you realize that for every major historical interpretation, there are multiple ways of viewing things. You can't sit back and watch this happen; you have to make up your own mind. You see, calling something an argument means that it must be defended, must be backed by evidence rather than committed unquestioningly to memory.

Consider this: the Industrial Revolution occurred in England during the years 1780 to about 1830. While historians might dicker over the precise dates of the Industrial Revolution, few dispute that something big and important took place. But the moment we turn from this fact to the question of "why"—why did the Industrial Revolution occur in England and not, for example, in China or India we've landed ourselves in the middle of a raucous argument.

On one side are the historians who claim that the key factor in the birth of the Industrial Revolution was chance and something called "contingency." According to their argument, the British were lucky enough to have vast coal deposits in their soil, which fueled the ravenous industrial machine by providing a steady stream of cheap fuel. England also had a convenient source of cheap cotton and a ready market for finished textiles in her American colonies. These factors, so the argument goes, were not destined or preordained but were contingent: They happily came together at the right time and the right place to produce the Industrial Revolution. There's only one reason why China and India didn't industrialize before England, according to this reasoning. In the words of one historian: "They simply did not have colonies or coal."

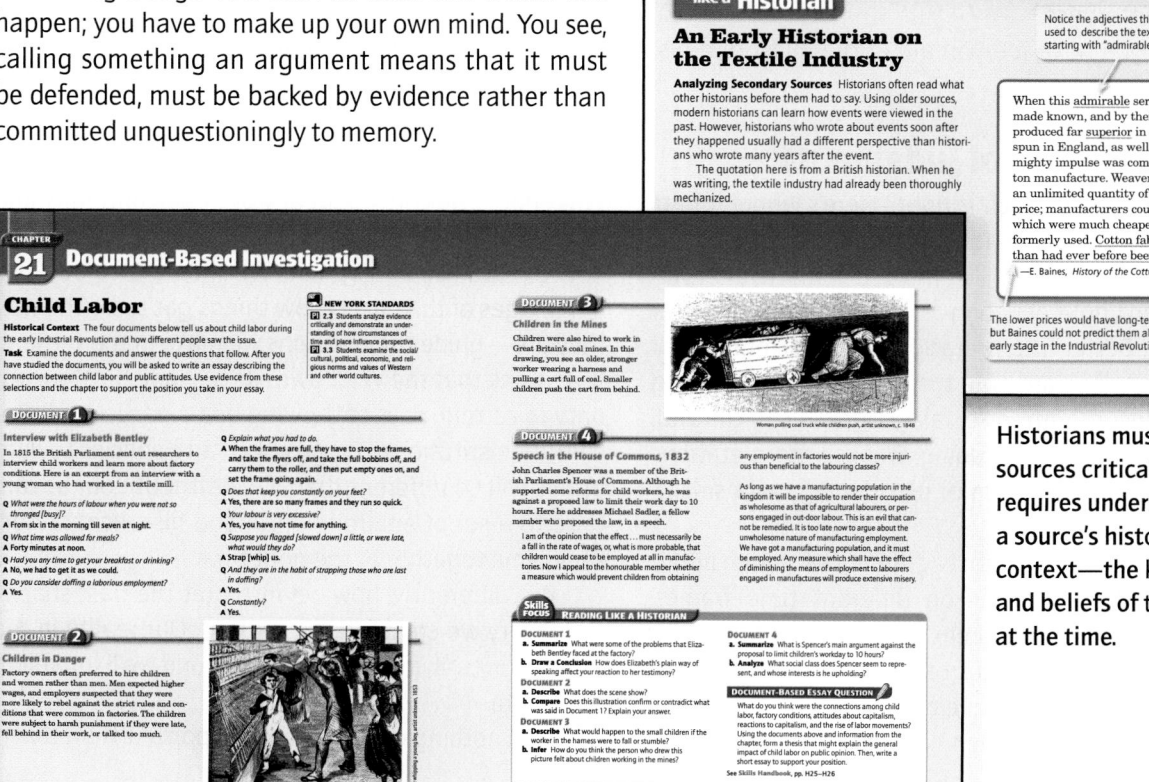

Historians must read sources critically. That requires understanding a source's historical context—the knowledge and beliefs of the people at the time.

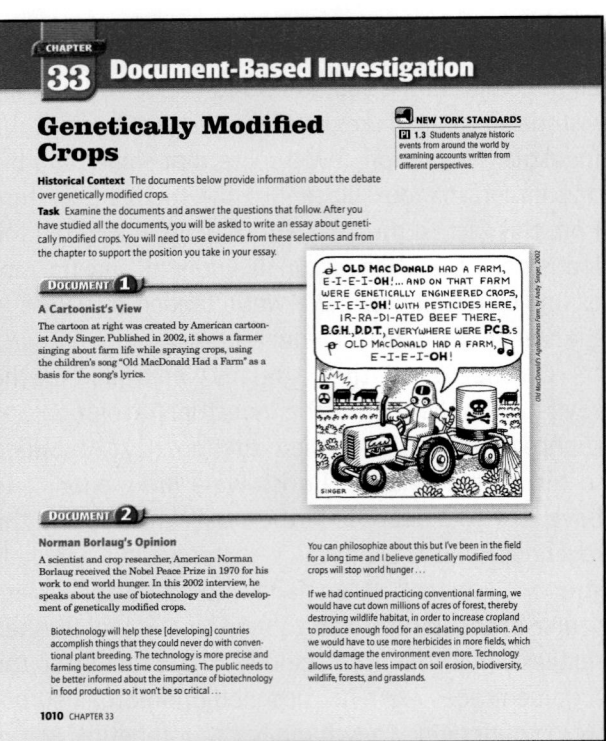

Historians need to be able to understand *continuity* and *change*. For example, people have always needed food, but the technology of food production changes.

are what historians call differences in **scale.** Where historians come down on the issue of the technological progress represented by the Industrial Revolution will depend on whether their focus is a 50 year period or a 500 year one. Scale determines not only what historians see but what they choose to look at.

Even though historians argue over the meaning of the past, they often draw on the same concepts in doing so. At the heart of almost every historical interpretation is the notion of **continuity and change**: the idea that the world before us is both the same and different from the one inhabited by people in the past. We see the interplay of continuity and change when we compare the world today with the world around 1500. Then, as now, most of the world's population lived on just under seven percent of the earth's 60 million square miles of land. Over the past 500 or so years, that hasn't changed much: 70% of the world still lives on the same 4.25 million square miles. But consider this change: Since 1500, the world's population has mushroomed from 350 million to 6 billion, an increase of 1700%. Most of these people are crammed into the same inhabited territory that was known to the world in 1500!

Hogwash, argue historians on the other side. The Industrial Revolution that swept England "was not a matter of chance, of 'things simply coming together.'" The scientific and technological superiority of Britain, writes a historian on this side, "was itself an achievement … the result of work, ingenuity, imagination, and enterprise."

There you have it—you are in the midst of a historical dogfight.

Making Historical Judgments

How do you know which is right? Here's where it gets dicey. There is no single right answer to big questions of historical interpretation like there is in math. Interpretations aren't right or wrong as much as they are better and worse. Better interpretations account for more of the evidence and are able to explain more of the big picture—incorporating social, geographical, cultural, and political factors in so doing. Weaker interpretations ignore pieces of evidence or use ideology as a substitute for hard thinking.

Sometimes interpretive differences come about because historians focus on different time frames. Even though they may seem to be arguing about the same thing, one may focus on what occurred during a decade or a century—while others may try to capture what happened over millennia. These time differences

Why History Matters

Why should we care about any of this—continuity and change, scale, contingency, the role of ideas, or even how to read like a historian? We should care because our images of the past—how things got to be the way they are—guide the decisions we make in the present. If we think that the West owes its technological superiority to certain ways of thinking and a particular set of cultural institutions, our positions and policies toward others will be different than if we attribute our advantage to a set of environmental and historical factors that came together at the right time.

Put differently, how we interpret the past shapes the reality we create in the present. Our reality in the present, in turn, gives birth to the world we'll inhabit in the future.

And nothing could be more important than that!

Analyzing Primary Sources

Define the Skill

Primary sources are documents or other artifacts created by people present at historical events either as witnesses or participants. Usually, you can identify a primary source by reading for first-person clues such as *I*, *we*, and *our*. These types of sources are valuable to historians because they give information about an event or a time period.

Primary sources can include:
- Letters
- Photographs
- Diaries
- Newspaper stories
- Pamphlets, books, or other writings
- Court opinions
- Autobiographies
- Pottery, weapons, and other artifacts
- Government data, laws, and statutes
- Speeches

Learn the Skill

Use the following strategies to analyze this primary source.

1 Identify the author or creator of the primary source and the date in which it was created.
The date gives you a historical context in which to place the primary-source document.

Vladimir Lenin issued his "Call to Power" speech on October 24, 1917, urging Russians to rise up and seize power from the provisional government. The Bolshevik Revolution began the next day.

❝I am writing these lines on the evening of the 24th. The situation is critical in the extreme. In fact it is now absolutely clear that to delay the uprising would be fatal.

With all my might I urge comrades to realize that everything now hangs by a thread; that we are confronted by problems which are not to be solved by conferences or congresses (even congresses of Soviets), but exclusively by peoples, by the masses, by the struggle of the armed people.

... [W]e must not wait. We must at all costs, this very evening, this very night, arrest the government, having first disarmed the officer cadets, and so on.

We must not wait! We may lose everything! ...❞

2 Compare details in the primary source to what you know about the historical event or time period.
The time frame of the primary source allows you to make connections between your previous knowledge and the information the document provides.

3 Determine what the author's intentions are in creating the primary source.
The document has a particular purpose and can be used by its author to inform, persuade, direct, or influence the audience.

Apply the Skill

1. What is Lenin's point of view?
2. How would this source help a historian write a historical interpretation of the Russian Revolution?

1. He wants to overthrow the current Russian government; he is a revolutionary.
2. Answers will vary; possible answer: The source was written a day before the revolution by one of the main players of the revolution and gives a first-hand account of the emotional tone of the time.

Analyzing Visuals

Define the Skill

Visuals, including paintings, drawings, photographs, and political cartoons, are another type of primary source. Like any primary source, they need to be analyzed critically. Sometimes visuals offer an accurate portrayal of the details of a historical figure or event. In other instances, they represent an exaggerated or biased point of view. Knowing and understanding an artist or photographer's point of view can sometimes reveal more to a historian than the actual image itself. By analyzing visuals, we are given an opportunity to see historical events through the eyes of the artist or photographer.

Learn the Skill

Use the following strategies to analyze visuals.

1 Identify the subject and determine the medium that is being used.
Visuals can be a photograph, a piece of fine art, an advertisement, or a cartoon. The type of visual being used can help you determine the audience.

3 Examine the details and the way in which the subject is depicted.
The details in the visual that surround the main subject can help you determine how the subject is depicted and what the artist wants you to know about the subject.

2 Identify the credit line and title.
The credit line tells you who created the image and the title can give you clues as to what the artist intended the image to show.

4 Place the image in a historical context.
The time frame in which the image was created gives you an idea of what the artist's possible intentions were in creating the image. You can draw on your knowledge of that particular time period to help further your understanding of the image.

Death of Marat, by Jacques-Louis David, 1793

Apply the Skill

1. What details of Marat's death are shown in this painting?
2. How does the artist portray Marat's death? What might his purpose be in portraying Marat in such a manner?

1. the knife, the tub, the letter
2. The artist portrays Marat as a victim, a martyr. Answers will vary; possible answer: to gain sympathy for the cause of the revolution

Interpreting Political Cartoons

Define the Skill

Political cartoons are another kind of visual used to help us understand a particular historical time period. These differ from visuals such as photographs and fine art because political cartoons express a point of view. They often exaggerate characteristics of subjects or events in order to convey a specific message, either about politics in particular or society in general. Historians use political cartoons to understand how a certain person or event was perceived at the time. To interpret political cartoons, examine all the elements while considering the social, political, and historical context of the time.

Learn the Skill

Use the acronym BASIC to interpret political cartoons.

caglecartoons.com/espanol

B **Background Knowledge**
Place the political cartoon in its historical context. Use your prior knowledge of what is being depicted to analyze the cartoon's message about that particular event or person.

A **Argument**
Determine what the artist is trying to say in the political cartoon. Analyze the message that the artist is sending to the audience.

S **Symbolism**
Analyze any symbols in the cartoon. Symbols can be used to represent large groups that can't be depicted easily or to stand for a person or an event. Symbols can also be used to simplify the cartoon or make its message clearer to the audience.

I **Irony**
Examine the irony that is present in the cartoon. Irony is the use of words to express something different from their literal meaning. Sometimes in political cartoons, examples of irony are implied through the various symbols and pictures.

C **Caricature (or exaggeration)**
Often in political cartoons, facial features or people's bodies are exaggerated. Analyze any exaggerations present in the cartoon and consider what the meaning of such exaggerations might be.

Apply the Skill

1. Who are the parties being depicted in this cartoon?
2. What is the artist trying to say about the relationship between NAFTA and Mexican industries?

1. the United States and Mexico
2. Answers will vary; possible answer: While NAFTA is meant to help countries in the Americas, it can lead to losses for local industries as imported goods take over domestic goods.

Interpreting Literature as a Source

Define the Skill

Historians can sometimes use **literature** written during a particular time period to gain detailed insights into certain people, places, and events. For example, a poem set in the Middle Ages, such as Chaucer's *Canterbury Tales*, can provide historical details about the lifestyle of people in England in the 1300s. However, because most literature is fiction, it needs to be approached with special caution. Literature, even historical fiction, cannot be taken at face value or treated as a reliable source of information.

Learn the Skill

Use the following strategies to interpret literature.

1 Identify the author and time period of the piece. The time period allows you to place the literary work into a historical context. You can then draw on your knowledge of that time period to interpret the meaning of the piece.

2 Look for descriptive passages that help you determine the author's tone, or manner of expression. The author's tone helps us to understand how the author feels about the subject he or she is writing about. In historical literature the tone can be used to demonstrate a widely felt emotion of people during that particular time period.

3 Determine whether the literature is meant to describe a certain historical event or to elicit an emotional response. Writers often try to elicit an emotional response from their audiences. Analyze the passage and decide whether or not the author is trying to make you feel one way or another about the subject matter.

Excerpt from *War and Peace*, by Leo Tolstoy, 1805

"Come on let's argue then," said Prince Andrew. "You talk of schools," he went on, crooking a finger, "education and so forth; that is you want to raise him (pointing to a peasant who passed by them taking off his cap) from his animal condition and awaken in him spiritual needs, while it seems to me that animal happiness is the only happiness possible, and that is just what you want to deprive him of. I envy him, but you want to make him what I am, without giving him my means. Then you say, 'lighten his toil.' But as I see it, physical labor is as essential to him, as much a condition of his existence, as mental activity is to you or me. You can't help thinking. I go to bed after two in the morning, thoughts come and I can't sleep but toss about till dawn, because I think and can't help thinking, just as he can't help plowing and mowing; if he didn't, he would go to the drink shop or fall ill. Just as I could not stand his terrible physical labor but should die of it in a week, so he could not stand my physical idleness, but would grow fat and die."

Apply the Skill

1. What is the author's point of view?
2. What is the goal of the literature selection?
3. What can historians learn about social classes in Russia by reading this selection?

1. Answers will vary; possible answer: Tolstoy is writing from the perspective of the elite upper class in Europe.
2. Answers will vary; possible answer: to show class distinctions in Russia in the early 1800s
3. Answers will vary; possible answer: There was a great gap in social classes in Russia in the 1800s, which is one reason for the revolutions and uprisings of the time.

Recognizing Bias in Primary Sources

Define the Skill

To develop an effective analysis of primary sources, historians must learn to recognize bias and the source of **bias in primary sources**. A bias is a preference or inclination that inhibits a person from making an impartial judgment. A person's bias can be influenced by political, social, cultural, or personal beliefs. Most primary sources reflect some type of bias, either from the person who created the source or the person viewing the source. Bias can give clues about an author's intent or background. For example, the author may be trying to justify an action or sway an opinion.

Sometimes an author expresses a personal view without knowing that it is biased. Bias can help historians understand the different attitudes during a certain time in history. To avoid bias, a historian must look at many sources on the same incident or issue.

Learn the Skill

Use the following strategies to recognize bias.

1 Identify the speaker or author.
The author's place in the context of a historical event or time period will give you an idea of what sort of bias he or she might have toward the subject.

Carelton Smith, visitor to the Lancashire mines, 1833

"The children, boys and girls, earned their wages by drawing the coals in tubs along the galleries by means of a belt and chain, which passed along their waists. Many girls were thus employed, and after a time became crooked and deformed."

2 Examine the author's point of view.
Analyze what beliefs the author is trying to convey to his or her audience.

3 Compare the primary source with other sources and with historical evidence.
Look to other sources available on this particular subject. Use a variety of sources to develop your own conclusions regarding the event or time period.

Apply the Skill

1. What is the author's goal in writing this passage?
2. Explain how a historian might use this document in preparing a historical account of child labor in coal mines.

1. to show the harsh conditions of children who were working in coal mines
2. Answers will vary; possible answer: This is an eyewitness account that a historian could use to prove that conditions in coal mines were unsuitable for children.

Analyzing Secondary Sources

Define the Skill

A **secondary source** is an account that is produced after a historical event by people who were not present at the actual event. These people rely on primary sources in order to write their secondary-source accounts. Secondary sources often contain summaries and analyses of events and time periods. Your textbook can be considered a secondary source.

Depending on the sorts of questions we ask, a document that we might have initially considered to be a secondary source can actually be a primary source. For example, a history textbook from the mid-1800s is normally considered to be a secondary source. But if we use that book to look at the ways in which history was written in the mid-1800s, the history text then becomes a primary source. It is important to pay attention to the ways in which a document is presented to us before determining whether it is a primary or secondary source.

> **Other kinds of secondary sources include**
> - Encyclopedia entries
> - Web sites
> - Articles and essays by historians
> - Biographies

Learn the Skill

Use the following strategies to analyze secondary sources.

1 **Identify the source.**
The author and the date give you a historical context for the source.

Einhard, the official biographer of Charlemagne, *The Life of Charlemagne*, 830

❝ Charlemagne practised the Christian religion with great devotion and piety. . . As long as his health lasted he went to church morning and evening with great regularity, and also for early-morning Mass, and the late-night hours. ❞

2 **Analyze the summary of historical events provided by the source.**
The author of a secondary source usually offers a summary of events or a time period.

3 **Primary-source possibilities.**
Determine whether or not this secondary source could also be considered a primary source. Use the date and your knowledge of the speaker to help you draw conclusions about how this source could be both primary and secondary.

Apply the Skill

1. What important information about Charlemagne can be found in this passage?
2. In what ways could this secondary source be viewed as a primary source?

1. He was very religious and went to church regularly.
2. Answers will vary; possible answer: This could be used as a primary source if someone wanted to look at the ways in which Charlemagne was viewed by historians over the centuries.

Recognizing Bias in Secondary Sources

Define the Skill

Most secondary sources, like most primary sources, contain some sort of bias based on the author's beliefs. Many secondary sources take a position on a historical event or time period and use that position to interpret the events that took place. Even secondary-source accounts that are meant to be neutral can reflect a bias of some sort. It is important to be able to notice when **bias exists in a secondary source** so that you can make your own assessment of the source's legitimacy.

Learn the Skill

Use the following strategies to recognize bias in secondary sources.

1 Identify the author and his or her purpose in writing the text. Secondary sources are written with a distinctive purpose toward the author's audience.

This excerpt is taken from a Chinese History textbook and is compiled by the Peoples' Education Company.

After the fight curtain was drawn back, the headquarters of the 29th troop of [the] Chinese defending army issued an order that they had to hold fast to Lugouqiao. Before this command was issued, the soldiers could not hold back their anger. So when the command reached them, the soldiers instantly ran out of the countryside, wishing they could wipe out the enemy immediately. The two lines of Chinese soldiers defended either side of the railroad bridge. Facing hundreds of Japanese attackers, they were not cowed in the least, and they engaged in intense hand-to-hand fights with [the] enemies. Nearly all of them died at the end of the battle of the bridge. Seeing their comrades fall in the battle, other soldiers, without showing much sorrow, clenched their teeth. They fought forward. Even the wounded who were ordered to retreat were still charging ahead.

2 Analyze the words the author uses to describe people, places, and events. The words or phrases that the author uses have a great deal to do with how he or she feels the subject. Identify and analyze these words in order to recognize what sort of bias the author has.

3 Determine the author's opinion about the subject being discussed. The author is looking at these events with particular feelings towards his or her subject. By analyzing where the author is coming from, you can recognize the bias in the writing.

Apply the Skill

1. What is the source?
2. Are there examples of emotional language in the excerpt? If so, what are they?
3. Is there bias in this passage? Explain your answer.

1. a Chinese history textbook
2. yes; "Japanese attackers;" "the soldiers could not hold back their anger;" "they were not cowed in the least;" "other soldiers, without showing much sorrow, clenched their teeth"
3. Yes; the author paints the Chinese in a very brave, positive light and the Japanese in a negative light, as the "attackers" and the "enemies."

Evaluating Historical Interpretation

Define the Skill

Historians and others **evaluate historical interpretations** to determine the credibility, level of bias, and relevance of the material. A historical interpretation is a way to explain the past. These interpretations can change over time as historians learn more about the people and events of the past.

Learn the Skill

Use the following strategies to evaluate historical interpretation.

1 **Identify the author or publisher of the source to determine credibility.**
The introduction tells you the author's name and his profession. You may have to do additional research to find out what the author's background is in order to determine credibility.

2 **Consider when the source was created.**
The more current the publishing date is, the more recent the scholarship is and, therefore, the more credible the source.

Excerpt from *The World of Rome*, by historians Peter Jones and Keith Sidwell, 1997

> **❝** Roman subjects have had a continuing appeal for cinema audiences. One thinks of *Ben-Hur* and *Spartacus*, for example, which established our view of galleys and chariot-races indelibly... There have been many novels devoted to Roman subjects. The best known in English, perhaps, are Robert Graves' *I, Claudius* and *Claudius the God*, adapted for TV in the 1960s...But it is not only the large-scale which shows the deep penetration of our consciousness by Roman images (even if these are merely images of images). All around, we can see trivial examples of this impact. There are Roman-style porticoes on fast-food stores and statue niches on minute houses on large estates. There are togas and gladiators in Bugs Bunny cartoons. There are Roman soldiers in Asterix books. There are Latin tags on British pound coins. There is a laurel wreath on the Whitehall cenotaph [a World War I monument in London].
>
> For all this, the world of Rome is ultimately responsible. **❞**

3 **Examine the level of bias in the interpretation.**
The author or authors of historical interpretations take a position on the particular time period or event that they are discussing. Analyze the way in which their bias affects their interpretation of the event or time period.

Apply the Skill

1. Who are the authors of the interpretation?
2. When was the source created? How does this affect the scholarship?
3. How does bias affect the interpretation?

1. historians Peter Jones and Keith Sidwell

2. 1997; Answers will vary: possible answer: It's fairly recent scholarship, only about 10 years old; there may be more recent scholarship that could be take into consideration when assessing the validity of the source.

3. Answers will vary; possible answer: The bias of the authors is that Rome's legacy left only positive images on popular culture and life today. They don't discuss any of the possible lasting negative effects.

Analyzing Points of View

Define the Skill

Interpretations of past events often come from differing **points of view.** Two historians given the same primary-source documents may, and often do, look at the historical event or time period in two completely different ways. These differing interpretations may reflect an extreme bias for one view or another, or they may reflect two different schools of thought. Historians are often faced with alternative points of view of a time or an event in the past when conducting their research. Good historians do additional research to find the accuracies in each account.

Learn the Skill

Use the following strategies to analyze points of view.

1 Identify information given about the authors and the time during which their research was conducted. Knowing the authors' background and when they conducted their work gives you an insight into where their scholarship lies in the grand scheme of the subject material.

Archaeologists Dennis Stanford and Bruce Bradley's views on migration to the Americas, 1999

"We reason that generations of Solutrean hunters learned to cope with ice and weather conditions to follow resources such as Harp seals and Great Auks that migrated north and westward along with retreating ice in late spring. Through such activities they ended up (by accident and/or design) along the exposed continental shelf of North America discovering a New Land."

2 Define and analyze the main points in each argument. Determine what each author is saying about the topic.

Archaeologist Stuart J. Fiedel's view on migration to the Americas, 1987

"The striking similarity of fluted points and associated artifacts across the whole expanse of North America suggests that the continent was rapidly filled by Paleo-Indian hunting bands, each retaining for several centuries the tool-making traditions of an ancestral population that originally entered through the ice-free corridor around 10,000-9500 BC. But the only place from which this hypothetical group could have come is Alaska, where there is hardly any existing evidence of Clovis occupation."

3 Compare the points of view. Based on the time period of their study and their conclusions, analyze the author's alternative points of view in order to draw conclusions about the topic.

Apply the Skill

1. What is the main point of each selection?
2. Which source do you feel has more credibility? Why?

1. Selection 1: The first people were Solutrean hunters who came to North America along the continental shelf. Selection 2: The first people came to North America from Alaska.

2. Possible answer: the first one because it is more recent

CREATING WRITTEN PRESENTATIONS

Biographical Writing

A biography is the story of a person's life as told by someone else. Historical accounts usually include a great deal of biographical writing. Personalizing history in this way makes it more interesting and easier to understand for many people. Follow these steps when you write a biography.

1. Prewrite

Identifying the Subject Sometimes you will be assigned a subject; sometimes you will have a choice. When choosing, pick a person who interests you, one that you would like to know more about. Be sure to get your choice approved by your teacher.

Identifying a Thesis Decide on your point of view toward the person. Is he or she a leader, an artist, a scientist? Was he or she a hero, a failure; famous or infamous? Focus your thoughts in a single statement, which can serve as your *thesis statement*. A thesis statement tells what your paper will be about.

Gathering Information and Details You will be able to find information about your subject in encyclopedias and other reference books, in articles, on CD-ROMs and Web sites, and through other informational sources. You want to check with your teacher or librarian to make sure your sources are reliable and objective. Choose facts, examples, anecdotes, and other details that relate directly to your thesis. It's better to have a few paragraphs of carefully explained, related information than a running list of dates and other facts.

Organizing Information and Details Almost all biographical writing is organized in *chronological*, or time, order. Use an outline to gather specific details under a main idea for each paragraph in your paper. Be prepared to revise your thesis as you gather information and learn more about your subject. You will not be able to use all the information you find. Pick only what best supports and illustrates your thesis and main ideas.

2. Write

Use a Writer's Framework to create a draft.

Introduction
- Start with a quotation, anecdote or fascinating fact.
- Identify your subject, giving facts and details that reflect your point of view toward him or her.
- Clearly express the main focus, or thesis, of your paper in a single statement.

Body
- Choose three or four main events from the person's life to develop into paragraphs supporting your thesis.
- Give specific facts and examples that directly support the main idea in each paragraph.
- Use chronological order to organize your paper.

Conclusion
- Restate the main focus (thesis) of your paper.
- Give additional biographical information about the person to strengthen or expand your thesis.
- Relate the person to historical events at that time or to someone else in history.

3. Revise and Publish

Evaluating and Revising Look back at each paragraph. Revise wording or sentence structure to strengthen the links between your thesis and the supporting information.

Proofreading and Publishing Double-check the spelling of all names of people, places, and events. Also, check all dates.

Many historical societies, service clubs, and other groups sponsor essay contests. Check the guidelines for entering any such contests.

Expository Writing

Essay questions on tests, book reports, and other assignments that require you to explain or present information about a particular subject are types of expository writing—explaining or giving information about a topic. The specific information you give and what you say about it depends on not only your topic, but also the organization, or structure, of your writing. Follow these steps when you write an expository paper.

1. Prewrite

Identifying a Topic Most expository writing assignments include a topic or choice of topics. Often, the structure is assigned, too. Much of your expository writing will involve at least one of the following three common structures, shown here with example topics.

> **Comparison-contrast topic:** *Explain three ways that the United Nations is like the League of Nations, and three ways they differ.*
>
> **Cause and effect topic:** *How did industrialization change British social structure, and what results of those changes are seen in today's society?*
>
> **Sequence of events topic:** *Trace the history of European exploration of the Americas.*

Writing a Thesis Statement Your response to your topic will guide the wording of your thesis statement. In a single sentence, state the main idea behind what you will write about the topic.

> **Comparison-contrast thesis:** *Though similar in origin, aims and hopes, the United Nations and the League of Nations differed in organization, scope, and authority.*

Gathering and Organizing Information Some expository writing assignments involve research. Books, CD-ROMs, the Web, and other information sources can provide facts, examples, and other details about your topic. As a rule, you will want to organize your information in an outline according to the structure you chose or were assigned.

> **Organize by comparison-contrast:** Sometimes you will want to give all your points of comparison first, then all the contrasting points. In other cases, you will give a point of comparison, then a contrast; then the next comparison, followed by the next contrast, etc.
>
> **Organize by cause and effect:** Usually, you will give the cause(s) first, then the effect(s).
>
> **Organize by sequence of events:** In most cases, you will use chronological, or time, order to organize a sequence of events.

2. Write

Use a Writer's Framework to create a draft.

Introduction
- Introduce your topic, providing any details or description readers will need to understand it.
- Briefly explain how you will develop your topic.
- Clearly state your thesis for your paper.

Body
- Follow your outline in presenting examples, facts, and other information in each paragraph.
- Use transitional words such as *then*, *as a result*, and *rather than* to relate ideas and information clearly.

Conclusion
- Briefly summarize (in a sentence or two) the key ideas and information in the body of your paper.
- Use information from the body of your paper to restate your thesis in more specific words.
- Expand on your thesis by explaining the importance, predicting future developments, or exploring some other aspect of your topic.

3. Revise and Publish

Evaluate and Revise Make sure that you have clearly introduced both your topic and the structure of your paper. Replace any weak transitional words with more precise words or phrases.

Proofread and Publish Proofread your paper to be sure that it is free of errors in punctuation, usage, and spelling. Transitional words often need to be set off by punctuation, so check them with special care.

Persuasive Writing

The purpose of persuasion is to convince others to believe something or do something. You'll most often find persuasive writing in advertisements, editorials written for newspapers and magazines, or in the speeches of political leaders. Persuasive writing turned into a speech is common in the great speeches of political leaders. Follow these steps when you write a persuasive paper.

1. Prewrite

Identifying an Issue One requirement for persuasion is a topic about which people disagree. If everyone agrees, there is no need to persuade. If you are asked to create a persuasive essay, an editorial, or a persuasive speech, start by identifying an issue with these characteristics:

1. You have an opinion about it.
2. There are clearly defined pro and con arguments about the issue.

Identifying a Thesis Once you have an issue, write a sentence that defines your opinion or position on it.
   Example thesis: *Wealthier countries should help poorer countries develop their economies.*

Building an Argument The support provided for an opinion or thesis is called an argument. A persuasive argument must be based on logical proof and evidence. It may also include appeals to emotions or to a person's ethics.
   Evidence: Facts, statistics, anecdotes, expert testimony, and precise examples
   Emotional Appeals: Appeals to ideas people care about, such as love of country or human life and welfare
   Ethical Appeals: Appeals to the readers' sense of right and wrong

Gathering and Organizing Support Unless you have already studied your topic, you will have to do some research for reasons and information to support your opinion. You can check online sources, textbooks, newspapers, etc.

   Once you have gathered the support, you'll need to think about the order in which you should present it. Sometimes you will want to put the strongest and most compelling information or reason first, to capture your reader's attention. At other times you may want to save it for the end, to make a strong final impression.

2. Write

Use a Writer's Framework to create a draft:

Introduction

- Start with a question, quotation, or interesting fact.
- Clearly state your thesis.
- Give background information so readers understand the issue.

Body

- Include at least three reasons to support your thesis.
- Support each reason with evidence, emotional appeals, or ethical appeals.
- Organize the reasons by order of importance—most to least or least to most.

Conclusion

- Summarize your argument.
- Restate your thesis in different words.
- Include a call to action—a sentence that tells readers what you want them to do.

3. Revise and Publish

Evaluate and Revise Turn the statements in the Writer's Framework into questions and ask yourself what changes you need to make. For example, "Do I have a clear statement of my thesis in the introduction to my paper?"

Proofread and Publish Proofread your paper to be sure that it is free of errors in punctuation, usage, and spelling. If you have a computer with spell-check, be sure to use it. You also need someone to read what you have written. You could submit a persuasive paper to the editorial page of your school or local newspaper.

Research Writing

Unlike other expository writing, research writing requires you to present not only your own ideas and knowledge on a topic but those of others. Consequently, the success of your research papers will depend on how well you find, select, and use information sources. Follow these steps when you write a research paper.

1. Prewrite

Identifying a Topic and Research Question

In some cases, your teacher will assign the general subject, or topic, of your report. Other times, you will choose your own. Topics often include time periods, places, people, and events in history. To shape your topic, turn it into a research question. For example, if your topic were the Bolshevik Revolution, you might ask "What were the causes of the Bolshevik Revolution?"

Gathering and Recording Information To answer your research question, you will need to seek information about your topic in sources such as books, articles, and CD-ROMs. Information from all sources needs to be factual, up-to-date, logical, and objective.

Keep a numbered list of the sources you use. Record each note on a separate piece of paper or note card, including the source number and the page number(s) where the information appears.

Writing a Thesis Statement Gathering information will guide you in answering your research question. That answer can serve as a statement of the main idea, or thesis, you will develop in your report.

> **Example thesis:** *The primary cause of the Bolshevik Revolution was long-term social unrest.*

Organizing Your Information Sort your notes into several major categories; then divide them further into subtopics. Organize all of these in an outline, according to how you want to present the information.

Depending on your thesis, you might organize by order of importance, chronological order, comparison and contrast, or cause and effect. With the example thesis on the Bolshevik Revolution, you might arrange causes in their order of importance or simply discuss causes before effects.

2. Write

Use a Writer's Framework to create a draft:

Introduction
- Grab readers' interest by opening with an interesting fact or anecdote.
- Give background information to acquaint readers with your topic and the research you've done.
- Clearly state your thesis.

Body
- Devote at least one paragraph to each main idea in your outline.
- Quote sources accurately and enclose all direct quotations in quotation marks.
- Insert a parenthetical source citation after each piece of research information that you use.

Conclusion
- Summarize your main points.
- Restate your thesis, relating it to your research.
- Create a Works Cited page listing your sources.

3. Revise and Publish

Evaluating and Revising Double check all quotations to make sure they're accurate. Where you have summarized or paraphrased information, make sure you have used your own words.

Proofreading and Publishing Proofread to be sure that you have enclosed each direct quotation in quotation marks. Check to be sure that you have given a parenthetical citation for the source for each piece of information used in your report.

Expository and Persuasive Speeches

Speeches are a common form of sharing information or persuading an audience. Preparing to give a speech usually involves the same steps as writing—planning, researching, organizing, drafting, and revising. Delivering a speech, however, requires an additional set of skills. Follow these steps when you prepare and deliver a speech about a historical event or issue.

1. Prepare the Speech

Identifying an Issue or Topic Sometimes you will be assigned a historical topic or issues for a speech. Other times you will be able to choose your own.

Identifying your Purpose

To Inform: Expository, or informative speeches, provide facts about and/or explain a historical event or situation.

To Persuade: Persuasive speeches attempt to change listeners' opinions about an issue on which there are clearly defined pro and con arguments. In addition to facts and examples, persuasive speeches rely on emotional appeals.

Identifying a Thesis A thesis statement is the statement of your main idea. You may be able to identify it as soon as you have a topic or an issue, but you may also wait until after you have done some research and gathered information. Here are examples of thesis statements.

Expository thesis: *Napoleon's Russian Campaign was troubled from the beginning, and it ended in failure.*

Persuasive thesis: *Napoleon's ego and pride were the cause of his failure in the Russian Campaign.*

Gathering Information Use reference books, history books, primary sources, and other sources to gather information. Persuasive speeches need *facts, statistics, anecdotes, expert testimony,* and *precise examples* just as much as expository speeches.

Organizing Your Notes Review the information you have gathered and identify the main points you want to make—the points that relate to and support your thesis. Then select a way to organize your presentation.

Typical ways to organize an *informative speech* include:

Organize by cause and effect: Discuss the cause(s) before the effect(s).

Organize by sequence: Discuss stages or actions in chronological order.

Organize by comparison-contrast: You might discuss one event or person and then discuss the other event and person. You can also organize by points of comparison. For example, you might compare two kings on political skills, military skills, and finally on their legacy to the world.

For a *persuasive speech*, you would typically:

Organize by order of importance: Save the most important and/or most dramatic point for last, to make a final impact on your audience.

Making Note Cards In most situations, you need to speak from a few note cards rather than a written paper. Make a separate card for:

- Each major point. Add reminder notes about facts, examples, or ideas you want to use to support that point.
- Direct quotations to be read word for word.
- When to show a map, chart, or other visual material to support your points.

Main Point: The Grand Army Dissolves
Describe how Napoleon's army dissolved on its retreat from Russia.
• Conditions: Winter; horrible, mud-soaked roads; no food, attacks from Russian army and partisans.
• How lon~~~~
• Statistic:
• Set up q~~

Key Facts:
• With no food, soldiers killed and ate their horses, which meant they had to walk.
• With no shoes, soldiers' feet bled on the snow
• Because many soldiers were not French, they more quickly abandoned the army

2. Practice the Speech

Practice will help build your self-confidence as well as help you spot and correct mistakes. You need to practice more than once, evaluating and changing your speech as you go.

Rehearse If possible, practice your speech in front of an audience—friends or family members. It is also helpful to practice in front of a mirror or make a video of your practice session. That way you can listen to the speech as well as observe the way you handled yourself while speaking.

Verbal Communication In a speech, it is not just the words that are important, it is also how the words are expressed. As you rehearse, adjust how well you do the following:

- Speak clearly and slowly
- Project your voice more loudly than in normal speech
- Stress words related to the main points
- Use small silences to suggest important points or give listeners time to think

Nonverbal Communication We use nonverbal signals whenever we speak, but when giving a speech, it is especially important to control and use these signals effectively. Practice controlling the following:

Facial Expressions: Frowning, smiling, etc. signal your feelings

Eye Contact: Maintaining eye contact with your audience makes them feel as though you are communicating directly to them

Gestures: Move your arms, hands, or head to emphasize your verbal message

Using Audiovisual Media Audiovisual media can make your speech more interesting and clarify your ideas. Audiovisual media include audio recordings, films, maps, charts, graphs, pictures, illustrations, power point presentations or anything else stored on a personal computer.

- Use visuals that are large enough for everyone in the audience to see and read.
- If you are going to use media as you present your speech, you need to include it when you rehearse.

3. Deliver the Speech

No matter how well you have planned and researched your topic—and you should know your topic inside and out—and how much you have practiced your presentation, actually standing in front of an audience and giving the speech is a challenge. Almost everyone is a little bit nervous when giving a speech, even people who have made a career as a speaker. Here are some things you can do to make speaking easier:

Check Your Audiovisual Media: Before the speech, make sure all electronic equipment is cued up and ready to go.

Read the Audience: Do they seem to be agreeing or disagreeing with the points you are making? Are they going to sleep or whispering to one another? You may need to adjust your verbal and nonverbal signals.

Slow Down: Force yourself to control the pace of your speech. Don't rush through it to get to the end.

Focus on What You Want to Say: Concentrate on your purpose for speaking. Don't be distracted or wander.

Finish with Finesse: Close your speech with emphasis on your main idea or point.

Multiple Choice

One of the most common questions you might see on a test is a **multiple-choice question.** These questions consist of a stem and several answer options. Use the strategies below to answer multiple-choice questions.

LEARN

❶ Read the stem carefully and review each of the answer options.

❷ Examine the question for key words and facts that indicate what the question is asking.

❸ Pay careful attention to questions that are phrased in the negative.
Some questions contain words such as *not* and *except*. In these cases, look for the answer option that is not true.

❹ Eliminate answer options that you know are incorrect
This will help you narrow down your choices.

❺ Consider options such as *all of the above* and *none of the above* as you would any other possible response.

❻ Watch for modifiers.
Answer options that include absolute words such as *always* or *never* are sometimes incorrect.

❼ Consider the options that remain and select the best.
If you are not sure of the answer, select the option that makes the most sense.

❷ The word *best* indicates that you should look for the option that best explains why Henry broke from the church.

1. Which of the following <u>best</u> explains why Henry VIII broke away from the Catholic Church?

Stem

Answer Options

 1 The pope refused to grant him an annulment.
 2 He was a close friend and follower of Martin Luther.
 3 He wanted to be head of the church.
 4 He strongly opposed the sale of indulgences.

❸

2. Which of the following was <u>not</u> a writer associated with the Renaissance?
 1 William Shakespeare
 2 Christine de Pisan
 3 Miguel de Cervantes
 4 Johannes Gutenberg

3. The Catholic Counter-Reformation led to
 1 improved relations between Catholics and Protestants.
 2 the formation of new religious orders.
 3 ~~the creation of the Lutheran Church.~~
 4 all of the above.

❹ You can eliminate option **C** if you recall that the Lutheran Church was a result of the *Protestant* Reformation.

4. Which of the following accurately describes Renaissance art?
 1 Renaissance art <u>never</u> focused on individuals.
 2 Renaissance art <u>always</u> had a religious theme.
 3 Renaissance artists rarely created sculptures.
 4 Renaissance paintings used a technique known as perspective.

❺ Absolute words such as *always, never, all, none,* and *every* often signal an incorrect option.

Answers: 1 (1), 2 (4), 3 (2), 4 (4)

Historical Sources

Often, test questions will include historical sources in order to assess your ability to analyze documents or images. **Historical sources** are written or visual sources that tell us about important events or people in history. Historical sources can be primary-source documents created by people present at historical events or during a historical time period, or secondary sources created after an event by a person who was not present. Use the strategies below to answer questions using historical sources.

LEARN

① Briefly examine the historical source and the questions that accompany it.
Look at the title and skim the source to identify the subject. Then read the questions to help you understand what information to focus on.

② Examine the source carefully.
Take note of when the source was created and by whom. Look for key events, persons, or other details that provide information about the subject.

③ Study the source to determine its purpose and point of view.
Look for clues that might indicate why the source was created. Was it intended to create a reaction in the audience? Is it for informational purposes?

④ Re-read the questions that accompany the historical source and review the source to find the answers.

①

Ferdinand Magellan

Magellan's greatness stands out, despite all attempts to disparage him. He not only had the gift of making the right decision at the right time; he was able to outwit enemies who were plotting to kill him, and to keep the loyalty of his men. And, as the Portuguese sailor who wrote the Leiden Narrative recorded, he was "an industrious man, and never rested," the kind of sea captain who slept little and woke at a moment's notice for anything like a change of wind. As a mariner and navigator he was unsurpassed; and although he did not live to complete the greatest voyage of discovery in the world's history, he planned it, and discovered the "Strait that shall forever bear his name," as well as the Marianas and the Philippines where no European had touched before.

—Samuel Eliot Morison, *The European Discovery of America: The Southern Voyages,* 1974, p. 320

②

② These words indicate that the author thought highly of Magellan.

1. Which of the following correctly identifies an accomplishment of Ferdinand Magellan?
   1 He wrote the Leiden Narrative.
   2 He was the first European to reach the Marianas and the Philippines.
   3 He was the greatest explorer who ever lived.
   4 He discovered a sea route from Europe to Asia.

2. What is the author's point of view toward the subject? **④**
   1 The author believes that Magellan's voyage was not very important in world history.
   2 He thinks that Europeans were wrong to colonize the Americas.
   3 The author thinks highly of Ferdinand Magellan.
   4 He believes that Magellan was a better sailor than Columbus

Answers: 1 (2), 2 (3)

Political Cartoons

Another common type of test question asks you to analyze a political cartoon. **Political cartoons** are primary sources that use images and symbols to make a point about political figures or issues. Because cartoons often provide insight into the opinions and values of a historical period, exams use political cartoons to test your knowledge of a particular period. Use the strategies below to answer test questions that deal with political cartoons.

LEARN

❶ Identify the cartoon's subject.
Read the cartoon's title and caption to help determine its subject. Information that indicates when the cartoon was created can also help you identify the subject matter.

❷ Interpret symbols and images used in the cartoon.
Political cartoons often use symbols to express ideas. For example, an olive branch might represent the idea of peace. Exaggerated images or facial expressions often indicate emotions.

❸ Determine the cartoonist's point of view.
Examine the cartoon to understand what point the artist is trying to make. Recognize whether the subject is portrayed positively or negatively. Does the cartoonist agree or disagree with the issue?

❹ Read the questions carefully and study the political cartoon to find the answers.

Taille, Impots et Corvee (Tithes, Taxes, and Labor), France late 1700s

❶ The title, place, and date of the cartoon help us identify the subject as France on the eve of the French Revolution.

❷ The priest and nobleman were common symbols of France's First and Second estates. The man under the rock represents the peasants and laborers of the Third Estate

❸ Showing the peasant being literally crushed might indicate that the artist believed the Third Estate was suffering.

❹ 1. The cartoon likely represents
  1 France's economic difficulties under King Louis XVI.
  2 religious disagreements that led to the French Revolution.
  3 political reasons for Napoleon's rise to power.
  4 social problems before the French Revolution.

2. What point is the artist most likely trying to make in this cartoon?
  1 The First and Second estates oppress the Third Estate.
  2 The First and Second estates share their wealth with the Third Estate.
  3 Members of the Third Estate should not pay their taxes.
  4 The three estates should work together to solve the country's economic problems.

Answers: 1 (4), 2 (1)

Line and Bar Graphs

Other test questions assess your ability to read graphs. Graphs are used to show statistical or numerical information in a visual way. **Line graphs** illustrate how quantities and trends change over time. **Bar graphs** compare groups of numbers within categories and sometimes show change over time. Use the strategies below to answer questions that cover line and bar graphs.

LEARN

1 **Read the title of the graph to determine its main idea**

2 **Read the questions that accompany the graph.**
Reading the questions first will help you focus in on the most important part of the graph.

3 **Study the label on the vertical axis.**
The vertical axis generally indicates what the graph measures.

4 **Examine the label on the horizontal axis.**
The horizontal axis usually tells you the time period the graph covers.

5 **Read any legends or additional labels on the graph.**
Legends and additional labels provide information about what the colors, patterns, or symbols on the graph mean.

6 **Identify any trends or patterns that the graph reveals.**

7 **Re-read the questions and review the graph to find the answers.**

6 The bars indicate that German production of steel and coal was rising.

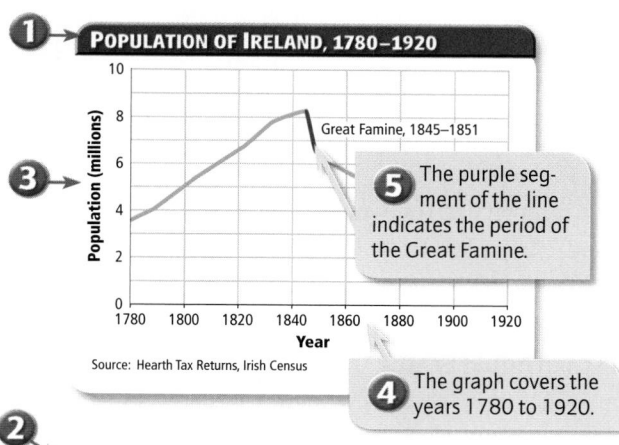

1 POPULATION OF IRELAND, 1780–1920

3 Population (millions)

Great Famine, 1845–1851

5 The purple segment of the line indicates the period of the Great Famine.

Year

Source: Hearth Tax Returns, Irish Census

4 The graph covers the years 1780 to 1920.

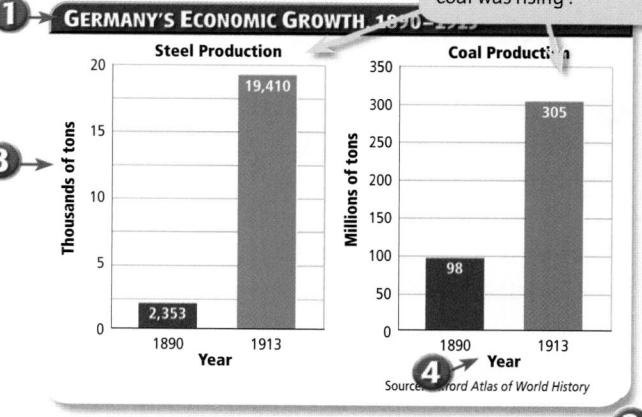

1 GERMANY'S ECONOMIC GROWTH, 1890–1913

Steel Production

Coal Production

3 Thousands of tons

19,410

2,353

1890   1913
Year

Millions of tons

305

98

1890   1913
4 Year

Source: Oxford Atlas of World History

2
1. Which statement *best* summarizes the information in the line graph?
   1. The Irish population declined dramatically around 1900.
   2. The population of Ireland has always been smaller than that of Great Britain.
   3. Ireland's population increased dramatically as a result of the Industrial Revolution.
   4. After years of population growth, the Irish population declined rapidly around the time of the Great Famine.

2
2. According to the graphs, between 1890 and 1913, Germany's
   1. coal production declined as a result of the Great Depression.
   2. steel production and coal production both experienced dramatic increases.
   3. coal production declined, while steel production increased.
   4. economy was relatively stable.

Answers: 1 (4), 2 (2)

Pie Graphs

Some tests include questions that require you to interpret information in pie graphs. A **pie graph** shows how parts are related to a whole. Slices of a pie graph should add up to 100% and are proportional to the percentage each represents. Sometimes exams will have two pie graphs side by side in order to show a comparison. Use the strategies below to answer questions about pie graphs.

LEARN

❶ **Read the title of the graph to learn the topic and time period it covers.**

❷ **Read the questions that accompany the pie graph.** Reading the questions first will help you focus in on the most important aspect of the graph.

❸ **Identify the different "slices" into which the pie graph is divided.** Look for a legend or labels to explain what the different slices represent. What percentage does each slice represent?

❹ **Draw conclusions about the information presented in the graph.** Consider why some slices are larger or smaller than others. What does the data tell you about the topic of the graph?

❺ **If there are two graphs, compare and contrast them to identify and understand trends.**

❻ **Re-read the questions and review the graph to find the answers.**

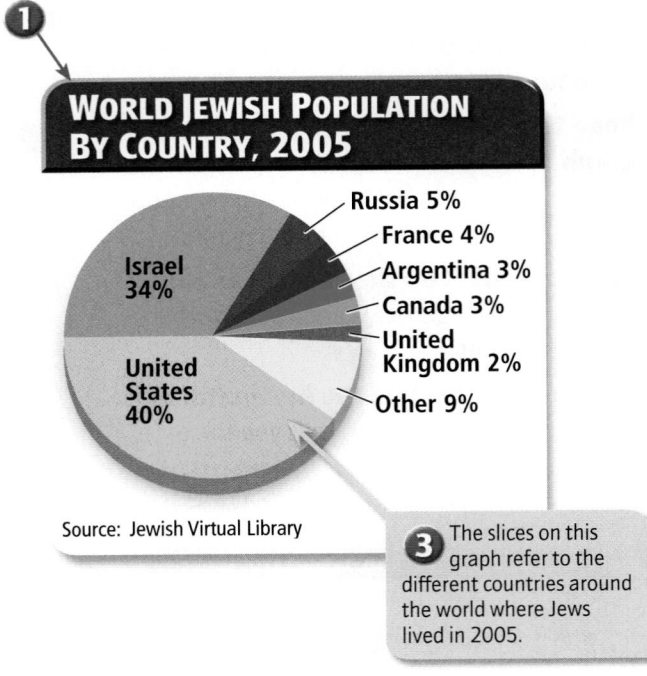

❶

WORLD JEWISH POPULATION BY COUNTRY, 2005

Israel 34%
United States 40%
Russia 5%
France 4%
Argentina 3%
Canada 3%
United Kingdom 2%
Other 9%

Source: Jewish Virtual Library

❸ The slices on this graph refer to the different countries around the world where Jews lived in 2005.

❷

1. In 2005 the majority of the world's Jewish population lived
   1 in Europe.
   2 in Israel.
   3 outside Israel.
   4 outside the United States.

❹

2. Which of the following conclusions can accurately be drawn from the graph above?
   1 In 2005 Jews lived in many different parts of the world.
   2 Jews make up the largest religious group in Israel today.
   3 A large number of Jews lived in Europe in 2005.
   4 In 2005 Judaism was the third largest religion in the world.

Political and Thematic Maps

Questions asking you to interpret maps frequently appear on tests. **Political maps** show countries and the political divisions within them. They may also highlight physical features such as mountains or bodies of water. **Thematic maps** focus on a specific topic and often show patterns of movement, distribution of resources, or location of events. Special symbols, such as icons or arrows, are often used on thematic maps. Use the strategies below to answer questions about political and thematic maps.

LEARN

❶ **Identify the map's subject and read the questions that accompany the map.**
The map's title will often indicate the subject. Reading the questions will help you identify information you need to focus on.

❷ **Study the map legend.**
The legend will help you identify what the different colors and symbols mean. These can give you details about the purpose of the map.

❸ **Examine the map's compass rose and scale.**
The compass rose can help you determine direction, while the scale can help you estimate the distance between two places.

❹ **Study the information provided on the map.**
Read all the labels and study the other information, such as colors, borders, or symbols.

❺ **Re-read the questions carefully and review the map to find the answers.**

MUGHAL EMPIRE, 1526–1707

❹ Note that each battle site on the map contains the name and the year of the battle.

❷ The legend tells you what territory was added to the Mughal Empire and indicates the symbols for battles and trading posts.

Legend:
- Mughal Empire, 1530
- Territory added, 1531–1605
- Territory added, 1606–1707
- European trading post, 1707
- Battle site
- 1504 Date of battle

1. In 1530 the Mughal Empire was centered
   1 around coastal cities.
   2 in the Himalayas.
   3 in northern India.
   4 in southern India.

2. Why might European trading posts have been located along India's coasts?
   1 to be close to valuable natural resources
   2 to be near shipping routes
   3 to be protected from invaders
   4 to be nearby large cities

Answers: 1 (3), 2 (2)

Constructed Response

Some tests include constructed-response questions. **Constructed-response** questions ask you to interpret a source and answer open-ended, short-answer questions. Unlike multiple-choice questions, the answers are not given. You have to construct them. Use the strategies below to answer constructed-response questions.

LEARN

❶ **Identify the subject of the document and read the questions that accompany it.**
Examine the title and any other information that might indicate the subject of the document. Reading the questions help you identify the information you need to focus on.

❷ **Study the document carefully.**
Documents can include written excerpts, graphs, charts, political cartoons, maps, or other visuals. Identify information presented in the document such as facts, figure, opinions, or points of view.

❸ **Read the directions that accompany the questions.**
Make sure you understand what you are expected to do to answer the questions. Some questions require answers that can easily be found in the source. Others ask you to connect pieces of information from different parts of the source. Others may require you to make inferences using information not in the source.

❹ **Re-read the questions and then use the document and your knowledge of the subject to find the answers.**

❺ **Write your answers.**
Use the space provided to write your answers to each question.

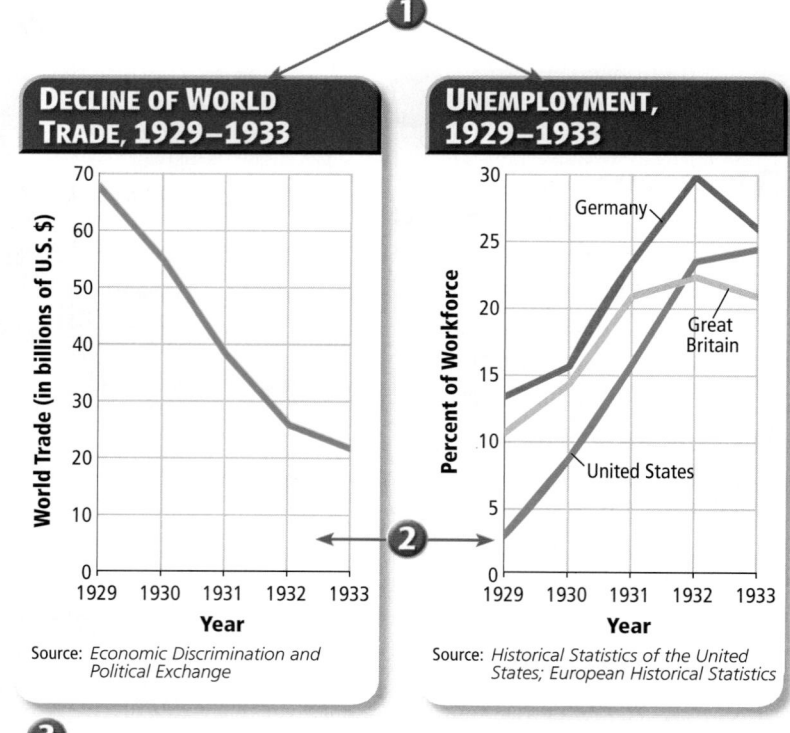

DECLINE OF WORLD TRADE, 1929–1933

World Trade (in billions of U.S. $)

Year

Source: *Economic Discrimination and Political Exchange*

UNEMPLOYMENT, 1929–1933

Percent of Workforce

Germany

Great Britain

United States

Year

Source: *Historical Statistics of the United States; European Historical Statistics*

❸

Directions *Examine the line graphs carefully and answer the questions that follow in complete sentences.*

1. What country had the highest unemployment rate between 1929 and 1933?

    Germany had the highest unemployment rate.

❹ 2. How might the decline in world trade have affected the unemployment rate? ❺

    The drop in world trade could have caused a

    decline in the number of available jobs.

3. What caused the decline of world trade and the rise of unemployment rates?

    The Great Depression caused world trade to

    decline and unemployment rates to rise.

Extended Response

Extended-response questions are similar to constructed-response questions in that they ask you to analyze information presented in a document such as a chart, graph, or map and then to write a response. Extended-response answers, however, usually consist of a paragraph or essay. You will be assessed partly on your ability to write a coherent, grammatically correct response. In addition to your interpretation and analysis of the document, your answer should also include some prior knowledge of the topic.

   To analyze and interpret the document, use the strategies you have already learned. To answer the question, use the strategies below.

LEARN

① Read the directions and question carefully to determine the purpose of your answer.
Be clear about what the question is asking you to do.

② Identify the subject and purpose of the document.
Examine the title, labels, and other details that can indicate a document's subject and purpose.

③ Study the document carefully.
Read the text and note facts or details that might help you answer the question.

④ Use the question and your notes to create a topic sentence.
Questions often point towards an effective topic sentence. However, avoid simply restating the question as a sentence.

⑤ Develop an outline or graphic organizer to help organize your main points.

⑥ Write your answer in complete sentences.
Start with your topic sentence. Then refer to your outline as you write. Be sure to use correct grammar, spelling, and punctuation.

② MAJOR TRADE ORGANIZATIONS AND AGREEMENTS
QUICK FACTS

ORGANIZATION [date formed]	Members (in 2006) and goals
General Agreement on Tariffs and Trade (GATT) [1948]	125 members (in 1995); worked to reduce tariffs and other international trade barriers; replaced by WTO
World Trade Organization (WTO) [1995]	Nearly 150 members; promotes lower trade barriers
Group of Eight (G-8) [1975, as G-6]	8 major industrial democracies; discuss international economic, environmental, and other issues ③
Organization of Petroleum Exporting Countries (OPEC) [1960]	11 major oil exporting countries, most in Middle East; coordinate oil policies of members
European Union (EU) [1993]	25 European nations; work for European economic and political integration

⑤ Use facts and examples from the document to help support your answer.

① Directions *Use the table and your knowledge of world trade to write an essay that answers the question below.*

1. How have regional and international trade organizations affected world trade? What are the advantages and disadvantages of such organizations?

   For the most part, international trade organizations have served to boost world trade. Some organizations, like the GATT were created to boost trade. Others, like OPEC, were created to strict oil sales of its members so that each will receive a high price for their products.

Document-Based Questions

Document-based questions ask you to analyze written and visual documents. Document-based questions usually consist of two parts. The first part asks short-answer questions about each document. The second part asks students to use their answers and information from the documents to produce an essay on a given topic. Use the strategies below to answer document-based questions.

LEARN

1 Read the Historical Context information carefully.
This section will help you understand the background of the issue and documents that you will read.

2 Review the Task information.
The task provides you with directions for answering the document-based question.

3 Read the essay question carefully.
Be sure to pay attention to what the question is asking you to do.

4 Skim each of the documents in Part A.
Briefly examine each document to get an idea of the issues it presents. Only two documents are shown here. Typically, document-based questions involve between four and eight documents.

5 Carefully examine and study each document.
Look for points that might help you answer the essay question. If you are allowed to mark up the exam, underline or otherwise identify key points. You may also want to make notes in the margin.

Historical Context In 1917 the United States was debating whether or not to enter World War I, then raging in its third year in Europe. There was strong sentiment to maintain neutrality.

Task Using information from the documents and your knowledge of world history, answer the questions that follow each document in Part A. Your answers to the questions will help you write the Part B essay, in which you will be asked to:

> **Discuss the positions both pro and con for United States entry into World War I and describe the eventual course of events.**

3 In this case, the question asks about United States neutrality in World War I.

Part A: Short-Answer Questions

Study each document carefully. Then answer the question or questions that follow each document in the space provided.

DOCUMENT 1

> *16 January 1917*
> "We intend to begin unrestricted submarine warfare on the first of February. We shall endeavor in spite of this to keep the United States neutral. In the event of this not succeeding, we make Mexico a proposal of an alliance on the following basis: Make war together, make peace together, generous financial support, and an understanding on our part that Mexico is to reconquer the lost territory in Texas, New Mexico, and Arizona...."
>
> Zimmermann

1. What did the Zimmermann telegram propose to Mexico?

The Zimmermann telegram proposed that Mexico join in an alliance

with Germany against the United States.

DOCUMENT **2**

2. What point about United States neutrality in World War I is this political cartoon attempting to make?

It makes the point that American patience is wearing thin.

Part B: Essay **9**

Using information from the documents and your knowledge of world history, write a well-organized essay recounting the debate over the United States's policy of neutrality in World War I and the events that altered that policy.

6 Read and answer each of the document-specific questions. As you answer the questions, think about how each connects to the essay topic.

7 Return to the essay question to help you form a topic sentence or thesis.

8 Create an outline or graphic organizer to help organize your main points. Review the document and any notes you made to find examples to support your points.

9 Write your essay. Include an introductory paragraph that frames your argument, a main body with details that explain it, and a closing paragraph that summarizes your position. Include specific details or documents to support your ideas.

Mastering the New York Social Studies Standards

Holt World History: Human Legacy, New York Edition was created specifically with the New York Learning Standards for Social Studies and the New York Core Curriculum in mind. These are documents that identify the skills and content you need to know to prepare for the Regents Exam.

The **New York Learning Standards for Social Studies, Standard 2—World History** are listed on pages NY3–NY4 of this textbook. Learning Standards are divided into Key Ideas and Performance Indicators.

- Key Ideas (KI): Key Ideas describe the kinds of skills that you will be learning. There are four Key Ideas.
- Performance Indicators (PI): Each Key Idea includes several Performance Indicators; these identify the skills you must use to show your understanding of world history.

At the beginning of each section in your textbook, you will see a code that refers to the specific Performance Indicator or Indicators that you will be covering in that section. For example, **PI** 1.1 means you will be using the first Performance Indicator under Key Idea 1.

The **New York Social Studies Core Curriculum** is listed on pages NY5–NY9. It is organized into eight units. Each unit identifies the specific content, concepts, and themes that you will need to learn in order to understand global history and geography. On certain pages in your textbook, you will see a code like the one below. This code refers to the content of the Core Curriculum covered by that part of the chapter. The diagram below shows how to read this code.

NEW YORK

CC Unit 8-B3

Economic interdependence

UNIT EIGHT: GLOBAL CONNECTIONS AND INTERACTIONS, continued

Content	Standards	Concepts/Themes	Connections
c. Political issues, e.g., participation in the political process		Factors of Production Environment Human Rights	need to understand how nations use and distribute scarce resources. Urbanization, modernization, and industrialization are powerful agents of social change in developing nations.
8. Ethnic and religious tensions: an analysis of multiple perspectives	2,4,5		- What factors determine whether or not a nation is overpopulated?
a. Northern Ireland			- What strategies are nations taking to overcome the adverse aspects of urbanization and overpopulation?
b. Balkans: Serbs, Croats, and Muslims			- To what extent has the status of women advanced throughout the 20th century?
c. Sikhs and Tamils		Conflict	Suggested Documents: Official United Nations documents from the Beijing Conference on Women (1995); Amnesty International, *Political Murder*; Paul Kennedy, *Demographic Explosion*
d. Indonesian Christians		Change	
e. China—Tibet			
f. Indonesia—East Timor			
B. Economic issues	1,2,4		TEACHER'S NOTE: Students should understand that as global economic systems become more interdependent, economic decisions made in one nation or region have implications for all regions. Economic development for all nations depends upon a wise use of globally scarce resources.
1. North/South dichotomy: issues of development (post-colonialism)			
a. Africa			
b. Latin America			
2. Korea's economic miracle		Change	
3. Economic interdependence		Economic Systems	
4. World hunger		Needs and Wants	- What is meant by the term "post-colonialism"?

New York Learning Standards for Social Studies

Standard 2—World History

Students will use a variety of intellectual skills to demonstrate their understanding of major ideas, eras, themes, developments, and turning points in world history and examine the broad sweep of history from a variety of perspectives.

KEY IDEA 1: The study of world history requires an understanding of world cultures and civilizations, including an analysis of important ideas, social and cultural values, beliefs, and traditions. This study also examines the human condition and the connections and interactions of people across time and space, and the ways different people view the same event or issue from a variety of perspectives.

PI 1.1 Students define culture and civilization, explaining how they developed and changed over time. Investigate the various components of cultures and civilizations, including social customs, norms, values, and traditions; political systems; economic systems; religions and spiritual beliefs; and socialization or educational practices.

PI 1.2 Students understand the development and connectedness of Western civilization and other civilizations and cultures in many areas of the world and over time.

PI 1.3 Students analyze historic events from around the world by examining accounts written from different perspectives.

PI 1.4 Students understand the broad patterns, relationships, and interactions of cultures and civilizations during particular eras and across eras.

PI 1.5 Students analyze changing and competing interpretations of issues, events, and developments throughout world history.

KEY IDEA 2: Establishing time frames, exploring different periodizations, examining themes across time and within cultures, and focusing on important turning points in world history help organize the study of world cultures and civilizations.

PI 2.1 Students distinguish between the past, present, and future by creating multiple-tier timelines that display important events and developments from world history across time and place.

PI 2.2 Students evaluate the effectiveness of different models for the periodization of important historic events, identifying the reasons why a particular sequence for these events was chosen.

PI 2.3 Students analyze evidence critically and demonstrate an understanding of how circumstances of time and place influence perspective.

PI 2.4 Students explain the importance of analyzing narratives drawn from different times and places to understand historical events.

PI 2.5 Students investigate key events and developments and major turning points in world history to identify the factors that brought about change and the long-term effects of these changes.

KEY IDEA 3: Study of the major social, political, cultural, and religious developments in world history involves learning about the important roles and contributions of individuals and groups.

PI 3.1 Students analyze the roles and contributions of individuals and groups to social, political, economic, cultural, and religious practices and activities.

PI 3.2 Students explain the dynamics of cultural change and how interactions between and among cultures have affected various cultural groups throughout the world.

PI 3.3 Students examine the social/cultural, political, economic, and religious norms and values of Western and other world cultures.

KEY IDEA 4: The skills of historical analysis include the ability to investigate differing and competing interpretations of the theories of history, hypothesize about why interpretations change over time, explain the importance of historical evidence, and understand the concepts of change and continuity over time.

PI 4.1 Students identify historical problems, pose analytical questions or hypotheses, research analytical questions or test hypotheses, formulate conclusions or generalizations, raise new questions or issues for further investigation.

PI 4.2 Students interpret and analyze documents and artifacts related to significant developments and events in world history.

PI 4.3 Students plan and organize historical research projects related to regional or global interdependence.

PI 4.4 Students analyze different interpretations of important events, issues, or developments in world history by studying the social, political, and economic context in which they were developed; by testing the data source for reliability and validity, credibility, authority, authenticity, and completeness; and by detecting bias, distortion of the facts, and propaganda by omission, suppression, or invention of facts.

The Great Sphinx was built next to the tomb of Pharaoh Khufu of Egypt.

New York Social Studies Core Curriculum

NEW YORK STATE STANDARDS

The Core Curriculum details what content and skills students need to master in their study of World History. The content of the Core Curriculum provides the basis for the New York State Regents examination in World History and Geography.

Methodology of Global History and Geography

A. History
1. Skills of historical analysis
2. Understand the concepts of change and continuity over time
3. The connections and interactions of people across time and space
4. Time frames and periodization
5. Roles and contributions of individuals and groups
6. Oral histories

B. Geography
1. Elements of geography
2. Critical thinking skills
3. Identifying and defining world regions

C. Economics
1. Major economic concepts (scarcity, supply/demand, opportunity costs, production, resources)
2. Economic decision making
3. The interdependence of economics and economic systems throughout the world
4. Applying critical thinking skills in making informed and well-reasoned economic decisions

D. Political science
1. The purposes of government
2. Political systems around the world
3. Political concepts of power, authority, governance, and law
4. Rights and responsibilities of citizenship across time and space
5. Critical thinking skills

Unit One:
Ancient World—Civilizations and Religions (4000 BC–500 AD)

A. Early peoples
1. Human and physical geography
2. Hunters and gatherers—nomadic groups
3. Relationship to the environment
4. Migration of early human populations
5. Early government

B. Neolithic Revolution and early river civilizations
1. Compare and contrast (Mesopotamia, Egypt, the Indus Valley, and Yellow River civilizations)
2. Identify demographic patterns of early civilizations and movement of people—Bantu migration (500 BC–1500 AD)

C. Classical civilizations
1. Chinese civilization
2. Greek civilization
3. Roman Republic
4. Indian (Maurya) Empire
5. Rise of agrarian civilizations in Mesoamerica—Mayan (200 BC–900 AD)
6. The status and role of women in classical civilizations
7. The growth of global trade routes in classical civilizations

D. The rise and fall of great empires
1. Han Dynasty
2. Roman Empire

E. The emergence and spread of belief systems
1. Place of origin and major beliefs
2. Expansion of Christianity, Islam, Confucianism, and Buddhism

Unit Two:
Expanding Zones of Exchange and Encounter (500–1200)

A. Gupta Empire (320–550 AD)
1. Human and physical geography
2. Artistic, scientific, and mathematical contributions
3. Ties to Hinduism
4. Organizational structure

B. Tang and Song Dynasty (618–1126 A D)
1. Human and physical geography
2. Contributions
3. Chinese influence on Korea and Japan
4. Cultural flowering
5. Growth of commerce and trade

C. Byzantine Empire (330–1453 AD)
1. Human and physical geography

NEW YORK STATE STANDARDS **NY5**

2. Achievements (law—Justinian Code, engineering, art, and commerce)
3. The Orthodox Christian Church
4. Political structure and Justinian Code
5. Role in preserving and transmitting Greek and Roman cultures
6. Impact on Russia and Eastern Europe

D. Early Russia
1. Human and physical geography
2. Trade
3. Kiev
4. Russian Orthodox Church

E. The spread of Islam to Europe, Asia, and Africa
1. Human and physical geography
2. Organizational structure
3. The development of Islamic law and its impact
4. Social class: women and slavery in Muslim society
5. Position of "people of the book"
6. The golden age of Islam
7. Trade

F. Medieval Europe (500–1400)
1. Human and physical geography
2. Frankish Empire—Charlemagne
3. Manorialism
4. Feudalism
5. Spiritual and secular role of the Church
6. Monastic centers of learning
7. Anti-Semitism
8. Art and architecture

G. Crusades
1. Causes
2. Impacts on Southwest Asia, Byzantium, and Europe
3. Perspectives
4. Key individuals—Urban II, Saladin, and Richard the Lion-Hearted

Unit Three:
Global Interactions (1200–1650)

A. Early Japanese history and feudalism
1. Human and physical geography
2. Early traditions (Shintoism)
3. Ties with China and Korea: cultural diffusion, Buddhism, and Confucianism
4. Tokugawa Shogunate
5. Social hierarchy and stratification
6. Comparison to European feudalism
7. Zen Buddhism

B. The rise and fall of the Mongols and their impact on Eurasia
1. Human and physical geography
2. Origins—Central Asian nomadic tribes
3. The Yuan Dynasty: a foreign non-Chinese dynasty

4. Extent of empire under Genghis Khan and Kublai Khan
5. Impact on Central Asia, China, Korea, Europe, India, Southwest Asia
6. Impact on the rise of Moscow
7. Interaction with the West and global trade, Pax Mongolia (e.g., Marco Polo)
8. Causes of decline

C. Global trade and interactions
1. Resurgence of Europe
2. Major trading centers—Nanjing/Calicut/Mogadishu/Venice
3. Ibn Battuta
4. Expansion of the Portuguese spice trade to Southeast Asia and its impact on Asia and Europe

D. Rise and fall of African civilizations: Ghana, Mali, Axum, and Songhai empires
1. Human and physical geography
2. Organizational structure
3. Contributions
4. Roles in global trade routes
5. Spread and impact of Islam—Mansa Musa
6. Timbuktu and African trade routes

E. Social, economic, and political impacts of the plague on Eurasia and Africa

F. Renaissance and humanism
1. Human and physical geography
2. Shift in worldview—otherworldly to secular
3. Greco-Roman revival (interest in humanism)
4. Art and architecture (e.g., da Vinci and Michelangelo)
5. Literature (e.g., Dante, Cervantes, Shakespeare)
6. Political science (e.g., Machiavelli)
7. New scientific and technological innovations (Gutenberg's moveable type printing press, cartography, naval engineering, and navigational and nautical devices)

G. Reformation and Counter Reformation
1. Human and physical geography
2. Martin Luther's *Ninety-Five Theses*: the challenge to the power and authority of the Roman Catholic Church
3. Anti-Semitic laws and policies
4. Henry VIII and the English Reformation
5. Calvin and other reformers
6. Counter Reformation (Ignatius Loyola, Council of Trent)
7. Roles of men and women within the Christian churches
8. Religious wars in Europe: causes and impacts

H. The rise and impact of European nation-states/decline of feudalism

Unit Four:
The First Global Age (1450–1770)

A. The Ming Dynasty (1368–1644)
1. Human and physical geography
2. Restoration of Chinese rule, Chinese world vision
3. The impact of China on East Asia and Southeast Asia
4. China's relationship with the West
5. Contributions
6. Expansion of trade (Zheng He, 1405–1433)

B. The impact of the Ottoman Empire on the Middle East and Europe
1. Human and physical geography
2. Contributions
3. Suleiman I (the Magnificent, the Lawgiver)
4. Disruption of established trade routes and European search for new ones
5. Limits of Ottoman Europe

C. Spain and Portugal on the eve of the encounter
1. Human and physical geography
2. Reconquista under Ferdinand and Isabella
3. Expulsion of Moors and Jews
4. Exploration and overseas expansion

D. The rise of Mesoamerican empires: Aztec and Incan empires before 1500
1. Human and physical geography
2. Organizational structure
3. Contributions
4. Trade

E. The encounter between Europeans and the peoples of Africa, the Americas, and Asia
1. Human and physical geography
2. European competition for colonies in the Americas, Africa, East Asia, and Southeast Asia—The "old imperialism"
3. Global demographic shifts
4. The extent of European expansionism
5. European mercantilism
6. Spanish colonialism and the introduction of the Encomienda system to Latin America
7. Dutch colonization in East Asia (Japan and Indonesia)
8. Exchange of food and disease

F. Political ideologies: global absolutism
1. Human and physical geography
2. Thomas Hobbes, *The Leviathan*
3. Jacques-Benigne Bossuet: Absolutism and Divine right theory
4. Case studies: Akbar the Great, Suleiman the Magnificent, Philip II, Louis XIV, Ivan the Terrible, and Peter the Great

Ottoman forces used cannons in their siege of Constantinople in 1453.

G. The response to absolutism: The rise of parliamentary democracy in England
1. Background—Magna Carta
2. Divine Right of Monarchy—Stuart rule
3. Puritan Revolution—Oliver Cromwell
4. Glorious Revolution—John Locke and the English Bill of Rights

Unit Five:
An Age of Revolution (1750–1914)

A. The Scientific Revolution
1. The development of scientific methods
2. The work of Copernicus, Galileo, Newton, and Descartes

B. The Enlightenment in Europe
1. The writings of Locke, Voltaire, Rousseau, and Montesquieu
2. The impact of the Enlightenment on nationalism and democracy
3. The enlightened despots—Maria Theresa and Catherine the Great

C. Political revolutions
1. Human and physical geography of revolutions
2. American Revolution
3. French Revolution
4. Independence movements in Latin America

D. The reaction against revolutionary ideas
1. Human and physical geography
2. Balance of power politics and the Congress of Vienna (Klemens von Metternich)
3. Revolutions of 1848
4. Russian absolutism: reforms and expansion

E. Latin America: The failure of democracy and the search for stability
1. Human and physical geography
2. Roles of social classes: land-holding elite, creoles, mestizos, native peoples, and slaves
3. Roles of the Church and military
4. Role of cash crop economies in a global market
5. The Mexican Revolution (1910–1930)

F. Global nationalism
1. Human and physical geography
2. Role in political revolutions
3. Force for unity and self-determination
4. Zionism
5. Force leading to conflicts

G. Economic and social revolutions
1. Human and physical geography
2. Agrarian revolution
3. The British Industrial Revolution
4. Mass starvation in Ireland (1845–1850)

H. Imperialism
1. Reasons for imperialism—nationalistic, political, economic, "The White Man's Burden," Social Darwinism
2. Spatial characteristics—"new imperialism"
3. British in India
4. British, French, Belgians, and Germans in Africa
5. European spheres of influence in China
6. Multiple perspectives toward imperialism

I. Japan and the Meiji restoration
1. Human and physical geography
2. The opening of Japan
3. Modernization, industrialization
4. Japan as an imperialist power

Unit Six:
A Half Century of Crisis and Achievement (1900–1945)

A. World War I
1. Europe: the physical setting
2. Causes
3. Impacts
4. Effects of scientific/technological advances on warfare
5. Armenian Massacre
6. Collapse of the Ottoman Empire
7. The war as reflected in literature, art, and propaganda

B. Revolution and change in Russia—causes and impacts
1. Czar Nicholas II
2. The Revolution of 1905

3. March Revolution and provisional government
4. Bolshevik Revolution
5. V. I. Lenin's rule in Russia
6. Stalin and the rise of a modern totalitarian state: industrialization, command economy, collectivization
7. Russification of ethnic republics
8. Forced famine in Ukraine
9. Reign of Terror

C. Between the wars
1. Human and physical geography
2. Treaty of Versailles and the League of Nations
3. Modernization and westernization of a secular Turkey—Kemal Atatürk
4. Women's suffrage movement
5. Great Depression—causes and impacts
6. Weimar Republic and the rise of fascism as an aftermath of World War I
7. Japanese militarism and imperialism
8. Policy of appeasement—Munich Pact
9. Colonial response to European Imperialism
10. Arabic and Zionist nationalism

D. World War II—causes and impact
1. Human and physical geography
2. The Nazi and Japanese states
3. Key individuals—Hitler, Mussolini, Stalin, Churchill, and Roosevelt
4. Key events—Dunkirk, the Blitz, D Day, Hitler's second front, the war in the Pacific
5. The Nazi Holocaust: the extermination of Jews, Poles, other Slavs, Gypsies, disabled, and others
6. Resistance
7. Japan's role—Nanjing, Bataan, Pearl Harbor
8. War in China—Long March
9. Impacts of technology on total war
10. Hiroshima and Nagasaki
11. War crime trials
12. Global spatial arrangements—post-World War II world

Unit Seven:
The 20th Century Since 1945

A. Cold War balance of power
1. Human and physical geography
2. The world in 1945: physical setting
3. United States occupation of Germany and Japan
4. Emergence of the superpowers
5. Political climate of the Cold War
6. Korean War

B. Role of the United Nations
1. Peace keeping
2. Social and economic programs
3. Contemporary social conditions

C. Economic issues in the Cold War and Post–Cold War era
1. Human and physical geography
2. A comparison of market versus command economies (Western Europe versus Soviet Union)
3. Economic recovery in Europe and Japan
4. Organization of Petroleum Exporting Countries (OPEC): oil crisis in the 1970s
5. Pacific Rim economies/economic crisis
6. North America Free Trade Agreement (NAFTA), 1997

D. Chinese Communist Revolution
1. Human and physical geography
2. Communist rise to power (1936–1949); Jiang Jieshi (Chiang Kai-shek), Mao Zedong
3. Communism under Mao Zedong
4. Communism under Deng Xiaoping
5. Return of Hong Kong—July 1, 1997
6. The social system in communist China versus dynastic China

E. Collapse of European imperialism
1. Human and physical geography
2. India—independence and partition
3. African independence movements and Pan Africanism
4. Southeast Asia

F. Conflicts and change in the Middle East
1. Human and physical geography
2. The creation of the State of Israel, Arab Palestinians, and Israel's Arab neighbors
3. Roles of individuals—Golda Meir, Yasir Arafat, Anwar Sadat, King Hussein, Yitzhak Rabin, Palestine Liberation Organization (PLO)
4. Role of terrorism
5. Turkey and Iraq—Kurds
6. Migration of Jews from Europe, the United States, the Soviet Union, and Africa
7. The Iranian Revolution
8. Persian Gulf War—Saddam Hussein
9. Islamic fundamentalism (Iran, Libya, Afghanistan, Algeria, Turkey)

G. Collapse of communism and the breakup of the Soviet Union
1. Human and physical geography
2. Background events, 1970 to 1987
3. Poland's Solidarity and Lech Walesa
4. Mikhail Gorbachev (perestroika and glasnost)
5. Fall of the Berlin Wall and the reunification of Germany—causes and impacts
6. Ethnic conflict in former satellite states, e.g., Kosovo, Bosnia
7. Changing political boundaries
8. Challenges faced by post-communist Russia—the world of Boris Yeltsin

H. Political and economic change in Latin America
1. Latin America: physical setting
2. Argentina
3. Fidel Castro's Cuban Revolution—causes and impact
4. Nicaragua and the Sandinistas
5. Guatemala and the indigenous peoples
6. Changing role of the Roman Catholic Church in Latin America
7. Latin American immigration to the United States
8. Return of the Panama Canal

Unit Eight:
Global Connections and Interactions

A. Social and political patterns and change
1. Human and physical geography
2. Population pressures and poverty (China, India, Africa, and Latin America)
3. Migration
4. Modernization/tradition—finding a balance
5. Scientific and technological advances
6. Urbanization—use and distribution of scarce resources (Africa, India, Latin America)
7. Status of women and children
8. Ethnic and religious tensions: an analysis of multiple perspectives

B. Economic issues
1. North/South dichotomy: issues of development (post-colonialism)
2. Korea's economic miracle
3. Economic interdependence
4. World hunger

C. The environment and sustainability
1. Pollution—air, water, toxic waste (Europe)
2. Deforestation (Amazon Basin)
3. Desertification (Sahel)
4. Nuclear safety (Chernobyl)
5. Endangered species (Africa)

D. Science and technology
1. Information age/Computer Revolution/Internet
2. Impact of satellites
3. Green Revolution
4. Space exploration
5. Literacy and education
6. Medical breakthroughs—disease control/life expectancy/genetics
7. Epidemics—AIDS
8. Nuclear proliferation

Preparing for the Regents Exam

Everyone wants to ace the big test, but doing well takes preparation and practice. *Holt World History: Human Legacy, New York Edition* provides many opportunities for you to prepare for the Regents Exam.

Countdown to Testing

The Countdown to Testing section will help you study and prepare during the weeks before your test.

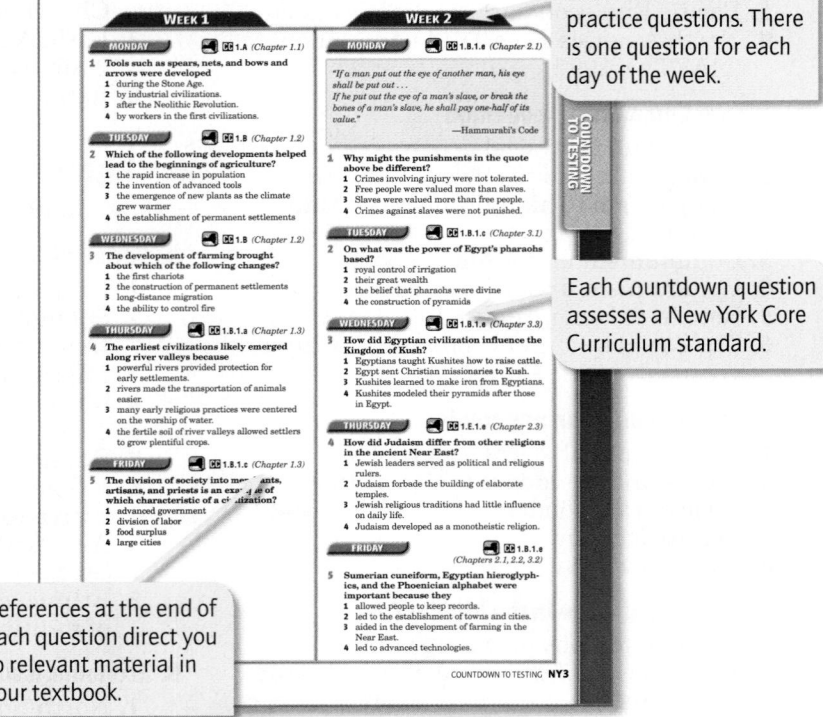

There are 24 weeks of practice questions. There is one question for each day of the week.

Each Countdown question assesses a New York Core Curriculum standard.

References at the end of each question direct you to relevant material in your textbook.

Other Test Prep and Practice

Other opportunities to practice and prepare for the Regents Exam include:

- Test-Taking Strategies Handbook in the Student Edition
- Unit-level Regents Practice in the Student Edition
- *Regents Review Workbook*

Test-Taking Tips

- **Use the Countdown to Testing questions to help you prepare.** Spend a few minutes every day answering that day's question.
- **Get plenty of sleep the night before the test.** A rested mind thinks more clearly and will help you focus during the test.
- **Arrive at the test prepared.** Remember your pencil and eraser and anything else you may need on test day.

- **Read each question carefully.** Be sure you know exactly what the question is asking.
- **Answer the easy questions first.** If you don't know the answer to a question, skip it and come back to it later.
- **Review your answers.** Before handing in your test, take a minute to look over your answers.

WEEK 1

MONDAY   **CC 1.A** *(Chapter 1.1)*

1 Tools such as spears, nets, and bows and arrows were developed
- **(1)** during the Stone Age.
- **2** by industrial civilizations.
- **3** after the Neolithic Revolution.
- **4** by workers in the first civilizations.

TUESDAY   **CC 1.B** *(Chapter 1.2)*

2 Which of the following developments helped lead to the beginnings of agriculture?
- **1** the rapid increase in population
- **2** the invention of advanced tools
- **(3)** the emergence of new plants as the climate grew warmer
- **4** the establishment of permanent settlements

WEDNESDAY   **CC 1.B** *(Chapter 1.2)*

3 The development of farming brought about which of the following changes?
- **1** the first chariots
- **(2)** the construction of permanent settlements
- **3** long-distance migration
- **4** the ability to control fire

THURSDAY   **CC 1.B.1.a** *(Chapter 1.3)*

4 The earliest civilizations likely emerged along river valleys because
- **1** powerful rivers provided protection for early settlements.
- **2** rivers made the transportation of animals easier.
- **3** many early religious practices were centered on the worship of water.
- **(4)** the fertile soil of river valleys allowed settlers to grow plentiful crops.

FRIDAY   **CC 1.B.1.c** *(Chapter 1.3)*

5 The division of society into merchants, artisans, and priests is an example of which characteristic of a civilization?
- **1** advanced government
- **(2)** division of labor
- **3** food surplus
- **4** large cities

WEEK 2

MONDAY   **CC 1.B.1.e** *(Chapter 2.1)*

> *"If a man put out the eye of another man, his eye shall be put out . . .*
> *If he put out the eye of a man's slave, or break the bones of a man's slave, he shall pay one-half of its value."*
>
> —Hammurabi's Code

1 Why might the punishments in the quote above be different?
- **1** Crimes involving injury were not tolerated.
- **(2)** Free people were valued more than slaves.
- **3** Slaves were valued more than free people.
- **4** Crimes against slaves were not punished.

TUESDAY   **CC 1.B.1.c** *(Chapter 3.1)*

2 On what was the power of Egypt's pharaohs based?
- **1** royal control of irrigation
- **2** their great wealth
- **(3)** the belief that pharaohs were divine
- **4** the construction of pyramids

WEDNESDAY   **CC 1.B.1.e** *(Chapter 3.3)*

3 How did Egyptian civilization influence the Kingdom of Kush?
- **1** Egyptians taught Kushites how to raise cattle.
- **2** Egypt sent Christian missionaries to Kush.
- **3** Kushites learned to make iron from Egyptians.
- **(4)** Kushites modeled their pyramids after those in Egypt.

THURSDAY   **CC 1.E.1.e** *(Chapter 2.3)*

4 How did Judaism differ from other religions in the ancient Near East?
- **1** Jewish leaders served as political and religious rulers.
- **2** Judaism forbade the building of elaborate temples.
- **3** Jewish religious traditions had little influence on daily life.
- **(4)** Judaism developed as a monotheistic religion.

FRIDAY   **CC 1.B.1.e**
(Chapters 2.1, 2.2, 3.2)

5 Sumerian cuneiform, Egyptian hieroglyphics, and the Phoenician alphabet were important because they
- **(1)** allowed people to keep records.
- **2** led to the establishment of towns and cities.
- **3** aided in the development of farming in the Near East.
- **4** led to advanced technologies.

MONDAY CC 1.B.1.d *(Chapter 4.1)*

1 Excavations at Mohenjo Daro and Harappa indicate that early Indian civilizations

1 practiced monotheism.
2 constructed large temple-pyramids.
(3) built large, advanced cities.
4 were destroyed by invaders from Egypt.

TUESDAY CC 1.B.1 *(Chapter 4.1)*

2 After the decline of the Indus civilization, what new civilization arose in India?

(1) Aryan civilization
2 Buddhist civilization
3 Sumerian civilization
4 Varnas civilization

WEDNESDAY CC 1.E.1 *(Chapter 4.2, 4.3)*

3 One similarity between Hinduism and Buddhism is that they both

1 encourage the practice of yoga to aid in meditation.
(2) believe in rebirth.
3 believe Brahman created and preserves the world.
4 spread throughout Africa.

THURSDAY CC 1.C.1.d *(Chapter 4.4)*

4 According to China's Mandate of Heaven

1 a powerful god created the first Chinese civilization.
2 rulers should obey the gods' wishes.
(3) the gods would not allow corrupt rulers to govern.
4 peasants should not participate in government.

FRIDAY CC 1.E.2 *(Chapter 4.3)*

5 Which of the following correctly describes the spread of Buddhism?

(1) Buddhism originated in India but later spread to Southeast Asia, China, and Japan.
2 Japanese missionaries introduced Buddhism to Southeast Asia.
3 Chinese merchants are credited with spreading Buddhism to India.
4 Buddhism originated in China and later spread to India.

MONDAY CC 1.C.2 *(Chapter 5.1)*

GREECE

Minoan settlement (c. 2000–1400 BC)
Mycenaean settlement (c. 1250 BC)

Aegean Sea
ASIA MINOR
Mycenae
Peloponnesus
Mediterranean Sea
Knossos
Crete
0 50 100 Miles
0 50 100 Kilometers

1 The map above illustrates

(1) the earliest known Greek civilizations.
2 Greek colonies in Asia Minor.
3 the empire of Alexander the Great.
4 the most powerful city-states in Greece.

TUESDAY CC 1.C.2.b *(Chapter 5.1)*

2 Loyalty, bravery, and discipline are values that would have been most highly prized by citizens of which city-state?

1 Athens
2 Corinth
3 Macedonia
(4) Sparta

WEDNESDAY CC 1.C.2.c *(Chapter 5.3)*

3 Aristotle is best known for his

1 discovery that Earth is round.
2 emphasis on thinking for oneself.
3 recording of the teachings of Socrates.
(4) logical study of most fields of science.

THURSDAY CC 1.C.2.e *(Chapter 5.4)*

4 Alexander the Great's empire extended from

1 Italy to Persia.
2 Asia Minor to the Caspian Sea.
(3) Greece to the Indus River.
4 Egypt to Mesopotamia.

FRIDAY CC 1.C.2.d *(Chapter 5.2)*

5 The government of the United States differs from that of ancient Athens in that

(1) U.S. citizens elect representatives to vote for them.
2 U.S. leaders can serve as many terms as they wish.
3 U.S. government is made up of only one branch.
4 foreigners cannot become citizens of the United States.

MONDAY **CC** 1.C.3.B *(Chapter 6.1)*

1 **The government of the Roman Republic resembles today's U.S. government in that**
  1 both give veto power to legislative leaders.
  2 both appoint powerful dictators in times of emergency.
  3 both are made up of only two branches.
  ④ both use a system of check and balances.

TUESDAY **CC** 1.D.2 *(Chapter 6.2)*

2 **The shift from republic to empire in Rome is credited to the efforts of**
  ① Augustus
  2 Constantine
  3 Diocletian
  4 Julius Caesar

WEDNESDAY **CC** 1.E.2 *(Chapter 6.4)*

3 **Emperor Constantine's conversion to Christianity helped**
  1 him win a decisive battle.
  2 introduce Christianity to non-Jews.
  ③ Christianity spread more rapidly throughout the empire.
  4 strengthen the Roman Empire.

THURSDAY **CC** 1.D.2.b *(Chapter 6.3)*

4 **The structure in the photo above is an example of the Romans' skill in**
  1 military conquest.
  ② engineering.
  3 law.
  4 science.

FRIDAY **CC** 1.D.2.d *(Chapter 6.5)*

5 **Which of the following was a key cause of the economic troubles that led to Rome's collapse?**
  1 A new capital at was constructed at Constantinople.
  2 The Visigoths sacked the city of Rome.
  ③ Emperors minted new coins that were not as valuable as they previously had been.
  4 Diocletian split the empire into two parts.

MONDAY **CC** 1.C.5 *(Chapter 7.2)*

1 **The discovery of elaborate tombs, giant stone head monuments, and pyramids in Olmec settlements *most likely* led scholars to believe that**
  1 the Olmec were skilled hunters.
  2 Olmec society was highly organized.
  3 the Olmec were polytheistic.
  ④ Olmec towns served as religious and ceremonial centers.

TUESDAY **CC** 4.D *(Chapter 7.2, 7.3)*

2 **Which of the following is a similarity between the Aztec and Inca civilizations?**
  ① Both created large and powerful empires.
  2 Trade played an important role in both civilizations.
  3 Slaves made up the lowest social class in both civilizations.
  4 Both civilizations were located in what is now Central Mexico.

WEDNESDAY **CC** 4.D.3 *(Chapter 7.2)*

3 **Which of the following is an example of Aztec achievements in astronomy?**
  1 the development of a writing system
  ② the creation of a 365-day calendar
  3 the use of *chinampas*
  4 the development of the concept of zero

THURSDAY **CC** 4.D
(Chapter 7.1, 7.2, 7.3)

4 **Which of the following identifies Mesoamerican civilizations from earliest to latest?**
  1 Anasazi, Aztec, Chavín, Inca
  ② Olmec, Maya, Aztec
  3 Zapotec, Aztec, Maya, Inca
  4 Maya, Hopewell, Aztec

FRIDAY **CC** 4.D.2 *(Chapter 7.3)*

5 **One way in which the Inca helped unify their large empire was to**
  ① build an extensive system of roads.
  2 demand a labor tax from all citizens.
  3 develop a uniform system of writing.
  4 maintain a powerful military.

COUNTDOWN TO TESTING

COUNTDOWN TO TESTING

MONDAY CC 1.D.1 *(Chapter 8.1)*

1 **Under Emperor Wudi, Confucianism became the official government philosophy. Why might Confucianism have appealed to Wudi?**
   1 It encouraged the use of strict laws and harsh punishments.
   2 It promoted the unification of the empire.
   ③ It emphasized obedience and loyalty.
   4 It stressed the importance of trade.

TUESDAY CC 1.C.7.b *(Chapter 8.2)*

2 **The Silk Roads played an important role during the Han dynasty because they**
   ① brought China into a global trade network.
   2 helped bring silk production to China.
   3 allowed China to export goods and ideas to Japan.
   4 helped to protect northern China from invaders.

WEDNESDAY CC 1.C.4 *(Chapter 8.3)*

3 **During his rule, Ashoka contributed to Indian society through all of the following ways *except***
   1 by improving roads and transportation.
   ② through his policy of taxation.
   3 in the construction of stone pillars.
   4 in his efforts to spread Buddhism.

THURSDAY CC 1.C *(Chapter 8.1, 8.2, 8.3, 8.4)*

4 **Which of the following correctly identifies an empire or dynasty with its achievement?**
   ① Han—created the civil-service system
   2 Gupta—built the Great Wall
   3 Maurya—invented the wheelbarrow
   4 Qin— invented paper

FRIDAY CC 1.C.7 *(Chapter 8.4)*

5 **During the Gupta period Indian trade helped link**
   ① the Mediterranean world and China.
   2 rich and poor.
   3 Hindus and Buddhists.
   4 north India and south India.

MONDAY CC 1.E.1.g *(Chapter 9.1)*

1 **Why did Muhammad leave Mecca for Yathrib, or Medina?**
   1 to avoid a war between the two cities
   ② his teachings had angered many people in Mecca
   3 he believed Medina was a holy city
   4 to relocate his trade business

TUESDAY CC 1.E *(Chapter 9.1)*

2 **Which of the following is a similarity between Islam, Judaism, and Christianity?**
   1 Each religion originated in Arabia.
   2 Each teaches followers to fast during its holy month.
   ③ Each is a monotheistic religion.
   4 Each believes that Muhammad is the last of God's prophets.

WEDNESDAY CC 1.E.2 *(Chapter 9.2)*

3 **The Muslim Empire expanded to all of the following areas *except***
   1 Spain
   2 Egypt
   3 Persia
   ④ Russia

THURSDAY CC 2.E.6.a *(Chapter 9.2)*

SUNNI AND SHIA DISTRIBUTION

4 **According to the map, the country with the most Shia Muslims is**
   ① Iran.
   2 Turkey.
   3 Saudi Arabia.
   4 Iraq.

FRIDAY CC 2.E.7 *(Chapter 9.3)*

5 **What role did Muslims play in global trade?**
   1 They traded gold to the rest of the world.
   ② They connected traders in the East and the West.
   3 They did not participate in global trade.
   4 They were the first to use coins in trade.

WEEK 9

MONDAY **CC 1.A.5** *(Chapter 10.1)*

1 Which of the following played the *most* important role in early African society?

1 village priests
2 the individual
3 kings and queens
④ the family

TUESDAY **CC 1.B.2** *(Chapter 10.1)*

BANTU MIGRATIONS

2 In what general direction did the Bantu migration routes travel?

① southeast
2 southwest
3 northeast
4 northwest

WEDNESDAY **CC 3.C.2** *(Chapter 10.2)*

3 What made the East African coast a center of world trade?

1 valuable trade items such as silk and glass
② its location on the Indian Ocean
3 large cities with walls for protection
4 powerful armies in Aksum and Ethiopia

THURSDAY **CC 3.D** *(Chapter 10.3)*

4 The power of West African kingdoms such as Ghana and Mali was largely based on their

1 use of camels for transportation.
2 conversion to Islam.
③ control of the salt and gold trades.
4 location along major trade routes.

FRIDAY **CC 3.D.5** *(Chapter 10.3)*

5 Mansa Musa's pilgrimage to Mecca was significant because it

① brought Mali's great wealth to the attention of other kingdoms.
2 caused the price of gold to rise.
3 brought great riches to the people of Mali.
4 introduced camels to Arabia and Europe.

WEEK 10

MONDAY **CC 2.B** *(Chapter 11.1)*

1 The Tang and Sui dynasties strengthened the power of the central government by

1 outlawing the production of weapons.
2 banning the export of silk.
③ reforming the bureaucracy.
4 encouraging new farming techniques to increase rice production.

TUESDAY **CC 2.B.2** *(Chapter 11.1)*

2 The compass and paper money were Chinese innovations that resulted from

1 the introduction of advanced warfare.
2 contact with Japan and Korea.
3 the creation of the civil-service system.
④ the increased importance of trade.

WEDNESDAY **CC 3.B.3** *(Chapter 11.2)*

3 Which of the following was an effect of Mongol rule in China?

① an increase in international trade
2 the spread of Mongol culture and religion
3 the invention of gunpowder
4 the introduction of horses to China

THURSDAY **CC 3.A.2** *(Chapter 11.3)*

4 The chief religion in early Japan was

1 Buddhism
② Shinto
3 Confucianism
4 Heian

FRIDAY **CC 2.B.3** *(Chapter 11.3)*

5 China influenced the development of Japan's

1 military.
2 social classes.
③ written language.
4 geography.

COUNTDOWN TO TESTING

COUNTDOWN TO TESTING

WEEK 11

MONDAY CC 2.C (Chapter 12.1)

1 **The Byzantine Empire emerged from**
- **①** the eastern portion of the Roman Empire.
- **2** Rus settlements along the Baltic Sea.
- **3** the union of the Angles and the Saxons.
- **4** barbarian tribes in Italy.

TUESDAY CC 2.C.2 (Chapter 12.1)

2 **Why was Justinian's law code significant?**
- **1** It outlawed slavery in the empire.
- **2** It gave Justinian the title of emperor.
- **3** It established Christianity as the official religion of the Byzantine Empire.
- **④** It collected Roman laws into a simple and clear system of law.

WEDNESDAY CC 2.C.5 (Chapter 12.1)

3 **Over time, the culture of the Byzantine Empire was increasingly influenced by**
- **1** China.
- **②** Greece.
- **3** Russia.
- **4** Western Europe.

THURSDAY CC 2.C.3 (Chapter 12.2)

4 **What led to the spread of Orthodox Christianity into Eastern Europe and Russia?**
- **1** the Byzantines' conquest of Kiev
- **2** Alexander Nevski's defeat of the Teutonic Knights
- **③** the development of the Cyrillic alphabet
- **4** the split between the Catholic Church and the Orthodox Eastern Church

FRIDAY CC 2.C.6 (Chapter 12.2)

5 **Which of the following is an example of Byzantine influence on Russia?**
- **1** the founding of Kiev
- **2** the rise of the Golden Horde
- **③** the establishment of the Russian Orthodox Church
- **4** the development of canon law

WEEK 12

MONDAY CC 2.F.4 (Chapter 13.3)

"I . . . shall be to you both faithful and true, and shall owe my Fidelity unto you, for the Land that I hold of you, and lawfully shall do such Customs and Services, as my Duty is to you, at the times assigned."

—from *The Manner of Doing Homage and Fealty*

1 **This quote *most likely* reflects the attitudes of what members of the feudal system?**
- **1** kings
- **②** vassals
- **3** peasants
- **4** lords

TUESDAY CC 4.C.2 (Chapter 13.4)

2 **Christians in what country defeated the Muslims and drove them from power in the Reconquista?**
- **1** France
- **②** Spain
- **3** Norway
- **4** Italy

WEDNESDAY CC 2.F.5 (Chapter 13.5)

3 **Which of the following explains the great power of medieval popes?**
- **1** Popes controlled the religious lives of almost everyone in Asia.
- **2** Popes developed the feudal system.
- **3** Popes had the power to name kings and emperors.
- **④** Popes held influence over politics and religion.

THURSDAY CC 2.G.2 (Chapter 14.1)

4 **What effect did the Crusades have on the economy of Europe?**
- **①** led to an increase in trade between East and West
- **2** ended the feudal system in Europe
- **3** led to the decline of towns and cities
- **4** introduced Islam to Europe

FRIDAY CC 3.E (Chapter 14.4)

5 **Historians believe the Black Death originated in**
- **①** Central Asia.
- **2** the Americas.
- **3** Italy.
- **4** Northern Europe.

MONDAY **CC** 3.F.3 *(Chapter 15.1)*

1 Renaissance art, literature, and education were greatly influenced by
 1 the invention of the compass.
 2 ancient Greek and Roman achievements.
 3 the love of beauty.
 4 a renewed emphasis on religion.

TUESDAY **CC** 3.F.4 *(Chapter 15.1)*

2 What Renaissance technique is illustrated by this painting?
 1 humanism
 2 movable type
 3 perspective
 4 predestination

WEDNESDAY **CC** 3.G.2 *(Chapter 15.3)*

3 Whose actions helped spark the Protestant Reformation?
 1 Michelangelo's
 2 Lorenzo de Medici's
 3 John Calvin's
 4 Martin Luther's

THURSDAY **CC** 4.C.4 *(Chapter 16.1)*

4 Which of the following was a reason for European overseas exploration?
 1 the desire to spread Christianity
 2 the need for more land for Europe's growing population
 3 the lack of resources in Europe
 4 the drive to compete with Chinese explorers

FRIDAY **CC** 4.E *(Chapter 16.3)*

5 How did the Columbian Exchange impact life in the Americas?
 1 Thousands of farmers in the Americas were left without lands to farm.
 2 Population in the Americas boomed as a result of the introduction of new foods.
 3 European diseases devastated the Native American population.
 4 Native empires were overthrown in the search for gold.

MONDAY **CC** 4.E *(Chapter 17.1)*

1 In the 1300s what Muslim empire expanded into Europe?
 1 the Ottoman Empire
 2 the Safavid Empire
 3 the Mughal Empire
 4 the Ming Empire

TUESDAY **CC** 4.B.1 *(Chapter 17.2)*

2 By the 1500s Muslim empires controlled all of the following regions *except*
 1 the Byzantine Empire.
 2 India.
 3 Japan.
 4 Persia.

WEDNESDAY **CC** 4.B.1 *(Chapter 17.3)*

3 Under what dynasty did China expand to its largest size?
 1 Ming
 2 Qing
 3 Tokugawa
 4 Yuan

THURSDAY **CC** 4.A.6 *(Chapter 17.3)*

4 China's Zheng He is significant because he
 1 created laws to limit contact with foreigners.
 2 moved the Chinese capital to Beijing.
 3 led the rebellion that overthrew the Yuan dynasty.
 4 led several voyages of exploration and trade.

FRIDAY **CC** 3.A.6 *(Chapter 17.4)*

5 Japanese feudalism differed from European feudalism in that it featured
 1 no code of ethics for samurai to follow.
 2 a shogun as a powerful central authority.
 3 a class of strong professional warriors.
 4 no exchange of land between lords and vassals.

WEEK 15

MONDAY **CC 4.G.4** *(Chapter 18.3)*

1 The English Bill of Rights is an important document because it
1 sparked the English Civil War.
② limited the power of the monarch.
3 restored the English monarch to power.
4 created the Estates General.

TUESDAY **CC 4.F.4** *(Chapter 18.2, 18.4)*

2 Which of the following is a similarity between Louis XIV and Peter the Great?
① They both fought wars to expand their empires.
2 They both made efforts to westernize their empires.
3 They both believed the people should have a say in government.
4 They both ruled with the help of the pope.

WEDNESDAY **CC 5.A** *(Chapter 19.1)*

3 Which of the following was a characteristic of the Scientific Revolution?
1 the Inquisition
② the belief in progress and the power of reason
3 the development of mass transportation systems
4 a growing desire to explore unknown parts of the world

THURSDAY **CC 5.B.1** *(Chapter 19.2)*

4 Which Enlightenment thinker argued that people were born with certain natural rights?
1 Adam Smith
2 Baron de Montesquieu
③ John Locke
4 Thomas Hobbes

FRIDAY **CC 5.C.2.a** *(Chapter 19.3)*

5 How did the American Revolution express the ideals of the Enlightenment?
1 American Patriots supported absolute monarchy.
② Colonists revolted against a government that failed to protect their rights.
3 The Patriots wanted to establish a free market economy.
4 The new American government granted equal rights to women.

WEEK 16

MONDAY **CC 5.C.3.a** *(Chapter 20.1)*

1 All of the following were causes of the French Revolution *except*
1 economic problems
2 support for Enlightenment ideas
3 social inequalities
④ the desire for a strong ruler

TUESDAY **CC 5.C.2.b** *(Chapter 19.3, 20.2)*

2 One similarity between the French and American revolutions was that they both
1 led to a period of terror and violence.
2 resulted in the execution of the monarch.
③ established basic rights and freedoms.
4 led to the establishment of constitutional monarchies.

WEDNESDAY **CC 5.C.3.c** *(Chapter 20.2)*

3 Which of the following areas did *not* experience counterrevolutionary activity?
1 Arras
2 Bordeaux
3 Nantes
④ Paris

THURSDAY **CC 5.C.3.d** *(Chapter 20.4)*

4 Which event played the *greatest* role in Napoleon's defeat?
① the Russian campaign
2 the Continental System
3 the Congress of Vienna
4 the Battle of the Nile

FRIDAY **CC 5.D** *(Chapter 20.4)*

5 Which of the following was a result of the Congress of Vienna?
1 It established democratic governments throughout Europe.
2 It created a powerful European Army.
3 It led to the downfall of Napoleon.
④ It restored monarchies to power in Europe.

WEEK 17

MONDAY **CC** 5.G.3 *(Chapter 21.1)*

1 **What factor explains Great Britain's industrialization?**
1. improvements in social equality
2. growth of private investment *(selected)*
3. increasing political instability
4. expansion of cottage industries

TUESDAY **CC** 5.C.3.b *(Chapter 21.2)*

2 **Which of the following *most likely* explains the rise of labor unions?**
1. Factory owners wanted better-trained workers.
2. Governments began regulating businesses.
3. The need for more workers was increasing.
4. Workers wanted their interests heard. *(selected)*

WEDNESDAY **CC** 5.G.3.a *(Chapter 21.3)*

3 **Which statement describes a market economy?**
1. Strict regulations govern businesses.
2. Businesses and individuals are free to compete for trade. *(selected)*
3. The government dictates what factories will produce.
4. Skilled workers are in high demand.

THURSDAY **CC** 5.G.3 *(Chapter 21.3)*

4 **In contrast to capitalism, socialism proposed that**
1. there should be no industry.
2. businesses and individuals should own and control industry.
3. society or the government should own and control industry. *(selected)*
4. the workers should own and control industry.

FRIDAY **CC** 5.G.3.d *(Chapter 22.3)*

5 **Which of the following was a result of the increase in leisure time?**
1. the demand for entertainment increased *(selected)*
2. the number of factory workers decreased
3. mass transportation improved
4. suburbs developed

WEEK 18

MONDAY **CC** 5.G.3.g *(Chapter 23.1)*

1 **How did industrialization lead to reform movements?**
1. Factory owners called for economic reforms.
2. The lack of industrialization in some industries led to a call for change.
3. The increased prosperity of factory workers and middle-class citizens led them to demand political change. *(selected)*
4. Industrialization did not affect the reform movement.

TUESDAY **CC** 5.G *(Chapter 23.2)*

> *"It is a crime to punish the minds of the lowly and the humble, to exasperate the passions of reaction and intolerance, while seeking shelter behind odious [horrible] anti-Semitism, which, if not suppressed, will destroy the great liberal France of the Rights of Man."*
>
> —Emile Zola, "J'accuse"

2 **Emile Zola was inspired to write "J'accuse" by what event in the late 1890s?**
1. nationalism
2. Zionism
3. the Civil War
4. the Dreyfus Affair *(selected)*

WEDNESDAY **CC** 5.C.4 *(Chapter 23.3)*

3 **Unlike the French revolutions of the 1800s, the revolutions in Latin America sought**
1. independence. *(selected)*
2. a return to absolute monarchy.
3. Communist government.
4. improvements in factory conditions.

THURSDAY **CC** 5.F.3.a *(Chapter 24.1)*

4 **What two European countries experienced unification movements in the mid-1800s?**
1. France and Germany
2. Portugal and Poland
3. Germany and Italy *(selected)*
4. Austria and Spain

FRIDAY **CC** 5.D.4.b *(Chapter 24.4)*

5 **Which of the following was a reform of Czar Alexander II?**
1. He funded the construction of the Trans-Siberian railroad.
2. He freed the Russian serfs. *(selected)*
3. He established a constitutional monarchy.
4. He granted women the right to vote.

MONDAY **CC** 5.H.3 *(Chapter 25.1)*

1 **Great Britain's most valuable colony was**
  1 China.
  2 Egypt.
  ③ India.
  4 Vietnam.

TUESDAY **CC** 5.H.4.a *(Chapter 25.1)*

2 **What allowed European empires to gain a foothold in Asia and Africa?**
  1 Asian and African rulers were eager to trade.
  2 European rulers negotiated for trade rights.
  3 Asian and African leaders began converting to Christianity.
  ④ European leaders took advantage of their military superiority.

WEDNESDAY **CC** 5.I.2 *(Chapter 25.2)*

3 **What effect did the opening of foreign trade have on Japan?**
  ① It encouraged Japan to modernize.
  2 It led to the establishment of democracy.
  3 It created tensions between Japan and China.
  4 It led to war between Japan and Great Britain.

THURSDAY **CC** 5.H.1 *(Chapter 25.3)*

> "My desire is to open a path to this district [of Africa], that civilization, commerce, and Christianity might find their way there."
> —David Livingstone's Cambridge Speech of 1857

4 **What reasons does Livingstone give for wanting to colonize Africa?**
  ① trade, religion, and to civilize the Africans
  2 gold, land, and slaves
  3 expansion of the slave trade and control of trade routes
  4 formation of alliances and trade

FRIDAY **CC** 5.H.6 *(Chapter 25.4)*

5 **During the age of imperialism, in what part of the world did the United States most frequently exert its influence?**
  1 Africa
  ② Latin America
  3 China
  4 Russia

MONDAY **CC** 6.A.2 *(Chapter 26.1)*

1 **What event triggered World War I?**
  1 Germany's invasion of Russia
  ② the assassination of Austria's archduke
  3 the sinking of the *Lusitania*
  4 the invention of trench warfare

TUESDAY **CC** 6.A.3 *(Chapter 26.2)*

2 **Which of the following is an example of total war?**
  ① Governments tell factories what to produce for the war effort.
  2 Civilians are drafted into the military.
  3 Governments spend millions to develop more powerful weapons.
  4 Neutral nations sell weapons to countries on both sides of the war.

WEDNESDAY **CC** 6.B *(Chapter 26.3)*

3 **What effect did the Russian Revolution have on World War I?**
  ① It forced Russia to withdraw from the war.
  2 It left Germany with no more allies.
  3 It led to the defeat of Austria-Hungary.
  4 It encouraged the United States to enter the war.

THURSDAY **CC** 6.B.5 *(Chapter 26.3)*

4 **Why is Vladimir Lenin a significant figure in Russian history?**
  1 He created Russia's first legislative body.
  ② He instituted a Communist regime in Russia.
  3 He curbed the government's control of the Russian economy.
  4 He was the commander of Russian forces in World War I.

FRIDAY **CC** 6.C.2 *(Chapter 26.4)*

5 **What was the main purpose of the Treaty of Versailles?**
  1 to ensure that another world war could not take place
  ② to punish Germany for its role in the war
  3 to punish Russia for withdrawing from the war
  4 to reward the Unites States for entering the war

MONDAY **CC** 6.C.9 *(Chapter 27.1)*

1 After World War I nationalist movements in European colonies increased as a result of
  1 the fear that colonists might be pulled into another costly war.
  2 the lack of financial support from Europe.
  3 the fear that European nations would demand more resources to rebuild after the war.
  (4) the colonists' belief that they had earned their freedom by fighting in the war.

TUESDAY **CC** 6.C.5 *(Chapter 27.2)*

2 Which of the following was a cause of the U.S. stock market crash in 1929?
  (1) increasing speculation in the stock market
  2 economic troubles brought on by the high cost of maintaining colonies
  3 government regulation of the economy
  4 lack of confidence in the government

WEDNESDAY **CC** 6.C.5 *(Chapter 27.2)*

3 How did the Great Depression in the United States affect foreign nations?
  1 U.S. companies stopped exporting goods abroad.
  2 Nations were forced to borrow money from the United States.
  (3) World trade slowed dramatically.
  4 It had little effect on most nations.

THURSDAY **CC** 6.D.2 *(Chapter 27.3, 27.4)*

4 In what way were Germany and Japan similar during the 1930s?
  1 Both joined an alliance with the Soviet Union.
  2 Both established colonies in the Pacific.
  (3) Both built up their military forces.
  4 Both had Communist governments.

FRIDAY **CC** 6.B.6 *(Chapter 27.4)*

5 Which of the following tactics did Joseph Stalin use to further his plan for economic modernization?
  1 He worked to improve political rights for women.
  (2) He instituted a policy of collectivization of small farms.
  3 He loosened government control of industry.
  4 He encouraged capitalist ideas and beliefs.

MONDAY **CC** 6.D *(Chapter 28.1)*

1 Which of the following is an example of German aggression prior to World War II?
  1 Germany remained neutral.
  (2) Germany reclaimed and militarized the Rhineland.
  3 Germany gave up control of Austria.
  4 Germany signed a treaty with Russia.

TUESDAY **CC** 6.D *(Chapter 28.1)*

2 What event triggered World War II?
  (1) Germany invaded Poland.
  2 Italy attacked North Africa.
  3 Japan bombed Pearl Harbor.
  4 Germany and the Soviet Union signed a nonaggression pact.

WEDNESDAY **CC** 6.D.4 *(Chapter 28.2)*

3 Which battle was a turning point in the war in the Pacific?
  1 Battle of El Alamein
  2 Battle of the Bulge
  (3) Battle of Midway
  4 Battle of Stalingrad

THURSDAY **CC** 6.D.5 *(Chapter 28.3)*

EUROPE'S JEWISH POPULATION

Source: United States Holocaust Memorial Museum

4 What was the likely cause of the population change depicted in the graph above?
  1 the dropping of atomic bombs
  (2) the Nazi's Final Solution
  3 the London Blitz
  4 the invasion of the Soviet Union

FRIDAY **CC** 7.A.4 *(Chapter 28.4)*

5 What two countries emerged from World War II as the world's most powerful nations?
  1 the United States and Japan
  2 Great Britain and the United States
  3 the Soviet Union and Germany
  (4) the United States and the Soviet Union

MONDAY **CC** 7.A.4 *(Chapter 29.1)*

1 **Which of the following was a cause of the Cold War?**
1. The Soviet Union set up Communist governments in Eastern Europe.
2. The United States refused to force Germany to pay reparations.
3. Soviet officials were charged with war crimes during the Nuremberg Trials.
4. The United States refused to loan money to the Soviet Union after the war.

TUESDAY **CC** 7.A.5 *(Chapter 29.1)*

2 **The goal of the Truman Doctrine was to**
1. permanently divide Europe between East and West.
2. rebuild the war-torn nations of Eastern Europe.
3. remove Stalin from power in the Soviet Union.
4. prevent the spread of communism.

WEDNESDAY **CC** 7.A.5.h *(Chapter 29.2)*

3 **All of the following are results of the U.S.-Soviet rivalry during the Cold War *except***
1. the Cuban missile crisis.
2. the development of a nuclear arms race.
3. the creation of Israel.
4. the Red Scare.

THURSDAY **CC** 7.G.5 *(Chapter 29.3)*

4 **The fall of the Berlin Wall in 1989 has become a symbol of**
1. the Cold War.
2. Germany's economic collapse.
3. the collapse of communism.
4. ethnic tensions in Eastern Europe.

FRIDAY **CC** 7.F *(Chapter 29.4)*

5 **Since the end of the Cold War, the United States has been chiefly involved in conflicts in**
1. the Middle East.
2. Southeast Asia.
3. Eastern Europe.
4. Africa.

MONDAY **CC** 7.E *(Chapter 31.1)*

1 **What impact did World War II have on independence movements in Africa and Asia?**
1. African natives gained political strength by ruling the colonies during the war.
2. The cost of the war made European nations more determined to hang on to their colonies' wealth.
3. Independence movements emerged as European countries lost power after the war.
4. The atrocities of the war led many Africans to oppose foreign control.

TUESDAY **CC** 7.F.2 *(Chapter 31.3)*

2 **The Zionist movement, immigration into Palestine, and the Holocaust led to**
1. the creation of a Jewish state in Palestine.
2. the Persian Gulf War.
3. the Iranian Revolution.
4. the OPEC oil embargo.

WEDNESDAY **CC** 7.H *(Chapter 32.1)*

3 **During the Cold War, the United States became involved in Latin America in order to**
1. support the rights of the poor.
2. gain valuable natural resources.
3. stop the spread of communism.
4. end the rule of brutal dictators.

THURSDAY **CC** 8.A *(Chapter 33.1)*

4 **The process by which countries are linked through trade and culture is known as**
1. urbanization.
2. international cooperation.
3. globalization.
4. free trade.

FRIDAY **CC** 8.A.3.a *(Chapter 33.2)*

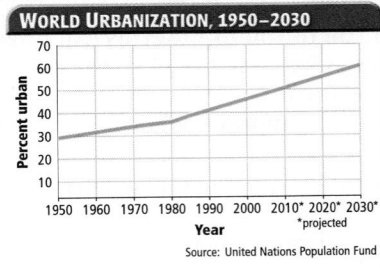

WORLD URBANIZATION, 1950–2030

Source: United Nations Population Fund

5 **According to predictions, what percent of the world will be urbanized by 2020?**
1. less than 30 percent
2. about 40 percent
3. about 60 percent
4. over 50 percent

The Dawn of Civilization
Prehistory–AD 300

This photograph shows the Chephren and Mycerinus pyramids in Egypt at sunrise.

CHAPTER 1
The Beginnings of Civilization
Prehistory–1000 BC

CHAPTER 2
The Ancient Near East
4000 BC–550 BC

CHAPTER 3
Nile Civilizations
5000 BC–AD 300

CHAPTER 4
Ancient India and China
2500 BC–250 BC

Themes

GEOGRAPHY AND ENVIRONMENT
Unique environmental and geographic features led to the development of civilizations with common characteristics in different parts of the world.

MIGRATION AND DIFFUSION
The migration of peoples spread ideas and goods from one part of the world to another. Migrating peoples also adopted and adapted the ideas and goods of the people they encountered.

BELIEF SYSTEMS
The belief systems of these early civilizations varied widely, and they helped shape the societies in which they arose.

1

Unit Preview

Introducing the Unit
Ask students what features they think of first when they hear the word *civilization*. List those features for the class to see. Which of those features were present in some form in early civilizations? Why or why not? Have students use the list to define *civilization*.

Connecting to Themes
Activity **Agriculture and Civilization** Ask students why civilizations arose independently in several different regions. Guide students in a discussion of the features those regions have in common. At what point did an agricultural society become a civilization? **LS** **Verbal-Linguistic**

Reading Like a Historian
Interpreting Visuals
The Pyramids Before the Egyptians began building pyramids, they marked their pharaohs' tombs with flat-roofed structures called *mastabas*. Sometimes a mastaba was topped with a mound of dirt. These mounds may have inspired the shape of the pyramids. However, scholars think it more likely that the pyramids' shape was modeled on the *benben*, a sacred pointed stone that symbolized the rays of the sun. The Egyptians believed that pharaohs traveled to heaven by way of sunbeams.

Unit Resources

Planning
- Differentiated Instruction Teacher Management System: Unit Pacing Guide
- OSP New York One-Stop Planner CD-ROM: Teacher Management System
- Power Presentations with Video CD-ROM

Standards Mastery
- Global History and Geography Regents Test Prep Workbook
- Regents Review Transparencies

Differentiating Instruction
- Differentiated Instruction Teacher Management System: Lesson Plans for Differentiated Instruction
- Differentiated Instruction Modified Worksheets and Tests CD-ROM

Enrichment
- A World History Teacher's Guide to Analyzing Movies
- Document-Based Activities for World History
- World History Outline Maps
- Reading Like a Historian: World History Toolkit
- World History Primary Source Library CD-ROM

Assessment
- PASS: Unit Test, Forms A and B
- Alternative Assessment Handbook
- OSP New York ExamView Test Generator correlated to NY SS Standards
- HOAP Holt Online Assessment Program (in the Premier Online Edition)

Chapter 1 Planning Guide

The Beginnings of Civilization

Chapter Overview	Reproducible Resources	Technology Resources
CHAPTER 1 pp. 2–29 **Overview: In this chapter, students will learn about the migration of early humans from Africa to other parts of the world, and the way early societies gave rise to the first civilizations.** KI 1, 2, 4; PI 1.1, 1.4, 2.5, 4.2 See pp. T32–T55 for a detailed correlation to the New York State Core Curriculum for Global History and Geography and the New York Learning Standards.	**Differentiated Instruction Teacher Management System:** • Pacing Guide • Lesson Plans for Differentiated Instruction **Interactive Reader and Study Guide:** Chapter Summary* **Chapter Resource File*** • Writing About History • Social Studies Skill • Chapter Review **World History Outline Maps**	**OSP New York One-Stop Planner CD-ROM:** Calendar Planner **Live Ink© Online Reading Help** **Student Edition on Audio CD Program** **Differentiated Instruction Modified Worksheets and Tests CD-ROM** **Interactive Skills Tutor CD-ROM** **World History Primary Source Library CD-ROM** **Power Presentations with Video CD-ROM** **History's Impact: World History Video Program (VHS/DVD):** The Beginnings of Civilization
Section 1: **The First People** **The Main Idea:** Scientific evidence suggests that modern humans spread from Africa to other lands and gradually developed ways to adapt to their environment. PI 2.5	**Differentiated Instruction Teacher Management System:** Section 1 Lesson Plan* **Interactive Reader and Study Guide:** Section 1 Summary* **Chapter Resource File*** • Vocabulary Builder: Section 1 • Literature: *Before Adam* • Biography: Marcel Ravidat • Primary Source: Painting at Lascaux Cave, France	**Regents Review Transparency:** Section 1* **Quick Facts Transparency:** Early Hominids* **Map Transparency:** The World, 2,000,000–3000 BC* **Map Transparency:** Migration of Early Humans* **Internet Activity:** Archaeology
Section 2: **The Beginnings of Agriculture** **The Main Idea:** The development of agriculture was a major turning point in human history and significantly changed the way in which many people lived. PI 2.5	**Differentiated Instruction Teacher Management System:** Section 2 Lesson Plan* **Interactive Reader and Study Guide:** Section 2 Summary* **Chapter Resource File*** • Vocabulary Builder: Section 2 • Biography: Kathleen Kenyon	**Regents Review Transparency:** Section 2* **Map Transparency:** Growth of Agriculture*
Section 3: **Foundations of Civilization** **The Main Idea:** From farming villages arose cities, and with them, the first civilizations, marking the beginnings of recorded history. PI 1.1, 1.4, 4.2	**Differentiated Instruction Teacher Management System:** Section 3 Lesson Plan* **Interactive Reader and Study Guide:** Section 3 Summary* **Chapter Resource File*** • Vocabulary Builder: Section 3 • Biography: Leonard Woolley • History and Geography: The First Civilizations	**Regents Review Transparency:** Section 3* **Quick Facts Transparency:** Economic Systems* **Map Transparency:** River Valleys and Civilizations* **Internet Activity:** Divisions of Labor

HOLT
History's Impact
World History Video Program (VHS/DVD)
The Beginnings of Civilization

Review, Assessment, Intervention

- **Global History and Geography Regents Test Prep Workbook**

- **Quick Facts Transparency:** The Beginnings of Civilization

- **Spanish Chapter Summaries Audio CD Program**

- **Progress Assessment Support System (PASS):** Chapter Test*

- **Differentiated Instruction Modified Worksheets and Tests CD-ROM:** Modified Chapter Test

- OSP **New York One-Stop Planner CD-ROM:** ExamView Test Generator (English/Spanish)

- HOAP **Holt Online Assessment Program (HOAP),** in the Holt Premier Online Student Edition

- **Alternative Assessment Handbook**

- **PASS:** Section 1 Quiz*
- **Online Quiz:** Section 1
- **Alternative Assessment Handbook**

- **PASS:** Section 2 Quiz*
- **Online Quiz:** Section 2
- **Alternative Assessment Handbook**

- **PASS:** Section 3 Quiz*
- **Online Quiz:** Section 3
- **Alternative Assessment Handbook**

Power Presentation with Video CD-ROM

Power Presentations with Video are visual presentations of each chapter's main ideas. Presentations can be customized by including Quick Facts charts, images and maps from the textbook, and video clips.

Holt
Online
Learning

go.hrw.com
Teacher Resources
KEYWORD: SHL TEACHER

go.hrw.com
Student Resources
KEYWORD: SHL BEG

- Document-Based Questions
- Interactive Multimedia Activities

- Current Events
- Chapter-Based Internet Activities
- and more!

Holt Premier
Online Student Edition

Complete online support for interactivity, assessment, and reporting

- Interactive Maps and Notebook
- Homework Practice and Research Activities Online

CHAPTER 1 PLANNING GUIDE

Before You Teach

The Big Picture

Peter N. Stearns

Early Stages of Humankind Without going into vast detail, and recognizing that a very long time period is involved, there are three major points here. First, the species developed a large number of variants of which Homo erectus and Homo sapiens ultimately proved the most important, yielding the species to which we all belong upwards of 200,000 years ago. This species ultimately predominated over competitors, and there has been no significant evolutionary change since its emergence. Second, tool use gradually improved, yielding new stone age technologies particularly from about 15,000 years ago onward. And third, the human species, including its latest version, migrated widely, reaching most inhabitable parts of the earth by 20,000 years ago. This migration (amid small overall populations) resulted from the economic needs of hunters-gatherers; it was facilitated by a different land-mass geography from what now exists.

Agriculture The Neolithic Revolution was one of the great changes in human history. Agricultural existence had a number of drawbacks compared to hunting-gathering, including greater inequalities, more vulnerability to disease and harder work. But it had huge advantages in terms of food supply, allowing rapid population increase. Different dates describe the advent and spread of agriculture in different places. Agriculture generated some similar changes wherever it developed, including patriarchal gender systems and (usually) village clustering.

Civilization This final major shift involves further changes in human organization. It resulted from further development in agriculture (though not all agricultural societies made the shift), plus new technologies such as the wheel, bronze use and, of course, writing. Reference to attributes of civilizations like more advanced cities, the state and so on must be balanced by three points: most people continued to be rural and illiterate; disadvantages also resulted, notably increased inequality; and important groups long maintained different forms of organization.

Recent Scholarship

David Christian's *Maps of Time: An Introduction to Big History* (2004) is a fascinating effort to place human history in the 13 billion year history of the cosmos. The emergence of Earth and life are further way stations to the arrival of humans, about a third of the way into the book. The approach offers important definitions of the decisive nature of agriculture and the long period of agricultural history, and somewhat more succinctly the advent of civilization, plus commentary on more recent changes away from agriculture. The effort is ambitious, but readable and provocative throughout.

Differentiating Instruction

 Differentiated Instruction Teacher Management System
- Pacing Guide
- Lesson Plans for Differentiated Instruction

 Interactive Reader and Study Guide

Spanish Chapter Summaries Audio CD Program

Student Edition on Audio CD Program

Differentiated Instruction Modified Worksheets and Tests CD-ROM
- Vocabulary Flash Cards
- Modified Vocabulary Builder Activities
- Modified Chapter Review Activity
- Modified Chapter Test

OSP One-Stop Planner CD-ROM
- ExamView Test Generator (English/Spanish)
- PuzzlePro
- Quiz Show for ExamView
- Transparencies and Videos

TE Differentiated Activities in the Teacher's Edition
- Studying the Past, p. 6
- Lives of Prehistoric People, p. 8
- Development of Agriculture, p. 15
- Early Villages and Cities, p. 19
- Early Civilizations Time Line, p. 20

Reading Like a Historian
Sam Wineburg

Studying the Distant Past How do you read something that has no words? This is precisely the dilemma of archaeologists who study "prehistoric" cultures that leave us with objects but no written records. Even without such records, we can ask questions of objects that allow us access to the societies that produced them thousands of years ago.

Take the example of a small bronze scale unearthed at Ban Chiang in southern Thailand, a site excavated by researchers of the University of Pennsylvania's Museum of Archaeology and Anthropology in the mid 1970s. (The scale can be viewed at http://chnm.gmu.edu/worldhistory sources/unpacking/objectsq1ex.php.) Ancient peoples had lived in the area around this site from 3600 BCE to the first or second century CE. Yet, despite this continuous settlement, we don't even know what these people called themselves! Archaeologists refer to this civilization as the Ban Chiang simply because this is geographic area in which objects were first found.

Until this excavation, archaeologists had assumed that bronze had developed in the Near East and spread west toward Europe. The societies of ancient Southeast Asia were considered technological backwaters, less sophisticated than the great empires of China and India. Most scholars thought that the peoples of Southeast Asia had not engaged in metalwork until as late as 500 BCE.

The finds at Ban Chiang changed those notions. Using carbon dating techniques, researchers learned that people at Ban Chiang were engaged in sophisticated metal work as early as the first half of the second millennium BC. Ancient peoples had long been working with copper, but copper is a weak metal that bends easily. But when copper is combined with tin, the resulting alloy, bronze, is stronger and more durable than either metal alone. In fact, a mixture of 10 percent tin and 90 percent copper produces a bronze that, when hammered sufficiently, can be stronger

than pure iron. The discovery of bronze objects at this site—not only the scale, but bracelets, rings, anklets, spearheads, axes, hooks and bells —showed that the ancient peoples of Ban Chiang possessed specialized knowledge of mining, smelting, and metallurgy thought to have developed much later.

Making Objects Speak What else does a scale adorned with twin figurines tell us? Given its size, it was probably used to weigh spices or small quantities of grain. Moreover, a scale with preset weights indicates a standardized system of measurements. The notion of standardization suggests another institution: some type of centralized authority responsible for determining that weights are uniform and consistent from place to place—not so different from governmental offices charged with the same function today.

The figurines that anchor the scale, two miniature men sitting back to back, point to artisans skilled in creating and maneuvering the clay casts into which molten metal was poured. Nor was the work of these artists purely functional. The detail on this scale shows highly specialized artisans whose work was shaped by aesthetic and possibly religious sensibilities. The exquisite pottery work found at Ban Chiang provides backing to this inference.

By interrogating ancient objects and asking questions similar to those we would ask of any historical find—Who produced it? What does it tell us of the society at large?—we can read objects that have no words. Just because objects don't talk doesn't mean they have no story. It is our job to make them speak.

(signature)

Chapter Main Ideas

Section 1 Scientific evidence suggests that modern humans spread from Africa to other lands and gradually developed ways to adapt to their environment.

Section 2 The development of agriculture was a major turning point in human history and significantly changed the way in which many people lived.

Section 3 From farming villages arose cities, and with them, the first civilizations, marking the beginnings of recorded history.

New York Standards

Key Idea 1 The study of world history requires an understanding of world cultures and civilizations, including an analysis of important ideas, social and cultural values, beliefs, and traditions. This study also examines the human condition and the connections and interactions of people across time and space and the ways different people view the same event or issue from a variety of perspectives.

Key Idea 2 Establishing timeframes, exploring different periodizations, examining themes across time and within cultures, and focusing on important turning points in world history help organize the study of world cultures and civilizations.

Key to Differentiating Instruction

Below Level

Basic-level activities designed for all students encountering new material

At Level

Intermediate-level activities designed for average students

Above Level

Challenging activities designed for honors and gifted and talented students

Standard English Mastery

Activities designed to improve standard English usage

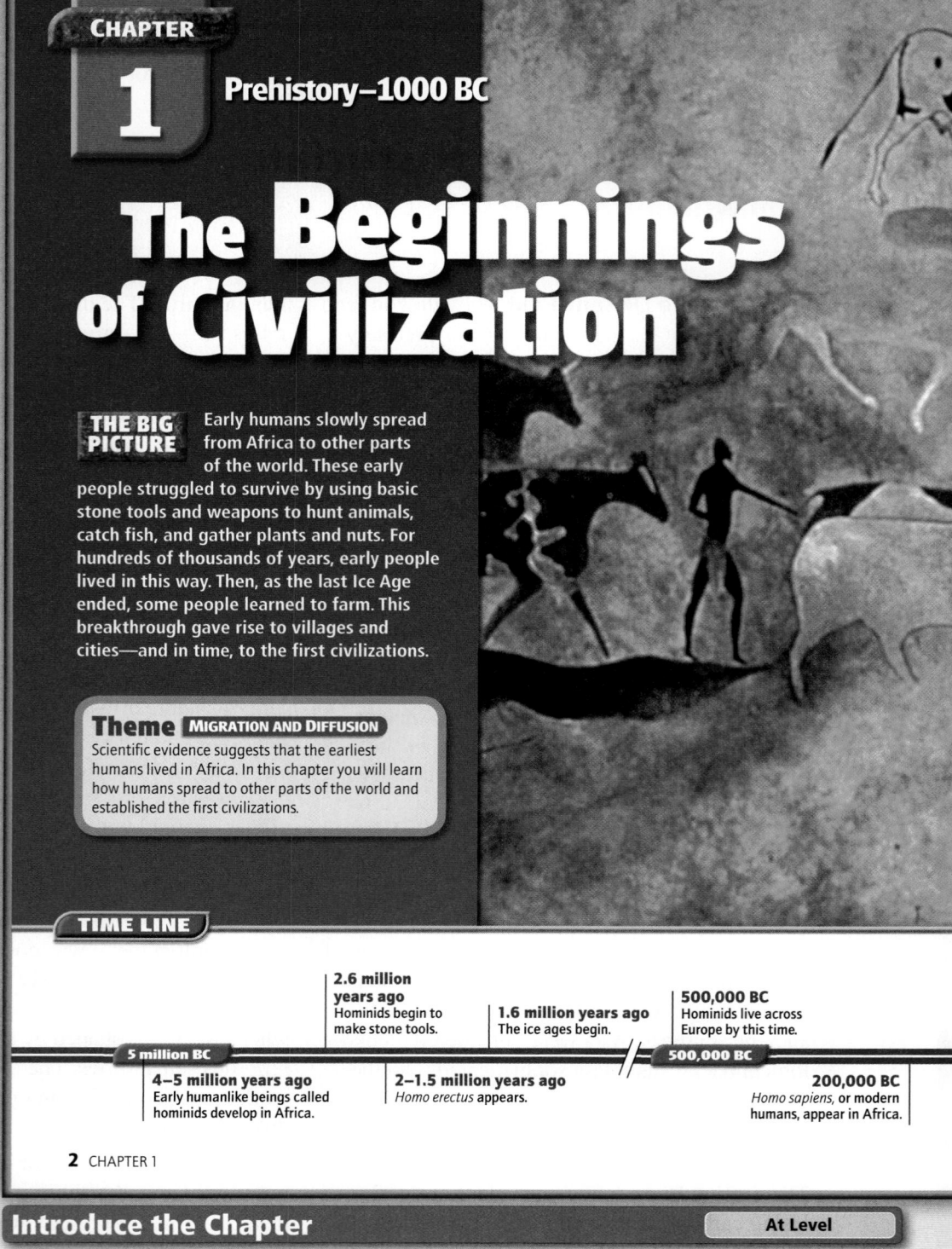

CHAPTER

1 Prehistory–1000 BC

The Beginnings of Civilization

THE BIG PICTURE Early humans slowly spread from Africa to other parts of the world. These early people struggled to survive by using basic stone tools and weapons to hunt animals, catch fish, and gather plants and nuts. For hundreds of thousands of years, early people lived in this way. Then, as the last Ice Age ended, some people learned to farm. This breakthrough gave rise to villages and cities—and in time, to the first civilizations.

Theme MIGRATION AND DIFFUSION
Scientific evidence suggests that the earliest humans lived in Africa. In this chapter you will learn how humans spread to other parts of the world and established the first civilizations.

TIME LINE

5 million BC

4–5 million years ago Early humanlike beings called hominids develop in Africa.

2.6 million years ago Hominids begin to make stone tools.

2–1.5 million years ago *Homo erectus* appears.

1.6 million years ago The ice ages begin.

500,000 BC Hominids live across Europe by this time.

500,000 BC

200,000 BC *Homo sapiens*, or modern humans, appear in Africa.

2 CHAPTER 1

Introduce the Chapter
At Level

The Beginnings of Civilization

1. Write the following question for students to see: What basic things do all humans have in common? Have students list all the answers they can think of.

2. Guide the class in a discussion of the conditions that need to be met for people not only to survive, but also to create societies. As students identify conditions necessary for creating societies, write them for the class to see.

3. Organize students into small groups. Have each group make a list of the ways in which early humans might have met the needs the class has identified.

4. Have volunteers from each group to share their lists with the class.

5. Tell students that in this chapter they will learn about early humans and the developments that led to the first civilizations. **LS** Interpersonal

Alternative Assessment Handbook, Rubric 14: Group Activity

History's Impact video program
Watch the video to understand the impact
of archaeology.

Reading like a Historian

This early rock painting shows African herders driving cattle in the Sahara. The rock painting was made between 5500 and 2000 BC in a region that borders what is now Algeria and Libya. The early art reveals that the Sahara was once more fertile than it is today.

Analyzing Visuals Based on the style of the art and the images shown, what might scientists be able to learn about early Africa from this painting?

See **Skills Handbook**, p. H26

9000 BC
Modern humans have spread to all of the continents except Antarctica.

7000 BC
Cattle herding begins in the Sahara in Africa.

3500 BC
The Bronze Age begins in some places.

11,000 BC ———————————————— 1000 BC

8000 BC
The Neolithic Era begins as agriculture develops.

6500 BC
More than 5,000 people live in Çatal Hüyük, in what is now Turkey.

THE BEGINNINGS OF CIVILIZATION **3**

• Chapter Preview •

HOLT
History's Impact
▶ Video Program: The Beginnings of Civilization
See the Video Teacher's Guide for strategies for using the video segment.

Reading Like a Historian

African Rock Paintings The Sahara Desert in North Africa was once fairly moist and has been inhabited since the beginnings of humankind. The earliest rock paintings from the area show hunting scenes. Men with clubs, sticks, axes, and bows are shown hunting animals that are now extinct in the region, such as the giant buffalo, elephant, rhinoceros, and hippopotamus. Between 6,000 and 8,000 years ago there was a shift from hunting to herding, as shown in paintings like the one on these pages. The cattle depicted here were the dominant herd animals at that time, but sheep and goats were also herded. Rock art created by the early people of North Africa appeared much later than the cave paintings that have been found in southwestern Europe, and probably developed independently.

go.hrw.com
Online Resources

Chapter Resources:
KEYWORD: SHL BEG
Teacher Resources:
KEYWORD: SHL TEACHER

Explore the Time Line

1. What were hominids? *early humanlike beings*
2. When did the ice ages start? *1.6 million years ago*
3. When and where did modern humans first appear? *about 200,000 BC, in Africa*
4. List two things that happened in 8000 BC. *The Neolithic Era began, and people began to develop agriculture.*

Info to Know

Prehistoric Tools For about 98 percent of the time since the appearance of the first hominids, or humanlike beings, scientists had little to help them determine how people lived except for the tools made from stone, flint, bone, and antler. Those tools developed slowly over time from single, all-purpose tools to tools that were designed to serve a single purpose.

Make Inferences Why do we get most of our clues to the prehistoric period from tools? *because early tools were made of materials that would not decay, such as stone and bone*

Answers

Reading Like a Historian *possible answers—that people in that part of Africa had domesticated cattle; that the Sahara was not the desert it is today*

3

Geography Starting Points

Origins of Modern Humans One hundred thousand years ago, several groups of early humans existed at the same time in different parts of the Earth. *Homo sapiens*—the human species as we know it today—lived in Africa and Southwest Asia. *Homo erectus* lived in Asia. Europe was inhabited by *Homo neanderthalensis*, or Neanderthals. There are two major theories of the origins of modern humans. Both of them suggest that the early human *Homo erectus* originated in Africa, but migrated to Asia and Europe.

One of these theories is known as the "Multiregional Continuity Model," which states that the early human *Homo erectus* species evolved into modern human *Homo sapiens* in several regions, leading to the development of different races.

The other major theory is known as the "Out of Africa Model." According to this theory, once outside Africa, *Homo erectus* sometimes evolved into separate species, such as the Neanderthals. This theory suggests that racial differences occurred relatively recently.

Scientists have used DNA to answer questions about human origins. Most scientists believe that DNA supports the "Out of Africa" theory, although there are some who disagree. Other recent finds have suggested that *Homo erectus* may in fact be descended from hominids that have been found in Asia.

- **Map Transparency:** Early People and Agriculture, 200,000–3000 BC
- **World History Outline Maps**

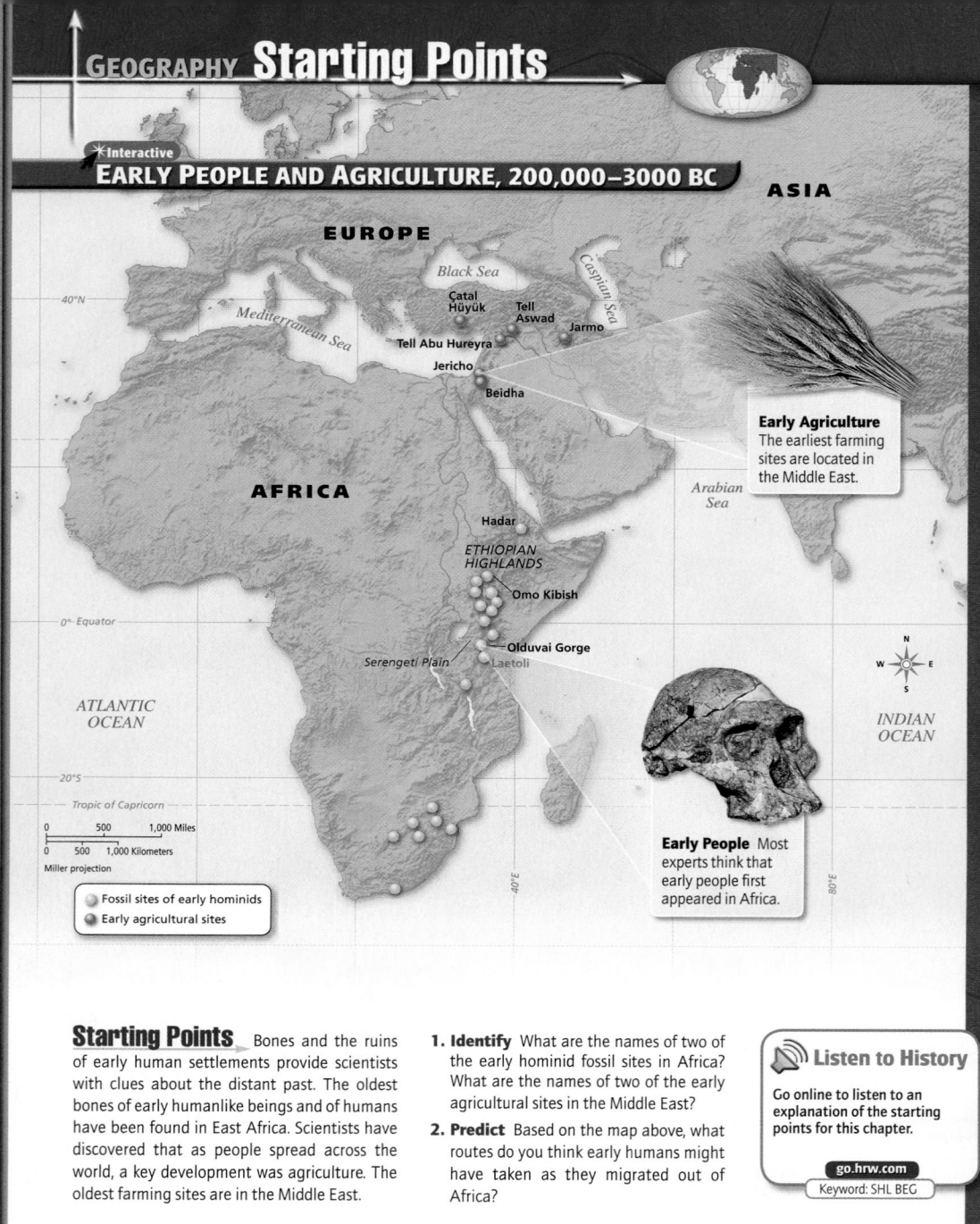

GEOGRAPHY Starting Points

Interactive
EARLY PEOPLE AND AGRICULTURE, 200,000–3000 BC

EUROPE

ASIA

Black Sea

Caspian Sea

Çatal Hüyük

Tell Aswad

Jarmo

Mediterranean Sea

Tell Abu Hureyra

Jericho

Beidha

Early Agriculture
The earliest farming sites are located in the Middle East.

AFRICA

Arabian Sea

Hadar

ETHIOPIAN HIGHLANDS

Omo Kibish

Olduvai Gorge

Serengeti Plain

Laetoli

ATLANTIC OCEAN

INDIAN OCEAN

Tropic of Capricorn

0   500   1,000 Miles
0   500   1,000 Kilometers
Miller projection

○ Fossil sites of early hominids
● Early agricultural sites

Early People Most experts think that early people first appeared in Africa.

Starting Points Bones and the ruins of early human settlements provide scientists with clues about the distant past. The oldest bones of early humanlike beings and of humans have been found in East Africa. Scientists have discovered that as people spread across the world, a key development was agriculture. The oldest farming sites are in the Middle East.

4 CHAPTER 1

1. **Identify** What are the names of two of the early hominid fossil sites in Africa? What are the names of two of the early agricultural sites in the Middle East?

2. **Predict** Based on the map above, what routes do you think early humans might have taken as they migrated out of Africa?

Listen to History

Go online to listen to an explanation of the starting points for this chapter.

go.hrw.com
Keyword: SHL BEG

Skills Focus: Analyzing Maps

At Level

Social Studies Skill
Early People

1. To help students understand information on the map, ask them to locate the following: fossil sites where the earliest early humans are believed to have appeared in East Africa; other sites where early human fossils have been discovered in South Africa.

2. Point out the Sinai Peninsula, which connects Africa to Southwest Asia and the Fertile Crescent.

3. Have students work in pairs to write down theories about the origins of humans and the development of farming. Have students consider how and why early humans would have moved from the oldest sites to other early fossil sites and from East Africa to Southwest Asia.

4. Have volunteers to read their theories to the rest of the class. **LS Interpersonal, Verbal-Linguistic**

Alternative Assessment Handbook, Rubrics 11: Discussions; and 21: Map Reading

Answers

Geography Starting Points
1. *Refer to map.* 2. *possible answer—They probably went north and crossed over by way of the Sinai Peninsula to Southwest Asia.*

1 The First People

BEFORE YOU READ

MAIN IDEA
Scientific evidence suggests that modern humans spread from Africa to other lands and gradually developed ways to adapt to their environment.

READING FOCUS
1. What methods are used to study the distant past?
2. What does evidence suggest about human origins?
3. How did early people spread around the world?
4. How did early people adapt to life in the Stone Age?

KEY TERMS AND PEOPLE
culture
artifacts
Mary Leakey
hominid
Donald Johanson
Louis Leakey
Paleolithic Era
nomads
hunter-gatherers
animism

 NEW YORK

P1 2.5 Students investigate key events and developments and major turning points in world history to identify the factors that brought about change and the long-term effects of these changes.

THE INSIDE STORY

How can footprints reveal facts about human history? In the 1970s anthropologist Mary Leakey took some fellow scientists to an archaeological site in Laetoli, Tanzania. Littered across the area were large piles of dried elephant dung. One scientist playfully picked up some dung and hurled it at another member of the group. Soon, dung was flying in all directions. As one man ran to avoid being hit, he tripped and fell. When he began to get up, he was amazed by what he saw. Before him were numerous animal tracks, hardened in volcanic ash. The tracks turned out to be around 3.5 million years old—a major find. An even greater find was still to come, however.

As Mary Leakey was examining the tracks one day she saw among them footprints that looked almost human. An analysis of the footprints revealed that two humanlike individuals had made them about 3.5 million years ago. The remarkable find showed that early people had walked upright on two legs long before scientists had thought, providing an important clue to the mystery of human origins. ▪

Studying the Distant Past

The human story goes back more than one million years, yet much of this story still remains a mystery. The reason is because writing, our main source of information about the past, has existed for only about 5,000 years. As a result, we know little about prehistory, the vast period of time before the development of writing. To study prehistory, scholars must be detectives, searching for clues and interpreting them to piece together the story of the distant past.

FOOTPRINTS FROM THE PAST

▲ A scientist studies the Laetoli footprints in Tanzania.

THE BEGINNINGS OF CIVILIZATION **5**

Teach the Main Idea

The First People

1. **Teach** Ask students the Reading Focus questions to teach this section.

2. **Apply** Have students create an outline of the section using the heads as main points. Have students identify at least two main ideas under each of the blue subheadings.

3. **Review** Review student outlines as a class. Have students identify the points in their outlines that they feel are most important or most interesting. Guide students in a discussion of life in the Stone Age.

4. **Practice/Homework** Tell students that they are television reporters covering the excavation of a site where archaeologists have found what they believe to be the earliest human ancestor. Have each student prepare a list of ten questions to ask the head of the archaeological expedition.
LS Verbal-Linguistic

📝 **Alternative Assessment Handbook**, Rubrics 1: Acquiring Information; and 11: Discussions

Preteach

Getting Started

Use the **Interactive Reader and Study Guide** to familiarize students with the section content.

📄 **Interactive Reader and Study Guide,** Section 1

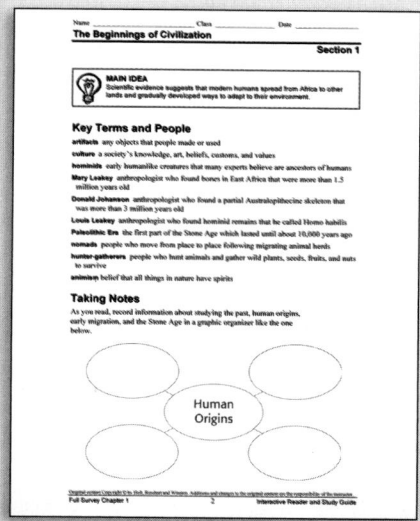

Academic Vocabulary

Review with students the high-use academic term in this section.

cycle to alternate among two or more things or events (p. 8)

📝 **CRF:** Vocabulary Builder: Section 1

Taking Notes

Studying the Past—paleontologists study fossils; archaeologists study artifacts and remains; anthropologists study human culture; Human Origins—early humans descended from hominids; Early Migration—humans originated in Africa; spread to the rest of world during ice ages; Stone Age—Stone Age humans used stone tools, developed clothing and shelter, and societies that included language, art, and possibly religion

go.hrw.com
Online Resources

KEYWORD: SHL BEG
ACTIVITY: Archaeology

1 What methods are used to study the distant past? *Archaeologists look for remains and objects used by early people, and anthropologists study fossils and human culture.*

Studying the Distant Past

Recall Why do we know little about prehistory? *because writing has existed for only about 5,000 years*

Contrast How do cultural anthropologists differ from archaeologists? *Cultural anthropologists study the cultures of past and present societies. Archaeologists dig into ancient settlements to find remains and objects used by early people.*

📝 **CRF: Literature:** *Before Adam*

Recent Scholarship

In *Ancestral Passions: The Leakey Family and the Quest for Humankind's Beginnings*, biographer Virginia Morell gives an in-depth account of the famous Leakey family, chronicling their adventures and groundbreaking scientific discoveries. Morell also delves into the personal lives of Mary and Louis Leakey, whose relationship, the author writes, evolved into more of a business partnership than a romantic one.

Ancestral Passions: The Leakey Family and the Quest for Humankind's Beginnings by Virginia Morell, Touchstone, 1996.

Answers

Faces of History *discovered 2-million-year-old artifacts*

Reading Check *by studying fossils, artifacts, and remains*

TAKING NOTES

As you read, take notes in a graphic organizer like this one. In the outer circles, record details about studying the past, human origins, early migration, and the Stone Age.

A variety of scientific fields analyze clues to learn about prehistory. One scientific field that contributes to our knowledge of prehistory is anthropology. This field includes a number of areas of specialization. For example, some anthropologists study fossils to learn about human origins. Fossils are the preserved remains or imprints of living things, such as preserved bones, teeth, or footprints. Other anthropologists study the cultures of past and present societies. **Culture** refers to a society's knowledge, art, beliefs, customs, and values.

Anthropologists called archaeologists study human material remains to learn about people in the past. Examples of human material remains include architectural ruins and artifacts. **Artifacts** are objects that people in the past made or used, such as coins, pottery, and tools. By analyzing material remains, archaeologists can make educated guesses about people's lives and cultures. For instance, by analyzing tools, archaeologists can draw conclusions about how technologically advanced a society was, what resources it had available, and some of the possible activities of people in the society.

FACES OF HISTORY

Mary and Louis LEAKEY
1913–1996 and 1903–1972

The husband-and-wife team of Mary and Louis Leakey made some of the most significant discoveries related to human origins. These discoveries—such as the Nutcracker Man skull, the Laetoli footprints, and the first *Homo habilis* fossils—have greatly expanded our understanding of early people.

Mary Leakey gained an interest in prehistoric archaeology during her childhood. While a teenager, she began working as an illustrator, drawing tools and other artifacts for an archaeologist. This work brought her in contact with Louis Leakey in 1933. Born and raised in Kenya, Louis Leakey had received a degree in anthropology and was working in that field.

After marrying in 1937, the Leakeys spent the next 30 years in East Africa searching together for clues to the origin and early development of humankind. Many of the Leakeys' greatest discoveries were made in the Olduvai Gorge, a steep-sided ravine in Tanzania. The sides of the gorge have yielded stone tools and fossils dating back some 2 million years.

Find the Main Idea How have Mary and Louis Leakey contributed to our knowledge of human origins?

Archaeologists excavate, or dig, at sites where people have left traces. At these sites, called archaeological digs, workers carefully excavate one small area at a time. They use tools such as trowels and small brushes to unearth objects without shifting or damaging them. Using screens, workers sift through removed soil for small items such as pieces of broken pottery. Researchers then use a variety of methods to date and analyze objects.

Anthropology and other scientific fields continue to expand and revise our picture of the prehistoric past. For example, scientists who study genetics have recently revised our understanding of human origins.

READING CHECK **Find the Main Idea** How do scientists learn about prehistory?

Human Origins

Throughout time, people have wondered about their origins. Where did the first people come from? When did they appear? Although we do not know all the answers, some key discoveries have provided important pieces to the puzzle. Not all scientists agree on the meaning of these discoveries, however; and future discoveries may lead to new ideas about human origins.

Key Discoveries In 1959 anthropologist **Mary Leakey** (LEE-kee) found skull fragments in East Africa that were more than 1.75 million years old. When put together, the fragments formed a skull with a heavy jaw and large teeth, earning it the nickname "Nutcracker Man." The skull was from an Australopithecine (ah-stray-loh-PITH-i-seen), an early humanlike being or **hominid** (HAH-muh-nuhd). This term refers to humans and early humanlike beings that walked upright.

In 1974 in Ethiopia, an anthropologist named **Donald Johanson** found a partial Australopithecine skeleton. He described his find.

HISTORY'S VOICES

❝We reluctantly headed back toward camp. Along the way, I glanced over my right shoulder. Light glinted off a bone. I knelt down for a closer look ... Everywhere we looked on the slope around us we saw more bones lying on the surface. .. The find launched a celebration in camp.❞

—Donald Johanson,
Ancestors: In Search of Human Origins

Differentiating Instruction

Below Level

Leaners Having Difficulty; English-Language Learners

Standard English Mastery

1. Have volunteers read aloud the paragraphs under the heading Studying the Distant Past. Have students use standard English to write a paragraph about the differences between archaeologists and anthropologists.

2. Have volunteers read their explanations to the class. Discuss necessary corrections to the paragraphs to align them with standard English usage. Guide students in a brief discussion of the differences between archaeologists and anthropologists.

3. Have another volunteer read aloud the paragraphs under the heading Human Origins. Then have students use standard English to write a paragraph describing how scientists date material remains.

4. Have volunteers read their explanations to the rest of the class. Guide the class in a brief discussion of the methods scientists use to date material remains. 🔲 **Verbal-Linguistic**

📝 **Alternative Assessment Handbook**, Rubric 40: Writing to Describe

Johanson named the partial skeleton Lucy. Tests showed that Lucy had lived more than 3 million years ago. Based on an analysis of her skeleton and knee joints, Johanson concluded that Lucy had been about 4 feet tall and walked upright. Walking upright is a major advance because it leaves the hands free to use tools.

In the 1970s Mary Leakey made yet another key discovery at a site called Laetoli in Tanzania. There, she and her team found hominid footprints preserved in hardened volcanic ash. Made by Australopithecines about 3.5 million years ago, the footprints provided the oldest evidence at the time of early hominids walking upright. Mary Leakey considered the discovery the most exciting of her career.

New finds continue to expand our knowledge of early people. In 2001 a scientific team found an early hominid skull in a desert region of Chad, a country in Central Africa. The skull has features of both an Australopithecine and a chimpanzee, and the creature it belonged to may have walked upright. The skull has been dated to between 6 and 7 million years old.

Later Hominids Based on the fossil record, more advanced hominids began appearing about 3 million years ago. In 1959 anthropologists Mary and **Louis Leakey** found a hominid fossil in Olduvai (OHL-duh-vy) Gorge, located in Tanzania. The hominid proved to be a new species, which became known as *Homo habilis*, or "handy man." *Homo habilis* first appeared about 2.4 million years ago in Africa. Compared to earlier hominids, *Homo habilis* had more humanlike features, such as smaller teeth and hands that were better able to grasp objects.

In addition, scientists think *Homo habilis* learned to make and use crude stone tools. These early tools were made by striking one rock against another to create a sharp edge. With these crude tools, hominids could cut meat, chop roots, or scrape meat from bones. The use of tools greatly improved survival.

Other hominids that scientists named *Homo erectus*, or "upright man," appeared some 2 to 1.5 million years ago in Africa. *Homo erectus* had a larger brain than earlier hominids and thus was probably more intelligent. For example, *Homo erectus* was a more skillful hunter than earlier hominids and created more advanced tools. One such tool was a hand ax made from flint, which is easy to shape into sharp edges.

Early Hominids

Groups of hominids appeared in Africa between about 5 million and 200,000 years ago. Later groups were more advanced than earlier groups and made better tools. ***What advantages did Homo erectus have over Homo habilis?***

AUSTRALOPITHECINE

- Name means "southern ape"
- Appeared in Africa about 4–5 million years ago
- Stood upright and walked on two legs
- Brain was about one-third the size of those of modern humans

HOMO HABILIS

- Name means "handy man"
- Appeared in Africa about 2.4 million years ago
- Used crude stone tools for chopping and scraping
- Brain was about half the size of those of modern humans

◄ An early Stone Age chopper

HOMO ERECTUS

- Name means "upright man"
- Appeared in Africa about 2–1.5 million years ago
- Used early stone tools such as the hand ax
- Learned to control fire
- Migrated out of Africa

A hand ax ►

HOMO SAPIENS

- Name means "wise man"
- Appeared in Africa about 200,000 years ago
- Migrated around the world
- Same species as modern humans
- Used a wide range of tools; learned to create fire; likely developed language

◄ A flint knife

THE BEGINNINGS OF CIVILIZATION **7**

7

Reading Focus

❸ How did early people spread around the world? *They migrated by using land bridges that were exposed when ice ages caused ocean levels to drop.*

Spreading Around the World

Explain What delayed human migration into northern Asia? *It was delayed by geographic features like high mountains and cold temperatures.*

Sequence Trace the migration of humans from their origin in East Africa. *They went to Southwest Asia. From Southwest Asia, they moved across southern Asia. From southern Asia, they moved to Australia, Europe, and northern Asia. From northern Asia, they moved into North America, and then South America.*

Predict How do you think patterns of human migration would have been different if the ice ages had not lowered ocean levels? *possible answer—People probably would not have settled some continents, such as the Americas until much later.*

Info to Know

Hobbit People Skeletons of a species of hobbit-like humans have been found on the remote island of Flores in Indonesia, halfway between Asia and Australia. They grew no taller than the height of a modern 3-year-old, but had skulls the size of grapefruits. One skeleton was that of a 30-year-old female who stood 3.3 feet (1 meter) tall and weighed 55 pounds (25 kilograms). These miniature people probably evolved from normal-size Homo erectus ancestors and may have interacted with modern humans. For centuries, myths about tiny creatures have circulated among the inhabitants of Flores.

Answers

Reading Check (left) *Australopithecine, Homo habilis, Homo erectus, Homo sapiens*

Reading Check (right) *The ocean level dropped, exposing land bridges that allowed early humans to migrate around the world.*

FOCUS ON NEW YORK

A notable prehistoric site in New York is located at West Athens Hill in Greene County. This site has yielded more than 1,400 artifacts, most of which were stone tools.

Flint hand axes enabled *Homo erectus* to dig more easily, chop through tree limbs, and cut through thick animal hides.

Scientists also think that *Homo erectus* was the first hominid to control fire. Once natural causes, such as lightning, had created a fire, *Homo erectus* learned to use the fire to cook food and to provide heat and protection. With the ability to control fire, *Homo erectus* could live in colder climates as well.

Modern Humans In time, hominids with the physical characteristics of modern humans appeared. Scientists call modern humans *Homo sapiens,* or "wise man." Every person alive today belongs to this species. With larger brains than earlier hominids, *Homo sapiens* developed more sophisticated tools and shelters and eventually learned to create fire.

Homo sapiens may have also been the first hominids to develop spoken language, perhaps because of improved brain and speech organs. With language, early people were better able to cooperate, hunt in groups, and resolve issues. Language also enabled people to form stronger relationships and interact with other groups.

READING CHECK **Identify Supporting Details** What four main types of hominids have scientists identified based on fossil evidence?

NEW YORK

CC **Unit 1-A4a** Migration of early humans out of Africa

ACADEMIC VOCABULARY

cycle to alternate among two or more things or events

Spreading Around the World

As later hominids learned to adapt better to the environment, they began to migrate, or move, out of Africa. This movement occurred gradually over hundreds of thousands of years. Scientists do not fully know why later hominids began to migrate, but one major reason was a change in the climate.

The Ice Ages About 1.6 million years ago, much of the world began experiencing long periods of freezing weather called ice ages. As the world climate cycled between colder and warmer periods, huge sheets of ice called glaciers advanced and retreated. When glaciers advanced, ocean levels fell, exposing areas that are today underwater. For example, during the ice ages, the Bering Strait that now separates Asia and North America was an exposed land bridge. Such land bridges helped early hominids spread around the world.

8 CHAPTER 1

Out of Africa Based on the fossil record, many scientists think that *Homo erectus* was the first hominid to migrate out of Africa. For example, *Homo erectus* fossils have been found throughout Asia and Europe. The ability to walk fully upright and to control fire may have enabled *Homo erectus* to make this migration.

Scientists hold different theories about the origins and migration of *Homo sapiens*. According to one theory, *Homo erectus* groups around the world gradually developed the characteristics of *Homo sapiens* over time. Recent genetic evidence does not support this theory, however. Based on the latest evidence, most scientists now think that *Homo sapiens* originated in Africa about 200,000 years ago. *Homo sapiens* then began to migrate out of Africa around 100,000 years ago.

The map "Migration of Early Humans" shows the possible migration routes of early *Homo sapiens*. After moving into Southwest Asia—the region of the Middle East—early modern humans likely spread across southern Asia and into Australia. Open sea may have separated Australia and Asia at the time, so early humans might have had to use some type of boat to make the crossing.

People took longer to move into Europe and northern Asia because high mountains and cold temperatures made it harder to live in those regions. As people improved their ability to create fire and adapt, though, they spread into Europe and northern Asia as well.

Scientists disagree on when and how the first people reached the Americas, but most scholars think that early people crossed a land bridge from northeast Asia to North America. By at least 9000 BC, humans had spread to all of the continents except Antarctica.

Adapting to New Environments As modern humans migrated around the world, they adapted to new environments. This process of adaptation caused humans to develop some of the genetic variety that exists today.

According to one view, two early groups of modern humans were Neanderthals and Cro-Magnons. Neanderthals lived about 200,000 to 30,000 years ago. After that time, though, they seem to have disappeared. Recent genetic research suggests they died out and may not have actually been *Homo sapiens*. Scientists continue to debate this point, however.

Differentiating Instruction

Below Level

Learners Having Difficulty

Background: Tell students that a major part of trying to understand the lives of prehistoric people is understanding the environment in which they lived.

1. Write the following headings for students to see:

- Tools and Technology
- Clothing and Shelter
- Stone Age Societies
- Language, Art, and Religion

2. Have students work in pairs to list all the facts they can find in the text and place them under the appropriate headings.

3. Have volunteers read the items from their lists to the class.

4. Guide students in a discussion of life in the Stone Age. **LS Interpersonal, Verbal-Linguistic**

📋 **Alternative Assessment Handbook**, Rubric 14: Group Activity

Cro-Magnons appeared about 40,000 years ago. Sturdy and muscular, Cro-Magnons were physically identical to modern humans. They made finely crafted tools, had superior hunting abilities, and were better able to survive. They also created figurines and haunting cave art.

READING CHECK **Analyze Information** How did the ice ages influence early human migration?

Life in the Stone Age

The first humans lived during the prehistoric period called the Stone Age. During this vast period, early people made tools mainly from stone. Scientists call the first part of the Stone Age the **Paleolithic** (pay-lee-uh-LI-thik) **Era**, or Old Stone Age. It lasted from around 2.5 million years ago to around 10,000 years ago.

FORENSICS in History

Can DNA Help Trace Our Origins?

Archaeological evidence suggests that modern humans appeared first in Africa and then slowly spread around the world, reaching the Americas last. However, not all scientists agree with this view. Could your DNA help prove where modern human globetrotters began their travels?

What facts do we have? People may differ on the outside, but genetically speaking all human beings are 99.9 percent identical. The 0.1 percent of genetic material, or DNA, that differs accounts for people's many variations. These genetic variations then get passed down from generation to generation.

Scientists are using people's genetic variations as markers to trace human ancestry. By taking DNA from people around the world, scientists have begun comparing genetic markers across populations.

So far, the results have traced everyone tested back to one woman in Africa who lived about 150,000 years ago, although other people lived at the time. Researchers think that perhaps no more than 1,000 people then made their way out of Africa between 50,000 and 70,000 years ago.

Draw Conclusions How can DNA be used to advance archaeological theories?

MIGRATION OF EARLY HUMANS

Yana River 30,000
20,000–15,000
40,000
Bering Strait
Cro-Magnon 35,000–10,000
40,000–30,000
Zhoukoudian 11,000
70,000–50,000
Qafzeh 92,000
Kennewick 9,000
Clovis 13,500
Meadowcroft 19,000–12,000
Omo Kibish 195,000 oldest *Homo sapiens* fossils
Niah Cave 40,000
50,000
Klasies River Mouth 100,000
Lake Mungo 45,000
Monte Verde 14,800
15,000–12,000

EUROPE · ASIA · AFRICA · AUSTRALIA · NORTH AMERICA · SOUTH AMERICA
ARCTIC OCEAN · PACIFIC OCEAN · ATLANTIC OCEAN · INDIAN OCEAN

0   2,000   4,000 Miles
0   2,000   4,000 Kilometers
Miller projection

- *Homo sapiens* fossil site
- Possible migration routes
- Glaciers, around 18,000 years ago
- Approximate land area during ice ages
- Present-day shoreline
- **9,000** Dates represent approximate number of years ago

THE BEGINNINGS OF CIVILIZATION **9**

Life in the Stone Age

Explain How did early people adapt to keep warm in cold areas? *learned to use fire and make clothing; found or built shelters*

Evaluate Which Stone Age development do you think is more important—language or art? Why? *possible answer—language, because it allows people to communicate with each other directly, enabling them to form relationships and solve problems*

 CRF: Biography: Marcel Ravidat

CRF: Primary Source: Painting at Lascaux Cave, France

Info to Know

Fossilized Skeleton Discovered in Europe in 2000, the fossilized skeleton of a 3-year-old girl is the oldest whole set of child's remains to date—approximately 3 million years older than other childhood fossils. It took several years before researchers completely uncovered and assembled the skeleton, which has provided them with new clues about early human development, movement, and speech.

Jewelry Researchers have found that humans wore jewelry at least 100,000 years ago, which is earlier than they had originally thought. Early jewelry consists of beads made from seashells. The first were found in 2004 in a cave in South Africa. More seashell jewelry has turned up in Israel and Algeria. Researchers believe that these shells were used as a kind of token for trade, and not just worn for decoration.

Answers

Reading like a Historian 1. *animals— a wild ox and horses;* **2.** *possible answer— The animals with more details may have been more important to the artists.* **3.** *drawing skills, skills at mixing pigments, and materials to use for the painting*

Reading Skills *possible answer— chisels, drills, saws, sharper knives*

Reading like a Historian

Stone Age Art

Analyzing Visuals The prehistoric people of Europe painted beautiful images deep within caves, where only flickering firelight would have lit the walls. The cave painting on the right is from Lascaux Cave, in France. This cave includes some 600 images of animals and symbols that people created between 17,000 and 15,000 years ago. In shades of yellow, red, brown, and black, the images cover the walls and ceilings of the cave complex.

To interpret what this cave art image suggests about the Stone Age, think about

- the subject of the image
- the details in the image
- the creation of the image

Skills FOCUS READING LIKE A HISTORIAN

1. **Subject** What is the subject of the art?
2. **Details** Why might the people who made the art have provided more details for some of the animals than others?
3. **Creation** What skills and materials would artists have needed to create these images?

See **Skills Handbook, p. H26**

The horned animal is an aurochs, a wild ox that is now extinct. Red symbols hover just before the beast.

A graceful horse in shades of orange and black overlaps the aurochs. Smaller black horses run past below.

THE IMPACT TODAY

Some people still live as hunter-gatherers. These groups include the San of the Kalahari Desert in southern Africa.

READING SKILLS

Predicting What types of new tools do you predict that prehistoric people developed to make survival easier?

Stone Age People During the Stone Age, people lived as **nomads**, moving from place to place as they followed migrating animal herds. These early people lived in small bands, or groups, and relied on the resources around them to survive. For shelter, people took cover in rock overhangs or caves when available. For food, people were **hunter-gatherers**, hunting, fishing, and gathering wild plants, berries, nuts, and other foods. In general, men hunted, while women collected plants and cared for the children. Because each role was important to survival, men and women likely were equals.

Stone Age Technology An important development for early people was the use of technology—the application of knowledge, tools, and materials to make life easier. The first tools that people made were crude chipped stones. Over time, people learned to make better tools out of wood and bone as well as stone.

For example, people learned to attach wooden handles to tools. By attaching a wooden handle to a stone arrow, people invented the spear. With spears, hunters could stand farther away from their prey and throw their weapons, which was safer. Another tool called a spear-thrower enabled Stone Age hunters to throw spears farther than by hand. As a result, hunters could take down larger prey, such as bison and mammoths, which resembled large elephants.

Early humans gradually learned to make more refined and specialized tools. Later Stone Age people learned to make string from plant fibers and animal sinew. People then used the string to make nets and other traps to capture fish and small animals. Other new tools and weapons included the bow and arrow, bone hooks, and fishing spears. To travel by water, some people learned to make canoes by hollowing out logs. Such developments greatly improved Stone Age life.

10 CHAPTER 1

Collaborative Learning

Prehistoric Art

Materials: butcher paper, paints or markers

Background: Tell students that ancient cave paintings give valuable clues about prehistoric life, attitudes, and events, just as modern art gives clues about an artist's life and times.

1. Guide students in a discussion of the similarities and differences between the image above and on the chapter opener pages of their text.

2. Organize students into small groups. Have each group create a mural illustrating some aspect of life that is important to them.

Student murals may either focus on a single activity or on several activities.

3. Display student murals for the class to see.

4. Guide students in a discussion of their murals. If these murals were all that remained about their lives, what conclusions might future archaeologists reach? Would their conclusions be accurate? **LS Visual-Spatial, Interpersonal**

Alternative Assessment Handbook, Rubrics 3: Artwork; and 14: Group Activity

As later Stone Age people migrated out of Africa, they encountered new environments with different climates or plants and animals. People had to develop new tools and skills to adapt to these new environments.

For example, in colder regions, later Stone Age people needed more than fire to keep them warm. As a result, people learned to make needles from bone and then used the needles to sew together animal skins for clothing. In time, people learned to use skins and other materials to make shoes, hats, and carrying sacks.

In addition to clothing, people learned to build shelters. The first human-made shelters were called pit houses, which were pits dug in the ground and covered with roofs of branches and leaves. Stone Age people eventually began to build shelters above ground as well. Early people used whatever was available to make their shelters. In some places, people used wood to create a frame and then covered it with animal skins. In eastern Europe, wood was scarce, so people used large mammoth bones instead. Still other people built more permanent shelters out of wood, stone, or other materials.

Stone Age Art and Religion Over time, bands of early humans began to form societies. A society is a community of people who share a common culture. Stone Age societies developed cultures that included not only language but also art and spiritual beliefs.

Cro-Magnons and other later Stone Age people produced a variety of art. They carved ornaments and figurines out of antlers, bone, coral, ivory, and shells. Later Stone Age people also painted and carved images on rocks and cave walls. Stunning examples of prehistoric rock and cave art exist around the world. In this art, bulls toss their heads, wounded bison charge at hunters, and horses leap majestically. Symbols and human hands appear as well. To create cave art, prehistoric artists used charcoal, clay, iron, and other materials to produce colors such as black, reds, and yellows.

Scholars are not certain what purpose this early art served. Prehistoric artists may have been representing the world as they saw and experienced it. They may have used cave art to chronicle hunts or to teach hunting skills. Symbols might have recorded the movements of the sun, moon, stars, or planets. Or, the art might have had a spiritual meaning.

Scholars know even less about the spiritual beliefs of early people. Anthropologists think that early people may have practiced **animism**, the belief that all things in nature have spirits. Cave paintings of animals might have been made to honor animal spirits. Early people might have believed in a life after death as well. Neanderthals and Cro-Magnons buried their dead and placed food and objects in the graves. These items might have been for the dead to use in an afterlife.

READING CHECK **Summarize** How did Stone Age people use technology to adapt and survive?

NEW YORK

CC Unit 1-A2
Early hunters and gatherers and nomadic groups and their relationship to the environment

---

SECTION 1 ASSESSMENT

go.hrw.com
Online Quiz
Keyword: SHL BEG HP

Reviewing Ideas, Terms, and People

1. **a. Recall** What is an **artifact**, and what are two examples of artifacts?
   b. Explain How do some anthropologists and archaeologists contribute to our understanding of prehistory?
   c. Make Judgments Based on what you have learned about archaeological digs, would you want to work on one? Use information from the text to support your answer.

2. **a. Identify** How have **Mary Leakey**, **Louis Leakey**, and **Donald Johanson** contributed to our knowledge of human origins?
   b. Contrast What set *Homo sapiens* apart from earlier **hominids**?
   c. Evaluate In your opinion, how did the development of language most benefit prehistoric people? Why?

3. **a. Describe** What possible routes did *Homo sapiens* use to spread from Africa throughout the world?
   b. Explain What do most scientists think helped contribute to some of the genetic variation seen among modern humans today?

4. **a. Define** What is a **hunter-gatherer**?
   b. Summarize What types of art did later Stone Age people create?
   c. Elaborate How did Stone Age technology improve over time?

Critical Thinking

5. **Summarize** Copy the graphic organizer below. Using your notes, complete the graphic organizer by describing what scientists have learned about human origins from each of the key discoveries listed.

Discovery	Importance
Nutcracker Man, 1959	
Lucy, 1974	
Laetoli Footprints, 1970s	
Chad fossils, 2001	

FOCUS ON WRITING

6. **Description** Write a paragraph describing the four main groups of early hominids. Your description should include the name of each hominid group, what scientists know about it, and how each group was more advanced than the previous one.

THE BEGINNINGS OF CIVILIZATION **11**

Direct Teach

Teaching Tip

Review with students the difference between BC and AD. Remind them that BC dates begin with 1 BC and increase in number as they go back in time. AD dates begin with AD 1 and increase in number as they go forward in time. BC is placed after a year, as in 500 BC, whereas AD is usually placed before a year, as in AD 500. So, the period from 500 BC to AD 500 is a span of 1,000 years.

Review & Assess

Close
Discuss the spread of early humans and life during the Stone Age.

Review
Online Quiz, Section 1

Assess
SE Section 1 Assessment
Progress Assessment: Section 1 Quiz
Alternative Assessment Handbook

Reteach/Intervene
Interactive Reader and Study Guide, Section 1
Interactive Skills Tutor CD-ROM

Answers
Reading Check *used fire, made tools and weapons*

Section 1 Assessment Answers

1. **a.** object that people in the past made or used; coins, pottery, tools
   b. make educated guesses about people's lives and cultures, expand and revise our picture of the prehistoric past
   c. possible answer—yes; to find new information about our ancestors.

2. **a.** expanded our knowledge of early peoples
   b. larger brains, developed sophisticated tools and shelters, created fire
   c. possible answer—Language helped them communicate and interact with others.

3. **a.** Southwest Asia to Asia and Australia; Bering Strait to Americas
   b. adaptation to new environments

4. **a.** person who hunted, fished, and gathered wild plants, berries, nuts for food
   b. ornaments and figurines, paintings, carvings, cave art
   c. they became more refined and specialized

5. Nutcracker man, 1959—early humanlike being with heavy jaw and large teeth that walked upright; Lucy, 1974—lived more than 3 million years ago; from her bones, scientists could tell that she had walked on two legs, freeing her hands to use tools; Laetoli Footprints, 1976—Humanlike individuals who had the ability to walk upright on two legs 3.5 million years ago ; Chad fossils, 2001—between 6 and 7 million years old, possessing features of both a chimpanzee and an Australopithecine, or hominid; may have walked upright

6. Students should mention Australopithecine, Homo habilis, Homo erectus, Homo sapiens, and include scientists' discoveries.

11

Getting Started

Use the **Interactive Reader and Study Guide** to familiarize students with the section content.

📝 **Interactive Reader and Study Guide,** Section 2

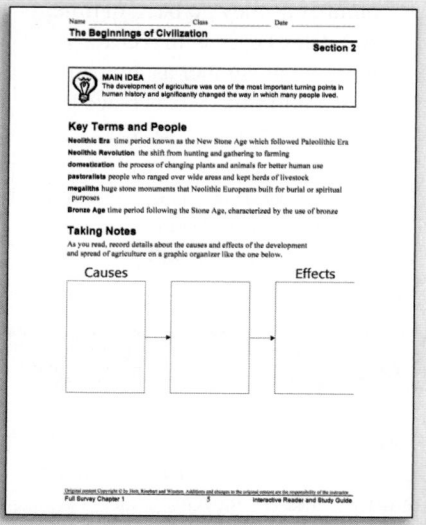

Academic Vocabulary

Review with students the high-use academic term in this section.

domestic relating to the home or to household activities (p. 17)

📝 **CRF:** Vocabulary Builder: Section 2

Taking Notes

Development of Agriculture—plants and animals domesticated; agriculture developed at different times in different places; Spread of Agriculture—people stayed in one place to raise crops; created permanent settlements; population grew; some farming communities grew into towns

---

SECTION

2 The Beginning of Agriculture

BEFORE YOU READ

MAIN IDEA

The development of agriculture was one of the most important turning points in human history and significantly changed the way in which many people lived.

READING FOCUS

1. What new tools and technologies did early humans develop during the New Stone Age?
2. How did early agriculture develop and spread?
3. In what ways did the development of agriculture change Stone Age society?

KEY TERMS

Neolithic Era
Neolithic Revolution
domestication
pastoralists
megaliths
Bronze Age

 NEW YORK

PI 2.5 Students investigate key events and developments and major turning points in world history to identify the factors that brought about change and the long-term effects of these changes.

THE INSIDE STORY

What might seeds reveal about the past? In Syria, on the banks of the Euphrates River, researchers carefully but quickly combed a prehistoric settlement to learn its secrets. A dam would soon flood the site, and time was running short. As the team of scientists raced to collect artifacts and other remains, a picture of the past began to emerge.

Flint and stone tools and the remains of houses showed that people had settled at the spot around 9,500 years ago. Using a specialized sifter, the scientists also found many seeds mixed among the dirt. An analysis of the seeds showed that they were cultivated, revealing that the people had known how to farm. The scientists were thrilled. They had found one of the first farming settlements.

Then, as the scientists continued to study the site, they had another major surprise. Beneath the first settlement was an even older one, dated to about 11,500 years ago. Once again, the scientists carefully sifted through the dirt and found numerous seeds—but with one major difference. These seeds were wild, yet they were still quite similar to the cultivated seeds from the later settlement. The excited scientists realized that the people who had once lived there might have learned the mysteries of farming in perhaps a single lifetime, far quicker than scientists had thought.

Today the settlements lie hidden beneath Lake Assad, but their secrets are hidden no more. There, people learned to farm. This development would radically change life and move people into the fast lane on the road to civilization. ◢

SEEDS OF CHANGE

The settlements the team found were located at this site, which is in Syria. The area now lies beneath Lake Assad. ▶

Teach the Main Idea

At Level

The Beginning of Agriculture

1. **Teach** Ask students the Reading Focus questions to teach this section.

2. **Apply** Have students work in pairs to make charts comparing hunter-gatherer societies and agricultural societies.

3. **Review** Review student charts as a class. Guide students in a discussion of other changes in Neolithic society that accompanied the development of agriculture. Which, if any, of these changes would have taken place without agriculture?

4. **Practice/Homework** Have students research one animal or plant that was domesticated in early times and write a brief report describing how domestication took place and what differences there were between the wild and domesticated versions.

LS Interpersonal, Verbal-Linguistic

📝 **Alternative Assessment Handbook,** Rubrics 7: Charts; 30: Research; and 42: Writing to Inform

The New Stone Age

With the development of more sophisticated tools, the Paleolithic Era gave way to a period that scientists call the **Neolithic Era**, or New Stone Age. In some places, such as parts of Southwest Asia, this period began as early as 8000 BC and lasted until about 3000 BC. In other places, the era began much later and lasted much longer.

Several advances in toolmaking defined the New Stone Age. Whereas before people had chipped stones to produce sharp edges or points, in the New Stone Age people learned to polish and grind stones to shape tools with sharper edges. These new methods enabled people to make more specialized tools, such as chisels, drills, and saws. However, the most significant advances of the Neolithic Era had to do with food, not tools.

READING CHECK Contrast How did toolmaking in the New Stone Age differ from toolmaking in the Old Stone Age?

Development of Agriculture

For tens of thousands of years—most of human history—people lived as nomads, surviving by hunting and gathering food. Then, around 10,000 years ago, some people learned to farm. The development of agriculture is one of the most important turning points in human history because it radically changed how people lived. As a result, historians refer to the shift to farming as the **Neolithic Revolution**.

Plants Around 10,000 years ago, a warming trend brought an end to last Ice Age. As the climate grew warmer and drier, sea levels rose. These changes caused many Ice Age plants and animals to become extinct, or die out. At the same time, new plants and animals appeared in some places. For example, wild grains such as barley and wheat began to spread throughout Southwest Asia.

In areas where wild grains spread, some people began to gather them for food. As people gathered grain each year, they may have noticed that new plants tended to grow where seeds fell. In time, people experimented with planting seeds and learned to farm. This process occurred gradually over a long period.

With the development of farming, people began to practice **domestication**, the selective growing or breeding of plants and animals to make them more useful to humans. Each year, people saved and planted the seeds from only the best plants, such as the hardiest. Slowly over time, wild plants became domesticated. Growing and domesticating plants provided people with larger food supplies.

Animals Before they domesticated plants, prehistoric people had already domesticated animals. As with plants, animal domestication required the careful selection and breeding of the best animals, such as the tamest or those that produced the most meat, milk, or wool.

TAKING NOTES

As you read, take notes in a graphic organizer like this one. Record details about the causes and effects of the beginning of agriculture.

Causes → → → Effects

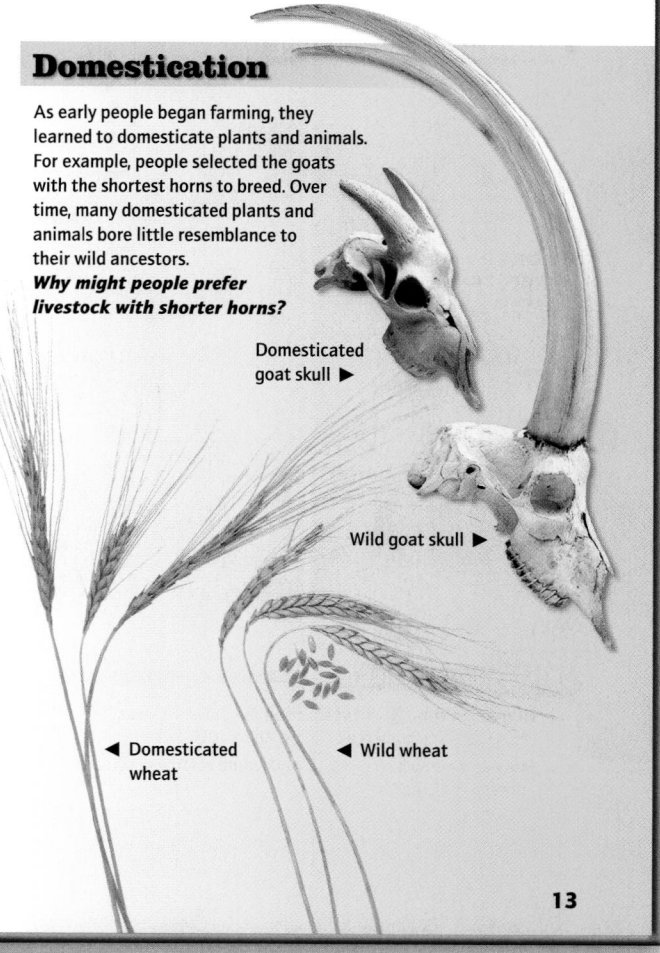

Domestication

As early people began farming, they learned to domesticate plants and animals. For example, people selected the goats with the shortest horns to breed. Over time, many domesticated plants and animals bore little resemblance to their wild ancestors.

Why might people prefer livestock with shorter horns?

Domesticated goat skull ▶

Wild goat skull ▶

◀ Domesticated wheat

◀ Wild wheat

13

13

Direct Teach

Reading Focus

Development of Agriculture

Identify Cause and Effect How did the domestication of animals help people settle in one place? *Animals provided meat, milk, skins, and wool, so people no longer had to follow wild herds.*

Evaluate Why might some people prefer to be hunter-gatherers rather than settle down to farm? *possible answer— They might like the opportunity to go to a cooler climate in the warmer months and to a warmer climate in the cooler months.*

🖐 **Map Transparency:** Growth of Agriculture

Info to Know

Domestication Plants were first domesticated in Southeast Asia around 10,000 years ago. The first plants to be domesticated included wheat, barley, and peas. They were easy to grow, could be harvested quickly, and could be easily stored. Most of them did not require much genetic change to make them suitable for growing as crops.

Most fruit and nut trees were not domesticated until around 4000 BC. The first to be domesticated were fruits such as olives, figs, dates, pomegranates, and grapes. The crops that were cultivated in a particular place depended on what wild plants were already there. In Southwest Asia, these included wheat, barley, rye, peas, walnuts, pistachios, grapes, and olives. People in Africa grew millet, sorghum, rice, and yams. In the Americas, people grew corn, squash, beans, potatoes, peppers, and sunflowers.

NEW YORK

CC Unit 1-B
Neolithic Revolution

Scientists think that the first animals that people domesticated were dogs. By 10,000 BC, people in North America and parts of Asia had tamed dogs, perhaps for use in hunting and as guard animals. In time, prehistoric people applied their knowledge of wild herd animals and learned to domesticate cattle, goats, pigs, and sheep.

By domesticating animals, people could raise livestock to provide a more stable supply of meat, milk, and skins or wool. In addition, people could use large animals such as cattle to carry or pull heavy loads and to help with farming. Like plant domestication, animal domestication provided prehistoric people with a larger and more reliable food supply.

Growth of Agriculture The development of agriculture occurred independently in different parts of the world at different times. In the regions where agriculture developed, people domesticated the plants and animals that were available. Those domesticated plants and animals then gradually spread to other areas.

In Southwest Asia, people domesticated barley, wheat, pigs, and sheep. In East Asia and South Asia, people grew barley, rice, and millet and raised cattle, goats, and water buffalo. In northern Africa, people domesticated sorghum and cattle. In Mexico and Central America, early crops included beans, corn, and squash; while in South America people domesticated potatoes and llamas.

GEOGRAPHY SKILLS | INTERPRETING MAPS

1. **Human-Environment Interaction** What were some of the crops that early farmers were growing by 7000 BC?
2. **Movement** In which areas did agriculture emerge or spread between 6000 and 3000 BC?

14 CHAPTER 1

Skills Focus: Sequencing

At Level

Reading Skill
Growth of Agriculture

1. Guide the class in a discussion of the map on this page by asking the following questions: Where on the map is the Fertile Crescent? *area in red;* What crop(s) did farmers grow in southeastern Europe? *olives;* When did agriculture spread to most of Europe? *by 3000 BC;* If there was no agriculture by 500 BC in most of North America, Australia, a large part of South America, southern Africa, northern Europe and Asia, what can you infer? *that people still relied on hunting and gathering in those regions*

2. Have students write a short essay tracing the growth of agriculture. Have volunteers read their essays to the class. **LS** **Visual-Spatial, Verbal-Linguistic**

📃 **Alternative Assessment Handbook**, Rubrics 21: Map Reading; and 42: Writing to Inform

---

Answers

Interpreting Maps 1. *Refer to map*
2. *Europe, North Africa, South Asia*

Eventually, agriculture spread throughout much of the world. People made the transition to agriculture gradually, however, and often continued to hunt and gather plants as they learned to farm. In addition, some people remained hunter-gatherers, perhaps because their territories were not suited to farming.

READING CHECK **Identify Cause and Effect** How did people benefit from farming and the domestication of plants and animals?

Agriculture Changes Society

Agriculture dramatically changed Stone Age societies. For one, the world population grew significantly because agriculture provided a larger and more reliable food supply. For another, people's ways of life changed. Some people began to live as nomadic **pastoralists**, people who ranged over wide areas and kept herds of livestock on which they depended for food and other items. Other people gave up the nomadic lifestyle and formed settlements. By living in settlements, people could farm and pool their labor and resources.

Early Farming Societies In early farming settlements, people often lived close together in houses made of mud bricks or other materials. On the land around their settlements, people grew crops and raised livestock. As populations grew, some settlements developed into villages and towns. By about 6000 BC, villages and towns of up to several hundred people had arisen in parts of the world.

With the growth of agricultural societies, people's everyday activities changed. Instead of hunting and gathering food, many people worked in the fields and tended livestock. Men, women, and children probably divided up the tasks involved in these activities. At the same time, with more food available, some people could spend more time doing activities other than food production. For example, some people became skilled at making crafts or tools.

As agriculture enabled people to produce extra food and products, trade increased. Settlements traded with one another to obtain raw materials and products that they lacked. For example, in Southwest Asia a popular trade good was obsidian, a dark volcanic glass used to make tools, jewelry, and mirrors.

Agriculture and trade made societies more complex and prosperous, and differences in social status began to emerge. Some people gained more wealth and influence than others. Other people rose to positions of authority, overseeing the planting and harvesting, running building projects, or planning defense. Men performed the heavier work in farming and often held positions of authority. As a result, men began to gain dominance and status over women in many agricultural societies.

Religion began to become more formalized in agricultural societies as well. Some societies began to construct structures for religious purposes. For example, in Europe some Neolithic societies built monuments out of **megaliths**, or huge stones, for burial or spiritual purposes. Some Neolithic people began to worship gods and goddesses associated with animals or the elements—air, water, fire, and earth. For example, one European tribe worshipped bulls, while another honored a thunder god. Other people may have worshipped their ancestors.

A more settled agricultural life had some negative effects as well. For example, warfare increased as societies began to fight over land and resources. As people became more dependant on farming, they were more affected by crop failure as a result of bad weather or other causes. In addition, disease increased. In settlements where people lived close together, disease spread more rapidly. Furthermore, increased contact between people and animals caused some animal diseases to cross over to humans. These diseases included the flu, measles, and smallpox.

New Technologies As their ways of life began to change, people developed new tools and methods to make life easier. Early farmers used hand tools such as hoes and sharpened sticks to prepare the soil for planting. Farmers scattered their seeds by hand and may have used animals to trample and loosen hard soil to work in the seeds. Then about 6000 BC, people began to use animals such as cattle to pull plows. With the plow, farmers could till larger areas to produce more crops.

To prepare foods such as grains, Neolithic people developed new tools such as pestles and grindstones. In addition, people learned to use clay to make pottery. Early pottery was used for cooking and to store grains, oils, and water.

READING SKILLS
Predicting How do you predict that agriculture changed Stone Age societies?

THE IMPACT TODAY
One of the most famous examples of **megaliths** can be seen at Stonehenge near Salisbury, England.

THE BEGINNINGS OF CIVILIZATION **15**

History Close-Up
Çatal Hüyük: An Early Farming Village

Early Paintings The discovery of Çatal Hüyük changed the way scientists thought about human life in Neolithic times. The site includes many shrines that provide the earliest evidence of religious beliefs. Paintings on the walls of these shrines resemble the Stone Age cave paintings found in Europe. They provide information about the way Neolithic people lived, including their daily activities, religion, appearance, and clothing. From these paintings and other remains, it appears that hunting was still an important part of the life of the inhabitants of Çatal Hüyük. Some murals depict the hunting of deer and there are also figures of leopards. The heads of bulls and rams are modeled on the walls of some of these shrines. Huge figures of goddesses giving birth appear to indicate that the main deity was a goddess. She is sometimes shown accompanied by leopards, and sometimes by male figures that may represent a husband and a son.

About the Illustration
This illustration is an artist's conception based on available sources. Historians, however, are uncertain exactly what this scene looked like.

HISTORY CLOSE-UP

Çatal Hüyük: An Early Farming Village

The village of Çatal Hüyük is among the oldest farming sites. Around 8,000 years ago the village was home to some 5,000 to 6,000 people, who lived in more than 1,000 houses. The houses were built so closely together that there were few if any streets. The people of Çatal Hüyük farmed, hunted, and fished; traded with people in distant lands; and built shrines.

Villagers used channels to move water from the river to their fields.

Villagers grew barley, peas, and wheat, and grazed livestock in fields and pastures around the village.

Because homes were built so close together, people entered their homes through rooftop openings.

Families buried ancestors beneath the floor of religious shrines in the main living area.

Inside their homes, families cooked food, stored grain, and used pottery and wooden bowls and cups.

Skills FOCUS INTERPRETING VISUALS

1. **Infer** Why might villagers have placed the entrances to their homes on the rooftops?
2. **Contrast** How were the houses in Çatal Hüyük different from modern American houses?

Collaborative Learning
At Level

Life in Çatal Hüyük

1. Organize students into small groups. Have each group use the History Close-Up on this page to prepare a short skit about life in Çatal Hüyük. Students may want to conduct additional research to help them with their skits. Have students frame their skits with a prologue and epilogue that discuss life in Çatal Hüyük.

2. Have each group present its skit to the class.

3. Guide students in a discussion of life in Çatal Hüyük. Ask students how life in Çatal Hüyük was similar to modern life and how it was different. then have students list similarities between Çatal Hüyük and any other cultures they know of, such as Native American cultures. **LS Interpersonal, Kinesthetic**

📋 **Alternative Assessment Handbook**, Rubrics 14: Group Activity; and 33: Skits and Reader's Theater

Answers

History Close-Up 1. *possible answer—to make it easier to defend their homes from other people and keep animals from wandering into them*
2. *possible answer—entrances were on the rooftops, houses had shared walls and were built around small courtyards, few or no streets, homes were made of wood covered with mud*

The domestication of animals made it possible for Neolithic people to use wool from goats and sheep to create yarn. Some early farming societies learned to spin yarn and weave it into cloth to make garments and blankets.

Eventually, people learned to use metal, first copper and then bronze, a mix of copper and tin. Bronze is harder than copper and produces stronger objects. As people began to make items from bronze, the Stone Age gave way to a time period that scientists call the **Bronze Age**. This transition occurred as early as 3000 BC in some areas, but much later in others.

Çatal Hüyük Archaeologists have found the remains of several Neolithic settlements and villages. One that has provided a wealth of information is Çatal Hüyük (cha-tal HOO-yuk). This Neolithic village was located in present-day Turkey and was home to some 5,000 to 6,000 people around 6000 BC. The village covered more than 30 acres, making it the largest Neolithic site that archaeologists have found.

The people of Çatal Hüyük grew crops such as barley, peas, and wheat in the fields around their village. In addition, they raised sheep and goats, hunted wild cattle, and fished in a nearby river. Based on artifacts found at Çatal Hüyük, such as shells, villagers traded with people as far away as the Red Sea.

The houses in Çatal Hüyük were built close together, and the village had few if any streets. Because of the closeness of the buildings, people entered their homes through openings in the roofs. Most homes had one main room in which a family lived, and one or two side rooms for storage. In the main room, areas were set aside for sleeping and for <u>domestic</u> tasks, such as cooking and making crafts. In some homes, areas were also set aside for religious shrines. These shrines often contained small female statues, large sculpted bulls' heads, and one or two bodies buried beneath the floor. In addition, families covered the interior walls of their homes with colorful, vibrant paintings.

Ötzi the Iceman Archaeological discoveries continue to add to our knowledge of Neolithic societies. In 1991 hikers in Italy's Ötztal Alps found a frozen male body that had been preserved by the cold, icy conditions. Scientific tests showed that the body was about 5,300 years old and from the Neolithic Era.

Nicknamed Ötzi the Iceman, the Neolithic man and his belongings were well preserved. Ötzi's outfit was made of three types of animal skins stitched together. In addition, he wore leather shoes padded with grass, a woven grass cape, a fur hat, and a sort of backpack. Among his belongings were a deerskin quiver with arrows, a flint dagger, and an ax with a copper blade. Heavy wear on Ötzi's front teeth suggest his diet included coarse grains.

Scientists do not think that Ötzi lived in the cold, mountainous location where he was found. Moreover, an arrowhead in his shoulder suggests he was murdered. Perhaps Ötzi had gone into the mountains to try to escape an enemy but then grew too weak to continue.

ACADEMIC VOCABULARY
domestic relating to everyday life or the home

READING CHECK **Summarize** How did the development of agriculture affect Neolithic societies?

SECTION 2 ASSESSMENT

go.hrw.com
Online Quiz
Keyword: SHL BEG HP

Reviewing Ideas, Terms, and People

1. **a. Recall** What characteristics define the **Neolithic Era**?
   b. Explain How did tools in the Neolithic Era differ from those in the Paleolithic Era?
2. **a. Describe** What is involved in plant and animal **domestication**?
   b. Summarize How did the development of agriculture benefit prehistoric people's lives?
   c. Elaborate How did geography contribute to the development and spread of agriculture?
3. **a. Identify** Who is Ötzi the Iceman, and why is he significant?
   b. Contrast How did life for early hunter-gatherers differ from that for people in early agricultural societies?
   c. Develop What have scientists learned about Neolithic farming societies by studying Çatal Hüyük?

Critical Thinking

4. **Identify Supporting Details** Create a graphic organizer like the one below. On the left side, describe the key facts related to the development of agriculture, including both plant and animal domestication. On the right side of the graphic organizer, note the ways in which the development of agriculture affected Neolithic societies.

FOCUS ON WRITING

5. **Persuasion** Write one or two paragraphs in support of the position that the Neolithic Revolution is one of the most important turning points in human history. Address both the positive and negative effects of the development of agriculture.

THE BEGINNINGS OF CIVILIZATION **17**

Section 2 Assessment Answers

1. **a.** specialized tools, development of agriculture/farming, domestication of animals and plants
   b. Paleolithic—chipped stones to make sharp points; Neolithic Era—polished and ground stones for sharp edges
2. **a.** selective growing or breeding of plants and animals
   b. provided larger, more reliable food supply
   c. People domesticated the plants and animals available in their regions.

3. **a.** Neolithic man whose remains were found in the Alps; body and possessions were preserved, reveals much about Neolitic society
   b. Early hunter-gatherers were nomadic and lived in caves; people in early agricultural societies formed settlements and raised crops and animals.
   c. they farmed, hunted, fished, traded with people from distant lands, built shrines
4. (left) end of last Ice Age, population growth, plant domestication, animal domestication; (right) larger, more stable supply of grains

and plants, meat, milk, skins, wool; animals could pull heavy loads and help with farming; settlements and villages developed; people's daily activities changed; trade increased; more complex societies led to differences in social status; development of religion; increase in warfare, disease; advances in toolmaking, including use of metal

5. Paragraphs should list positive aspects of Neolithic Revolution to justify its importance in history and negative aspects, such as increased warfare and disease.

Direct Teach

Info to Know

Avian Flu Recently scientists have been concerned about the spread of avian flu from birds to humans. If the virus mutates, as some scientists fear it will, it could be transmitted from human to human. Because air travel is so widespread, it could lead to a pandemic far worse than the Spanish flu pandemic of 1918–1919 in which tens of millions of people around the world died.

Review & Assess

Close

Guide students in a discussion of the change from hunting and gathering to agriculture.

Review

Online Quiz, Section 2

Assess

SE **Section 2 Assessment**
Progress Assessment: Section 2 Quiz
Alternative Assessment Handbook

Reteach/Intervene

Interactive Reader and Study Guide, Section 2
Interactive Skills Tutor CD-ROM

Answers

Reading Check *revolutionary changes; men and women assumed different roles; led to towns, government, religion, trade*

17

Getting Started

Use the **Interactive Reader and Study Guide** to familarize students with the section content.

📓 **Interactive Reader and Study Guide,** Section 3

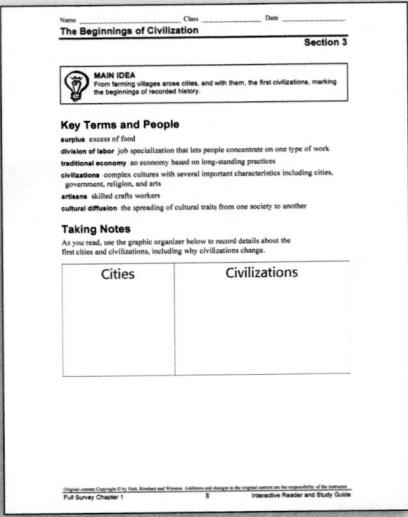

Academic Vocabulary

Review with students the high-use academic terms in this section.

acquistions something that has been obtained or bought (p. 20)

displace to cause a person, animal, or thing to move from its usual place (p. 23)

📓 **CRF:** Vocabulary Builder: Section 3

Taking Notes

Cities—new methods increased farm production; surplus food caused population to grow; division of labor; traditional economy; Civilizations—developed cities; organized government, formalized religion, specialization of labor, social classes, record keeping and writing, art

go.hrw.com
Online Resources
KEYWORD: SHL BEG
ACTIVITY: Divisions of Labor

Foundations of Civilization

BEFORE YOU READ

MAIN IDEA
From farming villages arose cities, and with them, the first civilizations, marking the beginnings of recorded history.

READING FOCUS
1. Why did some early villages develop into cities?
2. What characterized the world's first civilizations, and where did they develop?
3. What factors cause civilizations to change over time?

KEY TERMS
surplus
division of labor
traditional economy
civilization
artisans
cultural diffusion

 NEW YORK
PI 1.1 Students define culture and civilization, explaining how they developed over time. Investigate the components of civilizations.

THE INSIDE STORY

When is a town wall not enough? The townspeople of Jericho stood back to admire their hard work. A massive stone wall with a 30-foot high watchtower now encircled their town. Jericho's residents had every right to be proud. Around 8000 BC, when most people still lived as nomads, Jericho was the first walled town known to exist. To build such a wall took engineering skill, planning, and leadership.

Located in the Jordan Valley north of the Dead Sea, ancient Jericho was an oasis in an otherwise arid land. A spring at the site provided a continual source of water. With this water, the people of Jericho grew barley and wheat and herded sheep and goats. In addition, the townspeople traded across the region. Jericho's mighty wall, agriculture, and trade represented the first steps toward civilization.

Yet, Jericho's wall failed to protect the town. Sometime during the 7000s BC, the community at Jericho ceased to exist. Over time, many other groups settled at Jericho and rebuilt its wall. Even so, Jericho never developed into a civilization—the first civilization was still to come. ■

JERICHO'S MIGHTY WALL

▶ The site of ancient Jericho, located in the Jordan Valley, and some of the ruins that remain.

18 CHAPTER 1

Teach the Main Idea

At Level

Foundations of Civilization

1. **Teach** Ask students the Reading Focus questions to teach this section.

2. **Apply** Organize students into small groups. Have each group to conduct a discussion in which students create their own definition of the word *civilization*. Then have each group make a list of the characteristic institutions and features that they think a civilization should have.

3. **Review** Have volunteers from each group to read their definitions and lists to the class.

After each group has presented its definition and list of factors, compare their lists with the list of characteristics listed in this section under the heading The First Civilizations.

4. **Practice/Homework** Have each student to select one of the characteristics of civilizations listed in the text and write a brief essay about its role in modern civilization. **LS Interpersonal, Verbal-Linguistic**

📓 **Alternative Assessment Handbook,** Rubrics 14: Group Activity; and 42: Writing to Inform

From Villages to Cities

The development of agriculture and the growth of settlements marked a major advance in human history. As societies became more settled, and villages grew in size and complexity, the first cities began to appear.

Advances in farming and changing economies helped lead to the development of cities. Like the transition from a nomadic life to a settled agricultural life, the transition from villages to cities took place gradually.

Advances in Farming As time passed, early farmers continued to develop new methods to increase farm production. One of the most significant advances in farming was the development of irrigation systems. An irrigation system is a network of canals or ditches that links fields of crops to nearby streams or to storage basins of water.

The use of irrigation enabled early people to farm more land and to farm in drier conditions. As a result, farmers could plant more crops and produce more food. With irrigation, some farmers began to produce a **surplus,** or excess, of food. With surplus food, villages could support larger populations.

Changing Economies Because irrigation made farmers more productive, fewer people needed to farm to feed the growing population. As a result, some people were able to work full-time in jobs other than farming. For example, people skilled in making tools and weapons could devote all their time to that work. Other people became full-time weavers, potters, or religious leaders. The economic arrangement in which each worker specializes in a particular task or job is called a **division of labor**.

Food surpluses and a growing division of labor resulted in economic changes. Early farming villages had traditional economies. In a **traditional economy**, economic decisions are made based on custom, tradition, or ritual. In early villages, most people were farmers and relied on trade to obtain a few raw materials.

With the development of irrigation, however, villages could produce extra food as well as valuable trade products. In some villages, leaders began to make economic decisions based on fueling trade and feeding the growing population.

Characteristics of Cities As populations increased and economies became more complex, some villages grew into the first cities. These cities differed from early villages in several ways. First, cities were larger and more densely populated than villages. For example, the first known city was Uruk, located between the Tigris and Euphrates rivers in what is now Iraq. Around 3000 BC Uruk was home to some 40,000 to 50,000 people and covered more than 1,000 acres. In comparison, the village of Çatal Hüyük at its height had only about 5,000 to 6,000 people and covered about 30 acres.

Second, city—or urban—populations were more diverse than village populations. Early villages usually consisted of a few extended families or clans, whereas early cities usually included many unrelated people.

Third, early cities often had a more formal organization than villages. For example, most early cities had a defined center. City centers often contained palaces, temples, monuments, government buildings, and marketplaces. Many early cities had defined boundaries as well, marked by defensive walls, which separated the city from the surrounding villages. The large number of people living in cities provided the labor to create these large-scale building projects.

Finally, early cities served as centers of trade. Merchants and farmers from the surrounding villages traveled to city markets to exchange goods and raw materials. The people in the city produced goods to trade in turn. This trade fed city economies.

READING CHECK **Contrast** How did early cities differ from early farming villages?

The First Civilizations

The world's first civilizations formed from some of these early cities. A **civilization** is a complex and organized society. The first civilizations arose in fertile river valleys—the Tigris and Euphrates in Southwest Asia, the Nile in Africa, the Indus in South Asia, and the Huang He (also called the Yellow River) in China. In these river valleys, the rivers flooded annually. These floods spread mineral-rich silt from the river bottoms onto the nearby land. As a result, the river valleys had fertile land that could support a growing population.

TAKING NOTES
As you read, take notes in a graphic organizer like this one. Record key facts about the first cities and civilizations, including why civilizations change.

Cities	Civilizations

NEW YORK
CC Unit 1-B
Early river civilizations

NEW YORK
CC Unit 1-B.1b
Traditional economies

READING SKILLS
Predicting Based on what you have read so far, where do you predict that the first civilizations developed?

Reading Focus

1 Why did some early villages develop into cities? *They developed food surpluses that led to larger populations, job specialization, economic changes, and growth into cities.*

From Villages to Cities

Explain How did irrigation lead to a food surplus? *steady water supply, farmers could plant more crops*

Contrast How did the populations of cities differ from those of villages? *Most village populations consisted of a few families or clans. Cities were larger and more densely populated than villages, and included people who were not necessarily related to one another, as well as people who migrated from other areas.*

Elaborate How were irrigation and trade connected? *Irrigation led to food surplus, fewer farmers needed. Some people became weavers, potters, produced trade items.*

CRF: Biography: Leonard Woolley

Answers

Reading Check *Cities were larger, more diverse, more dense, and served as trade centers.*

Differentiating Instruction

Below Level

Learners Having Difficulty

1. Draw the chart for students to see. Omit the italicized answers. Have students work in pairs to copy and fill in the chart.

2. Have volunteers provide the facts from their charts, complete the class chart for all to see. Guide students in a discussion of the developments that took place as villages grew into cities. **LS** Visual-Spatial

Alternative Assessment Handbook, Rubric 7: Charts

Villages	• *food surpluses* • *a few crafts* • *priests* • *traditional economy*	• *Most people were farmers.* • *few families or clans* • *provided food for cities*
Cities	• *food surpluses* • *changing economies* • *improved farming* • *surpluses fuel trade* • *religious, economic, and cultural centers*	• *powerful leaders* • *large buildings* • *defensive walls* • *larger, more diverse population*

2 What characterized the world's first civilizations, and where did they develop? *record keeping and writing, specialized labor, government and religious institutions, the arts; along fertile river valleys*

The First Civilizations

Identify What and where were the world's first major cities? *Ur and Uruk near the Tigris and Euphrates rivers, Memphis on the Nile, Mohenjo-Daro on the Indus, and Anyang near the Huang He River.*

Summarize Why were priests powerful figures in early civilizations? *People in early civilizations believed gods and goddesses held power over the forces of nature; priests interpreted the will of gods and goddesses and performed rituals to gain the gods' favor. Because of this, priests often served as government officials.*

📄 **CRF:** History and Geography: The First Civilizations

Info to Know

Megaliths and Temples As people gathered into larger communities, their religious beliefs and practices became more formalized. They began building massive megaliths, or stone monuments, and temples. Some of these structures are astounding in their workmanship and sheer size, considering that, in most cases, the builders had nothing more than simple tools to help them.

Answers

Characteristics of Early Civilizations
possible answer—Each relied on an organized system in which some people had more power than others, and groups of people were interdependent.

20

Characteristics of Early Civilizations

As large cities began to form, the first civilizations appeared. A civilization is a complex society with a number of specific characteristics. *In what way are the characteristics of specialized labor and government and religious institutions connected?*

Record Keeping and Writing One early method of record keeping was a clay pouch that held clay tokens. Each token's shape and markings indicated a specific trade good, such as oil, perfume, or sheep.

Specialized Labor This model from the civilization of ancient Egypt depicts specialized laborers hard at work pounding grain into flour, rolling dough, and baking bread.

Although early civilizations differed, they had several characteristics in common:

- Developed cities
- Organized government
- Formalized religion
- Specialization of labor
- Social classes
- Record keeping and writing
- Art and architecture

Developed Cities Cities with developed social and economic institutions, or patterns of organization, formed the basis of early civilizations. Early cities served as political, economic, and cultural centers for surrounding areas. Major cities in the early river valley civilizations include Ur and Uruk near the Tigris and Euphrates rivers, Memphis on the Nile River, Mohenjo Daro on the Indus River, and Anyang near the Huang He.

🗽 **NEW YORK**
CC Unit 1-B.1c
Political systems of early river civilizations

Organized Government As cities grew, governments formed. Building large irrigation systems and feeding a growing population required planning, decision making, and cooperation. Early governments probably formed in response to such needs. The governments in the first civilizations created laws and established systems of justice. To help coordinate people's efforts, government officials supervised food production and building projects. In addition,

officials gathered taxes and organized defense. In some early civilizations, religious leaders such as priests held government power, while in other early civilizations, influential elders, warriors, or families held power.

Formalized Religion Early civilizations had formal religious institutions that included ceremonies, rituals, and other forms of worship. To gain the gods' favor, priests and other religious leaders performed rituals, such as sacrificing animals or offering gifts of food. To honor the gods, people built large temples and participated in various ceremonies.

Because religious leaders often interpreted the will of the gods, priests became powerful figures in many early civilizations. At the same time, priests and rulers sometimes competed for power. To prove their authority, some leaders claimed that they ruled by the will of the gods or that they represented one of the gods on Earth. As a result, government and religious institutions were often closely connected in early civilizations.

Specialization of Labor As cities became more complex, the division of labor increased and many new jobs developed. For instance, officials gathered taxes, engineers planned irrigation systems, and soldiers defended city walls. While some people farmed, others built large public works, such as temples and roads.

20 CHAPTER 1

Differentiating Instruction

Above Level

Research Required

Advanced Learners/Gifted and Talented
Materials: outline map of the world

1. Organize the class into seven groups. Give each group an outline map of the world and have students use maps or reference works to help them locate and label each of the following early cities: Ur and Uruk, Memphis, Mohenjo-Daro, and Anyang. Have each group make a time line showing when each civilization developed.

2. Assign one of the seven characteristics of civilizations listed in this section to each

group. Have groups research their assigned characteristic for each of the four civilizations. Then have each group prepare an oral report comparing and contrasting the development of that characteristic for each city.

3. Have volunteers from each group to present their report to the class. **LS** Interpersonal, **Verbal-Linguistic**

📋 **Alternative Assessment Handbook**, Rubrics 14: Group Activity; 24: Oral Presentations; and 36: Time Lines

Government and Religious Institutions
These figurines from the early civilization of Sumer depict praying holy men in sheepskin skirts. Such figurines were placed in temples.

The Arts China's Shang civilization created intricate works of bronze, such as the elephant below. A delicate Ibex decorates a pottery shard from India's Harappan civilization.

Artisans, or skilled craftspeople, devoted their time to crafts such as basketry, carpentry, metalwork, or pottery. Merchants and traders exchanged the products that artisans made and brought back <u>acquisitions</u> from other areas.

Social Classes As urban societies developed institutions and specialized labor, a social order developed as well. This social order was based on people's occupations, wealth, and influence. In early civilizations, rulers, priests, and nobles had the most power and ranked highest in the social order. Merchants and artisans usually ranked next. Below them, were farmers and unskilled workers, who made up the majority of the people. A class of enslaved people often formed the bottom of the social order. Some slaves were people who had been captured in war, while other had been sold into slavery.

Record Keeping and Writing As life in early cities grew increasingly complex, people needed ways to keep permanent records. For example, merchants needed to keep records of trade goods, and officials needed to track tax payments. In early civilizations people used a variety of methods of keeping records before the development of writing. For example, the early civilization of Sumer, which developed along the Tigris and Euphrates rivers, used clay tokens and pouches to keep records. The shape of each token and the markings on it

represented a specific item, such as a goat or a piece of pottery. The tokens were stored in a clay pouch. To retrieve the tokens, the pouch had to be broken open. The Inca civilization of Peru, which developed later in South America, used knotted colored strings to keep accounts.

Systems of writing began to develop about 5,000 years ago. The first writing systems used pictographs, or picture symbols, to represent objects or ideas. In time, people created more advanced writing systems that used abstract symbols to express a wider range of ideas. With the development of writing, early civilizations began to create a written record of their society. Such ancient texts and records are still important: they provide historians with a wealth of information about early civilizations.

Along with writing, people in early civilizations developed calendars. Because of the growing importance of farming, people needed to track the changing of the seasons and when it was time to plant or harvest. People in early river valley civilizations also needed to know when yearly floods would occur.

In response to such needs, some early civilizations created calendars. These calendars were based on the phases of the moon, which were easy for early people to see and track. Early lunar, or moon-based, calendars were inaccurate, though, because the lunar year is several days shorter than the solar year.

ACADEMIC VOCABULARY
acquisition something that has been obtained or bought

 NEW YORK

CC **Unit 1-B.1d**
Social structures and urbanization of early river civilizations

THE BEGINNINGS OF CIVILIZATION **21**

21

3 What factors cause civilizations to change over time? *geography, politics, and the movement of people and ideas*

Change in Civilizations

Explain Why could a lack of resources cause a civilization to change? *When resources run out, people are forced to seek alternative solutions, which in turn would likely cause an increase in different types of trade.*

Make Inferences How might the wealth and success of a civilization lead to its decline? *possible answer— Other civilizations may have wanted to acquire its resources, leading them to invade it. Prolonged war could deplete a civilization's wealth and cause it to decline, even if it wasn't conquered.*

Rank Which of the factors that change civilizations do you think has had the biggest effect? Why? *possible answer—cultural diffusion; has allowed different cultures to share ideas and develop better technology*

Quick Facts Transparency: Economic Systems

The Arts The people in early civilizations produced amazing works of art. The styles and techniques that artists used reflected each civilization's culture. Early artists created statues and paintings of gods and goddesses, heroes, and rulers. As the use of bronze spread, some artisans created intricate art pieces in bronze.

Works of art often adorned city squares, public buildings, and royal tombs. The most elaborate pieces of art, such as monumental statues of rulers, were meant to reflect a civilization's power and bring its ruler prestige.

READING CHECK **Draw Conclusions** What was the relationship between job specialization and the development of social classes in early civilizations?

Change in Civilizations

Once early civilizations developed, they continued to change over time. Factors such as the environment, conflicts, and the movement of people and ideas affected civilizations and led to change. While some changes weakened civilizations, others strengthened them and led to growth and expansion.

Environmental Influences Because of their dependence on farming, people in early civilizations relied on their environments. The forces of nature could easily bring destruction and ruin, however. Raging storms could destroy crops and leave people without enough food.

HISTORY and Economics

Needs and Wants

All people need certain things to survive, such as water, food, and shelter. In addition, people want things in addition to their needs, such as jewelry or cars. To satisfy their needs and wants, people make economic choices. In a society, the three basic economic choices are (1) what to produce, (2) how to produce it, and (3) for whom to produce it. Societies develop economic systems to make these choices. Understanding economic systems is essential for understanding history.

Economic Systems in History Prehistoric hunter-gatherers met their needs and wants simply. As cities and civilizations developed, though, satisfying needs and wants became more complex. People faced new choices: What do we need to prosper? What do we want that we cannot produce for ourselves? With whom will we trade to obtain those things? Such questions forged new economic relationships, and different economic systems developed.

Economic Systems in Your Life Much of history involves the interaction of societies in pursuit of their needs and wants. Conquests, revolutions, periods of artistic development—needs and wants and differing economic systems often

factor into such events. For example, imagine two countries each rich in what the other lacks. They form an alliance to meet their needs and wants together. In history you will find many such examples. Finding the "why" behind events, then, is often a matter of discovering the needs and wants involved and the economic systems used to pursue them.

Draw Conclusions How might an understanding of needs and wants and economic systems help you understand the causes of a war?

ECONOMIC SYSTEMS		QUICK FACTS
Traditional Economy	People make economic choices based on customs and traditions.
Command Economy	A central government makes all economic decisions.
Market Economy	Private individuals make economic choices based on competition.
Mixed Economy	Uses a mix of traditional, command, and market economies.

◄ Two merchants bargain in this carving produced sometime in the 900s to 700s BC.

Skills Focus: Drawing Conclusions

Reading Skill
Characteristics of Civilizations

1. Write the seven characteristics of civilizations listed in this section for students to see: developed cities, government, religion, job specialization, social classes, record keeping and writing, arts and architecture.

2. Have students choose one characteristic that they think was the most important. Have students write a brief essay describing the characteristic, explaining why it is necessary to civilization.

3. Poll students to see which characteristic each chose. Write each characteristic and the number of students who chose each one for students to see. Rank the characteristics by the number of students who chose each and discuss the results.

4. Have volunteers read their essays to the class.
   LS Verbal-Linguistic

   Alternative Assessment Handbook, Rubric 37: Writing Assignments

---

Answers

History and Economics *possible answer—Learning about what societies value and are willing to fight for can shed light on reasons for war.*

Flash floods could wipe out whole cities, and drought could kill off livestock. Farming used up the land, and after a period of time the soil lost fertility. Food shortages and other natural disasters could weaken a civilization and leave it open to outside attack.

A need for resources, such as metals, stone, and timber, could also cause civilizations to change. As early civilizations expanded, they began to use more resources. Some resources ran out. Other areas lacked needed resources. In such cases, people had to look for alternative solutions. In areas with few trees, for example, some people began to use dried animal dung as fuel for cooking. To obtain scarce resources, civilizations expanded trade.

Spread of People and Ideas The spread of people and ideas was another source of change in civilizations. Throughout history, the movement of people through trade, migration, and conquest has helped spread cultures and ideas. Traveling merchants learned new languages to conduct trade with foreign groups. Migrants brought their language, customs, and traditions with them when they moved to new areas. Civilizations often imposed their own cultures on the peoples they conquered.

The spread of ideas, beliefs, customs, and technology from one culture to another is called **cultural diffusion**. As a result of cultural diffusion, people adopted new customs, skills, and technologies. Advances such as writing, metalworking, and farming techniques spread from one civilization to another. Artists borrowed designs and materials from other cultures and blended them with their own styles to create new forms and designs. Religious beliefs spread as people adopted the gods and goddesses of other civilizations and made them their own.

Expansion and Warfare Expansion and warfare contributed to change in civilizations as well. As civilizations grew, they needed more land and other resources to support their growing populations. Conflicts over land, water, and other resources occurred and often led to war.

Civilizations waged war to gain control of rich farmland, important sea ports, or regions with valuable resources. Through conquest, civilizations expanded their control over land and people. Through such means, some civilizations developed into states and kingdoms.

Conflicts also arose between civilizations and nomadic groups. Not all people had chosen to live in settled communities. Nomadic pastoralists, or herders, traveled with their herds over wide-ranging territories. These nomadic groups were loosely organized into tribes led by chieftains. Nomadic societies had simple social organizations but developed rich cultures.

Toughened by the need to protect their herds, nomads were usually skilled warriors. In addition, once they learned to domesticate the horse, nomads became highly mobile. Although nomadic groups and settled communities often traded, nomads sometimes launched raids on villages and cities. Further conflicts arose as nomads and farmers competed over land.

READING CHECK Identify Cause and Effect
How did cultural diffusion affect early civilizations?

SECTION 3 ASSESSMENT

go.hrw.com
Online Quiz
Keyword: SHL BEG HP

Reviewing Ideas, Terms, and People

1. **a. Define** What is a **division of labor**?
   b. Identify Cause and Effect How did irrigation systems help contribute to the development of the first cities?

2. **a. Recall** Where did the world's first four **civilizations** develop?
   b. Summarize What conditions existed in river valleys that encouraged the development of the first civilizations?
   c. Evaluate Why do you think that record keeping and writing are necessary characteristics of civilization?

3. **a. Identify** What are some factors that cause civilizations to change?
   b. Explain What are some causes of **cultural diffusion**, and how did it affect early civilizations?
   c. Elaborate What are some possible ways that trade, migration, or invasion might lead to the spread of technology?

Critical Thinking

4. **Identify Supporting Details** Use your notes and a graphic organizer like the one shown below to identify and describe each of the characteristics that early civilizations had in common. You will need to add rows to your graphic organizer.

Characteristics	Description

FOCUS ON WRITING

5. **Exposition** Write two paragraphs that explain how migration and cultural diffusion contributed to civilizations changing over time. Consider the spread of both people and ideas.

THE BEGINNINGS OF CIVILIZATION **23**

River Valleys and Civilizations

Info to Know

The Nile Valley The climate around the Nile provided early Egyptians with ideal conditions for farming. The two main tributaries of the Nile, the Blue Nile and the White Nile, received heavy rainfall during the summer. When the Nile overflowed its banks, it flooded the Nile Valley and Delta. In October and November the water receded and the remaining moisture in the soil sustained the crops until harvest.

Tropical Civilizations Scientists can study water management strategies in still-existing civilizations such as Bali to see how early tropical civilizations developed. Scientists have noticed a consistent pattern of development that is far different from that of the civilizations that grew up along large rivers such as the Nile and the Indus. In tropical climates, there are so many species that each locale is unique. Because rain is seasonal, tropical states built reservoirs to store water for the dry season. Large reservoirs allowed a centralized population, and water could be used to increase power. For example, the Maya developed hilltop reservoirs to capture rainwater and as a result quickly gained political power.

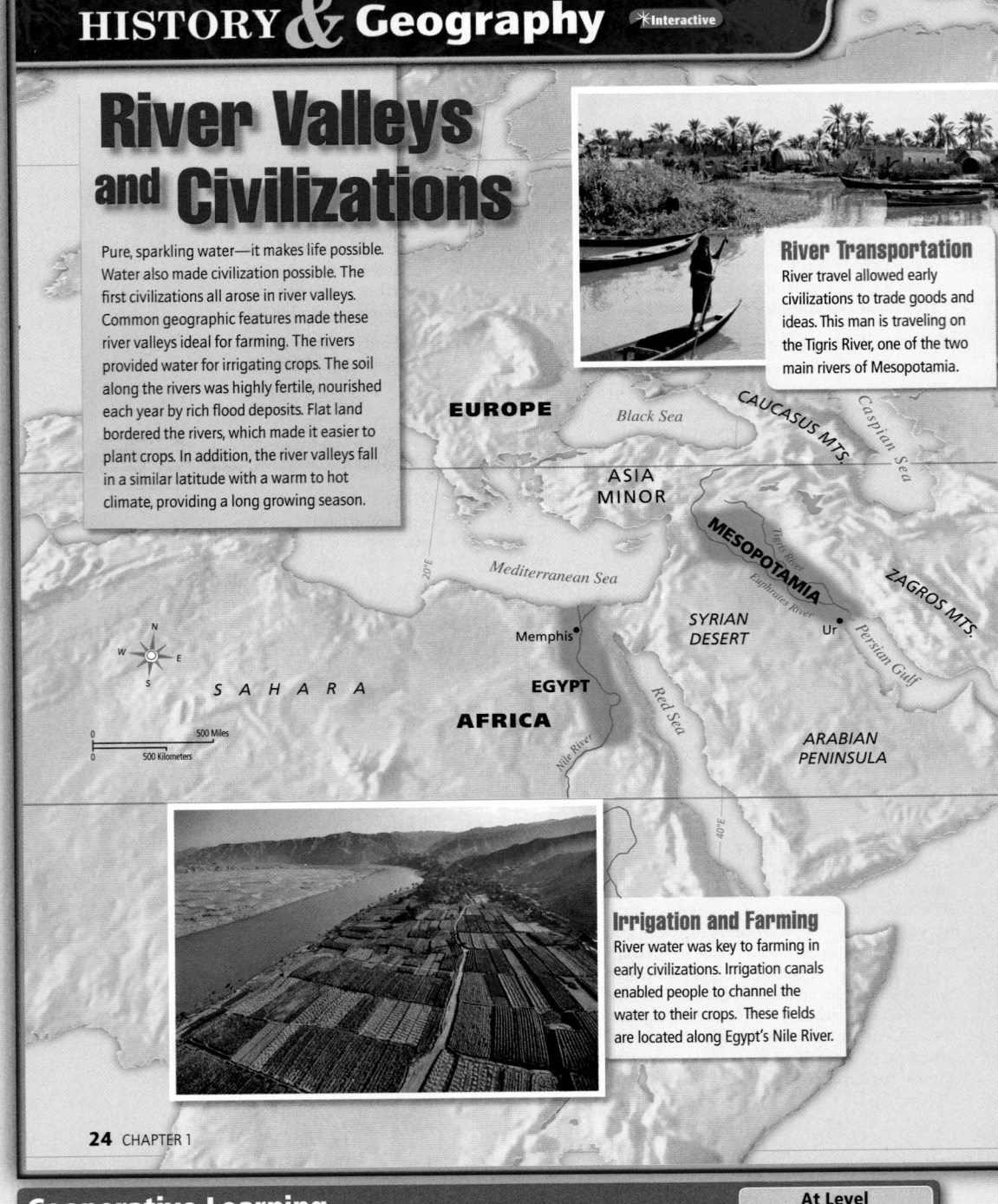

HISTORY & Geography   ✴Interactive

River Valleys and Civilizations

Pure, sparkling water—it makes life possible. Water also made civilization possible. The first civilizations all arose in river valleys. Common geographic features made these river valleys ideal for farming. The rivers provided water for irrigating crops. The soil along the rivers was highly fertile, nourished each year by rich flood deposits. Flat land bordered the rivers, which made it easier to plant crops. In addition, the river valleys fall in a similar latitude with a warm to hot climate, providing a long growing season.

River Transportation
River travel allowed early civilizations to trade goods and ideas. This man is traveling on the Tigris River, one of the two main rivers of Mesopotamia.

Irrigation and Farming
River water was key to farming in early civilizations. Irrigation canals enabled people to channel the water to their crops. These fields are located along Egypt's Nile River.

EUROPE

Black Sea

CAUCASUS MTS.

Caspian Sea

ASIA MINOR

MESOPOTAMIA

ZAGROS MTS.

Tigris River

Euphrates River

Mediterranean Sea

SYRIAN DESERT

Ur

Persian Gulf

Memphis

SAHARA

EGYPT

Red Sea

AFRICA

Nile River

ARABIAN PENINSULA

N W E S

0   500 Miles
0   500 Kilometers

24 CHAPTER 1

Cooperative Learning   At Level

Civilizations Then and Now

1. Organize students into small groups. Have each group make a list of the characteristics that were needed for a successful civilization 5,000 years ago. Then have students make a list of the characteristics needed for a successful civilization today.

2. Have each group analyze its lists using the following questions as a guide:
   - What do the similarities and differences of the two lists tell you about the changes that have occurred over the past 5,000 years?

   - Have those changes been for the better or worse?
   - Do you think you would have been more successful in one civilization than another? Why?

3. Have volunteers from each group share their lists and analyses with the class.
   LS Interpersonal

   Alternative Assessment Handbook, Rubric 14: Group Activity

Flooding The first civilizations all arose along rivers that flood their valleys each year. The receding floodwaters left behind fertile silt, enriching the soil and producing abundant crops. At the same time, flooding could be destructive, as in this scene of flooding on the Huang He (Yellow River) in China.

MONGOLIAN PLATEAU

G O B I

40°N

PLATEAU OF TIBET

KUNLUN MTS.

HINDU KUSH

Huang He (Yellow River)

Longshan

Yangshao

ASIA

CHINA

H I M A L A Y A S

Chang Jiang (Yangzi River)

Mohenjo Daro

INDUS VALLEY

Ganges River

Brahmaputra River

Arabian Sea

20°N

120°E

INDIA

The highlighted latitude lines mark the zone where the first civilizations arose.

Bay of Bengal

INDOCHINA PENINSULA

Mekong River

South China Sea

INDIAN OCEAN

80°E

60°E

GEOGRAPHY SKILLS INTERPRETING MAPS

go.hrw.com
Interactive Map
Keyword: SHL BEG

1. **Location** Where were each of the four river valley civilizations located? What do all the locations have in common?

2. **Human-Environment Interaction** What advantages did the locations of the first civilizations provide in addition to the advantages mentioned here?

0°Equator

THE BEGINNINGS OF CIVILIZATION **25**

History and Geography

Info to Know

The Indus River Pottery discovered by scientists at Mohenjo-Daro on the Indus indicates skillful artists capable of showing great detail in their work. Most pottery varied in shape and pieces were made of pinkish clay. Usual themes for pottery included animals, plants, and geometric motifs of intersecting circles and scales. Because scientists have found Indus objects on Mesopotamian sites, they believe trade existed between the two civilizations and have compared the pottery created by both populations.

Draw Conclusions Why would a civilization have developed beyond the flood plain of the Indus River? *possible answer—Such a location would avoid flooding and destruction of crops and buildings.*

Skills Focus: Identifying Main Idea and Details

At Level

Water: A Necessity of Life

Background: Explain to students that while water is still important for human life, major cities are not limited to river valleys, and communities no longer rely on regular flooding to raise food.

1. Guide students in a discussion of the importance of water in modern life. Have students name the ways in which we use water in modern civilization. As they do so, make a list for all to see.

2. Ask students if they know where the water they use every day comes from. What sources do we have for water today? As students name them, make a list for all to see.

3. Continue the discussion of water by asking students if supplies of clean water are unlimited. **LS** Verbal-Linguistic

🗒 **Alternative Assessment Handbook,** Rubric 11: Discussions

Answers

Interpreting Maps 1. *along the Nile in Egypt, along the Tigris and Euphrates rivers in Mesopotamia, along the Indus River in India, and along the Huang He in China; they were all at similar latitudes, so they probably had similar climates* **2.** *possible answer—They probably had a variety of edible plants that could be easily domesticated.*

25

Info to Know

Agatha Christie In 1929, having read of Leonard Woolley's excavations at Ur, the British mystery writer Agatha Christie traveled to Iraq. There she met Woolley and his wife Katharine, who had read Christie's 1926 novel *The Murder of Roger Ackroyd*. The visit was so successful that she returned a year later. On that trip she met Woolley's assistant, Max Mallowan, whom she married in September 1930. After their marriage Christie always accompanied her husband on his excavations. She assisted by photographing, cleaning, and recording finds. She particularly enjoyed restoring ceramics—often using her face cream to clean crevices! She also helped found the British School in Iraq. Agatha Christie's novel *Murder in Mesopotamia* (1936) was inspired by her visit to Woolley's excavation at Ur. She also used archaeological themes in several other books, including *Death on the Nile* (1937), *Appointment with Death* (1938), and *They Came to Baghdad* (1951).

 NEW YORK STANDARDS

PI 4.2 Students interpret and analyze documents and artifacts related to significant developments and events in world history.

Historical Context The four documents below describe some of the ways in which archaeologists learn about the past without the benefit of written records.

Task Study the selections and answer the questions that follow. After you have studied the documents, you will be asked to write an essay explaining how archaeologists learn about prehistory. You will need to use evidence from these selections and from the chapter to support your essay.

DOCUMENT 1

Excavating the Royal Cemetery of Ur

British archaeologist Sir Leonard Woolley excavated the ruins of Ur, an ancient city in Iraq, from 1922 to 1934. Woolley's excavation of the Royal Tombs of Ur provided a wealth of information about the ancient city and the people who lived there. Along with royalty the cemetery included the remains of court attendants and soldiers, sacrificed to serve their masters after death. The following passage describing Woolley's excavation is from the *Fundamentals of Archaeology*, a 1979 textbook by Robert J. Sharer and Wendy Ashmore.

The burials of King A-bar-gi and Queen Sub-ad were accompanied by interment [burial] of more than 80 other people, ... including soldiers with gold- and silver-headed spears, female attendants wearing headdresses of lapis, carnelian, and gold, ... and an array of spectacularly beautiful artifacts such as gaming boards and harps. Recovery was slow and painstaking; because of the quantity and in many cases the fragility of the remains, the overall area was divided into squares. Finds in each square were cleared and removed before work on the next square was begun. ... A nearly complete funerary scene could later be reconstructed by combining information from each square.

DOCUMENT 2

An Archaeological Dig in Syria

The photograph on the right shows a team of researchers and workers at an archaeological dig in Ebla, Syria. The team is excavating the ruins of a Hittite city from around 1600 BC. The person in the foreground is using a transit, a device for surveying a site. With this device, workers can determine location, plot a map of the site, and divide the site into specific units to map the location and depth where objects are found.

Collaborative Learning

At Level

The Present Through the Eyes of the Future

1. Organize students into small groups. Tell students that it is the year 5000 and archaeologists are excavating the site of your community. Have each group make a list of artifacts that might still remain buried at the site.

2. Have groups exchange their list of artifacts with other groups. Tell students that they are anthropologists in the year 5000 who are studying artifacts to reconstruct the lives of people at the beginning of the 21st century. Have each group use the list it received to write a profile of life in the present as it would appear to people in the future.

3. Have volunteers from each group read the list it received and its profile to the class.

4. Guide the class in a discussion of student lists and profiles. **LS Interpersonal, Verbal-Linguistic**

Alternative Assessment Handbook, Rubrics 14: Group Activity; and 40: Writing to Describe

DOCUMENT 3

Çatal Hüyük

Archaeologist Ian Hodder has led the excavation at Çatal Hüyük, a Neolithic farm village, since 1993. In the following passage from the article "This Old House" in the June 2006 edition of *Natural History* magazine, Hodder describes why the Çatal Hüyük site is such an archeological goldmine.

How much can be learned from what is perhaps the most intriguing feature of all about Çatalhöyük: that the site was built and rebuilt over the centuries in ways that provide an unusually rich record of the minutiae [small details] of daily life? The main reason for the abundance of the archaeological record [at Çatalhöyük] was that the Çatalhöyükans used a particular kind of construction material. Instead of making hard, lime floors that held up for decades (as was the case at many sites in Anatolia and the Middle East), the inhabitants of Çatalhöyük made their floors mostly out of a lime-rich mud plaster, which remained soft and in need of continual resurfacing. Once a year—in some cases once a month—floors and wall plasters had to be resurfaced. Those thin layers of plaster, somewhat like the growth rings in a tree, trap traces of activity.... The floors even preserve such subtle tokens of daily life as the impressions of floor mats.

DOCUMENT 4

Ötzi the Iceman

The 5,300-year-old body of a Neolithic traveler, nicknamed Ötzi the Iceman, has provided a wealth of information on Neolithic life in Europe. The passage below is from the article "Testimony from the Iceman" in the February 2003 edition of *Smithsonian* magazine. In the article, writer Bob Cullen describes how the long-dead Iceman still speaks.

Until Otzi, archaeologists had been required to reconstruct Neolithic civilization from skeletal remains, flint tools, and arrowheads, bits of pottery and the beginnings of metallurgy. The glacier's damp, freezing temperature had preserved not only Otzi himself but also a grove of organic artifacts—clothing, wooden handles for tools and weapons, feathered arrows never before seen by modern eyes.... The radiocarbon dating of Otzi's ax blade forced a revision in the generally accepted date for the advent [start] of copper smelting in the Alpine region. The feathers on two of his arrows showed that Neolithic man understood the ballistic principles that make an arrow rotate and fly more accurately. The embers that he carried wrapped in maple leaves in a birch-bark container suggested how Neolithic people transported fire from place to place.

Skills FOCUS — READING LIKE A HISTORIAN

DOCUMENT 1
a. Identify What method did Woolley use to excavate Ur's royal cemetery, and what objects did he find?
b. Draw Conclusions What types of conclusions do you think that archaeologists could draw about Ur based on the items found in the excavation of the royal cemetery?

DOCUMENT 2
a. Identify What are some of the tools and equipment that the workers are using at the excavation?
b. Interpret Based on the photograph, what are some of the activities that take place at an archaeological dig, and what are some of the difficulties that workers face?

DOCUMENT 3
a. Identify Main Ideas What aspect of Çatal Hüyük has provided archaeologists with a wealth of information?

b. Evaluate Based on this passage, do you think that luck plays a role in archaeological research? Explain your answer.

DOCUMENT 4
a. Describe What have scientists learned from Ötzi?
b. Explain Why is Ötzi such a significant find?

DOCUMENT-BASED ESSAY QUESTION

Archaeologists use many methods to learn about prehistory without the benefit of written records. Using the documents above and information from the chapter, form a thesis about the ways in which archaeologists learn about prehistory and some of the challenges they face. Then write an essay providing details to support your thesis.

See **Skills Handbook**, p. H25, H26

Skills Focus: Making Written Presentations   [At Level]

Reading Like a Historian Skill
Today's Artifacts

1. Have each student select one "artifact" from modern life, such as a cell phone, credit card, or skateboard. Have students choose artifacts that are meaningful to them. Then have students write an essay describing what the selected artifact says about American life at the beginning of the 21st century. In their essays have students explain why their chosen artifact is significant to them and what its significance

is to American life in general. Ask students if they think their artifacts will still be significant to them five years from now.

2. Have volunteers read their essays to the class. What kinds of things did students choose as their "artifacts"? **LS Verbal-Linguistic**

Alternative Assessment Handbook, Rubric 41: Writing to Express

Answers

Reading Like a Historian
Document 1. a. *He divided the area into squares and removed the finds from each square before going on to the next. He found spears, jewelry, gaming boards, and harps.* **b.** *possible answer—that it had a fairly advanced civilization that possessed great wealth;* **Document 2. a.** *a transit, bowls;* **b.** *One person is using a transit to survey the site. One person appears to be sifting through dirt looking for artifacts.;* **Document 3. a.** *the floors;* **b.** *possible answer—yes; easy to overlook;* **Document 4. a.** *a more accurate date for the advent of copper smelting in the alpine region; that Neolithic people understood ballistic principles; how they transported fire;* **b.** *He was preserved along with his clothing, tools, and weapons, allowing researchers to study more than the skeletal remains and nonperishable artifacts that they had previously had to work with.* **Essay** *Student essays should include details about how archaeologists learn from history and the challenges they face.*

Info to Know

Scientists have examined the contents of the Ötzi's transverse colon to determine what his last meal consisted of—a bit of unleavened bread, an herb or some other green, and meat. They also found many different varieties of pollen, which indicated that he had come from a valley to the south, five or six hours away by foot, and that he had left there within half a day of his death. However, they may never know what led him from the safety of that valley to try to cross the mountain in the snow with no food or water.

Visual Study Guide

Review and Inquiry Organize students into three groups. Have one group review the characteristics of the Paleolithic Era, one group the Neolithic Era, and one group Cities and Civilizations. Have each group prepare and present a brief lesson about the assigned topic to the class.

📚 **Quick Facts Transparency**: Visual Study Guide: The Beginnings of Civilization

Review Key Terms and People

1. Culture
2. Hunter-gatherers
3. Cultural diffusion
4. Civilization
5. Cycle
6. domestication
7. artifacts
8. Neolithic Revolution
9. artisans
10. nomads

Comprehension and Critical Thinking

11. a. by digging into ancient settlements to find artifacts
b. had to learn how to make tools, canoes, clothing, shelters
c. possible answer—The woman was an artisan or made jewelry from stone.

12. a. period in history that marked shift to farming; radically changed how people lived
b. led to more stable food supply, development of settlements and villages
c. possible answer—Scientists can conclude that Neolithic people ate coarse grains, used animals for food and clothing, used grass for weaving, and made weapons with stone and metal.

13. a. cities, organized government, formalized religion, specialization of labor, social classes, record keeping and writing; art and architecture
b. civilizations arose from the development of cities; grew along fertile river valleys

c. religious leaders, warriors, or influential elders held government power; social classes developed based on occupation, wealth, influence; rulers and priests were on top

Reading Skills

14. possible answer—Bronze tools were probably faster and easier to make than stone tools, so more time could be spent doing other things.

15. possible answer—I think organized government and writing were most beneficial to the first civilizations.

16. possible answer—There might have been conflict between the two groups or they may have become trading partners.

Analyzing Visuals

17. The prehistoric people who made the carvings felt bison were important to them. The artists were very talented.

18. The carvings may have had spiritual significance, or perhaps the people were representing the world as they saw it.

QUICK FACTS

VISUAL STUDY GUIDE

Key Discovery	Discoverer and Location
Nutcracker Man, 1959	Mary Leakey, East Africa
Lucy, 1974	Donald Johanson, Ethiopia
Laetoli footprints, 1970s	Mary Leakey, Tanzania
Homo habilis fossil, 1959	Mary and Louis Leakey, Olduvai Gorge in Tanzania
Chad skull, 2001	French Team, Chad

Hominid Group	Appeared About
Australopithecines (Southern Ape)	4–5 million years ago
Homo habilis (Handy Man)	2.4 million years ago
Homo Erectus (Upright Man)	2–1.5 million years ago
Homo Sapiens (Wise Man) • Neanderthals • Cro-Magnons	200,000 years ago • 200,000 years ago • 40,000 years ago

Paleolithic Era (Old Stone Age)
- nomadic bands of hunter-gatherers
- use of simple, chipped stone tools
- use of fire
- development of language
- creation of cave paintings and figurines
- burial of the dead

Neolithic Era (New Stone Age)
- farming and the domestication of plants and animals
- polishing of stone tools
- settlement of farming villages
- increases in types of activities, trade and differences in wealth
- pottery, weaving, and the plow

The First Cities and Civilizations
- irrigation leads to food surpluses
- development of division of labor
- rise of the first cities and civilizations
- development of government and religious institutions
- emergence of social classes
- invention of record keeping/writing

Review Key Terms and People

Complete each sentence by filling the blank with the correct term or person.

1. _____ refers to a society's knowledge, art, beliefs, customs, and values.
2. _____ are people who survive by eating animals that they have caught or plants they have collected.
3. _____ is the spreading of cultural traits from one society to another.
4. Characteristics of _____ include developed cities, record keeping and writing, and the specialization of labor.
5. To _____ is to alternate between two events.

6. By experimentation, people learned the practice of _____, or the selective growing or breeding of plants and animals for human use.
7. Pottery, tools, and weapons are examples of _____, or objects made and used by humans.
8. The development of agriculture is sometimes called the _____ because of the profound effects of agriculture on history.
9. Skilled craftspeople called _____ fashioned baskets, pottery, and metal goods by hand.
10. Herding societies did not establish permanent settlements but instead lived as _____, moving their herds from place to place in search of grazing land.

History's Impact video program

Review the video to answer the closing question:
How do archaeologists discover new ways of thinking about ancient cultures?

Comprehension and Critical Thinking

SECTION 1 *(pp. 5–11)*

11. a. Recall How do scientists study prehistory without the aid of written records from that time?

b. Summarize What are three ways in which early humans adapted to new environments during the Stone Age?

c. Develop If you were an archaeologist and found bead jewelry and stone chopping tools in an ancient woman's grave, what might you conclude?

SECTION 2 *(pp. 12–17)*

12. a. Identify What was the Neolithic Revolution, and why was it important?

b. Identify Cause and Effect How did the domestication of plants and animals change prehistoric societies during the Neolithic Era?

c. Make Judgments What can scientists conclude about life during the Neolithic Era from Ötzi the Iceman? Consider Ötzi's clothing, articles and weapons, location, and death in your answer.

SECTION 3 *(pp. 18–23)*

13. a. Recall What were the common characteristics of early civilizations?

b. Explain How did the world's first civilizations develop, and what did the four locations where they developed have in common?

c. Elaborate In early civilizations how were religion, government, and social classes all interconnected?

Reading Skills

Predicting *Use what you have learned about predicting to answer the questions below.*

14. As people began using bronze to create tools, the Stone Age gave way to the Bronze Age. What do you predict was one way in which the use of bronze tools affected early human societies?

15. Which characteristics of civilizations do you predict were most beneficial in helping the first civilizations grow and endure?

16. As early civilizations grew and expanded, how do you predict that nomadic pastoralists and more settled civilizations interacted?

Analyzing Visuals

Reading Like a Historian *The image shows two cave sculptures of bison, which prehistoric people carved out of the wall of a cave at Tuc d'Audoubert, Ariege, France.*

Bison Cave Sculpture, Tuc d'Audoubert, Ariege, France

17. Draw Conclusions Based on the carvings, what conclusions can you draw about the people who made them?

18. Infer Why do you think that early prehistoric people made these carvings?

Using the Internet

go.hrw.com
Practice Online
Keyword: SHL BEG

19. What would it be like to be an archaeologist and search for artifacts from the past? Using the keyword above, do research to learn about recent archaeological finds. Select two or more artifacts that interest you and write a short, informative article about them that could go in a school science magazine. Describe each artifact in detail.

WRITING ABOUT HISTORY

Exposition: Writing an Explanation *The Neolithic Revolution dramatically changed prehistoric societies.*

20. Assignment: In an essay, explain how the Neolithic Revolution affected the way in which people lived, the types of activities people performed, and the technology people used. To provide support for your explanation, use information from this chapter and from other research as needed. Be sure to collect facts and examples to illustrate your points.

THE BEGINNINGS OF CIVILIZATION **29**

Using the Internet

19. Go to the HRW Web site and enter the keyword shown to access a rubric for this activity.

> KEYWORD: SHL BEG

Writing About History

20. Student essays should explain how the Neolithic Revolution changed the way people lived, the activities they performed, and the technology they used. Facts and examples should be used to support their claims.

A rubric for the activity is provided in **CRF:** Writing for the SAT.

HOLT

History's Impact
► **Video Program: The Beginnings of Civilization**

See the Video Program Teacher's Guide for the answer to the closing question.

Review and Assessment Resources

Review and Reinforce

CRF: Chapter Review

Quick Facts Transparency: Visual Study Guide: The Beginnings of Civilization

Spanish Chapter Summaries Audio CD Program

OSP **Holt PuzzlePro:** Quiz Show for ExamView

Quiz Game CD-ROM

Assess

PASS: Chapter Test, Forms A and B

Alternative Assessment Handbook

OSP **ExamView Test Generator**, Chapter Test

Differentiated Instruction Modified Worksheets and Tests CD-ROM: Chapter Test

HOAP **Holt Online Assessment Program** (in the Premier Online Edition)

Reteach/Intervene

Interactive Reader and Study Guide

Differentiated Instruction Teacher Management System: Lesson Plans for Differentiated Instruction

Differentiated Instruction Modified Worksheets and Tests CD-ROM: Chapter Test

Interactive Skills Tutor CD-ROM

go.hrw.com
Online Resources

KEYWORD: SHL TEACHER

Chapter 2 Planning Guide

The Ancient Near East

Chapter Overview	Reproducible Resources	Technology Resources
CHAPTER 2 pp. 30–59 **Overview:** In this chapter, students will learn about the first civilizations, the rise of empires, and the influence of Hebrews and Judaism. KI 2, 3; PI 2.3, 2.4, 2.5, 3.1, 3.2, 3.3 See pp. T32–T55 for a detailed correlation to the New York State Core Curriculum for Global History and Geography and the New York Learning Standards.	**Differentiated Instruction Teacher Management System:** • Pacing Guide • Lesson Plans for Differentiated Instruction **Interactive Reader and Study Guide:** Chapter Summary* **Chapter Resource File*** • Writing for the SAT • Social Studies Skill • Chapter Review **World History Outline Maps**	OSP **New York One-Stop Planner CD-ROM:** Calendar Planner **Live Ink© Online Reading Help** **Student Edition on Audio CD Program** **Differentiated Instruction Modified Worksheets and Tests CD-ROM** **Interactive Skills Tutor CD-ROM** **World History Primary Source Library CD-ROM** **Power Presentations with Video CD-ROM** **History's Impact: World History Video Program (VHS/DVD):** The Ancient Near East
Section 1: **Mesopotamia and Sumer** **The Main Idea:** The first known civilization arose in Mesopotamia, and its culture and innovations influenced later civilizations in the region for thousands of years. PI 2.4, 2.5	**Differentiated Instruction Teacher Management System:** Section 1 Lesson Plan* **Interactive Reader and Study Guide:** Section 1 Summary* **Chapter Resource File*** • Vocabulary Builder: Section 1 • Biography: Sargon I • Literature: *Hymn to Innana*	**Regents Review Transparency:** Section 1* **Map Transparencies:** Fertile Crescent; Ancient Mesopotamia* **Quick Facts Transparency:** Mesopotamian Achievements*
Section 2: **Fertile Cresent Empire** **The Main Idea:** Indo-European invaders introduced new technologies to the Fertile Crescent while adapting earlier technologies developed by the civilizations they encountered there. PI 3.1	**Differentiated Instruction Teacher Management System:** Section 2 Lesson Plan* **Interactive Reader and Study Guide:** Section 2 Summary* **Chapter Resource File*** • Vocabulary Builder: Section 2 • Biography: Semiramis (Sammuramat)	**Regents Review Transparency:** Section 2* **Map Transparencies:** The Hittite Empire; The Assyrian Empire; The Chaldean Empire; Phoenician Trade* **Quick Facts Transparency:** Alphabet*
Section 3: **The Hebrews and Judaism** **The Main Idea:** The ancient Hebrews and their religion, Judaism, have been a major influence on Western civilization. PI 3.1, 3.3	**Differentiated Instruction Teacher Management System:** Section 3 Lesson Plan* **Interactive Reader and Study Guide:** Section 3 Summary* **Chapter Resource File*** • Vocabulary Builder: Section 3 • Biography: Abraham • Primary Source: Ancient Flood Narratives	**Regents Review Transparency:** Section 3* **Map Transparencies:** Kingdom of Israel, c. 930 BC; Divided Kingdoms, c. 920 BC*
Section 4: **The Persian Empire** **The Main Idea:** The Persians formed one of the largest and best governed empires in the ancient world and made great cultural achievements. PI 2.3, 3.2	**Differentiated Instruction Teacher Management System:** Section 4 Lesson Plan* **Interactive Reader and Study Guide:** Section 4 Summary **Chapter Resource File*** • Vocabulary Builder: Section 4 • Biography: Herodotus	**Regents Review Transparency:** Section 4* **Map Transparencies:** The Persian Empire* **Quick Facts Transparency:** Cyrus and Darius* **Internet Activity:** Ancient Leaders

go.hrw.com	Print Resource	Transparency
Learning Styles	Audio CD	CD-ROM
Video	SE Student Edition	TE Teachers Edition
OSP One-Stop Planner CD-ROM	NY Standards Mastery	

*also on One-Stop Planner CD-ROM

HOLT
History's Impact
World History Video Program (VHS/DVD)
The Ancient Near East

Review, Assessment, Intervention

- **Global History and Geography Regents Test Prep Workbook**
- **Quick Facts Transparency:** The Ancient Near East*
- **Spanish Chapter Summaries Audio CD Program**
- **Progress Assessment Support System (PASS):** Chapter Test*
- **Differentiated Instruction Modified Worksheets and Tests CD-ROM:** Modified Chapter Test
- OSP **New York One-Stop Planner CD-ROM:** ExamView Test Generator (English/Spanish)
- HOAP **Holt Online Assessment Program (HOAP),** in the Holt Premier Online Student Edition

---

- **PASS:** Section 1 Quiz*
- **Online Quiz:** Section 1
- **Alternative Assessment Handbook**

- **PASS:** Section 2 Quiz*
- **Online Quiz:** Section 2
- **Alternative Assessment Handbook**

- **PASS:** Section 3 Quiz*
- **Online Quiz:** Section 3
- **Alternative Assessment Handbook**

- **PASS:** Section 4 Quiz*
- **Online Quiz:** Section 4
- **Alternative Assessment Handbook**

Power Presentation with Video CD-ROM

Power Presentations with Video are visual presentations of each chapter's main ideas. Presentations can be customized by including Quick Facts charts, images and maps from the textbook, and video clips.

Holt Online Learning

go.hrw.com
Teacher Resources
KEYWORD: SHL TEACHER

go.hrw.com
Student Resources
KEYWORD: SHL ANE

- Document-Based Questions
- Interactive Multimedia Activities

- Current Events
- Chapter-Based Internet Activities
- and more!

Holt Premier
Online Student Edition
Complete online support for interactivity, assessment, and reporting
- Interactive Maps and Notebook
- Homework Practice and Research Activities Online

CHAPTER 2 PLANNING GUIDE

The Big Picture

Peter N. Stearns

The First Civilization Dealing with the emergence of civilization in Mesopotamia imposes several tasks. The concept of civilization as a form of human organization has already been defined, but now it can be fleshed out with more specific information about cities. There's also the question of Mesopotamia itself: what characteristics of the region help explain the advent of civilization and the specific forms it took. This leads, finally, to the main features of Sumerian civilization and its successors: what were the principal characteristics of art and culture, what kind of social and economic structure emerged, and what were the leading qualities of the state.

Successor Empires The succession of Babylonians, Hittites and Assyrians provides opportunities to talk about political and military changes, including the implications of the introduction of iron. These developments unfolded over a considerable period of time; the situation was not as unstable as a sequential list of empires might suggest. Dealing with the Phoenicians shifts attention to a different part of the Middle East and a different set of accomplishments. Finally, the great Persian Empire returns attention to the Mesopotamian heartland, though the empire was unusually large by the standards of the period and left a distinctive cultural and political legacy.

Jews and Judaism Early Jewish history imposes the delicate task of distinguishing between what is widely believed and what is known for sure: indisputable records about Jews trace back only to about 1100 BC. Jewish religious and ethical innovations properly draw the greatest attention, for they were unusual at the time and have had lasting impact. Folding this focus into a larger comparison of Jewish and Mesopotamian society can highlight the social and political characteristics of early Jewish history along with the religious emphasis.

The Question of Legacies Early civilizations in the Middle East offer two basic connections to later history. First, many innovations persisted as part of the apparatus of later societies in the region and beyond. This includes key technologies, the institutions of early states, including legal codes, basic concepts in math and science, and money and writing. Second, several specific societies contributed to ongoing political and cultural practice. This applies most obviously to Judaism, but also to the connections between Persia and present-day Iran.

Recent Scholarship

Robert Chadwick's *First Civilizations: Ancient Mesopotamia and Ancient Egypt* (2005) offers a stimulating recent view. The book embraces discussions of historical and archaeological methods, origins, early agriculture, and a clear account of the major stages of the history of both societies—with a strong emphasis on cultural achievements including science and death rituals. The account ends with the Persians, who had significant impact on both regions. Comparison is more implicit than explicit, but the book provides materials for this kind of analysis when Mesopotamia and Egypt are juxtaposed.

Differentiating Instruction

 Differentiated Instruction Teacher Management System
- Pacing Guide
- Lesson Plans for Differentiated Instruction

 Interactive Reader and Study Guide

Spanish Chapter Summaries Audio CD Program

Student Edition on Audio CD Program

 Differentiated Instruction Modified Worksheets and Tests CD-ROM
- Vocabulary Flash Cards
- Modified Vocabulary Builder Activities
- Modified Chapter Review Activity
- Modified Chapter Test

OSP One-Stop Planner CD-ROM
- ExamView Test Generator (English/Spanish)
- PuzzlePro
- Quiz Show for ExamView
- Transparencies and Videos

TE Differentiated Activities in the Teacher's Edition
- City Maps of Mesopotamia, p. 34
- The Death of Enkidu, p. 38
- Modern Indo-European Languages, p. 40
- The Persian Army in Battle, p. 52
- Hammurabi and The Kassites, p. 57

Reading Like a Historian
Sam Wineburg

Eye for an Eye Nothing from Hammurabi's Code is more recognizable than the phrase "eye for an eye," an image that calls up raging revenge seekers and a system of brutal justice.

Known in Latin as Lex Talionis (The Law of Retribution), the legal precept of "eye for an eye" is also found in the book of Exodus. Although the exact relationship between the Bible's legal code and Hammurabi's is hotly debated, the parallels between the two are clear. Indeed, an examination of Exodus 21:24 turns up the same language—"eye for eye, tooth for tooth"—that we find in Hammurabi's Code. Were the societies of the ancient Near East—the Babylonia of Hammurabi or the Canaan of the Hebrews—places of semi-blind, partially toothed madmen hell-bent on maiming each other in the name of "justice"?

Before we judge these ancient codes too harshly, we would be wise to ask the first question of historical analysis: What do these words mean in context? Here, the Bible offers a more nuanced view than our first impression.

Examining the four verses in Exodus 21:19-22 (which roughly parallel Hammurabi's Code, sections 196-214), we immediately see a division. The first two verses describe a struggle between two workers in which one rises up and strikes the other with his staff. In this act of premeditated, willful assault, the Bible does not demand that the aggrieved party deliver a similar blow in return. Rather, Exodus 21:20 explains that the injured party is due monetary compensation for his lost time on the job and treatment costs.

The next two verses describe a very different scenario. Men quarrel, but in this case, a pregnant woman gets caught in the cross-fire and is hurt accidentally. It is here, in a description of inadvertent injury, that the phrase "eye for an eye, tooth for a tooth" appears. Thus, if we take "eye for an eye" literally, we have a resulting legal code in which accidental injury exacts a stiffer penalty than one inflicted with raw malice. It doesn't add up.

The plot thickens when we examine how the Bible deals with the penalty for murder. Numbers 35:31 states: "No price may be given for the life of one who has taken life and whose right reward is death; he is certainly to be put to death." Here the Bible disallows monetary compensation for premeditated murder. However, in the cases of accidental death—a woodsman whose flying ax handle finds an unsuspecting victim—the implication is that compensation might be permissible. If compensation is allowed for accidental deaths, why would it be forbidden for a knocked out tooth?

Fair Compensation People did not run around in the name of "exact retribution" cutting off each other's hands and poking out each other's eyes either in Hammurabi's day or Biblical times. In fact, the precepts of Lex Talionis were designed to prevent just such chaos. As University of Michigan legal scholar William Ian Miller notes in his book *Eye for an Eye*, the meaning of this famous phrase is exactly the opposite of what many people think. Miller explains that "eye for an eye" served as an initial departure in suing for damages in ancient "honor" societies: a tooth was worth a tooth, not a hand or a leg. Indeed, Lex Talionis still guides tort law today: someone who winds up in a wheelchair after a collision with a drunk driver deserves more than someone who escapes with a broken leg. Lex Talionis, notes Miller, is "about setting price that constitutes exactly fair compensation for the loss."

It is compensation that restores peace, not primal revenge. This concept is preserved in the Hebrew word for peace, "Shalom," derived from the same root as the verb "to pay" and the adjective "complete" or "whole." By preventing people from acting on their impulses for revenge, Lex Talionis provided a guide for payment, which made things whole and paved the way to peace.

Chapter Main Ideas

Section 1 The first known civilization arose in Mesopotamia, and its culture and innovations influenced later civilizations in the region for thousands of years.

Section 2 Indo-European invaders introduced new technologies to the Fertile Crescent while adapting earlier technologies developed by the civilizations they encountered there.

Section 3 The ancient Hebrews and their religion, Judaism, have been a major influence on Western civilization.

Section 4 The Persians formed one of the largest and best-governed empires in the ancient world and made great cultural achievements.

New York Standards

Key Idea 2 Establishing timeframes, exploring different periodizations, examining themes across time and within cultures, and focusing on important turning points in world history help organize the study of world cultures and civilizations.

Key Idea 3 Study of the major social, political, cultural, and religious developments in world history involves learning about the important roles and contributions of individuals and groups.

Key to Differentiating Instruction

Below Level

Basic-level activities designed for all students encountering new material

At Level

Intermediate-level activities designed for average students

Above Level

Challenging activities designed for honors and gifted and talented students

Standard English Mastery

Activities designed to improve standard English usage

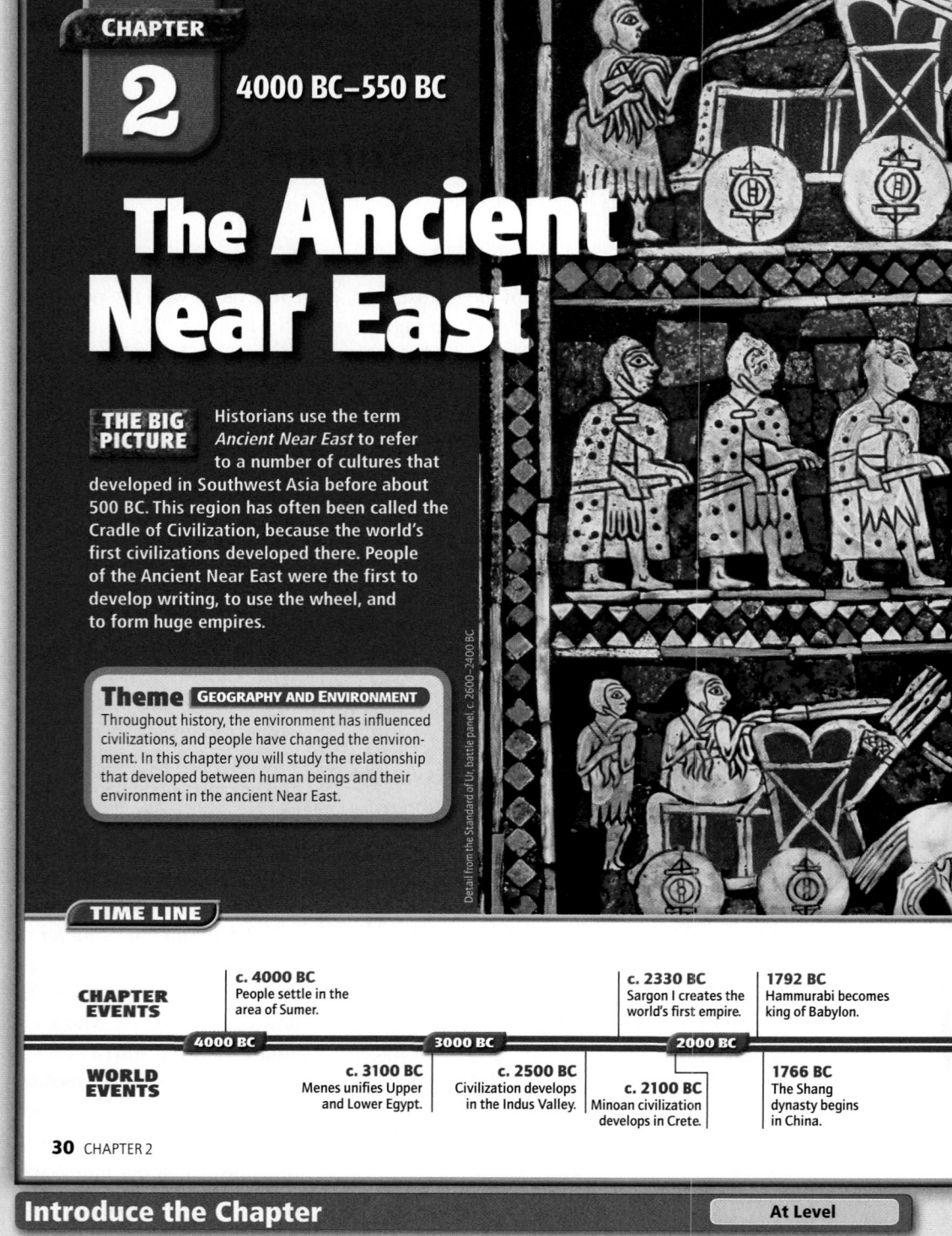

CHAPTER

2   4000 BC–550 BC

The Ancient Near East

THE BIG PICTURE Historians use the term *Ancient Near East* to refer to a number of cultures that developed in Southwest Asia before about 500 BC. This region has often been called the Cradle of Civilization, because the world's first civilizations developed there. People of the Ancient Near East were the first to develop writing, to use the wheel, and to form huge empires.

Theme GEOGRAPHY AND ENVIRONMENT
Throughout history, the environment has influenced civilizations, and people have changed the environment. In this chapter you will study the relationship that developed between human beings and their environment in the ancient Near East.

Detail from the Standard of Ur, battle panel, c. 2600–2400 BC

TIME LINE

CHAPTER EVENTS	**c. 4000 BC** People settle in the area of Sumer.	**c. 2330 BC** Sargon I creates the world's first empire. **1792 BC** Hammurabi becomes king of Babylon.

4000 BC — 3000 BC — 2000 BC

WORLD EVENTS	**c. 3100 BC** Menes unifies Upper and Lower Egypt. **c. 2500 BC** Civilization develops in the Indus Valley. **c. 2100 BC** Minoan civilization develops in Crete.	**1766 BC** The Shang dynasty begins in China.

30 CHAPTER 2

Introduce the Chapter

At Level

The Ancient Near East

1. Remind students that favorable geographic conditions are among the main reasons why people settle in a particular region.

2. Have students work in small groups to list various geographical features that might be attractive to settlers, including rivers for fertile soil, seas and rivers for fishing and trade, and mountains for protection. Also have students list features that might not be attractive to settlers, such as areas with extreme weather conditions. Have groups share their lists.

3. Guide students in a discussion of the advantages and disadvantages of various geographical features. Ask students to name man-made solutions that could help settlers adapt to various types of environments.

4. Tell students that in this chapter they will learn about an area known as the Fertile Crescent. **LS** Verbal-Linguistic

Alternative Assessment Handbook, Rubric 11: Discussions

History's Impact video program

Watch the video to understand the impact of Judaism throughout the world.

Reading like a Historian

This panel is part of a box that was found in a royal cemetery in the city of Ur. Made more than 4,000 years ago, the panel shows a scene of war. Soldiers in chariots rush off to battle, while others deliver prisoners they have captured to the king.

Analyzing Visuals What do the decorations on this panel suggest about the people of Ur? Based on this image, what can you conclude about their level of technology? Explain your answer.

See **Skills Handbook**, p. H26

965 BC
Solomon becomes king of Israel.

814 BC
The Phoenicians build the city of Carthage.

559 BC
Cyrus the Great founds the Persian Empire.

1000 BC

c. 750 BC
The city of Rome is established.

THE ANCIENT NEAR EAST **31**

Reading Like a Historian

Interpreting Visuals Have students take a moment to examine the image on these pages. Remind them that the image is part of an object found in a royal cemetery known as the Standard of Ur. Have students identify images that give clues that it is a battle scene. Ask students why this scene might have been on an object buried in a royal cemetery. *possible answers—The image shows soldiers in chariots, holding weapons, and taking prisoners. A victorious war scene might have been an important part of a ruler's legacy; putting this scene on a burial object may have been a way to commemorate an important military victory.*

Explore the Time Line

1. When did large cities begin to appear in Sumer? *4000 BC*

2. How many years elapsed between the time that cities began to appear in Sumer to the creation of the world's first empire? *1,670 years*

3. How long after the Phoenicians built the city of Carthage was the city of Rome built? *61 years*

4. Who unified Upper and Lower Egypt? *Menes*

Info to Know

Royal Tombs In the late 1920s, the British Museum and the University of Pennsylvania excavated almost 2000 burial sites in Mesopotamia. The majority of burials were simple; bodies were clothed in reed matting. Some burial sites, however, were more extensive, and showed evidence of wealth. The archaeologists called these sites "royal tombs."

Make Inferences Why do you think tombs of the wealthy were called "royal tombs"? *possible answer—Wealthier people may have been leaders, or possibly kings and queens.*

Answers

Reading Like a Historian *The decorations show that the people of Ur were involved with war, either defending themselves or attacking others. The level of technology was advanced for the time— they had wheels, chariots, and weapons.*

Geography Starting Points
Archaeological Conditions

Archaeological remains of Sumerian civilization are scarce, especially when compared to ancient Egypt. This is because the Sumerians used mud bricks and wood for building rather than stone. Some tombs in the shape of vaulted underground chambers have been found at Ur, but it does not appear that the Sumerians shared Egyptian concern with the afterlife.

📖 **Map Transparency:** Fertile Crescent

📄 **World History Outline Maps**

Teaching Tip

To help students understand where Mesopotamia is located, have students look at the small inset world map on this page. Then, have students compare this map to a modern map of the same area and list the modern-day countries that comprise this region. *Iraq, Kuwait, Jordan, Lebanon, Israel*

GEOGRAPHY Starting Points

Interactive
FERTILE CRESCENT

The valley of the Tigris and Euphrates rivers is the heart of the Fertile Crescent.

Surrounding the Fertile Crescent is some of the world's harshest desert.

Black Sea • ASIA MINOR • Caspian Sea • ASIA • PERSIA • ZAGROS MTS. • Amu Darya River • Euphrates R. • Tigris R. • 40°N • Mediterranean Sea • Sinai Peninsula • SYRIAN DESERT • NAFUD DESERT • Persian Gulf • Arabian Sea • 30°E • 60°E • SAHARA • Red Sea • Nile River • AFRICA • 20°N • RUB' AL-KHALI • ARABIAN PENINSULA • 40°E • 50°E • Gulf of Aden

0   150   300 Miles
0   150   300 Kilometers
Lambert conformal conic projection

Legend
- ☐ Fertile Crescent
- ---- Ancient coastline

ELEVATION

Feet		Meters
13,120		4,000
6,560		2,000
1,640		500
656		200
(Sea level) 0		0 (Sea level)
Below sea level		Below sea level

N • E • W • S

Starting Points The world's earliest civilization developed in Southwest Asia in the valley of the Tigris and Euphrates rivers. This river valley is at the heart of a larger region known through history as the Fertile Crescent. An oasis of fertile land in the midst of a barren desert, the Fertile Crescent saw the rise of many societies.

1. **Draw Conclusions** Why do you think the area outlined in purple on the map above is called the Fertile Crescent?

2. **Predict** What physical characteristics of the Fertile Crescent might have allowed early civilizations to develop and thrive there?

🔊 **Listen to History**

Go online to listen to an explanation of the starting points for this chapter.

go.hrw.com
Keyword: SHL ANE

32 CHAPTER 2

Skills Focus: Analyzing Maps

At Level

Social Studies Skill
Geography of the Fertile Crescent

1. Have students review the map on this page and note the elevation of various areas on this map. What is the highest elevation in the Fertile Crescent? *1,640 feet* What is the lowest elevation in the Fertile Crescent? *sea level*

2. Have students list the advantages and disadvantages of the low elevation of this area. *advantages— easy to access, mountains provide some protection from harsh climate;*

disadvantages—easy for invaders to access, no natural boundaries to thwart invaders

LS **Visual-Spatial**

📄 **Alternative Assessment Handbook**, Rubric 21: Map Reading

Answers

Geography Starting Points

1. *Rivers helped create fertile soil; land is fairly flat and outlined area is crescent-shaped.* **2.** *the Tigris and Euphrates rivers; fertile land*

Mesopotamia and Sumer

BEFORE YOU READ

MAIN IDEA
The first known civilization arose in Mesopotamia, and its culture and innovations influenced later civilizations in the region for thousands of years.

READING FOCUS
1. How did geography promote civilization in Mesopotamia?
2. What features defined the civilization of Sumer?
3. What were Sumer's main cultural achievements?
4. What events led to later empires in Mesopotamia?

KEY TERMS AND PEOPLE
Fertile Crescent
Mesopotamia
ziggurat
city-state
polytheism
dynasty
cuneiform
Sargon
Hammurabi

 NEW YORK

PI 2.5 Students investigate key events and developments and major turning points in world history to identify the factors that brought about change and the long-term effects of these changes.

THE INSIDE STORY

Why might a wedding be held to ensure a good harvest? In the city of Ur, crowds began filling the streets to celebrate New Year's Day, the last day of the spring festival. People made their way through Ur's mazelike streets, past mud-brick houses and shops, to the city center. There, an immense temple rose to the moon god, Nanna, and his wife.

A hush fell over the crowd. A small group was solemnly climbing a stairway to a shrine atop the temple. The time had come for the festival's main rite—the Sacred Wedding. In a symbolic ceremony the king of Ur was to marry a priestess. Surely this sacred rite would please the gods and lead to good harvests. Since their survival depended on the harvest, the people badly wanted the gods' favor. ■

Geography Promotes Civilization

In Southwest Asia a large band of fertile land forms an oasis in the midst of deserts and mountains. This region, sometimes called the **Fertile Crescent**, curves between the Mediterranean Sea and the Persian Gulf. Within the fertile region some of the richest soil lies between two rivers, the Tigris and the Euphrates (yoo-FRAY-teez). Both of these rivers begin in Turkey and flow south through Iraq to the Persian Gulf. For centuries, the area between the Tigris and Euphrates rivers has been called **Mesopotamia** (mes-uh-puh-TAY-mee-uh), which in Greek means "between the rivers." There, geographic conditions helped bring about the rise of the world's first civilization.

THE SACRED WEDDING

The ruins of the temple of Ur have been partially rebuilt. ▶

33

Teach the Main Idea

Mesopotamia and Sumer

1. **Teach** Ask students the Reading Focus questions to teach this section.

2. **Apply** Have students create one image that symbolizes each of the four headings in this section. For example, students could create maps of the Fertile Crescent to represent the heading Geography Promotes Civilization, or draw a picture of a ziggurat for Sumer.

3. **Review** Have volunteers share their drawings with the class, explaining their significance to Mesopotamia and Sumer.

4. **Practice/Homework** Have students write a short essay answering the following questions: How did geography help shape architecture and building practices in Mesopotamia? What role did geography play in the development of government? Why was religion important to all who lived in Sumer? How and why did Sumerians honor their gods? **LS Visual-Spatial, Verbal-Linguistic**

Alternative Assessment Handbook, Rubric 40: Writing to Describe

---

● ● **Preteach** ● ●

Getting Started

Use the **Interactive Reader and Study Guide** to familiarize students with the section content.

📖 **Interactive Reader and Study Guide**, Section 1

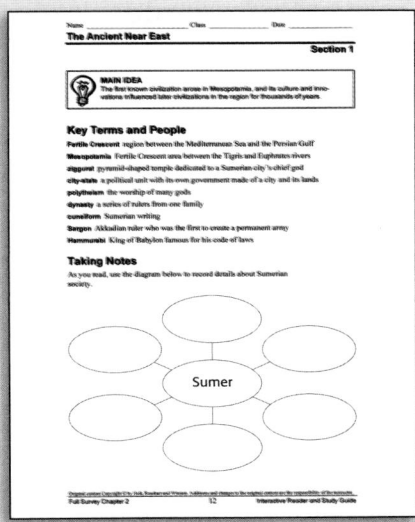

Academic Vocabulary

Review with students the high-use academic term in this section.

allocate to distribute for a particular purpose (p. 34)

📄 **CRF: Vocabulary Builder: Section 1**

Taking Notes

Sumer—built cities and ziggurats; polytheism; first writing system, called cuneiform; math system based on the number 60; famous works of art: cylinder seals with designs; invented the wheel and plow; traded grain for resources and building materials

---

THE ANCIENT NEAR EAST **33**

1 How did geography promote civilization in Mesopotamia? *The land was well suited to agriculture, and the flooding of rivers produced fertile soil.*

Geography Promotes Civilization

Identify Where was Mesopotamia? *between the Tigris and Euphrates rivers*

Summarize How were people in Mesopotamia able to control both flooding and drought? *built basins to store rainwater, canals to carry water to fields, and dikes to control flooding*

Evaluate How did the development of methods to control water lead to the formation of government? *Building canals, dikes, and basins to collect rainwater required organization, which developed into systems of leadership and government.*

🗄 **Map Transparency**: Ancient Mesopotamia

✳ **Interactive Map**: Ancient Mesopotamia

2 What features defined the civilization of Sumer? *cities with ziggurats, polytheism, kings, dynasties*

Sumer

Recall Why were ziggurats built? *to honor a city's chief god*

Contrast What is the difference between a city and a city-state? *A city-state is an organized political unit with its own government, controlled by the city. Early cities would not have been organized as a single, political unit.*

Answers

Interpreting Maps 1. *Tigris and Euphrates rivers;* **2.** *approximately 210 miles*

Reading Check *fertile land; plentiful food; need to organize people for jobs*

34

Use a diagram like this one to record details about Sumerian society.

ACADEMIC VOCABULARY
allocate to distribute for a particular purpose

As early as 5500 BC people were farming in southern Mesopotamia. This flat, swampy region was well suited for agriculture. The Tigris and Euphrates rivers often flooded there in spring. The floods left behind a fertile mud called silt, which enriched the soil. In this rich soil early farmers grew grains such as wheat and barley. With plenty of food, the population grew, and villages formed.

Farming in southern Mesopotamia posed challenges, though. The region received little rain. Thus, water levels in the Tigris and Euphrates depended on rainfall and snowmelt in distant mountains. Without warning, rivers could overflow, washing away crops and even villages. If river levels fell too low, crops would die during the hot, dry summers.

Over time, people in Mesopotamia developed methods to control water. They dug basins to store rainwater, canals to carry water to fields, and dikes to control flooding. These large projects required organization: people to assign jobs and allocate resources. As a result, leaders emerged and government formed. Slowly, a civilization developed.

READING CHECK **Summarize** What factors influenced the rise of civilization in Mesopotamia?

Sumer

The people who developed this first civilization were the Sumerians (soo-MER-ee-unz). They called their land Sumer. Sumerian civilization would influence many later civilizations.

The Cities of Sumer Large cities had begun to appear in Sumer by 3000 BC. Structures in these cities were built of mud bricks because other building materials were scarce. In each city center a large temple rose to the city's chief god. At the heart of the temple, a pyramid-shaped structure called a **ziggurat** rose to the sky. For defense, a massive wall circled each city. Fields surrounded the city.

Over time, each city and the land it controlled formed a **city-state**, a political unit with its own government. As the city-states grew, they increasingly fought over land and water.

Religion and Government Religion shaped life in the city-states. The Sumerians practiced **polytheism**, or the worship of many gods. They believed that the gods controlled all natural forces. The god Enlil, for example, ruled the air and storms. The Sumerians also believed that a god protected each city-state.

ANCIENT MESOPOTAMIA

Sumerian soldiers wore helmets like this one into battle.

GEOGRAPHY SKILLS **INTERPRETING MAPS**

go.hrw.com
Interactive Map
Keyword: SHL ANE

1. **Place** What bodies of water provided water to Sumer's farms?
2. **Regions** Approximately how many miles wide was Sargon's empire at its greatest extent?

34 CHAPTER 2

Differentiating Instruction

Below Level

Learners Having Difficulty

Materials: drawing paper, colored pencils

1. Have students review the information in the text about the importance of agriculture and the development of Sumerian city-states.

2. Have students work in pairs to select one of the cities shown on the map of ancient Mesopotamia. Have students create a city map for their chosen city. Students should include agricultural fields, the city's ziggurat, and city walls.

3. Have volunteers present and explain their maps to the class. **LS Visual-Spatial**

📝 **Alternative Assessment Handbook**, Rubric 20: Map Creation

The Sumerians believed that the gods were like humans in many ways. The gods ate and drank, fell in love and married, and fought. At the same time, the gods had enormous power. They could bring rich harvests or raging floods, depending on their whims.

Because of these beliefs the Sumerians worked hard to please the gods. The people built ziggurats and temples where priests and priestesses offered the gods food and drink and held ceremonies.

Priests held a high status in Sumer and initially governed the city-states. As city-states battled for dominance, however, war chiefs began to rule as kings. These kings, who served as the gods' chief representatives, performed ceremonies to please the gods. In time, many of the city-states' kings formed dynasties. A **dynasty** is a series of rulers from one family.

Sumerian Culture

Sumerian civilization produced great cultural achievements. Perhaps the greatest was the development of the first writing system. With the ability to write down events, humankind moved from prehistory into the historical age.

Writing Sumerian writing is called **cuneiform** (kyoo-NEE-uh-fohrm). To produce this writing, Sumerians used sharp tools called styluses to make wedge-shaped symbols on clay tablets.

Sumerians first used cuneiform to keep business accounts and other records. In time, they put their writing skills to new uses. They wrote works on law and grammar as well as works of literature, such as stories, poems, and songs. The best-known work of Sumerian literature is the *Epic of Gilgamesh*, the story of a legendary king.

Sumerians paid scribes, or writers, to create written documents. Becoming a scribe required years of schooling but was a way to move up in social class. Most scribes were men, but some upper-class women also learned to write.

Math and Sciences The Sumerians developed a math system based on the number 60. Because of their system we still divide an hour into 60 minutes and a circle into 360 degrees. The Sumerians also learned to use geometry, which was necessary to build elaborate structures and irrigation systems.

Reading like a Historian

A Cuneiform Tablet

Analyzing Primary Sources Early Sumerian writing used pictographs, or picture symbols. Each pictograph represented either an object, such as a tree, or a syllable. Reading a cuneiform inscription can teach us a great deal about the Sumerians. Look at the tablet below and read the translation provided. As you read, think about
• who might have written the document.
• why it was written.
• what we can learn about the Sumerians by reading it.

This symbol can mean "god," "goddess," or "heaven."

This complex symbol means "king."

Translation of the Tablet For Innana [a goddess] Lady of Eanna—His Lady. Shulgi, the mighty man, King of Ur, King of Sumer and Akkad.

 Skills FOCUS **READING LIKE A HISTORIAN**

1. **Creator** Who had this tablet created?
2. **Point of View** Why was this tablet created?
3. **Details** What can the inscription on this tablet tell us about ancient Sumerian society?

See **Skills Handbook**, p. H25

Reading Focus

3️⃣ What were Sumer's main cultural achievements? *writing (cuneiform), development of math system based on number 60, ziggurats, cylinder seals*

Sumerian Culture

Recall What was the initial purpose of cuneiform writing? *to keep business accounts and other records*

Make Inferences Why did scribes move up in social class? *scribes required years of schooling; was a respected job*

📖 **CRF:** Literature: Hymn to Innana: Loud Thundering Storm

Info to Know

Cuneiform The basis for cuneiform writing was pictograms, drawings of actual things. Over time, pictograms became simpler representations and then developed into more abstract wedge-shaped marks, cuneiform. Unlike pictograms, cuneiform could convey concepts and sounds. To create a cuneiform tablet, scribes used reed writing styluses and made their impressions on soft clay tablets.

Recent Scholarship

Ancient Mesopotamia by Susan Pollock provides an in-depth look at early Mesopotamia, from about 5000 to 2100 BC. Pollock uses current theory in anthropology to examine ancient Mesopotamia. Her study is based on settlement patterns, distribution of artifacts, texts, and burial sites.

Ancient Mesopotamia by Susan Pollock. Cambridge University Press, 1999.

Skills Focus: Making Generalizations

At Level

Reading Skill
Sumerian Society

1. Guide students in a discussion of the various roles in Sumerian society, including kings, priests and priestesses, scribes, merchants, craftspeople, and farmers.

2. Have each student select a Sumerian social role and write five daily journal entries about their lives and jobs. Have students include the importance of their role in Sumerian culture and their daily activities.

3. Have volunteers read their journal entries to the class.

4. As an extension, have students work in small groups to create graphic organizers that show the hierarchy in Sumerian social structure.
   LS Verbal-Linguistic, Visual-Spatial

📄 **Alternative Assessment Handbook**, Rubrics 15: Journals; and 13: Graphic Organizers

Answers

Reading Like a Historian 1. *Shulgi, King of Ur, Sumer, and Akkad;* **2.** *to honor the goddess Innana;* **3.** *Gods and goddesses were very important to Sumerians; specific gods were associated with individual city-states.*

Reading Focus

4 What events led to later empires in Mesopotamia? *creation of permanent armies; invaders conquered the region*

Empires in Mesopotamia

Describe How was Sargon I able to conquer all of Sumer and northern Mesopotamia? *created a permanent army and used it effectively*

Summarize What skills did Hammurabi have that made him an effective leader? *brilliant warrior, able administrator who created a code of laws, increased trade, and improved tax collection*

Make Judgments Do you think Hammurabi's Code was just? Why or why not? *possible answers—Yes, the "eye for an eye" idea is fair; no, it punished people from various classes differently for the same crime.*

Activity **Hammurabi's Code**
Organize a class debate on this topic: Are punishments in Hammurabi's Code fair or unjust?

CRF: Biography: Sargon I

Info to Know

Hammurabi and the Sun-God
Hammurabi's Code was engraved on a stele, or ancient stone slab. At the top of the stele is the image shown here. Hammurabi is facing the sun-god Shamash. Shamash is holding a ring and a rod, representing both royal authority and justice. The sun-god is distinguishable by the rays coming from his shoulders.

Answers

Reading Like a Historian 1. *That person's arm was broken.* **2.** *People were punished differently depending on their class.*

Reading Check *After the development of cuneiform, humankind moved from prehistory into the historical age.*

 NEW YORK
CC Unit 1-B1e
Contributions of Mesopotamia

The Sumerians also made many scientific advances. They invented the wheel, which they used both to make pottery and to build a variety of vehicles. Sumerians also invented the plow and learned to use bronze to make stronger tools and weapons. Archaeological remains show that Sumerians even built sewers. In addition, they collected and cataloged an impressive amount of medical knowledge. They even performed basic surgery.

The Arts Ruins and artifacts provide us with examples of the Sumerians' artistry and creativity. Sumerian architecture includes the use of arches, ramps, and columns, all visible on the ziggurats. Sumerian sculpture includes statues with large, wide-open eyes, as well as small objects carved out of ivory.

PRIMARY SOURCES

Hammurabi's Code

Hammurabi's Code listed 282 laws dealing with a variety of subjects. A few examples of these laws are listed below.

196. If a man put out the eye of another man, his eye shall be put out.

197. If he breaks another man's bone, his bone shall be broken.

198. If he put out the eye of a freed man, or break the bone of a freed man, he shall pay one [silver] mina.

199. If he put out the eye of a man's slave, or break the bones of a man's slave, he shall pay one-half of its value.

200. If a man knock out the teeth of his equal, his teeth shall be knocked out.

201. If he knock out the teeth of a freed man, he shall pay one-third of a [silver] mina.

202. If any one strike the body of a man higher in rank than he, he shall receive sixty blows with an ox-whip in public.

Skills FOCUS READING LIKE A HISTORIAN

1. **Analyze** How was a person who broke another's arm punished?

2. **Analyzing Primary Sources** What do these laws suggest about class equality in Babylon?

See **Skills Handbook**, p. H25

36 CHAPTER 2

Perhaps Sumer's most famous works of art are its cylinder seals, small stone cylinders engraved all around with detailed designs. Rolling a seal over wet clay left behind an imprint of its design. People used cylinder seals to "sign" documents or to show ownership.

Trade and Society Sumerians obtained many of the materials for their buildings and art through trade. Sumer lacked many raw materials, such as wood and metals. To obtain these materials, Sumerians traded with people across Southwest Asia and beyond, exchanging woven textiles for metals, timber, and stone.

As trade enriched Sumer, a distinct social hierarchy, or ranking, developed. At the top were the kings, priests, and their principal agents. Next were large landowners and wealthy merchants. Below them were the majority of Sumerians—artisans, farmers, and laborers. At the bottom were slaves, many of whom had been captured in battle.

Sumerian men and women developed distinct roles as well. Men held political power and made laws while women took care of the home and children. A few upper-class women received educations and served as priestesses in the temples.

READING CHECK **Draw Conclusions** Why was the Sumerians' development of cuneiform a major turning point in history?

Empires in Mesopotamia

Over time, frequent warfare weakened Sumer's city-states. Then one after another, invading peoples conquered the region. Because each new invader adapted aspects of Sumerian culture to its own society, Sumerian civilization continued to influence life in Mesopotamia.

Sargon's Empire To the north of Sumer lived the Akkadians (uh-KAD-ee-uhns). About 2330 BC the Akkadian ruler **Sargon I** created a permanent army, the first ruler to do so. From the city of Akkad (AH-kahd) on the Euphrates River, Sargon used this army to conquer all of Sumer and northern Mesopotamia. In doing so, he formed the world's first empire, a land that includes different kingdoms and people under one rule. The Akkadian Empire stretched from the Mediterranean Sea to the Persian Gulf.

Skills Focus: Analyzing Primary Sources   At Level

Reading Like a Historian Skill
Hammurabi's Code

1. Review the information in the text about Hammurabi's Code. Tell students that this code concerned all aspects of life in the Babylonian Empire, including commerce and industry, property rights, and working conditions. As noted in the primary source excerpt in the text, punishment for breaking a law could be severe.

2. Organize students into mixed-ability pairs. Have each pair create ten laws concerning working conditions and payment of wages, following the

style of Hammurabi's Code. Students should consider these questions: Is the law just? Does the punishment fit the crime? Are there different punishments for different people? If so, why? Have volunteers present their laws to the class.

3. As an extension, have students research and report on the actual laws in Hammurabi's Code. **LS** **Verbal-Linguistic**

Alternative Assessment Handbook, Rubric 38: Writing to Classify

The Akkadians adopted cuneiform from the Sumerians and used it to write their language, which became the official language of the government. Sumerian, though, remained the main language for religious and literary texts. Sargon also kept many aspects of Sumerian society, such as the power of the priesthood. The priests' influence in Akkadian society helped ensure the continuity of Sumerian culture.

Sargon's empire lasted about 140 years. During that time, the Akkadians helped spread Sumerian culture far beyond the Tigris and Euphrates valleys. In the end, however, Sargon's empire fell. Tribes from the east invaded and captured Akkad. A century of chaos followed during which several tribes battled for control of Mesopotamia.

The Babylonian Empire One such tribe was the Amorites. They settled in Babylon on the Euphrates, near modern Baghdad, Iraq. In 1792 BC the Amorite king **Hammurabi** became king of Babylon. A brilliant warrior, he united all of Mesopotamia in what became known as the Babylonian Empire, named for its capital.

Hammurabi's skills were not limited to the battlefield. He was also an able ruler and administrator who oversaw building projects and improved the tax-collection system to pay for them. He also increased trade so that the empire grew wealthy. Like Sargon before him, Hammurabi absorbed elements of the earlier cultures of the region. He honored the old Sumerian gods and allowed priests to retain their power and influence. During his reign, schools continued to teach the Sumerian language and cuneiform writing.

Hammurabi is most famous, though, for his code of laws. Hammurabi's Code consists of 282 laws dealing with everything from trade and theft to injury and murder. The code was important not only because it was thorough but also because it was written down for all to see. People across the empire could read exactly what actions were crimes.

During Hammurabi's long reign, Babylon became Mesopotamia's greatest city. Yet after his death, Babylonian power declined. In less than two centuries, the Babylonian Empire had fallen.

READING CHECK Sequence Who ruled Mesopotamia after Sumer, and in what order?

MESOPOTAMIAN ACHIEVEMENTS

Sumerians
Developed the world's first civilization
Created cuneiform writing
Invented the wheel and the plow
Wrote the *Epic of Gilgamesh*
Built cities and ziggurats

▼ Sumerian model of a wheeled cart

Akkadians
Established the world's first empire

Babylonians
Wrote Hammurabi's Code

SECTION 1 ASSESSMENT

go.hrw.com
Online Quiz
Keyword: SHL ANE HP

Reviewing Ideas, Terms, and People

1. **a. Define** Where is the **Fertile Crescent**, and which part of it is also known as **Mesopotamia**?
   b. Explain How did geographic conditions in southern Mesopotamia encourage the development of civilization there?

2. **a. Describe** What were some common features of Sumer's **city-states**?
   b. Infer How did geography influence religious beliefs in Sumer?
   c. Elaborate In what ways did religion shape all aspects of government and life in Sumer?

3. **a. Recall** What is **cuneiform**, and why is it historically significant?
   b. Draw Conclusions Why was trade important in Sumer?
   c. Make Judgments Was Sumerian society fair? Why or why not?

4. **a. Define** What is an empire, and what group of people created the world's first empire?
   b. Sequence What three tribes conquered and ruled Mesopotamia after the decline of Sumer's city-states? List the tribes in order.
   c. Evaluate Why was **Hammurabi**'s Code a significant achievement?

Critical Thinking

5. **Categorize** Draw a chart like the one below. Use your notes to complete each row with details about the Sumerians' achievements.

Category	Achievement or Innovation
Writing	
Technology	
Math & Science	
The Arts	

FOCUS ON WRITING

6. **Description** Write a journal entry from the point of view of a scribe who lives in ancient Sumer. Describe your work, your position in society, and some of the major features of life in your city.

Direct Teach

Primary Sources

"Do not speak ill, speak only good. Do not say evil things, speak well of people...Do not talk too freely, watch what you way...What you say in haste you may regret later. Exert yourself to restrain your speech."
—The Advice of an Akkadian Father to His Son, c. 2200 BC

🗎 **Quick Facts Transparency:** Mesopotamian Achievements

🗎 **CRF:** History and Geography: The Babylonian Empire

Review & Assess

Close

Guide students in a discussion of development within the Fertile Crescent. Have students list the empires and their achievements.

Review

🖥 **Online Quiz**, Section 1

Assess

SE Section 1 Assessment

🗎 **Progress Assessment:** Section 1 Quiz

🗎 **Alternative Assessment Handbook**

Reteach/Intervene

🗎 **Interactive Reader and Study Guide**, Section 1

💿 **Interactive Skills Tutor CD-ROM**

Section 1 Assessment Answers

1. **a.** in Southwest Asia; area between the Tigris and the Euphrates rivers
   b. Flooding created fertile soil for farming.

2. **a.** ziggurats, mud bricks, walled cities
   b. People believed gods controlled water.
   c. People believed gods controlled all aspects of life; priests had high status; kings led religious ceremonies

3. **a.** world's first known writing system
   b. provided building materials and wealth
   c. possible answer: No, it created inequality.

4. **a.** land that includes different kingdoms and people under one rule; the Akkadians
   b. Akkadians, Amorites, Babylonians
   c. first written code of laws; very thorough

5. cuneiform; wheel, plow, bronze weapons; geometry, math system based on 60; ziggurats, cylinder seals

6. Entries should describe the daily life and activities of a Sumerian scribe.

Answers

Reading Check *Akkadians, Amorities, Babylonians*

37

The Epic of Gilgamesh

Word Help

despair hopelessness

shimmering twinkling, sparkling

Meet the Writer

Many legends have been told about Gilgamesh, king of Uruk, who lived about 2700 BC. Stories and myths were written about him, beginning in about 2000 BC. There is no reliable evidence of a single author for the written stories; however, one version of the tablets found in the ruins of the library of King Ashurbanipal at Nineveh contains the name of an author for that particular version: Shin-eqi-unninni. He is the oldest known author known by name.

Teaching Tip

Explain to students that the *Epic of Gilgamesh* is widely considered the oldest form of literature, and it was originally written on eleven stone tablets. Guide students in a discussion abut how writing methods have changed throughout history.

Answers

Reading Like a Historian 1. *fear of death;* **2.** *Sumerians feared death and envied the immortality of the gods.*

World Literature

NEW YORK STANDARDS

PI 2.4 Students explain the importance of analyzing narratives from different times and places to understand historical events.

About the Reading Composed more than 4,000 years ago, the *Epic of Gilgamesh* tells of a hero called Gilgamesh. Though based on a real Sumerian king, the Gilgamesh of the epic is no ordinary man. He is part man and part god, with great powers but also with human weaknesses. In this passage, Gilgamesh reacts to the death of his friend Enkidu. He seeks out Utnapashtim, a man the gods had made immortal, hoping that he, too, can learn the secret of immortality.

Note how Gilgamesh expresses his emotions.

Excerpt from

The Epic of Gilgamesh

Bitterly Gilgamesh wept for his friend Enkidu; he wandered over the wilderness as a hunter, he roamed over the plains; in his bitterness he cried, "How can I rest, how can I be at peace? Despair is in my heart. What my brother is now, that shall I be when I am dead. Because I am afraid of death I will go as best I can to find Utnapishtim whom they call the Faraway, for he has entered the assembly of the gods." So Gilgamesh traveled over the wilderness, he wandered over the grasslands, a long journey, in search of Utnapishtim, whom the gods took after the deluge; and they set him to live in the land of Dilmun, in the garden of the sun; and to him alone of men they gave everlasting life.

At night when he came to the mountain passes Gilgamesh prayed: "In these mountain passes long ago I saw lions, I was afraid and I lifted my eyes to the moon; I prayed and my prayers wend up to the gods, so now, O moon god Sin, protect me." When he had prayed he lay down to sleep, until he was woken from out of a dream. He saw the lions round him glorying in life; then he took his axe in his hand, he drew his sword from his belt, and he fell upon them like an arrow from the string, and struck and destroyed and scattered them.

This image of Gilgamesh fighting a lion was made by rolling a cylinder seal over wet clay.

So at length Gilgamesh came to Mashu, the great mountains . . . At its gate the Scorpions stand guard, half man and half dragon; their glory is terrifying, their stare strikes death into men, their shimmering halo sweeps the mountains that guard the rising sun. When Gilgamesh saw them he shielded his eyes for the length of a moment only; then he took courage and approached. When they saw him so undismayed the Man-Scorpion called to his mate, "This one who comes to us now is flesh of the gods." The mate of the Man-Scorpion answered, "Two thirds is god but one third is man."

Skills FOCUS READING LIKE A HISTORIAN

go.hrw.com
World Literature
Keyword: SHL WRLIT

1. **Describe** What fear did Enkidu's death inspire in Gilgamesh?
2. **Interpret Literature as a Source** Based on this passage, what can you assume about the Sumerian view of death?

See **Skills Handbook**, p. H28

Differentiating Instruction

Learners Having Difficulty
Below Level

Review the excerpt with students. Have students explain why Gilgamesh is so upset about the death of Enkidu. Have students create a sequencing diagram or flow chart showing Gilgamesh's journey. **LS Visual-Spatial**

Alternative Assessment Handbook, Rubric 13: Graphic Organizers

Advanced Learners/ Gifted and Talented
Above Level

Have students reread this excerpt, noting the author's tone and what Gilgamesh's actions reveal. How does Gilgamesh express his emotions? What actions does he take after his friend's death? Have students write a short essay discussing whether immortality will solve Gilgamesh's problem. **LS Verbal-Linguistic**

Alternative Assessment Handbook, Rubric 42: Writing to Inform

BEFORE YOU READ

MAIN IDEA

Indo-European invaders introduced new technologies to the Fertile Crescent while adapting earlier technologies developed by the civilizations they encountered there.

READING FOCUS

1. What military advantages helped the Hittites establish an empire in Asia Minor?
2. What events led to the rise and fall of the Assyrian and Chaldean empires?
3. What were the main achievements of the Phoenicians?

KEY TERMS AND PEOPLE

Indo-Europeans
steppes
Nebuchadnezzar II

NEW YORK

PI **3.1** Students analyze the roles and contributions of individuals and groups to social, political, economic, cultural, and religious practices and activities.

THE INSIDE STORY

Why did the once mighty city of Babylon fall? Dust filled the sky as the army of heavy war chariots thundered toward the city of Babylon. Each chariot was drawn by two horses and carried three soldiers armed with spears and bows, ready for combat. Foot soldiers marched alongside the chariots, gripping spears, swords, and axes as they stared grimly ahead at the city of Babylon. The hardened warriors already had two victories to their credit, but Babylon would be their greatest prize. As they drew near the city, the Hittite chariots rushed ahead, breaking through the ranks of the Babylonian army that had set out to meet them. With their king himself leading the final charge, the Hittites captured the city in a lightning strike. The Babylonian soldiers were no match for the Hittites.

In celebration, the victorious Hittites looted Babylon of its wealth. Yet for reasons now lost to time, they chose not to stay and rule the city. Instead, the Hittites loaded up their booty and returned home, some 500 miles to the west. The people of Babylon heaved an amazed sigh of relief. True, they had suffered a great defeat, but the city was still theirs. However, the Hittites' stronger iron weapons had done their damage. In their weakened state, the Babylonians soon met defeat at the hands of other invaders, this time for good. ◼

THUNDER FROM THE WEST

Hittite soldiers stormed through Babylon in the 1500s BC. ▶

The Hittites

As the Babylonian Empire declined, other civilizations prospered in and around the Fertile Crescent. Nomadic tribes from the mountains and deserts moved into the region as well, drawn by its wealth. As tribes battled each other for land, a pattern slowly emerged in which control passed from one empire to another.

Teach the Main Idea

At Level

Fertile Crescent Empires

1. **Teach** Ask students the Reading Focus questions to teach this section.

2. **Apply** Have students work individually or in pairs to create a time line for the section. Have students find all the events that have dates and place them on their time lines in chronological order.

3. **Review** Review student time lines as a class. Have students name the events and dates in order, and create a class time line. The time line should include 2000 BC, Hittites settle in

Asia Minor; 1200 BC, Hittite Empire falls; 1300 BC, Assyrians build short-lived empire; 900 BC, Assyrians rise to power again; 612 BC, Chaldeans capture Nineveh

4. **Practice/Homework** Have students correct their own work and then illustrate their time lines. Students should also write a brief explanation of the significance of each event. **LS** **Verbal-Linguistic, Visual-Spatial**

📖 **Alternative Assessment Handbook**, Rubrics 36: Time Lines; and 37: Writing Assignments

Reading Focus

❶ What military advantages helped the Hittites establish an empire in Asia Minor? *mastery of ironworking, horse-drawn chariot*

The Hittites

Identify Where did the Hittites settle? *Asia Minor (now Turkey)*

Evaluate Why is the Hittite culture considered a blended culture? *The Hittites had their own culture, but used cuneiform to write their own language and developed laws similar to the Code of Hammurabi.*

📄 **CRF: Biography: Semiramis**

Interpreting Maps
The Hittite Empire

Location How much further north did the Hittite Empire extend past the Fertile Crescent? *approximately 300 miles*

Region Approximately what percentage of the Fertile Crescent was part of the Hittite Empire? *approximately 20 percent*

🖥 **Map Transparency**: The Hittite Empire

✳ **Interactive Map**: The Hittite Empire

Info to Know

Indo-European Languages Systematic resemblances between European languages and Sanskrit helped scholars recognize the existence of the Indo-European family of languages. Sanskrit is the oldest language of the Indian subcontinent, and the language appears in many written documents. English scholar Sir William Jones first proposed the common origin of European languages and Sanskrit when he was studying Oriental literature at Oxford.

Answers

Reading Check *With their military advantages, they were able to conquer people in surrounding areas.*

40

Conquering the Fertile Crescent

Waves of invaders swept into and ruled the Fertile Crescent after the fall of the Babylonian Empire. These invaders created huge empires and introduced new technologies to the region.

★**Interactive**
THE HITTITE EMPIRE

Hittite Empire, c. 1300 BC
Fertile Crescent
Ancient coastline

THE IMPACT TODAY

Indo-European languages, such as Greek, Hindi, and Russian, are still spoken in Europe, South Asia, and Southwest Asia.

ACADEMIC VOCABULARY

technique method, way for performing a task

Indo-Europeans The tribes who invaded Mesopotamia included the **Indo-Europeans**, several tribes who spoke related languages. The Indo-Europeans may have come from the **steppes**, or arid grasslands, north of the Black Sea, driven out by drought, conflicts, or a lack of resources. By studying modern languages, scholars can tell that Indo-Europeans gradually spread west and south from that area.

Hittite Military Might The Hittites, a warlike Indo-European tribe, developed in Southwest Asia. About 2000 BC, they settled in Asia Minor, which is now Turkey. There, the Hittites conquered the surrounding people to build a strong empire.

The Hittites' success came largely through their use of the horse-drawn war chariot. The Hittite chariot was heavy and slow, but very powerful. Whereas most chariots of the time held only two soldiers, Hittite chariots held three. As one man drove, a second fought, and a third held shields for defense. This extra defender enabled the Hittites to move their chariots in close to enemy forces while staying protected, easily crushing most foes.

With these advantages, the Hittites expanded their empire beyond Asia Minor. About 1595 BC, they sacked Babylon. This conquest weakened Babylon, which soon fell to another nomadic tribe, the Kassites, who ruled southern Mesopotamia for almost 400 years.

Hittite Culture The Hittites, like the Akkadians and Babylonians, blended their culture with the cultures around them. For example, they used Sumerian cuneiform to write their language. In addition, they developed a law code similar to that of Hammurabi.

The Hittites did make a crucial contribution of their own to Near Eastern culture. They were the first people in the region to master ironworking techniques. The Hittites used iron mostly for making ornaments, though later peoples adopted it for tools and weapons

Hittite rule reached its peak in the 1300s, but the Hittites remained a strong force in western Asia until about 1200 BC. Their empire then fell to powerful raiders, known to historians only as the Sea Peoples.

READING CHECK **Summarize** How were the Hittites able to build an empire in Asia Minor?

Differentiating Instruction

Above Level

Advanced Learners/Gifted and Talented

Research Required

1. Remind students that the Indo-European tribes that invaded Mesopotamia spoke related languages.

2. Have students conduct outside research and compile a list of modern Indo-European languages. Then have students choose ten words that would be common throughout the languages, such as *mother, father, son, daughter,* or *house.* Have students conduct further research and write these words in each of the languages on their list.

3. Guide students in a comparison of the words. How are they similar? How do they differ? What do they tell us about the evolution of language?

4. As an extension, have students prepare their word lists as large charts that can be displayed in the classroom. 🄻🅂 **Verbal-Linguistic**

📄 **Alternative Assessment Handbook**, Rubric 9: Comparing and Contrasting

THE ASSYRIAN EMPIRE

ASIA MINOR

Black Sea

Cyprus

Mediterranean Sea

EGYPT

Sinai Peninsula

Red Sea

Euphrates R.

Ashur • Nineveh

Syrian Desert

Babylon

Persian Gulf

0   150   300 Miles
0   150   300 Kilometers
Lambert conformal conic projection

■ Assyrian Empire, c. 650 BC
□ Fertile Crescent
---- Ancient coastline

THE CHALDEAN EMPIRE

ASIA MINOR

Black Sea

Cyprus

Mediterranean Sea

EGYPT

Sinai Peninsula

Euphrates R.

• Nineveh

Syrian Desert

Babylon

Persian Gulf

0   150   300 Miles
0   150   300 Kilometers
Lambert conformal conic projection

■ Chaldean Empire, c. 600 BC
□ Fertile Crescent
---- Ancient coastline

GEOGRAPHY SKILLS   INTERPRETING MAPS

go.hrw.com
Interactive Map
Keyword: SHL ANE

1. **Regions** Which group that invaded the Fertile Crescent also conquered Egypt?

2. **Human-Environment Interaction** Why do you think none of the empires extended far south of the Fertile Crescent?

The Assyrians and the Chaldeans

After the Hittite Empire fell, other peoples fought for dominance in western Asia. In time, the Assyrians (uh-SEER-i-unz) used fierce determination and military might to become the supreme power in the region.

The Assyrians The Assyrians were originally from northern Mesopotamia, near the city of Assur along the upper Tigris River. There, they grew barley and raised cattle. Like others in the region, the Assyrians also adopted many aspects of Sumerian culture.

Because the Assyrians' land received fairly good rainfall and lay along major trade routes, many tribes invaded, seeking to control the area. Over the centuries, the Assyrians had often been dominated by other people.

The Assyrians briefly gained power in the 1300s BC and built an empire, but it did not last. Then about 900 BC the Assyrians regained strength. They built a new empire, which came to include all of Mesopotamia as well as parts of Asia Minor and Egypt.

The Assyrian War Machine Assyria's power relied on its military. Frequent warfare had hardened Assyria into a fierce warrior society. Its army included not only war chariots and foot soldiers but also a cavalry, all armed with iron weapons. In addition, Assyrian soldiers were masters of siege warfare. They used battering rams to pound through city walls or dug beneath the walls to weaken them.

Assyrian warfare also relied on terror to awe enemies and to control conquered areas. To spread fear, the Assyrians often killed or maimed captives. An Assyrian king recalled,

HISTORY'S VOICES

❝Many of the captives I burned in a fire. Many I took alive; from some I cut off their hands to the wrist, from others I cut off their noses, ears, and fingers; I put out the eyes of many.❞

—Ashurnasirpal II, quoted in
Barbarian Tides, 1500–600 BC

Captives who lived were enslaved. In some cases, the Assyrians also split up and resettled conquered people to keep them from rebelling.

TAKING NOTES Use a chart like the one below to describe the empires of the Fertile Crescent.

THE ANCIENT NEAR EAST **41**

• Direct Teach •

Reading Focus

❷ What events led to the rise and fall of the Assyrian and Chaldean Empires? *Assyrian—the fall of the Hittite Empire and military strength; grew too large to control; Chaldean—fall of Assyrian Empire; Persians conquered Babylon*

The Assyrians and the Chaldeans

Recall What lands were controlled by the Assyrians? *all of Mesopotamia, parts of Asia Minor and Egypt*

Analyze Why did the Assyrians become such a fierce warrior society? *Many tribes had invaded their territory because of good rainfall and its place along major trade routes; the Assyrians kept power and control through military might.*

Interpreting Maps
The Assyrian and Chaldean Empires
Location Did the Assyrian Empire or the Chaldean Empire control more land? *The Assyrians controlled more land; their empire extended into Egypt and north into Asia Minor.*

Activity **Measuring Distance** Have students use the maps on this page to measure the distance between Nineveh and Babylon. *about 270 miles*

📦 **Map Transparencies:** The Assyrian Empire; The Chaldean Empire

---

Skills Focus: Comparing and Contrasting   **At Level**

Reading Skill
Assyrians and Chaldeans

1. Copy the Venn diagram for students to see. Have students copy it onto their own papers and complete it showing the differences and similarities between the Chaldeans and the Assyrians.

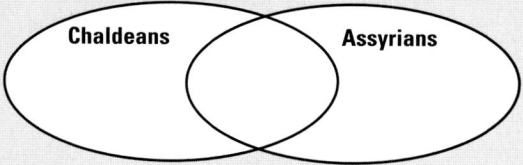

Chaldeans   Assyrians

Have volunteers share their answers, and complete the graphic organizer with the class.

2. Have students use the information in their charts to write a compare-and-contrast essay on the Assyrians and the Chaldeans. 🔤 **Verbal-Linguistic, Visual-Spatial**

📝 **Alternative Assessment Handbook**, Rubrics 9: Comparing and Contrasting; and 13: Graphic Organizers

Answers

Interpreting Maps 1. *the Assyrians;* **2.** *the Syrian desert had a harsh climate; no fresh water sources*

41

The Assyrians and the Chaldeans

Describe Describe the Assyrian system of government. *Kings ruled through local leaders who collected taxes, enforced laws, and raised troops.*

Draw Conclusions How were the Assyrians able to maintain peace in the empire? *efficient government and ruthless punishment of opposition*

Info to Know

Hanging Gardens of Babylon Archaeologists are still trying to unravel the mystery of the Hanging Gardens of Babylon. The gardens were documented by Greek historians, but they may not have seen them. The gardens were built on terraced palace roofs and irrigated by water pumped from the Euphrates. Babylonian tablets describe the palace and the city of Babylon, but they do not mention the gardens. Recent archaeological excavations reveal the existence of vaults and a chain pump, structures that might have been part of the substructure for the gardens.

Biography

Nebuchadnezzar, the Builder (c. 630–562 BC) While much is known of Nebuchadnezzar as military leader and diplomat, he is equally famous for his work in rebuilding Babylon. Nebuchadnezzar ruled for over 40 years, and built a deep moat around Babylon, as well as a new defense wall some 50 miles long. He also rebuilt temples, altars, and had canals dug.

Answers

The Splendor of Babylon *possible answer—from ancient writers' descriptions*

Faces of History *possible answer—to serve as a reminder of his leadership and legacy*

42

NEW YORK
CC Unit 1-B1c
Political systems of Mesopotamia

FOCUS ON NEW YORK
Two carved lions that once decorated the gates of Babylon are now in the Metropolitan Museum of Art in New York City.

Assyrian Rule The Assyrians created an efficient system to govern their vast empire. Kings ruled through local leaders, each of whom governed a small area of the empire. In that area, the local leader collected taxes, enforced laws, and raised troops for the army. A system of roads linked the distant parts of the empire. Over these roads, messengers on horseback raced with orders, troops moved with ease, and merchants carried on a thriving trade.

To maintain peace across the empire, the Assyrians ruthlessly punished anyone who opposed them. They were widely known and feared for their harsh treatment of anyone who opposed them. One Assyrian king boasted of his treatment of a group of rebels: "I fed their corpses—cut into small pieces—to the dogs, the swine, the wolves, the vultures." Such brutality fueled bitter hatred toward the Assyrians.

In spite of such brutality, the Assyrians produced great cultural achievements. Perhaps the greatest was the library in Assyria's capital, Nineveh (NI-nuh-vuh). This huge library included more than 20,000 cuneiform tablets collected from across the empire. Among them were many from Mesopotamia, including the *Epic of Gilgamesh.* Today the texts this library preserved are a valuable source of information for scholars.

Like many other empires, Assyria began to decline over time. As the empire grew larger, the Assyrians found it harder to control. Seeing their chance, the Chaldeans (kal-DEE-unz), who lived in southern Mesopotamia, and the Medes, who lived in what is now Iran, joined forces. In 612 BC they captured and torched Nineveh. With its capital and government gone, the Assyrian empire came to a sudden end.

The Splendor of Babylon

Babylon was one of the greatest cities of the ancient world. Archaeologists have found the ruins of the Ishtar Gate (below), but no trace of the Hanging Gardens (right) remains. *How might we know of the Hanging Gardens?*

FACES OF HISTORY
Nebuchadnezzar II
c. 630–562 BC

When he took the throne, Nebuchadnezzar II ordered the complete rebuilding of Babylon. Among its greatest structures was the Hanging Gardens. According to legend, he built this magnificent structure for his wife, who missed the mountains and forests of her birthplace.

Make Inferences Why might a ruler rebuild his capital city?

42 CHAPTER 2

Collaborative Learning

At Level

Seven Wonders of the World

Research Required

1. Organize students into seven groups. Assign each group one of the seven wonders of the ancient world: pyramids of Giza, Hanging Gardens of Babylon, statue of Zeus at Olympia, Temple of Artemis at Ephesus, Mausoleum at Halicarnassus, Colossus of Rhodes, and the Pharos (lighthouse) of Alexandria. Have students conduct outside research on their assigned "wonder of the world." Students should focus on the history and building process for their assigned topic.

2. Have each group prepare either a print or multimedia presentation on its assigned topic.

3. Have volunteers from each group present the information to the class.

4. As an extension, have students write a short essay summarizing their research and the information in their presentations. **LS Verbal-Linguistic, Visual-Spatial**

Alternative Assessment Handbook, Rubrics 24: Oral Presentations; and 42: Writing to Inform

The Chaldeans As Assyria crumbled, the Chaldeans swooped in to pick up the pieces. Taking much of southern and western Assyria, the Chaldeans formed their own empire.

The Chaldeans made the old city of Babylon the capital of their new Babylonian empire. **Nebuchadnezzar II** (neb-uh-kuhd-NEZ-uhr), the most famous Chaldean king, was known as both a warrior and as a builder. He fought the Egyptians and the Jews, capturing the Jewish capital of Jerusalem and taking many of its residents to Babylon as slaves. He also rebuilt Babylon into a place of splendor. Numerous palaces and temples, including an immense multistoried ziggurat, filled the city, and the Euphrates River flowed through the center. For himself, Nebuchadnezzar built a grand palace that, according to legend, featured the famous Hanging Gardens. There, thousands of trees and flowers grew on the terraces and roofs as if hanging in the air. Ancient writers listed the Hanging Gardens of Babylon as one of the seven wonders of the ancient world.

The Chaldeans, who like many others admired ancient Sumerian culture, studied the Sumerian language and built temples to Sumerian gods. The Chaldeans also developed a calendar based on the phases of the moon and made advances in astronomy. In Babylon, scholars charted the positions of the stars and used them to track economic, political, and weather events.

In spite of its achievements, the Chaldean Empire was short-lived. In 539 BC, less than a hundred years after they conquered the Assyrians, a people called the Persians conquered Babylon. With that event, the Chaldean Empire came to an end.

READING CHECK **Compare and Contrast** How were the Assyrian and Chaldean empires similar and different?

The Phoenicians

As great empires rose and fell, smaller states also emerged in western Asia. In an area called Phoenicia (fi-NI-shuh), city-states like Sidon and Tyre emerged as trading centers. Though the city-states of Phoenicia often came under the rule of foreign empires, the Phoenicians built a wealthy trading society whose legacy is still felt today.

PHOENICIAN TRADE, C. 800 BC

- Phoenicia
- Area of Phoenician settlement
- Phoenician colony
- Trade route

GEOGRAPHY SKILLS **INTERPRETING MAPS**

go.hrw.com
Interactive Map
Keyword: SHL ANE

1. **Movement** To what areas did Phoenician traders sail in their journeys?
2. **Location** How did Phoenicia's location help it become a major trading society?

Growth of a Trading Society Phoenicia lay at the western end of the Fertile Crescent, along the Mediterranean Sea. Today most of the region once know as Phoenicia is the nation of Lebanon.

The land of Phoenicia rose from a narrow coastal plain to rugged hills and mountains. Because farming was difficult and resources were limited, the Phoenicians turned to trade and the sea for their livelihood. They became expert sailors, dominating trade on the Mediterranean and sailing to ports in Egypt, Greece, Italy, Sicily, and Spain. Their ships even passed through the Strait of Gibraltar. Phoenician explorers sailed south along the west coast of Africa as far as modern Sierra Leone, and possibly even farther. Some historians also think that the Phoenicians sailed to the islands of Britain to obtain goods.

As trade grew, the Phoenicians founded colonies along their trade routes. One of the most famous colonies was Carthage (KAHR-thij), on the coast of northern Africa. Carthage later became a powerful city in the Mediterranean in its own right.

THE ANCIENT NEAR EAST **43**

Direct Teach

Reading Focus

The Phoenicians

Explain Why did the Phoenicians develop an alphabet? *Traders needed to record their activities.*

Contrast How was the Phoenicians' alphabet different from older writing systems? *more flexible and easier to use than pictographs or cuneiform*

🗄 **Quick Facts Transparency:** Alphabet

Review & Assess

Close

Have students list the major empires and city-states discussed in this section and one or two major achievements or notable characteristics about each group.

Review

 Online Quiz, Section 2

Assess

SE **Section 2 Assessment**

📄 **Progress Assessment:** Section 2 Quiz

📄 **Alternative Assessment Handbook**

Reteach/Intervene

📄 **Interactive Reader and Study Guide**, Section 2

💿 **Interactive Skills Tutor CD-ROM**

Answers

Alphabet *similar in shape; some letters have different sideways orientation*

Reading Check *purple dye, glassblowing, alphabet*

44

ALPHABET

QUICK FACTS

The Phoenician alphabet, adopted and modified by the Greeks and then the Romans, developed into our modern alphabet. *What similarities and differences can you see between the three sets of letters shown here?*

Phoenician

Greek

ΑΒΓΔΕΦΖΗ

Latin

ABCDEFGH

Trade brought Phoenicians great wealth. Local resources, although limited, included valuable export items. Giant cedar trees from Phoenicia were prized for timber. A local shellfish produced a purple dye used to color fabric, a fabric that was costly but popular with the rich. The Phoenicians invented glassblowing—the art of heating and shaping glass—and

glass objects became trade items as well. Other exports included ivory carvings, silverwork, and slaves.

The Phoenician Alphabet Trade was not the Phoenicians' only achievement. Perhaps their greatest achievement—and their most influential legacy—was their alphabet. To record their activities, Phoenician traders developed one of the world's first alphabets. Letters and alphabets, which can be combined to form countless words, are more flexible than writing systems that use symbols or pictographs to represent words or ideas.

The Phoenician alphabet consisted of 22 letters, all consonants. As Phoenician traders traveled from port to port, many people adopted their new alphabet because it made writing easier. Among these people were the Greeks, who expanded the alphabet to include vowels and modified some of the letters.

The Phoenician alphabet influenced not only the ancient world but the modern one as well. The Greeks' modified version of the old Phoenician alphabet is the ancestor of the modern alphabet we use to write the English language. Many civilizations, including our own, have benefited from the innovations of the seafaring Phoenicians.

READING CHECK **Find the Main Idea** What were the Phoenicians' most significant achievements?

SECTION 2 ASSESSMENT

go.hrw.com
Online Quiz
Keyword: SHL ANE HP

Reviewing Ideas, Terms, and People

1. **a. Identify** Who were the **Indo-Europeans**, and how have scholars traced their migrations?
   b. Identify Cause and Effect What was the major cause of the Hittites' success as empire builders in Asia Minor?
   c. Support a Position Do you agree or disagree with the position that ironworking was the greatest contribution of the Hittites? Support your answer.

2. **a. Recall** Who was **Nebuchadnezzar II**, and what legendary Chaldean achievement is associated with him?
   b. Summarize What were some of the key achievements of the Assyrian and Chaldean empires?
   c. Make Judgments Was the Assyrian use of terror and brutality as a means of control successful? Explain your answer.

3. **a. Describe** Where and what did the Phoenicians trade?
   b. Explain Why did the Phoenicians focus on trade by sea for their livelihood?

c. Elaborate Why is the Phoenicians' alphabet considered one of their greatest legacies?

Critical Thinking

4. **Identify Cause and Effect** Copy the chart below. Use it to list the causes and effects of the rise and fall of each empire.

Empire or State	Causes of Its Rise/Success

FOCUS ON WRITING

5. **Persuasion** Of the many cultural achievements described in this section, select the one that you think was the most important. Then write a letter to persuade a historian to agree with your position.

44 CHAPTER 2

Section 2 Assessment Answers

1. **a.** a group of several tribes that spoke related languages; by tracing modern languages
   b. use of horse-drawn chariot
   c. possible answer—agree; iron weapons allowed for expansion of empire

2. **a.** Chaldean king; built Hanging Gardens
   b. Assyrians—iron weapons, effective government structure, library in Nineveh; Chaldeans—Hanging Gardens, developed calendar, advances in astronomy
   c. possible answer—yes; used terror to gain power, build empire, keep order

3. **a.** Egypt, Greece, Italy, Sicily, Spain; glass, slaves, ivory works, timber, purple dye
   b. Resources were limited and trade allowed them to import necessary items.
   c. more flexible, influenced later alphabet

4. Hittite—military strength, new technology; fell to Sea Peoples; Assyrian—military strength, brutality; too big to control; Chaldean—captured Nineveh; Persians conquered Babylon

5. Letters might argue for the Code of Hammurabi, calendar, alphabet, sea trade.

SECTION 3 The Hebrews and Judaism

BEFORE YOU READ

MAIN IDEA

The ancient Hebrews and their religion, Judaism, have been a major influence on Western civilization.

READING FOCUS

1. What are the major events in the history of the early Hebrews?
2. How did the Kingdom of Israel develop, and who were some of its key leaders?
3. What are the basic teachings and sacred texts of Judaism?

KEY TERMS AND PEOPLE

Judaism
Torah
Abraham
covenant
patriarch
Moses
Exodus
Diaspora
monotheism

NEW YORK

P1 3.1 Students analyze the roles and contributions of individuals and groups to religious practices.

P1 3.3 Students examine the social/cultural and religious norms and values of Western and other world cultures.

JOURNEY to an UNKNOWN LAND

▲ According to the Bible, God promised to lead Abraham to a new homeland.

Abraham, Sarah, and an Angel, Jan Provost II, c. 1520

THE INSIDE STORY

Why might a man leave his home and move to a strange land?
Ancient accounts say that a shepherd named Abram lived near Ur during the time of the Babylonians. One day, God spoke to Abram: "Get thee out of thy country, and from thy kindred, and from thy father's house," God said, "unto the land that I will show thee. And I will make of thee a great nation, and I will bless thee, and make thy name great . . . and in thee shall all the families of the earth be blessed." (Genesis 12:1–4, Masoretic text)

So Abram took his family, herds, and belongings and began a long journey west. God led Abram to a land called Canaan, on the Mediterranean Sea. There, God gave Abram a new name—Abraham, meaning the "father of many." Abraham made a new home in Canaan, and his descendants multiplied. They became known as the Hebrews. ◼

The Early Hebrews

The Hebrews were the ancestors of the people called Jews. Originally nomadic pastoralists, they moved into the desert grasslands around the Fertile Crescent between 2000 and 1500 BC.

Much of what we know about the Hebrews comes from their own later writings, which contained not only the laws and requirements of their religion, **Judaism** (Joo-dee-i-zuhm), but also much of their early history. These writings later formed the foundation of both the Hebrew and Christian Bibles. The findings of Near Eastern archaeologists have also shed some light on early Hebrew history.

THE ANCIENT NEAR EAST **45**

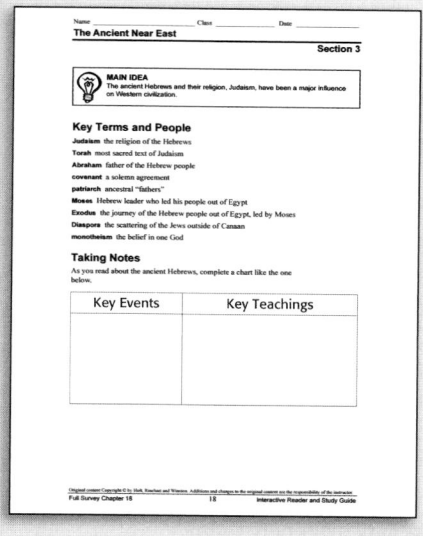

Reading Focus

1 What are the major events in the history of the early Hebrews? *Abraham leaving Ur for Canaan; Hebrews enslaved in Egypt; the Exodus; God giving Moses the Ten Commandments; the development of Israel*

The Early Hebrews

Describe What are the two sources of early Hebrew history? *work of archaeologists and written Hebrew accounts*

Explain Why did the Egyptian pharaoh finally agree to free the Hebrews? *A series of plagues befell Egypt.*

Elaborate How might monotheism have caused problems for the Hebrews? *Refusing to recognize various gods in local city-states may have caused conflict.*

 CRF: Biography: Abraham

 CRF: Primary Source: Ancient Flood Narratives

Info to Know

The Torah, Tanakh, Talmud, and Mishnah Torah refers to the first five books of the Bible, Genesis, Exodus, Leviticus, Numbers, and Deuteronomy. Tanakh refers to the Hebrew Bible, and is a Hebrew acronym that stands for three categories of books within it: Torah, Neviim (Prophets), and Ketuvim (Writings). Mishnah is a systematic anthology of rabbinic law based on the Torah, while Talmud is an extended commentary on the Mishnah that includes later rabbinic interpretation, legal rulings and discussion.

TAKING NOTES Use a chart like the one below to take notes on the ancient Hebrews.

Key Events	Key Teachings

The Hebrew Fathers The accounts of the Hebrews' early history appear in five books. Together, these books form the **Torah**, the most sacred text of Judaism. The Torah, along with other writings, is part of the Hebrew Bible. The Hebrew Bible is called the Old Testament in the Christian Bible.

The Torah traces the Hebrews back to a man named **Abraham**. A shepherd, he lived near Ur in Mesopotamia. The Torah says that God told Abraham to leave Mesopotamia and to abandon the polytheism he had grown up with. In return for Abraham's obedience, God made a **covenant**, or solemn promise, to him. God promised to lead Abraham and his descendants to a new home, a Promised Land, and to make those descendants a mighty people.

The land to which the Torah says God led Abraham was called Canaan (KAY-nuhn), a region along the eastern Mediterranean Sea. There, Abraham and his descendants lived for many years. In time, his grandson Jacob had 12 sons who were the ancestors of 12 tribes. Because Jacob was also called Israel, the tribes were called the Twelve Tribes of Israel, and the Hebrews became known as the Children of Israel or Israelites. Later Israelites all traced their roots to these twelve tribes. As a result, the Israelites—and modern Jews—considered Abraham, his son Isaac, and Isaac's son Jacob **patriarchs**, or ancestral "fathers."

In time, some Israelites left Canaan and went to Egypt, driven there by famine. The Israelites lived well there, and their population grew. Egypt's ruler, the pharaoh, began to fear that the Israelites might rise up against the Egyptians. To prevent an uprising, he made the Israelites slaves.

Moses and the Exodus The Torah tells of the Israelites' years of bitter toil as slaves in Egypt. Then a leader named **Moses** arose among them. According to the Torah, Moses had been born an Israelite but raised in the pharaoh's palace. One day God spoke to him and told him to lead the Israelites out of Egypt.

Moses went to the pharaoh and demanded the Israelites' freedom. But the pharaoh refused. God responded, the Torah says, by raining down a series of terrible plagues, or disasters, on Egypt. These plagues so terrified the pharaoh that he agreed to free the Israelites. In a journey called the **Exodus**, Moses

46 CHAPTER 2

led the Israelites out of Egypt. The Israelites believed that these events proved that God loved them and was watching over them.

The Exodus is a major event in Jewish history. Today Jews remember the Exodus by celebrating Passover in the spring of each year. During Passover, Jews eat a special meal called a seder (SAY-duhr) that includes foods symbolizing their hardships in Egypt and the escape from slavery to freedom.

After the Exodus the Israelites wandered through the desert for years. During this time, they came to a mountain called Sinai. The Torah says that, on that mountain, God gave Moses two stone tablets on which were 10 moral laws. These laws are the Ten Commandments.

The Ten Commandments state that only one God exists and stress the importance of life, self-control, and justice. The Israelites made a new covenant with God to follow the Commandments, which shaped their society. Over time, these laws had a major influence on the laws and values of Western civilization:

World Religions

SACRED TEXTS

The Torah

About the Reading The Torah, one of Judaism's most sacred texts, includes the first five books of the Hebrew Bible. It includes descriptions of the laws Jews are expected to follow and a history of the Jewish people up to the death of Moses. Among the events described in the Torah is the Exodus, the freeing of the Jews from slavery in Egypt. In this passage from the Torah, God instructs Moses to lead his people to freedom.

AS YOU READ Pay attention to the instructions God gives to Moses.

A Torah scroll encased in a decorative case ▶

Skills Focus: Analyzing Primary Sources

Above Level

Reading Like a Historian Skill
United States Law

Research Required

1. Have students read the Ten Commandments listed in the History's Voices feature. Have students work in small groups to read and write a brief explanation of each commandment.

2. Have students conduct outside research to find out which of the Ten Commandments are enforced by current state or federal laws.

3. Have students choose one commandment they have identified as current law. Have students research the history of that law, as well as the punishments for breaking it. Students should write a brief report of their findings. Have volunteers present their findings to the class.
LS Verbal-Linguistic

 Alternative Assessment Handbook, Rubrics 1: Acquiring Information; and 24: Oral Presentations

❝I am the Lord thy God, who brought thee out of the land of Egypt, out of the house of bondage.

Thou shalt have no other gods before Me. Thou shalt not make unto thee a graven image, nor any manner of likeness, of any thing . . .

Thou shalt not take the name of the Lord thy God in vain . . .

Remember the sabbath day, to keep it holy. Six days shalt thou labour, and do all thy work; but the seventh day is a sabbath unto the Lord thy God, in it thou shalt not do any manner of work. . .

Honour thy father and thy mother . . .

Thou shalt not murder.

Thou shalt not commit adultery.

Thou shalt not steal.

Thou shalt not bear false witness against thy neighbor.

Thou shalt not covet they neighbour's house; thou shalt not covet thy neighbour's wife . . . nor any thing that is thy neighbour's.❞

—Exodus 20:2–14, Masoretic Text

The Promised Land The Torah says the Israelites wandered in the desert for 40 years before entering Canaan. The Israelites believed that God had promised them this land, which was said to be "flowing with milk and honey."

Because other people now lived in Canaan, the Israelites battled for land for many decades. When they had once again gained control of Canaan, that land became known as Israel.

READING CHECK Sequencing What are some key events, in order, in early Israelite history?

The Kingdom of Israel

In Canaan, the Israelites settled in scattered communities where they farmed and raised livestock. The communities were organized loosely by the Twelve Tribes and did not have a central government. Instead, each community chose judges to enforce laws and settle disputes. The Hebrew Bible says that one of the most effective judges was a woman, Deborah.

And the LORD said: "I have surely seen the affliction of My people that are in Egypt, and have heard their cry by reason of their taskmasters; for I know their pains; and I am come down to deliver them out of the hand of the Egyptians, and to bring them up out of that land unto a good land and a large, unto a land flowing with milk and honey; unto the place of the Canaanite, and the Hittite, and the Amorite, and the Perizzite, and the Hivite, and the Jebusite. And now, behold, the cry of the children of Israel is come unto Me; moreover I have seen the oppression wherewith the Egyptians oppress them. Come now, therefore, and I will send thee unto Pharaoh, that thou mayest bring forth My people the children of Israel out of Egypt." And Moses said unto God: "Who am I, that I should go unto pharaoh, and that I should bring forth the children of Israel out of Egypt?" And He said: "Certainly I will be with thee; and this shall be the token unto thee, that I have sent thee: when thou hast brought forth the people out of Egypt, ye shall serve God upon this mountain." And Moses said unto God: "Behold, when I come unto the children of Israel, and shall say unto them: The God of your fathers hath sent me unto you; and they shall say to me: What is His name? what shall I say unto them?" And God said unto Moses: "I AM THAT I AM"; and He said: "Thus shalt thou say unto the children of Israel: I AM hath sent me unto you."

—Exodus 3:7–14, Masoretic Text

Analyze What does God promise to Moses?

▲ A Jewish teen holds a pointer called a yad as she reads from a Torah scroll.

Reading Focus

❷ How did the Kingdom of Israel develop, and who were some of its key leaders? *when the Philistines invaded Israel, the Israelites united to conquer them; Saul, David, and Solomon*

The Kingdom of Israel

Describe How were Canaan's communities organized? *loosely organized by the Twelve Tribes; no central government*

Make Inferences Deborah was one of the most effective Hebrew judges; what might this tell us about Hebrew society? *possible answers—Society was somewhat egalitarian; women could rise to positions of authority.*

Primary Source

In this passage, Solomon resolves a dispute between two women. "The king said, 'Divide the living boy in two; then give half to the one, and half to the other.'" But the woman whose son was alive said to the king—because compassion for her son burned within her—"Please, my lord, give her the living boy; certainly do not kill him!" The other said, "It shall be neither mine nor yours; divide it." Then the king responded: "Give the first woman the living boy; do not kill him. She is his mother."

—Hebrew 1 Kings.3:25-37

Answers

World Religions *If Moses brings the people out of Egypt, God will allow Moses to "serve God upon this mountain."*

Reading Check *Abraham traveled to Canaan, 1800 BC; Moses appeared among Hebrews in Egypt, 1200s BC; the Exodus; delivery of Ten Commandments to Moses; Hebrews wander desert for 40 years; invasion of Philistines to Israel, mid-1000s BC; Saul named first king of Israel, mid-1000s BC; David named second king of Israel, 1000 BC; Solomon named third king of Israel, 865 BC*

Skills Focus: Sequencing

Below Level

Reading Skill
Paraphrasing the Torah

Standard English Mastery

1. Have students read the excerpt from the Torah about the Exodus.

2. Organize students into mixed-ability pairs or small groups.

3. Have each group use standard English to rewrite the story in simple sentences. Tell students to check their work for correct spelling, punctuation, and grammar before writing a final draft.

4. Have volunteers share their final paraphrases with the class. Give students constructive criticism and feedback, and allow time for them to revise or rewrite their paraphrases.

LS Verbal-Linguistic

Alternative Assessment Handbook, Rubric 37: Writing Assignments

Reading Focus

The Kingdom of Israel

Explain What event marked start of the Diaspora? *Babylonion Captivity*

Summarize How did the Kingdom of Judah come into being? *conflict among the twelve tribes; two southern tribes formed the Kingdom of Judah*

Elaborate Why might the Kingdom of Israel have been a target for outside invaders? *proximity to the sea and other major waterways for trade and growing crops*

Interpreting Maps

Israel and Judah

Location What were the northern and western borders of the Kingdom of Israel in 930 BC? *Euphrates River to the north; Mediterranean Sea to the west*

Movement Why is the area of the Kingdom of Israel in 930 BC so much larger than the Divided Kingdoms? *Solomon expanded Israel and made it wealthy through trade; after he died, there was a power struggle over the new king; control of the land was less unified,*

🗺 **Map Transparencies:** Kingdom of Israel, c. 930 BC; Divided Kingdoms, c. 920 BC

Answers

Interpreting Maps 1. *Kingdom of Judah;* **2.** *approximately 200 miles*

Reading Check *They were the first kings of Israel; they unified the Israelites under the Kingdom of Israel.*

ISRAEL AND JUDAH

KINGDOM OF ISRAEL, C. 930 BC

Israel under Solomon

DIVIDED KINGDOMS, C. 920 BC

Kingdom of Israel
Kingdom of Judah

GEOGRAPHY SKILLS INTERPRETING MAPS

1. **Location** When Israel divided into two kingdoms, in which kingdom did Jerusalem lie?
2. **Regions** About how much farther north did Solomon's kingdom extend than the divided Kingdom of Israel?

From time to time during the period of the judges, prophets—holy men who were believed to carry messages from God—appeared among the Israelites. The goal of the prophets was to keep the Israelites focused on their faith.

Saul, David, and Solomon In the mid-1000s BC the Philistines, a powerful people who lived along the Mediterranean coast attacked Israel. The effort to drive out the Philistines led the Israelites to unite under one king.

Israel's first king was a man named Saul. Chosen for his military leadership, Saul had some success fighting against the Philistines. Described in the Hebrew Bible as a jealous and troubled ruler, Saul was never able to win the full support of the people.

David, who became Israel's second king in about 1000 BC, was well loved, and the people united behind him. A strong king and military leader, David was also a gifted poet and musician. Under David, Israel grew into a strong kingdom centered on the capital, Jerusalem.

Under David's son Solomon, the Kingdom of Israel reached the height of its wealth and influence. Solomon, praised in the Hebrew Bible for his great wisdom, traded with other powers of the Near East. Through this trade, Solomon became very rich. With his wealth, he built a magnificent temple in Jerusalem.

Division and Conquest Within a year of the death of Solomon about 931 BC, conflict over who should be king ripped Israel in two. The ten tribes in the north formed a new kingdom, also called Israel. The two tribes in the south formed the Kingdom of Judah and became known as Jews.

The two kingdoms lasted a few centuries. About 722 BC Israel fell to the Assyrians. The Assyrians then scattered the people of Israel across their empire. The second kingdom, Judah, fell to the Chaldeans in 586 BC. The Chaldeans destroyed Solomon's Temple and brought thousands of Jews to Babylon as slaves. The Jews called this enslavement the Babylonian Captivity. It lasted about 50 years. This event marked the start of the **Diaspora**, the scattering of the Jews outside Judah.

48 CHAPTER 2

Skills Focus: Analyzing Primary Sources [At Level]

Reading Like a Historian Skill
Mapping Canaan

Materials: outline map of Middle East, colored pencils

1. Have students study the maps of Israel and Judah on this page. Remind them that in Exodus, God tells Moses about "a land flowing with milk and honey..."

2. Guide students in a discussion about what is meant by "a land flowing with milk and honey." Point out that access to the sea and waterways make this region an attractive place to settle.

3. Review the locations of Mesopotamia and the Hittite, Assyrian, and Chaldean Empires.

4. Distribute outlines maps and have students use different colored pencils to shade the Kingdom of Israel, the Divided Kingdoms of Israel and Judah, Mesopotamia, and the different empires.
🅻🆂 **Visual-Spatial**

📋 **Alternative Assessment Handbook,** Rubrics 20: Map Creation; and 21: Map Reading

At that time a powerful new empire called Persia conquered the Chaldeans. The Persians let the Jews return to Jerusalem, where they rebuilt Solomon's Temple, which became known as the Second Temple. However, many Jews did not return to Jerusalem but stayed in Babylon or moved into Persia.

READING CHECK **Find the Main Idea** Why are Saul, David, and Solomon significant?

The Teachings of Judaism

Religion was the foundation upon which the ancient Hebrews, and later the Jews, based their whole society. Today Judaism's central beliefs continue to influence Jewish society.

Belief in One God The most important belief of Judaism is that only one God exists. The belief in one God is called **monotheism**. Most of the ancient world worshipped many gods, so the Jews' worship of one God set them apart. Many scholars believe that Judaism was the world's first monotheistic religion.

Justice and Righteousness Also central to Judaism are the beliefs of justice and righteousness. To Jews, being just means treating other people with kindness and fairness. Being righteous refers to doing what is right and proper, even when others do not.

The Jewish emphasis on righteousness has led to their creation of a strong code of ethics, or standards of behavior. For example, Jews are expected to respect their families, to tell the truth, not to cheat, and to treat all people equally. The Jewish ethical tradition was later carried forward into Christianity and became known as Judeo-Christian ethics.

Obedience to the Law Closely tied to the idea of righteousness is the Jewish emphasis on obedience to the law. The most important laws of Judaism are the Ten Commandments, but they are only part of the many laws that Jews believe Moses recorded. A whole system of laws, called Mosaic law, guides many areas of Jewish life. For example, Mosaic law governs how Jews pray and when they worship. The laws also limit what foods Jews may eat and how foods are prepared. Today food prepared according to these laws is called kosher, or fit.

Jewish Sacred Texts The beliefs and laws of Judaism are recorded in several sacred texts. As you have read, the most sacred of these texts is the Torah. The Torah is the first part of the Hebrew Bible. The other sections are the Prophets, which includes the teachings of early Israelite prophets, and the Writings, which contains lessons, history, poetry, songs, and proverbs, or sayings of wisdom.

Another sacred text of Judaism is the Talmud (TAHL-moohd). Written by Jewish scholars over several centuries and finished in the AD 500s, the Talmud contains explanations and interpretations of the other sacred texts. The beliefs in these sacred texts have helped the Jews remain a united religious community.

READING CHECK **Identify Supporting Details** What are the central beliefs of Judaism?

NEW YORK
CC Unit 1-E1e
The origins of Judaism

SECTION 3 ASSESSMENT

go.hrw.com
Online Quiz
Keyword: SHL ANE HP

Reviewing Ideas, Terms, and People

1. **a. Identify** Who were **Abraham** and Jacob, and what is their significance in early Hebrew history?
   b. Analyze Why is the **Exodus** a major event in early Jewish history?
   c. Elaborate In what ways do the Ten Commandments stress the values of human life, self-control, and justice?

2. **a. Define** What is the **Diaspora**?
   b. Sequence What happened to the Kingdom of Israel after Solomon's rule?
   c. Make Judgments Who do you think was the greater king of Israel—David or Saul? Why?

3. **a. Recall** What are the three sections of the Hebrew Bible? Which one do the Jews consider to be the most sacred?
   b. Summarize How do the central beliefs of **Judaism** shape Jewish life?

Critical Thinking

4. **Sequence** Draw a series of boxes like the one below. Using your notes, list and describe each key event in the history of the Hebrews from Abraham's migration to Canaan to the Babylonian Captivity.

☐ → ☐ → ☐ → ☐ → ☐ → ☐

FOCUS ON WRITING

5. **Exposition** Write a short newspaper article covering one of the following major events in Hebrew and Jewish history: the Exodus, the division of Israel into two kingdoms, the Babylonian Captivity, or the return of Jews to Jerusalem from Babylon. You should write the article from the point of view of an objective reporter who lived in the ancient world. Your article should be clear and address the questions of who, what, where, when, and how.

THE ANCIENT NEAR EAST **49**

• Direct Teach •

Reading Focus

3 What are the basic teachings and sacred texts of Judaism? *belief in one God, obedience to the Ten Commandments and Mosaic laws, justice and righteousness; Torah, Hebrew Bible, Talmud*

The Teachings of Judaism

Define What is belief in one God? *monotheism*

Contrast How did the beliefs of Judaism differ from other societies around this time? *Other societies were polytheistic, so people believed in many gods. Jews believed in one God.*

• Review & Assess •

Close

Have students summarize the early events that led to the development of the Kingdom of Israel. Then, have students list the main sacred texts of Judaism.

Review

Online Quiz, Section 3

Assess

SE Section 3 Assessment

📋 **Progress Assessment:** Section 3 Quiz

📋 **Alternative Assessment Handbook**

Reteach/Intervene

📋 **Interactive Reader and Study Guide**, Section 3

💿 **Interactive Skills Tutor CD-ROM**

Section 3 Assessment Answers

1. **a.** Abraham—shepherd, led his people to Canaan; Jacob—Abraham's grandson, had twelve sons that made up the Twelve Tribes
   b. Moses led Hebrews out of slavery; God gave Moses Ten Commandments.
   c. stress kindness and respect

2. **a.** scattering of Jews outside of Canaan after the Babylonian Captivity
   b. Israel divided into two nations; later conquered by Assyrians and Chaldeans
   c. possible answers—Saul: fought the Philistines, first king of Israel; David: unified

Twelve Tribes, grew Israel into strong kingdom

3. **a.** Torah, Hebrew Bible, Talmud; the Torah
   b. Ten Commandments guide actions and treatment of other people; Mosaic law guides worship, food, and other areas of life.

4. Abraham's migration to Canaan; the Exodus; Ten Commandments; Kingdom of Israel; Divided Kingdoms of Israel and Judah; Babylonian Captivity

5. Articles should reflect factual content of the section.

Answers

Reading Check *belief in one god; obedience to the Ten Commandments; justice and righteousness*

49

Getting Started

Use the **Interactive Reader and Study Guide** to familiarize students with the section content.

📄 **Interactive Reader and Study Guide,** Section 4

📄 **CRF:** Vocabulary Builder: Section 4

Taking Notes

Politics—Cyrus: tolerance for conquered people; ruled by himself; Darius: permanent army, created provincial governor, or satraps, who governed local regions; Religion—Zoroastrianism

go.hrw.com
Online Resources
KEYWORD: SHL ANE
ACTIVITY: Ancient Leaders

---

4 The Persian Empire

BEFORE YOU READ

MAIN IDEA
The Persians formed one of the largest and best-governed empires in the ancient world and made great cultural achievements.

READING FOCUS
1. Who shaped the growth and organization of the Persian Empire?
2. What were the main teachings of Zoroastrianism?
3. What were the most significant Persian achievements?

KEY TERMS AND PEOPLE
Cyrus the Great
Darius I
satrap
Xerxes
Zoroaster
dualism

🗽 **NEW YORK**

PI 3.2 Students explain the dynamics of cultural change and how interactions between and among cultures has affected various cultural groups throughout the world.

THE INSIDE STORY

Could a newborn infant be a threat to a king?
According to an ancient legend, the baby who grew up to be King Cyrus the Great of Persia was indeed a threat. Cyrus, the legend says, was the grandson of Astyages, king of the Medes. The king's daughter had married a prince of the Persians, a people the Medes had conquered. Shortly after the couple's first son, Cyrus, was born, the king had a dream that the baby would grow up to overthrow him. Afraid the dream would come true, he ordered his servants to kill young Cyrus.

Not wanting to kill a helpless baby, one of the servants took Cyrus out of the city and gave him to an old shepherd to raise. Under the shepherd's care, Cyrus grew to be a clever and capable leader who wanted to free his people from rule by the Medes. When he reached adulthood, Cyrus led a rebellion, overthrew his grandfather, and made himself the new king. ◼

The Infant Cyrus with the Shepherd, by Sebastiano Ricci, 1700s

A DANGEROUS BABY?

According to legend, Cyrus the Great was given as a baby to a shepherd to raise.

50 CHAPTER 2

Teach the Main Idea

At Level

The Persian Empire

1. **Teach** Ask students the Reading Focus questions to teach this section.

2. **Apply** Have students work in pairs or small groups to create brief summaries of the development of the Persian Empire, focusing on Cyrus the Great and Darius I. Tell students to list the achievements, leadership skills, and territorial expansions of each leader.

3. **Review** Have volunteers share their summaries with the class. Then guide

students in a discussion of the accomplishments of Cyrus the Great and Darius I.

4. **Practice/Homework** Have students write a brief, illustrated biography of either Cyrus the Great or Darius I. Advanced Learners may wish to conduct outside research or use primary source documents in their biography. **LS Verbal-Linguistic**

📄 **Alternative Assessment Handbook,** Rubrics 9: Comparing and Contrasting; and 40: Writing to Describe

THE PERSIAN EMPIRE

■	Persia under Cyrus, 559 BC
■	Conquered by Cyrus, 559–530 BC
■	Conquered by Cambyses, 530–522 BC
■	Conquered by Darius, 521–486 BC
—	Royal Road
⊛	Capital city

0   250   500 Miles
0   250   500 Kilometers
Two-point equidistant projection

CYRUS AND DARIUS — QUICK FACTS

Cyrus the Great
- Founded the Persian Empire
- Conquered many lands
- Let people keep their customs

Darius I
- Created a standing army
- Divided empire into satrapies
- Built the Royal Road

GEOGRAPHY SKILLS — INTERPRETING MAPS

1. **Place** What geographic features marked the Persian Empire's northern boundary?
2. **Regions** Which Persian ruler added the most territory to the empire?

Growth and Organization

Legends about the rise to power of Cyrus the Great have grown over time. Historians are not sure which of the legends' details are accurate. For example, they question whether Cyrus was really Astyages's grandson. What they do not question, however, is the greatness of his achievements. Cyrus conquered the Medes and established one of the largest empires of the ancient world, the Persian Empire.

Persia under the Medes The Persians and the Medes were both Indo-European tribes originally from Central Asia. Over time, both tribes settled on the plateaus of what is now Iran. There, the Medes created a new kingdom, Media, and set out to conquer their neighbors.

Among those conquered by the Medes were the Persians. The Medes allowed the conquered Persians to keep their own leaders as long as they did not rebel. In this way, the Persians remained subject to the Medes for centuries.

Cyrus the Great A new leader arose among the Persians in 559 BC, though, who would change everything. His name was Cyrus II, better known as **Cyrus the Great**. About 10 years after becoming the Persian king, Cyrus led a revolt against the Medes. He defeated the Median army and united the Persians and the Medes under his rule.

Once Cyrus had taken control of Media, he set out to expand his lands. He marched into Asia Minor and conquered the fabulously wealthy kingdom of Lydia. He also captured several Greek cities in Ionia, a region of Asia Minor along the Aegean Sea. From there, Cyrus moved south into Mesopotamia, where he defeated the Chaldeans and captured the city of Babylon.

When Cyrus conquered a region, he allowed people to keep their own customs rather than forcing them to adopt Persian ones. This tolerance for other people's customs won Cyrus the respect of those he conquered. The Jews, for example, admired Cyrus and considered him a hero. When he conquered Babylon, Cyrus freed the Jews from slavery and allowed them to return to Jerusalem and rebuild their temple.

TAKING NOTES Use a chart to take notes on the politics and religion of the Persian Empire.

The Persian Empire	
Politics	Religion

READING SKILLS
Questioning
As you read, ask yourself what Cyrus is doing and why.

THE ANCIENT NEAR EAST **51**

Reading Focus

❶ Who shaped the growth and organization of the Persian Empire? *Cyrus the Great, Cambyses, Darius I*

Growth and Organization

Identify Who were the Persians? *an Indo-European tribe from Central Asia*

Make Inferences How did the Medes maintain control over the Persians? *allowed the Persians to keep their own leaders as long as they did not rebel*

Evaluate Why was Cyrus considered an enlightened leader? *allowed people to practice their own religions and keep their own customs*

🖥 **Quick Facts Transparency:** Cyrus and Darius

🖥 **Map Transparency:** The Persian Empire

Info to Know

Persia and Iran The term *Persia* has long been used to describe the nation of Iran, its people, or its ancient empire. It derives from the name of a region in southern Iran, known as Persis, or *Fars* in the modern Persian language. The Greeks began to apply the name Persia to the Iranian plateau, which was the core of the original Persian Empire. Westerners referred to the state as Persia until March 21, 1935, when Reza Shah Pahlavi formally asked the international community to call the country by its native name, Iran, which means Land of the Aryans.

Skills Focus: Evaluating Historical Interpretation — Above Level

Reading Like a Historian Skill
Herodotus — Research Required

1. Have students review the legend of Cyrus and Astyages. Tell students that this story was written in several accounts of the Persian Empire, most famously by the Greek historian Herodotus in his nine-volume work *The Histories*.

2. Tell students that many philosophers in Herodotus's time criticized his work, arguing that there were exaggerations and lies in his books, but some scholars respect his accuracy. Guide students in a discussion of

why scholars have different opinions on the accuracy of primary sources. Remind students that archaeological excavation can unearth new evidence.

3. Have students research Persia in Herodotus's *The Histories* and in the Greek historian Xenophon's *Anabasis*. Have volunteers share their findings. 🄻🅂 **Verbal-Linguistic**

📄 **Alternative Assessment Handbook**, Rubric 1: Acquiring Information

Answers

Interpreting Maps 1. *Black Sea, Caucasus Mountains, Caspian Sea, Jaxartes River;* **2.** *Cyrus the Great*

51

Reading Focus

Growth and Organization

Explain Why was Cambyses disliked? *Compared to his father, he was intolerant and described as a tyrant.*

Make Inferences Why do you think the highly trained soldiers in Darius's army were called the Ten Thousand Immortals? *possible answer—elite of the Persian army, supported by other soldiers in battle*

Activity **Ten Thousan Immortals** Have students write a letter from a soldier to his family announcing that he has just been chosen to serve in the Ten Thousand Immortals. Remind students that this would have been considered a great honor.

 **Verbal-Linguistic**

Alternative Assessment Handbook, Rubrics 25: Personal Letters

CRF: Biography: Herodotus

Info to Know

Ten Thousand Immortals There were always 10,000 soldiers in this group of highly trained soilders. When one soldier was killed or died, he was immediately replaced so that the number remained constant.

The Persian Empire

Activity **Analyzing Maps** Have students use the map to calculate the size of the Persian Empire under Cyrus the Great in 530 BC. Tell students that they can divide the map up into rough rectangular areas, measure the height and width of each area, use the map key to calculate the area of each section, and then add the areas of each section to get the total area. *approximately 2.5 million square miles.* **Logical-Mathematical**

Alternative Assessment Handbook, Rubrics 21: Map Reading

Answers

The Persian Army *highly trained soilders, swift chariots*

52

The Persian Army

A strong army was the key to building a powerful empire. Led by Cyrus and Darius, the Persian army was one of the mightiest fighting forces in the ancient world. *What made the Persian army so strong?*

▼ **Cavalry and chariots were used to support the Immortals.**

Pulled by four horses, Persian chariots could move swiftly but could not easily turn.

◄ **A troop of highly trained soldiers called the Immortals was the heart of the army.**

 NEW YORK
CC Unit 1-B1c
Political systems of Mesopotamia

Cyrus died in 530 BC while fighting in Central Asia. At the time of his death, he ruled the largest empire in the world. According to a Greek historian, the Persians summed up Cyrus's achievements with this inscription carved on his tomb:

HISTORY'S VOICES

❝O man, I am Cyrus, son of Cambyses, who founded the empire of the Persians and was king of Asia. Do not therefore grudge me this monument.❞

—Arrian, *Anabasis,* Book VI

After Cyrus died, his son Cambyses II became emperor. Building on a plan first designed by his father, Cambyses invaded Egypt and added it to the Persian Empire.

Unlike Cyrus, who was admired for his tolerance, Cambyses was described as a tyrant and a madman. While in Egypt, he received word of a rebellion in Persia. On his way back home to crush the rebellion, Cambyses died and Persia was left without a ruler.

Darius I Out of the confusion surrounding the rebellion and the death of Cambyses rose a new leader for Persia. His name was **Darius I.**

For the first year of his reign, Darius had to fight to restore order in Persia. Many Persians did not like him and fought to keep him off the throne. Once he had extinguished the last flames of rebellion, Darius began a program to reorganize and strengthen his empire.

The first step Darius took to strengthen the empire was reforming the army. Under Cyrus, the Persians had had no permanent army. The emperor called people to fight for him when he went into battle, and they returned home when the fighting was done. Darius changed that system by creating a permanent army made up of paid soldiers. He also instituted a new training system for the army.

At the heart of Darius's army was a group of highly trained soldiers called the Ten Thousand Immortals. Hand picked for their skills and dedication, these soldiers often acted as a bodyguard for the emperor. In battle, they were supported by cavalry soldiers mounted on horses or camels and by chariots. The Persian chariots sometimes carried archers, who pelted their foes with arrows from a distance. With this army, Darius won new lands in the east and tried—but failed—to conquer Greece.

52 CHAPTER 2

Differentiating Instruction

Below Level

Special Education Students

Materials: drawing paper, colored pencils or markers

1. Have students work in mixed-ability pairs to review the information about Darius's army and the methods it used in battle. Review the information as a group so that all students understand the text.

2. Have students create a battle scene showing the Persian army going into battle. Student drawings should show cavalry and archers, horses, camels, and chariots, as well as armed foot soldiers.

3. Have volunteers share their drawings with the class. Post them for students to see.
   Visual-Spatial

   Alternative Assessment Handbook, Rubric 13: Artwork

Darius also made changes to the Persian government. For example, he surrounded the kingship with ceremony and ritual. As king, Darius was all powerful, and he wanted to demonstrate that power to everyone. Calling himself the Great King and the King of Kings, Darius surrounded himself with symbols of power. He wore embroidered robes and jewelry decorated with gold and gems. Anyone who came into his presence had to bow low to the ground, never looking directly at the king.

Powerful as Darius was, he could not personally control everything that happened in the empire. Persia was simply too large. To help him rule, Darius chose governors called **satraps** (SAY-traps). Each satrap governed a region, or satrapy, in the emperor's name.

Although satraps had considerable local authority, they had to obey the wishes of the king. To ensure that the satraps remained loyal, Darius sent officials called the king's eyes and king's ears on inspection tours. Satraps who received unfavorable reports from these inspectors were punished or replaced.

Darius's reforms also strengthened the Persian economy. Under his rule, the first coins ever minted in Persia were issued. He also encouraged trade by building roads throughout the Persian Empire. As a result of this increased trade, the empire grew richer.

Persia in Decline Most historians consider Darius's reign the high point of Persian culture. The emperors who followed never achieved the level of power and prestige he enjoyed.

Emperor **Xerxes** (ZUHRK-seez), the son of Darius I, tried to expand upon his father's success. Like Darius, he invaded Greece, hoping to succeed where his father had failed. His attempt failed, however, and Xerxes returned to Persia in defeat.

Xerxes was the last strong ruler of ancient Persia. Later emperors were mostly weak and could not maintain order. Rebellions were common, and trade slowed. Greatly weakened, the Persian Empire nonetheless survived for about 150 years after the death of Darius I. In the 330s BC, however, a Greek king named Alexander the Great conquered Persia in the course of building an empire of his own.

READING CHECK **Analyze** How did Persia grow and change under Cyrus and Darius?

FACES OF HISTORY

ZOROASTER
c. 628–c. 551 BC

Although Zoroaster founded a religion that attracted millions of followers, historians do not know much for certain about his life.

They are not even sure when Zoroaster, also known as Zarathushtra, lived. Ancient writings suggest that he was born in a rural community in what is now Iran and that he grew up to become a priest. The same sources say that he began to roam the world in search of wisdom in his early 20s. At age 30, Zoroaster received a vision from the god Ahura Mazda. In this vision, the god revealed teachings that Zoroaster was to share with other people. Zoroaster later recorded those teachings in writings that became the heart of the *Avesta*.

Spreading his new religion brought Zoroaster into conflict with many people. He faced opposition both from townspeople, who followed an older polytheistic religion, and from nomads, whose way of life Zoroaster distrusted. Despite the opposition from these groups, his teachings spread throughout the Persian Empire.

Draw Conclusions Why might historians know relatively little about the life of Zoroaster?

Zoroastrianism

During the reigns of Cyrus and Darius, a new religion took hold in parts of Persia. It was called Zoroastrianism and was based on the teachings of a man named **Zoroaster**.

Teachings Zoroaster taught that the world had been created by a god named Ahura Mazda. To Zoroaster, the god was the source of everything good, true, and pure in the world. He was, therefore, the only god that people should worship.

Opposing Ahura Mazda, however, was an evil spirit named Ahriman. The forces of Ahura Mazda were locked in an eternal struggle against the forces of Ahriman. Zoroastrianism was one of the first religions to teach **dualism**, the belief that the world is controlled by two opposing forces, good and evil.

Zoroaster believed that people had free will and could act as they chose. He encouraged people to join the forces of Ahura Mazda and to fight evil by telling the truth and avoiding bad deeds. Zoroaster's teachings on how people should best serve the god were eventually compiled and recorded in the *Avesta*, the sacred text of Zoroastrianism.

Reading Focus

❷ What were the main teachings of Zoroastrianism? *monotheism; dualism (struggle between good and evil); afterlife*

Zoroastrianism

Identify Who founded Zoroastrianism, and when did this person live? *Zoroaster (Zarathushtra); 628–551 BC*

Analyze What was unique about this new religion? *belief that world is controlled by good and evil*

Draw Conclusions Why did Zoroastrianism almost disappear? *The Persian Empire fell to the Greeks, who convinced Persians to convert to their religion.*

Info to Know

Weights and Measures Before weights and measures were standardized, different methods were used across the Persian Empire. This made trade difficult. To determine volume, Darius established the king's measure, which was similar to the modern bushel. The unit of length the royal cubit, which measured 18 inches; and the standard for weight was the karsha, about one-fifth of a pound.

Faces of History

Zoroaster

Comparing Religions Have students make a Venn diagram showing the differences between Zoroastrianism and Judaism. *both—monotheistic; Judaism—Torah, obedience to the Ten Commandments and Jewish law; Zoroastrianism—dualism, free will*

Answers

Faces of History *not much written; had little archaeological evidence; accounts of his life are cryptic or conflicting*

Reading Check *expanded rapidly under Cyrus; Darius also expanded the empire, organized empire into satraps, minted coins, built roads*

Skills Focus: Comparing and Contrasting

Below Level

Standard English Mastery

Reading Skill
The Persians in Greece

1. Review the information in the section about Persian attempts to invade and conquer Greece. Remind students that Cyrus captured several Greek cities in Ionia; however, the Persians were never successful in their Greek conquests.

2. Have students write two newspaper headlines and brief articles. One should be from the viewpoint of the Greeks who conquered the Persians. The other should reflect the viewpoint of the unsuccessful Persians.

Remind students to use standard English and to check grammar and spelling when they have finished writing their articles.

3. Have students share their newspaper articles and headlines with the class. As a class, discuss any corrections to the articles.

LS Verbal-Linguistic

Alternative Assessment Handbook, Rubric 23: Newspapers

Direct Teach

Reading Focus

③ What were the most significant Persian achievements? *roads, art objects, Persepolis*

Persian Achievements

Describe How did leaders of the Persian Empire encourage peace? *tolerance, blending of diverse customs*

Rank In your opinion, what was the most important achievement of the Persian Empire? *possible answers— Royal Road; minting coins; art and architecture*

Linking to Today
Roads and Armies

Eisenhower and Highways Long before he became president, Dwight Eisenhower understood the importance of good roads. In 1919, he participated in the U.S. Army's first transcontinental motor convoy from Washington, D.C., to San Francisco. The convoy experienced an ongoing series of mechanical difficulties. Vehicles got stuck in mud or sand, and trucks crashed through wooden bridges. During World War II, Eisenhower recognized the advantages of the German autobahn network. In 1954, Eisenhower signed the Federal-Aid Highway Act, a first step toward improving roads; it was followed by another major highway act in 1956.

Answers

Linking to Today *communication, transportation, national defense*

Reading Check *that the world is controlled by dueling forces of good and evil; those who live good lives will be rewarded; the wicked will be punished*

54

NEW YORK
CC Unit 1-B1d
Social structures and urbanization in Mesopotamia

The *Avesta* says that people who live good lives in the service of Ahura Mazda will be rewarded after death. They will enter a heaven filled with pleasures. Those who are wicked will be punished for their sins. However, the *Avesta* continues, at the end of time Ahura Mazda will defeat Ahriman and drive all evil from the world. When that happens, the wicked will be purified, and all souls will be restored to life to live happily together.

Spread By the time Darius I took the throne, Zoroastrianism had spread through much of the Persian Empire. The emperor himself worshipped Ahura Mazda, as did many of the emperors who followed him. Some emperors discouraged the practice of other religions.

When the Persian Empire fell to the Greeks, Zoroastrianism almost disappeared. The Greeks built temples to their gods and convinced many Persians to convert. The teachings of Zoroaster never completely disappeared, though, and gradually they began to spread again, both in Persia and to other parts of the world.

THE IMPACT TODAY

More than 2.6 million people practice Zoroastrianism today, mostly in Asia.

READING CHECK **Find the Main Idea** What does Zoroastrianism teach about good and evil?

Persian Achievements

The Persian Empire was huge, stretching across most of Asia. Dozens of peoples with their own customs and traditions lived within that vast area. When they became part of the empire, their diverse customs gradually blended into a single Persian culture. Leaders like Cyrus and Darius encouraged this blending, because they knew the importance of cultural unity.

One advantage of this shared culture was peace. For most of its early history, the Persian Empire was relatively peaceful. There were no major conflicts between peoples. Instead, they worked together to improve their empire. Together, the peoples of Persia made some amazing cultural achievements.

Communication Good communication was essential to ruling the Persian Empire. Rulers in the capital needed to know what was happening elsewhere in the empire in order to make decisions.

The heart of the Persian communication network was its high quality roads, which linked every part of the empire. The longest of these roads was the Royal Road, the world's first long highway. It stretched more than 1,500

Linking TO Today

Roads and Armies

When Darius the Great ordered the building of the Persian Royal Road, he was not simply creating an easy path for travelers to follow. He was thinking about the defense of the empire.

The Royal Road was a key factor in preventing and defeating attacks. Messengers on horseback could cross the empire swiftly to warn the emperor of imminent attacks. The road also allowed the Persian army to move quickly to any trouble spots in the empire.

Like Darius, U.S. president Dwight Eisenhower knew the importance of roads in national defense. In 1956 he convinced Congress to pass the Federal-Aid Highway Act, which created the interstate highway system. Like the ancient Persian Royal Road, interstate highways were planned as a crucial part of our national defense.

With more than 46,000 miles of roads in all 50 states, the interstate highway system allows the armed services to move troops quickly into any part of the country. If necessary, large numbers of forces could be moved completely across the country in only a few days.

In addition, the interstate highway system can be used to protect people in case of attack or natural disaster. Interstate highways provide routes for people to evacuate major cities.

Summarize What military advantages do roads provide to a country?

▲ Top: The foundation of the Persian Royal Road
Bottom: A modern highway interchange

54 CHAPTER 2

Skills Focus: Identifying Frame of Reference **Below Level**

Reading Like a Historian Skill
The Royal Road **Research Required**

1. Remind students that the Royal Road of the Persian Empire was over 1,500 miles long. Have students name places that are about 1,500 miles away from their homes. Have them name different ways to get to that place and then estimate how long it would take to travel the 1,500 miles.

2. Ask students to consider how they would get a message to this location and how long it would take.

3. Guide students in a discussion comparing the systems of communication and transportation used in the Persian Empire with modern-day systems. Have students write a brief essay describing the importance of modern transportation systems and communication technology. **LS Verbal-Linguistic, Interpersonal**

Alternative Assessment Handbook, Rubrics 11: Discussions; and 42: Writing to Inform miles and linked the major cities of Susa and Sardis. Smaller roads branched off the Royal Road to connect other key cities.

Following these roads, messengers on horseback could travel across the entire Persian Empire in a matter of days. To deliver urgent messages, the messengers worked in shifts. Like runners in a relay race, each one would travel only a short distance before passing the message to a partner with a fresh horse. After seeing this system in action, one Greek historian recorded his amazement:

HISTORY'S VOICES

❝Nothing mortal travels so fast as these Persian messengers . . . these men will not be hindered from accomplishing at their best speed the distance which they have to go, either by snow, or rain, or heat, or by the darkness of night.❞

—Herodotus, *History of the Persian Wars*, Book VIII

Art and Architecture The Persians were also widely admired for their art. Many of the objects their artists created were used in the royal court. For example, they crafted delicate drinking vessels out of gold set with precious gems. Many of these golden objects are shaped like animals, such as lions and bulls. Animals were a common subject in Persian art.

Animals were also common decorations in Persian architecture. The walls of the great palace in the capital city of Susa, for example, sported lions, bulls, and giraffes made of painted brick. Lions and bulls also appeared on the gates and columns of Persepolis, another of the empire's capitals.

Many archaeologists consider Persepolis the greatest example of Persian architecture. Designed as a ceremonial city by Darius I, the entire city of Persepolis was a monument to Persia's glory. At the center of the city was a high-ceilinged audience hall unlike anything else in the Ancient Near East. Larger than any other structure in the city, the hall was highly decorated. The columns that supported the ceiling were brightly painted and topped with stone figures. Carved soldiers and royal officials lined the walls, all bearing gifts for the mighty emperor in whose hall they stood.

READING CHECK Analyze How did Persian roads make communication faster and easier?

Persepolis
Built by Darius as a ceremonial capital, Persepolis was a grand city filled with art and sculpture.

SECTION 4 ASSESSMENT

go.hrw.com
Online Quiz
Keyword: SHL ANE HP

Reviewing Ideas, Terms, and People

1. **a. Identify** For what is Cyrus the Great best known?
   b. Identify Cause and Effect Why did Darius I appoint satraps to help rule his empire?
   c. Elaborate Why do you think the Persian Empire never again regained the heights it had reached under Darius I?
2. **a. Define** What is dualism? How is Zoroastrianism an example of a dualistic religion?
   b. Explain How did Zoroaster say people should act? Why did he think they should act this way?
3. **a. Describe** What were two features that made Persepolis an impressive city?
   b. Analyze Why did Darius I have the Royal Road built?
   c. Elaborate What might the Greek historian's amazement about the Persian messenger system tell you about communication in Greece?

Critical Thinking

4. **Summarize** Draw a chart like the one below. In each column, list the political or religious achievements of each person named.

Cyrus	Darius	Zoroaster

FOCUS ON WRITING

5. **Exposition** Write a paragraph explaining the governmental changes Darius I made in the Persian Empire. Be sure to include details of what he changed about the government and why he felt those changes were necessary.

THE ANCIENT NEAR EAST **55**

Section 4 Assessment Answers

1. **a.** conquering the Medes, expanding the Persian Empire
   b. empire was too big to be controlled by one person
   c. possible answers—weak emperors; empire too large to control
2. **a.** belief that the world is controlled by two opposing forces, good and evil; Ahura Mazda: source of good; Ahriman: evil spirit
   b. People should live good lives so that they will enter heaven.

3. **a.** large audience hall; highly decorated walls and columns
   b. for ease of communication within the empire
   c. possible answer—Communication was slow in Greece.
4. Cyrus—conquered the Medes, expanded Persian Empire; Darius—created permanent army; built system of roads, created satraps; Zoroaster—spread new religion
5. Paragraphs should focus on the size of the empire, establishment of provincial governors, satraps, and the building of roads.

Answers

Reading Check *roads linked cities; messengers could travel across empire in a few days*

55

Building Empires

besiege surround and attack

relief sculpture with raised details or features

Activity **Sargon's Empire** Have students either write a poem honoring the accomplishments of Sargon, following the style of the tablet excerpt about Sargon; or, have students create a drawing showing the details of Sargon's life as described in Document 1.

Info to Know

Sargon's Legend Sargon of Akkad was a respected military leader and ruler. One ancient legend says that Sargon's mother gave birth to him in secret, and then put him in a basket and sent him floating down the river. A man found him while drawing water from the river and raised Sargon as his son. The legend says Ishtar—the goddess of love, procreation, and war—blessed him and made him king.

Assyrian Military Images Assyrians, like the Sumerians, built using brick, but often lined gateways and interior walls with limestone. They decorated these long panels with reliefs that illustrated the conquests of the royal army. The reliefs show Assyrian forces on the march, always destroying enemy forces and taking prisoners. These detailed images depict a clear picture of the victorious Assyrian army.

MISCONCEPTION ///ALERT\\\

Although the Code of Hammurabi is often thought of as the first legal code, it was just one of many sets of laws in the Ancient Near East. Among other earlier examples, legal code from around 2050 BC has been found in Ur. Many of the law codes in the Ancient Near East, including the Code of Hammurabi, come from similar cultures and geographical areas, and have passages that are similar to one another.

Building Empires

Historical Context The Fertile Crescent was the home of the world's first empires. Over centuries, dozens of peoples invaded and built empires of their own.

Task Study the selections and answer the questions that follow. After you have studied all the documents, you will be asked to write an essay explaining how rulers in the Fertile Crescent built and kept order in their empires. You will need to use evidence from these selections and from Chapter 2 to support your position.

NEW YORK STANDARDS

PI 2.3 Students analyze evidence critically and demonstrate an understanding of how circumstances of time and place influence perspective.

DOCUMENT 1

Sargon's Empire

Archaeologists have found fragments of ancient documents that detail the life of Sargon, the Akkadian emperor. Though none of the fragments are complete, what we have found describes the building of Sargon's empire from the emperor's own point of view.

> Sargon, the mighty king, king of Akkad am I,
> My mother was lowly; my father I did not know;
> The brother of my father dwelt in the mountain.
> My city is Azupiranu, which is situated on the bank of the Purattu [Euphrates] . . .
> And for . . . years I ruled the kingdom.
> The black-headed peoples [Sumerians] I ruled, I governed;
> Mighty mountains with axes of bronze I destroyed.
> I ascended the upper mountains;
> I burst through the lower mountains.
> The country of the sea I besieged three times;
> Dilmun I captured.
> Unto the great Dur-ilu I went up . . .
> Whatsoever king shall be exalted after me . . .
> Let him rule, let him govern the black-headed peoples;
> Mighty mountains with axes of bronze let him destroy;
> Let him ascend the upper mountains,
> Let him break through the lower mountains;
> The country of the sea let him besiege three times;
> Dilmun let him capture;
> To the great Dur-ilu let him go up.

DOCUMENT 2

An Assyrian Conquest

This stone relief carving from Mesopotamia shows Assyrian soldiers attacking an enemy city. The Assyrians are using tall ladders to try to reach the top of the city walls, where defenders await with swords and bows.

Skills Focus: Analyzing Primary Sources

Below Level

Reading Like a Historian Skill
Understanding Ancient Documents

Standard English Mastery

1. Guide students in a discussion of the work by archaeologists and other scholars needed to decipher written texts, such as the one about Sargon or Hammurabi's Code. Remind students that when these documents were written, very few people could read or write.

2. Have students note the message that is conveyed in Documents 1 and 2. Have them write a brief essay in class explaining why military strength would be portrayed both in written and in pictorial form. Students should explain what these artifacts convey about the importance of military conquests.

3. Have volunteers share their essays with the class. As a class, review student essays and discuss any necessary corrections. **LS Verbal-Linguistic**

   Alternative Assessment Handbook, Rubrics 11, Discussions; and 15: Journals

DOCUMENT 3

Hammurabi's Authority

Known as a lawmaker, Hammurabi was one of the most powerful emperors of the ancient world. In this passage, taken from the same inscription as his laws, he explains that he was chosen to rule by the gods Anu, Bel, and Ea.

When Anu the Sublime, King of the Anunaki, and Bel, the lord of Heaven and earth, who decreed the fate of the land, assigned to Marduk, the over-ruling son of Ea, God of righteousness, dominion over earthly man, and made him great among the Igigi, they called Babylon by his illustrious name, made it great on earth, and founded an everlasting kingdom in it, whose foundations are laid so solidly as those of heaven and earth; then Anu and Bel called by name me, Hammurabi, the exalted prince, who feared God, to bring about the rule of righteousness in the land, to destroy the wicked and the evil-doers; so that the strong should not harm the weak; so that I should rule over the black-headed people like Shamash, and enlighten the land, to further the well-being of mankind.

DOCUMENT 4

A Modern Historian's View

The question of how and why ancient rulers gained their power is of great interest to modern historians. In this excerpt from *The Ancient Near East*, historian William Dunstan explains the power of the empire-building rulers of Assyria.

Assyria was essentially a military state depending on the ruthless efficiency of the army for exercising dominance. The overwhelming power of imperial Assyria was embodied in the king, regarded as the earthly representative and instrument of the supreme deity Assur. Almost all of the Assyrian kings were forceful figures who spent the campaign season in the field and much of the rest of the year hunting. The king was also a priest and as such was burdened by numerous time-consuming and complicated magico-religious duties. He presided over the chief religious celebrations of Assyria and Babylonia, most notably the New Year Festival, and took part in numerous rituals. The king consulted oracles on all matters of importance.

Skills FOCUS READING LIKE A HISTORIAN

DOCUMENT 1
a. Describe How does Sargon say he created his empire?
b. Draw Conclusions Who does Sargon suggest is worthy to take over his empire? What does this suggest about his opinion of kingship?

DOCUMENT 2
a. Identify Based on this carving, how did the Assyrians form their empire?
b. Compare Do you think the Assyrians would agree with Sargon's view of empire building? Why or why not?

DOCUMENT 3
a. Explain Why does Hammurabi say the gods gave him power?
b. Elaborate How do you think Hammurabi would have justified ruling a vast empire? Explain your answer.

DOCUMENT 4
a. Recall What does Dunstan say were the main duties of the Assyrian kings?
b. Compare Having read Document 4, look back at Document 2 again. Based on Dunstan's writing, what do you think led the Assyrians to conquer cities?

DOCUMENT-BASED ESSAY QUESTION

Over the centuries, dozens of empires ruled the Near East. Why did people think they had the right to rule over others? Using the documents above and information from the chapter, form a thesis that might explain why rulers felt this way. Then write a short essay to support your position.

See **Skills Handbook**, pp. H25–H26, H30

Info to Know

Hammurabi's Code Hammurabi's Code is inscribed on a block of black stone 7 feet, 5 inches high. The laws were considered of divine origin, which is perhaps why the relief at the top of the stele shows the king receiving the code from the sun-god, who is usually associated with justice. The inscribed stone was discovered by a group of French archaeologists during the winter of 1901-1902 in Iran. It is currently in the Louvre Museum in Paris.

Kassite Government Kassite kings ruled Babylonia for about 570 years, but they left very few written records about their history, and as a result little is know about their social structure or their culture. Their kingdom was organized into a series of provinces administered by governors, perhaps in a feudal system. The Kassites exported horses in exchange for raw materials. They established trade and had contacts with other groups, including the Hittites, the Egyptians, and the Assyrians.

Answers

Reading Like a Historian
Document 1. a. *by conquering lands using bronze weapons;* **b.** *someone willing to travel through the mountains and fight; kings should be strong military leaders;* **Document 2.** **a.** *through war;* **b.** *possible answer—Yes, it honors soldiers and war.* **Document 3.** **a.** *to bring justice to the land, destroy evil, protect the weak, further the well-being of mankind;* **b.** *He was chosen by the gods.* **Document 4.** **a.** *worked in fields, hunted, served as priests, performed religious ceremonies;* **b.** *probably rebelled against king who had too much power;* **Essay** *Student essays should include the ideas that rulers were chosen by the gods, power came from the gods, and that the gods supported those whose actions they favored.*

Differentiating Instruction
Below Level

Learners Having Difficulty

1. Have students reread Documents 3 and 4, and then write a short summary of each. Students may need help with Document 3.

2. Guide students in a discussion of the two documents. Focus the discussion on the purpose of the documents and how and when they were created.

3. Have students list Hammurabi and Kassites at the top of a piece of paper. Under each category, have students list specific differences in the reasons and ways that Hammurabi and the Kassites ruled their empires.

4. Have volunteers read their lists aloud and have students correct their own work.
LS **Verbal-Linguistic**

Alternative Assessment Handbook, Rubrics 9: Comparing and Contrasting; and 11: Discussions

Answers

Visual Summary

Review and Inquiry Have students create their own unique graphic organizers with the information shown in the Quick Facts: Peoples of the Fertile Crescent. Have students share their organizers with the class. Students should retain their organizers as a study tool.

Quick Facts Transparency: Visual Study Guide: The Ancient Near East

Review Key Terms and People

1. empire
2. Judaism
3. Cyrus the Great
4. cuneiform
5. Nebuchadnezzar II
6. Moses
7. city-state

Comprehension and Critical Thinking

8. **a.** the need to organize people into working groups
   b. Sumerians believed the gods controlled natural forces and the harvests.
   c. possible answers—military achievements, because he brought all of Mesopotamia into the Babylonian Empire; cultural achievements, because of his written code of laws

9. **a.** trade, development of the alphabet
   b. iron weapons instead of bronze; horse-drawn chariots
   c. possible answers—helped: people were intimidated and less likely to rebel; hindered: made people resent their rule and encouraged rebellion

10. **a.** belief in one God, obedience to the Ten Commandments and Jewish law, justice and righteousness
    b. According to the Torah, God told Abraham to leave Mesopotamia, and Abraham traveled to Canaan. Later following the Exodus, the Hebrews returned to Canaan.
    c. Hebrews believed that the events of the Exodus meant that God loved them and was watching over them.

VISUAL STUDY GUIDE

Civilization Develops in the Fertile Crescent

Flat land and river floods allow farming.

↓

Complex society with government and religion develops in Sumer.

↓

Military empires conquer and rule parts of the Fertile Crescent.

↓

Societies develop new laws, patterns of trade, and religions.

Main Teachings of Judaism

- Monotheism—the belief in only one God
- Justice and Righteousness—treating others well and always doing what is right
- Ethics—living according to a set standard of behavior
- Obedience—following God's laws as set forth in the Torah

Peoples of the Fertile Crescent

Sumerians
- Created world's first civilization
- Invented cuneiform and the wheel

Akkadians
- Built the world's first empire

Babylonians
- Built the city of Babylon
- Issued Hammurabi's Code

Hittites
- Made iron ornaments

Assyrians
- Formed a military society

Chaldeans
- Rebuilt Babylon

Phoenicians
- Traded across the Mediterranean
- Developed an alphabet

Hebrews
- Practiced Judaism
- Established the Kingdom of Israel

Persians
- Formed a huge empire
- Built roads

Review Key Terms and People

Complete each sentence by filling in the blank with the correct term or person.

1. By conquering and ruling many peoples, Sargon created the world's first _____.
2. The Hebrews practiced a religion called _____.
3. A ruler named _____ founded the Persian Empire.
4. The Sumerians developed a wedge-shaped system of writing called _____.
5. The greatest Chaldean ruler was _____, who built the famous Hanging Gardens.
6. According to the Hebrew Bible, _____ led the Hebrews out of slavery in Egypt.
7. A _____ is a political unit that includes a city and all the land around it.

58 CHAPTER 2

---

11. **a.** founder of Zoroastrianism
    b. with tolerance; in order to gain respect and keep peace throughout the empire
    c. Darius won new lands, strengthened the economy, built roads, developed a permanent army, and used local governors.

Reading Skills

12. the Hittites
13. capturing and looting Babylon
14. possible answers—add land to the empire, gain riches

Analyzing Primary Sources

15. bows and arrows, chariots
16. possible answer—The Assyrians had great military strength and battled with other groups.

Using the Internet

17. Go to the HRW Web site and enter the keyword shown to access a rubric for this activity.

KEYWORD: SHL ANE

History's Impact video program
Review the video to answer the closing question:
What impact has Judaism had on other cultures and religions?

Comprehension and Critical Thinking

SECTION 1 *(pp. 33–37)*

8. a. Identify What led to the creation of government in Sumer?

b. Analyze Why was religion so influential in Sumerian city-states?

c. Evaluate Do you think Hammurabi should be remembered for his military achievements or his cultural achievements? Why?

SECTION 2 *(pp. 39–44)*

9. a. Recall For what are the Phoenicians best known?

b. Explain Why were the Hittites able to defeat the Babylonians?

c. Make Judgments Did the Assyrians' cruelty help them or hinder them in ruling their empire? Explain your answer.

SECTION 3 *(pp. 45–49)*

10. a. Identify What are the main teachings of Judaism?

b. Sequence How did the Hebrew people come to live in Canaan?

c. Develop Why is the Exodus so significant in Hebrew history?

SECTION 4 *(pp. 50–55)*

11. a. Identify Who was Zoroaster?

b. Make Generalizations How did Cyrus the Great treat people he conquered? Why?

c. Evaluate Why is the reign of Darius I considered the high point of Persian culture?

Reading Skills

Questioning *Re-read the Inside Story feature that begins Section 2 of this chapter. As you read, ask yourself who the story is about, what they are doing, and why. After you have read the passage and questioned yourself, answer the questions below in your notebook.*

12. Who is the Inside Story feature about?

13. What are they doing?

14. Why are they doing that? What do they hope to gain or accomplish?

Analyzing Primary Sources

Reading Like a Historian *The bronze image below shows Assyrians attacking a city.*

Detail from bronze gate at palace of King Shalmaneser II, 800s BC

15. Identify What kinds of weapons are the Assyrians using?

16. Draw Conclusions What does this scene suggest about Assyrian culture?

Using the Internet

go.hrw.com
Practice Online
Keyword: SHL ANE

17. The ancient Near East was shaped by the actions of powerful leaders. Rulers like Sargon, Hammurabi, Nebuchadnezzar, and Cyrus the Great shaped history through their actions and ideas. Enter the activity keyword and choose one ancient ruler to learn more about. Then write a short newspaper article that describes your chosen subject's life and achievements.

WRITING FOR THE SAT ✎

Think about the following issue.

For centuries, people fought for control of the Fertile Crescent. From the earliest times of the Akkadians and the Babylonians through the Persians and the Greeks, rulers have fought and died to control this territory.

18. Assignment: Why were people so eager to live in and rule the Fertile Crescent? What made this area so appealing? Write a short essay in which you develop your opinion on this issue. Support your point of view with reasoning and examples from your reading and studies.

THE ANCIENT NEAR EAST **59**

Writing for the SAT

18. Student essays should be supported with information from the text and include details such as the geography of the Fertile Crescent, fertile soil for crops, and the accessibility of trade routes.

A rubric for the activity is provided in **CRF**: Writing for the SAT.

HOLT

History's Impact

▶ **Video Program**
Refer to the Video Program Teacher's Guide for a discussion of the closing question.

Review and Assessment Resources

Review and Reinforce

CRF: Chapter Review

Quick Facts Transparency: Visual Study Guide: The Ancient Near East

Spanish Chapter Summaries Audio CD Program

OSP **Holt PuzzlePro:** Quiz Show for ExamView

Quiz Game CD-ROM

Assess

PASS: Chapter Test, Forms A and B

Alternative Assessment Handbook

OSP **ExamView Test Generator,** Chapter Test

Differentiated Instruction Modified Worksheets and Tests CD-ROM: Chapter Test

HOAP **Holt Online Assessment Program** (in the Premier Online Edition)

Reteach/Intervene

Interactive Reader and Study Guide

Differentiated Instruction Teacher Management System: Lesson Plans for Differentiated Instruction

Differentiated Instruction Modified Worksheets and Tests CD-ROM: Chapter Test

Interactive Skills Tutor CD-ROM

go.hrw.com
Online Resources
KEYWORD: SHL TEACHER

Chapter 3 Planning Guide

Nile Civilizations

Chapter Overview	Reproducible Resources	Technology Resources
CHAPTER 3 pp. 60–88 **Overview:** In this chapter, students will learn about the development, growth, and achievements of civilizations along the Nile—the kingdom of Egypt and the Nubian kingdoms. KI 1, 4; PI 1.1, 1.4, 4.2, 4.4 See pp. T32–T55 for a detailed correlation to the New York State Core Curriculum for Global History and Geography and the New York Learning Standards.	**Differentiated Instruction Teacher Management System:*** • Instructional Benchmarking Guides • Lesson Plans for Differentiated Instruction **Interactive Reader and Study Guide:** Chapter Summary* **Chapter Resource File*** • Writing for the SAT • Social Studies Skill • Chapter Review **World History Outline Maps**	OSP **New York One-Stop Planner CD-ROM:** Calendar Planner **Live Ink© Online Reading Help** **Student Edition on Audio CD Program** **Differentiated Instruction Modified Worksheets and Tests CD-ROM** **Interactive Skills Tutor CD-ROM** **World History Primary Source Library CD-ROM** **Power Presentations with Video CD-ROM** **History's Impact: World History Video Program (VHS/DVD):** Nile Civilizations
Section 1: **The Kingdom of Egypt** **The Main Idea:** Egypt was one of the most stable and long-lasting civilizations of the ancient world. PI 1.1, 4.2	**Differentiated Instruction Teacher Management System:** Section 1 Lesson Plan* **Interactive Reader and Study Guide:** Section 1 Summary* **Chapter Resource File*** • Vocabulary Builder: Section 1 • History and Geography: Minerals in the Old Kingdom • Biography: Khufu	**Regents Review Transparency:** Section 1* **Map Transparency:** The Nile Valley* **Map Transparency:** New Kingdom Egypt* **Quick Facts Transparency:** Egypt in Nubia* **Internet Activity:** Explore the Pyramids
Section 2: **Egyptian Culture** The Main **Idea:** The Egyptians are famous for their religion, their burial practices, and their advances in art, writing, and science. PI 1.1	**Differentiated Instruction Teacher Management System:** Section 2 Lesson Plan* **Interactive Reader and Study Guide:** Section 2 Summary* **Chapter Resource File*** • Vocabulary Builder: Section 2 • Biography: Howard Carter • Literature: Book of the Dead	**Regents Review Transparency:** Section 2* **Internet Activity:** Ancient Art
Section 3: **The Nubian Kingdoms** **The Main Idea:** One of ancient Africa's most advanced civilizations, Kush developed along the Nile south of Egypt in a region called Nubia. PI 1.4, 4.4	**Differentiated Instruction Teacher Management System:** Section 3 Lesson Plan* **Interactive Reader and Study Guide:** Section 3 Summary* **Chapter Resource File*** • Vocabulary Builder: Section 3 • Primary Source: The Nubian Kingdom of Kush • Biography: Queen Shanakdakhete	**Regents Review Transparency:** Section 3* **Map Transparency:** Egypt and Kush* **Quick Facts Transparency:** Egypt in Nubia*

CHAPTER 3 PLANNING GUIDE

go.hrw.com	Print Resource	Transparency
LS Learning Styles	Audio CD	CD-ROM
Video	SE Student Edition	TE Teachers Edition
OSP One-Stop Planner CD-ROM	NY Standards Mastery	
	*also on One-Stop Planner CD-ROM	

HOLT
History's Impact
World History Video Program (VHS/DVD)
Nile Civilizations

Review, Assessment, Intervention

 Global History and Geography Regents Test Prep Workbook

 Quick Facts Transparency: Nile Civilizations*

 Spanish Chapter Summaries Audio CD Program

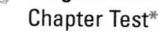 **Progress Assessment Support System (PASS):** Chapter Test*

Differentiated Instruction Modified Worksheets and Tests CD-ROM: Modified Chapter Test

OSP **New York One-Stop Planner CD-ROM:** Exam View Test Generator (English/Spanish)

HOAP Holt Online Assessment Program (HOAP), in the Premier Online Edition

 PASS: Section 1 Quiz*

 Online Quiz: Section 1

 Alternative Assessment Handbook

 PASS: Section 2 Quiz*

 Online Quiz: Section 2

 Alternative Assessment Handbook

 PASS: Section 3 Quiz*

 Online Quiz: Section 3

 Alternative Assessment Handbook

Power Presentation with Video CD-ROM

Power Presentations with Video are visual presentations of each chapter's main ideas. Presentations can be customized by including Quick Facts charts, images and maps from the textbook, and video clips.

Holt Online Learning

go.hrw.com
Teacher Resources
KEYWORD: SHL TEACHER

go.hrw.com
Student Resources
KEYWORD: SHL NIC

- Document-Based Questions
- Interactive Multimedia Activities

- Current Events
- Chapter-Based Internet Activities
- and more!

Holt Premier
Online Student Edition
Complete online support for interactivity, assessment, and reporting
- Interactive Maps and Notebook
- Homework Practice and Research Activities Online

The Big Picture

Peter N. Stearns

Ancient Egypt Egypt's early development and ongoing characteristics, as one of the major river valley civilizations, owed much to its particular geography. Major political institutions emerged, associated with the office of the pharaoh and the important government linkages with religion. Compared to many early civilizations, particularly those in neighboring Mesopotamia, Egypt enjoyed long periods of political stability and freedom from invasion. Egyptian society issued a few intriguing experiments, such as the flirtation with monotheism, which must not however be confused with the more durable patterns.

Egyptian Culture The standard focus on massive monuments is both inevitable and justifiable. But Egyptian beliefs about religion and the afterlife, and the approach toward death, deserve wider attention. Here too, comparisons particularly with Mesopotamia are rewarding. Egyptian religion and culture were more upbeat than those of the Mesopotamian neighbor; conditions for women and children differed as well. It was a Greek traveler, Herodotus, who noted with surprise that Egyptians did not practice infanticide. Egyptian science and mathematics also had some distinctive emphases. A key analytical challenge, besides comparison, involves assessment of legacies: some aspects of the Egyptian achievement, including specific religious beliefs, faded as the civilization declined, but elements of architecture and mathematics had wide influence in the eastern Mediterranean later on.

Other African Kingdoms South of Egypt, in the northeastern corner of sub-Saharan Africa, several important kingdoms developed in sequence, beginning with Kush. These kingdoms had a special relationship with Egypt but developed distinctive characteristics of their own. They influenced later African history particularly through the emergence of Ethiopia.

Recent Scholarship

Lost Discoveries: The Ancient Roots of Modern Science – from the Babylonians to the Maya (2002), by Dick Teresi, picks up, in very readable fashion, an earlier debate between Martin Bernal in *Black Athena: The Afroasiatic Roots of Classical Civilization* (1987) and Mary R. Lefkowitz in *Not Out of Africa: How Afrocentrism Became an Excuse to Teach Myth as History* (1997). The issue is how greatly Egyptian and Mesopotamian cultural achievements, including science, helped shape later civilizations, particularly in Greece. Teresi and Bernal argue that, partly because of anti-African bias, historians have exaggerated Greek originality; that Egyptian achievements carried over far more than we have realized. Lefkowitz, along with other critics of Teresi's book, contends that Greek culture was quite original; Egyptian accomplishments, though considerable, had little active connection to subsequent civilizations. The discussion deals with important issues—from the legacies of the river valley civilizations to the intrusion of more modern political concerns.

Differentiating Instruction

Differentiated Instruction Teacher Management System
- Pacing Guide
- Lesson Plans for Differentiated Instruction

Interactive Reader and Study Guide

Spanish Chapter Summaries Audio CD Program

Student Edition on Audio CD Program

Differentiated Instruction Modified Worksheets and Tests CD-ROM
- Vocabulary Flash Cards
- Modified Vocabulary Builder Activities
- Modified Chapter Review Activity
- Modified Chapter Test

OSP One-Stop Planner CD-ROM
- ExamView Test Generator (English and Spanish)
- PuzzlePro
- Quiz Show for ExamView
- Transparencies and Videos

TE Differentiated Activities in the Teacher's Edition
- Accomplishments of Early Egyptian Society, p. 77
- Tour of Ancient Nubia, p. 83
- Herodotus and Strabo Comparisons, p. 86

Reading Like a Historian
Sam Wineburg

Hollywood History For decades Cecil B. DeMille's *The Ten Commandments* (1956) defined the Hollywood extravaganza. With a cast of 12,000 actors and 15,000 animals, DeMille directed scenes by lofting himself on a giant crane towering high into the desert air. For the millions who watched the movie in theaters, or years later as TV reruns, DeMille indelibly shaped our image of this Biblical showdown: a venal and intransigent Ramses II (the bald but rippling Yul Brynner), worn down from lice, locusts, frogs and the death of his first-born. The strong, silent type Moses (Charlton Heston), now wearing the garb of his Hebrew brethren, but doing so with the panache that hinted at his regal upbringing.

For today's students, Pharaoh is more likely to have the deep baritone of Val Kilmer than the spiky rasp of Yul Brynner. Images of DeMille's *The Ten Commandments* have been replaced by the sleek, animated equivalents from DreamWorks' *The Prince of Egypt* (1998). Many of today's students will still associate the building of the pyramids with a staff-clutching Moses beseeching Pharaoh: "Let my people go!" Indeed, the notion that it was slaves who labored to build these giant structures was corroborated by the "father of history," the Greek Herodotus, who journeyed to the great pyramids in 450 BCE.

Yet, our chapter tells us that DeMille and Herodotus were mistaken—that the pyramids were not built by slaves, but by skilled workers. How could so many generations of storytellers be wrong? How is it, in short, that our conceptions of history get revised?

In this case, the credit goes largely to the efforts of one man, the North Dakota-born Egyptologist, Dr. Mark Lehner, who first ventured to Egypt on a year abroad program and ended up staying for 13.

Excavating the Truth Lehner and his Egyptian associate, the Director General of Giza and Saqqara, Dr. Zahi Hawass, pursued the question of who built the pyramids by excavating workers' settlements and doing scientific studies of what they found. One of the most striking discoveries was the enormous amount of cattle bone they uncovered—not those of aging herd cattle, but of young bulls, just the kind ready to be turned into juicy prime rib. Alongside bones were other traces of workers' meals, such as dried fish, bread, figs, dates, as well as the archaeological signs that these repasts were washed down with volumes of Pharohic ale. In other words, the archaeological evidence pointed to the kinds of feasts provided to skilled workmen, not impoverished slaves.

Lehner and Hawass also uncovered ancient graffiti in places few were supposed to see—like underneath foundations that would have been covered with bricks. These graffiti, the archaeologists believe, were the marks of work teams, ancient equivalents of "Joe was here." They took the form of "Friends of (Pharaoh) Khufu" and "Drunkards of Menkaura." Again, not quite the signs of oppressed slaves.

Lehner and Hawass's research suggests that the pyramids were built by rotating work teams that would work for a few months, and then be relieved by another team—a kind of national service. Lehner likened the system to the traditions of barn raising among the Amish, where an entire community is expected to contribute labor to a communal enterprise. "The pyramids were a national project, and they were sacred. Only Egyptians could work on them; slave labor was not used," noted Hawass. "It was like an army. Families from all over Egypt had to contribute individuals to work on the pyramids in the service of their pharaoh, and the families sent supplies of food and beer and clothing."

Today, the giant pyramids stand majestically in the Valley of Kings, as they have done for ages. But the story we tell about them—and how they came into being—is an ever-moving target.

Chapter Main Ideas

Section 1 Egypt was one of the most stable and long-lasting civilizations of the ancient world.

Section 2 The Egyptians are famous for their religion, their burial practices, and their advances in art, writing, and science.

Section 3 One of ancient Africa's most advanced civilizations, Kush developed along the Nile south of Egypt in a region called Nubia.

New York Standards

Key Idea 1 The study of world history requires an understanding of world cultures and civilizations, including an analysis of important ideas, social and cultural values, beliefs, and traditions. This study also examines the human condition and the connections and interactions of people across time and space and the ways different people view the same event or issue from a variety of perspectives.

Key Idea 4 The skills of historical analysis include the ability to investigate differing and competing interpretations of the theories of history, hypothesize about why interpretations change over time, explain the importance of historical evidence, and understand the concepts of change and continuity over time.

Key to Differentiating Instruction

Below Level

Basic-level activities designed for all students encountering new material

At Level

Intermediate-level activities designed for average students

Above Level

Challenging activities designed for honors and gifted and talented students

Standard English Mastery

Activities designed to improve standard English usage

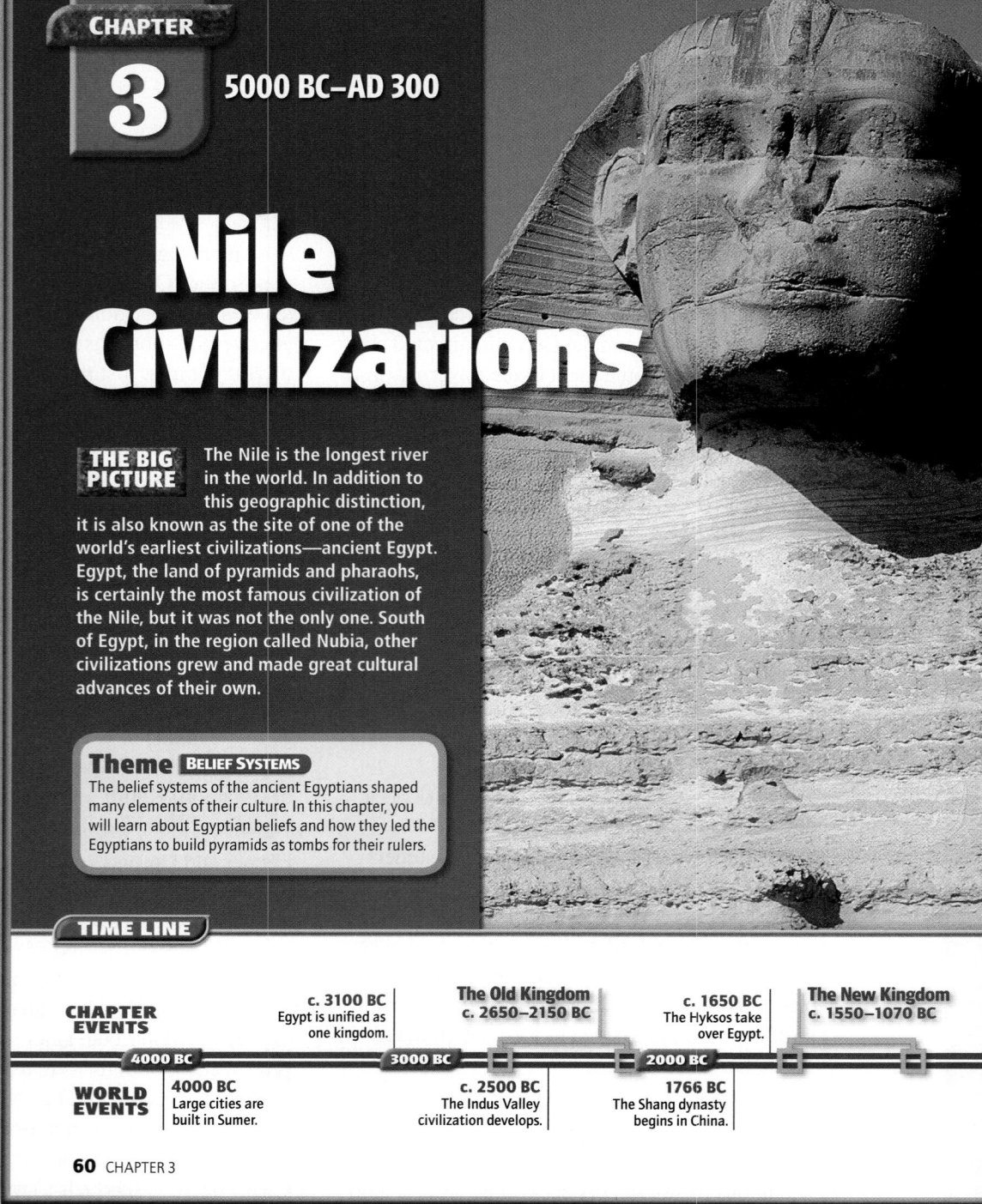

CHAPTER 3 5000 BC–AD 300

Nile Civilizations

THE BIG PICTURE The Nile is the longest river in the world. In addition to this geographic distinction, it is also known as the site of one of the world's earliest civilizations—ancient Egypt. Egypt, the land of pyramids and pharaohs, is certainly the most famous civilization of the Nile, but it was not the only one. South of Egypt, in the region called Nubia, other civilizations grew and made great cultural advances of their own.

Theme BELIEF SYSTEMS
The belief systems of the ancient Egyptians shaped many elements of their culture. In this chapter, you will learn about Egyptian beliefs and how they led the Egyptians to build pyramids as tombs for their rulers.

TIME LINE

CHAPTER EVENTS

c. 3100 BC Egypt is unified as one kingdom.

The Old Kingdom c. 2650–2150 BC

c. 1650 BC The Hyksos take over Egypt.

The New Kingdom c. 1550–1070 BC

4000 BC — 3000 BC — 2000 BC

WORLD EVENTS

4000 BC Large cities are built in Sumer.

c. 2500 BC The Indus Valley civilization develops.

1766 BC The Shang dynasty begins in China.

60 CHAPTER 3

Introduce the Chapter

At Level

Nile Civilizations

1. Organize the class into small groups. Ask each group to brainstorm and make a list of all the facts they can think of about ancient Egypt and Nubia.

2. Have volunteers from each group share their lists with the class. As they do so, make a master list for the class to see.

3. Guide the class in a discussion of the master list. Are there any facts that students disagree about? If so, circle them.

4. Review with students what they learned in the last chapter about the early civilizations in the Near East. How did those other early civilizations affect the civilizations of the Nile, or did they?

5. Tell students that in this chapter they will learn about Nile civilizations—the kingdom of Egypt and the Nubian kingdoms.
   LS Interpersonal

   Alternative Assessment Handbook, Rubrics 11: Discussions; and 14: Group Activity

HOLT
History's Impact
▶ **Video Program: Nile Civilizations**
See the Video Teacher's Guide for strategies for using the video segment.

Reading Like a Historian
Analyzing Visuals The Great Sphinx of Giza may be the most famous sculpture in the world. It has the body of an animal and a human head—the opposite configuration of most representations of Egyptian gods. The sphinx was a type of royal portrait used throughout most of ancient Egyptian history. The Great Sphinx of Giza is a portrait statue of King Khafre, who lived from about 2575–2465 BC.

Reading
like a Historian

The Great Pyramid at Giza, Egypt, was built as a tomb for King Khufu of Egypt. Next to the pyramid stands the Great Sphinx, a huge statue of a mythical creature with the head of a man and the body of a lion. Both the pyramid and the sphinx are among the largest structures built in the ancient world.

Analyzing Visuals Why do you think the Egyptians built structures like the Great Pyramid and the Great Sphinx? What does this say about Egyptian culture?

See **Skills Handbook**, p. H26

c. 280 BC
Meroë becomes the capital of Kush.

1000 BC

c. 600 BC
Nebuchadnezzar II rebuilds Babylon.

27 BC
The Roman Empire begins.

NILE CIVILIZATIONS **61**

go.hrw.com
Online Resources
Chapter Resources:
KEYWORD: SHL NIC
Teacher Resources:
SHL TEACHER

Explore the Time Line

1. How long after Egypt was unified as a single kingdom did the Old Kingdom begin? *about 450 years*

2. How long did the Old Kingdom last? *about 500 years*

3. When did Meroë become the capital of Kush? *about 280 BC*

4. Which civilization developed during the time of the Old Kingdom in Egypt? *the Indus Valley civilization*

Info to Know

Nubian Traders The Nubians, who were controlled by Egypt, acted as middlemen in trade along the Upper Nile. In time, they started asking for a tax on the goods that went through their land. In 1472 BC Queen Hatshepsut of Egypt had five ships carried across the desert to avoid the Nubian-controlled Upper Nile. Eventually the Nubians gained control of the trade routes from the Red Sea to the Nile and established the kingdom of Kush.

Make Inferences Why would Queen Hatshepsut want to avoid the Nubian-controlled Upper Nile? *to avoid paying tax to the Nubians*

Answers

Reading Like a Historian 1. *possible answers—because they were a wealthy civilization, held king in high regard; it was an advanced culture*

61

Geography Starting Points

The Nile Some of the most advanced civilizations of the ancient world grew up along the banks of the Nile. Water from the Nile is available throughout the year, making agriculture possible in a region that might otherwise be barren because of the high temperatures and low rainfall. The principal source of the Nile is Lake Victoria in east central Africa (not shown on this map), and the river flows north toward the Mediterranean Sea. Two branches, the White Nile and the Blue Nile, join at the present-day Sudanese capital of Khartoum. North of Khartoum—downstream—are six cataracts, or waterfalls. Five of these are in what is now Sudan but was known as Nubia in ancient times. The other cataract, which is referred to as the First Cataract, is near Aswan in Egypt. The First Cataract marked the ancient boundary between Egypt and Nubia. Above the First Cataract, the Aswan High Dam now harnesses the waters of the Nile for hydroelectric power and flood control. The Nile Delta begins north of Cairo. This is a triangular-shaped area where the prehistoric Mediterranean Sea has been filled in by silt that has been carried down the Nile. The soil of the Nile Delta is the most fertile in Africa.

- **Map Transparency:** The Nile Valley
- **World History Outline Maps**

Answers

Geography Starting Points
1. *along the Nile and in the Nile Delta;*
2. *possible answers—enabled them to create a distinct civilization; provided protection from invaders*

GEOGRAPHY Starting Points

Interactive
THE NILE VALLEY

A series of cataracts, or stretches of rapids, makes sailing the length of the Nile impossible.

Along the Nile's banks, Egypt is lush and fertile. Beyond the banks is harsh desert.

Legend:
- Fertile area
- Cataract

0   75   150 Miles
0   75   150 Kilometers
Lambert equal-area projection

Map labels: Mediterranean Sea, Dead Sea, Pe, Nile Delta, LOWER EGYPT, Memphis, Lake Moeris, Sinai Peninsula, WESTERN DESERT, Thebes, Nekhen, UPPER EGYPT, Elephantine, First Cataract, EASTERN DESERT, Second Cataract, SAHARA, NUBIA, Third Cataract, Fourth Cataract, Napata, KUSH, Fifth Cataract, Meroë, Sixth Cataract, White Nile River, Blue Nile River, Red Sea, ARABIAN PENINSULA, Tropic of Cancer, 25°N, 20°N, 15°N

Starting Points The Nile, the longest river in the world, flows northward from eastern Africa to the Mediterranean. Over much of its course, the Nile flows through the Sahara, the largest desert in the world and one of the harshest. The civilizations that developed along the Nile depended on the river to irrigate their lands and to make life possible.

1. **Predict** Look at the area labeled as fertile on the map. Based on this information, where do you think civilizations developed?
2. **Predict** Egypt is isolated from other regions by the desert and by cataracts on the Nile. How might this isolation have affected early Egyptian society?

Listen to History

Go online to listen to an explanation of the starting points for this chapter.

go.hrw.com
Keyword: SHL NIC

62 CHAPTER 3

Collaborative Learning

At Level

The Nile Valley

Research Required

1. Organize the class into small groups. Tell students that they are employees of a company that specializes in packaging tours. Their task is to design a brochure about cruises on the Nile, from the Nile Delta to the First Cataract. Have students conduct research to find out what sites tourists will be able to visit along the river, as well as to collect photographs of scenes along the river that they can use to illustrate their brochures.

2. Have each group put together its brochure, writing descriptive material, drawing maps, and using photographs to illustrate them.

3. Ask each group to present a "pitch" for its tour to the rest of the class. **Interpersonal, Visual-Spatial**

Alternative Assessment Handbook, Rubrics 3: Artwork; and 14: Group Activity

SECTION 1
The Kingdom of Egypt

BEFORE YOU READ

MAIN IDEA

Egypt was one of the most stable and long-lasting civilizations of the ancient world.

READING FOCUS

1. How did geography influence Egypt's early history?
2. What achievements were made in the Old Kingdom?
3. What happened during the Middle Kingdom?
4. What was Egypt like during the New Kingdom?

KEY TERMS AND PEOPLE

delta
cataracts
Menes
pharaoh
theocracy
bureaucracy
Hatshepsut
Ramses the Great

NEW YORK

P1 1.1 Students define culture and civilization, explaining how they developed and changed over time.
4.2 Students interpret and analyze documents and artifacts.

THE INSIDE STORY

What was the Nile's gift? Sometime in the 400s BC, a Greek historian named Herodotus traveled to Egypt. Like many people in Greece, he had heard of Egypt but knew very little of life there. What he saw on his journey both impressed and amazed him.

Of all the sights Herodotus witnessed in Egypt, none left more of an impression on him than the Nile itself. For a Greek who was took rain for granted, it was unthinkable that a society could depend on a river for all of its water. He was astounded at stories of the annual floods that brought water to the fields. These floods, he thought, made the work of Egyptian farmers incredibly easy. In contrast, the Egyptians to whom Herodotus spoke listened in disbelief to his descriptions of rain. They did not seem to trust the idea of water that did not come from a river.

Herodotus also could not believe the variety of animals that dwelled in or near the Nile, from fish and birds to crocodiles and hippopotamuses. Without the Nile, Herodotus concluded, Egypt could not exist: "For any one who sees Egypt, without having heard a word about it before, must perceive, if he has only common powers of observation, that the Egypt to which the Greeks go in their ships is an acquired country, the gift of the river." ▄

Geography and Early Egypt

As Herodotus noted, the Nile is the most important physical feature in Egypt. The river, the longest in the world, flows more than 4,000 miles through north Africa. For much of this length, the river flows through the Sahara, the world's largest desert. Without the Nile's waters, no one could live there.

THE GIFT OF THE NILE

▲ The Nile provided Egyptians not only with water for farming but with many types of animals and plants.

NILE CIVILIZATIONS **63**

---

❶ How did geography influence Egypt's early history? *The Nile flooded every year, leaving a band of fertile soil along its banks. This is where Egyptian civilization developed. Egypt was protected from invaders by the surrounding Sahara Desert and the Nile's cataracts to the south.*

Geography and Early Egypt

Recall How do historians organize Egyptian history? *by dynasties, or series of rulers from the same family*

Contrast How did the Nile's floods differ from those of Mesopotamia? *The Nile's floods were predictable, occurring every year at the same time, while the flooding of the Mesopotamian rivers was not predictable.*

Evaluate How might Egypt's natural defenses—the Sahara and the Nile's cataracts—also be viewed as limitations? *possible answer—They kept Egypt from expanding its borders, hindered it from learning about the rest of the world, and limited trade.*

📋 **CRF**: History and Geography: Minerals in the Old Kingdom

Info to Know

The Aswan Dam Completed in 1970, the Aswan High Dam was built to hold back the floodwaters of the Nile River, generate electricity, and to provide year-round irrigation for Egypt's agricultural fields. Since its construction, the dam has increased the amount of land irrigated each year by about 2.24 million acres and Egypt has doubled its agricultural production. On the other hand, the dam has also had serious effects on the environment causing erosion and an increased need for fertilization.

Answers

Reading Check *They lived in a narrow strip of fertile land where they could raise crops. It was surrounded by inhospitable desert, which would not easily support life.*

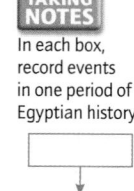

TAKING NOTES

In each box, record events in one period of Egyptian history.

NEW YORK

CC Unit 1-B1a Human and physical geography of Egypt

THE IMPACT TODAY

Since the building of the Aswan High Dam in the 1960s, the cataracts no longer prevent travel on the Nile.

The Geography of Egypt Like the Tigris and Euphrates in Mesopotamia, the Nile flooded every year. Unlike floods on the Mesopotamian rivers, however, the Nile's floods were predictable. These floods occurred every year when spring rains fed the river's sources south of Egypt. The floodwaters that poured over the river's banks covered the surrounding land with a rich black silt. Because of these floods, a narrow band of fertile soil stretched all along the Nile. It was in this band that Egyptian civilization developed.

The richest and most fertile soils in all Egypt were found in the Nile Delta. A **delta** is an area at the mouth of a river, often triangle-shaped, made up of silt deposits. Because the Nile is so long and carries so much silt, its delta is one of the largest in the world.

The dark color of the Nile river silt gave rise to the Egyptians' name for their country—the Black Land. In contrast, they called the surrounding desert the Red Land. Although the desert was mostly unlivable wasteland, its presence was something of a comfort to the Egyptians. The Sahara was so difficult to cross that it discouraged peoples from invading.

The Nile itself also helped prevent invasions. South of Egypt, the Nile flowed through a series of **cataracts**, rocky stretches marked by swift currents and rapids. Because of these dangerous currents and falls, boats could not sail through the Nile's cataracts. As a result, people from the areas south of Egypt could not use the Nile as an easy invasion route.

Two Kingdoms The first farming villages along the Nile appeared as early as 5000 BC. Over time, these villages consolidated into two kingdoms. The people of these kingdoms spoke different dialects, or versions of the same language, and had different customs.

The northern kingdom, Lower Egypt, was located downriver at the lower end of the Nile. It occupied most of the Nile Delta, where the climate was milder than it was in the south. The people of Lower Egypt worshipped a cobra goddess, and as a result that snake was a symbol of their kingdom.

South of Lower Egypt was Upper Egypt, which lay along the river's upper stretches. It stretched from south of the delta to about the first cataract. Upper Egyptians prayed to a vulture goddess, so a vulture was their symbol.

Unification The two kingdoms of Egypt were first unified around 3100 BC. Historians are not sure exactly how the unification came about, but ancient Egyptian legends say that a ruler named **Menes** (MEE-neez) from Upper Egypt conquered the north. Menes is also said to have founded the city of Memphis, the capital of unified Egypt.

As the ruler of both kingdoms, Menes adopted the symbols of both Upper and Lower Egypt, the cobra and the vulture. He also wore a crown that combined the traditional red and white crowns of the two kingdoms. Later Egyptian rulers likewise used both sets of symbols to show their power over all Egypt.

Menes founded Egypt's first dynasty, or series of rulers from the same family. Through its long history, Egypt was ruled by a string of dynasties. Historians use these dynasties as a tool for organizing their studies of Egyptian history. For example, they may refer to rulers of the Seventh dynasty or events that occurred during the Twenty-second dynasty. In total, 31 dynasties held power in Egypt.

READING CHECK **Draw Conclusions** How did geography affect where the early Egyptians lived?

Old Kingdom Pyramids

The famous pyramids of Egypt were built during the Old Kingdom. Mostly located along the lower Nile, the pyramids were built as tombs for kings.

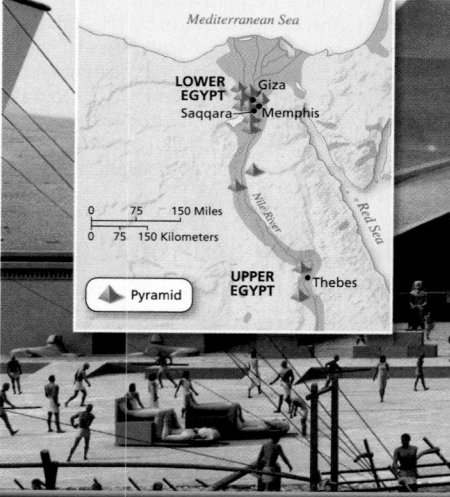

Mediterranean Sea

LOWER EGYPT · Giza
Saqqara · Memphis

0   75   150 Miles
0 75 150 Kilometers

UPPER EGYPT · Thebes

⬆ Pyramid

Nile River   Red Sea

Social Studies Skills
Cradles of Civilization

1. Guide students in a discussion of the geographic features that are necessary for agriculture, and thus for civilization. As students name each feature, write it for the class to see. Then discuss why it is important.

2. Have students review the map of the Nile Valley in the Geography Starting Points feature and identify the geographic features on their lists that were met by the Nile Valley. How did each feature contribute to the success of the Egyptian civilization?

3. Organize the class into small groups. Have each group make a chart listing the geographic features present in your town or region. Under each feature, have group members write a brief paragraph explaining how it has affected the local culture. **LS** Interpersonal

📋 **Alternative Assessment Handbook**, Rubrics 11: Discussions; and 14: Group Activity

The Old Kingdom

The rise of the Third dynasty in about 2650 BC marked the beginning of a long period of stable rule in Egypt. This period, known as the Old Kingdom, lasted about 500 years. Egyptians of the Old Kingdom created many of the institutions for which the civilization is best known.

The Pyramids The most famous symbols of ancient Egypt are the pyramids. Most of these huge structures were built during the Old Kingdom. The largest and most famous of the Old Kingdom pyramids are located near the town of Giza.

The pyramids were built as tombs for Egypt's rulers. Inside or below each pyramid was a hollow chamber in which a dead king was buried. To protect the bodies of their kings and the treasures that were buried with them, the Egyptians sometimes placed deadly traps within a pyramid.

Pyramid design changed greatly over time. The earliest pyramids did not have smooth sides. Instead, their sides looked like a series of steps. The smooth-sided pyramids with which we are familiar were built later.

However they changed, building pyramids took a great deal of planning and skill—and time. In fact, pyramids took so long to construct that kings usually ordered their pyramids begun soon after they took the throne. Workers built the pyramids from the inside out, carefully placing limestone blocks cut from nearby quarries. These blocks had to be dragged overland to the building site on rollers. Historians are not certain how workers hauled the heavy stone blocks up the sides of the pyramid, but some think that workers dragged the blocks up specially built ramps with ropes.

Despite what many people believe, the pyramids were not built by slaves. Most of the workers were peasants who were required to work for the government for one month out of the year. While they worked on a pyramid, the peasants received food and clothing and were sheltered in nearby villages.

Not all of the workers on a pyramid were peasants, though. Professional craftspeople were also hired to work on the tombs. Among them were the architects who actually designed the pyramid and surrounding buildings and the artists hired to decorate the interior of the finished tomb.

Tunnels through the Great Pyramid led to the inner chamber where the king's body was placed.

Rotating groups of laborers, mostly peasants, built the pyramids. Each group worked for one month of the year.

Skills FOCUS INTERPRETING VISUALS

Draw Conclusions Why do you think the Egyptians wanted to build such huge, permanent tombs for their kings?

go.hrw.com
COULD YOU HAVE SURVIVED?
Go online for a closer look at survival and this event.
Keyword: SHL NIC

65

Collaborative Learning

The Pyramids

1. Organize the class into small groups. Have each group conduct research and create an illustrated travel magazine article about the pyramids. The articles should include information on the following: the historical background of the pyramids; how the pyramids were built; what is inside the pyramids; how the pyramids were excavated. In addition to factual information, students should include the following pictures or illustrations of the pyramids and their contents and a map showing the location of the major pyramids.

2. Have volunteers from each group share their articles and then post them for the class to see. **LS Interpersonal, Visual-Spatial**

Alternative Assessment Handbook, Rubrics 14: Group Activity; and 19: Magazines

Reading Focus

2 What achievements were made in the Old Kingdom? *Most of the pyramids were built during that time, and Egypt's government took shape, with the pharaoh at the head and a bureaucracy headed by the vizier.*

The Old Kingdom

Explain Why were the pyramids built? *to serve as tombs for Egypt's rulers*

Contrast How did the first pyramids differ from the ones we are familiar with today? *The sides of the first pyramids looked like a series of steps. The ones we are familiar with today have smooth sides.*

Elaborate Why—other than for the pay—do you think peasants would have wanted to help build pyramids? *possible answer—They probably took pride in building a great monument, and were pleased to work on a structure honoring their rulers.*

Info to Know

Burial Tombs Around the time of the first dynasties, Egyptians began building tombs in which to bury their dead. Called *mastaba* in Arabic, these tombs had flat tops and sloped sides and were made of mud bricks. Within the tomb, and usually below the ground, were a chamber for the body and other chambers for burial goods. Over time, people began to build larger tombs, some with as many as 30 chambers.

Answers

Interpreting Visuals *possible answer—as a symbol of their wealth and power*

The Old Kingdom

Identify Who was the vizier? *the most powerful official of Egypt, who was usually a close relative of the pharaoh*

Make Inferences What gave the pharaohs absolute power? *They owned all the land in the country, they were judges and the leaders of Egypt's army, and they were believed to be gods.*

Predict Since the pharaoh was considered a god and given credit for Egypt's prosperity, how might people have reacted to widespread drought and famine? *possible answer—They might have lost faith in his divinity or realized he was only a human.*

📰 **CRF:** Biography: Khufu

Recent Scholarship

The Oxford History of Ancient Egypt is a sequential study of the Egyptian dynasties of Egypt. The authors also examine its cultural and social developments, including changes in art and architecture. The book traces the development of Egypt from the early Stone Age to the time of the Roman Empire. The book also examines the three "dark ages" of Egyptian history.

The Oxford History of Ancient Egypt edited by Ian Shaw. Oxford University Press, 2000.

TIME LINE

The Rulers of Egypt

◄ **This plaque is thought to show the fight to unify Egypt.**

c. 3100 BC Menes unifies Upper and Lower Egypt.

c. 2680 BC The oldest known pyramid is built at Saqqara for the Old Kingdom pharaoh Djoser.

c. 1900 BC Middle Kingdom pharaohs encourage merchants and sailors to trade with Nubia, Phoenicia, and Greece.

The Pharaohs Egypt's government also took shape during the Old Kingdom. At the head of the government was the king, who eventually became known as the **pharaoh** (FER-oh). The term *pharaoh* literally means "great house." Pharaohs had absolute power in Egypt. They owned all the land in the country, and their word was law. In addition, pharaohs acted as judges and as the leaders of Egypt's army.

One reason for the pharaoh's great power was the belief that he was a god. The ancient Egyptians believed that the pharaoh was really a god in human form. As such, people thought that the pharaoh was responsible for Egypt's prosperity. He and his priests had to perform elaborate rituals every day to ensure that the sun would rise, the Nile would flood, and crops would grow. For his role in keeping Egypt safe and secure, people honored the pharaoh:

HISTORY'S VOICES

❝Adore the king . . . living forever, in your innermost parts. Place His Majesty in friendly fashion in your thoughts . . . He is Re [the sun], by whose rays one sees, for he is one who illumines the Two Lands [Upper and Lower Egypt] more than the sun disk. He is one who makes [the land] green.❞

—Loyalty instructions from the Sehetepibre Stela

Because the pharaoh was thought to be a god, religion and government were closely intertwined in the Old Kingdom. Egypt was a **theocracy**, a state ruled by religious figures.

Egyptian Bureaucracy Powerful as the pharaoh was, he could not rule Egypt alone. The kingdom was simply too big and too complex for one person to govern. To aid him in ruling, the pharaoh was surrounded by a well-established **bureaucracy**, a highly structured organization managed by officials. In Egypt, many of these officials were the pharaoh's relatives.

Officially, members of the Egyptian bureaucracy had no power of their own. They simply acted upon the wishes of the pharaoh. In fact, however, many government officials were quite powerful. The most powerful official in Egypt was the vizier (VUH-zir), sometimes chosen for his ability but usually a relative of the pharaoh. He was responsible for advising the pharaoh, carrying out his orders, and trying court cases. The position of the vizier was hereditary. When a vizier died, his son took over his duties.

Serving below the vizier were hundreds of lesser officials. Their duties—and by extension, their influence—varied widely. Some officials served as governors of small territories within Egypt. Others were irrigation supervisors or crop inspectors. Census takers kept track of the kingdom's population, while tax collectors gathered the grain and goods that supplied the kingdom. All together, these officials kept Egypt running smoothly and efficiently.

READING CHECK **Summarize** What Egyptian institutions were developed during the Old Kingdom?

Skills Focus: Comparing and Contrasting   At Level

Reading Skill
Egyptian Government

Background: Explain to students that because of the belief that the pharaoh was a god, Egypt was a theocracy when it was ruled by pharaohs. In a monarchy, there is one ruler who has absolute power, usually a king or a queen.

1. Guide students in a discussion using the following questions as a guide: What problems might occur in theocracies? What similarities and differences are there between ancient Egyptian monarchies and present-

day monarchies? What similarities and differences are there between a monarchy and a democracy?

2. Have students create a chart comparing theocracies, monarchies, and democracies.

3. Have volunteers share their charts with the class.
   LS **Visual-Spatial**

📰 **Alternative Assessment Handbook**, Rubrics 7: Charts; and 11: Discussions

Answers

Reading Check *a government headed by the pharaoh, highly structured bureaucracy*

c. 1500 BC Hatshepsut increases trade between New Kingdom Egypt and other lands.

c. 1250 BC Ramses the Great rules over the last period of Egyptian glory.

c. 1350 BC Akhenaten introduces monotheism to Egypt by banning the worship of traditional gods.

◀ **Workers load grain onto a boat in this New Kingdom painting.**

Skills FOCUS **INTERPRETING TIME LINES**

Approximately how much time passed between the reigns of Menes and Ramses the Great?

See **Skills Handbook**, p. H14

The Middle Kingdom

Although the pharaohs of the Old Kingdom had tremendous authority, they eventually lost power. Powerful local nobles began to assert their own authority as rivals of the pharaoh. As a result, Egypt's internal order and stability gradually disappeared.

The government of the Old Kingdom collapsed around 2100 BC. For almost 200 years, economic problems, invasions, and civil wars racked Egypt. Famine and widespread disease added to the chaos. Finally, in about 2055 BC, a new dynasty rose to power and began the Middle Kingdom.

The strong leadership of this dynasty brought stability to Egypt. Along with this stability came economic prosperity. From their capital at Thebes, Middle Kingdom pharaohs encouraged sailors and merchants to import goods from surrounding lands. Historians have found evidence that Egyptians of the Middle Kingdom traded with the Nubians, who lived south of Egypt, the Phoenicians, the Minoans of Greece, and other peoples.

Trade routes into Egypt were not always safe, and bandits and hostile tribes sometimes attacked merchants. To protect their people, pharaohs sent armies to secure these routes. As part of this protection, the Egyptians built fortresses all along the Nile. They also took over Nubia as far south as the second cataract.

Despite these improved defenses, the Middle Kingdom fell to invaders around 1650 BC. Raiders from Syria whom the Egyptians called the Hyksos (HIK-sohs) invaded the Nile Delta and conquered Lower Egypt. The Hyksos had military technologies unknown in Egypt, including the horse-drawn chariot, armor, and a strong bow. Armed with these technologies, the Hyksos easily defeated the Egyptians.

READING CHECK **Summarize** How did the Middle Kingdom rise and fall?

The New Kingdom

The Hyksos ruled Egypt for almost 100 years. They were not harsh rulers, but the Egyptians resented being ruled by foreigners. Eventually, they rose up and drove the Hyksos out of their kingdom.

The army that defeated the Hyksos was led by nobles from Thebes, who declared themselves the new rulers of Egypt. Their reign marked the beginning of the New Kingdom.

Securing Egypt Years of Hyksos rule had taught the Egyptians a hard lesson: they could not depend solely on geographic barriers to protect them. The desert and the sea would no longer keep invaders out of Egypt. As a result, pharaohs had to find a new way to secure Egypt's borders and keep the kingdom safe.

READING SKILLS

Summarizing
After you read this paragraph, summarize it in one sentence using your own words.

NILE CIVILIZATIONS **67**

Reading Focus

The New Kingdom

Explain How did Akhenaten change Egyptian religious practices? *banned polytheism; worshipped one god, Aton*

Analyze How did Hyksos rule benefit the Egyptians? *The Egyptian army adopted Hyksos weapons and used them to conquer other nations.*

Elaborate Why do you think Hatshepsut's son tried to destroy all records of her reign? *possible answer— may have resented that she declared herself pharaoh and ruled in her own name, not in his; she kept him from the throne*

 Map Transparency: New Kingdom Egypt

 Interactive Map: New Kingdom Egypt

Info to Know

Warrior-Kings After the Hyksos were driven from Egypt, a new warrior tradition arose. It became the duty of Egyptian pharaohs to lead their armies into battle. The most famous of these warrior-kings was Thutmose III, who has been called the Napoleon of Egypt. Through Thutmose's military expertise and courage, Egypt conquered land in Southwest Asia and established it as part of the New Kingdom.

Answers

Interpreting Maps 1. *Punt—the Mediterranean Sea and the Nile River;* **2.** *gold, copper, gems, stone, luxury goods; eastern Mediterranean region—timber*

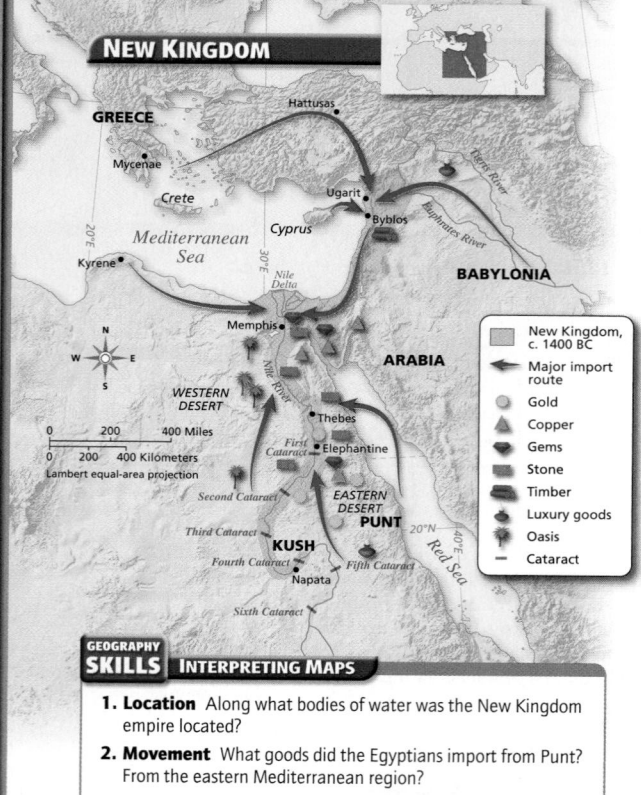

NEW KINGDOM

New Kingdom, c. 1400 BC	
Major import route	
Gold	
Copper	
Gems	
Stone	
Timber	
Luxury goods	
Oasis	
Cataract	

GEOGRAPHY SKILLS | **INTERPRETING MAPS**

1. **Location** Along what bodies of water was the New Kingdom empire located?
2. **Movement** What goods did the Egyptians import from Punt? From the eastern Mediterranean region?

New Kingdom pharaohs decided that the best way to protect Egypt from further invasions was to build a powerful military. To this end, they created the Egypt's first permanent army. In addition to traditional foot soldiers, the Egyptian army included archers and charioteers equipped with weapons adopted from the Hyksos.

To prevent a foreign people from taking over Egypt again, pharaohs decided to create an empire of their own. If Egypt ruled lands beyond the Nile Valley, they thought, then these lands would serve as a buffer between their kingdom and others. As part of their empire building, the pharaohs headed south into Nubia, which they had lost during the period of Hyksos rule. In Nubia, they conquered the kingdom of Kush and forced its rulers to pay tribute to Egypt.

68 CHAPTER 3

Even as their armies were invading Nubia, the pharaohs led campaigns east into Asia. They attacked and took over almost the entire Sinai Peninsula and parts of Phoenicia and Syria. As the map to the left shows, the Egyptians formed an empire that reached from southern Nubia all the way to the Euphrates.

The Reign of Hatshepsut While Egypt's territory was expanding, pharaohs were also increasing trade. As you can see on the map, goods poured into Egypt from as far away as Greece, Babylonia, and Africa south of Kush.

One of the pharaohs best known for encouraging trade was **Hatshepsut**, one of the few women to rule Egypt. She took power around 1500 BC when her husband, the pharaoh, died. Officially, Hatshepsut was only the regent, ruling in the name of her young son. Before long, however, she proclaimed herself to be Egypt's pharaoh, the only woman ever to do so.

Hatshepsut wanted to be treated like any other pharaoh, so she acted the part. She dressed like a man, even wearing the false beard that male pharaohs wore. She referred to herself as the son—not the daughter—of the sun god and had statues made in which she appeared to be a man.

The reign of Hatshepsut is best known for a huge trading expedition she sent to Punt, a kingdom on the Red Sea. This expedition returned to Egypt with such products as gold, apes and other wild animals, and myrrh, a valuable perfume. Hatshepsut had images of this magnificent journey carved on the walls of the temple in which she was buried.

When Hatshepsut died, her nephew took over as pharaoh. One of his first acts as ruler was to destroy nearly everything his aunt had created. He destroyed statues, removed her name from monuments, and tried to remove all record of her reign. Historians still do not know why he did this.

Monotheism in Egypt Around 1353 BC a new pharaoh took power in Egypt. His name was Amenhotep IV, but he is more commonly known by another name: Akhenaten, which means beloved of Aten. Egyptians had been worshipping many gods for centuries, but Akhenaten changed that. He worshipped only one god, Aten the sun god, and thought everyone should do the same.

Skills Focus: Summarizing

Reading Skill
Hatshepsut

1. Review the information in the text about Hatshepsut with students.

2. Have students make a list of her accomplishments. Have volunteers share their lists with the class and make a single class list for all to see.

3. Have students use the information from the class list to write an obituary honoring the pharaoh for her many accomplishments. Remind students to use standard English and check their obituaries for correct spelling and grammar. **LS Verbal-Linguistic**

Alternative Assessment Handbook, Rubric 40: Writing to Describe

As part of the changes he introduced in Egypt, Akhenaten banned the worship of any gods but Aten. He stripped power from the priests of other gods and ordered the gods' images destroyed. Out of respect for his god, he built a new capital called Akhetaten. He built a temple there to Aten and is thought to have written beautiful hymns to the god.

The worship of Aten did not survive Akhenaten's death. The very next pharaoh, Tutankhamon, or Tut, restored the worship of Egypt's traditional gods and moved the kingdom's capital back to Thebes.

Ramses the Great For most of the New Kingdom, the Egyptians continued to expand their empire, fighting campaigns in Nubia and Syria. By about 1250 BC, however, a new foe had appeared to threaten the empire. The Hittites from Mesopotamia invaded Egyptian-held Syria and began to take territory.

Pharaoh Ramses II (RAM-seez), also called **Ramses the Great**, led his army out to confront the Hittites. Accounts of the battle vary widely. According to Hittite records, the Egyptians lost the battle. Egyptian records, however, claimed a great victory for Ramses.

Hatshepsut, reigned c. 1503–1482 BC

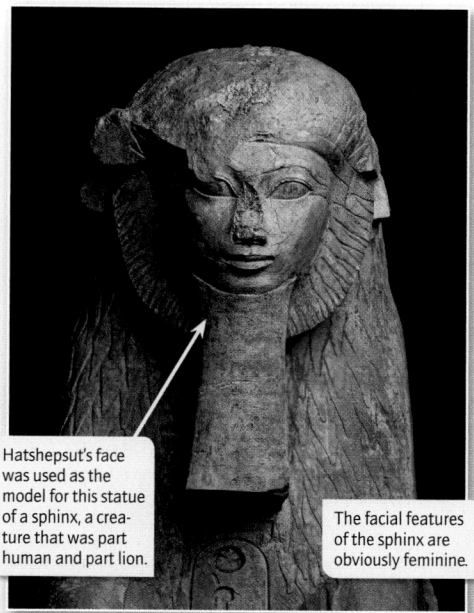

Hatshepsut's face was used as the model for this statue of a sphinx, a creature that was part human and part lion.

The facial features of the sphinx are obviously feminine.

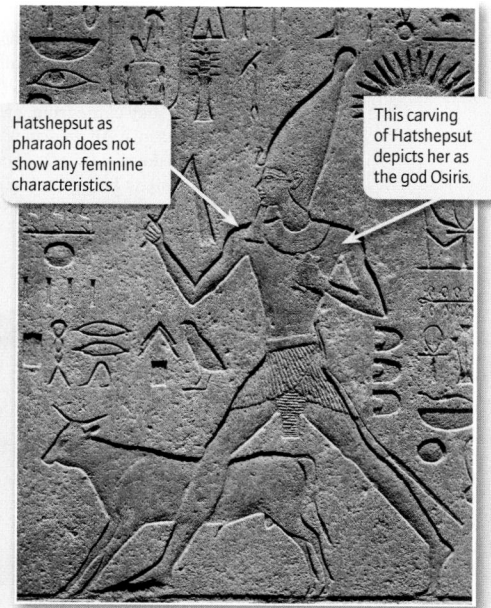

Hatshepsut as pharaoh does not show any feminine characteristics.

This carving of Hatshepsut depicts her as the god Osiris.

Hatshepsut is renowned as the only woman ever to rule Egypt as pharaoh. During her lifetime, she wanted to be portrayed as any other pharaoh would be. She frequently even had herself portrayed as male in statues.

As a result of the dual nature of Hatshepsut as a woman and as a pharaoh, images of her differ greatly. Compare the two representations of her above, and consider how each represents one aspect of her identity.

Skills Focus READING LIKE A HISTORIAN

1. **Identify** Which of these representations probably looks more like Hatshepsut really did?
2. **Explain** Why do you think Hatshepsut insisted that she be depicted as a man in many of her images?
3. **Analyze Visuals** How do these two representations portray different aspects of Hatshepsut's identity?

See **Skills Handbook**, p. H26

NILE CIVILIZATIONS **69**

The New Kingdom

Recall Who brought an end to Egypt's history as an independent kingdom? *Greek armies under Alexander the Great*

Summarize Why was Ramses II called Ramses the Great? *claimed victory over the Hittites, left architectual legacy, ruled for 67 years*

Review & Assess

Close

Have students summarize the history of ancient Egypt.

Review

Online Quiz, Section 1

Assess

SE Section 1 Assessment

Progress Assessment: Section 1 Quiz

Alternative Assessment Handbook

Reteach/Intervene

Interactive Reader and Study Guide, Section 1

Interactive Skills Tutor CD-ROM

Answers

Reading Check *built strong military, created own empire, increased trade*

However the battle turned out, the two armies agreed to a truce. As a sign of the peace, Ramses married a Hittite princess. With this marriage, the conflict with the Hittites ended.

Ramses ruled Egypt for more than 60 years. His reign was marked by extravagant splendor. With his great wealth, Ramses built more temples and monuments than any other pharaoh, including two huge temples at Abu Simbel in Nubia and another at Karnak in Egypt. Due to his political achievements and artistic legacy, no other pharaoh is as remembered or admired as Ramses.

Egypt's Decline The reign of Ramses II marked the last period of Egypt's greatness. His <u>successors</u> faced many challenges to their authority. Most of these challenges came in the form of invasions by foreign powers.

The first of the major invasions of Egypt was by a group that the Egyptians called the Sea Peoples. Today, no one is sure who the Sea Peoples were, where they came from, or even if they were a single people. All we know is that their invasions were devastating to empires in the area. Their invasions helped bring an end to the Hittite Empire and weakened Egypt's control of Syria.

ACADEMIC VOCABULARY

successors the people who follow others in an office or position

As the empire declined, priests and nobles struggled for power, and Egypt broke into small states. This breakup made the kingdom an easy target for foreign invasions. Over the next 700 years, many foreign rulers controlled Egypt. The Libyans from west of Egypt conquered Egypt and established themselves as a ruling dynasty, as did the Kushites from Nubia. Later, the Assyrians from Mesopotamia swept in and took over Egypt. In the late-500s BC, the Persians added Egypt to their huge empire.

After about 120 years of Persian rule, the Egyptians managed to drive the Persians out and once more rule Egypt themselves. Before long, however, the Persians returned. In 343 BC, they took over again and deposed the last Egyptian-born pharaoh. Never again would an Egyptian rule in ancient Egypt.

The second Persian conquest of Egypt did not last long, though. In 332 BC, a Greek army under Alexander the Great marched in and took over. The Greeks would rule Egypt for about 300 years before it fell to another power, perhaps the greatest power of the ancient world—Rome.

READING CHECK **Sequence** How did Egypt grow and change during the New Kingdom?

SECTION 1 ASSESSMENT

go.hrw.com
Online Quiz
Keyword: SHL NIC HP

Reviewing Ideas, Terms, and People

1. **a. Define** What were the **delta** and the **cataracts**? How did these features affect life in Egypt?
   b. Explain Why was the Nile so important to Egypt?
   c. Elaborate Why do you think many historians consider the unification of Egypt under **Menes** the beginning of Egyptian civilization?

2. **a. Identify** What was the purpose of Old Kingdom pyramids?
   b. Analyze How did the perception of **pharaohs** as gods add to their power?
   c. Elaborate How could a **bureaucracy** increase the speed and efficiency with which a government operates?

3. **a. Recall** What led to the end of the Middle Kingdom?
   b. Draw Conclusions Why were pharaohs able to increase trade during the Middle Kingdom?

4. **a. Identify Main Ideas** For what deeds are **Hatshepsut** and Akhenaten best known?
   b. Explain Why did some New Kingdom pharaohs want to build an empire?
   c. Evaluate Do you think Ramses II deserves to be known as **Ramses the Great**? Why or why not?

Critical Thinking

5. **Make Judgments** Draw a chart like the one below. For each period of Egyptian history listed in the first column, choose the event from your notes you think is most important. List that achievement in the second column, and tell why you think it is so important in the third.

Period	Achievement	Why Important
Early Egypt		
Old Kingdom		
Middle Kingdom		
New Kingdom		

FOCUS ON WRITING

6. **Description** Write a description of an Egyptian burial chamber as though you were part of the expedition that discovered it. Remember to use vivid details in your description.

Section 1 Assessment Answers

1. **a.** delta—area at the mouth of the Nile; cataracts— rocky river stretches with rapid currents and waterfalls; rich, fertile soil in delta helped give rise to the Egyptian civilization; cataracts kept the Nile from being an easy invasion route
   b. provided water; annual floods created rich black silt making agriculture possible
   c. Before unification there were two distinct kingdoms with different dialects and different customs.

2. **a.** tombs for Egypt's rulers
   b. People believed the pharaoh was responsible for Egypt's prosperity.
   c. by allowing specialization—each official was responsible for performing a certain task

3. **a.** The Hyksos conquered Lower Egypt.
   b. strong leadership brought stability to Egypt, encouraged sailors and merchants to import goods from surrounding lands

4. **a.** Hatshepsut—huge trading expedition; Akhenaten—establishing monotheism
   b. to prevent foreign invaders from taking over Egypt again; lands beyond the Nile Valley would serve as a buffer
   c. possible answer—yes; ruled Egypt for 67 years, built many temples and monuments, political achievements, artistic legacy

5. possible answers—Early Egypt: unification; created civilization that would endure for centuries; Old Kingdom: bureaucracy; provided a framework for ruling Egypt; Middle Kingdom: stability; economic prosperity; New Kingdom: created empire; increased trade

6. Students should discuss the number of rich, luxurious artifacts found with the bodies.

Belief Systems

Religion and government are two of the most influential factors in people's lives. Between them, religion and government shape how people act, live, and even think. In Egypt, as in most ancient societies, government and religion were closely intertwined. As you read in the previous chapter, priests in Mesopotamia held great political authority. In Egypt, the link between religion and government was even stronger—the pharaoh, the head of the government, was himself seen as a god.

▲ **NOW** The U.S. Constitution forbids the establishment of an official government religion.

GOVERNMENT AND RELIGION THEN As both the ruler and a god, the pharaoh was the central figure in both government and religion. In addition to his roles as the maker of laws and the leader of armies, the pharaoh also led the people of Egypt in their worship of the gods, including himself and his ancestors.

The pharaoh's divinity was the source of his political power, which was absolute. He was a necessary participant in the rituals that people believed would keep the sun rising, the crops growing, and the river flooding. In other words, the pharaoh was important not only for leadership but for ensuring the very survival of Egypt itself. To honor their leader, the Egyptians wrote hymns of praise to the pharaoh, built temples and statues to him, and held huge festivals in his honor. Nothing was considered too extravagant to honor a man who was both king and god.

GOVERNMENT AND RELIGION NOW Only a few countries in the world today have governments that are closely linked to religion. The Holy See, also known as Vatican City, is ruled by the pope, who is also the head of the Roman Catholic Church. Iran's government is strongly influenced by Muslim leaders called ayatollahs.

In most other countries, government and religion are kept at least somewhat separate. In the United States, for example, the government is forbidden by the Constitution from establishing an official religion or from restricting people's worship. At the same time, however, people's religious beliefs can influence government policies and decisions. Some of this influence stems from lawmakers' own beliefs, and some from the beliefs of the voters. The relationship between church and state is the subject of much debate in this country—debate that will continue for years to come.

Skills FOCUS UNDERSTANDING THEMES

1. **Describe** How were government and religion related in Egypt? How are they related in most countries today?
2. **Draw Conclusions** Why do you think people's religious beliefs can influence government decisions?
3. **Elaborate** Why do you think the relationship of government and religion is so debated today?

◀ **THEN** In this statue, the god Horus in falcon shape watches over a pharaoh, symbolizing the union of government and religion.

NILE CIVILIZATIONS **71**

Getting Started

Use the **Interactive Reader and Study Guide** to familiarize students with the section content.

📝 **Interactive Reader and Study Guide,** Section 2

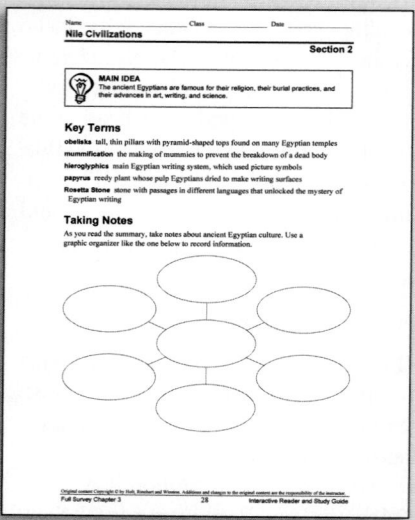

Academic Vocabulary

Review with students the high-use academic term in this section.

maximize to increase to the greatest possible level (p. 76)

📝 **CRF:** Vocabulary Builder: Section 2

Taking Notes

Ancient Egyptian Culture--worshipped hundreds of gods and goddesses; practiced mummification; dead buried with possessions, food, drink for afterlife; stratified social structure; most Egyptians were peasant farmers; created unique art; wrote using hieroglyphics and two other systems, papyrus; mathematical skills allowed them to build pyramids; had knowledge of human anatomy

go.hrw.com
Online Resources

KEYWORD: SHL NIC
ACTIVITY: Ancient Art

BEFORE YOU READ

MAIN IDEA
The ancient Egyptians are famous for their religion, their burial practices, and their advances in art, writing, and science.

READING FOCUS
1. What were the main principles of Egyptian religion?
2. Why did Egyptians practice mummification and burial?
3. What was daily life like in ancient Egypt?
4. What advances did Egyptians made in art, writing, and science?

KEY TERMS
obelisks
mummification
hieroglyphics
papyrus
Rosetta Stone

🗽 **NEW YORK**

PI 1.1 Investigate components of cultures including social customs, norms, values, and traditions; political systems; economic systems; religions and spiritual beliefs; and socialization or educational practices.

FROM ARCHITECT TO GOD

◀ **Imhotep, a great architect and physician, was later revered as a god.**

THE INSIDE STORY

How did a doctor and builder become a god? In the case of Imhotep, the most famous architect in Egyptian history, it was by helping shape Egyptian culture. Imhotep, who lived in the 2600s BC—early in the Old Kingdom—,designed the first pyramid ever built in Egypt. Located at Saqqara, the step-sided pyramid was the tomb of Imhotep's lord, the pharaoh Djoser.

Imhotep's contributions to Egyptian culture go far beyond pyramids, though. As an architect, he may have been the first person in the world to use columns in his designs, a style for which Egyptian architecture is famous. As a skilled physician, he is considered the founder of Egyptian medicine. He was believed to have written descriptions of cures for several diseases and instructions on how to perform surgery. Imhotep also acted as vizier to Djoser and as the high priest of the sun god Re. In these positions, he had great authority and considerable personal influence.

During Imhotep's lifetime, stories began to circulate in Egypt that he was the son of the god Ptah, the god of crafts and creation. Legends of Imhotep's brilliance continued to spread after he died, and over time people even began to worship him as a god. By about 2,000 years after his death, Imhotep had entered Egyptian religion as the god of medicine and healing. ■

Teach the Main Idea

At Level

Egyptian Culture

1. **Teach** Ask students the Reading Focus questions to teach this section.

2. **Apply** Have each student create a graphic organizer showing how the various aspects of Egyptian culture—religion, mummification, art, writing, math, and science—were related to each other

3. **Review** Review graphic organizers as a class. Guide students in a discussion of the relationships between the different aspects of Egyptian culture.

4. **Practice/Homework** Have each student select one aspect of Egyptian culture that seems to have been most important. Have students write a brief essay explaining how this aspect related to other parts of Egyptian culture. **LS Visual-Spatial, Verbal-Linguistic**

📝 **Alternative Assessment Handbook,** Rubrics 13: Graphic Organizers; and 43: Writing to Persuade

Egyptian Religion

Like the people of Mesopotamia, the Egyptians worshipped many gods. Some of the gods were ancient, worshipped from the earliest days of the Old Kingdom. Others, such as Imhotep, were added to the religion later. Egyptian religious beliefs were constantly evolving.

The Egyptians believed that gods controlled all natural events. As a result, a people dependent on the Nile's natural cycle of flooding for food and survival both feared and respected the awesome powers of the gods.

Chief Gods and Goddesses Although the Egyptians worshipped hundreds of gods and goddesses, a few were central to their religion. However, the gods that were central changed several times over the kingdom's long history.

The god of the sun was almost always a key figure in Egyptian religion. In the Old Kingdom, this god was called Re (RAY). Later, he became linked to a sky god called Amon and was known as Amon-Re. Amon-Re, the King of the Gods, was also thought to be the father of the pharaohs. The temple to him at Karnak was the largest ever built in Egypt.

Anubis, the protector of the dead, was also widely worshipped in Egypt. The Egyptians believed that he weighed the souls of the dead to decide their fate. Those who had light souls had been good in life and were rewarded after death, while those who were unworthy were fed to a terrible monster.

Also central were the trio of Osiris, Isis, and Horus. According to legend, the god Osiris introduced civilization into Egypt. Shortly afterward, however, Osiris was killed by his brother Seth, who cut the god's body into pieces that he scattered around Egypt. Isis, the wife and sister of Osiris, sought out the pieces of his body, reassembled them, and brought Osiris back to life. Afterward, they had a child, Horus, who grew up and sought revenge on his uncle Seth. Later, Osiris became the new judge of the dead, replacing Anubis, Isis became known as a goddess of nature and renewal, and Horus became the first king of Egypt.

Other important Egyptian gods included Hathor, the cow-headed goddess of love, and Thoth, the god of wisdom. In addition, the Egyptians worshipped local gods who had power over small areas or single households.

Temples and Religious Practices The Egyptians built temples to honor their gods and also to provide homes for them. The ruins of many such temples can still be seen around Egypt. Many of them were huge, decorated with massive statues, elaborate paintings, and detailed carvings. Many temples also featured **obelisks**, tall, thin pillars with pyramid-shaped tops. An obelisk was made from a single piece of stone and carved with intricate designs.

TAKING NOTES

In each oval, take notes about one aspect of ancient Egyptian culture.

Egyptian Gods

The ancient Egyptians worshipped hundreds of gods. Most gods were worshipped only in small areas within Egypt, but a few were honored throughout the kingdom. A few major gods are listed below.

◄ **Osiris** became the king and judge of the dead after he had been killed by Seth and restored to life by Isis. In art, he was portrayed as a green-skinned mummy.

► **Isis** was the sister and wife of Osiris. She was worshipped as a goddess of nature and the protector of women. She was usually drawn with a throne on her head.

◄ **Horus**, the son of Osiris and Isis, was the god of the sky. Pharaohs were thought to be human forms of Horus, who was usually depicted with a falcon's head.

► Like Osiris, **Anubis** was a judge of the dead and the protector of cemeteries and of mummy-makers. Images of Anubis had the head of a jackal.

NILE CIVILIZATIONS **73**

Direct Teach

Reading Focus

1 What were the main principles of Egyptian religion? *There were many gods who controlled all natural events. People who had been good in life were rewarded after death, while those who were unworthy were punished.*

Egyptian Religion

Recall What was the relationship between Osiris, Isis, and Horus? *They were a family—Osiris was the king and judge of the dead, Isis was Osiris's sister and wife, and Horus was the son of Isis and Osiris.*

Make Inferences How would the Nile's natural cycle of flooding lead the Egyptians to worship Isis? *Isis was the goddess of nature and renewal. She could be seen as representing the cycle of flooding, which renewed the land and nourished the crops.*

Evaluate Why would the god of the sun be one of the most important gods in Egyptian religion? *possible answer— because the sun was such a prominent feature in the Egyptian sky, as well as being important for growing food*

Info to Know

Canopic Jars The jars in which a mummy's internal organs were placed are called canopic jars. Each organ was identified with one of the four sons of the god Horus, whose head was depicted on the lid of its jar. Each of the gods had the head of a different animal. The liver was associated with Imset (human), the lungs with Hapy (baboon), the stomach with Duamutef (jackal), and the intestines with Kebechsenef (falcon).

Collaborative Learning

At Level

Designing an Egyptian Temple

Materials: poster paper, colored pens or markers

1. Organize the class into small groups. Tell students that they are architects in ancient Egypt, and have been put in charge of designing a new temple. Have each group select one of the gods discussed on this page. Then have them draw "blueprints" and pictures of what the interior and exterior of the temple will look like. Have them create designs for murals, statues, and other art that will be used in the temple. (You may wish to remind students that their designs should not resemble pyramids, which were tombs for the pharaohs.)

2. Have each group present its temple design poster to the rest of the class.

3. Guide the class in a discussion of the temple designs. Which features were used by all the groups? Which features were unique?
LS Interactive, Visual-Spatial

Alternative Assessment Handbook, Rubrics 28: Posters; and 29: Presentations

Reading Focus

Egyptian Religion

Describe How did the common people worship the gods? *During annual festivals, they sang hymns and other songs, danced, and paraded statues of the gods through the streets.*

Make Inferences In what way could Egyptian religious rituals be seen as supporting the monarchy? *Priests cared for the gods, in return for which the gods were supposed to grant the pharaohs immortality.*

📋 **CRF:** Biography: Howard Carter

Reading Focus

❷ Why did the Egyptians practice mummification and burial? *Mummification was an attempt to keep the body from decomposing, and thus to keep the ka, or life force, from shriveling away and vanishing.*

Mummification and Burial

Recall What was the Ka and why was it significant? *a life force that Egyptians believed separated from the body when a person died*

Explain In Egyptian religion, what happened after death? *Egyptians believed the soul lived on after death.*

Info to Know

Egyptian Burial Practices One of the world's most beautiful treasures is the life-size funeral mask of Pharaoh Tutankhamen, shown on this page. The mask shows the pharaoh as he was when he died in his late teens. It is made of beaten gold, with blue glass and beads. The beard is a symbol of the god Osiris, who judged the dead.

Answers

Egyptian Burial Practices *to accompany the pharaoh in the afterlife*

Reading Check *They built temples to honor them and provide homes for them. In the temples, priests performed rituals to fulfill the gods' needs.*

In Egyptian temples, priests performed rituals to fulfill the gods' needs. For example, each morning the priests placed a statue of their god on an altar, removed its clothing, and cleaned it by burning incense. They then dressed the statue in clean clothes, applied ointment to its face, and presented it with food. The Egyptians believed that such rituals refreshed the gods and kept them alive. In return for these rituals, the Egyptians believed that the gods would grant the pharaohs immortality and bring prosperity to all of Egypt.

Caring for the gods was the responsibility of the priests. Common people had no part in these religious rituals, and ordinary Egyptians never even entered temples. However, people did worship the gods during annual festivals. During these festivals, people sang hymns and songs, danced, and paraded statues of the gods through the streets.

READING CHECK **Analyze** What religious practices did the Egyptians follow to honor their gods?

Mummification and Burial

Central to Egyptian religion was the belief in an afterlife. The Egyptians believed that, after a person died, his or her soul would go to live in the land of the dead. Because of this belief in continued life after death, the Egyptians developed elaborate rituals regarding death and burial.

Teachings on the Afterlife The Egyptians believed that when the physical body died, a force called the *ka* escaped. The *ka* was essentially an individual's personality separated from the body. It was the *ka*, not the body, that would journey on to the land of the dead.

Although the *ka* had no physical presence, the Egyptians believed that it needed food and drink to survive. In addition, they believed that the *ka* might shrivel and vanish if the body decomposed. To keep this from happening, the Egyptians sought a way to prevent dead bodies from breaking down over time.

Egyptian Burial Practices

The tomb of pharaoh Tutankhamon, or King Tut, was one of the richest archaeological discoveries ever made. The tomb contained a wealth of treasures, including a magnificent golden coffin that held Tut's mummy. The tomb also held hundreds of items for the pharaoh to enjoy in the afterlife. *Why were such riches buried with the pharaoh?*

▼ King Tut's mummy (below) was buried in the magnificent coffin shown at right.

◄ Jars like these held the pharaoh's organs.

Collaborative Learning

At Level

Egyptian Religious Festivals

Note: If possible, have students get back into the same groups they were in for the activity on the previous page.

1. Organize the class into small groups. Tell students that they are in charge of organizing a festival program to honor one of the gods discussed in this section. Have students write songs about their assigned gods, create dances to honor them, and make pictures of the god to display. Their festival activities should have

an obvious relationship to the natural forces the god controlled.

2. Have each group present its festival program for the rest of the class.

3. Guide the class in a discussion of the festivals. How well did each group tailor its festival to the god it honored? **LS** Interpersonal, Kinesthetic

📋 **Alternative Assessment Handbook**, Rubric 14: Group Activity

Mummification The process that the Egyptians developed to prevent the breakdown of a dead body was **mummification**, or the making of mummies. Early in Egypt's history, only kings and members of the royal family could be mummified. Later, though, the process was made available to anyone whose family could afford it.

Mummification was a complex process that historians still do not fully understand. From what they have been able to discover, the first step in mummifying a body was to remove its internal organs. Most of the organs were taken out through an incision in the body's side, but the brain may have been liquefied and drawn out through the nose. The heart, which the Egyptians thought controlled a person's intellect and emotions, was left in the body. After removal, the organs were placed in jars to be buried with the mummy.

Next, the body was packed with various materials to help it keep its shape. Special salts were then used to dry out the body before it was wrapped in thin strips of linen. Once the mummy was wrapped, artists painted the dead person's features on the outside of the mummy itself or on a mask to ensure that the *ka* would be able to recognize its body.

Burial Mummification was only the first step in preparing the dead for the afterlife. Once a body was prepared, it still had to be buried.

Dead Egyptians were buried with all the possessions people thought they would need in the afterlife. For common people, this might include only some food and drink for the *ka*. The needs of pharaohs and nobles, however, were much greater. In addition to food, their bodies were surrounded with great treasures, riches to accompany them to the afterlife. Their tombs often sparkled with gold and gems.

THE IMPACT TODAY

Stories inspired by ancient Egyptian mummies are common in modern popular culture.

FORENSICS in History

What Can We Learn from Mummies?

People have been fascinated by mummies for centuries. Since the first mummies were uncovered in tombs and placed in museums, they have been among the most popular images of ancient Egypt. Recently, however, scientists have begun to ask whether mummies can be used as more than museum exhibits. Can we learn from them? The answer, they have discovered, is yes.

What facts do we have? By running tests such as CT scans on a body, forensic scientists can learn a great deal about a person's life. By running these same tests on a 3,000-year-old mummy, they can put together a clear image of Egyptian life.

For example, forensic scientists have learned about many diseases that were common in ancient Egypt. These diseases range from deadly conditions, such as smallpox and tuberculosis, to nonfatal ones like arthritis. Neither heart disease nor cancer appears to have been common in ancient Egypt.

▶ A scientist performs a CT scan on the mummy of Tutankhamon.

Studies of teeth from mummies have shed light on the Egyptians' diet. The teeth studied were greatly worn down, suggesting that the Egyptians ate coarse flour that had not been well ground. Scientists have also concluded that bread in Egypt included large amounts of sand that had gotten mixed in with the flour. Similar wear can be seen in teeth from members of all classes, from peasants to pharaohs, which suggests that everyone had a similar diet.

Forensics has even helped scientists learn about people's postures. By studying how people's bones grew, they can tell that scribes spent much of their time sitting with their legs crossed and that farmers were often hunched over. All of these discoveries have generated great interest and excitement among historians who study Egypt.

Draw Conclusions Why might historians be excited about the findings of forensic scientists?

Reading Focus

Mummification and Burial

Explain Why did the Egyptians bury food and possessions with the dead? *They believed the* ka *would need these things in the afterlife.*

Sequence What took place during mummification? *internal organs were removed and placed in jars; body was packed with various materials to help it keep its shape; body was dried out with special salts, then wrapped in strips of linen; artists painted the dead person's features on the outside so that the* ka *could recognize its body.*

Rank Where on the Egyptian social scale do you think the people who prepared mummies would have been? Why? *high on the scale, since mummification was so important*

📄 **CRF:** Literature: Book of the Dead

Info to Know

Book of the Dead Religious funerary texts have been found carved on the walls of pyramids dating from the 5th and 6th Dynasties of the Old Kingdom. After the Old Kingdom, private citizens had these texts painted on their coffins. Eventually, by the 18th Dynasty, these texts were written on papyrus and placed inside the mummy case. These texts are referred to as the "Book of the Dead," although they do not make up a single work. They contain formulas, hymns, and prayers that ancient Egyptians believed would help the *ka* on its journey to the afterlife.

Skills Focus: Making Inferences   At Level

Reading Skill
Death in Egypt

Background Tell students that the Egyptians did not believe that their life cycle ended with death. The Egyptians felt that the body needed to be preserved to make existence after death possible.

1. Have each student make a list of the things that people with beliefs like those of the Egyptians would consider to be necessary in the afterlife. Have them briefly explain why each item would be considered necessary.

2. Have each student write a paragraph describing ancient Egyptian religious beliefs and how these beliefs influenced their burial practices.

3. Ask volunteers to read their paragraphs aloud.

4. Guide students in a discussion of Egyptian burial practices. How did they compare with American burial practices of today? **LS Verbal-Linguistic**

📄 **Alternative Assessment Handbook**, Rubrics 11: Discussion; and 42: Writing to Inform

Answers

Forensics in History *allows them to learn much about how people lived in ancient Egypt, for example, that most bread in Egypt included large amounts of sand*

75

Reading Focus

❸ What was daily life like in ancient Egypt? *society was highly stratified, but less rigid than other civilizations; varied widely from class to class; largest group was peasant farmers who spent most of their time in the fields; Egyptian women had more rights than women in most other ancient civilizations; in free time enjoyed sports and games*

Daily Life

Explain How could getting an education change a boy's life in Egypt? *By getting an education, a boy could become a scribe, which was the fastest way to gain status.*

Contrast How did the institution of marriage differ from one class to another among the Egyptians? *Pharaohs usually married their sisters to keep the royal blood pure. Royalty often had more than one wife. Among the lower classes, a man would only have one wife, to whom he was not related.*

Draw Conclusions Why do you think Egyptian wigs and makeup also served as sun protection? *They lived in a hot desert, with intense sunshine most of the year. Farmers were outdoors most of the time.*

Info to Know

Women's Legal Rights Women had economic power in ancient Egypt. Women could write their own wills, and one woman, displeased with four of her children, disinherited them. Another court document records that a wife loaned some of her silver to her husband. The contract stated that he was required to repay it over three years at a 30 percent interest rate.

Answers

Reading Check *Egyptians believed in an afterlife for the* ka, *or life force. The* ka *needed food and drink to survive, so both were buried with bodies. Great care was taken to keep the body from decomposing so that the* ka *would not shrivel away and vanish.*

Besides treasures, dead pharaohs needed people to serve them. Royal tombs were filled with statues of servants that the Egyptians thought would come to life to serve the pharaoh's *ka*. Some tombs also contained models of animals, chariots, and boats to serve as transportation for the dead pharaoh.

The walls of Egyptian tombs were often painted with colorful scenes from the person's life or from stories about the gods. Egyptians believed the figures from these paintings would come to life to serve the *ka* and <u>maximize</u> its happiness in the afterlife.

ACADEMIC VOCABULARY
maximize to increase to the greatest possible level

READING CHECK **Summarize** How did beliefs about the afterlife shape Egyptian burial practices?

Daily Life

[NEW YORK icon] NEW YORK
CC Unit 1-B1d
Social structures of Egypt

The burial practices of ancient Egypt have taught us a great deal about people's daily lives. Archaeologists have uncovered thousands of items that had been buried in tombs to keep the *ka* happy, from furniture and tools to clothing and cosmetics. The images of daily life painted on tomb walls have also answered many questions about how the Egyptians lived. Coupled with the wealth of writings produced by the ancient Egyptians, these burial finds have given historians a fairly clear picture of Egyptian society and culture.

Social Structure Egyptian society was highly stratified, or layered. At the very top of society, of course, was the pharaoh and the royal family. Also prominent and influential in Egypt were key government officials, priests and priestesses, scribes, military leaders, landowners, and doctors. These people were all among the wealthiest in Egypt.

The next level of society included artisans, craftspeople, and merchants. These were the people who made and sold the goods, such as jewelry and clothing, used by others both in Egypt and in other lands.

The largest part of Egyptian society, about 90 percent of the population, was made up of peasant farmers. Although they spent most of their time in the fields, these farmers could also be recruited to build large public works, such as the pyramids, during the flood season. Farmers were also sometimes asked to work in quarries or mines or to serve in the army.

The Egyptians kept slaves, but slaves never made up a large part of the kingdom's population. Most slaves were convicted criminals or prisoners of war. They worked on public projects, in private households, or in temples. The number of slaves in Egypt increased during the later New Kingdom.

In some ways, Egyptian society was less rigid than other ancient civilizations. Although sons usually learned the same jobs their fathers had, it was possible—though rare—for people to become educated, to find better jobs, and to gain social status. Perhaps the fastest way to gain status was to become a scribe. Scribes' ability to write made them highly sought after. Scribes composed and copied religious texts, collected taxes, and kept public records.

Home and Family Life Egyptian family life varied widely from class to class. For example, marriage practices varied from one class to another. Pharaohs often married their sisters, a practice intended to keep the royal blood pure. In addition, while royalty often had more than one wife, most Egyptian men had only one wife.

Most Egyptians lived as family units. The father usually served as the head of the household, which included children and possibly unmarried relatives. Again, the houses in which families lived varied. Poor families might live in tiny huts, while slightly wealthier families had brick homes with a few rooms. Noble families often lived in huge palaces.

Women and Children As in most ancient societies, the primary duty of an Egyptian woman was to take care of the home and children. However, Egyptian women had more rights than women in most ancient civilizations. Women could be priestesses, own and inherit property, create wills, and divorce their husbands. Though many jobs were barred to them, women did often work outside the home. They worked as hairdressers, wigmakers, singers, and in other similar jobs.

Few children in Egypt received any kind of education, and most of those who were educated were boys learning trades. Girls, meanwhile, learned from their mothers how to raise children and run a household. When not in school, Egyptian children played with wooden toys and kept pets such as dogs, cats, monkeys, and ducks.

76 CHAPTER 3

Skills Focus: Analyzing Visuals   **Below Level**

Reading Like a Historian Skill
Tomb Design

Background: The most recognizable symbol of Egypt is probably the pyramid. Pyramids served as tombs for pharaohs.

1. Organize the class into small groups. Have each group choose a monument constructed in honor of a leader who died in the last 200 years. The monument does not need to be the leader's tomb. Each group should find a picture of the monument they have chosen.

2. Have each group create a chart comparing and contrasting the design and function of the modern monument it has chosen with the design and function of an Egyptian pyramid.

3. Have volunteers from each group share their pictures and charts with the class.
LS Interpersonal

[icon] **Alternative Assessment Handbook**, Rubrics 7: Charts; and 14: Group Activity

Daily Life in Ancient Egypt

Egyptian society was divided into social classes. About 80 percent of Egypt's people were peasant farmers. *How did the lives of rich Egyptians differ from the lives of the people seen here?*

Men did most of the manual labor in Egypt. They also served as the heads of households.

Many Egyptian women worked outside of the home. Women in Egypt had more rights than women in some other societies.

Appearance and Customs Most Egyptians paid close attention to their appearance. Many people of the upper class, both men and women, shaved their heads and wore wigs, both for fashion and to protect their heads and faces from the sun. Both men and women also wore perfume and makeup, including dark eyeliner that could double as sun protection. Women sometimes added lipstick and rouge.

Egyptian clothing was usually made from linen and wool. Peasant men wore short loincloths wrapped around their waists, while wealthy men wore longer skirts or robes. Women of all social classes wore long dresses that reached down to the floor. Wealthy men and women often decked themselves out in gold jewelry as well. Children, regardless of gender or social class, generally wore no clothes until they reached adolescence.

In their free time, the Egyptians enjoyed sports such as wrestling, javelin throwing, dancing, boating, and hunting. They also swam, fished, and sailed. Board games were also a popular form of entertainment in Egypt. Archaeologists have found many game boards and playing pieces, though they have not yet figured out the games' rules.

READING CHECK **Contrast** How did life differ for rich and poor Egyptians?

Art, Writing, and Science

Ancient Egyptian civilization lasted more than 2,000 years. During that time, the Egyptians made tremendous advances in many fields. Among the achievements for which the Egyptians are best remembered are those in art, literature, and science.

Egyptian Art Egyptian art is very distinctive. Both paintings and sculptures from Egypt are easily recognizable and quite distinct from the art of other ancient civilizations.

Egyptian paintings tend to be both detailed and colorful. The subjects of these paintings range widely, from illustrations of stories of the gods to pictures of daily life such as the painting shown on this page. Many of the paintings from ancient Egypt that have survived to today are found on the walls of tombs and temples, but illustrations in written manuscripts are also fairly common.

As you look through the Egyptian paintings shown in this chapter, you may notice some unusual characteristics. In many Egyptian paintings, people's torsos are seen straight on, but their heads, arms, and legs are seen from the side. In addition, major figures like gods and pharaohs are drawn much larger than other people. Together, these characteristics give Egyptian art a unique style.

NILE CIVILIZATIONS **77**

Reading Focus

4 What advances did Egyptians make in art, writing, and science? *Paintings are often very detailed. Statues tended to be large and imposing. The Egyptians were prolific writers, and developed several writing systems. Hieroglyphics were used on monuments, hieratic and demotic writing for business and literary texts. The Egyptians had a grasp of geometry and engineering, and they were masters of human anatomy.*

Art, Writing, and Science

Recall What subjects did Egyptian artists paint? *everything from illustrations of stories of the gods to pictures of daily life*

Analyze Why do you think that people's heads, arms, and legs are seen from the side in Egyptian paintings, even when their torsos are seen straight on? *possible answer—It was easier to paint them from the side.*

Primary Source

The Lansing Papyrus, quoted in the book *Pharaoh's People,* describes the life of an ancient Egyptian farmer: "Let me set out for you the farmer's state—that other hard calling. . . . He spends the day cutting tools for cultivating barley and the night twisting ropes. His midday hour even he is in the habit of spending in farmer's work. He sets about equipping himself to sally forth in the field like any warrior [that is, the farmer is burdened with many heavy tools]. The field is parched . . ."

Differentiating Instruction

Below Level

English-Language Learners

1. Tell students that they are illustrators for a book on ancient Egypt. Have each student produce a drawing for the book that will illustrate, without using words, one accomplishment or achievement of early Egyptian society.

2. Collect student drawings and have the class organize them to make a book.

3. Give students an opportunity to look at the book. Then guide students in a discussion of the images in the class book and review what students have learned about Egyptian society.
LS **Visual-Spatial**

Alternative Assessment Handbook, Rubrics 3: Artwork; and 11: Discussions

Answers

Daily Life in Ancient Egypt *Rich men wore longer robes; the rich also wore gold jewelry and would not have been farmers.*

Reading Check *Rich had large homes, poor might live in tiny huts; wealthy men wore longer skirts or robes than peasants; wealthy men and women often wore gold jewelry.*

Art, Writing, and Science

Define What was papyrus? *a reedy plant found along the Nile used by the Egyptians to make paper like sheets for writing*

Summarize Why do you think the Egyptians developed so many systems of writing, and what were their purposes? *possible answer—hieroglyphics: difficult to learn, took time to compose, used in formal writing and for religious texts, appreciated for their beauty; hieratic system: mostly for religious texts; demotic writing: mainly for legal and literary writings; both simpler and less attractive than hieroglyphics, could be written more quickly, more practical for everyday use*

Predict What would we have understood about Egyptian writing without the Rosetta Stone? *possible answer— might not ever have been able to figure out the meaning of Egyptian writings*

Info to Know

Sailing on the Nile Living along the Nile, the Egyptians were some of the earliest developers of water transportation. An image on a pot from about 3200 BC shows that Egyptians were already using the sail to travel on the Nile. Early boats floated downriver, and then their captains could raise a sail and be carried back upstream by the wind, which blows most often from the north. Rafts and barges carried goods up and down, and ferries traveled across the river and along the canals.

Answers

Reading Skills *possible answer-- Scholars used the Rosetta Stone to decipher Egyptian writing systems by comparing them with ancient Greek.*

78

Unlike the paintings, which often include tiny details, Egyptian statues are often large and imposing. Most large statues from ancient Egypt show gods or pharaohs and once stood in temples. These statues were designed to show the power and majesty of their subjects.

One of the most famous statues from Egypt is also the largest. The Great Sphinx is a huge stone statue of a creature with the body of a lion and the head of a person, 65 feet high and 260 feet long. It stands at Giza near the Great Pyramid of the pharaoh Khufu.

Egyptian Writing The Egyptians were prolific writers. They recorded the events of their society in great detail and composed beautiful songs and stories. Before they could create even the simplest tale, however, the Egyptians needed a system of writing.

The main Egyptian writing system was **hieroglyphics** (hy-ruh-GLIF-iks). This system, which uses picture symbols to represent objects, sounds, and ideas, was one of the world's first writing systems. Archaeologists have found examples of Egyptian hieroglyphics that date back to about 3200 BC. Only Sumerian cuneiform is thought to be older.

The Egyptians most often used hieroglyphics for formal writing, such as you might find on stone monuments, and for religious texts. Hieroglyphics were difficult to learn and took time to compose. Once written, however, they were appreciated for their beauty. Written words were appreciated as an art form.

For texts that needed to be written more quickly, the Egyptians had two other writing systems. The first was called hieratic (hy-RA-tik), and it was used mostly for religious texts. The other system, demotic (di-MAH-tik), was used mainly for legal and literary writings after about 500 BC.

Both simpler and less attractive than hieroglyphics, hieratic and demotic writings were seldom carved into stone. Instead, writings were made on wood, leather, pottery, and papyrus (puh-PY-ruhs) sheets.

Papyrus is a reedy plant that grew along the Nile. The Egyptians used the pulp of the papyrus to make paperlike sheets. Once dried, these sheets provided an excellent writing surface. Because Egypt's climate is so dry, papyrus did not decompose quickly. Many papyrus scrolls are still readable after thousands of years.

NEW YORK
CC Unit 1-B1e
Contributions of ancient Egypt

READING SKILLS
Summarizing After you read this paragraph, summarize it in a sentence using your own words.

78 CHAPTER 3

Egyptian Writing

The ancient Egyptians used three distinct forms of writing. The passage to the right from the sacred *Book of the Dead* is in hieroglyphics. The passage below is written in demotic.

For centuries after the decline of Egypt, no one could read Egyptian writing. Historians knew that the hieroglyphs they found in tombs were a form of writing, but they had no idea how to decipher it.

In 1799 a French soldier discovered a broken granite slab near the Nile Delta village of Rosetta. On this **Rosetta Stone**, as it came to be called, were long passages of ancient writing. In fact, the writing turned out to be the same text written in three different scripts: hieroglyphic, demotic, and ancient Greek. Using the Greek text as a guide, a French scholar managed to figure out the meaning of the hieroglyphs and of the demotic characters. This discovery unlocked the mystery of Egyptian writing, giving historians the key they needed to translate ancient texts.

Egyptian Math and Science The Egyptians were interested in math and science mainly for their practical applications. Rather than trying to understand how the world worked, they used science and math as tools to improve their lives. In doing so, however, they made many key discoveries.

In math, the Egyptians had a thorough understanding of basic arithmetic. They knew how to add, subtract, multiply, and divide. Also, the Egyptians obviously understood the basic

---

Reading Skill
Accomplishments Then and Now

1. Draw the chart for students to see. Omit the italicized answers.

2. Have volunteers call out the achievements they have listed in each cell. Fill in the master chart for the class to see. Have each student choose one category from the list and write a brief essay comparing and contrasting ancient Egyptian achievements with modern-day achievements in that area. **LS Visual-Spatial, Verbal-Linguistic**

Alternative Assessment Handbook, Rubrics 7: Charts; and 9: Comparing and Contrasting

	Then	Now
Architecture	pyramids	skyscrapers
Writing	hieroglyphics	books
Math	geometry	computers
Science	engineering	lasers
Medicine	anatomy	vaccines

Skills FOCUS **INTERPRETING VISUALS**

Drawing Conclusions Why do you think hieroglyphics were used only for sacred texts like the *Book of the Dead*?

principles of geometry. Without such an understanding, there is no way that they could have built the pyramids so precisely.

Building the pyramids also required a firm grasp of engineering. Engineers and architects had to understand how well buildings would stand and how much weight a column or wall could support. The fact that some of their buildings have stood for thousands of years is a testimony to their great building skills.

Perhaps the greatest Egyptian scientific advances, though, were in medicine. The Egyptians were masters of human anatomy. Doctors used this anatomical knowledge to treat patients, both at home and at certain temples regarded as healing centers. These doctors set broken bones, treated wounds, and performed simple surgical procedures, such as removing certain types of tumors. To cure simpler illnesses, they used medicines made from plants and animals. Doctors also prescribed regimens of basic hygiene, including regular bathing, in order to prevent people from getting sick. Written compilations of the Egyptians' medical knowledge were studied by doctors for many centuries after Egypt's decline.

READING CHECK **Find the Main Idea** What advances did the ancient Egyptians make in art, writing, and science?

SECTION 2 ASSESSMENT

go.hrw.com
Online Quiz
Keyword: SHL NIC HP

Reviewing Ideas, Terms, and People

1. **a. Describe** What were Egyptian temples like?
   b. Draw Conclusions Why were the Egyptians careful not to offend any of their gods?

2. **a. Identify Main Ideas** What were the Egyptians' burial practices?
   b. Explain How did the Egyptian idea of the afterlife lead to the beginning of **mummification**?

3. **a. Describe** What were the main social classes in ancient Egypt?
   b. Contrast How did the lives of women in ancient Egypt differ from the lives of women in other ancient societies?

4. **a. Define** What was the **Rosetta Stone**, and why was it important in translating **hieroglyphics**?
   b. Explain How did mummy-making advance Egyptian science?
   c. Elaborate What makes Egyptian painting and sculpture distinctive?

Critical Thinking

5. **Develop** Draw a graphic organizer like this one. In the outer circles, list one way in which each aspect of Egyptian culture was linked to Egyptian burial practices.

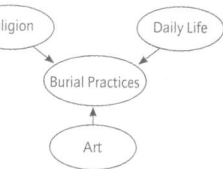

Religion — Daily Life — Burial Practices — Art

FOCUS ON WRITING

6. **Exposition** Write a report describing the three systems of writing used by the ancient Egyptians and how they differed. Note in your report what each writing system was used for.

NILE CIVILIZATIONS **79**

Direct Teach

Biography
Jean François Champollion (1790–1832)
Jean François Champollion was a French Egyptologist who became obsessed with deciphering hieroglyphics. After an English scientist had made a start in deciphering the hieroglyphic writing on the Rosetta Stone, Champollion finally began to make progress. He began to publish papers on the stone's hieroglyphics in 1821–1822, providing the key to understanding ancient Egypt.

Review & Assess

Close
Guide the class in discussing the role of religion in ancient Egyptian culture.

Review
Online Quiz, Section 2

Assess
SE **Section 2 Assessment**
Progress Assessment: Section 2 Quiz
Alternative Assessment Handbook

Reteach/Intervene
Interactive Reader and Study Guide, Section 2
Interactive Skills Tutor CD-ROM

Section 2 Assessment Answers

1. **a.** huge, decorated with massive statues, elaborate paintings, detailed carvings, obelisks
   b. Gods might disrupt the Nile's cycle of flooding on which the people's survival depended.

2. **a.** mummification; burial with possessions
   b. believed *ka* might vanish if body decomposed

3. **a.** pharaoh and royal family; government officials, priests, priestesses, scribes, military leaders, land owners, doctors; artisans, crafts workers, merchants; peasant farmers; slaves
   b. had more rights; could own and inherit property, create wills, divorce

4. **a.** a broken granite slab with the same passage in hieroglyphics, demotic, and ancient Greek; historians used the Greek text to translate
   b. gave them anatomical knowledge
   c. People drawn straight on, heads, arms, and legs from the side; gods, pharaohs drawn larger

5. possible answer—Religion: belief in the afterlife led to mummification; Daily Life: items buried with the dead; Art: many paintings found on the walls of tombs

6. Students should describe hieroglyphics, hieratic, and demotic writing.

Answers

Egyptian Writing *Appreciated for their beauty, difficult to learn, took time to compose*

Reading Check *detailed, colorful paintings, large, imposing statues, developed several writing systems, grasp of geometry and engineering, anatomy*

The Arts Around the World

Egyptian Temples

Info to Know

The Temple of Dendur New York's Metropolitan Museum of Art boasts an actual Egyptian temple as part of its collection. Moved from its original location in Egypt because of Nile River flooding, the Temple of Dendur was a gift from Egypt to the United States in 1965. Today it stands as the largest piece in the Metropolitan Museum's Egyptian art collection, spanning 82 feet from the front gate to the rear and weighing some 800 tons. Built during the period when Rome ruled Egypt, the Temple of Dendur features a figure of Caesar Augustus dressed in pharaoh clothing. It also depicts the traditional Egyptian gods Isis, Osiris, and Horus.

MISCONCEPTION ALERT

Remind students that Egyptian temples were not pyramid-shaped. Although many people mistakenly believe that the pyramids were built as temples, they were actually burial tombs for the pharaohs.

THE ARTS AROUND THE WORLD

Architecture

Egyptian Temples

What are they like? While pyramids are the most dramatic achievements of the Old Kingdom, temples are the greatest monuments of the New Kingdom. Some were built to honor gods and others to glorify the pharaohs who paid for them.

Some of the most magnificent temples still standing are at Karnak and Luxor—the northern and southern edges of the ancient capital of Thebes. The temples there are made up of courtyards and halls set behind tall, massive gateways called pylons. Within one of the halls, huge stone columns covered with intricate carvings stand close together. They once supported a stone ceiling, most of which is now gone. Although today bright sunlight pours in, the hall was dimly lit when the temple was built. The room may have seemed like a mysterious forest of stone.

Why are they important?
- The Egyptians built their huge temples without iron tools.
- Many of the temples' walls are covered with art that reveals much about Egyptian culture.
- Hieroglyphic texts on the walls tell the history of New Kingdom events and rulers.
- The New Kingdom temples rival the Old Kingdom pyramids as great monuments to Egyptian skill and power.

A granite obelisk and a statue of Ramses the Great stand near the First Pylon at the Temple of Luxor.

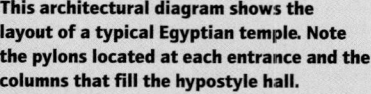

This architectural diagram shows the layout of a typical Egyptian temple. Note the pylons located at each entrance and the columns that fill the hypostyle hall.

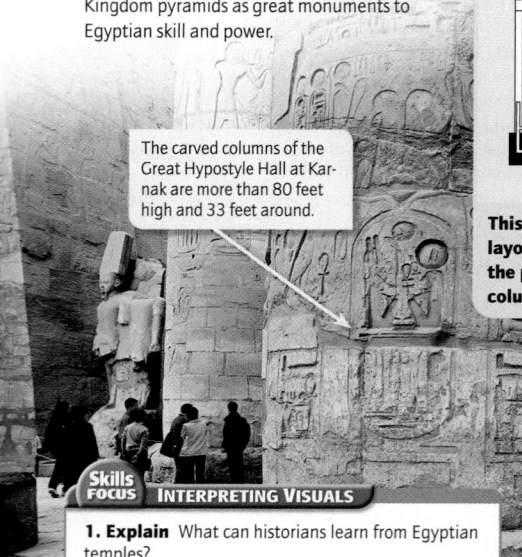

The carved columns of the Great Hypostyle Hall at Karnak are more than 80 feet high and 33 feet around.

Skills FOCUS INTERPRETING VISUALS

1. Explain What can historians learn from Egyptian temples?

2. Elaborate How could a temple glorify both the gods and the pharaoh who built it?

Activity Category Title

Below Level

Differentiating Instruction: Learners Having Difficulty

1. Have students create a list of facts about Egyptian temples using the photographs, diagram, and description on this page.

2. Then, have each student create a historically accurate drawing of an Egyptian temple, using the list of facts and any other resources they may need. Students may wish to do additional research using books or reliable Internet sites. Tell students they should not include any visual detail in their drawing unless they have confirmed it to be historically accurate.

3. When the drawings are complete, have students write a paragraph describing the Egyptian temple they have drawn. Student paragraphs should explain how the temple provides certain clues about Egyptian history and culture during the New Kingdom.
LS Learning Style

Alternative Assessment Handbook, Rubrics 1: Acquiring Information, 3: Artwork, and 39: Writing to Describe

Answers

Interpreting Visuals 1. *the history of New Kingdom events and rulers; information about building techniques and Egyptian culture;* **2.** *The pharaoh was believed to be a god.*

The Nubian Kingdoms

BEFORE YOU READ

MAIN IDEA

One of ancient Africa's most advanced civilizations, Kush developed along the Nile south of Egypt in a region called Nubia.

READING FOCUS

1. What were the land and people of Nubia like?
2. How did Kush grow into a major civilization?
3. How did Kushite society change in its later period?

KEY TERMS AND PEOPLE

Piankhi
smelt

NEW YORK

1.4 Students understand the broad patterns, relationships, and interactions of cultures and civilizations during particular eras and across eras.

THE INSIDE STORY

How could a man from outside of Egypt become pharaoh? In about 750 BC, a new king rose to power in Kush, a kingdom in the region of Nubia south of Egypt. His name was Piankhi. For centuries, the Nubians had lived in the shadow of their more powerful northern neighbors, and for much of that time had been ruled by them.

By Piankhi's time, however, Egypt was no longer so mighty. The powerful pharaohs of the New Kingdom had died, and there was no strong leader to keep order. Various nobles claimed to be the pharaoh and were tearing Egypt apart in their struggles for power.

Sensing an opportunity in this confusion, Piankhi sent a Kushite army north into Egypt. Steadily, this army marched northward, defeating army after army of Egyptians. Piankhi was not content to simply beat the Egyptians, though. He wanted them to know that they had been crushed. As he told his troops: "It is a year for making an end, for putting the fear of me in Lower Egypt, and inflicting on them a great and severe beating!"

Within a few years, Piankhi's army had reached the Nile Delta. From his capital deep within Kush, he now ruled all of Egypt. A foreigner had become Egypt's pharaoh. ◾

THE FOREIGN PHARAOH

▶ This model of Nubian soldiers was found in the tomb of an early pharaoh.

NILE CIVILIZATIONS **81**

Teach the Main Idea

`At Level`

The Nubian Kingdoms

1. **Teach** Ask students the Reading Focus questions to teach this section.

2. **Apply** Have students create an outline of the section using the heads as main points. Have students identify at least two main ideas under each of the blue subheadings.

3. **Review** Review student outlines as a class. Have students identify the points in their outlines that they feel are most important or most interesting. Guide students in

discussing whether being Egypt's neighbor was a blessing or a curse for Kush.

4. **Practice/Homework** Select one time when Kush was involved in a conflict with Egypt. Have each student write a brief newspaper article that explains the conflict and the result. **LS Verbal-Linguistic**

📝 **Alternative Assessment Handbook,** Rubric 23: Newspapers

Getting Started

Use the **Interactive Reader and Study Guide** to familiarize students with the section content.

📄 **Interactive Reader and Study Guide,** Section 3

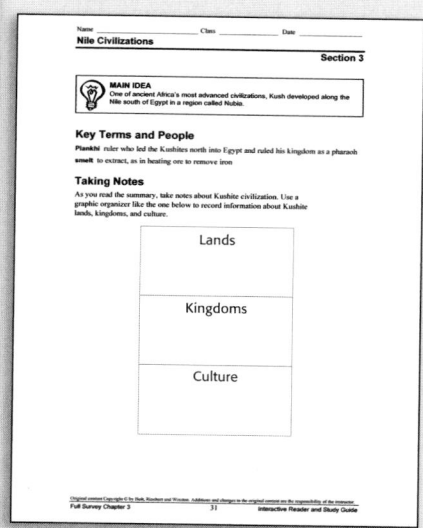

Academic Vocabulary

Review with students the high-use academic term in this section.

scope expanse or degree (p. 84)

📝 **CRF:** Vocabulary Builder: Section 3

Taking Notes

Lands--south of Egypt along Nile, farming almost impossible, great mineral wealth, ideal location for trade; Kingdoms--grew when Middle Kingdom collapsed around 1700 BC, Egypt ruled Kush for more than 400 years, Kush regained strength and power, later moved capital to Meroë, decline in trade led to downfall of Meroë in about 200 AD; Culture--Kush preserved Egyptian traditions, including burial practices, writing systems, did not adopt Egyptian dress, later Kush created own alphabet and writing system, women had high status

Reading Focus

❶ What were the land and people of Nubia like? *Nile flows through rocky mountains, land was not rich farmland, but had mineral wealth; people were expert traders, skilled potters, and expert archers; darker skinned than Egyptians*

The Region of Nubia

Identify What two rivers join to form the Nile? *the Blue Nile and the White Nile*

Identify Cause and Effect How did Nubia's geography affect its history? *Rocky landscape made farming almost impossible; location and gold, granite, and precious stones allowed Nubia to gain great wealth through trade.*

Evaluate What conclusions could be drawn from the fact that most of our knowledge of ancient Nubia comes from Egyptian writings? *possible answer—view could be biased*

📰 **CRF: Primary Source: The Nubian Kingdom of Kush**

Info to Know

Musawwarat The Great Enclosure of Musawwarat is a Kush ruin in modern Sudan. It consists of sandstone structures surrounding a temple. The temple is on a raised platform and can be entered only by climbing a ramp. Recent work by archaeologists shows that underground pipes for irrigation supplied water to gardens within the enclosure.

Answers

Reading Like a Historian 1. *inferior; cites the "lack of human necessities" in Nubia;* **2.** *one example: He describes the Nubians' use of butter and tallow instead of olive oil, which would have been used in Greece.* **3.** *possible answer—may have hoped to show that his culture was superior*

82

| Lands |
| Kingdoms |
| Culture |

The Region of Nubia

Nubia was located south of Egypt along the Nile. If you look at a map, you will see that two rivers, the Blue Nile and the White Nile, flow together to form the Nile. The point at which these rivers meet—near modern Khartoum, Sudan—may have been the southern boundary of Nubia. The region stretched north to the first cataract, Egypt's southern boundary.

Like the Egyptians, Nubians depended upon the Nile for its life-giving waters. However, Nubia's landscape made farming difficult. Unlike the flat riverbanks of Egypt, in Nubia the Nile flows through rocky mountains, making farming almost impossible.

A Wealth of Resources Although Nubia was not blessed with Egypt's rich farmland, it did have great mineral wealth. Mines in Nubia produced gold, granite, and precious stones that could be exported and sold.

Nubia's location was also a valuable resource. Goods from central Africa flowed into Nubia to be sent to Egypt, lands on the Red Sea, and elsewhere. Among the goods traded through Nubia were ostrich eggs and feathers, animal skins, ivory, ebony, and slaves.

Nubia's People Most of what we know about the people of Nubia is from Egyptian writings. The Nubians were expert traders and skilled makers of pottery. They were also regarded as expert archers. In fact, the Egyptians called Nubia the Land of the Nine Bows. They were so impressed by Nubian archers that some Egyptian rulers hired them as police and soldiers.

Early History The history of Egypt is so vast and so well documented that it often overshadows the history of its southern neighbor, Nubia. However, recent research into Nubian history has led to interesting findings. About the same time the Old Kingdom began in Egypt, the Nubians formed a kingdom of their own.

Reading like a Historian

A Description of Nubia

Analyzing Points of View Writers from one culture describing another often reveal their opinions of those other cultures in their works. For example, they may consider other cultures to be inferior to their own or their customs to be foolish. When reading such descriptions, it is important to take a writer's point of view into account. The description of Nubia on this page was written by the Greek geographer Strabo in the first century AD.

To recognize an author's point of view in this description or in another primary source, think about

- the author's opinions about the subject
- the author's background
- the author's goals in writing the work.

Skills FOCUS READING LIKE A HISTORIAN

1. **Author's Opinion** Based on this passage, did Strabo consider the culture of Nubia equal to or inferior to his own culture? How can you tell?
2. **Author's Background** How was Strabo's opinion shaped by his own background and experiences?
3. **Author's Goals** What do you think Strabo hoped to achieve by describing Nubia as he did?

See Skills Handbook, p. H33

> The word *inferior* shows an opinion.

In general, the extremities of the inhabited world, which lies alongside the part of the earth that is not temperate and habitable, because of heat or cold, must needs be defective and <u>inferior</u> to the temperate part; and this is clear from the modes of life of the inhabitants and from their lack of human necessities. They indeed live a hard life, go almost naked, and are nomads: and their domestic animals—sheep, goats, and cattle—are small; and their dogs are small though rough and pugnacious . . . The [Nubians] live on millet and barley, from which they also make a drink; but instead of olive oil they have butter and tallow.

—Strabo, *Geography*

> The author sees any differences from his own life as weaknesses.

Collaborative Learning

At Level

Daily Life in Ancient Nubia

Research Required

1. Organize the class into small groups. Have each group conduct research to prepare a brochure about daily life in ancient Nubia. Have students frame their brochures with a prologue and epilogue that discusses life in ancient Nubia.

2. Have groups present their brochures.

3. Guide students in a discussion of life in ancient Nubia. Ask students what similarities and differences they can see between life in ancient Nubia and life in ancient Egypt.
   LS Interpersonal, Visual-Spatial

📰 **Alternative Assessment Handbook**, Rubrics 3: Artwork; and 14: Group Activity

With its rich mineral resources, this early Nubian kingdom possessed great wealth and traded with Egypt and other lands. Before long, Nubia and Egypt became rivals, vying for control of land and resources. During Egypt's Middle Kingdom, the rivalry led to war as Egypt invaded and conquered much of Nubia. While under Egyptian rule, the Nubians adopted some elements of the Egyptians' culture, including their religion and building style.

READING CHECK Compare and Contrast How was Nubia similar to and different from Egypt?

The Growth of Kush

Although northern Nubia was controlled by Egypt during the Middle Kingdom, a powerful Nubian state began to develop at the same time. This state was called Kush, and it was based around the city of Kerma in southern Nubia, in what is now Sudan.

The Beginnings of Kushite Power
When the Middle Kingdom collapsed around 1700 BC, Kush seized the opportunity to grow. During this time, Kush expanded to rule all of Nubia, not just the southern part.

The rulers of Kush made an alliance with the Hyksos, the invaders who had ended the Middle Kingdom and now controlled Egypt. Under the Hyksos, Egyptian trade with Kush increased dramatically, and riches flowed into Kush. The Kushites used their wealth to build magnificent royal tombs in Kerma.

After Egyptian nobles drove the Hyksos out, in about 1550 BC, and began the New Kingdom, they also sought revenge on the Hyksos' allies. The Egyptians invaded Kush, destroyed Kerma, and added the land to their empire. As the top map on this page shows, Egypt ruled all of Kush by 1500 BC. Egyptian rulers, including Ramses the Great, built temples and other monuments throughout Kush.

The Kushites in Egypt
Egypt ruled Kush for more than 400 years, but eventually Kush regained its strength and power. This shift in power began as the New Kingdom weakened after the reign of Ramses the Great. By about 1100 BC, Kush was free from Egyptian control. Years of Egyptian control, however, had left the Kushites weak and disorganized.

EGYPT AND KUSH, 1500 BC

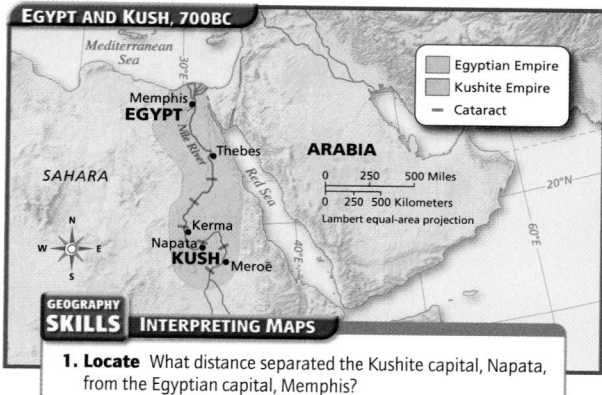

EGYPT AND KUSH, 700 BC

GEOGRAPHY SKILLS INTERPRETING MAPS

1. **Locate** What distance separated the Kushite capital, Napata, from the Egyptian capital, Memphis?
2. **Regions** How did the political relationship between Kush and Egypt change between 1500 and 700 BC?

Several centuries later, around 750 BC, a new Kushite kingdom began to grow and develop strength. The capital of this new kingdom was Napata, south of Kerma. Seeing the weakness that had beset Egypt after the fall of the New Kingdom, Kush's rulers decided to expand their power to the north.

The ruler who led the Kushites north into Egypt was named **Piankhi** (PYANG-kee), also known as Piye (PEE-yeh). Monument inscriptions from this period describe Piankhi as a compassionate ruler who granted pardons in exchange for loyalty. However, he could also be ruthless, as when he chased down fleeing soldiers after a battle to keep any from escaping.

NILE CIVILIZATIONS **83**

83

The Growth of Kush

Identify Who was Piankhi? *a Kushite ruler who conquered Egypt and made himself pharaoh*

Identify Cause and Effect What brought about the end of Kushite control of Egypt? *Assyrians from Mesopotamia swept into Egypt, Kushites fled back to Nubia.*

Evaluate Why do you think that Kushite rulers chose to be buried in pyramids rather than in temples? *possible answer —Pyramids were more impressive than temples.*

📜 **Quick Facts Transparency:** Egypt in Nubia

📄 **CRF:** Biography: Queen Shanakdakhete

3 How did Kushite society change in its later period? *Kushite culture changed dramatically; Meroitic kingdom sometimes referred to as a distinct culture, new capital built in a mountainous, forest area, most valuable resource was iron, rulers abandoned many of the elements of Egyptian culture*

Later Kush

Identify What was Kush's most valuable product? *iron*

Contrast How did the location of Meroë differ from the locations of the previous Kushite capitals? *farther south along the Nile, in a triangle formed by three rivers, area was mountainous and heavily forested, not as dry as other parts of Nubia*

Answers

Reading Check *Egyptians drove the Hyksos out and invaded Kush. As the New Kingdom weakened, Egyptian power over Kush declined. After a few centuries, Kushites pushed north into Egypt, eventually conquering all of it. When the Assyrians swept into Egypt, the Kushites fled back into Nubia.*

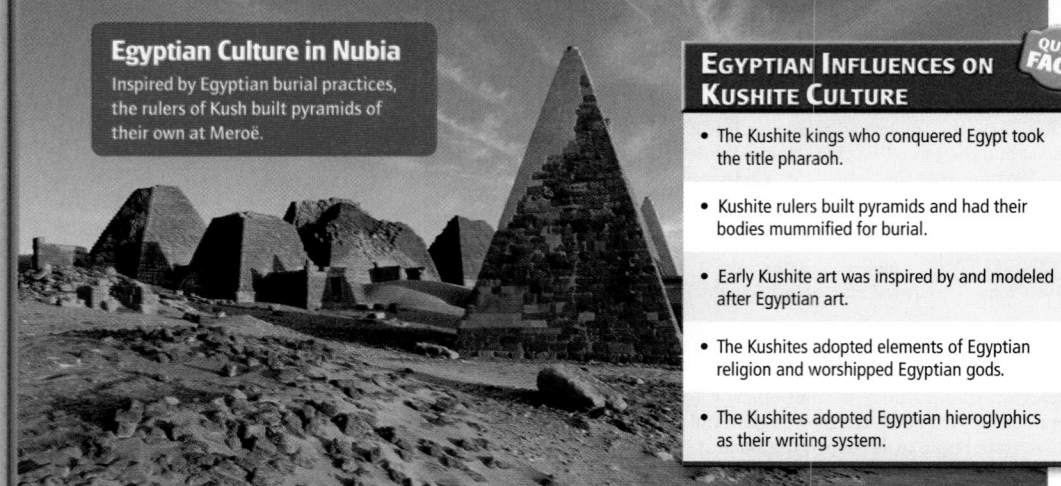

Egyptian Culture in Nubia
Inspired by Egyptian burial practices, the rulers of Kush built pyramids of their own at Meroë.

EGYPTIAN INFLUENCES ON KUSHITE CULTURE

QUICK FACTS

- The Kushite kings who conquered Egypt took the title pharaoh.
- Kushite rulers built pyramids and had their bodies mummified for burial.
- Early Kushite art was inspired by and modeled after Egyptian art.
- The Kushites adopted elements of Egyptian religion and worshipped Egyptian gods.
- The Kushites adopted Egyptian hieroglyphics as their writing system.

In the end, Piankhi conquered all of Egypt. However, Kushite rulers only held power in Egypt for about a century. In the mid-600s BC, the Assyrians from Mesopotamia swept into Egypt. Unable to stand up to the Assyrians, the Kushite pharaohs fled back into Nubia, to their old capital at Napata.

Kushite Culture Although they were not Egyptian, the Kushite pharaohs saw themselves as guardians of Egyptian tradition, and they tried to preserve Egyptian traditions. For example, they had their bodies mummified and buried in pyramids like Old Kingdom pharaohs, even though New Kingdom rulers had usually been buried in temples. (Kushite pyramids were smaller than Egyptian ones, though.) In addition, the Kushites adopted Egyptian hieroglyphics as their own writing system.

The Kushites did not abandon all their own customs when they ruled Egypt, however. For example, they did not adopt the Egyptian style of dressing to try to make themselves look Egyptian. Statues of Kushite pharaohs show distinctly Nubian features and clothing. These statues also show the pharaohs wearing a crown with two cobras, symbolizing the union of Egypt and Kush.

READING CHECK **Summarize** How did the relationship between Kush and Egypt change?

ACADEMIC VOCABULARY
scope extent or degree

Later Kush

The period immediately following the Kushite expulsion from Egypt by the Assyrians is a mystery to historians. There are few records from this period.

Our knowledge of Kushite history resumes in the mid-200s BC. At that time, the Kushites moved their capital to Meroë (MER-oh-wee), a city farther south along the Nile from Napata. No one is certain what led to the move, or even exactly when the move took place. However, it appears that Kushite culture changed substantially after the capital's move. In fact, the scope of the change was so great that some people refer to later Kush as a separate culture entirely from the earlier period.

The City of Meroë The new capital of Kush was located near the junction of two rivers. Because the city was near so much water, ancient writers often referred to the area as the island of Meroë, though the city did not actually lie on an island.

The area in which Meroë was built was not as dry as some parts of Nubia. The city's inhabitants used wood from nearby forests to build their homes and to obtain valuable trade goods such as ebony. In addition, the area was home to many species of wild animals:

Skills Focus: Sequencing

At Level

Reading Skill
Nubian Time Line

1. Have students create a time line for the Nubian kingdoms of Kush and its successor, the Meroitic Kingdom, from around 1700 BC to the first century AD. Have students show the events that mark growth in Nubian power above their time lines and those events that mark declines in Nubian power below their time lines.

2. Make a master time line for students to see. Have volunteers help fill in the dates.

3. Guide students in a discussion of Nubian history based on their time lines. Ask students if they can see any patterns of growth and decline in the time lines. **LS** **Visual-Spatial**

📄 **Alternative Assessment Handbook**, Rubric 36: Time Lines

"In the cities the dwellings are made of split pieces of palm-wood woven together, or of brick. And they have quarried salt, as do the Arabians. And, among the plants, the palm, the persea, the ebony, and the ceratia are found in abundance. And they have, not only elephants to hunt, but also lions and leopards."

—Strabo, *Geography*

Iron Industry One advantage to Meroë's location was the abundant mineral resources found nearby. In addition to copper, gold, and precious stones, iron was plentiful. The Kushites used the iron ore they found near Meroë to build a large and profitable iron industry.

Iron quickly became Kush's most valuable product. Archaeological evidence suggests that iron goods from Meroë were shipped throughout the Nile Valley. Rulers used the wealth they made from this trade to support building programs and the expansion of their kingdom.

Later Kushite Culture With the move to Meroë, Kush's rulers abandoned many of the elements of Egyptian culture they had adopted. They continued to build pyramids, but they no longer used hieroglyphics for writing. Instead, they created their own alphabet and writing system. Unfortunately, historians have not yet managed to translate their language, so many mysteries remain about later Kush's culture.

One of these mysteries is the role that women played in Kushite society. Based on carvings found on tombs, women appear to have enjoyed a fairly high status in Kush. In addition, the fact that many pyramids were built for women suggests that female rulers may not have been uncommon. However, historians have not yet been able to learn anything about the lives of these women. For example, they do not know whether they ruled Kush in their own right or as regents in the name of their children.

The Decline of Meroë As long as trade thrived and its economy stayed strong, Meroë prospered. However, a decline in trade in the AD 200s contributed to the kingdom's downfall. The decline in trade was caused by several factors. Increased competition for goods reduced the demand for Kushite exports. In addition, hostile peoples continually raided the Nile Valley, disturbing the trade routes that linked Meroë to the outside world. Environmental issues were also a factor. The Kushites needed wood for their forges in order to **smelt**, or refine, iron from its ore. Centuries of ironmaking had taken a toll on Nubia's forests, and eventually the Kushites could no longer work iron to make the tools they needed to survive as a kingdom.

As Meroë's economy declined, so did the kingdom. The weakened Kush was an attractive target for invaders. Finally, in about AD 350, the kingdom of Aksum, located in present-day northern Ethiopia, invaded and destroyed Meroë. With the collapse of the capital and nearby towns, Kushite civilization faded.

READING CHECK **Analyze** How did Kushite civilization change after the capital moved to Meroë?

SECTION 3 ASSESSMENT

go.hrw.com
Online Quiz
Keyword: SHL NIC HP

Reviewing Ideas, Terms, and People
1. **a. Describe** Where was the region of Nubia? What were the land and resources there like?
   b. Explain Why and how did the early Nubians come into contact with the Egyptians?
   c. Elaborate How did Nubia's location eventually lead to the growth of a wealthy civilization?
2. **a. Recall** What was Piankhi's major accomplishment?
   b. Make Generalizations How did Egypt influence Kushite culture after the Kushites conquered Egypt?
3. **a. Identify Main Ideas** What were two ways in which Meroë's location was beneficial to Kush?
   b. Contrast How was Kushite writing during the later Kushite kingdom different from what it had been in earlier Kush?
   c. Support a Position In the long run, do you think the mass production of iron was good or bad for Kush? Explain your answer.

Critical Thinking
4. **Analyze** Draw a graphic organizer like the one below. In the left box, list facts about the culture of Kush during the Napata period. In the right box, describe how Kush's culture changed during its later history.

FOCUS ON WRITING
5. **Exposition** Write a short paragraph explaining how Kush's location and physical setting were beneficial to the kingdom's economy. Use specific examples to support your main idea.

NILE CIVILIZATIONS **85**

Section 3 Assessment Answers

1. **a.** between the first cataract on the north and the point at which the Blue Nile and the White Nile meet on the south; rocky land, great mineral wealth, including gold, granite, and precious stones
   b. probably through trade; Egyptians hired Nubian archers as police and soldiers
   c. Goods from central Africa flowed into Nubia to be sent to Egypt, the Red Sea, and elsewhere.

2. **a.** conquered all of Egypt, made himself pharaoh

b. preserved Egyptian traditions, such as mummification and burial in pyramids, adopted Egyptian hieroglyphics

3. **a.** It had abundant mineral resources and was well located for trade with other parts of the world.
   b. abandoned hieroglyphics, created their own alphabet and writing system
   c. possible answer—bad, because of the environmental damage; Kush had grown rich from trade before, probably would

have continued to be wealthy without iron production

4. Napata—mummified pharaohs, buried them in pyramids, copied Egyptian styles of architecture and art, adopted Egyptian hieroglyphics; Later Kush—abandoned many elements of Egyptian culture, created own alphabet and writing system

5. Student answers should include Nubia's mineral wealth and that it was a crossroads for trade.

The Gift of the Nile

Word Help

restricted prevented, prohibited

first-fruits the earliest produce of the season

perpetuity permanence, forever

diverse different, varied

sustain nourish, support

suckle bring up or rear

Activity **Gifts of the Nile** Have students write a poem or song lyrics about the Nile and its gifts to the Egyptian people, as shown in Document 2.

Info to Know

Herodotus (c. 484–425 BC) Herodotus is considered the father of history, and his *History* may have been the first creative work written in prose rather than poetry. He spent many years traveling, going as far south as Elephantine in Egypt. He had an eye for detail, and tried to report accurately, and without bias.

Elephantine The island of Elephantine is in the area of Aswan. It was near the first cataract of the Nile, which divided Egypt from Nubia. Thus, the people who lived below Elephantine were Egyptians, while the people who lived above Elephantine were Nubians.

The Gift of the Nile

Historical Context The four documents below illustrate the importance of the Nile in various aspects of Egyptian culture.

Task Study the selections and answer the questions that follow. After you have studied all the documents, you will be asked to write an essay explaining the significance of the Nile to Egyptians. You will need to use evidence from these selections and from Chapter 3 to support the position you take in your essay.

DOCUMENT 1

The Nile and Egypt

The Greek historian Herodotus was intrigued by the importance of the Nile to Egypt. In his travels, he asked people about this subject. As an answer, a group of priests told him this story, which illustrated to Herodotus the idea that the Nile was the very definition of Egypt.

It happened that the people of the cities Marea and Apis, who live in the part of Egypt that borders on Libya, took a dislike to the religious usages of the country concerning sacrificial animals, and wished no longer to be restricted from eating the flesh of cows. So, as they believed themselves to be Libyans and not Egyptians, they sent to the shrine to say that, having nothing in common with the Egyptians, neither inhabiting the Delta nor using the Egyptian tongue, they claimed to be allowed to eat whatever they pleased. Their request, however, was refused by the god, who declared in reply that Egypt was the entire tract of country which the Nile overspreads and irrigates, and the Egyptians were the people who lived below Elephantine, and drank the waters of that river.

DOCUMENT 2

The Nile in Art

As the heart of Egyptian culture, the Nile was a common subject in the kingdom's art. This painting shows Egyptians in a boat sailing on the Nile, the gifts of which can be seen in the water and on the land around it.

Differentiating Instruction

Below Level

Learners Having Difficulty

Standard English Mastery

1. Go through Herodotus's anecdote (Document 1) with the class to make sure that they understand it. Make a class list of difficult words and then have students work in mixed-ability pairs to define them. Then guide students in a discussion of the passage, using the following questions as a guide: What does the passage reveal about Herodotus? Does he appear to be giving a fair and unbiased description of Egypt? Why or why not? What does the passage reveal about the Egyptians?

Do they appear to be tolerant of those who don't believe as they do? Why or why not?

2. Have students compare this passage with the Reading Like a Historian feature in this section: A Description of Nubia by Strabo.

3. Have students write a paragraph using standard English discussing the differences in the two passages. **LS** **Verbal-Linguistic**

   Alternative Assessment Handbook, Rubrics 11: Discussions; and 16: Judging Information

DOCUMENT 3

Hymn to the Nile

The Egyptians worshipped the Nile as a god, the bringer of life to their land. The following hymn, which dates back to the Old Kingdom, expresses the speaker's gratitude to the river.

Hail to thee, O Nile! Who manifests thyself over this land, and comes to give life to Egypt! Mysterious is thy issuing forth from the darkness, on this day whereon it is celebrated! Watering the orchards created by Re [the sun god], to cause all the cattle to live, you give the earth to drink, inexhaustible one! Path that descends from the sky, loving the bread of Seb [the Earth] and the first-fruits of Nepera, You cause the workshops of Ptah [the god of crafts] to prosper!

Lord of the fish, during the inundation [flood], no bird alights on the crops. You create the grain, you bring forth the barley, assuring perpetuity to the temples. If you cease your toil and your work, then all that exists is in anguish. If the gods suffer in heaven, then the faces of men waste away.

DOCUMENT 4

The Hymn to Aten

The Hymn to Aten was written by the pharaoh Akhenaten in praise of his god, Aten. The pharaoh believed in only one god, whom he believed had created everything in the world. Among the gifts for which Aten was most grateful was the Nile.

Each one has his food, and his lifetime is reckoned. Their tongues are diverse in speech and their natures likewise; Their skins are varied, for thou dost vary the foreigners. Thou dost make the Nile in the underworld, And bringest it forth as thou desirest to sustain the people . . .

For thou hast set a Nile in the sky, That it may descend for them, That it may make waves on the mountains like the sea, To water their fields amongst their towns. How excellent are thy plans, thou lord of eternity!

The Nile in the sky is for the foreign peoples, For the flocks of every foreign land that walk with (their) feet, While the (true) Nile comes forth from the underworld for Egypt. Thy rays suckle every field; When thou dost rise, they live and thrive for thee.

Info to Know

Hymn to the Nile The Hymn to the Nile dates from about 2100 BC. The entire hymn consists of 14 stanzas. Only the first two stanzas are given here.

Hymn to Aten Scholars have pointed to similarities between the Hymn to Aton and Psalm 104 from the Hebrew Old Testament. These similarities may be purely coincidental, or they may be an example of cultural diffusion.

Skills Focus — READING LIKE A HISTORIAN

DOCUMENT 1
a. Identify According to Herodotus, what defined Egypt?
b. Interpret Does this passage support Herodotus's belief that Egypt was the gift of the Nile? Why or why not?

DOCUMENT 2
a. Describe What kinds of plants and animals does this image suggest could be found in or near the Nile?
b. Draw Conclusions Based on this image, how did the Nile affect the daily lives of the ancient Egyptians?

DOCUMENT 3
a. Analyze What gifts does this hymn say the Nile brought to Egypt?
b. Elaborate Why do you think the ancient Egyptians saw the Nile as a god?

DOCUMENT 4
a. Explain Why does Akhenaten say Aten made the Nile?
b. Interpret What do you think Akhenaten meant by the phrase "Nile in the sky"? What does his use of this phrase suggest about the role of the Nile in Egyptian thought?

DOCUMENT-BASED ESSAY QUESTION

In a famous passage from his description of Egypt, Herodotus referred to Egypt as the "gift of the Nile." What did he mean by that phrase? Using the documents above and information from the chapter, form a thesis that might explain why Herodotus described Egypt the way he did. Then write a short essay to support your position.

See **Skills Handbook**, pp. H25–26

NILE CIVILIZATIONS **87**

Skills Focus: Comparing and Contrasting

At Level

Reading Skill
Ancient Egyptian Hymns of Praise

Background: Point out to students that the Hymn to Aten is supposed to have been written by the pharaoh Akhenaton, while the Hymn to the Nile would probably have been written by a priest.

1. Have each student write an essay comparing and contrasting the two hymns, Documents 3 and 4. What do they have in common? How do they differ?

2. Have volunteers read their essays to the class.

3. Guide the class in a discussion of the two hymns' similarities and differences.
   LS Verbal-Linguistic

   Alternative Assessment Handbook, Rubric 40: Writing to Describe

Answers

Reading Like a Historian
Document 1. a. *Egypt was "the entire tract of country which the Nile overspreads and irrigates."* **b.** *It would appear to support his belief, since he says that the god stated that Egypt was all the land overspread and irrigated by the Nile, and that anyone who lived below Elephantine and drank the waters of the river was an Egyptian.* **Document 2. a.** *possible answer—fish and green palm-like plants* **b.** *provided food and water, the necessities of life;* **Document 3. a.** *life, water, crops;* **b.** *possible answer—Life depended upon it; without the Nile, it would be impossible to live in Egypt.* **Document 4. a.** *because he wanted to sustain, or feed, the people of Egypt;* **b.** *possible answer—rain; it suggests that to the Egyptians, the Nile and water were synonymous.* **Essay.** *Student essays should emphasize that Nile was essential to life in Egypt and that hymns and art were created in its honor.*

87

Visual Summary

Review and Inquiry Egypt and Kush were neighboring civilizations on the Nile whose histories are intertwined. Have students create a point-by-point comparison of the civilizations of Egypt and Kush. Which of the two cultures exerted the greater influence on the other?

🎴 **Quick Facts Transparency**: Visual Study Guide: Nile Civilizations

Review Key Terms and People

1. dynasty
2. Piankhi
3. successor
4. Hatshepsut
5. mummification
6. scope
7. Menes
8. bureaucracy
9. pharaoh
10. smelt
11. Ramses

Comprehension and Critical Thinking

12. a. believed pharaohs were gods in human form, responsible for Egypt's prosperity
b. Without the Nile, there would have been no agriculture, and hence no civilization.
c. possible answer—the Old Kingdom: Most of the pyramids were built and Egypt's government took shape during this time.

13. a. hieroglyphics, mainly used for formal writing; hieratic writing, used for religious texts; demotic writing, used for legal and literary writings
b. to preserve bodies so that the *ka* would not shrivel and vanish; treasures were to accompany them to the afterlife
c. possible answer—agree; because people believed that the gods controlled all natural events, rulers were considered gods, and most art and architecture glorified gods

---

VISUAL STUDY GUIDE

QUICK FACTS

EGYPT

Location
- Along the lower stretches of the Nile and in the Nile delta

Government
- Ruled by pharaohs aided by a bureaucracy

Culture
- Polytheistic religion with emphasis on the afterlife
- Mummification and extravagant burials
- Hieroglyphic writing system
- Distinctive forms of art and sculpture
- Major advances in science and medicine

Nile Civilizations

KUSH

Location
- South of Egypt along the Nile

Government
- Ruled by kings who adopted Egyptian customs

Culture
- Religion borrowed from Egypt
- Pyramids built in Egyptian style
- As yet untranslated writing system
- Egyptian-influenced art and sculpture
- Powerful trading culture

Major Periods in Egyptian and Kushite History

Early Egypt
- Upper and Lower Egypt develop.
- Menes unifies all of Egypt.

Old Kingdom
- The first pyramids are built.
- Pharaohs take charge of Egypt.
- Egyptian bureaucracy forms.

Middle Kingdom
- Egypt conquers Kush.
- Trade increases.
- The Hyksos conquer Egypt.

New Kingdom
- Egypt builds an empire.
- Hatshepsut promotes trade.
- Akhenaten introduces monotheism.
- Ramses the Great builds monuments.

Early Kush
- Kush conquers Egypt.
- Kushites adopt Egyptian customs.

Later Kush
- The capital of Kush moves.
- Kush develops an iron industry.
- A new Kushite culture forms.

Review Key Terms and People

Identify the correct term or person from the chapter that best fits each of the following descriptions.

1. a group of rulers from the same family
2. Kushite ruler who conquered Egypt
3. a person who follows another in a position
4. female ruler of Egypt who encouraged the expansion of trade
5. the process of making mummies
6. expanse or degree
7. ruler who united Upper and Lower Egypt
8. highly structured organization run by officials
9. title given to the rulers of Egypt
10. to refine metal so it can be worked
11. Egyptian ruler who built great monuments in both Egypt and Kush

---

14. a. the Egyptian mode of burial (mummification and pyramids), hieroglyphics
b. Egyptian nobles pushed the Hyksos out of Egypt and sought revenge on the Hyksos' allies, invaded Kush and added it to their empire. After the fall of the New Kingdom, Kush's rulers took advantage of Egypt's weakness to expand to the north, and eventually took control of all of Egypt.
c. Much of what we know about Kush is from Egyptian writings; historians have not been able to translate the language of Kush's Meroitic culture.

Reading Skills

15. that the two kingdoms of Egypt were unified around 3100 BC, beginning the first Egyptian dynasty

16. possible answer—details about the crown, the definition and explanation of dynasties

17. Students should recognize that the two kingdoms of Egypt were unified around 3100 BC, that Menes conquered the north, founded Memphis, the capital of unified Egypt, and established Egypt's first dynasty.

History's Impact video program

Review the video to answer the closing question:
How has ancient Egyptian building design impacted
modern building design?

Comprehension and Critical Thinking

SECTION 1 *(pp. 63–70)*

12. a. Recall What views did Egyptians hold about their pharaohs?

b. Interpret Why has Egypt been called the "gift of the Nile?"

c. Rank During which period of Egyptian history do you think the greatest achievements were made? Support your answer.

SECTION 2 *(pp. 72–79)*

13. a. Describe What systems of writing did the Egyptians invent? What was each used for?

b. Explain Why did the Egyptians make mummies and bury them with treasures?

c. Support a Position Do you agree or disagree with this statement? "Egyptian belief in the afterlife affected every aspect of people's lives." Why?

SECTION 3 *(pp. 81–85)*

14. a. Identify What were two elements of Egyptian culture adopted by the Kushites?

b. Sequence How did Egypt come to rule Kush, and how did Kush later come to rule Egypt?

c. Elaborate Why do historians know less about Kush than they do about Egypt?

Reading Skills

Summarizing *Reread the passage in Section 1 of this chapter titled Unification. Then answer the questions below.*

15. What is the main idea of this passage?

16. What details included in this passage could you leave out of a summary?

17. Write a two or three-sentence summary of the passage that you just reread.

Using the Internet

18. Of all the achievements made by the ancient Egyptians, none is so well known as the building of the pyramids. Considered a symbol of Egyptian civilization, the pyramids are a major tourist destination today. Enter the activity keyword and research the pyramids. Then create an illustrated brochure that could be used to inform tourists about the pyramids' history.

> **go.hrw.com**
> **Practice Online**
> Keyword: SHL NIC

Analyzing Points of View

Reading Like a Historian *The selection below was copied on the wall of a temple built by Ramses the Great. It was written by a scribe named Pen-ta-ur and carved on the wall on the pharaoh's own orders. The passage describes a battle between Ramses and the Hittites. Read the passage and then answer the questions that follow.*

❝ Gracious lord and bravest king, savior-guard
Of Egypt in the battle, be our ward;
Behold we stand alone, in the hostile Hittite ring,
Save for us the breath of life,
Give deliverance from the strife,
Oh! protect us, Ramses Miamun!
Oh! save us, mighty King! ❞

19. Identify What was the author's inspiration in writing this passage?

20. Analyze What was the author's purpose in writing this poem? How did that affect his point of view?

21. Elaborate According to most accounts, the battle between Ramses and the Hittites ended in a draw. Is that fact evident in this passage? Explain your answer.

WRITING FOR THE SAT

Think about the following issue:

In the 1960s the Egyptian government built a new dam on the Nile. The construction of this dam caused a huge uproar around the world because the lake it created would have flooded the temple built by Ramses the Great at Abu Simbel. Faced with protests from historians, archaeologists, and tourists, the government physically moved the entire temple before building the dam.

22. Assignment: Should modern governments work to preserve historic monuments, even if it means passing up a chance for economic development? Write a short essay in which you develop your position on this issue. Support your point of view with reasoning and examples from your reading and studies.

NILE CIVILIZATIONS **89**

Answers

Using the Internet

18. Go to the HRW Web site and enter the keyword shown to access a rubric for this activity.

> KEYWORD: SHL NIC

Analyzing Points of View

19. the pharaoh's orders

20. to glorify the pharaoh; adds bias

21. It is impossible to tell from the passage. The passage does not give any indication that Egypt had won the battle. It just tells us that Ramses had saved Egypt. The wording gives the impression of having been written while the conflict was still taking place rather than after it was over.

Writing for the SAT

22. Student essays might include the argument that historic monuments should be saved whenever possible. Essays should be supported with logic and valid examples.

A rubric for the activity is provided in **CRF:** Writing for the SAT.

> **HOLT**
> ## History's Impact
> ► **Video Program: Nile Civilizations**
> See the Video Program Teacher's Guide for the answer to the closing question.

Review and Assessment Resources

Review and Reinforce

- **CRF:** Chapter Review
- **Quick Facts Transparency:** Visual Study Guide: Nile Civilizations
- **Spanish Chapter Summaries Audio CD Program**
- **OSP Holt PuzzlePro:** Quiz Show for ExamView
- **Quiz Game CD-ROM**

Assess

- **PASS:** Chapter Test, Forms A and B
- **Alternative Assessment Handbook**
- **OSP ExamView Test Generator,** Chapter Test
- **Differentiated Instruction Modified Worksheets and Tests CD-ROM:** Chapter Test
- **HOAP Holt Online Assessment Program** (in the Premier Online Edition)

Reteach/Intervene

- **Interactive Reader and Study Guide**
- **Differentiated Instruction Teacher Management System:** Lesson Plans for Differentiated Instruction
- **Differentiated Instruction Modified Worksheets and Tests CD-ROM:** Chapter Test
- **Interactive Skills Tutor CD-ROM**

> **go.hrw.com**
> **Online Resources**
> KEYWORD: SHL TEACHER

Chapter 4 Planning Guide

Ancient India and China

Chapter Overview	Reproducible Resources	Technology Resources
CHAPTER 4 pp. 90–117 **Overview:** In this chapter, students will learn about the early civilizations of India and China and how each developed their own governments, languages, customs, and religions. KI 1, 2, 3, 4; PI 1.5, 2.2, 3.1, 3.3, 4.1, 4.4 See pp. T32–T55 for a detailed correlation to the New York State Core Curriculum for Global History and Geography and the New York Learning Standards.	**Differentiated Instruction Teacher Management System:*** • Pacing Guide • Lesson Plans for Differentiated Instruction **Interactive Reader and Study Guide:** Chapter Summary* **Chapter Resource File*** • Writing for the SAT • Social Studies Skill • Chapter Review	OSP **New York One-Stop Planner CD-ROM:** Calendar Planner **Live Ink© Online Reading Help** **Student Edition on Audio CD Program** **Differentiated Instruction Modified Worksheets and Tests CD-ROM** **World History Primary Source Library CD-ROM** **History's Impact: World History Video Program (VHS/DVD):** Ancient India and China
Section 1: **Early India** **The Main Idea:** Early civilization arose in the Indus River Valley, flourished, and then mysteriously died out. Later India's Vedic civilization developed a culture based on old and new beliefs. PI 1.5, 4.1	**Differentiated Instruction Teacher Management System:** Section 1 Lesson Plan* **Interactive Reader and Study Guide:** Section 1 Summary* **Chapter Resource File*** • Vocabulary Builder: Section 1 • Biography: Vyasa • History and Geography: India's Geography	**Regents Review Transparency::** Section 1* **Map Transparency:** Eastern Asia* **Quick Facts Transparency:** The *Varnas** **Internet Activity:** Ancient India
Section 2: **Hinduism** **The Main Idea:** The religion of Hinduism developed and evolved over a long time in India, giving rise to a variety of beliefs and practices and to other religions, including Jainism. PI 3.1, 3.3	**Differentiated Instruction Teacher Management System:** Section 2 Lesson Plan* **Interactive Reader and Study Guide:** Section 2 Summary* **Chapter Resource File*** • Vocabulary Builder: Section 2 • Biography: Mahavira	**Regents Review Transparency:** Section 2*
Section 3: **Buddhism** **The Main Idea:** Buddhism, which teaches people that they can escape the suffering of the world through the Buddha's teachings, developed in India and spread to other parts of Asia and the world. PI 3.1, 3.3	**Differentiated Instruction Teacher Management System:** Section 3 Lesson Plan* **Interactive Reader and Study Guide:** Section 3 Summary* **Chapter Resource File*** • Vocabulary Builder: Section 3 • Biography: Ashoka • Literature: Siddhartha	**Regents Review Transparency::** Section 3* **Map Transparency:** Spread of Buddhism*
Section 4: **China's First Dynasties** **The Main Idea:** China's river valley civilizations built the foundations of a long-shared Chinese culture. The achievements of the Shang and Zhou dynasties can be felt to this day. PI 2.2, 4.4	**Differentiated Instruction Teacher Management System:** Section 4 Lesson Plan* **Interactive Reader and Study Guide:** Section 4 Summary* **Chapter Resource File*** • Vocabulary Builder: Section 4 • Biography: Zhuangzi	**Regents Review Transparency:** Section 4* **Map Transparency:** Shang and Zhou Dynasties* **Internet Activity:** Chinese Science and Philosophy

CHAPTER 4 PLANNING GUIDE

HOLT
History's Impact
World History Video Program (VHS/DVD)
Ancient India and China

Review, Assessment, Intervention

 Global History and Geography Regents Test Prep Workbook

 Quick Facts Transparency: Ancient India and China*

 Differentiated Instruction Modified Worksheets and Tests CD-ROM: Modified Chapter Test

OSP **New York One-Stop Planner CD-ROM:** Exam View Test Generator (English/Spanish)

 Holt Online Assessment Program (HOAP), in the Premier Online Edition

 PASS: Section 1 Quiz*

 Online Quiz: Section 1

 Alternative Assessment Handbook

 PASS: Section 2 Quiz*

 Online Quiz: Section 2

 Alternative Assessment Handbook

 PASS: Section 3 Quiz*

 Online Quiz: Section 3

 Alternative Assessment Handbook

 PASS: Section 4 Quiz*

 Online Quiz: Section 4

 Alternative Assessment Handbook

Power Presentation with Video CD-ROM

Power Presentations with Video are visual presentations of each chapter's main ideas. Presentations can be customized by including Quick Facts charts, images and maps from the textbook, and video clips.

Holt Online Learning

go.hrw.com
Teacher Resources
KEYWORD: SHL TEACHER

go.hrw.com
Student Resources
KEYWORD: SHL AIC

- Document-Based Questions
- Interactive Multimedia Activities

- Current Events
- Chapter-Based Internet Activities
- and more!

Holt Premier
Online Student Edition
Complete online support for interactivity, assessment, and reporting
- Interactive Maps and Notebook
- Homework Practice and Research Activities Online

CHAPTER 4 PLANNING GUIDE

The Big Picture

Susan Ramírez

The Value of the Great Books The *Vedas*, the *Ramayana*, the *Mahabharata*, the *Analects*, and the *Dao De Jing* represent more than religious source texts. These works explain, for example, why Indian society placed such a high value on performing one's duty and why the Chinese kings appointed advisors from his most qualified followers. They also remind us that our categorical distinctions between religion, politics, society, and culture do not always represent the worldviews of the early people we study.

The Concept of Legitimacy One of the great contributions of the Chinese was their concept of the "Mandate of Heaven" that explained and justified the rise and fall of governments. If rulers became corrupt or did not rule wisely, the ancestors sent signs, like floods, other natural disasters, and epidemics. If continued, these signs showed that an unjust ruler had lost the favor of the gods, opening the way for another to assume his place. In the United States, in contrast, the basis of legitimacy of public officials is determined by the judgment of the people, expressed through the ballot and the voting box.

Bronze and Iron Technology The Bronze Age was an aristocratic time because bronze was expensive and affordable only to the few. It was used mostly for arms that helped to guarantee the elite's position in society. Iron was cheaper and easier to produce. It became available to wider sectors of society who used it to make weapons and tools. Iron farm implements increased agricultural production, resulting in the growth of the population and cities. Furthermore, a surplus encouraged craft specialization and scholarship. Iron weapons in the hands of many also gave them the potential to rise up against the ruling elite.

Recent Scholarship

To make the history of early China come alive, I recommend "Ko Hung's Autobiography" from *Chinese Civilization and Society: A Sourcebook* (1993), edited by Patricia Buckley Ebrey. Ko Hung, an inwardly-directed and self-taught individual of humble birth, lived between 283 and 343 AD. His account describes such activities as farming, interacting with friends and family, following Daoist and Confucian doctrines, commanding an army, and watching chess players. His autobiography includes over 500 more chapters chronicling his life's work.

Differentiating Instruction

 Differentiated Instruction Teacher Management System
- Pacing Guide
- Lesson Plans for Differentiated Instruction

 Interactive Reader and Study Guide

Spanish Chapter Summaries Audio CD Program

Student Edition on Audio CD Program

Differentiated Instruction Modified Worksheets and Tests CD-ROM
- Vocabulary Flash Cards
- Modified Vocabulary Builder Activities
- Modified Chapter Review Activity
- Modified Chapter Test

OSP One-Stop Planner CD-ROM
- ExamView Test Generator (English/Spanish)
- PuzzlePro
- Quiz Show for ExamView
- Transparencies and Videos

TE Differentiated Activities in the Teacher's Edition
- Aryan Society, p. 96
- The Life of Siddhartha Guatama, p. 104
- Respect for Ancestors, p. 110

Reading Like a Historian
Sam Wineburg

Facing an imminent invasion from the north, the Emperor Taizu, our chapter tells us, uttered these words: "on our borders there is the constant threat of *barbarians*."

What's in a word? Barbarians. The word conjures up hordes of negative connotations: uncouth and uncivilized, crude in look and mien, lacking in refinement. In modern times, the phrase "barbarians at the gate" has been used to disparage everything from unscrupulous corporate takeovers to the proliferation of pop culture.

Barbarian comes to English by way of Latin, which borrowed the word from the original Greek. Grammatically, barbarian is an "imitative," repeating the same syllable twice to create an effect similar to onomatopoeia. Linguists are unsure if the repeated "bar-bar" referred to how Greek sounded to a non-Greek speaker, or how foreign languages sounded to the citizens of Greece. What is clear is that the word originally conveyed a linguistic deficiency, and it is in this sense that it appears in Homer's Iliad (2:867).

By the time of Aeschylus, writing after the Persian invasion of Greece, the word had already taken on meanings familiar to us today, not merely as description of linguistic capacity but as a statement of one's overall being. Unsophisticated, childlike in understanding, illiterate, brutish—in sum, morally and intellectually inferior to the suave denizens of Athens.

Although Taizu was steeped in the Confucian tradition, he knew neither Greek nor Latin. Thus, when we examine the words he supposedly uttered to the residents of his kingdom we can rule out that he used "barbarian" to warn them of a threat.

Translations as Interpretations In fact, Chinese had specific words to designate those who massed on her borders depending on the direction of the threat: the Dongyi, from the East, the Nanman from the South, the Xiong from the West, and the Beidi from the North. In Western languages, these terms are often translated as "barbarian", but depending on the context, it is possible to render them as "stranger" or "outsider," neither of which radiates the same disdain as barbarian. There are some who suggest that translating these Chinese words as "barbarian" may have been a deliberate attempt to cast the Chinese in a negative light—as a supercilious people who regarded all non-Chinese as inferior and uncivilized.

At the same time, we cannot dispute that a certain amount of ethnocentrism is built into China's own name for itself: Zhongguo, "the Middle Kingdom" or the "Capital of all States." Both locate the nation in the center of the known universe—the heart of civilization and human accomplishment. Given that those who invaded China were often unlettered and from places whose achievements in art, philosophy, and architecture paled in comparison to China's, it's not surprising that China viewed those beyond her borders as less developed and less cultured.

Whenever we encounter a source in another language—particularly one distant from the cognates of European languages—we should remember that the act of translation is never mechanical, but always involves choice and judgment. Choosing to render "barbarian" as "foreigner" or "stranger" or "outsider" is more than an aesthetic decision.

It constitutes, in itself, an act of interpretation.

Chapter Main Ideas

Section 1 Early civilization arose in the Indus River Valley, flourished, and then mysteriously died out. Later India's Vedic civilization developed a culture based on old and new beliefs.

Section 2 The religion of Hinduism developed and evolved over a long time in India, giving rise to a variety of beliefs and practices and to other religions, including Jainism.

Section 3 Buddhism, which teaches people that they can escape the suffering of the world through the Buddha's teachings, developed in India and spread to other parts of Asia and the world.

Section 4 China's river valley civilizations built the foundations of a long-shared Chinese culture. The achievements of the Shang and Zhou dynasties can be felt to this day.

New York Standards

Key Idea 3 Study of the major social, political, cultural, and religious developments in world history involves learning about the important roles and contributions of individuals and groups.

Key Idea 4 The skills of historical analysis include the ability to investigate differing and competing interpretations of the theories of history, hypothesize about why interpretations change over time, explain the importance of historical evidence, and understand the concepts of change and continuity over time.

Key to Differentiating Instruction

Below Level

Basic-level activities designed for all students encountering new material

At Level

Intermediate-level activities designed for average students

Above Level

Challenging activities designed for honors and gifted and talented students

Standard English Mastery

Activities designed to improve standard English usage

CHAPTER

4 2500 BC–250 BC

Ancient India and China

THE BIG PICTURE Like Mesopotamia and Egypt, India and China were each home to an early river valley civilization. The people of India and China developed their own governments, languages, customs, and social structures as well as religions and philosophies that still shape life in Asia.

Theme BELIEF SYSTEMS
Belief systems had a profound impact on the lives of people in ancient India and China. The teachings of Hinduism and Buddhism as well as the philosophies of Confucianism and Daoism shaped the way people lived, acted, and thought in those two regions.

TIME LINE

CHAPTER EVENTS

c. 2500 BC The Indus Valley civilization develops.

c. 1766 BC The Shang dynasty begins in China.

c. 1500 BC The Aryans gain power in India.

| 2500 BC | 2000 BC | 1500 BC |

WORLD EVENTS

c. 2330 BC Sargon I builds his empire in Mesopotamia.

1792 BC Hammurabi becomes king of Babylon.

c. 1500 BC Hatshepsut becomes Egypt's pharaoh.

90 CHAPTER 4

Introduce the Chapter

At Level

Ancient India and China

1. Draw a time line of the years 5000 BC to 0 BC for students to see. Label the time line in one thousand year increments (5000 BC, 4000 BC, etc.).

2. Have volunteers come forward and label the beginning of the world's oldest civilizations: Mesopotamia (4000 BC), Egypt (5000 BC), Indus Valley (2500 BC), and China (1766 BC). Tell students that one of the criteria used for calling a human society a civilization is the development of writing.

3. Tell students that in this chapter they will learn about the early development of civilization in two regions that are very important in world history—China and the Indian subcontinent.

4. Have students browse through the graphics and images in this chapter and make a list of questions about ancient India and China.
LS **Visual-Spatial, Kinesthetic**
Alternative Assessment Handbook, Rubric 1: Acquiring Information

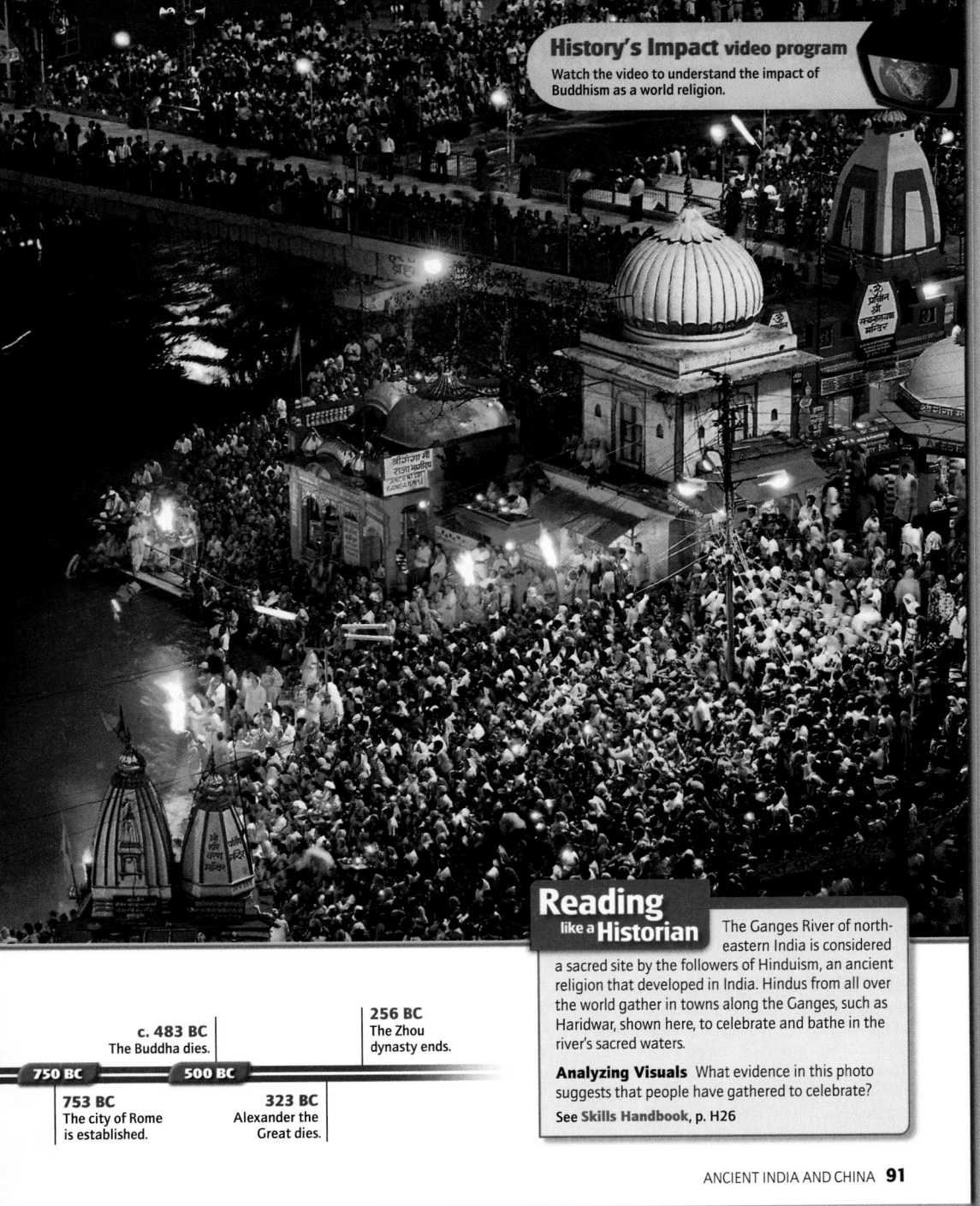

History's Impact video program
Watch the video to understand the impact of
Buddhism as a world religion.

Reading like a Historian

The Ganges River of north-eastern India is considered a sacred site by the followers of Hinduism, an ancient religion that developed in India. Hindus from all over the world gather in towns along the Ganges, such as Haridwar, shown here, to celebrate and bathe in the river's sacred waters.

Analyzing Visuals What evidence in this photo suggests that people have gathered to celebrate?

See Skills Handbook, p. H26

c. 483 BC
The Buddha dies.

256 BC
The Zhou
dynasty ends.

750 BC   500 BC

753 BC
The city of Rome
is established.

323 BC
Alexander the
Great dies.

ANCIENT INDIA AND CHINA **91**

● Chapter Preview ●

HOLT
History's Impact
▶ **Video Program: Ancient India and China**
See the Video Teacher's Guide for strategies for using the video segment.

Reading Like a Historian
Analyzing Visuals The Ganges River is one of the longest in the world. It begins in an ice cave high in the Himalaya mountains of northern India and flows some 1500 miles to the Bay of Bengal. One of India's largest cities, Kolkata, is located along the banks of the Ganges.

go.hrw.com
Online Resources
Chapter Resources:
KEYWORD: SHL AIC
Teacher Resources:
KEYWORD: SHL TEACHER

Explore the Time Line

1. When did the Indus Valley civilization develop? *about 2500 BC*

2. How long after Hammurabi became king of Babylon did the Shang dynasty begin? *about 26 years*

3. What happened around the same time that Hatshepsut became pharaoh in Egypt? *The Aryans gained power in India.*

4. What happened in about 483 BC? *The Buddha died.*

Info to Know

The Holy Ganges The Ganges River is considered sacred by the Hindus. Its soil is rich and the crops along the Ganges have always been plentiful, irrigated by the river and the seasonal monsoons. Earthly sins are thought to be washed away by a bath in the Ganges. Many Hindus hope to make a pilgrimage to the river at some point in their lives to experience its purification.
Elaborate Why do you think Hindus attach such importance to this river? *possible answer—It traditionally sustained crops, so people would benefit.*

Answers

Reading Like a Historian *possible answer—large crowds; people are facing the same direction; lit torches*

91

Geography Starting Points

Eastern Asia The ruins of Mohenjo Daro and Harappa, the two largest cities of the Indus Valley civilization, are located in present-day Pakistan.

🗺 **Map Transparency:** Eastern Asia

📋 **World History Outline Maps**

✳ **Interactive Map:** Eastern Asia

Recent Scholarship

For many years, Gregory Possehl has collected data and developed expertise in Indian archaeology. In his book *The Indus Civilization: A Contemporary Perspective*, he presents an overview of the most current knowledge on the ancient society, exploring technology, subsistence, political organization, religion, and other aspects. Possehl does not believe that Indus civilization was a unified state; he points to the absence of palaces, and lack of evidence for a state bureaucracy. Possehl describes what life was like in the Indus civilization. The book offers about 200 illustrations to accompany the text.

The Indus Civilization: A Contemporary Perspective by Gregory Possehl. AltaMira Press, 2003.

GEOGRAPHY Starting Points

✳ Interactive
EASTERN ASIA

EARLY INDIA, C. 1700 BC

ELEVATION

Feet	Meters
13,120	4,000
6,560	2,000
1,640	500
656	200
(Sea level) 0	0 (Sea level)
Below sea level	Below sea level

■ Indus Valley civilization
■ Shang dynasty
← Dry monsoon (Winter)
← Wet monsoon (Summer)
● Major settlement
· Other settlement

EARLY CHINA, C. 1050 BC

Starting Points → Like the valleys of the Tigris, Euphrates, and Nile rivers, the valleys of the Indus and the Huang He in eastern Asia supported the growth of complex civilization. These civilizations shared some characteristics that made the growth of civilizations possible, but their locations and other geographic features also led to unique developments.

1. **Draw Conclusions** What geographic features may have allowed civilizations to develop in ancient India and China?

2. **Predict** What geographic features do you think could have influenced the development of the Indus and Huang He civilizations?

🔊 **Listen to History**

Go online to listen to an explanation of the starting points for this chapter.

go.hrw.com
Keyword: SHL AIC

92 CHAPTER 4

Skills Focus: Evaluating Information on the Internet   Above Level

Social Studies Skill
Examining Artifacts

Research Required

1. Organize students into small groups. Assign half of the groups the Indus Valley civilization and the other half the civilization of ancient China.

2. Have groups use reliable online sources to conduct Internet research on artifacts from these civilizations. Have students choose three artifacts and learn about them. Have students evaluate conclusions that have been drawn from information learned about the artifacts.

3. Have groups use their findings to write a short essay about the results of their research.

🅛🅢 **Verbal-Linguistic**

📋 **Alternative Assessment Handbook**, Rubrics 12: Drawing Conclusions; and 30: Research

Answers

Geography Starting Points 1. *fertile river valleys;* **2.** *fertile river valleys; wet and dry monsoons*

SECTION 1 Early India

BEFORE YOU READ

MAIN IDEA

Early civilization arose in the Indus River Valley, flourished, and then mysteriously died out. Later India's Vedic civilization developed a culture based on old and new beliefs.

READING FOCUS

1. How did India's geography affect the development of civilization there?

2. What were the defining features of the Indus Valley Civilization?

3. What do we know about life in India's Vedic period?

KEY TERMS

subcontinent
monsoons
citadel
Vedas
rajas
varnas
castes

 NEW YORK

P1 1.5 Students analyze changing and competing interpretations of issues, events, and developments throughout world history.

P1 4.1 Students identify historical problems, pose analytical questions or hyphotheses, formulate conclusions or generalizations.

DECIPHERING AN ANCIENT CIVILIZATION

◀ More than 3,000 samples of Indus script have been found, including many seals that depict realistic animals alongside the writing.

 THE INSIDE STORY

What do all these characters mean? In the 1920s an archaeologist working in northwest India discovered a remarkable set of ruins, all that remained of a huge ancient city. His discovery was the first clue modern archaeologists had about the advanced civilization of the Indus River Valley that flourished thousands of years ago.

Since that original discovery, archaeologists have learned a great deal about the Indus civilization. Among the artifacts they have found are small seals like the ones above that contain what appears to be writing. Despite the best efforts of the archaeologists and linguists, however, no one has yet been able to decipher even one word from any of the seals.

Part of the challenge of deciphering the script is that linguists know of no related languages from which they can start their studies. In fact, no one knows even the first thing about the Indus language, though linguists have various theories. Some believe that the characters found in Indus writings are part of an alphabet, like that of the Phoenicians. Others believe that each character represents an object or an idea, like characters in Sumerian and Egyptian writing. Even among scholars who agree that characters represent objects, there is much disagreement. One symbol on the elephant tile above, for example, has been variously identified as a fish, a twist of rope, and a noble title. Until such disputes can be resolved, there is little chance that the language can be translated. ∎

ANCIENT INDIA AND CHINA **93**

Teach the Main Idea

At Level

Early India

1. **Teach** Ask students the Reading Focus questions to teach this section.

2. **Apply** Draw three ladders for students to see. Label the tops of the ladders with the names of the topics in this section: India's Geography, Indus Valley Civilization, and The Vedic Period. Have students copy the ladders onto their paper and fill in the rungs of the ladders with the main ideas of each topic.

3. **Review** As you review the section, have students explain how India's geography

influenced the development of the Indus Valley civilization.

4. **Practice/Homework** Have students write a letter from an archaeologist to a university, describing the first discovery of the Indus civilization. Student letters should be written in formal business style and should describe the discovery's significance.
LS Visual-Spatial

📝 **Alternative Assessment Handbook**, Rubrics 5: Business Letters; and 40: Writing to Describe

---

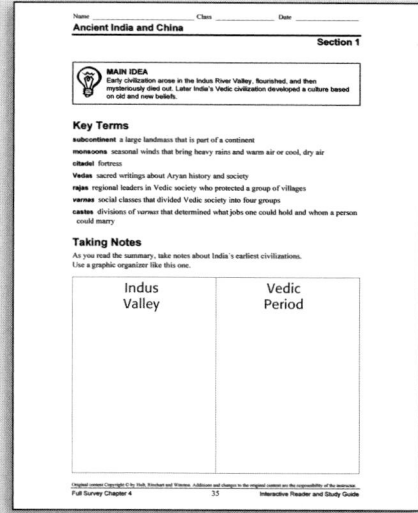

Preteach

Getting Started

Use the **Interactive Reader and Study Guide** to familiarize students with the section content.

📝 **Interactive Reader and Study Guide,** Section 1

Academic Vocabulary

Review with students the high-use academic term in this section.

assume believe to be true (p. 96)

📝 **CRF:** Vocabulary Builder: Section 1

Taking Notes

Indus Valley—flood deposits from rivers enrich Northern Plains, monsoons bring heavy summer rains, Indus Valley civilization developed writing 2500 BC, well-planned cities, citadel, agriculture and trade, writing system undeciphered, civilization declined; Vedic Period—sacred writings called Vedas provide information, villages banded together under rajas, social classes called varnas developed into castes, worshipped many gods

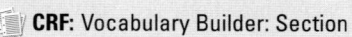 **go.hrw.com**

Online Resources

KEYWORD: SHL AIC
ACTIVITY: Ancient India

ANCIENT INDIA AND CHINA **93**

Reading Focus

❶ How did India's geography affect the development of civilization there? *Flood deposits from rivers enriched the soil, monsoons brought heavy rains to water crops.*

India's Geography

Identify What are the three geographic zones of India? *high mountains in north, fertile Northern Plains, Deccan Plateau in the south*

Explain How did the monsoons help the people of early India? *Winds brought in rains, rains flooded rivers, which deposited fertile silt.*

Interpret If you were a farmer in ancient India, when would you expect heavy rains to come? *during the summer months*

📄 **CRF:** History and Geography: India's Geography

Info to Know

Industry and Trade Trade was an important part of life in the Indus Valley. Artisans made both decorative and practical goods to trade. Decorative articles included ceramic beads, ornaments, and gold and silver jewelry. Useful goods included bronze and copper tools, pots and pans, and stone tools. Among the most impressive art objects are seals with writing. Indus-made seals have been found in the Tigris-Euphrates region near Sumerian sites, suggesting trade between the two civilizations.

Answers

Reading Check *flooding or drought*

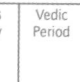

TAKING NOTES

As you read, take notes about India's earliest civilizations.

Indus Valley	Vedic Period

NEW YORK

CC Unit 1-B1a
Human and physical geography of the Indus Valley

India's Geography

The Indus River, home of one of the ancient world's great river valley civilizations, flows across the northwest edge of the Indian subcontinent. A **subcontinent** is a large landmass that is part of a continent. As its name implies, most of the Indian subcontinent is occupied by the country of India.

The Indian subcontinent includes three major geographic zones. In the far north are the Himalaya and Hindu Kush mountain systems, which separate India from the rest of Asia. In the south is the Deccan Plateau, a high plateau that receives less rain than other parts of the subcontinent. Between the mountains and the plateau are the Northern Plains, where society first developed in India. Flood deposits from three rivers—the Indus, Ganges, and Brahmaputra—enrich the soil of the plains, making it very fertile.

Heavy rains also add to the fertility of the Northern Plains. Much of this rain is brought to India by seasonal winds called **monsoons**.

Indus Valley Discoveries

The ruins of Mohenjo Daro were among the first remains archaeologists uncovered of the Indus Valley civilization. Within the ruins, they found hundreds of artifacts, including this statue, that can help us learn more about life in the ancient city.

94 CHAPTER 4

During the summer months, monsoon winds from the southwest bring warm air and heavy rains from the Indian Ocean. Most of India's annual rainfall occurs at this time. In the winter, northeast monsoons blow cool, dry air from Central Asia, resulting in drier months.

The people of India's first civilizations depended upon the monsoons to bring the water that their crops needed. Monsoon rains flooded rivers, which then deposited fertile silt in which farmers could grow their crops. But with the abundance of rainfall came the threat of devastation. If the monsoon rains were too heavy, crops, homes, and lives could be lost. In contrast, if the rains came too late or did not last long enough, people could not grow crops and famine became a danger.

READING CHECK **Describe** What problems could monsoons cause for early Indians?

Indus Valley Civilization

People have lived in the northern parts of the Indian subcontinent for thousands of years. At first, people lived as hunter-gatherers, but slowly people began to settle down in farming communities. In time, these communities gave rise to India's first civilization, which developed in the valley of the Indus River. Historians generally date the beginnings of this civilization to about 2500 BC, when people there first developed a system of writing.

Cities and Settlements The first ruins of the Indus Valley civilization found by archaeologists were the remains of two large cities. Harappa, named after a nearby modern city, and Mohenjo Daro, which means "mound of the dead," were both discovered in the 1920s. In fact, the civilization is sometimes called Harappan after the first ruins found. Since then, several large cities have been uncovered, as have hundreds of smaller towns and villages. Much of what we know about Indus society has come from studying their remains.

Indus settlements were well planned and carefully laid out. Streets ran in a grid pattern, north-south and east-west, with major avenues that were twice as wide as minor streets. People drew water from community wells or smaller wells dug in the courtyards of their homes, and public drainage systems carried away waste-

---

Skills Focus: Making Written Presentations
At Level

Reading Like a Historian Skill
Planned City

Materials: drawing paper, pencils

1. Review with students the information in the text about cities in the Indus Valley. You might wish to have students conduct additional research on the layout of these cities.

2. Have students draw a plan for an Indus city. Have students include all the elements mentioned in the text with labels. If students find actual plans of Indus cities, they should incorporate design elements, such as thick city walls.

3. Have students prepare a written presentation to accompany their drawings, in which they explain their design elements and the features of their city plans.

4. Have volunteers present their plans and read their written presentations to the class.
LS Visual-Spatial, Verbal-Linguistic,

📄 **Alternative Assessment Handbook**, Rubrics 3: Artwork; and 29: Presentations

Harappan Trade

Evaluating Historical Interpretation When a historian writes about the past, he or she must interpret the sources available to draw conclusions. As a reader, it is important to evaluate the writer's interpretation to determine whether or not it is valid. As you read, think about

- who wrote the document and what his or her credentials, or qualifications, might be.
- when the document was written and whether new evidence has been found that might affect the interpretation.
- whether the author is biased.

Skills FOCUS   READING LIKE A HISTORIAN

1. **Author** What do the author's credentials suggest about the validity of his interpretation?
2. **Date** This passage was written in the 1950s when archaeologists had only been working in the Indus Valley for 30 years. Why might interpretations of the civilization have changed since then?
3. **Bias** Does the author's interpretation of the past seem biased?

See **Skills Handbook**, p. H32

Though their culture extended nearly to the mouth of the Indus the people of Harappa and Mohenjo Daro seem to have cared little for the sea. Only two representations of ships have been found among their remains, and these are of small river vessels. But whether by sea or land, the products of the Indus reached Mesopotamia, for a number of typical Indus seals and a few other objects from the Indus Valley have been found in Sumer at levels dating between about 2300 and 2000 BC. Evidence of Sumerian exports to India is very scant and uncertain, and we must assume that they were mainly precious metals and raw materials.

—A. L. Basham,
The Wonder That Was India, 1954

> The interpretation of the past in this passage is based largely on the fact that archaeological evidence does not exist.

> A. L. Basham, the author of this text, was a professor of Indian history at a large, prestigious university.

---

water. In the largest cities, a walled, elevated **citadel**, or fortress, enclosed buildings such as granaries, warehouses, and meeting halls. Homes, workshops, and shrines were built outside the citadel. Such planning and uniformity among cities suggests that a central authority held power over the civilization.

Economy Historians believe the economy of the Indus civilization focused on agriculture and trade. Most people probably farmed and herded livestock. In cities, however, many people specialized in crafts such as pottery, metalwork, and jewelry. Example of all these crafts have been found in Harappan cities.

The Indus traded the goods they produced not only with people of nearby communities but with distant civilizations as well. Traders from the Indus Valley brought goods to locations as distant as Central Asia, the Arabian Peninsula, and Mesopotamia.

Society Unfortunately, archaeologists and historians have not been able to learn many details about Indus society. Although the people of the Indus Valley had a writing system, historians are not yet able to read it. The inability to read what people wrote makes it difficult to learn about society and daily life.

Based on material evidence, some scholars believe that Indus civilization was a single society rather than a collection of independent city-states. As you have already read, cities and towns throughout the Indus Valley were remarkably similar. In addition, the people of the Indus Valley apparently shared common tool designs and a standard set of weights and measures. These factors all suggest a single authority in control, though it is not yet possible to know for sure.

Decline The Indus Valley civilization thrived from about 2500 BC to 2000 BC. After that time, the civilization began to decline. For example, the city of Mohenjo Daro was abandoned.

NEW YORK
CC Unit 1-B1d
Social structures and urbanization of the Indus Valley

---

2 What were the defining features of the Indus Valley Civilization? *planned cities, citadel enclosed buildings, public drainage system; economy based on agriculture and trade; writing system*

Indus Valley Civilization

Describe What was the basic plan of an Indus settlement? *streets in a grid pattern, north-south and east-west, major avenues twice as large as minor streets*

Identify What items did Indus craftsmen make? *pottery, metalwork, jewelry*

Analyze Do you think the Indus civilization was a single society or a collection of independent city-states? Why? *possible answers—single society, planning and uniformity; independent city-states, not enough evidence to prove otherwise*

Teaching Tip

The Indus Valley civilization was completely forgotten until archaeologists discovered Harappa and Mohenjo Daro in 1925. Before the discovery, scholars had believed that the first Indian cities were built in the first millennium BC.

Skills Focus: Analyzing Primary Sources

At Level

Reading Like a Historian Skill
Excavating in the Indus Valley

Prep Required

1. Before the lesson, locate some images of Indus artifacts. Isolate the images from text and make several copies of each.

2. Tell students that in order to find impressive artifacts archaeologists must carefully sift through earth. Archaeology is a tedious process with great rewards.

3. Tell students they are archaeologists excavating a site in the Indus Valley.

4. Have students begin writing journal entries about the excavation process. As they write, randomly hand out images of artifacts. When students receive an image, they should write a careful description of the artifact, what testing might be done on it, and what information they think it can provide. **LS** Logical-Mathematical, Verbal-Linguistic

📝 **Alternative Assessment Handbook**, Rubrics 15: Journals; and 38: Writing to Classify

Answers

Reading Like a Historian 1. *that it is an expert opinion;* **2.** *possible answer— More evidence may have been found.* **3.** *possible answer—no, seems grounded in available facts*

Reading Focus

3 What do we know about life in India's Vedic period? *Aryans controlled India; villages banded together under rajas; society divided into four social classes; worship of gods through fire sacrifices and hymns*

The Vedic Period

Recall Who ruled much of India during the Vedic period? *the Aryans*

Make Inferences Why do you think villages banded together under rajas? *possible answer—suggests that it was a dangerous time period*

Develop Where do you think the Aryans were from? Why? *possible answers—Central Asia, linguistic ties; India, no evidence that they emigrated*

CRF: Biography: Vyasa

Info to Know

Daily Life Life in Aryan clans and families was somewhat freer and more open than in other societies. Although the Aryans were a patriarchal society, tribal chiefs were bound by their laws and customs. At the beginning of the Vedic period, women were free to choose their own husbands, rather than being told who they should marry. This practice, however, changed over time.

Answers

Counterpoints *linguistic ties to Central Asia; migration not mentioned in writing*
Reading Check *have not deciphered Indus writing*

96

ACADEMIC VOCABULARY
assume believe to be true

No one knows what led to the decline of the Indus civilization, or even if there was a single cause. Evidence from Mohenjo Daro suggests that the city suffered repeated flooding, which may indicate environmental reasons. Ancient records mention a river, the Sarasvati, that once flowed through the Indus Valley but later disappeared. The disappearance of that river could have had devastating effects on agriculture and sped the decline. Some historians also argue that invasion and disease helped end the civilization, though others argue that the available evidence does not support either conclusion. In truth, we may never know just why the Indus civilization disappeared.

READING CHECK **Analyze** Why do historians know relatively little about Indus society?

The Vedic Period

Sometime after 2000 BC, a new people took control of India. Historians often refer to this group as the Aryans, from a Sanskrit word meaning "noble." Eventually, the Aryans ruled over most of India, except for the far south.

Historians are not sure exactly when the Aryans arrived in India or where they came from originally. Some historians <u>assume</u> they moved from the area between the Caspian and Black seas, based on perceived linguistic ties to Indo-European languages spoken in that area. Others disagree, arguing that the Aryans developed in northern India itself and did not move into the area.

Little archaeological evidence remains to document the early Aryan period in India. Most of what we know comes from sacred writings called the **Vedas** (VAY-duhs), which include many details about Aryan history and society. As a result, this period in Indian history is often called the Vedic period.

Vedic Society According to the Vedas, people settled in villages much smaller than the cities of the Indus Valley. Later, groups of villages banded together under regional leaders known as **rajas** (RAH-juhz). According to the Vedas, the raja was primarily a war leader who was responsible for protecting the people. In return for this protection, he received payments of food or money.

COUNTERPOINTS

Two Sources on Indian Society

Many historians today believe that the Aryans moved to India from an original homeland, most likely in Central Asia. Their argument is based largely on linguistic ties between the Aryans and people of that region, ties that they say can be seen in Vedic writings.

❝Sometime during the second millennium . . . Aryan-speaking peoples invaded the Land of the Seven Rivers, the Punjab and its neighboring region. It has long been accepted that the tradition of this invasion is reflected in the older hymns of the Rigveda, the composition of which is attributed to the second half of the millennium.❞

Sir Mortimer Wheeler
—*The Indus Civilization*, 1968

Other historians believe that the Aryans developed within India and gradually rose to power. They point out that, had the Aryans come from another land, that land would certainly be mentioned in their writings. Debate over the issue has lasted for decades.

❝Neither in the Code (of Manu) nor, I believe, in the Vedas, nor in any other book that is certainly older than the code, is there any allusion [reference] to a prior residence or to a knowledge of more than the name of any country out of India. Even mythology goes no further than the Himalayan chain, in which is fixed the habitation of the gods.❞

Mountstuart Elphinstone
—*History of India*, 1841

Skills Focus **INVESTIGATING HISTORY**

Identify Supporting Details What evidence is used to support each theory of the Aryans' origins?

Differentiating Instruction

Above Level

Advanced Learners/Gifted and Talented

Research Required

1. Organize students into small groups.

2. Have each group use reliable online sources or traditional print sources to conduct research on one aspect of Aryan society. Examples might include social structure, religion, origins, and customs.

3. Have groups compile their research into a multimedia presentation.

4. Have groups make their presentations to the class. Allow time for a question/answer period following each presentation.

LS Visual-Spatial, Verbal-Linguistic

Alternative Assessment Handbook, Rubrics 14: Group Activity; 22: Multimedia Presentations; and 30: Research

Social Structure According to the oldest of the Vedas, the *Rigveda*, Vedic society was divided into four social classes called *varnas*. Each *varna* played a particular role in society, as described in the chart to the right. These roles are alluded to in a passage of the *Rigveda* that describes the creation of humans. According to this passage, people of the four *varnas* were created from the body of a single being:

HISTORY'S VOICES

❝ The Brahmin was his mouth, of both his arms was the Rajanya [Kshatriya] made. His thighs became the Vaisya, from his feet the Sudra was produced. ❞

—*Rigveda*, 10.90

The part of the body from which each *varna* was created was tied to its duties. For example, brahmins came from the mouth, the source of speech and wisdom, and thus were priests.

Over centuries, the four *varnas* of the Vedic period were divided into hundreds of smaller divisions called **castes**. Membership in a caste determined what jobs one could hold and whom one could marry. A social hierarchy developed in which some castes had more privileges than others, though the order of castes could and did change frequently. Not everyone in society belonged to a caste, though. A group commonly referred to as the untouchables had none of the protections of caste law and could perform only jobs that other castes did not, such as handling dead animals.

Vedic Religion Because the *Vedas* consist mostly of hymns in praise, we know a great deal about the religion of the Vedic period. For example, we know that people prayed to many aspects of a single eternal spirit, one such aspect being Indra, who ruled over heaven.

The *Vedas* described how people worshipped the gods through fire sacrifices and the chanting of sacred hymns. In the sacrifices, priests offered food and drink by placing them on a roaring fire. Over time, the rituals surrounding Vedic religion grew more complex. Priests claimed that order in the universe could only be maintained through the religious rituals that they performed. As a result, the brahmin *varna* gained more influence in society.

READING CHECK **Summarize** How was Vedic society organized?

THE VARNAS

During the Vedic period, Indian society was divided into four *varnas*, or classes. Members of each *varna* played specific roles in society.

Brahmins were the highest ranking *varna*, and the smallest numerically. Brahmins were Vedic society's priests and teachers.

Kshatriyas (ksha-TREE-uhs) were warriors and rulers.

Vaisyas (VYSH-yuhs) were the common people of Vedic society—traders, farmers, herders, and so on.

Sudras were servants who waited upon members of the other *varnas*.

SECTION 1 ASSESSMENT

go.hrw.com
Online Quiz
Keyword: SHL AIC HP

Reviewing Ideas, Terms, and People

1. **a. Define** What are **monsoons**, and how do they affect life on the Indian subcontinent?
   b. Explain Why did Indian civilization begin in the Northern Plains?
   c. Elaborate How might the geography of India have helped protect the Indus Valley civilization?

2. **a. Describe** What were two characteristics of cities built in the Indus River Valley?
   b. Identify Cause and Effect Why do many historians think that a single central authority ruled in the Indus Valley?
   c. Make Judgments Do you think it is important that historians learn to read Indus writing? Why or why not?

3. **a. Identify** What were the *varnas*?
   b. Explain Why did priests gain influence within Vedic society?
   c. Predict How do you think the development of the **caste** system affected India's social structure after the Vedic period?

Critical Thinking

4. **Analyze** Review your notes from this section and identify the main source of our knowledge about each of India's two earliest civilizations. Then identify one aspect of each society about which we know little and explain why it remains a mystery.

	Source	Unknown	Reason Unknown
Indus Valley			
Vedic Period			

FOCUS ON WRITING

5. **Describe** Write a brief description of India's geography, explaining how its physical features and climate affected the development of civilization on the subcontinent.

Reading Focus

The Vedic Period

Recall How did the caste system affect everyday life in India? *Caste membership determined possible jobs and marriage partners; some castes had more privileges.*

Make Generalizations What was Vedic religion like? *People prayed to many aspects of a single external spirit and worshipped the gods through fire sacrifices and chanting sacred hymns; priests placed food and drink in a roaring fire.*

QUICK FACTS
The Varnas

Analyze What are the advantages and disadvantages of the varnas system? *advantages—everyone knows their position in life, ensures certain jobs will be fulfilled; disadvantages— unfair to people in lower varnas, probably felt inferior*

Quick Facts Transparency: The Varnas

Review & Assess

Close

Have students compare and contrast the Indus Valley civilization and the Vedic civilization.

Review

Online Quiz, Section 1

Assess

SE **Section 1 Assessment**

Progress Assessment: Section 1 Quiz

Alternative Assessment Handbook

Reteach/Intervene

Interactive Reader and Study Guide, Section 1

Interactive Skills Tutor CD-ROM

Answers

Reading Check *into four social classes called* varnas

Section 1 Assessment Answers

1. **a.** seasonal winds; warm air and heavy rains in summer; cool, dry air in winter
   b. Flood deposits enriched the soil, rainfall provided water for crops.
   c. possible answer—Mountains kept out invaders

2. **a.** streets in a grid pattern; citadel enclosed buildings; community wells; public drainage system
   b. good planning; uniformity among cities
   c. possible answer—Yes, this will teach us a lot about Indus society

3. **a.** social classes during the Vedic period
   b. claimed that order in the universe could be maintained only through their rituals
   c. possible answer—divided society

4. Indus Valley—archaeology, Indus society, historians can't decipher writing system; Vedic—*Vedas*, origin of Aryans, conflicting evidence

5. Student descriptions should demonstrate an understanding of India's geography, including the effect of rivers, mountains, geographic zones, and monsoons.

Getting Started

Use the **Interactive Reader and Study Guide** to familiarize students with the section content.

📓 **Interactive Reader and Study Guide**, Section 2

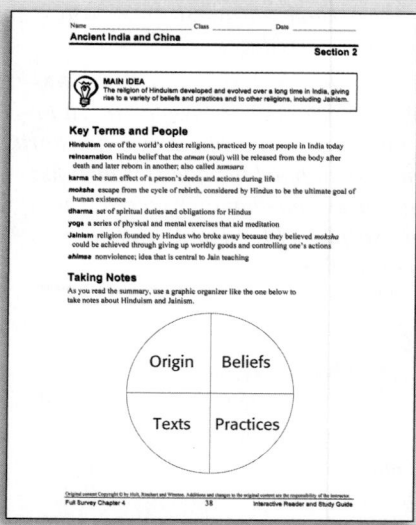

Academic Vocabulary

Review with students the high-use academic term in this section.

integrated blended together or combined (p. 101)

📓 **CRF:** Vocabulary Builder: Section 2

Taking Notes

Hinduism—evolved over thousands of years, diverse beliefs, belief in Brahman, devas, reincarnation, improving karma, goal is moksha or salvation; sacred texts are Vedas, related writings, and epics; diverse worship, yoga to focus mind and body; Jainism—broke away from Hinduism, led by Mahavira belief in ahimsa or nonviolence, tell the truth, devout Jains become monks or nuns, renounce violence, harm no living creature, avoid stealing, anger, prejudice, or gossip

---

SECTION 2 Hinduism

BEFORE YOU READ

MAIN IDEA

The religion of Hinduism developed and evolved over a long time in India, giving rise to a variety of beliefs and practices and to other religions, including Jainism.

READING FOCUS

1. What basic teachings do most Hindus share?
2. What are the sacred texts and religious practices of Hinduism?
3. What are the teachings of Jainism?

KEY TERMS

Hinduism
reincarnation
karma
moksha
dharma
yoga
Jainism
ahimsa

A LOVE FOR ALL TIME

Rama and Sita, by an artist of the Pahari school, c. 1740

◀ In the *Ramayana*, the prince Rama endures great hardships to rescue his wife Sita.

THE INSIDE STORY

What would Rama do to save his wife? For centuries, readers have considered Rama and Sita, the main characters of the sacred Hindu epic the *Ramayana*, a model of an ideal couple. In the *Ramayana*, both Rama and Sita are willing to face great hardships to remain loyal to each other.

Early in the *Ramayana*, the young prince Rama renounces his claim to his father's throne and becomes an exile from the kingdom at the demand of his father's wife. Facing a potentially difficult and dangerous life in the wilderness, Rama begs his wife Sita to remain in the city where she will be safe. However, Sita does not want to live without Rama, and she follows him into the forest to share his exile.

Their happiness is shattered, though, when Sita is kidnapped by the demon king Ravana. Distraught, Rama immediately sets out to find and rescue his beloved. Joined by powerful allies, Rama builds a mighty army with which he challenges the powerful Ravana. In the end, the prince kills the demon and, at long last, is reunited with Sita.

Rama and Sita are widely admired for their total devotion to each other. In addition, both are praised for their devotion to their duties and obligations. Rama, for example, does not complain when he is ordered to give up his claim to the throne, because he sees it as his duty. Likewise Sita considers it her duty to accompany him into exile. Fulfilling one's duties, or dharma, as Rama and Sita did is a central teaching of Hinduism, one of the world's major religions. ◼

98 CHAPTER 4

Teach the Main Idea

At Level

Hinduism

1. **Teach** Ask students the Reading Focus questions to teach this section.

2. **Apply** Have students create flashcards to learn the key terms and main ideas in this section. Have them write the definition or answer on one side of the card and the term or question on the other side.

3. **Review** As you review the section, have students use their flashcards to quiz each other on the main ideas and key terms.

4. **Practice/Homework** Have students write a letter to a friend explaining basic Hindu beliefs. **LS Visual-Spatial, Verbal-Linguistic**

📓 **Alternative Assessment Handbook**, Rubrics 25: Personal Letters; and 42: Writing to Inform

Basic Teachings of Hinduism

One of the world's oldest religions, **Hinduism** is practiced by most people in India today. Because it is so old, however, its origins are difficult to trace. Unlike other major religions, Hinduism has no founder. It evolved over thousands of years and was influenced by the cultures and traditions of many peoples.

Largely because it was influenced by so many cultures, the practice of Hinduism varies widely. Practices differ from place to place and even from person to person. However, a few fundamental teachings are shared by nearly all Hindus.

Brahman Among the most basic tenets of Hinduism is the belief in Brahman, the eternal being that created and preserves the world. Hindus believe that everything in the world is simply an aspect of Brahman.

Because Brahman is all-encompassing, literally including all of creation, many Hindus do not believe that the human mind is capable of understanding it. That is because people themselves are aspects of Brahman. Hindus also believe that each person has an *atman*, or soul, that is an aspect of Brahman. A person's *atman* shapes his or her personality and cannot be destroyed, even by death.

Most Hindus believe that various manifestations of Brahman called *devas* (DAY-vuhs) are active in the world, helping to maintain order in nature. For example, Ganesha is considered the lord of wisdom, while Lakshmi grants wealth. Like many teachings of Hinduism, people's views of the *devas* vary widely. For example, many Hindus recognize three *devas*—Brahma the Creator, Vishnu the Preserver, and Siva the Destroyer—as particularly influential. Some believe in thousands of *devas*, while others worship only one, usually Vishnu or Siva, as the true manifestation of Brahman.

Rebirth and Salvation Hindus believe that the universe and everyone in it are part of a continual pattern of birth, death, and rebirth. After death, they believe that the *atman* will be released from the body and later reborn in another, a process called **reincarnation**, or *samsara*. The nature of the person's new life will be shaped by his or her **karma**, the sum effect of his or her deeds and actions during life.

Hindu Beliefs

Hinduism teaches that everything in the world is a power of Brahman, the single great universal being. Most Hindus believe that various aspects of Brahman, called *devas*, are active in the world, helping to keep order in nature. Three of the *devas*, together called the Trimurti, have been particularly influential in the development of Hinduism. *How do the ways in which the* devas *are depicted in art reflect their powers and roles in the world?*

◄ Brahma
Brahma the Creator is often depicted with four heads, representing the four *Vedas*.

► Vishnu
Vishnu the Preserver holds in each of his four arms one of his symbols.

◄ Siva
Siva the Destroyer is often represented dancing upon the back of a demon, surrounded by a ring of fire.

BASIC HINDU BELIEFS

Dharma	A person's spiritual duties and obligations, which he or she must follow to achieve liberation
Karma	The sum effect of a person's actions, both good and bad, which helps shape future experiences
Moksha	Liberation; release from the cycle of reincarnation, and joining with the atman
Samsara	Reincarnation; the cycle of birth, death, and rebirth a person follows before achieving liberation

Reading Focus

❶ What basic teachings do most Hindus share? *Brahman is eternal spirit; devas are aspects of Brahman that are active in the world; reincarnation based on karma; goal is to fulfill dharma and reunite with Brahman*

Basic Teachings of Hinduism

Recall Why do Hindu beliefs vary widely? *influenced by many cultures*

Describe What are Hindu beliefs about Brahman? *created and preserves the world; everything in the world is an aspect of Brahman*

Make Inferences How might Hindu beliefs about karma and reincarnation affect the way that individuals live? *possible answer—behave well to improve karma, be reincarnated to a better life*

Info to Know

Sacred Animals Throughout their history, the people of India have respected and revered animals. The ancient Indus Valley dwellers carved the likenesses of animals, particularly bulls, on their beautiful trading seals. The Indo-Aryans, with nomadic herding roots, valued cattle so highly that they considered them to be the basic unit of wealth and used cattle as currency to purchase items of great value. Eventually the Hindus declared cows to be sacred and forbade killing them. The Hindus believed that souls could be reincarnated as humans or animals. Killing any creature—even an insect—was forbidden because any creature might house the soul of an ancestor or friend. Other animals that were highly revered in India included birds, monkeys, and elephants.

Answers

Hindu Beliefs *Brahman's four heads represent the four* vedas; *Vishnu has many arms, showing his diverse activities; Siva is surrounded by fire, showing destruction; all gods have many arms or heads, showing their ability to exercise control over many things at once.*

Collaborative Learning

At Level

Hinduism Scrapbook

Research Required

1. Organize students into small groups.

2. Have students conduct research in order to compile a scrapbook about Hinduism. Each group's scrapbook should include information about Hindu beliefs and sacred texts, as well as annotated images of Hindu gods, temples, holy sites, and worship practices.

3. Each group should assign specific tasks to its members: research, note taking, compiling information, layout of scrapbook, etc. Allow enough time for students to compile their scrapbooks.

4. Place the completed scrapbooks on one or two display tables in the classroom. Allow small groups of students to take turns examining the books. **LS Verbal-Linguistic, Kinesthetic**

📑 **Alternative Assessment Handbook**, Rubrics 14: Group Activity; and 32: Scrapbooks

❷ **What are the sacred texts and religious practices of Hinduism?** *texts the* Vedas, *writings inspired by the* Vedas, *sacred epics; practices offerings, prayers, meditation, yoga, pilgrimages*

Sacred Texts and Practices

Recall What do Hindus believe about the *Vedas*? *a collection of eternal knowledge; not written by humans but revealed to them by Brahman*

Contrast How are epics different from other sacred Hindu texts? *believed to be written by people; tell a story*

Evaluate Do you think epics are a good way to teach people about religious ideas? Why or why not? *possible answer—Yes, they can show examples of teachings in action, and can hold people's attention.*

Info to Know

The Upanishads The word *Upanishad* is derived from the Sanskrit words "sit," "down," and "near," referring to the fact that groups of students sat down near their teachers to hear their wisdom. The philosophy contained in the *Upanishads* is not thinking for its own sake; the goal is practical application to improve one's life.

Answers

Reading Check *escape from cycle of rebirth, reunion with Brahman; ultimate goal for Hindus; way to achieve* moksha *is to fulfill one's dharma*

100

Use two diagrams like the one below to take notes about Hinduism and Jainism.

| Origin | Beliefs |
| Texts | Practices |

NEW YORK

CC Unit 1-E1b
Origin and teachings of Hinduism

People who have behaved well will have good karma and can be reincarnated to a better station in the next life. Conversely, those who have bad karma will have a lower station.

For Hindus, the ultimate goal of human existence is **moksha,** escape from the cycle of rebirth. When a person achieves *moksha,* the *atman* leaves the world and reunites fully with Brahman. During their lives, Hindus work toward achieving *moksha* because it releases a person from worldly cares and the difficulties of life on Earth.

The way to achieve *moksha* is to fulfill one's **dharma,** or set of spiritual duties and obligations. Individuals' dharmas vary based on their class and their station in life. Fulfilling one's dharma allows a person to create good karma, to avoid suffering, and, eventually, to break free from the cycle of rebirth.

READING CHECK **Analyze** What is *moksha,* and how is it central to Hindu teachings?

Sacred Texts and Practices

As you have read, Hinduism has grown and evolved over centuries. Much of the religion's evolution stemmed from a number of sacred writings that have been produced during that time. These texts influenced not only what people believed about Hinduism, but how they practiced the religion in their own lives.

Sacred Texts The teachings and practices of Hinduism are based upon not one but many sacred texts. Most of these texts can be sorted into one of three categories:

- the *Vedas*
- later writings inspired by the *Vedas*
- sacred epics

The *Vedas,* sacred hymns of praise, were among the earliest sacred texts of Hinduism. The name *Veda* means "knowledge" in Sanskrit, an ancient Indian language used for many sacred texts. Hindus consider the *Vedas* to contain eternal knowledge not written by humans but revealed to them by Brahman. The written *Vedas,* parts of which date back more than 3,000 years, are considered the core of Hinduism even today.

As time passed, sacred texts that built upon the *Vedas* appeared in India. Some, such as the *Upanishads,* were also believed to have been

100 CHAPTER 4

SACRED TEXTS

Bhagavad Gita

About the Reading One of Hinduism's most sacred texts, the *Bhagavad Gita* was written as a dialogue between a warrior named Arjuna and Krishna, an avatar, or human form, of Vishnu. In this passage, Krishna, as a divine being, advises Arjuna about how to obtain *moksha* and eternal happiness.

AS YOU READ
Note how Krishna says one can achieve *moksha.*

An illustrated page from the *Bhagavad Gita* created in the 1700s or 1800s ▶

revealed to rather than written by people. The *Upanishads* are philosophical reflections on the *Vedas,* dealing with such questions as the nature of the world and the meaning of life.

Other sacred texts were based on themes found in the *Vedas* but composed by sages. Among them were two sacred epic poems, the *Ramayana* (rah-MAH-yuh-nuh) and the *Mahabharata* (muh-HAH-BAH-ruh-tuh). Each of these epics tells a story but at the same time reflects on what it means to live according to Vedic teachings. The *Ramayana* tells of the relationship between Rama—the *deva* Vishnu in human form—and his wife Sita. For centuries, Rama and Sita have been seen as a model for Hindu couples to follow, both for their devotion to each other and their willingness to obey their dharma. The *Mahabharata* tells of a war between two families who want to control part of the Ganges River Valley. As it tells the story, the epic also teaches about dharma and proper behavior for rulers, warriors, and others.

Reading Skill
Sacred Hindu Texts

1. Draw the chart for students to see. Omit the italicized answers.

2. Have students use information in the text to copy and complete the chart. Have volunteers fill in the class chart. **LS** Visual-Spatial

📖 **Alternative Assessment Handbook,** Rubric 7: Charts

Text	Importance to Hinduism
Vedas	*collection of eternal knowlege, believed to be revealed by Brahman*
Upanishads	*built upon the* Vedas, *deal with the nature of the world, meaning of life*
Ramayana	*sacred epic, model of devotion and dharma*
Mahabharata	*sacred epic, model of good behavior and dharma*
Bhagavad Gita	*one of the most sacred Hindu texts*

That devotee of mine, who hates no being, who is friendly and compassionate, who is free from egoism, and from (the idea that this or that is) mine, to whom happiness and misery are alike, who is forgiving, contented, constantly devoted, self-restrained, and firm in his determinations, and whose mind and understanding are devoted to me, he is dear to me. He through whom the world is not agitated, and who is not agitated by the world, who is free from joy and anger and fear and agitation, he too is dear to me. That devotee of mine, who is unconcerned, pure, assiduous, impartial, free from distress, who abandons all actions (for fruit), he is dear to me. He who is full of devotion to me, who feels no joy and no aversion, who does not grieve and does not desire, who abandons (both

what is) agreeable and (what is) disagreeable, he is dear to me. He who is alike to friend and foe, as also in honour and dishonour, who is alike in cold and heat, pleasure and pain, who is free from attachments, to whom praise and blame are alike, who is taciturn, and contented with anything whatever (that comes), who is homeless, and of a steady mind, and full of devotion, that man is dear to me. But those devotees who, imbued with faith, and (regarding) me as their highest (goal), resort to this holy (means for attaining) immortality, as stated, they are extremely dear to me.

—Bhagavad Gita

Summarize What qualities does Krishna say will help a person achieve eternal happiness when he or she dies?

A Hindu man reads sacred writings near a temple.

Included within the *Mahabharata* is a passage that many people consider the most sacred of all Hindu texts, the *Bhagavad Gita*. The *Gita*, as it is sometimes called, was written as a dialogue between the warrior Arjuna and Krishna, again Vishnu in human form. Their conversation addresses in great detail many aspects of Hindu belief and philosophy.

Hindu Religious Practices Because Hindu beliefs vary so widely, religious practices vary as well. Worship can take place anywhere—in large elaborate temples, in small village shrines, or at home. At temples, priests or other spiritual leaders might recite or read portions of the *Vedas* to worshippers. Sometimes an image of a *deva* is carried out of the temple and brought before the people. At home, individual worshippers might offer food, drink, or gifts to a *deva*. He or she might say special prayers, or meditate, or silently reflect upon the world and its nature.

To help them meditate, some Hindus also practice a series of integrated physical and mental exercises called **yoga**. The purpose of yoga is to teach people how to focus their bodies and minds, which will aid their meditation and help them attain *moksha*.

At some point during their lives, many Hindus desire to make a pilgrimage, or religious journey, to a holy location. Among the places considered sacred by many Hindus is the Ganges River, which is thought to flow from the feet of Vishnu and over the head of Siva. Through this contact with two *devas*, the river's waters become holy. As a result, many Hindus believe that bathing in the Ganges will purify them and remove some of their bad karma. Huge festivals held in towns along the Ganges each year attract millions of Hindu pilgrims from around the world.

ACADEMIC VOCABULARY
integrated
blended together or combined

READING CHECK **Categorize** What types of sacred texts help shape Hindu beliefs?

Reading Focus

Sacred Texts and Practices

Recall What are some places that Hindu worship can take place? *in temples, at shrines, in homes*

Explain What is the ultimate purpose of yoga? *to teach people how to focus their bodies and minds; help them attain moksha*

Interpret Why do Hindus make pilgrimages to the Ganges? *The river is believed to purify people and remove bad karma.*

Info to Know

Breath Control One of the earliest descriptions of yoga is of a group of musicians who used a type of breath control called *pranayama*. When they practiced *pranayama*, the musicians could sing better because they could control their breath and hold notes longer. Control of breathing still remains a fundamental part of many forms of yoga.

Skills Focus: Comparing and Contrasting
At Level

Reading Skill
Jainism

1. Review with students information in the text about Mahariva and the origin of Jainism.

2. Organize students into pairs. Have each pair create a script for a dialogue between Mahariva and a Hindu priest. The dialogue should convey the basic similarities and differences of each person's belief system.

3. After students have had enough time to write and rehearse their dialogues, have volunteers read their dialogues dramatically for the class.

LS Verbal-Linguistic

Alternative Assessment Handbook, Rubric 33: Skits and Reader's Theater

Answers

World Religions *faith, devotion, regarding Krishna as highest goal*

Reading Check Vedas, *writings inspired by the* Vedas, *sacred epics*

101

❸ What are the teachings of Jainism? *practice* ahimsa *or nonviolence toward living creatures; tell the truth; do not steal; try to eliminate greed, anger, prejudice, and gossip*

Jainism

Contrast How is Jainism different from Hinduism? *not as much emphasis on ritual, more emphasis on* ahimsa *or nonviolence*

Summarize How do Jain monks and nuns live? *give up all possessions, live outdoors, cover mouths and sweep the ground in front of them to avoid killing insects*

📄 **CRF:** Biography: Mahavira

● **Review & Assess** ●

Close

Have students describe the basic beliefs of Hinduism.

Review

🖥 **Online Quiz**, Section 2

Assess

SE Section 2 Assessment

📋 **Progress Assessment:** Section 2 Quiz

📋 **Alternative Assessment Handbook**

Reteach/Intervene

📋 **Interactive Reader and Study Guide,** Section 2

💿 **Interactive Skills Tutor CD-ROM**

Beliefs of Jainism
This Jain statue from the 1800s represents a soul that has been freed from the body and achieved *moksha.*

Jainism

Around 500 BC, a group of Hindus broke away from the religion and founded a new religion called **Jainism** (JYN-iz-uhm). Led by a teacher named Mahavira, the Jains thought that most Hindus of the time put too much emphasis on ritual. The Jains thought this ritual was unnecessary, because people could achieve *moksha* by giving up all worldly things and carefully controlling their actions.

Central to Jain teaching was the idea of *ahimsa,* or nonviolence. *Ahimsa* was not a new idea. In fact, most Hindus also practiced *ahimsa,* though not to the same extent as the Jains did. Jains carefully avoid harming any living creature, from people to insects. As a result, Jains are usually vegetarians, refusing to eat meat from any animal.

In addition to renouncing violence, Jains promise to tell only the truth and to avoid stealing. They strive to eliminate greed, anger, prejudice, and gossip from their lives. Any of these things, they believe, can prevent a person from achieving *moksha.*

The most devout of Jains give up all of their possessions and become monks or nuns. They live outdoors, seeking shelter only during the rainy season. Monks and nuns cover their mouths with masks and sweep the ground before them as they walk. In this way they avoid accidentally killing insects by inhaling them or by stepping on them.

Most Jains are not monks or nuns. However, their pledge to uphold the principles of *ahimsa* leads many Jains to careers that do not involve the harming of animals. Jainism calls upon those who are not monks to periodically fast, especially during festivals and on holy days, and to limit their worldly possessions.

READING CHECK **Find the Main Idea** What are the major principles of Jainism?

SECTION 2 ASSESSMENT

go.hrw.com
Online Quiz
Keyword: SHL AIC HP

Reviewing Ideas, Terms, and People

1. **a. Define** In Hindu teaching, what are *moksha* and **karma**? How are these two ideas related to **reincarnation**?
   b. Explain What is the nature of Brahman in Hindu belief?
   c. Elaborate Why would a Hindu consider it important to follow his or her **dharma**?

2. **a. Describe** What role does **yoga** play in Hindu religious practice?
   b. Analyze What spiritual lessons do the *Ramayana* and the *Mahabharata* teach?
   c. Elaborate How does the name *Veda* signify the importance of the *Vedas* to **Hinduism**?

3. **a. Define** What is *ahimsa*? How do the principles of *ahimsa* shape life for Jains?
   b. Compare and Contrast What is one way in which life is similar for Jains who are monks and those who are not? What is one way in which life is different?

Critical Thinking

4. **Compare and Contrast** Draw a Venn diagram like the one below. In the left circle, list teachings that are unique to Hinduism. In the right circle, list three teachings that are unique to Jainism. Where the two circles overlap, list one teaching that the two religions share.

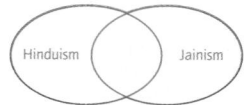

Hinduism   Jainism

FOCUS ON WRITING ✎

5. **Exposition** Write a short paragraph explaining one of the major teachings of Hinduism. You explanation should define the teaching and explain its role in Hindu teaching.

102 CHAPTER 4

Section 2 Assessment Answers

1. **a.** escape from the cycle of rebirth; sum effect of a person's actions; creating good karma results in reincarnation; *moksha* is an escape from reincarnation
   b. eternal spirit; created and preserves the world; everything is an aspect of Brahman
   c. to create good karma, avoid suffering

2. **a.** teaches people how to focus their bodies and minds, helps them achieve *moksha*
   b. models of devotion, behavior, dharma
   c. means "knowledge"; regarded as most important knowledge

3. **a.** nonviolence; Jains are vegetarians, have jobs which do not involve harming animals
   b. similar—practice *ahimsa*, seek *moksha*; different—monks live outdoors, sweep ground before them as they walk

4. Hinduism—more ritual, less focus on ahimsa; Jainism—less emphasis on ritual, practice *ahimsa* to a greater extent, monks give up all possessions; Both—seek *moksha*

5. Students should define one of the teachings in the section, using details and examples from the text.

Answers

Reading Check *practice nonviolence; tell the truth; do not steal; try to eliminate greed, anger, prejudice, and gossip*

SECTION 3 Buddhism

BEFORE YOU READ

MAIN IDEA

Buddhism, which teaches people that they can escape the suffering of the world through the Buddha's teachings, developed in India and spread to other parts of Asia and the world.

READING FOCUS

1. How did the early life of the Buddha lead to the beginnings of Buddhism?
2. What are the major teachings of Buddhism?
3. What areas were affected by the spread of Buddhism?

KEY TERMS AND PEOPLE

Buddhism
Buddha
Four Noble Truths
Eightfold Path
nirvana
Middle Way

NEW YORK

3.1 Students analyze the roles and contributions of individuals and groups to religious practices.

3.3 Students examine the social/cultural and religious norms and values of Western and other world cultures.

THE INSIDE STORY

Why would a prince abandon his old life and his chance to be a king? According to Buddhist tradition, young prince Siddhartha Gautama led a very sheltered life. On the day he was born, a seer predicted that the young prince would grow up to be either a mighty king or a great religious leader. His father the king, wanting Gautama to follow him as king, kept him isolated from all the hardships of the world. He was given three different palaces to live in, luxurious furnishings, and dutiful servants to attend to his every need.

When he was 29, Gautama asked to be taken out of the palace on a chariot ride. As he rode, he saw an old man among the crowd in the street. Never having seen the signs of old age, Gautama asked his servants what it meant. He was surprised to learn that everyone—even he himself—would eventually grow old. On later trips outside the palace, Gautama saw a sick man and a corpse being carried to its funeral. The idea of old age, sickness, and death profoundly affected him. Gautama had never known any sort of suffering and was shocked to learn that people had to endure it.

On a fourth chariot ride outside his palace, Gautama observed a holy man seeking enlightenment. This man had given up all of life's comforts in order to find a way to overcome old age, disease, and death. Gautama immediately decided to follow in the man's example. He asked his father for permission to leave the palace, but his father did not want him to go. Gautama left anyway, sneaking out in the night in what became known as the Great Departure, and became a monk. After years of meditation, Gautama found a path to enlightenment and became known as the Buddha, the founder of Buddhism. ■

The Great DEPARTURE

▲ In this painting of the Great Departure, spirits hold the hooves of Gautama's horse so he will not awaken anyone as he flees his father's palace.

Detail of a mural at Wat Ratchasitaram, Thailand, 1800s

ANCIENT INDIA AND CHINA **103**

Teach the Main Idea

At Level

Early Buddhism

1. **Teach** Ask students the Reading Focus questions to teach this section.

2. **Apply** Have students create a graphic organizer that sequences events in the life of Siddhartha Gautama and the spread of Buddhism.

3. **Review** As you review the section, have students describe the basic teachings of Buddhism.

4. **Practice/Homework** Have students write a short essay comparing and contrasting Hinduism and Buddhism. **LS Visual-Spatial, Verbal-Linguistic**

   Alternative Assessment Handbook, Rubric 9: Comparing and Contrasting

---

Preteach

Getting Started

Use the **Interactive Reader and Study Guide** to familiarize students with the section content.

Interactive Reader and Study Guide, Section 3

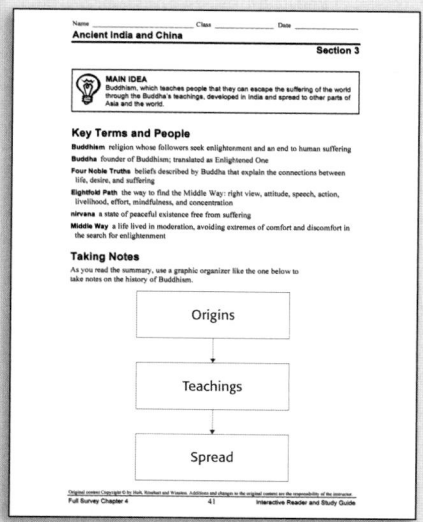

Academic Vocabulary

Review with students the high-use academic term in this section.

diverse made up of many elements, varied (p. 107)

CRF: Vocabulary Builder: Section 3

Taking Notes

Origins—founder was Siddhartha Gautama, also called the Buddha; began in 500s BC; the Buddha followed path to enlightenment for six years; Teachings—Four Noble Truths, the Eightfold Path, nirvana, the Middle Way; after the Buddha's death, divisions formed, including Theravada, Mahayana, and Tibetan Buddhism; Spread—reached peak in India in 200s BC, spread beyond India through missionaries, trade; spread to China, Korea, and Japan; today Buddhism a very diverse religion

1 How did the early life of the Buddha lead to the beginnings of Buddhism? *lived a sheltered early life; was deeply affected when he realized that there was suffering in life; resolved to find a way to overcome suffering, leading to the beginnings of Buddhism*

The Life of the Buddha

Identify What ideas did the Buddha learn while meditating and what are they called? *the four central truths; the Four Noble Truths*

Recall How did Gautama begin his search for enlightenment? *by living in forest, begging for food, studying with gurus*

📄 **CRF:** Literature: Siddhartha

TAKING NOTES

Use a graphic organizer like this one to take notes on the history of Buddhism.

Origins
↓
Teachings
↓
Spread

NEW YORK

CC Unit 1-E1c
Origin and beliefs of Buddhism

The Life of the Buddha

In addition to Hinduism, another of the world's major religions developed in ancient India. That religion was **Buddhism**. Unlike Hinduism, which evolved over thousands of years, Buddhism can be traced back to the teachings of a single founder, Siddhartha Gautama, also called the **Buddha**.

Early Life Much of what is known about the life of the Buddha comes from accounts told in Buddhist literature, some of which were written centuries after his death. According to these sources, Gautama was born in the 500s BC. He was a prince of a small kingdom in the very northern part of the Indian subcontinent in what is now Nepal.

The sources say that Gautama lived a very sheltered life free of any hardship or suffering. As a result, he was unaware that hardship existed in the world until he was almost 30. When Gautama realized that people grew old, got sick, and died, his life was changed. He resolved to find a way to overcome age and sickness, to keep people from having to suffer. As the first step toward finding this new path, he gave up his possessions and left his palace.

The Buddha's Enlightenment Tradition says Gautama sought enlightenment, or spiritual understanding, for six years. He began his search by living in the forest and begging for food. He studied with teachers called gurus and with monks who denied themselves food, drink, and other necessities. After a time, he decided that neither the gurus nor the monks could teach him the way to enlightenment.

Left alone with no teacher and no companions, Gautama sat under a tree, determined not to arise until he found the way to end human suffering. Stories say that he meditated all night, his resolve tested by violent storms and earthly temptations. When dawn broke, Gautama had been transformed. He had found enlightenment and became known from then on as the Buddha, or Enlightened One. The spot where the Buddha is believed to have sat in meditation is called Bodh Gaya. Later, a Buddhist temple was built there. It is one of Buddhism's most sacred places.

READING CHECK **Explain** How did Siddhartha Gautama become the Buddha?

The Teachings of Buddhism

After he achieved enlightenment, the Buddha remained at Bodh Gaya for seven weeks, deep in meditation. Then he set out to spread what he had learned to other people. His lessons became the basic teachings of Buddhism.

Buddhist Beliefs Among the ideas that the Buddha is said to have learned while meditating are four central truths. Together, these are called the **Four Noble Truths**:

- Suffering is a part of human life. No one can escape from suffering while alive.
- Suffering comes from people's desires for pleasure and material goods.
- Overcoming these desires during life eventually brings suffering to an end.
- Desires can be overcome by following the **Eightfold Path**.

World Religions

SACRED TEXTS

Dhammapada

About the Reading Many of the sacred texts of Buddhism record the words of the Buddha. Among them is the *Dhammapada*, which is believed to include the answers to questions asked of the Buddha on various occasions. The *Dhammapada* is particularly sacred to Theravada Buddhists, but Mahayana Buddhists read it as well.

AS YOU READ Note the qualities the Buddha says a person should have.

Buddhist scroll painted in Japan in the 1100s ▶

Differentiating Instruction

Below Level

Special Education Students

Materials: butcher paper, art supplies

1. Review with students the information in the text about Siddhartha Gautama's development from prince to enlightened teacher. Allow time for students to ask questions about the material to be sure they understand it.

2. Organize students into mixed-ability pairs.

3. Have each pair illustrate at least four scenes from the life of the Buddha on a piece of butcher paper. Tell students the scenes should be shown in chronological order, with the earliest scene on the far left.

4. Display the scenes in a classroom exhibit.
   LS Visual-Spatial

📄 **Alternative Assessment Handbook**, Rubric 3: Artwork

Answers

Reading Check *meditated under a tree, determined not to arise until he found solution to human suffering; was enlightened and transformed*

The Eightfold Path is a series of steps that Buddhists believe leads to enlightenment and salvation. It includes the following:

- Right view, or accepting the reality of the Four Noble Truths

- Right attitude, or striving for moderation in all things

- Right speech, or avoiding lies, boasts, and hurtful words

- Right action, or treating others fairly

- Right livelihood, or avoiding jobs that could bring harm to others

- Right effort, or constantly trying to improve oneself

- Right mindfulness, or remaining aware of the world around one, and

- Right concentration, or ignoring temptation and discomfort while meditating

The Buddha taught that those who followed the Eightfold Path could attain **nirvana**, a state of perfect peace in which the soul would be free from suffering forever. Those who do not attain nirvana will be reborn to live through the cycle of suffering again.

The basic teachings of the Eightfold Path can also be expressed as the **Middle Way**. In its simplest form, the Middle Way advises people to live in moderation, avoiding the extremes of either comfort or discomfort in the search for nirvana:

HISTORY'S VOICES

❝There are two extremes . . . which he who has given up the world ought to avoid. What are these two extremes? A life given to pleasures, devoted to pleasures and lusts: this is degrading, sensual, vulgar, ignoble, and profitless; and a life given to mortifications: this is painful, ignoble, and profitless.❞

—The Buddha, Sermon at Benares, c. 528 BC

READING SKILLS

Connecting How does the Buddhist teaching of reincarnation compare to the Hindu teaching you read about in the previous section?

All that we are is the result of what we have thought: it is founded on our thoughts, it is made up of our thoughts. If a man speaks or acts with an evil thought, pain follows him, as the wheel follows the foot of the ox that draws the carriage.

All that we are is the result of what we have thought: it is founded on our thoughts, it is made up of our thoughts. If a man speaks or acts with a pure thought, happiness follows him, like a shadow that never leaves him.

"He abused me, he beat me, he defeated me, he robbed me,"—in those who harbour such thoughts hatred will never cease.

"He abused me, he beat me, he defeated me, he robbed me,"—in those who do not harbour such thoughts hatred will cease.

For hatred does not cease by hatred at any time: hatred ceases by love, this is an old rule.

The world does not know that we all must come to an end here;—but those who know it, their quarrels cease at once.

He who lives looking for pleasures only, his senses uncontrolled, immoderate in his food, idle, and weak, Mâra (the tempter) will certainly overthrow him, as the wind throws down a weak tree.

He who lives without looking for pleasures, his senses well controlled, moderate in his food, faithful and strong, him Mâra will certainly not overthrow, any more than the wind throws down a rocky mountain.

—*Dhammapada*

Analyze What qualities does the Buddha say a person should try to master to find enlightenment?

A young monk studies Buddhist scripture.

Skills Focus: Comparing and Contrasting

At Level

Reading Skill
Comparing Religions

1. Review with students information in the text about Hinduism, Buddhism, and Jainism. Explain that each religion sought release from the cycle of rebirth.

2. Organize students into small groups. Have each group plan a newscast that will inform the public about each religion. Encourage students to include interviews with monks or priests in their newscasts.

3. Have students rehearse and perform their newscasts for the class. **LS Kinesthetic, Verbal-Linguistic**

   Alternative Assessment Handbook, Rubrics 14: Group Activity; and 33: Skits and Reader's Theater

❷ What are the major teachings of Buddhism? *the Four Noble Truths, the Eightfold Path, nirvana, the Middle Way*

The Teachings of Buddhism

Explain What is the relationship between the Four Noble Truths and the Eightfold Path? *The Four Noble Truths teach that overcoming desires for pleasure and material goods can bring suffering to an end. One overcomes those desires by following the Eightfold Path.*

Describe According to the Buddha, what happens to those who do not attain nirvana? *They are reborn to live through the cycle of suffering again.*

📄 **CRF:** Interdisciplinary Project

Info to Know

The Triptaka The oldest collection of Buddhist texts is called the Triptaka, meaning "three baskets," after the way the collection was originally written. The writing was done on long, narrow leaves, which were then sewn together, grouped into bunches, and stored in baskets. The original text was written in Pali, an Indian language that is no longer spoken.

The Twelve Great Deeds According to tradition, the life of the Buddha is divided into twelve defining moments. These moments are depicted in a series of paintings called *Twelve Great Deeds of the Buddha's Life*. These deeds include his renunciation of a worldly life, six years of self-denial, enlightenment, and proclamation of his teachings. These paintings are often beautifully decorated and use symbols to convey complicated ideas of Buddhism.

Answers

World Religions *pure thought, love, self-control*

Reading Focus

The Teachings of Buddhism

Compare What are the three main traditions of Buddhism, and how do they differ from one another? *Theravada—oldest of Buddhist traditions, teaches individual path to enlightenment; Mahayana—teaches that people can help each other find enlightenment; Tibetan Buddhism—teaches that one can use special techniques to achieve nirvana in a single lifetime.*

Explain According to Theravada, what is the best way to achieve nirvana? *to become a monk or a nun and spend all one's time in meditation*

Make Inferences Why are bodhisattvas worshipped by some Mahayana Buddhists? *They have found enlightenment.*

 Map Transparency: Spread of Buddhism

✱ **Interactive Map:** Spread of Buddhism

Info to Know

Meditation The practice of meditation forms a central part of Buddhism. Buddhists believe that meditation eventually leads to enlightenment and spiritual freedom. The two main types of Buddhist meditation are *vipassana*, which seeks to realize truths, and *samatha*, which trains the mind to concentrate.

Answers

Interpreting Maps 1. *China, Japan, and Korea;* **2.** *Refer to map.*

Reading Check *suffering comes from selfish desires; overcoming desire ends suffering; follow Eightfold Path to overcome desire*

106

✱ Interactive
SPREAD OF BUDDHISM

JAPAN

KOREA

CENTRAL ASIA

TIBET

CHINA

Yellow Sea

NEPAL
Bodh Gaya

Buddha from Afghanistan, c. 300

INDIA

SOUTHEAST ASIA

South China Sea

0   500   1,000 Miles
0   500   1,000 Kilometers
Two-point equidistant projection

Bay of Bengal

Sri Lanka

INDIAN OCEAN

Sumatra

Java

Buddha from Sui dynasty China, c. 600

Buddha from Khmer Thailand, c. 1400

⬅ Early spread of Buddhism
⬅ Spread of Mahayana
⬅ Spread of Theravada
☐ Mahayana Buddhism today
☐ Theravada Buddhism today
☐ Tibetan Buddhism today

GEOGRAPHY SKILLS | INTERPRETING MAPS

go.hrw.com
Interactive Map
Keyword: SHL AIC

1. **Regions** In what part of Asia is Mahayana Buddhism most common today?
2. **Movement** When was Buddhism introduced into Japan?

Divisions of Buddhism After the Buddha's death, differing opinions arose concerning the correct teachings and practices of Buddhism. Eventually, three main traditions formed—Theravada, Mahayana, and Tibetan Buddhism. Each sect believed that its teachings and practices most closely followed the way of the Buddha.

Theravada, meaning the Way of the Elders, is the oldest of the Buddhist traditions. It is based on the oldest known Buddhist writings. These writings are collectively called the Pali Canon, because they were written in the Pali language. Theravada teaches that the best way to attain nirvana is to become a monk or a nun and spend all of one's time in meditation. Through this meditation, each person must find his or her own path to enlightenment. As a result, Theravada is very much an individual religion. Those who do not become monks or nuns should support those who do, providing them with food and caring for temples.

In contrast, Mahayana teaches that people can help each other find enlightenment. This tradition incorporates teachings from texts that were written after the Buddha's lifetime. According to these teachings, it is not necessary to be a monk or a nun to reach nirvana. Anyone can do it, with some help. That help is provided by bodhisattvas, people who have found enlightenment but have not yet passed on to nirvana. Instead, they have remained on Earth to help others find their way. Because of their wisdom and compassion, bodhisattvas are worshipped by some Mahayana Buddhists.

The third Buddhist tradition, Tibetan Buddhism, shares many teachings with Mahayana. In addition to these teachings, however, Tibetan Buddhists believe that they can use special techniques to harness spiritual energy and achieve nirvana in a single lifetime.

READING CHECK **Summarize** What are the fundamental teachings of Buddhism?

106 CHAPTER 4

Reading Skill
Hinduism and Buddhism

1. Draw the Venn diagram as shown for students to see. Omit the italicized answers.

2. Have students copy the diagram onto their own paper and use information from the text about Hinduism and Buddhism to complete the diagram. Then have volunteers complete the class Venn diagram. **LS** Visual-Spatial

📝 **Alternative Assessment Handbook,** Rubric 13: Graphic Organizers

Two Religions of India

Hinduism   Buddhism

Hinduism: *Brahman, devas, dharma, caste system, ritual*

Both: *cycle of rebirth, seeking release from cycle, karma, nonviolence*

Buddhism: *Middle Way, Four Noble Truths, Eightfold Path*

The Spread of Buddhism

Unlike Hinduism, which largely remained an Indian religion, Buddhism spread into other parts of the world. Today, more than 350 million people are Buddhists, most of them concentrated in Asia, but relatively few people in India are Buddhists today.

Buddhism in India Throughout the Buddha's life, the Buddhist community in India grew. After his death, the Buddha's followers spread his teachings, though they were not written down until the first century BC. Once they had been recorded, Buddhist writings helped to preserve and spread the teachings of the Buddha throughout India.

Buddhism reached its peak in India in the 200s BC during the reign of the emperor Ashoka, whom you will read more about in a later chapter. During Ashoka's rule as emperor, he became a Buddhist and helped spread Buddhism into all parts of India. Ashoka also encouraged missionaries to carry the Buddha's message to lands outside of India.

Buddhism Beyond India One of the lands to which Ashoka sent missionaries was Sri Lanka, the large island off India's southern coast. He also sent missionaries north to lands along the Himalayas and east into the lands of Southeast Asia. There, Buddhism took a firm hold in the kingdoms that eventually became Myanmar, Thailand, and Vietnam. It also spread into the islands of Indonesia.

In addition to missionary work, trade helped to spread Buddhism beyond India. Merchants traveling routes from India to Central Asia introduced Buddhist teachings into that region in the 200s BC, about the same time that Ashoka was sending out missionaries.

Historians also believe that traders from both Central Asia and Southeast Asia took Buddhist teachings into China. In China, Buddhism slowly spread and blended with native Chinese philosophies.

From China, Buddhism eventually diffused into Korea and Japan. It was first introduced to Korea during the AD 300s, and Korean travelers then took the religion to Japan about 200 years later. By this time, Buddhism had become the leading religion in all of East and Southeast Asia.

As Buddhism encountered other religious traditions outside of India it continued to change and develop. Because of this blending, various smaller traditions developed within Theravada and Mahayana. For example, a branch of Mahayana known as Zen that emphasized self-discipline and meditation developed in China and spread to Japan. Buddhism today is a very <u>diverse</u> religion with a wide range of adherents and practices.

ACADEMIC VOCABULARY

diverse made up of many elements, varied

READING CHECK Sequence How did Buddhism spread through Asia?

SECTION 3 ASSESSMENT

go.hrw.com
Online Quiz
Keyword: SHL AIC HP

Reviewing Ideas, Terms, and People

1. **a. Describe** What was the early life of the **Buddha** like?
   b. Explain According to Buddhist texts, what happened to change the Buddha's outlook on life?
   c. Elaborate Why do you think many Buddhist consider Bodh Gaya to be a sacred place?

2. **a. Define** What is the **Middle Way**? How do Buddhists believe it will help them attain **nirvana**?
   b. Contrast What are the three major traditions of **Buddhism**, and how do they differ?
   c. Elaborate How are the **Four Noble Truths** and the **Eightfold Path** linked together in the teachings of Buddhism?

3. **a. Identify** Into what regions did Buddhism spread as it was carried out of India?
   b. Identify Cause and Effect What was the end result of Ashoka's conversion to Buddhism?
   c. Extend Why did Buddhism grow and change as it spread out of India into other parts of Asia?

Critical Thinking

4. **Analyze** Draw a graphic organizer like the one below. Using your notes, explain what each of the teachings listed in the left column is and how Buddhists believe each one will help them attain nirvana.

FOCUS ON WRITING

5. **Narration** Write a short biographical sketch of the Buddha. In your sketch, describe his early life, the changes that occurred when he was an adult, and his basic teachings. As you write, be sure to make the order of events clear.

ANCIENT INDIA AND CHINA **107**

Direct Teach

Reading Focus

3 What areas were affected by the spread of Buddhism? *Central Asia, Southeast Asia, Korea, and Japan*

The Spread of Buddhism

Explain How did Ashoka affect the spread of Buddhism? *He became a Buddhist; under his rule, Buddhism spread through the empire; he sent missionaries to other lands.*

Describe How did traders spread Buddhism? *Traders from Central Asia and Southeast Asia brought Buddhism to China.*

CRF: Biography: Ashoka

Review & Assess

Close

Guide a class discussion about the Four Noble Truths.

Review

Online Quiz, Section 3

Assess

SE Section 3 Assessment

Progress Assessment: Section 3 Quiz

Alternative Assessment Handbook

Reteach/Intervene

Interactive Reader and Study Guide, Section 3

Interactive Skills Tutor CD-ROM

Answers

Reading Check *through missionary work and trade*

107

Getting Started

Use the **Interactive Reader and Study Guide** to familiarize students with the section content.

📖 **Interactive Reader and Study Guide,** Section 4

📄 **CRF:** Vocabulary Builder: Section 4

Taking Notes

Shang dynasty—formed around 1766 BC; agricultural society; king with court; royal tombs show that Shang believed in an afterlife; ancestor worship; development of writing; ended with Zhou invasion in about 1100 BC; Zhou dynasty—Mandate of Heaven explained rise and fall of dynasties; learned to use iron; population grew; Warring States Period; Confucianism and Daoism became influential

go.hrw.com
Online Resources

KEYWORD: SHL AIC
ACTIVITY: Chinese Science and Philosophy

China's First Dynasties

BEFORE YOU READ

MAIN IDEA
China's river valley civilizations built the foundations of a long-shared Chinese culture. The achievements of the Shang and Zhou dynasties can be felt to this day.

READING FOCUS
1. How did China's geography affect its early civilization?
2. What were the achievements of the Shang dynasty?
3. How did China change during the Zhou dynasty?
4. What new philosophies were introduced in China?

KEY TERMS
loess
court
oracle bones
Mandate of Heaven
dynastic cycle
Confucianism
Daoism

NEW YORK

PI 2.2 Students evaluate the effectiveness of different models for the periodization of important historic events, identifying the reasons why a particular sequence for these events was chosen.

FATHER OF THE EMPERORS

The legendary emperor Fu Xi is said to have introduced civilization to China.

Fu Xi, by Ma Lin, c. AD 960–1279

108

THE INSIDE STORY

Who was China's first emperor? The answer to that question is shrouded in mystery. Whoever he may have been, China's first emperor lived so long ago that historians have not been able to learn anything about him. Ancient legends passed down through the centuries in China, however, tell of a great ruler named Fu Xi who brought civilization to the earliest people of the region.

According to these legends, Fu Xi lived in the 2800s BC. Part god and part man, he found the people of China living as barbarians and worked to bring civilization to the land. He taught people how to cook and to catch fish with nets as well as how to domesticate animals. Fu Xi is also credited with creating the I Ching, a system of predicting the future, and laying the foundation for China's writing system. For these deeds, ancient legends describe Fu Xi as a great hero and one of China's greatest emperors. ◢

China's Geography

The development of civilization in early China was aided greatly by certain geographic features. Long rivers, fertile soils, temperate climates, and isolated valleys all contributed to the growth and development of early China.

Teach the Main Idea
At Level

China's First Dynasties

1. **Teach** Ask students the Reading Focus questions to teach this section.

2. **Apply** Draw four rectangles for students to see. Label them with the names of the topics in this section: China's Geography, The Shang Dynasty, The Zhou Dynasty, and New Philosophies. Have students copy the rectangles onto their own paper and fill them in with the main ideas of each topic.

3. **Review** As you review the section, have students explain how the geography of China affected the development of Chinese civilization.

4. **Practice/Homework** Have students write a short dialogue between Confucius and Laozi. **LS** **Visual-Spatial, Verbal-Linguistic**

📄 **Alternative Assessment Handbook,** Rubric 37: Writing Assignments

Rivers, Soil, and Climates Like the civilizations of the Fertile Crescent, Egypt, and India, China's first civilizations developed in river valleys. Two major rivers supplied water for China's earliest civilizations: the Chang Jiang, also called the Yangzi, and the Huang He, or Yellow River. Both rivers flow east from the Plateau of Tibet to the Yellow Sea.

Annual floods along the Chang Jiang and the Huang He deposited rich soil on the rivers' flood plains. The valley of the Huang He was particularly fertile, due in large part to the type of soil that the river picked up. Called **loess** (LES), it was a fine dusty soil that had been carried into China by desert winds.

Although most of eastern China was covered with fertile soils, some regions were better suited for growing certain crops than others. Southern China along the Chang Jiang is warm and receives plenty of rainfall, which made it an excellent region for growing rice. Further north along the Huang He, the climate was cooler and drier. That region was suitable for grains such as wheat and millet.

Isolation The combination of rivers for irrigation and fertile soils for planting allowed the Chinese to thrive. In addition, China's relative isolation helped early civilization there develop and grow. Much of China is covered with mountains, hills, and desert. These features protected China from invasion. For example, the Himalayas—the world's tallest mountains—separate southern China from India and the rest of southern Asia. The Gobi, a vast desert, discouraged anyone from reaching China from the west.

Beginnings of Civilization Based on archaeological discoveries, historians believe that Chinese civilization began in the Huang He valley, where people started growing crops about 9,000 years ago. According to legend, the earliest Chinese were ruled by a dynasty known as the Xia (SHYAH). However, historians have not been able to find any evidence—either written or archaeological—that the Xia dynasty actually existed. As a result, most historians date the beginning of early Chinese civilization to the rise of the Shang dynasty.

READING CHECK **Summarize** What geographic features influenced life in early China?

Shang China

China's Shang dynasty was the first for which we have any historical evidence. The Shang are perhaps best known for their skill in making bronze objects, such as this tool.

The Shang Dynasty

According to ancient Chinese records, the Shang dynasty formed around 1766 BC, although many archaeologists believe it actually began somewhat later than that. Centered on the Huang He valley, Shang China created many institutions that carried over into later Chinese cultures.

Government and Society During the Shang period, China was ruled by a strong monarchy. At their capital city of Anyang, Shang kings were surrounded by a **court**, or gathering of wealthy nobles, who performed rituals intended to strengthen the kingdom and keep it safe.

To help keep order in China, the king appointed governors to rule distant parts of the kingdom. In addition, the king had at his disposal a large army. Besides fighting opponents from outside China, the army was responsible for preventing rebellions.

Shang China was largely an agricultural society. Most people spent their time in the fields tending to crops. From time to time, farmers were called upon to fight in the army or to work alongside slaves on building projects such as tombs, palaces, or walls.

In contrast to the majority of people in China, the Shang ruling elite had free time to spend in pursuit of leisure activities such as hunting for sport. Wealthy members of the elite also enjoyed collecting expensive objects made of bronze or jade.

TAKING NOTES Use a chart like the one below to take notes on the development and achievements of China's earliest dynasties.

Shang dynasty	Zhou dynasty

READING SKILLS

Connecting What connections can you see between the development of civilization in China and elsewhere?

ANCIENT INDIA AND CHINA **109**

Skills Focus: Drawing Conclusions

At Level

Reading Skill
Travels through Shang China

1. Review with students information in the text about the geography of China.

2. Tell students they are journalists who travel to Shang China. They will tour the country including the countryside and the royal court.

3. Have students write a magazine article about their travels in which they describe what they have seen. Students should draw conclusions

about the country, its people, and its royal court. Encourage students to include sketches to accompany their articles. **LS Verbal-Linguistic, Visual-Spatial**

Alternative Assessment Handbook, Rubric 19: Magazines

Direct Teach

Reading Focus

1 How did China's geography affect its early civilization? *Long rivers, fertile soil, temperate climates, isolated valleys helped civilization grow in China.*

China's Geography

Identify What natural features isolated China? *Himalayas separated China from Southern Asia; Gobi desert separated China from western lands.*

Identify Cause and Effect How did flooding of the Chang Jiang and the Huang He affect the region? *deposited rich soils in the river valleys*

Reading Focus

2 What were the achievements of the Shang dynasty? *development of Chinese writing; advances in working with bronze; precise calendar; money system*

The Shang Dynasty

Identify What type of government was China ruled by during the Shang dynasty? *monarchy*

Explain How did the king keep order in such a vast area? *appointed governors to rule distant parts of the kingdom*

Info to Know

The Chang Jiang The Chang Jiang is the world's third-longest river, after the Amazon and the Nile. It carries about 75 percent of China's domestic waterborne commerce and irrigates more than a third of the nation's agriculture. In addition, the river's watershed covers about 700,000 square miles, about a fifth of China's total land area.

Answers

Reading Skills *possible answers— development of monarchy; agriculture; development of writing system and calendar; bronze work; belief in afterlife*

Reading Check *Rivers deposited rich soil for farming; mountains, hills, and desert isolated the area.*

109

The Shang Dynasty

Recall What was the focus of Shang religion? *ancestor worship*

Explain How were oracle bones connected to early Chinese writing? *The earliest examples of writing are explanations of oracle bone readings, written on the bones themselves.*

Summarize What were some other achievements of the Shang dynasty? *made bronze vessels; built huge, stable structures; created precise calendar; may have created money system*

📓 **CRF:** Primary Source: Shang Dynasty Oracle Bones

Biography

The Hundred Schools of Thought

During the chaotic and violent Warring States Period, local lords struggled to survive and gain dominance. These lords sought out teachers and advisers to help them succeed in their quest for power. Confucius was one of many teachers who answered the lords' call for advice and wisdom. The various philosophies that these teachers formulated became known as the Hundred Schools of Thought. Other teachers included Mozi who preached equality of mankind and universal love, and Hanfeizi who developed the strict Legalist philosophy. Some teachers tried to explain all things through the dual principles of yin and yang, as well as the five elements: water, fire, wood, metal, and earth. The diverse ideas of this time period influenced Chinese thought for centuries.

Answers

Interpreting Visuals *ruler buried with large amounts of treasure, human sacrifice performed to ensure he is cared for in the afterlife*

110

Beliefs Much of what historians know about the Shang comes from studying royal tombs. From this study, they have drawn conclusions about Shang religious beliefs. For example, most Shang tombs contained valuable items made of bronze and jade. In addition, each tomb held the remains of hundreds of sacrificed prisoners of war who were buried with the ruler. From this, historians have concluded that the Shang believed in an afterlife in which a ruler would still need his riches and servants.

Shang religion centered on the idea of ancestor worship. The Shang offered gifts to their deceased ancestors in order to keep them happy and fulfilled in the afterlife. For example, they prepared ritual meals with their ancestors in mind. The family actually ate the food, but the steam from the food was believed to nourish the ancestors' spirits.

As part of their worship, the Shang often asked their ancestors for advice. They sought this advice through the use of **oracle bones,**

HISTORY CLOSE-UP

A Shang King's Tomb

Nearly all of the Shang artifacts that archaeologists have found have come from royal tombs. These tombs have not only been a source for material objects but have shed light on Shang beliefs and practices as well. For example, the presence of valuable objects and the remains of huge numbers of sacrificed people and animals in the tombs suggests that the Shang believed in an afterlife. Objects and people were probably placed in the tombs to serve the rulers after death.

The deceased ruler's coffin was buried in a pit and surrounded by treasures and sacrifices.

Valuable treasures of bronze and jade were buried with rulers, so they could be enjoyed in the afterlife.

Prisoners of war were sacrificed in the tomb so they could serve the ruler in the afterlife.

Skills FOCUS **INTERPRETING VISUALS**

Analyze What evidence can you see in this illustration that the people of Shang China honored and respected their rulers?

110 CHAPTER 4

Differentiating Instruction

Below Level

Learners Having Difficulty

Materials: drawing paper, art supplies

1. Review with students the information in the text about traditional Chinese beliefs about ancestors. Allow time for students to ask questions to be sure they understand the information.

2. Have students design a display honoring their families. Displays should include pictures, descriptions or drawings of important objects or heirlooms, and a sketch of a place to sit

and contemplate the pictures. Encourage students to feature the deceased or older family members prominently.

3. Have volunteers present their displays to the class. Place the completed designs in a classroom exhibit. 🔲 **Visual-Spatial, Intrapersonal**

📓 **Alternative Assessment Handbook,** Rubric 3: Artwork

inscribed bits of animal bone or turtle shell. First, the living person would ask a question of an ancestor. Then, a hot piece of metal was applied to the oracle bone, resulting in cracks on the bone's surface. Specially trained priests then interpreted the meaning of the cracks to learn the answer.

Shang Achievements The development of Chinese writing was closely tied to the use of oracle bones. The earliest examples we have of Chinese writing are the questions asked of oracle bones, actually written on the bones themselves. These early Shang texts used picture symbols to represent objects or ideas.

In addition to writing, Shang religion also led to great advances in working with bronze. Artists created highly decorative bronze vessels and objects, many of which were used in religious rituals. These bronzes are among the best known artifacts of the Shang dynasty.

The Shang made many other advances as well. They were able to build huge, stable structures such as tombs. In addition, Shang astronomers created a precise calendar based on the cycles of the moon. There is also evidence that the Shang may have created one of the world's first systems of money.

Decline of the Shang The Shang ruled China for more than 600 years, until about 1100 BC. In the end, however, ruling China's growing population proved to be too much for the Shang. Armies from a nearby tribe called the Zhou (JOH) invaded and established a new ruling dynasty.

READING CHECK **Summarize** How did religion influence other aspects of Shang culture?

The Zhou Dynasty

After taking over from the Shang around 1100 BC, the Zhou held China for several centuries. Historians often divide the Zhou dynasty into two periods. During the first period, called the Western Zhou, kings ruled from Xian (SHEE-AHN). This was generally a peaceful period, during which the Zhou made many cultural achievements. Later, however, conflict arose in China. In response, the kings moved east to Luoyang, marking the start of the Eastern Zhou period.

SHANG AND ZHOU DYNASTIES

0   200   400 Miles
0   200   400 Kilometers
Two-point equidistant projection

ASIA

GOBI

Huang He (Yellow River)

Ji

Yellow Sea

Xian
Luoyang
Shangqiu
Hao

Chang Jiang (Yangzi River)

East China Sea

Xi River

☐ Shang dynasty
c. 1500–1050 BC
☐ Zhou dynasty
c. 1050–400 BC

GEOGRAPHY SKILLS **INTERPRETING MAPS**

1. **Place** Which dynasty ruled earlier, the Shang or the Zhou?
2. **Location** Around which river valleys were both the Shang and the Zhou located?

Government When the Zhou conquered the Shang, their leaders worried that the Chinese people would not accept them. To gain acceptance for their rule, the Zhou introduced the idea that they ruled by the **Mandate of Heaven**. This principle stated that the gods would support a just ruler, but they would not allow anyone corrupt to hold power. The reason the Shang were overthrown, the Zhou explained, was because they had lost the gods' favor:

HISTORY'S VOICES

❝We do not presume to know and say that the lords of [Shang] received Heaven's mandate for so-and-so many years; we do not know and say that it could not have been prolonged. It was that they did not reverently attend to their virtue and so they prematurely threw away their mandate.❞

—Duke of Zhou, quoted in *Sources of Chinese Tradition*

Later Chinese rulers used the Mandate of Heaven to explain the **dynastic cycle**, the rise and fall of dynasties in China. Any dynasty that lost power, they claimed, had obviously become corrupt, and it was the will of the gods that it be overthrown. Historians still use the cycle of dynasties to organize their studies of early Chinese history.

NEW YORK
CC **Unit 1-C1**
Mandate of heaven and dynastic cycles

Direct Teach

Reading Focus

❸ How did China change during the Zhou dynasty? *began to use iron; population grew; beginnings of Confucianism and Daoism*

The Zhou Dynasty

Explain What was the significance of the Mandate of Heaven? *stated that gods would support a just ruler; would not allow corrupt one to hold power*
Recall What made the Zhou military stronger than previous forces? *iron weapons, catapult, cavalry*
Identify Cause and Effect How did the introduction of iron affect China? *backbone of new economy; strengthened the Zhou army*
📦 **Map Transparency:** Shang and Zhou Dynasties

Info to Know

Neighboring Peoples In about 1200 BC, herders from the harsh Gobi Desert and the Tian Shan foothills had begun to edge toward the Huang He valley. These people were probably attracted by the wealth and lifestyles of China proper. During the 1100s BC, the Shang almost continuously battled these warlike neighboring states.

Skills Focus: Identifying Main Idea and Details   At Level

Reading Skill
Ancient Chinese Dynasties

1. Draw the chart for students to see. Omit the italicized answers.
2. Have students copy the chart and complete it using information from the text. Have volunteers complete the class chart.
   🄻 **Visual-Spatial**
   📖 **Alternative Assessment Handbook**, Rubric 7: Charts

	Shang	Zhou
Government	*strong monarchy, court, appointed governors*	*used Mandate of Heaven to gain acceptance*
Achievements	*writing, bronze work, huge structures*	*iron work, coins, chopsticks*
Decline	*Zhou armies invaded*	*rebellions led to Warring States Period*

Answers

Interpreting Maps 1. *Shang;* **2.** *Chang Jiang, Huang He*

Reading Check *ritual meals for ancestors; oracle bones connected to early writing; bronze work for rituals; built stable tombs*

111

Reading Focus

④ What new philosophies were introduced in China? *Confucianism and Daoism*

New Philosophies

Recall Why were many new philosophies created during this period? *People tried to make sense of a chaotic time.*

Explain What did Confucius believe about human relationships? *People should treat each other humanely and express love and respect.*

Evaluate Do you agree with Confucius that respect for tradition is a good way to address problems? Why or why not? *possible answers—agree, time-honored ways are best; disagree—tradition is sometimes the source of the problem*

Primary Source

"The best [man] is like water.
Water is good; it benefits all things and does not compete with them.
It dwells in [lowly] places that all disdain.
This is why it is so near to Dao."
—Laozi, Dao De Jing

Answers

Faces of History *similarities—served in official positions; attracted followers for their philosophies; different—more is known about Confucius, Laozi was younger*

Reading Check *iron technology, population grew, new farm techniques, more food, cities grew, roads and canals built, coins and chopsticks introduced*

112

Zhou Achievements Before the Zhou dynasty, metalwork in China was done almost exclusively in bronze. The Zhou learned how to use iron, which became the backbone of their economy. Iron was strong and could be cast more cheaply and quickly than bronze. Iron weapons also helped strengthen the Zhou army, as did new weapons such as the catapult and the creation of China's first cavalry.

Under the Zhou, China's population grew. Farmers learned new techniques that increased the size of their harvests, thereby creating food surpluses. As the population grew, so too did cities. The growth of cities led to the building of roads and canals, allowing better transportation and communication throughout China. In addition, the Zhou introduced coins to China and began the use of chopsticks, which are still used as eating implements in China today.

THE IMPACT TODAY
Both Confucianism and Daoism are still influential in the countries of East Asia.

Decline of the Zhou As you have already read, conflict arose during the latter part of the Zhou dynasty. Clan leaders within China rose up against the king. As time passed, more and more local leaders turned against the Zhou, further weakening their rule.

The result of these rebellions was a time known as the Warring States Period. From 403 BC until 221 BC, a number of small states headed by nobles fought each other for land and power. Although the Zhou were still nominally in charge of China, their power was almost nonexistent by the mid-200s BC. Eventually, a new dynasty, the Qin, arose to bring an end to the Warring States Period and the Zhou dynasty.

READING CHECK **Analyze** How did China change under the Zhou?

New Philosophies

The conflicts of the late Zhou period led many Chinese thinkers to question the nature of society and of people's roles in it. The effort to make sense of the chaos led to the creation of many new Chinese philosophies, or ways of looking at the world. Of the many philosophies that were created during the late Zhou period, two became particularly influential in later Chinese history. These new philosophies were **Confucianism** and **Daoism** (DOW-iz-uhm).

FACES OF HISTORY **Chinese Philosophers**

CONFUCIUS
551–479 BC

Known in Chinese as Kongfuzi or Master Kong, the man known in the West as Confucius was born to a poor but noble family. From a young age, he was an eager student, constantly asking questions in order to learn more. As an adult, he became a teacher, the first in China to try to make education available to all children, regardless of their social class. He viewed education as the only way to improve oneself.

As he grew older, Confucius held several positions in local government. He also attracted followers to his teachings. By the time he died, Confucius had more than 3,000 followers.

LAOZI
500s BC

Little is known of the life of Laozi, the recorded author of the *Dao De Jing*, the major work of Daoist philosophy. According to one ancient historian who lived four centuries after Laozi is said to have died, Laozi had served as the official historian for a powerful noble. The same historian recorded that Laozi once met Confucius, who was younger than Laozi and quite pleased to meet the older philosopher.

Some historians believe that the *Dao De Ching* was not written by a single person but by several writers over a long period. Nonetheless, Daoists continue to honor the memory of Laozi as its creator.

Compare What similarities can you see in the lives of Confucius and Laozi? How were the two different?

Skills Focus: Comparing and Contrasting
At Level

Reading Skill
Twenty Questions: Confucianism or Daoism?

1. Have each student choose either Confucianism or Daoism and instruct students not to tell the philosophy they chose.

2. Have students take turns asking another student questions, which might include: What is the most important thing in life? How should people live?

3. Students should raise their hands when they think they know the student's chosen

philosophy. Once several students have raised their hands, ask the student being questioned to reveal his or her choice.

4. As a group, have students address this question: To what extent are these philosophies compatible? Tell students that both philosophies have co-existed in China for thousands of years. **LS** **Verbal-Linguistic**

Alternative Assessment Handbook, Rubric 11: Discussions

Confucianism Confucianism is based on the teachings of a scholar named Kongfuzi, better known in the West as Confucius. Born around 550 BC, Confucius believed that people should treat one another humanely. They should express love and respect for others by practicing traditional manners and rituals, which included the honoring of one's ancestors.

Confucius believed that this love and respect had disappeared during his lifetime and that its disappearance was responsible for the violence in society. He believed that by restoring a respect for tradition, society would once again become stable and orderly. His thoughts on how to improve society were later collected in a book called the *Analects*.

In the *Analects*, Confucius states that a ruler should treat his subjects fairly. In turn, subjects should reward their ruler with respect and loyalty. In addition, people need to respect the members of their family. Children must respect their parents and elder relatives, and parents have to care for their children with love and kindness. In addition, he writes, it is the duty of all educated people to devote themselves to public service.

Confucius's ideas were influential in Chinese history for centuries. For example, he wrote that a ruler should be advised by qualified, well-informed people, which led China's emperors to select their advisors based on merit rather than birth. In time, Confucian ideals spread to other parts of Asia as well, including Korea, Japan, and Vietnam.

Daoism Unlike Confucianism, which focuses on improving society, Daoism encourages people to retreat from the laws of society and yield to the laws of nature. At the heart of Daoism is the concept of the dao, or the way. According to Daoist teachings, the dao is the limitless force that is part of all creation. Through the dao, all things in nature are connected. By finding one's place in nature, it is possible for a person to achieve harmony with the universe.

Daoism embraced an ancient Chinese concept, the notion of yin and yang. Yin and yang represent the balancing aspect of nature: male and female, dark and light, hot and cold. Neither yin nor yang can exist without the other, so it is important that the two remain balanced. When balanced, yin and yang represent the perfect harmony of nature.

The exact origins of Daoism are unclear, but many Daoist teachings are attributed to a philosopher named Laozi (LOW-dzuh). He was among the first people in China to write about Daoist beliefs, which he did in a book called the *Dao De Jing*. This influential book includes a number of short sayings that summarize Daoist thought. The teachings of the *Dao De Jing* became so popular in China that some people began to worship Laozi as a god.

Though it eventually proved less influential that Confucianism in Chinese history, Daoism did play a major role in later dynasties. The idea of balance, for example, has been a key concept in China for centuries, largely as a result of Daoist teaching. Daoist philosophy has also led many of its followers to work for the preservation and protection of the natural environment.

NEW YORK
CC Unit 1-E1d Origin of Confucianism and Daoism

READING CHECK **Contrast** What is one difference between Confucianism and Daoism?

SECTION 4 ASSESSMENT
go.hrw.com
Online Quiz
Keyword: SHL AIC HP

Reviewing Ideas, Terms, and People

1. **a. Identify** On what rivers did Chinese civilization develop? Why?
   b. Predict How might Chinese civilization have developed differently if China had not been so isolated?

2. **a. Describe** What advances did the Shang dynasty make in China?
   b. Explain What was the purpose of **oracle bones**?
   c. Develop How have Shang burial sites improved historians' understanding of early Chinese culture?

3. **a. Define** What is the **dynastic cycle**?
   b. Interpret According to the **Mandate of Heaven**, what made it possible for a government to be overthrown?
   c. Evaluate Do you think the Zhou rulers were good for China? Why or why not?

4. **a. Describe** What role does balance play in Daoist teachings?
   b. Summarize What did Confucius think was the key to a happy society?

Critical Thinking

5. **Rate** Draw a graphic organizer like the one at right. Use your notes to identify the most significant achievement of each dynasty. Then write a sentence explaining why you think that achievement was so significant.

Early Dynasties of China	
Shang	Zhou

FOCUS ON WRITING

6. **Exposition** Write two paragraphs comparing and contrasting China under the Shang and Zhou dynasties. In your first paragraph, explain how the two were similar. In your second, tell how they were different.

ANCIENT INDIA AND CHINA **113**

CHAPTER 4 Document-Based Investigation

Changing Views of Early China

NEW YORK STANDARDS

PI 4.4 Students analyze different interpretations of important events, issues, or developments in world history by testing the data source for reliability and validity.

Historical Context The four documents that follow illustrate how historians' views of early Chinese civilization have changed over time based on new evidence.

Task Study the selections and answer the questions that follow. After you have studied all the documents, you will be asked to write an essay explaining how archaeology has changed our views of China. You will need to use evidence from these selections and from Chapter 4 to support the position you take in your essay.

DOCUMENT 1

From Legend to History

For hundreds of years, historians of ancient China assumed that the Shang dynasty was legendary. They had found no material evidence that the Shang had ever ruled, and so they concluded that the dynasty had been invented by later Chinese historians. However, major discoveries in the 1920s changed that view, as historians Edwin Reischauer and John Fairbank noted in their 1958 book *East Asia: The Great Tradition*.

> For a while, modern skepticism relegated even the Shang dynasty to the realm of pure fancy. Then, in the late 1920s, all this was reversed. For some time, so-called "dragon bones," some with writing incised on them, had been appearing on the Peking [Beijing] market, usually to be ground up for medicinal purposes. These were traced to the vicinity of the modern city of Anyang ... traditionally said to be the site of the Shang capital during the latter part of the dynasty. Now from deep in the ground of this capital emerged inscribed bones on which were found the names of practically all of the traditional Shang rulers. Study revealed that these were clearly Shang remains, dating approximately from 1400 to 1100 BC.

DOCUMENT 2

The Truth of the Xia

Ancient Chinese records list a dynasty that ruled China before the Shang called the Xia. Most historians still consider the Xia to be a legendary dynasty, as Reischauer and Fairbank did when they wrote the passage in Document 1. However, based on more recent research, Fairbank has revised his earlier ideas. In *China: A New History*, he states that the Xia may in fact have existed after all.

> In 1959 excavations at Erlitou (in the city of Yanshi not far from Luoyang and just south of the Yellow River) uncovered another site with large palaces that seems likely to have been a capital of the Xia dynasty. The Erlitou culture was widespread in the region of northwest Henan and southern Shanxi. It was a direct successor to the Longshan Black Pottery culture and preceded the early Shang, with radiocarbon dates of ca. 2100 to 1800 BC. With this all-but-final identification, the Xia and Shang components of the legendary Three Dynasties have taken tangible form. What do they tell us about China's origins?

Changing Views of Early China

Word Help

incised carved
vicinity surrounding area
tangible able to be touched

Primary Source

"I would have you stand by my side …to bring upon [the Xia ruler] Heaven's punishment. I will greatly reward you. Do not ye disbelieve me. I do not eat my words. If you do not follow the words of this vow, I will slay you and all your offspring and none will be forgiven."
—Legendary account of the Shang takeover of the Xia dynasty

Skills Focus: Evaluating Historical Interpretation

Above Level

Reading Like a Historian Skill
Archaeology Presentation

Research Required

1. Have students review the four documents. Organize students into groups of four to six. Groups should work together to develop a thesis based on the archaeological evidence shown here. The thesis should focus on the existence of the Xia dynasty or the spread of Chinese civilization.

2. Have groups conduct independent research to learn more about their topic. Students may wish to locate the original sources of these excerpts.

3. Have groups prepare multimedia presentations about the existence of the Xia dynasty or the spread of Chinese civilization. Presentations should include evidence to support the group's thesis statement.

4. Have groups give their presentations to the rest of the class. **LS Interpersonal, Visual-Spatial**

Alternative Assessment Handbook, Rubrics 14: Group Activity; and 22: Multimedia Presentations

DOCUMENT 3

Another Major Find

According to early records, both the Shang and the Xia ruled eastern China. As a result, that area has long been considered the birthplace of Chinese culture. Historians assumed that civilization gradually spread westward from the valleys of the Huang He and the Yangzi into the Asian interior. However, a recent find has challenged that theory. The bronze figure shown here was made during the time of the Shang dynasty, but it looks very different from anything made by the Shang. It was found outside of the area ruled by the Shang, at Sanxingdui.

SANXINGDUI, CHINA

0   250   500 Miles
0   250   500 Kilometers

Huang He (Yellow R.)

SHANG DYNASTY

Sanxingdui

Chang Jiang (Yangzi River)

PACIFIC OCEAN

DOCUMENT 4

The Meaning of Sanxingdui

The discovery at Sanxingdui created great excitement among archaeologists. This single discovery had changed much of what people assumed about China's history, as writer Peter Hessler noted in an article he wrote for *National Geographic* magazine.

> That summer a remarkable new culture came to light. Two pits contained hundreds of artifacts: elephant tusks, cowrie shells, and objects of jade, gold, and bronze. The pits, which had been buried around 1200 BC, were roughly contemporary to [Shang rulers] Wu Ding and Lady Hao.
>
> But Sanxingdui and Anyang are nearly 700 miles apart, and many Sanxingdui bronzes are unlike anything else ever discovered in China. There's a unique emphasis on the human form—the pits included more than 50 heads, 20 masks, and one enormous eight-and-a-half-foot-tall statue of a man. The heads are narrow and elongated, dominated by enormous eyes . . . "Even the diehards who believed in the diffusion model have given up in the face of Sanxingdui," said [archaeologist Robert] Bagley. "Nobody is claiming that this stuff comes from Anyang."

Skills FOCUS — READING LIKE A HISTORIAN

DOCUMENT 1
a. **Identify** What evidence convinced historians that the Shang dynasty was real and not legendary?
b. **Elaborate** Why might historians have been unwilling to believe that the Shang existed without evidence?

DOCUMENT 2
a. **Compare** How did Fairbank's view of early China change between the publication of Document 1 and Document 2? Why?
b. **Draw Conclusions** How could the evidence described in this document change our view of the Xia dynasty?

DOCUMENT 3
a. **Describe** Where is Sanxingdui located in relation to the Shang dynasty territory?
b. **Interpret** Why is Sanxingdui's location significant?

DOCUMENT 4
a. **Explain** How does Hessler say that the bronzes from Sanxingdui are different from those found elsewhere?
b. **Analyze** How might the discovery of the Sanxingdui bronzes change historians' view of early China?

DOCUMENT-BASED ESSAY QUESTION

As archaeologists uncover new evidence, our view of the past must be reshaped. Using the documents above and information from the chapter, form a thesis that explains how a single piece of new evidence can completely change our ideas about history. Then write a short essay to support your position.

See **Skills Handbook**, pp. H19, H30

ANCIENT INDIA AND CHINA **115**

Skills Focus: Comparing and Contrasting

At Level

Reading Like a Historian Skill
Comparing Artifacts

Prep Required

1. Show students photographs of bronze artifacts from the Shang dynasty. Examples might include artifacts from the tomb of Fu Hao, who lived during the late Shang period.

2. Have volunteers make comparisons between the Shang artifacts and the bronze figure shown in Document 3. List the comparisons for all to see. Students may point out that objects from both sites are made of bronze, but that the Sanxingdui object focuses on the human form.

3. Review Document 4. Ask how artifacts may provide evidence of different cultures.

4. Have students write a paragraph comparing the Sanxingdui bronze figure to the Shang artifacts. Students should tell what the differences suggest about early China.

LS Visual-Spatial, Verbal-Linguistic

Alternative Assessment Handbook, Rubric 9: Comparing and Contrasting

Info to Know

Discovery at Sanxingdui The ancient bronze shown on this page is one of more than 40 bronze heads discovered in 1986. Historians believe that the objects were likely buried as religious offerings. Significantly, the Sanxingdui site is believed to have existed at the same time as the late Shang dynasty. However, it differs in many ways from Shang burial sites. For example, Shang burial sites often contain evidence of human sacrifice, while the Sanxingudui site does not. Yet because no written records have been found, archaeologists have not yet been able to link the Sanxingdui findings conclusively to any other civilization in Bronze Age China.

Answers

Reading Like a Historian
Document 1 a. *Bones inscribed with the names of Shang rulers were discovered, dating to 1400 to 1100 BC.* **b.** *possible answer—The material evidence before the 1920s was unreliable.* **Document 2 a.** *In Document 2, Fairbank states that another dynasty, the Xia, may also have existed before the Shang; new artifacts were discovered dating from about 2100 to 1800 BC, which was even earlier than the Shang artifacts;* **b.** *possible answer—The archaeological evidence might suggest that the Xia dynasty was real and not legendary.* **Document 3 a.** *It is located outside the Shang dynasty territory.* **b.** *The location is significant because historians had previously assumed that civilization spread westward from the Shang. Yet the Sanxingdui artifacts suggest that a different civilization existed west of the Shang at about the same time.* **Document 4 a.** *They emphasize the human form.* **b.** *The discovery challenges the assumption that civilization spread westward from the Shang territory.* **Essay** *Student essays should describe how new archaeological evidence can change previously accepted historical interpretation. As supporting evidence, students should explain the impact of the excavations at Anyang, Erlitou, and Sanxingdui.*

Answers

Visual Summary

Review and Inquiry Organize students into three groups to review the chapter. Have the first group compare and contrast governments in ancient India and China. Have the second group prepare an outline of major achievements, indicating which they believe were the most important. Have the third group list the major religions and philosophies, and describe how each changed as it spread. Groups should use the Visual Study Guide as a starting point, and refer back to the chapter as needed.

Quick Facts Transparency: Visual Study Guide: Ancient India and China

Review Key Terms and People

1. Hindus believe that, after death, the soul is released from the body and reborn in another, in a process called reincarnation.

2. The Zhao used the Mandate of Heaven to explain the rise and fall of Chinese dynasties.

3. In Buddhism, nirvana is the state of perfect peace and freedom from suffering.

4. Monsoons are seasonal winds that brought water and fertile soil, leading to the development of India's first civilizations.

5. In Hinduism, karma is the sum effect of a person's actions during life.

6. Sacred writings called the *Vedas* provide details about Aryan history and society in India.

7. The Four Noble Truths are the central truths of Buddhism.

8. In Hinduism, *moksha* is the escape from the cycle of rebirth.

9. In India, *varnas* were the four social classes that later became known as castes.

10. Confucianism is a Chinese philosophy dealing with love and respect, traditional manners, and rituals.

11. In Buddhism, the Eightfold Path consists of the steps one must take to overcome desires.

VISUAL STUDY GUIDE

Two River Valley Civilizations

India

Indus Valley
- Urban civilization characterized by large cities, such as Harappa and Mohenjo Daro
- Uniformity of city planning and cultural elements suggests presence of a central authority.
- Traded manufactured goods with people of Central Asia, Arabia, and Mesopotamia
- Writing system never translated

Vedic Period
- Historians unsure where Aryan people came from
- Communities led by rajas
- Society divided into four *varnas* and hundreds of smaller castes
- Religious beliefs outlined in the *Vedas*

China

Shang Dynasty
- Developed in the valley of the Huang He with capital at Anyang
- Ruled by emperors
- Religion centered on ancestor worship
- Skilled at working with bronze
- Developed China's first writing system and a lunar calendar

Zhou Dynasty
- Took power from Shang, claiming authority under the Mandate of Heaven
- Learned to work iron, strengthened army
- Confucianism and Daoism helped shape patterns of Chinese thought.

Two Religions

Hinduism

- Brahman, the eternal spirit, created and preserved the world. Manifestations of Brahman called *devas* are active in the world.
- Each person has an *atman*, or soul. The ultimate goal of existence is *moksha*, the reunification of the *atman* with Brahman.
- The likelihood of achieving *moksha* is determined by one's dharma and karma.

Buddhism

- Suffering is unavoidable for people while they are alive. The only way to escape suffering is to attain enlightenment and nirvana.
- The way to find enlightenment is to follow a life of moderation as set forth in the Eightfold Path and the Middle Way.
- The various branches of Buddhism teach different paths to reaching enlightenment.

Review Key Terms and People

For each term or name below, write a sentence explaining its significance to ancient India or China or to the religions of Hinduism or Buddhism.

1. reincarnation
2. dynastic cycle
3. nirvana
4. monsoons
5. karma
6. Vedas
7. Four Noble Truths
8. *moksha*
9. *varnas*
10. Confucianism
11. Eightfold Path
12. Daoism

---

12. Daoism is a Chinese philosophy dealing with balance and the interconnectedness of nature.

Comprehension and Critical Thinking

13. **a.** provided water and fertile soil, encouraging the development of civilizations
b. large, well-planned cities; writing system
c. Society was divided into four *varnas*, or social classes.

14. **a.** the eternal being that created and preserves the world

b. Hinduism was influenced by many different cultures, over thousands of years.
c. because they have not yet fulfilled their dharma and achieved moksha

15. **a.** He found the way to end human suffering.
b. to overcome desire for pleasure and material goods
c. Different opinions developed regarding the correct teachings and practices of Buddhism.

16. **a.** Confucianism and Daoism
b. Historians were able to decipher pictures on oracle bones used in Shang texts
c. to explain the rise and fall of dynasties

History's Impact video program
Watch the video to answer the closing question:
What impact has Hinduism had on the world?

Comprehension and Critical Thinking

SECTION 1 *(pp. 93–97)*

13. a. Describe How did rivers and monsoons affect early civilizations in India?

b. Explain What evidence makes historians think the Indus Valley civilization was advanced?

c. Elaborate How did Indian social structures change during the Vedic period?

SECTION 2 *(pp. 98–102)*

14. a. Identify According to Hinduism, what is Brahman?

b. Explain Why do Hindu religious practices vary so widely?

c. Extend According to Hindu teachings, why are most people reincarnated after they die?

SECTION 3 *(pp. 103–107)*

15. a. Recall According to Buddhist tradition, what did the Buddha realize when he attained enlightenment?

b. Summarize What is the purpose of living by the Eightfold Path?

c. Elaborate Why did different Buddhist traditions develop after the Buddha's death?

SECTION 4 *(pp. 108–113)*

16. a. Identify What two major philosophies developed in China during the Zhou dynasty?

b. Explain How did oracle bones help historians learn more about ancient China?

c. Extend How did Chinese rulers use the idea of the Mandate of Heaven to justify rebellions?

Using the Internet

go.hrw.com
Practice Online
Keyword: SHL AIC

17. The cities of the Indus Valley civilization were highly advanced and featured many conveniences not found in other ancient cities. Large cities such as Harappa and Mohenjo Daro were particularly advanced, demonstrating superior planning abilities on the part of their builders. Enter the activity keyword and research more about life in these ancient cities. Then create a newspaper page that describes the advantages of living in such an advanced city.

Reading Skills

Connecting *Read the text below and then answer the questions that follow.*

“ The Huang He is the second longest river in China. The name Huang He means "Yellow River." That name stems from the yellowish color of the silt that the river picks up as it flows across China. However, the Huang He is also known by another name, China's Sorrow, because of the frequent floods on the river. These floods can be terribly destructive, drowning crops and people and burying entire villages in silt. ”

18. How does this passage connect to what you already knew about the Huang He?

19. What connections can you draw between floods on the Huang He and early Chinese civilization?

Evaluating Historical Interpretation

Reading Like a Historian *The passage below is a historian's view of one interpretation of Indian history held by earlier historians. Read the passage and then answer the questions that follow.*

“ The primitiveness of early Aryan society was much exaggerated by some 19th-century Indologists, who thought they found in the highly formalized and rigidly controlled style of the *Rig Veda* the first outpourings of the human spirit . . . In fact, by the time that even the earliest hymns were composed the Aryans were not savages, but were on the fringes of civilization. Their military technique was in advance of that of the Middle East, their priestly schools had raised the tribal sacrifice to a fine art, and their poetry was elaborate and formalized. ”

—A. L. Basham, *The Wonder That Was India*, 1954

20. Analyze What earlier interpretation of Indian history does Basham say was false?

21. Interpret How does Basham interpret the Aryan period? What evidence does he base this on?

WRITING ABOUT HISTORY

Exposition: Comparing and Contrasting *India and China were the sites of two of the world's oldest civilizations. Those civilizations shared some common characteristics but were in other ways very different.*

22. Assignment Write an essay in which you compare and contrast the civilizations of ancient India and China. Use information from this chapter and from other research as needed to provide specific similarities and differences between them.

Answers

Using the Internet

17. Go to the HRW Web site and enter the keyword shown to access a rubric for this activity.

KEYWORD: SHL AIC

Reading Skills

18. shows that river floods could bring destruction as well as fertile soil

19. The floods both hurt and helped early Chinese civilization.

Evaluating Historical Interpretation

20. that early Aryan society was primitive

21. believes early Aryan society was more advanced; military technique, religious rituals, poetry

Writing About History

22. Student essays should use details from the chapter to compare and contrast the civilizations described in the chapter. Essays should address the ancient civilizations of India and China in terms of their geography, history, government, society, religion, and philosophies. A rubric for the activity is provided in **CRF**: Writing About History

HOLT

History's Impact

▶ **Video Program**
Refer to the Video Program Teacher's Guide for a discussion of the closing question.

Review and Assessment Resources

Review and Reinforce

 CRF: Chapter Review

Quick Facts Transparency: Visual Study Guide: Ancient India and China

 Spanish Chapter Summaries Audio CD Program

OSP **Holt PuzzlePro**: Quiz Show for ExamView

 **Quiz Game CD-ROM**

Assess

 PASS: Chapter Test, Forms A and B

Alternative Assessment Handbook

OSP **ExamView Test Generator**, Chapter Test

Differentiated Instruction Modified Worksheets and Tests CD-ROM: Chapter Test

HOAP **Holt Online Assessment Program** (in the Premier Online Edition)

Reteach/Intervene

 Interactive Reader and Study Guide

Differentiated Instruction Teacher Management System: Lesson Plans for Differentiated Instruction

Differentiated Instruction Modified Worksheets and Tests CD-ROM: Chapter Test

Interactive Skills Tutor CD-ROM

go.hrw.com
Online Resources

KEYWORD: SHL TEACHER

You can use these pages to have students simultaneously review the unit and practice taking standardized tests.

Answers

1. 2
   The Ancient Near East, Section 1

2. 4
   The Beginnings of Civilization, Section 2

3. 2
   The Beginnings of Civilization, Section 2

4. 2
   Ancient India and China, Section 2

5. 2
   The Ancient Near East, Section 1

6. 4
   The Ancient Near East, Section 2

7. 1
   The Ancient Near East, Section 3

8. 3
   The Ancient Near East, Section 4

9. 2
   The Beginnings of Civilization, Section 1

10. 2
    Nile Civilizations, Section 1

UNIT 1
Regents Practice

Directions Write your answer for each statement or question on a separate answer sheet. Choose the number of the word or expression that best completes the statement or answers the question.

1 The type of building shown in the drawing below is

1 an Egyptian pyramid.
2 a ziggurat.
3 an Egyptian step pyramid.
4 a Hindu temple.

2 The agricultural revolution led to

1 slower population growth.
2 better health.
3 frequent moving.
4 population growth.

3 The practice of agriculture meant that

1 people had more free time.
2 not everyone had to produce food so there could be a division of labor.
3 everyone farmed so there was no division of labor.
4 people enjoyed equal status.

4 Hinduism is one of the world's oldest religions and

1 was founded by Vishnu.
2 had no single founder.
3 teaches that the goal of salvation is to achieve reincarnation.
4 is very uniform all across India.

5 Hammurabi's Code is important because

1 Hammurabi united all of Mesopotamia.
2 it was written down and displayed for all to see.
3 it dealt with everyone in the empire equally.
4 it was a system based on the number 60.

6 The Phoenicians were important because

1 they sailed to the British Isles to obtain goods.
2 they wrote the *Epic of Gilgamesh*.
3 they perfected ironworking techniques.
4 they invented an alphabet.

7 Many scholars think Judaism

1 is the world's first monotheistic religion.
2 was founded by King Solomon after the Diaspora.
3 has a long history that is recorded in the Book of the Patriarchs.
4 began as a response to the Babylonian Captivity.

8 What were some of Darius I's important accomplishments?

1 He founded a religion based on dualism.
2 He built a permanent army and defeated the Greeks.
3 He strengthened the economy, minted Persia's first coins, and built roads linking all parts of the empire.
4 He conquered Persepolis.

9 What is characteristic of Paleolithic peoples?

1 They stayed in one place and made very crude stone tools.
2 They were hunter-gatherers who moved from place to place.
3 They adapted to only one type of environment and lived in caves.
4 They were too busy getting food to engage in artistic activities.

10 Why is the Nile so important to Egypt?

1 The Sahara was difficult to cross.
2 The river created a delta with fertile soil.
3 It is the longest river in the world.
4 Its floods were infrequent and unpredictable.

11 The Egyptians developed the mummification process in order to

1 fulfill their gods' needs and bring prosperity to Egypt.

2 provide dead pharaohs with people to serve them.

3 avoid the need for burials.

4 keep the ka, or personality, from shriveling and vanishing.

12 The Rosetta Stone was important because it enabled scholars to

1 translate hieroglyphics.

2 learn how Egyptians developed papyrus scrolls.

3 understand how mummies were used.

4 discover the importance of the Egyptian god Osiris.

13 What was the most important factor in the growth of a wealthy civilization in Nubia?

1 good farmland provided by the Nile.

2 advancements in the arts and sciences.

3 a location that was a center for trade.

4 the Nubians' expertise in archery.

14 Most of what we know about Aryan history in India comes from

1 archaeological clues and evidence.

2 oral stories passed down from generation to generation.

3 records from traders who visited their lands.

4 sacred writings called Vedas.

15 The belief that the soul is released from the body at death and reborn in another body is known as

1 karma.

2 moksha.

3 reincarnation.

4 the belief that anger can prevent salvation.

16 The Buddha taught that those who live by the Eightfold Path can attain nirvana, or

1 pleasures and material goods.

2 life after death.

3 a state of perfect peace.

4 reincarnation.

17 The earliest examples of Chinese writing occurred

1 during the Zhou dynasty.

2 under the leadership of Confucius.

3 during the Warring States Period.

4 during the Shang dynasty.

18 Read the following quotation. Who is most likely to have written it?

"In serving his parents a filial son renders utmost respect to them while at home; he supports them with joy; he gives them tender care in sickness; he grieves at their death; he sacrifices to them with solemnity. If he has measured up to these five, then he is truly capable of serving his parents."

1 Laozi.

2 Confucius.

3 Hammurabi.

4 the Buddha.

REVIEWING THE UNIT

Constructed Response While the belief systems of early civilizations varied widely, they helped shape the societies where they arose. Recall what you have learned about the belief systems that developed in the ancient civilizations of the Near East, the Nile Valley, India, and China. Choose three belief systems that developed in those civilizations. Write an essay in which you summarize the most important beliefs of each religion and explain how those beliefs shaped the civilization in which they developed.

Answers

11. 4
Nile Civilizations, Section 2

12. 1
Nile Civilizations, Section 2

13. 3
Nile Civilizations, Section 3

14. 4
Ancient India and China, Section 2

15. 3
Ancient India and China, Section 2

16. 3
Ancient India and China, Section 2

17. 4
Ancient India and China, Section 5

18. 2
Ancient India and China, Section 4

Reviewing the Unit

Student essays should mention three of the following belief systems: polytheism (Mesopotamian, Sumerian, or Egyptian), monotheism (Egyptian or Hebrew), Hinduism, Buddhism, Confucianism, and Taoism. Student essays should indicate that polytheism, monotheism, and Hinduism are religions, or systems of worshipping one or more gods, whereas Buddhism, Confucianism, and Daoism do not directly involve the worship of gods but instead seek to teach people how to live.

Unit Review

Geography and Environment

Peas in a Pod Many of the changes that took place in the process of domestication were not the result of conscious choices. For example, the peas that humans eat are actually seeds, which are held in pods. Wild pea plants contain a gene that makes their pods burst, letting the peas fall to the ground. The mutant peas that do not pop open are the ones that humans eat. When humans started to plant peas, they planted them from these mutant pods, because these were the ones they had harvested. Thus, they unconsciously developed a new variety of peas that stayed in the pod (until they were taken out by humans).

Migration and Diffusion

Cyrillic Script While most of Europe uses an alphabet based on the Roman script, Greek script provided the model for the Cyrillic alphabet. The alphabet was named for St. Cyril, who was credited with developing the script in the 9th century for use by Eastern Orthodox Slavs. Russia, Ukraine, Belarus, Serbia, Bulgaria, and Montenegro all use alphabets based on Cyrillic script. The Central Asian republics and several smaller national groups within Russia use modified versions of the alphabet.

Info to Know

The Origins of the Alphabet In the summer of 1998 a team of archaeologists discovered written inscriptions in southern Egypt. Their discovery indicates that the first alphabet is at least two centuries older than originally believed, and that it originated in Egypt rather than Phoenicia. The inscriptions have not yet been completely translated, but the words *god* and *chief* have been identified, along with a few others. Scholars believe that the inscriptions include personal names, titles, and perhaps prayers to a local god.

Themes & Global Connections

THEME
GEOGRAPHY AND ENVIRONMENT

How did the geography and environment of various river valleys around the world make the rise of different civilizations possible?

Early civilizations arose in river valleys that had similarities in their geography and environment. The geography of those valleys provided water and fertile soil. The environment provided plants and animals that could be domesticated.

GEOGRAPHICAL AND ENVIRONMENTAL CHARACTERISTICS OF RIVER VALLEY CIVILIZATIONS

Reliable Source of Water
The rivers provided the water necessary for agriculture in regions without adequate rainfall. The Nile's flooding was predictable. Sometimes the Tigris and Euphrates, the Indus, and the Huang He did not have enough water, and sometimes disastrous floods struck. Building irrigations systems helped tame the rivers and provided the right amount of water to the fields.

Fertile Soil
Year after year, early peoples planted the same crops, depleting the soil of necessary nutrients. However, the annual flooding of the rivers replenished the soil by adding a new layer of silt to the fields.

Plants Suitable for Cultivation
Native grasses in the Near East and China were suitable for domestication. Once domesticated, these cereal grasses were adaptable to other areas such as the Nile valley.

Animals Suitable for Domestication
The ancestors of domesticated sheep, goats, pigs, and cattle are native to the Fertile Crescent. Also domesticated were native cattle in Egypt, pigs in Harappa, and pigs and silkworms in China.

THEME
MIGRATION AND DIFFUSION

How did migration and diffusion affect early civilizations?

When people migrate, or move from one place to another, they bring with them their beliefs, ways of life, and even domesticated plants and animals. In this way the diffusion, or spread, of ideas or things from one place to another takes place.

Consider the diffusion of writing. The advantages of writing were obvious, and writing diffused rapidly. The peoples who invaded Mesopotamia adopted cuneiform to their own languages, and it remained in use until the first century AD. Canaanite scribes used Egyptian hieratic and demotic scripts to represent the sound of the initial letter of Canaanite words. The Phoenicians used this system as the basis for their alphabet. A true alphabet, its individual symbols represented sounds rather than syllables or ideas. The Greeks adopted and changed the Phoenician alphabet to suit their language. The Romans adapted the Greek alphabet, and Roman scripts form the basis of most European scripts today.

Egyptian scripts → Canaanite scripts → Phoenician alphabet → Greek alphabet → Roman alphabet → Modern European alphabets

Differentiating Instruction
Above Level

Advanced Learners/Gifted and Talented

1. Have students name objects or ideas that could be spread through trade or migration. As they do so, create a list for students to see.

2. Have each student choose one item from the list and write a brief research paper on it. Students should use reliable online or print sources for their research. Their papers should answer the following questions:

- Where did the object or idea originate?
- Why, how, and where did it spread?
- Was the object or idea adapted by the recipient culture? If so, how?

3. Have volunteers read their papers to the class.
LS Verbal-Linguistic

Alternative Assessment Handbook, Rubrics 30: Research; and 42: Writing to Inform

THEME
BELIEF SYSTEMS

What were the belief systems of early civilizations like?

Belief systems associated with the river valley civilizations all concerned themselves with the need to control nature and secure a successful harvest. The ruler played a central role in both government and religion. In time, belief systems became more complex. Scholars think the Jews began the first monotheistic religion. Zoroaster founded another monotheistic religion and emphasized the concept of dualism. Three religions—Hinduism, Jainism, and Buddhism—began in India and are still practiced today. China was influenced by the philosophical ideas of Confucius and Laozi.

BELIEF SYSTEMS

CIVILIZATION/ PEOPLE	BELIEF SYSTEMS
Mesopotamia	People worship many gods.
Egypt	People worship many gods and emphasize the afterlife.
Canaan/Israel	The ancient Hebrews create Judaism.
Persia	Zoroaster founds Zoroastrianism; concept of Dualism.
India	Hinduism, Jainism, and Buddhism begin here.
China	The ruler needs the Mandate of Heaven and ancestors are venerated; the philosophies of Confucius and Laozi become important.

Skills FOCUS UNDERSTANDING THEMES

Choose one of the civilizations discussed in the unit to look at more closely. Use your textbook and other resources to answer the following questions and to complete the chart. How did geography and environment shape that civilization? How might migration and diffusion have influenced its development? What were the unique characteristics of the civilization's belief systems and have they had a lasting influence?

Theme	Contributions
Geography and environment	
Migration and diffusion	
Belief systems	

Global Connections

River valley civilizations were not the only ancient places with impressive sites such as the pyramids in Egypt. Stonehenge in England and New Grange in Ireland are two examples of prehistoric sites in Europe.

Making Connections Choose one of these sites or another ancient site and research what is known about how and why it was built. Prepare a presentation to explain what the site can tell us about the people who built it and their geography and environment, how migration and diffusion might have influenced the monument, and what the monument reveals about the belief systems of the people who built it.

▼Stonehenge and its megaliths, or huge stones, was once a sacred site.

121

Belief Systems

Zoroastrianism Zoroaster had an influence far beyond ancient Iran. Plato, Aristotle, and Pythagoras were interested in Zoroaster's ideas. Zoroastrianism greatly influenced development of Judeo-Christian beliefs about angels and demons, the afterlife, heaven and hell, and the idea of the resurrection. Zoroastrianism continues to be practiced today. Zoroastrians in Iran have been persecuted for centuries, although they experienced a few decades of well-being during the rule of the Pahlavi shahs. Under the Islamic Republic, their number has dropped to about 45,000. In India, where they are known as Parsis, Zoroastrians played an important role in building the country's modern economy.

Understanding Themes

Student charts will vary depending on the civilization they chose. Charts should demonstrate an understanding of how geography and environment shaped the civilization they chose.

Global Connections

Student presentations will vary depending on the sites chosen. Presentations should demonstrate knowledge of the site gleaned from adequate research.

Collaborative Learning

At Level

Ancient Belief Systems

1. Organize students into small groups. Assign each group one of the belief systems discussed in this chapter. Have groups create a chart showing the beliefs and how they corresponded to the society's needs at the time.

2. Have volunteers from each group present their charts to the class.

3. Guide the class in a discussion of ancient belief systems. Is the belief system still practiced today? Why or why not?
   LS Interpersonal, Visual-Spatial

   Alternative Assessment Handbook, Rubrics 7: Charts; 11: Discussions ; and 14: Group Activity

Unit Review

Summarizing the Unit

Remind students that many factors contributed to making a civilization. Review with students the basic characteristics of a civilization:
- Developed cities
- Organized government
- Formalized religion
- Specialization of labor
- Social classes
- Record keeping and writing
- Art and architecture

Then ask students to give examples of each characteristic as it is illustrated by one of the civilizations covered in this unit.

Answers

Thinking Like a Historian

Student charts, graphic organizers, or maps should compare and contrast the achievements of civilizations that arose in: Mesopotamia, the Nile valley, the Indus valley, and the Huang He river valleys.

UNIT 1
IN BRIEF

Below is a chapter-by-chapter summary of the main ideas in this unit, followed by a summary activity for the unit.

CHAPTER 1
The Beginnings of Civilization
Prehistory–1000 BC

MAIN IDEA Early humans spread from Africa to other parts of the world. All people survived by hunting and gathering until some people began to practice agriculture about the end of the last ice age.

SECTION 1 As scientists have made more discoveries, they have traced human origins to more than 3 million years ago. As early humans migrated into new areas, they adapted to new environments.

SECTION 2 The development of agriculture was a turning point in human history. It dramatically changed the way in which many people lived.

SECTION 3 Located along major rivers, the first farming villages gave rise to the first civilizations. These river valley civilizations shared some characteristics.

CHAPTER 2
The Ancient Near East
4000 BC–550 BC

MAIN IDEA The world's first civilizations developed in the Ancient Near East. The people of these civilizations not only formed empires but also developed writing and artistic as well as religious traditions.

SECTION 1 The first-known civilization arose in Mesopotamia, and for thousands of years it influenced civilizations that arose in the area. Sargon I created a permanent army and formed the world's first empire.

SECTION 2 Indo-European tribes invaded and conquered the Fertile Crescent peoples, bringing change to the region. The Phoenicians built a wealthy trading society and developed an alphabet.

SECTION 3 The religion of the ancient Hebrews was Judaism. Believed to be the first monotheistic religion, Judaism has been an important influence on Western civilization.

SECTION 4 The Persian Empire, one of the largest and best-governed of the ancient empires, was also known for its cultural achievements.

CHAPTER 3
Nile Civilization
5000 BC–AD 300

MAIN IDEA Ancient Egypt was one of the world's earliest civilizations. It developed a unique writing system and culture. To the south, in Nubia, other civilizations grew and made cultural advances of their own.

SECTION 1 Egypt was a remarkably stable and long-lasting civilization, in part because of its geography.

SECTION 2 Discoveries about ancient Egyptian burial practices and the translation of the writing system have added to our knowledge of ancient Egypt.

SECTION 3 Kush was another advanced civilization that developed along the Nile.

CHAPTER 4
Ancient India and China
2500 BC–250 BC

MAIN IDEA India and China each developed early river valley civilizations with lasting traditions.

SECTION 1 The Harappan civilization arose in the Indus River valley. Later civilizations developed based on old and new beliefs.

SECTION 2 Over the centuries, Hinduism developed in India, giving rise to a rich variety of beliefs and practices.

SECTION 3 According to tradition, a young Indian prince learned the path to enlightenment and founded Buddhism.

SECTION 4 China's river valley civilizations laid the foundations of Chinese culture. Important Chinese philosophies, Confucianism and Daoism, developed.

Thinking like a Historian
Summary and Extension Activity

The first civilizations developed in river valleys in different parts of the world. Create a chart, graphic organizer, or annotated map that compares and contrasts the achievements of the different river valley civilizations. Cover the following topics:

A. Social organization and form of government

B. Writing and technological and scientific achievements

C. Artistic achievements

122 UNIT 1

Unit Resources

Review and Reinforce

- **Global History and Geography Regents Test Prep Workbook**
- **Regents Review Transparencies**
- **CRF:** Chapter Review
- **Spanish Chapter Summaries Audio CD Program**
- OSP **Holt PuzzlePro:** Quiz Show for ExamView
- **Quiz Game CD-ROM**

Assess

- **PASS:** Unit Test, Forms A and B
- **Alternative Assessment Handbook**
- OSP **New York ExamView Test Generator** correlated to NY SS Standards
- **Differentiated Instruction Modified Worksheets and Tests CD-ROM:** Chapter Test
- HOAP **Holt Online Assessment Program** (in the Premier Online Edition)

Reteach/Intervene

- **Interactive Reader and Study Guide**
- **Differentiated Instruction Teacher Management System:** Lesson Plans for Differentiated Instruction
- **Differentiated Instruction Modified Worksheets and Tests CD-ROM:** Chapter Test
- **Interactive Skills Tutor CD-ROM**

UNIT 2

The Growth of Civilizations
2100 BC–AD 1500

CHAPTER 5
Classical Greece
c. 2100 BC–150 BC

CHAPTER 6
Rome and Early Christianity
750 BC–AD 500

CHAPTER 7
The Americas
1000 BC–AD 1500

CHAPTER 8
Empires of India and China
350 BC–AD 600

Themes

GOVERNMENT AND CITIZENSHIP
Each of the early empires had different ideas about government and citizenship. Even within an empire, these ideas changed over time.

SOCIETY
Each of the early empires made lasting contributions to architecture, the visual arts, and literature.

SCIENCE AND TECHNOLOGY
The early empires made significant advances in science and technical achievements.

Columns called caryatids support the roof of the Erechtheion temple on the Acropolis in Athens, Greece.

123

• Unit Preview •

Introducing the Unit
Have students think of technology or institutions that were developed by the civilizations covered in this unit. List them for the class to see. Which of those institutions or developments are still in use in our society? How have they changed over time, or have they?

Connecting to Themes
Activity **Creating Empires** Ask students why leaders may have wanted to create empires. Guide them in a discussion of empires. What advantages did empires have over smaller states? What disadvantages did empires have?
LS Verbal-Linguistic

Reading Like a Historian
Interpreting Visuals
Caryatids In the first century AD, the Roman architect Vitruvius wrote about the origin of the Caryatids in his book *De architectura:* "Carya, a city in the Peloponnese, allied herself with the Persian enemy against Greece. Later the Greeks were rid of their war by a glorious victory and, by common consent, declared war on the Caryates. So the town was captured, the males were killed and the Caryan state publicly disgraced. The victors led the matrons away into captivity…. [T]o ensure that they exhibited a permanent picture of slavery … the architects of those times designed images of them specially placed to uphold a load, so that a well-known punishment of the Caryates' wrongdoing might be handed down to posterity."

Unit Resources

Planning
- Differentiated Instruction Teacher Management System: Unit Pacing Guide
- **OSP** New York One-Stop Planner CD-ROM: Teacher Management System
- Power Presentations with Video CD-ROM

Standards Mastery
- Global History and Geography Regents Test Prep Workbook
- Regents Review Transparencies

Differentiating Instruction
- Differentiated Instruction Teacher Management System: Lesson Plans for Differentiated Instruction
- Differentiated Instruction Modified Worksheets and Tests CD-ROM

Enrichment
- A World History Teacher's Guide to Analyzing Movies
- Document-Based Activities for World History
- World History Outline Maps
- Reading Like a Historian: World History Toolkit
- World History Primary Source Library CD-ROM

Assessment
- **PASS**: Unit Test, Forms A and B
- Alternative Assessment Handbook
- **OSP** New York ExamView Test Generator correlated to NY SS Standards
- **HOAP** Holt Online Assessment Program (in the Premier Online Edition)

Chapter 5 Planning Guide

Classical Greece

Chapter Overview	Reproducible Resources	Technology Resources
CHAPTER 5 pp. 124–159 **Overview:** In this chapter, students will learn about the civilizations of ancient Greece, the impact of the founding of democracy, and the empire of Alexander the Great. KI 1, 3, 4; PI 1.1, 1.2, 3.1, 4.1, 4.2, 4.4 See pp. T32–T55 for a detailed correlation to the New York State Core Curriculum for Global History and Geography and the New York Learning Standards.	**Differentiated Instruction Teacher Management System:*** • Pacing Guide • Lesson Plans for Differentiated Instruction **Interactive Reader and Study Guide:** Chapter Summary* **Chapter Resource File*** • Writing About History • Social Studies Skill • Chapter Review **World History Outline Maps**	**OSP New York One-Stop Planner CD-ROM:** Calendar Planner **Live Ink© Online Reading Help** **Differentiated Instruction Modified Worksheets and Tests CD-ROM** **World History Primary Source Library CD-ROM** **Power Presentations with Video CD-ROM** **History's Impact: World History Video Program (VHS/DVD):** Classical Greece
Section 1: **Early Greece** **The Main Idea:** The earliest cultures in Greece, the Minoans and the Mycenaeans, were trading societies, but both disappeared and were replaced by Greek city-states. PI 1.1, 4.2	**Interactive Reader and Study Guide:** Section 1 Summary* **Chapter Resource File*** • Vocabulary Builder: Section 1 • Biography: Alice Kober • Primary Source: Life in Sparta • History and Geography: Trade in Early Greece • Literature: "The Spinning Contest"	**Regents Review Transparency:** Section 1* **Map Transparency:** The Early Greeks, 600 BC* **Internet Activity:** Ancient Minoans
Section 2: **The Classical Age** **The Main Idea:** The Classical Age of ancient Greece was marked by the great achievements, including the development of democracy, and by ferocious wars. PI 1.2	**Differentiated Instruction Teacher Management System:** Section 2 Lesson Plan* **Interactive Reader and Study Guide:** Section 2 Summary* **Chapter Resource File*** • Vocabulary Builder: Section 2 • Biography: Solon	**Regents Review Transparency:** Section 2* **Map Transparency:** Persian War* **Map Transparency:** Peloponnesian War* **Quick Facts Transparency:** Causes and Effects of the Peloponnesian War*
Section 3: **Greek Achievements** **The Main Idea:** The ancient Greeks made great achievements in philosophy, literature, art, and architecture that influenced the development of later cultures and ideas. PI 3.1, 4.2	**Differentiated Instruction Teacher Management System:** Section 3 Lesson Plan* **Interactive Reader and Study Guide:** Section 3 Summary* **Chapter Resource File*** • Vocabulary Builder: Section 3 • Biography: Aristophanes	**Regents Review Transparency:** Section 3* **Quick Facts Transparency:** Greek Philosophy* **Internet Activity:** Greek Art
Section 4: **Alexander the Great and His Legacy** **The Main Idea:** Alexander the Great formed a huge empire, spread Greek culture into Egypt and many parts of Asia, and paved the way for a new civilization to develop in those areas. PI 4.1, 4.4	**Differentiating Instruction Teacher Management System:** Section 4 Lesson Plan* **Interactive Reader and Study Guide:** Section 4 Summary* **Chapter Resource File*** • Vocabulary Builder: Section 4 • Biography: Archimedes	**Regents Review Transparency:** Section 4* **Map Transparency:** Alexander's Empire, 323 BC*

go.hrw.com	📄 Print Resource	🖥 Transparency
LS Learning Styles	🔊 Audio CD	💿 CD-ROM
📹 Video	**SE** Student Edition	**TE** Teacher's Edition

OSP One-Stop Planner CD-ROM   📕 NY Standards Mastery
*also on One-Stop Planner CD-ROM

HOLT
History's Impact
World History Video Program (VHS/DVD)
Classical Greece

Review, Assessment, Intervention

📕 **Global History and Geography Regents Test Prep Workbook**

🖥 **Quick Facts Transparency:** Classical Greece*

📄 **Progress Assessment Support System (PASS):** Chapter Test*

💿 **Differentiated Instruction Modified Worksheets and Tests CD-ROM:** Modified Chapter Test

OSP **New York One-Stop Planner CD-ROM:** Exam View Test Generator (English/Spanish)

HOAP **Holt Online Assessment Program (HOAP),** in the Premier Online Edition

---

📄 **PASS:** Section 1 Quiz*

🌐 **Online Quiz:** Section 1

📄 **Alternative Assessment Handbook**

📄 **PASS:** Section 2 Quiz*

🌐 **Online Quiz:** Section 2

📄 **Alternative Assessment Handbook**

📄 **PASS:** Section 3 Quiz*

🌐 **Online Quiz:** Section 3

📄 **Alternative Assessment Handbook**

📄 **PASS:** Section 4 Quiz*

🌐 **Online Quiz:** Section 4

📄 **Alternative Assessment Handbook**

Power Presentation with Video CD-ROM

Power Presentations with Video are visual presentations of each chapter's main ideas. Presentations can be customized by including Quick Facts charts, images and maps from the textbook, and video clips.

Holt Online Learning

go.hrw.com
Teacher Resources
KEYWORD: SHL TEACHER

go.hrw.com
Student Resources
KEYWORD: SHL GRE

- Document-Based Questions
- Interactive Multimedia Activities

- Current Events
- Chapter-Based Internet Activities
- and more!

Holt Premier
Online Student Edition

Complete online support for interactivity, assessment, and reporting

- Interactive Maps and Notebook
- Homework Practice and Research Activities Online

CHAPTER 5 PLANNING GUIDE

The Big Picture

Peter N. Stearns

Framework The development of ancient Greece primarily began to take shape after about 800 BC. Earlier societies, in Crete and on the mainland, provided some cultural precedents, along with contacts with civilizations in Egypt and the Middle East. These earlier societies declined, partly through the influx of Indo-European invaders and migrants. Geography played an important role for Greece, encouraging decentralized political units and a strong reliance on trade. Social forms developed around farming and had a tendency to rely on slavery. The aristocracy provided the governing elite in most Greek states. Women were strictly subordinate.

Politics Greek politics focused on the city-state. A variety of political forms emerged, including dictatorships and monarchies. The democratic impulse was important, particularly in Athens. City-states collaborated on occasions, such as in the staging of the Olympics. They also banded together to beat back Persian invaders. Sparta and Athens became particularly powerful after the Persian Wars. Each had a distinctive government and cultural outlook. Athenian democracy requires careful definition, for it combined what might be regarded as pure democratic forms with restricted citizenship. Athens and Sparta came to blows in the Peloponnesian War, triggered by Athenian imperial ambitions and Spartan resentment. The war ended the most creative period in classical Greece.

Culture The city-states, and most particularly Athens, generated important forms of art and literature, in spite of or because of a vigorous religious tradition. Greek philosophy and science played a major role at the time, and in setting the stage for developments in later civilizations in the Middle East and Europe.

The Hellenistic Empire After the decline of the city-states, Macedonian emperors conquered Greece and then, under Alexander, went on to build an empire of unprecedented magnitude, stretching through Egypt and the Middle East to the northeastern part of the Indian subcontinent. Hellenistic culture blended Greek achievements with the cultures of the Middle East and North Africa, producing new scientific work and a legacy that would affect later societies throughout the region.

Recent Scholarship

Despite huge advances in historical work on women and gender relations, figuring out how to move these topics into active engagement with other developments in world history remains a challenge. A recent collection edited by Fiona McHardy and Eireann Marshall, *Women's Influence on Classical Civilization* (2004), offers important insights into both Greece and Rome, including elements of the larger imperial holdings including North Africa. Topics range from women's images to political roles of individual women, with comments on artistic patronage and military inspiration as well. The range of subjects enlivens both women's history and a wider sense of the scope of the classical Mediterranean past.

Differentiating Instruction

 Differentiated Instruction Teacher Management System
- Pacing Guide
- Lesson Plans for Differentiated Instruction

 Interactive Reader and Study Guide

Spanish Chapter Summaries Audio CD Program

Student Edition on Audio CD Program

 Differentiated Instruction Modified Worksheets and Tests CD-ROM
- Vocabulary Flash Cards
- Modified Vocabulary Builder Activities
- Modified Chapter Review Activity
- Modified Chapter Test

OSP One-Stop Planner CD-ROM
- ExamView Test Generator (English/Spanish)
- PuzzlePro
- Quiz Show for ExamView
- Transparencies and Videos

TE Differentiated Activities in the Teacher's Edition
- Researching History: Minos, p. 128
- Mapping the Aegean Islands, p. 137
- Comparing Epic and Lyric Poetry, p. 145
- Understanding Cultural Diffusion, p. 157

Reading Like a Historian
Sam Wineburg

Credibility and Corroboration Historians rely on corroboration as a key tool in establishing the credibility of a historical source. The act of crosschecking and comparing accounts, corroboration takes various forms.

Two accounts of the same event can be corroborated provided that they were written independently. Depending on the topic, written accounts also can be corroborated by archaeological or forensic evidence. Geographers can also be consulted when a historical source lays out a particular travel route or notes place markers.

The Problem of One Voice What happens when only a single record remains from the past? This is the dilemma historians face when evaluating the credibility of the Greek historian Thucydides and his account of the Peloponnesian War.

But wait: Surely the Peloponnesian War had to leave behind some archaeological evidence. True, there are scattered remains from this time period, but what's left is pretty skimpy, an inscription here or a record of payment to a general there. As one historian put it, "Thucydides is still more useful for the restoration of the inscriptions than inscriptions are for the correction of Thucydides."

The same goes for the other accounts of the conflict between Athens and Sparta. Both Plutarch and Diodous Siculus chronicle the war, and both can be used to check Thucydides on certain details. But on those aspects for which we still turn to Thucydides' rich account—his description of Pericles' funeral oration, his keen insights in the motivations of its principle actors, his braided narrative on why these tragic events turned out as they did—Thucydides remains the historical source.

Internal Criticism How, then, does a historian evaluate his or her reliability? Faced with but a single source, historians employ a way of reading known as "internal criticism." In essence, Thucydides is checked against himself. Does his account cohere? Does he contradict himself? Is he one-sided? Does he strive for objectivity or revel in his biases? Does he describe his methods so that readers can make judgments as to his trustworthiness?

Let's begin with the last question. In Thucydides' entire account of the Peloponnesian War not a single footnote appears; in fact the very notion of a "documented claim" (complete with bibliographic references) is a feature of modern, not ancient, historiography.

At the same time, Thucydides was obsessed with historical method and felt compelled to share with his readers the back-story to his account. For example, here is how he described his method of recording speeches: "While keeping as closely as possible to the general sense of the words that were actually used to make the speakers say what, in my opinion, was called for by each situation."

However, instead of reassuring us, Thucydides' disclosure here provides little comfort. As we listen to Pericles, are we hearing a paraphrase of the ruler's actual words or Thucydides' view of what Pericles should have said—the historian, in effect, acting as ventriloquist?

Chapter Main Ideas

Section 1 The earliest cultures in Greece, the Minoans and the Mycenaeans, were trading societies, but both disappeared and were replaced by Greek city-states.

Section 2 The Classical Age of ancient Greece was marked by great achievements, including the development of democracy, and by ferocious wars.

Section 3 The ancient Greeks made great achievements in philosophy, literature, art, and architecture that influenced the development of later cultures and ideas.

Section 4 Alexander the Great formed a huge empire, spread Greek culture into Egypt and many parts of Asia, and paved the way for a new civilization to develop in those areas.

🖥 New York Standards

Key Idea 4 The skills of historical analysis include the ability to investigate differing and competing interpretations of the theories of history, hypothesize about why interpretations change over time, explain the importance of historical evidence, and understand the concepts of change and continuity over time.

Key to Differentiating Instruction

Below Level

Basic-level activities designed for all students encountering new material

At Level

Intermediate-level activities designed for average students

Above Level

Challenging activities designed for honors and gifted and talented students

Standard English Mastery

Activities designed to improve standard English usage

CHAPTER 5 2100 BC–150 BC

Classical Greece

THE BIG PICTURE The small, rugged peninsula in southern Europe called Greece was the home of a series of advanced civilizations. From the far-reaching trade of the early Minoans to the democracy of Athens and the empire of Alexander the Great, the Greeks left behind a legacy that helped define what we think of as Western civilization.

Theme GOVERNMENT AND CITIZENSHIP

Though the ancient Greeks practiced many forms of government during their long history, they are best known as the founders of democracy, or rule by the people. First created by the citizens of Athens in the 500s BC, Greek democracy helped inspire the creation of modern democracies, including our own government in the United States.

TIME LINE

CHAPTER EVENTS			
c. 2100 BC Minoan culture thrives in Crete.	**c. 1400 BC** Mycenaean civilization reaches its height.	**1200s BC** According to legend, the Trojan War is fought.

2000 BC — **1500 BC** — **1000 BC**

WORLD EVENTS		
c. 1770 BC Hammurabi issues his law code.	**c. 1237 BC** Pharaoh Ramses the Great of Egypt dies.

124 CHAPTER 5

Introduce the Chapter   At Level

Classical Greece

Materials: construction paper, marking pens

1. Remind students that the early Greeks laid the foundations for democracy in the western world and made many cultural advances that impacted today's art and philosophy. Organize the class into four groups. Assign each group a section of this chapter.

2. Have each group look for the main ideas in their assigned section. Students should look for pertinent, interesting information connected to the main ideas.

3. Have each group create a poster or brochure that "advertises" its assigned section. Have students record the section number and title at the top of the poster or on the front panel of the brochure, and create the advertisement.

4. Have groups share their advertisements and brochures. Students should take notes on each section during the presentations.
LS Verbal-Linguistic, Visual-Spatial

📋 **Alternative Assessment Handbook**, Rubrics 2: Advertisements; and 24: Oral Presentations

HOLT
History's Impact
► **Video Program: Classical Greece**
See the Video Teacher's Guide for strategies for using the video segment.

Reading Like a Historian
Analyzing Visuals Have students examine the photograph on these pages. Have students volunteer ideas about the location of the Parthenon and the Acropolis, which are on the top of the hill. Discuss the symbolism of locating buildings such as the Parthenon in higher elevations.

go.hrw.com
Online Resources
Chapter Resources:
KEYWORD: SHL GRE
Teacher Resources:
KEYWORD: SHL TEACHER

Reading like a Historian

The city of Athens, shown above, was one of the largest and greatest in ancient Greece. Rising above the city was the Acropolis, a rocky hill on which several temples and monuments stood. The most spectacular of them was the Parthenon, a marble temple to the goddess Athena and a symbol of Athens's glory.

Analyzing Visuals Why do you think the Athenians built their temples on the Acropolis?

See **Skills Handbook**, p. H27

478–431 BC
The Golden Age of Athens

c. 500 BC
Democracy begins in Athens.

323 BC
Alexander the Great dies.

500 BC

753 BC
The city of Rome is established.

c. 551 BC
Confucius is born in China.

325 BC
India's Mauryan Empire begins.

CLASSICAL GREECE **125**

Explore the Time Line

1. When did the Minoan culture thrive in Greece? *c. 2100 BC*

2. Who issued the first code of laws mentioned on this time line? *Hammurabi*

3. From what type of source do we know that the Trojan War was fought during the 1200s BC? *legend*

4. How long did the Golden Age of Athens last? *47 years*

Info to Know

Entasis The Parthenon overcomes an optical illusion suffered by buildings of its style. They tend to look heavier at the top. Master architect Pericles overcame this problem by making skilled use of an almost imperceptible progressive shrinking of the diameter of the columns from the middle to the point they reach the roof.

Make Generalizations How do you think architects learned about perspective? *possible answer—by observation, experimentation*

Answers

Reading Like a Historian *possible answer—so that the temples would be closer to the gods*

125

Geography Starting Points

Greece's Many Islands Why are there so many Greek sailors? The nation of Greece today includes some 2,000 islands, located in the Ionian and Aegean seas. So even if an islander is not a fisherman or ferryboat captain by trade, a boat might be more useful than a car. Most of the islands are located in the Aegean Sea, between Turkey and the Greek mainland. Though most large countries draw land boundaries for governing purposes, Greece organizes the islands in groups, because otherwise, keeping government records would be an administrative nightmare!

🗺 **Map Transparency:** The Early Greeks, 600 BC

📋 **World History Outline Maps**

✳ **Interactive Map:** The Early Greeks, 600 BC

Activity **Comparing Maps** Have students compare this map to a modern-day map of the Mediterranean region. Have students name the countries that surround Greece today. **LS Visual-Spatial**

📋 **Alternative Assessment Handbook**, Rubric 21: Map Reading

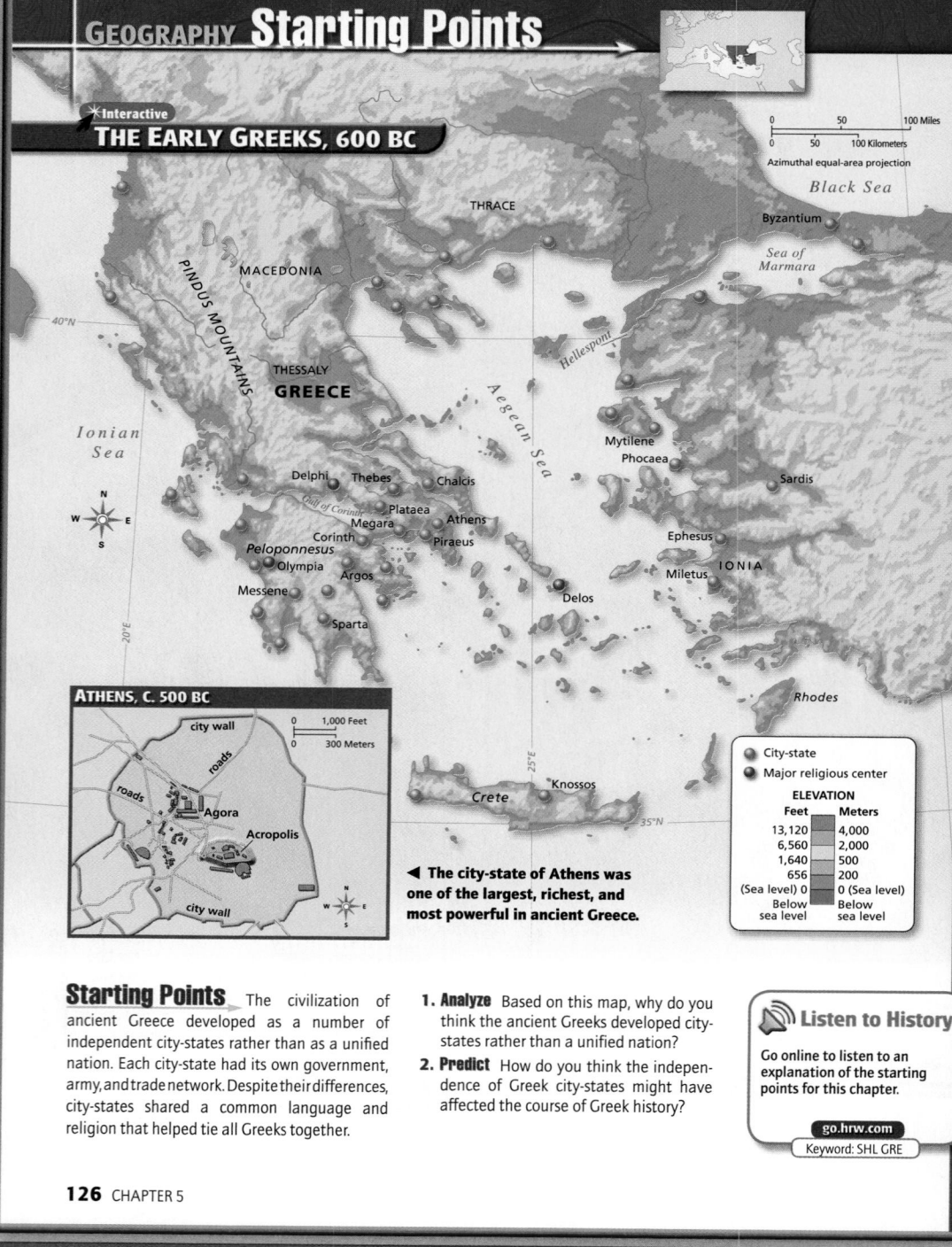

GEOGRAPHY Starting Points

✳ Interactive
THE EARLY GREEKS, 600 BC

◀ The city-state of Athens was one of the largest, richest, and most powerful in ancient Greece.

ATHENS, C. 500 BC
- city wall
- roads
- roads
- Agora
- Acropolis
- city wall
0 | 1,000 Feet
0 | 300 Meters

City-state
Major religious center

ELEVATION	
Feet	**Meters**
13,120	4,000
6,560	2,000
1,640	500
656	200
(Sea level) 0	0 (Sea level)
Below sea level	Below sea level

Starting Points The civilization of ancient Greece developed as a number of independent city-states rather than as a unified nation. Each city-state had its own government, army, and trade network. Despite their differences, city-states shared a common language and religion that helped tie all Greeks together.

1. **Analyze** Based on this map, why do you think the ancient Greeks developed city-states rather than a unified nation?

2. **Predict** How do you think the independence of Greek city-states might have affected the course of Greek history?

🔊 **Listen to History**

Go online to listen to an explanation of the starting points for this chapter.

go.hrw.com
Keyword: SHL GRE

126 CHAPTER 5

Skills Focus: Analyzing Maps

At Level

Social Studies Skill
Advantages and Disadvantages of Greek Geography

1. Remind students that the location and geography of nations influences their history.

2. Organize students into small groups. Have students create a list of Greece's geographic advantages and disadvantages. To do this, have students refer to the map on this page, other maps in this chapter and in the atlas of their texts. In their groups, students should discuss Greece's location in relation to other nearby influences.

3. Have groups record their ideas under the headings Advantages and Disadvantages.

4. When groups have finished their charts, have each group present its ideas to the class. Create a class list for all to see and have students add to and correct their work as needed. **LS Interpersonal, Visual-Spatial**

📋 **Alternative Assessment Handbook**, Rubrics 11: Discussions; and 21: Map Reading

Answers

Geography Starting Points
1. *possible answer—They were separated on different islands, and by mountains.* 2. *possible answer—Many different governments and societies probably developed.*

1 Early Greece

BEFORE YOU READ

MAIN IDEA
The earliest cultures in Greece, the Minoans and the Mycenaeans, were trading societies, but both disappeared and were replaced by Greek city-states.

READING FOCUS
1. What were Minoan and Mycenaean culture like?
2. What were the common characteristics of Greek city-states?
3. What role did stories of gods and heroes play in Greek culture?

KEY TERMS
polis
acropolis
agora
helots
hoplites
hubris

 NEW YORK

PI 1.1 Students define culture and civilization, explaining how they developed and changed over time. Investigate the various components of cultures and civilizations.

THE INSIDE STORY

Were the ancient stories about Crete based on fact? The wealthy King Minos, his deadly maze called the Labyrinth, and a half-man, half-bull beast called the Minotaur, who trapped prisoners in the maze and ate them alive—there are the tales Greek storytellers told. Many people have wondered whether they actually happened.

Beginning in the late 1890s a British archaeologist, Sir Arthur Evans, led an expedition to dig for ancient ruins on Crete. Evans's team found something amazing. They uncovered the ruins of a vast palace at Knossos, the site the myths named as the home of the Minos and his Minotaur. Evans found no signs of the beast, of course. But he did think he had found the history behind the legend. He called this lost civilization Minoan, after the legendary king. ■

Minoans and Mycenaeans

Until the discoveries by Evans and others in the 1800s, the earliest history of Greece had been lost to legend for centuries. Even now, after several major discoveries, many parts of that early history are a mystery to us. We do know, however, that two distinct cultures developed in early Greece, the Minoans and the Mycenaeans.

The Minoans of Crete The civilization we call Minoan developed on Crete as early as 3000 BC and lasted nearly 2,000 years. During that time, Minoan ships sailed all over the Aegean Sea—and perhaps further. Minoan colonies grew up on dozens of Aegean islands. Ships laden with trade goods sailed back and forth between these colonies and Crete.

IN SEARCH OF A MYTH

Minoan bull head from Knossos, 1700–1400 BC.

◀ Minoan statues of bulls, like this one, may have inspired tales of the legendary Minotaur.

CLASSICAL GREECE **127**

Preteach

Getting Started
Use the **Interactive Reader and Study Guide** to familiarize students with the section content.

📄 **Interactive Reader and Study Guide,** Section 1

📄 **CRF:** Vocabulary Builder: Section 1

Taking Notes
First Greeks—Minoans and Mycenaeans; advanced civilizations based on trade in the Aegean; became rich from trade; built huge palaces and temples; City-states—basic political unit in Greece; developed because Greece's rugged terrain made travel and communication difficult; built around area called acropolis; included agora, a public marketplace; Sparta was one of the mightiest city-states; Mythology—myths formed about hundreds of gods and goddesses; 12 were particularly influential; myths were also about heroes

---

Teach the Main Idea

At Level

Early Greece

Materials: wall map of Greece

1. **Teach** Ask students the Reading Focus questions to teach this section.

2. **Apply** Organize students into four groups. Assign each group one red heading from this section. Have each group list the main points discussed under its assigned heading.

3. **Review** Have each group share the main points. Use the wall map to identify the locations of cities important to the understanding of the material.

4. **Practice/Homework** Have each student make a list of the important things they look forward to learning in this section. When students have finished studying the section, have them add a short summary about each item on their lists. **LS Verbal-Linguistic, Visual-Spatial**

📄 **Alternative Assessment Handbook**, Rubrics 1: Acquiring Information; and 14: Group Activity

go.hrw.com
Online Resources
KEYWORD: SHL GRE
ACTIVITY: Ancient Minoans

Reading Focus

1 What were Minoan and Mycenean culture like? *advanced civilizations based on trade around the Aegean Sea; built huge palaces and temples*

Minoans and Mycenaeans

Identify Where did the early Minoans live? *Crete*

Recall How do we know about Minoan civilization? *from archeological excavations of buildings and objects; historians still cannot read Linear A, the Minoan writing*

Analyze Why do historians consider the Mycenaeans to be the first Greeks? *They spoke a form of the Greek language.*

Info to Know

Mysterious Minoan Art When we study the art a civilization leaves behind, we usually find its style grows or develops over time. This is not true for what we know of Minoan art. The decorative murals, sculptures, and pottery depict land and sea animals, and people singing while going about daily tasks, such as harvesting grain. On Minos, art achievements seem to have appeared and disappeared suddenly and repeatedly. This suggests that abrupt, violent changes occurred on the island. The whimsical art of the Minoans, however, does not reflect this.

Answers

Early Greek Civilizations *possible answer—They had easy access to ocean trade routes.*

128

TAKING NOTES

Use a graphic organizer like this to take notes on the first Greeks, city-states, and mythology.

Early Greece

Excavations at Knossos have revealed much about Minoan life. Buildings there were solidly constructed with many private rooms, basic plumbing, and brightly colored artwork on the walls. That artwork has likewise helped historians learn about the Minoan way of life. From images of ships, they can tell Minoan life was tied to the sea: sailing, trade, fishing, even playing in the waves were all common. Women seem to have played major roles in society. For example, most Minoan images of priests are women. Frescoes painted on the walls of Minoan houses suggest that the Minoans played dangerous games that involved leaping over charging bulls during festivals.

Much of what historians have written about Minoan civilization is the result of speculation and guesswork. Part of the problem stems from the Minoans' writing, which historians cannot read. Called Linear A, the language does not appear to be related to those of mainland Greece. Unless we learn to decipher their writing, all we know about the Minoans will come from the art and objects they left behind.

For reasons as yet unknown, the Minoan civilization fell apart rather suddenly. One possible cause was a world-shaking disaster. When a volcanic island near Crete blew itself apart—one of the largest eruptions ever—the blast may have affected weather patterns around the world. The damage this would have done to Minoan ports and crops may have substantially weakened the society. No matter what else happened, in the end the Minoans were conquered by the warlike Mycenaeans (my-suh-NEE-uhns) from the Greek mainland.

The Mycenaean States The Mycenaeans built small kingdoms that fought often with each other. The civilization's name comes from a fortress they built, Mycenae. Historians consider the Mycenaeans the first Greeks, because they spoke a form of the Greek language.

The earliest Mycenaean kingdoms owed much to the Minoans. They traded with them and copied Minoan writing to develop their own system, which somewhat resembled the earlier Minoan writing system. Unlike Minoan

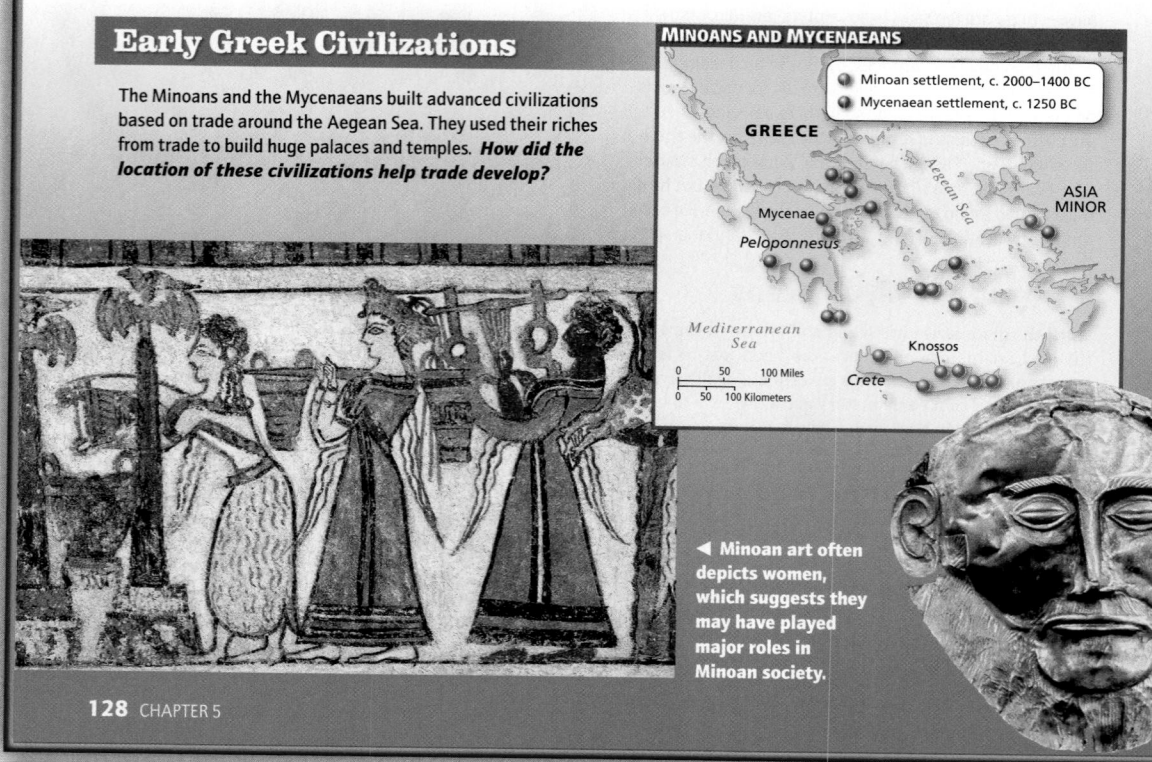

Early Greek Civilizations

The Minoans and the Mycenaeans built advanced civilizations based on trade around the Aegean Sea. They used their riches from trade to build huge palaces and temples. *How did the location of these civilizations help trade develop?*

MINOANS AND MYCENAEANS

- Minoan settlement, c. 2000–1400 BC
- Mycenaean settlement, c. 1250 BC

GREECE
Aegean Sea
ASIA MINOR
Mycenae
Peloponnesus
Mediterranean Sea
Knossos
Crete

0 50 100 Miles
0 50 100 Kilometers

◀ Minoan art often depicts women, which suggests they may have played major roles in Minoan society.

128 CHAPTER 5

Differentiating Instruction

Advanced Learners/Gifted and Talented

1. Remind students that even after studying Minoan artifacts, much of what historians know about the Minoans is guesswork. Have students conduct research to discover different scholars' opinions of Evans's conclusions from his excavations at Minos.

2. Discuss Internet search engines and procedures, as well as key words and terms that may be useful to students as they begin their research. Encourage students to use both online and print sources.

3. Have students prepare a multimedia presentation of their findings. Student reports should be accompanied by bibliographies.

4. Have volunteers report their findings to the class. Guide students in a discussion of bias in historical interpretations and in the problems associated with constructing history when evidence can be interpreted in different ways.

LS Verbal-Linguistic

Alternative Assessment Handbook, Rubrics 24: Oral Presentations; and 30: Research

writing, however, Mycenaean writing has been translated. Like the Minoans, the Mycenaeans also became great traders. Their trade only increased after they conquered Crete.

Despite their ties to Crete, the Mycenaeans' civilization developed in a very different direction. Mycenaean society was dominated by intense competition, frequent warfare, and powerful kings. To raise money to build great palaces and high walls, Mycenaean kings taxed trade and farming. To show off their strength, they built great monuments like the massive Lion's Gate at Mycenae.

The Mycenaean kings' constant quests for power and glory inspired many later legends. The most famous legend is the story of the Trojan War. The war supposedly involved early Greeks, led by Mycenae, fighting a powerful city called Troy in what is now Turkey. Although historians are not sure if the Trojan War really happened, they have found the ruins of a city they believe to be Troy. Evidence at these ruins suggests that the city was destroyed in battle, though it is impossible to be certain.

▼ Within the heavily fortified ancient walls of Mycenaean fortresses such as Mycenae, shown here, archaeologists have found artifacts like the gold mask at left.

Whatever the real Trojan story, war played a part in the end of Mycenaean civilization. Along with droughts and famines, invasion from outside, and the end of trade, war between Mycenaean cities sped up their downfall. By the end of the 1100s BC the Mycenaean cities were mostly in ruins. A dark age followed. People fled cities, struggled to farm enough to eat, fought their neighbors and outside invaders, and even lost the use of writing for several centuries. Greek civilization almost disappeared.

READING CHECK Compare and Contrast
How were Minoan and Mycenaean culture similar? How were they different?

Greek City-States

For more than 300 years, Greece was awash in confusion. By the 800s BC, however, life in Greece was stable enough for a new type of society to emerge. That society was centered on the **polis**, or city-state, which became the basic political unit in Greece. Because Greece was so rugged, travel and communication between city-states was difficult. As a result, each polis developed independently of its neighbors. Each developed its own form of government, laws, and customs.

Life in the Polis The polis was the center of daily life and culture for the ancient Greeks. One philosopher even defined a person as one who lived in a polis. Because it was so central to their lives, Greeks were fiercely loyal to their polis. In fact, people did not think of themselves as Greeks at all, but rather as residents of a particular city-state.

A typical polis was built around a high area called an **acropolis** (uh-KRAHP-uh-luhs). In addition to fortifications, the acropolis usually housed temples to the gods and spaces for public ceremonies. Below the acropolis were other public places, like the **agora** (A-guh-ruh), or marketplace, where people did business, gossiped, and discussed politics. Shops, houses, and more temples surrounded the agora. In quieter parts of the polis, one might find a gymnasium, a training ground and public bath for athletes. Surrounding the entire polis was a sturdy wall for defense. Beyond the wall were a few scattered houses and marketplaces as well as the fields where the city's food was grown.

🗽 **NEW YORK**
CC Unit 1-C2b
The rise of city-states

THE IMPACT TODAY
The word *polis* appears in the name of many American cities today, such as Annapolis, Indianapolis, and Minneapolis.

CLASSICAL GREECE **129**

129

Greek City-States

Recall Why did Spartans place such an emphasis on preparedness for war? *It was seen as the only way to keep order in society.*

Summarize What was the role of helots in Sparta? *farmed, performed manual labor for Sparta's citizens*

Rate Evaluate King Lycurgus's system for training boys. *possible answer—very harsh on such young children, probably very effective in creating tough soldiers*

Info to Know

Word Origins Many words have origins in ancient Greek and Latin. Many new words, however, are being coined by patching a Latin or Greek root onto a word or root from another language. An example of this is xeriscape; *xer-* means dry in Greek, and *-scape* is taken from the Dutch painters' term, *landschap*, a region of land with distinguishing characteristics. Thus, xeriscape, a trademarked term, is a tract of land characterized by the use of drought-resistant plants.

Both women and men in Sparta were expected to be in top physical shape. Women had to stay fit so they could bear strong, healthy children. Men had to stay in shape to fight in the army.

Each major polis had a different political system that developed over time. The trading polis of Corinth, for example, was an oligarchy, a city-state ruled by a few individuals. Athens, perhaps the most famous Greek polis, was the birthplace of democracy. To better understand how a city-state's government developed, we can study one state, Sparta, as an example.

NEW YORK

CC Unit 1-C2d
The Spartan political system

The Might of Sparta Sparta was one of the mightiest city-states in Greece, if one of the least typical. Located on the Peloponnesus, the large peninsula of southern Greece, Sparta was at first surrounded by smaller towns. Over time, Sparta seized control of the towns around it, including Messenia. Once they had conquered the town, the Spartans made the Messenians into **helots**, or state slaves. Helots were given to Spartan citizens to work on farms so that the citizens did not have to perform manual labor. As a result, Spartan citizens were free to spend all their time training for war.

The Spartan emphasis on war was not created out of any particular fondness for fighting. Instead, it was seen as the only way to keep order in society. The helots outnumbered Spartan citizens by about seven to one and were always ready to rebel against their rulers. The only way the Spartans could see to keep the helots in check was to have a strong army.

To support their military lifestyle, the Spartans demanded strength and toughness from birth. Babies, boys and girls alike, were examined for strength after birth. If a child was found unhealthy, he or she was left in the wild to die. Those who were healthy were trained as soldiers from a young age.

Boys were taught physical and mental toughness by their mothers until age seven. Then they entered a school system designed to train them for combat. This system had been created by a legendary king named Lycurgus whose goal was to toughen boys in preparation for the hardships they would face as soldiers:

HISTORY'S VOICES

❝Instead of softening their feet with shoe or sandal, his rule was to make them hardy through going barefoot. This habit, if practiced, would, as he believed, enable them to scale heights more easily and clamber down precipices with less danger. In fact, with his feet so trained the young Spartan would leap and spring and run faster unshod than another in the ordinary way. Instead of making them effeminate with a variety of clothes, his rule was to habituate them to a single garment the whole year through, thinking that so they would be better prepared to withstand the variations of heat and cold.❞

—Xenophon, *The Polity of the Spartans*, c. 375 BC

At the end of their training, groups of boys were sent into the wilderness with no food or tools and were expected to survive. Then, at age 20, boys became **hoplites**, or foot soldiers. They remained in the army for 10 years, after which time they were allowed to leave and take their place as citizens.

Sparta was rather unusual among Greek city-states in that women played an important role in society. Spartan women were trained in gymnastics for physical fitness. The Spartans thought women had to be fit to bear strong children. They had the right to own property, a right forbidden to women in most of Greece.

Politically, Sparta was led by two kings who served as military commanders. Over time, responsibility for making decisions fell more and more to an elected council of elders. It was considered an honor to take a seat on this council and help run the city.

READING CHECK **Identify Cause and Effect** Why did Sparta's political system develop?

Skills Focus: Analyzing Alternative Points of View | At Level |

The Spartans

1. Review the Spartan way of life with students. Then have volunteers paraphrase the quote from Xenophon and read their paraphrases to the class.

2. Have students prepare for a class debate on the following topic: Was the Spartan way of life good for its citizens? Organize students into an even number of small groups. Assign half of the groups to prepare statements to support the Spartan system. Assign the other groups to prepare statements against the Spartan system.

3. When groups have had time to prepare their arguments, call upon volunteers from each group to debate the topic. Have students take notes during the debate.

4. As an extension, have students use their notes to write a brief, persuasive essay explaining their own position on the topic. **LS** **Kinesthetic, Verbal-Linguistic**

📃 **Alternative Assessment Handbook**, Rubrics 10: Debates; 14: Group Activity; and 43: Writing to Persuade

Answers

Reading Check *Because of Sparta's emphasis on war, it was led politically by two kings who served as military commanders.*

Gods and Heroes

In addition to archaeological evidence, much of what we know or suspect about early Greece comes from studying the Greeks' legends and myths. Myths are stories told to explain natural phenomena or events of the distant past. The Greeks told myths to explain where they came from, how they should live, and how to cope with an uncertain world.

The Gods of Olympus The ancient Greeks believed in hundreds of gods and goddesses. Each of these deities governed one aspect of nature or life. For example, the god Apollo controlled the movement of the sun through the sky, while his sister Artemis did the same for the moon. Ares (AY-reez), the fierce god of war, frequently came into conflict with Athena (uh-THEE-nuh), the clever goddess of wisdom. The Greeks believed that the gods would protect them and their city-states in exchange for the proper rituals and sacrifices.

Although the Greeks believed in many gods, about 12 of them were particularly influential in their lives. The Greeks believed that these 12 gods and goddesses lived together on Mount Olympus, the highest mountain in Greece. As a result, they were called the Olympian gods.

Though they were thought to have great power, the Greeks did not consider their deities perfect. Indeed, myths say the gods were flawed and often unpredictable. They loved, hated, argued, made mistakes, got jealous, and played tricks on each other. For example, the chief god Zeus (zoos), lord of the skies and storms, and his wife Hera had a troubled marriage full of arguments. Poseidon (po-SY-duhn), god of the sea, was quick to anger but slow to think through his actions.

Although almost all Greeks worshipped the same gods, each polis claimed one god or goddess as its special protector. Corinth, for example, claimed Apollo's favor, while Athens considered itself sacred to Athena.

Mythological References Today

The ancient Greeks used myths to make sense of the world around them. Myths were created to explain everything from thunder to the changing of seasons.

Now that we know the science behind many of the phenomena that myths once explained, you might think that myths have no place in our modern world. If you thought that, however, you would be wrong. People all over the world still enjoy tales from Greek mythology, both in their classical ancient forms and in modern retellings as novels, films, or television programs.

In addition, myths have helped shape modern culture. For example, many companies use names or symbols from myths. Sporting goods giant Nike, for example, was named after the Greek goddess of victory. Many medical organizations use a staff and snake logo inspired by the symbols of Asclepius, the Greek god of medicine.

Words and phrases from myths have also entered our daily vocabulary. We sometimes call a person's greatest weakness his or her Achilles' heel, after a mythical warrior who could not be harmed anywhere on his body except one heel. Computer users have to watch out for trojan horses, malicious programs that are hidden inside or disguised as innocent programs. Their name is derived from a trick that Greek heroes used to win the Trojan War, hiding inside a giant wooden horse that the Trojans innocently brought into their city.

Draw Conclusions Why do you think references to Greek myths are still common today?

▲ The snake-twined staff of Asclepius, the Greek god of medicine, appears in the logo of the World Health Organization.

CLASSICAL GREECE **131**

Skills Focus: Interpreting Literature as Historical Evidence

Reading Like a Historian Skill
Literature Recounts History

Research Required   Above Level

1. Explain to students that some legends and myths of Greece are thought to be recorded history. Have students locate and read a myth or legend that historians believe depicts an actual event in Greek history. Remind students to use scholarly resources and to document their research in appropriate bibliographical form.

2. Have students write an explanation of the story and the real event it might portray.

3. Ask volunteers to share the legend or myth they read and the history it recounts and discuss as a class. **LS Verbal-Linguistic**

   Alternative Assessment Handbook, Rubric 16: Judging Information; and 30: Research

---

Reading Focus

③ What role did stories of gods and heroes play in Greek culture? *Stories about these heroes were used to teach Greeks where they came from and what sort of people they should try to be.*

Gods and Heroes

Explain How did various city-states honor the Olympian gods? *Every four years, citizens of various city-states would come together for the Olympic Games, where athletes met to compete and honor the gods.*

Contrast Explain the reasons for the telling of legends and of myths. *Legends are told to explain natural phenomena or events of the distant past. Myths explain where people came from, how they live, and how to cope in an uncertain world.*

Make Inferences How would the gods being flawed and unpredictable help the Greek people relate to them? *possible answer—gods would have seemed more real*

Activity The Greek Gods Have students select one of the Greek gods discussed in the section and write a poem or song describing and honoring the aspect of life governed by that god.
LS Musical-Auditory

Alternative Assessment Handbook, Rubric 26: Poems and Songs

Answers

Linking to Today *possible answer— Greek myths still are appreciated as entertaining stories, even though we now know the science behind many natural phenomena.*

131

Greek Gods and Goddesses

Explain What was the function of Greek mythical heroes? *provided examples of virtues and strength*

Describe Who was Theseus? *an Athenian prince who killed the Minotaur of Crete*

Make Inferences Why was hubris included in the stories of some heroes? *possible answer—story warns against excessive pride*

🗄 **Quick Facts Transparency:** The Greek Gods

● Review & Assess ●

Close

Review the development of Minoan and Mycenaean civilizations, the structure of the Greek city-states, and the function of gods in Greek life.

Review

🖥 **Online Quiz,** Section 1

Assess

SE **Section 1 Assessment**

📋 **Progress Assessment:** Section 1 Quiz

📋 **Alternative Assessment Handbook**

Reteach/Intervene

📋 **Interactive Reader and Study Guide,** Section 1

💿 **Interactive Skills Tutor CD-ROM**

Answers

Reading Check *explained natural phenomena; taught Greeks where they came from and how to act*

A few locations were considered sacred by all Greeks. One was Delphi, where priestesses of Apollo were thought to receive visions of the future. Another was Olympia. Every four years, Greeks from various city-states got together there for the Olympic Games. In these games, athletes met to compete against each other and to honor the gods.

FOCUS ON NEW YORK
Many cities in upstate New York, such as Attica, Delphi Falls, Ithaca, and Troy are named for places made famous in Greek myth.

Myths about Heroes Alongside the gods, Greeks also told myths about heroes. Stories about these heroes were used to teach Greeks where they came from and what sort of people they should try to be. Some heroes, such as Hercules, the son of Zeus who had godlike strength, were renowned throughout all of Greece. Others, such as Theseus, an Athenian prince who killed the Minotaur of Crete, were famous chiefly in their home cities.

The heroes of myths killed monsters, made discoveries, founded cities, and talked with gods on almost equal terms. With the right virtues they could rise above fear and uncertainty. Their examples could inspire individuals, and even whole city-states, to achieve great things. But even in legend, the Greeks' myths would only let them rise so far. **Hubris** (HYU-bruhs), or great pride, brought many heroes to tragic ends. Their deaths served as lessons to the Greeks not to overstretch their abilities.

READING CHECK **Describe** What role did mythology play in Greek culture?

THE GREEK GODS

The ancient Greeks worshipped hundreds of gods and goddesses. A few of the most important and most widely accepted are listed below.

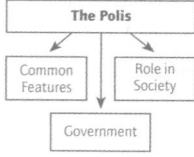

- **Zeus,** god of the sky and lightning, king of the gods ▶
- **Hera,** goddess of marriage and women, queen of the gods
- **Poseidon,** god of the sea and earthquakes
- **Hades,** god of the underworld
- **Demeter,** goddess of agriculture
- **Hestia,** goddess of the hearth and family
- **Athena,** goddess of wisdom
- **Apollo,** god of prophecy, healing, poetry, music, and the sun
- **Artemis,** goddess of hunting and the moon
- **Ares,** god of war
- **Aphrodite,** goddess of love
- **Hephaestus,** god of metalworking
- **Dionysus,** god of wine
- **Hermes,** the messenger god, god of trade

SECTION 1 ASSESSMENT

go.hrw.com
Online Quiz
Keyword: SHL GRE HP

Reviewing Ideas, Terms, and People

1. **a. Describe** What have historians learned by studying Minoan art?
   b. Compare and Contrast What is one way in which the Minoans and Mycenaean cultures were similar? What is one way in which they were different?
   c. Elaborate Why are historians not sure if the Trojan War really happened? What makes them think that it may have happened?

2. **a. Define** What roles did the **acropolis** and the **agora** play in a typical Greek **polis**?
   b. Identify Cause and Effect What led to the creation of a military society in Sparta?
   c. Evaluate Do you think the Spartan system was a good way to run a government? Why or why not?

3. **a. Describe** What were the gods of Greek mythology like?
   b. Explain Why did the ancient Greeks create myths?

c. Elaborate Why do you think the Greeks were interested in stories about great heroes?

Critical Thinking

4. **Analyze** Draw a graphic organizer like the one shown here. Using your notes, list details about the Greek polis, its typical features, its government, and its role in Greek society.

```
          The Polis
         /        \
   Common        Role in
   Features      Society
          \      /
        Government
```

FOCUS ON WRITING ✎

5. **Narration** Write a short paragraph-length legend about a hero, real or imaginary. As you write, think about what kind of life lesson readers could learn from your legend.

Section 1 Assessment Answers

1. **a.** about the Minoan way of life; life tied to sea; that women played major roles; games played
   b. similar—both trading states; different—Mycenaean language can be translated; Mycenaeans fought frequent wars
   c. only evidence is legend; there are ruins of a city believed to be Troy

2. **a.** acropolis—temples, public ceremonies; agora—marketplace, gathering place
   b. to preserve order
   c. possible answer—yes, it preserved order; no, it was harsh on the people

3. **a.** There were hundreds of gods. Twelve were particularly influential.
   b. to explain natural phenomena; to teach Greeks where they came from and how to live
   c. possible answer—taught them where they came from and how to act

4. Role in Society—central to Greeks' lives; Common features—housed temples; public places, walls for defense; Government—each had different political system

5. Student paragraphs should include a life lesson about valued Greek qualities.

World Literature

Homer (800s or 700s BC)

NEW YORK STANDARDS

PI 4.2 Students interpret and analyze documents and artifacts related to significant developments and events in world history.

About the Reading The *Odyssey*, one of two great Greek epics about the Trojan War, tells the story of Odysseus, the cleverest of all the Greek heroes who fought in the war. After the war, the gods forced Odysseus to spend 10 years wandering the seas before he could return to Greece. In the passage below, Odysseus, who has been shipwrecked, hears a minstrel singing of the end of the war and the fall of Troy, a feat accomplished through a clever trick Odysseus had planned.

AS YOU READ Ask yourself what elements of this story might have been based on actual events.

Excerpt from
The Odyssey
by Homer

The epic poems of Homer were the inspiration for the 2004 film *Troy*, a retelling of the Trojan War story.

"Now shift your theme, and sing that wooden horse
Epeios built, inspired by Athena—
the ambuscade Odysseus filled with fighters
and sent to take the inner town of Troy.
Sing only this for me, sing me this well,
and I shall say at once before the world
the grace of heaven has given us a song."

The minstrel stirred, murmuring to the god, and soon
clear words and notes came one by one, a vision
of the Akhaians [Greeks] in their graceful ships
drawing away from shore: the torches flung
and shelters flaring: Argive soldiers crouched
in the close dark around Odysseus: and
the horse, tall on the assembly ground of Troy.
For when the Trojans pulled it in, themselves,
up to the citadel, they say nearby
with long-drawn-out and hapless argument—
favoring, in the end, one course of three:
either to stave the vault with brazen axes,
or haul it to a cliff and pitch it down,
or else to save it for the gods, a votive glory—
the plan that could not but prevail.
For Troy must perish, as ordained, that day
she harbored the great horse of timber; hidden
the flower of Akhaia lay, and bore

slaughter and death upon the men of Troy.
He sang, then, of the town sacked by the Akhaians
pouring down from the horse's hollow cave,
this way and that way raping the steep city,
and how Odysseus came like Ares to
the door of Deiphobos, with Menelaos,
and braved the desperate fight there—
conquering once more by Athena's power.

The splendid minstrel sang it.
                              And Odysseus
let the bright molten tears run down his cheeks . . .

Skills FOCUS **READING LIKE A HISTORIAN**

go.hrw.com
World Literature
Keyword: SHL WRLIT

1. **Explain** How did the Greek army manage to get inside the walls of Troy?
2. **Interpret Literature as a Source** Do you think this text describes the end of a real war? Why or why not?

See **Skills Handbook**, p. H28

CLASSICAL GREECE **133**

Skills Focus: Making Generalizations

At Level

Research Required

Reading Skill
Evidence and the Trojan War

1. Remind students that we do not always have access to first-person accounts of historical events. However, sometimes legends such as the story of the Trojan War seem to match later discoveries and findings by historians and archaeologists.

2. Organize students into small groups, and have each group investigate the Trojan War story. Groups should use and document reliable online or print sources for their research.

3. Have groups prepare a poster or visual display that depicts their research findings.

4. Have volunteers present the posters to the class. **LS Interpersonal, Verbal-Linguistic**

Alternative Assessment Handbook, Rubrics 14: Group Activity; 28: Posters: and 30: Research

---

Excerpt from the *Odyssey*
Word Help

ambuscade equipment used for sneak attack
citadel fortress or stronghold

Meet the Writer
Homer (prior to 700 BC) History has left us with little information on the life of the man who is considered among the most influential and greatest writers ever. The dates of his birth and death remain obscure, but seven cities claim to be his birthplace. Historians are only certain that Homer lived in Ionia, on the western coast of modern Turkey. The numerous tales of his life confirm that he was a schoolmaster and poet in Smyrna, and that he became blind during a trip to Ithaca. Together, Homer's *Iliad* and *Odyssey* are the basis of Western epic poetry.

Primary Source
"And what he greatly thought, he nobly dared."
"But curb thou the high spirit in thy breast, for gentle ways are best, and keep aloof from sharp contentions."
"Be still my heart; thou hast known worse than this."
—Homer

Info to Know
Dactylic Hexameter Homer's epic poems were written in dactylic hexameter, a poetic form with 12 syllables in which one accented syllable is followed by two unaccented ones. It can be best illustrated by Longfellow's *Evangeline*: "THIS is the FORest primEVal. The MURmuring PINES and the HEMlocks."

Answers
Reading Like a Historian 1. *by hiding inside a hollow wooden horse;* **2.** *possible answer—this seems like a glorified account and therefore may not describe a real war*

Getting Started

Use the **Interactive Reader and Study Guide** to familiarize students with the section content.

📖 **Interactive Reader and Study Guide,** Section 2

Name _____ Class _____ Date _____
Classical Greece

Section 2

💡 **MAIN IDEA**
The Classical Age of ancient Greece was marked by great achievements, including the development of democracy, and by ferocious wars.

Key Terms and People

democracy government run by the people
Solon Athenian lawmaker who revised laws and created an elected council to help govern, the first step toward democracy
tyrant a leader who seizes power by force and claims to rule for the good of the people
Cleisthenes Athenian reformer, often called "the father of democracy"
direct democracy system of government in which all people vote directly on an issue
archon elected official who acted as the head of both the assembly and the Council of 500
phalanx a tight rectangle formation in which soldiers held long spears out ahead of their shields
Pericles military and political leader of Athens who is credited with most of the rebuilding of city after the Persian Wars

Taking Notes

As you read the summary, use a graphic organizer like the one below to take notes about the achievements and wars of Greece's classical age.

Achievements	Wars

Original content Copyright © by Holt, Rinehart and Winston. Additions and changes to the original content are the responsibility of the instructor.
Full Survey Chapter 5   51   Interactive Reader and Study Guide

---

Academic Vocabulary

Review with students the high-use academic term in this section.

commission to order the creation of something, such as a piece of art (p. 139)

📖 **CRF:** Vocabulary Builder: Section 2

Taking Notes

Achievements—development of democracy; Solon's law code; defense; rebuilt Athens as city of great sophistication; Wars—Persian Wars: Ionian city-states wanted independence; Persians put down revolt, attacked Greek mainland; after years of fighting Greeks eventually won; Peloponnesian War pitted Sparta against Athens; Sparta had strong army, but Athens had strong navy; nearly destroyed Athens; Sparta won; in the 340s BC, Macedonia took control of all Greece

---

SECTION
2 The Classical Age

BEFORE YOU READ

MAIN IDEA
The Classical Age of ancient Greece was marked by great achievements, including the development of democracy, and by ferocious wars.

READING FOCUS
1. What were the characteristics of Athenian democracy?
2. How did the Greeks manage to win the Persian Wars?
3. What advances were made in the golden age of Athens?
4. What led to the outbreak of the Peloponnesian War?

KEY TERMS AND PEOPLE
democracy
Solon
tyrant
Cleisthenes
direct democracy
archon
phalanx
Pericles

NEW YORK
PI 1.2 Students understand the development and connectedness of Western civilization and other civilizations and cultures in many areas of the world and over time.

THE INSIDE STORY

Why would the creator of a city's law code leave for 10 years? In the year 594 BC, the leaders of the polis of Athens asked an aristocrat named Solon to write a new law code for the city. The laws they had at that time were extremely harsh, and many people were unhappy with them. Solon drew up the law code that was requested from him, which tried to appeal to both nobles and the lower classes. According to legend, as soon as he was done with the code he left Greece and traveled for 10 years.

Why would Solon leave? The answer was simple. He wanted to be sure that his law code would be effective in keeping order in Athens even if he was not there to enforce it. When Solon returned after a decade's absence, he found his laws still in place and Athens prospering. ■

Solon Supporting His Laws, by Antoine Coypel, c. 1700

Themes Through Time

Democracy

GOVERNMENT AND CITIZENSHIP

Democracy is a form of government in which people govern themselves, either directly or through elected officials. Though democracy is now the most common form of government in the world, it was not always so. Though Athens had formed the world's first democracy in the 500s BC, democratic ideals did not truly take hold in Europe and the rest of the world until many centuries later.

134 CHAPTER 5

594 BC
Solon creates a new law code for Athens.

c. 430 BC Athenian democracy reaches its height under Pericles.

400 BC

508 BC
Cleisthenes reforms democracy in Athens.

▼ Athenians voted by writing candidates' names on shards of pottery.

Teach the Main Idea

At Level

The Classical Age

Materials: construction paper

1. **Teach** Ask students the Reading Focus questions to teach this section.

2. **Apply** Organize students into four groups. Assign each group a different part of this section. Have each group scan its assigned topic, plan a poster of the major events presented in that part, and then create a poster to present to the class

3. **Review** Have volunteers from each group present and explain their posters to the class. Place the posters on display for all to see.

4. **Practice/Homework** Have each student write a one paragraph summary of the events covered in this section.
   LS Interpersonal, Visual-Spatial

   📖 **Alternative Assessment Handbook**, Rubrics 14: Group Activity; 28: Posters

Athenian Democracy

The prosperity of Athens was due in large part to its stable and effective government. That government was the world's first **democracy**, a form of government run by the people. With the development of democracy around 500 BC, Athens entered its classical age, the period of its great achievements and triumphs.

The Development of Democracy Athens was the birthplace of democracy, but it had not always been a democratic city. Indeed, democracy developed slowly over a period of several centuries. Early in its history, Athens was ruled by kings. Later, the kings were replaced by aristocrats who had both money and power.

Most of Athens's subjects were poor, though, and had little power over their lives. The gap between rich and poor eventually led to conflict in Athens. To help resolve this conflict, an official named Draco reformed the city's laws. Draco thought the only way to end unrest was through harsh punishment, a belief reflected in his laws. In fact, however, the harshness of Draco's laws did not resolve the dispute between classes; they only made it worse.

Another lawmaker, **Solon**, revised the laws again in the 590s BC, overturning Draco's harshest laws. Solon outlawed debt slavery and tried to reduce poverty by encouraging trade. His most significant change, however, was in Athens's government. He allowed all men in Athens to take part in the assembly that governed the city and to serve on the juries that heard trials, but only wealthy men could run for or hold political office. Solon's laws were the first real step toward democracy in Athens, though it was a very limited democracy.

Solon's laws relieved the tension in Athens for a time but did not resolve it. Tensions flared up again after a few decades. In 541 BC a politician named Peisistratus (PY-sis-truht-uhs) took advantage of the renewed conflict to seize power. Peisistratus was a **tyrant**, a strongman who seized power by force and claimed to rule for the good of the people. Despite his violent rise to power, Peisistratus was popular. People liked that he pushed the aristocrats out of office and increased trade to make Athens richer.

After Peisistratus died, another reformer, **Cleisthenes** (KLYS-thuh-neez), took over Athens. His reforms set the stage for Athenian democracy. To break up the power of noble families, Cleisthenes divided Athens into 10 tribes based on where people lived. He made these new tribes, not families or social groups, the basis for elections. For example, each tribe elected 50 men to serve on a Council of 500 that proposed laws. Each tribe also elected one of the generals that led the Athenian army.

TAKING NOTES

As you read, take notes about the achievements and wars of Greece's classical age.

| Achievements |
| Wars |

NEW YORK

CC Unit 1-C2d
Growth of democracy in Athens

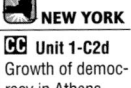

AD 930 The Althing, Europe's oldest Parliament, is founded in Iceland.

◄ **AD 1789** The U.S. Constitution is ratified.

1000   1500   2000

AD 1689
The English Bill of Rights is passed.

◄ **AD 1215** Magna Carta, a document protecting individual rights, is signed in England.

Skills Focus — **UNDERSTANDING THEMES**

Analyze Approximately how many years passed between the establishment of democracy in ancient Athens and the ratification of the U.S. Constitution?

CLASSICAL GREECE **135**

● **Direct Teach** ●

Reading Focus

❶ What were the characteristics of Athenian democracy? *direct democracy; only certain people allowed to vote; those people were expected to vote in all elections; serve in office if elected; serve on juries and in the military during war*

Athenian Democracy

Explain Why did Draco reform the laws in Athens? *to resolve conflicts between the rich and poor*

Make Generalizations What sort of leadership did Peisistratus provide? *possible answer—Though he was a tyrant, Peisistratus improved government and trade.*

Rate Which of Athens' early reformers was the most effective? Why? *possible answer—Solon, because he concerned himself with fairness in government, not punishment.*

Themes Through Time
Democracy

Analyze How many years passed between Solon's law code and Cleisthenes' establishment of democracy? *86*

Identify Where was Europe's oldest Parliament, the Althing, founded? *Iceland*

Answers

Themes Through Time *approximately 2300 years*

Skills Focus: Identifying Problem and Solution

At Level

Reading Skill
Tracing Democracy's Development

1. Have volunteers name each of the people who wrote Athenian laws. Then copy the chart for students to see, omitting the italicized answers. Have students complete the chart.

2. Have students use the information to write an informative paragraph about the development of democracy in early Athens.
LS Verbal-Linguistic, Visual-Spatial

Alternative Assessment Handbook, Rubrics 13: Graphic Organizers; and 42: Writing to Inform

Tracing Democracy's Development

Rulers	Problems	Solutions
Draco	*rich/poor gap*	*harsh punishment*
Solon	*harsh laws*	*jury trials, tax revision, members of any class allowed on council*
Peisistratus	*aristocrats in office*	*pushed aristocrats out, encouraged trade*
Cleisthenes	*power of noble families*	*established tribes based on where people lived, tribes elected counsil representatives equally*

135

Athenian Democracy

Describe Which people were allowed to vote? *free males over twenty who had completed military training*

Develop Why do you suppose Cleisthenes had the council of 500 work with the assembly? *possible answer— to ensure that the laws represented all of society fairly; the assembly was too large to be effective*

② How did the Greeks manage to win the Persian Wars? *defeated larger foe at Marathon; called on other Greek city-states for help; trapped Persians in Greece, far from home and short on supplies Sparta joined Greece to crush weakened Persian forces*

The Persian Wars

Identify Where did the Persian Wars start? *Ionia*

Elaborate How did the second invasion unify Greece? *possible answer —Sparta worked with Athens and the other city-states for their mutual defense.*

MISCONCEPTION
/////ALERT

Herodotus is sometimes referred to as the "Father of History." With a reputation like that, one would expect he was a factual reporter of historic events. However, his writings are not all accurate, and in his time, people sometimes called him the "Father of Lies."

Answers

Reading Check *direct democracy; only certain men could vote; consisted of assembly, Council of 500, and court system*

The Nature of Athenian Democracy As a democracy, Athens was ruled by the people. But not all people were able to take part in the government. Only free male Athenians over the age of 20 who had completed military training were allowed to vote. Women, children, and immigrants had no role in the government; nor did slaves. In the 300s BC only about 10 percent of the total population of Athens could participate in running the city.

Those people who were allowed to take part in the Athenian government were expected to do so fully. They had to

- vote in all elections
- serve in office if elected
- serve on juries
- serve in the military during war.

At its height, the Athenian democracy consisted of three main bodies. The first was an assembly that included all people eligible to take part in the government. This assembly made all of the laws and important decisions for Athens. It met on a particular hill within the city, and all members who were present voted on each measure. This type of system, in which all people vote directly on an issue, is called a **direct democracy**.

Working closely with the assembly was the second of the main bodies, the Council of 500. The main role of the Council, which had been created by Cleisthenes, was to write the laws that would be voted on by the full assembly.

The third body of the government was a complex series of courts that heard trials and sentenced criminals. Members of these courts, which could number up to 6,000 people, were chosen from the assembly.

Although most governing in Athens was done by the assembly, some elected officials had special roles to play. Among these elected officials were the generals who led the city in war. Another elected official was the **archon** (AHR-kahn), who served as the chief of state in Athens. The archon acted as the head of both the assembly and the Council of 500. Archons were elected for a term of one year, though they could be re-elected many times. The archon was seen as a public servant who could be removed from office or punished if he failed to serve the people well.

READING CHECK **Analyze** What were the key features of Athenian democracy?

The Persian Wars

Even as democracy was taking its final shape in Athens in the early 400s BC, the city—and the rest of Greece—was plunged into war. The Greek city-states came into conflict with the vast Persian Empire, bringing Greece into war with a much larger and stronger opponent.

Causes of the Conflict The roots of the Persian Wars lay not in mainland Greece but in the region called Ionia in what is now Turkey. Founded as Greek colonies, the Ionian city-states had become some of the largest and wealthiest Greek cities, but they had fallen under Persian rule in the 500s BC.

The Greeks of Ionia, unhappy with Persian rule and wanting independence, rebelled in 499 BC. Faced with a much larger Persian army, they asked their fellow Greeks for help. Among the cities that sent aid was Athens, who supplied ships to the Ionian rebels. Despite this assistance, the Persians put down the revolt. Furthermore, the revolt made Persian emperor Darius angry enough to seek revenge. He planned to punish the Ionians' allies, especially Athens, by attacking the Greek mainland.

The First Persian Invasion In 490 BC, the Persians set out to fulfill Darius's plans for revenge. A huge fleet carrying tens of thousands of Persian troops set out for Greece.

The fleet came ashore near a town called Marathon not far from Athens. Warned in advance of the Persians' approach, the Athenians set out to meet their foe.

The Athenians arrived at Marathon quickly and caught the Persians at work unloading their ships. The Athenians charged the beach in a **phalanx** (FAY-lanks), a tight rectangle formation in which soldiers held long spears out ahead of a wall of shields. The Persians, caught by surprise, counterattacked, but more Greeks closed in on them from the sides. Though they outnumbered their foe, the Persians retreated.

According to legend, an Athenian messenger ran from Marathon to Athens after the battle to announce the Greeks' victory. He completed the 26-mile run but died from exhaustion after he delivered the message. This legend inspired the modern marathon race, a 26-mile run that commemorates the messenger's dedication and athleticism.

Skills Focus: Comparing and Contrasting

Reading Skill

Democracy Then and Now

1. Tell students that their knowledge of the United States government is useful in understanding Athenian democracy. Have students list the branches of American government. Next to each branch, have students record the equivalent Athenian group. Create a class list for all to see.

2. Guide students in a discussion of the ways in which the structure of U.S. democracy is similar to the Athenian model, and how it has changed to accommodate our modern needs. Have students take notes during the discussion.

3. Have students use the list and their notes to write a paragraph about the similarities and differences in Athenian and U.S. democracies.

LS **Verbal-Linguistic**

Alternative Assessment Handbook, Rubrics 9: Comparing and Contrasting; and 37: Writing Assignments

Plataeans

Persians

Athenians

Persian retreat

Bay of Marathon

Marsh

persian flanking movement

Callidromus Mountains

Greek last stand

Main Persian advance

Ancient wall

Gulf of Malis

Persian encampment

Marathon The Athenians and their Plataean allies lured the Persian army forward and then sent more soldiers in from either side to trap the Persians.

Thermopylae A small Greek force was able to hold back a much larger Persian army for three days in a narrow mountain pass.

Wreck of Darius's Fleet

Thermopylae

Plataea

Marathon

Salamis

Sardis

Ionian Sea

Aegean Sea

IONIA

Athens

0   50   100 Miles
0   50   100 Kilometers
Azimuthal equal-area projection

•Sparta

Mediterranean Sea

Bay of Eleusis

Greeks

Persians

Salamis

Saronic Gulf

Persian Empire

Greek city-states allied against the Persians

Neutral and pro-Persian city-states

☆ Greek victory

✦ Persian victory

Darius's route

Xerxes's route

Salamis The Greeks led the larger Persian fleet into a narrow channel with little room to move, then used their smaller and more maneuverable ships to sink their opponents.

GEOGRAPHY SKILLS | **INTERPRETING MAPS**

go.hrw.com
Interactive Map
Keyword: SHL AIC

1. **Location** How did the local terrain help the Greeks at both Thermopylae and Salamis?

2. **Movement** Where did the Persian army head after it defeated the Greek force at Thermopylae?

CLASSICAL GREECE **137**

Reading Focus

The Persian Wars

Identify Which wars took place near marshes? *Thermopylae and Marathon*

Sequence Write the battles in the order they occurred and list their Persian leader. *Marathon—Darius, Thermopylae —Xerxes, Salamis—Xerxes*

Evaluate What advantages might there have been in Xerxes' routes? *possible answers— The Persians might not have been seen until they were very close to Athens. They avoided the dangers of traveling among islands with well-developed naval defenses. They could raid coastal cities and pick up supplies on their way.*

🗝 **Map Transparency:** Persian Wars

✷ **Interactive Map:** Persian Wars

Info to Know

The Plataeans Note that the Plataeans descended from the north to assist in the battles at Thermopylae and Marathon. These Greeks lived to the northwest of Athens and had voluntarily changed from the protection of Thebes to that of Athens prior to the Persian Wars. Plataea was the location of the 479 BC naval defeat of the Persians by the Greek fleet commanded by Aristedes.

Differentiating Instruction

Above Level

Advanced Learners/Gifted and Talented

Research Required

Materials: construction paper

1. Tell students that most nations extend their national borders to include islands that lie close to their shores. This is not the case in the Aegean Sea.

2. Organize students into small groups. Have students locate a map of the Aegean Islands and then create their own map of the region. Have students color code the islands in the region by group and nationality.

3. Have students discuss and record possible reasons the majority of the Aegean Islands were Greek in ancient times and remain so today. Have volunteers present their ideas to the class and guide students in a discussion of the Greek islands in the Aegean Sea.

LS **Visual-Spatial, Interpersonal**

✐ **Alternative Assessment Handbook**, Rubrics 12: Drawing Conclusions; and 20: Map Creation

Answers

Interpreting Maps 1. *Thermopylae— narrow mountain pass helped Greeks trap and hold back a larger Persian army; Salamis—trapped Persian fleet in a narrow channel, then attacked;* **2.** *Plataea*

137

Reading Focus

The Persian Wars

Make Inferences If the Persians were cut off from their supplies after the Battle of Salamis, how had the supplies been delivered? *by ship*

Understanding Cause and Effect What were the consequences of the Battle of Salamis? *Persian navy destroyed; Persian army crushed, led to peace settlement*

Activity **Thermopylae** Have students write a slogan for a sign to be placed near Thermopylae, to be seen by tourists to remind them of the action of ancient Spartans in the area.
LS Verbal-Linguistic

The Battle of Thermopylae

The Athenian historian Herodotus described the Persian Wars in his *History*. In this passage, he describes the efforts of the Spartans under King Leonidas to hold back the Persians at Thermopylae.

"So the barbarians under Xerxes began to draw nigh; and the Greeks under Leonidas, as they now went forth determined to die, advanced much further than on previous days, until they reached the more open portion of the pass. Hitherto they had held their station within the wall and from this had gone forth to fight at the point where the pass was the narrowest. Now they joined battle beyond the defile and carried slaughter among the barbarians, who fell in heaps. Behind them the captains of the squadrons, armed with whips, urged their men forward with continual blows. Many were thrust into the sea, and there perished; a still greater number were trampled to death by their own soldiers. No one heeded the dying. For the Greeks, reckless of their own safety and desperate, since they knew that as the mountain had been crossed their destruction was nigh at hand, exerted themselves with the most furious valour against the barbarians."

Skills Focus **READING LIKE A HISTORIAN**

Interpret What does Herodotus say inspired the Spartans to fight so fiercely at Thermopylae?
See **Skills Handbook, p. H25**

Preparations for a Second Invasion The Greek victory at Marathon shocked both Greeks and Persians. The Athenians could not believe that they had defeated a much stronger foe. The Persians, humiliated, were furious. Wanting revenge more than ever, Darius planned a second invasion of Greece, but he died in 486 BC, before he could launch that second invasion. His son Xerxes, vowing to get revenge for his father, continued planning another attack on Greece.

In 480 BC, 10 years after the first invasion, Xerxes set out for Greece. His army included hundreds of thousands of soldiers and sailors together with all their animals, weapons, food, and other supplies. According to ancient Greek accounts, the Persian army was so huge that it took them a week to cross a bridge they built into Greece, though this figure is certainly an exaggeration.

Faced with another invasion, the Athenians called on other Greek city-states to help fight off the Persians. Among the states that responded to the call was Sparta. Though the two cities were bitter rivals, Athens and Sparta agreed to work together to fight the Persians. Athens, which had recently built a large and powerful navy, took charge of the Greeks' fighting ships. Sparta took charge of the Greeks' armies.

The Second Persian Invasion As Persian forces marched into Greece, the Greeks worried that they would not have time to prepare their troops for battle. To slow down the Persians, a group of Spartans and their allies gathered in a mountain pass at Thermopylae (thuhr-MAH-puh-lee), through which the Persians would pass to get into Greece. There, the Spartans held off the entire Persian army for several days. In the end, a local resident showed the Persians an alternate path through the mountains, which allowed them to surround and kill the Spartans. Nevertheless, the Spartans' sacrifice bought time for the Greeks' defense.

After Thermopylae, the Persians marched south to Athens, which the Greeks had evacuated. The Persians attacked and burned the city but needed their fleet to bring them additional supplies. Not wanting the Persians to get what they needed, a clever Athenian commander lured the Persian fleet into the narrow Strait of Salamis near Athens. Because the Persian ships were so much larger than the Greek vessels, they could not maneuver well in the strait. With their opponents virtually helpless, the Greek warships cut them to pieces. They sank many ships and sent swarms of soldiers onto others. Xerxes, who had brought a throne to the shore to watch the battle from afar, saw his navy go down in defeat.

The Battle of Salamis changed the nature of the war. The Persian army was now stuck in Greece, far from home and short on supplies. Demoralized, they were no longer a match for the Greeks. The next year, in 479 BC, a huge Greek army led by the full might of Sparta crushed the Persians near Plataea. After Plataea, the Persians gave up on their invasion and agreed to a peace settlement. The Greeks had won the Persian Wars.

READING CHECK **Sequence** What events led to the Greek victory in the Persian Wars?

Skills Focus: Analyzing Alternative Points of View | At Level

Reading Like a Historian Skill
Reporting the Persian Wars

1. Guide students in a discussion of news reports in which the correspondent reports from the scene of battle.

2. Organize students into eight groups. Assign the Persian or Greek side of one of these topics to each group: The Ionian Rebellion, The Battle of Marathon, The Battle of Thermopylae, and The Battle of Salamis.

3. Have each group prepare a "live" news report of their assigned topic. Groups should make

sure their reporters describe the action from the point of view assigned to them. Groups should use information in the text so that they include pertinent details of their assigned event.

4. Have volunteers present the news reports to the class. **LS** Kinesthetic, Auditory-Musical

Alternative Assessment Handbook, Rubric 33: Skits and Reader's Theater

---

Answers

Reading Like a Historian *because they knew destruction was inevitable after the Persians crossed the mountain*

Reading Check *Athens and Sparta allied to fight the Persians; Spartans held off the Persians at Thermopylae, allowing Athens to prepare; Persian supplies were cut off when the Greek fleet destroyed their ships; Spartans led the Greek army to defeat the Persians at Plataea*

The Golden Age of Athens

As the leaders in the Persian Wars, Athens and Sparta became the two most powerful and influential city-states in Greece. Because the Spartans were not popular with the rest of Greece, Athens eventually became the leading city-state. After the Persian Wars, Athens entered a golden age, an age in which it was the center of Greek culture and politics.

Increased Influence After the Persian Wars, dozens of Greek city-states banded together to defend one another and to punish Persia for the invasion. In theory, this alliance was a league of equals; but as the largest and richest of its members, Athens actually controlled the entire alliance. Because the alliance's treasury was kept on the islands of Delos, the alliance became known as the Delian League.

As the Delian League's leader, Athens controlled its ships and money. Many cities were interested in league membership, so the league grew wealthier and more powerful. As its leader, Athens gained more influence in Greece.

Eventually, some league members began to resent Athenian dominance, but Athens would not allow these unhappy members to quit. Any league members who rebelled were attacked by the league fleet, led by Athens, and forced back into the alliance. Before long, the league, in effect, turned into an Athenian empire.

Rebuilding Athens After the Persian Wars, the people wanted to rebuild their city, which had been burned during the fighting. Some of the money for this rebuilding came from within Athens. A substantial amount, though, came from the treasury of the Delian League. The other members of the league were not happy that the Athenians used their collective funds to rebuild their own city, but none was powerful enough to stop Athens.

The rebuilding of Athens began at the top, with Athens' acropolis. The Athenians built a series of grand temples on the acropolis, the grandest of which was the Parthenon, a grand temple dedicated to the goddess Athena. The Athenians expanded their port, built new roads, and constructed high walls around the city itself. Many people considered the rebuilt Athens, a city of stone and marble, the height of Greek culture and sophistication.

The Age of Pericles Much of the rebuilding of Athens was due to one man—**Pericles** (PER-uh-kleez). A skilled politician and a gifted public speaker, Pericles was elected one of the city's generals in the 460s BC and was re-elected many times. Through his personal charisma and cleverness, Pericles became the most influential politician in Athens for many years.

Despite Pericles's own personal power, he was a great champion of democracy. To encourage more people to participate in government, he introduced payment for those who served in public offices or on juries. He also encouraged the Athenians to introduce democracy into other parts of Greece.

Besides being a skilled speaker and politician, Pericles was a great patron of the arts. It was he who <u>commissioned</u> the building of the Parthenon and several other monuments on the Acropolis, and it was his idea to hire great artists and sculptors to decorate them. Pericles wanted Athens to be the most glorious city in Greece, and he wanted its people to be proud of their city. He firmly believed that it had the best government and the noblest people, and he thought that it should have monuments to prove its superiority to other cities.

ACADEMIC VOCABULARY

commission to order the creation of something, such as a piece of art

FACES OF HISTORY

PERICLES
c. 495–429 BC

Born to a powerful Athenian family, Pericles showed interest in philosophy and art even as a young man. Once he had become an adult, Pericles became involved with a number of influential politicians who were working to make Athens more democratic. A gifted public speaker, Pericles used his talents to challenge aristocrats who thought their money and influence should allow them to rule the city.

Pericles was a firm believer in the superiority of Athens over other Greek city-states. He was instrumental in forming the Athenian Empire and ordered the building of the Parthenon.

When the Peloponnesian War between Athens and Sparta broke out, Pericles devised the Athenian strategy of withdrawing inside the city walls. The navy could bring food and supplies to Athens even if the Spartans surrounded the city. Ultimately, that plan led to his death. Overcrowding in the city led to the outbreak of plague, and Pericles was among its victims.

Draw Conclusions Why is the 400s BC in Athens sometimes called the Age of Pericles?

Reading Focus

3 What advances were made in the golden age of Athens?

The Golden Age of Athens

Recall Why did Athens become more influential than Sparta? *The Spartans were not popular with the rest of Greece.*

Analyze How did Athens come to control the Delian League? *Athens was the largest and richest member of the league, controlled both the ships and money*

Info to Know

Pericles the Olympian In Plutarch's *Lives*, he tells the following story about Pericles. Once, Pericles was doing business in the Athenian agora. All day long an annoying heckler followed him about. Pericles never lost his composure. Even when it became dark, the heckler still followed him home. Pericles simply ordered a servant to take a torch and guide the fellow home. Many other stories of Pericles' calm and wisdom are found in *Lives*. Pericles was nicknamed "the Olympian, " not because of athleticism, but because of his virtuous and godlike ability to rise above emotions.

Skills Focus: Making Generalizations

Below Level

Reading Skills
Rulers of Early Greece

Standard English Mastery

1. Review with students the rulers of Athens discussed in this section: Draco, Solon, Peisistratus, Cleisthenes, and Pericles. Have students write these names in a list or chart. Then have students work in mixed-ability pairs to write down key achievements of each ruler and problems each encountered.

2. Guide students in a discussion about the need for strong leaders and centralized power in the early formation of early nations.

3. Have students work in mixed-ability pairs to review their leader list. Then have students refer to their notes and write a paragraph describing the preparation of a nation for democratic rule. **LS Verbal-Linguistic**

📝 **Alternative Assessment Handbook**, Rubrics 11: Discussions; 40: Writing to Describe

Answers

Faces of History *because Pericles was a leader in creating the Athenian Empire and building the Parthenon*

The Peloponnesian War

Identify Cause and Effect What contributed to the Macedonian victory over Greece? *continual fighting between Athens and Sparta; the loss of wealth, resources, and power; Sparta's defeat by Thebes*

Make Judgments Would you rather have fought for Sparta or Greece? Why? *possible answer—the Greeks, because they had dominated the region militarily; Sparta, because they won the war*

(Activity) Traveling to War Have students use the map on this page to estimate about how far the Persians in Ionia had to travel to get to Athens by land and by sea. Have students refer to the illustrated plate to learn how the Persians might have been able to cross such enormous distances. **LS Logical-Mathematical**

🖙 **Map Transparency**: Peloponnesian War

❹ What led to the outbreak of the Peloponnesian War? *rivalry between Athens and Sparta*

The Peloponnesian War

Recall What natural event weakened Athens? *a plague*

Understanding Cause and Effect What fear caused the Peloponnesian League to declare war on the Delian League? *Peloponnesian Sparta feared the Athenians' fleet would stop it and its allies from trading.*

Answers

Interpreting Maps 1. *Crete*
2. *Peloponnesian League*

Reading Check *mutual fear; Sparta feared Athens would stop it from trading, Athens feared the military might of the Pelopponesian League*

140

Life in the Golden Age During the Golden Age, trade brought great wealth to Athens. Merchants from other parts of the world moved to the city, bringing their own foods and customs. As a result, Athens was a very cosmopolitan city. Adding to its appeal were grand festivals, public celebrations, and public events. Athenians could cheer on athletes in the city's religious games or watch great dramas played out in the city's theaters. Athens was the heart of Greek culture during this time.

READING CHECK Draw Conclusions What made the 400s a golden age in Athens?

The Peloponnesian War

As the leader of the Delian League, Athens was the richest, mightiest polis in Greece. Being rich and mighty, however, also brought the city many powerful rivals. The greatest of these rivals was Sparta, which wanted to limit Athens' power and end its dominance of Greece.

GREECE BEFORE THE PELOPONNESIAN WAR

MACEDONIA

Sea of Marmara

Aegean Sea

PERSIAN EMPIRE

Ionian Sea

Thebes
• Athens
ATTICA

IONIA

• Miletus

Peloponnesus
Sparta
SPARTA

Delos

Rhodes

Mediterranean Sea

Crete

- Delian League
- Peloponnesian League
- Neutral states

0   50   100 Miles
0   50   100 Kilometers
Azimuthal equal-area projection

GEOGRAPHY SKILLS INTERPRETING MAPS

1. **Place** What large island remained neutral during the Peloponnesian War?
2. **Regions** To which league did the city of Thebes belong?

140 CHAPTER 5

The Peloponnesian League Like Athens, Sparta was the head of a league of allied city-states. Called the Peloponnesian League, this alliance had been formed in the 500s BC to provide protection and security for its members.

For decades after the Persian Wars, tension built between the Delian and Peloponnesian leagues. Athens and its allies feared the military might of the other league. In return, Sparta feared that Athens's fleet would stop it and its allies from trading. This mutual fear led Athens and Sparta to declare war on each other in 431 BC. The resulting conflict, known as the Peloponnesian War, lasted many years.

War in Greece For the first several years of the war, neither side gained much of an advantage. Sparta and its allies dominated the land, while Athens and its allies dominated the sea. Realizing that the Spartan army was stronger, the Athenians avoided any battles on land. As a result, neither side could win more than minor victories against the other.

In 430 and 429 BC, a terrible plague struck Athens, changing the course of the war. Among those who died from the plague was Pericles, the city's leader through the beginning of the war. After the plague ended, fighting heated up for a few years before the Athenians and Spartans agreed to a truce in 421 BC. Peace had come to Greece, at least for a brief time.

▲ This ancient Athenian plate shows soldiers as they may have looked in the Peloponnesian War.

Skills Focus: Sequencing

At Level

Reading Skill
Time Lines of War in Greece

Materials: rulers

1. Review the information about the many wars and battles fought by the Greeks.

2. Have students work in mixed-ability pairs to create a chronological listing of the battles and dates discussed in the section.

3. Have students work individually to create a time line of the information. Have students calculate the scale they will use to accommodate the information on their papers.

4. Have volunteers present and describe their time lines to the class. Create a class time line for all to see and have students correct their work as needed. Have students retain their time lines as a study tool. **LS Logical-Mathematical, Visual-Spatial**

📝 **Alternative Assessment Handbook**, Rubric 36: Time Lines

Six years later, war broke out again, when Athens attacked one of Sparta's allies. The Spartans responded, but this time they took to the sea as well as the land. The Spartans destroyed the Athenian fleet, leaving Athens with no choice but surrender in 404 BC.

The Peloponnesian War nearly destroyed Athens. It lost thousands of soldiers, hundreds of ships, huge sums of money, and most of its allies. Sparta, too, was exhausted by the war. It had nearly lost several times and had suffered damage almost as great as Athens's.

After their victory, Sparta's army tried to act as Greece's dominant power. But Sparta's wealth and resources were badly strained, and its power had worn down. As a result of this strain, the Spartans could not keep control of Greece. The city-state of Thebes defeated Sparta, but it could not maintain control either. The struggle for power in Greece led to a long cycle of warfare that left all of Greece vulnerable to attack. Finally, in the 340s BC Macedonia, a Greek-speaking kingdom to the north, swept in and took control of all of Greece.

READING CHECK Identify Cause and Effect
What caused the Peloponnesian War?

CAUSES AND EFFECTS OF THE PELOPONNESIAN WAR

Causes

- After the Persian Wars, Athens used its influence with other city-states to establish the Delian League. Athens took advantage of its position as the head of the Delian League to create what amounted to an Athenian Empire.

- Sparta and its allies, the Peloponnesian League, resented the growing influence of Athens in Greece.

- Over decades, tensions built up between the two leagues.

Effects

- Athens lost its entire navy, most of its army, and most of its allies. For a short time, the city's government was replaced by an oligarchy chosen by Sparta, though democracy was soon reinstated.

- Sparta became the supreme power in Greece. However, the Spartan army was weakened and was defeated by Thebes in 371 BC.

- In the 340s BC, after years of bitter squabbling among city-states, all of Greece was conquered by Macedonia.

SECTION 2 ASSESSMENT

go.hrw.com
Online Quiz
Keyword: SHL AIC HP

Reviewing Ideas, Terms, and People

1. a. Identify What were the most significant elements of ancient Athenian **democracy**?
b. Sequence How did Athenian government change in the years leading up to the development of democracy?
c. Evaluate Do you think a **direct democracy** would work today? Why or why not?

2. a. Identify Who ordered the first Persian invasion of Greece? Why did he want to invade?
b. Identify Cause and Effect What was the ultimate result of the Battle of Marathon?
c. Predict How might the Persian Wars have ended differently if the Spartans had not held out at Thermopylae?

3. a. Identify Who was **Pericles**, and what did he do for the city of Athens?
b. Infer Why is the period after the Persian Wars considered a golden age of Athenian history?
c. Support a Position Do you think Pericles was justified in using the Delian League's money to rebuild Athens? Why or why not?

4. a. Describe What was Athens's strategy at the beginning of the Peloponnesian War?
b. Explain Why did the members of the Peloponnesian League resent Athens?
c. Elaborate How did Greece change after the Peloponnesian War?

Critical Thinking

5. Identify Cause and Effect Draw a graphic organizer like the one below. Using your notes, identify the causes and the effects of the Persian Wars.

Causes → The Persian Wars → Effects

FOCUS ON WRITING

6. Description Write an obituary such as you might find in a newspaper remembering the life of Pericles. The obituary should give a few facts about his life and detail his major accomplishments.

QUICK FACTS **Causes and Effects of the Peloponnesian War**

Activity **Heroic Art** Tell students that the ancient Greeks liked to honor warriors with heroic art, such as battle scenes. Organize students into eight groups. Assign each group a different Cause or Effect from the chart on this page and have each group create a visual to illustrate their assigned topic.
LS **Visual-Spatial**

Alternative Assessment Handbook, Rubric 6: Cause and Effect

Quick Facts Transparency: Causes and Effects of the Peloponnesian War

● Review & Assess ●

Close

Review the development of Athenian democracy, the events of the Persian Wars, the characteristics of Athens in the Golden Age, and the events of the Peloponnesian War.

Review

Online Quiz, Section 2

Assess

SE Section 2 Assessment

Progress Assessment: Section 2 Quiz

Alternative Assessment Handbook

Reteach/Intervene

Interactive Reader and Study Guide, Section 2

Interactive Skills Tutor CD-ROM

Section 2 Assessment Answers

1. a. direct democracy; only certain men allowed to vote; three separate bodies, including the assembly, the Council of 500, and the courts
b. code of laws changed
c. possible answer—Yes, a direct democracy would ensure that every vote was counted

2. a. The Persian emperor Darius; was angry about the Ionian rebels and wanted to punish their allies
b. The Persians retreated

c. possible answer—Greeks might not have won the Persian Wars

3. a. skilled politician and gifted speakers; helped rebuild Athens
b. Athens rose to glory and had great influence in Greece
c. possible answer—No, the money should have been used to benefit all members of the Delian League

4. a. avoided land battles
b. They supported Athens' rival, Sparta; feared Athens would stop trade

c. Sparta became the dominant power in Greece but lost control

5. Causes—Ionian rebellion, Persian invasion; Effects—Athens became the leading city-state; Athens entered a golden age; city-states banded together for defense

6. Obituaries should include details about Pericles' life and how he helped bring Athens into a golden age

Preteach

Getting Started

Use the **Interactive Reader and Study Guide** to familiarize students with the section content.

📖 **Interactive Reader and Study Guide**, Section 3

Academic Vocabulary

Review with students the high-use academic term(s) in this section.

irrelevant not appropriate or related to the subject (p. 145)

📑 **CRF:** Vocabulary Builder: Section 3

Taking Notes

Greek Philosophy—love of wisdom, three greatest were Socrates, Aristotle, and Plato; Greek Literature; Homer's epics include the Iliad *and the* Odyssey; *poetry often not written down; poets included Sappho and Pindar, Hesiod; playwrights included Aeschuylus, Sophocles, Euripedes, Aristophanes; history writers emerged including Herodotus and Thucydides; Arts— realistic and idealized style; Architecture— simple, clean, balanced*

go.hrw.com
Online Resources

KEYWORD: SHL GRE
ACTIVITY: Greek Art

SECTION
3 Greek Achievements

BEFORE YOU READ

MAIN IDEA
The ancient Greeks made great achievements in philosophy, literature, art, and architecture that influenced the development of later cultures and ideas.

READING FOCUS
1. How did Greek philosophy influence later thinking?
2. What types of literature did the Greeks create?
3. What were the aims of Greek art and architecture?

KEY TERMS AND PEOPLE
Socrates
Plato
Aristotle
reason
logic
Homer
lyric poetry
Herodotus
Thucydides

 NEW YORK

PI 4.2 Students interpret and analyze documents and artifacts related to significant developments and events in world history.

THE INSIDE STORY

Why was a peaceful philosopher condemned to die? In 399 BC, Socrates, considered by many to be the wisest man in Athens, was put on trial. The charges laid against him were impiety, or disrespect for religion, and corrupting the city's children. Some wealthy and powerful Athenians felt that Socrates's teaching led people, including children, to question the actions of the gods. Having only recently lost the Peloponnesian War, a loss they attributed to the displeasure of the gods, the Athenians did not want to do anything that might anger the gods further. Therefore, they decided Socrates had to be punished.

Many historians do not believe the charges laid against Socrates were valid. They think he was really arrested for political reasons and that the charges of impiety and corruption were only a cover. Several of Socrates's friends had been involved with a tyrannical government that had taken control of Athens, and historians think he was arrested to punish him for his connections to this group.

According to his student and friend Plato, Socrates accepted his death willingly and calmly. His friends were not so calm, grieving and urging Socrates to reconsider his decision. The old philosopher scolded them for their actions and asked them to let him die in peace. He then drank a cup of hemlock, a deadly poison and quietly passed away. ◼

A CUP OF DEATH

The philosopher Socrates (center) was condemned to die by drinking poison.

Teach the Main Idea

At Level

Greek Achievements

1. **Teach** Ask students the Reading Focus questions on the next page to teach this section.

2. **Apply** Have students scan the section and write a brief summary of each of the red headings in this section.

3. **Review** Allow time for volunteers to share their summaries with the class. Have students take notes and correct their own summaries as needed.

4. **Practice/Homework** Have each student write a short paragraph about Greek achievements and its influence on cultures that followed. **LS Verbal/Linguistic**

📖 **Alternative Assessment Handbook**, Rubrics 1: Acquiring Information; and 37: Writing Assignments

Greek Philosophy

Despite their condemnation of Socrates, the people of ancient Greece—especially Athens—were great believers in philosophy, the search for wisdom and knowledge. In fact, the word *philosophy* itself comes from the Greek word *philosophia*, which means "the love of wisdom." Philosophy played a key part in classical Greek life and culture.

While we can trace the earliest Greek philosophy to the 500s BC, it reached its height in Athens during the 400s and 300s. This golden age of Greek philosophy was inspired by the three greatest Greek philosophers: **Socrates** (SAHK-ruh-teez), **Plato** (PLAYT-oh), and **Aristotle** (ar-uh-STAH-tuhl).

Socrates Born in the mid-400s BC, Socrates was the first of the great Athenian philosophers. Though he was famous even in his own lifetime, we know very little about Socrates's personal life. What we know of his ideas comes from the writings of his students, like Plato. From those writings, we have obtained a clear picture of how Socrates thought and taught.

Socrates was interested in broad concepts of human life, such as truth, justice, and virtue. He thought that philosophers could learn what made good people and good societies. To learn such things, he thought that one had to ask questions. He started with basic questions such as, "What is truth?" When a person answered, Socrates followed up with more questions. By working through long series of questions, he thought people could discover the basic nature of life. Today we call this method of learning through questions the Socratic method.

Plato Plato, one of Socrates's students, became a great philosopher in his own right. Unlike Socrates, Plato left behind a great number of writings that record his ideas. These writings cover a wide variety of topics, from the nature of truth and goodness to the ideal form of government. Government is the topic of what may be Plato's most famous work, the *Republic*. In it, Plato argues that a government should be led by the people most qualified to make good decisions—philosophers. No one else, he argues, has the skills necessary to lead:

HISTORY'S VOICES

"Until philosophers are kings, or the kings and princes of this world have the spirit and power of philosophy, and political greatness and wisdom meet in one, and those commoner natures who pursue either to the exclusion of the other are compelled to stand aside, cities will never have rest from their evils—no, nor the human race."

—Plato, *Republic*

As this excerpt suggests, Plato did not support Athenian democracy, in which all men, philosophers or not, could take part.

To help spread philosophical ideas and thus improve the government, Plato wanted to make a philosopher's education more formal. To that end, he founded the Academy, a school where respected philosophers could teach their students and hold debates. In Plato's own lifetime the Academy became the most important site for Greek philosophers to do their work.

Aristotle Among the scholars who studied at the Academy was Aristotle, the third of the great Athenian philosophers. Unlike Socrates and Plato, who mostly studied human behavior, Aristotle was more concerned with the nature of the world around him.

TAKING NOTES

As you read, keep a list of key people and developments in Greek philosophy, literature, art, and architecture.

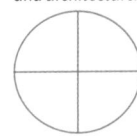

READING SKILLS

Visualizing Picture each philosopher in your mind. Think of two visual details to remind you of what each man stood for.

 NEW YORK

CC Unit 1-C2c Contributions of Greek civilization

Greek Philosophy

Recall How would you describe the Greek's belief in philosophy. *the search for wisdom and knowledge*

Contrast What is the difference between reason and logic? *Reason is clear and ordered thinking, which is applied to careful observations. Logic is the process of making inferences based on known facts.*

❷ What types of literature did the Greeks create? *epics, drama, poetry*

Greek Literature

Recall What is the subject of the *Iliad*? *the Trojan War*

Draw Conclusions Why would the story of Achilles be important to the early Greeks? *Achilles represents both the passion and the sense of honor Greeks revered.*

Archaeologists explain a preference for studying cultural groupings rather than political areas in *The Archaeology of Ancient Greece:* "Regional differences are apparent in virtually all areas of material easy to categorize. Roof construction techniques also attest to the value of cultural rather than political divisions . . ."

The Archaeology of Ancient Greece by James Whitley Cambridge University Press, 2001.

Answers

Literary Inspiration *possible answer— that literature was important because it was given to Greeks by the gods*
Reading Check *Socrates, Plato, and Aristotle*

144

Aristotle tried to apply philosophical principles to every kind of knowledge. He used these principles to study art and literature, to discuss politics, and to examine the natural world. His writings covered subjects that ranged from truth to biology to astronomy to poetry.

One of Aristotle's most valuable contributions to philosophy was his emphasis on reason and logic. **Reason** means clear and ordered thinking. Aristotle argued that people should use reason to help them learn about the world by making careful observations and thinking rationally about what they had seen. His emphasis on reason influenced the development of science in Europe.

Aristotle also helped develop the field of **logic**, the process of making inferences. He taught that people could use what they already know to infer new facts. For a simple example of Aristotle's logic, read the sentences below. Notice how the third sentence uses information from the first two to draw a conclusion.

- Birds have feathers and lay eggs.
- Owls have feathers and lay eggs.
- Therefore, an owl must be a type of bird.

READING CHECK **Identify** Who were the greatest philosophers of ancient Greece?

Literary Inspiration
The Greeks believed that writers were inspired by nine goddesses called Muses. The Muse in this image carries a stringed instrument called a lyre. *What does the belief in the Muses suggest about Greek attitudes toward literature?*

Greek Literature

Philosophers were not the only Greeks to leave written works. Many works of Greek literature also remain, a great many of them still popular today. Among the many forms of literature in which the Greeks excelled were poetry—both epics and other forms—history, and drama.

Homer's Epics Probably the most famous works of Greek literature are also some of the earliest. They are two epic poems, the *Iliad* and the *Odyssey,* both attributed to a poet named **Homer**. Epics, you may recall, tell stories about great events and heroes. Both of Homer's epics tell stories about the Trojan War, the legendary fight between the Mycenaean Greeks and the soldiers of Troy.

The *Iliad* tells the story of the last year of the Trojan War. It is largely the story of two mighty heroes: Achilles (uh-KIL-eez), the greatest of all Greek warriors, and Hector, a prince of Troy and leader of that city's army. Near the end of the epic, Achilles kills Hector in single combat, paving the way for the Greeks' ultimate victory over Troy.

Although the *Odyssey* tells the story of heroes from the Trojan War, it does not take place during the war itself. It tells of the hero Odysseus, who angers the gods and is forced to wander the sea for 10 long years before he can return to Greece. Along the way, he faces terrible dangers—including monsters, magicians, and even the gods—that threaten him and his crew, though he does eventually reach home.

Homer's epics had a tremendous influence in early Greece. Though they were not at first written down, poets recited and sang the epics throughout the Greek world. In time, the *Iliad* and the *Odyssey* became the basis for the Greek education system. Students were required to memorize long passages, and young men were encouraged to emulate the deeds of the heroes described in them. The heroic deeds described by Homer also inspired the subjects of many later Greek writers.

Other Forms of Poetry The Greeks wrote many types of poetry besides epics. For example, the poet Hesiod (HEE-see-uhd) wrote descriptive poetry. Among the subjects he described in his poems were the works of the gods and the lives of peasants.

Skill Focus: Making Inferences

Reading Skill
Aristotelian Logic

1. Read the example of Aristotle's logic on this page. Explain to students that Aristotle's design of the syllogism influenced the development of logic.

2. Explain that the sample syllogism's first statement expresses an established fact. The second expresses the similarity of something new to the first fact. The last statement uses the first two to make an inference.

3. Have students create several of their own syllogisms. If students have difficulty, assign them to work in mixed-ability pairs to complete the activity. Encourage students to consider using information they have learned in this chapter or in other classes.

4. Allow time for several volunteers to share their syllogisms. **LS** **Verbal-Linguistic**

📋 **Alternative Assessment Handbook**, Rubric 37: Writing Assignments

Greek History

Analyzing Primary Sources Thucydides is widely considered to be the greatest historian of ancient Greece. In his *History of the Peloponnesian War*, he included excerpts of speeches from leaders on both sides, including this passage from a speech by Pericles of Athens. The speech was given as part of a funeral for Athenian soldiers who had fallen during the war.

To understand why Thucydides included this speech as a primary source in his work, think about

- the author of the speech
- the purpose for which the speech was prepared and delivered
- Thucydides's own goals in writing his history.

Skills FOCUS **READING LIKE A HISTORIAN**

1. Author Who delivered this speech? Why might Thucydides have wanted to include one of his speeches?

2. Purpose What purpose does the speaker seem to have for giving this speech?

3. Goals Does the inclusion of this speech make Thucydides's work stronger? Why or why not?

See **Skills Handbook**, p. H25

> I would have you day by day fix your eyes upon the greatness of Athens, until you become filled with the love of her; and when you are impressed by the spectacle of her glory, reflect that this empire has been acquired by men who knew their duty and had the courage to do it, who in the hour of conflict had the fear of dishonor always present to them, and who, if ever they failed in an enterprise, would not allow their virtues to be lost to their country, but freely gave their lives to her as the fairest offering which they could present at her feast. The sacrifice which they collectively made was individually repaid to them; for they received again each one for himself a praise which grows not old, and the noblest of all sepulchres—I speak not of that in which their remains are laid, but of that in which their glory survives, and is proclaimed always and on every fitting occasion both in word and deed.
>
> —Pericles, quoted in Thucydides, *History of the Peloponnesian War*

The Greeks also created **lyric poetry**, named after a musical instrument called the lyre that was often played to accompany the reading of poems. Lyric poems do not tell stories. Instead, they deal with emotions and desires.

Among the earliest poets to gain fame for writing lyrics was Sappho (SAF-oh), one of the few Greek women to gain fame as a writer. Her poems deal with daily life, marriage, love, and relationships with her family and friends. In the poem below, Sappho begs the goddess of love to send her a new love:

HISTORY'S VOICES

> "Iridescent-throned Aphrodite, deathless
> Child of Zeus, wile-weaver, I now implore you,
> Don't—I beg you, Lady—with pains and torments
> Crush down my spirit"
>
> —Sappho, *Hymn to Aphrodite*

Another lyric poet, Pindar, who lived in the late 500s and early 400s, wrote poems to commemorate public events like the Olympic Games.

History In addition to poetry, the ancient Greeks also wrote works in other fields. Among the fields for which they are best known is history. The Greeks were one of the first people to write about and analyze their own past.

The first major writer of history in Greece was **Herodotus** (hi-RAHD-uh-tuhs), who lived in Greece during the wars with Persia. In his most famous work, *The Histories*, Herodotus described major events of the wars, such as battles and public debates. Some of these events he had witnessed himself, but some were reported to him by other people. Unfortunately, some of Herodotus's sources were unreliable, which led to errors in his history.

A second major historian likewise lived in Athens. **Thucydides** (thoo-SID-uh-deez) lived during the Peloponnesian War and wrote about it in detail. He included what we would today call primary sources, especially speeches that he heard delivered. Unlike Herodotus, Thucydides looked at his sources critically, ignoring those that seemed unreliable or underlined.

ACADEMIC VOCABULARY
irrelevant not appropriate or related to the subject

Differentiating Instruction

Below Level

Learners Having Difficulty

1. Write a two-column chart with the labels Hesiod and Sappho for students to see. Ask students to describe the subjects of each poet's writing and jot them down beneath each heading as students call them out.

2. Organize students into small groups. Tell students they will collaborate to write a poem using one of the above subjects and styles. Encourage groups writing epic poetry to focus on description and lauding heroism. Groups writing lyric poetry may choose a well-known song and write their own new words for the music.

3. When students have finished writing their poems, have them practice reading the poems aloud and then perform them for the class.

4. As homework, have students write a paragraph explaining which poems best represented the works of Hesiod and Sappho and why. **LS Auditory-Musical, Verbal-Linguistic**

Alternative Assessment Handbook, Rubrics 14: Group Activity; and 26: Poems and Songs

---

Reading Focus

Greek Literature

Identify Which poet wrote about the lives of peasants. *Hesiod*

Contrast What are some differences between Sappho and other poets? *Sappho was female, but almost all writers were male. She wrote about emotions, and personal lives and relationships, whereas other poets wrote about epic events or wrote descriptive poetry.*

MISCONCEPTION ALERT

Thucydides' History The vivid detail of Thucydides' writing gives the perception that he fought throughout the Peloponnesian War. He did indeed command forces in a region near Thrace, including seven warships, which he brought to defend an area north of Athens from Spartan attack. His forces failed to save an important site, however, and he was later exiled from Athens. Thucydides wrote during the leisure provided by exile, compiling information from a variety of points of view, but not from firsthand experience as a warrior.

Answers

Reading Like a Historian

1. *Pericles; because he was a very influential Athenian;* **2.** *to glorify Athens, motivate army;* **3.** *possible answers—No, this is a very biased source. Yes, this source shows us the opinions of a leading Athenian.*

Greek Literature

Compare In what way was Pindar's work similar to that of Sappho? *They were both lyric poets.*

Develop Why do you suppose Aeschylus chose to write about gods and heroes? *possible answer—He wrote during and after the Persian wars and must have known that his audiences would respond to tales of valor and strength.*

Activity **Parthenon Game**
Materials: 3" x 5" unlined index cards
Have students work in small groups to locate illustrations of architectural terms related to the Parthenon. Have groups create a set of cards drawing an illustration on one side, and the term on the other. Students may make several copies of each card. Have students stack their cards with the illustrations facing up. Two players take turns drawing cards and guessing the correct term. **LS Visual-Spatial**

Alternative Assessment Handbook, Rubric 1: Acquiring Information

The Parthenon

Built by Pericles, the Parthenon was the greatest example of Athenian architecture. *What evidence suggests that the Parthenon was an important monument?*

The carved friezes, now plain marble, were once painted in vibrant color.

Used to store ammunition in the 1600s, the Parthenon was heavily damaged in an explosion.

Xenophon (ZEN-uh-fuhn) is another early Greek historian whose work survives. Both a soldier and a philosopher, Xenophon had fought in Persia around 400 BC, long after the end of the Persian Wars. This service was the source for his major writing. Unlike Herodotus and Thucydides, Xenophon concentrated less on sources and debates and more on describing famous men. Despite his less critical style, Xenophon's work has helped us learn what life was like in Greece during the 300s BC.

Drama While the Greeks wrote histories to preserve the past and inform readers, they created another new form of writing for entertainment. That form was drama, the art of playwriting. Like many other elements of Greek culture, drama had its roots in Athens.

The earliest dramas were created as part of religious festivals honoring Dionysus, the god of wine and celebration. Most of these dramas consisted of a group of actors called a chorus who recited stories for the audience. Later,

as dramas became more complex, individual actors began to take on the roles of specific characters in the stories.

Over time, two distinct forms of drama were developed. The first was tragedy. Tragedies usually focused on hardships faced by Greek heroes. Three great writers of tragedies lived and wrote at about the same time in Athens:

- Aeschylus (ES-kuh-luhs) wrote plays based on ancient Greek myths and on events from Athenian history. His most famous series of plays, the *Oresteia*, tells of the tragedies that faced the leader of the Greek army when he returned home after the Trojan War.

- Sophocles (SAHPH-uh-kleez) concentrated his plays on the suffering that people brought upon themselves. Many of his characters had fatal flaws that brought tragedy to themselves and their families. For example, Oedipus, the main character of three plays by Sophocles, unknowingly killed his father and married his own mother.

146 CHAPTER 5

Skill Focus: Recognizing Bias in Primary Sources

At Level

Reading Like a Historian Skill
The Elgin Marbles Controversy

Research Required

1. Tell the students they will examine an ongoing controversy that began in the early 1800s involving the rightful home of the Parthenon's Elgin Marbles. Tell students they will create a time line of events using articles they find about the Elgin Marbles.

2. Organize students into an even number of small groups. As groups conduct research, have them record several quotations showing each point of view.

3. Remind students to keep in mind the attitude of the sources they discover.

4. Have each group display their time lines, quotations, and personal opinions.

5. When groups have finished, ask students to write a statement reflecting their own opinions. **LS Interpersonal, Verbal-Linguistic**

Alternative Assessment Handbook, Rubrics 16: Judging Information; 30: Research; and 36: Time Lines

Answers

The Parthenon *possible answers—the great size of the building; its location on top of the Acropolis*

- Euripides (yoo-RIP-uh-deez) wrote about characters whose tragedy was not brought about by flaws but by chance or irrational behavior. For example, *Medea* tells of a woman who swears revenge on her unfaithful husband, killing his new wife and family.

The second form of drama the Greeks created was comedy. Many of these comedies were satires, plays written to expose the flaws of their society. The greatest comedy writer was Aristophanes (ar-uh-STAHF-uh-neez). His plays poke fun at aspects of Athenian society ranging from government to the treatment of women. Aristophanes even mocks religion by having the clouds in the sky address the audience:

HISTORY'S VOICES

❝There exist no gods to whom this city owes more than it does to us, whom alone you forget. Not a sacrifice, not a libation is there for those who protect you! Have you decreed some mad expedition? Well! we thunder or we fall down in rain.❞

—Aristophanes, *The Clouds*

READING CHECK **Find the Main Idea** In what forms of writing did the Greeks excel?

Greek Architecture and Art

An important characteristic of the Athenians was that they enjoyed beauty, both written and visual. They expressed their love of written beauty through literature, and their love of visual beauty through architecture and art.

Architecture The Athenians wanted their city to be the most beautiful in all of Greece. To help reach this goal, they built magnificent temples, theaters, and other public buildings throughout the city. To enhance the appearance of these buildings, they added fine works of art, both painted and sculpted.

The grandest of all Athenian buildings were built on the acropolis at the city's center. Marble temples and bronze statues on the acropolis were visible from all over the city, gleaming in the sunlight. No other building on the acropolis, however, was as magnificent as the Parthenon, the massive temple to Athena that stood at the center of the acropolis. Begun by Pericles in 447 BC, the Parthenon took some 14 years to build. When finished, the marble temple was more than 200 feet long and 100 feet wide.

However, the Parthenon was impressive for its proportion, not for its sheer size. Its designers were careful not to make it either too tall, which would have made it look flimsy, or too wide, which could have made it appear squat.

Like most Greek temples, the Parthenon had doors but no windows. The structure was surrounded by tall, graceful columns, above which were slabs of marble carved with scenes from myths. Though the ruins of the Parthenon appear white today, parts originally were painted in vivid colors. A huge gold and ivory statue of Athena stood inside the temple.

Sculpture Impressive as they were on their own, buildings like the Parthenon would not have been quite so magnificent without the statues and carvings created to decorate them. Greek sculptors were among the finest the world has ever known.

Greek Sculpture

This statue from ancient Athens depicts an athlete throwing a discus. *What features of the statue imply that the man is moving?*

Discobolus, by Myron, c. 450 BC

CLASSICAL GREECE **147**

Skills Focus: Making Generalizations

Below Level

Prep Required

Reading Like a Historian Skill
Skill Focus: Analyzing Visuals

Materials: photographs of Greek sculptures dated 2000s to 400s BC, sticky notes

1. Display the photographs, covering the dates with sticky notes. Share the Info to Know from this page with students.

2. Have students record the order in which they think each sculpture was probably made. Have them write down the inferences that led to their choices and ask volunteers to read their inferences to the class.

3. Reveal the actual dates of each photograph and ask volunteers to arrange the photos in their proper order for students to see.

4. Have students write a paragraph about the characteristics of Greek sculpture.
   LS Visual-Spatial, Verbal-Linguistic

   Alternative Assessment Handbook, Rubrics 12: Drawing Conclusions; and 16: Judging Information

Direct Teach

Reading Focus

Greek Literature

Analyze In what way were the writing styles of Xenophon and Thucydides different? *Xenophon was less critical, and concentrated more on describing famous men than did Thucydides.*

Develop What reasons can you give that explain why satirical comedy developed in the 400s? *possible answers—Wealthy Athenians of the golden age felt secure enough to laugh at themselves. Comedy provided a good diversion from the worries of wartime.*

Reading Focus

❸ What were the aims of Greek art and architecture? *to express the Greek love of visual beauty*

Greek Architecture and Art

Recall Which art form did the Athenians feel would make their city more beautiful then others in Greece? *architecture*

Predict How would you expect Greek sculpture to look? Why? *possible answer—It would be idealistic, because the Greeks would have wanted their sculpture to reflect grace, beauty, and perfection.*

Info to Know

Contrapposto In one of his famous sculptures, *Kritios Boy*, the artist Kritios arranged the parts of the body asymmetrically, balanced around a central axis, making the figure appear to be transferring weight to the other leg, so the boy stands at ease. The technique, called *contrapposto*, was developed in the 400s BC, in which sculptors created works that conveyed movement in their figures.

Answers

Greek Sculpture *the position of the arms, legs; muscle definition*

Reading Check *epics, history, poetry, drama*

147

Direct Teach

Reading Focus

Greek Architecture and Art

Recall What characteristic of the Athenians led to the development of Greek art and architecture? *interest in visual beauty*

Analyze What were the two colors used in most Greek vases, plates, and vessels? Why were only two colors used? *red and black; the red was natural color; black was glaze*

Review & Assess

Close

Review with students the development of Greek philosophy, literature, fine arts, and scholarship.

Review

Online Quiz, Section 3

Assess

SE   Section 3 Assessment

Progress Assessment: Section 3 Quiz

Alternative Assessment Handbook

Reteach/Intervene

Interactive Reader and Study Guide, Section 3

Interactive Skills Tutor CD-ROM

Answers

Reading Check *architecture— proportion, columns, vivid colors; art— idealistic sculpture depicting the human form; red and black vessels with scenes conveying movement and depth; murals and wall paintings*

148

The Greeks were particularly adept at sculpting the human form. Sculptors carefully studied what people looked like, not only while they were still but also while they were moving. The sculptors then tried to re-create what they had observed, paying particular attention to how the subject's muscles looked. In most cases, the result was a statue that looks as if it could come to life. For example, look at the statue of the discus thrower pictured on the previous page. The athlete depicted in the statue looks as though he is in the process of launching his discus into the air.

While the Greeks wanted statues to look lifelike and active, they did not necessarily want them to look realistic. Greek sculptors were not interested in depicting people as they really looked. Instead, they chose to portray their subjects as physically perfect, without any blemishes or imperfections. As a result, Greek statues almost all depict figures of great beauty and grace.

Though we know a great deal about ancient Greek sculpture, very few original works remain. Much of what we do know about Greek sculpture is based on copies of Greek statues made by the Romans a few hundred years later. Roman artists made many copies of what they considered to be the greatest Greek statues, including the discus thrower shown in this chapter. Many of these copies survived even after the original statues were destroyed.

Painting As with Greek sculpture, only a few original Greek paintings survive. Of those that survive, the best preserved are paintings on vases, plates, and other vessels. These vessels are often decorated with scenes from everyday life or from myths or legends. Most of them use only two colors—red and black—for their illustration. The red was the natural color of the clay vessels, and the black was a glaze added to the finished pieces. Despite this limited palette, Greek artists were able to convey movement and depth in their paintings. This ability was important to the Greeks since they wanted objects to be both functional and beautiful.

Though we have little evidence of larger paintings, written sources tell us that the Greeks also created murals, or wall paintings, in many public buildings. According to these sources, the Greeks' murals often included scenes from the *Iliad* and the *Odyssey*. Such paintings often focused on the aftermath of battle rather than on the battle itself. One Athenian mural, for example, showed a scene from the day after the defeat of Troy. Fallen soldiers still dressed in full armor lay amid the ruins of once great Troy. Themes like this one, also common in tragic drama, were very popular with the Athenian people.

READING CHECK   Make Generalizations What were some characteristics of Greek architecture and art?

SECTION 3 ASSESSMENT

go.hrw.com
Online Quiz
Keyword: SHL GRE HP

Reviewing Ideas, Terms, and People

1. **a. Recall** How did **Socrates** think people should learn?
   b. Explain Why did **Plato** think that philosophers should be the leaders of governments?
   c. Extend How did **Aristotle**'s emphasis on **reason** and **logic** contribute to the development of science?

2. **a. Identify** Who was **Homer**? For what works is he known?
   b. Compare and Contrast How were Greek tragedies and comedies similar? How were they different?
   c. Elaborate Why might both **Herodotus** and **Thucydides** be considered fathers of history?

3. **a. Describe** What was most Greek painting like? On what types of objects did such painting appear?
   b. Make Generalizations What was the general goal of Greek sculptors?
   c. Elaborate Why was the Parthenon designed to be so impressive?

Critical Thinking

4. **Categorize** Use your notes and a chart like the one below. In the second column, write a description of each of the listed literary forms. In the third column, list a few Greek writers who used each form.

	Description	Writer
Epic		
Lyric Poems		
History		
Drama		
Comedy		

FOCUS ON WRITING

5. **Persuasion** Write a short letter to Plato in which you either agree or disagree with his belief that philosophers should rule cities. Whichever position you take, use evidence to support your argument.

148 CHAPTER 5

Section 3 Assessment Answers

1. **a.** by asking questions
   b. because they were most qualified
   c. emphasized making careful observations and thinking rationally

2. **a.** a poet; the Iliad and the Odyssey
   b. similar—forms of plays; different—tragedies focused on hardships of heroes; comedies exposed flaws in society
   c. possible answer—Both analyzed events.

3. **a.** scenes from every day life; on vases, plates, and other vessels
   b. to show beauty and grace

   c. possible answers—to represent the glory of Athens; to honor the gods

4. Epic—stories about great events and heroes; Homer; Lyric poetry—poems dealing with emotions and desires; Sappho, Pindar; History—writing that analyzes the past; Herodotus, Thucydides; Xenophon; Drama—art of playwriting; Aeschuylus, Sophocles, Euripedes; Comedy—plays written to expose flaws of society; Aristophanes

5. Student letters should use reason to agree or disagree with Plato's belief about philosophers

Drama

Greek Drama

What is it? Greek drama included comedies and tragedies. Hubris, a disregard for the limits that the gods had placed on people, was a key element of the tragedies. A character cursed with hubris offended the gods and suffered as a result. In contrast, the comedies were hilarious, sometimes crude, observations on human shortcomings.

Key facts:
- Greek drama developed from religious festivals.
- Plays were performed in verse and accompanied by music.
- A chorus, dressed all in black, provided more information on the characters and commented on the action throughout the play.
- Complete plays have survived from only four writers—Aeschylus, Sophocles, Euripides, Aristophanes.

Why is it important?
- Greek plays explore basic questions about people, their relationships, and their place in the world.
- The plays tell us about Greek mythology, philosophy, politics, and daily life.

Greek actors wore masks, probably of leather, wood, and linen. A mask's expression provided clues to the character's thoughts, since people in the last rows could not see an actor's face well. Masks also hid the fact that men played male and female roles, since women were not allowed on stage.

▲ A Greek actor portrays the tragic king in *Oedipus Rex*.

Performances are still held at the theater of Epidaurus. Built in a natural valley, the theater was enlarged by the Romans to hold 12,000 to 14,000 people. The acoustics are so good that words whispered on stage can be heard in the last rows.

NEW YORK STANDARDS

PI **3.1** Students analyze the roles and contributions of groups to social, political, economic, cultural, and religious practices and activities.

Skills FOCUS **INTERPRETING VISUALS**

1. **Compare and Contrast** How is the ancient theater shown on this page similar to theaters you have seen? How is it different?
2. **Analyze** What themes were common in ancient Greek plays?

149

Skill Focus: Analyzing Secondary Sources

At Level

Reading Like a Historian Skill
Dramatic Evidence

Materials: photographs of sculptures, painted pottery, and mosaics depicting Greek actors

1. Organize students into small groups to match the number of photos you have available. Distribute one photograph to each group.

2. Have groups carefully examine the artwork and neatly record a number of ideas about Greek drama depicted in the photographs.

3. Have each group display its observations next to the photograph, and post them on the classroom walls.

4. Hold a "museum exhibit," allowing time for students to view each display. **LS Kinesthetic, Visual-Spatial**

Alternative Assessment Handbook, Rubric 12: Drawing Conclusions

Answers

Interpreting Visuals 1. *possible answers—similar: rows of seating surrounding a stage; different: outdoors, very large;* **2.** *people, their relationships, their place in the world*

149

Getting Started

Use the **Interactive Reader and Study Guide** to familiarize students with the section content.

📝 **Interactive Reader and Study Guide,** Section 4

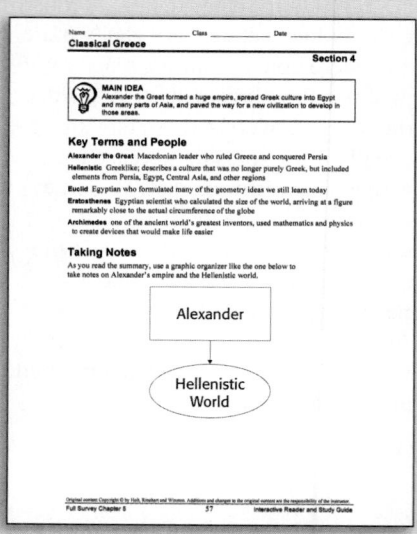

📝 **CRF:** Vocabulary Builder: Section 4

Taking Notes

Alexander—son of King Philip II of Macedonia; 20 years old when he became king; faced revolts in Greece; responded with harsh measures; built an empire in Persia, northern Africa, Central Asia; died without naming an heir; empire was divided; The Hellenistic World—a blended culture including Greek culture, plus ideas from Persia, Egypt, Central Asia, and other regions; city-state no longer the main political unit; women gained rights; new schools of philosophy including Cynicism, Epicureanism and Stoicism, advances in art, literature, science and technology

SECTION 4
Alexander the Great and His Legacy

BEFORE YOU READ

MAIN IDEA
Alexander the Great formed a huge empire, spread Greek culture into Egypt and many parts of Asia, and paved the way for a new civilization to develop in those areas.

READING FOCUS
1. How did Alexander the Great rise to power?
2. What was life like in the culture called the Hellenistic world that developed after Alexander's death?
3. What were some significant Hellenistic achievements?

KEY TERMS AND PEOPLE
Alexander the Great
Hellenistic
Euclid
Eratosthenes
Archimedes

 NEW YORK

PI **4.4** Students analyze different interpretations of important events, issues, or developments in world history by studying the social, political, and economic context in which they were developed.

THE INSIDE STORY

Could a 10-year-old boy tame the fiercest of stallions? According to the ancient biographer Plutarch, a horse trader approached King Philip of Macedonia with a beautiful stallion for sale named Bucephalus. However, none of Philip's servants could ride the wild horse. If anyone tried to mount him, the stallion reared high into the air and threw him off. He would allow no one to come near him.

Disappointed at the loss of so fine an animal, Philip prepared to send the trader away. Before the trader could leave, however, Philip's young son Alexander scoffed at the grooms. Only 10 years old, he claimed that he would be able to tame the fierce steed. Philip did not think it possible, but he agreed to allow Alexander to try. The young prince walked slowly to the horse, whispering calming words and

turning him to face the sun. Of all the people present, only young Alexander had noticed that Bucephalus was scared of his shadow. Once the horse was facing the sun and thus could no longer see his shadow, he allowed Alexander to climb on his back; and the two took off at a gallop. Philip, amazed at his son's cleverness, proclaimed, "O my son, look thee out a kingdom equal to and worthy of thyself, for Macedonia is too little for thee." ◾

A Horse Fit for a KING

▶ **Bucephalus was Alexander's favorite horse until its death in 326 BC.**

Teach the Main Idea
At Level

Alexander the Great and His Legacy

1. **Teach** Ask students the Reading Focus questions to teach this section.

2. **Apply** Draw a web diagram for students to see with the center oval titled Alexander the Great and His Legacy. Have students copy the diagram onto their own papers and write the red subheads in each of three surrounding ovals. Have students list the main ideas for each subhead on rays extending from each heading.

3. **Review** Display and discuss the web diagrams.

4. **Practice/Homework** Have each student write a one-paragraph summary of the major ideas in this section. **LS** **Verbal-Linguistic, Visual-Spatial**

📝 **Alternative Assessment Handbook**, Rubrics 1: Acquiring Information; and 13: Graphic Organizers

ALEXANDER'S EMPIRE, 323 BC

- Alexander's Empire
- ⚔ Major battle site
- Route of Alexander and his armies
- City founded by Alexander

GEOGRAPHY SKILLS | INTERPRETING MAPS

1. **Movement** Which did Alexander invade first, Egypt or India? How can you tell?
2. **Place** What name did Alexander give to most of the cities he founded? Why do you think this was so?

◀ Detail of Alexander from a Roman mosaic

Alexander the Great

In the years that followed the Peloponnesian War, a new power arose and took control of Greece. That power was Macedonia, a kingdom located just north of Greece. The Macedonian rise to power was led by a king named Philip II and his son, **Alexander the Great.**

The Rise of Macedonia Most Greeks considered the Macedonians somewhat backward: The Macedonians lived in villages rather than cities and spoke a form of Greek that was almost unintelligible to other Greek speakers. When Philip II took the throne in 359 BC, however, Macedonia's fortune changed.

One of Philip's first actions as king was reorganizing the Macedonian army. He adopted the phalanx system used by other Greeks, but he gave his soldiers much longer spears than others used. He also included larger bodies of cavalry and archers than most city-states used in their armies.

With his newly organized army, Philip set out to conquer Greece. Only a few city states, including Athens and Thebes, seemed to realize

the danger that Philip posed, and so he faced little opposition. The Macedonians quickly crushed the armies that stood against them in battle, and in time they conquered every major city-state in Greece except Sparta. Philip's conquests might have continued, but he was assassinated in 336 BC. His title and his plans for conquests fell to his son Alexander.

Alexander's Conquests Though very young—only 20 years old—when he became king, Alexander had been trained to rule almost from birth. He had learned both warfare and politics from several teachers: his father, his clever mother, and the philosopher Aristotle. When his father was killed, Alexander was both willing and able to take over the leadership of his kingdom.

Almost as soon as Alexander took over the kingdom, he was faced with revolts in Greece. He immediately set out to reestablish his control there, using harsh measures to show the Greeks that he would not tolerate rebellion. For example, when Thebes rebelled, Alexander totally crushed its army, sold the people into slavery, and burned the city to the ground.

TAKING NOTES

Use a graphic organizer like this to take notes on Alexander's empire and the Hellenistic world.

> Alexander
> ↓
> Hellenistic World

NEW YORK

CC Unit 1-C2e
Alexander and Hellenistic culture

CLASSICAL GREECE **151**

Direct Teach

Reading Focus

❶ How did Alexander the Great rise to power? *ended Greek revolts; conquered territory in Persia, Egypt, Phoenicia and Central Asia*

Alexander the Great

Recall How old was Alexander when he began his reign? *20*

Contrast What caused most Greeks to consider the Macedonians somewhat backward? *They lived in villages rather than cities and spoke a different form of Greek.*

Identify Cause and Effect What caused rebellion in Greece? *Alexander's father died, but Alexander needed to establish his own control.*

🗺 **Map Transparency:** Alexander's Empire, 323 BC

Interpreting Maps
Alexander's Empire, 323 BC

Location What city is located closest to due north of Alexandria? *Refer to map.*

Place Judging by the physical features on this map, what would attract people to establish a city at Pattala? *possible answers—mild climate, easy shipping access, convenient supply of fresh water*

Skill Focus: Making Written Presentations

At Level

Reading Like a Historian Skill
Historical Letters

Materials: unlined white paper

1. Tell students they are living in Asia Minor between 336 and 326 BC. Tell students they will write an informative letter with accurate historical details.

2. Have students refer to the map on this page and choose a place from which to write their letter. Then, have students write a rough draft, including appropriate historical details to reflect the time and place of their letters.

3. Distribute paper for students' final drafts. Remind students to add the recipient's address on the back of the paper so it might be seen when curled upward.

4. Tell students they can give the lower half of each letter a slight curl by drawing it over the edge of a table. Display the letters for all to see. **LS** Verbal-Linguistic, Visual-Spatial

📝 **Alternative Assessment Handbook**, Rubrics 25: Personal Letters; and 42: Writing to Inform

Answers

Interpreting Maps 1. *Egypt; he began in Macedonia, the route points to Egypt before he turned to India;*
2. *Alexandria; to show that he was the head of the empire*

151

Alexander the Great

Recall What event made Alexander the master of the Persian world? *the defeat of Darius*

Explain Why do you suppose the Egyptians viewed Alexander as a liberator? *possible answer—because he drove out the Persians, who had treated them poorly*

Make Inferences Why do you think Alexander did not name an heir? *possible answer—He did not expect to die so young.*

Info to Know

Greek Leadership When Alexander the Great died, the generals who took over the kingdom fought against each other. Seleucas joined Ptolemy against Antigonus. He spread his authority across the eastern part of the empire. His reach extended to India, where he made peace with an Indian ruler who gave him a herd of elephants to help wage a battle against Antigonus. It was Seleucus who attempted to imitate his former leader Alexander by founding Greek colonies within his territories.

Answers

Counterpoints *possible answer— Alexander could be viewed either as a hero or as a brutal conqueror, depending on whether the historian was of Greek descent or descended from ancestors who lived in one of the conquered kingdoms.*

152

Two Sources on Alexander

The Greek historian Plutarch lived and wrote about 400 years after Alexander died. In his account of the aftermath of the Battle of the Granicus, Plutarch portrays Alexander as a generous commander.

❝The Persians lost in this battle twenty thousand foot and two thousand five hundred horse. On Alexander's side, Aristobulus says there were not wanting above four-and-thirty, of whom nine were foot-soldiers; and in memory of them he caused so many statues of brass, of Lysippus's making, to be erected. And that the Grecians might participate in the honour of his victory he sent a portion of the spoils home to them particularly to the Athenians . . . All the plate and purple garments, and other things of the same kind that he took from the Persians, except a very small quantity which he reserved for himself, he sent as a present to his mother.❞

Plutarch
—*Life of Alexander*

The Zoroastrian writer Wiraz also lived centuries later than Alexander, though historians are not sure exactly when. His view of Alexander's victories against the Persians differs greatly from Plutarch's.

❝Then the accursed Evil Spirit, the sinful, in order to make men doubtful of this religion, misled the accursed Alexander the Roman, resident of Egypt, and sent him to the land of Iran with great brutality and violence and fear. He killed the Iranian ruler and destroyed and ruined the court and sovereignty.
That wicked, wretched, heretic, sinful, maleficent Alexander the Roman, resident of Egypt, took away and burnt those scriptures . . . he killed many of the high priests and the judges and Herbads and Mobads and the upholders of the religion and the able ones and the wise men of Iran.❞

Wiraz
—*Arda Wiraz Namag*

Skills FOCUS **INVESTIGATING HISTORY**

Interpret Why do Plutarch's and Wiraz's views of Alexander's Persian conquests differ so greatly?

With Greece firmly under his control, Alexander decided to build himself an empire. In 334 BC he led his army into Asia to take on the Persians. Alexander's army was relatively small, but his soldiers were well trained and fiercely loyal to him. In contrast, the Persian army was huge but disorganized.

Within a year, Alexander's army had won a major victory against the Persians in Asia Minor. From there, Alexander led his troops south into Phoenicia and Egypt, two territories ruled by Persia. In both places, Alexander was welcomed and praised as a liberator. In fact, the people of Egypt were so grateful that he had driven the Persians out that they named him their new pharaoh.

From Egypt, Alexander marched into what is now Iraq. In a huge battle near the city of Gaugamela, the Macedonians destroyed the Persian army and caused the Persian emperor, Darius III, to flee. Darius was later murdered by one of his own officers.

With the defeat of Darius, Alexander was essentially master of the Persian world. His troops marched to Persepolis, one of Persia's capitals, and burned it to the ground as a sign of their victory.

Alexander, however, was not yet satisfied with the size of his empire. He led his army deeper into Asia, winning more victories against the peoples of Central Asia. Still wanting more, he led his army to the Indus, perhaps intending to conquer India. His soldiers, however, had had enough. When they refused to proceed any farther from home, Alexander was forced to turn back to the west.

End of the Empire The empire Alexander had built was the largest the world had ever seen, but he did not rule that empire for very long. In 323 BC while in the city of Babylon, Alexander fell ill. After a few days, he died. At the time of his death, Alexander was only 33 years old.

Collaborative Learning

At Level

Alexander's Accomplishments

Materials: 12" x 18" construction paper

1. Remind students that after a great warrior died, people would create a monument and inscribe it with tales of the leader's mighty deeds. Tell students they will design an appropriate monument for Alexander.

2. Organize students into small groups. Have groups list the main accomplishments of Alexander. Then, have them sketch a three-dimensional monument accompanied by their lists.

3. Distribute paper for final copies and allow enough time for each group to complete its monument design. Display student work for all to see.

4. As an extension, have students write a paragraph evaluating Alexander's contribution to the development of civilization.
   LS Interpersonal, Visual-Spatial

    Alternative Assessment Handbook, Rubrics 3: Artwork; and 14: Group Activity

Alexander died without naming an heir. Within a short time, his generals began to fight among themselves for power. In the end, the empire was divided among three of the most powerful generals, who began to call themselves kings. Antigonus (an-TIG-uh-nuhs) became king of Macedonia and Greece, Seleucus (suh-LOO-kuhs) took over the Persian Empire, and Ptolemy (TAHL-uh-mee) ruled Egypt.

READING CHECK **Summarize** Why did Alexander's empire break apart after his death?

The Hellenistic World

By bringing together a number of diverse peoples in his empire, Alexander helped create a new type of culture. This new culture blended elements of Greek civilization with ideas from Persia, Egypt, Central Asia, and other regions. In other words, the civilization was no longer purely Greek, or Hellenic. (*Hellas* was the name Greeks used for their country.) As a result, historians call it **Hellenistic**, or Greeklike.

Blending Cultures The blending of cultures in Alexander's empire was no accident. Alexander made a conscious effort to bring people and ideas from different places together. For example, he married not one but two Persian princesses and encouraged his soldiers to marry Persian women as well. He appointed officials from various cultures to help rule the empire. He also built dozens of new cities—most of them named Alexandria—and encouraged Greek settlers to move into them.

The most famous of the new cities Alexander built was Alexandria, Egypt. Chosen as the capital of Egypt after Alexander's death, Alexandria was located at the mouth of the Nile where it met the Mediterranean. This location was ideal for trade, and at one time the city's harbor was the busiest in the world.

With the money that trade brought, the Alexandrians built great palaces and streets lined with grand monuments. The city was also home to centers of culture and learning. The Museum, a temple to the spirit of creativity, held many works of art. The Library of Alexandria contained works on philosophy, literature, history, and the sciences. Alexandria remained a center of culture and learning long after the Hellenistic rulers of Egypt fell from power.

Although Alexandria was one of the largest trading centers in the Hellenistic world, it was not the only one. Cities in Egypt, Persia, and Central Asia became trading centers. Traders went to Africa, Arabia, and India. In addition to goods from these regions, traders brought back new ideas. Among the ideas they carried were the teachings of Judaism, which influenced societies throughout the Hellenistic world.

Life in the Hellenistic World The shift from Hellenic Greece to the Hellenistic world brought many drastic changes to people's lives. Perhaps the most obvious change was in how people were governed. The city-state was no longer the main political unit of the Greek world, now replaced by the kingdom. Traditional Greek forms of government such as democracy had given way to monarchy.

The lives of women also changed significantly during the Hellenistic period. In most earlier Greek city-states, women had few rights. After Alexander, however, their lives began to improve. For the first time, some women gained the rights to receive an education and to own property. Legally, though, women were still not considered equal to men.

READING CHECK **Explain** How did society change in the Hellenistic age?

Alexandria

Alexandria was the greatest city of the Hellenist world. Towering above the city's busy harbor was a huge lighthouse called the Pharos, called one of the seven wonders of the ancient world.

Digital re-creation of Alexandria, by Francesco Reginato/TIPS Images

CLASSICAL GREECE **153**

THE IMPACT
TODAY

Alexandria is still the largest seaport in Egypt today.

3 What were some significant Hellenistic achievements? *new schools of philosophy; emotion conveyed in art; geometry; calculation of circumference of the globe; new inventions, including a pulley*

Hellenistic Achievements

Identify What new literary genre became popular in the Hellenistic world? *love stories*

Contrast How did Hellenistic sculpture differ from that of earlier Greeks? *It conveyed emotion and movement, and women became a much more common subject.*

Identify Cause and Effect What was the source of significant change in Hellenistic society? *the exchange of ideas by people from different cultures*

Info to Know

Mosaic Connections Hellenistic mosaics were usually simple, repetitive patterns. One way historians have learned about fragile Hellenistic paintings is through rare figurative mosaics. Researchers believe that because such scenes so closely resemble one another, some were copies of famous paintings. The changing status of women is also conveyed in mosaics. The mosaics were often designed to attract guests to increasingly elaborate scenes, leading them to the *andron*, or dining room, where only males were permitted to visit. In Hellenistic houses, mosaics covered multiple dining rooms, indicating that they were possibly used by women, a clear sign of women's increased status.

Answers

Hellenistic Math and Science
geometry, astronomy, physics

Reading Check *geometry; calculating the circumference of the globe; study of the movement of the stars; study of the human body; new inventions*

154

Hellenistic Achievements

The blending of cultures in the Hellenistic world brought significant changes to society. Some of the most dramatic changes were caused by the exchange of ideas by people from different cultures. This exchange led to new advances in philosophy, literature, and science.

Philosophy As Greek influence spread through Alexander's empire, so too did interest in Greek philosophy. Contact with other cultures led to changes in classical philosophy, which absorbed and reacted to ideas from these other cultures. Partly as a result of these changes, new schools of philosophy developed in the Hellenistic world.

One new school of philosophy created in the Hellenistic world was Cynicism. Its students, called Cynics, rejected the ideas of pleasure, wealth, and social responsibility. Instead, they believed that people should live according to nature, with none of humanity's created institutions. As a result, many Cynics gave away all their possessions, begged for food, and lived in public buildings.

Another new school of philosophy, the Epicureans, taught that people should seek out pleasure, which they equated with good, and try to avoid pain, which they considered evil. One way to find pleasure, the Epicureans believed, was to develop close friendships with people who shared similar ideas.

The most influential of the new schools of philosophy was Stoicism. The Stoics placed great emphasis on reason, self-discipline, emotional control, and personal morality. Unlike the Cynics, they did not believe that people should withdraw from society in order to find happiness. Instead, they argued that people should identify their proper role in society and strive to fulfill that role.

Hellenistic Math and Science

Hellenistic thinkers made great advances in many fields. The illustrations here represent only a small sample of the advances that they made. **What fields do the advances shown here represent?**

Hellenistic astronomers drew on earlier Greek works to form theories about the universe.

ARCHIMEDES INVENTS A WATER-RAISING DEVICE

Watertight tube

Threaded screw

With the lower end of the Archimedes screw resting in water, a handle attached to the upper end is rotated to turn the watertight tube. As the tube turns, water is carried up the threads of the screw to the top, where it spills into a collecting container. An Archimedes screw can be used to draw water from wells or to pump seawater out of the hold of a sinking ship.

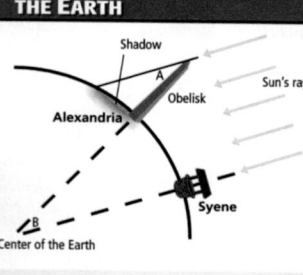

ERATOSTHENES MEASURES THE EARTH

Shadow

A

Obelisk

Sun's rays

Alexandria

Syene

B

Center of the Earth

As the sun shone on the city of Syene, Eratosthenes used an obelisk's shadow to figure the angle (A) at which the sun shone on Alexandria. Using geometry, he concluded that angles A and B were the same, about one fiftieth of a circle. He then multiplied the distance between Syene and Alexandria by 50 to figure out the Earth's circumference.

154 CHAPTER 5

Skills Focus: Making Oral Presentations

At Level

Reading Like a Historian Skill
Philosophy Skits

1. Review the three new schools of philosophy that developed in Hellenistic times: Cynics, Epicureans, and Stoics.

2. Organize students into several groups. Tell students they will convey all three philosophies in a skit. Tell students their skits may be humorous, but should be written based on factual material. Allow time for writing and rehearsing.

3. Have each group perform for the class. Discuss the pros and cons students have learned about each philosophy.

4. Select several skits to be performed for other classes. **LS Kinesthetic, Verbal-Linguistic**

Alternative Assessment Handbook, Rubric 33: Skits and Reader's Theater

Art and Literature Art and literature likewise changed during the Hellenistic period. Even more than earlier Greek artists had, Hellenistic artists learned to convey emotion and movement in their works, especially sculpture. In addition, women became much more common as the subject of art. Most earlier Greek statues had depicted men.

Women also became more common subjects in literature. Love stories, for example, became a popular form for the first time. Unlike earlier literature that dealt largely with the actions of the gods, Hellenistic writings often focus on common events in people's everyday lives.

Science and Technology The Hellenistic period witnessed tremendous advances in science and technology. Egypt in particular saw huge advances in science. Among the great scholars who lived there was **Euclid** (YOO-kluhd), who formulated many of the ideas about geometry that we still learn about today. Egypt was also the home of **Eratosthenes** (er-uh-TAHS-thuh-neez). He is best known for calculating the size of the world. Using careful observations and simple geometry, Eratosthenes arrived at a figure that was remarkably close to the actual circumference of the globe. Other Hellenistic scientists studied the movement of the stars through the sky and the makeup and inner workings of the human body.

Many of the Hellenistic period's greatest advances in technology were the work of one gifted man, **Archimedes** (ahr-kuh-MEED-eez). One of the ancient world's greatest inventors, Archimedes used his knowledge of mathematics and physics to create devices to make life easier. For example, he developed a compound pulley that could lift heavy loads. He also invented a mechanical screw for drawing water out of a ship's hold or out of a deep well. In a feat designed to prove the power of machines, Archimedes once used levers and pulleys to lift a fully loaded ship clear out of the water.

Other Hellenistic inventors were not so ambitious as Archimedes but were very clever in their own right. One lesser-known inventor, for example, built a tiny steam engine that he used to power mechanical toys. Such devices were representative of the Hellenistic fascination with mechanics and technology.

READING CHECK **Analyze** What advances did Hellenistic scholars make in science and technology?

Hellenistic Art
The statue *Nike of Samothrace*, often called *Winged Victory*, was carved in a flowing style common in Hellenistic art.

Nike of Samothrace, by an unknown artist, c. 200 BC

SECTION 4 ASSESSMENT

go.hrw.com
Online Quiz
Keyword: SHL GRE HP

Reviewing Ideas, Terms, and People

1. **a. Describe** What lands did **Alexander the Great** conquer?
   b. Identify Cause and Effect Why did Alexander destroy Thebes?
   c. Elaborate Why do you think Alexander agreed to head home rather than forcing his army to continue into India?

2. **a. Define** What does the word *Hellenistic* mean? Why is the society that Alexander formed called Hellenistic?
   b. Explain How did Alexander encourage the blending of cultures in his empire?
   c. Extend What made Alexandria such an impressive city?

3. **a. Identify** What new schools of philosophy developed in the Hellenistic world? What did each school teach?
   b. Contrast How was Hellenistic art different from earlier Greek art?
   c. Rank Which Hellenistic thinker do you think made the most impressive achievement? Support your answer.

Critical Thinking

4. **Summarize** Draw a graphic organizer like the one shown here. Using your notes, write one sentence in each box of the organizer to summarize Alexander's life, career, and legacy.

Life → Career → Legacy

FOCUS ON WRITING

5. **Narration** Write a short paragraph describing one incident in the life of Alexander the Great. Use chronological order to organize the actions within the incident.

Section 4 Assessment Answers

1. **a.** Persia, Egypt, Phoenicia, Central Asia
   b. Thebes had rebelled.
   c. possible answer—He realized he could not conquer India with his frustrated army.

2. **a.** Greeklike; reflects cultural blending
   b. married Persian princesses; appointed officials from various cultures; encouraged Greeks to move
   c. ideal location for trade; busiest harbor

3. **a.** Cynicism—rejected ideas of pleasure, wealth, and social responsibility; Epicureanism—seek pleasure, close friendships, avoid pain; Stoicism—emphasized reason, self-discipline, emotional control, morality
   b. conveyed more emotion and movement
   c. possible answer—Euclid, because geometry has since been used in countless practical applications

4. Life—became king at age 20, died at age 33 without an heir; Career—built enormous empire; Legacy— encouraged blending of cultures

5. Student paragraphs should describe one incident in the life of Alexander, paying careful attention to detail and sequence.

Diffusion of Greek Culture

Word Help

relocation: movement to another place
hierarchical: having different levels

(Activity) Cultural Diffusion Ask students to write down five important ways culture is spread today, and create a class list for all to see. Then have students write an essay, drawing parallels between the means of cultural diffusion in ancient Greece and how culture spreads today. **LS Verbal-Linguistic**

Alternative Assessment Handbook, Rubrics 9: Comparing and Contrasting; and 37: Writing Assignments

Info to Know

Cultures Change Technological advances can cause rapid change in societies where they are commonly employed. For example, nations primarily made up of city dwellers with access to Internet connections would be affected by cultural diffusion at a faster rate than nations where people are without such access. Thus, ancient cultures changed at a slower pace than more recent ones.

The Diffusion of Greek Culture

 NEW YORK STANDARDS

PI 4.1 Students identify historical problems, pose analytical questions or hypotheses, research analytical questions or test hypotheses, formulate conclusions or generalizations, raise new questions or issues for further investigation.

Historical Context The four documents that follow illustrate the diffusion of Greek culture from Greece into other parts of the world.

Task Study the selections and answer the questions that follow. After you have studied all the documents, you will be asked to write an essay identifying the type of diffusion that occurred in ancient Greece. You will need to use evidence from these selections and from Chapter 5 to support the position you take in your essay.

DOCUMENT 1

Cultural Diffusion

The term *cultural diffusion* refers to the spread of ideas or inventions through an area over time. Because diffusion is an ongoing process not restricted to the past, it is a subject of great interest to both historians and geographers. In this passage from their book *The Human Mosaic*, geographers Terry G. Jordan-Bychkov and Mona Domosh explain two main types of diffusion.

> Geographers . . . recognize several different kinds of diffusion. Two important types are expansion diffusion and relocation diffusion. In expansion diffusion, ideas spread throughout a population, from area to area, in a snowballing process, so that the total number of knowers and the area of occurrence increase. Relocation diffusion occurs when individuals or groups with a particular idea or practice migrate from one location to another, spreading it to their new homeland . . . Expansion diffusion can be further divided into subtypes . . . In hierarchical diffusion, ideas leapfrog from one important person to another or from one urban center to another, temporarily bypassing other persons or rural territory. We can see hierarchical diffusion at work in everyday life by observing the acceptance of new modes of dress or hairstyles. By contrast, contagious diffusion involves the wavelike spread of ideas, without regard to hierarchies, in the manner of a contagious disease.

DOCUMENT 2

Alexander as Diffuser

In his biography of Alexander, Plutarch observed that Alexander introduced many elements of Greek culture into the lands he conquered. The passage below outlines a few of those elements.

> But if you examine the results of Alexander's instruction, you will see that he educated the Hyrcanians to respect the marriage bond, and taught the Arachosians to till the soil, and persuaded the Sogdians to support their parents, not to kill them, and the Persians to revere their mothers and not to take them in wedlock. O wondrous power of Philosophic Instruction, that brought the Indians to worship Greek gods, and the Scythians to bury their dead, not to devour them! . . . when Alexander was civilizing Asia, Homer was commonly read, and the children of the Persians, of the Susianians, and of the Gedrosians learned to chant the tragedies of Sophocles and Euripides. . . . through Alexander Bactria and the Caucasus learned to revere the gods of the Greeks. . . . Alexander established more than seventy cities among savage tribes, and sowed all Asia with Grecian magistracies, and thus overcame its uncivilized and brutish manner of living . . . Those who were vanquished by Alexander are happier than those who escaped his hand; for these had no one to put an end to the wretchedness of their existence, while the victor compelled those others to lead a happy life.

156 CHAPTER 5

Skills Focus: Drawing Inferences   At Level

Critical Thinking Skill
Cultural Diffusion Experience Booklet

Materials: 8 ½" x 11" unlined white paper and construction paper

1. Tell students that they will create a booklet to record the effects of Greek culture in their lives.

2. Distribute one sheet of construction paper and four sheets of white paper to each student. Ask students to fold each neatly in half, forming an 8 ½" x 5 ½" booklet.

3. Have students create a cover. Then, have them mark the inside pages with the following headings: Architecture, Food, Government, Inventions, Music, Religion, and Education. Under each heading, have students record the ways Greek culture has influenced their lives.

4. Have volunteers share their booklets with the class. **LS Intrapersonal, Verbal-Linguistic**

   Alternative Assessment Handbook, Rubric 14: Group Activity

DOCUMENT 3

A Historian's View

Historians have long noted Alexander's role in spreading Greek culture, largely through his building of cities. Historian Charles Freeman described the influence of those cities in his book *Egypt, Greece, and Rome*.

Another of Alexander's legacies was the cities left behind him along the routes of his campaigns. At least twenty-five were founded during his lifetime. While one of them, Alexandria in Egypt, dedicated in the spring of 331, was destined to become the greatest city of the Mediterranean world, others were little more than military garrisons in the conquered territories. Most were east of the Tigris in regions where cities had been rare. Alexandria-in-Caucaso in the Hindu Kush, for instance, was made up of 3,000 Greco-Macedonian soldiers, some volunteer settlers, others discarded soldiers, supported by 7,000 locals who worked as labourers for them. Such cities were isolated, thousands of kilometers from Greece, among a hostile population, and with all the discomforts associated with pioneer life. Many failed completely, but others maintained themselves as enclaves of Greek culture for generations.

DOCUMENT 4

Modern Diffusion

The effects of Greek culture on other societies was not limited to the ancient world. The photograph below shows the U.S. Supreme Court building in Washington, D.C. The designers of the building modeled it after surviving structures from ancient Greek cities.

Skills FOCUS — READING LIKE A HISTORIAN

DOCUMENT 1
a. **Define** What is cultural diffusion? What is one example of cultural diffusion from your own life?
b. **Compare and Contrast** How are expansion diffusion and relocation diffusion similar? How are they different?

DOCUMENT 2
a. **Identify** What are some elements of Greek culture that Plutarch says Alexander introduced to conquered peoples?
b. **Analyze** What effect does Plutarch think the introduction of Greek culture had in conquered areas?

DOCUMENT 3
a. **Describe** What does Freeman say life was like in most of Alexander's cities?
b. **Interpret** What do you think Freeman meant when he called Alexander's cities "enclaves of Greek culture"?

DOCUMENT 4
a. **Identify** What elements of the Supreme Court building resemble ancient Greek structures?
b. **Draw Conclusions** Why do you think the building's designers wanted to model it after Greek structures?

DOCUMENT-BASED ESSAY QUESTION

Cultural diffusion occurs in many forms. What type of diffusion was the spread of Greek culture? Was it expansion or relocation diffusion, or a combination of multiple types? Using the documents above and information from the chapter, form a thesis identifying the type of diffusion at work. Then write a short essay to support your position.

See **Skills Handbook**, pp. H25–H26, H30

CLASSICAL GREECE **157**

Info to Know

From Wood to Stone and Back The earliest Greek builders created their buildings in wood. When they wanted to create more lasting public buildings, which are the ones that still remain today, they copied their wooden designs in stone. When Americans imitated Greek architecture between the late 1700s and the mid-1800s, their designs were also rendered in stone.

Activity **Greek Influence** Bring in one or more photographs of Greek Revival style houses. Tell students the Greek Revival style of American architecture was most prevalent between 1815 and 1860. Have students suggest reasons why Americans chose to imitate this Greek style. After students have called out ideas, remind them that America had achieved victory over England in the War of 1812, so they wanted to avoid architectural styles used by the English. Another reason Americans embraced Greek architecture was that they sympathized with the Greeks in their fight for independence from Turkish rule between 1812 and 1830. **LS Verbal-Linguistic**

Answers

Reading Like a Historian
Document 1 a. *the spread of ideas or inventions through an area over time; possible answer—any kind of food or celebration brought to the United States by an immigrant group from another country;* **b.** *similar—both involve spread of ideas through an area; different—relocation diffusion involves people moving from one place to another; expansion diffusion involves ideas spreading as more people know them;* **Document 2 a.** *marriage; Greek gods; burial practices; literature;* **b.** *made the conquered people happier than they otherwise would have been;* **Document 3 a.** *isolated, uncomfortable;* **b.** *places where Greek culture continued for years;* **Document 4 a.** *columns, frieze;* **b.** *possible answer—because the Greeks were known for their democracy;* **Essay** *Essays should define relocation diffusion and/or expansion diffusion and include examples.*

Differentiating Instruction

Below Level

Learners Having Difficulty

1. Draw a two-column chart for all to see. Label one column Expansion Diffusion and the other Relocation Diffusion.

2. Have a strong reader read Document 1 aloud. Meanwhile, have the other students listen for the definitions of each term you have written.

3. Have students share their definitions of relocation diffusion and expansion diffusion and write them in the class chart. Ask students: How are these two types of cultural diffusion different? How are they similar?

What are some examples of each type of diffusion? How do hierarchical diffusion and contagious diffusion relate to expansion diffusion? **LS Auditory-Musical**

Alternative Assessment Handbook, Rubrics 1: Acquiring Information; 7: Charts; and 18: Listening

Visual Summary

Review and Inquiry Review with students the difference between Classical Greece and the Hellenistic World. Then, have students review the list of Greek achievements and identify the one they think was most significant. Have volunteers explain their choices.

🖐 **Quick Facts Transparency**: Visual Study Guide: Classical Greece

Review Key Terms and People

1. Pericles
2. Hellenistic
3. polis
4. direct democracy
5. irrelevant
6. agora

Comprehension and Critical Thinking

7. **a.** People conducted business, gossiped, and discussed politics in the agora. They attended public ceremonies at the acropolis.
   b. trade, solidly constructed buildings, basic plumbing, artwork, a writing system called Linear A
   c. caused each city-state to develop independently, resulting in different societies

8. **a.** increased influence in Greece, a rebuilt city of Athens
   b. a rebellion in an area called Ionia
   c. possible answer—superior, because those who could vote had more rights

9. **a.** to show an appreciation of beauty
   b. Aristotle studied the world around him, rather than human behavior.
   c. possible answer—drama, because the famous Greek forms, tragedy and comedy, influence playwriting today

---

VISUAL STUDY GUIDE

Classical Greece

- Greek society was organized into independent city-states, each with its own government, laws, and customs.
- Two of the largest city-states were Athens, the birthplace of democracy, and Sparta, which developed a military society.
- The Greeks established colonies throughout the Aegean and Mediterranean worlds and came into conflict with the Persian Empire.
- Greek mythology taught that there were many gods whose actions controlled the forces of nature.
- The ancient Greeks, especially the Athenians, made huge contributions to many fields, especially the arts, philosophy, and science.

Hellenistic World

- Alexander the Great of Macedonia formed a huge empire that included all of Greece, the former Persian Empire, Syria, and Egypt.
- In his empire, Alexander encouraged the blending of native cultures with Greek.
- After Alexander died, his empire was divided among his generals. The result was three independent kingdoms, each with a Greek-influenced culture.
- Cities that Alexander founded such as Alexandria, Egypt, became great centers of learning and trade. Scholars in these cities made great advances in many fields.

Greek Achievements

Government
- Athens developed the world's first democracy.

Philosophy
- Classical thinkers like Socrates, Plato, and Aristotle laid the foundation for most later Western philosophy.
- Hellenistic thinkers founded new schools of learning.

Literature
- Poets wrote long, sweeping epics and beautiful lyric poems.
- Historians tried to record major events impartially.
- Athenian dramatists wrote the world's first tragedies and comedies.

Architecture
- The ancient Greeks built majestic and stately temples, like the Parthenon, that were characterized by proportional designs and the use of columns.

Art
- Painters used red clay and black glaze to create detailed scenes of daily life.
- Sculptors tried to capture perfect human forms that looked as though they could move.

Review Key Terms and People

Fill in each blank with the name or term that correctly completes the sentence.

1. The greatest of all Athenian politicians, _____ had the Parthenon built.
2. The term _____ , which means Greeklike, is used to describe the civilization that developed in Alexander's empire.
3. The basic unit of Greek society was the city-state, in Greek called a _____ .
4. A form of government like that of ancient Athens in which all people vote directly on an issue is called a _____ .
5. In his histories, Thucydides left out _____ , or unrelated, details.
6. The marketplace, or _____ , was often the center of life in a Greek town.

---

10. **a.** by ending rebellions, conquering new territory
    b. because he spread Greek culture over a large empire
    c. possible answer—the empire might have remained intact for much longer

Reading Skills

11. Accept all reasonable responses.
12. Accept all reasonable responses.

Analyzing Primary Sources

13. Athens; describes democracy
14. Yes, he says his form of government is "an example" to its neighbors.

History's Impact video program

Review the video to answer the closing question: How have the ideals of the Greek scholars influenced life today?

Comprehension and Critical Thinking

SECTION 1 (pp. 127–132)

7. a. Describe What was life like in a typical polis?

b. Summarize What achievements did the Minoans make?

c. Elaborate How did Greece's rugged geography affect the development of city-states?

SECTION 2 (pp. 134–141)

8. a. Identify What were two traits that marked the golden age of Athens?

b. Explain What led to the outbreak of the Persian Wars?

c. Support a Position Do you think the Athenian system of government was superior or inferior to the Spartan system? Support your answer.

SECTION 3 (pp. 142–148)

9. a. Identify Main Ideas What was the main goal of classical Greek art?

b. Contrast How did the basic philosophy of Aristotle differ from that of Socrates and Plato?

c. Evaluate In which field of literature do you think the Greeks had the most significant effect? Why?

SECTION 4 (pp. 150–155)

10. a. Describe How did Alexander build his empire?

b. Draw Conclusions Why is Alexander called "the Great"?

c. Predict How might European history have been different if Alexander had not died so young?

Reading Skills

Visualizing *Read the passage below, which is condensed from Section 4 of this chapter. Then use what you know about visualizing to answer the questions.*

❝With Greece firmly under his control, Alexander decided to build himself an empire. In 334 BC he led his army into Asia. Within a year, Alexander's army had won a major victory against the Persians in Asia Minor. From there, Alexander led his troops south into Phoenicia and Egypt. From Egypt, Alexander marched into what is now Iraq.❞

11. Visualize the area of the world in which Alexander is leading his army. Describe what you see.

12. Visualize Alexander and his army marching into Egypt. What details do you see?

Analyzing Primary Sources

Reading Like a Historian *The passage below is taken from a speech recorded by the historian Thucydides. Read the passage and then answer the questions that follow.*

❝Our form of government does not enter into rivalry with the institutions of others. We do not copy our neighbors, but are an example to them. It is true that we are called a democracy, for the administration is in the hands of the many and not of the few. But while the law secures equal justice to all alike in their private disputes, the claim of excellence is also recognized; and when a citizen is in any way distinguished, he is preferred to the public service, not as a matter of privilege, but as the reward of merit.❞

13. Analyze From what city-state do you think the speaker of this passage came? How can you tell?

14. Interpret Do you think the speaker admired his city's form of government? Support your answer with clues from the text.

Using the Internet

go.hrw.com
Practice Online
Keyword: SHL GRE

15. Aristotle, Archimedes, and other Greek thinkers helped inspire the modern concept of science. Without the Greeks, our views of the world might be substantially different. Enter the activity keyword and research the contributions of the ancient Greeks to modern science. Then use what you have learned to create a poster about the scientific advances made possible by ancient Greece.

WRITING ABOUT HISTORY

Narration: Writing a Biographical Essay *Great or not, Alexander of Macedonia was one of the most influential individuals of the ancient world. His actions in building and governing a huge empire shaped life not only in Greece but also in huge parts of Asia and Egypt.*

16. Assignment Write an essay describing the most important events and details of the life of Alexander of Macedonia. Remember to arrange the events in chronological order and to explain the significance of each event you include.

CLASSICAL GREECE **159**

Answers

Using the Internet

15. Go to the HRW Web site and enter the keyword shown to access a rubric for this activity.

KEYWORD: SHL GRE

Writing About History

16. Student essays should describe events in the life of Alexander of Macedonia from age 20 to age 33. Then, essays should go on to describe the legacy he left in the Hellenistic world.
A rubric for this activity is provided in **CRF: About History.**

HOLT

History's Impact
► **Video Program:**
Refer to the Video Program Teacher's Guide for an answer to the closing question.

Review and Assessment Resources

Review and Reinforce

CRF: Chapter Review

Quick Facts Transparency: Visual Study Guide: Classical Greece

Spanish Chapter Summaries Audio CD Program

OSP Holt PuzzlePro: Quiz Show for ExamView

Quiz Game CD-ROM

Assess

PASS: Chapter Test, Forms A and B

Alternative Assessment Handbook

OSP ExamView Test Generator, Chapter Test

Differentiated Instruction Modified Worksheets and Tests CD-ROM: Chapter Test

HOAP Holt Online Assessment Program (in the Premier Online Edition)

Reteach/Intervene

Interactive Reader and Study Guide

Differentiated Instruction Teacher Management System: Lesson Plans for Differentiated Instruction

Differentiated Instruction Modified Worksheets and Tests CD-ROM: Chapter Test

Interactive Skills Tutor CD-ROM

go.hrw.com
Online Resources

KEYWORD: SHL TEACHER

CLASSICAL GREECE **159**

Chapter 6 Planning Guide

Rome and Early Christianity

Chapter Overview	Reproducible Resources	Technology Resources
CHAPTER 6 pp. 160–195 **Overview:** In this chapter, students will learn how the spread of Christianity caused many of the changes ancient Rome experienced to both its government and culture. KI 1, 3; PI 1.1, 1.2, 1.4, 3.1, 3.3	**Differentiated Instruction Teacher Management System:*** • Pacing Guide • Lesson Plans for Differentiated Instruction **Interactive Reader and Study Guide:** Chapter and Section Summaries* **Chapter Resource File*** • Writing for the SAT • Social Studies Skill • Interdisciplinary Project: Comparing Greek and Roman Architecture • Chapter Review	**Live Ink© Online Reading Help** **Student Edition on Audio CD Program** **Differentiated Instruction Modified Worksheets and Tests CD-ROM** **World History Primary Source Library CD-ROM** **History's Impact: World History Video Program (VHS/DVD):** Rome and Early Christianity
Section 1: **The Foundations of Rome** **The Main Idea:** From a small town on the banks of an Italian river, Rome grew to control the entire Mediterranean region. PI 1.1	**Interactive Reader and Study Guide:** Section 1 Summary* **Chapter Resource File*** • Biography: Cincinnatus • Literature: Romulus and Remus	**Regents Review Transparency*** **Map Transparency:** Italy and the Mediterranean* **Quick Facts Transparencies:** Etruscan Influences; Checks and Balances in the Roman Government*
Section 2: **From Republic to Empire** **The Main Idea:** Governmental and social problems led to the end of the Roman Republic and the creation of a new form of government. PI 3.1	**Interactive Reader and Study Guide:** Section 2 Summary* **Chapter Resource File*** • Biography: Cleopatra • Primary Source: Views of the Roman Empire • History and Geography: Pax Romana Trade	**Regents Review Transparency:** Section 2* **Map Transparency:** The Roman Empire, AD 117*
Section 3: **Roman Society and Culture** **The Main Idea:** The Romans developed a complex society and pioneered cultural advances that, even today, affect life all over the world. PI 1.2	**Differentiated Instruction Teacher Management System:** Section 3 Lesson Plan* **Interactive Reader and Study Guide:** Section 3 Summary* **Chapter Resource File*** • Biography: Galen	**Regents Review Transparency:** Section 3* **Quick Facts Transparency:** Roman Society* **Internet Activity:** Destruction in Pompeii
Section 4: **The Rise of Christianity** **The Main Idea:** A new religion called Christianity developed within the Roman Empire and gradually spread throughout the Roman world. PI 3.1, 3.3	**Differentiated Instruction Teacher Management System:** Section 4 Lesson Plan* **Interactive Reader and Study Guide:** Section 4 Summary* **Chapter Resource File*** • Biography: Mary Magdalene	**Regents Review Transparency:** Section 4* **Map Transparency:** The Spread of Christianity*
Section 5: **The Fall of Rome** **The Main Idea:** Events and conditions inside as well as outside the Roman Empire weakened it and led to its collapse in the west in the 400s. 1.1, 1.2, 1.4	**Differentiated Instruction Teacher Management System:** Section 5 Lesson Plan* **Interactive Reader and Study Guide:** Section 5 Summary* **Chapter Resource File*** • Biography: Odoacer	**Regents Review Transparency:** Section 5* **Map Transparency:** Division and Invasion of the Roman Empire* **Quick Facts Transparency:** Causes and Effects of the Fall of Rome*

go.hrw.com go.hrw.com	**Print Resource**	**Transparency**		
LS Learning Styles	**Audio CD**	**CD-ROM**		
Video	**SE** Student Edition	**TE** Teachers Edition		
OSP One-Stop Planner CD-ROM		**NY Standards Mastery**		

*also on One-Stop Planner CD-ROM

HOLT
History's Impact
World History Video Program (VHS/DVD)
Rome and Early Christianity

Review, Assessment, Intervention

- **Global History and Geography Regents Test Prep Workbook**
- **Quick Facts Transparency:** Rome and Early Christianity*
- **Spanish Chapter Summaries Audio CD Program**
- **Progress Assessment Support System (PASS):** Chapter Test*
- **Differentiated Instruction Modified Worksheets and Tests CD-ROM:** Modified Chapter Test
- OSP **New York One-Stop Planner CD-ROM:** ExamView Test Generator (English/Spanish)
- HOAP **Holt Online Assessment Program (HOAP)**

- **PASS:** Section 1 Quiz*
- **Online Quiz:** Section 1
- **Alternative Assessment Handbook**

- **PASS:** Section 2 Quiz*
- **Online Quiz:** Section 2
- **Alternative Assessment Handbook**

- **PASS:** Section 3 Quiz*
- **Online Quiz:** Section 3
- **Alternative Assessment Handbook**

- **PASS:** Section 4 Quiz*
- **Online Quiz:** Section 4
- **Alternative Assessment Handbook**

- **PASS:** Section 5 Quiz*
- **Online Quiz:** Section 5
- **Alternative Assessment Handbook**

Power Presentation with Video CD-ROM

Power Presentations with Video are visual presentations of each chapter's main ideas. Presentations can be customized by including Quick Facts charts, images and maps from the textbook, and video clips.

Holt Online Learning

go.hrw.com
Teacher Resources
KEYWORD: SHL TEACHER

go.hrw.com
Student Resources
KEYWORD: SHL ROM

- Document-Based Questions
- Interactive Multimedia Activities

- Current Events
- Chapter-Based Internet Activities
- and more!

Holt Premier
Online Student Edition
Complete online support for interactivity, assessment, and reporting

- Interactive Maps and Notebook
- Homework Practice and Research Activities Online

CHAPTER 6 PLANNING GUIDE

The Big Picture

Peter N. Stearns

The Rise of Rome The early stages of what was initially a minor Italian city-state involve understanding the relationship between the estate-owning aristocracy and ordinary citizens, and how they built a set of republican institutions that balanced both interests while giving primacy to the patrician class. The initial expansion of the republic, through the Punic Wars, raises several topics. Understanding the basis of military organization is one. Seeing how Roman influence increasingly connected to the whole Mediterranean world is another. It is also important to see how expansion raised new issues and concerns in Roman culture, politics and social structure. The growth of slaveholding was a key example of how expansion began to alter the conditions on which the republic had been founded.

The Mature Empire and the Process of Decline The role of Roman law and its heritage to later societies command attention. It is also useful to note the strengths and weaknesses of Roman culture and technology: massive monuments and interesting art and literature fell short of earlier Greek originality; achievements in civil engineering combined with a production technology inferior to that of classical China and India. Rome's decline must be sketched, and of course it's an invitation to discuss the causes: how political deterioration, disease, economic change and invasion intertwined. The great differences among the different parts of the Mediterranean world at the end of the Empire must be emphasized, a world that has never since reunited. Wider comparison can also improve the grasp of what Rome was all about: comparing Rome and Han China, and their respective declines, is both feasible and illuminating.

Early Christianity The rise of a major new religion involves combining an understanding of what Christians believe about their origins with historical knowledge. Jewish roots and Roman context must also be combined. Christianity was not initially embraced by the empire but the empire helps explain how it spread and organized as it did; separation from official politics required the construction of a strong church organization. The adoption of Christianity by the later emperors created major new opportunities but also new problems. How and why the religion so easily survived the fall of the empire helps organize analysis of a vital transition in European history.

Recent Scholarship

The Rise of Western Christendom: Triumph and Diversity, AD 200–1000 (2003) is a masterful work by Peter Robert Lamont Brown, an accomplished scholar on Christianity and later antiquity. Despite the title, the book deals extensively with the early church and its relationship to wider Roman developments. Doctrine, church organization, and religious dissemination all receive attention. The book goes beyond the Roman period, of course, in dealing with the Middle Ages. Through this, it helps address questions about the relationship between Roman and Christian impulses in forming Western civilization.

Differentiating Instruction

Differentiated Instruction Teacher Management System
- Pacing Guide
- Lesson Plans for Differentiated Instruction

Interactive Reader and Study Guide

Spanish Chapter Summaries Audio CD Program

Student Edition on Audio CD Program

Differentiated Instruction Modified Worksheets and Tests CD-ROM
- Vocabulary Flash Cards
- Modified Vocabulary Builder Activities
- Modified Chapter Review Activity
- Modified Chapter Test

OSP One-Stop Planner CD-ROM
- ExamView Test Generator (English/Spanish)
- PuzzlePro
- Quiz Show for ExamView
- Transparencies and Videos

TE Differentiated Activities in the Teacher's Edition
- Etruscan Culture, p. 164
- Comparing the U.S. and Roman Constitutions, p. 165
- Mediterranean Trade, p. 175
- Building the Pont du Gard, p. 180

Reading Like a Historian

Sam Wineburg

Constantine's Conversion Fighting for the control of Rome and the helm of the Empire, Constantine's prospects looked dim. When his rival Maxentius left the security of Rome's walls to confront Constantine at the Milvian Bridge, things looked even dimmer. To emerge victorious Constantine needed "more powerful aid than his military forces could afford." He looked upward and, according to his biographer and contemporary Eusebius, witnessed a "most incredible sign":

"About noon, when the day was already beginning to decline, he saw with his own eyes the trophy of a cross of light in the heavens, above the sun, and an inscription, CONQUER BY THIS attached to it. At this sight he himself was struck with amazement, and his whole army also, which followed him on an expedition, and witnessed the miracle. . . . And while he continued to ponder and reason on its meaning, night overtook him; then in his sleep the Christ of God appeared to him with the sign which he had seen in the heavens."

Emboldened by this vision, Constantine routed his opponent, united the two parts of the empire, and in the Edict of Milan not only abrogated the laws persecuting Christians but became their patron. Above all, Constantine became the first pagan ruler of any importance to embrace Christianity and Jesus Christ. Or did he?

To Jacob Burckhardt, the great Swiss historian of the nineteenth century, the emperor's "conversion" was dubious from the get-go. Burckhardt's Constantine is a power-hungry tyrant who calculatingly used Christianity to unite a fragmented empire under a single standard. "In a genius driven . . . by ambition and lust for power there can be no question of Christianity or paganism . . . such a man is essentially unreligious." As Burckhardt pointed out, we know about Constantine's vision principally through Eusebius's *Life of Constantine*. And the Bishop of Caesarea was hardly a neutral bystander when it came to writing a history of the ruler who magnificently supported his pet projects, such as building churches and shrines in the Holy Land. Eusebius fared no better under Burckhardt's trenchant gaze: "the first thoroughly dishonest historian of antiquity."

Motivations Where does that leave us in trying to judge Constantine's spiritual transformation? If it is difficult to determine the sincerity of a conversion of someone in our own day, how much more so with someone who lived 1,700 years ago?

In recent years, Michael Grant, the British classicist and author of *Constantine the Great: The Man and His Times*, noted that there need not be a contradiction between Constantine's political motivations and his personal beliefs: one could see Christianity as a way of bringing diverse peoples together under a common faith and, on a personal level, passionately believe in that faith.

But ultimately the question of Constantine's sincerity may be one no historian can ever answer—unless he or she possesses an instrument that peers unflinchingly into the recesses of the heart. Even speculating as to the "real" motivations of Constantine earns the scorn of some scholars. Allen D. Callahan, a professor at Harvard's Divinity School, called this effort "one of the worst abuses of arm chair historiography of early Christianity."

In the end, we will never know Constantine's true motivation for embracing Christianity. But what is unassailable is its effect. In the course of the 300s, Christianity went from a small sect of passionate believers in a far flung outpost of the Roman Empire to the state religion of Rome. In this short period, Rome went from persecuting Christianity to persecuting all other religions except Christianity. Constantine's conversion set off this process. Of that, there can be no dispute.

Chapter Main Ideas

Section 1 From a small town on the banks of an Italian river, Rome grew to control the entire Mediterranean region.

Section 2 Governmental and social problems led to the end of the Roman Republic and the creation of a new form of government.

Section 3 The Romans developed a complex society and pioneered cultural advances that, even today, affect life all over the world.

Section 4 A new religion called Christianity developed within the Roman Empire and gradually spread throughout the Roman world.

Section 5 Events and conditions inside as well as outside the Roman Empire weakened it and led to its collapse in the west in the 400s.

🔲 New York Standards

Key Idea 1 The study of world history requires an understanding of world cultures and civilizations, including an analysis of important ideas, social and cultural values, beliefs, and traditions. This study also examines the human condition and the connections and interactions of people across time and space and the ways different people view the same event or issue from a variety of perspectives.

Key Idea 3 Study of the major social, political, cultural, and religious developments in world history involves learning about the important roles and contributions of individuals and groups.

Key to Differentiating Instruction

Below Level

Basic-level activities designed for all students encountering new material

At Level

Intermediate-level activities designed for average students

Above Level

Challenging activities designed for honors and gifted and talented students

Standard English Mastery

Activities designed to improve standard English usage

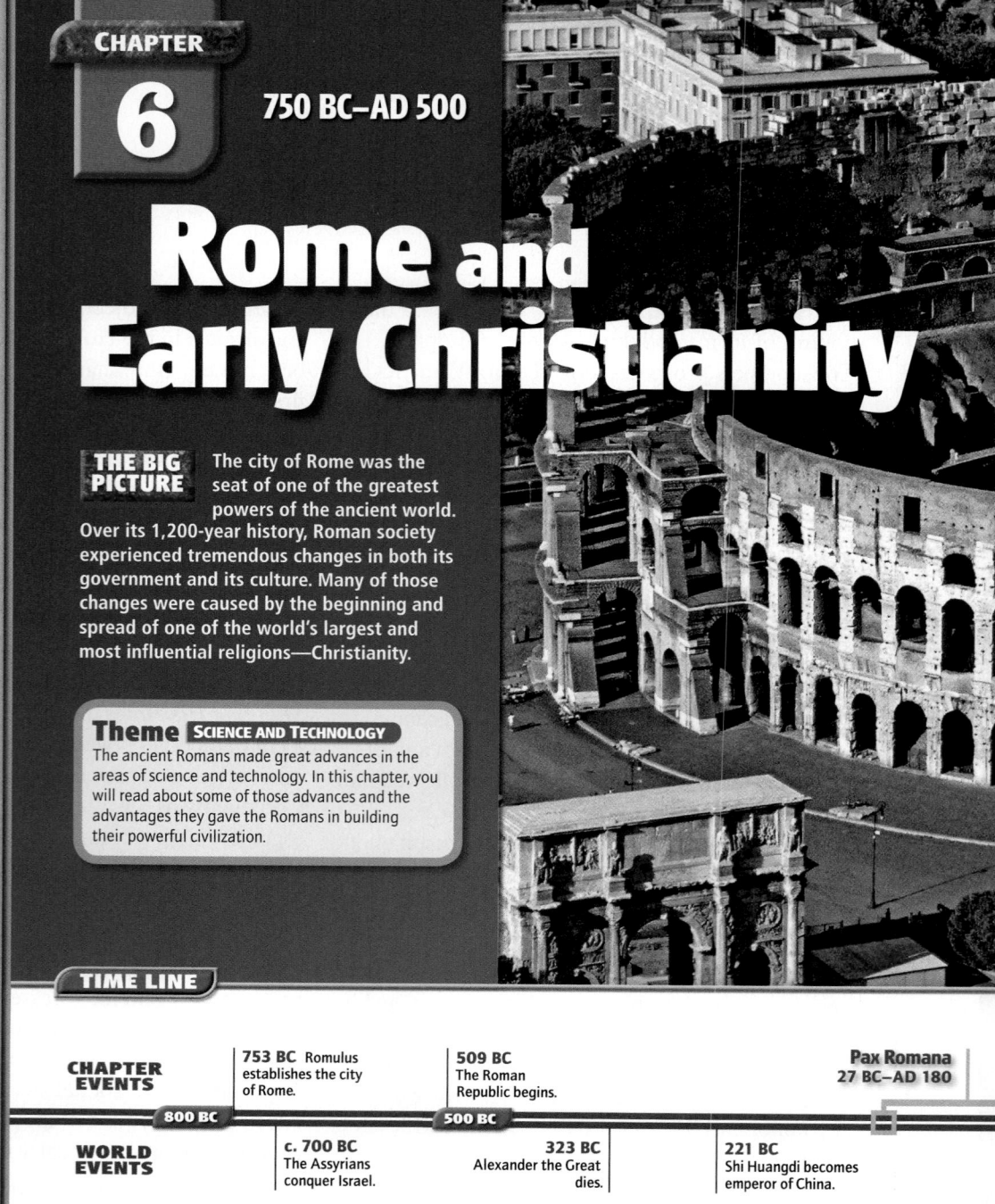

CHAPTER
6 750 BC–AD 500

Rome and Early Christianity

THE BIG PICTURE The city of Rome was the seat of one of the greatest powers of the ancient world. Over its 1,200-year history, Roman society experienced tremendous changes in both its government and its culture. Many of those changes were caused by the beginning and spread of one of the world's largest and most influential religions—Christianity.

Theme SCIENCE AND TECHNOLOGY
The ancient Romans made great advances in the areas of science and technology. In this chapter, you will read about some of those advances and the advantages they gave the Romans in building their powerful civilization.

TIME LINE

CHAPTER EVENTS	**753 BC** Romulus establishes the city of Rome.	**509 BC** The Roman Republic begins.		**Pax Romana** **27 BC–AD 180**
	800 BC	500 BC		
WORLD EVENTS	**c. 700 BC** The Assyrians conquer Israel.	**323 BC** Alexander the Great dies.	**221 BC** Shi Huangdi becomes emperor of China.	

160 CHAPTER 6

Introduce the Chapter

At Level

Rome and Early Christianity

Materials: five sheets large construction paper, marking pens

1. Remind students that the ideas of early Romans were especially advanced for that time, and those ideas and concepts continue to influence them today.

2. Organize students into five groups. Assign each group a section of this chapter. Have each group look for major events and developments in its assigned section.

3. Distribute one sheet of paper per group. Have students record their section number at the top, and write their findings below it to present to the class.

4. When groups are finished, have them share their findings while class members take notes. **LS Interpersonal, Verbal-Linguistic**

📄 **Alternative Assessment Handbook**, Rubrics 1: Acquiring Information; and 14: Group Activity

Reading like a Historian

The Roman Colosseum shown here was built in the first century AD. One of the largest structures in the Roman world, it was built as a site for public entertainments, especially vicious combats between professional gladiators.

Analyzing Visuals What kind of modern buildings does the Colosseum resemble? Why do you think this resemblance exists?

See **Skills Handbook**, p. H26

AD 313
Constantine ends all persecution of Christians.

AD 476
The last Western Roman Emperor is overthrown.

250

c. AD 250
The Maya Classic Period begins.

AD 320
The Gupta dynasty takes over India.

ROME AND EARLY CHRISTIANITY **161**

● **Chapter Preview** ●

HOLT
History's Impact
► **Video Program: Rome and Early Christianity**
See the Video Teacher's Guide for strategies for using the video segment.

Reading Like a Historian

Analyzing Visuals Have students examine the photograph on these pages. Have students compare the outside of the Colosseum to that of a sports arena they may have visited. Ask students why there does not seem to be very much parking. *Most people would have arrived on foot.* Tell students that there are many sites on the Internet that give different views of the ruins, and that it is now in the center of a large, metropolitan area.

go.hrw.com
Online Resources

Chapter Resources:
KEYWORD: SHL ROM
Teacher Resources:
KEYWORD: SHL TEACHER

Explore the Time Line

1. Who established the city of Rome? *Romulus*

2. How long did the Pax Romana last? *207 years*

3. What important historical figure died in 323 BC? *Alexander the Great*

4. If you were looking at a museum display of classic Mayan sculptures, after what year would you expect them to have been made? *AD 250*

Info to Know

Amazing Architecture The Colosseum in Rome was completed in AD 82. It could seat 50,000 spectators and had about eighty entrances, so crowds were able to enter and exit quickly. The vast arena covers approximately six acres and is 158 feet tall. Its enormous size and beautiful architectural details, using different styles of columns on each level, make it one of the finest pieces of architecture built in its time.

Explain What was practical about the Colosseum design? *possible answer—Many entrances made entering and exiting easy.*

Answers

Reading Like a Historian *possible answer—It looks like a modern sports arena; it was built so many people could watch the events that happened there.*

Geography Starting Points

Roman Shipbuilding Early Roman military officials were not experts in shipbuilding or navigation and may have only copied Greek vessel designs. However, between 70–68 BC, pirates threatened the corn supply, which was vital to the Romans. Pompey, a great military and political leader in ancient Rome, was commanded by the Senate to rid the sea of pirates. He did so in only three months by pressing Greek ships into service. Just three decades later, the military began constructing boats and training crews to work on them. Octavian, the emperor in 36 BC, was left with some 700 ships. The ships were powered by slaves. No Roman ever manned an oar.

- **Map Transparency:** Italy and the Mediterranean
- **World History Outline Maps**
- **Interactive Map:** Italy and the Mediterranean

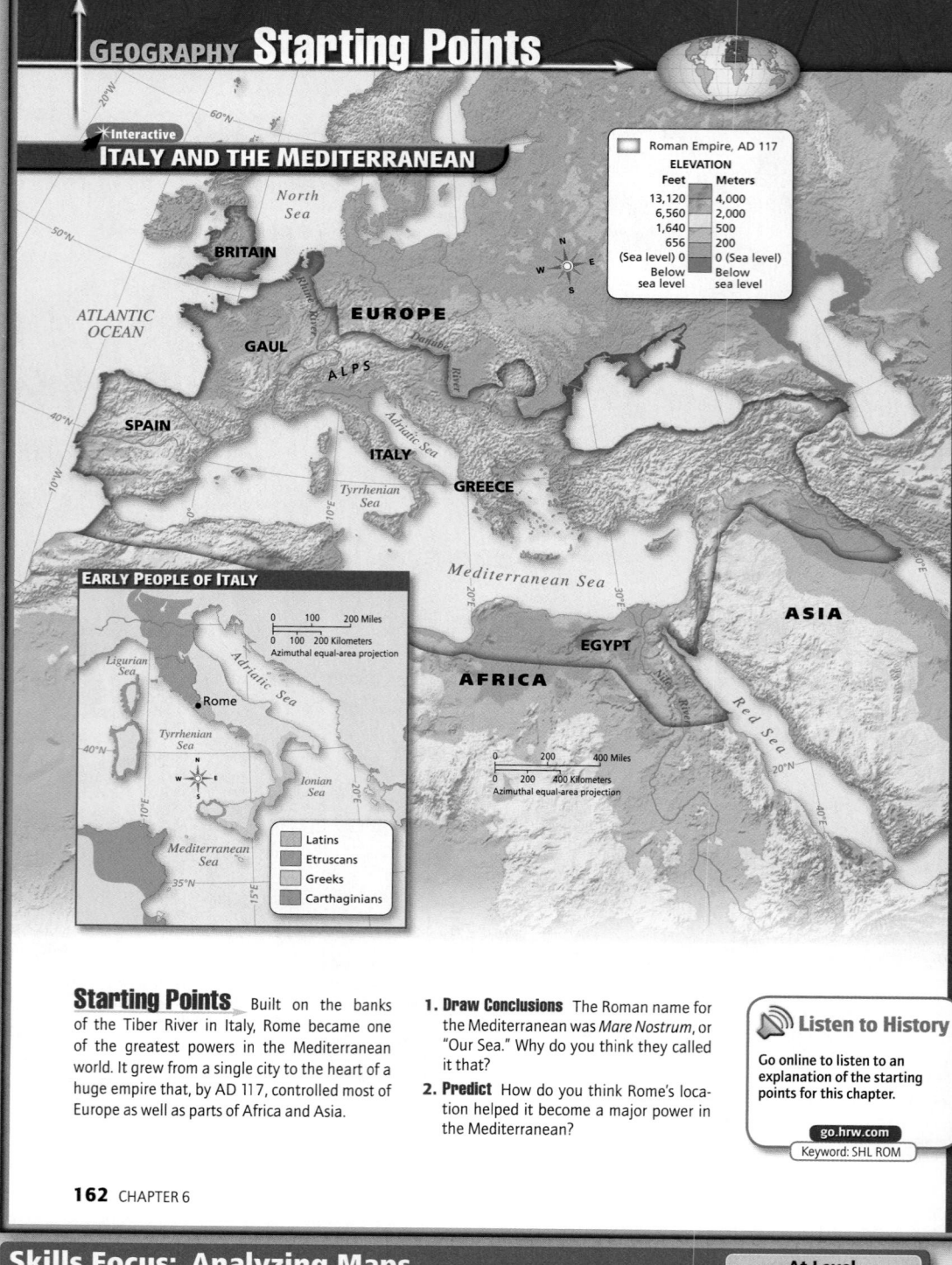

GEOGRAPHY Starting Points

Interactive
ITALY AND THE MEDITERRANEAN

Roman Empire, AD 117

ELEVATION

Feet	Meters
13,120	4,000
6,560	2,000
1,640	500
656	200
(Sea level) 0	0 (Sea level)
Below sea level	Below sea level

EARLY PEOPLE OF ITALY

0   100   200 Miles
0   100   200 Kilometers
Azimuthal equal-area projection

- Latins
- Etruscans
- Greeks
- Carthaginians

0   200   400 Miles
0   200   400 Kilometers
Azimuthal equal-area projection

Starting Points Built on the banks of the Tiber River in Italy, Rome became one of the greatest powers in the Mediterranean world. It grew from a single city to the heart of a huge empire that, by AD 117, controlled most of Europe as well as parts of Africa and Asia.

1. **Draw Conclusions** The Roman name for the Mediterranean was *Mare Nostrum*, or "Our Sea." Why do you think they called it that?

2. **Predict** How do you think Rome's location helped it become a major power in the Mediterranean?

Listen to History

Go online to listen to an explanation of the starting points for this chapter.

go.hrw.com
Keyword: SHL ROM

162 CHAPTER 6

Skills Focus: Analyzing Maps

At Level

Social Studies Skill
Roman Empire Charts

Materials: 12"x18" construction paper

Background: Remind students that the vast size of the Roman Empire gave it many advantages, but governing such a large area could also have disadvantages.

1. Organize students into small groups. Ask students to refer to the map on this page and discuss the opportunities and problems that Rome would have had with their far-reaching empire.

2. Distribute construction paper. Demonstrate folding the paper to form two 9"x12" sections. Have groups record their ideas under the headings Advantages and Disadvantages.

3. When groups have finished their charts, ask one member of each group to post the chart and have the other members present their ideas to the class. **Interpersonal, Visual-Spatial**

Alternative Assessment Handbook, Rubrics 7: Charts; 11: Discussions; and 24: Oral Presentations

Answers

Geography Starting Points

1. *possible answer—The Romans traveled throughout the region by boat, and controlled most of the Mediterranean Sea.* 2. *possible answer—Rome was located in the center of the Mediterranean Sea, so Romans could easily reach many areas by ship. This increased opportunities for trade and conquest.*

The Foundations of Rome

BEFORE YOU READ

MAIN IDEA

From a small town on the banks of an Italian river, Rome grew to control the entire Mediterranean region.

READING FOCUS

1. Where and how did Roman civilization develop?
2. What led to Rome's becoming a republic?
3. What were the major events in Rome's expansion?

KEY TERMS

republic
patricians
plebeians
veto
Forum
constitution
Senate
consuls
dictator

NEW YORK

PI 1.1 Students explain how cultures developed and changed over time, including social customs, norms, values, and traditions; political systems; economic systems; religions and spiritual beliefs; and socialization.

THE INSIDE STORY

Could a mighty civilization rise from the humblest of origins? According to legend, Rome did. The city traced its origins to twin brothers named Romulus and Remus, descendants of a Trojan hero named Aeneas who had fled to Italy after the Trojan War. As babies, the boys were placed in a basket and set adrift on the Tiber River at the order of their great-uncle. According to the legend, the basket washed ashore and was found by a wolf who cared for the boys. Eventually, the boys were discovered by a kind shepherd who adopted them as his own sons.

When the boys grew up, they decided to build a city on the Tiber, where they had been saved. The brothers fought about the exact location for the city, however. Eventually, Romulus won the argument and began to sketch out plans for the city's layout. Irritated that he had been overruled, Remus mocked his brother's plans. Enraged, Romulus attacked and killed Remus. He then built the city they had planned, which he named Rome, after himself. He made himself Rome's king and ruled for nearly 40 years. In time, the humble city of Romulus grew into a major power. ■

Roman Civilization Develops

"All roads lead to Rome." "Rome was not built in a day." "When in Rome, do as the Romans do." You have probably heard all of these expressions at some point in your life, but have you ever wondered why Rome features so prominently in popular sayings? How did the tiny city supposedly founded by Romulus grow into a major power and win a place in modern popular culture?

RAISED BY WOLVES

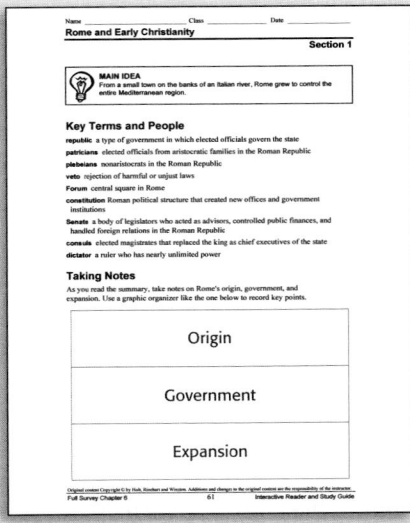

According to legend, Romulus and Remus were raised by a she-wolf.

Mosaic of Romulus and Remus from Aldborough, England, c. AD 100

ROME AND EARLY CHRISTIANITY **163**

Reading Focus

❶ Where and how did Roman civilization develop? *Located on a peninsula reaching into the center of the Mediterranean Sea, Rome was founded by Latins and heavily influenced by the Etruscan culture.*

Roman Civilization Develops

Explain How did the Alps north of Rome aid the growth of Roman civilization? *They protected Rome without isolating it.*

Identify What was unusual about the legendary founders of Rome, and what were their names? *According to legend, they were raised by wolves. The founders' names were Romulus and Remus.*

Evaluate In what way do you think the rule of the Etruscans might have been good for Rome? *built walls and sewers, introduced building techniques, and influenced culture and learning*

📝 **CRF:** Literature: Romulus and Remus

Info to Know

Etruscan Artists Though individual Etruscan artists' names weren't recorded, much of their remarkably advanced jewelry and sculpture survives today. Realistic sculptures of people with well-defined bodies beneath loosely draped clothing appeared as early as 510 BC. Later images were even more realistic, a quality seen in later Roman sculpture. Where did this rapid development of Etruscan art originate? Etruscan artists were influenced by the Greeks, but their own cultural identity is still reflected in their work.

📦 **Quick Facts Transparency:** Etruscan Influences

Answers

Reading Check *protected by mountains; sea provided protection and transportation; had rich soil, pleasant climate; located on major trade routes; Tiber River provided easy access to the sea*

164

TAKING NOTES

As you read, take notes on Rome's origin, government, and expansion.

| Origin |
| Government |
| Expansion |

🎬 **NEW YORK**
CC Unit 1-C3
The Roman Republic

Italy's Geography If you look at a map, the Italian Peninsula seems a logical place for the emergence of a mighty Mediterranean empire. The boot-shaped peninsula juts south from Europe far into the Mediterranean. It also lies almost halfway between the eastern and western boundaries of the Mediterranean Sea.

Italy's physical features aided the growth of a powerful civilization. To the north, the peninsula was protected, though not isolated, by the high mountains of the Alps. To the south, east, and west, the sea provided both protection and a means of rapid transportation. Much of the peninsula had rich soil and a mild climate, able to support a large population.

The Founding of Rome In the middle of this peninsula, the city of Rome grew up. According to legend, Romulus and Remus, twin brothers who were raised by a she-wolf, founded the city of Rome in 753 BC. Whether or not Romulus and Remus actually existed, the people who built Rome were members of an Indo-European tribe known as the Latins who had reached Italy in the 1000s BC.

Under the Latins, Rome grew into a bustling city. The city prospered at least partly from its location on the Tiber. This location not only lay across valuable trade routes between northern and southern Italy but also had easy access to the sea. Early Romans appreciated the location of the city, as one statesman explained:

HISTORY'S VOICES

❝It seems to me that Romulus must at the very beginning have [had] a divine intimation that the city would one day be the site and hearthstone of a mighty empire; for scarcely could a city placed upon any other site in Italy have more easily maintained our present widespread dominion.❞
—Cicero, *On the Republic* II.5

The Etruscans At first Rome was ruled by Latin kings. Around 616 BC, however, it came under the rule of the Etruscans of northern Italy. From evidence found at Etruscan cemeteries, scholars believe that they were great metalworkers and jewelers whose culture had been heavily influenced by Greece. The Etruscans had great influence on Roman society, as the chart below shows.

READING CHECK **Summarize** What advantages did Rome's location give the city?

ETRUSCAN INFLUENCES — QUICK FACTS

Built Rome's first city walls and sewer

Introduced building techniques such as the arch

Introduced alphabet and number system

Helped shape system of government

Introduced gladiator games and chariot races

Influenced styles of sculpture and painting

The Etruscans
Most of what historians know about the Etruscans has come from studying tombs like the one where this statue was found.

164

Differentiating Instruction

English-Language Learners

Above Level

Research Required

Materials: one sheet 12"x18" construction paper

1. Have students review the Geography Starting Points map at the beginning of this section. Point out that the Etruscans lived both to the north and to the south of Rome.

2. Organize students into six groups. Assign each group one Etruscan influence from the Quick Facts list on this page.

3. Have each group research the Etruscan culture to find specific information about its topic.

4. Have groups create a poster illustrating and explaining their findings, as well as their own ideas about how the Etruscans influence their lives today.

5. Allow time for groups to share their work and display for students to see. **LS Interpersonal, Visual-Spatial**

📝 **Alternative Assessment Handbook**, Rubrics 28: Posters; and 30: Research

Rome Becomes a Republic

According to ancient historians, the Etruscans ruled Rome until 509 BC, when the Romans revolted and threw out the last king, a tyrant. In place of the monarchy, the Romans established a new type of government—a **republic**, in which elected officials governed the state.

Patricians and Plebeians In the early days of the Republic, the heads of a few aristocratic families, known as **patricians**, elected officials from among themselves. Organized in clans, patrician families controlled every aspect of society—politics, religion, economics, and the military. Patricians maintained their power through a patronage system in which wealthy Romans provided financial, social, or legal support for lower ranking families in return for political backing and loyalty.

Almost from the beginning of the Republic, however, the common people, or **plebeians** (pli-BEE-uhns), challenged the patricians for power. When invaders threatened Rome in 494 BC, the plebeians seceded, or withdrew. They left Rome and refused to fight until changes were made. Realizing that they would not have an army without the plebeians, the patricians grudgingly expanded plebeian rights. Once they received these new rights, the plebeians returned to defend the city. Back in Rome, they formed their own assembly, the Plebeian Council. That assembly had the responsibility of overseeing and protecting plebeian affairs.

To guarantee their rights, the plebeians also gained the right to elect officials known as tribunes. It was the tribunes' job to protect the plebeians against unjust treatment by patrician officials. Eventually, these tribunes even gained the right to **veto**, or ban, laws that seemed harmful or unjust to the plebeians.

Later, around 450 BC, the plebeians forced the patricians to have all laws written down. The laws were displayed in the Roman **Forum**, or central square, on 12 large bronze tablets. As a result, the code became known as the Law of the Twelve Tables. Because the laws were posted, patrician judges could not make decisions based on their own opinions or on secret laws. However, one of the newly posted laws was a ban on marriage between patricians and plebeians—an attempt by the patricians to preserve their special status.

Reading like a Historian

The Law of the Twelve Tables

Analyzing Primary Sources The Law of the Twelve Tables, compiled sometime around 450 BC, was Rome's first written law code. Organized by patricians at the insistence of the plebeians, the laws included in the code deal largely with trials, a key issue in relations between the two classes in Roman society. As a result, studying the Law of the Twelve Tables can reveal a great deal about how the two classes got along, and thus about early Roman society. Read the sample laws from the tables below. As you read, think about

- who created the laws.
- the possible points of view of patricians and plebeians on each law.
- how the laws would have affected members of each class.

> This law protected the rights of both lenders and borrowers.

From Table I: If anyone summons a man before the magistrate, he must go. If the man summoned does not go, let the one summoning him call the bystanders to witness and then take him by force.

From Table III: One who has confessed a debt, or against whom judgment has been pronounced, shall have thirty days to pay it in. After that forcible seizure of his person is allowed. The creditor shall bring him before the magistrate. Unless he pays the amount of the judgment or some one in the presence of the magistrate interferes in his behalf as protector the creditor so shall take him home and fasten him in stocks or fetters. He shall fasten him with not less than fifteen pounds of weight or, if he choose, with more. If the prisoner choose, he may furnish his own food. If he does not, the creditor must give him a pound of meal daily; if he choose he may give him more.

> Patricians did not want to allow marriages between members of different classes, though this law was later repealed.

From Table XI: Marriages should not take place between plebeians and patricians.

—From the Law of the Twelve Tables

Skills FOCUS READING LIKE A HISTORIAN

1. **Creator** Who wanted the law from Table XI included in the code? Why do you think this was so?
2. **Point of View** Who do you think favored the idea that no one, patricians or plebeians, could ignore the law? Why?
3. **Details** How did the law from Table III protect both the rich and the poor?

See **Skills Handbook**, p. H25

Reading Focus

❷ What led to Rome's becoming a republic? *After a regionwide revolt against Etruscan rule, the Roman aristocrats established a republic.*

Rome Becomes a Republic

Explain How did rich patrician families maintain their power? *They provided financial, social, or legal support for their client families in return for political backing and loyalty.*

Contrast How did plebeian life change after 494 BC? *Plebeian Council formed; plebeians began to regulate their own affairs*

Evaluate How might having a flexible constitution be valuable? *possible answer—Laws could be changed to fit new circumstances.*

Reading Like a Historian
Analyzing Primary Sources
Recall What was Rome's first written law code called? *The Law of Twelve Tables*
Identify Which group of Romans insisted that the laws be written down? *the plebeians*

Differentiating Instruction

Above Level

Advanced Learners/Gifted and Talented

Standard English Mastery

Materials: one copy per group of the U.S. Constitution and Amendments

1. Ask students what they know about the U.S. Constitution and briefly discuss as a class.

2. Organize students into small groups. Have groups discuss and record the similarities they notice between the Roman constitution and the U.S. Constitution.

3. Distribute copies of the U.S. Constitution. Have students find and record text from it that supports their ideas.

4. Have students write a short paragraph expressing their conclusions about the relationship of the two constitutions.
   ◩ **Interpersonal, Verbal-Linguistic**

   ▱ **Alternative Assessment Handbook**, Rubrics 1: Acquiring Information; and 12: Drawing Conclusions

Answers

Reading Like a Historian 1. *the patricians; because they wanted to keep the classes separate;* **2.** *the plebeians; because the patricians might have thought they were above the law;* **3.** *It protected the rich by ensuring debts would be repaid, but also set rules for how to treat debtors.*

Reading Focus

Rome Becomes a Republic

Contrast Which of the duties of Roman censors are related to present-day census takers, and which duties are more closely related to the meaning of the modern English word, *censor*? *census —They recorded the wealth and residences of the entire population. censor—They had great influence in society because they appointed senators.*

Predict What is one way the Forum might have influenced Roman government? *possible answer—It provided a location for city leaders to encounter common citizens.*

Teaching Tip

To help students relate Roman government to American government, have them name the branches of the U. S. government. *executive, judicial, and legislative* Discuss the responsibilities of each branch and how they influence each other. Ask students to identify the system that protects citizens by giving each branch of government power over the others. *the system of checks and balances*

QUICK FACTS
Checks and Balances in the Roman Government

Identify What were the magistrates' responsibilities? *ran the city's daily affairs, led the army, issued edicts, and acted as judges and priests*
Explain How could tribunes influence magistrates? *Tribunes could veto the magistrates' actions.*
Contrast Even though the magistrates presided over the Senate, how could the Senate control the magistrates? *It could refuse to give them money.*

📜 **Quick Facts Transparency:** Checks and Balances in the Roman Government

---

Republican Government Working together, the patricians and plebeians created a practical and flexible unwritten **constitution**, or political structure. They were extremely proud of this system, as a statesman explained:

HISTORY'S VOICES

❝The reason for the superiority of the constitution of our city to that of other states is that the latter almost always had their laws and institutions from one legislator. But our republic was not made by the genius of one man, but of many, nor in the life of one, but through many centuries and generations.❞

—Cicero, *On the Republic* II.1

As part of their new Republican constitution, the Romans created new offices and institutions of government. Eventually, the government consisted of three parts:

(1) the **Senate**, a body of 300 members who advised elected officials, controlled public finances, and handled all foreign relations;

(2) various popular assemblies, in which all citizens voted on laws and elected officials;

(3) officials called magistrates, who put the laws into practice, governed in the name of the Senate and the people, and acted as priests.

Though initially dominated by patricians, all state offices, including the Senate, were later open to both patricians and plebeians.

ACADEMIC VOCABULARY
constraints
limitations

When the last king of Rome was thrown out, his place was taken by two magistrates called **consuls**. Elected for one year, the consuls were both chief executives and commanders of the army.

Next to the consuls, the most important magistrates were the censors. Censors recorded the city's population and how much property each person owned. They also appointed new Senators when vacancies appeared. The ability to select new Senators gave the censors great influence in Roman society.

In the 300s BC Romans also began to elect magistrates called praetors. Primarily judges, praetors could also act for the consuls when the consuls were away at war. As Rome expanded, both consuls and praetors were usually given military commands or were appointed as provincial governors after finishing their terms of office. To assist the consuls and praetors, many other officials were also elected to handle various other aspects of the city's administration.

One reason that Rome's government worked well was that it included a system of checks and balances, in which each part of the government could impose certain <u>constraints</u> upon the others. For example, the Senate could do little without the consent of the consuls, but at the same time consuls could not enact major changes without funding from the Senate.

CHECKS AND BALANCES IN THE ROMAN GOVERNMENT

Elected Magistrates
• Ran the city's daily affairs
• Led the army
• Issued edicts
• Acted as judges and priests

Magistrates presided over the Senate.

Senate could refuse to give magistrates money.

Senate
• Controlled finances
• Controlled foreign relations
• Reviewed proposed laws
• Advised magistrates

Assemblies and Tribunes
• Elected magistrates
• Approved laws
• Tried court cases
• Declared war

Tribunes could veto officials' actions.

Assemblies could reject laws approved by the Senate.

Collaborative Activity

At Level

Roman Government Debate

Research Required

1. Have students recall the basic job of the magistrates called consuls. Ask students who the consuls replaced.

2. Explain to students that they will conduct a debate on the following question: Who should rule Rome?

3. Organize students into an even number of small groups. Assign half of the groups to prepare statements representing those who supported the king. Assign the other groups to prepare statements representing those who support the two consuls.

4. When groups have had time to prepare a variety of statements, call up each pair of groups to debate the topic. **LS Interpersonal, Verbal-Linguistic**

📝 **Alternative Assessment Handbook**, Rubrics 10: Debates; and 14: Group Activity

The Forum Then and Now

The Forum was the center of Roman life. At its height, it was a splendid place of marble temples (left). Today, only ruins remain (below). *What evidence of the Forum's glory can you see in its ruins?*

Life in the Republic During the days of the Roman Republic, Rome was a thriving and vibrant city. At the heart of the city was the Forum, the public square and the site of the most important government buildings and temples. The Forum was nestled between two hills—the Palatine, on which many of Rome's wealthiest citizens lived, and the Capitoline, where the city's grandest temples were. Because of this location, city leaders could often be found in the Forum, mingling with the citizens. The Senate met in the Forum, and key public addresses were usually delivered from a speaking platform there.

The Forum was more than just a political center, though. It was also a popular place for shopping and gossip. Busy shops lined either side of the Forum, and public celebrations were commonly held there. Indeed, the Forum was the busiest place in an already busy city.

Despite the bustling nature of their city, the Romans prided themselves on their agrarian roots. Farming and land ownership were considered the noblest ways to make money. In fact, Senators were forbidden to participate in any career that did not involve land. They could not, for example, engage in commerce.

The Roman tie to the land is illustrated in a legend of the early Republic. In the story, the people of Rome turned to their greatest general, Cincinnatus, who was plowing his fields at the time, to save them from an invasion.

They made him **dictator**, an office that gave its holder nearly unlimited power but could only be held for six months. Dictators were chosen to resolve crises that faced Rome. As dictator, Cincinnatus defeated the enemies and returned to his farm. He had no interest in retaining power but simply wanted to get back to his normal life.

READING CHECK **Draw Conclusions** Why do you think the Romans established a republic?

The Republic Expands

As Rome's government changed, the Roman population continued to grow, and so too did the need for more land. Soon Rome began to settle its growing population on land it acquired by conquering its neighbors.

Military Might Rome's successful expansion would not have been possible without its powerful army. All Roman men between the ages of 17 and 46 with a minimum amount of property were required to serve in the army during times of war.

The Roman army was organized into units called legions. The backbone of the legions were centurions, commissioned officers who usually each commanded a century of 100 men. Above all, the Roman army was a highly disciplined and well-trained force that was capable of fighting in all types of terrain.

READING SKILLS

Identifying Stated Main Ideas What is the main idea of this paragraph?

ROME AND EARLY CHRISTIANITY **167**

The Republic Expands

Recall What led to the Romans' defeat of Carthage? *the building of a Roman navy*

Evaluate How might Romans have reacted when they saw Hannibal descending the Alps with a force of war elephants? Why? *possible answer— They must have been shocked and frightened, because most Romans had never seen an elephant, or any animal of that size.*

Info to Know

The Battle of Lake Trasimene A formidable leader, Hannibal led his troops through marshland to avoid the heavily guarded Roman roads. On the way to battle, there was a pass with a hill on one side and a lake on the other. Hannibal occupied the hill and concealed many troops on both sides. The early morning mist concealed the troops below, and as the Roman vanguard advanced, the mist lifted, revealing Carthaginian troops on both sides. Approximately 15,000 Romans were killed, and as many were captured. Hannibal's loss was only 1,500, though he himself lost an eye in the battle.

Answers

Faces of History *possible answer—The Carthaginians would have won and Hannibal might have become the ruler of Rome.*

168

The Conquest of Italy By about 265 BC the Romans had defeated the Etruscans and the Greek cities in southern Italy. As the Romans conquered Italy they generally imposed few conditions on their subject peoples. These subject peoples had to provide troops to the Roman army, but Rome rarely interfered with the domestic affairs of the peoples it conquered.

Once Rome had taken control of Italy, its attention was drawn to Sicily, a large island to the south of the peninsula. Roman allies in Sicily had come into conflict with Carthage—a powerful trading city in North Africa. Rome came to its allies aid, which brought it into direct conflict with Carthage. The conflict between these two cities eventually grew into a series of three wars. Called the Punic Wars, they continued on and off for nearly 80 years.

The Punic Wars Violence broke out between Rome and Carthage in 264 BC, the beginning of the First Punic War. Because the war was fought mostly at sea, Carthage's powerful navy dominated the fighting early on. Soon, however, the Romans built a navy of their own and were able to defeat Carthage.

Relations between Rome and Carthage were strained after the First Punic War, and violence soon broke out again. In 218 BC the Carthaginian general Hannibal led a well-trained army and a force of war elephants across the Pyrenees and the Alps to invade Italy. For many years Hannibal dominated the Italian countryside, defeating one Roman army after another. In a single battle, Hannibal's troops killed or wounded as many as 50,000 Romans, the worst defeat ever suffered by Rome.

FACES OF HISTORY **Two Commanders of the Punic Wars**

The commander of the Carthaginian army during the Second Punic War, Hannibal is widely considered one of the greatest military leaders in all of history. He was a master of strategy, managing to defeat the Roman army soundly time and again. In fact, the Romans respected his grasp of strategy so much that they ended up adopting elements of it themselves.

After Carthage lost the Second Punic War, the city's leaders exiled Hannibal. He moved to Syria and served as an advisor to the Hellenistic kings until Rome conquered the region. The Romans took Hannibal prisoner, but rather than live as a captive, he committed suicide.

During Hannibal's march through Italy, many Romans were considering surrendering to the Carthaginians. Thoughts of surrender outraged one noble, Publius Cornelius Scipio. So angry was Scipio that he is said to have stormed into the Senate and forced everyone at sword point to let the war go on.

Early in the Punic Wars, Scipio fought Hannibal's brother in Spain. After defeating him, Scipio raised an army of his own. It was his idea to attack Carthage, and it was his leadership that defeated Hannibal's army at Zama. For this victory, Scipio was given the honorary name Africanus, or conqueror of Africa.

Mediterranean Sea

Lake Trasimene 217 BC
Ilipa 206 BC
Rome
Cannae 216 BC
SCIPIO'S ROUTE
Carthage
Zama 202 BC
HANNIBAL'S ROUTE

■ Carthage
■ Roman Republic
✦ Carthaginian victory
✦ Roman victory

0 100 200 Miles
0 100 200 Kilometers
Azimuthal equal-area projection

Predict How might the history of the Mediterranean have been different had Scipio not forced the Romans to fight?

Skills Focus: Analyzing Maps

At Level

Social Studies Skill
Battles of the Punic Wars

Research Required

Materials: one sheet 12"x18" construction paper per group

1. Refer students to the map on this page. Ask students to name the other battles shown on the map.

2. Organize students into groups of five to six. Assign one of the battles shown on the map to each group.

3. Ask groups to conduct research on their assigned battle. Tell them to write an account of the battle, making it realistic and interesting. Next, have students draw an accurate map of the area based on their research.

4. Have groups present their findings to the class. **LS Verbal-Linguistic, Visual-Spatial**

📖 **Alternative Assessment Handbook**, Rubrics 20: Map Creation; and 30: Research

With Hannibal ravaging Italy and defeating every army sent to face him, the Romans needed a new strategy to win the war. After a major victory against the Carthaginians in Spain, Romans under Publius Cornelius Scipio (SIP-ee-oh) sailed to Africa and besieged Carthage itself. This siege forced Hannibal to withdraw from Italy and return to Carthage. In 202 BC Scipio routed Hannibal's forces on the plain of Zama outside Carthage and took the city, ending the Second Punic War.

As a result of the Second Punic War, Rome became the leading power of the western Mediterranean. The Romans stripped Carthage of its navy and the lands it had once held in Spain. However, the Romans did not destroy the city, as many citizens had wanted.

The huge losses of the Second Punic War remained in the memories of many Romans. For example, one Senator ended every speech he made with the phrase "Carthage must be destroyed." Finally, in 149 BC Rome decided to destroy its old enemy once and for all and declared war for the third time. After a siege of three years Carthage fell. The Romans enslaved the entire population and completely destroyed the city. They banned any people from living in the area.

The Conquest of Greece While the Punic Wars were raging in the western republic, Rome also became involved in the politics of the eastern Mediterranean. The Hellenistic kingdoms of Macedonia, Persia, and Egypt fought each other almost constantly, and Greek city-states feared that they would soon be conquered by their more powerful neighbors. For protection, the city-states sought an alliance with Rome.

Together with the Greeks, the Romans fought and defeated both Macedonia and Persia. Both kingdoms eventually became Roman provinces, as did many of their allies. After several more years of fighting within Greece itself, the Romans decided to annex Greece as a province as well.

Once Greece became a Roman province, the Romans adopted many elements of that culture. Even before they took over Greece, many Romans had admired Greek culture. After the conquest, Roman art and architecture began to reflect Greek ideals. In fact, many of the most famous works of Roman art are actually copies of earlier Greek pieces.

Another area in which the Romans borrowed ideas from the Greeks was religion. The Romans adopted the stories of the Olympian gods of Greece as their own, though they called the gods by Roman names. The Greek king of the gods Zeus became Jupiter, his wife Hera became Juno, and their brothers Poseidon and Hades became Neptune and Pluto. These gods became the heart of the Roman state religion, and temples were built to them in the city of Rome and in the provinces.

Not all Romans were happy with the growing influence of Greek culture in Rome. They thought that Rome should remain purely Roman and should maintain a simple culture like that of the early Republic. As a result, they fought to keep Greek styles out of Roman buildings. Despite their protests, however, the influence of the Greeks continued to grow in Rome for many years.

READING CHECK **Sequence** How did Rome come to dominate the Mediterranean world?

SECTION 1 ASSESSMENT

go.hrw.com
Online Quiz
Keyword: SHL ROM HP

Reviewing Ideas, Terms, and People

1. **a. Identify** Who were the Etruscans? What did the Romans learn from them?
   b. Infer How did Rome's location encourage both expansion and trade?
   c. Elaborate Why might the Romans have wanted to create stories about their city's humble origins?

2. **a. Describe** What were the parts of Rome's **republican** government?
   b. Explain Why did the **plebeians** want Rome's laws written down?
   c. Develop What are some places in our society that serve the same functions that the **Forum** did in Rome?

3. **a. Recall** How did Rome's army help it expand?
   b. Draw Conclusions Why do you think the Romans treated the Carthaginians so harshly at the end of the Punic Wars?
   c. Elaborate How did the conquest of Greece by Rome lead to major changes in Roman society?

Critical Thinking

4. **Analyze** Using your notes and a word web like the one shown here, analyze the structure of the Roman government. Make the lower circles large enough to hold details about the parts.

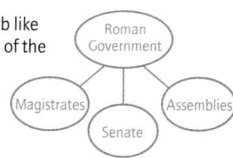

FOCUS ON WRITING

5. **Description** Write a short description of the Forum that might have appeared in a guidebook to ancient Rome. Use vivid details to try to bring the Forum to life for your readers.

ROME AND EARLY CHRISTIANITY **169**

Focus on Themes

Government and Citizenship

Recall How did early Romans think of participation in government? *It was both a right and a civic duty.*

Make Inferences What do you think the Social War indicates about the value of Roman citizenship? *possible answer—Citizenship must have been considered very valuable if people were willing to fight a war for it.*

Evaluate How might Rome have been different if the leaders had allowed all people to become citizens? *possible answers—less civil unrest, no Social War, greater equality*

Focus on Themes

Government and Citizenship

Citizenship, the right to take part in the government, was one of the most sought after rights in the Roman world. People from outside of Rome were so desperate to become Roman citizens that they even went to war for it—the Social War, for example, was fought by Italians who wanted Roman citizenship. What exactly did it mean to be a Roman citizen? How could one become a citizen if not born in Rome?

▲ **NOW** Newly sworn citizens of the United States celebrate by waving flags.

CITIZENSHIP THEN To a people for whom participation in the government was both a right and a civic duty, citizenship was essential. Only citizens could take part in the government of the Republic, and therefore only citizens were considered truly Roman. Noncitizens might live in Rome, but they were not Roman.

Roman citizenship carried with it many rights. Citizens could vote and take part in assemblies, they could make contracts, and they could file cases in court. In addition, only citizens could legally get married. Roman citizens could not be tortured or sentenced to death unless they were found guilty of treason.

Citizenship was desirable and eagerly sought after. Early in the Republic, people who performed some special service to the government were rewarded with citizenship. Later, laws passed by the Senate or—even later—the emperor gave citizenship to all residents of certain provinces except slaves, who had no rights.

CITIZENSHIP NOW Just as in ancient Rome, citizenship in the United States is a valuable and sought after right. Being an American citizen allows one to vote in elections, run for public office, and serve on juries to hear court cases.

The United States does not make citizenship difficult to obtain. As in Rome, the children of American citizens are automatically citizens, regardless of where in the world they are born. Any child born within the United States, regardless of his or her parents' citizenship, is considered a citizen as well. In addition, legal residents of the United States who are not citizens can apply for citizenship after living here for five years. In order to become a citizen, the resident must pass a test on American history and government, demonstrate basic fluency in English and swear an oath to support the U.S. Constitution.

Skills Focus UNDERSTANDING THEMES

1. **Draw Conclusions** What made citizenship so desirable to people in the Roman world?
2. **Summarize** What are the ways in which one can become an American citizen?
3. **Compare** How was ancient Roman citizenship similar to American citizenship? How did the two differ?

◀ **THEN** Only Roman citizens could wear the garment known as a toga.

170 CHAPTER 6

Answers

Understanding Themes 1. *Citizens could vote, take part in assemblies, make contracts, file cases in court, and legally get married. Citizens would not be tortured or sentenced to death unless found guilty of treason. Only citizens were considered truly Roman.* **2.** *by birth to American parents, birth within the United States, or by passing a test and swearing an oath of allegiance;* **3.** *Similar—Citizenship is highly valued and includes both rights and responsibilities; citizens can vote and take part in government; children of citizens are considered citizens. Different—Non-citizens in America have many rights denied to non-citizens in ancient Rome; all persons born in America are American citizens; citizenship is easier to obtain in the United States.*

170

Skills Focus: Making Oral Presentations

At Level

Reading Like a Historian Skill
Roman Citizenship Orations

1. Discuss with students the Understanding Themes questions on this page. Ask students to state in general terms how Rome was expanding during the formation of its governmental system.

2. Organize students into small groups. Ask groups to discuss the relationship Rome had with other nations around the Mediterranean.

3. Have groups list at least three reasons for limiting Roman citizenship.

4. Have groups write a Roman-style oration supporting the Roman point of view that citizenship must be limited.

5. Have volunteers present their group's orations.
   LS Interpersonal, Verbal-Linguistic

📖 **Alternative Assessment Handbook**, Rubrics 11: Discussions; and 24: Oral Presentations

From Republic to Empire

BEFORE YOU READ

MAIN IDEA

Governmental and social problems led to the end of the Roman Republic and the creation of a new form of government.

READING FOCUS

1. What problems did leaders face in the late Roman Republic?

2. How did Rome become an empire?

3. What helped tie the Roman empire together during the Pax Romana?

KEY TERMS AND PEOPLE

Gracchi
Gaius Marius
Lucius Cornelius Sulla
Julius Caesar
triumvirate
Augustus
Pax Romana

NEW YORK

PI 3.1 Students analyze the roles and contributions of individuals and groups to social, political, economic, and religious practices and activities.

THE INSIDE STORY

Why would a successful general break the law? In 50 BC Julius Caesar was one of the most powerful men in the Roman Republic. He was the governor of the province of Gaul—modern France—the winner of dozens of battles, a charismatic leader, and a powerful public speaker. To all appearances, his star was on the rise.

Caesar, however, had powerful enemies who were afraid of his ambition. Those enemies wanted him to leave Gaul and return to Rome—without his army. Caesar feared that they wanted to arrest him and drive him out of politics.

Torn between his ambition for power and caution, Caesar led his troops to the banks of the Rubicon River, the border between Gaul and Italy. Under Roman law, he could not take his army any farther. At the last minute, however, Caesar decided to take his army anyway, to protect him from his political opponents. As he led his horse into the river, he is said to have uttered, "The die is cast," meaning the game had begun. Caesar had made his first move, and there was no turning back. ■

Problems in the Late Republic

By the mid-100s BC, Rome had no rival anywhere in the Mediterranean world. However, the Romans soon found themselves faced on all sides by problems. The responsibilities of running their vast holdings stretched the Roman political system to its limits.

As the pressures of governing grew, a revolution began in Roman political and social institutions. The primary cause of this revolution was growing tension between the various classes of Roman society.

No Turning Back

▲ In this painting, the spirit of Rome appears to Julius Caesar and his soldiers as they prepare to cross the Rubicon.

The Goddess Roma Appearing to Julius Caesar at the Bank of the Rubicon, by Richard Westall, c. 1793

ROME AND EARLY CHRISTIANITY **171**

① What problems did leaders face in the late Roman Republic? *The responsibilities of running their vast holdings stretched the Roman political system to its limits; social unrest increased.*

Problems in the Late Republic

Explain How did Gaius Marius improve recruitment for the army? *He eliminated property restrictions and began to accept anyone into the army.*

Identify Cause and Effect What caused the Social War and what was the result? *Rome's Italian allies fought for citizenship; the Italians were defeated, but the Senate still granted them citizenship.*

Predict What problems might result from armies that were largely private forces devoted to their generals? *possible answer—Because they were not dedicated to Rome as a whole, their forces could undermine the Republic and lead to the rise of dictators.*

Primary Sources

The Death of Caesar

Recall How many times was Julius Caesar stabbed? *23*

Identify Who took the lead in Caesar's assassination? *Tillius Cimber*

Answers

Primary Sources *Yes, because he allowed them to come close, and he called Brutus "my child."*

Reading Check *slave revolts, social unrest, the Social War, and a civil war in which Sulla became dictator*

172

The Death of Caesar

Julius Caesar was killed in 44 BC by a conspiracy of Senators. This account of the act was written by historian Suetonius in the 100s.

> As he took his seat, the conspirators gathered about him as if to pay their respects, and straightway Tillius Cimber, who had assumed the lead, came nearer as though to ask something; and when Caesar with a gesture put him off to another time, Cimber caught his toga by both shoulders; then as Caesar cried, "Why, this is violence!" one of the Cascas stabbed him from one side just below the throat. Caesar caught Casca's arm and ran it through with his stylus, but as he tried to leap to his feet, he was stopped by another wound. When he saw that he was beset on every side by drawn daggers, he muffled his head in his robe, and at the same time drew down its lap to his feet with his left hand, in order to fall more decently, with the lower part of his body also covered. And in this wise he was stabbed with three and twenty wounds, uttering not a word, but merely a groan at the first stroke, though some have written that when Marcus Brutus rushed at him, he said in Greek, "You too, my child?"

Skills FOCUS READING LIKE A HISTORIAN

Analyze Primary Sources Do you think Caesar knew the men who killed him? Why or why not?

See **Skills Handbook**, p. H25

TAKING NOTES

Make a list of major events in Rome's change from a republic to an empire.

Social Unrest Among the first officials to notice the growing tension in Rome and try to resolve it were two brothers, the **Gracchi**. In 133 BC the tribune Tiberius Gracchus noted the treatment of soldier-farmers, who were being reduced to poverty. After long years of service, many legionnaires returned home to find their farms had been sold or were in such bad shape that they had to be abandoned.

Tiberius and his younger brother Gaius tried to help these soldiers by redistributing public land to small farmers. The Gracchi had public support, but the Roman elite reacted violently. Fearing that the Gracchi were trying to reduce its power, the Senate urged mobs to kill first Tiberius and later his brother, along with their supporters. For the first time, the blood of Roman citizens was intentionally shed in the Forum. Violence had become a political tool.

The Military in Politics In 107 BC the social unrest reached a new level when a talented military leader named **Gaius Marius** was elected consul. Anxious to improve recruitment for the army, he eliminated the property restrictions and began to accept anyone into the army who wanted to join. Poor people began to join the army, attaching themselves to a general in hopes of sharing the plunder and land at the end of a war. As a result of Marius's changes, armies largely became private forces devoted to the general. Ruthless generals soon realized that they could use the loyalty of their troops as a political tool to increase their own power.

The Social War For decades, Rome's allies in Italy had been trying to obtain Roman citizenship, but the Senate had stubbornly refused. In 91 BC conflict broke out. The conflict was known as the Social War, from *socius*, the Latin word for ally. In the end, the Italian rebels were defeated—but only after the Senate had finally agreed to give them citizenship.

Civil War The Social War revealed the talent of one general in particular, the ambitious **Lucius Cornelius Sulla**, who became consul in 88 BC. During Sulla's consulship, Marius and his supporters defied Roman custom by trying to prevent Sulla from taking a military command. Sulla responded by marching on Rome with his legions.

In the civil war that followed, Sulla emerged victorious and became dictator. In a bloody purge he executed those who had opposed him or whom he believed to be a danger to the state. He then carried out a program of reforms aimed at protecting the power of the Senate. Eventually, incorrectly believing he had preserved the old republic, Sulla voluntarily retired.

READING CHECK Summarize What challenges faced Rome in the late republic?

Rome Becomes an Empire

By establishing the example of dictatorship, Sulla had paved the way for major changes in Rome's government. Within a generation of his death, the old Republic was practically gone. The end of the Republic was the result of the ambitions of just a few influential individuals, the most powerful men in Rome.

Collaborative Activity

At Level

Skits About Problems in Rome

Prep Required

Materials: white bed sheets, tape

1. Remind students that in this period, the people of Rome experienced much upheaval. Have students to name important events from this period. Write them for students to see. Tell students they will perform skits about these events.

2. Organize students into six groups. Assign each group a different event. Tell students to emphasize factual details in their skits. Have

students make name tags for major players to increase audience understanding.

3. When students have had time to prepare and rehearse, offer sheets for togas and tape for name tags.

4. Have groups perform their skits in the order the events are covered in the textbook.
LS Interpersonal, Kinesthetic

Alternative Assessment Handbook, Rubric 33: Skits and Reader's Theater

The First Triumvirate Among those who helped bring an end to the republic were **Julius Caesar**, Gnaeus Pompey, and Licinius Crassus. Caesar and Pompey were both successful military commanders who had added huge amounts of territory to the republic. In the east, Pompey had conquered Syria and parts of Asia Minor. In the west, Caesar had added all of Gaul—modern France—to the republic. Crassus, not as successful a soldier, was one of the wealthiest people in Rome. In 60 BC the three men took over the Roman Republic as the First **Triumvirate**, or rule of three men.

Eventually Crassus died, and Caesar and Pompey faced off in a civil war. Caesar defeated Pompey and took full control of the Republic. Recognizing Caesar's power, the Senate declared him dictator for life in 44 BC.

As dictator, Caesar brought many changes to Rome. He gave citizenship to people in the provinces and gave public land to veterans. Caesar's reforms made him popular with the public, but many Senators thought he wanted to make himself king and destroy the Roman Republic. In a last desperate attempt to save the Republic, a group of Senators murdered Caesar on the Ides of March—March 15.

The Second Triumvirate Caesar's murder did not, however, save the Republic. In 43 BC the Second Triumvirate, composed of Caesar's adopted son and heir, Octavian; a loyal officer named Marc Antony; and the high priest Lepidus, took power. Soon Lepidus was pushed aside as Antony and Octavian agreed to govern half the empire each—Octavian in the west and Antony in the east.

When civil war between the two eventually broke out, Octavian defeated Antony and his ally, Queen Cleopatra of Egypt, at the naval battle of Actium in 31 BC. With the double suicide of Antony and Cleopatra the following year, Octavian alone controlled Rome. The Republic was effectively dead and a new period in Roman history was beginning.

From Octavian to Augustus As sole ruler, Octavian faced the task of restoring order in the empire. When he took power, Octavian had no intention of establishing a dictatorship, but he had later secretly decided that it would be impossible to return Rome to its old republican system of government.

Achievements of Augustus

Rome's first emperor, Augustus, introduced many changes to society. *What changes can you see illustrated in these photos?*

▲ Originally built under Augustus, the Pantheon, a temple to all the gods, was rebuilt later.

"I found Rome built of bricks; I leave her clothed in marble."

► As a military leader, Augustus added much territory to the empire.

► The peace Augustus brought to Rome allowed trade to grow.

Reading Focus

2 How did Rome become an empire? *Sulla's dictatorship set example; Rome ruled by Triumvirates; from Octavian on, Rome ruled by emperors*

Rome Becomes an Empire

Identify Who were the members of the First Triumvirate? *Julius Caesar, Gnaeus Pompey, and Licinius Crassus*

Explain Why was Caesar popular with the public? *He gave citizenship to people in the provinces and gave land to the poor.*

Develop What are some possible reasons Octavian did not return to the old republican system? *possible answer—He felt the government could be more effective if he held most of the power.*

📄 **CRF:** Biography: Cleopatra

MISCONCEPTION ALERT

Many people believe that Julius Caesar was born by Caesarian section, a surgical technique used to remove a baby from the womb. Because Caesar's mother, Aurelia, was involved in raising him, however, and since known surgical techniques of the day probably would have killed her, this account is quite unlikely.

Skills Focus: Evaluating Information on the Internet   `At Level`

Social Studies Skill
Finding Coins of the Empire

`Research Required`

1. Tell students that archaeologists have long sought Roman coins in archaeological digs and deep sea dives. Tell students they will conduct research using reliable Internet sites to locate recent finds.

2. Organize students into small groups. Have groups print out the text of one or more articles about Roman coin discoveries, including the bibliographic references page.

3. Have each group discuss the text and its source. Have students consider whether the writer could have been biased in any way, and if so, how. Tell students to write down their analyses.

4. Allow time for volunteers to share their discoveries and opinions. 🔲 **Interpersonal, Verbal-Linguistic**

📄 **Alternative Assessment Handbook,** Rubrics 16: Judging Information; and 30: Research

Answers

Achievements of Augustus *possible answer—temples, sculptures, coins*

173

Reading Focus

Rome Becomes an Empire

Explain What was the special name given to Octavian by the Senate, and what did it signify? *meaning "the revered one," the name Augustus signified the respect and admiration the Romans had for their leader*

Compare How did the Julio-Claudians differ from the Flavians? *Julio-Claudians—relatives of Julius Caesar, abilities varied widely; Flavians returned stability to the empire*

Make Inferences Do you think Augustus helped increase knowledge about ancient Rome? *possible answer—Yes, his support of Roman literature has helped us learn more about ancient Rome.*

Teaching Tip

Ask students if any of them have been to Rome. If so, have them share some of their photographs of ancient Roman buildings to help the class visualize ancient Rome.

Answers

Reading Check *The Roman Empire reached the limits of its territorial expansion and made developments in building, government, and culture.*

174

As Rome's ruler, Octavian created a new political order. Today it is known as the empire, but Octavian was careful to avoid the title of king or emperor. Instead, he called himself *princeps,* or "first citizen." The government he established is therefore known as the Principate. Despite this title, Octavian insisted that he had no powers greater than those of other magistrates and that he worked for the good of the people:

NEW YORK

CC Unit 1-D2b
Growth of the Roman Empire

HISTORY'S VOICES

❝ May I be privileged to build firm and lasting foundations for the government of the state. May I also achieve the reward to which I aspire: that of being known as the author of the best possible constitution, and of carrying with me, when I die, the hope that these foundations which I have established for the State will abide secure. ❞

—Augustus, quoted in Suetonius, *The Twelve Caesars*

In 27 BC the Senate gave Octavian a title of honor—**Augustus**, "the revered one." This title, a religious honor, is the name by which he is still known today. He was also given the right to wear a crown of laurel and oak leaves.

The Augustan Age For more than 40 years, Augustus remained at the head of the state. This very long reign made possible a smooth transition to the new imperial government. Augustus divided the power to rule Rome and its empire between himself and the Senate. However, most financial and administrative matters came under Augustus's control.

In foreign affairs Augustus started a vast program to bring peace to the west, particularly to Gaul and Spain. He also began a series of conquests that pushed the border of the empire eastward to the Danube River.

In Rome the legacy of the Augustan Age was even more impressive. Augustus took special care of Rome itself, creating a police force and fire brigades and stockpiling food and water supplies. Augustus also began a vast building program, boasting, "I found Rome built of bricks; I leave her clothed in marble." In addition, he presided over moral and religious reforms, arguing that since the gods had made the empire possible, it was wise to respect them. He restored old temples and built new ones.

Culturally, the Augustan Age was a great period of creativity in Latin literature. This period produced many of the greatest writers

in Roman history. Realizing that literature could enhance his fame, Augustus supported its development. Great writers flourished, including the poets Horace and Ovid, the historian Livy, and above all, the poet Virgil. In his epic poem the *Aeneid*, Virgil tried to imitate Homer by creating a national epic, Rome's answer to the *Iliad* and the *Odyssey*.

Julio-Claudians and Flavians Augustus died in AD 14. For the next 54 years, relatives of Julius Caesar, called the Julio-Claudian Emperors, ruled the empire. The abilities of these emperors varied widely. Tiberius, Augustus's adopted son, was a good soldier and a competent administrator. His brutal and mentally unstable successor, Caligula, however, once supposedly demonstrated his power to the Roman Senate by appointing his favorite horse as consul.

Nero, the last of the Julio-Claudians, committed suicide in AD 68. After his death, civil wars raged in Rome, and four military leaders claimed the throne in turn. The last of them, Vespasian, re-established order. During his reign and those of his two sons, stability returned to the empire. Together these three emperors are known as the Flavians.

The Good Emperors In AD 96 a new line of emperors established itself on the Roman throne. Called the Good Emperors, these five rulers governed Rome for almost a century. Almost all of the Good Emperors were from the provinces rather than from Rome. Consequently, they continued opening up Roman imperial society by admitting more members of the provincial elites into the Senate and the imperial administration.

Under the Good Emperors the empire grew tremendously. It reached the limits of its expansion under Trajan, who added present-day Romania, Armenia, Mesopotamia, and the Sinai Peninsula to the empire. Trajan's successor Hadrian, however, thought the empire had grown too large. He withdrew from almost all these eastern additions and built defensive fortifications along the frontiers to guard against invasions. In northern Britain, for example, Hadrian built a wall some 73 miles long.

READING CHECK **Explain** How did Rome grow and change after it became an empire?

Skills Focus: Analyzing Costs and Benefits   [At Level]

Social Studies Skill
Weighing the Changes of Augustus

Materials 12"x18" construction paper

1. Have students name a few of the various accomplishments of Augustus. Tell students they will chart the costs and benefits of the changes Augustus made to his empire. Remind students that costs and benefits are not always financial.

2. Organize students into small groups. Distribute paper to each group. Have students

create a three-column chart on lined paper, titled Weighing the Changes of Augustus.

3. When students have finished, display the charts and guide a class discussion of the material.

4. Have students write a paragraph about one of Augustus's accomplishments. **LS Verbal-Linguistic, Visual-Spatial**

📖 **Alternative Assessment Handbook**, Rubrics 13: Graphic Organizers; and 14: Group Activity

The Pax Romana

The period from the beginning of Augustus's reign in 27 BC until the death of the last of the Good Emperors in AD 180 is often called the **Pax Romana**—the Roman Peace. Several essential traits, such as stable government, a strong legal system, widespread trade, and, most importantly, peace characterized this long era. During the Pax Romana the smooth working of the imperial government was seldom interrupted by war or invasion.

Government The Roman government was the strongest unifying force in the empire. The government maintained order, enforced the laws, and defended the frontiers. Both in the central administration and in the provinces, members of the aristocracy participated in government, but emperors made all important decisions. By the AD 100s the supreme position of the emperor had been well established.

The Roman Empire was divided into provinces ruled by governors appointed from Rome. Provincial government was both fairer and more efficient than it had been under the Republic, largely because the government in Rome kept a closer check on the governors than before. Moreover, any citizen could appeal any unfair treatment directly to the emperor.

Through this provincial organization, the empire brought a certain uniformity to the cities of the Mediterranean world. Cities were governed in imitation of Rome, complete with their own local senates and magistrates. Similar theaters, amphitheaters, public baths, and temples, modeled on those in Rome, could be seen from Britain to Asia Minor.

NEW YORK

CC Unit 1-D2f
Pax Romana

THE ROMAN EMPIRE, AD 117

- Roman Republic, 100 BC
- Republic at Caesar's death, 44 BC
- Empire at Augustus's death, AD 14
- Greatest extent of empire, AD 117
- silk   Trade goods

GEOGRAPHY SKILLS **INTERPRETING MAPS**

1. **Location** What areas did Augustus add to the empire during his rule?
2. **Place** What types of trade goods were produced in northern Africa and Egypt?

ROME AND EARLY CHRISTIANITY **175**

Reading Focus

3 What helped tie the Roman Empire together during the Pax Romana? *stable government, law, and widespread trade and peace*

The Pax Romana

Explain What protected provincial citizens from unfair decisions by their governors? *Any citizen could appeal unfair treatment directly to the emperor.*

Draw Conclusions Why do you think you can see the ruins of ancient Roman style buildings in Britain and Asia Minor today? *possible answer— Provincial cities in those areas imitated Roman architecture.*

CRF: Primary Source: Contrasting Views of the Roman Empire

Interpreting Maps

The Roman Empire, AD 117

Movement Where might people from Jerusalem go to trade their wine for grain? *Egypt*

Map Transparency: The Roman Empire, AD 117

Differentiating Instruction

Below Level

Special Education Students

Materials 12"x18" construction paper

1. Tell students that they will learn about the lands of the Mediterranean based on the trade goods listed on the map on this page.

2. Based on the map, have students describe the regions where people would have produced each of the trade goods. Record answers for students to see.

3. Have each student prepare a three-column chart, filling in the first column with the names of trade goods, the second column with the description of the land where each item is produced, and the third column with all the regions of the Roman Empire that produced each item. **LS** **Visual-Spatial**

Alternative Assessment Handbook, Rubrics 4: Graphic Organizers; and 21: Map Reading

---

Answers

Interpreting Maps 1. *Egypt, northern Spain, and an area reaching from the Alps to northern Greece;* **2.** *grains, olives, olive oil*

175

Reading Focus

The Pax Romana

Identify How did landowners produce surplus for trade without using slaves? *They used tenant farmers who paid the owner for the use of his land with a certain amount of the harvest.*

Recall What manufactured goods were produced in the Roman Empire's cities? *pottery, textiles, and glassware*

Make Generalizations Why was trade with Alexandria particularly important? *Egypt produced grain surpluses with which the emperors fed Rome's urban population.*

📜 **CRF:** History and Geography: Trade During the Pax Romana

---

● Review & Assess ●

Close

Review with students the governmental and societal problems that ended the Roman Republic and led to the creation of the Roman Empire.

Review

🖥 **Online Quiz**, Section 2

Assess

SE Section 2 Assessment

📄 **Progress Assessment:** Section 2 Quiz

📄 **Alternative Assessment Handbook**

Reteach/Intervene

📄 **Interactive Reader and Study Guide**, Section 2

💿 **Interactive Skills Tutor CD-ROM**

Answers

Reading Check *The Roman government was the strongest unifying force, maintaining order, enforcing the laws, and defending the frontiers. Roman law provided stability and, with few exceptions, the same laws applied to everyone in the empire. Trade provided opportunities for commerce between people in different parts of the empire.*

176

Legal System Roman law also unified the empire. Stability in the Roman legal system was achieved by laws passed by assemblies, the Senate, or the emperor. These laws specified what could or could not be done and what the penalties were for breaking the law. With few exceptions, the same laws applied to all citizens in the empire, wherever they might live.

Trade and Transportation Throughout the Pax Romana, agriculture remained the primary occupation of people in the empire. Most farms were owned by independent farmers who seldom had surplus to sell. On large estates, however, a new type of agricultural worker, the tenant farmer, began to replace slaves. Each tenant farmer received a small plot of land from the estate's owner. In return he had to remain on the land for a set period of time and pay the owner with a certain amount of the harvest.

Meanwhile, manufacturing increased throughout the empire. In Italy, Gaul, and Spain, artisans made cheap pottery and textiles by hand in small shops. The most important manufacturing centers, however, were in the east, where cities such as Alexandria made products like fine glassware.

THE IMPACT TODAY
Many roads built by the Romans are still used today, some 2,000 years later.

The Roman Empire also provided many opportunities for trade. From the provinces, Italy imported grain, meat, and raw materials such as wool and hides. From Asia, merchants brought silks, linens, glassware, jewelry, and furniture to satisfy the wealthy. Rome and Alexandria became the empire's greatest commercial centers. Alexandria was particularly important, since Egypt produced grain surpluses with which emperors fed Rome's urban population.

All this commercial activity was possible largely because of two factors: the empire's location around the Mediterranean and its extensive road network. Ultimately there were about 50,000 miles of roads binding the empire together. Most roads, however, were built and maintained for military purposes. Local roads were not paved, and weather conditions often made overland travel impossible. It was actually cheaper to transport grain by ship from one end of the Mediterranean to the other than to send it 100 miles overland. Consequently, most goods went by sea.

READING CHECK **Analyze** How did government, law, and trade tie the Roman people together?

SECTION 2 ASSESSMENT

go.hrw.com
Online Quiz
Keyword: SHL ROM HP

Reviewing Ideas, Terms, and People

1. **a. Identify** Who were the Gracchi? What happened to them?
   b. Explain How did Lucius Cornelius Sulla pave the way for later changes in Roman government?
   c. Elaborate How do you think the military reforms made by Gaius Marius changed politics in Rome?

2. **a. Define** What is a triumvirate? What did the First Triumvirate do?
   b. Summarize What did Augustus achieve as Rome's first emperor?
   c. Evaluate Do you think Octavian earned the new name Augustus? Why or why not?

3. **a. Define** What was the Pax Romana? Why was it given that name?
   b. Analyze How did the imperial government help tie people throughout the Roman Empire together during the Pax Romana?
   c. Develop If it was generally cheaper to ship goods by sea than overland, why were roads still considered vital to the well-being of the Roman Empire?

Critical Thinking

4. **Identify Cause and Effect** Draw a graphic organizer like the one below. Use your notes to identify the causes or effects of the events listed in the boxes.

Causes	Effects
Poor soldiers lose land.	
	Sulla becomes dictator.
Senators fear Caesar.	
	Rome becomes an empire.

FOCUS ON WRITING ✏

5. **Narration** Write a diary entry as though you were a trader in Rome during the Pax Romana. In your entry, tell how you spent your day, including where you went, what you saw, and which goods you bought or sold.

176 CHAPTER 6

Section 2 Assessment Answers

1. **a.** The Gracchi were brothers who helped ex-soldiers by redistributing public land to small farmers. They were killed.
   b. by establishing the example of dictatorship
   c. possible answer—increased power of certain generals; less emphasis on republic

2. **a.** rule of three men; dominated the Roman state and helped bring an end to the Republic
   b. created a new political order, brought peace to the west, made cultural reforms
   c. possible answer—Yes, Octavian was revered and respected by people of his time.

3. **a.** a period of peace from 27 BC to AD 180; name means Roman Peace
   b. maintained order, enforced laws; provincial cities were governed in imitation of Rome
   c. Most roads were built for military use.

4. Causes—Sulla marches on Rome with his legions; Augustus becomes emperor; Effects—increased social unrest; Senators kill Caesar

5. Diary entries should include references to specific activities, locations, sights, and goods traded during the Pax Romana.

Roman Society and Culture

BEFORE YOU READ

MAIN IDEA

The Romans developed a complex society and pioneered cultural advances that, even today, affect life all over the world.

READING FOCUS

1. What social and cultural factors influenced life in imperial Rome?
2. What achievements shaped Rome's cultural legacy to the modern world?

KEY TERMS AND PEOPLE

villa
circuses
paterfamilias
augurs
Galen
Ptolemy
aqueducts
Latin
civil law

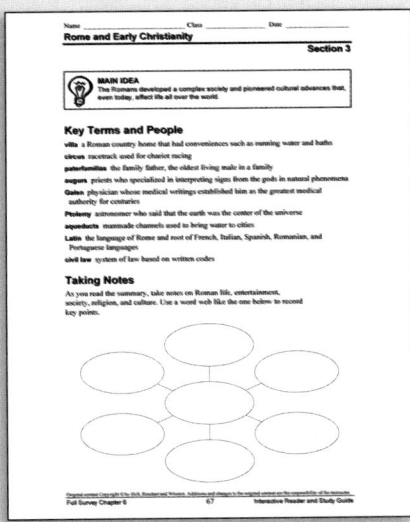

THE INSIDE STORY

Why would people risk their lives for others' enjoyment? Fights between gladiators, trained fighters who performed in public arenas, were a popular form of entertainment in Rome. The combat between gladiators was fierce, and many of them died in the arena. Why would anyone choose so dangerous a lifestyle?

Most gladiators did not choose the life. They were forced into it, either as slaves or as prisoners. A few individuals, however, did become gladiators voluntarily. Some were desperate for money and saw the arena as their only chance for survival. Others loved the thrill of danger. Still others became gladiators for the glory. Successful gladiators were among the most popular people in Rome, the equivalents to movie, television, and music stars of today. To some Romans, the potential for fame was worth the risk. ◼

Life in Imperial Rome

Gladiators locked in combat. Magnificent temples of marble. Soldiers marching off to war. These are a few of the images of Rome that have been carried down to the present by movies and stories. But what was life really like in the Roman Empire?

▼ **This Roman mosaic shows gladiators locked in combat.**

MORTAL COMBAT

177

Teach the Main Idea

At Level

Roman Society and Culture

Materials: chart paper or overhead projector

1. **Teach** Ask students the Reading Focus questions to teach this section.

2. **Apply** Ask students to write down each of the ten blue headings in this section. After each one, have them write a one-sentence generalization about the content.

3. **Review** Allow time for students to compare their sentences with others and make changes as necessary.

4. **Practice/Homework** Have each student write a short paragraph about Roman society and culture. **LS** Verbal-Linguistic

   📝 **Alternative Assessment Handbook**, Rubric 1: Acquiring Information

---

❶ What social and cultural factors influenced life in early Rome? *Wealth was distributed unevenly. The poor lived in crowded and dangerous conditions. People enjoyed public entertainment. They lived in patriarchal families, valued education, and believed in a variety of gods.*

Life in Imperial Rome

Recall How did wealthy Romans spend most of their time? *embroiled in politics*

Analyze What motive did the government have for giving free food and entertainment to the poor? *It kept the poor from rebelling against their living conditions.*

Predict What present-day sports may have descended from chariot racing? *possible answer—automobile or other vehicle racing*

MISCONCEPTION
ALERT

Many people believe that at the end of a gladiatorial event, a person of high status in charge was to turn his thumb up, indicating that one of the gladiators was to be allowed to live, or down if he was to be killed. The gesture was actually a turning of the thumb, which scholars believe imitated the movement of a sword.

TAKING NOTES
Use a word web to take notes on Roman life and culture.

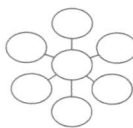

Life for the Rich The Pax Romana provided prosperity to many people, but citizens did not share equally in this wealth. Rich citizens usually had both a city home and a country home, or **villa**, that included conveniences such as running water and baths.

Wealthy Roman men spent much of their time embroiled in politics. Since public officials were not paid, only the wealthy could afford to hold office. Wealthy Romans could frequently be found meeting with public officials or with political groups with whom they held common interests. However, ties of marriage, friendship, and family alliances were as important as class interests. In addition, Roman politicians worked to perfect their public-speaking skills to better sway the opinions of members of the popular assemblies.

Life for the Poor Unlike the wealthy, most of the nearly 1 million residents of Rome lived in crowded three- and four-story apartment buildings. Fire posed a constant threat because of the torches used for light and the charcoal used for cooking. In part to keep poorer citizens from rebelling against such conditions, free food and public entertainment became a major feature of city life in Rome. A Roman poet once noted that only two things interested the Roman masses—bread and circuses.

Public Entertainment It was not only poor Romans who enjoyed public entertainments, however. Romans of all classes enjoyed the **circuses**, where chariot races took place. In Rome many such races were held in the Circus Maximus, a racetrack that could accommodate 250,000 spectators. Roman audiences particularly enjoyed the spectacular crashes that frequently occurred. They also liked theater, particularly comedies and satires. Performers such as mimes, jugglers, dancers, acrobats, and clowns also became quite popular.

Romans also enjoyed bloody spectacles in amphitheaters, where wild animals such as lions and bears were brought to battle each other or professional fighters. Often, condemned criminals were thrown into the arena to be torn to pieces by beasts. By far the most popular entertainment offered in the amphitheaters, however, were gladiatorial combats. Such shows often ended with the death of one or both of the fighters, who were usually slaves. In Rome such spectacles were performed in the Colosseum, a huge amphitheater that seated some 50,000 people.

Roman Life
Although only the rich could afford large estates like this one in Pompeii, Romans of all classes enjoyed the company of pets like the dog in this mosaic.

178 CHAPTER 6

Skills Focus: Analyzing Visuals

At Level

Reading Like a Historian Skill
Pompeii's Legacy

Research Required

1. Have students share what they know about Pompeii.

2. Organize students into small groups. Have each group conduct research about the Pompeii event, and why this particular archeological treasure is so important to historians.

3. Have groups document and compile bibliographic information as they go. Have

each group prepare a brief oral presentation about its findings.

4. Allow sufficient time for each group to give its presentation. Encourage students to accompany their presentation with visual items, such as posters or photographs.
LS **Interpersonal, Verbal-Linguistic**

Alternative Assessment Handbook, Rubrics 24: Oral Presentations; and 30: Research

Public baths were also popular places for recreation. The Romans were well aware of the importance of bathing and hygiene for health, but public baths offered far more than just a place to get clean. After bathing in a hot pool, people could retire to a cold pool to relax and socialize. In addition to the pools, many public baths included steam rooms, exercise facilities, and meeting rooms.

Family Like many other ancient peoples, Romans were patriarchal. The head of the family—the **paterfamilias**, or family father—was the oldest living male and had extensive powers over other members of the family. This included his wife, his sons with their wives and children, his unmarried daughters, and his family slaves. Within this family structure, Romans emphasized the virtues of simplicity, religious devotion, and obedience.

Adoption was an important aspect of Roman society. Some families with no sons would adopt a teenage boy or young man to serve as the heir to the paterfamilias. Adoption was one way of ensuring that the family name was carried on.

Roman women could do little without the intervention of a male guardian—her father or her husband—though women could own and inherit property. Among the lower classes, however, women had more freedom. Lower-class women often worked outside of the home as shopkeepers or at similar jobs.

Education The Romans, at least those of the upper classes, placed great value on education and literacy. In general, parents taught their children at home, though wealthy families might hire expensive tutors or send their sons to exclusive schools. In such schools, boys—and a few girls—learned Latin and Greek, law, math, and public speaking.

Religion As you have already learned, the Romans adopted many elements of Greek mythology. However, the Romans did not limit their belief to only a few gods. They made offerings to any gods who might exist to ensure Roman prosperity, including gods borrowed from the Egyptians, Mesopotamians, and Persians. Each Roman family also worshipped local household gods called *penates*. In addition, many Romans throughout the empire worshipped the emperor as a god.

ROMAN SOCIETY

QUICK FACTS

Roman society was highly stratified. The lives of rich and poor citizens differed greatly. However, there were a few common elements that virtually all members of Roman society shared. A few of them are described below.

Religion
The Romans were accepting of many gods. Among the most popular were the gods of Greece.

Education
Upper-class Romans placed a great value on education for their sons. Most schooling was conducted at home.

Entertainment
The Romans were great fans of public entertainment. Theater, chariot races, and gladiatorial combat were all popular forms.

Health
Baths were both a hygienic practice and a form of entertainment in Rome. Public baths like the ones below were popular gathering spots.

Roman public baths at Bath, England

The Romans believed that the gods sent signs and warnings to human beings in the form of natural phenomena, such as the flight of birds, or the color and arrangement of entrails in sacrificial animals. They paid particular respect to the priests known as **augurs**, who specialized in interpreting these signs. Nothing important was undertaken without first consulting the augurs.

 NEW YORK
CC Unit 1-C6
Status and role of women in Rome

READING CHECK Contrast How was life different for rich and poor citizens in Rome?

Reading Focus

Life in Imperial Rome

Identify Name the virtues emphasized in family life. *simplicity, religious devotion, and obedience*

Explain Why was adoption so important to Romans? *It ensured that the family name was carried on in families who had no sons.*

Quick Facts Transparency: Roman Society

Recent Scholarship

New evidence points to many *libertini*, or freed slaves, influencing Roman society. Lauren Hackworth Petersen's book *The Freedmen in Roman Art and Art History* describes Roman slaves' skillful accomplishments in art. Her book includes revealing information about a society called the Augustales, formed primarily of freedmen in Pompeii, who carefully bridged the gap between Pompeii's elite and commoners.

The Freedmen in Roman Art and Art History by Lauren Hackworth Petersen. Cambridge University Press, 2006.

Skills Focus: Comparing and Contrasting

At Level

Reading Skill
Roman Teen Booklet

Materials: 8-½"x11" unlined paper

1. Tell students they are teenagers living in ancient Rome. Tell students they will create a booklet that compares ancient Roman life to modern times.

2. Distribute three sheets of paper to each student. Have students fold them in half to form an 8-½"x5-½" booklet. Have them record a topic from the Quick Facts list on this page at the top of each two-page spread, until all four are listed.

3. Have students write realistic details about each topic as a Roman teen on the left and in their actual life on the right. Encourage students to "Romanize" their names, for example Larry Hill might become "Hill, Larius."

4. Collect booklets, and review before displaying for all to see. **LS** Intrapersonal

Alternative Assessment Handbook, Rubric 9: Comparing and Contrasting

Answers

Reading Check *Rich— often had two homes and spent time in politics, women's lives controlled by guardians; Poor—lived in crowded conditions, lower-class women had more freedom, often worked outside the home*

❷ What achievements shaped Rome's cultural legacy to the modern world? *The Romans advanced science, engineering, architecture, language and literature, and the law, all of which have influenced cultures around the world.*

Rome's Cultural Legacy

Identify Which Roman engineering contribution made large public structures possible? *concrete*

Compare What distinction can you make between the Greek approach to knowledge and the Roman one? *Greeks—preferred knowledge for its own sake; Romans—were practical and tried to apply their knowledge*

Make Inferences How would a new aqueduct influence city life? *possible answer—It would supply water and improve hygiene, keeping the population healthier.*

📝 **CRF:** Biography: Galen

Info to Know

The Getty Villa In 1974 American oil tycoon J. Paul Getty built a replica of a first century Roman country house in Malibu, California. This museum houses his extensive collection of Greek, Roman, and Etruscan antiquities—vases, sculptures, and artifacts. It also recently underwent a $275 million facelift. The public may visit the Getty villa, or view slide shows on the Internet.

History Close-Up
Roman Engineering
Analyze How did engineers protect their support structure? *They shaped the supports to avoid damage from running water.*

About the Illustration
This illustration is an artist's conception based on available sources. Historians, however, are uncertain exactly what this scene looked like.

Rome's Cultural Legacy

Although the Western Roman Empire fell in 476, much of Roman culture continued to influence life for centuries. In fact, we can still see many of the legacies of the great empire today.

Science and Engineering Among the areas in which the Romans influenced later people were science and engineering. On the whole, Romans were less interested in original scientific research to increase knowledge than in collecting and organizing information. **Galen**, a physician who lived in Rome during the AD 100s, wrote several volumes that summarized all the medical knowledge of his day. For centuries people regarded him as the greatest authority in medicine. **Ptolemy** synthesized the knowledge of others in a single theory in astronomy—that the earth was the center of the universe. Pliny the Elder observed and wrote about the eruption of Mount Vesuvius.

ACADEMIC VOCABULARY
synthesize to combine several parts into a whole

Unlike the Greeks, who were primarily interested in knowledge for its own sake, the Romans were very practical. They tried to apply the knowledge they gained from science to planning their cities, building water and sewage systems, and improving farming methods. Roman engineers constructed amazing roads, bridges, amphitheaters, public buildings, and **aqueducts**—man-made channels used to bring water to the cities. Without these aqueducts and a superior sewer system, Roman cities could not have grown as large as they did. Such advances would not have been possible without the development of concrete, which made such large public structures possible. From concrete, the Romans built amazing structures that still stand today, some 2,000 years later.

Interactive **HISTORY CLOSE-UP**

Roman Engineering

The Pont du Gard, a huge aqueduct and bridge in southern France, was built more than 2,000 years ago and still stands. More than 140 feet high and 800 feet long, its construction was a marvel of Roman engineering skill.

Arches made the overall structure incredibly strong.

Engineers used human-powered cranes to lift heavy blocks of stone into place.

180 CHAPTER 6

Differentiating Instruction

English-Language Learners

Materials: *Building Big*, by David Macaulay, or other illustrations of the Pont du Gard

1. Show several pages from *Building Big* to the class. Ask students to look at the drawing above and tell them they are in charge of building the Pont du Gard in ancient Gaul. Tell them they are contractors, developing a plan to get all the construction jobs completed in the correct sequence.

2. Organize students into groups of five or six. Have students list all the separate jobs that need to be done to build the bridge. Have students number each task in the order in which it needs to be completed.

3. Have each student in the group write a short paragraph describing the process of building this bridge over 2,000 years ago.

🔲 **Interpersonal, Verbal-Linguistic**

📝 **Alternative Assessment Handbook**, Rubrics 14: Group Activity; and 40: Writing to Describe

Roman bridges still span French, German, and Spanish rivers, and roads that connected Rome with its provinces still survive today. In many cities they conquered, the Romans added their own urban plan—a grid system of roads, temples, baths, theaters, and a central forum. Many European cities today reflect grid layouts originally planned by Roman engineers.

Architecture The Roman legacy in architecture is also strong. Many examples of Roman architecture can still be seen throughout the countrysides of southern Europe, North Africa, and Southwest Asia. The dominant Roman architectural advances, the round arch and the vault, allowed Romans to construct much larger buildings than earlier societies had. Following the Roman model, both advances have been used for many centuries and are still seen in the architecture of many countries.

The ruins of Roman buildings inspired generations of architects. Michelangelo used Roman models to design the dome of Saint Peter's Basilica in Rome in 1547, as did Thomas Jefferson when he built the library of the University of Virginia. Many other examples of Roman architecture abound throughout modern Europe and North America.

NEW YORK
CC Unit 1-D2c
Contributions of the Roman Empire

No mortar was used to hold the bricks together.

Workers stood on scaffolding built into the sides of the aqueduct.

The supports of the aqueduct were shaped to avoid damage from running water.

Water ran through a narrow channel at the top of the aqueduct.

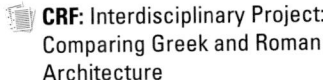

Skills FOCUS INTERPRETING VISUALS

go.hrw.com
Practice Online
Keyword: SHL ROM

Analyze How are the ancient Roman construction techniques seen in this image similar to modern techniques that you have seen? How are they different?

181

181

Direct Teach

Reading Focus

Rome's Cultural Legacy

Make Inferences How might the Roman system of law have reached New South Wales, a former British colony? *possible answer—England adopted the Roman law system and carried it to New South Wales, a British colony in Australia.*

Predict Name some benefits of learning Latin word roots. *possible answers—improved vocabulary and spelling; better knowledge of English language and other languages*

● Review & Assess ●

Close

Review with students the development of ancient Rome's complex society and cultural advances.

Review

 Online Quiz, Section 3

Assess

SE   Section 3 Assessment

📄 **Progress Assessment**: Section 3 Quiz

📄 **Alternative Assessment Handbook**

Reteach/Intervene

📄 **Interactive Reader and Study Guide**, Section 3

💿 **Interactive Skills Tutor CD-ROM**

Answers

Primary Sources *patriarchal family structure, religious devotion, obedience*

Reading Check *science, engineering, architecture, language, literature, and law*

182

PRIMARY SOURCES

Virgil's *Aeneid*

The *Aeneid*, an epic of the exploits of the Trojan warrior Aeneas whose descendants founded Rome, is one of the best known and most widely-read works from ancient Rome, still read in both English and Latin. In this passage, Aeneas takes his father Anchises and his son Ascanius, or Iulus, away from the destruction of Troy.

> "Then come, dear father. Arms around my neck:
> I'll take you on my shoulders, no great weight.
> Whatever happens, both will face one danger,
> Find one safety. Iulus will come with me,
> My wife at a good interval behind.
> Servants, give your attention to what I say.
> At the gate inland there's a funeral mound
> And an old shrine of Ceres the Bereft;
> Near it an ancient cypress, kept alive
> For many years by our fathers' piety.
> By various routes we'll come to that one place.
> Father, carry our hearthgods, our Penates.
> It would be wrong for me to handle them—
> Just come from such hard fighting, bloody work—
> Until I wash myself in running water."

Skills FOCUS   READING LIKE A HISTORIAN

Literature as a Source Which Roman values are stressed in this passage?
See **Skills Handbook**, p. H28

Language and Literature Another part of Rome's legacy is its language. Several languages, called Romance languages, developed from **Latin**, the language of Rome. Every person speaking French, Italian, Spanish, Romanian, or Portuguese is speaking a language with its roots in the language of Rome. Even English, which developed from other languages, owes much of its vocabulary to Latin. Examples of words of direct Latin origin in English are *et cetera*, *veto*, and *curriculum*.

Modern literature and drama also owe a great debt to Rome. For example, the technique of satire was derived from Roman authors. In addition, writers have for centuries borrowed themes from Roman authors such as Virgil.

Law Roman law also left its imprint on the world. The Romans used a system called **civil law**, a form of law based on a written code of laws. This civil law system was adopted by many countries in Europe after the empire fell. Centuries later, those nations carried their systems of law to colonies in Asia, Africa, and the Americas. As a result, many countries in these regions have civil law systems today. Thus, although it has been modified over time, the Roman influence can be seen in the legal systems of most of the world.

READING CHECK   Summarize What are some areas in which Rome's influence is still seen?

SECTION 3 ASSESSMENT

go.hrw.com
Online Quiz
Keyword: SHL ROM HP

Reviewing Ideas, Terms, and People

1. a. Identify What types of entertainment were held in the Circus Maximus and the Colosseum? What other types of entertainment were popular in Rome?
b. Explain In what ways was ancient Roman society patriarchal? What rights did Roman women have?
c. Develop What did the Roman poet mean when he said that the poor were only interested in bread and circuses? Do you think he approved of the lifestyle he was describing? Why or why not?

2. a. Describe How is the influence of Rome still felt in the area of language?
b. Analyze What were some of the advances made by the ancient Romans that allowed them to excel in engineering and architecture?
c. Elaborate How did the influence of ancient Rome spread through the world's legal systems?

Critical Thinking

3. Summarize Draw a word web like the one at right. Use your notes to write a sentence that summarizes the ancient Romans' views on the subject in each outer circle.

FOCUS ON WRITING ✏️

4. Exposition Write two paragraphs comparing and contrasting life for rich and poor Romans. In one paragraph, explain how the two lifestyles were similar. In the other paragraph, explain how they were different.

182 CHAPTER 6

Section 3 Assessment Answers

1. a. chariot racing; human and animal fights and gladiatorial combat; theatrical performances
b. paterfamilias had power over his family; women could do little without male guardian; lower class women had more freedom
c. The poor were kept from rebelling by being given free food and public entertainment. possible answer—The poet probably did not approve; he must have believed other things were more important.

2. a. Many languages have Latin roots.
b. arches, vaults, aqueducts

c. Roman laws were adopted in Europe and its colonies.

3. Family—A paterfamilias was head of the family. Education—Romans valued education. Women's Rights—Women could do little without a male guardian. Religion—Romans worshipped many gods and consulted augurs. Entertainment—Romans of all classes enjoyed public entertainment. Science—Roman advances in science influenced later cultures.

4. Student paragraphs should include details from the section.

The Rise of Christianity

BEFORE YOU READ

MAIN IDEA

A new religion called Christianity developed within the Roman Empire and gradually spread throughout the Roman world.

READING FOCUS

1. How was Christianity rooted in the teachings of Judaism?
2. What were the teachings of Jesus of Nazareth?
3. How did Christianity spread throughout the Roman world?
4. What was the early Christian church like?

KEY TERMS AND PEOPLE

Christianity
Messiah
Jesus of Nazareth
disciples
Apostles
martyrs
Paul
Eucharist
bishop
popes

 NEW YORK

PI 3.1 Students analyze the roles and contributions of individuals and groups to religious practices.

3.3 Students examine the social/cultural and religious norms and values of Western and other world cultures.

THE INSIDE STORY

Why had so many hungry people gathered in one place? The New Testament Book of Matthew describes how huge crowds would gather to hear Jesus of Nazareth preach. One day, the book says, a crowd of more than 5,000 people gathered and listened to his words, eating nothing.

The crowds remained all day with Jesus, who grew concerned for their well-being. He did not want to send people away without eating. Calling his closest followers, Jesus asked what food they had. All together, they had only five loaves of bread and two fish. Despite these meager portions, Matthew says that Jesus had his followers distribute food to the crowds and, miraculously, there was plenty of food for everyone. None of the people went hungry. ∎

Christianity and Judaism

Over time, the teachings of Jesus of Nazareth developed into a new religion—**Christianity**. Many of those teachings were rooted in the beliefs and customs of Jesus and his earliest followers, the teachings of Judaism.

Judaism in the Roman World In 63 BC, Roman forces under Pompey conquered Judea after months of brutal fighting. As the rulers of Judea, the Romans chose a new ruler for the region and installed him as king. Like other people the Romans conquered, the Jews had to pay tribute to the Romans. Unlike other peoples, however, the Jews were not willing to abandon their religion for the polytheistic religion of the Romans. To avoid trouble, Roman leaders allowed the Jews to practice their religion as long as they paid their tribute and maintained civic order.

Feeding the Masses

▲ **According to the Bible, hungry crowds gathered to hear Jesus preach.**
The Feeding of the Five Thousand, Hendrik de Clerck, c. 1600

183

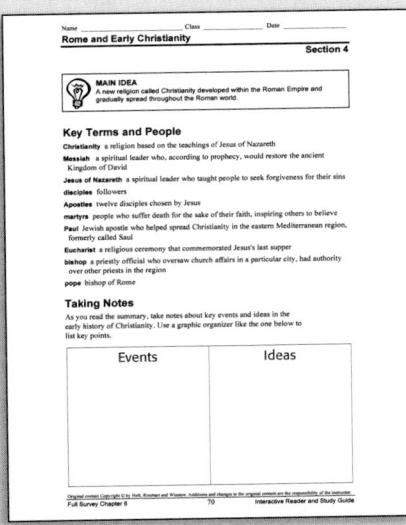

1 How was Christianity rooted in the teachings of Judaism? *Many of the teachings of Jesus teachings were rooted in the beliefs and customs of his childhood, the teachings of Judaism.*

Christianity and Judaism

Identify Which branch of Judaism was vocal about overthrowing Roman Rule? *the Zealots*

Contrast What was different about the Judeans, compared to other conquered peoples of the Roman Empire? *The Judeans were not willing to abandon their religion for the polytheistic religion of the Romans.*

2 What were the teachings of Jesus of Nazareth? *that people must repent and seek forgiveness, love God above all else, love others as they love themselves, and value humility, mercy, and charity*

Jesus of Nazareth

Recall What items make up the Christian Bible? *the New Testament, along with the books of the Hebrew Bible*

Explain Why did authorities arrest Jesus and sentence him to death? *His popularity made them fear political uprisings.*

Answers

Reading Check (left) *refused to give up religion; Zealots wanted to rise up against Roman rule;* **(right)** *Followers must love God above all else, and love others as they loved themselves.*

184

Keep a list of key events and ideas in the early history of Christianity.

Events	Ideas

NEW YORK

CC Unit 1-E1f Origins and major beliefs of Christianity

Reactions to Roman Rule Judaism, however, had many different branches, with varying ideas of whether they should cooperate with the Romans. For example, a group called the Zealots called on their fellow Jews to rise up, drive the Romans from Judea, and re-establish the Kingdom of Israel.

In time Zealots began to form pockets of armed resistance against the Romans of Judea. In response to a mass uprising in AD 66–70, the Romans sacked Jerusalem and killed thousands of Jews. They also destroyed the Second Temple, leaving part of the western wall intact. After another revolt in the 130s, all Jews were banned from Jerusalem entirely.

The Messianic Prophecies Not all Jews in Judea were willing to take up arms against the Romans. Others preferred to wait for the coming of the **Messiah**, a spiritual leader who, according to prophecy, would restore the ancient kingdom and bring peace to the world. As war and chaos rose up around them, many Jews eagerly awaited the Messiah's arrival.

READING CHECK **Make Generalizations** What were two Jewish reactions to Roman rule?

Jesus of Nazareth

Against this turbulent background, a spiritual leader named **Jesus of Nazareth** emerged. The message he taught was not one of armed revolt but of the need for people to seek forgiveness for their sins in preparation for the coming of God's Judgment Day.

Life Nearly all of our knowledge of Jesus comes from the Gospels—the first four books of the New Testament. The New Testament along with the books of the Hebrew Bible today make up the Christian Bible.

The Bible says Jesus was born in the town of Bethlehem, near Jerusalem, and grew up in Nazareth. As a boy, he learned carpentry, but also studied the writings of Jewish prophets.

In time, Jesus began to preach a message of redemption and warning. As he traveled through Judea, he gathered a small group of **disciples**, or followers. According to the biblical account, Jesus created a great deal of excitement by performing miracles of healing and by defending the poor and the oppressed.

184 CHAPTER 6

SACRED TEXTS

The New Testament

About the Reading The Christian Bible is made up of two parts—the Old Testament, which includes the Torah and the other books of the Hebrew Bible, and the New Testament. Included in the New Testament are the Gospels—accounts of the life and teachings of Jesus—the letters of Paul, and other writings by early Christians. This passage from the Gospel of Matthew describes a sermon given by Jesus to a gathering of disciples.

AS YOU READ Note who Jesus says is blessed.

Greek Bible from the 300s ▶

Above all, Jesus instructed people to repent of their sins and seek God's forgiveness. To obtain this forgiveness, he said that people must love God above all else and love others as they love themselves. In addition, they should practice humility, mercy, and charity.

Jesus's popularity and the crowds he drew alarmed authorities, who feared political uprisings. Before long, Jesus was arrested, tried, and sentenced to death.

Death and Resurrection According to the New Testament, after being crucified, or nailed to a cross, and buried, Jesus rose from the dead, spent another 40 days teaching his disciples on Earth, and then ascended into heaven. His followers believed that the Resurrection and Ascension revealed that Jesus was the Messiah. As a result, they called him Jesus Christ, after *Christos*, the Greek word for Messiah.

READING CHECK **Summarize** What was the main message of Jesus's teaching?

Skill Focus: Making Written Presentations

At Level

Reading Like a Historian Skill
First Century Newspapers

Materials: several newspapers, 12"x18" construction paper

1. Have students consider what would have been written in a newspaper about events developing in and around Jerusalem. Tell students they will create an original first century newspaper.

2. Point out to students the various elements of a typical newspaper: masthead, crime reports, community activities, political cartoons, letters to the editor, and so on.

3. Organize students into groups of four to six. Have students in each group divide the tasks among themselves and create sketches for their first drafts. Distribute paper on which students should create their final drafts.

LS **Verbal-Linguistic, Visual-Spatial**

Alternative Assessment Handbook, Rubrics 14: Group Activity; and 23: Newspapers

Then [Jesus] began to speak, and taught them, saying:

"Blessed are the poor in spirit, for theirs is the kingdom of heaven.

"Blessed are those who mourn, for they will be comforted.

"Blessed are the meek, for they will inherit the earth.

"Blessed are the merciful, for they will receive mercy.

"Blessed are the pure in heart, for they will see God.

"Blessed are the peacemakers, for they will be called children of God.

"Blessed are those who are persecuted for righteousness' sake, for theirs is the kingdom of heaven.

"Blessed are you when people revile you and persecute you and utter all kinds of evil against you falsely on my account. Rejoice and be glad, for your reward is great in heaven, for in the same way they persecuted the prophets who were before you.

"You are the salt of the earth; but if salt has lost its taste, how can its saltiness be restored? It is no longer good for anything, but is thrown out and trampled under foot.

"You are the light of the world. A city built on a hill cannot be hid. No one after lighting a lamp puts it under the bushel basket, but on the lampstand, and it gives light to all in the house. In the same way, let your light shine before others, so that they may see your good works and give glory to your Father in heaven."

—Matthew 5:1–16, NRSV

Analyze How does this passage support Jesus's emphasis on humility, mercy, and charity?

▲ Volunteers assemble Braille Bibles that can be read by Christians who are blind or visually impaired.

The Spread of Christianity

After Jesus's death, his disciples began teaching that all people could achieve salvation—the forgiveness of sins and the promise of everlasting life. Believing that God's judgment was close at hand, the disciples urgently set out to spread this message of salvation.

Among those who worked to spread Jesus's message were 12 disciples whom Jesus had specially chosen. Called the **Apostles**, these 12 men were the earliest Christian missionaries. Later, the term *apostle* was also applied to others who worked to spread Christianity. The first apostles traveled widely, teaching about Jesus's message. For the most part, they only taught in Jewish communities.

Paul of Tarsus Had it not been for the work of a Jewish apostle named **Paul**, Christianity might have remained a branch of Judaism. Paul, who was originally known as Saul, was born in the town of Tarsus in Asia Minor. As a young man, he had actively opposed those teaching that Jesus was the Messiah. During a trip to Damascus, however, Paul had a conversion experience and became a Christian.

Unlike many other early Christians, who thought only Jews should hear the teachings of Jesus, Paul believed that God had sent him to convert non-Jews, or Gentiles. With this mission in mind, Paul helped make Christianity a broader religion, attracting many new followers. Paul helped establish Christian churches throughout the eastern Mediterranean. His Epistles, or letters, to these churches later became part of the New Testament.

Finding that some Jewish customs, such as food prohibitions, were hindering missionary work among non-Jews, Paul dispensed with them as requirements for Christians. In place of these regulations, Paul emphasized new doctrines that helped distinguish Christianity from Judaism.

ROME AND EARLY CHRISTIANITY **185**

Reading Focus

3 How did Christianity spread throughout the Roman world? *Paul transformed Christianity, and with other disciples, established Christian churches throughout the eastern Mediterranean. Constantine's conversion led to Christians becoming the religious majority in the Roman world.*

The Spread of Christianity

Explain Why did disciples urgently set out to spread the message of salvation? *because they believed that God's judgment was close at hand*

Make Inferences Why do you suppose so many disciples worked to spread the message, given that they were often in danger? *possible answer—They may have thought their deaths would inspire others to believe, and they probably believed it was very important to spread Jesus's teachings.*

Evaluate Which of Paul's actions do you think was the most important to making Christianity a universal religion? Why? *possible answer—He dispensed with some of the Jewish customs, such as food prohibitions, which eased bringing non-Jews into the faith.*

📃 **CRF:** Biography: Mary Magdalene

Info to Know

Crucifixion The New Testament states that Jesus was crucified and historians believe that crucifixion was a common form of execution in ancient Rome. This cruel and inhumane type of punishment left its victims nailed to a cross and left to bleed to death, sometimes for as long as a week.

Skills Focus: Analyzing Secondary Sources
At Level

Reading Like a Historian Skill
Matthew's Message

1. Have students read the passage on this page from the Gospel of Matthew.

2. Organize students into small groups. Have each group discuss and record the following: genre, subject, author's point of view, and the final paragraph's main point.

3. When groups are ready, ask volunteers to share the answers that their group recorded.

4. Have students write a paragraph evaluating the significance of this writing as documentation of this event in Jesus's life.
LS Interpersonal, Verbal-Linguistic

📃 **Alternative Assessment Handbook**, Rubrics 14: Group Activity; and 16: Judging Information

Answers

World Religions *All those listed as blessed are humble, merciful, or charitable, or their condition would inspire that quality to surface in other people.*

The Spread of Christianity

Identify Which Roman tradition contributed to the spread of Christianity? *religious toleration*

Identify Cause and Effect What is the relationship between Theodosius and the end of polytheism? *He outlawed all non-Christian religious ceremonies, which made polytheism gradually disappear from the empire.*

Predict What do you imagine might have happened had Constantine not become Christian? *possible answers— Christianity would not have spread so rapidly; there would have been more persecution*

Biography

Theodosius (346–395) Born in Spain, Theodosius gained experience in military campaigns, eventually becoming commander, and then governor. After suffering from an illness that almost killed him, Theodosius was baptized. In the same year, he outlawed other religions. Theodosius the Great was the final emperor to reign over a united Roman Empire, dividing the empire to be ruled by his two sons.

Interpreting Maps
The Spread of Christianity

Movement On which journey did Paul visit Cyprus? *his first*

 Map Transparency: The Spread of Christianity

Roman Christianity Through the work of Paul and others, Christianity spread through the Roman world. There were many reasons for this growth. The Christian message of love and eternal life after death, regardless of social position, appealed to many. Roman religious toleration also contributed to its spread. Historians estimate that by about 300, some 10 percent of the Roman people were Christian.

 NEW YORK
CC Unit 1-E2
Spread of Christianity

Persecution As Christianity spread through the Roman world, some local officials feared that the Christians were conspiring against them. As a result, they arrested and killed many Christians. However, those killed were seen by the early Christians as **martyrs**, people who die for their faith and thus inspire others to believe. Even many nonbelievers were impressed by the martyrs' faith.

Although Christians often were persecuted at the local level, large-scale persecution by the Romans was rare during the first two centuries after Jesus's life. As it grew, however, some rulers came to see Christianity as a threat and began persecuting those who practiced it.

Imperial Approval The spread of Christianity through Rome was hastened by the conversion of the emperor Constantine to the religion in the early 300s. His conversion was apparently triggered by a vision that he claimed to have experienced just before a battle in 312. Before the battle, tradition says that the emperor saw a cross of light in the sky inscribed with the words "In this sign, conquer." After winning the battle, Constantine became a patron of Christianity. In 313 he issued the Edict of Milan, which made Christianity legal within the empire. Although Constantine did not actually ban the practice of other religions, his support for Christianity helped it to spread more rapidly through the Roman Empire.

Thus, from a tiny religious minority, Christians eventually grew to constitute a majority of the population. In 391 Emperor Theodosius outlawed public non-Christian sacrifices and religious ceremonies. As a result, polytheism gradually disappeared from the empire.

READING CHECK **Find the Main Idea** What helped spread Christianity through the Roman world?

THE SPREAD OF CHRISTIANITY

Christian areas, AD 300
Christian areas, AD 500
Boundary of Roman Empire, AD 395
← Paul's first journey
← Paul's second journey
← Paul's third journey
← Paul's fourth journey

EUROPE
GAUL
Tours
ATLANTIC OCEAN
SPAIN
Toledo
Corsica
Sardinia
ITALY
Rome
Sicily
Carthage
Malta
GREECE
Athens
Corinth
Crete
Constantinople
Nicaea
ASIA MINOR
Derbe
Tarsus
Antioch
Cyprus
SYRIA
Damascus
Black Sea
ASIA
Mediterranean Sea
Jerusalem
Alexandria
AFRICA
EGYPT
Red Sea

GEOGRAPHY SKILLS **INTERPRETING MAPS**

1. **Place** Did Christianity reach Alexandria before or after the year 300?
2. **Location** Where did Paul travel on his last journey?

0   300   600 Miles
0   300   600 Kilometers
Azimuthal equal-area projection

Skills Focus: Analyzing Maps

At Level

Social Studies Skill
Where Did Christianity Spread?

Materials: current wall map of the Mediterranean region, including northern Africa, Europe, and Asia; black line masters of the region

1. Tell students that the spread of Christianity affected the development of arts and architecture across the western world. Explain that they will discover which modern nations cover these areas.

2. Distribute black line masters. Have students refer to the map on this page and mark the boundary Christian areas reached by AD 500. Students should darken this border in red.

3. Next, have students draw the borders of present-day countries of the region.

4. Have students write a short paragraph describing what visitors might expect to see in these areas. **LS Visual-Spatial, Verbal-Linguistic**

Alternative Assessment Handbook, Rubrics 12: Drawing Conclusions; 21: Map Reading; and 42: Writing to Inform

Answers

Interpreting Maps 1. *before;* **2.** *from Jerusalem to Tarsus, to Crete, to Malta, to Rome*

Reading Check *the work of Paul and other disciples; the Edict of Milan; and the outlawing of other religions by Theodosius*

The Early Christian Church

The earliest Christian churches were not only spiritual organizations but also close-knit communities. These communities provided all kinds of support for their members, from burial services to food and shelter for the sick and poor. As Christianity grew and spread, however, its organization became more complex.

Part of the growing complexity came from the development of ceremonies that inspired people's faith and make them feel closer to Jesus. One such ceremony was the **Eucharist**, held in memory of Jesus's last supper with his disciples. During the Eucharist, Christians eat bread and drank wine in memory of Jesus's death and Resurrection. Another was baptism, by which people were admitted to the faith.

By about 100, priests trained in these ceremonies became prominent within Christianity. The authority of these priests was based on the authority given to the Apostles by Jesus. This spiritual authority distinguished the priests from the laity, or people who belonged to the general congregation of the Church.

As the church expanded, it began to develop an administrative structure. The most important official of the early Christian Church was the **bishop**. Bishops emerged to oversee church affairs in most cities and had authority over all other priests within the city. By the 300s the heads of the oldest and largest Christian congregations in Rome, Jerusalem, Antioch, Alexandria, and Constantinople were called patriarchs, and claimed spiritual authority over other bishops.

Many Christians believed that Peter the Apostle had founded the Roman Church and acted as its first bishop. As a result, later bishops of Rome, or **popes**, were seen as Peter's spiritual heirs. The popes interpreted a verse from the Gospel of Matthew, in which Jesus gives Peter the keys of the kingdom of heaven, to mean that all future popes would inherit the keys as well. They argued that all bishops should acknowledge the authority of the pope as the head of the entire church. Though other patriarchs did not at first recognize the pope's claims of supremacy, over time popes gained more influence within the Christian Church.

READING CHECK **Summarize** How did the Christian Church change as it grew?

Catacombs
Early Christians built elaborate burial chambers called catacombs under the city of Rome.

SECTION 4 ASSESSMENT

go.hrw.com
Online Quiz
Keyword: SHL ROM HP

Reviewing Ideas, Terms, and People

1. a. Define What was the **Messiah** for whom some Jews were waiting?
b. Sequence What happened to the Jews of Judea after the destruction of the Second Temple in AD 70?

2. a. Recall What do Christians believe happened to **Jesus of Nazareth** after he died?
b. Summarize How did Jesus say people should live?

3. a. Identify Who were the **martyrs**, and why were they honored?
b. Explain How did Constantine help **Christianity** gain a firm foothold in the Roman Empire?
c. Elaborate Why was **Paul** a key figure in the early history and development of Christianity?

4. a. Describe What types of officials developed in the early Christian church?
b. Explain Why did the **pope**, as the bishop of Rome, claim to have authority over all other bishops?

Critical Thinking

5. Sequence Draw a time line like the one below. Use your notes to identify the sequence of key events in the spread of Christianity through the Roman Empire.

←———|———|———|———→

FOCUS ON WRITING

6. Description Write a short description of the organization of the early Christian church. Be sure to include key officials in the church, their main responsibilities, and a statement about how their roles changed over time.

ROME AND EARLY CHRISTIANITY **187**

Section 4 Assessment Answers

1. a. a spiritual leader who would restore the ancient kingdom
b. Jews were banned from Jerusalem.

2. a. He rose from the dead.
b. love God above all else; love others as they love themselves; and practice humility, mercy, and charity

3. a. disciples who were honored for having suffered death for the sake of their faith
b. made Christianity legal
c. made changes that eased the spread of Christianity among non-Jews

4 a. priests, bishops, and the pope
b. by interpreting the Gospel of Matthew

5. AD 6: Zealots resist Roman forces; mid-to late first century: Disciples spread Christianity throughout Judea; AD 66-70: Zealots rebel in Jerusalem; 130s: all Jews banned from Jerusalem; 300: Paul spreads Christianity to Rome; 313: Constantine issues Edict of Milan; 391: Theodosius outlaws all religions but Christianity

6. Students should describe duties of priests, bishops, and popes.

● Direct Teach ●

Reading Focus

④ What was the early Christian church like? *spiritual organizations that acted as close-knit communities; developed special ceremonies and rituals; priests became a special class within Christianity; bishops had authority over priests; bishop of Rome became pope*

The Early Christian Church

Identify Who was likely the founder of the Roman church? *Peter the Apostle*

Identify Cause and Effect What were the expected effects of special Christian ceremonies and rituals? *inspired people's faith and made them feel closer to Christ*

Contrast In what way were the priests distinguished from the laity? *They derived their authority from Christ through the apostles.*

● Review & Assess ●

Close
Review the development and spread of Christianity within the Roman world.

Review

Online Quiz, Section 4

Assess

SE Section 4 Assessment

Progress Assessment: Section 4 Quiz

Alternative Assessment Handbook

Reteach/Intervene

Interactive Reader and Study Guide, Section 4

Interactive Skills Tutor CD-ROM

Answers

Reading Check *Special ceremonies and rituals developed; priests became a special class within Christianity; bishops had authority over priests; the bishop of Rome became a pope.*

187

Getting Started

Use the **Interactive Reader and Study Guide** to familiarize students with the section content.

📕 **Interactive Reader and Study Guide,** Section 5

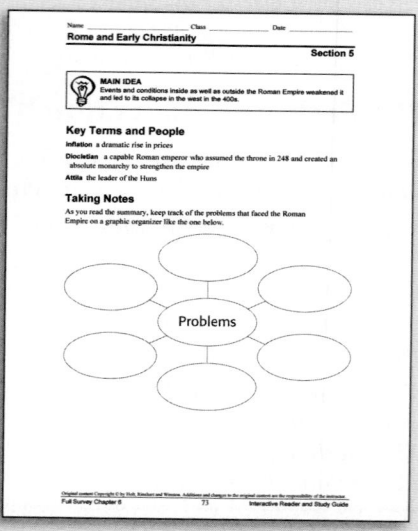

Academic Vocabulary

Review with students the high-use academic term in this section.

revenue money that a government uses to pay for public programs (p. 189)

📓 **CRF: Vocabulary Builder: Section 5**

Taking Notes

weak leaders, economic problems, and threats of invasion; series of military emperors, an increase in violent crime, and Rome stopped expanding; Diocletian made drastic reforms to increase army and protect Rome and its economy; Constantine converted to Christianity and built new capital in the east; Central Asian tribes pushed Germanic tribes who fled and eventually sacked empire; Pope Leo I persuaded Attila not to sack the city; Odoacer overthrew the last western emperor

---

SECTION 5

The Fall of Rome

BEFORE YOU READ

MAIN IDEA

Events and conditions inside as well as outside the Roman Empire weakened it and led to its collapse in the west in the 400s.

READING FOCUS

1. What problems weakened the empire in the 200s?
2. How did Diocletian and Constantine attempt to reform the empire?
3. What caused the invasion and ultimate fall of the empire in the 400s?

KEY TERMS AND PEOPLE

inflation
Diocletian
Attila

 NEW YORK

P1 1.1 Students explain how civilizations changed over time.
1.4 Students understand the broad patterns, relationships, and interactions of cultures and civilizations during particular eras.

LAST CHANCE FOR PEACE

◀ **Pope Leo I, called the Great, convinced the Huns not to invade Rome.**

The Meeting of Attila the Hun and Pope Leo I, by Raphael, 1511

THE INSIDE STORY

Could one man stop an invading army? In 452 a fierce army was headed toward Rome. They were the Huns, the most fearsome warriors the Romans had ever encountered. Unfortunately, the Roman army was in no state to stop them, and it seemed the Huns would destroy Rome itself.

In a desperate attempt to stop the Huns, Pope Leo I, the head of the Christian Church, rode out to meet them. Accompanied by only a few men, none of whom were warriors, he asked for a private audience with the leader of the Huns, the frightening Attila. The two men met on the shores of Lake Garda, in northern Italy. No one knows what they said to each other, but Attila and his army did not proceed any farther into Italy. Whatever Leo said, his words had managed to stop the invasion. ■

The Empire Weakens

The inability of the Roman army to stop the Huns was one symptom of the weakness that befell the empire after the end of the Pax Romana. After 180, the empire was confronted not only by challenges from outside but also by growing problems within.

Weak Leaders When the last of the Good Emperors died, Rome was left without a strong leader. The eventual result was a series of civil wars.

Part of the problem was that Rome found itself under increasing threat of invasion by tribal peoples along both the eastern and western frontiers. To meet this growing threat, emperors increased the size of Rome's army. Soon the growing demands on both the empire's

188 CHAPTER 6

Teach the Main Idea

At Level

The Fall of Rome

Prep Required

Materials: 8 ½"x11" unlined paper, a variety of political cartoons

1. **Teach** Ask students the Reading Focus questions to teach this section.

2. **Apply** Show students a variety of political cartoons. Emphasize that these types of cartoons are often characterized by exaggeration to convey a certain point of view. Tell students they will create their own political cartoon based on an issue or event in this section that led to the fall of Rome.

3. **Review** Have volunteers share their cartoons. Guide students in a discussion about the significance of the event or issue to which each cartoon relates.

4. **Practice/Homework** Have students write a one-paragraph explanation of their cartoons and the role the event or issue played in the fall of Rome. 📘 **Verbal-Linguistic, Visual-Spatial**

📗 **Alternative Assessment Handbook**, Rubric 27: Political Cartoons financial resources and its military caused a serious and prolonged economic crisis. This crisis lessened the stability and prosperity Rome had enjoyed during the Pax Romana.

As the crisis continued, the empire became a kind of military dictatorship. The legions had become the center of power, as they deposed emperors and elevated their own leaders to the throne. Twenty emperors ruled between 235 and 284; all but one died violently.

Economic Troubles The insecurity of civil wars and invasions affected many aspects of Roman life. Robbery and piracy increased, and travel became hazardous. Merchants feared to ship goods. Military needs required ever-increasing amounts of <u>revenue</u>, and to collect more money, emperors raised taxes.

As taxes rose, however, the value of money declined. Since Rome was no longer expanding, conquests no longer brought in new sources of wealth. To maintain the money supply, emperors minted new coins with copper and lead as well as silver. When people realized coins contained less silver, they refused to accept the currency at its face value. The result was growing **inflation**, or a dramatic rise in prices.

READING CHECK **Analyze** What problems faced Rome in the late 200s?

Attempts at Reform

The crises of the 200s shattered the Roman world. Drastic reforms had to be made if the empire were to survive. As luck would have it, two capable emperors rose to power and gave the empire another two centuries of life.

Diocletian The first of these emperors was **Diocletian** (dy-uh-KLEE-shuhn), who took power in 284. To slow the empire's decline, Diocletian changed the empire into an absolute monarchy. He placed himself far above his subjects and ruled with no accountability to anyone.

As part of his efforts to improve the efficiency of imperial administration, Diocletian divided the empire in two. Ruling the eastern half himself, he appointed a co-emperor to rule the western provinces. Both emperors named assistants, called Caesars, who were supposed to help run the empire.

Diocletian also forced Roman society into a rigid order. Almost every aspect of life was regulated by the imperial administration. Under Diocletian's decrees, sons were supposed to follow the trades and social positions of their fathers. Peasants were to be permanently tied to the land they farmed. In addition, Diocletian increased the army and gave the defense of the empire the bulk of his attention.

TAKING NOTES
As you read, keep track of the problems that faced the Roman Empire.

Problems

ACADEMIC VOCABULARY
revenue money that a government uses to pay for public programs

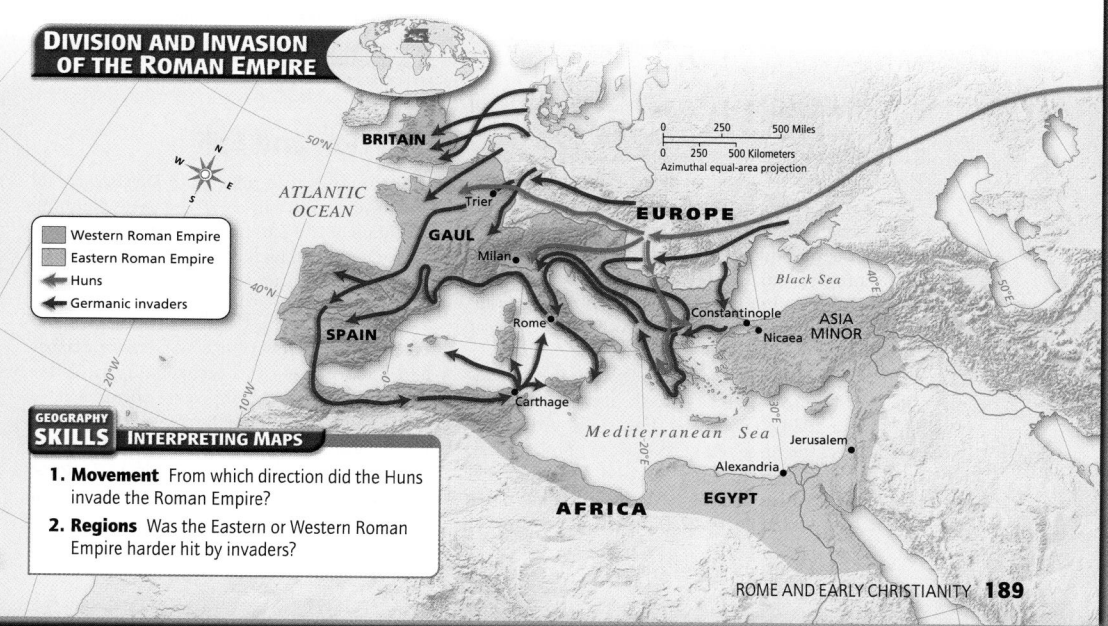

DIVISION AND INVASION OF THE ROMAN EMPIRE

0   250   500 Miles
0   250   500 Kilometers
Azimuthal equal-area projection

- Western Roman Empire
- Eastern Roman Empire
- Huns
- Germanic invaders

BRITAIN
ATLANTIC OCEAN
Trier
GAUL
Milan
EUROPE
Black Sea
Constantinople
Nicaea
ASIA MINOR
SPAIN
Rome
Carthage
Mediterranean Sea
Jerusalem
Alexandria
AFRICA
EGYPT

GEOGRAPHY SKILLS **INTERPRETING MAPS**

1. **Movement** From which direction did the Huns invade the Roman Empire?
2. **Regions** Was the Eastern or Western Roman Empire harder hit by invaders?

ROME AND EARLY CHRISTIANITY **189**

Reading Focus

1 What problems weakened the empire in the 200s? *weak leaders; economic problems, such as inflation; civil wars; threats of invasion*

The Empire Weakens

Explain Why did Rome need to increase its army? *to protect it from the growing threat of invasion*

Identify Cause and Effect What problems were a direct result of robbery and piracy? *Travel became hazardous and merchants feared to ship goods.*

Map Transparency: Division and Invasion of the Roman Empire

Reading Focus

2 How did Diocletian and Constantine attempt to reform the empire? *Diocletian—made drastic reforms to increase army and protect Rome and its economy; Constantine—converted to Christianity and built new capital in the east*

Attempts at Reform

Recall What new type of government did Diocletian create for Rome? *an absolute monarchy*

Rate What do you think most Romans thought of Diocletian? *possible answer—They probably thought he was a power-hungry ruler because he created so much bureaucracy and eliminated many personal freedoms.*

Skills Focus: Interpreting Movement Maps

Above Level

Social Studies Skills
Meet the Huns

Research Required

1. Ask students to compare the routes of the Germanic Invaders to those of the Huns on the map above.

2. Organize students into small groups. Have groups analyze the map and discuss possible explanations for the routes of the Hun invasions.

3. Have groups conduct research about the Huns' invasion routes. Tell students to use reliable online sources and to document bibliographic information as they go.

4. Have students prepare a brief oral presentation about their findings. Tell students they may use electronic visuals, hand-drawn or copied maps, and other materials. Allow sufficient time for each group to give their presentation. **LS** Interpersonal, Verbal-Linguistic

Alternative Assessment Handbook, Rubrics 24: Oral Presentations; and 30: Research

Answers

Interpreting Maps 1. *east;* **2.** *the western half*

Reading Check *The empire had weak leaders, civil wars, threats of invasion, and inflation led to a weak economy. Piracy and robbery made travel hazardous.*

Attempts at Reform

Explain Why did Diocletian and his co-emperor decide to retire at the same time? *so the two caesars could rise to become co-emperors at the same time*

Evaluate Do you think the steps Diocletian took to save the empire from collapse was worth the price? *possible answer—No; although he saved the empire from immediate collapse, in the long term, the reforms weakened the empire dramatically.*

3 What caused the invasion and ultimate fall of the empire in the 400s? *Many Germanic tribes, fleeing from the Huns and the Vandals, attacked Rome from North Africa. These attacks, and the economic instability and weak leadership of the empire, caused its collapse.*

Invasion and Fall

Recall What caused the Germanic tribes to invade the empire? *People from Central Asia began to move west, pushing the Germanic tribes into the empire.*

Judge What do you think about the tactics used by the Huns and the Vandals to conquer new lands? *possible answer—They were barbaric and unethical, because both tribes were destructive and violent with little regard for innocent human lives.*

FORENSICS in History

Did Disease Cause Rome's Fall?

Historians do not think disease alone caused the fall of Rome, but some think it may have helped. Some evidence suggests that a malaria epidemic swept through and weakened the Roman Empire in the 400s.

What facts do we have? The first hint that malaria may have struck Rome was found in a graveyard in the town of Lugnano, just outside Rome. Several young children had been buried there inside clay jars. Acting on a hunch, scientists tested the bodies' DNA and found traces of malaria. An outbreak of malaria in Italy could have reduced the population so much that harvesting crops and raising soldiers for the army would have been impossible.

Malaria is a tropical disease. How then did it strike Italy, which lies well north of the tropics? Historians speculate that traders who traveled to Africa became infected and brought the disease back with them. In addition, the larvae of mosquitoes—the carriers of malaria—could easily have lived in the water supplies of merchant ships.

Summarize How could disease have helped Rome's fall?

► A child's skeleton found at Lugnano

The imperial economy also came under state direction. Everywhere, commercial and manufacturing activities were geared toward the needs of imperial defense. A new tax system raised more money for the government and for the army. Though drastic, these reforms were successful, saving the empire from immediate economic collapse.

Constantine As long as Diocletian remained emperor, these arrangements worked reasonably well. However, in 305 he decided to abdicate. His co-emperor also retired so that the two Caesars could rise to become co-emperors at the same time. It was not long before the new emperors quarreled, and the empire plunged into civil war. Order was not restored until 312 when Constantine, the son of one of the original Caesars, was proclaimed the new emperor by his troops and put an end to the fighting.

Constantine continued Diocletian's policies of state control over society. At the same time, he made two decisions that would profoundly affect the direction of the future empire. First, as you have already learned, he supported Christianity. Second, he built a new capital—Constantinople, or "the city of Constantine"—

NEW YORK
CC Unit 1-D2d
Causes of the decline of Rome

on the site of the tiny village of Byzantium. It was located on the shore of the Bosporus, the strait separating Europe from Asia. Because the eastern half of the empire was richer and better defended than the west, Constantine wanted his capital located there.

READING CHECK **Analyze** How did Diocletian and Constantine try to save Rome?

Invasion and Fall

Unfortunately, the reforms of Diocletian and Constantine did not solve the overwhelming problems of the empire. During the 300s and 400s, these problems were only worsened by tribal peoples' increasing pressures on the empire's frontier.

The Invaders For centuries Germanic tribes had lived along—and occasionally raided—Rome's frontiers. As new peoples began to move west from Central Asia, however, they pushed these Germanic tribes into the empire. In the face of such challenges, rulers in both Rome and Constantinople tried desperately to hold the crumbling Roman Empire together.

190 CHAPTER 6

Skills Focus: Analyzing Alternative Points of View   At Level

Reading Like a Historian Skill
Diocletian Reform Debates

1. Remind students that Roman citizens often participated in their government. At the Forum, some of Diocletian's reforms may have been discussed. Tell students they will debate some of these reform ideas.

2. Organize students into three groups. Assign each group one of the following topics: The empire shall be split in two. Sons will follow the trades and social positions of their fathers. Peasants must remain on the land they farm.

3. Tell each group to organize its members into two groups: one will defend the statement, and one will oppose it.

4. When students are ready, have each group debate its assigned topic. **LS** **Interpersonal, Verbal-Linguistic**

   Alternative Assessment Handbook, Rubrics 10: Debates; and 11: Discussions

---

Answers

Forensics in History *An outbreak of malaria, carried by traders and in the supplies of merchant ships from North Africa, may have made harvesting crops and increasing the army impossible.*

Reading Check *Diocletian—tried to make governmental and economic reforms and build up the army; Constantine—moved capital to the eastern half of the empire*

In the late 300s a nomadic Central Asian people, the Huns, stormed out of the east and sent the Germanic tribes fleeing. Imperial defenses in the east managed to hold, but those in the west were soon overwhelmed. The speed and ferocity of the Huns struck terror in the people they attacked.

Under strong leadership, the Huns formed a vast empire among the nomadic steppe peoples of Eurasia. About 370 they attacked the Ostrogoths, a Germanic people living north of the Black Sea. This assault frightened the Visigoths, kinsmen of the Ostrogoths, and sent them fleeing into the Roman Empire and even into Italy. In 410 the Christian Visigothic king Alaric captured and sacked Rome itself.

Pushed by the Huns, other migrating tribes also soon attacked the Roman Empire. One group, the Vandals, crossed into North Africa, attacking Rome in the 450s. The Vandals were so infamous for destroying everything in their path that the term *vandal* came to mean "one who causes senseless destruction."

In the mid-400s **Attila** (AT-uhl-uh), the leader of the Huns, led an attack on Gaul. The Roman army alone could not repel him, so they allied with the Visigoths and defeated the Huns in a great battle in 451. Withdrawing from Gaul, Attila turned on Rome itself. Before the Huns reached the city, though, Pope Leo I persuaded Attila to leave Italy.

Fall of the West Despite the Huns' withdrawal, in their wake the Western Empire lay in a shambles. Germanic tribes ruled most of the western provinces, including Italy itself. Finally, in 476 the barbarian commander Odoacer (oh-doh-AY-suhr) overthrew the last emperor in the west. Many historians consider this the end of the Western Roman Empire.

Though the empire in the west collapsed, the Eastern Empire did not. It endured for several centuries. The people of the Eastern Empire always thought of themselves as Romans, but over time other influences, especially Greek, crept into their culture as well. As a result, historians refer to the later period of the Eastern Roman Empire by a new name, the Byzantine Empire. You will learn more about the Byzantines in a later chapter.

READING CHECK **Identify Cause and Effect** How did invaders contribute to Rome's fall?

CAUSES AND EFFECTS OF THE FALL OF ROME

CAUSES
- Weak leadership after AD 200
- Economic crises
- Social unrest and insecurity
- Invasions

EFFECTS
- In the west, the disappearance of central authority and the creation of small kingdoms
- In the east, the continuation of the Roman Empire ruled from Constantinople

---

SECTION 5 ASSESSMENT

go.hrw.com
Online Quiz
Keyword: SHL ROM HP

Reviewing Ideas, Terms, and People

1. **a. Describe** What problems faced the Roman Empire in the 200s?
   b. Explain What led to the rise of **inflation** in Rome?
   c. Elaborate Why do you think the growing influence of the military in choosing emperors was bad for Rome?

2. **a. Identify** What new capital did Constantine build for the empire? Why did he build it where he did?
   b. Draw Conclusions Why did **Diocletian** divide the Roman Empire?
   c. Evaluate Do you think Diocletian was justified in limiting people's freedoms to protect the empire? Defend your answer.

3. **a. Identify** Who was **Attila**, and why was he feared?
   b. Sequence What events made it possible for the Ostrogoths to conquer Rome?
   c. Make Judgments Do you think Rome would have fallen to invaders if it had not been weakened by other factors? Why or why not?

Critical Thinking

4. **Rate** Draw a chart like the one shown here. Using your notes, list in order of importance (from most important to least) the major problems or factors that contributed to Rome's fall. Next to each factor, write a sentence explaining the effect of that problem or factor.

Factor	Effect

FOCUS ON WRITING

5. **Persuasion** Write a letter as though you were an adviser to Constantine. In your letter, you must advise him either to move the empire's capital or to keep it at Rome. Support your argument with facts and examples.

ROME AND EARLY CHRISTIANITY **191**

Section 5 Assessment Answers

1. **a.** weak leaders, civil wars, threats of invasion, weak economy
   b. coins minted from less valuable metals
   c. possible answer—Military rulers deposed or killed so regime did not last, leaving empire vulnerable, weakening the army

2. **a.** Constantinople; eastern half of empire was richer and better defended than the west
   b. so he could rule one half and delegate co-emperors to run the other
   c. possible answer—No, such limitations caused unrest among the Romans.

3. **a.** a strong leader of the fierce Huns; led many successful attacks before coming to Rome
   b. previous invasions by Huns, Visigoths, Ostrogoths, and Vandals
   c. possible answer—No, political and economic factors caused it to fall. Their formerly strong army could have held off the invaders.

4. Student charts will vary but factors should include weak leaders, civil wars, economic troubles, and invasions.

5. possible answer—move the capital; new location easeir to defend; keep at Rome

Word Help

mere apart from anything else, pure
corruption inducement to wrong by bribery or other unlawful or improper means
apprehension suspicion or fear

Teaching Tip

Ask students what Thomas Jefferson meant when he referred to the Founding Fathers. Have students name the ones they know and review their accomplishments as a class.

Rome's Legacy

Historical Context The four documents below explore the enduring influence of Rome and Roman institutions on the world long after the end of the empire.

Task Study the selections and answer the questions that follow. After you have studied all the documents, you will be asked to write an essay explaining Rome's lasting legacy. You will need to use evidence from these selections and from Chapter 6 to support the position you take in your essay.

NEW YORK STANDARDS

PI 1.2 Students understand the development and connectedness of Western civilization and other civilizations and cultures in many areas of the world and over time.

DOCUMENT 1

A Republican Legacy

The Founding Fathers of the United States were quite familiar with Roman government and used it as a model for the republican government they created. In a letter to John Adams in 1796, Thomas Jefferson expressed a hope that the U.S. government could be like the early Roman one.

> This I hope will be the age of experiments in government, and that their basis will be founded on principles of honesty, not of mere force. We have seen no instance of this since the days of the Roman republic, nor do we read of any before that. Either force or corruption has been the principle of every modern government, unless the Dutch perhaps be excepted, and I am not well enough informed to except them absolutely. If ever the morals of a people could be made the basis of their own government, it is our case; and he who could propose to govern such a people by the corruption of their legislature, before he could have one night of quiet sleep, must convince himself that the human soul as well as body is mortal. I am glad to see that whatever grounds of apprehension may have appeared of a wish to govern us otherwise than on principles of reason and honesty, we are getting the better of them.

DOCUMENT 2

An Engineering Legacy

The Romans left behind a huge body of engineering knowledge as well as completed engineering projects. Ancient roads like the one shown here run through the former Roman world. Some 2,000 years after they were built, some of these roads still carry travelers. Perhaps more importantly, Roman construction techniques influenced how people built structures for centuries. The small image is a diagram showing the layers in which Roman roads were constructed.

Skills Focus: Analyzing Primary Sources

At Level

Reading Like a Historian Skill
Understanding Jeffersonian English

Standard English Mastery

1. Read Document 1 aloud to students. Explain that this style of writing was the mark of an educated individual. Point out that very little punctuation was used to break up long sentences. Tell students they will rewrite the document in their own words.

2. Organize students into small groups. Have groups copy each sentence at the top of a sheet of paper. Have students in each group divide the papers among themselves and write possible rewording below each sentence. Caution students to avoid changing the meaning.

3. Have students in each group review each others' work and make improvements as necessary.

4. Have students write a short paragraph about how this project increased their comprehension.
   LS Interpersonal, Verbal-Linguistic

   Alternative Assessment Handbook, Rubrics 14: Group Activity; and 37: Writing Assignments

DOCUMENT 3

A Social Legacy

Historians have long noted the social influence of Rome on later European society. Historian, C. Warren Hollister, described this influence in his book *Roots of the Western Tradition* (1966).

Notwithstanding the collapse of imperial government, the decline of cities, and the victory of a great Near Eastern religion, Greco-Roman culture never really died in the West. It exerted a profound influence on the fourth-century Doctors of the Latin Church and, through them, on the thought of medieval and early modern Europe. Even the Roman administration survived, through the Middle Ages and beyond, in the organizational structure of the Church. Just as papal Rome echoed imperial Rome, so too did the ecclesiastical 'dioceses' and 'provinces,' headed by bishops and archbishops, reflect imperial administrative units that had borne identical names . . . The Latin tongue remained the language of educated Europeans for well over a thousand years, while evolving in the lower levels of society into the Romance languages: Italian, French, Spanish, Portuguese, and Romanian. And the dream of imperial Rome has obsessed empire builders from Charlemagne to Napoleon.

DOCUMENT 4

A Popular Culture Legacy

The enduring legacy of Rome is not seen only in major areas like government and law. British historians Peter Jones and Keith Sidwell noted that Rome's influence extends into popular culture as well. They noted some of this influence in the 1997 book *The World of Rome*.

Roman subjects have had a continuing appeal for cinema audiences. One thinks of *Ben-Hur* and *Spartacus*, for example, which established our view of galleys and chariot-races indelibly . . . There have been many novels devoted to Roman subjects. The best-known in English, perhaps, are Robert Graves' *I, Claudius* and *Claudius the God* . . . But it is not only the large-scale which shows the deep penetration of our consciousness by Roman images (even if these are merely images of images). All around, we can see trivial examples of this impact. There are Roman-style porticoes on fast-food stores and statue niches on minute houses on large estates. There are togas and gladiators in Bugs Bunny cartoons . . . For all this, the world of Rome is ultimately responsible.

Skills FOCUS — READING LIKE A HISTORIAN

DOCUMENT 1
a. Describe How does Jefferson describe the government of the Roman Republic?
b. Interpret What evidence in this letter suggests that Jefferson wanted to model the new U.S. government after that of ancient Rome?

DOCUMENT 2
a. Explain Based on the diagram shown here, what steps did the Romans take to make their roads long-lasting?
b. Draw Conclusions Why do you think Europeans wanted to learn and copy ancient Roman engineering techniques?

DOCUMENT 3
a. Identify What are three areas in which Hollister saw Rome's enduring influence in Europe?

b. Interpret What does Hollister mean when he says that Greco-Roman culture never disappeared?

DOCUMENT 4
a. Recall How do Jones and Sidwell say that Rome has influenced movies and literature?
b. Elaborate What do the authors think it means that Roman images are common in modern society?

DOCUMENT-BASED ESSAY QUESTION

What is Rome's cultural legacy? Using the documents above and information from the chapter, form a thesis that summarizes Rome's influence. Then write a short essay to support your position.

See **Skills Handbook**, pp. H25–26, H30

Skills Focus: Drawing Inferences

At Level

Critical Thinking Skill
Ancient Rome's Influence

1. Remind students that the legacy of ancient Rome is far reaching. Tell students they will list ways that their own lives are influenced by ancient Rome.

2. Have students brainstorm to create a personal list of all the ways that their lives might somehow be connected to Roman concepts, ideas, or materials. Suggest that students consider things such as their clothing, money, faith, student government, and moral values.

3. Allow students to exchange their lists to give each other ideas.

4. Have students write a short essay about the different ways their lives are influenced by Roman concepts or ideas. **LS Intrapersonal, Verbal-Linguistic**

Alternative Assessment Handbook, Rubric 41: Writing to Express

---

Word Help

ecclesiastical of or relating to a church

indelibly inability to be removed or erased; permanently

penetration the ability to discern or understand clearly

Info to Know

The Adventures of Asterix Writer René Goscinny and cartoonist Albert Uderzo bring history to life in their series of children's books, *The Adventures of Asterix*. Since their first book was published in 1959, the French duo has seen remarkable success with their books, which have inspired movies and even a theme park. The series features the comic escapades of Asterix and his sidekick Obelix, whose adventures take them through different historic time periods. In *Asterix the Gladiator*, for example, the two characters disguise themselves as Roman gladiators.

Answers

Document 1. a. *that Rome was the only government ever founded on principles of honesty, not force;* **b.** *He states that Roman government was based on principles of honesty, and says that he is glad that they are succeeding in convincing those those who would want them to govern otherwise.*
Document 2. a. *constructed roads in interlocking layers;* **b.** *possible answer—Roman engineering techniques were superior.* **Document 3. a.** *the structure of the Church; influence on language; subsequent European empires;* **b.** *Greco-Roman cultural influences continue in the Western world today.* **Document 4. a.** *They say Roman stories and heroes, which appeal to the public, have inspired films and novels. They also point out widespread Roman influence in architecture.* **b.** *Roman culture is responsible for many of the ideas, images, and styles found throughout Western culture.* **Essay** *Student essays should state a clear thesis summarizing Rome's influence, which should be supported with reference to this chapter, and to the documents above.*

Visual Summary

Review and Inquiry Organize students into five groups, and assign each group one of these parts of the visual summary: The Roman Republic, The Roman Empire, Decline and Fall, Christianity in the Roman World, and Rome's Legacy. Have each group prepare a two-minute oral summary of its assigned topic.

🔖 **Quick Facts Transparency**: Visual Study Guide: Rome and Early Christianity

Review Key Terms and People

1. Augustus reigned for 40 years, bringing peace, improving public works and buildings, and encouraging creativity in Latin literature.

2. The Forum was a political, entertainment, and shopping center where plebeians and patricians mingled.

3. In order to save Rome from collapse, the emperor Diocletian divided the empire in two.

4. Two magistrates, called consuls, were elected for one year, and were the chief executives of the state.

5. During the late 200s, Roman emperors increased taxes in order to gain revenue for the military.

6. Constantine converted to Christianity and built the eastern capital, Constantinople.

7. Paul made reforms to spread Christianity and helped establish Christian churches throughout the eastern Mediterranean.

8. After Etruscan rule was overthrown, Rome became a republic governed by elected officials.

9. The Gracchi were two brothers who gave public land to poor farmers, but were killed because the Senate feared a loss of power.

10. The paterfamilias, the oldest male in a family, controlled other family members.

11. Julius Caesar, governor of Gaul, crossed the Rubicon with his standing army, broke the law, and was assassinated.

12. Inflation was caused by emperors who made coins from metals of low value.

VISUAL STUDY GUIDE

The Roman Republic
- Founded in 509 BC after the last Etruscan king of Rome was overthrown
- Governed by the Senate, elected magistrates, and popular assemblies working together
- During the Republic, the Romans conquered Italy, Greece, north Africa, and much of the eastern Mediterranean.
- Problems within the government led to the Republic's breakdown.
- Julius Caesar, one of the republic's last rulers, gained great power but was assassinated by his enemies.

The Roman Empire
- Founded in 27 BC when Augustus became the first emperor
- The beginning of the empire was marked by peace and prosperity, a period known as the Pax Romana.
- The empire continued to expand in both the east and west, completely surrounding the Mediterranean Sea and becoming the largest empire in the ancient world.
- Emperors gained more power as time passed, making all important government decisions themselves.

Decline and Fall
- Political and economic problems began to threaten the empire's stability in the late 200s and early 300s.
- Emperors became absolute rulers to try to stop the decline.
- Diocletian divided the empire in half in an effort to prevent its immediate collapse.
- Barbarian invasions and other factors led to the collapse of the Western Empire in 476.
- The Eastern Empire remained strong for several centuries, developing into the Byzantine Empire.

Christianity in the Roman World
- Based on the teachings of Jesus of Nazareth and spread by his disciples
- Taught that people should treat others well and seek forgiveness for their sins to achieve salvation
- Spread throughout the Roman world, especially after Constantine became Christian
- The Christian church began as small close-knit groups and became more complex as time passed.

Rome's Legacy
- Engineering and architecture techniques influenced later building practices.
- Art and literature influenced how people thought and wrote for centuries.
- Latin developed into the Romance languages and influenced English.
- Roman civil law is the basis for many of the world's modern law codes

Review Key Terms and People

For each term or name below, write a sentence explaining its significance to Roman history.

1. Augustus
2. Forum
3. Diocletian
4. consuls
5. revenue
6. Constantine
7. Paul
8. republic
9. Gracchi
10. paterfamilias
11. Julius Caesar
12. inflation

Comprehension and Critical Thinking

13. **a.** Roman territory expanded across the entire Mediterranean region and beyond.
   b. Rome lay across trade routes and had easy access to the sea.
   c. possible answer—Each part could balance the power of the others.

14. **a.** the period between 27 BC and AD 180, characterized by peace, stability, widespread trade and transportation
   b. Octavian (Augustus) became emperor and created a new political order.
   c. possible answer—his support of literary development and creativity because it preserved Rome's history

15. **a.** patriarchal; valued simplicity, religious devotion, and obedience
   b. The Romans preferred the practical application of knowledge.

16. **a.** Jesus—taught people to ask forgiveness and to love God, became known to followers as the Messiah; Paul—helped spread Christianity
   b. Disciples spread the faith; emperors supported it.

History's Impact video program

Watch the video to answer the closing question: How have Roman achievements impacted modern science and cultures today?

Comprehension and Critical Thinking

SECTION 1 *(pp. 163–169)*

13. a. Identify What were the results of the Punic Wars?

b. Explain How did Rome's location help the city grow into a major power in the Mediterranean?

c. Elaborate Why do you think the Roman government was made up of three separate parts?

SECTION 2 *(pp. 171–176)*

14. a. Define What was the Pax Romana?

b. Sequence How did Rome change from a republic to an empire?

c. Evaluate What do you think was Augustus's greatest achievement as emperor? Why?

SECTION 3 *(pp. 177–182)*

15. a. Identify Main Ideas What was family life like?

b. Analyze What was the Roman view toward science and engineering?

SECTION 4 *(pp. 183–187)*

16. a. Describe What roles did Jesus and Paul play in the early history of Christianity?

b. Draw Conclusions Why did Christianity spread so quickly through the Roman world?

SECTION 5 *(pp. 188–191)*

17. a. Identify What happened to the city of Rome in the year 476?

b. Summarize What problems helped weaken the Roman empire in the 200s and 300s?

c. Support a Position "Rome's final fall was caused solely by invasions." Do you agree or disagree with this statement? Support your answer.

Reading Skills

Identifying Stated Main Ideas *Read the passage below, which comes from Section 5 of this chapter. Then answer the question that follows.*

❝ The insecurity of civil wars and invasions affected many aspects of Roman life. Robbery and piracy increased, and travel became hazardous. Merchants feared to ship goods. Military needs required ever-increasing amounts of revenue, and to collect more money, emperors raised taxes. ❞

18. Which statement in this passage expresses the main idea of the passage?

Analyzing Primary Sources

Reading Like a Historian *The passage below comes from a letter written by a Roman statesman to his brother, who was a candidate for consul. In this letter, the statesman gives advice on how to win a Roman election.*

❝ In a word, you must secure friends of every class, magistrates, consuls and their tribunes to win you the vote of the centuries [people]: men of wide popular influence . . . The first and obvious thing is that you embrace the Roman senators and *equites* [nobles], and the active and popular men of all the other orders. There are many city men of good business habits, there are many freedmen engaged in the Forum who are popular and energetic: these men try with all your might, both personally and by common friends, to make eager in your behalf. ❞

19. Analyze According to this letter, who did a candidate have to appeal to in order to win an election?

20. Make Generalizations What does this letter suggest about the nature of Roman politics?

Using the Internet

21. Excavations at the ancient cities of Pompeii and Herculaneum have taught historians a great deal about Roman life. Both cities were buried by ash released by Mount Vesuvius, a volcano that erupted in AD 79. Enter the activity keyword and research the two cities. Then draw an annotated map of one of the cities, noting on the map what historians have learned from it about Roman life.

go.hrw.com
Practice Online
Keyword: SHL ROM

WRITING FOR THE SAT

Think about the following issue:

In a poem admiring the ancient world, Edgar Allan Poe wrote about "the glory that was Greece, the grandeur that was Rome." Poe's view of the past is similar to that held by many people, the view that the ancient Greco-Roman world was one of the high points of civilization.

22. Assignment: Why do modern people glorify the ancient world? What about Greco-Roman culture stirs up such positive feelings in people. Write a short essay in which you develop your position on this issue. Support your point of view with reasoning and examples from your reading and studies.

Answers

17. a. Odoacer overthrew the last Roman emperor.

b. a series of weak leaders, civil wars, invasions, economic troubles

c. possible answer—Disagree: Internal problems also contributed to the fall.

Reading Skills

18. the first sentence

Analyzing Primary Sources

19. people of every class

20. Politics were democratic.

Using the Internet

21. Go to the HRW website and enter the keyword shown to access a rubric for this activity.

KEYWORD: SHL ROM

Writing for the SAT

22. Possible answers should include details from the section about Rome's government system, vast empire, social structure, as well as its advances in architecture, engineering, and culture.

A rubric for the activity is provided in **CRF**: Writing for the SAT.

HOLT

History's Impact

▶ **Video Program: Rome and Early Christianity**
See the Video Program Teacher's Guide for the answer to the closing question.

Review and Assessment Resources

Review and Reinforce

📄 **CRF:** Chapter Review

📊 **Quick Facts Transparency:** Visual Study Guide: Rome and Early Christianity

🔊 **Spanish Chapter Summaries Audio CD Program**

OSP **Holt PuzzlePro:** Quiz Show for ExamView

💿 **Quiz Game CD-ROM**

Assess

📄 **PASS:** Chapter Test, Forms A and B

📄 **Alternative Assessment Handbook**

OSP **ExamView Test Generator**, Chapter Test

💿 **Differentiated Instruction Modified Worksheets and Tests CD-ROM:** Chapter Test

HOAP **Holt Online Assessment Program** (in the Premier Online Edition)

Reteach/Intervene

📄 **Interactive Reader and Study Guide**

📄 **Differentiated Instruction Teacher Management System:** Lesson Plans for Differentiated Instruction

💿 **Differentiated Instruction Modified Worksheets and Tests CD-ROM:** Chapter Test

💿 **Interactive Skills Tutor CD-ROM**

go.hrw.com
Online Resources
KEYWORD: SHL TEACHER

The Americas

Chapter Overview	Reproducible Resources	Technology Resources
CHAPTER 7 pp. 196–219 **Overview: In this chapter, students will learn about early American cultures and how they adapted to their environments.** KI 1; PI 1.1, 1.3, 1.4 See pp. T32–T55 for a detailed correlation to the New York State Core Curriculum for Global History and Geography and the New York Learning Standards.	**Differentiated Instruction Teacher Management System:*** • Pacing Guide • Lesson Plans for Differentiated Instruction **Interactive Reader and Study Guide:** Chapter Summary* **Chapter Resource File*** • Writing for the SAT • Social Studies Skill • Chapter Review **World History Outline Maps**	OSP **New York One-Stop Planner CD-ROM:** Calander Planner **Live Ink© Online Reading Help** **Student Edition on Audio CD Program** **Differentiated Instruction Modified Worksheets and Tests CD-ROM** **Interactive Skills Tutor CD-ROM** **World History Primary Source Library CD-ROM** **Power Presentations with Video CD-ROM** **History's Impact: World History Video Program (VHS/DVD):** The Americas
Section 1: **North America** **The Main Idea:** As people settled in North America, they adapted to different types of geography by developing different styles of housing and ways of getting food. PI 1.4	**Differentiated Instruction Teacher Management System:** Section 1 Lesson Plan* **Interactive Reader and Study Guide:** Section 1 Summary* **Chapter Resource File*** • Vocabulary Builder: Section 1 • Biography: Iroquois Confederacy Leaders	**Regents Review Transparency:** Section 1* **Map Transparency:** Environments of the Americas*
Section 2: **Mesoamerica** **The Main Idea:** Civilizations in Mesoamerica were some of the earliest and most advanced in the Americas. PI 1.1	**Differentiated Instruction Teacher Management System:** Section 2 Lesson Plan* **Interactive Reader and Study Guide:** Section 2 Summary* **Chapter Resource File*** • Vocabulary Builder: Section 2 • Biography: Montezuma II • Primary Source: Laws, Ordinances, and Statutes Decreed by King Montezuma I • Literature: *The Legend of La Llorona* • History and Geography: The Aztec Triple Alliance	**Regents Review Transparency:** Section 2* **Map Transparency:** Early Mesoamerican Civilizations **Internet Activity:** The Olmec Empire
Section 3: **South America** **The Main Idea:** Several early cultures in South America adapted to extreme environmental conditions. One of them, the Incas, built one of the biggest and most powerful empires in the Americas. PI 1.3, 1.4	**Differentiated Instruction Teacher Management System:** Section 3 Lesson Plan* **Interactive Reader and Study Guide:** Section 3 Summary* **Chapter Resource File*** • Vocabulary Builder: Section 3 • Biography: Atahualpa	**Regents Review Transparency:** Section 3* **Map Transparency:** South American Cultures* **Internet Activity:** Hike the Inca Trail to Machu Picchu

go.hrw.com   Print Resource   Transparency

LS Learning Styles   Audio CD   CD-ROM

Video   SE Student Edition   TE Teachers Edition

OSP One-Stop Planner CD-ROM   NY Standards Mastery
*also on One-Stop Planner CD-ROM

Review, Assessment, Intervention

Global History and Geography Regents Test Prep Workbook

Quick Facts Transparency: The Americas*

Spanish Chapter Summaries Audio CD Program

Progress Assessment Support System (PASS): Chapter Test*

Differentiated Instruction Modified Worksheets and Tests CD-ROM: Modified Chapter Test

OSP **New York One-Stop Planner CD-ROM:** ExamView Test Generator (English/Spanish)

HOAP **Holt Online Assessment Program (HOAP),** in the Holt Premier Online Student Edition

PASS: Section 1 Quiz*

Online Quiz: Section 1

Alternative Assessment Handbook

PASS: Section 2 Quiz*

Online Quiz: Section 2

Alternative Assessment Handbook

PASS: Section 3 Quiz*

Online Quiz: Section 3

Alternative Assessment Handbook

Power Presentation with Video CD-ROM

Power Presentations with Video are visual presentations of each chapter's main ideas. Presentations can be customized by including Quick Facts charts, images and maps from the textbook, and video clips.

Holt Online Learning

go.hrw.com
Teacher Resources
KEYWORD: SHL TEACHER

go.hrw.com
Student Resources
KEYWORD: SHL AMS

- Document-Based Questions
- Interactive Multimedia Activities

- Current Events
- Chapter-Based Internet Activities
- and more!

Holt Premier
Online Student Edition

Complete online support for interactivity, assessment, and reporting

- Interactive Maps and Notebook
- Homework Practice and Research Activities Online

CHAPTER 7 PLANNING GUIDE

The Big Picture

Peter N. Stearns

The Americas Dealing with American societies and civilizations before Columbus poses some clear problems. Not connected to societies in other parts of the world, American civilizations developed distinctively. Their economic, cultural and political achievements were impressive but they had different technological bases from their Afro-Eurasian counterparts and sustained the societies on vegetable crops native only to their regions. Some scholars compare American civilizations like the Maya to chronologically earlier river-valley civilizations like Mesopotamia, but this approach has limitations. Another issue involves how to understand the societies in North America that don't quite fit the definition of a full civilization, a form of human organization that many ancient Central American and Andean societies did fit.

Origins and Evolution Recent scholarship has dramatically recast our understanding of when and how humans reached the Americas—pushing the dates back while also suggesting rapid geographic dispersion down the Pacific coast of the two continents. Early civilization has also been more fully explored, notably with better grasp of the range of achievement of the Olmec, but also with new work on Chavin society in the Andes. Some standard issues remain important, particularly in comparing Maya society and culture with later Aztec, and in comparing imperial organization and social structure in Central America with counterparts in the Andes. Another classic topic, well worth discussion, involves religious sacrifice, and why societies continued to engage in the practice.

Change and Decline Another important focus involves understanding why certain American societies declined, often after a long period of high achievement. Maya decline is particularly intriguing, with a number of factors involved whose priority order is still debated. Recognizing the relatively brief ascendancy of Aztecs and Incas, with emerging problems that preceded the arrival of European conquerors, is another feature. It is vital to linger on the legacy of the American civilizations: it's easy to see that they are interesting, easy to see also that they would be radically suppressed by later Europeans and the erosion of disease; but what elements would persist nevertheless?

Recent Scholarship

Michael D. Coe's *The Maya* (2005 edition) is a major reworking of a well-established standard in a field that, in turn, deals with one of the most intriguing American civilizations. The book reflects the discovery of new archeological sites, at the early end of the Maya experience, and intriguing discussions of the conundrum of Maya decline, at the other end. In between, Coe sheds light on additional aspects of Maya culture, including newly accessible murals and regional political organization. Finally, assessment of Maya agriculture provides opportunities to talk about the crucial underpinnings of early American civilizations, well developed in spite of (by Old World standards) technological limitations.

Differentiating Instruction

 Differentiated Instruction Teacher Management System
- Pacing Guide
- Lesson Plans for Differentiated Instruction

 Interactive Reader and Study Guide

Spanish Chapter Summaries Audio CD Program

Student Edition on Audio CD Program

 Differentiated Instruction Modified Worksheets and Tests CD-ROM
- Vocabulary Flash Cards
- Modified Vocabulary Builder Activities
- Modified Chapter Review Activity
- Modified Chapter Test

OSP One-Stop Planner CD-ROM
- ExamView Test Generator (English /Spanish)
- PuzzlePro
- Quiz Show for ExamView
- Transparencies and Videos

TE Differentiated Activities in the Teacher's Edition
- Hohokam Irrigation and Anasazi Pueblos, p. 200
- The First Civilizations in Mesoamerica, p. 205
- Decline of the Maya, p. 206
- Rise of the Aztecs, p. 208
- Early Cultures of South America, p. 212
- The First Americans, p. 217

Reading Like a Historian
Sam Wineburg

Examining the Cultural Record Much of what we know about Tenochtitlán, the magisterial capital of the Aztecs and its ruler Montezuma, comes from the records of the conquering Spanish conquistadores. But because of the devoted efforts of a Franciscan monk, Bernardino de Sahagún, we also have oral histories collected from indigenous peoples who lived at the time, recorded in the Nahuatl language.

Having both Spanish and Nahuatl accounts allows us to understand how the different sides perceived events in this cultural encounter. For example, consider how Hernán Cortés describes his initial meeting with Montezuma. On seeing the Spaniard, the Aztec ruler delivers this speech: "We learned from our ancestors that neither myself nor any of those who inhabit this region were descended from its original inhabitants . . . We have always heard that [the descendants of the original ruler] would come to conquer this land, and reduce us to subjection as his vassals; and according to the direction from which you say you have come . . . and from what you say of the great lord or king, who sent you hither, we believe . . . that he is our natural sovereign."

The Nahuatl accounts record Montezuma's speech in this way: "Our lord . . . You have come here to sit on your throne, to sit under its canopy, which I have kept for awhile for you. For the rulers and governors . . . have gone . . . your poor vassal has been in charge for you, to govern the city of Mexico . . . For our rulers departed saying that you would come to your city and sit upon your throne. And now it has been fulfilled, you have returned."

Discrepancies in Accounts In Cortés's report, Montezuma emphasizes that the conquistador is an emissary of a "great lord or king, who sent you hither," a reference to King Charles of Spain. In the Nahuatl accounts, it is Cortés that Montezuma seats on the throne, not some distant ruler in Europe.

Even with these discrepancies, the impression conveyed from both is unmistakable: seemingly, the great Montezuma yields his authority and all his riches to this motley Spaniard and his crew of 400 fortune-seekers. When accounts from different perspectives corroborate, historians' confidence in the story they tell increases. Is this the case here?

Far from it. To historians, how a document comes into being is just as important as what that document says. Cortés had embarked on his voyage in brazen violation of the Spanish administration in Cuba. In this letter, Cortés goes over the heads of his immediate superiors and appeals to the king. Yes, Cortés may have disregarded orders, but he did so for the crown. Even Montezuma seems to know it!

Still, we have the troubling issue of Montezuma handing Cortés his throne on a silver platter. On that score, both accounts seem to agree. To understand why, we need to know how Sahagún's oral histories came into being.

Putting the Pieces Together While it is true that Sahagún's book drew on native accounts, it is also true that these accounts were put together some thirty years after the events in question. By this time the Aztecs were firmly under Spanish rule. In other words, these accounts were assembled and filtered by a Nahuatl-speaking Franciscan monk, part of the Spanish colonial administration.

Much of what we know about Mesoamerica comes from sources written by—or, in this case, preserved by—the conquerors. It is mistaken to regard these sources as mirrors that provide direct access to the past. Rather, these sources form only a rough contour of the picture of the Spanish conquest. If the past is a puzzle, it is a puzzle with missing pieces. Even the pieces that have survived are blurry and, in this case, very suspicious.

Chapter Main Ideas

Section 1 As people settled in North America, they adapted to different types of geography by developing different styles of housing and ways of getting food.

Section 2 Civilizations in Meso-america were some of the earliest and most advanced in the Americas.

Section 3 Several early cultures in South America adapted to extreme environmental conditions. One of them, the Incas, built one of the biggest and most powerful empires in the Americas.

New York Standards

Key Idea 1 The study of world history requires an understanding of world cultures and civilizations, including an analysis of important ideas, social and cultural values, beliefs, and traditions. This study also examines the human condition and the connections and interactions of people across time and space and the ways different people view the same event or issue from a variety of perspectives.

CHAPTER 7 1000 BC–AD 1500

The Americas

THE BIG PICTURE As an advanced civilization developed in Rome, other civilizations were developing in the Americas. These early American cultures found unique ways of adapting to the varied environments of the Americas. Some groups even developed sophisticated government structures and works of art and engineering that rivaled those of the ancient Romans.

Theme GOVERNMENT AND CITIZENSHIP
As civilizations emerged, they developed a number of ways to keep their societies orderly and productive. In this chapter, you will learn the different ways in which the early cultures of the Americas governed themselves.

TIME LINE

CHAPTER EVENTS

c. 400 BC The Moche culture develops in Peru's coastal desert.

Classic Age of Maya Civilization 250–900

c. 750 The Anasazi develop pueblo architecture.

500 BC — AD 1 — 500 — 1000

WORLD EVENTS

c. 500 BC Athens develops the world's first democracy.

206 BC The Han dynasty begins its rule of China.

476 The Roman Empire falls.

c. 1000 Murasaki Shikibu writes *The Tale of Genji*, the world's first novel.

196 CHAPTER 7

Introduce the Chapter

At Level

The Americas

1. Show students some, stereotypical images of Native Americans and associated cultural elements. Examples could include teepees, headdresses, Native Americans on horses, etc.

2. Ask students if they think these images are accurate. Tell students that although these images relate to real people and specific cultural elements, they are stereotypes, simplify culture, and can be insulting. Explain that early American cultures were much more complex and diverse than the images reveal.

3. Tell students that in this chapter they will learn about the diverse early civilizations of the Americas and their remarkable achievements.

4. Have students write a letter to the editor in which they address the issue of Native American stereotypes. **LS Verbal-Linguistic**

Alternative Assessment Handbook, Rubric 17: Letters to Editors

History's Impact video program

Watch the video to understand the impact of Maya achievements on math and astronomy.

Reading like a Historian This photograph shows the ruins of Machu Picchu, an ancient Inca city high in the Andes Mountains. Historians think this city was built as a retreat for Inca royalty. It lay all but forgotten for hundreds of years until its rediscovery in 1911.

Analyzing Visuals Why do you think the Inca chose to build a royal city in this location? What benefits and challenges do you think the geography presented?

See Skills Handbook, p. H26

1325
The Aztecs establish their capital at Tenochtitlán.

c. 1440
Pachacuti begins to expand the Inca Empire.

1500

1096
European Christians begin the Crusades for control of the Holy Land.

1453
Constantinople becomes part of the Ottoman Empire.

THE AMERICAS **197**

• **Chapter Preview** •

HOLT
History's Impact
► **Video Program: The Americas**
See the Video Teacher's Guide for strategies for using the video segment.

Reading Like a Historian

Make Inferences What advantages do you think the natural stone structures shown in this photograph gave the Incas? *possible answers—Stone structures provided a cool environment during hot weather; natural stone materials blended into surroundings, camouflaging the structures from enemies.*

go.hrw.com
Online Resources

Chapter Resources:
KEYWORD: SHL AMS
Teacher Resources:
KEYWORD: SHL TEACHER

Explore the Time Line

1. When did the Moche culture develop in Peru's coastal desert? *400 BC*

2. How long did the classic age of Maya civilization last? *650 years*

3. What happened to the Roman Empire during the Classic age of Maya civilization? *The Roman Empire fell.*

4. What event happened in the Americas shortly before Constantinople became part of the Ottoman Empire? *Pachacuti began to expand the Inca Empire.*

Info to Know

Machu Picchu Historians believe that Machu Picchu was probably planned and built under the supervision of master Inca architects. The buildings are made of granite blocks cut with stone or bronze tools and smoothed with sand. Although blocks are of different sizes, they fit together perfectly without mortar. The structures of Machu Picchu are well integrated with the landscape.

Make Inferences How might stone formations intergrate with the landscape? *possible answer— might be used as foundations for buildings*

Answers

Reading Like a Historian *because it is beautiful and isolated, seems spiritual; benefit—isolated from intrusions; challenge—difficult travel and transport*

197

Geography Starting Points

The Jicarillas The following quote is an excerpt from a Jicarilla Apache tale, and describes the settlement of the Jicarillas. "All the people came up. They traveled east until they arrived at the ocean; then they turned south until they came again to the ocean, and then they turned north. As they went, each tribe stopped where it wanted to. But the Jicarillas continued to circle the hole where they had come up from the underworld. Three times they went around it, when the Ruler became displeased and asked them where they wished to stop. They said, 'In the middle of the earth.' So he led them to a place very near Taos and left them, and there near the Taos Indians, the Jicarillas made their home."
—Jicarilla Apache tale, quoted in *American Indian Myths and Legends*

Analyzing Primary Sources How are myths useful to scholars? *possible answer—show a culture's values and beliefs and how early people view themselves; helpful in understanding culture*

🗺 **Map Transparency**: Environments of the Americas

📑 **World History Outline Maps**

✳ **Interactive Map**: Environments of the Americas

★Interactive
ENVIRONMENTS OF THE AMERICAS

Cold forest and tundra
Highland
Temperate forest
Grassland
Tropical forest
Desert and shrub land

NORTH AMERICA

ROCKY MOUNTAINS
GREAT PLAINS
APPALACHIAN MTS.
Hudson Bay
Missouri River
Ohio River
Gulf of Mexico
Yucatán Peninsula
West Indies
Caribbean Sea
PACIFIC OCEAN
ATLANTIC OCEAN

The Arctic region of North America is covered with glaciers and tundra.

Lush tropical forests make up most of Mesoamerica.

ANDES MOUNTAINS
AMAZON BASIN
SOUTH AMERICA

Equator — 0°
Tropic of Capricorn
20°S
40°S

0   500   1,000 Miles
0   500 1,000 Kilometers
Mercator projection

The Andes Mountains create a varied climate along the western coast of South America.

Starting Points North and South America have almost every possible type of environment—from frozen tundra to dusty deserts to lush tropical forests. In spite of the environmental differences, early people settled in almost every part of the Americas. They quickly learned to adapt to their region's unique climate, vegetation, and topography.

1. **Compare** What type of environments do you think would be most suitable for developing farming societies?
2. **Predict** In what ways might people adapt to living in cold forest and tundra areas? in highland areas?

🔊 **Listen to History**

Go online to listen to an explanation of the starting points for this chapter.

go.hrw.com
Keyword: SHL AMS

198 CHAPTER 7

Skills Focus: Evaluating Information on the Internet   At Level

Social Studies Skill   Research Required
Environments of the Americas

1. Review criteria for reliable Internet sites with students. Organize students into small groups.

2. Using reliable Internet sites, have groups conduct research to find information about one of the regions highlighted on the map: the Arctic, Mesoamerica, or the Andes Mountains. Tell students they will use presentation software to display facts based on their research.

3. Have students focus their research on the climate of the region, and wildlife found there. They should also be able to explain how people have traditionally lived in the environment.

4. Have groups make their multimedia presentations to the class. 🅛🆂 **Interpersonal, Visual-Spatial**

📑 **Alternative Assessment Handbook**, Rubrics 14: Group Activity; 22: Multimedia Presentations; and 30: Research

Answers

Geography Starting Points
1. *grassland;* **2.** *cold forest and tundra—hunt animals for food, use animal skins to keep warm, create shelters that trap heat; highland—grow different crops at different altitudes*

BEFORE YOU READ

MAIN IDEA
As people settled in North America, they adapted to different types of geography by developing different styles of housing and ways of getting food.

READING FOCUS
1. How did cultures adapt to the environment of the Desert West?
2. How have scientists learned about the mound builders?
3. How did geography affect the Inuit, the Iroquois, and the Plains Indians?

KEY TERMS
adobe
pueblo
kivas
maize
Iroquois League

 NEW YORK

PI 1.4 Students understand the broad patterns, relationships, and interactions of cultures and civilizations during particular eras and across eras.

THE FIRST AMERICANS

▶ Scientists have studied Kennewick Man's bones and developed this model of what he probably looked like.

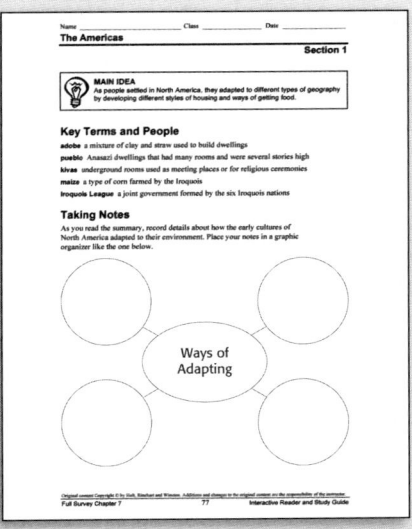

THE INSIDE STORY

Where did they come from and how did they get here? In 1996 two college students stumbled upon a human skull in the Columbia River near Kennewick, Washington. Later searches in the area turned up a nearly complete 9,000-year-old skeleton. Scientists nicknamed the skeleton Kennewick Man. Kennewick Man is helping scientists answer some questions about the first Americans.

Scientists have put forth many theories on how and when people first arrived in the Americas. According to one theory, the last ice age caused ocean levels to fall, exposing dry land across the Bering Strait, between present-day Russia and Alaska. At that time, sometime between 25,000 and 14,000 years ago, small bands of people from Asia could have crossed this "land bridge," known as Beringia, as they

followed the animals they were hunting into North America and formed settlements. From there, the people would have continued migrating southward as they looked for food.

Recent archaeological discoveries, such as Kennewick Man, suggest that the land bridge theory may not fully explain the arrival of the first Americans. One important recent discovery is the Monte Verde site in southern Chile. Remains found there are at least 12,500 years old—and may be as old as 30,000 years! If the remains are that old, it might have been impossible for humans to have migrated there from the Beringia land bridge. Many scientists now think that early people may have arrived to the Americas along the coasts, perhaps using boats. However they got here, as they spread across the continents, early Americans had to learn to adapt to many different environments. ■

THE AMERICAS **199**

Reading Focus

❶ How did cultures adapt to the environment of the Desert West? *learned how to farm in the dry environment, built homes from local materials*

Cultures of the Desert West

Describe How did the Hohokam manage water? *built irrigation canals, created dams to direct water, channeled water into villages, stored water*

Analyze What advantages did pueblo architecture have over pithouses? *easier to add on rooms than to dig new pithouse, cliff dwellings easy to defend*

Elaborate What disadvantages might cliff dwellings have? *possible answer—difficult to construct because all resources and building materials would have to be carried up steep hills*

QUICK FACTS — North American Cultures

Analyzing Visuals Which North American culture area are you most familiar with? Why? Which area do you think presented the most difficult challenges to its inhabitants? Why? Which area might have been the easiest to adapt to? Why? *possible answers—most familiar: people of the Great Plains because they have often been depicted in movies and images, but these are not usually true representations; most challenging: Arctic and Subarctic, because of extremely cold temperatures, permanent snow and ice; easiest: Great Plains because of fertile soil for farming*

Quick Facts Transparency: North American Cultures

Answers

North American Cultures *Arctic & Subarctic, Far West*

Reading Check *used local materials such as clay and straw, built pueblos in caves in high canyons*

200

TAKING NOTES
Take notes on the ways early cultures adapted to their environments.

(Ways of Adapting)

Cultures of the Desert West

Much of the southwestern United States and northern Mexico is desert. Early people in this region learned how to farm in the harsh, dry environment and to build their homes out of local materials.

Hohokam In the Desert West the Hohokam (ho-HO-kam) flourished from 300 BC to AD 1500. To farm in the desert, the Hohokam built shallow canals for irrigation. Next to the canals the Hohokam planted crops in a series of earthen mounds. Woven mats created dams in the canals that directed irrigation water toward the earthen crop mounds.

The Hohokam expanded their irrigation system to channel water into their villages. In addition to wells and other types of containers for storing water, Hohokam villages contained dwellings called pithouses. Pithouses were formed by digging shallow holes in the ground and building walls and roofs with a mixture of clay and straw called **adobe**.

Anasazi The Anasazi lived in the Desert West near the Hohokam from about 100 BC to AD 1300. Like their neighbors, they lived in pithouses. However, around the end of the first century AD the Anasazi developed a new kind of architecture called **pueblo**. Pueblos were several stories high and had many rooms, similar to modern apartment buildings. It was easier for the Anasazi to add rooms in pueblos than to dig pithouses. Most villages also had underground rooms called **kivas**. Kivas were used as meeting places or for religious ceremonies.

Also typical of Anasazi architecture were cliff dwellings. Pueblos were built in shallow caves high up in the walls of canyons. To enter their cliff dwellings, the Anasazi used staircases carved into the rock walls or ladders with notched footholds made from tree trunks. Because of their limited accessibility, cliff dwellings offered protection from attack.

READING CHECK **Make Generalizations** How did cultures of the Desert West adapt their architecture to their environment?

North American Cultures

North American cultures within certain regions shared similar characteristics. The geography of a region determined to a large extent what people ate, where they lived, and how their societies functioned. *Which cultures relied most on fishing?*

ARCTIC & SUBARCTIC

Ivory from walrus tusks was one of the few resources available to the Inuit for making ornaments.
- Peoples included the Inuit, Aleut, and Ingalik
- Environmental conditions included permanent snow and ice
- Relied on fishing and hunting sea mammals for food
- Built houses out of ice

FAR WEST

The bird and fish decoration on this spool shows two aspects of life for Native Americans in the far west.
- Peoples included the Haida, Chinook, Columbia, Miwok, and Chumash
- Geography included rivers, forests, and a long coastline
- Fishing in rivers and the ocean was a main method of getting food
- Built houses and canoes out of wood from the forests

Map labels: Arctic and Subarctic, Hudson Bay, PACIFIC OCEAN, Far West, Great Plains, Eastern Woodlands, Desert West, ATLANTIC OCEAN, Gulf of Mexico

200 CHAPTER 7

Differentiating Instruction

Above Level

Prep Required

English-Language Learners

Materials: photos of desert irrigation systems and pueblos, drawing paper, colored pencils

1. Review the information in the text about Hohokam irrigation and Anasazi pueblos. Show students images or slides of desert irrigation systems and pueblos.

2. Organize students into mixed-ability pairs.

3. Have each pair design a Hohokam irrigation system and an Anasazi pueblo. Have students sketch their designs and label each part of their sketch. Students should create design features that serve a purpose and label them.

4. Have volunteers share their designs with the class. **LS** Interpersonal, Visual-Spatial

Alternative Assessment Handbook, Rubric 3: Artwork

The Mound Builders

In the eastern woodlands of North America, near the Ohio and Mississippi river valleys, lived several societies known for the large earthen mounds they built. The mounds tell us about the sculptures of these societies.

Hopewell One early group of mound builders was the Hopewell, who lived from 200 BC to AD 500. They built large stone and earth mounds as burial sites. The size of the mounds suggests that Hopewell society included some form of organized labor. Buried inside the mounds were objects such as pottery and metal ornaments. These objects provide other clues to Hopewell society. For example, daggers of obsidian from the Rocky Mountains and shells from the Gulf of Mexico show that the Hopewell developed an extensive trade network.

In spite of their relatively organized society, the Hopewell culture gradually declined beginning around AD 400. Scientists are still unsure of the cause of this culture's decline.

Mississippian Later mound builders, the Mississippians, built some of the earliest cities in North America. Their largest city, Cahokia, had a population of up to 20,000 people and contained more than 100 mounds. Cahokia was a planned city. It was built by an organized Mississippian labor force using mathematical and engineering skills. For example, engineers used different types of soils in building the mounds to ensure proper drainage.

The layout of the city and the objects found in its mounds suggest that Mississippian society was complex and had clear divisions between social classes. Priests ruled Cahokia and surrounding villages, with the ruler living atop the largest mound in the city center. Rows of other houses surrounded a central plaza. In addition, artifacts found in some burial mounds show differences between common people and people who had elite status in society.

READING CHECK **Summarize** What do the mounds tell us about Hopewell and Mississippian society?

ACADEMIC VOCABULARY
status position or rank

DESERT WEST

The Cliff Palace at Mesa Verde in Colorado is the largest Anasazi cliff dwelling, containing 200 rooms.

- Peoples included the Hohokam, Anasazi, Apache, Shoshone, Tarahumara, and Yaqui
- Lived in a dry, rocky environment
- Used irrigation techniques to farm maize, beans, and squash
- Built houses out of adobe or into the sides of cliffs

GREAT PLAINS

This buffalo skin rattle shows the importance of the buffalo to the Plains Indians.

- Peoples included the Blackfoot, Sioux, Omaha, Comanche, and Crow
- Region consisted of treeless, grassy plains with fertile soil
- Hunted buffalo
- Lived in portable teepees made from buffalo skins

EASTERN WOODLANDS

Serpent Mound in Ohio was built by mound builders who lived about the same time as the Hopewell.

- Peoples included the Adena, Hopewell, Mississippian, Iroquois, Mohawk, and Seminole
- Warm and temperate forests were characteristic
- Relied on hunting and gathering, as well as farming some native crops
- Lived in log houses built from forest materials

THE AMERICAS **201**

201

❸ How did geography affect the Inuit, the Iroquois, and the Plains Indians? *each culture developed different ways of life based on local environment; geography determined the ways in which each obtained food, created shelter, and organized societies*

Other Cultures of North America

Recall How did the Iroquois get food? *trapped forest animals; grew beans, squash, and maize*

Identify Cause and Effect Explain how the horse changed the lives of the Plains Indians. *farmed and lived along rivers; then used horses to follow buffalo herds; buffalo became important*

📑 **CRF**: Biography: Iroquois Confederacy Leaders

Close

Have students give examples of how different peoples adapted to their environments.

Review

📕 **Online Quiz**, Section 1

Assess

SE Section 1 Assessment

📑 **Progress Assessment**: Section 1 Quiz

📑 **Alternative Assessment Handbook**

Reteach/Intervene

📑 **Interactive Reader and Study Guide**, Section 1

💿 **Interactive Skills Tutor CD-ROM**

Answers

Reading Check *Inuit lived in frozen, treeless landscape, no vegetation; Iroquois lived in forest environment, relied on trees and forest animals, farmed beans, squash, and maize; Plains Indians lived in treeless grassland, farmed along rivers, then used horses to hunt buffalo used for food, clothing, and tools*

202

Upstate New York was the heartland of the Iroquois League. From there, the League expanded in the 1600s to the east and west, subduing local tribes. Today, Cayuga, Seneca, and Oneida lakes in upstate New York recall three of the nations that made up the League.

Other Cultures of North America

In other areas of North America, cultures developed differently according to their different environments. The varied geography of the continent determined the way these peoples got food, made shelter, and organized their societies.

The Inuit The Inuit lived in the Arctic regions of North America. In this frozen, treeless landscape, the Inuit could not depend on vegetation for their food source. Instead, they became skilled hunters and fishers. Using kayaks, the Inuit hunted sea mammals such as seals. They also caught fish through holes in the ice. In the summer, the Inuit hunted land animals like caribou. Caribou skins and furs were important for making warm clothing. They also served as furniture in the Inuit igloos, or houses made from ice blocks.

The Iroquois To the south, in eastern North America, where it was warmer, the Iroquois relied on materials in their forest environment. They built their dwellings, called longhouses, from elm bark. For food, they trapped forest animals. The climate also allowed the Iroquois to farm crops such as beans, squash, and **maize**, which is another word for corn.

Although they shared many similar characteristics, the Iroquois were actually made up of five different nations. They included the Cayuga, Mohawk, Oneida, Onondaga, and Seneca. These tribes eventually formed a joint government called the **Iroquois League**. Each chief in the league had one vote. In the 1700s the Tuscarora were admitted to the League.

Plains Indians Like the Iroquois, the Plains Indians consisted of different tribes. However, not all spoke the same language, so communication was a problem. To solve the problem, the Plains Indians developed a form of sign language to communicate more easily when they met on the Great Plains.

The Great Plains region is a mostly treeless grassland. At first, the Plains Indians lived along rivers and streams, where they farmed the fertile land. After Europeans brought horses to the region, however, the lives of the Plains Indians changed. They began to use horses to follow buffalo herds over long distances. The buffalo became an even greater part of their lives. The Plains Indians ate buffalo meat, made clothing and portable tents from the skins, and used the bones and horns to make tools.

READING CHECK **Identify Supporting Details** What details show that the Inuit, Iroquois, and Plains Indians lived in different environments?

SECTION 1 ASSESSMENT

go.hrw.com
Online Quiz
Keyword: SHL AMS HP

Reviewing Ideas, Terms, and People

1. **a. Identify** What culture developed **pueblo** architecture?
   b. Explain How were the Hohokam able to grow crops in the desert?
2. **a. Recall** In what region did the mound builders live?
   b. Interpret What about the items found in burial mounds do you think led researchers to believe that the Hopewell had an extensive trade network?
   c. Elaborate How do you think the layout and mounds of Cahokia suggest that there were clear social divisions in Mississippian society?
3. **a. Describe** How did the Inuit adapt to their environment?
   b. Contrast What differed about the way the Iroquois and the Plains Indians dealt with the different nations within their regions?
   c. Predict How might the lives of the Plains Indians have been different if they had not started using horses?

Critical Thinking

4. **Evaluate** Using your notes on the section and a chart like the one below, list similarities and differences that developed in different cultures of North America. Note differences in climate and environment that may have affected cultures.

Similarities	Differences

FOCUS ON WRITING 🖊️

5. **Description** Choose one early North American culture and imagine you are visiting the people of that culture for the first time. Write a short paragraph describing unique characteristics of that culture.

202 CHAPTER 7

Section 1 Assessment Answers

1. **a.** Anasazi
   b. used irrigation canals, created dams to direct water towards crop mounds
2. **a.** eastern woodlands
   b. items were not available locally
   c. possible answer—layout suggests social ranking, ruler lived in largest mound; artifacts show difference between classes
3. **a.** became skilled hunters and fishers, used kayaks to hunt, used caribou skins and furs for clothes and furniture, made igloos out of ice blocks

b. Iroquois formed joint government; Plains Indians used sign language to communicate
   c. possible answer—would have remained farmers living by rivers

4. Answers should note differences and similarities of cultures discussed in this section.

5. possible answer—At the center of Mississippian territory stands the enormous city of Cahokia. Everywhere you walk, impressive mounds seem to rise up from the earth. The markets bustle with traders.

SECTION 2 Mesoamerica

BEFORE YOU READ

MAIN IDEA

Civilizations in Mesoamerica were some of the earliest and most advanced in the Americas.

READING FOCUS

1. What were the first civilizations in Mesoamerica like?
2. What were some characteristics of Maya civilization?
3. What made the Aztec empire one of the strongest in the ancient Americas?

KEY TERMS

elite
slash-and-burn agriculture
glyphs
codex
tribute
alliance

NEW YORK

PI 1.1 Students explain how culture and civilization developed and changed over time. Investigate the various components of cultures and civilizations.

GIANTS IN THE JUNGLE

THE INSIDE STORY

Was the Olmec civilization the "mother culture" of Mesoamerica? Among the ruins of an ancient Olmec city, archaeologists found some of the greatest sculptures in Mesoamerica—from tiny jade jaguar figures to giant stone heads up to 9 feet tall and weighing as much as 40 tons. This advanced artistic style led scholars to think that the Olmec were a relatively recent civilization in the region.

As more discoveries were made, however, scholars learned that the Olmec actually predated just about every other civilization in Mesoamerica. They were the first to develop what might be considered a writing system and the first to use an architecture style of pyramids and plazas that is common throughout the region. Because of all these "firsts," scholars once called the Olmec the "mother culture" of Mesoamerica, meaning they were the ones who gave rise to all later cultures in the region. ∎

The First Civilizations

Mesoamerica, a region that includes southern Mexico and northern Central America, was the site of the first farming settlements in the Americas. Warm temperatures, plentiful rainfall, and rich volcanic soils made the area ideal for growing crops. The first domesticated crop in the Americas, maize, was farmed in the region by around 5000 BC. Early Mesoamericans soon learned to farm beans and squash as well. Farming allowed some early peoples in Mesoamerica to create large cities and complex social structures and to advance culturally.

▼ An Olmec sculpture of a giant head may represent a ruler, a lord, or a god.

203

Teach the Main Idea

At Level

Mesoamerica

1. **Teach** Ask students the Reading Focus questions to teach this section.

2. **Apply** Draw three rectangles for students to see. Label the top of each rectangle with one of the three topics of this section: The First Civilizations, The Maya, and The Aztecs. Have students copy the rectangles on their papers and fill them in with key points from each topic.

3. **Review** As you review the section, guide students in a discussion about the social structure of the Maya and the Aztecs.

4. **Practice/Homework** Have students create a resume listing the achievements of one of the civilizations in this section.
   LS Visual-Spatial, Verbal-Linguistic

   Alternative Assessment Handbook, Rubric 31: Resumes

Reading Focus

1 What were the first civilizations in Mesoamerica like? *farming allowed for development of large cities, complex social structures, cultural achievements; civilizations included Olmec, Zapotec, and Toltec*

The First Civilizations

Recall What structures were found in the earliest Olmec town? *large pyramid, courtyard, eight giant stone heads, throne-like monuments*

Elaborate Why do you think Monte Albán is considered the first true city of Mesoamerica? *many people lived there, had more types of buildings; Olmec towns used mainly for ceremonies and meeting places*

Map Transparency: Early Mesoamerican Civilizations

Info to Know

Earliest Writing The discovery of an ancient stone tablet dates the earliest writing in the Western Hemisphere to about 900 BC, which is approximately 300 years earlier than what historians once believed was the earliest example of writing in the Americas. Analysis of the stone slab, which was unearthed in 1999 near an Olmec site in Veracruz, Mexico, has uncovered organized patterns of glyphs and symbols. While anthropologists say it is unlikely that the meaning of the text will ever be deciphered, its mere existence proves that the Olmec did, in fact, have a writing system.

Answers

Interpreting Maps 1. *Refer to map.*
2. *Refer to map.*

204

EARLY MESOAMERICAN CIVILIZATIONS

Gulf of Mexico

Tula • Teotihuacán
Lake Texcoco
Tenochtitlán • • Tlaxcala
Valley of Mexico
La Venta •
• Palenque
• Monte Albán
Bonampak •
• Tikal
Chichén Itzá •
Yucatán Peninsula
20°N

15°N
PACIFIC OCEAN
• Copán

0   300   600 Miles
0   300   600 Kilometers
Lambert azimuthal equal-area projection

— Olmec culture, 900 BC
— Zapotec culture, AD 200
— Toltec culture, AD 900
☐ Maya civilization, AD 900
☐ Aztec civilization, AD 1500

GEOGRAPHY SKILLS | **INTERPRETING MAPS**

1. **Place** Which civilization built cities on the Yucatán Peninsula?
2. **Movement** Which three cultures were located in the same area that the Aztecs were located?

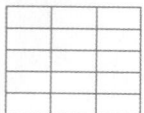

TAKING NOTES

Record details about the characteristics of the first civilizations, the Maya, and the Aztec societies.

Olmec The Olmec lived in the hot, humid, lowlands along the Gulf coast of southern Mexico from about 1200 BC to AD 300. They built the first large towns in Mesoamerica. The earliest Olmec town contained a large pyramid and a courtyard. It also contained eight giant stone heads and several other thronelike monuments. A later town, La Venta, had more giant stone heads as well as elaborate tombs and a pyramid. Because of the types of structures and monuments in the towns, scholars think Olmec towns served as ceremonial, political, and religious centers.

The towns may have also been where Olmec rulers and their families lived. The rulers led public ceremonies that symbolized their special relationship with the gods. People of lower social classes, such as artists and farmers, lived outside the towns and supported the rulers and priests.

In addition to leading ceremonies, the Olmec **elite**, or high-ranking members, controlled a large trade network that stretched to central Mexico and along the Pacific coast. Olmec traders traveled the network to obtain shells and certain types of valuable stones that could not be found nearby. They exported rubber, pottery, furs, and cacao.

Trade goods were not the only things exchanged along the network of trade routes. Knowledge, beliefs, and art styles spread in this way also. For example, the Olmec invented a calendar and were perhaps the first in Mesoamerica to use writing. They were also the earliest people in the region to play what became a popular ball game. These elements of Olmec civilization can be seen in many later Mesoamerican civilizations. As influential as the Olmec were, however, the reason for their decline remains a mystery.

Zapotec One later Mesoamerican people that may have had contact with the Olmec were the Zapotec. They lived in southern Mexico from about 1500 BC to AD 750. In the beginning, the Zapotec were farmers. Around 500 BC, however, they built a capital city, Monte Albán, high above the Valley of Oaxaca (wah-HAH-kah).

Monte Albán was the first true city in Mesoamerica. Its huge main plaza was lined with pyramids, temples, and palaces, some of which were decorated with carvings that showed Olmec influence. There was also a large ball court and even an observatory. Outside the main area, the city had fifteen residential neighborhoods, each with its own plaza.

204 CHAPTER 7

Skills Focus: Identifying Main Idea and Details | **At Level**

Reading Skill
Olmec, Zapotec, and Toltec

Materials: paper, three different colored markers

1. Draw the Venn diagram as shown for students to see. Omit the italicized words.

2. Have students copy and complete the Venn diagram on their own papers, using one colored marker for each oval. **LS** Visual-Spatial

Alternative Assessment Handbook, Rubric 13: Graphic Organizers.

First Cultures of Mesoamerica

Olmec: *stone heads, trade, calendar, writing*

Zapotec: *first true city, neighborhoods*

Zapotec and Olmec: *Olmec carvings, ball game*

All three: *pyramids and temples*

Toltec: *militaristic, near obsidian, mines*

Pyramids were often built on top of older, smaller pyramids. Over time, forest growth covered even the largest pyramids, making them difficult to find.

MAYA PYRAMID

▲ This Maya pyramid at Tikal was the tallest structure in the Americas before the arrival of the Europeans. Pyramids like these were often topped with temples.

At its height in the 700s, Monte Albán had a population of as many as 35,000 people. The city declined rapidly, however. Some scholars think that Zapotec leaders probably lost their people's support. When this happened, Mesoamerica's first urban population moved from Monte Albán to smaller communities. The site, however, was still used for high-status burials.

Toltec The Toltec, who lived in the highlands of central Mexico from AD 900 to 1200, formed another urban civilization. An early Toltec leader established a capital at Tula. Tula's location near obsidian mines made it a major trade center.

Like other early Mesoamerican cities, Tula had pyramids and temples. Unlike other cities, however, Tula's art and architecture showed the militaristic nature of its inhabitants. Statues and carvings of warriors celebrate the fierce Toltecs, who established military dominance over a large region. Toltec dominance did not last, however. Some combination of climate change and social conflict led to the abandonment of Tula in less than three centuries.

READING CHECK **Compare** What did the Olmec, Zapotec, and Toltec cultures have in common?

The Maya

The civilizations of the Olmec, Zapotec, and Toltec were small compared to the Maya civilization that developed in Mesoamerica around 1000 BC. At its height, Maya civilization consisted of some 10 million people spread among 40 cities.

Early Maya Civilization Before they built cities, the Maya lived in small villages where they grew corn, beans, and squash. While they benefited from good rainfall and rich soils, their rain forest environment presented some challenges to farming. To clear forest land for crops, the Maya practiced **slash-and-burn agriculture**. This method of farming involves burning vegetation to clear land for planting. Farmers who lived in the highlands built flat terraces into the hillsides so they could control erosion and more easily grow crops.

Farming did not provide everything the Maya needed. Villages started trading with one another to get goods such as cotton and jade that came from different parts of Mesoamerica. Trade and agriculture helped support larger populations, and the early Maya villages grew into cities.

Direct Teach

Reading Focus

❷ What were some characteristics of Maya civilization? *spectacular cities, trade networks, achievements in astronomy, math, writing and agriculture*

The Maya

Recall How big was Maya civilization at its height? *more than forty cities with 5,000 to 100,000 people each*

Summarize How did Maya farmers deal with environmental challenges? *used slash-and-burn agriculture, shaped hillsides into flat terraces*

Sequence Explain how trade affected the Maya civilization. *allowed people to get items from far away, supported larger population, caused civilization to grow*

Info to Know

Topiltzin In the AD 900s Topiltzin, a Toltec king, began building an empire in central Mexico. He introduced the religion of Quetzalcoatl and added the god's name to his own. Unfortunately, Topiltzin became involved in a civil war, which he and his followers lost. In AD 987, Topiltzin was forced out of the Toltec capital. According to legend, he went to Mexico's gulf coast, embarked on a raft made of snakes, and promised to return one day to save his people.
Draw Conclusions What does this legend suggest about the culture that produced it? *possible answers—later people hoping for salvation from hard times of cruel rulers; supporters of Topiltzin remained*

Differentiating Instruction

Below Level

Special Education Students

Materials poster paper, art supplies

1. Review with students the information in the text about the first civilizations in Mesoamerica.

2. Organize students into mixed-ability pairs and assign each pair a civilization covered in the section: the Olmec, Zapotec, Toltec, Maya, or Aztecs.

3. Have groups plan and create a poster documenting their civilization. Posters should include images of cities and artifacts, and text

explaining the images. Posters should also indicate when the civilization was at its height.

4. Display posters in a classroom exhibit. Arrange them from left to right in chronological order. Have students compare the images on the posters and identify similarities and differences between the civilizations. **LS Visual-Spatial, Interpersonal**

📖 **Alternative Assessment Handbook**, Rubric 29: Posters

Answers

Reading Check *They all built cities, pyramids, and temples; the Zapotec and Toltec cultures adopted some elements of Olmec culture.*

Reading Focus

The Maya

Recall How were Maya cities linked? *trade, warfare*

Describe What was the Maya ball game and how was it played? *religious ritual; players tried to get heavy rubber ball through stone ring; used only elbows, knees, or hips; losing team often killed*

Summarize What do scholars believe may have caused the decline of the Maya civilization? *long drought, increased warfare and competition for land, demands of powerful kings caused people to rebel and leave*

Recent Scholarship

In the southern Maya lowlands, rainfall was the main source of water for people and crops. Kings organized public ceremonies that showed their connection to the gods and precious water. In *Water and Ritual: the Rise and Fall of Classic Maya Rulers,* anthropologist Lisa Lucero describes Maya water policies. She explains how water was traded for tribute and goods, and theorizes that droughts ultimately caused the people to lose faith in their rulers. Lucero's work describes water as the central element in the rise, dominance, and fall of the Classic Maya kings.

Water and Ritual: the Rise and Fall of the Classic Maya Rulers, by Lisa Lucero. University of Texas Press, 2006

Answers

Reading Check *great cities; trade networks; achievements in astronomy, math, and writing; accurate calendar*

Cities and Government The Maya built most of their cities between AD 250 and 900, a period of Maya history known as the Classic Age. Maya cities such as Tikal and Copan were some of the most spectacular in Mesoamerica. They contained stone pyramids, temples, and palaces. Often built to honor gods or rulers, these monumental structures were brightly painted and decorated with stone carvings.

Maya cities functioned as city-states. Each had its own ruler and its own government. No ruler ever united the many cities into a single empire. Even without a central government, however, Maya cities were linked in several ways. One link was trade. Cities in the highlands traded local products such as jade and obsidian for cotton, rubber, and cacao from cities in the lowlands. Another link between cities was warfare. Neighboring Maya cities were often at war with each other. Through bloody battles, kings tried to gain land for their cities and power for themselves.

Society and Religion Kings had great influence in Maya society. The Maya believed kings communicated with the gods. The Maya worshipped many gods and believed they influenced daily life. To prevent disasters and keep the gods happy, the Maya performed private and public rituals for the gods. One common ritual involved offering blood to the gods, usually by piercing the tongue or skin. Another religious ritual involved playing a ball game common in Mesoamerica. In this game, players tried to get a heavy rubber ball through a stone ring using only their elbows, knees, or hips. Losing teams often lost their lives as well, with their hearts sacrificed to the gods. The Maya performed human sacrifice only on certain occasions.

Religious ceremonies were led by priests, who were part of the upper class. Also part of the upper class were professional warriors. They played an important role in Maya religion and society because they were responsible for getting war victims for use in human sacrifice.

Just below the upper class in Maya society were merchants and skilled craftspeople. Most men and women, however, were members of the lower class. They were the farmers and slaves whose labor supported the wealthier classes. They supported the upper classes by providing food and labor for public building projects.

206 CHAPTER 7

Achievements Impressive buildings and architecture, including canals, were a major achievement of the Maya. In addition, the Maya made advances in astronomy, math, and writing. They carefully observed the movements of the sun, moon, and planets. Based on what they observed, they created a calendar system. The Maya had two calendars—a 365-day farming calendar and a 260-day religious calendar. Priests consulted the calendars to determine what days would be lucky or unlucky for war, planting, and religious ceremonies. In spite of the way the Maya used their calendar system, it was more accurate than that used in Europe at the same time.

To go along with their calendars, the Maya created a number system that included some new concepts in math. For example, the Maya were among the first people in the world to use the concept of zero.

The Maya also developed a complex writing system to keep records. Their writing consisted of **glyphs**, or symbols, that represented both objects and sounds. The Maya carved their writing into large stone monuments called stelae. They also kept written records in a type of bark-paper book later referred to as a **codex**.

Decline A part of Maya history that is not clear from their written records is what caused their civilization to decline. Scholars think that a number of factors caused the decline. One factor may have been environmental damage from overuse of resources or a drought that made it difficult to feed everyone in the cities. A related theory says that warfare increased over competition for land. Increased warfare would have destroyed more crops. A third factor in the decline could have been the abuse of power by particularly strong kings, such as Yax Pak of Copán. The demands of kings could have caused people to rebel and leave their cities.

Although Maya civilization declined around 900, the Maya did not disappear. Evidence suggests that the Maya from forest cities moved to new cities, such as Chichén Itzá in the Yucatán Peninsula. Those cities remained powerful for several hundred years. Eventually, however, the Maya abandoned those cities as well and scattered into small villages in the region.

READING CHECK **Summarize** What were the main characteristics of Maya civilization?

Differentiating Instruction

Above Level

Advanced Learners/Gifted and Talented

Research Required

1. Have students conduct further research into the decline of Maya civilization.

2. Have students form a thesis explaining why Maya civilization declined and have them build a case to support it. Students may choose to use one of the explanations given in the chapter, but all students should gather evidence to support their theses.

3. Have students prepare short presentations in which they state their theses and give evidence to support them. Have students use presentation software to display support for their theses. Encourage students to ask questions following each presentation and discuss the issue as a class. **LS Verbal-Linguistic**

Alternative Assessment Handbook, Rubrics 22: Multimedia Presentations and 24: Oral Presentations

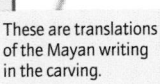

Reading like a Historian

Maya Carvings

Analyzing Primary Sources Whether they are primary or secondary sources, visual images can help us understand an event or a culture in history. Historians have learned a lot about the Maya from studying their carvings and writing. The image here is a Maya carving created about 770. The Maya typically wrote descriptions—much like captions—of the scenes in their carvings. The glyphs, or symbols, on the carving are Maya writing describing the scene. Historians are interested in studying Maya carvings to learn about their society.

To analyze what this carving has to say about Maya society, think about

- the subject of the image
- the details in the image
- the Maya description of the scene.

A bloodletting ritual was performed to celebrate the birth of Shield Jaguar II, son of Bird Jaguar

These are translations of the Mayan writing in the carving.

Bird Jaguar, he who took 20 captives, blood lord of Yaxchilan

The people in the image are a Maya king and his wife.

The lady is pulling a cord studded with stingray spines through her tongue to get blood.

Skills FOCUS — READING LIKE A HISTORIAN

1. **Creator** What does this carving tell us about the artist?
2. **Details** What does this carving reveal about Maya society?
3. **Subject** Why do you think the artist created this carving?

See **Skills Handbook**, p. H25

Direct Teach

Teaching Tip

To show students more examples of rubbings of Maya carvings, go to the following Web site: http://www.mesoweb.com/rub/rubbingsdatabase.html. Click on "Favorites" to see some elaborate representations of carvings.

Info to Know

Maya Astronomers The ancient Maya considered the stars and planets to be gods. They watched them to predict events on Earth that the gods controlled. As a result, the Maya made many accurate observations of the skies. For instance, they determined that Venus took 584 days to reappear at the same given point on the horizon. Maya observatories were carefully designed and positioned. Windows were lined up with various astronomical reference points, such as due west, where the sun sets on the vernal equinox.

Skills Focus: Analyzing Visuals

At Level

Reading Like a Historian Skill
Maya Carving

Materials: images of Maya carvings, drawing paper, pencils

1. Review with students the information in the text about Maya carvings. More images can be found at http://www.mesoweb.com/rub/rubbingsdatabase.html.

2. Have students sketch a plan for a carving that portrays some aspect of Maya daily life. Have students use the Maya style of art.

3. Have volunteers to present their drawings to the class. **LS Visual-Spatial**

Alternative Assessment Handbook, Rubric 3: Artwork

Answers

Reading Like a Historian 1. *that Maya rulers and religious ceremonies were important to artist;* **2.** *shows religious rituals and reveals significance of king; details show that rulers wore ornate clothing; people used writing system;* **3.** *possible answers—to honor the Maya king; to depict religious ritual*

207

3 What made the Aztec empire one of the strongest in the ancient Americas? *were fierce warriors, gained wealth through system of trade and tribute, ruled from the large city of Tenochtitlán*

The Aztecs

Recall When the Aztecs migrated south, where did they settle? *on a swampy island in Lake Texcoco*

Make Inferences Why do you think tribute was paid in different ways? *possible answer—probably because people could only pay based on what was available and valuable*

Evaluate Do you think merchants would make good spies? Why or why not? *possible answer—Yes, because they traveled throughout the empire and had contact with many people*

- **CRF:** Primary Source: Laws, Ordinances, and Statutes Decreed by King Montezuma I
- **CRF:** Literature: The Legend of La Llorona
- **CRF:** Biography: Montezuma II

Info to Know

Diego Rivera's Murals Diego Rivera created large mural paintings in public buildings in Mexico and the United States. One series depicts Mexico's history and the everyday life of its people. Rivera incorporated elements of native Mexican art into his work. Rivera's radical politics were often a source of controversy, but his murals have stood the test of time

Answers

Life in the Aztec Empire *possible answer—The foreground seems accurately depicted but the background reflects a more modern city.*

208

The Aztecs

About the time that the Maya cities in the Yucatán were declining, a group of people to the north, the Aztecs, began their rise to power. The early Aztecs were just a small group of unlucky farmers from northwestern Mexico who were searching for a new home. But in little time, they created the most powerful empire in Mesoamerica.

Rise of the Empire The Aztecs began as a group of separate tribes from northwestern Mexico. These farming tribes were probably subjects of the Toltecs. According to legend, the war god told one of the tribes' leaders that they should look for a place where they saw an eagle perched on a cactus eating a snake. It was there that they should settle and build a new capital.

The Aztecs migrated south to the Valley of Mexico in the 1100s. When they arrived, they found that other tribes had already taken all the good farmland. The Aztecs saw the eagle and the snake on a swampy island in Lake Texcoco. They founded a city there and called it Tenochtitlán. From there the Aztecs continued their rise to power.

NEW YORK
CC Unit 4-D1 Human and physical geography of the Aztec empire

In addition to being farmers, the Aztecs were also fierce warriors. They began fighting to control other towns around Lake Texcoco. The Aztecs gained strength in the 1420s when they formed an **alliance**, or partnership, with two other nearby city-states, Texcoco and Tlacopan. This alliance quickly gained control over a huge region that spread far beyond Lake Texcoco. The Aztecs came to rule 400 to 500 other city-states. At its height, about 5 million people were part of the Aztec Empire.

The Aztecs required the conquered people of their empire to pay **tribute**, or a type of tax. People in the empire paid tribute in many forms, from feathers and food crops to pottery and blankets. This tribute system was the basis of the Aztec economy. If any local ruler refused to pay tribute, the Aztecs used their military force to destroy the town.

The Aztec Empire gained wealth and strength through trade as well as through tribute. A system of roads aided trade. Merchants traveled throughout the empire to buy and sell luxury goods such as jade and cacao. Merchants sometimes acted as spies for the Aztec emperor. They could report any trouble they saw brewing in distant parts of the empire.

Life in the Aztec Empire

The famous Mexican muralist Diego Rivera painted this scene of Tenochtitlán in 1945. The title is *La Gran Tenochtitlán: Market Fair at Tenochtitlán*. It now hangs in Mexico City, the city built on the ruins of Tenochtitlán. **How accurately do you think this painting depicts Tenochtitlán?**

La Gran Tenochtitlán, by Diego Rivera, 1945
Courtesy SuperStock, Inc.

208 CHAPTER 7

Differentiating Instruction

Below Level

Struggling Readers

1. Review with students the story of how the Aztecs came from the north and settled on an island in Lake Texcoco.

2. Have students write poems, or song lyrics to tell this story and the story of the Aztecs' rise to power.

3. Have volunteers recite their poems or song lyrics for the class. Encourage students to accompany their poems or songs with a musical instrument. **LS Auditory-Musical**

   Alternative Assessment Handbook, Rubric 26: Poems and Songs

Tenochtitlán The glory of the Aztec Empire was most clearly seen in the capital city of Tenochtitlán. This amazing city covered five square miles and had a population of about 200,000. It was one of the largest cities in the world at that time.

At the center of the city was a huge walled compound that served as the political and religious heart of the entire empire. Within the walls rose a huge pyramid with two temples on top. The Aztec priests performed religious ceremonies at these temples. Other temples, as well as government buildings, palaces, and a ball court, filled the rest of the city center. It was such an impressive sight that one of the first Europeans to see Tenochtitlán said the city "seemed like an enchanted vision."

Since Tenochtitlán was built on a swampy island in the middle of a lake, there was not much land available for farming. To create more farmland for their corn, beans, and squash, the Aztecs built "floating gardens" called *chinampas* (chee-NAHM-pahs) around the edges of the city. They did this by piling soil on top of rafts anchored to reeds in the water. From the *chinampas*, farmers loaded crops onto canoes and floated them down canals to the market.

Tenochtitlán was connected by canals and causeways to the empire's biggest market at Tlatelolco, a smaller city just outside the Aztec capital. Tlatelolco attracted more than 60,000 people a day. Merchants brought goods such as cotton, jaguar pelts, and rubber to trade. Since the Aztecs had no coins, they sometimes used cacao beans or goose quills filled with gold as money. Vendors at the market had to pay a tax, usually in corn, to support the Aztec army.

Society and Religion Just as the economy of the Aztec Empire was highly organized, so was Aztec society. It was strictly divided into different social classes. At the top of the social order was the king. The king was part of a royal family, but he had to be elected by a group of nobles. The king displayed his power at his palace in Tenochtitlán, where he had gardens, a zoo, and thousands of servants. Certain nobles also served the king as government officials.

Just below the king in Aztec society were priests. They interpreted calendars and performed religious ceremonies. Aztec religious ceremonies were particularly bloody. Believing that the gods needed human blood, the Aztecs sacrificed as many as 20,000 victims a year. One European observer shared his perspective of a scene in a temple after a sacrifice.

ACADEMIC VOCABULARY
perspective personal point of view

HISTORY'S VOICES

❝All the walls of that shrine were so splashed and caked with blood that they and the floor too were black. Indeed, the whole place stank abominably.❞
—Bernal Díaz del Castillo, *The Conquest of New Spain*, 1568

The Aztecs usually used slaves or prisoners of war as sacrifices. Warriors were responsible for capturing these victims. Because of this tie to religion, certain highly trained warriors were also part of the Aztec upper class.

Not quite part of the upper class, but respected and wealthy nonetheless, were merchants and artisans. Merchants often became rich from trading in luxury goods. They lived in grand houses in Tenochtitlán, but they were not as wealthy as the king. Artisans were important because they made the goods required for tribute.

Most people in Aztec society were farmers. They made up the lower class and were very poor. They usually did not own their own land.

① The great temple stood in the center of Tenochtitlán. Other temples were scattered throughout the city.

② Slaves provided much of the labor in the Aztec Empire.

③ Canals and causeways linked Tenochtitlán to surrounding areas.

④ People from all over the empire came to the market to trade goods and food such as corn.

THE IMPACT TODAY

Mexico City, the capital of Mexico and one of the biggest cities in the world, was later built on the site of Tenochtitlán.

The Aztecs

Rank Which people in Aztec society had the most difficult lives? *slaves*

Rate How might Aztec civilization be considered advanced? *had writing system, kept written records, developed an accurate calendar, were master metal and stone workers*

• Review & Assess •

Close

Discuss achievements of early civilizations of Mesoamerica.

Review

Online Quiz, Section 2

Assess

SE **Section 2 Assessment**

📋 **Progress Assessment:** Section 2 Quiz

📋 **Alternative Assessment Handbook**

Reteach/Intervene

📋 **Interactive Reader and Study Guide,** Section 2

💿 **Interactive Skills Tutor CD-ROM**

Answers

Reading Check *good farmers, fierce warriors, founded capital of Tenochtitán, well-organized economy and society, created calendar*

Aztec Arts
This skull mask is made from turquoise and obsidian. Skulls and gods were common themes in Aztec art.

They often had to pay so much in tribute that they found it difficult to survive on what was left over.

Farmers could improve their lives, however, by becoming warriors or studying at special schools. All Aztec boys and girls had to attend school until the age of 15, but some people continued in special schools that enabled them to become government officials.

Those in Aztec society who suffered the most were slaves. Most slaves were people who had been captured in battle or those who could not pay their debts. Merchants also bought slaves from other towns in the region. Some slaves worked as farmers or laborers for nobles or merchants, and their children would be born free. Others became victims in human sacrifices.

NEW YORK

CC Unit 4-D3 Contributions of the Aztec empire

Achievements Like other Mesoamericans, the Aztecs are known for their achievements in art and science. Their artisans made bright feathers into headdresses, shields, and warrior costumes. Metalworkers fashioned gold, silver, and copper into jewelry and masks. In addition, master stoneworkers decorated temples and other buildings with elaborate sculptures depicting gods and stories from their history.

Like the Maya, the Aztecs kept written records. The Aztecs also used glyphs in their writing, but their system was not as advanced as Maya writing. The Aztecs used writing to keep track of tax records and business deals. They also composed poetry, riddles, and historical accounts. These were passed on orally from one generation to the next as well.

Using their knowledge of astronomy, the Aztecs created a 260-day religious calendar and a 365-day solar calendar much like the Maya calendar. They also accurately calculated the movements of some planets.

Although the Aztec Empire reached new heights of civilization in the Americas, it lasted a relatively short time. Tenochtitlán lasted less than 200 years. In the early 1500s contact with Europeans would quickly bring an end to the empire.

READING CHECK **Identify Supporting Details** What aspects of the Aztec Empire made it the strongest in Mesoamerica?

SECTION 2 ASSESSMENT

go.hrw.com
Online Quiz
Keyword: SHL AMS HP

Reviewing Ideas, Terms, and People

1. a. Describe What geographical features of Mesoamerica made it a good location for the development of early civilizations in the Americas?
b. Explain How did the Olmec influence knowledge and arts throughout Mesoamerica?

2. a. Define What is **slash-and-burn agriculture**?
b. Analyze In what ways was Maya religion linked to daily life?
c. Support a Position Defend or criticize the statement that the Maya civilization grew too fast for its own good.

3. a. Recall How did the **alliance** affect the Aztecs?
b. Interpret How did the Aztec system of **tribute** strengthen the empire?
c. Make Judgments How might an Aztec and a European view Aztec religion differently?

Critical Thinking

4. Compare and Contrast Use your notes on the section and a graphic organizer like the one below to show how the Maya and the Aztecs were similar and how they were different in their government, religion, society, and achievements.

	Maya	Aztec
Government		
Religion		
Society		
Achievements		

FOCUS ON WRITING

5. Description Imagine you are a visitor to a Maya city as the Classic Period is ending. Write a short letter home describing what you see. Include details about the environment, people's activities, what the city must have been like in earlier years, and what you expect it to look like in a few years.

Section 2 Assessment Answers

1. a. warm temperatures, rainfall, rich soil
b. along trade routes

2. a. a farming method in which vegetation is burned to clear land for planting
b. offered sacrifices to the gods
c. possible answer—defend: fast growth meant that many people had to be fed and provided for, which caused a decline; criticize: civilization declined because of war

3. a. allowed Aztecs control over large region, ruled hundreds of city-states, empire began

b. strengthened economy and increased power over neighbors
c. possible answer—European: might think religious ceremonies were barbaric; Aztec: would think that the gods needed blood

4. similar—large trade network, impressive cities with pyramids, human sacrifice, class system, writing and calendar; different—Maya: city-states, personal blood offering, number system; Aztec: unified empire, tribute system, human sacrifice common

5. possible details—city is breathtaking, has brightly painted pyramids, temples, and palaces; people are trading in marketplace, playing ball-game, priests are conducting blood ceremony; this city used to be a tiny plaza with a low pyramid, but will probably grow even larger and more impressive

3 South America

BEFORE YOU READ

MAIN IDEA

Several early cultures in South America adapted to extreme environmental conditions. One of them, the Inca, built one of the biggest and most powerful empires in the Americas.

READING FOCUS

1. How did early cultures of South America adapt to their environments?

2. How was the Inca Empire organized?

KEY TERMS AND PEOPLE

Pachacuti
quipu
census

 NEW YORK

PI 1.4 Students understand the broad patterns, relationships, and interactions of cultures and civilizations during particular eras and across eras.

THE INSIDE STORY

What are the gigantic designs in the desert of Peru? Since the 1920s scientists have studied some mysterious lines in the Peruvian desert. These lines formed images of plants and animals up to several hundred feet long. Some scholars think the Nazca people created the lines more than 2,000 years ago. But how did the Nazca create them and what purpose did they serve?

Scholars know that the lines were made by removing the top, darker layer of the desert floor to expose lighter ground underneath, but they can only theorize about their purpose. Perhaps the lines pointed to movements of the sun or planets. Or perhaps they were sacred pathways or had other religious functions.

An Ancient Desert Mystery

▼ **Although visible at ground-level, lines in the desert form designs so large they can only be clearly seen from the sky.**

THE AMERICAS **211**

Teach the Main Idea

At Level

South America

1. **Teach** Ask students the Reading Focus questions to teach this section.

2. **Apply** Have students create two web diagrams for the section, one for Early Cultures in South America and one for the Inca Empire. Have students write aspects of each culture in their diagrams.

3. **Review** As you review the section, have students explain how early cultures of South America survived in harsh environments.

4. **Practice/Homework** Have students write a speech from an Inca ruler to a conquered people, introducing them to the Inca system.
LS Visual-Spatial, Verbal-Linguistic

📝 **Alternative Assessment Handbook,** Rubric 42: Writing to Inform

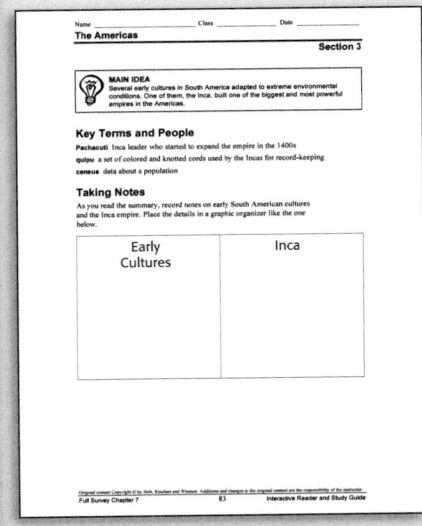

Preteach

Getting Started

Use the **Interactive Reader and Study Guide** to familiarize students with the section content.

📄 **Interactive Reader and Study Guide,** Section 3

Academic Vocabulary

Review with students the high-use academic term in this section.

stability resistance to change or destruction (p. 213)

📄 **CRF:** Vocabulary Builder: Section 3

Taking Notes

Inca government—replaced local leaders with loyal Inca, Pachacuti and other leaders used military for protection, required labor tax, distributed goods throughout empire, kept records, grouped families into communities, organized economy and society

go.hrw.com
Online Resources
KEYWORD: SHL AMS
ACTIVITY: Hike the Inca Trail to Machu Picchu

Early Cultures	Inca

Early Cultures in South America

The western region of South America is one of environmental contrasts. The coastal desert is one of the driest places on earth. The Andes, which run almost the length of the continent, form the second-highest mountain range in the world. On the eastern slopes of the Andes is a region of steamy rain forests. In spite of these geographical extremes, many early peoples learned to adapt to their environments and built advanced civilizations there.

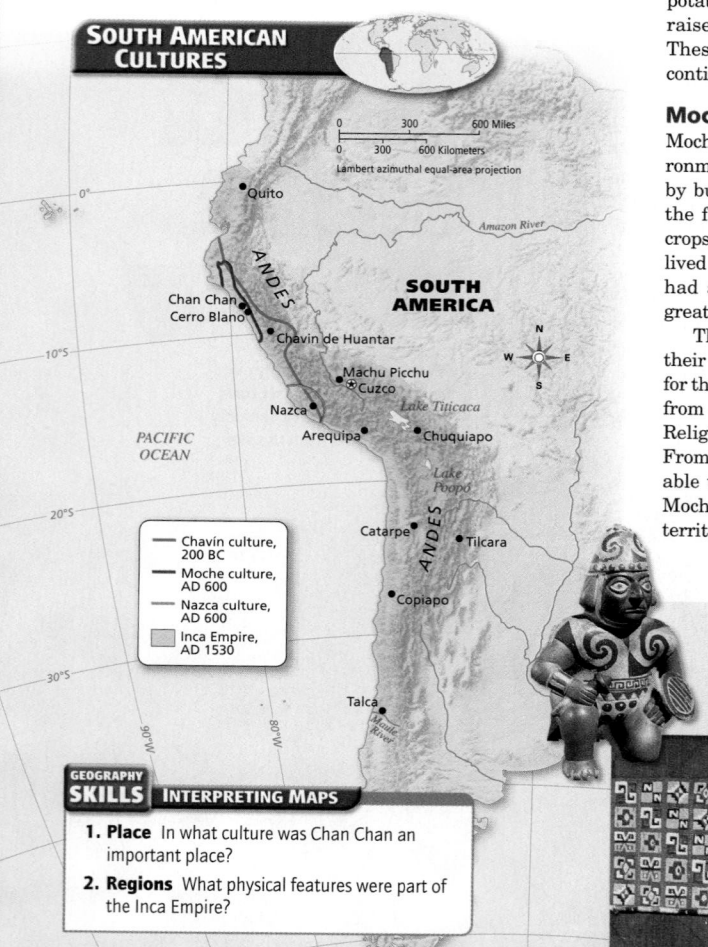

SOUTH AMERICAN CULTURES

Chavín culture, 200 BC
Moche culture, AD 600
Nazca culture, AD 600
Inca Empire, AD 1530

GEOGRAPHY SKILLS INTERPRETING MAPS

1. **Place** In what culture was Chan Chan an important place?
2. **Regions** What physical features were part of the Inca Empire?

212 CHAPTER 7

Chavín One early people, the Chavín (chah-VEEN), lived in the highlands of Peru from about 900 to 200 BC. The center of Chavín culture was a site called Chavín de Huantar. It was an urban religious and trading center with a population of about 3,000 farmers, craftspeople, and others.

Because Chavín de Huantar lay on the slopes of the Andes, farmers in the region had access to several distinct ecological zones. As a result, they were able to grow several different types of crops. In the warmer valleys, they built irrigation systems and grew corn. Higher in the mountains, where it was cooler, they grew potatoes. In the high-altitude grasslands, they raised animals such as llamas and alpacas. These same farming and herding strategies continued in later Andean societies.

Moche In the coastal desert of Peru, the Moche also learned how to adapt to their environment. They were able to farm in the desert by building irrigation canals that channeled the flow of streams from the Andes to their crops. From about 400 BC to 600 AD the Moche lived in farming and fishing villages. They also had an urban capital centered around two great pyramids.

The Moche were probably best known for their skilled metalwork in gold and silver and for their pottery. Moche pottery depicted scenes from daily life, such as weaving and hunting. Religion and war were also common themes. From Moche pottery, archeologists have been able to determine that warrior-priests ruled Moche society and that they expanded their territory through warfare.

Arts in South America
Pottery, such as this Moche warrior, and weaving, such as this Inca textile, were two of the most common forms of art among early cultures in South America.

Nazca Another desert people, the Nazca, lived from about 200 BC to AD 600. The Nazca are best known for the huge designs they made on the desert floor. These Nazca Lines show geometric shapes and outlines of animals such as a monkey, a hummingbird, and a spider. There are many theories as to why the Nazca created these large-scale drawings and designs. One theory is that they may have had something to do with the location of water.

Water was very important in the desert. The Nazca built irrigation canals and also relied on the natural springs and the annual flooding of streams to water their crops. This way, they were able to farm in the desert and support a large population.

READING CHECK **Identify Problem and Solution** What problems did the environments of South America create, and how did early cultures solve these problems?

The Inca Empire

Many years after the earliest civilizations began in western South America, the Incas brought the entire Andes region into one empire. They began as a small tribe in the Andes, but by the early 1500s their empire extended along almost the entire Pacific coast and throughout the Andes.

Government The Incas began their period of rapid expansion in the 1400s. From their capital at Cuzco, their leader **Pachacuti** used political alliances and military force to gain control of a huge territory. Later Inca leaders continued the expansion. At its height, in the early 1500s, the Inca Empire had a population of about 12 million.

To rule such a large empire, the Incas needed a strong government. The emperor had most of the power. However, he needed help to rule areas far from the capital because the Incas did not want people they conquered to gain too much power and rebel. To limit the power of various local leaders, the Incas made leaders of conquered areas move out of their villages. They then moved in new leaders who were loyal to the Inca Empire. This system of resettlement created <u>stability</u> in the empire. The military was also used to protect against internal rebellion and external attacks.

PACHACUTI
Died 1471

Pachacuti was the most powerful ruler in Inca history. He became emperor in about 1438. Under his rule, the Inca Empire had its period of greatest expansion. In addition to gaining territory, Pachacuti rebuilt the Inca capital at Cuzco.

Pachacuti was also responsible for many government reforms. For example, he began the policy of sending government officials to rule different areas of the empire. He also established an official religion and an official language, Quechua. These changes brought unity and stability to an empire that governed diverse groups of people.

Infer How would Pachacuti's establishing an official religion and language help him govern the Inca Empire?

Economy The government strictly controlled the economy in the empire. The common people in the empire were required to "pay" a labor tax called the *mita*. Women could fulfill the *mita* by activities such as weaving cloth for the army. Men worked on government-owned farms, in mines, or built roads. The government said what work would be done.

There were no merchants or markets as we know them in the Inca Empire. Instead, government officials distributed goods around the empire. This was how the Incas supplied their army and people who were old or sick with the goods they needed. Any extra food or goods were stored in government warehouses for use in emergencies.

To keep track of the movement of goods throughout the empire, the Inca used a **quipu**, or set of colored and knotted cords. The colors and knots represented numbers or dates. The quipu was the only system of record keeping in the empire because the Incas had no written language. The Inca used quipus to record information such as tax records, quantities of livestock, and **census**, or population, data. Only specially trained officials could read and use quipus. Scholars today have not been able to fully decipher these Inca records.

Quipu keepers, officials who distributed tribute goods, the army, and many other people relied on an extensive road network. Roads linked cities all over the empire. The Inca road system improved communication and helped the government control the economy.

READING SKILLS

Making Generalizations What generalization can you make about the Inca economy?

 NEW YORK

CC Unit 4-D4
Trade of the Incan empire

ACADEMIC VOCABULARY
stability resistance to change or destruction

THE AMERICAS **213**

Reading Focus

❷ How was the Inca Empire organized? *families grouped into communities called ayllus, group of ten ayllus had a chief who reported to higher official; chain of command stretched from local level up to emperor*

The Inca Empire

Explain How did the Inca create stability in the empire? *forced local leaders out of villages, used a system of resettlement by replacing them with loyal Inca leaders*

Summarize How did the *mita* system work? *government strictly controlled economy by requiring a labor tax of common people; people wove cloth for army, worked on government-owned farms or mines, built roads*

Evaluate Do you think the Inca had a good economic system? Why or why not? *possible answer—Yes, it distributed goods effectively.*

Skills Focus: Making Generalizations

At Level

Reading Skill
Conquered by the Inca

1. Review with students the information in the text about how the Inca conquered and controlled other peoples.

2. Have students write a series of seven journal entries from the point of view of a member of a tribe that has been conquered by the Inca. Suggest that students bring out positive and negative aspects of Inca rule.

3. Have volunteers read their journal entries to the class.

4. After students have read their journal entries, lead a class discussion about the accuracy of their entries. **LS** **Verbal-Linguistic**

📝 **Alternative Assessment Handbook**, Rubric 15: Journals

Answers

Faces of History *possible answer—would bring unity and stability and allow for communication*

Reading Skills *It was strictly controlled by government.*

Reading Check *extremely dry area, high mountain range, rain forest; planted crops based on zone, built irrigation canals so streams would flow from mountains to crops*

213

History Close-up
Inca Roads

Maintaining unity in the geographically long and mountainous Inca territory would have been impossible without a good road system. Since the Inca didn't use wheeled vehicles and the empire had no horses, roads were used only by pedestrians and pack llamas. Consequently, the roads did not need to be paved or even made especially flat.

Info to Know

Chasquis An important group of people who relied heavily on the Inca road system were Inca couriers called *Chasquis*. *Chasquis* were trained runners who carried messages throughout the empire. A relay system was set up that involved resting points at key locations along the roadway. One *Chasqui* would cover the distance from one resting point to the next, where he would hand off the message to another *Chasqui,* who was rested and could carry on. In this way, a message could be carried up to 250 miles per day.

About the Illustration

This illustration is an artist's conception based on available sources. Historians, however, are uncertain exactly what this scene looked like.

HISTORY CLOSE-UP

Inca Roads

The Incas built a network of roads, paved with stone blocks, that was about 14,000 miles long and crossed almost every kind of terrain imaginable. The roads stretched from sea level to almost 12,000 feet in elevation.

Stairs of cut stone linked roadways in higher and lower areas.

Terraces increased the amount of land available for agriculture.

Trained runners would carry messages and orders of the empire between carefully spaced *tambos,* or way stations, along the roads. This created a one-day delivery time for each 140 miles.

The first known suspension bridges spanned canyons, crevasses, and rivers. The bridges were woven out of fibers and vines.

SKILLS FOCUS **INTERPRETING VISUALS**

Roads were vital for transportation, communication, and government administration in the Inca Empire.

Analyze What challenges did the Incas face in building their roads?

214 CHAPTER 7

Skills Focus: Identifying Problem and Solution | At Level

Reading Skill
Inca Road Plans

Prep Required

Materials: photocopies of topographical maps

1. Before the lesson, obtain topographical maps, preferably of hilly or mountainous regions with rivers or streams.

2. Instruct students how to read topographical maps. Tell them that lines close together indicate a steep area and lines far apart indicate a flatter area.

3. Organize students into mixed-ability pairs. Give each pair a photocopy of a topographical map.

4. Have each pair plan an Inca road that will cross the map, roughly from north to south or from east to west. Students should consider geographic elements to design an effective road plan. Have students create a legend and show the location of rope bridges and steps.

5. Ask volunteers to present their plans to the class. **LS Logical-Mathematical, Visual-Spatial**

Alternative Assessment Handbook, Rubric 21: Map Reading

Answers

Interpreting Visuals *physical features such as mountainous landscape, rushing rivers, dense forests*

Society In the Central Andes, each family was grouped with others into a cooperative community called an *ayllu* (EYE-yoo). Members of the *ayllu* worked together in activities such as farming, building canals or terraces, and performing religious rituals. Under the Incas, each group of ten *ayllus* had a chief. That chief reported to a higher level government official and so on in groups of ten. In this way, the *ayllu* was at the end of a chain of command that stretched from the local level throughout the empire all the way to the emperor.

In spite of the cooperation in the *ayllus*, there were still clear class divisions in Inca society. There were no slaves in the Inca Empire, but most people belonged to the lower class. They were farmers, artisans, or servants. Inca laws required that they wear only plain clothes and restricted them from owning any more goods than they needed. The lower class had to serve the upper class.

The upper class, which included the king, government officials, and priests, lived in Cuzco, the capital. These elite, high-ranking members of society had good stone houses and wore fine clothes. They did not have to pay the labor tax. Sons of Inca nobles attended school where they studied religion, history, law, and the quipu to prepare for lives as government or religious officials.

Religion was a key element of Inca society. People throughout the empire were allowed to worship local gods, but the sun god was the most important god in the official Inca religion. The Incas believed their kings were related to the sun god. The mummies of dead kings were kept in Cuzco and worshipped. Priests performed ceremonies for this god at the main temple in Cuzco. These ceremonies often included sacrifices of llamas, cloth, or food. The Incas only sacrificed humans on rare occasions.

Achievements The level of organization of Inca government and society led to significant achievements in the areas of engineering and the arts. The Incas were particularly talented builders. They built temples, forts, and roads out of huge stone blocks. They cut the blocks to fit so precisely that they did not need mortar to hold them together. These Inca structures were built so well that many still stand today, and even today it is nearly impossible to slip a knife blade between the stones.

In the arts, the Incas were especially skilled in metalwork and weaving. Artisans made intricate ornaments out of gold and silver. They even created a life-sized field of corn out of gold and silver in a temple courtyard.

Inca weavers worked with both wool and cotton. They divided cloth into three categories—plain cloth used for households, finer cloth used for taxes and trade, and special cloth used only for royal and religious purposes. The Incas used a variety of patterns for their textiles. A particular pattern indicated an Inca's status in society.

In spite of the high level of organization and achievement, the Inca Empire lasted only about 100 years. It began to suffer from internal conflict. The arrival of the Spanish in Peru in 1532 would mark the end of the Inca Empire just as the Spanish arrival had for the Aztecs.

READING CHECK **Summarize** What methods did the government use to control the Inca Empire?

NEW YORK

CC Unit 4-D2
Organizational structure of the Incan empire

SECTION 3 ASSESSMENT

go.hrw.com
Online Quiz
Keyword: SHL AMS HP

Reviewing Ideas, Terms, and People

1. **a. Identify** What early culture is known for its pottery that showed scenes from daily life?
   b. Explain How were the Chavín able to raise different types of crops that grow in different climates?
   c. Develop How did the Nazca adapt their desert environment to grow crops?

2. **a. Identify** Who was Pachacuti?
   b. Infer Why do you think the Inca government wanted to keep records of **census** data?
   c. Evaluate Do you think the *mita* system was a good government policy? Why or why not?

Critical Thinking

3. **Evaluate** Use your notes on the section and the graphic organizer below to describe how you think people who were part of the Inca Empire benefited from living under the control of the Inca government.

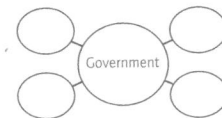

Government

FOCUS ON WRITING

4. **Persuasion** Imagine you are an Inca official who is trying to convince a group of people to peacefully become part of the Inca Empire. Write down three or four arguments you could use to persuade them.

THE AMERICAS **215**

Section 3 Assessment Answers

1. **a.** Moche
   b. Their land was located in various altitudes and environmental zones.
   c. built irrigation canals, used natural springs and flooding

2. **a.** Inca leader who used political alliances and military force to gain huge territory
   b. possible answer—It enabled accurate planning, allowed for the distribution of goods, and gave it control over society.
   c. possible answers—Yes, because it ensured work would be done, so goods and

food would flow to government; no, because it was unfair to lower classes.

3. possible answer—benefited from roads and received goods

4. possible arguments—everything you need will be distributed to you, even if you are old and sick; you will have protection of the military; you will have an excellent road system; you can still worship local gods; there is no slavery.

Theories on Migration to the Americas

Word Help

fluted marked by grooves
hypothetical supposed, not proven

Interpreting Maps

Early American Settlements

Movement Why do you think the land bridge may have encouraged people from Asia to move into North America? *possible answer—may have migrated to find resources available in other climates to meet basic needs such as food, clothing, and shelter*

Info to Know

Linguistics Scientists who study languages are known as linguists and their field is known as linguistics. These scientists examine the origins of human languages and how they are interrelated. Linguists often work closely with anthropologists to trace the origins of modern people. Before the arrival of large numbers of Europeans in the New World, about 300 Indian languages were spoken in North America. Though most of these languages were not written and some have been lost, the diversity that linguists find among the surviving languages is far greater than exists among modern European languages.

Make Inferences How do you think that studying languages helps linguists learn about various peoples' history and origins? *possible answer—If two modern languages are similar, the two peoples probably had close contact; languages with no similarities indicate separated development.*

Theories on Migration to the Americas

Historical Context The four documents below support different theories about when and how the first people migrated to the Americas.

Task Study the documents and answer the questions that follow. Then, using evidence from these selections and from the chapter, write an essay explaining why it is difficult for historians to agree on one theory.

DOCUMENT 1

The Traditionally Accepted Theory

Archaeologist Stuart J. Fiedel has studied hundreds of sites across the Americas to determine how and when the first people arrived in the Americas. The evidence he found supports the traditionally held theory that the first people, called Clovis, crossed the Bering Land Bridge and spread throughout the Americas.

> The striking similarity of fluted points and associated artifacts across the whole expanse of North America suggests that the continent was rapidly filled by Paleo-Indian hunting bands, each retaining for several centuries the tool-making traditions of an ancestral population that originally entered through the ice-free corridor around 10,000–9500 BC. But the only place from which this hypothetical ancestral group could have come is Alaska, where there is hardly any existing evidence of Clovis occupation. The earliest Alaskan cultures, which date to the period from 9000 to 6000 BC, are characterized by small-blade tools, derived from wedge-shaped cores. This "Paleo-arctic" tradition has clear ties to northeast Asia . . . . Unfortunately, there is no convincing evidence of a substantial human presence in Alaska before 9000 BC.

DOCUMENT 2

Archaeological Evidence

Archaeologists base their theories on migration to the Americas on the dates and locations of archaeological evidence of early human settlement.

EARLY AMERICAN SETTLEMENTS

Ice Age glaciers
Land exposed during Ice Age
● Settled 8,000–10,000 years ago
● Settled 11,000 years ago
● Settled 12,500 years ago

Skills Focus: Summarizing

Below Level

Reading Skill
Arrival of Peoples in the Americas

Standard English Mastery

1. Have students use standard English to write a short summary of each of the documents. Have students look up unfamiliar words in the dictionary.

2. Have volunteers read their summaries to the class. As a class, discuss any necessary corrections to the summaries to align them with standard English usage. Using individual student summaries, form a class summary of each document.

3. Guide students in a discussion about the various theories of first arrival in the Americas. Ask students which theory seems the most feasible. **LS Verbal-Linguistic**

Alternative Assessment Handbook, Rubrics 16: Judging Information; and 37: Writing Assignments

DOCUMENT 3

Another Side of the Debate

Archaeologist Thomas Dillehay has studied a site at Monte Verde, Chile. Evidence from that site raises questions about when people arrived in the Americas.

For most of the past century, archaeologists thought that all early sites in the Americas were Clovis, dating no earlier than about 11,200 years ago. If a site appeared to be earlier than Clovis and did not contain Clovis points, a debate ensued about misidentification of evidence from the site. As a result, the evidence from all pre-Clovis candidates was considered unconvincing and dismissed. Recently, however, the debate has taken a new turn because of a small number of sites excavated in the 1970s and 1980s, including Meadowcroft Rockshelter in Pennsylvania, probably the Cactus Hill site in Virginia and the Topper site in South Carolina, and several sites in eastern Brazil, Taima-Taima in Venezuela, Tibitó in Colombia, and Monte Verde in Chile. All these sites yielded more convincing pre-11,000-year dates and evidence suggestive of a generalized (non-big-game) hunter and gatherer lifeway. In other words, these sites contained not only more convincing radiocarbon dates, human-made artifacts, and reliable stratigraphic association but also evidence of early cultures that pre-dated Clovis.

DOCUMENT 4

A Newer Theory

Archaeologists Dennis Stanford and Bruce Bradley think that people have been so focused on the Beringia and Clovis-first theories that they have neglected other possible interpretations of the archaeological evidence.

We also point out that during Solutrean times [c. 20,000 years ago] lower sea levels greatly reduced the distance between the Celtic and the North American Continental Shelves and a connecting ice bridge eliminated the necessity of a 4,000-mile blue voyage between Lisbon and New York City. The southern margin of this ice bridge was a relative rich environment inhabited by migrating sea mammals, birds, and fish attracting Solutrean people. We reason that generations of Solutrean hunters learned to cope with ice and weather conditions to follow rich resources such as Harp seals and Great Auks that migrated north and westward along with retreating ice in late spring. Through such activities they ended up (by accident and/or design) along the exposed continental shelf of North America discovering a New Land.

Skills FOCUS — READING LIKE A HISTORIAN

DOCUMENT 1
a. **Describe** What evidence does Fiedel use to support the theory of Beringia migration by Clovis people?
b. **Draw Conclusions** Why does the lack of convincing evidence from Alaska not harm Fiedel's theory?

DOCUMENT 2
a. **Identify** What appear to be the sites of earliest human settlement?
b. **Analyze** Why might the earliest sites complicate the traditionally accepted theory about when people first arrived in the Americas?

DOCUMENT 3
a. **Identify Main Ideas** What does Dillehay say about the traditional theory that Clovis were the first Americans?
b. **Interpret** How does Dillehay think academic debate has influenced the development of theories on migration to the Americas?

DOCUMENT 4
a. **Describe** Where do Stanford and Bradley think the first Americans came from, and how did they get here?
b. **Compare and Contrast** How is Stanford and Bradley's theory similar to the traditionally accepted theory of the Bering Land Bridge? How is it different?

DOCUMENT-BASED ESSAY QUESTION

Although most scientists agree that the first people to come to the Americas came across the Bering Land Bridge about 11,000 years ago, there is increasing debate over this theory. Using the documents above and information from the chapter, form a thesis that explains why it is difficult for historians to agree on one theory. Then write a short essay to support your position.

See **Skills Handbook**, pp. H25–H26

THE AMERICAS **217**

Differentiating Instruction

Advanced Learners/Gifted and Talented

Above Level

Research Required

1. Have students conduct additional research on the topic of how the first people arrived in the Americas.
2. Have students form a thesis that explains how the first people arrived. Have them collect a body of evidence that supports their thesis.
3. Have students write a two-page persuasion paper, presenting their thesis and giving evidence to support it.
4. As an extension, guide students in a discussion of the various theories. Encourage them to debate the issue. **LS Verbal-Linguistic**

Alternative Assessment Handbook, Rubrics 11: Discussions; and 43: Writing to Persuade

217

Visual Summary

Review and Inquiry Organize students into three groups. Assign each group one of the regions in the visual summary: North America, Mesoamerica, and South America. Have each group make a brief oral presentation that includes information in the visual summary and at least two additional facts about their region.

Quick Facts Transparency: Visual Study Guide: The Americas

Review Key Terms and People

1. status
2. census
3. glyphs
4. Pachacuti
5. tribute
6. pueblo
7. slash-and-burn agriculture

Comprehension and Critical Thinking

8. **a.** to use as burial sites
   b. irrigation system, pithouses, adobe architecture, cliff dwellings
   c. possible answers—Mississippian, because they had a well planned city, engineering and math skills; Iroquois, because they had an advanced system of government

9. **a.** Zapotec
   b. similar—large trade network, cities with pyramids, human sacrifice, class system, writing and calendar; different—Maya: city-states, blood offering, number system; Aztec: unified empire, tribute system, human sacrifice common
   c. possible answer—No, because they had to pay tribute and captives could be human sacrifices.

10. **a.** built amazing temples, forts, and roads; were skilled metalworkers and weavers
    b. replaced local leaders with loyal Inca leaders, maintained road system, organized society into *ayullas*, had an official religion and official language
    c. benefit—ensured they would receive goods; burden—enforced

---

VISUAL STUDY GUIDE

QUICK FACTS

CIVILIZATIONS OF THE AMERICAS

North America
- Environments include deserts, woodlands, and icy tundra.
- Early peoples were the Hohokam, Anasazi, Mound Builders, Inuit, Plains Indians, and others.
- Architecture and hunting or farming depended on environment.

Mesoamerica
- Environment supported first farming in the Americas.
- Olmec, Zapotec, and Toltec built cities with pyramids.
- The Maya developed a large civilization of many cities between AD 250 and 900.
- In the 1300s, the Aztecs built one of the most powerful empires in the Americas.

Arctic and Subarctic

Far West   Great Plains

Desert West   Eastern Woodlands

Aztec   Maya

0   1,000 Miles
0   1,000 Kilometers
Mercator projection

Inca

N W E S

South America
- The Chavín, Moche, and Nazca learned to farm in the dry desert and rugged Andean highlands.
- The Inca Empire, with its strong government, controlled a huge area in the 1400s.

c. 12,000 BC Paleoindians arrive in the Americas

c. 5000 BC Maize first domesticated.

c. 1325 Aztecs establish Tenochtitlán.

c. AD 900 Height of Maya civilization

c. AD 100 Anasazi develop pueblo architecture.

c. 1400 Incas begin rapid expansion.

Chapter Review

Complete each sentence by filling the blank with the correct term or name.

1. Tombs often reflected a person's _____, or position or rank in society.
2. The Incas kept track of _____, or population, data.
3. Maya writing consisted of _____, or symbols.
4. The emperor _____ was mostly responsible for the great expansion of the Inca Empire.
5. The Aztecs forced the people they conquered to pay _____, a type of tax.
6. The Anasazi developed _____ architecture around AD 750.
7. The Maya practiced _____, a method of farming that involves burning vegetation to clear land for planting.

---

labor tax, could only wear plain clothes and own what they needed

Reading Skills

11. warlike people with a militaristic society
12. rainfall and rich soil allowed for good farming
13. trade and tribute, backed up by physical force
14. western region
15. strong government ruled over an expanded empire, limited power of local leaders, and strictly controlled the economy

Analyzing Visuals

16. the central figure; he wears an elaborate headdress and is attended by servants
17. The king's servants are attending to the king.

Using the Internet

18. Go to the HRW Web site and enter the keyword shown to access a rubric for this activity.

KEYWORD: SHL AMS

History's Impact video program
Review the video to answer the closing question:
How have Mayan achievements influenced math and
astronomy today?

Comprehension and Critical Thinking

SECTION 1 *(pp. 199–202)*

8. a. Recall Why did the Hopewell and Mississippian people build mounds?

b. Explain How did the Hohokam and the Anasazi adapt to their environment?

c. Make Judgments Based on what you know about early North Americans' different types of social organizations and ways of adapting to the environment, which culture do you think was the most advanced? Explain your answer.

SECTION 2 *(pp. 203–210)*

9. a. Identify Which group of people built the first true city in Mesoamerica?

b. Compare and Contrast In what ways were the Maya and the Aztec civilizations similar? How were they different?

c. Support a Position Do you think people who were conquered and became part of the Aztec Empire benefited by being part of the empire? Why or why not?

SECTION 3 *(pp. 211–215)*

10. a. Describe What were some of the main achievements of the Incas?

b. Explain What methods did the Inca use to maintain unity and stability in their empire?

c. Elaborate In what way did the organization of Inca society benefit members of the lower class? In what way did it burden them?

Reading Skills

Making Generalizations *Use what you have read in this chapter to make a one-sentence generalization to answer each question below.*

11. What do the Mississippian mounds tell us about the culture?

12. How did the early Maya benefit from the environment of Mesoamerica?

13. How did the Aztecs create one of the strongest empires in the Americas?

14. Based on the image and explanation on pages 208–09, what general statement could you make about life in the Aztec Empire?

15. Why was the Inca government strong?

Analyzing Visuals

Reading Like a Historian *The mural below shows a Maya king and his court.*

Mural from Structure 1, Bonampak, c. AD 700–800

16. Infer Which figure in the mural is the king? How can you tell?

17. Analyze What are the other figures doing?

Using the Internet

go.hrw.com
Practice Online
Keyword: SHL AMS

18. The Maya calendar had two wheels, one with 260 days and one with 365 days. Use the Internet to learn how Maya dates correspond to dates from our calendar system. Then calculate your birthday in the Maya calendar.

WRITING FOR THE SAT

Think about the following issue:

Exposition: Comparing and Contrasting The Aztecs and Inca both incorporated many different peoples into their large empires. There were similarities and differences in how these two empires treated their conquered subjects.

19. Assignment: Do you think conquered subjects had better lives in the Aztec Empire or the Inca Empire? Write a short essay in which you develop your position on this issue. Support your point of view with reasoning and examples from your reading and studies.

Review and Assessment Resources

Review and Reinforce

 CRF: Chapter Review

Quick Facts Transparency: Visual Study Guide: The Americas

🔊 **Spanish Chapter Summaries Audio CD Program**

OSP **Holt PuzzlePro**: Quiz Show for ExamView

💿 **Quiz Game CD-ROM**

Assess

PASS: Chapter Test, Forms A and B

Alternative Assessment Handbook

OSP **ExamView Test Generator**, Chapter Test

💿 **Differentiated Instruction Modified Worksheets and Tests CD-ROM**: Chapter Test

HOAP **Holt Online Assessment Program** (in the Premier Online Edition)

Reteach/Intervene

Interactive Reader and Study Guide

Differentiated Instruction Teacher Management System: Lesson Plans for Differentiated Instruction

💿 **Differentiated Instruction Modified Worksheets and Tests CD-ROM**: Chapter Test

💿 **Interactive Skills Tutor CD-ROM**

go.hrw.com
Online Resources
KEYWORD: SHL TEACHER

Chapter 8 Planning Guide

Empires of China and India

Chapter Overview	Reproducible Resources	Technology Resources
CHAPTER 8 pp. 220–245 **Overview: In this chapter, students will learn about the strong empires and dynasties that unified much of China and India, resulting in prosperity and cultural and scientific advancements.** KI 1, 3; PI 1.2, 1.4, 3.1, 3.2, 3.3 See pp. T32–T55 for a detailed correlation to the New York State Core Curriculum for Global History and Geography and the New York Learning Standards.	**Differentiated Instruction Teacher Management System:*** • Pacing Guide • Lesson Plans for Differentiated Instruction **Interactive Reader and Study Guide:** Chapter Summary* **Chapter Resource File*** • Writing for the SAT • Social Studies Skill • Chapter Review • Economics and History **World History Outline Maps**	**Live Ink© Online Reading Help** **Student Edition on Audio CD Program** **Differentiated Instruction Modified Worksheets and Tests CD-ROM** **Interactive Skills Tutor CD-ROM** **World History Primary Source Library CD-ROM** **Power Presentations with Video CD-ROM** **History's Impact: World History Video Program (VHS/DVD):** Empires of China and India
Section 1: **The Growth of China** **The Main Idea:** The Qin and Han dynasties created strong centralized governments that unified China and shaped Chinese civilization for thousands of years to follow. PI 3.1	**Differentiated Instruction Teacher Management System:** Section 1 Lesson Plan* **Interactive Reader and Study Guide:** Section 1 Summary* **Chapter Resource File*** • Vocabulary Builder: Section 1 • Biography: Liu Bang	**Regents Review Transparency:** Section 1* **Map Transparency:** China and India, c. 320s–220s BC* **Map Transparency:** Qin and Han Dynasties* **Internet Activity:** Imperial China
Section 2: **Chinese Society and Culture** **The Main Idea:** The Han dynasty was a time of social change, the growth of trade, and great achievements in the arts and sciences. PI 3.2	**Differentiated Instruction Teacher Management System:** Section 2 Lesson Plan* **Interactive Reader and Study Guide:** Section 2 Summary* **Chapter Resource File*** • Vocabulary Builder: Section 2 • Biography: Ban Zhao • Literature: *The Analects of Confucius* • Primary Source: The Sacred Duty of the Historian	**Regents Review Transparency:** Section 2* **Map Transparency:** The Silk Roads*
Section 3: **Early Indian Empires** **The Main Idea:** The Mauryas and Guptas created powerful empires that united much of India, while trading kingdoms thrived in southern India. PI 1.2	**Differentiated Instruction Teacher Management System:** Section 3 Lesson Plan* **Interactive Reader and Study Guide:** Section 3 Summary* **Chapter Resource File*** • Vocabulary Builder: Section 3 • Biography: Faxian • History and Geography: Alexander Invades India	**Regents Review Transparency:** Section 3* **Map Transparency:** Mauryan and Gupta Empires*
Section 4: **Indian Society and Culture** **The Main Idea:** The strength, prosperity, and stability of the Gupta Empire helped lead to a golden age in Indian society, trade and culture. PI 1.4, 3.1, 3.3	**Differentiating Instruction Teacher Management System:** Section 4 Lesson Plan* **Interactive Reader and Study Guide:** Section 4 Summary* **Chapter Resource File*** • Vocabulary Builder: Section 4 • Biography: Aryabhata	**Regents Review Transparency:** Section 4* **Map Transparency:** Nomads and Empires* **Quick Facts Transparencies:** Roman Empire and Nomads; Han China and Nomads*

HOLT
History's Impact
World History Video Program (VHS/DVD)
Empires of China and India

Review, Assessment, Intervention

 Global History and Geography Regents Test Prep Workbook

 Quick Facts Transparency: Empires of China and India*

 Spanish Chapter Summaries Audio CD Program

Progress Assessment Support System (PASS): Chapter Test*

 Differentiated Instruction Modified Worksheets and Tests CD-ROM: Modified Chapter Test

OSP **New York One-Stop Planner CD-ROM:** ExamView Test Generator (English/Spanish)

HOAP **Holt Online Assessment Program (HOAP),** in the Holt Premier Online Student Edition

 PASS: Section 1 Quiz*

 Online Quiz: Section 1

 Alternative Assessment Handbook

 PASS: Section 2 Quiz*

 Online Quiz: Section 2

 Alternative Assessment Handbook

 PASS: Section 3 Quiz*

 Online Quiz: Section 3

 Alternative Assessment Handbook

 PASS: Section 4 Quiz*

 Online Quiz: Section 4

 Alternative Assessment Handbook

Power Presentation with Video CD-ROM

Power Presentations with Video are visual presentations of each chapter's main ideas. Presentations can be customized by including Quick Facts charts, images and maps from the textbook, and video clips.

 Holt Online Learning

go.hrw.com
Teacher Resources
KEYWORD: SHL TEACHER

go.hrw.com
Student Resources
KEYWORD: SHL EIC

- Document-Based Questions
- Interactive Multimedia Activities

- Current Events
- Chapter-Based Internet Activities
- and more!

Holt Premier
Online Student Edition
Complete online support for interactivity, assessment, and reporting
- Interactive Maps and Notebook
- Homework Practice and Research Activities Online

CHAPTER 8 PLANNING GUIDE

Before You Teach

The Big Picture

Peter N. Stearns

The Classical Period India and China both matured their civilizations after about 300 BC, though they utilized cultural features—the Brahman religion (that would become Hinduism) in the case of India, Confucianism in China—developed even earlier. Both societies illustrated key features of the classical period more generally—features they broadly shared with Greco-Roman civilization in the Mediterranean and with Persia. Classical civilizations expanded territorially, as in the Chinese expansion south. They utilized superior iron tools and weapons and also persuasive cultural systems. Chinese growth under the Qin dynasty, with consolidation under the Han, illustrates the process clearly; the establishment of the Mauryan and then Gupta empires provide approximate analogues in India. To maintain their larger territories the classical civilizations worked hard at integration. They spread dominant belief systems to the newer regions, and in China spread the Mandarin Chinese language as well among elites. They developed internal transportation and commercial linkages, fostering domestic trade. And they built empires, providing direct political institutions for most or all of the territory embraced within the civilization.

Comparisons and Legacies China and India developed in different specific ways. The Chinese emphasis on politics and bureaucracy was more consistent than that of India, where religious interests and the caste system provided links beyond formal politics. While both societies developed new technologies, China stressed practical science and technology particularly effectively. Both societies assumed considerable social inequality, but India's caste system was different from China's somewhat less formal social layering. India and China interacted directly at the end of the classical period, particularly through the spread and adaptation of Buddhism in China. Before the decline of the Han and (later) Gupta empires, both societies had established artistic forms, patterns of belief, and political impulses that would continue to influence their respective regions long after the classical period had ended.

Recent Scholarship

Anne Behnke Kinney's *Representations of Childhood and Youth in Early China* (2004) is a fascinating effort to get beneath the surface of classical Chinese history, to deal with the nature of childhood. Here is an opportunity to consider how more familiar features, like Confucianism and the imperial state, related to more basic and personal human experience. Growing attention to children included concern about education and training, particularly by the time of the Han dynasty, and even embraced an interest in educating the fetus before birth. The book offers a chance to distinguish between Chinese and Western conceptions of childhood at a point when basic notions were taking root.

Differentiating Instruction

 Differentiated Instruction Teacher Management System
- Pacing Guide
- Lesson Plans for Differentiated Instruction

 Interactive Reader and Study Guide

 Spanish Chapter Summaries Audio CD Program

 Student Edition on Audio CD Program

 Differentiated Instruction Modified Worksheets and Tests CD-ROM
- Vocabulary Flash Cards
- Modified Vocabulary Builder Activities
- Modified Chapter Review Activity
- Modified Chapter Test

OSP One-Stop Planner CD-ROM
- ExamView Test Generator (English/Spanish)
- PuzzlePro
- Quiz Show for ExamView
- Transparencies and Videos

TE Differentiated Activities in the Teacher's Edition
- Civil Service Exam in Han China, p. 226
- Peasant Life In China, p. 230
- Han Products, p. 231
- Government Views, p. 244
- Virtuous Acts, p. 245

Reading Like a Historian
Sam Wineburg

Historical Constructs In Nu Jie (Lessons for Women), Ban Zhao, a woman who lived in China during the Han Dynasty from 45 – 116 CE, wrote the following:

"A woman ought to have four qualifications: (1) womanly virtue; (2) womanly words; (3) womanly bearing; and (4) womanly work.... To guard carefully her chastity; to control circumspectly her behavior; in every motion to exhibit modesty... this is womanly virtue. To choose her words with care; to avoid vulgar language... may be called the characteristics of womanly words. To wash and scrub filth away; to keep clothes and ornaments fresh and clean... may be called the characteristics of womanly bearing. With whole-hearted devotion to sew and weave; to love not gossip and silly laughter... may be called the characteristics of womanly work."

In light of these words, would we nominate Ban Zhao as China's first feminist?

If, by feminist, we mean the struggle for equal rights, the movement to gain entry to male-dominated professions, the right to vote, the achievement of equal pay for equal work—in short, the complete dismantling of cultural and institutional barriers to women's advancement in a patriarchal society, then it's clear from the above passage that Ban Zhao was no Betty Friedan.

But the question itself is wrongheaded.

Constructs from the present—"feminism," "equality," "racism," "liberty"—take shape in particular times and places. When we pluck them from their contemporary context and plop them down in distant times and place, we assume that history has no rhythm, no inner logic. Judging the past through the conceptual lenses of the present is what historians disdainfully call "presentism." Presentism distorts the logic of the past and thwarts historical understanding. The question to ask of Ban Zhao is not how she looks in our mirror—but in her own.

Radical Notions Ban Zhao was born into a Confucian society governed by strict notions of proper relations between husband and wife, elders and children, members of the Imperial court and commoners. Above all were notions of filial duty, in which individual needs were secondary to the broader needs of family and community. Women learned how to cook and sew but few learned to read or write. The classic texts of Confucianism provide extensive detail about the proper education of young men but say surprisingly little about a young woman's education. It was as if a woman's status was so well defined that it merited little comment.

It is against this backdrop that we must view Ban Zhao. The mere existence of her instructional manual reveals the contradiction between a woman of letters and the vast unlettered population for which she wrote. It is, however, on this point that we see Ban Zhao's radicalism. How were men and women to achieve the right balance of the feminine Yin with the masculine Yang if only men were instructed in proper behavior, not women? Husbands, wrote Ban Zhao, "teach their boys to read books and study histories.... Yet only to teach men and not to teach women—is that not ignoring the essential relation between them?... It is the rule to begin to teach children to read at the age of eight years... Only why should it not be that girls' education as well as boys' be according to this principle?"

The imperative to teach women to read and write was a radical notion for its time. In Ban Zhao's own case, literacy opened vistas to new worlds. In addition to her instruction manual, she composed official state histories and treatises on astronomy and travel. In her latter life, she received the prestigious appointment as personal tutor to Queen Deng.

Ban Zhao dwelled in a world of social codes that provided little space for women to maneuver. But within the space, she was a trailblazer.

Chapter Preview

Chapter Main Ideas

Section 1 The Qin and Han dynasties created strong centralized governments that unified China and shaped Chinese civilization for thousands of years to follow.

Section 2 The Han dynasty was a time of social change, the growth of trade, and great achievements in the arts and sciences.

Section 3 The Mauryas and Guptas created powerful empires that united much of India, while trading kingdoms thrived in southern India.

Section 4 The strength, prosperity, and stability of the Gupta Empire helped lead to a golden age in Indian society, trade, and culture.

New York Standards

Key Idea 1 The study of world history requires an understanding of world cultures and civilizations, including an analysis of important ideas, social and cultural values, beliefs, and traditions. This study also examines the human condition and the connections and interactions of people across time and space and the ways different people view the same event or issue from a variety of perspectives.

Key Idea 3 Study of the major social, political, cultural, and religious developments in world history involves learning about the important roles and contributions of individuals and groups.

Key to Differentiating Instruction

Below Level

Basic-level activities designed for all students encountering new material

At Level

Intermediate-level activities designed for average students

Above Level

Challenging activities designed for honors and gifted and talented students

Standard English Mastery

Activities designed to improve standard English usage

220 CHAPTER 8

CHAPTER 8
350 BC–AD 600

Empires of China and India

THE BIG PICTURE Beginning in the 300s and 200s BC, strong empires unified much of China and India. Under these empires, China and India grew and prospered. This prosperity helped lead to classical periods in their histories, during which China and India developed many of the characteristics that would come to define their civilizations into modern times.

Theme ARTS AND IDEAS
Throughout history, civilizations have produced classical, or golden, ages during which outstanding contributions have been made in cultural and intellectual life. In this chapter you will learn about golden ages in China and India.

TIME LINE

CHAPTER EVENTS

320 BC Chandragupta founds the Mauryan Empire in India.

221 BC Shi Huangdi unites China under the Qin dynasty.

206 BC Liu Bang founds the Han dynasty in China.

c. AD 65 Buddhism is introduced into China.

350 BC ———————————————————— BC 1 AD

WORLD EVENTS

326 BC Alexander the Great invades northwest India.

c. 100 BC The Silk Roads connect China and Southwest Asia.

c. AD 30 Jesus of Nazareth is crucified.

AD 70 Romans destroy the Second Temple in Jerusalem.

220 CHAPTER 8

Introduce the Chapter

At Level

Empires of China and India

1. Organize students into small groups that represent a small, fictional country.

2. Have each group design a flag and make up some facts about its country, such as natural resources, traditional clothing, and a national holiday. Have groups make very brief presentations about their countries. Ask: How would you feel about your country unifying with other countries represented here? If your country was conquered and made part of an empire, would you resist or accept it?

3. Tell students that in this chapter they will learn about the formation of empires in China and India that were formed not through cooperation, but by one kingdom conquering others.

4. Guide students in a discussion about the pros and cons of having a large empire.
LS Interpersonal, Verbal-Linguistic

Alternative Assessment Handbook, Rubrics 11: Discussions; and 14: Group Activity

HOLT
History's Impact
▶ **Video Program: Empires of China and India**
See the Video Teacher's Guide for strategies for using the video segment.

Reading Like a Historian
Analyzing Visuals In March 1974 farmers near the Chinese city of Xian were digging for a water well. What they uncovered was one of the most famous archaeological discoveries of the twentieth century. Measuring some 20 square miles, the tomb complex of Qin ruler Shi Huangdi is best known for the thousands of life-like terra-cotta soldiers that guard the tomb along with horses and chariots. While the inside of Shi Huangdi's actual tomb has yet to be excavated, historians believe it took some 700,000 workers more than 36 years to complete.

c. AD 320	c. AD 399
The Gupta Empire begins a golden age in India.	A Chinese monk named Faxian travels to India.

AD 500

AD 250	AD 476
The Maya classical age begins in Mexico.	The Western Roman Empire falls.

Reading like a Historian
The photograph shows ancient Chinese terra-cotta warriors and horses from the 200s BC. The life-sized figures were part of an army of more than 7,000 soldiers, horses, and chariots created to guard the tomb of China's first emperor, Shi Huangdi. Today the terra-cotta army provides historians with a lasting example of an ancient Chinese imperial guard.

Analyzing Visuals What can you learn from this photograph about ancient Chinese soldiers?

See **Skills Handbook**, p. H26

EMPIRES OF CHINA AND INDIA **221**

Online Resources

Chapter Resources:
KEYWORD: SHL EIC
Teacher Resources:
KEYWORD: SHL TEACHER

Explore the Time Line

1. How long after Alexander invaded northwest India was the Mauryan Empire founded? *6 years*

2. Which leader unified China under the Qin dynasty? *Shi Huangdi*

3. What religion was introduced into China about 35 years after Jesus of Nazareth was crucified? *Buddhism*

4. When did the Gupta Empire begin a golden age in India? *about AD 320*

Info to Know

International Dunhuang Project Thousands of manuscripts and artifacts dating from 100 BC to AD 1200 have been discovered in the caves of Dunhuang and at other sites along the Silk Road. The manuscripts are written in over 20 different languages. In 1994, the International Dunhuang Project was launched in an effort to conserve and catalog these treasures.

Make Inferences Why is it significant that the manuscripts are written in 20 different languages? *possible answer—shows the many cultures that interacted along the Silk Road.*

Answers

Reading Like a Historian *possible answers—They probably played an important role in ancient Chinese society; they may have served as guards for Shi Huangdi.*

221

Preteach

Geography Starting Points

India's Connections India had been linked by trade and culture to Southeast Asia for thousands of years. By the time of the first century BC, India had formed even closer connections to the Greek-controlled Middle East, and to China and Central Asia. As Greek power gave way to increased Roman power, trade paths to the west became even more extensive.

Draw Conclusions How did India's geography affect its connections to the rest of the world? *possible answers— long coastline could support ports, central location between Middle East and East Asia, rich resources*

- **Map Transparency:** China and India, c. 320s–220s BC

- **World History Outline Maps:** India and China

- **Interactive Map:** China and India, c. 320s–220s BC

★Interactive
CHINA AND INDIA, C. 320S–220S BC

As the Zhou dynasty declined, warring states fought for control in China.

Alexander the Great's army defeated an Indian force in 326 BC.

In India, kingdoms competed in the Ganges River valley in the 300s BC.

Legend:
- China warring states
- India kingdoms
- QIN Chinese state or Indian kingdom
- MIN-YUE Other peoples and states
- Battle site
- Route of Alexander the Great and his armies
- Defensive walls

Map labels: BACTRIA, Hindu Kush, GANDHARA, PUNJAB, Thar Desert, KOSALA, KASI, VRIJJI, ANGA, MAGADHA, KALINGA, Arabian Sea, Deccan Plateau, Bay of Bengal, INDIAN OCEAN, Sri Lanka, HIMALAYAS, Plateau of Tibet, INDIA, Tropic of Cancer, GOBI, XIONGNU, CHINA, ZHAO, YAN, WEI, ZHOU, QI, QIN, HAN, CHU, SHU, MIN-YUE, Yellow Sea, East China Sea, South China Sea

0 250 500 Miles
0 250 500 Kilometers
Two-point equidistant projection

Starting Points In the early 300s BC both India and China consisted of local states or kingdoms fighting one another for control. Unity was on the horizon, though. In India, a strong leader seized the kingdom of Magadha in the 320s BC. The empire he founded went on to unite much of India. In China, the state of Qin gained power, uniting the region by 221 BC.

1. **Analyze** Alexander the Great invaded northwest India in 326 BC. How do you think this event might have inspired empire-building in India?

2. **Predict** Based on the location of defensive walls in China, what do you think relations were like between the Chinese and the Xiongnu people to the north?

 Listen to History

Go online to listen to an explanation of the starting points for this chapter.

go.hrw.com
Keyword: SHL EIC

222 CHAPTER 8

Skills Focus: Analyzing Maps

At Level

Research Required

Social Studies Skill
India and China's Resources

Materials: outline maps of India and China, colored pencils

1. Organize students into small groups. Give half the groups outline maps of India. Give the other half outline maps of China.

2. Have groups conduct research using reliable online sources to find the location of resources in ancient China or India. Have students mark the location of resources on their maps as they go.

3. Have students prepare a final version of the resource map. Maps should include a legend and symbols for resources. Encourage students to make their final versions neat.

4. Have volunteers create large maps for students to see. Guide students in a discussion of how resources played a role in empire building.
LS Interpersonal, Visual-Spatial

Alternative Assessment Handbook, Rubrics 14: Group Activity; and 20: Map Creation

---

Answers

Geography Starting Points

1. *possible answers—His invasion might have inspired the idea of a large empire; Alexander's military tactics might have been copied.* **2.** *possible answer—probably a hostile relationship that involved frequent conflicts*

The Growth of China

BEFORE YOU READ

MAIN IDEA

The Qin and Han dynasties created strong centralized governments that unified China and shaped Chinese civilization for thousands of years to follow.

READING FOCUS

1. How did the Qin dynasty unify and expand China?
2. How did the Han dynasty restore unity and strengthen China's government?

KEY TERMS AND PEOPLE

Shi Huangdi
Legalism
Liu Bang
Wudi
civil service
Xiongnu

NEW YORK

PI 3.1 Students analyze the roles and contributions of individuals and groups to social, political, economic, cultural, and religious practices and activities.

THE INSIDE STORY

How might one man's paranoia astonish the modern world?

The emperor of China's Qin dynasty had grown increasingly paranoid. He distrusted his officials and moved often to evade assassins. In hopes of gaining immortality, he delved into Chinese alchemy and magic. At the same time, the emperor made elaborate plans for his tomb—just in case. Inside his tomb, he wanted mounted crossbows, loaded and ready to fire at invaders. He ordered that everyone who worked on the tomb be killed to keep its location secret. And to guard him in the afterlife, the emperor had artisans create a life-sized terra-cotta army with chariots, horses, and more than 7,000 soldiers. This army was placed in pits around the emperor's tomb.

The discovery in 1974 of this immense army of the dead awed the modern world. Each soldier was unique and realistic, the hands posed to hold weapons. An emperor's paranoia had led to one of the great artistic achievements of the ancient world. Today the terra-cotta warriors hint at the power of the Qin dynasty, the first to unify China. ◼

Army of THE DEAD

These terra-cotta warriors once guarded the tomb of Shi Huangdi. ▶

The Qin Dynasty

The Zhou dynasty, which had ruled China since the early 1100s BC, began to decline around 400 BC as power shifted to local nobles. By the 300s BC, several small states had developed and were battling for land and power. During this Warring States period, the state of Qin (CHIN) rose to power on China's western frontier. In a series of crushing military campaigns, the Qin state conquered the other states, swallowing them up "as a silkworm devours a mulberry leaf," in the words of one Chinese historian. In 221 BC the last rival state fell. The Qin state had become the first power to create a unified Chinese empire.

223

Teach the Main Idea

At Level

The Growth of China

1. **Teach** Ask students the Reading Focus questions to teach this section.

2. **Apply** Have students make note cards with key people, terms, events, and facts in this section. Have them write the answer on the back and one or more questions on the front.

3. **Review** As you review the section, have students quiz each other using their note cards.

4. **Practice/Homework** Have students write a one-page essay comparing and contrasting the Qin and Han dynasties. **LS Verbal-Linguistic**

Alternative Assessment Handbook, Rubric 9: Comparing and Contrasting

---

Preteach

Getting Started

Use the **Interactive Reader and Study Guide** to familiarize students with the section content.

📖 **Interactive Reader and Study Guide**, Section 1

Name _____ Class _____ Date _____
Empires of China and India

Section 1

MAIN IDEA
The Qin and Han dynasties created strong centralized governments that unified China and shaped Chinese civilization for thousands of years to follow.

Key Terms and People
Shi Huangdi "first emperor," title the Qin ruler gave himself when he unified China
Legalism a political philosophy that taught that a powerful and efficient state was the key to control and order
Liu Bang founder of the Han dynasty who defeated Qin forces in 206 BC
Wudi greatest Han ruler, brought the dynasty to new heights from 141 to 187 BC
civil service a system in which passing an exam is required to obtain government jobs
Xiongnu nomads who lived in the steppe, or grasslands, north of China and posed the biggest military threat to the Han dynasty under Emperor Wudi

Taking Notes
As you read the summary, take notes in the graphic organizer like the one below. Record the key people, events, and policies of each dynasty.

Qin	Han

Full Survey Chapter 8   87   Interactive Reader and Study Guide

Academic Vocabulary

Review with students the high-use academic term in this section.

distribution the spread of something among a group of people (p. 225)

📄 **CRF: Vocabulary Builder: Section 1**

Taking Notes

Qin—people: Shi Huangdi, Hanfeizi, Li Si; events and policies: China unified, Legalism, strong central government, systems standardized, building projects, Great Wall, rebellion; Han—people: Liu Bang, Empress Lü, Wudi, Wang Mang; events and policies: bureaucracy, court intrigue, Confucianism, civil service, Xiongnu attacked, economic problems, empire in chaos

go.hrw.com
Online Resources
KEYWORD: SHL EIC
ACTIVITY: Imperial China

Reading Focus

❶ How did the Qin dynasty unify and expand China? *conquered other states in military campaigns, subdued raiders to the north and south*

The Qin Dynasty

Recall How did Hanfeizi believe rulers should govern? *through force*

Explain Which people did Shi Huangdi see as a threat to his power? *nobles, Confucian scholars who opposed Legalism, nomadic warriors*

Elaborate What lessons could future rulers learn from Shi Huangdi? *possible answer—Oppressing people is a short-term solution and will eventually lead to revolt.*

Info to Know

The Mausoleum of Shi Huangdi Shi Huangdi's burial complex is designed to provide for his needs in the afterlife and to imitate his life on Earth. The mausoleum is patterned after a city, complete with walls, a palace, and even a cemetery. Amenities included a model of Shi Huangdi's capital, and a planetarium with constellations made of pearls. The actual tomb has not yet been found.

Primary Source

"Men have likes and dislikes; thus they can be controlled by the means of rewards and punishments…The ruler need only hold these handles [rewards and punishments] firmly, in order to maintain his supremacy…Force is the stuff that keeps the masses in subjection [under control]."
—Hanfeizi, quoted in *Chinese Thought from Confucius to Mao Tse-tung*

Answers

Reading Check *conquered other states; centralized government suppressed all criticism; subdued raiders to the north, constructed Great Wall*

224

TAKING NOTES

As you read, take notes in a graphic organizer like this one. Record the key people, events, and policies of each dynasty.

Qin	Han

NEW YORK

CC Unit 1-Eh
The emergence of the Chinese philosophy of Legalism

NEW YORK

CC Unit 1-D1b
Factors leading to the growth of the Han Dynasty

The Qin ruler of the new empire of China took the title **Shi Huangdi** (SHEE hwahng-dee), meaning "first emperor." He boasted that the Qin empire would last "unto one thousand and ten thousand generations."

Harsh Qin Rule Shi Huangdi unified China in part with the help of two advisors: Hanfeizi (HAN FAY-dzoo) and Li Si. Both men helped found the school of **Legalism**. This political philosophy taught that a powerful and efficient government was key to maintaining order and control over an empire.

Legalists rejected Confucianism, a Chinese philosophy that developed during the Zhou dynasty. Confucianists thought that rulers should be virtuous and provide a good example. In contrast, Legalists said that rulers should be strong and govern through force because people were naturally bad. Rulers, therefore, had to control people through strict laws based on rewards and punishments. The stress was on punishment, and Legalists supported the use of harsh penalties such as branding or mutilation for even minor crimes.

Shi Huangdi applied these Legalist ideas to build a strong, centralized government. To weaken rival nobles, he took their land and forced them to move to his capital at Xianyang, so he could watch them. To prevent rebellions, he seized all private weapons. He then divided China into 36 districts and appointed loyal officials who had no ties to noble families to govern the districts.

To maintain order, Shi Huangdi ruthlessly suppressed all criticism of his rule. For example, he ordered the burning of many books, including the Confucian classics, which conflicted with Legalist thinking. Only books on practical subjects such as agriculture and medicine were spared. Confucian scholars who discussed banned books or criticized the Qin government were tortured or killed. These actions earned Shi Huangdi the hatred of Confucianists.

Qin Reforms Although harsh, Qin policies unified and strengthened China. To decrease regional differences, Shi Huangdi standardized the different laws, writing, coins, and weights and measures used across China. He even made the width of cart axles the same so that all cart wheels traveled in the same ruts on China's roads.

To strengthen China, Shi Huangdi undertook massive building projects. An improved irrigation system increased farm production. An expanded network of roads and canals linked the Qin capital to other parts of the empire. As transportation improved, trade increased. However, peasants had to pay heavy taxes to fund these programs, and many people were forced to work on them.

Qin Growth and Defense While developing China internally, Shi Huangdi also worked to protect his empire from outside threats. The people who lived north of China were fierce nomadic warriors. Organized into loose tribes, they often raided the frontier. The Qin army battled these groups and pushed them farther north. The army also subdued areas to the south as far as Vietnam.

To strengthen security, Shi Huangdi had workers join the separate defensive walls in northern China. The united wall came to be known as the Great Wall of China. Hundreds of thousands of peasants were forced to toil on this wall for years, and many people died from the backbreaking labor. Later Chinese rulers rebuilt and extended the Great Wall to create the structure that winds across China today.

Fall of the Qin The Qin dynasty's harsh policies fueled anger and resentment among the people. After Shi Huangdi died in 210 BC, the Qin dynasty quickly crumbled. Peasants fed up with forced labor and high taxes rebelled, while nobles eager to regain their land and power raised armies against the new emperor.

In 206 BC **Liu Bang** (lee-OO-BAHNG), a peasant rebel leader, defeated the Qin forces. Liu went on to found the Han dynasty, one of the greatest dynasties in Chinese history.

READING CHECK **Summarize** How did Shi Huangdi unify China and build a strong empire?

The Han Dynasty

The Han dynasty ruled China from 206 BC to AD 220—more than 400 years. The dynasty would provide a model for later Chinese dynasties. In fact, the Han dynasty's influence on Chinese civilization was so great that, to this day, the main population of China still calls itself the Han people.

Skills Focus: Summarizing

At Level

Reading Skill
Obituary for Shi Huangdi

Materials: newspaper obituaries

1. Review with students information about the life and actions of Shi Huangdi. Share a few newspaper obituaries with students to serve as examples.

2. Have students write an obituary for Shi Huangdi that includes both positive and negative aspects of his actions and makes generalizations about his life and legacy.

3. Have volunteers read their obituaries to the class.

4. As an extension, have students design the layout of a one-page obituary of Shi Huangdi, including an illustration. **LS Verbal-Linguistic, Visual-Spatial**

Alternative Assessment Handbook, Rubric 23: Newspapers

Restoring Control By defeating the Qin ruler, Liu Bang (also known as Gaozu) showed that he ruled with the mandate of heaven, or the approval of the gods. The ancient Chinese believed that the gods supported virtuous rulers and opposed corrupt ones. When a ruler was defeated, the Chinese believed it was a sign that the ruler had lost the gods' support.

To cement control, however, Liu Bang had to gain the people's loyalty. He softened the Qin's harsh Legalist policies and lowered taxes. These actions helped earn him the loyalty of many peasants. In addition, he gave large blocks of land to his relatives and military supporters. This <u>distribution</u> of land earned him the military's loyalty.

To weaken his rivals, Liu Bang continued the Qin's strong, centralized government. In addition, he expanded the Qin bureaucracy, an organized body of appointed officials. Numerous officials were appointed to oversee the administration of the Han government. This system, combined with the regained loyalty of the people, helped restore stability to the Chinese empire.

Because of his peasant origins, Liu Bang was not well educated. However, he was a practical and effective ruler. He appointed Confucian scholars to advise him and to serve in the government. As a result, Confucianism regained popularity and shaped the Han government. Beneath this cloak of Confucianism, though, Liu Bang kept some Legalist policies to maintain firm control over his empire.

A Powerful Empress Liu Bang died in 195 BC, and his young son took the throne. The new emperor was too young to rule, so his mother, Empress Lü, ruled in his place. Empress Lü was only one of Liu Bang's many wives. When Liu Bang was alive, she had plotted to make certain her son became emperor.

ACADEMIC VOCABULARY

distribution
the spread of something among a group of people

QIN AND HAN DYNASTIES

- ☐ Qin dynasty, c. 221–202 BC
- ᴗᴗᴗ Great Wall under Qin
- ▨ Han dynasty, c. AD 100s
- ▨ Han protectorate
- ᴗᴗᴗ Han additions to Great Wall

MONGOLIA

ASIA

GOBI

Tian Shan

Taklimakan Desert

Dunhuang

CHOSON (KOREA)

JAPAN

Huang He (Yellow River)

Luoyang · Xianyang

Chang'an (Xian)

Chengdu

Hefei

Chang Jiang (Yangzi River)

Yellow Sea

PACIFIC OCEAN

East China Sea

Xi River

Guangzhou

South China Sea

ANNAM (VIETNAM)

INDIA

HIMALAYAS

TIBET

0   300   600 Miles
0   300   600 Kilometers
Two-point equidistant projection

FACES OF HISTORY

SHI HUANGDI
c. 259–210 BC

Qin emperor Shi Huangdi is remembered for unifying China as well as for his harsh Legalist policies and persecution of Confucianism. Later in life he grew paranoid, distrusting his advisors and increasingly isolating himself. His fears were not without merit. He escaped at least three assassination attempts on his life.

Draw Conclusions How might Shi Huangdi's Legalist policies have contributed to some people's desire to assassinate him?

GEOGRAPHY SKILLS   INTERPRETING MAPS

1. **Place** What human-made physical feature marked the northern boundary of both the Qin and Han dynasties?
2. **Location** Where was the Han protectorate located?

EMPIRES OF CHINA AND INDIA **225**

Skills Focus: Identifying Problem and Solution   At Level

Reading Skill
Press Conference with Liu Bang

1. Organize students into three groups: a small group of speechwriters, a medium-sized group of advisors, and a large group of the press.

2. Have speechwriters start working on Liu Bang's coronation speech. Have advisors learn as much as they can about Liu Bang's policies and prepare to answer questions on his behalf. Have the press quietly brainstorm questions to ask Liu Bang. Remind students that originally, Liu Bang's views and plans were not widely known.

3. Give a copy of the list of questions from the press (no more than one question per member of the press) to the advisors.

4. Choose one speechwriter to play the part of Liu Bang who will deliver the speech. Have members of the press ask their questions, and have the advisors respond. **LS Kinesthetic**

🖐 **Alternative Assessment Handbook**, Rubric 14: Group Activity

---

Reading Focus

2 How did the Han dynasty restore unity and strengthen China's government? *softened Legalist policies, lowered taxes, created large bureaucracy, restored stability, implemented civil service exams*

The Han Dynasty

Recall What did Liu Bang have to do to stay in power? *gain people's loyalty, cement control; show that he had mandate of heaven*

Draw Conclusions How did having infants on the throne benefit Empress Lü? *With weak rulers on the throne, she could maintain her power.*

Interpret Why were power plays and court intrigues common? *emperor had many wives; possibility to manipulate who would inherit the throne*

📦 **Map Transparency:** Qin and Han Dynasties

📄 **CRF:** Biography: Liu Bang

Info to Know

The Mandate of Heaven Using an older dynasty's Mandate of Heaven theory of divine authority, the Han emperors legitimized their claims to the throne by saying that the Mandate of Heaven had been reborn in their new ruler. Han philosophy established that a ruler should be responsible for the well-being of his subjects and for being an example of moral virtue. The emperor showed moral virtue by performing rituals and ceremonies.

Draw Conclusions Was this system an example of pure autocracy or did it place an obligation on both the ruler and the people? *possible answer—autocracy, no checks on power*

Answers

Faces of History *possible answer—People strongly opposed his strict policies and were willing to kill to put an end to them.*

Interpreting Maps 1. *in the Great Wall;* 2. *in the Taklimakan Desert*

225

The Han Dynasty

Recall How did Emperor Wudi promote economic growth? *built new roads and canals; set up monopolies on salt, iron, and alcohol; limited power of merchants and landowners*

Explain What was an advantage of having a civil service system? *Officials were selected based on merit, not family ties, which ensure that officials were qualified.*

Rank What do you think was the best way to deal with the feared Xiongnu? *possible answers—by military force because that's what they responded to; bribery may be more effective, saves trouble*

Recent Scholarship

Although the Qin and Han dynasties are well known to historians, information about "barbarian" groups such as the Xiongnu is much harder to come by. Nicola Di Cosmo bridges the gap into this lesser known subject in the recent work *Ancient China and its Enemies: the Rise of Nomadic Power in East Asian History*. Di Cosmo explores the beginning of hostilities between China and its northern neighbors and how the two powers drifted apart. The book describes the formation of a powerful nomadic empire in the north to match the settled Chinese empire in the south.

Ancient China and its Enemies: the Rise of Nomadic Power in East Asian History by Nicola Di Cosmo. Cambridge University Press, 2004.

Answers

Reading Skills *different—Han: Confucianist, land grants to supporters, bureaucracy, civil service; Qin: Legalist, nobles lacked power; similar—strong, centralized government, collected taxes*

226

TIME LINE

Qin and Han Dynasties

221 BC Shi Huangdi unifies China and founds the Qin dynasty.

c. 206 BC The Qin dynasty collapses four years after the death of Shi Huangdi. The rebel Liu Bang founds the Han dynasty.

c. 213 BC Shi Huangdi orders the burning of classic Confucian texts.

141 BC Wudi becomes emperor. Under him, a civil service system develops based on exams on Confucian texts.

▲ Bronze Qin dynasty coin, c. 200s BC

Examination of Country Magistrates, artist unknown, c. 1700s

NEW YORK

CC Unit 1-D1
Han Dynasty contributions, role of migrating nomadic groups from Central Asia in the Han Dynasty, and the causes of the decline of the Han Dynasty

READING SKILLS

Understanding Comparison and Contrast In what ways did the Han and Qin governments differ? In what ways were the two governments similar?

Once her son gained the throne, Empress Lü ruthlessly promoted her family's interests. When her son died young, she had a series of infants named emperor to maintain power. After Empress Lü died in 180 BC, a group of officials and princes had the entire Lü family killed. Such power plays and court intrigues became common throughout the Han and later Chinese dynasties. These court plots often distracted China's leaders and made it difficult for them to rule effectively.

The Greatest Han Emperor The Han dynasty reached its height under the emperor **Wudi** (woo-dee), who ruled from 141 to 87 BC. Energetic and aggressive, Wudi is considered perhaps the greatest of all Han rulers.

To strengthen China, Wudi promoted economic growth. New roads and canals made it easier for farmers and merchants to get products to market. To raise money, Wudi set up monopolies on salt, iron, and alcohol. In addition, he took land away from large landowners and placed limits on merchants to decrease the power and wealth of these groups.

Under Wudi, Confucianism became China's government philosophy. Wudi wanted his officials to hold Confucian values such as loyalty to the emperor. To obtain such officials, the Han government developed a **civil service** system. Under this system, candidates for government

226 CHAPTER 8

jobs had to pass an exam in the Confucian classics. An academy was founded to teach the Confucian classics to students. Because only the wealthy could afford the years of schooling needed to pass the exams, China's wealthy and influential families continued to control the government. Nonetheless, the civil service system proved efficient and remained in place until the end of China's imperial rule in 1912.

Expansion under Wudi On top of his domestic reforms, Wudi expanded the Chinese empire through warfare. As a result, he became known as the Martial Emperor. The biggest threat to security that Wudi faced was the **Xiongnu** (shee-OOHNG-noo), nomads who lived in the steppes, or grasslands, north of China. Like many pastoral nomads, the Xiongnu had excellent horse skills and were fierce warriors. They would sweep in off the steppe and raid settled areas along China's frontier.

To try to stop these raids, past Chinese emperors had sent the Xiongnu lavish gifts and married Chinese princesses to Xiongnu chiefs. Yet the raids had continued. Wudi decided the time had come to use force. In 133 BC he launched an aggressive military campaign against the Xiongnu. In addition, he sought military alliances with the Xiongnu's enemies. Over time, the Han military was able to weaken and push back some Xiongnu tribes.

Differentiating Instruction

Above Level

Advanced Learners/Gifted and Talented

1. Review with students the information in the text about the civil service exam.

2. Organize students into small groups.

3. Tell students that they are imperial advisors in Han China. Their assignment is to design a new civil service exam that will determine who can be a government official.

4. First, have each group come to a consensus on the qualities they want in government officials. Next, have them decide how these qualities should be tested. Finally, have them write one sample question and an appropriate answer for each quality. **LS Intrapersonal, Verbal-Linguistic**

Alternative Assessment Handbook, Rubrics 14: Group Activity; and 35: Solving Problems

◀ Han warrior figurine

AD 9 Wang Mang briefly seizes control. The Han regain control in AD 25.

AD 220 The Han dynasty falls, and China enters the Period of Disunion.

133 BC Wudi begins a series of military campaigns against the Xiongnu on the northern frontier.

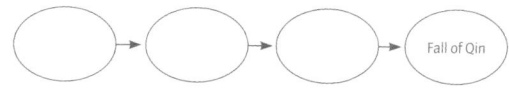

Skills FOCUS INTERPRETING TIME LINES

1. **Identify Cause and Effect** How did the death of Shi Huangdi affect imperial rule in China?
2. **Analyze** What conflict did the Han dynasty face from AD 9 to 25?

At the same time, Han armies colonized parts of Korea and Manchuria to the northeast and Vietnam to the south. To the west, Han forces extended Chinese control into Central Asia. Control of this region enabled Wudi to open up important trade routes, linking China to markets as far away as the Roman Empire.

Han Decline The Han dynasty faced a brief crisis in AD 9 when a rebel named Wang Mang seized the throne. By AD 25, however, the Han had regained control. This event marked the start of the Later Han dynasty.

Initially, the Later Han was stable and prosperous. In time, though, two problems began to weaken the empire. First, court intrigues increased, leading to weak rulers. Second, the gap between the rich and the poor increased as taxes rose to cover the cost of running the vast empire. Crushed by high taxes and debt, many peasants lost their land. With fewer landholders to tax, the Han government raised taxes even more, worsening the situation.

These problems paved the way for revolt. In 184 a Daoist sect called the Yellow Turbans rebelled, throwing the empire into chaos. As unrest spread, power shifted from the central government to local warlords. Nomads along the frontier swarmed southward, sacking and looting cities. As warfare tore the region apart, China entered a turbulent era called the Period of Disunion. It would last for some 350 years.

READING CHECK Identify Supporting Details Why is Wudi considered to be the greatest Han emperor?

SECTION 1 ASSESSMENT

go.hrw.com
Online Quiz
Keyword: SHL EIC HP

Reviewing Ideas, Terms, and People

1. **a. Identify** Who was **Shi Huangdi**, and why was he significant?
   b. Explain Why did Shi Huangdi move noble families to the capital and forbid the private ownership of arms?
   c. Evaluate What were the advantages and disadvantages of the harsh Legalist policies that Shi Huangdi used to govern the large Qin Empire?

2. **a. Recall** What different policies did Han emperors adopt in dealing with the **Xiongnu**?
   b. Compare and Contrast How did the political systems of the Qin and Han differ, and how were they similar?
   c. Evaluate Do you think that the Han **civil service** examination system was a good method for choosing government officials? Why or why not?

Critical Thinking

3. **Identify Cause and Effect** Create a graphic organizer like the one below. Using the graphic organizer and your section notes, list the causes of the fall of the Qin dynasty. Then create a second graphic organizer and list the causes of the fall of the Han dynasty.

○ → ○ → ○ → (Fall of Qin)

FOCUS ON WRITING

4. **Exposition** Write a brief history of the fall of the Qin dynasty and the rise of the Han dynasty from the point of view of a Confucian scholar working for the Han emperor Wudi. Make certain to include key events, people, and issues and to explain the belief in the mandate of heaven.

EMPIRES OF CHINA AND INDIA **227**

Section 1 Assessment Answers

1. **a.** powerful leader of Qin; unified and strengthened China, harsh ruler, built Great Wall
   b. watch over nobles, prevent rebellions
   c. advantages—strong government, controlled enemies; disadvantages—rebellion

2. **a.** launched military campaigns against them, formed alliances with their enemies
   b. similar—centralized government, collected taxes; different—Qin: Legalist, nobles without power; Han: Confucianist, land grants to supporters, bureaucracy, civil service

   c. possible answer—Yes, because a written test helps reduces favoritism.

3. Qin—oppressive Legalist policies, high taxes, forced labor; Han—weak rulers, high costs of large empire, high taxes

4. possible brief history—Shi Huangdi forced people to do back-breaking labor and criminals were punished by branding. This cruelty caused the Qin to lose the mandate of heaven. The people rebelled and Liu Bang rose to become emperor. He gained the Mandate of Heaven and won the hearts of the people.

Preteach

Getting Started

Use the **Interactive Reader and Study Guide** to familiarize students with the section content.

📖 **Interactive Reader and Study Guide,** Section 2

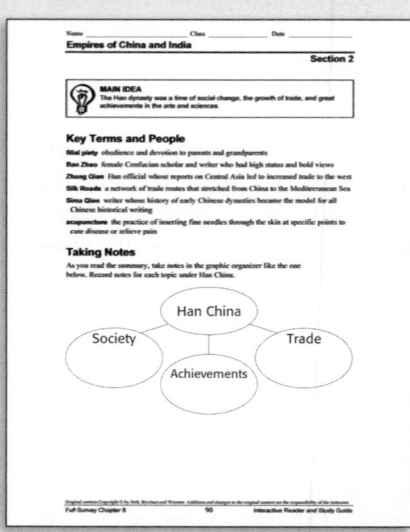

📖 **CRF:** Vocabulary Builder: Section 2

Taking Notes

Society—Confucianism, filial piety, lower status for women, social classes, hard lives for peasants; Trade—expansion to Central Asia; silk, spices, and luxury items on Silk Road; Buddhism in China; Achievements— skilled architecture, silk cloth, Buddhist art, cave temples, fu and shi poetry, paper, farm inventions, acupuncture, compass, sundial

---

Chinese Society and Culture

BEFORE YOU READ

MAIN IDEA

The Han dynasty was a time of social change, the growth of trade, and great achievements in the arts and sciences.

READING FOCUS

1. What features characterized Chinese society in the Han period?
2. How did trade and the spread of Buddhism affect Han society?
3. What were some achievements in art, science, and technology during the Han period?

KEY TERMS AND PEOPLE

filial piety
Ban Zhao
Zhang Qian
Silk Roads
Sima Qian
acupuncture

 NEW YORK

PI **3.2** Students explain the dynamics of cultural change and how interactions between and among cultures have affected various cultural groups throughout the world.

A PROFITABLE FAILURE

▲ Jade ornaments like the one above were valuable trade items in Han China.

THE INSIDE STORY

How might a mission be both a failure and a success? Zhang Qian, a Han official, stood before Emperor Wudi. Back home after 13 years, Zhang had to report that he had failed in his mission to form an alliance with nomads to the west. He and his men had barely set out when the Xiongnu had captured them. For 10 years the Xiongnu held him prisoner, until finally Zhang had escaped.

A truly dedicated official, Zhang then continued his mission. Eventually he reached the nomads to the west, but they had no desire to form an alliance with China. Although Zhang failed in his mission, there was a positive side to his adventure. Zhang told Wudi of the many amazing sights he had seen in Central Asia. In a land called Fergana, he had seen swift horses that sweated blood. And in a land called Bactria, he had seen merchants selling Chinese silks and bamboo. Learning of this new market for Chinese goods, Wudi rewarded Zhang for his information.

Zhang Qian's travels opened contact between China and Central Asia and paved the way for trade extending as far as the Roman Empire. As a Chinese historian of the time wrote, soon the people of the "distant west craned their necks to the east and longed to catch a glimpse of China." ■

Han Society

China's Han period was a time of great prosperity, growth, and achievement. During this period, China developed many of the social and cultural features that came to define imperial Chinese civilization for thousands of years.

Teach the Main Idea

At Level

Chinese Culture and Society

1. **Teach** Ask students the Reading Focus questions to teach this section.

2. **Apply** Draw three ladders for students to see. At the top of each ladder, write the name of a topic in this section: Han Society, Trade and Buddhism, and Han Achievements. Have students copy the ladders on their papers and fill in key points from each topic on the rungs of the appropriate ladder.

3. **Review** As you review the section, have students explain how various forces shaped life in Han China.

4. **Practice/Homework** Have students create a resumé listing the achievements of Han China **LS** **Visual-Spatial, Verbal-Linguistic**

📖 **Alternative Assessment Handbook,** Rubric 31: Resumes

Confucian Values in Han China

Album leaf from *Book of Filial Piety*, by Ma Hochich, c. 1100s

Filial piety stressed that children should honor and obey their parents. Here, a son and his wife serve his parents.

Confucianism valued close ties to the soil. Most families in Han China farmed to support themselves.

Confucianism valued children, which represented fertility.

SKILLS FOCUS **READING LIKE A HISTORIAN**

1. **Find the Main Idea** How did the Confucian principle of filial piety influence the roles of family members in Han China?

2. **Analyzing Visuals** Based on this image, what were some features of rural homes in Han China?

See **Skills Handbook**, p. H26

Family Life During the Han dynasty, the philosophy of Confucianism came to shape Chinese society. Confucius, the founder of Confucianism, taught that the family was central to the well-being of the state. As a result, Han officials promoted strong family ties, and the family grew in importance in Chinese society.

In keeping with Confucian values, the father served as the head of the family and had total authority over other family members. For example, fathers arranged their children's marriages and determined their sons' careers.

Children, in turn, were to obey their parents and respect their elders. Confucianism stressed **filial piety**, or obedience and devotion to parents and grandparents. Dutiful Chinese children not only obeyed their parents but also served them and cared for them as they aged. In addition, male family members were expected to honor dead parents and ancestors by making offerings to them at household shrines.

Han officials thought that dutiful children made respectful and obedient subjects. According to this view, children who obeyed their father and respected his authority would likewise obey the emperor and respect his authority. Some Chinese men even received government jobs because of the great respect that they showed their parents.

Women in Han China had fewer privileges and less status than men. For example, women rarely received an education or owned property. In addition, Chinese families valued sons more than daughters. Sons carried on the family line and remained part of their parents' household after marriage. In contrast, daughters married and joined their husbands' households. A Chinese proverb stated that "raising daughters is like raising children for another family."

Once they married, Chinese women were expected to obey their husbands and mothers-in-law. However, older women sometimes held power within the family because of the Confucian respect for elders and parents. Some older widows even became heads of families.

A few women did achieve positions of status in Han China. One of the best known is **Ban Zhao**, a Confucian scholar and writer. Ban Zhao wrote poems and essays and helped write a famous history of the Han dynasty. In her best known essay, titled *Lessons for Women*, she instructs women to be humble and obedient. Yet she also calls for harmony between husbands and wives and for some education for women—fairly bold views for the time.

TAKING NOTES

As you read, use a graphic organizer like this one to take notes on Han society, trade, and achievements.

NEW YORK

CC Unit 1-C6
The status and role of women in classical Chinese civilization

EMPIRES OF CHINA AND INDIA **229**

Direct Teach

Reading Focus

1 **What features characterized Chinese society in the Han period?** *Confucianism, filial piety, clearly defined social classes, most people were peasants*

Han Society

Recall According to Confucius, what was the relationship between the family and the state? *The family was central to the state's well-being.*

Summarize How were children supposed to treat their parents? *obey and serve them, take care of aging parents, make offerings to dead ancestors*

Contrast How was life more difficult for women than for men in Han China? *rarely educated or owned property; valued less by family; expected to obey husband and family; rarely gained status*

CRF: Literature: *The Analects of Confucius*

Info to Know

Extended Families The ideal of the extended family was very important in China. A typical upper-class family in China included a father, his wife, sons with their wives and children, and unmarried daughters. Often, all members of the family lived in the same house.

Evaluate What would you like about this arrangement? What would you dislike? *possible answers—Like: closer relationships with family members; Dislike: crowded, not much privacy*

Skills Focus: Comparing and Contrasting   At Level

Reading Skill
Filial Piety

1. Review with students the concept of filial piety as described by Confucius.

2. Organize students into groups of four to six. Have each group develop a script for two short scenes in a play about portraying the concept of filial piety. The first scene should show a family that is not exhibiting filial piety. The second scene should show the same characters exhibiting filial piety. Students might wish to assign the role of Confucius to narrate the play.

3. Allow adequate time for students to rehearse their scenes. Have students perform their plays for the class. **LS Kinesthetic, Interpersonal**

4. Guide students in a discussion about the concept of filial piety as it relates to Chinese society during the Han period.

Alternative Assessment Handbook, Rubrics 14: Group Activity; and 33: Skits and Reader's Theater

Answers

Confucian Values in Han China
1. *children honored, obeyed and cared for parents; women rarely received education or owned property; stressed order and harmony;* 2. *large area open to outside, vines growing on roof, fenced-in courtyard, little or no furniture, livestock nearby*

Han Society

Identify Who was in the third class of Han society? *artisans*

Cause and Effect How did social class structure affect peasants? *enormous value placed on the land, so peasants were forced to sell it; their families would become laborers, lose status*

🗺 **Map Transparency:** The Silk Roads

📝 **CRF:** Biography: Ban Zhao

Info to Know

Common Fabrics Grass fibers, hemp, and silk were the most common fabrics in use during the Han dynasty. While few examples of hemp cloth from the period still exist, historians believe that the majority of the population used hemp or other fibers for clothes. Silk was very expensive and was used to make imperial robes and other rich garments.

Draw Conclusions Why might soldiers' uniforms be made from a luxury fabric like silk? *possible answer—Soldiers represent the government so their expensive clothing would emphasize the wealth and power of the state.*

✳ **Interactive Map:** The Silk Roads

Teaching Tip

Guide a class discussion about the differences between Buddhism, Daoism, and Confucianism. Allow enough time for students to ask questions about the different philosophies pertaining to each "ism."

Answers

Reading Skills *rich—elegant homes, estates, hired laborers; poor—small houses, worked long hours in fields*

Reading Check *worked hard in fields, farmed, raised animals, often sold land to feed families, forced to work on building projects, easily forced into debt, worked for wealthy landowners*

230

Social Structure Han society was highly structured, with clearly defined social classes. At the top of society was the emperor, who ruled with the mandate of heaven. Beneath the emperor was an upper class consisting of the palace court, nobles, and the many government leaders, officials, and scholars.

The next and largest class consisted of China's peasants, valued because they grew the empire's food. Next came a class of artisans, who made practical items as well as luxury goods. Because Confucianism did not value trade, merchants occupied the fourth class. At the bottom of society were slaves.

The Rich and Poor Social class determined status but not necessarily wealth or power. For instance, merchants had a lower status than peasants but were usually far wealthier.

The wealthy in Han China lived well. Their elegantly furnished homes were spacious, with inner courtyards. Many of the wealthy owned large estates and hired numerous laborers.

READING SKILLS

Understanding Comparison and Contrast How did the lives of the rich and the poor differ in Han China?

In contrast, most Chinese during the Han dynasty led hard lives. Of the nearly 60 million people in China at the time, about 90 percent were peasants. Most of these peasants lived in small villages in simple wood-framed houses with walls and floors made of mud or stamped earth. For much of the year, peasants labored for long hours in the fields. In winter, peasants had to work on government building projects, such as canals and the Great Wall.

To survive, most peasants farmed and raised a few animals. For income, peasants sold extra crops and crafts at local markets. High taxes and bad weather could easily force peasants into debt, however. To worsen the situation, the Chinese had to divide their land equally among their heirs. In time, the land passed down was too small to feed a family. When farmers could not pay their debts or feed their families, they had to sell their land. Many peasants then became laborers for wealthy landowners.

READING CHECK **Summarize** What was life like for Chinese peasants during the Han dynasty?

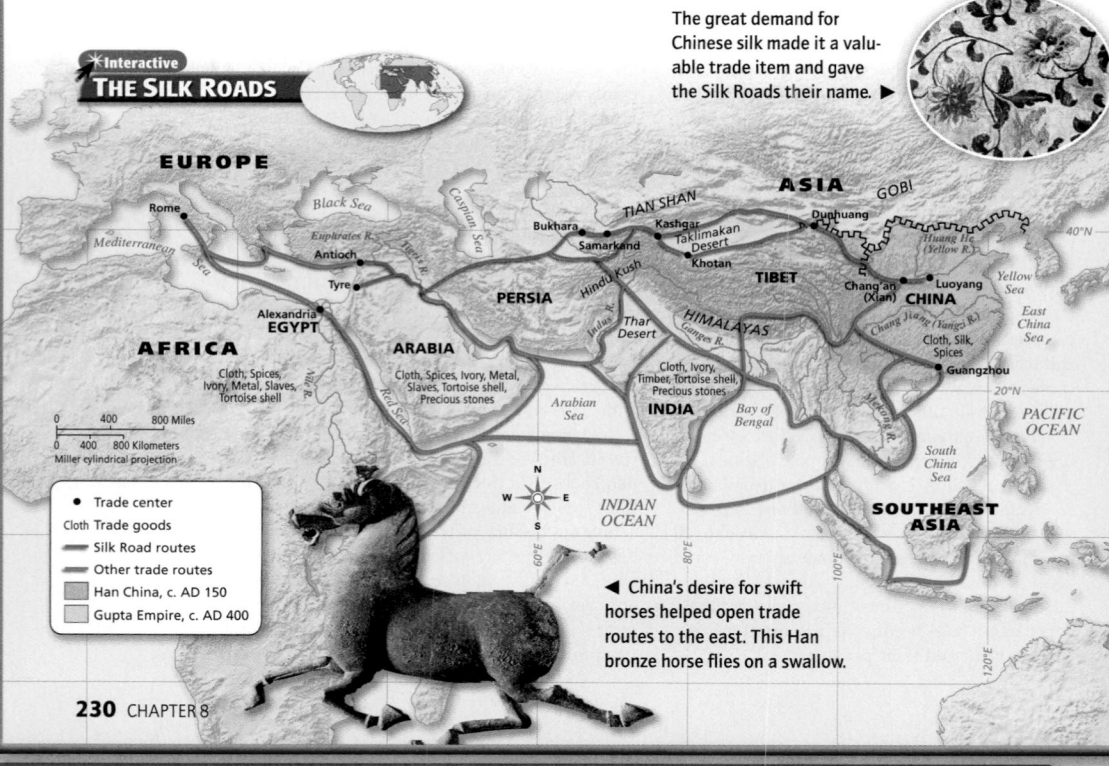

The great demand for Chinese silk made it a valuable trade item and gave the Silk Roads their name. ▶

THE SILK ROADS

✳ Interactive

◀ China's desire for swift horses helped open trade routes to the east. This Han bronze horse flies on a swallow.

- Trade center
- Cloth Trade goods
- ▬ Silk Road routes
- ▬ Other trade routes
- Han China, c. AD 150
- Gupta Empire, c. AD 400

230 CHAPTER 8

Differentiating Instruction

Below Level

Special Education Students

1. Review with students the information in the text about peasant life in China.

2. Organize students into mixed-ability pairs. Have each pair write song lyrics about the hardships of peasant life. Songs should be written in the first person. Explain to students that their songs do not have to rhyme, but they should depict an accurate portrayal of peasant life during the Han dynasty.

3. Have volunteers perform or recite their songs for the class. Encourage students to accompany their songs with a musical instrument they might know how to play, or to have musically inclined students accompany other student's songs. 🄻🄴 **Interpersonal, Auditory-Musical**

📝 **Alternative Assessment Handbook**, Rubric 26: Poems and Songs

Trade and Buddhism

Although agriculture formed the basis of the Han economy, manufacturing and trade grew in importance during the Han period. This growth increased prosperity and led to contact between China and other civilizations.

Han Products Artisans in the Han dynasty manufactured numerous products. Ironworkers made iron armor and swords. Artisans made fine pottery, jade and bronze objects, and lacquerware—wooden items that were coated with layers of hard varnish and often carved.

Perhaps China's most prized product was its silk. For centuries, the Chinese had known and carefully guarded the method for making silk. Revealing the secret was punishable by death. To produce silk, the Chinese raised silkworms and then unwound the threads of the worms' cocoons. Next, workers dyed the silk threads and wove them into fabric. Silk fabric was not only beautiful but also soft, strong, cool, and lightweight. As a result, silk fabric and clothing were costly and in high demand. During the Han dynasty, the production of silk fabric became a major industry in China.

▼ Below, a modern camel caravan on one Silk Road treks across barren land south of the Taklimakan Desert.

GEOGRAPHY **SKILLS** INTERPRETING MAPS

go.hrw.com
Interactive Map
Keyword: SHL EIC

1. **Place** Why do you think the Silk Roads divided to the west of China?
2. **Movement** What goods moved west from China over the Silk Roads?

Growth of Trade As they conquered areas of Central Asia, the Han learned that people farther west wanted Chinese goods. In addition, a Han official named **Zhang Qian** (jee-EN) returned from a mission to Central Asia in 126 BC. He told of the region's riches and the demand there for Chinese goods. These events led to increased Chinese trade with the West.

Emperor Wudi was highly interested in Zhang's tales of swift "blood-sweating" horses. Today we know that parasites caused these horses to have boils that bled, but the Han thought the horses were blessed by heaven. To obtain these heavenly horses, Wudi conquered more land to the west. As a result, Chinese trade with Central Asia increased even more.

The Silk Roads The merchants traveling between China and Central Asia used a series of overland routes. The most famous were called the **Silk Roads**. This network of routes eventually stretched from China 4,000 miles across the heart of Asia to the Mediterranean Sea. The Silk Roads linked China to India, the Middle East, and the Roman Empire.

Travelers on the Silk Roads crossed rugged, barren terrain and faced attacks by bandits. For protection, merchants traveled in huge camel caravans, stopping at way stations along the way. Most merchants traveled only part of the way and then traded their goods with other merchants from distant lands. As the map shows, most goods traded along the Silk Roads were luxury items, which were often small and valuable, and thus highly profitable.

Buddhism in China Traders carried ideas as well as goods over the Silk Roads and other trade routes. Among the ideas that spread to China from India was a religion—Buddhism.

Buddhism reached China in the first century AD. As the Han government became less stable, violence and suffering increased. For many Chinese, Buddhism's message of escape from suffering offered more hope than the Chinese beliefs of Confucianism or Daoism. By AD 200 Buddhism had spread across much of China. The spread of Buddhism from India to China is an example of cultural diffusion, the spread of ideas from one culture to another.

READING CHECK **Draw Conclusions** How did trade over the Silk Roads affect China's culture?

NEW YORK
CC **Unit 1-C1b**
Classical Chinese contributions such as silk

NEW YORK
CC **Unit 1-C7**
The growth of global trade routes, such as the Silk Road, in classical Chinese civilizations

NEW YORK
CC **Unit 1-Ec**
The spread of Buddhism

What were some achievements in the arts, science, and technology during the Han period? *skilled architecture, jade carvings, silk cloth, Buddhist artworks, poetry; paper, iron plow, seismograph, acupuncture, compass, water mill*

Han Achievements

Recall What is the first step in making paper? *grinding plant fibers into a paste*

Explain What is the significance of the Records of the Grand Historian? *became the model for Chinese historical writing*

📃 **CRF:** Primary Source: The Sacred Duty of the Historian

Close

Have students describe what it might be like to walk through a town or village in China during the Han period.

Review

Online Quiz, Section 2

Assess

SE **Section 2 Assessment**

📃 **Progress Assessment:** Section 2 Quiz

📃 **Alternative Assessment Handbook**

Reteach/Intervene

📃 **Interactive Reader and Study Guide,** Section 2

💿 **Interactive Skills Tutor CD-ROM**

Answers

Reading Check *paper, iron plow, wheelbarrow, acupuncture, compass, sundial, water mill, rudder*

232

NEW YORK

CC Unit 1-D1c
Contributions of the Han Dynasty

Han Achievements

The Han period was a classical age in China's history. During this period, the arts flourished, and advances in science and technology improved life.

The Arts Han China boasted magnificent palaces and multistoried towers. Although none of these structures has survived, ceramic models of buildings found in Han tombs show the skilled architecture of the period.

Han artisans produced ceramic and bronze figurines, exquisite jade carvings, and silk cloth with richly colored patterns. Han artists painted portraits and nature scenes on walls, scrolls, and room screens. During the Later Han, Buddhist art increased. Some of the most spectacular examples of Buddhist art of the period are found at cave temples in western China. These temples include wall paintings as well as thousands of Buddhist statues.

Han literature is known for its poetry. Han poets developed new styles of verse, including the popular *fu* style, which combined prose and poetry to create long works of literature. Another style of poetry, called *shi*, featured short lines of verse that could be sung.

Han writers also produced important works of history. The writer **Sima Qian** wrote *Records of the Grand Historian,* or *Shiji*. This early history became a model for Chinese historical writing. In the following passage, Sima Qian describes the fall of the Qin dynasty.

THE IMPACT TODAY

The practice of acupuncture is now used around the world and is gaining support among doctors in the West.

HISTORY'S VOICES

❝In the time of the Qin, the net of the law was drawn tightly about the empire and yet evil and deceit sprang up on all sides . . . Those who cared for justice and virtue were left to rot . . . When the Han arose, it lopped off the harsh corners of the Qin code and returned to an easy roundness.❞
—Sima Qian, *Records of the Grand Historian (Shiji)*

Science and Technology One of the most important Han inventions was an item still used every day—paper. The Chinese made paper by grinding plant fibers, such as hemp, into a paste. They then let the paste dry in sheets. To create "books," the Chinese connected several sheets of paper to create a long scroll.

In farming, Han inventions included the iron plow and the wheelbarrow. With an iron plow, a farmer could till more land. With a wheelbarrow, one farmer could haul far more.

In science, Han inventions included the seismograph, a device to measure earthquake tremors. Han emperors wanted to monitor earthquakes because they were seen as signs of heaven's disapproval.

In medicine, the Han made advances in the practice of **acupuncture**. This practice involves inserting fine needles into the skin at specific points to cure disease and relieve pain. Other Han inventions include the compass, the sundial, the water mill, and the ship's rudder.

READING CHECK **Summarize** What were some technological advances of the Han dynasty?

SECTION **2** **ASSESSMENT**

go.hrw.com
Online Quiz
Keyword: SHL EIC

Reviewing Ideas, Terms, and People

1. **a. Identify** Who was **Ban Zhao?**
   b. Explain Why did so many peasants lose their land during the Han period?

2. **a. Describe** What dangers and hazards did travelers face on the Silk Roads?
   b. Draw Conclusions Why was Buddhism so appealing to people in Later Han China?

3. **a. Recall** What were the major developments in the arts during the Han period?
   b. Cause and Effect How did technological advances improve farming during the Han period?
   c. Rank Which invention of the Han period do you think was most important? Why?

Critical Thinking

4. **Identify Cause and Effect** Create a graphic organizer like the one below. Use it and your section notes to list the causes and effects of the growth of trade in Han China.

Causes		Effects
	Silk Roads Trade →	

FOCUS ON WRITING ✏️

5. **Exposition** Write a paragraph that a Han emperor might have written instructing the Chinese people to display filial piety. You should describe filial piety and explain its benefits.

232 CHAPTER 8

 Section 2 Assessment Answers

1. **a.** female Confucian scholar and writer
   b. system of inheritance meant small plots; high taxes and bad weather could force them into debt; some had to sell land

2. **a.** rugged, barren terrain; bandit attacks
   b. Message of rebirth gave hope.

3. **a.** skilled architecture, ceramic and bronze figurines, Buddhist artworks, poetry
   b. farmer could till more land with iron plow; could haul huge loads with wheelbarrow
   c. possible answer—paper, because it has improved communication

4. causes—China's expansion into Central Asia, demand for Chinese goods, China's interest in swift horses; effects—camel caravans, profitable trade in luxury items, connections to Central Asia, spread of Buddhism into China

5. possible document—Gentlemen and ladies, you must show filial piety by respecting your parents and grandparents. Serve them and care for them at every opportunity, and when they pass on, make offerings to them at your family shrine. If family ties are strong, China will be strong.

BEFORE YOU READ

MAIN IDEA
The Mauryas and Guptas created powerful empires that united much of India, while trading kingdoms thrived in southern India.

READING FOCUS
1. How did the Mauryan Empire unify much of India, and who were its key rulers?
2. What regional kingdoms ruled India after the collapse of the Mauryan Empire?
3. Which key rulers and events shaped the Gupta Empire?

KEY PEOPLE
Chandragupta Maurya
Kautilya
Ashoka
Chandra Gupta II

NEW YORK

PI 1.2. Students understand the development and connectedness of Western civilization and other civilizations and cultures in many areas of the world and over time.

THE INSIDE STORY

Why might a great warrior become a supporter of peace?
Ashoka, the ruler of the Mauryan Empire in India, was a mighty conqueror. Under his rule, military campaigns expanded the empire that his grandfather had founded. Then in the 260s BC, Ashoka invaded Kalinga, a tribal kingdom on India's eastern coast. The invasion was a slaughter. According to reports from the time, some 100,000 people died during the fighting, and more died later from their wounds. In addition, Mauryan soldiers forced their way into Kalinga homes and took more than 150,000 people captive. According to Ashoka, the brutality of the invasion appalled him and filled him with remorse.

In response, Ashoka turned to Buddhism and became a strong supporter of nonviolence. He made it part of his duty as emperor to spread Buddhist teachings. Across his empire, he had messages inscribed on stone pillars and rocks urging people to engage in "right conduct." To spread his message to foreign lands, he sent out Buddhist missionaries. He even went on a 256-day pilgrimage to Buddhist holy sites. In this way, a man who began life as a mighty conqueror ended up becoming famous for promoting peace.

A MORE PEACEFUL WAY

This lion sculpture once topped one of Ashoka's inscribed pillars. An adaptation of this sculpture is now the national symbol of India. ▼

The Mauryan Empire

By the 300s BC a number of small kingdoms existed across India. Each kingdom had its own ruler, and no central authority united them. One of the dominant kingdoms was Magadha, located near the Ganges River in northeastern India. There, a strong leader named **Chandragupta Maurya** (shuhn-druh-GOOP-tuh MOUR-yuh) gained control and began conquering the surrounding kingdoms. His conquests led to the founding of India's first empire—the Mauryan Empire.

233

Getting Started
Use the **Interactive Reader and Study Guide** to familiarize students with the section content.

📄 **Interactive Reader and Study Guide,** Section 3

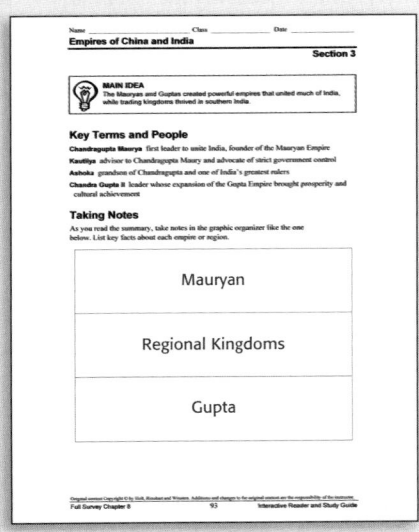

📄 **CRF:** Vocabulary Builder: Section 3

Taking Notes

Mauryan—Chandragupta Maurya built immense army, conquered northern India, united most of India, strong centralized government with secret spies, prosperous, little crime; Ashoka converted to Buddhism, believed in nonviolence and tolerance; Regional Kingdoms—Tamil kingdoms, sea trade with Southeast Asia, vibrant society; Gupta—Chandra Gupta I began dynasty, empire expanded under Chandra Gupta II, direct and indirect rule, did not control harshly, Hinduism

Teach the Main Idea

At Level

Early Indian Empires

1. **Teach** Ask students the Reading Focus questions to teach this section.

2. **Apply** Have students outline the section, using the red and blue heads as main points.

3. **Review** As you review the section, have students identify the key people and summarize their actions and accomplishments.

4. **Practice/Homework** Have students write ten journal entries from the point of view of Ashoka's chief of staff. Five entries should describe life before Ashoka's conversion to Buddhism; the other five should describe life in India after Ashoka's conversion. Have volunteers share their journal entries with the class. **LS Verbal-Linguistic**

📄 **Alternative Assessment Handbook,** Rubric 15: Journals

Direct Teach

Reading Focus

1 How did the Mauryan Empire unify much of India, and who were its key rulers? *built large army with soldiers, chariots, and war elephants, conquered territories; Chandragupta Maurya, Ashoka*

The Mauryan Empire

Recall What event marked the beginning of the Mauryan Empire? *Chandragupta Maurya seized the throne of Magadha, a kingdom along the Ganges River.*

Evaluate Do you think Chandragupta's policies were wise? Explain. *possible answers—No, policies were harsh and oppressive; yes, policies were effective, led to stability, prosperity and low crime.*

📄 **CRF:** History and Geography: Alexander Invades India

Info to Know

Lion Sculptures of Ashoka Ashoka built the first of his lion sculptures at Sarnath where the Buddha preached his first sermon. Historians believe that the original sculpture had a Wheel of Dharma on top of the lions and symbolized the triumph of virtue over worldly power.

Primary Source

"...for whoever imposes severe punishment becomes repulsive to the people; while he who awards mild punishment becomes contemptible. But whoever imposes punishment as deserved becomes respectable... [P]unishment, when ill-awarded under the influence of greed and anger or owing to ignorance, excites fury even among hermits and ascetics dwelling in forests, not to speak of householders."

–Kautilya, Arthashastra, Book I, Chapter 4

Answers

Linking to Today *possible answer—because of his decision to give up military conquest and pursue conquest by* dhamma, *or right conduct*

234

TAKING NOTES

As you read, take notes in a graphic organizer like this one to list key facts about each empire or region.

| Mauryan Empire |
| Regional Kingdoms |
| Gupta Empire |

🗽 **NEW YORK**

CC Unit 1-C4b
The government system of the Indian (Maurya) Empire.

Rise of the Mauryan Empire In 326 BC the military conqueror Alexander the Great marched his army into northwest India. In a fierce battle, Alexander's army defeated a powerful Indian force equipped with 200 war elephants. Alexander and his forces did not remain in India long, though. His battle-weary soldiers wanted to return to their homes, and Alexander and his army soon left India.

However, Alexander's brief conquest inspired Chandragupta Maurya. Around 321 BC he seized the throne of the kingdom of Magadha. Historians mark this event as the start of the Mauryan Empire.

Chandragupta built up an immense army that included some 600,000 soldiers as well as thousands of chariots and war elephants. With this mighty force, he began conquering northern India. In 305 BC he defeated Seleucus I, one of Alexander's generals who had invaded northwest India. By 303 BC the Mauryan Empire controlled northern India as well as much of what is now Afghanistan.

Mauryan Rule Like the Qin and Han rulers in China, Chandragupta Maurya established a strong, centralized government to control his empire and crush resistance to his rule.

For guidance, Chandragupta relied on a brilliant adviser named **Kautilya**, who was a Brahmin, or member of the priest caste. Historians think that Kautilya might have written the *Arthasastra*, a manual for statecraft. The *Arthasastra* called for strict state control, the use of spies, and even the use of assassination in some cases.

Under Kautilya's guidance, Chandragupta divided his empire into districts and appointed loyal relatives and generals to rule them. An organized bureaucracy of officials ran the government. To serve as the emperor's eyes and ears, a secret society of spies monitored officials, gathered information, and rooted out threats to the state.

During Chandragupta's rule, a Greek ambassador named Megasthenes visited the Mauryan Empire. He later wrote about his observations. Megasthenes describes a land of prosperity. The greatest city was Pataliputra, the Mauryan capital, which had magnificent palaces, temples, and parks. The government controlled the economy and operated mines and other enterprises. The emperor owned all the land, and farmers paid rent to use the land as well as taxes. This money helped fund the government and its massive army.

Linking TO Today

Ashoka's Lasting Fame

Mauryan emperor Ashoka lives on as one of India's most beloved historical figures. Wildly popular movies and television shows in India dramatize the events of his life. Companies and organizations have adopted his name as their symbol. Even India's national emblem is based on a lion statue that topped one of Ashoka's inscribed pillars.

Why has a ruler who lived more than 2,200 years ago remained so popular and influential in India? One answer might be the many roles that Ashoka played during his life. From warrior to empire-builder to peaceful Buddhist, Ashoka achieved greatness in many different ways. Today, however, Ashoka is most admired for his decision to give up

military conquest and pursue conquest by *dhamma*, or right conduct. According to the inscriptions he had made, Ashoka became a Buddhist after the brutal conquest of Kalinga. He then devoted his life to serving his subjects and spreading Buddhism.

Some historians question whether Ashoka was as idealistic a ruler as tradition holds. Nonetheless, Ashoka continues to hold a place in the hearts of the people of India today.

Draw Conclusions Why do you think that Ashoka remains such a beloved figure in India?

The statue on the left, made in the 1100s in Sri Lanka, shows Emperor Ashoka in a stately pose. The image above is a still from the 2001 film *Asoka*, depicting the young ruler as a mighty warrior.

234 CHAPTER 8

Skills Focus: Drawing Conclusions

At Level

Reading Skill
Kautilya's Policies

1. Review with students the information in the text about Kautilya's views of government.

2. Guide students in a discussion about these policies. Have students work in small groups to develop arguments to support Kautilya's views and arguments that criticize his views.

3. Organize students into two groups, one in support of Kautilya, the other opposing him. Have students use the arguments developed in their small groups to debate this question:

Did the need to exercise control in the empire justify Kautilya's policies?

4. As an extension, have students find other historical examples of strict state control, spying, and assassinations. Have them generalize about the effects of these policies.

LS **Verbal-Linguistic, Kinesthetic**

📄 **Alternative Assessment Handbook**, Rubrics 10: Debates; and 11: Discussions

Rule under Ashoka Chandragupta gave up his throne in 301 BC to become a Jainist monk. His son then became emperor followed by his grandson, **Ashoka**, in about 270 BC. Under Ashoka, considered to be one of India's greatest rulers, the Mauryan Empire reached its height.

Initially, Ashoka continued to expand the Mauryan Empire, which soon included most of India. However, a military campaign against the region of Kalinga in eastern India was especially brutal. The violence of the fighting appalled Ashoka. As a result, he abandoned his policy of conquest and became a Buddhist.

After converting to Buddhism, Ashoka began to promote a policy of right conduct. To spread this policy, Ashoka had his views and actions inscribed on rocks and stone pillars across his empire. In the following passage from one of these inscriptions, Ashoka urges the people to adopt religious toleration.

HISTORY'S VOICES

❝The Beloved of the Gods [Ashoka] . . . honors members of all sects [religions] . . . Whoever honors his own sect and disparages [speaks poorly about] another man's . . . does his own sect the greatest possible harm. Concord [harmony] is best, with each [person] hearing and respecting the other's teachings.❞

—Ashoka, Twelfth Major Rock Edict

Ashoka also worked to spread Buddhism. He supported Buddhist missionaries and funded the building of Buddhist stupas and monasteries. These efforts helped Buddhism spread throughout India and beyond.

In addition, Ashoka worked to improve the lives of his people. He founded hospitals, including hospitals for animals, and had new wells dug and more roads built. Along the empire's roads, he also had shade trees planted and rest houses built for weary travelers.

Decline of the Mauryan Empire After Ashoka died in 232 BC, the Mauryan Empire began to decline. As Ashoka's sons battled for power, central control weakened. Distant provinces began to slip away from the empire. About 184 BC the last Mauryan emperor was killed by one of his generals. The Mauryan Empire, which had lasted some 140 years, collapsed.

READING CHECK **Contrast** How did the reigns of Chandragupta and Ashoka differ?

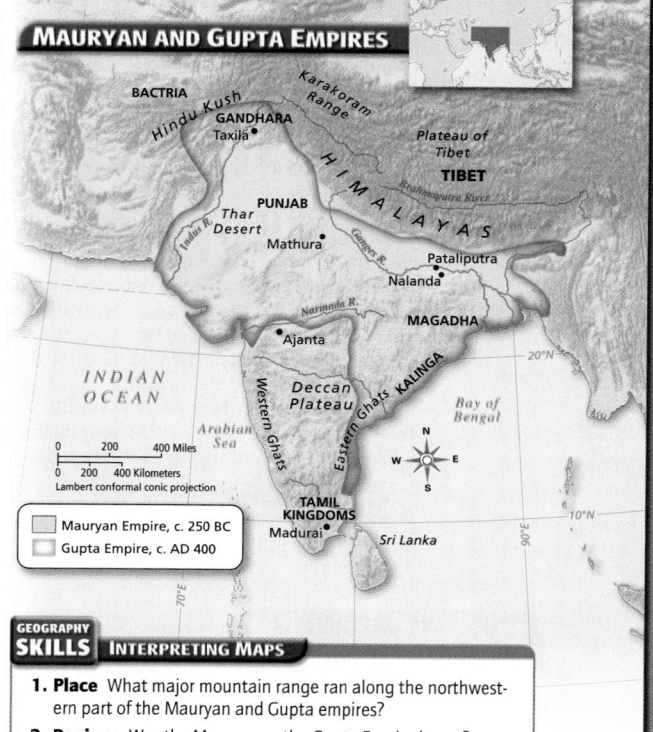

MAURYAN AND GUPTA EMPIRES

BACTRIA
Hindu Kush
Karakoram Range
GANDHARA
Taxila
Plateau of Tibet
TIBET
HIMALAYAS
Brahmaputra River
PUNJAB
Thar Desert
Indus R.
Mathura
Ganges R.
Pataliputra
Nalanda
Narmada R.
MAGADHA
Ajanta
INDIAN OCEAN
Deccan Plateau
Western Ghats
Eastern Ghats
KALINGA
20°N
Bay of Bengal
Arabian Sea
N W E S
0   200   400 Miles
0   200   400 Kilometers
Lambert conformal conic projection
□ Mauryan Empire, c. 250 BC
□ Gupta Empire, c. AD 400
TAMIL KINGDOMS
Madurai
Sri Lanka
10°N
70°E
80°E
90°E

GEOGRAPHY SKILLS **INTERPRETING MAPS**

1. **Place** What major mountain range ran along the northwestern part of the Mauryan and Gupta empires?
2. **Regions** Was the Mauryan or the Gupta Empire larger?

Regional Kingdoms

As the Mauryan Empire collapsed, India again divided into many regional kingdoms. These kingdoms <u>differed</u> in the north and south.

North India In northern India, groups of invaders from Central Asia established new dynasties. Many of these people had been displaced by the expansion of China. In addition, Greek invaders from what is now Afghanistan formed Greco-Indian dynasties in northern India. These dynasties introduced Greek art forms to India, which influenced local styles.

During the first century AD a people called the Kushans conquered much of northern India. The Kushans restored some of the grandeur of the Mauryan Empire to the region. By about AD 250 the Kushan dynasty had fallen, though, and northern India divided again.

READING SKILLS

Understanding Comparison and Contrast The verb *differed* tells you that the author is going to contrast North and South India. Read on to see how the two regions differ during this period.

Reading Focus

❷ What regional kingdoms ruled India after the collapse of the Mauryan Empire? *Greco-Indian dynasties, Kushan, Andhra, Tamil kingdoms*

Regional Kingdoms

Explain How did Greek sculptural forms come into India? *Greek invaders from Afghanistan introduced Greek forms of sculpture in India.*

Make Generalizations Describe life in the Tamil kingdoms. *active sea trade with Southeast Asia, wealthy, sophisticated culture, vibrant society, literature flourished*

Interpreting Maps
Mauryan and Gupta Empires

Location What was the only part of India not conquered by the Mauryan Empire? *southern tip*

 Map Transparency: Mauryan and Gupta Empires

Info to Know

High Commissioners of Equity To ensure peace in his empire, Ashoka established a group of "High Commissioners of Equity." These commissioners traveled the empire and addressed the complaints and needs of minorities and other groups.

Collaborative Learning
Ashoka's Conversion

Below Level

Materials: poster paper, art supplies

1. Review with students the information in the text about the ways in which Ashoka's conversion affected the Mauryan empire.

2. Organize students into small groups. Have each group create a poster that announces Ashoka's conversion, describes changes to be made in the empire, and urges people to practice right conduct.

3. Have groups present their posters to the class.

4. Display posters in a classroom exhibit.
   LS **Visual-Spatial**

   Alternative Assessment Handbook, Rubric 28: Posters

Answers

Interpreting Maps 1. *Hindu Kush;* **2.** *Mauryan*

Reading Skills *North—invaders started new dynasties, introduced Greek art forms, Kushans restored grandeur of Mauryan Empire; South—kingdoms expanded across south and central India, Tamil kingdoms traded and brought wealth and culture*

Reading Check *Chandragupta—strict state control, spies, conquest; Ashoka—nonviolence, public works, Buddhist teachings*

Direct Teach

Reading Focus

3 Which key rulers and events shaped the Gupta Empire? *Chandra Gupta I married into powerful clan; Samudra Gupta conquered 12 rulers in south India; Chandra Gupta II expanded territory; White Huns invaded*

The Gupta Empire

Identify Where did the Gupta dynasty rise to power? *the region of Magadha*

Identify Cause and Effect What were the effects of the Gupta dynasty takeover of northern India? *northern India reunited, Indian society prospered, Hinduism became popular*

Reading Like a Historian
A Tamil Poem
Activity **Tamil Poems** Have students write a prose poem in a similar style to the Tamil poem. The topic should be a street scene or a scene from a mall or shopping area that they have visited.
LS **Auditory-Musical**

Alternative Assessment Handbook, Rubric 26: Poems and Songs

Biography
The Tamil The Tamil people, or Tami-lars, still exist as an ethnic group who live mostly in Sri Lanka and South India. Many Tamil people desire their own nation on the island of Sri Lanka. A bloody civil war between Tamil fighters and the government of Sri Lanka has raged on and off since the 1980s.

Answers

Reading Like a Historian 1. *great gate, marketplace, royal procession, elephants, clothing and jewelry, worship; provides details of everyday life;* **2.** *entertain the reader with rich descriptions; perhaps he exaggerates to bring out best qualities*

Reading Check *They had been displaced from China by invasions of Qin and Han.*

236

South India Powerful kingdoms developed in India south of the Deccan Plateau. In the 100s BC the Andhra kingdom expanded across south and central India. This kingdom controlled the region until about AD 300.

In the far south, small kingdoms had ruled the region for some time. These kingdoms included the Chera, Chola, and Pandya. They were collectively called the Tamil kingdoms after the Tamil language spoken in the region.

The Tamil kingdoms carried on an active sea trade with Southeast Asia and other regions. This trade brought the kingdoms wealth, and they developed a sophisticated culture. For instance, the city of Madurai, the capital of the Pandya kingdom, became a center of Tamil poetry. This poetry is filled with descriptions of the vibrant society of ancient southern India.

READING CHECK **Identify Cause and Effect** Why did peoples from Central Asia invade northern India during the period after the collapse of the Mauryan Empire?

Reading like a Historian

A Tamil Poem

Interpreting Literature as a Source Historians sometimes use literature written during a particular time period to gain detailed insights into places, events, people, and attitudes of that period.

To interpret this Tamil poem about a festival in Madurai, the capital of the ancient kingdom of Pandya in southern India, think about

- the actions and events described in the poem
- the descriptive details in the poem, such as sights, sounds, and smells
- the author's goal in the poem, such as describing a meaningful event or drawing an emotional response from readers

Skills FOCUS **READING LIKE A HISTORIAN**

1. **Actions and Details** What actions and details in the poem might be useful to historians, and why?
2. **Goal** What do you think the author's goal was in this poem? How might this goal affect the poem's usefulness as historical evidence?

See **Skills Handbook**, p. H28

236 CHAPTER 8

The Gupta Empire

India remained divided into small kingdoms for about 400 years. Then around AD 320, the Gupta (GOOP-tuh) dynasty took over northern India. Under the Guptas, northern India was reunited, Indian society prospered, and the religion of Hinduism grew in popularity.

Rise of the Gupta Empire The Gupta dynasty, like the Mauryan dynasty, rose to power in the region of Magadha. The founder of the Gupta dynasty was Chandra Gupta I. He was not related to Chandragupta Maurya, although their names are similar. From his base in Magadha, Chandra Gupta I conquered neighboring lands to bring much of northern India under Gupta control.

India under Gupta Rule Gupta rule was less centralized than Mauryan rule. The Guptas divided the main part of their empire into units. Royal officials governed each unit.

Because the poem was written in Tamil, this English translation reads more like prose than a poem.

The poet enters the city by its great gate . . . It is a day of festival . . . The streets are broad rivers of people, folk of every race, buying and selling in the market-place or singing to the music of wandering minstrels. A drum beats, and a royal procession passes down the street, with elephants leading to the sound of conchs [shell trumpets] . . . Meanwhile stall keepers ply their trade, <u>selling sweet cakes, garlands of flowers, scented powder</u> . . . Noblemen drive through the streets in their chariots, their <u>gold-sheathed swords flashing</u>, wearing <u>brightly dyed garments</u> and <u>wreaths of flowers</u>. From balconies and turrets the many jewels of the <u>perfumed women</u> who watch the festival flash in the sunlight. The people flock to the temples to worship to the <u>sound of music</u>, laying flowers before the images and honoring the holy sages.

—excerpt from *The Garland of Madurai*, as appears in *The Wonder That Was India* by A. L. Basham

The details in this sentence describe some of the products and foods made in Madurai.

The author's use of sights, smells, and sounds helps bring the scene to life.

Skills Focus: Identifying Main Idea and Details   **Below Level**

Reading Skill
Mauryan and Gupta Empires

1. Draw the Venn diagram for students to see. Omit the italicized answers.

2. Have students copy and complete the diagram. Have volunteers share their completed diagrams, and have students correct their own work. **LS** **Visual-Spatial**

Alternative Assessment Handbook, Rubric 13: Graphic Organizers

Empires of India

Mauryan   Gupta

strict state control, spies, Buddhist

large territory, prosperity, same location

not harshly controlled, freedom, Hindu

In the more distant areas that they conquered, the Guptas governed through local rulers. Under this system, local rulers retained power but had to pay tribute to the Guptas and travel to the Gupta court on occasion.

Gupta power expanded under the heirs of Chandra Gupta I. His son Samudra Gupta extended the empire to the north and east and conquered several small kingdoms in southeastern India. Unable to maintain control over these distant lands to the southeast, however, he later restored the conquered rulers in that region to power.

The Gupta Empire reached its height under Samudra Gupta's son **Chandra Gupta II**, who ruled from 375 to 415. Chandra Gupta II further expanded the empire and strengthened its economy. His reign was a period of prosperity and cultural achievement in India.

During this period, a Chinese Buddhist monk named Faxian (FAH-shee-en) traveled to India. Faxian described the people of the empire as rich and prosperous. He also wrote that punishments were fair and that the government did not use capital punishment.

Support of Hinduism During the period between the Mauryan and Gupta empires, Buddhism had prospered and spread in India. Hinduism, meanwhile, had lost popularity. Under the Guptas, though, Hinduism again became the main religion in India.

The Gupta rulers supported the building of Hindu temples and promoted a revival of Hindu writings. At the same time, the Gupta rulers supported other religions, such as Buddhism and Jainism. Even so, Buddhism began to lose influence in India during this period.

End of Gupta Rule Gupta rule began to weaken in the late 400s. Because of the Guptas' loose control over conquered areas, some parts of the empire began to break away. In addition, Central Asian nomads called the White Huns began invading India.

These problems weakened the empire and disrupted trade. In addition, Gupta military efforts to defend the empire drained the treasury. Around 550, Gupta rule ended. Once again, India divided into a number of small, regional kingdoms.

READING CHECK **Identify Supporting Details** How did the Guptas rule their empire?

Hindu Architecture
This Hindu temple, built in the early 1000s, is located in Khajuraho in central India.

SECTION 3 ASSESSMENT

go.hrw.com
Online Quiz
Keyword: SHL EIC HP

Reviewing Ideas, Terms, and People

1. **a. Describe** What new policies did **Ashoka** adopt after his conversion to Buddhism?
   b. Explain How were the Mauryans able to rule such a large territory?
   c. Make Judgments Can Ashoka's ideals of nonviolence, right conduct, and tolerance help contemporary world leaders? Why or why not?

2. **a. Identify** What group of trading kingdoms ruled southern India?
   b. Explain How did invasions in northern India affect the region?

3. **a. Recall** How did the Chinese traveler Faxian describe India under the Gupta dynasty?
   b. Summarize How did Gupta rule affect religion in India?
   c. Support a Position Do you think that Gupta rulers were more tolerant than Mauryan rulers? Provide reasons to support your position.

Critical Thinking

4. **Compare and Contrast** Use your notes and a graphic organizer like the one here to explain the ways in which India's Mauryan and Gupta empires were similar and different.

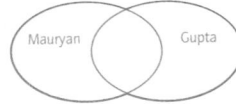

Mauryan   Gupta

FOCUS ON WRITING

5. **Narration** You are traveling through India during the reign of Ashoka. Write a journal entry describing interesting features of the Mauryan Empire, including the effects of Ashoka's conversion to Buddhism and the capital city at Pataliputra.

EMPIRES OF CHINA AND INDIA **237**

Getting Started

Use the **Interactive Reader and Study Guide** to familiarize students with the section content.

📖 **Interactive Reader and Study Guide,** Section 4

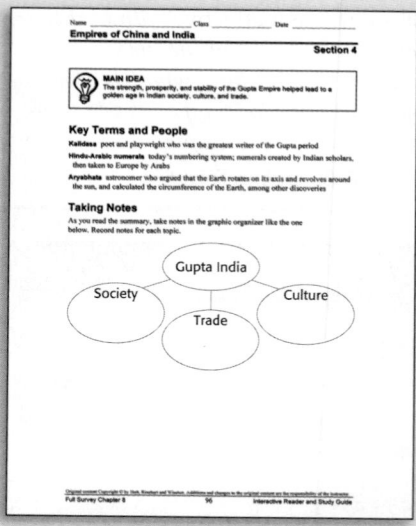

Academic Vocabulary

Review with students the high-use academic term in this section.

portray to show or depict something, such as a person or a scene (p. 240)

📝 **CRF:** Vocabulary Builder: Section 4

Taking Notes

Society—class and gender roles, jatis, women had limited status, thriving society and economy; Trade—network reached China, Silk Roads, Roman Empire, Southeast Asia; Culture—Kalidasa's poems and plays, architecture, religious art, Aryabhata's astronomy and mathematics

---

SECTION 4

Indian Society and Culture

BEFORE YOU READ

MAIN IDEA

The strength, prosperity, and stability of the Gupta Empire helped lead to a golden age in Indian society, trade, and culture.

READING FOCUS

1. What features defined Indian society and trade during the Gupta period?

2. What were major cultural and scientific achievements of the Gupta golden age?

KEY TERMS AND PEOPLE

Kalidasa
Hindu-Arabic numerals
Aryabhata

 NEW YORK

PI 3.1 Students analyze the roles and contributions of individuals and groups to social, political, economic, cultural, and religious practices and activities.

THE INSIDE STORY

How might a tiger turn into a treasure? In 1819 some British officers were stalking a tiger in the hills near Ajanta, India. As the group watched, the big cat blended into the forest and disappeared. Quickly the officers scanned the hills for their lost prey, but the tiger was gone. Then one man noticed a cave on an odd horseshoe-shaped cliff. With the tiger lost, the group decided to investigate. When the officers neared the cliff, though, they slowed in surprise. Before them was not a cave but an ornate temple hewn out

of the solid rock. Even more amazing, several other temples peeked out from beneath the thick overgrowth.

Excitedly the officers began ripping away vegetation to reveal intricate columns, huge arches, and statues of the Buddha. Eager to see more, the group entered one of the caves only to find an even greater treasure inside. All along the walls vibrantly colored murals glowed in the soft light filtering into the cave. The richly detailed scenes depicted bejeweled men and women, flying celestial beings, scenes from the life of the Buddha, animals, birds, and flowers.

The British officers had stumbled upon ancient Buddhist cave temples, long abandoned to nature. Today the Ajanta murals are considered masterpieces of Buddhist art, providing a glimpse into life in ancient India. ■

A TIGER LEADS TO Treasure

The image on the left is from a Buddhist mural located within the rock-cut temples of Ajanta, shown above.

238 CHAPTER 8

Teach the Main Idea

At Level

Indian Society and Culture

1. **Teach** Ask students the Reading Focus questions to teach this section.

2. **Apply** Have students create a graphic organizer for the section. They should use the three main heads as topics and then list main ideas and details under each head.

3. **Review** Have students share their graphic organizers with the class. Then have students describe various aspects of daily life during the time of the Gupta Empire.

4. **Practice/Homework** Have students write a one-act play about life during the Gupta Empire. **LS Verbal-Linguistic, Visual-Spatial**

📝 **Alternative Assessment Handbook,** Rubric 39: Writing to Create

Life in Gupta India

Indian civilization flourished during the period of the Gupta empire. Trade increased, and the economy strengthened. Cities prospered, and many Indian cultural traditions developed.

Growth of Trade During the Gupta period, foreign trade increased. Overland trade routes, such as the Silk Roads, linked India to markets from the Mediterranean Sea to Africa and China. Over these trade routes, Indian merchants exchanged goods such as cashmere, cotton, ivory, and spices for foreign goods such as Chinese silk and Roman ceramics.

The Gupta Empire and Tamil kingdoms in southern India traded actively by sea as well. Indian sailors used monsoons, or shifting seasonal winds, to reach foreign markets across the Arabian Sea. In addition, a sea trade between India and Southeast Asia developed at this time. This trade played a key role in the cultural diffusion of Indian culture to Southeast Asia. For example, trade helped spread Buddhism and Hinduism to Southeast Asia.

Daily Life The growth of trade strengthened the economy, and the Gupta Empire's cities reflected this prosperity. Shops and markets bustled with activity. As the use of money became more common, a new class of Indian bankers and moneylenders emerged. For the urban rich, a culture stressing luxury and pleasure developed, and young city dwellers enjoyed music, poetry, and art.

Most people during the Gupta period led simple lives in small villages, however. The majority of village dwellers were farmers. Other people provided the various services needed in each village. Most villages were self-sufficient, but trade did occur between villages. In addition, people from different villages got together for religious festivals and other events.

Social Structure Many rules and customs influenced Indian society during the Gupta period. As noted in an earlier chapter, most people in ancient India belonged to a specific caste, or social division. People's castes determined what jobs they could hold and how they should interact with others. During the Gupta period, the number of castes grew, and many castes developed their own rules and customs.

Faxian's Record of India

The Chinese Buddhist monk Faxian went on a journey to India from 399 to 414. In the following passage from his record of his journey, Faxian describes some aspects of life in Gupta India.

"The people are numerous and happy; . . . only those who cultivate the royal land have to pay [a portion of] the grain from it. If they want to go, they go; if they want to stay on, they stay . . . Throughout the whole country the people do not kill any living creature, nor drink intoxicating liquor, nor eat onions or garlic . . . In buying and selling commodities they use cowries [shells] . . . All who are diseased, go to . . . houses [of medicine], and are provided with every kind of help, and doctors examine their diseases. They get the food and medicines which their cases require, and are made to feel at ease."

—Faxian, *A Record of Buddhistic Kingdoms*

Skills Focus READING LIKE A HISTORIAN

1. **Summarize** How would you summarize life in Gupta India based on this primary source?
2. **Analyze Primary Sources** What conclusions can you draw from the primary source about medical knowledge in Gupta India?

See **Skills Handbook**, p. H25

In addition to the caste system, Hindu legal codes defined people's roles in Gupta India. For example, a legal code called *The Laws of Manu* was compiled sometime between 200 BC and AD 200. The laws in this code defined proper behavior for people of various stations.

Gender also shaped Indian society in the Gupta period. In general, men had more rights and authority than women did. For instance, most families were patriarchal, or headed by the father or eldest male. As in ancient China, marriages were arranged, and young women were taught that their role was to marry and have children. Once married, women were to obey their husbands. *The Laws of Manu* stated that, "In childhood, a female must be subject to her father, in youth to her husband." At the same time, men were expected to treat women with respect, and Hindu laws gave abused wives the right to leave their husbands.

READING CHECK Identify Cause and Effect How did trade affect city life in Gupta India?

TAKING NOTES

As you read, take notes in a graphic organizer like this one. Record notes for each topic.

Gupta India / Society / Culture / Trade

NEW YORK

CC Unit 1-C6
The status and role of women in classical civilizations

EMPIRES OF CHINA AND INDIA **239**

239

2 What were major cultural and scientific achievements of the Gupta golden age? *Sanskrit literature, religious art and architecture, temples and statues, metallurgy, advancements in mathematics, medicine, and astronomy*

A Gupta Golden Age

Explain What was the purpose of the *Panchatantra*? *meant to teach people lessons, such as thinking before acting*

Predict How do you think increased trade affected Indian culture? *possible answers—introduced new goods and ideas, connection to other lands, more diverse culture*

Activity **Trade Routes** Have students use the atlas in their text to create two maps, one showing the long route Indian traders had to take to reach the Roman Empire, the other showing the route across the Arabian Sea.
LS **Visual-Spatial**

Alternative Assessment Handbook, Rubric 20: Map Creation

Info to Know

Panchatantra The *Panchatantra* is an anonymous collection of fables most likely compiled before AD 500. The *Panchatantra* consists of one narrative thread that holds together several different stories. The stories, which combine both prose and verse, were originally intended for the instruction of the sons of royalty.

Answers

Gupta Achievements *possible answer—People can afford to devote time and money to the arts and to trading with distant cultures.*

240

Gupta Achievements

The stability and prosperity of the Gupta Empire ushered in a golden age for Indian trade, literature, art and architecture, and science and mathematics. *Why might a period of stability and prosperity help the arts and trade flourish?*

◀ **Trade** Under the Gupta Empire, Indian trade expanded widely, as illustrated by these Roman coins found in South India. The coins depict the emperor Caligula.

▲ **Sanskrit Literature** The manuscript cover above shows scenes from the play *Sakuntala*, by Kalidasa. The cover was made in Nepal during the 1100s, showing the wide and lasting popularity of Kalidasa's works.

Courtesy: The Kronos Collection

NEW YORK

CC **Unit 2-A2** Gupta Empire's artistic, scientific and mathematical contributions

A Gupta Golden Age

Like the Han period in ancient China, the Gupta period was a golden age of cultural and scientific achievements. During this period, Indian artists, writers, scholars, and scientists made great advances, some of which are still studied and admired today.

Sanskrit Literature Many great works of Sanskrit literature were created during the Gupta period. As you have learned, Sanskrit was the language of the ancient Aryans. One of the greatest writers of the time was **Kalidasa** (kahl-ee-DAHS-uh), a poet and playwright. His work was so brilliant that Chandra Gupta II hired him to write plays for the royal court. Kalidasa's writing has a lyricism and beauty with few equals in Sanskrit literature. His most famous play, *Sakuntala,* tells the story of a king who falls in love with a maiden named Sakuntala. The play combines myth, humor, court life, and lyric poetry to tell its story.

Another popular work of the period was the *Panchatantra* (PUHN-chuh-TAHN-truh), or "Five Books." This collection of stories was meant to teach people lessons. For instance, the following warns readers to think before acting.

ACADEMIC VOCABULARY

portray to show or depict something, such as a person or a scene

HISTORY'S VOICES

❝The good and bad of given schemes
Wise thought must first reveal:
The stupid heron saw his chicks
Provide a mongoose meal.❞
—*Panchatantra*, translated by Arthur William Ryder

Art and Architecture Much of the art and architecture of the Gupta period was religious. For instance, magnificent Hindu and Buddhist temples were built across India during this period. The Hindu temples created at this time often had huge towers and were covered with carvings. Buddhist temples of the period included stupas, temples that had domed roofs and were built to house sacred items from the life of Buddha. Like Hindu temples, many stupas were covered with detailed carvings.

Among the most spectacular architecture of the period were temples and monuments carved out of rock and cliff faces. The most famous are the cave temples at Ajanta and Ellora, located in west-central India. These temples have intricately carved columns and contain halls, rooms, and even windows.

The Gupta period also saw the creation of great works of art, both paintings and statues. Paintings of the time often portray beautiful and graceful Indians wearing fine jewelry and stylish clothing. Many of the finest paintings of ancient India are found in Buddhist and Hindu temples. Hindu artists decorated the walls and entrances of temples with *devas*, or aspects of Brahman. Buddhists covered the plaster walls and ceilings of cave temples with scenes from the life of the Buddha. Some of the finest examples are found in the Ajanta cave temples.

Many statues were made for temples as well. Buddhist temples featured statues of the Buddha and of kings. Hindu temples featured statues of Siva, Vishnu, and other *devas*.

240 CHAPTER 8

Collaborative Learning

The Gupta World

Materials: colored pencils or markers

1. Organize students into small groups.

2. Have each group put together a magazine called "The Gupta World." Magazines should include illustrated articles that reflect society, trade, and the culture of India during the Gupta period. For example, one article could contain "do's and don'ts" for high caste women. Another could discuss the new products available through trade. A third could feature Kalidasa's writings. Groups

may decide to conduct outside research to gather historical information to help them write their articles.

3. Have groups review their articles to check for alignment with standard English. Allow time for groups to make any necessary revisions to their articles.

4. Have groups present their magazines to the class. **LS** **Verbal-Linguistic, Visual-Spatial**

Alternative Assessment Handbook, Rubric 19: Magazines

Rock-cut Architecture The Gupta period is known for temples and monuments carved out of rock faces. The Kailasa temple, shown here, is located at the Ellora Caves in central India. Made during the AD 700s, the Hindu temple is dedicated to Siva.

Religious Art The rock-cut cave temples at Ajanta contain some of the finest examples of Buddhist art of the Gupta period. The Ajanta fresco on the left depicts two women playing flutes while a third woman dances.

Science and Technology In the fields of science and technology, the ancient Indians were pioneers of metallurgy (MET-uhl-uhr-jee), the science of working with metals. Indian iron was particularly valued for its hardness and purity. Gupta metalworkers built the famous Iron Pillar, located near Delhi. Unlike most iron, which rusts easily, this iron pillar is very resistant to rust. Scholars still study it today.

Gupta scholars were among the most advanced mathematicians of their day as well. They developed many of the elements of our modern math system. For example, the Indians were the first people to use a symbol for zero, without which modern math would not be possible. In addition, the numerals we use today are called **Hindu-Arabic numerals** because Indian scholars created them, after which Arabs brought the number system to Europe.

In medical science, the ancient Indians were quite advanced. They made medicines from plants and minerals and knew how to inject small amounts of viruses to inoculate, or protect, people against disease. When people were injured, Indian doctors could perform surgery, repair broken bones, and treat wounds. If all else failed, doctors cast magic spells.

In astronomy, the study of the stars and planets, Indians identified seven of the planets in our solar system. In addition, they could predict eclipses of the sun and the moon. One of the most famous Indian astronomers was named **Aryabhata**. He correctly argued that Earth rotates on its axis and revolves around the Sun. Aryabhata also knew that Earth was a sphere and calculated its circumference to remarkable accuracy. In addition, he made numerous contributions in mathematics.

 READING CHECK **Find the Main Idea** Why do historians consider the Gupta period to have been a golden age in the history of ancient India?

SECTION 4 ASSESSMENT

go.hrw.com
Online Quiz
Keyword: SHL EIC HP

Reviewing Ideas, Terms, and People

1. **a. Describe** How would you describe daily life in Gupta India?
   b. Compare and Contrast How did roles for men and women differ in Gupta India?
   c. Explain How did trade help contribute to the spread of Indian religions such as Hinduism and Buddhism?

2. **a. Identify** Who were **Kalidasa** and **Aryabhata**?
   b. Explain Why was the great literature of the Gupta period written in Sanskrit?
   c. Evaluate How did Indian mathematicians contribute to the development of our modern math system?

Critical Thinking

3. **Categorize** Use your notes and a copy of the graphic organizer shown here to identify key Gupta cultural achievements in art and architecture, literature, math, and science and technology.

Gupta Cultural Achievements

FOCUS ON WRITING

4. **Persuasion** Choose the one Gupta achievement that you think has had the most lasting influence on life today. Write a paragraph to persuade others to agree with your choice. Start by stating your choice clearly.

EMPIRES OF CHINA AND INDIA **241**

Nomads and Empires

Info to Know

Weapons of the Nomads The nomads used a combination of weaponry to succeed on the battlefield. Fighting on horseback, they used powerful composite bows made from strips of bone, and switched to sabers at close range. As the invasions continued, they obtained taller horses and used lances, making their attacks even deadlier.

 Roman Empire and Nomads

The Eastern Roman Empire was also attacked by nomadic invaders. The armies advanced on the capital, Constantinople, from the north and laid siege to the city. Leaders of Constantinople mobilized the people and inspired them with religious icons and hymns. Counterattacks on the invaders from land and sea soon ended the siege and saved the city.

Quick Facts Transparency: Roman Empire and Nomads

MISCONCEPTION ALERT

The invaders of this time period were not Mongols. The Mongol invasions were similarly devastating, but occurred approximately 700 years later.

HISTORY & Geography

Nomads and Empires

Nomadic tribes ranged throughout the steppes that extended across much of northern Europe and Asia. Fierce warriors, these nomads often raided empires to the south and drove other tribes before them. Such invasions contributed to the fall of the Western Roman Empire and the empire of Han China.

ROMAN EMPIRE AND NOMADS — QUICK FACTS

- Had ongoing conflicts with German-speaking tribes living along the frontier.
- Used defensive walls, alliances, and military force to try to stop nomadic raids and invasions.
- Westward movement of nomadic Huns drove German-speaking tribes to invade.
- Nomadic invasions contributed to the fall of the Western Roman Empire.
- The Eastern Roman Empire survived for another 1,000 years.

AD 453 Attila the Hun dies. The Huns soon retreat.

AD 370 Goths, pressed by the Huns, begin settling in the Roman Empire.

AD 410 Visigoths sack Rome.
AD 455 Vandals sack Rome.

Legend:
- Western Roman Empire, AD 454
- Eastern Roman Empire, AD 454
- Han Empire, AD 100
- Gupta Empire, AD 400
- Sassanian Empire, c. AD 400s
- Steppe
- Great Wall of China, AD 220

0   400 Miles
0   400 Kilometers
Miller cylindrical projection

Map labels: JUTES, ANGLES, SAXONS, FRANKS, Rhine R., BRITAIN, EUROPE, ATLANTIC OCEAN, GAUL, BURGUNDIANS, GOTHS AND VANDALS, HUNS, OSTROGOTHS, VISIGOTHS, Danube R., Black Sea, Constantinople, Nicaea, ASIA MINOR, Caspian Sea, Aral Sea, Rome, VISIGOTHS, Athens, Carthage, SPAIN, VISIGOTHS, GOTHS AND VANDALS, Mediterranean Sea, Alexandria, SYRIA, Jerusalem, Tigris R., Euphrates R., WHITE HUNS, PERSIA, Persian Gulf, Red Sea, EGYPT, AFRICA

Skills Focus: Identifying Problem and Solution   At Level

Reading Skill
Imperial Council

1. Organize students into small groups. Tell students that they are imperial advisors for an empire that is facing attacks by nomadic invaders.

2. Have groups discuss possible strategies for dealing with the invasion. Strategies might include building projects to defend key locations, bribing the invaders, attempting to form an alliance with nearby peoples, or a combination of these.

3. Have groups present their recommendations to the class.

4. Guide students in a discussion of the best strategies. Encourage students to debate their ideas. **LS Verbal-Linguistic, Interpersonal**

Alternative Assessment Handbook, Rubrics 11: Discussions; and 35: Solving Problems

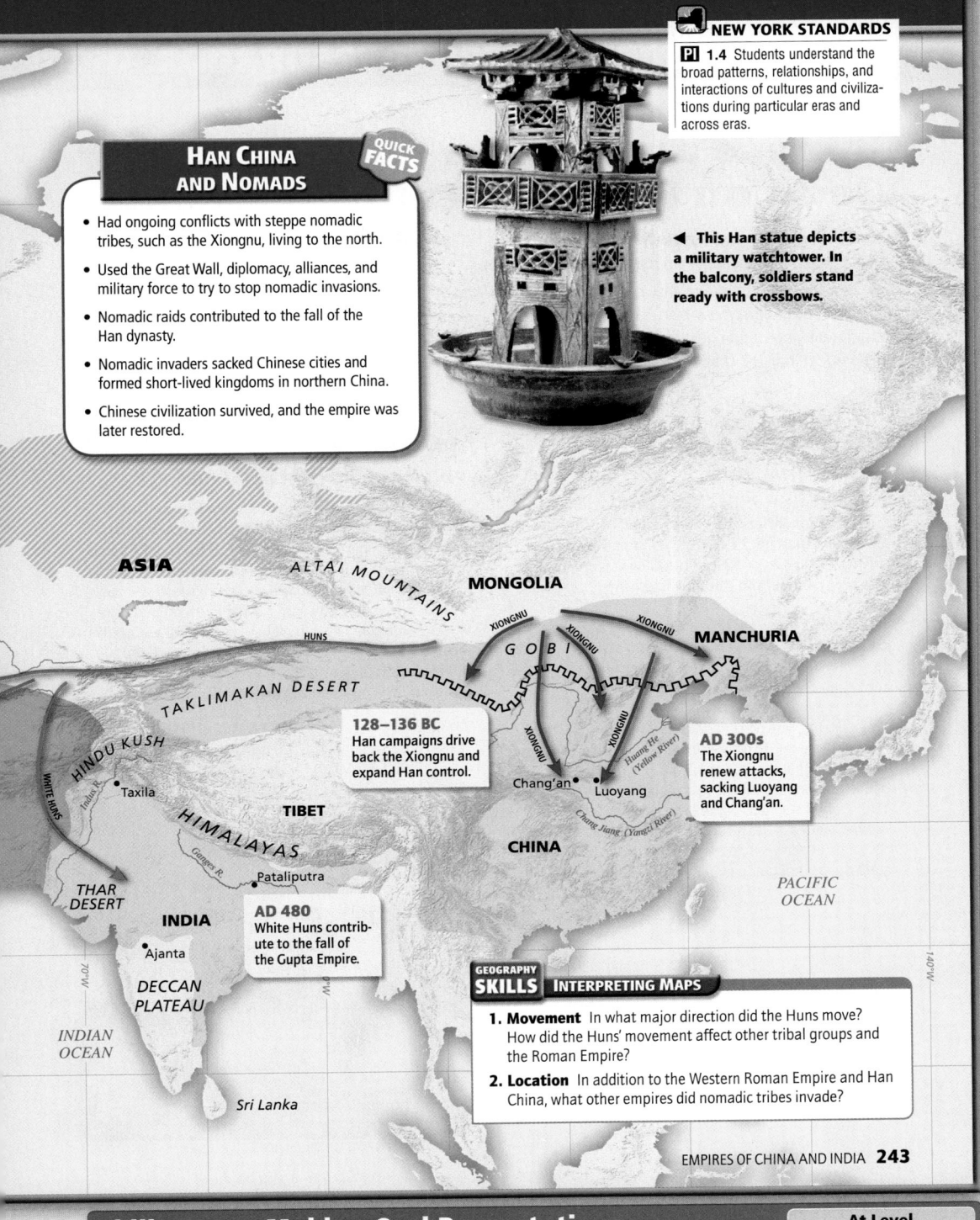

NEW YORK STANDARDS

P1 1.4 Students understand the broad patterns, relationships, and interactions of cultures and civilizations during particular eras and across eras.

HAN CHINA AND NOMADS
QUICK FACTS

- Had ongoing conflicts with steppe nomadic tribes, such as the Xiongnu, living to the north.
- Used the Great Wall, diplomacy, alliances, and military force to try to stop nomadic invasions.
- Nomadic raids contributed to the fall of the Han dynasty.
- Nomadic invaders sacked Chinese cities and formed short-lived kingdoms in northern China.
- Chinese civilization survived, and the empire was later restored.

◀ This Han statue depicts a military watchtower. In the balcony, soldiers stand ready with crossbows.

128–136 BC
Han campaigns drive back the Xiongnu and expand Han control.

AD 300s
The Xiongnu renew attacks, sacking Luoyang and Chang'an.

AD 480
White Huns contribute to the fall of the Gupta Empire.

ASIA
ALTAI MOUNTAINS
MONGOLIA
HUNS
GOBI
XIONGNU
MANCHURIA
TAKLIMAKAN DESERT
HINDU KUSH
WHITE HUNS
Taxila
Indus R.
TIBET
HIMALAYAS
Ganges R.
Pataliputra
Chang'an
Luoyang
Huang He (Yellow River)
CHINA
Chang Jiang (Yangzi River)
PACIFIC OCEAN
THAR DESERT
INDIA
Ajanta
DECCAN PLATEAU
INDIAN OCEAN
Sri Lanka

GEOGRAPHY SKILLS | INTERPRETING MAPS

1. **Movement** In what major direction did the Huns move? How did the Huns' movement affect other tribal groups and the Roman Empire?
2. **Location** In addition to the Western Roman Empire and Han China, what other empires did nomadic tribes invade?

EMPIRES OF CHINA AND INDIA **243**

History and Geography

Info to Know

Blended Culture When invaders set up kingdoms in northern China, they had no knowledge of how to govern an agricultural, non-nomadic people. Forced to turn to the Chinese for help, they incorporated Chinese principles of government. The nomads also learned to appreciate Chinese customs and literature. Intermarriage between upper class Chinese and former nomads formed a unique blended culture; out of this new nobility the Sui dynasty eventually emerged.

QUICK FACTS **Han China and Nomads**

Elaborate Were Chinese strategies to stop the invaders successful? Explain. *possible answers—only successful for a short time; invaders eventually sacked Chinese cities*

Quick Facts Transparency: Han China and Nomads

Skills Focus: Making Oral Presentations

At Level

Research Required

Reading Like a Historian Skill
Effects of the Invasions

1. Organize students into small groups. Assign each group an area in which a nomadic invasion occurred.

2. Have groups conduct research on the invasion that occurred in their area. Students should focus their research on the short- and long-term effects of the invasion.

3. Have groups make a brief oral presentation of their findings. **LS Kinesthetic, Verbal-Linguistic**

Alternative Assessment Handbook, Rubrics 29: Presentations; and 30: Research

Answers

Interpreting Maps 1.west; Huns drove German-speaking tribes to invade Roman Empire; **2.** Gupta Empire

243

CHAPTER

8 Document-Based Investigation

Chinese and Indian Views on Government

Chinese and Indian Views on Government

Word Help

conformers enforcements

sage wise person

 Book Burning Have students reread the information about Document 2 and study the painting portraying book burning. Then have students write a short, front-page newspaper article, complete with a headline, reporting on the event shown. Have volunteers share their articles with the class. **LS Verbal-Linguistic**

Alternative Assessment Handbook, Rubric 23: Newspapers

Info to Know

Daoism and Confucianism Daoism and Confucianism are sometimes referred to as religions, and sometimes as philosophies. These two ancient schools of thought have aspects of both, although Confucianism is usually associated with worldly matters, whereas Daoism is more concerned with nature and spirituality.

 NEW YORK STANDARDS

PI 3.3 Students examine the social/cultural, political, economic, and religious norms and values of Western and other world cultures.

Historical Context The four documents below express different views from ancient China and India about what defines good government.

Task Study the selections and answer the questions that follow. After you have studied the documents, you will be asked to write an essay explaining why people held different views about government. You will need to use evidence from these selections and from the chapter to support the position you take in your essay.

DOCUMENT 1

A Legalist View

Hanfeizi, a founder of the Chinese political philosophy of Legalism, briefly served as an advisor in the court of Shi Huangdi. In the following passages from *Hanfeitzu*, Hanfeizi describes his views on creating a strong government and maintaining control.

> If conformers to law are strong, the country is strong; if conformers to law are weak, the country is weak . . . Hence to govern the state by law is to praise the right and blame the wrong.

> When a sage [wise person] governs a state, he does not rely on the people to do good out of their own will. Instead, he sees to it that they are not allowed to do what is not good. If he relies on people to do good out of their own will, within the borders of the state not even ten persons can be counted on [to do good]. Yet, if one sees to it that they are not allowed to do what is not good, the whole state can be brought to uniform order. Whoever rules should . . . not devote his attention to virtue, but to law.

DOCUMENT 2

An Artist's View on Legalist Rule

The painting below, by an unknown Chinese artist, depicts Qin ruler Shi Huangdi's attempts to prevent opposition to his Legalist policies. While books burn in the foreground on the left, Shi Huangdi's servants execute Confucian scholars on the right. In the background, a scholar gives up a book to an official. The scene combines two separate events—Shi Huangdi's order in 213 BC to have most books burned and his alleged order a year later to execute 460 Confucian scholars who opposed his actions.

Confucian Scholars Being Thrown Into a Pit, by Hung Wu, date unknown

Differentiating Instruction

Below Level

Standard English Mastery

English-Language Learners

1. Have students work in pairs to write short summaries of Documents 1, 3, and 4. Have students look up unfamiliar words in the dictionary.

2. Have volunteers read their summaries to the class. As a class, discuss any necessary grammatical or stylistic revisions. Allow time for students to correct their summaries.

3. Guide students in a discussion about the various views of government presented here. Ask students these questions: Which view of government do you agree with most? Why? **LS Verbal-Linguistic**

Alternative Assessment Handbook, Rubric 11: Discussions

DOCUMENT 3

A Confucian View

Confucius and his followers taught that people and governments should value virtue and the ways of the past. A ruler should lead by example, inspiring good behavior in the people. The people, in turn, should honor and respect their superiors and learn from them. In the following passages from *The Analects,* Confucius expresses some of his ideas about good government.

> If a ruler himself is upright, all will go well without orders. But if he himself is not upright, even though he gives orders they will not be obeyed.

> Lead the people by laws and regulate them by penalties, and the people will try to keep out of jail, but will have no sense of shame. Lead the people by virtue and restrain them by the rules of decorum, and the people will have a sense of shame, and moreover will become good.

DOCUMENT 4

A Mauryan View

Chandragupta, founder of India's Mauryan Empire, relied on the *Arthasastra* as a guide for statecraft. Kautilya, an advisor to Chandragupta, is thought to have written the *Arthasastra.* The text supports a strong rule of law and the use of spies but also includes political advice based on his views of human nature.

> If a king is energetic, his subjects will be equally energetic. If he is reckless, they will not only be reckless likewise, but also eat into his works . . . In the happiness of his subjects lies [a king's] happiness; in their welfare his welfare; whatever pleases himself he shall not consider as good, but whatever pleases his subjects he shall consider as good. Hence the king shall ever be active and discharge his duties.

> Spies shall ascertain [determine] the fair or foul dealings of villagers . . . Spies under the disguise of old and notorious thieves may similarly associate with robbers and . . . cause the latter to be arrested. The Collector general shall exhibit these arrested robbers and announce to the public that their arrest is due to the instructions obtained from the king who has learned the divine art of catching robbers.

Info to Know

Kautilya and Machiavelli Kautilya has often been compared to the Italian thinker Niccolo Machiavelli, who also wrote a handbook of government. Like Kautilya, Machiavelli argues that the character or skill of a leader is what determines the success of the state. Machiavelli focuses on how to gain and maintain power and disregards traditional ideas of morality. For this reason, he is often associated with ruthlessness and deception.

Skills Focus — READING LIKE A HISTORIAN

DOCUMENT 1
a. **Recall** What does Hanfeizi state is the basis of a strong government?
b. **Draw Conclusions** Why might members of the lower classes in ancient China have supported a Legalist system?

DOCUMENT 2
a. **Describe** How does the artist depict the government servants and scholars?
b. **Infer** Do you think that the artist supported or opposed Shi Huangdi's policies and actions? Support your answer.

DOCUMENT 3
a. **Recall** What does Confucius state is the basis of a good government?
b. **Contrast** What are some key ways in which the views of Hanfeizi and Confucius differ regarding government?

DOCUMENT 4
a. **Interpret** What is the role of spies in Kautilya's model of government?
b. **Infer** Do you think that Hanfeizi would have agreed with Kautilya's view of government? Why or why not?

DOCUMENT-BASED ESSAY QUESTION

Philosophers and rulers in ancient China and India held a variety of views about government. Using the documents above and information from the chapter, form a thesis that explains why these people might have held such different views about government. Then write a short essay to support your position.

See **Skills Handbook,** p. H25

Differentiating Instruction

Above Level

Advanced Learners/Gifted and Talented

1. Have students write an explanation of what they believe virtue means and list one example of a virtuous act. Students should not list names, just actions they believe reflect virtuous behavior. You may wish to provide examples of virtuous acts: a football player decides to attend a charity event rather than a promotional one; a relative donates a kidney for a transplant, etc.

2. Organize students into small groups. Have students in each group share the actions they listed and create a group list.

3. Have each group discuss what all of the examples have in common. Have groups derive a definition of virtue from the examples.

4. Have groups present their definitions. Have students write an essay answering this question: How can leaders show virtue?
LS Intrapersonal, Verbal-Linguistic

Alternative Assessment Handbook, Rubrics 11: Discussions; and 12: Drawing Conclusions

Answers

Reading Like a Historian
Document 1. a. *clear, strong laws, strict penalties;* **b.** *same laws and punishments for all;* **Document 2. a.** *helpless; being executed;* **b.** *possible answer—opposed, shows scholars being brutalized;* **Document 3. a.** *virtue, conduct of ruler* **b.** *Hanfeizi—clear, strong laws and severe punishment more important than virtue; Confucius—virtue and good conduct more important than laws;* **Document 4. a.** *watch over villagers, catch robbers;* **b.** *No; Hanfeizi was not concerned with happiness of subjects, only law and order.*
Essay *Student essays should discuss motivations of rulers, different religious beliefs and philosophies, and different views of law and punishments.*

245

Visual Summary

Review and Inquiry Organize students into six groups. Assign each group one of the six headings shown on this page. Have each group write a paragraph summarizing the significant facts about the period.

Quick Facts Transparency: Visual Study Guide: Empires of China and India

Review Key Terms and People

1. Shi Huangdi united China under the state of Qin.

2. Legalism taught that a powerful and efficient state was the key to control and order

3. Wudi was the greatest of all Han rulers.

4. Wudi implemented the civil service system to obtain loyal officials

5. Poor distribution of wealth can lead to instability.

6. Sima Qian wrote an early history of China's dynasties.

7. Silk Roads were a network of trade routes that stretched across Central Asia.

8. Chandragupta Maurya established the Mauryan Empire in India.

9. Ashoka was the leader of the Mauryan Empire at its height of power.

10. Kalidasa, a poet and playwright, was the greatest writer of the Gupta period.

11. Indian scholars created Hindu-Arabic numerals.

12. Aryabhata was a famous Indian astronomer.

Comprehension and Critical Thinking

13. **a.** relocated nobles to capital; killed Confucian scholars who opposed him
b. Shi Huangdi died, peasants rebelled, nobles raised armies, Liu Bang defeated Qin forces and established the Han dynasty.
c. possible answers—Qin had a repressive system; Han enacted reforms, set up bureaucracy, more emphasis on merit through civil service

---

CHAPTER

8 Chapter Review

QUICK FACTS

VISUAL STUDY GUIDE

China

Qin Dynasty, 221–206 BC
- Founded by Shi Huangdi; united China for first time
- Strong, centralized government and harsh laws based on the Chinese philosophy of Legalism
- Persecution of Confucianists; burning of Confucian texts
- Standardization of laws, writing, weights and measures
- Many building projects, including Great Wall of China

Han Dynasty, 206 BC–220 AD
- Founded by Liu Bang; reunited China
- Government and society based on Confucian values
- Under Emperor Wudi, development of a civil service system and expansion of the empire
- Golden age of Chinese civilization
- Growth of trade over Silk Roads and other routes
- Spread of Buddhism from India to China

Period of Disunion, 220–589
- Shift of power from central government to local nobles
- Nomadic invasions by Xiongnu and others
- About 350 years of warfare and chaos
- Continuation of Chinese civilization despite disunity

India

Mauryan Empire, c. 320–185 BC
- Founded by Chandragupta Maurya; united much of India
- Under Chandragupta, strong government control with an organized bureaucracy and spy network
- Under Ashoka, expansion of empire, promotion of Buddhism, and building of new wells and roads
- Declined after Ashoka's death

Regional Kingdoms
- Division of India into many regional kingdoms
- North India: Invaders form small kingdoms; Kushan kingdom (c. 100 BC–c. AD 200)
- South India: Andhra kingdom (c. 100s BC–c. AD 300)
- Far South India: trade-based Tamil kingdoms

Gupta Empire, 320–c. 550
- Founded by Chandra Gupta I; reunited northern India
- Height of empire under Chandra Gupta II
- Golden age of Indian civilization
- Promotion of Hinduism and Hindu temples
- Declined in part because of invasions of White Huns

Review Key Terms and People

For each term or name below, write a sentence that explains its significance to the ancient empires of China and India.

1. Shi Huangdi
2. Legalism
3. Wudi
4. civil service
5. distribution
6. Sima Qian
7. Silk Roads
8. Chandragupta Maurya
9. Ashoka
10. Kalidasa
11. Hindu-Arabic numerals
12. Aryabhata

---

14. **a.** paper, iron plow, wheelbarrow, seismograph, acupuncture, sundial, compass, water mill, rudder
b. women—wives and mothers, generally low status, had to obey husbands; men—more authority and rights, sons valued
c. increased trade, connections to Central Asia, spread of Buddhism

15. **a.** brilliant advisor to Chandragupta Maurya, wrote handbook of government
b. policy of nonviolence and tolerance of other religions; encouraged right conduct; built roads and rest houses, dug wells

c. possible answers—yes, did not have to deal with faraway affairs, and people had their own local leaders; no, little centralized control over these areas

16. **a.** the language of ancient Aryans; many great works of Sanskrit literature created during Gupta period
b. time of peace, prosperity, booming trade, great works of art and literature
c. possible answer—Yes, the Guptas actively supported the arts; political stability and prosperity enabled arts to flourish.

History's Impact video program
Review the video to answer the closing question:
What impact has Buddhism had on the world?

Comprehension and Critical Thinking

SECTION 1 *(pp. 223–227)*

13. a. Recall How did Shi Huangdi assert his control over local nobles and potential rivals?

b. Sequence What series of events led to the fall of the Qin dynasty and to the rise of the Han dynasty? List the events in order.

c. Evaluate Why do you think the Han rulers were able to create an empire that lasted for 400 years, while the Qin dynasty lasted only 15 years?

SECTION 2 *(pp. 228–232)*

14. a. Recall What were the major scientific and technological achievements of the Han period?

b. Contrast How did the roles of women and men in Han China differ?

c. Elaborate How did the exchange of goods and ideas over the Silk Roads change the nature of Chinese society?

SECTION 3 *(pp. 233–237)*

15. a. Identify Who was Kautilya?

b. Summarize How did the Mauryan Empire change after Ashoka's conversion to Buddhism?

c. Evaluate Do you think that the Gupta policy of governing outlying conquered areas through local rulers was a wise policy? Why or why not?

SECTION 4 *(pp. 238–241)*

16. a. Define What is Sanskrit, and how was its use an important part of the Gupta golden age?

b. Explain Why is the Gupta period called the golden age of ancient India?

c. Make Judgments Do you think that the Gupta dynasty's policies contributed to the flourishing of art and literature during the Gupta golden age? Explain your answer.

Reading Skills

Understanding Comparison and Contrast *Use what you know about comparing and contrasting to answer the following questions.*

17. How were cultural and scientific achievements of the Han and Gupta periods similar?

18. Compare and contrast the roles of men and women in China and India during the period covered in this chapter.

Interpreting Literature as Evidence

Reading Like a Historian *A Han princess is thought to have written the following poem after she was sent as a gift to a nomadic chief. Han rulers hoped the gift would convince the chief to form an alliance with them.*

> My people have married me
> In a far corner of Earth;
> Sent me away to a strange land,
> To the king of the Wu-sun.
> A tent is my house,
> Of felt are my walls;
> Raw flesh my food
> With mare's milk to drink.
> Always thinking of my own country,
> My heart sad within.
> Would I were a yellow stork
> And could fly to my old home!

—Anonymous, *Chinese Poems*, edited by Arthur Waley

19. Identify What details in the poem describe life among the nomads?

20. Analyze What might historians learn from this poem about the role of women in Han China?

Using the Internet

21. The Great Wall of China is the largest human-made construction on earth. Using the keyword above, conduct research to learn about the Great Wall of China. Take notes and then write two to three paragraphs about the information that you gathered.

WRITING FOR THE SAT

Think about the following issue:

Han emperor Wudi is considered one of the greatest rulers of ancient China, while Mauryan emperor Ashoka is considered one of the greatest rulers of ancient India. Yet the two rulers and their achievements differed in many ways.

22. Assignment: What characteristics do you think define a great leader? Write a short essay in which you develop your position on this issue and explain why both Wudi and Ashoka might be considered great rulers. Support your point of view with reasoning and examples from your reading.

EMPIRES OF CHINA AND INDIA **247**

Answers

Reading Skills

17. Both periods had prosperity and cultural achievement.

18. similar—both had patriarchal families; men had more power, authority, and rights; different—older Chinese women could achieve power

Interpreting Literature as Evidence

19. tent house, raw meat as food, mare's milk to drink

20. possible answer—Women had little choice in marriage; they were unwilling participants in this form of diplomacy.

Using the Internet

21. Go to the HRW Web site and enter the keyword shown to access a rubric for this activity.

KEYWORD: SHL EIC

Writing for the SAT

22. Student essays should describe leadership qualities of Wudi and Ashoka

A rubric for this activity is provided in **CRF**: Writing for the SAT.

HOLT

History's Impact

► **Video Program: Empires of India and China**
Refer to the Video Program Teacher's Guide for a discussion of the closing question.

Review and Assessment Resources

Review and Reinforce

- **CRF**: Chapter Review
- **Quick Facts Transparency**: Visual Study Guide: Empires of China and India
- **Spanish Chapter Summaries Audio CD Program**
- OSP **Holt PuzzlePro**: Quiz Show for ExamView
- **Quiz Game CD-ROM**

Assess

- **PASS**: Chapter Test, Forms A and B
- **Alternative Assessment Handbook**
- OSP **ExamView Test Generator**, Chapter Test
- **Differentiated Instruction Modified Worksheets and Tests CD-ROM**: Chapter Test
- HOAP **Holt Online Assessment Program** (in the Premier Online Edition)

Reteach/Intervene

- **Interactive Reader and Study Guide**
- **Differentiated Instruction Teacher Management System**: Lesson Plans for Differentiated Instruction
- **Differentiated Instruction Modified Worksheets and Tests CD-ROM**: Chapter Test
- **Interactive Skills Tutor CD-ROM**

Online Resources

KEYWORD: SHL TEACHER

You can use these pages to have students simultaneously review the unit and practice taking standardized tests.

Answers

1. 3
The Americas, Sections 2 & 3

2. 2
The Americas, Section 2

3. 3
The Americas, Section 2

4. 2
Rome and Early Christianity, Section 1

5. 2
Rome and Early Christianity, Section 2

6. 2
Rome and Early Christianity, Section 3

7. 1
Rome and Early Christianity, Section 4

8. 3
Empires of China and India, Section 1

9. 1
Empires of China and India, Section 3

UNIT 2
Regents Practice

Directions Write your answer for each statement or question on a separate answer sheet. Choose the number of the word or expression that best completes the statement or answers the question.

1 Two societies of the Americas that the Spanish encountered were the
 1 Maya and Aztec.
 2 mound builders and Toltec.
 3 Aztec and Inca.
 4 Inca and Olmec.

2 Giant heads carved from stone were created by the
 1 mound builders.
 2 Olmec.
 3 Inca.
 4 Maya.

3 This is an example of a common theme in the art of

 1 Greece.
 2 Rome.
 3 the Aztecs.
 4 the Minoans.

4 During the Roman Republic, plebeians gradually gained
 1 equal status with patricians.
 2 more and more rights.
 3 the right to fight in the army.
 4 more power than the patricians.

5 Why did the Roman Republic come to an end?
 1 The Gracchi started a civil war.
 2 Social unrest and the ambitions of a few powerful men destroyed the republic.
 3 Octavian gained the title Augustus.
 4 Sulla, backed by his legions, refused to retire as dictator.

6 Rome's cultural legacy includes
 1 an interest in abstract reasoning or interest in knowledge for its own sake.
 2 architecture, language and literature, engineering, and law.
 3 augurs.
 4 an emphasis on public entertainment and education.

7 What helped Christianity spread throughout the Roman Empire?
 1 The Christian message appealed to the poor, and Paul of Tarsus's missionary work was extensive.
 2 Missionaries were sent only into Jewish communities.
 3 Paul of Tarsus converted the Roman emperor.
 4 The bishop of Rome became recognized as the pope.

8 The Han dynasty in China is significant because
 1 it lowered taxes and reversed Legalist policies.
 2 it was free of court intrigues so there was always a clear line of succession to the throne.
 3 it provided a model for all later Chinese dynasties and had a lasting influence on Chinese civilization.
 4 it was the first Chinese dynasty so it had lasting influence.

9 The Silk Roads were important because
 1 they helped Confucianism spread.
 2 they linked China with other civilizations and enabled trade.
 3 they brought an end to the Han dynasty.
 4 they helped China remain isolated.

10 Why did the Gupta Empire have a lasting influence on India?

1 It promoted Buddhism.
2 It extended its rule over small kingdoms in south India.
3 It ended the use of Sanskrit.
4 It promoted Hinduism.

11 During the Golden Age of Athens,

1 Pericles rebuilt the city with glorious monuments, patronized great artists and encouraged democracy.
2 Pericles saved the city from the Persians.
3 Athens became the leader of the Delian League, but its trade decreased.
4 Pericles built glorious monuments for Athens but discouraged democracy.

12 The lasting influence of Alexander the Great was

1 an empire that united most of the known world.
2 Hellenistic culture, which spread over the areas Alexander conquered.
3 the city of Alexandria, Egypt.
4 the end of the Persian Empire.

13 Cleisthenes is important to the history of Athenian democracy because

1 he favored harsh punishment for crime.
2 he opposed the reforms of Solon.
3 he was a tyrant.
4 he increased the size of the governing council and allowed men from every class the same rights.

14 Shi Huangdi and the Qin strengthened China by

1 allowing provinces a great deal of independence.
2 heavily taxing peasants to fund improvement projects.
3 expanding and improving irrigation systems, roads, and canals.
4 renouncing the philosophy of Legalism.

15 Mauryan emperor Ashoka is significant because

1 he expanded the empire and eventually worked to improved the lives of the people he ruled.
2 he has inspired modern moviemakers.
3 he converted to Buddhism.
4 as a devout Buddhist, he opposed religious tolerance.

16 The Incas promoted stability in their empire by

1 using the *mita* to keep track of taxes due so that everyone paid their share.
2 moving their capital from Cuzco to Machu Picchu.
3 replacing the leaders of conquered areas with leaders loyal to the empire.
4 conquering the Moche.

17 The Maya created

1 quipus for keeping records.
2 a complex but accurate calendar system and impressive temples.
3 a classless society.
4 a peaceful society of city-states.

18 Who is the speaker in the excerpt below describing?

"Our public men have, besides politics, their private affairs to attend to, and our ordinary citizens, though occupied with the pursuits of industry, are still fair judges of public matters; for, unlike any other nation, regarding him who takes no part in these duties not as unambitious but as useless."

1 Athenian democracy.
2 the Roman Republic.
3 Ashoka's kingdom.
4 the Inca Empire.

REVIEWING THE UNIT

Constructed Response During this period, Chinese, Indian, Greek, and Roman civilizations developed some of the characteristics that would come to define them for centuries. Select one of these civilizations and write a short essay discussing the civilization's unique characteristics. Mention features that had long-lasting effects on the development of the civilization.

CONNECTING TO THE PREVIOUS UNIT

Constructed Response Consider one the civilizations in this unit that began as a river valley civilization. Write a short essay describing how the key characteristics of the civilization developed from its earliest known beginning through its classical period.

THE GROWTH OF CIVILIZATIONS **249**

Answers

10. 4
Empires of China and India, Section 3

11. 1
Classical Greece, Section 2

12. 2
Classical Greece, Section 4

13. 4
Classical Greece, Section 2

14. 3
Empires of China and India, Section 1

15. 1
Empires of China and India, Section 3

16. 3
The Americas, Section 3

17. 2
The Americas, Section 3

18. 1
The Americas, Section 2

Reviewing the Unit

Student essays should discuss one civilization and the characteristics unique to it, and the lasting effects of its achievements on future civilizations.

Connecting to the Previous Unit

Student essays will vary depending on the civilization they chose, but should discuss either India or China, since they are the only two discussed in this unit that had their beginnings in the river valley civilizations covered in the previous unit. Essays should describe how the key characteristics of the civilization continued to develop.

Government and Citizenship

Alexander's Empire As he expanded his empire, Alexander the Great founded new cities. He encouraged his soldiers to marry local women, and set an example by marrying a daughter of the Persian king Darius III. He also began to substitute the pageantry of the Persian royal court for the simplicity of the Macedonian one, and at the time of his death he was planning to make Babylon the capital of his great empire. Alexander believed that he was creating the kind of government that his teacher Aristotle had thought best. He saw himself as a philosopher-king whose peoples would be united by a common culture.

Arts and Ideas

Hellenistic Culture The culture that was spread throughout Alexander's empire is referred to as Hellenistic to distinguish it from the Hellenic culture of classical Greece. Hellenistic religion combined Greek and Eastern deities in a process known as syncretism, or the mixing of religions. During the second and first centuries BC, the Romans extended their control over Greece and Southwest Asia. Roman civilization can be viewed as a continuation of Hellenistic culture, as it adopted many elements of Greek culture.

Info to Know

Deciphering the Quipu Researchers are working to shed light on Inca history and culture by deciphering quipu. The Incas used quipu to keep records of census, tribute, and other information. Some scholars think the quipu was the equivalent of writing, while others think it was merely a mnemonic device similar to a rosary. About 600 Inca quipu are still in existence.

THEME
GOVERNMENT AND CITIZENSHIP

What strategies did rulers devise to govern conquered territories and to maintain their empires from one generation to the next?

Governments during this period faced common problems. They had to integrate conquered territories into their empires and maintain a hold over them. They also had to govern an increasing number of people due to population growth. Empires not only expanded in terms of geographical area but their populations also grew due to increased agricultural productivity.

STRATEGIES FOR HOLDING ON TO EMPIRES

China	• Established the ruler as a divine person • Emphasized centralized administration and control • Promoted a common written language
Gupta	• Ruled through royal officials in core area of the empire • In outlying areas used local rulers who paid tribute • Promoted Hinduism • Gained support of Brahmans
Rome	• Appointed provincial governors • Established and enforced common laws • Maintained order and defended the frontier • Extended citizenship to conquered elites
Inca	• Replaced conquered leaders with leaders loyal to the ruler • Established a centrally controlled economy • Established a strong bureaucracy • Improved communication through a network of roads

THEME
ARTS AND IDEAS

What ideas united people within the different empires and gave people a sense of belonging?

The empires of this period are considered classical because features that came to characterize civilization in these areas became firmly established. These features helped define a sense of shared culture, which served to unite people. Many of these features still influence people in these regions today.

IDEAS UNITING AN EMPIRE

China	• Confucianism • Filial piety • Social hierarchy with duties and responsibilities owed to those above and below
Hellenistic	• Language • Culture
Rome	• Citizenship • Late in the empire, Christianity • The idea of law having a sense of fairness and objectivity
India	• Hinduism • Caste and a strongly patriarchal society

Collaborative Learning

At Level

Empire Builders' Round Table

1. Organize students into six groups. Assign each group one of the empire builders mentioned in this unit. Have each group make a list of the accomplishments of its assigned empire builder(s). (Students may want to conduct additional research to supplement the information in their texts.)

2. Guide a class discussion about the accomplishments of each empire builder using the following questions: What traits did they have in common? What traits did each have that were unique? What were the lasting effects of the empires they founded? How long did the empires continue to exist? What finally caused the empires to crumble?

LS Interpersonal

Alternative Assessment Handbook, Rubrics Rubric 11: Discussions; and 14: Group Activity

THEME
SCIENCE AND TECHNOLOGY

How did new discoveries in science and technology aid the expansion of empires?

During this period important technological advances, such as the iron plow, enabled farmers to feed more people. As a result, populations increased. Other advances improved communication. Engineering developments were put in service to the empire. The Romans in particular were interested in the practical application of new technologies.

TECHNOLOGICAL ADVANCES

China	• Paper made a lightweight writing surface. • Iron plows expanded the range of agriculture. • Wheelbarrows made it possible to move heavy loads.
Rome	• Roads allowed the army to move around the empire. • Arches made it possible to build aqueducts, bridges, and impressive public buildings. • Concrete made a versatile building material.
Inca	• Roads and bridges linked all parts of the empire.

Skills FOCUS
UNDERSTANDING THEMES

The great empires of this period eventually fell. Regardless of the system put in place to govern, imperial success depended in part on the talent of individual rulers. Consider the empires discussed in this unit. Create a chart that compares and contrasts the reasons for their collapse. Analyze your chart to determine whether or not there were common causes for the collapse of empires. Write a short essay detailing your findings.

	Differences	Similarities
China		
Gupta		
Hellenistic		
Rome		
Inca		

Global Connections

In this unit you learned about Greek and Roman ideas on citizenship and government. These ideas put forth in ancient Greece and Rome continue to help shape ideas about citizenship and government.

Making Connections Select a current democratic government and examine how it has been influenced by Greek and Roman traditions. Write a short essay detailing your findings.

The Pantheon in Rome was built as a temple at the beginning of the AD 100s. ▶

THE GROWTH OF CIVILIZATIONS **251**

Science and Technology

Zero The word *zero* is the term used to indicate naught, or nothing. Without a symbol for zero, modern mathematics would not be possible. However, a symbol for zero did not come into use until long after symbols for the other numbers. At first, it was used by the Babylonians as a placeholder to distinguish between numbers such as 123, 1023, 1203, and 1230. Indian mathematicians wrote numbers in columns, using the zero to indicate an empty column.

Understanding Themes

China—increasing court intrigues led to weak rulers, increasing gap between rich and poor as taxes rose to cover cost of running empire; Gupta—parts of empire began to break away due to loose control by Guptas, Central Asian nomads began invading India; military efforts to defend empire drained treasury; Hellenistic—Alexander the Great created huge empire, spread Greek culture into Egypt, after many conquests and further expansion, his death led to division of empire; Rome—series of weak leaders, economic problems, repeated attacks by Huns and other migrating tribes; Inca—internal conflict, invaded by Spanish conquistadors

Student essays should point out that there were multiple reasons for the collapse of empires, but that they usually included internal unrest that weakened the empires from within, diminishing their ability to withstand invaders from without.

Global Connections

Student essays should indicate how the modern government they chose has modified Greek and Roman traditions to fit contemporary society. For example, the United States is a representative democracy rather than a direct democracy like Greece.

Differentiating Instruction

Below Level

English-Language Learners

Materials: Poster paper, colored pencils or markers

1. Organize students into small groups. Have each group choose one of the technological developments discussed in this unit. Have students discuss why the advance was important. What technology, if any, did it replace?

2. Have each group create several posters that encourage people to make use of the new technology. Posters should indicate the ways in which the technological development will make people's lives easier or better.

3. Have each group display its posters for the rest of the class to see. **LS Interpersonal, Visual-Spatial**

Alternative Assessment Handbook, Rubrics 14: Group Activity; and 28: Posters

Unit Review

Summarizing the Unit

Guide the class in a discussion of the civilizations discussed in this unit. Then, to help them understand how perspective affects the writing of history, ask students the following questions:

- Why is so much more emphasis placed on classical Greece and ancient Rome than on the Americas or the empires of China and India?
- How do you think textbooks in China or India would organize the material in this unit?
- Why would people in other parts of the world place a different emphasis on historical events than we do?

Answers

Thinking Like a Historian

Answers will vary depending on the choice of civilization and the type of chart or graphic organizer used, but should cover all three areas: culture, the arts, and religion; technological innovation; and economy and government.

UNIT 2
IN BRIEF
Below is a chapter-by-chapter summary of the main ideas in this unit, followed by a summary activity for the unit.

CHAPTER 5
Classical Greece
c. 2100 BC–150 BC

MAIN IDEA Greece was the earliest great civilization in Europe. It made contributions that still influence the world.

SECTION 1 Two distinct cultures developed in early Greece—the Minoans and Mycenaeans. Most Greeks lived in city-states.

SECTION 2 During the Classical Age, Athenian democracy reached it height. Athens and its rival Sparta came together to defeat the Persians.

SECTION 3 Greek contributions to philosophy, literature, and the arts are still influential.

SECTION 4 Alexander the Great conquered the Near East, Egypt, and parts of central Asia. He did not build a lasting empire, but he spread Greek culture to conquered lands.

CHAPTER 6
Rome and Early Christianity
750 BC–AD 500

MAIN IDEA Rome was one of the greatest powers in the ancient world. It also made lasting contributions to the Western world.

SECTION 1 Rome's location on valuable trade routes helped it become a Mediterranean power.

SECTION 2 Government and social problems, and the ambitions of a few men, brought an end to the Republic. It was replaced by an empire.

SECTION 3 Roman accomplishments influenced the world long after the western empire fell.

SECTION 4 Christianity developed within the empire, and, in time, spread throughout the Roman world.

SECTION 5 Events inside and outside the empire led to its collapse in the west.

CHAPTER 7
The Americas
1000 BC–AD 1500

MAIN IDEA Early Americans found unique ways of adapting to the varied environments in which they lived. Some peoples developed advanced civilizations.

SECTION 1 People migrated to the Americas earlier than 14,000 years ago and established cultures throughout North America.

SECTION 2 Mesoamerica was the home of several early cultures that were influenced by the Olmec civilization, including the Aztec Empire.

SECTION 3 Peoples in South America developed agricultural methods for a variety of climates and were eventually united under the Inca Empire.

CHAPTER 8
Empires of India and China
350 BC–AD 600

MAIN IDEA Strong empires unified much of both China and India. During this classical period in their histories, both China and India developed many of the unique characteristics that would continue to define them in the modern era.

SECTION 1 The Qin and Han dynasties unified China and became the models for later dynasties.

SECTION 2 The Han dynasty saw the growth of trade and great achievements in the arts and sciences.

SECTION 3 The Mauryan and Gupta empires united much of India. In southern India, trading kingdoms thrived.

SECTION 4 The Gupta empire ushered in a golden age in Indian culture and society.

Thinking like a Historian
Summary and Extension Activity

Classical civilizations flourished during this period. Each one had lasting influence in the region it dominated. Select one of the classical civilizations and create a chart or graphic organizer that summarizes the developments in each of the following areas:

A. Culture, the arts, and religion

B. Technological innovation

C. Economy and government

252 UNIT 2

Unit Resources

Review and Reinforce

- **Global History and Geography Regents Test Prep Workbook**
- **Regents Review Transparencies**
- **CRF:** Chapter Review
- **Spanish Chapter Summaries Audio CD Program**
- OSP **Holt PuzzlePro:** Quiz Show for ExamView
- **Quiz Game CD-ROM**

Assess

- **PASS:** Unit Test, Forms A and B
- **Alternative Assessment Handbook**
- OSP **New York ExamView Test Generator** correlated to NY SS Standards
- **Differentiated Instruction Modified Worksheets and Tests CD-ROM:** Chapter Test
- HOAP **Holt Online Assessment Program** (in the Premier Online Edition)

Reteach/Intervene

- **Interactive Reader and Study Guide**
- **Differentiated Instruction Teacher Management System:** Lesson Plans for Differentiated Instruction
- **Differentiated Instruction Modified Worksheets and Tests CD-ROM:** Chapter Test
- **Interactive Skills Tutor CD-ROM**

go.hrw.com
Online Resources

KEYWORDS: SHL GRE, SHL ROM, SHL AMS, SHL EIC

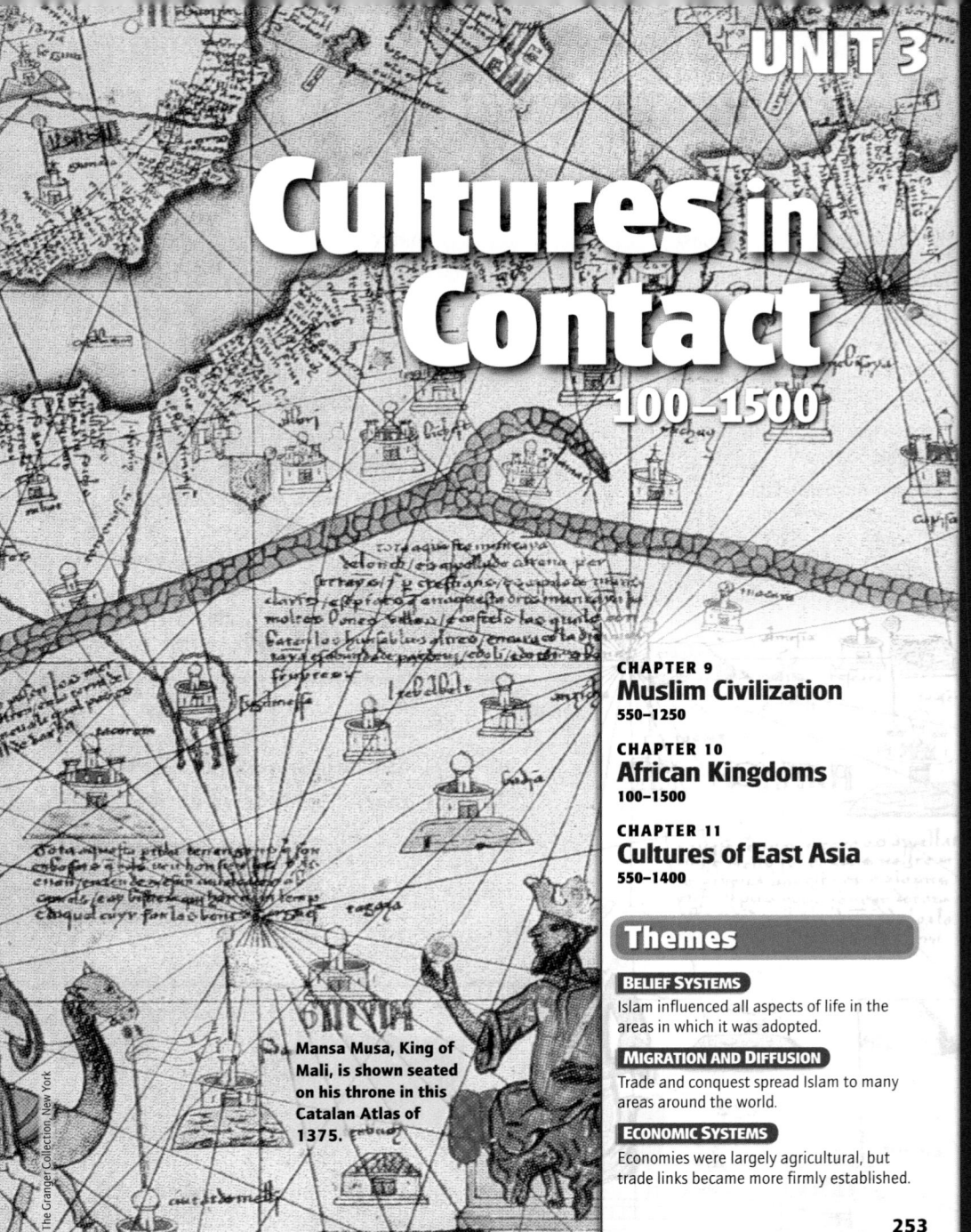

UNIT 3

Cultures in Contact
100–1500

CHAPTER 9
Muslim Civilization
550–1250

CHAPTER 10
African Kingdoms
100–1500

CHAPTER 11
Cultures of East Asia
550–1400

Themes

BELIEF SYSTEMS
Islam influenced all aspects of life in the areas in which it was adopted.

MIGRATION AND DIFFUSION
Trade and conquest spread Islam to many areas around the world.

ECONOMIC SYSTEMS
Economies were largely agricultural, but trade links became more firmly established.

Mansa Musa, King of Mali, is shown seated on his throne in this Catalan Atlas of 1375.

The Granger Collection, New York

253

Introducing the Unit
Have students give examples of the ways in which business and trade go beyond national boundaries. Then ask them how this has affected the modern world. Tell students that along with their wares, Muslim merchants carried ideas far beyond Arabia, east into Asia and west into Africa.

Connecting to Themes
Activity **Trade and Cultural Diffusion** Ask students how trade affected the interaction between vastly different cultures during the period covered in this unit. Guide the class in a discussion of the ways in which cultural diffusion took place between the Arabs and the peoples of Africa and Asia, and between the Chinese and their neighbors in East Asia. **LS** **Verbal-Linguistic**

Reading Like a Historian
Interpreting Visuals
The Catalan Atlas The Catalan Atlas is characterized by its use of brilliantly colored illustrations. The illustrations depict cities and important geographical features, accompanied by explanatory notes written in Latin. Christian cities are indicated with a cross, and other cities with a dome. The map also portrays rulers, including several African monarchs.

Unit Resources

Planning
📄 **Differentiated Instruction Teacher Management System:** Unit Pacing Guide
OSP **New York One-Stop Planner CD-ROM:** Teacher Management System
🔘 **Power Presentations with Video CD-ROM**

Standards Mastery
📄 **Global History and Geography Regents Test Prep Workbook**
📄 **Regents Review Transparencies**

Differentiating Instruction
📄 **Differentiated Instruction Teacher Management System:** Lesson Plans for Differentiated Instruction
🔘 **Differentiated Instruction Modified Worksheets and Tests CD-ROM**

Enrichment
📄 **A World History Teacher's Guide to Analyzing Movies**
📄 **Document-Based Activities for World History**
📄 **World History Outline Maps**
📄 **Reading Like a Historian: World History Toolkit**
🔘 **World History Primary Source Library CD-ROM**

Assessment
📄 **PASS:** Unit Test, Forms A and B
📄 **Alternative Assessment Handbook**
OSP **New York ExamView Test Generator correlated to NY SS Standards**
HOAP **Holt Online Assessment Program** (in the Premier Online Edition)

Muslim Civilization

CHAPTER 9 PLANNING GUIDE

Chapter Overview	Reproducible Resources	Technology Resources
CHAPTER 9 pp. 254–279 **Overview: In this chapter, students will learn about Muhammad and the spread of Islam, the spread of Muslim civilization, and its significant achievements in the arts and sciences.** KI 1, 3, 4; PI 1.3, 1.4, 3.1, 4.2 See pp. T32–T55 for a detailed correlation to the New York State Core Curriculum for Global History and Geography and the New York Learning Standards.	**Differentiated Instruction Teacher Management System:** • Pacing Guide • Lesson Plans for Universal Access **Interactive Reader and Study Guide:** Chapter Summary* **Chapter Resource File*** • Writing About History • Social Studies Skill • Chapter Review **World History Outline Maps**	OSP **New York One-Stop Planner CD-ROM:** Calendar Planner **Live Ink© Online Reading Help** **Student Edition on Audio CD Program** **Differentiated Instruction Modified Worksheets and Tests CD-ROM** **World History Primary Source Library CD-ROM** **Power Presentations with Video CD-ROM** **History's Impact: World History Video Program (VHS/DVD):** Muslim Civilization
Section 1: **The Origins of Islam** **The Main Idea:** Muhammad, a merchant whom Muslims believe was the last prophet, reported that he received messages from God. The religion he taught—Islam—drew many followers. PI 1.3	**Differentiated Instruction Teacher Management System:** Section 1 Lesson Plan* **Interactive Reader and Study Guide:** Section 1 Summary* **Chapter Resource File*** • Vocabulary Builder: Section 1 • Biography: Ibn Muqlah • Literature: "The Wonderful Bag" • History and Geography: Trade Along the Arabian Peninsula	**Regents Review Transparency:** Section 1* **Map Transparency:** Arabia, c. 550* **Map Transparency:** Islam in Arabia, 632*
Section 2: **The Spread of Islam** **The Main Idea:** After Muhammad's death, Islam spread beyond the Arabian Peninsula, shaping a major empire within 100 years. While the empire eventually broke into smaller parts, Islam continued to spread. PI 1.4, 3.1	**Differentiated Instruction Teacher Management System:** Section 2 Lesson Plan* **Interactive Reader and Study Guide:** Section 2 Summary* **Chapter Resource File*** • Vocabulary Builder: Section 2 • Biography: Razia • Primary Source: The Muslim Conquest of Spain	**Regents Review Transparency:** Section 2* **Map Transparency:** Spread of Islam, 632– 750* **Map Transparency:** Sunni and Shia Distribution* **Map Transparency:** Diffusion of a Civilization* **Quick Facts Transparency:** The End of Unity*
Section 3: **Society and Culture** **The Main Idea:** For the first Muslims, Islam was more than a religion. It was a guide to a political, social, and cultural life. The early Muslims responded with spectacular achievement in many fields. PI 1.3, 3.1, 4.2	**Differentiated Instruction Teacher Management System:** Section 3 Lesson Plan* **Interactive Reader and Study Guide:** Section 3 Summary* **Chapter Resource File*** • Vocabulary Builder: Section 3 • Biography: al-Razi	**Regents Review Transparency:** Section 3*

go.hrw.com	Print Resource	Transparency
LS Learning Styles	Audio CD	CD-ROM
Video	SE Student Edition	TE Teacher's Edition

OSP One-Stop Planner CD-ROM   NY Standards Mastery
*also on One-Stop Planner CD-ROM

Review, Assessment, Intervention

 Global History and Geography Regents Test Prep Workbook

Quick Facts Transparency: Muslim Civilization*

Program Assessment Support System (PASS): Chapter Test*

 Differentiated Instruction Modified Worksheets and Tests CD-ROM: Modified Chapter Test

OSP **New York One-Stop Planner CD-ROM:** ExamView Test Generator (English/Spanish)

Holt Online Assessment Program (HOAP), in the Holt Premier Online Student Edition

PASS: Section 1 Quiz*
Online Quiz: Section 1
Alternative Assessment Handbook

PASS: Section 2 Quiz*
Online Quiz: Section 2
Alternative Assessment Handbook

PASS: Section 3 Quiz*
Online Quiz: Section 3
Alternative Assessment Handbook

Power Presentation with Video CD-ROM

Power Presentations with Video are visual presentations of each chapter's main ideas. Presentations can be customized by including Quick Facts charts, images and maps from the textbook, and video clips.

Holt Online Learning

go.hrw.com
Teacher Resources
KEYWORD: SHL TEACHER

go.hrw.com
Student Resources
KEYWORD: SHL ISW

- Document-Based Questions
- Interactive Multimedia Activities

- Current Events
- Chapter-Based Internet Activities
- and more!

Holt Premier
Online Student Edition
Complete online support for interactivity, assessment, and reporting
- Interactive Maps and Notebook
- Homework Practice and Research Activities Online

CHAPTER 9 PLANNING GUIDE

The Big Picture

Peter N. Stearns

The Rise of Islam The development of Islam was one of the leading features of world history in the centuries after 600 AD. Islam spread more rapidly than any other religion in this time period, and today Islam is the world's second largest faith. The religion and the Islamic Caliphate helped unite the Middle East and North Africa, creating a durable cultural zone between 600 and 1450. Islam became an important force as well in Spain, sub-Saharan Africa, India, Central Asia, and Southeast Asia, though specific patterns varied in each case. Finally, it was under Islamic auspices that new patterns of interregional trade formed, linking many parts of Asia, Africa, and parts of Europe.

The Features of the Religion Islam's origins involve the story of Muhammad, as well as a complex relationship with elements of the other Middle Eastern religions, Judaism and Christianity. Key features involve the Qur'an and subsequent writings and laws, the determination of principal religious obligations, and the religion's political implications. Because Islam had a close relationship with governments from the outset, it developed a different set of political impulses from early Christianity. Rifts and changes within the religion, including the Sunni-Shiite split and the rise of Sufism, also warrant attention.

Islamic Society During the centuries after 600, political institutions developed through two major caliphates. The later stages of the Abbasid caliphate involved clear political decline. Interest in Islam combined with lively art, science and philosophy, creating one of the most vibrant intellectual communities of the period. Trade also flourished, providing support to religion and gaining support in turn. Islam's reforms in gender relations demand careful attention, because they involved some important and unusual new measures along with ongoing inequalities.

Recent Scholarship

The Formation of Islam: Religion and Society in the Near East, 600-1800 (2003) by Jonathan P. Berkey offers a very readable account of Islam's formation, evolution and dissemination. An initial chapter sets the stage in terms of prior religions and pre-Islamic Arabia. Treatment of early Islam captures major analytical issues, the relationship to the caliphates, key divisions, and treatment of non-Muslim communities. Berkey also pays careful attention to the emergence of Sufism.

Differentiating Instruction

 Differentiated Instruction Teacher Management System
- Pacing Guide
- Lesson Plans for Differentiated Instruction

 Interactive Reader and Study Guide

 **Spanish Chapter Summaries Audio CD Program**

 Student Edition on Audio CD Program

 Differentiated Instruction Modified Worksheets and Tests CD-ROM
- Vocabulary Flash Cards
- Modified Vocabulary Builder Activities
- Modified Chapter Review Activity
- Modified Chapter Test

OSP One-Stop Planner CD-ROM
- ExamView Test Generator (English/Spanish)
- PuzzlePro
- Quiz Show for ExamView
- Transparencies and Videos

TE Differentiated Activities in the Teacher's Edition
- Map of Arabian Trade Routes, p. 258
- Muslim Accomplishments, p. 268
- Contributions of Islamic Scholars, p. 272
- Pilgrimage to Mecca, p. 276

Reading Like a Historian
Sam Wineburg

In March 2001, Afghanistan's Taliban rulers loaded their rocket launchers and set out to do battle at Bamiyan Valley, 78 miles northwest of Kabul. They were certain their adversary could not plan an ambush. Their enemy, it turns out, was made of stone.

The Taliban aimed their artillery at two 1,500-year-old statues of the Buddha carved into Afghanistan's majestic mountain cliffs. The larger of the two, towering some 175 feet, was thought to be the tallest statue in the world. No matter. The Taliban's leader Mullah Muhammed Omar would not compromise: "Not a single pagan idol must remain."

The Western press exploded. "Cultural vandalism," fumed the *Wall Street Journal*; "A shocking act," blasted *The New York Times*, which claimed that the statues were not the Taliban's to destroy but belonged "to all humankind." An attempt to "kill [an] ancient heritage" accused London's *The Daily Telegraph*. The overall reaction of the Western press was a mixture of righteous indignation and astonished disbelief. What kind of religion could condone such brazen behavior?

Comparative History Ideally, knowledge of history should help us understand our present. If this is true, where might we go to gain insight into the Taliban's actions? Let's start by opening our Bibles. "He took the calf that they had made, burned it with fire, ground it to a powder, scattered it on the water, and made the people of Israel drink it. And Moses said to Aaron, 'What did this people do to you that you have brought so great a sin upon them,'" asks Exodus 32: 20-21. Remember the Second Commandment's prohibition against "graven images"?

Ah, but that's Judaism. Christianity has never had a problem with images. Here, too, a bit of history would introduce sobriety to our storytelling. With Christianity's ascendance as the state religion of Rome—a place littered with depictions of Emperors—various representations of Jesus, Mary and the Saints soon began to appear. With this proliferation came age-old worries about idolatry. Tensions reached a climax under Byzantine Emperor Leo III (717-741) the patron of the "iconoclasts"—those who advocated the smashing of "icons," or religious images. In 730, Leo signed an official edict forbidding all icons.

The Church's ban was repealed a century later. But icon tensions resurfaced with a vengeance during the Reformation. Anti-icon violence swept through Wittenberg in 1521, Zurich in 1523, and Strasbourg in 1524. Under Calvinist influence, wholesale destruction of churches raged through Holland in 1566, with protesters toppling statues, hacking away with axes at wooden crosses, and pelting stained-glass windows from Poperinghe to Amsterdam. Mobs destroyed not only religious icons, but organs, alters, pews. "Some set ladders to the walls, with hammers and staves battering the pictures. Others broke asunder the iron-work ....Others casting ropes about the great statues of Our Savior Christ, and the saints, pulled them to the ground," wrote the Jesuit historian Famiano Strada.

Iconoclasm soon spread to England, where a royal edict ordered reformers to "destroy all shrines… pictures, painting… so that there remain no memory of the same in wall, glass-windows, or elsewhere within their church or houses." Documents of this "memory cleansing," such as the account from William Dowsing in 1644, show that this house cleaning was anything but dainty.

This detour into Judeo-Christian history is neither an apology for the Taliban's destruction of the Buddhist statues nor an attempt to excuse it. What was wrong in the past is wrong in the present. Comparative history helps us render what is initially foreign and incomprehensible a bit more familiar. What at first glance appears to be a mutant strain in a distant culture turns out, under examination, to be present in our very own.

Chapter Main Ideas

Section 1 Muhammad, a merchant whom Muslims believe was the last prophet, reported that he received messages from God. The religion he taught—Islam—drew many followers.

Section 2 After Muhammad's death, Islam spread beyond the Arabian Peninsula, shaping a major empire within 100 years. While the empire eventually broke into smaller parts, Islam continued to spread.

Section 3 For the first Muslims, Islam was more than a religion. It was a guide to a political, social, and cultural life. The early Muslims responded with spectacular achievements in many fields.

New York Standards

Key Idea 1 The study of world history requires an understanding of world cultures and civilizations, including an analysis of important ideas, social and cultural values, beliefs, and traditions. This study also examines the human condition and the connections and interactions of people across time and space and the ways different people view the same event or issue from a variety of perspectives.

Key Idea 3 Study of the major social, political, cultural, and religious developments in world history involves learning about the important roles and contributions of individuals and groups.

Key to Differentiating Instruction

Below Level

Basic-level activities designed for all students encountering new material

At Level

Intermediate-level activities designed for average students

Above Level

Challenging activities designed for honors and gifted and talented students

Standard English Mastery

Activities designed to improve standard English usage

254 CHAPTER 9

CHAPTER
9 550–1250

Muslim Civilization

THE BIG PICTURE The Qur'an, Islam's holy book, states that Muhammad was the last prophet sent by God to humanity. In the centuries after his death, Islam spread across much of the Eastern Hemisphere, becoming one of the world's major religions. Muslim civilization developed states that touched three continents and produced some of history's most notable achievements in the arts and sciences.

Theme BELIEF SYSTEMS
Islam, one of the world's major monotheistic faiths, spread to a vast area over a very short time. In this chapter you will learn how Islam is a belief system that affects every aspect of a devout follower's life.

TIME LINE

CHAPTER EVENTS

c. 570 Muhammad is born in Arabia.

610 Muhammad reports the first revelations from Allah.

622 Muhammad flees to Medina—the hegira.

732 Muslim advance in Europe stopped in France at the Battle of Tours.

786 Harun al-Rashid leads the Abbasid caliphate to its height.

969 Fatimid rule extends to Egypt.

500

WORLD EVENTS

618 Tang dynasty begins in China.

750

768 Charlemagne begins his reign as king of the Franks.

c. 800 Ghana is a major trading empire in West Africa.

900 Mayan civilization reaches its peak.

254 CHAPTER 9

Introduce the Chapter

At Level

Muslim Civilization

1. Remind students that the advances made in Muslim Civilization centuries ago influence their lives today.

2. Have students write three questions they have about the inventions and developments within Muslim civilization.

3. Next, have students scan the chapter to find information that answers each of their questions. Have students record both the section number and red heading that apply to each question.

4. When students have finished, organize the class into small groups. Have them exchange and share their findings with the other students in the group.

5. Finally, have students write a short paragraph about what interests them most about the Islamic world. **LS Interpersonal, Verbal-Linguistic**

Alternative Assessment Handbook, Rubric 1: Acquiring Information

Reading like a Historian

The Great Mosque in Damascus, Syria, built between about 706 and 715, is one of the oldest and largest monuments in the Islamic world. When it was built, the mosque served not just as a place of worship, but also as a religious school, law court, hospital, homeless shelter, and place for political gatherings.

Analyzing Visuals Judging from the photo, what role do you think the mosque plays in its community?

See **Skills Handbook**, p. H26

1055
The Seljuk Turks take Baghdad.

1258
The Mongols capture Baghdad.

1000

1250

1066 The Norman Conquest ends Anglo-Saxon rule of England.

1215
King John signs the Magna Carta in England.

1000 Vikings settle on the coast of North America.

Chapter Preview

HOLT
History's Impact
▶ **Video Program: Muslim Civilization**
See the Video Teacher's Guide for strategies for using the video segment.

Reading Like a Historian
Analyzing Visuals Have students examine the photograph on these pages. After discussing the many functions of the Great Mosque, have students name the separate buildings in their own city that correspond to the functions of the mosque. Mention also that the call to prayer announced from the minarets served a bit like a clock. Have students name architectural details that might have been borrowed from other cultures. Students should recognize the arch, which was developed by the Etruscans and used in Roman architecture.

go.hrw.com
Online Resources

Chapter Resources:
KEYWORD: SHL ISW
Teacher Resources:
KEYWORD: SHL TEACHER

Explore the Time Line

1. When and where was Muhammad born? *in about 570 AD, Arabia*

2. What was the hegira, and when did it take place? *Muhammad fled to Medina; in 622*

3. When did Ghana emerge as a major trading empire? *about 800 AD*

4. What event happened in North America in 1000? *Vikings settled the coast of North America.*

Info to Know

Amazing Architecture Built on the site of the Aramean temple to the god Hadad, the first century Temple to Jupiter, and the 379 AD church of St. John the Baptist, the Umayyad mosque shown on this page is among the most beautiful ancient buildings in the world. A gift of four church sites elsewhere in Damascus compensated the Christians.

Explain Why was it important to compensate Christians for the site of the mosque? *The mosque was built on the site of the Christian church of St. John the Baptist.*

Answers

Reading Like a Historian *It is the community center, built to serve a wide variety of community needs. It is large enough to serve a very large number of people.*

255

Geography Starting Points

New Trade Routes In order to avoid being taxed by the governments of trade centers, Bedouins varied the routes of their camel caravans. *The Western Regions according to the Hou Han shu,* translated by Australian historian John Hill, shows that an ancient trade route linked Petra and Wadi Sirhan, and then went south to Gerrha and the Persian Gulf. Current maps, however, show no water source along this route. Using old maps, researchers were able to locate a huge underground water source labeled "Ancient Cistern or "Roman Pools" in just the right place, a strong indication that the ancient Chinese were familiar with the caravan routes.

- **Map Transparency:** Arabia, c. 550
- **World History Outline Maps**
- **Interactive Map:** Arabia, c. 550
- **CRF:** History and Geography: Trade Along the Arabian Peninsula

Info to Know

Food Crop Exchange During the Middle Ages and in later centuries, Persian Muslims spread agricultural advances as far as western India. This spread of ideas eventually led to a series of advanced agricultural methods. The Muslims spread advances in irrigation, farming techniques, and the exchange of new food crops, including sugar cane, rice various types of fruit, and saffron.

Answers

Geography Starting Points
1. *possible answer—benefited: access to Red Sea, Arabian Sea, Persian Gulf; Mediterranean Sea; hindered: deserts*
2. *possible answer—east to Asia; west to Spain*

256

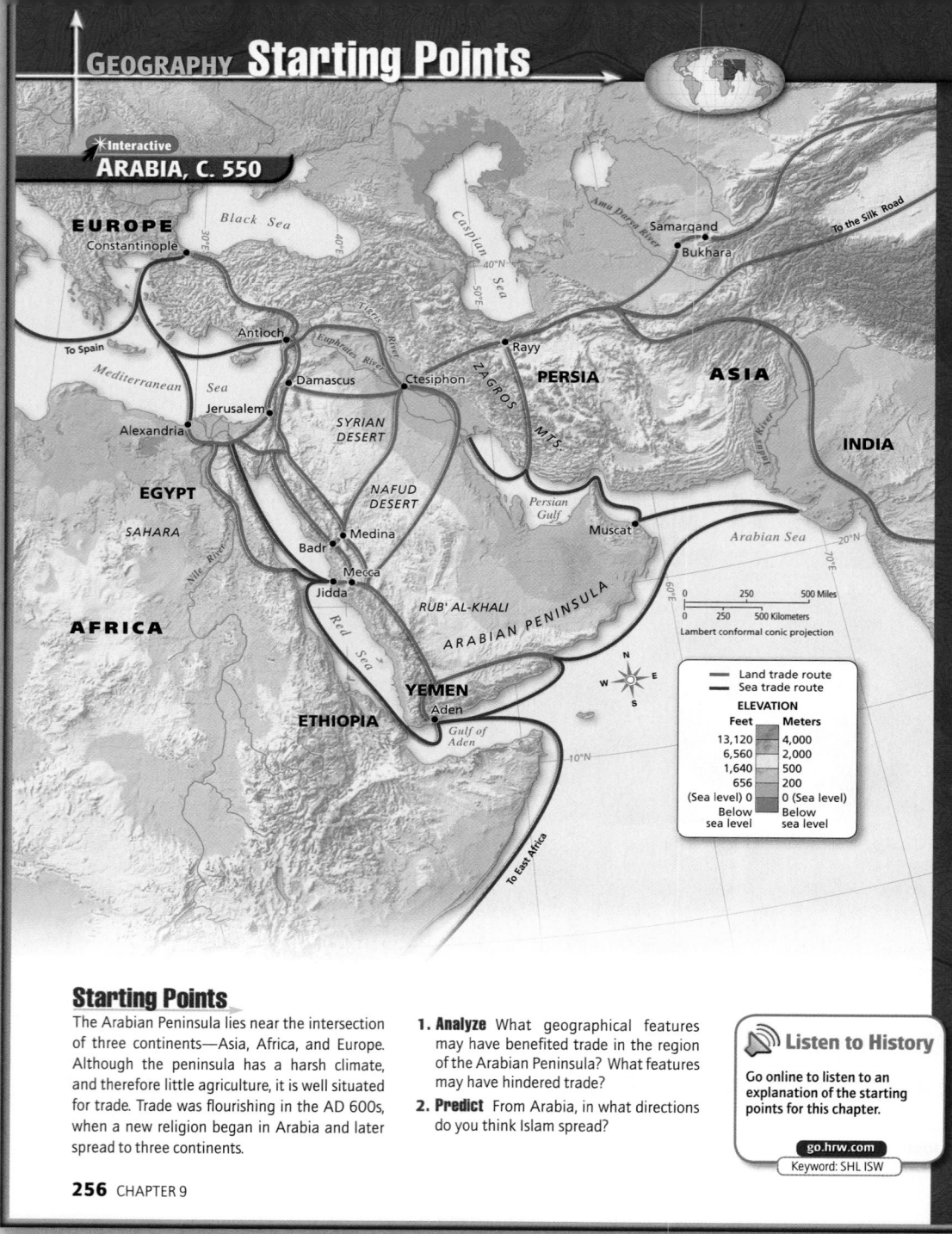

GEOGRAPHY Starting Points

ARABIA, C. 550

Starting Points

The Arabian Peninsula lies near the intersection of three continents—Asia, Africa, and Europe. Although the peninsula has a harsh climate, and therefore little agriculture, it is well situated for trade. Trade was flourishing in the AD 600s, when a new religion began in Arabia and later spread to three continents.

1. **Analyze** What geographical features may have benefited trade in the region of the Arabian Peninsula? What features may have hindered trade?
2. **Predict** From Arabia, in what directions do you think Islam spread?

Listen to History

Go online to listen to an explanation of the starting points for this chapter.

go.hrw.com
Keyword: SHL ISW

256 CHAPTER 9

Skills Focus: Analyzing Maps

At Level

Social Studies Skill
Arabian Trade Routes

1. Organize students into small groups. Remind students that trade routes were determined by a variety of factors. Have students refer to the map on this page and have each group determine three to six factors that may have influenced the particular routes shown on the map.

2. Have volunteers share one factor with the class, explain why they feel it is significant. Create a class list for all to see. If you have

a large map of the region or the world, have students use it to support their explanations.

3. When the class list is complete, have students add to their own work and retain the list as a study tool. Then, as an extension have students select one factor and write a paragraph explaining its influence on trade in the ancient Islamic world. **Verbal-Linguistic, Visual-Spatial**

Alternative Assessment Handbook, Rubrics 12: Drawing Conclusions; and 21: Map Reading

SECTION 1: The Origins of Islam

BEFORE YOU READ

MAIN IDEA

Muhammad, a merchant whom Muslims believe was the last prophet, reported that he received messages from God. The religion he taught—Islam—drew many followers.

READING FOCUS

1. What was Arabia like at the time of Muhammad's birth?
2. What were Muhammad's messages, and how were they received?
3. What are some basic ideas of Islam?

KEY TERMS AND PEOPLE

bedouins
Muhammad
hegira
Islam
Muslims
Qur'an
Five Pillars of Islam
mosque
jihad

 NEW YORK

PI 1.3 Students analyze historic events from around the world by examining accounts written from different perspectives.

THE INSIDE STORY

How did the city of Mecca come to be? According to Islamic teachings, Hagar and her son Ishmael were alone in the Arabian Desert. Ishmael's father, the biblical patriarch Abraham, had taken them there to keep them safe from Abraham's jealous wife. Yet the place where Abraham left Hagar and Ishmael was hot and dry. Hagar searched desperately for water but found none. In frustration, she fell to the ground and called out to God, who answered the call by bringing forth a spring of pure water.

Later, Abraham returned to the desert. Finding the spring, he built a cube-shaped stone structure to honor God. Over the centuries, the water continued to flow. People came from far and near to drink from the well and to visit the stone monument, called the Kaaba. A settlement built up around the two attractions. For more than a billion people, this story explains the origins of Mecca, a city with a central role in one of the world's major religions—Islam. ■

The Arabian Peninsula

The Arabian Peninsula is a harsh land with a vast desert interior. Some 1,500 years ago, Arabia was sparsely populated. In the desert, small bands of **bedouins**, or nomadic Arab peoples, moved their herds between scattered oases. Yet from this stark setting came a man whose teachings changed the world.

The Setting In Arabia, farming was limited, but commerce was lively because trade routes converged at the Arabian Peninsula. Along these routes ideas as well as merchandise were exchanged. Towns that depended on trade rose near the Arabian Peninsula's coasts.

▲ **The Kaaba in Mecca, from a painting of the 800s**
Detail showing the Kaaba from a Qur'an, 800s

MUSLIM CIVILIZATION **257**

Preteach

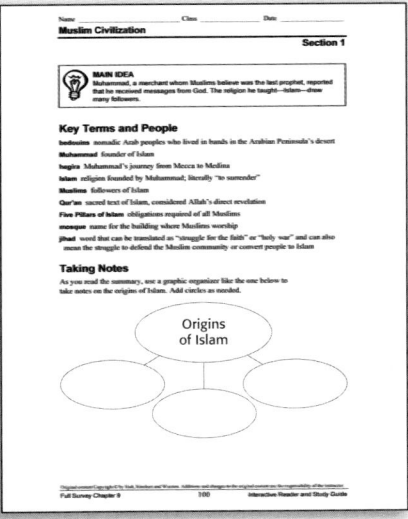

Getting Started

Use the **Interactive Reader and Study Guide** to familiarize students with the section content.

📖 **Interactive Reader and Study Guide**, Section 1

Academic Vocabulary

Review with students the high-use academic term in this section.

component part or element (p. 260)

📝 **CRF:** Vocabulary Builder: Section 1

Taking Notes

Muhammad was born in Mecca in about 570 on the Arabian Peninsula. On a spiritual retreat, Muhammad reported that an angel commanded him to speak messages, or revelations, from Allah. Muhammad reported many messages from the angel, and he became a political leader as well as a prophet. The message spread, giving rise to Islam.

Teach the Main Idea

At Level

The Origins of Islam

1. **Teach** Ask students the Reading Focus questions to teach this section.

2. **Apply** Organize students into groups of three. Within each group, assign each student one part of this section: The Arabian Peninsula, Muhammad the Messenger, or Basic Ideas of Islam. Have each student create an outline of the assigned part. When finished, have students share their outlines and add information about the other two

sections to their own work, so that each student has an outline of the entire section.

3. **Review** Create a master outline with input from volunteers. Have students correct their own work as needed.

4. **Practice/Homework** Have students use their outlines to write a brief essay about the rise of Islam and its basic tenets. **LS Verbal-Linguistic**

📋 **Alternative Assessment Handbook**, Rubric 40: Writing to Describe

MUSLIM CIVILIZATION **257**

Direct Teach

Reading Focus

1 What was Arabia like at the time of Muhammad's birth? *harsh land with desert interior; sparsely populated; limited farming; much commerce*

The Arabian Peninsula

Recall Why was commerce lively in Arabia? *Several trade routes converged there.*

Explain Why was Mecca an important town? *was a trade center; contained a building called the Kaaba that was considered sacred and drew religious pilgrims*

Reading Focus

2 What were Muhammad's messages, and how were they received? *Messages, or revelations, were received from Allah through an angel. Messages were that Allah was the only true God, and included instructions about how people shoul live in order to live in paradise after death.*

Muhammad the Messenger

Explain How do Judaism and Christianity fit into the teachings of Islam? *influenced Muhammad's thinking*

Identify Cause and Effect Why did Muhammad and his followers move to Yathrib? *Muhammad realized that they were not safe in Mecca, and the people in Yathrib were open to his message.*

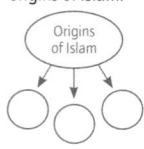

TAKING NOTES

Take notes on events and other facts about the origins of Islam.

Origins of Islam

NEW YORK

CC Unit 4-E1g
Human and physical geography

The most important of these towns was Mecca (ME-kuh), near the Red Sea. Besides being a trade center, Mecca also had a religious function. At Mecca's heart was a large cube-shaped structure called the Kaaba (KAH-bah). In the 500s, the Kaaba was an ancient building that was already considered sacred. Built into one of its walls was a stone, possibly a meteorite, said to be a relic from heaven. Inside the structure were idols—small statues of local gods. The site drew religious pilgrims.

Many gods and goddesses were worshipped in Mecca. One god was considered supreme, however, at least among members of the tribe that had founded Mecca. They called the supreme God Allah.

Muhammad the Messenger

Into this setting was born in about 570 Muhammad ibn Abd Allah—known as **Muhammad**. The boy's early life was marred by the death of both his parents. Muhammad was raised by his uncle Abu Talib, a powerful clan leader.

Muhammad's Early Life Muhammad grew up to have a successful career in Mecca as a merchant. He was respected by other merchants for his fairness and intelligence. At 25, he married an older widow named Khadijah (ka-DEE-jah). She had once been his employer. Together they had six children. The couple experienced tragedy, though. All the children except one daughter, Fatimah, died young.

As Muhammad traveled on business, he sometimes met followers of Judaism and Christianity. These faiths influenced his thinking. In addition, Muhammad probably knew of area preachers who were saying that there was only one God.

Muhammad had always been a religious man. He was in the habit of leaving his home to live for extended periods in a cave. There, he would pray and reflect on spiritual matters.

It was on one of these retreats, in about the year 610, that Muhammad had the first of the experiences that would change his life—and history. As he later explained it, he awoke from sleep to find himself in the presence of an angel who commanded him to speak messages, or revelations, from Allah—God. These words would become the first verses of the scripture that Muhammad brought to his followers.

Muhammad was at first deeply troubled by the visitation and unsure of its meaning. He told only Khadijah, who helped him in his effort to understand. After more visits from the angel, Muhammad concluded that God had chosen him, a humble merchant, to be his prophet. Eventually, Muhammad became a political leader as well as a prophet.

The Revelations Muhammad reported many messages from the angel. Among them was that Allah was the one and only true and all-powerful God. Other messages included instructions about how people should live if they hoped to please Allah and live in paradise after death.

For some time, Muhammad did not tell anyone besides his wife and a few close friends about his experiences. After about three years, though, he began to preach in public. He attracted a number of followers who accepted the new beliefs.

Some powerful Meccans did not accept his teachings. They disliked his criticism of their traditional beliefs in many gods. Muhammad had told them that their worship of idols was sinful. Local innkeepers and others who profited from the pilgrimage trade were also concerned that Muhammad's message would disrupt their business. Only the protection of Muhammad's uncle Abu Talib kept him safe. When Abu Talib died in 619, Muhammad knew that he and his followers were not safe in Mecca.

Sharing the Revelations In search of a new home, Muhammad visited the nearby city of Yathrib, where people were open to his preaching. In 622 Muhammad moved from Mecca to Yathrib, which came to be called Medina (muh-DEE-nuh), "the Prophet's city." Muhammad's journey from Mecca to Medina came to be known as the **hegira** (hi-JY-ruh) or hijra (HEEJ-ruh). Later, Muslims marked the year in which the hegira took place as the first year of the Islamic calendar.

Following the hegira, Muhammad spent a decade building up his community of fellow believers. Their faith was called **Islam**, which means "achieving peace through submission to God." The number of followers, who were known as **Muslims**, grew rapidly as Muhammad preached.

Differentiating Instruction

Above Level

Advanced Learners/Gifted and Talented

Research Required

Materials: construction paper, colored markers

1. Refer students to the Geography Starting Points map at the beginning of this chapter. Remind students that religious ideas and information about other cultures traveled on the same trade routes as commercial goods.

2. Have students use the construction paper to create a simple outline map of Arabia.

3. Have students use reliable sources to research the development of religions in neighboring regions and populations that may have traded

with Mecca in the late 500s. Students should prepare an annotated bibliography showing their sources.

4. Have students add the trade routes along which each religion would have traveled to their maps, using a different color for each faith. Maps should contain a key.

5. Have volunteers from each group share their work with the class. **LS** **Visual-Spatial**

Alternative Assessment Handbook, Rubrics 20: Map Creation; and 30: Research

Muhammad and Medina

In 622 Muhammad and his followers went to Medina. Today, the city's enormous mosque draws Muslims from around the world. *What does the size of the mosque indicate about the number of Muslims who come to Medina?*

ISLAM IN ARABIA, 632

- ← The hegira, 622
- ▨ Islamic lands at Muhammad's death, 632

Damascus
Jerusalem
Dead Sea
Medina
Mecca
ARABIAN PENINSULA
Persian Gulf
Red Sea
Gulf of Aden

0   200   400 Miles
0   200   400 Kilometers

The people of Mecca who wanted Muhammad stopped did not give up easily. They fought several battles with him and his followers. Ultimately, the Meccans lost ground. By 630, Muhammad controlled Mecca, and his influence in the western part of the Arabian Peninsula was unmatched.

READING CHECK **Sequence** What events led up to Muhammad's taking control of Mecca?

Basic Ideas of Islam

As Muhammad gained political power, the revelations continued. Since Muhammad could not read or write, he recited the revelations. His followers memorized the words and some followers wrote them down. These writings, which Muslims believe are direct revelations from God, were collected years later into the **Qur'an** (kuh-RAN), the sacred text of Islam.

Muslims read from the Qur'an to hear Allah's teachings. They also seek a religious experience in the rhythm and beauty of the words themselves. Muslims believe that only in its original Arabic language can one know the full meaning and beauty of the text. The Qur'an has been translated into other languages, but Muslims do not consider these translations to be true representations of the Qur'an.

The Five Pillars of Islam The Qur'an lays out five basic acts of worship that are central to Islam and that Muhammad himself fulfilled. These acts are called the **Five Pillars of Islam**.

The first pillar is the profession of faith. By affirming "There is no god but God [Allah], and Muhammad is the messenger of God," a Muslim signals his or her acceptance of the faith. This profession of faith denies the existence of the many gods and goddesses that many Arabs had worshipped. Moreover, the statement makes clear the belief that Muhammad was human—a prophet rather than a deity.

The second pillar is the performance of five daily prayers. Worshippers always face Mecca to pray, no matter where they are.

Another pillar is the giving of alms, or charity, to the poor and other needy people. Muslims are supposed to give a certain percentage of their income. Even people who have very little are encouraged to help others in some way.

Muslims are also required to fast—to go without food or drink—from dawn to dusk during the month of Ramadan. It was during Ramadan that Muhammad began to report the messages that were written down in the Qur'an. Muslims believe that fasting is a way to show that God is more important than one's own body.

MUSLIM CIVILIZATION **259**

Reading Focus

Basic Ideas of Islam

Identify What is a hadith? *An individual lesson or report on Muhammad's actions, contained in an important Muslim text called the Sunna.*

Contrast What is the difference between the Sharia and the Sunna? *The Sunna is the record of Muhammad's behavior and teachings; Sharia is the Muslim legal system.*

Analyze Why might there be differences in interpretation of Sharia? *law is not standardized; many schools of thought created it over several centuries*

📝 **CRF: Literature: "The Wonderful Bag"**

Info to Know

The Hadith To Muslims, the Qur'an is the most authoritative and important religious text. Second in line is the Sunna. Various followers of Muhammad recorded the hadith as they heard them, and by the 800s, there were over 600,000 recorded. Later readers edited this massive collection down to 25,000.

Answers

World Religions *possible answer— It lists the various parts of the world created by Allah and describes them as blessings.*

THE IMPACT TODAY

Today, up to 4 million people go to Mecca for the hajj each year.

ACADEMIC VOCABULARY

component part or element

Muslims who are physically and financially able are required at some point during their lives to go to Mecca. Such a journey is called the hajj. As part of the hajj, pilgrims gather by the thousands to pray in the city's immense **mosque**, the name for the building where Muslims worship. Pilgrims also perform various rituals, such as walking seven times around the Kaaba. One <u>component</u> of the hajj is walking to nearby Mount Arafat, where Muhammad is said to have delivered his last sermon.

Guidelines for Behavior The Qur'an, like holy books of other religions, provides guidelines for moral behavior. For example, Muslims are forbidden to eat pork or drink alcoholic beverages, and they must wash themselves before praying so that they will be pure before God. The Qur'an also provides guidelines for relationships among people. For example, the Qur'an prohibits murder, lying, and stealing.

Another requirement for the devout Muslim is **jihad**, a word that can be translated as "struggle for the faith." Jihad can also mean the struggle to defend the Muslim community, or historically, to convert people to Islam. The word has also been translated as "holy war."

The Sunna and Sharia The Qur'an describes the basic beliefs of Islam. Other texts written over many years provide models of behavior for Muslims to follow.

One of the texts tells how Muhammad acted in his daily life. The record of Muhammad's behavior and teachings is known as the Sunna (SOOH-nuh), which means "tradition." It includes hundreds of individual lessons or reports on Muhammad's actions. The Sunna provides Muslims with guidance in many areas, including personal relationships, business dealings, and religious practice. Each of the individual reports in the Sunna on Muhammad's actions is known as a hadith (huh-DEETH).

Over time, Muslims developed a legal system that reflects the various rules by which all Muslims should live. This system is called

World Religions

Sacred Texts

The Qur'an

About the Reading The Qur'an, the holy book of Islam, is divided into 114 chapters called *suras* (soo-ruhz). The *suras* vary widely in length. Each *sura* opens with the same phrase, translated here as "In the Name of Allah, the Compassionate, the Merciful."

AS YOU READ Look for words and phrases that are repeated within the text, and think about the reasons for the repetition.

▼ This copy of the Qur'an was produced in the 1400s.

The Granger Collection, New York

In the Name of Allah, the Compassionate, the Merciful

It is the Merciful who has taught the Qur'an.

He created man and taught him articulate speech.

The sun and moon pursue their ordered course. The plants and trees bow down in adoration.

He raised the heaven on high and set the balance of all things, that you might not transgress it. Give just weight and full measure.

He laid the earth for His creatures, with all its fruits and blossom-bearing palm, chaff-covered grain and scented herbs. Which of your Lord's blessings would you deny?

He created man from potter's clay and the jinn from smokeless fire. Which of your Lord's blessings would you deny?

The Lord of the two easts is He, and the Lord of the two wests. Which of your Lord's blessings would you deny?

He has let loose the two oceans: they meet one another. Yet between them stands a barrier which they cannot overrun. Which of your Lord's blessings would you deny?

Pearls and corals come from both. Which of your Lord's blessings would you deny?

His are the ships that sail like banners upon the ocean. Which of your Lord's blessings would you deny?

—Sura 55 (The Merciful): 1–25

Analyze Muslims believe that Allah created the world. How does this passage reflect that belief?

260 CHAPTER 9

Skills Focus: Analyzing Primary Sources

At Level

Reading Like a Historian Skill
Understanding a Hadith

Research Required

1. Remind students that the hadith are meant to guide people. Have students conduct research using reliable online or print sources to locate a hadith.

2. Have students read their hadith and write an explanation of its meaning. Have volunteers read their hadith and their explanations to the class.

3. Review students' explanations to be sue they understand their hadith's meaning.

4. As an extension, have students write a short essay on the usefulness of hadith in the lives of Muslims. 🖪 **Verbal-Linguistic**

📝 **Alternative Assessment Handbook**, Rubric 37: Writing Assignments

Sharia (shuh-REE-uh). Sharia law has never become standardized, but it does outline a method of reasoning and argument for legal cases. Numerous schools of thought contributed to the creation of Sharia law, which is not recorded in a single book. It is made up of opinions and writings over several centuries. Differences in interpretation vary among the many people within the Islamic world.

People of the Book Like the Jewish and Christian faiths, Islam is monotheistic—having only one God. The Qur'an teaches that Allah, the name of God in Arabic, is the same as God in the Jewish and Christian traditions. Muhammad considered Abraham, Moses, and Jesus to be messengers from God, but he saw himself as the last of God's prophets.

Muslims believe that the sacred texts of Judaism and Christianity also come from Allah—but that the Qur'an carries the greatest authority because it represents God's final message to humanity. Muslims are told

to respect Jews and Christians as "people of the book" because they share the tradition of prophets who taught and received revelation from God.

HISTORY'S VOICES

❝Do not argue with the followers of earlier revelation otherwise than in a most kindly manner—unless it be such of them as are bent on evil-doing—and say: 'We believe in that which has been bestowed from on high upon us, as well as that which has been bestowed upon you; for our God and your God is one and the same.'❞

—Qur'an 29:46

READING CHECK **Summarize** What are the acts of worship required of all Muslims?

NEW YORK

CC Unit 4-E5
Position of "people of the book"

Close

Have students describe the Arabian Peninsula in the time of Muhammad, the development of Islam, and the key features of the faith.

Review

📖 **Online Quiz**, Section 1

Assess

SE **Section 1 Assessment**

📄 **Progress Assessment**: Section 1 Quiz

📄 **Alternative Assessment Handbook**

Reteach/Intervene

📄 **Interactive Reader and Study Guide**, Section 1

💿 **Interactive Skills Tutor CD-ROM**

▲ **Muslim schoolgirls in a village in India read aloud from religious scriptures.**

SECTION 1 ASSESSMENT

go.hrw.com
Online Quiz
Keyword: SHL ISW HP

Reviewing Key Terms and People

1. a. Describe What were some of the major features of the Arabian Peninsula 1,500 years ago?
b. Explain In what two ways was Mecca an important settlement?
c. Evaluate What influence may his early years as a trader have had on Muhammad and his ideas?

2. a. Recall How was Muhammad's preaching received in Mecca?
b. Infer Based on its connection to the Muslim calendar, what can you infer about the importance of the **hegira** to Muslims?
c. Predict What does Muhammad's experience suggest about how Islam was to spread?

3. a. Recall What are the **Five Pillars of Islam**? What are some other requirements of devout Muslims?
b. Identify What are the key sources of religious wisdom and guidance for Muslims?
c. Compare What do Islam, Judaism, and Christianity have in common?

Critical Thinking

4. Sequence Use your notes and a graphic organizer like the one below to list events, in order, that led to the origins of Islam.

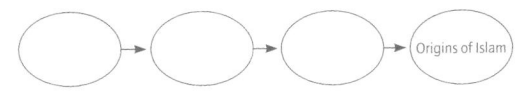

FOCUS ON WRITING

5. Narration Imagine that you are a bedouin who visited Mecca during Muhammad's conflict with some of the city's citizens. You have returned to your family's camp in the desert. Write a paragraph or two telling what you saw and heard in Mecca.

MUSLIM CIVILIZATION **261**

Answers

Reading Check *The Five Pillars of Islam—profession of faith, five daily prayers, giving of alms, fasting during Ramadan, and the hajj*

1. a. hot, dry land with limited farming, lively trade, nomads moving herds between scattered oases, few people
b. trading town; contained the Kaaba, an important religious pilgrimage site
c. He was exposed to Jews and Christians, whose faiths influenced him.

2. a. Many were angered by his criticism of their traditional beliefs; local innkeepers were afraid that Muhammad's preachings would disrupt the flow of pilgrims.
b. It represents the beginning of Islam.

c. possible answer—through his recitation of revelations and in the Qur'an

3. a. The Five Pillars of Islam—profession of faith, five daily prayers, giving of alms, fasting during Ramadan, and the hajj; Other requirements—no pork or alcoholic beverages, washing before prayer, no murder, lying, or stealing, jihad
b. the Qur'an, the Sunna, and the Sharia
c. Muslims believe in the same God as Jews and Christians; believe that the

sacred writings of Christians and Jews also came from Allah.

4. Muhammad reported revelations from Allah; Muhammad became a political leader and prophet; Muhammad made the hegira to Medina; number of followers grew; Muhammad and followers established control of Mecca; Islam spread

5. Student descriptions should include details from the section about why some of Mecca's citizens did not accept Muhammad's teachings.

MUSLIM CIVILIZATION **261**

Getting Started

Use the **Interactive Reader and Study Guide** to familiarize students with the section content.

▧ **Interactive Reader and Study Guide,** Section 2

📑 **CRF:** Vocabulary Builder: Section 2

Taking Notes

Abu Bakr became first caliph; Abu Bakr reunified Arabia and led forces north; by 661, territory under Muslim rule (caliphate) stretched from northern Africa to Persia; Umayyad dynasty expanded caliphate's borders still further

---

The Spread of Islam

BEFORE YOU READ

MAIN IDEA

After Muhammad's death, Islam spread beyond the Arabian Peninsula, shaping a major empire within 100 years. While the empire eventually broke into smaller parts, Islam continued to spread.

READING FOCUS

1. How did Islam evolve after Muhammad's death?
2. What were key events of the Umayyad dynasty?
3. What changes occurred under the Abbasid dynasty?
4. What led to the end of the caliphate's unity?

KEY TERMS AND PEOPLE

Abu Bakr
caliph
caliphate
Umayyad
Sunnis
Shia
Sufis
Abbasid
Harun al-Rashid

 NEW YORK

PI 3.1 Students analyze the roles and contributions of individuals and groups to social, political, economic, cultural, and religious practices and activities.

Muhammad's Death

◄ This illustration is an artistic depiction of Muhammad's name.

THE INSIDE STORY *How does a community choose a new leader?* For the first Muslims, Muhammad was more than God's messenger. He was also the unquestioned leader of their community. But Muhammad was a mortal man. Not long after he and his fellow Muslims regained control of Mecca, Muhammad saw that his death was approaching. "O people, lend me an attentive ear," he told his followers, "for I do not know whether, after this year, I shall ever be amongst you again." In 632, Muhammad died, leaving behind a community threatened by disunity. Some bedouin tribes that had been personally loyal to Muhammad began to break away, so strong leadership was needed. In the midst of this uncertainty, who would the community choose? ◢

Islam after Muhammad's Death

The death of Muhammad in 632 presented a challenge for the Muslim community. Who would lead the group and keep it unified? The answer affected the faith's spread and its future.

Muhammad's Successors Muhammad had not named a successor, and there was no clear candidate for the position. Although not everyone agreed, **Abu Bakr**, one of Muhammad's closest companions and one of the

---

Teach the Main Idea

At Level

The Spread of Islam

1. **Teach** Ask students the Reading Focus questions to teach this section.
2. **Apply** Have students scan the section and develop a time line for the spread of Islam from 632 to 1492. Students should include significant events and leaders discussed in the section.
3. **Review** Have volunteers share their time lines and create a class time line for all to see. As the class time line is being developed, have students explain the importance of each event and what each leader accomplished. Have students correct and add to their own time lines as needed.
4. **Practice/Homework** Have students select one event and one leader from the time line and write a one paragraph summary explaining the importance of the event and leader in the spread of Islam. **LS Visual-Spatial, Verbal-Linguistic**

📑 **Alternative Assessment Handbook**, Rubrics 36: Time Lines; and 42: Writing to Inform

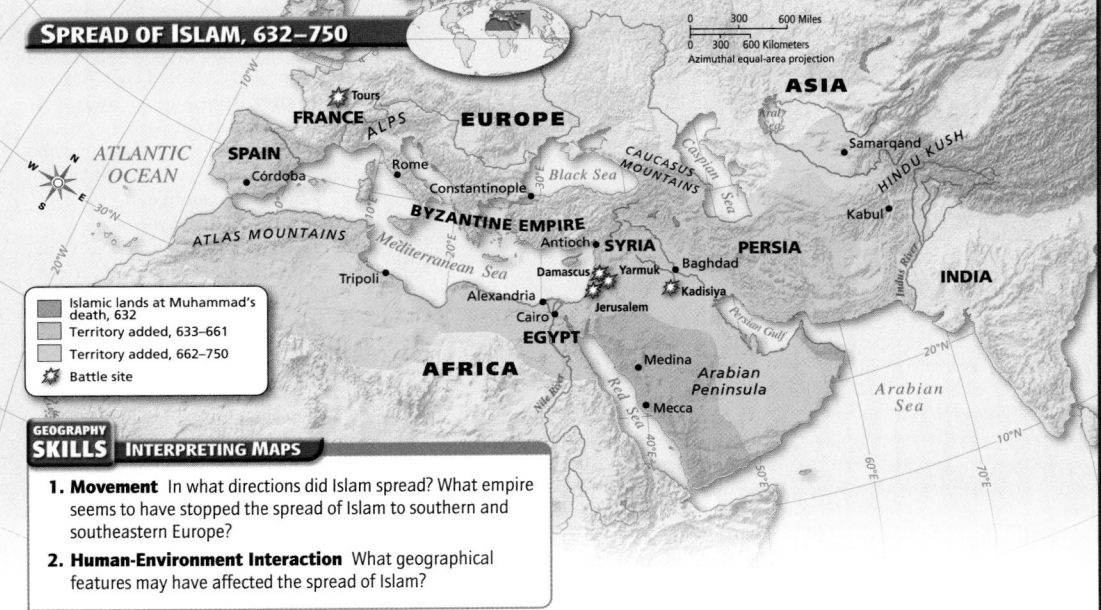

SPREAD OF ISLAM, 632–750

0   300   600 Miles
0   300   600 Kilometers
Azimuthal equal-area projection

Islamic lands at Muhammad's death, 632
Territory added, 633–661
Territory added, 662–750
⚔ **Battle site**

GEOGRAPHY SKILLS | **INTERPRETING MAPS**

1. **Movement** In what directions did Islam spread? What empire seems to have stopped the spread of Islam to southern and southeastern Europe?

2. **Human-Environment Interaction** What geographical features may have affected the spread of Islam?

---

earliest converts to Islam, was chosen. As the leader of the Muslim community, Abu Bakr and those who came after him were called **caliph** (KAY-luhf) or "successor."

When he took over leadership as caliph, Abu Bakr first focused on bringing back the bedouin tribes whose loyalty was slipping. To keep the tribes under control, Abu Bakr built up strong Arab fighting forces. After successfully reunifying Arabia, the caliph led his armies north.

Expansion of Territory Under Abu Bakr and his successor Umar, the territory under Muslim rule expanded rapidly. The weakness of neighboring empires, including Persia, contributed to the spread. In 637 Muslim forces defeated Persian forces in Iraq. Victory over the Persian Empire was complete by 642.

From Iraq and Persia, the Arab army turned west to face the wealthy Byzantine Empire, which was the eastern half of the old Roman Empire. The Byzantines first lost Damascus, Syria, and Jerusalem. In 639, the Byzantine province of Egypt fell. By 642, the rest of the Nile Valley came under Arab rule. Only 10 years after Muhammad's death, his followers had created an empire.

Conquests continued under later caliphs. By 661, the **caliphate**, or area ruled by a caliph, stretched all the way from northern Africa in the west to Persia in the east.

Internal Conflict and Division Although the Arab armies were successful in the field, there was deep conflict within the Muslim leadership. The tension had already begun when Abu Bakr was chosen as caliph. Some leaders had supported Ali, a cousin of Muhammad's and the husband of his daughter Fatimah.

In 644 another caliph had to be chosen. Ali lost again. The winner was Uthman, supported by the powerful **Umayyad** (oom-Y-yuhd) clan of Mecca. The Umayyads had converted reluctantly and had been Muhammad's enemies. They were unpopular, and rebels killed Uthman. Ali finally became caliph, but it was not long before civil war broke out between Ali's forces and the Umayyads. In the end, Ali was killed, and the Umayyads retook control.

Most Muslims reluctantly accepted the Umayyad caliph, Mu'awiya. They were called **Sunnis** (SOOH-neez), which meant "followers of the Sunna," or "way of the Prophet." Ali's supporters refused to go along with the Umayyads.

TAKING NOTES

Use a graphic organizer like this one to take notes on the spread of Islam.

NEW YORK

CC Unit 2-E2
Islam: Organizational structure

THE MUSLIM CIVILIZATION **263**

Direct Teach

Reading Focus

❶ How did Islam evolve after Muhammad's death? *The caliphs led the community. Muslim armies fought to spread their faith. The followers were split into the Shia and the Sunnis.*

Islam after Muhammad's Death

Explain Who were the caliphs, and what did they accomplish in the decade after Muhammad's death? *the leaders of the Muslim community and successors to Muhammad; created an empire*

Contrast Who were the Sunnis and the Shia? *Sunnis—followers of Umayyad clan of Mecca; Shia—followers of Ali, a cousin of Muhammad's and husband of his daughter*

Predict What do you think later caliphs might do with their armies? *possible answer—use them to continue to spread the faith*

📝 **CRF:** Primary Source: The Muslim Conquest of Spain

Interpreting Maps

Spread of Islam, 632–750

Location Where was Córdoba? *in Spain*

Movement Why might Islam have spread to Córdoba but not to other parts of Europe? *possible answer—connected by trade to Arabian Peninsula; not part of Byzantine Empire*

📦 **Map Transparency:** Spread of Islam, 632–750

Skills Focus: Making Generalizations   At Level

Reading Skill
Religious Freedom

1. Remind students that as Muslims expanded their territory, they generally respected religious freedom and granted religious rights to Christians and Jews. Remind students, too, that for the time, this was an enlightened idea. Some groups, however, were asked to pay a tax for their religious freedom.

2. Have students prepare two arguments, one supporting this type of taxation, and one opposing it.

3. Have volunteers read their arguments to the class. **LS Verbal-Linguistic**

📝 **Alternative Assessment Handbook**, Rubric 43: Writing to Pesuade

Answers

Interpreting Maps 1. *east, west, and north; the Byzantine Empire;* **2.** *large bodies of water, mountains*

263

❷ What were key events of the the Umayyad Dynasty? *expansion of caliphate's borders; defeat at the Battle of Tours in 732; spread of Muslim faith; strengthening of central government*

The Umayyad Dynasty

Recall What was the result of the Battle of Tours? *Muslim forces failed to push past Spain into what is now France.*

Describe How did the Umayyads treat the Jews and Christians they conquered? *allowed them to practice their religion; imposed taxes and some restrictions*

Reading like a Historian

Sufi Poetry

Interpreting Literature as a Source Rumi was an advocate of Sufism, a mystical branch of Islam. Like mystics of other faiths, Rumi believed that one needs to experience God personally. Sufis also believe that God exists in all things and that all things are essentially one, differing only in form. As you read this excerpt from one of Rumi's poems, think about:

- why the poem was written.
- what the poem tells us about Sufi beliefs.
- why the writer chose to write poetry rather than prose.

> The first two sentences state the poem's theme that the things we think we lose are replaced by other, often better, things.

> Don't grieve. Anything you lose comes round
> in another form. The child weaned from mother's milk
> now drinks wine and honey mixed.
>
> God's joy moves from unmarked box to unmarked box,
> from cell to cell. As rainwater, down into flowerbed.
> As roses, up from ground.
> Now it looks like a plate of rice and fish,
> now a cliff covered with vines,
> now a horse being saddled.
> It hides within these,
> till one day it cracks them open.
>
> —Rumi, "Unmarked Boxes," translated by
> John Moyne and Coleman Barks

> The second stanza details God's hidden presence in the ordinary; then the observer suddenly becomes aware of God's presence.

Skills Focus READING LIKE A HISTORIAN

1. **Creator** Why do you think Rumi wrote this poem?
2. **Details** What can this poem tell us about Sufi beliefs?
3. **Evaluate** Why do you think Rumi chose to write poetry rather than prose?

See **Skills Handbook**, p. H28

They became known as the **Shia**, from a phrase that means "party of Ali." The Shia believed that God had specially blessed Ali's descendants because they were Muhammad's true heirs. The Shia call each of Ali's successors *imam* (i-MAHM), which means "leader." For the Shia, only imams can interpret the Qur'an.

Conflict between the Sunni and Shia deepened after the deaths of Mu'awiya and Ali. Many thought Mu'awiya's son and successor, Yazid, had stolen the caliphate and was not a good Muslim. A grandson of Muhammad, Husayn, led a rebellion against Yazid. In 680, Yazid's army and Husayn's small band met in battle at Karbala, Iraq. Husayn was shot through with arrows while holding his infant son. Yazid's victorious forces slaughtered the survivors or took them prisoner. This battle became known as the martyrdom of Husayn. Since then, the Sunni and Shia split has remained bitter.

In addition to the Sunni and Shia division, a third group developed within Islam—the **Sufis** (SOO-feez). Sufis seek a mystical, personal connection with God. They use a range of practices, including breath control and meditation, in their rituals.

READING CHECK **Find the Main Idea** What was the result of the succession conflict?

The Umayyad Dynasty

Under the Umayyad caliphs, Muslim rule spread. Internal problems weakened the Umayyads, though, and led to their fall.

Continued Expansion Following the death of Husayn, the Umayyads strengthened their rule over the caliphate. Steps they took to strengthen their rule included establishing Arabic as the official language and making coinage uniform throughout the empire. They also began the first great work of Islamic architecture—the Dome of the Rock in Jerusalem.

Armies also extended the caliphate's borders. To the east, Muslim armies conquered territory all the way to the borders of China and the Indus River Valley. To the west, Muslim forces took northern Africa, crossed the Mediterranean, and took control of most of Spain.

Not all military expeditions were successful. Muslim forces failed to take Constantinople in 717. A small force also failed in an effort

---

Skill Focus: Analyzing Primary Sources

At Level

Reading Like a Historian Skill
Sunni and Shia Today

Research Required

1. Remind students that people have long fought over territory, but battles over faith seem to last longer than any other. Today, Sunni and Shia are still at odds.

2. Review with students what primary sources are and the types of materials they include. Then have students conduct outside research to locate primary source information about Sunni and Shia Muslims today.

3. Have students use their primary sources to create a collage of recent events involving one or both groups. Collages should include maps showing the countries featured in the primary source documents.

4. Have students present their work to the class.
   LS Verbal-Linguistic, Visual-Spatial

   Alternative Assessment Handbook, Rubrics 8: Collages; and 20: Map Creation

Answers

Reading Like a Historian 1. *to show mystical Sufi beliefs in a tangible way;* **2.** *shows that Sufis found a connection with God through nature;* **3.** *possible answer— Poetry allows for imagery that makes the mystical Sufi beliefs more tangible.*

Reading Check *Two different Muslim groups emerged—the Sunni and the Shia.*

The Sunni-Shia Divide

Newspaper headlines sometimes tell of violence between Shia and Sunni Muslims. Their disagreements may seem puzzling to non-Muslims.

The conflict dates back to the choice of the first successor to Muhammad and worsened with the death of Husayn, a descendant of Muhammad. Since then, the two groups have developed different beliefs, rituals, and laws. One crucial difference is in leadership. For the Sunni, no one stands between the individual believer and God. For the Shia, however, imams interpret religious issues. As a result, the imams have considerable influence and have even taken on political roles.

Today, the Shia still revere and mourn Husayn intensely. His martyrdom is a powerful symbol of brave opposition in the face of overwhelming odds. Consequently, Shia are more likely to interpret jihad as a violent fight for the faith. In recent years, such violence has been directed against governments led by Sunnis. Still, conflict between Sunni and Shia is not inevitable. The two groups often live and work together in peace.

Explain How does the Sunni-Shia split affect political action?

▼ Iran is the most populous Muslim country with a Shia majority. Several other countries have significant Shia minorities.

SUNNI AND SHIA DISTRIBUTION

to push beyond Spain into what is now France. It was defeated at the Battle of Tours in 732.

The conquests spread the Muslim faith as many conquered people converted to Islam. In general, Muslims allowed considerable religious freedom. They allowed Christians and Jews—People of the Book—to practice their religion. Non-Muslims did have to pay heavy taxes and endured some restrictions on their daily lives. For example, in some places, Muslims required synagogues to be built underground as a symbol of Judaism's inferior status.

Ruling the Empire As the caliphate grew in size, the Umayyads strengthened the central government. In the process, they created some dissatisfaction. Arab Muslims became a ruling class with power and privilege unavailable to those they conquered. This action conflicted with the strong Muslim ideal of equality. The wars over the succession were also deeply upsetting to many of the faithful. These Muslims were unhappy with the emphasis some placed on political ambition.

End of the Umayyads Displeasure with the Umayyads was widespread. The Shia continued their opposition. There was also unrest among some conquered people and among Arab tribes who thought the Umayyads favored certain families.

With the Umayyads weakened by discontent, the time was ripe for rebellion. A family known as the **Abbasids** (uh-BAS-idz) seized the opportunity. Led by a direct descendant of Muhammad's uncle, the Abbasids united many of the Umayyads' opponents by appearing to represent their causes. The Shia, for example, thought the Abbasids supported their position on the caliphate. Some devout Muslims thought the Abbasids would lead a return to pure Islamic values.

In a series of battles in the late 740s in Iran and Iraq, the Abbasids wiped out almost all of the Umayyad family. The caliphate thus entered a new phase—the Abbasid dynasty.

READING CHECK **Sequence** What events brought about the end of the Umayyad dynasty?

FOCUS ON NEW YORK

An estimated quarter of American Muslims live in New York State. The Islamic Center of New York in New York City is one of the country's largest mosques.

READING SKILLS

Identifying Implied Main Ideas What is the implied main idea of this paragraph? What details help you find the main idea?

Skills Focus: Analyzing Secondary Sources   Above Level

Reading Like a Historian Skill
Comparing Battle Accounts

Research Required

1. Tell students that historical accounts of battles are often written form the viewpoint of the victor, and that great victories are also great losses. Have students use reliable secondary source documents and find two accounts of the Battle of Tours. One should be written by a historian who believes that Charles Martel was a hero who stopped the Muslim invasion of Europe; the other should be from a historian who considers the Battle of Tours to be an insignificant loss for Muslim forces.

2. Have students read the documents carefully, write a summary of each, and then write an essay in which they discuss the bias shown in each account. Students should refer to actual passages within the documents to support their conclusions. **LS** Intrapersonal, Verbal-Linguistic

Alternative Assessment Handbook, Rubrics 16: Judging Information; and 30: Research

---

● **Direct Teach** ●

Reading Focus

The Umayyad Dynasty

Analyze Why were some Muslims unhappy with the Umayyad government? *Some Muslims were unhappy with the emphasis on politics and the growing power of Arab rulers.*

Rate Judge the use of armed forces in building the caliphate. *possible answer—The Qur'an does not support forcing people to accept the faith. Traveling missionaries might have caused less conflict between Muslim teachings and the caliphate's actions.*

Map Transparency: Sunni and Shia Distribution

Info to Know

A Warrior King's Nickname Charles Martel (688–741) gained his place in history when he led the forces that defeated the invading Muslim forces and killed their Spanish governor in battle. This pivotal battle, known as the Battle of Tours or the Battle of Poitiers, earned him the nickname "Martel," which means The Hammer, because of the ruthlessness with which he conquered the invaders.

Answers

Linking to Today *Shia sometimes direct violence toward Sunni governments.*

Reading Skills *possible answer—Abbasids and Umayyads were longtime enemies. Details —"series of battles," "wiped out"*

Reading Check *A family called the Abbasids took advantage of discontent with the Umayyads and established a new caliphate.*

265

3 What changes occurred under the Abbasid dynasty? *capital moved to Baghdad, government cut off from people, Islam became truly universal religion, Muslim culture flourished*

The Abbasid Dynasty

Identify What were some characteristics of Abbasid caliphs? *lived in luxury, had little direct contact with the people*

Explain How did Islam spread to West Africa and Southeast Asia? *through trade, which exchanged both goods and information*

Recent Scholarship

When Baghdad Ruled the Muslim World: The Rise and Fall of Islam's Greatest Dynasty is a fascinating look at Baghdad and the Islamic Empire during the eighth and ninth centuries. Author Hugh Kennedy focuses on the human dimension of the time, and he provides a thorough discussion of the flourishing culture of the empire. *When Baghdad Ruled the Muslim World: The Rise and Fall of Islam's Greatest Dynasty* by Hugh Kennedy. Da Capo Press, 2005.

Answers

Prosperity in Baghdad *Government and religion were central and connected; there was a large market area.*

Reading Check *The Abbasids focused more on prosperity and cultural advancement than on empire expansion.*

266

The Abbasid Dynasty

The Abbasids relocated the capital of the caliphate. They chose Baghdad, on the Tigris River, in what is now Iraq. In their new capital, the rulers lived in splendor.

Persian Influence The move to Baghdad marked the beginning of the end of Arab domination of the Muslim world. The Abbasids adopted a Persian style of government in which they cut themselves off from the people. In the throne room, for example, the caliph was hidden behind a beautiful screen so that he could not be seen. The Abbasids also relied on Persian government officials. A vizier (vuh-ZIR), or "deputy" oversaw affairs of state.

A Changing Culture Under the Abbasid dynasty, the nature of Islam changed also. Islam had been a religion that appealed mostly to Arabs. The Abbasids invited all peoples in the community to join in. In the process, they turned Islam into a truly universal religion that attracted people of many cultures.

Trade was one way that Islam spread. As Muslim traders journeyed from end to end of the caliphate, an exchange in both goods and information occurred. The exchange helped bring Islam to places such as West Africa and Southeast Asia.

Lively trade was also a source of funds for cultural achievements. Caliph **Harun al-Rashid** (hah-ROON ahl-rah-SHEED), the most prominent Abbasid caliph, helped bring Muslim culture to great heights during his reign from 786 to 809. His support of scholarship helped produce lasting achievements of Islamic arts and sciences.

READING CHECK **Contrast** How did the Abbasids differ from the Umayyads?

The End of Unity

Though Muslim culture thrived under Abbasid rule, Abbasid political power began to weaken as early as the 800s. By the 900s, a growing number of small, independent states broke away from the caliphate. Increasingly, the caliph became a powerless figurehead.

Prosperity in Baghdad

The Abbasids moved their capital to Baghdad. Under Caliph Harun al-Rashid, Baghdad attracted merchants, poets, scholars, and artists. *What does the map imply about the city's economy, government, and religion?*

BAGHDAD, 700–900

Syria Gate
Residential Area
Khurasan Gate
Tigris River
Palace — Mosque
Markets
Kufa Gate
Basra Gate

◀ This enameled pitcher from Iran is one of many luxury items traded during the Abbasid dynasty.

In this illustration from the early 1200s, Muslim astronomers study the works of Aristotle.

266 CHAPTER 9

Skills Focus: Identifying Main Idea and Details   At Level

Reading Skill
Comparing Two Dynasties

1. Draw the Venn diagram shown here for students to see. Omit the italicized words.

2. Have students copy and complete the diagram with details about the Umayyad and Abbasid dynasties. When students have finished, have volunteers share what they wrote in each section. **LS Visual-Spatial**

📖 **Alternative Assessment Handbook**, Rubric 13: Graphic Organizers

Umayyad and Abbasid Dynasties

Umayyad: *capital: Damascus; official language; official coinage; territory from edge of China to Spain; strong central government; emphasized politics over religion*

Both: *Muslims; powerful and privileged ruling class; spread Islam*

Abbasid: *capital: Baghdad; enabled great prosperity; advanced Islamic art, culture, and scholarship*

Challenges from Europe In some areas, European Christians weakened Muslim rule. Although Umayyads had kept control of Spain until the 1000s, Christian armies began to drive out Muslims at about that time.

Further east, European Christians went to war against Muslims in and around Jerusalem. The Europeans wanted to make the region, which they called the Holy Land, Christian. Although the Europeans won at first and ruled Jerusalem for a while, Muslim forces eventually retook the city. The wars to retake the Holy Land were called the Crusades. (See Chapter 14 for more information about the Crusades.)

Problems from Egypt A serious threat to the Abbasids emerged in 969 when a splinter group established the Fatimid dynasty in Egypt. The Fatimids claimed descent from Muhammad's daughter Fatimah. From Egypt, the Fatimids controlled the Mediterranean and Red seas, which disrupted Abbasid trade. As a result, the Fatimids were soon richer and more powerful than the Abbasids.

Seljuk Turks Among the peoples of the caliphate were many non-Arabs, including Turks. In 1055 a Turkish people known as the Seljuks rose to power and took control of Baghdad itself. The Seljuks were Sunni Muslims who supported the Abbasid caliph.

After defending the Abbasids against the Fatimids, the Seljuks went to war against the Byzantine Empire. In 1071 the Seljuks delivered a terrible defeat to the Byzantines at the Battle of Manzikert. Most of Anatolia fell under Turkish control. The Seljuk Turks would go on to create their own empire.

Mamluks and Mongols In the 1200s what remained of the caliphate was attacked from two directions. A group called the Mamluks, who had once been enslaved soldiers, took power in Egypt and Syria. Then in 1258 an Asian people, the Mongols, arrived at Baghdad after conquering China and Central Asia. The Mongols destroyed the city and killed the Abbasid caliph. The caliphate was finished.

Islam, however, was still a vital force. Islam spread beyond the Middle East and Africa to India, Central Asia, and Southeast Asia.

READING CHECK **Summarize** What forces ended the unity of the caliphate?

THE END OF UNITY

969 ■	Fatimid dynasty reaches the height of its power with the conquest of Egypt.
1055 ■	Seljuk Turks take control of Baghdad.
1071 ■	Seljuk Turks defeat Byzantines and take control of most of Anatolia.
1085 ■	Toledo, Spain, falls to Christian forces.
1099 ■	Jerusalem falls to the Crusaders.
1250 ■	Mamluks come to power in Egypt and Syria.
1258 ■	Mongols capture Baghdad and overthrow the Abbasid caliphate.

SECTION 2 ASSESSMENT

go.hrw.com
Online Quiz
Keyword: SHL ISW HP

Reviewing Key Terms and People

1. **a. Identify** Who was **Abu Bakr**?
   b. Compare and Contrast What are the basic differences between the **Sunni** and the **Shia**?
   c. Predict How might the death of Husayn affect later political conflicts between Sunni and Shia?

2. **a. Recall** What was the name of the first dynasty to gain control of the caliphate?
   b. Summarize What situation helped lead to the end of **Umayyad** rule?

3. **a. Describe** What features marked the **Abbasid** style of rule?
   b. Evaluate For what do you think the Abbasids should be remembered?

4. **a. Recall** Who were the Fatimids, Seljuk Turks, and Mamluks?
   b. Evaluate Evaluate this statement: "Even though the caliphate ended, its influence has lasted for hundreds of years."

Critical Thinking

5. **Summarize** Use your notes and a graphic organizer like the one below to write two important facts about key eras in the spread of Islam. The first one is started for you.

After Muhammad	Umayyad Dynasty	Abbasid Dynasty	End of Unity
• There was no clear successor after Muhammad died.			

FOCUS ON WRITING

5. **Description** Write a paragraph in which you describe the succession issues facing the Muslim community after Muhammad's death.

THE MUSLIM CIVILIZATION **267**

Diffusion of a Civilization

Info to Know

Protecting Ancient Treasures In 1977, graduate students Roderick and Susan McIntosh began excavating sites near the Mosque of Djenné in Mali. Djenné is located on the upper Niger River, about 220 miles south of Timbuktu, and was a major crossroads for the salt and gold trade. As word of the McIntosh excavation in Djenné spread, Western art collectors wanted to acquire some of the treasures. Soon, looters arrived in the Niger Delta, stealing precious treasures. The U.S. government placed import restrictions on cultural artifacts from Mali. It was the first and only African country to receive this protection.

- 📦 **Map Transparency:** Diffusion of a Civilization
- ✳ **Interactive Map:** Diffusion of a Civilization

MISCONCEPTION /// ALERT \\\

Careful archeological excavation of over fifteen feet of debris revealed that ancient Jenne-jeno, now Djenné, dates back as far as 200 BC. The organization of complex social systems in cities was thought to have begun only after the arrival of Arabs around 600-700 AD, but this new evidence showed the people of this area developed such systems far earlier. Jenne-jeno now joins Djenné on UNESCO's list of World Heritage sites.

HISTORY & Geography

Conquest
At first, Islam spread by conquest. This illustration shows a battle in Spain.

Missionary Journeys
Conversions led to the building of mosques far from Arabia, such as this one in Djenné, Mali.

Diffusion of a Civilization

Over a few hundred years, Islam extended from Africa's Atlantic coast to Southeast Asia—an example of cultural diffusion. Conquest, trade, and missionary journeys all contributed to the spread. Other aspects of Islamic civilization also developed in those lands—Islamic law and respect for learning, for examples.

268 CHAPTER 9

Map labels: EUROPE, Danube R., Black Sea, Caspian Sea, ATLANTIC OCEAN, Tours, 732, Medina, SPAIN, Córdoba, Las Navas de Tolosa, 1212, Constantinople, ASIA MINOR, Manzikert, 1071, Aleppo, SYRIA, Baghdad, Nehavend, 742, Tunis, Mediterranean Sea, Jerusalem, Euphrates R., Tigris R., Cairo, EGYPT, Nile R., Red Sea, Mecca, ARABIAN PENINSULA, S A H A R A, AFRICA, Timbuktu, Niger R., 0° Equator, 15°S, 30°S, 15°E, 30°E, Madagascar, 45°N, 15°W, 0 200 400 Miles, 0 200 400 Kilometers, Van der Grinten projection

---

Differentiating Instruction
Below Level

Learners Having Difficulty

1. Have students review Section 2 to locate important individuals discussed in the section.

2. Have volunteers name one person they learned about in this section. Write them on a strip of paper and hang them on the wall. Have other volunteers write one major fact associated with this person on the same paper. Add and post more names and facts as students think of them.

3. Have students copy the names and accomplishments onto their own paper. Then have students work in mixed-ability pairs to organize the names by groups and in chronological order. **LS Interpersonal, Visual-Spatial**

   📄 **Alternative Assessment Handbook,** Rubric 1: Acquiring Information

NEW YORK STANDARDS

PI 1.4 Students understand the broad patterns, relationships, and interactions of cultures and civilizations during particular eras and across eras.

ASIA

Talas River, 751

Samarqand

Kabul

HINDU KUSH

TAKLIMAKAN DESERT

PLATEAU OF TIBET

HIMALAYAS

Ganges R.

THAR DESERT

INDIA

DECCAN PLATEAU

INDIAN OCEAN

Bay of Bengal

MONGOLIA

GOBI

CHINA

PACIFIC OCEAN

South China Sea

Malacca

Sumatra

Borneo

Celebes

Jakarta

Java

Islamic lands in Muhammad's time, 632
Islamic Empire at its greatest extent, 750
Areas predominantly Islamic, c. 1500
Major battles won by Islamic armies
Major battles lost by Islamic armies
Trade routes

Trade Muslim merchants traveled thousands of miles from the Arabian Peninsula, bringing their faith with them.

GEOGRAPHY SKILLS   INTERPRETING MAPS

1. **Regions** What method of cultural diffusion seems to have affected Sumatra and Java?

2. **Movement** Which ocean in particular facilitated trade for Muslim travelers?

MUSLIM CIVILIZATION **269**

History and Geography

Info to Know

Paper and Progress At the end of the Umayyad period, a prisoner from China began manufacturing paper from hemp and linen in Samarkand. In the late 700s, a paper factory was established in Baghdad. The caliph Mamun (786–833) sent gifts to Byzantine emperors in exchange for books, which he had translated and studied. He shared his enthusiasm for learning and turned the caliphate library into a scholarly institution. Thanks to the ready supply of paper, manuscripts were copied and shared in libraries in Baghdad, and ideas were spread far away.

An Early Geographer One of the greatest Muslim geographers was Yaqut ibn-'Abdullah al-Hamawi, who lived from 1179 to 1229. Yaqut was a Greek slave. After he was given his freedom, Yaqut traveled from place to place, copying and selling manuscripts to support himself. He later wrote the *Dictionary of Cities*.

Activity **Code of Conduct** Have students form small groups and imagine they are Arab merchants in Medina. Tell them that they have employees traveling throughout North Africa and Persia buying, selling, and trading goods. Have each group develop a written code of conduct for these employees while away form home and in dealings with non-Muslim customers that will strengthen the perception of Islam in those regions.

Collaborative Learning

The Spread of Islam

At Level

Research Required

Materials: construction paper, markers

1. Tell students that several important advances made sea travel easier, allowing the further spread of Islam.

2. Organize students into small groups. Assign one of the following topics to each group: compass, astrolabe, lateen sails, and rudder.

3. Have each group research its innovation and then create two posters. The first poster should explain how the innovation works and the second poster should show how it affected sea travel in the period when it was first developed.

4. Have each group to present the posters to the class and then display them in the classroom.
   LS Verbal-Linguistic, Visual-Spatial

   Alternative Assessment Handbook, Rubrics 28: Posters; and 30: Research

Answers

Interpreting Maps 1. *trade;* **2.** *the Indian Ocean*

269

Preteach

Getting Started

Use the **Interactive Reader and Study Guide** to familiarize students with the section content.

📖 **Interactive Reader and Study Guide,** Section 3

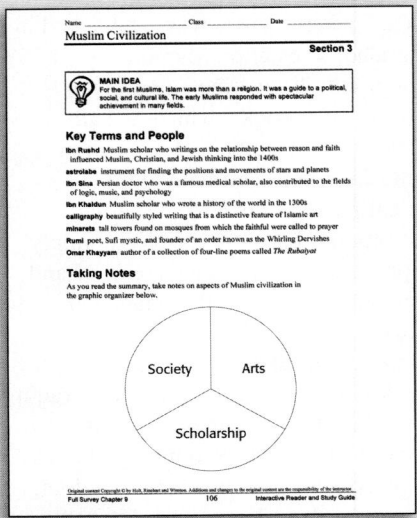

Academic Vocabulary

Review with students the high-use academic term in this section.

maintain keep up or support (p. 272)

📝 **CRF: Vocabulary Builder: Section 3**

Taking Notes

Society—man was head of family; during Abbasid dynasty women lost some status; slavery allowed; economy based on commerce; Arts—religious art does not contain human or animal figures; calligraphy; distinctive architecture includes minarets and domes; literature includes 1001 Nights *and the poetry of Rumi and Khayyam; Scholarship—culture of learning thrived; works translated into Arabic; advances in astronomy, mathematics, medicine, geography*

go.hrw.com

Online Resources

KEYWORD: SHL ISW
ACTIVITY: Islamic
Calligraphy

BEFORE YOU READ

MAIN IDEA

For the first Muslims, Islam was more than a religion. It was a guide to political, social, and cultural life. The early Muslims responded with spectacular achievement in many fields.

READING FOCUS

1. What were some key features of Muslim society?
2. What were some of the accomplishments of Muslim scholarship?
3. What were some contributions to the arts made by Muslim artists and writers?

KEY TERMS AND PEOPLE

astrolabe
Ibn Rushd
Ibn Sina
Ibn Khaldun
calligraphy
minarets
Rumi
Omar Khayyam

🗽 NEW YORK

PI 3.1 Students analyze the roles and contributions of individuals and groups to social, political, economic, cultural, and religious practices and activities.

Ibn Sina in an Ottoman miniature, 1600s

MAN OF MANY TALENTS

◀ **Ibn Sina directs preparation of a remedy for smallpox.**

THE INSIDE STORY

Was there anything Ibn Sina could not do? The Persian scholar Ibn Sina, also known as Avicenna, first mastered philosophy and religion. Then he gained fame as a physician and trained other doctors who came to him for guidance. While teaching and treating the sick, Ibn Sina began to study the law. After all these efforts, surely Ibn Sina had reached old age. But he was only 16 years old!

The next year, when he was all of 17 years old, Ibn Sina cured a powerful local leader of a disease that had frustrated other doctors. For his reward, the famous doctor asked only to use his patient's library. Ibn Sina contributed to medical libraries of the future by compiling a massive encyclopedia of known medical knowledge.

In addition to medicine, Ibn Sina contributed to mathematics, astronomy, music, poetry, and other fields. Ibn Sina's many lifelong achievements exemplify the tremendous accomplishments of Muslim scholars and artists. Their work left an enduring legacy. ▪

Muslim Society

Even though the Abbasid empire soon broke up into several independent units, Muslim civilization remained distinct. One reason is that Islam affected practically all aspects of daily life. Islamic texts provided guidance on how Muslims should deal with many issues, including family life, slavery, and the economy.

270 CHAPTER 9

Teach the Main Idea

At Level

Islamic Civilization

1. **Teach** Ask students the Reading Focus questions on the next page to teach this section.

2. **Apply** Organize the class into small groups. Assign one of these topics to each group: Muslim Society, Muslim Scholars, and Muslim Artists. Have each group design and assemble a collage made up of written work and sketches representing the information presented in this section.

3. **Review** Have volunteers from each group display and share their work with the class.

4. **Practice/Homework** Have each student write a short paragraph about Muslim society, scholarship, and arts.
   LS Interpersonal, Visual-Spatial

📋 **Alternative Assessment Handbook,** Rubrics 14: Group Activity; and 28: Posters

The Family and Women Islamic texts set forth roles within the family, the main social unit in Muslim society. The man was the head of the family. Men could have several wives. However, husbands were supposed to treat all their wives equally. Other aspects of the law sought to protect the rights of children and women.

At the time of Muhammad, the rights of women varied from clan to clan. There were no laws regarding the status of all women. That situation changed somewhat under Islam. According to the Qur'an, women are equal to men before Allah. In addition, Islam acknowledged that women could inherit property and could seek divorce in some circumstances.

Women played vital roles in the early Muslim community. Khadijah and several other women were among the first converts. Some of these women even went into battle. They also influenced political decisions. Women lost status during the Abbasid dynasty, however. Women of the Abbasid court were confined to a secluded part of the palace called the harem. Covering the hair and sometimes wearing a veil also became common during Abbasid rule.

Slavery Islamic texts also addressed slavery, which was common throughout Muslim lands. Most slaves came from non-Muslim regions. Some slaves who had been purchased by wealthy, privileged members of society became well educated.

Like the Bible, the Qur'an did not condemn slavery but required that slaves be treated fairly. Freeing slaves was praised as a religious act. Slaves were given some legal rights, including the right to buy their freedom. Although treatment of slaves improved under Islam, slavery remained a part not just of Muslim society but also of the economy. Muslim merchants traded in slaves over a wide area.

The Economy The economic life of the Muslim community was built largely on commerce, partly because ancient trade routes crossed the Arabian Peninsula. The Muslim merchants followed routes that extended northwest to Spain and southeast to the Spice Islands of Indonesia. Some merchants were "middlemen" who connected suppliers in the East to markets in the West. Others produced and traded agricultural products and goods such as finely crafted iron products.

Trade was one subject of Muhammad's teachings. In fact, a verse in the Qur'an commands, "Let there be amongst you traffic and trade by mutual goodwill." Such goodwill helped trade relationships, but Muslim merchants also developed practical business methods. They expanded the use of coinage, which eased long-distance commerce. Traders also used standardized weights and measures and extended credit to buyers over long distances.

Trade provided much of the wealth that maintained the empire and led to the growth of its splendid cities, such as Baghdad. Trade also helped spread the faith to distant lands and promoted the exchange of ideas.

READING CHECK **Identify** What are three aspects of life that are addressed in Islamic texts?

Muslim Scholarship

Learning, which was highly valued in all Muslim communities, added to cultural unity. Scholars made essential contributions in several fields. Indeed, many later European intellectual achievements grew out of the work of Muslim scholars.

A Culture of Learning Scholarship thrived throughout the Muslim world for a number of reasons. One reason was that Islam commanded its followers to examine their world and seek evidence of Allah in its wonders.

TAKING NOTES
Take notes in a graphic organizer like this one on aspects of Muslim civilization.

Society Arts
Scholarship

THE IMPACT TODAY
Women's roles vary widely in Islamic countries. For example, women are not allowed to drive in Saudi Arabia, while in Indonesia they can.

NEW YORK
CC Unit 2-E4
Social class: women and slavery in Muslim society

FACES OF HISTORY

al-KHWARIZMI
c. 780–c. 850

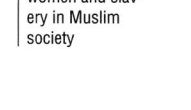

Some of today's students may not yet realize that algebra has practical uses. But when mathematician Muhammad ibn Musa al-Khwarizmi developed algebra, he did so to solve real problems. For example, Islamic law required that inheritances be divided according to proportions. Figuring out how much each heir should receive was made easier with algebra. Al-Khwarizmi also recommended using algebra to help with lawsuits, business deals, measuring land, and digging canals. In fact, we owe the word *algebra* to al-Khwarizmi, who used the Arabic word *al-jabr*, meaning "completion," in the title of a book on mathematics.

Analyze Why might al-Khwarizmi be characterized as a practical man and mathematician?

MUSLIM CIVILIZATION **271**

Direct Teach

Reading Focus

1 What were some key features of Muslim society? *Islam made men head of the family, set forth proper trade relations, and its laws protected women, children and slaves.*

Muslim Society

Recall What does the Qur'an say about slavery? *Slaves should be treated fairly; freeing slaves was praised as a religious act.*

Analyze How did trade affect Islamic society? *led to use of coinage, standardized weights and measures, enriched the empire*

Reading Focus

2 What were some of the major accomplishments of Muslim scholars? *translations of Greek texts, advances in astronomy, medicine, mathematics, philosophy, study of history*

Muslim Scholarship

Identify What was the House of Wisdom? *an academy in Baghdad, maintained by the government, where much translation of the works of ancient Greece took place*

Analyze Why was the translation of Greek works into Arabic of lasting importance? *saved works from being lost; stimulated further study in the Islamic world; eventually translated into Latin and available to European scholars*

Collaborative Learning   At Level

The Spread of Information

1. Remind students that they have already studied a number of empires and cultures that conquered others. Have volunteers name a few conquering cultures, and refer students to the text to refresh their memories. Write a list of conquests and results for all to see.

2. Organize students into an even number of groups. Have students in each group prepare for a debate on this issue: Scholars can make great advances when one country conquers another. Assign each group a pro or con side, and give students time to prepare. Have groups write as many arguments to support their position as they can, and have them consider points the other side might make.

3. Call pairs of groups to debate before the class.

4. As an extension, have students write a paragraph supporting the position they personally support. **LS** **Interpersonal, Verbal-Linguistic**

   Alternative Assessment Handbook, Rubric 10: Debates

Answers

Faces of History *possible answer—He used algebra to solve real problems.*

Reading Check *family life, slavery, and trade relationships*

271

Reading Focus

Muslim Scholarship

Explain Why did religion influence advances in astronomy? *Muslims needed to predict the phases of the moon in order to plan religious festivals, needed to pray in the direction of Mecca*

Make Inferences What do the establishment of hospitals and medical advances say about the leaders of this society? *possible answer—Human life was valued.*

Analyze Why was the study of geography important in Muslim civilization? *Pilgrims needed to find their way to Mecca; empire included many lands*

📝 **CRF:** Biography: al-Razi

Info to Know

The *Almagest* Ptolemy's second century *Mathematike Syntaxis*, or *System of Mathematics* was called the *Almagest*, which means "the Great Work." It not only gave tables of star movements, but told how to construct instruments to measure a star's position with precision. The *Almagest* became part of the great library in Córdoba, which held over 600,000 manuscripts in the tenth century. This was more than existed in all of France at the time. In 1105, Toledo fell and the vast library holdings stunned Christian Europeans. Italian Gerard of Cremona found Ptolemy's work in Córdoba and translated it into Latin. The *Almagest* soon became wildly popular in Europe.

This attitude promoted curiosity and inquiry. Another reason was the vastness of the caliphate and the many different cultures within it. Particularly influential were the Greek, Persian, and Indian civilizations.

One of the most valuable contributions of Muslim scholars was the translation into Arabic of works by scientists and philosophers of ancient Greece. During early Abbasid rule much of this work took place at an academy in Baghdad called the House of Wisdom that was <u>maintained</u> by the government. Through their translations, the resident scholars made texts from Hippocrates, Euclid, Galen, and Ptolemy available to a new audience. Once translated into Arabic, the Greek texts stimulated further study throughout the Muslim world.

The influence of these texts extended to Europe. The Arabic versions of many works were eventually translated into Latin. In this way, they became available to European scholars. In fact, much of the science and philosophy taught in European universities during the Middle Ages came from these translations.

Muslim Spain was the exchange point for much of this knowledge. For example, a Muslim scholar of Córdoba, Spain, named **Ibn Rushd** (IB-uhn ROOSHT), or Averroes (uh-VEER-uh-weez) wrote commentaries on Aristotle. Averroes' work on the relationship between reason and faith influenced not just Muslim but also Jewish and Christian thinking into the 1400s.

ACADEMIC VOCABULARY
maintain keep up or support

Astronomy and Mathematics
Among the many fields that Muslim scholars explored was astronomy, the study of the objects in space. In fact some stars, such as Aldebaran, still bear the names given them by their Muslim discoverers.

Astronomy first came to the Muslim world through texts from Persia and India. But the most important influence was Ptolemy's work, the *Almagest*, which was first translated into Arabic in the 800s. This work described the movements of heavenly bodies and gave tables for predicting their paths.

To expand their knowledge, Muslim astronomers built observatories for watching the sky. At an observatory in Persia, one astronomer completely revised a catalog of stars from Ptolemy's work. At another Persian observatory, scholars created such an accurate calendar that a version of it is still in use today.

The calendar was one way that astronomy served a practical purpose. It also helped with religious obligations. Muslims needed to predict the phases of the moon, in order to plan religious festivals, which were determined by the lunar calendar.

Knowledge of astronomy was essential to navigation. With their knowledge of the night sky, Muslims perfected the **astrolabe**, an instrument for finding the positions and movements of stars and planets. Sailors used astrolabes to calculate latitude, longitude, and the time of day. An astrolabe could also point the direction toward Mecca for daily prayers.

Muslim scholars made advances in mathematics. From India they adopted the symbols 0 through 9. by the time this system made its way to Europe, the numbers were known as Arabic numerals. Algebra and trigonometry also came from Muslim thinkers.

Medicine
Another science highly developed in the Muslim world was medicine. Doctors in Baghdad had to pass rigorous tests before they could practice. Baghdad also had the world's first school of pharmacy. Muslim doctors developed many skills. Perhaps the most remarkable was eye surgery, for which scores of different instruments were available. One instrument, a hollow needle, was used to draw out a film that caused blindness.

Ibn Sina (IB-uhn SEE-nah), a Persian doctor known also as Avicenna, was probably the most famous medical scholar of his time. He contributed to many fields besides medicine, including logic, music, and psychology.

Other Fields of Study
Geographers made strides, too, partly because the empire included so many different lands and peoples. Because pilgrims needed to find their way to Mecca, travel guides were written that describes the journey. One geographer measured the earth's circumference with considerable accuracy.

Muslim scholars also studied history. In the 1300s **Ibn Khaldun** (IB-uhn kal-DOON) wrote a history of the world. He made comments on general issues that still interest historians. For example, he warned historians against such basic errors as bias and praising rulers too highly in order to gain their favor.

READING CHECK **Summarize** What were some of the fields in which Muslim scholars excelled?

Differentiating Instruction

Below Level

Special Education Students

1. Review the information in the text about the many contributions of Islamic scholars. Have students work in mixed-ability pairs to make a list of the contributions and the scholars discussed.

2. Have students work individually or in pairs to transform the information in the list into a table or chart, organized by subject.

3. Have volunteers share their charts either with the class or in small groups. **LS Visual-Spatial**

📝 **Alternative Assessment Handbook**, Rubric 7: Charts

Answers

Reading Check *astronomy, medicine, mathematics, philosophy, history*

Arts and Literature

As with scholarly life, Muslim artistic expression was rich and varied. Influenced by the many cultures found in the vast empire, Islamic arts developed distinctive features.

Islamic Art Muslim artists worked in a range of materials, including wood, metal, ceramics, and textiles. Their works do share a stylistic feature. Islamic religious art generally does not contain any human or animal figures.

Muslims believe that portraying people or animals can tempt people to worship those images. Worshipping anything or anyone besides Allah would be the worst possible sin. Avoidance of figures led to using geometric patterns and floral designs in Islamic art. When the floral images are arranged in an intricate, interwoven geometric design, the result is known as an arabesque. Carpets, walls, and illustrated texts may all be decorated with arabesques.

Another distinctive feature of Islamic art is **calligraphy**, which is beautifully styled writing.

NEW YORK
CC Unit 2-E6a
Contributions to mathematics, science, medicine, art, architecture, and literature

HISTORY CLOSE-UP

Dome of the Rock

The Dome of the Rock is one of Islam's most revered sites. Built in Jerusalem on the holiest site in Judaism, where the First and Second Temples once stood, Muslims believe it is the spot from which Muhammad ascended to heaven to speak with Allah and receive instructions for Muslims.

Writing inside the dome commemorates Saladin, whose army won Jerusalem from European rulers in 1187.

Verses from the Qur'an are written in calligraphy on the mosque's outer walls.

Muslims believe that Muhammad ascended into heaven from this rock.

The interior walkway symbolizes the walk that pilgrims take around the Kaaba in Mecca.

Skills FOCUS INTERPRETING VISUALS

1. **Analyze** What is one feature of this building that is common to mosques?
2. **Draw Conclusions** What are some features of the Dome of the Rock that indicate it is considered a sacred building?

MUSLIM CIVILIZATION **273**

273

The artists who produced copies of the Qur'an sought perfection in their reproduction of the word of Allah. Over time, the artful representation of words became a central part of Islamic art. Calligraphy appears on the walls of mosques and adorns many household objects.

Architecture in the Muslim world also developed distinctive features. Although several forms and plans for building mosques developed, mosques have features in common. For example, **minarets**—tall towers from which the faithful are called to prayer—and domes are common features of mosques. Mosques from different parts of the empire or from different periods may show other influences, too, such as Persian or Turkish features.

Literature The most significant written work in Islam is the Qur'an itself. Its clear style and message have helped win millions of converts to the faith. In addition, the Qur'an influenced the later development of the Arabic language.

Nonreligious literature also has an important place in the Islamic world. One of the most popular works, *1001 Nights*, or the *Arabian Nights*, tells how a beautiful young woman named Shahrazad saved herself and other women from a murderous caliph. Each night she would withhold a story's ending until the next day. In this way, she postponed her execution so long that the caliph fell in love with her. The tales with which Shahrazad enchanted him make up *1001 Nights*. The stories were collected over time and include contributions from many Muslim countries. Even today, the stories appear in movies and other forms of popular culture.

Muslim poets produced works in several languages. One of them was Jalal ad-Din **Rumi**, whose Persian-language poems from the 1200s are still read and recited by many people. The following verse provides a glimpse of Rumi's appeal.

HISTORY'S VOICES

❝Lady, shall I tell thee where
Nature seems most blest and fair,
Far above all climes beside?—
'Tis where those we love abide:
And that little spot is best
Which the loved one's foot hath pressed.❞

—Rumi, *The Fairest Land,* c. 1250

Rumi was a Sufi mystic and founded a Sufi order whose members use music and dancing in their rituals. In the West, the order is known as the Whirling Dervishes.

Also writing in Persian was **Omar Khayyam**. His collection of four-line poems is called the *Rubaiyat*. The poems show a man pondering deep questions about God, life after death, and other serious topics. Unable to find answers, the poet celebrates simple pleasures.

READING CHECK **Identify Supporting Details** What are the some features that identify Islamic art?

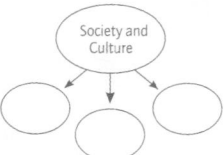

SECTION 3 ASSESSMENT

go.hrw.com
Online Quiz
Keyword: SHL ISW HP

Reviewing Key Terms and People

1. **a. Describe** How did the role of women change during the Abbasid caliphate?
   b. Evaluate Evaluate this statement: "The Qur'an and other Muslim scriptures deal strictly with religious topics." Explain your response.

2. **a. Recall** What were some contributions of Muslim scholars to astronomy?
   b. Explain What was the connection between Muslim scholars and the scholars of ancient Greece?

3. **a. Recall** What are **minarets**?
   b. Identify Cause and Effect Why was **calligraphy** a major means of artistic expression in the Muslim world?
   c. Evaluate **Omar Khayyam** is a popular poet in the West as well as in the Islamic world. Why do you think this is so?

Critical Thinking

4. **Identify Supporting Details** Use your notes and the graphic organizer to record details of Islamic society and culture.

Society and Culture

FOCUS ON SPEAKING

5. **Exposition** Write and deliver a brief speech in which you summarize the major achievements of Muslim scientists and scholars.

274 CHAPTER 9

Section 3 Assessment Answers

1. **a.** they lost status—were confined to harems, covered hair, and sometimes wore veils
   b. untrue—also defines family roles, sets rules for behavior, treatment of slaves, trade relations

2. **a.** discovered stars; predicted movements of heavenly bodies; created accurate calendar; perfected the astrolabe
   b. Many ancient Greek works were translated into Arabic and studied, which stimulated further study.

3. **a.** distinctive towers on mosques from which faithful are called to prayer
   b. artists copying the Qur'an sought perfection in reproducing the word of Allah; developed into its own art form
   c. possible answer—The questions Khayyam explored are universal.

4. society—defined family roles, people treated fairly, rules for trading relationships; scholarship—encouraged by faith, influenced by foreign civilizations, influenced European scholars, explored astronomy, mathematics, philosophy, history; arts—influenced by faith, used floral and geometric designs, calligraphy, distinctive architecture, literature

5. Student speeches should include examples and details from the section.

Decorative Arts

Islamic Calligraphy

What is it? Calligraphy is beautiful, artistic writing. Ever since the Qur'an was written down, the act of writing has played an important role in Islamic tradition. This importance is illustrated in an Arabic proverb that says "Purity of writing is purity of the soul." In fact, transcribing the Qur'an is considered a sacred act.

Why did it develop? Islamic teachings prohibit showing statues or pictures of anything that has a soul in religious contexts. Words and plants, however, may be shown. As a result, Muslim artists and artisans have lavished great care on calligraphy, often combined with plant forms. A primary use of calligraphy is transcribing sacred works of Islam. Calligraphy is also applied to buildings, pottery, textiles, and metalwork throughout the Islamic world.

Why is it important? Islamic calligraphy adds rich beauty wherever it appears. For Muslims, the use of calligraphy is also an expression of faith.

This panel on a mosque in Shiraz, Iran, displays a script called *kufic*, which is more squared off than the flowing cursive style. Kufic script is well suited to tilework.

▲ **A calligraphic tile panel in Iran**

▲ **A calligrapher in Medina writes out the Qur'an.**

These examples of calligraphy adorn the walls of Topkapi Palace in Istanbul, Turkey.

NEW YORK STANDARDS

PI 4.2 Students interpret and analyze documents and artifacts related to significant developments and events in world history.

Skills FOCUS INTERPRETING VISUALS

1. **Explain** What is the connection between the use of calligraphy and a basic Islamic belief?
2. **Draw Conclusions** Why do you think calligraphers developed the kufic style?

MUSLIM CIVILIZATION **275**

The Arts Around the World

Info to Know

Calligraphy Styles Some have called Islamic calligraphy "spiritual geometry produced with material tools." Since it acts both as decoration and as a carrier of ideas, it developed into a wide range of styles. Kufic, the earliest style, developed in 641. Because its lines are thick and bold, it is well suited to stone or metalwork, and was used to decorate mosque walls and coins. Thuluth, the most ornamental style, reached its height in the 800s. The form requires one third of each letter to slope. It is used for headings, princely titles, and engraved inscriptions. Nashki, a cursive form, became popular in the 900s, and was used by most educated Muslims. Nasta'liq script is so light and flowing that a story is told that its Persian designer was influenced by dreaming of the flight of geese. It was used in the 1400s–1600s mainly to copy literary works. There are still forms of Islamic calligraphy styles that exist today.

Activity Calligraphy Set up an area where you can allow students to experiment with calligraphy. Provide white paper, small paint brushes, and black ink or paint. Display samples of various calligraphic styles. Allow a few students at a time to try their hand at making the proper brushstrokes. As an extension, have students write a letter to a friend using calligraphy. You might want to ask art teachers if they can lend out a few calligraphy pens. **LS Visual-Spatial**

Alternative Assessment Handbook, Rubric 25: Personal Letters

Skills Focus: Comparing and Contrasting

At Level

Prep Required

Reading Skill
Analysis of Religious Decoration

1. Before class, find and make copies of illuminated manuscripts from Early European Bibles. Tell students that in many cultures, people enhance religious texts with decoration.

2. Distribute the copies of illuminated manuscript pages to each student. Have volunteers explain the purposes of illumination and calligraphy. Then have volunteers offer comparisons between the styles of the two. Create a class compare-and-contrast chart for all to see.

3. Have students use the information from the class chart to write an essay comparing and contrasting the use of decoration in religious works. **LS Verbal-Linguistic**

Alternative Assessment Handbook, Rubrics 9: Comparing and Contrasting; 37: Writing Assignments

Answers

Interpreting Visuals 1. *Islamic teachings prohibit depicting humans and animals in art, so calligraphy emerged as a form of art.* **2.** *Kufic was better suited to tilework than calligraphy was.*

Document-Based Investigation

Navigation and the Hajj

Word Help

Document-Based Investigation

Navigation and the Hajj

Word Help

retribution reward or punishment

traversed crossed

Activity Cultural Diffusion Have volunteers name the three ways that Islamic culture diffused as the civilization spread. *conquest, trade, and military activity* Write these answers with space below each for students to see. Have students copy the words and write examples of each method from this chapter. When students have had time to finish their work, discuss each method of cultural diffusion with the class, while students supplement or correct their entries. *possible answers—Conquest: Umayyad and Abbasid conquests from Persia to western Africa and Spain, and later caliphs' conquests into Southeast Asia, taxation of non-Muslims; Trade: trade routes passed through Mecca, trade in Baghdad during the reign of the Abbasid caliphs; Missionary Activity: Muhammad's teachings, his followers' move to Medina, the move of the capital to Damascus under the Abbasids, the influence of the Muslim Caliphs*

LS Verbal-Linguistic

Alternative Assessment Handbook, Rubric 11: Discussions

Teaching Tip

Explain to students the difference between the hegira, or hijra (Muhammad's journey to Medina) and the hajj (every Muslim's pilgrimage to Mecca once during their lifetime). Remind them that Mecca was the birthplace of Muhammad, and that it is the holiest city of Islam.

NEW YORK STANDARDS

PI 1.3 Students analyze historic events from around the world by examining accounts written from different perspectives.

Historical Context The four documents below describe the pilgrimage to Mecca, known as the hajj.

Task Study the selections and answer the questions that follow. After you have studied all the documents, you will be asked to write an essay about the hajj and the development of navigation in the Muslim world. You will need to use evidence from these selections and from the chapter.

DOCUMENT 1

The Importance of the Hajj

Muslims who are physically and financially able to do so are required at some point in their lives to travel to the city of Mecca in a pilgrimage known as the hajj. This passage from the Qur'an (Sura 2: 196) describes the importance of the pilgrimage.

> Fulfil the Pilgrimage and the Visitation unto God; but if you are prevented, then such offering as may be feasible. And shave not your heads, till the offering reaches its place of sacrifice. If any of you is sick, or injured in his head, then redemption by fast, or freewill offering, or ritual sacrifice. When you are secure, then whosoever enjoys the Visitation until the Pilgrimage, let his offering be such as may be feasible; or if he finds none, then a fast of three days in the Pilgrimage, and of seven when you return, that is ten completely; that is for him whose family are not present at the Holy Mosque. And fear God, and know that God is terrible in retribution.

DOCUMENT 2

The Journey to Mecca

Nasir Khusraw was a Persian scholar and poet who, from 1045 to 1052, traveled throughout the Muslim world. In this passage from his writings about his travels, Khusraw describes the route to Mecca.

> Whoever wants to go to Mecca from Egypt must go east. From Qulzum [modern-day Suez] there are two ways, one by land and one by sea. The land route can be traversed in fifteen days but it is all desert and three hundred parasangs long [about 1,050 miles]. Most of the caravans from Egypt take that way. By sea it takes twenty days to reach al-Jar, a small town in the Hijaz on the sea. From al-Jar to Medina it takes three days. From Medina to Mecca it is one hundred parasangs [about 350 miles].

Differentiating Instruction

Below Level

Learners Having Difficulty

Prep Required

1. Remind students that all Muslims who are physically and financially able are required to make the pilgrimage to Mecca at least once in their lifetime.

2. Have students refer to the Geography Starting Points map in this chapter and locate Mecca on the map. Tell students that the authors of Documents 2, 3, and 4 traveled to Mecca from Spain and Egypt. Have students identify which land and bodies of water these travelers would have had to cross. What navigational and geographic obstacles might travelers from Spain and Egypt have encountered?

3. Have a volunteer read Documents 2 and 3 aloud. Use the Word Help in the margin to clarify difficult words.

4. Have students write a paragraph from the point of view of a traveler making the hajj from Spain or Egypt. **LS** Visual-Spatial, Verbal-Linguistic

Alternative Assessment Handbook, Rubric 37: Writing Assignments

DOCUMENT 3

Traveling by Land

Ibn Jubayr was a Spanish Muslim traveler who wrote about his pilgrimage to Mecca, which began in 1183. In this passage Jubayr describes a large group of Iraqi pilgrims at Mecca.

The vast plain (at Khulays) was filled with [people], and the flat immensity of the desert was too narrow to encompass them. You could imagine the earth attempting to maintain its balance under the crowd's heaving and waves streaming from the force of its currents; you could picture in this crowd a sea swollen with waves, whose waters were the mirages and whose ships were the camels, their sails the lofty litters and round tents ... Who has not seen with his own eyes this Iraqi caravan has not experienced one of the genuine marvels of the world ...

This caravan travels at night to the light of torches, which people on foot carry in their hands, and you will not see one litter which is not preceded by a torch. Thus people travel as it were among wandering stars which illuminate the depth of the darkness and which enable the earth to compete in brightness with the stars of heaven.

DOCUMENT 4

Traveling by Sea

Here Ibn Jubayr describes his journey by ship across the Red Sea from Egypt to Arabia.

The ships that ply the Red Sea from Aydhab to Jidda are sewn together without a single nail. They are bound by cord made from coconut fiber, which the builders pound until it takes the form of thread ... The ships are caulked with palm-tree shavings, and when the construction is finished, they smear it with grease, castor oil, or shark oil, the last of which is best ...

Lightning bolts flashed off the mountains in the east and a rising storm darkened the skies, covering everything. The tempest raged, driving the ship off course and, finally, backward. The wind's fury continued. The darkness grew thick and filled the air so that we couldn't stay our course. Finally, a few stars reappeared to guide us ... In the morning God brought us relief. The wind fell, the clouds broke up, the sky grew clear ...

The entry [into Jidda's port] was made difficult by the presence of many reefs and winding shallows. We admired the dexterity with which these pilgrim captains and the sailors handled their ships among the reefs.

Skills FOCUS — READING LIKE A HISTORIAN

DOCUMENT 1
a. Identify Main Ideas What does the Qur'an require all Muslims to do once in their lifetimes?
b. Explain If a Muslim cannot make the pilgrimage to Mecca, what must he or she do??

DOCUMENT 2
a. Recall According to Khusraw, how many days did it take to travel to al-Jar from Egypt by sea?
b. Draw Conclusions What challenges might face pilgrims traveling to Mecca from Egypt by land, given that the land route crossed a desert?

DOCUMENT 3
a. Recall How does Ibn Jubayr describe the Iraqi pilgrims?
b. Analyze Why might it be difficult for so large a group of pilgrims to travel long distances across the desert at night?

What does this suggest about their navigation skills?

DOCUMENT 4
a. Describe How does Ibn Jubayr describe the ships?
b. Draw Conclusions What does Ibn Jubayr's description of the storm and voyage suggest about the sailors' skills?

DOCUMENT-BASED ESSAY QUESTION

Navigation and sailing were vital skills in the Muslim world. How might the requirements of the hajj have helped to develop those skills? Using the documents above and the chapter, form a thesis that explains your position. Then write a short essay to support your position.

See **Skills Handbook**, p. H25, H26

Skills Focus: Comparing and Contrasting

At Level

Reading Skill
Islamic Scholarship

1. Have students reread Documents 3 and 4. Draw a four-column chart for all to see. Have students name difficulties of land travel, and how the pilgrims overcame those difficulties. List student responses in columns 1 and 2. Then have students name difficulties of sea travel, and how the pilgrims overcame those difficulties. List student responses in columns 3 and 4.

2. Have students review the chart and guide them in a class discussion. Which mode of travel seems to have been more difficult? What inventions might have helped the pilgrims find their way to Mecca?

3. As homework, have students write a letter from the point of view of a Muslim traveler in the 1100s. Student letters should describe the journey to Mecca and the difficulties faced along the route. **LS Verbal-Linguistic**

Alternative Assessment Handbook, Rubric 25: Personal Letters

Document-Based Investigation

Word Help

immensity having large size or scale
litter type of covered seat with shafts used to carry a passenger
dexterity physical skill or grace

Primary Source

In 1853 the British explorer Sir Richard Francis Burton traveled in disguise to Mecca to learn about the city and its pilgrims. In his account, he wrote: "In the center of the square area rises the far-famed Kabah, the funereal shade of which contrasts vividly with the sunlit walls and precipices of the town. It is a cubical structure of massive stone, the upper two-thirds of which are mantled by a black cloth embroidered with silver, and the lower portion hung with white linen. At a distance of several yards it is surrounded by a balustrade provided with lamps, which are lighted in the evening, and the space thus enclosed is the circuit ground along which, day and night, crowds of pilgrims, performing the circular ceremony of Tawaf, realize the idea of perpetual motion."
—Sir Richard Burton, 1853

Answers

Reading Like a Historian
Document 1 a. *travel to the city of Mecca in a pilgrimage known as the hajj;* **b.** *make some other offering or sacrifice, such as fasting;* **Document 2 a.** *twenty days;* **b.** *possible answer—harsh climate; lack of water;* **Document 3 a.** *large, looks like an ocean with currents and waves; at night, people carry torches, which look like stars;* **b.** *possible answer—The only light at night would be from the torches they carried; navigation skills were limited;* **Document 4 a.** *They are bound together, caulked with palm-tree shavings, and smeared with some kind of oil.* **b.** *suggests only skilled sailors could make the sea voyage successfully;* **Essay** *Student essays should include details about the difficulty of the voyage and should list certain inventions, such as the astrolabe, that made the hajj possible.*

Visual Summary

Review and Inquiry Organize students into twelve groups. Assign each group one sentence from the Visual Study Guide. Have students write a paragraph expanding on the sentence they have been assigned. Have a volunteer from each group read the group's paragraph to the class.

Quick Facts Transparency: Visual Study Guide: Muslim Civilization

Review Key Terms and People

1. Muslims
2. astrolabe
3. Sufis
4. minarets
5. the hegira, or hijra
6. caliph
7. Abbasids
8. Abu Bakr
9. Omar Khayyam
10. Ibn Khaldun
11. kufic
12. mosque
13. Ibn Sina
14. bedouins

Comprehension and Critical Thinking

15. **a.** Mecca; a merchant and trader
    b. He and his followers were not safe in Mecca.
    c. possible answer—untrue, the Five Pillars of Islam describe very basic acts.

16. **a.** Muslims disputed who should succeed Muhammad.
    b. Their deaths deepened the split between Sunnis and Shia.
    c. possible answer—it was prosperous, emphasized scholarship, expanded trade, spread Islam widely.

VISUAL STUDY GUIDE

Five Pillars of Islam

1	2	3	4	5
State the profession of faith.	Pray five times a day while facing Mecca.	Give alms to the poor and other needy people.	Fast from dawn to dusk during Ramadan.	Go on a pilgrimage, or hajj, to Mecca.

The Spread of Islam

Muhammad reports revelations from Allah, attracts followers, and gains influence in Arabia.

⬇

After Muhammad's death, conflict surrounds the succession, leading to the Sunni-Shia split.

⬇

The Umayyad dynasty expands territory and strengthens the caliphate's central government.

⬇

The Abbasid dynasty stimulates trade, scholarship, and the arts, but ends with disunity and invasion.

Islamic Civilization

Society
Islamic texts influenced the structure of the family, the treatment of women and slaves, and trade.

Scholarship
Muslim scholars helped preserve ancient Greek texts and made original contributions to astronomy, mathematics, medicine, geography, history, and other fields.

Arts
Muslim art developed distinctive features, including calligraphy. The works of poets and other writers are still read today.

Review Key Terms and People

Identify the correct term or person from the chapter that best fits each of the following descriptions.

1. persons who follow Islam
2. instrument used to navigate at sea
3. group that seeks a mystical religious experience
4. tall towers from which the faithful are called to prayer
5. Muhammad's journey from Mecca to Medina
6. term that means "successor"
7. dynasty that defeated the Umayyads
8. the first caliph
9. poet whose poems were collected into the *Rubaiyat*
10. historian who warned later historians against bias and praising rulers in their works in order to gain favor
11. beautifully styled writing often applied to buildings, pottery, textiles, and metalwork
12. a building for Muslim worship
13. medical scholar who was also known as Avicenna
14. nomadic Arab peoples

---

17. **a.** Slaves should be treated fairly; freeing slaves is praised as a religious act.
    b. translated numerous texts written by Greeks into Arabic, which preserved them; these were later translated into Latin, helped promote European scholarship
    c. helped determine the phases of the moon for planning religious festivals; determined direction of Mecca so that Muslims could pray facing Mecca

Reading Skills

18. Women had vital roles in early Muslim civilization, but later lost status.

19. details about women being among the first converts; women influencing battles and politics; details about harems, hair covering, and veils

Interpreting Literature as a Source

20. Muhammad
21. enjoy life and the physical world
22. possible answer—probably would have disagreed with Khayyam's message

History's Impact video program
Review the video to answer the closing question:
What impact has Islam had on the world?

Comprehension and Critical Thinking

SECTION 1 *(pp. 257–261)*

15. a. Recall Where was Muhammad born, and what was his occupation as a young man?

b. Explain Why did Muhammad relocate from Mecca to Medina?

c. Evaluate Evaluate this statement: "The Five Pillars of Islam are very complicated and require years of study to determine their meaning."

SECTION 2 *(pp. 262–267)*

16. a. Describe What happened to the Muslim community following Muhammad's death?

b. Explain What roles did Ali and Husayn play in the split between the Sunni and the Shia?

c. Elaborate Why might a historian say that the Abbasid dynasty had a major impact on Islam as a world religion?

SECTION 3 *(pp. 270–274)*

17. a. Identify What do Islamic texts say about slavery?

b. Explain How did scholarship in the Muslim world affect Europe?

c. Develop What was the connection between Muslim expertise in astronomy and the requirements of the Islamic faith?

Reading Skills

Identifying Implied Main Ideas *Read the passage below from this chapter. Then answer the questions that follow.*

❝Women played vital roles in the early Muslim community. Khadijah and several other women were among the first converts. Some of these women even went into battle. They also influenced political decisions. Women lost status during the Abbasid dynasty, however. Women of the Abbasid court were confined to a secluded part of the palace called the harem. Covering the hair and sometimes wearing a veil also became common during Abbasid rule. ❞

18. What is the implied main idea of the paragraph?

19. What details help you find the implied main idea?

Interpreting Literature as a Source

Reading Like a Historian

The excerpt is from the Rubaiyat *by Omar Khayyam, who lived from about 1048 to 1131. Khayyam was both a poet and a scholar familiar with medicine, astronomy, and mathematics.*

❝Some for the Glories of This World; and some
Sigh for the Prophet's Paradise to come;
  Ah, take the Cash, and let the Credit go,
Nor heed the rumble of a distant Drum! ❞

—Omar Khayyam, *The Rubaiyat*

20. Infer In the second line, to whom does "the Prophet" refer?

21. Analyze What do you think Khayyam is recommending to the reader?

22. Develop The region where Khayyam lived was under the austere rule of the Seljuk Turks. How do you think the Seljuk Turks would have viewed Omar Khayyam's poem?

Using the Internet

go.hrw.com
Practice Online
Keyword: SHL ISW

23. Under Umayyad rule, Spain reached a golden age of both Muslim and Jewish culture. Advances in many fields, especially agriculture and architecture, were made, and Córdoba became one of the richest and grandest cities in Europe. Using the keyword above, do research to explore Muslim Spain. Then create a brochure that describes the main achievements of the era.

WRITING ABOUT HISTORY

Description: Writing a Comparison *In the Islamic world, architecture developed distinctive features. Many beautiful mosques from the early years of the caliphate still stand.*

24. Assignment: In an essay, compare the architecture of traditional mosques with the architecture of houses of worship that you have already studied, such as Egyptian, Greek, or Roman temples. To provide support for your comparison, use information from this chapter, previous chapters, and other research as needed. Use specific examples to describe ways that the buildings are similar and different.

Answers

Using the Internet

23. Go to the HRW Web site and enter the keyword shown to access a rubric for this activity.

KEYWORD: SHL ISW

Writing About History

24. Student essays should recognize the distinctive features of mosques, including minarets and domes. Essays should also compare and contrast the architecture of traditional mosques with that of Egyptian, Greek, or Roman temples, using details from previous chapters.

A rubric for this activity is provided in **CRF**: Writing about history

HOLT

History's Impact

▶ **Video Program: Muslim Civilization**
See the Video Program Teacher's Guide for the answer to the closing question.

Review and Assessment Resources

Review and Reinforce

 CRF: Chapter Review

 Quick Facts Transparency: Visual Study Guide: Muslim Civilization

 **Spanish Chapter Summaries Audio CD Program**

OSP **Holt PuzzlePro**: Quiz Show for ExamView

Quiz Game CD-ROM

Assess

PASS: Chapter Test, Forms A and B

Alternative Assessment Handbook

OSP **ExamView Test Generator**, Chapter Test

Differentiated Instruction Modified Worksheets and Tests CD-ROM: Chapter Test

HOAP **Holt Online Assessment Program** (in the Premier Online Edition)

Reteach/Intervene

Interactive Reader and Study Guide

Differentiated Instruction Teacher Management System: Lesson Plans for Differentiated Instruction

Differentiated Instruction Modified Worksheets and Tests CD-ROM: Chapter Test

Interactive Skills Tutor CD-ROM

go.hrw.com
Online Resources
KEYWORD: SHL ISW

Chapter 10 Planning Guide

African Kingdoms

Chapter Overview	Reproducible Resources	Technology Resources
CHAPTER 10 pp. 280–305 **Overview:** In this chapter, students will learn how the early societies of Africa grew into trading kingdoms and empires with strong leaders, religion and culture. **KI 1, 3; PI 1.4, 3.1, 3.2** See pp. T32–T55 for a detailed correlation to the New York State Core Curriculum for Global History and Geography and the New York Learning Standards.	**Differentiated Instruction Teacher Management System:*** • Instructional Benchmarking Guides • Lesson Plans for Differentiated Instruction **Interactive Reader and Study Guide:** Chapter Summary* **Chapter Resource File*** • Writing for the SAT • Social Studies Skill • Interdisciplinary Project • Chapter Review **World History Outline Maps**	OSP **New York One-Stop Planner CD-ROM:** Calendar Planner **Live Ink© Online Reading Help** **Student Edition on Audio CD Program** **Differentiated Instruction Modified Worksheets and Tests CD-ROM** **Interactive Skills Tutor CD-ROM** **World History Primary Source Library CD-ROM** **Power Presentations with Video CD-ROM** **History's Impact: World History Video Program (VHS/DVD):** African Kingdoms
Section 1: **Early Civilizations in Africa** **The Main Idea:** Africa's earliest people adapted to a wide range of geographic conditions to establish societies based on family ties, religion, iron technology, and trade. **PI 3.1**	**Differentiated Instruction Teacher Management System:** Section 1 Lesson Plan* **Interactive Reader and Study Guide:** Section 1 Summary* **Chapter Resource File*** • Vocabulary Builder: Section 1 • Biography: Salif Keita • History and Geography: Early Farming in Africa	**Regents Review Transparency:** Section 1* **Map Transparency:** Environments of Africa* **Map Transparency:** Bantu Migrations* **Internet Activity:** Congo Basin
Section 2: **Trading States of East Africa** **The Main Idea:** The growth of trade led to the development of wealthy kingdoms and city-states in East Africa. **PI 3.1**	**Differentiated Instruction Teacher Management System:** Section 2 Lesson Plan* **Interactive Reader and Study Guide:** Section 2 Summary* **Chapter Resource File*** • Vocabulary Builder: Section 2 • Biography: Queen of Sheba • Primary Source: Stela Inscription of King Ezana of Aksum	**Regents Review Transparency:** Section 2* **Map Transparency: Aksum and Ethiopia*** **Internet Activity:** African Languages
Section 3: **Kingdoms of West Africa** **The Main Idea:** An advanced civilization developed along the Nile south of Egypt in a region called Nubia. **PI 1.4, 3.2**	**Differentiated Instruction Teacher Management System:** Section 3 Lesson Plan* **Interactive Reader and Study Guide:** Section 3 Summary* **Chapter Resource File*** • Vocabulary Builder: Section 3 • Biography: Queen Amina • Literature: Sundiata: *An Epic of Old Mali*	**Regents Review Transparency:** Section 3* **Map Transparency:** West African Kingdoms*  **Quick Facts Transparency:** Trading Kingdoms of West Africa*

go.hrw.com go.hrw.com	Print Resource	Transparency	
LS Learning Styles	Audio CD	CD-ROM	
Video	SE Student Edition	TE Teacher's Edition	
OSP One-Stop Planner CD-ROM	NY Standards Mastery		

*also on One-Stop Planner CD-ROM

HOLT

History's Impact
World History Video Program (VHS/DVD)
African Kingdoms

Review, Assessment, Intervention

- **Global History and Geography Regents Test Prep Workbook**
- **Quick Facts Transparency:** African Kingdoms
- **Spanish Chapter Summaries Audio CD Program**
- **Program Assessment Support System (PASS):** Chapter Test*
- **Differentiated Instruction Modified Worksheets and Tests CD-ROM:** Modified Chapter Test
- OSP **New York One-Stop Planner CD-ROM:** Exam View Test Generator (English/Spanish)
- HOAP **Holt Online Assessment Program (HOAP),** in the Premier Online Edition

---

- **PASS:** Section 1 Quiz*
- **Online Quiz:** Section 1
- **Alternative Assessment Handbook**

- **PASS:** Section 2 Quiz*
- **Online Quiz:** Section 2
- **Alternative Assessment Handbook**

- **PASS:** Section 3 Quiz*
- **Online Quiz:** Section 3
- **Alternative Assessment Handbook**

Power Presentation with Video CD-ROM

Power Presentations with Video are visual presentations of each chapter's main ideas. Presentations can be customized by including Quick Facts charts, images and maps from the textbook, and video clips.

Holt Online Learning

go.hrw.com
Teacher Resources
KEYWORD: SHL TEACHER

go.hrw.com
Student Resources
KEYWORD: SHL AFK

- Document-Based Questions
- Interactive Multimedia Activities

- Current Events
- Chapter-Based Internet Activities
- and more!

Holt Premier
Online Student Edition
Complete online support for interactivity, assessment, and reporting
- Interactive Maps and Notebook
- Homework Practice and Research Activities Online

CHAPTER 10 PLANNING GUIDE

The Big Picture

Susan Ramírez

Ecological Change Environmental change affected African societies in important ways. The desiccation of the Sahara forced pastoralists to migrate in search of greener pastures and some of them to settle down and farm. Environmental degradation was also a factor in Aksum's decline. Iron tools allowed Aksum's farmers to cut down trees, enabling rain to erode the soil. As a consequence, food production fell below subsistence levels.

Long-distance Commerce Trade is an important factor in the history of the ancient kingdoms of both East and West Africa. Sea-faring merchants from Greece, India, and Southeast Asia landed on the East coast to exchange pottery, silk, cotton cloth, and wheat for ivory, gold, coconut oil, slaves, and other products. Traders also introduced food crops, like rice and bananas. In the West, Muslim traders crossed the Sahara to exchange salt for gold. The rulers of Ghana, Mali, and Songhai controlled and taxed this trade to fund their governments. Songhai, under strong rulers, proved the most successful in using tax revenue to centralize power and extending its authority farther than either of its predecessors.

Spread of Islam Traditionally, Africans worshipped their ancestors and believed in animism. As Africa's riches became known to the outside world, contact with Muslim traders led to conversions, especially among the ruling elites. Following Muslim teachings to be generous and to make a pilgrimage to Mecca once in a lifetime, rulers like Mansa Musa of Mali and Askia Muhammad of Songhai distributed gifts of gold along their routes, further stimulating the currents of trade. Such trips also attracted scholars turning cities like Timbuktu into major centers of learning and culture.

Recent Scholarship

For an excellent example of African oral history (in translation), as told by a griot, read *Sundiata, An Epic of Old Mali* by D.T. Niane. It is the story of Sundiata, the son of Sogolon, the hunchback princess, and Maghan, a handsome king, who as an adult fulfilled the soothsayers prophesies of uniting West African kingdoms into a powerful empire, which at the height of its power stretched from the Atlantic Ocean, across the savanna grasslands, to the city of Timbuktu. This short book is suitable reading for students and touches on the importance of family and age sets, ancestor worship, agriculture, iron work, trade, and government.

Differentiating Instruction

 Differentiated Instruction Teacher Management System
- Pacing Guide
- Lesson Plans for Differentiated Instruction

 Interactive Reader and Study Guide

Spanish Chapter Summaries Audio CD Program

Student Edition on Audio CD Program

Differentiated Instruction Modified Worksheets and Tests CD-ROM
- Vocabulary Flash Cards
- Modified Vocabulary Builder Activities
- Modified Chapter Review Activity
- Modified Chapter Test

OSP One-Stop Planner CD-ROM
- ExamView Test Generator (English/Spanish)
- PuzzlePro
- Quiz Show for ExamView
- Transparencies and Videos

TE Differentiated Activities in the Teacher's Edition
- Diseases of Africa, p. 285
- Trade in Africa, p. 289
- Life in Great Zimbabwe, p. 291
- Trading in Ghana, p. 297
- Cultural Blending in Africa, p. 303

Reading Like a Historian

Sam Wineburg

In any new situation, our assumptions, expectations, and beliefs filter what we see and shape the impressions that we form. It is important to remember this when reading the Ibn Battuta's fascinating *Rihla* (or *Travels*), the account of this 14th century Muslim traveler and his journey across 73,000 miles, stretching from his native Tangier to Sub-Saharan Africa, along Africa's eastern coast to Madagascar, to India and Sri Lanka, and by some accounts reaching as far as China. A member of the Muslim nobility, literate, cultured, possessing an intrepid spirit and a boundless curiosity, Ibn Battuta set down his impressions once he returned to his native Morocco with the help of his ghost writer, Ibn Juzayy.

Adventures in Mali Ibn Battuta's last journey, an eight-month sojourn in the kingdom of Mali and its capital Timbuktu, constitutes a remarkable historical source. According to Ross Dunn, author of *The Adventures of Ibn Battuta: A Muslim Traveler of the 14th Century*, the Mali accounts are priceless to historians because "we have no other surviving eyewitness accounts from the fourteenth-century . . . of the Empire of Mali which covered a huge part of the grasslands of West Africa. He is really the only eyewitness observer of Mali . . . at its imperial zenith."

Ibn Battuta's overall impressions of what he saw during his stay were mixed. As a devout Muslim, he was impressed with the piety he witnessed and notes with approval the Malians' "assiduity in prayer and their persistence in performing it in congregation." Likewise, he looked positively on the "zeal" this society showed in committing the Koran to memory. He describes an educational aid that modern readers, particularly your students, might find less attractive. To help the young learn the Koran, adults "put their children in chains if they show any backwardness in memorizing it, and they are not set free until they have it by heart."

Putting Perception in Its Place As we analyze Ibn Battuta's descriptions, we must recognize that he is not merely reporting what he sees, but coding it—right/wrong, pious/unholy, correct/deviant—according to the Islam of his homeland. To him, the world was split into two halves: Dar-al-Islam, the domain of Islamic rule, an immense swath of territory that today comprises 40 countries and which in the 14th century provided a web of security and unity, and everything beyond its pale—the territories of the non-believers.

Reserved for special scorn in Muslim Mali were practices that Ibn Battuta associated with non-Muslims, such as the eating of carrion or animals—like dog—forbidden by the Koran. However, what disturbed him most was this society's perceived immodesty compared to the Islamic practices he knew best:

"One of their disapproved acts," he wrote, "is that their female servants and slave girls and little girls appear before men naked, with their privy parts uncovered. During Ramadan I saw many of them in this state, for it is the custom of the *farariyya* to break their fast in the house of the sultan, and each one brings his food carried by twenty or more of his slave girls, they all being naked. Another is that their women go into the sultan's presence naked and uncovered, and that his daughters go naked. On the night of 25 Ramadan I saw about two hundred slave girls bringing out food from his palace naked, having with them two of his daughters with rounded breasts having no covering upon them."

Travel logs such as Ibn Battuta's are invaluable historical documents but they by no means offer a transparent window on the past. There is no such thing as 'immaculate perception' and, in this sense, we are no different from Ibn Battuta.

Chapter Main Ideas

Section 1 Africa's earliest people adapted to a wide range of geographic conditions to establish societies based on family ties, religion, iron technology, and trade.

Section 2 The growth of trade led to the development of wealthy kingdoms and city-states in East Africa.

Section 3 The expansion of trade across the Sahara led to the development of great empires and other states in West Africa.

📖 New York Standards

Key Idea 1 The study of world history requires an understanding of world cultures and civilizations, including an analysis of important ideas, social and cultural values, beliefs, and traditions. This study also examines the human condition and the connections and interactions of people across time and space and the ways different people view the same event or issue from a variety of perspectives.

Key Idea 3 Study of the major social, political, cultural, and religious developments in world history involves learning about the important roles and contributions of individuals and groups.

Key to Differentiating Instruction

Below Level

Basic-level activities designed for all students encountering new material

At Level

Intermediate-level activities designed for average students

Above Level

Challenging activities designed for honors and gifted and talented students

Standard English Mastery

Activities designed to improve standard English usage

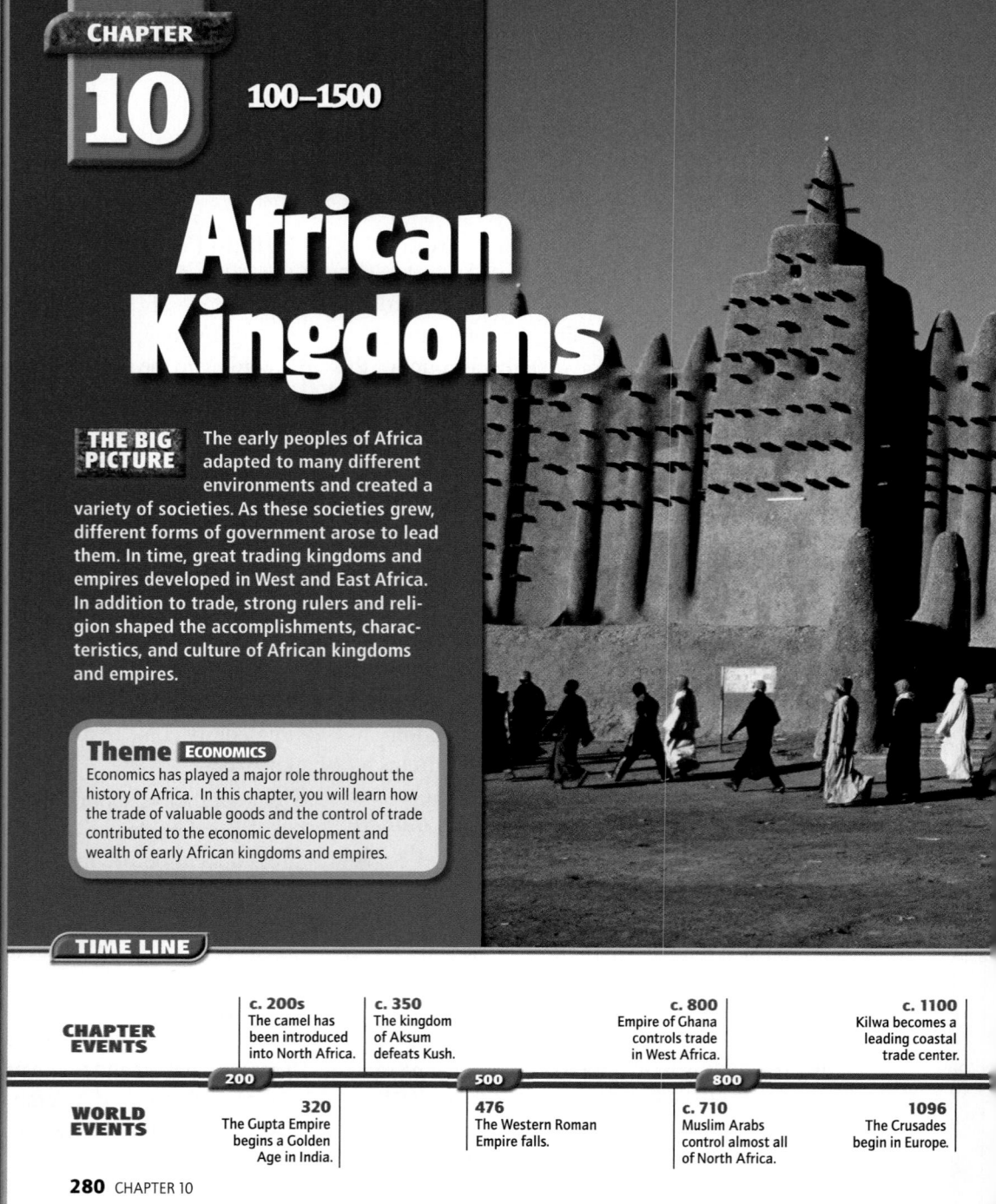

CHAPTER

10 100–1500

African Kingdoms

THE BIG PICTURE The early peoples of Africa adapted to many different environments and created a variety of societies. As these societies grew, different forms of government arose to lead them. In time, great trading kingdoms and empires developed in West and East Africa. In addition to trade, strong rulers and religion shaped the accomplishments, characteristics, and culture of African kingdoms and empires.

Theme ECONOMICS
Economics has played a major role throughout the history of Africa. In this chapter, you will learn how the trade of valuable goods and the control of trade contributed to the economic development and wealth of early African kingdoms and empires.

TIME LINE

CHAPTER EVENTS	**c. 200s** The camel has been introduced into North Africa.	**c. 350** The kingdom of Aksum defeats Kush.	**c. 800** Empire of Ghana controls trade in West Africa.	**c. 1100** Kilwa becomes a leading coastal trade center.
	200	**500**	**800**	
WORLD EVENTS	**320** The Gupta Empire begins a Golden Age in India.	**476** The Western Roman Empire falls.	**c. 710** Muslim Arabs control almost all of North Africa.	**1096** The Crusades begin in Europe.

280 CHAPTER 10

Introduce the Chapter

At Level

African Kingdoms

Materials: construction paper

1. Remind students that Africa is a huge continent, home to a wide variety of climates and cultures, and that the histories of regions differ greatly.

2. Organize students into three groups. Assign each group a section from the chapter: Early Civilizations in Africa, Trading States of East Africa, and Kingdoms of West Africa.

3. Have members of each group scan their section and work together to write a summary of that section. Group summaries should be based on images, photographs, and maps, as well as the red and blue headings within the section.

4. Have a volunteer from each group read the group summary to the class. 🄻 **Interpersonal, Verbal-Linguistic**

📝 **Alternative Assessment Handbook**, Rubric 1: Acquiring Information

Reading like a Historian

This photo shows the Djenné Mosque, located in the city of Djenné in the West African nation of Mali. Founded in the 1200s, Djenné was a center of trade and Muslim learning. The Djenné Mosque blends imported Muslim styles with mud-building styles native to West Africa.

Analyzing Visuals Based on the image, what are some features of West African mud-building?

See **Skills Handbook**, p. H24

Explore the Time Line

c. 1230s	1324	1464
Empire of Mali controls trade in West Africa.	Mansa Musa begins a hajj to Mecca.	Sunni Ali becomes ruler of the Songhai Empire.

1200

1325	1453
Aztecs found the city of Tenochtitlán.	The Ottoman Empire conquers Constantinople.

AFRICAN KINGDOMS **281**

HOLT

History's Impact
▶ **Video Program: African Kingdoms**
See the Video Teacher's Guide for strategies for using the video segment.

Reading Like a Historian

Analyzing Visuals Have volunteers describe buildings or pictures of buildings that they have seen that have beams or logs protruding from the walls. Then have students suggest the function of the poles in the mud mosque from the Upper Volta pictured here. Tell students that in this Western African mosque the wooden poles appear to be decorative, but they are useful. After the rainy season every year, workers use the poles as ladders to climb each tower and apply a new mud finish.

go.hrw.com
Online Resources

Chapter Resources:
KEYWORD: SHL AFK
Teacher Resources:
KEYWORD: SHL TEACHER

Explore the Time Line

1. What major world event occurred in 476? *The Western Roman Empire fell.*

2. What event would have brought Islam to the African continent? *In about 750, Muslim Arabs controlled part of North Africa.*

3. During which century did Mansa Musa live? *14th century (1300s)*

4. When was the Songhai Empire established? *1464*

Info to Know

Marvelous Mud Many cultures in Africa use mud as the main material in building. While some peoples baked mud into longer-lasting bricks, other builders created granaries, houses, mosques, and other structures from wet mud. Mud allows a great deal of artistic expression. The builder can make any shape he desires, and add decoration in relief, too. In European architecture, the work of Antoní Gaudí has sculptural qualities similar to those of African mud buildings.

Explain Why is mud considered an expressive medium? *It allows the builder to make any shape he desires, and add decoration in relief, too.*

Answers

Reading Like a Historian *Buildings are very tall and include wooden scaffolding.*

281

Geography Starting Points

Environments of Africa

Activity Map Game Have students refer to a current map of Africa and the map on this page. Have students locate areas with these environments: desert, dry woodland, Mediterranean, savanna, and tropical rain forest. Organize the class into several teams. The first team to supply the name of a present-day African country lying mostly within the climate zone will get a point. Call out the name of a climate and start the game! You may also wish to have several students in charge of recording the country names. The class will be amazed at the number of African nations there are.

🗄 **Map Transparency**: Environments of Africa

📃 **World History Outline Maps**

✴ **Interactive Map**: Environments of Africa

GEOGRAPHY Starting Points

★Interactive ENVIRONMENTS OF AFRICA

Desert The vast Sahara covers most of North Africa. Travelers often travel in camel caravans to cross the desert, as shown above.

Rain Forest Africa's dense rain forests are home to people as well as to many plants and animals.

Savanna Much of Africa is savanna, open grasslands with scattered shrubs and trees.

Legend:
- Desert
- Dry woodland
- Mediterranean
- Savanna
- Tropical rain forest
- ● Iron working sites, c. AD 300
- ➤ Possible spread of iron working

Starting Points Africa, the world's second-largest continent, has a broad range of environments, from barren deserts to lush tropical rain forests. These environments played a role in shaping the many cultures that arose in early Africa. In addition, Africa has a wealth of mineral resources, such as iron ore, which some Africans were forging into iron by 400 BC.

1. **Analyze** In what vegetation zone was Benin City located? How do you think that location affected life there?

2. **Predict** Iron working slowly spread from North Africa throughout the rest of the continent. Based on the map, how do you think the knowledge of iron working might have spread throughout Africa?

🔊 **Listen to History**

Go online to listen to an explanation of the starting points for this chapter.

go.hrw.com
Keyword: SHL AFK

282 CHAPTER 10

Skills Focus: Analyzing Maps

At Level

Social Studies Skill

Africa's Climates

Research Required

1. Remind students that the African continent is enormous and varied.

2. Organize students into small groups. Assign each group one of the climates depicted on the map in the Geography Starting Points feature. Have each group use reliable print and online sources to research the flora, fauna, and landforms that characterize such areas. Have students record the information they find using descriptive, vivid terms.

3. Have each group create a photomontage for the climate the group was assigned. Have groups write their climate name prominently and add captions to help others learn from their work.

4. When students are ready, have each group display and present its work to the class.
   🖥 **Interpersonal, Visual-Spatial**

📃 **Alternative Assessment Handbook**, Rubrics 3: Artwork; and 30: Research

Answers

Geography Starting Points

1. *tropical rain forest; possible answer—helped the development of agriculture;* **2.** *possible answer— through trade or migration*

Early Civilizations in Africa

BEFORE YOU READ

MAIN IDEA

Africa's earliest people adapted to a wide range of geographic conditions to establish societies based on family ties, religion, iron technology, and trade.

READING FOCUS

1. How does Africa's diverse geography shape life on the continent?

2. What cultural patterns did Africa's early societies share?

3. What major changes affected societies during Africa's Iron Age?

KEY TERMS

Sahel
savanna
griots
Nok
Bantu

NEW YORK

PI 3.1 Students analyze the roles and contributions of individuals and groups to social, political, economic, cultural, and religious practices and activities.

THE INSIDE STORY

Why might a storyteller be highly respected? "Listen to my word, you who want to know; by my mouth you will learn the history of Mali." A storyteller named Djeli Mamoudou Kouyaté began to relate the tale of the great warrior and king Sundiata, founder of the Mali Empire. "He was a lad full of strength; his arms had the strength of ten and his biceps inspired fear in his companions. He had already that authoritative way of speaking which belongs to those who are destined to command." Most early African civilizations did not develop a written language. Instead,

history was passed down orally by storytellers. Called griots, these storytellers memorized the tales of heroic kings and deeds and passed the information on from generation to generation. Because of their important role in passing on knowledge, griots were highly respected. The storyteller Kouyaté explained that "without us the names of kings would vanish into oblivion, we are the memory of mankind." Traditions such as storytelling were part of the cultural landscape of early Africa. ▪

Keeper of the MEMORIES

◄ A storyteller called a griot passes a legend on to the next generation in a village in Côte d'Ivoire in West Africa.

283

Teach the Main Idea

At Level

Early Civilizations in Africa

1. **Teach** Ask students the Reading Focus questions to teach this section.

2. **Apply** Have students list the three headings in this section on separate pieces of papers to use for taking notes: The Geography of Africa, Early African Societies, and Africa's Iron Age. Have students list several facts they already know about the topic under each heading and then add several things they want to learn about the topic.

3. **Review** Organize students into small groups and have them share what they already knew and what they want to learn about early Africa.

4. **Practice/Homework** Have each student write a brief statement about early civilizations in Africa. **LS Interpersonal, Verbal-Linguistic**

Alternative Assessment Handbook, Rubrics 9: Comparing and Contrasting; and 37: Writing Assignments

---

Preteach

Getting Started

Use the **Interactive Reader and Study Guide** to familiarize students with the section content.

Interactive Reader and Study Guide, Section 1

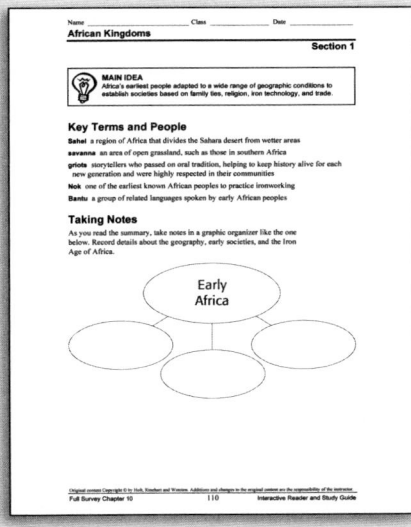

Academic Vocabulary

Review with students the high-use academic term in this section.

phase a period or stage within a longer process (p. 285)

CRF: Vocabulary Builder: Section 1

Taking Notes

three times the size of the United States, high and low plain, mountain ranges, Sahara, Congo, Zambezi, Niger rivers, Sahel, tropical savanna, tropical rainforests are near equator. Mediterranean climate is in far north and south; Early Societies—villages, extended families; age-sets, some beliefs based on animism; strong oral traditions; Iron Age—500 BC, iron used for farming; Nok practiced ironworking.

go.hrw.com
Online Resources

KEYWORD: SHL AFK
ACTIVITY: Congo Basin

Reading Focus

① How does Africa's diverse geography shape life on the continent? *Each region has a different climate and provides different resources for the people who live there. In each area, different cultures and ways of life developed.*

The Geography of Africa

Compare How large is Africa in comparison to the United States? *more than three times the size of the United States*

Make Inferences What sort of people might inhabit the Sahel? *possible answer—herders of hardy grazing animals*

Info to Know

Life in Mali The nation of Mali includes part of the inhospitable Sahara, a swath of the dry Sahel, and the remainder follows the course of the Niger River and its tributaries. In the Sahel, people live far apart so their animals can take advantage of the sparse vegetation. Farther south, there is more water, but infertile soil. Subsistence farmers manage to grow just enough millet, sorghum, corn, rice, cassava, and yams to feed themselves, with a little more to trade. Some are able to grow a few cash crops such as cotton, rice, peanuts, tobacco, and kola nuts. Though trade was lively in early Africa, today eighty percent of the population are subsistence farmers.

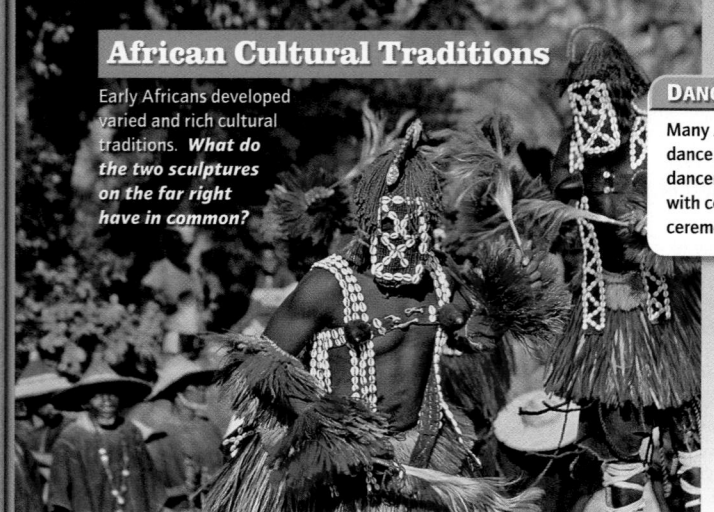

African Cultural Traditions

Early Africans developed varied and rich cultural traditions. **What do the two sculptures on the far right have in common?**

DANCE
Many African traditions involve dance and masks. These Dogon dancers wear masks decorated with cowrie shells for a harvest ceremony in Mali.

MUSIC
Traditional African music was performed with a variety of instruments, including stringed and wind instruments as well as drums, such as this one from Guinea.

TAKING NOTES

As you read, use a graphic organizer like this one to take notes on the geography, early societies, and Iron Age of Africa.

Early Africa

The Geography of Africa

Africa's location and large size—more than three times the size of the United States—have resulted in a wide variety of climates and vegetation. Each region of the continent has its own terrain and provides different resources for the people who live there. As a result, distinct cultures and ways of life developed.

Landforms If you look at a physical map of Africa you will see that the continent has a varied landscape. Low, wide plains run across Africa's northern and western interior. Vast plateaus, or high plains, cover much of Africa's central and southern interior. Farther east is the Great Rift Valley, a region of deep valleys, or rifts, and narrow lakes. Around the outer part of Africa are several mountain ranges, such as the Ethiopian Highlands in the northeast. Near the coastline, however, the land drops off sharply to coastal plains. Some of these coastal plains provide fertile farmland, while others are areas of desert, swamp, or sandy beaches.

Climate and Vegetation Africa's climate and vegetation are also quite varied. Northern Africa is dominated by the Sahara, the largest desert in the world. Stretching about 3,000 miles east to west and from 800 to 1,200 miles north to south, the Sahara includes mountains,

rocky plateaus, barren gravel plains, and sand dunes. Temperatures in the desert can climb above 120°F, and rain is rare. However, scattered throughout the desert are oases, or fertile areas, some large enough to support villages.

Just south of the Sahara, mighty rivers flow across Africa. These rivers include the Congo, Zambezi, and Niger. This region of Africa is called the **Sahel** (sah-HEL), a strip of land that divides the desert from wetter areas. Although the Sahel is fairly dry, it has enough vegetation to support hardy grazing animals.

Farther south is a band of tropical **savanna**, or open grassland, which extends east from Central Africa before wrapping back toward the south. Tall grasses, shrubs, and a few trees grow there. A variety of wild herd animals live on the savanna, as do the meat-eating animals that prey upon them. The majority of Africa's people live on the savannas as well.

Near the equator and on Madagascar, an island off the southeast coast, are tropical rain forests. The hot and humid climate and year-round rainfall of the rain forests supports a broad range of plant and animal life. Farther south, southern Africa consists mainly of hilly grasslands, deserts, and a high coastal strip of land. This region experiences a mild Mediterranean climate characterized by warm temperatures and both summer and winter rains.

Skills Focus: Comparing and Contrasting
Below Level

Reading Skill
Adapting to African Climates

1. Tell students that people have adapted in order to survive and thrive in each region of Africa. Students will conduct research on how people make their living in different climates.

2. Review the information in the text about the diverse geographic religions and climates in Africa. Have students predict and explain how people live in each area of Africa described in this section, how plants differ, and how some

people might rely on animals for food, and others on fish.

3. Have volunteers share their predictions and explanations with the class. Guide students in a discussion of the ways in which people adapt to their climate and geographic conditions. **🖪 Interpersonal, Verbal-Linguistic**

📝 **Alternative Assessment Handbook**, Rubric 11: Discussions

Answers

African Cultural Traditions *Both depict people wearing decorative neck jewelry.*

284

Adapting to Africa's Environment The first people to live in Africa had to adapt to the continent's varied climates and features. Insufficient water supplies and poor soil in some places made farming difficult. Rainfall—either too much or too little—presented problems that Africa's farmers continue to struggle with in modern times. Heavy rains can erode the soil and wash away nutrients important for growing crops. Insufficient rainfall can lead to drought and poor grazing land. As a result, farmers must decide which crops to grow based on the rainfall they expect to receive in a year. When rainfall is uncertain, such decisions become more difficult.

Another danger is caused by parasites, or small organisms, that thrive in Africa's tropical areas. Insects such as mosquitoes can transmit the parasites to humans or animals, leading to deadly diseases such as malaria. Another insect, the tsetse (TSET-see) fly, lives in some wooded areas and near lakes and streams in sub-Saharan Africa. This fly carries a parasite that can kill livestock and infect humans with sleeping sickness, a potentially fatal illness. The threat of disease makes areas inhabited by the tsetse fly unsuitable for settlement.

READING CHECK **Analyze** What challenges can Africa's environment pose to people living there?

Early African Societies

Based on excavations from Olduvai Gorge and other sites in the Great Rift Valley, anthropologists think that the first humans lived in East Africa. Over thousands of years, people spread out from that region into other parts of the continent to form distinct cultures and societies.

Early Farming Societies During the early phase of their history, Africans lived as hunter-gatherers. Around 9,000 years ago, though, some Africans began to farm, growing native crops such as sorghum, cotton, and yams. In some parts of Africa, pastoralism, or the practice of raising herd animals, arose before farming. Archaeological evidence shows that Africa's first farmers were likely pastoralists of the Sahara. About 8,000 years ago the Sahara's climate was much wetter than it is now.

About 5,000 years ago the climate changed, however; and the Sahara became drier. As more land became desert, people left areas where they could no longer survive. Pastoralists from the Sahara migrated to the Mediterranean coast, the Nile Valley, and parts of West Africa. By about 2500 BC many people in these regions practiced herding and mixed farming.

Social Structures Despite the diversity of early African societies, many of them shared some common features. For example, many early African societies developed village-based cultures built around clans, or families with common ancestors. Family ties were extremely important, and all family members were expected to be loyal to their clan. Often, extended family members—parents, children, and other close relatives—lived together.

In some areas people took part in another type of group called age-sets. In these groups men who had been born within the same two or three years formed special bonds. Men in the same age-set had a duty to help each other. Women, too, sometimes formed age-sets.

Loyalty to family and age-sets helped village members work together. Everyone had specific duties. The men hunted and farmed. Women cared for children, farmed, collected firewood, ground grain, and carried water. Even the very old and very young had their own tasks. For example, elders often taught traditions to the younger generations.

ACADEMIC VOCABULARY
phase a period or stage within a longer process

AFRICAN KINGDOMS **285**

Reading Focus

Early African Societies

Recall What were some religious beliefs of many early Africans? *spirits of their ancestors stayed nearby; natural objects have spirits*

Explain Why were oral traditions important in early Africa? *Many societies did not develop systems of writing, so oral traditions kept history alive.*

CRF: Biography: Salif Keita

Forensics in History

Can a Mutant Cell Stop a Killer Disease?

Recall How long has the sickle cell mutation existed? *4,000 years*

Explain Why is the sickle cell trait common in parts of Africa with high rates of malaria? *Carriers who inherited the trait from only one parent are resistant to malaria.*

Info to Know

Who Carries the Gene? One in 400 African American babies inherits the sickle cell gene from both parents. One out of twelve African Americans carries the trait and can pass it on to their offspring. But this trait is not restricted to descendants of Africa alone. Anyone whose ancestors came from areas where malaria is prevalent may also carry it. These regions include Greece, Italy, Sardinia, India, and the Arabian peninsula.

Answers

Forensics in History *when it protects a person from malaria*

Reading Check *Families were the heart of village life. Each person was expected to be loyal to his extended family, and each member of a family had his or her own tasks.*

Identifying Supporting Details What details support the statement that early African societies shared some features?

 NEW YORK

CC Unit 1-B2 The Bantu migration (500 BC– AD 1500), its causes, and its impact on other areas of Africa

Religion and Culture Many early Africans, shared similar religious beliefs. For example, many Africans believed that the unseen spirits of their ancestors stayed nearby. To honor these spirits, families marked certain places as sacred spaces by putting specially carved statues there. Family members gathered in these places to share news and food with the ancestors. Through these practices they hoped the spirits would protect them.

Many Africans also practiced a form of a religion called animism—the belief that bodies of water, animals, trees, and other natural objects have spirits. Animism reflected Africans' close ties to the natural world.

Many early African societies did not develop systems of writing either. Instead, they maintained their sense of identity and continuity with the past through oral traditions. These oral traditions included stories, songs, poems, and proverbs. The task of remembering and passing on oral traditions was entrusted to storytellers called **griots** (GREE-ohz). Griots helped keep history alive for each new generation and were highly respected in their communities.

Early Africans shared common features in the arts as well. In many African societies, music and dance were central to celebrations and rituals. In addition, elaborately carved masks were often worn during dances and other rituals.

READING CHECK **Generalize** What role did family ties play in early African societies?

Africa's Iron Age

Iron technology spread to parts of sub-Saharan Africa around the 500s BC. The development of Africa's Iron Age changed many aspects of life.

FORENSICS in History

Can a Mutant Cell Stop a Killer Disease?

The answer to this question is in human blood. Some 4,000 years ago, a genetic mutation that affects red blood cells resulted in a disease called sickle-cell anemia. The mutation has helped protect some Africans from another deadly disease—malaria.

What facts do we have? To have sickle-cell anemia, a person must inherit the sickle-cell trait from both parents. Normal red blood cells are smooth, flexible, and shaped like doughnuts. By contrast, sickle cells are hard, sticky, and shaped like quarter moons. Sickle cells die prematurely, resulting in a low red blood cell count, or anemia. They also have difficulty passing through small blood vessels. As a result, the cells form clots that deprive the body of blood and oxygen and cause painful episodes that can be fatal.

The red blood cells of people with the sickle-cell trait do not make good hosts for the malaria parasite transmitted by mosquitoes. Moreover, people who inherit the trait from only one parent have an extra advantage. They do not have sickle-cell anemia, yet they are resistant to malaria. Thus, the trait for sickle-cell anemia is most common in the parts of Africa with high rates of malaria.

Draw Conclusions When is the sickle-cell trait an advantage?

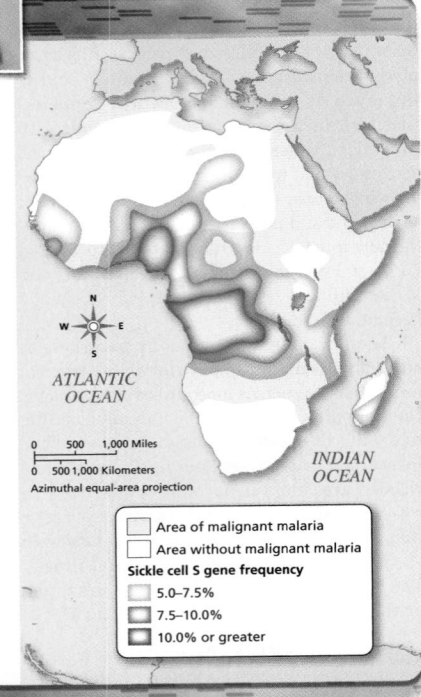

ATLANTIC OCEAN

INDIAN OCEAN

0   500   1,000 Miles
0 500 1,000 Kilometers
Azimuthal equal-area projection

☐ Area of malignant malaria
☐ Area without malignant malaria
Sickle cell S gene frequency
☐ 5.0–7.5%
☐ 7.5–10.0%
☐ 10.0% or greater

Skills Focus: Identifying Main Idea and Details   **At Level**

Reading Skill
Passing on History and Values

1. Remind students that griots and other elders taught family and community traditions, history, and values with songs, dances, and stories. In the absence of written historical records, the griots assumed a significant role.

2. Encourage students to choose a realistic subject that would have been common to an African family or community. Have students write down a lesson they would like to pass on to the family or village about this subject.

Then have students create a poem, song, dance, or story to convey the lesson.

3. When students have had time to prepare, have volunteers share their work.

4. As an extension, have students write a brief essay on the ways communities and families pass down their culture and values to their children. **LS Auditory-Musical, Kinesthetic**

Alternative Assessment Handbook, Rubrics 26: Poems and Songs; and 39: Writing to Create

Iron Technology Changes in technology helped early African communities grow. One change was the spread in sub-Saharan Africa, sometime around the 500s BC, of techniques for refining iron from iron ore. Knowledge of iron working made it possible for Africans to produce tools and weapons that were far superior to those they had made before.

One of the earliest known African societies to practice iron working was the **Nok**, who lived in what is now Nigeria in West Africa. The Nok produced iron tools and weapons, which made them better farmers, hunters, and warriors. As a result, the Nok grew in power. They also became known for producing fine sculptures out of terra-cotta, a type of clay.

With the ability to make iron tools, early Africans could live in places where they could not before. For example, with iron blades, people could cut down trees to clear land for farming. With more places to live and more land for growing food, Africa's population increased.

The Bantu Migrations Agriculture and iron working technology spread throughout Africa in part because of migration. A number of groups in Africa spoke related languages. These languages all originated from one language called Proto-Bantu, which developed in what is now Cameroon and Nigeria. Over time, hundreds of **Bantu** languages developed.

Beginning in the first century AD Bantu-speaking peoples gradually began to migrate east and south. Experts do not know why these migrations occurred. Perhaps as farming spread and West Africa's population grew, people needed more land. As they traveled, Bantu speakers spread their knowledge of farming. Later Bantu-speakers acquired the skill of iron working and helped spread this technology as well. In southern Africa, Bantu-speaking peoples soon became the dominant groups.

By the AD 900s Bantu-speaking peoples had developed complex social systems. Women farmed, while men mainly tended cattle. In fact, cattle were the most important resource in most Bantu societies. Cattle were an important food source and were used for ritual sacrifices. In addition, status in Bantu societies was often based on the size of one's cattle herds.

READING CHECK **Summarize** How did African societies change with the spread of iron working?

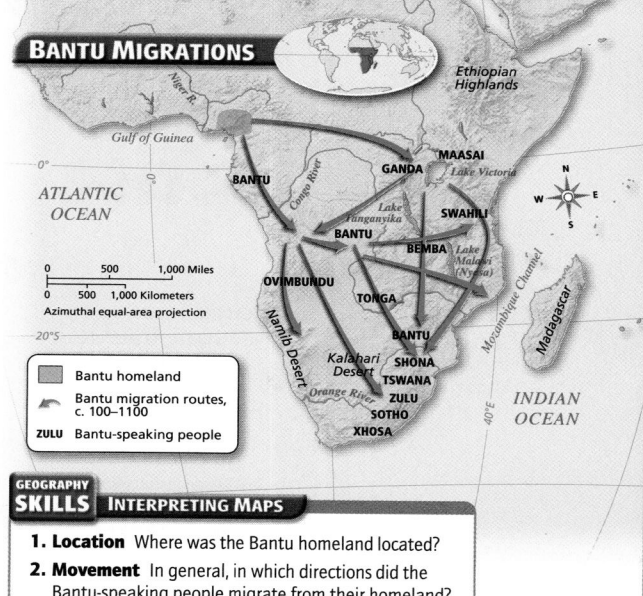

BANTU MIGRATIONS

- Bantu homeland
- Bantu migration routes, c. 100–1100
- **ZULU** Bantu-speaking people

0   500   1,000 Miles
0   500   1,000 Kilometers
Azimuthal equal-area projection

GEOGRAPHY SKILLS **INTERPRETING MAPS**

1. **Location** Where was the Bantu homeland located?
2. **Movement** In general, in which directions did the Bantu-speaking people migrate from their homeland?

SECTION 1 ASSESSMENT

go.hrw.com
Online Quiz
Keyword: SHL AFK HP

Reviewing Ideas, Terms, and People

1. **a. Recall** What are three vegetation regions found in Africa?
   b. Explain How did geography contribute to the development of many diverse cultures in early Africa?
   c. Rate In your opinion, which African region has the most favorable living conditions? Why?

2. **a. Define** What important societal role did **griots** fulfill in early Africa?
   b. Summarize What characteristics and cultural patterns did many early African societies share?
   c. Elaborate How did family ties shape life in early Africa?

3. **a. Identify** Who were the **Nok**, and why are they significant?
   b. Identify Cause and Effect What were the main effects of the **Bantu** migrations?

Critical Thinking

4. **Categorize** Using your notes and a graphic organizer like the one at right, identify the common social and cultural features of early societies in Africa. Add or delete circles as necessary.

East Africa

FOCUS ON WRITING

5. **Description** You are going to be leading an African tour that will go through two different vegetation regions of Africa. Write a paragraph describing some of the sights people can expect to see on the tour.

AFRICAN KINGDOMS **287**

Trading States of East Africa

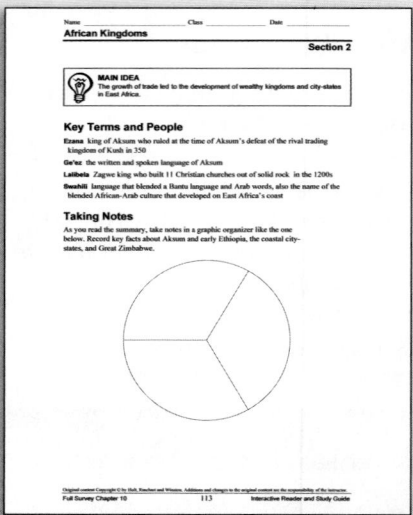
BEFORE YOU READ

MAIN IDEA

The growth of trade led to the development of wealthy kingdoms and city-states in East Africa.

READING FOCUS

1. How did trade and religion influence the development of Aksum and Ethiopia?
2. How did trade lead to the rise of coastal city-states in East Africa?
3. What do historians know about the African kingdom of Great Zimbabwe?

KEY TERMS AND PEOPLE

Ezana
Ge'ez
Lalibela
Swahili

NEW YORK

PI 3.1 Students analyze the roles and contributions of individuals and groups to social, political, economic, cultural, and religious practices and activities.

AKSUM AXES KUSH

◄ **Aksum's kings often had records of their conquests inscribed on stone monuments, known as stelae.**

288

THE INSIDE STORY

Why did early Ethiopians build stone towers? By the AD 200s the East African kingdom of Kush, which had once ruled the great civilization of ancient Egypt, had fallen into decline. Meanwhile, to the south, the early Ethiopian kingdom of Aksum was rising in power. As the two kingdoms competed for control of the region's trade, Kush's existence increasingly became a thorn in Aksum's side.

The Aksum king Ezana finally decided to eliminate Kush as a rival once and for all. Around AD 350, Aksum marched on Kush and inflicted a crushing defeat. In keeping with tradition, King Ezana had a record of the conquest inscribed on a stone monument called a stelae. "And [the Aksumites] slew and took prisoners and threw them into the water and [the Aksumites] returned safe and sound, after they had terrified their enemies and had conquered through the power of the Lord of the Land." With the defeat of Kush, Aksum became the most powerful kingdom in East Africa. ■

Aksum and Ethiopia

In East Africa, the kingdom of Aksum (AHK-soom) began to grow in power around the first century AD. Located mainly in what is now Ethiopia and Eritrea, Aksum lay south of Egypt and Kush and alongside the Red Sea. Thus, Aksum was ideally situated to control the Red Sea trade. Because of this trade, at its height Aksum was the most powerful kingdom in East Africa.

The Rise of Aksum The people of Aksum were descended from local African farmers as well as from people who had migrated from Arabia. By AD 100 Aksum had developed into a wealthy trading kingdom. Its two main cities were Aksum, the capital, and Adulis, a thriving port on the Red Sea.

The kingdom of Aksum extended from the Ethiopian Highlands to the coastal plain of the Red Sea. This geographic location provided several advantages. For one, the region was well suited to agriculture. For another, Aksum's proximity to the Red Sea was ideal for trade and gave the kingdom access to the Indian Ocean. Aksum's seaport at Adulis attracted traders from the African interior as well as from India, Persia, Arabia, Egypt, and the Mediterranean region. Traders from Africa's interior brought frankincense, gold dust, and ivory as well as enslaved Africans to Aksum's markets. At these markets, traders from abroad exchanged luxury goods such as cloth and spices for the goods of Africa. By about AD 300, Aksum had amassed great wealth from trade.

Aksum at Its Height Over time, Aksum became not only a wealthy trading kingdom but also a strong military power. The kingdom began to reach its height under King **Ezana**, whose reign began about 320. Like other kings of Aksum, Ezana's authority was mainly limited to the capital city. Outside of this city, the king collected tribute from the local rulers of other parts of Aksum but had little authority.

Under Ezana's rule, Aksum attacked and defeated the rival trading kingdom of Kush in about 350. This defeat gave Aksum control of trade in the region, and Aksum soon became the greatest power in East Africa.

Culture of Aksum Because of its thriving overseas trade, Aksum developed a diverse culture. The many merchants who came to Aksum from other areas brought new ideas with them as well as goods. Among the new ideas and beliefs brought to Aksum in the 300s was Christianity. King Ezana converted to Christianity and made it the official religion of Aksum. As a Christian ruler, Ezana recorded that he would "rule the people with righteousness and justice and will not oppress them, and may they preserve this Throne which I have set up for the Lord of Heaven."

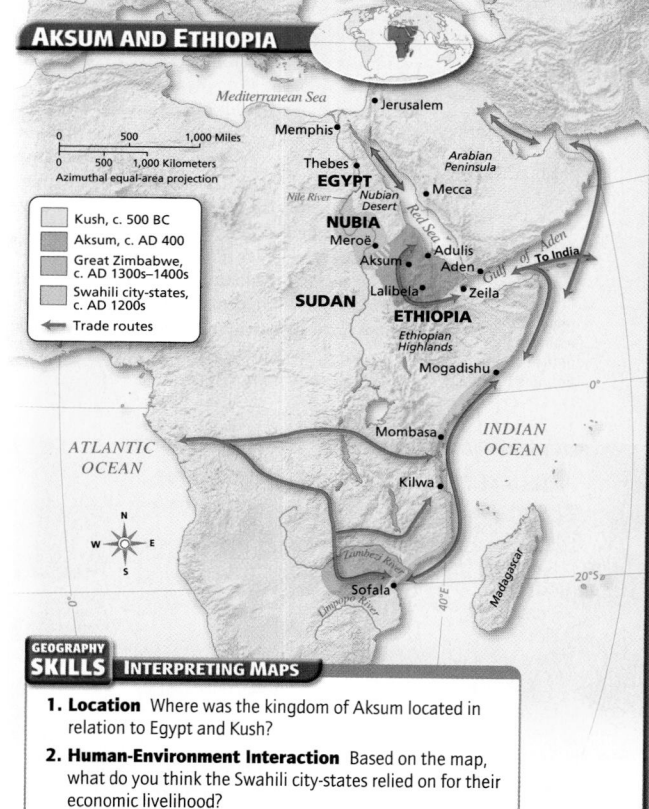

AKSUM AND ETHIOPIA

Kush, c. 500 BC
Aksum, c. AD 400
Great Zimbabwe, c. AD 1300s–1400s
Swahili city-states, c. AD 1200s
← Trade routes

Azimuthal equal-area projection

GEOGRAPHY SKILLS | **INTERPRETING MAPS**

1. **Location** Where was the kingdom of Aksum located in relation to Egypt and Kush?
2. **Human-Environment Interaction** Based on the map, what do you think the Swahili city-states relied on for their economic livelihood?

Historians know about Ezana's statement because it was inscribed on a stone monument called a stelae (STEE-lee). Aksum's kings often inscribed these stelae with records of important events. Several of Aksum's stelae still stand.

The stelae inscriptions provide examples of **Ge'ez** (GEE-ez), the written and spoken language of Aksum. Ge'ez was one of the first written languages developed in Africa and is the basis of the written language used in Ethiopia today. Although no longer spoken, Ge'ez is still used in Ethiopian religious ceremonies.

In addition to developing a written language, Aksum was the first African kingdom south of the Sahara to mint its own coins. Because of Aksum's thriving trade, merchants found it practical to use coins.

TAKING NOTES

As you read, use a graphic organizer like the one below to take notes on Aksum and Ethiopia, the coastal city-states, and Great Zimbabwe.

Reading Focus

❶ How did trade and religion influence the development of Aksum and Ethiopia? *Aksum's location was ideal for trade, brought it wealth and cultural influences, such as Christianity and Islam from Greece, India, and Persia.*

Aksum and Ethiopia

Identify Name one of the first written languages developed in Africa. *Ge'ez*

Explain How did Aksum rise to power? *developed as a wealthy trading kingdom along the Red Sea; defeated the rival trading kingdom of Kush in about 350*

Interpret How do historians know the words of King Ezana, who lived in the 300s? *His words were inscribed on stone monuments called stelae that still exist today.*

📝 **CRF:** Primary Source: Stelae Inscription of King Ezana of Aksum

Interpreting Maps
Aksum and Ethiopia
Human/Environment Interaction
How did traders move goods to and from East Africa? *They traveled by boat along the coast.*
Place How would Aksum's location have helped it prosper? *It controlled Adulis, a thriving port on the Red Sea.*
🗺 **Map Transparency:** Aksum and Ethiopia

Differentiating Instruction

Below Level

Learners Having Difficulty

Materials: large map showing the Mediterranean Sea to Africa, and east to India, sticky notes

1. Remind students that trade goods were transported more easily by boat than over land. Review the information in the text and have students name the exports of Aksum. Then have students name the imports of Aksum.

2. Organize students into mixed-ability pairs. Assign one product to each pair and have students find the locations where their product was probably produced and the routes such products likely traveled. Then have students show these locations on the large map.

3. As an extension, have students list and explain what they learned about Aksum's trade and trading partners. **LS** **Kinesthetic, Visual-Spatial**

📝 **Alternative Assessment Handbook,** Rubrics 21: Map Reading; and 30: Research

Answers

Interpreting Maps 1. *southeast of Egypt and Kush;* **2.** *trade*

Reading Focus

Aksum and Ethiopia

Identify Cause and Effect Why did Aksum decline? *Invaders destroyed its port city, cutting it off from trade.*

Compare How did the location of early Ethiopia compare to the location of Aksum? *It was inland, in the mountains, while Aksum had been located closer to the coast.*

📖 **CRF:** Biography: Queen of Sheba

Info to Know

Excavation to Yield Chronology An archaeologist at the University of Dar es Salaam, Professor Felix Chami followed the writings of Greek geographer Ptolemy, who had specified an exact location of a trade "metropolis," which was along the Rufiji River. This river's outflow points toward some tiny islands, just fifty miles south of Dar es Salaam. Chami has made earlier finds in the river region and clearly established that East Africans were part of a large community of Indian Ocean traders. But the new Iron Age site has been undisturbed, and its beads, pottery, and other materials, already dated as early as 1200 BC, may allow him to create a new cultural chronology. The Juani Island evidence supports Chami's opinion that Swahili traders interacted with other civilizations across the Indian Ocean long before the Islamic era.

🗽 NEW YORK

CC Unit 3-D3
Rise and fall of African civilizations: Axum and its role in global trade routes

THE IMPACT TODAY

Christianity remains the main religion in the nation of Ethiopia today.

The Decline of Aksum During the 600s Aksum began to decline primarily because of the arrival of Muslim invaders. In the 600s and 700s these invaders conquered parts of East and North Africa, although Aksum itself was never conquered. As nearby areas became Muslim, Christian Aksum was isolated. In time, Muslims destroyed Adulis, Aksum's port city, and took over the Red Sea trade. Cut off from trade, Aksum lost its main source of wealth.

The people of Aksum eventually retreated inland into the mountains and settled in what is now northern Ethiopia. Although Aksum's kingdom ended, its legacy lived on, shaping Ethiopia's later history.

Lalibela's Stone Churches

In the 1200s highly skilled Ethiopian architects and artisans carved 11 Christian churches out of solid rock in Lalibela. Some of the churches are set into the ground, and stairways provide access. The images here show the Church of St. George. *What Christian symbol does the shape of the church above resemble?*

290 CHAPTER 10

Ethiopia The name Ethiopia came to refer to the larger region around the kingdom of Aksum. By the 1100s the descendants of Aksum had established a new kingdom in Ethiopia. This kingdom began to truly develop under the rule of the Zagwe dynasty, which gained power around 1150.

The most famous of the Zagwe kings was King **Lalibela**, who ruled during the 1200s. He is known for building 11 stone Christian churches, many of which still stand. These Lalibela churches are carved out of solid rock and are impressive works of architecture. The churches show the remarkable technical knowledge and skill of Ethiopians at that time.

In addition, the Lalibela churches showed the continuing importance in Ethiopia of Christianity. Because many other peoples in East Africa were Muslim, Christianity provided a unifying identity for the Ethiopian people. Over time, Ethiopian Christianity developed its own unique characteristics, which included elements of local African customs.

In 1270 a second dynasty of Christian kings came to rule Ethiopia. In a text called "The Glory of Kings," these kings claimed to be descendants of the Hebrew king Solomon and the Queen of Sheba. For this reason, the dynasty is also known as the Solomonid dynasty. This long-lasting dynasty continued to rule Ethiopia for 700 years until 1974.

During the first centuries of Solomonid rule, the kings engaged in various religious wars. Although Ethiopia was Christian, Jews called Beta Israel lived there as well. During the 1400s Ethiopia's Christian kings began to fight the Beta Israel and make them leave. The effort was mostly unsuccessful. Jews remained in Ethiopia but faced continued persecution.

Meanwhile, a rival Muslim kingdom was forming to the east of Ethiopia near the Horn of Africa. This region of Africa juts out into the Indian Ocean south of the Arabian Peninsula. Muslim Arab merchants had settled in this region, which became known as the kingdom of Adal by the 1300s. Muslim Adal and Christian Ethiopia soon came into conflict and fought each other for many years. In the end, however, Muslim forces never conquered Ethiopia, which remained independent.

READING CHECK **Summarize** What religions had an effect upon Ethiopia during this period?

Skill Focus: Summarizing
At Level

Reading Skill
The Stelae of Aksum

Materials: cardstock strips, scissors, tape

1. Have students describe the stelae of King Ezana. Tell students that Ezana and others created stelae as a permanent record of history, or perhaps as a type of proclamation.

2. Distribute the cardstock strips and have students create their own three-dimensional stelae. Tell students to fold and unfold their stelae so the stelae can lie flat for writing.

3. Each stelae should be inscribed with a fact about Aksum or King Ezana.

4. When students have finished, have volunteers display their work to the class. **LS Visual-Spatial**

📖 **Alternative Assessment Handbook**, Rubrics 1: Acquiring Information; and 3: Artwork

---

Answers

Lalibela's Stone Churches *a cross*

Reading Check *Christianity, Islam, Judaism*

Coastal City-States

South of Ethiopia and the Horn of Africa, a number of Muslim city-states developed along the East African coast. Like the kingdom of Aksum, these coastal city-states made their wealth from overseas trade.

Rise of City-States Africa's East coast had drawn overseas traders from early times. The main reason was the influence of the Indian Ocean and its monsoon winds. Between November and March, the monsoons blew southwest from the coast of India toward Africa. From April to October, the monsoons reversed and blew northeast toward India and the Persian Gulf. Over time, sailors learned to take advantage of these winds to move around the Indian Ocean. A trade network soon developed that linked East Africa with Persia, Arabia, India, and even Southeast Asia. Market towns sprang up along the East African coast to take advantage of that trade.

Arab traders called this East African coastal region the land of Zanj and used the monsoon winds to visit these port towns. By AD 1100 several of these coastal market towns had grown into wealthy and thriving city-states. The main city-states were Mogadishu, Mombasa, Kilwa, and Sofala.

The coastal city-states linked merchants from overseas with traders from Africa's interior. In the city-states' markets, merchants from overseas sold luxury items such as glassware, East Asian porcelain, and silk and cotton from China and India. In exchange for these manufactured luxury items, foreign merchants obtained raw materials from Africa's interior. These goods included coconut oil, copper, leopard skins, and shells. African ivory, which was highly prized in many countries, was another valuable trade item along with gold from southern Africa.

In addition, enslaved Africans captured in the interior were exported through the coastal city-states to slave markets in Arabia, Persia, and India. These enslaved Africans were then sent to regions across Asia, many to work as domestic servants. The trade of enslaved Africans would later increase substantially after Europeans began coming to Africa. Many of the enslaved Africans in this later European slave trade would be exported to the Americas.

Ibn Battutah in Kilwa

An Arab named Ibn Battutah became famous for his extensive travels during the 1300s to Africa, China, and much of the Muslim world. From 1330 to 1332 Ibn Battutah sailed with a group along the eastern African coast. Below, he describes the trading city-state of Kilwa.

> Then I set off by sea from the town of Mogadishu for the land of the Swahili and the town of Kilwa, . . . the principal town on the coast, the greater part of whose inhabitants are Zanj . . . Kilwa is one of the most beautiful and well-constructed towns in the world. The whole of it is elegantly built. The roofs are built with mangrove poles. There is very much rain. The people are engaged in a holy war, for their country lies beside that of pagan [non-Muslim] Zanj. The chief qualities are devotion and piety [goodness].

—Translated by G. S. P. Freeman-Grenville, from *The East African Coast, Select Documents*

Skills FOCUS **READING LIKE A HISTORIAN**

1. **Identify Supporting Details** How did the people of Kilwa differ from some of the people living around them?
2. **Analyze Primary Sources** What do you think was Ibn Battutah's overall impression of Kilwa?

See **Skills Handbook**, p. H25

Trade along East Africa's coast reached its peak during the 1300s and 1400s. By this time, Kilwa had become the wealthiest and most powerful of the coastal city-states. Kilwa became a prosperous trading center because it was located at the southernmost point on East Africa's coast that a ship could reach in a single monsoon season. All African goods from south of Kilwa, therefore, were exported from Kilwa's market. Kilwa's power increased further in the late 1200s when it gained control of Sofala, through which much gold was exported.

Swahili Trade led to a blending of African, Arab, and Asian cultural influences along East Africa's coast. Over time, many Muslim Arabs and Persians settled in Africa's coastal city-states. These groups intermarried with the local African population and gradually influenced the local culture and ways of life.

 NEW YORK

CC Unit 3-C Global trade and the major trading center of Mogadishu; Ibn Battutah

AFRICAN KINGDOMS **291**

---

3 What do historians know about the African kingdom of Great Zimbabwe?

Great Zimbabwe

Recall What is a middleman? *a person who buys something from one person and sells it to another, making a profit*

Interpret What evidence suggests that Great Zimbabwe may have acted in the role of middleman for African trade? *its location; archaeologists' discovery of a coin minted at Kilwa and glass beads from India at the site of Great Zimbabwe*

Activity Trading Goods To demonstrate the role of a middleman, set up a model "trade" in the classroom. Have two students act as traders and a third student act as the middleman. Use cut pieces of paper as coins. The trade object will be a textbook. Separately, instruct the middleman to "charge" more for the object than the price he "pays" for it. Then, as the rest of the class observes, have one trader "sell" the textbook to the middleman, and the other trader "buy" it from the middleman. Ask students: how did the middleman profit from the sale?
LS Kinesthetic

Reading like a Historian

Great Zimbabwe's Walls Speak

Analyzing Secondary Sources A secondary source is a historical account produced by people who were not present at the time. For instance, this textbook is a secondary source. Often, secondary sources contain summaries, analyses, and interpretations of historical events, people, and periods.

The passage at right about Great Zimbabwe is from a secondary source. To analyze this passage, think about

- the author or source of the information.
- the facts and summaries provided.
- the objectivity of any interpretations made.

Skills FOCUS READING LIKE A HISTORIAN

1. **Author or Source** What is the source of the passage provided above about Great Zimbabwe?
2. **Interpretations** What interpretation does the passage provide about the purpose of the walls that surrounded the Great Enclosure at Great Zimbabwe? What support does the passage provide for this interpretation?

See Skills Handbook, p. H30

The writer gives one interpretation of the purpose of the walls of the Great Enclosure at Great Zimbabwe.

The enormous walls are the best-preserved testaments of Great Zimbabwe's past . . . The function of these stone walls, however, has often been misinterpreted. At first glance, these massive nonsupportive walls appear purely defensive. But scholars doubt they ever served a martial [warlike] purpose . . . The walls are thought to have been a symbolic show of authority, designed to preserve the privacy of royal families and set them apart from and above commoners . . . The remaining stone walls provide only partial evidence of the architecture's original appearance.

—from "Great Zimbabwe (11th–15th Century)," *Time Line of Art History,* The Metropolitan Museum of Art

The source of the text is shown here.

For example, local architecture featured coral stone walls and roofs of mangrove poles as well as Arab influences such as carved doors and decorative niches. In addition, local Africans, who spoke a Bantu language, adopted many Arab words. As the two languages blended, a new language called **Swahili** (swah-HEE-lee) developed. The term *Swahili* has also come to refer to the blended African-Arab culture that developed along East Africa's coast.

Because many foreign traders were Muslim, Islam gained hold along the East African coast as well. Many African rulers who governed the coastal city-states adopted Islam, and mosques appeared in cities and towns. At the same time, many Africans continued to practice local traditional religions such as animism.

READING SKILLS

Identifying Supporting Details What details support the statement that trade shaped life along the East African coast?

READING CHECK **Analyze** How did trade shape life in the East African coastal city-states?

Great Zimbabwe

The growing wealth of Africa's overseas trade stimulated developments in Africa's interior as well. There, ancestors of the Shona people established a kingdom called Great Zimbabwe (zihm-BAH-bway) around the 1100s. This kingdom was located between the Limpopo and Zambezi rivers in southeastern Africa. This area is now part of the nation of Zimbabwe, which was named for Great Zimbabwe.

Scholars think that Great Zimbabwe was part of Africa's thriving trade network because of the kingdom's location. Great Zimbabwe lay along a trade route linking Africa's interior gold mines to the city-states on the coast. In this location, Great Zimbabwe served as a middleman between gold miners and ivory hunters in southern Africa and the traders on the coast.

Answers

Reading Like a Historian 1. *The Metropolitan Museum of Art;* **2.** *that they were used to showing authority and protecting royal privacy; states that scholars believe this*

Reading Skills *Coastal city-states linked the merchants from overseas with interior trades; trade led to a blending of African, Arab, and Asian cultural influences.*

Reading Check *created wealth, brought Arab influences, contributed to the development of an Arab-Bantu language called Swahili*

Differentiating Instruction

At Level

English-Language Learners

1. Remind students that little is known about King Lalibela's churches, but their history is remarkably similar to that of Europe and the Mediterranean.

2. Copy the chart for students to see. Omit the italicized words. Have students copy and complete the chart. Review the answers and have students correct their work as needed. **LS Verbal-Linguistic**

Alternative Assessment Handbook, Rubric 17: Charts

During the Zagwe dynasty, where were 11 impressive stone churches built?	*Ethiopia*
About when were they built?	*the 1200s*
Who commanded the work?	*King Lalibela*
Who built them?	*artisans and architects*
How were they constructed?	*carved from solid rock*
What did these churches show about the importance of religion here?	*showed continuing importance of Christianity.*

A middleman is a person who buys something from one person and sells it to another, making a profit on the sale.

Archaeological discoveries support this role for Great Zimbabwe. For example, archaeologists have found glass beads from India and a coin minted in Kilwa at the site of Great Zimbabwe. The kingdom's rulers likely taxed the trade goods that passed through their territory. Through this control of trade, Great Zimbabwe rose to prosperity between 1200 and 1400.

The Great Enclosure The Shona word *zimbabwe* means "stone houses," and today all that remains of Great Zimbabwe are mainly stone ruins. The largest and most impressive of these ruins is a structure called the Great Enclosure. This structure, which is shown in the image on the left, includes a thick, circular, outer stone wall about 35 feet high. An inner wall runs along part of this outer wall and forms a narrow passage about 180 feet long. The stones used to build the walls were so well fitted together that no mortar was needed in the construction.

Inside the walls of the Great Enclosure is a 33-foot-high stone tower. In addition, archaeologists have discovered soapstone bird figurines within the enclosure. Experts are not certain of the purpose of the Great Enclosure, but think it may have been built to show the rulers' power or as an astronomical observatory.

The Mutapa Empire At its height, Great Zimbabwe may have had as many as 18,000 people. Yet, sometime during the 1400s they abandoned the area. Scholars are not certain exactly why this occurred. Because the people of Great Zimbabwe raised cattle, one plausible reason is that the land became overgrazed. The soil may have lost its fertility as well leading to poor harvests. Whatever the reason, by the time the first Europeans saw the site in the 1500s, Great Zimbabwe was already in ruins.

With Great Zimbabwe's abandonment, power in the region shifted to the Mutapa Empire. Based on oral tradition, this empire was founded by a former resident of Great Zimbabwe named Mutota. The oral tradition states that Mutota had gone north, where he founded a new kingdom. In the 1400s he gained control of much of the surrounding territory and built an empire. As a result, Mutota became known as *Mwene Mutapa,* meaning "master pillager" or "conqueror." His successors took the same title, from which the empire gained its name.

By 1500 the Mutapa Empire controlled much of what is now Zimbabwe. The empire grew wealthy by exporting gold and controlling trade through its territory. Eventually, though, Europeans would take control of the empire.

ACADEMIC VOCABULARY

plausible believable, reasonable

THE IMPACT TODAY
The bird on the flag of present-day Zimbabwe symbolizes the soapstone birds found at Great Zimbabwe.

READING CHECK **Find the Main Idea** How do scholars think Great Zimbabwe participated in trade?

SECTION 2 ASSESSMENT

go.hrw.com
Online Quiz
Keyword: SHL AFK HP

Reviewing Ideas, Terms, and People

1. **a. Identify** Who was King **Ezana**, and how did he contribute to the history of Aksum?
   b. Identify Cause and Effect How did the spread of Islam contribute to the decline of Aksum?
   c. Elaborate How did the legacy of Aksum shape later Ethiopian society?

2. **a. Recall** What were four of the trading city-states that arose along the East African coast?
   b. Explain How was the development of **Swahili** an example of cultural blending?
   c. Evaluate Do you think that the spread of Islam to East Africa affected Aksum or the coastal city-states more? Provide reasons to support your opinion.

3. **a. Describe** What remains of Great Zimbabwe?
   b. Summarize What role do scholars think that Great Zimbabwe played in the East Africa trading network?

Critical Thinking

4. **Compare and Contrast** Using your notes and a graphic organizer like the one below, compare and contrast the kingdom of Aksum with the later kingdom of Ethiopia.

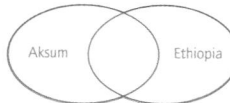

FOCUS ON WRITING

5. **Narration** You are a visitor to East Africa's coastal city-state of Kilwa at its height. Write a short journal entry in which you describe your tour of the city-state. Include information about the source of the city's wealth, some of the activities that are taking place there, and the culture there.

Reading Focus

Great Zimbabwe

Recall What does the word zimbabwe mean in Shona? *stone houses*

Explain What are some reasons the people of Great Zimbabwe may have abandoned the site? *The land may have become overgrazed by cattle; the soil may have lost its fertility.*

Review & Assess

Close

Review how the growth of trade led to the development of wealthy kingdoms and city-states in East Africa.

Review

Online Quiz, Section 2

Assess

SE Section 2 Assessment
Progress Assessment: Section 2 Quiz
Alternative Assessment Handbook

Reteach/Intervene

Interactive Reader and Study Guide, Section 2
Interactive Skills Tutor CD-ROM

Section 2 Assessment Answers

1. **a.** king of Aksum during its height; attacked and defeated Kush, converted Aksum to Christianity
   b. Muslim invaders arrived in East and North Africa, isolating Aksum.
   c. Ethiopia remained Christian and independent.

2. **a.** Mogadishu, Mombasa, Kilwa, Sofala
   b. It was a language that used both Bantu and Arab words.
   c. possible answer—the coastal city-states, because they adopted aspects of Arab culture into their own culture

3. **a.** stone ruins, including the Great Enclosure
   b. the role of middleman, taxing trade items as they passed from the interior to coastal trading states

4. Aksum—wealthy trading state; coastal; Ethiopia—Lalibela churches carved from solid rock; Jewish and Muslim influence; inland; Both—Christian

5. Student journal entries should describe the wealth and beauty of Kilwa and its location as the southernmost coastal city-state.

Answers

Reading Check *location served as the role of middleman, taxing trade goods that passed through its territory*

293

Focus on Themes

Economic Systems

Info to Know

Big Companies Use Old System Sometimes businesses need to limit their spending, avoiding actual purchases by bartering or trading to acquire what they need. This is facilitated by the use of a third party barter exchange, which keeps a record of the value of each transaction, allowing exchanges of goods of unequal value and reserving credits for the balance. In this way, companies may exchange carpeting for hotel rooms, dental work, or repairs for their company vehicles. Computer-assisted bartering is happening all over the world.

Recent Scholarship

A History of Money: From Ancient Times to the Present Day by Glyn Davies is full of fascinating facts about that troublesome commodity, money. The book provides a chronology of the development of money, as well as a history of banking, an accounting of the Euro and electronic money. According to Davies, between eight and eleven millennia ago, cattle were the earliest form of currency, and sometime around 3100 BC, writing was probably developed in order to help keep records of accounts.

A History of Money: From Ancient Times to the Present Day by Glyn Davies. Third revised edition, University of Wales Press, 2002.

Answers

Understanding Themes 1. *Barter was used instead of money to trade.*
2. A formal economy is regulated and taxed, while an informal economy is not.
3. possible answer—because it can be unfair to poorer people

294

Economic Systems

Early societies in Africa, as in much of the world, bartered instead of using money to trade. Barter is the direct trade of goods or services for other goods or services without the use of money. In early West Africa, for example, merchants often traded gold for salt. As trade increased in Africa, people began to use items such as gold dust and cowrie shells as money. Rulers began to regulate and tax trade as well. Much trade remained untaxed and informal, though, as people bartered for what they needed to live.

▲ **NOW** A street vendor sells bananas in Harare, Zimbabwe, in southern Africa.

BARTER AND ALTERNATIVE ECONOMIES THEN

In early West Africa, merchants often used a process called silent barter to trade gold and salt, both of which were highly valuable. In silent barter, people exchange goods without contacting each other directly. This method ensured that trade took place peacefully and kept the exact location of the gold mines a secret.

In the silent barter process, salt traders went to a specified location near the gold mines and left their salt. The traders then beat a drum to tell the gold miners that trading had begun. Afterward, the salt traders moved back several miles.

Next, the gold miners arrived and left what they considered a fair amount of gold in exchange for the salt. Then the gold miners also moved back several miles so that the salt traders could return. If the salt traders were happy with the amount of gold, they beat the drum again and left with the gold. The gold miners then returned and picked up their salt. Trading continued until both sides were happy with the result.

BARTER AND ALTERNATIVE ECONOMIES NOW

Today all nations use money as currency and have formal economies. In formal economies, the state regulates aspects of the economy and taxes goods and trade. In addition, people work for wages.

Informal, or alternative, economic activity still takes place, however. For example, in parts of Africa, much of the economic activity takes place outside of the control of the state. In other words, this economic activity is not regulated, reported, or taxed. In small villages, people still use barter to exchange crafts and surplus crops. People may work for food or other goods instead of for wages. In informal marketplaces, people sell and trade goods that are not reported or taxed. While most governments try to stop such activity, it enables poorer and less educated people to survive.

Skills FOCUS UNDERSTANDING THEMES

1. **Find the Main Idea** What role did barter play in early African societies?
2. **Contrast** How does a formal economy differ from an informal, or alternative, economy?
3. **Draw Conclusions** Why do you think that governments try to stop alternative economic activity?

◄ **THEN** At left are African cowrie shells and a box and spoon for storing and measuring gold dust.

294 CHAPTER 10

Skills Focus: Analyzing Costs and Benefits

At Level

Social Studies Skill
Understanding Barter

1. Remind students that the only way people could obtain goods from others before their society created money was to barter.

2. Have students name some items they own but cannot use, such as outgrown clothing. Next, have volunteers name the types of services they can provide, such as car washing. Have students create a list of the things they could use to barter for goods that they want or need. Have students identify what they might offer

a parent for privileges, favors, transportation, special clothing or sports equipment.

3. Guide students in a discussion of the relative values of things and services, and the limitations of barter as a means of trade.

 Verbal-Linguistic, Intrapersonal

Alternative Assessment Handbook, Rubrics 11: Discussions; and 35: Solving Problems

Kingdoms of West Africa

BEFORE YOU READ

MAIN IDEA

The expansion of trade across the Sahara led to the development of great empires and other states in West Africa.

READING FOCUS

1. How did trade contribute to the rise of Ghana?
2. How did strong rulers build the empire of Mali?
3. What were the greatest achievements of the Songhai Empire?
4. What other states developed in West Africa?

KEY PEOPLE

Sundiata
Mansa Musa
Sunni Ali
Askia Muhammad

NEW YORK

PI 1.4 Students understand the broad patterns, relationships, and interactions of cultures and civilizations during particular eras and across eras.

The Land of GOLD

THE INSIDE STORY

Was there really a kingdom of gold? In the 1700s stories began to circulate around Europe about a fabulous kingdom of gold in West Africa. One visitor noted that the king wore so much heavy gold jewelry on one hand that he had to support that hand on the head of a small boy. The kingdom thus described was ruled by the Asante people, who did indeed have huge amounts of gold.

The Asante were not the first West African kingdom to be known for their golden treasures, however. Centuries earlier, the rulers of Ghana surrounded themselves with gold as a sign of their power. A Muslim visitor to Ghana at that time described the gold displayed by the king's attendants: golden swords and shields, gold braided into people's hair, even gold and silver collars for the king's dogs. ▪

Empire of Ghana

As in the other kingdoms you have studied, trade was vital to the societies of West Africa. The region of West Africa produced valuable resources—most notably gold—that brought high prices. By the 800s, the rulers of Ghana had used the wealth from these products to create a huge, powerful empire.

▲ The rulers of Ghana gained great wealth by controlling the vast amounts of gold traded in their empire. The West African woman above is wearing gold jewelry and gold dust on her face.

AFRICAN KINGDOMS **295**

Preteach

Getting Started

Use the **Interactive Reader and Study Guide** to familiarize students with the section content.

📓 **Interactive Reader and Study Guide,** Section 3

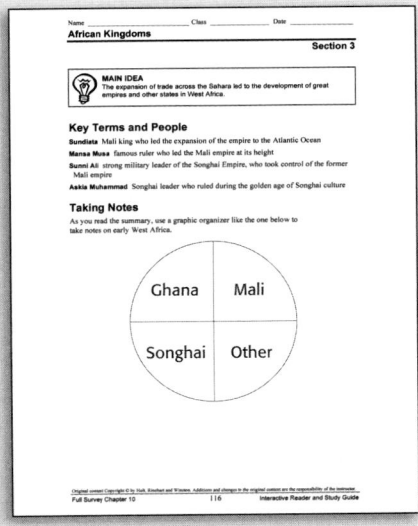

Academic Vocabulary

Review with students the high-use academic term in this section.

commerce trade, or the exchange of goods or services (p. 300)

📓 **CRF:** Vocabulary Builder: Section 3

Taking Notes

Ghana—located south of the Sahara; traders crossed the desert in caravans; Ghana controlled nearly all trade of gold and salt; kings had lavish lifestyle, kept supply of gold scarce; Mali—rose to power in the 1230s on same territory Ghana had ruled; first leader was Sundiata; Mansa Musa, a devout Muslim, ruled during height; Mansa Musa's hajj brought Mali to the attenion of Europe; Songhai—took control of former Mali empire by the 1460s, led by Sunni Ali; culture reached height under Askia Muhammad; Other West African Societies—Hausa city-states: economy based on trade, farming, manufacturing; Yoruba kingdoms: widely admired for artistic skill; Benin: came into contact with Europeans in 1400s also known for their arts

---

Teach the Main Idea

At Level

Kingdoms of West Africa

Materials: construction paper strips, colored markers, tape

1. **Teach** Ask students the Reading Focus questions to teach this section.

2. **Apply** Organize the class into four groups. Assign one of these topics to each: Empire of Ghana, Mali Empire, Empire of Songhai, and Other West African States. Have groups identify the main events in the development and decline of their assigned empire(s). Distribute materials. Have students write

events on the strips of construction paper and then tape them together in sequential order.

3. **Review** Have volunteers from each group display and share their work.

4. **Practice/Homework** Have each student write a short paragraph comparing the histories of West African empires discussed in this section. **LS Verbal-Linguistic, Visual-Spatial**

📓 **Alternative Assessment Handbook**, Rubrics 1: Acquiring Information; and 13: Graphic Organizers

Reading Focus

1 How did trade contribute to the rise of Ghana? *Ghana's gold-for-salt trade brought great wealth and introduced Islam to the empire.*

Empire of Ghana

Recall When were camels first used in desert caravans? *in the first few centuries AD*

Analyze Why would salt have been particularly valuable to sub-Saharan people? *Salt was used to preserve food, which would quickly spoil in the hot climate of the Sahel.*

CRF: Interdisciplinary Project: African Trade

Info to Know

Land Disputes For thousands of years, North African Berbers repelled Roman, French, and Arab invaders, preserving their language, land, and culture. In 2000, oil fields were discovered in Morocco by a joint American-Moroccan company. Berbers are not necessarily nomadic, and many strongly objected to the arrival of oil workers, who were claiming land for their own use. Morocco's King Mohammed VI faces the difficult task of managing the new wealth, satisfying displaced people, and negotiating with neighboring Algeria, across whose border the field may extend. Once more, trade in a scarce commodity may change the lives of African people.

Answers

History and Economics *If there are more people wanting something that is scarce, prices likely will go up.*

296

TAKING NOTES

As you read, use a graphic organizer like this one to take notes on early West Africa.

| Ghana | Mali |
| Songhai | Other |

The Rise of Ghana Although Ghana had many resources, its location delayed its development as a trading empire. Unlike the kingdoms of East Africa, Ghana had no easy access to the sea. In addition, a major obstacle blocked overland routes to potential trade partners—the Sahara. The largest desert in the world, the Sahara blocked travel between Ghana and other parts of Africa for centuries.

It was not until the first few centuries AD that North African traders learned how to cross the Sahara. Eventually, these traders began to travel in large caravans with camels, which were able to carry supplies over long distances. Because camels did not need much water, they could survive the trip across the harsh desert.

Once traders began to cross the Sahara, Ghana became a key player in African trade. Berber traders from the north went to Ghana in search of gold, for which they traded food, manufactured goods, and copper. The Berber traders also brought salt, which was produced in the desert of what is now Morocco. The people of Ghana then traded this salt to people to the south, where salt was scarce.

A Trading Empire By about AD 800, the kingdom of Ghana controlled nearly all trade of salt and gold in sub-Saharan Africa. Because Ghana's capital, Koumbi-Saleh, was located between Ghana's gold mines and the desert trade routes, it was a preferred trading place.

HISTORY and Economics

Scarcity, Supply, and Demand

Scarcity, the lack of a particular resource, exists because the world's resources are limited. The scarcity of resources affects everyone, but not always in the same way. For example, scarcity benefits those who can supply a desired limited resource, if those who demand the resource can pay the price.

Scarcity, Supply, and Demand in History
Ghana was a kingdom rich in gold—so rich that even the ruler's dogs wore gold-plated collars. This abundance of wealth lured traders from North Africa, where gold was scarce but in high demand. In exchange for the gold, the North Africans offered salt, which the people of West Africa needed in their diets to survive.

Ghana's kings gained wealth and power from the gold-salt trade. Major trade routes ran through the kingdom of Ghana, which enabled Ghana's kings to control and collect taxes on the trade. In addition, all of Ghana's gold was the kings' property. They kept all gold nuggets for themselves but allowed gold dust to be traded. In this way, the kings controlled the supply of gold and its price.

SUPPLY AND DEMAND

| supply > demand | = price falls |
| demand > supply | = price rises |

supply = amount available
demand = amount people want or need

Scarcity, Supply, and Demand Today
Consider how scarcity affects the world today. What countries benefit from supplying and controlling a limited resource just as Ghana did in the past? The world's oil-rich countries are a good example. These countries have greatly increased their wealth and global influence over the past 100 years by filling the demand for a single valuable resource that cannot be found in other places. As you study world history, look for ways that scarcity of resources affects supply and demand.

Explain How are some people able to benefit economically from scarcity?

▶ Raw salt is often formed into slabs for ease of transport. Here, a worker in a market in Mopti, Mali, in West Africa stacks slabs of salt to sell.

Skills Focus: Summarizing

At Level

Reading Skill
The Salt Trade

Research Required

1. Remind students that the salt-for-gold trade created great wealth in West African kingdoms, and that salt is still a valuable commodity to sub-Saharan peoples.

2. Organize students into small mixed-ability groups or have them work individually. Have students conduct research about the significance of the salt trade to various African cultures. Suggest to students that they search with keywords such as cultural survival and

salt trade. Have students create an annotated bibliography to accompany their research.

3. Have volunteers share their findings and their research techniques with the class. Have students take notes during the presentations.

4. As an extension, have students write a brief summary of the continuing importance of salt to indigenous people. **LS Verbal-Linguistic**

Alternative Assessment Handbook, Rubric 30: Research

Ghana's kings built great wealth by taxing the goods that were brought to their empire's markets. The majority of these taxes were charged on salt. The kings charged a fee for each load of salt brought into Ghana from the north and a larger fee for each load exported to the south. The kings did not tax gold in the same way, perhaps fearing that taxes would discourage traders from buying the gold at all.

To ensure that gold prices stayed high and trade remained profitable, Ghana's kings forbade anyone but them from owning gold nuggets. Other people could own only gold dust. The kings enforced this law by keeping the location of gold mines a strictly guarded secret. By keeping the supply of gold scarce, the kings kept the market from being flooded.

With money from trade and taxes, the kings of Ghana could afford a lavish lifestyle. The luxury that surrounded the kings was described by a Muslim writer who visited Ghana:

HISTORY'S VOICES

❝He sits in a pavilion around which stand ten pages holding shields and gold-mounted swords: and on his right hand are the sons of the princes of the empire, splendidly clad and with gold plaited into their hair.❞

—al Bakri, *The Book of Routes and Kingdoms*, c. 1067

To protect their wealth, Ghana's kings worked to keep the trade routes free from bandits. Ghana did not have a permanent army, but the king could raise a large force when needed. Ghana's kings used this power to conquer other peoples in the area. Captives were sold as slaves to Muslim traders.

Ghana's Decline By the mid-1000s, the empire of Ghana was rich and powerful. When the king tried to expand the empire to the north, however, Ghana came into conflict with the Almoravids, a Muslim Berber kingdom. This conflict led to a long war.

In 1076 the Almoravids captured Koumbi-Saleh, Ghana's capital. Although Almoravid control of the city did not last long, it left the empire of Ghana weakened. When people in part of the empire later rebelled, Ghana's king was unable to stop them. As Ghana fell into decline, a new empire rose to take its place.

READING CHECK **Summarize** How did the kings of Ghana become wealthy?

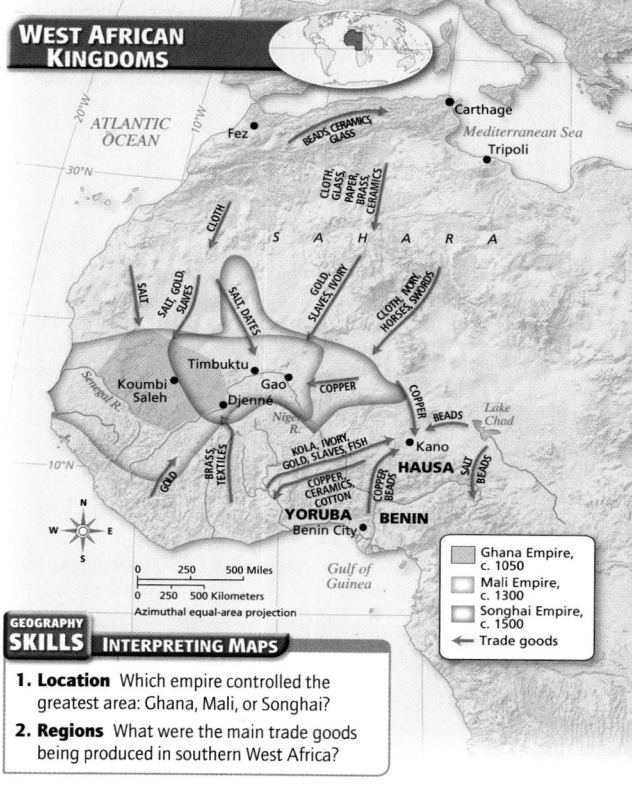

WEST AFRICAN KINGDOMS

	Ghana Empire, c. 1050
	Mali Empire, c. 1300
	Songhai Empire, c. 1500
←	Trade goods

GEOGRAPHY SKILLS **INTERPRETING MAPS**

1. **Location** Which empire controlled the greatest area: Ghana, Mali, or Songhai?
2. **Regions** What were the main trade goods being produced in southern West Africa?

Mali Empire

For about 150 years after Ghana's decline, no one kingdom controlled trans-Saharan trade. Then in the 1230s, a new empire, Mali, rose to power. Built on the same territory Ghana had ruled, Mali expanded to the Atlantic Ocean and became a wealthy and sophisticated empire.

Rise of Mali The founders of Mali, the Malinke people, had been active in Ghana's gold trade. Around 1230 the Malinke grew frustrated with the policies of neighboring peoples and rose up to conquer them. As a result, Mali became the leading power in West Africa.

The leader of Mali's rise to power was a king named **Sundiata** (soohn-JAHT-ah). After the conquest, Sundiata ruled for 25 years. The story of his reign and accomplishments is told in a great epic, also called *Sundiata*.

NEW YORK

CC **Unit 3-D**
Rise and fall of African civilizations: Ghana

Reading Focus

Empire of Ghana

Describe How did the kings control the value of gold? *made a law that only the king was allowed to own large gold nuggets, limiting the amount available for trade, raising its value*

Identify Cause and Effect How did the temporary control of Koumbi-Saleh by the Almoravids cause the decline of the kingdom of Ghana? *weakened control in Ghana, allowed local leaders to rebel*

Interpreting Maps
West African Kingdoms

Place How would rivers have made it easier for the three empires to develop? *provide irrigation and transportation*

Region Why did most trade happen between Ghana, Mali, and Songhai and traders from the north? *northern traders brought goods unavailable in the south, wanted gold, West Africa closer to Mediterranean region*

Map Transparency: West African Kingdoms

Differentiating Instruction

Below Level

Special Education Students

Materials: white paper, colored pencils or markers

1. Read aloud the quotation on this page describing the lavish lifestyle of Ghana's kings.

2. Have students draw the scene described in the quotation. Review student drawings as a class. What do the drawings suggest about who controlled the supply of gold in Ghana?

3. Guide students in a discussion of the importance of gold to Ghana and its kings. Remind students that Ghana was rich in

gold, but that only the king could own large amounts of it; the rest of the people could only own gold dust.

4. Have students work in mixed-ability pairs to list the advantages of keeping the supply of gold in the hands of the kings. **LS Visual-Spatial, Interpersonal**

Alternative Assessment Handbook, Rubric 3: Artwork

Answers

Interpreting Maps 1. *Mali;* **2.** *Refer to map.*

Reading Check *by taxing salt and gold, by controlling the price of gold*

297

Reading Focus

2 How did strong rulers build the empire of Mali? *Sundiata conquered and united several smaller kingdoms to form the kingdom of Mali. Mansa Musa brought culture, wealth, and fame to Mali.*

Mali Empire

Recall When did the Mali Empire rise to power? *in the 1230s*

Identify What one act made Mansa Musa especially famous? *his 1324 pilgrimage to Mecca*

CRF: Literature: *Sundiata: An Epic of Old Mali*

About the Illustration

This illustration is an artist's conception based on available sources. Historians, however, are uncertain exactly what this scene looked like.

Biography

Abu-Ishaq Ibrahim-es-Saheli (mid-1300s AD) A poet from Andalusia, Spain, named Abu-Ishaq Ibrahim-es-Saheli, met Mansa Musa during his famous hajj. Es-Saheli was well versed in techniques of mud and burnt-brick construction. The king offered him payment to convince him to travel to Mali and build a vast palace and mosque. Es-Saheli agreed to come and build Mansa Musa's palace. He also constructed the great Djingareyber Mosque and at Timbuktu, another one at Djenné, and a third in Gao. Es-Sahlei is credited with the introduction of burnt bricks, flat roofs, and the pyramid-shaped minaret to the area's architecture.

Answers

Reading Skills *territory expanded, population grew, wealth from taxation, army kept peace*

298

NEW YORK

CC Unit 3-D Rise and fall of African civilizations: Mali, its role in global trade routes, the spread and impact of Islam— Mansa Musa, and Timbuktu

READING SKILLS

Identifying Supporting Details What details support the statement that Mansu Musa was one of Mali's greatest rulers?

Mansa Musa Mali reached its height in the 1300s under the reign of a *mansa*, or king, named Musa. A relative of Sundiata, **Mansa Musa** came to power in 1307. During his reign, Mali's territory expanded, and its population may have reached as many as 40 million.

Also during Mansa Musa's reign, Mali grew wealthier than ever before. Much of this wealth came from taxation of the gold-salt trade. Like Ghana, Mali kept order along the Saharan trade routes by using a large army. This army also kept life in Mali relatively peaceful.

Like many of Mali's rulers after Sundiata, Mansa Musa was a devout Muslim. Islam had actually been introduced into West Africa by Muslim traders in Ghana, but it had never taken hold in the earlier empire. In Mali, however, the situation was different. Islam became a powerful influence there, especially among the ruling class.

In 1324 Mansa Musa set out on a hajj, or pilgrimage, to Mecca. He took along a huge entourage—more than 60,000 people. As they traveled, the pilgrims impressed the people they met with their lavish clothing and generous gifts. According to one Cairo official, the visitors gave away so much gold that the metal's value was severely reduced:

HISTORY'S VOICES

❝There was no person, officer of the [Cairo] court or holder of any office of the [Cairo] sultanate who did not receive a sum of gold from him . . . So much gold was current in Cairo that it ruined the value of money.❞

—Ibn Fadl Allah al-Omari, from *Sight-Seeing Journeys, c. 1300s*

In addition to fulfilling Mansa Musa's religious obligation, the trip to Mecca led to great changes in Mali. When he returned to his empire, Mansa Musa brought along artists and architects who designed beautiful mosques, some of which still stand. He also built schools and libraries where people could study the Qur'an and other Islamic writings. Many of these schools were located in the city of Timbuktu, which became West Africa's chief center of education, religion, and culture.

Mansa Musa's Pilgrimage

Mansa Musa's pilgrimage to Mecca in 1324 brought the wealth of Mali to the attention of the Muslim world and even medieval Europe. Based on historical accounts, Mansa Musa's impressive caravan included more than 60,000 people.

The baggage included huge amounts of gold to give away as gifts—gold valued at about $100 million today.

Some 500 people in the caravan carried staffs heavily decorated with gold to show Mali's wealth.

298 CHAPTER 10

Skills Focus: Interpreting Infographics

At Level

Social Studies Skill
Mansa Musa and his Pilgrimage

1. Remind students that the griots sang and told stories to share their history with children. Tell students that they are going to be griots and create a historical story or song about Mansa Musa's hajj.

2. Have students examine carefully the image in the History Close-Up feature. Have students look for details of the people, the architecture, and the obvious signs of wealth shown in the image. Remind students while this is a recreation of the event, it is based on historical accounts of Mansa Musa's pilgrimage.

3. Have students write their own brief story or poem about Mansa Musa's hajj, and have volunteers share their work with the class.
LS Verbal-Linguistic

Alternative Assessment Handbook, Rubric 39: Writing to Create

Mansa Musa's hajj also had effects outside of Africa. For example, it brought Mali to the attention of people in Europe, and Mali began to appear on European maps for the first time. Within a century, Europeans began to search West Africa for the source of Mali's riches.

The Decline of Mali The rulers who followed Mansa Musa were not as strong as he had been. A series of weak *mansas* left Mali's government in shambles in the 1300s. Without a strong authority in control, several peoples broke away from the empire and set up independent kingdoms. At the same time, peoples from outside of Mali invaded. Among these invaders were the Tuareg of North Africa. In 1433 the Tuareg captured Timbuktu, a blow from which Mali never recovered. The empire slowly slipped into decline.

READING CHECK **Analyze** What effects did Mansa Musa's travels have in Mali and in Europe?

Empire of Songhai

Songhai had existed as a small kingdom for centuries, paying tribute to the leaders of Ghana and Mali. Located in the eastern part of what had been Mali, Songhai grew wealthy trading goods along the Niger River. During this trade, the people of Songhai came into contact with Muslim traders who had settled in the city of Gao. As a result of this contact, Islam was introduced into Songhai, where it soon became a major influence on culture.

The Rise of Songhai By the 1460s the kingdom of Songhai had become strong and wealthy enough to begin to rival the empire of Mali. Songhai's rise took place largely under the leadership of a military leader, or *sunni*, named **Sunni Ali**. Ali's first act as leader was to take Timbuktu from the Tuareg. He then led a number of campaigns against neighboring peoples to build an empire.

Mansa Musa rode near the front. During his journey, he gained fame for his generosity.

Called "ships of the desert," camels could go for long periods without water and could withstand heat better than horses and donkeys.

FACES OF HISTORY

Mansa Musa
unknown–1332?

Mansa Musa was a descendant of Sundiata, the first emperor to rule a united Mali. Mansa Musa became emperor of Mali in 1307 and earned a reputation as an able administrator. He increased the territory of Mali and was a patron of education and the arts.

Summarize Why is Mansa Musa remembered as a great ruler?

Skills FOCUS **INTERPRETING VISUALS**

Draw Conclusions During his pilgrimage, Mansa Musa had to cross part of the Sahara. How do you think he prepared for this part of his journey?

go.hrw.com
COULD YOU HAVE SURVIVED?
Keyword: SHL AFK

Go online for a closer look at survival and this event.

AFRICAN KINGDOMS **299**

3 What were the greatest achievements of the Songhai Empire? *Askia Muhammad began Muslim dynasty, made pilgrimage to Mecca, Songhai became large, wealthy empire*

Empire of Songhai

Recall What means did Sunni Ali use to attack Mali? *a skilled cavalry and a navy of war canoes*

Explain How did Sunni Ali maintain control of smaller kingdoms? *replaced local leaders with his own representatives who were loyal to him*

Make Inferences Do you think the primary reason for Askia Muhammad's hajj was to show that he was a devout Muslim? *possible answer—no, may have wanted to restore relationship with Muslim traders, demonstrate wealth, be seen as Muslim king*

 Quick Facts Transparency: Trading Empires of West Africa

Info to Know

Europeans in West Africa The Portuguese established a chain of trade settlements on the "Gold Coast" of West Africa. The most important settlement was El Mina, where European ironware, cloth, food, and firearms were exchanged for African gold, ivory, and food beginning in the early 1400s.

TRADING EMPIRES OF WEST AFRICA

EMPIRE	KEY FACTS
GHANA (800s–1070s)	• Location: Near Niger and Senegal rivers • Key cities: Koumbi Saleh (capital) • Trade: Controlled gold-salt trade routes • Beliefs: Local beliefs; some Muslim influences
MALI (1230s–1430s)	• Location: Along upper Niger River • Key Cities: Niani (capital), Timbuktu • Key Rulers: Sundiata; Mansa Musa • Trade: Controlled gold-salt trade routes • Beliefs: Islam; local beliefs
SONGHAI (1460s–1591)	• Location: Near Niger River • Key Cities: Gao (capital), Timbuktu • Key Rulers: Sunni Ali; Askia Muhammad • Trade: Trans-Saharan trade • Beliefs: Islam; local beliefs

NEW YORK

CC Unit 3-D6 Rise and fall of African civilizations: Songhai, its role in global trade routes, and the spread and impact of Islam

Ali's military success was due to his army of skilled cavalry and navy of war canoes. According to oral tradition, his forces never lost a battle. As he conquered new territories, Sunni Ali replaced local leaders with his own loyal followers. This made revolts among conquered peoples, which had contributed to the downfall of Ghana and Mali, less likely.

Askia Muhammad Songhai reached its cultural height under **Askia Muhammad**, whose reign is considered a golden age. During the 35 years of his rule, Askia Muhammad expanded Songhai and strengthened its government.

Askia Muhammad was Songhai's first Muslim ruler as well. Islam had been introduced into Songhai earlier, but Sunni Ali had never become a Muslim. To show his commitment to Islam, Askia Muhammad decided to make a grand pilgrimage to Mecca. Like Mansa Musa before him, he traveled through Egypt, where he gained the support of the Muslim rulers.

During Askia Muhammad's pilgrimage, he made contact with traders from North Africa. As a result, the trans-Saharan trade that had slowed after the fall of Mali resumed once again. This increased <u>commerce</u> made Songhai a very wealthy kingdom. Askia Muhammad used his new wealth to once again make Timbuktu a center of culture and Islamic scholarship.

ACADEMIC VOCABULARY

commerce trade, or the exchange of goods or services

300 CHAPTER 10

To secure his control of the trans-Saharan trade, Askia Muhammad extended Songhai's borders north into the desert, the home of the Tuareg. He did not want raiders to interfere with traveling merchants. He also reformed Songhai's government to help keep order in the empire. For example, while he ruled the eastern part of the empire personally, he appointed an official called the *kurmina fari* to manage the western part. He also built offices in the capital city of Gao to oversee trade, agriculture, and the military.

Eventually, however, Askia Muhammad was overthrown by his son, who became king. He and the later kings did not manage the empire as well as Askia Muhammad had, and in 1591 the empire was conquered by Morocco.

READING CHECK **Describe** What kind of government did Askia Muhammad create in Songhai?

Other West African States

Although the trading empires of Ghana, Mali, and Songhai were the largest and wealthiest societies in West Africa, they were not the only ones. If you look at the map at the beginning of this chapter, you will see that other societies developed to the east and south of those empires. Though these other societies did not rival the size or power of the trading kingdoms, they made significant advances of their own.

Hausa City-States To the east of Songhai lived a people called the Hausa. The Hausa built a society based on independent city-states, which gained regional power between 1000 and 1200. Each city-state included a group of villages surrounded by wooden walls and extensive fields. These city-states never united into an empire, though they cooperated and traded with each other.

The economy of the Hausa city-states was based on farming, manufacturing, and trade. Much of the labor for farming was performed by enslaved people. Slave labor was also used to build new cities, and enslaved people became one of the Hausa's exports. Other important exports included cloth and leather goods. The Hausa were known as skilled weavers and dyers, and cotton cloth dyed in a dark blue color by Hausa artisans was in high demand throughout much of West Africa.

Skills Focus: Interpreting Charts

At Level

Reading Skill

Standard English Mastery

Trading Kingdoms of West Africa

1. Remind students that West Africa developed rapidly during the period of the trading kingdoms.

2. Have students refer to the Quick Facts chart on this page for information about Ghana, Mali, and Songhai.

3. Have students use their summaries and the information in the chart to write a four-paragraph essay comparing and contrasting the three trading kingdoms. Remind students to use

dictionaries and to follow proper grammatical conventions.

4. Have students work in pairs to review the draft manuscript of their essays and correct them as needed before turning in the work.

LS Verbal-Linguistic

Alternative Assessment Handbook, Rubrics 9: Comparing and Contrasting; and 42: Writing to Inform

---

Answers

Reading Check *strengthened the government, appointed an official to rule the western part of the empire*

Yoruba Kingdoms Another complex society developed to the south of Songhai among the Yoruba. The Yoruba were actually several peoples who lived in the same area and spoke related languages. Over time, the Yoruba established a number of strong kingdoms. The most powerful of these kingdoms were Ife and Oyo. Ife reached its height around the 1100s to 1400s, while Oyo rose in power around the 1400s to 1600s and eventually surpassed Ife.

The people of the Yoruba kingdoms were widely admired for their artistic skill. Yoruba artists produced realistic sculptures out of terra-cotta, bronze, brass, and copper. Many of these sculptures depict Yoruba leaders, or onis. The Yoruba imported the materials for these statues, especially copper, from Sahara traders, who also brought salt to the region. In return, the Yoruba sent food and ivory north.

Kingdom of Benin Southwest of the Yoruba kingdoms was the powerful kingdom of Benin. Located deep in the forests of the Niger delta, Benin grew into a powerful state perhaps as early as the 1000s. At the heart of the kingdom lay the capital city, also called Benin. Several miles wide, this city featured large houses and wide streets that impressed visitors.

In the mid-1400s, an ambitious *oba*, or ruler, named Ewuare came to power in Benin. Wanting to expand his kingdom, Ewuare built a powerful army and went to war. By his death, the kingdom of Benin stretched from the Niger River west to what is now central Nigeria.

Around this period, the people of Benin came into contact with Europeans. Portuguese sailors arrived in the late 1400s. Having been at war for several decades, the people of Benin had many captives whom they sold to the Portuguese as slaves. Trade between Benin and Portugal continued, though trade in slaves ceased for several centuries. Instead, Benin traded pepper, ivory, and cotton for gold.

Like the Yoruba, the people of Benin were known for their arts. Statues of bronze, brass, and copper were created to honor notable leaders, and copper plaques illustrated with scenes from Benin's history were displayed in cities. Brought home by the Portuguese, art from Benin also became popular in Europe.

READING CHECK **Identify** What was one result of contact between Benin and Portugal?

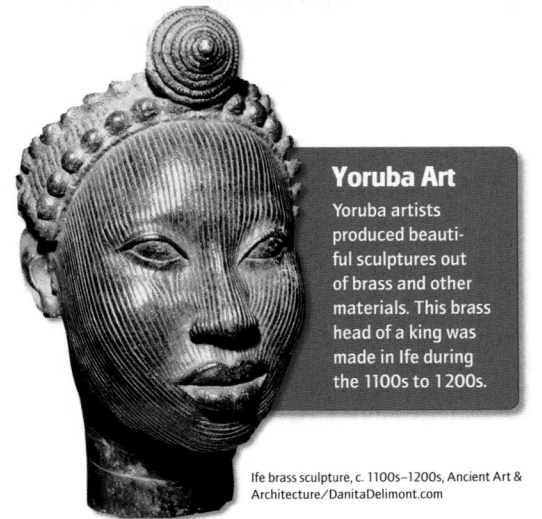

Yoruba Art
Yoruba artists produced beautiful sculptures out of brass and other materials. This brass head of a king was made in Ife during the 1100s to 1200s.

Ife brass sculpture, c. 1100s–1200s, Ancient Art & Architecture/DanitaDelimont.com

---

SECTION 3 ASSESSMENT

go.hrw.com
Online Quiz
Keyword: SHL AFK HP

Reviewing Ideas, Terms, and People

1. **a. Recall** What were the two major trade goods that made Ghana rich? From where did these two trade goods come?
   b. Explain Why did Ghana's rulers not want everyone to own gold?

2. **a. Identify** Who was **Sundiata**?
   b. Identify Cause and Effect How did **Mansa Musa**'s pilgrimage to Mecca affect the empire of Mali?
   c. Elaborate How did Muslim influences help turn Mali into a center of learning?

3. **a. Recall** What did **Sunni Ali** accomplish as ruler?
   b. Analyze How did Askia Muhammad's pilgrimage to Mecca contribute to the power of the Songhai Empire?
   c. Evaluate What do you think was Askia Muhammad's greatest accomplishment as a ruler?

4. **a. Recall** What were three smaller societies located in early West Africa?
   b. Compare What was one similarity between the Yoruba kingdoms and the kingdom of Benin?

Critical Thinking

5. **Compare and Contrast** Using your notes and a graphic organizer like the one at right, compare and contrast the West African empires of Ghana, Mali, and Songhai.

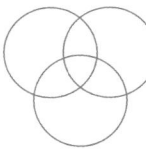

FOCUS ON WRITING

6. **Persuasion** Choose the West African ruler covered in this section who you think accomplished the most or was the greatest ruler. Write one paragraph in which you identify your choice and provide reasons to persuade others to agree with it.

AFRICAN KINGDOMS **301**

The Influence of Trade on African Culture

Word Help

Berber a North African group

Info to Know

Leo Africanus (c. 1465–1550) Born in Spain, Leo Africanus lived and was educated in Morocco. He made two journeys to West Africa between 1509 and 1513. His account of his travels was widely published in Europe in the 1500s, and his descriptions became Europe's primary source of information about West Africa. Leo Africanus himself was captured by pirates while traveling off the North African coast. His captors presented him as a slave to Pope Leo X. After a year, the pope set him free. Although Leo Africanus is said to have converted to Christianity, it is believed that he returned to his Muslim beliefs before his death in North Africa.

Teaching Tip

Tell students that the word *Swahili* means "coast people." Ask them why this term came to refer to the blended Arab-African culture of the East African coastal city-states.

The Influence of Trade on African Culture

Historical Context The documents in this investigation describe how trade contributed to cultural blending in early and medieval Africa.

Task Study the documents and answer the questions that follow. Then, using evidence from these documents and from the chapter, write an essay explaining how trade contributed to cultural blending in early and medieval Africa.

NEW YORK STANDARDS

PI 1.4 Students understand the broad patterns, relationships, and interactions of cultures and civilizations during particular eras and across eras.

PI 3.2 Students explain the dynamics of cultural change and how interactions between and among cultures have affected various cultural groups throughout the world.

DOCUMENT 1

Leo Africanus: City of Timbuktu

A Muslim traveler and scholar named Leo Africanus visited northern and western Africa in the early 1500s. In the book about his travels, titled the *History and Description of Africa,* Leo Africanus describes the city of Timbuktu, at the time part of the Songhai Empire.

The shops of the artisans, the merchants, and especially weavers of cotton cloth are very numerous. Fabrics are also imported from Europe to Timbuktu, borne by Berber merchants.

The women of the city maintain the custom of veiling their faces, except for the slaves . . . There are in Timbuktu numerous judges, teachers and priests, all properly appointed by the king. He greatly honors learning. Many hand-written books imported from Barbary [North Africa] are also sold. There is more profit made from this commerce [trade] than from all other merchandise.

Instead of coined money, pure gold nuggets are used; and for small purchases, cowrie shells which have been carried from Persia.

DOCUMENT 2

Kani Kombole Mosque

Muslims conquered parts of North Africa in the 700s, and over time North African traders helped spread Islam to West Africa. By the 1300s, mosques had become a common feature in many West African towns. Early West African mosques combined Muslim styles with West African building techniques, such as the use of dried mud reinforced with wooden poles. The mosque shown here is located in Kani Kombole, a Dogon village in what is now Mali. In addition to general West African characteristics, this mosque has specific Dogon characteristics such as niches along the outer wall.

Skills Focus: Comparing and Contrasting

At Level

Research Required

Reading Skill
African Mosques

1. Have students compare the photograph on this page with the photograph of the mosque that opens this chapter. Then, copy the Venn diagram for all to see.

2. Have students conduct research to find photographs of other mosques Have students copy and complete the Venn diagram.
   LS Visual-Spatial, Intrapersonal

   Alternative Assessment Handbook, Rubric 13: Graphic Organizers

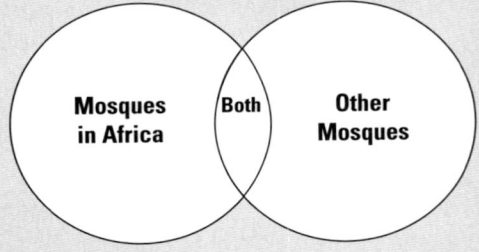

DOCUMENT 3

Ibn Battutah: Travels in Mali

Ibn Battutah, a famous Muslim traveler, visited the Mali Empire in 1352. In the following passage from his book, *Travels in Asia and Africa,* Battutah describes some traditional customs and Muslim practices of the people of the Mali Empire.

On feast-days ... the poets come in. Each of them is inside a figure resembling a thrush [a type of bird], made of feathers, and provided with a wooden head with a red beak, to look like a thrush's head. They stand in front of the sultan [king] ... and recite their poems ... I was told that this practice is a very old custom amongst them, prior to the introduction of Islam, and that they have kept it up ...

They are careful to observe the hours of prayer ... On Fridays, if a man does not go early to the mosque, he cannot find a corner to pray in, on account of the crowd ... Their prayer-mats are made of the leaves of a tree resembling a date-palm, but without fruit.

Another of their good qualities is their ... zeal for learning the Koran by heart. They put their children in chains if they show any backwardness in memorizing it, and they are not set free until they have it by heart.

DOCUMENT 4

Swahili Culture

In the following passage, writer Robert Caputo describes how trade and cultural blending led to the development of the Swahili culture. The passage is from the article "Swahili Coast," which appeared in *National Geographic* magazine in October 2001.

A string of ports that stretched along the East African coast from Mogadishu to present-day Mozambique ... evolved into powerful city-states as they grew rich from Indian Ocean trade ... Arabian sailors arriving in Africa found good harbors, a sea full of fish, fertile land, and opportunities for trade. Many of the Arabian sailors stayed to marry local women, and the melding [blending] is evident in the faces of the people ... Indeed, the interplay of African and Arabian languages and customs—the mingling of blood and ideas that permeated [spread throughout] every aspect of life created an urban and mercantile [trade-based] culture ... that is unique to this coast. Even its name, Swahili, is an adaptation of the Arabic word for coast, *sawahil* ...

Professor [Abdul] Sheriff in Zanzibar ... said ... "Swahili history is about adaptation and incorporation. We have always been middlemen—between the land and the sea, the producers and the buyers, the African and the Arabian. That is not a concern; it is our strength."

Skills FOCUS — READING LIKE A HISTORIAN

DOCUMENT 1
a. Identify What foreign goods and influences did Leo Africanus note in Timbuktu?
b. Draw Conclusions How do you think that foreign trade goods contributed to cultural blending in Timbuktu?

DOCUMENT 2
a. Describe How did trade influence religion and architecture in early West Africa?
b. Explain How does the architecture of the West African mosque in the photograph illustrate cultural blending?

DOCUMENT 3
a. Recall What traditional African custom did the people of Mali maintain despite their adoption of Islam?
b. Analyze How did the people of the Mali Empire adapt Islam to their own culture and environment?

DOCUMENT 4
a. Identify What two cultures blended together to form the Swahili culture and language?
b. Summarize Based on the passage, how do the Swahili people view the ways in which their culture has evolved?

DOCUMENT-BASED ESSAY QUESTION

Several strong trading kingdoms and empires developed in early and medieval Africa. Using the documents above and information from the chapter, form a thesis about how trade contributed to cultural blending in these kingdoms and empires. Then write an essay providing details to support your thesis.

See **Skills Handbook**, p. H48

AFRICAN KINGDOMS **303**

Differentiating Instruction

Above Level

Advanced Learners/Gifted and Talented

Research Required

1. Tell students that Ibn Battutah traveled not only in Mali, but throughout Asia and the rest of Africa. Have students conduct independent research to locate more excerpts from Battutah's *Travels in Asia and Africa.* The goal of their research should be to find further examples of cultural blending in Africa.

2. Organize students into groups of four to six. Each group should use its research to create a multimedia presentation showing the cultural

blending that occurred in East Africa as a result of trade. Multimedia presentations should include photographs or drawings of architecture and other cultural influences, and quotations from Ibn Battutah's account.

3. Have students give their presentations to the class. **LS Visual-Spatial, Interpersonal**

Alternative Assessment Handbook, Rubrics 22: Multimedia Presentations; and 30: Research

Primary Source

"There are many languages in the world, pronounced in different ways, and all the languages on earth have people who belong to them, in a special place
Not only in India, not only in Europe and America
[but everywhere] has the Almighty created language
I ask...
The Kamba have their own language which has been there since their genesis; and the British too [or the Europeans] have their own several languages; and the Meru people have their own, and the Somali are a different people again
and so they have their own language. And which language is ours?"
—from the poem "The Swahili Language," by Ahmad Bhalo

Answers

Document 1 a. *fabrics from Europe, books from North Africa, shells from Persia;* **b.** *These foreign trade items probably were valuable in Timbuktu. Books likely spread ideas from other cultures.* **Document 2 a.** *Trade brought the religion of Islam to Africa, along with its distinctive mosque architecture.* **b.** *possible answer—It appears to have adapted the Arab-style mosque architecture to work with local building materials, such as mud. This mosque also includes building characteristics of the Dogon people, an ethnic group in Africa.* **Document 3. a.** *They read poetry on feast-days, dressed as birds.* **b.** *Their prayer mats are made from local plants.* **Document 4 a.** *Arabian and African cultures;* **b.** *They seem to be proud of their culture of "adaptation and incorporation."* **Essay** *Student essays should describe how trade with Europe, Arabia, and other parts of the world led to cultural blending in African kingdoms and empires. Essays should be supported with details and examples from Documents 1–4 and the chapter.*

303

Visual Summary

Review and Inquiry Organize students into four groups. Assign each group one chart from the Visual Study Guide, which corresponds to the Reading Focus questions for each section. Have each group create a poster to demonstrate its assigned concept.

Quick Facts Transparency: Visual Study Guide: African Kingdoms

Review Key Terms and People

1. Sahel
2. griots
3. Nok
4. Ezana
5. Ge'ez
6. Lalibela
7. Swahili
8. Mansa Musa
9. Askia Muhammad
10. barter

Comprehension and Critical Thinking

11. a. the Sahel, savanna, tropical rain forests
b. village-based cultures, family ties, age-sets, religious beliefs, oral traditions
c. possible answer—positive, because the migration spread iron-working technology, which enabled societies to become more advanced

12. a. a blended African and Arabic language and culture; coastal East Africa
b. Trade helped both Aksum and the city-states grow wealthy. However, Aksum was a unified empire, while each of the city-states remained independent. Aksum was also Christian, while the city-states were Muslim.
c. Located along the trade routes between the coast and the interior gold mines, Great Zimbabwe could profit as a middleman for trade.

VISUAL STUDY GUIDE

QUICK FACTS

African Environments

Environment	Description
Desert	Arid wastelands; Sahara
Dry woodland	Wooded areas
Mediterranean	Mild, fertile areas; northern and southern coastal tips
Sahel	Semiarid land south of the Sahara
Savanna	Grasslands with scattered trees; dry and wet seasons; support farming; most populated region
Tropical rain forest	Hot, humid, and dense forests; high rainfall year-round

African Traditions

Characteristic	Description
Family ties	Extended families; clans; age-sets
Religions	Animism; ancestor worship
Oral traditions	Griots; history, stories, songs, poems, proverbs
Arts	Masks, dance, music

East African Civilizations

Society or State	Date	Key Rulers/City-States	Key Facts
Aksum	100s–500s (height)	King Ezana	Northeast trading kingdom; Christian
Early Ethiopia	1100s (founded)	King Lalibela	Northeast kingdom; Christian
Coastal trading city-states	1100s–1400s	Kilwa, Mogadishu, Mombasa, Sofala	Swahili; Arab and Muslim influence
Great Zimbabwe	1100s–1400s	—	Southeast inland trading kingdom

West African Civilizations

Society or State	Date	Key Rulers/City-States	Key Facts
Ghana Empire	800s–1070s	—	Gold-salt trade
Mali Empire	1230s–1430s	Sundiata, Mansa Musa	Gold-salt trade; Muslim
Songhai Empire	1460s–1591	Sunni Ali, Askia Muhammad	Trans-Saharan trade; Muslim
Benin Kingdom	1000s–1800s	—	Trade; bronze artwork

Review Key Terms and People

Identify the term or person from the chapter that best fits each of the following descriptions.

1. Semiarid region in Africa just south of the Sahara that separates the desert from wetter areas
2. West African storytellers
3. One of the earliest African cultures to practice iron working

4. Aksum king who conquered Kush
5. The written language developed in Aksum
6. Ethiopian king who built 11 Christian churches
7. East African language and culture that blends African and Arab influences
8. Mali ruler who made a famous hajj to Mecca
9. First Muslim ruler of Songhai
10. Trade or the exchange of goods

13. a. trade
b. Both were Muslim, and both made pilgrimages to Mecca.
c. They used available natural resources such as bronze, brass, and copper to create works of art.

Reading Skills

14. possible answer—details about the different landscapes, climates, and rainfall in different parts of Africa

15. possible answers—photographs and descriptions of African mosques, details about the actions of Muslim rulers, description of the Swahili culture

16. possible answers—details about the kings' supply of gold, maps of trade routes, archaeological evidence of trade items from faraway places found in Africa, description of Mansa Musa's lavish caravan

Comprehension and Critical Thinking

SECTION 1 *(pp. 283–287)*

11. a. Recall What are three different environments found in Africa?

b. Summarize What social structures and cultural traditions did many early African societies have in common?

c. Evaluate In your opinion, were the effects of the Bantu migrations positive, negative, or both? Explain your answer.

SECTION 2 *(pp. 288–293)*

12. a. Define What is Swahili, and in what area of Africa did it develop?

b. Compare and Contrast What did the kingdom of Aksum have in common with the coastal city-states of East Africa? How did Aksum differ from the coastal city-states?

c. Elaborate How did its location benefit the kingdom of Great Zimbabwe?

SECTION 3 *(pp. 295–301)*

13. a. Identify Main Ideas What did the empires of Ghana, Mali, and Songhai rely on for their economic prosperity?

b. Compare What did Mansa Musa and Askia Muhammad have in common as rulers?

c. Elaborate How did the smaller states of West Africa make use of their environments?

Reading Skills

Identifying Supporting Details *Use what you know about identifying supporting details to answer the following questions.*

14. What details support the statement that Africa is a large continent with a wide variety of climate and vegetation regions?

15. What details support the statement that the spread of Islam influenced the government, society, and culture of early Africa?

16. What details support the statement that trade contributed to the development, wealth, and power of many of the early kingdoms and empires in Africa?

Analyzing Secondary Sources

Reading Like a Historian *In the following passage, historian Basil Davidson describes some ways in which the camel affected the trans-Saharan trade in early Africa.*

❝ For centuries the lucrative [profitable] West African trade routes have depended on the camel caravan. Without the camel the barren expanses of the Sahara would have effectively blocked contact between the fertile northern coastland and the rich forests of the south . . . Though vital to trade, caravans were not a very efficient means of transport, largely because of the camels themselves. Ill-tempered, surly [rude] beasts, they balked at every attempt to bridle or load them, biting or spitting at the cameleers . . . And once on the move the caravan could not stop until evening for the camels would sit, spilling their loads onto the sand. ❞

—Basil Davidson, *African Kingdoms*

17. Analyze How did the use of camel caravans benefit trade in early Africa?

18. Summarize What were some drawbacks of using camel caravans to cross the Sahara?

Using the Internet

go.hrw.com
Practice Online
Keyword: SHL AFK

19. More than 800 different languages are spoken in Africa today. Using the keyword above, conduct research to learn about some of these languages. Then write two or three paragraphs about one African language or language group.

WRITING FOR THE SAT ✏

Think about the following issue:

All the gold produced in Ghana was officially the property of the king. Only the king could own gold nuggets, although Ghana's people could own and trade gold dust. Ghana's kings controlled the gold supply to regulate prices and keep the market from being flooded.

20. Assignment: *Do you think the economic control that Ghana's kings exercised benefitted the people of Ghana or not? Write a short essay in which you develop your position on this question. Support your point of view with reasons and examples from your reading.*

Answers

Analyzing Secondary Sources

17. allowed traders to cross the Sahara desert, which otherwise would have blocked trade

18. Camels were ill-tempered and difficult to manage; caravans could not stop during the day, fearing the camels would sit and spill their cargo.

Using the Internet

19. Go to the HRW Web site and enter the keyword shown to access a rubric for this activity.

KEYWORD: SHL AFK

Writing for the SAT

20. Student essays should explain the concept of scarcity as it relates to supply and demand. Essays should develop a position on whether the kings' control of Ghana's gold supply benefited the people of Ghana by keeping the price of gold high, or harmed them by limiting the amount of gold available for trade. Essays should be supported by details from the section.

A rubric for this activity is provided in **CRF: Writing for the SAT**.

HOLT
History's Impact
► **Video Program: African Kingdoms**
Refer to the Video Program Teacher's Guide for a discussion of the closing question.

Review and Assessment Resources

Review and Reinforce

- **CRF:** Chapter Review
- **Quick Facts Transparency:** Visual Study Guide: African Kingdoms
- **Spanish Chapter Summaries Audio CD Program**
- **OSP Holt PuzzlePro:** Quiz Show for ExamView
- **Quiz Game CD-ROM**

Assess

- **PASS:** Chapter Test, Forms A and B
- **Alternative Assessment Handbook**
- **OSP ExamView Test Generator,** Chapter Test
- **Differentiated Instruction Modified Worksheets and Tests CD-ROM:** Chapter Test
- **HOAP Holt Online Assessment Program** (in the Premier Online Edition)

Reteach/Intervene

- **Interactive Reader and Study Guide**
- **Differentiated Instruction Teacher Management System:** Lesson Plans for Differentiated Instruction
- **Differentiated Instruction Modified Worksheets and Tests CD-ROM:** Chapter Test
- **Interactive Skills Tutor CD-ROM**

go.hrw.com
Online Resources
KEYWORD: SHL TEACHER

Cultures of East Asia

CHAPTER 11 PLANNING GUIDE

Chapter Overview	Reproducible Resources	Technology Resources
CHAPTER 11 pp. 306–337 **Overview:** In this chapter, students will learn about China's various dynasties and their influence as they spread across East Asia. KI 1, 2; PI 1.1, 1.3, 1.4, 2.3, 2.4, 2.5 See pp. T32–T55 for a detailed correlation to the New York State Core Curriculum for Global History and Geography and the New York Learning Standards.	**Differentiated Instruction Teacher Management System:** • Pacing Guide • Lesson Plans for Differentiated Instruction **Interactive Reader and Study Guide:** Chapter Summary* **Chapter Resource File*** • Writing for the SAT • Social Studies Skill • Economics and History • Chapter Review **World History Outline Maps**	OSP **New York One-Stop Planner CD-ROM:** Calendar Planner **Live Ink© Online Reading Help** **Student Edition on Audio CD Program** **Differentiated Instruction Modified Worksheets and Tests CD-ROM** **Interactive Skills Tutor CD-ROM** **World History Primary Source Library CD-ROM** **Power Presentations with Video CD-ROM** **History's Impact: World History Video Program (VHS/DVD):** Cultures of East Asia
Section 1: **Chinese Empires** **The Main Idea:** The Sui dynasty reunified China, after which the Tang and Song dynasties produced an age of prosperity and achievement. PI 1.1	**Differentiated Instruction Teacher Management System:** Section 1 Lesson Plan* **Interactive Reader and Study Guide:** Section 1 Summary* **Chapter Resource File*** • Vocabulary Builder: Section 1 • Biography: Li Sixun • Literature: Spring Festival on the River	**Regents Review Transparency:** Section 1* **Map Transparency:** East Asia, c. 600* **Map Transparency:** Tang and Song Dynasties, 618–1279* **Quick Facts Transparency:** Innovations*
Section 2: **The Mongol Empire** **The Main Idea:** The Mongols built a vast empire across much of Asia, founded the Yuan dynasty in China, and opened China and the region to greater foreign contacts and trade. PI 2.5	**Differentiated Instruction Teacher Management System:** Section 2 Lesson Plan* **Interactive Reader and Study Guide:** Section 2 Summary* **Chapter Resource File*** • Vocabulary Builder: Section 2 • Biography: Sorghaghtani Beki • History and Geography: Mongol Military Might	**Regents Review Transparency:** Section 2* **Map Transparency:** Mongol Empire, 1294* **Internet Activity:** Genghis Khan: Leader of the Mongolian Empire **Internet Activity:** Marco Polo
Section 3: **Japan and Korea** **The Main Idea:** Geography and cultural borrowing from China shaped the early civilizations of Japan and Korea. PI 1.4, 2.4	**Differentiated Instruction Teacher Management System:** Section 3 Lesson Plan* **Interactive Reader and Study Guide:** Section 3 Summary* **Chapter Resource File*** • Vocabulary Builder: Section 3 • Biography: Murasaki Shikibu • Literature: Tanka Poems of Ancient Japan	**Regents Review Transparency:** Section 3* **Map Transparency:** Japan, 1300* **Map Transparency:** Korea, 918–1392*
Section 4: **Civilizations of Southeast Asia** **The Main Idea:** Geography and the cultures of India and China influenced the early civilizations of Southeast Asia. PI 1.3, 1.4, 2.3	**Differentiated Instruction Teacher Management System:** Section 4 Lesson Plan* **Interactive Reader and Study Guide:** Section 4 Summary* **Chapter Resource File*** • Vocabulary Builder: Section 4 • Biography: Sankara	**Regents Review Transparency:** Section 4* **Map Transparency:** Southeast Asian Kingdoms, 600–1350*

Review, Assessment, Intervention

Global History and Geography Regents Test Prep Workbook

Quick Facts Transparency: Cultures of East Asia*

Spanish Chapter Summaries Audio CD Program

Progress Assessment Support System (PASS): Chapter Test*

Differentiated Instruction Modified Worksheets and Tests CD-ROM: Modified Chapter Test

OSP New York One-Stop Planner CD-ROM: ExamView Test Generator (English/Spanish)

HOAP Holt Online Assessment Program (HOAP), in the Holt Premier Online Student Edition

---

PASS: Section 1 Quiz*

Online Quiz: Section 1

Alternative Assessment Handbook

PASS: Section 2 Quiz*

Online Quiz: Section 2

Alternative Assessment Handbook

PASS: Section 3 Quiz*

Online Quiz: Section 3

Alternative Assessment Handbook

PASS: Section 4 Quiz*

Online Quiz: Section 4

Alternative Assessment Handbook

Power Presentation with Video CD-ROM

Power Presentations with Video are visual presentations of each chapter's main ideas. Presentations can be customized by including Quick Facts charts, images and maps from the textbook, and video clips.

Holt Online Learning

go.hrw.com
Teacher Resources
KEYWORD: SHL TEACHER

go.hrw.com
Student Resources
KEYWORD: SHL CEA

- Document-Based Questions
- Interactive Multimedia Activities

- Current Events
- Chapter-Based Internet Activities
- and more!

Holt Premier
Online Student Edition
Complete online support for interactivity, assessment, and reporting

- Interactive Maps and Notebook
- Homework Practice and Research Activities Online

CHAPTER 11 PLANNING GUIDE

The Big Picture

Susan Ramírez

Cross-Cultural Encounters The many peoples of the vast area of East Asia did not live in isolation. Trade, conquest, migration, and religious proselytizing spread institutions from one group to another. India gave its neighbors and trading partners Hinduism and Buddhism, and served as one conduit for the spread of Islam. The Koreans and Japanese imported governing practices, like the civil service examination; script; and new crops, such as cotton, from China. By the end of the period, maritime and overland trade of silk, spices, porcelain, aromatics, and silver, linked the most far-flung kingdoms of East Asia to the heartland of Europe.

Early State Formation Enduring problems for early states included stability and the effective governance of distant peoples. Over the generations, the founding dynamism of early leaders faded. Taxes increased as governments grew. Other power contenders capitalized on discontent and eventually seized control. To break this cyclical rise and fall from power, leaders looked for means to improve their rule. One institution that the Chinese developed to this end was a civil service examination that opened government service to the best qualified individuals. This means of opening the opportunity structure to talent is one legacy from the past that is still important today.

Technological Innovation The peoples of East Asia, and especially the Chinese, were the inventors of their age. New agricultural techniques produced more rice. Shipbuilding advanced. Woodblock printing, movable type, paper money, gunpowder, and the compass were among their advances. These innovations spread throughout the region and eventually were adopted around the world.

Recent Scholarship

Some people focus on the voyages of Columbus and their aftermath in the Americas as the example of cross-cultural encounters. Jerry H. Bentley in his book *Old World Encounters: Cross-Cultural Contacts and Exchanges in Pre-Modern Times* puts the age of American exploration in perspective by examining life on the ancient Silk Road, the spread of world religions (like Buddhism), and the rise of nomadic empires. He shows that interactions across cultural frontiers could be complex and conflictive and that they had to be negotiated.

Differentiating Instruction

 Differentiated Instruction Teacher Management System
- Pacing Guide
- Lesson Plans for Differentiated Instruction

Interactive Reader and Study Guide

Spanish Chapter Summaries Audio CD Program

Student Edition on Audio CD Program

 Differentiated Instruction Modified Worksheets and Tests CD-ROM
- Vocabulary Flash Cards
- Modified Vocabulary Builder Activities
- Modified Chapter Review Activity
- Modified Chapter Test

OSP **One-Stop Planner CD-ROM**
- ExamView Test Generator (English /Spanish)
- PuzzlePro
- Quiz Show for ExamView
- Transparencies and Videos

TE **Differentiated Activities in the Teacher's Edition**
- Create Posters of Sang and Tang Achievements, p. 314
- Plan a Multimedia Presentation on the Mongols, p. 317
- Create Advertisements for Ancient Trade Goods, p. 332
- Research Women of the Heian Period, p. 335

Reading Like a Historian
Sam Wineburg

We are not even sure about the origin of her name, Sei Shonagon, since shonagon, "lesser counselor," was a title for a woman reflecting her father's status, and her father was not a shonagon. Her book at first glance seems strewn together, a random pastiche of lists mixed with brief vignettes and idiosyncratic impressions. The origin of the book's title is shrouded in mist. Even today no one even knows where she's buried.

But 1000 years after Sei Shonagon's death, the *Pillow Book* remains in print. Its opening lines, "In Spring, the dawn; The sky, dyed in morning light, slowly brightens and purple clouds stretch across the mountain," are recited by millions of Japanese school children, who memorize passages in junior high. It is a work whose words have maintained their "freshness and individuality a millennium after they were first conceived," writes Columbia's Donald Keene, author of *Seeds in the Heart: Japanese Literature from Earliest Times to the Late Sixteenth Century.*

A Voice from the Past When we first approach the *Pillow Book*, we are struck by the gap between the world of contemporary America and the court life of 10th century Imperial Japan. We can imagine few parallels between our students' instant-messengered lives and the cloistered existence of Sei Shonagon, much of it spent with other courtesans of the empress fanning themselves in dimly-lit rooms. The cultural codes that shape the *Pillow Book* seem impenetrable to anyone unstudied in Japanese culture. Comparing our modern lives to Sei Shonagon's invites anachronism and courts misunderstanding.

At the same time, the *Pillow Book* has withstood the test of time precisely because it bears the defining mark of every great writer: Voice. Across this 1000-year divide, even in translation, even in the face of cultural differences we can never fully fathom, we discern the unmistakable personality of Sei Shonagon. She's devilishly funny: "Things

that look hot and uncomfortable—fat people with hair plastered on their foreheads"; she possesses an acerbic wit: "Things that are the reverse of the other: summer and winter, the feeling I have seeing a man I once loved but now don't"; she's a snoop, but one we can't help identifying with: "Things that make me happy: I'm delighted when I find that, after putting the scraps together, I can read a letter someone threw away."

Her insights glisten. She weaves this example into her list of "Hateful Things": "A lover who is leaving at dawn announces he has to find his fan and his paper. 'I know I put them somewhere last night,' he says. Since it is pitch dark, he gropes about the room, bumping into the furniture and muttering, 'Strange! Where on earth can they be?' Finally he discovers the objects. He thrusts the paper into the breast of his robe with a great rustling sound; then he snaps open his fan and busily fans away with it. Only now is he ready to take his leave. What charmless behavior! 'Hateful' is an understatement."

We easily visualize the scene. The hush of intimacy shattered by the clunkiness of a bumbling lover trying to locate the 10th century equivalent of car keys. He starts to use his fan not because he's hot, but because he's on automatic pilot and can think of nothing better to do. He's oblivious to everything—most of all to the woman whose bed he has just left.

In the *Pillow Book*, we confront a radically different culture and vastly different era. Both aspects ordinarily pose insuperable barriers to historical understanding. But Sei Shonagon's words are an exception. Her extraordinary talent, honesty, and above all humanity radiate from the 10th century and make us smile even today.

Chapter Main Ideas

Section 1 The Sui dynasty reunified China, after which the Tang and Song dynasties produced an age of prosperity and achievement.

Section 2 The Mongols built a vast empire across much of Asia, founded the Yuan dynasty in China, and opened China and the region to greater foreign contacts and trade.

Section 3 Geography and cultural borrowing from China shaped the early civilizations of Japan and Korea.

Section 4 Geography and the cultures of India and China influenced the early civilizations of Southeast Asia.

New York Standards

Key Idea 1 The study of world history requires an understanding of world cultures and civilizations, including an analysis of important ideas, social and cultural values, beliefs, and traditions. This study also examines the human condition and the connections and interactions of people across time and space and the ways different people view the same event or issue from a variety of perspectives.

Key Idea 2 Establishing timeframes, exploring different periodizations, examining themes across time and within cultures, and focusing on important turning points in world history help organize the study of world cultures and civilizations.

Key to Differentiating Instruction

Below Level

Basic-level activities designed for all students encountering new material

At Level

Intermediate-level activities designed for average students

Above Level

Challenging activities designed for honors and gifted and talented students

Standard English Mastery

Activities designed to improve standard English usage

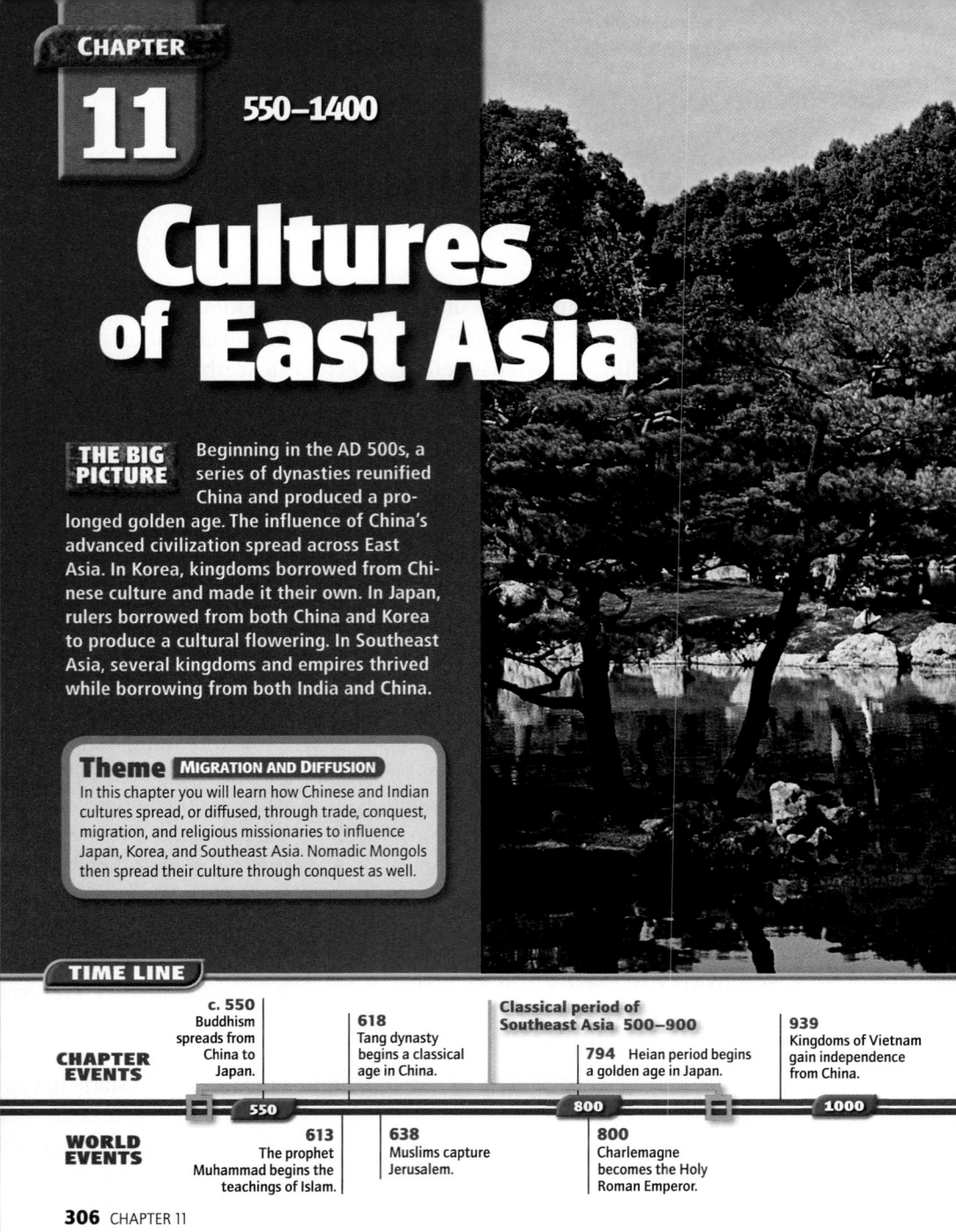

CHAPTER

11 550–1400

Cultures of East Asia

THE BIG PICTURE Beginning in the AD 500s, a series of dynasties reunified China and produced a prolonged golden age. The influence of China's advanced civilization spread across East Asia. In Korea, kingdoms borrowed from Chinese culture and made it their own. In Japan, rulers borrowed from both China and Korea to produce a cultural flowering. In Southeast Asia, several kingdoms and empires thrived while borrowing from both India and China.

Theme MIGRATION AND DIFFUSION
In this chapter you will learn how Chinese and Indian cultures spread, or diffused, through trade, conquest, migration, and religious missionaries to influence Japan, Korea, and Southeast Asia. Nomadic Mongols then spread their culture through conquest as well.

TIME LINE

CHAPTER EVENTS

| c. 550 Buddhism spreads from China to Japan. | 618 Tang dynasty begins a classical age in China. | Classical period of Southeast Asia 500–900 | 794 Heian period begins a golden age in Japan. | 939 Kingdoms of Vietnam gain independence from China. |

550 — 800 — 1000

WORLD EVENTS

| 613 The prophet Muhammad begins the teachings of Islam. | 638 Muslims capture Jerusalem. | 800 Charlemagne becomes the Holy Roman Emperor. |

306 CHAPTER 11

Introduce the Chapter
At Level

Cultures of East Asia

1. Write the phrases Classical Period and Golden Age for students to see. Have students write a few sentences about what they think these phrases mean.

2. Have volunteers read their sentences to the class. Write their responses below the phrases.

3. Guide students in a discussion about the meaning of the two phrases.

4. Tell students that in this chapter they will learn about a classical period and a period of foreign rule in China, a golden age in Japan, and the growth of various Southeast Asian kingdoms.

5. Have students scan the graphics and images in the chapter and make a list of questions they would like to ask about content in the chapter. **LS Verbal-Linguistic**

Alternative Assessment Handbook, Rubric 1: Acquiring Information

History's Impact video program

Watch the video to understand the impact of Chinese culture on Japan.

Reading like a Historian

The photograph above is of the Kinkaku-ji, or Golden Pavilion Temple, in Kyoto, Japan. Built during the 1300s as a residence, the building was converted to a Zen Buddhist temple in the 1400s. The gardens and architecture of the temple are meant to evoke paradise on Earth.

Analyzing Visuals Based on the photo, what were some features of Japanese architecture at the time?

See **Skills Handbook**, p. H26

c. 1100s
Angkor Wat built in the Khmer Empire.

1215
King John signs the Magna Carta in England.

1200

1279
Mongols take over China and found the Yuan dynasty.

1324
Mansa Musa begins his pilgrimage to Mecca.

1392
Choson dynasty begins in Korea.

1347
The Black Death strikes Europe.

1400

CULTURES OF EAST ASIA **307**

• Chapter Preview •

HOLT

History's Impact

▶ **Video Program: Cultures of East Asia**
See the Video Teacher's Guide for strategies for using the video segment.

Reading Like a Historian

Heian-jingu Shrine After making Kyoto, Japan its home from 794 to 1867, the Imperial Family relocated to Tokyo. This permanent departure left a great void in Kyoto. To make up for the loss the Kyoto people felt, the Heian-jingu Shrine was constructed, commemorating the city's 1,100th anniversary.

go.hrw.com

Online Resources

Chapter Resources:
KEYWORD: SHL CEA
Teacher Resources:
KEYWORD: SHL TEACHER

Explore the Time Line

1. When was the classical period of Southeast Asia? *500–900*

2. What happened in Japan shortly before Charlemagne became Holy Roman Emperor? *Heian period began its golden age*

3. When did Buddhism spread from China to Japan? *in about 550*

4. What people established the Yuan dynasty in China? *the Mongols*

Info to Know

Porcelain For many years, porcelain was one of the most valuable trade items in the world. First created in China during the Tang dynasty, porcelain is made from kaolin and petuntse, which are both forms of the mineral feldspar. Petuntse is ground into a powder and mixed with kaolin clay. The mixture is then fired in an extremely hot kiln, causing the two materials to fuse together.

Draw Conclusions Petuntse is found only in China. How does this fact affect the porcelain market? *gives China a monopoly on porcelain*

Answers

Reading Like a Historian *curved, pagoda-style roof lines, ornate structures with columns*

307

Geography Starting Points

Dong Son Drums Ancient bronze drums have been found in several places in Southeast Asia, especially concentrated in northern Vietnam, but also on the Malay Peninsula, in Sumatra, and in Java. These drums indicate that bronze-making technology existed in the region before the arrival of Indian or Chinese influence.

- **Map Transparency:** East Asia, c. 600
- **World History Outline Maps**
- **Interactive Map:** East Asia, c. 600

Info to Know

Indian Influence Around 600, Buddhist images and tablets and Sanskrit inscriptions began to appear in Southeast Asia. Although the cultures of Java and Sumatra had many Indian traits, they also sent tribute to China. By the 800s, Indian influence in the region had grown. Impressive temples in Cambodia, central Java, and southern Burma revealed the impact of Hinduism and Buddhism, religions that originated in India, on the people of Southeast Asia.

GEOGRAPHY Starting Points

Interactive
EAST ASIA, C. 600

China influenced early societies in Korea and Japan.

China controlled northern Vietnam until 939.

Through trade, India influenced societies in Southeast Asia.

Legend:
- Sui Dynasty (China)
- India kingdoms
- Yamato (Japan)
- Korea kingdoms
- PYU Cultural Group
- Great Wall of China
- ---- Grand Canal
- Trade routes

Starting Points The powerful empires of India and China had a strong influence on their less powerful neighbors. Through trade, conquest, and religious missionaries, Indian and Chinese culture spread to other parts of Asia. While India strongly influenced most of Southeast Asia, China influenced Korea, Japan, and northern Vietnam.

1. **Locate** Where are Korea and Japan located in relation to China?
2. **Predict** Most of the area to the east of India is the region called Southeast Asia. This region includes the islands to the south of the mainland as well. Why do you think that India influenced this region more than China?

Listen to History

Go online to listen to an explanation of the starting points for this chapter.

go.hrw.com
Keyword: SHL CEA

308 CHAPTER 11

Skills Focus: Analyzing Maps

At Level

Social Studies Skill
Indian Ocean Trader

Prep Required

1. Have students use the textbook to find what products were produced and traded in the 600s in the locations listed on the map. For instance, aromatics and spices were traded in various locations in Southeast Asia. You may wish to provide students with information about additional trade items, the monsoons, and wind directions.

2. Have students create a ship's log that describes a journey among some of the locations listed on the map, and lists the transactions that occurred at each location. A log might begin "May 26, 607: Left Ceylon with a cargo of tea; headed east across the Bay of Bengal towards the Strait of Malacca, following the summer monsoon."

3. Have volunteers present their logs to the class. **Verbal-Linguistic**

Alternative Assessment Handbook, Rubric 37: Writing Assignments

Answers

Geography Starting Points
1. *northeast of China;* 2. *possible answer—More trade routes connected India to Southeast Asia.*

Chinese Empires

BEFORE YOU READ

MAIN IDEA

The Sui dynasty reunified China, after which the Tang and Song dynasties produced an age of prosperity and achievement.

READING FOCUS

1. How did the Sui dynasty reunify China, and how did the Tang dynasty expand China?

2. How did the Song dynasty strengthen China?

3. What were some Tang and Song cultural achievements?

4. How was this period a time of prosperity and social change?

KEY TERMS AND PEOPLE

Wendi
Taizong
Wu Zhao
scholar-officials
porcelain
pagoda
woodblock printing
movable type
gentry

 NEW YORK

PI 1.1 Students investigate the components of cultures and civilizations including social customs, values, and traditions; political systems; economic systems; religions and spiritual beliefs; and socialization or educational practices.

THE INSIDE STORY

How might floating dragons show the power and unity of China? The Chinese peasants and officials standing along the canal stared in awe. A line of boats, many shaped like immense dragons, slowly floated toward them. On shore next to the boats, palace servants pulled on ropes to haul the boats forward, while royal guards rode along on horseback with banners flying. The amazing sight stretched as far as the eye could see.

The Chinese emperor Yang Di was making his royal tour down China's Grand Canal. To show his power, Yang Di had ordered boats built in the shape of dragons, the symbol of China's imperial family. In the top deck of the lead boat, the emperor sat dressed in golden silk robes, which only the Son of Heaven, as he was known, could wear. Behind his lead dragon-boat, which measured 200 feet from head to tail, followed thousands of smaller boats carrying royal attendants and other important officials.

The emperor's spectacular tour down the Grand Canal showed not only his great power but also the unity of his vast empire. For the Grand Canal, completed under his orders, had finally linked the northern and southern parts of his empire. This empire was the first to unify China in more than 350 years, since the fall of the Han dynasty. ■

Sui and Tang Dynasties

The Han dynasty ruled China from 206 BC to AD 220—more than 400 years. After the dynasty collapsed, however, military leaders split China into rival kingdoms. These events began a period of disorder and warfare that historians call the Period of Disunion.

THE EMPEROR'S DRAGONS

Chinese painting on silk, c. 1700s

▲ **Emperor Yang Di and his officials sail in a fleet of dragon boats down China's Grand Canal.**

CULTURES OF EAST ASIA **309**

Preteach

Getting Started

Use the **Interactive Reader and Study Guide** to familiarize students with the section content.

Interactive Reader and Study Guide, Section 1

Name _____ Class _____ Date _____
Cultures of East Asia
Section 1

MAIN IDEA
The Sui dynasty reunified China, after which the Tang and Song dynasties produced an age of prosperity and achievement.

Key Terms and People
Wendi Northern Chinese ruler who reunified China after the Period of Disunion in 589
Taizong Tang Dynasty emperor who took the throne in 626
Wu Zhao only female emperor of the Tang dynasty, reduced power of aristocratic families during her 15-year rule
scholar-officials elite, educated government workers who passed difficult civil service exams
porcelain a type of ceramic from China that was in demand by foreign traders
movable type metal blocks etched with symbols that could be rearranged for printing
pagoda multi-storied Chinese temples
woodblock printing text carved into wooden blocks and covered with ink; pages are then created when the blocks are pressed against paper
movable type faster form of printing than woodblock printing, uses etched metal blocks that could be rearranged and reused
gentry powerful class of scholar-officials and leading landowners

Taking Notes
As you read the summary, use a graphic organizer like the one below to list key facts for each of the four main parts of the section.

CRF: Vocabulary Builder: Section 1

Taking Notes

Sui and Tang Dynasties—reunified China; Grand Canal linked northern and southern China; Tang ruled from 618 to 907, a period of great brilliance, prosperity, and cultural achievement; expanded China and its influence; Wu Zhao the only female emperor in China's history; Buddhism came to China; Song Dynasty—reunified China after another split; enlarged government; Neo-Confucianism arose; in 1120s, Jin empire took over northern China and Song moved south; Cultural Achievements—art included literature, painted murals, pottery figurines, porcelain, innovations included gunpowder; magnetic compass, movable type; Prosperity and Society—agriculture and trade increased, cities grew, new class called the gentry developed, footbinding became a symbol of husband's authority over wife

---

Teach the Main Idea

At Level

Chinese Empires

1. **Teach** Ask students the Reading Focus questions to teach this section.

2. **Apply** Have students outline the section using the red and blue heads as main points. Have them include at least two key facts under each of the main points.

3. **Review** As you review the section, have students describe innovations that came about during the Tang and Song dynasties.

4. **Practice/Homework** Have students create a time line of the Sui, Tang, and Song dynasties. **LS Visual-Spatial**

   Alternative Assessment Handbook, Rubric 36: Time Lines

Direct Teach

Reading Focus

1 How did the Sui dynasty, and how did the Tang dynasty expand China? *built centralized government; restored order; created new legal code; built Grand Canal*

Sui and Tang Dynasties

Recall Why was Wu Zhao significant? *only woman to hold the title of emperor; ruled China after death of her husband, ruthless but effective ruler*

Explain Why is the Grand Canal considered the greatest accomplishment of the Sui dynasty? *huge waterway; probably aided reunification efforts; allowed for easier travel and trade between north and south*

Summarize What reforms did the Tang emperors carry out? *expanded civil service examination, created flexible law code, expanded China and increased contact with other peoples*

Info to Know

The Grand Canal China's Grand Canal is the world's oldest and longest canal system. It connects the Chinese cities of Hangzhou and Beijing, and is almost 1,000 miles long. Before the development of railroads, the canal was a convenient way to travel and transport goods between the northern and southern parts of China. The canal was created over many hundreds of years by digging trenches to link lakes, rivers, and other canals. Dams equalized water levels.

Answers

Faces of History *possible answer— She wanted advisers she could trust to do a good job.*

310

TAKING NOTES

As you read, use a graphic organizer like the one below to record the key facts for each of the four main parts of the section.

NEW YORK

CC Unit 2-B3
Tang Dynasty
Chinese influence
on Korea

The Period of Disunion During the Period of Disunion, nomads invaded northern China and formed their own kingdoms. Many northern Chinese, unwilling to live under the rule of the nomadic invaders, fled south to the region of the Chang Jiang (Yangzi River). There, a number of southern dynasties rose and fell.

Despite such events, Chinese civilization continued to thrive and develop. In northern China, the nomadic invaders adopted many aspects of Chinese civilization. Meanwhile, in the south, the culture of the northern Chinese immigrants blended with local cultures, and a flowering in the arts and philosophy occurred.

The Sui Dynasty The Period of Disunion lasted more than 350 years. The period ended in 589 when a northern ruler named **Wendi** reunified China. Also known as Yang Jian (YANG jee-EN), Wendi founded the new Sui (SWAY) dynasty and became its first emperor.

Using earlier dynasties as models, Wendi worked to build a centralized government. He restored order, created a new legal code, and reformed the bureaucracy. He also created policies to provide all adult males with land and to ensure the availability of grain.

The greatest accomplishment of the Sui dynasty, however, was the completion of the Grand Canal. This 1,000-mile waterway linked northern and southern China. As a result, northern China could more easily access the

resources of the south, such as the rice produced in the lower Chang Jiang valley. Begun during the reign of Yang Di, Wendi's son, the Grand Canal took several years to complete.

During his reign, Emperor Yang Di forced millions of peasants to work on the Grand Canal and other projects. Hundreds of thousands of laborers died, leading to discontent and rebellion. A series of failed military campaigns worsened the situation. In 618 an official assassinated Yang Di, and the short-lived Sui dynasty came to an end.

The Tang Dynasty A Sui general seized power and founded the Tang (TAHNG) dynasty. This dynasty ruled China from 618 to 907, nearly 300 years. Under Tang rule, China experienced a period of prosperity and cultural achievement. Chinese influence spread, and Tang government and other institutions served as models across East Asia.

The Tang rulers built on Sui foundations to create a strong government. They established one capital at Chang'an (chahng-AHN), the Sui capital, and a second capital at Luoyang. Government control remained centralized and based on a bureaucracy of officials. To obtain talented officials, the Tang expanded the civil service examination system. Under this system, people had to pass written exams to work for the government. In addition, Tang rulers created a flexible law code, which became a model for law codes in Korea and Japan.

In foreign affairs, the Tang significantly expanded China and its influence. Tang forces regained western lands in Central Asia and gained influence over Korea and other neighboring states. Chinese contact with Japan increased, and Japanese scholars came to China to study its government and culture. Expansion and increased contact with other peoples contributed to the growth of foreign trade, and the economy prospered.

Much of this expansion occurred during the reign of **Taizong** (TY-tzoong), who ruled from 626 to 649. One of China's most admired emperors, Taizong relied on talented ministers to help him govern. In addition to his military conquests, he had schools built to prepare students for the civil service exams.

After Taizong's death, one of his sons became emperor. The new emperor was weak and sickly, and his wife **Wu Zhao** gained power.

FACES OF HISTORY

WU Zhao
625–705

Married to the sickly emperor Kao Tsung, Wu Zhao became the virtual ruler of China. After her husband's death, Wu Zhao continued to hold virtual power while two of her sons ruled. She considered her sons to be poor rulers, however, and soon took the title of emperor for herself. She then became known as Empress Wu.

Empress Wu ruled with an iron fist. During her rise to power, she had ordered many of her rivals executed, which led many people to oppose her. Nonetheless, she was a gifted and respected ruler. Empress Wu filled her government with talented advisors and administrators who were chosen for their ability rather than their social rank.

Find the Main Idea Why was Wu Zhao respected as a ruler despite her harsh treatment of her political opponents?

310 CHAPTER 11

Skills Focus: Summarizing

At Level

Reading Skill
Sui and Tang Newspapers

1. Review with students the information in the text about the Sui and Tang dynasties.

2. Organize students into small groups. Assign each group either the Sui or Tang dynasty.

3. Have each group prepare a newspaper from the time period of its dynasty. Have students write articles on politics, innovations, and daily life of the period. Students should include at least one editorial about problems during that time.

4. Have groups present their newspapers to the class. **LS** **Verbal-Linguistic, Visual-Spatial**

Alternative Assessment Handbook, Rubric 23: Newspapers

TANG AND SONG DYNASTIES, 618–1279

Legend:
- Tang dynasty, 814
- Song dynasty, 1050
- Southern Song dynasty, 1145
- Jin dynasty, 1145
- Silk Roads
- Grand Canal
- Great Wall of China

Map labels: MANCHURIA, GOBI, Tian Shan, Kashi, Taklimakan Desert, Kunlun Shan, HIMALAYAS, Plateau of Tibet, Indus River, Ganges River, Brahmaputra River, INDIA, Huang He (Yellow River), Tianjin, Zhongdu (Beijing), KOREA, East Sea, Yellow Sea, Luoyang, Kaifeng, Chang'an (Xian), Wei River, Chengdu, Hangzhou, Chang Jiang (Yangzi River), CHINA, East China Sea, PACIFIC OCEAN, Xi River, Guangzhou, Taiwan, Mekong River, ANNAM (VIETNAM), INDOCHINA, South China Sea

0 300 600 Miles
0 300 600 Kilometers
Two-point equidistant projection

GEOGRAPHY SKILLS   INTERPRETING MAPS

1. **Movement** What important trade routes did China gain control of in Central Asia during the Tang dynasty?

2. **Location** How did the area of the Song dynasty differ from that of the Southern Song dynasty, and what major river did the dynasty lose access to when it moved south?

When her husband died, Wu Zhao continued to rule through her sons. Wanting full power, she became emperor herself—the only woman to hold the title in Chinese history. An effective but ruthless ruler, Empress Wu Zhao was overthrown in 705. The Tang dynasty then reached its height under Xuanzong (SHOO-AN-toong), who ruled from 712 to 756. During his reign, the empire prospered and culture flourished.

An Age of Buddhism Buddhism first came to China from India during Han times. Although few Chinese adopted the religion at first, during the Period of Disunion many Chinese turned to Buddhism. Because Buddhism taught that people could escape suffering and achieve peace, it appealed to people living in the midst of the turmoil of that period.

By the Tang dynasty, Buddhism was well established in China. Many of the Tang rulers were Buddhists and supported the religion. Buddhist temples appeared across the land, and Chinese missionaries spread Buddhism to other Asian lands. Because of Buddhism's importance, the period from about 400 to 845 in China is known as the Age of Buddhism.

The Age of Buddhism came to an end when the religion lost official favor in the mid-800s. A Tang emperor, seeing the growing power of the Buddhist religious communities as a threat, launched a campaign against Buddhism. His officials burned Buddhist texts and destroyed Buddhist temples. Although these actions weakened Buddhism in China, the religion survived. However, Buddhism began to change as the Chinese blended it with other beliefs, such as Confucianism and Daoism.

The Tang Decline The Tang dynasty began to decline in the 750s. Although the Tang put down a rebellion in 755, the government remained weak. At the same time, military defeats led to the loss of Tang lands in Central Asia and the north. Nomadic invasions and peasant rebellions over rising taxes created more problems. When a powerful general killed the emperor in 907, the Tang dynasty ended.

READING CHECK Summarize How did the Sui and Tang dynasties unite and expand China?

NEW YORK
CC Unit 1-E2
Expansion of Buddhism

---

2 How did the Song dynasty strengthen China? *centralized government control; enlarged government bureaucracy; used civil service exam to ensure good bureaucrats*

The Song Dynasty

Identify What philosophy experienced a revival during the Song dynasty? *Confucianism*

Explain How did the civil service exam affect the Song government? *ensured capable bureaucrats; not all candidates from wealthy families*

Identify Cause and Effect What effect did nomads have on the Song dynasty? *threatened borders; later conquered northern China and founded the Jin empire; Song continued to rule only in the south*

CRF: Economics and History: A Call for Reform in Song China

Tang and Song Achievements

The Tang and Song dynasties produced great achievements in the arts and technology, many of which had an influence around the world. *Which innovations listed in the chart do you think were most influential, and why?*

The Arts Tang artists made lively figurines, such as this female polo player, while Song artisans created elegant porcelain. The monastery at right has a curved pagoda roof.

The Song Dynasty

After the Tang dynasty, China again split apart and was not reunified until 960, with the Song dynasty. Like the Tang, the Song ruled for about 300 years, until 1279. Also like the Tang, the Song produced great achievements and prosperity. Under their rule, Chinese civilization became the most advanced in the world.

Government and the Civil Service The Song established a capital at Kaifeng and restored centralized government control. To manage their empire, they enlarged the government bureaucracy. In addition, they reformed the civil service examination system, which helped ensure that talented people ran the government. The exams tested students' grasp of Confucianism and related ideas. Under the Song, a new form of Confucianism, called Neo-Confucianism, gained favor. *Neo* means "new," and Neo-Confucianism emphasized not only Confucian ethics but also spiritual matters.

The civil service exams were extremely difficult to pass. Those who did pass the exams became **scholar-officials**—elite, educated members of the government. They received a good salary and were respected. Because the Song made civil service exams more open to ordinary people, the exams became a pathway to gaining wealth and status.

NEW YORK

CC Unit 2-B
Tang and Song Dynasty contributions and cultural flowering

The Southern Song Despite their many achievements, the Song rulers never regained the northern and western lands that the Tang had lost. Nomads in these lands threatened the Song borders. Like previous rulers, the Song tried to buy peace with the nomads by sending them lavish gifts.

Despite such efforts, in the 1120s a nomadic people called the Jurchen conquered northern China and founded the Jin empire. The Song continued to rule in the south, however, as the Southern Song dynasty for 150 more years.

READING CHECK **Analyze** How did the Song strengthen China's government?

Cultural Achievements

The Tang and Song dynasties were periods of great cultural achievement. Art and literature flourished, and many inventions and advances occurred in science and technology.

Literature and Art The Tang period produced some of China's greatest poets. The two most famous Tang poets are Du Fu and Li Bo. Du Fu wrote poems that expressed Confucian ideals or the horrors of war. Li Bo wrote poems about friendship, the joys of life, nature, and solitude. In the following poem, he expresses the homesickness a person can feel at night.

Skills Focus: Identifying Main Idea and Details   At Level

Reading Skill
Tang and Song Dynasties

1. Copy the Venn diagram for students to see. Omit the italicized answers.

2. Have students copy and complete the diagram. Have volunteers complete the class Venn diagram. **LS Visual-Spatial**

Alternative Assessment Handbook, Rubric 13: Graphic Organizers

Chinese Dynasties

Tang: *land reform, salt monopoly, expanding empire, tributary states*

Both: *thriving trade, innovations, poetry and arts*

Song: *threat of barbarians, civil service exam, Confucianism*

Answers

Tang and Song Achievements
possible answers—gunpowder: made future wars very deadly; movable type: made printing and communication more efficient; magnetic compass: allowed for navigation and world exploration

Reading Check *established capital at Kaifeng and restored centralized government control, enlarged bureaucracy, reformed civil service exam*

INNOVATIONS

Woodblock Printing Tang; printers could copy drawings or texts much faster than by hand

Movable Type Song; made printing much faster

Paper Money Tang, became popular during Song; improved trade because lighter and easier to use

Porcelain Tang; Chinese artisans became famous for this fragile and glossy ceramic

Gunpowder Tang or early Song; used mainly for fireworks and signals rather than for weapons

Magnetic Compass Tang improvements to this Han invention enabled farther sea travel

Printing The Chinese made major advances in printing during this period. The woodblock print above is of the Buddhist *Diamond Sutra*. Made in 868, it is the oldest known book. The blocks of moveable type at left each depict a different Chinese character.

HISTORY'S VOICES

❝Before my bed
there is bright moonlight
So that it seems
like frost on the ground:
Lifting my head
I watch the bright moon,
Lowering my head
I dream that I'm home.❞

—Li Bo, *Quiet Night Thoughts*

Chinese painting also reached new heights during this period. Tang artist Wu Daozi (DOW-tzee) painted murals that celebrated Buddhism and nature. His paintings were so lifelike that some people thought he had magical powers. Song artists focused on nature and produced landscapes of great beauty, though many of the artists painted using just black ink.

Chinese artisans created exquisite objects from clay. The Tang period is known for its pottery figurines, many made to go in tombs. Tang figurines often depicted horses or entertainment, such as girls dancing or people playing games like polo, popular among the Tang rich.

Song artisans also excelled at making **porcelain**, a type of ceramic often known as china. Song porcelain was frequently covered in white, black, or pale green glazes. Because of its fine quality, Song porcelain was admired and sought after around the world.

In architecture, Indian Buddhist temples influenced the design of the Chinese **pagoda**. These multistoried buildings featured roofs at each floor that curved upwards at the corners.

Inventions and Innovations During the Tang and Song periods, China led the world in achievements in technology and science. One major Chinese invention of the time was gunpowder. The Chinese used gunpowder mainly in fireworks, but as gunpowder spread around the world other people used it in weapons such as firearms and cannons. In time, gunpowder dramatically altered how wars were fought.

A major technical advance of Tang China was the perfection of the magnetic compass. This instrument, which uses Earth's magnetic field to show direction, revolutionized sea travel. With a compass, sailors could more accurately determine direction and navigate more easily. This advance would in time contribute to a dramatic increase in world exploration.

Two other inventions of the period related to printing. The Chinese had invented paper and ink much earlier. During the Tang period, they developed **woodblock printing**. In this method of printing, a page of text is carved into a block of wood. The block is then coated with ink and pressed against paper to create a printed page. These blocks could be recoated with ink and reused to create other prints.

CULTURES OF EAST ASIA **313**

Reading Focus

④ How was this period a time of prosperity and social change? *agriculture and trade increased; cities grew; social classes changed*

Prosperity and Society

Recall Who were China's trade partners during this period, and what routes did traders use? *Japan, Korea, and Southeast Asia, using sea routes; Central Asia, India, and beyond, using Silk Roads*

Summarize How was Chinese society changing during this period? *aristocratic families declined; gentry developed; cities grew; status of women declined*

Biography

Emperor Xuanzong and the Children of the Pear Garden The Tang Emperor Xuanzong was known for his patronage of the arts as well as for his own artistic talents. He gave money to several training schools for actors, the most famous of which was located in a pear garden just north of the Tang capital. In this location, young people practiced not only acting, but singing, dancing, and acrobatics. They were known as "children of the pear garden." Although these actors performed mostly for the emperor and other nobles, the beginning of Chinese opera began at this time. Traditionally, some incense is burned in honor of Xuanzong before performances of Chinese opera.

Answers

Reading Like a Historian **1.** *possible answer—People from different social classes interacted at festivals.*
2. *possible answer—shows the type of transportation working people used*

Reading Check *Gunpowder dramatically affected how wars were fought; the compass allowed for world navigation; printing innovations led to increased sharing of ideas.*

Inventors of the Song dynasty created another form of printing called **movable type**. This method uses blocks on which individual letters or characters are carved. The blocks can be rearranged and reused to print many things. Printing with movable type was faster than woodblock printing but infrequently used in China because of the vast number of Chinese characters. Later, the use of movable type in Europe would revolutionize printing.

Another invention of the time was paper money. For a long time, the Chinese had used bulky metal disks, which were placed on strings, as money. As the Song economy grew, however, a need for a more convenient form of currency developed. Paper money was light and easy to use, and its use quickly spread in Song China.

READING CHECK **Identify Cause and Effect**
How did Chinese innovations affect world history?

Prosperity and Society

In addition to cultural achievements, the Tang and Song periods were a time of growth and prosperity. Agriculture and trade improved, cities grew, and changes in society occurred.

Agriculture During this period, Chinese agriculture became more productive. New irrigation techniques increased the land people could farm, and a new variety of fast-ripening rice from Southeast Asia enabled Chinese farmers to grow two or three crops a year instead of just one. In addition, the production of cotton and tea increased, making them important crops. During the Song dynasty, tea became highly popular among the Chinese people.

Increased food production contributed to population growth. By the 740s, the population of Tang China was perhaps around 70 million.

Reading like a Historian

Song City Life

Analyzing Visuals This painting is part of a scroll titled *Going Upriver at the Qingming Festival*, made by Zhang Zeduan around the 1100s. The image shows a bustling city scene of streets lined with shops and restaurants and people going about their daily activities.

To analyze this image of Song city life, think about

- the subject of the image,
- the details in the image, and
- how the subject is portrayed.

Laborers use a donkey cart to haul goods into the city.

A man cooks food to sell to passersby.

The scene shows people of all social classes—the wealthy riding in sedan chairs, scholar-officials, monks, and laborers.

Skills FOCUS **READING LIKE A HISTORIAN**

1. **Subject** What can you learn about city life in the Song dynasty from this image?
2. **Details** The scroll is an important source of information on working people, who were not often included in the art of the period. What can you learn about working people from this image?

See **Skills Handbook**, p. H26

314 CHAPTER 11

Differentiating Instruction

Below Level

English-Language Learners

Materials: poster paper, art supplies

1. Review with students information in the text about innovations that occurred during the Tang and Song dynasties.

2. Organize students into mixed-ability pairs.

3. Have each pair create a poster that showcases innovations of the Tang and Song dynasties. The poster should include pictures and brief descriptions of the innovations.

4. Have volunteers present their posters to the class. **LS Visual-Spatial**

Alternative Assessment Handbook, Rubric 28: Posters

During the Song dynasty, the farmers of China fed nearly 100 million people, making China the most populous country in the world.

Trade Along with agriculture, trade expanded during the Tang and Song dynasties. Improvements in roads and canals helped increase trade within China. They made it possible for rural farm products and other goods to be transported to local markets and cities.

Foreign trade expanded as well. During the Tang dynasty, most foreign trade took place over land routes, such as the Silk Roads. These routes connected China to markets in Central Asia, India, and beyond. China also traded by sea with Japan, Korea, and Southeast Asia. With the loss of Central Asian lands during the late Tang dynasty, sea trade became more important to China. Advances in sailing and shipbuilding techniques contributed to this change. During the Song dynasty, ships from many regions visited China's port cities, and foreign merchants filled their markets.

The growth of trade helped create a strong, prosperous economy. During the Song dynasty, merchants became more important members of Chinese society, and the beginnings of a money and banking system began to develop.

City Life As farming and trade grew, so did China's cities. City streets were filled with people and lined with shops, teahouses, and restaurants. City markets bustled with activity and provided numerous foreign goods. Entertainment districts provided amusement.

China had the largest cities in the world at this time. The Tang capital of Chang'an had a population of more than 1 million, with another million people living around the city. A major trade center, Chang'an was filled with people of many cultures. During the Song dynasty, several cities had a million people or more, and sea trade caused China's port cities to boom. Despite this urban growth, though, most Chinese still lived in the countryside and farmed.

Society Chinese society underwent significant changes during this period as well. The power of China's aristocratic families began to decline while a new class, called the **gentry**, developed. The gentry included scholar-officials and leading landowners, who gained power during this time. As in the past, though, most

Chinese were peasants. These people farmed the land, paid most of the taxes, and received little, if any, formal schooling.

During the Song dynasty, the lives of Chinese women changed as well. In general, the status of women declined. This decline was most visible among upper class women, who were often encouraged to stay in the home.

In addition, a desire for small, dainty feet led to the custom of footbinding among Chinese women. This practice involved wrapping pieces of cloth around the feet, starting when a girl was young. Because the cloths kept the feet from growing, footbinding was painful and deformed the feet over time. Women with bound feet had difficulty walking or doing many other activities. As a result, bound feet became a symbol of a husband's authority over his wife.

READING CHECK **Draw Conclusions** How did footbinding reflect changes in attitudes toward women in China?

 THE IMPACT TODAY
China is still the world's most populous country, with more than 1.3 billion people.

NEW YORK
CC Unit 2-B
Growth of commerce and trade during the Tang and Song Dynasty

 SECTION 1 ASSESSMENT
go.hrw.com
Online Quiz
Keyword: SHL CEA HP

Reviewing Ideas, Terms, and People

1. **a. Identify** Who was **Wu Zhao**, and why is she significant in Chinese history?
   b. Sequence What events led to the decline of the Tang dynasty?
   c. Elaborate Why was the early part of the Tang period known as the Age of Buddhism, and how did Buddhism affect China during this time?

2. **a. Define** Why were **scholar-officials** highly respected in Song China?
   b. Make Generalizations What generalizations can you make about the rise and fall of Chinese dynasties based on the history of the Sui, Tang, and Song dynasties?

3. **a. Identify** Who were some well-known Tang poets and painters?
   b. Analyze How did economic needs lead to innovations in China?
   c. Support a Position What do you think was the greatest Tang or Song innovation or achievement? Provide reasons to support your position.

4. **a. Recall** What advances in farming occurred during this period?
   b. Summarize How did Chinese society change during this period?

Critical Thinking

5. **Categorizing** Using your notes and a graphic organizer like the one shown at right, categorize key facts about the Tang and Song dynasties.

	Tang Dynasty	Song Dynasty
Agriculture		
Cities		
Trade		
Art		
Inventions		

FOCUS ON WRITING

6. **Exposition** You are a historian during the Tang dynasty. Write a paragraph explaining what Tang rulers have accomplished. Consider political, economic, and cultural accomplishments.

CULTURES OF EAST ASIA **315**

Direct Teach

Reading Focus

Prosperity and Society

Describe What characterized the city of Chang'an? *over 1 million people; busy place for trade and commerce; many different cultures*

Identify Cause and Effect How did the increase in trade affect China? *created prosperous economy, led to money and banking system*

Review & Assess

Close
Guide students in a discussion about why the Tang and Song dynasties declined and eventually fell.

Review
Online Quiz, Section 1

Assess
SE Section 1 Assessment
Progress Assessment: Section 1 Quiz
Alternative Assessment Handbook

Reteach/Intervene
Interactive Reader and Study Guide, Section 1
Interactive Skills Tutor CD-ROM

Section 1 Assessment Answers

1. **a.** only female emperor in China's history
   b. invasions, rebellions, weak government
   c. more Chinese people turned to Buddhism; Buddhism became state religion

2. **a.** educated, passed difficult exams
   b. possible answer—China was large and difficult to govern; invasions and rebellions often threatened dynasties.

3. **a.** Du Fu, Li Bo, Wu Daozi
   b. expanding economy led to a need for money; heavy coins led to paper money

   c. possible answer—Tang's paper money; revolutionized monetary systems

4. **a.** irrigation techniques, new rice strains
   b. population grew; social classes changed; cities grew

5. Notes should list key facts from the section.

6. Student paragraphs should include details from the section about expansion, government, trade, religion (Buddhism), art, and inventions.

Answers

Reading Check *became symbol of husband's authority over wife, women's status declined*

315

The Mongol Empire

SECTION

BEFORE YOU READ

MAIN IDEA
The Mongols built a vast empire across much of Asia, founded the Yuan dynasty in China, and opened China and the region to greater foreign contacts and trade.

READING FOCUS
1. How did the nomadic Mongols build an empire?
2. How did China change under the Mongol rulers of the Yuan dynasty?
3. Why did the Yuan dynasty decline and finally end?

KEY TERMS AND PEOPLE
khan
Genghis Khan
Pax Mongolia
Kublai Khan
Marco Polo

NEW YORK
PI 2.5 Students investigate key events and developments and major turning points in world history to identify the factors that brought about change and the long-term effects of these changes.

THE INSIDE STORY

Why might people surrender to an enemy without a fight? Thousands of soldiers moved forward in a mass as much as 50 miles wide. Terror spread before them like a huge tidal wave. Their reputation and their appearance were so frightening that, at word of the Mongol approach, towns and cities surrendered without a fight.

The nomadic Mongols emerged in the 1200s as one of history's most brutal and efficient military forces. When on the move, the Mongols resembled a small, mobile city.

Soldiers traveled in divisions of 10,000 along with their families and herds. The full Mongol force moved only about five miles a day, but soldiers could quickly come together to attack when needed. Strike forces traveled at the front and rear, and scouts—who could cover as much as 100 miles a day—provided information. Mongol women carried out domestic tasks but could step into battle to provide help.

Borrowing from many groups, the Mongols combined superior tactics and weaponry with ruthless cunning and brutality. The world would not again see such military dominance until the modern era. ∎

★ Interactive
HISTORY CLOSE-UP

Mongols on the Move

A standard of horsetails stood by the Khan's tent. The horsetails were white when the Mongols were at peace; black when at war.

The felt tents, or *gers*, of the Khan and his wives and generals were set on wheeled platforms and pulled by teams of oxen.

Getting Started

Use the **Interactive Reader and Study Guide** to familiarize students with the section content.

📖 **Interactive Reader and Study Guide**, Section 2

📄 **CRF:** Vocabulary Builder: Section 2

Taking Notes

Mongols unify under Genghis Khan, conquer Asia; Kublai Khan conquers China, sets up Yuan dynasty; mixed economic results; discrimination against Chinese, expansion of trade, Marco Polo visits; power struggle after Kublai Khan dies, flood and economic crisis

go.hrw.com
Online Resources

KEYWORD: SHL CEA
ACTIVITY: Genghis Khan: Leader of the Mongolian Empire

Teach the Main Idea

At Level

The Mongol Empire

1. **Teach** Ask students the Reading Focus questions to teach this section.

2. **Apply** Have students scan the section, looking at all the visuals, graphics, and captions. Have students make a list of all the visuals and graphics. Ask students what these images reveal about the section and have them write a short paragraph explaining what they think the images will reveal.

3. **Review** As you review the section, have students describe the changes that occurred in China as a result of Mongol rule.

4. **Practice/Homework** Have students write a short biography of Genghis Khan. Stuents might also include an illustration of Genghis Khan to accompany their biographies.
LS Visual-Spatial, Verbal-Linguistic

📖 **Alternative Assessment Handbook**, Rubric 4: Biographies

The Mongols

Throughout its history, northern China had been attacked by nomadic peoples. These attacks became even more frequent during the Song dynasty. In the 1200s a nomadic people called the Mongols burst forth from Central Asia. They would create the largest land empire in history, and conquer China in the process.

Nomads from the Steppe Vast steppes, or grasslands, stretch across the north-central part of Eurasia. These steppes had long been home to nomadic peoples. Because the steppes were too dry for farming, these nomads lived as pastoralists, relying on herds of domesticated animals for their needs and moving frequently to find good pasture for their animals. To obtain items they lacked, they traded with settled peoples. Just as often, though, nomads swept down on settlements and took what they wanted from them.

Like the Huns and Turks, the Mongols emerged as a powerful nomadic people on the Central Asian steppes. They herded sheep and goats, which provided meat and milk for food and wool for clothing and shelter. Like many nomads, the Mongols were skilled with horses and learned to ride at an early age. Accustomed to living in a harsh environment and competing for scarce resources, they were a tough people and fierce warriors.

The Universal Ruler For centuries the Mongols were divided into separate clans, each led by a **khan**, or chief. A khan rose to power through his military skills and ability to lead. In the late 1100s, however, a powerful khan named Temujin began to conquer his rivals and unite the Mongol clans. In 1206 he succeeded, taking the title **Genghis Khan** (JENG-guhs KAHN), which means "Universal Ruler."

With the Mongols united under his rule, Genghis Khan set out to build an empire. He organized the Mongols into a powerful military machine, enforced strict discipline, and demanded complete loyalty. At the same time, he rewarded well those who pleased him.

Under his leadership, the Mongol forces began a bloody campaign of conquest. Genghis Khan's Mongol armies were highly mobile and could strike quickly. A cunning military leader, he used superb battle tactics to coordinate his armies to stalk and trap the enemy like prey. He reportedly told his men, "In daylight, watch with the vigilance [careful observation] of an old wolf, at night with the eyes of the raven. In battle, fall upon the enemy like a falcon."

TAKING NOTES

As you read, use a graphic organizer like this one to take notes about the key events during the period of the Mongol Empire. Add boxes as needed.

☐ ➡ ☐

NEW YORK

CC Unit 3-B
The rise of the Mongols, their human and physical geography, and their origins as Central Asian nomadic tribes

When on the move, scouts kept the khan informed.

Mongol fighters were skilled with the lance and bow and arrow. Stirrups kept riders stable in the saddle so they could fire arrows with accuracy.

Skills Focus INTERPRETING VISUALS
Infer How do you think the sight of the vast Mongol army on the move affected people in towns and cities?

go.hrw.com
COULD YOU HAVE SURVIVED?
Go online for a closer look at survival and this event.
Keyword: SHL CEA

317

Reading Focus

The Mongols

Identify Who were the Tartars? *the Golden Horde; conquered Russia in 1236*

Explain Why do historians refer to this period in history as Pax Mongolia? *means "Mongol Peace;" Mongols ruled empire peacefully, ensured safe travel and secure trade routes*

Reading Focus

❷ How did China change under the Mongol rulers of the Yuan dynasty? *Kublai Khan aimed to conquer all of China; used artillery to attack fortified cities; eventually controlled China, established Yuan dynasty*

The Yuan Dynasty

Recall Who was Kublai Khan and why was his rule significant? *Great Khan of the Mongol Empire, 1260; first foreigner to rule all of China*

Evaluate Do you think the Mongol attempts to gain Chinese loyalty were effective? Why or why not? *possible answers—no, Chinese still resented being ruled by outsiders and were not treated as equals; yes, tolerant policies helped*

📄 **CRF:** History and Geography: Mongol Military Might

Answers

Reading Skills *possible answer—resented them, thought they were rude and uncivilized*

Reading Check *army was skilled and well organized, rules promoted loyalty and obedience; tactics involved brutality and psychological warfare; built fear in those they conquered*

NEW YORK

CC Unit 3-B
Extent of the Mongol Empire under Genghis Khan and Kublai Khan, impact of the rise of the Mongols on Central Asia and China, Pax Mongolia, (e.g. Marco Polo), and the Yuan Dynasty: a foreign non-Chinese dynasty

The battle tactics of the Mongols included brutality and psychological warfare. To spread terror, the Mongols burned any town or city that resisted them and killed the inhabitants. They also sent agents ahead to tell of the Mongols' brutality and huge numbers as a way to build fear of the approaching forces. Soon, many people began to surrender without a fight.

The Mongol Empire Over the next 20 years, Genghis Khan led the Mongols in conquering much of Asia. In their fights against the Chinese and the Turks in Central Asia, the Mongols learned the art of siege warfare and the use of gunpowder. This knowledge helped the Mongols take city after city.

By the time Genghis Khan died in 1227, the Mongols controlled much of northern China and Central Asia. On his deathbed, Genghis Khan told his sons, "With Heaven's aid I have conquered for you a huge empire. But my life was too short to achieve the conquest of the world. That task is left for you." His sons and grandsons took up the challenge.

The Mongols divided Genghis Khan's vast empire into four khanates, or regions. An heir of Genghis Khan ruled each region, and a leader called the Great Khan ruled over the whole empire. Under grandson Kublai Khan, the Mongols resumed their efforts to complete the conquest of China and Korea. Another grandson, Hulegu, ruled the Ilkhan part of the empire. He and his forces conquered Persia, leaving a path of death and destruction in their wake. The Golden Horde under grandson Batu took up the task of conquering Russia in 1236. The Tartars, as the Russians called the Mongols, took Moscow and laid waste to the city of Kiev. The Mongols then stormed through Poland and Hungary. As they stood ready to invade Western Europe, the Mongols suddenly turned back on learning of the Great Khan's death. India and Western Europe escaped Mongol wrath, but most of Eurasia had been devastated. Millions of people had died, and entire cities had been annihilated.

The Mongol Peace Although brutal in building their empire, the Mongols ruled it peacefully. They tolerated local beliefs and ways of life. They often allowed local rulers to stay in power as long as they paid tribute, or riches, to the Mongols. In addition, some of the

READING SKILLS

Making Inferences Based on the text under "Kublai Khan Rules China," how do you think the Chinese felt about their Mongol rulers?

Mongols adopted aspects of the more civilized cultures they had conquered. For example, the Mongols in Central Asia and Persia adopted the religion of Islam.

The Mongol Empire established peace and stability across Asia. For this reason, some historians call this period the **Pax Mongolia**, meaning the "Mongol Peace." The Mongols guarded trade routes such as the Silk Roads and ensured safe travel across Asia. Secure trade routes allowed trade between the East and West to increase. People, goods, ideas, and Chinese innovations such as gunpowder, the compass, and printing spread westward. At the same time, most scholars think the Black Death, which wiped out much of Europe during the 1300s, also spread from Asia to the Middle East and Europe during this time.

READING CHECK **Identify Supporting Details** How were the Mongols able to build a vast empire across much of Eurasia?

The Yuan Dynasty

In 1260 **Kublai Khan** (KOO-bluh KAHN) became the Great Khan of the Mongol Empire. In actuality, though, he held power only over the Khanate of the Great Khan. He was, however, determined to complete the conquest of China, which he had begun in 1235. Although the Mongols ruled northern China, the Southern Song dynasty still ruled in the south. The Song fiercely resisted the Mongol invaders for many years. In 1279, though, the last Song ruler was defeated. Kublai Khan created the new Yuan dynasty and declared himself emperor. For the first time, foreigners ruled all of China.

Kublai Khan Rules China As emperor, Kublai Khan tried to gain the loyalty of his Chinese subjects. Many of the Chinese saw the Mongols as rude and uncivilized, and resented them as rulers. Kublai Khan did not force the Chinese to adopt Mongol ways of life. Instead, he adopted some Chinese practices, and even gave his dynasty a Chinese name.

To strengthen his control, Kublai Khan moved his capital from Mongolia to a new city in China. The new capital was located near what is now the city of Beijing, which is the modern capital of China. At his new capital, Kublai Khan had built a walled city in the Chinese

---

Skills Focus: Comparing and Contrasting

At Level

Reading Skill
Political Cartoons

Materials: drawing paper

1. Review with students information in the text about the conditions in China during the Yuan dynasty.

2. Organize students into mixed-ability pairs.

3. Have students create two political cartoons: one that portrays the Mongols as good rulers who brought peace and prosperity to China, and the other that shows them as selfish rulers who discriminated against the Chinese.

4. Have volunteers present their political cartoons to the class. **LS Visual-Spatial**

📄 **Alternative Assessment Handbook**, Rubric 27: Political Cartoons

MONGOL EMPIRE, 1294

EUROPE
- Moscow
- Kiev
- Vienna
- Venice
- Constantinople
- Danube
- Black Sea
- Caspian Sea
- Aral Sea

ASIA
- MONGOLIA
- Karakorum
- GOBI
- Khanbaliq (Beijing)

BYZANTINE EMPIRE
- Damascus
- Baghdad
- Bukhara
- Samarqand
- Kashgar
- Kabul
- SULTANATE OF DELHI

EGYPT
- ARABIAN PENINSULA
- Persian Gulf
- Red Sea
- Mediterranean Sea
- Tigris River
- Euphrates River
- Ganges River

CHINA
- Hangzhou
- Guangzhou
- HIMALAYAS
- Yellow R.
- Chang Jiang (Yangzi R.)

INDIA
- Arabian Sea
- Bay of Bengal
- KHMER
- Pagan
- VIETNAM
- Mekong River

KOREA
- JAPAN
- East Sea
- East China Sea
- South China Sea
- PACIFIC OCEAN

Legend:
- Khanate of the Great Khan
- Khanate of the Golden Horde
- Khanate of Chagatai
- Ilkhanate (Persia)
- Mongol border
- Mongol invasions, 1228–1281
- Route of Marco Polo, 1271–1295
- Great Wall of China

0   500   1,000 Miles
0   500   1,000 Kilometers
Robinson projection

GEOGRAPHY SKILLS   INTERPRETING MAPS

1. **Place** At its greatest extent about how many miles from west to east did the Mongol empire extend?

2. **Movement** How did Marco Polo's journey to China differ from his journey home to Venice?

style as well as a lavish palace. In his palace, he adopted many Chinese court ceremonies and tried to rule as a Chinese emperor.

At the same time, Kublai Khan took care to see that the Mongols were not absorbed into Chinese culture. The Mongols lived apart from the Chinese, individual friendships between Mongols and Chinese were discouraged, and Mongols were forbidden to marry Chinese. The Mongols created different laws and taxes for the Chinese and did not let them own weapons or serve in the military.

Although Kublai Khan left much of China's government in place, he distrusted the Chinese and limited their power. Only non-Chinese could hold higher government posts, for example. Because so few Mongols lived in China, though, Chinese officials still served at the local level. In addition, the Mongols invited other foreigners to hold government office.

The Mongols burdened the Chinese with heavy taxes, a large part of which went to support public-works projects. They used Chinese

laborers to build new roads and extended the Grand Canal to the capital city. These improvements made shipping rice and other goods from southern China to northern China easier and more reliable.

To keep the peace, the Mongols posted soldiers throughout China. The Mongol rulers took this action in part because they feared rebellions, particularly in the south where many of the Chinese remained loyal to the Song dynasty.

Foreign Trade Under Kublai Khan's rule, foreign trade increased. The Pax Mongolia had made travel across land much safer for merchants, and Kublai Khan had enormous ships built to improve trade across the seas. By welcoming foreign merchants to China's ports and offering some traders special privileges, Kublai Khan promoted foreign trade.

As a result of such policies, many travelers, merchants, and missionaries came to China. Most were from Southwest Asia and India.

CULTURES OF EAST ASIA **319**

Skills Focus: Making Generalizations

At Level

Reading Skill
Evaluating the Yuan Dynasty

1. Review with students information in the text about the Yuan dynasty.

2. Organize students into four groups: Mongols, other nomadic peoples, foreign merchants, and Chinese.

3. Write this question for students to see: How are the Yuan rulers doing? Have students write a paragraph evaluating the Yuan dynasty from their character's point of view.

4. Have volunteers share their responses with the class. Remind students to stay in character. Encourage students to debate the question. **LS Verbal-Linguistic**

   Alternative Assessment Handbook, Rubric 14: Group Activity

Direct Teach

Reading Focus

The Yuan Dynasty

Recall How did Marco Polo describe the grand palace of the Great Khan? *walls covered in silver and gold*

Evaluate Do you believe that Marco Polo actually reached China? Why or why not? *possible answers—Yes: he made a detailed written account of what he saw in China. No, he could have been passing along stories he heard.*

Info to Know

Marco Polo Marco Polo closely observed and later recorded many details about the people and places he encountered on his travels. He described cities, architecture, languages, diets, clothing, marriage customs, rituals, religions, and trade practices, as well as wildlife and terrain. Polo had a sense of wonder for all the things he saw.

go.hrw.com
Online Resources

KEYWORD: SHL CEA
ACTIVITY: Marco Polo

Answers

Counterpoints *possible answer—as powerful, ruthless killers*

320

 NEW YORK

CC Unit 3-B5
Causes of the Mongols' decline

However, a few visitors came all the way from Europe as well. One of the most famous of these Europeans was Marco Polo.

Marco Polo in China An Italian trader from Venice, **Marco Polo** traveled with his father to China. The Polos visited the Yuan court, where Kublai Khan took a liking to the younger Polo. The Yuan emperor sent Marco Polo on several missions, and for 17 years he traveled in and around China.

In 1295 Marco Polo and his father returned home to Venice. Not long after, Polo was captured during a battle and imprisoned. While in prison, he related the tales of his adventures in China to a fellow prisoner. The prisoner wrote them down and had them published as a book. Polo's tales of China fascinated many Europeans, and the book became a huge success.

In his accounts of China, Polo described the grand palace of the Great Khan, where the walls were covered in silver and gold. He noted the efficiency of the Chinese postal system and marveled over the use of paper money. He was also awed by the size and splendor of China's cities, as in this description of the capital.

HISTORY'S VOICES

" The city is the mercantile center of the world. All the most precious stones and pearls from India are brought there. The strangest and most valuable things come from Cathay [China] and other provinces. . . . At least 1,000 cartloads of silk are sent to Khan-balik every day. . . . There are more than 200 cities in the surrounding area from which the people come to Khan-balik to buy and sell. "

—Marco Polo, *Description of the World*, translated by Teresa Waugh

Some modern scholars question whether Marco Polo actually reached China or just related stories he had heard in his travels. These scholars note that Polo failed to mention common Chinese customs of the day such as tea drinking and footbinding, which would

COUNTERPOINTS

Two Views on the Mongols

For some, the Mongols evoked images of annihilated cities littered with the bones of the dead.

" The [Mongols] began to storm the city [of Riazan], some with firebrands, some with battering rams, and others with countless scaling ladders for ascending the walls of the city. And they took the city of Riazan on the 21st day of December . . . And the [Mongols] cut down many people, including women and children . . . And they burned this holy city with all its beauty and wealth . . . And not one man remained alive in the city . . . There used to be the city of Riazan, . . . but its wealth disappeared and its glory ceased, and there is nothing to be seen in the city excepting smoke, ashes, and barren earth. "

Anonymous
—*Tale of the Destruction of Riazan*

For others, the Mongols evoked images of peaceful, generous rule, and splendid cities.

" Inside the city [of Hangzhou] there is a Lake . . . and all round it are beautiful palaces and mansions, of the richest and most exquisite structure that you can imagine . . . In the middle of the Lake are two islands, on each of which stands a rich, beautiful and spacious edifice [building], furnished in such style as to seem fit for . . . an Emperor. And when any one of the citizens desired to hold a marriage feast, or to give any other entertainment, it used to be done at one of these palaces . . . The King made this provision for the gratification [enjoyment] of his people. "

Marco Polo
—*Description of the World*

Skills FOCUS **INVESTIGATING HISTORY**

Infer How do you think that most of the people conquered by the Mongols viewed them?

320 CHAPTER 11

Skills Focus: Summarizing

At Level

Standard English Mastery

Reading Skill
Marco Polo's Journal

1. Explain to students that when Polo returned from the east, many people did not believe he had traveled so far or done so many things.

2. Have students use standard English to write a series of journal entries from Marco Polo's point of view about his explorations and his discoveries. Have them write entries for his arrival in Yuan China, his meeting with Kublai Khan, his missions to India, his time in jail, and his freedom.

3. Have volunteers read their journal entries to the class. As a class, discuss any necessary corrections to the journal entries to align them with standard English usage.

4. Guide students in a discussion of how such people might be convinced that Polo was telling the truth about his explorations.

LS **Verbal-Linguistic**

Alternative Assessment Handbook, Rubrics 11: Discussions; and 15: Journals likely have intrigued his readers. True or not, Polo's tales increased European interest in the distant land of China to the east.

READING CHECK **Summarize** How did Mongol rule in the Yuan dynasty affect life for the Chinese?

End of the Yuan Dynasty

The Yuan dynasty began to weaken during the last part of Kublai Khan's reign. One cause was a number of military defeats. In an effort to expand his empire, Kublai Khan sent several invading forces into Southeast Asia. All of the invasions failed, and the Mongol armies suffered huge losses.

Meanwhile, Kublai Khan had also set his sights on conquering the islands of Japan. Twice he tried to invade Japan, each time with disastrous results. In the first attempt a fleet of some 900 Mongol ships attacked Japan. Although the Mongols won a brief land battle, a storm destroyed their fleet. More than 10,000 people died. Later, Kublai Khan sent an even larger battle fleet against Japan. For more than 50 days the Japanese held off the Mongol invasion. Then, a severe storm once again struck and wiped out the Mongol fleet. The Mongols never attempted to invade Japan again. The Japanese spoke reverently of the storms that had saved them, calling them the *kamikaze*, meaning the "divine wind."

These huge military losses weakened the Mongol forces that controlled and protected China. At the same time, the large amounts spent on public-works projects had weakened the economy. Such weaknesses, combined with Chinese resentment of the Mongols, left the empire ripe for rebellion.

After Kublai Khan died in 1294, several power struggles erupted over who would hold the throne. These struggles weakened Yuan rule, and Kublai Khan's successors lacked his talent for leadership. A series of disastrous floods and rising taxes further increased discontent in China. In the 1300s many Chinese factions rebelled against the Yuan dynasty, and in 1368 a rebel army defeated the Mongols. The Mongols fled to Manchuria, ending foreign rule in China.

READING CHECK **Identify Cause and Effect** What factors led to the end of the Yuan dynasty?

FACES OF HISTORY

KUBLAI Khan
1215–1294

Next to Genghis Khan, Kublai Khan was the greatest of the Mongol rulers. Much of his glory came late in life, and he was already in his mid-60s by the time he completed his conquest of China. Despite his age and being a barbarian in the eyes of the Chinese, Kublai Khan became the first ruler to unite China in more than 300 years. His further achievements as emperor of China include extending the Grand Canal and supporting advances in the arts and sciences.

The Venetian traveler Marco Polo described Kublai Khan as a great and noble ruler. At the same time, Polo noted that the emperor could display outbursts of cruelty. Kublai Khan adopted many aspects of Chinese culture. However, he remained a Mongol conqueror—he never stopped trying to enlarge his empire through conquest.

Find the Main Idea What was Kublai Khan's greatest achievement?

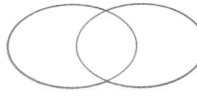

SECTION 2 ASSESSMENT

go.hrw.com
Online Quiz
Keyword: SHL CEA HP

Reviewing Ideas, Terms, and People

1. **a. Define** What was the **Pax Mongolia**, and how did it affect trade and the exchange of ideas across Asia?
   b. Explain What methods did **Genghis Khan** use to build his empire? Where were each of the empire's four khanates located?
   c. Elaborate How did the Mongol invasions and the creation of the Mongol Empire affect people across Eurasia?

2. **a. Identify** Who were **Kublai Khan** and **Marco Polo**, and what was their relationship with each other?
   b. Analyze Why was the period of the Yuan dynasty a significant time in Chinese history?
   c. Make Judgments Do you think that Kublai Khan ruled China well under the Yuan dynasty? Why or why not?

3. **a. Recall** When did the Yuan dynasty end?
   b. Analyze How effective was Yuan rule after the death of Kublai Khan?
   c. Evaluate Do you think the Mongols made a mistake in invading Japan? Why or why not?

Critical Thinking

4. **Compare and Contrast** Using your notes and a graphic organizer like the one shown, compare and contrast the accomplishments of Genghis Khan and Kublai Khan.

FOCUS ON WRITING

5. **Description** You are a member of a town that has just surrendered to a Mongol army. Write a short journal entry describing how the townspeople learned of the coming Mongol force, why they chose to surrender, and your thoughts and feelings about the events.

Section 2 Assessment Answers

1. **a.** time of peace, safety, increased trade
   b. brutality and psychological warfare
   c. inspired fear throughout Eurasia; brought many people under Mongol rule

2. **a.** Mongol ruler; Italian merchant who explored China; Kublai Khan liked Marco Polo, sent him on missions.
   b. It was a time of peace and expansion when the Mongol empire reached its greatest extent.
   c. possible answer—Yes, because he united China with many people under Mongol rule.

3. **a.** in 1368
   b. ineffective with discontent and rebellion.
   c. possible answer—Yes, the military losses significantly weakened the empire.

4. Genghis Khan—united Mongols; military leader; Kublai Khan—created Yuan dynasty; increased trade; Both—ruled during time of peace; united subjects; conquered new lands

5. Journals should include details fabout Mongol war tactics and how psychological warfare encouraged conquered peoples to surrender.

Preteach

Getting Started

Use the **Interactive Reader and Study Guide** to familiarize students with the section content.

📖 **Interactive Reader and Study Guide,** Section 3

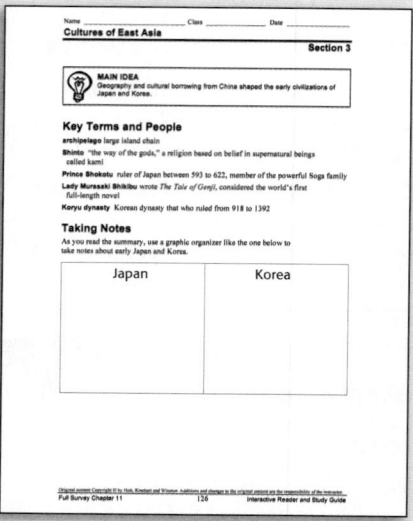

Academic Vocabulary

Review with students the high-use academic term in this section.

administer manage or to run (p. 324)

📝 **CRF: Vocabulary Builder: Section 3**

Taking Notes

Japan—islands, clan leadership, protected from invasion; Korea—peninsula, open to invaders

---

BEFORE YOU READ

MAIN IDEA
Geography and cultural borrowing from China shaped the early civilizations of Japan and Korea.

READING FOCUS
1. What factors shaped early Japanese civilization?
2. How did foreign influences shape life in early Japan?
3. What characteristics defined Japan's Heian period?
4. What were the main events in the history of early Korea?

KEY TERMS AND PEOPLE
archipelago
Shinto
Prince Shotoku
Lady Murasaki Shikibu
Koryo dynasty

 NEW YORK

PI 1.4 Students understand the broad patterns, relationships, and interactions of cultures and civilizations during particular eras and across eras.

▲ The legendary gods Izanagi and Izanami create the first island of Japan.

322

The Myth of Izanami and Izanagi, by Obayashi Eitaku, c. 1885; Photograph © 2007 Museum of Fine Arts, Boston

THE INSIDE STORY *How might geography shape a society's beliefs?* According to Japanese legend, the first gods appeared when the heaven and earth separated. The world still had no land, however. So the gods ordered Izanagi and Izanami, gods who were brother and sister, to form the land of Japan. "At this time the heavenly deities, all with one command, said to the two deities Izanagi-no-mikoto and Izanami-no-mikoto: 'Complete and solidify this drifting land!' Giving [Izanagi and Izanami] the Heavenly Jeweled Spear, they entrusted the mission to them."

Standing on the Heavenly Floating Bridge, the brother and sister dipped the Heavenly Jeweled Spear into the ocean of the world and stirred. "They stirred the brine [sea water] with a churning-churning sound; and when they lifted up [the spear] again, the brine dripping down from the tip of the spear piled up and became an island. This was the island Onogoro." After creating this first island, the brother and sister went on to create all the islands of Japan.

For the early people who lived on these islands, the ever-present nearness of the sea shaped their lives and beliefs. Today the legend of Izanagi and Izanami remains a popular Japanese creation myth. ■

Early Japanese Civilization

Northeast of China and some 100 miles east of the Asian mainland lies the island country of Japan. The Japanese call their land *Nippon,* meaning "Land of the Rising Sun." Japan sits on the western edge of the Pacific—what perhaps felt to the early Japanese like the origin of the sunrise. This location and the geography of Japan has shaped life in the region.

Teach the Main Idea

At Level

Japan and Korea

1. **Teach** Ask students the Reading Focus questions to teach this section.

2. **Apply** Draw four squares for students to see. Label them with the titles of the headings in this section: Early Japanese Civilization, Foreign Influences on Japan, The Heian Period, and Korea. Have students copy the squares onto their own paper. Students should write the main ideas of each topic in the appropriate square.

3. **Review** As you review the section, have students describe aspects of early Japan and Korea.

4. **Practice/Homework** Have students write an official letter from ancient Japan to ancient Korea, requesting information about Chinese culture and technology.
   LS Visual-Spatial, Verbal-Linguistic

📝 **Alternative Assessment Handbook,** Rubric 5: Business Letters

The Land The nation of Japan consists of thousands of islands. The largest four islands, from north to south, are Hokkaido (hoh-KY-doh), Honshu (HAWN-shoo), Shikoku (shee-KOH-koo), and Kyushu (KYOO-shoo). The islands form an **archipelago** (ahr-kuh-PE-luh-goh), or large island chain. This chain extends more than 1,500 miles—about the length of the eastern coast of the United States. The islands lie on the Ring of Fire—a zone of volcanoes and earthquakes that rings the Pacific. As a result, Japan is home to hundreds of volcanoes, many of them active, and has frequent earthquakes. Because of its island location, Japan is also subject to monster waves called tsunamis. These waves result from underwater earthquakes and can wash away everything in their path. In late summer and early autumn, massive storms called typhoons rage through the region.

The geography of Japan shaped the growth of civilization in the region. Much of the terrain is rugged, and steep mountains cover some 80 percent of the land. For this reason, only a small part of Japan is suitable for farming. Most of Japan's people have always lived in the river valleys and coastal plains, where farming is easier. Japan's farmland, while limited, is highly productive, in part because of the islands' fertile soil, mild climate, and abundant rainfall.

The Sea The nearness of the sea shaped the development of Japan as well. Even on Japan's larger islands, people were never far from the sea. Surrounded by water, the early Japanese turned to the sea for food and transportation.

In addition, the sea protected and isolated Japan during much of its history. Japan is separated from Korea by about 100 miles of water and from China by about 400 miles of water. These distances were large enough to prevent successful invasions from the mainland. In fact, no invasion of Japan ever succeeded until World War II. Separated from the mainland, the early Japanese were able to develop their own culture in relative isolation. At the same time, China and Korea were close enough to influence Japan's culture as time passed.

Early Japan Scientists think that the first people to settle in Japan migrated from the Asian mainland. These early people were likely hunters and gatherers. In time, they developed societies with distinct cultures.

JAPAN, 1300

⟵ Mongol invasion, 1274
⟵ Mongol invasion, 1281

ELEVATION

Feet	Meters
13,120	4,000
6,560	2,000
1,640	500
656	200
(Sea level) 0	0 (Sea level)
Below sea level	Below sea level

GEOGRAPHY SKILLS **INTERPRETING MAPS**

1. **Place** What are the four main islands of Japan, and what major bodies of water surround these islands?
2. **Location** How do you think the geographic terrain of Japan affected the location of its early cities?

One early Japanese culture is the Ainu (EYE-noo). Experts are not sure where the Ainu came from, but they do not resemble other East Asians. As more people migrated to Japan, they eventually drove the Ainu onto Japan's northernmost island, where their culture almost disappeared.

The people who lived on the islands south of the Ainu became the Japanese. Clans, or groups based on extended family ties, developed and came to rule many villages. Each clan worshipped nature spirits, called *kami* (KAH-mee), whom they believed were their ancestors.

These beliefs gradually developed into the religion of **Shinto**, which means "way of the *kami*." According to Shinto beliefs, everything in nature—the sun, trees, rocks, animals—has a *kami*. Unlike many religions, Shinto does not have a sacred text or a formal structure. Followers build shrines to *kami* and perform ceremonies to ask for their blessings. These shrines are located in natural settings and most are dedicated to a lovely or unusual tree, waterfall, or other natural object. A red gateway, called a *torii*, marks the entrance to each shrine.

TAKING NOTES
As you read, use a graphic organizer like this to take notes about early Japan and Korea.

Japan	Korea

NEW YORK

CC Unit 3-A
Japanese human and physical geography and early Japanese traditions (Shintoism)

CULTURES OF EAST ASIA **323**

Skills Focus: Making Generalizations — At Level

Reading Skill
The Sea and Land

1. Review with students the information in the text about the geography of Japan and its importance to the early settlers.

2. Have students write a poem or song lyrics from the point of view of an ancient Japanese person about the land of Japan and the sea surrounding it.

3. Have volunteers recite their poems or song lyrics to the class.

4. As an extension, encourage students to conduct research about the haiku form of Japanese poetry and present their findings to the class. Their presentations should include information about when the haiku was first developed, an original haiku about early Japan, and a haiku written by a Japanese poet.

LS Auditory-Musical, Verbal-Linguistic

📝 **Alternative Assessment Handbook**, Rubric 26: Poems and Songs

● **Direct Teach** ●

Reading Focus

① What factors shaped early Japanese civilization? *the sea was a source of food and protection, dangers of tsunamis and typhoons; Shinto religion; powerful clans*

Early Japanese Civilization

Recall How did the geography of Japan benefit early settlers? *sea was a source of food and transportation, offered protection from invasion; soil was fertile*

Describe What are the key beliefs of the Shinto religion? *nature spirits called kami; prayers and rituals to please the kami; no sacred text or formal structure*

Identify Cause and Effect How did Shinto beliefs influence life in Japan? *way of worship; also basis of clan division, people believed clan leaders were descended from kami*

 CRF: Literature: Tanka Poems of Ancient Japan

Info to Know

The Ainu of Japan The Ainu are indigenous people of Japan, similar in many ways to Native Americans. Contact with the Japanese has resulted in intermarriage and cultural assimilation. The Ainu have struggled to maintain their culture and traditional ways of life. Today most Ainu live on the northern island of Hokkaido where they hunt, fish, and farm.

Teaching Tip

Find slides of Shinto shrines to show how traditional Japanese architecture is well integrated with the natural environment.

Answers

Interpreting Maps 1. *Hokkaido, Honshu, Shikoku, Kyushu; Pacific Ocean, Sea of Japan (East Sea), Yellow Sea, East China Sea;* **2.** *cities formed in low elevations near water*

323

Direct Teach

Reading Focus

2 How did foreign influences shape life in early Japan? *iron tools, metalworking, weaving and pottery techniques introduced from Korea; learned Chinese writing from Koreans; Buddhism*

Foreign Influences on Japan

Summarize What changes did Prince Shotoku bring to Japan? *supported Buddhism; centralized government, using Chinese model*

Analyze Why do you think the Japanese adopted many aspects of Chinese government and culture? *possible answers—saw China as a more advanced society; aspects of Chinese culture became fashionable*

📃 **CRF:** Biography: Sankara

Info to Know

The Taiho Code In AD 702, the Taiho Code, based on the Chinese bureaucratic model, divided Japan into three levels of governmental administration: provinces, districts, and villages. Taxes were collected in the form of goods, such as grain or cloth, or in labor. Furthermore, all males were liable for enrollment in the military. However, a Chinese-style civil service examination system was not adopted by the Japanese. Thus, despite much borrowing from the mainland—religion, written language, government, laws, tax systems, and land reform—the aristocratic families retained ultimate authority.

Answers

Reading Check (left) *geologically active region; steep mountains, thick forests, limited but fertile farmland, islands surrounded by the sea; (right) gave Japan a written language; Buddhism spread from China to Japan; Chinese fashion and foods became popular; Japanese adopted some Chinese ideas about government*

324

📹 **NEW YORK**

CC Unit 3-A3
Early Japanese history and ties with China and Korea: cultural diffusion, Buddhism, and Confucianism

ACADEMIC VOCABULARY
administer to manage or to run

The Yamato Clan One of the most revered *kami* in Japan was Amaterasu, the sun goddess. According to legend, Japan's first emperor was the grandson of the sun goddess. This emperor belonged to the powerful Yamato clan, which claimed the sun goddess as its ancestor.

The Yamato clan lived on the Yamato plain, a rich farming region on the island of Honshu. By the AD 500s the clan controlled much of Honshu. Although they did not control all of Japan, the Yamato chiefs began to call themselves the emperors of Japan. In time, Japan's emperors claimed to be divine. Although this is no longer the case, Japan's emperor still claims to be descended from the Yamato clan.

Other clans eventually gained power over the Yamato. The leaders of these clans did not remove the Yamato emperor; instead they controlled him. As a result, the emperor often had no real authority, serving instead as a figurehead. This political system of an imperial figurehead controlled by the head of a powerful family continued in Japan until the 1900s.

READING CHECK **Identify Supporting Details** What geographic factors have influenced Japan's history and culture?

Foreign Influences on Japan

By the mid-500s Japan had increased contact with its neighbors Korea and China. As a result, Chinese culture in particular began to strongly influence Japan. The Japanese borrowed many Chinese ideas, which they modified to create their own unique culture.

Korean Influences Korean traders and travelers brought many foreign influences to Japan. Most of these influences originated in China. For instance, Korean scribes introduced Chinese writing to Japan. The early Japanese did not have a written language. As a result, many Japanese, particularly among the rich and well-educated, adopted Chinese writing.

Korean monks introduced the religion of Buddhism to Japan as well. Although some Japanese feared the new religion would offend the *kami,* Buddhist practices had spread throughout much of Japan by the 800s. Buddhism influenced Japanese art; and Buddhist temples, including pagoda architecture from China, were built across Japan.

324 CHAPTER 11

Chinese Influences One of the people who most helped spread Buddhism in Japan was **Prince Shotoku** (shoh-toh-koo). From 593 to 622 he served as regent to the Japanese empress, who was his aunt. A regent is a person who rules for someone who is unable to rule alone.

Besides supporting Buddhism, Shotoku greatly admired China. He decided to send scholars to learn from the Chinese directly. Over the next 200 years, many Japanese missions went to China, which was then under the Tang dynasty. The knowledge these missions brought back changed Japan in many ways.

In Japan, Chinese fashions, foods, and tea became popular along with Tang styles of art, music, dance, and gardening. The Japanese adopted many Confucian ideas about family, such as the ideas that wives should obey husbands and that children should obey parents.

The Japanese also adopted Tang ideas about government, including a stronger central government and a bureaucracy to <u>administer</u> government affairs. In addition, the Japanese adopted a law code similar to China's. However, Japan's nobles and clan leaders resisted a civil service system based on merit. Nobles continued to hold high offices, and clan leaders remained powerful.

Life in the Heian Period

Illustrated scene from *The Tale of Genji*

Skills Focus: Summarizing

At Level

Reading Skill
Korean Ambassadors

1. Review with students material in the text about information the ancient Japanese received from the Koreans.

2. Organize students into small groups. Have each group create a skit about an official visit of Korean ambassadors to the imperial court of Japan.

3. Allow enough time for students to write and rehearse their skits. Then, have students perform their skits for the class.

4. Conduct a brief critique session following the presentation of each skit. Remind students to use constructive criticism. **LS** **Kinesthetic, Verbal-Linguistic**

📃 **Alternative Assessment Handbook**, Rubric 33: Skits and Reader's Theater

When the Tang dynasty began to decline in the late 800s, the Japanese stopped sending missions to China. The Japanese took what they had learned and transformed it to create their own unique culture and society.

READING CHECK **Find the Main Idea** How did Chinese influences affect Japan during this period?

The Heian Period

In 794 Japan's emperor moved the capital to Heian (HAY-ahn), now called Kyoto (kee-OH-toh). Many of Japan's nobles moved to Heian, where they developed an elegant and stylish court society. At the Heian court, Japanese culture flowered. This era in Japanese history from 794 until 1185 is known as the Heian period.

Life in the Heian Period The nobles at Heian lived in beautiful palaces and enjoyed lives of ease and privilege. They loved elegance and beauty and passed the time strolling through lovely gardens or admiring art and poetry. Court life was so removed from that of Japan's common people that many nobles called themselves "dwellers among the clouds."

In this scene from *The Tale of Genji*, the women are hidden away inside the carriages. *How did travel differ for the noblemen of the Heian court?*

Rules of etiquette governed all aspects of court behavior and dress. Women often wore elaborate silk gowns made of 12 colored layers. The layers were cleverly cut and folded so that each one showed at the wrist. Nobles took great care with how they spoke and wrote. The proper way to write a note was an art form, and everyone was expected to write poetry. These poems often had five lines and focused on love or nature. The poem below recalls a past love.

HISTORY'S VOICES

❝Now that the fragrance
Rises from the orange trees
That wait till June to bloom,
I am reminded of those scented sleeves
And wonder about that person of my past.❞

—Anonymous, from *Kokinshu*, c. 905

PRIMARY SOURCES

The Pillow Book

Sei Shonagon (SAY shoh-nah-gohn) served as a lady-in-waiting to Japan's empress from 991 to 1000. During this period, Sei Shonagon wrote *The Pillow Book*, a journal in which she recorded observations, amusing stories, poems, and details about Heian court life. Here she describes things that please her.

I am most pleased when I hear someone I love being praised or being mentioned approvingly by an important person.

A poem that someone has composed for a special occasion or written to another person in reply is widely praised and copied by people in their notebooks. Though this is something that has never yet happened to me, I can imagine how pleasing it must be.

A person with whom one is not especially intimate refers to an old poem or story that is unfamiliar. Then one hears it being mentioned by someone else and one has the pleasure of recognizing it. Still later, when one comes across it in a book, one thinks, "Ah, this is it!" and feels delighted with the person who first brought it up.

Skills FOCUS **READING LIKE A HISTORIAN**

1. **Describe** What are some of the things that please Sei Shonagon?
2. **Interpret Literature as a Source** What details about court life does the excerpt provide?

See **Skills Handbook, p. H25**

CULTURES OF EAST ASIA **325**

READING SKILLS

Making Inferences Why do you think the nobles of the Heian court spent so much time on cultural activities and their appearance?

Direct Teach

Reading Focus

❸ What characteristics defined Japan's Heian period? *Japanese culture flourished; court society developed*

The Heian Period

Make Generalizations In what ways did Japanese culture flower during the Heian period? *An elaborate court society developed, and it valued art and poetry.*

Identify Cause and Effect What caused Japanese literature to flourish during the Heian period? *authors no longer copied Chinese models, used personal inspiration*

Activity **Heian Poetry** Have students conduct research to find other examples of poetry from the Heian period. As homework, have them write an original poem with similar style and content. **LS** **Verbal-Linguistic**

📝 **Alternative Assessment Handbook,** Rubric 26: Poems and Songs

📝 **CRF:** Biography: Murasaki Shikibu

Skills Focus: Making Generalizations

At Level

Reading Skill
Women of the Heian Court

1. Draw the chart for students to see. Omit the italicized answers.

2. Have students copy and complete the chart, filling the left column with specific details from this page, and filling the right column with a generalization they can make about women in the Heian court. **LS** **Visual-Spatial**

📝 **Alternative Assessment Handbook,** Rubric 7: Charts; and 12 Drawing Conclusions

Details	Generalization
• wore elaborate silk gowns, with 12 layers • enjoyed reading and writing • discouraged from learning Chinese • produced some of the best works of early Japanese literature, including Tale of the Genji	*Women's activities were important in the development of Japanese culture during the Heian period.*

Answers

Reading skills *possible answer— Elegance, beauty, and etiquette were important to them.*

Life in the Heian Period *women travelled inside carriages, men outside*

Reading Like a Historian 1. *praise; the idea of her writing becoming famous; recognizing the writings of others;* **2.** *Poems and stories were a part of the court culture.*

325

Reading Focus

4 What were the main events in the history of Korea? *Han dynasty defeated and colonized Korea, Confucianism and Buddhism introduced, ruled by three kingdoms, taken over by Silla until 1392, Koryo dynasty founded, Yuan invasion, new dynasty from 1392 to 1910*

Korea

Describe What is Korea's geography like? *a peninsula jutting out from East Asia; mostly covered by mountains; rivers running east to west*

Identify Cause and Effect What event led China to begin its influence on Korea? *The Han dynasty defeated and colonized part of Korea in 108 BC.*

Make Inferences Why do you think the word Korea comes from the name of the Koryo dynasty? *possible answer—because the Koryo dynasty is remembered for maintaining Korea's distinct culture*

Info to Know

Silla and China As the ancient tribal systems broke down, Silla's government and culture were heavily influenced by China. Silla regularly sent tribute missions to the Tang capital. In addition, many students and monks from Silla pursued their education and training in China. Thus, a flow of new ideas and philosophies arose. Eventually, the people of Silla embraced Buddhism and duplicated the Tang political system.

Answers

Reading Check *A court culture grew; writing and art flourished.*

326

The women of the Heian court enjoyed writing and reading. *Monogatari*, or fictional prose, was especially popular. Noblewomen were discouraged from learning Chinese, so many of them wrote and read in Japanese. By this time, the Japanese had developed a way to write their spoken language by combining Chinese characters with phonetic characters.

Heian women produced some of the best works of early Japanese literature. The greatest writer was perhaps **Lady Murasaki Shikibu** (moohr-ah-sahk-ee shee-kee-boo). Around 1000, she wrote *The Tale of Genji*, considered the world's first full-length novel. One of Japan's greatest novels, it tells the story of a prince named Genji and his quest for love. Lady Murasaki's writing is simple but graceful and describes Heian court life in great detail.

The Fujiwaras During most of the Heian period the Fujiwara family controlled Japan. Many Fujiwaras served as regent, and the Fujiwaras often married their daughters to the heirs to the throne. However, rich landowners with private armies eventually began to challenge the Fujiwaras and Japan's central government. You will read about how these changes affected Japan in a later chapter.

NEW YORK
CC Unit 3-B5
Impact of the rise of the Mongols on Korea

READING CHECK **Summarize** Why was the Heian period a golden age of culture in Japan?

Korean Celadon Pottery

During the Koryu period, Korean artisans became famous for their celadon pottery, such as this dragon-shaped vessel made in the 1100s.

326 CHAPTER 11

Korea

The Korean peninsula juts south from the East Asian mainland. To the north and southwest lies China, and to the east lies Japan. This location between China and Japan made Korea a bridge for the passage of people, culture, and ideas. At the same time, Korea's location left the region open to invasion, and both China and Japan have dominated Korea over time.

Geography Like Japan, much of the Korean Peninsula is covered by rugged mountains, which limits the amount of land for agriculture. The mountain ranges run north to south along the peninsula's east coast. As a result, Korea's main population centers are in the west, where the land flattens into plains. In general, Korea's climate is hot in the summer and cold in the winter.

Early Korea The first Koreans were nomadic peoples from northeastern Asia. As in Japan, the early Koreans formed clans and developed their own culture. China soon began to influence Korea, when the Han dynasty of China defeated and colonized part of Korea in 108 BC. During this period, the Koreans adopted Confucianism as well as Chinese writing, political institutions, and agricultural methods. Eventually, Chinese missionaries introduced Buddhism to Korea as well.

After China's Han dynasty declined, three rival kingdoms gained control of Korea. By 668 the rulers of one of these kingdoms, Silla, allied with China—then ruled by the Tang dynasty—and conquered the other two kingdoms. The Silla then turned on the Chinese and drove them from Korea. By about 670 the Silla ruled all of Korea.

Although independent, Silla's rulers agreed to pay tribute to China to ensure harmony and goodwill. Under Silla rule, the Koreans embraced many aspects of Chinese civilization. Silla's rulers promoted Buddhism, for example, and created a central government and bureaucracy based on the Tang model.

The Koryo Dynasty The Silla Kingdom eventually weakened, and around 935, rebels defeated it and founded the **Koryo dynasty**. This dynasty, whose name is the basis of the word *Korea*, lasted until 1392.

Skills Focus: Evaluating Information on the Internet   At Level

Reading Like a Historian Skill
Ancient Korea

Research Required

1. Organize students into small groups.

2. Have students conduct research on ancient Korean civilization using reliable online sources. You may wish to give groups different areas to focus on such as leaders, conflicts, relations with China, relations with Japan, religion, and language.

3. Have students use their research to create a poster depicting the findings of their research.

4. Have groups present their posters to the class.
LS Visual-Spatial

Alternative Assessment Handbook, Rubrics 28: Posters; and 30: Research

Koryo's rulers continued to adopt Chinese ideas but worked to maintain distinct Korean features. One Koryo ruler declared, "We have always had a deep adoration for Tang-style culture . . . But our country is a separate land, and our people's character is different." For instance, the Koryo adopted a civil service examination system similar to China's; in Korea, though, only nobles could take the test, and government positions were inherited. As a result, Korean society was divided between a powerful nobility and the rest of the people.

During the Koryo period, Korean culture thrived. Korean artisans created pottery covered with a blue-green glaze called celadon. This celadon pottery rivaled Song porcelain in beauty and was highly prized. In addition, the Koreans used Chinese methods of printing and carved some 80,000 wooden blocks to print Buddhist texts. The Koreans later improved the process by creating metal movable type.

In the 1200s the Mongols of Yuan China invaded and occupied Korea. They forced Koryo's rulers to pay immense tributes and enslaved many Koreans. They took artisans to China, and forced men to serve in the Yuan military. When the Yuan dynasty weakened, Koreans rebelled. In 1392 a Korean general founded a new dynasty, which ruled until 1910.

READING CHECK **Sequence** What were the major events and periods in early Korean history?

KOREA, 918–1392

GEOGRAPHY SKILLS **INTERPRETING MAPS**

1. **Place** What physical features help separate Korea from China?

2. **Movement** Did the Tang Chinese invade Korea by land or by water during the 660s?

SECTION 3 ASSESSMENT

go.hrw.com
Online Quiz
Keyword: SHL CEA HP

Reviewing Ideas, Terms, and People

1. **a. Recall** What is **Shinto**, and how does it differ from many other major religions?
   b. Explain How has Japan's location been both an advantage and a disadvantage?

2. **a. Identify** Who was **Prince Shotoku**, and how did he contribute to early Japanese history?
   b. Summarize What aspects of Chinese culture did the Japanese borrow?

3. **a. Describe** What was life like at the Heian court?
   b. Identify Cause and Effect How did the status of women in Japan influence the development of Japanese literature?

4. **a. Recall** Which kingdom first unified Korea?
   b. Analyze How did China's nearness to Korea affect the development of Korean culture?

Critical Thinking

5. **Identify Cause and Effect** Using your notes and a graphic organizer like this one, explain how China influenced Japan and Korea.

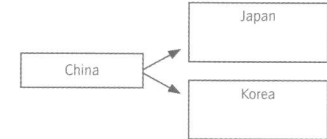

FOCUS ON WRITING

6. **Narration** You are a member of a Japanese mission sent to Tang China. Write a short diary entry in which you describe what you are doing and the purpose of your mission.

CULTURES OF EAST ASIA **327**

Section 3 Assessment Answers

1. **a.** religion that developed in Japan; does not have a sacred text or formal structure
   b. advantage: protection; disadvantage: isolation

2. **a.** regent to Japanese empress; supported Buddhism and brought Chinese influences to Japan
   b. fashion and foods, Confucian ideas, ideas about government

3. **a.** beautiful palaces, lives of privilege, art and poetry were important

   b. women were encouraged to write and read, produced many important works in early Japanese literature

4. **a.** the Silla
   b. was a bridge for culture and ideas

5. Japan—writing, Buddhism, Confucianism, government; Korea—Buddhism, government, printing methods

6. Student entries should include details from the section about Prince Shotoku's appreciation of China, Chinese fashion and foods, tea, Tang art, and Confucianism.

World Literature

The Tale of Genji

Meet the Writer

Lady Murasaki Shikibu (971–1016)

Born into the Fujiwara family, Murasaki Shikibu was the daughter of a provincial governor. She was married in her early twenties to an older man who died just a few years later. Because of Murasaki's brilliant mind and good connections, she was hired by the court to serve as an attendant of Empress Akiko. Around this time, she began writing *The Tale of Genji,* one of the world's earliest novels. Popular from the time of its release, the novel contains revealing observations on the actions and thoughts of members of upper class society. Murasaki also wrote a book of poems.

World Literature

Murasaki Shikibu (971–1016)

NEW YORK STANDARDS

P1 2.4 Students explain the importance of analyzing narratives drawn from different times and places to understand historical events.

About the Reading *The Tale of Genji,* a novel of more than 1,000 pages, traces the life, loves, and adventures of a prince known as "the shining Genji." Although Genji is the emperor's favorite son, he cannot inherit the throne because his mother is a commoner. In the following passage, Genji describes his impressions of some of the ladies at court. Except for Genji, all of the characters mentioned are women.

AS YOU READ Look for examples of the Japanese nobles' focus on beauty, elegance, and nature during the Heian period.

Excerpt from

The Tale of Genji

by Lady Murasaki Shikibu

This scene is from an illustrated scroll of *The Tale of Genji.* In the scene, Genji is reading a scroll aloud, while a woman listens.

It was the time of the month when the moon rises late. The flares at the eaves were just right, neither too dim nor too strong. Genji glanced at the Third Princess. She was smaller than the others, so tiny indeed that she seemed to be all clothes. Hers was not a striking sort of beauty, but it was marked by very great refinement and delicacy. One thought of a willow sending forth its first shoots toward the end of the Second Month, so delicate that the breeze from the warbler's wing seems enough to disarrange them. The hair flowing over a white robe lined with red also suggested the trailing strands of a willow. One knew that she was the most wellborn of ladies. Beside her the Akashi princess seemed gentle and delicate in a livelier, brighter way, and somehow deeper and subtler too, trained to greater diversity. One might have likened her to a wisteria in early morning, blooming from spring into summer with no other blossoms to rival it . . . Her hair fell thick and full . . . She had a most winning charm in the soft, wavering light from the eaves.

Over a robe of pink Murasaki wore a robe of a rich, deep hue, a sort of magenta, perhaps. Her hair fell in a wide, graceful cascade. She was of just the right height, so beautiful in every one of her features that they added up to more than perfection. A cherry in full bloom—but not even that seemed an adequate simile.

One would have expected the Akashi lady to be quite overwhelmed by such company, but she was not. Careful, conservative taste was evident in her grooming and dress. One sensed quiet depths, and an ineffable [indescribable] elegance which was all her own. She had on a figured "willow" robe, white lined with green, and a cloak of a yellowish green, and as a mark of respect for the other ladies, a train of a most delicate and yielding gossamer [a sheer, filmy fabric]. Everything about her emphasized her essential modesty and unassertiveness, but there was much that suggested depth and subtlety as well.

Skills FOCUS READING LIKE A HISTORIAN

go.hrw.com
World Literature
Keyword: SHL WRLIT

1. **Analyze** What comparisons does Genji use to describe the Third Princess and the Akashi princess?
2. **Interpret Literature as a Source** Based on this passage, what qualities were admired among women during the Heian period?

Skills Focus: Interpreting Literature as Historical Evidence

Reading Like a Historian Skill
Analyzing The Tale of Genji

At Level

1. Have students analyze the excerpt from *The Tale of Genji* focusing on the following aspects: writing style, attention to aesthetics, characters, and historical and cultural details. Have them write a few sentences about each aspect.

2. Have volunteers present their analyses to the class.

3. Guide students in a discussion about what historians can learn from *The Tale of Genji.*
   LS Verbal-Linguistic

   Alternative Assessment Handbook, Rubrics 11: Discussions, and 37: Writing Assignments

Answers

Reading Like a Historian 1. *Genji compares them to flowers. The Third Princess is like a willow, and the Akashi princess is like a wisteria.* **2.** *delicate appearance; refined behavior; beautiful hair and clothing*

SECTION 4
Civilizations of Southeast Asia

BEFORE YOU READ

MAIN IDEA
Geography and the cultures of India and China influenced the early civilizations of Southeast Asia.

READING FOCUS
1. What factors influenced early civilizations in the region of Southeast Asia?
2. What early kingdoms and empires developed in Southeast Asia?

KEY TERMS AND PEOPLE
Anawrahta
Angkor Wat
Trung Trac
Trung Nhi

NEW YORK
PI 1.4 Students understand the broad patterns, relationships, and interactions of cultures and civilizations during particular eras and across eras.

THE INSIDE STORY

Have explorers really found lost cities in the jungle? In 1858 a French explorer named Henri Mouhot was traveling through the jungles of Cambodia. He came across a missionary who told him that the people in the area spoke of a "lost city" in the jungle. Fascinated, Mouhot set out to find it. He hired local guides, who led him through the thick tropical forest to an amazing site. Hidden away in the Cambodian jungle were the remains of the city of Angkor, once the capital of the great Khmer Empire.

The most spectacular ruins in the city were those of Angkor Wat, a Hindu temple complex built in the early 1100s. Covering nearly one square mile, the complex was surrounded by a moat and walls within which sat a temple with soaring towers. Statues adorned the site, and lively Hindu carvings graced the walls. To the Khmer people, the temple in the center of the complex symbolized Mount Meru, a sacred mountain at the center of the Hindu cosmos. The temple's towers represented the mountain's peaks.

Henri Mouhot died of jungle fever before he could return to France. His vivid descriptions of the ruins of the city of Angkor were published, though, and caused a sensation in Europe. Today the ruins of Angkor are a reminder of the powerful empires that once ruled Southeast Asia. ◼

Uncovering A LOST JEWEL

▲ Beautiful carvings, like the one above, adorn the walls of Angkor Wat in Cambodia.

329

Preteach

Getting Started
Use the **Interactive Reader and Study Guide** to familiarize students with the section content.

📋 **Interactive Reader and Study Guide,** Section 4

[Worksheet reproduction: Cultures of East Asia — Section 4, Main Idea, Key Terms and People (Anawrahta, Angkor Wat, Trung Trac, Trung Nhi), Taking Notes graphic organizer with Southeast Asia box and boxes 1, 2, 3]

Academic Vocabulary
Review with students the high-use academic term in this section.

predominant most common or important (p. 330)

📋 **CRF:** Vocabulary Builder: Section 4

Taking Notes
Geography—mainland and islands; river deltas; rugged mountains; seas and straits; Cultural Influences—Indian and Chinese traders; Hinduism; Buddhism; Islam; Ancient Kingdoms—Pagan Kingdom; Khmer Empire; trading kingdoms; Vietnam

---

Teach the Main Idea

At Level

Civilizations of Southeast Asia

1. **Teach** Ask students the Reading Focus questions to teach this section.

2. **Apply** Have students create flashcards to learn the kingdoms, people, and key terms in this section. Have students write the definition or fact on one side of the card, and the kingdom, person, or term on the other side.

3. **Review** As you review the section, have students use their flashcards to quiz each other about the section.

4. **Practice/Homework** Have students write a short essay about the role religion played in ancient Southeast Asia.
   LS Verbal-Linguistic

📋 **Alternative Assessment Handbook**, Rubric 37: Writing Assignments

Reading Focus

1 What factors influenced early civilizations in the region of Southeast Asia? *river deltas supported farming; different cultures separated by mountains; ships relied on monsoon winds for trade*

Influences on Southeast Asia

Explain How did the rivers affect the development of Southeast Asia? *Fertile soil in the delta encouraged settlement.*

Summarize What were the positive and negative effects of monsoons on trade in Southeast Asia? *positive—Traders had to sit for months in ports, so port cities became important economic centers because they provided supplies and security to traders. negative—Traders lost time waiting for storms to pass.*

📦 **Map Transparency:** Southeast Asian Kingdoms, 600–1350

Primary Source

"It is from [Java] that the merchants of Zaitun and Manzi [southern China] in general have derived and continue to derive a great part of their wealth, and this is the source of most of the spice that comes into the world's markets."
—Marco Polo, *The Travels of Marco Polo*, c. 1298–1299

SOUTHEAST ASIAN KINGDOMS, 600–1350

Legend:
- Srivijaya Empire
- Pagan Kingdom (Myanmar)
- Khmer Empire (Cambodia)
- Dai Viet (Vietnam)
- Trade route
- (1351) Date founded

0   200   400 Miles
0   200   400 Kilometers
Miller projection

GEOGRAPHY SKILLS | **INTERPRETING MAPS**

1. **Location** Which three early kingdoms and empires were located on mainland Southeast Asia?

2. **Movement** Why do you think that trade became an important part of the economy of the islands of Southeast Asia?

TAKING NOTES
Use a graphic organizer like the one below. Take notes about the (1) geography, (2) cultural influences, and (3) ancient kingdoms of Southeast Asia.

Southeast Asia
→ 1   → 3
2

ACADEMIC VOCABULARY
predominant
most common or important

330 CHAPTER 11

Influences on Southeast Asia

The region of Southeast Asia is located between India and China. These two powerful neighbors shaped the development of civilization in the region. At the same time, geography and trade also played important roles in the region.

Geography Southeast Asia can be divided into two parts—mainland Southeast Asia and island Southeast Asia. The mainland area consists of the peninsulas that jut south from Asia between India and China. This area contains the modern nations of Cambodia, Laos, Myanmar (Burma), Thailand, and Vietnam as well as part of Malaysia. Island Southeast Asia consists of the islands south and east of the mainland, such as Sumatra, Borneo, and Java. These islands contain the rest of Malaysia as well as the nations of Brunei (brooh-NY), East Timor, Indonesia, the Philippines, and Singapore.

On the mainland, several major rivers flow south. The valleys and deltas of these rivers supported farming and became home to early civilizations in the area. Separating the rivers are rugged mountains. These mountains often limited contact among the people in the area, and many different cultures developed.

The islands of Southeast Asia are surrounded by seas and straits. These waterways provided the early people in the area with their main sources of food and travel. In addition, the seas came to serve as important trade routes.

Trade The waterways through Southeast Asia were the predominant trade routes between India and China. The two most important trade routes were the Malacca Strait, located between the Malay Peninsula and Sumatra, and the Sunda Strait, located between Sumatra and Java. Control of these and other important trade routes brought wealth and power.

Skills Focus: Interpreting Maps

Above Level

Social Studies Skill
The Geography of Southeast Asia

Research Required

1. Review with students information in the text about geographic and trade influences in Southeast Asia. Point out that the major cities were founded along bodies of water.

2. Have students name the major rivers, straits and seas of Southeast Asia. Then have them identify the trading partners of the Southeast Asian kingdoms, as shown on the map.

3. Guide students in a discussion about how culture can spread through trade. Point out

that India and China, the nearest neighbors of these Southeast Asian kingdoms, had great influence on these cultures.

4. Have students conduct research to learn about the present day nations of Myanmar, Cambodia, and Vietnam. What, if anything, do these countries have in common with the early empires? **LS Verbal-Linguistic**

📓 **Alternative Assessment Handbook**, Rubrics 11: Discussions; and 30: Research

Answers

Interpreting Maps 1. *Pagan Kingdom (Myanmar), Khmer Empire (Cambodia), Dai Viet (Vietnam);* **2.** *possible answer—The islands were centrally located along the sea trade routes.*

Monsoons, seasonal winds that blow northeast in summer and southwest in winter, shaped trade in Southeast Asia. Ships relied on the monsoons to sail from place to place. Once in port, ships often had to wait until the winds shifted to resume their voyage. As a result, many Southeast Asian port cities became important economic centers.

By the AD 100s merchants from India had begun a prosperous sea trade with Southeast Asia. After China's Han dynasty fell in 220, overland trade routes through central Asia became more dangerous. As a result, seaborne trade between India and China increased. These traders passed through Southeast Asia, where they exchanged goods for local products such as spices and aromatic woods.

India and China As Indian and Chinese traders came to Southeast Asia, they began to influence the region. Indian influence spread through trade and missionaries. For example, Indian missionaries introduced Hinduism and Buddhism to Southeast Asia, and many kingdoms adopted the religions. Some kingdoms built temples in the Indian style, such as the massive Buddhist monument at Borobudur, which is on the island of Java.

Over time, Indian ideas about writing, government, science, and art spread to Southeast Asia. Some local rulers, seeking to enhance their standing by embracing many of these new ideas, adopted Indian names and political ideas. The ancient Indian language of Sanskrit came into wide use. From the Malay Peninsula to southern Vietnam, many kingdoms showed strong Indian influences.

Eventually, Indian Muslims brought Islam to Southeast Asia as well. In the early 1000s Muslims gained control of much of northern India. Soon Muslim traders from India and other regions were spreading Islam throughout the islands of Southeast Asia. As a result, Islamic states formed in Sumatra, the Malay Peninsula, Borneo, and the Philippines.

Chinese influences spread to parts of mainland Southeast Asia through conquest, trade, and migration. For example, China controlled northern Vietnam at different times. As a result, China strongly influenced that region.

READING CHECK **Identify Cause and Effect** How did trade influence Southeast Asia?

Early Kingdoms and Empires

Several early kingdoms and empires arose across Southeast Asia. Although most of them were small, a few became quite powerful. As in Korea and Japan, the early kingdoms and empires of Southeast Asia blended influences from India and China to create their own unique societies and cultures.

The Pagan Kingdom Around the AD 840s a people called the Burmans established the kingdom of Pagan (puh-GAHN) in what is now Myanmar (Burma). The kingdom was located in the fertile Irrawaddy River valley, which was ideal for rice farming. Pagan's first great king was **Anawrahta**, who ruled from 1044 to 1077. King Anawrahta began to conquer the surrounding areas and by 1057 had united much of what is now Myanmar under his rule. His conquests provided Pagan with access to trading ports, and the kingdom prospered.

Anawrahta and his successors supported Theravada Buddhism. They built thousands of magnificent Buddhist temples, and Pagan became a center of Buddhist learning. The Venetian traveler Marco Polo, who visited the Mongol court in China, even mentioned the splendor of Pagan.

Borobudur Temple
The Buddhist monument of Borobudur on Java was built around the 800s by the rulers of the Sailendra Kingdom.

CULTURES OF EAST ASIA **331**

● **Direct Teach** ●

Reading Focus

Influences on Southeast Asia

Recall How did India and China influence Southeast Asian civilizations? *brought Hinduism, Buddhism, and Islam; architecture styles; ideas about writing, government, science, and art*

Make Inferences Why did local rulers embrace ideas from India? *India was seen as an advanced civilization, and some rulers wanted to enhance their images by adopting Indian ideas.*

Reading Focus

2 What early kingdoms and empires developed in Southeast Asia? *Pagan Kingdom, Khmer Empire, Sailendra, Srivijaya, Nam Viet*

Early Kingdoms and Empires

Identify Who was Anawrahta? *king of Pagan who united much of what is now Myanmar*

Analyze Why do you think the people of Myanmar consider Pagan to be the classical age of their history? *possible answer—the empire became united; it was a time of prosperity and splendor.*

Skills Focus: Identifying Main Idea and Details   At Level

Reading Skill
Southeast Asian Kingdoms

1. Copy the chart for students to see. Omit the italicized answers.

2. Have students copy and complete the chart. Have volunteers fill in the class chart. **LS** Visual-Spatial

📋 **Alternative Assessment Handbook,** Rubric 7: Charts

Kingdom	Pagan	Khmer	Srivijaya	Vietnam
Location	*modern nation of Myanmar*	*lower Mekong river*	*Sumatra, etc.*	*modern nation of Vietnam*
Notable Leaders	*Anawratha*	*Javayarman I and II*	*Not Listed*	*Trung Trac, Trung Ni, Ly Thai To*
Religion or Philosophy	*Theravada Buddhism*	*Hinduism*	*Buddhism*	*Confucianism*
Challenges	*declining power of kings*	*expensive projects, attacks*	*security from pirates*	*resisting Chinese occupation*

Answers

Reading Check *Ports became the economic centers of Southeast Asia; Indian and Chinese influence spread to Southeast Asia through trade.*

331

NEW YORK

CC Unit 3-B5
Impact of the rise of the Mongols on Southeast Asia

In the late 1200s the Mongols under the rule of Kublai Khan demanded tribute from Pagan. The king of Pagan refused and attacked the Mongols, who crushed the Pagan army. The Pagan king fled southward, after which one of his sons killed him and then agreed to pay the tribute to the Mongols. Pagan survived but lost its power. Nonetheless, the people of Myanmar consider Pagan their classical age because Pagan culture established principles that continue to influence their religion and society.

The Khmer Empire To the southeast of Pagan, the powerful Khmer (kuh-MER) Empire arose in what is now Cambodia. By the early 800s, the Khmer had begun to conquer the kingdoms around them to build a great empire.

Rice Cultivation

The farming of rice came to Southeast Asia perhaps around 2000 BC. Rice became a vital crop across much of the region, where the warm, wet climate is perfect for growing rice. *How did Southeast Asians and others adapt rice farming to hilly terrains?*

Farmers across Asia often built terraces in hilly areas to create level land for farming.

Rice seedlings were planted by hand in flooded fields called paddies. The fields were drained at harvest time.

332

This empire reached its height between about 850 and 1220, during which it controlled much of the Southeast Asian mainland.

The Khmer Empire reflected a strong Indian influence. The empire's rulers adopted both Hindu and Buddhist beliefs and ruled as gods. The design of the empire's capital city, Angkor, symbolized the shape of the Hindu universe, with a temple at its center.

In Angkor, the Khmer rulers had spectacular temple complexes built. The most famous is **Angkor Wat**, the ruins of which still stand. Built in the 1100s, this vast complex consists of walls surrounding a central temple with towers. Graceful carvings of Hindu myths and beliefs cover many of the walls. The temple's central tower rises some 200 feet and may have been used as an astronomical observatory.

The Khmer rulers could fund such impressive building projects because their empire had grown prosperous from rice farming. To improve agricultural production, the Khmer devised an irrigation system that covered millions of acres. With this system, the Khmer could grow several crops of rice a year. For some 400 years, the Khmer Empire prospered. In time, however, costly building projects and invaders contributed to the empire's decline.

Trading Kingdoms To the south of the mainland, several trading kingdoms developed on the islands of Southeast Asia. On the island of Java, the kingdom of Sailendra flourished from about 750 to 850. The people of this kingdom relied on agriculture and trade for their livelihood. The kingdom adopted Mahayana Buddhism and is known for its impressive Buddhist art and architecture. The Buddhist monument at Borobudur is the most famous Sailendra achievement. This monument has nine terraced levels that symbolize the stages of the Buddhist spiritual journey.

Centered on the island of Sumatra, the wealthy Srivijaya (sree-wi-jaw-yuh) Empire flourished from the 600s to the 1200s. At its height, the empire extended to the Malay Peninsula and Borneo. The Srivijaya Empire gained its wealth from its control of overseas traders through the Malacca and Sunda straits. Aware of the importance to trade to their continued prosperity, the rulers of Srivijaya worked to ensure that trade continued to pass through their empire.

The people of Srivijaya adopted Hinduism and Buddhism, which they blended with local beliefs. The Srivijaya capital, located at Palembang on Sumatra, became a center of Buddhist learning. It was such an important center of learning that one Chinese monk declared that Buddhist students should spend a year in study there before going on to study in India.

In 1025 an Indian kingdom attacked the Srivijaya Empire. Although the empire survived, it was severely weakened. Other nearby kingdoms grew in power, reducing Srivijaya's control of trade. In time, a Muslim kingdom on the Malay Peninsula came to dominate trade in the region. As Islam spread throughout the islands of Southeast Asia, Muslim traders developed a stable trade network that linked to other Muslim ports in Asia and Africa.

Vietnam While most of Southeast Asia was strongly influenced by India, Vietnam was strongly influenced by China. In 111 BC the Han dynasty of China conquered the kingdom of Nam Viet in what is now northern Vietnam. The Chinese ruled the region, which they called Annam, off and on for the next 1,000 years.

Under Chinese rule, Vietnam absorbed many aspects of Chinese civilization. Chinese rulers forced the Vietnamese to adopt the Chinese language and Chinese clothing and hairstyles. Confucianism and Daoism influenced Vietnamese society. The Vietnamese adopted many features of Chinese government as well, including a bureaucracy and a Confucian-based civil service system. Vietnam embraced Mahayana Buddhism, and Buddhist art and architecture influenced Vietnamese culture.

In spite of the many ways in which China influenced Vietnam, the Vietnamese still maintained many of their traditional customs. For example, the Vietnamese continued to worship nature spirits alongside other belief systems. The Vietnamese people remained determined to preserve their own culture and identity.

In hopes of regaining their independence, the Vietnamese sometimes rebelled when Chinese rule grew weak. One of the most famous rebellions took place in AD 39. That year, two sisters named **Trung Trac** and **Trung Nhi** raised an army and briefly drove the Chinese from Vietnam. The Chinese soon regained control of Vietnam, and the sisters drowned themselves. They still remain heroes in Vietnam today.

The fall of China's Tang dynasty in the early 900s provided the Vietnamese with another chance at independence. This time they succeeded. In 939 the Vietnamese established the independent kingdom of Dai Viet in what is now northern Vietnam.

The Chinese failed in their attempts to reconquer Vietnam. Although the rulers of Dai Viet sent tribute to China, the kingdom remained independent. In the late 1200s the Mongols invaded, but the Vietnamese defeated the Mongols and remained independent.

READING SKILLS

Making Inferences Why do you think the rulers of Dai Viet were willing to pay tribute to China?

READING CHECK **Contrast** How did the development of early Vietnam differ from the development of kingdoms and empires in the rest of Southeast Asia?

SECTION 4 ASSESSMENT

go.hrw.com
Online Quiz
Keyword: SHL CEA HP

Reviewing Ideas, Terms, and People

1. **a. Recall** How did monsoons shape trade in Southeast Asia?
   b. Identify Cause and Effect How did geography influence settlement patterns in mainland Southeast Asia?
   c. Elaborate How did Indian and Chinese influences differ in their spread and impact across Southeast Asia?

2. **a. Identify** Who were **Trung Trac** and **Trung Nhi**, and why are they still remembered today?
   b. Identify Cause and Effect How did trade shape the rise and fall of kingdoms and empires in the islands of Southeast Asia?
   c. Evaluate Which early kingdom or empire in Southeast Asia do you think produced the greatest achievements? Provide reasons to support your answer.

Critical Thinking

3. **Identify Cause and Effect** Using your notes and a graphic organizer like the one below, explain how geography affected the early kingdoms and empires of Southeast Asia. Consider the effects of the locations of kingdoms and empires in relation to their more powerful neighbors.

Kingdom or Empire

| Pagan |
| Khmer |
| Sailendra |
| Srivijaya |
| Vietnam |

Geography →

FOCUS ON WRITING

4. **Persuasion** You live in Vietnam during the early 900s. Write the text for a poster urging your fellow Vietnamese to rise up against their Chinese rulers. You should tell the Vietnamese why they should risk their lives to rebel against the Chinese. In addition, tell them why you think this is a good time to take such a course of action.

Status of Women in Asian Cultures

Info to Know

Results of Foot Binding In 1997 the University of California at San Francisco released a study of the effects of foot-binding on elderly women. The subjects of the study were women in Beijing who were in their 70s and 80s. Of the study's participants, 38% of women in their 80s and 18% of the women in their 70s had their feet bound as children. The study found that women whose feet had been bound were more likely to have fallen in the past year than women with normal feet. It also found that these women were more likely to have difficulty standing from a seated position, and were more likely to have difficulty squatting. However, the women with bound feet seemed to have no difficulty walking or climbing steps.

Status of Women in Asian Cultures

Historical Context The four documents below illustrate the changing status of women in China and Japan during this period.

Task Study the selections and answer the questions that follow. After you have studied the documents, you will be asked to write an essay about the status of women in Asian cultures. You will need to use evidence from these selections and from the chapter to support your essay.

NEW YORK STANDARDS

PI 1.3 Students analyze historic events from around the world by examining accounts written from different perspectives.

PI 2.3 Students explain the importance of analyzing narratives drawn from different times and places to understand historical events.

DOCUMENT 1

Women in Song China

During the Song dynasty, life for women in China began to change. While some changes were positive, others resulted in a loss of status for women. In the following passage, writer Patricia Buckley Ebrey describes some of these changes for women.

> With printing and the expansion of the educated class, more women [in Song China] were taught to read and write ... In the Song period women's legal claims to property were improved ... These changes can all be classed as favorable ... But there were concurrent [simultaneous] changes in Song times that are generally classed as detrimental [harmful] to women ... In the Tang [period], ... physical activity was fashionable enough that palace women played polo. In Song times, standards of beauty shifted to favor the delicate and restrained woman. Notions of female modesty became more rigid ... By the [1100s], ... doctors who called on women in elite households could neither view the woman nor question her; all they could do was take the pulse of a [woman's] hand extended through the bed curtains.

DOCUMENT 2

Foot Binding in China

Perhaps as early as the late Tang dynasty, the practice of foot binding began to spread among women in China. At a young age, girls' feet were tightly wrapped with pieces of cloth. The purpose of foot binding was to restrict the growth of the feet so that they appeared small and dainty. Foot binding was extremely painful and over time deformed the bones of the foot, as shown in the drawing at left. Above the drawing is a shoe that a Chinese woman with bound feet once wore.

Skills Focus: Drawing Conclusions

At Level

Reading Skill
Body Modification

1. Tell students that, although the process of foot binding is no longer practiced, people still make drastic changes to their bodies. Plastic surgery and the use of steroids are modern examples of body modification.

2. Organize students into small groups. Have each group discuss these questions: What are the pros and cons of making modifications to the body? What are some reasons people modify their bodies? Under what circumstances do you think making body modifications is acceptable? When should it be avoided?

3. Have one student in each group take notes and present a brief summary of the group's discussion to the class.

4. Guide students in a class discussion about these issues. **LS Verbal-Linguistic**

Alternative Assessment Handbook, Rubric 11: Discussions

DOCUMENT 3

A Chinese View of Women in Japan

The passage below is from a Chinese history written in the 500s. The history describes Japan, which the Chinese referred to as Wa at the time. As you read the passage, pay attention to any bias that the writer might show that reveals attitudes about the status of women in China. In addition, consider what the events in the passage imply about the status of women in Japan.

> During the reigns of Huan-di (147–168) and Ling-di (168–189), the country of Wa was in a state of great confusion, war and conflict raging on all sides. For a number of years, there was no ruler. Then a woman named Pimiko appeared. Remaining unmarried, she occupied herself with magic and sorcery and bewitched the populace. Thereupon they placed her on the throne. She kept one thousand female attendants, but few people saw her.

DOCUMENT 4

The Diary of Lady Murasaki

During Japan's Heian Period, the writer Lady Murasaki Shikibu, author of *The Tale of Genji,* kept a diary. In the following passage from the *Diary of Lady Murasaki,* she describes how she was affected by the Japanese view that women should not learn to read Chinese.

> When my older brother Korechika and I were still young, he received formal lessons in reading [the Chinese classics] while I had to settle for the privilege of sitting nearby. It was almost eerie as I could always recite whatever he was taught. That included those passages he forgot or could not comprehend readily. My father Tametoki was a learned man. He would sigh and say how sad he was that I was not born a boy . . .
> Afraid that someone might find out that I was literate [in Chinese], I refused to read a legend over a picture on a screen. The imperial consort Shoshi commanded me to read for her pieces from the *Selected Writings of Bo Zhuyi* (772–846). She showed a great deal of interest in a variety of topics. So starting two years ago, when no one else was around, I taught her ancient poems contained in volumes three and four of *Bo Zhuyi.*

Skills Focus — READING LIKE A HISTORIAN

DOCUMENT 1
a. **Identify** What positive changes did women experience during the Song dynasty?
b. **Summarize** In what ways did women lose status?

DOCUMENT 2
a. **Contrast** How did the size of a bound foot contrast to that of an unbound foot?
b. **Infer** How do you think having bound feet affected daily life for women in China?

DOCUMENT 3
a. **Draw Conclusions** What does the passage suggest about the status of women in Japan at that time?
b. **Interpret** Do you think that the author of the passage shows bias toward Pimiko as a ruler? List words or phrases from the passage that support your opinion.

DOCUMENT 4
a. **Explain** How did women in Japan's Heian Period get around restrictions that limited their education?
b. **Make Generalizations** What does the passage reveal about the status of women as compared to that of men in Japan's Heian Period?

DOCUMENT-BASED ESSAY QUESTION

In general, women in China and Japan lost status during this period. Using the documents above and information from the chapter, form a thesis about the changing status of women in China and Japan during this time. Then write an essay providing details to support your thesis.

See **Skills Handbook,** p. H48

Status of Women in Asian Cultures

Word Help

populace population
learned educated

Teaching Tip

Refer students to the time line at the beginning of this chapter, and have them identify China's Song dynasty, the Tang dynasty, and Japan's Heian period, in order to place the documents in historical context.

Info to Know

Sei Shonagon (c. 966–?) Like Lady Murasaki Shikibu, Sei Shonagon was a famous female Japanese writer of the Heian period. Her *Pillow Book* is remembered as a literary masterpiece detailing the intricacies of the Japanese court. The two women knew each other, and Lady Murasaki Shikibu even wrote about Sei Shonagon in her published diary. Shikibu noted that her fellow writer's sharp observations often angered others.

Answers

Reading Like a Historian
Document 1. a. *taught to read and write; could own property;* **b.** *ideas of female beauty restricted women's freedoms;*
Document 2. a. *The bound foot was about half the size of an unbound foot.* **b.** *possible answer—caused pain; made it difficult to walk and engage in regular activity;* **Document 3. a.** *not considered suitable rulers; remained out of view;* **b.** *possible answer—yes, seems to believe Pimiko did not deserve the throne, but that she used "magic and sorcery" and "bewitched" the people into making her their leader;* **Document 4. a.** *could learn by overhearing the lessons given to boys;* **b.** *It shows that they were not given equal education.* **Essay** *Student essays should describe the ways in which women in China and Japan lost status, using details and examples from the documents and the chapter.*

Differentiating Instruction

Advanced Learners/Gifted and Talented

Above Level

Research Required

1. Tell students that although women in Asian cultures generally lost status during this period, many of the most famous Japanese writers of the era were women. Ask students what might explain that contradiction. Why might women writers have achieved such success in Japan?

2. Have students conduct outside research about Japanese women writers of the Heian period. Students should develop a thesis about women writers and their status. Using this thesis, students should develop essays, using primary and secondary sources as evidence.

3. Have students share their findings with the class. Students may also wish to share with the class some of the primary sources or literature excerpts they found in their research. **LS Visual-Spatial, Verbal-Linguistic**

 Alternative Assessment Handbook, Rubric 30: Research; and 37: Writing Assignments

335

Answers

Visual Summary

Review and Inquiry Have students create a time line showing the major events in the Visual Study Guide or this page. Have students write a paragraph explaining how one of the Chinese or Mongol dynasties influenced a culture elsewhere in East Asia.

Quick Facts Transparency: Visual Study Guide: Cultures of East Asia

Review Key Terms and People

1. scholar-officials
2. porcelain
3. Wu Zhao
4. Genghis Khan
5. Yuan dynasty
6. Marco Polo
7. Shinto
8. Heian Period
9. Angkor Wat
10. administer

Comprehension and Critical Thinking

11. a. the Sui dynasty; completion of the Grand Canal
b. Expansion increased contact with other cultures.
c. possible answers—gunpowder: made future wars much more deadly; magnetic compass: allowed for world exploration; movable type: increased sharing of ideas

12. a. the steppes of Central Asia; they were nomads
b. They had a strong leader and a skilled army, and they intimidated other people.
c. He brought back an account of his travels in China.

13. a. clans
b. both formed clans; both developed own culture; both were influenced by China
c. possible answers—Yes, they lived a lavish lifestyle; no, women were denied some freedoms.

VISUAL STUDY GUIDE

QUICK FACTS

Cultural Influences

Japan: Chinese Influence
- Buddhism, Confucianism
- writing system
- government practices and code of laws
- tea drinking, fashions, foods, art, dance, music, gardening, pagoda architecture

Korea: Chinese Influence
- Buddhism, Confucianism
- writing system
- government practices
- agricultural techniques
- civil service examination system
- woodblock printing

Southeast Asia: Indian and Chinese Influence
- Vietnam: Chinese Confucianism, Daoism, culture, government practices
- other areas of Southeast Asia: Indian writing, government, science, architecture
- Buddhism, Hinduism, Islam

Cultures of East Asia, 550–1400

China
- Period of Disunion: 220–589
- Sui dynasty: 589–618
- Tang dynasty: 618–907
- Song dynasty: 960–1279
- Yuan (Mongol) dynasty: 1279–1368

Japan
- Yamato clan become emperors: c. 500s
- Prince Shotoku's rule as regent: 593–622
- Heian Period: 794–1185

Korea
- Three Kingdoms: c. 300s–c. 670
- Silla dynasty: c. 670–c. 935
- Koryu dynasty: c. 935–1392

Southeast Asia
Myanmar (Burma):
- Pagan Kingdom: c. 800s–1287
Cambodia:
- Khmer Empire (Angkor): height c. 800s–1250
Indonesia/Malaysia:
- Sailendra Kingdom: c. 750–c. 850
- Srivijaya Empire: height c. 600s–1200s
Vietnam:
- Chinese rule: 11 BC–939
- Dai Viet Kingdom: 939–1407

Review Key Terms and People

Identify the term or person from the chapter that best fits each of the following descriptions.

1. elite, educated members of China's government
2. type of fine ceramic at which the Song excelled
3. only woman to hold the title of emperor of China
4. the Mongol Universal Ruler
5. Chinese dynasty founded by the Mongols
6. European who served Kublai Khan
7. belief system whose followers worship *kami*
8. period of Japan during which culture flowered and an elegant court society developed
9. famous temple complex in the Khmer Empire
10. to manage or run, as in to run a government

---

14. a. Pagan's first great king; unified the Pagan Kingdom, ruled during time of great prosperity
b. because the area was located along major trade routes, and waterways provided access
c. possible answer—Yes, the fall of the Tang dynasty allowed Vietnam to win independence; Kublai Khan demanded tribute from the Pagan Kingdom during the height of the Mongol Empire.

Reading Skills

15. extended Chinese influence throughout East Asia

16. possible answer—India had more trade routes connecting it to Southeast Asia.

History's Impact video program
Review the video to answer the closing question:
How did Chinese culture influence the development
of Japanese culture?

Comprehension and Critical Thinking

SECTION 1 (pp. 309–315)

11. a. Recall What dynasty reunified China after the Period of Disunion? What is considered to be this dynasty's greatest accomplishment?

b. Analyze How did changes in the Tang dynasty affect trade and religion?

c. Evaluate Which Chinese innovation do you think had the greatest effect on world history—gunpowder, the magnetic compass, or moveable type? Explain your answer.

SECTION 2 (pp. 316–321)

12. a. Recall Where was the Mongols' homeland, and how did geography shape their life there?

b. Analyze How were the Mongols, a nomadic people, able to conquer more advanced civilizations?

c. Elaborate How did Marco Polo help shape European ideas about China?

SECTION 3 (pp. 322–327)

13. a. Describe What form of government system developed in early Japan?

b. Compare How were the histories of early Japan and early Korea similar?

c. Make Judgments Would you have wanted to be a member of the Heian court in Japan? Why or why not?

SECTION 4 (pp. 329–333)

14. a. Identify Who was Anawrahta, and why is he significant in the early history of Southeast Asia?

b. Explain Why was control of the waterways of Southeast Asia of strategic importance?

c. Support a Position Did major events in India and China affect life in Southeast Asia? Provide reasons to support your position.

Reading Skills

Making Inferences *Use what you know about making inferences to answer the following questions.*

15. What long-term contributions did the Mongols make to world history?

16. Why do you think India had more influence on Southeast Asia than China did?

Analyzing Visuals

Reading Like a Historian *The painting below depicts a Mongol warrior on horseback. The Mongols were highly skilled archers, able to fire accurately while on the move.*

Painting of Mongol rider, National Palace Museum, Taipei

17. Draw Conclusions How does the rider's position on the horse illustrate his skill as a mounted archer?

18. Analyze What other items did Mongol archers carry? How were these items likely used?

Using the Internet

go.hrw.com
Practice Online
Keyword: SHL CEA

19. The art of China, Japan, and Korea often celebrates myths and legends and the beauty of nature. Using the keyword above, do research to learn more about Asian art. Then create a brochure describing what you have learned about the topic.

WRITING FOR THE SAT

Think about the following issue:

Under the Mongol rule of the Yuan dynasty, the Chinese had to pay higher taxes and follow stricter laws than the Mongols did. At the same time, the Mongol rulers improved China's roads and canals and increased its foreign trade.

20. Assignment: Did the Yuan rulers govern China well? Write a short essay in which you develop your position on this question. Support your point of view with reasoning and examples from your reading.

CULTURES OF EAST ASIA **337**

Answers

Analyzing Visuals

17. The archer appears strong and stable even though the horse is moving quickly.

18. possible answer—lance, bow and arrows to fight enemies, shield to protect themselves

Using the Internet

19. Go to the HRW Web site and enter the keyword shown to access a rubric for this activity.

KEYWORD: SHL CEA

Writing for the SAT

20. possible answers— No, the Mongols treated their Chinese subjects unfairly; Yes, the Mongols accomplished great things despite their treatment of the Chinese. Essays should include details from the section about policies and accomplishments during the Mongol Empire. A rubric for this activity is provided in **CRF**: Writing for the SAT

HOLT

History's Impact

▶ **Video Program: Cultures of East Asia**
Refer to the Video Program Teacher's Guide for the answer to the closing question.

Review and Assessment Resources

Review and Reinforce

CRF: Chapter Review

 **Quick Facts Transparency:** Visual Study Guide: Cultures of East Asia

🔊 **Spanish Chapter Summaries Audio CD Program**

OSP **Holt PuzzlePro:** Quiz Show for ExamView

💿 **Quiz Game CD-ROM**

Assess

 PASS: Chapter Test, Forms A and B

Alternative Assessment Handbook

OSP **ExamView Test Generator,** Chapter Test

💿 **Differentiated Instruction Modified Worksheets and Tests CD-ROM:** Chapter Test

HOAP **Holt Online Assessment Program** (in the Premier Online Edition)

Reteach/Intervene

 Interactive Reader and Study Guide

Differentiated Instruction Teacher Management System: Lesson Plans for Differentiated Instruction

💿 **Differentiated Instruction Modified Worksheets and Tests CD-ROM:** Chapter Test

💿 **Interactive Skills Tutor CD-ROM**

go.hrw.com
Online Resources
KEYWORD: SHL TEACHER

You can use these pages to have students simultaneously review the unit and practice taking standardized tests.

Answers

1. 1
Muslim Civilizations, Section 3

2. 1
African Kingdoms, Section 1

3. 3
African Kingdoms, Section 2

4. 3
African Kingdoms, Section 3

5. 1
Muslim Civilizations, Section 1

6. 1
Muslim Civilizations, Section 2

7. 2
Muslim Civilizations, Section 2

8. 1
Muslim Civilizations, Section 3

9. 4
Muslim Civilizations, Section 3

UNIT 3
Regents Practice

Directions Write your answer for each statement or question on a separate answer sheet. Choose the number of the word or expression that best completes the statement or answers the question.

1 One reason this coin, like almost all coins from Muslim lands, is decorated with writing rather than a portrait is because

1 calligraphy was an important Muslim art form.
2 Muslim rulers were unpopular.
3 rulers wanted their coins to be used outside their own kingdoms.
4 rulers wanted their coins to be unlike Roman coins.

2 Why was the beginning of the Iron Age significant in Africa?
1 Iron tools enabled farmers to grow more food.
2 Iron was important in the practice of animism.
3 Iron weapons made it possible to conquer the Nok.
4 It helped North Africans build their economies.

3 Trading cities along the east coast of Africa grew and prospered because
1 the people were expert fishers.
2 the ancient Greeks had begun trading there.
3 the monsoon winds made it possible to trade with Arabia, India, and Southeast Asia.
4 the island of Madagascar was located off the east coast.

4 West Africa's gold and salt trade
1 was begun by the Almoravids.
2 made the kingdom of Ghana rich.
3 made the Berber kingdom rich.
4 was monopolized by Arab traders.

5 Muhammad's journey from Mecca to Medina is known as
1 the hegira.
2 the hajj.
3 the hadith.
4 the Sunna.

6 The split between the Sunnis and the Shia began over
1 who should be the leader of the Muslim community.
2 who should marry Muhammad's daughter Fatimah.
3 whether or not Muhammad had named Abu Bakr as his successor.
4 who could be considered a "People of the Book."

7 Muslim traders helped the caliphate prosper and
1 brought great art and artists back to Baghdad.
2 not only traded goods but also ideas, thus helping to spread Islam.
3 supported the Abbasid dynasty in expanding into Spain.
4 helped keep Muslim communities unified.

8 Muslim scholars made important contributions to knowledge by
1 translating the work of ancient Greek scientists and philosophers.
2 writing travel guides so people could visit the far-flung cities of the caliphate.
3 inventing the concept of zero.
4 becoming teachers in European universities during the Middle Ages.

9 Some of the characteristics of Muslim art are
1 using quotations from Rumi and geometric patterns to decorate objects.
2 using calligraphy and minarets to decorate paintings.
3 incorporating Turkish motifs in painting.
4 using calligraphy and geometric designs to decorate objects and buildings.

10 Historians consider the Tang dynasty to be one of the golden ages of Chinese civilization because

1 the Empress Wu was a great leader.

2 Wendi reunified China, restored order, reformed the bureaucracy, and created a new legal code.

3 Tang rulers expanded the empire and its influence and the arts flourished.

4 land reform freed more people to become artists.

11 Civil service exams under the Song made sure that

1 capable bureaucrats held office.

2 applicants from wealthy families received high grades.

3 capable shipbuilders, traders, and inventors were recruited for government positions.

4 only Legalists held office.

12 Genghis Khan was a successful warrior because

1 he was more interested in defeating enemies and seizing plunder than in ruling.

2 he was made ruler of all the Mongol tribes.

3 he organized his fighters to promote loyalty and obedience and created a messenger system.

4 he traveled with herds of horses so that the army could move quickly.

13 Why is Genghis Khan's grandson Kublai Khan important?

1 He conquered Japan and added it to the Mongol Empire.

2 He conquered all of China and founded the Yuan dynasty.

3 He conquered all of China and wrecked the Chinese economy.

4 He eliminated social classes in China.

14 A religion unique to Japan is called

1 Amaterasu.

2 Yamato.

3 *kami.*

4 Shinto.

15 During the Heian period in Japan,

1 wealthy landowners gained power at the expense of the emperor.

2 the samurai were disbanded.

3 Murasaki Shikibu became emperor.

4 increased contact with China led to greater Chinese influence on Japanese culture and society.

16 Southeast Asia's culture and society

1 developed in isolation because of the monsoons.

2 was influenced by Indian traders and scholars who brought Indian culture to Southeast Asia.

3 was shaped by Muslim settlers from the Near East.

4 was heavily influenced by Japan.

17 Korea was heavily influenced by China because

1 it was originally settled by the Chinese.

2 Chinese shamans dominated the Korean court.

3 the Han conquered the Koreans and spread Chinese technology and institutions.

4 many Koreans studied in China.

18 What conclusion can be drawn from this passage from Ibn Battuta's account of his travels?

"The sultan takes his seat on the pempi [ceremonial chair] after the midafternoon prayer. The armor-bearers bring in magnificent arms—quivers of gold and silver, swords ornamented with gold and with golden scabbards, gold and silver lances, and crystal maces … The interpreter Dugha comes with his four wives and his slave-girls, who are about a hundred in number. They are wearing beautiful robes, and on their heads they have gold and silver fillets."

1 Dugha is more important than the sultan.

2 All people are wealthy.

3 Ibn Battuta is not impressed by the sultan's wealth.

4 Mali is a wealthy kingdom.

REVIEWING THE UNIT

Constructed Response Recall what you have learned about the role of trade in spreading ideas and supporting empires. Write a brief essay on the role of trade in shaping Near Eastern, African, and Asian societies and cultures.

CONNECTING TO THE PREVIOUS UNIT

Constructed Response Recall what you have learned about new empires that formed in the Near East and China and the older empires in Persia, the Near East, and China. How were these new empires similar to the earlier empires in these areas? How were they different? Write a short essay showing how one of these empires changed and developed over this long time span. Include the factors that influenced change.

CULTURES IN CONTACT **339**

Unit Review

Answers

10. 3
Cultures of East Asia, Section 1

11. 1
Cultures of East Asia, Section 1

12. 3
Cultures of East Asia, Section 2

13. 2
Cultures of East Asia, Section 2

14. 4
Cultures of East Asia, Section 3

15. 1
Cultures of East Asia, Section 3

16. 2
Cultures of East Asia, Section 4

17. 3
Cultures of East Asia, Section 3

18. 4
African Kingdoms, Section 1

Reviewing the Unit

Student essays should mention the role of trade in spreading religion, especially Islam, throughout the Near East, Africa, and Southeast Asia. The riches brought in by trade helped support many kingdoms and empires.

Connecting to the Previous Unit

New powers took advantage of weaknesses in old empires. Muslims took over Persia, then turned their attention to the wealthy Byzantine Empire. The Mongols took over China. Like older empires, these new empires discovered that there were limits to the amount of expansion they could do before internal conflicts and divisions caused them to weaken.

Student essays should discuss how one of the empires changed and developed over time.

Belief Systems

Hinduism Like the three belief systems listed in the table on this page, Hinduism spread far beyond its place of origin. As Indian merchants settled in Southeast Asia, they brought their religion with them. Sanskrit inscriptions on Borneo provide the earliest physical evidence of Hinduism in Southeast Asia. However, Chinese histories refer to a Hindu kingdom in Vietnam two centuries earlier. Over time, Hinduism evolved into local variations. For example, the people of Bali, in Indonesia, practice a unique form of Hinduism.

Migration and Diffusion

Transmission of Knowledge Arabic scholars were not just the conduit through which Europeans learned of Indian advances. They also kept alive the heritage of ancient Greece. After the fall of Rome, the works of the Greek philosopher Aristotle were lost in the West. Arabic scholars translated his works from Greek into Arabic during the 9th century. In the 12th century the Spanish-Arab philosopher named Ibn Rushd, or Averroes wrote commentaries on Aristotle's works. Translated into Latin and Hebrew, they had a profound influence on both medieval Christian and Jewish philosophy.

Info to Know

The Mongols Historians believe the Mongols were a loose group of tribes before Genghis Khan united them in the early 13th century. At the height of their power, the Mongols ruled large areas of China and East Asia, Russia, Iran, and Turkey. After their power waned, they faded from history. Today, there are about 6 million Mongols, most of them Buddhists, found mainly in East Asia and parts of eastern Russia. They are still nomads, deriving their wealth from livestock.

UNIT 3 Cultures in Contact, 100–1500
Themes & Global Connections

THEME
BELIEF SYSTEMS

How did new belief systems spread across much of Africa, Asia, and Europe?

New religions replaced older polytheistic religions. One reason these religions spread so widely was that they were able to appeal to people of different cultures. While sometimes conversions were the result of conquest, most conversions were voluntary. Among those helping to spread these religions were missionaries. These religions also spread along trade routes as local people interacted with merchants.

BELIEF SYSTEMS		
RELIGION	**SPREAD FROM**	**SPREAD TO**
Buddhism	India	China, Japan, Korea, Central Asia, Southeast Asia
Christianity	Judea	North Africa, Europe, Russia
Islam	Arabia	North Africa, East Africa, West Africa, Southwest and Central Asia, Eastern Europe, Southeast Asia

THEME
MIGRATION AND DIFFUSION

How did nomadic peoples forge links between cultures?

Nomadic peoples helped move goods and ideas between rural and urban centers. By actively promoting trade, nomadic peoples such as the Mongols help forge contacts between the Mediterranean and India and China. In addition, Arab traders expanded their routes and helped spread knowledge as well as goods. Arabs translated Indian works on mathematics and astronomy into Arabic and adopted the Indian number system. Later, Europeans learned of these advances and adopted them from the Arabs.

Differentiating Instruction
Above Level

Advanced Learners/Gifted and Talented

1. Have students create a chart comparing and contrasting the three new belief systems listed in the chart at the top of the page—Buddhism, Christianity, and Islam. (Students may conduct additional research if needed.) Students should answer these questions as they fill in their charts: Who was its founder? When was it founded? How was it related to an earlier belief system? What were the major differences between each new belief system and the older system from which it arose?

2. Have volunteers create and fill in a master chart for the class to see.

3. Guide the class in a discussion of the three belief systems. What significant feature do these three belief systems have in common that sets them apart from earlier systems? *Each of them has a single founder.* **LS Visual-Spatial**

   Alternative Assessment Handbook, Rubrics 7: Charts; 9: Comparing and Contrasting; and 11: Discussions

THEME
ECONOMIC SYSTEMS

How did trading systems develop?

Economies remained overwhelming agricultural, and trade in agricultural products and nonluxury goods remained regional. Nonetheless, trade in luxury goods became more widespread as links between civilizations became more firmly established. Arab traders moved goods between Africa and India. By making travel safer, the Mongols promoted trade between Europe and Asia within the bounds of the vast Mongol Empire.

Inter-regional Trade

Regional Trade

Local Trade
agricultural products, raw materials

some agricultural products, raw materials and crafts, luxury goods

luxury goods

Skills FOCUS UNDERSTANDING THEMES

How did economic systems, migration and diffusion, and the spread of belief systems—in this case, world religions—affect society in one area? Choose a country or area in Africa, Europe, or Asia that was affected by these forces and answer this question. Then use your textbook and other resources to gather information about how new religions, migration, and trade affected your chosen area or country. Then create a chart like the one below that details your findings.

Theme	Effect on Country or Area
Spread of Belief Systems	
Migration and Diffusion	
Economic Systems	

Global Connections

Exposure to new ideas and inventions was closely linked to contacts between peoples and civilizations. Most of the contacts between civilizations occurred as a result of trade in luxury commodities.

Making Connections Select a luxury commodity such as silk, gold, or spices that was traded over long distances. Make a list of the peoples who would have been involved in trading the product and the new ideas the traders may have been exposed to or spread. Draw or trace an outline map of the regions involved in the trade of the product you have investigated. Then show the trade route on the map and annotate it with the information you collect.

This woman displays some of the gold that made Ghana such a wealthy trading state. ▶

341

Economic Systems

Caravans A caravan is a group of people who band together for travel. The term is most frequently used in connection with groups of merchants or pilgrims crossing the deserts of Africa and Asia. Groups of people traveled together to provide mutual protection. Trade caravans, such as those that plied the Silk Roads, have figured prominently in the history of Asia and Africa. Caravans crossing those regions have traditionally used camels as beasts of burden, but in more recent years special motor vehicles have largely replaced camels.

Understanding Themes

The way in which each of these factors affected society will vary depending on the country or area chosen. For example, spread of world religions often resulted in those religions replacing earlier, indigenous religions. Migration and diffusion led to other aspects of culture being exchanged. Trade often brought new wealth.

Global Connections

Answers will vary depending on the luxury commodity selected. For example, Berber traders would have exchanged salt and other goods for West African gold. Traders also brought their religion, Islam.

Skills Focus: Analyzing Visuals

Reading Like a Historian Skill
Patterns of Trade

1. Draw the graphic organizer for students to see.
2. Explain that local trade occurs within nearby shopping areas in your community. Regional trade refers to trade within your region—the entire state and region of the country. National trade is within the country. International trade is with other nations. Have students compare this graphic organizer with the one under Economic Systems above. Have

students list examples of goods traded at each level. Guide the class in a discussion about how these goods affect local culture.
LS Visual-Spatial

Alternative Assessment Handbook, Rubrics 9: Comparing and Contrasting; 11: Discussions; and 13: Graphic Organizers

International Trade

National Trade

Regional Trade

Local Trade

Summarizing the Unit

During the period covered by this unit, Islam was founded and spread throughout much of Asia and Africa. During the same time, China was extending its influence over Korea, Japan, and Southeast Asia. Ask students what part trade played in the spread of Islam and in contact between China and the West. *Muslim traders took ideas, including their religion, with them to Africa and other lands. The Silk Roads were trade routes for transporting luxury goods that linked China with the West.*

Answers

Thinking Like a Historian

Answers will vary depending on the choice of civilization and the type of chart or graphic organizer used, but should cover all three areas: culture and religion; technological innovation; and economy and government.

UNIT 3
IN BRIEF
Below is a chapter-by-chapter summary of the main ideas in this unit, followed by a summary activity for the unit.

CHAPTER 9 — Muslim Civilization
550–1250

MAIN IDEA Muslims believe that Muhammad was the last prophet that God sent to humanity. In the centuries after Muhammad's death, Islam spread across much of the Eastern Hemisphere, becoming one of the world's major religions. Muslim civilization developed states and produced notable achievements in the arts and sciences.

SECTION 1 In 610 a Meccan merchant named Muhammad began to report that he received messages from Allah, or God. The messages formed the basis of Islam, which first took hold in Arabia.

SECTION 2 After Muhammad's death, Islam spread, shaping a major empire within 100 years. The empire eventually broke into smaller parts, but Islam continued to spread.

SECTION 3 Islam deeply influenced the societies it touched and created a nurturing environment for learning and the arts.

CHAPTER 10 — African Kingdoms
100–1500

MAIN IDEA As Africa entered the Iron Age, people migrated throughout the continent. Trade and religion played strong roles in the development of kingdoms and empires in East and South Africa. Strong rulers and the trans-Saharan trade shaped the cultures of the kingdoms of West Africa.

SECTION 1 Africa's earliest people adapted to a wide range of geographic conditions. The spread of iron technology changed farming practices, and coastal cities flourished on trade.

SECTION 2 The growth of trade led to the development of wealthy kingdoms and city-states in East and South Africa.

SECTION 3 The expansion of trade across the Sahara led to the growth of new kingdoms in West Africa.

CHAPTER 11 — Cultures of East Asia
550–1400

MAIN IDEA China influenced life in much of East Asia. Trade and economic growth benefited many, but conflict and war also characterized the period. China profoundly influenced Korea, Japan, and the kingdoms of Southeast Asia.

SECTION 1 During the Tang and Song dynasties China enjoyed economic growth. Still, China struggled with domestic problems and the threat of foreign invasion.

SECTION 2 The Mongols built a huge empire across much of Asia and founded the Yuan dynasty in China. They opened the region to greater foreign contacts and trade.

SECTION 3 China's neighbors, especially Korea and Japan, borrowed from China. China's neighbors were also determined to remain independent.

SECTION 4 Geography and the cultures of China and India influenced the civilizations of Southeast Asia.

Thinking like a Historian
Summary and Extension Activity

Trade played an important role in spreading culture, religion, and technology. Choose one of the civilizations discussed in this unit, and create a chart or graphic organizer showing how trade influenced each of the following areas:

A. Culture and religion

B. Technological innovation

C. Economy and government

Unit Resources

Review and Reinforce

- Global History and Geography Regents Test Prep Workbook
- Regents Review Transparencies
- CRF: Chapter Review
- Spanish Chapter Summaries Audio CD Program
- OSP Holt PuzzlePro: Quiz Show for ExamView
- Quiz Game CD-ROM

Assess

- PASS: Unit Test, Forms A and B
- Alternative Assessment Handbook
- OSP New York ExamView Test Generator correlated to NY SS Standards
- Differentiated Instruction Modified Worksheets and Tests CD-ROM: Chapter Test
- HOAP Holt Online Assessment Program (in the Premier Online Edition)

Reteach/Intervene

- Interactive Reader and Study Guide
- Differentiated Instruction Teacher Management System: Lesson Plans for Differentiated Instruction
- Differentiated Instruction Modified Worksheets and Tests CD-ROM: Chapter Test
- Interactive Skills Tutor CD-ROM

go.hrw.com
Online Resources

KEYWORDS: SHL ISW, SHL AFK, SHL CEA

UNIT 4

Medieval Europe

300–1500

This scene for October is from *Les Tres Riche Heures du Duc de Berry* created by the Limbourg Brothers.

Les ... Heures du Duc de Berry–October, by the Limbourg Brothers, 1400s, courtesy of Musee Conde, Chantilly, France

CHAPTER 12
Kingdoms and Christianity
300–1250

CHAPTER 13
The Early Middle Ages
800–1215

CHAPTER 14
The High Middle Ages
1000–1500

Themes

ARTS AND IDEAS
Universities preserved knowledge in a period when most people did not have a formal education.

BELIEF SYSTEMS
Christianity influenced life during the Middle Ages

GOVERNMENT AND CITIZENSHIP
There was no strong central government; rather, feudal relationships exerted the strongest pull on loyalties.

343

Introducing the Unit
In this unit, students will read about the world that arose after the decline of the Roman Empire. Discuss with students the rise of Christianity and the role it played during the Middle Ages. Have students compare and contrast religion's role in society during the Middle Ages with the role it plays in American society today.

Connecting to Themes
Activity **Princes of the Church**
Guide students in a discussion of the ways in which, during the Middle Ages, the church took on many of the responsibilities and privileges that had traditionally been reserved to rulers. Ask students to list some of those responsibilities and privileges that the church assumed. What effects did this have on medieval society? **LS** **Verbal-Linguistic**

Reading Like a Historian
Interpreting Visuals
The *Très Riches Heures* The picture shown on this page is from the calendar section of the *Très Riches Heures*, a medieval book of hours—that is, a collection of prayers and texts for each liturgical hour of the day. This particular book of hours was commissioned by Jean, Duc (duke) de Berry, a brother of King Charles V of France and uncle of Charles VI. He was also one of the greatest art lovers of the medieval world. The painters were three Flemish brothers—Paul, Hermann, and Jean Limbourg. All three of the artists died in 1416, as did the Duc de Berry.

Unit Resources

Planning
- **Differentiated Instruction Teacher Management System:** Unit Pacing Guide
- **OSP New York One-Stop Planner CD-ROM:** Teacher Management System
- **Power Presentations with Video CD-ROM**

Standards Mastery
- **Global History and Geography Regents Test Prep Workbook**
- **Regents Review Transparencies**

Differentiating Instruction
- **Differentiated Instruction Teacher Management System:** Lesson Plans for Differentiated Instruction
- **Differentiated Instruction Modified Worksheets and Tests CD-ROM**

Enrichment
- **A World History Teacher's Guide to Analyzing Movies**
- **Document-Based Activities for World History**
- **World History Outline Maps**
- **Reading Like a Historian: World History Toolkit**
- **World History Primary Source Library CD-ROM**

Assessment
- **PASS:** Unit Test, Forms A and B
- **Alternative Assessment Handbook**
- **OSP New York ExamView Test Generator correlated to NY SS Standards**
- **HOAP Holt Online Assessment Program** (in the Premier Online Edition)

Chapter 12 Planning Guide

Kingdoms and Christianity

Chapter Overview	Reproducible Resources	Technology Resources
CHAPTER 12 pp. 344–369 **Overview: In this chapter, students will learn about the various kingdoms that appeared in Europe after the fall of Rome, and how Christianity spread and affected people's lives.** KI 1, 2, 3; PI 1.2, 2.3, 2.4, 2.5, 3.1, 3.2 See pp. T32–T55 for a detailed correlation to the New York State Core Curriculum for Global History and Geography and the New York Learning Standards.	**Differentiated Instruction Teacher Management System:** • Pacing Guide • Lesson Plans for Differentiated Instruction **Interactive Reader and Study Guide:** Chapter Summary* **Chapter Resource File*** • Writing for the SAT • Social Studies Skill • Chapter Review **World History Outline Maps**	OSP **New York One-Stop Planner CD-ROM:** Calendar Planner **Live Ink© Online Reading Help** **Student Edition on Audio CD Program** **Differentiated Instruction Modified Worksheets and Tests CD-ROM** **Interactive Skills Tutor CD-ROM** **World History Primary Source Library CD-ROM** **Power Presentations with Video CD-ROM** **History's Impact: World History Video Program (VHS/DVD):** Kingdoms and Christianity
Section 1: **The Byzantine Empire** **The Main Idea:** The Byzantine Empire, once the eastern half of the Roman Empire, was held together for centuries by strong leaders, profitable trade, and the influence of Christianity. PI 1.2, 3.1, 3.2	**Differentiated Instruction Teacher Management System:** Section 1 Lesson Plan* **Interactive Reader and Study Guide:** Section 1 Summary* **Chapter Resource File*** • Vocabulary Builder: Section 1 • Biography: Anthemius of Tralles • Literature: *The Alexiad of the Princess Anna Comnena* • History and Geography: The City of Constantine	**Regents Review Transparency:** Section 1* **Map Transparency:** Spread of Christianity, c. 1000* **Internet Activity:** Justinian Code
Section 2: **The Rise of Russia** **The Main Idea:** Starting as a blend of Slavs and northern Europeans, the Russians organized as a state, became Christian, and fought invaders. PI 2.4	**Differentiated Instruction Teacher Management System:** Section 2 Lesson Plan* **Interactive Reader and Study Guide:** Section 2 Summary* **Chapter Resource File*** • Vocabulary Builder: Section 2 • Biography: St. Olga	**Regents Review Transparency:** Section 2* **Map Transparency:** The Growth of Russia* **Internet Activity:** Yaroslav the Wise
Section 3: **Christianity in Western Europe** **The Main Idea:** The spread of Christianity, largely through the work of missionaries and monks, helped unify western Europe after the collapse of the Roman Empire. PI 2.3, 2.5	**Differentiated Instruction Teacher Management System:** Section 3 Lesson Plan* **Interactive Reader and Study Guide:** Section 3 Summary* **Chapter Resource File*** • Vocabulary Builder: Section 3 • Biography: Aethelflaed • Primary Source: The Angles and Saxons in Great Britain	**Regents Review Transparency:** Section 3* **Map Transparency:** Missionaries and Monasteries in Europe*

Review, Assessment, Intervention

- **Global History and Geography Regents Test Prep Workbook**

- **Quick Facts Transparency:** Kingdoms and Christianity*

- **Spanish Chapter Summaries Audio CD Program**

- **Progress Assessment Support System (PASS):** Chapter Test*

- **Differentiated Instruction Modified Worksheets and Tests CD-ROM:** Modified Chapter Test

- OSP **New York One-Stop Planner CD-ROM:** ExamView Test Generator (English/Spanish)

- HOAP **Holt Online Assessment Program (HOAP),** in the Holt Premier Online Student Edition

---

- **PASS:** Section 1 Quiz*
- **Online Quiz:** Section 1
- **Alternative Assessment Handbook**

- **PASS:** Section 2 Quiz*
- **Online Quiz:** Section 2
- **Alternative Assessment Handbook**

- **PASS:** Section 3 Quiz*
- **Online Quiz:** Section 3
- **Alternative Assessment Handbook**

Power Presentation with Video CD-ROM

Power Presentations with Video are visual presentations of each chapter's main ideas. Presentations can be customized by including Quick Facts charts, images and maps from the textbook, and video clips.

Holt Online Learning

go.hrw.com
Teacher Resources
KEYWORD: SHL TEACHER

go.hrw.com
Student Resources
KEYWORD: SHL CHR

- Document-Based Questions
- Interactive Multimedia Activities

- Current Events
- Chapter-Based Internet Activities
- and more!

Holt Premier
Online Student Edition
Complete online support for interactivity, assessment, and reporting
- Interactive Maps and Notebook
- Homework Practice and Research Activities Online

CHAPTER 12 PLANNING GUIDE

Before You Teach

The Big Picture

Peter N. Stearns

Context The fall of Rome left a huge vacuum of power in southern Europe. Even before the Empire disappeared in the West, European and Mediterranean unity had been compromised by the Emperor Constantine's decision to locate a second imperial capital in Byzantium. The Eastern portion of the Empire benefited from relatively high levels of trade and the still-active Greek scientific, artistic, and philosophical traditions, now combined with Christianity. It was less menaced by powerful invasions, though it did suffer Germanic incursions and endemic warfare on its eastern frontier. The Western empire, in contrast, literally collapsed. Here, the chief force for cohesion was long the Catholic Church based in Rome.

Byzantium and Russia Early Byzantine emperors attempted to reconquer wide territories. The emperors preserved many Roman imperial traditions. Withstanding Arab attacks, the Empire played an active role in world trade. Its political and cultural interests turned heavily toward largely Slavic lands in the Balkans and Russia. Missionary activities won wide success, and a Greek-derived Cyrillic alphabet was a vital cultural tool. Byzantine contacts, plus important trade between the Baltic and the Empire, provided new opportunities for rulers in western Russia, particularly around the city of Kiev. Russian kings converted to Orthodox Christianity and imported many artistic forms and political ideas. Byzantine decline after 1100 contributed to looser political and economic connections in Russia.

Western Christendom The final centuries of the Roman Empire saw important Christian scholarship, providing greater coherence Christian doctrine and beliefs, as well as literary flair. While scholarly levels declined with the fall of western Rome, the papacy remained capable of control over officials. A series of papal reforms bolstered these controls, even as Germanic kingdoms achieved regional success. Popes also sponsored active missionary endeavors, reaching northward to the British Isles, northern Germany and ultimately Scandinavia. The monastic movement helped spread Christianity in the east and in the west. Western monks, many operating under the Benedictine Rule, mixed piety with important work in scholarship, agriculture and charity.

Recent Scholarship

Byzantium and the Crusades (2003) by Jonathan Harris provides an excellent entry into the divisions between western and eastern Christianity, the complexities of Western motivation at a time of growing ambition, and the travails of the Byzantine empire in its final centuries. Several later crusades diverted from their stated purpose to advance Western interests in trade and political power at the expense of Byzantium. This was a power play primarily, but it also reflected real tensions between the two main branches of Christianity, and the results unquestionably weakened the Byzantine position.

Differentiating Instruction

 Differentiated Instruction Teacher Management System
- Pacing Guide
- Lesson Plans for Differentiated Instruction

 Interactive Reader and Study Guide

 Spanish Chapter Summaries Audio CD Program

 Student Edition on Audio CD Program

 Differentiated Instruction Modified Worksheets and Tests CD-ROM
- Vocabulary Flash Cards
- Modified Vocabulary Builder Activities
- Modified Chapter Review Activity
- Modified Chapter Test

OSP One-Stop Planner CD-ROM
- ExamView Test Generator (English/Spanish)
- PuzzlePro
- Quiz Show for ExamView
- Transparencies and Videos

TE Differentiated Activities in the Teacher's Edition
- Contrasting Rome and Constantinople, p. 348
- Justinian's and Theodora's Rule, p. 349
- Drawing the Hagia Sophia, p. 353
- Map of Russia, p. 358
- Doctors of the Church, p. 363

Reading Like a Historian

Sam Wineburg

Our students will be much better able to draw a line matching Saint Augustine's name with "battler of heresy" on a test than to offer an explanation of Augustine's doctrine of original sin or define the nature of heresy in the 5th century. The facts about Christianity's remarkable spread are fairly easy to memorize. What's harder is gaining even a sliver of understanding about the doctrinal disputes that the young church navigated on its road to dominance.

Remembering Doctrinal Disputes

This difficulty is evident when examining the ideas of Augustine, who, more than any other churchman, used his prolific pen, his boundless intelligence, and sometimes the forces of the emperor's army to uproot unorthodox beliefs. We are thrown headfirst into Augustine's world when we examine by way of example one of his most famous doctrinal battles: the disputes with his shrewd and able adversary, the monk Pelagius.

At the heart of the Augustinian project was man's falleness, his entry into the world as sinner. This sin was inherited from the primordial sinner, Adam, and transmitted to every human being via the quintessential act of human debasement: sexual union. Sex, an act to be tolerated but never celebrated, proved man's insatiable desire and frail will. Baptism might remove the taint of original sin but it could not rectify man's imperfection. In this system, humans are beyond repair and damned—except by the grace of the Savior.

The Life of an Idea

Pelagius burst onto the scene at a time of upheaval and legitimate soul-searching. Rome had been sacked and its citizens were receptive to a new message. Pelagius blasted optimism's trumpet: Human perfection was within our grasp. Original sin—and with it infant baptism—was bunk. How could a good God doom the soul of a baby because of the disobedience of some distant primordial ancestor? Why would God go to the trouble of revealing codes of conduct if He knew the deck was stacked? Pelagius wrote:

"Whenever I have to speak of laying down rules for behavior and the conduct of a holy life, I always point out, first of all, the power and functioning of human nature, and show what it is capable of doing . . . lest I should seem to be wasting my time, by calling on people to embark on a course which they consider impossible to achieve."

It was a winning message at first, appealing to the age-old desire for self-definition, the notion that humankind could pull itself up by its bootstraps and shout, "We can do it!" No more shifting the blame to Adam for our shortcomings. Take responsibility for your own actions, Pelagius exhorted.

At the end of the day, however, it was Augustine's message that prevailed. Our sins, he wrote, "are committed through pride, but not all happen proudly . . . they happen so often by ignorance, by human weakness; many are committed by men weeping and groaning in their distress."

As Princeton's Peter Brown, Augustine's biographer, noted, the doctrine of man's falleness had the weight of tradition and public opinion on its side. "The idea of a 'general collapse' of the human race above which no man might dare to claim to raise himself by his own merits" was at the core of ideas that set the course for the early Middle Ages. It spoke to the hardscrabble existence of ordinary people, and offered them in the dimness of the present the hope for a better life in the hereafter.

Pelagius died sometime in the early 5th century, but his ideas resurfaced centuries later, refashioned as the Bogomil heresy. Those who embraced notions of man's perfectibility in the face of Church doctrine forbidding it were not merely idealists: they were, given the forces the Church possessed for crushing heresy, putting their lives on the line.

Chapter Main Ideas

Section 1 The Byzantine Empire, once the eastern half of the Roman Empire, was held together for centuries by strong leaders, profitable trade, and the influence of Christianity.

Section 2 Starting as a blend of Slavs and northern Europeans, the Russians organized as a state, became Christian, and fought invaders.

Section 3 The spread of Christianity, largely through the work of missionaries and monks, helped unify western Europe after the collapse of the Roman Empire.

New York Standards

Key Idea 2 Establishing timeframes, exploring different periodizations, examining themes across time and within cultures, and focusing on important turning points in world history help organize the study of world cultures and civilizations.

Key Idea 3 Study of the major social, political, cultural, and religious developments in world history involves learning about the important roles and contributions of individuals and groups.

Key to Differentiating Instruction

Below Level

Basic-level activities designed for all students encountering new material

At Level

Intermediate-level activities designed for average students

Above Level

Challenging activities designed for honors and gifted and talented students

Standard English Mastery

Activities designed to improve standard English usage

CHAPTER 12 300–1250

Kingdoms and Christianity

THE BIG PICTURE After the fall of Rome, large and small kingdoms appeared in Europe. In most of these kingdoms, Christianity had a powerful influence on people's lives.

Theme BELIEF SYSTEMS
Christianity became a world religion in the centuries after the Roman Empire's fall. The faith was central to Byzantine culture for a thousand years. As missionaries brought Christianity to Europe and Russia, the faith had a deep impact on societies.

TIME LINE

CHAPTER EVENTS

330 Constantinople is founded as the new capital of the Roman Empire.

527 Justinian I begins rule of the Eastern Roman Empire.

871 Alfred the Great is crowned king of Wessex.

1019 Yaroslav the Wise becomes Grand Prince of Kiev.

1054 The Great Schism occurs.

WORLD EVENTS

300

600

900

320 Chandra Gupta I founds the Gupta dynasty in India.

476 The Western Roman Empire falls to invaders.

c. 570 Muhammad is born in Arabia.

c. 900 Mayan civilization is at its peak.

960 The Song dynasty begins in China.

344 CHAPTER 12

Introduce the Chapter

At Level

Kingdoms and Christianity

1. Write the following scenario for students to see: The new leaders of the region in which you live have different customs, culture, and religion than you do. They wish to spread their culture and religion to your region.

2. Have students meet in small groups to discuss ways that cultural diffusion takes place. How do customs spread through a population or a region? How do they evolve over time as new people come into a region? How do religions spread?

3. List student responses to these questions for the class to see. Encourage students to explain their reasoning and opinions.

4. Tell students that in this chapter they will learn about the spread of Christianity and the forming of new kingdoms in Europe.
   LS Verbal-Linguistic

   Alternative Assessment Handbook, Rubric 11: Discussions

Reading like a Historian

The Dormition Cathedral, pictured above, is known as the spiritual heart of Ukraine. A monastery was founded on the site in 1051, and construction began on the church in 1073. This cathedral in Kiev (also spelled Kyiv) is within the Russian Orthodox tradition.

Analyzing Visuals What features indicate that this building is a Christian church? How does the design differ from houses of worship in your region?

See **Skills Handbook**, p. H26

1242
Alexander Nevsky defends Russia against the Teutonic Knights.

1453
Constantinople falls, ending the Byzantine Empire.

1200

1281
The Mongol invasion of Japan fails.

KINGDOMS AND CHRISTIANITY **345**

• Chapter Preview •

HOLT
History's Impact
▶ **Video Program: Kingdoms and Christianity**
See the Video Teacher's Guide for strategies for using the video segment.

Reading Like a Historian

Analyzing Visuals The distinction today between western and eastern Christianity began over 1000 years ago, when the eastern and western Christian churches began to disagree over certain theological matters. One area of disagreement was over the use of icons, or religious pictures or representations. To this day, icons remain an important part of the Eastern Orthodox Christian tradition. The Russian Orthodox Church in this photograph is a good example of the highly visual Eastern Orthodox style.

go.hrw.com
Online Resources

Chapter Resources:
KEYWORD: SHL CHR
Teacher Resources:
KEYWORD: SHL TEACHER

Explore the Time Line

1. How many years passed between the founding of Constantinople and its fall? *1123 years*

2. How many years passed between the founding of Constantinople and the fall of the Western Roman Empire? *146 years*

3. When did the Great Schism in the Christian Church occur? *1054*

Info to Know

The Roman Empire When the Roman emperor Theodosius died in 395, he left the empire to his two sons. One became emperor of the eastern half of the empire, and the other became emperor of the western half. The Roman Empire was never united again. In 467, less than 100 years after the death of Theodosius, the Goths conquered Rome.
Evaluate If the Roman Empire had not split in 395, would it have remained a single, unified political entity? *possible answer—no: too large to govern, impossible to keep invaders out*

Answers

Reading Like a Historian *It includes crosses and scenes from the Christian Bible; possible answer—is decorated more elaborately*

345

Geography Starting Points

Spread of Christianity, c. 1000 Have students explain possible reasons for the spread of Christianity into Europe and North Africa. *possible answer—Missionaries and traders spread religion as they traveled to these regions.*

Activity **Time and Place** Have students copy this map onto their own paper. Then have them plot the events on the chapter time line on their maps. Guide students in a discussion connecting the time line key events with the cities and regions shown on the map.

LS Visual-Spatial

📋 **Alternative Assessment Handbook,** Rubric 21: Map Reading

📖 **Map Transparency:** Spread of Christianity, c. 1000

📰 **World History Outline Maps**

✳ Interactive Map: Spread of Christianity, c. 1000

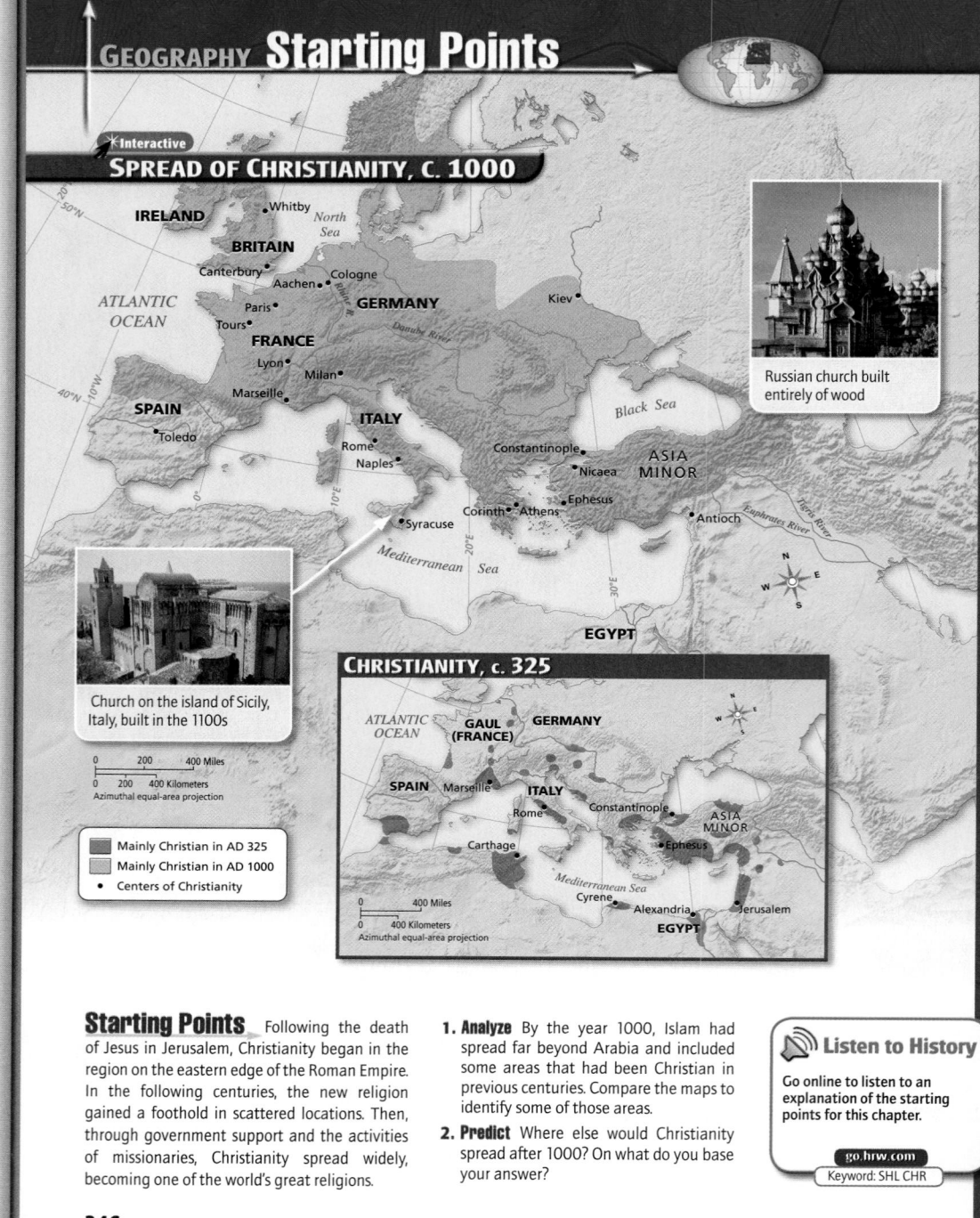

GEOGRAPHY Starting Points

Interactive
SPREAD OF CHRISTIANITY, C. 1000

Russian church built entirely of wood

Church on the island of Sicily, Italy, built in the 1100s

0   200   400 Miles
0   200   400 Kilometers
Azimuthal equal-area projection

■ Mainly Christian in AD 325
■ Mainly Christian in AD 1000
● Centers of Christianity

CHRISTIANITY, c. 325

0   400 Miles
0   400 Kilometers
Azimuthal equal-area projection

Starting Points Following the death of Jesus in Jerusalem, Christianity began in the region on the eastern edge of the Roman Empire. In the following centuries, the new religion gained a foothold in scattered locations. Then, through government support and the activities of missionaries, Christianity spread widely, becoming one of the world's great religions.

1. **Analyze** By the year 1000, Islam had spread far beyond Arabia and included some areas that had been Christian in previous centuries. Compare the maps to identify some of those areas.

2. **Predict** Where else would Christianity spread after 1000? On what do you base your answer?

🔊 **Listen to History**

Go online to listen to an explanation of the starting points for this chapter.

go.hrw.com
Keyword: SHL CHR

346 CHAPTER 12

Skills Focus: Analyzing Maps
At Level

Social Studies Skill
Spread of Christianity

1. Have students study the map on this page, and identify the areas where Christianity predominated in 325 and the areas where Christianity was predominant in 1000.

2. Have students compare this map to a current map of the region and identify the modern-day countries which were Christian in 1000.

3. Have students refer to the map in the feature and answer the following questions: How did Christianity spread? Why did Christianity spread to the areas that it did? Why did Christianity not spread to other areas?

4. Have students present and defend their ideas to the class. **LS** **Verbal-Linguistic, Visual-Spatial**

📋 **Alternative Assessment Handbook,** Rubrics 11: Discussions; and 21: Map Reading

Answers

Geography Starting Points

1. *southern Spain, northern Africa;*
2. *possible answer—might spread further into Russia and Asia; the fact that Islam was taking hold along the Mediterranean; the photograph of the Russian Orthodox church on the previous page*

SECTION 1
The Byzantine Empire

BEFORE YOU READ

MAIN IDEA

The Byzantine Empire, once the eastern half of the Roman Empire, was held together for centuries by strong leaders, profitable trade, and the influence of Christianity.

READING FOCUS

1. How did Byzantine emperors rule their empire from Constantinople?
2. What were some important features of Byzantine culture?
3. What led to the decline of the Byzantine Empire?

KEY TERMS AND PEOPLE

Byzantine Empire
Justinian I
Theodora
Belisarius
mosaics
icons
clergy
Orthodox Church

NEW YORK

PI 3.1 Students analyze the roles and contributions of individuals and groups to social, political, economic, cultural, and religious practices and activities.

THE INSIDE STORY

What did visitors experience in the most spectacular city of the Byzantine Empire? The exotic sights, sounds, and smells of Constantinople were unlike those in any other city. Visitors from other countries in the 400s and 500s were impressed by the sheer size of the city on the Bosporus, which had at least 400,000 residents and was built on seven hills. Its wide, bustling streets hummed with bazaars and food markets. Its sprawling palaces and churches glittered with gilded domes and high towers. Surrounded by high walls with ramparts and watchtowers, Constantinople impressed visitors as a beautiful, imposing fortress, with many treasures worth protecting. ◼

Emperors Rule in Constantinople

Constantinople—Greek for "The City of Constantine"—became the capital of the Roman Empire under Emperor Constantine I. For more than 1,000 years, from 395 to 1453, Constantinople was the seat of the Eastern Roman Empire—which became known as the **Byzantine Empire**.

A New Rome Constantinople remained the capital of the Eastern Empire long after Rome fell. Even before the fall of Rome, Constantinople was a larger, richer city than Rome. The city's location on the Bosporus not only put it in a position to control trade between Asia and Europe, but also helped guard it from attack. The sea protected the city on two sides, and heavily fortified walls protected the landward side. These factors allowed the empire centered in Constantinople to thrive for centuries.

VISIT TO A GLITTERING CITY

This medieval manuscript depicts the magnificent buildings of Constantinople.

Urbs Constantinopolitana Nova Roma, 1400s

Getting Started

Use the **Interactive Reader and Study Guide** to familiarize students with the section content.

📄 **Interactive Reader and Study Guide,** Section 1

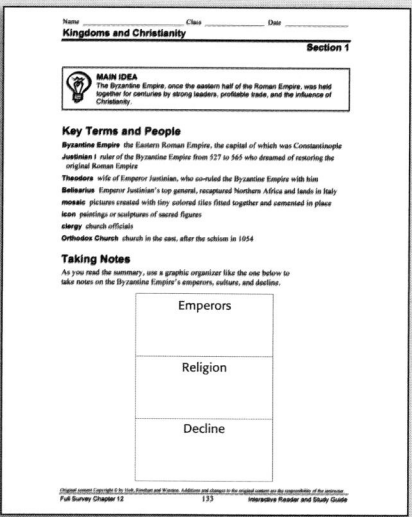

Academic Vocabulary

Review with students the high-use academic term in this section.

patriarch head of any of various eastern churches; also, a father-like leader (p. 351)

📖 **CRF:** Vocabulary Builder: Section 1

Taking Notes

Emperors—Constantine, Justinian and Theodora, Heraclius, Leo III; Culture—influenced by Christianity and Greek cultural influences, had ditinctive art and architecture, split from church in the west; Decline—pressure from Muslim invaders, internal conflict between military and aristocracy, fell to Turks

---

go.hrw.com
Online Resources

KEYWORD: SHL CHR
ACTIVITY: Justinian Code

Teach the Main Idea

At Level

The Byzantine Empire

1. **Teach** Ask students the Reading Focus questions to teach this section.

2. **Apply** Have students create an outline of the section using the heads as main points. Have students identify at least two main ideas under each of the blue subheadings.

3. **Review** Review student outlines as a class. Have students identify the points in their outlines that they feel are most important or most interesting.

4. **Practice/Homework** Have students write an in-depth magazine article summarizing the changes that occurred in the Eastern Roman Empire during the reign of Justinian and Theodora. **LS Verbal-Linguistic**

📄 **Alternative Assessment Handbook,** Rubric 19: Magazines

Direct Teach

Reading Focus

1 How did Byzantine emperors rule their empire from Constantinople? *Constantinople was hub of empire, established laws and constitutions*

Emperors Rule in Constantinople

Identify Who were Justinian and Theodora? *emperor and empress, co-rulers of the Byzantine Empire*

Analyze How did Justinian and Theodora end the Nika Revolt? *Theodora refused to flee or back down; their top general, Belisarius attacked rioters in the Hippodrome.*

Explain Why did Justinian decide to issue a new law code? *confusion over laws that arose from conflicting constitutions, different legal opinions about previous laws*

Info to Know

Justinian and Theodora Theodora's father died while she was still a child, and she began performing as a mime in the same arena that her father trained bears. Soon after she began miming Theodora began to act. At the age of 16, she moved to Africa where she lived for four years. In Africa she converted to the beliefs of Monophysitism, a form of Christianity that holds Jesus as completely divine as opposed to the Orthodox Christian belief that Jesus was both human and divine.

Answers

Faces of History *possible answer— From her own experience, Theodora saw what women could achieve when they were given the right to do so.*

Reading Check *put down the Nika Revolt, built the Hagia Sophia, reformed Roman law*

348

TAKING NOTES

Take notes in a diagram like this one on the Byzantine Empire's emperors, culture, and decline.

- Emperors
- Culture
- Decline

NEW YORK

CC Unit 2-C2 Achievements (law—Justinian Code, engineering, art)

CC Unit 2-C4 Political structure and Justinian Code

CC Unit 2-C5 Role in preserving and transmitting Greek and Roman cultures

Reclaiming the Western Empire After the fall of Rome, the eastern emperors did not give up their claim to the western part of the empire. The Byzantine emperor **Justinian I**, who reigned from 527 to 565, dreamed of restoring the original Roman Empire. In order to accomplish this feat, military action was necessary. The first task was to reconquer territories in northern Africa. These lands had been taken by a Germanic tribe called the Vandals.

In 533, Justinian sent a fleet of ships and troops led by his top general, **Belisarius**, to northern Africa. By 534, the fleet had recaptured the region, and it was absorbed back into the Roman Empire. The next year, Belisarius led troops into Italy to retake that region.

Rebellion at Home At home, Justinian and his wife **Theodora**, who served as co-ruler of the empire, faced a threat from rebels. Many people resented Justinian's efforts to reform the empire's administration. In 532 this opposition led to a rebellion called the Nika Revolt. Leading the revolt were two factions that took their names from popular chariot teams. The Greens represented the lower classes and the Blues the upper classes. Both sides wanted to oust Justinian. The uprising had Constantinople in flames, and Justinian prepared to flee.

FACES OF HISTORY

Justinian and Theodora
483–565 and c. 497–548

The emperor and empress came from very different backgrounds. Justinian was the previous emperor's nephew, but Theodora was a former actress, and her profession kept her from marrying an emperor. Justinian fell in love with her nonetheless. He raised her rank to that of patrician and then married her shortly before he became emperor. Her intelligence and political skill made her Justinian's most trusted adviser. In fact, some think she may have taken a more active role in governing than he did. It is known that she promoted the rights of women, changing divorce laws to give women more protection. Justinian is also known for his contributions to the law—the codification of Roman law. In addition, Justinian worked to extend the empire. Early in his reign he made peace with the Persians and concentrated his efforts on taking back the western provinces from invaders.

Infer Why might Theodora have been especially interested in winning more rights for women?

348 CHAPTER 12

The royal couple survived the crisis due largely to Theodora's determination. She stood firm, refusing to flee or back down, and convinced her husband to do the same. As a result, Belisarius and his troops attacked rioters who were assembled in a stadium called the Hippodrome and slaughtered them by the thousands.

Achievements The Nika Revolt destroyed parts of Constantinople, giving Justinian and Theodora a chance to rebuild the city with grand new monuments. The most important new building was the church known as Hagia Sophia (HAH-juh soh-FEE-uh), which in Greek means "Holy Wisdom." The building, a spectacular blend of domes and arches, still stands.

More important, however, were Justinian's initiatives to reform Roman law, which had fallen into a state of confusion. Previous emperors had not always kept good records. Justinian set up a commission that codified, or systemically arranged, the empire's existing laws and legal opinions into a clear system. The resulting document, called the Corpus Juris Civilis (Body of Civil Law), had four parts. The first part included all the existing constitutions from the time of Emperor Hadrian. The code was later updated and expanded to include laws created by Justinian himself. Together, the revised law code is called Justinian's Code.

Changes after Justinian Justinian's achievements were many, but they did not last. When he died in 565, he left the government nearly bankrupt from the expense of taking back the empire's territory. Furthermore, Justinian had expanded the empire beyond what the government could effectively administer. After his death, the western provinces once again fell to migrating tribes.

Pressures on the boundaries of the empire continued until the reign of Heraclius, which began in 610. Heraclius defeated the Persians, who had been a constant threat on the Byzantine Empire's eastern border. To the west, he settled migrating Croats and Serbs within the Balkan frontiers to act as buffers against new invaders. The Croats and Serbs were converted to Christianity. This conversion extended Byzantine influence into the region—an influence that would last for centuries.

READING CHECK **Summarize** What did Justinian accomplish during his reign?

Differentiating Instruction

Above Level

Advanced Learners/Gifted and Talented

Research Required

1. Have students research the origins and development of the Western and Eastern Roman Empires. Have students use traditional print sources, as well as reliable online sources for this activity. You might refer students to some of the classical works on the subject.

2. When students have completed their research, have them develop an essay or multimedia presentation comparing and contrasting Rome and Constantinople.

3. Have students read their essays or show their multimedia presentations to the class.

LS Verbal-Linguistic, Visual-Spatial

Alternative Assessment Handbook, Rubrics 9: Comparing and Contrasting; and 29: Presentations

Reading like a Historian

Justinian's Code

Analyzing Primary Sources Among the achievements for which Justinian is best known is his reorganization and simplification of Roman law. In the introduction to his simplified law code, reprinted at right, Justinian explained why he felt such an action was necessary. As you read the introduction, think about

- Justinian's goal in revising the legal code
- his perspective on the law as emperor
- the reasons he gives for his actions

Skills Focus — READING LIKE A HISTORIAN

1. **Author** What did Justinian hope to achieve by reorganizing and simplifying Roman law?
2. **Perspective** Why might it be important to a ruler to have a well-organized law code?
3. **Reasons** What reasons does Justinian give for wanting to revise Rome's law code? Which of these do you think was most important to him? Explain your answer.

See **Skills Handbook**, p. H25

Therefore, since there is nothing to be found in all things as worthy of attention as the authority of the law, which properly regulates all affairs both divine and human, and expels all injustice; We have found the <u>entire arrangement of the law which has come down to us from the foundation of the City of Rome and the times of Romulus</u>, to be so confused that it is extended to an infinite length and is not within the grasp of human capacity; and hence We were first induced to begin by examining what had been enacted by former most venerated princes, to correct their constitutions, and make them more easily understood; to the end that being included in a single Code, and <u>having had removed all that is superfluous in resemblance and all iniquitous discord</u>, they may afford to all men the ready assistance of true meaning.

—Justinian, Prologue to the *Digest*

> Some Roman laws dated back to the early days of the Roman Republic, more than 1,000 years before Justinian's time.

> Redundant or unfair laws were removed from the law code.

Byzantine Culture

Two institutions were central to Byzantine culture. The emperor and Christianity affected practically all aspects of Byzantine life.

The Role of the Emperor The emperor was a priest-king who was considered the deputy of Jesus Christ on earth and his co-ruler. Thus the emperor had responsibility for both civil and religious law, in effect, uniting the religious and civil spheres of Byzantine society.

An example of the emperor's influence is reflected in the empire's changing culture. Although the people of Constantinople referred to themselves as Romans, Greek cultural influences grew stronger. It was Emperor Heraclius, though, who brought an official end to Roman traditions in the Eastern Empire. He made Greek the official language, replacing Latin. He also replaced the old Roman imperial titles with Greek ones.

Religion and the Arts Christianity greatly influenced the artistic life of the Byzantines. Most Byzantine art, architecture, and literature was based on religious themes.

A large number of the human subjects in Byzantine art were of saints or figures from the Bible. Some portraits are of the emperor and empress. Much art was in the form of **mosaics**, pictures created with tiny colored tiles of glass, stone, or clay fitted together and cemented in place. Some of the tiles contained gold, making the whole picture glitter like a jewel. Mosaics decorated the floors, walls, and ceilings of many Byzantine buildings.

The nature of Byzantine mosaics and painting changed over time. Although the mosaics became more detailed, they did not become more realistic. Designs became more stylized, and artists used symbols to indicate common themes. For example, a hand above a cross symbolized the hand of God, and 12 lambs symbolized the Christian flock, or community, on earth.

KINGDOMS AND CHRISTIANITY **349**

Differentiating Instruction

Below Level

Learners Having Difficulty

Standard English Mastery

1. Have students work in mixed-ability pairs to review the information about the rule of Justinian and Theodora. You may wish to pair a student who has good writing skills with a struggling reader to complete this activity.

2. Have each pair develop a written summary of the information using standard English. Then have volunteers share their summaries with the class, and develop a brief summary for all students to see. Have each student copy the class summary.

3. Have students use the information from the summaries to write two journal entries describing events during the reign of Justinian and Theodora.

4. Have volunteers read one of their journal entries to the class. As a class, discuss any necessary corrections to align the journal entries with standard English usage. **LS Verbal-Linguistic**

   📄 **Alternative Assessment Handbook**, Rubric 15: Journals

---

Direct Teach

Reading Focus

2 What were some important features of Byzantine culture? *emperor as priest-king, Christian art, religious conflicts*

Byzantine Culture

Recall What was the main theme of most Byzantine art? *Christianity*

Analyze How did Greek culture become dominant in the Byzantine Empire? *Emperor Heraclius made Greek the official language, replacing Latin, and he replaced Latin imperial titles with Greek ones.*

Info to Know

Justinian's Code Comparing Justinian's Code with current laws is very interesting. Many of the laws that he codified or created are still pertinent today. For instance, women were allowed to own property, make contracts and wills, and bring forth a lawsuit. These are the same rights that women in many countries enjoy today. In Justinian's Code, the murder of another was punished by banishment; today, punishments for murder include prison sentences or death. In the Byzantine Empire, robbery was not a crime, but the victim could sue the robber. Today robbery is a crime that can be punished by fine and/or prison sentence. Even though Justinian's Code was created just under 1500 years ago, the laws that were codified are still relevant today. **Activity Comparing Codes** Have students review Hammurabi's Code in their texts and compare it to Justinian's Code. **LS Verbal-Linguistic**

Answers

Reading Like a Historian 1. *to make the law code more readily understandable to all men;* **2.** *to maintain order; to rule justly;* **3.** *to simplify the code and to remove redundant or unfair laws; possible answer—simplification was more important, because he describes it in greater detail*

349

Byzantine Culture

Describe How did the use of religious icons spark controversy? *Some Christians believed that the use of icons was too close to the non-Christian practice of worshipping idols. However, clergy found idols useful in teaching people who could not read.*

Summarize How did the controversy over icons relate to a larger issue? *There was a growing divide between the beliefs and practices of the eastern and western churches.*

Teaching Tip

Provide students with other pictures of famous Byzantine paintings, sculptures, and artwork to give them a better idea of the richness and variety of art at this time.

MISCONCEPTION
/// **ALERT** \\\

Byzantine art refers to the religious art that was created during the height of the Byzantine Empire. It was not just created within the empire. Many Byzantine artists were from other regions, including Italy and Russia.

Byzantine Religious Art

Most of the Byzantine art that has survived deals with religious subjects. Below is a mosaic of Jesus that glitters with gold. At right, a painter creates an religious icon. **Why was so much Byzantine art devoted to religious subject matter?**

Detail, *Deesis* mosaic, Hagia Sophia

Reliquary cross of Justinian, c. 500s.

St. Luje Paints the Mother of God Hodegetria, artist unknown, 1410

Religion was also the force behind Byzantine architecture. Early on, Byzantine architects began to build churches by placing a round dome over a square foundation. They did this by resting the dome on corner supports, instead of walls. The most striking example of this style is Hagia Sophia. This style of architecture influenced building styles across Europe and Asia.

Religious Conflicts In the 700s the use of art in churches deeply divided society. This religious controversy threatened the strength of both church and state.

The controversy involved the use of **icons**—paintings or sculptures of sacred figures. The churches contained many beautiful icons, but some Christians objected to their presence. They believed that the use of icons was too close to the non-Christian worship of idols. People who objected to icons were called iconoclasts, which means "icon breakers."

In 726, the Byzantine emperor Leo III issued a decree, or ruling, forbidding the use of holy images and ordering their destruction.

He even ordered the icon at the entrance to the imperial palace destroyed. Although some people embraced the movement against icons, others objected to it, even resorting to riots.

The iconoclast movement was unpopular with many officials within the church hierarchy, especially in the western church. Because few people could read, many of the **clergy**, or church officials, found sacred images useful for teaching people about Christianity.

By the time Leo III died in 780, a strong reaction against iconoclasm had set in. The movement raged on and off until a council in 843 settled the issue by accepting icons. The dispute over iconoclasm played a crucial role in the growing divide between the emperor in Constantinople and the pope in Rome.

The Church Splits Over time the number of issues that divided the eastern and western churches grew. The use of Greek was one, but theological differences also emerged. For example, the eastern church allowed members of the clergy to marry, whereas the western church did not.

Collaborative Learning

At Level

Byzantine Art

Materials: construction paper, colored pencils

1. Have students review the information in the text about Byzantine art and architecture, focusing on the information about the Hagia Sophia and the feature on Byzantine art. Guide students in a discussion of the connections among religion, society, and government in the Byzantine Empire. Remind students that in the United States, church and state are separated by law.

2. Organize students into small groups. Have each group design a mosaic representing the importance of education in the United States. Have students use colored pencils or markers to create a replica of the mosaic they designed. Remind students that each piece of the mosaic should represent a small, colored tile.

3. Have students present their finished mosaics to the class. **LS Kinesthetic, Visual-Spatial**

   Alternative Assessment Handbook, Rubrics 3: Artwork; and 14: Group Activity

Answers

Byzantine Religious Art *possible answer—because Christianity was an important part of the empire*

Ideas about church governance also split the eastern and western churches. In the east, the emperor oversaw church law, but he did not govern the church. Church leaders were the bishops of major cities—the pope in Rome and the patriarchs of Constantinople, Alexandria, Antioch, and Jerusalem. In the east, while the Byzantines acknowledged that the pope had special importance, they did not accept that he had supreme authority over religious issues. Instead, the Byzantines placed religious authority in the councils where church officials met to settle major issues.

In 1054 the differences became so large that a final schism (SI-zuhm), or split, occurred between the churches. The church in the east became the **Orthodox Church**, and the church in the west remained the Roman Catholic Church. (The word *orthodox* comes from Greek words that mean "right opinion.") At first, the break increased the emperor's authority. In later years the schism would prove dangerous to the Byzantine Empire, which could no longer rely on help from the west against invaders.

READING CHECK **Summarize** What led to the split between the eastern and western churches?

The Empire Declines

As far back as the reign of Heraclius, Muslims had been threatening the empire. Over time, Islam, pressure from migrating tribes, and internal conflict and corruption brought about the Byzantine Empire's fall.

Invaders in the Empire The Byzantines were constantly being attacked on their northern borders by migrating tribes such the Slavs and Bulgars. In the 600s the Byzantine provinces of Egypt and Syria, whose loyalty to Constantinople had been weakened by religious conflicts, fell to Muslim conquerors.

Leo III, who had issued the decree prohibiting icons, stopped advancing Muslim forces in 718 and again in 740. His successor, Constantine V, won great popularity with his victories against the Bulgars, but his successors failed to maintain those gains.

A Period of Calm By the 800s the Byzantines had endured a century of crises. The empire's fortunes improved, though, for about 200 years under a dynasty from Macedonia, northern Greece, which ruled from 867 to 1056.

ACADEMIC VOCABULARY
patriarch head of any of various eastern churches; also, a father-like leader

THE IMPACT TODAY

Today, more than 218 million people are included within the Orthodox tradition. Many countries have their own Orthodox churches.

Eastern and Western Christianity

The schism of 1054 left two churches—Roman Catholic in the west and Orthodox in the east—claiming to be the true Christian church. Although attempts have been made to unify the two, the division remains in effect.

A basic issue is that the Orthodox Church has some roots in Greek philosophy, while Roman Catholicism has roots in Roman law. These differences led to different interpretations of beliefs.

The nature of the pope's power continues to be one of the thorniest issues dividing the two churches. While Orthodox Christians recognize the pope's authority over bishops, they do not accept the pope as the ultimate authority over doctrine. For Roman Catholics,

these two forms of authority cannot be separated.

There are also subtle differences in the ritual practices of each church. For example, Roman Catholics use unleavened bread in their communion service, while Orthodox Christians view this as an uncalled-for innovation.

Summarize
How do the two churches view the pope's power?

▲ Easter service at a Greek Orthodox church, Istanbul, Turkey

◀ Roman Catholic service, St. Patrick's Cathedral in New York City

KINGDOMS AND CHRISTIANITY **351**

351

The Macedonian period was in some ways a golden age. The emperors improved the condition of the peasantry and established a law school to train officials in the art of government. They also recovered parts of Syria from the Arabs and annexed the Bulgarian kingdom to the north, extending Byzantine rule over the Balkan Slavs and Bulgars. In addition, missionary activity in southeastern Europe established Orthodox Christianity there.

Internal Weaknesses After about 150 years, the Macedonian dynasty began to decline. Factions were able to force emperors to step down. A series of incompetent emperors came and went—some with startling rapidity.

The conflicts of the Macedonian dynasty's last years were symptoms of a divide within Byzantine society. On one hand was the government located in Constantinople, which was made up of well-educated, cultured members of aristocratic families. They supported emperors who would restrain the military and enlarge the government. They used their energies to make Constantinople a center of culture and learning. But their focus on culture had a cost.

Members of the military aristocracy saw a different view. Based in the provinces, they were more aware of encroaching danger than the government in the capital. They supported emperors who had themselves been soldiers.

Final Decline Continuing strife between the military and the Constantinople government weakened the empire, making it vulnerable to challengers from the outside. And in fact, new enemies—the Seljuk Turks—were conquering areas on the empire's borders. In 1071 the Turks defeated the Byzantine army at Manzikert in eastern Asia Minor, permanently weakening the Byzantines in the region. In 1071 the Byzantines also lost their last outposts in Italy, ending their presence in the west.

The empire carried on, but by 1391 it had been reduced to Constantinople and a few outlying districts. In 1453 the Ottoman Turks attacked the great city. After a siege and fierce battle, Constantinople fell to the attackers. The Ottomans later renamed the city Istanbul. Hagia Sophia became a mosque.

The Ottomans had gained an important seat of power and spread their influence into Greece and the Balkans. Yet Byzantine influence left a strong imprint in that region, too. An important legacy was the Byzantine Empire's preservation of its ancient Greco-Roman heritage, benefitting later generations. It had also served as a buffer between the Christian West and the Muslim East.

READING CHECK **Identifying Cause and Effect** What was the connection between the rise of Islam and the fall of the Byzantine Empire?

SECTION 1 ASSESSMENT

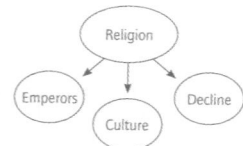

go.hrw.com
Online Quiz
Keyword: SHL CHR HP

Reviewing Ideas, Terms, and People

1. **a. Identify** Who was **Justinian I**, and what did he achieve regarding law?
   b. Describe How did the influence of **Theodora** affect the outcome of the Nika Revolt?
   c. Make Judgments How might Justinian I have ensured that his accomplishments lasted longer than they did?

2. **a. Recall** What are **mosaics**, and what role did they play in Byzantine art?
   b. Explain Why did the iconoclasts respond as they did to sacred paintings or carvings that showed human images?
   c. Develop Why did the split occur between the **Orthodox Church** and the Roman Catholic Church?

3. **a. Identify** Under what dynasty did the Byzantine Empire enjoy a 200-year golden age?
   b. Explain Why was the division between the aristocracies of city and countryside a problem?

c. Evaluate Evaluate this statement: "The Byzantines themselves, not the Turks, bear the greatest responsibility for the end of their empire."

Critical Thinking

4. **Categorize** Use your notes and a graphic organizer like this one to describe the impact of religion on the Byzantine Empire's emperors, culture, and decline.

Religion → Emperors, Culture, Decline

FOCUS ON WRITING

5. **Narration** Imagine that you are the official biographer of Theodora. Write a paragraph in which you describe her character, accomplishments, and role in the Nika Revolt.

352 CHAPTER 12

Architecture

Hagia Sophia

What is it? Hagia Sophia (HAH-juh soh-FEE-uh), which means "Holy Wisdom," is one of the world's most spectacular buildings. Its massive walls and half-domes rise over the old quarter of Istanbul. A dome high above the floor is pierced by many windows. On sunny days, so much light pours in that the dome seems to float on the light instead of on its thick stone supports.

What are some key facts?
- About 100,000 workers were hired to build Hagia Sophia.
- Construction lasted from 532 to 537—only five years!
- The main room is just slightly smaller than a football field.
- Hagia Sophia was built as a Christian church, became a mosque, and is now a museum.

Why is it important?
- Many Byzantine buildings and even mosques followed the same style as Hagia Sophia.
- Mosaics on the walls are exquisite examples of Byzantine art.
- The building's construction used an ingenious new technique, called pendentives, for supporting the dome.

▲ **This illustration shows Hagia Sophia's vast interior.**
Lithograph by Louis Haghe after a drawing by Chevalier Caspar Fussati, 1800s

☐ Pendetives   ☐ Squinches

▲ **Pendentives allow builders to create wider, more open spaces.**

NEW YORK STANDARDS

P1 1.2 Students understand the development and connectedness of Western civilization and other civilizations and cultures in many areas of the world and over time.

Skills FOCUS INTERPRETING VISUALS

1. **Contrast** How does the interior of Hagia Sophia compare to its exterior?
2. **Infer** How do pendentives create wider open spaces?

Differentiating Instruction

Below Level

Learners Having Difficulty

1. Have students review the information in the text and the images of the Hagia Sophia.

2. Have students draw the church as shown in the feature. Then have students work in pairs to identify each of the architectural elements of the church. Students should be able to recognize and mark the dome, the minarets, the pendentives, and the many sources of light. Then have students examine the artistic features shown on the painting of the interior. Have students identify mosaics and other artistic elements that they see.

3. Have volunteers share their drawings with the class. Then guide students in a discussion of the reasons the Hagia Sophia continues to be a world landmark. **LS Visual-Spatial**

📝 **Alternative Assessment Handbook,** Rubric 3: Artwork

Answers

Interpreting Visuals 1. *The interior is more richly decorated, both the exterior and interior are monumental, impressive pieces of architecture.* **2.** *The arches are stronger, can support more weight, and provide for open space and light.*

353

City at a Crossroads

Info to Know

Excavation at Constantinople In November of 2005, archeologists uncovered important keys in understanding the city of Constantinople. For example, they found a port that they named "Port of Theodosius." During their dig they also uncovered a church, a gated entrance to the city, and eight sunken ships. The ships are believed to have been victims of a giant storm and have been dated to around 1000. The site archaeologists excavated is about four city blocks long and two to three city blocks wide. The information gathered from the site has provided archaeologists and historians with a better picture of the ancient city of Constantinople.

CRF: History and Geography: The City of Constantine

HISTORY & Geography ★Interactive

City at a Crossroads

With its location where two continents meet and between two seas, Constantinople was well-placed for trade and communication. One aspect of the site, however, required a solution. Its only river was a small stream, so water had to be brought into the city and stored in more than 100 cisterns.

Roads to Europe
Roads extended west from Constantinople to European markets. Oil, wine, grain, and silk were among the products that merchants carried on these roads.

Areas of Interest
1. Harbors and Seawalls
2. Forum of Constantine
3. Hippodrome
4. Palace
5. Hagia Sophia

THE BYZANTINE EMPIRE

EUROPE

Black Sea

Bosporus Strait

Constantinople ★

ASIA

Aegean Sea

Sea of Marmara

ASIA MINOR

0   150   300 Miles
0   150   300 Kilometers
Azimuthal equal-area projection

Byzantine Empire, c. 1025

354 CHAPTER 12

Collaborative Learning

At Level

Archaeological Areas of Interest

1. Have students study the illustration of Constantinople, paying careful attention to the location of the five areas of interest that are pointed out in the text.

2. Organize students into five groups.

3. Assign each group one of the areas of interest. Have groups research their landmark using the text and other outside resources. Students should use both reliable Internet and print sources and create a bibliography.

4. Have groups prepare a multimedia presentation with information about their landmark and present it to the class.

LS Verbal-Linguistic

Alternative Assessment Handbook, Rubrics 14: Group Activity; and 22: Multimedia Presentations

NEW YORK STANDARDS

PI 3.2 Students explain the dynamics of cultural change and how interactions between and among cultures have affected various cultural groups throughout the world.

City Walls

About 13 miles of thick walls protected the city. Along the walls were 192 towers, some of which were 70 feet tall. A ditch beyond the walls could be flooded to create a moat.

Golden Horn Chain

When danger threatened from the sea, a huge chain was fastened across the mouth of the Golden Horn to keep out enemy ships.

Istanbul Today

Istanbul's location keeps the city of 10 million a busy place, but it poses a new hazard. Some 5,000 oil and gas tankers go through the Bosporus each year, making the city vulnerable to spills and accidents.

GEOGRAPHY SKILLS | INTERPRETING MAPS

go.hrw.com
Interactive Map
Keyword: SHL CHR

1. **Summarize** The site of Constantinople, now Istanbul, has probably been occupied for more than 2,600 years. Why has the location been so highly valued?

2. **Predict** More than once, ships have invaded the Golden Horn in spite of the chain. How do you think they did it?

355

History and Geography

Info to Know

Hippodrome The word hippodrome is derived from the Greek word *hippos* which means horse and *dromos* which means path or way. The Hippodrome in Constantinople was primarily a horse racing track that also featured other entertainment. It was very large, about 450 meters, or about 1,476 feet long, and 130 meters, or about 426.5 feet wide. It could seat about 100,000 audience members. The Hippodrome today is honored in Istanbul and is called Sultan Ahmet Square. Much of the original structure is located about two meters underground, but the track is marked by concrete. Other parts are still visible and surrounded by a landscaped garden.

Skills Focus: Analyzing Visuals

At Level

Reading Like a Historian Skill
Invading Constantinople

1. Have students study the illustration of Constantinople on these pages. Then have students review the information in the text about the city.

2. Have students use this information to develop an argument about why they think it would be difficult to invade and conquer Constantinople. Students should cite specific information from this feature to support their argument.

3. Have students present their arguments to the class. As an extension, you might wish to organize a class debate on the issue: Would it have been easy or difficult to invade Constantinople? **LS Verbal-Linguistic**

📝 **Alternative Assessment Handbook**, Rubric 37: Writing Assignments

Answers

Interpreting Maps 1. *Constantinople was strategically located on the Bosporus Strait, where it could control trade between Asia and Europe.* **2.** *possible answer—Invaders may have crashed their ships through the chain, or carried the ships over land.*

355

Getting Started

Use the **Interactive Reader and Study Guide** to familiarize students with the section content.

📄 **Interactive Reader and Study Guide,** Section 2

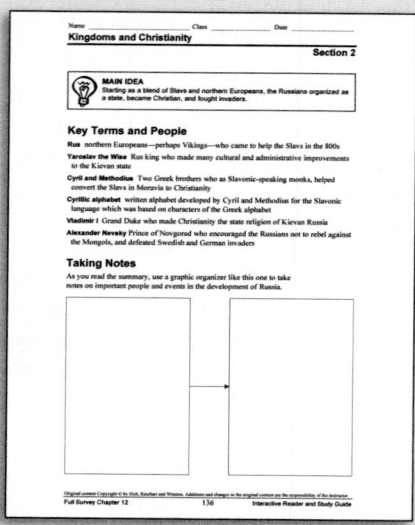

Academic Vocabulary

Review with students the high-use academic term in this section.

preliminary coming before something else, often as a necessary introduction (p. 358)

📄 **CRF:** Vocabulary Builder: Section 2

Taking Notes

People—*Yaroslav the Wise, Cyril and Methodius, Vladimir I, Alexander Nevsky; Events— invaded by the Rus, Kiev Rus weakened, Kiev fell to Mongols, Mongols attacked Swedes, Alexander fought Germans and Swedes, Russia freed from foreign rule, Muscovy becomes capital, Cyrillic alphabet developed; Christianity named the state religion; texts were translated; mass was performed in Slavonic*

go.hrw.com
Online Resources

KEYWORD: SHL CHR
ACTIVITY: Yaroslav the Wise

The Rise of Russia

BEFORE YOU READ

MAIN IDEA
Starting as a blend of Slavs and northern Europeans, the Russians organized as a state, became Christian, and fought invaders.

READING FOCUS
1. How did the Rus affect the early history of Kiev?
2. What factors helped establish Christianity in Russia?
3. What peoples attacked Russia?

KEY TERMS AND PEOPLE
Rus
Yaroslav the Wise
Cyril
Methodius
Cyrillic alphabet
Vladimir I
Alexander Nevsky

 NEW YORK

PI 2.4 Students explain the importance of analyzing narratives drawn from different times and places to understand historical events.

THE INSIDE STORY

Could a blessing create a city? Long, long ago, a man stood among a cluster of hills. He blessed the hills, predicting that a great city would rise there. Later, three brothers named Kiy, Shchek, and Khoriv, leaders of the Polyane tribe, arrived in the area and built settlements on the hills. One of the settlements became known as Kiev after Kiy, the oldest brother. The city grew, and Kiy rose in influence. He traveled all the way to Constantinople to meet with the Byzantine emperor, who treated him with great honor.

The man who blessed the hills became known in the Russian Orthodox Church as Saint Andrew. The story about him, the brothers, and the founding of Kiev is recorded in *The Russian Primary Chronicle,* written in the early 1100s.

Although the story is a legend, the city certainly played an important role in Russian history. From Kiev, which is now in Ukraine, and the surrounding region, Russia expanded to stretch across most of Asia. Kiev's central role in Russian history is still reflected in its nickname "the Mother of Cities." Now often called Kyiv or Kyyiv, the city remains a cultural center with deep significance for millions of people. ◾

A SAINT and Three BROTHERS

◀ This statue in Kiev, Ukraine, commemorates the city's founding by three brothers.

Teach the Main Idea

At Level

The Rise of Russia

1. **Teach** Ask students the Reading Focus questions to teach this section.

2. **Apply** Organize students into groups of three, and assign each student in the group one of the three topics in the section: The Rus and Kiev, Christianity in Russia, and Russia under Attack. Have each student create a graphic organizer to summarize or show the contents of the topic. Then have students share their graphics with the group and have students copy the graphic organizers.

3. **Review** Review student graphic organizers as a class. Have students add to or correct their own three graphic organizers.

4. **Practice/Homework** Have students create two maps of Russia, one showing its size in 912 and one showing its size today.
LS Visual-Spatial

📄 **Alternative Assessment Handbook,** Rubrics 13: Graphic Organizers; 14: Group Activity and 20: Map Creation

The Rus and Kiev

For thousands of years, hunter-gatherers managed to make a living in the sometimes harsh climate of the lands we now call Ukraine and Russia. Among the people who occupied the plains were the Slavs. They do not enter the historical record, however, until the AD 800s.

The Rus of Kiev The history of the Slavs is told in *The Russian Primary Chronicle*, written during the 1100s. According to this account, during the mid-800s, the Slavs along the Dnieper (NEE-puhr) River were fighting among themselves and asked for help from northern Europeans—perhaps Vikings—called the **Rus**.

HISTORY'S VOICES

❝'Our whole land is great and rich, but there is no order in it. Come to rule and reign over us.' They thus selected three brothers, with their kinsfolk, who took with them all the Rus, and migrated.❞
—*The Russian Primary Chronicle*, 860–862 (6368–6370)

The oldest of the three brothers, Rurik, took Novgorod, a trading center, and brought order to the Slavs there. In 882 Rurik's successor, Oleg, ventured farther south to a town called Kiev. He united the whole region and ruled over it. That state came to be called Kiev after the town on the Dnieper.

Oleg wanted to extend Kiev to the south, and in 907 he successfully attacked Constantinople. Legend claims that he nailed his shield to the city gates to celebrate his victory. That victory enabled Oleg to demand an advantageous trade agreement. The agreement was the beginning of a close connection between the Byzantine Empire and the Russian people.

The Growth of Kiev By the late 900s the Rus had extended their control far beyond Kiev. They defeated a people called the Khazars and freed several Slavic tribes that the Khazars had controlled. Although semi-independent princes ruled some areas, the Kievan region became a state called Kievan Rus.

During the height of Kievan Rus's power and prestige, the ruler was **Yaroslav the Wise**. Yaroslav became grand prince in 1019 and ruled until 1054. He made many cultural and administrative improvements to Kievan Rus. For example, he collected religious books and hired scribes to translate them from Greek into

THE GROWTH OF RUSSIA

- Novgorod
- Kiev
- Constantinople

Baltic Sea
Volga River
Dnieper River
Don River
Dniester River
Danube River
Black Sea
BYZANTINE EMPIRE

0   150   300 Miles
0   150   300 Kilometers
Azimuthal equal-area projection

☐	Russia in 912
▨	Russia in 972
▩	Russia in 1054

GEOGRAPHY SKILLS | **INTERPRETING MAPS**

1. **Movement** Why would people have fought over control of the Dnieper River?
2. **Location** By 1054 Russia extended from the Baltic Sea to the Black Sea. What advantage might this expansion have provided for the people who lived there?

the Slavic language. He began an ambitious building program to beautify Kiev. Also, under Yaroslav's rule, Russian law was codified.

Yaroslav's military record was mixed. He regained territory that had been lost and defeated a nomadic people called the Pechenegs. On the other hand, when he tried to attack Constantinople, his forces were crushed. In dealing with western Europe, Yaroslav was more clearly successful. He maintained good diplomatic and trade relationships with European countries, partly by arranging marriages between his daughters and European princes.

TAKING NOTES
Take notes on important people and events in the development of Russia.

People	Events

READING CHECK **Find the Main Idea** Who were the Rus, and what was their connection to Kiev?

KINGDOMS AND CHRISTIANITY **357**

Direct Teach

Reading Focus

❶ How did the Rus affect the early history of Kiev? *They ruled it for some time, were asked by feuding Slavs to rule them, built a trading center, and extended control beyond Kiev.*

The Rus and Kiev

Identify Who were the Rus? *northern Europeans—perhaps Vikings—who brought order to the Slavs living along the Dneiper River*

Describe How did friendly relations between the Slavic kingdom and Constantinople develop? *Oleg of Kiev attacked Constantinople. He demanded a trade agreement, which was the beginning of a close connection between the Russians and the Byzantines.*

Summarize What changes did Yaroslav the Wise make to help unify Russia? *translated religious books from Greek to Slavic, codified Russian law, regained territory, established diplomatic ties with western Europe*

The Growth of Russia
Interpreting Maps

Movement What are some of the factors that could have led to the growth of Russia? *possible answer—ambitious leaders, fought for more territory, became more organized, established ties with western Europe*

Map Transparency: The Growth of Russia

Skills Focus: Summarizing

At Level

Reading Skill
Russia Today

Prep Required

Materials: newspapers, news magazines

1. Have materials available for students, and have students work either individually or in small groups to read through the newspapers and magazines to find an article of interest about current events in Russia.

2. Have students prepare a summary of their chosen article in which they answer the following questions: Who are the people involved? What is the situation? Where is it?

When did it happen? Why is it important to know about?

3. Have students present their summaries to the class, and then guide students in a discussion of the political, economic, and social situation in Russia today. **LS Verbal-Linguistic**

Alternative Assessment Handbook, Rubric 37: Writing Assignments

Answers

Interpreting Maps 1. *possible answer—because it led to the Black Sea;* **2.** *possible answer—provided access to trade*

Reading Check *a group of northern Europeans—perhaps Vikings—who came to rule the Slavs*

357

Reading Focus

❷ **What factors helped establish Christianity in Russia?** *development of the Cyrillic alphabet and mass in the Slavonic language; Christianity made the state religion*

Christianity in Russia

Recall Describe the religion of the Slavs before they converted to Christianity. *It was based in nature and had many gods.*

Analyze What role did Cyril and Methodius play in the conversion of the Moravians to Christianity? *used native language which had great appeal*

CRF: Biography: St. Olga

Info to Know

Russian Orthodox Church The Russian Orthodox Church followed many of the same practices as the Orthodox Church in the Byzantine Empire. As in the Byzantine Empire, the Russian government was involved in church matters. There was no separation between church and state. During the Renaissance and the Reformation, the Russian Orthodox Church remained untouched by the cultural and religious changes in Europe. Today there are an estimated 40 to 80 million members of the Russian Orthodox Church throughout the world.

Answers

Reading Check *Monks from the Byzantine Empire traveled to Moravia and established the Cyrillic alphabet and a Slavonic mass to spread Christianity.*

358

NEW YORK

CC Unit 2-C6
Byzantine Empire: Impact on Russia

CC Unit 2-D3
Early Russia: Kiev

CC Unit 2-D4
Early Russia: Russian Orthodox Church

FOCUS ON NEW YORK
A Russian Orthodox monastery was established in Jordanville, New York, in 1930. The monastery uses the Slavonic language for services.

ACADEMIC VOCABULARY
preliminary
coming before something else, often as a necessary introduction

Christianity in Russia

Warfare and trade were not the only ways in which the Byzantine Empire affected Russia. Christianity spread to Russia from the Byzantine Empire.

Cyril and Methodius Before Rurik and Oleg arrived in Russia, the Slavs practiced a native religion. That belief system was based on nature and had many gods.

In 863 a churchman in Constantinople sent two Greek monks to Moravia (now in the Czech Republic) to convert the Slavs to Christianity. The monks, **Cyril** and **Methodius**, were brothers. They spoke the Slavonic language and used it instead of the traditional Greek to celebrate mass. Use of the native language helped Cyril and Methodius convert many Moravians to Christianity.

Cyril and Methodius did not travel far beyond Moravia. However, their desire to translate religious texts for a larger group of readers led them to develop a written alphabet for the Slavonic language. Based mainly on the characters of the Greek alphabet, it is called the **Cyrillic alphabet**.

Use of the Cyrillic alphabet and the Slavonic mass became widespread in what are now Serbia and Bulgaria, and their use eventually spread even farther. As a result of the Greek brothers' efforts, it was the Byzantine version of Christianity that spread to Russia.

Christian Russia Within some 100 years, Christianity was established and claimed an important convert. Grand Duke **Vladimir I** of Kiev gave up the old beliefs and was baptized a Christian. He then married the sister of a Byzantine emperor. Some historians say that Vladimir's conversion was just a preliminary step in gaining economic and political advantages from the Byzantine Empire. Even if his conversion was politically motivated, Vladimir did build libraries, schools, and churches afterwards. In 988 Vladimir made Christianity the state religion of Kievan Russia.

Christianity spread gradually, becoming common in the cities long before it did in the countryside. Meanwhile, tension between the eastern and western branches of the church had grown worse. Following the schism of 1054, the head of the church in Kiev set up a semi-independent church in Russia that would still be linked to the Orthodox Church in Constantinople. The new church eventually became the Russian Orthodox Church. Vladimir I was made a saint in the new church.

READING CHECK **Summarize** How did Christianity spread to Russia?

Russia under Attack

During the mid-1000s, Kievan Rus reached the height of its power as a center of trade and culture. But by the end of the 1200s, it had suffered a steep decline. Kievan Rus was under attack—first by princes within its borders, and later by invaders from beyond.

Kievan Rus Weakened After the death of Yaroslav the Wise in 1054, internal disputes became common among the Rus. The main threat was from princes whose lands were within the state's borders.

Many of the princes had grown steadily more powerful and wanted to enlarge their own lands. One of these was Prince Andrew Bogolyubsky. In 1169 he captured the City of Kiev and became the new grand prince. But Andrew insisted on ruling from his home city of Vladimir and installed relatives in the weakened post of prince of Kiev. This action further weakened Kiev's position as the capital. Power was no longer centralized, and the stage was set for fierce attacks from Europe and Asia.

A Threat from the East In the 1200s a new danger appeared. The Mongols, led by Genghis Khan, had swept across Asia to create an immense empire. Mongol raiders entered Rus lands in 1223. The Rus and their allies attacked the Mongols but were badly defeated.

In 1227 Genghis Khan died and his empire was divided into four regions. The empire's western edge was under the control of Batu Khan, a grandson of Genghis Khan. Batu's plan was to conquer Europe. Kiev fell to the Mongols in 1240, and Batu continued westward. He pulled back in 1241 but established a Mongol state in southern Russia. The era of Kievan Rus dominance was over.

Generally, the Mongols left local princes in charge and did not interfere with the church. Some local leaders saw that cooperating with

358 CHAPTER 12

Differentiating Instruction

Below Level

Learners Having Difficulty

Materials: outline maps of Russia

1. Have students refer to maps in this section and in the atlas of their text and draw their own maps of Russia. Have students work in mixed-ability pairs to locate the places discussed under the heading The Rus and Kiev.

2. On the outline maps, have students locate and mark the Baltic Sea, Novgorod, the Dnieper River, Kiev, and the Black Sea.

3. Have students share their maps in small groups, and explain what happened in each of these places.

4. As an extension, have students write a paragraph explaining how geography affected the movement of the Rus as they extended their reach into Kiev and beyond. **LS Visual-Spatial**

Alternative Assessment Handbook, Rubrics 20: Map Creation; and 37: Writing Assignments the Mongols was more practical than revolting against them. For example, Alexander, Prince of Novgorod, encouraged the Russians not to rebel against their new masters. As a result, the Mongols did not destroy as much as they had in other lands they had conquered, and complete disaster was avoided.

A Threat from the North At about the same time that the Mongols were attacking the Rus, danger also came from a different direction. In 1240 a band of Swedes invaded Russian territory north of Novgorod. The Swedes wanted to take control of the lucrative trade route between Russia and the Byzantine Empire. The same Prince Alexander who had calmed the Mongol threat now turned his attention to the Swedes.

On July 15, 1240, Alexander launched a surprise attack against the Swedish camp on the Neva River. In hand-to-hand fighting, the Swedes were completely defeated. The victory saved Russia from a full-scale invasion from the north.

FACES OF HISTORY **Alexander Nevsky,** c. 1220–1263

The halo indicates Alexander's status as a saint in the Russian Orthodox Church.

The soldier's uniform emphasizes Alexander's importance as the military hero who protected Russia from the Swedes and German knights.

Mosaic on Alexander Nevsky Cathedral, Yalta, Ukraine, no date

Alexander appears as a warrior in this 1940 painting.

Images similar to this one were used on WWII posters to rouse the Russians against the invading Germans.

Alexander Nevsky, by Afanasij Kulikow, 1940

To the Russians, Alexander Nevsky was both warrior and saint. His military genius protected Russia from invaders, and his intelligence made living under the Mongols tolerable. He was revered as a saint partly because his cooperation with the Mongols helped the Russian church thrive. The Mongols protected the church from taxation and from princes who plotted with the Roman Catholic pope. Centuries later, a third role was assigned to Alexander—as a symbol of resistance. When Nazi Germany invaded the Soviet Union during World War II, Soviet leaders used Alexander's name and image to rally the Russian people against the new invaders.

Skills Focus READING LIKE A HISTORIAN

1. **Draw Conclusions** Why do you think Alexander Nevsky is a powerful symbol for the Russian people?
2. **Analyze Visuals** Which image would you say is more historically accurate? Explain your answer.

KINGDOMS AND CHRISTIANITY **359**

Close

Have students summarize the expansion of Russia and how Christianity took hold in Russia.

Review

Online Quiz, Section 2

Assess

SE Section 2 Assessment

Progress Assessment: Section 2 Quiz

Alternative Assessment Handbook

Reteach/Intervene

Interactive Reader and Study Guide, Section 2

Interactive Skills Tutor CD-ROM

Answers

Reading Skills *"later," "again"*

Reading Check *Mongols; Swedes, Germans*

Mongols in Russia

This Persian painting from 1350 shows Mongol warriors at their portable dwellings, called yurts.

READING SKILLS

Understanding Sequencing In this paragraph, which words help you understand the sequence of events?

Invasion from the Baltic The victorious Alexander was later known as **Alexander Nevsky** ("of the Neva") for his accomplishment. Relying on his new status, Alexander began to meddle in Novgorod's internal affairs. The city banished him. But later, when another invader threatened Russia, Novgorod did not have a military leader to answer the threat. Alexander was again asked to save his people.

A German military order of knights called the Teutonic Knights wanted to force Russians to abandon the Orthodox Church and convert to Roman Catholicism. The knights invaded from the Baltic Sea. Having accepted the invitation to lead a defensive army, Alexander fought several battles with the Knights. Then, in April 1242, Alexander's army met the Teutonic invaders at a narrow strait between two lakes still covered with ice. During the battle, Alexander's forces lured the Teutonic Knights onto the thinning ice. The ice cracked, and men and horses fell through into the freezing water. The massacre on the ice, as the battle came to be called, remains one of the most famous in Russian history.

Alexander fought Germans and Swedes several more times, stopping a potential expansion into Russian territory. For his victories, Alexander was celebrated as a hero.

From Kiev to Muscovy For more than 200 years after Alexander's battles, Russia remained under the control of Asian nomadic peoples. The Tatars, a Central Asian people who spoke a Turkic language, emerged as Russia's rulers after the Mongols. Russia was eventually freed from foreign domination in 1480.

Within Russia, Muscovy, east of Kiev, grew in importance. It became the capital of a nation that gradually expanded to occupy much of Asia, the largest continent.

READING CHECK **Sequence** Which people first invaded Russia in 1223? What other groups invaded?

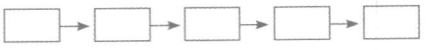

SECTION 2 ASSESSMENT

go.hrw.com
Online Quiz
Keyword: SHL CHR

Reviewing Ideas, Terms, and People

1. **a. Recall** Why did the Slavs ask for help from the **Rus**?
   b. Explain What were some accomplishments of **Yaroslav the Wise**?
   c. Develop How did physical geography affect the relationship between the Byzantine Empire and Kievan Rus? Use the map to help you answer the question.

2. **a. Identify** What did **Cyril** and **Methodius** do?
   b. Analyze What impact did **Vladimir I** have on Christianity in Russia?
   c. Infer Why do you think Christianity spread more rapidly in the cities than in the countryside?

3. **a. Identify** Who was **Alexander Nevsky**?
   b. Evaluate Which do you think caused more damage to the Kievan state—internal problems or invasions from outside? Explain your answer.

Critical Thinking

4. **Sequence** Use your notes and a graphic organizer like this one to list important events of pre-Christian and Christian Russia. Add more boxes as needed.

   □ → □ → □ → □ → □

FOCUS ON SPEAKING

5. **Persuasion** Imagine that you are Alexander, Prince of Novgorod, or one of the other local dignitaries who have an opinion on how the Russian people should respond to the Mongol conquest. Write and present the main argument you would make at a public meeting—either for rebelling against the Mongols or for living under their rule.

360 CHAPTER 12

Section 2 Assessment Answers

1. **a.** because they were fighting among themselves
   b. translated books from Greek to the Slavic language, beautified Kiev, codified Russian law, regained territory, maintained good relationships with Europe
   c. They were located across the Black Sea from each other, making contact fairly easy.

2. **a.** brought Christianity to Rus, developed an alphabet
   b. He made Christianity the state religion.

   c. possible answer—Slavonic religious texts and masses were probably more available in cities than in the country.

3. **a.** prince of Novgorod; protected Russians from invasions and encouraged them not to rebel against the Mongols, making life under Mongol rule more tolerable
   b. possible answer—internal problems, because strong central leadership might have made the Russians better able to withstand invasion

4. 882: Oleg unites the Slavs in Kiev; 1019: Yaroslav the Wise comes to power; 863: Cyril and Methodius bring Christianity to the Slavs; 988: Vladimir I makes Christianity the state religion of Kievan Russia; 1223: Genghis Khan invades Russia; 1240: Russians defeat Swedes; 1242: Russians defeat Germans

5. Student essays should use logic and details from the text to support argument. If written from Alexander's point of view, essays should argue that the Russians should not rebel.

3 Christianity in Western Europe

BEFORE YOU READ

MAIN IDEA

The spread of Christianity, largely through the work of missionaries and monks, helped unify western Europe after the collapse of the Roman Empire.

READING FOCUS

1. What new kingdoms arose in Europe, and how did they become Christian?
2. What characteristics defined Christian European society?
3. What roles did monks and monasteries play in European religion and society?

KEY TERMS AND PEOPLE

Alfred the Great
Clovis
medieval
Christendom
Gregory the Great
monasticism
Augustine of Hippo
Benedictine Rule
abbot

 NEW YORK

PI 2.5 Students investigate key events and developments and major turning points in world history to identify the factors that brought about change and the long-term effects of those changes.

THE INSIDE STORY

Why was a king on duty in a peasant's kitchen? In the 800s the Christians of southern England were locked in a long struggle against the Danes who ruled the north. Among the leaders of the English Christians was King Alfred, the ruler of the small kingdom of Wessex.

According to a legend, Alfred was separated from his troops after a battle and found himself wandering alone through the countryside. He came across a small cottage, where he asked for shelter. However, Alfred did not tell the owners of the cottage, a peasant and his wife, who he was.

One day Alfred was alone in the cottage with the woman. Busy with her chores, she asked Alfred to keep an eye on some cakes she was baking. Alfred agreed, but soon became lost in his thoughts and did not notice when the cakes burned. For his negligence, the wife scolded Alfred harshly, not realizing that he was actually her king. For his part, Alfred felt bad for abandoning his duty and calmly accepted the rebuke. The legend reveals Alfred's reputation for humility and sense of fairness. ■

New Kingdoms in Europe

The fall of Rome had very different results in eastern and western Europe. In the east, the Byzantine Empire grew out of the former Roman Empire and flourished. In the west, however, no single empire arose from Rome's ashes. Instead, the Germanic groups who had invaded Rome established many small kingdoms.

King OR Peasant?

▲ In an English folk tale, King Alfred was scolded severely for letting a peasant woman's cakes burn.

King Alfred Burning the Cakes, artist unknown, 1864

KINGDOMS AND CHRISTIANITY **361**

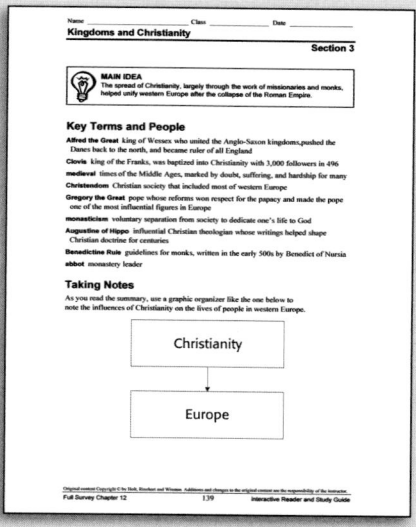
---

❶ What new kingdoms arose in Europe, and how did they become Christian? *Anglo-Saxons—group of monks led by Augustine of Canterbury, converted many people in Kent, and Christianity spread to the rest of England; Franks—king vowed to become Christian if he won in battle*

New Kingdoms in Europe

Recall Where did the name Anglo-Saxons come from? *two groups of Germanic peoples, the Angles and the Saxons*

Identify Cause and Effect What was the effect of the fall of the Western Roman Empire? *New kingdoms formed in western Europe; Byzantine Empire rose in the east.*

CRF: Primary Source: The Angles and Saxons in Great Britain

Charlemagne: Father of a Continent is a thematic look at the life and times of Charlemagne. The author, Alessandro Barbero, a professor of Medieval Studies at the University of Piemonte Orientale in Vercelli, Italy, recounts Charlemagne's life, but more importantly, examines his tactics in warfare and in spreading Christianity. The author also provides interesting and useful social and economic analyses of the period.

Charlemagne: Father of a Continent by Alessandro Barbero, translated by Allan Cameron. University of California Press, 2004.

Baptism of Clovis
The conversion of Clovis and the Franks helped bring Christianity to northwestern Europe.

TAKING NOTES
Use a graphic organizer like this one to note the influences of Christianity on the lives of people in western Europe.

Christianity
↓
Europe

THE IMPACT TODAY
The Archbishop of Canterbury is still considered the highest religious leader in England.

Anglo-Saxon England Among the Germanic peoples who established kingdoms in Europe were the Angles and the Saxons. Both groups had once lived in what is now Germany but had migrated to Britain in the 400s. In England they established seven small independent kingdoms. Together, the seven are known as the Anglo-Saxon kingdoms.

When the Angles and Saxons first moved to England, they were not Christian. Christianity had not made much headway in England. Then in the late 500s a group of monks led by Augustine of Canterbury arrived in the small kingdom of Kent. Augustine converted many of the people of Kent and was named Archbishop of Canterbury. From Kent, Christianity slowly spread through the rest of England.

The Anglo-Saxon kingdoms remained independent for several centuries. However, a threat arose that forced them to band together. The Danes, who had invaded northern England, began to march south. To fight them, the Anglo-Saxons united under **Alfred the Great**, king of Wessex, one of the seven Anglo-Saxon kingdoms. Under Alfred, the Anglo-Saxon forces pushed the Danes back to the north.

After a time, Alfred was recognized as the ruler of all England. As king, he reorganized the army, issued his own code of laws, and improved his court's financial system. Perhaps his greatest achievement, however, was establishing a system of schools that educated adults as well as children.

362 CHAPTER 12

The Franks Another Germanic kingdom was established in the former Roman province of Gaul—modern France—in the late 400s. That kingdom was established by the Franks. Led by a king named **Clovis**, the Franks defeated their neighbors to build a powerful kingdom.

According to legend, Clovis's victories also led him to adopt Christianity. During a particularly difficult battle, Clovis vowed to become a Christian if his troops won. The Franks did win, and Clovis did become a Christian. In 496 Clovis and 3,000 Franks were baptized in a massive public ceremony.

Under Clovis and his successors, the Franks became one of the major powers of western Europe. The height of Frankish power came in the 800s under a king named Charlemagne. You will read more about him in the next chapter.

READING CHECK **Summarize** How did the Anglo-Saxons and Franks become Christians?

Christian European Society

When Rome fell in the late 400s, Christianity was mostly confined to southern Europe. By about 600, however, the religion had spread northward into other parts of the continent. The conversion of peoples like the Anglo-Saxons and the Franks helped make western Europe into a largely Christian society.

Following Rome's fall, Christianity appealed to many Europeans. Early in this period, known as the Middle Ages or **medieval** (mi-DEE-vuhl) times, many people's lives were filled with doubt, suffering, and hardship. Christianity offered them comfort, the promise of a happy afterlife, and a sense of community.

Spreading Christianity The appeal of Christianity led many Europeans to want to share their beliefs with others. Some people became missionaries, or people who travel to spread their religion. In addition to Augustine of Canterbury, about whom you have already read, many others went to new lands to spread Christian beliefs.

Among the most famous missionaries was Patrick, who went from Britain to Ireland in the 400s. Though he faced opposition and even hostility from some Irish leaders, Patrick continued to preach. By the time he died around 460, nearly all of Ireland was Christian.

Skills Focus: Making Generalizations
Below Level

Reading Skill
Alfred the Great

1. Have students review the information in the text about Alfred the Great, including his many accomplishments.

2. Have students write a poem or a song praising the king and calling out his many accomplishments. In their poems or songs, students should explain why Alfred was called "the Great."

3. Have volunteers share their poems and songs with the class. **LS Auditory-Musical**

Alternative Assessment Handbook, Rubric 26: Poems and Songs

Answers

Reading Check *Monks brought Christianity to Kent, and it slowly spread throughout England.*

Clovis was king of the Franks. He vowed to become a Christian if his troops won.

Through the work of missionaries such as Augustine and Patrick, a Christian society formed that included most of western Europe. Historians call that society **Christendom** (CRI-suhn-duhm). Linked by a common religion and its customs, the people of Christendom saw themselves as a community of believers.

Strengthening the Papacy As the bishop of Rome, it might seem that the pope was in a position to exert great influence over all of Christendom. Early in the Middle Ages, however, most popes had little authority. Many people saw the pope as just another bishop.

This lack of authority ended with **Gregory the Great**, who worked to change views of the papacy. He thought that, as the successor to Peter—one of Jesus' Apostles and considered the first bishop of Rome—the pope was the supreme patriarch of the church. He undertook reforms that strengthened the papacy and canon law, or church law. He encouraged both missionary work and **monasticism**, or voluntary separation from society to dedicate one's life to God. He also encouraged people to care for the poor and less fortunate. Gregory's reforms won respect for the papacy and made the pope one of the most influential figures in Europe.

Sharing Beliefs As Christianity spread through the diverse population of Europe, the eastern Mediterranean, and northern Africa, people interpreted the faith in different ways. Debates arose over questions such as the humanity or divinity of Jesus. In order to prevent or resolve conflicts within the church over such issues, influential theologians, scholars who studied religion, wrote explanations that set forth the church's official positions.

The most influential of these medieval theologians was **Augustine of Hippo**, whose writings helped shape Christian doctrine for centuries. Augustine used ideas of the Greek philosopher Plato to support Christian teachings. In the greatest of his writings, the *City of God*, Augustine argued that people should pay less attention to the material world than they do to God's plan for the world. Written shortly after the sack of Rome by the Visigoths in 410, the *City of God* was an attempt to convince the Romans that God had not abandoned them.

READING CHECK **Infer** How did Christianity change in the early Middle Ages?

Monks and Monasteries

Among the reforms Pope Gregory the Great made was an increased emphasis on monasticism. Gregory, who had been a monk before he became pope, believed that monks played an important role in the church. Many Europeans agreed with him, and monasticism gained popularity in the early Middle Ages.

Monasticism was not new. The first Christian monks had lived in Egypt in the 200s. They usually lived alone as hermits or in small groups. During the Middle Ages, though, a new form of monasticism developed, characterized by groups of monks living in monasteries and abiding by a strict code of rules.

NEW YORK

CC Unit 2-F2
Frankish Empire

CC Unit 2-F5
Spiritual and secular role of the Church

PRIMARY SOURCES

Benedictine Rule

Most monks in Europe during the early Middle Ages lived by a strict set of guidelines called the Benedictine Rule, written by Benedict of Nursia. The rule governed nearly every aspect of monastic life, from how monks spent their time to how they dressed.

"Idleness is the enemy of the soul. And therefore, at fixed times, the brothers ought to be occupied in manual labour; and again, at fixed times, in sacred reading . . . There shall certainly be appointed one or two elders, who shall go round the monastery at the hours in which the brothers are engaged in reading, and see to it that no troublesome brother chance to be found who is open to idleness and trifling, and is not intent on his reading; being not only of no use to himself, but also stirring up others . . .

Vestments [clothing] shall be given to the brothers according to the quality of the places where they dwell, or the temperature of the air. For in cold regions more is required; but in warm, less. This, therefore, is a matter for the abbot to decide. We nevertheless consider that for ordinary places there suffices for the monks a cowl and a gown apiece—the cowl, in winter hairy, in summer plain or old—and a working garment, on account of their labours. As clothing for the feet, shoes and boots."

Skills FOCUS **READING LIKE A HISTORIAN**

1. **Describe** How did monks dress?
2. **Analyze** What activities took up a monk's time?
See *Skills Handbook*, p. H25

KINGDOMS AND CHRISTIANITY **363**

Reading Focus

2 What characteristics defined Christian European society? *missionaries, monasticism, Christians saw themselves as a community of believers, debates among theologians*

Christian European Society

Define What is meant by the term Christendom? *the Christian society that included most of western Europe, a community of believers*

Analyze Why did the message of comfort and promise of a meaningful afterlife appeal to people during the medieval period? *possible answer— Life was difficult; people suffered many hardships during their lives.*

Info to Know

St. Patrick St. Patrick, the patron saint of Ireland, lit hills on fire because the Irish were used to worshipping their gods with fire, and he incorporated the sun, an Irish symbol, into the cross which is now referred to as the Celtic cross. Many legends involve St. Patrick. For example, one legend claims that it was Patrick who drove snakes out of Ireland. It is also said that he used the shamrock as a tool for explaining the Trinity. St. Patrick's Day is celebrated on March 17, the anniversary of his death.

Differentiating Instruction

At Level

English-Language Learners

Standard English Mastery

1. Have students review the information in the textbook about Patrick, Gregory the Great, and Augustine of Hippo.

2. Guide students in a discussion of the accomplishments of these three figures, and have students take notes during the class discussion. You might wish to have students meet in mixed-ability pairs to review the class notes.

3. Have students select the individual they believe was the most influential. Then have students use the class notes to write

a brief essay or paragraph explaining the accomplishments of their selected individual. Remind students to use proper vocabulary, sentence structure, and grammar in their writing. You might wish to have students meet again in mixed-ability pairs to review and correct their writing, if necessary.

LS Verbal-Linguistic

Alternative Assessment Handbook, Rubric 37: Writing Assignments

Answers

Primary Sources 1. *a cowl, a gown, a working garment, shoes and boots;* **2.** *manual labor, sacred reading*

Reading Check *Christianity spread throughout Europe, the pope became one of the most influential figures in Europe, and different interpretations arose.*

3 What roles did monks and monasteries play in European religion and society? *Monks ran schools, copied ancient manuscripts, and served as political aides; monasteries became centers of wealth and power.*

Monks and Monasteries

Make Generalizations What did the different forms of monasticism have in common? *Monks led communal lives based on labor, worship, and scholarship.*

Summarize Who was Benedict, and what was his legacy? *a monk who lived in Italy in the early 500s; wrote the Benedictine Rule and established a monastery; eventually his teachings led to the Benedictine Order*

Interpreting Maps
Missionaries and Monasteries in Europe

Location What city has the highest concentration of monasteries? *Paris*

Movement Which missionary traveled the furthest? *Columban*

Human/Environment Interaction Based on this map, where do you think the largest centers of Christianity might be? *possible answer—around Paris, central, northeastern area of England, central Scotland*

 Map Transparency: Missionaries and Monasteries in Europe

Not all monks in Europe lived by the same rules. Two main forms of monastic life became common in Europe in the early Middle Ages. Although both forms had similar rules about a communal life based on labor, worship, and scholarship, the organization and details of life in their monasteries were quite different.

 NEW YORK

CC Unit 2-F6 Monastic centers of learning

Benedictines The most common form of monasticism in most of Europe during the Middle Ages was Benedictine monasticism. It was based on a rule written by a monk named Benedict of Nursia, who lived in Italy in the early 500s. This rule, or collection of guidelines for monks, is called the **Benedictine Rule**.

Benedict was the son of a Roman noble, but as a young man he abandoned the city to become a hermit. His dedication to God inspired a number of other Christians, who wanted to live as he did. In 529 they persuaded Benedict to establish a monastery at Monte Cassino in central Italy with himself as its first **abbot**, or leader. In time, other monasteries adopted Benedict's teachings as guides for their lives as well. This adoption marked the beginning of the Benedictine Order, or type, of monasticism. Each monk who joined the Benedictine Order had to take vows of poverty and obedience.

MISSIONARIES AND MONASTERIES IN EUROPE

Celtic monasteries were famed for their strictness, scholarship, and missionary efforts.

- Monastery
- c. 539 Date of monastery's founding
- Route of missionary
- (c. 863) Date of missionary's journey

Benedict of Nursia, who created the Benedictine Rule, is shown praying with monks in this painting from the 1500s.

GEOGRAPHY SKILLS INTERPRETING MAPS

1. **Location** In what parts of western Europe were most early monasteries located?
2. **Movement** Where did the missionary Columban come from? Where did he travel?

364 CHAPTER 12

Skills Focus: Making Generalizations

At Level

Reading Skill
Benedict of Nursia

1. Have students review the information on Benedict and his accomplishments. Guide students in a discussion of his importance in the history of the monasticism.

2. Have students write an obituary for Benedict, calling out his accomplishments and his place in history. If students are unfamiliar with obituaries, you might wish to bring in the local newspaper and share the obituary pages with students.

3. Have volunteers share their obituaries with the class. **LS Verbal-Linguistic**

Alternative Assessment Handbook, Rubric 37: Writing Assignments

Answers

Interpreting Maps 1. *England and France;* **2.** *He came from Ireland and traveled through France.*

The Benedictine Rule was based on a combination of prayer and labor. It outlined a schedule for a monk's day, including nine distinct prayer services and periods of work. Sometimes this work consisted of farm labor, and sometimes it involved copying manuscripts from the monastery library. The rule also set up the organization of the Benedictine Order. Each Benedictine monastery was a distinct entity. There was no central authority that governed them all. Instead, each monastery was run by an abbot chosen either by the monks themselves or by a local noble.

Benedictine monasticism made tremendous contributions to Europe. The monks ran schools that trained some of the finest minds of the Middle Ages, including theologians and other writers. By copying ancient manuscripts, they helped preserve the knowledge of Greece and Rome. In addition, their monasteries became centers of wealth and power, because kings and nobles donated money or gifts in exchange for prayers said on their behalf. As they became wealthier, the monasteries were drawn into local politics. Many monks acted as advisers and aides to local and national rulers in Europe.

Celtic Monasteries Not all European monasteries were run according to the Benedictine Rule. A second major branch of monasticism, which historians refer to as Celtic (KEL-tik) monasticism, developed in Ireland.

In general, Celtic monks were more ascetic, or severe, than Benedictines. Monks often took part in long fasts and spent days at a time in solitary contemplation. Many Celtic monasteries were built on small islands far offshore to more fully separate the monks from the rest of society. The monks believed that this isolation would help them stay focused on their faith.

Like Benedictine houses, Celtic monasteries were led by abbots. Celtic abbots had greater authority than their Benedictine counterparts. In mainland Europe, the most important religious officials were the bishops who headed the church in each city. Because Ireland had no large cities, people did not turn to bishops for spiritual guidance. Instead, they looked to the abbots of local monasteries.

One of the most famous Celtic monasteries was at Lindisfarne, a narrow peninsula that becomes an island at high tide, on the coast of England. Its fame stems from the Lindisfarne Gospels, a beautifully illustrated manuscript of the Gospels produced between 715 and 720. The Lindisfarne Gospels are among the greatest artistic achievements of the Middle Ages.

Many Celtic monks were scholars, running schools and preserving ancient knowledge. Other monks from Celtic monasteries were active missionaries, working to spread Christianity to the people of the British Isles. Some monks even traveled to the mainland to build Celtic monasteries in France and Germany.

ACADEMIC VOCABULARY

entity having an independent or separate existence

READING CHECK **Make Generalizations** What contributions did monks make to Europe?

SECTION 3 ASSESSMENT

go.hrw.com
Online Quiz
Keyword: SHL CHR HP

Reviewing Ideas, Terms, and People

1. **a. Identify** Who was **Alfred the Great**, and for what is he best known?
   b. Explain What led to the conversion of the Franks to Christianity?
   c. Elaborate Why do you think western Europe broke apart into small kingdoms rather than remaining unified after the fall of Rome?

2. **a. Recall** What did Patrick achieve in Ireland?
   b. Summarize What were the major achievements of Pope **Gregory the Great**?
   c. Extend How do you think the idea of **Christendom** affected life in **medieval** Europe?

3. **a. Describe** What was daily life like for the monks who lived in Celtic monasteries?
   b. Compare and Contrast How were Benedictine and Celtic monasteries similar? How were they different?
   c. Support a Position What do you think was the most significant role played by Benedictine monasteries in Europe? Support your answer.

Critical Thinking

4. **Analyzing** Use your notes and a concept map like the one below to describe how the spread of Christianity in western Europe affected various aspects of daily life. Add more ovals as necessary.

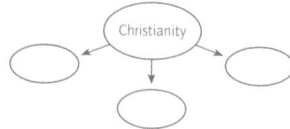

FOCUS ON WRITING

5. **Description** Write a paragraph describing a day in the life of a monk in a Benedictine or Celtic monastery. In your paragraph, explain what activities the monk performed throughout a typical day.

Section 3 Assessment Answers

1. **a.** ruler of England, united the Anglo-Saxons
   b. the king's vow to convert
   c. possible answer—With no central authority, it was easier for separate kingdoms to form.

2. **a.** converted the Irish
   b. made pope an influential figure in Europe
   c. possible answer—created a sense of community

3. **a.** severe, ascetic, solitary
   b. similar—focused on scholarship, faith; different—Celtic monks more ascetic.
   c. preserved ancient knowledge, provided spiritual guidance

4. common religion, customs, provided education

5. Student paragraphs should describe the daily life of a monk.

Answers

Reading Check *ran schools, preserved the knowledge of Greece and Rome, served as advisers and aides to European rulers*

Document-Based Investigation

Views of a Ruler

Word Help

amenable responsible; open to following advice

discrepancies areas of disagreement

dissembling concealing facts, intentions, or feelings

guileful deceitfully cunning

illustrious notably outstanding

Info to Know

Religion or Politics? The church of San Vitale in Ravenna, Italy, was built during Justinian's reign. The interior is richly decorated with fine mosaic work. Traditionally, the decoration of churches allows worshippers to focus on their faith and recall figures associated with their faith, such as the Holy Family and saints. Modest depictions of benefactors sometimes appear on church walls. In San Vitale, however, two large panels flank the altar itself. One depicts Justinian, and the other, Theodora, his empress. The design of the mosaics leads the viewer to imagine Justinian as a Christ figure, and Theodora as the Virgin Mary.

Justin and Justinian Emperor Justinian was not of noble background. He first came to Constantinople at the request of Justin, his uncle. Justin was an illiterate peasant from near Naissus (modern Serbia). He had entered the imperial army, rising to the position of officer, and finally become commander. When Anastasius I died without designating a successor, the senate made Justin the new Byzantine emperor. Justin named his nephew Justinian as his co-ruler. When Justin died a few months later, Justinian I became emperor.

Views of a Ruler

Historical Context The documents in this investigation describe different aspects of Justinian I and his rule of the Byzantine Empire.

Task Study the documents below and answer the questions that follow. Then, using evidence from the documents and from the chapter, write an essay about how to evaluate Justinian's rule.

NEW YORK STANDARDS

PI 2.3 Students analyze evidence critically and demonstrate an understanding of how circumstances of time and place influence perspective.

DOCUMENT 1

Justinian's Code

Early in his reign, Justinian ordered scholars to collect and organize all Roman laws into a single code of law. This excerpt is from *The Institutes*, the part of Justinian's Code that served as a guide for law students.

> Justice is the set and constant purpose which gives to every man his due. Jurisprudence is the knowledge of things divine and human, the science of the just and the unjust . . .

The precepts of the law are these: to live honestly, to injure no one, and to give every man his due. The study of law consists of two branches, law public and law private. The former relates to the welfare of the Roman State; the latter to the advantage of the individual citizen. Of private law then we may say that it is of threefold origin, being collected from the precepts of nature, from those of the law of nations, or from those of the civil law of Rome.

DOCUMENT 2

Justinian and His Attendants

This famous mosaic panel from the Church of San Vitale in Ravenna, Italy, was created in 547. It shows Emperor Justinian I surrounded by symbols of earthly and heavenly power. Justinian stands in the center, dressed in purple with a golden halo. He is flanked on the right by Bishop Maximian and the clergy and on the left by imperial officials and military officers. Although Justinian never visited Ravenna, the city was the seat of Byzantine authority in Italy.

Justinian and Attendants, Church of San Vitale, Ravenna, Italy, c. 547

366 CHAPTER 12

Skills Focus: Analyzing Primary Sources

At Level

Prep Required

Reading Like a Historian Skill
Justinian's Laws

Materials: translated copy of Justinian's *The Institutes* (can be found on the Internet)

1. Print out a copy of *The Institutes* and post it in the classroom for students to see. Remind students that Justinian is known for simplifying the legal code of his empire.

2. Organize students into small groups. Have each group choose one law and copy it down. Next, have groups discuss the merits and drawbacks of the law and record their

comments. If time allows, groups may select a second law for consideration.

3. Allow time for each group to present its law and comments to the class.

4. As homework, have students write their overall impression about Justinian's laws.

LS Interpersonal, Verbal-Linguistic

Alternative Assessment Handbook, Rubrics 11: Discussions; and 14: Group Activity

DOCUMENT 3

Procopius as Official Historian

Hailed as the last of the great ancient historians, Procopius served as Justinian's official historian. The excerpt below is from *On Buildings*, Procopius's account of the public works undertaken by Justinian.

In our own age there has been born the Emperor Justinian, who, taking over the State when it was harassed by disorder, has not only made it greater in extent, but also much more illustrious, by expelling from it those barbarians who had from of old pressed hard upon it . . . But this Sovereign does not lack the skill to produce completely transformed states—witness the way he has already added to the Roman domain many states which in his own times had belonged to others, and has created countless cities which did not exist before. And finding that the belief in God was, before his time, straying into errors and being forced to go in many directions, he completely destroyed all the paths leading to such errors, and brought it about that it stood on the firm foundation of a single faith. Moreover, finding the laws obscure because they had become far more numerous than they should be, and in obvious confusion because they disagreed with each other, he preserved them by cleansing them of the mass of their verbal trickery, and by controlling their discrepancies.

DOCUMENT 4

Procopius as Secret Historian

Between writing glowing accounts of Justinian's military successes and public works projects, Procopius wrote a book about Justinian commonly known as the *Secret History*. In this work, Procopius paints quite a different picture of the emperor.

Now such was Justinian in appearance; but his character was something I could not fully describe. For he was at once villainous and amenable; as people say colloquially, a moron. He was never truthful with anyone, but always guileful in what he said and did, yet easily hoodwinked by any who wanted to deceive him. His nature was an unnatural mixture of folly and wickedness . . . This Emperor, then, was deceitful, devious, false, hypocritical, two-faced, cruel, skilled in dissembling his thought, never moved to tears by either joy or pain, though he could summon them artfully at will when the occasion demanded, a liar always, not only offhand, but in writing, and when he swore sacred oaths to his subjects in their very hearing. Then he would immediately break his agreements and pledges, like the vilest of slaves, whom indeed only the fear of torture drives to confess their perjury.

Skills FOCUS — READING LIKE A HISTORIAN

DOCUMENT 1
a. **Describe** What basic rules guide Justinian's law?
b. **Elaborate** How does this excerpt affect your evaluation of Justinian's character?

DOCUMENT 2
a. **Describe** Which details from the mosaic symbolize Justinian's earthly and spiritual powers?
b. **Interpret** Some historians have called this mosaic an early example of political propaganda. Do you agree or disagree? Explain.

DOCUMENT 3
a. **Identify** According to Procopius, how did Justinian transform states?
b. **Explain** For what audience might Procopius have written this account?

DOCUMENT 4
a. **Compare** How does this description of Justinian compare to the one in Document 3?
b. **Evaluate** What may account for the difference between the opinions in *On Buildings* and the *Secret History*?

DOCUMENT-BASED ESSAY QUESTION

Historians often have to interpret contradictory, incomplete, and biased information. How does one balance evidence from different sources? How should the sources on Justinian be evaluated? Do they tell us that he was a tyrant or a great ruler? Using these documents and the chapter, write an essay evaluating Justinian's rule.

See **Skills Handbook**, pp. H25, H26

Skills Focus: Comparing and Contrasting

At Level

Reading Skill
Two Works by Procopius

1. Copy the chart for all to see. Omit the italicized answers. Have students copy and complete the chart.

2. Guide a class discussion about the two documents. Ask students what might account for the differences. Ask students about evidence of bias in both documents. **LS** **Visual-Spatial**

   Alternative Assessment Handbook, Rubrics 7: Charts; and 9: Comparing and Contrasting

Official History (Document 3)	Secret History (Document 4)
Justinian: *rid the empire of barbarians, added territory, created cities, strengthened religion, reformed the law code*	**Justinian:** *villainous and untruthful, easily fooled, a liar*

Document-Based Investigation

Biography

Procopius (c. 499–565) Procopius was a native of Palestine. Literary and legal training prepared him to serve as secretary and advisor to Belisarius, Justinian's top general. Procopius continued in civil service, and may have become a senator. He wrote eight books that provide a detailed history of several wars from about 527 to 554. Procopius then wrote a flattering treatise about the public works of Emperor Justinian, and six books of memoirs. One of these last volumes was so critical of Justinian that it wasn't translated or published until over a thousand years later. Procopius earned the honorary title, "illustris" and is recognized as the greatest historian of his time.

Answers

Reading Like a Historian
Document 1. a. *to live honestly, to injure no one, and to give every man his due;* **b.** *possible answer—It gives the impression that Justinian is a wise and compassionate ruler.* **Document 2. a.** *earthly power: purple robe, crown, jeweled robe clasp, imperial officials and military officers, shield; spiritual power: halo, religious text, incensory, clergy;* **b.** *possible answer—agree: the mosaic was placed for public viewing in a powerful city; presents Justinian as powerful ruler supported by the Church;* **Document 3. a.** *by enlarging them, expelling barbarians, creating new cities, unifying the faith, and simplifying the laws;* **b.** *for Justinian's approval, and by those people Justinian wished to influence;* **Document 4. a.** *Document 3 focuses on Justinian's power and achievements; Document 4 gives a negative view of his personality;* **b.** *Procopius might have written his* Secret History *in private, as it was critical of Justinian;* On Buildings *was likely written for the public;* **Essay** *Student essays should begin with an evaluation about Justinian's rule and be supported by details from the documents.*

367

Answers

Visual Summary

Review and Inquiry Have students complete a Venn diagram showing similarities and differences between the Roman Catholic Church and the Orthodox Church.

🖳 **Quick Facts Transparency**: Visual Study Guide: Kingdoms and Christianity

Review Key Terms and People

1. Cyrillic alphabet
2. icons
3. Yaroslav the Wise
4. Alexander Nevsky
5. monasticism
6. Theodora
7. Benedictine Rule
8. Alfred the Great
9. entity

Comprehension and Critical Thinking

10. a. It was a rebellion against Justinian's reforms; Theodora refused to back down and their top general slaughtered the rioters.
b. theological differences, including the role of icons in worship
c. The empire faced constant invasions, declined due to incompetent emperors, until finally Constantinople fell to the Ottoman Turks.

11. a. in the AD 800s
b. Alexander's forces lured the Teutonic Knights onto the ice, and they fell into the freezing water. The battle helped stop German expansion into Russia.
c. possible answer—The Mongol threat had the longest-lasting impact because it ended the dominance of Kievan Rus.

12. a. Clovis
b. Celtic monasteries had stricter rules than Benedictine monasteries. In both types of monasteries, monks led lives dedicated to scholarship and faith.
c. He used the ideas of the Greek philosopher Plato to support Christian teachings.

QUICK FACTS

VISUAL STUDY GUIDE

Christianity

Roman Catholic Church
- After the fall of the Western Roman Empire, Christianity was preserved in the east.
- The head of the church was, and still is, the pope.
- Monks and missionaries helped spread Roman Catholicism throughout western Europe.
- Roman Catholicism was the main form of Christianity in western Europe for centuries.

Orthodox Church
- The Orthodox Church separated from the western church in 1054 over issues of belief and governance.
- Authority is not centralized, and the pope is not the head of the church.
- Many countries have their own Orthodox churches.
- The Orthodox Church remains the main form of Christianity in southeastern Europe.

Western Christendom
- Establishment of small kingdoms by Germanic groups
- Anglo-Saxon kingdoms in England
- Alfred the Great and the Danes
- Franks in France, Christianized under Clovis
- Missionaries—example: Patrick
- Theologians—example: Augustine of Hippo
- Gregory the Great and power of the papacy
- Growth of monasticism
- Two types of monasteries—Benedictine and Celtic

Byzantine Empire
- Capital at Constantinople—well-situated for trade and defense
- Justinian and Theodora—territorial expansion, Nika Revolt, Justinian's Code
- Emphasis on religion in society and the arts
- Iconoclast movement
- Schism in church in 1054
- Golden age under Macedonian dynasty
- Decline due to internal problems and invasion
- Conquered by Ottoman Turks in 1453

Russia
- The Rus invited to rule over the Slavs on the Dnieper
- Kievan Rus under rule of Yaroslav the Wise
- Cyril, Methodius, the spread of Christianity, and Cyrillic alphabet
- Christianity made state religion under Vladimir I
- Mongol conquest
- Threats from Swedes and German knights averted by Alexander Nevsky
- Decline of Kiev and rise of Muscovy

Review Key Terms and People

Identify the term or person from the chapter that best fits each of the following descriptions.

1. alphabet developed for the Slavonic language
2. paintings or sculptures of sacred figures
3. ruler of Kievan Rus during its height
4. defended Russia from Teutonic Knights

5. voluntary separation from society in order to dedicate one's life to God
6. wife of Emperor Justinian I and his co-ruler
7. a list of rules that monks followed
8. king of Wessex who united the English to push the Danes back to the north
9. having an independent or separate existence

Analyzing Primary Sources

13. He hoped that if the temples were not destroyed, the people might be converted to Christianity.

14. by sprinkling their temples with holy water, setting up altars, and depositing relics

15. possible answer—This instruction may have helped increase Christianity's appeal in England.

History's Impact video program
Review the video to answer the closing question:
What impact has Christianity had on the world?

Comprehension and Critical Thinking

SECTION 1 *(pp. 347–353)*

10. a. Recall What was the Nika Revolt, and how did it end?

b. Explain What caused the split between the Orthodox Church and the Roman Catholic Church?

c. Elaborate Why did the Byzantine Empire eventually fall?

SECTION 2 *(pp. 356–360)*

11. a. Recall About when did the Slavs of Russia enter the historical record?

b. Describe What happened during the massacre on the ice, and why was the battle significant?

c. Evaluate Of the threats that Kievan Rus faced, which had the longest-lasting impact?

SECTION 3 *(pp. 361–365)*

12. a. Identify Which king united the Franks?

b. Compare How did Benedictine and Celtic monasteries differ? How were they alike?

c. Elaborate How did Augustine of Hippo influence Christian doctrine?

Analyzing Primary Sources

Reading Like a Historian *The following passage is from a message from Pope Gregory to a bishop in England. It advises the bishop not to destroy the pagan temples there.*

> **❝** [We] have come to the conclusion that the temples of the idols among [the English] people should on no account be destroyed. The idols are to be destroyed, but the temples themselves are to be aspersed [sprinkled] with holy water, altars set up in them, and relics deposited there . . . In this way, we hope that the people, seeing that their temples are not destroyed, may abandon their error . . . may come to know and adore the true God. **❞**
> —Pope Gregory the Great, *Message to Bishop Augustine,* 601

13. Why did Pope Gregory instruct the English bishop not to destroy pagan temples?

14. How did Pope Gregory hope to convert the residents of England to Christianity?

15. How do you think Pope Gregory's instruction to the English bishop affected the growth of Christianity in England?

Using the Internet

go.hrw.com
Practice Online
Keyword: SHL CHR

16. In the Byzantine Empire, new styles developed in art and architecture. Using the keyword above, do research to learn more about art and architecture of the Byzantine period. Then sketch a design for a picture or building in the Byzantine style.

Reading Skills

Understanding Sequencing *Use what you know about understanding sequencing to answer the questions below.*

17. Which of these events happened first?

A. the rise of Kievan Rus

B. the invitation from the Slavs to the Rus

C. the attacks by the Swedes and Teutonic Knights

D. the rise of Muscovy

18. Which of the following correctly describes the timing of the attack on Constantinople by Ottoman Turks?

A. occurred during the reign of Justinian

B. prevented the Nika Revolt

C. caused the final fall of the Byzantine Empire

D. preceded the split within the Christian Church

WRITING FOR THE SAT

Think about the following issue:

After the fall of Rome, the power of the Roman Empire shifted east to Constantinople and gave rise to the Byzantine Empire. The Byzantines played a key role in preserving and transmitting Greek and Roman culture. They are also remembered for their many contributions to law, art, architecture, and the development of Christianity.

19. Assignment: Was the Byzantine Empire primarily a conservative force that preserved Greek and Roman traditions, or was it mostly a creative force that gave rise to new political, religious, and cultural traditions? Or was it both? Write a short essay in which you develop your position on this issue. Support your point of view with reasoning and examples from your reading and studies.

Answers

Using the Internet

16. Go to the HRW Web site and enter the keyword shown to access a rubric for this activity.

KEYWORD: SHL CHR

Reading Skills

17. B.

18. B.

Writing for the SAT

19. Student essays should choose a position about the role of the Byzantine Empire. Essays should support the chosen position with logical reasoning and details from the chapter.
A rubric for this activity is provided in **CRF:** Writing for the SAT.

HOLT

History's Impact
▶ **Video Program: Kingdoms and Christianity**
Refer to the Video Program Teacher's Guide for the answer to the closing question.

Review and Assessment Resources

Review and Reinforce

📄 **CRF:** Chapter Review

🗄 **Quick Facts Transparency:** Visual Study Guide: Kingdoms and Christianity

🔊 **Spanish Chapter Summaries Audio CD Program**

OSP **Holt PuzzlePro:** Quiz Show for ExamView

💿 **Quiz Game CD-ROM**

Assess

📄 **PASS:** Chapter Test, Forms A and B

📄 **Alternative Assessment Handbook**

OSP **ExamView Test Generator,** Chapter Test

💿 **Differentiated Instruction Modified Worksheets and Tests CD-ROM:** Chapter Test

HOAP **Holt Online Assessment Program** (in the Premier Online Edition)

Reteach/Intervene

📄 **Interactive Reader and Study Guide**

📄 **Differentiated Instruction Teacher Management System:** Lesson Plans for Differentiated Instruction

💿 **Differentiated Instruction Modified Worksheets and Tests CD-ROM:** Chapter Test

💿 **Interactive Skills Tutor CD-ROM**

go.hrw.com
Online Resources

KEYWORD: SHL TEACHER

The Early Middle Ages

Chapter Overview	Reproducible Resources	Technology Resources
CHAPTER 13 pp. 370–399 **Overview:** In this chapter, students will learn about the widespread changes in religion and politics throughout Europe during the Early Middle Ages. KI 2, 3, 4; PI 2.4, 2.5, 3.1, 3.2, 4.2 See pp. T32–T55 for a detailed correlation to the New York State Core Curriculum for Global History and Geography and the New York Learning Standards.	**Differentiated Instruction Teacher Management System:*** • Pacing Guide • Lesson Plans for Differentiated Instruction **Interactive Reader and Study Guide:** Chapter Summary* **Chapter Resource File*** • Writing for the SAT • Social Studies Skill • Chapter Review **World History Outline Maps**	OSP **New York One-Stop Planner CD-ROM:** Calendar Planner **Live Ink© Online Reading Help** **Student Edition on Audio CD Program** **Differentiated Instruction Modified Worksheets and Tests CD-ROM** **Interactive Skills Tutor CD-ROM** **World History Primary Source Library CD-ROM** **History's Impact: World History Video Program (VHS/DVD):** The Early Middle Ages
Section 1: **Charlemagne's Empire** **The Main Idea:** Through conquest and social change, Charlemagne tied much of western Europe together in a single empire. PI 2.4, 2.5	**Interactive Reader and Study Guide:** Section 1 Summary* **Chapter Resource File*** • Vocabulary Builder: Section 1 • Biography: Einhard • Literature: Legends of Charlemagne	**Map Transparency:** Europe, 815* **Map Transparency:** Europe, 1215* **Quick Facts Transparency:** Charlemagne's Achievements* **Internet Activity:** Charlemagne
Section 2: **New Invaders** **The Main Idea:** Invasions and migrations changed the political and cultural landscapes of western Europe during the early Middle Ages. PI 3.2	**Interactive Reader and Study Guide:** Section 2 Summary* **Chapter Resource File*** • Vocabulary Builder: Section 2 • Biography: al-Masudi • Primary Source: A Viking Funeral	**Regents Review Transparency:** Section 2* **Map Transparency:** Vikings, Magyars, and Muslims, 800–1000*
Section 3: **The Feudal and Manorial Systems** **The Main Idea:** In Europe, during the Middle Ages, the feudal and manorial systems governed life and required people to perform certain duties and obligations. PI 3.1	**Differentiated Instruction Teacher Management System:** Section 3 Lesson Plan* **Interactive Reader and Study Guide:** Section 3 Summary* **Chapter Resource File*** • Vocabulary Builder: Section 3 • Biography: Chretien de Troyes	**Regents Review Transparency:** Section 3* **Quick Facts Transparency:** Feudal Obligations* **Internet Activity:** The Middle Ages
Section 4: **The Growth of Monarchies** **The Main Idea:** The power of kings grew and the nature of monarchy changed across Europe in the early Middle Ages. PI 2.5, 3.1	**Interactive Reader and Study Guide:** Section 4 Summary* **Chapter Resource File*** • Vocabulary Builder: Section 4 • Biography: Christine de Pizan • History and Geography: The Treaty of Verdun	**Regents Review Transparency:** Section 4* **Map Transparency:** The Holy Roman Empire*
Section 5: **Power of the Church** **The Main Idea:** Reform and changes swept through the Christian Church, one of the most influential institutions in medieval Europe. PI 2.5, 3.1, 4.2	**Differentiated Instruction Teacher Management System:** Section 5 Lesson Plan* **Interactive Reader and Study Guide:** Section 5 Summary* **Chapter Resource File*** • Biography: Thomas Becket	**Regents Review Transparency:** Section 5*

 go.hrw.com	 Print Resource	 Transparency
LS Learning Styles	 Audio CD	 CD-ROM
 Video	**SE** Student Edition	**TE** Teachers Edition

OSP One-Stop Planner CD-ROM   NY Standards Mastery
*also on One-Stop Planner CD-ROM

HOLT
History's Impact
World History Video Program (VHS/DVD)
The Early Middle Ages

Review, Assessment, Intervention

- **Global History and Geography Regents Test Prep Workbook**
- **Quick Facts Transparency:** The Early Middle Ages*
- **Program Assessment Support System (PASS):** Chapter Test*
- **Differentiated Instruction Modified Worksheets and Tests CD-ROM:** Modified Chapter Test
- **OSP New York One-Stop Planner CD-ROM:** ExamView Test Generator (English/Spanish)
- **HOAP Holt Online Assessment Program (HOAP),** in the Holt Premier Online Student Edition

---

- **PASS:** Section 1 Quiz*
- **Online Quiz:** Section 1
- **Alternative Assessment Handbook**

- **PASS:** Section 2 Quiz*
- **Online Quiz:** Section 2
- **Alternative Assessment Handbook**

- **PASS:** Section 3 Quiz*
- **Online Quiz:** Section 3
- **Alternative Assessment Handbook**

- **PASS:** Section 4 Quiz*
- **Online Quiz:** Section 4
- **Alternative Assessment Handbook**

- **PASS:** Section 5 Quiz*
- **Online Quiz:** Section 5
- **Alternative Assessment Handbook**

Power Presentation with Video CD-ROM

Power Presentations with Video are visual presentations of each chapter's main ideas. Presentations can be customized by including Quick Facts charts, images and maps from the textbook, and video clips.

Holt Online Learning

go.hrw.com
Teacher Resources
KEYWORD: SHL TEACHER

go.hrw.com
Student Resources
KEYWORD: SHL EMA

- Document-Based Questions
- Interactive Multimedia Activities

- Current Events
- Chapter-Based Internet Activities
- and more!

Holt Premier
Online Student Edition
Complete online support for interactivity, assessment, and reporting

- Interactive Maps and Notebook
- Homework Practice and Research Activities Online

CHAPTER 13 PLANNING GUIDE

The Big Picture

Peter N. Stearns

Early Medieval Politics The collapse of the Roman Empire led to chaotic political conditions in Western Europe, though a few tribal monarchies existed and in the Catholic Church provided some wider organization for the region. A brief but important exception emerged with Charlemagne, whose empire was not sustained after his death. Political division and frequent conflict were important parts of European history from this period until recently. Immediately after the Carolingian system broke down, additional invasions added to confusion. Two systems, along with the church organization, provided some political framework, though initially on a highly localized basis. Feudal ties linked levels of the military aristocracy with bonds based on loyalty and mutual obligation. Manorialism was a more economic system, providing some protection to peasants in return for payments and work service to their lords.

Political Change By about the 10th century, political conditions began to stabilize a bit, and invasions declined. European agriculture improved, population grew, and cities expanded. This was not yet an advanced economy, but there were resources available for more elaborate political structures. In several regions leaders were able to use feudal relationships to bolster the power of monarchies. Feudal monarchies very gradually developed some bureaucracy and greater independence of action; but resistance from feudal lords helped lead to the Magna Carta (not an important document at the time) and to the feudal version of parliaments, a significant innovation. Britain and France led the way here. Other parts of Europe remained more divided. Spain had been under Muslim rule during previous centuries, and considerable religious toleration flourished among Muslims, Jews and Christians, providing opportunities for other European scholars to borrow from Islamic society. But by the 10th century, Christian military leaders began to press the Muslims, establishing new Christian kingdoms in much of the peninsula.

Religion The spread and consolidation of Christianity was also a key feature of medieval Europe. Church institutions solidified, not only papacy, but also the monastic system. Clashes between church and state punctuated the period. Various reform movements periodically worked to restore religious devotion to an institution whose wealth and power often competed with spirituality.

Recent Scholarship

Old World Encounters: Cross-Cultural Contacts and Exchanges in Pre-Modern Times (1993), by one of the leading current world historians in the United States, Jerry H. Bentley, deals with travels and connections among different societies, mainly in Europe and Asia, from early civilizations until 1450. The book has helped stimulate a growing interest in the whole subject of contacts as a central way to approach world history. A major section treats the period 600-1000. The key topic here, the spread of missionary activity, helps put the dissemination of Christianity in western Europe, from Italian centers northward, in wider perspective. Bentley compares the process to the contemporary activities of Buddhist and Hindu merchants and missionaries, and to the intriguing history of Nestorian Christianity. Seeing early medieval Europe in the perspective of comparisons and wider contacts adds vital perspective.

Differentiating Instruction

Differentiated Instruction Teacher Management System
- Pacing Guides
- Lesson Plans for Differentiated Instruction

Interactive Reader and Study Guide

Spanish Chapter Summaries Audio CD Program

Student Edition on Audio CD Program

 Differentiated Instruction Modified Worksheets and Tests CD-ROM
- Vocabulary Flash Cards
- Modified Vocabulary Builder Activities
- Modified Chapter Review Activity
- Modified Chapter Test

OSP One-Stop Planner CD-ROM
- ExamView Test Generator (English/Spanish)
- PuzzlePro
- Quiz Show for ExamView
- Transparencies and Videos

TE Differentiated Activities in the Teacher's Edition
- Crowning of Charlemagne, p. 374
- Hero Sagas, p. 379
- The Magyar Regions Today, p. 380
- Feudal and Manorial Systems, p. 384
- Life on a Medieval Manor, p. 385
- Writing a Biography, p. 388
- Power of the Papacy, p. 394
- Paraphrasing Documents, p. 397

Reading Like a Historian
Sam Wineburg

Historical Inquiry History is told in words that reveal and conceal. Readers of historical narratives must pay careful attention to the words authors choose when describing past events. Behind seemingly minor choices lay a vast terrain of historical inquiry.

For example, when narrating Charlemagne's reign, our chapter notes that he "wanted to preserve and spread" his beliefs. We are told that Charlemagne "ordered the people he conquered to convert to Christianity. He then sent monks and missionaries to live among the conquered people to help Christianity take root."How was Christianity "spread"? What kind of "help" was offered? Is there any link between what conversion meant in the 8th century and how we use that term today, to denote a change in one's belief in God?

The longest military campaigns of Charlemagne's reign were against the Saxons, a pagan people from Northern Europe, organized into marauding bands and tribes. The Christian Franks had warred with the Saxons for generations. After each victory the Franks typically imposed a tribute on the Saxons, along with an agreement that Christian missionaries could proselytize unfettered in Saxon lands. In 782, however, all of this changed.

In that year, the charismatic Saxon rebel Prince Widukind led a revolt against Frankish rule. He scored a major victory at the Süntel Mountains, a battle in which Charlemagne's two closest advisors, Adalgisile and Geilo, were killed. Charlemagne had enough and set out to crush the Saxons once and for all. On a single day at Verden, Charlemagne not only vanquished the Saxons, but ordered his soldiers to assemble 4,500 men, women, and children and behead each in a bloodbath of epic proportions. Charlemagne likened himself to a Biblical King David justifying this murder as his own version of David eradicating the Moabites. But this was only the start of the work to be done. Religion became an arm of imperial policy.

Grave Consequences To Charlemagne and his advisors, the real problem with the Saxons was that their oaths meant little because they swore to a pagan god. Peace could only be realized between peoples who recognized the one true God. Therefore, Charlemagne imposed a legal code, the Capitulary of Saxony, intended to uproot paganism from Saxon lands.

Composed of 34 clauses, the Capitulary demanded that each Saxon accept baptism and profess faith in Christ: "If any one of the race of the Saxons hereafter concealed among them shall have wished to hide himself unbaptized, and shall have scorned to come to baptism and shall have wished to remain a pagan, let him be punished by death."

Beyond requiring conversion under penalty of death, the code meted out unyielding punishments for even the slightest infractions of Christian practice. Consider the fate of a meat-eater during Lent: "If any one, out of contempt for Christianity, shall have despised the holy Lenten fast and shall have eaten flesh, let him be punished by death." If a Saxon was caught cremating the body of a departed loved one instead of burying it, the punishment was also death. Likewise for refusing to fast on Fridays. Religious infractions that outside of Saxony would receive a penance or fine became capital offences.

The Capitulary of Saxony provides clues about the fate that awaited those who resisted Charlemagne's order. A court chronicler described the decision before the vanquished in the starkest of terms: "Either they were defeated and subjugated to the Christian religion or completely swept away."

In 8th century Saxony, conversion to Christianity had little to do with words like faith or belief. Disobeying Charlemagne's "order" carried the gravest consequences. It was literally a matter of life or death.

Chapter Main Ideas

Section 1 Through conquest and social change, Charlemagne tied much of western Europe together in a single empire.

Section 2 Invasions and migrations changed the political and cultural landscapes of western Europe during the early Middle Ages.

Section 3 In Europe, during the Middle Ages, the feudal and manorial systems governed life and required people to perform certain duties and obligations.

Section 4 The power of kings grew and the nature of monarchy changed across Europe in the early Middle Ages.

Section 5 Reform and changes swept through the Christian Church, one of the most influential institutions in medieval Europe.

New York Standards

Key Idea 2 Establishing timeframes, exploring different periodizations, examining themes across time and within cultures, and focusing on important turning points in world history help organize the study of world cultures and civilizations.

Key Idea 3 Study of the major social, political, cultural, and religious developments in world history involves learning about the important roles and contributions of individuals and groups.

Key to Differentiating Instruction

Below Level

Basic-level activities designed for all students encountering new material

At Level

Intermediate-level activities designed for average students

Above Level

Challenging activities designed for honors and gifted and talented students

Standard English Mastery

Activities designed to improve standard English usage

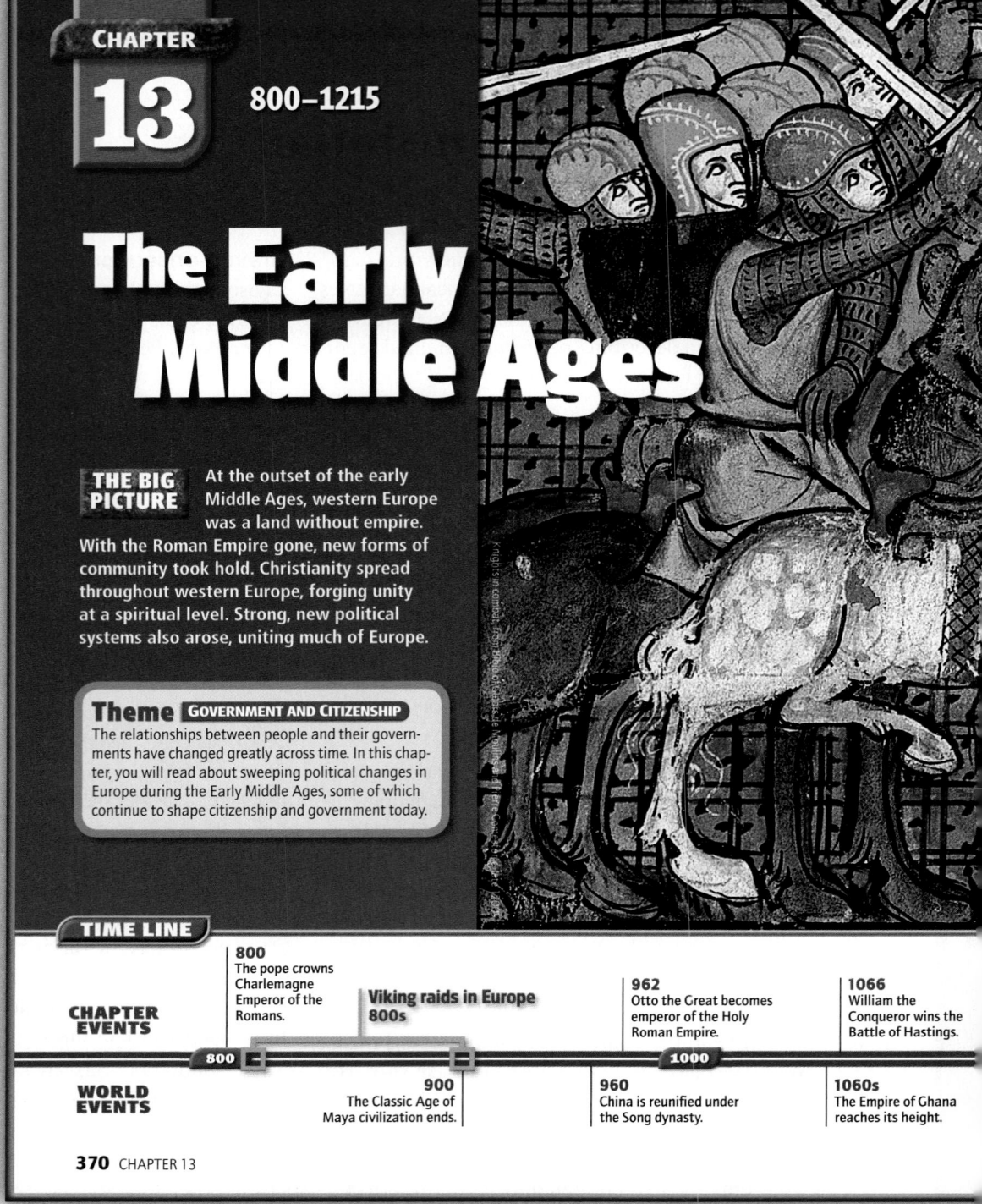

CHAPTER

13   800–1215

The Early Middle Ages

THE BIG PICTURE At the outset of the early Middle Ages, western Europe was a land without empire. With the Roman Empire gone, new forms of community took hold. Christianity spread throughout western Europe, forging unity at a spiritual level. Strong, new political systems also arose, uniting much of Europe.

Theme **GOVERNMENT AND CITIZENSHIP**
The relationships between people and their governments have changed greatly across time. In this chapter, you will read about sweeping political changes in Europe during the Early Middle Ages, some of which continue to shape citizenship and government today.

TIME LINE

CHAPTER EVENTS

800 The pope crowns Charlemagne Emperor of the Romans.

Viking raids in Europe 800s

962 Otto the Great becomes emperor of the Holy Roman Empire.

1066 William the Conqueror wins the Battle of Hastings.

800 — 1000

WORLD EVENTS

900 The Classic Age of Maya civilization ends.

960 China is reunified under the Song dynasty.

1060s The Empire of Ghana reaches its height.

370 CHAPTER 13

Introduce the Chapter

At Level

The Early Middle Ages

1. Tell students in this chapter they will learn about the beginning of the Middle Ages and the process of unification among the European kingdoms.

2. Have students work in pairs to make a list of the images they associate with the Middle Ages: princes, princesses, castles, knights, etc. Then create a class list of these ideas for all to see.

3. Have students copy the class list onto their own papers, and then have each student scan the chapter and add a list of the actual images shown in the chapter.

4. Guide students in a discussion of the similarities and differences between the two lists. If images were missing from the class brainstorm list, have volunteers try to explain the discrepancies. **LS** **Verbal-Linguistic**

Alternative Assessment Handbook, Rubrics 9: Comparing and Contrasting; and 12: Drawing Conclusions

Reading like a Historian

This illustration shows knights in conflict during the Middle Ages. Knights fought in service to kings and nobles, helping them to gain and maintain political power.

Analyzing Visuals What does this scene suggest about warfare in the Early Middle Ages? How accurate do you think this illustration is in showing a medieval battle? Explain your answer.

See **Skills Handbook**, p. H26

1215
King John signs Magna Carta.

1200

1192
The first shogun takes power in Japan.

THE EARLY MIDDLE AGES **371**

• **Chapter Preview** •

HOLT
History's Impact
▶ **Video Program: The Early Middle Ages**
See the Video Teacher's Guide for strategies for using the video segment.

Reading Like a Historian

Analyzing Visuals Remind students that some movies and books depict knights as glamorous individuals with shining armor, riding in the countryside on noble steeds, fighting their enemies. In reality, unless knights were able to make a profit from the land they received as payment from their lord, their armor was likely to be old and ill fitting.

go.hrw.com
Online Resources

Chapter Resources:
KEYWORD: SHL EMA
Teacher Resources:
KEYWORD: SHL TEACHER

Explore the Time Line

1. When did Charlemagne become Emperor of the Romans? *800*

2. Name three events that occurred in the 900s. *The Classic Age of Maya civilization ended; China was reunified under Song dynasty; Otto the Great became emperor of the Holy Roman Empire*

3. How much time passed between the Battle of Hastings and signing of the Magna Carta? *149 years*

Info to Know

The New Era When the pope crowned Charlemagne Emperor of the Romans, a new era began in Europe. Even when faced with Viking invasions, Charlemagne was able to hold onto most of the land. The spread of Christianity brought kingdoms together with a common goal, to preserve their Christian religion and to fight against non-Christian invaders.

Make Inferences Why do think Christianity was so important in achieving and maintaining a more unified Europe? *The majority of the people in Europe were becoming Christian; Christianity became a unifying factor among western Europeans.*

Answers

Reading Like a Historian *possible answers—Knights fought to the death for their lords and kings; image probably was created to glorify battles, and thus might not be completely accurate*

371

Preteach

Geography Starting Points

Europe, 815–1215 In 843, the Treaty of Verdun divided Charlemagne's empire into three, one for each of his grandsons. West Francia later became France; Middle Francia became the Netherlands, Belgium, Luxembourg and the Rhine lands; East Francia was the starting point for the Holy Roman Empire. Charlemagne is sometimes considered the first emperor of the Holy Roman Empire, or the father of Europe.

- **Map Transparencies:** Europe, 815; Europe, 1215
- **World History Outline Maps**
- **Interactive Map:** Europe, 815

MISCONCEPTION ALERT

The Kingdoms of Leon and Castile were not always separate. In 1037, Ferdinand I of Castile joined the two kingdoms as one; upon his death in 1065, the kingdom was split in two by his sons. In 1230, the kingdoms were joined once again and named the Kingdom of Leon and Castile or later the Crown of Castile.

★ Interactive
EUROPE, 815

England was divided into eight small kingdoms.

ANGLO-SAXON KINGDOMS

North Sea

Baltic Sea

SLAVIC STATES

ATLANTIC OCEAN

Paris •
Aachen •

Tours •

FRANKISH EMPIRE

Rhine R.

Danube River

Po River

Charlemagne built the Frankish Empire.

UMAYYAD CALIPHATE
• Córdoba

Tagus R.

Corsica

Rome •

Adriatic Sea

Constantinople •

BYZANTINE EMPIRE

Mediterranean Sea

AFRICA

0   200   400 Miles
0   200   400 Kilometers
Azimuthal equal-area projection

EUROPE, 1215

England was united as one kingdom.

ENGLAND

North Sea

Baltic Sea

POLAND

ATLANTIC OCEAN

FRANCE

HOLY ROMAN EMPIRE

What had been the Frankish Empire was divided into France and the Holy Roman Empire.

LEÓN

NAVARRE

CASTILE   ARAGON

PORTUGAL

ALMOHAD CALIPHATE

HUNGARY

Adriatic Sea

BYZANTINE EMPIRE

KINGDOM OF SICILY

Mediterranean Sea

0   200   400 Miles
0   200   400 Kilometers
Azimuthal equal-area projection

Starting Points In the 800s one major Christian kingdom, the Frankish Empire, ruled a huge portion of western Europe. This kingdom reached great heights under the rule of Charlemagne (SHAR-luh-mayn). By 1215 many kingdoms in Europe had divided, others had become unified, and even more had become Christian.

1. **Compare** What do you think caused the political boundaries in western Europe to change between 815 and 1215?

2. **Predict** What do you think happened during the Middle Ages to allow Christianity to spread so far in such a short period of time?

Listen to History

Go online to listen to an explanation of the starting points for this chapter.

go.hrw.com
Keyword: SHL EMA

372 CHAPTER 13

Skills Focus: Analyzing Maps

At Level

Social Studies Skill
Europe, 815–1215

1. To help students understand the information presented on the two maps, have them locate the following on the map dated 815 and then identify what the territory had become by 1215: Frankish Empire, *Holy Roman Empire;* Umayyad Caliphate, *Almohad Caliphate, Portugal, Castile, and Aragon;* Slavic states, *Poland and Hungary;* Anglo-Saxon Kingdoms, *England;* Byzantine Empire, *Byzantine Empire*

2. Have students work in pairs to brainstorm reasons Europe changed so dramatically between 815 and 1215. Have students answer the following questions: How had religion and politics changed in Europe? What challenges did Europeans face?

3. Have volunteers read their answers to the class. **LS Visual-Spatial**

- **Alternative Assessment Handbook**, Rubrics 12: Drawing Conclusions; and 21: Map Reading

---

Answers

Geography Starting Points

1. *possible answer—Territories merged together or were taken over by other leaders and were unified as kingdoms and empires.* **2.** *possible answer—More territory was conquered, allowing for Christianity to spread quickly.*

SECTION 1 Charlemagne's Empire

BEFORE YOU READ

MAIN IDEA

Through conquest and social change, Charlemagne brought much of western Europe together into a single empire.

READING FOCUS

1. How did Charlemagne and the Carolingians build the Frankish Empire?
2. How did Charlemagne's actions contribute to shaping a new society?

KEY TERMS AND PEOPLE

Charlemagne
Papal States
barons

NEW YORK

PI 2.5 Students investigate key events, developments, and major turning points in world history to identify factors of change and the effects of these changes.

THE INSIDE STORY

Could one man restore the lost glory of the Roman Empire? Cheers and excitement shattered the silence of Christmas morning in Rome in the year 800. From Saint Peter's Basilica—the city's most powerful church—word spread quickly through the city. For the first time in more than three centuries, Rome had a new emperor.

The new emperor was Charlemagne, the king of the Franks. His coronation was designed to surprise to everyone, perhaps even Charlemagne himself! During a Christmas mass, Pope Leo III walked to where Charlemagne was kneeling and lowered a golden crown onto the king's head. Addressing him as Emperor of the Romans, Leo hailed Charlemagne as the heir of Rome's ancient rulers.

Throughout Rome, people rejoiced. After more than 300 years, they had an emperor again! Even more exciting, however, was the fact that the emperor had been crowned by the pope, whom they saw as God's representative. To many people, the coronation was a sign that God had chosen their new emperor to restore the glory of their ancient empire. They thought Rome had been reborn. ■

A CHRISTMAS SURPRISE

▲ This medieval manuscript shows Pope Leo III crowning Charlemagne Emperor of the Romans.

Building an Empire

Though it was a surprise to some people, the crowning of **Charlemagne** as emperor was not a random decision. With the fall of Rome, Europe had entered into a period of political, social, and economic decline. Small kingdoms competed to control lands once under Rome's central authority. Among these were Charlemagne's predecessors, the kings of the Franks. By 800 the Franks ruled much of western and central Europe. The leaders most influential in the expansion of the Franks all belonged to one family. That family—the family to which Charlemagne belonged—was the Carolingians.

THE EARLY MIDDLE AGES **373**

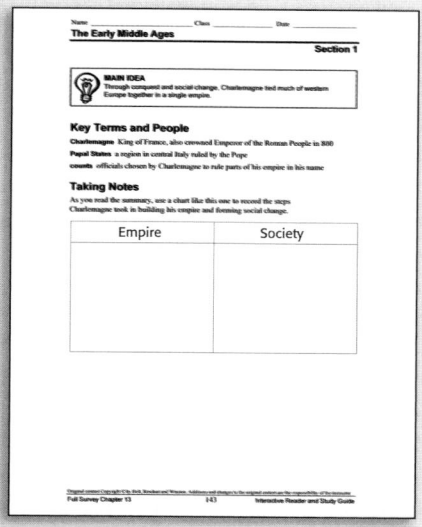

Teach the Main Idea

Charlemagne's Empire

1. **Teach** Ask students the Reading Focus questions to teach this section.

2. **Apply** Organize students into mixed-ability pairs. Have each pair review the answers to the Reading Focus questions. Have one student in each group write a new Reading Focus question for the text that falls under each blue head. The other student in the pair should write an answer to the new question.

3. **Review** Have students work in groups to ask and answer the new questions.

4. **Practice/Homework** Tell students it is the year 800, and they have just been named Emperor of Rome. Have students create a small poster showing the changes they intend to make, and what their rule will mean to the Roman people. Have volunteers share their posters with the class. **LS Verbal-Linguistic, Visual-Spatial**

📄 **Alternative Assessment Handbook**, Rubrics 3: Artwork; and 28: Posters

❶ How did Charlemagne and the Carolingians build the Frankish empire? *by serving the Frankish king and then taking the throne; they captured new lands and supported the pope; pope crowned Charlemagne Emperor of the Roman People*

Building an Empire

Define What were the Papal States? *a region in central Italy ruled by the pope*

Analyze Why was it important that the pope crowned Charlemagne emperor? *showed that Charlemagne had full support of the church, gave him tremendous power; also demonstrated that the pope would be selecting the emperor*

Predict What does the crowning of Charlemagne suggest about the relationship between emperor and pope in the future? *possible answer—They will be dependent upon each another.*

📓 **CRF:** Biography: Einhard

📓 **CRF:** Literature: Legends of Charlemagne

Info to Know

Charlemagne's Appearance
Charlemagne was tall for the Middle Ages. In the 18th century his skeleton was measured and found to be 1.9 m (6 feet, 3 inches) in length. Charlemagne has been described as having light colored hair and a large belly. He preferred to dress as a common man, but he always carried a sword.

Answers

Charlemagne in War and Peace
without his interest in improving the lives of his subjects, they might not have supported him

374

ACADEMIC VOCABULARY
incorporated combined or made into one body or unit

TAKING NOTES

As you read, take notes in a graphic organizer like this one. Take note of how Charlemagne's actions led to an empire and to social change.

Empire	Society

The Early Carolingians One of the first members of the Carolingian family to gain power was Charlemagne's grandfather, Charles Martel. Charles was not a king. Instead, he served as a political adviser and a war leader for the Frankish king. As war leader, he led the Frankish army in many crushing defeats of their opponents, most notably Muslims from Spain. From his skills in battle Charles earned the nickname Martel, which means "hammer."

Charles's son Pippin III was also a skilled leader. Like his father, Pippin won many battles and captured new lands for the Franks. Unlike Charles, Pippin would become king—the first king of the Carolingian dynasty. In 751 he forced the old king of the Franks to step down and Pippin took the throne for himself. When Pippin died in 768, he passed the kingdom on to his son, who was also named Charles. That son was the ruler we know today as Charlemagne.

Charlemagne's Rise to Power The name *Charlemagne* is from Old French for Charles the Great. In his case, the name was accurate, for Charlemagne was truly a great leader. In fact, many historians consider him one of the most important leaders in European history.

The foundation of Charlemagne's success was his military power. Each year, he assembled an army and led it into battle against one of his foes. When Charlemagne defeated a people, he incorporated their land into his sphere of influence and formed alliances with local rulers. In this way, he increased both the size and the power of the Carolingian kingdom.

Pope Leo III recognized Charlemagne's skill as a warrior and called on him for help when the Lombards attacked the **Papal States** in 774. The Papal States made up a region in central Italy that was under the control of the pope. Charlemagne answered the pope's call for help. The Franks swept into Italy and defeated the Lombards. Charlemagne became king of the Lombards, as well as the Franks.

The pope was grateful for Charlemagne's help against the Lombards, and his gratitude became even greater in the year 799. In that year, angry supporters of the previous pope attacked Leo and ran him out of Rome. Once again, Leo called on the Franks for help. Responding to his call, Charlemagne had Leo escorted back to Rome and restored to power.

The pope thanked Charlemagne by naming him Emperor of the Roman People. The pope's granting of this title put forward two ideas about Charlemagne. First, the title implied that Charlemagne had restored the glory of the Roman Empire in Europe. Second, the pope's action suggested that Charlemagne's rule had the full backing of the church and of God.

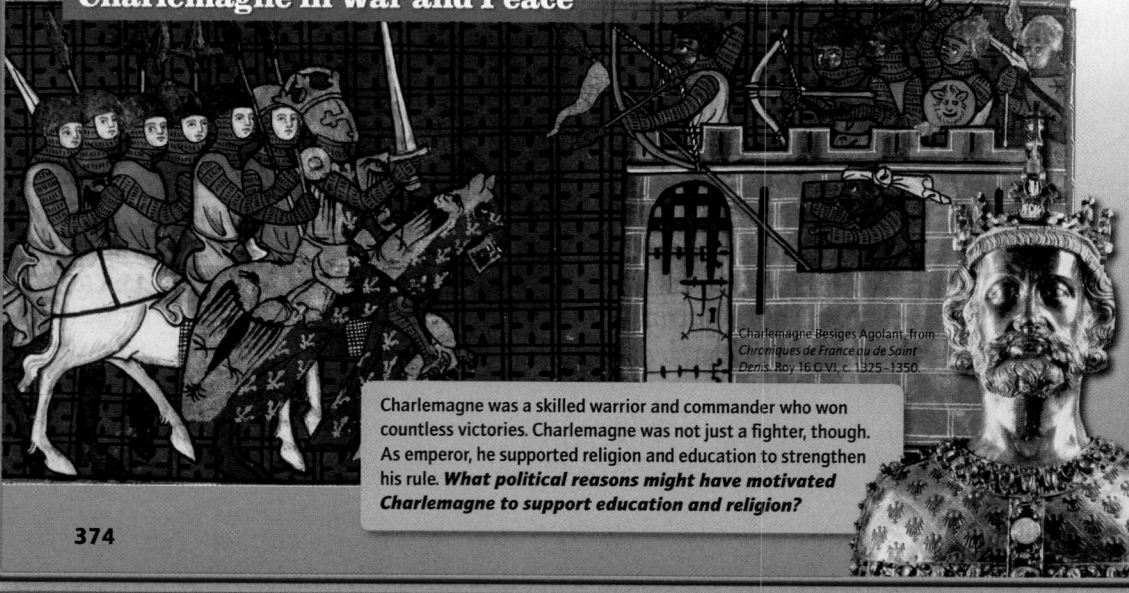

Charlemagne in War and Peace

Charlemagne Besieges Agolant, from Chroniques de France ou de Saint Denis, Roy 16 G VI, c. 1325–1350

Charlemagne was a skilled warrior and commander who won countless victories. Charlemagne was not just a fighter, though. As emperor, he supported religion and education to strengthen his rule. **What political reasons might have motivated Charlemagne to support education and religion?**

374

Differentiating Instruction

Below Level

Special Education Students

Materials: colored pencils or crayons

1. Review the crowning of Charlemagne with students. Then have students develop a series of five to ten pictures, in comic-book fashion, showing the crowning of Charlemagne.

2. Have students work in pairs, exchange their work, and have the other student write a caption for each picture.

3. Have volunteers share their finished work with the class. You might wish to display student work for all to see and discuss each picture as a class. 🅻🅂 **Visual-Spatial**

📓 **Alternative Assessment Handbook**, Rubric 3: Artwork

Charlemagne's Rule Charlemagne had tremendous power as emperor. However, the empire was so large that it was not easy to rule. Soon after taking power, Charlemagne made several changes to make his government both efficient and effective.

One step that Charlemagne took to improve his government was to select a center for his government. He established a permanent capital, which earlier Frankish kings had not done, at Aachen (AH-kuhn) in what is now Germany. There, Charlemagne built a huge palace and a cathedral to reflect his own greatness.

Because Charlemagne stayed in Aachen, he could not personally oversee his entire empire. He chose officials called **counts** to rule parts of the empire in his name. Counts were bound by oath to obey Charlemagne. In return, counts were granted large tracks of land and given considerable authority. Still, they had to answer to Charlemagne for their decisions.

To keep tabs on his counts, Charlemagne sent inspectors throughout the empire. The inspectors visited counts, rewarding those who did their jobs well and punishing those who did not. They helped ensure that counts remained loyal and that the empire was well run.

READING CHECK **Summarize** How did Charlemagne turn his kingdom into an empire?

A New Society

Although Charlemagne is known mostly as a warrior and a political leader, he also made sweeping changes to Frankish society. Some of the changes he introduced help shape life for hundreds of years.

Education One aspect of society in which Charlemagne was particularly interested was education. He was personally interested in learning and spent much of his time studying. In an era in which education was not widely appreciated, he wanted leaders in his empire to be able to read and write. To achieve this goal, Charlemagne ordered churches and monasteries to start schools staffed by educated priests and monks. Students in these schools studied religion, music, grammar, and other subjects.

To further encourage learning in his empire, Charlemagne invited noted scholars from all over Europe to Aachen. These scholars spent much of their time teaching. When they were not teaching, the scholars studied and copied ancient texts. They sent copies of the texts to monasteries all over Europe, where monks made more copies. Had the scholars and monks not done this, many valuable works from the ancient world might have been completely lost during the Middle Ages.

NEW YORK
CC Unit 2-F2
Charlemagne and the Frankish Empire

READING SKILLS
Using Word Origins If you know that cathedral comes from a Latin term meaning "of a bishop's seat," who would you expect to preside over a cathedral?

A devout Christian, Charlemagne built a huge cathedral in Aachen. ▼

Monk Eadwine at work on a manuscript, c. 1150.

◄ At Charlemagne's request, scholars and monks in Aachen spent hours studying and copying ancient writings.

THE EARLY MIDDLE AGES **375**

375

Reading Focus

A New Society

Draw Conclusions In what ways did Charlemagne's religious practices affect his rule as emperor? *possible answer—conquered people ordered to convert to Christianity; promoted religious education*

Make Inferences Why do you think that the empire did not last after Charlemagne's death? *possible answer —Without a single, strong leader, it was impossible to confront both internal conflict and external invaders.*

🗄 **Quick Facts Transparency:** Charlemagne's Achievements

● Review & Assess ●

Close

Guide students in a discussion of Charlemagne's rule and the changes that occurred within society during his reign.

Review

📟 **Online Quiz**, Section 1

Assess

SE Section 1 Assessment

📋 **Progress Assessment:** Section 1 Quiz

📋 **Alternative Assessment Handbook**

Reteach/Intervene

📋 **Interactive Reader and Study Guide**, Section 1

🖥 **Interactive Skills Tutor CD-ROM**

Answers

Reading Check *built an education system, preserved ancient writings, expanded religion, developed single law code*

376

Religion In addition to improving education, Charlemagne wanted to preserve and spread Christian teachings. The strength of the emperor's faith is described by his friend and biographer, Einhard:

HISTORY'S VOICES

 NEW YORK

CC Unit 2-F5
The Church in Medieval Europe

❝ Charlemagne practised the Christian religion with great devotion and piety . . . As long as his health lasted he went to church morning and evening with great regularity, and also for early-morning Mass, and the late-night hours. ❞

—Einhard, *The Life of Charlemagne*

As emperor, Charlemagne worked closely with the church to create a unified Christian empire. He accomplished this, in part, by force. During some military campaigns, Charlemagne ordered those he conquered to convert to Christianity, under penalty of death. He then sent monks to live among the conquered people to help Christianity take root.

Law Charlemagne honored the traditional laws of the tribes that he brought under his rule. Most of these laws had only existed in oral tradition. After Charlemagne became emperor, he had many of the tribal laws recorded, and he allowed tribal legal codes to maintain their separate existence. At the urging of the pope, Charlemagne also issued many new laws that enforced Christian teachings.

Unfortunately, with Charlemagne's death in 814, the empire lost its center. Charlemagne had not built a bureaucracy strong enough to maintain his vast holdings. Regional kings grew strong and, once again, disunity spread across western Europe. There was trouble in the Carolingian house, too. Charlemagne's grandsons fought amongst themselves for the throne. In 843 the grandsons agreed to divide the empire into three parts—a western, a middle, and an eastern kingdom. The empire was crumbling. To make matters worse, invaders challenged the empire from all sides.

READING CHECK Find the Main Idea How did Charlemagne change society in his empire?

CHARLEMAGNE'S ACHIEVEMENTS QUICK FACTS

As emperor, Charlemagne made sweeping changes to many aspects of Frankish society.

Politics
• Unified Europe for the first time since the fall of Rome

Education
• Built schools and preserved ancient writings

Religion
• Spread Christianity among conquered people

Law
• Developed a written legal code

SECTION 1 ASSESSMENT

 go.hrw.com
Online Quiz
Keyword: SHL EMA HP

Reviewing Ideas, Terms, and People

1. **a. Identify** What new title was **Charlemagne** given by Pope Leo III? What significance did that title have?
   b. Explain How did **counts** and inspectors help Charlemagne effectively rule his empire?
   c. Evaluate Do you think Charlemagne deserves the title Great? Why or why not?

2. **a. Describe** What changes did Charlemagne make to education in the Frankish Empire?
   b. Analyze How did Charlemagne's personal religious beliefs affect life in the empire?
   c. Make Judgments Which of Charlemagne's reforms do you think was the most significant? Why?

Critical Thinking

3. **Rank** Using your notes and a graphic organizer like the one below, rank Charlemagne's achievements in what you think was their order of importance in strengthening the empire.

   Achievements

FOCUS ON WRITING

4. **Narration** Write a letter describing Charlemagne's coronation as though you were a Roman who witnessed the event. In your letter, explain what happened and why.

Section 1 Assessment Answers

1. **a.** Emperor of the Romans; great honor, had full support of the church and pope
   b. counts ruled parts of empire for the emperor; inspectors supervised barons, made sure they were loyal and doing their jobs
   c. possible answers—yes, built kingdom into empire; no, used war to get power

2. **a.** built schools, encouraged scholars, had ancient writings copied
   b. He encouraged religious education, ordered conquered people to convert to Christianity, sent monks and priests to live

among conquered people, and issued laws that enforced Christian teachings|
   c. possible answers—law: unified the Roman Empire under one law; education: preserved writings and history

3. possible answers—unified Europe; reorganized law; built schools; spread Christianity

4. Letters might include descriptioins of Pope Leo III, the golden crown, and importance of naming a new emperor.

World Literature

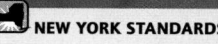 NEW YORK STANDARDS

PI 2.4 Students explain the importance of analyzing narratives drawn from different times and places to understand historical events.

About the Reading A popular form of entertainment in medieval Europe was storytelling. Through their craft, storytellers had the power to transform minor historical figures into heroes and insignificant events into legends. Such is the case with *The Song of Roland*, a story that dates back to the time of Charlemagne. The story is based on a real event, a minor skirmish between Charlemagne's forces and Christian Basques, a people who live in the Pyrenees Mountains that divide Spain from France. Over time, the story changed. The Basques were transformed into Muslims and Charlemagne's nephew Roland, who played only a minor role in the real battle, becomes a hero of epic proportions.

AS YOU READ Ask yourself which details are likely based on fact and which are literary creations.

Excerpt from
The Song of Roland

This stained-glass window from Chartres cathedral shows Roland in combat against an enemy warrior.

The battle is fearful and full of grief.
Oliver and Roland strike like good men,
the Archbishop, more than a thousand blows,
and the Twelve Peers do not hang back, they strike!
the French fight side by side, all as one man.
The pagans die by hundreds, by thousands:
whoever does not flee finds no refuge from death,
like it or not, there he ends all his days.
And there the men of France lose their greatest arms;
they will not see their fathers, their kin again,
or Charlemagne, who looks for them in the passes.
Tremendous torment now comes forth in France,
a mighty whirlwind, tempests of wind and thunder,
rains and hailstones, great and immeasurable,
bolts of lightning hurtling and hurtling down:
it is, in truth, a trembling of the earth.
From Saint Michael-in-Peril to the Saints,
from Besançon to the port of Wissant,

there is no house whose veil of walls does not crumble.
A great darkness at noon falls on the land,
there is no light but when the heavens crack.
No man sees this who is not terrified,
and many say: "The Last Day! Judgment Day!
The end! The end of the world is upon us!"
They do not know, they do not speak the truth:
it is the worldwide grief for the death of Roland.

Skills FOCUS **READING LIKE A HISTORIAN**

go.hrw.com
World Literature
Keyword: SHL WRLIT

1. **Identify Supporting Details** How does the storyteller use details about the day of Roland's death to communicate Roland's importance?

2. **Interpret Literature as a Source** What effect might changing the enemy army in the story from Basque to Muslim have had on listeners?

See **Skills Handbook**, p. H28

THE EARLY MIDDLE AGES **377**

World Literature

Excerpt from *The Song of Roland*

Word Help

strike hit sharply, attack
tempest a violent windstorm

Info to Know

The Song of Roland The epic poem *The Song of Roland* is based on the battle of Roncevaux Pass on August 15, 778. The poem tells the story of Charlemagne's army being attacked by Basques. *The Song of Roland* also played an important role during the First Crusade in the 1030s. The poem's last line refers to a Norman poet, Turold, who many scholars believe wrote the poem. Other historians believe that the work is a compilation of various story tellers.

Collaborative Learning   At Level

The Song of Roland

1. Read the poem aloud to the class while the students follow along with their textbooks.

2. Organize the students into small, mixed-ability groups.

3. Divide the poem into sections and give each group a section.

4. Have students in each group translate the excerpt into modern English. Have volunteers read their modern version to the class.
LS Verbal-Linguistic

Alternative Assessment Handbook, Rubric 40: Writing to Describe

Answers

Reading Like a Historian 1. *The poem describes Roland fighting valiantly, killing thousands. The world grieves when he dies.* **2.** *possible answer—Roland would probably have been depicted in a different light.*

377

Getting Started

Use the **Interactive Reader and Study Guide** to familiarize students with the section content.

📝 **Interactive Reader and Study Guide,** Section 2

[Worksheet image]

Name _____ Class _____ Date _____

The Early Middle Ages

Section 2

💡 **MAIN IDEA**
Invasions and migrations changed the political and cultural landscapes of western Europe during the early Middle Ages.

Key Terms and People
navigation planning a course of travel, such as the Vikings crossing the sea
sagas long Icelandic stories about great heroes and events
Leif Eriksson Viking who led settlers to the eastern shores of what is now Canada

Taking Notes
As you read the summary, use a graphic organizer like this one to list and describe the peoples that invaded Europe.

People	Description

Full Survey Chapter 13   146   Interactive Reader and Study Guide

---

📝 **CRF:** Vocabulary Builder: Section 2

Taking Notes

Vikings or Norsemen—ship builders and sailors; would steal anything of value; fierce invaders; some settled in Iceland; Magyars—invaded from the east; ancestors of present-day Hungarians; originally from central Asia; nomadic people but eventually settled in present-day Hungary; great warriors and skilled horseman; Muslims—invaded from the south; performed small, fast raids on Italy and southern France; pirates attacked ships sailing the Mediterranean

---

SECTION 2 New Invaders

BEFORE YOU READ

MAIN IDEA
Invasions and migrations changed the political and cultural landscapes of western Europe during the early Middle Ages.

READING FOCUS
1. Why did many Europeans fear the Vikings?
2. What made Magyar raids in eastern Europe so devastating to people there?
3. Why did Muslims raid towns in southern Europe?

KEY TERMS AND PEOPLE
navigation
sagas
Leif Eriksson

NEW YORK
PI 3.2 Students explain the dynamics of cultural change and how interactions between groups and among cultures has affected various groups throughout the world.

THE INSIDE STORY

"Where did they come from?" That question was on the minds of the monks of Lindisfarne Monastery on the morning of June 8, 793. Just a few hours before, the monks had been going about their daily business, tending crops, praying and copying manuscripts. Now many of them were dead, killed by the swords and spears of raiders. Those left alive watched as their monastery's precious treasures were loaded into ships that slipped quietly out to sea. Dazed, the monks wondered exactly what had led to this terrible destruction.

What the monks did not know was that the raiders were Vikings from what is now Denmark. Nor did they realize that the raid on their monastery was only the beginning of Europe's newest threat. The attack on Lindisfarne was the beginning of a 200-year period of raids on northern Europe, a period sometimes called the Age of Vikings. ∎

THE FIRST ATTACK

▼ The ruins of Lindisfarne Monastery lie on an island off Britain's coast.

378

The Vikings

The relative peace Charlemagne brought to western Europe did not last long. Even before Charlemagne died, invaders had begun nibbling at the edges of his empire. The invaders came from many directions, pouring across plains and seas into Europe. Of all these invaders, the fiercest were the warriors called the Vikings.

Origins of the Vikings The people we know as the Vikings came from northern Europe. They lived in Scandinavia, an area that today includes the countries of Norway, Denmark, and Sweden. Because of their northern homelands, the Vikings were also called the Norsemen or the Northmen.

Teach the Main Idea

At Level

New Invaders

1. **Teach** Ask students the Reading Focus questions to teach this section.

2. **Apply** Organize students into groups of three. Have each student within a group explain information about the Vikings, the Magyars, and the Muslims to other students in the group.

3. **Review** Have students use information from the group presentations to write a summary of the section. Guide students in a discussion about the invaders.

4. **Practice/Homework** Have students compile a list of interview questions they might ask a Middle Ages scholar, and create a class list for all to see. Questions might include the following: Where did the group come from? How did they attack? What areas in Europe did they attack? Have students write down the questions and use the text to answer them. **LS Verbal-Linguistic**

📝 **Alternative Assessment Handbook,** Rubrics 11: Discussion; and 14: Group Activity

In the Viking homelands, society was rural and agricultural. Most people worked as fishers or farmers. Although the sea provided plenty of fish, Scandinavia's soil was not very fertile. Viking farmers often had trouble growing enough grain to keep people fed. As Scandinavia's population grew, food shortages became a common problem. Looking for new sources of food and wealth, some Viking leaders decided to take what they needed from other people. Thus began the Viking raids.

Viking Raids The Vikings were superb shipbuilders and sailors. Their ships were capable of withstanding heavy ocean waves and carried crews of as many as 100 warriors. In addition, the Vikings' skills at **navigation**, or planning the course across the sea, allowed them to cross expanses of ocean in search of wealth, prestige, and new lands.

The first targets of Viking raids were England and northern France, neither of which is far from Scandinavia by sea. As time passed, the Vikings began raiding places farther and farther from their homeland, even Kiev and Constantinople were not safe. Nor were inland locations safe. The Vikings sailed their ships upriver, attacking cities such as Paris and Aachen. All over Europe, people lived in fear of the Vikings, and with good reason. Writings of the period are filled with haunting descriptions of fierce Viking raids:

HISTORY'S VOICES

❝The number of ships grows: the endless stream of Vikings never ceases to increase. Everywhere the Christians are victims of massacres, burnings, plunderings: the Vikings conquer all in their path, and no one resists them.❞

—A monk of Noirmoutier, quoted in *The Viking World* by James Graham-Campbell

People were constantly afraid because they had no warning that the Vikings were coming. Their fast-moving ships allowed the Vikings to approach a target quickly, so people had little time to prepare. Armed with swords, axes, spears, and shields, warriors leapt from the ships to attack. They killed or captured any defenders who stood against them, grabbed any precious items they could find, and returned to their ships to sail off. The people they captured were taken to distant lands and sold into slavery.

Reading like a Historian

Viking Raids

Analyzing Point of View Few historians would argue that the Viking raids were anything but savage. Still, historians may look at the raids in completely different ways. Interpretations of past events often come with differing points of view. These different interpretations may reflect differences in the historians' backgrounds, interests, and the sources that they use.

The earliest written accounts of the Viking raids were written by those who fell prey to Viking exploits. In this passage, present-day historian C.H. Lawrence discusses the Viking raids faced by monks in the Middle Ages. To analyze the author's point of view, think about

- the author's interests and sources
- the main points in the argument
- the use of emotional and factual language

> The author's use of *fearsome foes* suggests that he is telling the story from the monks' point of view.

> The monks had to face more <u>fearsome foes</u> in the heathen Vikings and Saracens [Muslims]. In the ninth century Christian Europe was under siege. Ireland, England, and the north of Gaul were ravaged by the Northmen. Abbeys near the coasts or on inland waterways of those areas were sitting targets. Lindisfarne, Clonfert, and Clonmacnoise were among the first to be sacked. The more accessible abbeys near the coast of northern Gaul and along the valleys of the Seine, the Meuse, and the Loire fell victims to the onslaught of the predators.
>
> —C. H. Lawrence, *Medieval Monasticism*, 1996

> The excerpt is taken from a book about medieval monasteries, many of which were destroyed by Viking raids.

 Skills FOCUS **READING LIKE A HISTORIAN**

1. **Author** What point of view might a historian writing about monasteries have of the Vikings?
2. **Details** Which details from the selection reveal the author's point of view?
3. **The Sources** Do you think the earliest written accounts of Viking raids would be a good source for understanding the Vikings' point of view? Explain.

See **Skills Handbook**, H32

Differentiating Instruction

English-Language Learners

Standard English Mastery   Prep Required

Materials: excerpts from different sagas, such as *The Saga of Eric the Red*

1. Have each student identify a hero, fictional or non-fictional, and write notes about why this person is a hero.
2. Review with the students what a saga is, and provide an excerpt. For example, you might choose a page from *t*.

3. Have students write a short saga about their hero. Students should first create a graphic organizer with the ideas from their notes, and use it to create the written saga.
4. Have volunteers share either their graphic organizers or their sagas with the class.
   LS **Verbal-Linguistic**
   Alternative Assessment Handbook, Rubrics 13: Graphic Organizers; and 39: Writing to Create

---

Reading Focus

1 Why did many Europeans fear the Vikings? *The Vikings traveled quickly, attacked their targets with little warning, and captured or killed anyone who tried to stop them.*

The Vikings

Explain What factors led to Viking raids on other countries? *need for food and supplies that Scandinavia could not provide*

Summarize What advantages did Vikings sailors have? *ships could carry large crews, withstand heavy waves; had excellent navigation skills*

Make Judgments Why do you think Vikings did not try to establish an empire in England or northern France? *possible answer—They were more interested in the riches they could take home; Viking warriors left their families at home during raids.*

Activity **Viking Ship** Have each student draw a picture of a Viking ship, using details from the text and other reliable sources. **LS** **Visual-Spatial**

Alternative Assessment Handbook, Rubric 3: Artwork

Info to Know

Leif Ericsson Leif Eriksson set out on a voyage to Greenland with his father, Eric the Red, to colonize the land. While there, they noticed land to the west. Leif left Greenland and started the journey toward North America landing in what is now Canada. The Greenlanders referred to North America as Vinland due to the many grapes that were growing there at the time.

Answers

Reading Like a Historian 1. *possible answer—They might share the monks' point of view.* **2.** *fearsome foes, heathen, ravaged, victims, predators, sacked;* **3.** *possible answer—No, authors would focus on or exaggerate the bad things that the Vikings did.*

The Vikings

Identify In what areas did the Vikings settle? *Iceland, Greenland, Canada, North America, northern France*

Explain How did the Vikings acquire land in northern France? *made a deal with the king of France; if raids stopped, king would grant land to Viking chief*

📋 **CRF:** Primary Source: A Viking Funeral

② What made Magyar raids in eastern Europe so devastating to people there? *skilled warriors, easily outmaneuvered opposing armies, attacked small settlements*

The Magyars

Identify Where did the Magyars settle? *in what is now Hungary*

Compare How did Viking and Magyar fighting styles differ? *Magyars fought on land, from horseback; Vikings attacked from the sea*

Interpreting Maps

Vikings, Magyars, and Muslims, 800-1000

Region Have students compare the climates that the Vikings encountered on their raids, from southern coasts to the colder climates of Iceland and Greenland. Have students compare current-day temperatures in various regions of Viking raids, and prepare the information in a chart. **LS Visual-Spatial**

📋 **Alternative Assessment Handbook,** Rubrics 7: Charts

🖥 **Map Transparency:** Vikings, Magyars, and Muslims, 800-1000

Answers

Interpreting Maps 1. *Muslims;*
2. *Vikings*

Reading Check *People did not know when they were coming, so could not prepare; Viking raids were brutal.*

380

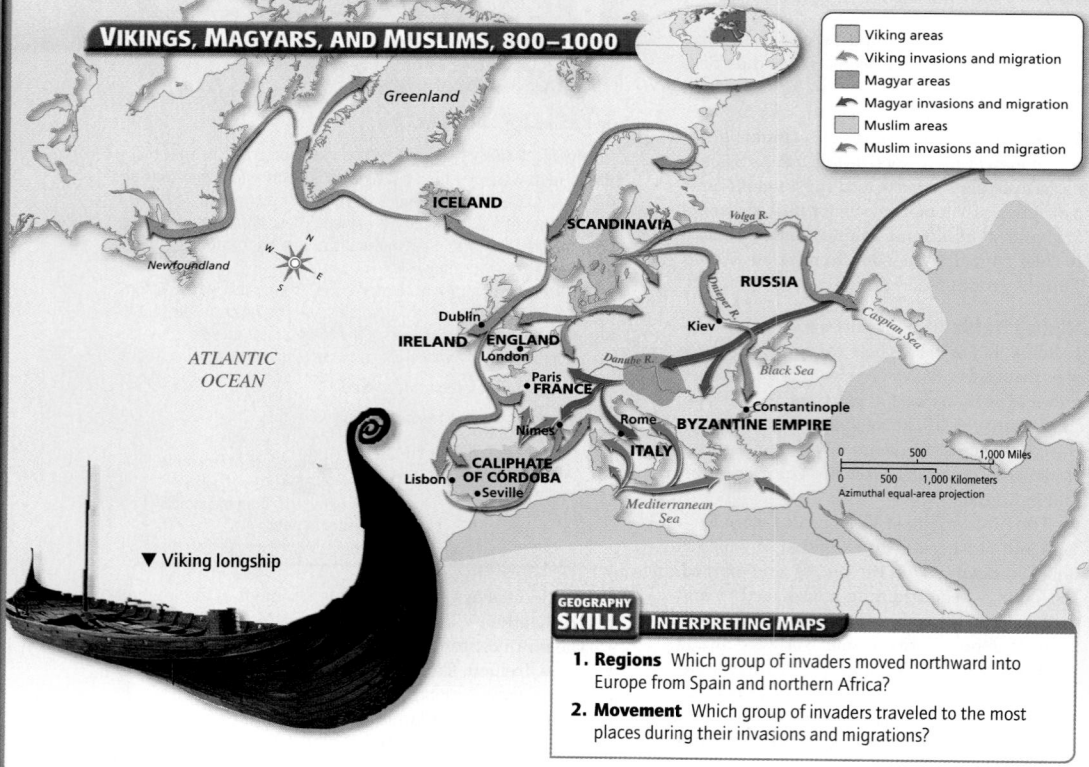

VIKINGS, MAGYARS, AND MUSLIMS, 800–1000

- Viking areas
- Viking invasions and migration
- Magyar areas
- Magyar invasions and migration
- Muslim areas
- Muslim invasions and migration

▼ Viking longship

GEOGRAPHY SKILLS | **INTERPRETING MAPS**

1. **Regions** Which group of invaders moved northward into Europe from Spain and northern Africa?
2. **Movement** Which group of invaders traveled to the most places during their invasions and migrations?

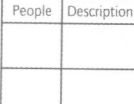

TAKING NOTES

As you read take notes in a graphic organizer like this one. List and describe the peoples that invaded Europe.

People	Description

Among the Vikings' favorite targets were monasteries. Because monks were not warriors, monasteries were generally easy to plunder. In addition, monasteries had fine treasures, such as jeweled crosses and gold or silver candlesticks. The Vikings, who were not Christian, saw nothing wrong with stealing these religious items to make themselves richer.

Viking Settlements Not all of the Vikings who left Scandinavia were raiders. Some were explorers in search of new lands. In time, some of these explorers settled down and established permanent settlements in far-off places.

Among the places settled by the Vikings was Iceland. According to old Icelandic sources, the first Vikings arrived there in the late 700s. Led by a council called the Althing, Viking society thrived in Iceland for centuries, much longer than the Vikings lasted in mainland Europe.

From Iceland, groups of Vikings set out to settle lands even farther from their homeland. According to the **sagas**—long Icelandic stories about great heroes and events—Viking explorers reached Greenland in 982. About 100 years later, Vikings under **Leif Eriksson** reached North America. They settled on the eastern shore of what is now Canada.

Viking warriors also settled in northern France. Led by a chief named Rollo, the warriors had raided France many times. The king of France, tired of the raids, made a deal with Rollo. If Rollo stopped his raids and defended Frankish lands against other Vikings, the king would give him land. Rollo accepted the deal. In time, the area he controlled became known as Normandy, or the land of the Northmen.

READING CHECK **Draw Conclusions** What made Viking raids so terrifying to Christian Europe?

380 CHAPTER 13

Differentiating Instruction

Above Level

Advanced Learners/Gifted and Talented

Research Required

1. Have students research current-day occurrences within the countries formed from Magyar regions. Students should use reliable major news Web sites such as the BBC, CNN, and the *New York Times*.

2. Have students identify a topic of interest and write a three-page examination and summary of their chosen topic. Students should include maps, charts, and other visuals as needed to support their research.

3. Have volunteers present their papers to the class. **LS Verbal-Linguistic**

📋 **Alternative Assessment Handbook,** Rubrics 30: Research; and 42: Writing to Inform

The Magyars

As the Vikings were terrorizing northern and western Europe, the Magyars were invading from the east. Originally from central Asia, the Magyars were nomads who settled in what is now Hungary. Like the Vikings, the Magyars were fierce warriors. Unlike the Vikings, they were not sailors. On horseback, the Magyars, who were skilled riders, could easily outmaneuver the armies of their opponents.

The Magyars planned their raids carefully. They never attacked heavily defended towns, choosing instead to attack smaller settlements. After looting these settlements, the Magyars fled, easily outrunning any armies sent to stop them. Using these tactics, they raided eastern France and Germany, northern Italy, and the western Byzantine Empire.

Eventually, the Magyars gave up their nomadic ways. In doing so, they lost their major advantage in battle. Once the Magyars had a permanent home, they could not easily run from opposing armies. In the mid-900s King Otto the Great of Germany crushed a huge Magyar army, ending the Magyar raids.

READING CHECK **Infer** Why were Magyar raids so difficult to stop?

The Muslims

Muslims first came to Europe in large numbers as conquerors. In 711 a Muslim army from northern Africa crossed the Strait of Gibraltar and made rapid conquest of Spain. The Muslims would rule the Iberian Peninsula for more than 700 years. Their capital city, Cordoba, became one of the wealthiest and most culturally advanced cities of the medieval world. Muslim Spain was also, for the most part, a land of tolerance, where Muslims, Christians, and Jews lived together in relative peace.

By 732 the Muslims had swept across the Pyrenees into France. There a Muslim raiding party was stopped short at the Battle of Tours by Charles Martel, Charlemagne's grandfather. Although later European accounts marked this as a major Muslim defeat, Muslims regarded this as only a minor skirmish.

In the 800s and 900s Muslim leaders changed their strategy. Instead of full-scale invasions, they ordered small, fast raids against cities and towns in southern France and Italy. Among the places the Muslims raided was Rome, the home of the pope and the spiritual center of Christianity in western Europe. The raiders destroyed many of the city's ancient churches, including Saint Peter's Basilica. The loss of these churches was a painful blow to European Christians.

In addition to raiding cities, Muslim fleets blocked Byzantine trade in the Mediterranean. Muslim pirates looted the ships and sold their crews into slavery. More importantly, they cut off trade routes between Italy and its eastern allies. The popes had little choice but to turn to the Franks for protection. As a result, the balance of power in western Europe shifted.

READING CHECK **Make Generalizations** Why did Muslims launch small, fast raids against Christian lands?

SECTION 2 ASSESSMENT

go.hrw.com
Online Quiz
Keyword: SHL EMA HP

Reviewing Ideas, Terms, and People

1. a. Identify What skills allowed the Vikings to conduct raids in locations far from their homeland?
   b. Draw Conclusions Why do you think the period between 800 and 1000 in western Europe is sometimes called the Age of Vikings?
   c. Evaluate Do stories like the Viking **sagas** make good sources for historical information? Why or why not?

2. a. Identify Who were the Magyars? What parts of Europe did they invade and settle?
   b. Explain How did the Magyars' decision to settle down in a permanent location help bring an end to their raids?

3. a. Describe Where did the Muslim raiders who attacked Europe in the 800s and 900s come from?
   b. Contrast How did Muslim attacks on Europe in the 800s differ from those in the 700s?
   c. Elaborate Which Muslim tactic do you think would have caused more problems for the people of southern Europe, small raids or a full-scale invasions? Explain your answer.

Critical Thinking

4. Compare and Contrast Use your notes and a graphic organizer like the one at right to compare and contrast the Viking, Magyar, and Muslim raiders.

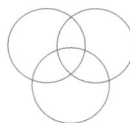

FOCUS ON WRITING

5. Description Write a description of a Viking, Magyar, or Muslim raid as though you are an inhabitant of the town being raided. Bring your description to life by choosing vivid adjectives to describe the sights, sounds, and emotions that surround you.

THE EARLY MIDDLE AGES **381**

Section 2 Assessment Answers

1. a. shipbuilding, sailing, navigation
   b. Vikings conducted raids throughout Europe.
   c. possible answer—Sagas may provide some useful information, but generally they are historically inaccurate, exaggerated stories.

2. a. a nomadic people from central Asia; eastern France and Germany, northern Italy, Western Byzantine empire
   b. could no longer run with opponents

3. a. Spain and northern Africa
   b. 800s—fast quick raids; 700s—tried to invade Europe

c. possible answer—small raids; they would not know when they would occur

4. None were Christian; all attacked Europe. Vikings—from Scandinavia, shipbuilders, attacked Christian buildings; Magyars—from central Asia, horsemen, nomadic; Muslims—from Spain and north Africa, attacked southern Europe, attacked Christian buildings

5. Student descriptions should include speed of the raid; difficulty of preparing; destruction of towns and villages

Getting Started

Use the **Interactive Reader and Study Guide** to familiarize students with the section content.

📝 **Interactive Reader and Study Guide,** Section 3

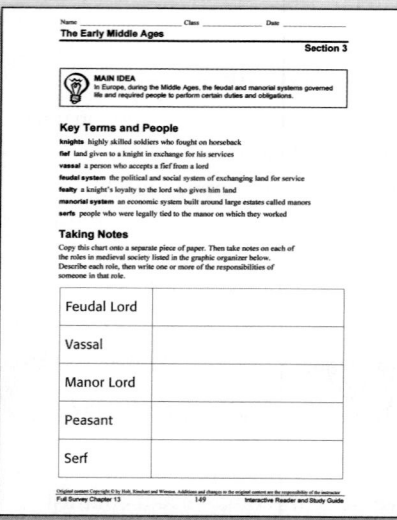

Academic Vocabulary

Review with students the high-use academic term in this section.

prohibition an order or law that forbids (p. 384)

📝 **CRF:** Vocabulary Builder: Section 3

Taking Notes

Feudal Lord—nobles who paid knights with a fief, or parcel of land, in return for protection and loyalty; some nobles more powerful than king; Vassal—person who received land from his lord; Manor Lord—wealthy lords or knights who owned manors; Peasant—farmed land in exchange for land and protection from invaders; Serf—peasant who was legally tied to manor; hereditary position

go.hrw.com

Online Resources

KEYWORD: SHL EMA
ACTIVITY: The Middle Ages

The Feudal and Manorial Systems

BEFORE YOU READ

MAIN IDEA

In Europe, during the Middle Ages, the feudal and manorial systems governed life and required people to perform certain duties and obligations.

READING FOCUS

1. What duties and obligations were central to the feudal system?
2. How did the manorial system govern the medieval economy?
3. What was daily life like for people on a manor?

KEY TERMS AND PEOPLE

knights
fief
vassal
feudal system
fealty
manorial system
serfs

 NEW YORK

PI 3.1 Students analyze the roles and contributions of individuals and groups to social, political, economic, cultural, and religious practices and activities.

THE INSIDE STORY

What did it mean to be a knight? For William Marshal, knighthood did not convey the same image of dashing heroes in shining armor that we imagine today. For William, knighthood meant a lifetime of military and political service. As a young knight, he gained fame and wealth by besting other knights in tournaments all over France and England. From there, William went on to serve the first of four English kings. He fought in dozens of battles, risking his life to protect the English crown.

William was handsomely rewarded for his service. Kings and queens respected William, and he was even granted the honor of knighting one of England's crown princes. He was named Earl of Pembroke and his marriage to one of England's wealthiest women made him lord over vast lands and a castle. However, William's career was not always easy. Despite his skill as a warrior, William was badly wounded many times. He also spent considerable time as a prisoner. For his sacrifices and his successes, many people consider William Marshal the greatest knight who ever lived. ◼

The Feudal System

Knights like William Marshal did not exist at the beginning of the Middle Ages. Soldiers fought mostly on foot, not on horseback, and were part of large armies headed by kings. As the Middle Ages progressed, however, knights began to emerge as key figures in Europe. What was responsible for this change in society?

THE GREATEST KNIGHT

▲ This medieval manuscript shows a knight pledging himself in service to a lord.

Teach the Main Idea

At Level

The Feudal and Manorial Systems

1. **Teach** Ask students the Reading Focus questions to teach this section.

2. **Apply** Have students develop an outline of the section. Students should use the main red and blue subheads as the main points in their outlines. Under each subheading there should be at least two details.

3. **Review** Have students contribute to a class outline that all can see. Have students check and correct their own work.

4. **Practice/Homework** Have students write a paragraph explaining how feudalism and the manorial system worked during the Middle Ages. **LS Verbal-Linguistic**

📝 **Alternative Assessment Handbook,** Rubric 37: Writing Assignments

◄ Knights in battle at the Battle of Hastings in 1066

Battle of Hastings, from Chronique de Normandie, c. 1450, courtesy of The British Library.

The Origins of Feudalism Feudalism in Europe originated, in part, as a result of the Viking, Magyar, and Muslim invasions. In the face of these invaders, kings all over Europe found themselves unable to defend their lands and the lands of their nobles from attack.

The nobles, who could no longer count on their kings' armies for protection, had to find a way to defend their own lands. To achieve this defense, nobles built castles. Often, castles were built on hills because hilltop locations were easier to defend. Most early castles were not the elaborate structures we see in movies and books. They were usually built of wood, not stone, and were simply a place for the noble and his family to take shelter in case of attack.

Knights and Lords To defend their castles, nobles needed trained soldiers. The most important of these soldiers were **knights**, highly skilled soldiers who fought on horseback. Mounted knights in heavy armor were the best defenders nobles could have.

Being a knight was expensive. Knights needed weapons, armor, and horses, all of which were expensive to acquire and maintain. For this reason, knights demanded payment for their services. This payment did not usually take the form of money. Instead, most knights were paid for their services with land.

The land given to a knight for his service was called a **fief** (FEEF). Anyone who accepted a fief was called a **vassal**, and the person from whom he accepted it was his lord. Historians sometimes call this system of exchanging land for service the **feudal system**, or feudalism.

Feudal Obligations Lords and vassals in the feudal system had duties to fulfill to one another. These duties were the ties that bound people together.

For example, a knight's chief duty as a vassal was to provide military service to his lord. He had to promise to remain loyal to his lord and not turn against him. This promise was called an oath of **fealty**, or loyalty:

HISTORY'S VOICES

❝ Hear you my Lord [name] that I, [name] shall be to you both faithful and true, and shall owe my Fidelity unto you, for the Land that I hold of you, and lawfully shall do such Customs and Services, as my Duty is to you, at the times assigned. So help me God and all his Saints. ❞

—from *The Manner of Doing Homage and Fealty*

A knight also had certain financial obligations to his lord. If the lord was captured in battle, for example, the knight was obliged to help pay ransom for his release. A knight also gave money to his lord on special occasions.

THE EARLY MIDDLE AGES **383**

2 How did the manorial system govern the medieval economy? *economy based on agriculture; lords employed peasants and serfs to farm land, in return got food and place to live*

The Manorial System

Describe What was the advantage of the three-field crop rotation system? *improved soil led to better harvests*

Contrast What was the difference between serfs and peasants? *peasants— free people, worked on manors to have a safe place to live; serfs—legally tied to the manor; serfdom is hereditary*

Summarize In what ways did a manor resemble a small town? *was self-sufficient, produced food, included a church, a mill, blacksmith*

Teaching Tip

Explain the difference between the feudal system (a social system) and the manorial system (an economic system).

Recent Scholarship

In *Those Terrible Middle Ages: Debunking the Myths,* French historian and archivist Regine Pernoud discusses many of the myths associated with the Middle Ages. She makes a strong argument that the Middle Ages were not dark, but instead produced a number of scholars of both genders.

Those Terrible Middle Ages: Debunking the Myths by Regine Pernoud. Ignatius Press, 2000.

Answers

Reading Check (left) *lord gave land to knight in return for protection and loyalty* **(right)** *lords' farmlands were taken care of, produced food; peasants were provided protection from invaders*

One such occasion was the knighting of the manor lord's eldest son.

In return for this loyalty and service, a lord had to meet certain duties to his knights. He had to treat them fairly, not demanding too much of their time or money. The lord also had to protect a knight that was attacked by enemies. In addition, the lord had to act as a judge in disputes between knights.

A Complicated System The feudal system in Europe was incredibly complex. Only in rare cases was it clear who owed service to whom. This complexity of the feudal system stemmed from many factors.

First, a person could be both a lord and a vassal at the same time. Some knights who were given large fiefs subdivided their fiefs into smaller parts. They gave small pieces of their land to other knights in exchange for their loyalty. These other knights could even subdivide their land further if they chose, creating many levels of obligations.

Second, one knight could serve many lords. There was no prohibition against a knight accepting fiefs from more than one noble. Indeed, such occurrences were common. If the two lords that a knight served went to war with each other, he had to choose which to follow into battle.

In theory, almost everyone who was part of the feudal system served more than one lord. Everyone in a country was supposed to be loyal to the king. In fact, most fealty oaths were careful to note that the knight would be loyal to both his lord and to the king. In practice, however, not everyone was so loyal. Across Europe, powerful nobles sometimes found themselves to be as strong as the kings they were supposed to serve. Some of these nobles, who might bear the title duke, count, earl, or baron, ignored their duties as vassals. In their lands, the central authority of the king gradually faded.

Third, the rules guiding feudal obligations were specific to time and place. For example, the rules that bound a knight and a lord in England might not apply to the same relationship in France. These rules could also change over time. Just keeping track of one's duties required a great deal of effort.

ACADEMIC VOCABULARY

prohibition an order or law that forbids

READING CHECK **Summarize** How did the feudal system work?

The Manorial System

The feudal system was essentially a political and social system. A related system was at the heart of medieval economics. This system was called the **manorial system** because it was built around large estates called manors.

Lords, Peasants, and Serfs Manors were generally owned by wealthy lords or knights. Bound by feudal duties, lords were too busy to farm their own lands. Instead, peasants farmed the manor fields. Manor lords gave peasants protection and plots of land to cultivate for themselves. In exchange, peasants had to provide the lord with labor and other services.

Most of the peasants on a manor were **serfs**, workers who were legally tied to the manor on which they worked. Serfs not slaves, meaning that they could not be sold away from the manor. Still, serfs were not free to leave a manor or marry without their lord's permission. In addition, serfdom was hereditary: if a child's parents were serfs, so was the child.

Manors also had some free people who rented land from the lord. Free people might also have included land-owning peasants and skilled workers, such as millers and blacksmiths. Most manors also had a priest to provide for spiritual needs.

A Typical Manor Most of a manor's land was occupied by fields for crops and pastures for animals. Farmers in the Middle Ages learned that leaving a field empty for a year helped improve the soil, thus improving the size and quality of harvest. In time, this practice developed into the three-field crop rotation system. In this system, one field was planted in spring for a fall harvesting. Another field was planted in winter for spring harvesting, and the last field remained unplanted for a year.

Besides fields, each manor included a fortified manor house for the noble family and a village where the peasants and serfs lived. It was the goal of each manor lord to make his manor self-sufficient, or able to produce everything people there needed to live. As a result, a typical manor would also include a church, a mill to grind grain, and a blacksmith.

READING CHECK **Analyze** How did lords and peasants benefit from the manorial system?

Differentiating Instruction

Below Level

Learners Having Difficulty

Materials: colored markers, poster paper

1. Have students work in mixed-ability pairs to summarize the information in the text about feudal and manorial systems. Have volunteers share their summaries with the class.

2. Have each student use the information from their summaries to make an illustrated chart comparing and contrasting the feudal and manorial systems.

3. Have students consider the following when making the poster: Is it a social system or economic system? Who is involved in each system? What are their duties and responsibilities of all the people involved?

LS Verbal-Linguistic, Visual-Spatial

Alternative Assessment Handbook, Rubrics 9: Comparing and Contrasting; and 28: Posters

A Typical Manor

Manors were large estates owned by wealthy lords. Peasants and serfs lived and worked on manors. Most manors produced most of the food and other goods that people living there needed.

The manor house or castle provided protection from attack for all people of the manor.

Peasants worked on the lord's lands and also farmed their own. They had to give the lord part of their crop.

In return for the privilege of living on the lord's land, peasants often had to pay a tax on grain ground at the mill.

Even people's spiritual needs were provided for on a manor, which typically had its own church.

New farming tools, such as the heavy plow, and techniques, such as crop rotation, helped farmers grow more food in the Middle Ages.

Skills FOCUS **INTERPRETING VISUALS**

Peasants and lords had different duties and obligations on a manor.

Compare and Contrast How was life on a manor similar and different for peasants and lords?

See **Skills Handbook**, p. H28

THE EARLY MIDDLE AGES **385**

Biography

Gerald of Wales (c. 1146–1223)? Gerald of Wales wrote seventeen books and was a well-known churchman, rising to the position of Archdeacon of Brecon in Wales. He was present at the uncovering of a grave, reportedly that of King Arthur. Gerald wrote two separate accounts of the discovery of the body at Glastonbury. One account reads, "Many tales are told and many legends have been invented about King Arthur and his mysterious ending. In their stupidity the British people maintain that he is still alive. Now that the truth is known…The fairy-tales have been snuffed out…so that what really happened must be made crystal clear to all and separated from the myths…"

Info to Know

Life on a Manor In order to be successful, a manor would have to consist of at least 900 to 2000 acres of farmable land. A manor could consist of more than one village. A typical manor would have a castle, church, mill, an oven for baking, a pond for fishing, an orchard for fruit and vegetable garden. The manor would also raise sheep for wool and keep bees for honey.

About the Illustration

This illustration is an artist's conception based on available sources. Historians, however, are uncertain exactly what this scene looked like.

Differentiating Instruction

Above Level

Advanced Learners/Gifted and Talented

Research Required

1. Tell students they will be researching and reporting on daily life on a Middle Ages manor.

2. Have students conduct outside research, using both traditional print and reliable Internet sources to learn more about manors, medieval farming practices, and the relationships between the social classes. Students should find and include primary source material in their research.

3. Have students create a visual or multimedia presentation showing the results of their research. In addition, students should create a piece of art symbolizing life on a manor or write a poem describing manorial life.

4. Have the students present their work to the class. **LS Verbal-Linguistic, Visual-Spatial**

   Alternative Assessment Handbook, Rubrics 3: Artwork; and 30: Research

Answers

Interpreting Visuals *similar—both had safe place to live; different—lords lived in larger homes, did not have to work the field, were responsible for overall maintenance of the manor; peasants had to work hard in the fields, pay taxes to the lord, provide him with food*

3 What was daily life like for people on a manor? *very hard work with little leisure time*

Daily Life in the Middle Ages

Describe What were the early castles like? *dark, stuffy, cold, crowded; little privacy*

Make Generalizations What do you think would be the hardest part of living on a manor for a peasant? *possible answer—working continually, paying lord with portions of food*

Review & Assess

Close

Have students describe how feudalism and the manorial system shaped society during the Middle Ages.

Review

Online Quiz, Section 3

Assess

SE Section 3 Assessment

Progress Assessment: Section 3 Quiz

Alternative Assessment Handbook

Reteach/Intervene

Interactive Reader and Study Guide, Section 3

Interactive Skills Tutor CD-ROM

Answers

Reading Check *castle life more comfortable, people did not have to work in the fields; village life was very difficult, no comforts, whole family had to work continually*

386

Daily Life in the Middle Ages

Life in the Middle Ages was not easy. People did not enjoy many of the comforts we have today, and most died relatively young. Of course, the lives of nobles and peasants differed greatly.

Life in a Castle Medieval castles sometimes doubled as manor houses. Early castles were built for defense, not for comfort. Most castles had few windows and tended to be stuffy in the summer, cold in the winter, and dark inside almost all of the year. Because the nobles of the castle had to share space with many other people, including soldiers and servants, private rooms were very rare.

The main room of a castle was the hall. The nobles of the castle used this large room for dining and entertaining. Carpets often hung on the walls, but they were not used on the floors. In the earliest castles, the noble family slept at one end of the hall, with their bedrooms separated from the main living area by sheets. Later castles often had separate bedrooms.

Near the bedrooms were the latrines. Waste traveled either down a long pipe that emptied onto the ground or down a chute directly into a moat or river. Instead of toilet paper, people used hay. People bathed in an area of the castle that was separate from the latrines. Usually a wooden bathtub was placed in the garden in warm weather and indoors near a fireplace in cold weather.

Life in a Village In villages, peasant families lived in small, one to two room cottages that they built themselves. The floor was made of packed dirt. The windows were kept small to prevent heat loss. The straw thatch roof was the most critical part of the construction. It had to be layered thick enough to be waterproof, but not so heavy as to collapse on those living inside.

The inside of a peasant's cottage was quite simple. Other than wooden stools and benches, peasants had few pieces of furniture. For bedding, they used straw, sometimes stuffing it into a sack to make a rough mattress. Bedding straw had to be replaced regularly as unwelcome guests, bedbugs and lice, favored it.

Peasant families cooked their meals over an open fire set in the middle of the floor. A typical meal might include brown bread, cheese, vegetables and, on occasion, pork or bacon. Because there were no chimneys, the house was often full of smoke. In addition, sparks from the fire could easily ignite the straw roof and start a massive blaze.

The whole family had to rise before dawn to start their day. Men and boys—and sometimes women—went to work in the fields. Women and girls cooked, sewed, cared for animals, and grew vegetables. During harvest times, the entire family worked in the field all day.

READING CHECK **Contrast** How was life in a castle different from life in a village?

NEW YORK
CC Unit 2-F3
Manorialism in medieval Europe

---

go.hrw.com
Online Quiz
Keyword: SHL EMA HP

Reviewing Ideas, Terms, and People

1. a. Define What was the **feudal system?** What roles did lords and **vassals** play in it?
b. Analyze How did oaths of **fealty** and feudal obligations tie knights to their lords?
c. Elaborate Why was the feudal system so complicated?

2. a. Define What was the **manorial system?** Who participated in this system?
b. Compare and Contrast How were the lives of nobles and peasants similar? How were they different?
c. Elaborate Why do you think most lords wanted their manors to be self-sufficient?

3. a. Describe What was village life like in the Middle Ages?
b. Explain What made the **manorial system** an effective economic system?

Critical Thinking

4. Summarize Draw a graphic organizer like the one below. In each box, list the responsibilities that each group had toward the other.

| Lords | → ← | Knights | → ← | Peasants |

FOCUS ON WRITING

5. Narration Write a journal entry from the point of view of a man or woman in the early Middle Ages. In your entry, describe what your daily life is like and what duties and obligations you fulfill.

386 CHAPTER 13

Section 3 Assessment Answers

1. a. Lords gave land to vassals in return for protection and loyalty.
b. knights required to remain loyal, provide military service when needed
c. different rules in every area; some knights had multiple lords; duties always changing

2. a. economic system of large estates; lords, knights, peasants, serfs
b. Both were farm workers; serfs were legally tied to the manor, peasants were free.
c. possible answer—so people would not leave

3. a. primitive housing, difficult work for all family members
b. built for defense, not comfort

4. Lords—gave land to knights and protected them; Knights—gave military service to lords, provided safe place for peasants to live; Peasants—farmed land on manors owned by knights and lords

5. Journals should mention the never-ending work, that whole families had to work, and the very primitive living conditions.

4 The Growth of Monarchies

BEFORE YOU READ

MAIN IDEA
The power of kings grew and the nature of monarchy changed across Europe in the early Middle Ages.

READING FOCUS
1. How did the power of the English monarchy grow and change?
2. How did kings increase their powers in the other monarchies of Europe?

KEY TERMS AND PEOPLE
Alfred the Great
William the Conqueror
Domesday Book
Eleanor of Aquitaine
Magna Carta
Parliament
Hugh Capet
Otto the Great
Reconquista

NEW YORK
2.5 Students investigate key events in history to identify the factors and effects of change.

3.1 Students analyze the contributions of individuals and groups to social, political, economic, cultural, and religious practices and activities.

THE INSIDE STORY

Did a comet foretell the Norman Conquest of England? In 1066 King Harold of England was traveling with several of his knights. A comet, the one we know today as Halley's comet, appeared in the sky above. Thinking it was a new star, the men stared at the comet in wonder. They had never seen such a sight before. What could it mean?

Harold and his men soon decided that the new star was a sign that change was coming to England. They were right. However, the coming change was not one that Harold and his knights would appreciate. Within the year the Normans, under the command of Duke William of Normandy, invaded England and took the English throne. ◼

A SIGN FROM THE HEAVENS

The appearance of Halley's comet was recorded in the Bayeux Tapestry. It was created before 1476 but when and by whom is unknown. ▼

ISTI MIRANT STELLA

HAROLD

387

Teach the Main Idea

At Level

The Growth of Monarchies

1. **Teach** Ask students the Reading Focus questions to teach this section.

2. **Apply** Have students copy the map of the Holy Roman Empire in this section onto their own papers. Have students add Spain and Portugal to their maps. Then have students scan the section, and write notes on their maps about the growth of monarchies discussed in the section.

3. **Review** Have students work in pairs or small groups to share and discuss their

notes. Have volunteers share notes about each country with the class, and have students check and correct their own work.

4. **Practice/Homework** Have students write a brief essay explaining why the Magna Carta is considered to be the first step toward democracy in England. **LS Visual-Spatial, Verbal-Linguistic**

Alternative Assessment Handbook, Rubrics 20: Map Creation; and 42: Writing to Inform

---

Preteach

Getting Started
Use the **Interactive Reader and Study Guide** to familiarize students with the section content.

Interactive Reader and Study Guide, Section 4

Name _____ Class _____ Date _____
The Early Middle Ages
Section 4

MAIN IDEA
The power of kings grew and the nature of monarchy changed across Europe in the early Middle Ages.

Key Terms and People
Alfred the Great first king of the united England and who drove out the Vikings
William the Conqueror Duke of Normandy, conquered England in 1066
Domesday Book the record of William's survey of England's people and their property
Eleanor of Aquitaine powerful French duchess; divorced the king of France to marry Henry II of England and ruled all of England and about half of France with him
Magna Carta document that restricted the king of England's power, considered to be the first step toward democracy in England
Parliament governing body that was the result of the king's council in the 1260s and which still makes England's laws today
Hugh Capet first ruler from the Capetian dynasty that ruled and expanded France
Otto the Great Saxon duke who became emperor of the Holy Roman Emperor in the early 900s
Reconquista Christian leaders' effort to retake the Iberian peninsula from the Moors

Taking Notes
Copy this chart on a separate piece of paper. As you read the summary, take notes on the growth of monarchies in Europe. In the second box, show how they changed over time.

England	
France	
Holy Roman Empire	
Spain	
Portugal	

Original content Copyright © by Holt, Rinehart and Winston. Additions and changes to the original content are the responsibility of the instructor.
Full Survey Chapter 13   152   Interactive Reader and Study Guide

CRF: Vocabulary Builder: Section 4

Taking Notes

England—William the Conqueror divided England into fiefs, created Domesday book, central tax system; France—Hugh Capet gradually acquired more land and power; Holy Roman Empire—elected ruler, needed support of dukes to make decisions and laws; Spain—Reconquista pushed Moors south, rulers of Aragon and Castile married, united Spain; Portugal—drove the Moors out, claimed independence

❶ How did the power of the English monarchy grow and change? *nobles loyal to the king; king had great power, expanded territory through marriages and conquests; later, the Magna Carta was created to limit king's power; Parliament formed*

The English Monarchy

Explain Why was King William I of England known as William the Conqueror? *He fought the Battle of Hastings and won the crown of England.*

Draw Conclusions Why did William I create a new nobility in England? *to reward Norman soldiers who fought with him; make sure that nobles were loyal to him, instead of King Harold*

Make Judgments Do you think William should have insisted that his nobles learn the Anglo-Saxon language? *possible answers—Yes, not learning English led to a division within English culture; no, eventually English became the language of the land, French enriched the English language.*

Faces of History

Eleanor of Aquitaine Tending Soldiers Eleanor of Aquitaine was an unusual woman, especially for the Middle Ages. During the Second Crusade she and hundreds of her female friends volunteered to follow the soldiers and tend to them throughout the war. She was described as wearing armor and carrying a lance.

Answers

Faces of History *took strong leadership role, divorced, governed her own lands*

Reading Skills *Danish Vikings*

388

FACES OF HISTORY

ELEANOR of Aquitaine
c. 1122–1204

Eleanor of Aquitaine was one of the most powerful people of the Middle Ages. Having inherited a fief about one-third the size of present-day France, she was wealthy in her own right. She gained more power by marriage. At age 15 she married the king of France. The couple, however, grew apart and ended their marriage in 1152.

Soon after, she married Henry II of England, adding her lands to his kingdom. In the early years of their marriage, Eleanor ruled the couple's French territories. Over time, Eleanor and Henry's relationship soured, and Henry imprisoned Eleanor for 15 years. Upon Henry's death in 1189, Eleanor helped her son Richard I rule England.

Infer In what ways was Eleanor an unusual woman?

TAKING NOTES

As you read take notes about the growth of monarchies in Europe.

Monarchy	Details
England	
France	
Holy Roman Empire	
Spain	
Portugal	

READING SKILLS

Using Word Origins If you know that Danelaw comes from combining the Old English words for "the Danes" and "law," whose laws do you think applied in the lands north of London?

The English Monarchy

England was one of the first countries in Europe to develop a strong central monarchy. Under the Anglo-Saxons, who first unified the country, and then under the Normans, who conquered the Anglo-Saxons, the English kings exercised considerable power.

Anglo-Saxon England The Anglo-Saxon rulers of England were descendants of the Angles and Saxons who invaded the island in the 400s. For most of the Anglo-Saxon period, England was divided into seven small kingdoms, each with its own laws and customs.

In the 800s Danish Vikings invaded England and conquered several of these kingdoms. The Vikings never conquered all of England. Their campaign was cut short in 878 by **Alfred the Great**, then king of Wessex in southern England. Alfred drove the Viking forces north of London to what became the Danelaw, a territory under Viking control.

The Norman Conquest Alfred's descendants ruled England for most of the next two centuries. In 1066, however, the king died without an heir, and two men claimed the crown. One was Harold, an Anglo-Saxon nobleman from England. The other was William, the duke of Normandy in France and a distant relative of the dead king. Supported by the English nobility, Harold was named the new king.

Angry at being passed over, William decided to take the crown by force. He gathered an army and sailed to England. Harold marched out to meet him, and the two armies fought in the Battle of Hastings. William won. He became King William I of England, but he is better known as **William the Conqueror**.

William was a stronger king than Anglo-Saxon rulers had been. One of his first acts was to claim all the land in England as his personal property. He then divided the land into fiefs to give to his Norman soldiers and thus created a new nobility. The new nobles owed their positions and their loyalty directly to the king.

To learn more about his kingdom, William ordered a survey taken. He wanted to know who lived in each part of England, what they owned, and how much they could afford to pay in taxes. The survey results were collected in the **Domesday Book**, a book that William used to create a central tax system for England.

William and the Normans introduced many elements of French culture into England. Because most of England's new nobles had been born in France, they spoke French and practiced French customs. Most of the lower classes, on the other hand, kept their old Anglo-Saxon language and habits. Still, the link to French culture would last for centuries.

The English in France As king, William had considerable power. The kings who followed him, though, gained even more power as time passed. This new power came largely from the acquisition of new lands, many of them in France.

William's descendants inherited his position as the duke of Normandy, so they ruled that region in France. In addition, William's great-grandson Henry II was the son of a French duke. When his father died, Henry also inherited his father's lands in France, which became part of England.

Even more territories in France were added to the English crown when Henry married **Eleanor of Aquitaine**, a powerful French duchess. Together, the two ruled all of England and about half of France. In theory, their French holdings made the English kings vassals of the king of France. In practice, however, the kings of England were much stronger than their French counterparts and ignored any feudal obligations they were supposed to have.

Differentiating Instruction

At Level

English-Language Learners

Standard English Mastery | **Research Required**

1. Have students work in pairs to scan the section and create a list of all the people mentioned.

2. Have each student select one person from the list who interests them. Then have students conduct outside research on that person. Students should consult at least two sources for their research.

3. Have students prepare an outline for a biography of that person, and then write a short biography of their chosen person.

Biographies should include an illustration of the person and a bibliography citing all the sources used.

4. Have volunteers share their biographies with the class. 🖎 **Verbal-Linguistic**

📝 **Alternative Assessment Handbook**, Rubrics 4: Biographies; and 29: Presentations

Magna Carta By about 1200 the power of the English king had started to worry some nobles. They feared that kings would abuse their powers and take away the nobles' rights.

The nobles' concerns reached a crisis point in 1215 under King John. Caught up in a war with France in which he lost almost all of England's French holdings, John found himself short of money. He tried to raise money with a new tax on the nobility, but the nobles refused and, instead, took up arms against the king.

Eventually, the rebellious nobles forced John to accept a document outlining their rights. This document was called **Magna Carta**. It contained many provisions that restricted the king's power. For example, Magna Carta stated that the king had to obtain the consent of the nobles before raising taxes. The document also ended the king's ability to arrest and punish people without cause or to take their property without following legal procedures.

The importance of Magna Carta grew in the years after its signing. It set forth ideas about limiting government and rights above executive power. For example, by restricting the king's power, Magna Carta suggested that even kings were not above the law. Because of this, many people today consider Magna Carta one of the most important historical documents to the formation of modern democracies.

Parliament Although Magna Carta addressed many of the nobles' concerns, some nobles were still not satisfied. The king was constantly asking for their approval to raise taxes to finance wars or debts of which they disapproved. To obtain a say in how the kingdom was run, the nobles started another rebellion in the 1260s.

As part of the agreement that ended the rebellion, the king agreed to meet with members of the nobility, the clergy, and the middle class to discuss key issues facing the country. The resulting council eventually developed into **Parliament**, the governing body that still makes England's laws today.

For several years the powers of Parliament remained undefined. One of the first kings to clarify the role of Parliament and to work effectively with this new governing body was Edward I. The Parliament he summoned in 1295 included not only nobles and clergy members but representatives from every county and town in England. It had the power to create new taxes and to advise the king on lawmaking. Members of Parliament also advised the king on other matters of royal policy.

With the help of Parliament, Edward strengthened England's central government and reformed its system of laws. However, Edward saw Parliament as a tool for strengthening the monarchy rather than limiting it. He maintained the power of the king over Parliament, keeping Parliament in a secondary role.

THE IMPACT TODAY
Today the British Parliament is the highest legislative body in the United Kingdom.

READING CHECK **Summarize** How did Magna Carta and Parliament change the English monarchy?

PRIMARY SOURCES

A Summons to Parliament

Parliament took on a greater role in English government during the rule of King Edward I. This letter, sent by the king in 1295 to call a noble to a meeting of Parliament, shows the nature of this new form of government.

"The king to his beloved and faithful relative, Edmund, <u>Earl</u> of Cornwall, greeting. Because we wish to have a consultation and meeting with you and with the rest of the principal men of our kingdom, as to provision for remedies against the dangers which in these days are threatening our whole kingdom; we command you, strictly enjoining you in the fidelity and love in which you are bound to us, that on the Lord's day next after the feast of St. Martin, in the approaching winter, you be present in person at Westminster, for considering, ordaining and doing along with us and with the prelates [high-ranking clergy], and the rest of the principal men and other inhabitants of our kingdom, as may be necessary for meeting dangers of this kind."

> Earl is a title of nobility.

> Similar letters were sent to important people throughout England.

Skills FOCUS **READING LIKE A HISTORIAN**

1. **Explain** Why is the king calling a meeting of Parliament?
2. **Analyze Primary Sources** What does the king's choice of words suggest about his relationship with nobles?

See **Skills Handbook**, p. H25

Reading Focus

The English Monarchy

Recall Why did nobles rebel against King John? *He wanted to place new taxes on them.*

Analyze What was most unusual about the council that became Parliament? *It was composed of nobles, the clergy, and members of the middle class, and commoners, who worked together to form a governing body.*

Draw Conclusions What was the most revolutionary part of the Magna Carta? *the idea that no one, not even the king, was above the law*

📄 **Alternative Assessment Handbook**, Rubrics 3: Artwork

📄 **CRF:** Biography: Christine de Pizan

Info to Know

Parliament Today Parliament is the governing body in the United Kingdom, while the monarchy plays a mostly symbolic role. Parliament consists of two houses, the House of Lords and the House of Commons. Members in the House of Lords are not elected; the position is based on title and heredity. The House of Commons is composed of elected officials who serve regional constituencies. Both houses debate and discuss governmental issues; however, members of the House of Lords do not have a say in matters of taxes and finance.

Collaborative Learning

At Level

The Magna Carta Debate

1. Organize students into small groups, and have each group prepare arguments supporting and opposing the Magna Carta. Students should consider King John's position, the role of kings in the Middle Ages, and the position about new taxes and government taken by nobles, clergy, and the English commoners.

2. Have volunteers stage a short class debate about whether or not the Magna Carta was fair to all.

3. Have students write a short essay explaining if and why the Magna Carta was revolutionary for its time. 🄻🄢 **Kinesthetic, Verbal-Linguistic**

📄 **Alternative Assessment Handbook**, Rubrics 10: Debates; and 43: Writing to Persuade

---

Answers

Reading Like A Historian 1. *to discuss how to prepare for coming dangers;* **2.** *The tone is formal but very polite. He seems respectful.*

Reading Check *reduced the king's power, formed a council (Parliament) that would create new taxes and advise the king on lawmaking*

2 How did kings increase their powers in other monarchies of Europe? *France—gradually acquired more lands by treaties, marriage, and conquest; Holy Roman Empire—gained support from German nobles, had pope's support; Spain—began to drive the Moors out of the Iberian Peninsula, Aragon and Castile united; Portugal—drove the Moors out and declared independence*

Other European Monarchies

Recall Before the Capetians, what territory was ruled by the kings of France? *area around Paris and Orléans*

Draw Conclusions Why do you think the emperor of the Holy Roman Empire was elected? *possible answer—because the Holy Roman Empire was not a unified kingdom; each new emperor needed support from each separate state*

Analyze Why do you think the Holy Roman emperor had to travel to Rome to be crowned by the pope? *demonstrated that pope and the church had power and authority over the emperor*

🗝 **Map Transparency:** The Holy Roman Empire, 1100

Have students look at a current map of Europe in the textbook atlas. Here students locate the current borders of France, Germany, Poland and Hungary, and compare them to the borders of the Holy Roman Empire.

Answers

Interpreting Maps 1. *14*
2. *making sure states would not declare independence or fight with one another for land*

390

THE HOLY ROMAN EMPIRE, 1100

North Sea

ENGLAND FRIESLAND
SAXONY
LORRAINE
FRANCONIA POLAND
BOHEMIA
FRANCE
SWABIA BAVARIA
BURGUNDY Danube
CARINTHIA HUNGARY
LOMBARDY Po River
TUSCANY Adriatic Sea
CORSICA SPOLETO
SARDINIA Mediterranean Sea

| | Holy Roman Empire |
| | Papal States |

0   100   200 Miles
0   100   200 Kilometers
Azimuthal equal-area projection

◀ Created in the 900s, the crown of the Holy Roman emperors was made of gold and gems.

GEOGRAPHY SKILLS | INTERPRETING MAPS

1. **Place** About how many states made up the Holy Roman Empire in 1100?
2. **Regions** What difficulties might have been part of governing the Holy Roman Empire because of its political divisions?

Other European Monarchies

NEW YORK
CC Unit-2
Human geography of medieval Europe

The changes in the English monarchy were unique. During the Middle Ages, kings in other European countries also worked to gain more power, but their experiences were very different from those of the English rulers.

France After Charlemagne's reign, the kings of France did not rule much territory at all. Their rule was largely limited to an area around the cities of Paris and Orléans. The rest of what we think of as France was in the hands of powerful nobles, including the king of England. Many of these nobles, who owned more land and had more power than the king, ignored the king's wishes and ruled as they pleased.

390 CHAPTER 13

In the mid-900s one noble family rose to power in France when one of its members was elected king. This family was called the Capetians, named after the first family member to hold power, **Hugh Capet** (kuh-PAY). Hugh and his successors gradually managed to extend the power of their monarchy throughout France. Sometimes they fought local nobles for power, while at other times they created allegiances with other powerful nobles through treaties or arranged marriages. By about 1300 the Capetians ruled almost all of modern France.

Holy Roman Empire Recall that the emperor Charlemagne managed to unify most of western Europe into one empire. After he died, however, his empire split into two parts. The western part of the empire became France. The eastern part became known as Germany. Unlike France, which remained somewhat unified under one king, Germany separated into several small states. Each state had its own ruler, most of whom used the title of duke.

In 936, **Otto the Great**, the duke of Saxony, gained enough support from other German nobles to succeed his father, Henry I, as king of the Germans. Otto worked to unite German lands, and he conquered parts of northern Italy. When nobles challenged Pope John XII, he turned to Otto for help. The pope rewarded Otto's support by crowning him Emperor of the Romans in 962. In time, the territories united under Otto became known as the Holy Roman Empire. It was called holy because the empire had the pope's support. It was called Roman because Charlemagne, when he had ruled over the area, had held the title Emperor of the Roman People.

For the most part, Holy Roman Emperors made decisions and passed laws with the

---

Skills Focus: Sequencing

Below Level

Reading Skill
Holy Roman Empire Charts

1. Have students review the information in the text about the Holy Roman Empire.

2. Copy the graphic organizer for students to see, omitting the italicized answers. Have students copy and complete it showing the sequence of development within the Holy Roman Empire.

📝 **Alternative Assessment Handbook**, Rubric 7: Charts

Charlemagne unifies central Europe.
↓
Charlemagne dies, empire splits
↓
Germany separates into small states.
↓
Otto the Great gains support from German nobles; takes title of emperor
↓
Otto has pope's support, Germany becomes Holy Roman Empire

help dukes, who maintained full authority in their own lands. Support from the dukes was needed not only to make laws but also to become emperor. Beginning in the 1100s, Holy Roman emperors did not inherit their position. Instead, they were elected. A select group of electors—the dukes of certain powerful states and a few archbishops—met when an emperor died to choose his successor. The person chosen to be the new emperor then had to travel to Rome to be crowned by the pope before his power was fully recognized.

Spain and Portugal In Spain and Portugal, the growth of the monarchy was coupled with religious struggles. Today these two countries share the Iberian Peninsula, which had been conquered by Muslims in the early 700s. Called Moors by Christians, these Muslims had built a powerful state centered in the city of Córdoba. Christians ruled only a few small kingdoms in the far northern part of the peninsula.

As early as 722 Christian rulers expanding westward had begun to fight the Moors, trying to drive them out of Europe. Over time, Christian rulers continued their westward push, but they met with little success until the early 1000s. By this time, a civil war had broken out in Muslim Spain, weakening the Moorish leaders. Watching from afar, Christian leaders took advantage of this weakness.

Christian states embarked on a series of campaigns to retake the Iberian Peninsula, an effort called the **Reconquista** (reh-kahn-KEES-tuh), or reconquest. The largest of the Christian kingdoms in the Iberian Peninsula and the leader of the Reconquista was Castile (ka-STEEL). In 1085 the king of Castile won a great victory over the Moors by capturing the city of Toledo. His victory inspired the rulers of two other Christian kingdoms, Aragon and Portugal, to join in the Reconquista.

Together, the three Iberian kingdoms won victory after victory over the Moors. In the early 1100s the Portuguese drove the Moors completely out of their lands and established the Kingdom of Portugal. Meanwhile, the rulers of Aragon and Castile continued to push south. In 1236 they captured Córdoba itself. Within a few years, the Christians had pushed the Moors almost all the way out of Spain. Of the once powerful Moorish state, only a small kingdom called Granada, protected by mountains in the far south, remained.

The Moors were not driven completely off the Iberian Peninsula until 1492, when they were finally forced to surrender Granada. Modern Spain also has its origins in the late 1400s. A royal marriage between the rulers of Aragon and Castile had united the two kingdoms. By combining their countries and their power, the two found that they ruled one of the strongest countries in all of Europe.

READING CHECK **Analyze** How did rulers in France, the Holy Roman Empire, and Spain gain power?

SECTION 4 ASSESSMENT

go.hrw.com
Online Quiz
Keyword: SHL EMA HP

Reviewing Ideas, Terms, and People

1. **a. Describe** How did **William the Conqueror** come to rule England? How did the English government change after he took the throne?
   b. Explain How did **Magna Carta** and the development of **Parliament** limit the power of England's kings?
   c. Predict How might England's history have been different if the Normans had not arrived and England had remained an Anglo-Saxon kingdom?

2. **a. Identify** What family gained power in France in the 900s? How did that family gain power?
   b. Draw Conclusions How did the **Reconquista** lead to the growth of the Spanish and Portuguese monarchies?
   c. Elaborate How do you think having elected emperors affected the balance of power between emperors and nobles in the Holy Roman Empire?

Critical Thinking

3. **Identify Cause and Effect** Use your notes to create a chart like the one below. For each monarchy, describe the growth of the king's power and its effects.

King's Power	→	Effects
	→	
	→	
	→	

FOCUS ON WRITING

4. **Persuasion** Write a letter to King John of England as though you were one of his advisors. In your letter, you must advise him either to accept or reject Magna Carta. Remember to use logical reasons to support your position.

THE EARLY MIDDLE AGES **391**

Section 4 Assessment Answers

1 **a.** won the Battle of Hastings, reclaimed England; new nobility created
   b. developed council with power to tax, king discussed key issues with council
   c. might not have turned into powerful, unified kingdom with a Parliament

2. **a.** Capetians; through treaties, conquest, and marriage
   b. created a strong Christian military; united three Iberian kingdoms against the Moors
   c. possible answer—Each new emperor needed the support of all the dukes.

3. England—William the Conqueror centralized power; nobility fought back; France—Capetians acquired land and power, enlarged and unified country; Holy Roman Empire—elected ruler with support of pope; became very powerful; Spain—pushed Moors south; rulers of Aragon and Castile married, uniting Spain; Portugal—drove Moors out, claimed independence

4. Letters should mention that the Magna Carta, would allow the king to retain many of his powers.

• **Direct Teach** •

Reading Focus

Other European Monarchies

Recall What was the Reconquista? *Christian effort to remove Muslims from the Iberian Peninsula*

Summarize How was Spain united and what the result? *Rulers of Aragon and Castile married; Spain became one of the strongest countries in Europe.*

CRF: History and Geography: The Treaty of Verdun

• **Review & Assess** •

Close

Have students compare and contrast the development of the monarch in England with those in other European countries.

Review

Online Quiz, Section 4

Assess

SE Section 4 Assessment

Progress Assessment: Section 4 Quiz

Alternative Assessment Handbook

Reteach/Intervene

Interactive Reader and Study Guide, Section 4

Interactive Skills Tutor CD-ROM

Answers

Reading Check *by acquiring new land and territories through alliances, marriage, and conquest*

391

Preteach

Getting Started

Use the **Interactive Reader and Study Guide** to familiarize students with the section content.

📝 **Interactive Reader and Study Guide,** Section 5

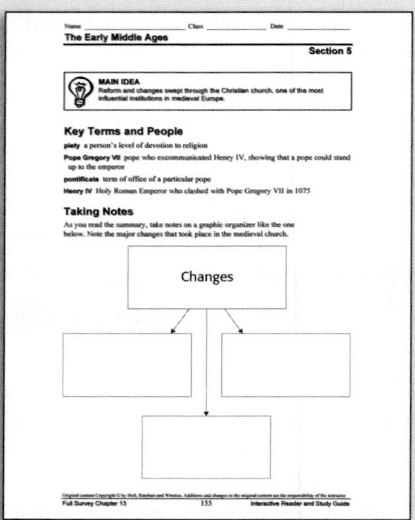

Academic Vocabulary

Review with students the high-use academic term in this section.

resolved determined (p. 394)

📝 **CRF: Vocabulary Builder: Section 5**

Taking Notes

pope became political figure; religion united Europe; upswell of piety as members became more active and devoted; Leo IX reformed church; split in church, Roman Catholic and Orthodox; papal armies; reforms in monasteries; emergence of the Cistercian Order

BEFORE YOU READ

MAIN IDEA

Reform and changes swept through the Christian Church, one of the most influential institutions in medieval Europe.

READING FOCUS

1. What was the nature and influence of religion in the Middle Ages?
2. What led to the growth of papal power in Europe?
3. What changes in monasticism were introduced in the Middle Ages?

KEY TERMS AND PEOPLE

piety
pontificate
Pope Gregory VII
Henry IV

🟦 **NEW YORK**

PI **3.1** Students analyze the roles and contributions of individuals and groups to social, political, economic, cultural, and religious practices and activities.

BAREFOOT in the SNOW

▲ **Emperor Henry IV waited three days to meet with Pope Gregory VII and the Countess Matilda.**
Henri IV asking Countess Matilda to intervene in the conflict with the pope, from a poem by Donizon, Italian school, 1100s.

392 CHAPTER 13

THE INSIDE STORY

Who would have the power to make an emperor wait in the snow, begging for an audience?
Late in January 1077, Henry IV, the Holy Roman emperor, left Germany. He was headed to Canossa, a castle in northern Italy. Once he arrived at Canossa, Henry stripped off all his royal finery and donned a simple shirt woven from rough cloth. Shoeless, Henry waded into the deep snow before the castle and waited for an invitation to enter. For three days he stood there, shivering and eating nothing, before the castle's huge gates were finally opened to him.

Canossa was the home of Matilda, the countess of Tuscany, but Henry had not come to see her. He was there to see the only man powerful enough to make the mighty Holy Roman emperor wait—the pope, Gregory VII. ◼

Religion in the Middle Ages

The pope is the head of the Roman Catholic Church. Early popes were seen as spiritual leaders, but during the Middle Ages they became powerful political figures as well. How did this change come about?

While manorialism and feudalism encouraged local loyalties, Christian beliefs brought people across Europe together in the spiritual community of Christendom. The majority of people in Europe were, at least in name, Christian, and religion touched almost every aspect of their lives. Major life events—baptism, marriage, death—were marked by religious ceremonies. Monks acted as peacemakers in disputes and prayed for the safety of rulers and armies. Church officials also served as teachers and record keepers. As the people's main connection to the church, members of the clergy had great influence.

Teach the Main Idea

At Level

Power of the Church

1. **Teach** Ask students the Reading Focus questions to teach this section.

2. **Apply** Have students scan the section and create a Web diagram showing the main headings and subheadings. For each blue subheading, students should list at least two details.

3. **Review** Have volunteers display their diagrams to the class. Have students select the diagrams that they feel best represent the content of the section.

4. **Practice/Homework** Have students write a brief essay explaining the influence of religion, the growth of papal power, and the changes in monasticism during the Middle Ages. 🄻🅂 **Visual-Spatial, Verbal-Linguistic**

📝 **Alternative Assessment Handbook,** Rubric 40: Writing to Describe

Sometime around 1000 the influence of the church increased dramatically. At that time, there was a great upwelling of piety in Europe. **Piety** is a person's level of devotion to his or her religion. For centuries Europeans had been members of the Christian church, but at this time many believers became more devout. Across Europe, people's participation in religious services increased, and thousands flocked to monasteries to join religious orders.

READING CHECK Identify Cause and Effect Why was the medieval clergy so influential?

Growth of Papal Power

The common people of Europe were not the only ones inspired by a new sense of piety in the Middle Ages. Within the Christian Church itself, many clergy members sought ways to improve conditions and end corrupt practices.

Church Reforms In the 900s and 1000s, popes had little authority. Although the pope was considered the head of the entire church, local bishops actually made most important religious decisions. As a result, the papacy was not held in high regard. Adding to this lack of esteem was the fact that few popes during this time were noted for their religious devotion. Most of them were nobles who were more concerned with increasing their own power than overseeing spiritual matters.

In 1049 the first of a series of clever and capable popes dedicated to reforming the papacy came to power. His name was Leo IX. A man of high ideals, Leo believed that Europe's clergy had become corrupt and set out on a mission to reform it. Among Leo's top concerns was simony, the buying and selling of church offices. He traveled throughout Europe, seeking out and replacing bishops suspected of such offenses.

Bishops guilty of particularly bad offenses were excommunicated, or cast out of the church. For Christians in the Middle Ages, there was no greater punishment. A person who had been excommunicated could not take part in the Eucharist, and the belief was that one who died while excommunicated would not be saved. Through his reforms, Leo became more active in governing the church than any other pope had been for centuries.

Leo's reforms brought him into conflict with both political and religious leaders. Kings resented what they saw as interference with the bishops in their kingdoms. Many bishops, too, believed the pope had no authority to tell them how to act. Among those who rejected Leo's authority was the patriarch, or bishop, of Constantinople. Leo excommunicated the patriarch in 1054, an action that split the Christian Church in two. Those who agreed with Leo were Roman Catholics, and those who sided with the patriarch were called Orthodox.

Popes and Politics Popes gained influence not only over people's religious lives but also over politics in Europe. The pope became the head of a huge network of ecclesiastical, or church, courts, that heard cases on religious or moral matters. Popes also ruled territories, such as the Papal States in Italy. To defend their territories, popes had the ability to raise armies. For example, several popes hired the Normans to fight wars on their behalf. The Crusades, a series of wars launched against the Muslims of Southwest Asia, were launched by popes.

TAKING NOTES
Take notes on the major changes in the medieval church.

Changes

NEW YORK

CC Unit 2-F5
The role of the church in medieval Europe

Papal Authority
Some medieval popes had enough authority to summon nobles and even kings to councils, such as this one that launched the Crusades.

Pope Urban II presiding over the Council of Clermont, France, c. 1490. Courtesy of Bibliotheque Nationale

THE EARLY MIDDLE AGES **393**

Direct Teach

Reading Focus

1 What was the nature and influence of religion in the Middle Ages? *almost every European was Christian; religion touched almost every part of life, unified Europeans; church members became more active, more people joined religious orders*

Religion in the Middle Ages

Recall What two roles did popes have during the Middle Ages? *head of the Roman Catholic Church, political leaders*

Make Inferences Why did Europeans' devotion to the church increase? *upswelling of piety; church touched almost every aspect of people's lives*

Reading Focus

2 What led to the growth of papal power in Europe? *Popes became involved in governing church, ruled territories, raised armies, retained power to name bishops, and could excommunicate kings.*

Growth of Papal Power

Identify Who made most of the decisions for the church during the early Middle Ages? *the bishops*

Summarize What led to the split in the Catholic Church? *bishop of Constantinople refused to accept Pope Leo's authority over the bishops; Leo excommunicated him; Orthodox Church formed*

Skills Focus: Identifying Cause and Effect

At Level

Reading Skill
Split in the Catholic Church

1. Have students review the information in the text about the split in the Catholic Church and write a quick summary of what occurred.

2. Have students use their summaries to write two letters or petitions. The first letter should be from Pope Leo to the bishop of Constantinople. This letter should tell the bishop that if he does not begin to follow the pope's policies, he will be excommunicated. The letter should describe the consequences of excommunication. The second letter or petition should be from the bishop to the pope, announcing that he does not intend to follow the pope's orders and intends to split and form the Orthodox Church. In this letter students should predict consequences for the Roman Catholic Church if a split occurs.

3. Have volunteers share their letters with the class. **LS** Verbal-Linguistic

Alternative Assessment Handbook, Rubrics 9: Comparing and Contrasting; and 41: Writing to Express

Answers

Reading Check *Christian church had strong influence over daily lives of most Europeans; clergy were the people's link to the church*

393

Reading Focus

Growth of Papal Power

Recall Before Pope Gregory, who chose religious leaders? *Kings chose most bishops; Holy Roman emperors had named several popes.*

Explain How did the pope gain authority over the Holy Roman emperor? *excommunicated him, called for his overthrow*

📄 **CRF:** Biography: Thomas Becket

Counterpoints

Two Sources on the Power of the Papacy

Make Inferences Why do you think the emperor wanted the power to appoint the pope? *possible answers— emperor wanted power over church; did not want a more powerful leader than himself to exist*

Info to Know

Investiture Controversy Those who were appointed to serve as bishop by a king received large tracts of land and could accumulate great wealth. The sale of church offices was known as simony, but the Church considered the practice sinful. Pope Gregory VII wanted to return the right of investiture, awarding church offices, to the papacy. The Roman Catholic Church developed the College of Cardinals to initiate the appointment of bishops.

Answers

Counterpoints *Gregory, the pope, believes that priests should be considered fathers and masters of kings; Henry, the emperor, believes that popes were not called to priesthood, but got their positions by cunning or by buying the position; He also believes that the Lord calls kings to their positions, so they should appoint the popes.*

Reading Skills *possible answer— probably defensive and angry*

Reading Check *eliminated corrupt clergy, appointed bishops, became political leaders, built armies, ruled territory*

394

COUNTERPOINTS **Two Sources on the Power of the Papacy**

Holy Roman Emperor Henry IV believed that he and other rulers had been chosen by God. He denounced the political power of popes, whom he did not believe had the authority to pass judgment on kings.

❝Our Lord, Jesus Christ, has called us to kingship, but has not called you to the priesthood. For you have risen by these steps: namely, by cunning, which the monastic profession abhors, to money; by money to favor; by favor to the sword . . . You have also touched me, one who, though unworthy, has been anointed to kingship among the anointed. This wrong you have done to me, although as the tradition of the holy Fathers has taught, I am to be judged by God alone.❞

Emperor Henry IV
—from a letter to Pope Gregory VII, 1076

Pope Gregory VII argued that the pope's spiritual authority was greater than the secular power wielded by kings. He believed that the pope's power came from God, but a king's came from more worldly sources.

❝Who does not know that kings and princes derive their origin from men ignorant of God who raised themselves above their fellows by pride, plunder, treachery, murder—in short, by every type of crime—at the instigation of the Devil, the prince of this world, men blind with greed and intolerable in their audacity? . . . Does anyone doubt that the priests of Christ are to be considered as fathers and masters of kings and princes and of all believers? Would it not be regarded as pitiable madness if a son should try to rule his father or a pupil his master?❞

Pope Gregory VII
—from a letter to the bishop of Metz, Germany, 1081

Skills Focus INVESTIGATING HISTORY

Analyze How did Gregory's and Henry's views of the papacy differ? How did each man's view relate to his own position?

ACADEMIC VOCABULARY

resolved
determined

READING SKILLS

Understanding Word Origins If you know that scathing comes from an Old Norse word meaning "to injure," what do you think was the tone of Gregory's letter?

Conflict over Bishops Although popes had increased their power, they still came into conflict with political leaders. Popes of the late 1000s were firmly <u>resolved</u> to change the way members of the clergy were chosen. For years, kings and other leaders had played an active role in choosing clergy. Kings chose most of the bishops who served in their lands, and the Holy Roman emperor had named several popes. The reform popes did not think that anyone except the clergy should choose religious officials.

The issue of clergy selection became critical during the **pontificate**, or papal term in office, of **Pope Gregory VII** in the late 1000s. At that time, the Holy Roman emperor was **Henry IV**. In 1075 Henry chose a new bishop for the city of Milan in northern Italy. Gregory did not approve of his choice and removed the bishop. In response, Henry wrote a <u>scathing</u> letter to the pope, stating that Gregory had no authority over him or any other ruler.

Gregory's response was to excommunicate Henry. He also called on the clergy and nobility of Germany to replace the emperor with a more suitable candidate. This response frightened Henry. Fearing that he would lose his throne, he traveled to Canossa, Italy, where Gregory was staying to beg forgiveness. Though reluctant, Gregory lifted the excommunication.

Gregory and Henry continued to fight over bishops for years. In fact, the conflict over this issue outlived both men. Later popes and emperors finally reached a compromise: local clergy would choose bishops, but their choices could be vetoed by secular rulers. More important than the details of the conflict, though, was the fact that Gregory had been able to stand up to the emperor. The pope had become one of the strongest figures in Europe.

READING CHECK **Analyze** In what ways did popes become stronger in the Middle Ages?

Differentiating Instruction

Below Level

Learners Having Difficulty

1. Review with students the two quotes from the Counterpoints feature. Have students work in mixed-ability pairs to write a quick summary of each argument. Have students chart the arguments on a graphic organizer like the one shown.

2. As an extension have advanced students to conduct research on the conflict and report their findings to the class. **LS** Visual-Spatial

 Alternative Assessment Handbook, Rubric 13: Graphic Organizers

Pope Gregory VII	Emperor Henry IV

Changes in Monasticism

In the early Middle Ages, monasteries had been founded all across Europe by men seeking lives of contemplation and prayer. These monasteries were often paid for by local rulers, who then helped to choose the abbots who led the monasteries. By about 900, however, rulers had stopped choosing qualified abbots. Far from being religious, many abbots held their positions just for the prestige it brought to them or their families. In monasteries led by these abbots, the strict Benedictine Rule was largely abandoned.

In the early 900s a small group of monks sought to return monasticism to its strict roots. They established a new monastery at Cluny, France, where they would live strictly according to the Benedictine Rule. To prevent the onset of corruption, the monks of Cluny reserved the right to choose their own abbot, rather than having one appointed to them.

Over time, Cluny became the most influential monastery in Europe. Monks from Cluny established daughter houses, whose leaders had to answer to the abbot of Cluny. In addition, other monasteries in France, Spain, and Italy adopted Cluny's customs and agreed to follow the direction of its abbots. Over time, Cluny became the core of a network of monasteries that stretched across western Europe.

For some monks, however, even the Benedictine life was not strict enough. These monks wanted lives free from any worldly distractions. Not finding what they wanted in Benedictine houses, they created new orders.

The most popular of these new monastic orders was the Cistercian (sis-TUHR-shuhn) order. Cistercian monasteries were usually broad estates built outside of towns to ensure isolation. These monasteries were undecorated and unheated, even in winter. The monks who lived there divided their time between prayer and labor, such as farm work or copying texts.

Some other new orders were even stricter than the Cistercians. Members of these orders lived like hermits in tiny cells, having no contact with other people. Those who joined such orders were widely admired for their piety and dedication to their faith.

READING CHECK **Find the Main Idea** What changes were introduced to monasticism?

Cistercian Life
As shown in this medieval manuscript, the Cistercian order was dedicated to leading simple lives. Monks spent part of each day in prayer and part at work.

SECTION 5 ASSESSMENT

go.hrw.com
Online Quiz
Keyword: SHL EMA HP

Reviewing Ideas, Terms, and People

1. a. Define What is **piety**? How did increased piety affect religion in the Middle Ages?
   b. Draw Conclusions Why did a shared religion make people feel like part of a larger community?

2. a. Identify What goals did Leo IX have as pope? How did he achieve those goals?
   b. Make Generalizations What was the relationship between Pope Gregory VII and Emperor **Henry IV** like? Why?
   c. Elaborate Explain why both kings and popes wanted the right to choose bishops.

3. a. Describe How was Cluny different from earlier monasteries?
   b. Summarize Why were monks frustrated in the early Middle Ages, and what steps did they take to change things?

Critical Thinking

4. Summarize Draw a chart like the one at right. Use your notes on changes in Christianity to identify how those changes affected different types of people in the Middle Ages.

Popes	Kings
Monks	Other Christians

FOCUS ON WRITING

5. Description Write a paragraph describing what life was like in a Cistercian monastery. Use vivid language and specific details to make your writing more interesting.

THE EARLY MIDDLE AGES **395**

Direct Teach

Reading Focus

3 What changes in monasticism were introduced in the Middle Ages? *stricter rules, monks stayed out of politics, simplified lives*

Changes in Monasticism

Describe How did the monks at Cluny reform monasticism? *Monks strictly followed Benedictine Rule and kept right to choose their abbot.*

Analyze Why might monks want to join the Cistercian Order? *possible answer—live simple lives dedicated to God; avoid politics*

Review & Assess

Close

Have volunteers describe the changes in religious life during the Middle Ages.

Review

Online Quiz, Section 5

Assess

SE Section 1 Assessment
📄 **Progress Assessment**: Section 5 Quiz
📄 **Alternative Assessment Handbook**

Reteach/Intervene

📄 **Interactive Reader and Study Guide**, Section 5
💿 **Interactive Skills Tutor CD-ROM**

Section 5 Assessment Answers

1. a. religious devotion; strengthened the Roman Catholic Church
   b. unified people within Europe

2. a. reform the church; eliminated corrupt clergy, met with nobles, made political decisions, limited power of kings in religious matters
   b. It was heated; pope excommunicated Henry; Henry had to beg pope to change excommunication.
   c. powerful job; bishops would owe loyalty to person who appointed them

3. a. very strict, followed Benedictine Rule
   b. believed monasteries did not follow the Benedictine Rule, monks pulled into politics; developed stricter new orders and rules

4. Popes—acquired more political power; Kings—owed allegiance to pope; Monks—reformed monastery life; Other Christians—unified through religion, more devoted

5. Student paragraphs should include descriptions of stark, bare conditions and regimented lifestyle.

Answers

Reading Check *stricter rules, monks stayed out of politics, simplified lives*

395

Document-Based Investigation

CHAPTER 13

Document-Based Investigation

Perspectives on Magna Carta

Historical Context The four documents below reveal different aspects of and attitudes toward Magna Carta.

Task Study the selections and answer the questions that follow. Then, using evidence from these selections and from the chapter, write an essay explaining whether Magna Carta is truly a foundation of democratic government or just another document that upheld feudal relationships.

Word Help

heir one who inherits

livelihood living, income

gravity seriousness, significance

exiled banished, stripped of citiznship

Info to Know

The Magna Carta King John was forced to meet with his nobles at Runnymede, and on June 15, 1215, he signed the Articles of the Barons, which became known as the Magna Carta. Today the Runnymede meadows are owned by the National Trust, and a memorial commemorates the signing of the charter.

Activity Magna Carta Posters
Have students design a poster commemorating the signing of the Magna Carta.

LS Visual-Spatial

Alternative Assessment Handbook, Rubrics 28: Posters

DOCUMENT 1

Selections from Magna Carta

Magna Carta outlined the rights of nobles and limited the king's power, which a group of nobles thought he was abusing. The excerpts below describe just some of the new agreements between king and nobles.

> To all free men of our kingdom we [the monarchy] have also granted, for us and our heirs for ever, all the liberties written out below, to have and to keep for them and their heirs, of us and our heirs:

20. For a trivial offence, a free man shall be fined only in proportion to the degree of his offence, and for a serious offence correspondingly, but not so heavily as to deprive him of his livelihood.

21. Earls and barons shall be fined only by their equals, and in proportion to the gravity of their offence.

29. No constable may compel a knight to pay money for castle-guard if the knight is willing to undertake the guard in person, or with reasonable excuse to supply some other fit man to do it. A knight taken or sent on military service shall be excused from castle-guard for the period of this service.

39. No free man shall be seized or imprisoned, or stripped of his rights or possessions, or outlawed or exiled, or deprived of his standing in any other way, nor will we proceed with force against him, or send others to do so, except by the lawful judgement of his equals or by the law of the land.

396 CHAPTER 13

DOCUMENT 2

An Artist's View

The painting below was created by an unknown artist who copied an engraving by artist Alonzo Chappel. Created several hundred years after the signing of Magna Carta, it shows the artist's view of the mood at the historic event.

King John signing Magna Carta, undated illustration after painting by Chappel.

Skills Focus: Analyzing Primary Sources

At Level

The Magna Carta

1. Organize students into small mixed-ability groups.

2. Have students review and summarize each of the documents. You may wish to work with students to ensure that they understand the content of each document.

3. Have each group answer the following question: Is the Magna Carta the foundation for a democratic government or for a feudal contract? Each group should discuss the question and then agree on the answer.

4. Have each group present the reasoning behind its answer to the class. Guide the class in a discussion about each group's answer.

LS Verbal-Linguistic

Alternative Assessment Handbook, Rubrics 12: Drawing Conclusions; and 14: Group Activities

DOCUMENT 3

A Contemporary's Account

Roger of Wendover was a monk and a historian, who lived at the time of the signing of Magna Carta. The excerpt below is from his account of the signing.

King John, when he saw that he was deserted by almost all, so that out of his regal superabundance of followers he scarcely retained seven knights, was much alarmed lest the barons would attack his castles and reduce them without difficulty, as they would find no obstacle to their so doing; and he deceitfully pretended to make peace for a time with the aforesaid barons . . . and told them that, for the sake of peace, and for the exaltation and honour of the kingdom, he would willingly grant them the laws and liberties they required . . . Accordingly, at the time and place pre-agreed on, the king and nobles came to the appointed conference, and when each party had stationed themselves apart from the other, they began a long discussion about terms of peace and the aforesaid liberties. . . . At length, after various points on both sides had been discussed, king John, seeing that he was inferior in strength to the barons, without raising any difficulty, granted the underwritten laws and liberties, and confirmed them by his charter.

DOCUMENT 4

A Historian's View

C. Warren Hollister is one of many historians today to explore the different meanings of Magna Carta in its historical context.

Its authors were looking neither forward nor backward but were contending with problems of the moment. Magna Carta's most important clauses were designed to keep the king within the bounds of popular and feudal custom. Royal taxes not sanctioned by custom, for example, were to be levied only with the consent of the great men of the kingdom. But implicit in the traditional doctrine that the lord had to respect the rights of his vassals and rule according to good custom was the constitutional principle of government under the law. In striving to make John a good feudal lord, the barons in 1215 were moving uncertainly toward constitutional monarchy. Thus Magna Carta expresses the notion that the king is bound by traditional legal constraints in his dealings with all classes of free English people.

Word Help

superabundance excessive

exaltation praise, honor

aforesaid stated before

charter contract

clauses specific articles, terms, or conditions in a formal document

sanctioned approved

levied imposed, collected

doctrine belief, principle

Info to Know

Roger of Wendover (?–1236) Roger of Wendover spent most of his adult life at St. Albans abbey. He wrote a chronicle called *Flores Historiarum* (Flowers of History), a world history that he compiled from information that he found at St. Albans. In his work he reports on the signing of the Magna Carta.

Skills FOCUS — READING LIKE A HISTORIAN

DOCUMENT 1

a. Identify To what people do the agreements described in Magna Carta apply?

b. Infer What kinds of problems do you think were going on in England that led to the writing of Magna Carta?

DOCUMENT 2

a. Describe What groups of people does the artist represent as present at the signing of Magna Carta?

b. Analyze How does the artist portray King John's emotions at the signing of Magna Carta? Why would the king have felt that way?

DOCUMENT 3

a. Identify Main Ideas According to Roger of Wendover, why did King John agree to sign Magna Carta?

b. Analyze What circumstances might affect the accuracy of Roger of Wendover's account?

DOCUMENT 4

a. Identify According to Hollister, what was the main goal of the framers of Magna Carta?

b. Explain Why does Hollister describe Magna Carta as a feudal document?

DOCUMENT-BASED ESSAY QUESTION

Magna Carta has been referred to as a document that simply defined the relationship of lord and vassal. It has also been referred to as a great step toward democratic government. Which interpretation is correct? Or are both valid? Using the documents and information from the chapter, form a thesis to support your interpretation of Magna Carta. Then write a short essay to support your position.

See **Skills Handbook**, p. H25

Differentiating Instruction

Below Level

Standard English Mastery

Learners Having Difficulty

Materials: construction paper, colored markers

1. Have students reread each of the documents and select one that interests them the most.

2. Have students paraphrase the document in modern terms and language. Remind students to use standard English, and to check for speling and grammatical errors.

3. Have students write their paraphrase on the construction paper. Post student work for all to see on a piece of poster board to be displayed in the classroom.

4. Allow class time for students to look at the posters. **LS Visual-Spatial, Verbal-Linguistic**

Alternative Assessment Handbook, Rubric 28: Posters

Answers

Reading Like a Historian
Document 1. a. *all free men in the kingdom;* **b.** *abusive punishments and fines, people stripped of possessions and exiled;* **Document 2. a.** *King John and his nobles;* **b.** *upset, angry; did not want to give up power;* **Document 3. a.** *knew that he had lost support, knew he could lose the crown;* **b.** *possible answer—his opinion about the Magna Carta and his loyalties to the king;* **Document 4. a.** *to limit the power of the king, ensure fairness;* **b.** *it was a contract between a lord (king) and his vassals (barons);* **Essay** *Student essays should reflect the content and viewpoints in the documents and be supported with logic and concrete details.*

Visual Summary

Review and Inquiry Have students write a summarizing paragraph for each of the four Quick Facts boxes on this page.

Quick Facts Transparency: Visual Study Guide: The Early Middle Ages

Review Key Terms and People

1. navigation
2. feudal system
3. William the Conqueror
4. incorporate
5. Charlemagne
6. serfs
7. fief
8. manorial system
9. Parliament
10. piety
11. sagas

Comprehension and Critical Thinking

12. a. defeated Lombards; pope crowned him emperor

b. brought unity to the empire; barons helped govern empire, using same laws for all people

13. a. central Asia

b. needed food and supplies; their farmlands were not fertile

c. caused people to be afraid, motivated them into becoming organized in order to fight off the invaders

14. a. lords—provided land to vassals in return for protection, resolved disputes between knights, protected knights; vassals—provided a military service, loyal and faithful, gave money on special occasions

b. possible answer—similarity: both knights and serfs served a lord; difference: knights given land in return for service, serfs given a place to live, could not leave the land

c. possible answer—fortunate; had place to live, could grow food

15. a. an effort by Christians to retake the Iberian Peninsula from Muslims

b. William the Conqueror had lived in France, granted nobility to French sol-

diers who fought with him during the Battle of Hastings

c. restricted the power of the kings; gave nobles and middle class voice in taxation and England's affairs of state

16. a. almost everyone in Europe was Christian; popes could excommunicate kings

b. pope believed that he should appoint bishops so that loyalty of bishops would be to the pope and the Church, not to their kings

c. possible answer—the pope; he is in charge of church and religious affairs, not political issues

---

QUICK FACTS

VISUAL STUDY GUIDE

Political Changes in the Early Middle Ages

Charlemagne and the Frankish Empire
- Charles Martel leads the Franks to victory at the Battle of Tours
- Pope Leo III crowns Charlemagne Emperor of the Romans
- Charlemagne unites much of Western Europe into a Christian empire
- Viking, Magyar, and Muslim invasions and migrations bring change to the Frankish Empire
- After Charlemagne, the Frankish Empire declined

Monarchies Grow and Change
- William the Conqueror takes England by force and increases the power of the king
- Henry II and Eleanor of Aquitaine rule all of England and about half of France
- Magna Carta limits the English monarchy
- Hugh Capet extends of the French monarchy
- Otto the Great starts the Holy Roman Empire
- Christian monarchies in Spain and Portugal unite to drive out the Moors

The Church in the Early Middle Ages

Everyday Life
- Church officials serve as teachers and record keepers
- Religious ceremonies important to everyday life
- Christianity unifies most parts of western Europe

Popes Gain Power
- Replace corrupt bishops
- Threaten to excommunicate
- Raise armies
- Call kings and nobles to council
- Rule the Papal States

Monasteries Change
- Wealthy monasteries spark reform
- Benedictine Rule regains followers
- New, stricter, orders form
- Monks retreat from politics

Feudalism

Lords
- Provide fief, or land
- Offer protection
- Resolve disputes between knights

Vassals
- Provide military service
- Remain loyal and faithful
- Give money on special occasions

Manoralism

Lords
- Own manors
- Provide protection from attacks
- Provide land for farming

Peasants
- Live on the lord's land
- Give a portion of their crops to the manor lord
- Farm the lord's land

Review Key Terms and People

Identify the term or person from the chapter that best fits each of the following descriptions.

1. planning a course across the sea
2. the system of exchanging land for service
3. duke of Normandy who fought in the Battle of Hastings and became king of England
4. to unite or work into something that already exists
5. emperor of the Frankish Empire
6. workers who were legally tied to the manor on which they worked
7. the land given to a knight for his service
8. an economic system built around large estates
9. governing body that still makes England's laws
10. a person's level of devotion to his or her religion
11. Icelandic stories about great heroes and events

Reading Skills

17. From the Greek word for hermit's cell, the word means to live alone; monasteries were places for secluded life where monks would spend their lives worshiping God, away from the outside world.

18. From the Latin word for loyalty, the word refers to the faithfulness, or trust, and loyalty between a vassal and his lord.

19. From the Latin word for *navis*, ship, and *-igare*, to drive, it means to drive the ship. The Vikings had excellent navigation skills.

Comprehension and Critical Thinking

SECTION 1 *(pp. 373–376)*

12. a. Describe How did Charlemagne rise to power?

b. Explain How did the changes Charlemagne made to education strengthen his empire?

SECTION 2 *(pp. 378–381)*

13. a. Recall Where did the Magyars come from?

b. Explain Why did the Vikings go on raids throughout Europe?

c. Draw Conclusions What effects do you think Viking raids might have had on Europe?

SECTION 3 *(pp. 382–386)*

14. a. Identify Main Ideas What were the main obligations of lords and vassals in the feudal system?

b. Compare and Contrast What was one similarity and one difference between the feudal system and the manorial system?

c. Make Judgments Do you think peasants were fortunate or unfortunate to be part of the manorial system? Explain your answer.

SECTION 4 *(pp. 387–391)*

15. a. Recall What was the Reconquista?

b. Analyze Why did French culture flourish in England after 1066?

c. Elaborate How did Parliament strengthen the reforms made in Magna Carta?

SECTION 5 *(pp. 392–395)*

16. a. Identify Main Ideas Why did popes have so much power in medieval Europe?

b. Summarize What issues were at the root of the conflict over selection of clergy?

c. Make Judgments Who do you think should have appointed bishops in the Middle Ages, the pope or the emperor?

Reading Skills

Understanding Word Origins *Using a dictionary, find the origins of the following words and explain how the origin of each relates to the use of the word in the chapter.*

17. monastery

18. fealty

19. navigation

Analyzing Points of View

Reading Like a Historian *The selection below was written by English historians in 1963.*

❝ For half a century or so from 1066 the English way of life was not sensibly altered [changed]. The Normans had very little to teach, even in the art of war, and they had very much to learn. They were barbarians who were becoming conscious of their insufficiency. ❞

—H. G. Richardson and G. O. Sayles, *The Governance of Medieval England*

20. Identify What main point of view do the historians express about the Norman conquest of England in the selection?

21. Analyze How might the information provided about the authors help explain the authors' point of view?

22. Elaborate What details do the authors use to support their point of view? What details from the chapter provide an alternative point of view of the influence of the Normans in England?

Using the Internet

go.hrw.com
Practice Online
Keyword: SHL EMA

23. During the Middle Ages, daily life differed greatly for nobles and peasants. Using the keyword above, do research to learn more about the daily life of either peasants or nobles. Then create a poster illustrating the different aspects of the daily life experienced by of the group you choose.

WRITING FOR THE SAT

Think about the following issue:

Charlemagne greatly expanded his empire through conquest. He also made sweeping changes to Frankish society. Through his roles as both a warrior and a political leader, he created one of the largest and strongest kingdoms of the Early Middle Ages.

24. Assignment Which were more important to the creation of a strong empire—Charlemagne's conquests or his social reforms? Write a short essay in which you develop your position on this issue. Support your point of view with reasoning and examples from your reading and studies.

Answers

Analyzing Points of View

20. The author tells us the Normans "had very little to teach. . . and had very much to learn." Words such as *barbarians* and *insufficiency* also show bias.

21. possible answer—The English lost the Battle of Hastings, so this English historian might be biased against the conquerors.

22. the date 1066, English way of life for most people probably did not change much; Normans able to teach the English better military ways

Using the Internet

23. Go to the HRW Web site and enter the keyword shown to access a rubric for this activity.

KEYWORD: SHL EMA

Writing for the SAT

24. Student essays should discuss that conquest and social reform are both important factors in creating and maintaining a strong empire.

A rubric for this activity is provided in **CRF**: Writing for the SAT.

HOLT

History's Impact

▶ **Video Program: The Early Middle Ages**
See the Video Program Teacher's Guide for the answer to the closing question.

THE EARLY MIDDLE AGES **399**

Review and Assessment Resources

Review and Reinforce

CRF: Chapter Review

Quick Facts Transparency: Visual Study Guide: The Early Middle Ages

Spanish Chapter Summaries Audio CD Program

OSP **Holt PuzzlePro:** Quiz Show for ExamView

Quiz Game CD-ROM

Assess

PASS: Chapter Test, Forms A and B

Alternative Assessment Handbook

OSP **ExamView Test Generator**, Chapter Test

Differentiated Instruction Modified Worksheets and Tests CD-ROM: Chapter Test

HOAP **Holt Online Assessment Program** (in the Premier Online Edition)

Reteach/Intervene

Interactive Reader and Study Guide

Differentiated Instruction Teacher Management System: Lesson Plans for Differentiated Instruction

Differentiated Instruction Modified Worksheets and Tests CD-ROM: Chapter Test

Interactive Skills Tutor CD-ROM

go.hrw.com
Online Resources

KEYWORD: SHL TEACHER

Chapter 14 Planning Guide

The High Middle Ages

Chapter Overview	Reproducible Resources	Technology Resources
CHAPTER 14 pp. 400–427 **Overview:** In this chapter, students will discover the many changes that occurred during the High Middle Ages: the growth of trade, new business practices, bigger towns, and cultural achievements. **KI 3; PI 3.1, 3.2, 3.3** See pp. T32–T55 for a detailed correlation to the New York State Core Curriculum for Global History and Geography and the New York Learning Standards.	**Differentiated Instruction Teacher Management System:** * • Pacing Guide • Lesson Plans for Differentiated Instruction **Interactive Reader and Study Guide:** Chapter Summary* **Chapter Resource File*** • Writing About History • Social Studies Skill • Economics and History • Chapter Review **World History Outline Maps**	**OSP New York One-Stop Planner CD-ROM:** Calendar Planner **Live Ink© Online Reading Help** **Student Edition on Audio CD Program** **Differentiated Instruction Modified Worksheets and Tests CD-ROM** **World History Primary Source Library CD-ROM** **History's Impact: World History Video Program (VHS/DVD):** The High Middle Ages
Section 1: **The Crusades** **The Main Idea:** The Crusades, a series of attempts to gain Christian control of the Holy Land, had a profound economic, political, and social impact on the societies involved **PI 3.1**	**Differentiated Instruction Teacher Management System:** Section 1 Lesson Plan* **Interactive Reader and Study Guide:** Section 1 Summary* **Chapter Resource File*** • Vocabulary Builder: Section 1 • Biography: Saladin • History and Geography: Third Crusade	**Regents Review Transparency:** Section 1* **Map Transparencies:** Europe, 1095*; The First Crusades, 1095–1204* **Quick Facts Transparency:** Causes and Effects of the Crusades*
Section 2: **Trade and Towns** **The Main Idea:** Towns and cities grew during the high Middle Ages as the amount of trade increased between Europe and other continents. **PI 3.3**	**Differentiated Instruction Teacher Management System:** Section 2 Lesson Plan* **Interactive Reader and Study Guide:** Section 2 Summary* **Chapter Resource File*** • Vocabulary Builder: Section 2 • Biography: Marco Polo	**Regents Review Transparency:** Section 2* **Map Transparency:** Medieval Trade*
Section 3: **Art and Culture of the Middle Ages** **The Main Idea:** During the Middle Ages, great achievements were made in the visual arts, literature, and thinking and learning. **PI 3.2**	**Differentiated Instruction Teacher Management System:** Section 3 Lesson Plan* **Interactive Reader and Study Guide:** Section 3 Summary* **Chapter Resource File*** • Vocabulary Builder: Section 3 • Biography: Hildegard of Bingen • Literature: *Morte Darthur* • Primary Source: The Question of Usury	**Regents Review Transparency:** Section 3*
Section 4: **Challenges of the Late Middle Ages** **The Main Idea:** In the late Middle Ages, Europeans faced many challenges, including religious crises, wars, and a deadly plague. **PI 3.1**	**Differentiating Instruction Teacher Management System:** Section 4 Lesson Plan* **Interactive Reader and Study Guide:** Section 4 Summary* **Chapter Resource File*** • Vocabulary Builder: Section 4 • Biography: Joan of Arc	**Regents Review Transparency:** Section 4* **Map Transparency:** Hundred Years' War* **Quick Facts Transparency:** Effects of the Plague* **Internet Activity:** The Black Death

go.hrw.com   Print Resource   Transparency

LS Learning Styles   Audio CD   CD-ROM

Video   SE Student Edition   TE Teachers Edition

OSP One-Stop Planner CD-ROM   NY Standards Mastery
*also on One-Stop Planner CD-ROM

HOLT
History's Impact
World History Video Program (VHS/DVD)
The High Middle Ages

Review, Assessment, Intervention

 Global History and Geography Regents Test Prep Workbook

 Quick Facts Transparency: The High Middle Ages*

 Process Assessment Support System (PASS): Chapter Test*

Differentiated Instruction Modified Worksheets and Tests CD-ROM: Modified Chapter Test

OSP **New York One-Stop Planner CD-ROM:** ExamView Test Generator (English/Spanish)

HOAP **Holt Online Assessment Program (HOAP),** in the Premier Online Edition

 PASS: Section 1 Quiz*

 Online Quiz: Section 1

 Alternative Assessment Handbook

 PASS: Section 2 Quiz*

 Online Quiz: Section 2

 Alternative Assessment Handbook

 PASS: Section 3 Quiz*

Online Quiz: Section 3

Alternative Assessment Handbook

 PASS: Section 4 Quiz*

 Online Quiz: Section 4

Alternative Assessment Handbook

Power Presentation with Video CD-ROM

Power Presentations with Video are visual presentations of each chapter's main ideas. Presentations can be customized by including Quick Facts charts, images and maps from the textbook, and video clips.

Holt Online Learning

go.hrw.com
Teacher Resources
KEYWORD: SHL TEACHER

go.hrw.com
Student Resources
KEYWORD: SHL HMA

• Document-Based Questions
• Interactive Multimedia Activities

• Current Events
• Chapter-Based Internet Activities
• and more!

Holt Premier
Online Student Edition
Complete online support for interactivity, assessment, and reporting
• Interactive Maps and Notebook
• Homework Practice and Research Activities Online

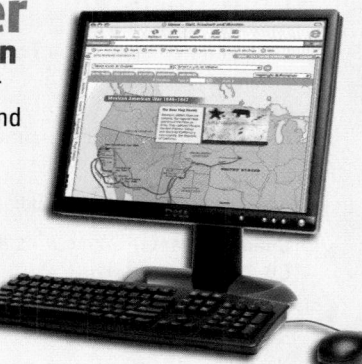

CHAPTER 14 PLANNING GUIDE

The Big Picture

Peter N. Stearns

High Middle Ages Various factors combined to generate new levels of economic and intellectual-artistic vitality after about 900 or 1000 in Western Europe, particularly in contrast to earlier conditions. Population growth surged, which both caused and reflected new economic activity. Improvements in agricultural productivity were crucial, permitting some significant urban growth. Political conditions stabilized somewhat with the reduction of invasions and the construction of larger political units, including feudal monarchies in several regions.

Societal Relationships Western Europe still lagged behind major Asian civilizations by measurements such as city size or levels of government bureaucracy. On the other hand, efforts to reach out increased. Europeans borrowed intellectual models from other societies these were combined with European cultural forms including Catholicism. Trade levels increased with the Middle East, but European taste for Asian imports increased more rapidly than development of export goods. In this context, the Crusades expressed new dynamism, a more vigorous hostility to Islam, and a desire to expand commercial contacts. While the Crusades did not lead to permanent conquest, they did increase European consumer interests and helped weaken the Byzantine Empire. Durable results on the Islamic side were less marked.

Culture and Economy Medieval cultural forms emphasized religious art and scholarship. Philosophers worked to develop more rational structures under the discipline of religious faith. New scientific research emerged, based in part on the inspiration of Islamic models. Economic activity featured new roles for cities and for merchants, though in an economy still predominantly agricultural. Clear signs of commercial capitalism emerged, but they were balanced by other kinds of organizations, notably the guilds, that were more concerned with protections of group interest and assurances of quality than with maximizing profits.

Synthesis and Decline By the 14th century, various factors combined to reduce the vitality of distinctively medieval forms. Population stagnated, thanks to new disease levels and a limited food supply. In politics, heightened military conflict, reduced stability in some regions and also began to undermine the principles of feudal warfare. Religious dissent increased, along with new problems of corruption in some branches of the church. Characteristic medieval forms such as scholastic philosophy began to decline.

Recent Scholarship

Michael D. Bailey uses biographical materials of Johannes Nider (c.1380–1438) to discuss major features of popular belief and religious activity as the Middle Ages began to wind down in *Battling Demons: Witchcraft, Heresy, and Reform in the Late Middle Ages* (2003). This is a specific study, in other words, that abundantly and explicitly reveals some of the major religious issues of the later Middle Ages, on the eve of even more fundamental transformations. It particularly explores the complicated connections between popular belief and practice, on the one hand, and the views of the Catholic officialdom on the other.

Differentiating Instruction

 Differentiated Instruction Teacher Management System
- Pacing Guide
- Lesson Plans for Differentiated Instruction

 Interactive Reader and Study Guide

 Spanish Chapter Summaries Audio CD Program

 Student Edition on Audio CD Program

 Differentiated Instruction Modified Worksheets and Tests CD-ROM
- Vocabulary Flash Cards
- Modified Vocabulary Builder Activities
- Modified Chapter Review Activity
- Modified Chapter Test

OSP One-Stop Planner CD-ROM
- ExamView Test Generator (English/Spanish)
- PuzzlePro
- Quiz Show for ExamView
- Transparencies and Videos

TE Differentiated Activities in the Teacher's Edition
- Time Lines of the Crusades, p. 405
- Daily Life in Medieval Towns, p. 411
- Hundred Years' War Charts, p. 421
- Creating Coats of Arms, p. 422
- Preparing for Outbreak of Disease, p. 425

Reading Like a Historian
Sam Wineburg

Several years ago I participated in a reading group with local high school teachers. In one session we discussed Stephen Ambrose's *Undaunted Courage,* a retelling of Lewis and Clark's epic journey to the Pacific Coast. We invited a prominent historian to our discussion. He said little during the meeting but managed to ask a question that puzzled us: "In telling the story of this journey," the historian asked, "where was Steven Ambrose sitting?"

No one rushed to answer. At first, the question made little sense. Obviously Ambrose told the story sitting at his desk, with his assistants brewing coffee. But this historian was aiming for something different—and in so doing provided deep insight into what it means to read like a historian.

Like fictional narrators, historical storytellers also make choices. The choices most apparent to us, as readers, are the words and phrases authors use. Such choices are visible and easy analyzed. But a question like "where was Ambrose seated" is not immediately apparent to the eye. In thinking about Lewis and Clark's journey was the author on the shore with native peoples watching these strange explorers travel up the Missouri, or was he sitting right there in Corps of Discovery keelboat, looking over Meriwether Lewis's shoulder? By asking this question, the historian invited us to consider something far broader than "what was the bias" of Stephen Ambrose. The question reminded us that it is impossible to narrate history standing on the moon. Historical narrators have to sit somewhere.

"Where is the narrator sitting" is a useful question to help students see things they might otherwise overlook. Unlike historical monographs, history textbooks contain no visible authors who insert themselves into the text with personal pronouns. But that doesn't mean that we—the authors of your text—are "seatless." In considering how our chapter tells the story of the Crusades ask your students, "Where are the authors of your book sitting?"

Start with the map on page 404. The center of the map is dotted with names we recognize—the Holy Roman Empire, France, England, Sicily, Paris—but aside from a few city names in the "Holy Land," the Muslim East appears as an undifferentiated blur. As readers, we are marching east alongside the Crusaders (from the French *croisode* or "marked by the cross"), leaving homes in Paris, Lyon and Vienna heading south through the Serbian Forests, crossing over to Constantinople, and heading south to liberate Jerusalem from the "Turks." (Would our enemies call themselves "Turks," or defenders of Islam, the seat of the Sultanate?)

How might our narrative change if we were to play narrative musical chairs? Our chapter describes the defeat of Richard the Lion-Hearted like this: "Although Richard won several battles against the Muslims, he was not able to drive them out of the Holy Land or to take Jerusalem. In the end, he had to admit defeat and return to England." As readers, standing next to Richard, we too hang our head in shame. But if we switched chairs and placed ourselves next to Saladin, our narrative would sound quite different: "Despite early set-backs, Saladin ultimately defeated Richard, driving the Christians out of Muslim lands and back to the European countries from which they came."

Not only would our prose change but so would its emphasis. Rather than focusing on the dashed hopes of the Europeans, we might accentuate the success of Ayyubid rulers who, after absorbing the loss of Jerusalem in the First Crusade, were able to overcome the fragmentation of their patchwork territories, regain lost land and prevent a new European invasion.

Writers of history make narrative choices that often go unnoticed by readers until they ask the simple question "where is the author sitting?" Every author—even the authors of textbooks—has to sit somewhere. By asking this question, you and your students become more astute readers of history.

Chapter Main Ideas

Section 1 The Crusades a series of attempts to gain Christian control of the Holy Land, had a profound economic, political, and social impact on the societies involved.

Section 2 Towns and cities grew during the high Middle Ages as the amount of trade increased between Europe and other continents.

Section 3 During the Middle Ages, great achievements were made in the visual arts, literature, and thinking and learning.

Section 4 In the late Middle Ages, Europeans faced many challenges, including religious crises, wars, and a deadly plague.

New York Standards

Key Idea 3 Study of the major social, political, cultural, and religious developments in world history involves learning about the important roles and contributions of individuals and groups.

CHAPTER
14 1000–1500

The High Middle Ages

THE BIG PICTURE During the High Middle Ages, many changes took place in Europe. The growth of trade brought about new business practices and bigger towns. As people's lives changed, one element remained constant: Religion continued to play a huge role in people's lives. Religion inspired the arts and, at times, caused conflict among different groups.

Theme ARTS AND IDEAS
The High Middle Ages was a time of advances in arts and learning. New art forms, such as the stained glass windows like the one on the right, became more prominent. Also, medieval thinkers emerged to challenge former methods of teaching and learning.

Chartres Cathedral , Chartres, France, 1220–1230

TIME LINE

CHAPTER EVENTS	**1096** The first Crusaders leave Europe to battle for the Holy Land.	**1163** The Building Notre of Dame begins.	**1347** The Black Death begins to spread through Europe.
	1000	1200	1300
WORLD EVENTS	**1076** Ghana falls to Muslim invaders.	**1192** The first shogun rules Japan.	**1279** Mongols found the Yuan dynasty in China.	**c. 1325** The Aztec capital of Tenochtitlán is established.

400 CHAPTER 14

Introduce the Chapter

At Level

The High Middle Ages

1. Have students make a list of the section titles and the headings that fall within each section of the chapter. Then have students write one main idea and one supporting detail under each of the headings.

2. Organize students into small groups. Have students compare and share their main ideas and supporting details. Student should add new facts and additional information provided by the other students in the group onto their own papers.

3. Have volunteers from each group share their work with the class. Write the headings, main ideas, and details for all to see. Have students add any additional information from the class list to their own papers. Have students retain their work as a study tool. **LS** **Visual-Spatial, Interpersonal**

Alternative Assessment Handbook, Rubric 1: Acquiring Information

History's Impact video program

Watch the video to understand the impact of the Black Death.

Reading like a Historian This stained glass window from Chartres Cathedral in France shows sculptors and stonemasons making decorations for a cathedral. Religion and the development of professional groups of skilled craftspeople both influenced life in the High Middle Ages.

Analyzing Visuals What do you think that stonemasons and sculptors were used to decorate a church window? What might a stained glass window like this tell you about the artist's intentions?

See **Skills Handbook**, p. H26

The Hundred Years' War
1337–1453

1500

1492
Christopher Columbus lands in America.

THE HIGH MIDDLE AGES **401**

Explore the Time Line

1. When did the first Crusaders leave for the Holy Land? *1096*

2. What disease began to spread early during the Hundred Years' War? *the Black Death*

3. How long did the Hundred Years' War last? *116 years*

4. How many years after the end of the Hundred Years' War did Columbus land in America? *39 years*

Info to Know

Stained Glass The art of stained glass in Europe reached its height between 1150 and 1500. Artisans made clear glass by mixing sand and wood ash and heating the mixture into molten liquid, which became glass when it cooled. To color the glass, powdered metals were added to the mixture. Artisans created pictures by cutting the glass and arranging the different pieces in a design. The edges of each piece were fitted with strips of lead, which held the panel together.

Draw Conclusions Why do you think stained glass is still used to decorate churches? *possible answer—to keep the look of older churches*

● Chapter Preview ●

HOLT
History's Impact
▶ **Video Program: The High Middle Ages**
See the Video Teacher's Guide for strategies for using the video segment.

Reading Like a Historian
Analyzing Visuals Chartres Cathedral contains 176 stained glass windows. Some windows portray scenes from the New Testament. Others portray scenes from the Old Testament. Have students consider the fact that, throughout the Middle Ages, most people could not read. Ask students to explain what functions stained glass panels might have served besides their beauty. *taught illiterate people about the Bible; communicated ideas*

go.hrw.com
Online Resources

Chapter Resources:
KEYWORD: SHL HMA
Teacher Resources:
KEYWORD: SHL TEACHER

Answers

Reading Like a Historian 1. *possible answers—scenes from the Bible; respected and revered their religion*

401

Geography Starting Points

Old Forests of Europe In the year 1000 huge, thick forests still covered the majority of Europe. In the following century, large portions of the land were cleared. There were three main forces at work in this change to the environment. First, peasants slowly cleared forest land to enlarge their fields. Second, land-hungry settlers moved to uninhabited highlands and created fields and enclosures there. Third, lords and monasteries cleared land in order to start villages in hopes of increasing their income. New land under cultivation resulted in an agricultural surplus which became available for trade, leading to the growth of towns, markets and fairs.

Info to Know

Growth of Islam Most people who lived in lands conquered by Muslims converted to Islam. The primary exception was Christians, who retained their own religion. By 1350 Islam was the prevailing religion from North Africa to China. Muslims controlled the main trade routes, and they supplied Western Europe with African, Eastern, and Chinese luxuries, including Persian rugs, Chinese silks, precious jewels, gold, perfumes, and spices.

- Map Transparency: Europe, 1095
- World History Outline Maps
- Interactive Map: Europe, 1095

Answers

Geography Starting Points
1. *Roman Catholic;* 2. *possible answer—conflict over access to and control of holy sites*

GEOGRAPHY Starting Points

★Interactive
EUROPE, 1095

Eastern and western Europe were both mostly Christian.

Jerusalem, in the Holy Land, was under Muslim control.

- ☐ Roman Catholic lands
- ☐ Eastern Orthodox lands
- ☐ Muslim lands

Starting Points In 1095, around the start of the High Middle Ages, three religions competed for territories and believers in Europe and the Middle East. Christianity had been the most common religion in Europe for hundreds of years, but Islam was slowly spreading to lands that bordered Christian territories.

1. **Analyze** To which religion did most Europeans belong?
2. **Predict** What consequences might result from the competing goals of these different religions?

Listen to History

Go online to listen to an explanation of the starting points for this chapter.

go.hrw.com
Keyword: SHL HMA

402 CHAPTER 14

Skills Focus: Analyzing Maps
                                                               At Level

Social Studies Skill
Routes to the Holy Land

1. Tell students that even before the Crusades, Christian pilgrims visited Jerusalem, which they considered a holy city. During the First Crusade, armies traveled over land because there was no fleet in Western Europe that could carry them.

2. Have students find the shortest land route from Paris to Jerusalem. How far is it from Paris to Constantinople? Why is the shortest land route not always the best one?

3. Have students find the shortest route to Jerusalem that includes land and sea travel. Tell to students that this type of route was expensive because ship captains demanded payment.

4. Have students explain what route they would take if they were traveling from Paris to Jerusalem and why. **LS Visual-Spatial**

Alternative Assessment Handbook, Rubric 21: Map Reading

The Crusades

BEFORE YOU READ

MAIN IDEA

The Crusades, a series of attempts to gain Christian control of the Holy Land, had a profound economic, political, and social impact on the societies involved.

READING FOCUS

1. Why did Europeans launch the Crusades?
2. What happened during the Crusades?
3. What were the effects of the Crusades?

KEY TERMS AND PEOPLE

Crusades
Holy Land
Pope Urban II
Saladin
Richard the Lion-Hearted

NEW YORK

PI 3.1 Students will analyze the roles and contributions of individuals and groups to political and religious practices and activities.

DISASTER AND TREACHERY

▶ **Richard the Lion-Hearted fights in a Crusade battle.**

Richard the Lion-hearted and the Emperor of Cyprus in Battle

THE INSIDE STORY

Why did three powerful men fail to reach a common goal? In the late 1180s, three of the most powerful men in Europe set out on a mission to Jerusalem. They were King Richard the Lion-Hearted of England, King Philip Augustus of France, and Emperor Frederick Barbarossa of Germany. Their goal was to retake Jerusalem, a city sacred to Christians, Jews, and Muslims but at that time ruled by Muslims. The kings of Europe wanted to drive the Muslims out and make Jerusalem a Christian city.

Trouble began almost immediately. While crossing a river, Frederick drowned. The exact circumstances surrounding his death are unknown, but it is believed that he fell into the river and the weight of his armor pulled him down. Frederick's death broke the morale of the German army.

Arrogance also caused problems for the kings. Soon after they reached the vicinity of Jerusalem, Richard and Philip quarreled. Philip decided to return to France, and much of his army went with him. This departure left Richard, his army, and the few remaining French to fight the Muslims.

Although Richard's army won several victories against the Muslims, personality conflicts continued to trouble the war effort. Richard alienated several of the nobles who fought at his side, leading to the breakdown of the army's discipline. Eventually, the English were forced to abandon some of the lands they had captured and head home.

On his way home, Richard was taken prisoner by one of the nobles he had alienated. What had begun as a common goal shared by Europe's most powerful men had ended in disaster and treachery. ▪

THE HIGH MIDDLE AGES **403**

Teach the Main Idea

The Crusades

1. **Teach** Ask students the Reading Focus questions to teach this section.

2. **Apply** Draw a blank sequencing diagram or flow chart for students to see. Label the appropriate parts of the diagram with the topics in this section: Launching the Crusades, Fighting the Crusades, and Effects of the Crusades. Have students copy the diagram onto their own papers. Then have students complete the diagram with the main ideas of each topic.

3. **Review** As you review the section, have students explain the events that led to the Crusades and the results.

4. **Practice/Homework** Have students write six journal entries from a point of view of a knight in the First Crusade. Entries should include their experiences during travel, arrival, and fighting. **LS Visual-Spatial, Verbal-Linguistic**

   Alternative Assessment Handbook, Rubrics 7: Charts; and 15: Journals

Preteach

Getting Started

Use the **Interactive Reader and Study Guide** to familiarize students with the section content.

📝 **Interactive Reader and Study Guide**, Section 1

Academic Vocabulary

Review with students the high-use academic term in this section.

despite in spite of (p. 406)

📝 **CRF: Vocabulary Builder: Section 1**

Taking Notes

Causes—Seljuk Turks took Holy Land and threatened Byzantines; pope called on Christians to capture Holy Land; Fighting— knights took Jerusalem, established kingdoms, Muslims began retaking lands, fierce fighting in the Third Crusade, Crusaders sacked Constantinople, Christians driven out of Holy Land; Results—increased trade, kings more powerful, Christians less tolerant, tension between religions

go.hrw.com

Online Resources

KEYWORD: SHL HMA
ACTIVITY: Crusades

1 Why did Europeans launch the Crusades? *Muslim Seljuk Turks conquered the Holy Land and attacked the Byzantine Empire; Byzantine emperor called on pope for assistance; pope called on Christians to capture Holy Land*

Launching the Crusades

Recall What was the goal of each Crusade? *to take Jerusalem and the Holy Land away from the Muslims who controlled it*

Draw Conclusions Were the Byzantine emperor's fears reasonable? *possible answer—Yes, Turks had destroyed the Byzantine army; he had no way to fight the Turks.*

Analyze Why do you think so many people joined the Crusade? *possible answer—People believed it was God's will to retake the Holy Land.*

🗺️ **Map Transparency:** The Crusades, 1095–1204

✴️ **Interactive Map:** The Crusades, 1095–1204

Primary Source

"Christian warriors, who seek without end for vain pretexts for war, rejoice, for you have today found true ones. You who have been so often the terror of your fellow-citizens, go and fight against the barbarians, go and fight for the deliverance of the holy places…"
—Pope Urban, Council in Clermont

Answers

Reading Check *Seljuk Turks conquered Holy Land, threatened Byzantines; Byzantine emperor called on pope for assistance*

404

 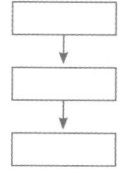
As you read, take notes on the causes, the course of, and the results of the Crusades.

🗽 **NEW YORK**
CC Unit 2-G1
Crusades: Causes

Launching the Crusades

During the Middle Ages, European Christians launched a series of religious wars called the **Crusades**. The goal of each Crusade was the same: to take Jerusalem and the area around it, known as the **Holy Land**, away from the Muslims, who also considered it holy. Jerusalem was holy to Jews because of the Holy Temple, and for Christians, it was the place where Jesus was crucified and buried. Many Christians also believed that Christ would come again only once Christians held Jerusalem. Thus it was vital to Christians that they control the city.

Muslims Control the Holy Land By the late 1000s, the city of Jerusalem had fallen to North African Muslims called the Fatimids. Turkish Muslims also swept through southwest Asia, taking control of Persia and other lands. After the Turkish conquest, stories spread throughout Europe that the Turks were persecuting Christians visiting the region.

Once in control of Persia, the Turks attacked the Byzantine Empire. In 1071, they destroyed the Byzantine army in the Battle of Manzikert. With most of his army gone, the emperor feared that the Turks would soon destroy Constantinople. Desperate, he turned to Western Europe and **Pope Urban II** for help.

The Council of Clermont In response to the emperor, Urban called church leaders to a council in Clermont, France. There he described to them the dangers faced by the Byzantines. He called on all Christian warriors, including knights and nobles, to put aside their differences and fight against the Turks. Urban's call was effective. By the hundreds, people volunteered to take part in the Crusade. Calling out their slogan, "God wills it!" they set out to meet their foes.

READING CHECK **Sequence** What events led to the call for a Crusade?

✴️ Interactive
THE CRUSADES, 1095–1204

A Crusader fortress located in Tripoli that still stands today.

Roman Catholic lands, 1095
Eastern Orthodox lands, 1095
Muslim lands, 1095
States established by Crusaders, c.1142
First Crusade, 1096–1099
Second Crusade, 1147–1149
Third Crusade, 1189–1192
Fourth Crusade, 1201–1204

404 CHAPTER 14

Skills Focus: Making Inferences

Reading Skill
Calls for a Crusade

1. Review with students the information from the text about the Byzantine emperor's call to the pope for assistance, the council of Clermont, and Pope Urban's speech to the knights and nobles of France.

2. Have half of the students recreate the Byzantine emperor's letter asking for assistance. Have the other half recreate the pope's speech. Remind students that the pleas should contain factual information and that

they should also convey the passion of all Christians for recapturing the Holy Land.

3. Have volunteers read their documents to the class.

4. As an extension, students may wish to conduct outside research and read the speech that Pope Urban gave to the council in Clermont.

🔲 **Verbal-Linguistic**

📝 **Alternative Assessment Handbook,** Rubrics 24: Oral Presentations; and 37: Writing Assignments

Fighting the Crusades

The Crusaders inspired by Urban left France in 1096 in what is known as the First Crusade. All in all, nine organized Crusades set out from Europe between 1096 and 1291. Though they had different leaders and met with varying degrees of success, each Crusade had the same goal—claiming or protecting the Holy Land.

First Crusade The Crusaders that set out in 1096 fell into two groups. The first group was made up of peasants who had answered the pope's call. Unskilled in war, these peasants did not fare well.

As they traveled through Germany, the peasant Crusaders passed several large Jewish communities. Eager to fight non-Christians in the Holy Land, some Crusaders decided to attack non-Christians in Europe as well. They slaughtered entire communities of Jews, in spite of protests by local officials and clergy.

CRUSADER STATES

COUNTY OF EDESSA — Edessa
Antioch — PRINCIPALITY OF ANTIOCH
COUNTY OF TRIPOLI — Tripoli
Acre
Jerusalem
KINGDOM OF JERUSALEM

Crusader Fortress

0 — 100 Miles
0 — 100 Kilometers

GEOGRAPHY SKILLS INTERPRETING MAPS

go.hrw.com
Interactive Map
Keyword: SHL HMA

1. **Movement** Where did the Second Crusade begin? Where did it end?
2. **Regions** Why do you think the Crusaders failed to hold on to the Crusader states?

Those peasants who did make it to Jerusalem fell quickly to the army of the Seljuk Turks.

The other group of Crusaders that set out from Clermont were trained knights. Somewhat better prepared than the peasants, the knights were still unprepared for the hardship of their journey. Food and water ran low, and many knights resorted to looting towns and farms to get needed supplies.

After almost three years of traveling, the Crusaders finally reached Jerusalem. Faced with a well-prepared Muslim army, the Crusaders nevertheless laid siege to several cities along the eastern Mediterranean. The siege of Jerusalem, while it was a victory for the Crusaders, involved terrible fighting and ended in disaster for the city's inhabitants.

HISTORY'S VOICES

❝ It was necessary to pick one's way over the bodies of men and horses . . . In the Temple and porch of Solomon, men rode in blood up to their knees and bridle reins . . . The city was filled with corpses and blood. **❞**

—Raymond d'Aguilers, *History of the Franks Who Captured Jerusalem*

After the conquest of Jerusalem, the Crusaders created four states in the Holy Land. Centered on the cities of Jerusalem, Edessa, Antioch, and Tripoli, these states were intended to be Christian strongholds against future Muslim conquests in the region.

Second Crusade Within a few years the Muslims began to recapture lands that they had lost in the First Crusade. In 1144, they took the city of Edessa, the capital of one of the Crusader states. Upon learning that Edessa had been lost, European leaders called for a second Crusade. Among the Crusaders were King Louis VII of France and his wife, Eleanor of Aquitaine.

Launched in 1147, the Second Crusade was a failure. The Crusaders took no lands from the Muslims and were forced to return to Europe empty-handed.

Third Crusade About 30 years after the Second Crusade, a new leader arose in the Muslim world. His name was Salah ad-Din, but he was known to Europeans as **Saladin**. Saladin overthrew the Fatimids and took the title of sultan for himself.

READING SKILLS

Understanding Causes and Effects What was the effect of the Muslims' retaking Edessa?

Direct Teach

Reading Focus

❷ **What happened during the Crusades?** *After travel and siege, knights took Jerusalem; Crusaders established four kingdoms; Muslims began retaking lands including Jerusalem; the Second Crusade failed; fierce fighting occured in the Third Crusade; Crusaders sacked Constantinople; Muslims drove Christians completely out of the Holy Land.*

Fighting the Crusades

Explain Why did European Jews become targets of some Crusaders? *Crusaders decided to attack non-Christians in Europe on their way to the Holy Land.*

Analyze Why do you think the Crusaders eventually established four states in the Holy Land? *possible answer—easier to administer four small territories than rule one large one*

Summarize How did Saladin change the situation in the Holy Land? *overthrew Seljuk Turks; conquered Crusader states; drove Christians out of Jerusalem*

📄 **CRF:** Biography: Saladin

Info to Know

Over Land and Sea During the First and Second Crusades, knights traveled to Constantinople over land because Western Europe did not yet possess a fleet capable of transporting a large army across the Mediterranean. The Third Crusade marked the first usage of such fleets, notably from the Italian trade cities.

Differentiating Instruction

At Level

English-Language Learners

Materials: butcher paper, art supplies

1. Organize students into small groups.

2. Have each group create an illustrated time line of the Crusades. Provide students with additional events and dates from the Crusades or have students conduct outside research to locate this information themselves. Each time line should include four or more illustrations.

3. Have volunteers share their time lines with the class and explain why they chose the specific events shown.

4. Display time lines in the classroom.
   📘 **Visual-Spatial**

   📄 **Alternative Assessment Handbook**, Rubrics 3: Artwork; and 36: Time Lines

Answers

Reading Skills *European leaders called for a second Crusade, but it failed.*

Interpreting Maps 1. *Paris; Antioch and Acra;* **2.** *possible answer—kingdoms surrounded by Muslim territory, far from most Christian support*

405

Reading Focus

Fighting the Crusades

Compare What did Richard the Lion-Hearted and Saladin have in common? *respected each other; strong military leaders; were courteous*

Evaluate Would the Crusades have been successful if the Crusaders had had strong, centralized military leadership? *possible answers—no, too far away from supplies and support; yes, they were able fighters*

📝 **CRF:** History and Geography: Third Crusade (1189–1192)

Info to Know

The Children's Crusade A twelve year-old French shepherd named Stephen began preaching outside the abbey of St. Denis, France, announcing that he would lead a band of children to the Holy Land and that God would grant them victory where adults had failed. The message spread, and several thousand children gathered to follow the young man. Another large group of children gathered in Germany. The French children arranged for a sea passage to the Holy Land, but were tricked and sold into slavery in North Africa. The German children reached Rome, but the pope told them to return home. Many of the children had died along the way. Others stayed in the lands they had reached, too exhausted to return. Few of those who set out ever returned to their homes.

Reading like a Historian

The Crusades

Recognizing Bias in Primary Sources Primary sources often contain bias. Biased primary sources may not give us a complete and balanced understanding of a historical event, but they can help us to understand opinions and attitudes of the time.

To recognize bias in this Crusader's description of the capture of Jerusalem, think about

- the source or occasion of the document
- the writer's point of view
- the writer's goal

Skills Focus   READING LIKE A HISTORIAN

1. **Point of View** What is the writer's point of view? How do you know?
2. **Emotional Language** Why do you think the writer includes the details that he mentions? What does he hope to convey with these details?

See **Skills Handbook**, p. H29

But now that our men had possession of the walls and towers, wonderful sights were to be seen. Some of our men (and this was more merciful) cut off the heads of their enemies; others shot them with arrows, so that they fell from the towers; others tortured them longer by casting them into the flames . . . Indeed, it was a just and splendid judgment of God that this place should be filled with the blood of the unbelievers, since it had suffered so long from their blasphemies.

In this case, "the unbelievers" are the Muslims.

—Raymond d'Aguilers, quoted in *The First Crusade*, edited by Edward Peters

Raymond d'Aguilers was a chaplain who was present at the First Crusade.

Saladin set out to take back the Crusader states. He succeeded in his conquest and drove European Christians out of Jerusalem. Christians responded to this loss by launching the Third Crusade. As you read in the Inside Story, three kings set out from Europe on the Third Crusade, but only King **Richard the Lion-Hearted** of England fought in the Holy Land.

Richard and Saladin had great respect for each other even though they never met. Both were admired as military leaders and also for their knightly behavior. Stories spread about Saladin sending horses to Richard and offering the use of his doctor when Richard was ill. The two men also made proposals for peace—including a marriage alliance between Richard's sister and Saladin's brother, which never took place because of religious differences.

ACADEMIC VOCABULARY
despite in spite of

Despite their mutual admiration, Richard and Saladin fought fiercely for control of the Holy Land. Although Richard won several battles against the Muslims, he was not able to drive them out of the Holy Land or to take Jerusalem. In the end, he had to admit that the Crusade was a draw and return to England.

Fourth and Later Crusades With Jerusalem still in Muslim hands, Europeans set out on the Fourth Crusade in 1201. But the Crusaders found that they could not afford to pay the Venetians who had arranged to take them to the Holy Land. In lieu of payment, the Crusaders agreed to attack the city of Zara, a port that had once belonged to Venice but was now held by the Christian king of Hungary. Angry that the Crusaders had attacked a Christian city, the pope excommunicated them all.

Nevertheless, the Crusaders pushed on toward the Holy Land. When they reached the Christian city of Constantinople, though, they decided to attack it instead. The Crusaders ransacked the city and made one of their leaders the new emperor. Disorganization and a lack of strong leadership made the Fourth Crusade another failure.

Five other Crusades followed the sack of Constantinople, but none was successful. By 1291, the Muslims had once more driven the Christians completely out of the Holy Land.

READING CHECK **Find the Main Idea** What was the goal of the Crusades?

Skills Focus: Summarizing   At Level

Reading Skill
After the Crusades

1. Review with students information in the text about Saladin and Richard the Lion-hearted.

2. Organize students into small groups.

3. Have each group write a skit in which Saladin and Richard meet years after the Third Crusade. Among other things, the characters should discuss the conflict, their proposed alliance, and what happened to them after the Third Crusade.

4. Have students rehearse and perform their skits. 🄻 **Kinesthetic, Auditory-Musical**

📝 **Alternative Assessment Handbook**, Rubric 33: Skits and Reader's Theater

Answers

Reading Like a Historian 1. *supports the Crusaders and their actions; sees killings as "wonderful sights";* **2.** *possible answer—wants to illustrate the carnage; show that unbelievers were being punished for their crimes*

Reading Check *to take Jerusalem and the Holy Land away from the Muslims who controlled it*

Effects of the Crusades

Although the Crusades did not accomplish their main goal, they had long-lasting effects. They changed both Europe and the Holy Land economically, politically, and socially.

Economic Changes Historians know that Muslims, Byzantines, and western Europeans traded with one another before the Crusades. The Crusades enhanced existing trade as returning Crusaders brought even more goods, such as spices and textiles, to Europe. The increase in trade following the Crusades added to the changing European economy of the Middle Ages.

Political Changes The Crusades led to the deaths of many knights and nobles. Those who did not return to their homes left their lands vulnerable. In some cases, kings took control of the lands left unoccupied. By controlling more land, the kings had more power in Europe.

Social Changes The Crusades brought knowledge of Muslim culture to Europe, which had a great impact on European society. Some European Christians who had participated in the Crusades grew to respect other cultures. Others, especially those who had not participated, became more intolerant. Many Europeans began to view all non-Christians as enemies. This led to an increase in the perse-

cution of Jews in Europe. Jews and Muslims in the Holy Land, in turn, saw the Crusaders as invaders. After the Crusades, many people held on to these views of one another.

READING CHECK   Draw Conclusions Why did people's attitudes change after the Crusades?

CAUSES AND EFFECTS OF THE CRUSADES
QUICK FACTS

Causes

- Muslims controlled the Holy Land.
- The Byzantine emperor feared Muslim Turks would destroy Constantinople.
- Pope Urban II called for Christians to join a Crusade at the Council of Clermont.

Effects

- Trade increased.
- Kings gained more power.
- Knowledge of Muslim culture spread throughout Europe.
- Relations between Christians and Jews became increasingly strained.

Reviewing Ideas, Terms, and People

1. **a. Define** What were the **Crusades**?
   b. Identify Cause and Effect What were two causes of the First Crusade?
   c. Evaluate Why do you think people were willing to join the Crusades and fight in the Holy Land?

2. **a. Identify** Who were **Saladin** and **Richard the Lion-Hearted**?
   b. Analyze In what ways did Saladin help Richard during the Crusades?
   c. Evaluate Why do you think the relationship between these two leaders is still talked about today?

3. **a. Identify** What kinds of changes did the Crusades bring to Europe?
   b. Explain How did the Crusades affect the economy?
   c. Elaborate Why might some Christians who participated in the Crusades have grown more respectful of other cultures?

Critical Thinking

4. **Analyze** Draw a concept map like the one to the right. Use your notes from the section and the circles drawn for you to outline the courses of the Crusades. From each of the circles draw more circles containing details about the effects of the Crusades.

(Crusades)

FOCUS ON WRITING

5. **Narration** Write a journal entry from the perspective of Richard the Lion-Hearted during the Crusades. Describe what the fighting is like and what you feel are the strengths and weaknesses of your army. You may also wish to discuss some of the emotions that a king in battle might be feeling.

THE HIGH MIDDLE AGES **407**

Section 1 Assessment Answers

1. **a.** series of wars launched by Christians to take the Holy Land from Muslims who controlled it
   b. Turks threatened Byzantine Empire; Pope Urban called for Crusade
   c. believed it was God's will

2. **a.** leaders during Third Crusade
   b. Saladin provided Richard with horses and a physician; planned an alliance
   c. fierce, heroic military leaders; both were gentlemen, courteous to each other

3. **a.** economic, political, and social; strained, intolerant relations among religions

   b. new products introduced, increased trade
   c. possible answer—Learning about other cultures made them more tolerant.

4. new products and increased trade; kings more powerful, temporarily reduced fighting in Europe; Christians became more intolerant of other religions; strained relations among people of different religions

5. Journal entries should discuss the difficult conditions, being far from home, lack of supplies, and the brutality of the fighting.

407

Getting Started

Use the **Interactive Reader and Study Guide** to familiarize students with the section content.

📋 **Interactive Reader and Study Guide,** Section 2

📋 **CRF:** Vocabulary Builder: Section 2

Taking Notes

Trade—Italian merchants traded around Mediterranean; Hanseatic League promoted trade; trade fairs; increased use of currency and credit; Cities and towns—technology reduced need for farm workers, people moved to towns; towns grew under merchant leadership

---

SECTION

2 Trade and Towns

BEFORE YOU READ

MAIN IDEA

Towns and cities grew during the high Middle Ages as the amount of trade increased between Europe and other continents.

READING FOCUS

1. Which cities saw the initial growth of trade in the Middle Ages?
2. What led to the growth of towns and cities in the Middle Ages?
3. What was daily life like in medieval cities?

KEY TERMS

Hanseatic League
credit
guilds
apprentice
journeyman

NEW YORK

PI 3.3 Students will examine the social, cultural, and economic norms and values of Western and other world cultures.

THE INSIDE STORY

What would it have been like to grow up in London in the 1100s?

Most people of today would find the London of the 1100s to be dirty, smelly, and dangerous. However, a person who actually lived during that time might not share this opinion. According to at least one medieval writer, William fitz Stephen, London was the most magnificent city in the world. Writing in the late 1100s, he recalled his childhood in the city: "Among the noble and celebrated cities of the world, London, the capital of the kingdom of the English, extends its glory farther than all others and sends its wealth and merchandise more widely into far distant lands. It holds its head higher than all the rest."

Among fitz Stephen's most vivid memories of London were the busy merchants who made their fortune there. He recalled a particular neighborhood and restaurant he had often visited: "Each day, at this cook shop, you will find food according to the season—dishes of meat, roasted, fried, and boiled; large and small fish; coarser meats for the poor and more delicate for the rich, such as venison and large and small birds."

So, although we might not want to live in London as it was in the 1100s, some people who did live there saw it as a wondrous place with lots to see and do. And as trade increased and merchants became more common, European cities, like London, began to grow and expand as well. ■

The Lure of LONDON

▼ **London was a bustling city in the Middle Ages.**
Royal Manuscript, from the *Poems of Charles Duke of Orleans,* 1394–1465

408

Teach the Main Idea

At Level

Trade and Towns

1. **Teach** Ask students the Reading Focus questions to teach this section.

2. **Apply** Draw a large triangle for students to see. On each side of the triangle, write the name of one of the topics in this section: Growth of Trade, Growth of Towns and Cities, and Daily Life in Cities. Have students copy the triangle onto their papers. Have them write the main ideas of each section on the appropriate side of the triangle.

3. **Review** As you review the section, have students describe the growth and changes in trade and towns that occurred during the High Middle Ages.

4. **Practice/Homework** Have students write a description of a walk through a medieval town. **LS Visual-Spatial, Verbal-Linguistic**

📋 **Alternative Assessment Handbook,** Rubric 40: Writing to Describe

MEDIEVAL TRADE

— Routes controlled by Hanseatic League
— Routes controlled by Italian city-states
FURS Trade goods

GEOGRAPHY SKILLS INTERPRETING MAPS

1. **Movement** Which group controlled most of the trading routes in medieval Europe?
2. **Place** Which countries produced textiles? What sorts of goods were these countries likely to trade in exchange for the textiles that they produced?

Growth of Trade

Large cities, like London, became more common in the High Middle Ages than ever before. After the Crusades, trade began to grow in Europe. Most of this trade was controlled by merchants from Italy and northern Europe.

Italian Trade Cities The Italians were among the first people in medieval Europe to build a thriving trade economy. Skilled sailors, they set out from their home on the Mediterranean and Adriatic seas to find valuable goods from distant lands.

The most important of the early trading cities in Italy was Venice. The city was protected by powerful warships from the Venetian fleet, one of the largest fleets in the area. Venetian traders traveled to ports in the Byzantine Empire and in Muslim lands. There, they picked up goods from those areas and places

farther east. Among these goods were silk and spices from China and India. Back in Venice, merchants loaded the goods onto wagons and headed north to sell them. Because they came to the Italian ports across lengthy Asian trade routes, these goods were very expensive, and thus, very profitable. Seeing Venice grow rich from trade, other Italian cities—Genoa, Florence, Pisa, and Milan—created trade routes of their own. Soon, Italians controlled almost all trade in southern Europe.

Hanseatic League While the Italians were dominating trade in the south, another group was actively trading in northern Europe. This group was the **Hanseatic League**, a group of northern German cities and towns that worked together to promote and protect trade. The league controlled most of the trade between Europe, Russia, and the Baltic region.

TAKING NOTES

As you read, take notes on the growth of trade and cities or towns.

READING SKILLS

Understanding Causes and Effects What was an effect of trade in the High Middle Ages?

THE HIGH MIDDLE AGES **409**

Direct Teach

Reading Focus

❶ **What cities saw the initial growth of trade in the Middle Ages?** *Italian cities, including Venice, Genoa, Florence, Pisa, and Milan; cities and towns in northern Germany that belonged to the Hanseatic League*

Growth of Trade

Recall Which group began trading at locations around the Mediterranean? *Italian merchants*

Explain How did the Venetians build such a strong trade network? *protected by warships; traveled to Byzantine Empire and Muslim lands; brought goods back to Europe*

Make Inferences Why did the Hanseatic League form? *Cities and towns found that they could improve and promote trade by cooperating.*

🗺 **Map Transparency:** Medieval Trade

📄 **CRF:** Biography: Marco Polo

Skills Focus: Making Oral Presentations

At Level

Reading Like a Historian Skill
Venice and the Sea

Research Required

1. Organize students into small groups.

2. Have students conduct outside research on the history of Venice. Students should focus their research on the period when the city-state of Venice dominated the Mediterranean trade and on the cultural life that developed in Venice.

3. Have students use their research to prepare a multimedia presentation about the city-state.

4. Have groups make their presentations to the class. 🆂 **Verbal-Linguistic, Kinesthetic**

📄 **Alternative Assessment Handbook**, Rubrics 22: Multimedia Presentations; and 30: Research

Answers

Reading Skills *Italians eventually controlled almost all trade in southern Europe.*

Interpreting Maps 1. *Italian city-states;* **2.** *Refer to map*

409

Reading Focus

Growth of Trade

Recall Where were trade fairs usually held? *near towns or monasteries*

Make Generalizations What were trade fairs like? *attracted huge crowds; people traveled long distances to get there; large variety of goods; could last for months*

Evaluate Did the increased use of currency and credit have positive or negative effects? *positive; stimulated trade; led to the creation of banks*

🗎 **CRF:** Economics and History: Taxes in the Kingdom of Jerusalem

History Close-up

A Trade Fair Champagne Fairs In the 1100s and 1200s, a cycle of six fairs developed in Champagne, starting with a fair at Lagny in January and ending with the "cold fair" in December at Troyes. Available goods included luxury items as well as raw and finished wool, furs, crafted goods, grain, and wine. The travels of merchants helped open new routes of communication and exchange. In the 1200s, Italian traders regularly made the overland journey north to attend the fairs at Champagne. Italian traders were thus able to sell their goods to the many inhabitants of the lands around eastern France. A century later, however, Italian merchants typically traveled by ship instead. Ships sailed from Venice and Genoa to northern ports. This shift in travel routes made Flanders the most important location for merchants to do business.

About the Illustration

This illustration is an artist's conception based on available sources. Historians, however, are uncertain exactly what this scene looked like.

Answers

Reading Check *Italian merchants traded around Mediterranean; Hanseatic League promoted trade; trade fairs brought together buyers and sellers; increased use of currency and credit*

Trade Fairs and Markets As goods poured into Europe through Italian and German cities, merchants needed ways to get the goods to customers. One place where buyers and sellers could meet was a trade fair.

Trade fairs were held in towns and drew huge crowds because merchants were willing to travel long distances to visit them. Trade fairs were generally places for sales between merchants who serviced different parts of the economy. The merchants offered a great variety of goods, ranging from rare fabrics to aromatic spices to trained animals.

Trade fairs were held once a year at specific locations. Some could last for months. The schedule of the fairs was staggered so that merchants could travel from one to the next. As a result, some merchants spent most of their time on the road, traveling from one trade fair to another in search of profits.

Trade fairs were not events attended by the average person. For everyday needs, people visited their weekly local markets. At these markets, people could buy locally-produced goods.

THE IMPACT TODAY

In today's world, people buy many of their goods using credit cards. Having good credit also allows people to purchase large items like cars and houses.

Money and Credit Trade encouraged people to use money once more, which had not been common in Europe for many years. Previously, workers had been paid with goods. As cities began minting their own coins, though, money became a more accepted method of exchange. Workers began to demand coins for payment and coins were also used to pay taxes to lords.

Some merchants even allowed their customers to buy goods on **credit**, or the promise of later payment. In return for goods, a customer signed a document that stated when and how payment would be made.

The increased use of money and credit eventually led to the creation of Europe's first banks. People could deposit money in a bank for safekeeping, or they could request loans. Because religious laws prevented Christians from charging interest on loans, most moneylenders were Jews. As non-Christians, Jews were barred from many other occupations.

READING CHECK Summarize How did trade grow and develop in the Middle Ages?

★Interactive
HISTORY CLOSE-UP

A Trade Fair

Merchants traveled from all over to sell their goods at trade fairs. Here, they bought and sold goods from other merchants to sell in their local markets.

Banking increased when goods were being purchased with coins and credit.

Traders from foreign countries brought their goods to the fair along sea and land routes.

410 CHAPTER 14

Skills Focus: Summarizing

At Level

Reading Skill
Medieval Trade Fair Advertisements

Materials: paper, art supplies

1. Review with students the information in the text about products available at medieval trade fairs.

2. Organize students into mixed ability pairs.

3. Have each pair create an advertisement for a product or products to be sold in a medieval town trade fair. Remind students to make the pictures dominant, because the majority of people in the Middle Ages could not read. Students might try to mimic the paper of the time—vellum, thin sheets made from animal skin, which was also a fairly valuable commodity.

4. Have volunteers present their advertisements to the class. **LS Visual-Spatial**

🗎 **Alternative Assessment Handbook**, Rubric 2: Advertisements

Growth of Towns and Cities

Thriving trade and the increase in the use of money in Europe helped lead to the expansion of towns and cities. Hoping to make money, many peasants left their farms and villages for cities where most of them worked as laborers.

New Technologies Advances in farm technology contributed to the move to cities. The heavy plow, for example, increased the amount of crops people could grow on their land. Other new technologies included the water mill and the windmill, which used the power of nature to grind wheat into flour. These improved technologies meant that fewer people were needed to work on farms. This, in turn, enabled more people to move to cities and try to build a life for themselves.

Free Towns Looking for places to conduct trade, merchants moved into medieval towns. Most of these towns were run by local lords who could charge any fees or taxes they wished. Merchants, however, did not want to pay high fees or taxes on their goods. To avoid these fees, merchants appealed to kings for special charters for new towns. These charters allowed the merchants to run towns in any way they wanted. In return, they paid taxes to the king.

Towns grew quickly under the leadership of merchants. In the High Middle Ages, more people than ever before were migrating to European cities. By 1300, Paris and Rome each had about 100,000 residents while London and Florence each had about 75,000. In time, these towns began to be referred to as cities.

Guilds With so many people living in towns and cities, craftspeople began to see a need to organize themselves in order to protect their own interests. Eventually, they created trade organizations called **guilds**. All the members of a guild had the same occupation. One of the primary functions of a guild was to restrict competition. Working together, members of a guild set standards and prices for their products. In this way, guilds provided mutual protection and also insured quality control.

NEW YORK

CC Unit 3-C1bc
Global trade and interactions: Trade fairs and towns; Medieval guilds

Trade fairs were often held near churches.

Merchants from nearby villages brought their animals and other goods to sell at the trade fairs.

Skills FOCUS **INTERPRETING VISUALS**

go.hrw.com
Practice Online
Keyword: SHL HMA

Draw Conclusions A trade fair was an excellent way to buy goods, but it only occurred once a year. What sort of competition might have arisen between the trade fair and everyday markets?

Only members of a guild could run a business. Here an apprentice works with a tailor.

THE HIGH MIDDLE AGES **411**

411

3 What was daily life like in medieval cities? *crowded, dirty, dangerous places; also provided places for people to socialize, entertainment, sports*

Daily Life in Cities

Summarize Why were medieval cities unpleasant? *little sunlight; crowded streets, trash and waste; vermin and disease; thieves and murderers*

Rate If you lived in medieval times, would you prefer to be a farmer or a city merchant? Why? *possible answers— farmer: country life is cleaner, more wholesome; merchant: opportunities to socialize, entertainment in the city*

● Review & Assess ●

Close

Have students explain the factors that led to the growth of cities.

Review

Online Quiz, Section 2

Assess

SE **Section 2 Assessment**

Progress Assessment: Section 2 Quiz

Alternative Assessment Handbook

Reteach/Intervene

Interactive Reader and Study Guide, Section 2

Interactive Skills Tutor CD-ROM

Answers

Reading Check (left) *technology reduced need for farm workers, people moved to towns; towns grew under merchant leadership;* **(right)** *narrow winding streets; trash and waste in the street; smelly and smoky; lots of animals; places for people to socialize; plays and festivals; sports*

Guilds also trained children in their crafts. A child who wanted to learn a craft started out as an **apprentice**. As an apprentice, he spent several years working with a master craftsperson, learning the basic skills of the craft. Most apprentices lived in their masters' homes.

Once an apprentice had learned the basics of his career, he became a **journeyman**. Some journeymen traveled from workshop to workshop, learning from many masters. It was difficult for journeymen to become masters themselves due to some of the guild restrictions.

Most medieval guilds were open only to men, but some accepted female members as well. In fact, a few industries, such as textiles, had a great number of women workers.

READING CHECK **Identify Cause and Effect** Why did towns grow in the Middle Ages?

Daily Life in Cities

According to today's standards, the cities that grew up in Europe in the Middle Ages were small and crowded. At times, life in these cities could be very unpleasant.

Streets in many cities were narrow and winding. Shops and houses, often three to four stories high, lined both sides of the street. Because these tall buildings blocked sunlight,

these buildings were often dark inside. City streets were crowded, not only with people but with horses, pigs, and other animals. Most cities lacked public sanitation facilities, so trash and other waste piled up in the streets. Rats and insects lived in this waste, making disease a common threat.

In addition to the threat of disease, fire and crime made medieval cities dangerous. The air was hazy with smoke from cooking fires, forges, glass factories, and tanneries. Such fires were necessary, but they were also potential disasters—most buildings were made of wood that easily caught fire. Violence was also common, as criminals frequented city streets.

However, not all aspects of city life were so dismal. Cities provided benefits for the people who lived there. Churches, eating halls, and markets were common places for people to meet and socialize. Guilds provided public entertainment in the form of plays and festivals for religious holidays. Sports were also common, and teams of players from guilds competed in ball games. The growth of cities helped bring about a greater familiarity with the wider world. Cities also allowed for the spread of arts and new ideas in medieval Europe.

READING CHECK **Describe** What was life like in a medieval town?

SECTION 2 ASSESSMENT

go.hrw.com
Online Quiz
Keyword: SHL HMA HP

Reviewing Ideas, Terms, and People

1. a. Define What was the **Hanseatic League**?
  b. Summarize What took place at a trade fair?
  c. Evaluate How might the use of money and **credit** have helped to increase trade in the Middle Ages?

2. a. Describe What are **guilds**?
  b. Contrast What is the difference between an **apprentice** and a **journeyman**?
  c. Elaborate How did merchants help influence the growth of towns?

3. a. Identify What major issues faced people living in medieval cities?
  b. Compare What were the good aspects and bad aspects of city life in the Middle Ages?
  c. Evaluate What do you think about daily life in a medieval city? Explain.

Critical Thinking

4. Analyze Draw a causes-and-effects chart like the one below. Use your notes from the section to list causes and effects of the movement to towns and cities during the Middle Ages. Look at the ways in which the increase in trade and the growth of towns and cities were connected.

Causes	Effects

FOCUS ON SPEAKING

5. Persuasion Write and deliver a short speech in which you try to convince farming peasants of the Middle Ages to move to a medieval city.

Section 2 Assessment Answers

1. a. group of towns in northern Germany that worked together to promote and protect trade
b. Merchants sold goods from around the world.
c. made it easier to purchase goods

2. a. group of people with same occupation who band together to protect their own interests
b. apprentice—learned a craft from a single master; journeyman—practiced and worked in craft
c. Merchants brought trade, which brought people to towns.

3. a. crowded streets, animals, lack of public sanitation, disease
b. places to meet and socialize, entertainment, sports; disease and pollution, violence
c. possible answer—Despite problems, cities offered economic opportunities.

4. Causes—desire for goods, technological advances, economic opportunities; **Effects**—trade increased; merchants led towns; currency, credit, guilds

5. Speeches should discuss the economic and social advantages of city life.

Art and Culture of the Middle Ages

BEFORE YOU READ

MAIN IDEA

During the Middle Ages, great achievements were made in the visual arts, literature, and thinking and learning.

READING FOCUS

1. What were the major achievements of the visual arts during the Middle Ages?

2. What were the great literary works of the Middle Ages?

3. What new developments were made in medieval thinking and learning?

KEY TERMS AND PEOPLE

Gothic
flying buttress
illumination
Hildegard of Bingen
troubadours
Geoffrey Chaucer
Dante Alighieri
Thomas Aquinas
Scholasticism

 NEW YORK

PI 3.2 Explain the dynamics of cultural change and how interactions between and among cultures has affected various cultural groups.

THE INSIDE STORY

What inspired a man to create a new style of architecture? When Maurice de Sully became bishop of Paris in 1160, he was unimpressed with the church in which he was to hold services. He wanted to build a new church, one that would help make Paris one of Europe's greatest cities. But what should the new church look like?

According to legend, the answer came to de Sully in a dream. When he awoke, he sketched out a plan for his new church in the dirt. He then ordered workers to begin the demolition of the old church as well as several nearby buildings. The new church was going to need lots of room.

The new church—the cathedral of Notre Dame—was an architectural marvel. The church was huge, its ceiling soaring much higher than any other building in Paris. Enormous windows allowed light, tinted by stained glass, to flood the interior. Accustomed to small, dark, crowded churches, the people of Paris were amazed at this new style of building. They viewed their new church as a symbol of God's glory. ◼

Visual Arts

Soaring cathedrals, such as the Cathedral of Notre Dame in Paris, are the most striking legacy of the importance of Christianity in the Middle Ages. In the deeply religious period of the Middle Ages, many artists created glorious works of art. These works were most commonly displayed in churches and cathedrals.

Spires in the Sky

▲ The Cathedral of Notre Dame in Paris

THE HIGH MIDDLE AGES **413**

---

❶ What were the major achievements of the visual arts during the Middle Ages? *Gothic cathedrals, illuminated manuscripts, beautifully woven tapestries*

Visual Arts

Explain What was the purpose of art during the Middle Ages? *to show the glory of God*

Contrast How were Gothic churches different from previous churches? *taller and brighter; used flying buttresses to support walls from outside; allowed higher ceilings, fewer columns, larger windows*

Draw Conclusions Why were architects and engineers needed during the Middle Ages? *new forms of architecture; new designs for buildings*

Activity **Help Wanted** Have students write a help-wanted ad for a church master builder. Students should include a complete job description.

🔲 **Verbal-Linguistic**

📋 **Alternative Assessment Handbook**, Rubric 37: Writing Assignments

Info to Know

The Builders The construction of a large church or cathedral required the services of a master builder. Master builders needed both technical expertise and managerial abilities. Masons, carpenters, roofers, metalworkers, glassmakers and sculptors were all involved in the construction. Many of these workers came from great distances and lived on-site during construction. From plans to consecration, building a church could take up to thirty years.

Religious Art & Architecture

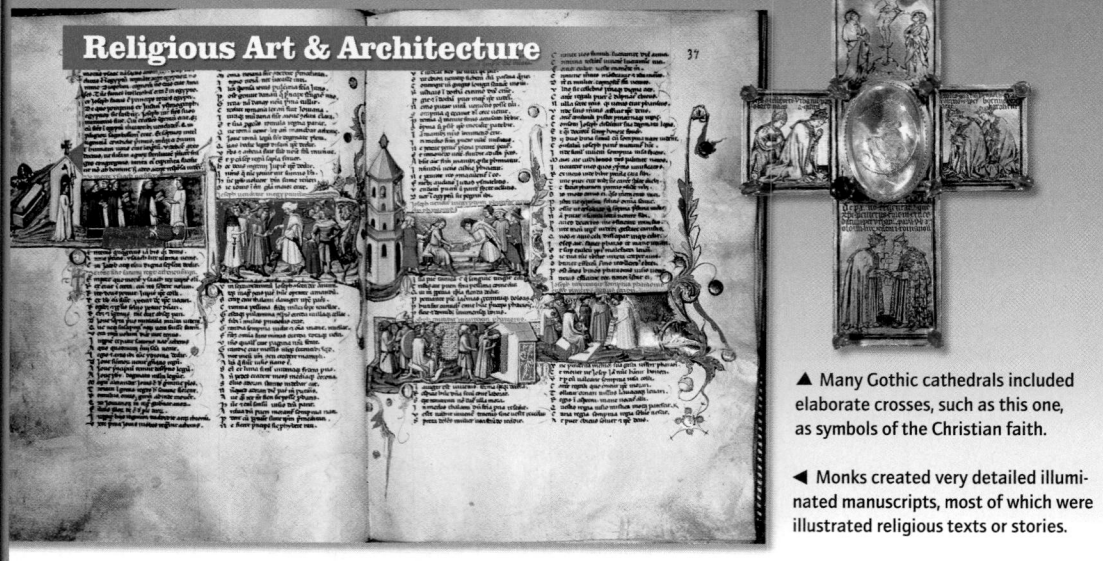

▲ Many Gothic cathedrals included elaborate crosses, such as this one, as symbols of the Christian faith.

◄ Monks created very detailed illuminated manuscripts, most of which were illustrated religious texts or stories.

TAKING NOTES

As you read, take notes on the great achievements in visual arts, literature, and learning in the Middle Ages.

Visual Arts	
Literature	
Thinking and Learning	

FOCUS ON NEW YORK

Medieval architecture continued to be a favored style for church buildings for centuries. New York City has two of the largest and most famous American churches built in the medieval style: St. Patrick's Cathedral and the Cathedral of St. John the Divine.

Gothic Architecture In the Middle Ages, some of the greatest examples of the religious feelings were found in churches like Notre Dame. These churches were built in the new **Gothic** style. Gothic churches were both taller and brighter than earlier churches had been.

The design of Gothic churches was made possible by advances in engineering. The most important of these advances was a new type of support called the **flying buttress**. Earlier churches had used interior columns and braces to support the roof, which meant that ceilings were low. Flying buttresses supported a church's walls from the outside, allowing much higher ceilings and largely eliminating the need for columns. This gave churches a much more airy feeling.

Flying buttresses relieved some of the stress that would otherwise have been placed on the walls of earlier churches. As a result, church builders were able to include much larger windows than ever before. In order to take advantage of this light, church officials hired artists to create panels of stained glass for the windows. Many of these stained glass windows showed scenes from the Bible or depicted the lives of saints.

Another advantage of the light and the windows was that windows were larger. These

larger windows made it possible to use stained glass for a greater effect inside the church.

Cathedrals were lavishly decorated, inside and out. On the exterior of many cathedrals stood statues of saints, kings, and figures from the Old Testament. There were also fanciful gargoyles, or spouts to drain rainwater off the roof. In the Middle Ages, many gargoyles were carved into the likenesses of hideous beasts.

The interiors of cathedrals included a number of decorative elements. Walls were sometimes painted with elaborate murals of religious scenes. In addition, candleholders, crosses, and statues were often intricate works of art decorated with gold and precious stones. Even the clothes worn by priests were works of art, often heavily embroidered and woven with threads made of gold.

Illumination Like churches, religious texts were often richly decorated in the Middle Ages. The process of decorating a written manuscript with pictures or designs is called **illumination**.

Illuminators used their art to bring pages to life. These artists painted scenes from the manuscript they were decorating or added purely decorative designs. One common technique was to decorate the first letter that occurred on a page. These letters were painted in a very large script and often colorful and

414 CHAPTER 14

Skills Focus: Analyzing Visuals

Reading Like a Historian Skill

Illuminated Manuscript

Materials: paper with faint lines, rulers, thin or wedge-tipped markers Before the lesson, make copies of several short selections from either Chaucer or Dante

1. Review the information in the text about illuminated manuscripts. You may wish to show students some examples of illuminated manuscripts. Provide students with one medieval selection and an old calligraphy alphabet.

2. Have students copy the medieval selection onto their own papers in calligraphy. Students should start with a square in the upper left corner. This will be the space for the first letter.

3. When students are finished with the lettering, have them illuminate their manuscript. Encourage them to integrate a relevant picture into the first letter. 🔲 **Visual Spatial**

📋 **Alternative Assessment Handbook**, Rubric 3: Artwork

◄ Cathedrals often featured carvings of religious subjects. The west entrance to the Cathedral of Notre Dame depicts the Last Judgment.

◄ Although built with heavy stone, the interiors of Gothic cathedrals seemed light and airy. New building techniques such as the exterior flying buttresses supported the walls, allowing windows to let light stream in.

 Skills FOCUS **INTERPRETING VISUALS**

Making Generalizations Most of the visual arts during the Middle Ages had religious themes. Why do you think religion was the main focus of the visual artwork of the time?

flowing. Inside the books, illuminators would paint plants, animals, or people. For some special texts, they might apply thin sheets of gold leaf to the painted surface.

Tapestry Although most medieval art was religious in nature, some artists created works dealing with daily life, history, or fantasy. Among these works are tapestries, or large woven wall hangings. Tapestries were hung in castles to prevent drafts. Many medieval tapestries that still survive show scenes from daily life or fantastic creatures such as unicorns and dragons. One famous tapestry is the Bayeux Tapestry, which tells the story of William the Conqueror and his conquest of England in 1066.

READING CHECK **Find the Main Idea** What were three forms of medieval art?

Literature

Just as the art forms practiced in the Middle Ages introduced new ideas and practices, so too did the types of literature created. Writers from the period produced works of varying styles on topics that covered the entire spectrum of human life, including religion, romance, and epic adventures.

Religious Texts As you might expect, many of the writings created in the Middle Ages dealt with religion. This was especially true in the Early Middle Ages, when few people other than monks and priests could read or write. After 1200, more people were literate, especially in cities.

Religious writers of the Middle Ages created all sorts of works, from sermons about how people should live to interpretations of passages from the Bible. Another popular topic was the lives of saints. These tales were compiled into collections during this period and widely read by the literate nobility, merchants, and clergy.

Medieval writers also created religious songs and poems. One of the most famous medieval poets was a nun, **Hildegard of Bingen**. An artist, poet, and a composer, she wrote dozens of poems and music to accompany them. Like other Christian writers in Europe at the time, Hildegard wrote in Latin, the language of the Roman Catholic Church.

Epics and Romances In addition to writings on religious topics, literature of the Middle Ages included epics and romances. Epics and romances are both long poems that tell stories of heroes and villains, but these works differ in their subject matter.

THE HIGH MIDDLE AGES **415**

Reading Focus

❷ What were the great literary works of the Middle Ages? *Canterbury Tales, the* Divine Comedy; *also poems of Hildegard of Bingen*

Literature

Recall What kinds of religious writing appeared during the Middle Ages? *sermons, interpretations of Bible passages, lives of saints, songs and poems*

Analyze Why do you think Hildegard of Bingen wrote in Latin? *She was a nun; Latin was the language of the Church.*

Make Generalizations What were medieval romances like? *tales of true love and chivalry; had heroes and villains; performed by troubadours*

📄 CRF: Biography: Hildegard of Bingen

Teaching Tip

Review with students the information in the text about sagas. Then have students explain the differences and similarities between sagas and epic poems.

Info to Know

Artists and Craftsman People in the Middle Ages made no distinction between fine artists and craft workers. Master painters often went from creating portraits to painting banners or designing clothes. During the late 1300s, the court painter of the Duke of Burgundy also decorated chairs and made mechanical repairs.

Skills Focus: Interpreting Literature as Historical Evidence

Reading Like a Historian Skill
King Arthur Stories

Research Required **At Level**

1. Review with students what an epic poem is. Then have students locate two King Arthur stories. You may wish to assign them chapters from T.H. White's classic "The Once and Future King."

2. Have students summarize the stories and tell what they thought about them.

3. Tell students that many of these stories are extremely old and have been passed down for generations. Guide students in a discussion about how —and what—historians might learn from these stories. **LS** **Verbal-Linguistic**

📄 **Alternative Assessment Handbook**, Rubric 12: Drawing Conclusions

Answers

Interpreting Visuals *The Church and worship were important during this time period.*

Reading Check *architecture, illumination, and tapestries*

Literature

Identify Cause and Effect What effect did Chaucer and Dante have on their respective languages? *increased usage of English and Italian; shaped development of these languages*

Evaluate Should Chaucer's work be considered a reliable source for historians? Why or why not? *possible answer—yes, shows many details of everyday life at the time*

CRF: Literature: *Morte Darthur*

Info to Know

Dante and Beatrice Dante first saw Beatrice when they were nine years old. His love for here was the purely spiritual *amor amicitae* defined by Thomas Aquinas as a love in which the beloved "is loved in love of friendship...simply and for its own sake." Dante married another woman, but always thought highly of Beatrice. He wrote of Beatrice as his guide through Paradise in the *Divine Comedy*.

Biography

Peter Abelard (1079–1142) and Heloise (1101–1162) Peter Abelard was a respected medieval lecturer and theologian, with many students. A powerful man named Fulbert asked Abelard to tutor his niece, Heloise. Although many years younger than Abelard, Heloise was a promising scholar and masterful writer. Their relationship grew into love. They were married in secret, but Fulbert soon discovered the truth. Enraged, he hired men to beat and mutilate Abelard. Abelard and Heloise separated and took religious vows, withdrawing to a convent and a monastery. Both continued their scholarly work and wrote letters to each other for many years afterward.

Answers

Primary Sources 1. *way of life;*
2. *possible answer—People were concerned with living life correctly so that they would enter heaven.*

Reading Check *religious subjects; heroes, villains, love; chivalry*

The epic poems of the Middle Ages tell exciting tales related to war and its heroes. *The Song of Roland*, for example, is an epic that tells the story of Charlemagne's fight against the Muslims in Spain. Romances, on the other hand, tell exciting tales of true love and chivalry. Chivalry was a code of honor that knights were supposed to live by; it required knights to be generous and courteous to women and other knights. The subjects of some medieval romances remain familiar to us even today. Many of them, for example, tell stories of King Arthur and his knights of the Round Table.

Epics and romances were often performed by wandering singers called **troubadours**. These troubadours wandered from court to court, performing and spreading news. Because epics and romances were intended to be entertainment,

PRIMARY SOURCES

The Divine Comedy

In the *Inferno*, the first part of Dante's *The Divine Comedy*, Dante describes his imaginary journey through Hell. The passage below describes how his journey begins and the fear that he is experiencing.

"When I had journeyed half of our life's way,
I found myself within a shadowed forest,
for I had lost the path that does not stray.
Ah, it is hard to speak of what it was,
that savage forest, dense and difficult,
which even in recall renews my fear:
so bitter—death is hardly more severe!
But to retell the good discovered there,
I'll also tell the other things I saw.
I cannot clearly say how I had entered
the wood; I was so full of sleep just at
the point where I abandoned the true path.
But when I'd reached the bottom of the hill—
it rose along the boundary of the valley
that had harassed my heart with so much fear."

Skills FOCUS READING LIKE A HISTORIAN

1. **Define** The word *path* shows up twice in this passage. What does Dante mean by "path"?
2. **Interpret Literature as a Source** How does Dante's work reflect the thoughts and feelings of people during the Middle Ages?

See **Skills Handbook, p. H25**

416 CHAPTER 14

they were not written in Latin. These poems were in the vernacular, the language that people spoke every day. English and French were vernacular languages, as opposed to Latin, which was the language of the church.

Major Works Two noteworthy works of the High Middle Ages are *The Canterbury Tales*, by **Geoffrey Chaucer** and the *The Divine Comedy*, by **Dante Alighieri** (DAHN-tay ahl-eeg-YEH-ree). *The Canterbury Tales* is a collection of stories that tells the tale of a group of pilgrims traveling to the town of Canterbury, England. Along the way, each pilgrim agrees to tell a story to entertain the other travelers.

The Canterbury Tales is significant as more than just a collection of stories. Chaucer's characters come from a wide range of social backgrounds, from a wealthy knight to a humble farmer. His descriptions of these characters help historians picture what life was like for people in the Middle Ages. Also, the fact that Chaucer wrote in English helped increase the use of this written language in England. Since the Norman Conquest, many people in England, especially nobles, had been speaking French.

The other major work, Dante's *The Divine Comedy* is composed of three parts, or *cantos*: *Inferno* (Hell), *Purgatorio* (Purgatory), and *Paradiso* (Paradise). Together they tell the story of an imaginary trip that Dante took through the afterlife. During the course of his trip, Dante meets people from his own life, as well as great figures from history. For example, the ancient Roman poet Virgil acts as his guide for part of the way.

Dante served much the same function for Italian as Chaucer did for English. Dante's writing led to the increased use of written Italian and helped shape the development of the Italian language for centuries after his death.

READING CHECK Summarize What subjects did medieval authors write about?

Thinking and Learning

The many religious writers of the Middle Ages helped spread new ideas throughout Europe. These new ideas helped give rise to new ways of thinking and learning. Science and universities shaped these new systems of thought.

Skills Focus: Identifying Main Idea and Details   At Level

Reading Skill
Medieval Literature

1. Draw the Venn diagram for students to see. Omit the italicized answers. Have students copy and complete the diagram.

2. Have volunteers share their completed Venn diagrams, and complete the class diagram for all to see. Have students retain their charts as a study tool. **LS Visual-Spatial**

Alternative Assessment Handbook, Rubric 13: Graphic Organizers

Canterbury Tales: *Chaucer, English, tales told by people on a pilgrimage*

Both: *developed languages, clues for historians*

Divine Comedy: *Dante, Italian, journey through afterlife*

Alchemy Curious about how the world worked, people in the Middle Ages began to conduct scientific experiments. In doing so, they practiced an early form of chemistry called alchemy.

Some alchemists, people who practiced alchemy, thought that they could find a way to turn base metals, like lead, into gold. As they sought to solve this problem, they heated materials to dissolve or vaporize them. In this way they gained practical experience in chemical reactions that aided later scientists.

Universities The growth of European universities increased the flow of Greek learning into Europe. Scientific, philosophical, mathematical, astronomical, as well as medical texts were translated into Latin. Lecturers taught Latin grammar, rhetoric, logic, geometry, arithmetic, astronomy, and music. Together, this course of study was called the liberal arts. Universities also taught theology, medicine, and law. Universities helped create a new educated class, who spoke and wrote in Latin and shared a common culture.

The Teachings of Thomas Aquinas The teachers in medieval universities included some of the greatest scholars of the age. Perhaps the most influential of all these scholars was **Thomas Aquinas** (uh-KWY-nuhs), a teacher at the University of Paris.

Aquinas was keenly interested in the works of ancient philosophers, especially Aristotle. The revival of interest in the Greek philosophers sparked a major controversy in the church over how humans could learn about the world. Aristotle believed that truth could be discovered only through human reason. Christians, on the other hand, believed that truth was revealed by God and depended on faith. Aquinas tried to reconcile the two approaches. He argued that both reason and faith were necessary for an understanding of truth. His approach, known as **Scholasticism**, tried to show that Christian teachings were also knowable and provable through the use of logic and reason. Thus Aquinas ensured that in western Europe human reason would remain a primary element in determining truth.

READING CHECK **Analyze** How did thinking and learning change in the Middle Ages?

FACES OF HISTORY

Thomas AQUINAS 1225–1274

Thomas Aquinas was born to a noble Italian family. As a young man, he chose a life of poverty and joined the Dominican order. He spent much of his life in France—studying, teaching, and writing.

In one of his most important works, the *Summa Theologica*, Aquinas explored many questions of philosophy and theology. For each subject he studied, he tried to consider every possible argument—both for and against it. In doing so, he wished to show how opposing views were related. Although some people of his time did not approve of his ideas, many now consider him the one of the greatest thinkers of the Middle Ages.

Infer Why might some people have objected to Aquinas's ideas?

SECTION 3 ASSESSMENT

go.hrw.com
Online Quiz
Keyword: SHL HMA HP

Reviewing Ideas, Terms, and People

1. a. Define What is a flying buttress?
   b. Explain How did illumination help bring religious texts to life?
   c. Evaluate Why do you think religious art was so important to people in the Middle Ages?

2. a. Identify Who was Hildegard of Bingen? What is she known for?
   b. Contrast What are the differences between epics and romances?
   c. Evaluate What effect did writers like Geoffrey Chaucer and Dante Alighieri have on literature in the Middle Ages?

3. a. Define What is alchemy?
   b. Make Generalizations What are some characteristics of the first universities?
   c. Elaborate How were the ideas and teachings of Thomas Aquinas new and different to people in the Middle Ages?

Critical Thinking

4. Summarize Copy the graphic organizer below and fill in the achievements of the Middle Ages in art, literature, thinking, and learning.

Medieval Achievements

FOCUS ON SPEAKING

5. Description Write and deliver a speech that describes the new artistic and cultural achievements of the Middle Ages. Choose one achievement that you feel has had the largest impact and discuss why you think so.

THE HIGH MIDDLE AGES **417**

Arts and Ideas

Info to Know

Early Universities The earliest Western school that could be called a university was actually a medical school in Salerno, Italy. The University of Bologna, the first true university, was founded late in the 11th century. The University of Paris, founded between 1150 and 1170, was the first to be established in northern Europe, and it served as a model for England's Oxford University. The universities of Oxford and Paris were composed of colleges, which were actually residence halls. Universities had to finance themselves, so instructors charged fees; if students did not like their teachers, they could move to other schools. The first universities in the Western Hemisphere were the University of Santo Domingo, begun by the Spanish in 1538, and the University of Michoacán, founded in Mexico in 1539. The first American colleges were Harvard (1636), William and Mary (1693), Princeton (1746), and King's College, now known as Columbia University (1754).

Activity **University Brochures**
Have students design an advertising brochure for a medieval university, and one for a current university. Tell students to use the information in the section, including the information on illumination, as they design their brochures. **LS** **Visual-Spatial**

Alternative Assessment Handbook, Rubric 2: Advertisements

Answers

Understanding Themes **1.** *students met with teachers, no campus, liberal arts;* **2.** *similarities—students come to learn, better selves, prepare for a job, socialize with each other; differences— early European university students were Christian, studied liberal arts and theology; today women and people from different backgrounds attend; public and private universities; courses of study greatly expanded*

Focus on Themes

Arts and Ideas

During the High Middle Ages, universities became more and more commonplace as use of the written word increased and the ability to reason, read, and compute became of greater importance to Europeans. As knowledge came to be of greater value, people went to universities to learn more about the world around them. Universities, both then and now, offer people the chance to expand their minds through lectures and discussion amongst their peers.

▲ **NOW** Students participate in a seminar on the lawn of a modern-day university.

UNIVERSITIES THEN Universities in the Middle Ages were products of the growing cities. The term *university* broadly meant "a group of persons associated for any purpose." The medieval university had neither a campus nor a set of buildings. Rather, students met with their teachers at designated places throughout the city.

The medieval university was one of the first ways in which Europeans were exposed to a liberal arts education. Students were expected to take seven liberal arts courses. A master of arts program took six years to complete; it took an additional eight years to earn a degree in theology. University students of the time were all men, and most came to study at about the age of 17. The students were mostly Christian, and they did not come from the nobility. Instead, the majority of students were recently migrated peasants who had come to live in cities.

UNIVERSITIES NOW In many respects, universities today are similar to those of the Middle Ages. Students at a liberal arts college are expected to take a wide range of courses, and the age at which students usually begin their studying is about the same as it was in the Middle Ages.

However, there are some important differences in the way modern universities operate. Today's universities are open to women and people from any religious background. Most universities have their own campuses, and the large number of private and public universities allow students to choose the programs and the schools that are right for them. People around the world place a great value on higher education, and that value has only grown since the Middle Ages.

Skills FOCUS **UNDERSTANDING THEMES**

1. **Summarize** What were some characteristics of the medieval university?
2. **Compare and Contrast** What are some of the similarities and differences between universities of the Middle Ages and universities today?

◀ **THEN** A teacher from the Middle Ages lectures his students on the liberal arts.

418 CHAPTER 14

Skills Focus: Summarizing

Below Level

Standard English Mastery

Reading Skill
Universities Now and Then

1. Review the information in the feature about university studies, and guide students in a discussion of the similarities and differences between universities now and then.

2. Guide students in a discussion of the reasons a college education is valuable. Have students take notes during the discussion or create a class list of the advantages of attending college. Write the list for all to see.

3. Guide students in a discussion about the difficulties of attending universities during the Middle Ages—expenses, finding a place to live, etc. Have students compose a letter from a young man living during the 1300s to his family explaining why he wants to go to a university and how it will change his life. **LS** **Verbal-Linguistic**

Alternative Assessment Handbook, Rubric 25: Personal Letters

Challenges of the Late Middle Ages

BEFORE YOU READ

MAIN IDEA

In the late Middle Ages, Europeans faced many challenges, including religious crises, wars, and a deadly plague.

READING FOCUS

1. What sorts of religious crises did Europe face during the late Middle Ages?
2. What were the causes of war and conflict in the late Middle Ages?
3. What was the Black Death, and how did it affect people?

KEY TERMS AND PEOPLE

heresy
Inquisitions
friars
Hundred Years' War
Joan of Arc
Wars of the Roses
Henry VII
Black Death

NEW YORK

PI 3.1 Students will analyze the roles and contributions of individuals and groups to social, political, and religious practices and activities.

THE INSIDE STORY

When is a nosebleed a good thing? In 1346 a huge fleet set out from England for France. The fleet was led by King Edward III of England, who was hoping to defeat the French king and claim the throne for himself. When Edward's ship reached land, the king hopped out. Unfortunately for his dignity, the land was uneven and the king fell, striking his head on the ground.

Blood gushed out of the king's nose. His knights saw the king's fall as a bad omen and begged him to get back on board the ship, but the king disagreed. He thought the nosebleed was a good sign. He believed that his blood on the French soil meant that the land was truly his. ■

Religious Crises

When King Edward III of England, invaded France in 1346, Europe was in turmoil. Europe faced challenges to its religious, political, and social order. Because Christianity was the one element that tied most Europeans together, religious crises were a grave threat to all of society.

Heresy One issue facing the church in the High Middle Ages was increasing **heresy**, beliefs that opposed the official teachings of the church. Heretical beliefs had begun appearing in Europe around the first millennium. Even though most people remained faithful, by the 1100s cases of heresy were increasing rapidly enough to cause church officials alarm.

SIGN OF BLOOD

◄ **A battle scene between the English and the French during the Hundred Years' War**

Battle of Crécy, from a medieval manuscript, 1346

Teach the Main Idea

At Level

Challenges of the Late Middle Ages

1. **Teach** Ask students the Reading Focus questions to teach this section.

2. **Apply** Draw three rectangles for students to see. Label them with the names of the topics in this section: Religious Crises, Wars and Conflict, and Black Death. Have students copy the rectangles onto their papers. Have them write the main ideas of each topic in the appropriate rectangle.

3. **Review** As you review the section, have students use their rectangles to describe the difficult challenges of the Late Middle Ages.

4. **Practice/Homework** Have students write a song about life during the Late Middle Ages. **LS** **Visual-Spatial, Auditory-Musical**

   Alternative Assessment Handbook, Rubric 26: Poems and Songs

---

Getting Started

Use the **Interactive Reader and Study Guide** to familiarize students with the section content.

📄 **Interactive Reader and Study Guide**, Section 4

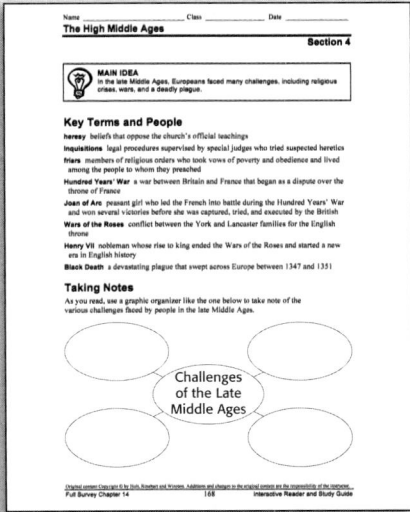

Academic Vocabulary

Review with students the high-use academic term in this section.

sacraments solemn Christian rites believed to have been instituted by Jesus (p. 420)

📄 **CRF: Vocabulary Builder: Section 4**

Taking Notes

people questioned faith, led to heresy, Inquisitions, religious crises; Hundred Years' War, War of the Roses, the Black Death

go.hrw.com
Online Resources

KEYWORD: SHL HMA
ACTIVITY: The Black Death

❶ What sorts of religious crises did Europe face during the late Middle Ages? *the Inquisition; disputes over the papacy*

Religious Crises

Compare and Contrast How could friars fight heresy more effectively than monks? *Friars lived among the people in cities, could relate to the people and teach them; monks lived in monasteries.*

Summarize What events led to the dispute over the papacy? *political fighting caused pope to flee Rome and live in Avignon, France; a future pope moved back to Rome; when he died, two rival popes emerged, one in Rome and one in Avignon*

Primary Source

"Where there is charity and wisdom, there is neither fear nor ignorance. Where there is patience and humility, there is neither anger nor vexation."

—Francis of Assisi, *The Chronicles of the Holy Father Saint Francis, Admonition 27*

Recent Scholarship

William Jordan describes the Middle Ages as the best and worst of times. In *Europe in the High Middle Ages*, he explores Gothic art and architecture, the beginnings of universities, and the literature that emerged. He also examines the struggles within in the Church, political conflicts and wars, and the Black Death.

Europe in the High Middle Ages by William C. Jordan. Allen Lane, 2001.

Answers

Inquisition and Heresy *possible answer—The events were public spectacles. Deaths were violent.*

Reading Check *the Inquisition, location of the papacy, who would be the next pope*

ACADEMIC VOCABULARY

sacraments solemn Christian rites believed to have been instituted by Jesus

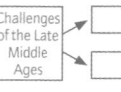

TAKING NOTES

As you read, take notes on the various challenges faced by people in the late Middle Ages.

Challenges of the Late Middle Ages → ☐ ☐

In many instances, people accused of heresy were de-emphasizing the role of the clergy and the sacraments. These beliefs frightened religious officials as it threatened social order in the church. Determined to stop the spread of heresy, the clergy tried several ways to stamp it out.

The primary method used to fight heresy was **Inquisitions**. The Inquisitions were legal procedures supervised by special judges who tried suspected heretics. Accused people came before the court and anyone found guilty of heresy was punished by local authorities.

The church also tried fighting heresy through Christian education. In the early 1200s two men, Francis of Assisi and Dominic of Osma, created new religious orders to spread Christian teachings. Members of these orders, called **friars**, took vows of poverty and obedience, like monks did. Unlike monks, though, friars lived in cities among the people to whom they preached. The teachings of the friars was believed to be a great weapon against heresy.

Inquisition and Heresy

The Supplication of the Heretics in 1210, by Jean Fouquet, c. 1420–1480, courtesy of Bibliotheque Nationale, Paris, France

Skills Focus **READING LIKE A HISTORIAN**

Church officials put to death people convicted of heresy.

Analyzing Visuals What does this painting suggest about the nature of executions during the Inquisition?

See **Skills Handbook**, p. H26

Another method used in the fight against heresy was war. In 1208, Pope Innocent III called for a crusade against a group of heretics who believed in dualism, in southern France. Christian soldiers from northern France joined in the war, a war that spent 21 years trying to eliminate heretics in the region.

The Papacy in Dispute Adding to the turmoil in the medieval church was a dispute over the papacy. In 1309, after political fighting in Rome forced the pope to flee the city, he moved to Avignon (ah-vee-NYAWN) in southern France. Consequently, the next several popes lived at Avignon in a huge palace they had built.

Seventy years later, Pope Gregory XI decided to return to Rome. When Gregory died later that same year, though, there was disagreement over who should become the new pope. As a result, two men, one in Rome and one in Avignon, claimed papal power. The conflict went unresolved for nearly 40 years. The resulting confusion weakened the church's influence.

READING CHECK **Find the Main Idea** What religious challenges did Europeans face in the later Middle Ages?

Wars and Conflict

While Europeans were facing uncertainty in their religious leadership, political leaders were also fighting numerous wars to gain more power for themselves. The two most violent and destructive of these wars, the Hundred Years' War and the Wars of the Roses, both involved the kings of England.

Hundred Years' War In 1328 the French king died without a son. His nearest living male relative was a nephew, King Edward III of England. But, the late king also had a cousin who had served as his regent. The English wanted to rule both countries, and the French, not wanting to be ruled by an English monarch, favored the regent. The French decided that the regent was the rightful heir, and he was thus crowned King Philip VI of France.

This decision did not please the English king. At the head of a huge army, Edward invaded France in 1337. This invasion marked the beginning of the **Hundred Years' War**.

Skills Focus: Identifying Problem and Solution | **At Level**

Reading Skill
Clerical Council

1. Organize students into small groups.

2. Tell students that they are members of the clergy during the late Middle Ages. They will be attending a council to decide the best way to deal with the problem of heresy. Their choices will be the Inquisition, sending friars into cities, or some combination of these options. Students could also come up with an original solution to the problem. Remind students that this was not a time of religious tolerance.

3. Have students discuss the problem and try to arrive at a consensus about the best solution.

4. Have volunteers share the results of their discussions, and whether or not they reached a consensus. Tell students that many clerical councils ended in bitter disagreements.

🅛🅢 **Verbal-Linguistic**

📝 **Alternative Assessment Handbook**, Rubric 11: Discussions

HUNDRED YEARS' WAR

ENGLAND
Agincourt, 1415
FLANDERS
English Channel
Formigny, 1450
Crécy, 1346
BRITTANY
NORMANDY
Patay, 1429
Orléans, 1429
Poitiers, 1356
BURGUNDY
Bay of Biscay
FRANCE
Bordeaux, 1453
AQUITAINE
ATLANTIC OCEAN
HOLY ROMAN EMPIRE
Mediterranean Sea

0   100   200 Miles
0   100   200 Kilometers
Azimuthal equal-area projection

Land held by England, 1337
Land held by England, 1429
English victory
French victory
Boundary of France, 1453

GEOGRAPHY SKILLS INTERPRETING MAPS

1. Location Where did the French stop the English invasion? What battle was fought in the southern part of France, and which region of France was it fought in?

2. Regions Why did the English want to control France? What benefits would they have if they won the war?

FACES OF HISTORY

Joan of Arc
c. 1412–1431

Joan of Arc was only 17 years old when she led the French forces into battle. She managed to rally the French troops, who had been morally defeated by their losses. A strict Catholic, Joan required her soldiers to go to church and to confession. These men were willing to follow her because she claimed to be sent by saints.

After she was captured in 1430, Joan was condemned as a heretic by the English. At the age of 19, she was burned at the stake. Twenty five years later, she was cleared of all charges, and in 1920 she was made a Catholic saint.

Summarize Why did the soldiers follow Joan?

Edward and his troops won victory after victory, largely because they used better weapons, like the longbow and cannon. In the Battle of Crécy, the English weapons devastated both the French fighters and their Genoese allies.

HISTORY'S VOICES

> "The English archers took one pace forward and poured out their arrows on the Genoese so thickly and evenly that they fell like snow . . . The English continued to shoot into the thickest part of the crowd, wasting none of their arrows. They impaled or wounded horses and riders, who fell to the ground in great distress."

—Jean Froissart, *Chronicles*

As the war progressed, new leaders took over the fight. Heartened by victories like Crécy, the English marched deeper into France, and under a new king, Henry V, the English army advanced all the way to the gates of Paris.

In 1429 a young peasant girl, **Joan of Arc**, helped change the course of the war. Joan claimed that the saints had told her to lead the French into battle. Even though French prince was skeptical of Joan's story, he allowed her to take command of an army. Joan and her army

marched to the town of Orléans and defeated a huge English army. She led the French in several more victories before being captured, tried, and executed by the English.

After Joan's death, King Charles VII of France rallied his army. The French steadily took back the land they had lost to the English, and by 1453 had driven the English almost completely out of their country. After more than 100 years, the war was finally over.

Wars of the Roses The end of the Hundred Years' War did not mean the end of political fighting in England. Shortly after peace was made with France, two families began a war over the English throne: the Lancasters, who used a red rose as their emblem, and the Yorks, who used a white rose. Because both families had rose symbols, the conflict became known as the **Wars of the Roses**.

At first the Yorkists were successful. Edward IV, a member of the York family, took the throne in 1461 and won victories over the Lancastrians. Trouble began again, though, after Edward's death. The king's sons disappeared, and Edward's brother became king.

READING SKILLS

Understanding Causes and Effects What was a cause of the War of the Roses?

THE HIGH MIDDLE AGES **421**

Reading Focus

Wars and Conflict

Recall What marked the end of the Wars of the Roses? *Henry Tudor (Henry VII) was related to the Lancasters by blood and rose to power.*

Summarize Were the Yorks successful? Explain. *possible answer—No, after Edward's death, many problems emerged; Richard III was faced with uprisings, and killed in battle. Eventually a Tudor, Henry VII, took the throne.*

Reading Focus

❸ What was the Black Death, and how did it affect people? *a deadly plague, perhaps a combination of bubonic and pneumonic plagues, that killed as many as 25 million people and caused the medieval manor system to fall apart*

Black Death

Explain How did merchant ships spread the plague? *Rats carrying infected fleas which bit sailors, and spread the disease to distant ports.*

Make Generalizations Why were the sick often not treated? *Doctors and priests who tended the sick usually caught the plague and died.*

Answers

Forensics in History *possible answer—They may have been murdered.*

Reading Check *heirs unclear; dispute over French throne led to Hundred Years' War; dispute over English throne led to Wars of the Roses*

422

Almost as soon as he was crowned, however, the new king, Richard III, faced a number of uprisings. One of them was a rebellion led by the Duke of Buckingham, who had originally helped Richard gain the throne. Richard was eventually killed in the battle of Bosworth Field in 1485, while trying to fight off another uprising.

With Richard's death, a nobleman from one of the most important families in England, the Tudors, claimed the throne. Furthermore, Henry Tudor, who became **Henry VII**, was related to both warring factions. He was married to Edward IV daughter, Elizabeth of York, and related to the Lancasters by blood. His rise to power marked the end of the Wars of the Roses and began a new era in English history.

READING CHECK **Summarize** How did fights over the thrones of England and France lead to conflict in medieval Europe?

Black Death

While the Hundred Years' War was taking its toll on the armies of England and France, another crisis struck the people of Europe. That crisis was the **Black Death**, a devastating plague that swept across the continent between 1347 and 1351.

Historians are still not sure what disease the Black Death was, or even if it was a single disease. One theory is that the disease took two different forms. One, called bubonic plague, was spread by fleas that lived on rats and other animals. The other, pneumonic plague, could be spread through the air from person to person.

Origins In 1346 plague struck Mongol armies laying siege to a Black Sea port. From there infected rats and fleas made their way onto ships. Infected fleas bit humans transferring the disease to them. As merchants traveled,

FORENSICS in History

What Happened to the Princes?

One of history's fascinating mysteries is what happened to Edward V and his brother Richard. Can forensic science help find the answer?

▶ The Tower of London

What facts do we have? Edward V, a boy of 12, became king upon the death of his father, Edward IV, in April 1483. His uncle Richard, duke of Gloucester, was appointed as the boy's protector to rule in his place until he matured. Not satisfied with temporary rule, though, the duke took possession of Edward and his younger brother, Richard, and had them imprisoned in the Tower of London. In June, the boys' uncle had their births declared illegitimate. Richard, duke of Gloucester, was then crowned Richard III. By August, the two princes were missing, never seen again.

This drama led many to believe that Richard III had the young princes killed. Unfortunately, the existing physical evidence offers only limited clues. In 1674, workmen digging in the Tower of London found two small skeletons. Presumed to be the two princes, the bones were deposited in an urn in Westminster Abbey. In 1933 they were examined by a dental surgeon, who concluded that they were indeed the bones of the young princes.

Since that time, though, forensic anthropologists have found that the conclusions from the 1933 examination were not valid given the science that was available at the time. It is believed that modern DNA tests could determine if the bones in the urn belong to members of the royal family, and other examinations might shed some light onto how the pair died. However, Queen Elizabeth II will not allow the remains to be tested.

Draw Conclusions What do you think happened to the princes in the tower?

Differentiating Instruction

Special Education Students

Materials: drawing paper, art supplies

1. Remind students that in the Wars of the Roses, one family, the Yorks, had a white rose emblem, and the other family, the Lancasters, had an emblem with a red rose. Tell students that in the Middle Ages, such symbolism was extremely important.

2. Show students examples of coats of arms. Point out various symbols that they use, such as animals, the cross, and the fleur de lis.

3. Have students create their own personal coat of arms, using symbols that they feel represent them. Below the coat of arms, have students write a few sentences describing what the symbols mean.

4. Have volunteers present their coat of arms to the class. **LS** **Visual-Spatial**

📖 **Alternative Assessment Handbook**, Rubric 3: Artwork

so did the plague. It spread quickly throughout Europe, first striking coastal regions and then moving inland. By 1351, almost no part of Europe remained untouched by the Black Death.

Course of the Disease The Black Death was almost always fatal. Usually, a sign that a person was infected was the development of large dark splotches on the skin. Accompanying the splotches were other symptoms, including high fever, vomiting, and severe headaches. Most people who caught the plague died within a few days. Because it spread so easily, priests and doctors who tended the sick usually caught the plague and died themselves.

Historians estimate that as many as 25 million Europeans—one-third of the population—died during the Black Death. The plague not only devastated the European population but also ravaged Central Asia, North Africa, and the Byzantine Empire. In China, the population dropped from about 125 million in the late 1200s to about 90 million in the late 1300s.

Effects People had varying responses to the plague. People's most common reaction was to think God was punishing them for their sins. Some of these people took to beating or otherwise harming themselves. Some people turned to witchcraft in the hope of using magic to cure themselves. In some areas people blamed the Jews, saying that they poisoned wells. Some frightened mobs massacred entire Jewish communities. These reactions led to an increase in anticlericalism and also added to the already increasing anti-Semitic feelings in Europe.

Because of the loss of population, plague also helped bring an end to the manorial system. Because so many workers had died, those who survived were able to demand higher wages. Some peasants moved to cities where they became manufacturing workers. In rural areas, lords tried to fix wages at pre-plague levels, but these efforts failed.

Vacant land was bought up by people with money. These people were then able to create more efficiently organized estates that used less labor. This reorganization of estates also helped to end the manorial system..

READING CHECK **Analyze** How did the Black Death help end the manorial system?

EFFECTS OF THE PLAGUE

- Europe and China both lost one-third of their populations.

- People blamed God for the plague; anti-clericalism began to rise.

- Anti-Semitic beliefs increased in Europe.

- The manor system collapsed as people left their manors.

Danse Macabre, Eglise Saint-Germain La Ferté-Loupiére, late 15th to early 16th century

go.hrw.com
Online Quiz
Keyword: SHL HMA HP

Reviewing Ideas, Terms, and People

1. **a. Define** What is **heresy**?
   b. Identify Cause and Effect What were some of the methods used to combat heresy in the late Middle Ages?
   c. Evaluate How did the papal dispute weaken the Catholic Church?

2. **a. Identify** Who was **Joan of Arc**, and what did she do for France?
   b. Compare What are the similarities between the **Hundred Years' War** and the **Wars of the Roses**?
   c. Make Judgments What do you think about the reasons for war in the late Middle Ages? Explain.

3. **a. Describe** What was the **Black Death**, and how did it spread?
   b. Summarize How did the Black Death spread so quickly through the European population?
   c. Evaluate What were the ways in which the Black Death brought about the end of the manorial system?

Critical Thinking

4. **Categorize** Copy the chart to the right and, using your notes, fill in the chart with the challenges faced by people during the late Middle Ages.

Challenges of the Late Middle Ages

5. **Exposition** Imagine that you are a person living during the late Middle Ages. Write a letter in which you describe some of the difficulties that you face in your everyday life. You may write to someone in your family who lives in a different country or to a friend who lives in the same town or city as you do.

Direct Teach

Reading Focus

Black Death

Recall What fraction of Europe's population died as a result of the Black Death? *one-third of the population*

Explain Why could farmers demand wages for their work after the Black Death came to Europe? *because there was a smaller labor supply after the Black Death killed many workers*

Quick Facts Transparency: Effects of the Plague

Review & Assess

Close

Have students explain the reasons behind the Hundred Years' War and the Wars of the Roses.

Review

Online Quiz, Section 4

Assess

SE Section 4 Assessment

Progress Assessment: Section 4 Quiz

Alternative Assessment Handbook

Reteach/Intervene

Interactive Reader and Study Guide, Section 4

Interactive Skills Tutor CD-ROM

Section 4 Assessment Answers

1. **a.** beliefs that opposed the Church's official teachings
   b. the Inquisition; sending friars into cities to preach and teach
   c. Two rival popes claimed authority, leading to weakness in the Church.

2. **a.** French peasant girl; led French to victory in battle during the Hundred Years' War
   b. Both were fought over who would be king.
   c. possible answer—showed people's concern about the heir to the throne

3. **a.** a deadly plague that devastated Europe; spread by sailors, merchants, fleas, rats
   b. Infected merchants spread disease.
   c. reduced labor supply on farms; survivors demanded wages; farm workers left

4. religious crises, Hundred Years' War, Wars of the Roses, plague

5. Student letters should include a discussion of the religious problems, the political unrest and wars between England and France, and the devastation caused by the Black Death.

Answers

Reading Check *reduced labor supply; survivors demanded wages; left manors for cities; manor system collapsed*

423

The Black Death

Word Help

Word Help

chemists those who prepared medicine; today, pharmacists

mallow a flowering plant

nettles a plant with stinging hairs

poultice a moist object, typically of plant material, applied to a sore spot on the body

abscesses swollen areas on the body

Info to Know

Medical Treatments Treatments for the plague included bleeding, purging with laxatives, lancing the swollen areas, or buboes, or applying hot plasters. Doctors prescribed medicines such as powdered stag's horn, saffron, myrrh, and potions of potable gold. None of these treatments proved effective. Others tried to hold back the plague by burning sweet herbs to purify the air. The personal physician of Pope Clement VI had two large fires lit in the papal apartments and ordered the pope to sit between them, even during the hot Avignon summer. This method actually worked, not because of purification, but because it kept fleas away and required the pope to remain in his chambers.

MISCONCEPTION ALERT

Plagues are not just a thing of the past. An outbreak of pneumonic plague—a more serious and almost always fatal form of the Black Death—hit western India in 1994, killing many people. Agencies such as the Centers for Disease Control track current outbreaks of such highly infectious diseases.

The Black Death

Historical Context The four documents below reveal how the Black Death affected people in Europe and how they reacted to the spread of the disease.

Task Study the selections and answer the questions that follow. After you have studied the documents, you will be asked to write an essay describing how the Black Death affected people in the Middle Ages. You should use evidence from these selections and from the chapter to support your essay.

 NEW YORK STANDARDS

P1 3.1 Students will analyze the roles and contributions of individuals and groups to social, political, and religious practices and activities.

DOCUMENT 1

A Politician's Account

Some three decades after the plague, Italian politician Marchionne wrote the following account of Florence, Italy, during the Black Death.

> No industry was busy in Florence; all the workshops were locked up, all the inns were closed, only chemists and churches were open. Wherever you went, you could find almost nobody; many rich good men were borne from their house to church in their coffin with just four undertakers and a lowly cleric carrying the cross, and even then they demanded a florin apiece. Those who especially profited from the plague were the chemists, the doctors, the poulterers, the undertakers, and the women who sold mallow, nettles, mercury plant and other poultice herbs for drawing abscesses. And those who made the most were these herb sellers. Woollen merchants and retailers when they came across cloth could sell it for whatever price they asked. Once the plague had finished, anybody who could get hold of whatsoever kind of cloth, or found the raw materials to make it, became rich; but many ended up moth-eaten, spoilt, and useless for the looms, and thread and raw wool lost in the city . . . This plague began in March as has been said, and finished in September 1348. And people began to return to their homes and belongings. And such was the number of houses full of goods that had no owner, that it was amazing. Then the heirs to this wealth began to turn up. And someone who had previously had nothing suddenly found himself rich and couldn't believe it was all his, and even felt himself it wasn't quite right.

DOCUMENT 2

Map of Affected Areas

The map shows the spread of the Black Death through Europe over a period of time. Plague made its way from Central Asia to the Black Sea ports. From there it spread along European shipping routes to almost all of Europe.

SPREAD OF THE BLACK DEATH

- 1347
- 1348
- 1349
- 1350
- 1351
- Areas relatively lightly affected
- Approximate route of disease

Skills Focus: Identifying Problem and Solution
At Level

Reading Skill
Monument for Plague Victims

1. Review with students the estimates of the number of people who died in the Black Death.

2. Organize students into mixed-ability pairs.

3. Have each pair design a monument to the victims of the Black Death. Monuments should be tasteful, but should also express the idea that a huge amount of suffering took place during the Black Death.

4. The design concept should include sketches of the monument from several angles and any text that will be placed on the monument.

5. As an extension, have a group of students from another class judge the designs, choose the best one, and award two honorable mentions. **LS Visual-Spatial**

Alternative Assessment Handbook, Rubric 3: Artwork

A Writer's Description

The following description of the Black Death appears in a major literary work called *The Decameron*. It was written by Giovanni Boccaccio between 1350 and 1353, just a few years after the plague hit Florence.

Tedious were it to recount, how citizen avoided citizen, how among neighbors was scarce found any that shewed [showed] fellow-feeling for another, how kinsfolk held aloof, and never met, or but rarely; enough that this sore affliction entered so deep into the minds of men and women, that in the horror thereof brother was forsaken by brother, nephew by uncle, brother by sister . . . Mothers were found to abandon their own children, untended, unvisited, to their fate, as if they had been strangers. Wherefore the sick of both sexes, whose number could not be estimated, were left without resource but in the charity of friends (and few such there were), or the interest of servants, who were hardly to be had at high rates and on unseemly terms, and being, moreover, one and all, men and women of gross understanding, and for the most part unused to such offices, concerned themselves no further than to supply the immediate and expressed wants of the sick, and to watch them die; in which service they themselves not seldom perished with their gains.

DOCUMENT **4**

An Artist's View

This painting was created by Thomas of Stitny around 1376. It depicts death in a grotesque human form strangling a victim of the plague.

Skills FOCUS READING LIKE A HISTORIAN

DOCUMENT 1
a. **Identify Main Ideas** What effect did the Black Death have on the economy in Italy?
b. **Analyze** Why do you think a politician would focus on the economic effects of the Black Death?

DOCUMENT 2
a. **Identify** Where did the Black Death come from?
b. **Make Generalizations** What areas were among the first to experience the Black Death? Why?

DOCUMENT 3
a. **Describe** How did the Black Death affect relationships among people in Florence?
b. **Analyze** Consider the source for this selection. What does the type of source tell you about the lasting influence of the Black Death?

DOCUMENT 4
a. **Describe** What is happening in the painting?
b. **Interpret** What do you think the artist was trying to convey by showing the plague as a human killing another human?

DOCUMENT-BASED ESSAY QUESTION

The Black Death had profound effects on most of Europe during the Middle Ages. Who did the Black Death affect, and in what ways did people's lives change? Using the documents above and information from the chapter, form a thesis that describes the effects of the Black Death. Then write a short essay with details to support your thesis.

See **Skills Handbook**, pp. H25, H26

Visual Summary

Review and Inquiry Guide students in a discussion about the challenges people faced during the High Middle Ages and how trade, guilds, and cultural achievements affected the growth of towns and cities.

📖 **Quick Facts Transparency**: Visual Study Guide: The High Middle Ages

Review Key Terms and People

1. guild
2. Dante Alighieri
3. heresy
4. Hanseatic League
5. Joan of Arc
6. Crusades
7. illumination
8. sacraments
9. Richard the Lion-Hearted

Comprehension and Critical Thinking

10. a. sultan who overthrew the Seljuk Turks; fought Richard the Lion-Hearted in the Third Crusade
b. First—one group finally took Jerusalem, established four states in the Holy Land; Second—Christians failed to take any land from Muslims; Third—conquered Crusader states, drove Christians out of Jerusalem; fought Richard the Lion-Hearted; Muslims maintained control of Holy Land; Fourth—Crusaders invaded and sacked Constantinople, failed to retake Holy Land; four Crusades followed, none successful
c. possible answers—far from home, lacked supplies, no real way of resupplying armies, lacked centralized military command

11. a. a special occasion at a central location where buyers and sellers met; goods came from around the world, people traveled to attend trade fairs
b. medieval cities were polluted, crowded, streets filled with farm animals; lacked public sanitation; buildings made of wood with straw roofs, fire a constant threat; theft and murder common

---

VISUAL STUDY GUIDE

Key Events of the Crusades

1071 ■ Turks attack the Byzantine Empire.

1095 ■ Pope Urban II calls for the Council of Clermont.

1096 ■ The First Crusade is launched.

1144 ■ Muslims retake Edessa.

1147 ■ The Second Crusade begins.

1169 ■ Saladin comes to power in the Muslim world.

1189 ■ The Third Crusade sets out to retake Jerusalem from Saladin.

1201 ■ The Fourth Crusade is launched from Venice.

1291 ■ The Crusades come to an end.

Challenges of the High Middle Ages

- Heresy threatens the Christian church; the Inquisition and new religious orders, such as the friars, are intoduced to society in order to help eliminate heretics in Europe.
- A dispute over the rightful claim to the papacy leads to confusion and disorganization in the Roman Catholic Church.
- The Hundred Years' War is fought between England and France over the heir to the French throne. Joan of Arc emerges as a leader among the French troops.
- The Wars of the Roses are fought to determine which family would rule England. Henry VII of the Tudor family takes the throne.
- The Black Death wipes out one-third of the populations of Europe and China and brings about the end of the manorial system in Europe.

Growth of Towns and Cities

Trade increases between Europe and Asia. Trade fairs become a part of the economic system of medieval towns.

Guilds are established, which allow for greater organization of merchants and craftspeople in the ever-expanding towns.

Cultural achievements are made. Great works of art and literature as well as new types of learning become a part of people's lives.

Review Key Terms and People

Identify the term or person from the chapter that best fits each of the following descriptions.

1. A trade organization
2. Author of *The Divine Comedy*
3. Beliefs that opposed the church's official teachings
4. A group of cities and towns in northern Germany that worked together to promote and protect trade
5. A peasant girl who led French troops during the Hundred Years' War
6. A series of religious wars fought to take Jerusalem and the Holy Land
7. The process of decorating a written manuscript with pictures or designs
8. Solemn Christian rites believed to have been instituted by Jesus Christ
9. English king who fought in the Third Crusade

---

c. People who had the same occupation banded together, set prices and standards for their products, and trained new people in the craft.

12. a. Gothic architecture, illumination of manuscripts, tapestries
b. Aquinas said that science and religion were related; he believed that people should study classic writings to improve their understanding of Christian teachings.
c. possible answers—written in English; included descriptions of people from all walks of life and social classes

13. a. England wanted its king to rule France; France chose a French person, the regent, for the throne.
b. About one third of Europe's population was killed; the number of deaths devastated the economy; and it eventually led to higher wages for farm workers, who moved to cities, and ended the manorial system.
c. possible answers—yes, the Church was right to be concerned when people began to oppose official teachings; no, the Church should have tried to understand why people were not following its teachings.

History's Impact video program
Review the video to answer the closing question:
How did the Black Death impact Europe?

Comprehension and Critical Thinking

SECTION 1 *(pp. 403–407)*

10. a. Identify Who was Saladin? What role did he play in the Third Crusade?

b. Sequence What were happened during the first four Crusades?

c. Make Judgments Why do you think the Crusades were unsuccessful for the Christian armies?

SECTION 2 *(pp. 408–412)*

11. a. Define What is a trade fair? How did it differ from an everyday market in the Middle Ages?

b. Compare How do medieval cities compare with cities of today?

c. Elaborate How did guilds help to bring about a more organized way of doing business?

SECTION 3 *(pp. 413–417)*

12. a. Recall What three new forms of visual art were first introduced in the Middle Ages? What was a common theme of these artworks?

b. Contrast What was distinctive about Thomas Aquinas' way of viewing Christian doctrine?

c. Evaluate Why do you think *The Canterbury Tales* was such an important work to people of the Middle Ages? Explain.

SECTION 4 *(pp. 419–423)*

13. a. Describe Why did the French and English fight the Hundred Years' War?

b. Analyze In what ways did the Black Death affect people in the late Middle Ages?

c. Rate Do you think the church's reaction to heresy was a legitimate one? Why or why not?

Reading Skills

Understanding Causes and Effects *Use what you know about causes and effects to answer the questions below.*

14. Why did European Christians launch the Crusades? What social effects did the Crusades have on Europe and the Holy Land?

15. Why did Europe experience an increase in trade during the High Middle Ages? What were some of the effects of this increased trade?

16. List the causes of the Black Death and its effects on Europeans during the late Middle Ages.

Analyzing Bias in Secondary Sources

Reading Like a Historian *The selection below was written by William fitz Stephen, a man who lived in London during the High Middle Ages. He describes the grandness of the city and the buildings that made London superior to other cities. Read the passage below and then answer the questions that follow.*

 On the east the Tower of London, very great and strong. . . On the west there are two powerful castles, and from there runs a high and massive wall with seven double gates and with towers along the north at regular intervals. "

—William fitz Stephen, quoted in *Medieval Europe: A Short History*, by C. Warren Hollister

17. Identify What words does the author use to express his feelings about how London is constructed?

18. Explain Does the author feel as though London is a strong or a weak city? How can you tell?

19. Evaluate How might someone else describe the city of London during the High Middle Ages?

Using the Internet

go.hrw.com
Practice Online
Keyword: SHL HMA

20. As a young teenager, Joan of Arc was visited by saints urging her to help liberate France from England's control. She was a woman of amazing faith and vision. Using the keyword above, research the life of Joan of Arc, her accomplishments, and significance in history. Use an interactive template to write a biography on Joan of Arc. Be sure to use proper grammar, punctuation, and sentence structure.

WRITING ABOUT HISTORY

Exposition: Writing an Explanation *During the High Middle Ages, people experienced many different social, political, and economic changes. New technologies, new art forms, new ways of thinking, and changes in the church and in government all contributed to the movement of Europe into the modern world.*

21. Assignment: In an essay, explain how the varying social, political, and economic changes of the High Middle Ages contributed to the emergence of the modern era. To provide support for your explanation, use information from the chapter and other research as needed. Use specific reasons and examples to illustrate the points you are making.

Answers

Reading Skills

14. to retake Holy Lands from Muslims; led to conflict between Muslims and Christians

15. towns and cities merchants travelled, grew; currency developed

16. spread by traveling merchants and rats; devastated population, led to great fear of disease, devastated economy of Europe ended manorial system

Analyzing Bias in Secondary Sources

17. "very great and strong," "powerful," "high and massive"

18. strong; word choices

19. Someone else might see the walls, gates, and towers as evidence that the city was fearful of invasion.

Using the Internet

20. Go to the HRW Web site and enter the keyword shown to access a rubric for this activity.

KEYWORD: SHL HMA

Writing About History

21. Student essays should discuss some of the major events and changes that occurred during the high Middle Ages

A rubric for the activity is provided in **CRF:** Writing About History.

Review and Assessment Resources

Review and Reinforce

CRF: Chapter Review

Quick Facts Transparency: Visual Study Guide: The High Middle Ages

Spanish Chapter Summaries Audio CD Program

OSP **Holt PuzzlePro:** Quiz Show for ExamView

Quiz Game CD-ROM

Assess

PASS: Chapter Test, Forms A and B

Alternative Assessment Handbook

OSP **ExamView Test Generator,** Chapter Test

Differentiated Instruction Modified Worksheets and Tests CD-ROM: Chapter Test

HOAP **Holt Online Assessment Program** (in the Premier Online Edition)

Reteach/Intervene

Interactive Reader and Study Guide

Differentiated Instruction Teacher Management System: Lesson Plans for Differentiated Instruction

Differentiated Instruction Modified Worksheets and Tests CD-ROM: Chapter Test

Interactive Skills Tutor CD-ROM

go.hrw.com
Online Resources
KEYWORD: SHL TEACHER

You can use these pages to have students simultaneously review the unit and practice taking standardized tests.

Answers

1. 1
The Early Middle Ages, Section 5

2. 3
The Early Middle Ages, Section 5

3. 4
Kingdoms and Christianity, Section 1

4. 1
Kingdoms and Christianity, Section 3

5. 2
The Early Middle Ages, Section 1

6. 2
The Early Middle Ages, Section 1

7. 3
The High Middle Ages, Section 1

8. 2
The High Middle Ages, Section 4

9. 2
Kingdoms and Christianity, Section 1

10. 4
Kingdoms and Christianity, Section 1

UNIT 4
Regents Practice

Directions Write your answer for each statement or question on a separate answer sheet. Choose the number of the word or expression that best completes the statement or answers the question.

1 This map shows Europe

  1 after Charlemagne.
  2 before Charlemagne.
  3 during Charlemagne's reign.
  4 during Charles Martel's reign.

2 During the Middle Ages, popes were able to exercise power over nobles because of
  1 the fealty oath.
  2 the Benedictine Code.
  3 the threat of excommunication.
  4 the ability to choose bishops.

3 A major accomplishment of Justinian I was
  1 founding the city of Constantinople.
  2 leading the Nika Revolt.
  3 defeating his enemies in battle at the Milvian Bridge.
  4 having Roman law codified.

4 The early monasteries of Europe were
  1 instrumental in spreading Christianity.
  2 clustered in major cities.
  3 ruled directly by the pope.
  4 closed by barbarian raids in the AD 300s.

5 The person who first unified most of the Christian lands in western Europe after the fall of Rome was
  1 Henry II.
  2 Charlemagne.
  3 Charles Martel.
  4 William the Conqueror.

6 Charlemagne changed Frankish society by
  1 destroying Roman texts.
  2 encouraging learning and codifying laws.
  3 encouraging the Crusades.
  4 developing separate laws to suit each conquered tribe.

7 A European king who fought in the Crusades was
  1 Philip Augustus.
  2 Saladin.
  3 Richard the Lion-Hearted.
  4 Frederick Barbarossa.

8 The religious crises during the Middle Ages were the result of
  1 The Hundred Years' War.
  2 an increase in the amount of heresy against the church.
  3 the creation of friars.
  4 the growth of trade and towns.

9 Byzantine art is characterized by
  1 secular themes.
  2 Christian themes.
  3 Muslim themes.
  4 classical Greek themes.

10 Constantinople's location was important because it was
  1 a rich prize for invading peoples.
  2 near the Bosporus.
  3 well fortified and had a good water source.
  4 on the land route from Europe to Asia.

11 Yaroslav the Wise was known for

1 codifying Byzantine law.

2 developing the Cyrillic alphabet.

3 codifying Russian law.

4 defeating Constantinople.

12 Gregory the Great worked to

1 expand the power of the pope.

2 expand the power of the kings over the church.

3 convert the Roman emperor to Christianity.

4 complete an important work of philosophy.

13 Viking raiders from Scandinavia

1 defeated the Magyars.

2 eventually settled in France.

3 defeated the Normans in England.

4 eventually settled the coast of northern Italy.

14 Which of the following best explains the change in European population shown on the graph?

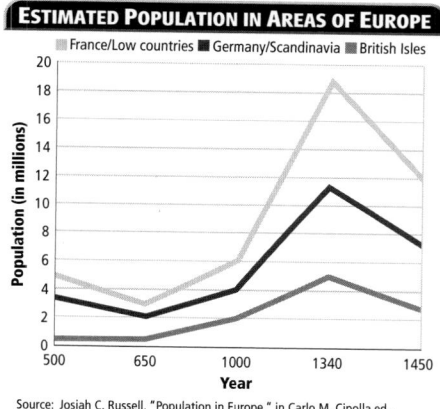

ESTIMATED POPULATION IN AREAS OF EUROPE

France/Low countries ■ Germany/Scandinavia ■ British Isles

Population (in millions)

Year

Source: Josiah C. Russell, "Population in Europe," in Carlo M. Cipolla ed., *The Fontana Economic History of Europe, Vol. 1: The Middle Ages,* (Glasgow: Collins/Fontana, 1972), 25–71

1 the Crusades

2 a smallpox epidemic

3 the plague

4 drought and poor harvests

15 The growth of trade in Europe was

1 controlled by merchants from northern Europe and Italy.

2 set back by the Crusades.

3 controlled by the Hanseatic League.

4 hindered by guilds that prohibited the used of credit.

16 Feudalism was a response to

1 unemployed knights pillaging the countryside.

2 the need for vassals to provide fealty to lords.

3 attempts to improve the manorial system.

4 the inability of kings to defend their lands from attack.

17 What does the following excerpt from the will of Francis of Assisi indicate about him?

"When the Lord gave me the care of some brothers, no one showed me what I ought to do, but the Most High himself revealed to me that I ought to live according to the model of the holy gospel . . . Those who presented themselves to follow this kind of life distributed all they might have to the poor."

1 He would be concerned with the needs of the poor.

2 He would be concerned with the needs of the rich.

3 He would want to build magnificent churches.

4 He wanted to increase the church's wealth.

REVIEWING THE UNIT

Constructed Response After the fall of Rome and during the Middle Ages, the church, feudalism, and manorialism played important roles in Europe. Recall what you learned about each topic. Then write a brief essay in which you summarize how the church, feudalism, and manorialism affected life in Europe.

CONNECTING TO THE PREVIOUS UNIT

Constructed Response Muslim traders and the Mongols were important in moving goods and ideas from Asia into Europe. Recall what you have learned about the diffusion of goods and ideas between Asia and Europe. Write a brief essay on how these contacts affected Europe during the Middle Ages.

MEDIEVAL EUROPE **429**

Answers

11. 3

Kingdoms and Christianity, Section 2

12. 1

Kingdoms and Christianity, Section 3

13. 2

The Early Middle Ages, Section 2

14. 3

The High Middle Ages, Section 4

15. 1

The High Middle Ages, Section 2

16. 4

The Early Middle Ages, Section 3

17. 1

The High Middle Ages, Section 4

Reviewing the Unit

Student essays should mention that the church was a central part of nearly everyone's life during the Middle Ages. In the absence of strong states, it provided stability. Feudalism also provided some stability, with its system of mutual protection and support in which vassals pledged allegiance to lords in return for favors, including land. Under the manorial system, lords left the farming of their land to peasants who worked the land in return for a place to live and a share of their crops, or serfs who were legally tied to the land.

Connecting to the Previous Unit

Student essays should demonstrate an understanding of the diffusion of goods and ideas between Asia and Europe and the impage on Europe during the Middle Ages.

Unit Review

Belief Systems

The Russian Orthodox Church

Byzantine missionaries introduced Christianity to the Kievan Rus in the 9th century. After the baptism of Vladimir, prince of Kiev, in 988, Christianity was accepted as the official religion of the state that would become Russia. During Mongol rule from the 13th through the 15th century, the Russian church flourished. It was not only exempted from taxation, but the monastic system grew remarkably.

Arts and Ideas

Scholasticism Scholasticism was a movement that attempted to combine Aristotle's science and philosophy with Christianity. From the middle of the 11th century to the middle of the 15th century, the movement dominated philosophical and theological thought. It took its name from the fact that it arose in the monastic or cathedral schools that developed into universities. The best-known theologian of the movement was Saint Thomas Aquinas. He wrote his *Summa Theologica* in the 13th century, at the height of scholasticism.

Themes & Global Connections

THEME
BELIEF SYSTEMS

How did the expansion of Christianity affect Europe?

Papal missionaries took Roman Catholic Christianity beyond the bounds of the old Roman Empire into Germany, northern Britain, and Scandinavia. The church promoted the building of monasteries, and the spread of Benedictine monasteries helped unify Christian practice. The Byzantine Empire was the spiritual center of Orthodox Christianity, which dominated Eastern Europe and Russia and expanded the range of civilization in these areas.

THEME
ARTS AND IDEAS

How did the arts and ideas of the Middle Ages reflect people's beliefs?

European art of the period was primarily religious. Religious themes dominated painting, sculpture, and illuminated manuscripts. Gothic architecture, with its tall spires and high arched windows with beautiful stained glass, seemed to reach for the heavens. Religious subjects were common in universities, but toward the end of the period the curriculum expanded to include the works of ancient philosophers such as Aristotle.

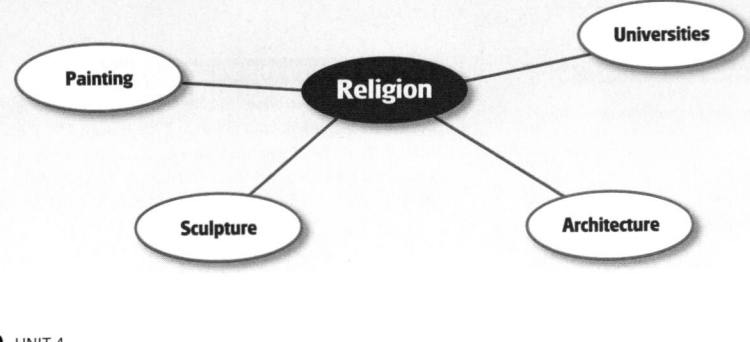

Skills Focus: Comparing and Contrasting

At Level

Reading Skill
East and West

1. Have students create charts comparing and contrasting the arts and culture of the Byzantine Empire with the arts and culture of medieval Western Europe. Student charts should include the following headings: Painting, Sculpture, Architecture, Literature, and Universities.

2. Create a master chart for students to see. Then have volunteers fill it in.

3. Guide the class in a discussion of the art and culture of the Middle Ages. What were the biggest similarities between Byzantine art and Western European art and culture during that period? What were the biggest differences?
LS Visual-Spatial, Verbal-Linguistic

Alternative Assessment Handbook, Rubrics 7: Charts; 9: Comparing and Contrasting; and 11: Discussions

THEME
GOVERNMENT AND CITIZENSHIP

What tensions existed in medieval government?

Tensions existed between European monarchs' efforts to centralize power in their hands and the nobility's efforts to limit the kings' power. When Charlemagne's empire fell apart under the onslaught of Viking, Magyar, and Muslim attackers, feudal lords had the opportunity to seize more power for themselves. In England, William the Conqueror reversed this trend by conquering England and consolidating power in his hands. However, some 150 years later English nobles rebelled and forced the king to sign Magna Carta, which limited the king's power, and again reversed the trend.

King
Conquest
Consolidation of Realms

Power

Nobles
Viking Attacks
Magna Carta

Skills Focus
UNDERSTANDING THEMES

Western Europe had been touched but not fundamentally changed by the Roman Empire, and northern Europe had remained beyond Rome's influence. After the fall of Rome, any unifying political control that had existed was gone. The Roman Catholic Church, however, did provide a sense of unity in Europe. Throughout Christendom, the arts and architecture of the time reflected similar religious themes. Monasteries promoted better agricultural techniques learned through contact with Eastern Europe and from Asian invaders. Create a chart like the one below to show how religion provided a sense of unity.

Unifying Factors	
Art	
Monasteries	
Language	
Architecture	
Church government	

Global Connections

The Byzantine Empire lasted almost a thousand years after the fall of Rome, and Constantinople's location made it a crossroads between Europe and Asia. The empire controlled territory in eastern Europe, the eastern Mediterranean, and the northern Middle East. It also spread civilization northward to new areas and played a role in the preservation of Greek and Roman culture and learning.

Making Connections Create a chart that details the contributions the Byzantine Empire made to the spread of civilization.

THE BYZANTINE EMPIRE

EUROPE

Black Sea

Bosporus Strait

Constantinople

Sea of Marmara

Aegean Sea

ASIA

ASIA MINOR

0 150 300 Miles
0 150 300 Kilometers
Azimuthal equal-area projection

Byzantine Empire, c. 1025

MEDIEVAL EUROPE **431**

Government and Citizenship

The Domesday Book After taking over England, William the Conqueror ordered an inventory of his new domain. The was known as "the description of England." By the mid-12th century, it was more commonly known as the Domesday Book, a reference to "doomsday," or judgment day. It got that nickname because its judgments of levies and assessments were as binding as the final judgment. The Domesday Book consists of two volumes that list all the feudal estates that owed allegiance—and revenues—to the English king.

Understanding Themes

Unifying Factors	
Art	Religious themes dominated.
Monasteries	helped spread Christianity
Language	Latin was a universal language.
Architecture	Gothic churches provided some of the greatest expressions of Christian feeling.
Church government	maintained order in the absence of strong state system

Global Connections

Student charts should include the following contributions: codified and expanded Roman laws, modernized government, traded with China and other lands, established universities and preserved ancient Greek learning, helped spread Christianity, Byzantine art and architecture provided a bridge between ancient Greece and the Renaissance.

Differentiating Instruction

Below Level

Learners Having Difficulty; Struggling Readers

1. Draw the graphic organizer for students to see. Tell students that it shows feudal relationships. Label the top circle *King* and the small circles at the bottom *Serfs*. Explain that below the king were lords (vassals). Lords also had vassals (knights). Peasants and serfs were at the bottom.

2. Ask students which level of circles represents knights and which circles represent lords.
LS Visual-Spatial

Alternative Assessment Handbook, Rubric 13: Graphic Organizers

Summarizing the Unit

During the period covered by this unit, Christianity spread across Europe. In a time of weak kingdoms, new institutions and systems—the church, the feudal system, and the manorial system—arose to provide stability. Have students create a chart showing how each of these institutions or systems helped shape life in the Middle Ages.

Answers

Thinking Like a Historian *Student charts or graphic organizers will vary, depending on which period they selected, but should summarize developments in all three areas—government, intellectual life and the arts, and religious institutions.*

UNIT 4
IN BRIEF
Below is a chapter-by-chapter summary of the main ideas in this unit, followed by a summary activity for the unit.

CHAPTER 12 — Kingdoms and Christianity
300–1250

MAIN IDEA With its capital at Constantinople, the Byzantine Empire kept Christianity alive after the Western Roman Empire's fall. Byzantine traditions affected the development of Russia. Missionaries and monks helped spread Christianity throughout Europe.

SECTION 1 Constantine established the Christian Byzantine Empire in the 330s. After over 1,000 years, the empire ended in 1453.

SECTION 2 Slavs and Vikings created the first Russian state, which eventually became Christian. Mongols took over Russia for a while but did not interfere much with Russian culture.

SECTION 3 After the fall of the Western Roman Empire, new kingdoms arose in Europe. Missionaries spread Christianity throughout Europe and established monasteries.

CHAPTER 13 — The Early Middle Ages
800–1215

MAIN IDEA The early Middle Ages brought sweeping change throughout Europe. Most Europeans adopted Christianity, and Charlemagne forged an empire.

SECTION 1 Charlemagne unified much of western Europe under a great empire that laid a foundation for European politics and culture.

SECTION 2 Invasions and migrations changed the cultural and political landscape of Europe.

SECTION 3 Two distinct systems, feudalism and manorialism, shaped the political, social, and economic order of the Middle Ages.

SECTION 4 Following Charlemagne's death, the breakup of his lands resulted in a number of small kingdoms, which grew in power and faced many changes.

SECTION 5 The power of the Roman Catholic Church grew, making it central to daily life and an influential political institution.

CHAPTER 14 — The High Middle Ages
1000-1500

MAIN IDEA During the high Middle Ages the pace of change began to quicken. The Crusades exposed more people to the wider world as well as to the benefits of trade. Religion continued to play a important role in people's lives.

SECTION 1 Europeans fought in the Crusades from 1096 to 1291 but ultimately failed to take Jerusalem and the Holy Land from Muslim control.

SECTION 2 During the Middle Ages an increase in trade from Europe to other lands led to the growth of towns and cities.

SECTION 3 The late Middle Ages saw a surge in art and thinking that ranged from masterful religious art to great works of literature to the dawn of liberal arts universities.

SECTION 4 Religious crises, war, and disease threatened and challenged the people living in Europe during the high Middle Ages.

Thinking like a Historian
Summary and Extension Activity

From the fall of the Roman Empire until the end of the Middle Ages, Europe saw enormous change. Select one time period and create a chart or graphic organizer that summarizes the developments in:

A. Government
B. Intellectual life and the arts
C. Religious institutions

432 UNIT 4

Unit Resources

Review and Reinforce
- Global History and Geography Regents Test Prep Workbook
- Regents Review Transparencies
- CRF: Chapter Review
- Spanish Chapter Summaries Audio CD Program
- OSP Holt PuzzlePro: Quiz Show for ExamView
- Quiz Game CD-ROM

Assess
- PASS: Unit Test, Forms A and B
- Alternative Assessment Handbook
- OSP New York ExamView Test Generator correlated to NY SS Standards
- Differentiated Instruction Modified Worksheets and Tests CD-ROM: Chapter Test
- HOAP Holt Online Assessment Program (in the Premier Online Edition)

Reteach/Intervene
- Interactive Reader and Study Guide
- Differentiated Instruction Teacher Management System: Lesson Plans for Differentiated Instruction
- Differentiated Instruction Modified Worksheets and Tests CD-ROM: Chapter Test
- Interactive Skills Tutor CD-ROM

go.hrw.com
Online Resources
KEYWORDS: SHL CHR, SHL EMA, SHL HMA

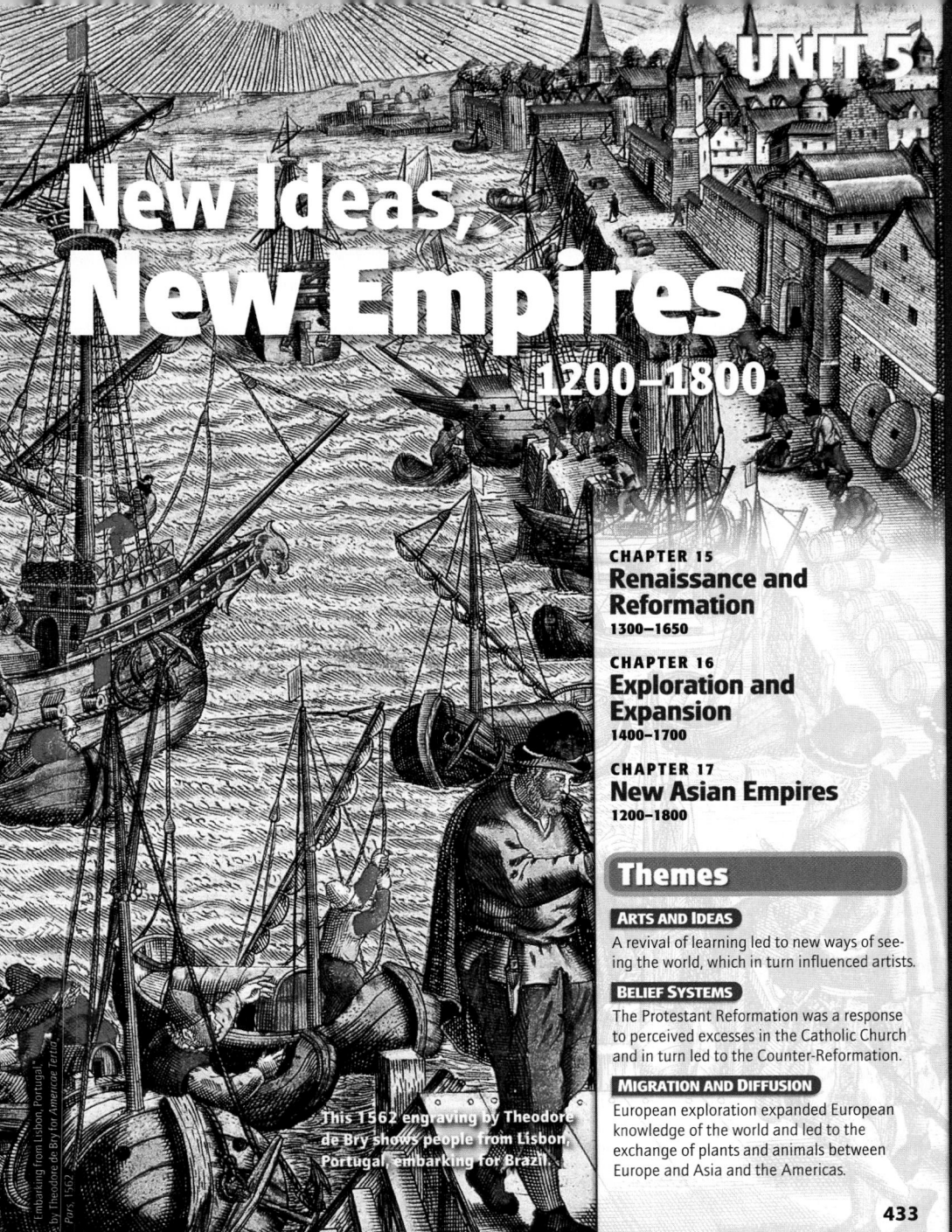

UNIT 5

New Ideas, New Empires
1200–1800

CHAPTER 15
Renaissance and Reformation
1300–1650

CHAPTER 16
Exploration and Expansion
1400–1700

CHAPTER 17
New Asian Empires
1200–1800

Themes

ARTS AND IDEAS

A revival of learning led to new ways of seeing the world, which in turn influenced artists.

BELIEF SYSTEMS

The Protestant Reformation was a response to perceived excesses in the Catholic Church and in turn led to the Counter-Reformation.

MIGRATION AND DIFFUSION

European exploration expanded European knowledge of the world and led to the exchange of plants and animals between Europe and Asia and the Americas.

This 1562 engraving by Theodore de Bry shows people from Lisbon, Portugal, embarking for Brazil.

"Embarking from Lisbon, Portugal" by Theodore de Bry for *Americae Tertia Pars*, 1562.

433

Unit Preview

Introducing the Unit

Ask students to consider what it would be like to discover another planet that was suitable for human habitation. Have students make a list of the ways in which humans could use a new world. Write each item for the class to see. Then guide the class in a discussion of the items. Tell students that Europeans viewed the discovery of the Americas in much the same way—hence the nickname "New World."

Connecting to Themes

Activity Renaissance to Reformation Ask students how the Renaissance paved the way for the Protestant Reformation. Guide students in a discussion of the ways that a new focus on the secular and the individual led some people to question the Catholic Church.
LS Verbal-Linguistic

Reading Like a Historian
Interpreting Visuals
Voyages to Brazil The engraving shown on this page is part of a series illustrating voyages of discovery and exploration around the world. This engraving shows Portuguese caravels leaving Lisbon for Brazil. It comes from Part 3 of De Bry's *Grand Voyages*, which covered voyages to Brazil.

Unit Resources

Planning

📓 **Differentiated Instruction Teacher Management System:** Unit Pacing Guide

OSP **New York One-Stop Planner CD-ROM:** Teacher Management System

🔘 **Power Presentations with Video CD-ROM**

Standards Mastery

📓 **Global History and Geography Regents Test Prep Workbook**

📦 **Regents Review Transparencies**

Differentiating Instruction

📓 **Differentiated Instruction Teacher Management System:** Lesson Plans for Differentiated Instruction

🔘 **Differentiated Instruction Modified Worksheets and Tests CD-ROM**

Enrichment

📓 **A World History Teacher's Guide to Analyzing Movies**

📓 **Document-Based Activities for World History**

📓 **World History Outline Maps**

📓 **Reading Like a Historian: World History Toolkit**

🔘 **World History Primary Source Library CD-ROM**

Assessment

📓 **PASS:** Unit Test, Forms A and B

📓 **Alternative Assessment Handbook**

OSP **New York ExamView Test Generator** correlated to NY SS Standards

HOAP **Holt Online Assessment Program** (in the Premier Online Edition)

Chapter 15 Planning Guide

Renaissance and Reformation

Chapter Overview	Reproducible Resources	Technology Resources
CHAPTER 15 pp. 434–465 **Overview:** In this chapter, students will learn how the rediscovery of classical knowledge led to a period of creativity and learning known as the Renaissance. As emphasis was placed on the individual, new ideas about religion emerged, which led to the Reformation. KI 1, 2, 4; PI 1.3, 2.5, 4.1, 4.2	**Differentiated Instruction Teacher Management System:** • Pacing Guide • Lesson Plans for Universal Access **Interactive Reader and Study Guide:** Chapter Summary* **Chapter Resource File*** • Writing for the SAT • Social Studies Skill • Chapter Review **World History Outline Maps**	**Live Ink© Online Reading Help** **Student Edition on Audio CD Program** **Differentiated Instruction Modified Worksheets and Tests CD-ROM** **World History Primary Source Library CD-ROM** **Power Presentations with Video CD-ROM** **History's Impact: World History Video Program (VHS/DVD):** Renaissance and Reformation
Section 1: **The Italian Renaissance** **The Main Idea:** In Italy the growth of wealthy trading cities and new ways of thinking helped lead to a rebirth of the arts and learning. This era became known as the Renaissance. PI 1.3, 4.2	**Differentiated Instruction Teacher Management System:** Section 1 Lesson Plan* **Interactive Reader and Study Guide:** Section 1 Summary* **Chapter Resource File*** • Vocabulary Builder: Section 1 • Biography: Sofonisba Anguissola • Primary Source: The School of Athens	**Regents Review Transparency:** Section 1* **Map Transparency:** Europe, c. 1300* **Quick Facts Transparency:** Causes of the Renaissance*
Section 2: **The Northern Renaissance** **The Main Idea:** Renaissance ideas soon spread beyond Italy to northern Europe by means of trade, travel, and printed material, influencing the art and ideas of the north. PI 1.3, 4.2	**Differentiated Instruction Teacher Management System:** Section 2 Lesson Plan* **Interactive Reader and Study Guide:** Section 2 Summary* **Chapter Resource File*** • Vocabulary Builder: Section 2 • Biography: Jan van Eyck • History and Geography: Trade Fuels City Growth • Literature: *The Canterbury Tales*	**Regents Review Transparency:** Section 2* **Internet Activity:** The Printing Press
Section 3: **The Protestant Reformation** **The Main Idea:** Criticism of the Roman Catholic Church led to a religious movement called the Protestant Reformation and brought changes in religion and politics across Europe. PI 2.5	**Differentiated Instruction Teacher Management System:** Section 3 Lesson Plan* **Interactive Reader and Study Guide:** Section 3 Summary* **Chapter Resource File*** • Vocabulary Builder: Section 3 • Biography: Jan Hus	**Regents Review Transparency:** Section 3* **Map Transparency:** Spread of Protestantism* **Internet Activity:** Reformation Leaders
Section 4: **The Counter-Reformation** **The Main Idea:** Catholics at all levels recognized the need for reform in the church. Their work turned back the tide of Protestantism in some areas and renewed the zeal of Catholics everywhere. PI 4.1	**Differentiated Instruction Teacher Management System:** Section 4 Lesson Plan* **Interactive Reader and Study Guide:** Section 4 Summary* **Chapter Resource File*** • Vocabulary Builder: Section 4 • Biography: Teresa of Avila	**Regents Review Transparency:** Section 4* **Map Transparency:** Religions in Europe, 1600* **Quick Facts Transparency:** The Reformation*

HOLT
History's Impact
World History Video Program (VHS/DVD)
Renaissance and Reformation

Review, Assessment, Intervention

Global History and Geography Regents Test Prep Workbook

Quick Facts Transparency: Renaissance and Reformation*

Progress Assessment Support System (PASS): Chapter Test*

Differentiated Instruction Modified Worksheets and Tests CD-ROM: Modified Chapter Test

OSP **New York One-Stop Planner CD-ROM:** ExamView Test Generator (English/Spanish)

HOAP **Holt Online Assessment Program (HOAP),** in the Holt Premier Online Student Edition

PASS: Section 1 Quiz*

Online Quiz: Section 1

Alternative Assessment Handbook

PASS: Section 2 Quiz*

Online Quiz: Section 2

Alternative Assessment Handbook

PASS: Section 3 Quiz*

Online Quiz: Section 3

Alternative Assessment Handbook

PASS: Section 4 Quiz*

Online Quiz: Section 4

Alternative Assessment Handbook

Power Presentation with Video CD-ROM

Power Presentations with Video are visual presentations of each chapter's main ideas. Presentations can be customized by including Quick Facts charts, images and maps from the textbook, and video clips.

Holt Online Learning

go.hrw.com
Teacher Resources
KEYWORD: SHL TEACHER

go.hrw.com
Student Resources
KEYWORD: SHL REN

- Document-Based Questions
- Interactive Multimedia Activities

- Current Events
- Chapter-Based Internet Activities
- and more!

Holt Premier
Online Student Edition
Complete online support for interactivity, assessment, and reporting
- Interactive Maps and Notebook
- Homework Practice and Research Activities Online

CHAPTER 15 PLANNING GUIDE

The Big Picture

Peter N. Stearns

The Big Changes Western Europe between 1350 and 1600 began to participate in two or three really big changes, all in a context in which Europe's world role began gradually to expand. First, the European economy began to become more commercial. Second, stronger governments began to emerge, and feudal controls weakened. Third, culture began to shift away from a primary emphasis on traditional religious values. The Renaissance, Reformation, and Counterreformation can be seen in terms of these big changes, though they had their own flavors and complexities. The Renaissance built on and encouraged growing trade and urbanism. The Reformation did ultimately contribute to more focus on economic life as a means of demonstrating God's favor. The Renaissance encouraged new political functions and values, initially in the Italian city-states; the Reformation, by cutting the power of the papacy, gave new leeway to secular rulers. The Renaissance encouraged a more secular culture; and while the Reformation sought exactly the opposite, its weakening of Christian unity encouraged some cultural change as well.

The Renaissance The Renaissance began in the particular context of late-medieval Italy, with unusual ties to the classical past and fewer feudal controls. The Renaissance achievements showed particularly in dramatically new cultural and artistic forms, and the more general sentiments described in humanism. How much the movement affected politics and, particularly, daily life must be debated. The Renaissance spread northward after about 1450. It was encouraged by the printing press and rising literacy. Encouragement to some of the great vernacular writers of all time showed the power of cultural change in Britain and France as well as Spain.

The Reformation and Counterreformation Concern about church corruption, national sentiment, and new readings of the Bible prompted Luther's defiance of the Catholic Church. Reformation leaders did not intend to destroy Christian unity but rather redefine it. Lutheranism, Calvinism, and Anglicanism produced a dramatically new religious map. Catholic revival, and new tools such as the powerful Jesuit order, preserved much territory for Catholicism, but it could not stem division. The result was a period of confusion and considerable conflict, including concern about witchcraft.

Recent Scholarship

Daily Life in Renaissance Italy (2001) by Elizabeth S. Cohen and Thomas V. Cohen shows the dramatic improvements in historians' ability not only to find out about patterns of daily life, but also to show why they deserve serious attention and not just antiquarian interest. Urban conditions produced new aspirations and some strikingly modern-seeming protest, though economic life was not fully transformed. Gender, family life, and sexuality showed a similar combination of change and continuity. The book takes its analysis up to about 1500, as the peak Renaissance impulses began to decline in Italy.

Differentiating Instruction

 Differentiated Instruction Teacher Management System
- Pacing Guide
- Lesson Plans for Differentiated Instruction

Interactive Reader and Study Guide

 Spanish Chapter Summaries Audio CD Program

Student Edition on Audio CD Program

Differentiated Instruction Modified Worksheets and Tests CD-ROM
- Vocabulary Flash Cards
- Modified Vocabulary Builder Activities
- Modified Chapter Review Activity
- Modified Chapter Test

OSP **One-Stop Planner CD-ROM**
- ExamView Test Generator (English/Spanish)
- PuzzlePro
- Quiz Show for ExamView
- Transparencies and Videos

TE **Differentiated Activities in the Teacher's Edition**
- Machiavelli's Theories, p. 441
- Political Cartoons: The Protestants, p. 450
- The Council of Trent, p. 457

Reading Like a Historian
Sam Wineburg

The Prince Few political theorists in history are immortalized with their own adjective. But Nicolo Machiavelli has bequeathed to us "Machiavellian"—unscrupulous, lacking morals, bereft of conscience, an out-and-out rogue. There's even an online Machiavellian personality quiz: "Are you a cutthroat or a pussycat?" Agree or disagree: "Never tell anyone the real reason you did something unless it is useful to do so." Agree and you earn the right to be in the Machiavellian Club.

But there was more than one side to this Italian author and statesman. How do we reconcile the autocratic Machiavelli of *The Prince* with the life-long republican and author of *The Discourses*, an extended panegyric on the virtues of liberty and the advantages of representative government? This is the puzzle of reading Machiavelli.

One way to solve it is to cast *The Prince* as satire, so over the top that we have no choice but to conclude that it means the opposite of what it says—a view held by Garrett Mattingly, longtime professor of European history at Columbia University. Mattingly drew inspiration from Spinoza, who read *The Prince* as a cautionary tale that warns us what happens when rulers forswear morality to ensure the survival of the state. Others, like the German philosopher Fichte, read *The Prince* as an anti-religious tract, a frontal assault on Christianity. Benedetto Croce, the 20th century Italian philosopher, saw in Machiavelli the humanist. For him, *The Prince* embodied the author's view of the nobility of man and contained its own moral code.

But overwhelmingly, the most common reading of Machiavelli and his famous book is the one we already know: the chilling statement of statecraft by a philosophizing sociopath. In this vein, the British philosopher and public intellectual Bertrand Russell coined the most unforgettable epithet. Russell damned *The Prince* as a "handbook for gangsters."

Misreading Machiavelli? How is it that a book that has been widely acknowledged as lucid and transparent, a "model of clear Renaissance prose," one whose own author proclaimed that he had "not ornamented this work, nor filled it with fulsome phrases" is given to so many divergent readings? What other philosopher could we imagine being defended with the words—the title of a piece appearing on the webpage of New York's Italian American society—"Machiavelli was not Machiavellian"?

In a magisterial review that appeared in the New York Review of Books, Sir Isaiah Berlin claimed that Machiavelli challenged a core assumption of the Western tradition—and it is this challenge, never explicitly stated in *The Prince*—that has given rise to so many misreadings of the text. According to Berlin, at the heart of the Western tradition is the "idea of the world and of human society as a single intelligible structure," an organic whole whose pieces with much human toil can ultimately be aligned. "It is this rock, upon which Western beliefs and lives had been founded, that Machiavelli seems, in effect, to have split open."

In Berlin's reading, Machiavelli is not saying, as many would have him, that there is a conflict between the private realm of morality and the public realm of statecraft. Rather—and this is *The Prince's* most radical point—Machiavelli claimed that the two spheres are incommensurate. They can never be reconciled. "If Machiavelli is right, this entire tradition—the central current of Western thought—is fallacious. For if his position is valid then it is impossible to construct even the notion of a perfect society, for there exists at least two sets of virtues—let us call them the Christian and the pagan—which are not merely in practice, but in principle, incompatible."

If Berlin is right, we have misread Machiavelli because we have yet to read him correctly. *The Prince* called the bluff of the Western tradition, and it is easier to misread this book than to wrestle with the implications of its claim.

Chapter Main Ideas

Section 1 In Italy the growth of wealthy trading cities and new ways of thinking helped lead to a rebirth of the arts and learning. This era became known as the Renaissance.

Section 2 Renaissance ideas soon spread beyond Italy to northern Europe by means of trade, travel, and printed material, influencing the art and ideas of the north.

Section 3 Criticism of the Roman Catholic Church led to a religious movement called the Protestant Reformation and brought changes in religion and politics across Europe.

Section 4 Catholics at all levels recognized the need for reform in the church. Their work turned back the tide of Protestantism in some areas and renewed the zeal of Catholics everywhere.

New York Standards

Key Idea 4 The skills of historical analysis include the ability to investigate differing and competing interpretations of the theories of history, hypothesize about why interpretations change over time, explain the importance of historical evidence, and understand the concepts of change and continuity over time.

Key to Differentiating Instruction

Below Level

Basic-level activities designed for all students encountering new material

At Level

Intermediate-level activities designed for average students

Above Level

Challenging activities designed for honors and gifted and talented students

Standard English Mastery

Activities designed to improve standard English usage

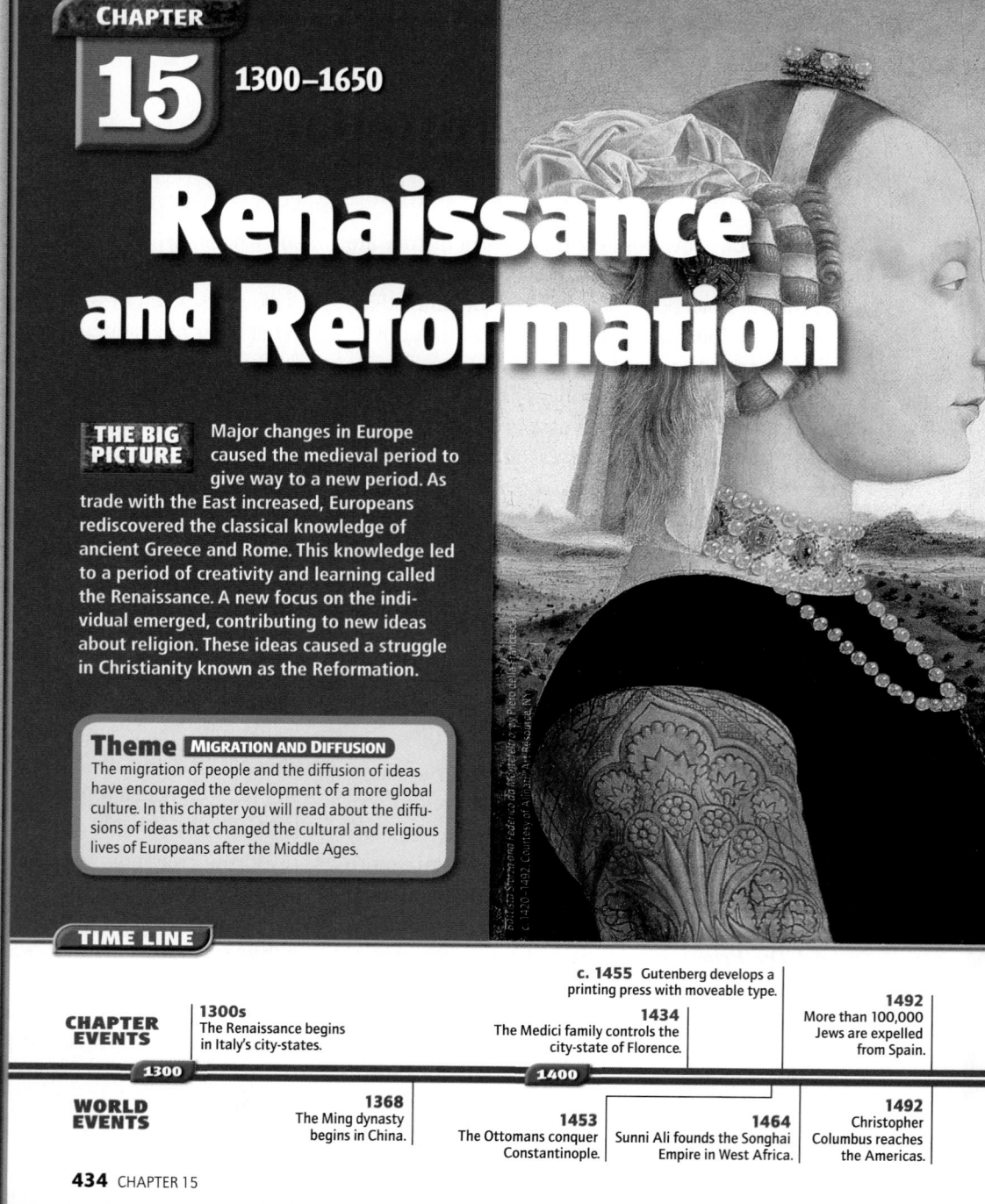

CHAPTER 15 1300–1650

Renaissance and Reformation

THE BIG PICTURE Major changes in Europe caused the medieval period to give way to a new period. As trade with the East increased, Europeans rediscovered the classical knowledge of ancient Greece and Rome. This knowledge led to a period of creativity and learning called the Renaissance. A new focus on the individual emerged, contributing to new ideas about religion. These ideas caused a struggle in Christianity known as the Reformation.

Theme MIGRATION AND DIFFUSION
The migration of people and the diffusion of ideas have encouraged the development of a more global culture. In this chapter you will read about the diffusions of ideas that changed the cultural and religious lives of Europeans after the Middle Ages.

TIME LINE

CHAPTER EVENTS

1300s The Renaissance begins in Italy's city-states.

1434 The Medici family controls the city-state of Florence.

c. 1455 Gutenberg develops a printing press with moveable type.

1492 More than 100,000 Jews are expelled from Spain.

1300

1400

WORLD EVENTS

1368 The Ming dynasty begins in China.

1453 The Ottomans conquer Constantinople.

1464 Sunni Ali founds the Songhai Empire in West Africa.

1492 Christopher Columbus reaches the Americas.

434 CHAPTER 15

Introduce the Chapter

Renaissance and Reformation

At Level

Prep Required

1. Have students skim the chapter and list all the artwork depicted, noting the artists who created the pieces.

2. Guide students in a discussion of the similarities and differences of the pieces in terms of visual effects such as shadow and perspective, realism, and subject matter.

3. Tell students that in this chapter they will learn about a period of stunning advances in the arts and other fields. Around the same time, people began challenging some basic elements of Catholic doctrine.

4. Have students write a paragraph describing the different and similar styles used by artists mentioned in this chapter. **LS** Visual-Spatial, Verbal-Linguistic

Alternative Assessment Handbook, Rubrics 11: Discussions; and 40: Writing to Describe

Reading like a Historian

The Renaissance saw a rebirth in artistic creativity. New themes and techniques, such as perspective, made Renaissance art more realistic and three-dimensional than medieval art. During the 1400s Renaissance artist Piero della Francesca painted the portraits above of the Duke of Urbino and his wife.

Analyzing Visuals What aspects of the portraits show realism and a three-dimensional perspective?

See **Skills Handbook**, p. H26

1508
Michelangelo starts painting the Sistine Chapel.

1500

1537
Spanish conquistadors conquer the Inca Empire in South America.

RENAISSANCE AND REFORMATION **435**

• Chapter Preview •

HOLT

History's Impact
▶ **Video Program: Renaissance and Reformation**
See the Video Teacher's Guide for strategies for using the video segment.

Reading Like a Historian

Analyzing Visuals This Italian couple ruled in Urbino, Italy, during the 1400s. What about these two portraits might indicate that these people were rulers? *possible answers—The woman's clothing is formal and she wears jewels, indicating her wealth and status; the man wears a hat that may signify power.*

go.hrw.com
Online Resources

Chapter Resources:
KEYWORD: SHL REN
Teacher Resources:
KEYWORD: SHL TEACHER

Answers

Reading Like a Historian *realistic details and shadows in faces, clothing, and jewelry; scale of natural features diminishes in background, showing distance*

Explore the Time Line

1. What city-state was controlled by the Medici family? *Florence*

2. What important device was developed around the same time that the Ottomans conquered Constantinople? *printing press with movable type*

3. How many years after Michelangelo began painting the Sistine Chapel was the Inca Empire conquered? *about 29 years*

4. In what century did the Renaissance begin in Italy? *1300s*

Info to Know

Condotierri: The Mercenaries As the Italian city-states grew wealthy from trade, wars became nearly constant. City-states fought to maintain control over their holdings. Italian leaders turned to condotierri, who were mercenary generals. The Duke of Urbino, pictured above, was one of the most successful condotierri. As a young fighter, he lost his right eye and the bridge of his nose. Therefore, all portraits of him are profiles, presenting his left side.

Draw Conclusions What qualities would make an effective condotierre? *good military leader; no firm loyalty*

435

Geography Starting Points

Mediterranean Trade In the late Middle Ages, wealth and urban development were concentrated in cities around the Mediterranean Sea, especially in Italy. With the exception of Paris, the only European cities with more than 10,000 people were Naples, Venice, Milan, and Constantinople. Venice financed trading ventures and organized fleets of ships that traded around the Mediterranean. Meanwhile, Arab caravans arrived in the Near East with silks, spices, and cotton. North African traders brought gold and ivory across the Sahara and within reach of the Mediterranean.

- **Map Transparency:** Europe, c. 1300
- **World History Outline Maps**
- **Interactive Map:** Europe, c. 1300

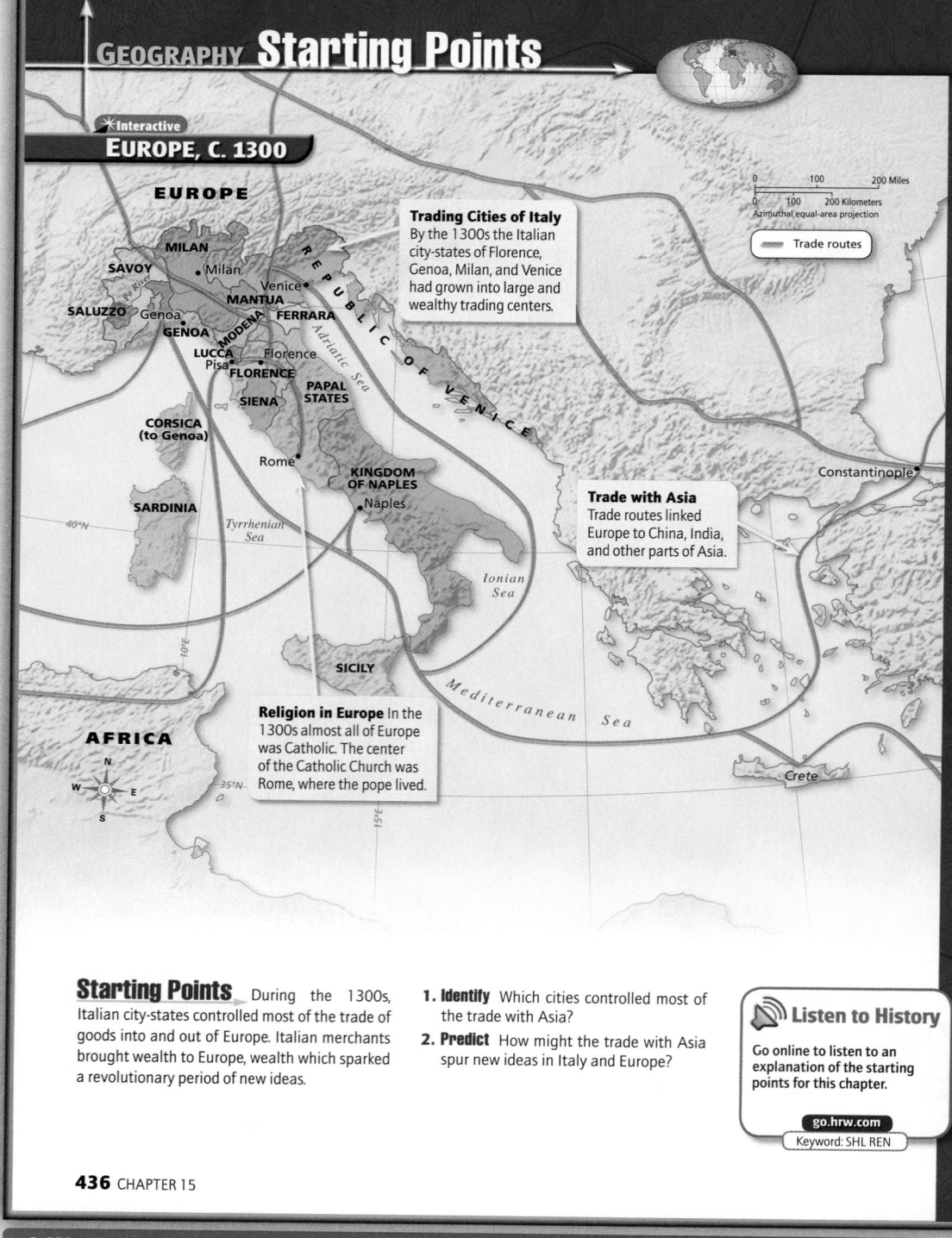

GEOGRAPHY Starting Points

★ Interactive
EUROPE, C. 1300

Trading Cities of Italy By the 1300s the Italian city-states of Florence, Genoa, Milan, and Venice had grown into large and wealthy trading centers.

Trade routes

0   100   200 Miles
0   100   200 Kilometers
Azimuthal equal-area projection

Trade with Asia Trade routes linked Europe to China, India, and other parts of Asia.

Religion in Europe In the 1300s almost all of Europe was Catholic. The center of the Catholic Church was Rome, where the pope lived.

Starting Points During the 1300s, Italian city-states controlled most of the trade of goods into and out of Europe. Italian merchants brought wealth to Europe, wealth which sparked a revolutionary period of new ideas.

1. **Identify** Which cities controlled most of the trade with Asia?
2. **Predict** How might the trade with Asia spur new ideas in Italy and Europe?

Listen to History

Go online to listen to an explanation of the starting points for this chapter.

go.hrw.com
Keyword: SHL REN

436 CHAPTER 15

Skills Focus: Analyzing Maps

At Level

Social Studies Skill
Trader's Log

Research Required

1. Have students conduct research to find what products were produced and traded in the 1300s in the locations listed on the map. For instance, Florence was well known for its woolen cloth.

2. Have students create a trader's log that describes a journey among some of the locations listed on the map. Tell students to list the transactions that occurred at each location. A log might begin "Jan. 26, 1307: Left Florence, via horse-drawn cart, headed north to Venice with a cargo of fine cloth."

3. Have volunteers present their logs to the class. **LS Verbal-Linguistic**

Alternative Assessment Handbook, Rubric 37: Writing Assignments

Answers

Geography Starting Points
1. *Naples, Venice;* 2. *possible answer—Asian traders might bring new ideas about religion, society, and government.*

The Italian Renaissance

BEFORE YOU READ

MAIN IDEA

In Italy the growth of wealthy trading cities and new ways of thinking helped lead to a rebirth of the arts and learning. This era became known as the Renaissance.

READING FOCUS

1. What changes in society and in cities stimulated the beginning of the Renaissance?
2. What ideas formed the foundation of the Italian Renaissance?
3. What contributions did artists make to the Renaissance?

KEY TERMS AND PEOPLE

Renaissance
humanism
secular
Baldassare Castiglione
Niccolò Machiavelli
Lorenzo de Medici
Leonardo da Vinci
Michelangelo Buonarroti
Raphael

NEW YORK

PI **1.3** Students evaluate the effectiveness of different models for the periodization of important historic events, identifying the reasons why a particular sequence for these events was chosen.

A VISION OF GOD

◀ **This painting by Michelangelo shows a Christian-inspired view of God creating the stars and planets. The painting decorates part of the ceiling of the Sistine Chapel in Rome.**

Michelangelo, Creation of the Stars and Planets. Detail of God.

THE INSIDE STORY

How did one man's vision turn a ceiling into a masterpiece? Weak light filtered through the arched windows of the Sistine Chapel in Rome. High above the ground, the artist Michelangelo stood on a platform. He looked up, raised his brush to the ceiling, and carefully applied paint to the wet plaster. For almost four years, this ceiling had been his canvas. Across it, he had painted vivid scenes of events and people from the Bible. The expressive, detailed figures were monumental, so they could be seen from far below.

Each day, Michelangelo and his assistants climbed a 40-foot ladder to a scaffolding. From there, steps rose another 20 feet to a platform 7 feet beneath the chapel's immense, vaulted ceiling. All day Michelangelo stood, his head craned back, his arm raised high to the ceiling.

Yet when the agony of the work was finally done, Michelangelo had created one of the world's great masterpieces. One observer wrote that the Sistine Chapel was so beautiful "as to make everyone astonished." ◼

The Beginning of the Renaissance

Michelangelo's painting was not only beautiful but also very different from the art of the Middle Ages. A new direction in art was only one of the ways in which European society began changing after the 1300s.

Changes in Society The Black Death, starvation, and warfare had overtaken Europe about 1300. These catastrophic events and the enormous loss of life may have led to some of the changes of the 1300s.

RENAISSANCE AND REFORMATION **437**

Preteach

Getting Started

Use the **Interactive Reader and Study Guide** to familiarize students with the section content.

📘 **Interactive Reader and Study Guide,** Section 1

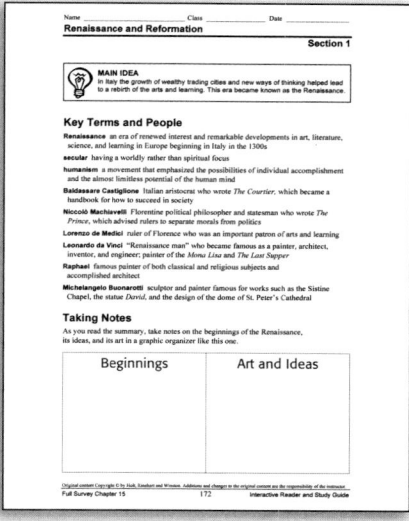

Academic Vocabulary

Review with students the high-use academic term(s) in this section.

deviate to turn away from a course or topic (p. 441)

📝 **CRF:** Vocabulary Builder: Section 1

Taking Notes

Beginnings:—thriving cities, increased trade, wealthy merchant class, renewed interest in art, literature, science, and learning, desire to beautify cities; Ideas and Art:— rebirth in art, literature, and science, secular focus, humanism, individualism, vernacular literature, interest in ancients

---

Teach the Main Idea

At Level

The Italian Renaissance

1. **Teach** Ask students the Reading Focus questions to teach this section.

2. **Apply** Have students scan the section, examine the pictures and charts, and read the captions. Tell students to make a list of these elements, leaving space for notes. Ask students what these elements reveal about the section.

3. **Review** As you review the section, have students take notes about each picture or chart, describing its significance to the broader themes of the Renaissance.

4. **Practice/Homework** Have students create a resumé for one of the artists or writers of the Italian Renaissance.
   🔲 **Visual-Spatial, Verbal-Linguistic**

   📋 **Alternative Assessment Handbook**, Rubric 31: Resumés

1 What changes in society and in cities stimulated the beginning of the Renaissance? *growth of important city-states; increased trade; new wealth*

The Beginning of the Renaissance

Identify Which groups dominated society in the city-states? *the Roman Catholic Church, nobles, merchants, artisans*

Recall How did the merchants of northern Italy use their wealth? *built up their cities, made them magnificent*

Draw Conclusions What advantage might banking have over other industries? *possible answer—easy access to money, money can be used for investment*

Info to Know

Communication Speed Although Venice established connections with ports around the Mediterranean Sea, the rate of travel and communication remained quite slow by today's standards. It took 9 days for news from Venice to reach Naples, 22 days to reach Sicily, and 37 days for it to reach Constantinople. Even by the year 1500, journeys were typically measured by weeks, not days.

Answers

Reading Skills *possible answer— The wealthy classes might sponsor art and science.*

Florence and the Medici Family *possible answers—His appearance suggests that he is wealthy, he sits perched on a chair with Florence behind him.*

Reading Check *Specialization in agriculture increased, resulting in more trade; urban areas became centers of commerce; merchants and artisans became important; some cities became displays of wealth.*

438

TAKING NOTES

In a graphic organizer like this one, take notes on the beginnings of the Renaissance, its ideas, and its art.

Beginnings	Ideas and Art

READING SKILLS

Predicting How might the change in economic structure change other parts of society?

NEW YORK

CC Unit 3-F1 Human geography during the Renaissance

The decrease in population allowed farmers to produce more food than they needed. Food prices declined, allowing people more money to spend on other things. The demand for agricultural goods increased, allowing various areas of Europe to begin to specialize in the products that were best suited to their environment. For example, England began to produce more wool and areas of Germany, more grain. As specialization increased, regions had to trade for the products they did not produce.

The Rise of City-States Urban areas also began to specialize, particularly in Italy. The territory that today makes up Italy was divided into several large city-states in the north and various kingdoms and the Papal States in the south. The northern city-states of Venice, Milan, and Florence became bustling centers of commerce. In these city-states, the Roman Catholic Church, nobles, merchants, and artisans dominated society. Merchants were usually either bankers or traders. Artisans practiced such crafts as goldsmithing. Knowledge of arts such as painting, sculpture, and architecture increased as nobles and merchants sought to display their new wealth.

Venice, a city with access to the sea, built its economy and reputation on trade. Its people had a long history of trading with other ports along the Mediterranean Sea. Shipbuilding prospered, and sailors traveled to the Near East. As a result, Venetian merchants became some of the wealthiest in the world. They used this wealth to build a unique city that has been described as "a work of art."

Milan, to the west of Venice, based its economy on agriculture, silk, and weapons. Florence, to the south, was famous for its banking and cloth. Monarchs appealed to Florentine bankers for money to fund wars or other endeavors. Merchants refined raw wool into fine cloth and sold it abroad. The leading merchants and bankers poured their wealth into creating a city that rivaled any other in Europe. A citizen of Florence expressed his admiration:

HISTORY'S VOICES

❝What wealth of buildings, what distinguished architecture there is in Florence! Indeed, how the great genius of the builders is reflected in these buildings, and what a pleasure there is for those who live in them.❞

—Leonardo Bruni, *Panegyric to the City of Florence*, 1403

READING CHECK **Find the Main Idea** How did society and cities change in the 1300s?

Florence and the Medici Family

Lorenzo the Magnificent, Anonymous

The Medici family helped finance many new buildings in Florence. This portrait depicts the influential Lorenzo de Medici. *How does Lorenzo's portrait show his importance?*

Detail from "Catena Map"

438

Skills Focus: Summarizing

At Level

Research Required

Reading Skill
City-State Newspapers

1. Review with students the information in the text about Italy in the 1300s. Tell students that bitter rivalry existed between the Italian city-states.

2. Organize students into small groups. Assign each group an Italian city-state.

3. Have each group prepare a newspaper from its city-state in the 1300s. Have students write articles on politics, current events, and daily life of the period. Have them include at least one editorial about how society has changed after the Black Death. Remind students to include some references to appreciation of ancient Greece and Rome.

4. Have groups present their newspapers to the class. **LS** **Verbal-Linguistic, Visual-Spatial**

Alternative Assessment Handbook, Rubrics 14: Group Activity; and 23: Newspapers

Renaissance Ideas

As the economy and social structure changed, new ideas began to appear. The ideas led to a sustained period of renewed interest and remarkable developments in art, literature, science, and learning. This era became known as the **Renaissance**. (The word *renaissance* is French for "rebirth.") The Renaissance arose in Italy, in part because of its thriving cities, increased trade, and wealthy merchant class.

Inspiration from the Ancients Along with goods for trade, the ships of Venice carried Greek scholars seeking refuge in Italy from the Ottomans. These scholars brought works by ancient writers that the Italians had thought to be lost.

Suddenly the doors to a new world of ideas opened to Italians who could read. They began looking for more information, reading Arabic translations of original texts and searching the libraries and finding lost texts. As they read, they began to think about art, philosophy, and science in different ways. Along the way they began to think more like the classical thinkers who had believed in the human capacity to create and achieve.

Humanism The interest in ancient Greek and Roman culture drove scholars to think about the characteristics of a good education. Under their influence, the church's scholastic education began to give way to the classics: rhetoric, grammar, poetry, history, and Latin and Greek. These subjects came to be known as humanities, and the movement they inspired is known as **humanism**.

In contrast with Church teachings that individuality and achievement were relatively unimportant, humanists emphasized individual accomplishment. They believed that the potential of the human mind was almost limitless. A humanist from Florence, Giovanni Pico della Mirandola (mee-RAN-oh-lah) wrote about the importance of the human mind:

HISTORY'S VOICES

❝On Man . . . the father conferred the seeds of . . . every way of life . . . If [a man is] rationale, he will grow into a heavenly being. If [a man is] intellectual, he will be an angel and the son of God.❞
—Giovanni Pico della Mirandola,
On the Dignity of Man, 1486

CAUSES OF THE RENAISSANCE

- Increased trade with Asia and other regions as a result of the Crusades
- Growth of large, wealthy city-states in Italy
- Renewed interest in the classical learning of ancient Greece and Rome
- Rise of rich and powerful merchants, who became patrons of the arts
- Increased desire for scientific and technical knowledge
- Desire to beautify cities

The roots of humanism are sometimes traced back to the work of Dante Alighieri, a Florentine poet of the late middle ages. His work contains glimpses of what would become the humanist focus on human nature. Many historians believe the Renaissance itself began with two humanists who lived a generation after Dante. Giovanni Boccaccio (bo-KAH-chee-oh) and Francesco Petrarch (PEHT-rahrk) both wrote literature in the vernacular, or everyday language of the people. In the past, most writing had been done in formal Latin.

Humanists rediscovered ancient texts on anatomy, geography, and astronomy. Advances were made in medicine—notable among them were Leonardo da Vinci's studies of human anatomy. Progress was also made in astronomy. Philosophers and writers produced works that would influence Europeans for centuries.

Secular Writers After a period of war in the early 1500s, life in Italy seemed insecure and precarious. The church no longer served as a source of stability and peace. Looking for comfort and guidance in the midst of this instability, some people turned to a form of humanism developed from Petrarch's ideas. Their focus was also **secular**; that is, they had a worldly rather than a spiritual focus.

These humanists argued that individual achievement and education could be fully expressed only if people used their talents and abilities in the service of their cities. Under their influence, the ideal Renaissance man came to be the "universal man," accomplished in the classics, but also a man of action. Such a man could respond to all situations.

RENAISSANCE AND REFORMATION **439**

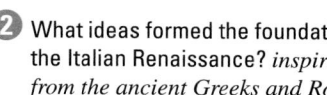

Renaissance Ideas

Identify Cause and Effect How did *The Courtier* influence society? *It was used as a handbook for how to succeed in society.*

Analyze How were Machiavelli's views shaped by his experiences? *possible answer—saw political violence; came to believe that morals should play no part in politics*

Make Judgments Do you think Machiavelli was right when he said that a ruler must do whatever is necessary to maintain power? Why or why not? *possible answers—Yes, if not, the state would cease to exist. No, a ruler must always be fair and just, even if it means losing power.*

Primary Source

"[A gentleman should] speak not always of serious subjects, but also of amusing things such as games and jests and jokes, according to the occasion. He should always of course, speak out fully and frankly and avoid talking nonsense … [A gentlewoman should] know how to choose topics suitable for the kind of person she is addressing … She should not introduce jests and jokes into a discussion about serious things. She should not … [pretend] to know what she does not know, but she should seek modestly to win credit for knowing what she does."

—Baldassare Castiglione, *The Courtier*

One of these humanists, the Italian diplomat **Baldassare Castiglione** (cas-steel-YOH-nay) wrote a book called *The Courtier*. Published in 1528, it describes how the perfect Renaissance gentleman—and gentlewoman—should act. In the book Castiglione creates a fictional conversation between a duke and his guests. They discuss how courtiers and court ladies should behave, suggesting that they should

- Speak of serious subjects as well as amusing ones,
- Have a knowledge of Latin and Greek,
- Be well-acquainted with poetry and history,
- Be able to write prose as well as poetry.

Merchants also used Castiglione's book as a guide to behavior. They hoped that if they acted like courtiers, they would raise their status.

At about the same time that Castiglione was finishing *The Courtier*, a fellow Italian, **Niccolò Machiavelli** (mahk-ee-uh-VEL-ee) of Florence, was writing another influential book. Machiavelli was a political philosopher and statesman whose experiences with violent politics of the time influenced his opinions about how governments should rule. He set down his ideas in a book called *The Prince*.

Much of Machiavelli's advice seemed to encourage harsh treatment of citizens and rival states. He describes men as "ungrateful, fickle, liars, and deceivers" and advises rulers to separate morals from politics. Power and ruthlessness, Machiavelli says, are more useful than idealism to a ruler. He insists that a ruler must do whatever is necessary to maintain political power, even if it is viewed as cruel, for without it the state will cease to exist.

THE ARTS AROUND THE WORLD

Art and Architecture
The Italian Renaissance

What is it? Art and architecture of the Italian Renaissance did not follow a single style or method. Instead, works from the period of about 1350 to 1550 display a change in attitudes. Renaissance attitudes about the value of people affected artists and architects. These talented individuals competed with one another for paid assignments and for fame. Subject matter went beyond religious scenes to real people and their places in the natural world. Moreover, the works produced were for people to enjoy, not solely for the glory of God.

What are the key characteristics?
- Realistic portrayals of people and other subjects
- Use of perspective
- Influence of classical Greece and Rome
- Beauty, balance, and harmony
- Value of the individual

Why is it important?
With the Italian Renaissance, art and architecture entered the modern era. Not only are the paintings, sculptures, and buildings beautiful and inspiring, but they also reflect modern people's interest in competition, achievement, and the world we see around us.

▶ **The Individual** Leonardo da Vinci painted this portrait of an upper-class woman with her pet ermine in about 1490. The emotion shown on the woman's face, her clothing and jewelry, and the way she holds her pet express her unique personality.

Cecilia Gallerani, Leonardo da Vinci, c. 1490

◀ **Realism and Classical Influence** This statue by Michelangelo is of the Israelite king David. The muscular statue realistically portrays the human body. Its natural pose and perfection show the influence of classical Greek and Roman statues.

David, Michelangelo, 1501–1504

Collaborative Learning
At Level

Design Competition
Materials: drawing paper

1. Organize students into groups of four to six students. Each group should designate a sculptor, a painter, at least one architect, and a detail person to work out design elements.

2. Tell students that they will compete with other groups to design a city hall for an Italian town during the Renaissance. Have students sketch concepts for each element of the building. Students may need to create several sketches before they arrive at their final design. The design proposal should include doors, an entry hall, a conference room, and a sample of the exterior façade.

3. Have groups present their design proposals to the class. You may wish to show students' proposals to another class and have them vote on the best design. **LS Visual-Spatial, Interpersonal**

Alternative Assessment Handbook, Rubrics 3: Artwork; and 14: Group Activity

❝A prudent ruler cannot, and must not, honor his word when it places him at a disadvantage and when the reasons for which he made his promise no longer exist.❞

—Niccolò Machiavelli, *The Prince*, 1513

Machiavelli's theory that "the end justifies the means" <u>deviated</u> from accepted views of correct behavior. However, its idea that the state was an entity in itself, separate from its ruler, became the foundation for much later political philosophy.

Science of the Renaissance As humanists searched archives and Arab translations for classical texts, they discovered a wealth of scientific information. Although the majority of humanist scholars and writers during the Renaissance focused on human sciences such as history, geography, and politics, new ideas about the natural world were beginning to be explored. Science would soon become an important avenue of inquiry, challenging the church's teachings about the world.

Among other scientists who challenged the church's ideas about nature, viewers of the night sky began to claim that Earth was not the center of the universe as the church taught. Nicholas Copernicus, a Polish astronomer, suggested that the Sun sat at the center of the universe, orbited by the planets and stars. Galileo Galilei, an Italian astronomer who wrote that Earth orbited the Sun, was placed under house arrest by church officials for expressing his views.

ACADEMIC VOCABULARY

deviate to turn away from a course or topic

READING CHECK **Draw Conclusions** What were some important new ideas of the Renaissance?

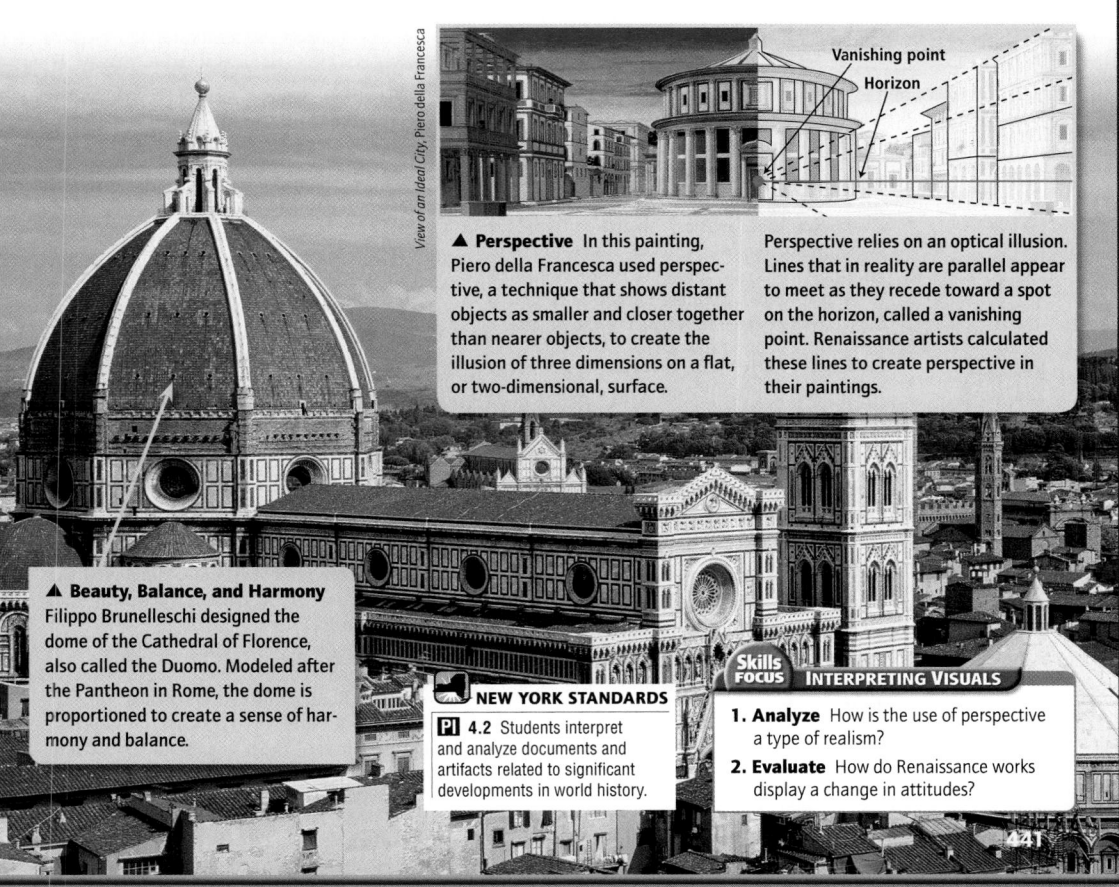

View of an Ideal City, Piero della Francesca

Vanishing point

Horizon

▲ **Perspective** In this painting, Piero della Francesca used perspective, a technique that shows distant objects as smaller and closer together than nearer objects, to create the illusion of three dimensions on a flat, or two-dimensional, surface.

Perspective relies on an optical illusion. Lines that in reality are parallel appear to meet as they recede toward a spot on the horizon, called a vanishing point. Renaissance artists calculated these lines to create perspective in their paintings.

▲ **Beauty, Balance, and Harmony** Filippo Brunelleschi designed the dome of the Cathedral of Florence, also called the Duomo. Modeled after the Pantheon in Rome, the dome is proportioned to create a sense of harmony and balance.

NEW YORK STANDARDS

PI 4.2 Students interpret and analyze documents and artifacts related to significant developments in world history.

Skills FOCUS **INTERPRETING VISUALS**

1. **Analyze** How is the use of perspective a type of realism?
2. **Evaluate** How do Renaissance works display a change in attitudes?

441

Differentiating Instruction

Above Level

Advanced Learners/Gifted and Talented

Prep Required

Materials: excerpts from Machiavelli's *The Prince*

1. Hand out excerpts from *The Prince* to each student. Allow enough time for students to read the excerpts.

2. Guide students in a discussion of the ideas Machiavelli presents in *The Prince*.

3. Ask students whether they agree with Machiavelli that morals should be separated from politics. What would be the results of this type of rule?

4. Have students write a short essay in which they defend Machiavelli's theories, or disagree with them. Essays should include a clear thesis and several supporting statements.

LS Verbal-Linguistic

Alternative Assessment Handbook, Rubrics 11: Discussions; and 37: Writing Assignments

441

3 What contributions did artists make to the Renaissance? *new styles and techniques; focus on human personality; works inspired by Greek and Roman art*

Renaissance Art

Identify How did wealthy patrons support Renaissance art? *purchased artwork; gave money to artists, intellectuals, and musicians*

Contrast How did the subject matter of Renaissance art differ from the subject matter of medieval art? *included scenes from Greek and Roman myths; focused as much on human personality as on religious significance*

Info to Know

Renaissance Rivalry According to several sources, there was a bitter rivalry between Leonardo da Vinci and Michelangelo. When the two artists met in Florence, the young Michelangelo jokingly referred to one of da Vinci's failed projects, a bronze statue of a horse and rider. The comment apparently offended the old master. The two great artists' mutual dislike for one other only increased when they were commissioned to paint battle scenes on opposite walls of the city hall in Florence.

Answers

Faces of History *alike—served as artists to important figures, lived in Florence, careers affected by power struggles in Italy; different—Leonardo da Vinci also known for accomplishments in physics, engineering, anatomy*

442

FACES OF HISTORY   **Two Renaissance Masters**

LEONARDO Da Vinci
1452–1519

MICHELANGELO Buonarroti
1475–1564

Leonardo was born in Vinci and moved to Florence when he was 15. He was apprenticed to an artist, but Leonardo's skill soon surpassed his master's. He left for Milan, where he served the duke. While continuing as a painter, he advised the duke on architecture and weaponry.

Leonardo spent time in Milan, Florence, and Rome as power struggles gripped Italy. Today he is remembered for his masterful painting and for his wide-ranging knowledge of many topics, including anatomy, physics, and engineering.

Analyze How did Leonardo achieve fame?

Michelangelo considered himself a "son of Florence," although he was born in Caprese. His father was an official who relied on the Medici family for support. As a young artist, Michelangelo studied in the Medici garden school.

When Lorenzo de Medici died in 1492, Florence was torn into political factions. Michelangelo's art career became tied up with power struggles there and in Rome. The artist continued to receive important commissions, however, and to create what many consider to be the finest art in the world.

Infer Why was Michelangelo a successful artist?

Compare and Contrast How were the careers of these two artists alike and different?

NEW YORK

CC Unit 3-F4
Art and architecture of the Renaissance

THE IMPACT TODAY

Today the U.S. government helps support artists and art education through grants and special programs. The National Endowment for the Arts oversees many of these programs.

Renaissance Art

Even more than politics, the arts reflected the new humanist spirit. Whereas medieval artists had used idealized and symbolic representations of religious themes, Renaissance artists depicted the things they observed in nature.

Patrons of the Arts In medieval times, artwork was created by anonymous artists who worked for the church. During the Renaissance, artists worked for whoever offered them the highest price. The buyers of art, or patrons, might be wealthy individuals, city governments, or the church. Wealthy individuals competed against one another, displaying their wealth and modernity through the purchase of artworks.

In Florence, the Medici—a wealthy and powerful family who ruled the city—supported the arts. They gave huge sums of money to artists, intellectuals, and musicians. **Lorenzo de Medici**, himself a well-educated poet, supported some of the most talented artists of the day. The Sforza family, rulers of Milan, were also benefactors of artists and others.

Styles and Techniques Renaissance artists wanted to paint the natural world as realistically as possible, which was a change from the style of the Middle Ages. To help with this goal, they studied perspective. Using perspective, artists could represent three-dimensional objects on flat surfaces. Painters also experimented with new ways of using color to portray shapes and textures accurately.

Renaissance art also differed from that of the Middle Ages in its subject matter. Although many artists continued to choose religious subjects, artists began to paint and sculpt scenes from Greek and Roman myths. In addition, religious paintings focused as much on the human personality of the figures as their religious significance. This shift in themes displayed the humanist interest in classical learning and human nature.

During the Renaissance, the design of buildings also reflected humanist reverence of Greek and Roman culture. Churches, palaces, and public buildings incorporated columns and domes inspired by those of classical Greek and Roman architecture.

Skills Focus: Identifying Main Idea and Details   [At Level]

Reading Skill
Artists and their Works

1. Draw the chart for students to see. Omit the italicized answers.

2. Have students copy and complete the chart. Have volunteers fill in the class chart. **LS** Visual-Spatial

Alternative Assessment Handbook, Rubric 7: Charts

Artist	Field(s)	Achievement
Raphael	*painter, architect*	*"The School of Athens"*
Leonardo da Vinci	*painter, architect, engineer, mathematician, musician, etc.*	*"The Last Supper"; "The Mona Lisa"; observations and designs*
Bramante	*architecture*	*designed St. Peter's Basilica*
Michelangelo Buonarroti	*painter, sculptor, architect, poet*	*Sistine Chapel; "Pieta"; "David"*

Leonardo da Vinci The genius **Leonardo da Vinci** was a highly talented painter; but he was also a writer, an inventor, an architect, an engineer, a mathematician, a musician, and a philosopher. Two of his paintings, *The Last Supper* and the *Mona Lisa*, continue to be studied and admired today. *The Last Supper* shows a gathering of the disciples of Jesus the night before his crucifixion. The *Mona Lisa* tries to capture the complexity of the human spirit with its mysterious smile.

Leonardo filled some 20,000 pages with notes recording his ideas for building an armored tank and a flying machine, sketches of human anatomy, and countless other things. He designed and built canals, developed a machine to cut threads in screws, and designed the first machine gun. His interests and enthusiasms were boundless.

Michelangelo The sculptors of the Renaissance studied anatomy to make their statues more lifelike. One of the most accomplished of these was Michelangelo.

In Rome at the age of 24, **Michelangelo Buonarroti** won fame with his *Pietà*, a sculpture of Mary, the mother of Jesus, holding her son after his death. Michelangelo's *Pietà* communicates themes of grief, love, acceptance, and immortality. Michelangelo soon amazed Rome again with his 13-foot marble statue of *David*.

The statue's representation of the human form, suppressed energy, and depth of expression are unsurpassed.

In painting, Michelangelo is most famous for his artwork on the ceiling of the Sistine Chapel in Rome. The ceiling shows sweeping scenes from the Old Testament of the Bible. Many art historians consider it one of the greatest achievements in the history of painting because of the personalized characterizations of Biblical figures.

Raphael Raffaello Sanzio, who became known as **Raphael**, was a renowned painter and an accomplished architect. His most famous work, *The School of Athens*, is a fresco, a painting made on fresh, moist plaster. The fresco shows Plato and Aristotle surrounded by philosophers from the past and present who were admired by the humanists. He is also well known for his many paintings of the Madonna, or mother of Jesus.

Bramante Renaissance architecture reached its height with the work of Donato Bramante. He had already achieved fame with his designs when he was chosen architect of Rome. His design for St. Peter's Basilica influenced the appearance of many smaller churches.

READING CHECK **Find the Main Idea** What was the ideal of Renaissance art?

---

go.hrw.com
Online Quiz
Keyword: SHL REN HP

SECTION 1 ASSESSMENT

Reviewing Ideas, Terms, and People

1. **a. Recall** Which groups came to dominate Italian city-states in the 1300s and 1400s?
   b. Identify Cause and Effect How did the Black Death influence the economic system of Europe?

2. **a. Define** What is **humanism**?
   b. Draw Conclusions How did **Machiavelli's** *The Prince* reflect humanist and Renaissance ways of thinking?
   c. Evaluate How did Castiglione's book reveal a new idea about the role of achievement?

3. **a. Describe** How were Renaissance artists funded?
   b. Explain For what reason(s) is Leonardo da Vinci considered a Renaissance man?
   c. Predict How might the new ideas of the Renaissance affect society?

Critical Thinking

4. **Identify Cause and Effect** Using your notes on the section and the graphic organizer below, show what effect humanism had on arts and ideas during the Renaissance.

Painting	Sculpture	Architecture	Thinkers

FOCUS ON WRITING

5. **Exposition** Choose a person from the chapter and write a short paragraph explaining why he was important in the Renaissance. You should include a list of his achievements.

RENAISSANCE AND REFORMATION **443**

Direct Teach

Reading Focus

Renaissance Art

Identify What important sculpture did Michelangelo create when he was twenty-four? *Pietà, sculpture of Jesus and Mary*

Explain Why is Michelangelo's work on the Sistine Chapel considered so amazing? *showed personalized characterizations of Biblical figures*

Predict What do you think it would be like to meet Michelangelo? *possible answer—he would offer fascinating information about the process he used to create his masterpieces.*

CRF: Biography: Sofonisba Anguissola

CRF: Primary Source: The School of Athens by Raphael

Review & Assess

Close

Have students explain how the Italian Renaissance represented a major shift from the period before it.

Review

Online Quiz, Section 1

Assess

SE Section 1 Assessment

Progress Assessment: Section 1 Quiz

Alternative Assessment Handbook

Reteach/Intervene

Interactive Reader and Study Guide, Section 1

Interactive Skills Tutor CD-ROM

Section 1 Assessment Answers

1. **a.** church, nobles, merchants, artisans
   b. transformed it from farm-based system to commerce-based system

2. **a.** a school emphasizing the potential of the human mind
   b. possible answer—emphasized individual accomplishment, lacked idealism
   c. described new rules for social behavior

3. **a.** wealthy individuals, city governments, the church
   b. He pursued knowledge and achieved success in many subjects.

   c. possible answer—might encourage people to question accepted teachings

4. Painting—captured the human spirit; Sculpture—more lifelike, showed depth of expression; Architecture—reflected humanist love of Greek and Roman culture; Thinkers—human mind is almost limitless, focus on individualism

5. Student paragraphs should provide details about one of the artists, thinkers, or political figures in this section.

Answers

Reading Check *capturing the human personality, realism, human form*

443

Getting Started

Use the **Interactive Reader and Study Guide** to familiarize students with the section content.

📖 **Interactive Reader and Study Guide**, Section 2

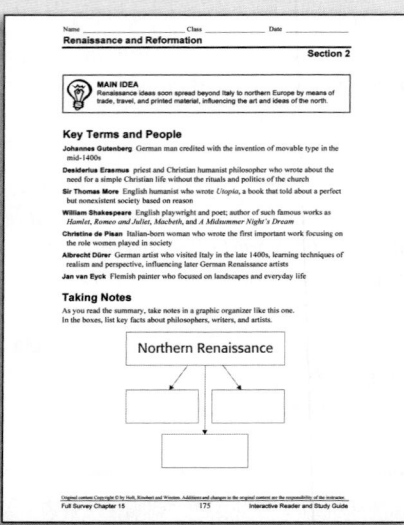

📋 **CRF:** Vocabulary Builder: Section 2

Taking Notes

Northern European cities and trade grow, trade spreads ideas to northern Europe, printing press speeds spread of ideas; Dürer brings Renaissance techniques to Germany, van Eyck and Brueghel use techniques for everyday subjects; Christian humanism, Erasmus writes about simple Christian life, More's history and philosophy; Shakespeare's plays and sonnets

go.hrw.com
Online Resources

KEYWORD: SHL REN
ACTIVITY: The Printing Press

The Northern Renaissance

BEFORE YOU READ

MAIN IDEA

Renaissance ideas soon spread beyond Italy to northern Europe by means of trade, travel, and printed material, influencing the art and ideas of the north.

READING FOCUS

1. How did the Renaissance spread to northern Europe?
2. What contributions did writers and philosophers make to the northern Renaissance?
3. How did the works of northern artists differ from those of the Italian Renaissance?

KEY TERMS AND PEOPLE

Johannes Gutenberg
Desiderius Erasmus
Sir Thomas More
William Shakespeare
Christine de Pisan
Albrecht Dürer
Jan van Eyck

NEW YORK

PI **1.3** Students interpret and analyze documents and artifacts related to significant developments and events in world history.

▲ **Albrecht Dürer, son of a Nuremberg goldsmith, is well known for his woodcuts.**

Self Portrait at the Age of Twenty-Eight, by Albrecht Dürer, 1500

THE INSIDE STORY

How did a German artist find hope in Italy? In 1506, the German artist Albrecht Dürer was soon to end a visit to Italy. He wrote to a friend, "I want to ride to Bologna to learn the secrets of the art of perspective, which a man is willing to teach me. I will stay there about eight or ten days and then return to Venice . . . Here I am a gentleman; at home only a parasite." Dürer's letter provides evidence of the spread of Renaissance techniques and ideas to other parts of Europe. It also comments on the low position of artists in most parts of Europe during the 1400s and 1500s. That would soon change, as the Renaissance passion for art and culture raised the status of artists everywhere. Dürer's 1500 self-portrait shows his view of the importance of artists by portraying himself as the subject of a painting. ◢

The Renaissance Spreads North

In the 1200s and 1300s, most cities in Europe were in Italy. By the 1500s, however, large cities had also sprouted in northern Europe. Soon the ideas of the Renaissance reached the growing cities of London, Paris, Amsterdam, and others. Trade, the movement of artists and scholars, and the development of printing helped spread Renaissance ideas northward.

Trading Goods and Ideas As cities grew, a vast trading network spread across northern Europe. This network was dominated by the Hanseatic League, a merchant organization that controlled trade throughout northern Europe. The league operated from the 1200s to the 1400s, working to protect its members from

---

Teach the Main Idea
At Level

The Northern Renaissance

1. **Teach** Ask students the Reading Focus questions to teach this section.

2. **Apply** Have students create flashcards to learn the names of the important writers and artists in this section. Have students write the name on one side of the card and a description of the person's achievements or famous work on the other side.

3. **Review** As you review the section, have students use their flashcards to quiz each other on the different writers and artists.

4. **Practice/Homework** Have students write a short compare-contrast paper on the Italian Renaissance and the Northern Renaissance.
   LS Visual-Spatial, Verbal-Linguistic

   📋 **Alternative Assessment Handbook**, Rubric 9: Comparing and Contrasting pirates and other hazards. It also made shipping safer by building lighthouses and training ship captains. Along with goods, northern Europeans exchanged ideas with people from other places. Thus, trade helped the ideas of the Italian Renaissance spread to the north.

Renaissance ideas were also spread by Italian artists who fled to northern Europe to escape violent clashes between the armies of northern monarchs and the wealthy Italian cities. The artists brought their humanist ideas and new painting techniques with them.

In addition, some northern scholars traveled to Italy for an education. When these scholars returned home, they brought the humanist ideas they had learned with them. As newly wealthy northern Europeans became able to afford higher education, universities were established in France, the Netherlands, and Germany.

A Book Revolution In the mid-1400s, the German **Johannes Gutenberg** cast the letters of the alphabet onto metal plates and locked those plates into a wooden press. This movable type, which had its roots in China and Korea, resulted in one of the most dramatic upheavals the world has ever known. Other people had made steps toward this invention, but Gutenberg is traditionally given the credit.

With movable type, text could be quickly printed on both sides of a sheet of paper. Until this time, the only way to reproduce writing was by hand, which was a long, painstaking process. Movable type made producing books and other printed material faster and cheaper, making them available to more people.

Gutenberg's first publication was a 1,282-page Bible. Soon printers in other cities, such as Rome and Venice, appeared. Within 35 years, a Gutenberg press appeared as far away as Constantinople. Books could now be made quickly and inexpensively. A scholar wrote that "thirty buyers rise up for each volume . . . tearing one another's eyes out to get hold of them." Printed books provided more rapid access to new ideas. With easier access to books, more people learned to read and more books were printed. The explosion of printed material quickly spread Renaissance ideas.

READING CHECK **Find the Main Idea** How did Renaissance ideas spread to northern Europe?

Philosophers and Writers

As Renaissance ideas spread beyond Italy, northern humanists expressed their own ideas in works that combined the interests of theology, fiction, and history. They created philosophical works, novels, dramas, and poems.

Erasmus Some northern philosophers combined Christian ideas with humanism to create Christian humanism. The leading Christian humanist was **Desiderius Erasmus**. Working as a priest in what is now the Netherlands, Erasmus wrote extensively about the need for a pure and simple Christian life, stripped of the rituals and politics of the church on earth. He also advised readers on educating children.

Erasmus's writings fanned the flames of a growing discontent with the Roman Catholic Church. He himself was dismayed by this effect, but his works were later censored in Paris and condemned by the Church.

FOCUS ON NEW YORK
Gutenberg Bibles are among the rarest books in the world. There are four in New York City libraries—one at the New York Public Library and three at the Morgan Library and Museum.

Advances in Printing

The illustration above shows Johannes Gutenberg in his printing shop, inspecting a page that has just been printed. The book to the right is one of the Bibles printed by Gutenberg in the 1400s. *Why was Gutenberg's printing press such an important invention?*

RENAISSANCE AND REFORMATION **445**

445

---

❷ What contributions did writers and philosophers make to the northern Renaissance? *created Christian humanism; fanned flames of discontent with Church; introduced humanism to England, spread Renaissance ideas to a mass audience*

Philosophers and Writers

Recall Explain the effects of Erasmus' writings. *fanned flames of discontent with Catholic Church*

Summarize What is *Utopia* about? *criticizes English government; describes perfect society based on reason*

Analyze In what ways is Shakespeare's work a good example of Renaissance ideals? *drew inspiration from ancient works; explored topics of humans and nature; included realistic characters*

📝 **CRF:** Literature: *The Canterbury Tales*

Info to Know

The Praise of Folly Erasmus was an educated man and was also a great satirist. He took a light-hearted approach in writing a book called *The Praise of Folly*. In the book, Folly is personified as a woman, who explains why people of various rank and status choose her over common sense. Erasmus used this clever device to critique the church as well as society at large.

Answers

Reading Check *expressed humanist ideas, scientific knowledge, realistic experiences, and social conditions*

Northern Renaissance Art

Return of the Hunters, by Pieter Brueghel the Elder, 1565

The Promenade, by Albrecht Dürer, 1495

NEW YORK
CC Unit 3-F5
Literature of the Renaissance

TAKING NOTES

Using a graphic organizer like this one list key facts about philosophers, writers, and artists.

Northern Renaissance

Sir Thomas More Humanism was introduced to England by Italians living there and by English people who had studied in Italy. Erasmus also lived in England for a time. During his stay, he became friends with an important fellow humanist and English statesman, **Sir Thomas More**.

More's best-known humanist work is the novel *Utopia*. The book was meant for a humanist audience, and it was widely read across Europe. More's book contains both a criticism of English government and society and a vision of a perfect, but nonexistent, society based on reason. The title of his work has become a common word for any ideal society.

William Shakespeare In an age of great writers, many scholars believe the greatest was English playwright **William Shakespeare**. As one contemporary writer noted, Shakespeare "was not of an age, but for all time."

Shakespeare drew inspiration from ancient and contemporary works of literature. A wide knowledge of natural science and humanist topics, as well as a deep understanding of human nature, were expressed in his plays. His use of language and choice of themes, however, made his plays appeal even to uneducated people.

Through his plays, Shakespeare helped spread the ideas of the Renaissance to a mass audience. His dramatic plays were a shift from the religious morality plays that had become popular during the Middle Ages. Unlike morality plays, which focused on teaching ideal behavior, Shakespeare focused on the lives of realistic characters. The first public theaters were not built in London until the end of the 1500s, but by Shakespeare's death in 1616, London was the scene of a thriving theater district, with some theaters able to hold up to 2,000 spectators. Shakespeare's plays were a popular pastime for people from every class.

Christine de Pisan Italian-born writer **Christine de Pisan** wrote important works focusing on the role women played in society. Pisan grew up in the French court of Charles V. After she was widowed, she turned to writing as a way of supporting herself and her three children. Her writings included poetry, a biography of Charles V, and works that guided women on proper morality.

Pisan was recognized as a great writer during her lifetime. In her book *The City of Women*, she discusses different views of women and their roles in society. She was one of the few to champion equality and education for women.

READING CHECK **Summarize** What were some characteristics of Renaissance writers' work?

Skills Focus: Making Generalizations
At Level

Research Required

Reading Skill
Becoming a Docent

1. Tell students that docents are people who give tours of art and historical museums, so they need to be experts in art and history.

2. Have students choose a work of art from the Renaissance to research. Research should focus on the artist's approach to the subject matter, techniques and visual effects, and when the piece was created. Encourage students to locate unusual or anecdotal information about the artist or the work that a crowd of museum visitors would find interesting.

3. Have students present the artwork as a docent would in an art museum. Encourage students to use a pointer to refer to specific elements in the piece. **LS** **Verbal-Linguistic, Kinesthetic**

📝 **Alternative Assessment Handbook**, Rubric 24: Oral Presentations

The Merchant Georg Gisze, by Hans Holbein the Younger, 1532

Northern Renaissance art contains more realistic scenes than Italian Renaissance art does. The hunting scene on the left portrays daily life, while the woodcut and portrait display intricate details and textures of clothing and objects. ***How did northern artists adapt Italian techniques to their own subject matter?***

Artists

Like their literary counterparts, the artists of northern Europe were influenced by the Italian Renaissance. They adopted Italian techniques, but their works reflected a more realistic view of humanity. Whereas Italian artists tried to capture the beauty of Greek and Roman gods in their paintings, northern artists often tried to depict people as they really were.

German artist **Albrecht Dürer** (DOOR-uhr) visited Italy in the late 1400s. On his return

to Germany, he used the Italian techniques of realism and perspective in his own works.

Dürer's paintings also exhibit features that were unique to the northern Renaissance. For example, Dürer painted in oils, a medium that characterized the art of northern Europe. Oil paints also suited the northern artists' love of detail. They reproduced the texture of fabric, wood, and other material; the reflection of objects in a room in a mirror; scenes outside a window; and other tiny details.

Northern artists in the area of the Netherlands known as Flanders developed their own distinct style. Known as the Flemish School, they used a technique of oil painting that had been perfected in the 1400s by the Flemish painter **Jan van Eyck**. Van Eyck's work often focused on landscapes and domestic life. Northern artists fused the everyday with the religious through the use of symbolism in their paintings. A single lit candle or the light streaming through a window are representations of God's presence. German painter Hans Holbein used objects as symbols to characterize the subjects of his portraits.

In the 1500s Flemish artist Pieter Brueghel (BROY-guhl) the Elder used Italian techniques. In subject matter, however, Brueghel's art followed that of earlier northern artists. His paintings showed scenes from everyday peasant life, very different from the mythological scenes of Italian paintings.

READING CHECK **Contrast** How did northern Renaissance artwork differ from that of Italian artists?

SECTION 2 ASSESSMENT

go.hrw.com
Online Quiz
Keyword: SHL REN HP

Reviewing Ideas, Terms, and People

1. **a. Identify** Name four ways in which Renaissance ideas spread to northern Europe.
   b. Make Judgments Was the printing press or trade networks more important in spreading Renaissance ideas? Explain your answer.

2. **a. Define** What is Christian humanism?
   b. Interpret Explain the meaning of the description of William Shakespeare as "not of an age, but for all time."

3. **a. Identify** Who was **Albrecht Dürer**, and how did he influence German painting?
   b. Explain What was new in the subject matter of Northern Renaissance painting?

Critical Thinking

4. **Sequence** Using your notes and the graphic organizer below, describe some of the differences between Italian and northern Renaissance painting.

Italian Renaissance	Northern Renaissance

FOCUS ON SPEAKING

5. **Persuasion** Write a short speech that an Italian might make to a northern European to convince him or her that the Renaissance would bring beneficial changes to the culture. Give at least three reasons.

RENAISSANCE AND REFORMATION **447**

Reading Focus

3 How did the works of northern artists differ from those of the Italian Renaissance? *Northern artists tried to depict things as they actually were*

Artists

Identify What Renaissance techniques did Dürer learn in Italy? *realism, perspective*

Evaluate What do you think Italian Renaissance artists would think about the Northern Renaissance artists' works? *possible answer—They probably would be impressed by the northern artists' techniques, but would find the subject matter strange.*

CRF: Biography: Jan van Eyck

Review & Assess

Close

Have students explain how Christian humanism was connected to the ideas of the Renaissance.

Review

Online Quiz, Section 2

Assess

SE Section 2 Assessment

Progress Assessment: Section 2 Quiz

Alternative Assessment Handbook

Reteach/Intervene

Interactive Reader and Study Guide, Section 2

Interactive Skills Tutor CD-ROM

Answers

Northern Renaissance Art *showed a more realistic view of humanity*

Reading Check *depicted everyday objects, people as they actually were*

447

Section 2 Assessment Answers

1. **a.** Trade spread new ideas; Italian artists went north; northern scholars went to Italy; printing press quickened the spread of ideas.
   b. possible answers—Printing press made books accessible; trade spread ideas faster.

2. **a.** school of thought seeking to simplify Christian life, separating it from rituals and politics of the church on earth
   b. possible answer—Works can always be appreciated; themes are timeless.

3. **a.** German painter; incorporated techniques of Italian Renaissance

   b. focused on people as they actually were

4. **a.** Italian Renaissance: try to capture beauty of Greek and Roman gods, used realism and perspective, mythological scenes

   b. Northern Renaissance: more realistic, showed people as they were, love of details, used oils, showed scnes of everyday life

5. possible answers—will encourage new ways of thinking about the world; will inspire great writers; will inspire artists to try new techniques

Petrarch and Shakespeare

Meet the Writers

Petrarch (1304–1374) Francesco Petrarca, better known as Petrarch, grew up in the Italian province of Tuscany, and later in Avignon, France. He studied law and entered the service of the church around 1330. Petrarch spent much of his life traveling through Italy, France, Germany, and the Low Countries as a diplomat; his duties involved writing formal speeches. He wrote in Latin and Italian and produced poems, historical pieces, and artful personal letters.

William Shakespeare (1564–1616) Known for his many sonnets and plays, Shakespeare displays an impressive knowledge of human motivation and behavior through his characters. Born in the English town of Stratford-upon-Avon, he was married at the age of eighteen to Anne Hathaway. Shakespeare arrived in London around 1588 and acted in a theater troupe. He began writing plays to be staged by the troupe; he also produced sonnets. The company became successful, opened the Globe Theater in 1599, and frequently performed at the courts of Queen Elizabeth I and King James I.

Activity **Poetic Letters** Have students write a letter to one of their friends. Tell students to use poetic language in the style of Petrarch or Shakespeare.

LS Verbal-Linguistic

Alternative Assessment Handbook, Rubric 25: Personal Letters

World Literature

NEW YORK STANDARDS

PI 4.2 Students interpret and analyze documents and artifacts related to significant developments and events in world history.

About the Reading A form of poem called a sonnet became popular during the Renaissance, when poets began writing about more worldly matters, such as love or politics. A sonnet is a 14-line lyric poem that follows a strict pattern of rhyme and rhythm. Italian poet Francesco Petrarch perfected the Italian sonnet, which consists of two sections. English poets created their own version of the sonnet, perfected by English poet and playwright William Shakespeare. The English sonnet consists of three sections followed by two lines, called a couplet. A major theme in Renaissance sonnets is how the best things in life, such as youth and beauty, are fleeting and should be enjoyed before they fade away.

AS YOU READ Think about how each poet expresses his personal feelings about love.

Sonnet 61 (1329)
Petrarch

1304–1374

Blest be the day, and blest the month and year,
Season and hour and very moment blest,
The lovely land and place where first possessed
By two pure eyes I found me prisoner;
And blest the first sweet pain, the first most dear,
Which burned by heart when Love [Cupid, the god
    of love] came in as guest;
And blest the bow, the shafts which shook my breast,
And even the wounds which Love delivered there.
Blest be the words and voices which filled grove
And glen [valley] with echoes of my lady's name;
The sighs, the tears, the fierce despair of love;
And blest the sonnet-sources of my fame;
And blest that thought of thoughts which is her own,
Of her, her only, of herself alone.

—translated by Joseph Auslander

Sonnet 116 (1609)
Shakespeare

1564–1616

Let me not to the marriage of true minds
Admit impediments [barriers]. Love is not love
Which alters when it alteration finds,
Or bends with the remover to remove:

O no! It is an ever-fixed mark [navigational beacon]
That looks on tempests [storms] and is never shaken;
It is the star [North Star] to every wandering bark [ship],
Whose worth's unknown, although his height be taken.

Love's not Time's fool, though rosy lips and cheeks
Within his bending sickle's compass come:
Love alters not with his brief hours and weeks,
But bears it out even to the edge of doom.

    If this be error and upon me proved,
    I never writ, nor no man ever loved.

Skills FOCUS **READING LIKE A HISTORIAN**

go.hrw.com
World Literature
Keyword: SHL WRLIT

1. **Find the Main Idea** How would you summarize the main idea of Petrarch's sonnet?

2. **Analyze** In what ways does Shakespeare's sonnet explore the theme of the nature of love?

3. **Interpret Literature as a Source** Both sonnets focus on worldly romantic love. How might the focus of these sonnets have been different if they had been written during the Middle Ages? Explain your answer.

See **Skills Handbook**, p. H28

Skills Focus: Analyzing Primary Sources
At Level

Reading Like a Historian Skill
Analyzing Sonnets
Standard English Mastery

Background: Tell students that sonnets follow strict guidelines. The two main forms of sonnets are represented here: the Italian or Petrarchan sonnet, and the English or Shakespearian sonnet.

1. Have students analyze the rhyme scheme of each sonnet.

2. Tell students that Shakespeare wrote in iambic pentameter, a line of verse with five metrical "feet," in which unstressed and stressed syllables alternate. You may want to demonstrate the meter to students by tapping on your desk.

3. Have students copy some lines of Shakespeare's sonnet onto their own papers. Then, have them divide the feet with vertical lines, placing an accent mark above accented syllables. Then have students use iambic pentameter to write their own sonnets. **LS Verbal-Linguistic**

Alternative Assessment Handbook, Rubric 26: Poems and Songs

Answers

Reading Like a Historian

1. *possible answer—Love is a blessed thing.* **2.** *explains that love does not change with the passage of time* **3.** *possible answer—might have focused on love for God instead of love for another human*

The Protestant Reformation

BEFORE YOU READ

MAIN IDEA

Criticism of the Roman Catholic Church led to a religious movement called the Protestant Reformation and brought changes in religion and politics across Europe.

READING FOCUS

1. What was the state of Catholicism in the 1400s?
2. How did Martin Luther challenge the Catholic Church?
3. How did Protestantism spread to other areas?
4. What were the effects of the Reformation in England?

KEY TERMS AND PEOPLE

Protestant Reformation
indulgences
Martin Luther
theocracy
John Calvin
predestination
Henry VIII
annulled
Elizabeth I

 NEW YORK

P1 2.5 Students investigate key events and developments and major turning points in world history to identify the factors that brought about change and the long-term effects of these changes.

THE INSIDE STORY

Why did a humble monk defy the Holy Roman Emperor? In the fall of 1517 a monk nailed a list of items to the door of Castle Church in Wittenberg. He listed certain financial and religious practices he wanted to debate with Catholic leaders and bring to an end. His list of complaints, posted where many people could see them, shocked the people who read it. In the early 1500s no one criticized the church publicly, certainly not a monk.

As people read the list, word spread around Germany. The complaints, called the Ninety-Five Theses, were soon printed and distributed around Europe. The pope, upset by the monk's defiance, banned the work, telling Roman Catholics not to read it.

Eventually the Holy Roman Emperor and German parliament got involved, demanding that the monk take back his words. The monk refused, saying that he must obey his conscience and stand by his work. The actions of that monk, named Martin Luther, are considered the beginning of the movement called the Protestant Reformation.

Catholicism in the 1400s

Over the centuries since its beginning, the Roman Catholic Church had gained power and wealth in Europe. As the influence, extravagance, and worldliness of the church grew, some people thought it had strayed too far from its spiritual roots. By the early 1500s, the concerns crystallized into a reform movement that eventually came to be called the **Protestant Reformation**.

A MONK Defies THE EMPEROR

▼ In 1517 a Catholic monk named Martin Luther posted Ninety-five Theses criticizing the Roman Catholic Church.

Martin Luther, by Hugo Vogel, 1890

449

Preteach

Getting Started

Use the **Interactive Reader and Study Guide** to familiarize students with the section content.

📖 **Interactive Reader and Study Guide,** Section 3

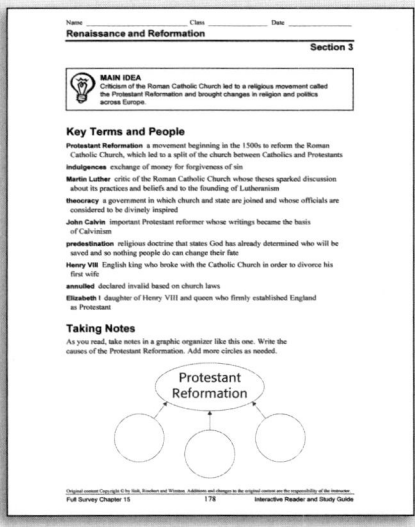

📄 **CRF:** Vocabulary Builder: Section 3

Taking Notes

Causes—financial corruption, abuses of power, immorality, unfair taxes, rise of nationalism

go.hrw.com
Online Resources

KEYWORD: SHL REN
ACTIVITY: Reformation Leaders

Teach the Main Idea

At Level

The Protestant Reformation

1. **Teach** Ask students the Reading Focus questions to teach this section.

2. **Apply** Draw four ladders for students to see. Label the tops of the ladders with the names of the topics in this section: Catholicism in the 1400s, Martin Luther, The Spread of Protestantism, and Protestantism Spreads to England. Have students copy the ladders onto their own paper and fill in the rungs of the ladders with the main ideas of each topic.

3. **Review** As you review the section, have students explain how the actions of Protestant reformers challenged traditional Catholic doctrine.

4. **Practice/Homework** Have students write a letter to the editor about church problems during the 1400s. **LS Visual-Spatial, Verbal-Linguistic**

📋 **Alternative Assessment Handbook**, Rubrics 13: Graphic Organizers; and 17: Letters to Editors

Direct Teach

1 What was the state of Catholicism in the 1400s? *Church was wealthy and powerful, involved in politics, had moved away from spiritual roots, often financially corrupt, immorality of some clergy*

Catholicism in the 1400s

Recall What were common criticisms of the Church? *financially corrupt, abusive of power, immoral, taxed unfairly*

Develop If you had been a Church official during this period, what would you have done to fend off criticism and controversy? *possible answers—would try to reform Church from inside; would try to suppress criticism by focusing on positive aspects of the Church*

📝 **CRF:** Biography: Jan Hus

Info to Know

Example of Corruption Most Germans who bought indulgences believed that the money would go to the construction of St. Peter's Basilica. The public didn't realize, however, that some of the money was going to Albert of Brandenburg. Albert had purchased the position of archbishop of Mainz, but was too young to occupy it according to church law. Pope Leo decided that Albert could take the office provided that he pay the church a large sum of money, which he did by borrowing. Half the money raised by indulgences went to Albert to pay off his debt.

TAKING NOTES

Use a graphic organizer like this one. Take notes about the causes of the Protestant Reformation.

READING SKILLS

Predicting How might reformers change the Catholic Church?

NEW YORK

CC Unit 3-G2
Martin Luther's
Ninety-Five Theses

Dissatisfaction with the Church As the wealth and worldliness of the Church grew, so did instances of financial corruption, abuse of power, and immorality. In return, people's respect for priests, monks, and even popes weakened. Heavy taxation also caused discontent. The church financed Renaissance artists in elaborate projects, but it was the middle class and peasants who were taxed to pay for those projects.

In the early 1500s Pope Leo X needed money for the construction of Saint Peter's Basilica in Rome. To help raise money, he approved the sale of **indulgences**. Indulgences were pardons issued by the pope that people could buy to reduce a soul's time in purgatory. For almost a thousand years, Catholics had believed that after dying people went to purgatory, where their souls worked off the sins they had committed. The sale of indulgences, however, was one of the church's most criticized practices.

As unhappiness with taxation, the sale of indulgences, and other church practices grew, another major shift was occurring in Europe. Nationalism, or the devotion to a particular state or nation rather than to the church, began to grow. People began to consider themselves citizens of a government separate from the church.

Early Reformers Earlier, two men had stepped forward to challenge the church. The first, John Wycliffe, was born in England about 1330. He believed that the church should give up its earthly possessions. His views proved unpopular with church officials, who removed him from his teaching position.

Another reformer, Jan Hus (yahn HOOS), was born in southern Bohemia about 1370. He became a priest and was soon preaching against the immorality and worldliness of the Catholic Church. In 1412 Hus was excommunicated by Pope Gregory XII. Hus was later arrested, tried for heresy, and burned at the stake.

These two men were some of the first and most influential theologians to openly criticize the church. Their views, though condemned by the church and not widely accepted by ordinary people, began a discussion that would eventually lead to reform.

READING CHECK **Summarize** What conditions led to the Protestant Reformation?

Reading like a Historian

Reformation Woodcuts

Analyzing Visuals Historians can learn about how events or people were viewed by analyzing visuals that convey a point of view. Some German Protestant reformers used woodcuts to spread their ideas. Woodcuts were cheap to produce and easy to print, and people did not have to be able to read to understand them. The two woodcuts here, made in 1521, attack Pope Leo X by comparing him unfavorably to Jesus.

To interpret these woodcuts, think about
- the subject of each illustration
- the details and symbols in each illustration
- the overall message of the pair of illustrations

Skills FOCUS **READING LIKE A HISTORIAN**

1. **Subject** How are the subjects of the two woodcut illustrations related?
2. **Details** What details in each of the woodcut illustrations show how Jesus and Pope Leo X view themselves and live their lives?
3. **Message** What is the overall message of the pair of woodcut illustrations?

See **Skills Handbook**, p. H26

Martin Luther

Although scholars, priests, and laypeople had criticized the church before 1517, this year symbolically marks the beginning of the Protestant Reformation. It was in this year that **Martin Luther** made public his complaints about the church.

The Ninety-five Theses To Martin Luther, selling indulgences was sinful. In his theses, Luther flatly denied that indulgences had any power to remit sin. He also criticized the power of the pope and the wealth of the church.

Luther's theses were not intended for the common people of his parish but for church leaders. They were written in academic Latin, which most people did not understand. In nailing them to the church door, Luther was following a common practice of the time. Church doors then served much as community bulletin boards do today.

Differentiating Instruction

Below Level

English-Language Learners

1. Review with students the information in the text about church abuses, Protestant criticisms of the Church, and various Protestant groups.

2. Organize students into mixed-ability pairs.

3. Have students create two political cartoons, one that portrays Protestants as crusaders against the evils of the Church, and the other that minimizes the Church problems and shows Protestants as fanatics.

4. Have volunteers present their political cartoons to the class. 🖼 **Visual-Spatial**

📝 **Alternative Assessment Handbook**, Rubric 27: Political Cartoons

---

Answers

Reading Like a Historian 1. *Both involve leaders; but the leaders' attitudes toward their followers differ.* **2.** *Jesus is on his knees washing a disciple's feet; pope is sitting high above his visitors in a throne; they are kissing his feet.* **3.** *possible answer—The pope has departed from the original teachings of Jesus.*

Reading Check *Church's financial corruption; immorality; abuse of power*

Jesus is washing the feet of his disciples. He taught that people should serve others and not put themselves above others.

The pope has visiting world leaders kiss his feet. He raises himself above others and has them serve him.

The Pope as the Antichrist, by Lucas Cranach the Elder, 1521

Luther's theses, as he had intended, stimulated a discussion among university intellectuals. Soon, thanks to the newly invented printing press, the theses were published. The work spread across Europe and was widely read by intellectuals, clergy, and laypeople. The ideas expressed in the theses made sense to many people, and the desire for reform grew.

Luther's Message Following the publication of the theses, Luther continued to study and debate. He contradicted basic Catholic beliefs when he insisted that God's grace cannot be won by good works. Faith alone, he said, was needed. In Leipzig in 1519, he shocked many when he declared that the only head of the Christian Church is Jesus himself, not the pope. He also insisted that individual Christians should be their own interpreters of scripture and that Christian practices should come only from the Bible. To further this aim, Luther translated the Bible into German. The translation enabled many more people to read the Bible without the aid of the clergy.

Reactions to Luther In 1520 Pope Leo X excommunicated Luther, or expelled him from the Church. In 1521 Martin Luther was summoned to appear before the newly crowned Holy Roman emperor, Charles V, and the German Diet, or assembly, at the city of Worms. Luther refused to change his opinions.

The Holy Roman emperor handed down the Edict of Worms. This decree declared Luther to be an outlaw and condemned his writings. The edict did not prevent Luther's ideas from spreading, however. Although Martin Luther himself had not intended to begin a new religion, by 1530, Lutheranism was a formally recognized branch of Christianity.

In 1529, Charles V moved to suppress Lutherans in Germany. Lutheran princes in the German assembly issued a *protestatio*, or protest, against these measures. This is how the term *Protestant* came into being.

READING CHECK **Identify Supporting Details** Describe the ideas of Martin Luther and how they contradicted the church's teachings of his day.

Reading Focus

2 How did Martin Luther challenge the Catholic Church? *wrote Ninety Five Theses; claimed Christ was the only head of the Church, salvation by faith alone, questioned basic beliefs of Catholicism*

Martin Luther

Identify Cause and Effect What was Luther's intention when he posted his theses? *to spark a discussion among intellectuals*

Make Inferences Do you think that Luther's writings put him in physical danger? *Definitely, he was challenging the most powerful institution of his time.*

Info to Know

"The Daughter of Printing" The invention of the printing press greatly affected change during the Renaissance and Reformation. Martin Luther's religious ideas spread quickly by print. Some historians have called the Reformation, "the daughter of printing." During Luther's lifetime, about 4,000 editions (books printed from one set of type) of his writings were published. In fact, one third of the books in Germany were written by him. Luther's Address to the Christian Nobility, which appeared in the 1520s, sold 4,000 copies in one week.

Skills Focus: Summarizing   At Level

Reading Skill
Press Conference with Martin Luther

1. Organize students into three groups: a small group of speechwriters, a medium-sized group of colleagues, and a large group of the press.

2. Have speechwriters write a speech for Martin Luther to be given a few months after he posted his theses. Have colleagues learn as much as they can about Luther's ideas and prepare to answer questions on his behalf.

3. Guide the press in narrowing down their questions to no more than one question per

reporter. Give a copy of the questions to the advisors. Have colleagues discuss how they will answer any tricky questions.

4. Begin the press conference. Choose one of the speech writers to present the speech. Have members of the press stand up, ask their questions, and have colleagues answer them.
LS **Kinesthetic, Verbal-Linguistic**

📖 **Alternative Assessment Handbook**, Rubric 14: Group Activity

Answers

Reading Check *God's grace cannot be won by good works but by faith; leader of church is Jesus, not pope; people can interpret scripture; practices come from Bible; challenged Catholic practices and the authority of the pope*

❸ How did Protestantism spread to other areas? *Luther's stand against the Church opened the door for others to make differing ideas known*

The Spread of Protestantism

Describe What was the basis of Zwingli's church in Switzerland? *theocracy; government in which church and state are joined*

Compare What did John Calvin's church have in common with Zwingli's? *Protestant, in Switzerland, based on theocracy*

Evaluate Why do you think Calvin's church was successful when Zwingli's was not? *possible answer—Luther opposed Zwingli, Zwingli open to attack from Church because they lacked Lutheran support; Calvin had larger power base from citizens who embraced strictness*

Info to Know

Religion in Switzerland Today the population of Switzerland is approximately half Catholic and half Protestant. The country also has a small Jewish community.

Answers

Faces of History *Calvin created religious government; strict laws, and controlled people's lives.*

Reading Check *some were more radical; included ideas of theocracy, predestination*

John CALVIN 1509–1564

Born into the French middle class, John Calvin studied law and the humanities. Calvin, unlike Martin Luther, was never a monk or priest in the Catholic Church. Calvin and Luther disagreed on several points of theology, but both rejected Catholicism.

Calvin arrived in Geneva in 1536 and became an influential leader of the reform movement there. Under his influence, his followers created a system of worship they called "the religion." He and his supporters instituted a religious government in Switzerland that controlled almost every aspect of people's lives. Calvin's ideas soon spread. People still follow his ideas today through religious denominations called "Reformed."

Infer How did Calvin approach to reform differ from Luther's?

The Spread of Protestantism

Martin Luther's stand against the Roman Catholic Church opened the door for others to put forth their differing ideas on religious matters. As Lutheranism arose in Germany, new religious movements began in Switzerland and other places in Europe.

NEW YORK

CC Unit 3-G5 Calvin and other reformers

Ulrich Zwingli Another Reformation priest, Ulrich Zwingli, was born in Switzerland within months of Luther. Zwingli entered the priesthood at the age of 22 and soon began preaching similar ideas to those of Martin Luther. His proposed reforms, however, went even farther than those of Luther.

Many of Zwingli's ideas about religion were viewed as radical. The church he established in Switzerland had the notion of theocracy at its base. A **theocracy** is a government in which church and state are joined and in which officials are considered to be divinely inspired.

Although Zwingli's movement gained support throughout Switzerland, some areas of the country opposed him and his supporters. His opponents included Martin Luther, who accused Zwingli of tampering with the word of God. Since the Swiss Protestants could not win the Lutherans' support, they were vulnerable to attack by the Catholics. When the disagreement between Swiss Protestants and Catholic officials erupted in war, Zwingli was one of the casualties. He died in battle in 1531.

John Calvin Next to Luther, **John Calvin** was the most important Protestant reformer. Born in 1509 and educated in France, Calvin was influenced by Erasmus and other Renaissance humanists. He also supported the reforms of Martin Luther in Germany.

Inspired by the ideas of Augustine, Calvin preached the doctrine of **predestination**. Predestination holds that God knows who will be saved, even before people are born, and therefore guides the lives of those destined for salvation. Thus, nothing humans can do, either good or bad, will change their predestined end.

Calvinism took root in Geneva, Switzerland, and the city became a theocracy under Calvin's leadership. Calvinists viewed people as sinful by nature, and strict laws were enacted that regulated people's behavior. In Geneva, church attendance was mandatory, and even matters such as the number of courses in each meal and the color of clothing were the subject of laws. Amusements such as feasting, dancing, singing, and wearing jewelry were forbidden.

This strictness was actually the heart of Calvinism's appeal. It gave its followers a sense of mission and discipline. Calvinists felt they were setting an example and making the world fit for the "elect," those who had been chosen for salvation.

Other Reformers Other reformers took the ideas of Martin Luther, Ulrich Zwingli, and John Calvin and adapted them to their own beliefs. John Knox became the spokesman for the Reformation in Scotland after spending time in John Calvin's Geneva. After years of religious turmoil in Scotland, Knox's Reformed Church replaced the Roman Catholic Church. His church structure laid the ground for the Presbyterian denomination that arose later.

Another group separated itself from the Lutherans, Calvinists, and other Protestant Reformers by its beliefs about baptism. The Anabaptists insisted on rebaptizing adults, which was a crime punishable by death at that time. The Anabaptist Church later evolved into several religious factions, including the Hutterites (named for their founder, Jakob Hutter), the Mennonites, and the Amish Mennonites.

READING CHECK **Make Generalizations** How did the ideas of reformers who came after Luther differ from those of Luther?

Reading Skill
Protestant Movements

1. Draw the Venn diagram for students to see. Omit the italicized answers.

2. Have students copy and complete the diagram. Have volunteers complete the class Venn diagram. **LS** Visual-Spatial

Alternative Assessment Handbook, Rubric 13: Graphic Organizers

Protestant Movements

Zwingli's Movement *condemned by Luther; attacked by Church*

Both: *influenced by Luther; Switzerland; theocracy*

Calvinism *predestination; strict laws regulating people's behavior*

Protestantism Spreads to England

The Protestant Reformation began with criticism of the Catholic Church by priests and other religious thinkers. In England, the Reformation began with the king.

A King's Protest Henry VIII became king of England in 1509 at the age of 17. As a young king, he was a devout Catholic who wrote angry protests against the "venomous" ideas of Luther. Henry's actions won him the title "Defender of the Faith."

By 1525, Henry's wife, Catherine of Aragon, had borne only one child, a girl named Mary. This presented a problem for Henry, who wanted a male heir. It was thought that a female monarch could weaken England politically, and he believed Catherine would produce no male heir. Henry decided to have the marriage **annulled**, or declared invalid based on church laws, so that he could marry again.

The pope offered Henry several solutions to his problem but would not agree to the annulment because Catherine and her nephew, Holy Roman Emperor Charles V, opposed it. The dilemma became known as "the king's great matter." While Henry argued with the pope over his annulment, he fell in love with Anne Boleyn. Henry soon took matters into his own hands.

The Reformation Parliament Henry summoned Parliament. Known as the Reformation Parliament, the gathering led to a declaration that England no longer considered itself under the authority of the pope. Instead, Henry himself became the head of the Church of England. He changed the rituals of the church very little, but Henry closed Catholic monasteries and convents and distributed much of the land to nobles. This helped build more public support for the split from the Church.

In 1533, Anne Boleyn and Henry VIII were secretly married. Later that year, after Parliament had declared Henry's marriage to Catherine null and void, Anne gave birth to a girl, Elizabeth. The next year Parliament passed the Act of Supremacy, which required subjects to take an oath declaring Henry VIII to be "Supreme Head of the Church of England." The break with Rome was complete.

Religious Conflicts in England

The desire of King Henry VIII to end his marriage led to religious conflict in England. **Why is King Henry VIII a key figure of the Reformation?**

Portrait of Henry VIII, by Hans Holbein the Younger, 1540

▶ **1527** King Henry VIII asks the pope to annul his marriage, but the pope refuses.

▶ **1534** Henry VIII breaks from the Catholic Church. He founds the Church of England and serves as its head.

▲ **1553** Queen Mary I restores the Catholic Church in England and executes many Protestants.
Execution of Protestants at Smithfield, 1557, Unknown, c. 1720

◀ **1558** Queen Elizabeth I restores the Church of England and support for Protestantism.
Elizabeth I, by Nicholas Hilliard

Direct Teach

Reading Focus

4 What were the effects of Protestantism in England? *Henry VIII broke from Catholic Church; Church of England formed*

Recall What was the "king's great matter"? *that the pope would not agree to annul his marriage to Catherine of Aragon*

Contrast How did Henry VIII's break with the church contrast with his actions as a young man? *As a young man he had supported the Catholic Church against Luther; was called "Defender of the Faith"*

Info to Know

Religious Conflicts in England When he organized the Church of England, Henry VIII changed little in the way of doctrine or ritual. The main difference was that the monarch, not the pope, was the head of the church. A generation later, Archbishop Thomas Cranmer wrote the first version of the Book of Common Prayer, which replaced the Latin liturgical books with prayers in English.

Skills Focus: Drawing Conclusions

At Level

Reading Skill
The King's Great Matter

1. Review with students the information in the text about "the king's great matter."

2. Organize students into two groups. Pose the following question to students: Was King Henry VIII justified in doing what he did to resolve this dilemma?

3. Have students in each group brainstorm ideas in support of their argument. Students in one group should list reasons they feel the king was justified in his actions; students in the other group should list reasons opposing the king's actions. One student in each group should take notes and compile a group list.

4. Serving as moderator, conduct a class debate, instructing students in each group to provide at least two reasons why they either support or oppose King Henry VIII's actions.
LS Verbal-Linguistic

Alternative Assessment Handbook, Rubrics 10: Debates; and 14: Group Activity

Answers

Religious Conflicts in England
broke from Catholic Church; founded Church of England

Interpreting Maps
Spread of Protestantism

Summarize What does this map show about the spread of Protestantism? *possible answer—Protestantism changed as it spread to different areas.*

Predict What might happen between Protestant nations and Catholic nations? *possible answers—might try to convert each other; might go to war*

📦 **Map Transparency:** Spread of Protestantism

• Review & Assess •

Close

Have students compare and contrast official church doctrines and Luther's viewpoints.

Review

📶 **Online Quiz,** Section 3

Assess

SE Section 3 Assessment

📑 **Progress Assessment:** Section 3 Quiz

📑 **Alternative Assessment Handbook**

Reteach/Intervene

📑 **Interactive Reader and Study Guide,** Section 3

💿 **Interactive Skills Tutor CD-ROM**

Answers

Interpreting Maps 1. *Geneva;*
2. *Lutheran*

Reading Check *the desire of Henry VIII to annul his marriage*

454

SPREAD OF PROTESTANTISM

Anglican
Anglican spread
Calvinist
Calvinist spread
Lutheran
Lutheran spread

GEOGRAPHY SKILLS **INTERPRETING MAPS**

1. **Place** What city was the center of the Calvinist movement?

2. **Regions** Which Protestant movement spread to the largest area, according to this map?

Henry's Heirs In the end, Henry VIII had six wives. Henry's third wife, Jane Seymour, gave England its male heir, Edward VI. None of Henry's later three marriages produced any children.

When Edward VI took the throne in 1547 at age nine, Protestantism gained more ground under the guidance of his guardians. Edward died before his 16 birthday, and Henry's daughter Mary became queen of England.

Mary returned England to the authority of the pope. Hundreds of people were burned at the stake for their Protestant beliefs, earning the queen the title Bloody Mary. The news of Mary's death caused little sorrow among Protestants. Her 25-year-old half-sister Elizabeth, the daughter of Anne Boleyn, became queen.

Elizabeth's Reign Elizabeth I was a Protestant at heart. One of her first acts as queen was to draft a new Supremacy Act in 1559, splitting England once again from Rome.

Throughout her reign, Elizabeth was threatened by Catholics who plotted to place Mary, Queen of Scots, on the throne. In turn, Elizabeth persecuted any who dared to worship as Catholics. A strong queen, Elizabeth survived these struggles, firmly establishing the Church of England.

READING CHECK **Summarize** What caused the Reformation to spread to England?

SECTION 3 ASSESSMENT

go.hrw.com
Online Quiz
Keyword: SHL REN HP

Reviewing Ideas, Terms, and People

1. **a. Identify** Name three criticisms that were made of the Catholic Church in the 1500s.
   b. Summarize What other factors contributed to a weakening of the power of the Church in the 1500s?

2. **a. Recall** What were the **Ninety-five Theses**?
   b. Analyze What criticisms did **Martin Luther** have of the Catholic Church?

3. **a. Recall** Which Protestant reformer preached the doctrine of predestination?
   b. Draw Conclusions Why did Zwingli's followers wish to form an alliance with the Lutherans?

4. **a. Describe** What led to **Henry VIII**'s break with the Catholic Church?
   b. Make Judgments Based on the response to Henry VIII's break with Rome, what was likely to be the future relationship between the church and England? Explain your answer.

Critical Thinking

5. **Identify Cause and Effect** Using your notes and a graphic organizer like the one below, record the major reforms brought about by each reformer.

Reformers	Reforms

FOCUS ON WRITING ✏️

6. **Narration** Write a short paragraph that tells how England became a Protestant nation. Include important people, dates, and events.

454 CHAPTER 15

Section 3 Assessment Answers

1. **a.** financially corrupt, abused power, immoral
   b. high taxes for middle class and peasants; rise of nationalism

2. **a.** Luther's propositions regarding the Church
   b. criticized power of the pope and church's wealth, the selling of indulgences

3. **a.** Calvin
   b. possible answer—to form a unified front against the Catholic Church

4. **a.** his desire to annul his marriage
   b. possible answer—There might be a power struggle between the king and the pope

5. Luther—began Protestant Reformation with the Ninety-five Theses; Zwingli—theocracy; Calvin—predestination, strict laws; Knox—his church replaced Catholic Church in Scotland; Anabaptist—rebaptism of adults

6. Student answers should include and explain the following events: Henry tries to get marriage annulled; pope won't agree to annulment; Henry forms Church of England.

The Counter-Reformation

BEFORE YOU READ

MAIN IDEA
Catholics at all levels recognized the need for reform in the church. Their work turned back the tide of Protestantism in some areas and renewed the zeal of Catholics everywhere.

READING FOCUS
1. What reforms were made in the Catholic Church?
2. What were the religious and social effects of the Counter-Reformation?
3. What wars occurred because of the Counter-Reformation?

KEY TERMS AND PEOPLE
Counter-Reformation
Jesuits
Ignatius of Loyola
Council of Trent
Charles Borromeo
Francis of Sales
Teresa of Avila

 NEW YORK

PI 4.1 Students identify historical problems, pose analytical questions or hypotheses, research analytical questions or test hypotheses, and formulate conclusions or generalizations.

From SOLDIER to Saint

Saint Ignatius Loyola, anonymous

THE INSIDE STORY

How does a soldier change his life to become a saint? A Spanish soldier, whose legs had been shattered by a cannonball, was taken by litter to a castle. His right leg had to be rebroken in order to be set correctly, and, eventually, part of the bone had to be sawed off. During the long months of recovery, the soldier's life changed.

The soldier needed something to occupy his time until he could walk again, so he read the only material available to him in the castle—biographies of saints. At first the soldier and former courtier in the Spanish royal court was bored by the stories of penance. But the ideas in the books soon filled his mind with the desire to find a religious purpose, and he began to see religious visions.

The books and visions inspired the soldier, whose name was Ignatius, to change his life—to become a "soldier of God" rather than a "soldier of man." Ignatius later founded a religious teaching order still active today—the Jesuits.

◀ This painting by an unknown artist shows Saint Peter offering a key to Ignatius of Loyola. The key allows one to enter Heaven.

RENAISSANCE AND REFORMATION **455**

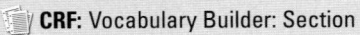
---

❶ What reforms were made in the Catholic Church? *Savonarola's preaching against abuses in the Church; new religious orders such as the Jesuits*

Reforming the Catholic Church

Recall What reforms did Savonarola call for? *called for churches to melt down ornaments to provide food for the poor; convinced others to burn jewelry, mirrors, and trinkets, new religious orders worked to reform the Church*

Identify How did the Jesuits spread Catholicism? *by establishing missions, schools, and universities*

Analyze Why do you think Savonarola was first encouraged, then condemned? *possible answers—The Church feared he might become too powerful.*

Info to Know

Spiritual Exercises Ignatius of Loyola wrote a guide for meditation and discipline called "Spiritual Exercises." This book asked the reader to picture a thought or prayer, then to think of Jesus's actions, and sometimes to visualize oneself doing those actions. Loyola wanted the members of his order to be spiritual, but also to take an active role in the world.

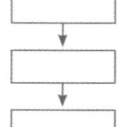

TAKING NOTES

Use a graphic organizer to take notes on the reforms, effects, and wars related to the Counter-Reformation.

THE IMPACT TODAY

Several Jesuit colleges are today ranked among the best in the United States, including Fordham, Georgetown, and Loyola.

NEW YORK
CC Unit 3-G6
Counter Reformation

Reforming the Catholic Church

Protestant reformers were not the only ones who were dissatisfied with the state of the Catholic Church. Even before Martin Luther posted his theses, some Catholics had been working toward reform of the church itself. Later, in response to the spread of Protestantism, the church began a series of reforms known as the **Counter-Reformation.**

Early Reformers A monk named Girolamo Savonarola (sahv-oh-nuh-ROH-luh) was one of the first reformers to try to change the church from within. During the late 1400s, he preached fiery sermons against the abuses of the church. He called for churches to melt down their gold and silver ornaments to buy bread for the hungry and poor members of the church.

Savonarola convinced people to gather and burn jewelry and trinkets. This enormous fire was known as "the bonfire of the vanities." Pope Alexander at first allowed Savonarola's work but eventually excommunicated him for spreading ideas the pope thought dangerous. In 1498, Savonarola was executed at Florence.

Jesuits Other leaders formed new religious orders whose members worked to reform the church. Their work renewed the church's emphasis on spirituality and service. The most influential of these groups was the Society of Jesus, or the **Jesuits.**

The Jesuit order was founded in 1534 by **Ignatius of Loyola**, a Basque nobleman and former soldier. The order was approved by the pope in 1539. Loyola, the Father General, ran the Jesuits like a military organization, emphasizing obedience to the church above all. The Jesuits concentrated on education as a means of combating the Protestant Reformation. They established missions, schools, and universities. With such effective organizations, the Catholic Church began to regain ground against Protestantism.

The Council of Trent Recognizing the need to redefine the doctrines of the Catholic faith, Pope Paul III convened the **Council of Trent** in 1545. It met on and off until 1563. Its delegates examined the criticisms made by Protestants about Catholic practices. In doing so, they clarified Catholic teaching on important points.

The delegates addressed the abuses that had weakened the church over the past century. A series of reforms addressed the corruption of the clergy. The training of priests was regulated and financial abuse was curbed. The sale of indulgences was abolished.

Above all, the Council of Trent rejected the Protestants' emphasis on self-discipline and individual faith. The council argued that the

The Council of Trent
Members of the Catholic clergy met in the Italian city of Trent to decide how to react to the rise of Protestantism. Members of the council signed decrees that outlined specific rules that Catholics were to follow.

The First Chapter of the 25th Council of Trent, anonymous, 1630

Skills Focus: Identifying Main Idea and Details [At Level]

Reading Skill
The Jesuits

1. Draw the graphic organizer below for students to see. Omit the italicized answers.
2. Have students copy and complete the chart. Have volunteers fill in the class chart.
   LS Visual-Spatial

📖 **Alternative Assessment Handbook**, Rubric 7: Charts

The Jesuits

started by	*Ignatius of Loyola*
goals	*obedience to Church and, above all, renewal of Church's spirituality and science, concentrated on education*
achievements	*starting schools and universities, missionary activity, knowledge of other cultures*

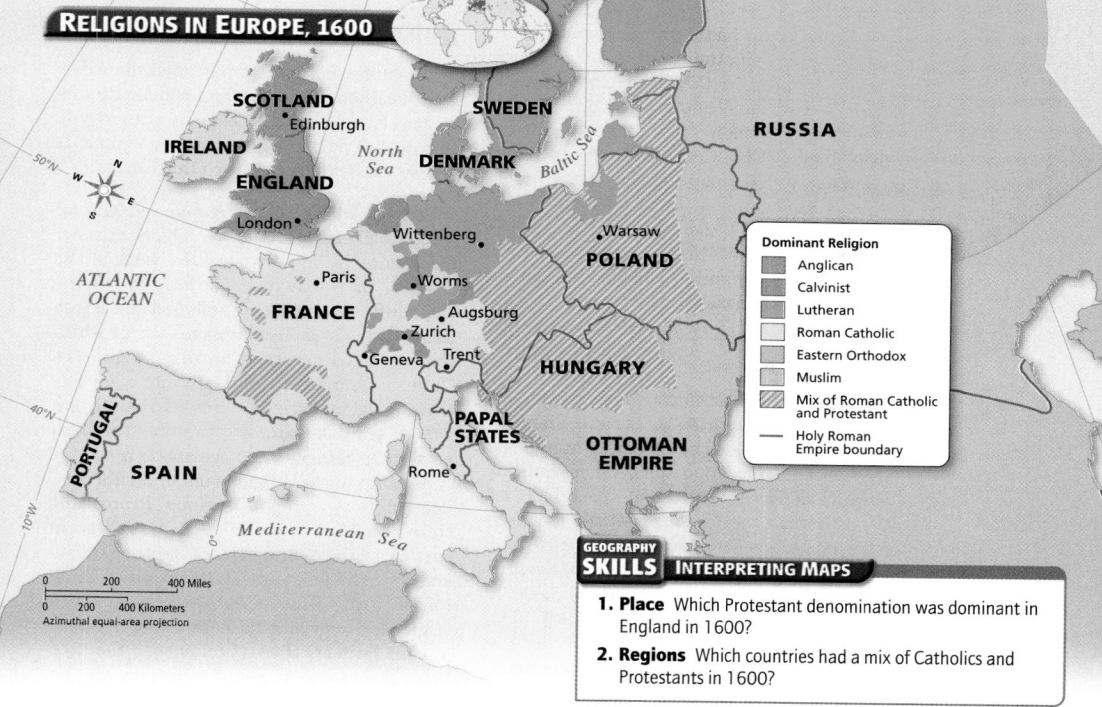

RELIGIONS IN EUROPE, 1600

Dominant Religion
- Anglican
- Calvinist
- Lutheran
- Roman Catholic
- Eastern Orthodox
- Muslim
- Mix of Roman Catholic and Protestant
- Holy Roman Empire boundary

SCOTLAND · Edinburgh
IRELAND
ENGLAND · London
SWEDEN
DENMARK
North Sea
Baltic Sea
RUSSIA
Wittenberg
Warsaw
POLAND
ATLANTIC OCEAN
Paris · Worms
FRANCE · Augsburg · Zurich
Geneva · Trent
HUNGARY
PORTUGAL
SPAIN
PAPAL STATES
Rome
OTTOMAN EMPIRE
Mediterranean Sea

0 200 400 Miles
0 200 400 Kilometers
Azimuthal equal-area projection

GEOGRAPHY SKILLS INTERPRETING MAPS

1. **Place** Which Protestant denomination was dominant in England in 1600?

2. **Regions** Which countries had a mix of Catholics and Protestants in 1600?

church could help believers achieve salvation by using mystery and magnificent ceremonies to inspire faith. This was consistent with the beliefs of millions of people, indeed the majority of Europeans, who remained Catholic.

The pronouncements of the Council of Trent meant that would be no compromise between Catholicism and Protestantism. The council's bold action was a great boost to Catholicism. Austria, Poland, and other parts of Europe returned to the Catholic Church. In addition, Catholics everywhere felt renewed energy and confidence.

The Jesuits used this renewed spirit to expand the scope of the church. By 1700, they operated 669 colleges in Italy, Germany, and other places. Many future leaders were educated at Jesuit schools. In this way, the order had some influence over political affairs. As they worked in India, Japan, China, and other places, the Jesuits also gained and passed along information about the cultures of other lands.

Reforming Catholics Several important figures in the Catholic Church helped to carry out the reforms decreed by the Council of Trent. **Charles Borromeo** (bohr-roh-MAY-oh) was the archbishop of Milan from 1560 to 1584. He took decisive steps to implement the reforms ordered by the council, such as building a new school for the education of priests.

In France, **Francis of Sales** worked to regain the district of Savoy, which had largely turned to Calvinism. As a result of his missionary work, most of the people of Savoy returned to the Catholic Church. He later founded a religious teaching order for women.

Women and the Church During the Renaissance, women in religious orders began to take on more active roles in the Church. Before the Renaissance, they lived in secluded convents. By the late Middle Ages, it was acceptable for nuns to help the poor, orphaned, or sick.

RENAISSANCE AND REFORMATION **457**

Reading Focus

Reforming the Catholic Church

Identify What reforms were passed by the Council of Trent? *addressed clergy's corruption, regulated priests' training, curbed financial abuses, condemned sale of indulgences*

Predict How do you think Protestants would view the decisions of the council? *possible answer—good decisions, but didn't go far enough*

Map Transparency: Religions in Europe, 1600

Recent Scholarship

Girolamo Savonarola raged against church abuses such as profiting from the poor and charged the Medicis as accomplices. In *Fire in the City: Savonarola and the Struggle for the Soul of Renaissance Florence*, Lauro Martines has written about this pivotal moment in the Renaissance.

Fire in the City: Savonarola and the Struggle for the Soul of Renaissance Florence by Lauro Martines. Oxford University Press, 2006.

Differentiating Instruction

Below Level

English-Language Learners

1. Review with students the information in the text about the Council of Trent.

2. Organize students into mixed-ability pairs.

3. Have students create a poster that summarizes the decisions made at the Council of Trent. You may wish to have students write the first letter of each line in Renaissance-era calligraphy.

4. Have volunteers present their posters to the class. Display the posters in a classroom exhibit for all to see. **LS Verbal-Linguistic, Visual-Spatial**

Alternative Assessment Handbook, Rubric 28: Posters

Answers

Interpreting Maps 1. *Anglican;*
2. *France, Poland, Hungary, Russia, Holy Roman Empire*

457

Reading Focus

Reforming the Catholic Church

Identify Name some women who began religious orders during this period. *Angela Merici, Jane of Chantal, Teresa of Avila*

Evaluate Why was the Inquisition considered an abuse of power? *people put on trial; torture and executions*

📄 **CRF:** Biography: Teresa of Avila

Reading Focus

❷ What were the religious and social effects of the Counter-Reformation? *changes in both Catholicism and Protestantism; persecution of non-Catholics, Jews, and Muslims; formation of independent states and nations*

Religious and Social Effects

Recall What groups were most often executed for alleged witchcraft? *women and the poor*

Describe Name three ways in which the Reformation and Counter-Reformation affected politics and government. *softened harsh rule of colonial governments; encouraged independent states; political power separated from churches*

Answers

Reading Skills *possible answer—that the church might gain a broader following due to reforms*

Reading Check *spreading Catholicism through mission work and education reforms of the Council of Trent; Inquisition put people on trial, punished them*

READING SKILLS
Predicting Look at the head in the second column. What might be the effects of the Counter-Reformation?

ACADEMIC VOCABULARY
proportion the size or amount of a thing in relation to another thing

Many women had a profound and important influence on others through their work with the church. In 1535 Italian nun Angela Merici began the Company of Saint Ursula, an order of women dedicated to teaching girls. Jane of Chantal and Francis of Sales cofounded the Visitation of Holy Mary order, which trained women to be teachers. Mary Ward of England began a network of schools for girls throughout Europe. At first her work was denounced by anti-Jesuits and the church because Ward's ideas about women were considered dangerously new. Later, however, her missionary influence was formally recognized by the church.

Perhaps the most famous female spiritual leader was **Teresa of Avila**. Born in Spain in 1515, Teresa decided to become a nun about the age of 20. Her father opposed her plan, but Teresa ran away to a convent about 1536. At the convent, after deciding that the practices were too lax, she followed her own strict rules regarding fasting, prayer, and sleep. Eventually the church gave her permission to reform the Carmelite order. Teresa's deep spirituality, reported visions of Christ, and fervor for the Catholic faith inspired many would-be Protestants to remain in the church.

The Inquisition To counter the Reformation, the church established a church court, called the Roman Inquisition, in 1542 to fight Protestantism. Later popes increased the Inquisition's power. They tried people who were accused of being Protestants, of practicing witchcraft, or of breaking church law.

The Spanish monarchs set up and controlled the much harsher Spanish Inquisition in 1478. They used the Inquisition to impose religious uniformity, especially on converted Jews and Muslims, and later, on Protestants.

The church also tried to stamp out rebellion through its *Index of Forbidden Books*. The church warned the people not to read books on the lists or they would lose their souls. Accounts of torture and executions by the courts damaged the church's image. The Inquisition's actions during the Counter-Reformation are still seen as an abuse of the church's power.

READING CHECK **Summarize** What methods did the Catholic Church use to stop the spread of Protestantism?

Religious and Social Effects

The Counter-Reformation affected the whole world. Although the Roman Catholic Church was no longer the only religious authority in Europe, its policies influenced governments and societies wherever the church existed.

Changes in Religion A renewed zeal for the Catholic faith spread the religion to other continents, largely through the work of the Jesuits. In North America and elsewhere, their influence at times softened the harsh colonial rule of the governments under which they worked. Protestants broke away from the Catholic Church and then split into many factions. Religious turmoil increased as Catholics persecuted non-Catholics and non-Catholics persecuted Catholics and one another.

Adding to the religious discord, rifts soon opened between the various Protestant churches. Martin Luther and his followers denounced the radical ideas of the Anabaptists and Zwingli's followers. Those whose thinking coincided with John Calvin disapproved of some of the ideas on which Lutheranism was based. Martin Luther's theses had opened the door to religious freedom. That freedom brought an equal proportion of conflict and turmoil.

Persecution and Hysteria Both Catholics and Protestants, including Luther, viewed Jews and Muslims as heretics. In 1492, Jews and, in 1500, Muslims were forced to convert to Catholic Christianity or leave Spain. Many Jews resettled in eastern and southern Europe. The majority of the Jews who had earlier converted to Christianity and who were members of the educated elite, stayed in Spain.

In many of the areas in Europe where Jews were allowed to stay, they were not as restricted as they had been during the Middle Ages. However, in some places they were forced to live in a particular part of the city, called a ghetto. The ghettos were walled and their gates closed at a certain time each evening.

Across Europe, many people feared that witches roamed the land, killing children and cattle and working with the devil. Their fears increased in times of poor harvests or other hardships. The fears inspired hysteria in which accused witches were rounded up and tried for their alleged wrongdoing.

Skills Focus: Making Oral Presentations

At Level

Reading Like a Historian Skill
Women and the Church

Research Required

1. Tell students that women have always been involved in the Catholic Church, although their roles have changed over the years. Certain types of involvement by women have been and continue to be controversial.

2. Assign each student a famous Catholic woman, such as Mother Teresa or Catherine of Sienna.

3. Have students conduct research on their assigned person. Research should focus on the person's actions, her faith, and her relationship to the Catholic leadership.

4. Have students make a short presentation about their assigned person. **LS Verbal-Linguistic**

📄 **Alternative Assessment Handbook**, Rubrics 24: Oral Presentations; and 30: Research

Christianity

The Reformation divided Christians in western Europe into Catholic and Protestant. Today Catholics, Protestants, and Orthodox Christians form the three main branches of Christianity.

Origins of Christianity The Christian faith is rooted in the beliefs of Judaism. Christians believe that a man named Jesus of Nazareth who lived in the first century AD was the promised Jewish Messiah and the Son of God. Jesus taught that all people who believe that he is the Son of God and follow his teachings will receive salvation—the forgiveness of sins and the promise of everlasting life.

The life and teachings of Jesus are described in the Gospels, the first four books of the New Testament. The New Testament along with the Hebrew Bible make up the Christian Bible, the sacred text of Christianity.

Christianity Today Christianity is now the religion with the most followers worldwide, with 2.1 billion followers. The nations with the highest percentages of Christians are in the Americas and Europe. In the United States, 85 percent of the population identifies themselves as Christian.

The chart breaks down Christianity into its major branches. Within these branches are many smaller groups called denominations. In all, Christianity has some 1,000 denominations in North America alone. Protestants account for most of these.

Some Christian denominations, including Catholics, perform the Eucharist, or Communion, which reenacts Jesus' Last Supper. An important holy day is Easter. On this day, Christians remember the Resurrection, when they believe Jesus rose from the dead.

Find the Main Idea What are the three main branches of Christianity?

Guell Colony Chapel, Antoni Gaudi

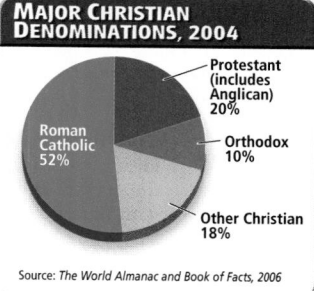

MAJOR CHRISTIAN DENOMINATIONS, 2004

- Roman Catholic 52%
- Protestant (includes Anglican) 20%
- Orthodox 10%
- Other Christian 18%

Source: The World Almanac and Book of Facts, 2006

The penalty for practicing witchcraft at this time was often death, and many innocent victims were executed for alleged witchcraft. The majority of executions for witchcraft occurred between 1580 and 1660. Thousands of people, most of them women or poor, were killed.

Political Effects A rising sense of national identity was interwoven with a decline in the power of the Catholic Church. The Protestant Reformation indirectly encouraged the formation of independent states and nations. Rulers and merchants both wanted the church to be less involved in state and business affairs, which they sought to control on their own. Political power became separated from churches, although nations and churches often aligned themselves with one another to increase their own influence in a region.

READING CHECK **Generalize** How did religious turmoil affect society during the 1500s?

Religious Wars and Unrest

In 1494, shortly before Michelangelo sculpted his *Pietà* and Savonarola was executed, King Charles VIII of France invaded Italy. This began a series of wars in which France and Spain vied for control of the Italian peninsula.

The Italian Wars During the Italian Wars, control of Italy bounced between these two powers. England also eventually became involved, as did several popes. The fighting finally culminated in the sack of Rome by the Spaniard and Holy Roman Emperor Charles V in 1527.

The Italian Wars officially ended in 1559. The real significance of the Italian Wars was that they were credited with expanding the Italian Renaissance throughout Europe. Troops returned home carrying ideas they had been exposed to in Italy. In addition, artists from Italy fled to the north, bringing new techniques and styles with them.

NEW YORK

CC Unit 3-G8
Religious wars in Europe

Skills Focus: Interpreting Pie and Bar Graphs

At Level

Social Studies Skill
Religious Denominations

Research Required

1. Have students review the pie graph on this page.

2. Have students conduct Internet research using reliable Web sites to find the percentages of religious followers in the United States in these categories: Protestants, Roman Catholics, Nonreligious or Atheists, Orthodox, Independent Christian, and Other Religions. Then, have them research these percentages in your home state.

3. Have students create basic pie graphs of their findings.

4. Have students write a paragraph describing how the percentages of religious followers worldwide compares to percentages in the United States and in your home state.
LS **Verbal-Linguistic, Visual-Spatial**

Alternative Assessment Handbook, Rubrics 7: Charts, and 30: Research

---

459

Direct Teach

📖 **Quick Facts Transparency:** The Reformation

• Review & Assess •

Close

Have students describe Catholic actions in response to the Protestant Reformation.

Review

🖥️ **Online Quiz,** Section 4

Assess

SE **Section 4 Assessment**

📄 **Progress Assessment:** Section 4 Quiz

📄 **Alternative Assessment Handbook**

Reteach/Intervene

📄 **Interactive Reader and Study Guide,** Section 4

💿 **Interactive Skills Tutor CD-ROM**

THE REFORMATION *QUICK FACTS*

Causes

- Humanist values led people to question church authority.
- Some clergy were corrupt, worldly, or poorly educated.
- Martin Luther posted his Ninety-five Theses.
- The printing press helped spread Reformation ideas.

Effects

- Many Protestant sects developed.
- Church leaders reformed the Catholic Church.
- Religious intolerance and anti-Semitism increased.
- Religious conflicts spread across Europe.

Conflicts among Germans With new ideas circulating amongst a growing population, peasants were becoming more unhappy with high taxes and a lack of power. At the same time, Reformation preachers were giving backing to the idea of freedom. Stirred by these factors, in 1524 tens of thousands of German peasants stormed castles and monasteries, a rebellion known as the Peasants' War. The nobles harshly suppressed the uprising.

Martin Luther, accused of beginning the unrest, denounced it. The peasants, he wrote, "rob and rage and act like mad dogs." Luther's refusal to side with the peasants prevented the Reformation from spilling over into a social revolution that encouraged social equality.

Holy Roman Emperor Charles V, a devout Catholic, was determined to turn back the tide of Protestantism. In 1546 he began a war against the Lutheran princes of Germany. After years of battles, enthusiasm for the war waned, and the Peace of Augsburg was signed in 1555. Charles, who scorned religious compromise, would not attend the meeting.

The agreement reached in Augsburg allowed each prince to choose the religion that his subjects would practice. The only choices were Catholicism or Lutheranism, and the subjects had no say in the choice. Still, the seeds of religious freedom had been planted.

Conflicts between Religions In France the Huguenots, the Protestant minority, fought for years against the Catholics. The fighting ended when their leader, Henry of Navarre, became Catholic. His conversion led to political stability by encouraging Catholics to accept him as king. In 1598 Henry's Edict of Nantes granted religious freedom to Protestants.

READING CHECK **Identify Cause and Effect** What factors led to the Peasants' War?

SECTION 4 ASSESSMENT

go.hrw.com
Online Quiz
Keyword: SHL REN HP

Reviewing Ideas, Terms, and People

1. a. Recall On what issues did the reformer **Ignatius of Loyola** focus?
   b. Explain How did the Catholic Church try to keep people from becoming Protestant?
   c. Evaluate In your opinion, what was the main importance of the **Counter-Reformation** in European history?

2. a. Describe What were some of the effects of the Counter-Reformation on European society?
   b. Summarize What led to the persecution of witches across Europe during the 1500s?

3. a. Identify Who were the Huguenots?
   b. Interpret How did the Peace of Augsburg encourage religious toleration?
   c. Elaborate How did Luther's reaction to the Peasants' War affect the Counter-Reformation?

Critical Thinking

4. Compare Using your notes from the section and a graphic organizer like the one below, analyze causes, characteristics, and effects of the Counter-Reformation.

Counter-Reformation	
Causes	
Characteristics	
Effects	

FOCUS ON WRITING

5. Exposition Which Counter-Reformation reform do you think was most important? Write a paragraph identifying the reform and exploring why it was so important.

Answers

Reading Check *peasants' high taxes, lack of power; Reformation ideas of freedom*

Section 4 Assessment Answers

1. a. obedience to the church above all, renewed emphasis on spirituality and service
   b. Counter-Reformation, redefined doctrine at Council of Trent
   c. possible answer—reformed the Church; brought people back to the faith; new converts

2. a. the Church's influence was restored, spirituality and service emphasized
   b. fear of different religious practices

3. a. French Protestants
   b. allowed each prince to choose the religion his subjects would practice; allowed different religions to coexist
   c. prevented Reformation from becoming a social revolution as well

4. Causes: response to spread of Protestantism, some Catholics left reform was overdue; Characteristics: Council of Trent redefined doctrines, Jesuits taught spirituality and service, worked to bring about reform, women took on more active roles; Effects: church regains supports of Catholics in many European countries, majority of Europeans remained Catholic

5. Student paragraphs should include one of the reforms and support their choice with logic and details from the section.

Focus on Themes

Migration and Diffusion

Before Gutenberg's press, books were rare and expensive. New ideas usually spread by word of mouth as people traveled from place to place. Although clergy and nobles might have been able to read the few books that existed, the majority of books were philosophical and religious works with little practical knowledge in them. Political ideas, technical knowledge about agriculture or medicine, and even laws, were usually learned directly from others.

DIFFUSION OF IDEAS THEN The movable type that Gutenberg developed changed the way people shared information. New forms of literature began to appear in Europe for new kinds of audiences. Novels were published for pleasure reading. Manuals on agriculture were published to help farmers learn techniques that produced more and better crops. Political tracts began appearing and changed the way people thought about their place in society. Printed sheets of news, the first European newspapers, appeared in German cities in the late 1400s. Italian news sheets were purchased for a small coin called a *gazeta*.

As printing presses spread throughout Europe and literacy rates grew, anyone who could read had access to ideas previously known only to the elite. For the first time, religious and political authorities had little control over the spread of information between people and places, although many tried to institute a measure of censorship.

▲ NOW A Sotho woman in South Africa uses a laptop to access information on the Internet.

DIFFUSION OF IDEAS NOW Today a similar revolution is occurring with the spread of computers and access to the Internet. An immense amount of information is available to people in areas that have no libraries or universities.

In addition, new forms of communication are being created that take advantage of the new technology. Music and graphics can accompany text in a way books do not allow and can make certain ideas more easily understood. Hyperlinked text allows readers instant access to more information on certain topics.

As with the technology of printing, Internet technology raises issues for modern authorities, who struggle to maintain a flow of information that respects the legal rights of all concerned. The illegal downloading of copyrighted material is one such issue.

Skills Focus UNDERSTANDING THEMES

1. **Summarize** Why was the printing press such a revolutionary technology?
2. **Compare and Contrast** What are some similarities and differences between the printing revolution and the Internet revolution?
3. **Predict** Do you think the problems created by the technology of the Internet will be solved?

◀ THEN A woodcut shows printers working on a printing press, a revolutionary technology at the time.

The Printer's Workshop, by Jost Ammann, 1568

Focus on Themes

Info to Know

Copyrights and the Internet Copyright law seeks to protect the rights of creators of music, books, and many other original works, so that the creators may profit from their own work. With the Internet revolution, new challenges for copyright law arose. For example, in the 1990s, Internet music-sharing services arose, allowing people to share music files, sometimes without paying for them. Courts in the United States ruled that these services violated copyright laws, while courts in Canada ruled that the use of these services does not violate copyright. Distributors of electronic books and other electronic content have faced similar challenges.

Skills Focus: Comparing and Contrasting   At Level

Reading Skill
Diffusion of Ideas, Then and Now

1. Copy the graphic organizer for all to see, omitting the italicized answers.
2. Have students fill in the boxes of the flow chart. Then use the flow charts to compare the Internet revolution and the printing revolution. **LS Visual-Spatial**

   📝 **Alternative Assessment Handbook**, Rubric 7: Charts

| Idea in era of printing revolution | → | printed on: *paper in book form* | → | idea accessible by: *anyone who could read* |

| Idea in era of Internet revolution | → | printed on: *Web site* | → | idea accessible by: *anyone with computer* |

Answers

Understanding Themes 1. *allowed all readers access to new ideas; made spread of ideas faster;* **2.** *similarities—both increased speed of communication; differences—Internet revolution does not involve physical printing;* **3.** *possible answer—Yes, the problem is still quite new, and will probably take more time to solve.*

461

Document-Based Investigation

The Renaissance and Individualism

Info to Know

Anamorphosis The painting "The Ambassadors" contains one particularly unusual element—the object protruding from under the table. To create this object, artist Hans Holbein used a technique called anamorphosis. Looking at the object from straight ahead reveals nothing, but looking at it from a sharp angle, in this case from the right, reveals a human skull. It is possible that the painting was meant to be hung above and to the left of a doorway so that the viewer would see the skull upon entering the room. Although many have debated the symbolic meaning of the skull in this painting, no one is certain of Holbein's intent.

The Renaissance and Individualism

NEW YORK STANDARDS

PI 4.1 Students identify historical problems, pose analytical questions or hypotheses, research analytical questions or test hypotheses, formulate conclusions or generalizations, raise new questions or issues for further investigation.

Historical Context The documents below illustrate the changing view of individuals that occurred during the Renaissance.

Task Study the documents and answer the questions that follow. After you have studied all of the documents, you will be asked to write an essay explaining changes that occurred during the Renaissance.

DOCUMENT 1

A Medieval View

In 1195 Pope Innocent III published a work entitled *On the Misery of the Human Condition*. In it, he described all of humanity as sinful people who should focus all their energy on receiving God's forgiveness.

> [Man] does depraved [evil] things by which he offends God, offends his neighbors, offends himself. He does vain and shameful things by which he pollutes his fame, pollutes his person, pollutes his conscience. He does vain things by which he neglects serious things, neglects profitable things, neglects necessary things.

DOCUMENT 2

Individuals and Accomplishment

Wealthy people with access to education began learning not just religious or practical things, but things that interested them. Geography, music, art, and mathematics were learned because they interested the student, not in order to obtain employment or gain salvation. This painting of two French ambassadors by Hans Holbein shows items associated with subjects that the two men have studied.

The Ambassadors, Hans Holbein the Younger, 1533

Skills Focus: Analyzing Alternative Points of View   Below Level

Reading Like a Historian Skill
Pre- and Post-Renaissance Viewpoints

1. Explain to students that the introduction to each document is designed to help them gain a frame of reference. Write the following words and phrases for all to see: "1195," "focus all their energy on receiving God's forgiveness," "not in order to obtain employment or gain salvation."

2. Tell students that these words and phrases provide clues about the point of view conveyed in each document. Ask students to identify other clues, and write them for all to see.

3. Have students use these clues and their reading to determine which document represents a pre-Renaissance view, and which represents a post-Renaissance view. Have volunteers identify the documents, and explain how they arrived at their answer.

LS Visual-Spatial, Interpersonal

Alternative Assessment Handbook, Rubrics 12: Drawing Conclusions; and 16: Judging Information

DOCUMENT 3

The Dignified Man

In 1487 an Italian nobleman and scholar, Giovanni Pico della Mirandola, prepared a speech called "Oration on the Dignity of Man." The work assumes the point of view of God speaking to Adam after his creation.

The nature of all other beings is limited and constrained within the bounds of laws prescribed by Us. Thou [you], constrained by no limits, in accordance with thine own free will, in whose hand We have placed thee, shalt ordain for thyself the limits of thy nature. We have set thee at the world's center that thou mayest from thence more easily observe whatever is in the world. We have made thee neither of heaven nor of earth, neither mortal nor immortal, so that with freedom of choice and with honor, as though the maker and molder of thyself, thou mayest fashion [make] thyself in whatever shape thou shalt prefer.

DOCUMENT 4

Christian Humanism

The writings of Desiderius Erasmus brought together the ideas of Christianity and the ideas of humanism. In a preface to his Latin version of the New Testament, he discusses why it is important for humanists to study Christianity.

And in the first place, it's not pleasant to raise the complaint, not altogether new but all too just and never more timely than in these days when men are applying themselves singlemindedly each to his own studies, that the philosophy of Christ is singled out for derision [mockery] even by some Christians—is ignored by most and cultivated [studied] (coldly at that—I won't say insincerely) by only a few. In all other disciplines where human energy is invested, there's nothing so obscure and elusive that lawless curiosity has not explored it. Yet how does it happen that even those of us who lay claim to the Christian name fail to embrace this philosophy in full sincerity, as we should? Platonists, Pythagoreans, Academics, Stoics, Cynics, Peripatetics, and Epicureans all know the doctrines of their particular sects, they learn them by heart, and fight fiercely for them, ready to die rather than abandon the cause of their particular patron. Why then don't we stand up even more spiritedly on behalf of our maker and our leader, Christ?

Document-Based Investigation

Primary Source

"… we do not intend to tear up the old and commonly accepted edition, but to amend it in some places where it is corrupt, and to make it clear where it is obscure; and this not by the dreams of my own mind, nor, as they say, with unwashed hands, but partly by the evidence of the earliest manuscripts, and partly by the opinion of those whose learning and sanctity have been confirmed by the authority of the Church…"
—Erasmus, letter to Pope Leo X about his version of the New Testament

Skills FOCUS — READING LIKE A HISTORIAN

DOCUMENT 1
a. **Interpret** How does Pope Innocent III's description of humanity view the individual?
b. **Infer** Why was secular learning discouraged before the Renaissance?

DOCUMENT 2
a. **Describe** What subjects are the ambassadors interested in learning?
b. **Interpret** How might this painting be different from earlier paintings of important officials?

DOCUMENT 3
a. **Identify** Why does humanity have a special place in the universe, according to Mirandola?
b. **Compare** How has the view of the relationship between God and humanity changed in Mirandola's eyes?

DOCUMENT 4
a. **Analyze** Why does Erasmus say humanists should study Christianity?
b. **Interpret** How does Erasmus equate spiritual and secular learning?

DOCUMENT-BASED ESSAY QUESTION

The change in the view of humanity during the Renaissance was a subtle and gradual shift that would have a profound effect. What changes occurred in the view of the individual? Using the documents above and information from the chapter, note some changes. Then write an essay about how they may have affected the way people lived.

See **Skills Handbook**, p. H22

RENAISSANCE AND REFORMATION **463**

Skills Focus: Analyzing Primary Sources

At Level

Reading Like a Historian Skill
The Life of Erasmus

1. Explain to students that in order to understand Erasmus's introduction to the New Testament, they must understand some facts about his life.

2. Have students review the information about Erasmus in the chapter. Individually or in groups, have them conduct additional research to answer the following questions: Why did Erasmus create a Latin version of the New Testament? What was his relationship with the Church? How did

Erasmus react to the teachings of Luther? What were some of Erasmus's other writings and what topics did they address?

3. Have students write several paragraphs to inform what they have learned about Erasmus. Have volunteers share their paragraphs with the rest of the class, in order to help them better understand Document 4. **LS Verbal-Linguistic**

Alternative Assessment Handbook, Rubric 42: Writing to Inform

Answers

Document 1 a. *sinful;* **b.** *because it was believed people should only focus on receiving God's forgiveness for sins;* **Document 2 a.** *geography, music, art, mathematics;* **b.** *possible answers—earlier officials were probably painted as being close to God, chosen by God;* **Document 3 a.** *because of free will;* **b.** *possible answer—God gave Adam free will, but in Mirandola's time, the Church controlled people's actions.* **Document 4 a.** *because secular groups are studying their areas with passion and singlemindedness, and Christianity is no less important;* **b.** *Christianity should be stood up for more spiritedly.* **Essay** *Student essays should use the documents and the chapter to identify that the role of the individual before the Renaissance was to cultivate a relationship with God, and that the individual had more freedoms and activities after the Renaissance. Essays should go on to explain the effect this shift would have on the way people lived.*

463

Answers

Visual Summary

Review and Inquiry Have students choose one of the lists in the Visual Study Guide on this page. Have students write a one-sentence summary of each person's accomplishments or each event's significance.

Quick Facts Transparency: Visual Study Guide: Renaissance and Reformation

Review Key Terms and People

1. The Renaissance was a period of renewed interest in art and science.
2. Humanism emphasized individual accomplishment.
3. Leonardo da Vinci was a Renaissance artist and inventor.
4. Johannes Gutenberg invented movable type.
5. Albrecht Dürer was a German painter who used techniques of the Italian Renaissance.
6. William Shakespeare's plays helped spread ideas of the Renaissance.
7. The Protestant Reformation reformed the Catholic Church.
8. The Reformation symbolically began in 1517 when Martin Luther posted the Ninety-five Theses.
9. Indulgences were pardons issued by the pope in exchange for money.
10. Henry VIII began the Church of England.
11. The Catholic Reformation followed the Protestant Reformation.
12. The Council of Trent reformed church practices.

Comprehension and Critical Thinking

13. **a.** a school of thought emphasizing the individual and the human mind
    b. religious subjects; idealized
    c. Wealthy patrons supported artists.
14. **a.** controlled trade throughout northern Europe; protected merchants; built lighthouses
    b. trade, travel, printing
    c. possible answer—works were censored, condemned by Church

---

VISUAL STUDY GUIDE

People of the Renaissance

Lorenzo de Medici	Ruler of Florence and patron of many artists
Leonardo da Vinci	Italian artist, engineer, and scientist
Michelangelo	Italian painter and sculptor
Baldassare Castiglione	Italian writer and courtier
Niccolo Machiavelli	Italian political writer and statesman
Albrecht Dürer	German painter
Johannes Gutenberg	German creator of movable type
Desiderius Erasmus	Christian humanist philosopher and writer
William Shakespeare	English playwright and poet
Martin Luther	German religious reformer
John Calvin	Swiss religious reformer
Henry VIII	King of England
Elizabeth I	Queen of England and daughter of Henry VIII
Ignatius of Loyola	Spanish monk and founder of the Jesuits
Teresa of Avila	Spanish nun and reformer of the Carmelite order

Events of the Renaissance

mid-1300s	Italy experiences a rise of city-states.
1435	Alberti writes an explanation of perspective for other artists.
1455	Gutenberg develops a printing press with moveable type.
1506	Dürer returns to Germany from a trip to Italy.
1508	Michelangelo starts painting the Sistine Chapel.
1517	Luther posts his Ninety-Five Theses at Wittenberg.
1518	Castiglione completes *The Courtier*.
1533	Henry VIII marries Anne Boleyn.
1537	Teresa of Avila runs away from home to join a convent.
1540	Ignatius of Loyola founds the Jesuits.
1542	The Inquisition is established.
1545	Pope Paul III convenes the Council of Trent.
1558	Elizabeth I comes to the throne of England.
1593	Shakespeare appears in London records.

Review Key Terms and People

For each term or name below, write a sentence explaining its significance to the Renaissance or Reformation.

1. Renaissance
2. humanism
3. Leonardo da Vinci
4. Johannes Gutenberg
5. Albrecht Dürer
6. William Shakespeare
7. Protestant Reformation
8. Martin Luther
9. indulgences
10. Henry VIII
11. Catholic Reformation
12. Council of Trent

464 CHAPTER 15

---

15. **a.** the list of complaints that Martin Luther publicized in 1517
    b. the wife of Henry VIII did not produce a male heir; Henry VIII wanted an annulment; pope refused to grant annulment; Henry VIII founded Church of England
    c. possible sentence—Yes, earlier writers had also begun to criticize the Church.
16. **a.** to redefine Catholic doctrines; to examine criticisms made by Protestants
    b. possible answer—the Jesuits, because they used positive methods, such as education

    c. possible answer—The two religions would continue to disagree with each other, leading to wars and further differences.

Reading Skills

17. possible answer—The Catholic Church might decline in power as a result of the Protestant Reformation.
18. possible answer—more wars between Catholic and Protestant

Comprehension and Critical Thinking

SECTION 1 *(pp. 437–443)*

13. a. Recall What was humanism?

b. Explain How did medieval artwork differ from the artwork created during the Renaissance?

c. Evaluate How did the success of Italian city-states help make the Renaissance possible?

SECTION 2 *(pp. 444–447)*

14. a. Identify Name the functions of the Hanseatic League.

b. Summarize What were the various ways that Renaissance ideas were spread?

c. Elaborate Why did it become dangerous to own a book by Erasmus?

SECTION 3 *(pp. 449–454)*

15. a. Define What were the Ninety-Five Theses?

b. Sequence Describe the sequence of events that led to England's break with the Roman Catholic Church.

c. Support a Position If Martin Luther had not posted his theses back in 1517, would the Reformation ever have happened? Take a position on this question and write a few sentences in support of that position.

SECTION 4 *(pp. 455–460)*

16. a. Identify Main Ideas What was the purpose of the Council of Trent?

b. Compare The Catholic Church used many methods to stop the spread of Protestantism. Compare the methods of the Jesuits to those of the Inquisition. Which had more far-reaching effects?

c. Predict "The pronouncements of the Council of Trent meant that no middle ground between Catholicism and Protestantism existed." Predict the future of both religions based on this statement and the other information in this chapter.

Reading Skills

Predicting *Use what you know about predicting to answer the following questions.*

17. If you know that the Catholic Church played an important role in society before the Renaissance and Reformation, what might you predict would happen to the church after these movements?

18. After studying the religious wars in Europe during this time what do you think might happen next on this continent?

Analyzing Visuals

Reading Like a Historian *The painting below shows wealthy Italians at a daily meal during the Renaissance.*

Concert, by Ambrosius Benson

19. Draw Conclusions The musicians on the left side of the painting are performing a concert for the diners. What does this painting tell you about what wealthy Italians valued during the Renaissance?

Using the Internet

go.hrw.com
Practice Online
Keyword: SHL REN

20. Certain religious practices caused a number of people to call for change. Using the keyword above, do research to learn about leaders of the Reformation. Then use the information you learned to create a pamphlet on the topic.

WRITING FOR THE SAT ✐

Think about the following issue:

Although drastic changes occurred during the Renaissance, most people's lives changed very little. The elite and nobles benefitted the most from the changes of the Renaissance.

21. Assignment: Why would the poor not benefit as much as nobles from changes of the Renaissance? Write a short essay discussing this issue. Support your point of view with examples.

RENAISSANCE AND REFORMATION **465**

Answers

Analyzing Visuals

19. possible answer—shows wealthy Italians valued art and music

Using the Internet

20. Go to the HRW Web site and enter the keyword shown to access a rubric for this activity.

KEYWORD: SHL REN

Writing for the SAT

21. Student essays should demonstrate an understanding of the Renaissance and its effects on people's lives. Essays should also point out that the lives of the wealthy were improving and that wealthy patrons financed art and music.

A rubric for this activity is provided in **CRF:** Writing for the SAT.

HOLT

History's Impact
▶ **Video Program: Renaissance and Reformation**
Refer to the Video Program Teacher's Guide for a discussion of the closing question.

Review and Assessment Resources

Review and Reinforce

📄 **CRF:** Chapter Review

🖳 **Quick Facts Transparency:** Visual Study Guide: Renaissance and Reformation

🔊 **Spanish Chapter Summaries Audio CD Program**

HOAP **Online Chapter Summaries in Six Languages**

OSP **Holt PuzzlePro:** Quiz Show for ExamView

💿 **Quiz Game CD-ROM**

Assess

📄 **PASS:** Chapter Test, Forms A and B

📄 **Alternative Assessment Handbook**

OSP **ExamView Test Generator**, Chapter Test

💿 **Differentiated Instruction Modified Worksheets and Tests CD-ROM:** Chapter Test

HOAP **Holt Online Assessment Program** (in the Premier Online Edition)

Reteach/Intervene

📄 **Interactive Reader and Study Guide**

📄 **Differentiated Instruction Teacher Management System:** Lesson Plans for Differentiated Instruction

💿 **Differentiated Instruction Modified Worksheets and Tests CD-ROM:** Chapter Test

💿 **Interactive Skills Tutor CD-ROM**

go.hrw.com
Online Resources

KEYWORD: SHL TEACHER

Chapter Overview	Reproducible Resources	Technology Resources
CHAPTER 16 pp. 466–495 **Overview:** In this chapter, students will learn about the explorations, conquests, and expansion that occurred between 1400 and 1700. KI 1, 4; PI 1.1, 1.2, 1.4, 4.3;	**Interactive Reader and Study Guide:** Chapter Summary* **Chapter Resource File*** • Writing About History • Social Studies Skill • Chapter Review	**Live Ink© Online Reading Help** **Differentiated Instruction Modified Worksheets and Tests CD-ROM** **World History Primary Source Library CD-ROM** **History's Impact: World History Video Program (VHS/DVD):** Exploration and Expansion
Section 1: **Voyages of Discovery** **The Main Idea:** During the 1400s and 1500s European explorers—inspired by greed, curiosity, and the desire for glory and aided by new technologies—sailed to many previously unknown lands in the 1400s and 1500s. PI 1.2;	**Differentiated Instruction Teacher Management System:** Section 1 Lesson Plan* **Interactive Reader and Study Guide:** Section 1 Summary* **Chapter Resource File*** • Vocabulary Builder: Section 1 • Biography: Vasco da Gama • History and Geography: Portuguese Explorers in Africa	**Regents Review Transparency:** Section 1* **Map Transparency:** European Discovery, 1400–1700* **Map Transparency:** Explorers and Their Routes* **Internet Activity:** Navigation Tools
Section 2: **Conquest and Colonies** **The Main Idea:** The countries of Europe established colonies in the lands they had discovered but, in some cases, only after violently conquering the native people who lived there. PI 1.1;	**Differentiated Instruction Teacher Management System:** Section 2 Lesson Plan* **Interactive Reader and Study Guide:** Section 2 Summary* **Chapter Resource File*** • Vocabulary Builder: Section 2 • Biography: Isabella I • Primary Source: An Aztec Account of the Spanish Arrival of Tenochtitlán	**Regents Review Transparency:** Section 2* **Map Transparency:** Colonies in the Americas* **Quick Facts Transparency:** Causes and Effects of the French and Indian War* **Internet Activity:** Exploration and Expansion
Section 3: **New Patterns of Trade** **The Main Idea:** The creation of colonies in the Americas and elsewhere led to the exchange of new types of goods, the establishment of new patterns of trade, and new economic systems in Europe. PI 1.4;	**Differentiated Instruction Teacher Management System:** Section 3 Lesson Plan* **Interactive Reader and Study Guide:** Section 3 Summary* **Chapter Resource File*** • Vocabulary Builder: Section 3 • Biography: Pocahontas	**Regents Review Transparency:** Section 3* **Quick Facts Transparency:** The Columbian Exchange* **Quick Facts Transparency:** Basic Principles of Mercantilism*
Section 4: **The Atlantic Slave Trade** **The Main Idea:** Between the 1500s and the 1800s millions of Africans were captured, shipped across the Atlantic Ocean, and sold as slaves in the Americas. PI 1.2, 4.3;	**Interactive Reader and Study Guide:** Section 4 Summary* **Chapter Resource File*** • Vocabulary Builder: Section 4 • Biography: Olaudah Equiano • Literature: *The Interesting Narrative and Other Writings*	**Regents Review Transparency:** Section 4* **Map Transparency:** The Atlantic Slave Trade*

HOLT
History's Impact
World History Video Program (VHS/DVD)
Exploration and Expansion

Review, Assessment, Intervention

Global History and Geography Regents Test Prep Workbook

Quick Facts Transparency: Exploration and Expansion*

Progress Assessment Support System (PASS): Chapter Test*

OSP **New York One-Stop Planner CD-ROM:** ExamView Test Generator (English/Spanish)

PASS: Section 1 Quiz*
Online Quiz: Section 1
Alternative Assessment Handbook

PASS: Section 2 Quiz*
Online Quiz: Section 2
Alternative Assessment Handbook

PASS: Section 3 Quiz*
Online Quiz: Section 3
Alternative Assessment Handbook

PASS: Section 4 Quiz*
Online Quiz: Section 4
Alternative Assessment Handbook

Power Presentation with Video CD-ROM

Power Presentations with Video are visual presentations of each chapter's main ideas. Presentations can be customized by including Quick Facts charts, images and maps from the textbook, and video clips.

Holt
Online
Learning

go.hrw.com
Teacher Resources
KEYWORD: SHL TEACHER

go.hrw.com
Student Resources
KEYWORD: SHL EXP

- Document-Based Questions
- Interactive Multimedia Activities

- Current Events
- Chapter-Based Internet Activities
- and more!

Holt Premier
Online Student Edition
Complete online support for interactivity, assessment, and reporting
- Interactive Maps and Notebook
- Homework Practice and Research Activities Online

CHAPTER 16 PLANNING GUIDE

Before You Teach

The Big Picture

Peter N. Stearns

The European Surge Beginning as early as the 13th century Europeans began to undertake a widening series of sea voyages. There was great desire to gain direct access to the products of Asia without having to use Islamic traders as middlemen. Europeans had trouble paying for the Asian goods they wished, and direct trade and a desire to find new sources of gold were key responses. But political motives added in: explorations soon became part of interstate rivalry within Europe, particularly as France, Holland, and England joined the parade.

The Columbian Exchange European exploration of the Americas had a host of consequences. New food products were available to other parts of the world. To the Americas the same exchange brought new animals and grains, as well as new tools and weapons, with results that greatly changed the nature of life. Most important however were new diseases, like measles and chicken pox, which gradually killed off about 80 percent of the Native American population. The resultant labor shortage helped encourage the final component of the exchange, the importation of African slaves by the millions.

Colonies Spain formed colonial centers in Central America and the Andes, overtaking Aztec and Inca governments. Spanish control also loomed large in the Caribbean. Portugal's American empire focused on Brazil. Later, Britain, France and Holland gained colonial holdings in North America and the Caribbean. Colonial holdings also formed in several parts of Asia and Africa, where Europe's advantage in naval weaponry was particularly relevant.

A World Economy Europe's growing dominance over key ocean trade routes and its role in brokering American products, like silver, gained new profits for trading companies and governments alike. Capitalism spread, as did government involvement, later enshrined in the politically competitive doctrine of mercantilism. American economies were increasingly geared to produce crops and raw materials for world trade. European profits grew, and manufacturing opportunities expanded as well. Asian economies prospered through their strong manufacturing output.

Recent Scholarship

Several recent books have captured key elements of the new world economy that resulted from European ventures and the inclusion of the Americas. *White and Deadly: Sugar and Colonialism* (1999) does an excellent job in showing vital new connections. Sugar was a product that had already caught European fancy; it now became a mass consumer item dependent on global production and trade. Essays show the efforts to spread production of sugar not only in the Americas but in Africa and Indonesia. Labor systems receive appropriate attention, as does the rise of corporate involvement in sugar colonies.

Differentiating Instruction

 Differentiated Instruction Teacher Management System
- Pacing Guide
- Lesson Plans for Differentiated Instruction

 Interactive Reader and Study Guide

Spanish Chapter Summaries Audio CD Program

Student Edition on Audio CD Program

 Differentiated Instruction Modified Worksheets and Tests CD-ROM
- Vocabulary Flash Cards
- Modified Vocabulary Builder Activities
- Modified Chapter Review Activity
- Modified Chapter Test

OSP **One-Stop Planner CD-ROM**
- ExamView Test Generator (English/Spanish)
- PuzzlePro
- Quiz Show for ExamView
- Transparencies and Videos

TE **Differentiated Activities in the Teacher's Edition**
- Explorers throughout History, p. 470
- Europeans Encounter the Aztecs and Incas, p. 477
- Markets and Manufactured Goods, p. 485
- Columbus and the Native Americans, p. 492

BEFORE YOU TEACH

Reading Like a Historian
Sam Wineburg

Understatement can sometimes distance us from the grit of historical understanding, shaving off the very details that provide a toehold to insight. This may be the case with our chapter's description of the Aztecs and their neighbors. "Though the Aztec were very powerful," we are told, "they were very unpopular with the people they had conquered." Perhaps because they ate them?

The Scale of Aztec Sacrifice That the Aztecs practiced human sacrifice is widely known, but its dimensions—unless you've studied this culture—will be beyond you or your students' wildest calculations. The priestly blood cult was anything but a "remote, top of the pyramid" affair in the words of Inga Clendinnen, author of *Aztecs: An Interpretation*. Rather, the blood of sacred killing leached into all levels of Aztec society.

On the inauguration of the temple to Huitzilopochtli, Aztec god of war and sun, the air around Lake Texcoco was especially thick with the smell of fresh blood (could it be otherwise, when as many 20,000 humans were given over to the killing stone in a single day?). Such massive killings were special events. But smaller sacrifices—to lesser gods—stained the 18 months of the Aztec calendar. These killings were conducted locally in neighborhood temples, each staffed with its own team of priests. The priests themselves would pin down the victim's limbs as a flint knife punctured the chest below the rib cage to extract a still-pulsating heart. In the maintenance of this cult, all of the work leading up to and following the sacrifice, members of the Aztec laity were involved at every stage.

Prior to their sacrifice, victims had to be tended to and cared for, groomed in special cages that the Spanish, when they entered the capital Tenochtitlán, a thriving metropolis of about 200,000 people, mistakenly took for fattening cages. Commoners in the city's different wards were responsible for tending to the victims-to-be before their appointed date, dressing them up in the special sacrifice regalia, even plying them with wine on the night before "in order that they would not dread death."

It is afterwards, after victims' hearts were extracted and their skin flailed (so that warriors, draping the blood-drenched flesh over their backs, could parade through the streets), that we see how the cult of sacrifice infused all levels of Aztec society. As victims' bodies cascaded down the steps of the temple, old men collected the corpses and deposited them at the cultic butcher shops. Carvers severed the limbs—hands, feet and arms—and messengers would deliver the flesh to the waiting hearths of the commoners. For all, elite and commoner alike, the devouring and digesting of neighbors was a providential sign of their gods' favor. When these morsels of flesh came from close neighbors, the gods were especially pleased.

Bad Neighbors Sometimes war was waged for no other reason than to gain captives to feed this flesh industry and, as one might imagine, Tenochtitlán's unslakable blood-thirst made for bad neighbor policy. So, when Cortés laid siege to Tenochtitlán for four months in 1520, he had a lot already going for him as a recruiter. "The Indian empire," wrote Walter Prescott Webb some 150 years ago, "was in a manner conquered by Indians." According to Ross Hassig, author of three books on the Spanish conquest, the final defeat of Tenochtitlán was carried out by a small band of 350-400 Spaniards backed by an estimated 200,000 allies—Tlaxcalans, Huejotzincans, and other neighboring peoples—"even though they went virtually unacknowledged and certainly unrewarded."

The Aztec were "very unpopular" indeed. Eating your neighbors has never been a recipe for winning friends.

Chapter Main Ideas

Section 1 During the 1400s and 1500s European explorers—inspired by greed, curiosity, and the desire for glory and aided by new technologies—sailed to many previously unknown lands in the 1400s and 1500s.

Section 2 The countries of Europe established colonies in the lands they had discovered but, in some cases, only after violently conquering the native people who lived there.

Section 3 The creation of colonies in the Americas and elsewhere led to the exchange of new types of goods, the establishment of new patterns of trade, and new economic systems in Europe.

Section 4 Between the 1500s and 1800s millions of Africans were captured, shipped across the Atlantic Ocean, and sold as slaves in the Americas.

🖳 New York Standards

Key Idea 1 The study of world history requires an understanding of world cultures and civilizations, including an analysis of important ideas, social and cultural values, beliefs, and traditions. This study also examines the human condition and the connections and interactions of people across time and space and the ways different people view the same event or issue from a variety of perspectives.

Key Idea 4 The skills of historical analysis include the ability to investigate differing and competing interpretations of the theories of history, hypothesize about why interpretations change over time, explain the importance of historical evidence, and understand the concepts of change and continuity over time.

Key to Differentiating Instruction

Below Level

Basic-level activities designed for all students encountering new material

At Level

Intermediate-level activities designed for average students

Above Level

Challenging activities designed for honors and gifted and talented students

Standard English Mastery

Activities designed to improve standard English usage

CHAPTER

16 1400–1700

Exploration and Expansion

THE BIG PICTURE Between 1400 and 1700, a new world opened up for Europe. Sailors set out on great voyages of discovery to lands that the people of Europe had not previously known existed. As news of the discoveries spread, countries scrambled to claim new lands, setting up colonies in hopes of gaining wealth and power. Once colonies were established, ships crossed the Atlantic in both directions laden with goods of all kinds.

Theme MIGRATION AND DIFFUSION
The arrival of Christopher Columbus in the Americas in 1492 was a turning point in world history. In the years that followed Columbus's voyage, European migration to the Americas took off, and the diffusion of goods and ideas changed societies worldwide.

Map showing the last voyage of Willem Barents, by Gerrit de Veer, 1596–97

TIME LINE

CHAPTER EVENTS

1419 Prince Henry the Navigator begins to support Portuguese exploration.

1488 Bartholomeu Dias rounds the tip of Africa.

1492 Christopher Columbus reaches the Americas.

1520 Magellan's ships sail around the southern tip of South America.

1400 — 1450 — 1500

WORLD EVENTS

1453 The Hundred Years' War ends.

1453 Constantinople falls to the Ottoman Turks.

1517 The Protestant Reformation begins.

466 CHAPTER 16

Introduce the Chapter

At Level

Exploration and Expansion

1. Tell students that during the period covered by this chapter, the nations of western Europe entered an Age of Exploration that resulted in the European discovery and colonization of the Americas.

2. Have each student prepare a list of reasons why one country would want to conquer another and colonize it. Then have volunteers share their lists with the class.

3. Guide students in a discussion of the reasons presented using the following questions: What advantages did the home country obtain from having colonies? What challenges might the home country face in ruling its colonies? What advantages, if any, would the colony get from foreign rule? What challenges would the colony face?

4. Tell students that in this chapter they will learn about how European nations established colonies in the New World. **LS** Verbal-Linguistic

📝 **Alternative Assessment Handbook**, Rubrics 6: Cause and Effect; and 11: Discussions

Reading like a Historian

This map, drawn in the late 1500s, shows the region called Nova Zembla, a cluster of islands in the Arctic Ocean off the northern coast of Russia. This region was one of the many explored and mapped by Europeans in the Age of Discovery.

Analyzing Visuals What evidence on this map suggests the European drive to find and explore new lands and regions?

See **Skills Handbook**, p. H26

1602
Dutch capitalists form the East India Company.

1600

1644
The Ming dynasty ends in China.

1649
King Charles I is beheaded during the English Civil War.

EXPLORATION AND EXPANSION **467**

Explore the Time Line

1. When did Prince Henry begin to support navigation? *1419*

2. How long after Columbus reached America did the Protestant Reformation begin? *25 years*

3. What event happened in 1520? *Magellan's ships sailed around the southern tip of South America.*

Info to Know

Nova Zembla Not all nautical expeditions looking for a shorter northern route to China sailed west to find a Northwest Passage. The English and Dutch also searched for a Northeast Passage, but never got any farther than Nova Zembla. The island, off the north coast of Russia, was first sighted by an English ship in 1553. Nova Zembla is shown on the right side of the map above.

Make Inferences Why did the English and Dutch hope to find a Northeast Passage to China? *They thought it would be shorter than the usual route.*

● **Chapter Preview** ●

HOLT
History's Impact
► **Video Program: Exploration and Expansion**
See the Video Teacher's Guide for strategies for using the video segment.

Reading Like a Historian

Analyzing Visuals Novaya Zemlya, or "new land," is the Russian name for Nova Zembla. In the 1950s, the Soviet Union used these islands as a nuclear test site.

Answers

Reading Like a Historian *ships, navigation instruments, sea animals appear happy*

467

Geography Starting Points

Ptolemy's *Geography* The Greek astronomer Ptolemy was also famous for his treatise on cartography, or map-making. In it, he drew a map of the world as it was known to the Greeks and Romans of his time, around AD 100–150. The known world stretched from the Atlantic Ocean to China and southeast Asia, and from the Baltic Sea to central Africa. Ptolemy's *Geography* also included instructions for reconstructing his map based on the longitudes and latitudes of some 8,000 localities. Early manuscripts and printings of the *Geography* often included beautifully detailed maps based on his instructions. His book was an early best seller. A Latin translation with maps was published in the 15th century. It inspired Columbus's fateful decision to try to reach Asia by sailing west.

- 📦 **Map Transparency:** European Discovery, 1400–1700
- 📖 **World History Outline Maps**
- ✺ **Interactive Map:** European Discovery, 1400–1700

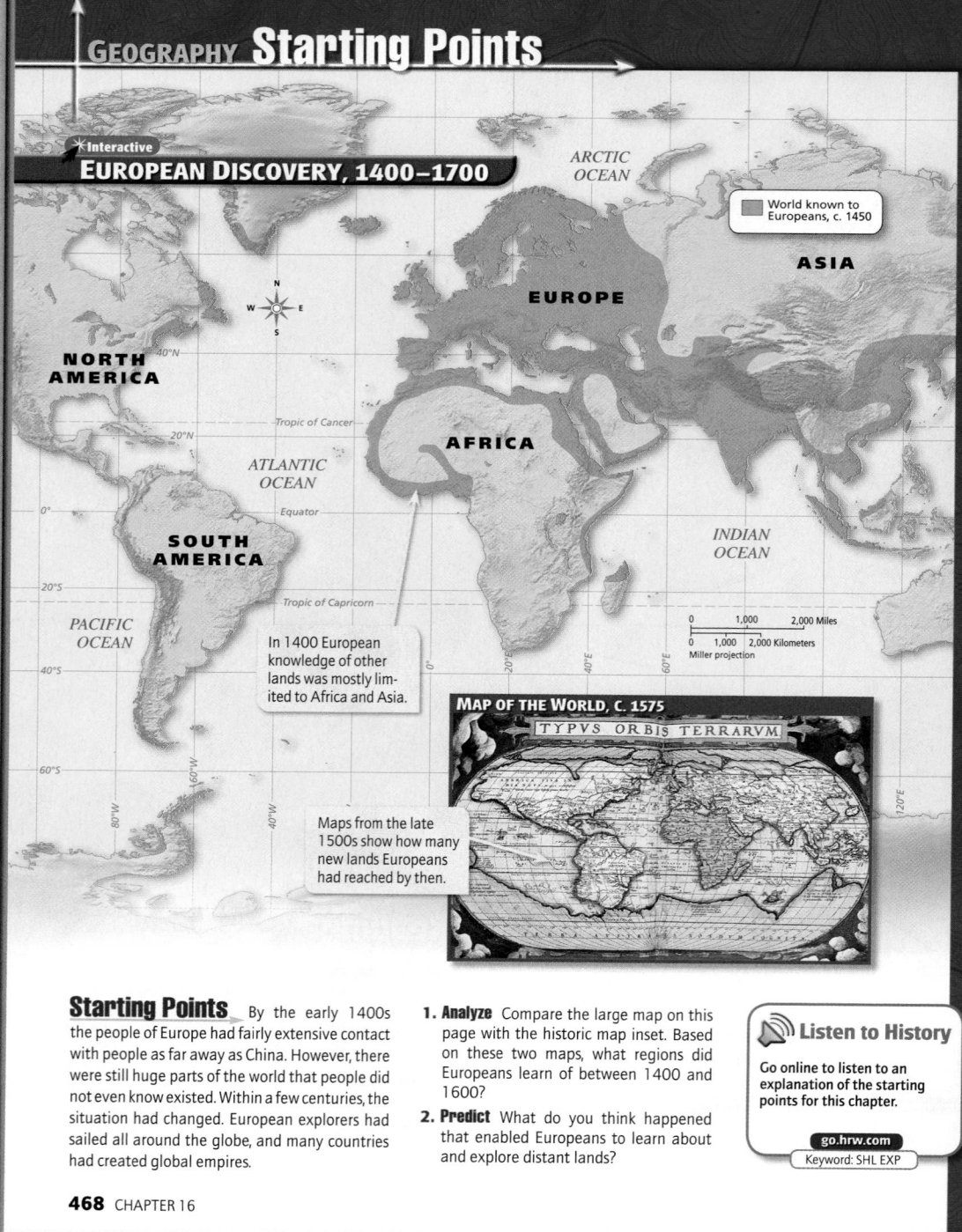

GEOGRAPHY Starting Points

✺Interactive EUROPEAN DISCOVERY, 1400–1700

World known to Europeans, c. 1450

In 1400 European knowledge of other lands was mostly limited to Africa and Asia.

MAP OF THE WORLD, C. 1575
TYPVS ORBIS TERRARVM

Maps from the late 1500s show how many new lands Europeans had reached by then.

Starting Points By the early 1400s the people of Europe had fairly extensive contact with people as far away as China. However, there were still huge parts of the world that people did not even know existed. Within a few centuries, the situation had changed. European explorers had sailed all around the globe, and many countries had created global empires.

1. **Analyze** Compare the large map on this page with the historic map inset. Based on these two maps, what regions did Europeans learn of between 1400 and 1600?

2. **Predict** What do you think happened that enabled Europeans to learn about and explore distant lands?

🔊 **Listen to History**

Go online to listen to an explanation of the starting points for this chapter.

go.hrw.com
Keyword: SHL EXP

468 CHAPTER 16

Skills Focus: Making Inferences

At Level

Reading Skill
A Different World

1. Have students consider what the world would be like if Europeans had never sailed west and discovered the Americas. Have students write a short essay describing what their lives might be like today if the Old World and New World had never come into contact. Where might they live? How might they live?

2. Have volunteers read their essays to the rest of the class.

3. Guide students in a discussion of the profound changes that were brought about as a result of the European voyages of discovery between 1400 and 1700. 🆂 **Verbal-Linguistic**

📖 **Alternative Assessment Handbook**, Rubrics 11: Discussions; and 40: Writing to Describe

Answers

Geography Starting Points
1. *southern Africa and North and South America;* 2. *possible answer—better ships and navigational skills*

Voyages of Discovery

BEFORE YOU READ

MAIN IDEA

During the 1400s and 1500s European explorers—Inspired by greed, curiosity, and the desire for glory and aided by new technologies—sailed to many previously unknown lands.

READING FOCUS

1. What were the foundations upon which the Age of Exploration was built?
2. What discoveries were made by explorers from Portugal and Spain?
3. What drove explorers from the rest of Europe?

KEY TERMS AND PEOPLE

caravel
Henry the Navigator
Vasco da Gama
Christopher Columbus
Ferdinand Magellan
circumnavigate
Sir Francis Drake
Henry Hudson

NEW YORK

 1.2 Students understand the development and connectedness of Western civilization and other civilizations and cultures in many areas of the world and over time.

THE INSIDE STORY

How wide was the sea? When Christopher Columbus set out to reach Asia by sailing across the Atlantic in 1492, he did not expect the voyage to be long. Like many Europeans, Columbus was aware that the earth was round, but he did not realize how large it was. Nor did he realize that two continents—the Americas—lay between him and his goal.

For nearly a month, Columbus and his crew sailed with no land in sight. After weeks without even a glimpse of land, many of Columbus's sailors were getting restless. They feared that the small fleet would run out of food or water, and they wanted to return home to Spain.

Columbus convinced the crew to sail on for a few more days. Before long, watchful sailors began to spot signs of land, such as birds flying overhead. Finally, on October 12, the shout that the crew had been waiting for rang out: land had been spotted. That land was the Caribbean island now called San Salvador. Columbus was in a land previously unknown to Europeans, but he did not realize it. He firmly believed he had achieved his goal of reaching Asia by sailing west, a belief he held for the rest of his life. ■

Foundations of Exploration

During the Renaissance, a spirit of discovery and innovation had been awakened in Europe. In the later part of the 1400s and 1500s, that spirit led Europeans to set sail on voyages of discovery to find new lands or new routes to places already known. Such voyages were so frequent and influential that the period is sometimes called the Age of Exploration.

LAND AHOY!

A statue of Christopher Columbus in the Dominican Republic commemorates his arrival in the Caribbean in 1492.

EXPLORATION AND EXPANSION **469**

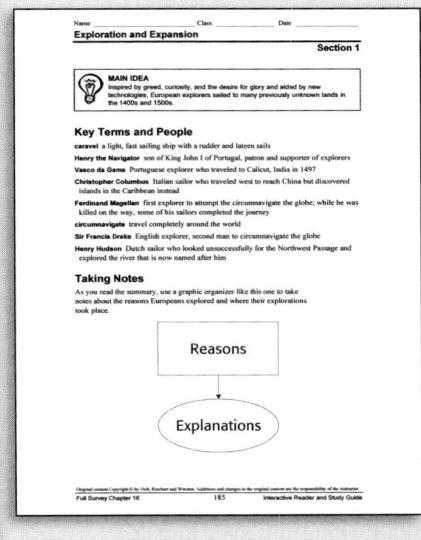

Teach the Main Idea   **At Level**

Voyages of Discovery

1. **Teach** Ask students the Reading Focus questions to teach this section.

2. **Apply** Have students create charts of the explorers mentioned in this section. Student charts should include the explorers' names, dates, country for which they explored, and achievements or discoveries.

3. **Review** Review student charts as a class, and create a master chart for students to see. Guide students in a discussion of the accomplishments of the early explorers.

4. **Practice/Homework** Have each student choose one of the explorers and write a resumé of his accomplishments. (If necessary, review standard resumé formats with students or provide sample resumés for them to imitate.) **LS** **Visual-Spatial, Verbal-Linguistic**

🗐 **Alternative Assessment Handbook**, Rubrics 7: Charts; and 31: Resumés

1 What were the foundations upon which the Age of Exploration was built? *a spirit of discovery and innovation during the Renaissance, technology borrowed from other cultures*

Foundations of Exploration

Summarize What changes in technology helped improve navigation? *compass to determine direction, astrolabe to determine distance from equator, new type of ship called the caravel*

Rank What do you think was the main motive that drove the Age of Exploration? Why? *possible answer— Money was probably the motive; merchants outside Italy wanted to get expensive luxury goods without having to pay the high prices demanded by Italian merchants who controlled trade with Asia.*

 CRF: Interdisciplinary Project: Geometry, Math, and Navigation

---

 TAKING NOTES
Use a graphic organizer like this one to take notes on the reasons Europeans explored and where their explorations took place.

> Reasons
> ↓
> Explorations

The Drive to Explore Like many other events in history, the Age of Exploration was driven in large part by the search for wealth. For years, Europeans had desired expensive luxury goods such as spices, silk, perfume, and jade from China and India. The flow of these goods to Europe was controlled by Italian merchants, who charged high prices for the rare goods. Many of the explorers who set out from Europe in the 1400s and 1500s hoped to find new, faster routes to Asia that they could use to gain a foothold in this trade.

Wealth was not the only goal that drove people to explore, though. Some people set out on voyages to find fame and glory. They hoped that making a great discovery would bring honor to their names.

Other explorers hoped to spread their faith into new lands. The Reformation and Counter-Reformation had brought a new religious zeal to Europe, and some Europeans saw the search for new lands as a chance to introduce new populations to Christian teachings.

One final motive for braving uncharted ocean waters was simple curiosity. Writings by medieval travelers such as Marco Polo, who had lived in the Mongol court of China for many years, were very popular in Europe. These writings intrigued many explorers with their tales of exotic lands and peoples.

Advances in Technology Whatever their reasons for exploring, Europeans could not have made their voyages of discovery without certain key advances in technology. Some of these advances were made in Europe during the Renaissance, and others were borrowed from people with whom the Europeans had contact, especially the Chinese and Muslims.

To make long voyages, sailors needed precise means to calculate their location. This means was provided by the introduction of the compass and the astrolabe to Europe. Brought to Europe from China, the compass let sailors know at any time which direction was north. The astrolabe, which Europeans first learned how to use from Muslims, allowed navigators to calculate their location based on the position of the sun and stars in relation to the horizon. Together, the compass and the astrolabe allowed sailors to plot courses even when they were out of sight of land.

Just as important as these advances in navigation were the advances Europeans made in shipbuilding. First, Europeans learned to build ships that rode lower in the water than earlier ships. These deep-draft ships, as they were called, were capable of withstanding heavier waves than earlier ships could. These ships also typically had larger cargo holds and thus could carry more supplies.

Themes Through Time

Exploration

MIGRATION AND DIFFUSION Though the spirit of exploration that struck Europe in the 1400s was new, exploration itself was not a new idea. People have been exploring the world around them since ancient times, and the drive to explore affects people even today.

c. 600 BC Phoenician sailors explore the west coast of Africa.

c. 1325–1350 Muslim writer Ibn Battutah travels through Southwest Asia, Africa, India, and China.

1200

1271–1292 European merchant Marco Polo travels through China and southeast Asia.

Marco Polo arriving at Hormuz, by the Boucicaut Master, c. 1400s

470

Differentiating Instruction

Learners Having Difficulty

1. Have students name as many explorers from this time period as they can. Write the explorers' names for all students to see.

2. Group students together in mixed-ability pairs and have each pair choose one name from the list. Then have pairs write answers to the following questions: What discoveries did the explorer make? What country did he represent? When did he make his explorations? What were the immediate and long-term results of the explorer's discoveries?

3. Have pairs use the answers to write a paragraph about their chosen explorers.

4. Guide students in a discussion of exploration. What characteristics did all the explorers have in common? Where do today's explorers travel? How does exploration today differ from exploration in previous centuries?
LS **Verbal-Linguistic**

Alternative Assessment Handbook, Rubric 42: Writing to Inform

Another new ship that aided in exploration was the **caravel**, a light, fast sailing ship. The caravel had two features that made it highly maneuverable. First, it was steered with a rudder at the stern, or rear, of the ship rather than the side oars used on earlier ships. In addition, it was equipped with lateen sails, triangular sails that could be turned to catch wind from any direction. Lateen sails could even be used to sail directly into a headwind.

Another advantage of the caravel was that it could be equipped with weapons, including cannons. Armed with cannons, the ship's crew could face off against hostile ships at sea. Based on its maneuverability and defensive ability, the caravel quickly became the most popular ship for exploratory voyages.

READING CHECK **Summarize** How did advances in technology spur exploration?

Explorers from Portugal and Spain

Portugal and Spain share the Iberian Peninsula, the westernmost extent of continental Europe. As a result of their location facing the Atlantic Ocean, these two countries were well suited to kicking off the Age of Exploration.

The Portuguese Portugal was the first country to launch large-scale voyages of exploration. These voyages were begun largely due to the efforts of one man, Prince Henry, the son of King John I of Portugal. Though he is often called **Henry the Navigator**, the prince was not himself an explorer. Instead, he was a patron and supporter of those who wished to explore.

In the early 1400s Henry established a small court to which he brought sailors, mapmakers, astronomers, and others who were interested in navigation. From this court, Henry sent expeditions west to islands in the Atlantic and south to explore the western coast of Africa. As a result of these voyages, the Portuguese began to settle the Azores and Madeira Islands in the Atlantic. Portuguese sailors also learned a great deal about Africa's coast, including the fact that both gold and slaves were available in the area.

Prince Henry's ultimate goal was to find a water route around Africa to India. He died before that goal could be accomplished, but. Portuguese explorers did not abandon their attempts to find such a route. In 1488 Bartolomeu Dias became the first European to attempt to sail around the southern tip of Africa, a point today known as the Cape of Good Hope. Dias and his crew might have sailed farther, but violent storms forced to turn back.

READING SKILLS
Questioning As you read, ask yourself how Prince Henry supported exploration.

Reading Focus

② What discoveries were made by explorers from Portugal and Spain? *learned about Africa; found sea route to India; landed in the Americas; circumnavigated the world*

Explorers from Portugal and Spain

Explain Why did Portugal turn toward the Atlantic Ocean rather than the Mediterranean Sea for exploration? *possible answer—because Portugal borders the Atlantic instead of the Mediterranean*

Identify Cause and Effect What was Prince Henry's reason for bringing together people interested in navigation? *to raise his sailors' chances of success in exploring the African coast*

📄 **CRF**: Biography: Vasco da Gama

📄 **CRF**: History and Geography: Portuguese Explorers in Africa

1405–1433 Chinese admiral Zheng He explores lands all around the Indian Ocean.

1492 Christopher Columbus sails to the Americas.

1768–1779 Captain James Cook explores the South Pacific.

Mid-1800s Large-scale exploration of the polar regions begins.

Mid-1900s New technology allows the exploration of space to begin.

1600

1900

Skills FOCUS **UNDERSTANDING THEMES**

1. **Draw Conclusions** How does exploration lead to migration and the diffusion of ideas?
2. **Elaborate** How have recent advances in technology encouraged exploration?

EXPLORATION AND EXPANSION **471**

Skills Focus: Summarizing

At Level

Reading Skill
The Technology of Exploration

1. Have students create a four-column chart about technology that aided overseas exploration in the 1400s. The first column should identify the technological advances. The second column should describe each advance and the third column should explain how it aided exploration. In the fourth column, students should number the advances to rank their importance, with 1 being most important.

2. Review student charts as a class, creating a master chart for all to see. How did students rank the advances? Was there a consensus, or did student opinions vary widely?

3. Guide students in a discussion of the ways in which technological advances combined with the drive to explore. **LS Visual-Spatial, Logical-Mathematical**

📄 **Alternative Assessment Handbook**, Rubric 7: Charts

Answers

Reading Skills *possible response—He brought together people interested in exploration and navigation; financed expeditions*

Themes Through Time 1. *causes new lands to become available for settlement, causes different cultures to come into contact and share ideas;* **2.** *New technology has made the exploration of space possible.*

Reading Check *new ships faster and more maneuverable, could better handle sea voyages; navigational instruments allowed for voyages of exploration*

Info to Know

The Astrolabe Sailors of the 1500s had only a few simple tools—such as the astrolabe—to guide them. Using the position of the sun and stars, these explorers sailed the oceans of the world. They could plot and hold a course and measure their progress. Astrolabes helped them estimate where they were with respect to land. These devices, which take their name from the Greek word for "star," were usually made of brass or iron. To use the astrolabe, a sailor would sight a star along the attached bar. By lining up the bar with markings on a disk, he could figure out the latitude of his ship's position. Astrolabes were used until the 18th century, when they were replaced by the more accurate sextant.

Pedro Cabral On his visit to Calicut, Pedro Cabral encountered problems with the Arab merchants controlling the port. The Arabs attacked the Portuguese trading booths, killing some of the sailors. Cabral bombarded the city and then sailed south to the rival city of Cochin to trade.

Ferdinand Magellan Ferdinand Magellan was convinced that he could reach the Spice Islands in East Asia by sailing west. The circumnavigation of the globe by his fleet was not only a great achievement of navigation and courage, it was also the first proof that the world was round.

🗺 **Map Transparency:** Explorers and Their Routes

✳ **Interactive Map:** Explorers and Their Routes

Interactive
EXPLORERS AND THEIR ROUTES

Christopher Columbus sailed across the Atlantic to the Caribbean in 1492.

Vasco da Gama of Portugal sailed around the southern tip of Africa to India.

Excited by Dias's success, another Portuguese explorer, **Vasco da Gama**, set out for India in 1497. On the way da Gama stopped at several African ports, where he learned that Muslim merchants were already actively involved in trade. Though the journey took more than 10 months, da Gama and his crew eventually reached the city of Calicut in India.

The return of da Gama caused great excitement among the Portuguese, who hurried to send another expedition to India. This second trip was led by Pedro Cabral, who sailed far to the west to avoid the windless Gulf of Guinea. Not only did Cabral keep the wind behind his sails, but he and his men sighted and claimed the land that became known as Brazil.

In India, the Portuguese established trading centers from which they could ship goods back to Europe. In addition, Portuguese sailors from India sailed out to find other lands, such as Indonesia, that could supply valuable goods. As a result of this lucrative trade, Portugal became one of the richest and most powerful nations in Europe.

472 CHAPTER 16

Collaborative Learning

At Level

School for Navigators

Materials: poster paper, colored pencils or markers

1. Organize students into small groups. Tell students they work for the admissions department of a navigation school in the late 1400s. Have each group create a set of posters, brochures, advertisements, and other materials to recruit students for the school. Recruitment materials should provide information about the school's programs and explain how they will prepare students for a maritime career.

2. Have volunteers from each group share their recruitment materials with the rest of the class. **LS Visual-Spatial, Interpersonal**

📝 **Alternative Assessment Handbook**, Rubrics 28: Posters; and 43: Writing to Persuade

Portuguese exploration ← English exploration
Spanish exploration ← Dutch exploration
French exploration

EUROPE

ASIA

CHINA

JAPAN

Ferdinand Magellan's crew was the first to sail completely around the world.

Arabian Peninsula

INDIA

PHILIPPINES

MAGELLAN, 1519–1521

PACIFIC OCEAN

DA GAMA, 1497–1499

CABRAL, 1500–1501

DRAKE, 1577–1580

INDIAN OCEAN

EAST INDIES

TASMAN, 1642–1643

TASMAN, 1642–1643

TASMAN, 1644

DRAKE, 1577–1580

AUSTRALIA

ELCANO, 1521–1522

TASMAN, 1642–1643

Sir Francis Drake of England sailed around the world a few years after Magellan.

GEOGRAPHY SKILLS INTERPRETING MAPS

go.hrw.com
Interactive Map
Keyword: SHL EXP

1. **Place** Which country's explorers were most active in the area of the Caribbean Sea?

2. **Movement** How many years did Magellan's crew take to complete their journey around the world?

The Spanish Like Portugal, Spain was eager to seek out new routes to the riches of the East. In 1492 the Spanish rulers, King Ferdinand and Queen Isabella, agreed to pay for a voyage by Italian sailor **Christopher Columbus**. Columbus believed that he could sail west around the world from Spain to reach China.

Although Columbus was correct in theory, the figures he presented to the king and queen about the earth's size were wrong. He also had no idea that the Americas lay across the Atlantic. As a result, when Columbus reached

an island in the Caribbean after about two months at sea, he thought he had reached the Asian islands known as the Indies. As a result, he called the people living there Indians.

Columbus returned to Spain in March 1493 with many exotic items from the lands he had explored, including parrots, jewels, gold, and plants unknown in Europe. In addition, he brought several Native Americans back to Spain, where they were baptized as Christians. Believing that he had found a new route to Asia, the Spanish hailed Columbus as a hero.

NEW YORK

CC Unit 3-C4a
Exploration by Columbus

EXPLORATION AND EXPANSION **473**

Explorers from Portugal and Spain

Recall Which nation financed Columbus's voyages? *Spain*

Analyze Why did Columbus believe he had reached Asia? *His figures about the size of the earth were wrong; he did not know the Americas lay across the Atlantic.*

Interpret Why did mapmakers name America after Amerigo Vespucci and not Christopher Columbus? *Vespucci was the first to conclude the Americas were a new land and not part of Asia.*

Activity **Slogans** Have students create a slogan for Prince Henry's school for navigators. **Verbal-Linguistic**

Alternative Assessment Handbook, Rubric 24: Slogans and Banners

3 What drove explorers from the rest of Europe? *desire for shorter route to Asia, new trading partners, search for Northwest Passage*

Explorers from the Rest of Europe

Identify What other European nations undertook voyages of exploration? *England, France, the Netherlands*

Explain What common goals did explorers from these nations share? *quicker passage to Asia via a Northeast Passage, and through the Americas via a Northwest Passage*

Answers

Primary Sources *no fresh food or water; rats, worms; sickness and death*

Reading Check *da Gama—reached India via sea; Columbus—landed in the Americas; Magellan—circumnavigated the earth*

474

Columbus made three more voyages to the Americas, still believing that he had reached Asia. His error was not realized until about 1502, when explorer Amerigo Vespucci sailed along the coast of South America and concluded that it was not Asia but a new land. Later mapmakers named the land America in his honor.

Now knowing that they had found a new land, the Spanish set out to explore it. In 1513 Vasco Núñez de Balboa led an expedition across the Isthmus of Panama. After more than three weeks of difficult travel, Balboa became the first European to see the Pacific Ocean.

After Balboa's discovery, the Spanish realized they needed to cross another ocean to reach Asia. What they did not know was how large that ocean might be. To answer that question, a daring adventurer named **Ferdinand Magellan** decided to sail west around the world.

NEW YORK

CC Unit 3-C4b Exploration by Magellan

PRIMARY SOURCES

An Explorer's Journal

Life on an explorer's ship was harsh. Supplies were scarce, and many sailors grew ill. The passage below was written by an Italian writer who accompanied Magellan on his trip around the world. It describes the hardships the crew faced as they crossed the Pacific Ocean.

"We were three months and twenty days without getting any kind of fresh food. We ate biscuit, which was no longer biscuit, but powder of biscuits swarming with worms, for they had eaten the good. It stank strongly of the urine of rats. We drank yellow water that had been putrid for many days. We also ate some ox hides that covered the top of the mainyard to prevent the yard from chafing the shrouds, and which had become exceedingly hard because of the sun, rain, and wind. We left them in the sea for four or five days, and then placed them for a few moments on top of the embers, and so ate them; and often we ate sawdust from boards. Rats were sold for one-half ducado [gold coin] apiece, and even we could not get them. But above all the other misfortunes the following was the worst. The gums of both the lower and upper teeth of some of our men swelled, so they could not eat under any circumstances and therefore died."

Skills FOCUS READING LIKE A HISTORIAN

Interpret What made the trip across the Pacific so difficult for Magellan's sailors?

See **Skills Handbook, p. H25**

474 CHAPTER 16

Born in Portugal but sailing for Spain, Magellan set out in 1519 with five ships and about 250 men. His journey was long and difficult, and some of his men mutinied, or rebelled. After months at sea, Magellan's fleet reached the Philippines, where Magellan was killed in a fight against the native people. His men sailed on, however, led by Juan Sebastián de Elcano. In early September 8, 1522, 18 survivors of the original fleet arrived in Spain. They were the first people ever to **circumnavigate**, or sail completely around, the world.

READING CHECK Analyze What did da Gama, Columbus, and Magellan accomplish?

Explorers from the Rest of Europe

Though the Spanish and Portuguese were the first to launch voyages of discovery, they did not remain alone in their efforts. By the early 1500s the English and French were exploring the northern parts of the Americas, and within a century the Dutch had joined the efforts.

The English The first major English voyage of discovery was launched just a few years after Columbus reached the Caribbean. In 1497 a sailor named John Cabot sailed from England to the Atlantic coast of what is now Canada. Like Columbus, Cabot thought that he had reached Asia. After returning to England, Cabot set out once more to repeat his voyage, but he never returned. His entire fleet vanished, presumably sunk.

Like the Spanish, the English soon realized that they had not reached Asia but a previously unknown land. In response, the English queen sent **Sir Francis Drake** to round the tip of South America and explore its west coast. After a stop in what is now California, Drake sailed north to seek a route around North America back to the Atlantic. However, the weather proved too cold, and he ended up heading west around the world to get back to England. He became the second man to circumnavigate the globe.

Eager for success, England's rulers wanted to find a shorter route to Asia than Magellan had found. In search of this route, they sent a Dutch-born sailor named **Henry Hudson**. In 1607 Hudson set out to the north, hoping to

---

Collaborative Learning

At Level

Explorers Wanted

1. Organize students into small groups. Tell students it is 1481 and King John II of Portugal has asked them to help him recruit explorers. Have each group think of characteristics that would make a good explorer—personality, education, background, etc.—and write a job description for the position. Job descriptions should mention risks involved in the profession, as well as compensation (salary, bonuses, and other benefits such as insurance and pension plans).

2. Next, have each group create a newspaper display advertisement to attract applicants. Student display ads might include artwork, and should list main points from the job description.

3. Have volunteers from each group share their job descriptions and newspaper ads with the rest of the class. **Interpersonal, Visual-Spatial**

Alternative Assessment Handbook, Rubrics 2: Advertisements; and 14: Group Activity find a Northeast Passage around Europe. Finding nothing but ice, he returned to England. Later, Hudson set out on two more voyages for the English and one for the Dutch.

The French Like the English, the French wanted to find a passage to Asia. They sent explorers to look for a Northwest Passage that would take them around the northern reaches of North America. One of the French explorers who sought this passage was Jacques Cartier, who left France in 1534. Cartier sailed past the island of Newfoundland into the St. Lawrence River. He claimed all the land along the river as the province of New France, or as it came to be called later, Canada. Later French explorers added to Cartier's claims, but none ever found a Northwest Passage.

The Dutch By the early years of the 1600s, the Netherlands—once a Spanish possession—had become a powerful trading nation. Already heavily involved in trade with Asia but hoping to find new products and new trading partners, the Dutch soon became involved in the exploration of the Americas as well.

One of these Dutch explorers was Henry Hudson, the same man who had sailed for the English before. In 1609, he once again set out to find a Northeast Passage around Asia. Once again unsuccessful, he instead headed west to seek a Northwest Passage through the

Henry Hudson greeted by Native Americans, The Granger Collection, New York

Henry Hudson
Henry Hudson, who sailed for both England and the Netherlands, explored the area we now call New York.

Americas. Though he did not find the passage he sought, he did explore the river that now bears his name. Though the river is named for Hudson, it had actually been discovered years earlier by Giovanni da Verazzano, an Italian explorer sailing for France. Hudson also reached and explored Hudson Bay.

READING CHECK **Find the Main Idea** What did English, French, and Dutch explorers hope to find?

---

go.hrw.com
Online Quiz
Keyword: SHL EXP HP

SECTION 1 ASSESSMENT

Reviewing Ideas, Terms, and People

1. a. Identify What were four reasons that drove people to explore new lands?
   b. Explain How did devices like the astrolabe, compass, and caravel help promote exploration?
   c. Support a Position Do you agree or disagree with this statement: "The Age of Exploration could not have occurred without the Renaissance"? Support your answer.

2. a. Describe For what is **Vasco da Gama** best known? For what is **Ferdinand Magellan** known?
   b. Summarize Why was **Christopher Columbus** mistaken about the land he had found?
   c. Elaborate What role did **Henry the Navigator** play in launching the Age of Exploration?

3. a. Recall What goal did English, French, and Dutch explorers share with the Spanish and Portuguese? How was their approach to the Americas different?

   b. Explain Why did **Sir Francis Drake** end up sailing completely around the world?

Critical Thinking

4. Categorize Draw a chart like the one below. Using your notes, identify the major explorers that sailed for each country and the areas that they explored.

European Explorers				
Portugal	Spain	England	France	Netherlands

FOCUS ON WRITING

5. Persuasion Write a letter as though you were a European explorer trying to convince a monarch to fund your expedition. Your letter should point out why you want to explore.

EXPLORATION AND EXPANSION **475**

• **Review & Assess** •

Close
Have students explain the impact of technology on exploration in the 1400s.

Review
Online Quiz, Section 1

Assess
SE Section 1 Assessment
Progress Assessment: Section 1 Quiz
Alternative Assessment Handbook

Reteach/Intervene
Interactive Reader and Study Guide, Section 1
Interactive Skills Tutor CD-ROM

Answers
Reading Check *a shorter route to Asia*

Section 1 Assessment Answers

1. a. search for wealth, fame and glory, desire to spread faith, curiosity
   b. made longer sea voyages possible, improved navigation
   c. possible answer—agree: The Renaissance awakened a spirit of discovery and innovation in Europe.

2. a. da Gama—sea route to India; Magellan—circumnavigation of the world
   b. He believed he was in Asia.

c. brought together people interested in exploration and navigation, financed expeditions

3. a. trade with Asia; sought a shorter route
   b. The weather was too cold to return the way he came, and he continued sailing west.

4. Portugal—Dias: southern Africa; da Gama: India; Cabral: India, Brazil; Spain—Columbus: Caribbean; Vespucci: South America; Balboa: Panama, Pacific

Ocean; Magellan: circumnavigation of world; England—Drake: southern tip of South America, circumnavigation of world; Hudson: North America; France—Cartier: Newfoundland, Canada; Netherlands—Hudson: Hudson Bay

5. Student letters should include the major reasons for exploration during this period, including religious zeal, curiosity, and the search for wealth, fame, and glory.

Conquest and Colonies

Preteach

Getting Started

Use the **Interactive Reader and Study Guide** to familiarize students with the section content.

📋 **Interactive Reader and Study Guide,** Section 2

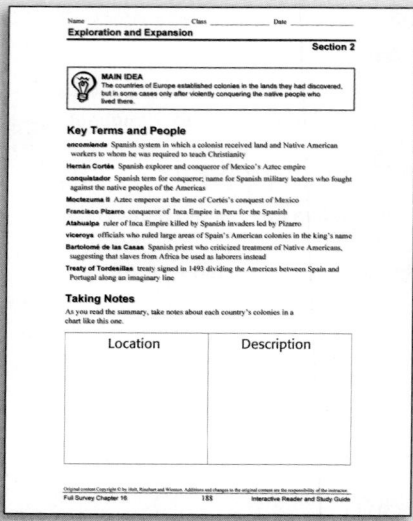

📋 **CRF:** Vocabulary Builder: Section 2

Taking Notes

Spain—Location: Caribbean, Mexico, South America; Description: Aztec Empire, Inca Empire, gold, silver, farming; Portugal—Location: Brazil; Description: heavy jungles made mining and farming difficult; France—Location: New France, or Canada, south into North America; Description: rich in fish, furs, fewer colonists sent there; Netherlands—Location: Hudson River valley; Description: small settlement; England—Location: Virginia, Massachusetts; Description: marshy ground, impure water

go.hrw.com
Online Resources

KEYWORD: SHL EXP
ACTIVITY: Exploration and Expansion

BEFORE YOU READ

MAIN IDEA

The countries of Europe established colonies in the lands they had discovered but, in some cases, only after violently conquering the native people who lived there.

READING FOCUS

1. How did Spain build an empire in the Americas?
2. What kind of colony did the Portuguese establish in Brazil?
3. What was life like in the French, Dutch, and English colonies in the Americas?

KEY TERMS AND PEOPLE

encomienda
Hernán Cortés
conquistador
Moctezuma II
Francisco Pizarro
Atahualpa
viceroys
Bartolomé de Las Casas
Treaty of Tordesillas

 NEW YORK

PI 1.1 Students define culture and civilization, explaining how they developed and changed over time. Investigate the various components of cultures and civilizations, including social customs, political systems, and economic systems.

A FATEFUL MEETING

◄ The meeting between Cortés and Moctezuma was marked by the exchange of gifts.

Miniature of the meeting of Cortés and Moctezuma, from *History of the Indians*, by Diego Duran, 1579

THE INSIDE STORY

What happened when the Aztec king met Europeans for the first time? In 1519 Spaniard Hernán Cortés led a small force of soldiers into the interior of Mexico. His intention was to establish a Spanish colony there. Once in Mexico, he heard many tales of the powerful Aztec Empire and its mighty leader, Emperor Moctezuma II. Cortés and his troops set out to meet the emperor for themselves.

Just as Cortés had heard tales of Moctezuma, so the Aztec emperor had heard of the Spaniard. As Cortés neared the Aztec capital of Tenochtitlán, Moctezuma and his advisers headed out to meet him. According to one account, the two men met for the first time on one of the bridges that linked the island city to the mainland. Moctezuma, carried

on a litter by four servants, was a magnificent sight. Draped in gold and precious stones, he was shaded by a canopy of green feathers decorated with more gold and stones.

As he approached Moctezuma, Cortés dismounted from his horse and bowed deeply. Moctezuma returned the bow, and the two leaders exchanged gifts. Cortés presented Moctezuma with an elaborate necklace of perfumed glass beads, receiving in return wreaths and garlands of flowers, gold collars, and other items. Through interpreters, the men exchanged greetings and respectful comments.

The meeting of the Aztecs and the Europeans changed society in the region forever. Before long, Moctezuma was dead, and the Spanish and Aztecs were at war. Aztec dominance was ending, and a new society was forming. ■

476 CHAPTER 16

Teach the Main Idea

At Level

Conquest and Colonies

1. **Teach** Ask students the Reading Focus questions to teach this section.

2. **Apply** Have students create a time line of the major events in this section. Student time lines should begin with Cortés's expedition in 1519 and end with war between the British and French in 1754.

3. **Review** Review student time lines as a class. Have students identify the kinds of conflicts that might be expected to arise among the European nations colonizing the Americas.

4. **Practice/Homework** Each of the European nations that established colonies in the Americas had its own distinct system of governing its colonies. Have each student decide which nation's colony he or she would have preferred to live in and write a brief essay explaining why. **LS Visual-Spatial, Verbal-Linguistic**

📋 **Alternative Assessment Handbook,** Rubrics 36: Time Lines; and 40: Writing to Describe

Spain Builds an Empire

After European explorers reached the Americas, countries began to scramble to establish colonies and empires in the lands they had found. Among the first countries to successfully settle in the Americas was Spain, which eventually conquered the two greatest native empires of the Americas, the Aztecs and Incas.

Spain in the Caribbean The first areas settled by the Spanish were Caribbean islands such as Hispaniola and Cuba. When Columbus first arrived in the area, he had hoped to find huge quantities of gold. In this, he was disappointed. However, the Spanish still hoped to make his discovery profitable by introducing the *encomienda* system to the Caribbean.

In the *encomienda* system, a colonist was given a certain amount of land and a number of Native Americans to work the land for him. In exchange, the colonist was required to teach the native workers about Christianity. This system became the basis for nearly all Spanish settlements on the mainland as well.

The *encomienda* system was disastrous for Native Americans. Overwork and mistreatment took a horrendous toll on the native population. Even worse, however, were the diseases spread by Europeans. Smallpox, tuberculosis, measles, and other deadly diseases had previously been unknown in the Americas. For this reason, Native Americans had no resistance to these illnesses, and millions died.

The Conquest of Mexico From the Caribbean some Spaniards moved to the mainland to set up colonies. One such person was **Hernán Cortés**, who led an expedition to Mexico that ended with the conquest of the Aztec Empire. Cortés was a **conquistador**, or conqueror, a term applied to Spanish military leaders who fought against the native peoples of the Americas.

At the time of the Spanish arrival in Mexico, the Aztec emperor was **Moctezuma II**. Though the Aztecs were very powerful and ruled much of Mexico, they were unpopular with those they had conquered. Cortés was able to use this lack of popularity to his advantage. By the time he reached the Aztec capital, Tenochtitlán, Cortés's small band of Spanish soldiers had been joined by thousands of Native Americans who wanted to defeat the Aztecs.

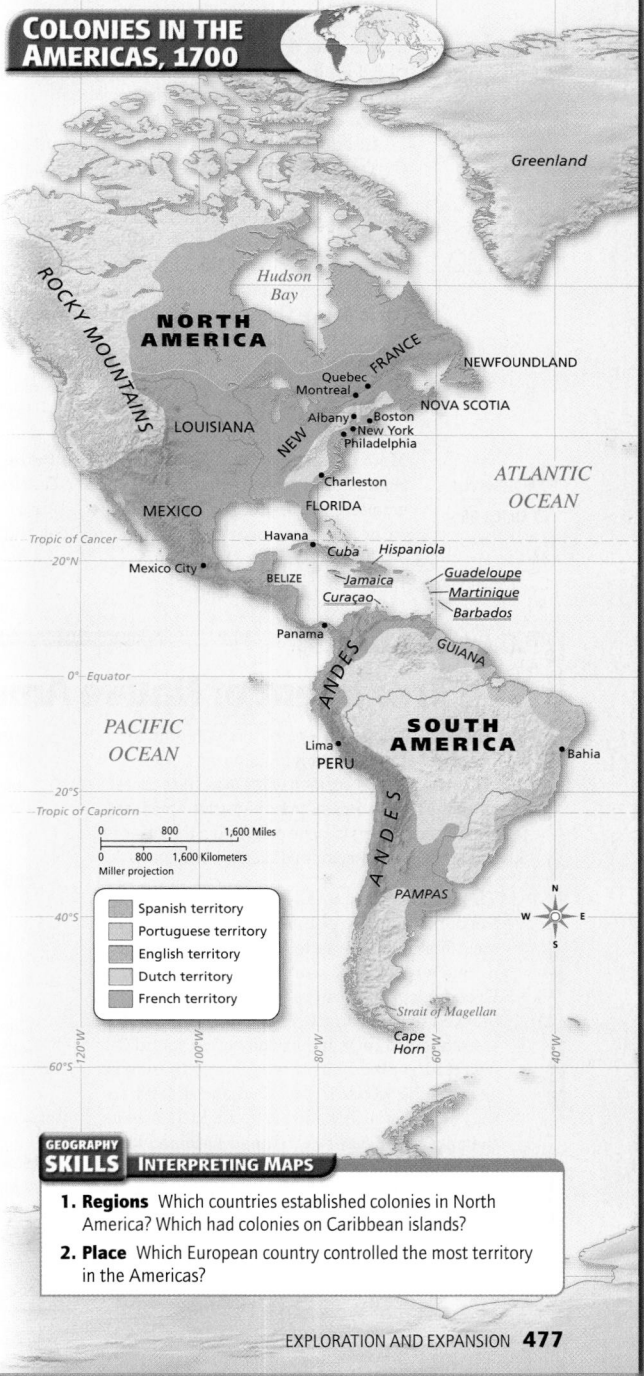

COLONIES IN THE AMERICAS, 1700

Spanish territory
Portuguese territory
English territory
Dutch territory
French territory

GEOGRAPHY SKILLS | INTERPRETING MAPS

1. **Regions** Which countries established colonies in North America? Which had colonies on Caribbean islands?

2. **Place** Which European country controlled the most territory in the Americas?

EXPLORATION AND EXPANSION **477**

Differentiating Instruction

Above Level

Advanced Learners/Gifted and Talented

Research Required

1. Have students research at least one aspect of either the Aztec or Inca civilization at the time the conquistadors first arrived, such as religion, architecture, or agriculture.

2. Tell students that they are members of either Cortés's expedition in Mexico or Pizarro's expedition in Peru, depending on the civilization they researched. Have students write a series of journal entries describing the civilization they discovered from the point of view of a 16th-century European encountering it for the first time.

3. Have volunteers read their journal entries to the class.

4. Guide students in a discussion of the Aztec and Inca cultures based on their research. How were these cultures different than the culture of the Europeans who conquered them? **LS Verbal-Linguistic**

Alternative Assessment Handbook, Rubrics 30: Research; and 42: Writing to Inform

Reading Focus

❶ How did Spain build an empire in the Americas? *introduced* encomienda *system, conquered Aztec and Inca empires, viceroys governed land*

Spain Builds an Empire

Identify What was the *encomienda* system? *system in which a colonist was given land and Native Americans to work the land for him*

Make Inferences Why did Cortés find Malinche useful? *because she could serve as a translator between the Spanish and the Aztecs*

Predict What will be the outcome of Cortés's conquest of Tenochtitlán? *Mexico will become a major Spanish colony.*

🔲 **Map Transparency:** Colonies in the Americas

📄 **CRF:** Biography: Isabella I

📄 **CRF:** Primary Source: An Aztec Account of the Spanish Arrival in Tenochtitlán

Info to Know

Tenochtitlán In his letters, Hernán Cortés described Tenochtitlán: "This city has many squares where trading is done and markets are held continuously. There is also one square ... where every kind of merchandise produced in these lands is found.... There are shops like apothecaries', where they sell ready-made medicines as well as liquid ointments and plasters. There are shops like barbers' where they have their hair washed and shaved, and shops where they sell food and drink."

Answers

Interpreting Maps 1. *North America—France, Spain, England; Caribbean—France, Spain, England, the Netherlands;* **2.** *Spain*

477

Reading Focus

Spain Builds an Empire

Recall What two major empires did the conquistadors encounter in the Americas? *Aztec and Inca*

Evaluate What do you think was the motive of the Spanish in seeking to convert the Indians to Christianity? *possible answer—They probably believed that they were saving the Indians' souls and "civilizing" them.*

Info to Know

Aztec and Inca Unrest in the Aztec and Inca Empires contributed to their defeat by the Spanish. Both groups had built their empires in the 1400s, often through the conquest of their neighbors, and both had to put down frequent rebellions in the decades that followed. The Inca were in the midst of a civil war when the Spanish arrived in 1530. Cortés and Pizarro exploited such tensions among native peoples to gain control of both empires.

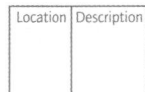
For each country you read about, take notes about its colonies in a chart like this one.

Location	Description

NEW YORK

CC Unit 3-E6
Spanish colonialism

Among the Native Americans who joined Cortés was a woman named Malintzin, also called Malinche. Because she was able to speak the Aztec language, Malintzin became invaluable to Cortés as a translator.

In addition to his Native American allies, Cortés had several other advantages that helped him defeat the Aztecs. He had metal weapons and heavy armor, neither of which was known to the Aztecs, as well as guns. Also, Cortés and a few of his soldiers rode horses, animals never before seen in the Americas. Some Aztecs were so scared at their first sight of the horses that they fled in terror. As it had in the Caribbean, disease also swept through the Aztec Empire, killing thousands of people.

On November 8, 1519, Cortés and his army entered Tenochtitlán. Though Cortés and Moctezuma greeted each other respectfully, the Spanish soon took the emperor prisoner. Battle erupted, during which Moctezuma was killed. After months of heavy fighting, Cortés took the city and the entire Aztec Empire.

The Conquest of Peru About 10 years after the conquest of the Aztecs, a conquistador named **Francisco Pizarro** led an expedition to Peru. Pizarro had heard of the fabulous wealth of Peru's Inca Empire, and he hoped to win some of that wealth for himself.

The Inca Empire that Pizarro found was already weakened significantly. Smallpox had recently swept through, killing many people, including the emperor. In the wake of the emperor's death, civil war had broken out. A new ruler, **Atahualpa**, had only just taken control of the empire when the Spanish arrived.

Atahualpa heard of the Spaniards' arrival and agreed to meet with them in 1532. At that meeting, Pizarro demanded that Atahualpa accept Christianity and hand over his empire to Spain. Atahualpa refused, and the Spanish took him prisoner. Though Atahualpa gave Pizarro a huge fortune in gold and silver, the Spanish killed him and headed south to Cuzco, the Inca capital. There they destroyed the Inca army and took over the empire.

PRIMARY SOURCES

The Treatment of Native Americans

Bartolomé de Las Casas was vocal in his protests of the treatment of Native Americans by Europeans. In his *Brief Account of the Destruction of the Indies,* Las Casas described the terrible ordeals that the Native Americans faced as forced laborers, despite orders from the king of Spain that they be protected and taught Christianity.

"The Indians were totally deprived of their freedom and were put in the harshest, fiercest, most horrible servitude and captivity which no one who has not seen it can understand. Even beasts enjoy more freedom when they are allowed to graze in the fields. When the Indians were allowed to go home, they often found it deserted and had no other recourse than to go out into the woods to find food and die. When they fell ill, which was very frequently because they are a delicate people unaccustomed to such work, the Spaniards did not believe them and pitilessly called them lazy dogs, and kicked and beat them; and when illness was apparent they sent them home as useless. I sometimes

came upon dead bodies on my way, and upon others who were gasping and moaning in their death agony, repeating "Hungry, hungry." And this was the freedom, the good treatment, and the Christianity that Indians received.

Is there a single nation which would not think that the world is full of just such evildoers as the Spaniards if their first experience with that outside world was with a people who entered territories by force, killed the people, and deprived them of their rights? Just because the Spaniards told them to obey the King of Castile [Spain], supposing they understood, what obligation did they have to obey since they already had their own kings?"

SKILLS FOCUS **READING LIKE A HISTORIAN**

1. **Analyze** According to Las Casas, how have the Spanish mistreated Native Americans?
2. **Draw Conclusions** For what audience do you think Las Casas was writing? What makes you think so?

See **Skills Handbook**, p. H25

Skills Focus: Identifying Problem and Solution   At Level

Reading Skill
Governing the Spanish Colonies in America

1. Guide students in a discussion of the *encomienda* system. How did the intentions of the *encomienda* system compare with the reality of it?

2. Organize students into small groups. Tell students they are advisers to the Spanish monarchs charged with developing a new system to replace the *encomienda* system. Have each group write a plan that will treat Native Americans well and still allow

development of the colonies. Each system should have a means of enforcing the requirement to treat natives well.

3. Have volunteers from each group share their plans with the rest of the class.
LS Interpersonal, Verbal-Linguistic

Alternative Assessment Handbook, Rubrics 14: Group Activity; and 35: Solving Problems

---

Answers

Primary Sources 1. *deprived them of freedom and made them slaves; mistreated them when they were ill and dying;* **2.** *possible answer—future Spanish colonists, because he implies that the Indians may fight back if they continue to suffer mistreatment*

Life in the Spanish Empire With the conquests of Mexico and Peru, Spain gained control of a huge empire in the Americas. To govern his American holdings, the Spanish king chose officials called **viceroys**, each of whom ruled a large area in the king's name.

The Spanish colonial economy was based largely on the mining of gold and silver, though farming was also common. For labor in both mines and on farms, the Spanish drafted Native Americans. However, disease and mistreatment took a toll on the native population, which dropped by more than 90 percent from an estimated 50 million to only 4 million.

Some Spaniards were appalled at the treatment of Native Americans and called on others to protect those who remained. The most vocal of these reformers was a priest named **Bartolomé de Las Casas**. In seeking to protect the Native Americans, however, Las Casas recommended replacing them as laborers with imported African slaves. Slave labor soon became a common practice in the Americas.

READING CHECK **Summarize** How did the Spanish create an empire in the Americas?

The Portuguese in Brazil

Like the Spanish, the Portuguese built an empire in the Americas. However, because of a treaty signed early in the Age of Exploration, their empire was not nearly as large as the Spanish one. The **Treaty of Tordesillas**, signed in 1494, drew an imaginary line through the Atlantic. Everything to the west of this line, including most of the then-undiscovered Americas, would belong to Spain. Everything to the east would be Portuguese. Of the Americas, only Brazil remained as a Portuguese colony.

Brazil's heavy jungles made both mining and farming difficult, so the Portuguese were in no hurry to settle there. Only in the 1530s did colonists slowly begin to move in, mostly along the Atlantic coast. When colonists did finally arrive, they established huge farming estates similar to those in the Spanish lands. Like the Spanish, the Portuguese first used Native American labor and then African slaves to work on their farms.

READING CHECK **Explain** Why did few colonists originally move to Brazil?

French Traders
Most people who moved to French colonies in North America were traders, not settlers. *What does this image suggest about life in French colonies?*

Shooting the Rapids, by Frances Anne Hopkins, c. 1879

French, Dutch, and English Colonies in the Americas

As silver and gold from Spain's and Portugal's American colonies began to circulate throughout Europe, other European countries paid close attention. Leaders in France, England, and the Netherlands decided that they, too, needed to establish colonies in the Americas.

New France French explorers had established several colonies in an area known as New France, or Canada. The French hoped that this colony would be as rich a source of gold and silver as the Spanish lands to the south.

Although the French were disappointed in their hope of finding gold, silver, and other riches, they found other potentially valuable trade goods. For example, the waters of the North Atlantic were swarming with fish, a staple of the European diet. In addition, the forests yielded valuable furs. Fox, lynx, otter, and other furs, especially beaver, sold for high prices in Europe.

Unlike the Spanish and Portuguese, the French did not send large numbers of colonists to the Americas. Only small groups of traders moved across the sea. As a result, the French population in North America remained small.

THE IMPACT TODAY
Portuguese is still the official language of Brazil today.

French, Dutch, and English Colonies in the Americas

Identify What were the major French possessions in North America, and where were they located? *New France included possessions along the St. Lawrence River, Newfoundland, and Nova Scotia. Louisiana was the region of the Mississippi River and its tributaries.*

Draw Conclusions Why do you think the French did not enslave the Native Americans? *possible answer—Native Americans were important allies, helping the French to hunt animals.*

Activity **Attracting Settlers** Have students design their own recruiting slogan or flyer to attract settlers to Virginia. **LS Visual-Spatial**

Alternative Assessment Handbook, Rubric 34: Slogans and Banners

---

Also unlike the Spanish and Portuguese, the French did not enslave Native Americans. In fact, Native American hunters were the French traders' main source of furs, and they often became allies. Many French traders even married Native American women, intermingling the two cultures.

From New France, a few French explorers headed south to seek out more lands they could claim. Samuel de Champlain, for example, founded the city of Quebec in 1608. The French also explored the Mississippi River, which they believed flowed to the Pacific and thus would provide them with a route to Asia. Eventually, they realized their error. In 1682 René-Robert La Salle canoed down the entire Mississippi River to the Gulf of Mexico. La Salle claimed the enormous Mississippi region and its tributaries for France. He named this huge, fertile area Louisiana, after the king, Louis XIV.

NEW YORK

CC Unit 3-E3 European competition for colonies

The Dutch of New Netherland Like the French, the Dutch colonists who came to North America were mostly interested in trade. The only large Dutch colony in North America was New Netherland, located in the Hudson River valley. In 1626 the governor of New Netherland bought the island of Manhattan from the Wappinger people and founded the city of New Amsterdam, which later became New York City. The settlement remained small for some time, with fewer than 4,000 people in all of New Netherland in the 1650s.

One reason that New Netherland did not grow was that the Dutch were more focused on developing their colonies in other parts of the world. Those colonies were more profitable for the Dutch because they produced goods that could not be obtained in Europe or the Americas. For example, Dutch colonies in the Caribbean produced sugar. Even more valuable were the spices that the Dutch imported from their colonies in southeast Asia.

Reading like a Historian

Nova Britannia, or New England, was a name given to the English colonies in North America.

Recruiting Colonists

Analyzing Primary Sources Posters and pamphlets can be important sources of information about the past. Such documents can tell us about what people considered important and how they tried to persuade others to agree with them.

To examine the meaning of a poster or a pamphlet, think about

- the creator of the document
- the purpose of the document
- the facts and evidence used to support the creator's ideas

Skills FOCUS **READING LIKE A HISTORIAN**

1. **Creator** Who was the creator of the pamphlet shown here? Who was the pamphlet's intended audience?

2. **Purpose** For what purpose was this pamphlet created?

3. **Facts and Evidence** What facts did the creators of the pamphlet use to try to convince people to listen to them?

See **Skills Handbook**, p. H25

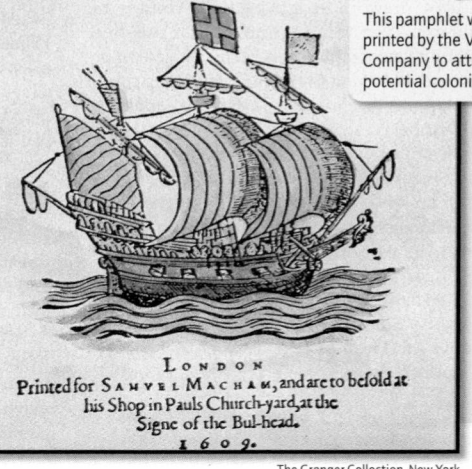

NOVA BRITANNIA.

OFFERING MOST
Excellent fruites by Planting in
VIRGINIA.

Exciting all such as be well affected
to further the same.

LONDON
Printed for SAMVEL MACHAM, and are to be sold at
his Shop in Pauls Church-yard, at the
Signe of the Bul-head.
1609.

This pamphlet was printed by the Virginia Company to attract potential colonists.

The Granger Collection, New York

Collaborative Learning

At Level

Colonial Life

Research Required

1. Organize students into small groups. Have each group research life in the early Spanish, Portuguese, French, Dutch, or English colonies in the Americas. Then have students write skits portraying scenes from everyday life in one of the colonies, including typical interactions between native people and the colonists. To ensure variety, you might wish to assign a nation to each group.

2. Have each group present its skit to the class.

3. Guide students in a discussion of life in the various early European colonies in the Americas. **LS Interpersonal, Kinesthetic**

Alternative Assessment Handbook, Rubrics 30: Research; and 33: Skits and Reader's Theater

---

Answers

Reading Like a Historian 1. *the Virginia Company; potential colonists;* **2.** *to attract potential colonists;* **3.** *that farming was good, that the colonial life was exciting*

The English Colonies The English, too, set out to establish colonies in America. The first English colony was established at Jamestown, Virginia, in 1607. The settlers of Jamestown hoped to find gold and silver and possibly a river route to the Pacific. Instead, they found marshy ground and impure water. Some 80 percent of the settlers of Jamestown died during their first winter in America. Nevertheless, the colony endured.

In 1620 another group of settlers called the Pilgrims sailed from England. The Pilgrims, who had been persecuted in England for their religious beliefs, established a colony at Plymouth, Massachusetts. Despite initial difficulties, the Pilgrims persevered, and the settlement was self-sufficient within five years.

The English settlers did not share the same relationship with Native Americans as the French and Dutch. Although both the Jamestown and Plymouth colonies had received aid from local peoples during their early years, most English colonists viewed the Native Americans with distrust or even anger.

British-French Conflict The English also ran into conflict with French settlers in the Americas. In the mid-1700s English colonists began attempting to settle in French territory in the upper Ohio River valley. Tension between English and French settlers in the region grew, until war broke out in 1754. On one side were the English, and on the other were the French, though each side also had Native American allies. For that reason, the English named the conflict the French and Indian War.

At first, the war went badly for the British. The French had many more soldiers in America than they did. Before long, however, the British had turned the tide, taking the city of Quebec. Eventually, the French surrendered, yielding to England not only Canada but all French territory east of the Mississippi River.

Although the British now controlled much more of North America than they had before, the war had been very costly. The English king tried to place the costs of the war on his American colonists, which led to resentment on their part. Eventually, this resentment helped bring about the American Revolution.

READING CHECK **Sequence** What series of events led to the French and Indian War?

CAUSES AND EFFECTS OF THE FRENCH AND INDIAN WAR

CAUSES

- The English tried to settle on land in the Americas that had been claimed by the French.
- Native American groups allied with each side to fight their opponents.

EFFECTS

- The French lost nearly all of their territory in North America, including Canada.
- Great Britain amassed huge debts, which the British tried to recoup from the colonies.

SECTION 2 ASSESSMENT

go.hrw.com
Online Quiz
Keyword: SHL EXP HP

Reviewing Ideas, Terms, and People

1. **a. Identify** Who were **Hernán Cortés** and **Francisco Pizarro**? How did their actions shape Spain's empire in the Americas?
   b. Explain Why was the *encomienda* system originally created? What effect did it ultimately have on American society?
   c. Elaborate How might the history of Mexico and South America have been different if the Spanish had not discovered gold and silver there?
2. **a. Describe** What economic activities took place in Portuguese Brazil?
   b. Compare and Contrast What was one way in which Portuguese and Spanish colonies were similar? What was one way in which they differed?
3. **a. Describe** What was the main resource in France's colonies?
   b. Make Generalizations How did French and Dutch colonists relate to Native Americans? How did the English relate to Native Americans?
   c. Extend How did the French and Indian War shape American history?

Critical Thinking

4. **Analyze** Draw a chart like the one below. Using your notes, fill in the chart with details about each country's colonies: their locations, the activities that took place, and the colonists' relations with Native Americans.

	Location	Activities	Relations
Spain			
Portugal			
France			
Netherlands			
England			

 FOCUS ON WRITING

5. **Exposition** The opinions of Bartolomé de Las Casas were influential in alerting Europeans to the treatment of Native Americans. Write a short paragraph explaining what his opinions were and how they affected attitudes in Europe.

EXPLORATION AND EXPANSION **481**

481

Getting Started

Use the **Interactive Reader and Study Guide** to familiarize students with the section content.

📖 **Interactive Reader and Study Guide,** Section 3

Academic Vocabulary

Review with students the high-use academic term in this section.

intermittent happening from time to time, not constant (p. 484)

📄 **CRF:** Vocabulary Builder: Section 3

Taking Notes

Columbian Exchange—widespread exchange of plants, animals and disease between the societies of Europe and the Americas; effects also felt in Africa and Asia; Mercantilism—system based on the idea that a nation's strength depended upon its wealth; needed favorable balance of trade; colonies helped provide raw materials, new markets; Capitalism—system in which most economic activity is carried on by private individuals or organizations seeking profit; joint-stock companies were one example of capitalism in the colonies

---

SECTION 3 New Patterns of Trade

BEFORE YOU READ

MAIN IDEA

The creation of colonies in the Americas and elsewhere led to the exchange of new types of goods, the establishment of new patterns of trade, and new economic systems in Europe.

READING FOCUS

1. How did exploration result in a new exchange of plants and animals?
2. What was mercantilism, and how did it push the drive to establish colonies?
3. How did global trade lead to the rise of capitalism in Europe?

KEY TERMS

Columbian Exchange
mercantilism
balance of trade
subsidies
capitalism
joint-stock companies

NEW YORK

PI 1.4 Students understand the broad patterns, relationships, and interactions of cultures and civilizations during particular eras and across eras.

Painted tile showing chocolate drinkers, from Barcelona, Spain, 1790

▲ **Chocolate was first introduced in Europe as a drink, not as a candy or dessert.**

482 CHAPTER 16

THE INSIDE STORY

Why didn't many Europeans like chocolate? Before the 1500s the people of Europe had never tasted chocolate. Cacao, the bean from which chocolate is made, is native to the Americas. Until the Europeans arrived in South America during the Age of Exploration, they had never had a chance to sample the sweet treat.

Chocolate did not make much of an impression on Europeans at first. Christopher Columbus actually brought a few cacao beans back to Europe after his first voyage, but because the beans looked unimpressive—few people even noticed them. In the Americas, however, cacao was not only used in a popular beverage but also as a form of currency.

The use of cacao beans as money brought them to the attention of Hernán Cortés during his conquest of the Aztecs. Cortés actually sampled chocolate but did not like it; the chocolate drink made by the Aztecs included neither sugar nor milk and was considered bitter by the Europeans.

Chocolate did not come to the attention of many people in Europe until a few years later. Later, Europeans thought to mix the bitter drink with milk and sugar to produce something similar to modern hot chocolate. When a group of Dominican friars brought this new, sweeter chocolate drink to the court of Prince Philip of Spain, it became an instant hit. Chocolate became one of the favored drinks of the Spanish nobility. Because cacao was grown only in the Americas, the drink was very expensive, which added to its prestige. Chocolate remained a treat that only the very rich could afford, and drinking it was a sign of high status. ■

Teach the Main Idea

At Level

New Patterns of Trade

1. **Teach** Ask students the Reading Focus questions to teach this section.

2. **Apply** Have students create an outline of the section using the heads as main points. Have students identify at least two main ideas under each of the red subheadings.

3. **Review** Review student outlines as a class. Have students identify the points in their outlines they feel are most important or most interesting. Guide students in a discussion of the ways in which new business practices

affected European nations' desire for colonial empires.

4. **Practice/Homework** Have students answer the following question in a brief essay: Which side gained the most as a result of the Columbian Exchange, or did both sides benefit equally? **LS Visual-Spatial, Verbal-Linguistic**

📄 **Alternative Assessment Handbook,** Rubrics 11: Discussions; and 43: Writing to Express

THE COLUMBIAN EXCHANGE

From the Americas

Animals
- guinea pigs
- llamas
- turkeys

Plants
- avocados
- beans
- cashews
- chili peppers
- chocolate
- corn
- papayas
- peanuts
- pecans
- pineapples
- potatoes
- rubber
- squash
- strawberries
- sweet potatoes
- tobacco
- tomatoes
- vanilla

From Europe, Africa, and Asia

Animals
- cattle
- chickens
- donkeys
- goats
- horses
- housecats
- mice and rats
- pigs
- rabbits
- sheep

Plants
- bananas
- black pepper
- citrus fruits
- coffee
- garlic and onions
- lettuce
- peaches and pears
- sugar
- wheat, rye, and oats

Diseases
- cholera
- influenza
- malaria
- measles
- smallpox

The Columbian Exchange

The voyages of Christopher Columbus and those that followed launched a period of large-scale contact between the societies of Europe and of the Americas. The arrival of colonists and their interaction with Native Americans led to sweeping cultural changes in both societies. Over time, contact between the two groups led to the widespread exchange of plants, animals, and disease. Historians call this global transfer the **Columbian Exchange**.

The Exchange of Goods Because of the physical isolation between the Eastern and Western Hemispheres, plants and animals had developed in very different ways. As a result, before contact with the Americas Europeans had never known foods like potatoes, corn, sweet potatoes, or turkeys. Peoples in the Americas had not known coffee, oranges, rice, wheat, sheep, or cattle.

The arrival of Europeans in the Americas changed that. Previously unknown foods were brought from the Americas—what Europeans of the time called the New World—back to Europe, as colonists were eager to share new discoveries. At the same time, colonists brought familiar foods from the so-called Old World to the Americas with them, which resulted in items previously unknown in the Americas being introduced there.

New foods were not the only benefit that resulted from the Columbian Exchange. The introduction of beasts of burden, especially horses, to the Americas was a significant development. Before European contact, almost the only domesticated beast of burden in the Americas was the llama, which lived only in the Andes. The introduction of the horse provided people in the rest of the Americas with a new source of labor and transportation.

Effects of the Columbian Exchange

The exchange of foods and animals had a dramatic impact on later societies. Over time, crops native to the Americas, such as corn and potatoes, became staples in the diets of people in Europe and other parts of the world. These foods provided substantial nutrition and helped people live longer. Also, later economic activities such as Texas cattle ranching or Brazilian coffee growing would not have been possible without the Columbian Exchange, since both cows and coffee were native to the Old World.

Even traditional cuisines changed because of the Columbian Exchange. Who today could imagine Italian food without tomatoes? Until contact with the Americas, however, Europeans had never tried tomatoes. In fact, most Europeans viewed tomatoes with suspicion when they first arrived from America, thinking them poisonous. By the late 1600s, however, tomatoes had begun to be included in Italian cookbooks.

TAKING NOTES

Take notes on the Columbian Exchange, mercantilism, and capitalism in a graphic organizer like this one.

Trade Patterns

NEW YORK

CC Unit 3-E8
Exchange of food and disease

Direct Teach

Reading Focus

1 How did exploration result in a new exchange of plants and animals? *As contact increased between Europe and the Americas, plants, animals, and disease traveled from one part of the world to another.*

The Columbian Exchange

Explain How did the Columbian Exchange work? *Europeans transported plants, animals, people, and diseases between the Eastern and Western hemispheres.*

Identify Cause and Effect What were the results of the Columbian Exchange? *New economic activities grew up and national cuisines changed. However, diseases brought to the Americas by Europeans wiped out much of the native population.*

Make Judgments If the Columbian Exchange had not taken place, would you rather have lived in the Old World or the New World? Why? *possible answer—the New World; the fruits, nuts, and vegetables found there tasted better than those found in the Old World*

Quick Facts Transparency: The Columbian Exchange

CRF: Biography: Pocahontas

Teaching Tip

Some students may not know what the items are on the Columbian Exchange chart. Review each term on the chart or have students use an illustrated dictionary to look up each new term.

Skills Focus: Comparing and Contrasting

Below Level

Reading Skill
The Columbian Exchange

Materials: blank note cards, tacks, or tape

1. Organize students into small groups. Give each group a list of plants and/or animals from the two lists in the Quick Facts chart on this page along with a stack of note cards. Each member of the group should have one item and one card.

2. Have groups find pictures of the plants and animals on their lists. Have each student draw and label one of the plants or animals on a card.

3. Create two display areas for all to see and label them "New World" and "Old World."

4. Collect all the cards, shuffle them, and hand them back so that each student gets one card. Have students tack or tape their cards in the appropriate area. **LS Interpersonal, Visual-Spatial**

Alternative Assessment Handbook, Rubrics 3: Artwork; and 14: Group Activity

Reading Focus

❷ What was mercantilism, and how did it push the drive to establish colonies? *system based on the idea that a nation's strength was based on its wealth; colonies helped provide wealth*

Mercantilism

Summarize How did the desire to create a favorable balance of trade help lead to the establishment of colonies? *European powers wanted to establish colonies so that they could control sources of raw materials and to provide new markets for manufactured goods.*

Elaborate How did the establishment of colonies in the New World lead to inflation? *Shiploads of gold and silver flowed to Europe from the Americas. They were made into new coins, increasing the amount of money in circulation. The increase of money pushed the prices of goods higher.*

Quick Facts Transparency: Basic Principles of Mercantilism

Effects of the Columbian Exchange were felt not only in Europe and the Americas. Africa and Asia, too, changed as a result of the exchange. For example, the arrival of corn, an easy-to-grow, nutritious crop, in China helped that country's population grow tremendously. China was also one of the main consumers of the silver mined in the Americas. In Africa, two crops native to the Americas, corn and peanuts, are still among the continent's most widely grown products. In fact, scholars estimate that a full one-third of all food crops grown around the world today are of American origin.

ACADEMIC VOCABULARY

intermittent happening from time to time, not constant

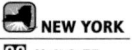

NEW YORK

CC Unit 3-E5 European mercantilism

The Introduction of New Diseases Even more disastrous than overdependence on new foods were the diseases brought to the Americas by Europeans. As you read in the previous section, the Native Americans had no natural resistance to European diseases such as small-pox, measles, influenza, and malaria. Those diseases killed millions of Native Americans. A few new diseases were introduced in Europe as well, but they were much less deadly.

Often, the first epidemics following the arrival of Europeans were the most severe. By 1518 or 1519, for example, smallpox had killed perhaps one-half of the population of Santo Domingo. Historians have estimated that the population of central Mexico decreased by more than 30 per cent in the 10 years following the first contact with Europeans.

Epidemics returned again and again, with even more devastating effects. The Native American population continued to decline in subsequent centuries. Some historians estimate that the Inca Empire decreased from about 13 million people in 1492 to 2 million in 1600. The North American population fell from around 2 million in 1492 to 500,000 by 1900. Disease was not the only factor that led to such a dramatic decrease. Intermittent warfare and other violence contributed. But without question, diseases from Europe had a devastating impact on Native American populations.

READING CHECK **Find the Main Idea** What were two lasting effects of the Columbian Exchange?

Mercantilism

The founding of colonies in the Americas and the introduction of new goods to Europe led to significant changes in the European economy. During the 1500s, for example, Europeans developed a new type of economic policy called **mercantilism**. The basic principle of mercantilism was that a nation's strength depended on its wealth. A wealthy nation had the power to build a strong military to protect itself and expand its influence.

During the mercantilist era, wealth was measured by the amount of gold and silver that a nation possessed. Mercantilists believed that there was a fixed amount of wealth in the world. For one nation to become wealthier—and therefore more powerful—it had to take wealth and power away from another nation. As a result, mercantilism led to intense competition between nations for wealth during the 1500s and 1600s.

Balance of Trade Mercantilists believed that a nation could build wealth in two ways. It could extract gold and silver from mines at home or in its colonies, or it could sell more goods than it bought from foreign countries, thus creating a favorable **balance of trade**. With a favorable balance of trade, a country received more gold and silver from other nations than it paid to them. In the mercantilists' view, this situation increased the nation's power and weakened its foreign competitors. Therefore, a favorable balance of trade became a central goal for many mercantilist countries.

BASIC PRINCIPLES OF MERCANTILISM — QUICK FACTS

A nation's strength depends on its wealth as measured in gold and silver.

Only a fixed amount of wealth exists in the world, and nations have to compete for their share of that wealth.

A favorable balance of trade is an important step in gaining wealth.

Countries should seek to limit imports and maximize exports.

A country should have its own source for raw materials and precious metals to avoid dependence on others.

Colonies exist only as a way for the mother country to make profit.

A country's colonies should not trade with any other countries.

---

484 CHAPTER 16

Skills Focus: Analyzing Primary Sources

Below Level

Reading Like a Historian Skill
The Columbian Exchange and Cuisine

1. Have students obtain or make copies of menus from local Chinese, Italian, or Mexican restaurants.

2. Have each student choose a meal to "order." Then have students find recipes for each item on his or her "order" and make a list of the ingredients. (Tell students they can ignore the amounts needed for each recipe.)

3. Next, have students identify which ingredients came from the New World and which originated in the Old World.

4. Have volunteers share their lists with the class.

5. Guide students in a discussion of ways in which these recipes illustrate how cuisines were affected by the Columbian Exchange.

LS Verbal-Linguistic

Alternative Assessment Handbook, Rubrics 11: Discussions; and 30: Research

---

Answers

Reading Check *possible answers— changes in cuisine, changes in crops grown around the world, epidemics*

Two Sources on Colonies

European economists believed that the sole purpose of colonies was the make their mother countries rich. If a colony was unprofitable, then it should be abandoned.

Colonists, on the other hand, felt that they were risking their lives for king and country and should be cared for regardless of the colony's overall profitability.

❝If it should be found impracticable for Great Britain to draw any considerable augmentation of revenue from any of the resources above mentioned; the only resource which can remain to her is a diminution of her expense . . . The expense of the peace establishment of the colonies was, before the commencement of the present disturbances, very considerable, and is an expense which may, and if no revenue can be drawn from them ought certainly to be saved altogether.❞

Adam Smith
—*The Wealth of Nations*, 1776

❝Look here, King of Spain! Do not be cruel and ungrateful to your vassals, because while your father and you stayed in Spain without the slightest bother, your vassals, at the price of their blood and fortune, have given you all the kingdoms and holding you have in these parts. Beware, King and lord, that you cannot take, under the title of legitimate king, any benefit from this land where you risked nothing, without first giving due gratification to those who have labored and sweated in it.❞

Lope de Aguirre
—Letter to King Philip II of Spain, 1561

Skills Focus INVESTIGATING HISTORY

Analyze What was the driving force behind Smith's view of colonies? What force drove Aguirre's views?

A country could do several things to achieve a favorable balance of trade. One approach was to reduce the amount of goods imported from other countries by placing tariffs, or import taxes, on those goods. The importer of a particular good paid the tariff and added that cost to the price of the good. Imported goods were thus often more expensive than similar goods produced within the nation. The higher price, therefore, discouraged people from buying imported goods.

Another approach was to encourage exports that could sell for high prices. For example, manufactured goods sold to other nations fat highers prices than raw materials did. So woolen cloth could be sold at a higher profit than raw wool could. Countries therefore encouraged manufacturing and the export of manufactured goods. Governments provided **subsidies**, or grants of money, to help businesspeople start new industries.

A third approach to achieving a favorable balance of trade was to control overseas sources of raw materials and precious metals. A nation that controlled its own sources of these goods would not need to import them from competing nations. Why was this important? There were two main reasons. First, a country did not need to spend any of its own money on obtaining raw materials. Second, foreign countries were always considered rivals. At any time, a rival might become an active enemy and cut off supplies of raw materials. To minimize that risk, European nations worked to become more self-sufficient. For example, they began to establish colonies in the lands they controlled.

Colonies The building of colonial empires was essential to the mercantilist system. European powers wanted to establish colonies in order to control sources of raw materials and provide new markets for manufactured goods.

READING SKILLS

Questioning As you read, ask yourself how each mercantilist approach could lead to a favorable balance of trade.

EXPLORATION AND EXPANSION **485**

485

Mercantilism

Explain How did European monarchs restrict economic activities in their colonies to make sure that the colonies benefited only the home country? *by forbidding them to sell raw materials to any nation other than the home country; by forcing colonies to buy manufactured goods only from their home countries and forbidding them from manufacturing goods themselves*

Identifying Cause and Effect What was the impact of colonization on European societies? *growth of cities and towns; new class of wealthier merchants who wielded more power*

Info to Know

The New Commercial Economy World exploration led to a new kind of economy in Europe. Goods brought from Africa, Asia, and the New World made many countries in Europe rich. Spices, silks, gold, silver, and precious stones were some of the most sought-after items. The Portuguese, Spanish, and Dutch were the first European powers to build trading empires. Trade and commerce eventually replaced farming as the leading economic activity in Europe. Over time, the new commercial economy generally helped to spread wealth and improve living standards.

Saving and Investing In recent years the U.S. household savings rate has been declining. The household savings rate in Japan is double that of the United States, and Europe's savings rate is four times greater than the United States.

Answers

History and Economics *profitable— might earn a lot of money; risky—might lose a lot of money*

In the mercantilist view, colonies existed only to benefit the home country. In 1697 the English economist Charles D'Avenant explained how colonies benefited England.

HISTORY'S VOICES

❝Our plantations . . . consume more of our home manufactures . . . they produce commodities indispensably necessary to this part of the world, and not to be produced elsewhere, and, with industry and conduct, may be made an inexhaustible mine of treasure to their mother kingdom.❞
—Charles D'Avenant, "An Essay on the East-India Trade"

To make sure that colonies benefited only the home country, European monarchs restricted economic activities in the colonies. People living in the colonies could not sell raw materials to any nation other than the home country or buy manufactured goods from other nations. Governments passed strict laws that forbade colonies from manufacturing goods. So colonies were forced to buy manufactured goods only from their home country. Mercantilists argued that such laws were justified because colonies existed to benefit the home country.

Impact on Society The changes taking place because of colonization also had an impact on European societies. Towns and cities grew as business activity increased. A new class of wealthier merchants emerged who began to wield more power in their towns.

HISTORY and Economics

Saving and Investing

What should you do with any money you have left over after paying for necessities? Consider making your money work for you by saving or investing it.

Saving and Investing in History Before the late 1500s opportunities for saving and investing were limited. Then banks began offering other services to customers, including a secure place for keeping money. Opportunities for investment also became available at that time. For example, many joint-stock companies were established to engage in the lucrative trade in Asian spices and textiles. These companies, in turn, played a significant role in financing exploration and trading voyages. The companies were frequently able to return large profits to investors when their ships came back from the East Indies laden with valuable merchandise.

Saving and Investing in Your Life One of the most important financial responsibilities you will have to learn is how to use your money wisely. Begin by opening a savings account. This is a risk-free way to finance your goals, because deposits are insured by the government. Saving is also profitable, since banks pay interest.

ENGLISH JOINT-STOCK COMPANIES, 1688			
Company	Date of Creation	Value of Each Share	Number of Investors
East India	1600	£100	511
Royal African	1672	£100	203
Hudson's Bay	1670	£100	32
White Paper	1686	£50	unknown
Royal Lustring	1688	£25	134

Another option is investing in stocks or bonds. Investing money is riskier but can provide richer rewards. However, because you risk losing all your money if an investment fails, you should invest money only if you have adequate savings.

Analyze How can investing in a company be profitable? How can it be risky?

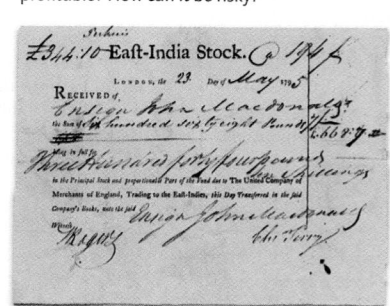

◀ Stock certificate from the East India Company, an early joint-stock company

---

Skills Focus: Identifying Cause and Effect

At Level

Reading Skill
The Effects of Mercantilism

1. Have students draw editorial cartoons that illustrate one of the effects of mercantilism, such as the accumulation of gold and silver, creating a favorable balance of trade, establishment of colonial empires, or policies that restricted trade and manufacturing in the home country's colonies. Since these are editorial cartoons, students should take a clear stand for or against the policy they illustrate.

2. Display student cartoons for the class to see.

3. Guide students in a discussion of the effects of mercantilism on society and the world.
   LS Visual-Spatial

   Alternative Assessment Handbook, Rubrics 11: Discussions; and 27: Political Cartoons

The impact of colonization was not felt throughout society, though. Rural life continued much as it had for centuries. Generations would pass before many began to grow new foods from the Americas. In towns and cities, wealthy merchants enjoyed some social mobility, but most people remained poor.

READING CHECK **Summarize** What were the main principles of mercantilism?

The Rise of Capitalism

Increasing trade between European nations and their colonies resulted in the creation of new business practices during the 1500s and 1600s. These practices would have a profound impact on the economies of European nations.

Capitalism Emerges During this period, an economic system known as **capitalism** expanded. In capitalism, most economic activity is carried on by private individuals or organizations in order to seek a profit. Individuals, not just the government, began to amass great fortunes through overseas trade.

Merchants began to supply colonists with goods from Europe and, in return, brought back products and raw materials from the Americas. This overseas trade made many merchants rich, and this wealth enabled them to invest in still more business ventures. Business activity in Europe increased markedly.

Rising Prices Investors willingly took the risks of investing in overseas trade because of inflation, or a steady increase in prices. Demand for goods increased because of a growing population and a relative scarcity of goods. The rising demand drove prices higher.

Another factor leading to higher prices was the increase of the money supply in Europe. Shiploads of gold and silver flowed into Europe from the Americas to be made into new coins. Over time, the increase of money in circulation pushed prices for goods still higher.

A New Business Organization Overseas business ventures were very costly, often too expensive for individual investors. Soon, investors began to pool their money into **joint-stock companies** to fund ever-larger businesses. In a joint-stock company, investors bought shares of

stock in the company. If the company achieved a profit, each shareholder would receive a portion of that profit, based on the number of shares owned. If the company failed, investors would lose only the amount of money they had invested in the business.

One of the first joint-stock companies was the British East India Company, founded in 1600 to import spices from Asia. Other joint-stock companies formed to bear the enormous cost of establishing new colonies. In 1607, for example, the Virginia Company of London established the first successful English colony in the Americas at Jamestown, Virginia.

READING CHECK **Identify Cause and Effect** Why did new business practices develop in Europe?

THE IMPACT TODAY
The notion of investors sharing profits and risk is the norm in the business world today.

SECTION 3 ASSESSMENT

go.hrw.com
Online Quiz
Keyword: SHL EXP HP

Reviewing Ideas, Terms, and People

1. **a. Define** What was the **Columbian Exchange**? What were some of the products exchanged?
   b. Explain How did the exchange of plants and animals change life in both Europe and the Americas?
   c. Elaborate What effect did the introduction of new diseases into the Americas have on Native American populations?
2. **a. Describe** What was the most important principle of **mercantilism**?
   b. Make Generalizations Why were colonies important under the principles of mercantilism?
   c. Extend How did the quest for a favorable **balance of trade** push the drive to establish colonies?
3. **a. Recall** Why did people form **joint-stock companies**?
   b. Elaborate How did the drive to establish colonies lead to the growth of **capitalism**?

Critical Thinking

4. **Compare and Contrast** Draw a Venn diagram like the one below. Using your notes, write three facts about mercantilism in the left oval. Then write three facts about capitalism in the right oval. Where the ovals overlap, identify one feature that the two systems have in common.

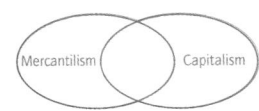

Mercantilism   Capitalism

FOCUS ON WRITING

5. **Persuasion** Write a short letter as though you were one of the founders of a joint-stock company trying to convince a friend to invest his or her money in your venture. In your letter, explain what you hope your company will accomplish and why you feel it would be beneficial to your friend to take part.

EXPLORATION AND EXPANSION **487**

Direct Teach

Reading Focus

3 How did global trade lead to the rise of capitalism in Europe? *It provided opportunities for individuals to invest money and build wealth.*

The Rise of Capitalism

Define What is capitalism? *system in which most economic activity is carried on by private individuals or organizations in order to seek a profit*

Make Generalizations How was the Virginia Company of London an example of capitalism? *Investors pooled their money in order to make a profit by establishing American colonies.*

Review & Assess

Close

Guide students in a discussion of the ways in which mercantilism encouraged European nations to establish colonial empires.

Review

Online Quiz, Section 3

Assess

SE Section 3 Assessment

Progress Assessment: Section 3 Quiz

Alternative Assessment Handbook

Reteach/Intervene

Interactive Reader and Study Guide, Section 3

Interactive Skills Tutor CD-ROM

Section 3 Assessment Answers

1. **a.** exchange of plants and animals between Europe and Americas; possible answers— tomatoes, cows, coffee, corn, peanuts
   b. changed cuisines, crops
   c. Millions died from the diseases.

2. **a.** that a nation's strength depended on its wealth
   b. Colonies could provide raw materials and new markets.
   c. allowed nations to control overseas sources of raw materials and precious metals

3. **a.** to pool their money in an attempt to make a profit
   b. Colonies provided opportunities for individuals to build wealth.

4. Mercantilism—nation's strength depended on wealth; favorable balance of trade; Capitalism—most economic activity carried on by private individuals or organizations seeking profit; Both—benefited from establishment of colonies

5. Student letters should explain how investors can make a profit in the venture.

Answers

Reading Skills (left) *nation's strength depended upon its wealth; needed a favorable balance of trade;* **(right)** *because of increasing trade between Europe and its colonies*

487

Getting Started

Use the **Interactive Reader and Study Guide** to familiarize students with the section content.

📖 **Interactive Reader and Study Guide**, Section 4

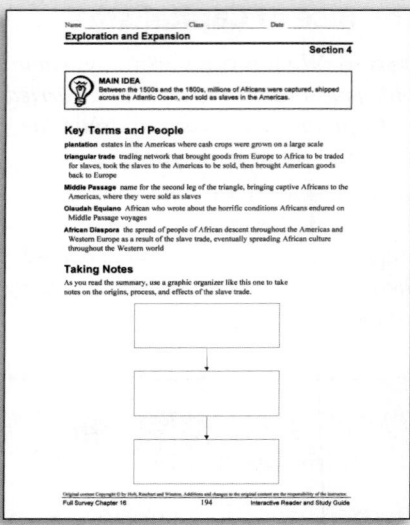

📝 **CRF:** Vocabulary Builder: Section 4

Taking Notes

Origins—need for workers on plantations in the Americas; Process—triangular trade began; Middle Passage brought Africans to Americas under inhumane conditions; Effects—an estimated 15 to 20 million Africans were shipped to the Americas; millions of people deprived of their freedom; resulted in countless deaths; harmed Africa; divided Africans from one another; enriched other parts of the world; led to African Diaspora and spread of African culture

---

SECTION 4

The Atlantic Slave Trade

BEFORE YOU READ

MAIN IDEA

Between the 1500s and the 1800s millions of Africans were captured, shipped across the Atlantic Ocean, and sold as slaves in the Americas.

READING FOCUS

1. Where did the Atlantic slave trade originate?
2. How did slavery evolve in the American colonies?
3. What were the consequences of the slave trade?

KEY TERMS AND PEOPLE

plantations
triangular trade
Middle Passage
Olaudah Equiano
African Diaspora

NEW YORK

PI 1.2 Students understand the development and connectedness of Western civilization and other civilizations and cultures in many areas of the world and over time.

THE INSIDE STORY

How did the door of a Senegalese house become a powerful symbol for millions of people worldwide?

On rocky Gorée Island off the coast of Senegal stands the House of Slaves. Millions of African captives spent their last days in Africa in this house or houses like it. Crowded into dark, dungeonlike rooms, they awaited the ships that would carry them into slavery in the Americas. Their last steps in Africa were through the Door of No Return, a narrow doorway facing the Atlantic Ocean. Once through it, they would leave behind everything they knew—to face an uncertain and terrifying future.

Though historians today are not sure how prominent a role Gorée Island played in the slave trade, the history of the House of Slaves draws about 200,000 people to visit each year. However many slaves actually departed through the Door of No Return, it remains a powerful symbol of the tragedy of slavery. ◼

Origins of the Slave Trade

Throughout history, slavery has existed in many parts of the world, including Africa. The people who were forced into slavery came from various walks of life. Many were farmers, merchants, priests, soldiers, or musicians. They were fathers and mothers, sons and daughters.

The Atlantic Slave Trade A shortage of labor in the Americas led to the beginning of the Atlantic slave trade. European planters in the Americas needed large numbers of workers on their **plantations**, estates where

The view through the door of the House of Slaves on Gorée Island is a profound symbol of the slave trade.

488

Teach the Main Idea

At Level

The Atlantic Slave Trade

1. **Teach** Ask students the Reading Focus questions to teach this section.

2. **Apply** Have students make a cause-and-effect chart about slavery in the Americas. Tell students that the reasons the slave trade was started are the causes, while the results, or consequences, of the slave trade are the effects.

3. **Review** Review student charts as a class. Guide students in a discussion of how the development of the American colonies

would have been different if slavery had never been introduced in the New World.

4. **Practice/Homework** Have students write about the causes and effects of the African slave trade. 🄻🅂 **Visual-Spatial, Verbal-Linguistic**

📝 **Alternative Assessment Handbook**, Rubrics 7: Charts; and 41: Writing to Express cash crops such as sugar or tobacco were grown on a large scale. Planters had first used Native Americans as workers, but European diseases had killed millions of them. In the 1600s planters used indentured servants—people who worked for a set period in exchange for passage to the Americas—from Europe, but such workers were expensive to support.

As a result, millions of Africans were forcibly taken to the Americas before the slave trade ended in the 1800s. Most came from the coast of West Africa, between Senegal and Angola. Some slaves were supplied by African rulers in exchange for European firearms or other goods. Others were kidnapped on slave raids organized by European traders.

Captured Africans were marched to slave ships where they became part of a network called the **triangular trade**. The first leg of the triangle consisted of ships carrying European goods to Africa to be exchanged for slaves. The second leg, or **Middle Passage**, brought Africans to the Americas to be sold as slaves. The third leg carried American products such as sugar, tobacco, and rice to Europe. Some slave traders from the Americas sailed directly to Africa, however, not following the triangular route.

The Middle Passage The Middle Passage was a terrifying ordeal. Captive Africans were chained together and forced into dark, cramped quarters below the ship's decks. In many cases, the Africans were packed into such a small space that they could neither sit nor stand. One African, **Olaudah Equiano**, later wrote about these horrific conditions.

HISTORY'S VOICES

❝The stench of the hold . . . was so intolerably loathsome, that it was dangerous to remain there for any time . . . The closeness of the place, and the heat of the climate . . . almost suffocated us . . . The shrieks of the women, and the groans of the dying, rendered the whole scene of horror almost inconceivable.❞

—Olaudah Equiano, *The Interesting Narrative of the Life of Olaudah Equiano*, 1789

TAKING NOTES

Use a graphic organizer to take notes on the origins, process, and effects of the slave trade.

Origins → Process → Effects

NEW YORK

CC Unit 3-E3
The triangular trade

THE ATLANTIC SLAVE TRADE

NORTH AMERICA
ATLANTIC OCEAN
BRITISH NORTH AMERICA 453,000
SPANISH EMPIRE 1,553,000
BRITISH WEST INDIES 1,665,000
FRENCH WEST INDIES 1,600,000
DUTCH WEST INDIES 528,000
BRAZIL 3,596,000
PACIFIC OCEAN
SOUTH AMERICA
AFRICA
St. Louis
James Island
Elmina
Accra
Assini
Whydah
INDIAN OCEAN

British North America
Spanish Empire
British West Indies
French West Indies
Dutch West Indies
Brazil
Slave fort
Direction of slave trade

0   800   1,600 Miles
0   800   1,600 Kilometers
Miller projection

EXPLORATION AND EXPANSION **489**

GEOGRAPHY SKILLS INTERPRETING MAPS

1. **Location** From what region were most African slaves taken?
2. **Movement** Which colony received the most slaves?

❷ How did slavery evolve in the American colonies? *By the end of the 1600s, England dominated the slave trade; living conditions for slaves were harsh; some enslaved people rebelled.*

Slavery in the Colonies

Describe Describe the living conditions for enslaved people. *They were harsh. Many owners and overseers inflicted degrading physical punishment for minor offenses. Enslaved people frequently had to endure brutal treatment and abuse.*

Summarize How did Africans resist slavery? *by slowing work, destroying equipment, committing acts of sabotage, revolting, or running away*

The journey to the Americas usually lasted three to six weeks. Between 10 and 20 percent of all captive Africans did not survive the voyage. When those who survived arrived in the Americas, they faced still more terrors—the auction block and an uncertain future.

READING CHECK **Describe** What was the Middle Passage of the slave trade like?

Slavery in the Colonies

Slave traders carried captive Africans to many parts of the Americas. Spanish traders took slaves to their Caribbean sugar plantations. Portuguese traders brought millions to Brazil. The English took most of their captives to the West Indies but also brought large numbers to colonies in North America. By the end of the 1600s England dominated the slave trade.

Living Conditions Most enslaved Africans worked on plantations, but others worked in mines, in towns, and in the countryside. Those

who had been skilled craft workers—such as carpenters, metalworkers, or coopers—often continued their crafts in the Americas. Women were sometimes given domestic duties as servants and cooks.

Slaves had to meet their own basic needs in the short hours at the end of the workday. Daily tasks such as cooking, mending clothing, and tending the sick had to be fit in around the work they performed for the slaveholder.

Living conditions for many enslaved people were harsh. Owners and overseers inflicted physical and degrading punishment for minor offenses. As a result, many slaveholders lived in constant fear of rebellion by angry slaves who could not take the harsh treatment they faced on plantations anymore.

Resistance Laws in the Americas considered enslaved Africans to be property. Slaves had no rights and no freedoms, and slaveholders controlled most of the conditions under which they lived. In many cases, enslaved people endured brutal treatment and abuse.

FORENSICS in History

How Were Slaves Treated in the North?

In the United States, most people think of slavery as a southern phenomenon. Many more slaves lived in the American South than in the North, and, for many years, people assumed that those slaves who did live in the North were better treated than their southern counterparts. A recent discovery, however, has led many people to change their minds.

What facts do we have? In 1991 workers in Manhattan laying the foundation for a new skyscraper found a graveyard that dated back to the 1700s. Buried in the graveyard were the remains of 427 African slaves.

The remains were sent to Howard University in Washington, D.C., to be studied. The results of that study showed that many of the slaves had been pushed to their physical limit or beyond—literally worked to death. The strain of their labors had resulted in deformed muscles and broken bones. In addition, the fact that many of the slaves buried

in the graveyard were children—several less than six months old—suggests that the slaves lived under terrible conditions.

Infer How could this study challenge the idea that northern slaves were well treated?

▶ The slaves found in the New York City graveyard were reburied in a special ceremony in 2003.

Skills Focus: Analyzing Alternative Points of View   At Level

Reading Like a Historian Skill
The Slave Trade

Materials: poster paper, colored markers or pencils

1. Organize students into small groups. Have each group discuss the advantages and disadvantages of the slave trade for one of the following individuals: a plantation owner in the Americas, an enslaved person, the owner of a slave ship, or the ruler of an African kingdom.

2. Have each student write an essay analyzing the different points of view involved in the slave trade.

3. Guide students in a discussion of the slave trade from the points of view that have been presented. **LS** **Interpersonal, Visual-Spatial**

📝 **Alternative Assessment Handbook**, Rubric 37: Writing Assignments

---

Answers

Forensics in History *It shows that the slaves in New York had been worked to their physical limits and probably lived under terrible conditions.*

Reading Check *a terrifying ordeal; people were cramped, chained together; as many as one in four people did not survive the voyage*

Enslaved Africans and their descendants coped with these inhumane conditions in many different ways. Some resisted by trying to keep their cultural traditions alive. Others turned to religion for strength and hope for a better life.

Some slaves also fought back by slowing down their work or destroying equipment. Occasionally they revolted, attacking slave-holders and their families. Some slaves were able to flee plantations and establish communities of runaways in remote areas.

READING CHECK **Summarize** Why did many slaves fight back against their owners?

Effects of the Slave Trade

The Atlantic slave trade continued for 400 years and devastated societies in West Africa. Historians have estimated that about 15 to 20 million Africans were shipped to the Americas against their will. Millions more were sent to Europe, Asia, and the Middle East.

The human cost of the slave trade was enormous. Countless people died marching from the interior to the coast or crammed aboard slave ships. Slavery deprived millions of people of their freedom and doomed their descendants to lives of forced servitude.

In Africa, the effects of the slave trade were profound. Slave raiders captured many of the strongest young people—the future leaders of their societies. The slave trade also divided Africans from one another. For example, some African rulers waged wars against their own people and their neighbors to gain captives.

The forced labor of millions of Africans did not enrich Africa, but it did enrich other parts of the world. The labor of African slaves helped build the economies of many American colonies. Their knowledge of agriculture contributed to the growth of the rice industry in the southern English colonies.

As a result of the slave trade, people of African descent spread throughout the Americas and Western Europe. This dispersal is called the **African Diaspora**. The African Diaspora eventually led to the diffusion of African culture—including music, art, religion, and food—throughout the Western world.

READING CHECK **Explain** What effects did the Atlantic slave trade have in Africa?

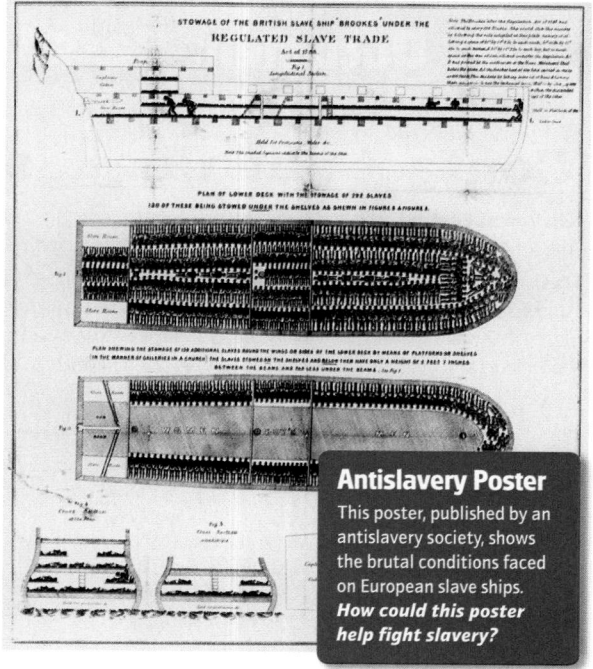

STOWAGE OF THE BRITISH SLAVE SHIP 'BROOKES' UNDER THE REGULATED SLAVE TRADE

PLAN OF LOWER DECK WITH THE STOWAGE OF 292 SLAVES

Antislavery Poster
This poster, published by an antislavery society, shows the brutal conditions faced on European slave ships. *How could this poster help fight slavery?*

SECTION 4 ASSESSMENT

go.hrw.com
Online Quiz
Keyword: SHL EXP HP

Reviewing Ideas, Terms, and People

1. **a. Identify** From where did most of the slaves involved in the Atlantic slave trade come? Where were the slaves taken?
   b. Explain Why was the **triangular trade** developed?
   c. Elaborate How did the **plantation** system lead to the slave trade?
2. **a. Describe** What were living conditions like for most African slaves?
   b. Analyze What were three reactions of slaves to their loss of freedom?
3. **a. Define** What is the **African Diaspora**? How did it affect the world?
   b. Make Judgements What do you think was the most tragic result of the African slave trade? Why?

Critical Thinking

4. **Identify Cause and Effect** Draw a graphic organizer like the one below. Using your notes, identify the social, economic, and cultural effects of the Atlantic slave trade.

```
                    ┌─────────────┐
                    │   Social    │
┌──────────────┐    ├─────────────┤
│   Atlantic   │───▶│  Economic   │
│ Slave Trade  │    ├─────────────┤
└──────────────┘    │  Cultural   │
                    └─────────────┘
```

FOCUS ON WRITING

5. **Description** Write a short description of the Middle Passage experienced by enslaved Africans. Include in your description the conditions slaves had to endure and the effects of the passage on those slaves.

Section 4 Assessment Answers

1. **a.** West Africa; the Americas
   b. to form a trade network between Europe, Africa, and Asia
   c. It required large numbers of workers.
2. **a.** harsh conditions, lack of freedom
   b. keeping cultural traditions alive, religion, rebellion
3. **a.** the spread of people of African descent throughout the Americas and Western Europe; spread African culture

   b. possible answer—the fact that millions of people were deprived of freedom; because freedom is a basic right
4. Social—led to lack of freedom for certain people in the Americas, separated Africans from one another, caused wars; Economic—enriched other parts of the world, but did not enrich Africa; Cultural—led to spread of African culture, the African Diaspora
5. Student descriptions should include details about inhumane treatment and point out that many people died on the voyage.

Answers

Antislavery Poster *might make people realize how brutal the conditions were and thus begin to oppose slavery*

Reading Check (top) *to cope with inhumane conditions;* **(bottom)** *took away future leaders; divided Africans from one another*

491

Document-Based Investigation

Contact and Change

Info to Know

The Dark Side of the Columbian Exchange Although few European explorers had active diseases, they still carried many germs that were highly contagious to Native Americans. Passing these germs to just a few people could rapidly infect large areas. Large, prosperous towns discovered by Spanish explorers in the early 1540s in what is now the southeastern United States no longer existed in 1560. During this time, Spanish colonists in Florida tried to find these towns to acquire food but diseases brought by the explorers had destroyed them. It is estimated that by the early 1600s, the Mesoamerican Indian population was 90 to 95 percent smaller than it had been a hundred years before.

Recent Scholarship

In his book *1491: New Revelations of the Americas Before Columbus*, Charles C. Mann makes many revelations. One of the chief of these is his assertion that the Americas were much more urban, more populated, and more technologically advanced than has generally been assumed. Far from living in harmony with nature, Native Americans engineered the landscape to meet their needs. The empty landscape that greeted later settlers was a result of the diseases carried by the first Europeans.

1491: New Revelations of the Americas Before Columbus by Charles C. Mann. Knopf, 2005.

Contact and Change

 NEW YORK STANDARDS

PI 4.3 Students plan and organize historical research projects related to regional or global interdependence.

Historical Context The four documents here describe changes that occurred in the Americas as a result of the arrival of Europeans in the region.

Task Study the selections and answer the questions that follow. After you have studied all the documents, you will be asked to write an essay describing how the year 1492 was a turning point in history. You will need to use evidence from these documents and from the chapter to support the position you take in your essay.

DOCUMENT 1

The Arrival of Europeans

The arrival of Christopher Columbus in the Caribbean in 1492 had a tremendous impact on the future of that region. The passage below describes that arrival. It is taken from an abridgment of Columbus's personal journal made by Bartholomé de las Casas.

> The Admiral . . . called them as witnesses to certify that he in the presence of them all, was taking, as he in fact took possession of said island for the King and Queen his masters, making the declarations that were required as they will be found more fully in the attestations then taken down in writing. Soon after a large crowd of natives congregated there. What follows are the Admiral's own words in his book on the first voyage and discovery of these Indies. "In order to win the friendship and affection of that people, and because I was convinced that their conversion to our Holy Faith would be better promoted through love than through force, I presented some of them with red caps and some strings of glass beads which they placed around their necks, and with other trifles of insignificant worth that delighted them and by which we have got wonderful hold on their affections."

DOCUMENT 2

The Impact of Disease

Among the most disastrous effects of the arrival of Europeans in the Americas was the rapid spread of disease. Historians estimate that about 90 percent of the Native American population was killed by diseases like smallpox, influenza, and malaria. The image shown here was drawn in the mid- to late 1500s by a Spanish friar named Bernardino de Sahagún, who had befriended many Aztecs. In his *General History of the Things of New Spain*, from which this image is taken, Sahagún describes the effects of these diseases on Aztec populations. The image shows Aztecs suffering through various stages of smallpox.

American Museum of Natural History

Differentiating Instruction

Below Level

Learners Having Difficulty

Materials: white paper, colored pencils or markers

1. Have students draw the scene that takes place in Document 1. Tell students that in order to create a detailed drawing, they will need to pay careful attention to the Admiral's quote.

2. Review student drawings as a class. Ask students: Do the people in their drawings appear to be getting along with one another? Why or why not?

3. Guide students in a discussion of the relationship of Columbus's men with Native Americans, and how it changed over time.
LS Visual-Spatial

Alternative Assessment Handbook, Rubric 3: Artwork

DOCUMENT 3

A New Economic System

When they established colonies in the Americas, the Spanish created a new economic system, the *encomienda* system, in which Native Americans worked on Spanish-owned estates. The basis for that system was laid out in a letter from King Ferdinand and Queen Isabella to the governor of Hispaniola in 1503.

> Our desire is that the Christians not lack people to work their holdings and to take out what gold there is. It also is our desire that the Indians be converted. All this can be better done by having the Indians live in community with the Christians, because they then will help each other cultivate and settle the island, take out the gold, and bring profit to Spain. Therefore, we command you, our governor, to compel the Indians to associate with the Christians. The Indians should work on the Christians' buildings, mine the gold, till the fields, and produce food for the Christians. This the Indians shall perform as free people, which they are, and not as slaves. Also, see to it that the Indians are well treated, with those who become Christians better treated than the others. Do not consent or allow any person to do them any harm or oppress them.

DOCUMENT 4

Changes in Society

The detail below comes from a map drawn by explorer Sebastian Cabot in 1544. The illustrations on the map depict many changes that had occurred in American society over the previous 50 years.

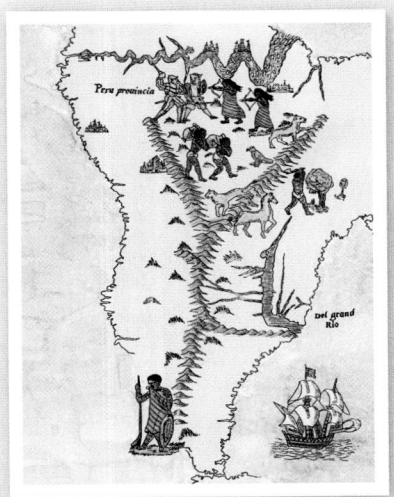

Map of Peru and South America, by Sebastian Cabot, 1544

Skills Focus: READING LIKE A HISTORIAN

DOCUMENT 1
a. Describe What was Columbus's first act upon arriving on the Caribbean island he had discovered?
b. Explain Why does Columbus say he gave gifts to the Native Americans he encountered?

DOCUMENT 2
a. Analyze What symptoms appear in this image?
b. Make Judgments Do you think Sahagún sympathized more with the Spanish or with the Aztecs? Why?

DOCUMENT 3
a. Interpret Why did Ferdinand and Isabella want Native Americans and Christians to live together?
b. Infer Do you think the governor of Hispaniola followed the monarchs' instructions fully? Why or why not?

DOCUMENT 4
a. Describe In what activities are the people shown on this map engaged? How do these activities reflect changes in American society?
b. Summarize What other changes are shown?

DOCUMENT-BASED ESSAY QUESTION

The year 1492 has been described as a turning point in world history. What does this phrase mean? Using the documents above and information from the chapter, form a thesis that might explain its meaning. Then write a short essay to support your position.

See **Skills Handbook**, pp. H25–H26

Info to Know

Stamina and Nutrition Levels of nutrition in the New World were probably much lower than in Europe, which would account for the smaller stature and lower energy levels in Native Americans. When Europeans tried to force Native Americans to do Old World levels of work, many were literally worked to death.

Answers

Reading Like a Historian
Document 1. a. *gave gifts to the Native Americans;* **b.** *because he could more easily convert them to Christianity through love than by force;* **Document 2. a.** *vomiting, spots on skin;* **b.** *with the Aztecs; the depiction of the disease makes it look painful;* **Document 3. a.** *because the Native Americans could help the Spanish Christians and might convert to Christianity themselves;* **b.** *no, because we know Native Americans were treated harshly under the* encomienda *system;* **Document 4. a.** *fighting and working; shows the natives fighting Europeans, and making use of horses;* **b.** *Native Americans are also shown laboring under heavy loads, possibly as slaves.* **Essay** *Student essays should use details from the documents and the chapter in order to show the changes in Europe and the Americas after 1492. Essays should discuss the effects of the Columbian Exchange, exploration, conquest, and colonization.*

Skills Focus: Sequencing

At Level

Reading Skill
After 1492

1. Have students create a time line of events in the Americas in the years immediately following Columbus's arrival.

2. Tell students that their time lines should include the conquest of the Aztec and Inca Empires, as well as important explorations that took place during this time. Students should also indicate on the time line when Documents 1, 2, 3, and 4 were created.

3. Guide a class discussion about what happened in the Americas between 1492 and 1550. What effects did these events have on Native Americans and Europeans? **LS** **Visual-Spatial, Intrapersonal**

Alternative Assessment Handbook, Rubrics 11: Discussions; and 37: Time Lines

Answers

Visual Study Guide

Review and Inquiry Organize students into three groups. One group will cover the Columbian Exchange, the second group will cover New Economic Systems, and the third group will cover the Atlantic Slave Trade. Have each group review the chart in the visual summary and write a brief explanation of how exploration and colonization led to its assigned topic.

Quick Facts Transparency: Visual Study Guide: Exploration and Expansion

Review Key Terms and People

1. Columbian Exchange
2. Vasco da Gama
3. caravel
4. African Diaspora
5. Ferdinand Magellan
6. subsidy

Comprehension and Critical Thinking

7. **a.** the Caribbean; Asia
   b. for fame and glory, in search of wealth, to spread Christianity, because they were curious about the world
   c. possible answer—Yes, because there was the appeal of wealth, fame, and glory.

8. **a.** building colonial empires
   b. based on different trade goods (fish and furs); fewer colonists; allied with Native Americans
   c. possible answer—Spain, because millions of Native Americans died in Spain's colonial empire.

9. **a.** the relationship between a nation's imports and exports; because having more exports than imports brought wealth
   b. exchanged plants, animals, and disease between Europe and the Americas
   c. possible answer—They probably disliked mercantilism because it focused on building the wealth of the mother country, not building the wealth of the colonies.

VISUAL STUDY GUIDE

Exploration
- Explorers from countries throughout Europe set out in search of new routes to Asia.
- Instead of Asia, many explorers ended up in the Americas.

Colonization
- Europeans established colonies in the lands they had discovered.
- The Spanish conquered Native American tribes to build an empire.
- The Portuguese settled Brazil.
- The French, Dutch, and English established colonies in North America and the Caribbean.

Columbian Exchange
- New plants and animals were introduced to both Europe and the Americas.
- Diseases from Europe killed millions of Native Americans.
- The exchange of goods had effects worldwide.

New Economic Systems
- Mercantilism was based on the idea that a nation's power was determined by its wealth.
- Capitalism was based on businesses owned by individuals or groups of investors rather than the government.

Atlantic Slave Trade
- Millions of Africans were captured and shipped to the Americas as slaves.
- Slaves worked on plantations in various European colonies.
- Slaves endured horrific conditions once they arrived.

Review Key Terms and People

Finn each blank with the name or term that correctly completes each sentence.

1. The exchange of new plants, animals, and diseases between Europe and the Americas was called the _____.

2. A Portuguese explorer named _____ was the first person to sail around Africa to reach India.

3. A fast new type of ship, the _____, helped begin the Age of Exploration.

4. The spread of people of African descent through the Western world is called the _____.

5. The first voyage completely around the world was originally led by _____.

6. A _____ is a government grant of money intended to promote a business.

10. **a.** the trading of goods and people between Europe, Africa, and the Americas
    b. They were denied freedom and basic rights and lived under very poor conditions.
    c. in Africa—led to loss of future leaders; wars; divisions between Africans; outside Africa—led to the loss of freedom for millions of enslaved people; enriched countries other than Africa

Using the Internet

11. Go to the HRW Web site and enter the keyword shown to access a rubric for this activity.

KEYWORD: SHL EXP

Comprehension and Critical Thinking

SECTION 1 *(pp. 469–475)*

7. a. Recall Where did Christopher Columbus travel on his first voyage? At what place did he think he had arrived?

b. Explain Why did Europeans of the 1400s and 1500s want to explore the world?

c. Develop Would you have wanted to leave Europe to explore? Why or why not?

SECTION 2 *(pp. 476–481)*

8. a. Identify Main Ideas What was main goal of Spanish and Portuguese colonists?

b. Contrast How did French colonies in the Americas differ from Spanish colonies?

c. Elaborate Which country's colonization efforts do you think had the greatest impact on Native American cultures? Why?

SECTION 3 *(pp. 482–487)*

9. a. Define What is a balance of trade? Why did countries want a favorable balance of trade?

b. Make Generalizations How did the Columbian Exchange change both Europe and the Americas?

c. Extend How do you think most colonists felt about mercantilism? Why do you think so?

SECTION 4 *(pp. 488–491)*

10. a. Describe What was involved in the triangular trade?

b. Summarize How were slaves treated in the American colonies?

c. Elaborate How did the slave trade affect people in Africa? How did it affect people outside of Africa?

Using the Internet

go.hrw.com
Practice Online
Keyword: SHL EXP

11. In order to attract settlers, many colonists in the Americas created posters and pamphlets that advertised the benefits of living in their colonies. Some posters, for example, pointed out pleasant climates or readily available land. Using the keyword above, do research to learn more about one of the colonies discussed in this chapter. Then create a poster that could have been used to attract new settlers.

Analyzing Primary Sources

Reading Like a Historian *The poster below was printed in Charleston, South Carolina, in 1769. Examine the poster and then answer the questions that follow.*

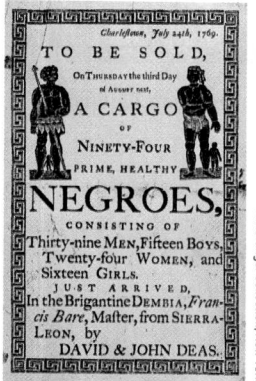

The Granger Collection, New York

12. Analyze What was the purpose of this poster?

13. Interpret Why did the creator of this poster include the details that he did?

Reading Skills

Questioning *Re-read the Inside Story feature that opens Section 3 of this chapter. As you read, ask yourself questions about what is happening in the story. Then answer the questions below.*

14. Where was chocolate originally made?

15. Who brought chocolate to Europe?

16. How was chocolate first received in Europe?

WRITING ABOUT HISTORY ✎

Narration: Writing a Biographical Essay *Many of the explorers who set out in search of new lands during the Age of Exploration did so to seek fame and fortune. As you have read, a number of explorers found the fame they sought and are still known today.*

17. Assignment: In an essay, write a biographical sketch of an explorer from the Age of Exploration. You can choose one of the explorers discussed in this chapter or another about whom you wish to learn more. Use information from this chapter and from other research in your sketch.

Answers

Analyzing Primary Sources

12. to sell the slaves listed on the poster

13. It states that the slaves are healthy in order to show that they will be strong workers.

Reading Skills

14. in the Americas

15. Christopher Columbus

16. People did not like chocolate at first; they considered it bitter.

Writing About History

17. Student biographical sketches should focus on one explorer of the Age of Exploration and provide details about that explorer's life and motivations for exploration, the area he explored, and the effects of his voyage.

A rubric for this activity is provided in **CRF**: Writing for the SAT.

HOLT

History's Impact
► **Video Program: Exploration and Expansion**
Refer to the Video Program Teacher's Guide for the answer to the closing question.

Review and Assessment Resources

Review and Reinforce

🗒 **CRF**: Chapter Review

🖥 **Quick Facts Transparency**: Visual Study Guide: Exploration and Expansion

🔊 **Spanish Chapter Summaries Audio CD Program**

OSP **Holt PuzzlePro**: Quiz Show for ExamView

💿 **Quiz Game CD-ROM**

Assess

🗒 **PASS**: Chapter Test, Forms A and B

🗒 **Alternative Assessment Handbook**

OSP **ExamView Test Generator**, Chapter Test

💿 **Differentiated Instruction Modified Worksheets and Tests CD-ROM**: Chapter Test

HOAP **Holt Online Assessment Program** (in the Premier Online Edition)

Reteach/Intervene

🗒 **Interactive Reader and Study Guide**

🗒 **Differentiated Instruction Teacher Management System**: Lesson Plans for Differentiated Instruction

💿 **Differentiated Instruction Modified Worksheets and Tests CD-ROM**: Chapter Test

💿 **Interactive Skills Tutor CD-ROM**

go.hrw.com
Online Resources
KEYWORD: SHL TEACHER

Chapter 17 Planning Guide

New Asian Empires

Chapter Overview	Reproducible Resources	Technology Resources
CHAPTER 17 pp. 496–525 **Overview:** In this chapter, students will learn about the great empires and shifts in power that occurred in Asia from 1200 to 1800. KI 1, 3; PI 1.4, 3.1, 3.2, 3.3 See pp. T32–T55 for a detailed correlation to the New York State Core Curriculum for Global History and Geography and the New York Learning Standards.	**Differentiated Instruction Teacher Management System:** * • Pacing Guide • Lesson Plans for Differentiated Instruction **Interactive Reader and Study Guide:** Chapter Summary* **Chapter Resource File*** • Writing for the SAT • Social Studies Skill • Chapter Review **World History Outline Maps**	**Live Ink© Online Reading Help** **Student Edition on Audio CD Program** **Differentiated Instruction Modified Worksheets and Tests CD-ROM** **World History Primary Source Library CD-ROM** **Power Presentations with Video CD-ROM** **History's Impact: World History Video Program (VHS/DVD):** New Asian Empires
Section 1: **The Ottoman and Safavid Empires** **The Main Idea:** The Ottoman and Safavid empires flourished under powerful rulers who expanded the territory and cultural influence of their empires. PI 1.4	**Differentiated Instruction Teacher Management System:** Section 1 Lesson Plan* **Interactive Reader and Study Guide:** Section 1 Summary* **Chapter Resource File*** • Vocabulary Builder: Section 1 • Biography: `Abbas • History and Geography: Muslim Rule in India Gains Foothold • Primary Source: Soldiers of the Ottoman Empire	**Regents Review Transparency:** Section 1* **Map Transparency:** Asian Empires, c. 1600's* **Map Transparency:** The Ottoman Empire, 1300–1683* **Map Transparency:** The Safavid Empire, 1500–1639*
Section 2: **The Mughal Empire** **The Main Idea:** Mughal rulers created a powerful empire in which military might and artistic culture flourished. PI 3.2	**Differentiated Instruction Teacher Management System:** Section 2 Lesson Plan* **Interactive Reader and Study Guide:** Section 2 Summary* **Chapter Resource File*** • Vocabulary Builder: Section 2 • Biography: Nur Jahan	**Regents Review Transparency:** Section 2* **Map Transparency:** Mughal Empire, 1526–1707* **Quick Facts Transparency:** Achievements of the Mughal Emperors*
Section 3: **The Ming and Qing Dynasties** **The Main Idea:** During the Ming and Qing dynasties China prospered, but the empire entered a period of isolation in response to increasing European contact. PI 3.1, 3.2, 3.3	**Differentiated Instruction Teacher Management System:** Section 3 Lesson Plan* **Interactive Reader and Study Guide:** Section 3 Summary* **Chapter Resource File*** • Vocabulary Builder: Section 3 • Biography: Zhang Juzheng	**Regents Review Transarency:** Section 3* **Map Transparency:** Ming and Qing Dynasties, 1368–1911* **Map Transparency:** The Voyages of Zheng He* **Internet Activity:** Ming and Qing Art
Section 4: **Medieval Japan and Korea** **The Main Idea:** During the medieval period, a feudal warrior society developed in Japan, while Korea's rulers endured invasion and turned to isolation. PI 1.4, 3.1, 3.3	**Differentiating Instruction Teacher Management System:** Section 4 Lesson Plan* **Interactive Reader and Study Guide:** Section 4 Summary* **Chapter Resource File*** • Vocabulary Builder: Section 4 • Biography: Tomoe Gozen • Literature: Hokku Poems	**Regents Review Transarency:** Section 4* **Map Transparency:** Japan and Korea, 1592–1597* **Internet Activity:** Japanese Theatre

go.hrw.com	Print Resource	Transparency	
LS Learning Styles	Audio CD	CD-ROM	
Video	**SE** Student Edition	**TE** Teacher's Edition	
OSP One-Stop Planner CD-ROM	NY Standards Mastery	

*also on One-Stop Planner CD-ROM

HOLT
History's Impact
World History Video Program (VHS/DVD)
New Asian Empires

Review, Assessment, Intervention

 Global History and Geography Regents Test Prep Workbook

Quick Facts Transparency: New Asian Empires*

Progress Assessment Support System (PASS):
Chapter Test*

Differentiated Instruction Modified Worksheets and Tests CD-ROM: Modified Chapter Test

OSP **New York One-Stop Planner CD-ROM:** ExamView Test Generator (English/Spanish)

HOAP **Holt Online Assessment Program (HOAP),** in the Holt Premier Online Student Edition

---

 PASS: Section 1 Quiz*

 Online Quiz: Section 1

 Alternative Assessment Handbook

 PASS: Section 2 Quiz*

 Online Quiz: Section 2

 Alternative Assessment Handbook

 PASS: Section 3 Quiz*

 Online Quiz: Section 3

 Alternative Assessment Handbook

 PASS: Section 4 Quiz*

 Online Quiz: Section 4

 Alternative Assessment Handbook

Power Presentation with Video CD-ROM

Power Presentations with Video are visual presentations of each chapter's main ideas. Presentations can be customized by including Quick Facts charts, images and maps from the textbook, and video clips.

Holt Online Learning

go.hrw.com
Teacher Resources
KEYWORD: SHL TEACHER

go.hrw.com
Student Resources
KEYWORD: SHL NAS

- Document-Based Questions
- Interactive Multimedia Activities

- Current Events
- Chapter-Based Internet Activities
- and more!

Holt Premier
Online Student Edition
Complete online support for interactivity, assessment, and reporting
- Interactive Maps and Notebook
- Homework Practice and Research Activities Online

CHAPTER 17 PLANNING GUIDE

The Big Picture

Peter N. Stearns

Gunpowder Empires The emergence of large new empires in Asia, embracing many different cultures and language groups, was a crucial development during the early modern period. Based in part on the use of land-based guns, particularly siege cannons, new groups of invaders seized power in the Middle East/southeastern Europe, Persia, and India. Empire also revived in China. Japan did not form an empire, but did develop more centralized rule within the feudal system. For several centuries, the Asian empires maintained substantial political power, opulent cities, and a variety of new contributions in the arts. They also played a vigorous economic role.

The Ottoman, Safavid and Mughal Empires Three empires were Muslim-ruled, giving some renewed political coherence to Islam. During their initial phases, the empires were also tolerant, which contributed to their success. The empires made significant contributions to bureaucratic development, as well as to military strength. They also had a major cultural impact, through new artistic and architectural combinations and even linguistic innovation.

East Asia Generalizations about China in this period often miss the mark. Two major dynasties flourished during the early modern centuries. The second, the Qing, was imposed from the outside and had characteristics of the gunpowder empires of southern and western Asia. A brief flurry of international trade was followed by greater internal focus. Still China remained a center for global production and profited from European-mediated exchanges with the Americas. Japan adopted a more systematic policy of isolation, but even here trade with the Dutch persisted. The Tokugawa shogunate maintained the feudal social system and Confucianism gained ground, leading to educational expansion.

Decline Several of the gunpowder empires faltered by around 1700. The Mughal Empire fell into serious trouble because of military overextension and growing intolerance. The Ottoman Empire reached peak expansion in the 17th century. China displayed some new problems by the 18th century.

Recent Scholarship

India before Europe (2006) is a sympathetic and readable study of the varieties of Indian development in the early modern period, from the establishment of the Mughal Empire to important regional kingdoms. Catherine B. Asher and Cynthia Talbot deal well with Muslim-Hindu relationships, including the vitality of Indian Islam, as well as with urban, artistic, economic patterns. Also vital for the period and hugely influential in recent world history, is Kenneth Pomeranz's *The Great Divergence: China, Europe, and the Making of the Modern World Economy* (2000), which shows the vitality of Chinese world trade and challenges conventional interpretations of Europe's economic gains.

Differentiating Instruction

 Differentiated Instruction Teacher Management System
- Pacing Guide
- Lesson Plans for Differentiated Instruction

 Interactive Reader and Study Guide

Spanish Chapter Summaries Audio CD Program

Student Edition on Audio CD Program

 Differentiated Instruction Modified Worksheets and Tests CD-ROM
- Vocabulary Flash Cards
- Modified Vocabulary Builder Activities
- Modified Chapter Review Activity
- Modified Chapter Test

OSP One-Stop Planner CD-ROM
- ExamView Test Generator (English/Spanish)
- PuzzlePro
- Quiz Show for ExamView
- Transparencies and Videos

TE **Differentiated Activities in the Teacher's Edition**
- Map of Constantinople, p. 501
- The Death of Akbar, p. 505
- The Mongols, p. 510
- Social Structure of Feudal Japan, p. 520

Reading Like a Historian

Sam Wineburg

Historical Imaginings Some seventy years before Columbus reached the New World, the fleet of Admiral Zheng He, the eunuch mariner and emissary of the Ming Emperor Yongle, set out on a remarkable voyage. From China, Zheng He's captains sailed their massive 500-feet long junks to the western coast of Africa, then crossed the Atlantic to modern day Mexico, Brazil, Patagonia, and California. Along the way they brought horses to the Americas, smelted copper in Greenland, and mined for lead and saltpeter in Australia.

Fantastic? Not according to former British submarine commander and amateur historian, Gavin Menzies, whose *1421: The Year China Discovered the World*, published in 2002 climbed to the top of best-seller lists and became a media sensation. It's not everyday that a thick book packed with multiple-page explanations of celestial navigation makes front-page news ("Did the Chinese beat out Columbus?" asked the *International Herald Tribune*, June 25, 2005.) Even if a fraction of Menzies' claims are true, then the textbook you are holding will have to undergo substantial revision.

On his website (http://www.1421.tv) Menzies has amassed over 100,000 notes from supporters, the preponderance of which are from like-minded enthusiasts eager to debunk accepted history. One scans the list in vain for endorsements by serious historians—Western, Chinese, or otherwise. They have not been forthcoming.

"Alternative History" Why have historians been slow to warm to what *1421*'s publisher calls "the incredible true story of the discovery of America before Columbus was even born"? The response can be summed up in one word: evidence.

Consider just a few of the hundreds of claims *1421* puts forth: that Ming voyagers reached South and North America, Antarctica and Australia, even though no Ming artifacts have been located and documented in those regions; that, while visiting the tip of Patagonia, sailors captured giant ground sloths, even though by *1421* such beasts had been extinct for about a thousand years; that animals aboard these ships were nourished by foods mixed with desalinated sea water, even though there's no evidence the Chinese had mastered this technology; or that during long stretches at sea, Ming mariners replenished their own food supply by impressing "trained otters working in pairs to heard shoal into nets" even though no evidence is provided of such miraculous creatures. And this is just the tip of a Patagonian iceberg.

Reviewing the book in the *Journal of World History*, University of Arkansas historian Robert Finlay called Menzies a man "gripped by a mania to bend everything to his purposes," someone who "flouts the basic rules of both historical study and elementary logic." University of London's T. H. Barrett goes one step further. He claims that Menzies' imagination casts him "upon the desolate shores of Alternative History. There spacemen, Altanteans, and Templars jostle endlessly … in a picture of the past that never was."

Not all historians see *1421* without use. Writing in *World History Connected*, John E. Wills suggests that the book's greatest value may lay as a tool to "teach students about the use and misuse of historical evidence."

Zheng He was a remarkable mariner whose bold expeditions to the Indian Ocean are well documented by historical sources. Unfortunately, the eunuch admiral died at sea and was thus denied the custom of being reunited with his missing parts, long sealed in a jar, so that he would not remain impotent in the next life.

A historical interpretation unbound by evidence remains impotent in this life.

Chapter Main Ideas

Section 1 The Ottoman and Safavid empires flourished under powerful rulers who expanded the territory and cultural influence of their empires.

Section 2 Mughal rulers created a powerful empire in which military might and artistic culture flourished.

Section 3 During the Ming and Qing dynasties, China prospered, but the empire entered a period of isolation in response to increasing European contact.

Section 4 During the medieval period, a feudal warrior society developed in Japan, while Korea's rulers endured invasion and turned to isolation.

New York Standards

Key Idea 1 The study of world history requires an understanding of world cultures and civilizations, including an analysis of important ideas, social and cultural values, beliefs, and traditions. This study also examines the human condition and the connections and interactions of people across time and space and the ways different people view the same event or issue from a variety of perspectives.

Key Idea 3 Study of the major social, political, cultural, and religious developments in world history involves learning about the important roles and contributions of individuals and groups.

Key to Differentiating Instruction

Below Level

Basic-level activities designed for all students encountering new material

At Level

Intermediate-level activities designed for average students

Above Level

Challenging activities designed for honors and gifted and talented students

Standard English Mastery

Activities designed to improve standard English usage

CHAPTER 17 1200–1800

New Asian Empires

THE BIG PICTURE In Asia, the period from 1200 to 1800 was a time of great empires and shifts in power. From east of the Mediterranean Sea to India, strong Muslim rulers built large empires. In China a new dynasty sought to revive the traditions neglected under the Mongols, while a military society arose in Japan.

Theme ARTS AND IDEAS
The civilizations of Asia have contributed many lasting achievements in the arts and ideas throughout history. In this chapter, you will learn about the contributions of China, Japan, and Muslim empires in Asia in the arts, learning, science, and technology.

TIME LINE

CHAPTER EVENTS

c. 1300 Osman founds the Ottoman state.

1368 China's Ming dynasty begins.

1392 The Choson dynasty begins in Korea.

1453 Ottomans conquer Constantinople.

1501 Safavid Empire founded.

1526 Mughal Empire founded.

1300 **1400** **1500**

WORLD EVENTS

1279 Mongols found the Yuan dynasty in China.

1347 Black Death begins to spread through Europe.

1492 Columbus reaches the Americas.

1517 Protestant Reformation begins.

496 CHAPTER 17

Introduce the Chapter

At Level

New Asian Empires

Materials: 4 large sheets of paper, colored markers

1. Tell students that through fierce competition for power, rulers gained control over different parts of Asia. Organize the class into four groups, and assign each group a section of this chapter.

2. Have each group look for major power struggles that are described within their assigned section.

3. Distribute one sheet of paper and one marker to each group. Have students record their assigned section number at the top, and record their findings on the paper.

4. When groups have finished their work, have them share their findings. Have students take notes during the presentations and ask them to retain their notes as a study tool.

LS Interpersonal, Verbal-Linguistic

Alternative Assessment Handbook, Rubrics 1: Acquiring Information; and 14: Group Activity

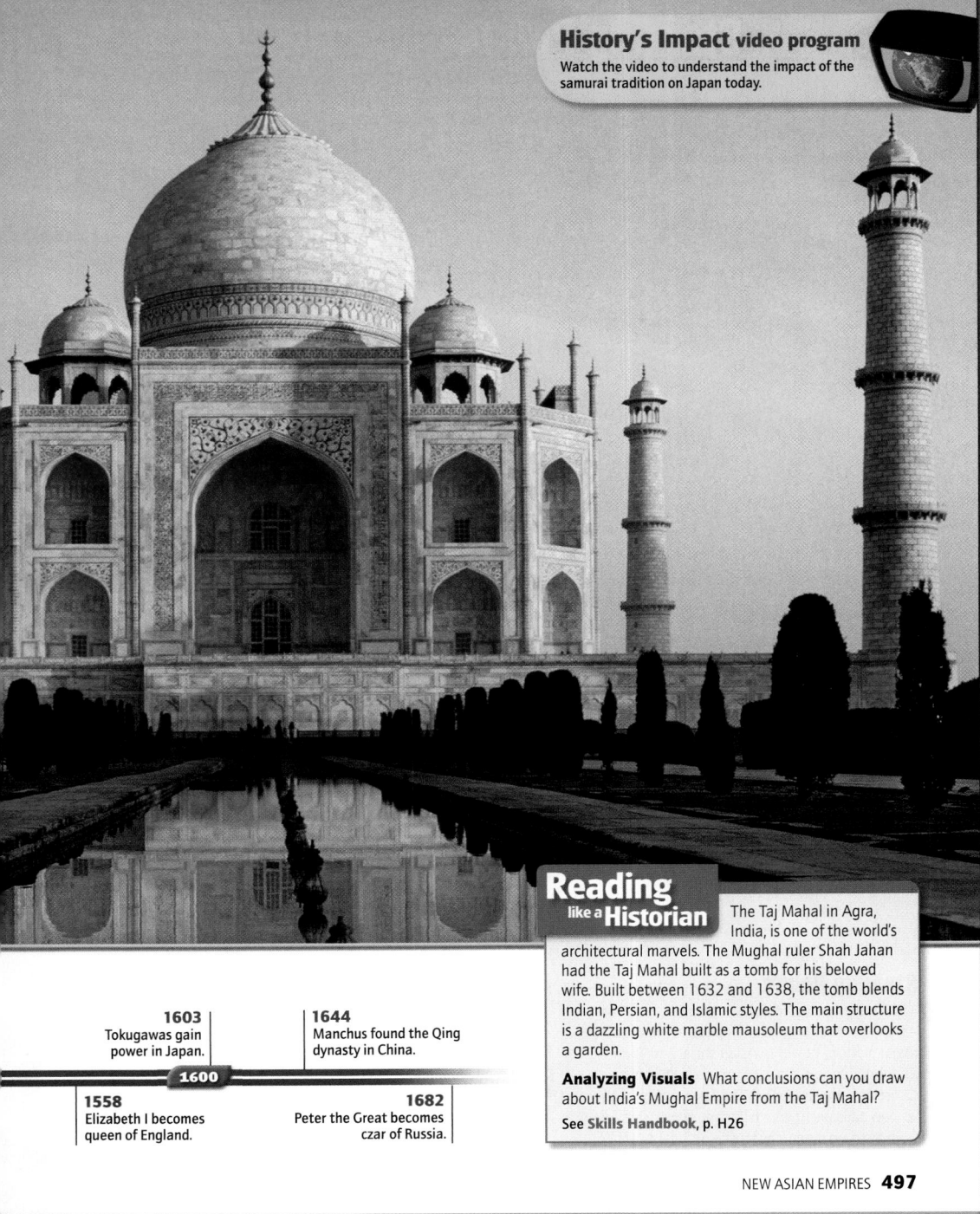

History's Impact video program
Watch the video to understand the impact of the samurai tradition on Japan today.

Reading like a Historian

The Taj Mahal in Agra, India, is one of the world's architectural marvels. The Mughal ruler Shah Jahan had the Taj Mahal built as a tomb for his beloved wife. Built between 1632 and 1638, the tomb blends Indian, Persian, and Islamic styles. The main structure is a dazzling white marble mausoleum that overlooks a garden.

Analyzing Visuals What conclusions can you draw about India's Mughal Empire from the Taj Mahal?

See **Skills Handbook**, p. H26

1603	1644
Tokugawas gain power in Japan.	Manchus found the Qing dynasty in China.

1600

1558	1682
Elizabeth I becomes queen of England.	Peter the Great becomes czar of Russia.

▶ **Video Program: New Asian Empires**
See the Video Teacher's Guide for strategies for using the video segment.

Reading Like a Historian

Analyzing Visuals This memorial mausoleum expresses not only love for the departed, but reminds the faithful to pray. Point out to students that the minarets are part of the overall plan, and that the spires atop the buildings guide one's eyes upward. Have students describe the effect of the reflecting pond and explain how the desert location of the Taj Mahal adds to the pond's importance.

Explore the Time Line

1. Which dynasty was founded in 1279? *the Yuan dynasty in China*

2. How much time elapsed between the founding of the Safavid Empire and the Mughal Empire? *25 years*

3. What event began in Europe in 1517? *the Protestant Reformation*

4. Who gained power in 1603 in Japan? *the Tokugawas*

Info to Know

The Taj Mahal The Taj Mahal was built during the reign of Shah Jahan, who brought workers from all over India and central Asia to work on the building. It took more than 20,000 workers and over 20 years to finish the job.

Make Inferences What statement does this building make about the reign of Shah Jahan? *possible answer—that he was a powerful ruler with unlimited financial resources, and that his reign lasted a long time*

go.hrw.com
Online Resources

Chapter Resources:
KEYWORD: SHL NAS
Teacher Resources:
KEYWORD: SHL TEACHER

Answers

Reading Like a Historian *possible answer—that the Mughals were wealthy and Muslim*

Geography Starting Points

The Caucasus Mountains The name of these mountains is at the root of the term that is used to identify people with fair skin (Caucasian). In 1795, Johann Blumenbach, a German anthropologist, introduced the term, because he erroneously assumed that the ancestors of such people had originated somewhere in the Caucasus range. Though it is not a scientific term, it is still in use for want of a better one. The mountains themselves received their name from the Greek word *kaukhasis*, which came from the Scythian *kroy-khasis*, which literally means "(the mountain) ice-shining."

- **Map Transparency:** Asian Empires, c. 1600's
- **World History Outline Maps**
- **Interactive Map:** Asian Empires, c. 1600's

Answers

Geography Starting Points
1. *The Ming Dynasty and the Tokugawa Shogunate;* 2. *New leaders would bring new styles of leadership, laws would change, and reforms would be introduced*

GEOGRAPHY Starting Points

✱Interactive
ASIAN EMPIRES, c. 1600s

The Christian Byzantine Empire fell to Sunni Muslim Turks called Ottomans in the 1400s.

China's Yuan dynasty fell to the Ming dynasty in 1368, while in Japan the Heian government gave way to military dynasties called shogunates.

In the early 1500s Shia Muslims conquered Persia, while Sunni Muslims took power in India.

Map labels: ATLAS MOUNTAINS, Algiers, Vienna, Rome, EUROPE, Tripoli, Mediterranean Sea, Constantinople (Istanbul), Black Sea, CAUCASUS MOUNTAINS, Caspian Sea, Aral Sea, ASIA, AFRICA, Jerusalem, Baghdad, Esfahan, Nile River, Medina, Red Sea, Mecca, Persian Gulf, ARABIAN PENINSULA, Delhi, Agra, Fatehpur Sikri, HIMALAYAS, Ganges River, Indus River, GOBI, Beijing, Edo (Tokyo), Kyoto, Osaka, Yellow Sea, Nanjing, East China Sea, Chang Jiang (Yangzi River), Tropic of Cancer, Arabian Sea, Bay of Bengal, South China Sea, Sri Lanka, INDIAN OCEAN

Scale: 0 500 1,000 Miles / 0 500 1,000 Kilometers / Two-point equidistant projection

Legend:
- Ming Dynasty, c. 1600
- Mughal Empire, 1707
- Ottoman Empire, 1683
- Safavid Empire, 1683
- Tokugawa Shogunate, mid-1600s
- ✱ Capital
- ⌇⌇ Great Wall

Starting Points Between 1300 and 1500 several powerful new empires arose in Asia. The rise of these empires represented major shifts in power in Asian society. In Turkey and India, for example, power shifted from the Christians and Hindus who had previously ruled to new Muslim rulers. In Japan, power shifted from a strong monarchy to rule by local rulers.

1. **Analyze** According to the map, what new dynasties took power in China and Japan during this period?
2. **Predict** What effects do you think the changes in government of the 1300s and 1400s had on Asian societies? Why do you think these changes took place?

Listen to History

Go online to listen to an explanation of the starting points for this chapter.

go.hrw.com
Keyword: SHL NAS

498 CHAPTER 17

Skills Focus: Analyzing Maps

At Level

Social Studies Skill
Borders of Asian Empires

1. Tell students that they will identify the natural borders of each of the five Asian Empires.

2. Draw the chart for students to see. Omit the italicized answers. Organize students into small groups, and have groups focus on one map area at a time as they fill in the chart. **Interpersonal, Visual-Spatial**

- **Alternative Assessment Handbook**, Rubrics 13: Graphic Organizers; and 21: Map Reading

Asian Empires	Natural Borders
Mughal	*Arabian Sea, Bay of Bengal, Indian Ocean, Himalaya's*
Ottoman	*Black Sea, Mediterranean Sea, Red Sea, Persian Gulf, Atlas Mountains, Caucasus Mountains*
Safavid	*Persian Gulf, Caspian Sea, Caucasus Mountains*
Ming	*Yellow, East China and South China Seas, Gobi Desert*
Tokugawa	*Yellow or East China Seas*

SECTION 1
The Ottoman and Safavid Empires

BEFORE YOU READ

MAIN IDEA

The Ottoman and Safavid empires flourished under powerful rulers who expanded the territory and cultural influence of their empires.

READING FOCUS

1. How did the Ottomans build a powerful empire, and what were their cultural accomplishments?

2. How was the Safavid Empire founded and enlarged, and what cultural elements did it combine?

KEY TERMS AND PEOPLE

ghazis
Ottomans
sultan
Janissaries
Mehmed II
Suleyman I
shah
'Abbas

 NEW YORK

PI 1.4 Students understand the broad patterns, relationships, and interactions of cultures and civilizations during particular eras and across eras.

THE FALL OF NEW ROME

Siege of Constantinople, 1455

▲ Ottoman forces use massive cannons in their siege of Constantinople in 1453.

THE INSIDE STORY

How might a black powder alter history? For more than 1,000 years, Constantinople had been the capital—the New Rome—of the Byzantine Empire, the eastern half of the old Roman Empire. By 1453, though, the once-great empire was crumbling, falling to invaders called Ottomans.

The 21-year-old Ottoman ruler, Mehmed II, burned with desire to take Constantinople. But how to break through its massive walls? The answer was an explosive black powder called gunpowder. Invented by the Chinese, gunpowder had slowly spread west. There, the Ottomans were among the first to use gunpowder weapons, such as cannons—weapons that changed warfare and the course of history.

Mehmed II surrounded Constantinople and aimed massive cannons at its walls. After some two months of battering, the city fell. Waves of Ottoman soldiers flooded in, killing and enslaving thousands. One witness said the "blood flowed through the streets like rainwater after a sudden storm." With Constantinople's conquest, the Ottoman Empire had become one of the great world powers. ■

The Ottoman Empire

The Mongol conquests of the 1200s had ripped apart the Seljuk Turk empire in Anatolia, a region also known as Asia Minor. A number of small, independent Turkish states then formed in the region. In the late 1200s a great chieftain, who was from one of these states, arose and went on to found the powerful Ottoman Empire.

NEW ASIAN EMPIRES **499**

Direct Teach

Reading Focus

1 How did the Ottomans build a powerful empire, and what were their cultural accomplishments? *rich, diverse culture, many religious practices, built magnificent mosques and palaces*

The Ottoman Empire

Identify What were two advantages of the Ottoman military? *elite soldiers loyal to sultan, had superior new weapons*

Explain What was special about the location of Anatolia? *It lay at the strategic intersection of Asia and Europe.*

Develop What are some possible reasons the Ottomans might have shown cultural and religious tolerance? *possible answer—They would have faced less opposition from the conquered and benefited from their knowledge.*

📋 **CRF:** Primary Source: Soldiers of the Ottoman Empire

Interpreting Maps
The Ottoman Empire, 1300–1683

Human/Environment Interaction Why do you think the Ottomans never expanded their territory west of the Nile? *It is a desert area without water or other resources needed to support human life.*

Movement In the expansion of 1451 to 1520, in which direction did the Ottomans travel to add territory that was not contiguous to their own? *north, to Crimea*

🗺 **Map Transparency:** The Ottoman Empire, 1300–1683

Answers

Interpreting Maps 1. *Balkans, Greece, Anatolia;* **2.** *Africa, Asia, Europe*

500

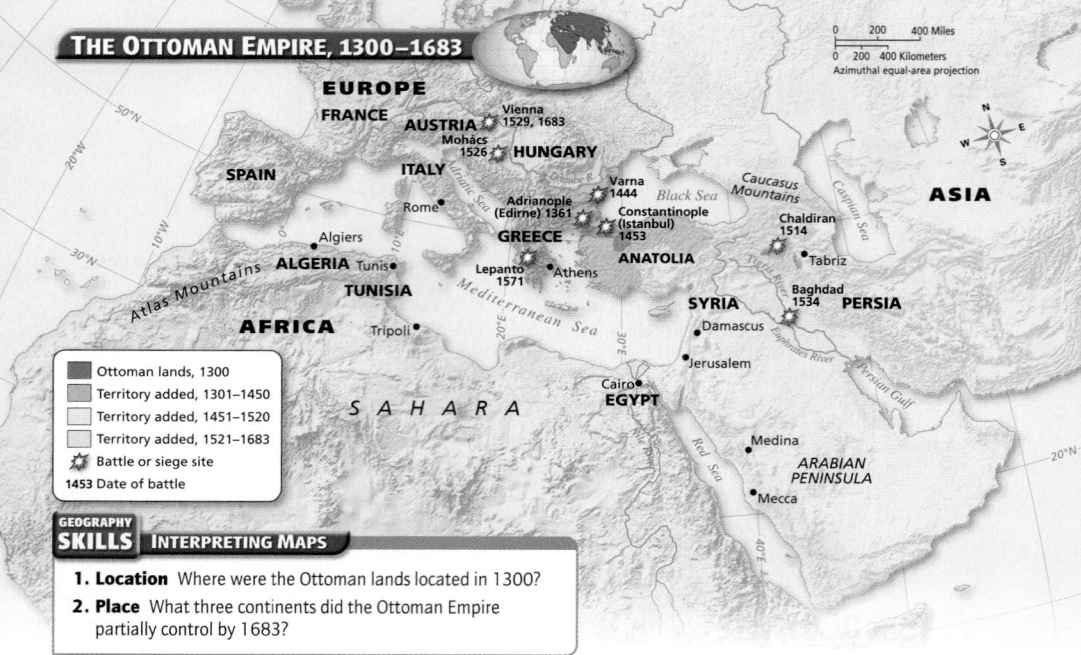

THE OTTOMAN EMPIRE, 1300–1683

- Ottoman lands, 1300
- Territory added, 1301–1450
- Territory added, 1451–1520
- Territory added, 1521–1683
- ✹ Battle or siege site
- **1453** Date of battle

GEOGRAPHY SKILLS | **INTERPRETING MAPS**

1. **Location** Where were the Ottoman lands located in 1300?
2. **Place** What three continents did the Ottoman Empire partially control by 1683?

TAKING NOTES

Take notes in a graphic organizer like this one to record key facts about the Ottoman and Safavid empires.

Ottoman	Safavid

Growth of the Empire Anatolia lies at the strategic intersection of Asia and Europe. In the early 1300s, the region was bordered by the declining Christian Byzantine Empire to the west and by Muslim empires to the east. To the north, beyond the Black Sea, lay Russia.

The Turks of Anatolia were mainly Muslim. A nomadic people with a militaristic society, they saw themselves as *ghazis,* or "warriors for the Islam faith." One of the ablest *ghazi* leaders was Osman I. By 1300 he had built a strong state in Anatolia. Westerners came to refer to Osman and his descendants as the **Ottomans**. Their power grew quickly, and by the mid-1300s the Ottomans controlled much of Anatolia.

Orhan I, Osman's son, became the second Ottoman ruler and declared himself **sultan**, Arabic for "ruler." Under Orhan and later sultans, Ottoman forces swept into the Balkans in southeastern Europe to attack the Byzantine Empire. In 1361 the Ottomans took Adrianople, the second-most important Byzantine city, renamed it Edirne, and made it their capital. By the early 1400s the Ottomans controlled

much of the Balkan Peninsula. Within about 100 years, the Ottoman state had grown into a true empire and become a European power.

The key to the Ottomans' success was their military. As their empire grew, the Ottomans enslaved Christian boys from conquered areas. The boys were converted to Islam and trained as elite soldiers called **Janissaries**, who were loyal only to the sultan. Many Christians called this practice a blood tax. In addition, the Ottomans adopted gunpowder weapons such as cannons. The force of these weapons made it possible to take cities defended by heavy walls.

Invasion and Decline Despite their strong military, the Ottomans experienced a setback when the great Central Asian conqueror Timur (TEEM-uhr) attacked. Because of an old leg injury, Timur was known as Timur the Lame and in Europe as Tamerlane. At the Battle of Ankara in 1402, his army crushed the Ottoman forces. Timur soon withdrew, but the Ottoman Empire was left in shambles, its ruler dead. A bloody power struggle followed, which weakened the empire.

500 CHAPTER 17

Skills Focus: Identifying Main Idea and Details | At Level

Reading Skill | **Research Required**
The Ottomans

1. Remind students that the Ottomans were remarkably tolerant of other cultures and religions. Review the information in the text about the treatment of conquered people.

2. Have students design an illustrated, public relations brochure explaining the changes that will be coming to a people that cannot withstand the Ottoman army. Have students first sketch their ideas and plan the layout for their brochures. Remind students that the

illustrations are crucial, as not everyone spoke the same language.

3. Have volunteers present their work to the class.

4. As an extension, have students write a generalization statement about the Ottoman treatment of conquered peoples.
LS Interpersonal, Visual-Spatial

📋 **Alternative Assessment Handbook**, Rubric 3: Artwork

Fall of Constantinople Following a period of decline, a spectacular phase of expansion began with the reign of **Mehmed II** in the mid-1400s. A strong military leader, Mehmed was determined to take Constantinople, the Byzantine capital. The Ottomans had failed to capture this city despite conquering the lands around it. Constantinople controlled the Bosporus Strait, a major trade route between Asia and Europe. Control of this vital waterway not only provided the Byzantines with great wealth but also divided the Ottoman Empire.

In 1453 the Ottomans led a major land and sea assault against Constantinople. Using massive cannons, Ottoman forces battered the city's walls. After a siege of almost two months, Constantinople fell. The Byzantine Empire no longer existed. Mehmed became known as "the Conqueror," and, in triumph, claimed the center of eastern Christianity for Islam.

Mehmed made Constantinople his capital, which became known as Istanbul. In keeping with tradition, he allowed his soldiers to pillage the city for three days, during which many residents were killed or enslaved. Mehmed then rebuilt Constantinople into a Muslim city. He had palaces and mosques built and even had Hagia Sophia, the great Orthodox Christian cathedral, turned into a mosque. To repopulate the city, he had people moved there from across the empire. Soon, the city was again a major trade center with people of many cultures.

Height of the Empire Under the next three sultans, expansion continued. The Ottomans expanded their empire east through the rest of Anatolia. They also addressed a new threat in Persia—the Safavid Empire. In 1514 Ottoman forces crushed the Safavids at the Battle of Chaldiran. The Ottomans then swept through Syria and into Egypt in North Africa. Soon afterward, the Ottoman army captured Mecca and Medina, the holy cities of Islam.

The Ottoman Empire reached its height under **Suleyman I** (soo-lay-MAHN), known in the West as Suleyman "the Magnificent." During his reign, from 1520 to 1566, Ottoman forces pushed through Hungary up to Vienna. Meanwhile, the navy gained control of the eastern Mediterranean and the North African coast.

Suleyman's domestic achievements were equally impressive. He reformed the tax system and overhauled the government bureaucracy.

In addition, he improved the court system and legal code and had new laws issued to reduce corruption. For these actions, he earned the title Suleyman "the Lawgiver."

Society and Culture The Ottoman sultan ruled over a vast and diverse empire. As head of this empire, the sultan had immense power and issued all laws and made all major decisions. Numerous officials advised the sultan, however. These officials were considered his slaves—that is, they had to be completely loyal to the sultan and the empire, and they had to practice Islam and follow Ottoman customs.

This privileged ruling class formed one of two classes in Ottoman society. The second class consisted of everyone else in the empire. This group included people of many cultures who spoke many different languages and practiced many different religions.

In general, the Ottomans governed their diverse subjects with tolerance. At the same time, Non-Muslims had to pay heavy taxes and endure restrictions, although they did not have to serve in the military. Muslims did have to join the military but they were not taxed. Following Islamic law, the Ottomans allowed religious freedom. They required some religious groups, such as Christians and Jews—People of the Book to Muslims—to form millets, or religious communities. Each millet could follow its own religious laws and choose its own leaders, who were responsible to the sultan.

 NEW YORK

CC Unit 4-B3
The impact of the Ottoman Empire and Suleyman 1 (the Magnificent, the Lawgiver)

FACES OF HISTORY

SULEYMAN
c. 1494–1566

Suleyman was named for the Hebrew king Soloman, whom the Qur'an considers to be the wisest ruler of antiquity. Energetic, calm, and intelligent, Suleyman studied subjects from architecture to geography to poetry. He used his vast knowledge to improve the Ottoman Empire in many ways. His military campaigns extended the empire to the east and west. He had many bridges and mosques built and reformed the empire's administration and laws, for which his subjects gave him the title *Kanuni*, or "Lawgiver." In addition, some historians consider Suleyman's rule to have been the height of Ottoman cultural achievements.

Summarize How did Suleyman improve the Ottoman Empire?

Reading Focus

The Ottoman Empire

Describe How were Janissaries created? *In the Balkans, some Christian boys were taken from their families and converted to Islam and trained soldiers.*

Evaluate What is your opinion of Mehmed II's conquest of Constantinople? *possible answer—It was cruel to kill so many and it was not necessary to destroy a great city.*

Recent Scholarship

Osman's Dream: The History of the Ottoman Empire by Caroline Finkel is an overview of an empire that lasted over six centuries. Finkel describes the richness and the complexity of the Ottoman Empire. She looks at the Ottomans as they saw themselves and their empire, not as a Westerner looking at the empire from the outside. Osman's Dream is a careful, well-researched history, complete with descriptions of the richness, complexity, and change that occurred in the empire over the centuries.

Osman's Dream: The History of the Ottoman Empire by Caroline Finkel. Basic Books, 2006.

Differentiating Instruction

Below Level

Learners Having Difficulty; English-Language Learners

1. Remind students that Constantinople was a well-defended city and only fell because Sultan Mehmed II carried out an effective siege plan.

2. Have students use the maps in this chapter or in the atlas of their textbook to create a map showing the location Byzantium, the Black Sea, and the Bosporus Straits.

3. Have students show the path that Mehmed II took when he laid siege to the city. Students should show the probable positions of forts, armed forces, and the armada which felled the city. Student maps should include a key and a means for measuring distance. **LS Visual-Spatial**

📖 **Alternative Assessment Handbook**, Rubrics 1: Acquiring Information; and 20: Map Creation

---

Answers

Faces of History *expanded the empire; built mosques and bridges; reformed the empire's administration and laws*

501

NEW YORK

CC Unit 4-B2
Contributions of the Ottoman Empire

Reading Focus

2 How was the Safavid Empire founded and enlarged, and what cultural elements did it combine? *through conquest; blended the Shía religion with Persian tradition, built magnificent cities, palaces, and mosques and produced a golden age*

The Safavid Empire

Identify Who was the founder of the Safavid Empire? *a 14-year old boy named Esma'il*

Explain How did religion bring the Safavid Empire into conflict with the Ottoman Empire? *The Safavids were Shia Muslims, while most other Muslims were Sunnis.*

 Map Transparency: The Safavid Empire, 1500–1639

Primary Source

"I gave my orders—make a dress for my beloved.
Use the sun to make the top,
Use the moon to make the lining, Use the white clouds for the trimmings,
Use the blue of the sea to make the threads.
Use the stars for buttons, And make the fastenings out of me."

—excerpt of a letter from Suleyman to his wife, former Ukrainian slave, Roxolana

✳ **Interactive Map:** The Safavid Empire, 1500–1639

The mixing of many peoples created a rich Ottoman culture, which reached its peak under Suleyman. Architects built magnificent mosques and palaces. Many buildings showed a Byzantine influence, such as in the use of domes. One master designer was Sinan. His Mosque of Suleyman in Istanbul shows a graceful solution to the problem of combining a round dome with a rectangular building.

The Empire's Decline After Suleyman's reign, the Ottoman Empire gradually declined. One cause was the practice of dealing with heirs. Until the 1600s, new sultans had their brothers killed to eliminate rivals. Later, princes and heirs were locked up in the royal palace. When a prince or heir was released to become sultan, he had no experience with governing. Though there were periodic efforts to reform the system, a series of weak sultans resulted. Even so, the empire lasted until the early 1900s.

READING SKILLS

Summarizing
After you read the information on the Safavid Empire, summarize the key points in three to five sentences.

READING CHECK **Analyze** Why is Suleyman's reign considered the height of the Ottoman Empire?

The Safavid Empire

East of the Ottomans, Persian Muslims called the Safavids (sah-FAH-vuhds) began building an empire around 1500. The Safavids soon came into conflict with the Ottomans and other Muslims. The conflict related to Islam's split into the rival Sunni and Shia sects. The Safavids were Shia; most other Muslims were Sunnis.

Growth of the Empire The founder of the Safavid Empire was a 14-year-old boy named Esma'il (is-mah-EEL). His father had died fighting Sunni Muslims, and in 1501 Esma'il took up the sword. Joined by his father's supporters, Esma'il led his army on a sweep of conquest in Persia. In a series of victories, he gained control of what is now Iran as well as part of Iraq. Esma'il then took the Persian title of **shah,** or "king," of the Safavid Empire.

As shah, Esma'il made Shiism the official Safavid religion. This act worried his advisers because most people in the empire were Sunnis. Unconcerned, Esma'il said the following:

Interactive
THE SAFAVID EMPIRE, 1500–1639

Safavid Persia, 1629
Border set by treaty, 1639
Safavid advance
Ottoman advance
Uzbek advance
Battle site
1514 Date of battle

0   100   200 Miles
0   400   200 Kilometers
Azimuthal equal-area projection

GEOGRAPHY SKILLS **INTERPRETING MAPS**

go.hrw.com
Interactive Map
Keyword: SHL NAS

1. **Location** What empire lay east of the Safavid Empire?
2. **Regions** In what region of the Safavid Empire were the main battles against the Uzbeks fought?

502 CHAPTER 17

Skills Focus: Comparing and Contrasting

At Level

Reading Skill
Expansion by Conquest

1. Review the rapid expansion of the Ottoman Empire with students. Use both the text and the maps in this section to help students understand the immensity of the Safavid Empire.

2. Organize students into an even number of groups, and have groups prepare for a debate on the topic "A civilization that expands by conquest will maintain power and spread their beliefs." Assign half of the groups to prepare statements to represent those who support this

position. Assign the other groups to prepare statements to represent those who disagree.

3. When groups have prepared their statements, call upon pairs of groups to debate the issue.

4. When the debates are finished, have students write a short essay explaining their position on this topic. **LS** **Interpersonal, Verbal-Linguistic**

Alternative Assessment Handbook, Rubrics 10: Debates; and 14: Group Activity

---

Answers

Reading Skills *Student summaries should show an understanding of the Safavid Empire.*

Interpreting Maps 1. *The Mughal Empire;* **2.** *in the northeast*

Reading Check *because Suleyman expanded the empire, built bridges and mosques, and reformed the administration and laws of the empire*

> ❝I am committed to this action; God and the Immaculate Imams [pure religious leaders] are with me, and I fear no one; by God's help, if the people utter one word of protest, I will draw the sword and leave not one of them alive.❞
>
> —Esma'il, quoted in *A Literary History of Persia, Volume 4*, by Edward G. Browne

The blending of Shia religion and Persian tradition gave the Safavid state a unique identity and laid the foundation for the national culture of present-day Iran. At the same time, Shiism sharply distinguished the Safavid state from its Sunni neighbors, notably the Ottomans to the west and the Uzbeks to the northeast.

Esma'il dreamed of converting all Sunnis to Shiism. He battled the Uzbeks with some success but suffered a crushing defeat by the Ottomans in 1514 at the Battle of Chaldiran. The Safavid army was no match for the Ottomans' superior gunpowder weapons. Esma'il died in 1524, and later Safavid shahs struggled to keep the empire together.

Then in 1588 the greatest Safavid leader, **'Abbas**, became shah. 'Abbas reformed the government, strengthened the military, and acquired modern gunpowder weapons. Copying the Ottoman model, 'Abbas had slave youths captured in Russia trained to be soldiers. Under 'Abbas's rule, the Safavids defeated the Uzbeks and gained back land lost to the Ottomans.

Culture and Economy 'Abbas's achievements produced a golden age in Safavid culture. Abbas brought in Chinese potters to improve the quality of glazed tiles and ceramics. The Safavids created public spaces with graceful arches and lush gardens. Colorful tiles and domes decorated mosques. During the 1600s the capital, Esfahan (es-fah-HAHN), was one of the world's most magnificent cities.

Safavid culture played a role in the empire's economy because 'Abbas encouraged the manufacturing of traditional products. Hand-woven Persian carpets became an important industry and export. Such trade goods brought wealth to the Safavid Empire and helped establish it as a major Muslim civilization. The empire lasted until 1722.

READING CHECK Compare and Contrast How were the achievements of Esma'il and 'Abbas similar, and how were they different?

Safavid Culture
The dome of Madrasa Mader-e Shah college, built in the 1700s in Esfahan, blends Chinese tilework with the Muslim tradition of using calligraphy for decoration with stunning results.

SECTION 1 ASSESSMENT

go.hrw.com
Online Quiz
Keyword: SHL NAS HP

Reviewing Ideas, Terms, and People

1. **a. Identify** Who were the **Janissaries**, and what was their role in the success of the **Ottomans**?
   b. Draw Conclusions Why do you think Westerners referred to Suleyman I as "the Magnificent"?
   c. Elaborate What impact did the Ottoman Empire and its expansion have on European history? Support your explanation with examples from the reading.
2. **a. Recall** Why did the Safavid Empire come into conflict with other Muslim empires around it?
   b. Explain How did events of the Safavid period shape culture in the present-day country of Iran?
   c. Evaluate Who do you think was the better Safavid ruler—Esma'il or 'Abbas? Provide reasons to support your opinion.

Critical Thinking

3. **Categorize** Using your notes and a graphic organizer like the one below, categorize and organize the information that you recorded about the Ottoman and Safavid empires.

	Ottoman	Safavid
Location		
Key People		
Key Events		
Society		
Culture		

FOCUS ON WRITING

4. **Persuasion** Write a short letter from the Ottoman sultan Mehmed II to his military advisors stating that he wants to attack the Byzantine capital of Constantinople. The letter should explain why capturing the city is so important to the Ottoman Empire and persuade the military advisors to support the campaign.

NEW ASIAN EMPIRES **503**

Direct Teach

Reading Focus

The Safavid Empire

Recall What were some achievements of 'Abbas? *He reformed the government, strengthened the military, and acquired gunpowder weapons.*

Interpret How did the Ottoman Empire defeat the Safavids in 1514? *by using superior gunpowder weapons*

CRF: Biography: 'Abbas

Review & Assess

Close

Review the development of the Ottoman and Safavid dynasties, the means with which they expanded their territories, and the cultural influence of their empires.

Review

Online Quiz, Section 1

Assess

SE Section 1 Assessment
Progress Assessment: Section 1 Quiz
Alternative Assessment Handbook

Reteach/Intervene

Interactive Reader and Study Guide, Section 1
Interactive Skills Tutor CD-ROM

Section 1 Assessment Answers

1. **a.** Christian boys taken by the sultan, converted to Islam, trained to fight; became an elite fighting corps
   b. developed a code of laws, was responsible for empire's immense expansion
   c. led to the fall of Byzantine Empire
2. **a.** The Safavids were Shia Muslims, while most other Muslims were Sunnis.
   b. blended the Persian culture with Shia religion, laying the foundation for Iran's culture
   c. possible answer—'Abbas, because he gained back land that had been lost.
3. Ottoman—Anatolia, spreading into Africa, Asia, Europe; Mehmed II, Suleyman; fall of Constantinople; diverse society, two classes, religious tolerance; blended cultures; Safavid—east of the Ottomans, in Persia; Esma'il, 'Abbas; defeat by the Ottomans in 1514; 'Abbas's achievements brought a golden age in culture; magnificent city of Esfahan
4. Student letters should emphasize that Constantinople divided the Ottoman Empire. Acquiring it would provide great wealth and a trade route between Asia and Europe.

Answers

Reading Check *Both leaders focused on military. 'Abbas had more success in battle because he acquired gunpowder weapons.*

503

Preteach

Getting Started

Use the **Interactive Reader and Study Guide** to familiarize students with the section content.

📖 **Interactive Reader and Study Guide,** Section 2

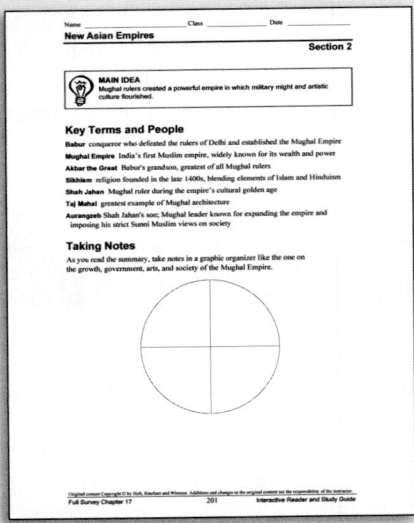

Academic Vocabulary

Review with students the high-use academic terms in this section.

stance attitude, position, or view about someone or something (p. 506)

regime a specific and often harsh government (p. 508)

📝 **CRF:** Vocabulary Builder: Section 2

Taking Notes

Growth— defeated rulers of Delhi by 1526, established Mughal Empire, Akbar organized the empire, empire reached greatest size under Aurangzeb; Government—Akbar: won people's loyalty, fought to prevent rebellion, had firm grasp of government and finances; Shah Jahan imposed heavy taxes; Arts—cultural golden age during the reign of Shah Jahan, Taj Mahal built, along with other monuments of Mughal majesty such as the Peacock Throne; Society—religious tolerance, Jahangir came into conflict with Sikhs.

BEFORE YOU READ

MAIN IDEA
Mughal rulers created a powerful empire in which military might and artistic culture flourished.

READING FOCUS
1. How was Muslim rule first established in India?
2. What was the new empire created by Babur and Akbar like?
3. What achievements were made by the rulers who held power at the height of the Mughal Empire?

KEY TERMS AND PEOPLE
Babur
Mughal Empire
Akbar the Great
Sikhism
Shah Jahan
Taj Mahal
Aurangzeb

 NEW YORK

P1 **3.2** Students explain the dynamics of cultural change and how interactions between and among cultures have affected various cultural groups throughout the world.

A Tiger Stalks INDIA

504

THE INSIDE STORY

How did a young prince and his outnumbered army create an empire? From birth, Prince Babur seemed destined to be a conqueror. Babur, whose name means "tiger," was a descendant of both Timur, the great general from Central Asia, and Genghis Khan, perhaps the greatest conqueror in Asian history. At 11 Babur became king of Fergana, a small territory in Central Asia. By 14 he had led a victorious army to take the city of Samarqand.

Babur's ambition was to build a huge empire that rivaled that of his ancestor Timur. As part of his empire building, Babur set out to conquer India in 1525. He and his army marched deep into India, heading for the capital, Delhi. In response, the Indian army came out to meet them. The two armies faced off near the small village of Panipat.

Babur's army was vastly outnumbered by the Indians. He had only about 12,000 troops with which to fight an estimated 100,000 foes. In addition, the Indian army included some 1,000 elephants, while Babur's had none. At first glance, the battle appeared to be hopeless.

However, Babur's army was better trained and better disciplined than the Indians'. In addition, Babur had a secret weapon—cannons—never before used in India. The first cannon shots astounded the Indians and terrified the elephants, who turned and stampeded through the Indian army. Within a few hours, Babur had won. Historians mark this victory as the beginning of a new empire in India. ◼

◀ **Babur's cannons helped him overcome overwhelming odds to win the Battle of Panipat and create a new empire.**

Battle of Panipat illustration from the *Baburnama*, c. 1598

Teach the Main Idea

At Level

The Mughal Empire

1. **Teach** Ask students the Reading Focus questions to teach this section.

2. **Apply** Organize students into three groups. Assign each group one of the three topics in the section: Muslim Rule in India, A New Empire, Height of the Mughal Empire. Have each group plan a set of drawings to illustrate the main points of its assigned topic. Each member of the group should have one main point to illustrate. When students have finished their drawings, have them record the

main point at the bottom of their papers.

3. **Review** Have each group present its work in the same order the topics are presented in the text. Create a class display of the drawings.

4. **Practice/Homework** Have students write a short summary of what they learned about the Mughal Empire. **LS Interpersonal, Visual-Spatial**

📖 **Alternative Assessment Handbook,** Rubrics 3: Artwork; and 24: Oral Presentations

Muslim Rule in India

After the fall of the Gupta Empire in the 500s, India broke apart into a number of small kingdoms. For several centuries, no single ruler emerged to take charge of all India.

The Arrival of Islam During this period of small kingdoms, Arab Muslim traders arrived in India for the first time. These traders sailed to ports along India's west coast in search of goods such as spices. Over time, some Muslim traders settled in Indian towns, where they peacefully lived beside Hindus and Buddhists.

The next Muslims to arrive in India, however, were not so peaceful. In the early 700s Muslim raiders invaded and conquered the region of Sind in what is now Pakistan. About 300 years later, Muslims poured into north India from Afghanistan. By the 1200s, most of northern India was under Muslim control.

The Delhi Sultanate Once the Muslims had taken control of north India, they established a new government for the region. Because this new government was based in the city of Delhi, it became known as the Delhi sultanate.

The rulers of the Delhi sultanate were tolerant and allowed the Indian people to practice their traditional customs and religions. At the same time, though, they worked to spread Muslim culture through India by inviting artists and scholars from other parts of the Islamic world to Delhi. As a result, a new culture formed that blended Muslim and Indian elements. For example, a new language, Urdu, formed from a combination of Arabic and Sanskrit.

READING CHECK **Sequence** How did Muslims come to rule India?

A New Empire

The Delhi sultanate remained strong for about 300 years. By the early 1500s, however, its power was weakening. This weakening left India open to invasion.

Babur The man who took advantage of India's weakness was a young Central Asian conqueror named Zahir ud-Din, but better known as **Babur**, or "the tiger." After trying and failing to create an empire in Central Asia, Babur turned to India. By 1526 he had defeated the rulers of Delhi and founded the **Mughal Empire**. The Mughals—whose name comes from the Persian word *Mogul* for "Mongol"—reigned as India's first Muslim empire and were one of the great civilizations of history. The Mughal Empire was known for its wealth and power.

Akbar the Great Babur died shortly after his conquest of India, and the task of organizing what he had conquered fell to his descendants. Most of this organization was done by Babur's grandson **Akbar the Great**. Despite being only 13 when he took the throne in 1556, Akbar became the greatest of all Mughal rulers.

FACES OF HISTORY

AKBAR
1542–1605

A Mughal emperor of India, Akbar united Indian territory north of the Vindhya Range under one empire. His rule is noted for many reforms, including the abolition of slavery and the development of trade. He was a patron of the arts and encouraged the development of science. Although himself a Muslim, his tolerance for non-Muslims in his empire was remarkable. His enlightened leadership became a model for later Mughal rulers.

Analyze Why was Akbar considered a great ruler?

Akbar built a new capital called Fatehpur Sikri, or the "City of Victory," to commemorate his achievements as emperor.

505

❸ What achievements were made by the rulers who held power at the height of the Mughal Empire? *supported literature and arts; built Taj Mahal and other monuments to Mughal greatness; expanded empire's borders*

Height of the Mughal Empire

Describe What was the architectural style of the Taj Mahal? *greatest example of Mughal architecture, included elements of Indian, Persian, Muslim architectural styles*

Evaluate In what ways, if any, did the golden age of architecture play a role in the decline of the Mughal Empire? *possible answer—The building projects were very costly, probably led to the taxation, resentment, and loss of prosperity within the empire.*

📝 **CRF:** Biography: Nur Jahan

Interpreting Maps

Mughal Empire 1526–1707

Movement Of the three groups living in the northern section of the map, which one's descendants have a nation named after them today, and what is it called? *Uzbecks, Uzbekistan*

Place What are some possible reasons that trading centers were grouped close together in some areas? *possible answers —safe ports, concentration of available goods, political stability in the area*

📦 **Map Transparency:** Mughal Empire, 1526–1707

Answers

Interpreting Maps 1. *the northern region; the southern region; 1606–1707;*
2. *possible answer—to connect to Indian Ocean trade routes*

Reading Check *by commitment to justice, religious tolerance, and the expansion of the empire.*

506

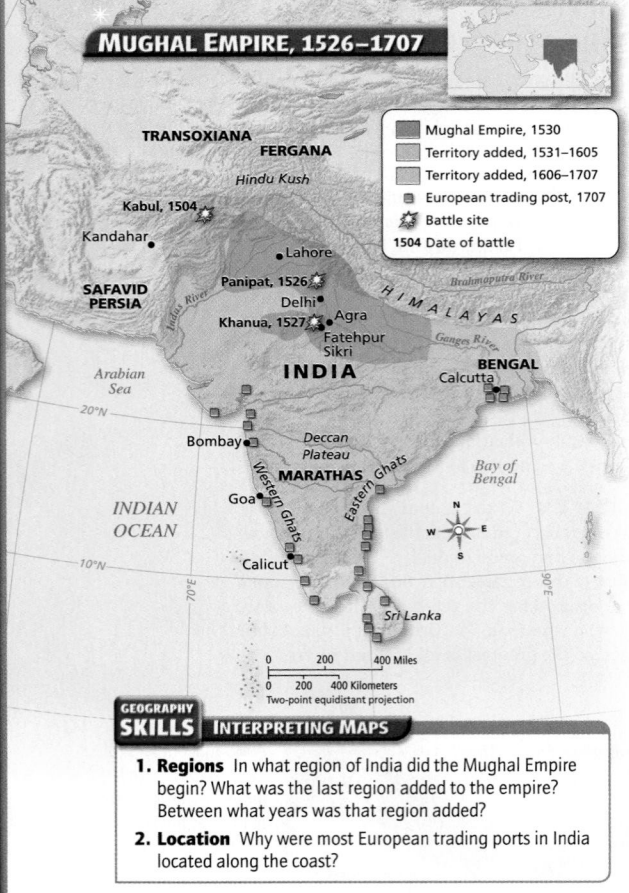

MUGHAL EMPIRE, 1526–1707

TRANSOXIANA
FERGANA
Hindu Kush
Kabul, 1504
Kandahar
Lahore
SAFAVID PERSIA
Panipat, 1526
Delhi
Khanua, 1527
Agra
Fatehpur Sikri
HIMALAYAS
Brahmaputra River
Ganges River
INDIA
BENGAL
Calcutta
Arabian Sea
20°N
Deccan Plateau
Bombay
Bay of Bengal
MARATHAS
Western Ghats
Eastern Ghats
INDIAN OCEAN
Goa
10°N
Calicut
70°E
90°E
Sri Lanka

Legend:
- Mughal Empire, 1530
- Territory added, 1531–1605
- Territory added, 1606–1707
- ▪ European trading post, 1707
- ⚔ Battle site
- **1504** Date of battle

0   200   400 Miles
0   200   400 Kilometers
Two-point equidistant projection

GEOGRAPHY SKILLS | INTERPRETING MAPS

1. **Regions** In what region of India did the Mughal Empire begin? What was the last region added to the empire? Between what years was that region added?

2. **Location** Why were most European trading ports in India located along the coast?

Akbar realized that India had a diverse population, which he feared could lead to the breakdown of his empire. As a result, he did everything he could think of to win the people's loyalty. For example, he married the daughter of a local noble to win the noble's support and brought the sons of other nobles to live at his court. At the same time, Akbar was not hesitant to fight to prevent rebellion. By the time Akbar died in 1605, the Mughals ruled most of north India and much of the interior.

Akbar also worked to unify his diverse empire by promoting religious tolerance. His personal *stance* was that no single religion—including Islam, which he had been raised

ACADEMIC VOCABULARY

stance an attitude, position, or view about someone or something

506 CHAPTER 17

to practice—could provide all the answers to life's problems. As a result, he did not want to discourage people from practicing any religion or to discriminate against anyone for their beliefs. He abolished taxes that earlier rulers had placed on non-Muslims and appointed Hindus to several influential positions in his government. He also encouraged discussions and debates among Muslims, Hindus, Christians, and members of other religions.

Although flexible and generous in his support of different religions, Akbar kept a firm grasp on his government and its finances. He established a centralized government framework that gave him supreme civil and military authority over his empire. To keep better track of the empire's finances, Akbar reformed the tax system and appointed officials to oversee it. To try to prevent officials with regional loyalties, only about one-third of these officials were from India. The majority were from outside of the Mughal Empire.

READING CHECK **Explain** How did Babur and Akbar the Great help create a new empire in India?

Height of the Mughal Empire

Babur and Akbar laid the foundation for a powerful empire. The rulers who followed them built upon that foundation and raised Mughal India to new heights of power and wealth.

Jahangir Intelligent and impatient to rule, Akbar's son Jahangir rebelled against his father. The two later reconciled, and Jahangir became emperor after Akbar's death in 1605. Despite his ruthless start, Jahangir was known as a good ruler. He continued Akbar's practice of religious tolerance, appointing both Muslim and Hindu officials. He supported the arts and adopted many Persian influences into Indian society. Jahangir's acceptance of Persian customs was inspired by his wife, Nur Jahan, who had been born in Persia. A powerful woman, Nur Jahan actually ruled for several years while her husband was ill.

During his reign, Jahangir came into conflict with a religious group known as the Sikhs (SEEKS), some of whom had supported a rebellion against him. **Sikhism**, which had been founded by Guru Nanak (1469–c. 1539), blended elements of both Islam and Hinduism.

Skills Focus: Making Inferences | At Level

Reading Skill
The Mughal Shahs

1. Tell students that political cartoonists use their talent to express their opinions and beliefs, both positive and negative, about the actions of national rulers.

2. Have students select one of the shahs discussed in this section and create a political cartoon that makes a clear, visual political statement about his actions.

3. When students have had time to complete their work, have volunteers share their political cartoons to the class. Students should explain the reasoning for the viewpoint shown. **LS** Visual-Spatial

📝 **Alternative Assessment Handbook**, Rubric 27: Political Cartoons

Like Muslims, Sikhs believe that there is only one God, that God created the world, and that he has no physical form. But unlike Muslims, who believe in an afterlife, Sikhs believe in the Hindu concept of reincarnation. They believe that the goal of existence is to be freed from the cycle of rebirth and to attain unity with God. Sikhs do not practice rituals such as pilgrimage and yoga that came from the earlier religions.

Shah Jahan Jahangir's son and successor, **Shah Jahan** shared his father's love of literature and art. During his reign the Mughal Empire experienced a cultural golden age. The greatest example of Mughal architecture, the **Taj Mahal** in Agra, was built during his reign. Designed by Persian architects and displaying elements of Indian, Persian, and Muslim architectural styles, the Taj Mahal was built as a tomb for Shah Jahan's beloved wife.

In addition to the Taj Mahal, Shah Jahan built a new capital for India at Delhi. At the heart of the capital was a chamber that held the magnificent Peacock Throne. Flanked by two sculpted peacocks and encrusted with gold, diamonds, emeralds, and other gems, the throne became a symbol of Mughal majesty.

The cost of building monuments such as the Taj Mahal and the palaces of Delhi was enormous. To pay for the monuments, Shah Jahan imposed heavy taxes on the people of India. He demanded half of all crops grown in the country, which led to hardship and famine for many people. Adding to Shah Jahan's need for money was a series of wars he launched against India's neighbors. Many of these wars were fought in the name of Islam against Christians and Hindus because, unlike his father and grandfather, Shah Jahan was a Muslim who did not practice religious tolerance.

Aurangzeb In 1657 Shah Jahan grew terribly ill. His sons, thinking their father near death, began to maneuver to take the throne. Before long, war broke out between them. When Shah Jahan unexpectedly recovered, his son **Aurangzeb** captured him and locked him in a prison in Agra. Aurangzeb then killed his rivals, and brought the head of one brother in a box to show his father. With the way clear, Aurangzeb then declared himself emperor.

Early in his reign, Aurangzeb was chiefly concerned with expanding India's borders. The empire reached its greatest size at this time.

READING SKILLS

Summarizing
After you read the information on the Height of the Mughal Empire, summarize the key points of the reigns of Jahangir, Shah Jahan, and Aurangzeb in four to six sentences.

Linking TO Today

The Sikhs

Today more than 20 million people identify themselves as Sikhs, making Sikhism the world's fifth-largest religion. The majority of Sikhs live in the Punjab region of India, where about 500 years ago a young spiritual teacher named Guru Nanak founded the faith. Nanak wrote his teachings as poems. These poems, along with the teachings of nine other gurus, or prophets, now form part of the holy book of Sikhism.

Sikhs strive to live according to these teachings, which they believe to be the living word of a single, all-powerful God. Serving others, living a truthful life, and the belief that all people are equal, regardless of gender or social class, are core to Sikh spirituality.

As an expression of their faith, Sikhs wear special clothing. The turban, for example, symbolizes the Sikhs' strong belief in social equality. In the early years of Sikhism, before India was under Mughal rule, only kings and noblemen could wear turbans. In response, a Sikh guru commanded all Sikhs, both men and women, to wear the turban as a symbol of their social equality. Today this tradition continues. Wearing the turban is required for all Sikh men but is optional for Sikh women.

Why do Sikhs continue to wear turbans today?

▲ Like the turban, uncut hair is a symbol of Sikh identity and faith. To honor the human form as created by God, Sikhs do not cut their hair or beards.

NEW ASIAN EMPIRES **507**

Skills Focus: Analyzing Costs and Benefits

Social Studies Skill

Weighing the Value of Patronage

1. Have students name a few of the artistic achievements of the Mughals they read about in this section. Make a class list for students to see.

2. Have students select one shah they have studied in this section and identify one particular arts project he supported. Have students record these two pieces of information on a piece of paper that has been divided into a three-part chart.

3. On the bottom third of the paper, have students list the costs of the patronage on the left and the benefits on the right.

4. When students have finished, display the charts and guide the class in a discussion of the costs and benefits of art patronage.
   LS Verbal-Linguistic, Visual-Spatial

   Alternative Assessment Handbook, Rubrics 6: Cause and Effect; and 13: Graphic Organizers

Reading Focus

Height of the Mughal Empire

Recall What foundation did Babur and Akbar build for rulers who suceeded them? *legacy of wealth and power*

Explain In what ways did Sikhism blend elements of Islam and Hinduism? *Like Muslims, Sikhs believe in only one God, that God created the world, and that he has no physical form. Like Hindus, they believe in reincarnation.*

Make Inferences Why were there so many influences in Mughal cultural development? *possible answer— geographic location, trade, acceptance of foreign cultures and faiths, invasion and assimilation of neighboring people*

Activity **Shah Facts** Have students make a list of the shahs they have studied so far and record facts they have learned about each of them.
LS Verbal-Linguistic

Teaching Tip

Help students develop a connection to the Mughal Empire by holding an "East India Traders' Day." Students may bring examples or drawings of cotton fabrics, teas, and spiced goods to class. Suggest saris, teas, and food made with spices from India and Sri Lanka.

Answers

Reading Skills *Student summaries will vary, but should show a clear understanding of each ruler's reign.*

Linking to Today *as an expression of their faith and a symbol of their belief in social equality*

507

Direct Teach

Info to Know

Women of Influence Women's patronage of the arts became significant under the rule of Shahs Jahangir and Jahan. During the reign of Shah Jahangir, his wife, Queen Nur Jahan, gained more influence in politics and the arts. She made many political decisions, introduced new styles of dress, and commissioned many buildings and gardens. She also arranged her son's marriage. When her son's wife died, his unmarried daughter, Jahanara assumed royal duties and commissioned many artistic works.

 Quick Facts Transparency:
Achievements of the Mughal Emperors

Review & Assess

Close

Have students describe the Mughal rulers, their achievements, and the characteristics of their reigns.

Review

Online Quiz, Section 2

Assess

SE Section 2 Assessment

Progress Assessment: Section 2 Quiz

Alternative Assessment Handbook

Reteach/Intervene

Interactive Reader and Study Guide, Section 2

Interactive Skills Tutor CD-ROM

THE IMPACT TODAY
Persecution would later lead many Sikhs to move to California.

Later, however, Aurangzeb turned more to domestic affairs. A strict Sunni Muslim, he worked to impose his religious views on society. He issued strict decrees about morality and personal behavior and appointed officials to enforce them. He also persecuted Hindus and Sikhs, taxing them, forbidding them high positions in government, and destroying their temples. When crowds of Shia and Sufi Muslims gathered to protest his actions, Aurangzeb ordered soldiers mounted on elephants to crush them.

Aurangzeb's restrictions and his persecution of his subjects led many peasants to rebel. One rebellious subject wrote to the emperor:

HISTORY'S VOICES

❝Your subjects are trampled underfoot; every province of your Empire is impoverished . . . If Your Majesty places any faith in those books by distinction called divine, you will be there instructed that God is the God of all mankind, not the God of Mussalmans [Muslims] alone.❞

—Anonymous Mughal citizen, quoted in *History of Aurangzeb* by Jadunath Sarkar

ACADEMIC VOCABULARY
regime a specific and often harsh government

Decline of the Mughals Although Aurangzeb had enlarged the Mughal Empire, his actions marked the beginning of its end. Due to the harsh measures of Aurangzeb's regime, frequent rebellions broke out in the later 1600s. When Aurangzeb died, rival claims to the throne led to civil war. Soon, invaders poured into India from the north.

Although the Mughals continued to rule for about 150 more years, they held little power and controlled far less territory. In time, India fell under the sway of the British, who made it a colony and part of their global empire.

READING CHECK   Summarize How did Aurangzeb contribute to the Mughals' decline?

SECTION 2 ASSESSMENT

go.hrw.com
Online Quiz
Keyword: SHL NAS HP

Reviewing Ideas, Terms, and People

1. **a. Identify** What was the first Muslim government established in India? Where did its name come from?
   b. Explain How did relationships between Muslims and members of other religions change in India?
   c. Elaborate How did the arrival of Islam in India lead to later changes in society?

2. **a. Describe** How did Babur establish the Mughal Empire?
   b. Make Generalizations What qualities helped Babur and Akbar the Great create a successful and prosperous empire in India?
   c. Rate Which of Akbar's accomplishments as emperor do you think was most impressive? Why?

3. **a. Identify** What were two artistic achievements made in India under Shah Jahan?
   b. Compare and Contrast How were Shah Jahan and Aurangzeb similar? How were they different?

   c. Extend How did the policies of Shah Jahan and Aurangzeb lead to the decline of Mughal civilization?

Critical Thinking

4. **Identify Cause and Effect** Using your notes and a graphic organizer like the one here, explain the reasons for the growth and decline of the Mughal Empire. List reasons for growth in the left arrow and reasons for decline in the right arrow.

FOCUS ON WRITING

5. **Narration** Write a short paragraph about the founding of the Mughal Empire. In your paragraph, trace the key events in the empire's early history.

Section 2 Assessment Answers

1. **a.** Delhi sultanate; because the new government was based in Delhi
   b. possible answer—In the beginning of the empire, there was religious tolerance, but later, different religions clashed.
   c. A new culture formed, blending Muslim and Indian elements.

2. **a.** defeated the rulers of Delhi
   b. ambition, capable leaders
   c. possible answer—keeping peace among many different religions, because later emperors were unable to do this

3. **a.** Taj Mahal; Peacock Throne
   b. similar—did not believe in tolerance; different—Aurangzeb more interested in expansion
   c. possible answer—Policies led to rebellions.

4. Growth: religious tolerance, strong government, expansion of borders, wealth; building of great monuments; Decline: use of wealth for building projects, violence, heavy taxation, religious persecution, lack of religious tolerance

5. Student paragraphs should be supported by the text.

Answers

Reading Check *His harsh regime led to rebellions.*

The Ming and Qing Dynasties

BEFORE YOU READ

MAIN IDEA

During the Ming and Qing dynasties China prospered, but the empire entered a period of isolation in response to increasing European contact.

READING FOCUS

1. How did the Ming dynasty bring stability, prosperity, and isolation to China?

2. How did the Manchus of the Qing dynasty rule China?

3. What cultural developments occurred during the Ming and Qing periods?

KEY PEOPLE

Hongwu
Yonglo
Zheng He
Matteo Ricci
Kangxi
Qianlong
Lord George Macartney

 NEW YORK

P1 3.1 Students analyze the role and contributions of individuals and groups to social, political, economic, cultural, and religious practices and activities.

THE INSIDE STORY

Why might a ruler build a city within a city? The Gate of Divine Might, the Hall of Supreme Harmony, the Palace of Heavenly Purity—these structures are part of China's Forbidden City. Set in the heart of Beijing, China's capital, the Forbidden City was built in the early 1400s for China's Ming emperor and his family, court, and servants. The vast complex is surrounded by a moat and a 35-foot-high wall, and includes dozens of imperial palaces, halls, temples, residences, and other buildings. This amazing city within a city earned its name because China's common people were not allowed to enter it.

For centuries, the golden-colored rooftops of this hidden city—all that China's people could see of it—symbolized China's imperial glory. ◼

The Ming Dynasty

In 1279 the Mongol leader Kublai Khan conquered China and founded the Yuan dynasty. After Kublai Khan's death in 1294, however, the Yuan dynasty weakened. This weakness, combined with Chinese resentment of Mongol rule, made China ripe for rebellion—and the rise of a new dynasty.

A FORBIDDEN City

◀ The Hall of Supreme Harmony in China's Forbidden City

509

Reading Focus

1 How did the Ming dynasty bring stability, prosperity, and isolation to China? *gained independence from Mongol rule, rebuilt China, passed beneficial reforms, government officials were educated, corruption reduced; protected China from Mongol invasions, built the Great Wall, developed agriculture, industry, and the arts, set up trade with foreign nations; developed China's sea power; became a stable, prosperous time in history of China*

The Ming Dynasty

Recall Who led seven sea voyages for China during the early 1400s? *Zheng He*

Summarize Why was Hongwu considered a great emperor? *passed reforms; increased stability and prosperity; worked to eliminate Mongol influence and restore traditional Chinese values*

Analyze Why do you think the Ming emperors limited sea voyages and European trade? *possible answer— After years of Mongol rule, it was important to the Ming emperors to preserve China's traditions and keep away foreign influences.*

Activity **The Forbidden City** Tell students that a new capital on the site of the Mongol Yuan dynasty's capital city, now called Beijing, was built between 1406 and 1420. During most of the Ming and Qing dynasties, commoners were forbidden to enter the building. For this reason it became known as the Forbidden City. Ask students how the isolation of the Ming emperors inside the walls of the Forbidden City might have affected the way in which they governed. *Students should recognize the potential problems that arise when rulers are out of touch with the people they govern.*

CRF: Biography: Zhang Juzheng

TAKING NOTES
As you read, use a graphic organizer like the one below to take notes on the Ming and Qing dynasties and their culture.

Ming	Qing

NEW YORK
CC Unit 4-A
The relationship of the Ming dynasty (1368–1644) with the West and the Ming expansion of trade (Zheng-He, 1405–1453)

China under Ming Rule In 1368 a peasant named Zhu Yuanzhang (JOO YOO-AHN-jahng) and his rebel army overthrew the last Mongol emperor. Zhu took the name **Hongwu**, meaning "vastly martial," and founded the Ming dynasty. *Ming* means "brilliant," and Ming China lasted nearly 300 years until 1644. During this period, China's rulers gained control of Korea, Mongolia, and parts of Central and Southeast Asia.

Having expelled the Mongols, Hongwu worked to rebuild China. He reduced taxes and passed reforms to improve agriculture and trade, increasing stability and prosperity in China. In addition, Hongwu worked to eliminate Mongol influences and to revive traditional Chinese values and practices, such as Confucian principles. For example, to obtain government officials educated in Confucian ideas, he restored and improved the civil service examination system. To root out corruption, he increased the influence of censors, officials who monitored government.

At the same time, Hongwu greatly expanded his power as emperor. He did away with the positions of some high-level officials and took over more control of the government. As a result, the Ming emperors were much more powerful than emperors of previous dynasties. In addition, Hongwu eliminated anyone whom he saw as challenging his authority, and over time he had thousands of his rivals killed.

Hongwu died in 1398. Following a power struggle, his son **Yonglo** (YOOHNG-LOH) became emperor, ruling from 1402 until 1424. Yonglo moved the Ming capital to Beijing, a city in the northeast of China. At the center of Beijing, he built a vast imperial city, which was surrounded by high walls. This city complex became known as the Forbidden City because most people were forbidden from entering it.

Ming Sea Voyages To extend China's influence, Yonglo sponsored overseas voyages. Between 1405 and 1433 **Zheng He** (juhng HUH), a Chinese Muslim admiral, led seven voyages around the Indian Ocean as far as Africa. To show China's power, Zheng He sailed with huge fleets of as many as 300 ships. These fleets included trading ships called junks as well as immense treasure ships, each about 400 feet long. Wherever he went, Zheng He presented gifts from China, and in return several foreign leaders sent tribute to China's emperor.

The Great Wall of China

Zheng He's voyages demonstrated Ming China's growing sea power. After 1433, however, a new emperor stopped the overseas voyages. They had been highly expensive, and some officials complained that China's resources would be better used to defend the frontiers.

Ming Foreign Relations The policy to end the voyages was part of a move in Ming China toward isolation from the outside world. This move toward isolation gained full force in the 1500s, when the Ming heavily restricted foreign trade and travel to limit outside contacts. Foreign merchants were allowed to trade only at a few Chinese ports, such as Canton, and only during certain times. Such policies were impossible to enforce, however. All along China's coast, ambitious Chinese smugglers carried out a brisk trade with foreign merchants.

One reason for the Ming emperors' decision to isolate China was the arrival of European traders and Christian missionaries in the 1500s. The Europeans introduced many new goods and ideas—including new products from the Americas. In fact, Europeans often paid with silver from the Americas. The Ming disliked the influence of the Europeans, though, and sought to preserve China's traditions.

Differentiating Instruction

Below Level

Learners Having Difficulty

1. Remind students that the Mongols were powerful, skilled warriors who had much success in battle, and they viewed Europeans as suspicious barbarians.

2. Remind students that the primary reason the Chinese had contact with Europeans was to acquire gold and silver, not to learn more about Europe or European culture. Review the information in the text about foreign merchants being allowed in China only during specific times.

3. Have students write a banner headline telling foreign merchants that they have to leave China because trading season is over.
   LS Verbal-Linguistic

   Alternative Assessment Handbook, Rubric 34: Slogans and Banners

MING AND QING DYNASTIES, 1368–1911

Legend:
- Ming dynasty, 1368–1644
- Qing dynasty, 1644–1911
- Qing vassal state
- Grand Canal
- Great Wall

0   400   800 Miles
0   400   800 Kilometers
Two-point equidistant projection

The Great Wall ran along the northern Ming frontier.

RUSSIA

MONGOLIA   MANCHURIA   JAPAN

GOBI   KOREA   Beijing

Yellow Sea

HIMALAYAS   TIBET   Xi'an   Nanjing   Hangzhou   East China Sea

Chengdu   Chongqing   Chang Jiang (Yangzi River)   Tropic of Cancer

NEPAL

BURMA   CHINA   Guangzhou (Canton)   Taiwan   PACIFIC OCEAN

Xi River   Macao (Portuguese colony, 1557)

ANNAM (VIETNAM)

SIAM   South China Sea

Much of the Great Wall of China that you see today was built during the Ming dynasty.

GEOGRAPHY SKILLS | INTERPRETING MAPS

1. **Location** In what region of the Ming empire was Beijing, the capital, located?
2. **Regions** What regions did China gain under Qing rule?

Even so, some Europeans gained influence in China. One such European was **Matteo Ricci** (mah-TAY-oh REE-chee), an Italian Jesuit priest, who arrived in 1583. To gain acceptance, Ricci learned the Chinese language and adopted many Chinese customs. His efforts gained him entry to the Ming court, where he became highly respected. There, Ricci introduced European learning in mathematics and science.

In addition to dealing with the Europeans, the Ming faced a renewed Mongol threat to the north. To improve defense, the Ming restored China's Great Wall. Parts of earlier walls were repaired but most of the construction was new. In fact, much of the Great Wall that is seen today was built during the Ming period.

Ming Economy and Society Ming rule brought prosperity to China. Improved methods of irrigation increased farm production, and peasants produced huge crops of rice in the southern river valleys. In addition, new crops from the Americas, such as corn and sweet potatoes, reached China in the 1500s. These crops further increased farm output.

Stability and plentiful food led to substantial population growth. As the population grew, so did China's cities. In these cities, industries such as the manufacture of porcelain and silk expanded in response to a growing European demand for Chinese goods. At the same time, China remained a mainly agricultural society.

Ming Decline In the late 1500s, the Ming dynasty began to decline. Several weak rulers took the throne, and under their rule corruption increased. As defense efforts drained the treasury, Ming rulers raised taxes. High taxes combined with crop failures in the 1600s led to famine and hardship. Rebellions broke out.

As Ming China weakened, the Manchu—a people to the northwest in Manchuria—saw their chance. In 1644 the Manchu swept into Beijing and took the capital. The last Ming emperor killed himself to avoid capture. The Manchu then formed their own dynasty and gave it a Chinese name—Qing (CHING).

READING CHECK **Analyze** What were some of the strengths and weaknesses of the Ming dynasty?

READING SKILLS

Summarizing
After you read the information on the Ming Dynasty, summarize the key points in five to seven sentences.

NEW ASIAN EMPIRES **511**

511

② How did the Manchus of the Qing dynasty rule China? *with respect for Chinese traditions; keeping Manchu separate from Chinese; with isolation from foreign influence*

The Qing Dynasty

Recall What territory did Qianlong add to the empire? *Taiwan, Mongolia, Tibet*

Analyze Why do you think the Qing empire was stable? *possible answer— The Qing rulers showed respect for the Manchus traditions and gave them government positions.*

③ What cultural developments occurred during the Ming and Qing periods? *developments in art, literature*

Ming and Qing Culture

Identify Cause and Effect What development led to a growth in popular fiction? *rising literacy rates*

Explain What made Ming porcelain so valuable in Europe? *its beauty and superb quality*

Counterpoints

Two Sources on China and Trade

Activity **Trade Discussions** To ensure that students understand the quotes, have them work individually or in pairs to write paraphrases of each quote. Have volunteers share their paraphrases with the class.

Answers

Counterpoints *possible answer— Macartney does not understand why the Chinese do not wish to trade and think that view is a mistake. Qianlong explains that the Chinese have everything they need and do not want his trade goods.*

512

The Qing Dynasty

The Qing dynasty, which ruled from 1644 to 1911, became the last dynasty in 3,500 years of imperial rule in China. Under the Qing dynasty's Manchu rulers, China again grew prosperous and expanded to its largest size in history.

China under Qing Rule As foreigners, the Manchu initially faced heavy resistance from their Chinese subjects, especially in the south. To win the support of the Chinese, the Manchu showed respect for Chinese customs and maintained China's Confucian traditions. The Manchu rulers carried over much of the Ming government structure and continued the civil service examination system. In addition, government positions were distributed equally among Chinese and Manchu officials. These actions eventually earned the Manchu the respect and loyalty of many of their Chinese subjects and restored stability to the empire.

At the same time, the Manchu remained separate from the Chinese and placed some restrictions on them. Manchu were not allowed to marry Chinese, and Manchu women were forbidden to bind their feet as Chinese women did. In addition, Chinese males had to wear their hair in the Manchu style—shaved in the front with a queue, or braid, in the back.

Qing China flourished under two outstanding emperors: **Kangxi** (KAHNG-SHEE) and his grandson **Qianlong** (chee-UHN-LOOHNG). Kangxi, who ruled from 1661 to 1772, reduced taxes for peasants and expanded the empire into parts of Central Asia. An intellectual, he supported the arts and entertained Jesuit priests at court. The Jesuits were highly educated, and Kangxi enjoyed learning from them about European advances in science and other areas.

Kangxi's grandson Qianlong brought the Qing dynasty to its height. Ruling from 1736 to 1796, Qianlong expanded the empire of China to its largest size by conquering Taiwan, Mongolia, and Tibet. During his reign, agricultural production continued to rise; and China's population boomed, surging to more than 300 million by 1750. The economy thrived as well, benefiting from improved transportation and from growing domestic and foreign markets.

NEW YORK
CC Unit 4-A5
Ming Dynasty
(1368–1644)
contributions

COUNTERPOINTS
Two Sources on China and Trade

In a letter to King George III of England, Qing emperor Qianlong explains his refusal of the king's gifts and request for trade.

❝Swaying the wide world, I have but one aim in view, to maintain a perfect governance and to fulfill the duties of the State: strange and costly objects do not interest me... Our dynasty's majestic virtue has penetrated unto every country under Heaven, and Kings of all nations have offered their costly tribute by land and sea. As your Ambassador can see for himself, we possess all things. I set no value on objects strange or ingenious [clever], and have no use for your country's manufactures [products].❞

QIANLONG
—from a letter to King George III

Lord George Macartney led Great Britain's first attempt to expand trade relations with China. The Macartney Mission of 1792–1794 ended in failure.

❝They receive us... with the highest distinction [and] show us every external mark of favour... Yet, in less than a couple months, they plainly discover that they wish us gone, refuse our requests without reserve..., and dismiss us dissatisfied... I must endeavour [try] to unravel this mystery if I can. Perhaps they have given way to impressions which they could not resist, but are ashamed to confess; perhaps they begin to find their mistake, and wish to make amends.❞

LORD MACARTNEY
—from an entry in Macartney's diary

Skills Focus **INVESTIGATING HISTORY**

Analyze How does Lord Macartney's view of the trade discussions compare with Emperor Qianlong's view?

512 CHAPTER 17

Skills Focus: Identifying Problem and Solution   `At Level`

Reading Skill
Strengthening China

1. Explain to students that under the Mongols, China grew weak. Tell students that they will act as advisers to Hongwu.

2. Organize students into small, mixed-ability groups. Have students use information from the text to list things that needed to be improved in China during the late 1300s. Have students use their ideas to create a plan to improve the Chinese government and economy. When students have prepared their plans, have them create a petition that they could present to the Chinese emperor.

3. Have volunteers share their petitions with the class. You might wish to provide students with parchment paper and have them write their petitions in black ink. **LS** **Verbal-Linguistic**

📝 **Alternative Assessment Handbook**, Rubrics 24: Oral Presentations; and 35: Solving Problems

Qing Foreign Relations Qianlong continued the Ming policy of isolation and restricting foreign trade. The Manchu, like the Chinese, saw Chinese civilization—and products—as superior and expected foreigners to trade on China's terms. Accepting these terms, the Dutch began a thriving trade in Chinese goods. Dutch traders obtained Chinese porcelain and silk along with a new good, tea. In fact, tea soon became the main Chinese export to Europe.

Other Europeans continued to try to change China's trade restrictions. In 1793 a British official, **Lord George Macartney**, came to China to discuss expanding trade. The Chinese found the British goods that he brought inferior to their own products. In addition, the Chinese demanded that Macartney show respect to Emperor Qianlong by kowtowing—kneeling in front of the emperor and touching the forehead to the ground nine times. Macartney refused, and the Chinese sent him away.

At the time, China was one of the most advanced civilizations in the world. Isolation, however, would help prevent the Chinese from keeping up with European advances. In the 1800s European efforts to open China's closed society would eventually topple the Qing dynasty—and imperial rule.

READING CHECK **Draw Conclusions** How did cultural differences hamper trade relations between the British and the Chinese during the Qing period?

Ming and Qing Culture

Under Ming and Qing rule, the Chinese made many developments in the arts and literature. Ming artisans produced exquisite blue-and-white porcelain. The beauty and superb quality of Ming porcelain made it a valuable trade item, especially in Europe.

During the Ming period, rising literacy rates contributed to the growth of popular fiction, or fiction written in everyday language for the common people. Short stories became more popular, and the first Chinese novels were published. In the 1700s the Qing writer Cao Zhan wrote the novel *Dream of the Red Chamber*. Considered China's greatest novel, it examines the decline of an upper-class Chinese family.

READING CHECK **Analyze** How did literature change during the Ming period?

Ming Porcelain
Ming porcelain was often richly decorated with blue-and-white abstract or floral designs. A bearded dragon wraps around the vase shown here.

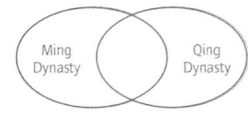

SECTION 3 ASSESSMENT

go.hrw.com
Online Quiz
Keyword: SHL NAS HP

Reviewing Ideas, Terms, and People

1. **a. Identify** Who were **Hongwu** and **Yonglo**, and what were their main achievements?
   b. Draw Conclusions How did **Zheng He**'s voyages demonstrate Ming China's sea power and increase China's influence?
   c. Evaluate How did interaction with foreigners affect China during the Ming period?

2. **a. Recall** How did the Manchu rulers of the Qing dynasty earn the support and loyalty of many of the Chinese people?
   b. Explain Why did the British fail in their efforts in the 1790s to expand trade relations with Qing China?
   c. Rank Based on what you have learned about the major Ming and Qing emperors, how would you rank them? Explain your reasoning.

3. **a. Identify** Which book is considered to be China's greatest novel, and when was it written?
   b. Analyze How did Ming porcelain contribute to China's economy?

Critical Thinking

4. **Compare and Contrast** Using your notes and a graphic organizer like the one here, compare and contrast the main accomplishments and challenges of the Ming and Qing dynasties.

Ming Dynasty   Qing Dynasty

FOCUS ON WRITING

5. **Exposition** You are a Dutch merchant who conducts trade with China in the 1700s. Write a short letter to another European merchant giving the merchant advice on how to gain the right to trade with China.

NEW ASIAN EMPIRES **513**

• **Review & Assess** •

Close
Have students identify the changes that occurred in China during the Ming and Qing dynasties.

Review
Online Quiz, Section 3

Assess
SE **Section 3 Assessment**
Progress Assessment: Section 3 Quiz
Alternative Assessment Handbook

Reteach/Intervene
Interactive Reader and Study Guide, Section 3
Interactive Skills Tutor CD-ROM

Answers
Reading Check (top) *The British official who came to trade did not perform a traditional gesture of respect to the emperor, and was sent away.* **(bottom)** *Popular fiction was written in everyday language; short stories became popular.*

Section 3 Assessment Answers

1. **a.** Ming emporor; Hongwu—extended China's influence, stabilized China, began building the Great Wall; Yonglo—moved the capital to Beijing, large-scale diplomatic and economic contact with the Europeans, developed the world's largest commercial navy, launched historic trade expeditions under Zheng He
   b. He traveled with huge fleets of ships loaded with treasures, made contact with leaders who sent tribute to the emperor.
   c. It introduced European learning in mathematics and science.

2. **a.** showed respect for Chinese customs and traditions
   b. Chinese thought the British goods were inferior; British official refused to kowtow to the emperor.
   c. possible answer—Kangxi and Qianlong would rank highest because they reduced taxes, expanded the empire, and brought the Qing dynasty to its height.

3. **a.** Dream of the Red Chamber was written in the 1700s.

b. It was a valuable trade item, especially in Europe.

4. Ming—built Forbidden City; Zheng He led sea voyages; built Great Wall of China; prosperity, population growth; Qing—China grew prosperous; showed respect for Confucian traditions; largest empire in China's history; Both—emphasized Chinese culture; isolated from foreign influence

5. Student letters should explain the importance of showing respect to the emperor and bringing quality items for trade.

513

The Voyages of Zheng He

Teaching Tip

The travels of Zheng He are recounted in a film titled *Ghost Fleet: The Epic Voyage of Zheng He*. Photojournalist Michael Yamashita, director Jonathan Finnigan, and a film crew covered over 10,000 miles to retrace these epic voyages. They began in Yunan, China and traveled all the way to the Swahili coast of Africa. Director Finnigan made a two-hour documentary from the lengthy shoot, which made its debut Asia in December 2005. It debuted in New York City in May 2006.

Activity **Understanding Climate**
Have students compare the latitude of their hometown with that of the areas Zheng He traveled. Discuss the similarities and differences in the climate of various locations based on your own and students' experiences. Travel Web sites frequently offer a weather report for various destinations. Have volunteers locate several of Zheng He's stops on a weather Web site and report on current weather in those locations. **LS Visual-Spatial**

Activity **Zheng He's Travels** Have students compare the distance traveled by Zheng He with the distance across the continental United States (approximately 2,500 miles) or the distance from their town to the nearest large city. Have students estimate the number of times they would have to travel back and forth to equal the length of Zheng He's voyage. **LS Logical-Mathematical**

HISTORY & Geography ★Interactive

The Voyages of Zheng He

Between 1405 and 1433 the Chinese admiral Zheng He led seven grand voyages throughout the Indian Ocean. During the seven voyages, Zheng He visited ports in Southeast Asia, India, Persia, the Arabian Peninsula, and Africa. The voyages consisted of huge fleets, some with hundred of ships. These ships were like traveling cities; and their crews included not only sailors but also astrologers, blacksmiths, cooks, doctors, officials, royal guards, and translators.

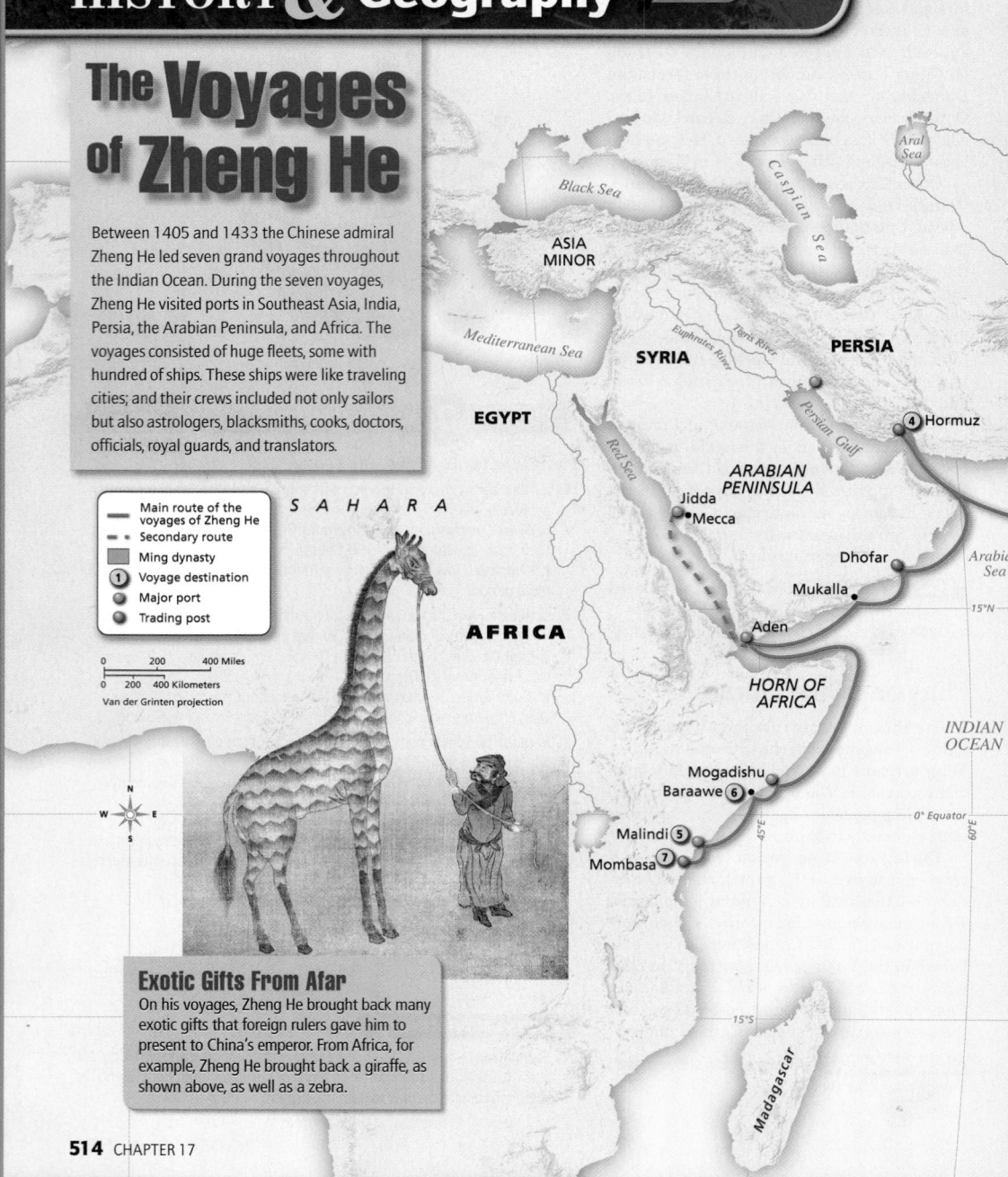

Legend:
— Main route of the voyages of Zheng He
--- Secondary route
■ Ming dynasty
① Voyage destination
● Major port
● Trading post

0   200   400 Miles
0   200   400 Kilometers
Van der Grinten projection

Exotic Gifts From Afar
On his voyages, Zheng He brought back many exotic gifts that foreign rulers gave him to present to China's emperor. From Africa, for example, Zheng He brought back a giraffe, as shown above, as well as a zebra.

514 CHAPTER 17

Skills Focus: Analyzing Secondary Sources   At Level

Reading Like a Historian   **Research Required**
Comparing Ships

1. Remind students that many explorers sailed in search of land and wealth. They sailed different ships and traveled to different areas. Have students compare the voyages of Zheng He with those of Christopher Columbus.

2. Organize students into small groups. Have students collect data about the ships of each explorer on the list. Students should document the sources of their data, especially when it conflicts with another source.

3. Next, have students record their information in bar graph form. Display completed work.

4. Discuss the difference in the estimated ship sizes. Finally, have students write a paragraph discussing whether size matters when comparing ships of Columbus and Zheng He. **LS Logical-Mathematical, Visual-Spatial**

📖 **Alternative Assessment Handbook**, Rubrics 13: Graphic Organizers; and 30: Research

NEW YORK STANDARDS

PI 3.2 Students explain the dynamics of cultural change and how interactions between and among cultures have affected various cultural groups throughout the world.

PI 3.3 Students examine the social/cultural, political, economic, and religious norms and values of Western and other world cultures.

ASIA

MONGOLIA

G O B I

"We have set [our] eyes on barbarian regions far away . . . while our sails loftily unfurled like clouds."

–Zheng He, Pillar inscription

Huang He

Beijing

JAPAN
Edo (Tokyo)
Kyoto

KOREA

Yellow Sea

HINDU KUSH

TIBET

HIMALAYAS

Ganges River

Nanjing
Changshu

Zhang Jiang Yangtze River

CHINA
Fuzhou
Changle
Quanzhou
Guangzhou

Home Base
All seven of the voyages departed from the city of Nanjing, one of China's main ports at the time.

Thar Desert

INDIA

Chittagong

Deccan Plateau

Bay of Bengal

South China Sea

Manila

CHAMPA

BURMA
Ayutthaya
SIAM
ANNAM
(Vietnam)

Philippines

① ② ③

Kozhikode (Calicut)

Sri Lanka
Galle

Banda Aceh

MALAY PENINSULA
Malacca
Singapore

Borneo

China's Treasure Ships
Zheng He's fleets included immense treasure ships, called *baochuan*. These ships were some 400 feet in length and carried crews of nearly 1,000.

Palembang
Sumatra

Celebes

Java

Java Sea

Surabaya

Image courtesy of Mr. Chung Chee Kit and National Library Board, Singapore, 2006

75°E

105°E

135°E

GEOGRAPHY SKILLS | INTERPRETING MAPS

go.hrw.com
Interactive Map
Keyword: SHL NAS

1. **Movement** On which of his seven voyages did Zheng He first visit Africa?

2. **Place** What Muslim religious center on the Arabian Peninsula did Zheng He visit on one of his side trips during his voyages?

NEW ASIAN EMPIRES **515**

History and Geography

Info to Know

A Special Place of Honor The amazing voyages of Zheng He were nearly lost to history, at least to western historians. However, in China, he was famous enough to inspire a special honor on the 580th anniversary of his voyage. In 1985, in recognition of the importance of his accomplishment, a new tomb was crafted. The memorial hall at the Ming-style entrance includes paintings of the navigator and his maps. The steps to the tomb are divided in four sections of seven each, likely representing the four cardinal directions and the number of his voyages.

The Spice Islands The fabled Spice Islands attracted many sailors and explorers from afar. Zheng He was no exception. The Moluccas are located in eastern part of Indonesia and are now called the Maluku Province. Cloves, nutmeg, and mace are all grown on the small volcanic islands. Archaeologists have discovered evidence that cloves were traded in Persia over 3,000 years ago. In medieval Europe, spices were prized for their medicinal use, as well as to add interesting flavors to edibles. Spices were very expensive because of the great distance they had to be shipped. Many voyages of exploration were inspired by the desire to find an easier route to the Spice Islands.

Social Studies Skill
Zheng He and Spices

Materials: sticky notes, large world map

1. Tell students that several common spices come from India. It is likely that Zheng He's travels along the Malabar Coast led to the spread of spices.

2. Have students make a list of at least five of their favorite spices. Then have students conduct outside research to discover the origins of the spices. Students should record the sources of their information.

3. Have students share their lists and the results of their research with the class. As volunteers provide the information, place a label on the map for the origins of each spice discussed.

4. Have students write a paragraph about the spices, explaining why they think explorers were interested in finding them.
LS Intrapersonal, Verbal-Linguistic

Alternative Assessment Handbook, Rubrics 12: Drawing Conclusions; and 30: Research

Answers

Interpreting Maps 1. *on his fifth voyage* **2.** *Mecca*

Preteach

Getting Started

Use the **Interactive Reader and Study Guide** to familiarize students with the section content.

📓 **Interactive Reader and Study Guide,** Section 4

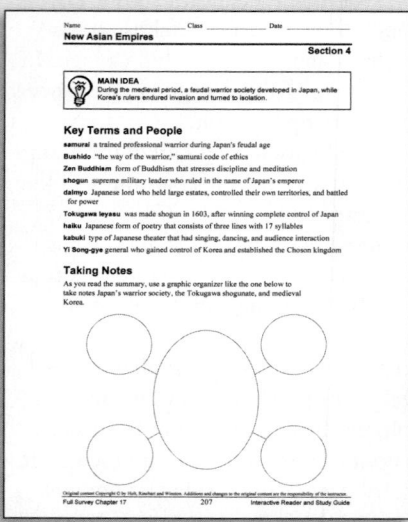

Academic Vocabulary

Review with students the high-use academic term in this section.

preclude to prevent somthing or someone from acting (p. 519)

📓 **CRF:** Vocabulary Builder: Section 4

Taking Notes

Japan—in feudal system, large landowners hired samurai, trained professional warriors; samurai were highly respected, followed code of ethics known as Bushido, adopted Zen Buddhism; shoguns: generals who ruled in emperor's name; daimyo: powerful warlords; Tokugawa shogunate ruled with strong central government, brought about period of peace and stability, increased contact with Europeans; haiku and kabuki were popular; Korea—Choson kings formed a government based on Confucianism; Korea became isolated

---

Medieval Japan and Korea

BEFORE YOU READ

MAIN IDEA

During the medieval period, a feudal warrior society developed in Japan, while Korea's rulers endured invasion and turned to isolation.

READING FOCUS

1. What were the key characteristics of the feudal warrior society in Japan?
2. How did the Tokugawa Shogunate rule Japan, and in what ways did culture flourish during the period?
3. How did the Choson dynasty shape events in medieval Korea?

KEY TERMS AND PEOPLE

samurai
Bushido
Zen Buddhism
shogun
daimyo
Tokugawa Ieyasu
haiku
kabuki
Yi Song-gye

 NEW YORK

PI 3.1 Students analyze the role and contributions of individuals and groups to social, political, economic, cultural, and religious practices and activities.

This image shows a portion of a famous Japanese folding screen of the summer siege of Osaka.

Siege of OSAKA CASTLE

Japanese Folding Screen of Summer War of Osaka

THE INSIDE STORY

Would the castle be strong enough to withstand the attack?
In 1614 a human wall of some 200,000 Japanese warriors stormed toward Osaka Castle. The castle, one of the greatest in Japan, had a five-story tower and was surrounded by double walls more than 100 feet high. Inside this fortress, Toyotomi Hideyori, the lord of the castle, grew desperate. He was surrounded and knew that Tokugawa Ieyasu, Japan's new military leader, was determined to defeat him to wipe out any possible rivals.

As some 300 cannons battered the castle's double walls, Hideyori sent his army out to meet the enemy. The two forces met in bloody engagement on the battlefield. Arrows flew, swords slashed with deadly force, and guns— a fairly new arrival in Japan—blasted away.

The winter siege of Osaka castle terrified the Toyotomi clan trapped within the two-mile-wide compound. Unable to endure any more, Hideyori finally signed a truce. But Ieyasu broke the truce and laid siege to Osaka Castle again in the summer of 1615. In June the castle's weakened walls finally fell. Ieyasu's forces overran the gates, burned the castle to the ground, and slaughtered the occupants. The victors took the head of Hideyori's son as a trophy. In defeat, Hideyori took his own life rather than be captured. ◼

516 CHAPTER 17

Teach the Main Idea

At Level

Medieval Japan and Korea

1. **Teach** Ask students the Reading Focus questions to teach this section.

2. **Apply** Have students make a list of the visuals in the section. Make a class list for all to see. Then have students work in pairs to scan the section and write a caption or information box about each of the visuals and how it relates to the section.

3. **Review** Have volunteers share their captions and information boxes with the class. Add the information to the class list.

4. **Practice/Homework** Have students select one of the visuals and write a paragraph about it and its relationship to the history of Japan and Korea. **LS Verbal-Linguistic, Visual-Spatial**

📓 **Alternative Assessment Handbook,** Rubric 37: Writing Assignments

Japan's Warrior Society

By the 1100s Japan's central government had begun to lose control of the empire. Local clans began to fight each other for power and land. Law and order gave way to conflict and chaos, and bandits roamed the countryside. For protection, large landowners hired armies of **samurai** (SA-muh-ry), or trained professional warriors. Gradually, a feudal warrior society developed in Japan that was similar to that of medieval Europe—yet, uniquely Japanese.

Feudalism and the Samurai In Japan, as in medieval Europe, a feudal system gradually developed. In exchange for allegiance and military service, noble landowners gave property or payment to samurai warriors. Unlike in Europe, where knights were usually paid with land grants, only the most powerful samurai received land. Most of them were paid with food, generally rice. Those samurai who did receive land did not work or live on that land, but they did profit from it. The samurai's lands were worked by peasants, who gave the samurai money or food as payment each year.

The main role of the samurai was that of a warrior, and so they were highly skilled in that role. Like the medieval knights of Europe, samurai wore armor, were skilled with many weapons, and often fought on horseback. At all times, samurai were expected to be in fighting form, ready to do battle should the need arise. As time passed, samurai rose in status in Japanese society and enjoyed many privileges. When samurai strutted along Japan's streets, crowds parted to let them pass. People dropped their eyes out of respect—and fear—because a samurai had the right to kill anyone who showed him disrespect.

In addition to training as warriors, samurai had to follow a strict code of ethics known as **Bushido** (BOOH-shi-doh), which means "the way of the warrior." Bushido required samurai to be courageous, honorable, obedient, and most of all loyal. The Japanese word *samurai* means "those who serve," and each samurai had to serve and obey his lord without hesitation, even if the samurai or his family suffered as a result. Samurai who failed to obey or protect their lord were expected to commit seppuku—suicide by ritual disembowelment—rather than live with their shame.

JAPAN AND KOREA, 1592–1597

- Tokugawa-controlled land
- Daimyo boundary
- Five highways
- Choson (Yi) dynasty
- Japanese invasion
- Chinese invasion

CHINA
Pyongyang
Wonsan
Kaesong
KOREA
Seoul
Yellow Sea
Mokpo
Pusan
Korea Strait
Hirado
Shimabara
Nagasaki
Kyushu
Hokkaido
Sea of Japan (East Sea)
Honshu
JAPAN
Mt. Fuji
Kyoto
Edo (Tokyo)
Osaka
Shikoku
PACIFIC OCEAN

0   200   400 Miles
0   200   400 Kilometers
Lambert conformal conic projection

GEOGRAPHY SKILLS INTERPRETING MAPS

Movement What two major Japanese cities did the Five Highways connect?

Samurai strove to live disciplined lives, which they thought made them better warriors. To improve their self-discipline, many samurai pursued activities that required great focus, such as writing poetry, arranging flowers, and performing tea ceremonies. In addition, many samurai adopted **Zen Buddhism**, a form of Buddhism that spread from China to Japan in the 1100s. Zen stressed discipline and meditation as ways to focus the mind and gain wisdom.

Both men and women of samurai families learned to fight, though only men usually went to war. Like male samurai, female samurai had to follow Bushido and were prepared to die to protect their home and family honor. Honored in Japanese society, samurai women could inherit property and participate in business.

Rise of the Shoguns For most of the 1100s, Japan had no strong central government. The emperor was nominally in charge, but he had little control over the country. Local nobles, the heads of powerful clans, fought for power.

TAKING NOTES

Use a graphic organizer like this one to take notes on Japan's warrior society, the Tokugawa Shogunate, and medieval Korea.

NEW YORK

CC Unit 3-A6
Comparison of Japanese feudalism to European feudalism

NEW ASIAN EMPIRES **517**

Direct Teach

History Close-Up
The Way of the Warrior

Make Inferences Why was it important for samurai to follow Bushido? *It was expected that these men would be self-disciplined.*

Develop What are some possible reasons the samurai's protective clothes were not made of metal like those of knights? *possible answer— Japan may not have had sufficient metal resources; bamboo and leather may have provided adequate defense.*

 CRF: Biography: Tomoe Gozen

About the Illustration
This illustration is an artist's conception based on available sources. Historians, however, are uncertain exactly what this scene looked like.

Info to Know

Japanese Swordmaking When Fujiyasu Masahira makes a sword, he follows the exacting traditional method of master craftsmen from hundreds of years ago. He makes his own charcoal, which he uses to smelt iron oxide sand into steel. When he has made a sufficient amount of steel with the right carbon content, he stacks pieces to form the blade. He wraps the stack in rice paper and dips it in clay before heating it in the forge. Some silicon from the rice straw ash becomes part of the steel. The metal is heated, folded and pounded flat repeatedly. It is then filed into a rough shape and tempered by repeated heating and quenching in water. After careful shaping and polishing, a custom sword guard and scabbard are made. Masahira is one of only fourteen Mukansa smiths. Mukansa smiths have won so many first prizes in their craft that they can no longer take part in competition.

Answers

Interpreting Visuals 1. *armor, helmets;* **2.** *possible answer—to make themselves more intimidating*

518

The Way of the Warrior

The elite, highly trained samurai followed a strict code of ethics called Bushido, or "the way of the warrior." Samurai were expected to serve with honor and loyalty in battle and to value duty and death over defeat. Terrifying and bloodthirsty in war, a samurai also found time to meditate, write poetry, and arrange flowers to focus his mind and body.

All samurai were skilled in the use of the longbow.

The samurai below are writing poetry. Writing poetry helped train the samurai to concentrate.

Samurai wore colorful armor and fierce-looking helmets. Most samurai carried and sometimes fought with two swords.

Skills Focus INTERPRETING VISUALS

go.hrw.com
Interactive
Keyword: SHL NAS

1. **Find the Main Idea** What equipment did the samurai use to protect themselves in battle?
2. **Draw Conclusions** Why do you think that samurai wore fierce-looking helmets with horns or other terrifying features?

518

Skill Focus: Analyzing Primary Sources

At Level

Reading Like a Historian Skill

Prep Required

Samurai Sayings

1. Before class, print out a variety of quotes or samurai sayings. They are easily found on the Internet. Remind students that samurai considered themselves to be philosophers, and have left behind a number of their ideas.

2. Have students choose one samurai quotation to analyze. Have students copy their chosen quote and explain its meaning. Remind students to consider the time it was written and if it might still be meaningful to people today.

3. Have volunteers share the quotations they selected and their analyses.

4. As an extension, have students illustrate their quotation. **LS Intrapersonal, Verbal-Linguistic**

Alternative Assessment Handbook, Rubrics 12: Drawing Conclusions; and 37: Writing Assignments

After decades of warfare between clans, the Minamoto family defeated a rival to become Japan's most powerful clan. In 1192 the clan leader, Minamoto Yoritomo, forced the emperor to name him **shogun**, or "general." Japan's supreme military leader, the shogun ruled in the emperor's name. Although the emperor remained at the top of Japanese society, he became a mere figurehead. For nearly 700 years following, shoguns would rule Japan.

Yoritomo allowed the emperor to continue to hold court at Heian, which in time became known as Kyoto. The new shogun then formed a military government at Kamakura. The Kamakura Shogunate (SHOH-guhn-uht), or military dynasty, ruled Japan until 1333.

In the 1200s the Kamakura Shogunate faced a major threat—the Mongols. In 1274 and again in 1281, large Mongol fleets attacked Japan. Each time, the Japanese defeated the Mongols with the help of a powerful storm that wiped out the enemy fleet. The Japanese referred to these storms as the *kamikaze*, or "divine wind," and believed they showed that the gods favored Japan.

The Mongol invasions weakened the Kamukura Shogunate, however. Many lords did not think the shogun had rewarded them well enough for their part in the fighting and grew to resent the shogun's power over them. Loyalties began to break down, and in 1338 the Kamakura Shogunate was overthrown.

Rebellion and Order A new shogunate took power but was too weak to gain control of Japan. With the loss of centralized rule, Japan splintered into many competing factions. Numerous local **daimyo** (DY-mee-oh), powerful warlords who held large estates, gained control of their own territories and battled for power.

To defend their lands, the daimyo built large fortified castles. As in medieval Europe, these castles were often on hills, protected by walls, and surrounded by water. People came to the castles for protection, and towns often grew up around them. In time, the daimyo began to use peasants as foot soldiers in their armies in addition to samurai on horseback. After 1543 Portuguese traders introduced firearms to Japan. The daimyo gradually began to arm their soldiers with these weapons. Some samurai refused to use guns and later died wielding swords against superior firepower.

During the 1500s, three strong daimyo worked to take control of Japan. The first of these ambitious daimyo was Oda Nobunaga (ohd-ah noh-booh-nah-gah), who was the first daimyo to arm his soldiers with guns. With these weapons, Oda easily defeated his opponents' traditional samurai cavalry. By Oda's death in 1582 he controlled half of Japan.

Toyotomi Hideyoshi, Oda's greatest general, continued his leader's efforts and by 1590 controlled most of Japan. A few years later in 1600, **Tokugawa Ieyasu** (toh-koohg-ah-wuh ee-e-yahs-ooh) won a decisive battle to gain complete control of Japan. In 1603 the emperor made Tokugawa shogun. This event began the Tokugawa shogunate, which ruled until 1867.

READING CHECK **Find the Main Idea** What features defined Japan's feudal warrior society?

The Tokugawa Shogunate

Tokugawa Ieyasu established his capital at a quiet fishing village named Edo (AY-doh), which is now the city of Tokyo. By establishing a strong, central government, he and the later Tokugawa shoguns brought about a period of relative unity, peace, and stability in Japan.

Tokugawa Rule The Tokugawa shoguns closely controlled the daimyo, who still held power at the local level. To keep the daimyo loyal, the shoguns required them to live in Edo periodically and to leave their families there year-round as "hostages." These requirements forced the daimyo to maintain two residences, which was expensive, and were an attempt to preclude the daimyo from rebelling.

The stability and peace of Tokugawa rule brought prosperity to Japan. Agricultural production rose, the population and cities grew, and economic activity increased. New roads called the Five Highways linked the main cities and castle towns, further improving trade.

Under Tokugawa rule, Japan's strict feudal social structure became even more rigid. At the top of society was the emperor, in truth a figurehead. Next was the shogun, who held the real power as the top military ruler. Below the shogun were daimyo, who owed him their loyalty, and then samurai, who served the daimyo. Together, the emperor, shogun, daimyo, and samurai made up the ruling warrior class.

NEW YORK
CC **Unit 3-A4**
Japanese history and the Tokugawa Shogunate

ACADEMIC VOCABULARY
preclude to prevent something or someone from acting

Direct Teach

Reading Focus

Japan's Warrior Society

Identify Who were the daimyo? *warlords who held large estates and battled one another for power*

Identify Cause and Effect How did the Mongol invasions affect the Kamukura Shogunate? *weakened the power of the shogunate, led to rebellions*

Reading Focus

2 How did the Tokugawa Shogunate rule Japan, and in what ways did culture flourish during this period? *required daimyos live in Edo periodically, requiring them to establish two residences, some family members were kept hostage in Edo, a strict social structure was maintained, cities became centers of culture in art, literature, and theater*

The Tokugawa Shogunate

Recall What were the Five Highways? *new roads linking the main cities and castle towns, increasing trade*

Make Inferences Why do you think the Tokugawa rulers found it necessary to impose such strict rules? *possible answer—The previous shogunate had lost power when it lost centralized rule; Tokugawa rulers wanted to keep this from happening again.*

Skills Focus: Identifying Cause and Effect

At Level

Reading Skill
Changes in Political Stability

1. Tell students that the rise and fall of power were the result of chains of events. Tell students they will create two such chains in class.

2. Write the following title for all to see: The Collapse of Central Government. Have volunteers share an event or situation that led to the collapse of centralized government in Japan during the feudal period, and add each event to the chain. When finished, arrange

the events in order of occurrence and have students copy the information.

3. Next, repeat this process with the following title: The Establishment of Peaceful Rule.

4. Have students write a paragraph about the causes and effects involved in changes in political stability. **LS** **Verbal-Linguistic**

Alternative Assessment Handbook, Rubric 9: Comparing and Contrasting

Answers

Reading Check *Samurai gave military service in exchange for property or payment; shoguns ruled in the name of the emperor; daimyo were powerful warlords.*

519

Reading Focus

The Tokugawa Shogunate

Identify What three classes were below the warrior class during the time of the Tokugawa Shogunate? *peasants, artisans, merchants*

Contrast What was the role of women during the Tokugawa period? *led restricted lives, obedient to male head of household, lost many rights and freedoms*

Describe How did relations with the West change during the Tokugawa Shogunate? *Initially European traders were welcomed, but the shoguns grew concerned with the spread of Christianity in Japan and began to restrict trade and travel. By 1650 Japan was again mostly closed to European trade.*

📝 **CRF:** Literature: Hokku Poems

Info to Know

Korean Alphabet Hangul (Korean for "Great Script") is the name of the 24-letter Korean alphabet. Developed during the reign of Sejong in the mid-1440's, Hangul became the official writing system of the Korean language. However, Chinese influence and Japanese rule kept the language from being used by scholars or the upper class until the end of Japanese rule of Korea in 1945.

Answers

Reading Like a Historian 1. *possible answer—The servant's costume is very simple, while the woman's costume is elaborate and expensive-looking.*
2. *possible answer—that kabuki continues to be performed today*

Below the warrior class were three classes—peasants, artisans, and merchants. Members of these lower classes could not rise in social status, serve in the military or government, or hold government positions that might challenge the power of the warrior class.

Peasants made up the vast majority—about 80 percent—of Japan's population. Forbidden from doing anything but farming, they supported themselves by growing rice and other crops on daimyo and samurai estates. In Japan, farming was considered an honorable trade, and peasants enjoyed a relatively high status, just below samurai. At the same time, peasants paid most of the taxes and led hard lives.

Below the peasants were artisans, who often lived in castle towns and made goods such as armor and swords. At the bottom of society were the merchants, not honored because they did not produce anything. Yet merchants often grew wealthy and could use their wealth to improve their social position.

During the Tokugawa period, women's status gradually declined. Many women led restricted lives and had to obey the male head of the household absolutely. Even women in the samurai class lost many rights and freedoms, such as the right to inherit property.

While male samurai continued to command respect, their role changed. Peace put many samurai out of work. Because samurai were not allowed to engage in trade, many ronin—masterless samurai—fell on desperate times. Some became farmers, others warriors-for-hire, and still others roaming bandits.

Relations with the West The prosperity of the Tokugawa Period went hand in hand with Japan's increasing contact with Europeans. The Portuguese had arrived in Japan in 1543, and other Europeans soon followed. Initially, the Japanese welcomed European traders and missionaries and the new ideas, products, and technologies that they brought.

Reading like a Historian

Kabuki Theater

Analyzing Visuals Kabuki plays combine dance, song, music, dialogue, and pantomime with elaborate costumes and make-up to tell stories about historical events as well as everyday life. The photograph at right is a still from a 2001 London performance of Tsuri Onna, or "Fishing for a Wife," a kabuki comedy about a servant tricked into marrying an unattractive woman. To interpret this image think about

- the subject of the image
- the details of the image
- the creation of the image

Skills FOCUS   READING LIKE A HISTORIAN

1. **Details** What details from the costumes of the two characters suggest a difference in social class?
2. **Creation** What does the date and information about the photograph's creation suggest about kabuki as an artform?

See Skills Handbook, p. H26

Actors in female roles cover their face, hands, and feet with a thick white make-up that symbolizes delicate skin.

Some kabuki costumes can weigh up to 40 pounds. The servant's simple costume is an indicator of his social status.

520 CHAPTER 17

Differentiating Instruction

Below Level

English-Language Learners

1. Organize students into mixed-ability pairs. Tell students that the feudal social structure under the Tokugawa Shogunate was quite rigid.

2. Copy the chart for students to see, omitting the italicized items. Have students copy and complete the chart.
   LS Verbal-Linguistic, Visual-Spatial
   📋 **Alternative Assessment Handbook**, Rubric 1: Acquiring Information

Feudal Social Structure	
Title	**Role**
Emperor	*Figurehead ruler*
Shogun	*True ruling power*
Daimyo	*Warlord landowners, owed loyalty to shogun*
Samurai	*Warriors, served the daimyo*
Peasants	*Farmers*
Artisans	*Made goods like armor and swords*
Merchants	*Sold goods, not honored*

Most important ↑ Least important ↓

While trade with Europe boosted Japan's economy, Christian missionaries changed Japanese society. Many Japanese became Christian, and soon samurai could be heard chanting Christian prayers in battle. Over time, though, the Tokugawa shoguns grew concerned with the spread of Christianity in Japan. Shoguns began to persecute Christians and kill missionaries or force them to leave. At the same time, the shoguns began to restrict foreign trade and travel. For example, they banned the building of all large ships. By 1650 Japan had shut its doors to all Europeans except the Dutch. Japan continued this policy for more than 200 years.

Feudal Culture Japan's growing cities became centers of culture during the feudal period. In art, colorful woodblock prints called Ukiyo-e, or "pictures of the floating world," became popular. Many of these prints showed vibrant scenes of city life.

In literature, realistic stories became popular as well as a form of poetry called **haiku**. A haiku consists of three lines with 17 syllables. Many haiku, including the one below, deal with themes of nature and harmony.

HISTORY'S VOICES

❝An old silent pond . . .
A frog jumps into the pond,
splash! Silence again.❞

—Matsuo Basho, translated by Harry Behn

In theater, Noh drama developed in the 1300s. Slow-moving, Noh plays told stories through the use of masks, stylized dance, and music. For more action, plot, and humor, Japanese audiences turned to a new type of theater in the 1600s— **kabuki**. A kabuki play could last all day as actors sang and danced, pausing to interact with the audience. Although women initially performed kabuki, they were later banned from performing and replaced by men.

READING CHECK **Summarize** What changes did Tokugawa rulers impose on Japanese society?

Medieval Korea

In 1392 a powerful general named **Yi Song-gye** gained control of Korea and established the Choson kingdom. The Choson, or Yi, dynasty that ruled the kingdom became one of Korea's longest ruling dynasties, lasting until 1910.

The Choson kings formed a government based on Confucianism. During this period, Korea prospered and produced many cultural achievements, including the creation of a Korean alphabet. Then in the late 1500s the Japanese invaded Korea twice. The Koreans held off the Japanese by using advanced Turtle ships—ironclad warships with cannons—and receiving help from Ming China. The fighting left Korea in ruins, though. In the early 1600s Korea faced another threat when the Chinese invaded. By the 1640s Korea had become a vassal state to the Qing dynasty in China.

As a result of these events, the Choson kings increasingly isolated Korea from the world except for trade with China. In the West, Korea became known as "the Hermit Kingdom" because of its isolation.

READING SKILLS

Summarizing
After you read the information on Medieval Korea, summarize the key points in two to four sentences.

READING CHECK **Analyze** How did foreign influences both help and hurt Korea?

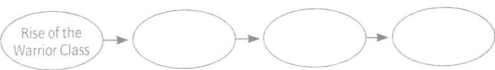

go.hrw.com
Online Quiz
Keyword: SHL NAS HP

Reviewing Ideas, Terms, and People

1. **a. Identify** Who were Minamoto Yoritomo and **Tokugawa Ieyasu**, and why were they each significant in Japanese history?
   b. Compare How were the **samurai** of medieval Japan similar to the knights of medieval Europe?
   c. Elaborate How did the rise of the **daimyo** alter Japanese society?

2. **a. Describe** What was life like for Japanese peasants, merchants, women, and ronin during the Tokugawa Period?
   b. Summarize What actions did Tokugawa Ieyasu and later Tokugawa shoguns take to secure Japanese unity?
   c. Evaluate How did **kabuki** and **haiku** contribute to Japanese culture?

3. **a. Recall** Who founded the Choson dynasty in Korea, and when?
   b. Analyze How do you think isolation might have benefited Korea's development, and how might it have hurt it?

Critical Thinking

4. **Sequence** Using your notes and a graphic organizer like the one below, explain the sequence of events from the development of a feudal warrior society in Japan to the rise of the Tokugawa Shogunate. You may need to add circles to your graphic organizer.

Rise of the Warrior Class → ◯ → ◯ → ◯

FOCUS ON WRITING

5. **Exposition** Write a letter that a Tokugawa shogun might have sent to a European ruler explaining the relationships among the emperor, shogun, daimyo, samurai, and peasants in Japan's feudal warrior society.

NEW ASIAN EMPIRES **521**

Feudalism in Japan and Europe

Word Help

fealty the loyalty of a vassal or feudal tenant to his lord

fluid likely to change; variable

practicable possible to practice or perform

Activity **Analyzing Primary Sources** Ask students to volunteer what they know about European knights' code of chivalry. Tell students that *bushido* is roughly the samurai equivalent to chivalry. Write the following ten virtues of bushido for all to see: loyalty, self sacrifice, justice, sense of shame, refined manners, purity, modesty, frugality, martial spirit, honor, and affection. Ask students which of these Hojo Shigetoki discussed in Document 1. *loyalty and self sacrifice*

Info to Know

Matsumoto Castle Now a National Treasure of Japan, Matsumoto Castle was originally designed to withstand attack from *teppo*, the firearms used at that time. Construction of the castle began in the 1580s. It has three moats and small openings in the walls allowed the use of weapons. The castle also has a secret third floor, which invaders were unaware of until they were captured in the dark, windowless room. The fourth floor was the lord's chamber where he attended to castle business. The fifth floor provides excellent visibility on all sides, as does the tiny room on the top floor.

Feudalism in Japan and Europe

Historical Context The documents in this investigation describe different aspects of feudalism in medieval Japan and in medieval Europe.

Task Study the documents and answer the questions that follow. Then, using evidence from these documents and from the chapter, write an essay comparing and contrasting feudalism in Japan and in Europe.

NEW YORK STANDARDS

PI **1.4** Students understand the broad patterns, relationships, and interactions of cultures and civilizations during particular eras and across eras.

PI **3.3** Students examine the social/cultural, political, economic, and religious norms and values of Western and other world cultures.

DOCUMENT 1

The Ideal Samurai in Medieval Japan

In about 1256, Hojo Shigetoki, a Buddhist monk and former deputy to the Kyoto Shogunate, wrote a series of essays outlining the ideal behavior and moral character of Japan's warrior class, the samurai.

> When one is serving officially or in the master's court, he should not think of a hundred or a thousand people, but should consider only the importance of the master. Nor should he draw the line at his own life or anything else he considers valuable. Even if the master is being phlegmatic [slow to rise to action] and one goes unrecognized, he should know that he will surely have the divine protection of the gods and Buddhas. While in the midst of duties, one should keep this principle in mind concerning service at the master's court, too. To think of receiving the blessings of the master without fulfilling the duties of court service is no different from trying to cross a rough sea without a boat.

DOCUMENT 2

Fortresses of Feudalism

Medieval fortresses such as Matsumoto Castle (left) in Japan and Bodiam Castle (right) in England were often built on hills and surrounded by water for defensive purposes. As in medieval Europe, the need for castles in Japan arose in a time marked by the absence of a strong central government and intense competition between local rulers. During this period of disorder and division in Japan, dozens of warlords fought each other and built castles to defend their lands.

522 CHAPTER 17

Collaborative Learning

At Level

Fortresses of Feudalism

Research Required

1. Review with students the characteristics shared by Matsumoto and Bodiam castles. Tell students they will compare and contrast the physical characteristics of European and Japanese medieval fortresses.

2. Organize students into small groups. Have each group conduct research to locate information about the two castles pictured in Document 2. Have each group create a list of facts about the defensive structural advantages of each castle, and a bibliography of references for the facts it recorded.

3. Next, have each group mark list entries that have strong similarities.

4. Have groups post their lists for display and allow students time to circulate the room to view each group's results. **LS** **Interpersonal, Visual-Spatial**

Alternative Assessment Handbook, Rubrics 9: Comparing and Contrasting; and 14: Group Activity

DOCUMENT 3

Duties of a Knight in Medieval Europe

In about 1023 Duke William of Aquitaine, in present-day France, asked Bishop Fulbert of Chartres to advise on the duties of vassals and lords. The following excerpt is from the bishop's reply.

To William most glorious duke of the Aquitanians ... Asked to write something concerning the form of fealty, I have noted briefly for you on the authority of the books of the things we follow. He who swears fealty to his lord ought always to have these six things in memory; what is harmless, safe, honorable, useful, easy, practicable. Harmless, that is to say that he should not be injurious to his lord in his body; safe, that he should not be injurious to him in his secrets or in the defences through which he is able to be secure; honorable, that he should not be injurious to him in his justice or in other matters that pertain to his honor; useful, that he should not be injurious to him in his possessions; easy or practicable , that that good which his lord is able to do easily, he make not difficult, nor that which is practicable he make impossible to him.

DOCUMENT 4

A Historian's View

In the 1960s Peter Duus was one of many historians who debated whether or not "feudalism" was a valid concept for understanding Japanese history. In the following passage from his book *Feudalism in Japan,* published in 1969, Duus examines feudalism in Japan and Europe.

Of course, we should not expect feudal Japan to be a mirror image of feudal Europe, either in its pattern of development or in its institutional structure. The history of Japan was conditioned by a geographic, economic, social, and intellectual environment vastly different from that of Europe. What we should expect to find is a family resemblance, not an exact likeness. Equally important we should not think of European feudalism as being more "normal" than Japanese feudalism. Building a model on the basis of the European experience is simple a convenience; a close study of both Japan and Europe may mean that we will have to modify the model. It may be that some things we assume to be indispensable aspects of feudalism were not present in both cultures and that certain things we had not assumed to be so were in fact common to both. In short, we are still at the beginning of the comparative study of feudalism, and our definition of it will have to remain a fluid one.

Skills FOCUS READING LIKE A HISTORIAN

DOCUMENT 1
a. Identify According to Hojo Shigetok, what should be the foremost concern of a samurai?
b. Explain What does Hojo Shigetok mean when he says that expecting a master's blessing without fulfilling one's duties is like trying to cross a rough sea without a boat?

DOCUMENT 2
a. Describe What architectural features suggest that both castles were defensive structures?
b. Elaborate Why were castles important to the development and maintenance of feudalism in Europe and Japan?

DOCUMENT 3
a. Identify Main Ideas According to Bishop Fulbert, how should a knight in service to a lord act?

b. Compare Based on this document and Document 1, how did a knight's duties compare to those of a samurai?

DOCUMENT 4
a. Describe According to Duus what might account for the differences in feudalism in Japan and Europe?
b. Interpret How would a fluid definition of feudalism help historians study feudalism in Japan and Europe?

DOCUMENT-BASED ESSAY QUESTION

Using details from the documents and information from this chapter and other resources, write a short essay comparing and contrasting feudalism in Japan and Europe.

See **Skills Handbook**, p. H48

Skills Focus: Making Inferences

[At Level]

Reading Skill
A Samurai Journal

1. Remind students that the life of a samurai was quite different from that of his European counterpart.

2. Have students write a journal entry for a samurai living at Matsumoto Castle in the 1600s. Students should review each document to help them infer what a samurai's life may have been like. Suggest that students include specific duties that would have been

performed by the samurai or his servant, and describe specific places he would go.

3. When students have had time to write, have several volunteers share their work.

4. As homework, have students write a short essay about their new understanding of feudalism in Japan. **LS Verbal-Linguistic**

Alternative Assessment Handbook, Rubric 15: Journals

Biography

Bishop Fulbert, (c. 950s–1028) Bishop Fulbert of Chartres overcame a humble background by excelling as a student and then establishing a school at Chartres Cathedral. The school attracted students from across Europe, who held such respect for him that they referred to Fulbert as "the venerable Socrates." When Chartres burned down in 1020, Fulbert received help from various European kings to rebuild it. His writings are valued by the Catholic Church because they describe the liturgy and discipline of the church at the time.

Answers

Reading Like a Historian
Document 1. a. *the importance of the master;* **b.** *possible answer—The fulfillment of one's duties to his master is a source of protection in bad times, just like a boat protects one during harsh seas;* **Document 2. a.** *moats, protective walls with narrow openings for defense;* **b.** *Castles protected people who lived and worked together, cooperating with each other under a behavioral code and the law of a single ruler. This protection allowed people to survive invasions.* **Document 3. a.** *A knight must remember what is harmless, safe, honorable, useful, easy, and practicable.* **b.** *A knight must concern himself with what is harmless, safe, and easy, but a samurai's focus is on the importance of his master, even disregarding his own safety.* **Document 4. a.** *The history of Japan was conditioned by a geographic, economic, social, and intellectual environment vastly different from that of Europe.* **b.** *possible answer—We should allow the definition of feudalism to change as we learn more.* **Essay** *Student essays should include several similarities and differences in feudalism in Japan and Europe.*

Answers

Visual Summary

Review and Inquiry Organize students into six groups. Assign one region from the Visual Study Guide to each group. Have groups create an oral presentation about their assigned region.

Quick Facts Transparency: Visual Study Guide: New Asian Empires

Review Key Terms and People

1. sultan
2. Suleyman
3. Akbar the Great
4. Shah Jahan
5. Zheng He
6. Qing dynasty
7. Bushido
8. haiku
9. Yi Song-gye
10. stance

Comprehension and Critical Thinking

11. a. 1453; provided Ottoman Empire with a trade route between Asia and Europe; marked the fall of the Byzantine Empire
b. Safavids were Shia Muslims, Ottomans were Sunni. Safavid emperors went to war with the Ottoman Empire to convert it.
c. Ottoman Empire defeated the Safavids at the Battle of Chaldiran, spread of Safavid Empire.

12. a. won loyalty of diverse population, promoted religious tolerance.
b. Later Mughal rulers did not practice religious tolerance.
c. possible answer—Yes, during his reign the empire experienced a golden age.

13. a. After European traders arrived, Ming rulers isolated China from the outside world to preserve China's traditions.
b. possible answer—stability, prosperity
c. possible answer—Yes, it helped preserve China's traditions.

14. a. by re-establishing a strong central government in Japan
b. Samurai gave military service in exchange for property or payment; shoguns ruled in the name of the emperor; daimyo were powerful warlords.
c. Rulers in both Japan and Korea were concerned about how foreign influence would affect their cultures.

VISUAL STUDY GUIDE

QUICK FACTS

Asian Empires, 1200–1800

Ottoman Empire
- Muslim Turks built the empire from a state in Anatolia in the 1300s.
- Under Mehmed II, the Ottomans captured Constantinople in 1453.
- Suleyman I brought the empire to its height and reformed law codes.
- Tolerated but restricted non-Muslims and enslaved Christian boys.
- Ottoman culture combined Persian, Muslim, and Byzantine influences.

Safavid Empire
- Esmai'il founded this Muslim empire in Persia in the 1500s.
- Esmai'il strictly enforced Shiism and came into conflict with Sunni Muslims such as the Ottomans.
- 'Abbas, the greatest Safavid shah, strengthened the military and expanded the empire.
- Safavid culture blended Chinese, Muslim, and Persian styles.

Mughal Empire
- Babur founded this Muslim empire in India by 1526.
- Akbar and Jahangir encouraged tolerance and cooperation between Muslims and Hindus.
- Shah Jahan and Aurangzeb tried to eliminate non-Muslims.
- Mughal art combined influences from India, Persia, and Muslim lands in structures like the Taj Mahal.

China
- Ming dynasty (1368–1644) rulers provided prosperity and stability, built the Forbidden City in Beijing, funded sea voyages, and isolated China as European influences rose.
- Qing dynasty (1644–1911) rulers expanded China to its largest size and continued isolation.
- Cultural developments included Ming porcelain and Chinese novels.

Japan
- A feudal warrior society arose in which a shogun ruled over daimyo with private armies of samurai.
- Samurai followed Bushido, a code stressing loyalty and bravery.
- The Kamakura shogunate unified Japan and defeated the Mongols.
- The Tokugawa shogunate reunified Japan in 1603, and later isolated Japan as European influences rose.

Korea
- General Yi Song-gye founded the Choson, or Yi, dynasty in 1392.
- Choson kings created a government built on Confucian principles.
- Japanese invasions in the late 1500s left Korea in ruins.
- After Manchu invasions, Korea became a Qing vassal state.
- Korea was isolated from the world for much of this period.

Reviewing Key Terms and People

Identify the correct term or person from the chapter that best fits each of the following descriptions.

1. title of the rulers of the Ottoman Empire
2. Ottoman ruler who reformed the legal code
3. Considered to be the greatest Mughal emperor
4. Mughal emperor who had the Taj Mahal built
5. Chinese admiral who led seven sea voyages for China during the 1400s
6. series of Manchu rulers who governed China
7. code of ethics for Japanese samurai
8. Japanese poetry with three lines and 17 syllables
9. general who founded Korea's Choson dynasty
10. attitude or position about someone or something

524 CHAPTER 17

Reading Skills

15. key points—Ottomans built vast empire in Europe, Asia, and Africa; had strong military ruled by sultan; conquered Constantinople; diverse cultures created rich Ottoman culture

16. key points—Qing dynasty were Manchus who overthrew the Ming dynasty; last dynasty in China's history and the largest empire; respected Chinese customs and traditions; maintained Ming policy of isolation

History's Impact video program
Review the video to answer the closing question: Describe some
influences of the samurai on the traditions of contemporary Japan.

Comprehension and Critical Thinking

SECTION 1 *(pp. 499–503)*

11. a. Recall When did the Ottomans capture the city of Constantinople, and why was the city's conquest significant?

b. Analyze How did religion divide the Ottoman and Safavid empires, and how did this division affect the two empires' relationship?

c. Elaborate How did the Ottoman Empire influence the Safavid Empire, and what was the outcome of this influence?

SECTION 2 *(pp. 504–508)*

12. a. Recall How did Akbar bring stability to the Mughal Empire?

b. Contrast How did the religious stances of later Mughal rulers differ from those of earlier rulers?

c. Evaluate Do you think Shah Jahan was a good emperor for India? Why or why not?

SECTION 3 *(pp. 509–513)*

13. a. Describe How did China's relationship with the outside world change during the Ming dynasty?

b. Make Generalizations What common factors contributed to population and city growth during the Ming and Qing dynasties?

c. Make Judgments Do you think that China's Ming emperor made the right decision to stop making overseas voyages? Why or why not?

SECTION 4 *(pp. 516–521)*

14. a. Recall How did the Tokugawa Shogunate bring stability, peace, and prosperity to Japan?

b. Summarize What were the main features that characterized Japan's feudal warrior society?

c. Elaborate What common factors motivated rulers in medieval Japan and Korea to close their societies to the outside world?

Reading Skills

Summarizing *Use what you know about summarizing to answer the questions below:*

15. Review the information on the Ottoman Empire and summarize the key points in four to five sentences.

16. Review the information on the Qing dynasty and summarize the main points in a few sentences.

Analyzing Visuals

Reading Like a Historian *The painting below, made during the 1700s shows young women relaxing and playing on swings during the Mughal Empire.*

Mughal miniature, c. 1700s

17. Infer What can you infer about Mughal art from this image?

18. Analyze What can you learn about Mughal women's fashions in the 1700s from this image?

Using the Internet

go.hrw.com
Practice Online
Keyword: SHL NAS

19. The Ottoman Empire lasted more than 500 years. Using the keyword above, conduct research on the history of the Ottoman Empire. Then create an illustrated time line of the major events of the empire.

WRITING FOR THE SAT

Think about the following issue:

Some of the most successful Asian rulers during this period governed with almost absolute power. Two examples are the Ottoman sultan Suleyman and the Mughal emperor Akbar. These two rulers used their power to improve and expand their empires.

20. Assignment: *What did these two rulers have in common in the ways in which they used their power? Write a short essay in answer to this question. Support your answer with examples from your reading and studies.*

Answers

Analyzing Visuals

17. possible answer—that Mughal art depicted daily life

18. Mughal women wore long, colorful skirts, blouses, and dresses.

Using the Internet

19. Go to the HRW Web site and enter the keyword shown to access a rubric for this activity.

KEYWORD: SHL NAS

Writing for the SAT

20. Student essays should include details from the chapter about the reigns of the Ottoman sultan Suleyman and the Mughal emperor Akbar. Essays should point out what the two rulers had in common. A rubric for this activity is provided in **CRF:** Writing for the SAT.

HOLT

History's Impact

▶ **Video Program: New Asian Empires**
See the Video Program Teacher's Guide for the answer to the closing question.

Review and Assessment Resources

Review and Reinforce

- **CRF:** Chapter Review
- **Quick Facts Transparency:** Visual Study Guide: New Asian Empires
- **Spanish Chapter Summaries Audio CD Program**
- OSP **Holt PuzzlePro:** Quiz Show for ExamView
- **Quiz Game CD-ROM**

Assess

- **PASS:** Chapter Test, Forms A and B
- **Alternative Assessment Handbook**
- OSP **ExamView Test Generator**, Chapter Test
- **Differentiated Instruction Modified Worksheets and Tests CD-ROM:** Chapter Test
- HOAP **Holt Online Assessment Program** (in the Premier Online Edition)

Reteach/Intervene

- **Interactive Reader and Study Guide**
- **Differentiated Instruction Teacher Management System:** Lesson Plans for Differentiated Instruction
- **Differentiated Instruction Modified Worksheets and Tests CD-ROM:** Chapter Test
- **Interactive Skills Tutor CD-ROM**

go.hrw.com
Online Resources
KEYWORD: SHL TEACHER

You can use these pages to have students simultaneously review the unit and practice taking standardized tests.

Answers

1. 4
   Exploration and Expansion, Section 3

2. 2
   Renaissance and Reformation, Section 3

3. 4
   Renaissance and Reformation, Section 4

4. 1
   Renaissance and Reformation, Section 1

5. 3
   Renaissance and Reformation, Section 1

6. 1
   Renaissance and Reformation, Section 3

7. 3
   Exploration and Expansion, Section 1

8. 2
   Exploration and Expansion, Section 1

9. 4
   Exploration and Expansion, Section 3

UNIT 5
Regents Practice

Directions Write your answer for each statement or question on a separate answer sheet. Choose the number of the word or expression that best completes the statement or answers the question.

1 The illustration shows the effects on Aztecs of the

American Museum of Natural History

1 Mayan attacks.
2 famine.
3 Spanish weapons.
4 Columbian exchange.

2 Why were many people in the 1500s unhappy with the Roman Catholic Church?

1 People wanted the Catholic Church to sell indulgences so they could have their sins forgiven.
2 People thought that the Catholic Church had become too worldly, too wealthy, and had strayed from its spiritual roots.
3 The newly invented printing press enabled heresy to spread quickly.
4 They opposed the Diet of Worms.

3 One response of Catholics to the Reformation was

1 the sack of Rome by the soldiers of the Holy Roman Emperor Charles V.
2 Ignatius of Loyola calling the Council of Trent.
3 encouraging people to read and criticize Luther's work.
4 the formation of new religious orders, such as the Jesuits, who worked to reform the church.

4 Some of the factors that helped bring about the Renaissance are

1 increased trade, the growth of wealthy city-states, and an interest in classical ideas and styles.
2 decreased trade as a result of the Crusades.
3 decreased interest in secular themes in literature.
4 increased focus on finding ways to glorify God.

5 One of the characteristics of the Renaissance was

1 a focus on religious art.
2 a lack of trade among towns and cities.
3 an emphasis on the individual.
4 a return to traditional religious ideas.

6 Martin Luther taught that

1 faith alone can lead to salvation.
2 faith and good works lead to salvation.
3 God has already chosen those who will be saved.
4 the Bible and church tradition are both sources of truth.

7 During the 1300s and 1400s, Europeans set out on voyages of exploration to find

1 a cure for the plague and other serious illnesses.
2 the North and South poles.
3 wealth and fame.
4 the American continents.

8 The monarch who established a school for navigators was

1 King John II of Portugal.
2 Prince Henry of Portugal.
3 Queen Isabella of Spain.
4 King Henry VII of England.

9 The global transfer of plants, animals, people, and diseases between the Eastern and Western hemispheres became known as the

1 mercantile exchange.
2 European-Western Exchange.
3 balance of trade.
4 Columbian Exchange.

10 The Spanish conquistador Hernán Cortés
1 captured and destroyed the Aztec capital, Tenochtitlan.
2 conquered the Incas, who were weakened by disease.
3 respected and admired the Aztec emperor Montezuma II.
4 established the first Spanish colony in Hispaniola.

11 The voyage of enslaved Africans across the Atlantic Ocean was known as the
1 African-American Passage.
2 Middle Passage.
3 Long Voyage.
4 Passage of the Enslaved.

12 When the Ottomans conquered Constantinople they renamed it
1 Byzantium.
2 Adrianople.
3 Anatolia.
4 Istanbul.

13 Suleyman I (the Great) is best known for
1 expanding the Ottoman Empire to its height of power.
2 leading the Ottomans into Europe.
3 defeating a crusade at the Battle of Nicopolis.
4 conquering Constantinople.

14 During his reign as shah of the Mughal Empire, Akbar
1 gained a foothold in India.
2 established a religion that blended Muslim, Christian, and other beliefs.
3 pursued artistic interests and allowed his wife and her family to govern.
4 destroyed Hindu temples and kept Hindus out of high positions in government.

15 One of the achievements of the Ming dynasty under Hongwu was
1 diplomatic and economic contact with Europeans.
2 a dramatic increase in taxes.
3 the complete defeat of the Mongols.
4 shared government control between the emperor and the chief minister.

16 Japanese feudalism was similar to European feudalism in that it
1 had a central governing figure.
2 was governed by church and civil authorities.
3 gave land to vassals who swore allegiance to a lord.
4 had a code of ethics called the bushido.

17 One characteristic of Japanese life during the Tokugawa period was the
1 respect and high social rank given to merchants.
2 continued need for samurai.
3 strictness of the social structure.
4 power of the daimyo over the shogun.

18 Read this excerpt from Leonardo da Vinci's writings. What is his opinion about the art of painting?

"The painter will produce pictures of small merit if he takes for his standard the pictures of others, but if he will study from natural objects he will bear good fruit. As was seen in the painters after the Romans who always imitated each other and so their art constantly declined from age to age… Those who take for their standard any one but nature… weary themselves in vain."

1 He recommends studying other painters' works.
2 He supports copying Roman works.
3 He thinks that an artist must study nature.
4 He thinks that painting required little talent.

REVIEWING THE UNIT

Constructed Response From the 1300s through the 1600s, some empires expanded, some fell, and others closed their borders. Recall what you have learned about European, Asian, and American empires during this period. Choose one empire and write a brief essay identifying the causes and effects of its expansion, its fall, or its retreat from the outside world.

CONNECTING TO THE PREVIOUS UNIT

Constructed Response During the Renaissance and Reformation, Europeans began to change how they looked at the world. Recall what you learned about Europe during the Middle Ages. Then write a brief essay about medieval events that set the stage for the Renaissance, Reformation, and exploration.

Answers
10. 1
Exploration and Expansion, Section 2
11. 2
Exploration and Expansion, Section 4
12. 4
New Asian Empires, Section 1
13. 1
New Asian Empires, Section 1
14. 2
New Asian Empires, Section 2
15. 3
New Asian Empires, Section 3
16. 3
New Asian Empires, Section 4
17. 3
New Asian Empires, Section 4
18. 3
Renaissance and Reformation, Section 1

Reviewing the Unit
Students essays will vary depending on the empire they chose to write about.

Connecting to the Previous Unit
Student essays should discuss the influence that medieval events had on the Renaissance, the Reformation, and exploration.

Unit Review

Migration and Diffusion

The Columbian Exchange One area in which the New World came out ahead in the Columbian Exchange was in terms of the exchange of animals. In the New World there were 25 species of large mammals, but none of them except the llama and alpaca were suitable for domestication. On the other hand, Europe and Asia had 72 large animal species, of which 13 were suitable for domestication, including horses, cattle, sheep, goats, and pigs.

Arts and Ideas

The Development of Printing Perhaps the most important development of the Renaissance took place in Northern Europe rather than in Italy: the printing press. In the first 50 years after the invention of movable type, more than 6,000 separate works were printed. The first books printed in Northern Europe were Bibles and other religious texts. In Italy, on the other hand, printers published Greek and Roman classics, as well as new literary and scientific works by Renaissance scholars. The religious and political controversies of the 16th and 17th centuries were spread largely by printed pamphlets.

Activity **The Importance of Printing** Tell students to envision what the world would be like without printing. How would it affect their lives? Have students write a paragraph about what life would be like without books, magazines, or newspapers.

LS Verbal-Linguistic

Themes & Global Connections

THEME
MIGRATION AND DIFFUSION

Why can 1492 be considered a turning point in world history?

The encounters among the Americas, Africa, and Europe had profound affects on the populations, food sources, and diseases all over the world. For example, American foodstuffs introduced into Asia resulted in an increase in the population of China.

THEME
ARTS AND IDEAS

How did the Renaissance influence Europeans' world view?

The Renaissance brought a shift in most Europeans' focus from spiritual concerns characteristic of the Middle Ages to a more secular and individualistic focus. Religion still played an important role in people's lives, but people increasingly focused their attention on their own interests and achievements.

RESULTS OF EUROPEAN EXPLORATION

Europe	• New food sources enriched diets and led to a population boom. • Spain was enriched with American gold and silver, leading to global dominance and inflation. • Europeans raced to establish colonies. • European-American trade led to increased European business activity. • Mercantilist and capitalist ideas took hold.
Americas	• European diseases devastated Native American populations, which lacked immunity. • Millions of Africans were forcibly enslaved and brought to the Americas. • Europeans emigrated in great numbers to the Americas. • The wheel, iron tools, and guns were introduced. • New domesticated plants and animals were introduced.
Africa	• The Atlantic slave trade forcibly removed millions of Africans from the continent. • New food crops were introduced. • Guns were introduced into West Africa.
China	• New food sources enriched diets and led to a population boom. • China received American silver in payment for Chinese luxury goods.

Renaissance World View

Arts
Painters and sculptors treated secular and religious subjects realistically. Painters used perspective. Classical influences stressed perfection, harmony, and balance.

Government
Rulers abandoned the ideal of Christian unity and peace, and instead used diplomacy and politics to enhance their own power.

Religion
Thinkers became more willing to question religious teachings. This questioning helped lead to the Reformation.

Literature and Learning
An interest in ancient Greek and Roman cultures stimulated learning. The printing press made books more available and thus contributed to the spread of Renaissance ideas. Writers began to use vernacular languages instead of Latin.

528 UNIT 5

Differentiating Instruction

Below Level

English-Language Learners

1. Organize students into four groups. Assign each group one of the four areas affected by the Renaissance world view, as shown in the graphic organizer on this page. Have groups find or draw pictures that illustrate the area assigned to them and create a collage showing how that area affected the way people looked at the world.

2. Have volunteers from each group present their collages to the class. Place each collage on display for the class to see.

3. Guide the class in a discussion of the ways in which the Renaissance changed the way people looked at the world around them.
   LS Interpersonal, Visual-Spatial

   Alternative Assessment Handbook, Rubrics 8: Collages; 11: Discussions; and 14: Group Activity

THEME
BELIEF SYSTEMS

How did conquest affect people's belief systems?
During this period conquest resulted in a change in the dominant religion in several areas of the world.

CONQUEST AND BELIEF SYSTEMS

Ottomans conquered Constantinople.	Orthodox Christian Constantinople became Muslim Istanbul.
Safavids expanded their empire.	Shia Islam became the state religion in what is today Iran, replacing a number of existing traditions.
Mughals conquered northern India.	Islam was promoted, but Hinduism remained dominant and Buddhism nearly disappeared.
Europeans conquered the Americas.	Christianity replaced Native American religions.

Skills FOCUS UNDERSTANDING THEMES

Conquest by Ottoman Turkish armies was a major factor in the diffusion of Ottoman culture. The Ottoman military kept Italian traders out of the eastern Mediterranean, took over much of Hungary, and laid siege to Vienna. Following the conquest of Constantinople, the Ottomans forced people of other cultures to migrate to the city. Use your textbook and other resources to gather information about how Europeans responded to the Ottoman expansion. Then create a chart like the one below to explain how Europeans responded. Add as many rows as you need.

Ottoman Empire	European Response
Control of the eastern Mediterranean ports through which Asian trade passed	
Conquest of Hungary	
Siege of Vienna	

Global Connections

Japan's feudal period bears some similarities to European feudalism. The samurai were the at the center of the warrior class much as knights had been. They served their daimyo, or lord, and received land for their services. The shogun was at the top of the hierarchy and the real ruler of Japan.

In the last unit you learned about European feudalism. There are similarities between the systems, but they are not identical. What in European and Japanese society might account for the differences and similarities? Use your textbook and other sources to create a chart that compares and contrasts Japanese and European feudal systems.

Making Connections Analyze your chart to determine whether or not you think the two systems were similar. Then state your conclusions in a short essay of two to three paragraphs explaining your position.

▼ **Matsumoto Castle is located in Japan.**

▼ **Bodiam Castle is located in England.**

529

Skill Focus: Identifying Problem and Solution

At Level

Reading Skill
The New World: An Alternate Version

1. Tell students that it is 1492, and Columbus has just discovered the Americas, but in this version of history, he realizes that he has not reached Asia but instead a new, previously unknown land. Instead of landing, he goes back to Spain and tells of his discovery.

2. Organize students into small groups. Tell them they are advisers to the Spanish monarchs who want to make sure that the people of the Americas are treated fairly and that their safety is guaranteed. Have each group develop a set of guidelines designed to protect the Native Americans from possible contamination and exploitation.

3. Have volunteers from each group present their guidelines to the rest of the class.
LS Interpersonal

Alternative Assessment Handbook, Rubrics 14: Group Activity; 35: Solving Problems

---

Belief Systems

The Catholic Monarchs Ferdinand of Aragon and Isabella of Castille ruled over the most diverse country in western Europe, which had large Muslim and Jewish populations. Spanish civilization owed much to this fact. The Jews had made their mark in business and government, while Muslims had dominated in the visual arts and architecture. The leader of the Spanish Inquisition, Tomás de Torquemada, began a campaign against the Jews. In 1492—the year Columbus discovered the Americas—the Catholic Monarchs conquered the Muslim kingdom of Granada in southern Spain, finally uniting Spain. After Muslims rebelled in 1499–1500, they were given the choice of converting to Catholicism or leaving the country. The expulsion of the Jews and Muslims deprived Spain of much of its educated middle class, which would have serious repercussions in the future.

Understanding Themes

Ottoman Empire	European Response
Control of eastern Mediterranean ports through which Asian trade passed	One last crusade ended in a European defeat at Nicopolis, on the Danube.
Conquest of Hungary	For the next 200 years there was near-constant warfare in Hungary between the Hapsburg and Ottoman empires.
Siege of Vienna	Europe reacted with fear and resolved to fight to the death to turn back the Ottomans.

Global Connections

Student charts and essays should indicate the following similarities: both were systems in which lords gave lands to vassals in exchange for service. Differences include the fact that there was a single central authority, the shogun, in Japan. Also, in Japan military leaders governed, rather than civil or religious authorities.

Summarizing the Unit

During the period covered in this unit, the world experienced great changes. Guide the class in a discussion of those changes. Have students identify the ways in which the Renaissance, Protestant Reformation, Counter-Reformation, European voyages of discovery, and the formation of Asian empires and dynasties were related to each other.

Answers

Thinking Like a Historian

Student charts or graphic organizers will vary, depending on which area students selected, but should summarize developments in all three areas—government, trade and the economy, and the arts.

UNIT 5
IN BRIEF

Below is a chapter-by-chapter summary of the main ideas in this unit, followed by a summary activity for the unit.

CHAPTER 15
Renaissance and Reformation
1300–1650

MAIN IDEA As trade with the East increased, Europeans rediscovered the classical knowledge of ancient Greece and Rome. This knowledge led to a period of creativity and learning known as the Renaissance. A new focus on the individual emerged, leading to new ideas about religion, and ultimately the Reformation.

SECTION 1 In Italy the growth of wealthy trading cities and new ways of thinking led to a rebirth of the arts and learning known as the Renaissance.

SECTION 2 Trade and printing helped spread the Renaissance beyond Italy to Northern Europe, where it affected artists and writers in many ways.

SECTION 3 The Protestant Reformation was a response to criticisms of the Roman Catholic Church. The Reformation led to changes in politics as well as religion.

SECTION 4 Many Catholics recognized the need for reform of the church, and their work renewed the faith of Catholics.

CHAPTER 16
Exploration and Expansion
1400–1700

MAIN IDEA Between 1400 and 1700 explorers set out on great voyages of discovery, and as the news of new lands spread, countries scrambled to set up colonies in hopes of gaining wealth.

SECTION 1 Aided by new technologies and inspired by greed, curiosity, and the desire for glory, European explorers sailed to previously unknown lands.

SECTION 2 The countries of Europe established colonies in the lands they had discovered but in some cases only after conquering the people who lived there.

SECTION 3 The creation of colonies in the Americas and elsewhere led to the establishment of new patterns of trade and new economic systems in Europe.

SECTION 4 Millions of Africans were captured, transported across the Atlantic Ocean, and sold as slaves in the Americas between the 1500s and the 1800s.

CHAPTER 17
New Asian Empires
1200–1800

MAIN IDEA Several new Muslim empires arose in Asia. In China, Mongol rule came to an end with the rise of the Ming dynasty. In Japan, the Tokugawa Shogunate created a strong central government.

SECTION 1 The Ottomans conquered Constantinople and developed a rich culture. The Safavid dynasties expanded their territories.

SECTION 2 Mughal rulers in India created a powerful empire and saw an artistic flowering.

SECTION 3 China's power and size reached new heights during the Ming and Qing dynasties, and trade and culture flourished.

SECTION 4 Japan's feudal system unified under a shogunate that also produced a cultural blossoming.

Thinking like a Historian
Summary and Extension Activity

The Renaissance and Reformation set the stage for European expansion into previously unknown lands. In Asia, new empires formed and expanded, and the arts flourished. Choose one of these areas and create a chart or graphic organizer that shows the developments in:

A. Government

B. Trade and the economy

C. The arts

Unit Resources

Review and Reinforce

- **Global History and Geography Regents Test Prep Workbook**
- **Regents Review Transparencies**
- **CRF:** Chapter Review
- **Spanish Chapter Summaries Audio CD Program**
- OSP **Holt PuzzlePro:** Quiz Show for ExamView
- **Quiz Game CD-ROM**

Assess

- **PASS:** Unit Test, Forms A and B
- **Alternative Assessment Handbook**
- OSP **New York ExamView Test Generator** correlated to NY SS Standards
- **Differentiated Instruction Modified Worksheets and Tests CD-ROM:** Chapter Test
- HOAP **Holt Online Assessment Program** (in the Premier Online Edition)

Reteach/Intervene

- **Interactive Reader and Study Guide**
- **Differentiated Instruction Teacher Management System:** Lesson Plans for Differentiated Instruction
- **Differentiated Instruction Modified Worksheets and Tests CD-ROM:** Chapter Test
- **Interactive Skills Tutor CD-ROM**

go.hrw.com
Online Resources

KEYWORDS: SHL REN, SHL EXP, SHL NAS

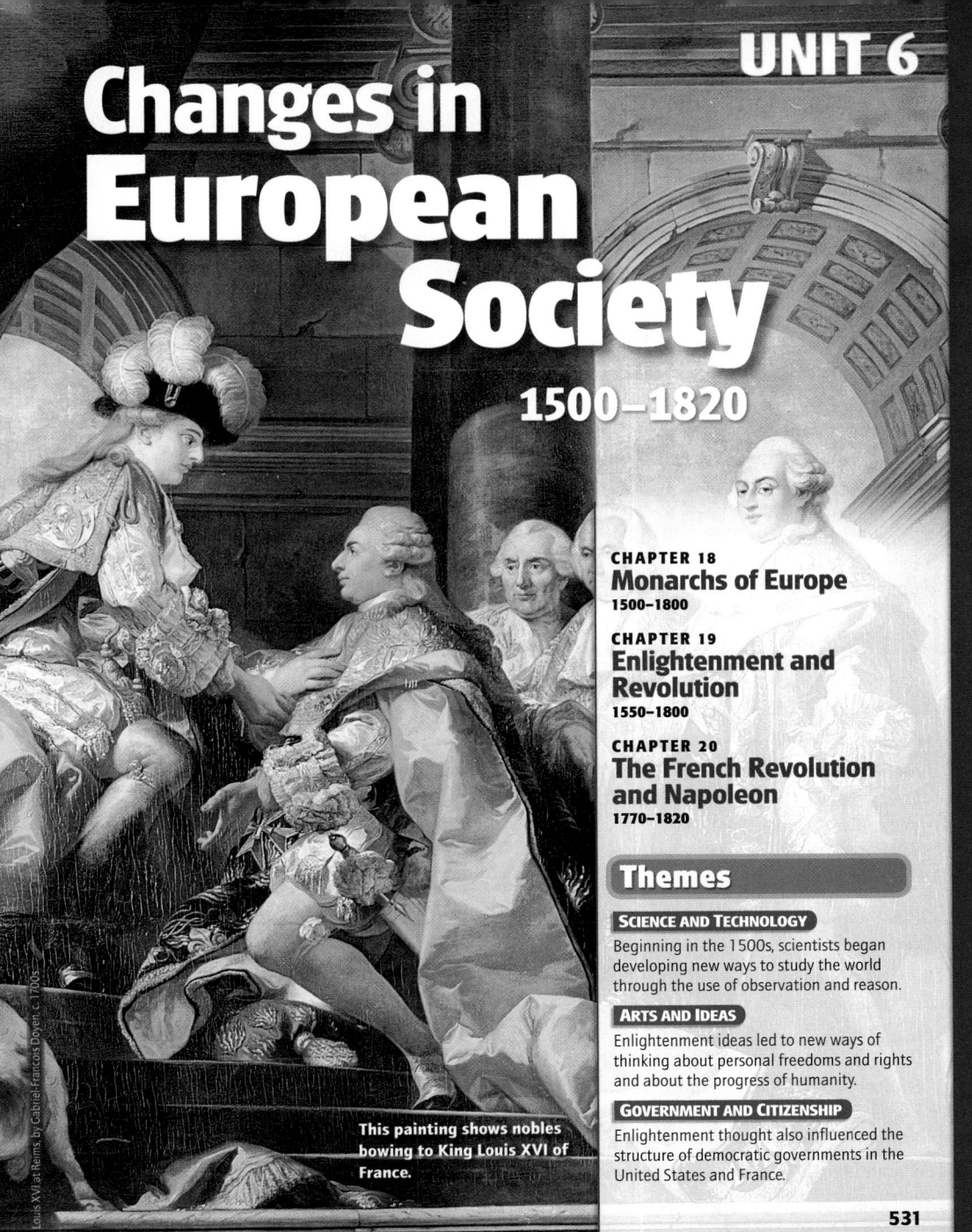

UNIT 6

Changes in European Society

1500–1820

CHAPTER 18
Monarchs of Europe
1500–1800

CHAPTER 19
Enlightenment and Revolution
1550–1800

CHAPTER 20
The French Revolution and Napoleon
1770–1820

Themes

SCIENCE AND TECHNOLOGY
Beginning in the 1500s, scientists began developing new ways to study the world through the use of observation and reason.

ARTS AND IDEAS
Enlightenment ideas led to new ways of thinking about personal freedoms and rights and about the progress of humanity.

GOVERNMENT AND CITIZENSHIP
Enlightenment thought also influenced the structure of democratic governments in the United States and France.

This painting shows nobles bowing to King Louis XVI of France.

Louis XVI at Reims, by Gabriel-François Doyen, c. 1700s

531

• **Unit Preview** •

Introducing the Unit
Ask students to name a societal, economic, or political issue they feel strongly about, such as homelessness, hunger, war, or terrorism. Then have students list factors that might cause people involved in the issue to rebel against authority. Have students list what might have caused revolts against monarchs during the 1500s to 1800s.

Connecting to Themes
Activity New Ideas Bring Change
Ask students how changes in personal beliefs and in economic systems led to individualism and to changes in European society. Guide students in a discussion about the ways in which belief systems and economic systems changed during the Enlightenment.

Reading Like a Historian
Interpreting Visuals
Louis XVI When he came to the throne, Louis XVI was an awkward, timid twenty-year old, who was ill equipped to rule a country. Throughout his reign, he often expressed his desire to have been born a common man, free of his great responsibility. Louis' propensity to listen to self-interested advisors and give in to the extravagant demands of Queen Marie-Antoinette eventually cost him his life.

Unit Resources

Planning
- **Differentiated Instruction Teacher Management System:** Unit Pacing Guide
- OSP **New York One-Stop Planner CD-ROM:** Teacher Management System
- **Power Presentations with Video CD-ROM**

Standards Mastery
- **Global History and Geography Regents Test Prep Workbook**
- **Regents Review Transparencies**

Differentiating Instruction
- **Differentiated Instruction Teacher Management System:** Lesson Plans for Differentiated Instruction
- **Differentiated Instruction Modified Worksheets and Tests CD-ROM**

Enrichment
- **A World History Teacher's Guide to Analyzing Movies**
- **Document-Based Activities for World History**
- **World History Outline Maps**
- **Reading Like a Historian: World History Toolkit**
- **World History Primary Source Library CD-ROM**

Assessment
- **PASS:** Unit Test, Forms A and B
- **Alternative Assessment Handbook**
- OSP **New York ExamView Test Generator correlated to NY SS Standards**
- HOAP **Holt Online Assessment Program** (in the Premier Online Edition)

Chapter 18 Planning Guide

The Monarchs of Europe

Chapter Overview	Reproducible Resources	Technology Resources
CHAPTER 18 pp. 532–563 **Overview: In this chapter, students will learn about the power of European monarchs and the various challenges they faced.** KI 1, 2, 3, 4; PI 1.4, 2.5, 3.1, 4.1, 4.2, 4.4 See pp. T32–T55 for a detailed correlation to the New York State Core Curriculum for Global History and Geography and the New York Learning Standards.	**Differentiated Instruction Teacher Management System:*** • Pacing Guide • Lesson Plans for Differentiated Instruction **Interactive Reader and Study Guide:** Chapter Summary* **Chapter Resource File*** • Writing for the SAT • Social Studies Skill • Economics and History • Chapter Review	OSP **New York One-Stop Planner CD-ROM:** Calendar Planner **Live Ink© Online Reading Help** **Student Edition on Audio CD Program** **Differentiated Instruction Modified Worksheets and Tests CD-ROM** **World History Primary Source Library CD-ROM** **History's Impact: World History Video Program (VHS/DVD):** The Monarchs of Europe
Section 1: **The Power of Spain** **The Main Idea:** Spain experienced a golden age during the 1500s, but economic problems and military struggles decreased Spanish power by the 1600s. PI 4.1	**Differentiated Instruction Teacher Management System:** Section 1 Lesson Plan* **Interactive Reader and Study Guide:** Section 1 Summary* **Chapter Resource File*** • Vocabulary Builder: Section 1 • Biography: Diego Velázquez	**Regents Review Transparency:** Section 1* **Map Transparency:** Monarchs of Europe*
Section 2: **Absolute Monarchy and France** **The Main Idea:** Henry IV, Louis XIII, and Louis XIV strengthened the French monarchy, with Louis XIV setting the example of an absolute monarch for the rest of Europe. PI 4.4	**Differentiated Instruction Teacher Management System:** Section 2 Lesson Plan* **Interactive Reader and Study Guide:** Section 2 Summary* **Chapter Resource File*** • Vocabulary Builder: Section 2 • Biography: Louis de Rouvroy • Primary Source: The Edict of Nantes	**Regents Review Transparency:** Section 2* **Internet Activity:** Louis XIV
Section 3: **Monarchy in England** **The Main Idea:** In contrast to the absolute monarchies of Spain and France, the English monarchy was limited by Parliament; following a civil war, Parliament became even more powerful. PI 2.5, 4.2	**Differentiated Instruction Teacher Management System:** Section 3 Lesson Plan* **Interactive Reader and Study Guide:** Section 3 Summary* **Chapter Resource File*** • Vocabulary Builder: Section 3 • Biography: William and Mary • History and Geography: A King at War • Literature: *The Life of King Henry V*	**Regents Review Transparency:** Section 3*
Section 4: **Rulers of Russia and Central Europe** **The Main Idea:** The czars of Russia struggled with the westernization of their empire, while powerful families battled for control of Central Europe. PI 1.4, 3.1, 4.4	**Differentiated Instruction Teacher Management System:** Section 4 Lesson Plan* **Interactive Reader and Study Guide:** Section 4 Summary* **Chapter Resource File*** • Vocabulary Builder: Section 4 • Biography: Maria Theresa	**Regents Review Transparency:** Section 4* **Map Transparency:** The Expansion of Russia* **Map Transparency:** Central Europe, 1763* **Internet Activity:** Peter the Great and Catherine the Great

HOLT
History's Impact
World History Video Program (VHS/DVD)
The Monarchs of Europe

Review, Assessment, Intervention

 Global History and Geography Regents Test Prep Workbook

 Quick Facts Transparency: The Monarchs of Europe

 Progress Assessment Support System (PASS): Chapter Test*

Differentiated Instruction Modified Worksheets and Tests CD-ROM: Modified Chapter Test

OSP New York One-Stop Planner CD-ROM: ExamView Test Generator (English/Spanish)

HOAP Holt Online Assessment Program (HOAP), in the Premier Online Student Edition

---

 PASS: Section 1 Quiz*

 Online Quiz: Section 1

 Alternative Assessment Handbook

 PASS: Section 2 Quiz*

 Online Quiz: Section 2

 Alternative Assessment Handbook

PASS: Section 3 Quiz*

Online Quiz: Section 3

Alternative Assessment Handbook

 PASS: Section 4 Quiz*

 Online Quiz: Section 4

 Alternative Assessment Handbook

Power Presentation with Video CD-ROM

Power Presentations with Video are visual presentations of each chapter's main ideas. Presentations can be customized by including Quick Facts charts, images and maps from the textbook, and video clips.

Holt Online Learning

go.hrw.com
Teacher Resources
KEYWORD: SHL TEACHER

go.hrw.com
Student Resources
KEYWORD: SHL MON

- Document-Based Questions
- Interactive Multimedia Activities

- Current Events
- Chapter-Based Internet Activities
- and more!

Holt Premier
Online Student Edition
Complete online support for interactivity, assessment, and reporting
- Interactive Maps and Notebook
- Homework Practice and Research Activities Online

CHAPTER 18 PLANNING GUIDE

Before You Teach

The Big Picture

Peter N. Stearns

Politics and Diplomacy Three features predominate in the early modern period. First, major shifts occurred in the balance of power among nations. Second, important innovations occurred in the institutions of monarchy. In the 17th century, however, monarchical strength increased, notably in the rise of absolute monarchs. Absolutism also influenced Prussia and Russia, and to a degree the Hapsburgs. After Tudor gains, the English monarchy encountered new opposition. Through the English civil wars and the Glorious Revolution, a quite different parliamentary monarchy model emerged. Finally, European states gained new powers that outlasted the era of absolutism. Bureaucracies grew and became more specialized, and governments more actively intervened in the economy.

The Spanish Era Fueled by the Hapsburg dynastic link and the resources from the Americas, Spain served as Europe's major power during the 16th century. But naval defeat at British hands, economic lag, and overextension in other parts of Europe reduced Spain's power.

French Absolutism After the weaknesses of the later 16th century, the French monarchy rebounded and developed the clearest model of absolutism, with claims of untrammeled royal authority and divine right. Centralization increased, though in fact there were many limitations from the aristocracy and provincial institutions. Louis XIV's reign featured cultural and ritual splendor that reduced aristocratic interference. Mercantilist policies justified state economic intervention, new taxes, and colonialism.

Russia and Central Europe Absolutist policies and pomp spread to the Hapsburg monarchy and successful expansion against the Ottoman Empire was a distinctive theme. Prussian power increased, again with some territorial expansion as the result of careful wars and diplomacy. The Russian state shook off Tartar overlords and began a systematic policy of territorial expansion, making it a major player in central and east Asia as well as in Europe. Under Peter the Great, a very selective pattern of westernization emerged, designed to create a new elite culture, enhance the power of the czar, and create a more powerful and effective military.

Recent Scholarship

Absolutism in Central Europe (2000) provides a well-informed definition of absolutism in practice and its operation in central Europe. Author Peter H. Wilson reviews the major aspects of the historiography, in a subject that has gone through several interpretations. The focus on central Europe allows comparisons of different forms and attention to a region that can be somewhat slighted in general coverage, in favor of the showier developments in France. The book also allows discussion of the consequences of absolutism in the later political experience of the region, a subject on which the author is well versed.

Differentiating Instruction

Differentiated Instruction Teacher Management System
- Pacing Guide
- Lesson Plans for Differentiated Instruction

Interactive Reader and Study Guide

Spanish Chapter Summaries Audio CD Program

Student Edition on Audio CD Program

 Differentiated Instruction Modified Worksheets and Tests CD-ROM
- Vocabulary Flash Cards
- Modified Vocabulary Builder Activities
- Modified Chapter Review Activity
- Modified Chapter Test

OSP One-Stop Planner CD-ROM
- ExamView Test Generator (English/Spanish)
- PuzzlePro
- Quiz Show for ExamView
- Transparencies and Videos

TE Differentiated Activities in the Teacher's Edition
- Monarch Family Trees, p. 534
- Designing a Royal Compound, p. 543
- The English Civil War: Board Game, p. 548
- Imperial St. Petersburg Charts, p. 559
- Absolute Power Debate, p. 561

Reading Like a Historian
Sam Wineburg

Tyndale's Translation Biblical translation is a contact sport and sometimes—as William Tyndale learned the hard way—the results can be fatal.

Inspired by Erasmus, whose ideas he encountered at Cambridge at the beginning of the 16th century, Tyndale believed that the way to God was through study of His word. A master of Greek and Hebrew, Tyndale was determined to produce a Biblical translation so accessible that even "a boy that driveth the plough" could understand it.

Tyndale's freethinking ways ran afoul of Henry VIII, and he took flight to Germany and then to Holland, where he was betrayed by an English spy. As he awaited death at the stake for heresy on October 6, 1536, he is reputed to have uttered the words, "Lord, open the King of England's eyes."

King Henry's eyes remained shut. A new translation would have to wait until 1604, when King James I, in an attempt to make peace between warring factions of Anglicans and Puritans, convened translators representing a wide swath of religious views and interests. Their charge was to produce a translation all sides of this religiously divided kingdom could approve.

At the end of the day, however, the resulting "King James Version" looked surprisingly like the text produced by that heretic William Tyndale. About 83 percent of the King James Bible was identical to Tyndale's, including such unforgettable phases as "Let there be light" (Genesis 1:3) and "In the beginning God created the Word" (John 1:1). Acknowledging this contribution, Biblical scholars today refer to the King James Bible as the "Tyndale-King James Version."

Comparing Translations There have been too many translations of the Bible to count, starting as early as the 7th century when the poet Caedmon rendered Biblical stories into Old English verse.

One of the most widely used modern translations is the much-heralded 1952 Revised Standard Version (RSV) of the National Council of Churches, produced by America's most eminent Biblical scholars. Yet the RSV's reception, at least in its early days, showed that Biblical controversies die a hard death—an impression impossible to miss by scanning the titles of various reviews: "The Devil's Masterpiece," "Modernism's Unholy Bible," "A Sad Travesty," and—reflecting 1950s Cold War passions—"The New Communist Bible."

To almost all of these commentators, the touchstone remained the King James Version. Writing in *The New Yorker*, critic Dwight Macdonald noted that, "Literature,... and especially religious literature is not primarily concerned with being clear and reasonable; it is connotative rather than direct, suggestive rather than explicit.... To make the Bible readable in the modern sense means to flatten out, tone down and convert into tepid expository prose what in the King James Version is wild, full of awe, and passionate."

Four hundred years after its first appearance, the King James Bible is the metric for any attempt to render this Bible into English. Its hold is due, in part, to Tyndale's unique touch, seen unmistakably in his rendering of Psalm 23, which begins, "The Lord is my Shepard, I shall not want." Compare the elegance of Tyndale-King James to the Living Bible's clunky "Because the Lord is my Shepard, I have everything I need" or the New International Version's strained "The Lord is my Shepard, I shall not be in want."

The King James Bible is the most widely read book in the English language. Without it, King James, and his otherwise uneventful reign, would have been long forgotten.

Chapter Main Ideas

Section 1 Spain experienced a golden age during the 1500s, but economic problems and military struggles decreased Spanish power by the 1600s.

Section 2 Henry IV, Louis XIII, and Louis XIV strengthened the French monarchy, with Louis XIV setting the example of an absolute monarch for the rest of Europe.

Section 3 In contrast to the absolute monarchies of Spain and France, the English monarchy was limited by Parliament; following a civil war, Parliament became even more powerful.

Section 4 The czars of Russia struggled with the westernization of their empire, while powerful families battled for control of Central Europe.

🗽 New York Standards

Key Idea 1 The study of world history requires an understanding of world cultures and civilizations, including an analysis of important ideas, social and cultural values, beliefs, and traditions. This study also examines the human condition and the connections and interactions of people across time and space and the ways different people view the same event or issue from a variety of perspectives.

Key Idea 4 The skills of historical analysis include the ability to investigate differing and competing interpretations of the theories of history, hypothesize about why interpretations change over time, explain the importance of historical evidence, and understand the concepts of change and continuity over time.

Key to Differentiating Instruction

Below Level

Basic-level activities designed for all students encountering new material

At Level

Intermediate-level activities designed for average students

Above Level

Challenging activities designed for honors and gifted and talented students

Standard English Mastery

Activities designed to improve standard English usage

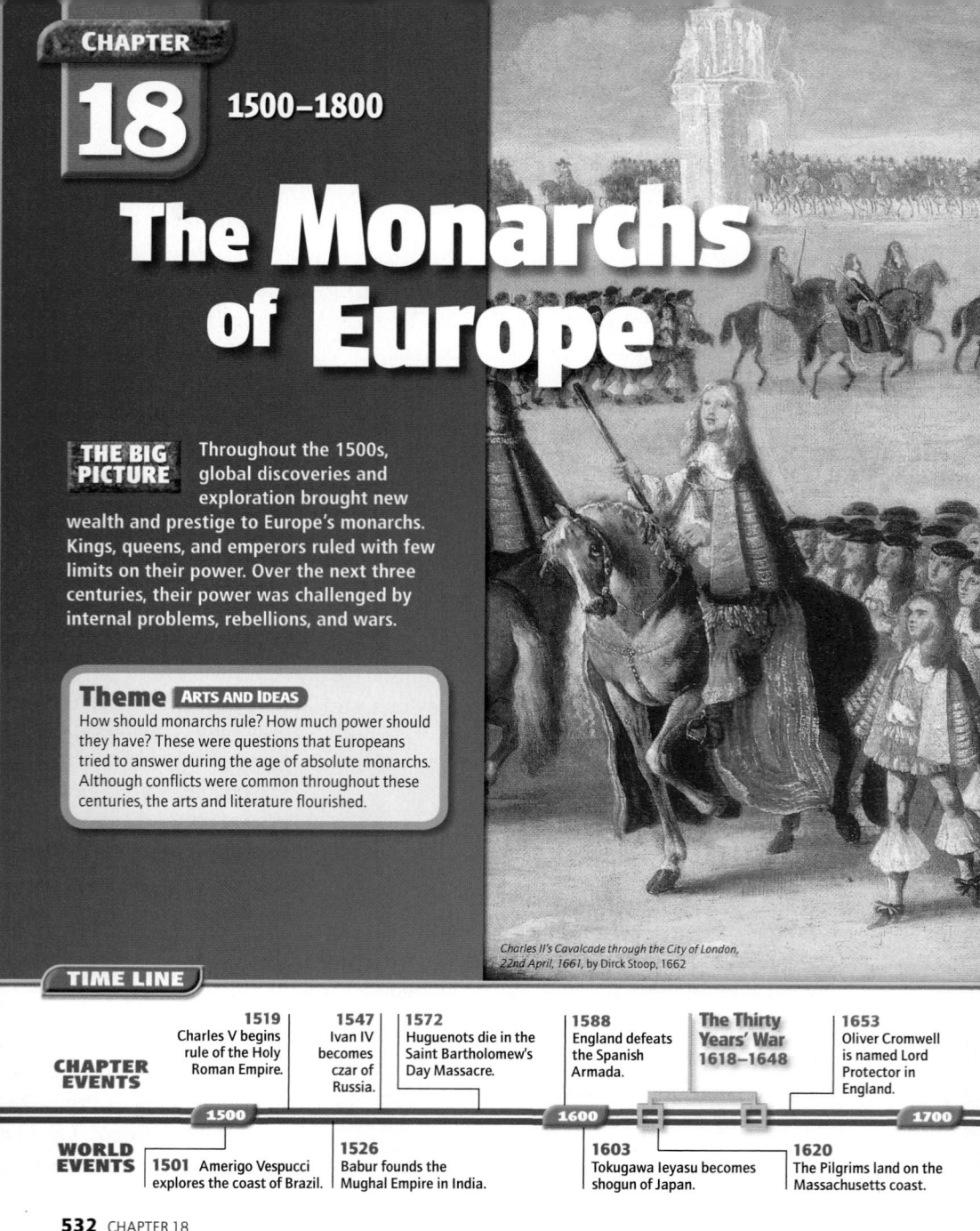

CHAPTER

18 1500–1800

The Monarchs of Europe

THE BIG PICTURE Throughout the 1500s, global discoveries and exploration brought new wealth and prestige to Europe's monarchs. Kings, queens, and emperors ruled with few limits on their power. Over the next three centuries, their power was challenged by internal problems, rebellions, and wars.

Theme ARTS AND IDEAS
How should monarchs rule? How much power should they have? These were questions that Europeans tried to answer during the age of absolute monarchs. Although conflicts were common throughout these centuries, the arts and literature flourished.

Charles II's Cavalcade through the City of London, 22nd April, 1661, by Dirck Stoop, 1662

TIME LINE

CHAPTER EVENTS

1519	1547	1572	1588	The Thirty Years' War 1618–1648	1653
Charles V begins rule of the Holy Roman Empire.	Ivan IV becomes czar of Russia.	Huguenots die in the Saint Bartholomew's Day Massacre.	England defeats the Spanish Armada.		Oliver Cromwell is named Lord Protector in England.

1500 **1600** **1700**

WORLD EVENTS

1501	1526	1603	1620
Amerigo Vespucci explores the coast of Brazil.	Babur founds the Mughal Empire in India.	Tokugawa Ieyasu becomes shogun of Japan.	The Pilgrims land on the Massachusetts coast.

532 CHAPTER 18

Introduce the Chapter

At Level

The Monarchs of Europe

1. Tell students that during the period covered by this chapter, the map of Europe continued to change as strong monarchs consolidated their control over their kingdoms and extended their territories through marriage or through conquest. At the same time, the spread of Protestantism created new conflicts, both within and between nations.

2. Organize students into small groups. Have each group prepare a list of the advantages and disadvantages of having a strong

monarch in the historical context of the time. Have volunteers from each group share their lists with the class.

3. Guide the class in a discussion of the ideas presented. Did the advantages of having a strong monarch outweigh the disadvantages? Why or why not? In what ways could strong monarchs abuse their power? How could such abuses be remedied? **LS** Interpersonal, Verbal-Linguistic

Alternative Assessment Handbook, Rubric 11: Discussions

Reading like a Historian

Throughout the centuries from 1500 to 1800, monarchs liked to display their grandeur. In this painting, Charles II of England parades through London the day before he is crowned.

Analyzing Visuals What do you think historians can learn from this painting?

See **Skills Handbook**, p. H26

Time Line

1714
The War of the Spanish Succession ends.

1762
Catherine the Great becomes czarina of Russia.

1800

1707
The Mughal Empire of India begins to disintegrate.

1776
The British colonies of North America declare their independence.

THE MONARCHS OF EUROPE **533**

• **Chapter Preview** •

HOLT

History's Impact

► **Video Program:
The Monarchs of Europe**
See the Video Teacher's Guide for strategies for using the video segment.

Reading Like a Historian

Analyzing Visuals When Charles II returned to England to become king, he did so in grand style. His cavalcade, or large procession consisted of many men and horses. They passed through many arches along their route.

go.hrw.com
Online Resources

Chapter Resources:
KEYWORD: SHL MON
Teacher Resources:
KEYWORD: SHL TEACHER

Explore the Time Line

1. When did Ivan IV become czar of Russia? *1547*

2. When did the Thirty Years' War take place? *1618–1648*

3. Who was Oliver Cromwell? *Lord Protector in England*

4. How long after the defeat of the Spanish Armada did the Pilgrims land on the Massachusetts coast? *about 32 years*

Info to Know

An Exiled King Charles II lived in exile for about a decade after his father, Charles I, was executed. Then, in 1660 Charles II was named King of England. The years that followed are known as the Restoration because monarchy was restored in England.

Make Inferences How do you think the people in the painting above felt about Charles's return? Why? *possible answer—happy; believed the restored monarchy would mean a return to stability*

Answers

Reading Like a Historian *possible answers—the conditions under which Charles II returned to England as king; information about regal ceremonies, clothing, and weapons*

533

Geography Starting Points

Primary Source

"It appears from all this that the person of the king is sacred, and that to attack him in any way is sacrilege. . . . Kings should be guarded as holy things, and whosoever neglects to protect them is worthy of death. . . ."

—Jacques Benigne Bossuet, on the divine right of kings

Teaching Tip

Remind students that the Protestant Reformation began in 1517 when Martin Luther publicized his complaints against the Roman Catholic Church. Have students predict how the Protestant Reformation might have affected the monarchs shown on the map.

📖 **Map Transparency:** Monarchs of Europe
📄 **World History Outline Maps**
✴ **Interactive Map:** Monarchs of Europe

GEOGRAPHY Starting Points

✴ **Interactive**
MONARCHS OF EUROPE

Henry VIII (1491–1547) wanted to make England independent of the pope and increase his personal power.

Catherine the Great (1729–1796) wanted to expand Russia's territory and make Russia more European.

Louis XIV (1638–1715) wanted fame for himself and glory for France.

Maria Theresa (1717–1780) wanted to strengthen Austria and reclaim lost territory.

Philip II (1527–1598) wanted to spread the Roman Catholic faith and conquer England.

0   200   400 Miles
0   200   400 Kilometers
Azimuthal equal-area projection

ATLANTIC OCEAN, NORWAY, RUSSIA, SCOTLAND, North Sea, DENMARK, IRELAND, PRUSSIA, ENGLAND, NETHERLANDS, POLAND AND LITHUANIA, SMALL GERMAN STATES, AUSTRIA, FRANCE, SWITZERLAND, SPAIN, SMALL FRENCH AND ITALIAN STATES, Mediterranean Sea, Baltic Sea

☐ Spain and its possessions

Starting Points European monarchs, some of whom are pictured above, began to increase their power in about 1500. The kings, queens, emperors, and empresses had conflicting goals, though. As a result, wars were common. This map of Europe in 1650 gives clues to some of the issues these monarchs faced.

1. **Analyze** How might the location of Spain's possessions have been both an advantage and a disadvantage for Spain?

2. **Predict** Based on the map and the monarchs' goals described in the captions, what conflicts do you think developed? Where do you think wars broke out?

🔊 **Listen to History**

Go online to listen to an explanation of the starting points for this chapter.

go.hrw.com
Keyword: SHL MON

534 CHAPTER 18

Differentiating Instruction

Above Level

Advanced Learners/Gifted and Talented

Research Required

1. Explain to students that many of the monarchs of Europe were related to one another by blood or marriage. Tell them that marriages between royal families were often used to strengthen alliances or prevent wars.

2. Have students conduct independent research to find out which of the monarchs shown on this page had family relationships, whether by blood or marriage. Remind students that these monarchs ruled at different times, so some of them will be generations apart.

3. Have students draw a simple family tree to illustrate one of the family connections they discovered. Have students write an essay analyzing the relationship they chose. Have students predict the effect the monarchs' connection might have upon their nations.
🔤 **Visual-Spatial, Verbal-Linguistic**

📄 **Alternative Assessment Handbook**, Rubrics 30: Research; and 37: Writing Assignments

Answers

Geography Starting Point

1. *possible answer—advantage: gave Spain a foothold in Central Europe; disadvantage: hard to govern and protect the small, separate territories;*
2. *possible conflicts and wars—Roman Catholic monarchs might struggle against Protestant monarchs; Spain might try to conquer England; Austria and Russia might try to expand; France might try to claim territory to add to its glory*

SECTION 1
The Power of Spain

BEFORE YOU READ

MAIN IDEA

Spain experienced a golden age during the 1500s, but economic problems and military struggles decreased Spanish power by the 1600s.

READING FOCUS

1. What challenges did King Charles I face when he became Emperor Charles V?
2. What were some artistic achievements of Spain's golden age?
3. How did Spain rise and then decline under Philip II?

KEY TERMS AND PEOPLE

absolute monarch
divine right
Charles V
Peace of Augsburg
Philip II
El Greco
Diego Velázquez
Miguel de Cervantes
Sister Juana Ines de la Cruz
Spanish Armada

NEW YORK

PI 4.1 Students identify historical problems, pose analytical questions or hypotheses, raise new questions or issues for further investigation.

Fasti Farnesiani, by Taddeo Zuccari, c. 1560s

The KING of SPAIN SPEAKS NO SPANISH

THE INSIDE STORY *Why did the king of Spain speak no Spanish?* In 1516, a thin and sickly 16-year-old boy named Charles became king of Spain. In some ways, Charles would not seem to be a likely candidate for the Spanish throne. After all, he was born in Belgium, raised by Austrian relatives, and grew up speaking French. When Charles became king, his ignorance of the Spanish language made him a foreigner in the eyes of the Spanish. Charles proved to everyone that he could learn quickly, though. He mastered Spanish along with other languages. In fact, Charles is said to have spoken "Spanish to God, Italian to women, French to men, and German to his horse." He needed all those languages, because Charles became not only king of Spain but also Holy Roman Emperor. In that role, he ruled an empire that stretched across much of Europe. ■

The King Becomes Emperor

In 1516 the teenaged Charles became King Charles I of Spain. Although he was inexperienced, Charles had at least one kingly trait. As a member of the ancient and powerful Hapsburg family, he was prepared to rule as an **absolute monarch**—a ruler whose power was not limited by having to consult with the nobles, common people, or their representatives. Moreover, absolute monarchs generally believed that they ruled by **divine right**. This concept held that the monarchs received their power from God and therefore must not be challenged. From about 1500 through the 1700s, absolute monarchs tried to impose their will across much of Europe and even to lands far beyond. In Spain, Charles struggled to keep the territories within his empire under control.

THE MONARCHS OF EUROPE **535**

Teach the Main Idea

At Level

The Power of Spain

1. **Teach** Ask students the Reading Focus questions to teach this section.

2. **Apply** Have students create charts comparing and contrasting the reign of Charles V with that of his son, Philip II.

3. **Review** Review student charts as a class. What similarities did they find between the reigns of the two monarchs? What differences were there? Guide students in a discussion of the two leaders' reigns. Which was a better ruler?

4. **Practice/Homework** Have students write an essay explaining why they think Charles V divided his empire between his brother and his son rather than passing it on intact.

LS Visual-Spatial, Verbal-Linguistic

Alternative Assessment Handbook, Rubrics 7: Charts; and 9: Comparing and Contrasting

---

Preteach

Getting Started

Use the **Interactive Reader and Study Guide** to familiarize students with the section content.

Interactive Reader and Study Guide, Section 1

Academic Vocabulary

Review with students the high-use academic term in this section.

region an area with one or more common features (p. 536)

CRF: Vocabulary Builder: Section 1

Taking Notes

Strengths—American possessions brought great wealth; strong military; Golden Age of Spanish art; Weaknesses—unrest and revolts; constant fighting; economic problems

1 What challenges did King Charles I face when he became Emperor Charles V? *ruling all the separate states, with enemies on all sides; the Protestant Reformation led to rebellions against Catholic rule*

The King Becomes Emperor

Explain Why did monarchs of this time believe their authority should never be questioned? *ruled by divine right, power came directly from God*

Evaluate Why do you think Charles V had more success in the Americas than in Europe? *possible answer—because there his explorers had superior weapons with which they could conquer huge empires; in Europe he was surrounded by enemies who had access to the same weapons*

Info to Know

The Peace of Augsburg The Peace of Augsburg was a temporary settlement that allowed each German prince to determine a state religion, either Catholicism or Lutheranism. Anyone who adhered to the other religion could move to a territory where that religion was recognized. Other Protestant sects, such as Calvinism, were not recognized by the agreement.

Answers

Achievements in Art and Literature *possible answer—provided money to pay for court painters*

Reading Check *successful—exploration of the Americas, which brought fabulous wealth to Spain; unsuccessful—did not maintain religious control over Europe; constant wars brought financial problems*

Achievements in Art and Literature

Spain's prominence in European affairs in the 1500s and 1600s is reflected in the important role it had in art and literature. *How might wealth from the Americas have affected Spain's artistic achievements?*

View of Toledo, by El Greco, c. 1597

◄ Plate made of gold acquired in the Americas ►

▲ Stormy skies over Toledo in an El Greco painting

TAKING NOTES

Take notes to record examples of Spain's strengths and weaknesses during the 1500s and 1600s.

Strengths
Weaknesses

ACADEMIC VOCABULARY

region an area with one or more common features

Charles V and the Empire When Charles became king of Spain, his territory also included the Low Countries of Belgium and the Netherlands, along with colonies in the Americas. He had inherited all these lands. Then in 1519 the throne of the Holy Roman Empire became vacant. The position was elective, so Charles borrowed money to buy the votes. He became Holy Roman Emperor as **Charles V**. As a result, his holdings expanded to parts of Italy, Austria, and various German states. The resulting empire was so vast that Charles liked to say the "sun never set" over it.

Ruling all the separate states was not an easy task. Charles faced enemies on all sides. Ottoman Turks, the French, and rebellious German princes all fought him.

At the same time, Charles was fighting for religious control over Europe. As Holy Roman Emperor, Charles wanted Europe to be Roman Catholic. His power was closely connected to the power of the Catholic Church, so the growing Protestant movement threatened his influence. In 1521 Charles confronted Protestant leader Martin Luther directly, declaring him an outlaw. In spite of Charles's efforts, Protestants gained influence, and rebellions against Catholic rulers spread.

After years of devastating wars between Catholics and Protestants, Charles V had to sign the **Peace of Augsburg**. The agreement, signed in 1555, gave each German prince the right to decide whether his state would be Catholic or Protestant. Thus, Charles's vision of a Catholic Europe never became reality. Moreover, constant warfare had brought him to the brink of bankruptcy.

Charles V achieved more success in the Americas than he did in Europe. During his reign, Spanish explorers claimed much of the Americas for Spain. Among the explorers he supported were Hernán Cortés, who conquered the Aztec Empire, and Francisco de Coronado, who explored the American Southwest region. Within 20 years of those early explorations, silver and gold began to flow from the American colonies—especially those in Bolivia, Peru, and Mexico—bringing Spain fabulous wealth.

Dividing the Empire Charles V gave up his thrones in 1556, frustrated by his failures in Europe. He decided to divide his large empire between his brother and his son. His brother took over the old Hapsburg holdings in Austria. His son, who became **Philip II**, ruled the Netherlands, Spain, Sicily, and Spain's colonies in the Americas. Charles V lived the rest of his life in a Spanish monastery, his dream of a unified empire unfulfilled.

READING CHECK **Draw Conclusions** In what ways was Charles V successful as an emperor? In what ways was he unsuccessful?

Skills Focus: Interpreting Historical Maps

At Level

Social Studies Skill
The Empire of Charles V

Research Required

Materials: outline maps of Europe and the Americas, colored markers

1. Organize students into small groups. Give each group a copy of each of the two outline maps and colored markers.

2. Have each group use descriptions and historical maps to create detailed maps of Charles V's empire. Write the following instructions for students to see: Use pink to show lands Charles V inherited. Use orange to show lands he acquired during his rule. Use green to show countries with which Charles V formed alliances through marriages. Use red to outline the Holy Roman Empire as it existed in his lifetime.

3. Review student maps as a class.
   LS **Interpersonal, Visual-Spatial**

Alternative Assessment Handbook, Rubrics 20: Map Creation; and 30: Research

◀ The painter can be seen before his easel in this scene of court life.

Las Meninas, or *The Maids in Waiting*, by Diego Velázquez, c. 1656

Sister Juana Ines de la Cruz with the small picture that was part of her nun's habit, or clothing

EL INGENIOSO
HIDALGO DON QVI-
XOTE DE LA MANCHA,
Compuesto por Miguel de Ceruantes
Saauedra.

DIRIGIDO AL DVQVE DE BEIAR,
Marques de Gibraleon, Conde de Benalcaçar, y Baña-
res, Vizconde de la Puebla de Alcozer, Señor de
las villas de Capilla, Curiel, y
Burguillos

Año, 1605.

CON PRIVILEGIO,
EN MADRID Por Iuan de la Cuesta.

Vendese en casa de Francisco de Robles, librero del Rey nro señor.

▲ The title page of the first edition of *Don Quixote*

Artistic Achievements

Just as Spain exerted political power, it also influenced European culture. From about 1550 to 1650 Spain had a golden age, known as the Golden Century, of artistic achievement.

Art One of the most prominent painters was a Greek, Domenicos Theotocopoulos, who became known as **El Greco**. Much of his work was religious and reflected Spain's central role in the Counter-Reformation. El Greco's style is famous for elongated human figures.

Another Spanish painter, **Diego Velázquez**, created masterpieces that portray people of all social classes with great dignity. Velazquez had the privilege of being the court painter.

Literature The Spanish golden age also produced fine writers, the greatest being **Miguel de Cervantes**. His most famous work, *Don Quixote de la Mancha*, is about a man who is caught between the medieval and modern worlds.

Writers in Spain's colonies also produced works of merit. A Mexican nun named **Sister Juana Ines de la Cruz** wrote poetry, prose, and plays. Church officials criticized Sister Juana for some of her ideas, for example, her belief that women had a right to education.

READING CHECK **Summarize** What were some achievements of Spain's Golden Century?

Spain under Philip II

Spain reached the peak of its grandeur during the reign of Philip II. One reason for this prosperity was the steady stream of gold and silver that flowed from its American colonies. With this immense wealth, Spain's power grew considerably. Eventually, though, American gold could not solve Spain's problems.

Religion and Revolt Like his father, King Philip II was a devout Catholic and saw himself as a leader of the Counter-Reformation. A chance to spread Catholicism came when Philip married Queen Mary I of England, who was also Catholic. She died, though, before she could give birth to an heir who could have returned England to the Catholic faith.

Philip also wanted to secure the position of Catholicism in his European territories. But his faith clashed with the Calvinist Protestantism that was spreading through the northern provinces of the Low Countries (the Netherlands, Belgium, and Luxembourg). A bloody revolt began in the 1560s when the Dutch refused to declare allegiance to Philip. To punish them, he sent an army under the command of the Duke of Alba. Alba set up a court, known locally as the Court of Blood, that tortured and executed thousands of people suspected of being rebels. Such cruelties only made the situation worse, and rebellion broke out anew.

THE MONARCHS OF EUROPE **537**

Skills Focus: Identifying Problem and Solution
At Level

Reading Skill
Spain's Troubles

1. Organize students into small groups. Tell groups they are advisers to Philip II of Spain. Have each group choose one of the following topics for discussion: the revolt in the Netherlands, the attempt to invade England with the Spanish Armada, or Spain's economic problems.

2. Have each group write a memorandum to Philip discussing the situation of their choice and examining the advantages and disadvantages of possible actions. Students should then make recommendations to Philip based on their analysis of the situation.

3. Have volunteers from each group read their memorandums to the class. **LS** **Interpersonal, Verbal-Linguistic**

📄 **Alternative Assessment Handbook**, Rubrics 35: Solving Problems; and 37: Writing Assignments

Answers

Reading Check *paintings by El Greco and Velázquez, writings by Miguel de Cervantes and Juana Ines de la Cruz*

537

Reading Focus

Spain under Philip II

Judge Why do you think the Spanish did not want the Netherlands to break away from the empire? *possible answer—They may have feared that other parts of the empire would follow the example of the Dutch and seek independence.*

Make Inferences What do you think Philip II could have done differently to prevent the decline of his empire? *possible answer—use some of the wealth from the American colonies for economic development in Spain*

● Review & Assess ●

Close

Guide students in a discussion of the successes and failures of Charles V and Philip II.

Review

Online Quiz, Section 1

Assess

SE Section 1 Assessment

Progress Assessment: Section 1 Quiz

Alternative Assessment Handbook

Reteach/Intervene

Interactive Reader and Study Guide, Section 1

Interactive Skills Tutor CD-ROM

Answers

Reading Check *revolt in the Netherlands; defeat of the Spanish Armada*

NEW YORK

CC Unit 4-F4
Case studies:
Philip II

The revolt dragged on for decades. Finally, in 1609, a truce was reached. The seven northern provinces formed the independent nation of the Netherlands, while the southern provinces remained in Spanish hands.

Spain and England Long before the Dutch revolt ended, it had deepened another rivalry. That conflict was between Spain and England. As fellow Protestants, the English had sent aid to the Dutch rebels. England's assistance to the Dutch infuriated Philip, but he was also worried about English attacks on his ships. England's Queen Elizabeth I was allowing her ship captains to attack Spanish treasure ships coming from America. These ship captains, known as the sea dogs, stole the gold and silver for England. Sir Francis Drake was one of the most infamous sea dogs. Drake even destroyed 30 ships in a Spanish harbor.

King Philip II wanted to stop England from raiding his ships and to return England to the Catholic Church, from which it had broken in 1534. He decided to invade England.

Philip ordered his navy to assemble a great fleet, the **Spanish Armada**. It totaled about 130 ships and 20,000 soldiers and sailors. The fleet, which was called invincible, or unbeatable, sailed into the English Channel in 1588. Queen Elizabeth I rallied her troops, and the English prepared for attack.

The Spanish had packed the ships with soldiers for a land invasion. They had also planned to be joined by Spanish forces in the Netherlands. Instead, they faced a series of fierce naval battles that severely damaged their fleet. Then, the English set eight ships on fire and aimed them at the remaining ships of the Armada. In panic and disarray, the Spanish ships fled before the English fireships. As the damaged ships made their way home the long way around, several were wrecked. King Philip's Armada was not invincible.

An Empire in Decline The defeat of the Armada was not the end for Spain, which recovered from the loss. But England remained Protestant, defiant, and undefeated.

Spain's real problems were internal. Philip's government was so centralized that he insisted on approving every decision himself. In addition, because Philip trusted no one, the court was riddled by factions and suspicion. As a result, government action practically came to a standstill. Moreover, Philip spent the wealth from the Americas on constant warfare. It was never enough, though—he borrowed money often and went bankrupt four times. The flood of American gold and silver also drove up prices, leading to inflation. Nor did Spain develop industries, relying instead on its traditional agricultural economy. Therefore, the economy lagged behind that of other countries. Spain gradually declined as a major power.

READING CHECK **Recall** What were two events that caused problems for Spain?

SECTION 1 ASSESSMENT

go.hrw.com
Online Quiz
Keyword: SHL MON HP

Reviewing Ideas, Terms, and People

1. **a. Define** Write a brief definition of the following terms: absolute monarch, divine right.
   b. Explain How did Charles I become Holy Roman Emperor Charles V?
   c. Analyze How did the size of his empire affect the rule of Charles V?
2. **a. Identify** Who were El Greco and Diego Velázquez?
   b. Infer Why might church officials have been particularly critical of some works by Sister Juana Ines de la Cruz?
3. **a. Recall** What region of Spain's European territories rebelled, starting in the 1560s?
   b. Explain Why did Philip II want to invade England?
   c. Evaluate A Spanish official in the Americas is said to have commented, "If Death had to come from Spain, I would live forever." What was the official implying?

Critical Thinking

4. **Identify Cause and Effect** Use your notes and a graphic organizer like the one below to describe the rise and decline of the Spanish empire, paying particular attention to the role that strengths and weaknesses played.

Rise → Spanish Empire → Decline

FOCUS ON SPEAKING

5. **Narration** Imagine that you are a Spanish or English sailor who survived the Spanish Armada's attempted invasion of England. Prepare and deliver the tale you tell other sailors when you return home.

538 CHAPTER 18

Section 1 Assessment Answers

1. **a.** absolute monarch: ruler whose power was not limited; divine right: idea that monarchs received their power from God
   b. He bought the necessary votes.
   c. faced enemies on all sides; could not maintain religious control

2. **a.** painters during Spain's Golden Century
   b. Some of her beliefs were controversial, including women's right to education.

3. **a.** the Low Countries (the Netherlands, Belgium, and Luxembourg)

   b. to stop England from raiding his ships; to return England to Catholicism
   c. possible answer—that the transport of people and goods from Spain to the New World was very slow

4. Rise: Colonies in America sent a steady stream of gold and silver to Spain; Decline: caused by a series of wars, the defeat of the Spanish Armada, and economic problems

5. Student tales should show an understanding of the Spanish Armada's attempted invasion of England.

The Wreck of the Spanish Armada

A series of battles in the English Channel had weakened the Armada. Then, when the English launched fireships at the enemy, some of the Spanish sailors cut their anchor lines so they could escape. It was a fateful decision, because the Spanish ships were then at the mercy of storms in the North Atlantic, and many ships were wrecked. This illustration combines several events into one scene.

ROUTE OF THE ARMADA

Storms were perhaps the Spaniards' worst foes. Many ships wrecked off the coasts of Ireland and Scotland.

SCOTLAND
North Sea
IRELAND
SPANISH NETHERLANDS
ENGLAND
London
Dover ● ● Graveline
ATLANTIC OCEAN
Calais
FRANCE
La Coruña ● ● Santander
PORTUGAL SPAIN
Lisbon ●

— Route of the Spanish Armada
✦ Storms
✦ Battles
▢ Controlled by Philip II

Rebels closed the Dutch harbor where Spanish ships were waiting to launch a second force against England.

The Spanish sailors were already suffering from overcrowding, hunger, and disease by the time they encountered the English.

The English set fire to ships rigged so that their cannons would fire automatically.

Skills FOCUS INTERPRETING VISUALS

Analyze What tactics did the English use against the Armada? How did those tactics, combined with poor weather, defeat the Armada?

go.hrw.com
COULD YOU HAVE SURVIVED?
Go online for a closer look at survival and this event.
Keyword: SHL MON

THE MONARCHS OF EUROPE **539**

History Close-Up

The Wreck of the Spanish Armada

"I have the heart and stomach of a king, and of a king of England, too; and think foul scorn that Parma or Spain or any prince of Europe should dare to invade the borders of my realm; to which rather than any dishonour should grow by me, I myself will take up arms, I myself will be your general, judge, and rewarder of every one of your virtues in the field."

—Speech by Queen Elizabeth I, 1588

Activity **Analyzing Primary Sources** Write the Queen Elizabeth quote above for all to see. Tell students that the queen gave this speech to the English army as it prepared for the Spanish invasion. Have a strong reader read the quote aloud. Then ask students the following questions: Why does Elizabeth call herself a king of England? How might this speech have motivated the army? **LS** Verbal-Linguistic

About the Illustration

This illustration is an artist's conception based on available sources. Historians, however, are uncertain exactly what this scene looked like.

Skills Focus: Identifying Cause and Effect

At Level

Reading Skill
What Caused the Armada's Defeat?

1. Draw the graphic organizer for all to see. Omit the italicized answers.

2. Have students copy and complete the graphic organizer. Guide a class discussion about what caused the wreck of the Spanish Armada.
LS Visual-Spatial

✎ **Alternative Assessment Handbook**, Rubrics 6: Cause and Effect; and 13: Graphic Organizers

Causes	Effects
1. *overcrowding, hunger, and disease on Spanish ships*	*Wreck of the Spanish Armada*
2. *storms*	
3. *English set fires on ships.*	
4. *Rebels closed Dutch harbor.*	

Answers

Interpreting Visuals *The storms wrecked many of Spain's ships, helping England, which was a Protestant nation; the Spanish were trying to escape by heading into the North Sea.*

Absolute Monarchy and France

BEFORE YOU READ

MAIN IDEA
Henry IV, Louis XIII, and Louis XIV strengthened the French monarchy, with Louis XIV setting the example of an absolute monarch for the rest of Europe.

READING FOCUS
1. How did Henry IV end France's wars of religion?
2. How did Louis XIII and Cardinal Richelieu strengthen the French monarchy?
3. What were the main events in the monarchy of Louis XIV?

KEY TERMS AND PEOPLE
Huguenot
Saint Bartholomew's Day Massacre
Henry IV
Edict of Nantes
Louis XIII
Cardinal Richelieu
Louis XIV
War of the Spanish Succession
Treaty of Utrecht

NEW YORK

PI 4.4 Students analyze different interpretations of important events, issues, or developments in world history by studying the social, political, and economic context in which they were developed.

THE INSIDE STORY

Why did the streets of Paris run with blood? It was August 24, 1572, the Catholic feast day of Saint Bartholomew. Many Protestant nobles were in Paris for the wedding of Henry of Navarre, a Protestant nobleman, to Marguerite de Valois, a Catholic princess. The marriage was supposed to calm the hostilities between Catholics and Protestants that had been tearing France apart. But just two days before, Catherine de' Medici, the queen of France and the bride's mother, had ordered the murder of a prominent Protestant leader. The attempt failed, but then Catherine had another idea. While so many Protestants were in the city, she ordered their massacre. Just before dawn on August 24, the killing began, with a bloodbath as the result. ◼

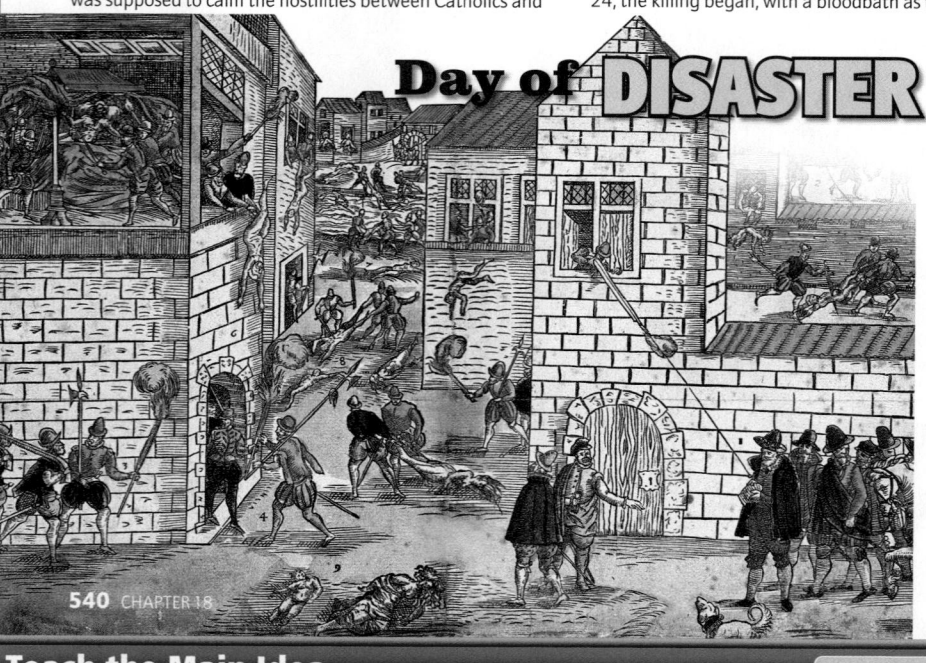

Day of DISASTER

◀ **In Paris alone, some 3,000 Protestants were killed in the Saint Bartholomew's Day Massacre.**

St. Bartholomew's Day Massacre in Paris, artist unknown, c. 1572

540 CHAPTER 18

Religious War and Henry IV

Soon after the Protestant Reformation began in Germany, it spread to France. By the 1560s, about one in ten French men and women was a **Huguenot** (HYOO-guh-NAHT), or French Calvinist Protestant. Many noble families were Huguenots. Such a large number of Protestants, especially among the nobles, threatened the Catholic French monarchy. The monarchy adhered to the idea that all loyal citizens of France should share *un roi, une loi, une foi*—"one king, one law, one religion." The religious conflict was a challenge to absolute monarchy.

Conflict and a New King Just as wars between Catholics and Protestants shook Germany, in France fighting broke out between Catholics and Huguenots in 1562 and raged for years. Hostilities took a particularly horrible turn in 1572, when the Catholic queen of France ordered the killing of Huguenots in Paris. Her assassins started with the Huguenot nobles who were in the city for the wedding of Henry of Navarre, a French nobleman. The event became known as the **Saint Bartholomew's Day Massacre**. From Paris, the violence spread to other parts of France. Estimates of the final death toll range from 10,000 to 70,000.

Henry of Navarre escaped death by denying his religion. Years later, he was in line to become king, but as a Huguenot in a heavily Catholic country, he had to fight Catholic troops to claim the throne. Finally, in 1593 Henry won acceptance by converting to Catholicism and was crowned **Henry IV**. According to some accounts, he explained his conversion by saying, "Paris is well worth a mass."

Compromise and Progress Henry knew that a compromise was needed to restore peace. In 1598 he granted some rights to Huguenots by issuing the **Edict of Nantes** (NAHNT). It gave Huguenots limited freedom of worship. Among other freedoms granted was the right of Huguenots to hold office and to rule 200 towns where they were already in the majority.

At the time, the Edict of Nantes was a remarkable document in that it represented a clear break with the conformity of the past. No longer were all the people forced to follow the monarch's religion. The concept of "one king, one law, one religion" was no longer in effect.

French Catholics accepted the edict because it ended the religious wars but still declared Catholicism the official religion of France. In addition, the edict required that Huguenots support the Catholic Church financially.

Following the edict's success, King Henry IV focused on repairing his war-torn country. A major achievement was improving France's financial situation. Henry eliminated France's debt and even built up a surplus. He also created new industries, drained swamps, built canals and roads, stimulated trade, and encouraged agriculture. Over time he became one of France's most respected monarchs.

TAKING NOTES Take notes on how Henry IV, Louis XIII, and Louis XIV increased the power of absolute monarchy in France.

Henry IV	
Louis XIII	
Louis XIV	

READING CHECK **Summarize** What were some high points and low points in the life of Henry IV?

Louis XIII and Richelieu

Henry had only about 10 years to enjoy being king of France. In 1610 a fanatic Catholic stabbed him while his carriage was stopped in traffic. The next king, **Louis XIII**, was very young when he was crowned. For several years he depended upon his mother to serve as regent, that is, to govern in his place.

Once Louis XIII was old enough to rule, a Catholic churchman named **Cardinal Richelieu** (REESH-uhl-oo) became his chief minister and most trusted adviser. Louis XIII was a relatively weak ruler, but Cardinal Richelieu was determined to strengthen the monarchy. Doing so required that its opponents be crushed.

FACES OF HISTORY

Cardinal RICHELIEU 1585–1642

Armand-Jean du Plessis, duc de Richelieu, was determined to strengthen the monarchy and France. He used ruthless methods to fulfill his goal. To weaken the nobility's military power, Cardinal Richelieu demanded that all fortified castles not necessary for the defense of France be torn down. The nobles protested, but their precious castles were demolished anyway. In addition, Richelieu attacked the nobles' political power by appointing only local officials who supported the king. For some positions, he even appointed middle-class common people who disliked the nobles. These officials knew they served at his pleasure and behaved accordingly.

Analyze Why would the demolition of the nobles' castles diminish their military power?

THE MONARCHS OF EUROPE **541**

Reading Focus

Louis XIII and Richelieu

Recall Why did Richelieu become involved in the Thirty Years' War? *He wanted to bring down the Hapsburg family.*

Identify Cause and Effect What was one effect of Richelieu's victory at La Rochelle? *It gave the message to the Huguenots not to resist the monarchy.*

Recent Scholarship

Cardinal Richelieu: And the Making of France is a detailed biography of Richelieu. Author Anthony Levi gives a detailed look at the ways Richelieu made France into a great power, perhaps the most powerful nation in continental Europe. Levi discusses Richelieu's accomplishments within France and examines his determination to unify the nation.

Cardinal Richelieu: And the Making of France by Anthony Levi. Constable and Robinson, 2001.

FOCUS ON NEW YORK
New Rochelle, New York, was named after the city of La Rochelle, France. It was founded in 1688 by Huguenot settlers fleeing religious persecution in France.

NEW YORK
CC Unit 4-F4
Case studies:
Louis XIV

Both Louis XIII and Richelieu wanted to reduce the recently won power of the Huguenots. To teach the Huguenots a lesson, in 1627 Richelieu used a situation at La Rochelle, a Huguenot port city. The people of La Rochelle had sided with English forces that had taken a nearby island. Richelieu's troops laid siege to the walled city, cutting off its supplies. After 14 months, the starving citizens surrendered. Richelieu ordered the city walls to be torn down and all the city's churches to become Catholic. His victory was a signal to all Huguenots that resistance to the monarchy carried risks.

Richelieu and the king also saw the nobles as a threat, so Richelieu turned to suppressing them. His spies uncovered a series of planned revolts by some nobles. Punishments were severe. For example, Richelieu had three prominent nobles publicly executed for treason.

As the king's chief minister, Richelieu also directed foreign policy. The Thirty Years' War, about which you will read more later, pitted Catholics against Protestants in Central Europe. Because he wanted to bring down the Hapsburg family, which led the Catholic side of the conflict, Richelieu involved France on the side of the Protestants.

READING CHECK **Identify** Who did Louis XIII and Cardinal Richelieu see as their enemies?

The Monarchy of Louis XIV

Richelieu died in 1642, and Louis XIII died one year later. In 1643 the son of Louis XIII was crowned **Louis XIV**. History's best example of an absolute monarch, Louis led France during a time of great power, prosperity, and glory. His reign had a lasting impact on France—both positive and negative.

Rise of the Sun King Like his father, Louis XIV became king, with his mother as regent, at a very young age. A churchman named Cardinal Mazarin, who became chief minister after Cardinal Richelieu, provided advice.

Louis was raised to be king. From childhood, he was taught all the skills that a king would eventually need—from interviewing foreign ambassadors and interpreting state papers to hunting and dancing.

The young king was quite different from his father. For example, he was supremely confident in his ability to rule. When Cardinal Mazarin died, Louis XIV, who was only 18 years old, declared that he would run the government himself. He declared, "L'état, c'est moi," meaning "I am the state." Louis chose the sun as his personal symbol, implying that the world revolved around him. He thus became known as the Sun King.

The Palace at Versailles
The royal family and some 10,000 officials, servants, and nobles lived at Versailles—making the place more a city than a palace.

The king pointing to plans for Versailles

Louis XIV, artist unknown, 1600s

View of Versailles, artist unknown, 1668

542 CHAPTER 18

Skills Focus: Identifying Main Idea and Details   At Level

Reading Skill
The Monarchy of Louis XIV

1. Have each student write a series of newspaper headlines that report the course of Louis XIV's policies and actions as king. Student headlines may either be supportive or critical, but each student should express a consistent point of view.

2. Have volunteers read their headlines to the class.

3. Guide students in a discussion of their headlines. What do the events of Louis XIV's reign reveal about his attitude toward power?
LS Verbal-Linguistic

Alternative Assessment Handbook, Rubric 23: Newspapers

Answers

Reading Check *Huguenots, nobles, the Hapsburg family*

HISTORY & Economics

Making Economic Decisions

Making economic decisions requires balancing benefits and costs. Often a decision has costs that one does not see at first. When you spend money on one thing, you cannot spend that money on something else. Those things that one cannot have as a result of an economic decision are called opportunity costs.

Economic Decisions in History Louis XIV faced opportunity costs when he decided to spend so much money on building the palace at Versailles. A major cost was in lost goodwill. The French people felt resentment when they saw their money going to build a huge, grand palace while they paid high taxes and sometimes went hungry. This resentment would help cause a revolution years later.

Economic Decisions and Your Life Your economic decisions have opportunity costs, too. Consider the decision of whether or not to buy the latest electronic gadget when it first comes on the market. Should you rush out to buy it, or should you wait for the price to come down? Either decision carries opportunity costs. Buying now means spending money that you could use for a long-term goal, such as building your college fund. Buying later means giving up the pleasure you might get from joining the newest fad.

Explain Why should you consider opportunity costs when making economic decisions?

BUILDING VERSAILLES	
COSTS	**BENEFITS**
• Cost five percent of the country's annual revenue • Created resentment among the people • Helped cause revolution years later	• Kept court safer from Paris crowds • Was clear symbol of king's power • Allowed the king to keep the nobles in check

▲ The decision to build Versailles had both costs and benefits.

Absolutism at Versailles For the rest of his long reign, Louis XIV retained absolute power. He began a tradition of absolute monarchy in France that would last for more than a century. Louis demanded that he be in charge of all military, political, and economic initiatives. The religion of his subjects was also to be under his direct control.

By drawing so much power to himself and the central government, Louis deprived the nobles of influence. They declined further in status when Louis built an enormous palace at Versailles (ver-SY), a few miles outside of Paris, and required that his nobles visit him there regularly. Nobles gained prestige by becoming servants in the king's Versailles court instead of by fighting or building local influence far from Paris. In addition, Louis urged the nobles to develop expensive new habits of dressing, dining, and gambling. As the nobles thus grew poorer, they had to depend on the king's generosity just to survive.

An immense complex of buildings and gardens, Versailles was a grand spectacle of kingly power. Louis XIV's style and ceremony emphasized his political strength. Practically every moment of the king's day required rituals performed by bowing courtiers. Eating, dressing, walking in the garden—all required a ritual. And Louis always knew who had given what he considered proper attention, as described in one courtier's memoir.

HISTORY'S VOICES

❝If anyone habitually living at Court absented himself he insisted on knowing the reason; those who came there only for flying visits had also to give a satisfactory explanation; any one who seldom or never appeared there was certain to incur his displeasure.❞

—Duc de Saint-Simon, *The Court of Louis XIV*, 1746

THE MONARCHS OF EUROPE **543**

Reading Focus

❸ What were the main events in the monarchy of Louis XIV? *building of Versailles, cancellation of Edict of Nantes, War of the Spanish Succession, Treaty of Utrecht*

The Monarchy of Louis XIV

Identify Who was Cardinal Mazarin? *the adviser who became chief minister after Cardinal Richelieu's death*

Analyze How did Louis XIV work at building his image? *created elaborate rituals to emphasize his power, built a grand palace at Versailles*

Evaluate Do you think that Louis XIV's extravagant lifestyle was worth the cost? Why or why not? *possible answer—Yes, it probably helped keep France politically stable by symbolizing his power.*

🗎 CRF: Biography: Louis de Rouvroy

Info to Know

The Boy King Louis XIV became king of France at the age of four. Although he was surrounded by the luxury of the French court, the first years of his reign were not easy. When he was just nine, Louis had to flee Paris when rebellions broke out between the French nobility and the monarch. From 1648 to 1652, Louis kept moving through France, suffering from hunger, cold, and fear. The memory of that hardship stayed with Louis forever. He never again trusted the people of Paris or the nobility.

The Arts in France Catherine de Medici introduced ballet into France in 1581, but under Louis XIV, ballet became a serious art form. He founded the first school for ballet in 1661. In 1681 female dancers first performed at the Paris Opera.

Answers

History & Economics *possible answer—While they are not immediately apparent, they help you make a more informed decision.*

Below Level

English-Language Learners

Materials: construction paper

1. Organize students into small groups. Tell students they have been chosen by the king to design a royal compound in the country with a royal palace, palaces to house members of the court, theaters, stables, and other buildings, as well as formal gardens, lawns, woods, and recreational spaces. Have each group draw up a plan and make illustrated displays of court life, including art, dance, dress, and social etiquette. Have students decide where the money should come from to build their royal compounds.

2. Display student designs for the class to see.

3. Guide students in a discussion of the finished designs. How do they think their royal compounds compare to Louis XIV's Versailles? **LS Interpersonal, Visual-Spatial**

🗎 **Alternative Assessment Handbook**, Rubrics 3: Artwork; and 14: Group Activity

543

Reading Focus

The Monarchy of Louis XIV

Recall What country benefited most from the War of Spanish Succession? *England*

Identify Cause and Effect What were the causes and effects of the War of the Spanish Succession? *caused when other European powers did not want to see Louis XIV's son become king of Spain; resulted in giving Louis's grandson the Spanish throne, but keeping France and Spain from being ruled by the same monarch, and making France give up territory. England ended up benefiting at the expense of France and Spain.*

● **Review & Assess** ●

Close

Guide students in a discussion of the reasons for the increasing power of the monarchy from Henry IV to Louis XIV.

Review

 Online Quiz, Section 2

Assess

SE **Section 2 Assessment**

📋 **Progress Assessment**: Section 2 Quiz

📋 **Alternative Assessment Handbook**

Reteach/Intervene

📋 **Interactive Reader and Study Guide**, Section 2

💿 **Interactive Skills Tutor CD-ROM**

Answers

Reading Skills *possible answer— Another problem of succession was Henry IV becoming King of France.*

Reading Check *building of Versailles, cancellation of Edict of Nantes, War of the Spanish Succession, Treaty of Utrecht*

Louis and Protestantism Another way that Louis established absolute monarchy was by smashing the power of the Huguenots once and for all. Since the reign of Henry IV, the Edict of Nantes had protected the Huguenots. For all Richelieu's efforts, even he had not been able to eliminate that protection.

In 1685 Louis made his move. He revoked, or canceled, the edict and outlawed Protestantism in his realm. Over 200,000 Huguenots fled France, including many prosperous merchants and artisans. The loss of their skills and wealth helped cause a financial crisis.

READING SKILLS

Connecting How does the War of the Spanish Succession connect to other problems related to succession about which you have already read?

Money and the Military Louis's finances were always a matter of concern because the grand lifestyle he demanded required a great deal of money. The treasury was saved primarily by the efficient policies of the minister of finance, Jean-Baptiste Colbert (kawl-BER). Colbert limited imports and increased exports. In addition, he simplified the tax system. Colbert even reduced the government's debt. Still, Louis always wanted more money.

Louis needed cash to fulfill his greatest ambition—to build up the military and expand French territory. He succeeded in this goal, certainly, by enlarging the army from some 70,000 men to more than 200,000 disciplined soldiers. Louis also spent money on good equipment for his new army. With this mighty force, Louis became the most powerful ruler in Europe, taking France into war four times.

War over a Throne Louis XIV wanted to increase his power beyond the borders of France. He went to war to reclaim territory that France had lost, but his wars cost France dearly. In fact, they cost so much that Louis had to melt down royal silver to pay for army supplies. The most costly of his wars was the **War of the Spanish Succession**. It began when the Spanish king died without an heir. Three rulers claimed that they should name the successor. Louis was one of the three, because he wanted the Spanish throne for his oldest son.

The other European monarchs did not want France and Spain to be so closely connected. Such an alliance could cause economic and political problems for several countries. Therefore, in 1701 England, the Netherlands, and the Holy Roman Empire went to war against France. Fighting was not limited to Europe. In North America, the conflict was connected to a phase of the French and Indian Wars.

After many defeats, in 1713 Louis accepted the **Treaty of Utrecht**. Although the treaty said that Louis's grandson got the Spanish throne, it also said that France and Spain would never be ruled by the same monarch. Louis also had to give up most of the territory he had taken. The war benefited England at the expense of France and Spain. Despite the setback, Louis XIV remained in power until his death in 1715—still an absolute monarch.

READING CHECK **Find the Main Idea** What were some main events during Louis XIV's reign?

SECTION 2 ASSESSMENT

go.hrw.com
Online Quiz
Keyword: SHL MON HP

Reviewing Ideas, Terms, and People

1. **a. Define** Write a brief definition of the following terms: Huguenot, Saint Bartholomew's Day Massacre, Edict of Nantes.
   b. Sequence List in order the major events in the conflict between French Huguenots and Catholics.
   c. Elaborate Attributed to **Henry IV** is the quotation, "Paris is well worth a mass." What does this statement mean?

2. **a. Identify** Who was **Cardinal Richelieu**, and why was he significant?
   b. Interpret What were the effects of the siege of La Rochelle?

3. **a. Identify** What was Versailles? Why was it important?
   b. Explain What did **Louis XIV** mean by "L'état, c'est moi"?
   c. Evaluate How could Louis XIV have improved his legacy?

Critical Thinking

4. **Sequence** Copy the graphic organizer below and use it to describe how the power of the French monarchy increased under Henry IV, Louis XIII, and Louis XIV.

   Henry IV → Louis XIII → Louis XIV

FOCUS ON WRITING ✎

5. **Description** Study the illustrations in this section. Then write a brief description of either the St. Bartholomew's Day Massacre or the palace that Louis XIV built at Versailles. Use details that will help your reader visualize the scene.

544 CHAPTER 18

Section 2 Assessment Answers

1. **a.** Huguenot: French Protestant; St. Bart's Day Massacre: killing of 10,000 to 70,000 Huguenots; Edict of Nantes: document giving certain rights to Huguenots
   b. St. Bartholomew's Day Massacre, Henry IV converted to Catholicism, Edict of Nantes, Thirty Years' War
   c. France was worth converting to Catholicism

2. **a.** chief minister, trusted adviser of Louis XIII
   b. all churches became Catholic; gave signal to Huguenots that resistance was unwise

3. **a.** Louis XIV's palace; symbol of king's power
   b. "I am the state"; could rule by himself
   c. possible answer—by placing less emphasis on appearance, and more on strategy

4. Henry IV: issued Edict of Nantes, made reforms; Louis XIII: took power from Huguenots, nobles; Louis XIV: absolute monarch, built Versailles

5. Student descriptions should include details about the illustration of a chosen event.

BEFORE YOU READ

MAIN IDEA

In contrast to the absolute monarchies of Spain and France, the English monarchy was limited by Parliament; following a civil war, Parliament became even more powerful.

READING FOCUS

1. How did the Tudors work with Parliament?

2. What led the first two Stuart kings to clash with Parliament?

3. What were the causes and results of the English Civil War?

4. What happened when monarchy returned to England?

KEY TERMS AND PEOPLE

Puritans
Charles I
Royalists
Oliver Cromwell
commonwealth
Restoration
Charles II
William and Mary
Glorious Revolution
constitutional monarchy

NEW YORK

PI 2.5 Students investigate key events and developments and major turning points in world history to identify the factors that brought about change and the long-term effects of these changes.

A BOLD QUEEN

Portrait of Elizabeth I, by unknown artist, 1500s

◄ Queen Elizabeth at the height of her glory, as shown by the richness of her clothing and jewels

THE INSIDE STORY

How did a queen get her way?
Queen Elizabeth I had a very strong personality—and it showed in her relationship with England's Parliament. Early in her reign, the members of Parliament asked Elizabeth I when she planned to marry. In response, she told them that she planned to die without a husband, and that it was none of Parliament's business anyway. She was not interested in sharing power with a king. Elizabeth's close relationship with Parliament was assisted by her fierce and obvious love for England. In her last speech to Parliament she said, "Though you have had, and may have, many princes more mighty and wise sitting in this seat, yet you never had, nor shall have, any that will be more careful and loving." Later monarchs would not be as close to Parliament, or so skillful in dealing with it. ■

The Tudors and Parliament

Two prominent members of the Tudor dynasty, Henry VIII and his daughter Elizabeth I, ruled during the time when absolutism was common on the European continent. In England, though, Parliament placed curbs on absolute monarchy. Both father and daughter had to learn how to work with Parliament to fulfill their goals for England.

THE MONARCHS OF EUROPE **545**

Getting Started

Use the **Interactive Reader and Study Guide** to familiarize students with the section content.

📖 **Interactive Reader and Study Guide,** Section 3

📄 **CRF:** Vocabulary Builder: Section 3

Taking Notes

Tudors worked with Parliament to get what they wanted; Parliament forced Charles I to sign the Petition of Right; English Civil War resulted in Parliament defeating and executing Charles I; Parliament restored monarchy but continued to develop its role; Parliament invited William and Mary to replace James II; Parliament passed the Bill of Rights, further limiting royal power.

Teach the Main Idea

At Level

Monarchy in England

1. **Teach** Ask students the Reading Focus questions to teach this section.

2. **Apply** Have students create a time line of the major events in this section. Student time lines should begin with the passage of the Act of Supremacy in 1534 and end with the passage of the English Bill of Rights in 1689.

3. **Review** Guide students in a discussion of the events on their time lines. What events could be considered milestones in England's road to democracy? What events were setbacks?

4. **Practice/Homework** Tell students that it is the time of the English Civil War. Have each student decide whether he or she would have been on the side of the Cavaliers or the Roundheads and write an essay explaining why. Have students take into consideration the leadership of Charles I and Oliver Cromwell and the issues at stake.

LS Visual-Spatial, Verbal-Linguistic

📄 **Alternative Assessment Handbook**, Rubrics 36: Time Lines; and 40: Writing to Describe

1 How did the Tudors work with Parliament? *Henry VIII teamed with Parliament to pass a series of laws to convert England to Protestantism and name him head of the Church of England. Elizabeth I needed the help of Parliament to re-establish herself as the head of the Church of England.*

The Tudors and Parliament

Summarize What measures did Henry VIII take to convert England to Protestantism? *teamed with Parliament to pass a series of laws, Act of Supremacy made the king head of the Church of England*

Predict What do you think would have happened if Elizabeth I had married? *possible answer—might have lost power because her husband would have wanted to play a part in governing England.*

CRF: Literature: *The Life of King Henry V*

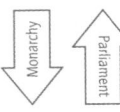

TAKING NOTES
As you read, take notes to record details about the decreasing power of the monarchy and increasing power of Parliament.

Monarchy ↓ Parliament ↑

Henry VIII created the Protestant Church of England so he could divorce his first wife. To effect the split with the Roman Catholic Church, Henry had Parliament pass laws ending the power of the pope in England. In 1534 the Act of Supremacy named the king as the head of the Church of England.

After Henry's death and the short reign of his son Edward, Henry's daughter Mary I became queen. Often called Bloody Mary, she briefly made England Catholic again. When Mary died in 1558, Elizabeth was crowned queen and returned England to the Anglican, or English Protestant, Church. Parliament helped her do so by passing laws that favored Protestantism.

Tension developed between Parliament and the queen when Parliament pressured her to marry so that she would have an heir to the throne. She refused, knowing that marriage to either an Englishman or a foreigner could limit her freedom. Still, she managed to talk Parliament into approving the funds she needed.

A major reason for Elizabeth's good relationship with Parliament was her willingness to let the members speak their minds without fear of punishment. Her close ties to Parliament show in the fact that she called it into session 10 times during her 45-year reign.

While Elizabeth was clearly in charge, she had some difficulty keeping her subjects from questioning her actions. For example, in 1601 one of her favorite courtiers, the Earl of Essex, rebelled against the queen's authority. He asked publicly, "Cannot princes err? Cannot subjects receive wrong? Is an earthly power or authority infinite?" Essex was tried and executed, but he was not the last to question the English monarch's authority.

READING CHECK Recall What did Henry VIII and Elizabeth I work with Parliament to do?

The Stuarts and Parliament

The Tudors' success with Parliament was not repeated by their successors. When Elizabeth I died in 1603, a relative of the Tudors from Scotland became king. James I was the first member of the Stuart dynasty to rule in England. His view of absolute monarchy caused conflict with Parliament.

James I Clashes with Parliament James faced problems from the start. He believed firmly in the divine right of kings and wanted to rule as an absolute monarch. But wars waged

---

Linking TO Today

The British Monarchy

Should the United Kingdom still have a king or queen? Ever since the conflict between king and Parliament in the 1600s, the monarch has had a restricted role in the government.

Critics of the monarchy sometimes claim that the royal family is an expensive luxury. Monarchy's defenders reply that Queen Elizabeth II's wealth—perhaps about $500 million—allows her to pay her own way. Her accountants agree. In 2006 a report from the office of Royal Public Finances stated that Queen Elizabeth II and her family cost each citizen of the United Kingdom only about $1.13 per year. In addition, the monarchy's supporters point out that the tourist industry, which is worth more

than $300 billion per year, would suffer if the romance of royalty were eliminated. Elizabeth II can also sometimes defuse a touchy situation with other heads of state, since she does not represent a particular political viewpoint.

Perhaps the best argument for the monarchy is its power as a symbol. It represents continuity—the ability of the kingdom's people to survive centuries of global turmoil and still live in relative peace with each other.

Draw Conclusions Should the monarchy continue? Why or why not?

Queen Elizabeth II greets crowds celebrating her eightieth birthday. ▶

Answers

Linking to Today *possible answers—Yes, it is a symbol of continuity, it encourages tourism; No, the royal family is expensive to maintain.*

Reading Check *to pass laws to help the monarch achieve desired results*

Collaborative Learning [At Level]

The Reign of Queen Elizabeth I

1. Organize students into two groups for a classroom debate on the reign of Queen Elizabeth I. Have one side support her policies and the other side argue against them. Have students consider the historical context in evaluating the policies. Why did Elizabeth refuse to marry, re-establish herself as the head of the Church of England, and allow English captains to attack Spanish ships coming from America laden with treasure? Give each side time to prepare arguments.

2. Conduct a classroom debate on Elizabeth's policies. Which side presented the most convincing arguments? **LS Interpersonal**

Alternative Assessment Handbook, Rubric 10: Debates

by his predecessors, combined with his own spending, left him low on funds. In addition, because he was from Scotland, he was considered an outsider. For all of these reasons, he had difficulty getting along with Parliament. Although James called Parliament repeatedly during his reign, he was rarely able to get Parliament to approve all the money he wanted.

As Parliament increased its influence, another group was starting to make itself known. The **Puritans**, a group of strict Calvinists, demanded that the Church of England be further reformed. They wanted to "purify" the English church of practices they thought were still too Catholic. For example, priests still dressed in elaborate robes, and worshippers knelt during services.

Another of the Puritans' goals was to take power away from church officials. James saw this stance as a threat to his power because the church leadership supported him. As a result, he refused to pass most of the Puritans' requests for reform. One reform James agreed to was the publication of an English version of the Bible that became known as the King James Bible.

Charles I Defies Parliament When James I died in 1625, his younger son was crowned king as **Charles I**. He was popular at first, but married a Catholic princess and involved England in military adventures overseas.

In 1628 Charles summoned Parliament to request money. Parliament refused to grant it until Charles signed a document, called the Petition of Right, that placed limits on the king's power. Among the document's provisions was a statement that the king could not levy taxes without Parliament's approval. Nor could he imprison anyone without legal justification, force citizens to house soldiers, or declare martial law in peacetime. The Petition of Right was a direct challenge to absolute monarchy.

When Parliament refused to give him money again later, Charles taxed the English people on his own and forced bankers to loan him money. The members of Parliament were furious. In response, Charles dismissed Parliament and in 1629 decided to rule without consulting Parliament ever again.

READING CHECK Find the Main Idea Why did the Stuarts have trouble with Parliament?

The English Civil War

Conflict continued between a king who believed in absolute monarchy and a Parliament that saw itself as independent of the king. The conflict became so severe that it led to war and even the king's death.

Parliament Reconvened In 1640 Charles I was badly in debt, thanks to a religious rebellion in Scotland. He finally had to reconvene Parliament so he could ask for more money.

This session became known as the Long Parliament because it did not disband for many years. After being ignored for 11 years, the members of Parliament were in no mood to bow to the king's wishes, and they took the opportunity to further limit the king's powers. They demanded that Parliament must be called at least every three years, and the king could no longer dismiss Parliament. Charles I accepted these new rules, but he awaited the right moment to overturn them.

War with Parliament That moment came when a radical Puritan group within Parliament moved to abolish the appointment of bishops in the Anglican Church. The king, whose power was connected to the power of the church, was outraged.

For this insult, Charles decided to arrest the Puritan leaders for treason. He led troops into the House of Commons to make the arrest, but the men had already escaped. Now Charles had given away his intentions to take back power. Some members of Parliament decided to rise up against the king. Charles I called for the support of the English people. Within months, in 1642, the English Civil War began.

Without funding from Parliament, the king had to rely on contributions to pay for an army. His supporters, mainly wealthy nobles, were called **Royalists** for their allegiance to his royal person. On the other side, Parliament could back its army by voting for funding. Supporters of Parliament were called Roundheads, from their short, bowl-shaped haircuts, which contrasted with the Royalists' long wigs. The Roundheads included Puritans, merchants, and some members of the upper classes.

Leading the Roundhead forces was a member of Parliament named **Oliver Cromwell**. He had risen to leadership as an army general.

READING SKILLS
Connecting
How does this information about the Puritans connect to what you already know about Puritans in America?

THE IMPACT TODAY

Today, England's monarch is allowed to enter the Houses of Parliament only once a year, to open a session of Parliament.

THE MONARCHS OF EUROPE **547**

• **Direct Teach** •

Reading Focus

❷ What led the first two Stuart kings to clash with Parliament? *went to Parliament to raise money, rarely able to get the money they wanted*

The Stuarts and Parliament

Recall What did Charles I do when Parliament refused to give him money after he signed the Petition of Right? *He taxed the English people and dismissed Parliament.*

Evaluate Do you think the English would have accepted James I as an absolute monarch if he had not been an "outsider"? Explain your answer. *possible answer—no; because they were used to having monarchs work with Parliament*

Reading Focus

❸ What were the causes and results of the English Civil War? *causes—Long Parliament limited Charles I's powers and refused to give him money; results—Charles I executed; monarchy and House of Lords abolished; England became a commonwealth*

The English Civil War

Recall Why did Charles I call Parliament into session in 1640? *He needed money following a religious rebellion in Scotland*

Summarize How did Oliver Cromwell's role in government change over time? *started as member of Parliament; became army general and commander-in-chief; seized power as Lord Protector*

📄 **CRF:** History and Geography: A King at War with Parliament

Skills Focus: Summarizing

Below Level

Reading Skill
The Role of Religion in English Politics

1. Have students work in mixed-ability pairs to make a chart summarizing the relations between religion and government during the reigns of Henry VIII, Mary, Elizabeth I, and James I.

2. Review student charts as a class, and make a class chart for all to see. Have students correct their own work as needed.

3. Guide students in a discussion of religious conflicts in England using the following questions: How did religious conflicts in

England compare with conflicts elsewhere in Europe? What factors might account for differences in England? How did the fact that the English monarch was also the head of the Church of England affect English religious conflicts? **LS Visual-Spatial**

📄 **Alternative Assessment Handbook**, Rubrics 7: Charts; and 11: Discussions

Answers

Reading Skills *Many Puritans left England and settled in America.*

Reading Check *Both wanted to rule as absolute monarchs.*

547

Reading Focus

The English Civil War

Sequence List, in order, the events leading to the establishment of the commonwealth. *Cromwell led Roundheads in battle against Royalists; king surrendered; Cromwell dismissed members of Parliament who disagreed with him; king tried and executed; monarchy and House of Lords outlawed*

Make Judgments Do you think that England was better off under the commonwealth or under the monarchy? Explain. *possible answer—under the monarchy: in the end Cromwell proved to be as much of a tyrant as the king he had deposed by passing many restrictive laws*

Info to Know

Charles I Charles I originally attempted to marry the daughter of the Spanish king in order to form an alliance between Spain and England. When he failed to negotiate the marriage, he married the French princess Henrietta Maria instead, forming an alliance with France against Spain. His marriage to Henrietta, a Catholic, angered his Protestant subjects.

Answers

Reading Like a Historian 1. *no; shows he is not an effective leader;* **2.** *They were expensive and harmful to England.*

548

A View of Oliver Cromwell

Interpreting Political Cartoons England faced problems both at home and abroad during the mid-1600s. Under Charles I, fighting had broken out in Ireland and Scotland. Oliver Cromwell inherited those tensions—and expenses. In addition, he had Parliament pass a law that damaged Dutch trade. A war with the Dutch was the result. Cromwell was also in conflict with the Royalists, of course.

Cromwell's foreign exploits made him very unpopular in the other countries. In England, though, Cromwell was popular enough that in 1657 Parliament offered him the crown, which he declined. As you study this Dutch cartoon about Cromwell titled "The Horrible Tail Man," consider:

- the identities of the characters in the cartoon
- what the various characters are doing
- where Cromwell's attention is focused
- the country where it was published

Cromwell is portrayed in a negative way. His face is ugly, and he has a long, fat tail filled with coins.

A Royalist, a Dutchman, an Irishman, and a Scot are cutting off sections of Cromwell's money-filled tail.

Skills Focus · READING LIKE A HISTORIAN

1. **Details** Is Cromwell aware of what is going on behind him? How does this affect the meaning?
2. **Message** What was the cartoonist saying about the impact of Cromwell's foreign involvements?

See **Skills Handbook**, p. H27

In 1644, at the first truly decisive battle of the war, he led a victory in which 4,000 of the king's soldiers died. Cromwell continued to rise in power until he became commander-in-chief of Parliament's army.

The Royalist army was outmatched by Cromwell's disciplined troops. In 1646 the king surrendered. Now in full control, Cromwell dismissed all members of Parliament who disagreed with him. Those who were left made up what was called the Rump Parliament.

Trial and Execution Eventually the Rump Parliament charged the king with treason and put him on trial. During his trial, Charles defended himself with great eloquence but refused to even recognize Parliament's authority to try him. "I do stand more for the liberty of my people than any here that come to be my pretended judges," he declared. In the end, the king was sentenced to death for treason. On January 30, 1649, Charles I was publicly beheaded in front of his own palace—the first European monarch to be formally tried and sentenced to death by a court of law. To some people he was a martyr, to others a tyrant who got what he deserved.

England under Cromwell For the next 11 years, England's government changed completely. The House of Commons abolished the House of Lords and outlawed the monarchy.

England became a **commonwealth**, which is a republican government based on the common good of all the people. In 1653 Cromwell was given the title Lord Protector of England,

---

Differentiating Instruction

Above Level

Advanced Learners/Gifted and Talented

Research Required

Materials: poster board; colored markers

1. Organize students into small groups. Have each group create a board game for the English Civil War. The playing board should be a map of Great Britain and Ireland with major cities and sites of major battles marked on it. Game pieces should represent the Royalist forces (Cavaliers) and Parliamentary forces (Roundheads), with special pieces representing King Charles I and Oliver Cromwell.

2. Have each group conduct research about the progress of the English Civil War to mark the major battle sites on the map and to write rules for playing the game. Game rules should allow either two people or two teams to play.

3. Have each group demonstrate its board game for the rest of the class. Guide students in a discussion about the English Civil War.

LS Visual-Spatial, Kinesthetic

Alternative Assessment Handbook, Rubrics 20: Map Creation; and 30: Research

Scotland, and Ireland. Although Cromwell was a skilled leader, he demanded complete obedience. He clamped down on English social life by closing the theaters and limiting other forms of popular entertainment.

Cromwell had to deal with foreign issues, too. He led military expeditions to Scotland and Ireland. His economic policies led to a war with the Dutch over trade. To limit Spanish activity in the Americas, he also warred on Spain.

A Defender of Absolutism Cromwell, the king's death, and the war troubled many of the English people. One of them was Thomas Hobbes, a Royalist who fled to France during Cromwell's rule. Hobbes wrote what is now a classic work of political science, *Leviathan*. In it, Hobbes described humans as being naturally selfish and fearful. Life in nature, he wrote, was "solitary, poor, nasty, brutish, and short." Hobbes argued that people needed an all-powerful monarch to tell them how to live. His views sparked controversy during a time when England was trying to find a balance between government by the people's representatives and the monarchy.

> **READING CHECK** Identify Cause and Effect
> What were some effects of the English Civil War?

The Monarchy Returns

Hobbes's ideas reflected the fact that many people were unhappy under Cromwell, especially when he dismissed Parliament to rule. Attitudes were changing so much that a return to monarchy became possible.

The Restoration When Cromwell died in 1658, his son took his place. Richard Cromwell lacked his father's leadership abilities, though, and his government collapsed. Eventually Parliament reconvened and voted to bring back the monarchy—an event known as the **Restoration**.

In the spring of 1660, Parliament invited the son of the dead Charles I, also named Charles, to be the new king. Parliament laid out certain conditions, which Charles accepted, along with the invitation. He would be crowned King **Charles II**. As he rode into London upon his return, the people shouted their good wishes. The writer Samuel Pepys recorded his impressions of the day in his diary:

The Reign of Charles II Charles knew that as king he had to watch his step. When his policies were opposed, he usually gave in. Still, he had to address many issues. Conflict with the Dutch continued. Religious tensions remained. And the role of Parliament was still being developed. Charles supported religious toleration for Catholics, for example, but Parliament insisted upon laws to strengthen the Church of England.

The Restoration years were a mixture of positive and negative events. On one hand, Charles reopened the theaters, with a flowering of English drama as the result. Another positive event was passage of the Habeas Corpus Act of 1679. This act guaranteed that someone accused of a crime had the right to appear in court to determine if the accused should be held or released. The act is one of the most important in English history.

England also suffered setbacks during the reign of Charles II. In 1665 the bubonic plague returned, killing perhaps 100,000 people in London alone. The next year, the Great Fire of London destroyed large parts of the city—but also killed the rats that had spread the deadly plague. After the fire, though, Charles supported public construction projects.

James II Later in Charles's reign the question of who would succeed him remained. His brother, James, was next in line, but he was Catholic. In addition, James had married a Catholic princess whose Catholic son would outrank James's Protestant daughters from his first marriage. When Charles died in 1685, James II was crowned king. Many people wondered if another destructive war would follow.

James was not popular. Besides being a Catholic, he believed wholeheartedly in his right to rule as an absolute monarch. The English people, however, would no longer tolerate such a belief.

THE MONARCHS OF EUROPE **549**

NEW YORK

CC Unit 4-F2
Thomas Hobbes, *The Leviathan*

CC Unit 4-G3
Puritan Revolution—Oliver Cromwell

Reading Focus

4 What happened when monarchy returned to England? *Charles II took the throne, followed by his brother, James II, a Catholic. Then, Protestants William and Mary became king and queen in the Glorious Revolution.*

The Monarchy Returns

Identify Cause and Effect Why did Parliament vote to bring back the monarchy? *People were unhappy with new Puritan laws, and Cromwell's son was an uninspiring leader.*

Evaluate What were the positive and negative aspects of the Restoration years? *positive—the theaters reopened, Habeas Corpus Act passed; negative— conflict with Dutch, religious tension, bubonic plague, Great Fire of London*

Analyze Why are the events of 1688 known as the Glorious Revolution? *A new king and queen took power without bloodshed.*

 CRF: Biography: William and Mary

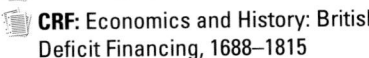 **CRF:** Economics and History: British Deficit Financing, 1688–1815

Info to Know

Hobbes and *Leviathan* When the struggle between Charles I and Parliament broke out, Thomas Hobbes began work on a defense of the powers of the monarch, using ideas that he later developed in *Leviathan*. Fearing arrest by Parliament, he fled to Paris. From 1646 to 1648 he taught mathematics to Charles I's son, the future King Charles II, who was living in exile in Paris. *Leviathan* was viewed by Prince Charles's advisers as justifying the Commonwealth, and by French authorities as attacking the papacy. Fearing arrest again, he returned to England. When Charles II came to the throne in 1660, he welcomed his former teacher back to his court.

Answers

Reading Check *temporarily ended monarchy and House of Lords, restricted English social life in certain ways*

Skills Focus: Identifying Main Idea and Details   At Level

Reading Skill
The Puritan Commonwealth

1. Guide students in a discussion of the effectiveness of Cromwell's Commonwealth using the following questions: Why was the monarchy abolished? How does the idea of a commonwealth fit in with Cromwell's dismissal of Parliament and seizure of power? How did Cromwell's behavior compare with that of King Charles? Did the English just replace one tyrant with another?

2. Have each student write a "job evaluation" assessing Oliver Cromwell's performance as the leader of England. First have students create an evaluation form with questions about different aspects of job performance, then have students fill in the answers.

3. Have volunteers read their job evaluations to the class. **LS Verbal-Linguistic**

   Alternative Assessment Handbook, Rubrics 11: Discussions; and 40: Writing to Describe

549

Analyzing Primary Sources

The English Bill of Rights

Activity **Comparing Documents**
Provide students with copies of the Bill of Rights from the United States Constitution. Have them search for similarities between the American Bill of Rights and the English Bill of Rights. **LS** Verbal-Linguistic

Review & Assess

Close

Have students summarize the important events in English history from the time of the Tudors to the Glorious Revolution.

Review

Online Quiz, Section 3

Assess

SE Section 3 Assessment

Progress Assessment: Section 3 Quiz

Alternative Assessment Handbook

Reteach/Intervene

Interactive Reader and Study Guide, Section 3

Interactive Skills Tutor CD-ROM

PRIMARY SOURCES

The English Bill of Rights

These excerpts from The Bill of Rights illustrate the limits placed on the monarchy by Parliament. In the document, the members of Parliament made several declarations, including:

1. That the pretended power of suspending laws, or the execution of laws, by regal authority, without consent of parliament is illegal. . .

5. That it is the right of the subjects to petition the king, and all commitments and prosecutions for such petitioning are illegal. . .

8. That election of members of parliament ought to be free.

9. That the freedom of speech, and debates or proceedings in parliament, ought not to be impeached or questioned in any court or place out of parliament.

10. That excessive bail ought not to be required, nor excessive fines imposed, nor cruel and unusual punishments inflicted.

Skills Focus **READING LIKE A HISTORIAN**

1. **Analyze** In the fifth declaration, what does "petition the king" mean?

2. **Draw Conclusions** Which of these rights do we enjoy today?

See **Skills Handbook, p. H25**

The Glorious Revolution In 1688 a group of nobles invited James's daughter Mary and her husband William to become king and queen of England. **William and Mary** were both Protestants, living in the Netherlands. James, knowing that it was pointless to fight, fled to France. Parliament gave the throne to William III and Mary II as joint rulers. This transfer of power became known as the **Glorious Revolution**.

Changes in Government With the Glorious Revolution, Parliament had essentially crowned the new king and queen. More important was a document that William and Mary had to sign before taking the throne—the English Bill of Rights. This document prevented the monarch from levying taxes without the consent of Parliament, among many other provisions. Decades later, the Bill of Rights was reflected in the U.S. Constitution.

The Bill of Rights was central to England's growth as a **constitutional monarchy**, the term for a monarchy limited by law. The document's approval came after decades of dramatic changes in English government. England had rejected the concept of an absolute monarch who supposedly ruled by divine right for a monarchy ruled by law.

READING CHECK **Describe** What happened during the Glorious Revolution?

SECTION 3 ASSESSMENT

go.hrw.com
Online Quiz
Keyword: SHL MON HP

Reviewing Ideas, Terms, and People

1. **a. Identify** Which monarch separated England from the Roman Catholic Church?
   b. Explain Why did Elizabeth I need to get along with the English Parliament?

2. **a. Recall** How did the **Puritans** get their name?
   b. Summarize What was the basic conflict between James I and Parliament?

3. **a. Identify** When did the **English Civil War** begin?
   b. Explain Why did **Charles I** have a hard time raising money for an army, while Parliament did not?
   c. Develop Why did the English people differ in their views on the execution of Charles I?

4. **a. Recall** What is a **constitutional monarchy**?
   b. Compare and Contrast How were the **Restoration** and the **Glorious Revolution** similar and different?
   c. Make Judgments Why is the English Bill of Rights important to both the English and American people?

Critical Thinking

5. **Identify Cause and Effect** Using your notes and a graphic organizer like the one below, identify the causes of the decreasing power of the monarchy. Add more boxes as needed.

| Cause |
| Cause | → | Decreased power of the monarchy |

FOCUS ON WRITING

6. **Exposition** Imagine that you are a guide in a museum that has a copy of the English Bill of Rights. As a handout for museum visitors, write a brief explanation of the importance of this document.

550 CHAPTER 18

Section 3 Assessment Answers

1. **a.** Henry VIII
   b. to pass laws supporting her policies

2. **a.** wanted to "purify" the Church of England
   b. James I could not get money from Parliament.

3. **a.** 1642
   b. Parliament was able to levy taxes.
   c. People who supported the monarchy believed Parliament did not have the authority to execute the king.

4. **a.** monarchy limited by law

b. similar—both did not involve violence; different—in Glorious Revolution, the king and queen had to accept limits on their power
c. provided rights that are important to this day; some rights later included in U.S. Bill of Rights

5. Kings believed in absolute monarchy while Parliament wanted to remain independent of King, Charles I overthrown by Parliament, English Bill of Rights passed

6. Student handouts should point out that Parliament's role was still being developed

---

Answers

Primary Sources 1. *speak freely when asking for political change;* 2. *free speech; free elections; no cruel and unusual punishment*

Reading Check *William and Mary were given the English throne by Parliament.*

550

Music

Classical Music

What is it? The term "classical music" means different things to different people. It can describe a certain era of European music that began in the mid-1700s. Most people, though, probably think of classical music as beautiful concert music of any time period played by an orchestra—a large group of musicians.

Key characteristics:
- Includes many different forms—symphonies, operas, string quartets, art songs sung by individuals, and more
- Involves many different instruments—violins, violas, cellos, clarinets, horns, drums, pianos, drums, and many more
- Usually performed by highly trained musicians and singers

Why is it important?
- Classical music expresses the entire range of human emotions, from deep religious reverence to wild passion.
- It is an always-evolving form of musical expression that incorporates new instruments and modern topics.
- Although the performers are trained, one does not need to be trained to enjoy classical music.

Maestro Seiji Ozawa conducts the Boston Symphony.

This is an original score from one of classical music's greatest masters—Wolfgang Amadeus Mozart.

Composer Franz Josef Haydn was Austrian but visited London often. His many musical works inspired later composers.

NEW YORK STANDARDS

PI 4.2 Students interpret and analyze documents and artifacts related to significant developments and events in world history.

Skills Focus INTERPRETING VISUALS

1. **Compare and Contrast** What do the performances pictured have in common? How are they different?

2. **Rank** What modern issues do you think would be good topics for symphonies or operas?

THE MONARCHS OF EUROPE **551**

The Arts Around the World

Biography

Franz Joseph Haydn (1732–1809)

Joseph Haydn was one of the creators of the Classical style in music. During most of his career, he was the musical director at the court of the Esterhazys, one of the wealthiest families in the Austrian empire. During his regular visits to Vienna, Haydn developed a close friendship with Wolfgang Amadeus Mozart. In 1791 he visited England. After he returned to Vienna, Ludwig van Beethoven went there to study with him. Haydn recognized his student's greatness, saying: "I shall be proud to be called his teacher." He visited England a second time in 1794. His 12 London symphonies won over British audiences and led King George III to invite him to stay, but he decided to return to Austria instead. In 1797 Haydn wrote the national anthem of the Austrian monarchy, which was also used as the national anthem of Germany. "Papa" Haydn died in 1809, a famous and wealthy man.

Teaching Tip

Collaborate with the school music department or a local orchestra to present examples of classical music to students. Explain the history behind each piece of music presented.

Skills Focus: Comparing and Contrasting

At Level

Prep Required

Reading Skill
Classical Music

Materials: CDs featuring works of a classical composer such as Beethoven, and a modern orchestral composer such as Bela Bartok; CD player

1. Explain that the word "classical" can refer generally to orchestral music, or specifically to the Classical period.

2. Play a short selection from both CDs. Ask students which music came from the Classical period, and which is modern. Have volunteers give their guesses and explain their reasoning. Reveal who composed each selection.

3. Organize students into small groups. Play the CDs again. Have each group create a list of details about each piece, and compare the lists with the class. **LS Auditory-Musical, Interpersonal**

Alternative Assessment Handbook, Rubric 9: Comparing and Contrasting

Answers

Interpreting Visuals 1. *possible answer—both include conductors; one is a painted scene, the other is a photograph; one seems to be a large group; the other is a smaller group;* **2.** *Student answers will vary.*

551

Getting Started

Use the **Interactive Reader and Study Guide** to familiarize students with the section content.

📋 **Interactive Reader and Study Guide,** Section 4

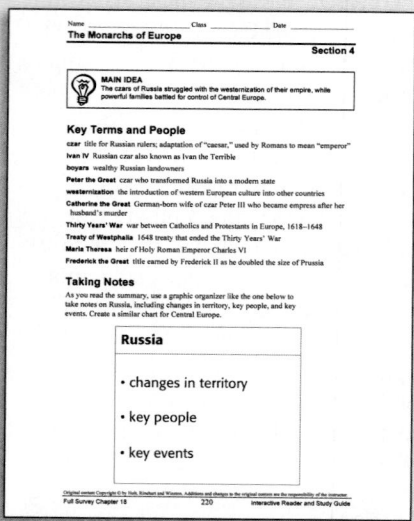

Academic Vocabulary

Review with students the high-use academic term in this section.

legitimacy the right to rule (p. 555)

📋 **CRF:** Vocabulary Builder: Section 4

Taking Notes

Russia—Territory: expansion into Siberia, warm-water port at St. Petersburg; Key People—Ivan IV; Peter the Great; Catherine the Great; Events: Time of Troubles; Great Northern War, building of St. Petersburg; Central Europe—Territory: possessions of Hapsburgs and Hohenzollerns; Key People: Frederick I; Maria Theresa, Frederick the Great; Events: Thirty Years' War; Treaty of Westphalia; Seven Years' War

---

go.hrw.com
Online Resources

KEYWORD: SHL MON
ACTIVITY: Peter the Great
and Catherine the Great

SECTION 4
Rulers of Russia and Central Europe

BEFORE YOU READ

MAIN IDEA

The czars of Russia struggled with the westernization of their empire, while powerful families battled for control of Central Europe.

READING FOCUS

1. How did Ivan IV strengthen the Russian monarchy?
2. What reforms did Peter the Great make in Russia?
3. How did the rule of Catherine the Great affect Russia?
4. What states formed in Central Europe in the 1600s and 1700s?

KEY TERMS AND PEOPLE

boyars
czar
Ivan IV
Peter the Great
westernization
Catherine the Great
Thirty Years' War
Treaty of Westphalia
Maria Theresa
Frederick the Great

NEW YORK

PI 3.1 Students analyze the roles and contributions of individuals and groups to social, political, economic, cultural, and religious practices and activities.

IVAN THE Terrible

Tsar Ivan IV Vasilyevich the Terrible (1530–84), by Victor Mikhailovich Vasnetsov, 1897

552 CHAPTER 18

THE INSIDE STORY

How did a ruler earn such a bad reputation? The young Russian emperor, Ivan IV, seemed reasonable at first and made several positive reforms. He also went to war to expand Russia's territory. When he seized the city of Kazan, the Russian people gave him the nickname *groznyi,* which means "fearsome" or "stern." However, the word has also been translated as "terrible." Ivan's actions did indeed become terrible, as he slipped into periods of uncontrollable rage, suspicion, and violence. Whole towns were burned and their people sent away. Ivan killed some enemies while they were in church. He had leading citizens publicly executed in grisly ways designed to horrify the many witnesses. Ivan even mortally wounded his own son in an argument. This incident probably sealed his reputation for all time as "Ivan the Terrible." ■

The Monarchy of Ivan IV

In the 1500s Russia was far behind western Europe in technological advancement and centralized government. At the time, Russia was run, in effect, by church officials and **boyars**, or landowners, usually with conservative viewpoints. Then, in 1546 a young prince claimed the title of **czar** (ZAHR) and put Russia on a different course. The title was a version of the Latin word *caesar,* or emperor, the title used by the Romans. The new czar, whose name was Ivan, intended to rule without limits on his power. But his own madness created chaos.

Teach the Main Idea

At Level

Rulers of Russia and Central Europe

1. **Teach** Ask students the Reading Focus questions to teach this section.

2. **Apply** Have students create an outline of the section using the heads as main points. Have students identify at least two main ideas under each of the red subheadings.

3. **Review** Review student outlines as a class. Guide students in a discussion of the relationship between Austria and Prussia during this period.

4. **Practice/Homework** Tell students that it is 1618 and they are mediators trying to prevent war after Protestants threw the Holy Roman Emperor's representatives out of the palace windows. Have students use the terms of the Peace of Augsburg and any other arguments they can think of to try to convince the emperor to negotiate rather than go to war.
LS Visual-Spatial, Verbal-Linguistic

📋 **Alternative Assessment Handbook**, Rubrics 11: Discussions; and 43: Writing to Persuade

Reforms of Ivan IV During the early years of his rule, **Ivan IV** made many reforms. He created a general council that included merchants and lower-level nobles. He also began to promote military officers on merit rather than status and drew up a new legal code. These and similar reforms reduced the boyars' power.

Ivan also expanded Russia's borders and trade. He defeated the Tatars, who had succeeded the Mongols, and expanded Russian territory east to the Volga River. Controlling the length of the Volga to the Caspian Sea increased trade. As a result of such achievements, the years from 1547 to 1563 are known as Ivan's "good period."

Ivan the Terrible During the 1560s, Ivan changed. It was during this time that his strict policies and violent actions sealed his reputation as Ivan the Terrible. First, he became suspicious of his closest advisers and sent them away, killing many of their supporters. When his wife Anastasia died, he became convinced that she was murdered and that people were conspiring against him.

To investigate and punish the opposition, Ivan created a private police force of some 6,000 men. These men dressed in black and rode black horses. They controlled almost half of Russia's territory in Ivan's name and brutally punished anyone who spoke out against the czar's policies.

Ivan's harshness continued when in 1565 he seized land from 12,000 boyars. Soon after, he ordered the killing of thousands of people in the city of Novgorod because he suspected that they wanted to separate from Russia. Ivan's descent into mental illness seemed complete when in 1581 he killed his own son, who was next in line to be czar.

Although it may have been an accident, the death of Ivan's son left Russia without an heir to the throne. As a result, power changed hands many times. Uncertainty about the succession, economic problems, and foreign invasions added up to a chaotic period known as the Time of Troubles. It lasted until 1613, when Michael, a relative of Ivan's first wife, was crowned czar. Michael was the first of the Romanov dynasty, which ruled Russia until 1917.

READING CHECK **Contrast** How did the early rule of Ivan IV differ from his later years?

Peter the Great

About 70 years later, Peter I was crowned czar. Known later as **Peter the Great** for his efforts to transform Russia into a modern state, Peter had the strength to regain absolute power for the Russian monarchy.

Early Rule Peter became czar in 1682 while he was still a child, so his sister insisted on ruling in his place. At the age of 17, Peter removed his sister from the throne and took power for himself.

Peter was an impressive man. He was about six and a half feet tall, and it was said that he was so strong he could roll up a heavy silver platter as if it were foil. Peter also had a strong personality and boundless energy.

One of Czar Peter's first acts was to storm Azov, a Black Sea port held by Turks. The attack was a disaster, but it inspired Peter to build a navy. Peter labored side-by-side with thousands of carpenters to build hundreds of ships. When Peter's new navy took up the campaign against Azov, the Turks surrendered.

Modernization and Reform As Russia's ruler, Peter realized that his country needed to modernize to catch up with the rest of Europe. He was determined to bring elements of Western culture to Russia. This process is known as **westernization**.

In 1697 Peter began a journey to western Europe to see for himself what Russia needed to modernize. He traveled in disguise but was sometimes recognized anyway. Wherever Peter went, he learned hands-on skills, especially shipbuilding. He also recruited European experts to bring their skills to Russia.

This historic trip was cut short, though, by a rebellion among the *streltsy*, a military corps that also had political influence. Certain that the *streltsy* wanted to put his sister back on the throne, Peter had many members tortured and then executed. Finally, he disbanded the *streltsy* and organized a more modern army.

In addition to modernizing the army, Peter made many other reforms. He brought the church under state control, built up Russian industry, started the first newspaper in Russia, and sponsored new schools. Peter modernized the calendar and promoted officials based on service instead of their social status.

THE MONARCHS OF EUROPE **553**

TAKING NOTES

Take notes on Russia in a chart like this one, including changes in territory, key people, and key events. Create a similar chart for Central Europe.

Russia
• changes in territory
• key people
• key events

 NEW YORK

CC **Unit 4-F4**
Political ideologies: global absolutism
Case studies: Ivan the Terrible and Peter the Great

Peter the Great

Recall What were some ways in which Peter the Great attempted to westernize Russia? *encouraged Russians to adopt European styles of clothing and grooming, gained a warm-water port to keep Russia open to western trade year-round*

Analyze In what ways was St. Petersburg significant? *provided warm-water port for Russia, symbolized westernization of Russia*

Teaching Tip

The word *czar* is sometimes spelled *tsar*. In American usage, *czar* is the more common spelling. However, most scholars of Slavic studies prefer the *tsar* spelling, which more closely follows the Russian spelling.

Answers

Faces of History 1. *possible answer—yes, because he looks regal, wealthy, and strong;* **2.** *possible answer—They illustrate that Peter the Great was willing to go to great lengths to westernize Russia.*

Reading Check *by encouraging men to shave off their beards, encouraging people to adopt European styles of dress, building a new capital with Western-style architecture*

554

Peter also supported education, believing that Russians needed to learn more about science and other critical fields from the West.

Some reforms were less important but did affect people's daily lives. For example, Peter wanted Russians to adopt European styles of clothing and grooming. Peter even personally cut off the boyars' traditional long coats and beards so they would look more European. The boyars resented and resisted such actions.

Through these and other reforms, Peter tried to impose his will on the Russian people and make Russia a more modern country. Although he was not always successful, Peter the Great is often considered the founder of modern Russia for his efforts.

THE IMPACT TODAY

St. Petersburg is Russia's second-largest city and is still a cultural and educational center.

Founding of St. Petersburg In addition to his many reforms, Peter also founded a new city. In the early 1700s, Peter fought Sweden to acquire a warm-water port. Russia's other ports were choked by ice much of the year. A port farther south on the Baltic Sea would keep Russia open to western trade all year long and help connect Russia to the west.

On land he won from Sweden, Peter built a new capital, St. Petersburg, and Russia's government was moved to the new city. St. Petersburg featured Western-style architecture, rather than traditional Russian styles.

READING CHECK **Recall** Name three ways in which Peter the Great attempted to westernize Russia.

FACES OF HISTORY Peter the Great, 1672–1725

Portrait of Peter I the Great, by Jean Marc Nattier, 1717

Notice the regal posture, shining armor, and rich fabrics in this official portrait.

This Dutch painting shows Peter in a casual pose, with unkempt hair, beard stubble, and the clothing of a laborer.

Portrait of Peter the Great, Dutch school, no date

Do these two portraits really show the same person—the powerful Peter the Great? They do indeed! The portrait on the left shows him as Peter I, Czar of Russia. On the right, he is shown as a common Dutch shipbuilder, a disguise he adopted on a trip to Europe to learn firsthand the secrets of Western technology. Under an assumed name, Peter even earned a certificate as a qualified shipwright. Also in Europe, Peter learned new printing methods and participated in surgical operations. He even learned basic dentistry and enjoyed pulling his servants'

teeth. To learn additional skills from the West, Peter persuaded hundreds of craft workers, doctors, engineers, naval officers, and other experts to come to Russia.

Skills Focus READING LIKE A HISTORIAN

1. **Analyze** If Peter had seen the portrait on the right, do you think he would have liked it? Why or why not?
2. **Evaluate** How do these portraits affect your evaluation of Peter the Great?

554 CHAPTER 18

Skills Focus: Identifying Main Idea and Details   At Level

Reading Skill
The Greats

1. Tell students they are newspaper reporters in czarist Russia preparing to interview either Peter the Great or Catherine the Great. Have each student choose one of the two "great" Russian rulers and write that ruler's name at the top of a sheet of paper. Have students write a series of questions that they would like to ask that ruler.

2. Have students exchange questions. Now tell students they are the ruler whose name is at the top of the list of questions. Have students answer the questions as they think that ruler would have.

3. Have volunteers share the questions they answered, along with their answers, with the rest of the class.

4. Guide students in a discussion of the two rulers based on their interviews. **LS** **Verbal-Linguistic**

Alternative Assessment Handbook, Rubric 23: Newspapers

THE EXPANSION OF RUSSIA

GEOGRAPHY SKILLS **INTERPRETING MAPS**

1. **Regions** During what time period was most of Siberia added to Russia?
2. **Movement** What was the general direction of Russian expansion?

Expansion of Russia

By 1462	By 1689
By 1505	By 1762
By 1598	By 1796

— Borders of present-day Russia

— Borders of other present-day countries

Lambert equal-area projection

Catherine the Great

Russia's next important ruler was actually a German princess who came to Russia to marry a grandson of Peter the Great. She became known as **Catherine the Great**.

Catherine Takes Power After her husband became Czar Peter III in 1761, Catherine and many Russian nobles grew angry at his weak and incompetent rule. With the help of her allies, Catherine seized power from the new czar, who was murdered. Catherine II was declared czarina of Russia. The word *czarina* is the female form of "czar."

Early Reforms Catherine saw herself as the true successor of Peter the Great and worked to build on his westernization efforts. To emphasize the legitimacy of her claim, she built a bronze statue in St. Petersburg honoring Peter. It was inscribed "To Peter the First, from Catherine the Second."

Catherine began an ambitious plan of reforms. She was influenced by major European thinkers of the time who believed that a strong and wise ruler could improve life for his or her subjects. Catherine reformed Russia's legal and education systems and removed some restrictions on trade. She also promoted science and the arts.

Challenges to Catherine's Rule As Catherine tried to reform Russia, she was soon distracted by conflict. A few years after taking power, she faced war in Poland, where people wanted freedom from Russian influence. In 1768 the Ottoman Empire joined the Polish cause. Eventually, Russia won the war and took over half of Poland and territory on the Black Sea, a valuable outlet for sea trade.

While the war was still raging, Catherine faced a popular rebellion inside Russia. A man named Yemelyan Pugachev was traveling the countryside claiming that he was Peter III and had not been murdered after all. Pugachev gained support among Russia's peasants and led a ragtag army that took over many areas before the rebellion was put down. In the end, Pugachev was captured and beheaded.

The revolt convinced Catherine that she needed to strengthen the authority of the monarchy in rural areas. She completely reorganized local governments and put their administration in the hands of area landowners and nobles. In return for their service as government officials, Catherine reduced their taxes and gave them absolute control over their lands and peasants.

READING CHECK **Analyze** What was one way that Catherine showed she was an absolute monarch?

NEW YORK
CC **Unit 5-B3**
The enlightened despots—Catherine the Great

ACADEMIC VOCABULARY
legitimacy
the right to rule

THE MONARCHS OF EUROPE **555**

Reading Focus

4 What states formed in Central Europe in the 1600s and 1700s? *Estonia, Latvia, Lithuania, Belarus, Moldova, Ukraine, Georgia*

Monarchy and Conflict in Central Europe

Identify What was the Thirty Years' War? *a religious clash between Catholics and Protestants that began in 1618, involved the powerful empires of Central Europe*

Identify Cause and Effect What was one major effect of the Thirty Years' War? *The map of Europe changed.*

📝 **CRF:** Biography: Maria Theresa

Info to Know

Balance of Power The emergence of Prussia as a major military power after the War of the Austrian Succession affected the balance of power in Europe. When England allied itself with Prussia, an alarmed France allied itself with Austria, and rivalries intensified.

Monarchy and Conflict in Central Europe

Unlike the monarchs of Russia and Western Europe, rulers in Central Europe in the 1500s and 1600s never became absolute monarchs. The Holy Roman Empire, which included most of Central Europe at that time, was headed by a single emperor, but he did not have total authority. His empire included dozens of small states, each with its own ruler, who fought vigorously against increased imperial power.

Since the 1450s, all of the Holy Roman Emperors had come from a single family, the Hapsburgs. In the early 1600s, an attempt

A Deadly Assault

The Holy Roman Emperor's forces stormed Magdeburg, Germany, in 1631 and butchered two-thirds of the townspeople. Outrage over the slaughter inspired the Swedes under Gustavus Adolphus to fight harder. ***Why could it be said that the battle of Magdeburg was both a victory and defeat for its conquerors?***

556 CHAPTER 18

by one of the Hapsburg emperors to exert his authority launched a terrible conflict known as the **Thirty Years' War.** Alliances between the Hapsburgs and other European monarchs helped make the war a continent-wide affair.

The Thirty Years' War The Thirty Years' War began as a religious dispute. In 1618 in Prague (now in the Czech Republic) an official representing Holy Roman Emperor Ferdinand II, who was Roman Catholic, ordered that two Protestant churches be shut down. Local Protestants were furious. They responded by throwing the emperor's representatives out of the palace windows. Although the men landed on a rubbish heap and were unhurt, their dignity was damaged.

The emperor's attempt to control people's religion sparked revolt throughout the region. Nobles in the German states of Bavaria and Austria rebelled against the emperor, and nobles from other states soon joined them. The rulers of other countries became involved in the war as well. The monarchs of Spain, who were also members of the Hapsburg family, joined the war on Ferdinand's side. In response, the king of France, Spain's rival, joined the Protestant opposition. The kings of Denmark and Sweden also joined on the Protestant side.

The Thirty Years' War dragged on until 1648, with devastating effects on Germany. Several million Germans died—in battle, from disease, or starvation because their fields were ruined. In the end, the two sides agreed to the **Treaty of Westphalia,** which ended the war. In addition to extending religious toleration to both Catholics and Protestants, the treaty further reduced the power of the Holy Roman emperor and strengthened the rulers of the states within it.

Austria and Prussia Among the rulers who gained from the treaty were the leaders of Austria and Prussia. Austria was governed by the Hapsburg family, while Prussia's rulers came from a rival family, the Hohenzollerns.

In 1740 the Hapsburg Holy Roman Emperor Charles VI died without a male heir. But before he died he had approved a document called the Pragmatic Sanction, which stated that the empire could be passed to a female heir. It seemed his daughter, **Maria Theresa**, would take the throne.

Skills Focus: Comparing and Contrasting   At Level

Reading Skill
The Hapsburgs and the Hohenzollerns

1. Maria Theresa and Frederick II came to power at the same time. Have students make charts comparing and contrasting the two rulers, including comparisons of their families and the history and geography of the nations they led.

2. Review student charts as a class.

3. Guide students in a discussion of the Hapsburgs and the Hohenzollerns based on their charts. Use the following questions: What effect did the histories of Austria and Prussia have on

their rulers' behavior? How did their family backgrounds influence them? How did the fact that Maria Theresa was a woman affect relations between Austria and Prussia? Do you think her gender was really a factor, or just an excuse? Which ruler do you think was more effective? Why? Under which ruler would you rather have lived? Why? 🄛 **Visual-Spatial**

📝 **Alternative Assessment Handbook**, Rubrics 7: Charts; and 11: Discussions

Answers

A Deadly Assault *because many people died, but the loss inspired the Swedes to fight even harder*

The Hohenzollerns had a different plan. Frederick II of Prussia, also called **Frederick the Great**, seized the Austrian province of Silesia, which had minerals and industries. To avoid a long war, Frederick offered Maria Theresa an alliance. He also promised to help her husband become Holy Roman Emperor. Maria Theresa turned him down, and the War of the Austrian Succession broke out in 1740. Soon Spain, France, and two German states entered the war on Prussia's side, each hoping to gain territory. With so much against her, Maria Theresa asked for peace in 1748. Prussia kept Silesia, launching Prussia to a position of real power.

Continued Rivalry Prussia's victory only intensified the rivalry between Austria and Hungary, and it was not long before war broke out again. In 1756 the Seven Years' War began. On one side were Prussia—still ruled by Frederick the Great—and Great Britain. On the other were Austria, France, and Russia. Fighting occurred not just in Europe, but also in the enemies' colonies in North America and India.

During the first part of the war, Prussia was on the verge of defeat. At one point, Austrian and Russian forces even occupied the capital, Berlin. But then Russia pulled out of the war, allowing Prussia to regain strength. Eventually, Prussia emerged as the strongest military power in Europe. With his newfound might, Frederick pushed his opponents out of Prussia. As a result, the war ended in 1763 with both sides exhausted. However, the rivalry between Austria and Prussia was far from over. Hapsburgs and Hohenzollerns struggled for control of Central Europe for many more years.

READING CHECK **Recall** What were three wars that affected Central Europe?

CENTRAL EUROPE, 1763

- Possessions of the Austrian Hapsburgs
- Possessions of the Hohenzollerns

GEOGRAPHY SKILLS **INTERPRETING MAPS**

Location Why might the locations of Hapsburg and Hohenzollern holdings have caused conflict with other powers?

---

go.hrw.com
Online Quiz
Keyword: SHL MON HP

SECTION 4 ASSESSMENT

Reviewing Ideas, Terms, and People

1. a. Define Write a brief definition for the following terms: czar, boyars.
   b. Explain Why was **Ivan IV** known as Ivan the Terrible?
   c. Develop Why would uncertainty about who would be czar contribute to a Time of Troubles?

2. a. Identify What was the significance of Russia's new capital at St. Petersburg?
   b. Draw Conclusions Do you think Peter I earned the name Peter the Great? Why or why not?

3. a. Recall How did **Catherine the Great** become czarina?
   b. Explain How did Pugachev's revolt affect her reign?

4. a. Describe How did the **Thirty Years' War** begin?
   b. Identify Cause and Effect How did the rivalry between the Hapsburgs and Hohenzollerns affect Central Europe?

Critical Thinking

5. Compare and Contrast Use your notes and a chart like the one below to identify major figures in Russia and Central Europe, key events, and the roles they played in those events.

Person	Event	Role

FOCUS ON WRITING

6. Persuasion Imagine that you are a German engineer who has moved to Russia to help Peter the Great build St. Petersburg. Write a letter in which you try to persuade another professional back home to come work with you in Russia.

Info to Know

The Art of Governing Frederick William I worried about the worthiness of his son to rule because of Frederick II's interest in the arts and philosophy rather than in the military or government.

Map Transparency: Central Europe, 1763

Review & Assess

Close

Have students create a time line to place important events in Russia and Central Europe in chronological sequence.

Review

Online Quiz, Section 4

Assess

SE **Section 4 Assessment**

Progress Assessment: Section 4 Quiz

Alternative Assessment Handbook

Reteach/Intervene

Interactive Reader and Study Guide, Section 4

Interactive Skills Tutor CD-ROM

Answers

Interpreting Maps *possible answer—The Hapsburg and Hohenzollern lands bordered strong powers on all sides, and many of those powers hoped to expand.*

Section 4 Assessment Answers

1. a. czar: the title chosen by Ivan IV for himself, adapted from the word *caesar*, which the Romans used to mean "emperor"; boyars: wealthy Russian landowners
   b. latter part of his rule marked by terror
   c. possible answer—There was no strong leadership to keep order.

2. a. symbolized Peter the Great's efforts to modernize and westernize Russia, featured western-style architecture
   b. possible answers—yes, he expanded Russia's borders and increased trade, brought Russia into closer contact with western Europe, modernized Russia; no, cruel actions undermined achievements

3. a. married a grandson of Peter the Great
   b. showed Catherine she needed to strengthen her authority in rural areas

4. a. Most of Europe became involved for either religious or political reasons.
   b. intensified other European rivalries; led to War of Austrian Succession and Seven Years' War

5. Peter the Great—Events: Great Northern War; building of St. Petersburg; Role: westernizer and modernizer of Russia; Catherine the Great—Event: Pugachev's rebellion; Role: absolute ruler; Maria Theresa—Events: War of Austrian Succession; Seven Years' War; Roles: heir to Austrian throne; ally of France, Russia; Frederick the Great—Event: Seven Years' War; Role: ally of Great Britain, emerged as strongest power in Europe

6. Student letters should focus on the importance of St. Petersburg, both as a warm-water port and a symbol of westernization.

Imperial Saint Petersburg

Info to Know

A Changing City Peter designated St. Petersburg his capital in 1712, but Russia's capital returned to Moscow after the Bolsheviks seized power in 1917. After Lenin's death in 1924, the Communists renamed the city Leningrad. With the collapse of communism and the breakup of the Soviet Union, Leningrad became St. Petersburg again in 1991. Today St. Petersburg remains an important cultural center in Russia. The city is home to the Hermitage, a museum housed in the Winter Palace of Catherine the Great.

HISTORY & Geography

Imperial St. Petersburg

Cities reflect the history of the rulers who built and ruled them. St. Petersburg certainly reflects the determination of Peter the Great to create a grand new capital with a warm-water port. Peter started construction on the city in 1703—even before he had truly won the land from Sweden. The site he chose was actually a dank swamp—a place so hazardous that some 40,000 Swedish prisoners of war died while building the city. Their bones went into the city's foundations. After Peter's rule, his successors added more features that were heavily influenced by Western European styles.

▼ **This 1712 map shows Peter's original plan for the city.**

ST. PETERSBURG

☐ Central St. Petersburg

Gulf of Finland   St. Petersburg   Neva River

0   2   4 Miles
0   2   4 Kilometers

The Fortress of Saints Peter and Paul
Among the buildings within the fortress walls are a mint, Saints Peter and Paul Cathedral, a prison, and museums.

The Admiralty
The Admiralty began as a shipyard, where some 10,000 men worked at building the ships for Peter's new navy. It is now the home of the Naval Engineering School.

The Neva River
Although the Neva provides advantages, it floods badly. In 1703 a flood swept the building materials away only three months after construction of the city had begun.

558 CHAPTER

Skills Focus: Interpreting Historical Maps

At Level

Social Studies Skill
St. Petersburg in 1712

1. Explain to students that the map on this page is an actual historical map showing Peter the Great's plan for his capital city. Direct students' attention to the inset map. Ask students to identify why this location was chosen for St. Petersburg. What challenges might it have presented to city builders?

2. Organize students into groups of four to six. Tell them they are city planners for Peter the Great and will be presenting their plans for St. Petersburg to the czar, using this map as a visual source.

3. Have groups prepare oral presentations, which should answer the following questions: What advantages does the new capital provide to Russia? How have city planners overcome challenges, such as

flooding? What buildings in the new city represent the glory and strength of Russia? Tell students they must convince the czar that these plans fulfill his dreams for a capital city.

4. Have groups give their presentations to the rest of the class. **LS Visual-Spatial, Interpersonal**

📄 **Alternative Assessment Handbook,** Rubric 24: Oral Presentations

NEW YORK STANDARDS

PI **1.4** Students understand the broad patterns, relationship, and interactions of cultures and civilizations during particular eras and across eras.

Topographische Vorstellung der Neuen
SCHEN HAUPT-RESIDENZ und SEE-STADT
PETERSBURG
samt ihrer zu erst aufgerichteten Vestung

▼ This view of a bridge over the Neva River shows the grandeur of St. Petersburg.

View of Troizko Bridge, by J. Schroeder, 1800s

▲ Several palaces make up the Hermitage. The original palace was built for Peter's daughter Elizabeth, who took the Russian throne in 1741. Today, the Hermitage is one of the world's finest art museums.

▲ Peterhof, Peter the Great's own palace, is outside the city, linked directly to the Gulf of Finland by a canal. Pictured above is the Grand Cascade.

THE MONARCHS OF EUROPE **559**

GEOGRAPHY SKILLS **INTERPRETING MAPS**

1. **Location** Peter's original plan was for Vasilevskiy Island, at the far left, to be the city's center. That plan was abandoned, and the city grew up around the Admiralty. What may have accounted for the change in plans?

2. **Place** How do you think early visitors to St. Petersburg reacted to the buildings pictured here?

Differentiating Instruction

Below Level

Learners Having Difficulty

1. Draw the chart for all to see. Omit the italicized answers.

2. Have students copy and complete the chart individually or in small groups, using the visuals on this spread. When charts are completed, review them as a class. Have students use their charts to make general observations about St. Petersburg. **LS Visual-Spatial**

Alternative Assessment Handbook, Rubrics 7: Charts; and 21: Map Reading

Imperial St. Petersburg		
Buildings	**Geography**	**Building Challenges**
• *The Admiralty* • *Saints Peter and Paul Cathedral* • *Mint* • *Prison* • *Museums* • *Hermitage* • *Peterhof*	• *swampland* • *warm-water port* • *Neva River*	• *flooding* • *death of workers*

Answers

Interpreting Maps 1. *possible answers—island might have flooded, might have wanted city center closer to the Fortress of Saints Peter and Paul;* **2.** *possible answer—Visitors were probably awed by the grandeur of the buildings.*

559

Views of Absolutism

Document-Based Investigation

Views of Absolutism

Activity Political Cartoons

Review Document 1 with students, and have them answer the related questions. Then, have students draw the same political cartoon from the opposite point of view. Tell students they can do this simply by changing or removing certain elements of the original cartoon.

LS Visual-Spatial

Teaching Tip

Remind students that Louis XIV is famous for saying "L'état, c'est moi." In English this translates to "I am the state." Discuss with students how this short phrase captures the idea of absolutism.

NEW YORK STANDARDS

PI 4.4 Students analyze different interpretations of important events, issues, or developments by studying the social, political, and economic context in which they developed.

Historical Context These documents reveal different reactions to absolutism, a dominant political theory in the 1500s through 1700s in parts of Europe.

Task Study the selections and answer the questions that follow. After you have studied all the documents, you will be asked to write an essay supporting or criticizing absolutism. You will need to use evidence from these selections and from the chapter to support the position you take in your essay.

DOCUMENT 1

Queen Catherine's Dream

This English cartoon shows Catherine the Great being offered the cities of Warsaw and Constantinople by the devil. The title is "Queen Catherine's Dream." Catherine claimed to be fighting the Turks to free Constantinople and the Ottoman Empire from Muslim rule. The English had a different view. They accused her of simply wanting more territory.

Queen Catherine's Dream, by Richard Newton, 1791

DOCUMENT 2

The Sun King's Emblem

Louis XIV chose the sun as his emblem because of the "unique quality of the radiance . . . the good it does in every place." He believed that "the profession of king is great, noble, a fount of delight" and that "God who made you king will give you the necessary guidance." The golden emblem shown here is from Versailles, the elaborate palace that Louis built outside the city of Paris.

Réunion des Musées Nationaux / Art Resource, NY

560 CHAPTER 18

Skills Focus: Analyzing Visuals

Above Level

Reading Like a Historian Skill
The Treasure of Versailles

Materials: blank paper or posterboard

1. Explain to students that the gold emblem shown in Document 2 is just one of the many luxurious objects found in the palace of Louis XIV. Have students conduct independent research about the treasures of Versailles.

2. Have students create posters illustrating some of the treasures they found. Posters should

include accompanying text that describes the objects and how they symbolize the power of the French monarchy.

3. Display student posters for all to see.
   LS Visual-Spatial, Intrapersonal

   Alternative Assessment Handbook, Rubrics 28: Posters; and 30: Research

DOCUMENT 3

On the Divine Right of Kings

Jacques Benigne Bossuet, Bishop of Meaux, served as tutor to the French heir to the throne. Bossuet strongly supported absolutism in this excerpt from his treatise titled *Politics Derived from Holy Writ*.

> We have already seen that all power is of God ... Rulers then act as the ministers of God and as his lieutenants on earth. It is through them that God exercises his empire ... The royal throne is not the throne of a man, but the throne of God himself ...
>
> Note what is said in Ecclesiasticus: "God has given to every people its ruler." ... He therefore governs all peoples and gives them their kings ...
>
> But kings, although their power comes from on high, ... must employ it with fear and self-restraint, as a thing coming from God and of which God will demand an account ...
>
> God is infinite, God is all. The prince, as prince, is not regarded as a private person: he is a public personage, all the state is in him; the will of all the people is included in his. As all perfection and all strength are united in God, so all the power of individuals is united in the person of the prince.

DOCUMENT 4

Why Did Charles I Fight the Civil War?

Here British historian Conrad Russell expresses his views on the limitations that monarchs faced.

> The belief that it was the duty of a ruler to enforce uniformity in the true religion was one which caused difficulties ... Philip II in the Netherlands failed in this task for reasons not altogether different from those of Charles I. Both felt themselves obliged to fight rather than give up the struggle ...
>
> For him, [Charles I] then, the problem of religious unity was one of unity between kingdoms ... On this point, Charles's Scottish opponents agreed with him. They too thought that unless there was unity of religion and church government between England and Scotland, there would be permanent instability ... Charles, moreover, did not only have a King of England's resistance to Scottish notions of Presbyterianising England: he also had to view such a proposal through the eyes of the King of Ireland. A religious settlement in which it would have been a key point that no papists were to be tolerated would hardly have led to stability in Ireland ... Of all the participants in the crisis of 1640–42, Charles was the only one whose position forced him to a genuinely British perspective.

Skills FOCUS · READING LIKE A HISTORIAN

DOCUMENT 1
a. **Describe** What elements of the cartoon suggest that the cartoonist is suspicious of Catherine's motives?
b. **Infer** How does the cartoon reflect the history of absolutism in England, in contrast to its history in Russia?

DOCUMENT 2
a. **Analyze** Why do you think Louis chose this emblem? Is it an appropriate emblem for Louis XIV?
b. **Infer** What do you think the effect of this emblem might have been on the people who saw it at Versailles?

DOCUMENT 3
a. **Identify** On what basis does Bossuet justify absolutism?
b. **Analyze** Does Bossuet think there are any limitations on the king's power? Why or why not?

DOCUMENT 4
a. **Describe** What limited Charles I's choices?
b. **Infer** How does the writer view Charles I's decisions?

DOCUMENT-BASED ESSAY QUESTION

People held different views on the proper role of the monarch and the limits of royal authority. Using the documents above and information from the chapter, form a thesis that supports a role for absolute monarchy or argues for limits on royal power. Consider if there were both benefits and hazards of absolutism. Then write a short essay to support your position.

See **Skills Handbook**, pp. H25, H26

THE MONARCHS OF EUROPE **561**

Differentiating Instruction

Below Level

Learners Having Difficulty

1. Review each document with students. Have students summarize the message or significance of each document in their own words.

2. Tell students that the four documents represent different perspectives on absolute rule. Have students classify each document as either supporting absolute rule or supporting limits on royal power.

3. Organize a class debate on whether monarchs should rule with absolute power, or whether they should have limits on their power. Have students base their arguments on each document and the text in this chapter.
   LS Interpersonal

   Alternative Assessment Handbook, Rubrics 10: Debates; and 38: Writing to Classify

Word Help

personage person of distinction
papist disparaging, or degrading term for a Roman Catholic

Info to Know

The Divine Right In England, the execution of Charles I symbolizes the end of divine right. Although the monarchy would eventually return to England, future monarchs were forced to accept limits on their power. Elsewhere in Europe, however, absolutism and the idea of divine right continued for many years. As late as the 1900s, Czar Nicholas II of Russia and Emperor Wilhelm II of Prussia claimed to receive their power from God.

Answers

Document 1. a. *She is being given territory by the devil.* **b.** *possible answer—By the time Catherine the Great ruled Russia, monarchs in England had been forced to accept limits on their power.* **Document 2. a.** *possible answer—Yes, the sun is present everywhere and affects almost everything.* **b.** *possible answer— might have inspired them to believe in the power of their king;* **Document 3. a.** *that God gave rulers their absolute power;* **b.** *Yes, God will punish rulers if they misuse their power.* **Document 4. a.** *the political and religious views of Scotland and Ireland;* **b.** *as genuinely British;* **Essay** *Student essays should either argue for limits on royal power, using examples from England and their reading in the chapter, or for absolute monarchy, using examples from Document 2, Document 3, and the chapter. Essays should be supported by detail and logic.*

Visual Summary

Review and Inquiry Organize students into five groups. Assign each group one of the areas shown in the Visual Study Guide. Have groups prepare an oral presentation to give to the rest of the class, reviewing key rulers and events of their area.

Quick Facts Transparency: Visual Study Guide: The Monarchs of Europe

Review Key Terms and People

1. Thirty Years' War
2. Glorious Revolution
3. Peace of Augsburg
4. Cardinal Richelieu
5. Huguenots
6. legitimacy
7. Spanish Armada
8. divine right
9. Royalists

Comprehension and Critical Thinking

10. a. its large size; conflict between Protestants and Catholics
b. naval battles, English fireships, and storms
c. possible answer—Despite great wealth, Spain faced economic failure and decline.

11. a. The Saint Bartholomew's Day Massacre began.
b. These groups threatened the absolute power of the monarch.
c. Over 200,000 Huguenots fled France after the edict was revoked, causing an economic crisis.

12. a. He placed restrictions on English social life.
b. because many people were unhappy during Cromwell's reign and the reign of his son
c. English monarchs accepted limits on their power.

VISUAL STUDY GUIDE — Monarchs of Europe: 1500–1800

Spain

Ruler	Major Events	Results of Reign
Charles V	Many enemies, Reformation, Peace of Augsburg	Spain powerful; empire divided between heirs
Philip II	Dutch revolt, Armada defeat	Spain weakened

France

Ruler	Major Events	Results of Reign
Henry IV	Survived massacre, issued Edict of Nantes	Calmed religious conflict, repaired war-torn country
Louis XIII	La Rochelle, clash with nobles, Thirty Years' War	Huguenots and nobles weakened
Louis XIV	Versailles built, revocation of the Edict of Nantes, military buildup	Absolutism firmly established, economic growth, expensive wars

Central Europe

Ruler	Major Events	Results of Reign
Maria Theresa (Austria)	War of Austrian Succession, Seven Years War	Continued competition with Hohenzollerns
Frederick II (the Great) (Prussia)	War of Austrian Succession, Seven Years War	Prussia as major European power

England

Ruler	Major Events	Results of Reign
Henry VIII	Split with pope	Parliament strengthened
Elizabeth I	War with Spain	England undefeated
Charles I	Led troops into Parliament	Executed amid English Civil War
Cromwell	Civil War, conflicts abroad	Ruled alone, created resentment
Charles II	Restoration	Habeas Corpus Act
William and Mary	Glorious Revolution, English Bill of Rights	Parliament's power greatly increased

Russia

Ruler	Major Events	Results of Reign
Ivan IV	Reforms, expanded territory, terror	Time of Troubles
Peter I (the Great)	Reforms, *streltsy* rebellion, St. Petersburg built	Beginning of westernization
Catherine II (the Great)	Rebellion, rural government reform	More power for nobles over serfs

---

Review Key Terms and People

Identify the correct term or person from the chapter that best fits each of the following descriptions.

1. war that lasted from 1618 to 1648 and devastated Germany
2. transfer of power to William III and Mary II
3. treaty that gave the rulers of German states the right to decide the religion of their states
4. the most trusted adviser of King Louis XIII
5. French Protestants
6. the right to rule
7. fleet that tried to invade England in 1588
8. belief that God grants absolute power to monarchs
9. supporters of Charles I

---

13. a. Ivan the Terrible
b. high points—reforms, winning Great Northern War, building St. Petersburg; low points—storming of Azov, rebellion of *strelsky*
c. because most fighting took place in Germany, and several million Germans died in the war

Reading Skills

14. possible answer—that the Reformation began in Germany in 1517 and spread throughout Europe; key terms such as "Protestant Reformation" and "Calvinist"

History's Impact video program
Review the video to answer the closing question:
When was Spain's Golden Century, and how was it financed?

Comprehension and Critical Thinking

SECTION 1 (pp. 535–538)

10. a. Recall What were two reasons why Charles V had a difficult time ruling his empire?

b. Sequence What events foiled the Spanish Armada's invasion of England?

c. Elaborate Why might a historian title a book about Spain from 1550 to 1650 *A Glorious Failure*?

SECTION 2 (pp. 540–544)

11. a. Identify What happened in Paris early in the morning on August 24, 1572?

b. Explain Why did Cardinal Richelieu want to crush the power of the nobles and the Huguenots?

c. Elaborate Why was the revocation of the Edict of Nantes a problem for more people than just the Huguenots?

SECTION 3 (pp. 545–550)

12. a. Describe How did Cromwell change English society?

b. Infer Why did the people of London cheer Charles II when he returned from exile?

c. Develop The English monarchy developed in a very different direction than did the monarchies of Spain and France. How did it differ?

SECTION 4 (pp. 552–557)

13. a. Identify By what name is Ivan IV often remembered?

b. Compare and Contrast What were some high points and low points of Peter the Great's rule?

c. Draw Conclusions Why was the Thirty Years' War one of the worst disasters in German history?

Reading Skills

Connecting *Read the passage below from this chapter. Then answer the question that follows.*

❝ Soon after the Protestant Reformation began in Germany, it spread to France. By the 1560s, about one in ten French men and women was a Huguenot, or French Calvinist Protestant. ❞

14. How does this passage connect with what you learned in a previous chapter about the Reformation? Which words help you remember what you have learned?

Interpreting Political Cartoons

Reading Like a Historian *Peter the Great wanted to westernize Russia. He even ordered Russian men to cut their beards so they would look more European.*

Woodcut showing Russian official cutting off a beard, artist unknown

15. Analyze Do you think the artist approved of Peter's rule? Why or why not?

Using the Internet

go.hrw.com
Practice Online
Keyword: SHL MON

16. The era of absolute monarchs was also a key period for the extension of government functions. Rulers set up more effective administrations and got involved in new activities, such as building hospitals. Using the keyword above, research expansion of the government's role in one country and write a report on your findings.

WRITING FOR THE SAT ✎

Think about the following issue:

The concept of absolutism influenced monarchs to varying degrees, and the monarchs' reigns affected their countries long after their deaths.

17. Assignment: Some monarchs left their countries in better condition than when they began their rule, while others left lasting damage. Choose three of the monarchs from the chapter and, in a brief essay, compare and contrast how absolutism affected those rulers' impact on their countries.

THE MONARCHS OF EUROPE **563**

Interpreting Political Cartoons

15. possible answer—The artist probably approved of Peter's rule because the tone of the cartoon is light, and he makes fun of the nobleman being forced to change his formal appearance.

Using the Internet

16. Go to the HRW Web site and enter the keyword shown to access a rubric for this activity.

KEYWORD: SHL MON

Writing for the SAT

17. Student essays should discuss three of the monarchs covered in the chapter. Essays should use supporting details and examples to make a logical argument about the rulers' impact on their countries. A rubric for this activity is provided in **CRF:** Writing for the SAT.

HOLT

History's Impact

▶ **Video Program: The Monarchs of Europe**
Refer to the Video Program Teacher's Guide for a discussion of the closing question.

Review and Assessment Resources

Review and Reinforce

📑 **CRF:** Chapter Review

🖥 **Quick Facts Transparency:** Visual Study Guide: The Monarchs of Europe

🔊 **Spanish Chapter Summaries Audio CD Program**

OSP **Holt PuzzlePro:** Quiz Show for ExamView

💿 **Quiz Game CD-ROM**

Assess

📑 **PASS:** Chapter Test, Forms A and B

📑 **Alternative Assessment Handbook**

OSP **ExamView Test Generator,** Chapter Test

💿 **Differentiated Instruction Modified Worksheets and Tests CD-ROM:** Chapter Test

HOAP **Holt Online Assessment Program** (in the Premier Online Edition)

Reteach/Intervene

📑 **Interactive Reader and Study Guide**

📑 **Differentiated Instruction Teacher Management System:** Lesson Plans for Differentiated Instruction

💿 **Differentiated Instruction Modified Worksheets and Tests CD-ROM:** Chapter Test

💿 **Interactive Skills Tutor CD-ROM**

go.hrw.com
Online Resources

KEYWORD: SHL TEACHER

Enlightenment and Revolution

CHAPTER 19 PLANNING GUIDE

Chapter Overview	Reproducible Resources	Technology Resources
CHAPTER 19 pp. 564–587 **Overview: In this chapter, students will study the effect of new discoveries and ideas about government and society during the Enlightenment. They will also learn how the influence of Enlightenment ideas led to the establishment of the United States.** KI 1, 2, 3; PI 1.2, 1.3, 1.4, 2.5, 3.1, 3.3 See pp. T32–T55 for a detailed correlation to the New York State Core Curriculum for Global History and Geography and the New York Learning Standards.	**Differentiated Instruction Teacher Management System: *** • Pacing Guide • Lesson Plans for Differentiated Instruction **Interactive Reader and Study Guide:** Chapter Summary* **Chapter Resource File*** • Writing About History • Social Studies Skill • Chapter Review **World History Outline Maps**	OSP **New York One-Stop Planner CD-ROM:** Calendar Planner **Live Ink© Online Reading Help** **Student Edition on Audio CD Program** **Differentiated Instruction Modified Worksheets and Tests CD-ROM** **Interactive Skills Tutor CD-ROM** **World History Primary Source Library CD-ROM** **Power Presentations with Video CD-ROM** **History's Impact: World History Video Program (VHS/DVD):** Enlightenment and Revolution
Section 1: **The Scientific Revolution** **The Main Idea:** New ways of thinking led to remarkable discoveries during the Scientific Revolution. PI 2.5, 3.1	**Differentiated Instruction Teacher Management System:** Section 1 Lesson Plan* **Interactive Reader and Study Guide:** Section 1 Summary* **Chapter Resource File*** • Vocabulary Builder: Section 1 • Biography: Carl Linnaeus • Primary Source: The Compatibility of Science and Religion	**Regents Review Transarency:** Section 1* **Map Transparency:** European Centers of Learning, c. 1750* **Quick Facts Transparency:** The Scientific Method* **Quick Facts Transparency:** Causes and Effects of the Scientific Revolution*
Section 2: **The Enlightenment** **The Main Idea:** European thinkers developed new ideas about government and society during the Enlightenment. PI 3.3	**Differentiated Instruction Teacher Management System:** Section 2 Lesson Plan* **Interactive Reader and Study Guide:** Section 2 Summary* **Chapter Resource File*** • Vocabulary Builder: Section 2 • Biography: Madame Geoffrin	**Regents Review Transparency:** Section 2* **Quick Facts Transparency:** Key Enlightenment Ideas* **Internet Activity:** John Locke
Section 3: **The American Revolution** **The Main Idea:** Enlightenment ideas led to revolution, independence, and a new government for the United States. PI 1.2, 1.3, 1.4	**Differentiated Instruction Teacher Management System:** Section 3 Lesson Plan* **Interactive Reader and Study Guide:** Section 3 Summary* **Chapter Resource File*** • Vocabulary Builder: Section 3 • Biography: Benjamin Franklin • Literature: *Rip Van Winkle* • History and Geography: Battles in the War for Independence	**Regents Review Transparency:** Section 3* **Map Transparency:** The Revolutionary War* **Internet Activity:** The Enlightenment

go.hrw.com	Print Resource	Transparency
LS Learning Styles	Audio CD	CD-ROM
Video	SE Student Edition	TE Teachers Edition

OSP One-Stop Planner CD-ROM   NY Standards Mastery
*also on One-Stop Planner CD-ROM

HOLT
History's Impact
World History Video Program (VHS/DVD)
Enlightenment and Revolution

Review, Assessment, Intervention

- **Global History and Geography Regents Test Prep Workbook**
- **Quick Facts Transparency:** Enlightenment and Revolution*
- **Spanish Chapter Summaries Audio CD Program**
- **Progress Assessment Support System (PASS):** Chapter Test*
- **Differentiated Instruction Modified Worksheets and Tests CD-ROM:** Modified Chapter Test
- OSP **New York One-Stop Planner CD-ROM:** ExamView Test Generator (English/Spanish)
- HOAP **Holt Online Assessment Program (HOAP),** in the Holt Premier Online Student Edition

---

- **PASS:** Section 1 Quiz*
- **Online Quiz:** Section 1
- **Alternative Assessment Handbook**

- **PASS:** Section 2 Quiz*
- **Online Quiz:** Section 2
- **Alternative Assessment Handbook**

- **PASS:** Section 3 Quiz*
- **Online Quiz:** Section 3
- **Alternative Assessment Handbook**

Power Presentation with Video CD-ROM

Power Presentations with Video are visual presentations of each chapter's main ideas. Presentations can be customized by including Quick Facts charts, images and maps from the textbook, and video clips.

Holt Online Learning

| go.hrw.com |
| **Teacher Resources** |
| KEYWORD: SHL TEACHER |

| go.hrw.com |
| **Student Resources** |
| KEYWORD: SHL ENL |

- Document-Based Questions
- Interactive Multimedia Activities

- Current Events
- Chapter-Based Internet Activities
- and more!

Holt Premier
Online Student Edition
Complete online support for interactivity, assessment, and reporting
- Interactive Maps and Notebook
- Homework Practice and Research Activities Online

CHAPTER 19 PLANNING GUIDE

The Big Picture

Peter N. Stearns

Scientific Revolution The Scientific Revolution was a big development in world history, and certainly in European history. European science had not been very advanced, but now it surged forward. New discoveries overturned traditions and provided unprecedented knowledge about the physical universe and the workings of the human body. Clear definitions of scientific methods emerged. The result was not only great innovation, but also the establishment of science as the basis for human knowledge—the first time science had held this position in any culture. Of course there were struggles with established religions, some of which continue, but the basic trend was clear.

Implications of the Scientific Revolution: The Enlightenment Growing literacy and weariness with earlier religious quarrels set a context for wide popular interest in the new science. Various intellectuals also began to apply new thinking to political and social topics. John Locke held a central role in setting up the Enlightenment, both in his praise of popular sovereignty and religious tolerance and in his belief in the educability of children. Enlightenment thinkers, centered in France, applied new methods to the study of government, praising constitutions, legal equality, and, in some cases, democracy. Criticism of older institutions like the church and the aristocracy ran strong. Enlightenment figures also praised technological progress, urged a reform of criminal justice, and established new social sciences, including economics. A few maverick voices claimed even more, staking out feminist and socialist arguments. The Enlightenment set an intellectual basis for a wide variety of reform and protest movements.

The American Revolution New ideas, the examples of the earlier English civil wars, and new, widely resented colonial measures by the British government set the context for the American Revolution and the ultimate establishment of national independence. Enlightenment ideas figured strongly in the new United States Constitution, including its protection of personal freedoms in the Bill of Rights. In turn, the American Revolution helped spur political change in other regions, including France.

Recent Scholarship

In *The Household and the Making of History: A Subversive View of the Western Past* (2004), Mary S. Hartman offers a challenging interpretation of gender relations in European society. She argues that distinctive family patterns set up unusual collaborations and tensions between men and women that paralleled more familiar developments in the early modern centuries, including science, in establishing distinctive Western institutions and ideas.

Differentiating Instruction

 Differentiated Instruction Teacher Management System
- Pacing Guide
- Lesson Plans for Differentiated Instruction

 Interactive Reader and Study Guide

Spanish Chapter Summaries Audio CD Program

Student Edition on Audio CD Program

 Differentiated Instruction Modified Worksheets and Tests CD-ROM
- Vocabulary Flash Cards
- Modified Vocabulary Builder Activities
- Modified Chapter Review Activity
- Modified Chapter Test

OSP One-Stop Planner CD-ROM
- ExamView Test Generator (English/Spanish)
- PuzzlePro
- Quiz Show for ExamView
- Transparencies and Videos

TE Differentiated Activities in the Teacher's Edition
- Foundations of Modern Science, p. 568
- Scientific Method Experiments, p. 569
- Odes to Reason, p. 575
- Discussing the Declaration of Independence, p. 584

Reading Like a Historian
Sam Wineburg

Our chapter quotes the Declaration of Independence and words familiar to many: "We hold these truths to be self-evident, that all men are created equal." However, as some of our students will point out, this documents' author, Thomas Jefferson, was himself a slaveholder. How could Jefferson write about equality while holding African Americans in bondage? Students will often see only one logical conclusion: Jefferson was a hypocrite.

Confronted with documents from the Mayan empire, we have little trouble recognizing the differences between that world and our own. But the Declaration of Independence presents a different kind of problem. Its language is so familiar that we presume it speaks directly to us. If there is a discrepancy between the words of this document and the behavior of its author, we conclude that the problem is not our understanding—but Jefferson's own moral failings.

The challenge in reading history is to understand what documents meant to the people who actually wrote them. This means trying to set aside our present-day conceptions long enough to ask what an author two hundred years ago might have meant. Is it possible that Jefferson intended something different by "all men are created equal" than how we understand the same words today?

The historian and journalist Garry Wills asks this question in his exhaustive study, *Inventing America: Jefferson's Declaration of Independence.* To understand Jefferson, Wills immersed himself in the same works of philosophy that Jefferson read.

Understanding Jefferson We should begin by recognizing that Jefferson shared in many of the taken-for-granted prejudices of his day—particularly in the way that European societies assumed intellectual superiority to those in Africa and Asia. However, Jefferson wrote this statement: "Whether further observation will or will not verify the conjecture that nature has been less bountiful to [Blacks] in the endowments of the head, I believe that in those of the heart she will be found to have done them justice."

Here Jefferson assumes a skeptical stance regarding differences in intellect between Blacks and Whites. But he concludes by stating that "nature" has done Africans "justice" —has put them on an equal footing—in issues of the heart. What are we to make of this curious statement? Is it a throw away line—a patronizing consolation prize in a world that valued head over heart?

Wills points out that this distinction was crucial to Jefferson. To him and the philosophers he drew on, it was the human heart that united humanity far more than the head. Blacks, for Jefferson, were equal to Whites in moral qualities that resided in the heart, in "benevolence, gratitude, and unshaken fidelity," and it is these qualities that represented the highest of human achievements. To the moral philosopher Thomas Hutcheson, whose thought influenced Jefferson's, all men are created equal in their moral capacity, "these natural rights equally belong to all. . . . Nature makes none masters, none slaves."

To us, the separation of head from heart seems like a cynical apology that permitted Jefferson to proclaim equality while enforcing bondage. But in Jefferson's world, this was a real distinction. To Jefferson, according to Wills, "accidental differences of body and mind were dwarfed by an all-important equality in the governing faculty of man. There is no inconsistency in his theory, whatever one may think of its validity. For him it was valid, and everything he wrote about Blacks . . . is derived from its principles."

Chapter Main Ideas

Section 1 New ways of thinking led to remarkable discoveries during the Scientific Revolution.

Section 2 European thinkers developed new ideas about government and society during the Enlightenment.

Section 3 Enlightenment ideas led to independence and a new government for the United States.

📖 New York Standards

Key Idea 1 The study of world history requires an understanding of world cultures and civilizations, including an analysis of important ideas, social and cultural values, beliefs, and traditions. This study also examines the human condition and the connections and interactions of people across time and space and the ways different people view the same event or issue from a variety of perspectives.

Key Idea 2 Establishing timeframes, exploring different periodizations, examining themes across time and within cultures, and focusing on important turning points in world history help organize the study of world cultures and civilizations.

Key Idea 3 Study of the major social, political, cultural, and religious developments in world history involves learning about the important roles and contributions of individuals and groups.

Key to Differentiating Instruction

Below Level

Basic-level activities designed for all students encountering new material

At Level

Intermediate-level activities designed for average students

Above Level

Challenging activities designed for honors and gifted and talented students

Standard English Mastery

Activities designed to improve standard English usage

CHAPTER

19 1550–1800

Enlightenment and Revolution

THE BIG PICTURE Beginning in the late 1500s, new discoveries and the use of reason in Europe during the Scientific Revolution and the Enlightenment led to changing ideas about government and society. Influenced by Enlightenment ideas, British colonists in North America established a new nation—the United States.

Theme SCIENCE AND TECHNOLOGY
Between about 1550 and 1800 scientists in Europe made advances in science through observation and experimentation. In this chapter you will study these discoveries in science and learn how they affected the world.

A Philosopher Giving a Lecture at the Orrery, by Joseph Wright of Derby, 1776

TIME LINE

CHAPTER EVENTS

1609 In Italy, Galileo develops the first telescope used for astronomy.

1690 John Locke publishes *Two Treatises on Civil Government*, arguing that government should protect people's natural rights.

1759 Voltaire publishes *Candide*, a novel attacking the church and other institutions of his time.

1600

1700

1750

WORLD EVENTS

1652 Dutch colonists arrive at the Cape of Good Hope.

1707 The Mughal Empire ends in India.

1769 Spanish missionaries begin founding missions in California.

564 CHAPTER 19

Introduce the Chapter

At Level

Enlightenment and Revolution

1. Write this John Locke quote for students to see: "New opinions are always suspected, and usually opposed, without any other reason but because they are not already common."

2. Guide students in a discussion of the meaning of the quote. When students understand the quote, ask them if they agree. Have them brainstorm examples, real or hypothetical, in which new ideas and opinions have been summarily rejected. As volunteers give responses, write them for students to see.

3. Tell students that in this chapter they will learn about a shift in ideas and opinions about nature and society.

4. Have students write a newspaper op-ed column in which they argue that new ideas should be given a fair chance and not rejected outright. Have students use examples from the class list to prove their point. **LS Verbal-Linguistic**

📝 **Alternative Assessment Handbook**, Rubrics 23: Newspapers; and 43: Writing to Persuade

• Chapter Preview •

HOLT
History's Impact
► **Video Program: Enlightenment and Revolution**
See the Video Teacher's Guide for strategies for using the video segment.

Reading Like a Historian
Analyzing Visuals Why do you think astronomers build models such as the one in the painting? *possible answers— to work out problems in three dimensions; to aid understanding; to educate others*

go.hrw.com
Online Resources

Chapter Resources:
KEYWORD: SHL ENL
Teacher Resources:
KEYWORD: SHL TEACHER

Reading like a Historian In this painting, a scientist gives a demonstration of an orrery, a device that shows the movement of the planets around the sun. The spectators respond to their new understanding of the universe with wonder and awe.

Analyzing Visuals What do you think the darkened room and the illuminated faces of the spectators symbolize?

See **Skills Handbook**, p. H26

1775	1783	1787
The American Revolutionary War begins.	The Treaty of Paris recognizes the United States as a nation.	American leaders write the U.S. Constitution.

1775

1780	1789
Tupac Amaru leads a peasant revolt in Peru.	The French Revolution begins.

ENLIGHTENMENT AND REVOLUTION **565**

Explore the Time Line

1. Who published an important work first, Voltaire or Locke? *Locke*

2. What was the argument of *Two Treatises on Civil Government*? *Government should protect people's natural rights.*

3. What happened in 1775? *The American Revolution began.*

4. About how many years after the Treaty of Paris recognized the United States as a nation was the U.S. Constitution written? *four years*

Info to Know

The Music of the Spheres During medieval times, people believed that Earth and the heavens were a series of huge spheres, one within the next. They also believed that Earth was at the center, the planets and stars were in the two closest spheres, and the outer spheres were inhabited by angels and other spirits. They thought that as these spheres revolved one inside another, they made heavenly music.

Make Inferences Where do you think these ideas about the solar system might have originated? *possible answers—based on descriptions in the Bible; opinions of scholars*

Answers

Reading Like a Historian *possible answer—The darkened room probably symbolizes lack of knowledge; the illuminated faces symbolize the enlightenment and knowledge that scientists experienced.*

Geography Starting Points

The Scientific Community For the thinkers during the Enlightenment, a remarkable amount of communication occurred through letters. Scientists wrote to each other and to friends who were scientifically inclined. Science and math scholar Father Marin Mersenne, a close friend of Descartes, would compile many of the letters and ideas for scientists during the Enlightenment.

Make Inferences Look at the map on this page. Why do you think these scientists did not simply meet each other face to face? *possible answers—lived far away from one another; travel was difficult; may have had local commitments*

🖨 **Map Transparency:** European Centers of Learning c. 1750

📖 **World History Outline Maps**

✳ **Interactive Map:** European Center of Learning, c. 1750

GEOGRAPHY Starting Points

✱ Interactive
EUROPEAN CENTERS OF LEARNING, c. 1750

● Observatories
● Leading academic centers

At Cambridge University in the late 1600s, Isaac Newton lectured on mathematics.

In Poland in the late 1400s Copernicus began his study of astronomy.

In Paris by the mid-1700s, people were reading Voltaire's philosophical works.

In Padua in 1609 Galileo created the first working telescope for astronomy.

Starting Points In Europe, beginning about 1550, a period of revolutionary scientific discovery began that would change the world forever. Later, in an era known as the Enlightenment, philosophers introduced new ways of thinking about government and society. By 1750, academic centers and observatories thrived throughout Europe.

1. **Analyze** Which nation had a concentration of leading academic centers in 1750?

2. **Predict** How do you think centers of learning influenced how Europeans viewed the world in the 1700s?

🔊 **Listen to History**

Go online to listen to an explanation of the starting points for this chapter.

go.hrw.com
Keyword: SHL ENL

566 CHAPTER 19

Skills Focus: Analyzing Maps

At Level

Social Studies Skill
Tour of the Enlightenment

Research Required

1. Review with students the various activities and events that occurred during the Enlightenment and Scientific Revolution.

2. Organize students into small groups. Tell them that they are members of the Royal Society of London, philosophers and scientists. Have students plan a trip that begins in London and travels to four other centers of the Enlightenment.

3. To make plans accurate, have students conduct research on cities, everyday life, and modes of travel in the 1600s and 1700s. Itineraries should include destinations, modes of travel, people to meet, and activities to undertake.

4. Have volunteers present their itineraries to the class. **LS Interpersonal**

📖 **Alternative Assessment Handbook**, Rubric 40: Writing to Describe

Answers

Geography Starting Points 1. *Great Britain;* **2.** *possible answer—probably changed their views dramatically and made them more open to new ideas*

1 The Scientific Revolution

BEFORE YOU READ

MAIN IDEA
New ways of thinking led to remarkable discoveries during the Scientific Revolution.

READING FOCUS
1. What changes led to the dawn of modern science?
2. What discoveries occurred in astronomy, physics, and math during the Scientific Revolution?
3. How did early scientists advance knowledge in biology and chemistry?
4. How did scientific ideas move beyond the realm of science and affect society?

KEY TERMS AND PEOPLE
geocentric theory
Scientific Revolution
scientific method
René Descartes
Nicolaus Copernicus
heliocentric theory
Galileo Galilei
Isaac Newton

NEW YORK

PI 2.5 Students investigate key events and developments and major turning points in world history.

PI 3.1 Students analyze the roles and contributions of individuals and groups to social, political, economic, cultural, and religious practices and activities.

THE INSIDE STORY

How was a college student inspired to change the future of science?

Nicolaus Copernicus seemed destined to become an astronomer. He began his studies in Poland, where he studied many subjects, including astronomy. At that time, astronomy courses taught little more than methods of calculating the dates of holy days. But for Copernicus, the course ignited a passion for astronomy.

However, his uncle Lucas, a bishop, wanted Copernicus to have a church career. He soon sent Copernicus to the university in Bologna, Italy, to study church law. Copernicus rented a room from an astronomy professor and assisted with his research. In 1497 Copernicus observed the moon eclipse the sun. As a result, his excitement for astronomy continued to grow.

Copernicus eventually made a living as a doctor, but his first love was always astronomy. Throughout his life Copernicus carefully observed the heavens, made calculations, and developed a mathematical formula that proved the earth rotated around the sun. The world of science would never be the same. ■

In the late 1400s astronomer Nicholas Copernicus proved the earth rotated around the sun. ▶
The Astronomer Copernicus: Conversation With God, by Jan Matejko, 1800s

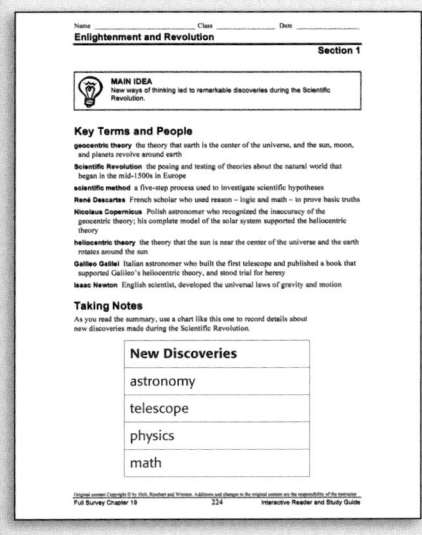

DESTINED TO STUDY THE STARS

Teach the Main Idea

At Level

The Scientific Revolution

1. **Teach** Ask students the Reading Focus questions to teach this section.

2. **Apply** Draw four rectangles for students to see. Label them with the names of the four topics in this section: Dawn of Modern Science; Discoveries in Astronomy, Physics, and Math; Discoveries in Biology and Chemistry, and Science and Society. Have students copy the rectangles onto their papers and fill them in with discoveries, names of key scientists, and other important details.

3. **Review** As you review the section, have students describe how scientific discoveries changed the way people viewed the world.

4. **Practice/Homework** Have students write a research proposal from the point of view of Galileo, Newton, or Vesalius. **LS Visual-Spatial, Verbal-Linguistic**

Alternative Assessment Handbook, Rubric 1: Acquiring Information

---

Getting Started

Use the **Interactive Reader and Study Guide** to familiarize students with the section content.

📖 **Interactive Reader and Study Guide**, Section 1

Name _____ Class _____ Date _____
Enlightenment and Revolution

Section 1

💡 **MAIN IDEA**
New ways of thinking led to remarkable discoveries during the Scientific Revolution.

Key Terms and People

geocentric theory the theory that earth is the center of the universe, and the sun, moon, and planets revolve around earth

Scientific Revolution the posing and testing of theories about the natural world that began in the mid-1500s in Europe

scientific method a five-step process used to investigate scientific hypotheses

René Descartes French scholar who used reason – logic and math – to prove basic truths

Nicolaus Copernicus Polish astronomer who recognized the inaccuracy of the geocentric theory; his complete model of the solar system supported the heliocentric theory

heliocentric theory the theory that the sun is near the center of the universe and the earth rotates around the sun

Galileo Galilei Italian astronomer who built the first telescope and published a book that supported Galileo's heliocentric theory, and stood trial for heresy

Isaac Newton English scientist, developed the universal laws of gravity and motion

Taking Notes

As you read the summary, use a chart like this one to record details about new discoveries made during the Scientific Revolution.

New Discoveries
astronomy
telescope
physics
math

Original content Copyright © by Holt, Rinehart and Winston. Additions and changes to the original content are the responsibility of the instructor.
Full Survey Chapter 19   224   Interactive Reader and Study Guide

---

📄 **CRF:** Vocabulary Builder: Section 1

Taking Notes

Astronomy—heliocentric theory, elliptical orbits; Telescope—Galileo confirms that planets orbit the sun with first telescope used for astronomy in 1609; Physics and Math—calculus, universal laws of gravity and motion

Reading Focus

❶ What changes led to the dawn of modern science? *traditional authorities challenged; new theories posed and tested; exploration led to closer study of natural world; development of scientific method*

Dawn of Modern Science

Define What is the geocentric theory? *earth is center of universe; sun, moon, and planets revolve around earth*

Identify Cause and Effect How did exploration affect the development of modern science? *discoveries outside the realm of ancient scholars; led to closer study of natural world; need for accurate knowledge*

Contrast How was the scientific method different from previous methods of understanding? *reliance on testing ideas by experimentation, rather than accepting the view of traditional authorities*

Info to Know

Scientists or Philosophers? During the 1600s, those who investigated nature were not referred to as scientists. Instead, they were called "natural philosophers." Their tools were referred to as "philosophical instruments." Mathematicians were usually called "geometers" after the most advanced branch of math at the time.

Primary Source

"The truth is the science of Nature has been already too long made only a work of the brain and the fancy: It is now high time that it should return to the plainness and soundness of observations on material and obvious things."
—Robert Hooke, *Micrographia*, 1665

Answers

Linking to Today *It allowed biologists to see whole cells for the first time.*

568

TAKING NOTES
Take notes on new discoveries during the Scientific Revolution.

New Discoveries
astronomy
telescope
physics
math

NEW YORK
CC Unit 5-A1
The development of scientific methods

Dawn of Modern Science

When some scholars in the Middle Ages had questions about the natural world, they sought answers from traditional authorities—the church and ancient scholars. In the mid-1500s, however, scholars began to challenge tradition as they began to think in new ways.

The Old View One example of how scholars relied on traditional authorities was in their beliefs about the structure of the universe. People believed that the earth was the center of the universe and that the sun, moon, and planets revolved around the earth. This viewpoint was called the **geocentric theory**.

The Greek philosopher Aristotle proposed the geocentric theory in the 300s BC. The Greek astronomer Ptolemy expanded upon Aristotle's ideas in the AD 200s. These ideas were upheld by the church, which taught that God put the earth at the center of the universe. For centuries, scholars and the church were the accepted authorities for European intellectuals.

New Viewpoints In the Middle Ages, scholars in Europe learned about scientific advances in the Arab world. By the mid-1500s, they began to challenge traditional authorities.

They posed theories about the natural world and developed procedures to test those ideas. Historians have called this new way of thinking the **Scientific Revolution**.

Why were Europeans open to new ideas at this time? One reason was exploration. When explorers journeyed to Africa, Asia, and the Americas, they found people and animals they had never seen before. The ancient scholars could provide no information about these new lands. Perhaps there were other things to be discovered that the ancients had not known.

The Age of Exploration also led scientists to study the natural world more closely. Navigators, for example, needed more accurate instruments and geographic knowledge to help find their way across vast oceans. The more that scientists examined the natural world, however, the more they found that it did not match ancient beliefs.

The Scientific Method Scientists eventually developed a new approach to investigation and discovery called the **scientific method**. The scientific method consists of five basic steps. First, scientists identify a problem. Next, they form a hypothesis that can be tested. They then perform experiments to test the hypothesis.

Linking TO Today

The Science of Cells

Since the Scientific Revolution, scientists have continued to use the scientific method to make remarkable discoveries. Mary Osborn, a cell biologist in Göttingen, Germany, researches cytoskeletons, or the structures that form the skeleton of cells. In the 1970s she focused her research on microtubules, tiny tubes that move important substances throughout cells. She developed a new microscopic technique that allowed her to see that microtubules form continuous lines that snake through cells.

One of her colleagues in the scientific community, however, dismissed her findings as false. At that time, biologists used electron microscopes to study cells. Electron microscopes required scientists to slice cells very thinly to view them. For this reason, biologists had never before seen microtubules intact.

Mary Osborn's microscopic technique allowed biologists to see whole cells for the first time. Scientists now use her technique widely, most notably for improved cancer diagnoses. More reliable diagnoses allow doctors to treat cancer patients more effectively than ever before.

Analyze How did Osborn's technique allow scientists to see cells in an entirely new way?

Mary Osborn in her laboratory in Göttingen, Germany ▶

Differentiating Instruction

Below Level

Special Education Students

Materials: poster paper, current science and technology magazines, scissors, glue

1. Review with students the idea that the foundations of modern science were built during the Scientific Revolution.

2. Organize students into mixed-ability pairs.

3. Have students search current magazines for images of things made possible by modern science, particularly in the realm of astronomy, math, physics, biology, and chemistry. Possible images could include machines and people engaged in scientific study.

4. Have students create a collage with images they find. Display collages for students to see.
LS Visual-Spatial

Alternative Assessment Handbook, Rubric 8: Collages

They record the results of the experiments. Finally, they analyze the results of the experiments to form a conclusion that either proves or disproves the hypothesis.

Two of the most important scholars who helped develop the scientific method were Francis Bacon and René Descartes (day-KAHRT). In England, Francis Bacon wrote in 1620 that the only true way to gain scientific knowledge was through experimentation—observing, measuring, explaining, and verifying. In France, meanwhile, René Descartes placed more emphasis on reason. He believed that everything should be doubted until it could be proven by reason. Descartes relied on mathematics and logic to prove basic truths.

The ideas of Bacon and Descartes continue to influence modern scientific methods. Scientists today use observation and experimentation along with mathematical logic to achieve a deeper understanding of the natural world.

READING CHECK **Find the Main Idea** What was the Scientific Revolution?

Discoveries in Astronomy, Physics, and Math

Early scientists made significant contributions in astronomy, physics, and math. Their work began to explain the complexities of the solar system and the limits of the physical world.

Copernicus In the early 1500s Polish astronomer **Nicolaus Copernicus** recognized that the geocentric theory did not explain the movements of the sun, moon, and planets accurately. After years of careful observation, he came to the conclusion that the sun, not the earth, was near the center of the solar system. Copernicus's discovery that the earth revolves around the sun is called the **heliocentric theory.**

The idea that the earth orbits the sun was not completely new. But Copernicus developed a detailed mathematical explanation of how the process worked. In addition, Copernicus was the first scientist to create a complete model of the solar system that combined physics, astronomy, and mathematics.

Copernicus did not publish his conclusions in his most famous book, *On the Revolutions of the Heavenly Spheres*, until the last year of his life. He knew the church would oppose his work

because his work contradicted the teachings of the church. He was also concerned about the weaknesses of his theory. His mathematical formulas did not predict the positions of the planets very well, and Copernicus did not want to face ridicule for these weaknesses.

Copernicus died in 1543, shortly after his revolutionary work was published. Other scientists would further develop and expand upon Copernicus's ideas.

Brahe and Kepler One of those scientists was Tycho Brahe (brah), a Danish astronomer. When a bright object appeared in the sky over Denmark in 1572, Brahe wrote a book proving that the object was a newly visible star that was far away. He called it a supernova, the name still used for distant exploding stars that suddenly become visible on earth.

Brahe's book impressed King Frederick II of Denmark, who gave Brahe money to build two observatories. There, Brahe developed his own system to explain planetary movement. He believed that the sun revolved around the earth, but that the other five known planets in the solar system revolved around the sun.

Brahe later moved to Prague and hired a German mathematician named Johannes Kepler as his assistant. Brahe needed help to form a mathematical theory from the detailed measurements he had made of the planets.

READING SKILLS

Visualizing
To help you understand the heliocentric theory, draw a circle in the center of a piece of paper to represent the sun. Then draw circles around the "sun" to represent the earth and the planets.

THE SCIENTIFIC METHOD **QUICK FACTS**

The Scientific Method is a set of techniques for acquiring new knowledge about the natural world based on observable, measurable evidence.

Step 1 Identify a problem or a research question to be answered.

Step 2 Form a hypothesis that can be tested. A hypothesis is a proposed answer to the research question and is based on previous knowledge.

Step 3 Perform experiments to test the hypothesis.

Step 4 Record the results of the experiments.

Step 5 Analyze the results of the experiments to form a conclusion that either proves or disproves the hypothesis.

Direct Teach

Reading Focus

② What discoveries occurred in astronomy, physics, and math during the Scientific Revolution? *heliocentric theory; planets orbited sun; predictable laws of movement; law of universal gravitation; calculus*

Discoveries in Astronomy, Physics, and Math

Recall Why did Copernicus not publish his work until the last year of his life? *he knew the Church would oppose it; uncertain about weaknesses of theory*

Contrast What set Copernicus's work apart from that of previous scientists? *created a complex model of solar system that combined physics, astronomy, and mathematics*

Make Generalizations Based on Frederick II's actions, what role do you think rulers and patrons played in the Scientific Revolution? *financed projects and experiments*

CRF: Primary Source: The Compatibility of Science and Religion

QUICK FACTS **The Scientific Method**
Evaluate Why must scientists analyze results instead of skipping the final step and going on to the next experiment? *They must determine the meaning of results before deciding what the next experiment should be.*

Quick Facts Transparency: The Scientific Method

Differentiating Instruction

Above Level

Advanced Learners/Gifted and Talented

1. Review with students the steps in the scientific method. Briefly discuss the concept of a controlled experiment.

2. Give students some examples of simple experiments they could do at home. Have students generate short lists of experiments they would like to try.

3. Check student lists to make sure they are appropriate. Experiments should be controlled, relatively simple, safe, and ethical.

4. Have students choose an experiment, document their question, and form a hypothesis. Then, have them document their experiment and results. Remind students not to falsify data if the experiment did not go how they expected.

5. Have students create visuals to show the steps of their experiment. Have volunteers present their experiments to the class. **LS** **Logical-Mathematical, Visual-Spatial**

Alternative Assessment Handbook, Rubric 1: Acquiring Information

Answers

Reading Check *a new way of thinking about the natural world that challenged traditional views and instead relied upon experimentation*

Discoveries in Astronomy, Physics, and Math

Identify What valuable contribution did Kepler make? *proved that planets had elliptical orbits around the sun*

Make Inferences Why were Galileo's books so controversial? *They contradicted the official Church viewpoint that the sun orbited Earth.*

Evaluate What do you think was Newton's most important discovery? Why? *possible answers—idea that planets and stars move according to predictable laws, expressed mathematically; new view of the universe*

MISCONCEPTION ///ALERT\\\

Though it is often perceived that scientists rely purely on facts and data, early scientists had a good measure of what might be perceived as superstition. Girolamo Cardano, a doctor, natural philosopher, and mathematician, supposedly had the gift of prophesy and predicted the date of his own death. Isaac Newton studied alchemy and spent his time searching the Bible for clues about the end of the world.

After Brahe's death, Johannes Kepler published the result of Brahe's measurements of the orbit of Mars. These measurements led Kepler to solve the main problem of Copernican theory. Copernicus had assumed that the planets orbited the sun in a circle. Kepler found through the Mars measurements that this assumption was not true. He was the first astronomer to prove that the planets orbited the sun in an oval pattern, or ellipse.

Brahe had wanted to prove Copernicus wrong. Instead, his measurements led Kepler to prove that the heliocentric theory was right. Kepler's mathematical model of the solar system was also correct.

📹 **NEW YORK**
CC Unit 5-A2
The work of Galileo and Newton

Galileo Copernican theory was supported and by **Galileo Galilei**, an Italian scientist. After learning about a sailor's spyglass that allowed one to see distant objects, Galileo built the first telescope used for astronomy in 1609, which he used to scan the heavens.

Galileo was the first scientist to observe Saturn, the craters on the moon, sunspots, and the moons of Jupiter. He also discovered that the Milky Way was made up of stars. He described these amazing discoveries in 1610 in a book called *Starry Messenger*.

Sir Isaac Newton The English scientist **Isaac Newton** changed the world of science by bringing together astronomy, physics, and mathematics. As a young man, Newton wondered if gravity affected the universe the way that it affected objects on earth. Years later, his assistant wrote about Newton's questioning.

HISTORY'S VOICES

❝Whilst he was musing in a garden it came into his thought that the same power of gravity (which made an apple fall from the tree to the ground) was not limited to a certain distance from the earth, but must extend much farther than was usually thought—Why not as high as the Moon[?]❞
—John Conduitt, *Conduitt's Account of Newton's Life at Cambridge*, 1727

In 1687 Newton published his greatest work, *The Mathematical Principles of Natural Philosophy*, also known as the *Principia*. In this book, he explained his law of universal gravitation. This law states that gravity affects objects in the universe as well as on earth. Just as gravity causes an apple to fall from a tree, gravity keeps the planets in their orbits.

From these findings, Newton developed a new kind of mathematics called calculus, which he used to predict the effects of gravity. Controversy soon erupted, however. The German philosopher Gottfried von Leibniz independently developed calculus at the same time. Leibniz and Newton accused each other of plagiarism and feuded for many years. Historians now believe that it was simply a case of independent discovery by two very talented men.

READING CHECK **Contrast** How did Copernicus and Brahe differ in their views of the universe?

Themes Through Time

ASTRONOMY

SCIENCE AND TECHNOLOGY Early astronomers studied the sun, moon, and planets to help create calendars or assist with navigation. After the Scientific Revolution, the science of astronomy expanded to include the study of the solar system, the stars in the Milky Way galaxy, and other more distant galaxies and stellar formations.

c. 150 Ptolemy writes that the earth is the center of the universe. He remains the authority on astronomy until the 1600s.

499 During the Gupta Empire in India, the astronomer Aryabhata writes that the spherical earth rotates on its axis.

500

c. 600 Mayan astronomers compile detailed observations of the heavens and acquire the knowledge to predict solar eclipses.

570 CHAPTER 19

Skills Focus: Identifying Main Idea and Details   [At Level]

Reading Skill
Astronomers and Their Achievements

1. Draw the graphic organizer for students to see. Omit the italicized answers.

2. Have students copy and complete the graphic organizer. Then, have volunteers fill in the class graphic organizer. **LS** **Visual-Spatial**

📝 **Alternative Assessment Handbook**, Rubric 13: Graphic Organizers

Astronomers and Their Achievements

- *heliocentric model of solar system*
- *made detailed measurements*
- Copernicus
- Brahe
- **Astronomers**
- Kepler
- Galileo
- *planets' orbits are ellipses*
- *first working telescope, Milky Way made of stars*

Answers

Reading Check *Copernicus—all planets orbit the sun; Brahe—sun orbits Earth, other planets orbit sun*

Discoveries in Biology and Chemistry

Just as astronomers moved away the works of ancient Greeks, other scientists used the scientific method to acquire new knowledge. As a result, during the Scientific Revolution, scientists made great discoveries in the fields of biology and chemistry.

Biology In the Middle Ages, European doctors relied on the works of the ancient Greek physician Galen. But Galen's works were inaccurate. He had assumed that human anatomy was similar to that of animals, because he had never dissected a human body.

Andreas Vesalius, a Flemish doctor, became known for his work in anatomy at the University of Padua in Italy. In 1539 a judge learned of his work and made the bodies of executed criminals available to Vesalius for dissection. Vesalius hired artists to produce accurate drawings. He published his greatest work, *On the Workings of the Human Body*, in 1543.

Vesalius laid the groundwork for English physician William Harvey to observe and explain the workings of the human heart in the early 1600s. Harvey described how blood and the circulatory system functioned.

Later in the 1600s Dutch scientist Antony van Leeuwenhoek used his interest in developing a magnifying lens to invent the micro-

scope. He was the first person to describe the appearance of bacteria, red blood cells, yeast, and other microorganisms.

English physicist and inventor Robert Hooke used an early microscope to describe the appearance of plants at a microscopic level. In addition to his many achievements in physics and mathematics, Hooke is credited with creating the term *cell*.

Chemistry Robert Boyle is often called the father of modern chemistry. Boyle was the first chemist to define an element. His 1661 work, *The Sceptical Chemist*, described matter as a cluster of tiny particles (now called atoms or molecules). Boyle stated that changes in matter happened when these clusters were rearranged. His most significant contribution to chemistry was Boyle's law, which describes how temperature, volume, and pressure affect gases.

French chemist Antoine-Laurent Lavoisier (lah-vwaH-zee-ay) developed methods for precise measurements in the 1700s. He discovered the law of Conservation of Mass, which proved that matter could not be created or destroyed. Lavoisier recognized and named oxygen, introduced the metric system of measurements, and invented the first periodic table, which included 33 elements.

THE IMPACT TODAY

To pass a scuba diving certification test, divers must answer questions about how Boyle's law relates to safely ascending and descending underwater.

READING CHECK Summarize
What were the major contributions made in biology and chemistry?

1610 Using a telescope, Galileo confirms that the planets orbit the sun and observes that the moon's surface is not smooth but rough and jagged.

1453 Nicolaus Copernicus publishes a book proposing that the sun is the center of the universe.

1500

2000

1990 The Hubble Telescope is launched and starts recording spectacular images of the universe like this one of a dying star.

1905 Albert Einstein's theory of relativity changes the world's views on time and space.

Skills Focus UNDERSTANDING THEMES

Infer What impact did the invention and refinement of the telescope have on the field of astronomy?

ENLIGHTENMENT AND REVOLUTION **571**

4 How did scientific ideas move beyond the realm of science and affect society? *Science and religion combined to produce artistic achievements of the Renaissance; scientists also challenged some of the traditional ideas of the Church.*

Science and Society

Contrast How did the basis of Christianity differ from the basis of science? *Christianity was based on faith; science was based on the pursuit of knowledge.*

Analyze How did Renaissance artists combine science and religion? *studied anatomy, experimented with chemistry of paints and nature of light, used math to create balance; works dedicated to God*

Info to Know

Other Discoveries During the Scientific Revolution, the barometer was developed and used to prove that air pressure varies with altitude. Newton and Descartes found that light occurs in waves and that colors result from varying frequencies of light. Boyle discovered that chemicals interact mechanically, and not through some spirit or principle within them. Finally, advances in medicine showed that wounds should be treated with a dressing rather than a red-hot iron, and that instruments should be used to aid difficult births.

Primary Source

"Cogito ergo sum." (Latin)
("I think, therefore I am.")
—René Descartes

Answers

Faces of History *possible answer— because his discoveries advanced science*

572

▼ Standing before Church officials, Galileo defended his belief that the planets orbit the sun.

Galileo Galilei Before the Inquisition, 1633, by Joseph-Nicolas Robert-Fleury, 1847

FACES OF HISTORY

Galileo GALILEI
1564–1642

Many people considered the sentencing of Galileo in 1633 to life imprisonment a great tragedy. Efforts to clear his name continued for centuries after his death. But as late as 1822, the Vatican still banned Galileo's *Dialogue concerning Two Chief World Systems.*

The church gradually changed its views toward Galileo. A church commission reopened his case in 1983. In 1992 Pope John Paul II declared that the church had wrongfully condemned Galileo.

Infer Why do you think the Catholic Church decided to reexamine Galileo's case in the 1980s?

Science and Society

As science began to assume greater significance in society, the question of the role of the Roman Catholic Church in a changing culture became important. At this time the church opposed the views of many scientists, such as Galileo. However, the church benefitted from the new scientific discoveries that made Renaissance art and architecture possible.

Science and the Church As the most powerful institution in Europe during the Middle Ages, the church had also been the primary resource for knowledge and learning. The church had established cathedral schools, many of which became universities, to train people to run the church. How did scientists and their innovative views fit into the church's established structure?

Most European scientists were Christian and did not want to challenge the role of Christianity in society. However, conflicts between the church and science developed. The church explained the world through inspiration and revealed truth. Early science sought to explain the world through the accumulation of facts and logical reasoning.

The early church rejected some of the beliefs of ancient Greek scholars because they were not Christians. Some leaders in the

church also feared reason as an enemy of faith. But, the church leaders eventually became convinced that reason could be used to serve the needs of the church instead of undermining them. To a limited extent, the church began to embrace some of the achievements of the Scientific Revolution.

Galileo's theories, however, brought him into direct conflict with the church. Church leaders pressured Galileo not to support the ideas of Copernicus. Still, Galileo continued his studies. In 1632 he published *Dialogue concerning Two Chief World Systems.* Although this book included the views of both Ptolemy and Copernicus, it clearly showed Galileo's support of Copernican theory. Pope Urban VII angrily ordered Galileo to Rome to stand trial before the Inquisition—the church institution to stamp out heresy, or dissenting views.

In April 1633 Galileo stood trial before the Inquisition. Galileo reluctantly stated that he would not use Copernican theory in his work so that he would receive a lenient sentence. The pope ordered Galileo placed under house arrest in his villa near Florence, where he spent the remainder of his life.

Science and Art During the Renaissance, the study of art and architecture were not separate from the study of science. Artists learned human anatomy so they could paint the body.

Skills Focus: Summarizing

At Level

Reading Skill
The Trial of Galileo

1. Review the information in the text about the trial of Galileo. You may wish to give students more information about the Inquisition.

2. Organize students into small groups. Have each group write a skit about Galileo's trial. Characters could include Galileo, a few inquisitors, and few spectators.

3. Allow enough time for students to prepare and rehearse their skits. Then, have students perform their skits for the class.

LS **Kinesthetic, Interpersonal**

Alternative Assessment Handbook, Rubric 33: Skits and Reader's Theater

Artists experimented with the chemistry of paints and the nature of light. Painters used mathematics to create compositions of perfect balance. The use of mathematics and physics were crucial to the great architecture and engineering achievements of the time.

Science and religion thus combined to produce the great artistic achievements of the Renaissance. Much of the great art and architecture of the Renaissance was dedicated to the glory of God and would have been impossible without reason and science. But the artists and architects had not challenged a basic belief of the church. Rather, astronomers such as Galileo did.

Science and Community The Scientific Revolution had firmly established a new way of thinking about the physical world. Great advances had been made in the disciplines of astronomy, physics, biology, and chemistry. In turn, those advances had influenced developments in the arts and architecture. As the Scientific Revolution spread, its impact would reach far beyond the laboratories and observatories of scientists.

Soon, philosophers and scholars would seek new understandings about society. They would reexamine old ideas government, religion, education, and economics. They would

also wonder if reason could solve the age-old problems of poverty, war, and ignorance. The new ways of thinking that emerged from the Scientific Revolution would lead to even more dramatic changes, as you will read about in the next section.

READING CHECK **Draw Conclusions** How did the Scientific Revolution have an impact beyond the realm of science?

CAUSES AND EFFECTS OF THE SCIENTIFIC REVOLUTION   QUICK FACTS

CAUSES

- Exploration and expansion of trade
- Continuing study of ancient authorities
- Development of the scientific method

EFFECTS

- Beginnings of modern science
- Belief in progress and the power of reason
- New view of the universe as a well-ordered system

Reading Focus

Science and Society

Identity What were some of the long-term effects of the Scientific Revolution? *development of modern science; belief in progress and the power of reason*

Predict How might other parts of society be affected by the ideas of the Scientific Revolution? *possible answers—Government might be affected because people would become less willing to accept authority without reason; religion might become affected because people would be more likely to look for experimental proof.*

Quick Facts Transparency: Causes and Effects of the Scientific Revolution

---

Close

Have students describe the changes in ideas brought about by the Scientific Revolution.

Review

Online Quiz, Section 1

Assess

SE **Section 1 Assessment**

Progress Assessment: Section 1 Quiz

Alternative Assessment Handbook

Reteach/Intervene

Interactive Reader and Study Guide, Section 1

Interactive Skills Tutor CD-ROM

SECTION 1 ASSESSMENT

go.hrw.com
Online Quiz
Keyword: SHL ENL HP

Reviewing Ideas, Terms, and People

1. **a. Define** What was the **geocentric theory** of the universe?
   b. Analyze How did the **scientific method** change the way people learned about the natural world?
   c. Evaluate What effect would the scientific method have on the acceptance of the geocentric theory?

2. **a. Identify** What was the **heliocentric theory**?
   b. Contrast In what way did Galileo's view of the universe differ from Aristotle's view?
   c. Elaborate Why do you think the Catholic Church objected to the Galileo's theories so strongly?

3. **a. Recall** Who was the traditional authority on human anatomy before the Scientific Revolution?
   b. Explain How did Vesalius acquire more accurate knowledge about human anatomy?

4. **a. Describe** What effects did the Scientific Revolution have on art and architecture?
   b. Draw Conclusions Why do you think artists and architects were eager to embrace the ideas of the Scientific Revolution?

Critical Thinking

5. **Identify Cause and Effect** Copy the graphic organizer below and use it to list the causes and the effects of new discoveries made during the Scientific Revolution.

Causes → New Discoveries → Effects

FOCUS ON WRITING

6. **Persuasion** Suppose that you are an astronomer during the mid-1500s. Write a short speech explaining why the scientific method would reveal truth more accurately than reliance upon traditional authorities.

ENLIGHTENMENT AND REVOLUTION **573**

Section 1 Assessment Answers

1. **a.** The earth was at the center of the universe.
   b. gave them step-by-step process to test their hypotheses
   c. possible answer—would disprove the geocentric theory

2. **a.** The sun was the center of universe.
   b. Aristotle—geocentric theory; Galileo—heliocentric theory
   c. possible answer—because his ideas challenged Church teachings

3. **a.** Galen
   b. by dissecting human bodies

4. **a.** New knowledge led to artistic achievement
   b. provided new way of depicting physical world

5. Causes—traditional theories challenged, age of exploration, examination of natural world, accurate instruments; Effects—scientific method, new models of solar system, advances in math, anatomy, and chemistry; conflicts with Church

6. Student speeches should explain the process of the scientific method.

Answers

Reading Check *led people to question the Church, inspired great artistic achievements, led to new ideas about government, religion, education, and economics*

573

Preteach

Getting Started

Use the **Interactive Reader and Study Guide** to familiarize students with the section content.

📖 **Interactive Reader and Study Guide,** Section 2

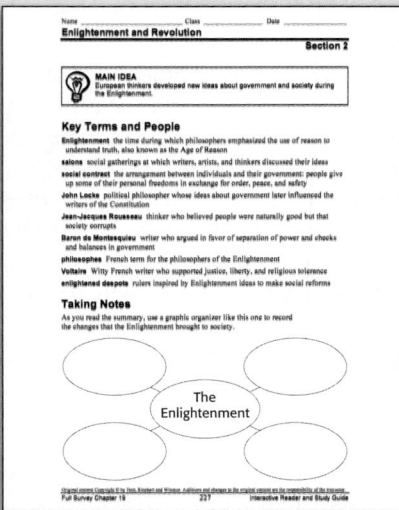

Academic Vocabulary

Review with students the high-use academic term in this section.

rational having reason or understanding (p. 576)

📝 **CRF:** Vocabulary Builder: Section 2

Taking Notes

belief in reason as the key to all; new views on government—social contract, government's purpose to protect rights, otherwise it is in breach of contract, checks on power of king; new views on society

go.hrw.com
Online Resources

KEYWORD: SHL ENL
ACTIVITY: John Locke

The Enlightenment

BEFORE YOU READ

MAIN IDEA
European thinkers developed new ideas about government and society during the Enlightenment.

READING FOCUS
1. How was the Enlightenment influenced by reason?
2. What new views did philosophers have about government?
3. What new views did philosophers have about society?
4. How did Enlightenment ideas spread?

KEY TERMS AND PEOPLE
Enlightenment
salons
social contract
John Locke
Jean-Jacques Rousseau
Baron de Montesquieu
philosophes
Voltaire
enlightened despots

 NEW YORK

PI 3.3 Students examine the social, cultural, political, economic, and religious norms and values of Western and other world cultures.

Engraving of Voltaire imprisoned in the Bastille, by François Bouchot, 1800s.

▲ **Voltaire began writing an epic poem in prison.**

THE INSIDE STORY
Why was a French philosopher jailed for his writings? In the early 1700s François-Marie Arouet was the toast of Paris. His witty, satirical verses delighted Parisian aristocrats. But in 1717 he may have mocked the wrong man. The Duke of Orleans, who ruled France as regent until the young king Louis XV came of age, believed Arouet made fun of him. Outraged, the Duke of Orleans imprisoned Arouet in the Bastille prison for 11 months.

While in prison, Arouet began writing more serious works. He wrote his first play, called *Oedipe*, which would secure his reputation as the greatest French playwright of his time. He also completed an epic poem about Henry IV called *La Henriade*. But Arouet would be best known for his philosophical works, which he would write under the pen name Voltaire. ■

The Age of Reason

The Scientific Revolution convinced many European thinkers about the power of reason. With the scientific method and reason, scientists had made countless discoveries about the physical world. Could reason be used to study human nature and society as well?

In the 1600s a new generation of philosophers began to view reason as the best way to understand truth. They came to the remarkable conclusion that reason could be used to solve all human problems. This exciting time of optimism and possibility is now called the **Enlightenment,** or the Age of Reason.

Ideas of the Enlightenment inspired educated people throughout Europe and beyond. People gathered in cof-

---

Teach the Main Idea
At Level

The Enlightenment

1. **Teach** Ask students the Reading Focus questions to teach this section.

2. **Apply** Have students create flashcards to learn the ideas of the philosophers in this section. Have them write the idea on one side of the card and the philosopher's name on the other side. Some ideas are similar, so students should write them as they appear in the text.

3. **Review** As you review the section, have students use their flashcards to quiz each other on the philosophers and their ideas.

4. **Practice/Homework** Have students create a resume for one of the philosophers in this section. **LS Visual-Spatial, Verbal-Linguistic**

📝 **Alternative Assessment Handbook**, Rubric 31: Resumés

feehouses and public spaces to debate the new ideas. Many writers published their ideas in books, magazines, and inexpensive pamphlets to help spread their ideas among educated readers. They were all inspired by the exciting notion that the problems of the world could be solved by educated people.

By the time the Enlightenment reached its peak in the 1700s, Paris was a center of intellectual activity. Eager to promote the new ideas, many wealthy Parisian women began hosting social gatherings called **salons**. These women brought together philosophers, artists, scientists, and writers regularly to discuss their ideas.

READING CHECK Find the Main Idea What exciting conclusion did philosophers reach during the Enlightenment?

New Views on Government

As the Enlightenment began, European thinkers began looking for ways to apply reason in order to improve the human condition. Some of these thinkers began to examine the organization of government.

Thomas Hobbes The English thinker Thomas Hobbes wrote about his views on government in his 1651 book, *Leviathan*. His experience of the violence and upheaval of the English civil war persuaded him that people were selfish and greedy. In the natural state, he wrote, people would lead lives that were "solitary, poor, nasty, brutish, and short."

Hobbes believed that people needed governments to impose order. He argued that people in a society should agree to give up some freedoms to a strong leader in exchange for the peace, safety, and order that government could provide. Hobbes called this exchange between society and government the **social contract**. He believed that absolute monarchy was the best form of government because an absolute monarchy had the power of a leviathan, a massive sea monster. That strong, centralized power could be used to impose law and order.

John Locke Another English philosopher, John Locke, believed that people were naturally happy, tolerant, and reasonable. He argued that all people were born equal with the natural rights of life, liberty, and property.

Locke stated that the purpose of government was to protect people's natural rights. He believed that monarchs were not chosen by God. Instead, the people consented to the government, whose power was limited by laws. In *Two Treatises on Government*, Locke described the importance of the fairness of law.

HISTORY'S VOICES

❝Those who are united into one body, and have a common established law and judicature [court system] to appeal to, with authority to decide controversies between them, and punish offenders, are in civil society one with another . . .❞

—John Locke, *Two Treatises on Government*, 1690

Locke believed that if a government failed to protect its citizens' natural rights, they had the right to overthrow it. Locke's belief in government by consent became a foundation for modern democracy. His ideas inspired later revolutionaries in Europe and the Americas.

Jean-Jacques Rousseau The French philosopher **Jean-Jacques Rousseau** (roo-soh) believed that people were basically born good.

TAKING NOTES
Take notes on the changes that the Enlightenment brought to society.

The Enlightenment

NEW YORK
CC Unit 5- B1
The writings of Locke and Rousseau

PRIMARY SOURCES

Rousseau's Social Contract

Jean-Jacques Rousseau believed that the social contract was not just between the governors and the governed but between all members of society.

"What then is government? It is an intermediary body established between the subjects and the sovereign [king] to keep them in touch with each other. . . The government's power is only the public power vested in it. . . . when the [government] has a particular will of its own stronger than that of the sovereign. . . at that moment the social union will disappear and the body politic will be dissolved."

—Jean-Jacques Rousseau, *The Social Contract*, 1763

Skills FOCUS **READING LIKE A HISTORIAN**

1. **Define** What did Rousseau mean by "an intermediary body" in the first line of this excerpt?

2. **Analyzing Primary Sources** What would happen if government carried out its own wishes in opposition to those of the people?

See **Skills Handbook**, p. H25

ENLIGHTENMENT AND REVOLUTION **575**

Direct Teach

Reading Focus

❶ How was the Enlightenment influenced by reason? *like scientists, philosophers emphasized use of reason to understand truth; used reason to study human condition*

The Age of Reason

Recall What was the Enlightenment? *a time of optimism and possibility when people used reason to attempt to solve the problems of the world*

Describe What role did salons play in the Enlightenment? *brought together philosophers, artists, scientists, and writers to discuss new ideas*

Reading Focus

❷ What new views did philosophers have about government? *Hobbes—social contract, limits to freedom, monarchy is best; Locke—people of equal value, government protects rights, people can rebel against government; Rousseau—government is for common good; Montesquieu—separation of powers*

New Views on Government

Analyze How did the views of Hobbes and Locke about humans in their natural state affect their political ideas? *Hobbes—people naturally bad, need all-powerful monarch to protect them; Locke—people naturally good, need government to protect rights*

Elaborate If applied, how would Locke's economic theory affect taxes? *possible answer—state has no natural right to property or money*

Differentiating Instruction

Below Level

Learners Having Difficulty

1. Review with students the importance of reason for the philosophes.

2. Have students write a poem or song called "Ode to Reason" that could have been written by a philosophe. Encourage students to find creative ways to praise reason and all of the things that could be accomplished through it.

3. Have volunteers recite their poems for the class. **LS** **Verbal-Linguistic, Auditory-Musical**

Alternative Assessment Handbook, Rubric 26: Poems and Songs

Answers

Primary Sources 1. *a group created to keep the subjects and the kings in touch with each other;* **2.** *The social contract would cease to exist.*

Reading Check *Reason could be used to solve all human problems.*

575

Reading Focus

New Views on Government

Describe What is separation of powers? *power divided among several branches of government*

Explain According to Montesquieu, how was Great Britain's government an example of separation of powers? *divided into branches: parliament made laws, king carried out laws, court interpreted laws*

Reading Focus

3 What new views did philosophers have about society? *religious toleration, women's right's; an economic system without government regulation*

New Views on Society

Recall Why was Voltaire imprisoned? *criticisms of nobility, government, and the Church*

Explain How did Voltaire express his ideas? *by writing with sharp wit*

Info to Know

The Encyclopedia The word encyclopedia means "circle of teachings." Although a slim three-volume set was produced in English, French philosopher Denis Diderot edited perhaps the first work that is truly worthy of that name. *Encyclopedia or Systematic Dictionary of the Arts, Sciences, and Crafts* filled 35 volumes by the time it was completed in 1777. Contributors included many leading thinkers of the Enlightenment.

Answers

Counterpoints *Hobbes—human nature is violent; Locke—human nature is governed by natural laws*

Reading Check *Each philosopher had strong opinions about the power and purpose of government.*

COUNTERPOINTS

Two Views on Society

After living through the English civil war, Thomas Hobbes became convinced that society needed a strong central authority to control and contain the natural barbarism of humans.

❝In [a state of nature], there is . . . no Knowledge of the face of the Earth; no account of Time; no Arts; no Letters; no Society; and which is worst of all, continuall feare, and danger of violent death; And the life of man, solitary, poor, nasty, brutish, and short.❞

Thomas Hobbes
—Leviathan, 1651

John Locke believed that under ideal conditions, people lived according to a law of nature. Because people could interpret the law differently, they needed an authority to enforce it.

❝The state of nature has a law of nature to govern it. . . no one ought to harm another in his life, health, liberty, or possessions: . . . Every one . . . may not . . . take away, or impair . . . the life, the liberty, health, limb, or goods of another.❞

John Locke
—Two Treatises on Government, 1690

Skills FOCUS **READING LIKE A HISTORIAN**

Contrast How do Hobbes's and Locke's views of human nature differ?

ACADEMIC VOCABULARY

rational having reason or understanding

NEW YORK

CC Unit 5-B1
The writings of Montesquieu and Voltaire

Rousseau also believed that society corrupted people. In *The Social Contract*, he wrote, "Man is born free but everywhere he is in chains."

Rousseau believed that government should work for the benefit of the common good, not for the wealthy few. He argued that individuals should give up some of their freedoms for the benefit of the community as a whole.

Rousseau despised inequality in society. He believed that all people were equal and should be recognized as equal in society. His view would inspire revolutionaries in years to come.

Baron de Montesquieu Another French thinker, **Baron de Montesquieu** (MOHN-tes-kyoo), argued that the best form of government included a separation of powers. Dividing power among branches of government, he believed, would prevent any individual or group from abusing its power.

In 1748 Montesquieu published *The Spirit of the Laws*. In this book he wrote about his admiration for Great Britain's government, because its powers were divided into branches. Parliament (the legislative branch) made the laws. The king and his advisers (the executive branch) carried out the laws. The court system (the judicial branch) interpreted the laws.

In truth, Montesquieu had misunderstood the structures of the British government. His misunderstanding, however, led him to a <u>rational</u> conclusion. The separation of powers allowed each branch of government to serve as a check against the power of the others—a concept known as the system of checks and balances. This concept would become an important part of the structure of later democratic governments, especially that of the United States.

READING CHECK **Make Inferences** Why was the subject of government so important to Hobbes, Locke, Rousseau, and Montesquieu?

New Views on Society

While some Enlightenment philosophers focused their attention on government, others chose to deal with issues in society, such as religious toleration, women's rights, and economic systems.

Voltaire One of the most outspoken French philosophers, or **philosophes**, was François-Marie Arouet, who wrote under the name **Voltaire** (vohl-TAYR). With biting wit, Voltaire attacked injustice wherever he saw it—among

---

Skills Focus: Identifying Main Idea and Details   **At Level**

Reading Skill
Philosophers of the Enlightenment

1. Draw the chart for students to see. Omit the italicized answers.

2. Have students copy and complete the chart. Then, have volunteers fill in the class chart. Guide students in a discussion about the differences of each philosopher's beliefs.
   LS Visual-Spatial

   Alternative Assessment Handbook, Rubrics 7: Charts; and 11: Discussions

Philosophers of the Enlightenment

Philosopher	Hobbes	Locke	Rousseau	Montesquieu
Main Work	*Leviathan*	*Two Treatises of Civil Government*	*Social Contract*	*The Spirit of Laws*
Idea of Government	*imposes order, prevents violence*	*protects rights, political equality*	*sovereignty comes from the people*	*democracy must be carefully maintained*
Preferred Government	*Monarchy*	*Democracy*	*Democracy*	*Republican (Democracy)*

the nobility, in the government, and in the church. His sharp wit created enemies, however, and Voltaire was imprisoned twice. He was later exiled to England for two years.

Voltaire used his pen to defend every principle that he held dear and to fight superstition and ignorance. Despite making enemies, Voltaire continued the struggle for justice, religious toleration, and liberty during his entire life.

Diderot and the *Encyclopedia* By the mid-1700s the great expansion of human knowledge convinced French philosophe Denis Diderot (DEE-de-roh) to compile it all into a single work, the *Encyclopedia*. This extensive 35-volume work explained new ideas about art, science, government, and religion. Its purpose was the promotion of knowledge.

Diderot worked on the *Encyclopedia* for 27 years, publishing the last volume in 1772. French leaders attacked the *Encyclopedia* because it criticized the church, the government, and the legal system. The government tried to stop publication in 1759, and Diderot completed the remaining volumes in secret. The *Encyclopedia* was an immediate success, and it helped spread Enlightenment ideas across Europe and to North America.

Mary Wollstonecraft Although Enlightenment thinkers questioned many established beliefs, they usually held traditional views about women. Many believed that women's proper roles were as wives and mothers, and that women should receive only enough education to prepare them for those roles.

The English writer Mary Wollstonecraft rejected that view. Wollstonecraft demanded equal rights for women, especially in education—a radical view at the time. In her 1792 book, *A Vindication of the Rights of Woman*, she argued that if men and women had equal education, they would be equal in society.

Adam Smith Some thinkers such as Scottish economist Adam Smith, used reason to analyze economic systems. In his 1776 book, *The Wealth of Nations*, Smith argued that business activities should take place in a free market. Smith was a strong believer in laissez-faire (les-ay FAYR) economics, an economic system that worked without government regulation. In French, laissez-faire means "leave alone".

Smith believed that the economy would be stronger if the market forces of supply and demand were allowed to work freely.

READING CHECK Summarize How did philosophers apply reason to issues in society?

Reading like a Historian

Voltaire's *Candide*

Interpreting Literature as a Source Works of fiction can be very revealing about the times in which they were written. Through the actions and words of the characters, the writer may include information about how people lived, worked, and interacted with each other.

The main character in *Candide* is a young man named Candide who is on a journey around the world in search of enlightenment and wisdom. In the excerpt below, Voltaire describes Candide's view of the aftermath of an earthquake in Lisbon, Portugal. When analyzing a work of fiction, think about

- the details in the literature and known facts
- the author's point of view

An auto-da-fe was a ritual of penance for condemned heretics, who were usually executed afterward.

> After the earthquake, which had destroyed three-fourths of the city of Lisbon, the sages [wise men] of that country could think of no means more effectual to preserve the kingdom from utter ruin than to entertain the people with an auto-da-fe, it having been decided by the University of Coimbra, that the burning of a few people alive by a slow fire, and with great ceremony, is an infallible preventive of earthquakes.
>
> —Voltaire, *Candide*, 1759

Universities were controlled by the church and existed primarily to prepare students for church careers.

Skills FOCUS   READING LIKE A HISTORIAN

1. Details What action did Portuguese leaders believe would save the country from further devastation?

2. Author's Point of View How does the phrase "entertain the people with an auto-da-fe" reveal Voltaire's disdain for Portuguese leaders?

See **Skills Handbook**, p. H28

ENLIGHTENMENT AND REVOLUTION **577**

4 How did Enlightenment ideas spread? *Monarchs across Europe began to adopt Enlightenment ideas in their social policies.*

Enlightenment Ideas Spread

Recall Who were the enlightened despots? *monarchs who made reforms based on Enlightenment ideas*

Explain Why did Catherine the Great shift her focus from reform to building a Russian empire? *because she realized that if her reforms were too liberal she would lose the support of the wealthy landowners*

📄 **CRF:** Biography: Madame Geoffrin

Arrange the classroom like a salon for a discussion. Place chairs or desks in a circle and sit in the circle with students. Keep pressure low, and ask thought-provoking questions that will encourage students to get involved. This will work well if you treat the activity as an incentive and make guidelines ahead of time. Afterwards, ask students how the reorganization of desks and chairs affected the discussion.

Enlightenment Society

In the late 1700s, Madame Geoffrin hosted some of the most popular salons and frequently invited Voltaire, Diderot, and Montesquieu.

An actor entertains the salon's guests by reading Voltaire's play *The Orphan of China*.

Salons were intellectually stimulating social gatherings held in the homes of wealthy Parisian women. Philosophers, writers, artists, and scientists gathered there to share their ideas. *How do you think salons helped women gain more rights in Enlightenment society?*

Enlightenment Ideas Spread

The spirit of optimism and change was not confined to the salons and the coffeehouses of Europe. Enlightenment ideas quickly spread throughout Europe to Prussia, Russia, Austria, and beyond. Many philosophes appealed directly to European monarchs for change. As a result, a few monarchs developed a system of government in which they ruled according to Enlightenment ideas. These monarchs became known as **enlightened despots**.

NEW YORK

CC Unit 5-B3
The enlightened despots

Prussia Frederick II, the king of Prussia from 1740 to 1786, believed that his duty was to rule with absolute power in order to build Prussia's strength. But he was also strongly influenced by the ideas of Voltaire. While Frederick was building Prussia a military power in Europe, he also introduced a number of reforms.

Frederick ambitiously tried to establish a system of elementary education for all Prussian children. He abolished torture and supported

most forms of religious tolerance. Frederick also reduced censorship.

Frederick's reforms were limited, however. For example, he did not extend religious tolerance to Jews; he tried to limit the number of Jews that could live in Prussia. Frederick also opposed serfdom, but he did not abolish it because he needed the support of the aristocracy. Like other enlightened despots, Frederick did not make reforms simply to achieve justice. He did so to build Prussia's strength and make his own rule more powerful.

Russia When Catherine II became the ruler of Russia in 1762, she dreamed of establishing order and justice in Russia while supporting education and culture. Catherine not only read the works of the philosophes also corresponded with both Voltaire and Diderot.

Inspired by the philosophes, Catherine set about reforming Russia. She drafted a Russian constitution and a code of laws, but they were considered far too liberal and were never put

578 CHAPTER 19

Skills Focus: Make Inferences

At Level

Reading Skill
Recommendations for a Despot

1. Review with students the basic ideas of the Enlightenment philosophers.

2. Organize students into mixed-ability pairs.

3. Have each pair make a list of five recommendations for rulers who wanted to implement Enlightenment ideas. For example, rulers should not confiscate a person's property unless that person owes a large amount of money in taxes.

4. Have volunteers read their recommendations to the class. **LS Verbal-Linguistic**

📄 **Alternative Assessment Handbook**, Rubric 35: Solving Problems

Answers

Enlightenment Society *possible answer—Intellectual gatherings probably inspired them to push for more rights.*

into practice. Before Catherine came to power, she intended to free the serfs but quickly realized that she would lose the support of wealthy landowners if she did. Catherine had no intentions of giving up power and she became a tyrant. During her reign she actually imposed serfdom on more Russians than ever before.

Austria The most radical enlightened despot was Joseph II, the son of Maria Theresa of Austria. When he became emperor in 1780, Joseph embarked upon an ambitious reform program. He eliminated torture and the death penalty and provided free food and medicine for poor citizens. As a Catholic emperor, he granted religious tolerance to Protestants and Jews. His most significant reform was abolishing serfdom and requiring that laborers be paid for their work.

These dramatic changes were resisted by the nobility and the church. They forced Joseph to revoke some of his reforms shortly before his death in 1790.

Later Times and Places During the Enlightenment, writers and philosophers questioned ideas that had been long held as absolute truths. They challenged beliefs in absolute monarchy, questioned the relationship between the church and state, and debated the roles and rights of people in society. Enlightenment philosophers promoted ideas that reformers and revolutionaries would later use to change society.

The Enlightenment belief in progress would spur many generations to enact reforms. People began to believe that human reason could solve any problem. Instead of accepting poverty, ignorance, and inequality as part of the human condition, people debated new ways of making society more just.

Enlightenment ideas about power and authority would inspire not only reforms but revolutions. For example, leaders in Great Britain's American colonies would use those ideas as inspiration to break free from the British monarchy. Strongly influenced by the political views of Locke and Rousseau, the colonists began to experience a new sense of national identity.

READING CHECK Draw Conclusions How successful were the reforms of the enlightened despots?

KEY ENLIGHTENMENT IDEAS

- The ability to reason is what makes humans unique.

- Reason can be used to solve problems and improve people's lives.

- Reason can free people from ignorance, superstition, and unfair government.

- The natural world is governed by laws that can be discovered through reason.

- Like the natural world, human behavior is governed by natural laws.

- Governments should reflect natural laws and encourage education and debate.

SECTION 2 ASSESSMENT

go.hrw.com
Online Quiz
Keyword: SHP ENL HP

1. **a. Define** What was the **Enlightenment**?
   b. Explain Why did philosophers believe reason was important?
   c. Elaborate Why would **salons** be an effective way to spread Enlightenment ideas?

2. **a. Identify** Who wrote *Leviathan*?
   b. Analyze How did Hobbes and Locke differ in their ideas about government?

3. **a. Recall** Who were the **philosophes**?
   b. Explain What radical idea did Mary Wollstonecraft support?
   c. Predict Why might Adam Smith's economic ideas appeal to business owners?

4. **a. Identify** What was an **enlightened despot**?
   b. Draw Conclusions How were Frederick II's reforms limited?
   c. Evaluate What do you think is the most significant legacy of the Enlightenment?

Critical Thinking

5. **Analyze** Use a concept map like this one below and your notes from this section to describe how Enlightenment ideas affected government.

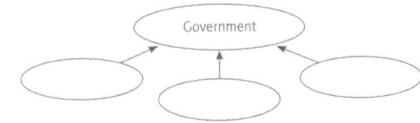

FOCUS ON SPEAKING

6. **Persuasion** Suppose you are a philosophe who would like your monarch to make reforms based on Enlightenment ideas. Prepare a speech in which you try to convince Frederick the Great, Catherine the Great, or Joseph II to support your ideas. Be sure to include reasons why you believe it would be in the monarch's best interests to make your reforms.

ENLIGHTENMENT AND REVOLUTION **579**

Section 2 Assessment Answers

1. **a.** a time of optimism in which people used reason to solve human problems
   b. because it helped people to abandon traditional beliefs
   c. possible answer—Salons brought together many different groups of people to share ideas.

2. **a.** Thomas Hobbes
   b. Hobbes—government imposes order, monarch should be obeyed; Locke—government protects rights, should be limited

3. **a.** French philosophers of the Age of Reason
   b. equal rights for women

c. did not want government regulations

4. **a.** a ruler who made reforms based upon Enlightenment ideas
   b. only helped certain people; made some reforms to increase his own power
   c. possible answer—American and French revolutions would not have occurred.

5. Notes should mention that people began to question traditional authorities.

6. Speeches should show an unerstanding of Enlightment ideas.

Getting Started

Use the **Interactive Reader and Study Guide** to familiarize students with the section content.

📓 **Interactive Reader and Study Guide,** Section 3

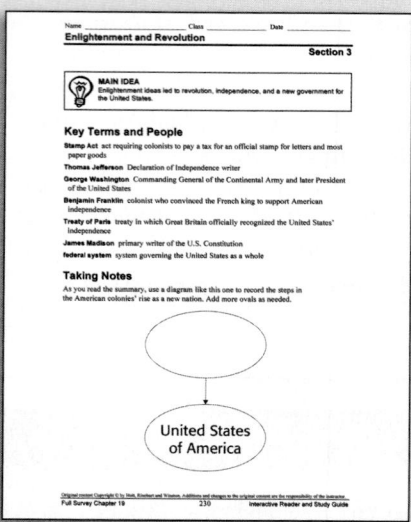

Academic Vocabulary

Review with students the high-use academic term in this section.

regulation a law designed to control or govern conduct (p. 581)

📓 **CRF:** Vocabulary Builder: Section 3

Taking Notes

first successful English colonies; Seven Years' War and new tax policies; opposition and increase in tensions; fighting breaks out; Common Sense; Declaration of Independence; America wins war

go.hrw.com
Online Resources

KEYWORD: SHL ENL
ACTIVITY: The
Enlightenment

The American Revolution

BEFORE YOU READ

MAIN IDEA
Enlightenment ideas led to revolution, independence, and a new government for the United States.

READING FOCUS
1. What were some of the causes of change and crisis in the American colonies?
2. How was the struggle for independence affected by Enlightenment concepts?
3. How did American colonists form a new government?

KEY TERMS AND PEOPLE
Stamp Act
Thomas Jefferson
Benjamin Franklin
George Washington
Treaty of Paris
James Madison
federal system

NEW YORK
PI 1.4 Students understand the broad patterns, relationships, and interactions of cultures and civilizations during particular eras and across eras.

THE INSIDE STORY

How did Enlightenment ideas influence an American leader?
Benjamin Franklin was one of the great Enlightenment philosophers in America. Like Voltaire, Rousseau, and other Enlightenment philosophers, Franklin believed that reason and intelligence could be used to improve the lives of everyone.

Franklin was not just a philosopher; he was a scientist as well. His methodical observations and experiments led him to invent a number of useful items, such as the lightning rod, bifocals, and the Franklin stove. Through his inventions, Franklin showed that practical applications of scientific knowledge could be used to improve people's lives.

Although Franklin may be best remembered today for his inventions and experiments, his commitment to Enlightenment ideals would have an even longer-lasting impact. In the 1770s Franklin came together with other American Enlightenment thinkers, such as Thomas Jefferson, to put Enlightenment ideals into practice to create a new government and nation—the United States. ■

◀ **French engraving of three titans of the Enlightenment: Voltaire, Jean-Jacques Rousseau, and Benjamin Franklin**

580 CHAPTER 19

Teach the Main Idea

At Level

The American Revolution

1. **Teach** Ask students the Reading Focus questions to teach this section.

2. **Apply** Draw three ladders for students to see. Label the tops of the ladders with the names of the topics in this section: Change and Crisis, Struggle for Independence, and Forming a New Government. Have students copy the ladders and fill in the rungs of the ladders with the main ideas of each topic.

3. **Review** As you review the section, have students explain the various ideas that made an impact during the American Revolution.

4. **Practice/Homework** Have students write an open letter from an Enlightenment philosopher to the American colonists, encouraging them in their struggle against England. **LS Visual-Spatial, Verbal-Linguistic**

📓 **Alternative Assessment Handbook,** Rubric 25: Personal Letters

Change and Crisis

By the mid-1700s dramatic new Enlightenment ideas had spread as far as North America. These ideas inspired Great Britain's colonists to seek independence and forge a new nation founded on the ideals of the Enlightenment.

Forming a New Identity Since the establishment of the first English settlement in North America in the early 1600s, the British colonies had expanded rapidly along the east coast. By 1770 the colonies had a population of more than 2.1 million people.

The colonies offered many opportunities that simply were not available in Great Britain. Land was plentiful and cheap. The English class system was largely absent, and individuals could more easily advance themselves through intelligence and hard work.

By the mid-1770s the colonies had been established for nearly 150 years. Although the colonists were British subjects, they were allowed a large measure of independence. Each colony had its own government and made most of its own laws. Over time, the colonists began to identify more closely with the colonies and less with Britain itself.

Opposing British Policies Trouble erupted when Britain began to assert its right to impose laws on the colonies. In the 1760s conflict between some colonists and Britain escalated rapidly.

Britain defeated France in the French and Indian War in 1763, and France had to give up its North American colonies. The war had been very expensive for Britain. Because removing the French benefited the colonists, Britain decided to make the colonies pay part of the cost in the form of new taxes.

In 1765 Parliament passed the **Stamp Act**, which required colonists to pay a tax for an official stamp on all newspapers, legal documents, and other public papers. Colonial leaders were outraged that Parliament taxed them without representatives there to plead their case. They called for a boycott of English goods, which caused Parliament to repeal the act in 1766.

The British, in 1767, imposed a new series of taxes on glass, paper, paints, and tea. Furious merchants in Boston, Massachusetts, one of the largest colonial cities and a major port,

called for another boycott of English goods. The British sent in troops to keep order in the city. As a result, Bostonians harassed the troops constantly on the city's streets.

Finally, in 1770 British discipline snapped. Troops shot and killed five men in an incident known as the Boston Massacre. Most of the Townshend Acts were partially repealed after another colonial boycott. However, the tax on tea remained.

In 1773 a group of rebellious Bostonians called the Sons of Liberty boarded three ships in Boston Harbor. Led by Samuel Adams and Paul Revere, the Sons of Liberty dumped hundreds of crates of tea into the harbor to protest the tax, an act known as the Boston Tea Party. The British closed the port of Boston and passed the so-called Intolerable Acts, regulations that limited the freedoms of the colonists.

The colonists called the First Continental Congress in Philadelphia in 1774 to list their grievances against the British government. A plan to reconcile their differences with the British was presented, but it was voted down.

Revolution Begins The Sons of Liberty in Massachusetts expected a war. As a consequence, they hid weapons in the countryside and towns west of Boston. In April 1775 hundreds of British troops marched out of Boston toward the towns of Lexington and Concord, intending to find these weapons. At dawn on April 19, British troops confronted about 75 colonial militiamen in Lexington. Shots rang out, and the American Revolution began.

ENLIGHTENMENT AND REVOLUTION **581**

FACES OF HISTORY
George WASHINGTON
1732–1799

George Washington's leadership was crucial to an American victory in the Revolutionary War. When he took command of the American forces in 1775, he faced the daunting task of leading an army of untrained militia men against one of the world's strongest military forces.

But Washington's leadership skills won him the loyalty of his troops. He enforced strict discipline, but he also demanded better food, clothing, and pay for them from the Continental Congress. Washington knew that if he looked after his soldiers' needs, they would be better prepared to defeat the British army.

Identify Supporting Details What were some of the ways in which Washington created an effective army against the British?

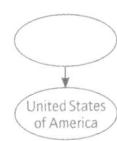

TAKING NOTES
Take notes on the steps in the American colonies' rise as a new nation. Add more ovals as needed.

United States of America

ACADEMIC VOCABULARY
regulation a law designed to control or govern conduct

NEW YORK
CC Unit 5-C2a
Impact of the Enlightenment on the American Revolution

Reading Focus

② How was the struggle for independence affected by Enlightenment concepts? *The concept of the social contract led colonists to believe Great Britain could not rule the colonies without their consent; Enlightenment ideas were used in the Declaration of Independence.*

Struggle for Independence

Identify Who was on the committee to write the Declaration of Independence? *Thomas Jefferson, John Adams, Benjamin Franklin, and others*

Analyze Did the Declaration of Independence present new or old ideas? Explain your answer. *possible answer—was influenced by Magna Carta, English Bill of Rights, and Enlightenment ideas, but Declaration presented those ideas in a new way*

Predict How do you think the English government reacted to the Declaration? *possible answer—views unchanged; still needed to keep colonies under control for economic reasons*

📄 **CRF:** Biography: Benjamin Franklin

About the Illustration

This illustration is an artist's conception based on available sources. Historians, however, are uncertain exactly what this scene looked like.

Info to Know

Indentured Servants Approximately half of the new settlers in the North American colonies were indentured servants. These people signed a contract called an indenture in order to gain passage to the colonies. Indentured servants were fairly expensive to obtain, but they worked on their employer's land from four to seven years. After they finished their term, they were given food, clothing, tools, and some money, and could stake their own claim to land.

Answers

Reading Check *Both imposed taxes on the colonies.*

FOCUS ON NEW YORK
When the Declaration of Independence was read for the first time in New York City on July 9, 1776, excited residents marched down to Bowling Green Park and destroyed a statue of King George III. Metal from the statue was melted down and made into bullets for the Continental Army.

Not all colonists were Patriots, or those who wanted independence from Britain. Many colonists remained loyal to the British. Others thought that such a war was too risky.

In his January 1776 pamphlet, *Common Sense*, writer Thomas Paine argued that the colonies had matured to the point that they no longer needed British rule. Instead, he argued, they deserved independence. Widely read, Thomas Paine's *Common Sense* helped the Patriots gain popular support for the cause of independence.

READING CHECK **Compare** What did the Stamp Act and the Townshend Acts have in common?

Struggle for Independence

The American Revolution was the first war in which old ideas about government were challenged by the ideas of the Enlightenment. The Patriots created a nation based on these ideas.

Declaring Independence During the meeting of the Second Continental Congress in 1776, a committee formed to write a document declaring the colonies' independence from Britain. Members of the committee were well-educated leaders, such as John Adams, **Thomas Jefferson**, and **Benjamin Franklin**, who were familiar with Enlightenment concepts. Jefferson wrote a draft of the Declaration, incorporating ideas from Locke and Rousseau. On July 4, 1776, the Continental Congress adopted the Declaration of Independence.

The Declaration of Independence was an elegant expression of Enlightenment political philosophy. Many of these ideas were presented in the Preamble.

HISTORY'S VOICES

❝That to secure these rights, Governments are instituted among Men, deriving their just powers from the consent of the governed,—That whenever any Form of Government becomes destructive of these ends, it is the Right of the People to alter or to abolish it, and to institute new Government . . .❞
—The Declaration of Independence, 1776

★Interactive **HISTORY CLOSE-UP** **Valley Forge**

From December 1777 to June 1778 the Continental Army camped at Valley Forge, a hilltop near Philadelphia. Here soldiers endured a harsh winter, very little food, and disease. Despite these hardships, the soldiers who left Valley Forge were a more unified and disciplined army.

Women at the camp cooked and took care of sick soldiers.

As many as 12 men shared a tiny hut like this one.

582 CHAPTER 19

Skills Focus: Comparing and Contrasting   At Level

Reading Skill
British Policies and Taxes

1. Review with students the information in the text about British policies and taxes leading up to the American Revolution.

2. Have students create two political cartoons— one that opposes British policies, implying they are unjust, and the other that supports them, implying that the colonists are complaining unnecessarily.

3. Have volunteers present their political cartoons to the class.

4. Guide a class discussion about the differing viewpoints expressed in students' cartoons.
   LS **Visual-Spatial**

📄 **Alternative Assessment Handbook**, Rubric 27: Political Cartoons

The Declaration of Independence drew ideas from the English Bill of Rights of 1689, which protected citizens' right to a trial, the right to elect members of Parliament, and the right to an independent judicial system.

The Revolutionary War Before independence had been declared, the Second Continental Congress assigned **George Washington** as the commanding general of the army in June 1775. The Americans had little money. However, they had a courageous and resourceful leader in General Washington, as well as the advantage of fighting in their own land.

The American Revolution began poorly for the British, who evacuated Boston in June 1775 after the Americans positioned cannons overlooking the city. British troops later defeated Washington in the Battle of Long Island, and the Continental Army was driven into New Jersey. Beaten and bruised, Washington engineered a surprising and daring victory by crossing the icy Delaware River and defeating British forces at Trenton.

In 1777 the British defeated Washington's forces in New Jersey, and Washington moved into Pennsylvania. Philadelphia fell to the British, and Washington's army spent a bitter and deadly winter at Valley Forge.

In upstate New York, the British were also winning battles in the summer of 1777. In October, however, the Americans trapped British general Burgoyne's army at the Battle of Saratoga. The British surrendered and the victory was a crucial win for the Americans. At the same time, Benjamin Franklin was in Paris seeking aid from the French. The victory at Saratoga was exactly the news he needed. Franklin was able to convince the French to contribute heavily to the American cause. This alliance became a turning point in the war.

Over the next two years, the Americans strengthened their forces. The British adopted a strategy to divide the colonies in two. They captured Savannah, Georgia in 1778 and Charleston, South Carolina in 1780. In South Carolina, the Americans made numerous attacks on the British.

In September 1781 the French and American armies surrounded the British army under Lord Cornwallis in Yorktown, Virginia. After a siege of several weeks, Cornwallis grew tired of waiting for the British reinforcements. Lord Cornwallis and his troops surrendered to General Washington on October 19, 1781. The American colonists had won their independence from Great Britain.

FOCUS ON NEW YORK
Today, thousands of people visit the battlefield at Saratoga National Historic Park near Victory, New York.

General George Washington led the Continental Army.

With marching drills and weapons training, General Steuben from Prussia helped transform the American soldiers into a professional army.

Skills Focus INTERPRETING VISUALS

Draw Conclusions How do you think surviving a harsh winter with few clothes and little food helped unite the soldiers in the Continental Army?

go.hrw.com
COULD YOU HAVE SURVIVED?
Keyword: SHL ENL

Go online for a closer look at survival and this event.

ENLIGHTENMENT AND REVOLUTION **583**

Reading Focus

3 How did American colonists form a new government? *replaced Articles of Confederation with a new Constitution and Bill of Rights*

Forming a New Government

Identify What powers did the government lack under the Articles of Confederation? *had no power to tax or negotiate with foreign powers*

Contrast How did the Constitution differ from the Articles of Confederation? *created a federal system of government, divided power among three branches of government*

Explain How did the Bill of Rights become part of the Constitution? *A group of opponents wanted protection for individual rights to be added to the Constitution.*

📖 **Map Transparency:** The Revolutionary War

Info to Know

Young Patriots Patriots of all ages fought in the Revolutionary War. Many boys between the ages of 14 and 16 enlisted in the American army. Other boys, some who were as young as 6, served as drummers for the troops. The job of drummer boys was to signal commands from generals to troops, which sometimes put them in the midst of battle. The American navy had its share of young sailors as well; these boys served as deckhands or "powder monkeys" who carried ammunition to the gunners during battle.

Answers

Interpreting Maps 1. *Massachusetts;* **2.** *The Atlantic Ocean*

Reading Check *Second Continental Congress declares colonies' independence from Britain; Washington assigned commander of army; American forces strengthened; French and American armies defeat British army; colonists win independence*

THE REVOLUTIONARY WAR

Major Battles
- Lexington, April 1775
- Bunker Hill, June 1775
- New York, August 1776
- Trenton, December 1776
- Brandywine, September 1777
- Saratoga, October 1777
- Camden, August 1780
- Kings Mountain, October 1780
- Guilford Courthouse, March 1781
- Yorktown, October 1781

⚔ British victory
⚔ Colonial victory

0   250   500 Miles
0   250   500 Kilometers
Azimuthal equal-area projection

GEOGRAPHY SKILLS | **INTERPRETING MAPS**

1. Location In which state were the first two major battles of the Revolutionary War fought in 1775?

2. Regions What physical feature served as a natural boundary for the thirteen colonies?

In September 1783 the British government formally recognized the independence of the United States by signing the **Treaty of Paris**. Benjamin Franklin and other American leaders signed the document in Paris. This treaty set the geographic boundaries for the new United States. The treaty gave the Americans not only independence but also much greater territory than the original 13 colonies. The Americans gained all land east of the Mississippi River and north of the 31st parallel.

The end of the war was just the beginning, however. The Americans now faced the daunting and difficult task of building a new nation.

READING CHECK **Sequence** What events led to the signing of the Declaration of Independence?

Forming a New Government

The American Revolution was over. Now the colonists had to figure out how to band together to form a new government and nation. Meanwhile, in France, revolutionaries inspired by the success of the American Revolution began to oppose the French monarchy.

The Articles of Confederation The first government of the new United States was established by the Articles of Confederation, approved in 1781. The framers of the Articles deliberately made the national government weak to avoid abuses of power. For example, the government had no power to tax. It also could not negotiate with foreign nations. The Articles of Confederation produced a government that proved too weak to govern effectively.

The Constitution In 1787, delegates met at a Constitutional Convention in Philadelphia to revise the Articles. Instead, they wrote a new constitution. The U.S. Constitution remains the oldest written constitution still in use today.

George Washington presided over the convention, but **James Madison** played a leading role in negotiating the main points. Delegates met for nearly four months, and the Constitution that emerged was a product of skillful compromise. The delegates signed the Constitution in 1787, which then went to the states to be ratified. The Constitution went into effect in 1789.

The Constitution created a **federal system** of government. In a federal system, certain powers are held by the federal government, and other powers are reserved for the state governments. The Constitution divides the national government's powers among three branches of government. The executive branch includes the president, who has the power to carry out laws. The judicial branch interprets the laws. Congress, the legislative branch, makes the laws. Congress consists of a lower house, called the House of Representatives, and an upper house, called the Senate. A system of checks and balances ensures that no branch of government becomes too powerful.

The influence of Enlightenment thought on the Constitution was very powerful. The founding principle of the Constitution is that government exists for the people. This principle

---

Differentiating Instruction

Above Level

Advanced Learners/Gifted and Talented

Prep Required

Materials: copies of the Declaration of Independence, the Constitution and Bill of Rights, various Enlightenment writings, the English Bill of Rights, and Magna Carta

1. Organize students into small groups. Give each group copies of the Declaration of Independence, the preamble to the Constitution, the Bill of Rights, and one other document. You may wish to find annotated versions.

2. Tell students that the early leaders of the United States were influenced by many earlier

documents. Have students search for similarities in the documents. Suggest that students first read the American documents and then split up the other selection and search for similar language and ideas. Have students compile the similarities into an annotated list.

3. Have groups present their lists to the class.
🗣 **Verbal-Linguistic**

📄 **Alternative Assessment Handbook**, Rubrics 9: Comparing and Contrasting; and 30: Research reflects Locke's and Rousseau's idea of government by consent of the people. The division of government into three branches reflects Montesquieu's idea of the separation of powers.

The Bill of Rights A group of opponents to the Constitution argued that it failed to protect the rights of citizens. They wanted protection for individuals' rights to be added to the Constitution. Congress responded with the Bill of Rights, the first 10 amendments to the Constitution. The Bill of Rights protected the natural rights advocated by Voltaire, Locke, and Rousseau, such as the freedoms of speech and religion. The Bill of Rights protected a number of other rights, but most important, it guaranteed people equality, or due process, of law.

Impact of American Government News of the American colonies' successful revolution had a tremendous impact on other governments, especially in France. The French king Louis XVI had supported the American Revolution. However, his form of government could not have been further from the ideals of the colonists. He was an absolute monarch who taxed his people without mercy and cared nothing for their suffering. The loss of the Seven Years' War had also added to France's troubles. Additionally, the king's support of the American war effort had been expensive and contributed to France's economic problems.

France would experience the upheaval of revolution beginning in 1789. One of the many

Scene at the Signing of the Constitution, by Howard Chandler Christy, 1940

Signing the Constitution
George Washington presided over the Constitutional Convention, held in Philadelphia from May to September 1787.

reasons for that revolution was the inspiration of the American example. A group of distant British colonies had adopted the ideals of the Enlightenment and shown that it was possible to oppose tyranny. This new government was created based on the principles of liberty and equality. The courage and determination of the soldiers who fought in the Revolution, and the wisdom of the framers of the Constitution, have stood as shining examples to movements against oppression ever since.

NEW YORK
CC Unit 5-C2b
Impact of the American Revolution on other revolutions

READING CHECK **Find the Main Idea** How did the Constitution and the Bill of Rights change the government and society of the United States?

SECTION 3 ASSESSMENT

go.hrw.com
Online Quiz
Keyword: SHL ENL HP

Reviewing Ideas, Terms, and People

1. **a. Identify** Who was Thomas Paine, and what did he write?
   b. Analyze How did opposition to British tax policies affect the American colonies?
   c. Evaluate Do you think you would have joined the colonial rebellion in 1770? Why or why not?

2. **a. Recall** What was the Treaty of Paris?
   b. Draw Conclusions How did Enlightenment ideas influence the Continental Congress in 1776?

3. **a. Recall** When were the Articles of Confederation approved?
   b. Explain Why was a Constitutional Convention called in 1787?
   c. Make Judgments Do you think it was a wise decision to add the Bill of Rights to the Constitution? Why or why not?

Critical Thinking

4. **Categorize** Use the graphic organizer below to show four key events that led to the formation of the United States. Be sure to explain why you chose those four events.

United States

FOCUS ON WRITING

5. **Persuasion** You are a young American colonist in the early 1770s. Write a short letter to your newspaper's editor stating why you support independence from Great Britain. Explain your reasons.

ENLIGHTENMENT AND REVOLUTION **585**

Right sidebar

Direct Teach

Reading Focus

Forming a New Government

Compare In what ways were the American and French revolutions similar? *people rebelled against absolute monarchs and unfair taxation; replaced governments with Enlightenment principles of liberty, equality, democracy*

Analyze Why do you think the French king supported the American Revolution even though his own government was similar to Great Britain's? *possible answer—wanted to gain an advantage over Great Britain*

Review & Assess

Close
Have students explain the connections between Enlightenment ideas and the American colonial struggle.

Review
Online Quiz, Section 3

Assess
SE Section 3 Assessment
Progress Assessment: Section 3 Quiz
Alternative Assessment Handbook

Reteach/Intervene
Interactive Reader and Study Guide, Section 3
Interactive Skills Tutor CD-ROM

Answers

Reading Check *caused anger about taxation without representation; colonial leaders supported creation of new nation; committee formed at Continental Congress; Jefferson wrote draft; adopted by the Congress*

585

Documents of Democracy

Historical Context The four famous and significant documents below provide different views on the relationship between government and the people.

Task Examine the selections and answer the questions that follow. After you have studied the documents, you will be asked to write an essay about the ideal of democratic government. You will need to use evidence from these selections and from the chapter to support the position you take in your essay.

Word Help

allay reduce, relieve

redress compensation, payment

assail fight against

arbitrary unrestrained in the exercise of power

Info to Know

The Magna Carta and Democracy The Magna Carta is often cited as the first document in the development of modern democracy. While it is true that the Magna Carta did establish a foundation for later democratic documents, the document King John signed in 1215 was not so much democratic as it was a limitation of the powers of the king by the nobles. Nowhere in its pages did the Magna Carta provide for fully representative government, nor did it grant many rights to ordinary English people. Nevertheless, the Magna Carta did establish an important point: that even a king had to obey the law. Some of the rights granted to the nobles within the Magna Carta were later used to support modern political ideas such as due process of law, no taxation without representation, and the right to trial by jury.

NEW YORK STANDARDS

PI **1.2** Students understand the development and connectedness of Western civilization and other civilizations and cultures in many areas of the world and over time.

PI **1.3** Students analyze historic events from around the world by examining accounts written from different perspectives.

DOCUMENT 1

The Magna Carta, 1215

In 1215 a group of English noblemen demanded that King John sign the Magna Carta to protect their rights. This document established that the power of the king could be limited by a written document.

> Since we have granted all these things for God, for the better ordering of our kingdom, and to allay the discord that has arisen between us and our barons, . . . we give and grant to the barons the following security:
>
> The barons shall elect twenty-five of their number to keep . . . the peace and liberties granted and confirmed to them by this charter.
>
> If we . . . offend in any respect against any man . . . , and the offence is made known to four of the said twenty-five barons, they shall come to us . . . to declare it and claim immediate redress. If we . . . make no redress within forty days, . . . the twenty-five barons . . . may distrain upon and assail us in every way possible . . . by seizing our castles, lands, possessions, or anything else . . . until they have secured such redress as they have determined upon. Having secured the redress, they may then resume their normal obedience to us.

DOCUMENT 2

The Spirit of the Laws, 1748

In his 1748 work, *The Spirit of the Laws*, Baron de Montesquieu explained his views on the separation of powers.

> Again, there is no liberty, if the power of judging be not separated from the legislative and executive powers. Were it joined with the legislative, the life and liberty of the subject would be exposed to arbitrary control, for the judge would then be the legislator. Were it joined to the executive power, the judge might behave with all the violence of an oppressor.
>
> There would be an end of every thing were the same man, or the same body, whether of the nobles or of the people to exercise those three powers that of enacting laws, that of executing the public resolutions, and that of judging the crimes or differences of individuals.

Collaborative Learning

At Level

Debating the King's Power

Research Required

1. Organize students into two groups. Assign the first group to represent the point of view of a king. The second group will represent the point of view of the king's subjects.

2. Have students in the first group make a list of reasons why a king should have absolute power. Have students in the second group make a list of reasons why subjects should limit a king's power. Students should develop their lists by using their textbooks, other reference books, and their own ideas. Both groups should examine the four Documents as they develop their lists.

3. Have each group choose one or two representatives to serve as debaters. Then, lead a class debate on the following topic: Do people have the right to limit the power of a ruler? **LS** **Interpersonal, Verbal-Linguistic**

📝 **Alternative Assessment Handbook**, Rubrics 1: Acquiring Information, and 10: Debates

DOCUMENT 3

Common Sense, 1776

Thomas Paine argued for independence in his 1776 pamphlet, *Common Sense*.

Were a manifesto to be published, and despatched to foreign courts, setting forth the miseries we have endured, and the peaceable methods we have ineffectually used for redress; declaring, at the same time, that not being able, any longer, to live happily or safely under the cruel disposition of the British court, we had been driven to the necessity of breaking off all connections with her; at the same time, assuring all such courts of our peaceable disposition towards them, and of our desire of entering into trade with them: Such a memorial would produce more good effects to this Continent, than if a ship were freighted with petitions to Britain.

Under our present denomination of British subjects, we can neither be received nor heard abroad: The custom of all courts is against us, and will be so, until, by an independence, we take rank with other nations.

DOCUMENT 4

Declaration of Independence, 1776

Thomas Jefferson wrote the Declaration of Independence in June 1776. The Declaration proclaimed the political philosophy of the American people—a philosophy drawn from Enlightenment ideals—and listed a set of grievances against the British king George III. The document was intended to justify the breaking of ties with Great Britain and the establishment of a newly independent United States.

We hold these truths to be self-evident, that all men are created equal, that they are endowed by their creator with certain unalienable rights, that among these are life, liberty, and the pursuit of happiness. That to secure these rights, governments are instituted among men, deriving their just powers from the consent of the governed, that whenever any form of government becomes destructive of these ends, it is the right of the people to alter or to abolish it, and to institute new government, laying its foundation on such principles, and organizing its powers in such form, as to them shall seem most likely to effect their safety and happiness.

Skills Focus: READING LIKE A HISTORIAN

DOCUMENT 1

a. Recall What was the role of the 25 barons in relation to the Magna Carta?

b. Analyze How did the Magna Carta limit the power of the monarch?

DOCUMENT 2

a. Identify Which three powers did Montesquieu believe should be separated among branches of government?

b. Draw Conclusions What would be the consequences of not separating the three powers?

DOCUMENT 3

a. Describe What complaints of the colonists does Paine want foreign nations to know about?

b. Interpret Why does Paine want foreign nations to know

about the colonies' unhappiness of living under British rule?

DOCUMENT 4

a. Define What did "unalienable rights" mean?

b. Explain What options are available to citizens whose government no longer protects their rights?

DOCUMENT-BASED ESSAY QUESTION

What were some key elements of the Enlightenment ideal of democratic government? Using the documents above and information from the chapter, form a thesis that explains your position. Then write a short essay to support your position.

See **Skills Handbook**, p. H25

ENLIGHTENMENT AND REVOLUTION **587**

Skills Focus: Interpreting Time Lines

At Level

Social Studies Skill

Key Documents of Democracy

Research Required

1. Draw a time line for students to see. The time line should begin at 1200 and continue in hundred-year increments to 1800. Have students copy the time line onto their own papers.

2. Have students add the Declaration of Independence (1776), *The Spirit of the Laws* (1748), Magna Carta (1215) and *Common Sense* (1776) to their time lines.

3. Write the following additional examples for students to see: Mayflower Compact (1620);

English Bill of Rights (1689); *Two Treatises on Government* (1690); Virginia Declaration of Rights (1776); United States Constitution (1789). Have students add the new examples to their time lines.

4. Have students conduct research about each document and then write a one-sentence summary of each one. **LS Visual-Spatial**

🖎 **Alternative Assessment Handbook**, Rubric 36: Time Lines

Answers

Reading Like a Historian
Document 1. a. *elected officials responsible for bringing the barons' complaints to the king and securing payment for any wrongdoing; could seize property from the king if necessary;* **b.** *showed that the king could be punished for his actions;* **Document 2. a.** *the judicial, legislative, and executive;* **b.** *If power were not separated, it could become arbitrary and oppressive.* **Document 3. a.** *that the colonists cannot live happily or safely under British rule;* **b.** *in order to justify the call for independence;* **Document 4. a.** *rights that have been given to people by God and cannot be taken away;* **b.** *They may change their government, or get rid of it and start a new government.* **Essay** *possible answer—governments should rule with the consent of the governed; power of government should be limited*

587

Visual Summary

Review and Inquiry Organize students into three groups, and assign each group one of the topics in the Spread of Ideas flow chart: Scientific Revolution, Enlightenment, and American Revolution. Have each group write a short summary of its assigned topic.

Quick Facts Transparency: Visual Study Guide: Enlightenment and Revolution

Review Key Terms and People

1. Declaration of Independence
2. Catherine the Great
3. Nicolaus Copernicus
4. Stamp Act
5. John Locke
6. rational
7. heliocentric theory
8. Baron de Montesquieu
9. George Washington
10. scientific method

Comprehension and Critical Thinking

11. **a.** that the earth rotated around the sun
    b. He supported Copernican theory, even though the Church pressured him not to support it.
    c. possible answer—It inspired people to question old views; ideas also spread to government, society, and art.

12. **a.** period when philosophers believed in using reason to understand truth
    b. believed in social contract; Hobbes believed human nature was violent, while Locke believed human nature followed natural laws
    c. possible answer—Yes, they instituted some Enlightenment reforms, though often for their own reasons.

VISUAL STUDY GUIDE

QUICK FACTS

The Spread of Ideas

Scientific Revolution
- Francis Bacon and René Descartes develop the scientific method.
- Scientists learn more about the solar system and the limits of the physical world.
- Biologists learn more about the human body, and chemists define matter.
- Advances in science influence developments in art and architecture.

Enlightenment
- Enlightenment thinkers apply reason to the study of human nature.
- Thinkers develop new ways of organizing government.
- Philosophers use reason to deal with religious toleration, women's rights, and economic systems.

American Revolution
- Enlightenment ideas inspire American colonists to declare independence from Great Britain.
- The success of the American Revolution inspires people in France to revolt against their monarchy.

Major Scientists and Thinkers

Nicolaus Copernicus
- Developed the heliocentric theory of the solar system

Galileo Galilei
- Built first working telescope for astronomy

Sir Isaac Newton
- Developed calculus to explain all movement in the universe

Thomas Hobbes
- Believed people needed governments to impose order

John Locke
- Believed the purpose of government was to protect people's natural rights

Jean-Jacques Rousseau
- Believed all people should be equal in society

Voltaire
- Believed in justice and religious toleration in society

Denis Diderot
- Compiled the *Encyclopedia*, 28 volumes on art, science, government, and religion

Mary Wollstonecraft
- Believed women should have the same educational opportunities and rights as men

Review Key Terms and People

Identify the term or person from the chapter that best fits each of the following descriptions.

1. Document proclaiming that the United States was a free and independent nation
2. Enlightened despot from Russia
3. Polish astronomer who developed the heliocentric theory of the solar system
4. British policy that taxed newspapers and other public documents
5. English philosopher who believed in government by consent
6. Having reason or understanding
7. Theory that the sun was the center of the universe
8. French philosopher who believed in the separation of powers
9. Commander of colonial army during the American Revolution
10. Five-step process for testing theories in order to acquire new knowledge

---

13. **a.** the first ten amendments to the Constitution; protected individual liberties
    b. incorporated Enlightenment philosophers' ideas of the social contract, natural rights, equality, toleration
    c. possible answer—John Locke, because his phrases were used in the Declaration of Independence; idea of social contract lay behind the entire Revolution

Reading Skills

14. had lived apart from Great Britain; had been allowed to rule themselves somewhat
15. caused tension
16. Causes—new identity for colonists, opposition to British policies; Enlightenment philosophy; Effects—independence for United States; other revolutions began

History's Impact video program
Review the video to answer the closing question:
How does the Declaration of Independence affect
American life today?

Comprehension and Critical Thinking

SECTION 1 *(pp. 567–573)*

11. a. Recall What did Nicolaus Copernicus discover about the universe?

b. Explain How did Galileo's beliefs about Copernican theory bring him into conflict with the church?

c. Elaborate Did the Scientific Revolution bring about a modern way of thinking? Explain your answer.

SECTION 2 *(pp. 574–579)*

12. a. Define What was the Enlightenment?

b. Compare and Contrast Both Thomas Hobbes and John Locke believed in a social contract. How were their views similar? In what ways were they different?

c. Support a Position Were enlightened despots an improvement over traditional monarchs? Why or why not?

SECTION 3 *(pp. 580–585)*

13. a. Identify What was the Bill of Rights?

b. Analyze How did the Constitution and the Bill of Rights incorporate some of the ideas of Enlightenment thinkers Montesquieu, Voltaire, Locke, and Rousseau?

c. Rate Which Enlightenment thinker had the greatest influence on the framers of the U.S. Constitution? Explain your answer.

Reading Skills

Understanding Causes and Effects *Use what you know about understanding causes and effects to answer the questions below.*

14. Why did the colonists in the British colonies begin to develop a new identity?

15. What effects did the Stamp Act, Townshend Acts, and other British taxes have on the relationship between Great Britain and its colonies in North America?

16. List the causes and effects of the American Revolution.

Interpreting Literature as a Source

Reading Like a Historian *Voltaire wrote the short story "Micromégas" in 1752. In this early work of science fiction, visitors from outer space observe and comment on the frequency with which Europeans go to war.*

> ❝I assure you, at the end of 10 years, not a hundredth part of those wretches will be left; even if they had never drawn the sword, famine, fatigue, or intemperance will sweep them almost all away. Besides, it is not they who deserve punishment, but rather those armchair barbarians, who from the privacy of their cabinets, and during the process of digestion, command the massacre of a million men, and afterward ordain a solemn thanksgiving to God.❞

—Voltaire, "Micromégas"

17. Explain Who does Voltaire blame for the evils of warfare?

18. Analyze What does Voltaire reveal about his view of European leaders?

Using the Internet

go.hrw.com
Practice Online
Keyword: SHL ENL

19. The U.S. Constitution was a result of skillful negotiation and compromise. Using the Internet, research the major issues that arose during the weeks of the Constitutional Convention. Then write a report about the issues and the compromises achieved, using eyewitness accounts and other documents to support your work.

WRITING ABOUT HISTORY ✏

Exposition: Writing an Explanation *The Scientific Revolution resulted in a dramatic change in the way in which scientists viewed the natural world and the way in which they acquired knowledge about it. Most people, however, were not scientists. Nevertheless, the Scientific Revolution led to changes far beyond the realm of science.*

20. Assignment: In an essay, explain how the new ways of thinking that arose out of the Scientific Revolution led to the Enlightenment. To provide support for your explanation, use information from this chapter and from other research as needed. Be sure to use facts and examples to clearly illustrate the points you are making about the ways in which ideas led to concrete changes in the world.

ENLIGHTENMENT AND REVOLUTION **589**

Answers

Interpreting Literature as a Source

17. government leaders

18. He believes they are heartless and deserve punishment for their actions.

Using the Internet

19. Go to the HRW Web site and enter the keyword shown to access a rubric for this activity.

KEYWORD: SHL ENL

Writing About History

20. Student essays should include examples of concrete changes that occurred after the Age of Reason, including the women's rights movement, Adam Smith's laissez-faire economic system, new governments based on democracy and equality, and developments in art and architecture.

A rubric for the activity is provided in **CRF:** Writing about History.

HOLT

History's Impact

▶ **Video Program: Enlightenment and Revolution**
See the Video Program Teacher's Guide for the answer to the closing question.

Review and Assessment Resources

Review and Reinforce

- 🗒 **CRF:** Chapter Review
- 🖥 **Quick Facts Transparency:** Visual Study Guide: Enlightenment and Revolution
- 🔊 **Spanish Chapter Summaries Audio CD Program**
- **OSP** 🗒 **Holt PuzzlePro:** Quiz Show for ExamView
- 💿 **Quiz Game CD-ROM**

Assess

- 🗒 **PASS:** Chapter Test, Forms A and B
- 🗒 **Alternative Assessment Handbook**
- **OSP** **ExamView Test Generator**, Chapter Test
- 💿 **Differentiated Instruction Modified Worksheets and Tests CD-ROM:** Chapter Test
- **HOAP** **Holt Online Assessment Program** (in the Premier Online Edition)

Reteach/Intervene

- 🗒 **Interactive Reader and Study Guide**
- 🗒 **Differentiated Instruction Teacher Management System:** Lesson Plans for Differentiated Instruction
- 💿 **Differentiated Instruction Modified Worksheets and Tests CD-ROM:** Chapter Test
- 💿 **Interactive Skills Tutor CD-ROM**

go.hrw.com
Online Resources
KEYWORD: SHL TEACHER

ENLIGHTENMENT AND REVOLUTION **589**

Chapter 20 Planning Guide

The French Revolution and Napoleon

| --- | --- | --- |
CHAPTER 20 pp. 590–623 **Overview:** In this chapter, students will learn about events in France that led to a revolution, a period of chaos, and the emergence of a dictator. KI 2, 3; PI 1.2, 1.3, 2.3, 2.4, 2.5, 3.3 See pp. T32–T55 for a detailed correlation to the New York State Core Curriculum for Global History and Geography and the New York Learning Standards.	**Differentiated Instruction Teacher Management System:** • Pacing Guide • Lesson Plans for Differentiated Instruction **Interactive Reader and Study Guide:** Chapter Summary* **Chapter Resource File*** • Writing for the SAT • Social Studies Skill • Chapter Review **World History Outline Maps**	**Live Ink© Online Reading Help** **Student Edition on Audio CD Program** **Differentiated Instruction Modified Worksheets and Tests CD-ROM** **World History Primary Source Library CD-ROM** **Power Presentations with Video CD-ROM** **History's Impact: World History Video Program (VHS/DVD):** The French Revolution and Napoleon
Section 1: **The Revolution Begins** **The Main Idea:** Problems in French society led to a revolution, the formation of a new government, and the end of the monarchy. PI 2.3, 2.4	**Differentiated Instruction Teacher Management System:** Section 1 Lesson Plan* **Interactive Reader and Study Guide:** Section 1 Summary* **Chapter Resource File*** • Vocabulary Builder: Section 1 • Biography: Marie-Antoinette • Biography: Georges-Jacques Danton • Literature: *Les Misérables*	**Quick Facts Transparency:** Causes of the Revolution* **Regents Review Transparency:** Section 1* **Internet Activity:** Revolutions
Section 2: **The Republic** **The Main Idea:** An extreme government changed French society and tried through harsh means to eliminate its critics within France. PI 2.5	**Differentiated Instruction Teacher Management System:** Section 2 Lesson Plan* **Interactive Reader and Study Guide:** Section 2 Summary* **Chapter Resource File*** • Vocabulary Builder: Section 2	**Quick Facts Transparency:** Governments of Revolutionary France* **Regents Review Transparency:** Section 2*
Section 3: **Napoleon's Europe** **The Main Idea:** Napoleon Bonaparte rose through military ranks to become emperor over France and much of Europe. PI 1.3	**Differentiated Instruction Teacher Management System:** Section 3 Lesson Plan* **Interactive Reader and Study Guide:** Section 3 Summary* **Chapter Resource File*** • Vocabulary Builder: Section 3 • Biography: Pope Pius VII • Primary Source: *The Plumb-pudding in Danger*	**Map Transparency:** Napoleon's Empire, 1812* **Regents Review Transparency:** Section 3* **Internet Activity:** Napoleon Bonaparte
Section 4: **Napoleon's Fall and Europe's Reaction** **The Main Idea:** After defeating Napoleon, the European allies sent him into exile and held a meeting in Vienna to restore order and stability to Europe. PI 1.2, 3.3	**Differentiated Instruction Teacher Management System:** Section 4 Lesson Plan **Interactive Reader and Study Guide:** Section 4 Summary **Chapter Resource File*** • Vocabulary Builder: Section 4 • Biography: Czar Alexander I • History and Geography: Napoleon Invades Russia	**Quick Facts Transparency:** Soldiers in Napoleon's Russian Campaign* **Map Transparency:** Russian Campaign, 1812* **Map Transparency:** Europe After the Congress of Vienna, 1815* **Regents Review Transparency:** Section 4*

HOLT

History's Impact
World History Video Program (VHS/DVD)
The French Revolution and Napoleon

Review, Assessment, Intervention

- **Global History and Geography Regents Test Prep Workbook**
- **Quick Facts Transparency:** The French Revolution and Napoleon*
- **Spanish Chapter Summaries Audio CD Program**
- **Program Assessment Support System (PASS):** Chapter Test*
- **OSP New York One-Stop Planner CD-ROM:** ExamView Test Generator (English/Spanish)
- **HOAP Holt Online Assessment Program (HOAP),** in the Holt Premier Online Student Edition

- **PASS:** Section 1 Quiz*
- **Online Quiz:** Section 1
- **Alternative Assessment Handbook**

- **PASS:** Section 2 Quiz*
- **Online Quiz:** Section 2
- **Alternative Assessment Handbook**

- **PASS:** Section 3 Quiz*
- **Online Quiz:** Section 3
- **Alternative Assessment Handbook**

- **PASS:** Section 4 Quiz*
- **Online Quiz:** Section 4
- **Alternative Assessment Handbook**

Power Presentation with Video CD-ROM

Power Presentations with Video are visual presentations of each chapter's main ideas. Presentations can be customized by including Quick Facts charts, images and maps from the textbook, and video clips.

Holt Online Learning

go.hrw.com
Teacher Resources
KEYWORD: SHL TEACHER

go.hrw.com
Student Resources
KEYWORD: SHL NAP

- Document-Based Questions
- Interactive Multimedia Activities

- Current Events
- Chapter-Based Internet Activities
- and more!

Holt Premier
Online Student Edition
Complete online support for interactivity, assessment, and reporting
- Interactive Maps and Notebook
- Homework Practice and Research Activities Online

CHAPTER 20 PLANNING GUIDE

Before You Teach

The Big Picture

Peter N. Stearns

Causes and Outcomes of the French Revolution Explaining the factors that prompted people to revolt against a longstanding political and social regime involves crucial historical issues. Political policy, ideas, social tensions and short-term economic problems feed the equation. Once launched, the Revolution went through several crucial stages, becoming for a time particularly bloodthirsty (though at levels tame by more recent standards). A key challenge is to understand the durable changes introduced by the Revolution, from the initial liberal phase through the more democratic Terror, without getting lost in the sequence of events or totally distracted by the Revolution's drawbacks and limitations. Changes in the position of the aristocracy and other legally privileged groups; recasting the relation between religion and state; and developing new bases for nationalism and for national military conscription are among the key results, though new constitutional freedoms, key voting systems, the attack on monarchy and even the introduction of the metric system deserve attention as well. The French Revolution also displayed classic patterns of revolution more generally, which can be teased out for comparison with similar events including the American Revolution.

Napoleon Napoleon's stormy rule invites another balancing act, between short-term conquests and ultimate failures, and the longer term role in spreading revolutionary achievements, including nationalism. Napoleon permanently installed some features of the Revolution in France—but not all of them. He spread key principles more widely, particularly in adjacent territories but also in more distant parts of Europe. The Vienna settlement that followed Napoleon's final defeat must be interpreted as a recognition of change along with a clear effort to install a more conservative diplomatic and political order. The settlement created issues for the future, but it has also been hailed as far more constructive than many more modern peace treaties. In the wake of Napoleon, it's important, finally, to think about how elements of the French Revolution spread across the Atlantic, but not, until much later, to Asia and Africa.

Recent Scholarship

Explaining the Revolution *Making Democracy in the French Revolution* (2001) by James Livesey is a much discussed recent effort to explain major features of the revolutionary achievement. Livesey puts some emphasis on new ideas, but also looks to the social base—the kinds of groups that supported dramatic political change—with particular reference to commercial practices. Not surprisingly, scholars have been trying to pinpoint causes of the French Revolution for a long time, and until recently, focus seemed to have shifted from social issues to ideologies. Livesey represents a new start on a more comprehensive approach. Acknowledging other interpretations while working beyond them, Livesey contributes to one of the great causation questions in modern history.

Differentiating Instruction

 Differentiated Instruction Teacher Management System
- Pacing Guide
- Lesson Plans for Differentiated Instruction

 Interactive Reader and Study Guide

Spanish Chapter Summaries Audio CD Program

Student Edition on Audio CD Program

 Differentiated Instruction Modified Worksheets and Tests CD-ROM
- Vocabulary Flash Cards
- Modified Vocabulary Builder Activities
- Modified Chapter Review Activity
- Modified Chapter Test

OSP One-Stop Planner CD-ROM
- ExamView Test Generator (English /Spanish)
- PuzzlePro
- Quiz Show for ExamView
- Transparencies and Videos

TE Differentiated Activities in the Teacher's Edition
- France in the 1780s, p. 594
- National Assembly, p. 597
- Bastille Day, p. 597
- Concept of Irony, p. 600
- French Government and Society, p. 603
- Characteristics of Napoleon, p. 610
- Napoleon's Last Campaigns, p. 616
- Execution Debate, p. 621

Reading Like a Historian
Sam Wineburg

A Fairy Tale Ending? Few students will come to your class already knowing about the storming of the Bastille. But you can be fairly certain that they'll know a story about a little girl dressed in red, whose visit to grandma goes terribly awry. "What big teeth you have Grandma," says an unsuspecting Little Red Riding Hood to the beast disguised as grandma. "Better to eat you with," replies the wolf. As the wolf lunges toward his prey, the girl's screams alert a woodsman who, on entering the house, forces the wolf to spit out grandma (miraculously intact). The woodsman kills the beast and then goes on his way. In the words of one modern version: "Little Red Riding Hood and her grandma had a nice lunch and a long chat."

What in the world does Little Red Riding Hood have to do with the French Revolution? This is precisely the question asked by Princeton historian Robert Darnton, whose research draws on early versions of common folktales to reconstruct the worldviews of the people in the past. Darnton contrasts the happy ending of our familiar story with the same tale as recounted by peasants in pre-Revolutionary France. Accosting grandma, our French wolf does not swallow her whole, but kills her, then pours "her blood into a bottle" and slices "her flesh onto a platter." When little granddaughter arrives, the wolf-as-grandma invites her to a feast: "There is meat and wine in the pantry." The unsuspecting little cannibal dines on meat and wine and, sated, crawls into bed with grandma-wolf. In the French version no woodsman appears handily to save the little girl. Indeed, "What big teeth you have," are Little Red Riding Hood's parting words before she, too, becomes dinner. Hardly a happy ending.

Folktales as Historical Sources Darnton shows that it is not just this story that casts a dark shadow, but the antecedents to other familiar tales as well: Hansel and Gretel, Puss n' Boots, Cinderella. "Storytellers of 18th century France," he writes, "portrayed a world of raw and naked brutality."

And why should we expect otherwise? Peasants of the Third Estate eked out a hardscrabble existence. Our chapter describes the particularly harsh winter of 1788. But the truth is that this winter only made a bad situation worse. Hunger for the peasants of the Third Estate was a way of life and, for many, a way of death. A watery porridge seasoned by a wilted vegetable served as the daily staple. Meat was virtually unheard of, reserved for the few occasions when a holiday or marriage brightened the calendar. An oppressive tax system, ground rents, and forced tithes added to the peasant's burden. Life was dominated by basic needs, a fact which brings us back to Little Red Riding Hood.

Food—especially the height of extravagance, a meat meal—was an obsession for French peasants and major theme in their tales. Rather than offering an escape from their grim reality, the peasants' stories mirrored their bleak existence. As Darnton writes, such tales "erect warning signs around the seeking of fortune: 'Danger!' 'Road Out,' 'Go Slow!' 'Stop!'" The sin of our ill-fated French heroine was that she blithely avoided these warning signs and let her guard down. Instead of becoming suspicious by the offer of a meat and wine during an otherwise uneventful visit to grandma, she let her stomach triumph over her good sense—a mistake for which she paid dearly.

Viewing these early folktales as historical sources aquaints us with a world vastly different from our own. Often their precise meaning escapes us because of our inability to span the abyss separating our two worlds. But when we listen closely to an early version of a common folktale we can discern clues about the life of the voiceless masses of the Third Estate. In the process, we gain insight into the despair and misery that ultimately fueled the forces of the French Revolution.

Chapter Main Ideas

Section 1 Problems in French society led to a revolution, the formation of a new government, and the end of the monarchy.

Section 2 An extreme government changed French society and tried through harsh means to eliminate its critics within France.

Section 3 Napoleon Bonaparte rose through military ranks to become emperor over France and much of Europe.

Section 4 After defeating Napoleon, the European allies sent him into exile and held a meeting in Vienna to restore order and stability to Europe.

▣ New York Standards

Key Idea 2 Establishing timeframes, exploring different periodizations, examining themes across time and within cultures, and focusing on important turning points in world history help organize the study of world cultures and civilizations.

Key Idea 3 Study of the major social, political, cultural, and religious developments in world history involves learning about the important roles and contributions of individuals and groups.

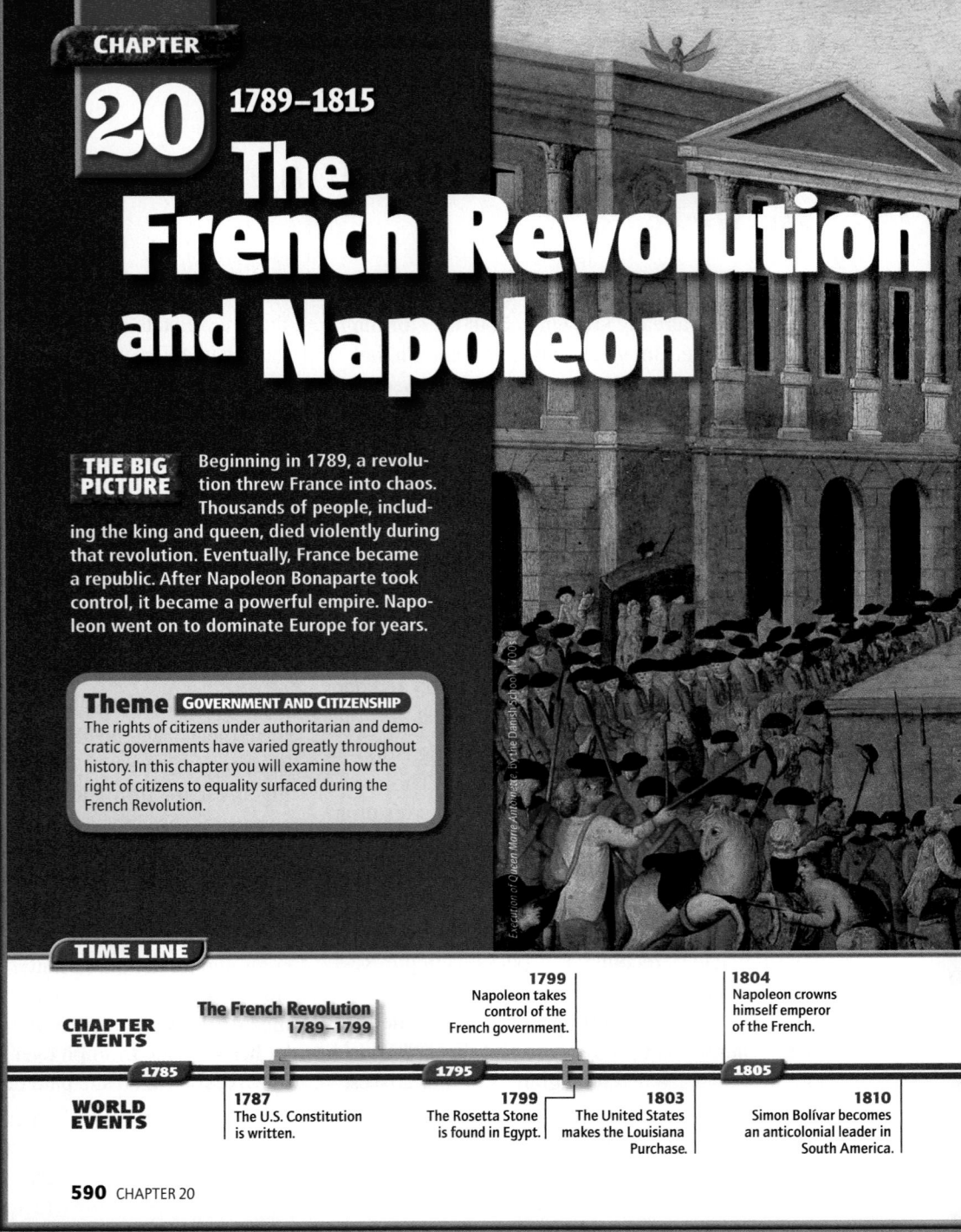

CHAPTER

20 1789–1815
The French Revolution and Napoleon

THE BIG PICTURE Beginning in 1789, a revolution threw France into chaos. Thousands of people, including the king and queen, died violently during that revolution. Eventually, France became a republic. After Napoleon Bonaparte took control, it became a powerful empire. Napoleon went on to dominate Europe for years.

Theme GOVERNMENT AND CITIZENSHIP
The rights of citizens under authoritarian and democratic governments have varied greatly throughout history. In this chapter you will examine how the right of citizens to equality surfaced during the French Revolution.

Execution of Queen Marie-Antoinette, by the Danish School, 1793

TIME LINE

CHAPTER EVENTS
The French Revolution 1789–1799

1799 Napoleon takes control of the French government.

1804 Napoleon crowns himself emperor of the French.

1785 — 1795 — 1805

WORLD EVENTS
1787 The U.S. Constitution is written.

1799 The Rosetta Stone is found in Egypt.

1803 The United States makes the Louisiana Purchase.

1810 Simon Bolívar becomes an anticolonial leader in South America.

590 CHAPTER 20

Introduce the Chapter

At Level

The French Revolution and Napoleon

1. Tell students that in this chapter they will learn about events in France that led to a revolution, a period of chaos, and the emergence of a dictator.

2. Write these terms for students to see: liberty, equality, brotherhood/sisterhood. Then have students write a few sentences about what each of the words means to them. Have volunteers read their sentences to the class.

3. Guide students in a discussion about why some people might be willing to sacrifice everything for these principles, especially in an unjust society.

4. Have students scan the chapter and develop a list of the main topics and a list of the charts and maps that appear in the chapter.

5. Guide students in a review of the maps and charts. Have students explain what the maps and charts reveal about this time period.
LS Verbal-Linguistic

Alternative Assessment Handbook, Rubrics 1: Acquiring Information; and 11: Discussions

Reading like a Historian

This painting shows the execution by guillotine of Queen Marie-Antoinette in 1793. The queen was killed during the French Revolution's Reign of Terror, an especially bloody time.

Analyzing Visuals How do you think the painter who created this picture felt about the queen's execution? Explain your answer.

See **Skills Handbook**, p. H27

1815
Allied forces defeat Napoleon at the Battle of Waterloo.

1821
Napoleon dies in exile.

1813
Mexico declares its independence from Spain.

THE FRENCH REVOLUTION AND NAPOLEON **591**

Explore the Time Line

1. How many years did the French Revolution last? *ten*

2. What event happened the same year that the Rosetta Stone was found in Egypt? *Napoleon took control of the French government.*

3. What did Napoleon do in 1804? *crowned himself emperor of the French*

4. In which battle was Napoleon defeated? *Battle of Waterloo*

Info to Know

The Diamond Necklace Affair Before the revolution, a young adventuress named Madame Lamotte hatched a plot to advance her own place in society and gain wealth. Her plot involved the queen, Marie-Antoinette, a prominent clergyman, a jeweler, and a diamond necklace worth about $100 million today. Although Marie-Antoinette was innocent of involvement in the scheme, her reputation among the French was severely damaged.

Draw Conclusions Why was Marie-Antoinette's reputation damaged? *because she was implicated in a crime though she was innocent*

● **Chapter Preview** ●

HOLT
History's Impact
► **Video Program: The French Revolution and Napoleon**
See the Video Teacher's Guide for strategies for using the video segment.

Reading Like a Historian

Analyzing Visuals Have students take a moment to examine the image on these pages. Ask students to look at the crowd. What kinds of people are represented? *soldiers, poor people* What are their reactions to the execution? *Some are excited and celebrating, others stand silently.*

go.hrw.com
Online Resources

Chapter Resources:
KEYWORD: SHL NAP
Teacher Resources:
KEYWORD: SHL TEACHER

Answers

Reading Like a Historian *possible answer—felt that the execution was barbaric; executioner parades head, shows blood*

591

Preteach

Geography Starting Points

Where are Italy and Germany? By 1789, the outlines of the modern nations of Spain, France, and Portugal were clearly recognizable. At this time in history, Germany and Italy were divided into dozens of small states, although the German states were still organized into the Holy Roman Empire. During the Napoleonic Wars, France conquered or subjugated these small states, but could not hold them for long. Italy and Germany did not achieve complete unification until the 1870s.

🗺 **Map Transparency**: Europe, 1789

📖 **World History Outline Maps**

★Interactive
EUROPE, 1789

France was a powerful European country at the start of the French Revolution.

FRENCH EMPIRE, 1812

The French Empire controlled much of Europe.

0   150   300 Miles
0   150   300 Kilometers
Azimuthal equal-area projection

— Holy Roman Empire
▨ Habsburg possessions

Starting Points In the late 1700s France was one of Europe's large and powerful kingdoms. At that time, Europe was made up of a few large kingdoms and empires as well as many smaller states and territories. Then in 1789, the French Revolution set off a chain of events that reshaped Europe's political map.

1. **Analyze** Compare France on the large map to the French Empire on the inset map. What might have happened to allow France to become an empire?

2. **Predict** How do you think leaders of other European countries might have reacted as France expanded into other parts of Europe?

🔊 **Listen to History**

Go online to listen to an explanation of the starting points for this chapter.

go.hrw.com
Keyword: SHL NAP

592 CHAPTER 20

Skills Focus: Analyzing Maps   At Level

Social Studies Skill
French Expansion

Materials: outline maps, colored pencils

1. Give each student an outline map of Europe.

2. Have students use the information from the map on this page to create a new map that shows French expansion. Students should start by carefully outlining the 1789 French border and coloring in France.

3. Have students draw arrows that show the various directions of the French conquest. Then, have students outline the 1812 borders

and color in the new territories with a different color. Tell students that most of this territory did not become part of France, but was controlled by France.

4. Have students locate major battles that occurred during the French conquest and add this information to the map. LS **Visual-Spatial**

📖 **Alternative Assessment Handbook**, Rubric 20: Map Creation

Answers

Geography Starting Points

1. possible answers—a strong military leader took control; values of country shifted to building an empire; weaker neighbors; **2.** possible answers—felt threatened; challenged French conquest

SECTION 1 — The Revolution Begins

BEFORE YOU READ

MAIN IDEA

Problems in French society led to a revolution, the formation of a new government, and the end of the monarchy.

READING FOCUS

1. What caused the French Revolution?
2. What happened during the first events of the Revolution?
3. How did the French create a new nation?

KEY TERMS AND PEOPLE

Old Order
King Louis XVI
Marie-Antoinette
First Estate
Second Estate
Third Estate
bourgeoisie
sans culottes
Declaration of the Rights of Man and of the Citizen
radical

NEW YORK

PI 2.3 Students analyze evidence critically and demonstrate an understanding of how circumstances of time and place influence perspective.

THE INSIDE STORY

What drove a Paris mob to fury? In April 1789 a rumor was flying through the Paris workers' neighborhoods: Réveillon the wallpaper manufacturer was about to slash his employees' wages in half. Although the rumor was probably false, an angry crowd of unemployed workers from various industries gathered at Réveillon's home. The home was famous for its gorgeous furnishings. Such wealth was in sharp contrast to the miserable poverty of the thousands of Parisians assembled there. When the crowd pushed into the house, Réveillon's family fled. Seeing the home's splendor—evidence of wealth that workers could never even hope for—the crowd went on a rampage, breaking and burning everything in sight. This event was just the beginning. Poverty and inequality would drive French workers to violence again and again. ■

Causes of the Revolution

In the 1780s, long-standing resentments against the French monarchy fueled anger throughout France. The source of the French people's ill will could be found in the unequal structure of French government and society.

Inequalities in Society A social and political structure called the **Old Order**, or ancien régime (ahns-yan ray-ZHEEM), created inequalities in French society. Under the Old Order, the king was at the top, and three social groups called estates were under him.

A Wallpaper Maker's BAD LUCK

▼ Poor laborers riot in the streets of Paris.

THE FRENCH REVOLUTION AND NAPOLEON **593**

Now the right column "Preteach" section.

Preteach

Getting Started

Use the **Interactive Reader and Study Guide** to familiarize students with the section content.

📝 **Interactive Reader and Study Guide**, Section 1

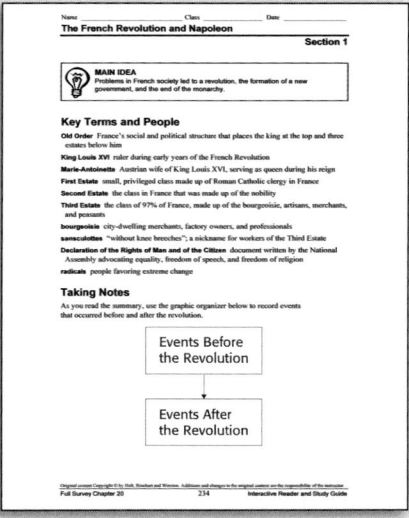

Academic Vocabulary

Review with students the high-use academic term in this section.

privileges special rights granted to certain people because of their position in society (p. 594)

📝 **CRF:** Vocabulary Builder: Section 1

Taking Notes

Before Revolution— inequalities in society, Enlightenment ideas, poor leadership, financial crisis, hunger; After Revolution— National Assembly completed constitution, restricted king's power, gave citizens broad rights, formed Legislative Assembly, disbanded and formed National Convention, ended monarchy, declared France a republic

---

Teach the Main Idea

The Revolution Begins

1. **Teach** Ask students the Reading Focus questions to teach this section.

2. **Apply** Write the following question for students to see: How do you know when a system is unfair? Have students work in pairs to brainstorm answers to this question. Have each pair volunteer its best answer, and write all the answers for students to see. Have students provide brief examples of unfair systems they have encountered.

3. **Review** As you review the section, have students explain how the conditions in France led to the revolution.

4. **Practice/Homework** Have students write a one-page petition to the king of France in which they suggest reforms that might help France avoid revolution. **LS Verbal-Linguistic**

📝 **Alternative Assessment Handbook**, Rubric 43: Writing to Persuade

Reading Focus

1 What caused the French Revolution? *inequalities in society, Enlightenment ideas, poor leadership, financial crisis, hunger and cold*

Causes of the Revolution

Recall What groups made up the First and Second Estates? *First Estate —clergy; Second Estate—nobility*

Making Inferences Why do you think church lands and properties were exempt from taxes? *possible answer—tradition of the importance of the church in society; immoral to tax religious property*

Evaluate What are some possible reasons for the reluctance of the First and Second Estates to eliminate their tax exemptions? *possible answers— pride, tradition, lack of empathy for Third Estate*

CRF: Biography: Marie-Antoinette

CRF: Literature: *Les Misérables* by Victor Hugo

CRF: Social Studies Skills: Interpreting Charts

Info to Know

Population Growth In 1700, France's population hovered around 20 million. As diseases and food shortages diminished, the population increased by 8 to 10 million over the next hundred years. This rapid growth contributed to social stress that in turn led to revolution.

Answers

Reading Like a Historian 1. *the First and Second Estates;* **2.** *possible answer—First and Second: anger at this portrayal; Third: agreement and motivation to take action*

NEW YORK

CC Unit 5-C3b
Key individuals in the French Revolution (Louis XVI)

ACADEMIC VOCABULARY
privileges special rights granted to certain people because of their position in society

The king at the time of the Revolution was **King Louis XVI**. He lived at the extravagant palace of Versailles, 10 miles outside of Paris. King Louis XVI was shy and indecisive but not cruel. His queen, **Marie-Antoinette**, was from Austria—a country that was a traditional enemy of France. Marie-Antoinette's nationality made her unpopular with the French, but she was also frivolous and self-indulgent. She enjoyed lavish parties and fancy clothes while many of the common people wore rags.

The rest of French society was divided into three classes, called estates. These groups varied widely in what they contributed to France, in terms of both work and taxes.

The **First Estate** was made up of the Roman Catholic clergy, about 1 percent of the population. The clergy had held several <u>privileges</u> since the Middle Ages. For example, only church courts could try priests and bishops for crimes, so the clergy did not have to answer to the same laws as everyone else. Furthermore,

neither the clergy nor the Roman Catholic Church had to pay taxes. Land belonging to the Roman Catholic Church was also exempt from taxes. In addition, the church owned about 10 percent of France's land, which produced vast sums of money in rents and fees. Bishops and some other higher clergy controlled this wealth and became very rich. Although many of the priests who ministered to the common people were poor, many people resented the wealth and privileges of the clergy.

The **Second Estate** was made up of the nobility, less than 2 percent of the population. Although the nobility controlled much of the country's wealth, they paid few taxes. Members of the Second Estate held key positions in the government and military. Many lived on country estates where peasants did all the work and were forced to pay high fees and rents to the landowner. Some nobles lived in luxury at the king's court, where their only real jobs were ceremonial.

PRIMARY SOURCES

The Three Estates

This cartoon shows a member of the Third Estate crushed beneath a stone that represents taxes, land rent and fees, and labor the peasants had to perform without pay. Nobles paid some fees, but no taxes. The clergy did not pay taxes either. The graph below shows that the Third Estate contributed much more money to the country's treasury than the other estates.

REVENUE PAID BY ESTATES

First Estate — 0.5%   Second Estate — 1.5%

Third Estate **98%**

Source: Simon Schama, Citizens

The First and Second Estates, represented by a priest and nobleman, stand on the stone and add to the peasant's misery.

The man under the rock represents the peasants and laborers of the Third Estate.

Taille, Impots et Corvee, anonymous, 1700s

Skills FOCUS   READING LIKE A HISTORIAN

1. **Analyze** In the cartoon, which two estates appear to be allies?
2. **Analyze Primary Sources** How do you think members of the three estates might have reacted to this cartoon? Explain your answer.

See Skills Handbook, p. H25

Differentiating Instruction

Below Level

Special Education Students

Guide students in a discussion about the various types of people who lived in France during the 1780s. Copy the three-column chart at right for students to see. Omit the italicized words. Have students copy and complete the chart. **LS Visual-Spatial**

Alternative Assessment Handbook, Rubrics 7: Charts; and 11: Discussions

Estate	Title	Roles
First	*Clergy*	*control of 1/10th of the land; minister to common people*
Second	*Nobility*	*controlled much of country's wealth; ran government; served in military*
Third	*Bourgeoisie, sansculottes, peasants*	*merchants, factory owners, professionals, artisans, workers, farmers, laborers*

The **Third Estate**, by far the largest group of people, included about 97 percent of the population. The Third Estate was itself made up of several groups. At the top of the Third Estate was the **bourgeoisie** (boorhzh-wah-ZEE)—city-dwelling merchants, factory owners, and professionals such as lawyers and doctors. Although they had no role in the government, some of the bourgeoisie were highly educated and quite rich. Their wealth, however, did not buy them any influence in the government.

Below the bourgeoisie were the artisans and workers of the cities. These were the shoemakers, carpenters, bricklayers, dressmakers, and laborers. If these people had no work, they went hungry. The workers of the Third Estate were known as **sans culottes** (sanz-kooh-laht), or those "without knee breeches." They wore long pants—in contrast to the tight knee-length breeches, or pants, worn by the nobility. Sans culottes became a nickname of pride for the workers.

At the bottom of the Third Estate were the peasants who farmed the nobles' fields. Not only did they pay rents and fees to the landowners, but they also paid a tenth of their income to the church. In addition, they had to perform labor, such as working on roads, without pay. Many peasants were miserably poor and had no hope for a better life.

Enlightenment Ideas While social inequalities were driving poor people toward revolt, new ideas from the Enlightenment were also inspiring the French Revolution. Many educated members of the bourgeoisie knew about the writings of the great Enlightenment philosophers John Locke, Baron de Montesquieu, and Jean-Jacques Rousseau. Members of the bourgeoisie also knew that Great Britain's government limited the king's power. More recently, they had learned that American colonists, inspired by Enlightenment ideas, had successfully rebelled against Britain's king. Seeing how these ideas were transforming government and society in other countries, some of the bourgeoisie began to consider how these ideas might be used in France.

A Financial Crisis A third cause of the Revolution was a financial crisis, severe economic problems that affected much of the country.

CAUSES OF THE REVOLUTION

- Inequalities in society
- Ideas of Enlightenment writers
- Poor leadership from Louis XVI
- Financial crisis
- Widespread hunger and record cold

TAKING NOTES

As you read, take notes in a graphic organizer like this one. Record details of the events that led up to the revolution and the events that occurred immediately after it.

Events Before the Revolution → Events After the Revolution

 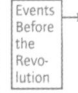

The Bread Famine and the Pawnbroker by Le Sueur brothers, 1700s

First, France was deeply in debt. Over the previous centuries, France had borrowed huge sums of money to spend on wars, including the American Revolution. But the king and his court continued to spend lavishly, leading to even more borrowing and debt. By the 1780s, this pattern of spending and borrowing had taken the country deeply into debt.

By 1787 King Louis XVI was desperate for money. He tried to tax the Second Estate, but the nobles refused to pay. The king, incapable of the strong leadership the situation required, backed down. A year later the country faced bankruptcy. Half the taxes collected were needed just to pay the country's debt.

At the same time, nature was creating other economic problems. First, a hailstorm and a drought ruined the harvest. Then the winter of 1788 was the worst in 80 years. Frozen rivers prevented waterwheels from powering the mills that ground wheat into flour. Food and firewood were scarce and expensive. As hunger and cold made life wretched for thousands of French citizens, misery grew into anger.

The country was broke, and people were hungry and angry. Eliminating the tax exemptions for the First and Second Estates could have helped the situation, but the clergy and the nobility resisted all such efforts.

READING CHECK **Summarize** What were the causes of the French Revolution?

FOCUS ON NEW YORK

While France was careening toward a revolution, the framers of the U.S. Constitution were using parts of the New York State Constitution as a model for their new document.

 NEW YORK

CC **Unit 5-C3a**
Causes of the French Revolution

Reading Focus

Causes of the Revolution

Recall Who were the sansculottes? *workers of the Third Estate who wore long pants instead of fashionable knee breeches; became a nickname of pride for workers*

Summarize What spending patterns put France into deep debt by the 1780s? *borrowing huge sums of money to spend on wars; lavish spending by king and his court*

Predict What actions could King Louis have taken to avoid an economic crisis? *possible answer— eliminated tax exemptions for the First and Second Estates*

Activity **Reform Slogans** Have students create three slogans that members of the Third Estate might use to encourage reform in France. List slogans for the class to see. **LS Verbal-Linguistic**

Alternative Assessment Handbook, Rubric 34: Slogans and Banners

Quick Facts Transparency: Causes of the Revolution

Skills Focus: Identifying Problem and Solution

At Level

Reading Skill
Problems in France

Materials: butcher or poster paper, colored markers

1. Guide students in a discussion of the problems that France faced in the 1780s. Develop a class list of these problems and write them for students to see.

2. Organize students into six groups and assign each group a role: monarch, clergy, nobility, bourgeoisie, artisans, and peasants.

3. Have each group develop a plan to address three of France's problems. Remind students to suggest plans in accordance with their roles. Have groups write their plans on the poster paper.

4. Have volunteers share their plans with the class, and display their posters for the class to see. Have students discuss which plans seem most feasible. **LS Visual-Spatial, Interpersonal**

Alternative Assessment Handbook, Rubrics 11: Discussions; and 35: Solving Problems

Answers

Reading Check *inequalities in society, Enlightenment ideas, poor leadership, financial crisis, hunger and cold*

595

❷ What happened during the first events of the Revolution? *Members of the Third Estate demanded more representation and rights; a mob stormed the Bastille; rumors of retaliation spread.*

First Events of the Revolution

Recall Why did a mob storm the Bastille? *to look for weapons to defend themselves; the Bastille was a symbol of oppression*

Contrast How was the 1789 meeting of the Estates General different from previous meetings? *Members of the Third Estate had a new sense of their importance; they demanded, and eventually received, increased voting rights.*

Make Judgments Did the National Assembly created by the Third Estate have the right to make laws for all of France? *possible answer—Yes, they represented 97 percent of the people in France.*

📑 **CRF:** Biography: Georges-Jacques Danton

Primary Source
Louis XVI: "Is it a revolt?"
François Alexandre Frederic, Duc de La Rochefoucauld-Liancourt: "No, Sire, it is a revolution."
–Upon learning at Versailles of the fall of the Bastille, 1789

Answers

Reading Like a Historian 1. *possible answer—Cholat participated in the storming and thought it was important.* **2.** *possible answer—He wanted to tell the story in one painting.* **3.** *possible answer—to show the perspective of the people moving toward the Bastille*

596

First Events of the Revolution

By the spring of 1789, no group was happy. The First and Second Estates—the upper clergy and the nobility—resented that they had lost power to the monarchy. The wealthy bourgeoisie resented government regulations that hampered the growth of businesses as well as being barred from government and military positions. The poorer members of the Third Estate resented the hunger and unemployment that plagued them now more then ever.

Meeting of the Estates-General One of the first events of the Revolution was a meeting that the nobility pressed Louis to call. The nobles wanted a meeting of the Estates-General, an assembly made up of the three estates, to approve new taxes on the Third Estate. In August 1788 Louis agreed that the Estates General should meet the following spring.

In the tense atmosphere that existed in the spring of 1789, representatives of the Estates-General came to Paris. Because the Estates-General had not met for 175 years, this was the first such meeting for all of the representatives. In preparation for the event, the representatives wrote "notebooks," called cahiers (kah-YAYZ), to document their grievances. As the notebooks arrived in Paris, excitement grew. It became clear that people wanted the Estates-General to pass sweeping reforms. However, the voting process threatened the possibility of reforms.

Each of the three estates had always had only one vote in the Estates-General. Usually the First and Second Estates voted together, outvoting the Third Estate. This time, though, the ideas of the Enlightenment philosophers had given members of the Third Estate a new sense of importance. The Third Estate wanted to change the voting process.

At the start of the first meeting, King Louis instructed the assembly to follow the old rules of voting by estate. But the Third Estate, which had more representatives than the First or Second, refused the king's order. When Louis did nothing to have the order enforced, the Third Estate acted. On June 17, 1789, they proclaimed themselves a legislature, the National Assembly, with the right to make laws for France.

Storming the Bastille

Analyzing Visuals One way we can learn about the past is by carefully analyzing works of art. The watercolor image on the right is Claude Cholat's *Storming the Bastille*. Even though Cholat was not a professional artist his painting interests historians because he was at the storming of the Bastille.

To interpret what this painting suggests about the French Revolution, think about

• the subject of the painting
• the title of the work
• the details in the painting

Skills FOCUS READING LIKE A HISTORIAN

1. **Subject and Title** Why do you think Cholat chose to paint the storming of the Bastille rather than some other event in the Revolution?

2. **Details** Why do you think Cholat included details of the entire day—from the initial attack on the Bastille to the flag of surrender—in this one image?

3. **Details** Why do you think Cholat put the scene in the courtyard in the foreground and the Bastille itself in the background?

See Skills Handbook, p. H26

Only then did the king take action, by locking the Third Estate out of their meeting place. Not to be defeated, the representatives of the Third Estate met in an indoor tennis court. There they swore what became known as the Tennis Court Oath—that they would not leave the court until they had written a constitution for France. In the face of this event, Louis relented and allowed each representative to have a vote.

The Storming of the Bastille The next major event of the Revolution occurred because Louis made a serious mistake. He started ordering troops to Paris and Versailles in case he needed to preserve the monarchy by force. Seeing this, members of the National Assembly feared that the king would use violence to end their meetings. The people of Paris, in sympathy with the National Assembly, sought to arm themselves against any action the king might take.

Differentiating Instruction

Below Level

Learners Having Difficulty

1. Review the information in the text about the storming of the Bastille. Have students closely examine the painting by Claude Cholat.

2. Organize students into mixed-ability pairs. Have each pair write a poem or song lyrics that tell the story of the storming of the Bastille from the point of view of a member of the mob, the commander, the prison guard, or one of the prisoners.

3. Have volunteers recite their poem or song lyrics to the class. 🄻🅂 **Auditory-Musical**

📑 **Alternative Assessment Handbook**, Rubric 26: Poems and Songs

Cholat compressed all the day's events into this single image.

A soldier atop the Bastille is waving a white flag to surrender. Other accounts of the day support this detail.

The men on the wall are cutting the chains that will lower the drawbridge leading to the Bastille.

Storming the Bastille, by Claude Cholat, 1789

On July 14, 1789, a mob of Parisians went to the Bastille, an ancient prison, looking for weapons. In the past, the French government imprisoned people at the Bastille who spoke out against the monarchy. However, at the time, the prison held only seven prisoners, but the people viewed the huge medieval building as a powerful sign of the people's oppression. At first, the mob tried to negotiate with the Bastille's commander for weapons. When negotiations broke down, the angry mob and the prison guard exchanged fire and the mob swarmed into the prison. The mob killed the commander, stuck his head on a long stick, and paraded it through the streets. The action of the storming of the Bastille became a powerful symbol of the French Revolution.

The Spread of Fear After the fall of the Bastille, many people were shocked by what they had done. They feared that the king would punish them and end the Revolution.

Some people spread rumors that the king had hired foreign soldiers to punish the Third Estate. As a result, a panic later called the Great Fear swept through France. This panic was based on both fiction and fact. For example, rumors of massacres spread from village to village, and many people believed all kinds of wild stories. In the region of Champagne, for example, 3,000 men tried to find a gang of thugs reportedly seen in their neighborhood. However, the gang turned out to just be a herd of cattle.

As a result of the years of abuse by landowners, some peasants took revenge. The peasants destroyed records listing feudal dues and rents and burned nobles' houses. There was violence in the countryside, but the violence did not come from foreign soldiers.

THE IMPACT TODAY

July 14, called Bastille Day, is now France's national holiday.

READING CHECK **Identify Cause and Effect** What was the connection between the fall of the Bastille and the Great Fear?

THE FRENCH REVOLUTION AND NAPOLEON **597**

Differentiating Instruction

Advanced Learners/ Gifted and Talented   Research Required   Above Level

Have students conduct research on the National Assembly, including its decisions and individual members. Each student should write a short essay in which they evaluate decisions of the National Assembly on an item-by-item basis. Have volunteers read selections from their essays to the class. **LS Verbal-Linguistic**

📝 **Alternative Assessment Handbook**, Rubric 37: Writing Assignments

English-Language Learners
                                                    Below Level

Materials: poster paper, colored markers

Have students review the material about the storming of the Bastille. Guide students in a discussion about the significance of Bastille Day and why it was made a national holiday in France. Have students create a poster in honor of Bastille Day. Display posters in a classroom exhibit. **LS Visual-Spatial**

📝 **Alternative Assessment Handbook**, Rubric 28: Posters

Reading Focus

First Events of the Revolution

Recall What did people fear after the fall of the Bastille? *that the king would punish them and end the revolution*

Explain How were rumors of massacres misleading? *Some stories were untrue, such as a reported gang of thugs in Champagne that was really a herd of cattle.*

Reading Like a Historian
Storming the Bastille

Activity Guide students in a discussion about how this painting celebrates the storming of the Bastille. Have students create an illustration that portrays the same events in a negative light. **LS Visual-Spatial**

📝 **Alternative Assessment Handbook**, Rubrics 3: Artwork; and 11: Discussions

---

Answers

Reading Check *possible answer— After the fall of the Bastille, people were terrified that the king would punish them.*

597

3 How did the French create a new nation? *National Assembly completed constitution; restricted king's power; created Legislative Assembly; gave citizens broad rights; ended monarchy*

Creating a New Nation

Recall What was the outcome of the women's march on Versailles? *Louis made peace with the crowd by promising to return to Paris.*

Make Inferences Why did the National Assembly turn the clergy into public employees? *possible answer—They wanted the clergy to be accountable to the public, not part of a separate institution.*

Teaching Tip

Highlight the lasting importance of the Declaration of the Rights of Man and of the Citizen by having students compare it with the Universal Declaration of Human Rights, passed by the United Nations after World War II. The similarities will be striking.

Answers

Reading Like a Historian 1. *liberty, property, security, resistance to oppression;* **2.** *equality of man; listing basic human rights; free speech, innocent until proven guilty*

Reading Skills *possible answer—those who have a love of wisdom*

598

Declaration of the Rights of Man and of the Citizen

This excerpt from the Declaration states the principles of the French Revolution and shows the strong influence of Enlightenment ideals.

"The representatives of the French people, . . . believing that the ignorance, neglect, or contempt of the rights of man are the sole cause of public calamities and of the corruption of governments, have determined to set forth in a solemn declaration the natural, unalienable, and sacred rights of man. . .

1. Men are born and remain free and equal in rights. . .

2. The aim of all political association is the preservation of the . . . rights of man. These rights are liberty, property, security and resistance to oppression. . .

5. Law can only prohibit such actions as are hurtful to society. . .

6. Law is the expression of the general will. Every citizen has a right to participate personally, or through his representative, in its formation. It must be the same for all. . .

7. No person shall be accused, arrested, or imprisoned except in the cases and according to the forms prescribed by law. . .

9. As all persons are held innocent until they shall have been declared guilty. . .

11. The free communication of ideas and opinions is one of the most precious of the rights of man. . . .

12. A common contribution [tax] is essential. . . . This should be equitably distributed among all the citizens in proportion to their means."

Skills FOCUS READING LIKE A HISTORIAN

1. Explain According to the Declaration, what are the natural rights of man?

2. Analyze What ideas do the Declaration and the American Declaration of Independence and U.S. Bill of Rights share?

See **Skills Handbook,** p. H25

Creating a New Nation

The violence that marked the beginning of the Revolutions eventually lessened.. At this stage, in the Revolution the National Assembly began transforming centuries of French tradition. The Assembly formed a new government and France's monarchy eventually crumbled.

Legislating New Rights By early August 1789, the National Assembly had eliminated all the feudal dues and services that the peasants owed the landowners. The Assembly also eliminated the First Estate's legal privileges.

In late August the National Assembly adopted the **Declaration of the Rights of Man and of the Citizen**. The Declaration laid out the basic principles of the French Revolution—"liberty, equality, fraternity [brotherhood]." Writers of the Declaration took their inspiration from the English Bill of Rights, the American Declaration of Independence, and the writings of Enlightenment <u>philosophers</u>.

READING SKILLS

Understanding Word Parts If you know that *philo* means "love" and *sophia* means "wisdom," how would you define *philosophers*?

The document stated that all men are born equal and remain equal before the law. Like the U.S. Bill of Rights, the Declaration guaranteed freedom of speech, the press, and religion.

However, these rights did not extend to women. A famous Paris playwright, Olympe de Gouges (duh-goozh), wrote a declaration of rights for women, but the National Assembly turned it down.

Restrictions on Power Alarmed by the National Assembly's actions, Louis made the same mistake he had made earlier in the summer. He called troops to Versailles to protect his throne. This angered the common people of Paris, who feared that the king would crush the Revolution. In October a crowd of perhaps 7,000 women marched through the rain from Paris to Versailles. Demanding bread, the mob broke into the palace. To make peace with the crowd, Louis agreed to return to Paris and live in the Tuileries Palace with his family.

598 CHAPTER 20

Skills Focus: Analyzing Primary Sources

At Level

Reading Like a Historian Skill
French Revolution Principles

1. Guide students in a discussion about the main points of the Declaration of the Rights of Man and of the Citizen.

2. Organize students into eight groups. Assign each group one of the principles listed in the Declaration.

3. Have students in each group work together to paraphrase the principle in their own words. Remind students that assembly members felt strongly about the ideas they discussed.

4. Have a volunteer from each group read its paraphrased principle and discuss as a class.

LS Interpersonal, Verbal-Linguistic

Alternative Assessment Handbook, Rubrics 11: Discussions; and 14: Group Activity

The seizure of the royal family encouraged the Revolution's leaders to take bolder steps, and they passed several anticlerical measures. In November, the National Assembly seized church lands and sold them to pay off France's huge debt. All religious orders were disbanded. The Assembly also passed an act that turned the clergy into public employees. This action outraged most members of the clergy and also horrified many peasants.

Formation of a New Government In 1791 the National Assembly finally completed its constitution. It created a new legislative body called the Legislative Assembly. Citizens gained broad voting rights, but only taxpaying men at least 25 years old had the right to vote. The constitution kept the monarchy but severely restricted the king's power. In June 1791 the king and queen suspected that they were not safe, so they put on disguises and fled Paris. However, they were recognized and brought back to the Tuileries Palace.

The Intervention of Foreign Powers In July 1792 Austria and Prussia issued a declaration warning against harming the French monarchs and hinting that any such action would provoke war. Although the declaration was not meant to be read as a serious threat, Austria sent 50,000 troops to the French border. In response, the Legislative Assembly declared war. France's army was in disarray, however, and was defeated.

In Paris the financial strain of war, food shortages and high prices, and foreign troops marching toward the city led to unrest. Many people blamed the army's defeats on the king. Parisians feared that the achievements of the Revolution would be overturned, and they decided they had nothing to lose from extreme action.

The End of the Monarchy Extreme action came on August 10, 1792, when a mob marched on the Tuileries Palace and slaughtered the guards. Louis, Marie-Antoinette, and the children—now demoted to commoners—were thrown in prison.

Faced with mob violence and foreign invasion, the Legislative Assembly felt powerless. It voted itself out of existence and called for the election of a new legislature, the National Convention. The violence in August helped put the **radical** faction, or those who favored extreme change, in control. Among the National Convention's first acts were abolishing the monarchy and declaring France a republic.

The same day the new National Convention met, the French won a battle against the foreign invaders. This victory inspired hope in the revolutionary troops. The French Republic had held its ground against Europe's Old Order.

READING CHECK **Sequence** What steps did National and Legislative Assemblies take to create a new nation?

go.hrw.com
Online Quiz
Keyword: SHL NAP HP

SECTION 1 ASSESSMENT

Reviewing Ideas, Terms, and People

1. **a. Recall** What was the **Old Order**, and who was at its top?
   b. Explain Why did members of the **Third Estate** feel they were treated unfairly by the **First** and **Second Estates**?
   c. Predict What do you think might have happened if, in the fall of 1789, harvests had been larger than usual?

2. **a. Explain** What happened on July 14, 1789?
   b. Analyze Why did **Third Estate** members of the Estates-General feel that the Tennis Court Oath was necessary?
   c. Evaluate Do you think the Great Fear was a logical reaction to the fall of the Bastille? Why or why not?

3. **a. Describe** What rights did the **Declaration of the Rights of Man and of the Citizen** grant?
   b. Sequence List the events that directly affected the royal family.

Critical Thinking

4. **Identify Cause and Effect** Copy the graphic organizer below and use it to list causes of the French Revolution and the immediate effects. Add rows as needed.

Causes	Effects

FOCUS ON WRITING

5. **Persuasion** You are a member of one of the French estates. Write a short letter to the editor of the newspaper, arguing for or against each representative to the Estates-General having one vote.

THE FRENCH REVOLUTION AND NAPOLEON **599**

Section 1 Assessment Answers

1. **a.** structure of French society in 1780s; King Louis XVI
   b. First and Second Estate—small tax burden, powerful positions and privileges; Third Estate—large tax burden, few rights
   c. possible answer—tensions would have eased, conflict would have been postponed

2. **a.** The Bastille was stormed.
   b. believed France needed a constitution soon
   c. possible answer—Yes, French peasants could expect punishment.

3. **a.** freedom of speech, press, and religion, right to participate in government, receive fair trial
   b. women's march to Versailles, 1791 constitution, march on Tuileries palace

4. Causes—huge inequalities, Enlightenment ideas, economic problems, poor harvest; Effects—resentment of upper class, gave people hope, country desperate for money, hunger and anger, end of monarchy

5. possible answers—letters for: balances interests of France; letters against: unfair because 97 percent of people are in Third Estate

World Literature

CHARLES DICKENS (1812–1870)

NEW YORK STANDARDS

ST 2.4 Students explain the importance of analyzing narratives drawn from different times and places to understand historical events.

Excerpt from *A Tale of Two Cities*

Word Help

latter the second of two, last
basement lower part
Monsieur mister or sir
Marquis title of nobility
submissive obedient, compliant

Meet the Writer

Charles Dickens (1812-1870) One of the most celebrated English authors, Charles Dickens wrote such classic novels as *Oliver Twist* and *A Christmas Carol*. To highlight the injustices of the 19th century, Dickens depicted the harsh treatment of the poor in a society divided along lines of wealth. Rather than stating his critique directly, Dickens skillfully used his characters to bring out social issues. Dickens pioneered the serial method of publication, which was later widely copied. Magazines printed monthly installments of his novels, making the stories available to those who could not afford books.

About the Reading The French Revolution is the setting for *A Tale of Two Cities*, but the book was written many years later, in 1859. In both cities—London and Paris—the reader meets people who show the best and worst of human qualities. The passage below introduces one of the book's villains, here called Monsieur the Marquis, as he rides through Paris in his carriage. The scene takes place before the Revolution has truly begun.

AS YOU READ Think about why the poor people in the street react as they do.

Excerpt from

A Tale of Two Cities

by Charles Dickens

Driving his Mail Coach in Nice, by Alphonse de Toulouse-Lautrec-Monfa, 1881

With a wild rattle and clatter, and an inhuman abandonment of consideration not easy to be understood in these days, the carriage dashed through streets and swept round corners, with women screaming before it, and men clutching each other and clutching children out of its way. At last, swooping at a street corner by a fountain, one of its wheels came to a sickening little jolt, and there was a loud cry from a number of voices, and the horses reared and plunged.

But for the latter inconvenience, the carriage probably would not have stopped; carriages were often known to drive on, and leave their wounded behind, and why not? But the frightened valet had got down in a hurry . . .

"What has gone wrong?" said Monsieur, calmly looking out.

A tall man in a nightcap had caught up a bundle from among the feet of the horses, and had laid it on the basement of the fountain, and was down in the mud and wet, howling over it like a wild animal.

"Pardon, Monsieur the Marquis!" said a ragged and submissive man, "it is a child."

"Why does he make that abominable noise? Is it his child?"

"Excuse me, Monsieur the Marquis—it is a pity—yes." . . .

The people closed round, and looked at Monsieur the Marquis. . . [He] ran his eyes over them all, as if they had been mere rats come out of their holes.

He took out his purse.

"It is extraordinary to me," said he, "that you people cannot take care of yourselves and your children. One or the other of you is for ever in the way. How do I know what injury you have done my horses?"

Skills FOCUS **READING LIKE A HISTORIAN**

go.hrw.com
World Literature
Keyword: SHL WRLIT

1. **Explain** What was the Monsieur's main concern?
2. **Interpret Literature as a Source** What bias may show in Dickens's novel? What sources do you think Dickens used for information on the Revolution?

See **Skills Handbook**, p. H28

600 CHAPTER 20

Differentiating Instruction

Above Level

Advanced Learners/Gifted and Talented

1. Guide the class in a discussion about the concept of irony using the following example: Later in A Tale of Two Cities, the Marquis is killed to avenge the death of the young child. The killer leaves this note on the body: "Drive him fast to his tomb. This, from JACQUES."

2. Have students brainstorm ways in which a person unapologetically commits a crime or does something wrong and meets an ironic fate. For example, a thief leaves stolen goods in the trunk of his car and, ironically, his car is stolen.

3. Have students write down their ideas and have volunteers share their ideas with the class. Discuss how well the students captured the concept of irony. **LS Verbal-Linguistic**

Alternative Assessment Handbook, Rubric 11: Discussions

Answers

Reading Like a Historian 1. *his horses;* **2.** *bias against French nobility; sources sympathetic to the Third Estate*

BEFORE YOU READ

MAIN IDEA
An extreme government changed French society and tried through harsh means to eliminate its critics within France.

READING FOCUS
1. What changes did the radical government make in French society and politics?
2. What was the Reign of Terror, and how did it end?

KEY TERMS AND PEOPLE
Maximilien Robespierre
guillotine
counterrevolution
Reign of Terror

NEW YORK

PI 2.5 Students investigate key events and developments and major turning points in world history to identify the factors that brought about change and the long-term effects of these changes.

Death of Marat, by Jacques-Louis David, 1793

◀ Jacques-Louis David painted the *Death of Marat* in 1793. The painting provides a narrative of Marat's murder, showing Corday's letter and knife and Marat's wound and blood.

THE INSIDE STORY

How did a skin disease help destroy a radical leader?
On July 13, 1793, Charlotte Corday, who hated the radicals, set out on what she saw as a patriotic mission. Believing that only Jean-Paul Marat's death would save France's republic, the young woman made her way to Marat's home in Paris. A member of the National Convention, Marat was a leader of the radicals who had taken over the French government. Because he was suffering from a severe skin disease, he had taken to working at home while soaking in the tub. At Marat's

home, Corday said that she had information about traitors. She was taken to Marat, who sat partially covered by a table across his tub. As the two talked, Corday slowly reached into a fold of her dress. Suddenly, she pulled out a large kitchen knife, leaned over, and plunged the blade into Marat's chest. Blood gushed from the wound, and Marat sank slowly into the water. The radical leader's skin disease gave an enemy the chance to destroy him. With his murder, Marat became a martyr to his followers. ∎

THE FRENCH REVOLUTION AND NAPOLEON **601**

Preteach

Getting Started

Use the **Interactive Reader and Study Guide** to familiarize students with the section content.

📄 **Interactive Reader and Study Guide**, Section 2

📄 **CRF:** Vocabulary Builder: Section 2

Taking Notes

A radical government—three factions in government: Mountain, Girondins, and Plain; king executed, control tightened society transformed; The Reign of Terror—opposition to Revolution, civil war, trials and executions, Directory formed

---

Teach the Main Idea

At Level

The Republic

1. **Teach** Ask students the Reading Focus questions to teach this section.

2. **Apply** Draw two large circles for students to see. Label each circle with one of the topics of the section: A Radical Government and The Reign of Terror. Have students copy the circles. Then have students work in pairs and write the main ideas of each topic in the appropriate circle.

3. **Review** As you review the section, use the circles as a graphic organizer, and

have students identify the main ideas they have written in their circles. Have students identify the links between the two circles.

4. **Practice/Homework** Have students write an editorial for a Paris newspaper, cautioning the people about excessive violence in the revolution. **LS Visual-Spatial, Verbal-Linguistic**

📄 **Alternative Assessment Handbook,** Rubrics 13: Graphic Organizers; and 37: Writing Assignments

1 What changes did the radical government make in French society and politics? *tried and executed king; set up Committee of Public Safety and the Revolutionary Tribunal; closed churches; tried to undo old ways*

A Radical Government

Identify What were the three factions in the National Convention? *the Mountain or Montagnards, the Girondins, and the Plain*

Contrast How were the Jacobins different from the Girondins? *Jacobins were most radical, support came from the poor; Girondins were moderate; support came from provinces, supported a constitutional monarchy*

Interpret When the National Convention decided to try and execute the king, what message were they sending to France? *possible answer—The monarchy is over and cannot return.*

Info to Know

Slavery and the Haitian Revolution
Revolutionary leaders had proclaimed liberty as their highest ideal, which raised the issue of colonial slavery. France had several colonies in the Caribbean that followed a plantation system with a labor force of black slaves. After the Revolution began, free blacks and people of mixed race began calling for full rights and an end to the slave trade. Their cause was promoted in France by some National Assembly members and radical journalists. The white planters fought back, however, and a 1790 decree did nothing to change things. In 1791, tensions reached a breaking point; a huge slave revolt began and eventually led to the independence of Haiti.

Answers

Reading Like a Historian *possible answer—wanted to ridicule all monarchs as nothing more than entertainers*

As you read, take notes on the changes made in French government and society and the Reign of Terror.

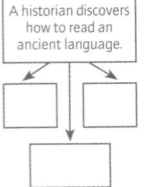

A historian discovers how to read an ancient language.

A Radical Government

When the National Convention convened on September 20, 1792, the radical representatives were in control. Under their direction the Revolution took an extreme turn. France would no longer be a constitutional monarchy. It would be a republic.

Factions in the New Government All of the members of the National Convention supported the Revolution. They grouped themselves into three political factions, however. The Mountain, whose members were called Montagnards, were the most radical. Many Montagnards also belonged to the radical Jacobin (JAK-uh-bihn) Club, or Jacobins. The Montagnards support came from lower middle class and poor people. This support pushed the Montagnards to adopt more radical policies.

Death of a King

Matière à Reflection pour les Jongleurs Couronnées, anonymous, 1793

Skills Focus READING LIKE A HISTORIAN

This poster of Louis XVI's execution was titled "Matter for Reflection for the Crowned Jugglers of Europe," appeared throughout Europe.

Draw Conclusions Why do you think the artist used the phrase "crowned jugglers" instead of "kings"?

See **Skills Handbook**, p. H27

A second political faction, the Girondins, were moderates. They came mainly from the provinces and resented what they considered the excessive influence of the Paris mob on the Revolution. The Girondins generally supported a constitutional monarchy and resisted extremes on either side.

The third political faction, the Plain, was made up of the swing voters. In general, the members of the Plain originally supported the Girondins but later switched their support to the Mountain.

These groupings had no formal organization. They did not put forth programs or promote plans of action. Each member acted as an individual and was often strongly influenced by personal rivalries.

Radical Leaders Three members of radical groups played particularly important roles in the new government.

1. Jean-Paul Marat, an advocate of violence and a leader of the Paris sans culottes, was one of the National Convention's most radical leaders.

2. Georges-Jacques Danton, a violent agitator in the early days of the Revolution, was very popular with the public. A compromiser, he came to oppose what he considered the Revolution's excesses.

3. Maximilien Robespierre was known for his intense dedication to the Revolution. He became increasingly radical and led the National Convention during its most bloodthirsty time.

The Execution of the King Shortly after the National Convention convened, the king was placed on trial. The Girondins had hoped to avoid a trial, but they were in the minority. The more powerful Montagnards were eager to try and execute the king in order to prevent a return of the monarchy and to defend the Revolution from its enemies.

Quickly condemned, the king was scheduled to die the next day, January 21, 1793. That morning, the Paris streets were quiet. Soldiers lined the way to the place of execution, in case any supporters of the monarchy caused trouble. At the scaffold, Louis began to deliver a speech proclaiming his innocence, but a drumroll drowned out his voice. He was pushed into place on the **guillotine**, a device that dropped a sharp, heavy blade through the victim's neck.

Collaborative Learning

At Level

The King on Trial?

1. Guide students in a discussion of the trial of the king, including the possible effects on France if the king were executed.

2. Organize students into mixed-ability pairs. Have half of the pairs write a letter to the National Convention explaining why the king should be put on trial. Have the other half write letters arguing against a trial.

3. Have volunteers read their letters to the class. As they read, make a list of arguments for and against a trial for students to see.

4. Tell students that they are the members of the National Convention and will vote on whether or not to put the king on trial. Remind students that they are not voting on the outcome of the trial.

5. Maintain a secret ballot and tally the votes for students to see. **LS Verbal-Linguistic, Interpersonal**

Alternative Assessment Handbook, Rubric 43: Writing to Persuade

When the deed was done, a young guard held up the dripping head for all to see.

Reports of the king's execution quickly spread across Europe. Outside of France, Europeans reacted with horror to the news of the French Revolution. The London *Times* newspaper condemned the Revolution and the execution of the king as savagery.

HISTORY'S VOICES

❝ Every [heart] burns with indignation in this kingdom, against the ferocious savages of Paris . . . A Republic founded on the blood of an innocent victim must have but a short duration. ❞

—*London Times*, January 25, 1793

Tightening Control After the king's execution, the National Convention began to tighten its hold on France. First, it set up the Committee of Public Safety to manage the country's military defense against the foreign forces on France's borders. The committee promptly created an unprecedented draft of all able-bodied, unmarried men between 18 and 45 for military service. In addition, the National Convention established a court called the Revolutionary Tribunal. This court was supposed to root out and eliminate people who threatened the Revolution from within.

Transforming Society The Revolution not only transformed the French government but also attempted to completely transform French society. The leaders of the new government wanted to erase all connections to old ways of life, including religion. Many clergy members lost their positions. In Paris the local government closed the churches. To replace Roman Catholicism, Robespierre created the cult of the Supreme Being, in which enthusiasm for the Revolution was the object of worship.

Anticlerical feeling took many forms. Even statues of people holding Bibles were not safe. Workers changed the titles on the Bibles to read "Declaration of the Rights of Man."

A metric system replaced the old system of weights and measures. A new calendar also cut ties to the past. The months were renamed, and every month had 3 weeks of 10 days. The revolutionary calendar fell out of use, but the metric system was one change that was kept.

READING CHECK Explain Why did the National Convention want to change French government and society?

Daily Life and the French Revolution

Ideals of the Revolution influenced the design of many kinds of everyday objects. *Why might objects such as playing cards have helped spread revolutionary ideas?*

► To erase connections with royalty, makers of playing cards replaced the traditional images of kings and queens with revolutionary ideals. For example, in place of the queens were the freedoms of worship, marriage, the press, and the professions.

French School, 1700s

◄ Instead of stiff fussy dresses, women began to wear light, loose ones that recalled the styles of ancient Greece—much admired for its democracy.

Incroyable and Merveilleuse in Paris, by Louis Leopold Boilly, 1801

► Household items also showed revolutionary themes. Here, a wallpaper panel displays revolutionary slogans and a red Phrygian (FRI-jee-uhn) cap. The Phrygian cap became a popular symbol of the Revolution because freed slaves of ancient Rome wore such caps.

UNITÉ·INDIVISIBILITÉ DE·LA·REPUBLIQUE. LIBERTÉ·ÉGALITÉ FRATERNITÉ·OU·LA·MORT

French School, 1700s

THE FRENCH REVOLUTION AND NAPOLEON **603**

2 What was the Reign of Terror, and how did it end? *a period of accusations, trials, and executions that created a wave of fear; when those who began the terror were killed*

The Reign of Terror

Recall Where did the main opposition to the Revolution come from? *the countryside*

Explain Why did peasants generally oppose the Revolutionary government? *peasants were devoutly Catholic, some supported monarchy, opposed anticlerical moves*

Summarize What dramatic events occurred in the Vendée? *civil war; violence between counterrevolutionary and government forces*

Primary Source

"Anarchy within, invasion from without. A country cracking from outside pressure, disintegrating from internal strain. Revolution is at its height. War. Inflation. Hunger. Fear. Hate. Sabotage. Fanaticism. Hopes. Boundless idealism . . . and the dread that all the gains of the Revolution would be lost. And the faith that if they won, they would bring Liberty, Equality, Fraternity to the world."—R. R. Palmer, *Twelve Who Ruled*

Answers

The Reign of Terror *northwestern and southeastern corners of France, areas far from Paris*

604

FOCUS ON NEW YORK

American Thomas Paine joined the Girondists and published a defense of the French Revolution. In 1792, Paine moved to France where he barely escaped death in the Terror. In 1802, Paine moved to New York City and died several years later. He is buried in New Rochelle.

The Reign of Terror

By the middle of 1793, many people were concerned about the course of the Revolution. Many of the French themselves were criticizing it. Outside France, the countries of Great Britain, Holland, Spain, Austria, and Prussia were worried enough about the Revolution to form a coalition and make war against France.

As a result, some of the revolutionary leaders feared that they would lose control. They decided to take drastic actions to avoid a possible **counterrevolution**, a revolution against a government that was established by a revolution. The Mountain began a series of accusations, trials, and executions that became known as the **Reign of Terror**, creating a wave of fear throughout the country.

An Outbreak of Civil War In France, real resistance to the Revolution lay in the countryside. Shortly after the peasants won their main goal—the end of feudal dues—they returned to their essentially conservative views. In general, they remained devoutly Catholic and opposed the Revolution's anticlerical moves.

When the National Convention instituted a draft, the peasants' hatred for the government erupted. Village rebels declared, "They have killed our king; chased away our priests; sold the goods of our church; eaten everything we have and now they want to take our bodies . . . no, they shall not have them."

In a region of western France called the Vendée (vahn-day), resistance to the government was so strong that it led to civil war. A counterrevolutionary force called the Catholic and Royal army, a name showing support for the Roman Catholic Church and the monarchy, fought government forces. Savage fighting spread across the region. The government eventually regained control of the Vendée, destroying everyone and everything it could.

Accusations and Trials Back in Paris, the Mountain, the leaders of the campaign to eliminate any resistance to the Revolution, used the Revolutionary Tribunal to rid the country of dissent. Robespierre declared the need to use terror to defend the republic from its many enemies.

The Reign of Terror

The Committee of Public Safety unleashed the Reign of Terror in the summer of 1793. The committee used its broad powers to eliminate all the Revolution's enemies—real and imagined. One member went so far as to accuse losing generals of treason and answered critics with the cry, "heads! heads! and more heads!" *According to the map, where did most counterrevolutionary activity take place?*

Maximilien Robespierre He dominated the Committee of Public Safety.

A model shows Dr. Guillotin's machine, designed to make execution quick and painless.

FRANCE, 1793

Arras 400
Paris 1,500 JUNE-JULY, 1794
Nantes 3,000
Angers 2,000
VENDÉE
Bordeaux 300
Orange 300
Marseille 300
Toulon 800

- Cities with many executions
- 300 Approximate number of people executed
- Areas of sustained counterrevolutionary resistance, 1793

0   100 Miles
0   100 Kilometers
Lambert conformal conic projection

SPAIN
Mediterranean Sea

Skills Focus: Identifying Problem and Solution   At Level

Reading Skill
City Folk and Country Folk

Materials: three sheets of butcher paper, markers

1. Organize the class into three groups. The first group will represent revolutionaries in Paris, the second will represent people of the Vendée, and the third will represent a group of mediators.

2. Have the first two groups make a list of complaints about each other on the butcher paper. The third group will "float" between the first two, observe, and draft a list of proposals for compromise.

3. Have representatives from the first two groups read their lists to the class.

4. Have the third group read its proposals for compromise. Then allow the first and second groups to make suggestions to improve the compromise. Arrive at a consensus and write the final compromise on the third piece of butcher paper. **Visual-Spatial, Interpersonal**

Alternative Assessment Handbook, Rubric 14: Group Activity

"Now, what is the fundamental principle of the democratic or popular government? . . . It is virtue . . . which is nothing other than the love of country and of its laws. . . If the spring of popular government in time of peace is virtue, the springs of popular government in revolution are at once virtue and terror: virtue, without which terror is fatal; terror, without which virtue is powerless. Terror is nothing other than justice, prompt, severe, inflexible; it is therefore an emanation of virtue."

—Robespierre, *Justification of the Use of Terror,* speech February 5, 1794

The Revolutionary Tribunal started its campaign with the Girondists, who were seen as a threat to the Revolution because they had once favored a constitutional monarchy. Soon, anyone who had ever criticized the Revolution or who had had any connection to the Old Order was in danger of being hauled in for a trial. Some people were tried merely because they were suspected of counterrevolutionary activity. The accused had few rights and some were even forbidden to defend themselves.

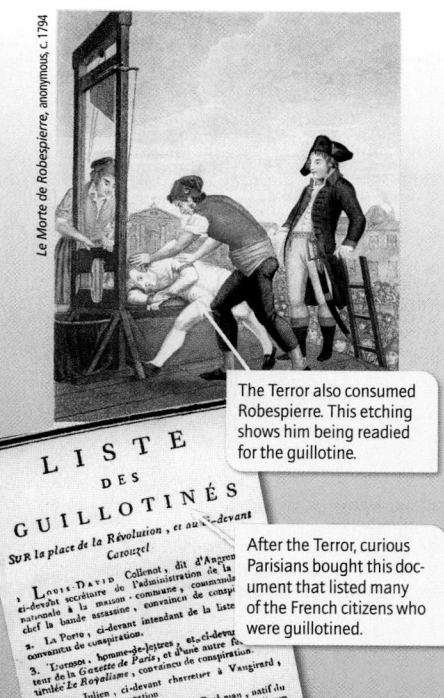

Le Morte de Robespierre, anonymous, c. 1794

The Terror also consumed Robespierre. This etching shows him being readied for the guillotine.

LISTE DES GUILLOTINÉS
SUR la place de la Révolution, et au ci-devant Carouzel

After the Terror, curious Parisians bought this document that listed many of the French citizens who were guillotined.

Death by Guillotine The most common sentence was death by guillotine. Such a death was quick, in contrast to the agonizing methods of execution in use for centuries. To get to the scaffold where the guillotine waited, the condemned rode in an open cart that paraded through the streets of Paris. Crowds gathered along the cart's route to jeer at or sometimes cheer for the passengers. At the scaffold, mobs watched the gruesome executions. Women with radical sympathies sometimes sat near the scaffold and quietly knitted while the victims went to their deaths.

The guillotine was so efficient that the executioner could execute more than one person per minute. Executions became so common in Paris that residents complained about the blood overflowing the city's drainage ditches.

The Terror's Victims The Reign of Terror did not spare any particular class, occupation, or gender. Though many more common people than nobles were killed, the nobility was not entirely spared. The peasants and laborers—the same people the Revolution was supposed to aid—formed the largest group of victims. Nor did the Terror spare women. Marie-Antoinette, was one of the early victims, as were many women of the lower classes. Olympe de Gouges, who wrote the Declaration of the Rights of Woman and the Female Citizen, also went to the guillotine. Even the nuns who refused to close their convents were also sent to the guillotine.

Those who launched the Reign of Terror eventually fell victim themselves. Robespierre sent Danton and his followers to the guillotine for suggesting that the rule of terror might be relaxed. Then Robespierre himself became a victim. On July 27, 1794, Robespierre and his supporters were surrounded by National Convention soldiers and taken into custody. Soon after their arrest, the heads of Robespierre and about 100 of his supporters fell into the guillotine's basket where so many heads had fallen before.

How many victims had the Terror claimed? During the 10 months of the Terror, some 300,000 people were arrested, and about 17,000 were executed. Even though the dead were a small percentage of France's population, the widespread violence shocked the French and increased foreign opposition to the Revolution.

NEW YORK
CC Unit 5-C3b Key individuals in the French Revolution (Robespierre)

THE FRENCH REVOLUTION AND NAPOLEON **605**

Direct Teach

Reading Focus

The Reign of Terror

Identify What was the new governing board called? *the Directory*

Explain Why was the new government ineffective? *directors were weak and corrupt, argued amongst themselves, fell into patterns of Old Order*

📦 **Quick Facts Transparency:** Governments of Revolutionary France

---

Review & Assess

Close

Have students explain how the radical government disintegrated into the Reign of Terror.

Review

📕 **Online Quiz**, Section 2

Assess

SE Section 2 Assessment

📋 **Progress Assessment:** Section 2 Quiz

📋 **Alternative Assessment Handbook**

Reteach/Intervene

📋 **Interactive Reader and Study Guide,** Section 2

💿 **Interactive Skills Tutor CD-ROM**

GOVERNMENTS OF REVOLUTIONARY FRANCE

QUICK FACTS

Throughout the Revolution, legislative bodies dissolved to create new governments. Methods of electing the legislatures differed.

National Assembly, created June 17, 1789
- Ended feudalism and privileges of the First and Second Estates
- Approved the Declaration of the Rights of Man and of the Citizen
- Seized church lands and made clergy paid employees
- Wrote constitution that reduced the king's power

Legislative Assembly, first met September 1791
- Inexperienced representatives, often deadlocked on domestic issues
- Declared war on Austria in April 1792

National Convention, first met September 1792
- Ended monarchy, proclaimed France a republic
- Tried and executed Louis XVI for treason
- Instituted draft to increase size of army
- In power during Reign of Terror
- Began codifying laws and creating public education system
- Abolished slavery in French colonies
- Wrote a new constitution, and created the Directory

Directory, first met in 1795
- Run by an executive branch of five directors
- Weak, corrupt, and inefficient
- Ended in 1799 when Napoleon seized power

The actions of the Reign of Terror were intended to protect the Revolution but had in fact weakened it. As one woman shouted as she went to her death, "Oh Liberty, what crimes are committed in your name!"

After the Terror When the Terror ended, France had to start over with a new government. In 1795 the National Convention wrote yet another constitution. It restricted voting rights given in the previous constitution. Now, only men who owned property could vote.

After the new constitution was adopted, voters elected a governing board. Called the Directory, this governing board was made up of five men called directors. The directors did pass some financial reforms that helped farmers and improved trade, but the Directory was not an effective government.

Partly because the directors were weak and corrupt, France's troubles continued. The directors argued among themselves, failing to lead the exhausted country forward. Eventually, their rule shared many characteristics of the Old Order's—high prices, bankruptcy, citizen unrest. The result was a power vacuum. With no one really in control, something in France had to change.

READING CHECK **Summarize** Why was the period of mass executions called the Reign of Terror?

SECTION 2 ASSESSMENT

go.hrw.com
Online Quiz
Keyword: SHL NAP HP

Reviewing Ideas, Terms, and People

1. **a. Identify** Who was **Maximilien Robespierre**, and why is he important?

   b. Analyze How did anticlerical sentiment affect France's church and society?

   c. Support a Position What is your opinion about Louis XVI not having the opportunity to speak to the crowd before his execution? Explain your answer.

2. **a. Recall** What was the most common sentence given by the Revolutionary Tribunal?

   b. Identify Cause and Effect What are two reasons that many peasants opposed the Revolution?

   c. Make Judgments If you had been the king of Great Britain in 1793, would you have been nervous? Why or why not?

Critical Thinking

3. **Categorize** Copy the chart below and fill it in with ways in which the French Revolution affected the daily lives of the French people.

French Revolution

FOCUS ON SPEAKING

4. **Description** You are a peasant in the French countryside. Write and present a short speech describing the ways you think the Reign of Terror has changed your life.

Section 2 Assessment Answers

1. **a.** radical leader dedicated to the Revolution, led France during Reign of Terror

   b. clergy lost positions, Parisian churches closed, new cult created, statues altered

   c. possible answer—Louis might have given a passionate speech, captured public sympathy, and have been spared.

2. **a.** death by guillotine

   b. peasants were devoutly Catholic and supported the monarchy; opposed the draft

   c. possible answer—Yes, what happened in France could also happen in Britain.

3. military draft; anticlerical activity; metric system; new clock and calendar; Reign of Terror

4. possible ways life changed—live in environment of fear and despair, widespread violence, loss of life by guillotine

Answers

Reading Check *It was a period of accusations, trials, and executions that led to a wave of fear.*

Government and Citizenship

The 1789 Declaration of the Rights of Man and of the Citizen described how the French government would treat its citizens. The first article of the declaration states, "Men are born and remain free and equal in rights." The declaration uses the word *men*, but many asserted that the article applied to women, too. That women were equal to men was a truly revolutionary idea, and it frightened many people in France and the rest of Europe.

▲ **NOW** Young workers in Rennes, France, protest unfair working conditions.

EQUALITY THEN Equality was a key goal of the National Convention, which took control of France in 1792. Determined that everyone should be treated the same, the Convention went so far as to ban the titles *monsieur* and *madame*, the French equivalents of *Mr.* and *Mrs.* These titles, Convention leaders argued, had been derived from the words for *lord* and *lady*—noble titles—and should be abolished. Instead, people were required to address one another as "Citizen". For example, when King Louis XVI was overthrown, he became Citizen Capet, after his family's ancient name.

Despite the government's intentions, however, people were not treated equally. Women in particular had few rights. Although many women had taken part in the Revolution, they were not allowed to participate in the new government. Other people banned from the government included servants, men under 25, and people who did not pay taxes.

▶ **THEN** Parisians marching on the Legislative Assembly.

EQUALITY NOW Just as it was in France during the French Revolution, the idea that all people are equal is important in democracies around the world today. In most modern democracies, all citizens—men and women—are free to take part in the government. In addition, laws have made it illegal to discriminate against people based on their gender, race, occupation, or income.

In spite of the progress made by many democracies, equality for all is still a goal—not a reality—for many governments and their citizens. In many places, for example, women cannot vote, hold office, drive cars, or even appear in public alone. Consequently, groups of people all around the world are working hard to make equality a reality. The ideal of equality supported in the French Revolution, though not fully achieved, is alive in the world today.

Skills Focus **UNDERSTANDING THEMES**

1. **Summarize** What does the Declaration of the Rights of Man and of the Citizen say about equality?
2. **Analyze** How did the treatment of women during the French Revolution differ from the Declaration's goals?
3. **Predict** Do you think women around the world will gain rights or lose rights in the future? Why?

THE FRENCH REVOLUTION AND NAPOLEON **607**

Differentiating Instruction

At Level

English-Language Learners

Research Required

1. Organize students into pairs. Have each pair conduct research on women's participation in government in various countries around the world, including the United States.

2. Students should investigate local, regional, and national offices held, as well as voting statistics. Statistics for women should be compared with those for men.

3. Have students compile their findings in a one-page report that includes a brief summary of their findings.

4. Have pairs present the results of their research to the class. **LS Logical-Mathematical, Verbal-Linguistic**

📄 **Alternative Assessment Handbook,** Rubrics 1: Acquiring Information; and 30: Research

Getting Started

Use the **Interactive Reader and Study Guide** to familiarize students with the section content.

📝 **Interactive Reader and Study Guide,** Section 3

Name _____ Class _____ Date _____
The French Revolution and Napoleon
Section 3

💡 **MAIN IDEA**
Napoleon Bonaparte rose through military ranks to become emperor over France and much of Europe.

Key Terms and People
Napoleon Bonaparte ambitious military leader who became emperor of France
Admiral Horatio Nelson British naval commander who won the Battle of the Nile
coup d'état a forced transfer of power
plebiscite a question put before all voters
Continental System a blockade that stopped French and allied ships from trading with Great Britain to prevent that nation from funding the rebellion against Napoleon
nationalism a sense of identity and unity as a people

Taking Notes
As you read the summary, use a graphic organizer like the one below to record the steps in Napoleon's rise to power. Add more boxes as needed.

Original content Copyright © by Holt, Rinehart and Winston. Additions and changes to the original content are the responsibility of the instructor.
Full Survey Chapter 20   240   Interactive Reader and Study Guide

Academic Vocabulary

Review with students the high-use academic term in this section.

blockade to isolate an enemy by using troops or warships (p. 610)

📝 **CRF:** Vocabulary Builder: Section 3

Taking Notes

forced British out of Toulon; defeated Austrians in Italy; dispersed mob of royalists; assigned to defend French interior; defeated Austrians and Italians; won control of Egypt; lost battle with British, but covered it up; staged coup d'état in France; crowned himself emperor; began a series of wars to conquer Europe

go.hrw.com
Online Resources
KEYWORD: SHL NAP
ACTIVITY: Napoleon Bonaparte

BEFORE YOU READ

MAIN IDEA
Napoleon Bonaparte rose through military ranks to become emperor over France and much of Europe.

READING FOCUS
1. How did Napoleon rise to power?
2. How did Emperor Napoleon come to dominate Europe?
3. What were Napoleon's most important policies?

KEY TERMS AND PEOPLE
Napoleon Bonaparte
Admiral Horatio Nelson
coup d'état
plebiscite
Continental System
nationalism

 NEW YORK
PI 1.3 Students analyze the roles and contributions of individuals and groups to social, political, economic, cultural, and religious practices and activities.

THE INSIDE STORY

How did a young officer's chance to prove himself change Europe's future?

Sometimes achieving greatness requires a little luck. For a young soldier named Napoleon Bonaparte, the lucky break came in the summer of 1793. British troops held the vital French port of Toulon. The French artillery battled courageously to retake the port but made little headway. During the fighting the French captain was wounded, and young Napoleon Bonaparte was chosen to take the wounded captain's place.

Napoleon made the most of his chance. He came up with a daring plan to retake the port by surrounding the harbor with 80 cannons. Napoleon convinced the officers above him that his plan would succeed. Within 48 hours, the port was his. The victory showed Napoleon's genius for military strategy and brought him both notice and promotion. There now appeared to be no stopping him. Within 20 years, he would rule most of Europe. ■

WITH A LITTLE LUCK...

▼ Napoleon led French forces in a fierce battle for Toulon, a port on the Mediterranean Sea.

608 CHAPTER 20

Teach the Main Idea

At Level

Napoleon's Europe

1. **Teach** Ask students the Reading Focus questions to teach this section.

2. **Apply** Have students draw a ladder that shows Napoleon's rise to power. Have students list Napoleon's policies at the top of their ladders.

3. **Review** As you review the section, have students discuss what steps Napoleon took to gain power and the policies he pursued when he was in power.

4. **Practice/Homework** Have students prepare a short illustrated biography of Napoleon. **LS** Visual-Spatial, Verbal-Linguistic

📝 **Alternative Assessment Handbook,** Rubrics 13: Graphic Organizers; and 37: Writing Assignments

Napoleon's Rise to Power

Napoleon Bonaparte was a ruthlessly ambitious young man. The turmoil of the French Revolution gave him a prime opportunity to rise quickly to power. Within a few short years, he would rise from a mere army captain to become the ruler of France.

Opportunities for Glory Napoleon was a brilliant military leader who achieved many early successes. In 1793 he forced British troops out of the port of Toulon. The following year he won a dazzling victory over Austrian troops in Italy.

In 1795 Napoleon faced off against a mob of royalists trying to regain power in Paris. Using artillery to shoot into the crowd, Napoleon forced the royalists to flee. As a reward for stopping the uprising, Napoleon was put in charge of defending the French interior. He was only 26 years old.

The following year, the Directory placed Napoleon in command of French forces invading Italy. Poorly supplied, his troops had to take their food from the countryside. But Napoleon turned this hardship to his advantage. Because his troops were not slowed down by a supply train, they could strike quickly. In Italy, Napoleon won battles against the Austrians and Italians. His victories not only kept France's borders secure but also won territory for France. Napoleon's future looked very bright.

Next, Napoleon turned his attention to Egypt, where he wanted to disrupt the valuable trade between Great Britain and India. He took the French fleet and a large army across the Mediterranean Sea in 1798. Napoleon's forces quickly defeated Egypt's Ottoman defenders and won control of much of Egypt. But the British navy, under the command of **Admiral Horatio Nelson**, was on Napoleon's trail. Nelson trapped the French ships. In the long Battle of the Nile, the British destroyed most of the French fleet.

After his loss in the Battle of the Nile, Napoleon wanted to cover up his disastrous defeat. He left his army in Egypt under the command of another officer and sailed back to France. He kept his defeat out of the press and exaggerated the successes of the French army, becoming a national hero in the process.

Young Napoleon
As a young general, Napoleon showed great courage and leadership in battles against Austrian and Italian armies.

Le General Bonaparte a Arcole, by Antoine Jean Gros, 1797

Destruction of the French Fleet at Toulon, by T. Sutherland, 1816

Napoleon Seizes Power Napoleon's ambitions continued to grow. Capitalizing on his status as a national hero, he decided to seize political power.

By this time, the Directory had grown weak and ineffective. As a result, some French leaders feared that royalists might conspire to place a monarchy in power. Others feared the growing opposition of European nations, such as Great Britain and Austria, against France. As a result, a group of conspirators began to plot to seize more power for Napoleon.

Armed supporters of Napoleon surrounded the Directory legislature and forced members to turn the government over to Napoleon in November 1799. This event was a **coup d'état** (koo day-TAH), a forced transfer of power.

A group of three consuls, called the Consulate, would replace the Directory as the government of France. Members voted Napoleon in charge as first Consul. The structure of a republic was still in place, but Napoleon had become a dictator.

Why would a nation that had overthrown its king now welcome a new dictator? Exhausted by the chaos of the Revolution and constant warfare, the French craved the order and stability Napoleon promised. Napoleon also pledged to uphold some key revolutionary reforms. The people would willingly give up some freedoms if Napoleon could bring peace, prosperity, and glory to France.

TAKING NOTES

As you read, take notes in a diagram like this one to record the steps in Napoleon's rise to power. Add more boxes as needed.

NEW YORK

CC Unit 5-C3d
Napoleon's rise to power

READING CHECK **Summarize** What events led to Napoleon's rise to power?

Reading Focus

1 How did Napoleon rise to power? *achieved military successes, showed courage and leadership, covered up his defeat, his supporters staged coup d'état*

Napoleon's Rise to Power

Recall What was the outcome of Napoleon's campaigns in Italy? *He was victorious, kept France's borders secure and won territory for France.*

Explain How did Napoleon become the dictator of France? *His supporters staged a coup d'état; Napoleon was set up as first Consul, clearly in charge.*

Evaluate Did Napoleon achieve more by his victories or by covering up his defeats? *possible answer—Covering up his defeats made him seem invincible.*

MISCONCEPTION ALERT

Though Napoleon is often described by historians as a short man, he would not have been considered short during the time in which he lived. He stood about 5'6", which was an average height in early 19th century France.

Skills Focus: Sequencing

At Level

Reading Skill
Life of Napoleon

Research Required

Materials: butcher paper, art supplies

1. Organize students into small groups. Have each group use information in the text to create an illustrated time line of Napoleon's life.

2. Have students conduct additional research to find events and dates that are not in the text, and have them add this information to their time lines. Each time line should include at least four illustrations.

3. Display students time lines in the classroom. Ask students which events in Napoleon's life made a large impact on the course of history.
LS Interpersonal, Visual-Spatial

Alternative Assessment Handbook, Rubric 36: Time Lines

Answers

Reading Check *stopped royalists from regaining power, defended French interior, won battles in Italy, kept borders secure, won territory for France, covered up Battle of Nile, coup d'état*

Reading Focus

❷ How did Emperor Napoleon come to dominate Europe? *strengthened control over France; began a series of wars to conquer Europe*

Emperor Napoleon

Recall What question was submitted in the plebiscite? *whether France should be declared an empire*

Explain Why was Napoleon unable to conquer Great Britain? *Admiral Nelson and the British Navy defeated a combined French and Spanish force in the Battle of Trafalgar.*

Make Judgments Was a blockade of Great Britain a good strategy? *possible answers—Yes, because British economy depended on overseas trade; no—because it was hard to enforce trade restrictions.*

 CRF: Biography: Pope Pius VII

 CRF: Primary Source: *The Plumb-pudding in Danger*

Info to Know

Napoleon and Josephine As Napoleon entered the political realm, he began searching for a wife. He was introduced to Marie-Josephe-Rose de Beauharnais at a party and soon fell in love with her, calling her "Josephine." Although she had reservations at the beginning, she eventually agreed to marry him. During Napoleon's long absences for military campaigns, Josephe entertained other men and the rumors eventually reached him. Initially heartbroken, he began taking mistresses. The two remained married for many years, but the issue of an heir eventually arose; Josephine was barren. Napoleon divorced her and married Maria-Louisa of Austria.

Emperor Napoleon

As first consul, Napoleon moved quickly to strengthen his power over France. Once France was firmly under his control, he set about conquering Europe.

Napoleon Crowns Himself Napoleon wanted to make his own power permanent and hereditary. He submitted a **plebiscite**, a question put before all the voters, in 1804: Did they want to declare France an empire? French voters supported him and voted yes. Thus, Napoleon became Emperor Napoleon I.

Pope Pius VII came from Rome to crown Napoleon emperor in Paris. As the pope was about to place the crown on the new emperor's head, Napoleon grabbed the crown and placed it on his own head. This action told the world that no one gave Napoleon his authority—he took it for himself.

Desire for Empire Once Napoleon became emperor of France, he moved to build an empire. He wanted to rule Europe and to extend French power in the Americas. France controlled a number of territories in the Americas, including Louisiana, Florida, and the sugar-producing colony of Saint Domingue (now called Haiti). When civil war erupted in Saint Domingue, Napoleon sent an expedition to take back the colony and restore its profitable sugar industry. But the French expedition failed miserably.

This failure led Napoleon to abandon his dream of empire in the Americas. He sold the Louisiana Territory to the United States and turned his focus to Europe.

The Napoleonic Wars Begin In his quest to conquer Europe, Napoleon began a series of wars that became known as the Napoleonic Wars. These wars were an extension of the ones fought between France and other European nations during the French Revolution. During this period of warfare, France became the dominant European power. Although it grew rapidly under Napoleon's leadership, the French empire would fall apart even more quickly. The Napoleonic Wars lasted until 1815, keeping France in a state of near-continuous warfare for more than a decade.

Throughout the Napoleonic Wars, Great Britain remained France's greatest enemy.

ACADEMIC VOCABULARY
blockade to isolate an enemy by using troops or warships

Britain helped organize a series of coalitions of European nations against France, and British funds helped strengthen resistance to Napoleon across Europe. Napoleon knew that until he could defeat Great Britain, he would have no peace in Europe.

Napoleon hoped to invade Britain and defeat it. However, Admiral Nelson and the British navy, the commander and fleet that had earlier defeated Napoleon in Egypt, stood in his way. The British navy proved its worth in October 1805 when it defeated a combined French and Spanish navy off the coast of Spain in the Battle of Trafalgar.

On land, Napoleon was more successful. Two months after his defeat at the Battle of Trafalgar, he won a devastating victory over Russian and Austrian troops at the Battle of Austerlitz, near Vienna, Austria.

The Continental System Great Britain continued to defy Napoleon. But this "nation of shopkeepers," as Napoleon disdainfully called the country, was vulnerable. Britain's economy depended on overseas trade. If Napoleon could disrupt that trade, he would weaken Britain's ability to fund rebellion in Europe against him.

In an effort to disrupt Great Britain's trade with other nations, he planned a blockade. This plan, called the **Continental System**, prohibited French or allied ships from trading with Britain. The British responded by requiring all ships from neutral countries to stop in British ports for permission to trade with the French.

While trying to enforce these trade restrictions, Britain and France were drawn into other conflicts. One conflict was the Peninsular War, which drew Portugal and Spain into the conflict between France and Great Britain.

The Peninsular War Portugal, which shares the Iberian Peninsula with Spain, was neutral during the Napoleonic Wars. The Portuguese refused to comply with the Continental System because they depended on trade with Britain. To enforce his power, Napoleon sent French troops into Portugal to take control and drive out the king. Napoleon then quickly conquered Spain and placed his brother Joseph on the Spanish throne. But the Spanish resented having a foreign ruler and revolted in 1808.

To support the Spanish revolt of French rule, Great Britain sent its military forces to Spain.

610 CHAPTER 20

Differentiating Instruction

Below Level

Special Education Students

Prep Required

Materials: magazines, poster paper, paste, scissors, small photocopied images of Napoleon

1. Review the text about Napoleon's rise to power. Have students brainstorm adjectives, both positive and negative, that could be used to describe Napoleon. Create a class list for students to see.

2. Give each student a piece of poster paper and a photocopied image of Napoleon. The image should be pasted in the center or at the top of

the poster paper. The title of the poster should be: Words that Describe Napoleon.

3. Have students search the magazines for images that could be used to illustrate the adjectives on the class list. Students should write the term on their poster paper and paste the image above it.

4. Display posters for students to see. **LS** Visual-Spatial

Alternative Assessment Handbook, Rubrics 3: Artwork; and 28: Posters

Now battling two military forces, Napoleon faced a serious threat. He responded by sending troops from central Europe, and they quickly won several victories over the British and Spanish troops.

Yet a more deadly enemy still threatened—the Spanish people. They began a guerrilla war in which bands of peasants ambushed French troops and raided French camps. To punish the Spanish guerrilla fighters, the French slaughtered many innocent Spanish civilians. Nevertheless, the war kept the French army pinned down, and eventually Napoleon had to pull his troops out of Spain.

Napoleon Dominates Europe In spite of this setback in Spain, Napoleon managed to take control of most of Europe through treaties, alliances, and victories in battle. The only nations free of his control were Great Britain, Sweden, Portugal, and the Ottoman Empire.

In many of the European nations Napoleon conquered, he put his relatives in power. He gave his brothers the thrones of Holland, the Italian states of Naples and Sicily, and the German state of Westphalia. His sisters, and even his stepson, also held powerful positions.

READING CHECK **Summarizing** What regions of Europe did Napoleon dominate?

FACES OF HISTORY **Napoleon Bonaparte,** 1769–1821

Napoleon actually rode a mule across the Alps instead of a fine horse like the one in this painting.

Napoleon looks like a big, impressive man in this portrait. In fact, he was 5'6" or shorter.

Napoleon on Horseback at the St. Bernard Pass, by Jacques-Louis David, 1801

Contrast Napoleon's slumped posture in this painting with his pose in the other one.

Notice the scuffed, dusty boots and rumpled coat.

Napoleon at Fontainebleau, by Paul Delaroche, 1814

The people who knew or met Napoleon held different opinions about him. He inspired fierce loyalty in his troops. His wife Josephine adored him. Some other observers, though, saw Napoleon as cold and unfeeling.

As is the case with famous people, historians and artists have also portrayed Napoleon in different ways, depending on their points of view. Compare the two portraits of Napoleon above and how the artists' viewpoints differed.

Skills Focus **READING LIKE A HISTORIAN**

1. **Draw Conclusions** Which of the portraits do you think is a more realistic painting?
2. **Analyze Visuals** How does each painting reflect different aspects of Napoleon's personality and the rise and fall of his fortunes?

See **Skills Handbook,** p. H26

THE FRENCH REVOLUTION AND NAPOLEON **611**

Emperor Napoleon

Identify In what countries did Napoleon place his relatives? *Spain, Holland, Italy, and Germany*

Make Judgments Do you think placing one's relatives in power is an effective way to lead a nation or territory? *possible answers—Yes, they can be manipulated and will do what the leader tells them; no, because they might be inexperienced or ineffective.*

📋 **Map Transparency:** Napoleon's Empire, 1812

Info to Know

Napoleon's Empire, 1812 In all of the "satellite kingdoms" of France, efforts were made to introduce elements of French government. This meant trying to remove the old feudal privileges of the nobility and diminish the importance of the Church in society. Conscription, or a military draft, also occurred in regions throughout the empire.

✳ **Interactive Map:** Napoleon's Empire, 1812

✳Interactive
NAPOLEON'S EMPIRE, 1812

Napoleon put his relatives into positions of power throughout Europe, and they helped him control the empire. Though some of these relatives were popular with the people they governed, the fact that each had the same last name served as a constant reminder that Napoleon ruled over them.

Louis-Napoleon, a younger brother, was king of Holland.

Jerome-Napoleon, the youngest brother, was king of Westphalia.

Joseph-Napoleon, the oldest brother, was king of Spain.

Eugene-Napoleon, a stepson, ruled the Kingdom of Italy.

Elisa-Napoleon, a sister, was grand duchess of Tuscany.

Joachim-Napoleon, a brother-in-law, ruled the Kingdom of Naples.

French Empire
States controlled by Napoleon
States allied with Napoleon
State opposed to Napoleon

0   150   300 Miles
0   150   300 Kilometers
Albers equal-area projection

GEOGRAPHY SKILLS **INTERPRETING MAPS**

go.hrw.com
Interactive Map
Keyword: SHL NAP

1. **Location** How did the strategic placement of Napoleon's relatives affect his control of Europe?

2. **Movement** Was Napoleon's empire protected on all sides? If not, from where might enemies have attacked?

612 CHAPTER 20

Collaborative Learning

At Level

Nepotism Debate

1. Discuss with students Napoleon's policy of placing relatives in control of conquered territories.

2. Organize students into two groups. Pose the following question to students: Is nepotism an effective leadership tool?

3. Have students in each group brainstorm ideas in support of their argument. One group should list reasons in favor of nepotism and

the other group should list reasons against it. One student in each group should take notes and compile a group list.

4. Conduct a class debate, instructing students in each group to provide at least three reasons why they either support or oppose nepotism.

🔵 **Interpersonal, Verbal-Linguistic**

📋 **Alternative Assessment Handbook**, Rubrics 10: Debates; and 14: Group Activity

Answers

Interpreting Maps 1. *enabled Napoleon to control the entire empire, and relatives had same last name, a constant reminder of who was in power;* **2.** *No, it was vulnerable to attack on the east-central border; the Mediterranean Sea*

Napoleon's Policies

As Napoleon ruled his empire, he also strengthened the power of France's central government. He developed a plan to establish order and efficiency throughout France, which involved reforms in many areas of French society.

Reform of Church-State Relations

Many French citizens had despised the antireligious nature of the French Revolution. Napoleon soothed these feelings by making an agreement with the pope. Called the Concordat, this agreement acknowledged that most French citizens were Roman Catholics. The agreement did not require that they be Catholics, because religious toleration was still the law. The Concordat recognized the influence of the Roman Catholic Church in France but did not return any control over national affairs to the church.

Economic Reforms

Because Napoleon knew that a good financial system was essential for the stability of France, he established the Bank of France to regulate the economy. He also set up a more efficient tax collection system. These measures ensured that the government would not face the kinds of financial crises that occurred before the Revolution.

Legal and Educational Reforms

Under Napoleon's leadership, scholars revised and organized French law and created the Napoleonic Code. This code made laws uniform across the nation and eliminated many injustices. However, it also promoted order and authority over individual rights. Freedom of the press, for example, was restricted by censors who banned books and newspapers for certain political content. In addition, the code was limited in that it only applied to male citizens. The code denied rights for women and allowed for husbands to have authority over their wives.

Napoleon also believed that a strong state depended on having strong leaders in government and military positions. He established a network of high schools, universities, and technical schools to educate young men in preparation for those jobs.

Napoleon's Legacy

Napoleon left a legacy in France as well as throughout Europe. In France, Napoleon ensured that some basic ideas of the revolution would remain part of the French government. Historians speak of this period of Napoleon's domination of Europe as the Age of Napoleon.

Napoleon made some basic revolutionary ideas part of the French government. These democratic ideas included equality before the law and a representative system of government. In fact, these revolutionary principles were those that Napoleon had approved and supported.

Throughout Europe, Napoleon's actions helped fuel the spread of **nationalism**—a sense of identity and unity as a people. During the Revolution, the French people developed a new loyalty to France as a whole. In addition, similar feelings of nationalism spread to peoples that Napoleon had conquered.

READING CHECK Identify Cause and Effect
How did Napoleon's reforms affect French society?

NEW YORK

CC Unit 5-C3d
Napoleon's impact
(Napoleonic Code)

SECTION 3 ASSESSMENT

go.hrw.com
Online Quiz
Keyword: SHL NAP HP

Reviewing Ideas, Terms, and People

1. a. Identify What happened in November 1799?
b. Analyze How did Napoleon use French citizens to gain power?
c. Evaluate Do you think you would have welcomed Napoleon as a dictator? Why or why not?

2. a. Recall Who fought the battles at Trafalgar and Austerlitz? Which side won each battle?
b. Analyze How did the **Continental System** affect countries beyond Europe?
c. Make Judgments How do you think you would have reacted if you had been present at Napoleon's crowning?

3. a. Define What is **nationalism**, and how did it spread?
b. Contrast In what way did Napoleon's support of revolutionary ideals contrast with other actions that he took?
c. Elaborate Why do you think historians may hold different views of Napoleon?

Critical Thinking

4. Sequence Use the graphic organizer below to show the sequence of events that led to Napoleon's rise to power.

FOCUS ON WRITING

5. Exposition Write a one-paragraph letter to Napoleon from the viewpoint of a French officer stationed in Spain during the Peninsular War. In your letter, make suggestions about how to win the war.

THE FRENCH REVOLUTION AND NAPOLEON **613**

Section 3 Assessment Answers

1. a. Supporters of Napoleon staged a coup d'état.
b. submitted a plebiscite asking whether France should be an empire
c. possible answers—Yes, he established order; no—dictators take power from the people.

2. a. Trafalgar—British defeated French and Spanish; Austerlitz—French defeated Russians and Austrians.
b. prohibited trade with Britain; created other conflicts
c. possible answer—shocked that Napoleon crowned himself

3. a. sense of patriotism, identity, and unity as a people; through Napoleon's conquests
b. Napoleon often suppressed individual freedoms.
c. possible answer—Napoleon was a complex figure who took many diverse actions.

4. stopped royalists from regaining power, won battles and territory, secured borders, staged a coup d'état

5. Students' letters might mention attacks from peasants and propose reasonable ways to deal with guerrillas.

Getting Started

Use the **Interactive Reader and Study Guide** to familiarize students with the section content.

📄 **Interactive Reader and Study Guide,** Section 4

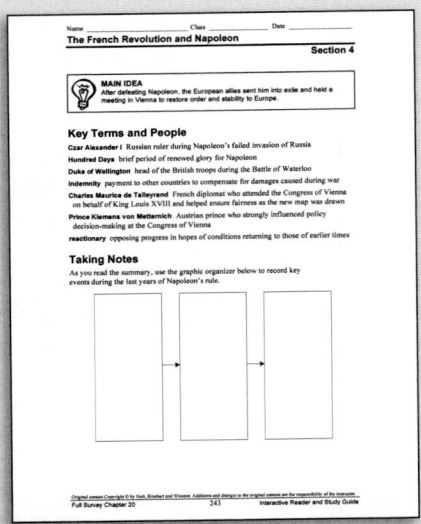

📄 **CRF:** Vocabulary Builder: Section 4

Taking Notes

disastrous Russian campaign; defeat at Battle of Nations; exile to Elba; the Hundred Days; Battle of Waterloo; France returned to original size; map of Europe redrawn; monarchies restored; people's rights restricted

SECTION 4
Napoleon's Fall and Europe's Reaction

BEFORE YOU READ

MAIN IDEA

After defeating Napoleon, the European allies sent him into exile and held a meeting in Vienna to restore order and stability to Europe.

READING FOCUS

1. What events caused disaster and defeat for Napoleon?
2. What were Napoleon's last campaigns?
3. What did the Congress of Vienna achieve?
4. What is the legacy of the French Revolution?

KEY TERMS AND PEOPLE

Czar Alexander I
Hundred Days
Duke of Wellington
Prince Klemens von Metternich
Charles Maurice de Talleyrand
indemnity
reactionary

 NEW YORK

PI 1.2 Students understand the development and connectedness of Western civilization and other civilizations and cultures in many areas of the world and over time.

Catastrophe!

THE INSIDE STORY *Did a bad omen doom an invasion from the start?* On a moonlit June evening in 1812, Napoleon camped with his army near the Neman River in an area now known as Lithuania and Belarus. The army was ready to cross the river and invade the powerful empire of Russia.

With a few officers as company, Napoleon was riding his horse through a field. Suddenly, a rabbit sprang out between the legs of the emperor's horse. The horse swerved, and Napoleon lost his hold, tumbling to the ground. Only slightly bruised, Napoleon quickly stood and remounted his horse—all without speaking a word. The event worried the officers, who could not shake off their leader's tumble as a harmless accident. One officer said to another: "We should do better not to cross the Neman. That fall is a bad sign." ◼

614 CHAPTER 20

Teach the Main Idea

At Level

Napoleon's Fall and Europe's Reaction

1. **Teach** Ask students the Reading Focus questions to teach this section.

2. **Apply** Draw a four-column chart for students to see. Label the columns with the topics of this section—Disaster and Defeat, The Last Campaigns, The Congress of Vienna, and The Revolution's Legacy. Have students copy the chart and have them write the main points of each topic in the corresponding column.

3. **Review** As you review the section, have students explain the effects of the French Revolution and Napoleon over the short term and the long term.

4. **Practice/Homework** Have students write a one-page essay on the continuing importance of the French Revolution.
   LS Visual-Spatial, Verbal-Linguistic

📄 **Alternative Assessment Handbook,** Rubrics 7: Charts; and 37: Writing Assignments

Disaster and Defeat

While some of Napoleon's officers believed they had seen a "bad sign" before they invaded Russia, Napoleon himself apparently did not see the sign. He decided to invade Russia.

The Russian Campaign When Napoleon stationed troops near the western border of Russia, **Czar Alexander I**, the Russian ruler, became very nervous. The czar, who was also concerned about the effects of the Continental System on his country's need to import goods, began to gather his own troops. Napoleon noticed those troop movements. To teach the czar a lesson, he decided to turn his troops east and move into Russia.

In June, Napoleon and an army of some 600,000 men marched across the Russian border. However, this invasion was troubled from the beginning. First, many of the soldiers were new recruits from conquered territories who felt no loyalty to Napoleon. Also, many of the army's supplies were lost or spoiled along the rough roads. In addition to those problems, the July heat made men and horses miserable. As a result, many men suffered from disease, desertion, and hunger, which thinned the army's ranks.

Napoleon wanted a quick victory over Russia, but there was no one for Napoleon to fight. The Russian troops withdrew as he advanced. Russian peasants, too, moved east after setting fire to their fields in order to leave nothing behind that the French troops could use. To Napoleon and his troops, all of western Russia seemed deserted.

In August, the French army was still moving east toward Moscow. Napoleon's troops finally clashed with the Russians. The French won the battle, but their casualties were very high. The Russian army, still 90,000 men strong, retreated.

What remained of the French army pushed on to Moscow in September. The troops found the city nearly deserted and in flames. No one knows whether the Russians or French looters lit the fires. Regardless of the cause, Napoleon could not support his troops in the ruined city through the winter. In October he had no choice: He left Moscow.

Napoleon's weary troops began the long retreat homeward. The Russians forced the French army to return the way it had come—across the same scorched fields Napoleon had crossed earlier in the summer. To make the journey even worse, Russian peasants attacked isolated French soldiers.

TAKING NOTES
As you read, record key events during the last years of Napoleon's rule in boxes like the ones below. Then summarize the changes after his fall.

This painting shows Napoleon leading French troops to Moscow.

RUSSIAN CAMPAIGN, 1812

UNITED KINGDOM
North Sea
Baltic Sea
Neman River
Moscow
PRUSSIA
RUSSIAN EMPIRE
ATLANTIC OCEAN
Beresina River
Dnieper River
Don River
Paris
NAPOLEON'S EMPIRE
AUSTRIAN EMPIRE
PORTUGAL
Black Sea

0 200 400 Miles
0 200 400 Kilometers
Azimuthal equal-area projection

→ Napoleon's invasion
→ Napoleon's retreat

The First Sight of Moscow, by Laslett John Pott, undated

QUICK FACTS
SOLDIERS IN NAPOLEON'S RUSSIAN CAMPAIGN
- 600,000 began the campaign
- 250,000 died in Russia
- 94,000 taken prisoner
- 150,000 wounded or deserted
- 100,000 survived

Analyze What factors do you think contributed to the huge loss of men?

615

615

2 What were Napoleon's last campaigns?
The Hundred Days, Battle of Waterloo

The Last Campaigns

Identify After Napoleon's exile, who became leader of France? *Louis XVIII, brother of Louis XVI*

Make Inferences Why do you think Napoleon was exiled rather than placed in prison? *possible answer—so that he would be far away, unable to bribe his way out or influence politics in any way*

Make Judgments If you lived in France at the time, would you have supported Napoleon's return? *possible answers—Yes, he made reforms and won glory for France; no—he dragged France through years of bitter warfare.*

Info to Know

War and Peace Leo Tolstoy's *War and Peace* is one of the greatest—and longest—novels ever written. Tolstoy relates a dramatic story of fictional characters against the backdrop of the Napoleonic Wars. The main characters are members of Russian nobility and the military who get caught up in the wars. Much of the book takes place during Napoleon's Russian campaign.

Answers

Reading Skills *face, meet*

Reading Check (left) *soldiers lacked loyalty to Napoleon, extreme heat, supplies lost or spoiled, disease, desertion, hunger, Russian troops withdrew, harsh Russian winter* **(right)** *hired a ship to return him to France and won the support of people and the army*

616

Understanding Word Origins If the root word *contra* means "against," what do you think the word *encounter* means?

Then true horror set in. The harsh Russian winter was the most terrifying enemy that the French army had <u>encountered</u>. As the exhausted men marched west, starvation and freezing temperatures killed thousands. The brutal Russian winter did what no military power had been able to do before. It decimated Napoleon's army.

What was left of French army staggered back to French territory without a leader. Napoleon had rushed back to Paris by sleigh, leaving his troops to face much of the awful trip without him. In the end, only about 94,000 out of the original 600,000 French troops made the journey back.

Defeat and Exile to Elba Napoleon's disaster in Russia gave his enemies new hope. Russia, Prussia, Austria, and Great Britain allied themselves against France. Meanwhile, Napoleon raised another army, but his troops were inexperienced. In October 1813 the allies met Napoleon's new troops near the German city of Leipzig. This battle was a clear defeat for Napoleon. In March 1814, the allies entered Paris in triumph.

As one of the terms of surrender, Napoleon had to give up his throne. The victors allowed him to keep the title of emperor, but his new empire was tiny—a small Mediterranean island named Elba, off the coast of Italy. He went into exile with a small pension and about 400 guards.

READING CHECK Identify Cause and Effect What factors contributed to Napoleon's failure in Russia?

The Last Campaigns

THE IMPACT TODAY

Waterloo has come to mean any sort of crushing defeat. The phrase to meet one's Waterloo means "to face a final and decisive moment."

By exiling Napoleon and sending him to Elba, the allies believed they had ended any threat from him. But Napoleon would not go quietly. He waited for an opportunity to regain control of France.

Meanwhile, the allies restored the French monarchy. They recognized Louis XVIII, the brother of the executed king Louis XVI, as the rightful king of France. In addition, the allies returned the borders of France to what they had been in 1792. But the king quickly grew unpopular, and many French citizens feared a return to the Old Order.

616 CHAPTER 20

The Hundred Days After about a year in exile on Elba, Napoleon managed to hire a ship that took him and many supporters back to France. He landed on the north coast and headed for Paris.

As rumors of Napoleon's return spread, people began to react. Louis XVIII panicked and fled to Belgium, and the allies declared Napoleon an outlaw. The French people who despised Napoleon for dragging France through years of bitter warfare were not happy. Thousands of other French citizens, however, were excited to hear that Napoleon was back. They still adored their emperor for the reforms he had made and the glory he had won for France. In fact, the troops sent to arrest Napoleon pledged their loyalty to him instead. On March 20 Napoleon arrived in Paris to cheering crowds. This was the beginning of the **Hundred Days**, a brief period of renewed glory for Napoleon and of problems for his enemies.

The Battle of Waterloo Across Europe, Napoleon's enemies were gathering their troops for another showdown with Napoleon. After some indecisive battles, the final confrontation pitted Napoleon's troops against British troops led by the **Duke of Wellington**. Belgian, Dutch, and German troops increased Wellington's ranks. On June 18, 1815, the armies met near Waterloo, a Belgian village.

Heavy rain delayed the battle until late morning. The British forces stood their ground, but the fighting was ferocious all day. One of Britain's allies, Prussia, came to their aid. As Prussian troops arrived to help the British soldiers, Napoleon's army was no match for the combined strength of the two armies. They drove the French army off the field by the end of the day.

The French and the British both suffered huge losses at the Battle of Waterloo. Casualties totaled about 50,000 men. But for Napoleon, the Battle of Waterloo was a crushing defeat. It was the end of his military career and the end of the Napoleonic Wars.

Napoleon's Final Days Napoleon evaded the victors briefly. Having fled to a port, he tried to escape to America, but he was soon captured. This time, Napoleon's captors sent him much farther away than Elba.

Differentiating Instruction

Below Level

English-Language Learners

1. Review the information in the text about Napoleon's final campaigns. Remind students that Napoleon had been a popular figure in France for many years before his downfall.

2. Organize students into mixed-ability pairs. Have each pair work together to write a summary of Napoleon's last campaigns. Summaries should include campaigns from the end of the Russian campaign up until Napoleon's death.

3. Have volunteers present their summaries to the class. **LS Verbal-Linguistic**

Alternative Assessment Handbook, Rubric 37: Writing Assignments

Was Napoleon Murdered?

Does it matter whether Napoleon was murdered? Perhaps not, but at the time it certainly did matter. Many French were sure that the British had something to do with his death. The English were equally anxious to prove that they had not mistreated him.

What facts do we have? The official autopsy results reported a perforated, or punctured, stomach and stomach cancer. However, that report also documented a high level of poisonous arsenic in Napoleon's hair.

Does the presence of arsenic prove that the British had Napoleon killed? Not necessarily. There are two possible sources for the arsenic other than deliberate poisoning. One source of arsenic was medicine, since arsenic was an ingredient in many 19th-century medicines. Because doctors treated Napoleon for many ailments, the arsenic may have come from drugs.

Napoleon could also have been poisoned by the wallpaper in his sitting-room. It included a green color made with copper arsenite. Although copper arsenite is usually harmless, mold can convert it to a poisonous vapor. The climate on Saint Helena is humid enough for this to have occurred.

▲ Wallpaper from Napoleon's room

Recently, Paul Fornes, a French forensic scientist, reviewed the old autopsy report. Fornes concluded that while Napoleon had cancer, the cancer did not kill him. Fornes also pointed out that the source of the arsenic in the hair sample remains unknown. Thus, whether Napoleon was murdered is still one of history's mysteries.

Draw Conclusions Why might the cause of Napoleon's death still be a topic of international interest today?

They exiled him to Saint Helena, a bleak volcanic island in the South Atlantic, some 1,200 miles from the nearest mainland.

Napoleon never escaped from his remote prison on Saint Helena. Nor did Napoleon serve a long sentence; he died six years later at the age of just 51. The cause of his death has never been determined definitively.

READING CHECK **Draw Conclusions** How was Napoleon able to escape exile in Elba and return to command the French army?

The Congress of Vienna

Just before Napoleon's escape from Elba, hundreds of diplomats had gathered in the city of Vienna. The purpose of this grand meeting, called the Congress of Vienna, was to create a plan to restore order and stability to Europe after the turmoil of the Napoleonic Wars. The diplomats' plan redrew the map of Europe.

The Negotiators Although about 700 diplomats attended the Congress, only a few played crucial roles in the negotiations: Lord Castlereagh (KAS-uhl-ray) of Great Britain, Czar Alexander I of Russia, King Frederick William III of Prussia, and **Prince Klemens von Metternich** (MET-ern-ik) of Austria. **Charles Maurice de Talleyrand** attended on behalf of King Louis XVIII, who had retaken the French throne.

Metternich, who had a strong distrust of democracy and political change, dominated the Congress of Vienna. He wanted to restore a balance of power, make Europe peaceful again, restore old monarchies, and compensate the Allies for their losses. Like Metternich, the other decision makers wanted to make sure that France could never again rise to such power. Perhaps more than anything, worried members of the Congress wanted to put down revolution wherever it might appear.

THE FRENCH REVOLUTION AND NAPOLEON **617**

Direct Teach

Reading Focus

❸ What did the Congress of Vienna achieve? *redrew map of Europe; formed the German Confederation; took and distributed France's conquered territories; restored some monarchies*

The Congress of Vienna

Identify Who was the most important figure at the Congress of Vienna? *Prince Klemens von Metternich*

Draw Conclusions Why did the Congress of Vienna want to suppress all revolutions? *saw revolutions as destabilizing force; wanted to stabilize Europe*

Forensics in History

Copper Arsenite Copper arsenite is a known carcinogen. It affects the central nervous system, the gastrointestinal tract, and the kidneys. Symptoms include coughs and headaches, as well as cardiac disorders and shock. When the chemical is heated, toxic fumes are released, and exposure to the chemical can lead to death.

Answers

Forensics in History *possible answer—could lead to a different understanding of political or social events in history*

617

The Congress of Vienna

Explain How was it decided which nations gained territory and which nations lost it? *Those which aided France lost territory; those which opposed France won territory.*

Make Judgments Do you think France was treated fairly by the Congress of Vienna? *possible answers— Yes, France caused much suffering in Europe; no—other countries plundered French holdings.*

🖳 **Map Transparency**: Europe After the Congress of Vienna, 1815

Interpreting Maps

Europe After the Congress of Vienna, 1815

Movement Which countries were never controlled by France? *Great Britain, Russia*

Answers

Interpreting Maps 1. *Netherlands, Prussia, Spain, Lesser German States, Switzerland, Kingdom of Sardinia;* **2.** *Italy, Germany*

Reading Check *restore order, stability, and balance of power; ensure France could not rise again; suppress revolution*

They wanted to remove all traces of the French Revolution and Napoleon's rule. To do so, they changed boundaries across Europe.

Redrawing the Map The Congress of Vienna changed many national borders in order to strengthen the nations near France. Strengthening the states surrounding France was supposed to lessen the chance that France would invade its neighbors again.

The Dutch Republic and the Austrian Netherlands were united as the Kingdom of the Netherlands. Austria joined with 38 German states to form a loose organization of states called the German Confederation. Great Britain received overseas territories, rather than land in Europe.

The process of redrawing the map required complicated trades. Countries that had aided France lost territory. Those that had fought France gained territory. If one country seemed to be getting too much, it had to give up something else. Talleyrand was instrumental in arranging these trades.

In the end, France lost all its conquered territory. Its boundaries were pulled back to where they had been in 1792. France also had to pay a large **indemnity**—a payment to other countries to compensate them for damages.

Restoring Monarchies In addition to redrawing the map, the Congress of Vienna restored some of the monarchies that Napoleon had eliminated. Members of the old Bourbon royal family were returned to the thrones of Spain and Sicily. Monarchies were also restored in Portugal and the island nation of Sardinia.

Metternich's Influence After Napoleon's fall, reactionary attitudes deeply influenced politics and society. People with **reactionary** ideals not only oppose progress but also want conditions to return to those of an earlier time.

Metternich was a reactionary who wanted to return Europe to the years before 1789. He believed in absolute monarchy. Constitutions, voting rights, freedom of religion and the press—Metternich despised them all. In the areas where Metternich's influence was strong—Austria, the German states, and northern Italy—all such liberal ideas were suppressed. Secret police spied on people who disagreed with Metternich's ideas, and his opponents were often imprisoned or fined.

⭐ Interactive
EUROPE AFTER THE CONGRESS OF VIENNA, 1815

GEOGRAPHY SKILLS INTERPRETING MAPS

go.hrw.com
Interactive Map
Keyword: SHL NAP

1. **Location** What countries surrounded France after the Congress of Vienna?
2. **Regions** Which regions were broken up into small states?

618 CHAPTER 20

Collaborative Learning

At Level

Delegates in Vienna

1. Review with students the main representatives and viewpoints at the Congress of Vienna.

2. Organize students into groups of five. Four of the students will represent figures at the congress and the fifth will serve as a note-taker. If there are remaining students, they should represent the fifth important figure at the congress in their respective groups.

3. Have students in each group brainstorm and create a list of goals each of the congressional representatives wants to achieve.

4. Have the note-taker in each group summarize the goals of the congress for the class.
   LS **Interpersonal**

📖 **Alternative Assessment Handbook**, Rubric 14: Group Activity

In addition, newspapers were not allowed to publish opposing views. For about 30 years, Metternich's conservative influence helped silence the liberal ideals of the Revolution.

READING CHECK **Summarize** What were the main goals of the Congress of Vienna?

The Revolution's Legacy

Given the results of the Congress of Vienna, was the French Revolution a failure? At first glance, you might think so. After the Congress of Vienna, monarchs ruled much of Europe once again. Citizens' rights were again restricted, and nobles enjoyed the privileges of a glittering lifestyle. Had so many revolutionaries died in vain? Had the principles of the Enlightenment died with them?

In fact, the French Revolution had changed many things. Never again would Europe's monarchs and nobles be secure in their privileged positions. They knew that Enlightenment ideas about human dignity, personal liberty, and the equality of all people would not go away.

The common people also remembered something important—that they could change the world. In the Revolution, French workers and peasants had taken control of their own destinies. No longer did people have to assume that nothing would ever change to make their lives better.

Though the Revolution was over within 10 years, the ideals that inspired it influenced

FACES OF HISTORY

Prince Klemens von METTERNICH
1773–1859

Metternich hated the republican form of government. This hatred most likely stemmed from an event during the French Revolution. The Metternich estate, which his family had held for 800 years, was seized by the French in 1794.

Metternich believed only monarchies working together could keep the peace: "Union between the monarchs. . . must . . . save society from total ruin." His repressive policies, however, helped bring on revolutions in 1848. During the revolution in Austria, Metternich fled Vienna in a laundry cart, but he eventually retired in peace.

Draw Conclusions Why do you think Metternich's policies sparked revolutions in 1848?

people around the world for the next 200 years. Those ideals were so powerful that they could survive the worst horrors that the French Revolution and the Napoleonic Wars could create. Only a few years after Napoleon's empire ended, massive revolutions began from France to Romania. Enlightenment ideals crossed the Atlantic and inspired people in Latin America to throw off colonial rule. Eventually, the same ideals would inspire political movements in Asia and Africa.

READING CHECK **Draw Conclusions** Why could it be said that the French Revolution is still being fought today?

NEW YORK

CC Unit 5-C3c
The French Revolution's impact on France and other nations.

go.hrw.com
Online Quiz
Keyword: SHL NAP HP

SECTION 4 ASSESSMENT

Reviewing Ideas, Terms, and People

1. **a. Explain** What challenges did the French army face in the Russian campaign?
   b. Infer How did Russia's physical geography affect Napoleon's invasion?

2. **a. Recall** What was the **Hundred Days**?
   b. Draw Conclusions How do you think the results of the Battle of Waterloo affected morale on both sides?

3. **a. Identify** Who was Metternich, and why was he important?
   b. Make Generalizations Use the maps in this section to make a general statement about how Europe's boundaries changed between 1812 and 1815.

4. **a. Describe** What did Europe after the Congress of Vienna have in common with Europe before 1789?
   b. Make Judgments Do you think the French Revolution was effective? Why or why not?

Critical Thinking

5. **Analyze** Use the concept map below to describe possible long-term results of the French Revolution.

French Revolution → Napoleon → Congress of Vienna

FOCUS ON WRITING

6. **Persuasion** Write a brief conversation between two leaders of the Congress of Vienna—Metternich and Talleyrand. In your conversation, have the speakers debate what the Congress should do to maintain peace in Europe.

THE FRENCH REVOLUTION AND NAPOLEON **619**

Section 4 Assessment Answers

1. **a.** supplies lost or spoiled, difficult to find Russian army, harsh Russian winter
   b. size of country meant long marches; harsh winter killed thousands

2. **a.** period when Napoleon returned from exile
   b. possible answer—French: heartbroken; British and Prussian: joyful

3. **a.** Austrian prince; guided decisions at the Congress of Vienna
   b. France shrank to original size; empires splintered into smaller countries; confederations formed

4. **a.** monarchs ruled much of Europe; citizens' rights restricted; nobles enjoyed privileges
   b. possible answer—Yes, high ideals inspired others worldwide.

5. Enlightenment ideals and nationalism spread, uniform government efficient, monarchy returns, people's rights restricted, territories redistributed

6. Students' conversations might include the following debate points: Metternich—absolute monarchy to ensure peace; Talleyrand—redistribution of land; balance of power.

Direct Teach

Reading Focus

4 What is the legacy of the French Revolution? *monarchs no longer secure in their positions, people realized they could change their governments and destinies*

The Revolution's Legacy

Recall In what way was the French Revolution unsuccessful? *Monarchs again ruled Europe; citizens' rights were restricted; nobles enjoyed a privileged lifestyle.*

Elaborate Why is the French Revolution considered so important? *ideals of revolution inspired people worldwide; gave knowledge that people could change their own destinies*

Review & Assess

Close

Have students discuss the lasting impact of the French Revolution.

Review

Online Quiz, Section 4

Assess

SE **Section 4 Assessment**

Progress Assessment: Section 4 Quiz

Alternative Assessment Handbook

Reteach/Intervene

Interactive Reader and Study Guide, Section 4

Interactive Skills Tutor CD-ROM

Answers

Faces of History *His policies were undemocratic and repressive; people wanted more control.*

Reading Check *People still fight for the basic ideals of liberty and equality.*

619

Document-Based Investigation

Reactions to Revolution

Word Help

conspiracies plots to do harm

treason betraying one's country

fancy imagine, perceive

torpid powerless to move

Info to Know

Chappe's Mechanism During the French Revolution, inventor Claude Chappe devised a way to communicate quickly across long distances. Chappe's system was made up of tall towers, up to 10 miles apart, topped by moveable mechanical arms that could be arranged in dozens of different positions. Each arrangement signified a different message. Once a message had been posted, an operator on the nearest tower "read" it through a telescope. He then set his own mechanism with the same message, to be read farther down the line. In this way, a message could travel at more than 100 miles an hour. Unfortunately for Chappe, angry crowds twice attacked his equipment, thinking that he was communicating with enemies of the Revolution.

Activity **Analyzing Visuals** Have students closely examine Delaroche's painting. Have them write a list of adjectives that describe the people depicted in the painting. *possible answers—determined, angry, desperate, tired* **LS Verbal-Linguistic**

Reactions to Revolution

Historical Context The four documents here reveal the reactions of people from various parts of the world to the events of the French Revolution.

Task Study the selections and answer the questions that follow. After you have studied all the documents, you will be asked to write an essay explaining why people's reactions to the revolution differed. You will need to use evidence from these selections and from the chapter to support the position you take in your essay.

 NEW YORK STANDARDS

PI 3.3 Students examine the social, cultural, political, economic, and religious norms and values of Western and other world cultures.

DOCUMENT 1

A French Writer's Recollections

François-Auguste-René de Chateaubriand is one of the most famous authors in French history. A member of the nobility, he fled France when the Revolution began. Writing in England, he described how the upheaval in France, including changes to the names of days and months, affected the people still living there.

> The people, now hearing of nothing but conspiracies, invasion, and treason, were afraid of their own friends, and fancying themselves upon a mine which was ready to burst beneath them, sunk into a state of torpid terror. The unfortunate confounded [confused] people no longer knew where they were, nor whether they existed. They sought in vain for their ancient customs—these had vanished. They saw a foreign nation in strange attire, wandering through the public streets. As if condemned for ever to this new order of misery, the unknown months seemed to tell them that the revolution would extend to eternity; and in this land of prodigies, they had fears of losing themselves even in the midst of the streets, the names of which they no longer knew.

DOCUMENT 2

An Artist's View

The painting at right was created by French artist Paul Delaroche. Painted in the 1830s, it shows the artist's idea of what the mob that stormed the Bastille in 1789 may have looked like. The figure in white with the sword holds the keys to the Bastille. Other members of the crowd are carrying or dragging objects that they have taken from the prison.

The Conquerors of the Bastille before the Hotel de Ville in 1789, Paul Delaroche, 1839

620 CHAPTER 20

Skills Focus: Recognizing Bias in Primary Sources   `At Level`

Reading Like a Historian Skill
Chateaubriand the Nobleman

1. Guide students in a discussion about Chateaubriand's writing. Ask students how Chateaubriand's position as a nobleman might have made him biased as an observer.

2. Have students write a one-page response to Chateaubriand's writing from a member of the National Convention or from a French worker. The response should acknowledge

   that things are not perfect under the Republic, but they are better than they were under the Old Order.

3. Have volunteers read their responses to the class. **LS Verbal-Linguistic**

   📖 **Alternative Assessment Handbook**, Rubric 37: Writing Assignments

DOCUMENT 3

A British Newspaper's Response

The trial and execution of King Louis XVI of France in 1793 shocked people around Europe. Descriptions of the execution were printed by newspapers around the world, many of them clearly expressing their opinions of the revolutionaries who had overthrown Louis. The following passage was printed in *The Times*, a London newspaper, on January 25, 1793.

> The Republican tyrants of France have now carried their bloody purposes to the uttermost diabolical stretch of savage cruelty. They have murdered their King without even the shadow of justice, and of course they cannot expect friendship nor [dealings] with any civilized part of the world. The vengeance of Europe will now rapidly fall on them; and, in process of time, make them the veriest wretches on the face of the earth. The name of Frenchman will be considered as the appellation [name] of savage, and their presence will be shunned as a poison, deadly destructive to the peace and happiness of Mankind.

DOCUMENT 4

An American Reaction to British Critics

Thomas Paine, one of the heroes of the American Revolution, was living in Europe when the French Revolution broke out. There, he read British writings (like Document 3) on events in France. Paine, in response to these writings, published his own thoughts on the French Revolution. The excerpt below is one of his published reactions.

> It was not against Louis XVI. but against the despotic principles of the Government, that the nation revolted. These principles had not their origin in him, but in the original establishment, many centuries back: and they were become too deeply rooted to be removed, and the ... parasites and plunderers too abominably filthy to be cleansed by anything short of a complete and universal Revolution. When it becomes necessary to do anything, the whole heart and soul should go into the measure, or not attempt it. That crisis was then arrived, and there remained no choice but to act with determined vigor, or not to act at all...

Skills FOCUS — READING LIKE A HISTORIAN

DOCUMENT 1
   a. Describe How does Chateaubriand describe the lives of French people during the French Revolution?
   b. Infer Do you think Chateaubriand supported the Revolution? Why or why not?

DOCUMENT 2
   a. Identify Which elements of the image suggest that the people are not happy with the revolutionary government?
   b. Compare Do you think the artist who created this image would agree with Chateaubriand's opinions? Why or why not?

DOCUMENT 3
   a. Recall What does the author predict will happen to France?
   b. Analyze What words or phrases in this selection reveal the author's bias? What impact do these words have?

DOCUMENT 4
   a. Interpret Why does Paine say that a revolution was needed? Support your answer.
   b. Interpret Does Paine agree with the writer of Document 3 about the execution of King Louis XVI? What words or phrases support your answer?

DOCUMENT-BASED ESSAY QUESTION

Responses to the French Revolution varied from country to country, and from person to person. Why do you think people had such different reactions to the idea of revolution? Using the documents above and information from the chapter, form a thesis that might explain these differences. Then write a short essay to support your position.

See *Skills Handbook*, pp. H25, H26, H30, H34

Differentiating Instruction

Above Level

Advanced Learners /Gifted and Talented

1. Organize students into two groups. One will support the opinion expressed in the British newspaper. The other will support the opinion expressed by Thomas Paine. Give students time to go over the documents and organize their arguments.

2. Pair students from one group with members of the other group. If there is a remaining student, make one grouping of three.

3. Have students debate the following question: Was the execution of the king a necessary part of the Revolution?

4. Guide students in a discussion about strong points that were made on both sides.
   LS Verbal-Linguistic

   Alternative Assessment Handbook, Rubrics 10: Debates; and 14: Group Activity

Word Help

veriest wretches most awful people
despotic having absolute power
parasite a person who receives help from another without giving anything in return

Info to Know

Thomas Paine Thomas Paine praised the French for setting up a constitutional government. Britain, he argued, did not have a true constitution, only a set of monarchical and aristocratic claims backed up by force. The French were so impressed with Paine's ideas that he was elected to the National Congress, even though he didn't speak French.

Teaching Tip

Have students conduct research about Chappe's mechanism and discuss their findings as a class. As an extension activity, have students build scale models to demonstrate how the mechanism worked.

Answers

Reading Like a Historian
Document 1. a. *afraid of friends, terrified, confused, felt they were in a foreign country;* **b.** *possible answer—no, because he was a displaced nobleman, saw only chaos and fear;* **Document 2. a.** *People hold swords and have sad, angry expressions.* **b.** *possible answer—yes, because the people depicted may be confused and were reacting to the Revolution;* **Document 3. a.** *Other countries will take vengeance, all French will be considered savages.* **b.** *tyrants, bloody purposes, murdered; get an emotional response from reader;* **Document 4. a.** *Revolution was the only way to destroy despotic principles of government.* **b.** *no; cleansed, complete and universal Revolution, act with determined vigor;* **Essay**

Visual Summary

Review and Inquiry Organize students into six groups, and assign each group one of these parts of the visual summary: short-term causes, long-term causes, short-term effects, long-term effects, 1789-1795, 1799-1815. Have each group prepare a two-minute oral summary of its assigned topic.

Quick Facts Transparency: Visual Study Guide: The French Revolution and Napoleon

Review Key Terms and People

1. coup d'état
2. Continental System
3. plebiscite
4. guillotine
5. indemnity
6. estates
7. nationalism
8. reactionary

Comprehension and Critical Thinking

9. **a.** bourgeoisie, artisans and workers, peasants
   b. stormed by mob, commander killed
   c. declaration by Austria and Prussia provoked war with France; war led to shortages and financial strain

10. **a.** shocked and horrified
    b. clergy became elected public employees or lost positions, Parisian churches closed, new cult
    c. No, directors were weak and corrupt.

11. **a.** made a compromise agreement with the pope, the Concordat
    b. efficient tax collecting system, revised and organized law, established schools
    c. possible answers—intense hatred of invaders, carefully planned ambushes, inability of French army to fight guerrilla war

12. **a.** so soldiers could not get any of the food, adding to challenges of invasion
    b. France reduced to original size, territories redistributed, German Confederation formed
    c. possible answers—yes, revolution had caused disorder; no—suppressing rights does not create order for long.

VISUAL STUDY GUIDE

Causes and Effects of the Revolution

CAUSES

Short-Term Causes
- Poor harvests, food shortage
- Massive government debt
- Louis XVI's refusal to accept financial reforms
- Fall of the Bastille

Long-Term Causes
- Great inequalities in society
- Spread of Enlightenment ideas
- Weak leadership from King Louis XVI

French Revolution

EFFECTS

Short-Term Effects
- A written constitution for France
- End of the monarchy and execution of the king and queen
- European alliance against France
- Reign of Terror

Long-Term Effects
- Napoleon's seizure of power
- Growth of nationalism in Europe
- Congress of Vienna
- Spread of revolutionary ideas to Latin America, Asia, and Africa

Major Events of the Revolution and Napoleonic Era

1789
- National Assembly forms
- Fall of the Bastille
- Declaration of the Rights of Man and of the Citizen

1791
- Legislative Assembly forms
- France declares war against Austria and Prussia

1792
- National Convention forms
- Monarchy ends

1793
- Louis XVI executed
- First coalition forms against France
- Reign of Terror begins

1795
- The Directory forms

1799
- Napoleon seizes power

1805
- French defeat at Trafalgar, victory at Austerlitz

1812
- Disastrous Russian campaign

1813
- Napoleon exiled to Elba

1815
- Napoleon's Hundred Days
- French defeat at Waterloo
- Napoleon exiled to Saint Helena
- Congress of Vienna

Review Key Terms and People

Identify the term or person from the chapter that best fits each of the following descriptions.

1. a forced transfer of power
2. Napoleon's plan for cutting off trade to enemy countries
3. a question put before all voters
4. execution device that dropped a heavy blade through the victim's neck
5. a payment to other countries to compensate them for damages
6. classes of French society
7. a sense of patriotism and unity as a people
8. opposing progress; wanting conditions to return to those of an earlier time

Reading Skills

13. Noblilty are those who are in a state or condition of being noble.
14. against the clergy
15. possible answer—concord; means agreement or harmony

History's Impact video program
Review the video to answer the closing question:
How did the French Revolution impact the world?

Comprehension and Critical Thinking

SECTION 1 (pp. 593–599)

9. a. Identify What were the groups within the Third Estate?

b. Summarize What happened at the Bastille on July 14, 1789?

c. Elaborate How did events in other countries affect the development of the French government?

SECTION 2 (pp. 601–606)

10. a. Recall How did other European countries react to the execution of Louis XVI?

b. Analyze In what ways did the Revolution change religion in France?

c. Make Judgments Was the Directory an improvement on the National Convention? Why or why not?

SECTION 3 (pp. 608–613)

11. a. Explain How did Napoleon make peace with the Roman Catholic Church?

b. Draw Conclusion How did Napoleon's policies affect common people?

c. Predict What are some possible reasons for the success of the Spanish peasants' guerrilla war against Napoleon's troops?

SECTION 4 (pp. 614–619)

12. a. Explain Why did the Russian people burn their fields as they retreated eastward?

b. Contrast How did the Congress of Vienna change the map of Europe?

c. Rate Do you think Metternich's reaction to the French Revolution and Napoleon's rule was a logical one? Why or why not?

Reading Skills

Understanding Word Origins *Use what you know about prefixes, suffixes, and root words to answer the questions below.*

13. If you know that the suffix *–ity* means "state or condition," how do you explain the relationship between the word *nobles* and the word *nobility*?

14. What does the prefix *anti–* tell you about the meaning of the word *anticlerical*?

15. What do you think is the root of the word *concordat*? What does this root word suggest about the meaning of *concordat*?

Analyzing Visuals

Reading Like a Historian *The cartoon below shows Napoleon in front of his home, the palace at Fontainebleau.*

From High to Low… or the Causes and the Effects, artist unknown, c. 1814

16. Explain Does this cartoon show a period early in Napoleon's career or late in his career? Explain.

17. Draw Conclusions The buildings in the left corner are symbols for Spain. Those in the right corner stand for Russia. What do you think the cartoonist was trying to say by using these symbols?

Using the Internet

go.hrw.com
Practice Online
Keyword: SHL NAP

18. During the French Revolution, many political parties competed for power. Using the keyword above, do research to learn about the beliefs, leaders, and activities of some of these political parties. Then create a chart to clarify what the parties had in common and how they differed.

WRITING FOR THE SAT

Think about the following issue:

The Revolution threw France into chaos and cost thousands of lives. Still, millions of French people were fiercely loyal to the Revolution and believed that it offered a better life than they had known under King Louis XVI.

19. Assignment: Why were so many French willing to risk everything for revolutionary ideals? Write a short essay in which you develop your position on this issue. Support your point of view with reasoning and examples from your reading.

THE FRENCH REVOLUTION AND NAPOLEON **623**

Answers

Analyzing Visuals

16. late; he is struggling to maintain his reach over the empire and has dropped his crown and scepter

17. that Napoleon has lost control over his empire

Using the Internet

18. Go to the HRW Web site and enter the keyword shown to access a rubric for this activity.

KEYWORD: SHL NAP

Writing for the SAT

19. possible reasoning—The French were willing to risk everything because the Old Order took their labor and tax money and gave them nothing in return. possible example—wanted the right to participate in government

A rubric for the activity is provided in **CRF: Writing for the SAT.**

HOLT

History's Impact

▶ **Video Program**
Refer to the Video Program Teacher's Guide for a discussion of the closing question.

Review and Assessment Resources

Review and Reinforce

- **CRF:** Chapter Review
- **Quick Facts Transparency:** Visual Study Guide: The French Revolution and Napoleon
- **Spanish Chapter Summaries Audio CD Program**
- OSP **Holt PuzzlePro**; Quiz Show for ExamView
- **Quiz Game CD-ROM**

Assess

- **PASS:** Chapter Test, Forms A and B
- **Alternative Assessment Handbook**
- OSP **ExamView Test Generator,** Chapter Test
- **Differentiated Instruction Modified Worksheets and Tests CD-ROM:** Chapter Test
- HOAP **Holt Online Assessment Program** (in the Premier Online Edition)

Reteach/Intervene

- **Interactive Reader and Study Guide**
- **Differentiated Instruction Teacher Management System:** Lesson Plans for Differentiated Instruction
- **Differentiated Instruction Modified Worksheets and Tests CD-ROM:** Chapter Test
- **Interactive Skills Tutor CD-ROM**

go.hrw.com
Online Resources
KEYWORD: SHL TEACHER

You can use these pages to have students simultaneously review the unit and practice taking standardized tests.

Answers

1. 4
Monarchs of Europe, Section 1

2. 3
Monarchs of Europe, Section 1

3. 1
Monarchs of Europe, Section 1

4. 1
Monarchs of Europe, Section 2

5. 2
Monarchs of Europe, Section 4

6. 1
Monarchs of Europe, Section 3

7. 4
Enlightenment and Revolution, Section 1

8. 1
Enlightenment and Revolution, Section 1

9. 1
Enlightenment and Revolution, Section 1

10. 1
Enlightenment and Revolution, Section 2

UNIT 6
Regents Practice

Directions Write your answer for each statement or question on a separate answer sheet. Choose the number of the word or expression that best completes the statement or answers the question.

1 Throughout the 1500s and 1600s, many European monarchs worked to
1 create large trade associations throughout Europe.
2 spread democracy in Europe.
3 allow religious freedom in their kingdoms.
4 centralize their political power.

2 King Philip II of Spain saw himself as a leader of the
1 Protestant Reformation.
2 Renaissance.
3 Catholic Reformation.
4 Spanish Succession.

3 In 1588 the Spanish Armada was defeated by
1 England.
2 France.
3 Italy.
4 Germany.

4 Absolute monarchy in France is most associated with which king?
1 Cardinal Richelieu
2 Philip II
3 Louis XIV
4 Henry IV

5 A key goal of Peter the Great was to
1 isolate Russia.
2 modernize Russia.
3 democratize Russia.
4 divide Russia.

6 With the Glorious Revolution in England in 1688,
1 Parliament gained more power.
2 England became less democratic.
3 Parliament revoked the English Bill of Rights.
4 William and Mary left England.

7 The work of which Scientific Revolution thinker produced this understanding of the solar system?

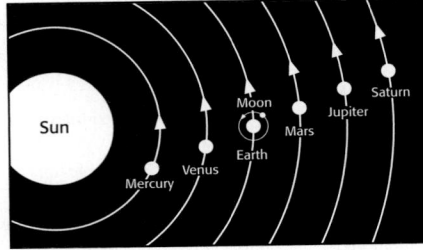

1 Voltaire
2 Thomas Aquinas
3 Descartes
4 Copernicus

8 Francis Bacon and René Descartes are credited with developing
1 the scientific method.
2 the law of motion.
3 the theory of relativity.
4 the geocentric model.

9 Which famous physicist studied the laws of motion and gravity?
1 Isaac Newton
2 William Harvey
3 Ptolemy
4 Robert Boyle

10 John Locke is best known for advancing which idea?
1 People have a natural right to life, liberty, and property.
2 Government power should not be limited.
3 Governments should be separated into different branches.
4 Monarchy is the best form of government.

11 The Enlightenment idea that government should be created and controlled by the people is called

1 divine right of kings.

2 enlightened despotism.

3 absolutism.

4 popular sovereignty.

12 The passage below from *The Social Contract*, published in 1762, was written by which Enlightenment thinker?

"Man is born free; and everywhere he is in chains. One thinks himself the master of others, and still remains a greater slave than they. How did this change come about? I do not know. What can make it legitimate? That question I think I can answer."

1 Voltaire

2 Locke

3 Montesquieu

4 Rousseau

13 The Declaration of Independence put forth the idea that

1 monarchs had more rights than their subjects.

2 monarchy should be abolished everywhere.

3 people had a right to overthrow unjust governments.

4 people should have no say in the independence of nations.

14 The U.S. Constitution established a system of

1 separation of powers into different branches of government.

2 constitutional monarchy in the colonies.

3 equal voting rights for men and women.

4 strategic military and trade alliances.

15 Both the American and French revolutions

1 resulted in a lasting constitution.

2 failed to overthrow their governments.

3 happened before the Enlightenment.

4 inspired others seeking democracy.

16 One cause of the French Revolution was

1 the strong leadership of Louis XVI.

2 nearby revolutions in Germany and Austria.

3 record government surpluses.

4 inequalities in society.

17 Which person was a leader of France's Reign of Terror?

1 Napoleon

2 Louis XVI

3 Robespierre

4 Prince Klemens von Metternich

18 In his rise to power, Napoleon

1 defeated British troops at the French port of Toulon.

2 defeated the British navy at the Battle of the Nile.

3 decided not to replace the Directory with a Consulate.

4 chose not to lead French forces invading Italy.

REVIEWING THE UNIT

Constructed Response Enlightenment ideas influenced key government documents that were created in the 1600s and 1700s. Recall what you have learned about the English Bill of Rights, the U.S. Declaration of Independence, the U.S. Constitution, and the French Declaration of the Rights of Man and of the Citizen. Then write a brief essay in which you summarize how each document reflected Enlightenment ideas.

CONNECTING TO THE PREVIOUS UNIT

Constructed Response The Protestant and Catholic Reformations affected many European monarchs, their governments, and their relations with other countries. Choose one country from this unit that was deeply affected by religious changes and divisions in Europe. Then write a brief essay explaining how the Protestant or Catholic Reformation affected the country's history, government, and society.

11. 4

Enlightenment and Revolution, Section 2

12. 4

Enlightenment and Revolution, Section 2

13. 3

Enlightenment and Revolution, Section 3

14. 1

Enlightenment and Revolution, Section 2

15. 4

The French Revolution and Napoleon, Section 4

16. 4

The French Revolution and Napoleon, Section 1

17. 3

The French Revolution and Napoleon, Section 2

18. 1

The French Revolution and Napoleon, Section 3

Reviewing the Unit

Student essays should mention that the English Bill of Rights gave citizens important civil rights, which reflected Enlightenment ideals about liberty, rights, equality, the social contract, and the limits of government. The Declaration of Independence reflected Enlightenment ideals such as the demand for certain unalienable rights. The U.S. Constitution reflected Enlightenment ideas about checks and balances. The Declaration of the Rights of Man and of the Citizen stated that all men are born equal and remain equal before the law, and it guaranteed freedom of speech and religion.

Connecting to the Previous Unit

Student essays will vary depending on choice of country, but essays should discuss one country from this unit that was affected by religious changes and divisions in Europe. Essays should explain how the Protestant or Catholic Reformation affected the country's history, government, and society.

Science and Technology

Deductive Reasoning René Descartes' life-long obsession with *how* we know what we know may have begun when he studied under the Jesuits. The Jesuits used reason to interpret and comprehend Christian teachings. This method of gaining knowledge may have inspired Descartes to ask questions like "How do you know what is true?" and "How can you tell what is true from what is false?" These are the fundamental questions that Descartes spent most of his career investigating to outline his methods of deductive reasoning.

Arts and Ideas

Tolerance Another important and influential idea to come out of the Enlightenment was the idea of tolerance. Tolerance was especially important to the *philosophes,* a group of French thinkers most active in the 18th century. As far as the *philosophes* were concerned, the worst crimes against humanity were instigated and carried out in the name of religion. They believed that without religious tolerance, a just and fair society was impossible.

Analyzing Primary Sources

Activity **Rousseau** Write the following quote by Rousseau for students to see: "Man is born free but everywhere is in chains." Explain that though Rousseau was describing the state of Europe, his statement still rings true today. Have students write a paragraph in which they explain how Rousseau's statement can be applied to recent global events.

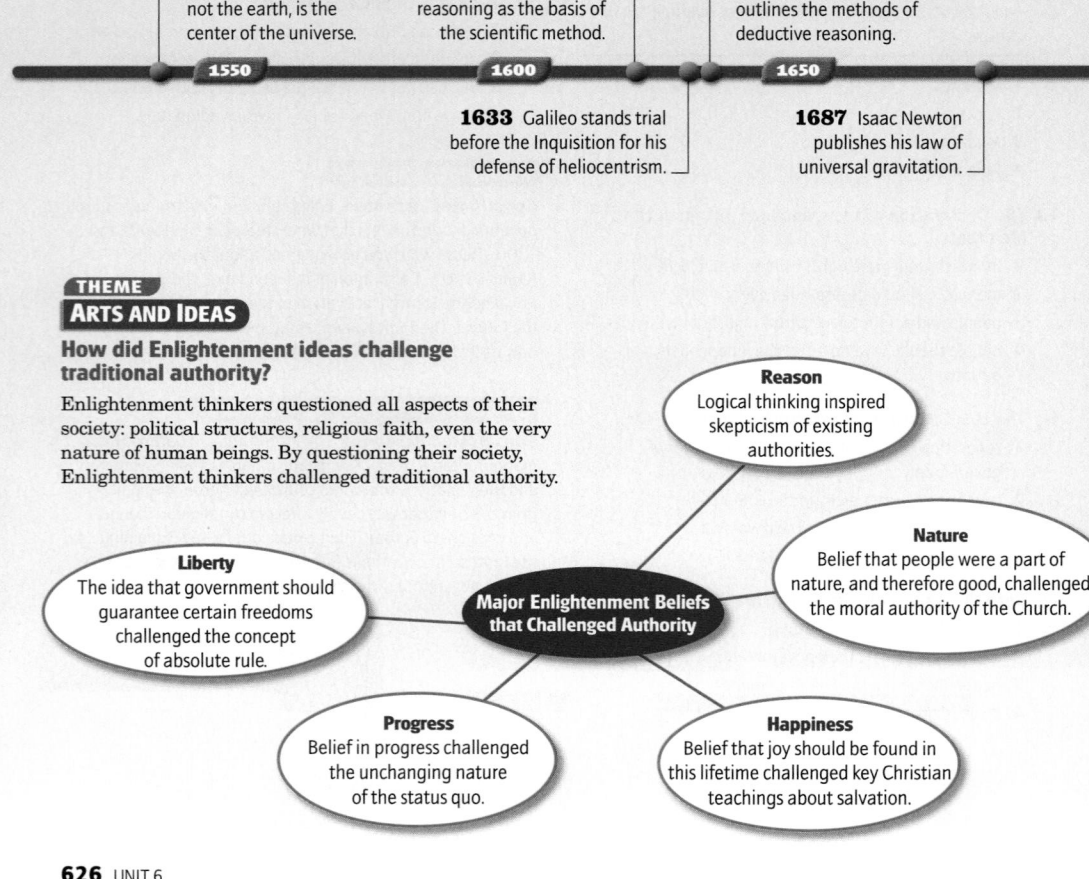

THEME
SCIENCE AND TECHNOLOGY

How did advances in science lead to new ways of thinking?

For more than a thousand years, scientific thought in Europe had been dominated by the ideas of the ancient Greeks. But beginning in the 1500s, people began using reason to study the world in new ways. As a result, scientists made major advances that led to new ways of thinking about the world.

1543 Copernicus argues that the sun, not the earth, is the center of the universe.

1620 Francis Bacon proposes inductive reasoning as the basis of the scientific method.

1637 René Descartes outlines the methods of deductive reasoning.

1550 · 1600 · 1650

1633 Galileo stands trial before the Inquisition for his defense of heliocentrism.

1687 Isaac Newton publishes his law of universal gravitation.

THEME
ARTS AND IDEAS

How did Enlightenment ideas challenge traditional authority?

Enlightenment thinkers questioned all aspects of their society: political structures, religious faith, even the very nature of human beings. By questioning their society, Enlightenment thinkers challenged traditional authority.

Reason
Logical thinking inspired skepticism of existing authorities.

Nature
Belief that people were a part of nature, and therefore good, challenged the moral authority of the Church.

Liberty
The idea that government should guarantee certain freedoms challenged the concept of absolute rule.

Major Enlightenment Beliefs that Challenged Authority

Progress
Belief in progress challenged the unchanging nature of the status quo.

Happiness
Belief that joy should be found in this lifetime challenged key Christian teachings about salvation.

626 UNIT 6

Differentiating Instruction

Above Level

Advanced Learners/Gifted and Talented

Standard English Mastery

1. Organize students into five groups. Assign each group one of the five items listed on the time line.

2. Have each group conduct additional research on the event using reliable online or traditional print sources. Students should take notes about the significance and impact of the event as it related to society at the time.

3. Have students use information from their research to write a newspaper article announcing the event to the public. The article should explain the event's significance and its likely impact on society. Remind students to use the pyramid structure of journalism (information should be presented from most to least significant), and to use the five Ws and one H (who, what, where, when, why, and how).

4. Have a student from each group read the article to the class. **LS Interpersonal, Verbal-Linguistic**

Alternative Assessment Handbook, Rubric 23: Newspapers

THEME
GOVERNMENT AND CITIZENSHIP

How did the ideas of the Enlightenment influence the emergence of democratic government?

The ideas of the Enlightenment had a huge influence on the leaders of the American and French revolutions. When these leaders began to form new democratic governments in France and the United States, they built the ideas of thinkers like Locke, Montesquieu, Rousseau, and Voltaire into the very structures of their governments.

IMPACT OF ENLIGHTENMENT THOUGHT ON GOVERNMENT IN FRANCE AND THE UNITED STATES

John Locke	Wrote that government and the people were bound by a social contract	The U.S. Declaration of Independence upheld the social contract by stating that "governments are instituted among men, deriving their just powers from the consent of the governed."
John Locke	Argued that government should protect citizens' natural rights, which included life, liberty, and property	The French National Assembly protected citizens' rights in the Declaration of the Rights of Man and of the Citizen. The U.S. Declaration of Independence defined natural rights as "life, liberty, and the pursuit of happiness."
Montesquieu	Wrote that power in a republican democracy should be divided to avoid tyranny	Both the U.S. Constitution and the French Declaration of the Rights of Man and of the Citizen called for the separation of powers in government.
Rousseau	Argued that true democracy would require many people to share political power	Citizens in France and the United States voted for their representatives in government. Many participated directly as elected government officials.
Voltaire	Argued in favor of free speech and religious toleration	Both the United States and French governments protected the freedoms of speech and religion.

Skills Focus
UNDERSTANDING THEMES

How did the Scientific Revolution and the Enlightenment result in a new view of human beings and their world? Use your textbook and other resources to gather information about how people's views changed after the Scientific Revolution and Enlightenment. Then create a chart like the one below to contrast these changing views.

Changing Views		
	Old Ways and Ideas	**New Ways and Ideas**
Methods used to explain the world		
Relationship between the ruler and the people		
Importance of the individual		

Global Connections

Political revolutions have one common characteristic—they result in the overthrow of one government or ruler and the substitution of another. But each revolution has its own specific causes that arise because of particular conditions in that nation.

In this unit, you learned about three significant revolutions: the Glorious Revolution in England, the American Revolution, and the French Revolution. Create a chart that compares and contrasts their political, economic, and social causes.

Making Connections Analyze your chart to determine what the most common causes of revolution were. Then write a short essay of two to three paragraphs explaining your understanding of why those causes so frequently led to revolution.

CHANGES IN EUROPEAN SOCIETY **627**

Government and Citizenship

The Social Contract Locke's idea of the social contract formed the foundation of his thoughts about government and those who are governed. Locke put forth that, in the social contract, government exists to protect those it governs. When government does not protect, it breaks the contract, leaving the governed free to choose new rulers or a new government. The idea of the social contract was the driving influence behind the Declaration of Independence.

Understanding Themes

Student charts should include the following information:
Method used to explain the world—old ways and ideas dominated by ideas of ancient Greek new ways and ideas: relied on systematic observation, precise instruments, and reasoning
Relationship between the ruler and the people—old ways and ideas: divine right of kings, absolutism; the governed supported their rulers, rulers did not support their subjects; new ways and ideas: social contract, government exists to protect the governed
Importance of the individual—old ways and ideas: community, authority, and tradition were foundation of society; new ways and ideas: individuals are in control of their own destiny; individual has ability to change the world

Global Connections

Student charts should compare and contrast the political, economic, and social causes of the Glorious Revolution, the American Revolution, and the French Revolution. Student essays will vary, but should demonstrate an understanding of the causes that led to each revolution.

Skills Focus: Making Oral Presentations　　　　　　　At Level

Reading Like a Historian Skill
Philosophers' Conference

1. Have students reread the chart on this page outlining the impact of Enlightenment and then tell them to choose one of the four philosophers.

2. Using the information in the chart, have students create a speech from the point of view of their chosen philosopher, asserting that philosopher's Enlightenment idea. Tell students they will present their speech at a philosophers' conference, which will be attended by French and American citizens and government officials.

3. Have volunteers present their speeches to the class, which will represent conference participants. Encourage students to use clear and loud voices, and to speak persuasively and passionately when presenting their speeches. **LS Verbal-Linguistic**

Alternative Assessment Handbook, Rubric 24: Oral Presentations

Summarizing the Unit

Remind students that although many of America's customs and traditions come from British roots, other countries have also shaped American culture. Have students create a class chart of contributions from the other people discussed in this unit. To begin list ways that French philosophers of the Enlightenment influenced American social thought.

Answers

Thinking Like a Historian *Student charts or graphic organizers should show an understanding of causes and effects of Enlightenment ideas and how they influenced modern government structures, citizens' rights, and the use of reason to solve problems.*
possible responses—
A. *Modern governments reflect checks and separation of powers advocated by Enlightenment thinkers. Democratic governments are structured to ensure popular sovereignty.*
B. *Governments are expected to protect citizens' rights, such as the right to their own property. Many believe that governments should reflect peoples' right to popular sovereignty.* **C.** *Philosophes emphasized education and used reason to study the human condition, which continues today in the social sciences.*

UNIT 6
IN BRIEF
Below is a chapter-by-chapter summary of the main ideas in this unit, followed by a summary activity for the unit.

CHAPTER 18
Monarchs of Europe
1500–1800

MAIN IDEA Between 1500 and 1800, Europe's rulers in Spain, France, Russia, and other kingdoms held absolute power over their subjects.

SECTION 1 During the 1500s Spain grew powerful under the rule of absolute monarchs like Philip II and entered a Golden Age of art and literature. But beginning in the late 1500s, wars, revolts, and economic problems began to weaken Spain's empire.

SECTION 2 After a period of religious violence, Henry IV reunified France in the late 1500s. During the 1600s, French kings such as Louis XIV consolidated their political power as absolute rulers.

SECTION 3 In England, monarchs clashed with Parliament in the English Civil War. After the war, England became a constitutional monarchy, and Parliament limited the power of monarchs with the peaceful Glorious Revolution.

SECTION 4 Russia became a world power under Peter the Great and Catherine the Great, as they reformed and modernized the county. In Central Europe, powerful families ruled new states.

CHAPTER 19
Enlightenment and Revolution
1550–1800

MAIN IDEA New ideas and discoveries in Europe during the Scientific Revolution and the Enlightenment led to significant changes in government and society. Enlightenment ideas inspired a revolution, independence, and democracy in the United States.

SECTION 1 The beginnings of modern science can be traced back to the discoveries and methods of the Scientific Revolution.

SECTION 2 During the Enlightenment, philosophers began to argue that people have basic natural rights and governments are responsible for protecting them.

SECTION 3 Inspired by Enlightenment ideas, colonists in America rebelled against England, gaining independence and becoming the world's first modern democracy.

628 UNIT 6

CHAPTER 20
The French Revolution and Napoleon
1770–1820

MAIN IDEA The French Revolution of 1789 overthrew the French monarchy and established a democracy based on Enlightenment ideas. But instability after the revolution allowed Napoleon Bonaparte to take power and create a large European empire until he was finally defeated.

SECTION 1 Inequalities in society and other problems led to the French Revolution and a democratic government in France. The new government worked to protect people's rights and to put an end to the monarchy.

SECTION 2 The French government soon became radical and began a Reign of Terror. Political opponents were put on trial and executed as the government tried to maintain power.

SECTION 3 As France's new government struggled, the young general Napoleon Bonaparte rose to power and seized control. Napoleon waged wars across Europe to build an empire and increase French power and influence.

SECTION 4 Napoleon was eventually defeated in Russia and at the Battle of Waterloo by an alliance of European powers. After his defeat, European leaders met at the Congress of Vienna to restore the balance of power in Europe, redraw Europe's borders, and restore European monarchies.

Thinking like a Historian
Summary and Extension Activity

Enlightenment ideas of the 1600s and 1700s caused changes in government and society that still influence the world today. Choose one of the following topics and create a chart or graphic organizer to show how Enlightenment ideas have influenced the modern world.

A. Structures of modern governments
B. Rights of citizens
C. Use of reason to solve problems

Unit Resources

Review and Reinforce

📋 **Global History and Geography Regents Test Prep Workbook**
🖐 **Regents Review Transparencies**
📢 **Spanish Chapter Summaries Audio CD Program**
OSP **Holt PuzzlePro:** Quiz Show for ExamView
💿 **Quiz Game CD-ROM**

Assess

📋 **PASS:** Unit Test, Forms A and B
📋 **Alternative Assessment Handbook**
OSP **New York ExamView Test Generator** correlated to NY SS Standards
💿 **Differentiated Instruction Modified Worksheets and Tests CD-ROM:** Chapter Tests
HOAP **Holt Online Assessment Program** (in the Premier Online Edition)

Reteach/Intervene

📋 **Interactive Reader and Study Guide**
📋 **Differentiated Instruction Teacher Management System:** Lesson Plans for Differentiated Instruction
💿 **Differentiated Instruction Modified Worksheets and Tests CD-ROM:** Chapter Tests
💿 **Interactive Skills Tutor CD-ROM**

go.hrw.com
Online Resources

KEYWORDS: SHL MON, SHL ENL, SHL NAP

UNIT 7
Industrialization and Nationalism
1700–1920

CHAPTER 21
The Industrial Revolution
1700–1900

CHAPTER 22
Life in the Industrial Age
1800–1900

CHAPTER 23
Reforms, Revolutions, and War
1800–1900

CHAPTER 24
Nationalism in Europe
1800–1920

CHAPTER 25
The Age of Imperialism

Themes

ECONOMIC SYSTEMS
The Industrial Revolution changed the economic systems of many countries and led to the development of a world economy.

SCIENCE AND TECHNOLOGY
New inventions and technologies caused changes in how people lived, worked, and traveled and set the stage for the modern technological age.

GOVERNMENT AND CITIZENSHIP
Nationalism and imperialism in Europe affected governments and citizens around the world as European countries competed for colonies and resources.

Women and children work in a coal-sifting room in France during the Industrial Revolution.

The Blanzy Mine, by J.F. Bonhomme, c. 1860

629

Introducing the Unit
Have students list the factors that characterize modern society. As they do so, write them for the class to see. As a class, go through the list to determine which of those factors first evolved during the period covered by this unit. For example, globalization can be viewed as an outgrowth of the imperialism that led European nations to colonize much of Africa and Asia.

Connecting to Themes
Activity **The Effects of Industrialization** Have students identify the effects of the Industrial Revolution. Guide the class in a discussion of the ways in which industrialization led to urbanization, improvements in education, a rise in democracy at home, and imperialist policies abroad. **LS** **Verbal-Linguistic**

Reading Like a Historian
Interpreting Visuals
The French Industrial Revolution
Industrial development took place later in France than in Great Britain. At the time when Britain was rapidly industrializing, France was embroiled in a revolution. France had become an industrial power by 1848, but even after great growth during the Second Empire, it lagged behind Britain.

Unit Resources

Planning
- **Differentiated Instruction Teacher Management System:** Unit Pacing Guide
- OSP **New York One-Stop Planner CD-ROM:** Teacher Management System
- **Power Presentations with Video CD-ROM**

Standards Mastery
- **Global History and Geography Regents Test Prep Workbook**
- **Regents Review Transparencies**

Differentiating Instruction
- **Differentiated Instruction Teacher Management System:** Lesson Plans for Differentiated Instruction
- **Differentiated Instruction Modified Worksheets and Tests CD-ROM**

Enrichment
- **A World History Teacher's Guide to Analyzing Movies**
- **Document-Based Activities for World History**
- **World History Outline Maps**
- **Reading Like a Historian: World History Toolkit**
- **World History Primary Source Library CD-ROM**

Assessment
- **PASS:** Unit Test, Forms A and B
- **Alternative Assessment Handbook**
- OSP **New York ExamView Test Generator correlated to NY SS Standards**
- HOAP **Holt Online Assessment Program** (in the Premier Online Edition)

Chapter 21 Planning Guide

The Industrial Revolution

Chapter Overview	Reproducible Resources	Technology Resources
CHAPTER 21 pp. 630–655 **Overview:** In this chapter, students will learn how new processes and machines led to dramatic changes in industry–a period in history known as the Industrial Revolution. **KI 2, 3; PI 2.3, 2.5, 3.2, 3.3** See pp. T32–T55 for a detailed correlation to the New York State Core Curriculum for Global History and Geography and the New York Learning Standards.	**Differentiated Instruction Teacher Management System:*** • Pacing Guide • Lesson Plans for Differentiated Instruction **Interactive Reader and Study Guide:** Chapter Summary* **Chapter Resource File*** • Writing About History • Social Studies Skill • Chapter Review • Interdisciplinary Project **World History Outline Maps**	**OSP New York One-Stop Planner CD-ROM:** Calendar Planner **Live Ink© Online Reading Help** **Student Edition on Audio CD Program** **Differentiated Instruction Modified Worksheets and Tests CD-ROM** **Interactive Skills Tutor CD-ROM** **World History Primary Source Library CD-ROM** **Power Presentations with Video CD-ROM** **History's Impact: World History Video Program (VHS/DVD):** The Industrial Revolution **Online Resources**
Section 1: **A New Kind of Revolution** **The Main Idea:** In the 1700s, conditions in Great Britain led to the rapid growth of the textile industry, which in turn led to huge changes in many other industries. **PI 2.5**	**Differentiated Instruction Teacher Management System:** Section 1 Lesson Plan* **Interactive Reader and Study Guide:** Section 1 Summary* **Chapter Resource File*** • Vocabulary Builder: Section 1 • Biography: Norbert Rillieux • Primary Source: Machines Transform the English Textile Industry	**Regents Review Transparency:** Section 1* **Map Transparency:** Resources of Great Britain, 1800* **Quick Facts Transparency:** New Machines for an Old Industry*
Section 2: **Factories and Workers** **The Main Idea:** The transition from cottage industries changed how people worked in factories, what life was like in factory towns, labor conditions, and, eventually, processes within factories. **PI 3.2**	**Differentiated Instruction Teacher Management System:** Section 2 Lesson Plan* **Interactive Reader and Study Guide:** Section 2 Summary* **Chapter Resource File*** • Vocabulary Builder: Section 2 • Biography: Nelly Bly • Literature: *Hard Times*	**Regents Review Transparency:** Section 2* **Map Transparency:** Effects of the Factory System* **Internet Activity:** Labor Unions
Section 3: **New Ideas in a New Society** **The Main Idea:** The Industrial Revolution inspired new ideas about economics and affected society in many ways. **PI 2.3, 3.3**	**Differentiated Instruction Teacher Management System:** Section 3 Lesson Plan* **Interactive Reader and Study Guide:** Section 3 Summary* **Chapter Resource File*** • Vocabulary Builder: Section 3 • Biography: : Louis Pasteur • History and Geography: The First Modern Railroad	**Regents Review Transparency:** Section 3* **Quick Facts Transparency:** Effects of Industrialization on Women* **Map Transparency:** Industrialized Europe, 1900* **Internet Activity:** Historic Origins of Socialism and Capitalism

HOLT
History's Impact
World History Video Program (VHS/DVD)
The Industrial Revolution

Review, Assessment, Intervention

Global History and Geography Regents Test Prep Workbook

Quick Facts Transparency: The Industrial Revolution*

Spanish Chapter Summaries Audio CD Program

Progress Assessment Support System (PASS): Chapter Test*

Differentiated Instruction Modified Worksheets and Tests CD-ROM: Modified Chapter Test

OSP **New York One-Stop Planner CD-ROM:** ExamView Test Generator (English/Spanish)

HOAP Holt Online Assessment Program (HOAP), in the Holt Premier Online Student Edition

---

 PASS: Section 1 Quiz*

 Online Quiz: Section 1

 Alternative Assessment Handbook

 PASS: Section 2 Quiz*

 Online Quiz: Section 2

 Alternative Assessment Handbook

 PASS: Section 3 Quiz*

 Online Quiz: Section 3

 Alternative Assessment Handbook

Power Presentation with Video CD-ROM

Power Presentations with Video are visual presentations of each chapter's main ideas. Presentations can be customized by including Quick Facts charts, images and maps from the textbook, and video clips.

Holt Online Learning

go.hrw.com
Teacher Resources
KEYWORD: SHL TEACHER

go.hrw.com
Student Resources
KEYWORD: SHL IND

- Document-Based Questions
- Interactive Multimedia Activities

- Current Events
- Chapter-Based Internet Activities
- and more!

Holt Premier
Online Student Edition
Complete online support for interactivity, assessment, and reporting
- Interactive Maps and Notebook
- Homework Practice and Research Activities Online

CHAPTER 21 PLANNING GUIDE

Before You Teach

The Big Picture

Peter N. Stearns

The Industrial Revolution The Industrial Revolution is one of the big changes in human history, deservedly compared with the Neolithic Revolution much earlier in the course. Both the Industrial and the Neolithic revolutions fundamentally altered the ways people worked, where they lived, even what kinds of families they had. At the same time the Industrial Revolution is not quite like the set of events that make up a development such as the French Revolution. There are specific developments, like the key inventions, but the main focus is on broader processes that unfold over several decades. A good start involves basic definitions of early industrial technology including transportation, organizational forms beginning with the factory, and changes in levels of material goods. Discussion must also deal with the question of causes, including what distinctive factors existed in Great Britain.

Extensions and Impacts of Industrialization Britain led the world's industrial pack until the later 19th century. At the same time, it's vital to highlight broader participation in the process by 1850, with much of Western Europe and key parts of the United States joining in. How this expansion occurred, why these areas and not others, and what implications expanding industrialization had for the rest of the world are all important questions. Industrialization was a force that forever changed the human experience and gave rise to new forms of social organization and new social divisions, such as, the emergence of modern working class and middle class. A focus on how work and work values changed can help students understand human impact and the extent of change, while also raising questions about why people protested and also how many could accommodate to new experience. Western industrialization also had gender implications, rather different from what might be expected by more contemporary standards, which can help organize discussion of the broader consequences for family life. Finally, the Industrial Revolution occurred in an ideological framework, with the rise of liberal economics but also the emergence of Marxist critique. The two ideological systems need to be discussed through comparison but also through understanding of the political and social results of ideological competition during the industrialization process.

Recent Scholarship

My latest book, *The Industrial Revolution in World History* (2006), looks at industrialization from a global perspective. The book defines industrialization technologically and organizationally; it looks at social consequences, with particular reference to work, family and leisure; it deals with environmental impact. Discussions about causation issues, and particularly the balance between global and internal British or Western factors, are phrased in terms of active debates. The book looks at the Industrial Revolution in three phases, from Britain's launch to current globalization: early, with emphasis of course on Britain, Western Europe and the United States; late 19th to early 20th centuries, with attention to Russia and Japan along with further Western and global developments; and recent decades, when an additional 40 percent of the world's population are becoming more actively involved in the industrialization process. In all stages, global consequences and new inequalities play a crucial role.

Differentiating Instruction

 Differentiated Instruction Teacher Management System
- Pacing Guide
- Lesson Plans for Differentiated Instruction

Interactive Reader and Study Guide

Spanish Chapter Summaries Audio CD Program

Student Edition on Audio CD Program

 Differentiated Instruction Modified Worksheets and Tests CD-ROM
- Vocabulary Flash Cards
- Modified Vocabulary Builder Activities
- Modified Chapter Review Activity
- Modified Chapter Test

OSP One-Stop Planner CD-ROM
- ExamView Test Generator (English/Spanish)
- PuzzlePro
- Quiz Show for ExamView
- Transparencies and Videos

TE Differentiated Activities in the Teacher's Edition
- Britain's Industrial Success, p. 634
- Cottage Industries vs. Factory Work, p. 641
- Conditions in Manchester, p. 642
- Discontented Workers, p. 644
- New Industrialists, p. 647
- Rebuttal to Spencer, p. 653

Reading Like a Historian
Sam Wineburg

Accident or Achievement? Why did the Industrial Revolution take place in England? This seemingly inoffensive question hurls us into the epicenter of historical argument.

Consider how Robert B. Marks, author of *The Origins of the Modern World*, answers it. England did not achieve industrial eminence because of some inherent quality or essence of thought. "The West certainly did not 'rise' over other parts of the world because of cultural (or racial) superiority." For Marks, the engine in the machine is historical accident and a set of contingent circumstances. England was blessed with huge coal deposits, providing her with a steady supply of cheap fuel. That and the fact that Britain used slave labor to grow cheap cotton in her American colonies (which it then sold back at a handsome profit as finished textiles) kept the whole thing going. There was only one reason why the Chinese or the Indians didn't industrialize first: "They simply did not have colonies or coal."

David S. Landes, professor of history and economics at Harvard and author of *The Wealth and Poverty of Nations*, argues that there was nothing accidental about England's ascendance. The Industrial Revolution that swept this island nation "was not a matter of chance, of 'things simply coming together.'" The superiority of Britain "was itself an achievement . . . the result of work, ingenuity, imagination, and enterprise." For Landes, Britain possessed cultural and institutional features that created unique opportunities for industrial development. These included an ethos of inquiry, the development of a shared scientific language, and the building of a scholarly community that "routinized discovery" and in so doing elevated scientists and inventors to the status of rock stars. It was this cultural environment that gave birth to a technological hothouse that world had never before seen.

Marks focuses on the accident of cheap coal and pooh-poohs the role of scientific innovation. Landes places scientific and rational thinking at the center.

Who's Right? Historical arguments that address "big" questions resist pat answers. Such arguments are never-ending, embracing earlier arguments as well as adopting new data and explanations that come in and out of fashion. Understanding all sides brings us closer to complexity, and helps us understand multi-faceted phenomena.

There's another reason why such arguments cannot be settled once and for all. They are as much about the present as the past. What stings Marks is the hubris of "Eurocentrism," the notion that "the West has some unique historical advantage . . . which gave this human community a permanent superiority." For him, Eurocentrism blinds us to unequal distribution of resources that have often come about by exploitation (slavery), greed (capitalism), and, in this case, the fickleness of historical accident (living atop huge coal deposits).

Landes views such thinking as a politically correct mist that obscures one enduring fact: "culture makes all the difference." And the culture that lead to technological innovation and prosperity? One that rewarded individual achievement, honesty in government, the protection of private property; that "afforded opportunity to individual or collective enterprise" and "encouraged initiative, competition, and emulation." England.

If you hear echoes of contemporary debates—clashing views about free markets, globalization, the policies of the G-8 and the World Bank, the inherent goodness or evil of capitalism—you should. To better understand why historians argue over the past, we must also ask why they, and we, argue over the present. Debates about what happened in the past will be settled only when we sign on to a collective vision for the future.

Don't hold your breath.

Chapter Main Ideas

Section 1 In the 1700s, conditions in Great Britain led to the rapid growth of the textile industry, which in turn led to huge changes in many other industries.

Section 2 The transition from cottage industries changed how people worked in factories, what life was like in factory towns, labor conditions, and eventually, processes within factories.

Section 3 The Industrial Revolution inspired new ideas about economics and affected society in many ways.

📖 New York Standards

Key Idea 2 Establishing timeframes, exploring different periodizations, examining themes across time and within cultures, and focusing on important turning points in world history help organize the study of world cultures and civilizations.

Key Idea 3 Study of the major social, political, cultural, and religious developments in world history involves learning about the important roles and contributions of individuals and groups.

Key to Differentiating Instruction

Below Level

Basic-level activities designed for all students encountering new material

At Level

Intermediate-level activities designed for average students

Above Level

Challenging activities designed for honors and gifted and talented students

Standard English Mastery

Activities designed to improve standard English usage

CHAPTER
21 1700–1900

The Industrial Revolution

THE BIG PICTURE The Scientific Revolution and Enlightenment led people to develop new ways of doing things. Among these new ways were processes and machines for raising crops, making cloth, and other jobs. These developments led to dramatic changes in industry and the world of work. Because so much changed, this era is called the Industrial Revolution. It began in Great Britain and then spread to other parts of the world.

Theme SCIENCE AND TECHNOLOGY
Industrialization made a dramatic impact on the world. In this chapter you will learn the remarkable ways in which technology altered how people worked and lived between 1700 and 1900.

TIME LINE

CHAPTER EVENTS

1701 Jethro Tull invents the seed drill.

1764 James Hargreaves develops the spinning jenny.

1793 Eli Whitney introduces the cotton gin.

1802 Richard Trevithick builds the first steam locomotive.

1700   1750   1800

WORLD EVENTS

1762 Catherine the Great becomes czarina of Russia.

1776 The Thirteen Colonies declare their independence.

1815 Napoleon is defeated at Battle of Waterloo.

630 CHAPTER 21

Introduce the Chapter

At Level

The Industrial Revolution

1. Have students write their own definitions of the word *revolution*. Have volunteers share their definitions, and write the responses for students to see. If student definitions focus on political revolts, ask leading questions that will guide students toward other types of major economic, social, or technological changes.

2. Have students create a single class definition for the term *revolution* using elements of various responses. Display the class definition in the classroom.

3. Tell students that in this chapter they will learn about a revolution in the ways that goods were produced. Industrialization is called a revolution because of the sweeping changes it brought.

4. Have students give examples of items they use in their daily lives that are produced by machines and items produced without solely relying on machines. **LS Verbal-Linguistic**

📖 **Alternative Assessment Handbook,** Rubric 11: Discussions

• Chapter Preview •

HOLT
History's Impact
▶ **Video Program: The Industrial Revolution**
See the Video Teacher's Guide for strategies for using the video segment.

Reading Like aw Historian

Analyzing Visuals Many of Adoph von Menzel's paintings are historical in theme, and he created a series of paintings about the accomplishments of Frederick the Great. In this painting, von Menzel captures a sense of the grim colors and harsh conditions of workers in an iron factory.

Reading like a Historian

The painting shown here is of workers in a German factory flattening a sheet of hot iron. The artist, Adoph von Menzel, visited factories like this one so he could reproduce the details correctly.

Analyzing Visuals How many different tasks or activities can you see in the painting? How do you think the artist felt about the industry pictured? Explain your answer.

See **Skills Handbook**, p. H26

1848
Marx and Engels publish *The Communist Manifesto*.

1850

1848
Revolutions occur throughout Europe.

1871
Trade unions are legalized in Britain.

THE INDUSTRIAL REVOLUTION **631**

go.hrw.com
Online Resources

Chapter Resources:
KEYWORD: SHL IND
Teacher Resources:
KEYWORD: SHL TEACHER

Explore the Time Line

1. Who invented the seed drill? *Jethro Tull*

2. What did Richard Trevithick accomplish in 1802? *built the first steam locomotive*

3. What occurred the same year that *The Communist Manifesto* was published? *Revolutions occurred throughout Europe.*

4. How many years after *The Communist Manifesto* were trade unions legalized in Britain? *twenty-three years*

Info to Know

British Cloth Cloth production was the most important business activity in 18th century Britain. Families did much of the work in their homes, and they farmed as well. Woven cloth was sold to merchants who then took the cloth to the nearest market town. Many merchants also exported cloth to America, Russia, Sweden, Holland, and Germany.

Draw Conclusions Why do you think cloth makers sold their finished cloth to merchants, rather than taking cloth to market towns by themselves? *possible answers—could not leave farms, towns were far away, lack of transportation*

Answers

Reading Like a Historian *possible answers—three; felt that industry was a noble activity because workers are in heroic poses, but the work is very hard*

631

Preteach

Geography Starting Points

The Canal Builder One of the great canal-builders in Britain was Thomas Telford. He built the Ellesmere Canal in Wales, which included two giant aqueducts. Telford also built the Caledonian Canal, a waterway that connects the east coast of Scotland to the west coast.

🏺 **Map Transparency:** Resources of Great Britain, 1800

✹ **Interactive Map:** Resources of Great Britain, 1800

📑 **World History Outline Maps**

★Interactive
RESOURCES OF GREAT BRITAIN, 1800

North Sea

Glasgow

Newcastle upon Tyne

Irish Sea

IRELAND

Bradford · Leeds
Manchester
Liverpool
Sheffield
Nottingham

Kingston upon Hull

Birmingham

GREAT BRITAIN

London

Bristol

English Channel

FRANCE

Major canal
Coal field
Iron ore

0   50   100 Miles
0   50   100 Kilometers
Lambert conformal conic projection

Coal had been a useful fuel for centuries. In the 1700s, mines starting producing large amounts of coal.

Interior of a mine in South Staffordshire

Throughout Great Britain, rushing streams could be used to power waterwheels like the one shown here.

River Scene with Overshot Mill, by Charles Towne, 1833

Starting Points In 1800, much of Europe's economy was still based on farming. Times were changing, though, particularly in Great Britain. There, fewer people were working on farms, and more were working in manufacturing. Great Britain's natural resources, such as coal and iron, were major factors in the growth of British industry.

1. **Analyze** What do you think is the connection between canals and rivers and industry?
2. **Predict** Based on the map, where do you think Great Britain's first industries grew?

🔊 **Listen to History**

Go online to listen to an explanation of the starting points for this chapter.

go.hrw.com
Keyword: SHL IND

632 CHAPTER 21

Skills Focus: Analyzing Maps

At Level

Social Studies Skill
Resource Development

Materials: drawing paper, colored pencils

1. Have students draw a map of a large island nation. Islands should not resemble England. Have students include one river, two cities, mountains and other natural features. Have students divide their islands into a grid system of 16 zones and label them A1, A2, B1, B2, etc.

2. Label six scraps of paper with zone names and place the papers in a hat. Draw three out and read the zone names. These will be the locations of coal deposits. The last three will be the locations of iron ore deposits. Have students create a map legend for the coal and iron deposits.

3. Based on the location of the iron and coal deposits, have students place two new towns, three canals, and two railroads on their maps.
LS Visual-Spatial

📑 **Alternative Assessment Handbook,** Rubric 20: Map Creation

Answers

Geography Starting Points
1. *canals and rivers used to bring natural resources to industrial sites, transport goods;* **2.** *in the south central region, some coastal areas*

632

1 A New Kind of Revolution

BEFORE YOU READ

MAIN IDEA
In the 1700s, conditions in Great Britain led to the rapid growth of the textile industry, which in turn led to huge changes in many other industries.

READING FOCUS
1. Why did the Industrial Revolution begin in Great Britain?
2. How did industrialization cause a revolution in the production of textiles?
3. How did steam power the Industrial Revolution?
4. Where did industrialization spread beyond Great Britain?

KEY TERMS AND PEOPLE
Industrial Revolution
enclosure movement
factors of production
cottage industry
factory
industrialization
Jethro Tull
Richard Arkwright
James Watt
Robert Fulton

NEW YORK

PI 2.5 Students investigate key events and developments and major turning points in world history to identify the factors that brought about change and the long-term effects of those changes.

THE INSIDE STORY
How did one farmer's frustration help start a revolution? Jethro Tull had never planned to be a farmer. He had trained to be a lawyer but inherited the family farm. While running the farm, Tull was often annoyed by the workers' sloppy habits. For example, when planting, they wasted seeds by throwing big handfuls onto the ground. Sure that the job could be done more efficiently, Tull invented a horse-drawn machine that planted seeds one by one. He called it a seed drill. Without knowing it, Tull was helping to start a revolution—an agricultural revolution that would bring changes to nearly all aspects of life. ◾

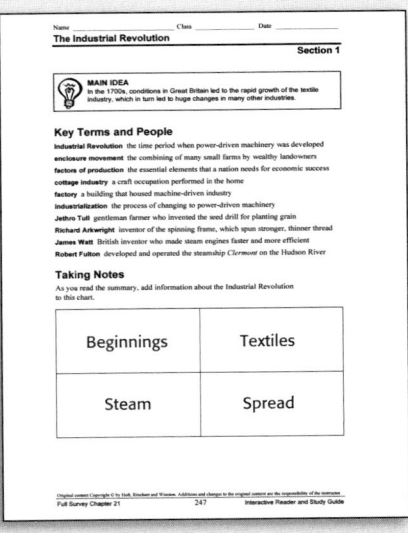

From Muscle to Machines

For centuries, workers had used muscle power to farm the land.

The Mowers, by Sir George Clausen, 1891

THE INDUSTRIAL REVOLUTION **633**

A Revolution in Great Britain

During the 1700s changes in technology began that would transform the world. These changes were based on a shift in how people worked. For centuries people had used human and animal power as their main energy sources. Then they began to develop water and steam power to drive new machines and perform countless tasks. This era, when the use of power-driven machinery was developed, is called the **Industrial Revolution.** For several reasons, it started in Great Britain.

Factors for Success By the 1700s several factors had come together to set the scene for the development of industry in Great Britain. Those factors included a range of political and economic events.

---

① Why did the Industrial Revolution begin in Great Britain? *colonies provided raw materials, political stability encouraged commerce, powerful navy defended shipping, government supported business, agricultural factors, factors of production*

A Revolution in Great Britain

Recall Where did many of Britain's raw materials come from? *colonies held by Britain*

Make Inferences Why do you think rich farmers experimented with agricultural methods? *possible answers—to farm more efficiently, to find ways to increase crop yields*

Summarize Why was water initially more important to Britain's growing industry than coal or iron? *Water was readily available; it did not have to be mined or transported; waterways provided transportation among mines, factories, and markets.*

Info to Know

Enclosure Movement The enclosure movement greatly changed rural England as communal use and care of the land changed to private ownership. As individual landowners and tenants took control of defined areas of land, communities lost their land use rights. Open, unfenced fields and meadows were turned into privately owned hedged, fenced, or walled fields. Acts of Parliament, as well as private agreements between lords and their tenants, helped speed the change.

Answers

History and Economics 1. *fossil fuels not found in Britain, skilled labor supply from China and India, investors from Asia and Middle East;* **2.** *possible answer—renewable power sources, more emphasis on technically skilled workforce*

634

As you read, take notes on the early years of the Industrial Revolution.

| A. In Britain |
| B. In Textiles |
| C. Steam Power |
| D. Spread |

- **Exploration and colonialism** Great Britain claimed colonies around the world that provided vast amounts of raw materials, such as cotton fiber. In addition, the colonies became new markets for British goods. (However, India's own textile industry was severely damaged by British competition.)
- **Seapower** Britain could bring in raw materials and send finished goods around the world because it had the largest, most powerful navy and merchant fleet in the world.
- **Political stability** Although Great Britain fought wars in Canada and North America during the 1700s, at home the country was at peace, and commerce thrived.
- **Government support** Parliament passed laws that favored business, helping the country compete successfully against other nations.
- **Growth of private investment** Private businesses funded experiments for creating better products—what we would call "research and development" today.

Agricultural Factors Much of the research and development took place on farms as some of Britain's so-called gentlemen farmers began to experiment with agricultural methods.

Jethro Tull was among these wealthier farmers. In about 1701 Tull invented the seed drill, a machine that made planting grain much more efficient.

Farmers experimented with other aspects of agriculture also. For example, they improved livestock breeding methods to raise healthier animals. Better varieties of food crops, such as potatoes, were developed. These improvements increased Britain's food supply. Since more food can support more people, Britain's population grew rapidly.

Another agricultural development had mixed results. Wealthy landowners could buy up fields that had previously been shared by rich and poor farmers alike. The new landowners combined the small fields to create large farms and fenced them, a transformation

HISTORY and Economics

Factors of Production

The basic factors of production are the essential elements that a nation needs to achieve economic success. They are land (natural resources), labor, and capital. The places where these factors can be found change over time.

Factors of Production in History In the 1700s the factors of production that sparked the Industrial Revolution were all in place in Great Britain. From these factors—coal, iron ore, waterways, unemployed farmers, cash, and human talent—the British built an industrial empire.

Factors of Production Today Much has changed since the 1700s. The land, labor, and capital that made Great Britain an industrial leader no longer have the same value. For example, running water is not as important as a power source as it once was. Today, the industrial world depends more on fossil fuels, especially oil. Countries other than Great Britain provide most of the

world's supply of the precious fuel. Labor resources can also be found elsewhere. Today, China and India have huge numbers of skilled workers. Capital resources have shifted, too. Investors from Asia and the Middle East now fund many factories in Western countries.

All these shifts in where the factors of production are located affect wealth and, therefore, political power. As you study different countries, keep track of how the factors of production have affected their economies—and their histories.

▲ A worker in Malaysia assembles TVs for a Japanese company.

1. Summarize How has the location of the factors of production changed in current times?
2. Predict How might the factors of production continue to change?

Differentiating Instruction

Below Level

Special Education Students; Learners Having Difficulty

Materials: construction paper, markers

1. Review what the term *industrialization* means and then guide students in a discussion of Britain's factors for success in industrialization. Make a list of Britain's five factors for industrial success for students to see.

2. Organize students into mixed-ability pairs.

3. Have each pair design a series of Web pages that explain the five factors of Britain's

industrial success. There should be a home page and a separate page for each factor. Pages should include text and a picture or icon that illustrates the factor.

4. Have volunteers share their pages with the class. **LS** Visual-Spatial

Alternative Assessment Handbook, Rubric 3: Artwork

called the **enclosure movement**. The movement allowed for more efficient farming methods and, therefore, further increased the food supply. However, enclosure also threw countless farmers off the land. Unable to make a living in the countryside, these poor farmers went to the cities for jobs. There they would form the workforce for growing industries.

Britain's Big Advantage These conditions all point to the basic reason why the Industrial Revolution began in Great Britain. The country had the essential elements that a nation needs to achieve economic success—what economists call the **factors of production**. There are three factors: land, labor, and capital.

Land, in this context, means all of a place's natural resources. Great Britain had all the resources it needed for industry. It had coal to burn as fuel and iron to make into steel and machinery. But to get industry started, no resource was more important than water. People used Britain's streams and rivers to turn waterwheels and generate power, and many of those same waterways provided transportation between mines, factories, and markets. A network of canals connected major rivers. In the mid-1700s England already had about 1,000 miles of canals, which grew to about 4,000 miles by 1800. Also, for long-distance shipping, Great Britain had good deepwater harbors.

For _labor_, Britain had the growing population made possible by a greater food supply. Within this growing population were the thousands of people who had lost their farmland because of the enclosure movement. These were often entire families, and entire families would go to work in industry.

Britain's last factor of production was capital, which refers to funds for investment in business. The country was generally prosperous, and people had money to spend. Britain also had "human capital"—people with abilities and skills that are needed in industry. For example, Jethro Tull and later inventors were among this group of capable people. With all these factors of production in place, Great Britain was ready for a boom in business.

READING CHECK **Find the Main Idea** Why was Great Britain in the 1700s ideally suited to be the birthplace of the Industrial Revolution?

New Machines for an Old Industry

The inventors who revolutionized the textile industry improved on each other's ideas. The spinning frame shown here, invented by Richard Arkwright, twisted fibers together. As a result, it made thread that was much stronger than thread made by an earlier machine.

The Granger Collection, New York

A Revolution in Textiles

The Industrial Revolution began with the British cloth-making, or textile, industry. British workers had been handweaving woolen cloth for centuries. Weaving was a **cottage industry**— a craft occupation performed in the home. But the old ways of making cloth were completely transformed by **industrialization**, or the process of changing to power-driven machinery.

A New Way of Making Cloth In Great Britain most fabric was made of wool or cotton. During the 1700s the supply of both fibers increased. The wool supply increased because the enclosure movement converted so many farms to pastures for raising more sheep. Shipments of cotton fiber came from the British colonies, particularly in India and North America. In the southern American colonies the trade in cotton had a tragic result. Slave labor helped make cotton farming more profitable. Therefore, as Great Britain bought more and more American cotton, slavery became more entrenched throughout the South. A new invention also helped keep the American cotton industry—and slavery—profitable.

ACADEMIC VOCABULARY
labor work, or people who do the work

NEW YORK
CC Unit 5-G2
Agrarian revolution

THE INDUSTRIAL REVOLUTION **635**

Direct Teach

Reading Focus

2 How did industrialization cause a revolution in the production of textiles? _new devices allowed faster and less labor-intensive production of cloth_

A Revolution in Textiles

Explain Why did the supply of wool and cotton increase in the 1700s? _enclosure movement converted farms to pastures for more sheep, cotton came from British colonies, including those in America_

Identify Cause and Effect How did Britain's demand for cotton affect the United States? _made growing cotton very profitable; increased the spread of slavery in the American South_

Quick Facts Transparency: New Machines for an Old Industry

CRF: Primary Source: Machines Transform the English Textile Industry

Skills Focus: Identifying Main Idea and Details At Level

Reading Skill
Land, Labor, Capital

1. Draw the chart below for students to see. Omit the italicized answers.

2. Have students copy and complete the chart. **LS** Visual-Spatial

Alternative Assessment Handbook, Rubric 7: Charts

Factors of Production in Britain

Factor of Production	Land	Labor	Capital
what it means	_all natural resources_	_people available to work_	_funds for investment_
how it was an advantage	_had coal for fuel, iron for steel_	_growing population, people who had lost farmland_	_country prosperous, money to spend, people with abilities_

Answers

Reading Check _Colonies around the world supplied raw materials, powerful navy and merchant fleet facilitated trade, waterways provided power and transportation, enclosure movement led to large labor supply, private investors provided funds for investment, coal and iron deposits provided needed resources._

635

A Revolution in Textiles

Recall What problem did Eli Whitney solve? *the slow, tedious process of pulling seeds from raw cotton; invented the cotton gin*

Identify What machines were developed to spin fiber into thread or yarn? *spinning jenny, spinning frame*

Evaluate Did inventors like Kay and Arkwright deserve to be honored or scorned? *possible answers—honored: their inventions changed the world; scorned: many people lost their jobs*

Activity **Weavers Wanted** Have students design a "Jobs Wanted" flyer inviting workers to leave their farms and come to work at a weaving factory. Remind students that many farm workers might not have been able to read or write at this time in history.
LS Visual-Spatial

📝 **CRF:** Biography: Nobert Rillieux

Reading Like a Historian

Analyze Ask students how they think Baines might have described pre-industrial methods of production. *primitive, backward*

Teaching Tip

If students have trouble grasping the changes brought by the Industrial Revolution, ask them to name products that have revolutionized their lives, such as cell phones and other technological devices that they consider necessities.

Answers

Reading Like a Historian 1. *possible answer—No, Baines could not have understood the long-term effects during his own lifetime.* **2.** *positive adjectives, general tone*

Reading Check *spinning jenny and spinning frame spun thread into yarn, "flying shuttle" and power loom made weaving faster*

Reading like a Historian

An Early Historian on the Textile Industry

Analyzing Secondary Sources Historians often read what other historians before them had to say. Using older sources, modern historians can learn how events were viewed in the past. However, historians who wrote about events soon after they happened usually had a different perspective than historians who wrote many years after the event.

The quotation here is from a British historian. When he was writing, the textile industry had already been thoroughly mechanized.

> Notice the adjectives the author used to describe the textile industry, starting with "admirable."

When this <u>admirable</u> series of machines was made known, and by their means yarns were produced far <u>superior</u> in quality to any before spun in England, as well as lower in price, a mighty impulse was communicated to the cotton manufacture. Weavers could now obtain an unlimited quantity of yarn at a reasonable price; manufacturers could use warps of cotton, which were much cheaper than the linen warps formerly used. <u>Cotton fabrics could be sold lower than had ever before been known.</u>

—E. Baines, *History of the Cotton Manufacture in Great Britain*, London, 1835

> The lower prices would have long-term results, but Baines could not predict them all at this early stage in the Industrial Revolution.

Skills FOCUS   READING LIKE A HISTORIAN

1. **Credibility** Would Baines be an authority on the long-term effects of industrialization? Why or why not?
2. **Details** What details show the author's attitude about the textile industry?

See **Skills Handbook**, p. H30

Pulling seeds from raw cotton blossoms was time-consuming when done by hand. An American named Eli Whitney solved the problem. He built a machine, called the cotton gin, that removed the seeds efficiently.

The fiber was then spun into thread or yarn. James Hargreaves, a weaver, revolutionized the spinning process with a machine he called the spinning jenny, which spun several threads at once. Hargreaves' machine was not perfect. The thread it produced was still thick and prone to break when woven into cloth. **Richard Arkwright**, another inventor, solved this problem with the spinning frame, which spun stronger, thinner thread.

Finally, the thread was woven into fabric. The traditional in-home weaving loom was about six feet wide—the width a man could reach from side to side to push the thread back and forth on a shuttle. The "flying shuttle," patented by John Kay, doubled the speed at which a weaver could do the job. Because many workers lost their jobs as a result, Kay was attacked and fled to France. He died in poverty.

Nevertheless, the ever-faster spinning machines soon created a demand for better weaving machines. To meet that demand, in 1785 Edmund Cartwright patented the power loom, a larger, faster weaving system.

Cloth-Making in Factories The new machines were too big for the weaver's cottage. They had to be housed in large buildings constructed specially for that purpose. A building that housed industrial machines became known as a **factory**, from the old word *manufactory*. Factories needed ready supplies of power. Arkwright built early factories to house a spinning system driven by water power. His system was known as the water frame.

From this flurry of invention and innovation, an industry was born. In 1770 England produced about 50,000 bolts of cloth. By 1800 the textile output had increased to 400,000 bolts.

READING CHECK **Identify Problem and Solution** How did machines solve problems that weavers faced?

Skills Focus: Making Oral Presentations

At Level

Research Required

Reading Like a Historian Skill
Inventors Showcase

1. Assign each student the role of an inventor mentioned in the section, such as Jethro Tull, James Hargreaves, or Robert Fulton.

2. Have each student conduct outside research on the assigned person and his most famous invention.

3. Have students prepare and present short, first-person accounts of their assigned inventor's most famous invention. Students should give

some background on why they created the device and demonstrate how it works with drawings or models.

4. Hold an Inventors Showcase in which students present their inventions.
LS Intrapersonal, Kinesthetic

📝 **Alternative Assessment Handbook**, Rubrics 24: Oral Presentations; and 30: Research

Steam Powers the Revolution

A simple fact of physics powered the Industrial Revolution: when water is heated and changes into steam, it expands. British inventors learned how to harness the force of steam to drive machines that transformed the world.

Development of the Steam Engine The first commercially successful steam engine was built in England in 1712, but it was very slow. Then an inventor named **James Watt** came up with crucial innovations. His engine was faster and more efficient at driving machinery. By 1800 about 500 of Watt's steam engines were chugging and hissing in mines and factories throughout Britain.

The widespread use of steam engines began when inventors put them to use in the textile mills. Using steam power instead of water power meant that factories no longer had to be built near ready supplies of water. Instead, they could be located where fuel was readily available and where workers already lived. Also, factories could be built closer to roads and ports from which raw materials and finished products could be shipped.

Steam was soon applied to other uses, eventually producing a revolution in transportation. In about 1802 Richard Trevithick used a steam engine to power the first locomotive. Steam-powered trains soon became essential to the Industrial Revolution. They made possible the fast shipment of finished goods even to faraway markets.

Steam also provided a power source for ships. An Irish-born American, **Robert Fulton**, became famous for developing a steamship called the *Clermont*. In 1807 the *Clermont* began operating on the Hudson River between New York City and Albany. Fulton's business was the first profitable use of steam navigation. Steamships would replace sailing ships on the open sea and the horse-drawn barges that hauled goods along canals.

Coal for British Steam Engines Steam engines required immense amounts of fuel to heat water. Wood was scarce, though, because most of England's forests had been cut down for farming. But the country had a big supply of another valuable fuel—coal. Consequently, as more factories were built to run on steam,

the coal mining industry in northern and western England grew. By 1800, Great Britain produced 80 percent of Europe's coal.

Naturally, many factories were built near Britain's northern coal mines. Quiet agricultural landscapes changed into busy, noisy boom towns dotted with factories and surrounded by endless rows of workers' and miners' homes.

The miners' families often experienced tragedy. Working in the mines was a dangerous job. Mine explosions, coal dust, collapsing shafts, and the sheer hard labor took a heavy toll. Children were often hired to slip down the narrow shafts and pick and haul coal. Their lives were hard, as one account describes:

HISTORY'S VOICES

❝The children, boys and girls, earned their wages by drawing the coals in tubs along the galleries by means of a belt and chain, which passed around their waists. Many girls were thus employed, and after a time became crooked and deformed.❞
—Carelton Smith, visitor to the Lancashire mines, 1833

Such reports caught the public's attention. Industrialization continued for some time, though, before the situation changed.

READING CHECK Make Generalizations
What impact did the steam engine have on the growth of British industry?

FACES OF HISTORY

James WATT 1736–1819

As a young man, Watt was an instrument maker at Scotland's Glasgow University. There he was given an early steam engine to repair. It was a slow contraption that wasted fuel. One day in 1765, as Watt strolled across the campus, he got an idea for how to improve the old engine. Watt built his new engine in secrecy, patented his design, and began manufacturing it. The engine was very popular and set off a revolution in the production of textiles, paper, and flour, in mining, and in transportation. Thanks to his steam engine and other inventions, Watt became rich and famous. Today in Glasgow, a stone marks the place where young Watt had his "Aha!" moment—the spark of inspiration that helped launch the Industrial Revolution.

A tribute to James Watt can be found on every light bulb in your home. The inventor played such a central role in the development of power generation that today we measure electric power in watts.

Identify Problem and Solution How did James Watt make sure that he would profit from his valuable design?

FOCUS ON NEW YORK
On August 17, 1807, the Clermont made its first trip up the Hudson River from New York City to Albany. The 150-mile trip took about 30 hours, including an overnight stop.

NEW YORK
CC Unit 5-G3e
Changing roles of men, women, and children

4 Where did industrialization spread beyond Great Britain? *America, continental Europe, Asia*

Industrialization Spreads

Explain How did Britain try to keep its discoveries secret? *outlawed export of certain machines, forbade skilled craftsmen from leaving the country*

Make Inferences What do Samuel Slater's accomplishments reveal about him? *possible answer—that the was technically skilled, highly motivated, and had a good memory*

Info to Know

Spread of Industry Britain remained a manufacturing powerhouse in the 19th century, but other nations began developing their own industrial bases, as well. In 1809 a visitor to the Ruhr and Wupper valleys in present-day Germany described them as a "miniature England." Large coalfields in France, Belgium, and present-day Germany became important centers of industrial growth.

Biography

William Blake (1757–1827) William Blake was a British artist and poet who defied convention. Apprenticed to an engraver, he drew copies of monuments in London's churches. After trying unsuccessfully to establish a print shop, Blake made a modest living as an engraver and illustrator. He developed a method of "illuminated printing," which combined art and text on a single plate of etching. Blake was also a poet, and he illustrated and printed his own poems with assistance from his wife. Inspired by nature and mystical vision, Blake rejected industrialization and political themes. In one poem, he writes of Britain's "dark Satanic mills." The greatness of Blake's works was not generally recognized during his lifetime, but he is now regarded as one of England's most original and lyric writers.

Industrialization Spreads

With steam driving British factories, industrialization increased rapidly and soon spread to western Europe and the United States. Other regions, including Asia and Africa, did not industrialize in the 1800s. Why did industry not take hold in some areas? What was it about Western countries that encouraged them to embrace industry?

Industry and the West Today's scholars have many ideas about why industrialization did not spread quickly to all parts of the world. Among those ideas is the impact of individual freedom on economic activity.

In Western countries, individual freedom was becoming a significant force in society. Although during the 1800s even Western countries were not truly democratic, the individual citizens enjoyed more political liberty than people elsewhere. People with a degree of freedom can compete against each other. Western societies saw competition as good. Wealth and fame rewarded those who competed well. For example, explorers raced to find new lands where merchants could do business. Fierce competition even led some Westerners to exploit other countries in their search for raw materials and markets. Then, during the Industrial Revolution, Western industrialists competed to improve on inventions and processes.

Industry Comes to America Although industrialization spread far beyond Great Britain, it was not because the British wanted to share the wealth. In fact, Britain outlawed the export of certain machines and even forbade some skilled craftsmen from leaving the country. As a result of these restrictions, from about 1760 to 1830, the Industrial Revolution took place mainly in Great Britain, giving the country a head start in economic development. But it was just a matter of time before knowledge of the machines and how to run them leaked out. The United States was one of the first places to benefit from that knowledge.

In his 1791 *Report on Manufactures*, U.S. Treasury Secretary Alexander Hamilton argued that industrialization would help the young United States gain economic independence from Great Britain. He even wanted the U.S. government to bribe British citizens into bringing their knowledge to this country.

Fortunately for the United States, Samuel Slater, a highly skilled young millworker, had already arrived from Britain. To avoid arrest, Slater had disguised himself as a farmworker and boarded a ship to America in 1789.

Slater had a dream—of making a fortune in America. He had detailed knowledge of the

Steamships and the Spread of Industrialization
Steamships helped spread industrialization. They carried raw materials to industrialized countries, finished products to markets, and immigrants to countries where they could get factory jobs. The ship in this print is the *Great Eastern* under construction in the 1850s. It was built to carry passengers and cargo from Europe to Australia.

638 CHAPTER 21

Collaborative Learning

Prep Required | **At Level**

Interviewing Slater and Lowell

1. Find and provide students with supplementary information on Samuel Slater and Francis Cabot Lowell.

2. Organize students into small groups. Provide each group with the information about Slater and Lowell.

3. Have groups brainstorm interview questions that could be asked of Slater and Lowell. Questions should focus on the most important details of their lives.

4. Have groups develop their questions into a script for a radio round-table interview featuring Slater and Lowell and two interviewers. Encourage students to include dialogue and discussion between Slater and Lowell. Have groups rehearse and then present the interviews to the class.

LS Auditory-Musical, Kinesthetic

Alternative Assessment Handbook, Rubric 33: Skits and Reader's Theater machinery created by water frame inventor Richard Arkwright for combing and spinning cotton in a single, efficient process. But Slater did not have a copy of the English machines to use as a model. In a remarkable feat of memory, Slater built the complex Arkwright machinery from scratch at a Rhode Island mill.

Slater's bold move resulted in a big success. In 1793 he built what is known today as Slater's Mill in Pawtucket, Rhode Island. For his contribution, Slater became known as the Father of American Industry.

Textile mill technology spread rapidly throughout the northeast United States. The mill city of Lowell, Massachusetts, became the jewel of American industry. The mill's principle founder, Francis Cabot Lowell, used the power of a nearby waterfall to run his machinery. Lowell's mills, situated in 40 multi-story brick buildings on a network of six miles of canals, were models for modern industry.

Lowell had the world's first all-in-one mill that took raw cotton through the various processes from fiber to finished cloth. He hired young, single girls from nearby farms to work in the mills, providing good wages and clean, safe housing for them. Some 10,000 workers were employed there by 1850.

Industry Spreads to Europe A British engineer named William Cockerill brought industry to continental Europe. In 1807 he founded a textile factory in Belgium, which became the second industrialized European country after Great Britain.

Political unrest delayed the industrialization of France. In 1789 revolution erupted in France. The Napoleonic Wars further delayed the process. After Napoleon was defeated in 1815 the French government gave financial support for building industry. By 1848 France had become an industrial power.

In Germany, there was no central government to support industry. Railroads were being built, however, among the many small German states. The railroads paved the way for industrialization after about 1850. Treaties that dropped trade barriers among the states also helped industry grow.

Industry in Asia Eventually, industry spread to Asia. Although today Japan is one of the world's industrial leaders, the Industrial

Revolution spread to Japan fairly late. Industrialization took hold there after 1868, when the Meiji government came to power and modernized Japan's economy. Within just a few decades, Japan had thriving industries.

Japan was far ahead of its Asian neighbors. The industrialization of other major world powers—including China, India, and Russia—would not occur until the 1900s.

READING SKILLS
Drawing Conclusions
If you know the Meiji modernized Japan's economy, what can you conclude about the previous government's role in the country's economy?

READING CHECK Compare and Contrast
How did industrialization in Britain compare to the process in America and Europe?

SECTION 1 ASSESSMENT

go.hrw.com
Online Quiz
Keyword: SHL IND HP

Reviewing Ideas, Terms, and People

1. **a. Describe** What were the factors of production that helped produce an Industrial Revolution in Great Britain?
   b. Identify Cause and Effect What effect did changes in agriculture have on the Industrial Revolution?
   c. Rate Which condition in mid-1700s England do you think was most crucial to the birth of the Industrial Revolution? Explain your answer.

2. **a. Identify** What did Richard Arkwright invent?
   b. Infer Why did some people not like the arrival of machines?
   c. Predict What effect might the shift from cottages to factories have on the lives of textile workers and on towns and cities?

3. **a. Recall** What industry stimulated the widespread use of steam engines?
   b. Evaluate How do you think people justified the use of children doing hard labor in coal mines?

4. **a. Identify** Why is Samuel Slater known as the Father of American Industry?
   b. Draw Conclusions How do you think visitors reacted when they saw the Lowell mills?

Critical Thinking

5. **Categorize** Use your notes and a graphic organizer like the one below to show how various factors helped start the Industrial Revolution.

Factors in the Start of the Industrial Revolution				
Government	Agriculture	Land	Labor	Capital

FOCUS ON WRITING

6. **Persuasion** Imagine that you are a highly skilled millworker living in Great Britain in about 1800. Write an outline for the main points you would make to government officials to persuade them that you should be allowed to go to the United States to start a textile business.

Section 1 Assessment Answers

1. **a.** land, labor, and capital
   b. seed drill improvements in breeding increased food supply, population grew; evicted farmers joined industrial workforce
   c. possible answers—powerful navy protected shipping; enclosure movement

2. **a.** the spinning frame
   b. caused job loss, changed work pattern
   c. work under close supervision, unsafe conditions; rapid growth of towns and cities

3. **a.** textile industry
   b. possible answers—Families needed the

money; children could fit into mine shafts.

4. **a.** brought industrial knowledge to America
   b. possible answer—amazed by the size of the operation and the advanced technology

5. Government—laws favored businesses; Agriculture—experimental farming methods; enclosure movement; Land—Britain had coal, iron, and water; Labor—growing population supplied a large workforce; Capital—Britain prospered, had skilled workers and inventors

6. Outlines should show an understanding of the textile industry during the Industrial Revolution.

Getting Started

Use the **Interactive Reader and Study Guide** to familiarize students with the section content.

📖 **Interactive Reader and Study Guide,** Section 2

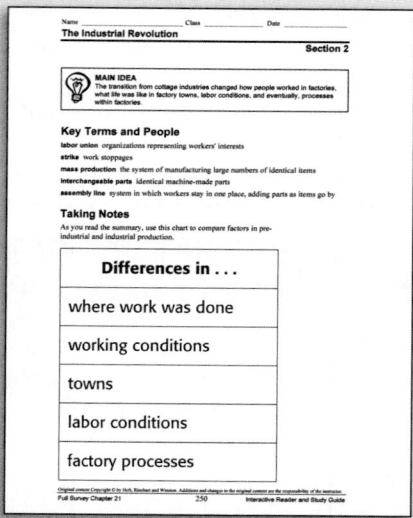

Academic Vocabulary

Review with students the high-use academic term in this section.

invest to commit money in order to make a financial return (p. 643)

📝 **CRF:** Vocabulary Builder: Section 2

Taking Notes

where work was done—homes vs. factories; working conditions—comfortable vs. unsanitary and noisy; towns—small towns and villages vs. large cities; labor conditions—direct contact with merchants vs. contact with managers and factory owners; factory processes—required wide range of skills vs. mass production, repetitive tasks

go.hrw.com
Online Resources

KEYWORD: SHL IND
ACTIVITY: Labor Unions

Factories and Workers

BEFORE YOU READ

MAIN IDEA

The transition from cottage industries changed how people worked in factories, what life was like in factory towns, labor conditions, and, eventually, processes within factories.

READING FOCUS

1. How was production organized before factories?
2. What were factories and factory towns like?
3. How did the factory system affect workers?
4. What was mass production, and what were its effects?

KEY TERMS

labor union
strike
mass production
interchangeable parts
assembly line

 NEW YORK

PI 3.2 Students explain the dynamics of cultural changes and how interactions between and among cultures has affected various cultural groups throughout the world.

THE INSIDE STORY

How did the early Industrial Revolution affect families? In 1795 writer Hannah More told a story about a large family in Lancashire, in northern England. The father worked in the coal mine, and the wife and children worked at home spinning fiber into thread and running a small dairy farm. There was not enough work at home to keep all the children busy, though, so three of them, including nine-year-old Mary, went to work with their father in the coal mine. Gradually the family's income increased, thanks to the children's hard work. But tragedy soon struck. The father died in a mine accident, the mother lost her mind from so much grief, and Mary struggled to keep her sisters and brothers fed. Although we do not know if this story of Mary's family was true, the problems it describes were true for many real families. The early years of the Industrial Revolution brought hardships to many British families, whether they worked in the mines or the factories. ■

This scene of textile workers making cloth at home was a common one until the late 1700s.

FROM HOME TO WORK

640 CHAPTER 21

Teach the Main Idea

At Level

Factories and Workers

1. **Teach** Ask students the Reading Focus questions to teach this section.

2. **Apply** Organize students into pairs. Have each pair create a two-column chart and write short descriptions of production, labor, and family life before and after industrialization.

3. **Review** As you review the section, have students describe the changes that industrialization brought to individuals, families, workplaces, and towns.

4. **Practice/Homework** Have students write a series of journal entries from the point of view of a worker who has been forced to switch from a cottage industry to factory work. **LS Verbal-Linguistic**

📝 **Alternative Assessment Handbook,** Rubric 15: Journals

Production before Factories

Production of goods for others did not begin with the Industrial Revolution. Instead, it began many years earlier with cottage industries, when workers produced goods at home.

Work in the Home In cottage industries, workers who produced finished goods dealt directly with merchants. Like other such industries, the manufacturing of textiles followed several steps.

In the first step, a merchant delivered raw materials to the weaver's cottage. In the early textile industry, the raw material was usually wool. Next, the weavers and their families processed the wool in several stages, from raw material to finished product. They hand-spun the fiber into thread and wove the thread into cloth. When the cloth was finished, the merchant picked it up and took it to market.

Work at home had some clear benefits. The weavers controlled their work schedules and product quality. They could work faster when they needed to earn more money. Or, they could work more slowly to make cloth of the highest quality. Also, family life revolved around the business. Weavers made their own decisions on when to work and rest, depending on the family's needs. They could make adjustments for illness, holidays, and the seasons.

Problems for Cottage Industries Even though working in the home had benefits for workers such as weavers, it also had disadvantages. A fire or flood that destroyed the home's equipment could ruin a family in an instant. Also, cloth-making demanded a range of technical skills for the various steps—skills that took a long time to learn. Moreover, only adults had the physical strength that some jobs, such as weaving on a loom, required. The typical home loom was at least six feet wide and required strength to operate. So, if the parents fell ill or died, the children could not take their places. As textile production and then other occupations moved from the cottage to the factory, business owners were able to take advantage of the problems these drawbacks caused for workers.

READING CHECK Find the Main Idea What were some benefits of the cottage system of production?

Factories and Factory Towns

A major change from the cottage industry system to the factory system was where employees worked. A factory laborer had to leave his or her home and work in a place built especially for industry. For some workers, a job in a factory was a welcome way to support the family. For many workers, however, the factory system caused real hardship.

Working in a Factory Factory work was divided into several separate, easily learned tasks, and each worker was assigned to one task. As a result, children could learn jobs as well as adults could. Many families fleeing poverty in the countryside would send their boys and girls—some as young as six years old—to work in the factories. In fact, some factory owners preferred hiring children because they could pay them lower wages. Still, the majority of factory workers were adult men.

Factory work was dangerous for all workers, but children faced special hazards. For example, one problem with early weaving looms was that the threads often snapped. Children, with their small hands, could reach into the still-running machines to retrieve the broken threads more easily than adults. Some children lost fingers in the process. Because there was no safety protection from the massive machines, such severe injuries were common.

The workday was long—more than twelve hours for even very young children. Noise, lack of ventilation, poor sanitation, and inadequate food added to the hardship.

Poor factory conditions were common throughout the late 1700s and into the 1800s. In the 1830s, however, the public began to take notice and ask for improvements. Some of the requests came from the child workers:

HISTORY'S VOICES

❝We respect our masters, and are willing to work for our support, and that of our parents, but we want time for more rest, a little play, and to learn to read and write. We do not think it right that we should know nothing but work and suffering, from Monday morning to Saturday night, to make others rich. Do, good gentlemen, inquire carefully into our concern.❞

—submission from the Manchester's Factory Children Committee to the House of Commons, 1836

THE INDUSTRIAL REVOLUTION **641**

TAKING NOTES

Create a table to compare the differences in pre-industrial and industrial production in terms of the factors listed.

Differences in . . .
labor relations
working conditions
land
society
economy

Reading Focus

❶ How was production organized before factories? *in small cottage industries; a family worked together to produce goods such as cloth or barrels*

Production before Factories

Describe What happened after a merchant dropped off wool at a weaver's cottage? *family hand-spun the fiber into thread, wove threads into cloth; merchant picked up cloth, took it to market*

Evaluate Would you choose to work in a cottage industry or in a factory? Explain. *possible answers—cottage industry: time with family, freedom of work schedule; factory: easier to learn single task, some security in employment*

Reading Focus

❷ What were factories and factory towns like? *factories—often dangerous; work divided into separate, easily-learned tasks; low wages; long hours; factory towns—comprised of shoddy, close-packed company dwellings; polluted; poor sanitation*

Factories and Factory Towns

Summarize What hardships were part of factory work? *dangerous conditions, long work days, noise, lack of ventilation, poor sanitation, inadequate food*

Draw Conclusions Why were children sent to work in factories? Explain. *Families desperately needed money; some factory owners preferred hiring children.*

Differentiating Instruction

Below Level

English-Language Learners

Materials: construction paper, colored markers

1. Review with students the information in the text about cottage industries and factory work.

2. Have each student create a two-panel drawing. The first panel should feature a family at work in a cottage industry. The second panel should show the same family members after they have begun working in a factory. Encourage students to highlight the differences between the two systems in their drawings. Have students present their drawings to the class.

3. As an extension, have students write a paragraph explaining why the family was forced to switch to factory work. **LS Visual-Spatial**

Alternative Assessment Handbook, Rubric 3: Artwork

Answers

Reading Check *workers made decisions about when to work, rest, and eat, how much to produce; family could adjust work schedule, all family members could be involved*

Factories and Factory Towns

Explain Why did companies provide housing to employees? *Families from the countryside needed housing.*

Identify What were the hazards of coal as a power source? *thick, dark soot; poisonous chemicals in the air*

Make Generalizations Why do you think conditions in Manchester became so terrible? *possible answer— city unable to cope with overcrowding; factory owners didn't care about conditions or the environment*

Activity **Manchester Poem** Have students write a poem lamenting the conditions in Manchester. **LS Auditory-Musical**

📝 **Alternative Assessment Handbook,** Rubric 26: Poems and Songs

Primary Source

"How little can the rich man know
Of what the poor man feels,
When Want like some dark demon foe,
Nearer and nearer steals!...

He never saw his darlings lie
Shivering, the grass their bed;
He never heard that maddening cry,
'Daddy, a bit of bread!'"
—"Manchester Song", quoted by
 Elizabeth Gaskell in
 *Mary Barton: A Tale of
 Manchester Life*

Find several images that illustrate life before and after industrialization. Display them for students to see.

Answers

Reading Check *injuries, long workdays, noise, lack of ventilation, poor sanitation, inadequate food*

642

Life in Factory Towns Factories changed not just the lives of their workers, but also the towns where the factories were located. Along rivers, large mill operations sprang up quickly. Whole towns grew up around the factories. Some companies provided housing to their employees, many of whom arrived from the countryside with few belongings and nowhere to stay. Families crowded into shoddy, close-packed company dwellings.

When water power changed to steam power, manufacturing towns rose near the coal mines also. The hazards of burning coal for producing steam quickly became apparent. Thick soot from the burning coal blanketed towns, turning day into night. The smoke sent sulfur and other poisonous chemicals into the air.

Factories for smelting, or refining, iron were often built near coal mines. They sent more dark, smoky pollution into the air. The iron smelting factories in one region of northwestern England emitted so much pollution that the region was nicknamed "black country." Because the iron-smelting required fires, one American visitor to the region called it "black by day and red by night."

North of this region lay the textile city of Manchester—the British city that came to symbolize the problems of industrialization. Sanitation statistics provide detail. According to one account, some neighborhoods of Manchester had only two toilets for every 250 residents. Under such conditions, disease spread easily. As a result, about six children in ten died before the age of five.

READING CHECK **Identify Supporting Details** What are some facts that illustrate the difficulties of factory work?

*Interactive
HISTORY CLOSE-UP

Factory Work

With industrialization, more and more people went to work in factories to produce goods such as textiles. Although factory jobs were difficult and dangerous, they provided a living.

In the large image you see what it was like to work in a textile factory in about 1835. The smaller drawing shows a cut-away view of a similar factory of a few years earlier.

Ventilation was poor. Dust and fibers drifting in the air caused tuberculosis and other illnesses.

Workers who arrived at the factory late were punished. Keeping track of the time was hard for families who could not afford a clock.

Foremen sometimes beat children who talked too much or worked too slowly.

Children often had to scramble under the still-running machines, and accidents were common. One hospital reported that each year it treated 1,000 injuries caused by factory machines.

642 CHAPTER 21

Differentiating Instruction

Above Level

Advanced Learners/Gifted and Talented

Materials: butcher paper, art supplies

1. Review the effects that industrialization had on towns such as Manchester.

2. Organize students into small groups. Have each group write an official petition to city officials in Manchester and a petition to Parliament asking for improved conditions within the city. Student petitions should focus on the need for improved sanitation, working conditions, child labor laws, and environmental conditions.

3. Have students share their petitions with the class.

4. Guide students in a discussion of the petitions. Did the petitions address all the needs of Manchester residents and workers? **LS Intrapersonal, Verbal-Linguistic**

📝 **Alternative Assessment Handbook,** Rubric 43: Writing to Persuade

The Factory System and Workers

Factories changed more than just families and towns. They also transformed the very nature of labor, as industry moved from the home to the factory.

Workers in a New Economy The factory system required large amounts of capital, or money, to pay for building the factories and installing the machinery. This produced three main levels of participants within the system:

- wealthy business people to <u>invest</u> in and own the factories
- mid-level employees to run the factories and supervise the day-to-day operations
- low-level employees to run the machines.

Employers who invested their money expected to make a profit. They shared little of their profits with their employees, who were paid only for the hours they worked. At the same time, no one worker was responsible for the product's quality, and factory workers had little incentive to improve their job performance. Quality could decline.

Also, workers were plentiful. British factories had no trouble finding former farm workers displaced by the enclosure movement. In the United States, immigrants were glad to find any work they could.

Employers often preferred hiring women and children because men expected higher wages. Men were also seen as not taking orders as readily. In addition, many people saw unskilled factory jobs as inappropriate for men. Factory work was seen as "women's work."

NEW YORK
CC Unit 5G3b
Factory system

ACADEMIC VOCABULARY
invest to commit money in order to make a financial return

On the factory's top floor, looms wove the thread into finished cloth.

A giant waterwheel below ground drove all the factory's machines.

On the middle floor, the threads were twisted to make them stronger.

Inside a Textile Factory This illustration is based on the inner workings of a cotton-processing factory in Bedworth, England, in about 1800.

Workers had to stand for hours. Many children were gradually deformed because their growing bones could not tolerate the constant strain.

Skills FOCUS INTERPRETING VISUALS

Draw Conclusions What hazards did children face while working in the factory? What features of the Bedworth factory's construction helped make it efficient?

go.hrw.com
COULD YOU HAVE SURVIVED?
Keyword: SHL IND
Go online for a closer look at survival and this event.

THE INDUSTRIAL REVOLUTION **643**

Skills Focus: Identifying Problem and Solution
Below Level

Reading Skill
Company Meeting

Materials: butcher paper, markers

1. Review with students the different levels of employees within the factory system and the working conditions within the factories.

2. Organize students into three groups: business owners, mid-level employees, and lower-level employees. Have each group work together to make a list of complaints to present at the company meeting. Have students write the complaints on butcher paper.

3. Hold a company meeting during class. Have volunteers from each group read its list of complaints to the class.

4. Post the lists for students to see, and guide students in a discussion about whether compromises could be reached on any common issues among the three groups.
LS Interpersonal, Verbal-Linguistic

Alternative Assessment Handbook, Rubrics 14: Group Activity; and 35: Solving Problems

---

643

The Factory System and Workers

Explain How did British workers react to the government's unwillingness to change labor conditions? *organized, formed labor unions, went on strike*

Draw Conclusions Why did the British government ignore the problems of workers and the unemployed? *did not believe these were government problems; thought people would lose incentive to work harder*

 CRF: Biography: Nellie Bly

QUICK FACTS Effects of the Factory System

Evaluate What effects do you think the factory system had on families? *possible answer—unable to spend much time together, informal education interrupted for children*

🖳 **Quick Facts Transparency:** Effects of the Factory System

Info to Know

Chartism The Reform Act of 1832 widened voting rights in Britain but included property requirements that excluded people of the lower classes. In 1836 organizers formed the London Working Men's Association and drew up a charter of political demands. The so-called Chartists used public meetings, petitions, and strikes to draw attention to their cause. Some Chartists even threatened physical force if their demands were not met. Although the movement eventually died out, its goals were taken on by others and many reforms were passed in the second half of the 19th century.

Answers

Reading Check *Different groups that were part of the factory system became part of the middle class.*

644

Cottage Workers' Unrest One group of people faced a particular challenge caused by the factory system. These were the weavers and other cottage industry workers still trying to earn their living by making goods at home. Their handmade goods were more expensive than factory-made items, so they had a hard time selling them. Facing ruin, some of these workers turned to violence.

One night in 1811, masked workers attacked a textile factory in Nottingham, England. The incident marked the beginning of the Luddite movement. The Luddites, named after a General Ned Ludd who probably did not exist, opposed machines that were "hurtful to the commonality"—in other words, that put them out of work. Luddites burned factories and smashed machines but tried to avoid injuring people. During 1812 the movement quickly spread to other cities. Several Luddites were caught and hanged, though, and the Luddite movement ended quickly.

THE IMPACT TODAY
People who resist using today's new technologies are sometimes called Luddites.

Changing Labor Conditions The severe treatment of the Luddites illustrates that the British government did not want to get involved in factory problems. Government leaders did not see regulating business as their job. Many citizens thought that if the government helped poor people too much, they would lose their incentive to work harder. As a result, the government did not pass laws relating to work hours, safety, or child labor.

Because the government took no action, in the early 1800s British workers started to organize. They formed the first **labor unions**, which are organizations representing workers' interests. To urge employers to raise wages and improve conditions, unions in Britain organized **strikes**, or work stoppages. At first, Parliament banned unions and strikes, fearing social and economic trouble.

Slowly, pressure from the public and unions brought change. Hearings in Parliament in 1832 produced the Sadler Report, which described abuses in the factories. Eventually Britain passed laws that limited work hours for adults and children. Another law required child workers to be at least nine years old. In 1871 Parliament legalized labor unions.

American workers also organized. In the United States, the first nationwide labor unions developed in the mid-1800s.

A New Class of Workers While factory conditions were slowly improving, another process was also taking place—the growth of the middle class. The middle class included the various groups, or types, of workers that were in the middle income range, between the rich factory owners and the poor factory workers.

Several groups of workers who were essential to the factory system became part of the middle class. Managers and accountants kept

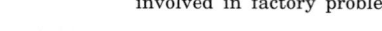

EFFECTS OF THE FACTORY SYSTEM (QUICK FACTS)

Before the Factory System

- Goods were produced in the home.
- Work required a wide range of skills.
- Children did chores at home with the family.
- Families worked directly with merchants.
- Few people were members of the middle class.

After the Factory System

- Good were produced in factories.
- Work required a few easily learned skills.
- Children were employed in large numbers in factories.
- Workers dealt with managers and, sometimes, factory owners.
- More people joined the middle class.

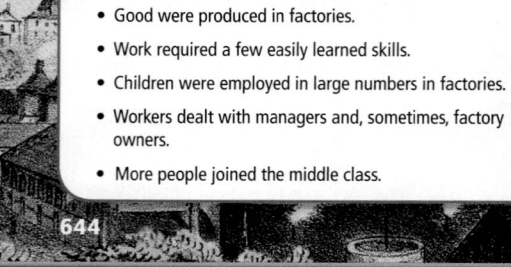

Factories, Le Creusot, France, artist unknown, c. 1855

Differentiating Instruction

Above Level

Advanced Learners/Gifted and Talented

1. Have students consider these questions: If you were a discontented worker in industrial Britain, what options would you have? What actions would you take to change your situation? Have students write a half-page response to these two questions.

2. Organize students into small groups. Have groups discuss their responses and select the one that they believe might be most effective and achievable.

3. Guide students in a discussion about the various options that discontented workers had. Also discuss the probable outcome of various actions.

4. As an extension, have students watch the classic silent film *Metropolis* and then discuss its imagery and symbolism. 🅛 **Intrapersonal, Verbal-Linguistic**

📝 **Alternative Assessment Handbook,** Rubrics 11: Discussions; and 41: Writing to Express the factories running and their books balanced. Engineers designed the machines, and mechanics kept them in good repair. Other workers transported the goods to market while still others were engaged in sales of those goods. As the income from increased manufacturing, buying, and selling spread throughout the economy, more people entered the middle class.

READING CHECK **Identify Cause and Effect** How the factory system affected different groups?

Factories and Mass Production

The factory system certainly changed the world of work. In addition, new processes further changed how people worked in factories and what they could produce.

The Process of Mass Production Many changes in industry evolved fully in the United States. One of these changes was the development of **mass production**—the system of manufacturing large numbers of identical items. Elements of mass production, including interchangeable parts and the assembly line, came to be known as the American system.

Interchangeable parts are identical machine-made parts. They made production and repair of factory-made goods more efficient. Before industrialization, one skilled worker might have made an entire gun, clock, or other product by himself. He would make or gather all the parts and assemble them. The process could be slow, and because the parts were all handmade, the finished products were a little different from each other. With interchangeable parts, though, one worker could put together many identical products in a short time. Making repairs was easier, too, because replacement parts did not have to be custom-made to fit.

The other element of mass production related to movement within factories. In early workshops, the product stayed in one place and workers moved around it, adding parts and making refinements. An innovation was the **assembly line**. In an assembly line, the product moves from worker to worker, as each one performs a step in the manufacturing process. With this division of labor, workers can make many items quickly.

Effects of Mass Production Mass production had advantages and disadvantages. A big advantage was a dramatic increase in production. Businesses that made many items quickly could charge less per item. As a result, more people could afford to buy these mass-produced goods.

For employees, however, mass production could lead to more repetitious jobs. At first, some workers protested, refusing to work quickly. But the changes could not be stopped, and mass production became the norm in factories.

READING CHECK **Summarize** What was mass production?

NEW YORK

CC Unit 5-G3d
Changes in social classes

SECTION 2 ASSESSMENT

go.hrw.com
Online Quiz
Keyword: SHL IND HP

Reviewing Ideas, Terms, and People

1. **a. Describe** How did the textile business work when it was a cottage industry?
   b. Compare List some advantages and disadvantages of cottage industry.

2. **a. Recall** Why were early factory towns unhealthy?
   b. Explain Why was factory work especially dangerous for children?
   c. Infer If working in factories and living in the cities was so terrible, why did people stay?

3. **a. Identify** What was the structure of authority within the new factories?
   b. Infer What factors combined to keep workers' wages low?
   c. Evaluate Why might workers have been reluctant to hold a **strike** in the early years of the factory system?

4. **a. Define** What were the two main components of the **American system** of mass production?
   b. Develop Why would the American system help many industries grow larger and richer?

Critical Thinking

5. **Analyze** Use your notes to fill in a chart like the one below by analyzing the effects of the factory system. Who do you think benefited the most and least from the changes?

Industrial Production	
Advantages	Disadvantages

FOCUS ON WRITING

6. **Narration** Write a paragraph or two in which you describe the changes that a typical English town and its residents might have experienced in the 1800s as industries developed in the town.

THE INDUSTRIAL REVOLUTION **645**

Getting Started

Use the **Interactive Reader and Study Guide** to familiarize students with the section content.

📖 **Interactive Reader and Study Guide,** Section 3

Academic Vocabulary

Review with students the high-use academic term in this section.

stance attitude or position (p. 648)

📓 **CRF:** Vocabulary Builder: Section 3

Taking Notes

new ideas about economics; entrepreneurs built fortunes; new industries developed; lives of women changed; migration of job seekers from countryside to city; cities became crowded and dangerous; pollution of air and water; population grew rapidly; standard of living in industrialized countries improved; Great Britain, France, and Germany emerged as global leaders; United States benefited from industrialization

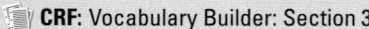

---

go.hrw.com
Online Resources

KEYWORD: SHL IND
ACTIVITY: Historic Origins of Socialism and Capitalism

BEFORE YOU READ

MAIN IDEA

The Industrial Revolution inspired new ideas about economics and affected society in many ways.

READING FOCUS

1. What new ideas about economics developed during the Industrial Revolution?

2. What competing economic ideas arose as a result?

3. How did the Industrial Revolution affect society?

KEY TERMS AND PEOPLE

laissez-faire
Adam Smith
Thomas Malthus
entrepreneur
Andrew Carnegie
socialism
Karl Marx
communism
standard of living

NEW YORK

PI 3.3 Students examine the social/cultural, political, economic, and religious norms and values of Western and other cultures.

THE INSIDE STORY

What marvels of industry were displayed in a glass palace? In 1851 the Great Exhibition in London drew residents and visitors to a huge glass and iron building called the Crystal Palace. Inside the marvelous structure were nearly 14,000 exhibits, many of which displayed industrial products and processes. English writer Charlotte Brontë was dazzled by the exhibition: "It is a wonderful place—vast, strange, new, and impossible to describe. Its grandeur does not consist in *one* thing, but in the unique assemblage of *all* things." Brontë was impressed by the wide range of exhibits, including "great compartments filled with railway engines and boilers, with mill machinery in full work . . ." All these remarkable exhibits showed the accomplishments of the Industrial Revolution. People came from far away to gawk at those achievements. In fact, some 6 million visitors from across Europe and elsewhere attended the exhibition. ◼

A PALACE FOR INDUSTRY

◀ Visitors crowded into the Crystal Palace to view the displays.

Dickinsons' Pictures of Great Exhibition, 1851

New Ideas about Economics

During the late 1700s and early 1800s industrialization was changing not just products and work, but also how people thought about economics. One change was that mercantilism was giving way to capitalism and competition.

Capitalism and Competition Under the old mercantile system, governments restricted trade to protect their own industries from foreign competition. Then, starting in the late 1700s, some people said that governments should not interfere in business. This idea is called **laissez-faire** (lehz-ay-FEHR) economics, from a French phrase meaning "free to do."

Teach the Main Idea

At Level

Results of the Industrial Revolution

1. **Teach** Ask students the Reading Focus questions to teach this section.

2. **Apply** Have students create two Web diagrams for the section, one that shows the key people and their ideas and the other that shows the costs and benefits of industrialization.

3. **Review** As you review the section, have students explain the different political and economic ideas that came out of the Industrial Revolution.

4. **Practice/Homework** Have students write a one-page essay on the positive and negative results of the Industrial Revolution.
   LS Visual-Spatial, Verbal-Linguistic

📓 **Alternative Assessment Handbook,** Rubric 37: Writing Assignments

Adam Smith became the leading advocate of laissez-faire economics. In 1776 he published *The Wealth of Nations*, in which he analyzed the definition and creation of wealth. Smith wrote that markets free from government interference benefited all. Such an economic system free from regulation is called a market economy. Also in a market economy, businesses can compete freely against each other for trade. The British government agreed with Smith's ideas and ended most regulations by the 1840s.

Smith influenced **Thomas Malthus**, who was concerned about population growth caused by the development of industry. Malthus wrote that the population would always grow faster than food production. Therefore, he concluded, poverty and misery would never go away. Population growth, Malthus said, was slowed only by war, disease, famine, and decreased reproduction. Because many people agreed that these problems were unavoidable, Malthus' ideas were used to justify low wages and laws that limited charity to the poor.

In time, Malthus was proved wrong. The disasters he predicted did not happen, but the population did grow. Still, the ideas of Smith and Malthus affected attitudes. As Smith predicted, industrialization succeeded and spread. Industrial capitalism emerged as the main economic pattern in the Western world.

New Roles for Business Leaders Industrialization also changed the roles that business leaders played in public life. Before the Industrial Revolution, people who owned land controlled the wealth and power. But by the mid-1800s, the leaders of industry began taking away the landowners' influence. Some industrialists became extremely wealthy, and their new wealth bought them political power.

The Industrial Revolution also highlighted the role of the **entrepreneur**, someone who starts a new business. Among the entrepreneurs were financiers, bankers, and investors who pooled their money to create large corporations. As demand increased for capital to build factories, banking and finance became more important occupations. Some industrialists made fortunes simply by buying and selling companies for a profit.

A few industrialists, mainly in the United States, built some of the largest corporate empires ever seen—and acquired wealth that

A View of Andrew Carnegie

Andrew Carnegie, who took the steel industry to new heights, gave away some $350 million to fund various charities. This cartoon from *Punch*, a satirical British magazine, shows Carnegie giving $2 million to Scottish universities. The original title is "The MacMillion."

Carnegie's clothing is a combination of the traditional Scottish kilt and the American flag.

Punch, May 29, 1901

The mortarboards, which are the headgear for college graduates, are labeled with the names of Scottish universities.

Skills FOCUS READING LIKE A HISTORIAN

1. **Analyze** What might Carnegie's clothing have meant to people at the time?
2. **Evaluate** How do you think the artist felt about Carnegie's donation? Explain your answer.

See **Skills Handbook**, p. H25

few people could imagine. In the late 1800s, their stories helped make them famous.

Andrew Carnegie, who was born in Scotland, was an example of "rags to riches" success. His father, a weaver, was driven out of work by the textile mills. The family moved to America, and Carnegie started working in a mill at age 12. With hard work, creativity, intelligence, and tough business practices, he led the expansion of the American steel industry.

NEW YORK

CC Unit 5-G3g
Shift from mercantilism to laissez-faire economics

THE INDUSTRIAL REVOLUTION **647**

Reading Focus

① *What new ideas about economics developed during the Industrial Revolution?* laissez-faire economics, The Wealth of Nations, *increased role of entrepreneur*

New Ideas about Economics

Describe What is *The Wealth of Nations* about? *analyzes wealth and how it is created; states that markets free from regulation would benefit all*

Make Inferences How were Malthus's ideas used to justify low wages? *Poverty would never go away, so there was no reason to combat it with higher wages.*

Make Generalizations How did industrialists and entrepreneurs become extremely powerful? *took away influence of landowners, pooled money to create corporations, used tough business practices, acquired enormous wealth*

Primary Source

"Upon the sacredness of property civilization itself depends—the right of the laborer to his hundred dollars in the savings bank, and equally the legal right of the millionaire to his millions."
—Andrew Carnegie, "Wealth" from the *North American Review*, June 1889

Primary Source

"In a sense, the theory of the Communists may be summed up in a single sentence: Abolition of private property."
—Karl Marx and Friedrich Engels, *The Communist Manifesto*, 1848

Differentiating Instruction

Below Level

Learners Having Difficulty

1. Draw the graphic organizer for students to see. Omit the italicized answers.

New Industrialists		
Who were they?	What did they do (positive)?	What did they do (negative)?
Carnegie, Rockefeller, Vanderbilt	*built large businesses, gave to charity*	*drove competitors out of business, did not allow unions*

2. Organize students into mixed-ability pairs. Have pairs copy and complete the graphic organizer. **LS** Visual-Spatial

Alternative Assessment Handbook, Rubric 13: Graphic Organizers

Answers

Reading Like a Historian 1. *His traditional Scottish clothing indicates he was pro Scottish.* **2.** *possible answer— thought Carnegie was too generous because artist shows him throwing money*

Reading Focus

② What competing economic ideas arose as a result? *socialism, communism*

Competing Economic Views

Contrast How is socialism different from capitalism? *Under capitalism, individuals own property and control industry, whereas under socialism, the government or society does.*

Interpret How were Robert Owen's ideas applied in New Lanark? *emphasis on good of all, good working conditions, nonprofit stores, free schooling, strict rules*

Predict What factors might have led to the failure of New Harmony? *possible answer—economic failure, conflicts within community*

Info to Know

Robert Owen Robert Owen began his career as an entrepreneur in the textile industry. When he purchased New Lanark, one of his first actions was to set up a school nearby. He stopped employing children under the age of ten, and sent them to school instead. Fearing a loss of money, Owen's partners protested. In response, Owen borrowed money to buy out his partners' shares of the business.

Answers

Primary Sources 1. *high wages cause population to increase, laborers increase, wages fall;* **2.** *possible answer—Yes, he writes about the workers' happiness, health, and "enjoyments of life."*

Reading Check *mercantilism gave way to capitalism and competition, laissez-faire economics and The* Wealth of Nations *allowed for increased role of entrepeneur*

PRIMARY SOURCES

The Iron Law of Wages

The ideas of Adam Smith and Thomas Malthus had many admirers. Among them was David Ricardo (1772–1823), an English banker. In an 1817 work, Ricardo argued that natural economic forces would keep wages low—so low that workers barely had enough to survive. Ricardo's theory came to be called The Iron Law of Wages, indicating that the "law" was real and unchangeable. The theory was popular with factory owners, since it justified their paying low wages to their employees.

"It is when the market price of labour exceeds its natural price that the condition of the labourer is flourishing and happy, that he has it in his power to command a greater proportion of the necessaries and enjoyments of life, and therefore to rear a healthy and numerous family. When, however, by the encouragement which high wages give to the increase of population, the number of labourers is increased, wages again fall to their natural price, and indeed from a reaction sometimes fall below it."

—David Ricardo, *On Wages*, 1817

> Like Malthus, Ricardo predicted a rise in population. According to Ricardo, what encourages population growth?

Skills FOCUS **READING LIKE A HISTORIAN**

1. **Sequence** According to Ricardo, what is the sequence of the rise and fall of wages?
2. **Draw Conclusions** Do you think Ricardo felt some sympathy with workers? Why or why not?

See **Skills Handbook,** p. H25

TAKING NOTES

Take notes on the new ideas of the Industrial Revolution.

New Ideas

NEW YORK

CC Unit 5-G3g
Responses to industrialization

ACADEMIC VOCABULARY

stance attitude or position

Other industrialists achieved similar feats. Examples include Cornelius Vanderbilt in railroads and John D. Rockefeller in oil. These men built giant corporations that drove out their competitors. They were both admired for their contributions to human progress and criticized for their treatment of workers. For example, they were generally against their employees' joining labor unions. Although some, like Andrew Carnegie, gave generously to charity, people who disapproved of their methods sometimes called them "robber barons."

READING CHECK **Summarize** What were some of the new ideas about economics?

Competing Economic Views

Not everyone agreed that laissez-faire capitalism was a good thing. Some thinkers blamed capitalism for bad working conditions and big gaps between the rich and poor. They took a different <u>stance</u> on economic sytems. Two of these men were Robert Owen and Karl Marx.

Robert Owen In contrast to the gloomy views of Thomas Malthus, Robert Owen had a more hopeful view of how industry might affect people. He thought that for the good of all, society or the government, instead of individuals, should own property and control industry—a theory called **socialism**. The theory was a clear contrast to capitalism.

To demonstrate his ideas, Owen built a mill complex at New Lanark, Scotland, that gained widespread praise as a model industrial town. The workers there enjoyed good working conditions, shopped at nonprofit stores, lived in decent houses, and could earn sick pay. Because he felt that education improved character, Owen even provided free schooling for the workers' children. He also imposed strict rules on workers' personal lives, including curfews and bathing requirements.

Owen brought his ideas to the United States in 1825, when he founded a community called New Harmony in Indiana. New Harmony was to be a utopia, an ideal community where poverty and other evils of society did not exist. The belief that such communities can solve society's problems is called utopianism.

The efforts of Owens and other people who believed in socialism led to a movement called social democracy. Those who advocated social democracy wanted to move from capitalism to socialism by democratic means.

Skills Focus: Drawing Conclusions   Above Level

Reading Skill
Economic Issues of the Industrial Revolution

Background: Explain to students that for countries to determine whether their economics will be based on free enterprise or on socialism, they must decide what goods will be produced, how goods will be produced, and for whom. Other economic factors arose during the Industrial Revolution, such as monetary systems, and measures of wealth and value determination, which today include such indicators as CPI and GNP.

1. Organize students into small groups.

2. Have groups discuss why these various economic issues arose during the Industrial Revolution, and why different methods of value determination emerged.

3. Guide students in a class discussion about each group's conclusions. **LS Interpersonal, Verbal-Linguistic**

Alternative Assessment Handbook, Rubrics 11: Discussions; and 14: Group Activity

Karl Marx A more radical view of socialism was put forth by two Germans, Friedrich Engels and **Karl Marx**. They declared that as capitalism grew, more and more workers would sink into poverty. In time they would rebel, seize control of the "means of production"—such as factories and farms—and govern themselves. Capitalism would collapse. Workers would establish a society based on cooperation and equal distribution of wealth. Such a revolution was inevitable, the authors claimed.

In time, Marx would be better known than Engels. In 1867 Marx produced the first volume of *Das Kapital*. In this three-part work, he put forth his arguments against capitalism. One of its evils, Marx said, was how capitalism disrupts the relationship between labor and profit. He thought there should be a direct connection between one's work and one's pay. For example, he thought it was not fair that one worker could toil all day at back-breaking labor and make very little money while another person got rich doing nothing more than sitting in an office speculating on future markets.

Marx thought that socialism could help rid the world of these injustices. However, he believed that the transition to socialism would not happen quickly because many people, especially the wealthier classes, would not see any benefit for themselves. For that reason, he thought the workers would have to control the government. Because the government would then control the economy, a command economy would result. The system in which the government owns almost all the means of production and controls economic planning is called **communism**. Years later, some governments would adopt communism and use it to violate basic human rights and freedom of choice.

> **READING CHECK** **Infer** Why did capitalism provoke strong response from the socialists?

Effects on Society

The rise of new economic ideas was among the countless effects of the Industrial Revolution. Other effects were felt in small and large ways, from how families lived to how countries dealt with each other. For example, the shift away from cottage industries affected home life and the roles of women in society.

Effects on Home Life When work was done in the home, women often worked alongside their husbands. Then when industry drew workers away from home, women were usually the ones who stayed home to care for children. The worlds of work and home began to separate. Women and men were seen as occupying "separate spheres"—the woman in the home and the man in the workplace to support the home and family.

EFFECTS OF INDUSTRIALIZATION ON WOMEN
QUICK FACTS

Women Who Went from Cottage Industries to Factory Work
- Earned low wages in low-skill jobs
- Separated from their families
- No real improvement in their status

Other Working-Class Women
- Found jobs as cooks, maids, and child-care workers because more families could afford to hire them
- Found some new educational and cultural opportunities in cities
- Overall improvement for many women

Middle-Class Women
- Freed from chores because many could afford to hire domestic help
- Began to attend college and get jobs as teachers and nurses
- Those who did work often criticized by people who said that they should not work outside the home
- Most affected by idea of separate spheres

Time for Tea, by Valentine Prinsep, 1800s

The Terrace, by Silvestro Legato, 1868

THE INDUSTRIAL REVOLUTION **649**

649

Reading Focus

Effects on Society

Recall How did industrialization positively affect Great Britain, France, and Germany? *became leaders in global economy; mass produced ships and weapons*

Elaborate How might industrialization lead to cultural clashes and discrimination? *possible answer—limited number of jobs, housing, waves of immigrants looking for work*

Map Transparency: Industrialized Europe, 1900

CRF: History and Geography: The First Modern Railroad

✴ Interactive Map: Industrialized Europe, 1900

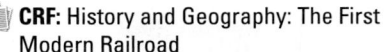

Many male writers who lived through the Industrial Revolution expressed a longing for an idealized past. According to Susan Zlotnick, professor of English at Vassar College, British women writers had a very different perspective. In her book *Women, Writing, and the Industrial Revolution*, Zlotnick argues that writers like Elizabeth Gaskell and Charlotte Brontë were more willing to accept industrialism and foresaw the possibility of improvement in the changes that it brought.

Women, Writing and the Industrial Revolution, by Susan Zlotnick, The Johns Hopkins University Press, 2001.

Answers

Interpreting Maps 1. *Britain, Belgium, parts of Germany and eastern Europe, northern Italy;* **2.** *industrial area grew up around a mine or power source*

650

✴Interactive

INDUSTRIALIZED EUROPE, 1900

Railroad
Industrialized area

Coal mines helped make the Ruhr area of Germany one of the world's largest industrial regions.

Although some countries, such as Sweden, did not develop industry early, their natural resources fed the factories of other countries. For example, Sweden had major iron deposits.

Great Britain's industrial strength brought with it wealth and power.

While much of central and western Europe became heavily industrialized, most of southern Europe lagged behind.

go.hrw.com
Interactive Map
Keyword: SHL IND

GEOGRAPHY SKILLS **INTERPRETING MAPS**

1. **Regions** What areas were heavily industrialized by 1900?
2. **Human-Environment Interaction** Some areas were heavily industrialized but did not have major cities. What do you think explains that situation?

The idea of separate spheres had another effect. Although so many people enjoyed what the new industrialized economy provided, in general they saw the business world as without moral controls. Women were expected to provide moral guidance in the home.

Middle-class families were more affected by this division between home and work than were lower-class families. Poorer families that depended on two incomes to survive could not afford for the wife to say home. However, belief in the home as society's moral center was equally powerful among lower-class families.

Effects on Countries On a scale much larger than the family home, industrialization also affected entire countries. For some nations, industry brought with it great power. For example, Great Britain, France, and Germany became leaders in the global economy.

650 CHAPTER 21

Skills Focus: Analyzing Costs and Benefits

Above Level

Social Studies Skill
Analysis of Industrialization

1. Organize students into small groups.

2. Have groups discuss the following questions: How has the Industrial Revolution changed everyday life? How has it changed the way you view the world? Who has it benefited most and who has it benefited least? How might the negative impact of industrialization be diminished? For example, what could be done to reduce pollution that continues to occur? How might industry be refocused in the future to achieve the maximum benefits with minimum costs?

3. Guide students in a large group discussion of these questions. **LS Intrapersonal**

Alternative Assessment Handbook, Rubric 11: Discussions

Mass production increased their ability to build ships and make weapons. With increased military strength, some countries were able to conquer and control sources of raw materials around the world.

The powerful industrial giants could even control the economy of a place thousands of miles away. For example, India had made and exported cotton cloth for centuries already when Britain took control of the region. Indian textile workshops were not mechanized, however, so cotton cloth imported from Britain was cheaper. The Indian textile industry could not compete and was practically destroyed.

Back on this side of the world, the effect of industrialization on the United States was very dramatic. With its huge size, wealth of natural resources, and spirit of independence, the United States industrialized rapidly. Like the major industrial powers of Europe, the United States gained global political power based on its industrial strength. In addition, industry helped the country's population grow quickly. A large number of the new Americans had moved from other lands around the world, drawn by jobs in American factories. The immigrants, both skilled and unskilled, contributed to the nation's economic success and its cultural variety.

Long-Term Effects on Societies Overall, industrialized societies saw an increase in wealth. It is true that much of the wealth flowed into the pockets of a few rich industrialists. But manufacturing also created a new middle class of clerks, merchants, and managers. In general, the **standard of living**, or level of material comfort, for people in industrialized countries improved. Even many of the poorest people gradually benefited from labor-saving devices and cheap, machine-made goods.

The Industrial Revolution introduced something new to the middle class: leisure. People had more time on their hands and more money in their pockets. They could enjoy public sports events, a concert in the park, a day at the beach, or even a vacation. With increased leisure time, they could become more educated or participate more deeply in politics.

You will soon read how industrialization brought big changes to almost all aspects of daily life—from art to transportation. We are still experiencing those changes in our lives today. The full story of the Industrial Revolution has yet to be written.

FOCUS ON NEW YORK

Coney Island, in the Brooklyn borough of New York City, was one place where people spent their leisure time. In the mid-1800s, rail service brought New Yorkers to the Coney Island beach, boardwalk, and other attractions.

READING CHECK Identify Cause and Effect What were some of the major effects industrialization had on families and countries?

SECTION 3 ASSESSMENT

go.hrw.com
Online Quiz
Keyword: SHL IND HP

Reviewing Ideas, Terms, and People

1. **a. Identify** What is the connection between **Adam Smith** and **laissez-faire** economics?

   b. Draw Conclusions Why do you think some economists believed that unrestricted capitalism would help all of society?

   c. Predict What are some of the groups of people who might have called the big industrialists "robber barons"? Who might have called them "captains of industry"?

2. **a. Describe** What was the role of **Karl Marx** and Friedrich Engels in the development of socialism?

   b. Analyze How would someone who advocated social democracy have responded to Marx's prediction?

3. **a. Recall** How did the Industrial Revolution affect the **standard of living** for people in industrialized countries?

   b. Interpret Why do you think Americans' spirit of independence encouraged the growth of capitalism?

   c. Predict How do you think the idea of separate spheres affected the children of middle-class families?

Critical Thinking

4. **Compare and Contrast** How did each of the major economic theories propose to change or benefit society? Fill in a table like the one below with as many changes as you can.

Theory	Proposed Social Change
Capitalism	
Utopianism	
Socialism	
Communism	

FOCUS ON WRITING

5. **Description** Imagine that you belong to a middle-class family in the late 1800s. Write a conversation that you have with your great-grandfather about the changes that your family has experienced over the years.

THE INDUSTRIAL REVOLUTION **651**

651

Word Help

doffing removing completed spools from machinery

bobbins spools of thread

Child Labor

NEW YORK STANDARDS

PI 2.3 Students analyze evidence critically and demonstrate an understanding of how circumstances of time and place influence perspective.
PI 3.3 Students examine the social/cultural, political, economic, and religious norms and values of Western and other world cultures.

Historical Context The four documents below tell us about child labor during the early Industrial Revolution and how different people saw the issue.

Task Examine the documents and answer the questions that follow. After you have studied the documents, you will be asked to write an essay describing the connection between child labor and public attitudes. Use evidence from these selections and the chapter to support the position you take in your essay.

DOCUMENT 1

Interview with Elizabeth Bentley

In 1815 the British Parliament sent out researchers to interview child workers and learn more about factory conditions. Here is an excerpt from an interview with a young woman who had worked in a textile mill.

Q *What were the hours of labour when you were not so thronged [busy]?*
A From six in the morning till seven at night.

Q *What time was allowed for meals?*
A Forty minutes at noon.

Q *Had you any time to get your breakfast or drinking?*
A No, we had to get it as we could.

Q *Do you consider doffing a laborious employment?*
A Yes.

Q *Explain what you had to do.*
A When the frames are full, they have to stop the frames, and take the flyers off, and take the full bobbins off, and carry them to the roller, and then put empty ones on, and set the frame going again.

Q *Does that keep you constantly on your feet?*
A Yes, there are so many frames and they run so quick.

Q *Your labour is very excessive?*
A Yes, you have not time for anything.

Q *Suppose you flagged [slowed down] a little, or were late, what would they do?*
A Strap [whip] us.

Q *And they are in the habit of strapping those who are last in doffing?*
A Yes.

Q *Constantly?*
A Yes.

DOCUMENT 2

Children in Danger

Factory owners often preferred to hire children and women rather than men. Men expected higher wages, and employers suspected that they were more likely to rebel against the strict rules and conditions that were common in factories. The children were subject to harsh punishment if they were late, fell behind in their work, or talked too much.

Supervisor whipping a young boy, artist unknown, 1853

Skills Focus: Analyzing Secondary Sources

At Level

Research Required

Reading Like a Historian Skill
Child Labor

1. Tell students that child labor is still very common in the world.

2. Have students conduct research about an aspect of child labor and prepare a short research paper on their findings. Tell students to use secondary sources about their chosen topic, and to analyze each source for accuracy and potential bias. Possible topics include industries and corporations that employ children, hours and working conditions, children's access to education, connections to economic and political factors, and how child labor is justified by employers and families.

3. Have volunteers present their findings to the class.

4. Guide students in a discussion about things that can be done to abolish child labor.
   LS Verbal-Linguistic

   Alternative Assessment Handbook, Rubrics 29: Presentations; and 30: Research

DOCUMENT 3

Children in the Mines

Children were also hired to work in Great Britain's coal mines. In this drawing, you see an older, stronger worker wearing a harness and pulling a cart full of coal. Smaller children push the cart from behind.

Woman pulling coal truck while children push, artist unknown, c. 1848

DOCUMENT 4

Speech in the House of Commons, 1832

John Charles Spencer was a member of the British Parliament's House of Commons. Although he supported some reforms for child workers, he was against a proposed law to limit their work day to 10 hours. Here he addresses Michael Sadler, a fellow member who proposed the law, in a speech.

> I am of the opinion that the effect . . . must necessarily be a fall in the rate of wages, or, what is more probable, that children would cease to be employed at all in manufactories. Now I appeal to the honourable member whether a measure which would prevent children from obtaining any employment in factories would not be more injurious than beneficial to the labouring classes?
>
> As long as we have a manufacturing population in the kingdom it will be impossible to render their occupation as wholesome as that of agricultural labourers, or persons engaged in out-door labour. This is an evil that cannot be remedied. It is too late now to argue about the unwholesome nature of manufacturing employment. We have got a manufacturing population, and it must be employed. Any measure which shall have the effect of diminishing the means of employment to labourers engaged in manufactures will produce extensive misery.

Info to Know

The Chadwick Report A report written by Edwin Chadwick, the secretary of the royal commission on reform of the poor laws and commissioner on the Board of Health, and published in 1842, stated that in his research of the living conditions in poor neighborhoods, he found that 43,000 women had become widows. His research also found that 112,000 children had become orphans as a result of poor sanitary conditions.

Skills FOCUS — READING LIKE A HISTORIAN

DOCUMENT 1
- **a. Summarize** What were some of the problems that Elizabeth Bentley faced at the factory?
- **b. Draw a Conclusion** How does Elizabeth's plain way of speaking affect your reaction to her testimony?

DOCUMENT 2
- **a. Describe** What does the scene show?
- **b. Compare** Does this illustration confirm or contradict what was said in Document 1? Explain your answer.

DOCUMENT 3
- **a. Describe** What would happen to the small children if the worker in the harness were to fall or stumble?
- **b. Infer** How do you think the person who drew this picture felt about children working in the mines?

DOCUMENT 4
- **a. Summarize** What is Spencer's main argument against the proposal to limit children's workday to 10 hours?
- **b. Analyze** What social class does Spencer seem to represent, and whose interests is he upholding?

DOCUMENT-BASED ESSAY QUESTION

What do you think were the connections among child labor, factory conditions, attitudes about capitalism, reactions to capitalism, and the rise of labor movements? Using the documents above and information from the chapter, form a thesis that might explain the general impact of child labor on public opinion. Then, write a short essay to support your position.

See **Skills Handbook**, pp. H25–H26

THE INDUSTRIAL REVOLUTION **653**

Differentiating Instruction

Above Level

Advanced Learners/Gifted and Talented

1. Have students write a one-page rebuttal to Spencer's speech. Rebuttals should address Spencer's assumptions and flawed reasoning. They should also make original points in support of Sadler's proposal.

2. Have volunteers read their rebuttals aloud to the class. Encourage students to make their points dramatically.

3. As an extension, have pairs of students play the roles of Spencer and Sadler and participate in an extemporaneous debate on the subject of Sadler's proposal. **LS Verbal-Linguistic, Kinesthetic**

Alternative Assessment Handbook, Rubric 10: Debates

Answers

Reading Like a Historian

Document 1. a. *long hours, only one break time, continuous, fast-paced work, possibility of whipping;* **b.** *possible answer—She appears to be matter of fact, which makes her testimony shocking because it shows that she had gotten used to working in such deplorable conditions.* **Document 2. a.** *a child being punished;* **b.** *confirms; boys are being whipped for stopping work;* **Document 3. a.** *They would be injured* **b.** *sympathetic to their suffering by calling attention to the horrendous conditions;* **Document 4. a.** *Preventing children from working would hurt working classes by denying them jobs and money.* **b.** *seems to represent wealthy class because he states that the law might cause injury to "laboring classes"; upholds interests of business and factory owners;* **Essay** *Students essays should explain the differences in public opinion in reaction to child labor, such as the views of John Spencer in Document 4.*

653

Visual Summary

Review and Inquiry Organize students into small groups. Randomly choose bulleted phrases or items from the time line in the visual summary, and have groups take turns explaining the phrase's significance to the Industrial Revolution.

Quick Facts Transparency: Visual Study Guide: The Industrial Revolution

Review Key Terms and People

1. standard of living
2. factors of production
3. Jethro Tull
4. invest
5. entrepreneur
6. cottage industry
7. laissez-faire
8. industrialization

Comprehension and Critical Thinking

9. **a.** coal, iron, streams, rivers
   b. made cotton production and slavery profitable
   c. possible answers— Steam engine allowed factories to spread, and also created a transportation revolution; other machinery might have been used.

10. **a.** a group of workers who violently protested new machines
    b. dangerous machines, pollution, long hours, abuse
    c. possible answers— cottage industry, because loss of family business means loss of income for all family members; factory, because of the terrible working conditions

11. **a.** Andrew Carnegie, Cornelius Vanderbilt, John D. Rockefeller
    b. Communism is a more radical view of socialism.
    c. increased their ability to build ships and weapons, and thereby conquer and control new sources of raw materials

---

QUICK FACTS

VISUAL STUDY GUIDE

Causes and Effects of the Industrial Revolution

CAUSES

- Availability of raw materials and markets in colonies
- Great Britain's seapower and political stability
- Parliament's support of free enterprise
- Agricultural improvements in Great Britain
- Enclosure movement in Great Britain
- Great Britain's factors of production
- Invention of new machines in the textile industry
- Development of the steam engine
- Increased individual freedom in the West
- Western attitudes toward competition

Industrial Revolution

EFFECTS

- Development of labor-saving, time-saving machines
- The factory system
- Poor working conditions in factories
- Overcrowding, pollution, disease in cities
- Competing ideas about economics
- Rise in standard of living, growth of middle class
- Rise of new industries and powerful industrialists
- New emphasis on middle-class home life
- Increased power of industrialized countries

Key Events of the Industrial Revolution

1701 ■ Jethro Tull invents the seed drill.

1765 ■ James Watt develops idea for practical steam engine.

1776 ■ Adam Smith publishes *The Wealth of Nations*.

1785 ■ Edmund Cartwright patents the power loom.

1789 ■ Samuel Slater arrives in the United States.

1793 ■ Slater's Mill is established in Rhode Island.

1802 ■ Richard Trevithick uses a steam engine to drive the first locomotive.

1807 ■ William Cockerill builds a factory in Belgium.

1811 ■ The Luddites stage their first attack on textile factories.

1832 ■ The Sadler Report details the conditions in British factories.

1851 ■ The Great Exhibition displays the marvels of industry to the world.

1867 ■ Karl Marx publishes the first volume of *Das Kapital*.

1871 ■ The British Parliament legalizes labor unions.

Reviewing Key Terms and People

Identify the correct term or person from the chapter that best fits each of the following descriptions.

1. level of material comfort
2. the essential elements that a nation needs to achieve economic success
3. invented a seed drill that made planting more efficient
4. to commit money in order to make a financial return
5. person who starts a business
6. a craft occupation performed in the home
7. economic system in which government does not regulate business and commerce
8. the process of changing to power-driven machinery

Reading Skills

12. Children were hired as mine workers because of their small size.
13. Cotton production likely increased.

Analyzing Secondary Sources

14. possible answer—Yes, because livestock and farming changed dramatically.
15. He describes the appearance of the sheep with a lot of visual detail.

History's Impact video program
Review the video to answer the closing question:
How did industrialization affect the United States?

Comprehension and Critical Thinking

SECTION 1 *(pp. 633–639)*

9. a. Recall What natural resources enabled the Industrial Revolution to begin in Great Britain?

b. Sequence How did the cotton gin affect slavery in the United States?

c. Support a Position Defend or refute this statement: "Without the steam engine, the Industrial Revolution would not have amounted to more than a pile of rickety machines."

SECTION 2 *(pp. 640–645)*

10. a. Identify Who were the Luddites, and what did they do?

b. Explain What were some of the hazards of working in the early factories?

c. Rank Which family do you think faced more potential problems—a cottage industry family, or one whose members worked in a factory? Explain.

SECTION 3 *(pp. 646–651)*

11. a. Identify Who were some of the industrialists who gained wealth and power in the United States?

b. Compare How do socialism and communism differ?

c. Evaluate In what ways did industrialization give countries such as Great Britain and Germany an advantage over some of their neighbors?

Reading Skills

Drawing Conclusions *Use what you know about drawing conclusions to answer the questions below.*

12. If you know that coal mines had narrow passageways and low ceilings, what can you conclude about why many children were hired to work in the mines?

13. If you know that Eli Whitney's cotton gin speeded up the process of pulling seeds from raw cotton blossoms, what can you conclude about a change in the rate of cotton production during the 1800s?

Analyzing Secondary Sources
Reading Like a Historian

"Early breeders of better animals succeeded not because of a knowledge of chemistry, which was in its infancy, or of genetics, which did not exist, but because they backed hunches. Even so, the results were remarkable. The appearance of the livestock inhabiting the landscape changed; the scraggy medieval sheep whose backs resembled, in section, the Gothic arches of the monasteries which bred them, gave way to the fat, square, contented-looking animal familiar today."

—J. M. Roberts, *History of the World,* 1993

14. Explain Do you think Roberts would agreed that the changes in agriculture could be called an agricultural revolution? Why or why not?

15. Analyze How does Roberts's description of the sheep help the reader understand the change in their appearance over time?

go.hrw.com
Practice Online
Keyword: SHL IND

Using the Internet

16. The cities of Manchester and Birmingham, England, suffered some of the worst effects of the Industrial Revolution. The two cities also contributed much to Great Britain's rise to power and wealth. Choose one of these cities and use the Internet to research the role it played in industrialization. Then, create a chart showing the city's contributions and problems.

WRITING ABOUT HISTORY

Exposition: Writing an Explanation *The Industrial Revolution changed life in every society it touched. It affected individuals as well as groups, the rich as well as the poor, the cities as well as the rural areas.*

17. Assignment: In an essay, explain how this revolution affected people in three ways: how they worked, how they conducted business, and how they lived at home. To provide support for your explanation, use information from this chapter and from other research sources as needed. Be sure to use facts and examples to clearly illustrate the points you are making about the ways in which life changed.

THE INDUSTRIAL REVOLUTION **655**

Answers

Using the Internet

16. Go to the HRW Web site and enter the keyword shown to access a rubric for this activity.

KEYWORD: SHL IND

Writing for the SAT

17. Student essays should discuss how the Industrial Revolution affected the way people worked, conducted business, and lived at home. They should compare pre-industrial conditions to those observed during the process of industrialization. Possible answers may include that before industrialization, work was based in the home; after industrialization, work was based in factories.

A rubric for the activity is provided in **CRF:** Writing for the SAT.

HOLT

History's Impact
► **Video Program: The Industrial Revolution**
See the Video Program Teacher's Guide for the answer to the closing question.

Review and Assessment Resources

Review and Reinforce

 CRF: Chapter Review

 Quick Facts Transparency: Visual Study Guide: The Industrial Revolution

 Spanish Chapter Summaries Audio CD Program

OSP **Holt PuzzlePro:** Quiz Show for ExamView

Quiz Game CD-ROM

Assess

 PASS: Chapter Test, Forms A and B

Alternative Assessment Handbook

OSP **ExamView Test Generator,** Chapter Test

 Differentiated Instruction Modified Worksheets and Tests CD-ROM: Chapter Test

HOAP **Holt Online Assessment Program** (in the Premier Online Edition)

Reteach/Intervene

 Interactive Reader and Study Guide

Differentiated Instruction Teacher Management System: Lesson Plans for Differentiated Instruction

Differentiated Instruction Modified Worksheets and Tests CD-ROM: Chapter Test

Interactive Skills Tutor CD-ROM

go.hrw.com
Online Resources
KEYWORD: SHL TEACHER

Chapter 22 Planning Guide

Life in the Industrial Age

Chapter Overview	Reproducible Resources	Technology Resources
CHAPTER 22 **pp. 656–681** **Overview:** In this chapter, students will learn about the far-reaching effects of the Industrial Revolution and its effects on many aspects of daily life. **KI 3, 4; PI 3.1, 4.1, 4.2, 4.4** See pp. T32–T55 for a detailed correlation to the New York State Core Curriculum for Global History and Geography and the New York Learning Standards.	**Differentiated Instruction Teacher Management System:*** • Pacing Guide • Lesson Plans for Differentiated Instruction **Interactive Reader and Study Guide:** Chapter Summary* **Chapter Resource File*** • Writing for the SAT • Social Studies Skill • Chapter Review **World History Outline Maps**	**OSP** **New York One-Stop Planner CD-ROM:** Calendar Planner **Live Ink© Online Reading Help** **Student Edition on Audio CD Program** **Differentiated Instruction Modified Worksheets and Tests CD-ROM** **Interactive Skills Tutor CD-ROM** **World History Primary Source Library CD-ROM** **Power Presentations with Video CD-ROM** **History's Impact: World History Video Program (VHS/DVD):** Life in the Industrial Age
Section 1 **Advances in Technology** **The Main Idea:** The technological breakthroughs of the Industrial Age included advances in electric power, transportation, and communication. **PI 3.1**	**Differentiated Instruction Teacher Management System:** Section 1 Lesson Plan* **Interactive Reader and Study Guide:** Section 1 Summary* **Chapter Resource File*** • Vocabulary Builder: Section 1 • Biography: Granville Woods	**Regents Review Transparency:** Section 1* **Map Transparency:** Growth in the Industrial Age* **Map Transparency:** U.S. Railroads, 1870* **Internet Activity:** The Inventions of Thomas Edison
Section 2: **Scientific and Medical Achievements** **The Main Idea:** Advances in science, medicine, and the social sciences led to new theories about the natural world and human mind, an improved quality of life, and longer life spans. **PI 4.1**	**Differentiated Instruction Teacher Management System:** Section 2 Lesson Plan* **Interactive Reader and Study Guide:** Section 2 Summary* **Chapter Resource File*** • Vocabulary Builder: Section 2 • Biography: Elizabeth Blackwell • Literature: *Frankenstein*	**Regents Review Transparency:** Section 2 **Quick Facts Transparency:** New Ideas in the Sciences* **Internet Activity:** Introduction of Anesthesia to Surgery
Section 3: **Daily Life in the Late 1800s** **The Main Idea:** During the late 1800s, cities grew and changed, while education, leisure time activities, and the arts reflected those changing times. **PI 4.2, 4.4**	**Differentiated Instruction Teacher Management System:** Section 3 Lesson Plan* **Interactive Reader and Study Guide:** Section 3 Summary* **Chapter Resource File*** • Vocabulary Builder: Section 3 • History and Geography: The Growth of Cities • Biography: Sarah Winnemucca	**Regents Review Transparency:** Section 3* **Quick Facts Transparency:** Increase in Leisure Activities*

HOLT
History's Impact
World History Video Program (VHS/DVD)
Life in the Industrial Age

Review, Assessment, Intervention

- **Global History and Geography Regents Test Prep Workbook**
- **Quick Facts Transparency:** Life in the Industrial Age*
- **Spanish Chapter Summaries Audio CD Program**
- **Progress Assessment Support System (PASS):** Chapter Test*
- **Differentiated Instruction Modified Worksheets and Tests CD-ROM:** Modified Chapter Test
- **OSP** **New York One-Stop Planner CD-ROM:** ExamView Test Generator (English/Spanish)
- **HOAP** **Holt Online Assessment Program (HOAP),** in the Holt Premier Online Student Edition

---

- **PASS:** Section 1 Quiz*
- **Online Quiz:** Section 1
- **Alternative Assessment Handbook**

- **PASS:** Section 2 Quiz*
- **Online Quiz:** Section 2
- **Alternative Assessment Handbook**

- **PASS:** Section 3 Quiz*
- **Online Quiz:** Section 3
- **Alternative Assessment Handbook**

Power Presentation with Video CD-ROM

Power Presentations with Video are visual presentations of each chapter's main ideas. Presentations can be customized by including Quick Facts charts, images and maps from the textbook, and video clips.

Holt Online Learning

go.hrw.com
Teacher Resources
KEYWORD: SHL TEACHER

go.hrw.com
Student Resources
KEYWORD: SHL LIF

- Document-Based Questions
- Interactive Multimedia Activities

- Current Events
- Chapter-Based Internet Activities
- and more!

Holt Premier
Online Student Edition
Complete online support for interactivity, assessment, and reporting

- Interactive Maps and Notebook
- Homework Practice and Research Activities Online

CHAPTER 22 PLANNING GUIDE

The Big Picture

Peter N. Stearns

Industrial Society From the 1830s onward, new social forms that constituted the essence of industrial society developed in Western Europe and the United States. Urbanism was a vital feature of the new industrial society and new technologies changed life outside as well as within the workplace. New forms of transportation and communication and electric lighting are key examples. Public health measures reduced urban disease and infant mortality rates.

Industrial Culture Scientific discoveries dominated the intellectual scene. The theory of evolution helped redefine biology. For many people, a general sense of scientific explanations of the natural world and a belief in the link between science and technological progress shaped basic outlooks in powerful new ways. Scientific thought spilled over into the social sciences and psychology. Artistic developments, such as impressionism, were somewhat separate. In literature, realism captured the scientific spirit, in seeking an objective examination of the human condition. Major artistic and scientific developments, though not easily compatible, created a common cultural framework from Russia to the United States.

Popular Culture Crucial changes occurred in ordinary life, too. Despite major social divisions, consumerism increased. Education spread more widely, and the majority of people in Western society were literate by the 1890s. Educational opportunities for women expanded as part of this general development. New leisure forms emerged, often emphasizing pleasure-seeking and spectatorship, or the enjoyment of professional sports and entertainments.

Assessment Obviously, many of these developments created a recognizably modern world—technology, suburbs, commercialized leisure, improved health. The developments correspondingly challenge assessment. They represented progress in many ways, as contemporaries often insisted, but they did not resolve all older problems—poverty remained, for example—and they created some new ones, such as more regimented leisure.

Recent Scholarship

In *Marianne in the Market: Envisioning Consumer Society in Fin-de-Siècle France* (2001), Lisa Tiersten deals with some of the leading developments of the later 19th century, obviously in a single national context. She discusses the new consumer role of women and how it related to living conditions and to the new criticisms levied both against women and consumerism. Aesthetic issues also figure in, as new products challenged older ideas of taste and artistry. Consumerism is portrayed as a major change in living standards and personal beliefs, but also as an unsettling process for many groups.

Differentiating Instruction

 Differentiated Instruction Teacher Management System
- Pacing Guide
- Lesson Plans for Differentiated Instruction

 Interactive Reader and Study Guide

Spanish Chapter Summaries Audio CD Program

Student Edition on Audio CD Program

 Differentiated Instruction Modified Worksheets and Tests CD-ROM
- Vocabulary Flash Cards
- Modified Vocabulary Builder Activities
- Modified Chapter Review Activity
- Modified Chapter Test

OSP One-Stop Planner CD-ROM
- ExamView Test Generator (English/Spanish)
- PuzzlePro
- Quiz Show for ExamView
- Transparencies and Videos

TE Differentiated Activities in the Teacher's Edition
- Comparing Theories of Evolution, p. 667
- Leisure Activities in the 1800s, p. 674
- Examining Art of the 1800s, p. 679

Reading Like a Historian
Sam Wineburg

Reading Without Words How do historians read something without words—for example, Claude Monet's 1874 painting *Sunrise*, which inspired the term "impressionism"? They can use words to describe this seascape's most distinguishing features—its radiant sun or its contrast of serenity and movement. But in so doing historians are typically no better than anyone else. What they can do, however, is build a context for a work by asking about the circumstances of its creation. How and when did a painting come into being and for what purpose? What cultural forces did it draw on or react against?

The school of painting known as impressionism arose in Paris in the second half of the 19th century, a time of dizzying social change and unprecedented urbanization. It was in this environment that Monet quit the studio and took his canvas outside—a bold act that spurned artistic convention. His scenes of everyday life contrasted with the ornate designs of traditional painting, the castles, mythological figures, church scenes, and formal portraits that defined the French Academy of Fine Arts.

The word impressionism was first used as a term of disparagement, something unfinished, superficial, or half-baked. It appeared in a biting review of Monet's work by Louis Leroy, who ridiculed *Sunrise* by quipping that "wallpaper in its embryonic state is more finished than that seascape!" Monet and others adopted the term as the name of their new movement, pointing out that impression also carried the sense of leaving an indelible mark—of appealing directly and unrepentantly to the senses.

Impressionists became famous for their use of color—raw, bold, and thick stroked—applied directly to the canvas. Hamlin Garland, one of the first American critics to offer a defense of impressionism, noted that the "impressionist does not believe that nature needs toning.... He paints with nature's colors—red, blue, and yellow; and he places them fearlessly on the canvas side by side, leaving the eye to mix them as in nature." In a society becoming increasingly mechanized, impressionists created images no machine could imitate. If urbanization had separated Europeans from nature by breaking agricultural rhythms, painting a canvas *en plein air* restored the relationship between the artist and nature.

Technology and Change That the impressionists rebelled against the changes brought about by industrialization is true—but only to a point. No artist is an island. This is illustrated most vividly in their response to the new technology of photography.

The impressionists' renunciation of "copying" nature in all its detail can be interpreted as a response to photographic realism. Impressionism did not need to compete with the camera because its goal was to teach the eye to see in a way no photo could. Like many other Parisians of his day, Monet himself was a camera enthusiast who noticed that pictures taken at slow shutter speeds resulted in blurred images. These insights led him to experiment with their equivalents on the canvas: smudged images that resembled photographic blurs and afterimages. Photography opened up the eyes of the artist and taught him a new way of seeing.

Artists both react to and are subsumed by the forces of their age. Reading a painting does not mean reducing Monet or others to the material conditions of industrialization. Rather, placing art in time and space reminds us that creative forms arise in settings with their own particular stories. Reading a work of art historically means reuniting that work with its rightful story.

Chapter Main Ideas

Section 1 The technological breakthroughs of the Industrial Age included advances in electric power, transportation, and communication.

Section 2 Advances in science, medicine, and the social sciences led to new theories about the natural world and human mind, an improved quality of life, and longer life spans.

Section 3 During the late 1800s, cities grew and changed, while education, leisure time activities, and the arts reflected those changing times.

New York Standards

Key Idea 3 Study of the major social, political, cultural, and religious developments in world history involves learning about the important roles and contributions of individuals and groups.

Key Idea 4 The skills of historical analysis include the ability to investigate differing and competing interpretations of the theories of history, hypothesize about why interpretations change over time, explain the importance of historical evidence, and understand the concepts of change and continuity over time.

Key to Differentiating Instruction

Below Level

Basic-level activities designed for all students encountering new material

At Level

Intermediate-level activities designed for average students

Above Level

Challenging activities designed for honors and gifted and talented students

Standard English Mastery

Activities designed to improve standard English usage

CHAPTER

22 1800–1900

Life in the Industrial Age

THE BIG PICTURE During the 1700s and 1800s, the Industrial Revolution changed practically everything about the world of work. Many of the changes were technological advances. As the rate of advances increased, many other aspects of daily life besides work were also transformed.

Theme SCIENCE AND TECHNOLOGY
Changes in science and technology accelerated rapidly during the 1800s. One discovery or invention led to another. The process repeated over and over, until practically every aspect of human experience was affected.

TIME LINE

CHAPTER EVENTS

1803 John Dalton develops modern atomic theory.

1817 Beethoven begins composing his Ninth Symphony.

1837 Samuel Morse invents the telegraph.

1849 Steamship service around South America begins.

1800 | 1820 | 1840

WORLD EVENTS

1813 Mexico declares its independence from Spain.

1816 Shaka Zulu founds the Zulu Empire in southern Africa.

1850 The Taiping Rebellion, which claims 20 million lives, begins in China.

1851 India's first railroad is built.

656 CHAPTER 22

Introduce the Chapter

At Level

Life in the Industrial Age

1. Write the following words for students to see: electricity, telephone, radio, automobile, airplane, vaccines, anesthesia, antiseptics. Remind students that all of these developments had their origins in the Industrial Age.

2. Organize students into small groups. Have each group choose from the list of developments the one that they think is most important. Then have students in each group make a list of the ways in which the development changed life.

3. Have volunteers from each group share their lists with the class. Guide students in a discussion of the ideas presented. Which development was chosen by the most groups? Why?

4. Tell students that in this chapter they will learn about the technological advances of the Industrial Age and how they changed everyday life in the 19th century. **LS Interpersonal**

📖 **Alternative Assessment Handbook**, Rubrics 11: Discussions; and 14: Group Activity

History's Impact video program
Watch the video to understand the impact of the Industrial Age.

Reading like a Historian

During the 1800s, a revolution in transportation occurred as railroads made travel faster and easier. At the same time, the middle class grew, and more people could take advantage of railroad service.

Analyzing Visuals This painting shows a crowded railroad platform in England in about 1860. What evidence of prosperity do you see in the painting?

See **Skills Handbook**, p. H26

1879
Thomas Edison invents the lightbulb.

1885
Louis Pasteur develops a vaccine against rabies.

1860

1880

1861
The Civil War begins in the United States.

1884 The Berlin Conference begins the partition of Africa.

Chapter Preview

HOLT
History's Impact
► **Video Program: Life in the Industrial Age**
See the Video Teacher's Guide for strategies for using the video segment.

Reading Like a Historian

Steam Power In 1802, British engineer Richard Trevithick designed a steam-powered coach. However, because they were so heavy, steam vehicles were soon banned from public roads, and their owners were forced to run them on tracks. Eventually, they were replaced by locomotives running on iron rails.

Explore the Time Line

1. How many years after the invention of the telegraph did the Civil War begin in the United States? *24 years*

2. When was the lightbulb invented, and by whom? *1879, by Thomas Edison*

3. How many years passed between the invention of the telegraph and the invention of the light-bulb? *42 years*

Info to Know

Industrial Revolution The Industrial Revolution is a term originally used to describe the transformation of England from a largely rural population to an urban manufacturing power. Other nations began to go through the same process soon afterward. Some nations, such as Japan and Russia, did not become industrialized until the first half of the 20th century. Today there are still nations that have not yet begun the process of industrialization.
Identify Where did the Industrial Revolution begin? *in England*

go.hrw.com
Online Resources

Chapter Resources:
KEYWORD: SHL LIF
Teacher Resources:
KEYWORD: SHL TEACHER

Answers

Reading Like a Historian 1. *fine clothing; travelers have many pieces of luggage filled with belongings; people appear content*

Geography Starting Points

Activity **Analyzing Maps** Have students use a large map of the United States to locate the U.S. cities shown on the map in the text. Have students identify the waterways that are adjacent to each city. Then have students explain why early industrial cities developed along rivers, lakes, and oceans.

LS Visual-Spatial

Alternative Assessment Handbook, Rubric 21: Map Reading

Map Transparency: Growth in the Industrial Age

World History Outline Maps

Interactive Map: Urban Growth in the Industrial Age

GEOGRAPHY **Starting Points**

Interactive
URBAN GROWTH IN THE INDUSTRIAL AGE

Starting Points

By the 1800s industrialization was causing cities in Europe and the United States to grow at a tremendous rate. In addition, society was changing rapidly in the cities. However, advances in technology, science, medicine, and other fields soon changed daily life far beyond the cities.

658 CHAPTER 22

1. **Analyze** By about how many people did London grow from 1800 to 1890? What factors may have caused the population increase?

2. **Predict** How do you think the growth of cities affected the people who lived in them?

Listen to History

Go online to listen to an explanation of the starting points for this chapter.

go.hrw.com
Keyword: SHL LIF

Skills Focus: Analyzing Maps

At Level

Social Studies Skill
The Industrial Age

Research Required

1. Have students conduct outside research and compare the population of the cities shown on the map in three time periods, 1820, 1880, and 1920.

2. Have students calculate the percentages of growth or decline and show their results in tabular format, using the graphs above as a model.

3. Have students find photographs from one of these cities in the 1800s. Have students create multimedia presentations combining their graphs and photographs. Presentations should illustrate how population growth affected life in industrial cities during the 1800s.

LS Visual-Spatial, Logical-Mathematical

Alternative Assessment Handbook, Rubrics 7: Charts, and 22: Multimedia Presentations

Answers

Geography Starting Points

1. *about 4 million people; people may have moved to cities to work in industrial jobs;* **2.** *possible answer—crowded living conditions, unhealthy environment*

Advances in Technology

BEFORE YOU READ

MAIN IDEA

The technological breakthroughs of the Industrial Age included advances in electric power, transportation, and communication.

READING FOCUS

1. How did electric power affect industry and daily life?
2. What advances in transportation occurred during the Industrial Age?
3. What were the advances in communication, and how were they achieved?

KEY TERMS AND PEOPLE

Michael Faraday
Thomas Edison
Bessemer process
Henry Ford
Wilbur and Orville Wright
telegraph
Samuel Morse
Alexander Graham Bell
Guglielmo Marconi

NEW YORK

P1 3.1 Students analyze the roles and contributions of individuals and groups to social, political, economic, cultural, and religious practices and activities.

THE INSIDE STORY

What new technology wowed the world in 1900? As visitors approached the gates to the Paris Exhibition of 1900, they wondered what was lighting up the night sky so brilliantly. Many had heard about a new technology that was a great improvement over the oil and gas lighting they currently used in their homes. But what they saw was amazing—a spectacular display of electricity as 5,000 multicolored lights lit up an enormous steel and glass building. None of the 50 million people who visited the exhibition had ever before seen such a spectacle of electric power. Few could imagine how electricity would transform their lives. ∎

In 1900, lights of the Palace of Electricity turned part of Paris into a fantasy land.

Palais de Electricité, artist unknown, c. 1900

LIGHTS FANTASTIC

Preteach

Getting Started

Use the **Interactive Reader and Study Guide** to familiarize students with the section content.

📖 **Interactive Reader and Study Guide,** Section 1

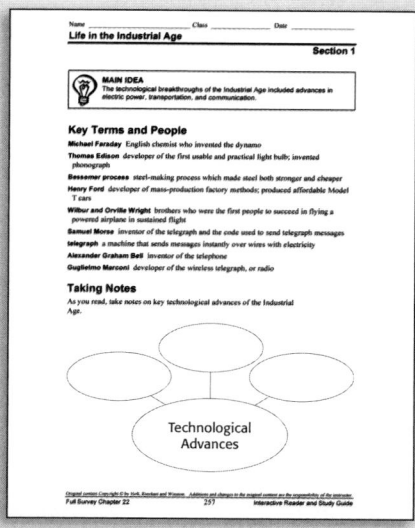

📋 **CRF:** Vocabulary Builder: Section 1

Taking Notes

Technological Advances—lightbulb; steam-powered trains; Bessemer process; steamships; automobile; airplane; telegraph; telephone; radio and phonograph

go.hrw.com
Online Resources

KEYWORD: SHL LIF
ACTIVITY: The Inventions of Thomas Edison

Teach the Main Idea

At Level

Advances in Technology

1. **Teach** Ask students the Reading Focus questions to teach this section.

2. **Apply** Have students make a chart with the following headings: Electric Power, Transportation, Communication. Under each heading, have students list the important 19th-century developments in that area.

3. **Review** Review student charts as a class. Then have students identify the one change under each heading that they believe was the most important.

4. **Practice/Homework** Have students write editorials from the point of view of a 19th century editor. They should try to convince the public that the federal government should help fund a transcontinental railroad system. Student editorials should describe the benefits of such a system and explain why it will be worth the money to build it.
   LS Visual-Spatial, Verbal-Linguistic

📝 **Alternative Assessment Handbook**, Rubrics 7: Charts; and 43: Writing to Persuade

Reading Focus

1 How did electric power affect industry and daily life? *drastically changed them; industry—factories no longer relied on steam engines powered by waterways, work day could extend past sunset; daily life—provided cheaper, convenient light source, led to other inventions*

Electric Power

Define What is a dynamo? *a machine that generates electricity by moving a magnet through a coil of copper wire*

Make Generalizations Why did inventors and scientists want to develop new power sources in the 1800s? *Water, coal, and steam were not very efficient sources of power.*

Recent Scholarship

Light! The Industrial Age 1750–1900, Art & Science, Technology & Science examines how the electric light bulb changed the way people live, work, and shop. It also describes how light influenced other inventions, including microscopes and cameras. The book identifies how the use of light led to dramatic changes in painting, with emphasis on the Romantics and the Impressionists.

Light! The Industrial Age 1750–1900, Art & Science, Technology & Science by Andreas Bluhm and Louise Lippincott. Thames & Hudson, 2001.

Answers

Faces of History *possible answer— No, he credited hard work more than inspiration for his discoveries.*

Reading Check *Factories no longer needed steam engines or water sources to power them; production increased; people could light their homes and businesses more safely and effectively with electric lighting.*

TAKING NOTES

Use a graphic organizer like the one below to take notes on key technological advances of the Industrial Age.

Technological Advances

Electric Power

Before the late 1880s water, coal, and steam had powered industry. As the Industrial Age progressed, though, inventors and scientists were inspired to develop new technologies. One technology drastically changed industry and daily life more than any other—electricity.

Early Attempts at Electric Power For many centuries, scientists had known of and been interested in electricity. During the 1700s Benjamin Franklin and other scientists had performed important experiments. Still, no one had developed a way to harness electricity and put it to use. In 1831, however, English chemist **Michael Faraday** discovered the connection between magnetism and electricity. His discovery led to the dynamo, a machine that generated electricity by moving a magnet through a coil of copper wire. Faraday used the electricity to power an electric motor, and his discoveries led to the development of electrical generators.

During the 1800s other scientists also created devices that used electric power. For instance, in 1860 British chemist Joseph Swan developed a primitive electric lightbulb that gave off light by passing heat through a small strip of paper. However, Swan's lightbulb did not shine for very long, and its light was too dim. Swan's work was a beginning, but it was nearly 40 more years before the invention of a usable lightbulb.

FACES OF HISTORY

Thomas EDISON
1847–1931

Thomas Edison, one of the world's most brilliant inventors, came from a humble background. He had only a few months of formal schooling. After working as a newsboy, Edison became a telegraph operator, where he got involved in electronic communication. In fact, improvements in the telegraph system were among his first inventions. Eventually, Edison held more than 1,090 patents for new inventions. His goal was to make things that could succeed on the market and, by doing so, prove their usefulness. He also believed in hard work, as he explained in this famous quote. "Genius is one percent inspiration and ninety-nine percent perspiration."

Draw Conclusions Do you think Edison saw himself as a genius? Why or why not?

Edison's Lightbulb Based on the work of Faraday and Swan, **Thomas Edison** developed the first usable and practical lightbulb in 1879. The new invention caused a sensation.

HISTORY'S VOICES

"Edison's electric light, incredible as it may appear, is produced from a tiny strip of paper that a breath would blow away. Through this little strip of paper is passed an electric current, and the result is a bright, beautiful light . . . and this light, the inventor claims, can be produced cheaper than that from the cheapest oil."

—Marshall Fox, *New York Herald*, 1879

This invention did not come easily, even to Edison. Instead, it came through trial and error and many hours of work in his laboratory in Menlo Park, New Jersey. As Edison's research became known, young people who shared his passion for inventing flocked to his lab to work for him. In addition to the lightbulb, Edison and his team made generators, motors, light sockets, and other electrical devices.

Edison also played a major role in the development of city electrical utility systems. He built the world's first central electric power plant in New York City. The plant produced enough power to light several city blocks. As a result of Edison's work, many aspects of life became easier.

Effects on Industry and Daily Life The wide availability of electric power transformed industry in both the United States and Europe. Electric power improved industry in three significant ways. First, by using electric power, factories no longer had to rely on large steam engines to power machines. Second, factories did not have to depend on waterways to power the steam engines. Third, factory production increased as factories became less dependent on sunlight. With electric lighting in factories, workers could stay on the job late into the night.

In addition to changing industry, electricity transformed daily life. Before people had electricity, they lit their homes with candles, gaslights, or oil lamps. Electricity provided a cheaper, more convenient light source. Inventors soon created other electrical devices that made daily life more convenient.

READING CHECK **Analyze** How did electricity change industry and daily life?

Skills Focus: Identifying Problem and Solution

Level Tag

Reading Skill
Edison's Invention Factory

1. Organize students into small groups. Tell students that it is the 1890s and each group is a research team at Thomas Edison's "invention factory." Have each group decide on a new invention they want to work on. Students should get approval before proceeding with their invention.

2. Have groups write a proposal that explores the market for their product and the feasibility of producing it affordably. Then have groups develop sketches and diagrams of their product and write an explanation of how the invention will work.

3. Ask volunteers from each group to present their invention to the rest of the class. The rest of the class will represent potential investors. Which inventions would they invest in?

LS Kinesthetic, Visual-Spatial

Alternative Assessment Handbook, Rubrics 3: Artwork; and 14: Group Activity

Railroads
Present-day boundary

Boston
Chicago
New York
Philadelphia
San Francisco
Kansas City
ATLANTIC OCEAN
Houston
New Orleans
Gulf of Mexico

0   200   400 Miles
0   200   400 Kilometers
Albers equal-area projection

30°N
70°W
Tropic of Cancer

U.S. RAILROADS, 1850

0   400 Miles
0   400 Kilometers

go.hrw.com
Interactive Maps
Keyword: SHL LIF

GEOGRAPHY
SKILLS INTERPRETING MAPS

1. **Regions** Where did railroads expand rapidly?
2. **Human-Environment Interaction** How do you think the railroad to San Francisco affected population growth and economic development?

Advances in Transportation

In addition to power technology, the late 1800s brought improvements in transportation. The development of efficient steam engines led to trains and steamships, while the internal combustion engine led to cars and airplanes.

Steam-Powered Trains Throughout the early 1800s boats on canals and rivers provided the best means for long-distance travel. Then, with the development of efficient steam engines, trains began to replace boats. Trains could carry heavy loads, did not require waterways, and traveled faster than watercraft. By 1830 the world's first rail line linked two major British cities, Manchester and Liverpool. By 1840 about 3,000 miles of railroad tracks crisscrossed the eastern United States.

Improvements in steel production contributed to the expansion of the railroad system. A new process made steel stronger and was also cheaper and more efficient. Working separately, Englishman Henry Bessemer and American William Kelly developed the new process in

the late 1850s. The **Bessemer process** involved forcing air through molten metal to burn out carbon and other impurities that make metal brittle. The process came to be named for Bessemer because he made it a financial success.

Using the Bessemer process, factories increased their production of locomotives and railroad tracks. In addition, engineers used the stronger steel to build bridges that allowed the trains to cross any type of terrain.

As the new steel-making process made building railroads easier, they expanded rapidly. By 1860 a 30,000-mile network of tracks linked the major American cities. West of the Mississippi River, new railroads brought people to unsettled or thinly settled areas of the country. As a result, cities in the American West grew and prospered along the tracks.

Engineers also took railroad technology around the world. India's first train ran in 1851. Just one year later, the first African railroad was built in Egypt. Construction on the world's longest railroad, the Trans-Siberian in Russia, began in 1891.

NEW YORK

CC Unit 5-G3f
Urbanization

LIFE IN THE INDUSTRIAL AGE **661**

661

Reading Focus

Advances in Transportation

Summarize How did expansion of the railroad benefit trade? *Markets for goods increased, travel time decreased, and new products became available.*

Predict How will Henry Ford's "motor car for the great multitude" change life in the United States? *Affordable cars will give Americans freedom to travel anywhere at any time.*

Activity Modern Transportation
Have students sketch modern-day versions of each mode of transportation shown in the transportation feature. How are they similar? How are they different? **LS** **Visual-Spatial**

CRF: Biography: Granville Woods

Info to Know

Assembly Lines Ransom Eli Olds founded the first automobile factory in 1897. The Olds Motor Vehicle Company was also the first to use an assembly line. In 1913, Henry Ford became the first manufacturer to use a conveyor belt on an assembly line, more than tripling production. Assembly lines with conveyor belts soon became the norm.

NEW YORK

CC Unit 5-G1
Human and physical geography

THE IMPACT TODAY

The auto industry continues its technological innovations. For example, in 2002 the Ford Motor Company began production of a car that runs on fuel cells powered by hydrogen. Water is the only emission.

The rapid expansion of the railroad helped both travel and trade. As a result, markets for goods increased. Because trains could move huge loads efficiently, transportation costs declined, bringing a wide range of low-cost products to market. In addition, new products became available. Shoppers had more food choices. Perishable foods could get to market before they spoiled. For example, merchants in the United States shipped frozen beef by rail from the west to the east.

Steamships Just as trains revolutionized land transportation, steamships changed ocean travel. Sailing ships depended on wind for power, but steamships could travel through any kind of weather.

In 1849 regular U.S. steamship service began, traveling from the west coast, around South America, to the east coast. Within a few years, engineers had made mechanical improvements to steamships. By 1870, long-distance movement of goods by steamship was economically viable. People also came on board. A long ocean voyage became an option for people looking for jobs or for fun.

The Automobile As early as 1769, several Europeans had tried to build a form of personal transportation. For more than a century only small advances were made. Finally, German engineers Carl Benz and Gottlieb Daimler both developed practical automobiles. In 1885 Benz built a three-wheeled vehicle. A year later, Daimler put an internal combustion engine on a horse carriage. Daimler also developed the carburetor, which mixed fuel with air for proper combustion in the engine.

At about the same time, several Americans developed their own automobile models. These early cars were too expensive for most buyers, but **Henry Ford** wanted to change that. In 1908 he announced, "I will build a motor car for the great multitude." He did it. Using mass-production methods in modern factories, Ford built a line of affordable cars called the Model T.

By 1920 the Model T made up 40 to 50 percent of U.S. automobile production. With cars, Americans gained a new freedom that allowed them to travel anywhere at any time. Road builders had to keep up. By 1915 American roads spanned more miles than rail lines.

New Ways to Travel

New modes of transportation revolutionized travel in the 1800s and early 1900s. One of the new ways to travel was introduced by Orville and Wilbur Wright, pictured below, when they flew their airplane at Kitty Hawk, North Carolina, in 1903.

A train arriving in a New Mexico station

The Train at Glorieta Summit, by Roy Anderson, 1800s

Model T Fords in a St. Louis park in the 1920s

The Wright Brothers at Kitty Hawk, N. Carolina, artist unknown, 1900s

The Granger Collection, New York

Skills Focus: Comparing and Contrasting

Above Level

Research Required

Reading Skill
Powering Transportation

1. Organize students into small groups. Have the groups conduct outside research using reliable Internet or print sources to find out how steam engines and internal combustion engines work. Students should investigate the kinds of fuels that can be used to power steam engines and internal combustion engines.

2. Have each group make a before-and-after chart describing why internal combustion engines quickly replaced steam engines.

3. Have volunteers share the information from their charts with the entire class. Guide students in a discussion of the changes that were made possible as a result of the internal combustion engine. What, if any, alternatives are there to using internal combustion engines powered by fossil fuels? **LS** **Interpersonal, Visual-Spatial**

Alternative Assessment Handbook, Rubrics 7: Charts; and 30: Research

Telephone Technology

Although Alexander Graham Bell and Thomas Watson made the first telephone in 1876, improvements were gradual. Rural areas and small towns, especially, were often behind the cities in technological progress.

For example, only 50 years ago many calls still required the help of a live operator. To place a call, a person picked up the receiver, and an operator said "Number, please." The caller replied with a series of numbers. The operator made the connection, the other phone rang, and the call was completed.

The first telephone operators were boys who had experience as telegraph operators. But customers complained that the boys were rude to them. In 1878 the telephone companies began hiring women operators. Emma Nutt, a Boston woman, was the first one hired.

Today, of course, we can talk, send instant messages, surf the Internet, and take photos on our phones—without any help.

Analyze How would your daily life be different if you did not have access to advanced telephone technology?

A modern cell phone ▶

An operator connects two callers on a switchboard in about 1900.

The Airplane Advances in transportation were not limited to land and sea. People also wanted to fly. Hot air balloons made their debut in 1783 and became useful for wartime spying and aerial photography. However, balloons were at the mercy of the wind.

A big step forward in controlled flight happened at Kitty Hawk, North Carolina, on December 17, 1903. On that date, American brothers **Wilbur and Orville Wright** succeeded in flying a powered airplane in sustained flight.

Drawing from the work of earlier aviation engineers, the Wrights had spent four years developing their lightweight airplane. They used principles of aerodynamics, which is the study of how forces act on solid surfaces moving through the air. The Wrights designed a glider with specially shaped wings. To power their plane, they attached a version of the internal combustion engine. The first powered flight went only 120 feet, but the plane's performance improved rapidly. This first flight paved the way for the use of airplanes to travel the globe, transport goods, and fight wars.

READING CHECK **Identifying Cause and Effect** What effect did advances in transportation have on daily life?

Advances in Communication

Today, news and messages travel around the world in mere seconds by e-mail and telephone. In the early 1800s, though, news traveled much more slowly, by boat or by messenger on foot, horseback, or carriage. As a result, entrepreneurs and inventors started to look for better and faster ways to communicate.

The Telegraph Putting electricity to use made possible the invention of the **telegraph**, a machine that sent messages instantly over wires. American **Samuel Morse** is credited with inventing the telegraph in 1837. Morse also developed a "language," which became known as Morse code, for sending telegraph messages. Morse code is a series of long and short signals that represent letters and numbers. These telegraph messages were transmitted as electrical pulses of different lengths.

In 1844 Morse received funding from the United States government to lay 35 miles of telegraph wires between Washington, D.C., and Baltimore., Maryland The first telegraph message Morse tapped out was, "What hath God wrought?" With this message, a new era in communication technology began.

FOCUS ON NEW YORK

The telegraph helped secure New York City's status as the country's corporate capital, partly because it allowed the New York Stock Exchange to connect distant buyers and sellers.

LIFE IN THE INDUSTRIAL AGE **663**

Skills Focus: Identifying Cause and Effect

At Level

Advances in Communication

Standard English Mastery

1. Guide students in a discussion of the advances in communication that were made during the 1800s.

2. Tell students that it is 1850 and they are writing a magazine article about the effects of the telegraph. Have students use the following questions to guide them: How have changes in the speed of communication changed life? Would these changes constitute a revolution in communication? Why or why not? What other changes might occur as the country is linked by telegraph wires? What might happen if telegraph wires someday link the United States with Europe and England with India? What future developments might further revolutionize communication?

3. Have students check their articles for correct spelling and grammar. Ask volunteers to read their articles to the class. **LS Verbal-Linguistic**

Alternative Assessment Handbook, Rubrics 11: Discussions; and 40: Writing to Describe

---

Direct Teach

Reading Focus

3 What were the advances in communication, and how were they achieved? *telegraph, telephone, radio; made possible by the invention of electricity; telephone and telegraph sent messages over wires, radio provided wireless communication*

Advances in Communication

Recall Where did funding for the first telegraph wires come from? *the United States government*

Make Inferences Why could the telegraph not have been invented earlier? *It relied on electricity.*

Linking to Today
Telephone Technology

Predict Remind students that cellular telephone technology is relatively new, and currently changing. Have students predict what the next generation of cell phones will look like—and what they will do.

Answers

Linking to Today *possible answers— much more complicated, harder to communicate quickly, more in-person contact*

Reading Check *better and faster means of transportation; made it possible to get more goods to market at lower costs, increasing consumers' choices*

Advances in Communication

Sequence In what order were the major developments in communication made? *telegraph, telephone, radio*

Make Judgments Which of the three advances in communication had the biggest impact? Why? *possible answer—telegraph, first to make communication instantaneous*

● **Review & Assess** ●

Close

Have students summarize the technological breakthroughs that took place during the Industrial Age.

Review

 Online Quiz, Section 1

Assess

SE **Section 1 Assessment**

📋 **Progress Assessment:** Section 1 Quiz

📋 **Alternative Assessment Handbook**

Reteach/Intervene

📋 **Interactive Reader and Study Guide,** Section 1

💿 **Interactive Skills Tutor CD-ROM**

Answers

Reading Check *telegraph transmitted coded messages; telephone transmitted voice*

664

As the United States grew, the importance of the telegraph increased. By 1851 more than 50 telegraph companies were in operation in the United States. About 10 years later, telegraph wires strung on poles along established railroad tracks linked much of the country. At railroad stations, passengers could send messages, or telegrams, to friends and family.

Communication between the United States and Europe also improved with the laying of a telegraph cable on the floor of the Atlantic Ocean in 1866. By 1870 telegraph wires stretched from England to India.

The telegraph revolutionized more than personal communication. In many countries, businesses could keep in close contact with suppliers and markets. News traveled around the world in hours instead of weeks. Newspapers sent correspondents to the front lines of wars, from where they telegraphed back vivid reports of victories and defeats. The reading public was very impressed by these timely reports. The reports were one way in which the telegraph globalized communication.

The Telephone As use of the telegraph spread around the world, inventors tried to improve on it. American **Alexander Graham Bell**, a teacher of hearing-impaired students, was one of the scientists working in sound technology. Bell tried to create a way to send multiple telegraph messages at the same time.

While working on that device, Bell made a remarkable discovery. One day in 1876 he was in one room and his assistant Thomas Watson was in another. Bell said, "Mr. Watson, come here, I want to see you!" Watson could hear Bell's voice not just through the air but also through the device's receiver. The telephone was born.

During the 1880s demand for telephones increased. Telephone companies laid thousands of miles of phone lines across the United States. By 1900 almost 1.5 million telephones were installed in American homes and offices.

The Radio and Phonograph Although the telephone revolutionized communication, the technology was limited. Wires could only stretch so far. A new wireless technology was based on theories about electromagnetic waves. In 1895 Italian physicist **Guglielmo Marconi** used the discoveries to build a wireless telegraph, or radio. First used as a communication method for ships, the radio was later used for entertainment and news. Entertainment options increased when Thomas Edison recorded sound with one of his many inventions. It was the phonograph, which became the record player. With these inventions, music was available to everyone.

READING CHECK **Contrast** How did the telegraph differ from the telephone?

SECTION 1 ASSESSMENT

go.hrw.com
Online Quiz
Keyword: SHL LIF HP

Reviewing Ideas, Terms, and People

1. **a. Recall** What did Michael Faraday invent?
   b. Draw Conclusions What impact did electricity have on industry?
   c. Evaluate Assess the validity of this statement: **Thomas Edison** contributed to all aspects of electrical technology.
2. **a. Define** What is the **Bessemer process**?
   b. Explain What advantages did rail travel have over canal and river travel?
   c. Develop What advantages did the automobile provide?
3. **a. Define** What is the **telegraph**?
   b. Analyze How did advances in communication technology change the way people lived in the late 1800s?
   c. Evaluate Do you think the telegraph, telephone, radio, and phonograph could have had both positive and negative effects on daily life in the late 1800s? Explain your answer.

Critical Thinking

4. **Identify Supporting Details** Use your notes and a graphic organizer like this one to record details that support the main idea about one type of technological advance. Write the subsection's main idea in the center circle.

FOCUS ON WRITING ✏️

5. **Narrative** Write a paragraph that tells the story of one of the advances in technology during the 1800s. Include details from this section.

Section 1 Assessment Answers

1. **a.** the dynamo,
   b. Factories no longer relied on steam engines or water sources; production increased as workday lengthened.
   c. possible answer—valid, he created many different electrical inventions
2. **a.** a steel-making process that made steel stronger
   b. faster, not tied to waterways
   c. gave Americans the freedom to travel
3. **a.** a machine that sends messages instantly over wires with electricity

   b. revolutionized communication, allowing news to travel quickly
   c. possible answer—revolutionized communication, made life complicated

4. electric power—transformed industry and daily life; transportation—increased availability of products; people free to travel; communication—allowed news to travel quickly

5. Paragraphs should discuss the innovation's development and impact.

Focus on Themes

Science and Technology

Humanity's fascination with electricity has a long history. The first people were probably awed by lightning. In the 600s BC a Greek scholar noticed that rubbing a piece of amber produced a spark. More than 2,000 years later a German physicist made a device that generated static electricity. Then in 1831 Michael Faraday saw the connection between magnetism and electricity, and a new technology was born. Since then, electricity has changed practically all aspects of daily life in industrialized countries.

▲ **Now** This NASA image shows where artificial lights shine from the earth at night. The composite of satellite images took a year to complete.

BEFORE ELECTRICITY Before the development of electricity, people depended on several sources of power for their daily needs. They burned candles and oil lamps for light. To drive machines, they used the power of muscle, water, coal, and steam. For other activities, people depended on themselves and each other. For entertainment, audiences attended live performances. To communicate long distances, they wrote letters. Today, it is hard for us to imagine what life was like before the widespread use of electricity.

◄ **THEN** This lightbulb is a replica of the one invented by Thomas Edison in 1879.

The Granger Collection, New York

AFTER ELECTRICITY What aspect of daily life has not been transformed by electricity? Think about how electricity makes your daily routine possible, starting with the alarm clock that wakes you in the morning. Drying your hair, cooking breakfast, checking the weather on the Internet before you decide what to wear—electricity makes it all possible. Throughout your whole day, from lighted classrooms and the computer lab to instant messages on your cell phone and late-night TV talk shows, electricity powers your modern lifestyle.

There is a price to pay for all this convenience. Much of the world's electricity is generated by burning fossil fuels, which pollute air around the world. As a result, even people who live where electricity is not available are affected by its use. Another type of pollution is the result of so much light. In big cities, people cannot see the stars because the lights are so bright. To avoid this light pollution, astronomers must build their telescopes in remote locations or send them into space. Still, there are probably few among us who would want to go back to the "dark" ages.

 Skills Focus — **UNDERSTANDING THEMES**

1. **Contrast** How would your daily life be different if you did not have electricity?
2. **Support a Position** Would you give up some conveniences to reduce the burning of fossil fuels? Explain your answer.

Science and Technology

Info to Know

Life Before Electricity Before electricity, artificial light was dim, sooty, and smelly. Even regular cleaning could not get rid of the grime and odor left throughout the house by candles, kerosene lamps, and gas lights. Because of their flames, these light sources could cause fires. In addition, gas lights released dangerous fumes if the flame went out.

Houses were designed to be functional, with doors to shut off individual rooms for airing and to minimize draft. Rooms were decorated in dark colors to hide soot.

Skills Focus: Identifying Problem and Solution

At Level

Reading Skill
The Impact of Electricity

Research Required

Background: In addition to polluting the air, fossil fuels are becoming increasingly expensive, driving up the cost of generating electricity.

1. Organize students into six groups. Have each group research one of the following alternatives to fossil fuels for creating electricity: nuclear energy, solar energy, geothermal energy, wind power, water power, burning wood or other biomass such as garbage. Have students make a list of the pros and cons of using each.

2. Have volunteers from each group share their lists with the class. Ask members of the class to name any additional benefits or disadvantages they can think of for each energy source.

3. Guide students in a discussion of the best ways to reduce dependency on fossil fuels.

LS **Interpersonal**

Alternative Assessment Handbook, Rubrics 14: Group Activity; and 30: Research

Answers

Understanding Themes 1. *Answers will vary. Students should recognize that almost every device in their homes is powered by electricity.* **2.** *possible answers—Yes, giving up some conveniences would be worth it if pollution decreased; no, it would be difficult to give up the conveniences to which we are accustomed.*

Getting Started

Use the **Interactive Reader and Study Guide** to familiarize students with the section content.

📄 **Interactive Reader and Study Guide,** Section 2

BEFORE YOU READ

MAIN IDEA

Advances in science, medicine, and the social sciences led to new theories about the natural world and human mind, an improved quality of life, and longer life spans.

READING FOCUS

1. What were some of the new ideas in the sciences?
2. What medical breakthroughs affected the quality of life?
3. What new ideas developed within the social sciences?

KEY TERMS AND PEOPLE

Charles Darwin
Marie and Pierre Curie
radioactivity
Albert Einstein
Louis Pasteur
pasteurization
anesthetic
Ivan Pavlov
Sigmund Freud

 NEW YORK

P1 4.1 Students identify historical problems, pose analytical questions or hypotheses, research analytical questions or test hypotheses, formulate conclusions or generalizations, raise new questions or issues for further investigation.

[Interactive Reader and Study Guide worksheet showing:]

Name _____ Class _____ Date _____

Life in the Industrial Age

Section 2

💡 **MAIN IDEA**
Advances in the natural world and human mind, an improved quality of life, and longer life spans.

Key Terms and People

Charles Darwin scientist who developed the theory of natural selection

Marie and Pierre Curie Married French chemists who discovered the elements polonium and radium and described the process of radioactivity

radioactivity the process through which certain elements break down, releasing energy

Albert Einstein German scientist who developed the theory of relativity to describe the relationship between space, time, and motion

Louis Pasteur French chemist who showed the link between germs and disease and developed the process of pasteurization

pasteurization heating liquids to high temperatures to prevent fermentation

anesthetic something given to a medical patient to reduce pain or cause unconsciousness

Ivan Pavlov Russian physiologist who proved that dogs could be conditioned to have certain reflex actions

Sigmund Freud Austrian doctor who introduced the concept of the unconscious mind

Taking Notes

Record basic information on new ideas in the sciences, medicine, and the social sciences in a graphic organizer like this one.

Sciences	
Medicine	
Social Sciences	

Original content Copyright © by Holt, Rinehart and Winston. Additions and changes to the original content are the responsibility of the instructor.

Full Survey Chapter 22   260   Interactive Reader and Study Guide

---

Academic Vocabulary

Review with students the high-use academic term in this section.

theories plausible general principles offered to explain what has been observed (p. 667)

📄 **CRF: Vocabulary Builder: Section 2**

Taking Notes

Sciences—theory of evolution; modern atomic theory; periodic table; radioactivity; relativity; Medicine—pasteurization, new vaccinations; anesthetics; more modern hospitals; decline in infant mortality; Social Sciences—new fields of study including psychology, archaeology, anthropology, sociology

go.hrw.com
Online Resources

KEYWORD: SHL LIF
ACTIVITY: Introduction to Anesthesia to Surgery

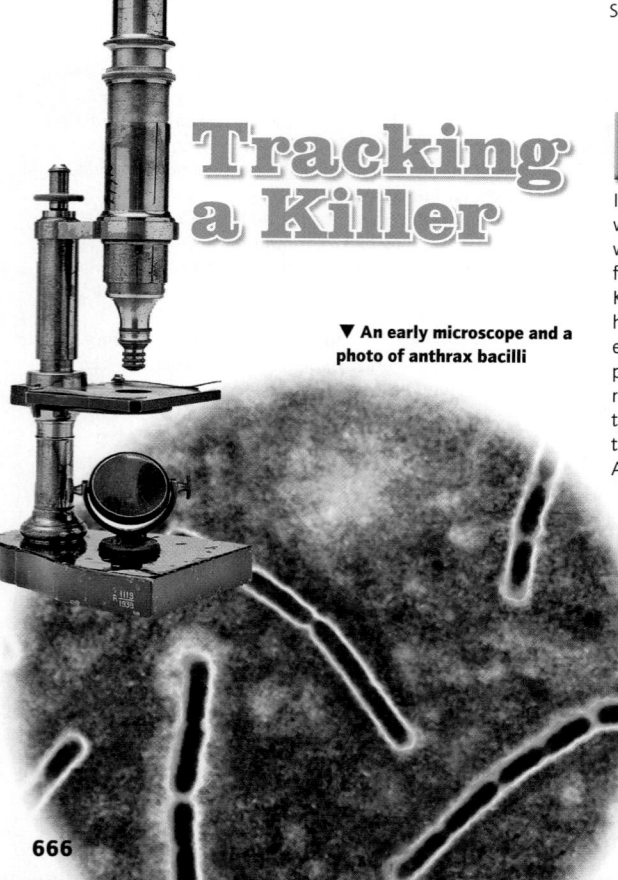

Tracking a Killer

▼ **An early microscope and a photo of anthrax bacilli**

THE INSIDE STORY

How did a poorly equipped country doctor make major discoveries about disease?

In the 1870s a military doctor named Robert Koch was stationed in the German countryside. The region was plagued by anthrax, a disease that killed many farm animals and could be transmitted to people. Koch wanted to learn more about the disease. But he had no library, no assistants, and practically no equipment besides a microscope. He first hoped to prove that a previously discovered bacillus, or bacterium, did indeed cause anthrax. To do so, Koch carved tiny wood slivers to inject mice with anthrax bacillus taken from the blood of animals killed by the disease. All the mice died. Then he injected other mice with blood from healthy animals, and they all survived. In this way, Koch proved that anthrax could be transmitted by the blood of infected animals.

Koch went on to discover that the anthrax bacillus produced seedlike bodies called spores that could spread the disease. Later, Koch made additional discoveries that led to treatments for malaria, tuberculosis, and other diseases. Koch's discoveries are among countless scientific advances made during the 1800s. ■

666

Teach the Main Idea

At Level

Scientific and Medical Achievements

1. **Teach** Ask students the Reading Focus questions to teach this section.

2. **Apply** Have students create an outline of the section using the red headings as main points. Have students identify at least two main ideas under each of the blue subheadings.

3. **Review** Review student outlines as a class. Have students identify the points in their outlines that they feel are most important or most interesting. Guide students in a

discussion of the similarities and the differences between science and social science.

4. **Practice/Homework** Have students write letters to the editor of a scientific journal about an important scientific or medical achievement described in this section. Letters should persuade readers that the achievement is of utmost importance.

LS Verbal-Linguistic

📄 **Alternative Assessment Handbook,** Rubrics 11: Discussion; and 17: Letters to Editors

Reading like a Historian

A Scientist's Report on Island Animals

Analyzing Primary Sources During his long voyage on the HMS *Beagle*, Charles Darwin recorded his observations on practically everything he saw and experienced. In the passage given here, he describes the iguanas and birds of the Galapagos Islands, which lie in the Pacific Ocean about 600 miles west of South America.

As you read, think about how a report from 1835 might differ from a present-day scientific report from the same islands. Consider:

- the author's background
- scientific knowledge at the time
- details of scientific observation

Darwin's comments about the birds' behavior indicate that few if any people had ever visited the islands.

> These islands appear paradises for the whole family of Reptiles . . . The black Lava rocks on the beach are frequented by large (2–3 ft) most disgusting, clumsy Lizards. They are as black as the porous rocks over which they crawl & seek their prey from the Sea. Somebody calls them "imps of darkness." They assuredly well become the land they inhabit . . . The birds are Strangers to Man & think him as innocent as their countrymen the huge Tortoises. Little birds within 3 & four feet, quietly hopped about the Bushes & were not frightened.
>
> —*Charles Darwin's Beagle Diary*, 1835

Skills FOCUS — READING LIKE A HISTORIAN

1. **Author** What does the passage reveal about Darwin's previous experiences? about knowledge at the time?
2. **Details** What details demonstrate Darwin's skills of scientific observation?

See **Skills Handbook**, p. H25

New Ideas in Science

Among the many new ideas of the 1800s were those developed by a young geologist named **Charles Darwin**. He had taken a long voyage during which he studied variations among plants and animals. Many years later, Darwin published his theories in a book titled *On the Origin of Species*.

Darwin's Theories Through careful observation of what he saw on his journey, Darwin developed the concept of natural selection. According to this theory, creatures that are well adapted to their environments have a better chance of surviving to produce offspring. The offspring will inherit the physical features that help the creatures survive. Over time, Darwin argued, the species will evolve, or change to improve its survival chances. This idea became known as the theory of evolution.

Darwin's theory was controversial, however. The theory indicated that human beings were descended from other animals. Many people thought this possibility was simply ridiculous. Others opposed Darwin because his theory differed from the creation story in the Bible.

Advances in Chemistry and Physics In the early 1800s chemists and physicists also made landmark discoveries. For centuries, scientists had proposed that tiny particles, or atoms, made up chemical elements. Moreover, most scientists thought that all elements were made of the same kinds of atoms. But in 1803 English chemist John Dalton developed modern atomic theory. An essential part of this theory is the idea that atoms of different elements are themselves of different size and mass.

In 1871 Russian chemist Dmitri Mendeleyev arranged all the chemical elements into a chart called the periodic table. The table revealed previously unknown patterns among the elements. Mendeleyev left gaps in the periodic table, knowing that some elements were yet to be discovered. He even described what those elements would be like.

As Mendeleyev had predicted, scientists that came after him discovered more elements that fit into the periodic table. For example, in France in 1898 chemists **Marie and Pierre Curie** discovered polonium and radium. The Curies also concluded that certain elements release energy when they break down. Marie Curie called this process **radioactivity**.

ACADEMIC VOCABULARY
theories plausible general principles offered to explain what has been observed

TAKING NOTES
Use a graphic organizer like this one to record new ideas in the sciences, medicine, and the social sciences.

| Sciences |
| Medicine |
| Social Sciences |

Reading Focus

1 What were some of the new ideas in the sciences? *ideas that provided a much better understanding of the way the universe works, including the origins of species, atomic structure, and the relationships between space, time, and motion*

New Ideas in Science

Identify What is the periodic table? *a chart in which all the chemical elements are arranged*

Explain Why was Darwin's theory of evolution controversial? *Some people thought the idea that humans descended from animals was ridiculous. The theory differed from the creation story in the Bible.*

Evaluate How important were Einstein's ideas to science? *revolutionary—overturned what Newton and many others had said about how the universe worked*

Info to Know

Birds in the Galapagos Darwin collected a large number of animal specimens on the Galapagos Islands. After analyzing the specimens, he realized that several Galapagos birds, which he had first thought to be totally different kinds of birds, were actually closely related to a species of finches. The beaks of the different birds varied greatly in size and shape. Darwin realized the beaks were specialized according to what the birds ate.

Differentiating Instruction

Above Level

Advanced Learners/Gifted and Talented

Research Required

Background: Tell students that in the early 1800s French biologist Jean-Baptist Lamarck set forth a theory of evolution, which stated that living things changed their form in response to their environments. For example, giraffes developed long necks because they always had to stretch high up in trees. He believed that such acquired changes were then passed on by inheritance to offspring. Many of Lamarck's ideas were later proven wrong, but he did influence Charles Darwin.

1. Have students construct a Venn diagram showing the major ideas of Lamarck and Darwin and what points the two scientists had in common.

2. Have volunteers share their Venn diagrams.

3. Guide students in a discussion of the theories of Lamarck and Darwin. On what points did they agree? On what points did they disagree?
LS Visual-Spatial

Alternative Assessment Handbook, Rubrics 13: Graphic Organizers; and 30: Research

Answers

Reading Like a Historian
1. *suggests he and many others had not seen birds and animals like this before;*
2. *the many descriptive details about the size, appearance, and behavior of the animals and birds; shows that he feels superior to the people he is describing, and pities them for their "miserable" life*

667

Direct Teach

Reading Focus

New Ideas in Science

Describe According to Ernest Rutherford, what is the nucleus of an atom like? *a heavy core at the center of an atom, made up of positively charged particles called protons*

Analyze Where does the relativity in Einstein's theory of relativity come into play? *the idea that motion can only be measured relative to a particular observer*

Reading Focus

2 What medical breakthroughs affected the quality of life? *Pasteur discovered methods of preventing disease through pasteurization and vaccines. Other scientists developed anesthetics and antiseptics.*

Medical Breakthroughs

Recall What was the concept of spontaneous generation? *the idea that bacteria, flies, or other tiny animals could spring to life out of nonliving matter*

Evaluate In addition to being useful in combating diseases, how could an understanding of bacteria have negative effects? *Bacteria can be used in biological warfare.*

Primary Source

"I am one of those who think like Nobel, that humanity will draw more good than evil from new discoveries." –Marie Curie

Answers

Faces of History *because she helped stockpile radioactive materials for use in health care and research; because she won the Nobel Prize*

Reading Check *evolution, radioactivity, relativity*

668

Other scientists developed theories based on the Curies' work. In 1911 British chemist Ernest Rutherford realized that in the center of an atom lay a core called a nucleus. In addition, he found that the nucleus is made up of positively charged particles, which he called protons. These findings disproved the long-held belief that an atom is a solid piece of matter.

Einstein's Genius In 1905 German-Jewish scientist **Albert Einstein** revolutionized physics. In an early work, Einstein used mathematics to show that light can act not only as a wave, but also like tiny particles of energy. In another paper, Einstein developed the special theory of relativity, based on two crucial ideas. One was that no particle of matter can move faster than the speed of light. The other is that motion can be measured only from the viewpoint of a particular observer. Therefore, scientists cannot speak of absolute motion, space, or time.

Among Einstein's ideas was a now-famous formula: $E = mc^2$. The formula means that a small amount of mass can be converted into a huge amount of energy. Einstein also proposed that space itself is curved and that one must include time in the study of space. These theories overturned what Sir Isaac Newton and many scientists who came after Newton had said about how the universe worked.

READING CHECK **Summarize** What new theories revolutionized science?

THE IMPACT TODAY

Pasteurization technology is still improving. With ultra-high-temperature (UHT) pasteurization, milk is heated to above the boiling point for one or two seconds. If in a sterile container, UHT milk can be stored without refrigeration for months.

FACES OF HISTORY

Marie CURIE 1867–1934

Marie Curie's accomplishments went beyond her discoveries related to radioactivity. At a girls' school, she introduced the idea of teaching science through experiments. Curie was the first woman to teach at the Sorbonne, the oldest university in Paris. She also helped stockpile rare and valuable radioactive minerals for use in health care and further research.

Curie shared the Nobel Prize for Physics in 1903 with her husband and another physicist. Then in 1911, she received the Nobel Prize for chemistry on her own. Although Curie's work was brilliant, it was ultimately fatal. She died from leukemia caused by exposure to radiation.

Draw Conclusions Why do you think Marie Curie is respected and revered by workers in many health care professions?

668 CHAPTER 22

Medical Breakthroughs

During the late 1800s breakthroughs in medicine occurred as a result of the scientific advances made earlier in the century. Fundamental concepts of disease, medical care, and sanitation were revealed.

Preventing Disease For thousands of years, people had been mystified by what caused disease. Part of the mystery was solved in 1870 when French chemist **Louis Pasteur** showed the link between microbes and disease. He also disproved a concept called spontaneous generation—the idea that bacteria, flies, or other tiny animals could spring to life out of nonliving matter. Instead, Pasteur showed that bacteria are always present in the air, although we cannot see them, and reproduce like other living things.

Pasteur also discovered that bacteria present in the air cause fermentation, the process that makes grape juice turn into wine and milk turn sour. By heating liquids and foods to high temperatures, Pasteur killed the bacteria and prevented fermentation. His process became known as **pasteurization**. The process also destroys bacteria that cause disease. Today, most milk, cheese, and juice on our grocery shelves has been sterilized, or made germ-free, through pasteurization.

Pasteur next targeted a deadly disease that was a constant threat to people and their livestock—anthrax. To prevent anthrax, Pasteur injected animals with a vaccine containing weakened anthrax germs, which prevented the animals from getting sick. His vaccine worked because the body builds up substances called antibodies to fight weakened germs when they enter the body.

Preventing rabies was Pasteur's next goal. He developed a vaccine in 1885 and saved the life of a young boy who had been bitten by a rabid dog. Pasteur's fame was secured.

Improving Medical Care Other medical practices improved also. One was the treatment of pain. Surgery patients suffered terribly. American surgeon Crawford W. Long discovered a solution. Long had his patients breathe in a gas called ether. It was an **anesthetic**, a drug that reduces pain and in large doses makes the patient unconscious.

Collaborative Learning

At Level

Emergency Room in the 1800s

1. Organize the class into small groups. Have each group write a skit illustrating the state of medicine in the early 1800s, before the development of anesthetics and antiseptics. Each of the students in the group should have a role in the skit. (Students may wish to conduct additional research to find out more about medical practices of the early 1800s.)

2. Have each group present its skit to the rest of the class.

3. Guide students in a discussion of advances in medical science between the early 1800s and today. What further developments can students envision? **LS** **Interpersonal, Kinesthetic**

Alternative Assessment Handbook, Rubrics 14: Group Activity; and 33: Skits and Reader's Theater

FORENSICS in History

Do the Prints Match?

Forensics advanced in the 1800s along with the other sciences. The use of fingerprints in solving crimes was a major development.

Who solved the crimes? Around the world today, fingerprints are the most commonly used forensic evidence. Scientists and law enforcement officers in many countries contributed to their use.

In the 1820s a Czech scientist classified fingerprints into categories but did not note that fingerprints were unique. Decades later, a British official in India required fingerprints on contracts. Over time, he noticed that a person's prints did not change with age. A Scottish doctor working in Japan is probably the first person to prove a suspect's innocence by showing that fingerprints left at the crime scene did not match those of the suspect. In Argentina in 1892, a police officer matched a bloody fingerprint to a woman who had killed her sons but cut her own throat to avoid arrest. By the end of the 1800s, police around the world were using fingerprints to solve crimes.

Analyze Why do you think the value of fingerprints was not recognized more quickly?

▲ The police record of the thief who stole the *Mona Lisa* in 1911 includes his fingerprints.

In 1842 Long performed the first painless operation by administering ether. Other types of anesthetics were soon developed.

Still, many surgical patients later died from infections. In the 1860s English surgeon Joseph Lister began cleaning wounds and equipment with an antiseptic—a germ-killing agent containing carbolic acid. By using the antiseptic, Lister reduced post-surgery deaths in one hospital ward from 45 to 15 percent.

Another improvement in public health was the building of more modern hospitals. More physicians, nurses, and other medical professionals were trained. Nursing schools trained large numbers of women as nurses or physicians' assistants. Some women even enrolled in medical school to become doctors. By 1900, 5 percent of American physicians were women.

A major result of these developments in medical care and public health was a dramatic decline in infant mortality, or deaths in infancy. Statistics from Sweden provide a clear example. In 1800 Sweden reported 240 deaths of infants under one year old per 1,000 live births. By 1898 that figure had dropped to 91 deaths.

READING CHECK Identify Cause and Effect
What medical advances allowed people to live longer?

New Ideas in Social Sciences

In the late 1800s scientists expanded their focus to include the study of the mind and human societies. These new fields became known as the social sciences and include psychology, archaeology, anthropology, and sociology.

Psychology In the 1890s the study of the mind and human behavior emerged as a separate field known as psychology. Observation and experiments helped psychologists explore their subject.

To better understand human behavior some scientists studied animal behavior. Russian physiologist **Ivan Pavlov** used dogs as research subjects to prove that animals could be conditioned, or taught, to have certain reflex actions. In his study, Pavlov rang a bell each time he fed the dogs. Over time Pavlov discovered that instead of only salivating at the sight or smell of food, the dogs salivated when they heard the bell. Pavlov called this reaction the conditioned reflex. By studying the dogs' behavior, Pavlov concluded that human behaviors are also a series of connected conditioned reflexes.

Direct Teach

New Ideas in Social Sciences

Identify Why was Freud interested in dreams? *He believed dreams revealed repressed thoughts, thoughts that might cause mental illness.*

Contrast How did archaeology change in the 1800s? *Early excavations were little more than treasure hunts; modern archaeology takes a scientific approach, recording and carefully preserving all the work.*

📝 **CRF**: Literature: *Frankenstein*

🗄 **Quick Facts Transparency**: New Ideas in the Sciences

Review & Assess

Close

Guide students in a discussion of 19th-century achievements in science, medicine, and the social sciences.

Review

🖥 **Online Quiz**, Section 2

Assess

SE Section 2 Assessment

📄 **Progress Assessment**: Section 2 Quiz

📄 **Alternative Assessment Handbook**

Reteach/Intervene

📄 **Interactive Reader and Study Guide**, Section 2

💿 **Interactive Skills Tutor CD-ROM**

Answers

Reading Skills *the first sentence; supporting sentences detail the contributions Freud made to the study of human behavior*

Reading Check *Ideas of human behavior and societies led to new fields of study, including psychology, archaeology, anthropology, and sociology.*

670

New Ideas in Science	Natural selection and evolution Modern atomic theory Mendeleyev's periodic table Radioactivity Atomic nucleus Theory of relativity
Advancements in Medicine	Pasteurization and vaccination Anesthetics Antiseptics Modern hospitals More training for nurses and doctors
Developments in the Social Sciences	Pavlov's theories of conditioned response Freud's theories of the unconscious Scientific approach to archaeology Anthropology Sociology

READING SKILLS

Identifying Stated Main Ideas Which sentence states the main idea of this paragraph? How do details contribute to the main idea?

Studies of human behavior continued with the work of Austrian-Jewish physician **Sigmund Freud** (FROYD). Freud argued that an unconscious part of the mind contains thoughts of which one is unaware. Hypnotism was one of the techniques Freud used to explore the unconscious with his patients. He wrote his first paper on hypnotism in 1893. Freud also encouraged patients to tell him about their dreams. He felt that repressed thoughts revealed in dreams could cause mental illness. Freud called his method of therapy psychoanalysis.

Other Social Sciences Just as Freud studied individuals, other scientists studied people as members of groups. These scholars were interested in societies, or communities of people who share a common culture.

One field that received much attention was archaeology, the study of the past based on artifacts. Archaeology was not an entirely new field of study. Many early archaeological expeditions, however, had been little more than treasure hunts. Then, starting in the mid-1800s, archaeologists started to take a more scientific approach to their investigations. They carefully recorded all stages of their work and preserved their finds for education, not just for riches.

As more evidence of the human past was unearthed, anthropology became an organized discipline. Anthropology is the study of humanity and human ancestors. Physical anthropologists are interested in how *Homo sapiens* developed as a species over time. In the 1920s cultural anthropology, which deals more with the structures of societies, became a separate field. In general, cultural anthropologists study cultures other than their own.

Closely related to anthropology is sociology, which emerged as a social science in the late 1800s. Sociologists also study people in groups. More often, though, the groups are in their own societies. As part of their work, sociologists examine societies' institutions and sub-groups, such as those organized around racial or ethnic identity, gender, or age.

READING CHECK Draw Conclusions How did new ideas contribute to the social sciences?

SECTION 2 ASSESSMENT

go.hrw.com
Online Quiz
Keyword: SHL LIF HP

Reviewing Ideas, Terms, and People

1. a. Define What are theories?
   b. Explain What did **Albert Einstein** say about the connection between space and time?
   c. Evaluate Why would later discoveries in physics and chemistry depend on Dalton's conclusion?

2. a. Describe How does **pasteurization** affect bacteria?
   b. Draw Conclusions How do you think people's opinion of surgery changed after the development of **anesthetics**?

3. a. Describe How did **Sigmund Freud** contribute to the field of psychology?
   b. Identify Cause and Effect What effect did **Ivan Pavlov's** study of dog behavior have on the study of human behavior?

Critical Thinking

4. Infer Using your notes and a chart like this one, record the effects of key scientific advances.

Advance	Effects

FOCUS ON WRITING

5. Persuasive Imagine you are a scientist in the late 1800s working on cures for diseases. Write a letter to a U.S. senator asking for help with funding for your research. Explain how you think your research will benefit society.

Section 2 Assessment Answers

1. a. plausible general principles offered to explain what has been observed
   b. that one must include time in the study of space
   c. because it showed that atoms of different elements have different size and mass

2. a. destroys bacteria
   b. probably feared it much less

3. a. introduced the idea of the unconscious mind and therapy through psychoanalysis
   b. It suggested that human behaviors are a series of connected conditioned reflexes.

4. evolution—contributed to field of physical anthropology; atoms—led to periodic table, discovery of radioactivity, knowledge of structure of atoms; germs—pasteurization and vaccines; advances in medical care—saved lives, led to more modern hospitals, more physicians and nurses; psychology—led to knowledge of the way human minds work, allowing mental illness to be treated

5. Letters will vary but should include logical reasons for funding research.

Daily Life in the Late 1800s

BEFORE YOU READ

MAIN IDEA

During the late 1800s, cities grew and changed, while education, leisure time activities, and the arts reflected those changing times.

READING FOCUS

1. How did cities grow and change in the late 1800s?
2. What developments affected education, leisure, and the arts?

KEY TERMS AND PEOPLE

urbanization
romanticism
William Wordsworth
Ludwig van Beethoven
realism
Charles Dickens
Leo Tolstoy
Henrik Ibsen
impressionism

 NEW YORK

PI 4.2 Students interpret and analyze documents and artifacts related to significant developments and events in world history.

THE INSIDE STORY

How did a new garment and a new sport give women more freedom? In 1850 American social reformer Amelia Jenks Bloomer wore a startling new outfit in public. Instead of the floor-length skirt that most women wore, Bloomer had on long, baggy pants that showed beneath her short skirt. Although she did not invent this new costume, called bloomers, she helped popularize it.

By the 1890s the term "bloomers" referred to a different version of the outfit—short, baggy pants worn with knee-high stockings. Women often wore bloomers for a new

sport—bicycling. With clothing that allowed freedom of movement and with the availability of bicycles that were light and safe, thousands of women in Europe and the United States began cycling through city streets and parks. Cycling gave women the freedom to leave their homes alone and travel long distances. Although some people claimed that bike riding might be harmful to women's health because of "the organic weakness of women," riding bikes was fun and provided women with a new form of exercise. Women did give up floor-length skirts, but they did not give up their bikes. ◼

Bicyclists on the Digue Ze, Ostend, by Carl Kuechler, 1800s

BIKES AND BLOOMERS

In this illustration, women and men enjoy bicycling along the seashore in Belgium.

671

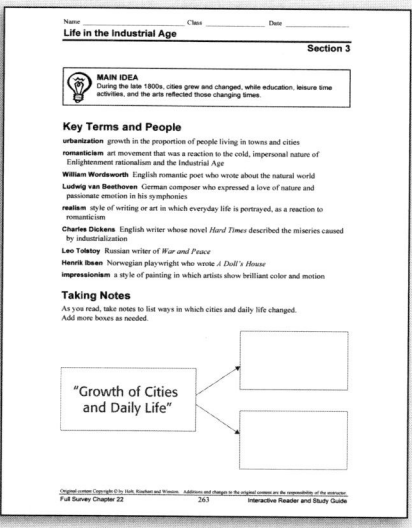

Preteach

Getting Started

Use the **Interactive Reader and Study Guide** to familiarize students with the section content.

📄 **Interactive Reader and Study Guide**, Section 3

Academic Vocabulary

Review with students the high-use academic term in this section.

immigrate move to another country to live (p. 673)

📄 **CRF:** Vocabulary Builder: Section 3

Taking Notes

growth of industrial factories; migration of workers; cities became crowded; unhealthy conditions; increase in education, leisure and arts; improvements in city life; suburbs less crowded, cleaner

Teach the Main Idea

At Level

Daily Life in the Late 1800s

1. **Teach** Ask students the Reading Focus questions to teach this section.

2. **Apply** Have students write a brief summary of the section. Student summaries should include at least two main ideas from under each of the red subheadings.

3. **Review** Review student summaries as a class. Have students identify the points in their summaries that they feel are most important or most interesting. Guide students in a

discussion of the ways in which life changed as a result of urbanization.

4. **Practice/Homework** Have students write a journal entry from the point of view of a teenager in the 1800s. The entry should describe some recent changes in the teenager's daily life. **LS Verbal-Linguistic**

📄 **Alternative Assessment Handbook**, Rubric 37: Writing Assignments

Direct Teach

Reading Focus

1 How did cities grow and change in the late 1800s? *Industrial cities grew rapidly. They required a large workforce to gather raw materials, produce manufactured goods, and distribute those goods, and attracted many people to fill those jobs.*

Cities Grow and Change

Define What is urbanization? *the growth in the proportion of people living in towns and cities*

Contrast How did industrial cities differ from traditional cities? *Traditional cities served political, military, religious, or trade functions. Industrial cities gathered raw materials, manufactured goods, and distributed them.*

Make Judgments Was the enormous growth of cities in the late 1800s a good or bad thing? Explain. *possible answer—a bad thing; cities became overcrowded, and living conditions were not healthy*

History Close-up
New York City in the Late 1800s

Transportation In 1883 the Brooklyn Bridge was completed, linking New York City with Brooklyn across the East River. It was the longest suspension bridge in the world. Urban mass transit improved steadily in the second half of the 19th century. Horse-drawn streetcars were introduced by the 1850s, elevated trains by the 1870s, and electric trolleys by the 1890s. The first subway was opened in 1904.

About the Illustration
This illustration is an artist's conception based on available sources. Historians, however, are uncertain exactly what this scene looked like.

★ Interactive
HISTORY CLOSE-UP

New York City in the Late 1800s

Like many cities of the late 1800s New York was a busy, crowded place. To make city life more pleasant and convenient, the age's new technologies were put to use.

The first elevated trains ran on steam, but they were later converted to electricity.

Streetlights were first used on Broadway. Within a few years, streetlights were common. As a result, after dark the city was safer and more lively.

In 1884 the legislature required that utility lines be placed underground.

672 CHAPTER 22

Cities Grow and Change

New activities like reading by electric light and riding bicycles were signs of the changes that occurred during the Industrial Age. Many of the changes took place in the cities. Throughout the 1800s, much of Europe and the United States experienced rapid **urbanization**—the growth in the proportion of people living in towns and cities. Not only did cities grow, but they underwent a transformation.

Skills FOCUS INTERPRETING VISUALS

1. **Compare and Contrast** Which of the improvements shown were also made in the area where you live?
2. **Draw Conclusions** How would the technological advances shown have affected the daily life of a city's residents?

go.hrw.com
Interactive
Keyword: SHL LIF

Skills Focus: Analyzing Costs and Benefits   Above Level

Social Studies Skill
The Growth of Cities

1. Organize students into small groups. Tell them that it is 1825 and they are industrialists planning a new factory town. Have each group develop a plan for the city, including a map showing the location of the factory, housing, public buildings, and recreational opportunities. Remind students that in 1825 industrialists needed to take into consideration the power needs of factories as well as transportation, recreation, and services that would be available. At the same time,

they needed to try to keep factories profitable and cities affordable.

2. Have volunteers from each group share their plans with the rest of the class.

3. Guide the class in comparing and contrasting the "ideal" cities designed by students with the actual cities that developed during the Industrial Age. **LS Kinesthetic, Visual-Spatial**

Alternative Assessment Handbook, Rubrics 14: Group Activity; and 20: Map Creation

The Industrial City Before the Industrial Age, most cities existed to serve trade, political, military, or religious functions. The industrial city, in contrast, did more. In the industrial city raw materials had to be sent to factories, new products manufactured in the factories, and the products distributed to buyers. To meet these functions, industrial cities needed factories, a large workforce, a reliable transportation network, warehouses, stores, and offices.

One of the first cities to have all these supports for industry was Lowell, Massachusetts. At the heart of Lowell's growth was its textile factories, which employed young women from the surrounding countryside and newcomers from Europe.

Other industries besides textiles fueled the growth of cities. Meat-packing was one of several industries that lured workers to Chicago. As a result, Chicago's population grew from 30,000 in 1850 to 1.7 million in 1900. Another example is Pittsburgh, Pennsylvania, where jobs in the steel industry attracted workers.

Industrial cities were lively, fast-paced places. For example, in growing cities a constant stream of pedestrians competed with electric streetcars and horse-drawn carriages for space on the streets. Merchants advertised their wares by shouting out prices from their doorways. Construction crews produced a constant sound of hammering as they built new banks, office buildings, and homes for the growing population.

With high population density, the health of many city residents suffered. One of the hazards was smoky air from the coal that was burned to run steam engines and to warm homes. London had a special problem with smoke that combined with the fog that is common in damp climates. The word *smog* was coined to describe the thick, choking, lung-burning result. In 1873 a smog episode caused 268 deaths. An 1879 episode lasted for four long months.

Migration to Cities Despite the cities' unhealthy conditions, people kept arriving during the late 1800s. They wanted not just jobs, but also to escape hunger, political oppression, or discrimination.

Just as the goals of the new city residents differed, so did their origins. Some people came to the cities from the countryside. Boatloads of people, though, left their own countries behind and went to cities in a different country. Many Europeans sailed to Latin America, Australia, and other places. But the United States drew the most people.

Between 1870 and 1900, about 12 million people immigrated to the United States. Many came from Ireland, England, Germany, Italy, Russia, and China. In 1890, 42 percent of New Yorkers were foreign-born. Immigrants poured into other major U.S. cities, including Boston, Chicago, and San Francisco, where the newcomers gradually created their own unique communities.

When they first arrived, though, most of the immigrants lived in miserable, crowded conditions. Journalist and photographer Jacob Riis described what he saw in New York's dismal apartment buildings, or tenements.

HISTORY'S VOICES

❝Bedrooms in tenements were dark closets, utterly without ventilation. There couldn't be any. The houses were built like huge square boxes, covering nearly the whole of the lot. Some light came in at the ends, but the middle was always black.❞

—Jacob Riis, *The Battle with the Slum*, 1902

TAKING NOTES
Take notes on the ways in which cities and daily life changed. Add more boxes as needed.

Growth of Cities and Daily Life

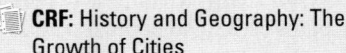
NEW YORK
CC Unit 5-G3f
Urbanization

ACADEMIC VOCABULARY
immigrate to move to another country to live

By the 1880s the city's sky was criss-crossed with telephone wires.

Trolley car lines spurred the development of suburbs. Trolleys also took passengers to holiday spots like Coney Island.

Reading Focus

Cities Grow and Change

Explain Why did suburbs develop? *Public transportation made it possible to move outside a city, where it was less crowded, quieter, and cleaner.*

Summarize How did reforms make cities more livable? *improved sanitation, clean water made cities healthier and cleaner; transportation improved, parks were built*

📄 **CRF:** Primary Source: The Public Park Movement

Info to Know

Leisure Time In the Industrial Age, shorter workdays and higher wages gave people more free time. Team sports became favorite pastimes. As these sports became more popular, increasing numbers of people came to cheer for their team. Families played games together or went bicycling. Trips to the beach, parks, and museums were also popular activities.

Football The teams of the earliest football games usually consisted of whole villages, and the field could cover more than a dozen square miles. The ball was advanced by kicking, punching, and carrying. The game was very violent and could lead to injury and even death. In the 1600s a less violent form of football was played in England in schools, although many authorities thought it too rowdy.

Answers

Reading Check *to work in factories*

The Livable City Eventually, reforms eased the squalid conditions. Improvements were made in cities' infrastructure. For example, cities modernized their water and sewer systems. These improvements also extended to the home. Better plumbing allowed more families to have clean drinking water, toilets, and bathtubs. Sanitation and overall health improved as a result.

Electricity also made homemaking more convenient. In the early 1900s appliances such as vacuum cleaners, refrigerators, and electric stoves became available.

With more people moving to the cities, working and living space became scarce. Constructing taller buildings was one solution. In 1883 architect William Le Baron Jenney designed the first multistory steel-framed building, or skyscraper, in Chicago. It was 10 stories tall. Four years later, the high-speed elevator was perfected. Skyscrapers could get taller still.

Growing populations caused congestion on city streets. Underground railway systems, or subways, helped relieve the crowding. In 1863 London opened the world's first subway line. Other cities followed. For example, the city of Budapest, Hungary, opened its subway in 1896. The original purpose of this subway was so residents could get to a city park easily.

As cities spread out, city planners made an effort to preserve green spaces within the city. In the 1860s Napoleon III created parks in

FOCUS ON NEW YORK

New Yorker Frederick Law Olmsted (1822–1903) is considered the father of American landscape design. Some of his more notable parks are Central Park in Manhattan and Prospect Park in Brooklyn.

Paris to give working people places for healthy recreation. In the United States, Frederick Law Olmsted designed city parks that were equally accessible to all residents.

The Suburbs As cities in Europe and the United States became more congested, their boundaries expanded to include surrounding areas. As a result, people moved out of the cities to new areas called suburbs.

People moved to the suburbs because they were less crowded, quieter, and cleaner than the central city. Public transportation helped suburbs grow. In the early 1800s streetcar and ferry transportation linked cities to the suburbs. Later, suburbs developed along railroad and bus lines.

READING CHECK **Identify Cause and Effect** Why did people migrate to cities?

Education, Leisure, and Arts

With the growth of cities in the 1800s, new educational opportunities developed. In addition, new sports, other leisure activities, and changes in the arts world affected society.

A Day at the Beach

Blackpool, in northwestern England, offered working families a holiday. In the background, the photo shows an observation tower modeled on the Eiffel Tower in Paris and a gigantic Ferris wheel. In the foreground, couples enjoy rides along the beach in horse-drawn carts.

Differentiating Instruction

Learners Having Difficulty

1. Ask students what types of activities they enjoy doing in their spare time. As students mention activities, write them for the class to see.

2. Tell students that people in the 1800s did some of these same activities for fun. After students have read the text titled Education, Leisure, and Arts, ask how people in the 1800s spent their leisure time. As students mention activities, make a new list for students to see.

3. Guide the class in a discussion of the ways in which leisure activities of the 1800s differed from those of today.

4. Have students write a paragraph summarizing the class discussion. Tell students to check their paragraphs for correct grammar, spelling, and punctuation to align them with standard English usage. 🄻🄢 **Verbal-Linguistic**

📄 **Alternative Assessment Handbook**, Rubrics 9: Comparing and Contrasting; and 11: Discussions

Education and Information During the 1800s increased industrialization created a need for a more educated workforce. Factories wanted managers who could read and write and engineers with technical skills. Armed forces grew larger, and military leaders wanted officers who knew about the wider world. Because people became more involved in politics they supported public education as a way to develop informed, patriotic citizens.

After 1870 governments in western Europe and the United States passed laws requiring education for all children. Many countries required only elementary education. Eventually, some governments funded education through high school.

Not all social classes were educated equally, however. Most children of the lower classes stayed in school only as long as the law required. Then, many of them quit school to go to work. However, the establishment of vocational and technical training schools gave some members of the working class more opportunities. For instance, in Tuskegee, Alabama, in 1881, Booker T. Washington founded a private school to train African Americans to be teachers.

Just as education for lower classes lagged behind, so did education for girls. Although more industrialized countries guaranteed free public education, some countries did not require that girls go beyond elementary school. Even in countries that provided basic education for girls, few girls in high schools took the science and math classes that could lead directly to careers in the industrialized world. Because few colleges allowed women to enroll as students, educators who thought women should have more opportunities began founding colleges just for women.

With a more educated populace, more cities began printing newspapers. The new papers expanded their coverage from current events to the arts and sciences. Lively stories published in weekly installments kept readers coming back to follow the adventures of favorite fictional characters. Political cartoons often poked fun at public figures. Because newspapers usually held specific viewpoints, one could choose a newspaper that agreed with a certain political or religious stance. For example, some French papers supported the king, while others supported a republican form of government.

INCREASE IN LEISURE ACTIVITIES

QUICK FACTS

CAUSES

- Higher incomes, more free time
- Public transportation to recreational areas
- Public funding of cultural activities

EFFECTS

- Time for sports: soccer, rugby, football, baseball
- More people enjoying vacation spots and resorts
- More opportunities to hear music, enjoy art

New technology, including the linotype machine and the electric press, improved newspaper printing processes. Reporting of foreign affairs improved when the telegraph made up-to-date coverage possible. Foreign correspondence was just one area within a growing profession—journalism.

Leisure Time As leisure time increased, people had more time to play and watch sports. In Britain, football—known as soccer in the United States—became more popular. Rugby and American football were also developed. Baseball became a popular pastime for troops during the American Civil War and grew quickly as an amateur and professional sport. With the growth of railroads, sports fans could travel to see their favorite teams play.

In fact, railroads allowed more families to enjoy a range of activities. For example, in Britain in the mid-1800s, working-class families could take the train to vacation spots. Seaside resorts such as Blackpool provided entertainment, relaxation, and fresh air.

Cultural activities, too, became available to more people. Before the 1800s musicians usually performed in private homes or at religious services. During the 1800s, though, city governments began building new concert halls and theaters and supporting more orchestras, bands, and choral groups. With public funding, ticket prices were within the budget of more audience members.

READING SKILLS

Identifying Stated Main Ideas In the first paragraph about leisure time, what indicates that the first sentence contains the main idea?

Reading Focus

2 What developments affected education, leisure, and the arts? *factory workers could afford leisure activities; with railroad, people could travel; the arts idealized nature, then turned to realistic works and impressionism; educated workforce developed, which led to an increase in number of newspapers and magazines*

Education, Leisure, and Arts

Compare How are the novels of Dickens similar to photographs? *They are both examples of the realist movement.*

Analyze How did railroads contribute to leisure activity? *They led to the development of tourist resorts and professional sports, as people could travel to watch their favorite teams play.*

Predict What industries besides newspapers might have been affected as the population became increasingly educated? *possible answer—the publishing industry; more people would read books, and books are necessary for schools*

 Quick Facts Transparency: Increase in Leisure Activities

Biography

Émile Zola (1840–1902) Émile Zola was the chief proponent of French naturalism. He applied scientific techniques to his novels, observing characters and their surroundings objectively. He tried to show how heredity and the environment affected his characters and shaped their behavior.

Skills Focus: Identifying Cause and Effect

At Level

Reading Skill
The Importance of Education

1. Remind students that education was not always compulsory, and was once the luxury of those who could afford it. Then guide the class in a discussion of the ways in which education affects their daily lives.

2. Point out to students that life is much more complex today than it was in the 1800s. What skills do they think are needed in today's society and workplaces? How can they best learn those skills?

3. Have students write an essay describing what life would be like today for someone who could not read or write. How would the inability to read and write affect their own lives? Conversely, what kinds of changes could learning to read and write make in their lives?

4. Have volunteers read their essays to the class.
   LS Verbal-Linguistic

   Alternative Assessment Handbook, Rubric 40: Writing to Describe

Answers

Reading Skills *possible answer—It is a general statement; other sentences give details.*

Education, Leisure, and Arts

Recall What was realism? *a movement in the arts that revealed the details in everyday life, no matter how unpleasant*

Interpret What characteristics did the romantic movement value, and why? *love of nature, deep emotions, the individual, the past, and imagination; a response to Enlightenment rationalism and problems of the Industrial Revolution*

● Review & Assess ●

Close

Have students explain how industrialization contributed to urbanization.

Review

 Online Quiz, Section 3

Assess

SE Section 3 Assessment

📋 **Progress Assessment:** Section 3 Quiz

📋 **Alternative Assessment Handbook**

Reteach/Intervene

📋 **Interactive Reader and Study Guide,** Section 3

💿 **Interactive Skills Tutor CD-ROM**

Answers

Reading Check *The arts reflected the struggle between the ways of the past and the new inventions of the Industrial Age.*

676

Just as performances moved from private homes to new spaces, so did art. Museums such as the Louvre (LOOV) in Paris made great works of art available to all. Public libraries also opened their doors. For example, the reading room of London's British Museum opened, making its huge collection of books accessible to scholars.

Changes in the Arts With all the discoveries, inventions, and new ideas of the 1800s, it is no wonder that the world of the arts underwent change as well. Artists, writers, and musicians developed new styles in response to what was going on around them.

A literary and artistic development of the early 1800s was called **romanticism**. With an emphasis on intuition and feeling, the romantic movement was a reaction to Enlightenment rationalism and the early abuses of the Industrial Revolution. Major characteristics of the movement were love of nature, deep emotions, value of the individual, affection for the past, and the importance of the imagination. Political revolutions that swept through Europe in the 1800s released a spirit of liberty and equality that were also common in works of the romantic era.

Poet **William Wordsworth** expressed the romantic spirit in his definition of poetry as "the spontaneous overflow of powerful feelings from emotions recollected in tranquility." In music, nature inspired composers such as German **Ludwig van Beethoven**, who also celebrated human freedom in his work. Among

THE IMPACT TODAY
Original impressionist paintings are still immensely popular—and expensive. For example, in 1990 a painting by Auguste Renoir sold for more than $78 million.

many great romantic painters was Frenchman Theodore Gericault (zhay-REE-KOH), whose scenes of suffering heroes caught the public's attention. William Blake, an English artist and writer, painted scenes of mystical beauty.

In the mid-1800s, a movement known as **realism** developed in reaction to romanticism. The realist movement revealed the details of everyday life, no matter how unpleasant. For example, in his novel *Hard Times* Englishman **Charles Dickens** wrote about the struggles of London's poor. That novel also described pollution, exploitation, and miseries caused by industrialization. In the novel *War and Peace,* Russian writer **Leo Tolstoy** showed that war is chaotic and horrible. Norwegian playwright **Henrik Ibsen** broke new ground in *A Doll's House*. The play revealed the unfair treatment of women within families.

Painters also turned to realism as a reaction against romanticism. Instead of painting imaginary or emotional scenes, they painted ordinary working people as they really lived. Many realist paintings show people of the lower classes as possessing quiet dignity.

Later in the century, beginning in the 1860s, a group of French painters introduced a new way of looking at the world. They started a movement that came to be called **impressionism**. These artists wanted to capture an impression of a scene using light, vivid color, and motion, rather than just showing its realistic details.

READING CHECK Find the Main Idea How did the arts reflect how people viewed the world in the 1800s?

SECTION 3 ASSESSMENT

go.hrw.com
Online Quiz
Keyword: SHL LIF HP

Reviewing Ideas, Terms, and People

1. a. Describe What were industrialized cities of the 1800s like?
   b. Explain How did technological innovations help make cities more livable?
   c. Evaluate Do you think the industrialized cities were better places to live than the countryside in the late 1800s? Why or why not?

2. a. Identify What literary style did **William Wordsworth** follow? What style did **Charles Dickens** follow?
   b. Contrast How did **realism** differ from **romanticism**?
   c. Elaborate How might increased educational opportunities have benefited society in general in the 1800s?

Critical Thinking

3. Identifying Cause and Effect Copy the chart below. Use it and your notes to describe causes and effects of urbanization.

Causes of Urbanization	Effects of Urbanization

FOCUS ON WRITING

4. Persuasive Imagine that you live in a big city in the 1880s. Write a letter to the editor of your local newspaper arguing for or against the development of suburbs.

Section 3 Assessment Answers

1. a. contained factories, transportation network, stores and offices; attracted large workforce; lively and fast-paced; high population density; unhealthy living conditions
b. water and waste systems improved, improving sanitation and health; electricity led to invention of home appliances; taller buildings created more living space; public transportation improved travel; parks enabled recreation
c. possible answer—yes, work was available and life was fast-paced

2. a. Wordsworth—romanticism; Dickens—realism
b. realism—details of everyday life, romanticism —life idealized
c. educated society, stronger workforce

3. causes—growth of industrial factories, migration of workers; effects—crowded cities, unhealthy conditions, increase in education, leisure and arts, improvements in city life

4. Student letters should include details from the section to support their arguments.

Painting

Impressionism

What is it? Several painters caused a sensation in the French art world in the 1860s. They were rebelling against the definition of art promoted by France's official art school, the Academy of Fine Arts. The Academy wanted the subject matter to be clear and the painting method to be realistic. The rebel painters, who shared a style of painting called impressionism, were more concerned about the effects of shadows and light, the use of color, and the suggestion of movement. They tried to capture these effects by painting outdoors, rather than in a studio. They wanted to show an "impression" of the scene rather than an exact record of it, and they experimented with different kinds of brushstrokes to achieve that effect. Although impressionism was controversial when it first developed, it has become one of the best-loved artistic styles of all time.

Why is it important?
• Impressionism helped artists and the general public see the world in new ways.
• The new style freed artists to paint as they wished, not as they were told.

Key characteristics:
Impressionist painters focused on
• everyday life and ordinary people
• outdoor settings
• light, weather, and atmosphere
• visible brushstrokes

Young Girl Lying in the Grass, **by Auguste Renoir**

The scene in this painting by Auguste Renoir is dappled with light and shade, and the outline of the figure is blurry. The combination of these techniques gives the impression of a warm, hazy, summer day.

Claude Monet painted many views of water lilies. The play of light on water was a favorite subject of the impressionist painters.

Banks of the Loing River, **by Alfred Sisley, 1885**

NEW YORK STANDARDS
PI 4.2

Skills Focus — INTERPRETING VISUALS

1. **Summarize** How did the impressionists' style vary from the style that the Academy approved?
2. **Predict** How do you think the impressionists' rebellion affected other artists over time?

Skills Focus: Analyzing Visuals
At Level

Reading Like a Historian Skill
Impressionism

1. Guide students in a discussion of the two paintings shown on this page using the following questions: What similarities do you notice? What differences do you notice? Which key characteristics does each display? What makes both of these pictures examples of impressionism?

2. Have each student choose one of the two paintings and write a poem or song lyrics based on it.

3. Have volunteers share their poems or lyrics with the class. **LS** **Auditory-Musical**

   Alternative Assessment Handbook, Rubrics 9: Comparing and Contrasting; and 26: Poems and Songs

---

The Arts Around the World

Impressionism

Info to Know

Impressionism The term *impressionist* was first used in 1874 by a French art critic, Louis Leroy, in a review of an exhibit of paintings by "The Anonymous Society of Painters, Sculptors, Engravers, etc." The name was suggested by one of the paintings in the show, *Impression, Sunrise,* by Claude Monet. In his satirical review, Leroy argued that the artists were satisfied with the impression given by a few quick brushstrokes and had left their paintings unfinished. In spite of its original negative connotations, the term impressionism stuck. The term was also used to describe a style of classical music that emerged in the late 1800s. It is most strongly identified with the music of French composer Claude Debussy. The dreamlike qualities of Debussy's music reminded critics of impressionist paintings. Other composers, including Maurice Ravel, Paul Dukas, and Albert Roussel, adopted the impressionist style.

Answers

Interpreting Visuals 1. *The French Academy wanted subject matter to be clear and the painting method to be realistic. Impressionists were more interested in capturing an "impression" of a scene rather than an exact record of it.* **2.** *possible answer—It probably freed other artists from the constraints of painting in an officially accepted style, allowing them to give free rein to their imaginations.*

677

Word Help

list a field or arena designed for jousting
recoil jump back
visor front piece of a helmet

Info to Know

Caspar David Friedrich Friedrich is considered to be one the greatest German Romantic artists. His landscapes and seascapes usually depict a sense of the helplessness of man in the face of nature. He is known for capturing quiet, isolated landscapes, and his scenes of nature usually show some element of mystery or awe, as in the painting on this page.

Activity **Analyzing Visuals** Have students write a short description of the view shown in Friedrich's painting *Wanderer Above the Sea of Fog*.

Teaching Tip

Before reading the excerpt from *Ivanhoe*, you might wish to review the chapter, Early Middle Ages, so that students can refresh their memories about kings, knights, and jousting.

Artistic Responses to the Industrial Age

Historical Context These four documents show examples of two major artistic movements of the Industrial Age—romanticism and realism.

Task Study the selections and answer the questions that follow. After you have studied the documents, you will be asked to write an essay analyzing why writers and artists responded to the Industrial Age in various ways.

DOCUMENT 1

Wanderer Above the Sea of Fog, by Caspar David Friedrich, 1818

A German Painter's View

Caspar David Friedrich was one of Germany's foremost artists in the early 1800s. The painting shown is one of his most famous. But Friedrich did not just paint. He also wrote about painting. On the issue of subject matter, Friedrich had this to say:

> The artist should paint not only what he sees before him, but also what he sees within him. If, however, he sees nothing within him, then he should also refrain from painting that which he sees before him.

DOCUMENT 2

A Medieval Tale

Sir Walter Scott wrote several novels set during the Middle Ages. One of the most famous, *Ivanhoe*, was published in 1819. It relates the adventures of bold knights, fair ladies, and wicked nobles. In the passage here, the author describes the scene as a tournament, or contest between knights, begins.

The trumpets had no sooner given the signal, than the champions vanished from their posts with the speed of lightning, and closed in the centre of the lists with the shock of a thunderbolt. The lances burst into shivers up to the very grasp, and it seemed at the moment that both knights had fallen, for the shock had made each horse recoil backward upon its haunches. The address of the riders recovered their steeds by use of the bridle and spur; and having glared on each other for an instant with eyes which seemed to flash fire through the bars of their visors, each . . . received a fresh lance from the attendants.

Recognizing Bias in Primary Sources

Above Level

Prep Required

Reading Like a Historian Skill
Realism and Romanticism

1. Prepare copies of a short excerpt or scene from a novel written in the style of realism for students. Works by Charles Dickens, such as *Hard Times,* work well for this activity.

2. Have students read the excerpts, and then rewrite the scene in a romantic style. Rewrites can take the form of poems, scenes for a play, or prose.

3. Have volunteers share their writings with the class. Then guide students in a discussion of

the differences between the two styles. Which style do they prefer? Which style do they feel has less bias?

4. Have students reread the excerpt from Scott and explain if they believe it is a biased or factual account of a joust. **LS** **Verbal-Linguistic**

   Alternative Assessment Handbook, Rubrics 9: Comparing and Contrasting; and 41: Writing to Express

DOCUMENT 3

A French Painter's View

Gustave Courbet (koor-BAY) painted common people he saw in the French countryside. The painting here is titled *Girls Sifting Corn*. Like Friedrich, Courbet had something to say about an artist's subject matter:

"An *abstract* object, invisible or nonexistent, does not belong to the domain of painting."

"Show me an angel and I'll paint one."

Girls Sifting Corn, by Gustave Courbet, 1855

DOCUMENT 4

A Norwegian Playwright's View

Henrik Ibsen's 1883 play *An Enemy of the People* focuses on Dr. Stockman, a man who has found that his town's public baths are badly polluted. He feels that people should be alerted to the danger. However, because the baths are a major source of income, the townspeople agree that Dr. Stockman must be silenced. In fact, they insist that he be declared "an enemy of the people." In this excerpt, Stockman defends himself at a public meeting and attacks the townspeople's way of thinking.

No, it's ignorance and poverty and ugliness in life that do the devil's work! In a house that isn't aired and swept every day—my wife Katherine maintains that the floors ought to be scrubbed as well, but that's debatable—anyway—I say in a house like that, within two or three years, people lose all power for moral thought and action. Lack of oxygen dulls the conscience. And there must be a woeful dearth of oxygen in the houses of this town, it seems, if the entire solid majority can numb their consciences enough to want to build this town's prosperity on a quagmire [swamp] of duplicity and lies.

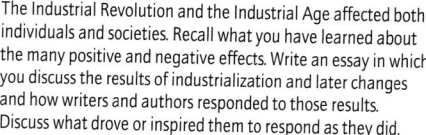

READING LIKE A HISTORIAN

DOCUMENT 1

a. Explain To which movement did Friedrich belong? What elements in the painting provide clues?

b. Infer What connections can you make between the quote from Friedrich and the scene in the painting?

DOCUMENT 2

a. Categorize How does Scott's choice of words show that he wrote within the romantic movement?

b. Develop How might a realist writer have described the scene? Provide examples to illustrate your answer.

DOCUMENT 3

a. Explain How does Courbet's choice of subject matter indicate the movement he helped found? How does the style of painting indicate the movement?

b. Compare and Contrast How do Courbet's statements about subject matter compare to Friedrich's statements?

DOCUMENT 4

a. Identify According to Dr. Stockman, what does "the devil's work"?

b. Support a Position Defend or dispute this statement: "Ibsen probably thought that the new middle class was too pleased with its own success." Support your argument.

DOCUMENT-BASED ESSAY QUESTION

The Industrial Revolution and the Industrial Age affected both individuals and societies. Recall what you have learned about the many positive and negative effects. Write an essay in which you discuss the results of industrialization and later changes and how writers and authors responded to those results. Discuss what drove or inspired them to respond as they did.

See **Skills Handbook**, pp. H25–H26

LIFE IN THE INDUSTRIAL AGE **679**

679

Visual Summary

Review and Inquiry Organize students into groups of three. Have each group prepare a visual and written summary of the New Ideas of the Industrial Age, including technology, science and medicine, and daily life. Have volunteers share their work with the class.

Quick Facts Transparency: Visual Study Guide: Life in the Industrial Age

Review Key Terms and People

1. Samuel Morse
2. Ludwig van Beethoven
3. anesthetic
4. Guglielmo Marconi
5. Louis Pasteur
6. Marie Curie
7. Albert Einstein
8. impressionism
9. immigrate

Comprehension and Critical Thinking

10. a. light bulb, electric motors, generators, light sockets, first permanent electric power plant
b. markets for goods increased, travel time decreased, transportation costs declined, low-cost products became available, new products became available
c. possible answer—Communication improved dramatically so that diplomats could talk to each other, resolve conflicts and problems quickly, rather than waiting for weeks for mail to arrive.

11. a. heating liquids and foods to high temperatures to kill bacteria and prevent fermentation; destroys bacteria that cause disease
b. first systematic arrangement of chemical elements; revealed unknown patters among elements, and gaps showed that some elements had yet to be discovered
c. that human behavior may be a series of connected conditioned reflexes

---

VISUAL STUDY GUIDE

QUICK FACTS

New Ideas of the Industrial Age

Technology
- Faraday and electrical power
- Swan, Edison, and the lightbulb
- Bessemer process
- Expansion of railroads
- Steamships
- Benz, Daimler, Ford, and cars
- Wright Brothers and the airplane
- Morse and the telegraph
- Bell and the telephone
- Marconi and the radio
- Edison and the phonograph

Science and Medicine
- Darwin and evolution
- Dalton and atomic theory
- Mendeleyev and periodic table
- Curies and radioactivity
- Einstein's theories
- Pasteur's fight against disease
- Anesthetics and antiseptics
- Pavlov, Freud, and the mind
- Advances in archaeology
- Anthropology and sociology

Daily Life
- Growth of industrial cities
- Migration to cities
- Improvements in utilities
- Skyscrapers, subways, parks
- Growth of suburbs
- More education and newspapers
- Sports, other uses of leisure time
- Public museums and libraries
- Romanticism
- Realism
- Impressionism

Key Events of the Industrial Age

1803 ■ John Dalton develops modern atomic theory.
1830 ■ Railroad links Manchester and Liverpool.
1831 ■ Michael Faraday discovers connection between magnetism and electricity.
1835 ■ Charles Darwin's *Beagle* diary describes discoveries made about animals on voyage.
1842 ■ Crawford W. Long performs surgery using ether as anesthetic.
1844 ■ Samuel Morse sends telegram.
1871 ■ Dmitri Mendeleyev's periodic table reveals patterns among elements.
1873 ■ London smog kills 268 people.

1876 ■ Bell and Watson invent the telephone.
1881 ■ Booker T. Washington opens school.
1883 ■ First skyscraper is built in Chicago.
1885 ■ Carl Benz builds three-wheeled vehicle.
　　　 ■ Pasteur develops vaccine against rabies.
1891 ■ Trans-Siberian Railroad construction starts.
1893 ■ Sigmund Freud publishes first paper on use of hypnotism.
1898 ■ Curies discover polonium and radium.
1900 ■ Paris Exhibition displays power of electricity.
1903 ■ Wright Brothers fly at Kitty Hawk.
1908 ■ Henry Ford announces the Model T.

Review Key Terms and People

Identify the correct term or person from the chapter that best fits each of the following descriptions.

1. invented the telegraph and a code for sending messages by telegraph
2. great German composer of the romantic movement
3. a drug that dulls pain
4. Italian who invented the radio

5. French scientist who used his knowledge of germs to develop vaccines against anthrax and rabies
6. scientist who died because of her research with radioactivity
7. scientist whose new theories about the universe disagreed with those of Sir Isaac Newton
8. artistic style that used light, movement, outdoor settings, and ordinary people as subject matter
9. to take up residence in a new country

---

12. a. the growth in the proportion of people living in towns and cities; new factories in cities attracted millions of workers, who left the countryside to work in the factories
b. Romanticism is an idealized view of life, as writers and painters imagined life might or could be; artists of the realism movement showed realistic, often harsh details from everyday life.
c. possible answer—Not all social classes were educated equally. Education for lower classes and girls lagged behind.

Reading Skills

13. the first sentence, especially the phrase, "...scientists that came after him discovered additional elements that fit into the periodic table."

Comprehension and Critical Thinking

SECTION 1 *(pp. 659–664)*

10. a. Summarize What were Thomas Edison's contributions to advances in technology?

b. Explain How did the expansion of railroads affect commerce?

c. Predict How might the invention of the telegraph have affected global diplomacy?

SECTION 2 *(pp. 666–670)*

11. a. Identify What is pasteurization?

b. Explain Why was Mendeleyev's chart of elements important?

c. Draw Conclusions What did Pavlov's experiment with dogs seem to indicate about people?

SECTION 3 *(pp. 671–676)*

12. a. Recall What is urbanization, and why did it increase during the 1800s?

b. Analyze Why did some artists and writers turn to romanticism?

c. Make Judgments What is one way that advances of the 1800s did not apply equally to all people?

Reading Skills

Identifying Stated Main Ideas *Read the passage below from this chapter. Then answer the question that follows.*

"As Mendeleyev had predicted, scientists that came after him discovered additional elements that fit into the periodic table. For example, in France in 1898 chemists Marie and Pierre Curie discovered polonium and radium. The Curies also concluded that certain elements release energy when they break down. Marie Curie called this process radioactivity."

13. Which statement in this passage expresses the main idea of the paragraph?

Using the Internet

go.hrw.com
Practice Online
Keyword: SHL LIF

14. The chapter discusses just a few of the advances of the Industrial Age. Use the keyword to explore the Internet for other inventions and discoveries. Choose one and research it fully. Then create a report that includes information on the person(s) responsible for the discovery, the process he or she went through to make the discovery, and graphics that help explain it to a nonexpert audience.

Analyzing Primary Sources

Reading Like a Historian *The excerpt below is from the records of a doctor who treated the poor people of Manchester, England, during an outbreak of cholera, a devastating intestinal disease.*

❝I had requested the younger members of the staff, charged with the visitation of the outpatients of the infirmary, to give me the earliest information of the occurrence of any cases indicating the approach of cholera. I had a scientific wish to trace the mode of its propagation [origin], and to ascertain if possible by what means it would be introduced into the town. My purpose also was to discover whether there was any, and if so what, link or connection between the physical and social evils, to which my attention had been so long directed.❞

—Sir James Kay-Shuttleworth,
The Moral and Physical Condition of the Working Classes Employed in the Cotton Manufacture in Manchester, 1832

15. Draw Conclusions What was an important piece of information about cholera that doctors did not yet know in 1832?

16. Elaborate Think about what you learned in this chapter and the previous one about the effects of the Industrial Age. What do you think Sir Kay-Shuttleworth meant by "physical and social evils"?

✎ **WRITING FOR THE SAT**

Think about the following issue.

The development of railroads, steamship lines, automobiles, and air travel during the late 1800s and early 1900s has been called the Transportation Revolution.

17. Assignment: Think about the events and trends throughout your study of world history that have been characterized as revolutions. Some were quick and violent, while others happened over many years and were relatively peaceful. What qualities do these two types of revolutions have in common? Do the changes in transportation qualify as a revolution? Why or why not? Write an essay in which you develop your position on this issue. Support your point of view with reasoning and examples from your reading and studies.

● Answers ●

Using the Internet

14. Go to the HRW Web site and enter the keyword shown to access a rubric for this activity.

KEYWORD: SHL LIF

Analyzing Primary Sources

15. Doctors wanted to know how cholera was introduced into towns.

16. possible answer—He was probably referring to problems that were caused by rapid expansion of towns and cities, including child labor, illiteracy, and unhealthy living and working conditions.

Writing for the SAT

17. Students should discuss the meaning of the term revolution, and how changes in transportation dramatically changed commerce, trade, and travel. A rubric for the activity is provided in **CRF:** Writing for the SAT.

HOLT

History's Impact

▶ **Video Program: Life in the Industrial Age**
See the Video Program Teacher's Guide for the answer to the closing question.

Review and Assessment Resources

Review and Reinforce

📄 **CRF:** Chapter Review

📊 **Quick Facts Transparency:** Visual Study Guide: Life in the Industrial Age

🔊 **Spanish Chapter Summaries Audio CD Program**

OSP **Holt PuzzlePro:** Quiz Show for ExamView

💿 **Quiz Game CD-ROM**

Assess

📄 **PASS:** Chapter Test, Forms A and B

📄 **Alternative Assessment Handbook**

OSP **ExamView Test Generator**, Chapter Test

💿 **Differentiated Instruction Modified Worksheets and Tests CD-ROM:** Chapter Test

HOAP **Holt Online Assessment Program** (in the Premier Online Edition)

Reteach/Intervene

📄 **Interactive Reader and Study Guide**

📄 **Differentiated Instruction Teacher Management System:** Lesson Plans for Differentiated Instruction

💿 **Differentiated Instruction Modified Worksheets and Tests CD-ROM:** Chapter Test

💿 **Interactive Skills Tutor CD-ROM**

go.hrw.com
Online Resources

KEYWORD: SHL TEACHER

Chapter 23 Planning Guide

Reforms, Revolutions, and War

Chapter Overview	Reproducible Resources	Technology Resources
CHAPTER 23 pp. 682–709 **Overview: In this chapter, students will learn about the reforms that took place in Europe and the Americas during the 1800s. They will also study the causes and effects of the Civil War.** KI 2, 3, 4; PI 2.5, 3.1, 3.2, 3.3, 4.2 See pp. T32–T55 for a detailed correlation to the New York State Core Curriculum for Global History and Geography and the New York Learning Standards.	**Differentiated Instruction Teacher Management System:** • Pacing Guide • Lesson Plans for Differentiated Instruction **Interactive Reader and Study Guide:** Chapter Summary* **Chapter Resource File*** • Writing About History • Social Studies Skill • Chapter Review **World History Outline Maps**	OSP **New York One-Stop Planner CD-ROM:** Calendar Planner **Live Ink© Online Reading Help** **Student Edition on Audio CD Program** **Differentiated Instruction Modified Worksheets and Tests CD-ROM** **World History Primary Source Library CD-ROM** **History's Impact: World History Video Program (VHS/DVD):** Reforms, Revolutions, and War
Section 1: **Reforms in the British Empire** **The Main Idea:** During the 1800s Great Britain passed many democratic reforms that changed the way people lived and worked. PI 3.2, 3.3	**Differentiated Instruction Teacher Management System:** Section 1 Lesson Plan* **Interactive Reader and Study Guide:** Section 1 Summary* **Chapter Resource File*** • Biography: Sir Apirana Tupura Ngata • Literature: *A Vindication of the Rights of Woman*	**Regents Review Transparency:** Section 1* **Map Transparency:** European Possessions, 1800* **Quick Facts Transparency:** British Reforms*
Section 2: **Revolution and Change in France** **The Main Idea:** During the 1800s opposing groups in France struggled to determine what kind of government France would have—a republic, a constitutional monarchy, or an absolute monarchy. PI 2.5	**Differentiated Instruction Teacher Management System:** Section 2 Lesson Plan* **Interactive Reader and Study Guide:** Section 2 Summary* **Chapter Resource File*** • Vocabulary Builder: Section 2 • Biography: Gustave Eiffel	**Regents Review Transparency:** Section 2*
Section 3: **Independence in Latin America** **The Main Idea:** Revolutionary ideas took hold in Latin America as colonies fought for independence from Europe. PI 3.1	**Differentiated Instruction Teacher Management System:** Section 3 Lesson Plan* **Interactive Reader and Study Guide:** Section 3 Summary* **Chapter Resource File*** • Vocabulary Builder: Section 3 • Biography: José Martí	**Regents Review Transparency:** Section 3* **Map Transparency:** Independence in Latin America* **Quick Facts Transparency:** Causes and Effects of Revolution in Latin America*
Section 4: **Expansion and War in the United States** **The Main Idea:** As the United States began to expand west, conflicts erupted over territory and slavery. PI 2.5, 4.2	**Interactive Reader and Study Guide:** Section 4 Summary* **Chapter Resource File*** • Vocabulary Builder: Section 4 • Biography: Harriet Tubman • Primary Source: The Secession of South Carolina • History and Geography: Slavery Divides States	**Regents Review Transparency:** Section 4* **Map Transparency:** Westward Expansion of the United States* **Quick Facts Transparency:** Causes and Effects of Westward Expansion*

HOLT
History's Impact
World History Video Program (VHS/DVD)
Reforms, Revolutions, and War

Review, Assessment, Intervention

- **Global History and Geography Regents Test Prep Workbook**
- **Quick Facts Transparency:** Reforms, Revolutions, and War*
- **Spanish Chapter Summaries Audio CD Program**
- **Progress Assessment Support System (PASS):** Chapter Test*
- **Differentiated Instruction Modified Worksheets and Tests CD-ROM:** Modified Chapter Test
- **OSP New York One-Stop Planner CD-ROM:** ExamView Test Generator (English/Spanish)
- **HOAP Holt Online Assessment Program (HOAP),** in the Holt Premier Online Student Edition

- **PASS:** Section 1 Quiz*
- **Online Quiz:** Section 1
- **Alternative Assessment Handbook**

- **PASS:** Section 2 Quiz*
- **Online Quiz:** Section 2
- **Alternative Assessment Handbook**

- **PASS:** Section 3 Quiz*
- **Online Quiz:** Section 3
- **Alternative Assessment Handbook**

- **PASS:** Section 4 Quiz*
- **Online Quiz:** Section 4
- **Alternative Assessment Handbook**

Power Presentation with Video CD-ROM

Power Presentations with Video are visual presentations of each chapter's main ideas. Presentations can be customized by including Quick Facts charts, images and maps from the textbook, and video clips.

Holt Online Learning

go.hrw.com
Teacher Resources
KEYWORD: SHL TEACHER

go.hrw.com
Student Resources
KEYWORD: SHL REF

- Document-Based Questions
- Interactive Multimedia Activities

- Current Events
- Chapter-Based Internet Activities
- and more!

Holt Premier
Online Student Edition
Complete online support for interactivity, assessment, and reporting
- Interactive Maps and Notebook
- Homework Practice and Research Activities Online

CHAPTER 23 PLANNING GUIDE

Before You Teach

The Big Picture

Peter N. Stearns

Currents of Reform The aftermath of the French and American revolutions spawned a number of movements to broaden social and political reform. New ideas about human improvability and equality, social tensions generated by expanding industrialization, and efforts by newly vigorous conservatives to forestall further change created the context for a variety of new efforts on both sides of the Atlantic. Four key cases, each with roots early in the 19th century, important in their own right, illustrate the larger processes involved.

Britain and France The British adopted the reform route, beginning with the gradual expansion of voting rights from 1832 through the rise of feminism toward the century's end. British politics also contended with demands from Ireland, Canada and Australia. Patterns of revolution resumed in France in 1830, with the uprising of 1848 and then the establishment of the Third Republic after 1871. Changes in education and some social reform followed from political change, along with new efforts to resolve old tensions between church and state. Britain and France can be usefully compared: why reform in one, revolutions in another, and did the long-term results point essentially in the same directions?

Latin America While Haiti ventured a genuine and important revolution, much of Latin America produced wars for independence. The causes of these wars can be compared with the causes of reform and revolution in Europe, as can the goals. But independence movements must be seen as somewhat different from revolution. Political independence ushered in a new era in Latin American history, even though the dreams of many leaders foundered on ensuing territorial divisions and frequent political instability.

The United States Reform impulses in the United States showed in the advent of Jacksonian democracy, dramatic expansion of education, and some social reform. Great energy also went into territorial expansion, with results that did not always mesh easily with the reform impulses. Slavery focused the most important set of political and social issues, and ultimately the Civil War responded to the bitter divisions involved.

Recent Scholarship

The abolition of slavery was one of the key developments in 19th-century world history. Seymour Drescher's *From Slavery to Freedom: Comparative Studies in the Rise and Fall of Atlantic Slavery* (1999) focuses both on the extended geography and chronology of emancipation, and at basic causes. His essays chart the beginning of the process, through attacks on West Indian slavery and the slave trade—attacks closely associated with the age of revolution and reform. He also treats later emancipations, which became such a central part of United States and Latin American history. Drescher considers many factors in the emancipation process, but highlights the rise of a new kind of humanitarian ideology, also closely linked to the revolutionary era but capable of spreading more widely in place and time. Several sections also treat what happened to workers after slavery ended.

Differentiating Instruction

 Differentiated Instruction Teacher Management System
- Pacing Guide
- Lesson Plans for Differentiated Instruction

 Interactive Reader and Study Guide

 Spanish Chapter Summaries Audio CD Program

 Student Edition on Audio CD Program

⊙ **Differentiated Instruction Modified Worksheets and Tests CD-ROM**
- Vocabulary Flash Cards
- Modified Vocabulary Builder Activities
- Modified Chapter Review Activity
- Modified Chapter Test

OSP One-Stop Planner CD-ROM
- ExamView Test Generator (English/Spanish)
- PuzzlePro
- Quiz Show for ExamView
- Transparencies and Videos

TE Differentiated Activities in the Teacher's Edition
- Arts and Culture of the Victorian Era, p. 687
- France's Road to Democracy, p. 692
- Brazil's Steps to Independence, p. 699
- Charting the Expansion of U.S. Territory, p. 702

Reading Like a Historian
Sam Wineburg

Haitian Independence Drawing inspiration from the American Revolution, in 1797 the former slave Toussaint L'Ouverture and his force of black and mulatto soldiers set out to cast off French rule on the island of Saint Domingue, present-day Haiti.

Despite his capture by the 20,000-strong force sent by Napoleon to quell the rebellion, and his imprisonment in France's Jura Mountains, L'Ouverture predicted that his brethren in bondage would soon be free. Some 7,000 French and an estimated 200,000 to 300,000 Haitian deaths later, L'Ouverture was proven right. On January 1, 1804, the Republic of Haiti was born.

One might assume that the two western hemisphere countries that had overthrown European rule—one against the British, the other against the French—would have much in common. But from the start, Haiti's neighbor to the north cast a suspicious eye on this nation of former slaves. The young American government—still under the Washington administration—provided aid ($726,000 for the purchase of guns and ammunition) to French planters to suppress the revolt.

The author of the Declaration of Independence, Thomas Jefferson, believed that it would be against American interests for former slaves to achieve self-government, fearing that if they did they would send "black crews, & supercargoes & missionaries" to the southern states to foment rebellion. Jefferson wrote, "If this combustion can be introduced among us under any veil whatever, we have to fear it."

American Policy As president, Jefferson did more than fear. He sought to isolate the black nation. American policy toward the newly independent Haiti was summarized by Jefferson's Secretary of the Treasury Albert Gallatin: "San Domingo is a French colony, recognized as such by the United States and by every European nation, a colony in a state of rebellion against the mother–country." Continuing to trade with Haiti would be "altogether illegal."

With the help of Congress, Gallatin's stance became law. On February 28, 1806, President Jefferson signed a trade ban, putting an embargo on commerce with Haiti. In so doing, Jefferson supported his son-in-law, John W. Eppes, congressman from Virginia, who argued that American businessmen should have little to do with a race that Americans needed "to depress and keep down."

Congress hoped that an isolated Haiti might become so desperate that it would seek the protection of its former French rulers. This didn't happened. The only lasting effect of the trade ban (which disintegrated four years later—Haitian sugar was too valuable) was that it "firmly established American hostility toward the black republic," in the words of historian Donald R. Hinkey.

Americans wanted Haitian sugar but southern lawmakers could not tolerate establishing relations with a nation of slaves that rose up and killed many of their masters. It wasn't until after the outbreak of the Civil War—when it was no longer necessary to placate the south—that Congress finally recognized Haiti and the hypocrisy of denying it the very rights that Americans claimed in 1776.

Chapter Main Ideas

Section 1 During the 1800s Great Britain passed many democratic reforms that changed the way people lived and worked.

Section 2 During the 1800s opposing groups in France struggled to determine what kind of government France would have—a republic, a constitutional monarchy, or an absolute monarchy.

Section 3 Revolutionary ideas took hold in Latin America as colonies fought for independence from Europe.

Section 4 As the United States began to expand west, conflicts erupted over territory and slavery.

🔖 New York Standards

Key Idea 2 Establishing timeframes, exploring different periodizations, examining themes across time and within cultures, and focusing on important turning points in world history help organize the study of world cultures and civilizations.

Key Idea 3 Study of the major social, political, cultural, and religious developments in world history involves learning about the important roles and contributions of individuals and groups.

Key Idea 4 The skills of historical analysis include the ability to investigate differing and competing interpretations of the theories of history, hypothesize about why interpretations change over time, explain the importance of historical evidence, and understand the concepts of change and continuity over time.

Key to Differentiating Instruction

Below Level

Basic-level activities designed for all students encountering new material

At Level

Intermediate-level activities designed for average students

Above Level

Challenging activities designed for honors and gifted and talented students

Standard English Mastery

Activities designed to improve standard English usage

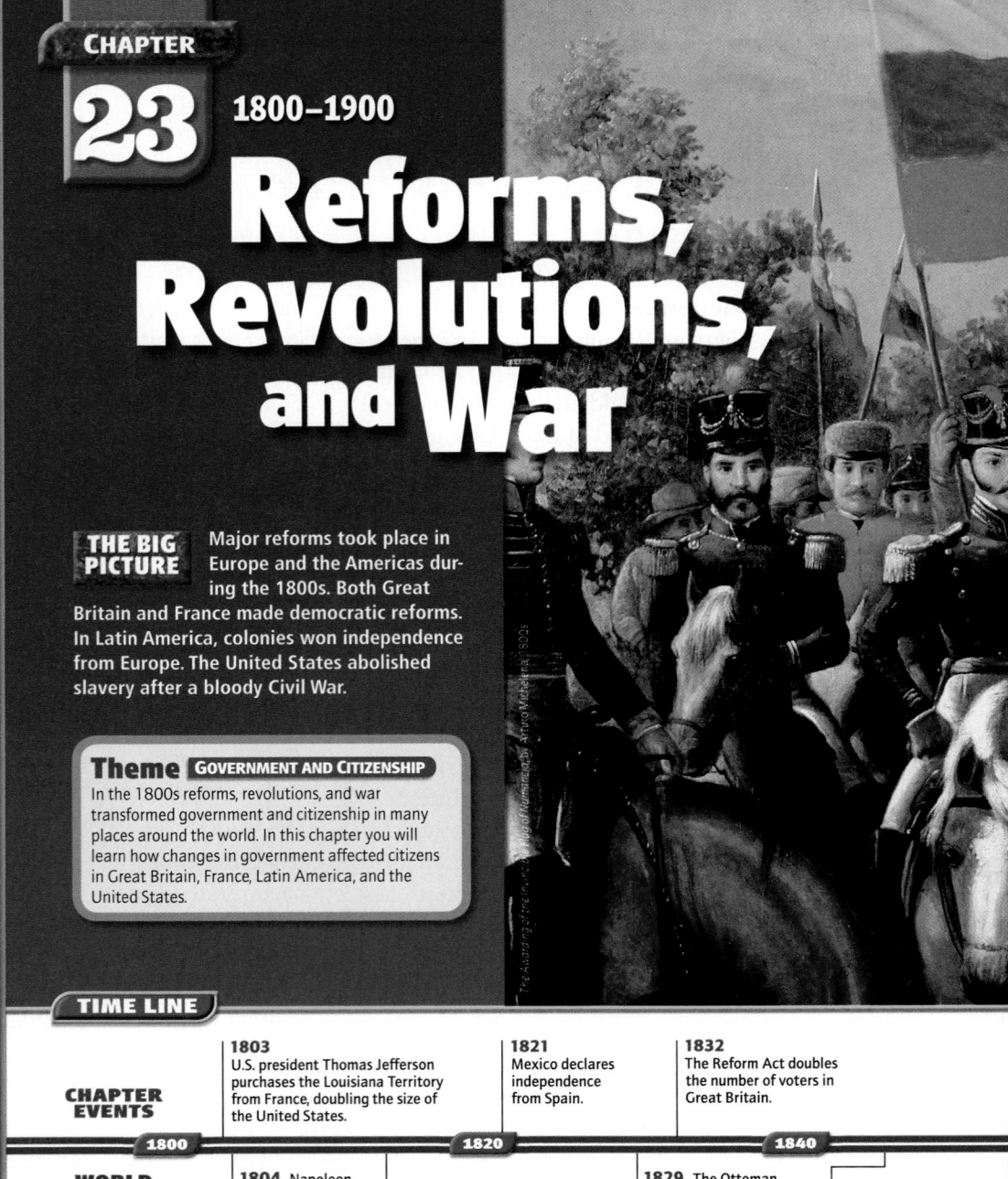

CHAPTER

23 1800–1900

Reforms, Revolutions, and War

THE BIG PICTURE Major reforms took place in Europe and the Americas during the 1800s. Both Great Britain and France made democratic reforms. In Latin America, colonies won independence from Europe. The United States abolished slavery after a bloody Civil War.

Theme GOVERNMENT AND CITIZENSHIP

In the 1800s reforms, revolutions, and war transformed government and citizenship in many places around the world. In this chapter you will learn how changes in government affected citizens in Great Britain, France, Latin America, and the United States.

TIME LINE

CHAPTER EVENTS

1803 U.S. president Thomas Jefferson purchases the Louisiana Territory from France, doubling the size of the United States.

1821 Mexico declares independence from Spain.

1832 The Reform Act doubles the number of voters in Great Britain.

1800 **1820** **1840**

WORLD EVENTS

1804 Napoleon is crowned emperor of France.

1812 Egyptian forces capture Mecca and Medina.

1829 The Ottoman Empire recognizes Greece's independence.

1852 The Republic of South Africa is formed.

682 CHAPTER 23

Introduce the Chapter

At Level

Reforms, Revolutions, and War

1. Remind students that the Industrial Revolution changed life profoundly. Not only was it accompanied by rapid urbanization, but it also brought about revolutions in science, medicine, transportation, and communication.

2. Organize students into small groups. Have each group prepare a list of possible changes or reforms—both political and social—that they would expect to come about as a result of the Industrial Revolution. Have volunteers from each group share their lists with the class.

3. Guide the class in a discussion of the ideas presented.

4. Tell students that in this chapter they will learn about the wars, revolutions, and reforms that helped shape the modern world.
LS Interpersonal

📖 **Alternative Assessment Handbook**, Rubrics 11: Discussions; and 14: Group Activity

Reading like a Historian

This painting shows Simón Bolívar and members of the Venezuelan army after they defeated Spanish troops at the Battle of Carabobo on June 24, 1821. Bolívar is shown congratulating one of his generals by presenting him with a flag of liberation.

Analyzing Visuals How did the artist make Simón Bolívar the focal point of this painting? Explain your answer.

See **Skills Handbook**, p. H26

1861
The Civil War begins in the United States.

1863
U.S. president Abraham Lincoln signs the Emancipation Proclamation, freeing slaves in the Confederate states.

1860 ——————— 1880

1864 The Taiping Rebellion in China leaves 20 million Chinese dead.

REFORMS, REVOLUTIONS, AND WAR **683**

• **Chapter Preview** •

HOLT
History's Impact
► **Video Program: Reforms, Revolutions, and War**
See the Video Teacher's Guide for strategies for using the video segment.

Reading Like a Historian

Simón Bolívar Simón Bolívar was born into an aristocratic Venezuelan family of Spanish descent. Raised in wealth and privilege, Bolívar received an excellent education, in the course of which he was influenced by the thinking of John Locke, Thomas Hobbes, and the French writers of the Enlightenment. He led popular revolutions against Spanish rule in what is now Bolivia, Colombia, Ecuador, Peru, and Venezuela. Today Bolívar is known throughout Latin America as El Libertador—"The Liberator."

Explore the Time Line

1. What did the Reform Act accomplish? *doubled the number of voters in Britain*

2. When was Napoleon crowned emperor of France? *1804*

3. How did the United States double in size? *Thomas Jefferson bought the Louisiana Territory from France.*

4. What did the Emancipation Proclamation do? *freed the slaves in the Confederate states*

Info to Know

An Early Revolutionary Among the first serious rebellions against Spain's rule was an Indian uprising in the Viceroyalty of Peru in 1780. Led by Tupac Amarú, who claimed descent from an Inca emperor of the same name, a poorly armed force of more than 10,000 Indians attacked the city of Cuzco. Although Tupac was captured the revolt continued and spread to Bolivia.

Make Judgments Why do you think claiming descent from an Inca emperor would have helped Amarú's cause? *possible answer —It would have made others more likely to follow him.*

go.hrw.com
Online Resources

Chapter Resources:
KEYWORD: SHL REF
Teacher Resources:
KEYWORD: SHL TEACHER

Answers

Reading Like a Historian *possible answer—The artist depicted Bolívar on a white horse to make him the focal point of the painting. Bolívar is also shown in brighter light than the other figures in the painting.*

Geography Starting Points

The British Empire In 1897 Queen Victoria celebrated her Diamond Jubilee—60 years on the throne of Great Britain. Her empire comprised one-fourth of the earth and over 400 million people. British influence was evident in virtually every country on Earth. Today little remains of the British Empire, but Britain's legacy is still apparent. Capitalism was a British invention, and English has become the international language for business and culture. Britain's successor on the world stage, the United States, continues to export the message of democracy that was first learned from the British.

Primary Source

"If France were to establish itself permanently in North Africa, to penetrate to central Africa, to make its influence felt in the entire Sahara and to win the [Western] Sudan; if in these immense regions where only fanaticism and brigandage [plundering by roving bands] reign today, it were to bring—even at the price of spilled blood—peace, commerce, tolerance, who could say this was a poor use of force? … Having taught millions of men civilization and freedom would fill it with the pride that makes great peoples."
—Gabriel Charmes

🗝 **Map Transparency:** European Possessions, 1800

📖 **World History Outline Maps**

✳ **Interactive Map:** European Possessions, 1800

GEOGRAPHY Starting Points

★ Interactive
EUROPEAN POSSESSIONS, 1800

Britain still possessed a large area of North America.

NORTH AMERICA — CANADA

UNITED STATES

GREAT BRITAIN

EUROPE

FRANCE

PORTUGAL SPAIN

Spain controlled a large part of the Americas.

ATLANTIC OCEAN

PACIFIC OCEAN

AFRICA

Portugal controlled territory in Africa and South America.

BRAZIL

SOUTH AMERICA

| 0 | 1,000 | 2,000 Miles |

| 0 | 1,000 2,000 Kilometers |
Miller cylindrical projection

■ British
■ French
■ Spanish
□ Portuguese

ASIA AND THE PACIFIC WORLD

INDIA
PHILIPPINES
PACIFIC OCEAN
INDIAN OCEAN
AUSTRALIA
Sydney

| 0 | 2,000 Miles |
| 0 | 2,000 Kilometers |
Miller cylindrical projection

Starting Points In 1800 Great Britain, France, Spain, and Portugal controlled territories around the world. Most of the Americas was colonial territory that provided valuable natural resources to European nations.

1. **Analyze** How do you think Spain was able to control much of Latin America?

2. **Predict** How might the people in far-away colonies like India react to being ruled by a European country?

🔊 **Listen to History**

Go online to listen to an explanation of the starting points for this chapter.

go.hrw.com
Keyword: SHL REF

Skills Focus: Analyzing Maps [At Level]

Social Studies Skill
European Possessions in 1800

1. Have students compare the map on this page with a map of the world in 1900. Guide the class in a discussion of the differences using the following questions as a guide: What happened to the great colonial empires? Which empires virtually disappeared? Which empires expanded greatly? How would having an empire affect the ruling nation? How would being part of an empire affect a colony?

2. Have each student write an essay describing how history might have been different if Spain, Portugal, France, Great Britain, and other European nations had *not* built empires.

3. Have volunteers read their essays to the class.
   LS Visual-Spatial, Verbal-Linguistic

📝 **Alternative Assessment Handbook**, Rubrics 21: Map Reading; and 40: Writing to Describe

---

Answers

Geography Starting Points

1. *possible answers—may have signed treaties with other European nations; may have used force to defend colonies in Latin America;* **2.** *possible answer— They probably resented being controlled by a country so far away.*

684

SECTION 1
Reforms in the British Empire

BEFORE YOU READ

MAIN IDEA

During the 1800s Great Britain passed many democratic reforms that changed the way people lived and worked.

READING FOCUS

1. How did social and political reforms change life in Britain during the early 1800s?

2. What reforms helped to shape the Victorian Era?

3. What changes transformed the British empire?

KEY TERMS AND PEOPLE

Queen Victoria
Victorian Era
Benjamin Disraeli
suffrage
Emmeline Pankhurst

NEW YORK

PI 3.2 Students explain the dynamics of cultural change and how interactions between and among cultures have affected various cultural groups.

PI 3.3 Students examine the social/cultural, political, economic, and religious norms and values of cultures.

THE INSIDE STORY

What did British women have to endure to gain the right to vote? Some British women took extreme measures in the their fight for voting rights. In the late 1800s and early 1900s, hundreds of British women protested Parliament's refusal to grant women voting rights through criminal acts. They broke windows, set fires, and assaulted police officers. As a result, British police arrested the women and brought them to the Holloway prison in London. In prison, some of the women went on hunger strikes and refused to eat. They thought they would have to be released from prison if they starved themselves. But to their surprise, instead of releasing them, prison officials force fed them, holding the women down and sticking feeding tubes up their noses.

Some British citizens protested this harsh treatment. As a result, Parliament passed an act that allowed women who were sick from hunger to leave prison to recover. Once they were well, the police would then take them back to the prison. Still, this act ensured that the women could not use hunger strikes to shorten their prison times. ◼

STARVING FOR THE VOTE

A group of British women celebrate their release from Holloway prison in 1908. ▶

REFORMS, REVOLUTIONS, AND WAR **685**

Teach the Main Idea

At Level

Reforms in the British Empire

1. **Teach** Ask students the Reading Focus questions to teach this section.

2. **Apply** Guide students in a discussion of the ways in which democracy changed in the British Empire during the 1800s. Why is it significant that a British possession, New Zealand, was the first nation in which women gained the right to vote? Have students make a time line of the major voting reforms that led to universal adult suffrage in 1928.

3. **Review** Review student lists as a class, writing each reform for students to see.

4. **Practice/Homework** Britain has been called the "mother of democracies" and the "mother of nations." Have students write a brief essay based on material in this section explaining why they think those nicknames either fit or do not fit. **LS Visual-Spatial, Verbal-Linguistic**

Alternative Assessment Handbook, Rubrics 11: Discussions; and 43: Writing to Persuade

Preteach

Getting Started

Use the **Interactive Reader and Study Guide** to familiarize students with the section content.

Interactive Reader and Study Guide, Section 1

Academic Vocabulary

Review with students the high-use academic term in this section.

liberal supporter of political and social reform (p. 686)

CRF: Vocabulary Builder: Section 1

Taking Notes

Social—Factory Acts of 1833 and 1839, abolition of slavery; Political—Reform Act of 1832, some self-government granted to British possessions; Voting—voting reforms of 1867–1885 give more men of all classes the right to vote, New Zealand becomes the first country in which women gain the right to vote, British women gain right to vote on the same basis as men in 1928

go.hrw.com
Online Resources
KEYWORD: SHL REF
ACTIVITY: The Settling of Australia

❶ How did social and political reforms change life in Britain during the early 1800s? *reformed parliamentary representation, expanded voting rights; abolished slavery, improved conditions of workers, legalized trade unions*

Social and Political Reforms

Recall Why were some British prevented from voting? *They were poor, did not meet property requirements.*

Evaluate What was the significance of the People's Charter? *It was a petition sent to Parliament in 1839 demanding a number of additional reforms, such as voting rights for all men and a secret ballot. Although it was rejected by Parliament, Chartists gained wide support, and by the end of the century Parliament had passed many of its reforms.*

TAKING NOTES

Take notes on the three types of reforms discussed in this section.

Reforms	
Social	
Political	
Voting	

NEW YORK

CC Unit 5-G3g Responses to industrialization (legislative reform)

ACADEMIC VOCABULARY

liberal supporter of political and social reform

Social and Political Reforms

Before the 1800s Britain was dominated by the interests of wealthy landowners and aristocrats. During the 1830s, however, industrialization led to rapid changes in society. The growth of factories created a new class of workers, but these new industrial workers were not well represented in government. Recognizing the changing times, some British citizens began to call for social and political reform.

Reform Act of 1832 The growing prosperity of the working and middle classes produced by the Industrial Revolution in Britain led to greater demands for political reform. In 1800 landowning aristocrats made up most of Parliament. Some industrial cities, such as Birmingham and Manchester, had no representatives at all. Throughout Britain, only wealthy male property owners could vote. Catholics, Jews, and other minority groups could hold few political offices. In addition, members of Parliament's House of Commons were not paid for their services, so public office was largely restricted to men of great wealth.

By the 1830s, however, demands for reform became too strong to ignore. In Britain, as in the rest of Europe, liberals were challenging the old aristocratic and conservative order. Unrest increased throughout the country as ordinary people demanded greater political participation. Finally, Parliament agreed to change the electoral laws.

The Reform Act of 1832 gave industrial cities representation in Parliament for the first time. The bill also gave the vote to middle-class men, which increased the number of eligible voters by about 50 percent and significantly reduced the power of the aristocracy. However, political leaders continued to assume that only men with property and education would be responsible voters. Consequently, the bill stated that only men with a certain amount of property could vote. This requirement effectively prevented many working-class men from voting. Furthermore, British law continued to exclude women from voting.

Sadler and the Factory Act At the same time Parliament was debating the Reform Act of 1832, one of its members set out to investigate the treatment of children in Britain's textile factories. This member of Parliament, Michael Sadler, showed the harmful conditions endured by child workers—including physical mistreatment, long hours, and low wages.

In Sadler's report, one former child worker, who had worked in a mill in the early 1830s, remembered what it was like to work 13-hour days as a young boy.

Themes Through Time

Women's Suffrage

SOCIETY It was not until the late 1800s and early 1900s that women began to receive the right to vote. Before that, women fought to gain equal voting rights with men. Today, women exercise the freedom to vote in democratic countries around the world.

1792 Mary Wollstonecraft publishes a book advocating women's rights in Britain.

1848 Elizabeth Cady Stanton and Lucretia Mott organize the first women's rights convention in Seneca Falls, New York.

1800 — 1900

1888 Supporters of women's voting rights from Europe and the United States meet in Washington, D.C.

1893 New Zealand becomes the first country to grant women voting rights.

Skills Focus: Analyzing Alternative Points of View [At Level]

Reading Like a Historian Skill
Chartists

1. Guide the class in a discussion of the demands made by the People's Charter using the following questions as a guide: What demands did the Chartists make? Do any of their demands seem radical or unreasonable? Why do you think the Chartists did not request voting rights for women as well as for men?

2. Tell students that they are newspaper editors in 1839 who oppose the People's Charter. Have each student write an editorial giving reasons why the provisions of the People's Charter should not be passed by Parliament.

3. Have volunteers read their editorials to the class. **LS Verbal-Linguistic**

📖 **Alternative Assessment Handbook**, Rubrics 11: Discussions; and 43: Writing to Persuade

---

❝My school life came to an end when I was about eight years old . . . I now went to work at John Sharpe's mill at the bottom of the town and close to the school I had left . . . We could count whole families of children who worked with us who had gone to an early grave.❞

—Thomas Wood, child mill worker, quoted in *Useful Toil*

Because of Sadler's report, Parliament passed the Factory Act in 1833. This act limited the working hours of children in textile factories. The act made it illegal for teenagers to work more than 12 hours a day. In addition, children between the ages of 9 and 13 had to receive two hours of schooling a day.

Other Reforms As workers gained more rights, the British Parliament also passed other social reforms. In 1833 Parliament abolished slavery in Great Britain and all of the British Empire. However, the Slavery Abolition Act did not immediately free slaves. For another four years, slaves over the age of six remained only partly free. In addition, the act stated that the British government would compensate slave owners depending on how many slaves they freed. Parliament also passed new public health and crime laws to improve living conditions in industrial cities.

Chartism By 1839 many people still could not vote. To remedy this problem, a group called the Chartists worked for universal manhood suffrage: voting rights for all men.

The Chartists got their name from the People's Charter, a petition sent to Parliament in 1839. The People's Charter demanded voting rights for all men, vote by secret ballot, annual elections, and pay for representatives in Parliament. The secret ballot was important because it meant people could not be intimidated to vote in a certain way. Pay for representatives in Parliament meant that working people could become members.

Parliament rejected the People's Charter. In response, the Chartists gained wide popular support and staged uprisings, including one large revolt in 1848. Based on the number of signatures on the 1848 petition, there may have been several million Chartist supporters.

Although the Chartists did not see immediate results of the petition they sent to Parliament, they did draw attention to their cause. By the end of the 1800s, many reforms in the original People's Charter had been passed in Parliament.

READING SKILLS
Identifying Implied Main Ideas What is the main idea of this paragraph?

READING CHECK Compare How did the demands of Chartism compare to the voting reforms passed in 1832?

1914 Activist Emmeline Pankhurst is arrested in London for speaking out on women's rights.

1920 American women gain the right to vote with the passage of the Nineteenth Amendment.

2006 Kuwaiti women vote for the first time in their country's national election.

2000

Skills Focus **UNDERSTANDING THEMES**

Identify Cause and Effect What early events in the history of the women's suffrage movement affected voting rights for women around the world?

REFORMS, REVOLUTIONS, AND WAR **687**

Differentiating Instruction

Above Level

Advanced Learners/Gifted and Talented

Research Required

Background: Tell students that Queen Victoria's reign was not only marked by political and social reforms and economic progress, but also by the development of a distinct culture.

1. Have students use reliable primary and secondary sources to search for information on the arts and culture of the Victorian Era.

2. Have students make a collage or multimedia presentation based on their findings. Presentations may either focus on a particular aspect of Victorian culture, such as architecture, furniture, fashions, art, literature, religion, or morality, or they may take a more general approach.

3. Have volunteers share their presentations with the class.

4. Guide students in a discussion of Victorian culture based on the presentations.
LS Visual-Spatial

Alternative Assessment Handbook, Rubrics 22: Multimedia Presentations; and 30: Research

---

❷ What reforms helped to shape the Victorian Era? *voting rights expanded for men, secret ballot created*

Victorian Era Voting Reforms

Recall What was Queen Victoria's attitude toward women's suffrage? *She was opposed to it.*

Summarize What reasons did Disraeli give for believing that women should have the right to vote? *Women were considered capable of other responsibilities connected with both church and state.*

Predict Do you think that the Women's Social and Political Union's use of destructive means will help or hurt the cause of women's suffrage? Explain. *possible answers—may hurt the cause by making women appear to be irrational and their opponents justified; may help the cause by gaining recognition*

🗃 **Quick Facts Transparency:** British Reforms

📄 **CRF:** Literature: *A Vindication of the Rights of Woman*

Info to Know

British Labor Movement Only about 10 to 15 percent of British laborers enjoyed high pay, regular employment, and membership in trade unions during the late 1800s. This so-called "labour aristocracy" —consisting of skilled artisans such as engineers, cotton spinners, printers, and cabinet-makers—provided the leadership of the working class. Although its members generally adopted a lower-middle-class lifestyle, the leadership of radical reform movements frequently came from this "aristocracy."

BRITISH REFORMS

During the 1800s and early 1900s, the British Parliament passed a series of reforms that gave more rights and freedoms to its citizens.

Reform Act of 1832 Redrew political boundaries to give more equal representation in Parliament

Abolition of Slavery, 1833 Abolished slavery in both Britain and its colonies

Factory Acts of 1833 and 1839 Limited the working hours of women and children in factories

People's Charter, 1839 Charter sent to Parliament that called for voting rights for all men and for voting by secret ballot

Voting Reforms, 1867–1885 Several different acts that gave more men of all classes voting rights

Women's Suffrage, 1918 and 1928 Granted women over 30 the right to vote (1918) and all British women the right to vote (1928)

NEW YORK

CC Unit 5-G3g Parliamentary reforms and expansion of suffrage

Victorian Era Voting Reforms

In 1837 **Queen Victoria** became the ruler of Great Britain. Her reign, the longest in British history, lasted until 1901 and is known as the **Victorian Era**. It was a time of great change in Britain, including voting reforms that made the country more democratic. Britain had long been a constitutional monarchy, but the voting reforms of the Victorian Era made it increasingly democratic.

Disraeli and Gladstone During the years 1868–1885, two influential prime ministers, **Benjamin Disraeli** and William Gladstone, were elected prime minister several times. Disraeli was a member of the Conservative party, which wanted to preserve the best traditions of the past. The Conservatives were slow in accepting modern reforms. Gladstone was a member of the Liberal party, which adopted a more progressive approach to solving society's problems.

Voting Rights for Men Disraeli put forth a new reform bill that would extend voting

---

rights to more working men. Passed in 1867, the bill meant about one out of every three men could now vote. Another law created the secret ballot, to ensure voters would not be bribed or intimidated. In 1885 Gladstone pushed through a reform bill that extended voting rights still further.

Women's Suffrage While Gladstone and Disraeli were trying to extend voting rights for men, some members of Parliament were also pushing for women's **suffrage**, or the right to vote. The question of women's rights had first been raised during the Enlightenment. But during most of the 1800s, women were still not seen as equals. They could not own property and they were not even considered the legal guardians of their children.

Many women thought the right to vote could increase their power in society. In contrast, Queen Victoria was against women's suffrage, calling it "mad, wicked folly."

In spite of the Queen's opposition, Disraeli argued in favor of women's voting rights in a speech before the House of Commons in 1866. He argued that if a woman could be queen or own land, she should be able to vote:

HISTORY'S VOICES

❝I say that in a country governed by a woman . . . [and] where a woman by law may be a churchwarden and overseer of the poor—I do not see, when she has so much to do with the state and the Church, on what reasons . . . she has not a right to vote.❞

—Benjamin Disraeli, speech before House of Commons, 1866

Disraeli and other members of Parliament tried to add women's suffrage to the 1867 reform bill. But they did not succeed.

For nearly 40 years, suffragists—people who work to achieve voting rights for women—made little progress, but not from lack of trying. One group of suffragists, led by Millicent Garrett Fawcett, used a gradual approach to winning the vote. They lobbied members of Parliament, signed petitions, and worked on educating the public. But the government largely ignored their efforts.

By the early 1900s, some women grew frustrated with the slow pace of the suffrage movement. **Emmeline Pankhurst**, founder of the Women's Social and Political Union (WSPU),

---

Skills Focus: Analyzing Alternative Points of View   At Level

Reading Like a Historian Skill
Women's Suffrage

1. Review the information in the text about women's suffrage with students. Organize students into two groups. Have one group represent the point of view of British citizens who supported women's suffrage. Have the other group represent British citizens who opposed women's suffrage. Have each group prepare arguments to support its position.

2. Conduct a classroom debate on women's suffrage.

3. Guide the class in a discussion of the results of the debate. What reasons were students able to give for denying the vote to women? Why do they think that Queen Victoria—a woman— would want to deny equal rights to other women? 🅛🅢 **Interpersonal, Verbal-Linguistic**

📄 **Alternative Assessment Handbook,** Rubrics 10: Debates; and 11: Discussions said that in order to achieve reform, "You have to make more noise than anybody else." As the government continued to ignore the issue of women's suffrage, the WSPU adopted more destructive tactics, such as breaking windows and arson. For these acts, many suffragists went to prison.

Finally, in 1918, Parliament granted the vote to women over the age of 30. Not until 1928, however, did British women gain the right to vote on the same basis as men.

READING CHECK **Summarize** What reforms were passed during the late 1800s?

Changes in the British Empire

Beyond Britain, people living in other parts of the British Empire were also moved by the spirit of reform. In the mid-1800s people in Ireland, Canada, Australia, and New Zealand took steps to rule themselves.

Ireland Since 1801 Ireland had been part of the United Kingdom after the Act of Union joined it with England, Scotland, and Wales. Some Irish hated their British rulers, especially British landlords. These landlords owned much of Ireland's land and had the power to evict Irish farmers. In addition, policies created to help British industry hurt Irish agriculture.

Several times in the mid-1800s, the potato crop failed. Because many Irish peasants depended on potatoes as their main food source, famine swept Ireland. The failure of the potato crop left many with no food and no income. Without the money to pay rent, many peasants were evicted from their homes.

HISTORY'S VOICES

❝In many places the wretched people were seated on the fences of their decaying gardens, wringing their hands and wailing bitterly the destruction that had left them foodless.❞

—Father Matthew, Irish priest, in a letter to Prime Minister Trevelyan

NEW YORK

CC Unit 5-G3
Mass starvation in Ireland, growth of Irish nationalism, and global migration

Ireland's Potato Famine

In the early 1800s, about half of Ireland's population depended on potatoes as their main food source. Beginning in 1845, a disease, or blight, struck Ireland's potato crop. As a result, about 1 million people died from starvation or famine-related diseases. To make matters worse, the British government did little to help the starving Irish. *Based on the graph below, when did the Irish population finally stop declining after the famine?*

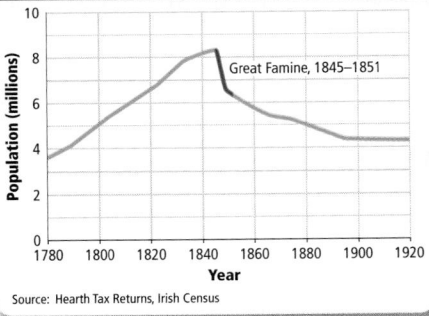

POPULATION OF IRELAND, 1780–1920

Great Famine, 1845–1851

Source: Hearth Tax Returns, Irish Census

This British cartoon from 1846 shows a wealthy British landowner offering potatoes to a poor Irish family. ▼

"Union is Strength," *Punch*, 1846

REFORMS, REVOLUTIONS, AND WAR **689**

689

Changes in the British Empire

Recall In what year were women in New Zealand allowed to vote? *1893*

Infer What kind of society do you think resulted from Britain sending criminals to Australia? *possible answer—probably chaotic and dangerous*

CRF: Biography: Sir Apirana Tupura Ngata

● **Review & Assess** ●

Close

Have the class summarize the growth of democracy in Great Britain.

Review

Online Quiz, Section 1

Assess

SE **Section 1 Assessment**

Progress Assessment: Section 1 Quiz

Alternative Assessment Handbook

Reteach/Intervene

Interactive Reader and Study Guide, Section 1

Interactive Skills Tutor CD-ROM

Answers

Reading Check *potato famine left Irish resentful, 1920: limited self-rule; 1867: British granted some Canadian colonies self-rule; Australia granted self-rule; Maoris in New Zealand exchanged land for self-rule*

Of the 2 million Irish who emigrated to escape the famine, most came to the United States. By 1860 Irish immigrants made up about 25% of New York City's population. Other Irish immigrants settled in Rochester, Syracuse, and Buffalo, New York.

During the years of the famine, about 1 million people starved, and about 1.5 million others emigrated—many to the United States.

Tragically, Ireland continued to export food throughout the famine years. Food shipments left Irish ports for England under heavy guard by British soldiers. British officials encouraged this trade because they believed that interfering with this trade would harm the British economy.

The famine left many Irish people more resentful of British rule than ever. By the 1860s, many Irish began to fight for change. Some wanted independence and staged violent protests. Others struggled for home rule, in which Ireland would govern itself within the United Kingdom. Parliament debated several bills to grant home rule to Ireland in the 1800s, but they did not pass. Ireland did not receive limited self-government until 1920.

Canada Like Ireland, Canada was also controlled by Britain. Britain's colonies in Canada were very different, however. Some were mainly French-speaking, and others were mainly English-speaking. This diversity created a lack of unity in Canada and led to calls for reform. Rebellions in the Canadian colonies in 1837 convinced the British that reform was necessary. In 1838 the British government sent Lord Durham to serve as governor-general to Canada. Durham wanted the Canadian colonies to unite to form "a great and powerful people."

By 1867 the British Parliament united several Canadian colonies and granted them the power to govern themselves. With this act, Canada became a dominion, or a self-governing colony. For Canada, this was the first step toward independence from Britain.

The new dominion continued to expand westward until it eventually reached the Pacific coast. Although Canada was developing its own identity, it remained closely tied to Britain.

Australia and New Zealand Canada became a model for self-government in other British colonies on the other side of the globe—Australia and New Zealand. Since the late 1700s, Britain had used Australia as a place to send its criminals. In the mid-1800s, however, other British colonists, attracted by the discovery of rich copper and gold deposits, began to settle in Australia. In 1901 Britain granted self rule to the Commonwealth of Australia, which established its own parliament but still remained part of the British empire.

In New Zealand, the British government made an agreement with the local Maori people for land in exchange for self rule. In this way, New Zealand became a dominion of Great Britain. In 1893 New Zealand became the first country to give women the vote.

READING CHECK **Compare and Contrast** How did self-rule come about in Ireland, Canada, Australia, and New Zealand?

SECTION 1 ASSESSMENT

go.hrw.com
Online Quiz
Keyword: SHL REF HP

Reviewing Ideas, Terms, and People
1. **a. Recall** What was Chartism?
   b. Analyze Why did the Chartists fail to gain universal manhood suffrage in 1848?
   c. Evaluate Why do you think the first labor reforms dealt with child labor?
2. **a. Identify** Name two reforms of the late 1800s.
   b. Explain What reforms did **Benjamin Disraeli** argue for?
   c. Evaluate Do you think **Emmeline Pankhurst** was right when she said reformers had to "make more noise than anybody else" in order to be successful? Why or why not?
3. **a. Recall** What was the purpose of the Act of Union?
   b. Compare and Contrast How were New Zealand and Australia similar and how were they different?

Critical Thinking
4. **Categorize** Copy the graphic organizer below and use it to list social, political, and voting reforms in Great Britain during the 1800s. Identify how each reform affected people's lives.

Social	Political	Voting

FOCUS ON WRITING

5. **Exposition** Choose a reform discussed in the section and decide whether you think it was a beneficial reform or not. Write a paragraph explaining the reasons for your decision.

Section 1 Assessment Answers

1. **a.** a movement that got its name from the People's Charter, a voting rights petition sent to Parliament in 1839
   b. Parliament rejected the People's Charter.
   c. possible answer— It was a cause that might appeal to all people.
2. **a.** extension of voting rights to all men; creation of the secret ballot
   b. extending voting rights to more working men; women's suffrage

c. possible answer—no, destructive and violent acts may have convinced some people to oppose women's suffrage

3. **a.** to create a United Kingdom joining England, Scotland, and Wales to Ireland
   b. similar: far from Britain; Australia—place to send criminals, immigrants attracted by minerals, granted self-rule in 1901; New Zealand—Maoris exchange land for self rule

4. Reform Act of 1832—eliminated unequal representation in Parliament; extended vote to middle class; abolition of slavery—freed many slaves; public health and crime laws—improved conditions in cities; Factory Act of 1833—limited women and children's hours in textile factories; made working all night illegal; voting reforms—extended vote to men of all classes; created secret ballot

5. Paragraphs should focus on one reform and its benefits or drawbacks.

2 Revolution and Change in France

BEFORE YOU READ

MAIN IDEA
During the 1800s opposing groups in France struggled to determine what kind of government France would have—a republic, a constitutional monarchy, or an absolute monarchy.

READING FOCUS
1. What happened during the Revolution of 1830?
2. What were the results of the birth of the French republic?
3. How did the Dreyfus affair reveal divisions within French society?

KEY TERMS AND PEOPLE
Louis Philippe
Louis Napoleon
Dreyfus affair
anti-Semitism
Theodor Herzl
Zionism

NEW YORK
PI 2.5 Investigate key events and developments and major turning points in world history to identify the factors that brought about change and the long-term effects of these changes.

Combat Before the Hotel de Ville, July 28, 1830, by Victor Schnetz, 1800s

During the Revolution of 1830, Parisians built barricades in the streets. ▲

DOWN WITH THE KING!

THE INSIDE STORY

What led France to revolution again?
The year was 1830. Fifteen years had passed since the Congress of Vienna. Charles X—the last of the French Bourbon monarchs—was now king of France.

Liberals had just won a majority of seats in the French legislature, but Charles was a conservative. To prevent the liberals from exercising power, he passed laws that broke up the legislature and called for new elections. The new laws also limited the freedom of the press.

The king's actions reminded some people of the absolute monarchs who had ruled before the French Revolution. In 1830 the people revolted, and protesters took over the center of Paris. They built large barricades and waved the tricolor flag, shouting "Down with the Bourbons!" Another revolution was underway. ▪

REFORMS, REVOLUTIONS, AND WAR **691**

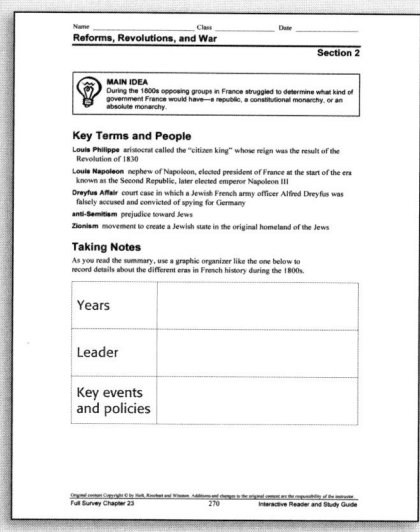

Teach the Main Idea

At Level

Revolution and Change in France

1. **Teach** Ask students the Reading Focus questions to teach this section.

2. **Apply** Have students create an outline of the section using the heads as main points. Have students identify at least two main ideas under each of the blue subheadings.

3. **Review** Review student outlines as a class. Have students identify the points in their outlines that they feel are most important or most interesting. Have students explain why anti-Semitism would emerge so forcefully during the Third Republic.

4. **Practice/Homework** Write the following statement for students to see: It is acceptable for the government to limit civil liberties if more jobs and a stronger France are the result. Have each student write an editorial either supporting or opposing the statement. Student editorials should support opinions with facts and examples from this section.
   LS Visual-Spatial, Verbal-Linguistic

📝 **Alternative Assessment Handbook,** Rubrics 11: Discussions; and 17: Letters to Editors

1 What happened during the Revolution of 1830? *King Charles X abdicated and was replaced by King Louis Philippe, the "citizen king"*

The Revolution of 1830

Explain Why was Louis Philippe known as the "citizen king"? *He was popular with the middle class; he appeared to live like ordinary people; he dressed in long pants rather than the knee-length breeches worn by the nobility.*

Evaluate Why was Metternich so upset with the Revolution of 1830? *A revolution—especially one to overthrow an absolute monarch—went against his reactionary ideals.*

2 What were the results of the birth of the French republic? *King Louis Philippe abdicated. A new republican government formed, with Louis Napoleon as president.*

Birth of a Republic

Recall What positive effects did the Revolution of 1848 have in France? *gave French men the right to vote; created support for republican government; fueled a new women's movement in France*

Explain What was unusual in the way that Napoleon III became emperor? *He was elected by the voters.*

📝 **CRF:** Biography: Gustave Eiffel

Answers

Time Line *1848*

Reading Check *King Charles X abdicated and was replaced by King Louis Philippe, the "citizen king"*

TAKING NOTES

Take notes on the different eras in French history during the 1800s.

Years	
Leader	
Key events and policies	

🗽 **NEW YORK**

CC Unit 5-D3
Revolutions of 1848

The Revolution of 1830

At the end of the Napoleonic era, the Congress of Vienna restored Louis XVIII to the French throne. The French had a constitution and a legislature, but most power remained with the king. The French people would not remain content with their government for long.

A King Abdicates After Louis XVIII died, his brother Charles X inherited the throne. Charles tried to rule as an absolute monarch. But when he suspended the power of the legislature, angry citizens revolted in an uprising known as the Revolution of 1830. Within days they controlled Paris. Charles abdicated, or gave up the throne, and fled to England.

News of the revolution in France quickly reached Klemens von Metternich in Austria. "My life's work is destroyed!" he exclaimed. The reactionary ideals and absolute monarchies he had supported at the Congress of Vienna were beginning to crumble. Metternich feared that revolution threatened to spread throughout the continent. His fears would soon come true.

The Reign of Louis Philippe Having rid the country of King Charles, moderate liberal leaders formed a constitutional monarchy and chose **Louis Philippe** to be the new king. Louis Philippe was an aristocrat who was popular with the middle class. He dressed like them, wearing long pants rather than the knee-length breeches worn by the nobility. Because he appeared to live simply, like ordinary citizens, many French people referred to him as the "citizen king."

Over time, however, Louis Philippe seemed less like a citizen and more like a king. He increased the number of voters—but only by extending the vote to more wealthy citizens. To protect the power of the government, he limited the freedom of the press. His rule became increasingly repressive, and he silenced most people who opposed him.

During Louis Philippe's reign, working people grew poorer, while the middle class and aristocracy became more prosperous. The popularity of the king deteriorated rapidly in 1846 when an economic depression made life even more difficult for all but the wealthiest French people. Discontent would lead France to revolution once more.

READING CHECK Identify Cause and Effect
What were the effects of the Revolution of 1830?

Birth of a Republic

The economic troubles and general unhappiness simmered in France until 1848. Then revolution exploded again, and another republic was born.

The Revolution of 1848 The Revolution of 1848 was sparked when the French government banned a banquet planned by reformers. Angry protesters, both middle and working class, took to the streets.

Louis Philippe quickly abdicated and the monarchy came to an end. The French citizens formed a new government, a republic headed by a president. Voters elected Napoleon's nephew, **Louis Napoleon** as president.

TIME LINE

Changes in France's Government

1830 King Charles X flees France during the Revolution of 1830. Louis Philippe is crowned king.

1848 In the Revolution of 1848, Louis Philippe abdicates and the Second Republic is formed with Louis Napoleon as president.

1852 Louis Napoleon dissolves the National Assembly and is elected emperor by the people.

1870 After the Franco-Prussian War, a democratic government is restored during the Third Republic.

Second Republic · **Second Empire** · **Third Republic**

Skills FOCUS INTERPRETING TIME LINES
In which year did the French government replace a king with a president?

Differentiating Instruction

Below Level

Learners Having Difficulty

1. Organize students into mixed-ability pairs. Have students use the information in their texts to create a chart comparing and contrasting the rise to power, rule, and fall from power of Louis XVI, Napoleon, Louis Philippe, and Louis Napoleon (Emperor Napoleon III).

2. Review student charts as a class. Create a master chart for students to see and fill it in as students call out the points of comparison. Ask students what parallels existed among the rule of these four men.

3. Guide the class in a discussion of France's rocky road to democracy during the 1800s. What do the repeated returns to monarchy indicate about the nation? **LS** Visual-Spatial

📝 **Alternative Assessment Handbook,** Rubrics 7: Charts; and 9: Comparing and Contrasting

Reading like a Historian

The Dreyfus Affair

Interpreting Political Cartoons In 1894 the French government put Alfred Dreyfus, a captain in the French army, on trial for spying for Germany, even though he was innocent. At the time, many French were anti-Semitic, or prejudiced toward Jews. Because Dreyfus was Jewish, he suffered from this anti-Semitism.

To interpret what this cartoon suggests about anti-Semitism, think about

- the details of the cartoon
- the message or point of the cartoon
- the message versus known facts

Skills FOCUS

READING LIKE A HISTORIAN

1. **Details** What details do you see in the cartoon? How do the details dehumanize Dreyfus?
2. **Message** What is the message of the cartoon? How is that message contradicted by facts?

See **Skills Handbook**, p. H28

MUSÉE DES HORREURS n:6

le Traitre!

Alfred Dreyfus is shown as a mythical dragon in this anti-Semitic cartoon.

The French government called Dreyfus *le traitre*, the traitor.

The era that followed was known as the Second Republic; the First Republic had existed during the years between the French Revolution and the reign of Napoleon.

The Revolution of 1848 had far-reaching effects. From that point on, all adult French men had the right to vote and never lost it again. The Revolution of 1848 also created support for republican government, fueled a new women's rights movement, and inspired other revolutions across Europe.

Napoleon III and the Second Empire

The French constitution allowed the president to serve only four years, but Louis Napoleon wanted to remain in office. In 1851 he sent his troops to Paris and arrested members of the National Assembly who opposed him. Then he called for a national vote to decide whether he should be given the power to draft a new constitution. Voters approved the measure.

In another vote the following year, the French people elected him emperor Napoleon III. Thus began the period known as the Second Empire. During the Second Empire Napoleon III made some reforms, such as

increasing voting rights, but he always kept absolute power as emperor. He ruled during a time of economic prosperity and built many miles of railroads, which helped increase trade and improve communications in France.

The Third Republic

In 1870 Napoleon III drew France into a war with Prussia. In the Franco-Prussian War, Napoleon III was captured in battle and surrendered to the Prussians. This shameful defeat led the French Assembly to depose Napoleon and proclaim the Third Republic. The new republic immediately faced a crisis as the Prussians invaded France and began a siege of Paris.

Despite this troubled beginning, the Third Republic made some important reforms. In 1882 the government made primary education available for children between the ages of 6 and 13. In 1884 trade unions were legalized, and by 1900 working hours had been reduced. In addition, in 1906 a new act required employers to give their workers one day off per week.

READING CHECK **Draw Conclusions** Why did the French elect Louis Napoleon as their president?

REFORMS, REVOLUTIONS, AND WAR **693**

Direct Teach

Recent Scholarship

The Dreyfus Affair by Leslie Derfler contains primary sources, reference material and background information that put the affair into context. Derfler examines the tension that developed in France over the incident and addresses the history of anti-Semitism in France.

The Dreyfus Affair by Leslie Derfler. Greenwood Press, 2002.

Info to Know

Louis Napoleon A liberal who was influenced by his uncle Napoleon I's ideas, Louis Napoleon was deeply involved in revolutionary activities. In 1836, he attempted a military coup against King Louis Philippe and was exiled to the United States. Returning to France in 1840 he launched another uprising against the king, for which he was sentenced to life in prison.

Skills Focus: Making Inferences

At Level

Reading Skill
The Dreyfus Affair

1. Review the information in the text and the political cartoon about the Dreyfus affair. Tell students that they are foreign correspondents in the 1890s covering the Dreyfus affair for an American newspaper. Have each student write an article about the affair from the perspective of an American reporter of the time.

2. Have volunteers read their articles to the class.

3. Guide the class in a discussion of the Dreyfus affair using the following questions as a guide:

Could something like the Dreyfus affair have happened in the United States in the 1890s? Could something like that happen today? What other groups have been singled out for similar treatment in the United States? What other instances of scapegoating—fixing the blame on someone other than the perpetrator—can students name? **LS** **Verbal-Linguistic**

Alternative Assessment Handbook, Rubrics 11: Discussions; and 42: Writing to Inform

Answers

Reading Like a Historian 1. *the words "le traitre" (traitor) attached to the dragon's body, the snakes around Dreyfus's head depict him as a monster;* **2.** *The message depicts Dreyfus as a traitor, but he was innocent.*

Reading Check *possible answer— because of his famous name and family legacy*

3 How did the Dreyfus affair reveal divisions within French society? *It was at the bottom of the Dreyfus affair. The controversy split the French into those who sided with Dreyfus, a Jewish army officer, and those who were against him.*

The Dreyfus Affair

Recall What effect did Zola think the Dreyfus affair would have on France? *Anti-Semitism would destroy the liberal France of the Rights of Man.*

Identify Cause and Effect What were some effects of the Dreyfus affair, both inside and outside of France? *in France—set off anti-Semitic riots; united many political groups into just two—supporters and opponents of Dreyfus; outside France—Zionist movement began and gained strength*

Close

Guide the class in a discussion about democracy in 19th-century France.

Review

 Online Quiz, Section 2

Assess

SE Section 2 Assessment

 Progress Assessment: Section 2 Quiz

 Alternative Assessment Handbook

Reteach/Intervene

📄 **Interactive Reader and Study Guide**, Section 2

💿 **Interactive Skills Tutor CD-ROM**

Answers

Reading Check *polarized the French into two groups; inspired Theodor Herzl to begin the movement called Zionism, with the objective of creating a Jewish state in Palestine*

694

The Dreyfus Affair

These reforms did not solve all of France's problems. Divisions continued to split French society. In 1894 these divisions came to a head over the controversial court case known as the **Dreyfus affair**. The Dreyfus affair revealed the extent of **anti-Semitism**, or prejudice toward Jews, in France.

In 1894 Alfred Dreyfus (DRAY-fuhs), a captain in the French army who was Jewish, was falsely accused and convicted of betraying French military secrets to Germany. Even though they knew he was not guilty, anti-Semitic military officers let Dreyfus take the blame rather than admit their error.

A month after Dreyfus was found guilty a public military ceremony was held to humiliate him. The stripes on his uniform were removed, and his sword was broken. A crowd that had gathered to watch shouted, "Kill him! Kill him!" Later evidence suggested that another officer may actually have done the spying. But the second officer, who was not Jewish, was found not guilty in court. A few years later army officers came forward with the real story, but Dreyfus was not cleared until 1906.

The Dreyfus affair divided people in France. One famous French writer, Émile Zola came to Dreyfus's defense. Zola published a letter in 1898 called "J'accuse" (I accuse). This letter accused the French government of anti-Semitism and led the French courts to reopen Dreyfus's case.

NEW YORK
CC Unit 5-F4
Zionism

❝ It is a crime to poison the minds of the lowly and the humble, to exasperate the passions of reaction and intolerance, while seeking shelter behind odious [horrible] anti-Semitism, which, if not suppressed, will destroy the great liberal France of the Rights of Man. ❞

—Émile Zola, "J'accuse"

Zola's letter set off anti-Semitic riots in more than 50 towns. Zola eventually went to trial himself and was found guilty of libel, or publishing false information.

The Dreyfus affair had an important effect on the growth of Jewish nationalism. **Theodor Herzl** was a Hungarian-born Jewish journalist who covered the trial. He was shocked by the anti-Semitism he saw in France and in other parts of Europe. Herzl came to believe that the root of the problem was that Jews in Europe did not have a nation of their own. In 1896 Herzl published *The Jewish State*, which outlined plans for an independent Jewish country developed with the support of the international community. Herzl's work helped spark **Zionism**, a Jewish nationalist movement to re-create a Jewish state in its original homeland.

By the early 1900s, a growing number of Jews were returning to their ancient homeland in the eastern Mediterranean. These settlements encouraged other Jews to follow, and the Zionist movement gained strength.

READING CHECK **Identify Cause and Effect** What were two major effects of the Dreyfus affair?

SECTION 2 ASSESSMENT

go.hrw.com
Online Quiz
Keyword: SHL REF HP

Reviewing Ideas, Terms, and People

1. a. Identify Who was **Louis Philippe**?
 b. Analyze Why was it significant that Louis Philippe wore long pants and lived more simply than other aristocrats?
 c. Develop Why do you think it was important to some people that the new king be a "citizen king"?

2. a. Recall What reforms were made during the Second and Third republics?
 b. Identify Cause and Effect What effect did the Revolution of 1848 have on the rest of Europe?
 c. Evaluate In your opinion, was Napoleon III a good leader for France? Why or why not?

3. a. Describe Describe the events of the Dreyfus affair.
 b. Analyze What is **Zionism** and how was it related to anti-Semitism in Europe?

Critical Thinking

4. Compare and Contrast Use your notes and the graphic organizer below to compare achievements of each era of French government. How do they compare with one another?

Government	Achievement

FOCUS ON SPEAKING

5. Narration Using information in the section, write a short speech that tells the story of the creation of the Third Republic and its goals.

694 CHAPTER 23

Section 2 Assessment Answers

1. a. king of France who replaced Charles X
 b. It made him popular with the middle class.
 c. possible answer—reassured them that he didn't wasn't an absolute monarch.

2. a. all French men gained right to vote, primary education established, trade unions legalized, working hours reduced
 b. It inspired similar revolutions across Europe.
 c. possible answer—yes, had support of people, reign marked by economic prosperity

3. a. French army officer accused of spying for Germany because he was Jewish; charges

polarized France, led to Zionism movement
 b. Theodor Herzl believed anti-Semitism arose because Jews in Europe did not have their own nation.

4. Second Republic—all French men gained right to vote; Second Empire—increased voting rights, built railroads; Third Republic—primary education established; trade unions legalized; working hours reduced

5. Speeches should include details about the Third Republic.

Independence in Latin America

BEFORE YOU READ

MAIN IDEA
Revolutionary ideas took hold in Latin America as colonies fought for independence from Europe.

READING FOCUS
1. How did early struggles in Latin America affect Haiti and other colonies?
2. What events led to independence in Mexico?
3. Who were the key revolutionary leaders in South America, and what did they achieve?

KEY TERMS AND PEOPLE
Toussaint L'Ouverture
creoles
peninsulares
Miguel Hidalgo
José María Morelos
Simón Bolívar
José de San Martín
Pedro I

 NEW YORK

PI 3.1 Analyze the roles and contributions of individuals and groups to social, political, economic, cultural, and religious practices and activities.

FROM SLAVE TO SOLDIER

THE INSIDE STORY

How did a former slave become a military hero?
Toussaint L'Ouverture (Too-san loo-vehr-Toor) was born into slavery in a French colony on the Caribbean island of Hispaniola. As a young man, Toussaint was chosen to be a house servant. He learned to read and write in the slaveholder's home. Toussaint read about Enlightenment philosophers and their ideas of liberty and equality, as well as about military heroes such as Julius Caesar and Alexander the Great.

In 1771 Toussaint was legally freed. His life changed dramatically in 1791 when a major slave revolt broke out on the island. Toussaint helped his former slaveholder escape, then joined the rebellion. Soon afterward, he became a soldier in the Spanish army. During that time Toussaint took the last name L'Ouverture, which means "an opening" in French. Toussaint went on to become a military leader. Well respected for his leadership, he soon commanded a force of more than 4,000 men. ◢

◀ **Toussaint L'Ouverture presents a document to French army officers.**

REFORMS, REVOLUTIONS, AND WAR **695**

Teach the Main Idea

At Level

Independence in Latin America

1. **Teach** Ask students the Reading Focus questions to teach this section.

2. **Apply** Have students make a time line showing the major events from this section, beginning with the slave revolt in Haiti (1791) and ending with San Martín's death (1850).

3. **Review** Review student time lines as a class. Guide the class in a discussion of the events on their time lines. How do the time lines clarify what was happening concurrently in different parts of Latin America?

4. **Practice/Homework** Tell students that Latin American independence movements were inspired by the ideas of Enlightenment philosophers but used the political turmoil in Europe to their advantage. Have students write a short essay explaining what they think was the primary reason that Latin American colonies sought independence when they did, and why. **LS Visual-Spatial, Verbal-Linguistic**

Alternative Assessment Handbook, Rubrics 36: Time Lines; and 43: Writing to Express

---

Preteach

Getting Started
Use the **Interactive Reader and Study Guide** to familiarize students with the section content.

Interactive Reader and Study Guide, Section 3

Name _____ **Class** _____ **Date** _____
Reforms, Revolutions, and War
Section 3

MAIN IDEA
Revolutionary ideas took hold in Latin America as colonies fought for independence from Europe.

Key Terms and People
Toussaint L'Ouverture a former enslaved African who led the Haitian independence movement against the French in Saint Domingue
creoles people of European descent who were born in the colonies
peninsulares colonists born in Spain
Miguel Hidalgo creole priest who was the first to call for Mexican independence
José María Morelos creole priest who led the revolutionary movement in Mexico
Simón Bolívar revolutionary leader known as the Liberator because of his key role in liberating Spain's colonies in South America
José de San Martín revolutionary leader who fought for independence from Spain in Argentina, Chile, and Peru
Pedro I prince from Portugal who declared Brazil independent then became its emperor

Taking Notes
As you read, use a graphic organizer like the one below to record details about independence movements in Latin America in the 1800s.

Full Survey Chapter 23   273   Interactive Reader and Study Guide

---

Academic Vocabulary

Review with students the high-use academic term in this section.

export item sent to other regions for trade (p. 696)

CRF: Vocabulary Builder: Section 3

Taking Notes

Independence Movements—Haiti gains independence in 1804; conflict between creoles and peninsulares in Latin America; Napoleon invades Spain and Portugal in 1807; several Latin American countries gain independence in 1831; Revolutionary Leaders—Miguel Hidalgo, José Maria Morelos, and Agustín de Iturbide, Mexico; Simón Bolívar and José de San Martín, South America; Pedro I, Brazil

Reading Focus

1 How did early struggles in Latin America affect Haiti and other colonies? *Haiti declared independence in 1804 after a war against France. In Spain's Latin American colonies, creoles resented the* peninsulares *and their Spanish rulers.*

Early Struggles in Latin America

Recall Where is Haiti? *on the western part of the island of Hispaniola*

Contrast What was the difference between creoles and* peninsulares? *Creoles—colonists of European descent who were born in the colonies; Peninsulares—colonists who had been born in Spain*

Info to Know

Toussaint L'Ouverture Although there are many sketches and engravings of Toussaint L'Ouverture, there are no existing portraits that were done from life. Many engravings were based on oral descriptions of the man, and some of these drawings reflect the artists' biases.

Teaching Tip

Explain to students that in Spanish America, creoles were people of pure European descent. People of mixed European and native heritage were referred to as mestizos.

Answers

Reading Check *A rebellion of slaves and mulattoes became a revolution against France after Napoleon tried to take power from the revolutionary leader Toussaint L'Ouverture.*

TAKING NOTES

Take notes on independence movements and revolutionary leaders in Latin America during the 1800s.

Independence Movements	
Revolutionary Leaders	

ACADEMIC VOCABULARY

export item sent to other regions for trade

 NEW YORK

CC Unit 5-C4 Independence movements in Latin America (Toussaint L'Ouverture)

Early Struggles in Latin America

By the early 1800s growing tensions among the different ethnic and social groups of Latin American society, as well as reforms imposed by colonial authorities in Europe, were leading to demands for change. The Enlightenment and the American and French Revolutions also inspired some in Latin America to seek greater freedom. Soon new nations began to emerge from colonial domination throughout Latin America.

Haiti Becomes Independent The first Latin American territory to break its ties with Europe was Saint Domingue, located on the western half of the Caribbean island of Hispaniola. Sugar <u>exports</u> had made Saint Domingue one of France's richest possessions. But this prosperity was built on slave labor.

The French Revolution had had a dramatic effect on Saint Domingue. The Declaration of the Rights of Man and of the Citizen gave the right to vote to all free men, including mulattoes, people of mixed African and European ancestry. French settlers on Saint Domingue, however, resisted the new law. As tensions rose, **Toussaint L'Ouverture**, a former enslaved African, led a group of mulattoes and slaves in a bloody revolt against the French settlers.

Toussaint's military and political actions made him a hero in Hispaniola. Back in France, the emperor Napoleon was worried. Napoleon sent a French general to Hispaniola to take control of the colony away from Toussaint. The island forces struggled for months, but in 1802 Toussaint agreed to an armistice. The French broke the agreement and sent him to prison in France, where he died in 1803.

Still the fight for independence continued. In 1804 the revolutionaries of Saint Domingue declared their independence from France and named their new nation Haiti.

Colonies of Spain and Portugal At the same time, another kind of independence movement was beginning to form in the colonies of Spain and Portugal. In the 1800s, Spain controlled most of Latin America, including what is today Mexico and a large portion of Central and South America. Portugal governed the huge colony of Brazil.

696 CHAPTER 23

In the 1700s Spanish kings had made improvements in their colonies, building roads and regulating trade. As a result, the colonies grew in wealth and prosperity. This wealth gave some in Latin America greater access to education and new ideas. As a result, educated colonists read the works of Enlightenment philosophers and learned about revolutions in France and America. One scholar named Antonio Nariño translated the Declaration of the Rights of Man and of the Citizen into Spanish.

At the same time, tensions were growing between two groups in Latin America: **creoles** (KREE-ohlz), people of European descent who were born in the colonies, and **peninsulares** (peh-neen-soo-LAHR-ayz), colonists who were born in Spain. A similar distinction was made between Brazilian-born and Portuguese-born colonists. Creoles were excluded from the highest-level government or church positions, which were reserved for *peninsulares*. Together, creoles and *peninsulares* made up the highest social class; lower on the social scale were people of mixed race, Africans, and Indians.

As their prosperity grew, creoles began to resent the *peninsulares*. Creoles also resented their faraway Spanish rulers. One bishop said that if the Creoles "could empty their veins of the Spanish part of their blood, they would gladly do so."

In 1807 the French emperor Napoleon invaded Spain and Portugal. The king of Spain went to prison and the king of Portugal fled to Brazil. This invasion seriously weakened the power of Spain and Portugal in Latin America. Some creole revolutionaries decided the time was right to fight for independence.

READING CHECK **Sequence** How did Haiti win independence from France?

Independence in Mexico

Napoleon's conquest of Spain was the spark for independence in the colony of New Spain, as Mexico was known at the time. Mexico was a Spanish colony with a mixture of creoles, *peninsulares*, Indians, and people of mixed race.

Father Hidalgo In 1810 in a small town in southern Mexico, a creole priest named Father **Miguel Hidalgo** (mee-GEHL ee-DAHL-goh) made the first public call for Mexican independence.

Skills Focus: Identifying Problem and Solution
At Level

Reading Skill
Colonial Reforms

1. Have students write letters to the king of Spain urging him to make reforms in his American colonies. Tell students to choose a point of view from one of the following classes: creoles, *peninsulares*, or one of the other social classes who made up the population of Spain's American colonies. Student letters should discuss specific problems and propose solutions.

2. Have volunteers read their letters to the class. How well does each letter fit the point of view of the selected social class?

3. Discuss with students how history might have been different if Spain had made changes in the way its colonies were run. **LS** Verbal-Linguistic

Alternative Assessment Handbook, Rubric 43: Writing to Persuade

INDEPENDENCE IN LATIN AMERICA

During the early 1800s, revolutionary leaders Simón Bolívar and José de San Martín led independence movements across South America. Inspired by their efforts, other revolutions flared up across the region, and neither Spain or Portugal could hold onto their empires in the Americas. By 1831 a dozen nations had declared their independence.

LATIN AMERICA, 1790

NEW SPAIN
UNITED STATES
Mexico City
BAHAMAS (U.K.)
CUBA   HISPANIOLA
BRITISH HONDURAS (U.K.)
MOSQUITO COAST (U.K.)
DUTCH GUIANA
FRENCH GUIANA
Caracas
NEW GRANADA
Quito   Bogotá
Lima
La Paz
BRAZIL
PERU
LA PLATA
Santiago
Rio de Janeiro
Buenos Aires

- Spanish
- Portuguese
- Dutch
- French
- British

0   1,000 Miles
0   1,000 Kilometers

UNITED STATES
40°N
MEXICO 1821
Gulf of Mexico
Mexico City
20°N
Tropic of Cancer
BAHAMAS (U.K.)
BRITISH HONDURAS (U.K.)
CUBA (SPAIN)
JAMAICA (U.K.)
HAITI 1804
DOMINICAN REPUBLIC 1844
HONDURAS 1838
GUATEMALA 1838
EL SALVADOR 1838
NICARAGUA 1838
COSTA RICA 1838
MOSQUITO COAST (U.K.)
Caribbean Sea
PUERTO RICO (SPAIN)
Caracas
1812–14
TRINIDAD (U.K.)
BRITISH GUIANA (U.K.)
DUTCH GUIANA (NETH.)
FRENCH GUIANA (FRANCE)
PACIFIC OCEAN
COLOMBIA 1819
VENEZUELA 1830
Bogotá
1819
GRAN COLOMBIA
ECUADOR 1822
Quito
0° Equator
1823–26
PERU 1824
Lima
1820–22
1823–26
La Paz
BOLIVIA 1825
1820–22
BRAZIL 1822
ATLANTIC OCEAN
PARAGUAY 1811
Tucumán
Rio de Janeiro
20°S
Asunción
Tropic of Capricorn
1817–18
ARGENTINE CONFEDERATION 1816
Santiago
URUGUAY 1828
CHILE 1818
Buenos Aires
Montevideo
PATAGONIA
40°S
Falkland Islands (U.K.)

- Independent nations
- **1811** Year of Independence
- San Martín's route
- Bolívar's route
- Major battle

0   500   1,000 Miles
0   500   1,000 Kilometers
Azimuthal equal-area projection

120°W   100°W   80°W   60°W   40°W   20°W

Panel of the Independence, by Juan O'Gorman, 1961

In 1810 Father Miguel Hidalgo inspired Mexicans to fight for independence from Spain.

GEOGRAPHY SKILLS   INTERPRETING MAPS

1. **Regions** Which areas of South America remained under European control in the 1800s?
2. **Movement** Describe the routes of Bolívar and San Martín.

REFORMS, REVOLUTIONS, AND WAR **697**

Direct Teach

Reading Focus

2 **What events led to independence in Mexico?** *Father Hidalgo called for the peasants to revolt against the peninsulares, beginning a revolution in 1810. In 1821, Mexico finally won independence after a revolutionary war when the leader of the royalists, Agustín de Iturbide, switched sides.*

Independence in Mexico

Recall How did Mexico's fight for independence begin? *with a speech by Father Miguel Hidalgo calling the peasants to fight for their independence from the peninsulares*

Evaluate Why do you think the Spanish authorities in Mexico investigated Father Hidalgo for leading discussions of literature and art in his home? *They may have thought the discussions were about Enlightenment ideas, or that they served as a cover for subversive plans.*

🗺 **Map Transparency:** Independence in Latin America

📄 **CRF:** Biography: José Martí

Info to Know

Fanny Calderón de la Barca (1804–1882)
Frances ("Fanny") Erskine Inglis was born in Edinburgh, Scotland, but grew up in the United States. In 1838 she married the Spanish-born Don Angel Calderón de la Barca, who was appointed Minister to Mexico. The historian William H. Prescott assembled her letters from Mexico into a book, which was published in 1843. *Life in Mexico* was so accurate American officers used it as a guide four years later during the Mexican-American War.

Answers

Interpreting Maps 1. *Trinidad, British Guiana, Dutch Guiana, French Guiana;* **2.** *Bolívar began in the north and moved southward; San Martín began in the south and moved northward; the two leaders met in Lima, Peru.*

Reading Focus

Independence in Mexico

Compare Describe the similarities between Hidalgo and Morelos. *Both were priests; both included people of all races and backgrounds in their plans; both were captured and executed by the Spanish.*

Identify Cause and Effect Why did Iturbide change sides in the Mexican war for independence? *There was a liberal revolution in Spain that he thought might reduce his power.*

Evaluate Why do you think Mexico lost so much of its territory so soon after becoming independent? *possible answer—It was too large to be easily governed, especially by inexperienced leaders.*

Info to Know

Agustín de Iturbide An officer in the colonial forces in Mexico, Iturbide supported the Spanish government after his hacienda was sacked by Hidalgo's Indian army. However, he was denied a promotion because he was a creole. Iturbide rethought his loyalties and switched to the rebel side, where he quickly rose to a leadership position. After he was overthrown in 1823, he was bribed to accept exile in Europe. When the payments were not made, he disguised himself and slipped back into Mexico, ignoring the advice of fellow exile José de San Martín to not return. Despite Iturbide's disguise, a soldier recognized him by his style of mounting a house. He was arrested, tried, and shot.

Answers

Faces of History (left) *Bolívar freed Venezuela, helped free Bolivia, and served as president of Gran Colombia.* **(right)** *San Martín liberated Chile by crossing the Andes Mountains and defeating royalist forces.* **(bottom)** *Together, the two leaders helped liberate much of South America from colonial rule.*

698

FACES OF HISTORY **Two Revolutionary Leaders**

Simón BOLÍVAR
1783–1830

Known as the "George Washington of South America," Simón Bolívar was a revolutionary general. In the early 1800s he liberated several South American colonies from Spanish rule.

Beginning in 1811 Bolívar helped free his native Venezuela. He was president of Gran Colombia (present-day Venezuela, Colombia, Panama, and Ecuador) and then Peru. Because Bolívar also helped free Bolivia, the country was named in his honor. Today Bolívar's birthday is a national holiday in both Venezuela and Bolivia.

Summarize What were Bolívar's accomplishments?

José de SAN MARTÍN
1778–1850

José de San Martín was the son of a royal official in the colony of La Plata, which later became Argentina. San Martín was the main leader against Spanish rule in southern South America. By 1821 he had liberated not only La Plata but also Chile and much of Peru. As Spanish resistance continued, San Martín helped fellow revolutionaries such as Simón Bolívar.

San Martín is perhaps best known for skillfully leading his troops into Chile through the difficult terrain of the Andes Mountains. There, he defeated royalist troops and liberated Chile.

Analyze How did San Martín liberate Chile?

Granger Collection, New York

Draw Conclusions What impact did the accomplishments of Bolívar and San Martín have on Latin America?

Hidalgo had a history of challenging authority. He had been investigated by Spanish authorities for leading discussions of literature and art in his home. Hidalgo invited many people to these discussions, including creoles, *peninsulares*, Indians and people of mixed race. Eventually he met creoles who wanted to take power from the *peninsulares*. Hidalgo became a leader and helped to plan a rebellion.

THE IMPACT TODAY

Mexicans celebrate Mexican Independence Day on September 16.

NEW YORK

CC Unit 5-C4 Independence movements in Latin America (causes and impacts)

On September 16, 1810, Hidalgo rang a bell in his home town, calling the members of his church to the churchyard. There he delivered a famous speech calling on peasants to fight for their independence against the Spanish *peninsulares* in Mexico. He shouted, "Death to bad government and death to Spaniards!"

Hidalgo was calling for the peasants to revolt against the *peninsulares*, not against Spain. In fact, in his speech he said he was loyal to the Spanish king. But the Spanish authorities realized Hidalgo was behind the growing revolution. He was captured and executed, but the Mexican independence movement had begun. Hidalgo would later become known as the Father of Mexican Independence.

698 CHAPTER 23

Morelos Continues the Revolution

After the death of Hidalgo, another creole priest, **José María Morelos**, became the leader of the revolutionary movement. He organized a Mexican congress with representatives from many places in Mexico. Morelos wanted all people born in Mexico, whether they were Indian, mixed race, or creole, to be called Americans. He also wanted Mexico to be an independent republic with guaranteed freedoms.

Morelos was a strong military leader. He led troops and took control of parts of Mexico for the independence movement. But eventually he too was captured. The Spanish authorities found him guilty of treason and executed him.

A Creole King for Mexico Not all creoles in Mexico wanted independence from Spain. Some remained royalists, people who were loyal to the Spanish king. One of these creole royalists was a military officer named Agustín de Iturbide (ah-goos-TEEN day ee-toor-BEE-day).

In 1820 the Spanish authorities asked Iturbide to lead a final battle against the revolutionaries. They believed he could end the Mexican independence movement for good.

Skills Focus: Comparing and Contrasting   [Below Level]

Reading Skill
Wars of Independence

1. Have students make a chart comparing and contrasting the wars of independence in Mexico and in South America.

2. Have volunteers use the information from their charts to make a master chart for all students to see. Have students correct their own work as needed.

3. Guide the class in a discussion about the Latin American wars of independence. Ask students why they think the leaders of the independence movements were creoles and not peasants. Which form of government—a monarchy or a republic—would have been the more common choice in those days?

LS Visual-Spatial

Alternative Assessment Handbook, Rubrics 7: Charts; and 9: Comparing and Contrasting

However, that same year a liberal revolution was underway in Spain. Iturbide believed this revolution might take away some of his power, so he decided to switch sides and fight for the Mexican revolutionaries.

Iturbide made a three-part proposal to the leader of the revolution. First, Mexico would gain its independence but would be ruled by a monarch. Second, creoles and *peninsulares* would have equal rights. Third, the Roman Catholic Church would be the official church of Mexico. This independence proposal was very different from the ideas of Hidalgo and Morelos. But after 10 years of fighting, the compromise brought together many different groups, including the creoles and the *peninsulares* and the revolutionaries and the royalists. Both royalist and rebel troops joined Iturbide to win independence from Spain.

In 1821 Mexico declared its independence from Spain. That same year Mexico named as its emperor the creole military leader who had made independence happen. Iturbide became Emperor Agustín I of Mexico.

READING CHECK Compare and Contrast
How were the goals of Hidalgo, Morelos, and Iturbide different, and how were they similar?

Revolutionary Leaders in South America

The revolutions in Haiti and Mexico, as well earlier revolutions in the United States and France, inspired leaders in South America. Soon, independence movements began to form in these colonies, and several capable revolutionary leaders emerged.

Simón Bolívar The most influential leader in the South American independence movement was **Simón Bolívar** (see-MOHN boh-LEE-vahr) He is known as simply "the Liberator" because of his key role in liberating Spain's colonies in South America.

Bolívar was born into a wealthy creole family in what is now Venezuela. He often traveled to Europe and was an admirer of Napoleon's leadership. Once, while in Rome, he made a famous pledge to liberate South America.

In 1811 Venezuela declared independence from Spain. For the next 10 years, Bolívar led a series of military campaigns against Span-

ish forces. Finally, in 1821, Bolívar's troops had defeated the Spanish in most of northern South America.

Bolívar had a dream for the newly independent South America. He wanted to form one large, united country called the Federation of the Andes. That dream, however, never became reality. Bolívar did set up the state of Gran Colombia, which included what are now Venezuela, Colombia, Panama, and Ecuador. But other leaders set up separate countries in Peru, Bolivia, and other places. "America is ungovernable," Bolívar complained.

José de San Martín While Simón Bolívar was fighting for independence in the north, **José de San Martín** was fighting for independence from Spain in the south. San Martín was a soldier who had fought against Napoleon in Spain. Born in Argentina, he returned home when he learned that his country was rising up against Spanish rule. Eventually, San Martín would lead the independence movement not only in Argentina, but in most of southern South America.

READING SKILLS
Identifying Implied Main Ideas What is the main idea of this paragraph?

NEW YORK
CC Unit 5-C4
Simón Bolívar and José de San Martín

PRIMARY SOURCES

Bolívar's Message to the Congress of Angostura

In 1819 Simón Bolívar wrote to members of Congress in the city of Angostura asking for the abolition of slavery.

"Americans by birth and Europeans by law, we find ourselves engaged in a dual conflict: we are disputing with the natives for title of ownership, and at the same time we are struggling to maintain ourselves in the country that gave us birth against the opposition of the invaders . . . As our role has always been strictly passive and political existence nil, we find our quest for liberty is now even more difficult to achieve; for we, having been placed in a state lower than slavery, had been robbed not only of our freedom but also of the right to exercise an active domestic tyranny."

Skills FOCUS **READING LIKE A HISTORIAN**

Draw Conclusions Who is Bolívar referring to when he mentions the "invaders"?

See **Skills Handbook**, p. H25

REFORMS, REVOLUTIONS, AND WAR **699**

Direct Teach

Reading Focus

❸ Who were the key revolutionary leaders in South America, and what did they achieve? *Bolívar and San Martín, Pedro I; Venezuela declared independence in 1811, took 10 years before independence became reality; Argentina won independence in 1816; Bolívar and San Martín led fight for independence in northern and western South America; Pedro I declares Brazil independent in 1822.*

Revolutionary Leaders in South America

Identify What was the Federation of the Andes? *the nation that Bolívar hoped to establish in western South America; would have included Venezuela, Colombia, Ecuador, Peru, and Bolivia*

Contrast How did Bolívar and San Martín's opinions of Napoleon differ? *Bolívar admired Napoleon's leadership, but San Martín had fought against Napoleon's armies in Spain.*

Differentiating Instruction

Below Level

Learners Having Difficulty

1. Copy the sequence chart for students to see. Omit the italicized answers. Have students work individually or in pairs to fill in the steps by which Brazil gained its independence.

2. Guide the class in a discussion of the similarities and differences between the way Brazil and the Spanish colonies gained independence. **LS** Visual-Spatial

   Alternative Assessment Handbook, Rubrics 7: Charts; and 9: Comparing and Contrasting

1807: Napoleon invades Portugal.
↓
Portuguese royal family flees to Brazil.
↓
Prince João changes status of the colony.
↓
Napoleon falls from power.
↓
King João returns to Portugal, leaving Prince Pedro to rule Brazil
↓
1822: Prince Pedro declares Brazil independent
↓
Prince Pedro crowned Emperor Pedro I of Brazil.

Answers

Primary Sources peninsulares

Reading Skills *Despite his establishment of the state of Gran Colombia, Bolívar's dream for an independent South America never became a reality.*

Reading Check *Hidalgo wanted the peasants to revolt against the* peninsulares, *not against Spain; Morelos wanted independence from Spain and an "American" identity to unify all people born in Mexico; Iturbide wanted to create an independent monarchy, give creoles and* peninsulares *equal rights, make the Roman Catholic Church the official church of Mexico*

699

Revolutionary Leaders in South America

Recall What changes came about in Brazil as a result of the king's residence there? *Rio de Janeiro was named capital of the Portuguese empire; Brazil was allowed to trade directly with the rest of the world.*

Identify Cause and Effect What effect did the independence movements in Spain's colonies have on Brazil? *Brazilian colonists wanted their independence, too.*

📦 **Quick Facts Transparency:** Causes and Effects of Revolution in Latin America

---

• Review & Assess •

Close
Have students summarize the paths to freedom that were taken by the nations of Latin America.

Review
🖥 **Online Quiz**, Section 3

Assess
SE Section 3 Assessment

📑 **Progress Assessment:** Section 3 Quiz

📑 **Alternative Assessment Handbook**

Reteach/Intervene
📑 **Interactive Reader and Study Guide,** Section 3

💿 **Interactive Skills Tutor CD-ROM**

Answers
Reading Check *Brazil won independence more smoothly and without violence.*

FOCUS ON NEW YORK
New York honors the heroes of Latin American independence in Central Park in New York City. Statues of Simón Bolívar, José de San Martín, and José Martí stand at the head of the Avenue of the Americas.

After declaring independence for Argentina in 1816, San Martín moved on to Chile. There he helped lead troops over a 15,000-foot summit in the Andes Mountains. The feat helped his forces surprise the Spanish troops and win independence for Chile.

Next San Martín moved on to Gran Colombia. There he met the northern revolutionary leader Simón Bolívar. Historians do not agree on what the two men discussed when they met. What is known is that San Martín resigned his position after the meeting. This left Bolívar in power. San Martín returned to Europe, where he lived until his death in 1850.

Pedro I The story of independence was a bit different in the Portuguese colony of Brazil. When Napoleon invaded Portugal in 1807, the reigning Portuguese monarch John VI and his family fled. They took a long journey to their colony in Brazil, where they lived for more than 10 years. Having the Portuguese monarch in Brazil raised the status of the colony. John VI named the Brazilian city of Rio de Janeiro as the capital of the entire Portuguese empire. He also allowed Brazil to trade directly with the rest of the world, rather than through Portugal.

After a revolution in Portugal in 1820, John VI returned to Portugal. He left his son Pedro to rule Brazil. Then, at about the time that Bolívar and San Martín were liberating the rest of South America, Brazil-ian-born colonists began to protest their colonial status. Brazil wanted independence too. But the transition to independence happened more smoothly in Brazil than anywhere else in Latin America. In September 1822, Prince Pedro simply declared Brazil independent. Soon afterward, he was crowned Emperor **Pedro I** of Brazil. Brazil had achieved independence with very little violence.

READING CHECK **Contrast** In what ways was the independence movement in Brazil different from independence movements elsewhere in South America?

CAUSES AND EFFECTS OF REVOLUTION IN LATIN AMERICA

CAUSES
- Tensions between ethnic and social groups
- The French Revolution and American Revolution
- Limited freedoms under Spanish rule

EFFECTS
- Independence from Spain
- New nations and governments formed
- Ethnic and social groups work together

---

go.hrw.com
Online Quiz
Keyword: SHL REF HP

SECTION **3** ASSESSMENT

Reviewing Ideas, Terms, and People

1. **a. Identify** Who was **Toussaint L'Ouverture**?
   b. Identify Cause and Effect What effect did Napoleon's invasion of Spain and Portugal have on independence movements in Latin America?

2. **a. Identify** Whose speech launched the Mexican independence movement?
   b. Interpret Why was the congress organized by **José María Morelos** important?
   c. Evaluate Why do you think Agustín de Iturbide's plan for Mexican independence worked?

3. **a. Identify** Which two generals led independence movements in much of South America?
   b. Infer What do you think happened in the meeting between **Simón Bolívar** and **José de San Martín**?

Critical Thinking

4. **Sequence** Use the graphic organizer below to show the sequence of events that led to Latin American nations gaining independence.

   [graphic organizer with four boxes connected by downward arrows]

FOCUS ON WRITING ✏

5. **Description** Choose a revolutionary leader from this section and write a paragraph on his life, his achievements, and his goals for revolution.

Section 3 Assessment Answers

1. **a.** former slave, military leader, appointed governor of Hispaniola for life
   b. It led some creole revolutionaries to decide to fight for independence.

2. **a.** Father Miguel Hidalgo
   b. It included representatives from many places in Mexico.
   c. it was a compromise; brought together many different groups, including creoles and *peninsulares*, revolutionaries, and royalists

3. **a.** Simón Bolívar and José de San Martín

   b. possible answer—probably argued about South America's future, since San Martín resigned after the meeting

4. Students should list key events, in order of their occurrence, that led to Latin American countries' independence.

5. Paragraphs should contain details about Toussaint L'Ouverture, Father Miguel Hidalgo, José María Morelos, Agustín de Iturbide, Simón Bolívar, or José de San Martín.

4 Expansion and War in the United States

BEFORE YOU READ

MAIN IDEA

As the United States began to expand west, conflicts erupted over territory and slavery.

READING FOCUS

1. How did the United States expand during the first half of the 1800s?
2. What issues led to civil war in the United States?

KEY TERMS AND PEOPLE

Louisiana Purchase
Monroe Doctrine
manifest destiny
Trail of Tears
abolition
Abraham Lincoln
secession
Emancipation Proclamation

 NEW YORK

PI 2.5 Investigate key events and developments and major turning points in world history to identify the factors that brought about change and the long-term effects of these changes.

 THE INSIDE STORY

Did the president of the United States have the power to purchase foreign territory? That was the question on Thomas Jefferson's mind in 1803. The French emperor, Napoleon, had offered to sell the enormous Louisiana Territory to the United States for about $15 million. Napoleon no longer wanted to build a French empire in North America, and the United States wanted to expand westward. It seemed like the perfect deal. But did the U.S. Constitution give the president the power to buy it?

Jefferson, who believed in a strict interpretation of the Constitution, thought that buying territory was "an act beyond the Constitution." He wanted to amend the Constitution to include such a purchase. Others in the government, however, believed there was no need for an amendment. Eventually, American diplomats in Paris signed the Louisiana Purchase treaty on April 30, 1803. The treaty gave more than 800,000 square miles of land to the United States and doubled the size of the young country. ∎

A PRESIDENT'S PURCHASE

▲ The Louisiana Purchase included this stretch of land near the edge of the Great Plains.

REFORMS, REVOLUTIONS, AND WAR **701**

Teach the Main Idea

At Level

Expansion and War in the United States

1. **Teach** Ask students the Reading Focus questions to teach this section.

2. **Apply** Have students create a sequence chart showing how westward expansion led to increased tensions in the United States during the 19th century.

3. **Review** Review student charts as a class. Have students describe how the following groups were affected by manifest destiny: white settlers, African Americans, Native Americans.

4. **Practice/Homework** Have students write scenarios describing what they think would have happened if the South had been allowed to secede and the Civil War had never taken place. **LS Visual-Spatial, Verbal-Linguistic**

   Alternative Assessment Handbook, Rubrics 7: Charts; and 40: Writing to Describe

Reading Focus

1 How did the United States expand during the first half of the 19th century? *bought Louisiana from France in 1803, annexed Texas in 1845, then annexed the Mexican Cession after winning the Mexican-American War*

Growth of the United States

Identify Cause and Effect How did manifest destiny affect Native Americans? *The Indian Removal Act made Native American lands available to white settlers by relocating Indian nations to Indian Territory. Subsequent laws moved Native Americans onto reservations.*

Make Judgments Do you think that the United States was justified in annexing Texas and forcing Mexico to give up the Mexican Cession? Why or why not? *possible answers—No, Americans essentially stole the land from Mexico; yes, the Texas settlers wanted to be part of the United States.*

🗺 **Map Transparency:** Westward Expansion of the United States

Info to Know

Florida The Adams-Onís Treaty formalized the United States' acquisition of Florida in 1819. It also settled a 16-year-old dispute between the United States and Spain over the western boundary of the Louisiana Purchase.

Answers

Interpreting Maps 1. *the Rocky Mountains;* **2.** *Refer to map.*

702

CC Unit 5-G1
Human and physical geography

TAKING NOTES
Take notes on the causes and effects of westward expansion and civil war in the United States.

Growth of the United States

In 1803 the United States completed the **Louisiana Purchase** with France, an agreement that gave the United States a huge territory in central North America. During the rest of the 1800s, the United States would continue to grow and expand westward.

A Young Nation At the beginning of the 1800s the United States was still a young nation. It had only recently won independence from Great Britain. Yet Britain was still harassing its former colony, seizing American sailors to use in its naval war against Napoleon. This angered Americans. In addition, Britain was helping Native Americans fight American settlers in the Northwest. As a result, Great Britain and the United States went to war in 1812. When the fighting ended, no territory had changed hands, but some Americans felt they had proved their country to be an independent nation.

By the 1820s the young nation was growing in national pride and beginning to build a world reputation. President James Monroe went so far as to declare the Americas off limits to further European colonization. This policy became known as the **Monroe Doctrine**.

Texas and Mexico In 1820 an American named Moses Austin got permission from Spain to found small settlements in Texas. Texas was a part of Mexico at this time. But when Mexico gained its independence from Spain, strict laws were imposed on the settlers in Texas. Eventually these settlers fought for and achieved independence for the Republic of Texas.

In 1845 the United States admitted Texas as a state. The Mexican government, however, claimed Texas was still part of Mexico. This dispute and others led to the Mexican-American War from 1846 to 1848, which the United States won. The result of the war was that the United States gained a large territory that is now the southwestern United States.

Westward Expansion of the United States

From 1803 to 1853, the United States expanded westward all the way to the Pacific Ocean. Some new territories were bought, while others were acquired through annexation and war.

GEOGRAPHY SKILLS **INTERPRETING MAPS**

1. **Movement** What major physical feature did people moving west have to cross over?
2. **Regions** Which region did the United States acquire from Mexico?

702 CHAPTER 23

Differentiating Instruction

At Level

English-Language Learners

1. Copy the chart for students to see. Omit the italicized information. Have students copy and fill in the chart. Have students use the maps on this page to identify the states formed either completely or partly from each land acquisition. Students may need to consult another U.S. map to identify the states.

2. Fill in the master chart and have students correct their charts as needed. **LS Visual-Spatial**

 Alternative Assessment Handbook, Rubrics 7: Charts; and 21: Map Reading

Territory	How Obtained	States
Louisiana	*bought from France*	*Minnesota, Iowa, Missouri, Arkansas, Louisiana, Oklahoma, Kansas, Nebraska, South Dakota, North Dakota, Montana, Wyoming, Colorado*
Texas	*annexed by United States*	*Texas, Oklahoma, Kansas, Colorado, Wyoming, New Mexico*
Mexican Cession	*war with Mexico*	*New Mexico, Colorado, Wyoming, Utah, Arizona, Nevada, California*

The Move West By 1850 the westward expansion of the United States had been ongoing for more than half a century. The United States had claimed territory all the way to the Pacific Ocean, including the Louisiana Territory, Florida, Texas, the Mexican Cession, and the Oregon Territory.

This rapid expansion led some Americans to believe that they had a God-given right to settle land all the way to the Pacific Ocean. One journalist arguing for Texas annexation came up with the term **manifest destiny** to describe this belief:

HISTORY'S VOICES

❝Other nations have tried to check . . . the fulfillment of our manifest destiny to overspread the continent allotted by Providence [God] for the free development of our yearly multiplying millions.❞
—John O'Sullivan, editorial, 1845

Settlers headed west for many reasons. In 1848 gold was discovered in California, which led to massive immigration. In addition, a national law promised 160 acres of free land to anyone who made the trip west. Thousands of Americans packed all of their belongings into covered wagons and traveled west.

Effects on Native Americans By moving west, American settlers were often moving onto land that had been inhabited for thousands of years by Native Americans. Conflict between Native Americans and settlers was frequent. Some people believed the solution was to push Native Americans further west.

In 1830 the Indian Removal Act called for the relocation of five Indian nations to Indian Territory, part of the Louisiana Territory in the Great Plains. Under the control of the United States army, Indians from the Cherokee, Choctaw, Chickasaw, Seminole, and Creek nations were forced from their homes and moved into Indian Territory.

The Cherokee march to the Indian Territory was so deadly that it became known as the **Trail of Tears**. It is estimated that a quarter of the Cherokees who made the trip died. As Americans moved further west, subsequent laws moved Native Americans into designated areas, called reservations.

READING CHECK **Summarize** What territories did the United States acquire between 1803 and 1850?

Causes and Effects of Westward Expansion
QUICK FACTS

CAUSES
- United States acquires new territories
- Desire for land and opportunity
- Discovery of gold in California

EFFECTS
- Millions of people move to new territories
- Native Americans are forcibly relocated
- Population of California explodes

The Civil War

As the United States expanded west, the issue of slavery became a national problem. Since colonial times Americans had used enslaved Africans and African Americans as unpaid workers. Slave labor helped support the American economy, especially in the South. Yet many Americans believed denying freedom to enslaved people was wrong. Some fought for **abolition**, or the end of slavery.

The Road to War As new territories and states were added to the country, Americans had to decide whether the new states would allow slavery or not. Some Southerners worried that new states where slavery was not allowed might cause a shift of power in congress, which could end slavery in all states. For the first half of the 1800s, however, a series of compromises preserved the balance between slave states and free states.

In 1854 the Kansas-Nebraska Act created two new territories in the west, Kansas and Nebraska. The decision of whether to allow slavery or not in each state was left to the residents. This act set off a bitter debate. Tensions were so great between antislavery and proslavery Americans that after the election of **Abraham Lincoln** as president, South Carolina decided to secede, or separate from the Union. This separation is called **secession**.

REFORMS, REVOLUTIONS, AND WAR **703**

The Civil War

Analyze Why was the Battle of Gettysburg important? *The victory made Union troops think that they could win the war.*

Evaluate How many slaves were immediately freed by the Emancipation Proclamation? *none, actually, since it applied only to Confederate states, which were not under Lincoln's control at the time it was issued*

📄 **CRF:** History and Geography: Issue of Slavery Divides States

Biography

Mathew Brady (c. 1823-1896) While Mathew Brady began as a portrait photographer in New York, he is perhaps best known today for his groundbreaking photographs of the Civil War. In 1862 Brady shocked New Yorkers with his photographs of the bloody aftermath of the Battle of Antietam, showing northerners the war's gruesome results. Though he never gained financial success, his work showed that photography could be used for more than just portraits: it could document real-life events.

Info to Know

Legalized Segregation After the Civil War, most southern states passed "Jim Crow" laws to enforce racial segregation in businesses, buses and trains, and public institutions such as schools. Under these laws, it was also illegal to marry someone of a different race.

Answers

A Nation Divided *Causes—conflicts over slavery and states' rights, Lincoln's election, secession, attack on Fort Sumter; Results—end of slavery, 500,000 deaths, South left in ruins, a reunited nation*

A Nation Divided

From 1861 to 1865 the Civil War war between the North, or Union states, and the South, or Confederate states, tore the country apart. *What were some main causes and results of the Civil War?*

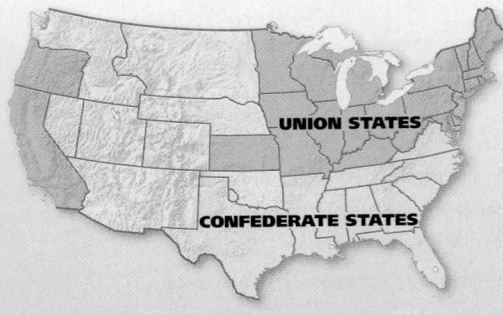

UNION STATES

CONFEDERATE STATES

Causes of the Civil War
- Conflicts over slavery and states' rights
- Lincoln's election as president
- The secession of southern states
- The attack on Fort Sumter

Battle of Lookout Mountain, by Kurz and Allison, 1889

The Civil War In November 1863 the Union army defeated the Confederate army in battles near Chattanooga, Tennessee.

Results of the Civil War
- The end of slavery
- More than 500,000 dead
- The South left in ruins
- A reunited nation

Other states soon followed. The states that seceded from the Union adopted the name the Confederate States of America and elected Jefferson Davis as their president. Soon after, the leaders of the Confederate states drafted a constitution.

War Begins President Lincoln did not believe that the Constitution gave states the right to secede. In April 1861 he gave orders to bring supplies to an American fort in South Carolina. There, at Fort Sumter, the first shots of the Civil War were fired.

The Civil War continued for four years. During the war more than 500,000 soldiers died from battle or disease—more soldiers than in any other American war before or since. As the deadly conflict grew and spread, the future of the country was in the balance.

The Emancipation Proclamation In January 1863 Lincoln took a historic step. With the **Emancipation Proclamation**, Lincoln declared all slaves free in some areas of the Confederate states. The proclamation did not apply to areas that had already been conquered by Union armies.

The Emancipation Proclamation helped the North in several ways. First, many Southern slaves fled to the North, which hurt the Southern economy. The proclamation also gave renewed purpose to Union soldiers, who now saw their cause as abolition as well as the preservation of the Union. In addition, the Emancipation Proclamation caused European powers to withdraw support for the Confederacy.

The Union Prevails Later in 1863, the Battle of Gettysburg in Pennsylvania represented a turning point in the war. In this battle, Union soldiers defeated Confederate troops and began to believe they could actually win the war. Later that year Lincoln delivered a famous speech at a cemetery dedication ceremony for the soldiers killed in the Battle of the Gettysburg.

HISTORY'S VOICES

❝We here highly resolved that these dead shall not have died in vain—that this nation, under God, shall have a new birth of freedom—and that government of the people, by the people, for the people, shall not perish from the earth.❞

—Abraham Lincoln, Gettysburg Address, 1863

Skills Focus: Making Inferences

Reading Skill
Social Changes Following the Civil War

1. Have students identify three major social changes that resulted from the Civil War. Have students explain which of these changes affected women, and how they affected women.

2. Have each student write a short essay predicting how the Fifteenth Amendment will affect women. Tell students to explain their predictions in the body of their essays.

3. Have volunteers read their essays to the class.

4. Guide the class in a discussion of student essays. 🄛 **Verbal-Linguistic**

📄 **Alternative Assessment Handbook**, Rubrics 11: Discussions; and 40: Writing to Describe

The war continued for about one and half more years with the Union forces gradually gaining an advantage. Finally, after several significant Union victories in the South, Confederate general Robert E. Lee surrendered to Union general Ulysses S. Grant at Appomattox, Virginia, in 1865. The Civil War was over, but the issues that caused it still plagued the United States.

Effects of the Civil War After the Civil War much of the South lay in ruins. Large areas were destroyed, and economies were ruined. The final battles of the war had also damaged railroads, roads, and bridges. Many Americans wondered how the federal government would treat the former Confederate states.

How would the slavery issue be resolved? How would the South rebuild? In an era known as Reconstruction—the period of rebuilding in the South—congress and the president sought to answer these questions.

Reconstruction was a difficult time for the United States because people had different ideas on how to solve the problems caused by the war. Despite these disagreements, however, the government passed several important laws and constitutional <u>amendments</u>.

The Civil Rights Act protected some rights of formerly enslaved people. The Fourteenth Amendment granted citizenship to all freed African Americans and "equal benefit of all laws and proceedings for the security of person and property, as is enjoyed by white citizens."

FACES OF HISTORY

Abraham LINCOLN
1809–1865

Abraham Lincoln is considered one of the best presidents in U.S. history. He kept the Union together during the war and ended slavery.

Before his presidency, Lincoln ran against Senator Stephen Douglas for a senate seat in Illinois. In a series of debates with Douglas, Lincoln expressed his views on slavery and defended democracy and the Union. As president, Lincoln opposed extending slavery into the territories. In addition, in the Emancipation Proclamation, he proclaimed the freedom of slaves in the Confederate states. As a result, about 180,000 African-American men volunteered to fight in the Union army during the Civil War.

Find the Main Idea How did Lincoln's efforts help end slavery?

The Fifteenth Amendment stated that voting rights could not be denied based on race.

Reconstruction did not fully achieve the goal of equal rights for former slaves, however. Some Southern states continued to pass discriminatory laws. In reality many freed African Americans were still prevented from making a decent living after the war. Nevertheless, the constitutional amendments passed during Reconstruction did provide a foundation for later civil rights movement in the United States during the 1900s.

ACADEMIC VOCABULARY
amendment a written change to a legal document

READING CHECK **Contrast** In what ways did Reconstruction succeed and in what ways did it fail?

SECTION 4 ASSESSMENT

go.hrw.com
Online Quiz
Keyword: SHL REF HP

Reviewing Ideas, Terms, and People

1. a. Define What is manifest destiny?
b. Analyze Why did President James Monroe issue the Monroe Doctrine?
c. Elaborate How do you think the idea of manifest destiny influenced the settlement of the west?

2. a. Recall What did the Kansas-Nebraska Act say about expansion and slavery?
b. Analyze What were the main causes of the Civil War, and what were the war's effects?
c. Evaluate How successful was Reconstruction? Provide reasons for your answer.

Critical Thinking

3. Analyze Use the graphic organizer below and your notes to analyze ways in which westward expansion and the Civil War were related.

Westward Expansion	
Civil War	

FOCUS ON WRITING

4. Persuasion Using information from the section, write a paragraph persuading others how the expansion of the United States will be good for the country.

REFORMS, REVOLUTIONS, AND WAR **705**

705

Document-Based Investigation

Independence in Latin America

Info to Know

Diego Rivera Diego Rivera is considered to be the greatest Mexican painter of the 20th century. Rivera studied art in Mexico City and then in Paris where he became acquainted with the work of the impressionists, post-modernists, and Cubists. He also studied the Italian Renaissance frescoes, and using frescoes, brought art to everyday people.

Activity Analyzing Visuals Have students work together in pairs to name the various groups of people shown in the mural on this page.

Primary Source

"The painter can and must abstract from many details in creating his painting. Every good composition is above all a work of abstraction. All good painters know this. But the painter cannot dispense with subjects altogether without his work suffering impoverishment."
—Diego Rivera

Independence in Latin America

NEW YORK STANDARDS

PI 4.2 Students analyze the roles and contributions of individuals and groups to social, political, economic, cultural, and religious practices and activities.

Historical Context These four documents are accounts of several Latin American revolutions by people involved in or affected by these revolutions.

Task Study the documents and answer the questions that follow. After you have studied all the documents, you will be asked to write an essay outlining similarities and differences between several Latin American revolutions.

From the Conquest to 1930, by Diego Rivera, 1900s

DOCUMENT 1

Mexico's History Reflected in Art

In the 1900s Mexican artist Diego Rivera painted enormous murals throughout Mexico City. This section of Rivera's mural in the city's National Palace shows the history of Mexico. Rivera depicts Father Hidalgo and other prominent figures in Mexico's struggle for independence standing above the eagle in the center of the mural.

DOCUMENT 2

Freedom in Haiti

Several months after he seized power in France in 1799, Napoleon issued a proclamation to the people of Haiti promising to respect the rights of the colony's free black citizens. He decreed that the words "Remember, brave blacks, that the French people alone recognize your freedom and equality of rights" should be written on the flags of the colony. But Toussaint L'Ouverture refused to follow the order and responded with the following words.

It is not a circumstantial freedom conceded to ourselves alone that we want. It is the absolute adoption of the principle that any man born red, black or white cannot be the property of his like. We are free today because we are the stronger party. The Consul maintains slavery in Martinique and Bourbon; we will thus be slaves when he will be stronger.

706 CHAPTER 23

Collaborative Learning

At Level

Independence Mural

Materials: poster paper, colored markers

1. Organize students into small groups. Assign each group one of the countries that fought for independence discussed in this chapter.

2. Have students reexamine the Diego Rivera mural shown on this page. Guide students in a discussion of the style, the groups of people shown, and the emblem in the foreground. Then have students review the information in the text about their assigned country.

3. Have students work together to design and then sketch that country's fight for independence in the same style as the Rivera mural.

4. Have students use the art supplies to create their own mural. Have volunteers from each group share the finished mural with the class.
LS Visual-Spatial

Alternative Assessment Handbook, Rubric 3: Artwork

DOCUMENT 3

A Bolivian Supports Independence

In 1885 Bolivian writer and statesman Nataniel Aguirre published *The Memoirs of Juan de la Rosa*, a novel about a fictional soldier in the Bolivian revolution. In the excerpt below, de la Rosa's teacher tells him about some of the motivations behind the revolution.

The country where we were born, as well as many other countries in this part of the world, obey a king who is two thousand leagues away, on the other side of the ocean. It takes one year for our complaints to reach his feet, and we never know when—if at all—the resolutions that his Council dictates, or even his sovereign dispositions, will arrive here. His agents believe that they are demigods, high above us. His subjects who come from there consider themselves nothing more and nothing less than our masters and lords. Those of us who are their very children —the criollos [Bolivian-born people with only Spanish blood]—are looked upon with disdain; they think that we should never aspire to the honors and public positions that are reserved just for them. The mestizos [people with mixed Spanish and Indian blood], whose blood is half like theirs, are scorned and condemned to suffer innumerable humiliations.

DOCUMENT 4

A Cuban's View of San Martín

José Martí, a supporter of the Cuban revolution, published an article in 1891 describing José de San Martín. In the article Martí describes the life of the liberator of Argentina, Chile, and Peru through the eyes of a Cuban revolutionary.

His veins flowed with the blood of a soldier from León and a granddaughter of conquistadors; his father was governor of Yapeyú on the banks of one of America's great rivers. He learned to read on the mountain slopes and grew up in the town as a gentleman's son in the shade of the palms and the urundays [kinds of trees]. He was taken to Spain to learn dancing and Latin in a school for the sons of noblemen. At the age of 12 the child "who seldom laughed" became a cadet. When as a Spanish lieutenant-colonel of 34 he returned to fight against Spain, he was no longer the man forged by the wind and rain of the pampas [grasslands] deep in his America, but the soldier who, in the glow of his native memories, had nurtured in the shadows of the Masonic Lodge of Lautaro, among young patricians and noblemen from Madrid, the will to work systematically and according to plan for American independence.

Skills FOCUS READING LIKE A HISTORIAN

DOCUMENT 1
a. **Describe** How does Rivera represent the leaders of the Mexican Revolution?
b. **Analyze** How does Rivera represent the people of Mexico in this mural?

DOCUMENT 2
a. **Interpret** Why did Toussaint L'Ouverture refuse to follow Napoleon's order?
b. **Analyze** How do Toussaint L'Ouverture's words indicate that a rebellion in Haiti might occur in the future?

DOCUMENT 3
a. **Interpret** How does Aguirre characterize the Spanish?
b. **Identify Main Ideas** Why should Bolivians support the revolution, according to Aguirre?

DOCUMENT 4
a. **Interpret** Do you think Martí respects San Martín? Why or why not?
b. **Compare and Contrast** What are some similarities and differences between San Martín and other revolutionaries you have read about?

DOCUMENT-BASED ESSAY QUESTION

People supported independence in the Americas for many reasons. What were some of these reasons, and how did they affect Latin American independence? Using the documents above and information from this chapter, form a thesis that expresses your opinion. Then write a short essay to support your opinion.

See **Skills Handbook**, pp. H25, H28

Skills Focus: Interpreting Literature as Historical Evidence

Reading Like a Historian Skill
The Memoirs of Juan de la Rosa

> At Level

1. Remind students that Document 3 is an excerpt from a novel written during the period of the Latin American independence movements. Then, have them reread Document 3. Ask the following questions: What makes the excerpt seem like a novel? Can this novel be considered historical evidence as well?

2. Have students review the material in this chapter about creoles and peninsulares.

Then, copy this chart for all to see. Have students complete the chart with facts from the textbook and facts from Document 3. What do the two columns of the chart suggest about Document 3? After comparing the two columns, ask students if they would consider *The Memoirs of Juan de la Rosa* to be a good source of historical evidence. Why or why not? **LS Visual-Spatial, Interpersonal**

Alternative Assessment Handbook, Rubrics 7: Charts, and 9: Comparing and Contrasting

Word Help

demigod person with more power than a mortal, but with less power than a god
innumerable countless
patrician person of noble birth

Activity. **Drawing José de San Martín** Have students create drawings of José de San Martín based on the description provided in Document 4 and details in the chapter. When the drawings are complete, have volunteers share their drawings, noting what features the drawings share. **LS Visual-Spatial**

Alternative Assessment Handbook, Rubric 3: Artwork

Answers

Reading Like a Historian

Document 1. a. *The mural represents the leaders of the Mexican Revolution as just one part of Mexico's long history from empire, to conquest, to independence.* **b.** *The people of Mexico are looking up to the revolutionary leaders and looking back on their history.* **Document 2. a.** *because slavery still existed in other areas of the French empire;* **b.** *L'Ouverture lists several demands for change.* **Document 3. a.** *The Spanish believe they are almost gods, and that they should be the masters of the Bolivians.* **b.** *because they have suffered scorn and humiliation under Spanish rule;* **Document 4. a.** *possible answer—yes, seems to respect San Martín; traces his educational background and development as a leader;* **b.** *possible answer—came from a background of prosperity and was well-educated;* **Essay** *possible thesis—Latin American independence movements brought together people with many different goals, including independence from colonial rulers, change in Latin America's social structure, and an end to slavery.*

Visual Summary

Review and Inquiry Remind students that the title of the chapter is Reforms, Revolutions, and War. Have students classify the events in Great Britain, France, Latin America, and the United States as reforms, revolutions, or wars. Some events may fit in more than one category. As a class, discuss the reasons that change sometimes happens peacefully, and sometimes through revolution and war.

Quick Facts Transparency: Visual Study Guide: Reforms, Revolutions, and War

Review Key Terms and People

1. Simón Bolívar
2. Emancipation Proclamation
3. potato famine
4. creole
5. manifest destiny
6. liberal
7. suffrage
8. Victoria
9. anti-Semitism
10. abolition

Comprehension and Critical Thinking

11. a. limited working hours of children and teenagers, children aged 9 to 13 had to receive two hours of schooling per day
b. broke windows, set fires, assaulted police officers, went on hunger strikes
c. possible answer—might not have established different cultures

12. a. reactionary leader in Austria
b. extended vote to wealthy citizens; limited freedom of the press, silenced opposition caused economic depression and discontent
c. possible answer—Dreyfus was a scapegoat because he was Jewish.

13. a. He led a slave revolt that became an independence movement.
b. liberated several South American colonies, served as president of Gran Colombia

---

VISUAL STUDY GUIDE

Reforms, Revolutions, and War

Great Britain
- The British Parliament passes many social reforms.
- British women gain the right to vote.
- About 1 million Irish die from starvation in the potato famine, and more than 1 million emigrate.

France
- Louis Philippe is crowned king in 1830.
- The Second Republic is established in 1848.
- Louis Napoleon becomes emperor in 1852.
- The Third Republic passes reforms in the late 1800s.
- Alfred Dreyfus is falsely accused of spying in 1894.

Latin America
- Haiti gains independence from France in 1804.
- Tensions grow between creoles and *peninsulares*.
- Mexico gains independence from Spain in 1821.
- Other nations gain independence.

United States
- The United States expands in the 1800s.
- Americans move westward.
- The North defeats the South in the Civil War.

Key People

Queen Victoria
- Ruled Great Britain from 1837 to 1901 during an era of reform

Benjamin Disraeli
- Influential British prime minister who argued for women's suffrage

Emmeline Pankhurst
- Led the British women's suffrage movement

Louis Philippe
- French monarch who expanded voting rights

Louis Napoleon
- Ruled France during the Second Republic

Toussaint L'Ouverture
- Liberated Haiti from the French

Miguel Hidalgo
- Mexican priest who made the first public call for independence from Spain

José María Morelos
- Mexican military leader who led the fight for independence

Simón Bolívar
- Leader of several independence movements in South America

José de San Martín
- Leader of independence movements in southern South America

Pedro I
- Declared Brazil independent in 1822

Review Key Terms and People

Identify the correct term or person from the chapter that best matches each of the following descriptions.

1. Venezuelan leader who was called "the Liberator"
2. American Civil War document that freed slaves in states that were in rebellion
3. disaster that killed nearly 1 million Irish
4. term for a colonist of European descent who was born in the Americas
5. the belief that Americans had a God-given right to settle the North American continent all the way to the Pacific Ocean
6. supporter of political and social reform
7. the right to vote
8. the British monarch who had the longest reign
9. prejudice towards Jews
10. the movement to end slavery

---

c. possible answer—It was unfair that colonists born in Spain had more rights and opportunities.

14. a. encouraged westward expansion as a "God-given" right
b. forced Native Americans from their homes; many died on march west, the Trail of Tears
c. ended slavery; killed more than 500,000 Americans; left South in ruins; reunited the nation

Reading Skills

15. that the Factory Act of 1833 improved working conditions for children and teenagers

16. details about limited working hours and mandatory schooling

History's Impact video program
Watch the video to answer the closing question: How have voting rights for women affected politics around the world today?

Comprehension and Critical Thinking

SECTION 1 *(pp. 685–690)*

11. a. Recall How did the Factory Act of 1833 change working conditions?

b. Explain What extreme measures did women take to gain the right to vote in Britain?

c. Predict How might British colonies be different today if they had not become independent?

SECTION 2 *(pp. 691–694)*

12. a. Identify Who was Klemens von Metternich?

b. Explain In what ways did Louis Philippe change France?

c. Evaluate What do you think about how the French government treated Alfred Dreyfus?

SECTION 3 *(pp. 695–700)*

13. a. Describe How did Toussaint L'Ouverture free Haiti from French rule?

b. Identify Cause and Effect How did Simón Bolívar gain independence for South America?

c. Evaluate What do you think of the peninsulares' role in Latin American society during the 1800s?

SECTION 4 *(pp. 701–705)*

14. a. Recall What effect did manifest destiny have on the westward expansion of the United States?

b. Cause and Effect How did the Indian Removal Act change the way Native Americans lived?

c. Elaborate In what ways did the Civil War affect the United States?

Reading Skills

Identifying Implied Main Ideas *Read the passage below and use what you know about identifying implied main ideas to answer the questions that follow.*

> ❝ Because of Sadler's report, Parliament passed the Factory Act in 1833. This act limited the working hours of children in textile factories. The act made it illegal for teenagers to work more than 12 hours a day. In addition, children between the ages of 9 and 13 had to receive two hours of schooling a day. ❞

15. What is the implied main idea of this paragraph?

16. What details help you find the implied main idea?

Interpreting Political Cartoons

Reading Like a Historian *The 1863 cartoon below shows Lady Liberty representing the Union by defending herself against members of Congress who are represented by snakes.*

The Granger Collection, New York

17. Draw Conclusions Why do you think the cartoonist chose to use Lady Liberty to represent the Union?

18. Explain Why are the members of congress attacking the Union?

Using the Internet

go.hrw.com
Practice Online
Keyword: SHL REF

19. Beginning in the early 1800s, Mexicans fought for their independence from Spain. Several leaders led the fight, including Father Miguel Hidalgo, José María Morelos, and Agustín de Iturbide. Using the Internet, research more about one of these revolutionary leaders. Then write a report about how the leader helped Mexico gain its independence from Spain.

 WRITING ABOUT HISTORY

Exposition: Analyzing Causes and Effects *In Great Britain during the 1800s political and social reforms changed people's lives for the better.*

20. Assignment: In an essay, analyze the causes and effects of British reforms during the 1800s. To provide support for your essay, use specific examples from the chapter and from other research sources if needed.

REFORMS, REVOLUTIONS, AND WAR **709**

Answers

Interpreting Political Cartoons

17. possible answer—to represent the Union's fight for freedom and emancipation

18. possible answer—were against Lincoln's anti-secession belief's

Using the Internet

19. Go to the HRW Web site and enter the keyword shown to access a rubric for this activity.

KEYWORD: SHL REF

Writing About History

20. possible answer—Student essays should discuss how industrialization created a new class of workers and new problems in Great Britain. This led to calls for increased representation and certain factory reforms. In turn, those early reforms led to further social and political reforms. A rubric for the activity is provided in **CRF: Writing About History.**

HOLT

History's Impact

▶ **Video Program: Reforms, Revolutions, and War**
See the Video Program Teacher's Guide for the answer to the closing question.

Review and Reinforce

 CRF: Chapter Review

 Quick Facts Transparency: Visual Study Guide: Reforms, Revolutions, and War

 **Spanish Chapter Summaries Audio CD Program**

OSP **Holt PuzzlePro:** Quiz Show for ExamView

Quiz Game CD-ROM

Assess

 PASS: Chapter Test, Forms A and B

Alternative Assessment Handbook

OSP **ExamView Test Generator,** Chapter Test

 Differentiated Instruction Modified Worksheets and Tests CD-ROM: Chapter Test

HOAP **Holt Online Assessment Program** (in the Premier Online Edition)

Reteach/Intervene

Interactive Reader and Study Guide

Differentiated Instruction Teacher Management System: Lesson Plans for Differentiated Instruction

Differentiated Instruction Modified Worksheets and Tests CD-ROM: Chapter Test

Interactive Skills Tutor CD-ROM

 go.hrw.com
Online Resources

KEYWORD: SHL TEACHER

Chapter 24 Planning Guide

Nationalism in Europe

Chapter Overview	Reproducible Resources	Technology Resources

CHAPTER 24
pp. 710–737
Overview: In this chapter, students will learn how nationalism led to revolutions across Europe, causing monarchies to fall and dramatically changing the map of Europe.

KI 2, 3; PI 2.3, 2.4, 2.5, 3.1
See pp. T32–T55 for a detailed correlation to the New York State Core Curriculum for Global History and Geography and the New York Learning Standards.

Differentiated Instruction Teacher Management System:*
• Pacing Guide
• Lesson Plans for Differentiated Instruction

Interactive Reader and Study Guide:
Chapter Summary*

Chapter Resource File*
• Writing for the SAT
• Social Studies Skill
• Economics and History
• Chapter Review

OSP **New York One-Stop Planner CD-ROM:** Calendar Planner

Live Ink© Online Reading Help

Student Edition on Audio CD Program

Differentiated Instruction Modified Worksheets and Tests CD-ROM

Interactive Skills Tutor CD-ROM

World History Primary Source Library CD-ROM

History's Impact: World History Video Program (VHS/DVD): Nationalism in Europe

---

Section 1:
Italian Unification
The Main Idea: In the 1800s, Italian states rebelled against Austria and unified as the Kingdom of Italy.
PI 2.3, 3.1

Differentiated Instruction Teacher Management System: Section 1 Lesson Plan*

Interactive Reader and Study Guide: Section 1 Summary*

Chapter Resource File*
• Vocabulary Builder: Section 1
• Biography: Giuseppe Verdi

Regents Review Transparency: Section 1*

Map Transparency: Europe, 1815; The Unification of Italy, 1858–1870*

Quick Facts Transparency: Elements of Nationalism*

Internet Activity: The Making of a Hero: Giuseppe Garibaldi

Section 2:
German Unification
The Main Idea: In the late 1800s, Otto von Bismark transformed Germany from a loose confederation of separate states into a powerful empire.
PI 3.1

Differentiated Instruction Teacher Management System: Section 2 Lesson Plan*

Interactive Reader and Study Guide: Section 2 Summary*

Chapter Resource File*
• Vocabulary Builder: Section 2
• Biography: Johann Gottlieb Fichte

Regents Review Transparency: Section 2*

Map Transparency: The Unification of Germany, 1865–1871*

Quick Facts Transparencies: Steps to Unification in Germany; Germany's Economic Growth, 1890–1913*

Section 3:
Austria-Hungary and the Ottoman Empire
The Main Idea: Nationalism broke down two old European empires—the Austrian Hapsburg Empire and the Ottoman Empire.
PI 3.1

Differentiated Instruction Teacher Management System: Section 3 Lesson Plan*

Interactive Reader and Study Guide: Section 3 Summary*

Chapter Resource File*
• Vocabulary Builder: Section 3
• Biography: Mustafa Kemal
• Primary Source: Hungary's National Song, 1848

Regents Review Transparency: Section 3*

Map Transparencies: Ethnic Groups in Austria-Hungary, 1867; The Ottoman Empire*

Section 4:
Unrest in Russia
The Main Idea: In the early 1800s and early 1900s, Russians rebelled against the absolute power of the czar and demanded social reforms
PI 2.3, 2.4, 2.5

Differentiated Instruction Teacher Management System: Section 4 Lesson Plan*

Interactive Reader and Study Guide: Section 4 Summary*

Chapter Resource File*
• Biography: Karl Marx
• Literature: *Dead Souls*
• History and Geography: Russian Expansion

Regents Review Transparency: Section 4*

Quick Facts Transparencies: Last Czars of Russia; Russian Revolution of 1905*

Internet Activity: Russian Revolution

HOLT
History's Impact
World History Video Program (VHS/DVD)
Nationalism in Europe

Review, Assessment, Intervention

🏴 **Global History and Geography Regents Test Prep Workbook**

💾 **Quick Facts Transparency:** Nationalism in Europe*

🔊 **Spanish Chapter Summaries Audio CD Program**

📇 **Progress Assessment Support System (PASS):** Chapter Test*

💿 **Differentiated Instruction Modified Worksheets and Tests CD-ROM:** Modified Chapter Test

OSP **New York One-Stop Planner CD-ROM:** ExamView Test Generator (English/Spanish)

HOAP **Holt Online Assessment Program (HOAP),** in the Premier Online Edition

---

📇 **PASS:** Section 1 Quiz*

💻 **Online Quiz:** Section 1

📇 **Alternative Assessment Handbook**

📇 **PASS:** Section 2 Quiz*

💻 **Online Quiz:** Section 2

📇 **Alternative Assessment Handbook**

📇 **PASS:** Section 3 Quiz*

💻 **Online Quiz:** Section 3

📇 **Alternative Assessment Handbook**

📇 **PASS:** Section 4 Quiz*

💻 **Online Quiz:** Section 4

📇 **Alternative Assessment Handbook**

Power Presentation with Video CD-ROM

Power Presentations with Video are visual presentations of each chapter's main ideas. Presentations can be customized by including Quick Facts charts, images and maps from the textbook, and video clips.

 Holt Online Learning

go.hrw.com
Teacher Resources
KEYWORD: SHL TEACHER

go.hrw.com
Student Resources
KEYWORD: SHL NAT

- Document-Based Questions
- Interactive Multimedia Activities

- Current Events
- Chapter-based Internet Activities
- and more!

Holt Premier
Online Student Edition
Complete online support for interactivity, assessment, and reporting
- Interactive Maps and Notebook
- Homework Practice and Research Activities Online

CHAPTER 24 PLANNING GUIDE

The Big Picture

Peter N. Stearns

The Nature of Nationalism Nationalism became such a powerful force around the world that it is hard to remember how new it is. While hints of nationalism can be found earlier, the force was only fully defined in the late 18th century. Intellectuals, especially in Germany, helped define the importance of national cultures. Social changes spurred many groups to seek new loyalties, as opposed to more traditional regional and religious identities. The French Revolution aided nationalism by breaking down barriers between citizens and the state and by causing nationalist resistance in places like Spain, Italy and Germany. By the early 19th century, nationalism was a powerful force in European politics, despite conservative efforts to keep it under control. Nationalist revolts occurred in Greece, Poland, and Belgium.

Unification Nationalism caused major intellectual and political movements in Italy and Germany. The revolutions of 1848 in these countries highlighted demands for national unification and though they failed, the efforts continued. Leaders like Cavour and Bismarck took advantage of nationalist sentiments to increase their power and to use force to cement loyalty to moderate-liberal and conservative governments. Such unions provided the leading diplomatic developments of the third quarter of the 19th century. After unifications, nationalism helped maintain domestic stability, amid some new foreign adventurism, though it could not prevent a growing challenge from socialism.

Disruption In the Hapsburg, Ottoman, and, to an extent, Russian empires nationalism proved to be a disruptive force. It became increasingly difficult to maintain multinational empires against demands by smaller groups for cultural and political independence. Austria tried to compromise with Hungarian nationalism, but faced growing agitation from Slavic groups. The Ottomans could not prevent independence movements in the Balkans; around 1900 a Turkish nationalist group arose as the Ottoman Empire visibly declined. Russia faced some nationalist pressure, but social issues loomed larger. Peasant reforms did not suffice, and Marxist and other movements gained ground against a tsarist regime that refused fundamental political change. The revolution of 1905 foreshadowed larger upheaval.

Recent Scholarship

Benedict Anderson's *Imagined Communities: Reflections on the Origin and Spread of Nationalism* (1991) is not brand new, but it remains the most widely cited recent work on nationalism. Using various European and Southeast Asian examples, Anderson discusses how nations came to be defined, despite no really objective prior existence. This leads in turn to a discussion of what other interests nationalism served. The emphasis is on nationalism as a historic product, not some inevitable force of nature. An important companion piece, heavily focused on nationalist traditions in various parts of the world, is *The Invention of Tradition* (1983) edited by Eric Hobsbawm and Terence Ranger.

Differentiating Instruction

 Differentiated Instruction Teacher Management System
- Pacing Guide
- Lesson Plans for Differentiated Instruction

 Interactive Reader and Study Guide

Spanish Chapter Summaries Audio CD Program

Student Edition on Audio CD Program

 Differentiated Instruction Modified Worksheets and Tests CD-ROM
- Vocabulary Flash Cards
- Modified Vocabulary Builder Activities
- Modified Chapter Review Activity
- Modified Chapter Test

OSP **One-Stop Planner CD-ROM**
- ExamView Test Generator (English and Spanish)
- PuzzlePro
- Quiz Show for ExamView
- Transparencies and Videos

TE **Differentiated Activities in the Teacher's Edition**
- German Unification Chart, p. 719
- Serfdom in Europe Chart, p. 729
- Causes and Effects of the Revolution of 1905, p. 731
- Analyzing Prince Andrew's Attitudes, p. 773

Reading Like a Historian
Sam Wineburg

Siege of Paris By New Year's Eve, 1870, Bismarck's siege of Paris was coming onto three months. With food deliveries halted from the country-side, Parisians took to drastic measures. Today, a plaque at the Paris zoo commemorates one of them. "Famine required the sacrifice of any animal which would be a contribution, however small, to the public food supply; it was necessary . . . to slaughter the two elephants, Castor and Pollux."

In the first weeks of 1871, rich Parisians wolfed down elephant. The poor, however, took to a more gruesome sort of protein seeking—the most desperate form short of cannibalism. They hunted and roasted flea-infested rats—or "rat pâté" as it was known.

On January 28, the siege ended. Old, beaten, suffering from gallstones that gave him little respite, a haggard Napoleon III capitulated to Bismarck. Paris was in shambles and France shamed. On the other hand, intoxicated by his stunning victory, Bismarck seized the French provinces of Alsace and Lorraine. But the Prussian victory had greater internal ramifications than this territorial conquest. Victory cemented German unification, providing the glue that would bind Europe's German-speaking states into the continent's most formidable fighting machine. A French defeat paved the way to German unification.

The Franco-Prussian war was a historical oil spill, the consequences of which were not felt for decades. Forty years later, France would again go to war to regain its pride—and Alsace-Lorraine—in World War I. This war was the prelude to World War II, the Holocaust, and the carving up of Europe into new spheres of superpower influence. Nearing the midpoint of the 20th century, blood stained the European continent.

Counterfactual History What if this whole chain of events had been stopped at its source? Let's go back to that decisive moment in 1870 before the siege. The French attaché pays a visit to the Prussian king seeking assurance that he will not try to place a minor German prince, one of several possible candidates, on Spain's throne. The king pays the attaché no heed and snubs him by refusing to speak further about the issue. An account of the meeting, a telegram actually, is released. French newspapers have a field-day playing up this diplomatic slight. Their passions enflamed by lurid headlines, crowds gather in Paris feverously chanting "À Berlin."

Instead of yielding to this warmongering, suppose that Napoleon proceeds with caution. Who knows what will happen to Spain? Instead of fanning flames, Napoleon chooses to turn the other cheek.

This thought experiment is what historians call a "counterfactual," a "what if" that lays out an alternative history that might have occurred had a different path been pursued. This particular scenario is the brainchild of historian Alistair Horne, the author (with Richard Cobb) of *The Fall of Paris: The Siege and the Commune 1870-71.*

Had Napoleon ignored Bismarck's slight, the ramifications would have been greater than saving Castor and Pollux. Bismarck would have been deprived of his crowning victory, and German unification would have been stalled. Catholic Bavaria, imagines Horne, may have joined with Catholic Austria, counterbalancing Prussian might and the military titan known as Germany would be stillborn. No World War I, no World War II, and that little boy Adolf, born in Braunau am Inn, would have died a second-rate artist and small-town rabble-rouser.

The counterfactual teaches us that the past could have been different. In so doing, it reminds us that the future is ours to make.

Chapter Main Ideas

Section 1 In the 1800s, Italian states rebelled against Austria and unified as the Kingdom of Italy.

Section 2 In the late 1800s, Otto von Bismarck transformed Germany from a loose confederation of separate states into a powerful empire.

Section 3 Nationalism broke down two old European empires—the Austrian Hapsburg Empire and the Ottoman Empire.

Section 4 In the 1800s and early 1900s, Russians rebelled against the absolute power of the czar and demanded social reforms.

New York Standards

Key Idea 3 Study of the major social, political, cultural, and religious developments in world history involves learning about the important roles and contributions of individuals and groups.

Key Idea 2 Establishing timeframes, exploring different periodizations, examining themes across time and within cultures, and focusing on important turning points in world history help organized the study of world cultures and civilizations.

Key to Differentiating Instruction

Below Level

Basic-level activities designed for all students encountering new material

At Level

Intermediate-level activities designed for average students

Above Level

Challenging activities designed for honors and gifted and talented students

Standard English Mastery

Activities designed to improve standard English usage

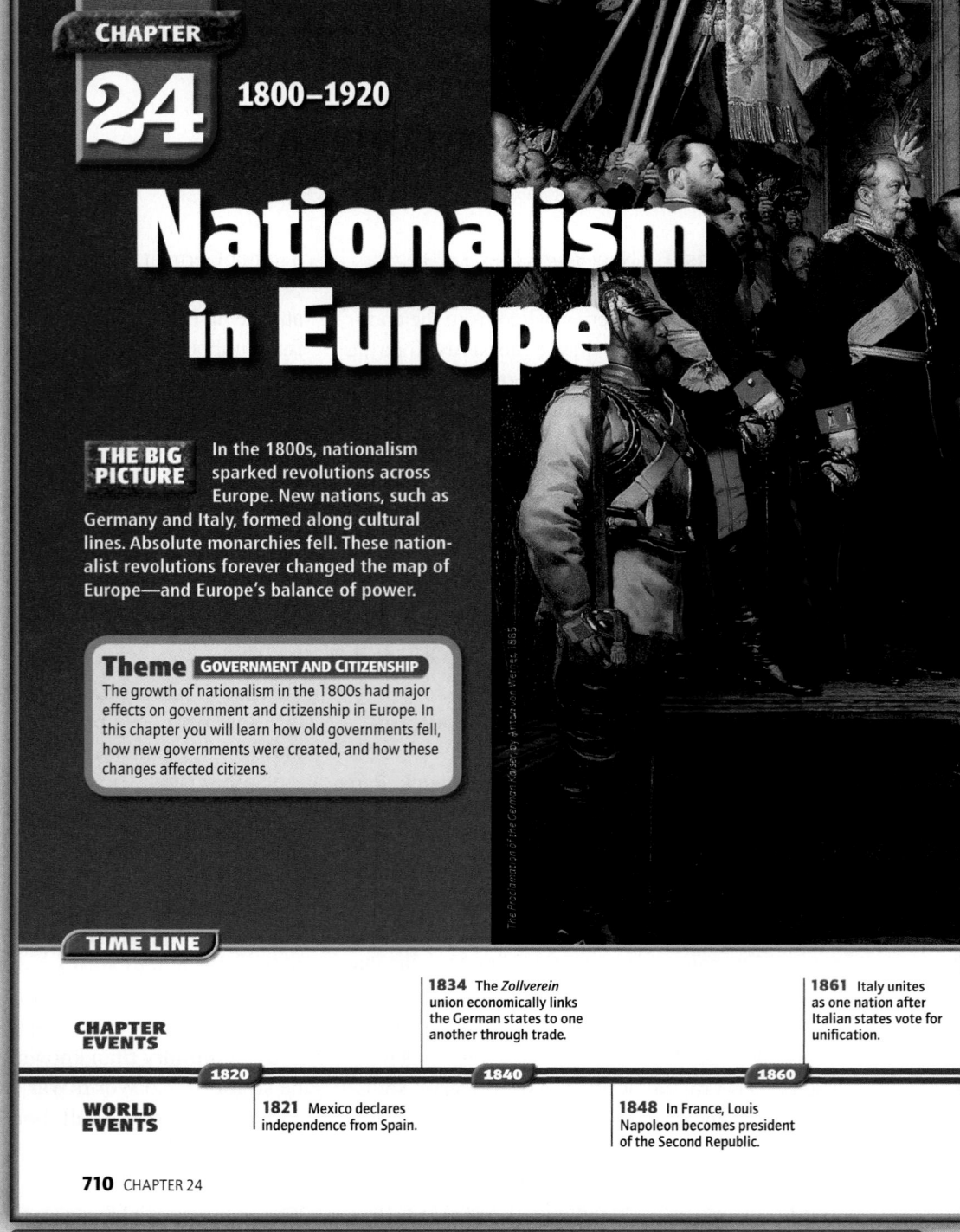

CHAPTER

24 1800–1920

Nationalism in Europe

THE BIG PICTURE In the 1800s, nationalism sparked revolutions across Europe. New nations, such as Germany and Italy, formed along cultural lines. Absolute monarchies fell. These nationalist revolutions forever changed the map of Europe—and Europe's balance of power.

Theme GOVERNMENT AND CITIZENSHIP
The growth of nationalism in the 1800s had major effects on government and citizenship in Europe. In this chapter you will learn how old governments fell, how new governments were created, and how these changes affected citizens.

The Proclamation of the German Kaiser by Anton von Werner, 1885

TIME LINE

CHAPTER EVENTS

1834 The *Zollverein* union economically links the German states to one another through trade.

1861 Italy unites as one nation after Italian states vote for unification.

| 1820 | 1840 | 1860 |

WORLD EVENTS

1821 Mexico declares independence from Spain.

1848 In France, Louis Napoleon becomes president of the Second Republic.

710 CHAPTER 24

Introduce the Chapter

At Level

Nationalism in Europe

1. Remind students that in 1815 Europe was recovering from the Napoleonic wars. The Congress of Vienna had tried to restore the old order, but the seeds of nationalism had been planted.

2. Organize students into small groups. Have each group try to define nationalism and write predictions of the ways in which nationalism would change the map of Europe.

3. Review student predictions as a class. Then guide students in a discussion of nationalism and its probable outcomes.

4. Tell students that in this chapter they will learn what effects nationalism had and how it changed the map of Europe. **LS** Interpersonal

Alternative Assessment Handbook, Rubrics 14: Group Activity; and 38: Writing to Classify

HOLT

History's Impact
▶ **Video Program: Nationalism in Europe**
See the Video Teacher's Guide for strategies for using the video segment.

Reading Like a Historian

Analyzing Visuals During the Franco-Prussian War, the Prussian army captured the French emperor, Napoleon III. The French formed a Government of National Defense to carry on the war until it ended in January 1871. Prussian statesman Otto von Bismarck rubbed in his victory by annexing the provinces of Alsace and Lorraine, demanding an indemnity of 5 billion francs, and organizing a victory march through Paris. He also proclaimed Wilhelm I of Prussia the new German emperor in the Hall of Mirrors at Versailles, just outside of Paris.

1867 Austria and Hungary become two separate, equal states under the Dual Monarchy.

1905 Revolution breaks out in Russia after troops kill some protesters on Bloody Sunday.

1880

1910

1869 Suez Canal opens in Egypt.

1901 Theodore Roosevelt becomes president of the United States.

Reading like a Historian

In this painting, Prussian prime minister Otto von Bismarck (in white) proclaims the Prussian king Wilhelm I (on podium) to be Emperor of Germany on January 18, 1871. This ceremony marked the creation of the German Empire following Prussia's defeat of France in the Franco-Prussian War.

Analyzing Visuals How can you tell that this painting commemorates an important event?

See **Skills Handbook**, p. H26

NATIONALISM IN EUROPE **711**

Explore the Time Line

1. What was the purpose of the *Zollverein*? *to link the German states through trade*
2. When did Italy unite as one nation? *1861*
3. When did the Dual Monarchy begin? *1867*
4. Who became president of the United States in 1901? *Theodore Roosevelt*

Info to Know

German Nationalism During the early 1800s, many Germans associated nationalism with liberalism. They believed that representative government and individual freedoms would advance along with nationalistic principles. However, Otto von Bismarck used nationalism mainly as a tool to help Prussia gain control over the rest of Germany. **Analyze** How did different people view the connection between nationalism and government rule in Germany? *Some believed nationalism would advance representative government; Bismarck believed it would advance the power of the kaiser.*

go.hrw.com
Online Resources

Chapter Resources:
KEYWORD: SHL NAT
Teacher Resources:
KEYWORD: SHL TEACHER

Answers

Reading Like a Historian *The men are wearing dress uniforms and raising their swords to the new emperor. Their facial expressions reflect their intense interest in the event.*

711

Geography Starting Points

Switzerland Switzerland is a confederation of cantons that has traditionally been neutral in times of war. The country was occupied by France under Napoleon, who forced upon the Swiss a constitution and a strong central government. After Napoleon's downfall, Switzerland once more became a confederation of states. A new constitution expanded federal power in 1848. In 1874 the constitution was revised to change Switzerland into a unified nation.

Info to Know

Confederations Frederick K. Lister served for 34 years in the secretariat of the United Nations. He recently studied three confederations—the early United States, the Swiss Confederation, and the German Confederation. None of those confederations succeeded in the long run, but he blames their failure on the lack of modern means of communication, which forced them to create more centralized federal governments. Today, he believes that they could serve as a model for such international organizations as the European Union, NAFTA, and the United Nations.

🗺 **Map Transparency:** Europe, 1815

📋 **World History Outline Maps**

✳ **Interactive Map:** Europe, 1815

GEOGRAPHY Starting Points

Interactive EUROPE, 1815

— Boundary of the German Confederation

The German Confederation was made up of the lesser German states and parts of Prussia and the Austrian Empire.

Italy was split into many separate states.

Starting Points In 1815 the Congress of Vienna divided Europe with little regard for the nationalities of the people who lived there. By the mid-1800s, nationalist movements arose which would lead to the breakup of empires and the creation of new nations. In Russia, a revolution threatened the power of the czar.

1. **Analyze** How would you describe the political geography of Germany and Italy at this time?

2. **Predict** Based on the map, what challenges do you think Italy would face as it unified?

🔊 **Listen to History**

Go online to listen to an explanation of the starting points for this chapter.

go.hrw.com
Keyword: SHL NAT

712 CHAPTER 24

Skills Focus: Analyzing Maps

At Level

Social Studies Skill
Europe, 1815

1. Have students compare the map on this page with a map of Europe after World War I. Guide students in a discussion of the following questions: What nations disappeared between 1815 and 1918? What new nations emerged between 1815 and 1918? Which nations lost the most land?

2. To help students see the continuing effects of nationalism, have them compare the 1918 map of Europe with a present-day map of Europe. Discuss the differences using the following questions: What new nations have emerged since 1918? What nations have lost land since 1918? What nations have gained land since 1918?

3. Finally, ask students how nationalism continues to play a part in world affairs today.
LS Verbal-Linguistic

📋 **Alternative Assessment Handbook**, Rubrics 9: Comparing and Contrasting; and 21: Map Reading

Answers

Geography Starting Points
1. *Each consisted of many separate states.* 2. *possible answer—many of the separate Italian states did not border one another, so it might prove difficult to govern them as one nation.*

Italian Unification

BEFORE YOU READ

MAIN IDEA
In the 1800s, Italian states rebelled against Austria and unified as the Kingdom of Italy.

READING FOCUS
1. How did nationalism stir in Italy after the Congress of Vienna?

2. What role did Cavour and Sardinia play in the path toward Italian unification?

3. How did Garibaldi and the Red Shirts help unite Italy?

4. What challenges did Italy face after unification?

KEY TERMS AND PEOPLE
Giuseppe Mazzini
Camillo di Cavour
Giuseppe Garibaldi
Red Shirts
Victor Emmanuel

NEW YORK

2.3 Students analyze evidence critically and demonstrate an understanding of how circumstances of time and place influence perspective.

3.1 Students analyze the roles and contributions of individuals and groups.

THE INSIDE STORY

How did the lyrics of an opera help unite all Italians? During the 1800s most Italians were unhappy being part of the Austrian Empire. They were beginning to yearn to have their own nation, an Italian nation.

Someone had to put these yearnings into words, however, and that someone was Giuseppe Verdi, an Italian composer. In the lyrics to some of his operas, Verdi called for the Italian people to unite. Italians especially identified with his opera, *Nabucco*. It featured singers praising their homeland with the lyrics, "Go, settle on the cliffs and hills, where the sweet breezes bring the warm, soft fragrances of your native land. . . Oh my fatherland so beautiful and lost!" These words reminded Italians of the beauty of their own land and the fact that it was under Austria's control.

Verdi's music became a kind of national anthem for Italians seeking unification, inspiring them and urging them to act. The popularity of his music not only made Verdi an international star, but also helped spread the message of Italian nationalism. ■

A COMPOSER INSPIRES A NATION

▶ **Giuseppe Verdi conducts an orchestra in Paris in 1880.**

Illustration of Giuseppe Verdi conducting in Paris, by Stefano Bianchetti, 1800s

NATIONALISM IN EUROPE **713**

Getting Started

Use the **Interactive Reader and Study Guide** to familiarize students with the section content.

📖 **Interactive Reader and Study Guide,** Section 1

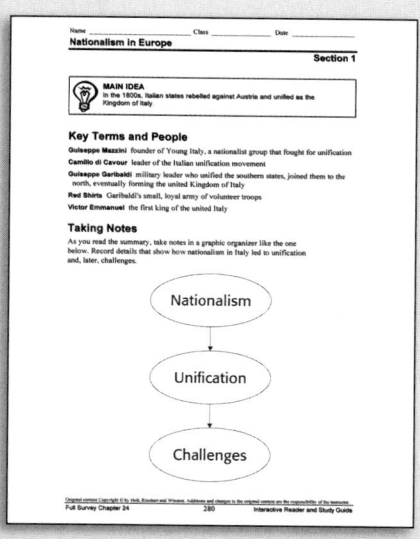

Academic Vocabulary

Review with students the high-use academic term in this section.

ethnic common background or culture (p. 714)

📄 **CRF:** Vocabulary Builder: Section 1

Taking Notes

Nationalism—It inspired uprisings in 1848; some states rebelled against Austrian rule; by 1860 northern Italy had freed itself from the control of the Austrian Empire.
Unification—Cavour and Garibaldi united Italy with the Two Sicilies; most of Papal States joined soon after.
Challenges—Regional differences kept nation from being truly united; Pope forbade Catholics from voting; social tensions were building; widespread poverty caused many Italians to emigrate; only wealthy males could vote; working class was beginning to campaign for change.

go.hrw.com
Online Resources
KEYWORD: SHL NAT
ACTIVITY: The Making of a Hero: Giuseppe Garibaldi

Teach the Main Idea

At Level

Italian Unification

1. **Teach** Ask students the Reading Focus questions to teach this section.

2. **Apply** Have students work in pairs to make visual representations of the events that led to Italian unification. Encourage students to use visual symbolism such as two rivers flowing toward unification.

3. **Review** Review student visual representations as a class. Guide students in a discussion of Italian unification. Ask students to name what they consider to be

the most important event on the road to unification.

4. **Practice/Homework** Have students write an essay that describes what might have happened in Italy if Garibaldi and Cavour had not been able to reach an agreement to unite Italy under the king of Sardinia.

LS Visual-Spatial, Verbal-Linguistic

📄 **Alternative Assessment Handbook,** Rubrics 14: Group Activity; and 40: Writing to Describe

Reading Focus

1 How did nationalism stir in Italy after the Congress of Vienna? *Some Europeans believed that people of the same background should form separate nation-states. Mazzini's Young Italy attracted tens of thousands of Italians to the cause of unification.*

Stirrings of Nationalism

Summarize What had happened to Italy since the fall of the Roman Empire? *It had consisted of a number of competing states for most of that time until it was united briefly by Napoleon.*

Evaluate Why do you think a nationalist movement arose in Italy in the mid-1800s? *possible answer —because Napoleon had united many of the Italian states into the Kingdom of Italy, which was later divided once again under the rule of other nations*

Quick Facts Transparency: Elements of Nationalism

Teaching Tip

Explain to students that nationalism can take many forms. In one form, national groups broke away from larger nations or empires that included people of many different back grounds. Greece, which broke away from the Ottoman Empire, is an example of this type of nationalism. In another form, smaller states that shared a language and culture united to form larger states. Italy and Germany are examples of this type of nationalism.

Answers

Elements of Nationalism *possible answer—A shared past connects people.*

714

ELEMENTS OF NATIONALISM

QUICK FACTS

In Europe in the 1800s, devotion to one's national group, or nationalism, swept through the continent. The elements of nationalism listed below help bond a nation together.
How is history an element of nationalism?

Culture Shared beliefs and a way of life create a common bond.

History A shared past connects people as a group.

Religion A common religion helps unite people.

Language A common language is a key element of nationalism.

Territory A shared land gives people a sense of unity.

History The accomplishments of the Roman Empire are a source of national pride for Italians.

TAKING NOTES

Take notes on how nationalism in Italy led to unification and, later, challenges.

Nationalism

↓

Unification

↓

Challenges

NEW YORK

CC Unit 5-F Global nationalism

ACADEMIC VOCABULARY

ethnic common background or culture

Stirrings of Nationalism

The Italian Peninsula had not been unified since the fall of the Roman Empire. Although most people spoke the same language, the peninsula was divided into several competing states, each with its own government. When Napoleon invaded Italy, he united many of these states under one government, but that unification did not last.

After Napoleon was defeated, the Congress of Vienna split the Italian states apart once more. This time, however, a spirit of nationalism, or a devotion to one's national group, was on the rise throughout Europe.

After the Congress of Vienna Prince Metternich of Austria had wanted the Congress of Vienna to maintain the old Europe with its old relationships. But just 15 years after the Congress met, a tired Metternich admitted that "the old Europe is nearing its end." Despite his efforts to halt change, the old order had been destroyed beyond repair.

Nationalism was a growing force in Europe during the 1800s, fostered in part by some of the decisions made at the Congress of Vienna. The Congress had created political boundaries that ignored national groups, instead placing these groups under the control of large empires. Some of Europe's empires included people of different <u>ethnic</u> groups. For example, the

Austrian Empire was home to Croats, Czechs, Germans, Hungarians, Italians, Poles, Serbs, Slovaks, and Slovenes. The Italians were split into three groups. The Congress of Vienna had placed much of northern Italy under Austrian rule, other Italian states under control of the Hapsburgs, and still others under control of a French ruler. Italian nationalism grew in opposition to these conditions.

Mazzini and Young Italy As Italian artists, writers, and thinkers became interested in celebrating Italy's cultural traditions, other Italians in Austria formed secret societies to work for political change. They began plotting to overthrow the Austrian government in Italy.

In 1831 a popular writer launched a nationalist group called Young Italy to fight for unification of the separate Italian states. This writer, **Giuseppe Mazzini**, had been exiled because of his outspoken nationalism, but he smuggled his patriotic pamphlets into Italy. Mazzini believed that Europe needed to redraw the lines set by the Congress of Vienna in 1815.

HISTORY'S VOICES

❝ Europe no longer possesses unity of faith, of mission, or of aim . . . The question of nationality can only be resolved by destroying the treaties of 1815 and changing the map of Europe and its public law. ❞

—Giuseppe Mazzini, "On Nationality," 1852

Skills Focus: Making Oral Presentations

At Level

Reading Like a Historian Skill
Italian Nationalists

Research Required

1. Organize students into four groups. Have each group research one of the following leaders in the Italian independence movement: Giuseppe Mazzini, Camillo di Cavour, Giuseppe Garibaldi, or King Victor Emmanuel. Each student within the group should find a different source, and each group's sources should include both print and online sources. Sources should include visuals such as pictures of the leaders and maps. Have students look for reliable sources of information and get approval before continuing.

2. Have each group prepare a multimedia presentation on its assigned leader.

3. Have each group give its presentation to the class. **LS Interpersonal, Verbal-Linguistic**

Alternative Assessment Handbook, Rubrics 22: Multimedia Presentations; and 30: Research

Mazzini's Young Italy attracted tens of thousands of Italians to the cause of unification. Italians were ready to unite behind a strong nationalist leader.

READING CHECK **Define** What is nationalism?

The Path Toward Unity

As Italian nationalism grew, some Italians led unsuccessful rebellions. Then two men, Camillo di Cavour and Giuseppe Garibaldi, rose to lead a successful movement to unify Italy.

Uprisings and Revolutions Nationalist-inspired revolutions spread throughout Europe in 1848, and Italian nationalists led rebellions of their own. In some of the Italian states, citizens rebelled against Austrian rule. For example, the state of Piedmont declared war against Austria. That war lasted only a year and ended in Piedmont's defeat.

In 1849 other revolutionaries seized Rome and set up a republic that Mazzini and two others leaders governed. French troops, however, helped the pope gain control of Rome again.

The only successful revolt was in Sardinia. The rebellion there forced the rulers of Sardinia to grant a new constitution, and Sardinia remained independent.

Cavour and Sardinia The failures of the rebellions of 1848 and 1849 did not seriously weaken the nationalist movement. One of the most important leaders of the Italian unification movement, **Camillo di Cavour**, emerged at this time.

Before the rebellions Cavour had expressed his belief that the Italian nationalist movement was strong enough to unite Italy, despite differences among the many Italian states.

HISTORY'S VOICES

❝Nationalism has become general; it grows daily; and it has already grown strong enough to keep all parts of Italy united despite the differences that distinguish them.❞

—Camillo di Cavour, 1846

Cavour founded a nationalist newspaper called *Il Risorgimento*, which means "resurgence" or "rebirth." The movement for Italian unification and freedom from Austrian control also became known as *Il Risorgimento*.

In 1852 Cavour became prime minister of the independent Kingdom of Sardinia. He believed that a thriving economy was important in order for the nation of Italy to be reborn. Therefore, he worked to build the Sardinian economy. He also believed that Italy should be reborn as a monarchy.

By this time, Cavour was in a position to cultivate a powerful ally. He supported France in a war with Russia and gave France the provinces of Savoy and Nice. France, in turn, agreed to support Sardinia in its planned war against Austria. The plan worked. By 1860 the northern Italian states were liberated from the control of the Austrian Empire.

READING CHECK **Identify Cause and Effect** How did Cavour help Sardinia break free from the Austrian Empire?

NEW YORK
CC Unit 5-F3a
Camillo Cavour

PRIMARY SOURCES

Mazzini's Young Italy

In 1831 the Italian writer Giuseppe Mazzini founded a nationalist movement called Young Italy. In just a few years, Young Italy had about 60,000 members. This excerpt is from Mazzini's instructions to new members of the movement:

"Young Italy is a brotherhood of Italians who believe in Progress and Duty, and are convinced that Italy is destined to become one nation—convinced also that she possesses sufficient strength within herself to become one, and that the ill success of her former efforts is to be attributed not to the weakness, but to the misdirection of the revolutionary elements within her—that the secret of force lies in constancy and unity of effort. They join this association in the firm intent of consecrating both thought and action to the great aim of reconstituting Italy as one independent sovereign nation of free men and equals."

Skills FOCUS **READING LIKE A HISTORIAN**

1. **Interpret** Why do you think Mazzini links a united Italy with "Progress and Duty"?

2. **Analyze Primary Sources** From reading this excerpt, what can you learn about Mazzini's goal to unite Italy?

See **Skills Handbook**, p. H25

NATIONALISM IN EUROPE **715**

Direct Teach

Reading Focus

2 **What role did Cavour and Sardinia play in the path toward Italian unification?** *Cavour supported France in a war in return for France's support of Sardinia in its planned war against Austria.*

The Path Toward Unity

Identify What was *Il Risorgimento*? *a nationalist newspaper founded by Cavour as well as the name for the Italian movement for unification*

Identify Cause and Effect How did the revolutions of 1848 indirectly help Cavour? *Cavour was able to get support in Italy's fight against Austria; support for nationalism grew.*

Make Judgments If a nation is trying to unite, does it make sense to give some of its territory to another nation in exchange for support? Explain. *possible answer—No, it would be better to have the other nation's support without resorting to bribery, since a nation that would take a bribe of land from one group might also accept bribes from the opposition.*

Skills Focus: Comparing and Contrasting

At Level

Reading Skill
Cavour and Garibaldi

1. Have each student make a chart comparing and contrasting Camillo di Cavour and Giuseppe Garibaldi.

2. Review student charts as a class. Guide students in a discussion of the similarities and differences between the two leaders.

3. Have students explain how Italy's history might have been different if Cavour and Garibaldi had not been willing to cooperate.

Have each student write a paragraph describing the possible outcome.

4. Have volunteers read their paragraphs to the class. **LS** **Visual-Spatial, Verbal-Linguistic**

Alternative Assessment Handbook, Rubrics 9: Comparing and Contrasting; and 40: Writing to Describe

Answers

Primary Sources 1. *possible answer—to inspire people to follow him;* **2.** *He hopes that people will dedicate themselves wholeheartedly to that goal.*

Reading Check (left) *devotion to one's national group*

Reading Check (right) *He cultivated an alliance with the French.*

715

❸ **How did Garibaldi and the Red Shirts help unite Italy?** *Garibaldi led the Red Shirts to victory in Sicily and Naples; gained control of the southern Italian states, led to a united Italy*

Garibaldi and the Red Shirts

Identify Who was Giuseppe Garibaldi? *military commander, rose to lead a successful unification movement in Italy*

Contrast How did Garibaldi's approach to Italian unification differ from Cavour's approach? *Cavour worked through the political system in the north; Garibaldi led a military revolt in the south.*

Predict What do you think would have happened if Garibaldi had invaded the Papal States? *possible answer—It would have set the pope more firmly against unification, and might have alienated Catholics in other parts of Italy.*

📽 **Map Transparency:** The Unification of Italy, 1858–1870

🗽 **NEW YORK**
CC Unit 5-F3a
Unification of Italy

Garibaldi and the Red Shirts

Many Italians consider Cavour the "brain" of Italian unification and Mazzini its "heart." Equally important was **Giuseppe Garibaldi** (GAR-uh-BAWL-dee), whom many have called the "sword" of Italy.

Garibaldi joined Mazzini's Young Italy movement in 1833. Because of his nationalist activities, however, he was forced to flee from Italy twice. While living in exile in South America, he learned the techniques of guerrilla warfare. He then returned to Italy several times to continue the fight to free Italy from Austrian domination.

Garibaldi returned to Italy for good in 1854. Five years later, Cavour asked him to lead part of the Sardinian army in the war against Austria. Garibaldi accepted. After a few months of bitter fighting, the Austrians agreed to give up Lombardy, while keeping Venetia.

The Red Shirts Garibaldi and his followers, known as the **Red Shirts** because of their colorful uniforms, next turned their attentions to the Kingdom of the Two Sicilies. Using tactics of guerrilla warfare, Garibaldi and the Red Shirts gained control of the island of Sicily by July 1860. Then they crossed to the mainland. Meanwhile, Cavour had annexed territory in central Italy. In September, Sardinian troops helped Garibaldi conquer Naples. The Red Shirts now controlled the southern part of the Italian peninsula.

Unification Though he favored a republic, Garibaldi offered the Kingdom of the Two Sicilies to King **Victor Emmanuel** of Sardinia. The territories throughout Italy held elections in 1861, and all agreed to unification. The only holdouts were Venetia, which still belonged to Austria, and the Papal States, where French troops supported the pope.

THE UNIFICATION OF ITALY, 1858–1870

Kingdom of Sardinia, 1858
Austrian territory annexed by Sardinia, 1859
Territory annexed by Sardinia, 1860
Austrian territory annexed by Italy, 1866
Territory annexed by Italy, 1870
← Route of Garibaldi, 1860

0   100   200 Miles
0   100   200 Kilometers
Azimuthal equal-area projection

GEOGRAPHY SKILLS INTERPRETING MAPS

1. Movement In what city did Garibaldi end his military campaign through Italy?

2. Regions Which territory did Italy gain from Austria in 1866?

In 1860, on the island of Sicily, Garibaldi led the Red Shirts to victory against foreign troops in the Battle of Catalafimi.

Collaborative Learning

At Level

Unifying Italy

Background: With Camillo Cavour as prime minister, the Kingdom of Sardinia led the movement to unify Italy. Giuseppe Garibaldi united the Kingdom of the Two Sicilies with the Kingdom of Sardinia.

1. Organize students into two groups. Have one group represent people of the Kingdom of Sardinia supporting the unification. Have the other group represent people of the Kingdom of the Two Sicilies opposing unification. Give each side time to do research and prepare arguments in support of its position.

2. Conduct a classroom debate on Italian unification.

3. Guide students in a discussion of the debate. Which group was able to make the most convincing arguments for its position? What reasons did supporters of unification present? What reasons were opponents able to present?
🔲 **Interpersonal, Verbal-Linguistic**

📋 **Alternative Assessment Handbook,** Rubrics 10: Debates; and 14: Group Activity

---

Answers

Interpreting Maps 1. *Naples;*
2. *Venetia*

Those territories, however, did not hold out for long. In 1866 war broke out between Austria and Prussia. The Italians sided with the Prussians, and after Austria's defeat, Prussia gave Venetia to Italy. In 1870 war between France and Prussia forced the French to withdraw their troops from Rome. Italian troops entered Rome later that year, thus completing the unification of Italy under King Victor Emmanuel.

READING CHECK **Find the Main Idea** What actions led Garibaldi to be called the "sword" of Italian unification?

Challenges After Unification

In the years after unification, Italy faced many new challenges. Although politically unified, Italy had to deal with a number of social and economic problems. During the late 1800s, the new nation would take steps to catch up with the rest of Europe in industrialization, foreign policy, and social reform.

Social and Economic Problems

Although Italy was now politically united, strong regional differences still led to a lack of unity among many Italians. For example, some southern Italians resented being governed by Rome, which became the new capital of Italy in 1871. Meanwhile, the Catholic Church did not recognize Italy as a legitimate nation, and the pope prohibited Catholics from voting.

Widespread poverty was a serious problem. Unemployment and rising taxes often led to rioting in the towns, and violence was common. Poverty also led many Italians to emigrate. In the 1880s, large numbers of Italians began to leave Italy, many headed for the Americas. By 1920, some 4.5 million Italians had emigrated.

Reforms The Italian government soon began to address some of the problems facing the new nation. Voting reform was a major priority. At the time of unification, only the wealthiest Italian men could vote. By the late 1800s, most adult male taxpayers could vote.

As Italy industrialized, particularly in the north, the government passed reforms, including laws limiting working hours and prohibiting child labor. The government also encouraged the building of transportation and water systems to improve cities and encourage industry.

A New Foreign Policy In 1882 Italy formed a military alliance with Austria-Hungary and Germany. The three nations agreed to defend each other against any possible attack. This mutual arrangement was known as the Triple Alliance. As you will read in the next chapters, this alliance and others combined with political developments brought most of Europe to war in 1914.

Italy also tried to build an empire. It tried to gain control over Ethiopia, but failed after being defeated by a larger Ethiopian army in 1896. Then, in 1911, Italy declared war on the Ottoman empire. As a result, Italy gained territory in Africa.

READING CHECK **Summarize** What problems did Italy face after unification?

SECTION 1 ASSESSMENT

go.hrw.com
Online Quiz
Keyword: SHL NAT HP

Reviewing Ideas, Terms, and People

1. **a. Describe** What was Young Italy?
   b. Analyze Why did **Mazzini** think the territory lines set by the Congress of Vienna needed to be changed?
   c. Elaborate What effect did the Congress of Vienna have on the development of nationalism in Italy?

2. **a. Recall** Who was **Camillo di Cavour**?
   b. Interpret Why did Cavour form an alliance with France?
   c. Develop What role could a newspaper like *Il Risorgimento* play in the Italian unification movement?

3. **a. Identify** Who were the **Red Shirts**?
   b. Interpret Given that he favored a republic, why do you think **Garibaldi** handed over the southern states to **Victor Emmanuel**?

4. **a. Recall** Name two problems Italy faced after unification.
   b. Contrast How did social reform in Italy compare to reforms in Great Britain and France during the same period?

Critical Thinking

5. **Identify Cause and Effect** Use your notes from the section and a graphic organizer like this one to list causes and effects of Italian unification. Which effects were positive? Which were negative?

Causes	→	Italian Unification	→	Effects

FOCUS ON WRITING

6. **Persuasion** Suppose you are Giuseppe Garibaldi. Write a letter to Camillo di Cavour, explaining why you believe a unified Italy would be better off as a republic than a monarchy.

NATIONALISM IN EUROPE **717**

Section 1 Assessment Answers

1. **a.** a nationalist group
   b. He believed that people of the same background needed to form separate nation-states.
   c. possible answer—encouraged the development of nationalism by drawing political boundaries that ignored national groups

2. **a.** a leader of the Italian unification movement
   b. He wanted France's support in Italy's fight against Austria.
   c. might spread the message of nationalism

3. **a.** volunteer troops led by Garibaldi
   b. possible answer—for the sake of Italian unity

4. **a.** regional differences, poverty
   b. possible answers—There was still a lack of unity in Italy; Italy needed strong allies.

5. Causes—dissatisfaction with Congress of Vienna, nationalism, international politics; Effects—regional political differences (negative), industrialization (positive), voting reforms (positive), widespread poverty and mass emigration (negative)

6. Student letters should show an understanding of the characteristics of republics and monarchies.

717

Getting Started

Use the **Interactive Reader and Study Guide** to familiarize students with the section content.

📓 **Interactive Reader and Study Guide,** Section 2

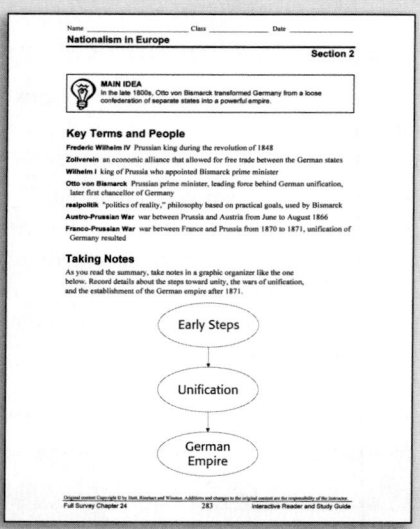

📝 **CRF:** Vocabulary Builder: Section 2

Taking Notes

Early Steps—German Confederation; revolutions of 1848; creation of Zollverein; Bismarck's wars with Denmark and Austria;

Unification—Austro-Prussian War joined together north German states; Franco-Prussian War united southern German states with the north;

German Empire—created a federalist government of 25 separate states with Wilhelm I as head of the government; Bismarck worked to limit the power of the Catholic Church in Germany; joined in alliances with Austria-Hungary, Italy, and Russia

---

SECTION 2

German Unification

BEFORE YOU READ

MAIN IDEA

In the late 1800s, Otto von Bismarck transformed Germany from a loose confederation of separate states into a powerful empire.

READING FOCUS

1. What steps did Germany take toward unification?
2. What was Bismarck's plan for Germany and how did he hope to achieve it?
3. How did wars lead to the unification of a German Empire?
4. In what ways did Germany grow and change after unification?

KEY TERMS AND PEOPLE

Frederick Wilhelm IV
Zollverein
Otto von Bismarck
Wilhelm I
realpolitik
Austro-Prussian War
Franco-Prussian War

NEW YORK

P1 3.1 Students analyze the roles and contributions of individuals and groups to social, political, economic, cultural, and religious practices and activities.

THE INSIDE STORY

How did a revolution help lead to the unification of Germany? In 1848 revolution spread through Europe. At this time, German liberals also revolted. When the people of Berlin heard that Metternich had been ousted in Vienna, they encircled the royal palace to hear the response of the Prussian king, Frederick Wilhelm IV. The crowd erupted when edgy soldiers accidently fired two shots. They felt tricked that a peaceful celebration had turned into a confrontation. To fight the royal soldiers, the Berliners set up wooden barricades, which forced the soldiers to retreat. Hundreds died in the two days of fighting.

Soon after the revolt, the king gave in to nationalist demands and proclaimed, "From now on Prussia merges with Germany!" However, the king quickly reasserted his power. Even though the revolution failed, German unification would eventually be accomplished with new policies enacted by a king and his powerful chancellor. ■

BARRICADES IN BERLIN

In 1848 Berliners fight Prussian troops in the city's streets.

Teach the Main Idea

At Level

German Unification

1. **Teach** Ask students the Reading Focus questions to teach this section.

2. **Apply** Tell students that in the mid-1800s Germany was divided into numerous independent states. Have students work in pairs to make lists of reasons for and against unification.

3. **Review** Review student lists as a class. Guide students in a discussion of the ways in which both liberal nationalists and conservative rulers seemed to get what they wanted.

4. **Practice/Homework** Have students write a paragraph predicting how German unification will unfold, using what they have read about Italian unification to form their predictions. Remind students that the two nations might not necessarily have unified in the same manner. **LS Interpersonal, Verbal-Linguistic**

📝 **Alternative Assessment Handbook,** Rubrics 11: Discussions; and 43: Writing to Persuade

Steps Toward Unification

Like Italy, Germany was not a unified nation in 1848. However, the patchwork of independent German states did have a common language and culture. In addition, Napoleon had nurtured nationalism when he united the German states into a confederation. Following Napoleon's defeat in 1815, the leaders at the Congress of Vienna retained that organization but renamed it the German Confederation. Thus, a group of 39 separate states with a common language and culture was poised for the movement to unite.

Revolution in Prussia As revolution swept through Europe in 1848, German liberals in the state of Prussia also took the opportunity to revolt. Though liberals differed over whether to support a republic or a constitutional monarchy, they agreed that German unity would promote individual rights and liberal reforms.

Facing calls for increased democracy, Prussian king **Frederick Wilhelm IV** quickly promised a constitution and other reforms. These changes did not become reality, however. By the end of 1848, the king went back on many of his promises. "Now I can be honest again," he told one of his ambassadors. He banned publications and organizations that supported democracy, and the constitution was never written.

Economic and Cultural Unity Another early step toward creating a unified Germany was an economic alliance between some of the German states. Created in 1834, the **Zollverein**, (TSOHL-fer-yn) or customs union, allowed for the removal of tariffs, or taxes, on products traded between the German states. The Zollverein inspired businesspeople to support unification and encouraged the growth of railroads connecting the German states. It also helped join Germans economically, if not yet politically, to each other. By 1844 the Zollverein included almost all of the German states.

As the German economy was growing, the sense of a distinctly German culture was growing. For example, German composers such as Richard Wagner wrote music glorifying German myths and traditions.

READING CHECK **Identify** What was the outcome of the revolution of 1848 in Prussia?

STEPS TO UNIFICATION IN GERMANY

In the mid-1800s many Germans were driven by nationalistic feelings to support a unified Germany.

The Revolution of 1848
• Inspired by revolution in France and a desire for a united Germany, Germans revolt against the Prussian king.

The Promise of Reforms
• At first, the Prussian king Frederick Wilhelm IV agrees to bring about democratic reforms, but later breaks his promises.

The Zollverein
• Germans create an economic alliance between the German states, the Zollverein, which promotes trade and a strong economy.

German Unification
• Otto von Bismarck leads Germany towards unification using his political philosophy of realpolitik, or "the politics of reality."

Bismarck's Plan for Germany

Otto von Bismarck, a conservative and a politician, was the leading force behind German unification. He became prominent in Prussian politics in 1847 when he gave a strongly conservative speech at the National Assembly. In 1862 **Wilhelm I**, the new Prussian king, chose Bismarck as Prussia's prime minister.

Bismarck's Philosophy Bismarck was not a liberal like the people involved in the revolution. Instead, he was a conservative who supported the king of Prussia and believed that it was Prussia's destiny to lead the German people to unification. Bismarck's philosophy about government was practical rather than idealistic. Practicing what would later be known as **realpolitik** (ray-AHL-poh-luh-TEEK), he developed policies based on the interests of Prussia.

"Blood and Iron" Bismarck's politics of reality were soon made evident in his push to increase the power of the Prussian military. In a speech to the Prussian parliament, he argued that German unity would not be won by speeches and majority vote but by "blood and iron." When the liberal parliament would not approve funds to expand the military, he dismissed the assembly and collected the taxes anyway. He then built the Prussian army into a great war machine, one that could use force to unite Germany.

TAKING NOTES

Take notes on the steps toward unity, the wars of unification, and the establishment of the German Empire after 1871.

Early Steps
↓
Unification
↓
German Empire

NEW YORK

CC Unit 5-F3a
Otto von Bismarck

• Direct Teach •

Reading Focus

1 What steps did Germany take toward unification? *German Confederation formed by Congress of Vienna; German revolt, Prussian king promises reform, but breaks promises, Zollverein allowed for free trade among German states*

Steps Toward Unification

Identify What was the German Confederation? *a group of 39 separate states, including Austria and Prussia, set up by the Congress of Vienna*

Analyze What did Frederick Wilhelm IV mean when he said "Now I can be honest again"? *that he did not have to pretend to support a republic*

Elaborate How would free trade help in the development of railroads? *would encourage trade, which would increase the need for transporting goods*

Quick Facts Transparency: Steps to Unification in Germany

Reading Focus

2 What was Bismarck's plan for Germany and how did he hope to achieve it? *to lead the German people to unification by increasing the power of the Prussian military.*

Bismarck's Plan for Germany

Define What was realpolitik? *Bismarck's "politics of reality," a belief in practical goals instead of theory*

Contrast How did Bismarck's beliefs differ from those of the German revolutionaries? *did not believe in liberal democracy; was a conservative who supported the king*

Answers

Reading Check *failed to bring democratic reform to Prussia*

719

Reading Focus

3 How did wars lead to the unification of a German Empire? *Austro-Prussian War joined northern German states; Franco-Prussian War declared unification of all German states*

Unification and Empire

Recall What were the results of the Austro-Prussian War? *dissolved German Confederation; forced Austria to give territory to Prussia; joined together the north German states*

Identify Cause and Effect What caused the south German states to join together with the north German states in the Franco-Prussian War? *feelings of nationalism over Alsace and Lorraine*

Make a Judgment Why do you think that Wilhelm I chose to be proclaimed emperor of Germany at Versailles? *possible answer—to get revenge against France; Versailles associated with French kings*

Bismarck's First War A disagreement over two border states, called Schleswig and Holstein, eventually gave Bismarck a way to start a war with Denmark. In 1864 Bismarck formed a military alliance with Austria against Denmark, believing both Schleswig and Holstein should be controlled by the German Confederation. After a brief fight, Denmark gave the territory to Austria and Prussia. Prussia would control Schleswig, and Austria would control Holstein. However, this meant that Austria now held a small bit of territory inside Prussia's borders. Bismarck knew that if he were to unite Germany, war with Austria was inevitable.

READING SKILLS

Understanding Word Origins If you know that the term *confederate* comes from the Latin word *confoederare* meaning "to unite by a league," how would you define confederation?

READING CHECK **Describe** What was the plan of Bismarck to unite Germany?

Unification and Empire

Bismarck could not increase Prussia's power as long as Austria was in the way. Austria was a leader in the German Confederation and it had influence over some of the German states that opposed Prussia's leadership. With two short wars, Bismarck moved Austria out of the way and established a unified German Empire.

The Austro-Prussian War To prepare for the war with Austria that he knew he had to wage and win, Bismarck worked behind the scenes. He met with the Italian prime minister and promised that, in exchange for support against Austria, Italy could have the territory

FACES OF HISTORY

Otto von BISMARCK
1815–1898

The revolutions of the mid-1800s gave Otto von Bismarck his first taste of power. In 1847, Bismarck gave a strongly conservative speech to the German National Assembly. He soon became the leader of the conservative politicians who supported the king and opposed the liberal revolution of 1848.

In 1862 Wilhelm I, the new Prussian king, appointed Bismarck as head of the Prussian cabinet. Bismarck believed it was Prussia's destiny to lead the German people to unification. Bismarck is perhaps best known for his build up of the Prussian army into a great war machine. With this army, Bismarck forcibly united the German states.

Draw Conclusions How did Bismarck's beliefs affect Germany?

---

of Venetia. He also persuaded Napoleon III to keep France neutral if war broke out between the German states. Then, to provoke Austria, Bismarck sent Prussian troops into the Austrian state of Holstein. In response, Austria declared war against Prussia.

The skirmish in Holstein was just what the Prussian leaders needed to gain support for the war with Austria. In an address to the Prussian people, king Wilhelm I blamed Austria for starting the war. His address clearly appealed to the people's sense of nationalism.

The war between Prussia and Austria unfolded just as the king and Bismarck planned. The highly skilled and well-equipped Prussian army defeated the Austrians in only seven weeks. The treaty ending the **Austro-Prussian War** dissolved the German Confederation and forced Austria to surrender the state of Holstein. When several other states in the North united with Prussia, only three states in the South remained outside Prussian control.

Together, Bismarck and Wilhelm used the victory to rally other German states around Prussia. The German Confederation, which had joined Austria to Prussia, had been destroyed by the war. By joining together the North German states, the Austro-Prussian War was the first step toward German unification.

The Franco-Prussian War Despite the victory in the Austro-Prussian War, it would take another war to create a unified Germany. The southern German states were still not included in the North German Confederation.

In 1870 a conflict was brewing with France over the disputed territory of Alsace and Lorraine. These provinces had been a part of the Holy Roman Empire, which included Prussia. The issue over Alsace and Lorraine sparked feelings of nationalism in the south German states. As a result, these states supported Prussia and the north German states in a war against France. In 1871 with the southern German states' help, Bismarck secured a Prussian victory in the **Franco-Prussian War**. Prussia won the war, and the peace treaty declared the unification of Germany.

Creating the German Empire The peace treaty following the Franco-Prussian War had far-reaching consequences. For example, the victory established a unified German empire.

Skills Focus: Comparing and Contrasting
At Level

Reading Skill
Roads to Unification

1. Have students work in pairs to create charts that compare and contrast unification in Germany and Italy. Student charts should show the causes of unification in each nation, which state led the unification process, leaders of the unification processes, the methods they used to bring unification about, who ruled the unified nations, and the aftereffects of unification.

2. Review student charts as a class. Guide students in a discussion of the similarities and differences between unification in Germany and Italy. **LS** **Interpersonal, Visual-Spatial**

   Alternative Assessment Handbook, Rubrics 7: Charts; and 9: Comparing and Contrasting

Answers

Faces of History *believed government policies should be based on realistic interest, not idealism; led to unification*

Reading Skills *a league of united states*

Reading Check *increase the Prussian military, go to war with Austria*

THE UNIFICATION OF GERMANY, 1865–1871

Legend:
- Kingdom of Prussia, 1865
- States annexed by Prussia, 1866
- States joining Prussia to form the North German Confederation, 1867
- States joining the German Empire, 1871
- → Route of Prussian armies in Austro-Prussian War, 1866
- → Route of German armies in Franco-Prussian War, 1870–1871
- ✳ Battles

GEOGRAPHY SKILLS — INTERPRETING MAPS

1. **Movement** From which German states did the Prussian armies begin their march during the Austro-Prussian War?
2. **Regions** When did the region of southern Germany join the German Empire?

Representatives of the allied German states met at Versailles, near Paris. The representatives proclaimed Wilhelm I the first kaiser, or emperor, of the German Empire. Wilhelm then appointed Bismarck as his first chancellor. The German victory also significantly changed the balance of power in Europe. With Napoleon III gone, France was no longer as powerful. As Germany grew economically, a new empire rose in power.

READING CHECK **Sequence** How did the Austro-Prussian and the Franco-Prussian War lead to German unification?

The Empire's Growth and Change

In the years after 1871, Germany prospered. Under the leadership of Wilhelm I and Bismarck, Germany developed into a strong empire. This period was known as the Second Reich, or empire, because Germans considered the Holy Roman Empire to be the First Reich.

A New Government Germany's 25 separate states wanted to retain some power. As a result, the government of the new German empire took a federalist form. Similar to the United States government, power was shared between state and national governments. Wilhelm I led the government. According to the law, all men in Germany over the age of 25 could vote. But in reality the government placed many restrictions on voters. Political parties also developed.

The Government and the Church Bismarck also believed that the Roman Catholic Church posed a threat to his government. He believed the government and not the church should control aspects of culture such as education. Bismarck worked to pass laws limiting the influence of the Catholic Church in Germany. This struggle between the government and the church was known as Kulturkampf, which in German means "the struggle for culture."

Economic Growth After unification Germany experienced a time of economic growth.

NEW YORK
CC Unit 5-F3a
Unification of Germany

NATIONALISM IN EUROPE **721**

GERMANY'S ECONOMIC GROWTH, 1890–1913

QUICK FACTS

Steel Production

Thousands of tons

- 1890: 2,353
- 1913: 19,410

Coal Production

Millions of tons

- 1890: 98
- 1913: 305

Source: Oxford Atlas of World History

Skills FOCUS INTERPRETING GRAPHS

Infer How do you think the growth in steel and coal production between 1890 and 1913 affected life in Germany?

France had paid reparations, or money for damages, to Germany after the Franco-Prussian War. German leaders used some of the money to build railroads to link the German states. Other funds helped build German businesses. Over the next half century, the new empire quickly caught up with the other industrial countries of Europe. Coal mines and steel factories flourished in Germany's major cities.

The Path to Social Reforms As in other nations, industrialization had its critics in Germany. German socialists protested against harsh factory conditions and called for state control of all industries. In the late 1870s Bismarck blamed socialists for two assassination attempts made on the emperor.

Even as Bismarck tried to destroy socialism, he also sought to reduce its appeal among the German people by enacting his own reforms. Beginning in the early 1880s, Bismarck pushed through legislation that provided benefits for health, accidents, old age, and disability.

Bismarck and the Wilhelm II After unification, Bismarck did not want to expand Germany's borders any further. He did, however, believe that France remained a threat. To counteract that threat, he entered a number of alliances with other European nations, including Austria-Hungary, Italy, and Russia. These nations agreed to help protect one another from a possible attack.

In 1888 Wilhelm I's grandson became kaiser of Germany. After a disagreement, the new kaiser, Wilhelm II, fired Bismarck as prime minister. In the early 1900s, the Wilhelm II continued to make alliances with other European nations and build up the most powerful military forces in Europe.

READING CHECK **Describe** How did Germany change both economically and politically in the years following unification?

SECTION 2 ASSESSMENT

Reviewing Ideas, Terms, and People

1. **a. Define** What was the **Zollverein**?
   b. Explain What did German liberals in Prussia want?
2. **a. Identify** Who was **Otto von Bismarck**?
   b. Explain Why were the states of Schleswig and Holstein significant?
   c. Evaluate In your opinion, what are the pros and cons of the policy of **realpolitik**? List two pros and two cons.
3. **a. Identify** What was the North German Confederation?
   b. Explain How did the **Franco-Prussian War** affect German unification?
4. **a. Identify** What was the structure of government in the new German Empire?
   b. Summarize How did Bismarck struggle with the church?
   c. Elaborate Why do you think Germany's economy grew so quickly in the years after unification?

Critical Thinking

5. **Identify Cause and Effect** Use your notes from this section and a graphic organizer like the one below to list causes and effects of German unification.

   Causes → German Unification → Effects

6. **Exposition** Imagine you are a reporter and are about to interview Otto von Bismarck. Write three short questions you will ask him about German unification.

Austria-Hungary and the Ottoman Empire

BEFORE YOU READ

MAIN IDEA

Nationalism broke down two old European empires—the Austrian Hapsburg Empire and the Ottoman Empire.

READING FOCUS

1. In what ways did the Austrian Empire struggle with nationalism in 1848 and beyond?

2. What was the dual monarchy of Austria-Hungary, and why was it created?

3. How did nationalism create conflict in the Ottoman Empire?

KEY TERMS AND PEOPLE

Franz Joseph I
Magyars
Dual Monarchy
Crimean War
Balkan Wars
Young Turks

NEW YORK

PI 3.1 Students explain the dynamics of cultural change and how interactions between and among cultures has affected various cultural groups throughout the world.

THE INSIDE STORY

How did a British woman revolutionize the field of nursing? The Crimean War, fought in the 1850s between Russia on one side and Great Britain, France, the Ottoman Empire, and Sardinia on the other, has been called "the most unnecessary war in history." Fierce battles took a heavy toll on soldiers. In addition, conditions in the crowded and filthy field hospitals caused diseases to spread. Florence Nightingale, a British nurse, described one hospital by stating, "Civilians have little idea, from reading the newspapers, of the horror and misery in a military hospital of operating upon these dying exhausted men . . . We have now 4 miles of beds and not 18 inches apart."

When she arrived at the war hospitals in 1854, Nightingale immediately took charge. She had the hospital wards cleaned to control the spread of disease. She obtained food, eating utensils, clothes, and bedding for wounded soldiers. These supplies, and the care given by the nurses, helped improve morale and reduce the mortality rate.

After the war, Nightingale helped set up training programs for nurses and worked to reform British military hospitals. She received the British Order of Merit for her dedication to nursing. ■

Florence Nightingale at Scutari, Crimean War

A NURSE'S CARE SAVES LIVES

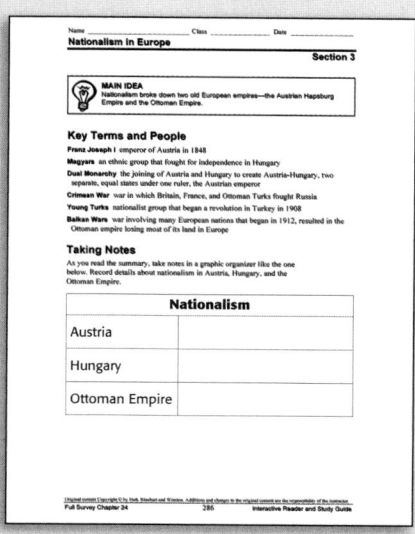

▲ Florence Nightingale and other nurses tend to patients during the Crimean War.

NATIONALISM IN EUROPE **723**

Preteach

Getting Started

Use the **Interactive Reader and Study Guide** to familiarize students with the section content.

Interactive Reader and Study Guide, Section 3

CRF: Vocabulary Builder: Section 3

Taking Notes

Austria—against nationalist activities; Congress of Troppau attempted to unite European nations against nationalist revolutions; resignation of Metternich and the Austrian emperor;

Hungary—1848 revolution stopped by Austria; Dual Monarchy created in 1867, making Austria and Hungary two separate and equal states under one ruler; ethnic groups remained divided

Ottoman Empire—nationalist groups began revolutions in the Balkans, war cost Ottoman Empire most of its land in Europe; Young Turks began revolution in 1908, leading to more representative and liberal government

---

Teach the Main Idea

At Level

Austria-Hungary and the Ottoman Empire

1. **Teach** Ask students the Reading Focus questions to teach this section.

2. **Apply** Have students create an outline of the section using the heads as main points. Have students identify at least two main ideas under each of the red subheadings.

3. **Review** Review student outlines as a class. Have students identify the points in their outlines that they feel are most important or most interesting. Guide students in a discussion comparing the problems of the Austrian and Ottoman empires.

4. **Practice/Homework** Tell students that it is 1867 and Franz Josef has asked them to write a speech for him to explain how the Dual Monarchy will work and how it will benefit the people of Austria, Hungary, and the Austro-Hungarian Empire. Have students present their speeches. **LS Visual-Spatial, Verbal-Linguistic**

Alternative Assessment Handbook, Rubrics 13: Graphic Organizers; and 43: Writing to Persuade

Reading Focus

❶ In what ways did the Austrian Empire struggle with nationalism in 1848 and beyond? *rebellions in Vienna led to resignations by Metternich and Ferdinand, empire unstable, continued rebellion; despite efforts, naturalist movement continued to grow*

The Austrian Empire

Identify What steps did Metternich take to confront liberal movements within the Austrian Empire? *prohibited reforms conflicting with absolute monarchy; formed alliances*

Analyze How was Metternich able to maintain control over Europe during the first half of the 19th century? *The Austrian Empire was one of the strongest and largest in Europe, and as leader of the German Confederation Metternich kept nationalism in check.*

Reading Focus

❷ What was the Dual Monarchy of Austria-Hungary, and why was it created? *agreement that made Austria and Hungary two separate, equal states under one ruler, Austrian emperor and Hungarian nationalist leaders created Dual Monarchy as compromise*

The Dual Monarchy

Recall What were the economic advantages of the Dual Monarchy? *Hungary could provide raw materials to Austria; Austria could provide industrial products to Hungary.*

Evaluate Was the Dual Monarchy successful? Explain. *possible answer —yes: there were economic and political advantages.*

Answers

Reading Check *to unite European powers in trying to prevent nationalist revolutions*

724

TAKING NOTES

Take notes about nationalism in Austria, Hungary, and the Ottoman Empire.

Nationalism
Austria
Hungary
Ottoman Empire

NEW YORK

CC Unit 5-D2
Klemens von Metternich

The Austrian Empire

The Hapsburg family, rulers of the Austrian Empire at the beginning of the 1800s, had controlled much of the region for nearly four centuries. When the Congress of Vienna met after the fall of Napoleon, Prince Metternich of Austria was a powerful voice in determining how to restore the balance of power in Europe. Nevertheless, this powerful empire would not remain intact through the remainder of the 1800s.

Resistance to Change After the Congress of Vienna, the Austrian emperor, Franz I, and his foreign minister, Prince Metternich, worked together to maintain the power of the Austrian Empire and the Hapsburg monarchy. They were determined to hold onto the empire and resist liberal ideas and movements that might endanger it.

As revolts spread through other parts of Europe, Metternich clamped down on the universities, accusing them of creating "a whole generation of revolutionaries." As leader of the German Confederation, he called a meeting at Carlsbad and helped pass the Carlsbad Decrees. These decrees, or laws, prohibited any reforms that conflicted with absolute monarchy. In addition, the decrees established censorship of newspapers and created a secret police force that spied on students who were suspected of liberal or nationalist revolutionary activities.

In addition to creating these restrictive laws for the empire, Metternich formed alliances with other European powers that were trying to prevent nationalist revolutions. In 1820 he and the leaders of these powers convened a meeting called the Congress of Troppau. At that Congress, the leaders agreed to provide military intervention to support governments against internal revolution.

Turmoil in Europe and Austria Metternich was able to protect the power of the Austrian Empire for a few years. But events in Europe and changes within the empire itself eventually caught up with him.

Revolutions in France, Italy, and the German states set off revolts in the Austrian Empire. People of many different nationalities living within the Austrian Empire wanted independence. In Vienna, demonstrators and the army clashed in the streets. A frightened

---

emperor Ferdinand ordered Metternich to resign, and Metternich fled Austria. Later in 1848 Ferdinand abdicated, and the throne went to his young nephew, **Franz Joseph I**.

Response to Revolution During his long reign, Franz Joseph I ruled over an unstable empire. In 1848 the Hungarian **Magyars** rebelled against Austrian rule, and for a long time it looked as though they would win their independence. However, czar Nicholas I of Russia sent Russian troops to help Austria crush the revolt. Franz Joseph I then abolished the liberal reforms enacted in 1848, but he could not stamp out nationalism in his multiethnic empire. Franz Joseph I revoked the new constitution. The revolutions had been stopped, at least for a while.

READING CHECK **Find the Main Idea** What was the purpose of the Congress of Troppau?

The Dual Monarchy

Although Franz Joseph I abolished the liberal reforms of 1848 and restored the power of the monarchy, he could not stop the nationalist movement. Change had to come to the Austrian Empire. It came in the form of the **Dual Monarchy**, also known as Austria-Hungary.

Forming a New Government As the nationalist movement continued in Europe, Austria lost the province of Lombardy to Italy in 1859. In 1866 Austria's defeat in the war with Prussia brought new demands from the Hungarians. Finally, Franz Josef I and leaders of the Hungarian nationalist movement reached an agreement. Known as the Compromise of 1867, this agreement created the dual monarchy of Austria-Hungary.

Under the dual monarchy, Austria and Hungary became two separate, equal states. They would have one ruler, Franz Joseph I, whose title would be emperor of Austria and king of Hungary. Austria and Hungary shared the ministries of war, finance, and foreign affairs, but each had its own parliament.

An Uneven Solution The Dual Monarchy lasted for about 50 years, until 1918. In addition to easing some of the pressure for nationalism, the Dual Monarchy had other benefits.

Collaborative Learning

At Above

The Congress of Troppau

Research Required

Background: The Congress of Troppau was convened to decide what action to take in response to liberal uprisings across Europe.

1. Organize students into five groups. Assign each group one of the nations that met at the Congress of Troppau: Austria, Prussia, Russia, Great Britain, and France. Tell each group that it is the delegation from its country to the Congress of Troppau. Have each group research its country's position toward repressing nationalist revolutions.

2. Tell students that the Congress of Troppau is called to order. Act as moderator as each group presents its case either for or against suppressing revolutions.

3. Guide students in a discussion of the results of the Congress of Troppau. Why did Austria, Prussia, and Russia vote to suppress nationalist revolutions? Why did France and Great Britain refuse to go along with them? **LS** **Interpersonal**

Alternative Assessment Handbook, Rubrics 11: Discussions; and 14: Group Activity

ETHNIC GROUPS IN AUSTRIA-HUNGARY, 1867

Slavs
- Croats and Serbs
- Czechs and Slovaks
- Poles
- Slovenes
- Ukrainians

Others
- Germans
- Magyars
- Romanians
- Italians

THE DUAL MONARCHY, 1867

GEOGRAPHY SKILLS INTERPRETING MAPS

1. **Location** Where were Germans and Magyars located in the empire?

2. **Regions** How did the borders of the Dual Monarchy follow the distribution of ethnic groups?

For example, there were some economic advantages to the arrangement. Hungary, mostly rural and agricultural, could provide raw materials and food to Austria. Austria, which was more industrialized, could in turn provide industrial products to Hungary.

The unrest in the empire did not go away, however. Divisions remained among the various nationalities. Austrian Germans and Hungarian Magyars did not speak the same language. Also, ethnic minorities received little benefit from the Dual Monarchy and continued to seek self-government.

READING CHECK **Describe** What was the basic structure of the government in Austria-Hungary?

The Ottoman Empire

Like the Austrian Empire, the Ottoman Empire had existed for centuries and controlled a vast multiethnic territory. Within its borders were many different religious and ethnic groups, including Greeks, Bulgarians, Turks, Kurds, Arabs, and Jews. This empire had been in decline since the late 1600s, and it could not survive the winds of change blowing across Europe in the 1800s.

The Eastern Question In the early 1800s, it became clear that the Ottoman Empire could no longer defend itself against independence movements or against external threats.

NATIONALISM IN EUROPE **725**

725

The Ottoman Empire

Identify Cause and Effect What were the results of the Crimean War? *ended in a stalemate; resulted in approximately half a million deaths*

Analyze Why were the Balkans important to Russia? *The area would provide access to the Mediterranean.*

Info to Know

The Balkans The Balkan region has often been at the center of conflict over the centuries because it is strategically located at the southern crossroads of Europe and Asia, just across the Adriatic Sea east of Italy. From the 300s BC until modern times, the Balkans have been invaded and conquered or contested by the Roman, Byzantine, Slav, Bulgar, Venetian, Ottoman, and Austro-Hungarian empires.

Answers

Linking to Today *Civil war and ethnic and religious violence have plagued this region for hundreds of years. Yugoslavia broke up in the early 1900s; violence in Bosnia and Herzegovina, new countries created in peace accord*

The Balkans Today

Montenegrins rally for independence in 2006.

The ethnic diversity in the Balkans that led to the Balkan Wars has also led to ethnic conflicts in more recent times. This incredibly diverse region, which includes Croats, Serbs, Montenegrins, Bosnians, Macedonians, and many other ethnic groups, has unfortunately had a long history of conflict.

After World War I, European leaders created the country of Yugoslavia. It included many formerly independent countries and ethnic groups under one government. Yugoslavia did not last. In the early 1990s, it broke up amidst civil war and ethnic and religious violence.

The violence in Yugoslavia was so severe that other countries stepped in to help put an end to the conflict. In 1995 countries around the world sent troops to one of the hardest hit regions, Bosnia and Herzegovina, to help bring an end to the fighting. A peace accord was later signed which resulted in the end of the former Yugoslavia and the creation of five new countries that had been Yugoslav republics.

In 2006 another country was born. Montenegro, which was part of the former Yugoslav republic of Serbia and Montenegro, narrowly voted to declare its independence. It became the world's newest nation without conflict.

Draw Conclusions How has ethnic diversity affected the political history of the Balkans?

NEW YORK

CC Unit 5-F5a
Balkans before World War I

CC Unit 5-F3b
Young Turks

By 1830, for example, Greece had gained independence. Russian had forced the Ottomans to accept Russian control of territory in the Caucasus and self-rule for Serbia.

This situation greatly worried European powers and created what they called "The Eastern Question." What would happen if the Ottoman Empire collapsed? In particular, what would happen to the city of Constantinople? Russia wanted to control that city so that it would have access to the Mediterranean. To keep Russia from gaining control of Constantinople, the French and British propped up the Ottoman Empire.

The Crimea The situation between the Ottomans and Europeans grew worse in the 1850s with a dispute over the Holy Land. The Ottomans, who controlled the region, gave Roman Catholics the control of the holy places in Palestine. When the Ottomans denied Orthodox Christians these same rights, the Russians invaded Ottoman territories. In addition, Great Britain saw Russia's move as a potential threat against its interests in India and joined in an alliance with France. Great Britain and France then joined with the Ottoman Empire in a war against Russia.

This war, most of which was fought in the Russian Crimea on the shores of the Black Sea, accomplished almost nothing. The **Crimean War** lasted about two years, ended in a stalemate, and resulted in approximately half a million deaths. Many of those deaths were the result of disease and crowded, filthy conditions in field hospitals. British nurse, Florence Nightingale, is well-known for her work to save lives during the Crimean War.

The Balkans The Balkans were another hot spot in the Ottoman Empire. The rise of nationalism in Europe had created discontent among the diverse ethnic groups in the region. Serbs, Romanians, Bulgarians, Albanians, and Greeks all wanted independence and their own nation state. These conditions, along with the competing interests of several European countries, let to a series of conflicts and wars in the 1800s and early 1900s.

Russia was involved in several of these conflicts in the Balkans. The Russians saw the Balkans as a route to the Mediterranean, which they wanted to gain. Great Britain and France were looking after their own interests in the region, so they sometimes sided with the Russians and sometimes sided with the Ottomans.

Skills Focus: Analyzing Alternative Points of View · At Level

Reading Like a Historian Skill
Balkan Nationalism

1. Organize students into five groups. Assign each group one of the following: the Ottoman Empire, the Austrian Empire, Russia, Prussia, France. Tell students that it is 1865 and they are newspaper editors in the country they represent. Have each student write an editorial discussing the situation in the Balkans. Students should consider the balance of power and attitudes of their nation toward nationalism in general and toward Balkan nationalism in particular.

2. Have volunteers read their editorials to the class. How well did students grasp the probable attitudes of their nation toward the Balkan nationalist revolutions?

3. Guide students in a discussion of the causes and effects of the Balkan nationalist movements. **LS Verbal-Linguistic**

Alternative Assessment Handbook, Rubric 23: Newspapers

Germany and Austria wanted to secure Austrian control over the various ethnic groups. When all was said and done, the **Balkan Wars** had cost the Ottoman Empire most of its land in Europe and the Balkan issues were far from settled.

With Russian troops almost at the gates of Constantinople, however, the other European powers became alarmed. In 1878 Prussian chancellor Bismarck hosted the Congress of Berlin to discuss the situation. In fact, the real purpose of the Congress was to overturn the gains Russia had made against the Ottomans.

The Congress of Berlin also gave Austria-Hungary land in the Balkans with no consideration of ethnic or national ties. As a result, conflicts between ethnic groups would erupt in the region for many years to come.

Political Reform One conflict occurred in 1908 when a nationalist group called the **Young Turks** began a revolution. The Young Turks were fighting against the absolute power of the sultan, the ruler of the Ottoman Empire. Mainly educated men, the Young Turks were devoted to restoring the constitution. Their revolution helped ensure a more representative, liberal government. Education improved, and the government took steps to provide some individual liberties.

READING CHECK **Recall** How were European nations involved in the affairs of the Ottoman Empire?

THE OTTOMAN EMPIRE

Territory lost, 1699–1878
Territory lost, 1879–1913
Ottoman Empire in 1913

Azimuthal equal-area projection

GEOGRAPHY SKILLS **INTERPRETING MAPS**

1. **Location** Where was Russia located in relation to the Ottoman Empire?
2. **Regions** Where did the Ottoman Empire lose territory between 1699 and 1913?

Direct Teach

Info to Know

The Ottoman Empire The Ottoman Empire was once feared as the conqueror of Europe. However, beginning with the unsuccessful Siege of Vienna in 1683, its domination of eastern Europe declined. Failure to centralize power led local officials to take control of many provinces.

 Map Transparency: The Ottoman Empire

● Review & Assess ●

Close

Have students summarize the ways in which the Austrian and Ottoman empires dealt with nationalist movements.

Review

 Online Quiz, Section 3

Assess

SE Section 3 Assessment

 Progress Assessment: Section 3 Quiz

 Alternative Assessment Handbook

Reteach/Intervene

 Interactive Reader and Study Guide, Section 3

 Interactive Skills Tutor CD-ROM

Reviewing Ideas, Terms, and People

1. **a. Recall** What were the Carlsbad Decrees?
   b. Analyze Why was Metternich's resignation significant?
   c. Evaluate Why do you think the revolution of 1848 failed in Austria?

2. **a. Define** What was the Dual Monarchy?
   b. Interpret How did Hungary benefit from Austria-Hungary's economy?
   c. Evaluate Do you think the dual monarchy of Austria-Hungary would have been formed if Austria had won the Austro-Prussian War? Explain your answer.

3. **a. Identify** What was the Eastern Question?
   b. Identify Cause and Effect What was the major effect of the Balkan Wars?

Critical Thinking

4. **Identify Cause and Effect** Copy the graphic organizer below and use it and your notes on the section to identify the effects of nationalism in Austria, Hungary, and the Ottoman Empire.

Nationalism

Austria | Ottoman Empire | Hungary

FOCUS ON WRITING

5. **Persuasion** You belong to a minority ethnic group in Austria-Hungary. Write a letter to Emperor Franz Joseph I outlining why your group should have independence. Use details from the chapter in your notes.

NATIONALISM IN EUROPE **727**

Section 3 Assessment Answers

1. **a.** a series of restrictive laws to censor and investigate liberal and nationalist groups
   b. possible answer—Ferdinand might have hoped it would end the revolution; instead it led to further demands.
   c. possible answer—because the revolutionaries could not win against military action

2. **a.** the two nations of Austria and Hungary, with a government led by Franz Joseph I
   b. Austria provided industrial products.
   c. possible answer—No, Austria probably would have remained an independant nation.

3. **a.** concern over how the fate of the Ottoman Empire would affect the rest of Europe
   b. The Ottoman Empire lost most of its land in Europe.

4. Austria and Hungary—creation of Dual Monarchy; Ottoman Empire—loss of territory

5. Student letters should discuss the benefits of independence for separate ethnic groups.

Answers

Interpreting Maps **1.** *to the east and northeast;* **2.** *in north Africa and the Balkans*

Reading Check *became involved in wars to protect their own territorial interests and the overall balance of power*

Preteach

Getting Started

Use the **Interactive Reader and Study Guide** to familiarize students with the section content.

📋 **Interactive Reader and Study Guide**, Section 4

Academic Vocabulary

Review with students the high-use academic term in this section.

sector a subdivision of society (p. 732)

📋 **CRF:** Vocabulary Builder: Section 4

Taking Notes

Government and Society—czars were autocrats, serfdom was a problem in Russian society; Reform and Repression—Decembrist Revolt fought against czar's rule, Alexander II freed the serfs, pogroms were violent attacks against Jews, industry developed rapidly under Nicholas II, Trans-Siberian Railroad built; War and Revolution—Russo-Japanese War; Marxist ideas spread; Bloody Sunday killings inspired Revolution of 1905 against the czar; October Manifesto promised reform and democratic government after revolution, but czar still maintained significant power

go.hrw.com
Online Resources

KEYWORD: SHL NAT
ACTIVITY: Russian Revolution

BEFORE YOU READ

MAIN IDEA

In the 1800s and early 1900s, Russians rebelled against the absolute power of the czar and demanded social reforms.

READING FOCUS

1. What was government and society like in Russia in the first half of the 1800s?
2. What were some examples of reform and repression in Russia?
3. How did war and revolution affect Russia in the early 1900s?

KEY TERMS AND PEOPLE

autocracy
serfs
Alexander II
pogroms
Trans-Siberian Railroad
Russo-Japanese War
socialist republic
Vladimir Lenin
Bloody Sunday
Duma

 NEW YORK

PI 2.5 Students investigate key events and developments and major turning points in world history to identify the factors that brought about change and the long-term effects of these changes.

THE INSIDE STORY

Why did terrorists kill Russia's leader? It was the same day that Czar Alexander II signed a document granting major political reforms to the people. The czar was traveling through the snow in his iron-clad carriage to the Winter Palace in St. Petersburg. His guards kept close by him on open sleighs. Terrorists had already tried to assassinate the czar several times. As the carriage approached a street corner, a bomb exploded, and some of the guards were wounded.

Alexander II stepped out of the carriage to check on the wounded guards' condition. After he got out, a terrorist threw another bomb—fatally injuring the czar.

The terrorist who assassinated Alexander II belonged to a radical group called The People's Will. Members of The People's Will believed that Russian society needed radical reforms, and the only way to make that happen was to overthrow the government and start over. Alexander II had made many reforms during his rule, but it was not enough. ◼

Contemporary drawing of the assassination of Alexander II at St. Petersburg, 1881

▲ A terrorist explodes a bomb as Czar Alexander II and his guards travel outside the Winter Palace.

Teach the Main Idea

At Level

Unrest in Russia

1. **Teach** Ask students the Reading Focus questions to teach this section.
2. **Apply** Have students make a time line showing the major events from this section. Student time lines should begin with the death of Czar Alexander I in 1825 and end with the October Manifesto of 1905.
3. **Review** Review student time lines as a class. Guide students in a discussion of the events on their time lines. Call students' attention to the swing back and forth from

repression to reform, to repression under different czars.

4. **Practice/Homework** Tell students that they are advisers to the czar of Russia. Have students make a list of proposed reforms to improve the economic and social conditions of the country. **LS Visual-Spatial, Verbal-Linguistic**

📋 **Alternative Assessment Handbook**, Rubrics 36: Time Lines; and 42: Writing to Inform

LAST CZARS OF RUSSIA

QUICK FACTS

The last czars of Russia passed some reforms but still ruled with nearly unlimited power.

Nicholas I (ruled 1825–1855) put down the Decembrist Revolt and led Russia during the Crimean War.

Alexander II (ruled 1855–1881) enacted social and economic reforms and freed Russia's serfs.

Alexander III (ruled 1881–1894) used the secret police and censorship to quell unrest.

Nicholas II (ruled 1894–1917) led Russia during the Russo-Japanese War and issued the October Manifesto promising reforms.

▲ Nicholas II and his wife, Alexandra, are crowned in 1896.

Government and Society

In the first half of the 1800s, Russia was one of the great powers of Europe. Russian troops helped defeat Napoleon, and Russia's leaders helped reorganize Europe after his fall. Yet Russia was very different from Europe's other powers. The Russian Empire was huge. It stretched eastward far into Asia and included many different ethnic groups.

To govern this large and diverse empire, Russian monarchs ruled with absolute power. They were called czars and they had control over most aspects of Russian life. The czars believed in **autocracy**, or government by one ruler with unlimited power.

Russian society under the czars was mainly agricultural. Unlike many other countries in Europe, Russia had not industrialized very much. Much of the country's population consisted of peasants. Many of these Russian peasants were **serfs**—agricultural workers who were considered part of the land on which they worked.

Serfs were controlled by lords, the wealthy nobles who owned the land. Technically, serfs were not slaves because they were not legally considered property. However, their poor living conditions and lack of freedom resembled slavery. For example, serfs were not allowed to leave the property on which they were born and they did not own the land on which they worked.

In addition, serfs had to make regular payments of both goods and labor to their lords.

Some government leaders wanted to improve conditions for the serfs, but they were unable to make reforms. Russian serfdom remained a way of life for many people and was a major problem in Russian society.

READING CHECK **Summarize** What was Russian government and society like in the first half of the 1800s?

Reform and Repression

As in other European countries at this time, revolutionary ideas began to grow in Russia. Russians wanted more freedoms and more democracy. But Russia's conservative czars were resistant to reform, which led to revolts, unrest, and repression.

The Decembrist Revolt Some revolutionaries formed secret societies to fight against the czar's rule. When Czar Alexander I died in 1825, they saw it as an opportunity for change.

A group of revolutionaries later referred to as the Decembrists rebelled against the government. The Decembrists included many military officers. They led a group of some 3,000 soldiers that assembled near the Winter Palace, publicly refusing to declare their allegiance to the new czar, Nicholas I.

TAKING NOTES

Take notes on government and society, reforms and repression, and war and revolution in Russia.

NEW YORK
CC Unit 5-D4b
Russian serfdom

READING SKILLS

Understanding Word Origins If you know that the term *serf* comes from a Latin word meaning "slave," what might that tell you about their status in society?

NATIONALISM IN EUROPE **729**

729

Reading Focus

❸ How did war and revolution affect Russia in the early 1900's?
Russia's defeat in the war with Japan amplified social unrest and led to protests against the czar's strict rules. In response, some reforms were made but the czar still held absolute power.

War and Revolution

Recall Why did Japan attack Russia in what became known as the Russo-Japanese War? *Japan viewed Russia as a threat to its growing empire.*

Make Inferences Why do you think Marx's ideas gained popularity in the late 1800's? *possible answer—his ideas probably appealed to the large working class*

Identify Cause and Effect Why did Czar Nicholas issue the October Manifesto? *in response to Bloody Sunday and other protests, in hopes of quelling future rebellions and strikes*

Info to Know

Emperor Nicholas When news of Czar Alexander's death reached his family, his brother Nicholas declared loyalty to their other brother Konstantin, as the new emperor. However, Alexander had named Nicholas heir apparent in a manifesto. Konstantin had married a Polish woman not of royal blood and had renounced his rights to the throne. Nevertheless, Nicholas swore allegiance to Konstantin but eventually took the throne anyway because the threat of revolt was spreading.

Answers

Reading Check *freeing of serfs; system whereby peasants could buy the land they worked; reformed judicial system and some local self-government*

730

Nicholas responded by crushing the rebellion. Many of the Decembrists were captured and sent to Siberia, an isolated region in far eastern Russia. Five were executed. The Decembrist revolt had failed, but it began a revolutionary movement in Russia that would only grow in the years ahead.

Reforms of Alexander II The next czar, **Alexander II**, came to power in 1855 near the end of the Crimean War, which Russia lost to Great Britain, France, the Ottoman Empire, and Sardinia. The loss showed how far behind Russia was from the rest of Europe. Russia did not have the modern technology and industry necessary to build a military that could compete with Europe's powers. To solve these problems, Alexander II began a program of reforms.

In 1861 Alexander II took the historic step of freeing Russia's serfs and giving them the right to own land as part of a commune. He believed that if the terrible living conditions continued for the serfs, a rebellion was likely. In addition, he hoped that giving serfs their own land would help build a market economy in Russia. The government set up a system in which peasants would buy the land they worked on from the landowner, usually with government help.

Alexander II made other reforms to modernize Russia. He set up a new judicial system and allowed some local self-government. In addition, he reorganized the army and navy.

Despite these reforms, revolutionary movements continued to gain strength and call for more radical changes. In 1881 a radical group called the People's Will assassinated Czar Alexander II.

Unrest Under Alexander III Alexander's son, Alexander III, became the next czar. He was a reactionary, or a person who wants to go back to the way things were in the past. Alexander III ended the reforms of his father. He responded to revolutionary threats by going after individuals and groups suspected of plotting against the government.

Meanwhile, a different sort of unrest was building. Mobs of people started attacking Jews, killing them and destroying their property. These widespread violent attacks were known as **pogroms**, and there were several waves of them in Russia.

NEW YORK
CC Unit 5-D4c
Expansion of Russia into Siberia

FOCUS ON NEW YORK
From 1881 to 1914, many Russian Jews fleeing pogroms settled in New York City and Brooklyn. The Russian language newspaper founded to serve the new immigrants, *Novoe Russkoe Slovo*, is still published today.

730 CHAPTER 24

The first wave of pogroms began after Alexander II was assassinated. Some people in the government and in society wrongly blamed Jews for the assassination. As a result, groups of anti-Semitic rioters attacked and killed innocent Jews, and the authorities did nothing to stop them.

Industrialization under Nicholas II Nicholas II was crowned czar in 1894. Like his father, he ruled as an autocrat. Early in his reign, industry developed rapidly in Russia. During the 1890s Russia began building the **Trans-Siberian Railroad** to link western Russia with Siberia. But Russian expansion in the east would soon led to a conflict and war.

READING CHECK **Identify** What were some key reforms in Russia during the 1800s?

War and Revolution

As Russia expanded in the east, it came into conflict with another imperial power—Japan. At the same time, revolutionary ideas were growing again, and revolution was brewing.

War with Japan In the early 1900s, Japan was building an empire in the east and viewed Russia as a threat to its plans. As a result, in 1904 Japanese forces attacked and eventually defeated Russia in the **Russo-Japanese War**. The defeat shocked many Russians and added to growing unrest and calls for change.

Marxist Ideas One group calling for change in Russia was the Marxists, Russians who followed the communist theories of Karl Marx. In the late 1800s, Marx's ideas gained popularity in Russia. Marx's followers wanted to create a **socialist republic**, a society in which there would be no private property and the state would collectively own and distribute goods.

In 1902 a Marxist named **Vladimir Lenin** published a work supporting the overthrow of the czar. He called for revolutionaries to rise up against "the shame and the curse of Russia."

The Revolution of 1905 By 1905 many Russians were ready to rebel against the czar. On January 22, 1905, an Orthodox priest named Father Gapon planned to bring a petition to the czar at the Winter Palace. The petition listed a number of demands.

Reading like a Historian

Bloody Sunday in St. Petersburg

Analyzing Visuals One source that historians study to learn about the past is art. The painting below, *Death in Snow,* is by Russian artist Vladimir Makovsky. It shows protesters in St. Petersburg, Russia, on January 22, 1905—an event known as Bloody Sunday.

To analyze what this painting suggests about this event and about the Russian Revolution of 1905, think about
• the subject of the painting
• the details in the painting
• the title of the work

On Bloody Sunday, Russian troops killed and wounded hundreds of peaceful protesters, igniting the Russian Revolution of 1905.

Father Gapon, a Russian priest, led the march.

The protesters included poor workers, women, and children. They had marched to the czar's Winter Palace to ask for better working conditions.

Skills FOCUS READING LIKE A HISTORIAN

1. **Subject** Why do you think Makovsky chose to paint this event? What might his decision indicate about the importance of Bloody Sunday?
2. **Details** How would you describe the expressions and body language of the people shown?
3. **Title** What statement did Makovsky make by titling the painting *Death in Snow*?

See Skills Handbook, p. H26

Biography

Nikolay Rimsky-Korsakov (1844–1908)

Nikolay Rimsky-Korsakov was educated at the Russian naval academy in St. Petersburg but began to compose a symphony in 1861. After his graduation in 1862, he sailed on a clipper ship to the United States at the height of the American Civil War. He finished his first symphony after returning to St. Petersburg, and it was premiered in 1865. In the 1860s Rimsky-Korsakov joined four other composers to create a truly national school of Russian music known as "The Five." By 1871 he was hired to teach composition at the St. Petersburg Conservatory. One of his biggest services to Russian music was as editor of many of his colleagues' musical scores for publication; his work guaranteed the survival of those works.

Quick Facts Transparency: Russian Revolution of 1905

● **Review & Assess** ●

Close

Have students summarize the periods of repression and reform in Russia between 1825 and 1905.

Review

Online Quiz, Section 4

Assess

SE Section 4 Assessment

Progress Assessment: Section 4 Quiz

Alternative Assessment Handbook

Reteach/Intervene

Interactive Reader and Study Guide, Section 4

Interactive Skills Tutor CD-ROM

Answers

Reading Check *growing unrest, pogroms, crack down on revolutionary movements, defeat in Russo-Japanese War led to discontent, Bloody Sunday inspired rebellions against czar*

732

When Gapon and the protesters neared the Winter Palace, troops fired at the group, and hundreds died. The day became known in Russian history as **Bloody Sunday**.

Bloody Sunday inspired many <u>sectors</u> of society to rise up against the czar. In the cities and across the countryside, rebellions broke out. Workers went on strike, and university students protested in the streets. Peasants rebelled against their landlords. People everywhere began to disobey the czar's strict rules. The Russian Revolution of 1905 had begun.

At first the czar firmly supported the autocracy. Then he promised reform but did not follow through with his promises. Finally, in October, a massive worker's strike seemed to be the final straw. Some 2 million workers protested in the streets of Russia. Railroads stopped because of lack of workers. Czar Nicholas II had to do something.

ACADEMIC VOCABULARY

sector a subdivision of society

The October Manifesto In response to the rebellions and strikes, Nicholas II issued the October Manifesto, an official promise for reform and a more democratic government. The October Manifesto promised a Russian constitution. It guaranteed individual liberties to all Russians, including freedom of speech and freedom of assembly. Many Russians also gained the right to vote.

The October Manifesto stated that voters would elect representatives to the **Duma** (doomuh), an assembly that would approve all laws. Although the czar would continue to rule Russia, he promised not to pass any laws without the approval of the elected Duma.

Nicholas II hoped that the October Manifesto would end the revolution. But he still did not want to give up the absolute power he had always known. In 1906 when the first Duma met, the czar ended the meeting when the Duma made too many demands.

Nicholas II and his advisers did make more reforms in the years after the Russian Revolution of 1905. However, it was clear that the czar had not achieved a balance between his own power and the growing support for democracy. People still wanted reform and change. Eventually they would get it.

READING CHECK **Cause and Effect** What were some causes of the Russian Revolution of 1905?

QUICK FACTS

RUSSIAN REVOLUTION OF 1905

CAUSES

- The slow pace of reforms by Russia's czars
- Desire for better living conditions and freedoms
- The growth of revolutionary groups

EFFECTS

- Nicholas II issues October Manifesto promising some reforms, Duma as representative body
- Political parties and voting rights are allowed, but czar maintains absolute power

---

SECTION **4** ASSESSMENT

go.hrw.com
Online Quiz
Keyword: SHL NAT HP

Reviewing Ideas, Terms, and People

1. **a. Define** What is an **autocracy**?
   b. Explain What was life like for Russia's **serfs**?
   c. Evaluate Why do you Russia's czars failed to improve living conditions for serfs?

2. **a. Recall** What historic action did **Alexander II** take in 1861?
   b. Contrast In what ways did Alexander II differ from Russia's other czars?
   c. Evaluate Why do you think the Decembrist Revolt failed?

3. **a. Identify** What was the **Duma**?
   b. Interpret Why was **Bloody Sunday** a significant event?
   c. Predict How do you think the refusal of Russia's czars to make lasting reforms would affect Russia?

Critical Thinking

4. **Rank** Use your notes from the section and a graphic organizer like this one to rank three major problems facing Russian society in the late 1800s and early 1900s.

   (1)   (2)   (3)

FOCUS ON WRITING

5. **Narration** Write a short paragraph from the point of view of a newspaper reporter describing the events of Bloody Sunday.

732 CHAPTER 24

Section 4 Assessment Answers

1. **a.** government by one ruler with unlimited power;
   b. poor living conditions; lack of freedom
   c. possible answer—There were so many serfs that it was difficult to make a change.

2. **a.** freed the serfs
   b. Nicholas I's rule was marked by repression, whereas Alexander II's rule was marked by liberal reforms.
   c. possible answer—did not have widespread support

3. **a.** the Russian legislative assembly set up after the Revolution of 1905
   b. It led to the October Manifesto promising reforms and more democratic government.
   c. possible answer—might result in another revolution

4. Possible answer—serfdom; military defeats; growth of revolutionary groups

5. Student paragraphs should include details from the section about the protest and the response.

World Literature

NEW YORK STANDARDS

PI **2.4** Students explain the importance of analyzing narratives drawn from different times and places to understand historical events.

Leo Tolstoy (1828–1910)

About the Reading Leo Tolstoy's novel *War and Peace*, published from 1865 to 1869, is considered one of the greatest novels of all time. It follows the lives of five Russian families in the early 1800s and presents a picture of Russian society during this time. In the passage below, two of the novel's characters, Pierre Bezukhov and Prince Andrew Bolkonsky, argue about whether or not people should live their lives to help others or to help themselves.

AS YOU READ Think about how Prince Andrew views Russia's serfs.

Excerpt from

War and Peace

by Leo Tolstoy

"Come on let's argue then," said Prince Andrew. "You talk of schools," he went on, crooking a finger, "education and so forth; that is you want to raise him" (pointing to a peasant who passed by them taking off his cap) "from his animal condition and awaken in him spiritual needs, while it seems to me that animal happiness is the only happiness possible, and that is just what you want to deprive him of. I envy him, but you want to make him what I am, without giving him my means. Then you say, 'lighten his toil.' But as I see it, physical labor is as essential to him, as much a condition of his existence, as mental activity is it to you or me. You can't help thinking. I go to bed after two in the morning, thoughts come and I can't sleep but toss about till dawn, because I think and can't help thinking, just as he can't help plowing and mowing; if he didn't, he would go to the drink shop or fall ill. Just as I could not stand his terrible physical labor but should die of it in a week, so he could not stand my physical idleness, but would grow fat and die. The third thing—what else was it you talked about?" and Prince Andrew crooked a third finger. "Ah, yes, hospitals, medicine. He has a fit, he is dying, and you come and bleed him and patch him up. He will drag about as a cripple, a burden to everybody, for another ten years. It would be far easier and simpler for him to die. Others are being born

and there are plenty of them as it is. It would be different if you grudged losing a laborer—that's how I regard him—but you want to cure him from love of him. And he does not want that. And besides, what a notion that medicine ever cured anyone! Killed them, yes!" said he, frowning angrily and turning away from Pierre.

This painting shows Russian serfs in the 1800s.

Dinner at the Zemstvo, by Grigori Mjasoedov, 1872

Skills FOCUS **READING LIKE A HISTORIAN**

go.hrw.com
World Literature
Keyword: SHL WRLIT

1. **Describe** How would you describe Prince Andrew's attitude toward Russia's serfs?

2. **Interpret Literature as a Source** Do you think this novel accurately portrays the views of some upper-class Russians toward serfs? Why or why not?

See **Skills Handbook**, p. H28

NATIONALISM IN EUROPE **733**

World Literature

War and Peace

Word Help

condition state of being
toil work

Meet the Writer

Leo Tolstoy (1828–1910) Tolstoy was born into a noble family. In about 1876 he experienced a religious conversion, after which he preached nonviolence and advocated a simple life. He considered any organizations that ruled by force—including both the government and the church—to be wrong. A Tolstoy cult developed, attracting pilgrims to his estate. The Russian Church excommunicated Tolstoy in 1901. Because of his prestige, however, the government left him alone. Tolstoy's belief in practicing what he preached led him to abandon all earthly goods, including his home. In 1910, with no destination, he left home with his youngest daughter, caught a chill, and died.

Info to Know

War and Peace Many people consider *War and Peace* to be the one of the greatest novels ever written. It combines three kinds of material—an actual history of the Napoleonic wars, biographies of fictional characters, and essays in which Tolstoy attempts to formulate laws of history. In his view, history is not a result of major decisions by great men, but is the sum total of all the little decisions made by ordinary people.

Differentiating Instruction

English-Language Learners
Below Level

Review through this passage with students to make sure that they understand its meaning. Have each student write a paragraph responding to Prince Andrew. Have volunteers read their paragraphs to the class. Then guide students in a discussion of Prince Andrew's attitudes toward the peasants and their responses. **LS** **Verbal-Linguistic**

Alternative Assessment Handbook, Rubrics 11: Discussions; and 37: Writing Assignments

Advanced Learners/ Gifted and Talented
Above Level

Have students write a brief essay analyzing Prince Andrew's attitudes toward peasants. Which of the two men would probably be considered a conservative? Which would probably be a liberal nationalist? Have volunteers read their essays to the class. Then guide students in a discussion of the condition of peasants in Russia at the time. **LS** **Verbal-Linguistic**

Alternative Assessment Handbook, Rubrics 11: Discussions and 37: Writing Assignments

Answers

Reading Like a Historian **1.** *He is not sympathetic about their living conditions; believes serfs are meant to live the way they do.* **2.** *possible answer—probably accurate, the upper-class Russians probably looked for a justification to the way the serfs were treated.*

733

Revolution and Unification

Word Help

prolongation a lengthening in time
intolerable unbearable

Primary Source

"The passions of the mob broke loose like a bursting dam. The people, seeing the dead and dying carried away in all directions, the snow on the streets and pavements soaked with blood, cried aloud for vengeance . . . Men, women, and children fell at each volley, and were carried away in ambulances, sledges, and carts. The indignation and fury of every class were aroused. Students, merchants, all classes of the population alike were inflamed. At the moment of writing, firing is going on in every quarter of the city."

—*Eyewitness account of Bloody Sunday, published in London Weekly Times, January 1905*

Revolutions and Unification

NEW YORK STANDARDS

PI 2.3 Students analyze evidence critically and demonstrate an understanding of how circumstances of time and place influence perspective.

Historical Context The four documents below provide different views and accounts of revolutions and unification in Europe during the late 1800s and early 1900s.

Task Study the documents and answer the questions that follow. After you have studied the documents, you will be asked to write an essay about the causes of revolutions and unification in Europe. You will need to use evidence from these selections and from the chapter to support the position you take in your essay.

DOCUMENT 1

Petition to the Czar

In St. Petersburg, Russia, in 1905, Father Gapon wrote a petition to Russian Czar Nicolas II expressing the desires of the Russian people for more equal rights under the law.

> Oh Sire, we working men and inhabitants of St. Petersburg, our wives, our children and our parents, helpless and aged women and men, have come to you our ruler, in search of justice and protection. We are beggars, we are oppressed and overburdened with work, we are insulted, as slaves. The moment has come for us when death would be better than the prolongation of our intolerable sufferings. We are seeking here our last salvation. Do not refuse to help your people. Destroy the wall between yourself and your people.

DOCUMENT 2

Germany's Military Might

In the early 1900s, as kaiser of a united Germany, Wilhelm II built up a powerful military as a show of strength and national pride. This 1914 Russian cartoon shows Wilhelm II surprised by an invasion of Germany by the Russian army.

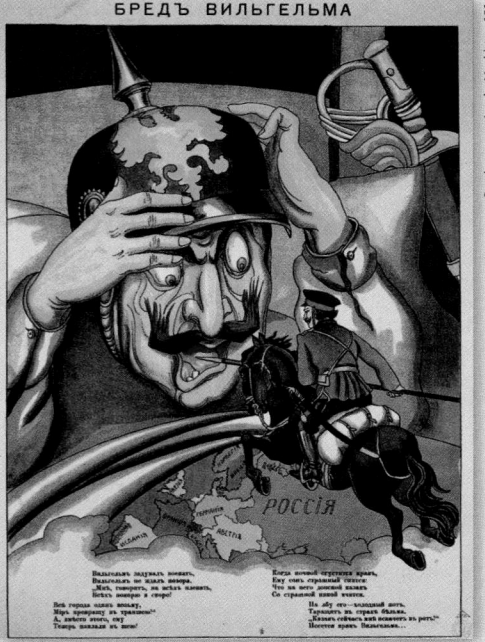

Russian engraving, by Machistov, 1914

Skills Focus: Analyzing Alternative Points of View   At Level

Reading Like a Historian Skill
Petition to the Czar

1. Remind students that Father Gapon led the Bloody Sunday protest of 1905.

2. Ask students what words Gapon uses to describe the Russian working people. How does he get his message across? Which words show his point of view? How might the Russian czar describe the situation from his point of view?

3. Have students compare Document 1 with the artwork *Death in Snow* in Section 4 of this chapter. Do Vladimir Makovsky and Father Gapon share the same point of view? How can you tell?

4. Have students write a brief essay comparing the points of view expressed in "Petition to the Czar" and *Death in Snow*, focusing on the portrayal of the protesters. **LS Verbal-Linguistic**

   Alternative Assessment Handbook, Rubrics 9: Comparing and Contrasting, and 38: Writing to Classify

DOCUMENT 3

Bismarck's "Blood and Iron" speech

In this speech to the Prussian parliament in 1862, Otto von Bismarck argues for a buildup of the Prussian military. Bismarck went on to build the Prussian army into a great war machine that would use "blood and iron" to forcibly unite the German states under Prussia.

> Public opinion changes, the press is not [the same as] public opinion; one knows how the press is written; members of parliament have a higher duty, to lead opinion, to stand above it. We are too hot-blooded, we have a preference for putting on armor that is too big for our small body; and now we're actually supposed to utilize it. Germany is not looking to Prussia's liberalism, but to its power; Bavaria, Württemberg, Baden may indulge liberalism, and for that reason no one will assign them Prussia's role; Prussia has to coalesce and concentrate its power for the opportune moment, which has already been missed several times; Prussia's borders according to the Vienna Treaties [of 1814–1815] are not favorable for a healthy, vital state; it is not by speeches and majority resolutions that the great questions of the time are decided—that was the big mistake of 1848 and 1849—but by iron and blood.

DOCUMENT 4

Revolution Spreads to the German States

In his memoir, Carl Schurz describes the excitement he witnessed on the streets of Berlin during the German Revolution of 1848.

> Great news came from Vienna! There the students of the university were the first to assail the Emperor of Austria with the cry for liberty and citizens' rights . . . In the Prussian capital the masses surged upon the streets, and everybody looked for events of great import.
>
> On the 18th of March we too had our mass demonstration. A great multitude gathered for a solemn procession through the streets of the town [Berlin] . . . At the head of the procession Professor Kunkel bore the tricolor—black, red, and gold—which so long had been prohibited as the revolutionary flag. He spoke with wonderful eloquence, his voice ringing out in its most powerful tones as he depicted a resurrection of German unity and greatness and new liberties and rights of the German people, which now must be conceded by the princes or won by force by the people. And when at last he waved the black-red-gold banner, and predicted to a free German nation a magnificent future, enthusiasm without bounds broke forth. People clapped their hands; they shouted; they embraced one another; they shed tears.

Skills FOCUS — READING LIKE A HISTORIAN

DOCUMENT 1
a. Describe How does Father Gapon describe the people of St. Petersburg?
b. Explain What is Father Gapon asking the czar to destroy?

DOCUMENT 2
a. Identify How does the artist reveal his views about Russia in this cartoon?
b. Infer Why do you think the artist chose to show the German kaiser so surprised?

DOCUMENT 3
a. Describe What does Bismarck want most from Prussia?
b. Interpret What kind of mistake do you think Bismarck is referring to that occurred in 1848 and 1849?

DOCUMENT 4
a. Explain What event in Vienna inspired people to march in Berlin?
b. Evaluate What symbol was the professor using to show the crowd his national pride?

DOCUMENT-BASED ESSAY QUESTION

What were some reasons that people in Prussia and Russia wanted change? Using the documents above and information from the chapter, form a thesis to explain the desires and causes of revolution and unification. Then write a short essay to support your position.

See Skills Handbook, pp. H25, H27, H29

Differentiating Instruction

Above Level

Advanced Learners/Gifted and Talented

Research Required

1. Draw a time line for all to see, beginning in 1850 and ending in 1920, with marks at 10-year increments. Have students add Documents 1, 2, 3, and 4 to the class time line and copy the time line onto their own papers.

2. Have students conduct research to add several important events to the time line, including Bloody Sunday, the Franco-Prussian War, German unification, the revolutions of 1848, and the beginning of World War I.

3. Using the time lines as a starting point, ask students what new observations they can make about the documents. Ask students the following questions: What was Bismarck trying to accomplish with the blood and iron speech? Did Russia and Germany go to war? What happened after Gapon's petition? How are Documents 3 and 4 related? **LS Visual-Spatial**

Alternative Assessment Handbook, Rubrics 12: Drawing Conclusions, and 36: Time Lines

---

Document-Based Investigation

Info to Know

Carl Schurz After participating in the unsuccessful revolutions of 1848 in Berlin, Carl Schurz emigrated to the United States, where he became an American citizen. He was involved in the antislavery movement in the United States and served as a brigadier general in the Union army during the American Civil War. Schurz was also elected as a United States senator and, later, named secretary of the interior. As secretary of the interior, Schurz fought for the rights of Native Americans as the United States expanded westward.

Teaching Tip

Remind students that revolution broke out in Vienna in March 1848. That year, protesters called for a constitution and the resignation of Austria's foreign minister, Prince Metternich. As a result Metternich fled Austria. Have students connect these events in Austria to the events described in Document 4.

Answers

Reading Like a Historian
Document 1 a. *as suffering beggars, slaves;* **b.** *the division between the czar and the people;* **Document 2 a.** *shows Russia as a strong force to be feared by Germany;* **b.** *possible answer—because Germany did not expect to be invaded by Russia; kaiser thought German military was unbeatable, thought fighting would take place in the west;* **Document 3 a.** *power, a unified Germany;* **b.** *the resignation of Metternich, the revolutions of 1848 and calls for liberal reform;* **Document 4 a.** *protests calling for liberty and citizens' rights;* **b.** *a black, red, and gold flag;* **Essay** *Student essays should explain that revolutions of the 1800s were caused both by nationalism and the call for liberal reforms. Using examples from the documents and the chapter, students might choose to argue that the forces of nationalism and liberal reform were often in conflict in Prussia and Russia during this period.*

Answers

Visual Summary

Review and Inquiry Organize students into five groups. Have each group review the history of nationalism in one of the countries shown in the Visual Study Guide. Have groups create and perform a skit summarizing the key events in their country.

Quick Facts Transparency: Visual Study Guide: Nationalism in Europe

Review Key Terms and People

1. Guiseppe Mazzini
2. Red Shirts
3. Zollverein
4. Otto von Bismarck
5. Balkan Wars
6. autocracy
7. Duma
8. ethnic

Comprehension and Critical Thinking

9. **a.** growing nationalism; opposition to Austrian rule; Cavour unified Kingdom of Sardinia; Garibaldi unified Kingdom of Two Sicilies
   b. regional differences; widespread poverty; emigration; industrialization and reform; new foreign policy
   c. led Italians to support their actions

10. **a.** first kaiser, or emperor, of the German Empire
    b. similarity—both examples of realpolitik; difference—Austro-Prussian war fought only by Prussia; Franco-Prussian war also involved the southern German states
    c. encouraged trade between them

11. **a.** Austria and Hungary were two separate, equal states, with one ruler as both emperor of Austria and king of Hungary
    b. set off revolts in the Austrian empire
    c. possible answer—disagree; ultimately led to conflict between ethnic groups

---

VISUAL STUDY GUIDE

Nationalism in Europe, 1800–1920

Italy

- In 1815 the Congress of Vienna split the Italian states apart.
- In 1831 Giuseppe Mazzini formed a nationalist group called Young Italy to fight for the unification of Italy.
- In 1852 Camillo di Cavour united states in northern Italy.
- In the 1860s Giuseppe Garibaldi continued the fight for unification of the rest of the Italian states.
- In 1861 under Victor Emmanuel's reign, Italians voted for unification.

Germany

- In 1834 the German states formed the Zollverein, or customs union, that made trade easier between the states.
- In 1848 German liberals revolted in the state of Prussia.
- In the mid-1800s Otto von Bismarck built up the Prussian military and pushed for the unification of Germany.
- In 1866 Prussia defeated Austria in the Austro-Prussian War.
- In 1871 Prussia defeated France in the Franco-Prussian War, and Germany was unified.

Austria-Hungary

- After the Congress of Vienna in 1815, Austrian foreign minister Metternich passed laws limiting reforms and formed alliances with other European powers to deter uprisings.
- In 1848 Hungarian Magyars made an unsuccessful attempt at a revolution.
- In 1867 the Dual Monarchy was set up, and Austria and Hungary became two separate, equal states.

Ottoman Empire

- The power of the Ottoman Empire declined during the 1800s.
- In the 1850s the Ottomans fought with Great Britain, France, and Sardinia against Russia in the Crimean War.
- The Ottoman Empire lost much territory in Europe after the Balkan Wars.
- In 1908 a nationalistic movement called the Young Turks began a revolution against the Ottoman sultan.

Russia

- In the first half of the 1800s, many Russian peasants were serfs—agricultural workers who were considered part of the land on which they worked.
- In 1825 Russian revolutionaries rebelled against the Czar Nicholas I but were defeated.
- From the 1860s to the 1880s Czar Alexander II freed the serfs and made other reforms.
- The Russian Revolution of 1905 began after Bloody Sunday because people were upset with the slow pace of reform.

Review Key Terms and People

Identify the correct term or person from the chapter that best matches each of the following descriptions.

1. Founded the Italian nationalist movement called Young Italy

2. Followers of Giuseppe Garibaldi

3. German customs union that allowed for the removal of tariffs between the German states

4. Prussian leader who helped unify Germany by "blood and iron"

5. wars that cost the Ottoman Empire most of its land in Europe

6. government by one ruler with unlimited power

7. an assembly in Russia that approved all laws

8. common background and culture

---

12. **a.** guaranteed individual liberties to all Russians, including freedom of speech and freedom of assembly; some Russians gained the right to vote
    b. regular payments of goods and labor
    c. by staging rebellions across Russia

Reading Skills

13. nation: from roots meaning "birth" or "race;" examples of nationalism in the chapter involve people of common background

14. empire: from roots meaning "absolute authority" or "to command;" empires in the chapter had absolute rulers

15. autocrat: from roots meaning "one" and "rule;" autocracy means rule by one person with absolute power

Analyzing Visuals

16. They are pulling it by a rope and appear to be tied together.

17. that the serfs lived under extremely poor conditions

Comprehension and Critical Thinking

SECTION 1 *(pp. 713–717)*

9. a. Describe What led to the unification of Italy?

b. Analyze What new challenges did Italians face after unification ?

c. Evaluate How did feelings of nationalism affect the actions of Italian leaders such as Giuseppe Mazzini and Camillo di Cavour?

SECTION 2 *(pp. 718–722)*

10. a. Identify Who was Wilhelm I?

b. Compare and Contrast What was one similarity and one difference between the Austro-Prussian War and the Franco-Prussian War?

c. Elaborate How did the Zollverein strengthen ties between the German states?

SECTION 3 *(pp. 723–727)*

11. a. Describe What was the government of Austria-Hungary like under the Dual Monarchy?

b. Identify Cause and Effect How did revolutions elsewhere in Europe affect uprisings in the Austrian Empire?

c. Make Judgments Do you agree or disagree on how the Congress of Berlin ignored ethnic groups when they gave land to Austria-Hungary?

SECTION 4 *(pp. 728–732)*

12. a. Recall How did the October Manifesto benefit Russians?

b. Explain What did serfs owe to the lords who owned the land they worked on?

c. Elaborate How did Russians react to the news of violence on Bloody Sunday?

Reading Skills

Understanding Word Origins *Using a dictionary, find the origins of the following words. Then explain how the origin of each word relates to the use of the word in this chapter.*

13. nation

14. empire

15. autocrat

Analyzing Visuals

Reading Like a Historian *The painting below shows Russian serfs on the banks of the Volga River.*

The Bargemen on the Volga, by Ilya Repin, 1870s

16. Identify How are the serfs pulling this ship down the river?

17. Draw Conclusions Many of the serfs in the painting have ragged clothing, no shoes, and look exhausted. What do you think the artist was trying to say by showing the serfs in this condition?

Using the Internet

go.hrw.com
Practice Online
Keyword: SHL NAT

18. During the 1800s in Italy and Germany, several key people led nationalist movements that resulted in their country's unification. Enter the activity keyword and choose one Italian or German leader to learn more about. Then write a short newspaper article that describes this person's life and achievements.

WRITING FOR THE SAT

Think about the following issue:

Nationalism was a major force in Europe during the 1800s as people began to feel an allegiance to others who shared a common language, religion, and history. As a result, the nations of Italy and Germany achieved unification, and old multinational empires started to crumble. In some places, representative government began to replace the absolute power of monarchs.

19. Assignment: In your opinion, what was the most important effect of European nationalism in the 1800s? Write an essay in which you develop your position on this issue. Support your point of view with reasoning and examples from the chapter.

Answers

Using the Internet

18. Go to the HRW Web site and enter the keyword shown to access a rubric for this activity.

KEYWORD: SHL NAT

Writing for the SAT

19 Student essays might address liberal reforms, the formation of new nations, the new balance of power in Europe, or some other effect of nationalism. Essays should be supported by logic and specific examples from the chapter.

A rubric for this activity is provided in **CRF**: Writing for the SAT

HOLT

History's Impact

▶ **Video Program: Nationalism in Europe**
Refer to the Video Program Teacher's Guide for the answer to the closing question.

Review and Assessment Resources

Review and Reinforce

 CRF: Chapter Review

Quick Facts Transparency: Visual Study Guide: Nationalism in Europe

Spanish Chapter Summaries Audio CD Program

OSP **Holt PuzzlePro**: Quiz Show for ExamView

Quiz Game CD-ROM

Assess

 PASS: Chapter Test, Forms A and B

Alternative Assessment Handbook

OSP **ExamView Test Generator**, Chapter Test

Differentiated Instruction Modified Worksheets and Tests CD-ROM: Chapter Test

HOAP **Holt Online Assessment Program** (in the Premier Online Edition)

Reteach/Intervene

 Interactive Reader and Study Guide

Differentiated Instruction Teacher Management System: Lesson Plans for Differentiated Instruction

Differentiated Instruction Modified Worksheets and Tests CD-ROM: Chapter Test

Interactive Skills Tutor CD-ROM

go.hrw.com
Online Resources

KEYWORD: SHL TEACHER

Chapter 25 Planning Guide

The Age of Imperialism

Chapter Overview	Reproducible Resources	Technology Resources
CHAPTER 25 pp. 738–769 **Overview:** In this chapter, students will learn about the age of imperialism from 1800 to 1920, when European powers ruled over much of Africa and Asia, and the United States influenced its neighbors. **KI 2, 3; PI 2.3, 2.5, 3.1, 3.2** See pp. T32–T55 for a detailed correlation to the New York State Core Curriculum for Global History and Geography and the New York Learning Standards.	**Differentiated Instruction Teacher Management System:** • Pacing Guide • Lesson Plans for Differentiated Instruction **Interactive Reader and Study Guide:** Chapter Summary* **Chapter Resource File*** • Writing About History • Social Studies Skill • Chapter Review **World History Outline Maps**	**OSP** **New York One-Stop Planner CD-ROM:** Calander Planner **Live Ink© Online Reading Help** **Student Edition on Audio CD Program** **Differentiated Instruction Modified Worksheets and Tests CD-ROM** **World History Primary Source Library CD-ROM** **Power Presentations with Video CD-ROM** **History's Impact: World History Video Program (VHS/DVD):** The Age of Imperialism
Section 1: **The British in India** **The Main Idea:** One of the first examples of European imperialism in Asia, the British rule over India changed Indian politics, economics, and society and led to the rise of Indian nationalism. **PI 2.5, 3.2**	**Differentiated Instruction Teacher Management System:** Section 1 Lesson Plan* **Interactive Reader and Study Guide:** Section 1 Summary* **Chapter Resource File*** • Vocabulary Builder: Section 1 • Biography: Ramanujan	**Regents Review Transparency:** Section 1* **Map Transparencies:** European Imperialism*; The British in India, 1767–1858* **Quick Facts Transparency:** Forms of Imperialism*
Section 2: **East Asia and the West** **The Main Idea:** While Western nations focused their imperial ambitions on East Asia, the reactions and results differed in China, Japan, and Southeast Asia. **PI 2.5**	**Differentiated Instruction Teacher Management System:** Section 2 Lesson Plan* **Interactive Reader and Study Guide:** Section 2 Summary* **Chapter Resource File*** • Vocabulary Builder: Section 2 • Biography: Hokusai • History and Geography: Japan Opens Trade Routes	**Regents Review Transparency:** Section 2* **Map Transparencies:** Imperialism in China, 1842–1900*; Southeast Asia, 1895*; Imperialism and a Global Economy* **Quick Facts Transparency:** The Meiji Reforms*
Section 3: **The Scramble for Africa** **The Main Idea:** In the late 1800s and early 1900s, European powers claimed land in much of Africa. **PI 2.3, 3.1**	**Interactive Reader and Study Guide:** Section 3 Summary* **Chapter Resource File*** • Vocabulary Builder: Section 3 • Biography: Samuel Ajayi Crowther • Literature: *Heart of Darkness*	**Regents Review Transparency:** Section 3* **Map Transparency:** Imperialism in Africa* **Quick Facts Transparency:** The New Imperialism in Africa* **Internet Activity:** Democratic Republic of the Congo Today
Section 4: **Imperialism in Latin America** **The Main Idea:** Imperialism in Latin America involved the United States and European nations seeking to strengthen their political and economic influence over the region. **PI 2.5, 3.2**	**Differentiated Instruction Teacher Management System::** Section 4 Lesson Plan* **Interactive Reader and Study Guide:** Section 4 Summary* **Chapter Resource File*** • Vocabulary Builder: Section 4 • Biography: José Guadalupe Posada • Primary Source: U.S. Imperialism	**Regents Review Transparency:** Section 4* **Map Transparency:** United States Intervention in the Caribbean* **Internet Activity:** Report on Imperialism

HOLT
History's Impact
World History Video Program (VHS/DVD)
The Age of Imperialism

Review, Assessment, Intervention

Global History and Geography Regents Test Prep Workbook

Quick Facts Transparency: The Age of Imperialism*

Progress Assessment Support System (PASS): Chapter Test*

Differentiated Instruction Modified Worksheets and Tests CD-ROM: Modified Chapter Test

OSP **New York One-Stop Planner CD-ROM:** ExamView Test Generator (English/Spanish)

HOAP **Holt Online Assessment Program (HOAP),** in the Holt Premier Online Student Edition

---

PASS: Section 1 Quiz*

Online Quiz: Section 1

Alternative Assessment Handbook

PASS: Section 2 Quiz*

Online Quiz: Section 2

Alternative Assessment Handbook

PASS: Section 3 Quiz*

Online Quiz: Section 3

Alternative Assessment Handbook

PASS: Section 4 Quiz*

Online Quiz: Section 4

Alternative Assessment Handbook

Power Presentation with Video CD-ROM

Power Presentations with Video are visual presentations of each chapter's main ideas. Presentations can be customized by including Quick Facts charts, images and maps from the textbook, and video clips.

Holt Online Learning

go.hrw.com
Teacher Resources
KEYWORD: SHL TEACHER

go.hrw.com
Student Resources
KEYWORD: SHL IMP

- Document-Based Questions
- Interactive Multimedia Activities

- Current Events
- Chapter-Based Internet Activities
- and more!

Holt Premier
Online Student Edition
Complete online support for interactivity, assessment, and reporting

- Interactive Maps and Notebook
- Homework Practice and Research Activities Online

CHAPTER 25 PLANNING GUIDE

The Big Picture

Susan Ramírez

Forms of Imperialism In contrast to the conquest and annexation style of imperialism common in the Americas earlier in history, this era saw new forms of international control. Protectorates and spheres of influence were important types involving not only Europeans and the nations of Africa and Asia, but also Japan in Korea and China.

The Benefits of Imperialism Foreigners benefited disproportionately from imperialism. Foreign governments collected taxes. Foreign traders sold manufactured goods in distant markets and entrepreneurs exported gold, diamonds, silk, tea, cotton, indigo, spices, sugar, coffee, and jute to supply industry and consumption at home. The peoples of India, Asia, and Africa benefited from the extent that they found employment in the export-import sector or worked on the railroads, canals, and roads constructed in their countries. Too many, however, especially in the rural areas, lost land or were saddled with paying the high taxes that paid for the infrastructure built to service world trade.

Resistance to Foreign Domination The inequality that developed in colonized states was not accepted by all. The control of a country by foreigners generated local protests, rebellion, and more subtle forms of resistance. Eventually, these movements coalesced into a rising tide of nationalism.

Recent Scholarship

The necessary brevity and synthesis of a textbook sometimes sacrifices the impact of great events or trends on ordinary people. "Everyday Forms of Resistance" by James C. Scott (a chapter in *Everyday Forms of Peasant Resistance* (1989), edited by Forrest D. Colburn restores the popular perspective to history. He analyzes the sometimes disguised opposition to domination by persons with little formal power. Individual and small group resistance include poaching, squatting [on land], desertion, evasion [of taxes], and foot dragging. Revenge, smuggling, folk religion, social banditry, and class heroes are other forms.

Differentiating Instruction

 Differentiated Instruction Teacher Management System
- Pacing Guide
- Lesson Plans for Differentiated Instruction

Interactive Reader and Study Guide

Spanish Chapter Summaries Audio CD Program

Student Edition on Audio CD Program

 Differentiated Instruction Modified Worksheets and Tests CD-ROM
- Vocabulary Flash Cards
- Modified Vocabulary Builder Activities
- Modified Chapter Review Activity
- Modified Chapter Test

OSP One-Stop Planner CD-ROM
- ExamView Test Generator (English/Spanish)
- PuzzlePro
- Quiz Show for ExamView
- Transparencies and Videos

TE Differentiated Activities in the Teacher's Edition
- The Scramble for Africa, p. 740
- The East India Company and the Raj, p. 743
- Downfall of the Qing Dynasty, p. 750
- Effects of Rubber in a Global Economy, p. 755
- U.S. Actions in Foreign Countries, p. 764
- Chinese Nationalist Editorials, p. 766

Reading Like a Historian
Sam Wineburg

Our students have come of age when wars are fought with infrared night goggles, and terrorist groups, using cell phones to detonate road-side explosives, send live video feed via satellite back to their mountain hideouts. Technology so defines modern warfare that it will be difficult for today's students to imagine anything different. Few will be able to grasp the true import of our chapter's statement that "repeating rifles, machine guns and exploding shells made European armies more lethal." What exactly did "more lethal" mean?

Outgunned! Technology and Power So lop-sided were the contests between Africans and European imperialists that these encounters "resembled hunting more than war" in the words of Daniel R. Headrick, author of the *Tools of Empire: Technology and European Imperialism in the Nineteenth Century*. Fatality rates provide a rough sense of this mismatch. In the 1898 Battle of Omdurman, a force of 50,000 Sudanese soldiers, armed with spears and the previous decade's collection of European arms, faced a combined British and Egyptian force half that size. The British possessed the Maxim machine gun. The first automatic machine gun in history, the Maxim could fire up to 600 rounds of ammunition a minute. At the end of five hours of battle, 11,000 Sudanese lay dead, versus 20 British soldiers and 20 Egyptian allies.

Still, such numbers fail to convey the full horror of this bloodbath. Winston Churchill, a 24-year-old officer with the British forces, documented this battle by sending accounts back to London's *Morning Post* (he got around the prohibition forbidding dispatches from the front by writing letters to his mother, who then forwarded them to the newspaper). Churchill wrote: "At the critical moment the gunboat arrived on the scene and began suddenly to blaze and flame from Maxim guns, quick-firing guns and rifles. The range was short; the effect tremendous . . . The charging Dervishes sank down in tangled heaps."

These Maxim-equipped soldiers held such an upper hand that the adrenaline of warfare eventually dissipated into boredom: "The infantry fired steadily and stolidly, without hurry or excitement . . . Besides, the soldiers were interested in the work and took great pains. But presently the mere physical act became tedious."

To the Sudanese, British tedium spelled hellish fury: "Bullets were shearing though flesh, smashing and splintering bone; blood spouted from terrible wounds; valiant men were struggling on through a hell of whistling metal, exploding shells, and spurting dust—suffering, despairing, dying." With more than a hint of bravado, Churchill summarized the tally sheet at the end of day: "The strongest and best-armed savage army yet arrayed against a European power had been destroyed and dispersed, with hardly any difficulty, comparatively small risk, and insignificant losses to the victors."

Similar scenes with only slight variations in detail would be repeated many times. To give just one example, in 1899 in Chad, a French force of 320 vanquished the armies of Rabah, 12,000 strong and armed with 2,500 antiquated firearms.

A Moral Compass Gone Awry The irony of these bloodbaths was that the victors explained their ease of conquest not as the consequence of Hiram Maxim figuring out how to cool the exploding chamber of his weapon with a constant stream of water so that it would continue to fire unabated. Rather, the Europeans interpreted technological prowess as proof of their inherent moral and cultural superiority.

As our chapter notes, the encounters between Europeans and Africans were fatal in terms of human cost. But the first fatality was the moral compass of the European invaders.

Chapter Main Ideas

Section 1 One of the first examples of European imperialism in Asia, the British rule over India changed Indian politics, economics, and society and led to the rise of Indian nationalism.

Section 2 While Western nations focused their imperial ambitions on East Asia, the reactions and results differed in China, Japan, and Southeast Asia.

Section 3 In the late 1800s and early 1900s, European powers claimed land in much of Africa.

Section 4 Imperialism in Latin America involved the United States and European nations seeking to strengthen their political and economic influence over the region.

New York Standards

Key Idea 2 Establishing timeframes, exploring different periodizations, examining themes across time and within cultures, and focusing on important turning points in world history help organize the study of world cultures and civilizations.

Key Idea 3 Study of the major social, political, cultural, and religious developments in world history involves learning about the important roles and contributions of individuals and groups.

Key to Differentiating Instruction

Below Level

Basic-level activities designed for all students encountering new material

At Level

Intermediate-level activities designed for average students

Above Level

Challenging activities designed for honors and gifted and talented students

Standard English Mastery

Activities designed to improve standard English usage

CHAPTER
25 1800–1920
The Age of Imperialism

THE BIG PICTURE European powers came to rule a large portion of Africa and Asia between 1800 and 1920. Only Japan emerged as an independent power capable of challenging the West. In the Americas, the United States exercised greater influence over the affairs of its neighbors.

Theme ECONOMIC SYSTEMS
In the 1800s industrialized nations looked beyond their own borders for ways to build their economic and political strength. In this chapter you will examine how this economic drive contributed to an intense competition for global empire.

TIME LINE

CHAPTER EVENTS	**1842** The first Opium War ends in China.	**1862** France gains control of Vietnam.	**1884–1885** The Berlin Conference sets the rules for dividing Africa.	**1885** The Indian National Congress is founded.	
	1840	1860		1880	
WORLD EVENTS	**1845** The Irish Potato Famine begins.	**1861** The American Civil War begins.	**1871** German unification is complete.		

738 CHAPTER 25

Introduce the Chapter   At Level

The Age of Imperialism

1. Tell students that imperialism involves nations gaining power by gaining territory. Have students name some reasons why European nations might have wanted to build empires in the years between 1880 and 1920. Tell students about the economic, political, and cultural reasons for the rise of imperialism.

2. Organize students into small groups. Assign one group economic reasons, one group political reasons, and one group cultural reasons.

3. Have each group scan the chapter to find reasons for imperialism that relate to its category. Have a volunteer from each group explain some of their reasons to the rest of the class. **LS** Interpersonal

   Alternative Assessment Handbook, Rubric 1: Acquiring Information

HOLT
History's Impact
▶ Video Program: The Age of Imperialism
See the Video Teacher's Guide for strategies for using the video segment.

Reading Like a Historian
Analyzing Visuals Indian nationalism was rising in the late 1800s. Prince Edward's visit to India in 1875-1876, as shown in this painting, was intended to improve the relationship between Britain and India.

Reading like a Historian

This painting shows Great Britain's Edward, Prince of Wales, being greeted by Indian princes during an official visit to India in 1875.

Analyzing Visuals The artist painted this scene in 1917, when Britain's position as a major world power was being threatened by the events of World War I. Why do you think the artist chose to look back at this particular moment?

See **Skills Handbook**, p. H26

1895
Japan wins the Sino-Japanese War.

1898
The United States gains control of Cuba and the Philippines.

1900
1920

1901
Edward VII becomes king of the United Kingdom.

1914
World War I begins.

THE AGE OF IMPERIALISM **739**

go.hrw.com
Online Resources

Chapter Resources:
KEYWORD: SHL IMP
Teacher Resources:
KEYWORD: SHL TEACHER

Explore the Time Line

1. How many years passed between the end of the Sino-Japanese War and the beginning of World War I? *19 years*

2. In what year was the Indian National Congress founded? *1885*

3. When did the United States gain control of Cuba and the Philippines? *1898*

4. What was the purpose of the Berlin Conference? *to set the rules for dividing Africa*

Info to Know

Economics and Imperialism Britain experienced a slight economic depression from 1873 to 1896. Feeling the effects of this decline, the country's leaders intensified the policies of imperialism. They hoped to claim an empire before other nations did.

Make Inferences Why might an economic depression have intensified policies of imperialism? *Colonies could provide resources and new markets.*

Answers

Reading Like a Historian *possible answer—This painting probably was created to remind people of Britain's glory, because it depicts a scene at the height of the British empire's power and wealth.*

739

Geography Starting Points

Different Kinds of Imperialism Imperialists from Britain and France held vastly different views about the future of their African colonies. Britain expected them to mature into independent nations. Some French imperialists, on the other hand, wanted to merge the colonies with their home country. Colonized peoples were later represented in France's legislature.

The Economics of Imperialism Whether their colonial holdings were of substantial economic value to the imperialist powers remains unclear. A look at three Western countries provides an interesting counterargument. Before the height of imperialism in the 1890s, Britain had reached its economic peak. Despite continued imperial expansion throughout the early twentieth century, Britain continued to lose its economic lead. Germany, which held barely any important colonies, was ready to surpass Britain and become Europe's richest power. Meanwhile, the United States, with fewer overseas colonial possessions, was richer still than Germany.

Interactive
EUROPEAN IMPERIALISM

1850

India became the centerpiece of the British Empire.

0   1,500   3,000 Miles
0   1,500   3,000 Kilometers
Robinson projection

European Colonies
- Belgian
- British
- Danish
- Dutch
- French
- German
- Italian
- Portuguese
- Spanish

1914

By 1914 much of West Africa had been claimed by France.

King Leopold of Belgium controlled the Congo until 1908.

0   1,500   3,000 Miles
0   1,500   3,000 Kilometers
Robinson projection

Starting Points Starting in the late 1700s, European nations began a renewed campaign of competitive empire building that would eventually span the globe. By the early 1900s, European nations controlled territory on nearly every continent. The legacy of imperialism would affect the world for decades to come.

1. **Analyze** Why do you think there were more European colonies in 1914 than in 1850?

2. **Predict** How do you think the change in political control in Africa between 1850 and 1914 affected Africa's people?

Listen to History

Go online to listen to an explanation of the starting points for this chapter.

go.hrw.com
Keyword: SHL IMP

740 CHAPTER 25

Differentiating Instruction

Above Level

Advanced Learners/Gifted and Talented

Research Required

1. Remind students that most of Africa was colonized by European nations between the years 1850 and 1914. Have students predict how they think colonization affected Africa, and how Africans reacted to it.

2. Organize students into small groups. Have each group pick an African colony and research its history from colonization to independence, if applicable. Student research should help answer the following questions: which country controlled this part of Africa

from 1850-1914? Did the Africans eventually gain independence? How?

3. Have groups create a multimedia presentation showing how imperialism affected the part of Africa they researched.

LS **Interpersonal, Visual-Spatial**

Alternative Assessment Handbook, Rubric 22: Multimedia Presentations

Answers

Geography Starting Points 1.
The nations of Europe were competing for colonies during those years, and each probably wanted to claim as much territory as possible. **2.** *possible answer—probably influenced by European culture; may also have resisted colonization*

1 The British in India

BEFORE YOU READ

MAIN IDEA

One of the first examples of European imperialism in Asia, the British rule over India changed Indian politics, economics, and society and led to the rise of Indian nationalism.

READING FOCUS

1. What changes set the stage for European imperialism in Asia and Africa?

2. What role did the British East India Company play in British imperialism in India?

3. What was life like in India when it became a British colony?

KEY TERMS

British East India Company
Sepoy Mutiny
Raj
Indian National Congress
Muslim League

Robert Clive and Mir Jaffar after the Battle of Plassey, by Francis Hayman, 1857

GREAT BRITAIN'S DECEIT

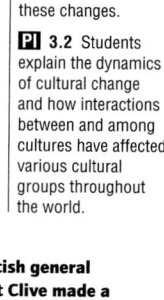

◄ **British general Robert Clive made a secret deal to gain territory for Britain.**

THE INSIDE STORY

When does a secret work better than an army? The year was 1756, and British power in India was rising. To secure their position in India, the British began fortifying their position in the rich trading city of Calcutta. This effort angered the ruler of Bengal, the region in which Calcutta lay, and he sent his army to attack the British fortifications at Fort William. The fort fell quickly, and more than 140 British defenders were imprisoned in a small, poorly ventilated jail cell for the night. All but 23 of the prisoners died of dehydration and suffocation.

Outraged, the British sent general Robert Clive to recapture Calcutta. Clive secretly met with a commander of the Bengal army. Later, when the British met the Bengal army, the commander refused to join in the battle. Why did the commander not fight? He and Clive had made a secret deal. The deal helped the British recapture Calcutta, and the commander became the ruler of Bengal.

By taking control of Calcutta, the British had essentially become the rulers of the richest province in the Mughal Empire. Remarkably, the conquest of Bengal had been won not through military might, but through deceit. ■

THE AGE OF IMPERIALISM **741**

THE AGE OF IMPERIALISM **741**

Reading Focus

1 What changes set the stage for European imperialism in Asia and Africa? *The Industrial Revolution introduced new technologies that increased the European military advantage over the rest of the world, and the great empires of Asia and North Africa all had severe internal problems at the time when European power was rising.*

Setting the Stage

Define What is imperialism? *the process of one people ruling or controlling another*

Make Inferences Why do you think Europeans did not try to control Africa and Asia earlier? *possible answer—lacked technology to compete with empires of Asia and North Africa*

Quick Facts Transparency: Forms of Imperialism

Reading Focus

2 What role did the British East India Company play in British imperialism in India? *controlled trade between Britain, India, and East Asia; ruled India in Britain's name*

British East India Company

Identify Who were the Sepoys? *Indian soldiers who had fought in the British armyn*

Summarize How was the British Empire in India built? *British East India Company established trading posts; after decline of Mughal Empire placed allies on the thrones of Indian states and waged wars against the most powerful kingdoms of India; after Sepoy Mutiny British Crown took direct control*

Answers

Reading Check *Europeans had an advantage in the quality of their weapons and military training, and took advantage of the decline of the great empires in Asia and Africa.*

742

TAKING NOTES

As you read, take notes on the development and effects of British rule in India.

Development
↓
British Rule in India
↓
Effects

NEW YORK

CC Unit 5-H3
British East India Company and the Sepoy Mutiny

THE IMPACT TODAY

English is still widely spoken in India today and serves as a major language of government and business.

Setting the Stage

The arrival of the British in India was an example of European imperialism, the process of one people ruling or controlling another. By 1700, Spain, Great Britain, France, and Portugal ruled vast territories in the Americas. Europeans had less success, however, in ruling territory in Asia and Africa. While Europeans had built trading posts along those continents' coasts, they held little territory farther inland.

By the late 1700s, however, European states began expanding their power in Asia and Africa. Two factors that made this possible were new technologies and the weakening of the great empires of Asia and North Africa.

New Technologies Advances in technology gave Europeans a huge military advantage over Africans and Asians. Steam-powered gunboats could attack even inland targets, while repeating rifles, machine guns, and exploding shells made European armies more lethal than ever. Asian and African weapon makers simply could not match these new technologies.

Weakening Empires Meanwhile, the great empires of Asia and North Africa were weakening, and Europeans took advantage. The Mughal Empire in India entered a deep decline after 1707. The Ottoman Empire lost strength throughout the 1700s and had a weak grasp on its North African provinces. The Qing dynasty in China faced several major rebellions. By the late 1700s, European armies faced limited resistance as they claimed new territories.

READING CHECK **Summarize** Why did European power begin to expand in the late 1700s?

FORMS OF IMPERIALISM

QUICK FACTS

Imperial nations developed several different ways of organizing and governing the many territories in their empires.

- **Colony** a territory governed by a foreign power
- **Protectorate** a territory that has its own government but is controlled by a foreign power
- **Sphere of influence** a territory in which a country claims exclusive political or economic rights.

742 CHAPTER 25

British East India Company

Early British imperialism in India was not carried out by the government but by a trading company, the **British East India Company.** Created to control trade between Britain, India, and East Asia, the company soon became embroiled in Indian politics. By 1800 it had come to rule much of India in the name of Great Britain.

The British Take Control As long as the Mughal Empire remained strong in India, the East India Company's activity was limited to coastal trading cities. When the empire began to break apart into small states in the mid-1700s, though, leaders of the East India Company sensed a chance to take over Indian lands. They manipulated the rulers of these new states, suggesting to each ruler that he needed British support to keep his throne. By playing rulers against each other and keeping them from cooperating, the British kept India in chaos. The company then swept in with its own armies and took over much of India, claiming to have done so just to restore order.

Changes in India Once in control, the East India Company made changes to Indian society. They introduced a new education system and the English language. They also introduced British laws that banned certain customs, such as sati, the practice of Hindu widows throwing themselves on their husbands' funeral fires. The British also invited Christian missionaries to spread their beliefs through India.

Eventually, some Indians began to believe the British were trying to destroy their society. They thought the British wanted to eliminate Indian customs and Hinduism completely. As a result, relations between Indians and British became increasingly strained.

The Sepoy Mutiny In 1857 these strained relations exploded into a rebellion, the **Sepoy Mutiny.** Sepoys were Indian soldiers who fought in the British army. The spark that set off their rebellion was the introduction of a new type of British rifle. Before inserting a cartridge into the rifle, a soldier had to bite off the end of an ammunition cartridge, which was greased with pork and beef fat. This offended both Muslim sepoys, who did not eat pork, and Hindu sepoys, who did not eat beef.

Skills Focus: Identifying Main Idea and Details

At Level

Prep Required

Reading Skill
European Imperialism

1. Organize the class into small groups. Have each group create a chart showing the causes of European imperialism between 1800 and 1920. Tell students to group the causes under the following headings: Technology and Weakening Empires.

2. Review student charts as a class, creating a master chart for students to see.

3. Guide students in a discussion of the causes of the new wave of European colonization.
   LS Interpersonal, Visual-Spatial

   Alternative Assessment Handbook, Rubrics 7: Charts; and 11: Discussions

British controlled in 1767
British controlled in 1805
British controlled in 1858
— Area of Sepoy Mutiny

KASHMIR
PUNJAB
Delhi
RAJPUTANA
NORTHWEST PROVINCES
SIND
BIHAR
ASSAM
BENGAL
Calcutta
BERAR
ARAKAN
Bombay
HYDERABAD
Bay of Bengal
Arabian Sea
Goa (Portugal)
MYSORE
Madras
Pondicherry (France)
Andaman Islands

0   250   500 Miles
0   250   500 Kilometers
Albers equal-area projection

CEYLON (SRI LANKA)

The Sepoy Mutiny, unknown Indian artist, c. 1860, The Granger Collection, New York

This Indian artwork shows soldiers rebelling against British rule in the Sepoy Mutiny of 1857.

GEOGRAPHY SKILLS | **INTERPRETING MAPS**

Movement How did the territory controlled by Great Britain change between 1805 and 1858?

Already resentful of the British efforts to westernize India, many sepoys balked. Thinking that the new cartridges were a plot to make them abandon Hinduism and Islam, sepoys in the town of Meerut refused to use them. For their protest, these sepoys were punished. In response, sepoys all over northern India rose up against British officers. Before long the rebellious sepoys had gained control of Delhi.

The violence of this rebellion was ferocious, with both sides committing atrocities. Sepoys killed not only their officers but also British women and children. The British responded with extreme brutality. Captured mutineers were strapped to cannons and shot. Villages suspected of supporting rebels were burned. The fighting continued for two years.

As a result of the mutiny, the British ended the rule of the East India Company in 1858. From then on, the British government would rule India directly. Although the British moved away from some of the social regulations that had angered many Indians, distrust continued between the British and the Indians.

READING CHECK **Identify Cause and Effect** How did the decline of the Mughal Empire contribute to the rise of British power in India?

India as a British Colony

India was Britain's most important colony—the "jewel in the crown" of the British Empire. Ruling India gave the British great political and financial rewards, as well as national pride. But for many Indians, British rule was a source of frustration and humiliation. This frustration gave rise to powerful feelings of nationalism.

The Raj The era of British rule in India is often called the British **Raj** (RAHZH), a Hindi word meaning "rule." The administration of India was carried out by a government agency called the Indian Civil Service (ICS). Though they were ruling India, most officials of the ICS were British. The ICS employed very few Indians, leaving many educated Indians frustrated at having no say in their own government.

Many British officials in India believed themselves superior to the people they governed. As a result, they lived in segregated neighborhoods and belonged to exclusive clubs. Most of these officials believed that they were improving the lives of the Indian people through westernization. Yet many prejudiced British officials believed that Indians were utterly incapable of governing themselves.

ACADEMIC VOCABULARY
prejudiced biased against a racial, religious, or national group

THE AGE OF IMPERIALISM **743**

India as a British Colony

Identify Who was Ram Mohun Roy and what was his message? *an Indian nationalist; believed that Indians should have the same rights as Europeans*

Identify Cause and Effect What were the effects of the swadeshi boycott movement? *convinced the British to make concessions to the Indian people; formation of Muslim League*

Evaluate In what ways did British rule help India? In what ways did it harm India? *possible answer—helped: built railroads, roads, and canals; harmed: devastated India's pre-existing industry, kept Indians from participating in government*

CRF: Biography: Ramanujan

Info to Know

British Rule Under the Raj, the British ruled India through a network of Indian politicians and civil servants. While it appeared to be stable, the Raj was constantly under threat from within as Indians aspired to self-rule, as well as from the plotting of other imperialist nations. Russia also had designs on the subcontinent. The competition between Britain and Russia for control came to be called "the great game."

Answers

Impact of the Raj on India *possible answer—new technology and industry; because those things helped modernize India, a lasting effect even after independence*

744

Impact of the Raj on India

The era of British control in India brought many changes. The British introduced their own governmental, legal, and educational systems, the English language, and new forms of technology and industry. These changes to India's economy and society, combined with unhappiness over foreign control, led to the growth of nationalism in India. **Which of these changes do you think had the longest lasting effects in India? Why?**

Ram Mohun Roy, an Indian nationalist, argued for India's right to govern itself.

The British encouraged the growth of commercial agriculture, India's main industry during the Raj.

During the Raj the British built railroads, roads, and canals in India. By 1910 India had the fourth-largest railroad network in the world. Britain invested in transportation for two reasons: to move troops to trouble spots more easily and to help sell British products throughout India.

India was an important market for British manufactured goods, but that was not its only economic significance. It was a source of raw materials, such as cotton, tea, indigo, and jute. In fact, India became one of the most significant sources of raw cotton for British textile factories in the 1860s, after cotton from the United States became unavailable during the American Civil War. In addition, taxes collected from Indian landowners paid for the administration of India and the Indian army.

Though it was profitable for Britain, the introduction of British manufactured goods, especially textiles, devastated India's pre-existing industry. Although India had been a major exporter of textiles to Asia until the early 1800s, the British closed Indian textile factories to prevent competition with British companies. By the mid-1800s, India primarily exported raw materials rather than manufactured goods.

The Rise of Indian Nationalism Many groups in India found the changes that came with British rule deeply disturbing. Indian elites and middle classes resented having so few opportunities to participate in government. Although the British allowed Indians to participate in town and district councils after 1861, Indians had little power to influence decisions at higher levels of government.

Still, it took more than resentment to build a nationalist movement. That movement did not take off until Indians began to see themselves as having the same rights as Europeans. This idea was first expressed by the reformer Ram Mohun Roy in the 1820s. Roy, an activist who wanted to abolish several aspects of traditional Indian society, felt that the British were violating the Indian people's rights, including the rights of free speech and religion. Roy wrote texts and opened schools to spread his nationalist ideas throughout India.

Despite Roy's efforts, it took several decades for the nationalist movement to become active. The first Indian nationalist organization, the **Indian National Congress**, was not founded until 1885. A popular organization, the Indian National Congress was established by English-speaking Indians, most of whom were Hindu. In the early years, the requests of the Congress to the British were modest, such as more positions for Indians in the ICS and better representation on government councils.

Indian nationalism became more radical, though, when the British announced plans to partition Bengal. Officials claimed that breaking Bengal into two provinces would make it

Collaborative Learning

At Level

The British in India

Research Required

1. Organize students into two groups. Have each group prepare for a classroom debate about the positive and negative effects of British rule on India. Have students use reliable print and online sources to gather information for the debate. Each group should be prepared to either defend or attack the overall effects of British rule.

2. After each group has had time to conduct its research and prepare its arguments, hold a classroom debate. Which side was able to present the more convincing arguments?

3. Guide students in a discussion of the overall effects of British rule on India. How did researching both sides of the issue help them understand the ongoing controversy over it?

LS Interpersonal, Kinesthetic

Alternative Assessment Handbook, Rubrics 10: Debates; 11: Discussions; and 30: Research

Under British rule, thousands of miles of railroads were built across India. Here, workers build the East Bengal Railway around 1870.

A lingering effect of the Raj is the prevalence of the English language in India today. One of the country's most widely spoken languages, English is often used in politics and business.

easier to govern, but some nationalists thought the partition was an attempt to break up Bengal's Hindu population. In response, radicals in the Congress called for a boycott of British goods. This boycott, or *swadeshi* ("own country"), movement lasted from 1905 to 1908.

Participants in the *swadeshi* boycotts vowed to wear only Indian-made garments. As part of their protest, some publicly burned piles of British cloth. A few militant nationalists, not thinking the boycott to be a strong enough statement of their feelings, attacked British officials. The militants were punished, but the *swadeshi* movement convinced the British to make concessions to the Indian people.

In addition to political concessions, the *swadeshi* movement had some unintended consequences. One was the formation of the **Muslim League** in 1906. Many Muslim leaders feared that Hindus had opposed the partition of Bengal for political reasons—to preserve the power of Hindus at the expense of Muslims. As a result, the Muslim League sought to protect the interests of Indian Muslims. The Indian National Congress and the Muslim League later became the main organizations in the struggle for Indian independence.

NEW YORK

CC Unit 5-H6
Immediate and long-term changes made under European rule

 READING CHECK **Infer** Why did Indian nationalists respond to the plan to partition Bengal with a boycott of British goods?

SECTION 1 ASSESSMENT

go.hrw.com
Online Quiz
Keyword: SHL IMP HP

Reviewing Ideas, Terms, and People

1. **a. Recall** What military technologies did the Industrial Revolution provide to Europeans?
   b. Identify Cause and Effect How did internal problems in Asian empires contribute to the success of European imperialism?

2. **a. Identify** What was the **Sepoy Mutiny**?
   b. Explain How did Britain gain control over most of India by 1858?

3. **a. Define** What was the **Raj**?
   b. Explain How did the *swadeshi* movement lead to the creation of the **Muslim League**?

Critical Thinking

4. **Categorize** Using the chart below and your notes from this section, summarize the effects of British rule on India in each category listed. Which effect was most significant?

Category	Effects
Politics	
Economics	
Society	

 FOCUS ON SPEAKING

5. **Persuasion** Write a short speech arguing that British rule helped India or harmed India. Use details from the section.

Direct Teach

Info to Know

Gandhi's Spinning Wheel Mohandas Gandhi, the great leader of the Indian independence movement, was often photographed at his spinning wheel. His spinning wheel represented resistance to the forced importation of British textiles that had undermined the Indian weaving industry. It also represented resistance to the British rulers and the way of life they had tried to impose on India.

Review & Assess

Close

Guide students in a discussion of the overall effects of British rule on India's economy, society, and government.

Review

Online Quiz, Section 1

Assess

SE **Section 1 Assessment**

Progress Assessment: Section 1 Quiz

Alternative Assessment Handbook

Reteach/Intervene

Interactive Reader and Study Guide, Section 1

Interactive Skills Tutor CD-ROM

Section 1 Assessment Answers

1. **a.** steam-powered boats, repeating rifles, machine guns, and exploding shells
   b. by weakening them so that they could only offer limited resistance to European armies

2. **a.** Muslim and Hindu soldiers refused to use a rifle that had a cartridge greased with animal fat. They were punished, leading to mutiny.
   b. by placing allies on the thrones of Indian states, and through a series of wars against the most powerful kingdoms of India

3. **a.** the age of British rule in India
   b. because the boycotts seemed to protect the rights of Hindus at the expense of Muslims

4. Politics—introduced British system of government; Economics—hurt India's existing industry, made India an exporter of raw materials rather than manufactured goods; Society—introduced English language, led to growth of Indian nationalism

5. Students should support their arguments with information from the text.

Answers

Reading Check *They thought the partition was intended to weaken the Hindu population.*

Getting Started

Use the **Interactive Reader and Study Guide** to familiarize students with the section content.

📖 **Interactive Reader and Study Guide,** Section 2

[Worksheet image: "The Age of Imperialism" Section 2, with Main Idea box, Key Terms and People, Taking Notes graphic organizer with rows for China, Japan, Indochina, Siam and column "Western Actions"]

📖 **CRF:** Vocabulary Builder: Section 2

Taking Notes

China—Treaty of Nanjing; Taiping Rebellion; Boxer Rebellion; 1911 Revolution; Japan— Treaty of Kanagawa; Meiji Restoration and reforms; modernization and industrialization; Dutch East Indies—established large plantations in Southeast Asia; British took control parts of the Malay Peninsula; Indochina—French conquered Indochina; Vietnam—French controlled most of the South; Siam—retained independence; served as buffer between British Burma and French Indochina

---

SECTION 2 East Asia and the West

BEFORE YOU READ

MAIN IDEA

While Western nations focused their imperial ambitions on East Asia, the reactions and results differed in China, Japan, and Southeast Asia.

READING FOCUS

1. How did Western nations gain power and influence in China in the 1800s?
2. What led to the rise of Japan as a major power?
3. How did European power and influence increase in Southeast Asia?

KEY TERMS AND PEOPLE

unequal treaties
extraterritoriality
Taiping Rebellion
Boxer Rebellion
Sun Yixian
Treaty of Kanagawa
Emperor Meiji
Sino-Japanese War

NEW YORK

PI 2.5 Students investigate key events and developments and major turning points in world history to identify the factors that brought about change and the long-term effects of these changes.

THE INSIDE STORY

Why did Great Britain go to war over the sale of illegal drugs?
During the 1700s tea became a popular drink among the British. China was the sole source of tea. Despite Britain's position as the world's greatest industrial power, China had little interest in buying anything Britain produced. So, to pay for its tea habit, Britain sent vast quantities of silver to China. Year after year, silver was leaving Britain for China, and little money was coming back.

To correct the imbalance, Britain needed to find a product that the Chinese would buy, and it found one—opium. Opium had been grown in Asia for centuries, but the Chinese emperor had outlawed the opium trade in 1729. Even so, British traders had been smuggling in small quantities of opium from Britain's territories in India for years. Because of the desire to send silver back to Britain, the British East India Company increasingly ignored opium smuggling in the territory it controlled.

Opium had a devastating effect on China. Workers and peasants fell victim to the drug. It is impossible to know exact figures, but some historians estimate that as many as 1 out of every 10 Chinese were addicted to opium.

The drug's destructive effects on Chinese society led the emperor to stand firm against the British smuggling. Commissioner Lin Zixu wrote a letter to Queen Victoria, stating the Chinese case.

"Let us ask, where is your conscience? I have heard that the smoking of opium is very strictly forbidden by your country; that is because the harm caused by opium is clearly understood. Since it is not permitted to do harm to your own country, then even less should you let it be passed on to the harm of other countries—how much less to China!"

The British never responded to Lin's letter. When Lin ordered the destruction of British opium stored in the city of Guangzhou, the British struck back by sending warships to China. The Opium War had begun. ◼

THE OPIUM WAR

British ships attacking Chinese warships during the Opium War ▶
Iron Steam Ship Nemesis Destroying the Chinese War Junks, by Edward Duncan, 1841

Teach the Main Idea

At Level

East Asia and the West

1. **Teach** Ask students the Reading Focus questions to teach this section.

2. **Apply** Have students create an outline of the section using the headings as main points. Have students identify two main ideas under each of the blue subheadings.

3. **Review** Review student outlines as a class. Have students identify the points in their outlines that they feel are most important to the section entitled East Asia and the West. Then guide students in a discussion of the ways in which China, Japan, and Southeast Asia were affected by Western imperialism.

4. **Practice/Homework** Have students write a paragraph explaining why a government might try to limit its people's trade and contact with other nations. **LS Visual-Spatial, Verbal-Linguistic**

📖 **Alternative Assessment Handbook,** Rubric 42: Writing to Inform

Western Nations Gain Power

In 1800 trade with European merchants was profitable for the Chinese, but the Chinese did not view the Europeans as particularly important. They were just another set of foreigners who might pay tribute to the emperor.

All of that changed in the 1800s. Little by little, the Qing dynasty lost its power, its prestige, and its sovereignty over China.

The Opium War Chinese rulers had long believed that all nations outside China were barbaric, and they wanted little contact with the outside world. When Europeans pushed for trading rights in China, the Chinese restricted their trade to a single city, Guangzhou.

The Chinese did not want European goods, but they did want silver. They were pleased when tea became popular in Britain and British silver flowed into China. But the British were distressed by the imbalance of trade.

In the late 1700s the British discovered a solution to the trade imbalance—opium. In China there was a great demand for the drug, and opium addiction became such a problem that the Chinese government banned the import of opium in 1796. But foreign merchants continued to smuggle the drug into China.

In 1839 Chinese officials ordered the destruction of British opium in Guangzhou. The British responded by sending a naval force to launch an attack. After capturing Shanghai in 1842, the British forced the Chinese to sign a peace treaty, the Treaty of Nanjing.

The Treaty of Nanjing was the first of the **unequal treaties**—so called because they benefited European countries at the expense of China. The treaty opened five more ports to Western trade. It also gave **extraterritoriality** to the British, meaning that British citizens accused of crimes had the right to be tried in British courts rather than in Chinese courts.

In the next two decades, China was forced to sign more treaties with Britain, France, the United States, and Russia. Slowly but surely, the Qing dynasty was losing control over China to Western intruders.

The Taiping Rebellion The failure of the Qing dynasty to resist the Western powers led some Chinese to believe that the dynasty had lost the mandate of heaven. That belief led to a series of rebellions starting in 1850.

TAKING NOTES
Take notes about the actions of Western nations and the responses of nations in East Asia.

Western Actions	Response of East Asian Nations

 NEW YORK
CC Unit 5-14
Opium Wars and the Treaty of Nanjing

IMPERIALISM IN CHINA, 1842–1900

Spheres of Influence
- Russian
- British
- German
- French
- Japanese
- ● Treaty port
- — Area of Boxer Rebellion, 1900

RUSSIAN EMPIRE

MANCHURIA

Vladivostok

OUTER MONGOLIA

MONGOLIA

INNER

Beijing
Tianjin

Port Arthur
Weihai
Qingdao

KOREA

JAPAN

Sea of Japan (East Sea)

CHINA

Huang He (Yellow R.)

Nanjing
Wuchang
Wuhan
Ningbo

Shanghai

East China Sea

Chang Jiang (Yangtze R.)

Fuzhou

Amoy

Guangzhou (Canton)
Xi Jiang

MACAO (Port.)
HONG KONG (U.K.)

Taiwan

South China Sea

GEOGRAPHY SKILLS | **INTERPRETING MAPS**

Regions Which two nations controlled the largest spheres of influence?

 Direct Teach

Reading Focus

❶ How did Western nations gain power and influence in China in the 1800s?
Britain smuggled opium to China; forced Chinese to sign unequal treaties benefiting Europeans at China's expense

Western Nations Gain Power

Describe How did the Chinese view Europeans in the 1800s? *as just another set of foreigners who might pay tribute to the emperor*

Make Inferences Why did the Chinese restrict trade with Europe? *believed all nations outside China were barbaric*

Make Judgments Were Chinese fears about Western intentions warranted? Explain. *possible answer— Yes; by the end of the 19th century, China had lost much of its sovereignty to Western powers, and the Chinese empire was overthrown in 1911.*

Activity **Asia Past and Present**
Have students compare this map of Asia with a current map in the atlas of their text. Have students identify what has changed between 1900 and the present. **LS Visual-Spatial**

🗺 **Map Transparency:** Imperialism in China, 1842–1900

Answers
Interpreting Maps *Great Britain*

747

Reading Focus

Western Nations Gain Power

Identify Cause and Effect What were the effects of the Taiping Rebellion? *more than 20 million Chinese died; Qing dynasty ended the rebellion*

Explain How did the Boxer Rebellion start and end? *In 1899, the Boxers started attacking Christians in China; 20,000 foreign troops captured Beijing and suppressed the uprising*

Info to Know

Hong Kong The Chinese island of Hong Kong was ceded to Great Britain after the first Opium War in 1842. Hong Kong and the peninsula of Kowloon were leased to Great Britain for 99 years. The lease expired in 1997, and the area reverted to Chinese control.

In the 1850s the most serious rebellion was led by Hong Xiuquan (shee-oo-CHOO-ahn), who believed that he was the brother of Jesus. He wanted to create a "Heavenly Kingdom of Great Peace," (*Taiping Tianguo*) where no one would be poor. His followers formed a movement called the **Taiping Rebellion**.

Hong and his followers captured large territories in southeastern China and by 1853 controlled the city of Nanjing. Qing soldiers, as well as British and French armies, attacked the Taiping army and finally defeated it in 1864. Although the Qing dynasty emerged victorious, the cost was great—more than 20 million Chinese died in the Taiping Rebellion.

Foreign Influence Takes Hold After the Taiping Rebellion, reform-minded officials of the Qing dynasty tried to make changes. For example, they pushed to build coal mines, factories, and railroads. They encouraged the government to make modern weapons and ships. They tried to introduce Western knowledge and languages to China. This movement, called the self-strengthening movement, ultimately failed because of strong resistance from traditional Confucian scholars and powerful officials.

While China struggled to reform, Japan was emerging as a major military power. China went to war with Japan over Korea in 1894, but the Japanese soundly defeated China.

Noting the weakness of the Chinese military, Western powers rushed to claim more territory in China. Germany, Russia, Great Britain, and France all carved out spheres of influence there.

By the late 1890s the United States got involved. Americans feared that European nations would divide China among themselves and the United States would lose its profitable trade in China. To prevent such a loss, U.S. secretary of state John Hay proposed the Open Door Policy, which would allow free trade in the Chinese ports under European control. This policy would allow the United States to continue its trade in China. Although the European nations never formally agreed to the Open Door Policy, they did allow free trade in their ports.

READING SKILLS

Identifying Supporting Details What kind of reforms did Qing officials make?

HISTORY CLOSE-UP

Shanghai, 1900

Located near the mouth of the Chang Jiang (Yangzi River), the city of Shanghai became an international financial and trade center in the late 1800s. As a treaty port, Shanghai was open to free trade with the West.

The Chinese area of the city centered around Nanjing Road, where Chinese merchants sold goods to both Chinese and Europeans.

Chinese merchants sold a variety of goods, including tea, leather goods, and gift items.

748 CHAPTER 25

Reading Skill
Chinese Isolationism

1. Have students create charts summarizing the ways in which contact with Europeans affected China. Have students list advantages and disadvantages of contact with the West.

2. Review student charts as a class, creating a master chart for students to see. Have students correct their own charts as needed.

3. Tell students they are editors of an early Western-style Chinese newspaper. Have each student write an editorial discussing whether China should have remained isolated from Westerners. Student editorials should take a stand either for or against isolationism, and should include valid arguments.

LS **Visual-Spatial, Verbal-Linguistic**

Alternative Assessment Handbook, Rubrics 7: Charts; and 17: Letters to Editors

Answers

Reading Skills *pushed to build coal mines, factories, and railroads; encouraged government to make modern weapons and ships; tried to introduce Western knowledge and languages to China*

By the end of the 1800s, China was in a desperate position. The war with Japan had exposed China's military weakness, and Europeans now controlled large portions of Chinese territory. Something had to be done if China were to remain independent.

In 1898 the Chinese emperor decided to enact a series of reforms, including changing the civil service examinations and building a modern army. But Empress Dowager Cixi, the most powerful person in China, stopped the reforms because she believed they threatened the rule of the Qing dynasty. People who believed the reforms were necessary now began to call for an end to the Qing dynasty.

The Boxer Rebellion The humiliation of China by the West produced several nationalist movements intent on restoring China's glory. The most important was the Harmonious Fists, or Boxers. This secret society combined martial arts training, hatred of foreigners, and a belief that they were invulnerable to Western weapons. The **Boxer Rebellion** began in 1899 when the Boxers started attacking missionaries and Chinese converts to Christianity.

In June 1900 the Boxers laid siege to the foreign compounds in Beijing and held the foreigners hostage for 55 days. A few weeks later, an army of 20,000 foreign troops captured Beijing and suppressed the uprising. The foreign powers imposed a heavy fine on the Chinese government for secretly supporting the Boxers. The result was more humiliation for the Chinese government at the hands of foreigners.

NEW YORK

CC Unit 5-H5b
Boxer Rebellion

The 1911 Revolution With the defeat of the Boxers, Qing officials finally began to enact reforms. They eliminated the system of examinations for officials and tried to establish primary and secondary schools. Qing officials took steps to create a new national army. They even created elected provincial assemblies, which began to meet in 1909.

Still, these reforms were too little, too late. Radicals living in Japan and the United States called for the overthrow of the Qing dynasty and the creation of a new Chinese republic.

Skills FOCUS INTERPRETING VISUALS

Draw Conclusions Why do you think Europeans considered Shanghai an important trading port?

Europeans controlled the area of the city along the river. This stretch of land included European banks, hotels, clubs, and restaurants.

Chinese merchants sold raw materials such as cotton and silk to European traders, who shipped the goods to Europe by steamship.

THE AGE OF IMPERIALISM **749**

Info to Know

Shanghai Today Today Shanghai is a bustling, modern city with a population well over 16 million. It is China's leading scientific and technological research center, and one of China's largest industrial centers.

The Taiping Rebellion The Taiping rebel force at its greatest consisted of about one million people. After they captured the city of Nanjing in 1853, they made it the capital of their kingdom. They were not driven out of Nanjing until 1864.

The Rise of the Chinese Press Toward the end of the 1800s, many Chinese scholars shifted from traditional to modern ideas and practices. Western religious texts were translated, along with a variety of other written works. The 1870s brought newspapers and magazines that circulated information about current events—a distinct break from the Confucian focus of the past. Large numbers of people were able to read the same periodicals at the same time. The press included satirical and critical pieces aimed at the government and foreign nations, which provoked reactions from the mass populace.

About the Illustration
This illustration is an artist's conception based on available sources. Historians, however, are uncertain exactly what this scene looked like.

Reading Skill
Western Influence and the Qing Dynasty

1. Have students make two lists, one describing Western influence on China and the other identifying problems with Qing rule.

2. Review student lists as a class, creating a master list for students to see. Have students identify examples of each type of Western influence or each problem with Qing rule.

3. Have each student write an analysis of the economic, political, and social problems of Qing rule. Which of the problems were directly attributable to Western influence? How might history have been different if China had been able to successfully resist foreign influence? **LS Verbal-Linguistic**

Alternative Assessment Handbook, Rubric 38: Writing to Classify

Answers

History Close-Up *was open to free trade with the West; traded tea, leather goods, and gift items, as well as raw materials such as cotton and silk*

749

Western Nations Gain Power

Recall What were the three principals of Sun Yixian's ideology? *nationalism, democracy, and "people's livelihood"*

Analyze How did Sun Yixian's philosophy incorporate both democracy and socialism? *possible answer— belief in independence, elected rulers, and individual freedoms, but also in equality in land ownership to remedy problems of the past in China*

Primary Sources

"An individual should not have too much freedom. A nation should have absolute freedom."
—Sun Yat-Sen

FACES OF HISTORY

SUN Yixian
1866–1925

Known as the Father of Modern China, Sun Yixian first became interested in pursuing a political career after China's disastrous defeat in the Sino-Japanese War. By 1905 he began developing a plan to restore economic and political strength to China. His ideas centered around the concept of political tutelage—that a strong government would teach the Chinese people the principles of representative government until a true democracy could emerge. Sun Yixian was practical and formed many alliances—even with Russian Communists—in an effort to unite the Chinese people.

Draw Conclusions What was Sun Yixian's main goal throughout his career?

FOCUS ON NEW YORK

Chinese had lived in New York since at least the 1820s. During the early 1900s, most of New York's Chinese community, which was concentrated in Manhattan's Chinatown, supported Sun Yixian, giving money and even returning to China to fight.

Sun Yixian, known in the West as Sun Yat-sen, was the most prominent of these radicals. Sun based his revolutionary ideology on three basic principles—nationalism, democracy, and "people's livelihood." The last of these principles involved equality in landownership and was often translated as socialism.

Sun believed that China should eventually become a democracy, but that the Chinese people were not ready yet. First, he called for the overthrow of the Qing dynasty and its replacement by a ruling nationalist party. He wanted this party to act as a guardian of the Chinese people until they were ready for democracy.

Other people in China also began to call for the overthrow of the Qing dynasty. Revolutionary ideas took root among intellectuals and junior officers in military academies. In October 1911 a group of young officers led a revolt in the city of Wuchang. Support for the revolt grew rapidly. In January 1912 the revolutionaries declared a republic.

The Qing wanted a general named Yuan Shikai to quash the rebellion. Instead of crushing the rebels, though, Yuan negotiated peace with them. At the peace talks, Yuan convinced the Chinese emperor to abdicate. This event brought an end to the 268-year rule of the Qing dynasty. After the abdication, Yuan Shikai agreed to become the first president of the new Republic of China.

READING CHECK **Find the Main Idea** How did European intervention in China contribute to the downfall of the Qing dynasty?

The Rise of Modern Japan

Japan learned from the Chinese example about how *not* to respond to the West. Like China, Japan resisted contact at first. But once that contact was made in the mid-1800s, Japan reacted differently. Instead of descending into turmoil and revolution, Japan emerged as a great military and imperial power.

The U.S. Renews Contact The Tokugawa regime ruled Japan from 1603 to 1867 and tried to limit contact with the outside world. Yet American and European merchants wanted to trade with Japan. To open up trade, in 1852 U.S. president Millard Fillmore sent Commodore Matthew Perry on a mission to Japan. Perry appeared in Edo (Tokyo) Bay in 1853 with four warships and again in 1854 with nine ships.

The threat of the U.S. navy convinced Japanese officials to sign the **Treaty of Kanagawa** in 1854. This treaty allowed American ships to stop at two Japanese ports. Another treaty in 1858 opened five more Japanese ports to Western merchants. This treaty also established extraterritoriality for Westerners in Japan.

Many Japanese found these treaties deeply humiliating. They were especially angry that Westerners committing crimes in Japan received extremely mild punishments or no punishment at all. These treaties contributed to the rise of Japanese nationalism.

The Meiji Restoration Throughout the Tokugawa period, the emperor had been little more than a symbolic figure. The shogun, or supreme military ruler, was the real power in Tokugawa Japan. But many Japanese people, resenting the way that the shogun had given in to Western demands, forced the shogun to step down. This ended the military control of the Japanese government.

The young emperor, Mutsuhito, took back the power of the government in 1868, taking the name **Emperor Meiji**, which means "enlightened rule." The period of his reign from 1868 to 1912 is called the Meiji period, and the emperor's return to power is called the Meiji Restoration.

From China's example, the Meiji emperor learned about the risk of resisting Western demands. China had clung to its traditional ways and had been unsuccessful in keeping

---

Below Level

Learners Having Difficulty

1. Have students work in mixed-ability pairs to review the information in the text about the Qing dynasty. Then have students work in pairs to create a sequence diagram showing the steps that led to the dynasty's downfall.

2. Review student sequence charts as a class, creating a master chart for students to see. Have volunteers explain steps on the chart. Have students correct their work as needed.

3. Guide students in a discussion of the downfall of the Qing dynasty. Have volunteers suggest measures that could have been taken at each step to help strengthen the dynasty.
LS Visual-Spatial

Alternative Assessment Handbook, Rubric 7: Charts

Answers

Faces of History *to restore economic and political strength to China*

Reading Check *Western actions in China led to nationalist movements and rebellions. In 1911 Chinese revolutionaries ended the 268-year Qing dynasty and declared the Republic of China.*

its sovereignty, or independent control of its government. The Meiji emperor believed that the best way to preserve and build Japan's strength was to modernize and reform.

Meiji Reforms The reforms undertaken during the Meiji era were far-reaching. A group of Japanese officials made a two-year journey called the Iwakura Mission, in which they traveled to the United States and Europe to learn about Western society, military practices, and economics. The officials were to determine which aspects of Western life would help Japan modernize efficiently.

Japan soon required all children to attend school and allowed some students to study abroad. Japanese military officials adapted practices of the U.S. and European armed forces to strengthen their own military.

Most significantly, the emperor supported rapid industrialization. The government financed the construction of the infrastructure necessary for a modern industrial economy. It built telegraph lines, set up a postal service, established a national currency, and helped build a railroad system. By the 1890s, the Japanese economy was booming. In fact, between 1895 and 1915, manufacturing grew more rapidly in Japan than in the United States. Japan was quickly becoming one of the world's great industrial powers.

Becoming an Imperial Power Now that Japan had modernized, it was ready to take its place on the world stage. It began by strengthening its influence over Korea. In the 1870s Japan forced Korea to open three ports to Japanese merchants—even though Korea had traditionally pledged its allegiance to China. When a rebellion broke out in Korea in 1894, Japan and China both sent troops to Korea. This action led to the **Sino-Japanese War**, which lasted only a few months and ended in a humiliating defeat for China.

NEW YORK

CC Unit 5-I
Japan and the Meiji restoration

Japan Reacts to U.S. Military Might

Commodore Matthew Perry Arrives in Japan, by Yoshitoshi Taiso

Skills FOCUS   READING LIKE A HISTORIAN

In this print, artist Yoshitoshi Taiso depicts the arrival of Commodore Perry in Edo Bay in 1853. Perry's hulking black warships sent the Japanese a strong message about U.S. military power.

Analyzing Visuals How did the artist show the difference between Japanese and American power?
See **Skills Handbook**, p. H26

Reading Focus

❷ What led to the rise of Japan as a major power? *During the Meiji period, Japan made reforms and modernized.*

The Rise of Modern Japan

Identify What was the main point of the Treaty of Kanagawa? *allowed American ships to stop at two Japanese ports*

Interpret Why did Japan agree to the Treaty of Kanagawa? *The threat of the U.S. navy convinced Japan to sign the treaty, even though many Japanese found the treaty humiliating.*

Contrast How did Japan's response to the West differ from China's response? *Instead of rebelling against Western influences, Japan made reforms and modernized.*

📄 **CRF:** Biography: Hokusai

📄 **CRF:** History and Geography: Japan Opens Trade Routes

Info to Know

Modernizing the Silk Industry In the late 1800s Japan acquired Western techniques and machinery to mechanize its silk industry. Using steam or water power instead of turning the reel by hand produced silk filaments of uniform size and greater strength at faster speed. A large labor force was still required to prepare silkworm cocoons and tend the machines. Most of the employees were women. Under Meiji rule, the silk industry progressed due to the use of more advanced methods of production and numerous mills.

Skills Focus: Identifying Problem and Solution   At Level

Reading Skill
Japan Responds to Perry

1. Tell the class that they are daimyo, and the Japanese shogun has asked for their advice on how to respond to Commodore Perry's demands for U.S. trading privileges in Japan.

2. Organize the class into small groups, and have the daimyo discuss among themselves whether opening trade with the United States is in Japan's best interests.

3. Then have the daimyo propose courses of action that might satisfy the United States but still preserve Japan's culture and desire for isolation.

4. Have each daimyo write a draft of a letter of response for Perry to take back to the American president. Each letter should include the reasoning behind that daimyo's decision. **LS Interpersonal, Verbal-Linguistic**

📄 **Alternative Assessment Handbook**, Rubrics 14: Group Activity; and 41: Writing to Express

Answers

Reading Like a Historian *possible answer—Perry's ship appears large and intimidating in comparison to the small Japanese boats in the foreground.*

Direct Teach

Reading Focus

3 How did European power and influence increase in Southeast Asia? *Dutch, British, and French claimed colonies in Southeast Asia.*

Europeans in Southeast Asia

Recall Where did Great Britain and France claim colonies in Southeast Asia? *Great Britain—Malaysia; France—Indochina*

Contrast How was Siam different from other parts of Southeast Asia? *It was the only Southeast Asian country to retain its independence in the 1800s.*

🗏 **Quick Facts Transparency:** The Meiji Reforms

🗏 **Map Transparency:** Southeast Asia, 1895

Info to Know

Government Reforms The new Japanese government abolished feudalism. Most of the feudal lords willingly gave up their privileges, but those who resisted were ruthlessly crushed. As compensation for their losses, former lords were awarded European titles and public offices. Thus counts, barons, and marquises began to appear as key figures in the Japanese government.

Answers

Reading Check *Japan modernized and industrialized, which gave it the power to begin expanding.*

752

 QUICK FACTS

THE MEIJI REFORMS

During the Meiji era, a number of significant reforms quickly transformed Japan into a modern industrialized nation.

Governmental Reforms
- Ended feudalism; local government based on prefectures (districts)
- Enacted European-style constitution

Rapid Industrialization
- Government invested in transportation and communication
- Government directly supported businesses and industries

Military Reforms
- Modeled army and navy after those of Prussia and Britain
- Required three years' military service from all men

▲ **Factory workers during the Meiji era**

Meiji Reform Silk Factory, by Ichiyosai Kuniteru, c. 1875

🗽 **NEW YORK**

CC Unit 5-14
Japan as an imperialist power

The Japanese victory established Japan as the most powerful state in Asia. As a result of the war, China recognized Korea's independence. Japan gained control of Taiwan, which became its colony, and won the right to build factories in China. Western powers treated Japan with a newfound respect, giving in to Japan's request to end extraterritoriality.

Japan's status as a great power was confirmed by its victory in the Russo-Japanese War of 1904–1905. This war was caused by Russian competition with Japan over influence in Manchuria and Korea. Although the Japanese won a series of battles, they could not get the Russians to surrender. Instead, the two sides asked U.S. president Theodore Roosevelt to help negotiate a peace treaty, called the Treaty of Portsmouth.

The treaty gave Japan control over Russian railway lines in southern Manchuria and transferred Russian leases on two Manchurian ports to Japan. The treaty also recognized Korea as under Japanese influence.

Japan's victory over Russia was celebrated all over Asia. It showed that an Asian power could defeat a European power. But growing Japanese power also presented a threat to its Asian neighbors. In 1910 Japan annexed Korea as a Japanese colony, demonstrating that its power in Asia was growing.

READING CHECK **Draw Conclusions** How did Japan gain the strength to become an imperial power?

752 CHAPTER 25

Europeans in Southeast Asia

Southeast Asia had long been a source of spices, such as cloves and pepper, that Europeans valued highly. To get these spices, Europeans established colonies there in the 1500s.

In the 1600s and 1700s, the Dutch controlled the spice trade by holding key Southeast Asian ports and fortifications. The Dutch began to grow sugar and coffee on large plantations in their Southeast Asian colonies. This shift to plantation agriculture set the pattern for future colonies in Southeast Asia.

In the 1800s the British began to compete with the Dutch in Malaysia. The British attained control of Malacca (part of modern-day Malaysia) from the Dutch in 1824. Britain already controlled the port cities of Singapore and Penang on the Malay Peninsula. In the late 1800s, the British moved into the interior of the peninsula. There, they established rubber plantations to provide raw material for bicycle-tire factories in Britain.

While the British increased their control over Malaysia, the French conquered part of Indochina. French missionaries and traders were active in Vietnam in the early 1800s. The ruling Nguyen (NGWEEN) dynasty saw the French as a threat and tried to expel French missionaries from the country. They also tried to crack down on Vietnamese converts to Christianity. In response, French emperor Napoleon III sent a fleet to Vietnam. The French defeated the Vietnamese forces in the Mekong

---

Skills Focus: Identifying Problem and Solution

At Level

Reading Skill
The Meiji Reforms

1. Tell students they will act as advisers to Emperor Meiji. Direct students' attention to the Quick Facts chart on this page.

2. Organize students into small groups and have them come up with several good reasons behind each of the reforms listed on the chart. Remind students to think about the reforms as a response to Western influence and to consider the long-term effects of each reform for Japan.

3. Have students write drafts of a letter to Emperor Meiji. Letters should propose that he enact several of the reforms and explain why each one will be beneficial to Japan.

LS Interpersonal, Verbal-Linguistic

📝 **Alternative Assessment Handbook**, Rubrics 14: Group Activity; and 41: Writing to Express

Delta and forced the Vietnamese ruler to sign the Treaty of Saigon in 1862. This treaty gave the French control of most of the territory in southern Vietnam.

France took control of the rest of Vietnam in 1884 and annexed neighboring Laos and Cambodia, creating a territory known as French Indochina. Like the British in India, the French built roads, railroads, and irrigation systems in Indochina. They also introduced some reforms in education and medical care.

French colonialism in Indochina largely benefited the French, however. Many French citizens became rich from their large tea and rubber plantations. Meanwhile, many Vietnamese farmers fell into debt when they were unable to pay high taxes. Due to these factors, Vietnamese peasants often lost their farms and were forced to become wage laborers. Vietnamese resentment against the French rulers grew throughout the 1800s and early 1900s.

Siam (called Thailand today) was the only Southeast Asian country to retain its independence in the 1800s. Siam served as a buffer between British-controlled Burma and French Indochina. By skillful exploitation of European rivalries and by careful modernization, the monarchs of Siam preserved the nation's freedom.

READING CHECK **Summarize** Why were Europeans interested in colonizing Southeast Asia?

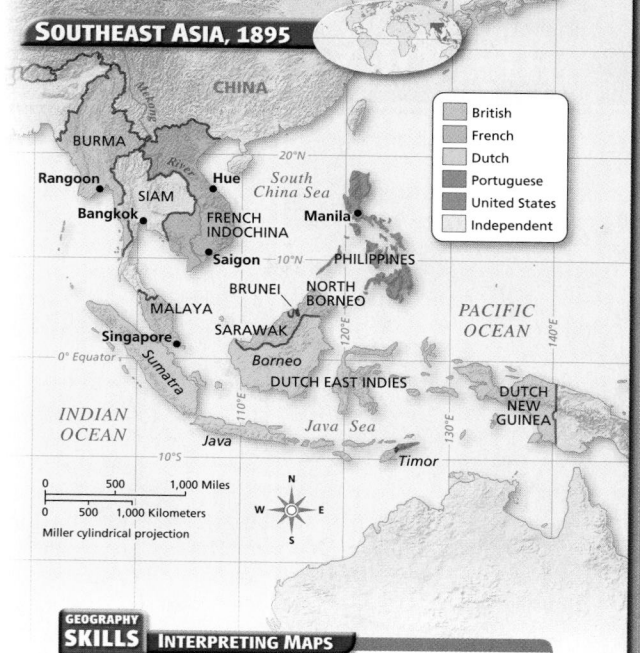

SOUTHEAST ASIA, 1895

British	
French	
Dutch	
Portuguese	
United States	
Independent	

GEOGRAPHY SKILLS **INTERPRETING MAPS**

1. **Location** Which nation served as a buffer state between British-controlled Burma and French Indochina?

2. **Place** According to the map, which nation controlled the most land area in Southeast Asia?

SECTION 2 ASSESSMENT

go.hrw.com
Online Quiz
Keyword: SHL IMP HP

Reviewing Ideas, Terms, and People

1. **a. Recall** What were the unequal treaties?
   b. Draw Conclusions How did European imperialism lead to problems for the Qing dynasty?
   c. Elaborate How did the Chinese people react to the growing influence of Westerners in China?

2. **a. Identify** Who was Emperor Meiji?
   b. Contrast How did Japan's reaction to Western imperialism differ from China's?
   c. Evaluate Why was Japan more successful than China in maintaining its independence?

3. **a. Recall** What was the Treaty of Saigon?
   b. Make Generalizations How did Siam retain its independence?

Critical Thinking

4. **Compare and Contrast** Using your notes from the section and the chart below, compare and contrast European imperialism's effects on China and Japan.

	Effects on Japan	Effects on China
Political		
Economic		
Cultural		
Military		

FOCUS ON SPEAKING

5. **Persuasion** Suppose you are an official at the court of the Chinese emperor, just after China's defeat in the Sino-Japanese War. Prepare a short presentation to the emperor explaining the types of reforms China needs to make to become a great power again.

THE AGE OF IMPERIALISM **753**

Close

Have students summarize the ways in which China, Japan, and Southeast Asia responded to Western influences.

Review

Online Quiz, Section 2

Assess

SE **Section 2 Assessment**

Progress Assessment: Section 2 Quiz

Alternative Assessment Handbook

Reteach/Intervene

Interactive Reader and Study Guide, Section 2

Interactive Skills Tutor CD-ROM

Answers

Interpreting Maps **1.** *Siam;* **2.** *The Netherlands*

Reading Check *to obtain valuable spices such as cloves and pepper*

Section 2 Assessment Answers

1. **a.** treaties that benefited Europeans at the expense of the Chinese
   b. Humiliating defeats at the hands of European imperialists weakened the Qing dynasty, causing rebellions.
   c. They rebelled against their leaders.

2. **a.** the young emperor who returned to power in Japan in 1868
   b. Japan made reforms; Chinese resisted change.
   c. possible answer—Japan's modernization and industrialization allowed it to protect itself and expand its borders.

3. **a.** treaty that gave France control of most of the territory in southern Vietnam
   b. by exploiting European rivalries; modernizing

4. Political—Japan: rise in nationalism led to Meiji Restoration; China: rise in nationalist movements led to rebellions that weakened government; Economic—Japan: modernized industry, economy; China: British introduced opium, weakening China's economy Cultural—Japan: Meiji emperor made all children attend school, allowed some study abroad—China: Christian missionaries indirectly influenced rebellions; Military—Japan: modernized military; China: weak military led to loss of Sino-Japanese War and carving out of spheres of influence by Western nations

5. Student presentations might recommend reforms similar to the Meiji Reforms, which helped Japan emerge as a world power.

THE AGE OF IMPERIALISM **753**

Imperialism and a Global Economy

Info to Know

Before Imperialism Western trade with China from 1760 to 1842 was considered by the Chinese to be a gracious grant by the Son of Heaven to foreigners. However, the Chinese government would not directly involve itself in dealings with Western traders. Instead, this task was assigned to special Chinese merchants known as the Cohong. Foreigners were allowed to live in specific areas in the port of Guangzhou only while engaged in trade, were not allowed the company of their wives, and were discouraged from learning Chinese. Foreign merchants could only communicate with government officials through Cohong intermediaries. Western traders endured these cumbersome regulations and restrictions. The end of the Cohong system was a major British goal in negotiating the Treaty of Nanjing.

HISTORY & Geography

Africa, a source for raw materials such as a wide range of metals, was almost entirely controlled by European powers by the early 1900s.

Imperialism and a Global Economy

One result of the growth of imperialism was the creation of a global economy. As European nations competed for power and influence, they set up colonies around the world, especially in Africa and Asia. The colonies provided Europe's powers with the raw materials they needed for their rapidly industrializing economies. At the same time, the colonies provided new markets for European exports of manufactured goods. As a result, global trade grew dramatically, and a two-way traffic of goods developed—raw materials went to Europe, and manufactured goods went to the colonies.

754 CHAPTER 25

Skills Focus: Identifying Cause and Effect — At Level

Reading Skill
The Effect of the Suez Canal

Research Required

1. Review with students the information about the Suez Canal. Remind them that control of the Suez Canal was an important goal of imperialists, and that the canal was strategically located for shipping between Asia and Europe.

2. Have students conduct independent research on the impact to shipping of the 1867 opening of the Suez Canal.

3. Organize students into groups of four to six. Each group will prepare a multimedia

presentation that explains the importance of the Suez Canal. Students may use photographs, graphs and charts, and/or time lines in their presentations.

4. Have groups give their presentations to the rest of the class. **LS Interpersonal, Visual-Spatial**

Alternative Assessment Handbook, Rubrics 14: Group Activity; 22: Multimedia Presentations; and 30: Research

European Colonies

- Belgian
- British
- Dutch
- French
- German
- Italian
- Portuguese
- Spanish

← Main trade in raw materials
← Main trade in manufactured goods
COAL Raw materials

0   1,000   2,000 Miles
0   1,000   2,000 Kilometers
Robinson projection

Colonies in Asia produced valuable goods like rubber, silk, and spices.

ASIA

SILK

SILK
SUGAR
SILK
METALS
SPICES
TEA
TEA
COTTON
SILK
METALS
SILK
RICE
RICE
RICE
RUBBER
RICE
RICE
SPICES
COFFEE
METALS
RUBBER
RICE
SPICES
METALS
RUBBER
METALS
RUBBER
RUBBER
RICE

PACIFIC OCEAN

INDIAN OCEAN

METALS
COAL
AUSTRALIA
METALS
COAL

Raw Materials and Industry

As industry in Europe grew, so did the need for raw materials, such as rubber to make bicycle tires. Rubber is a tropical crop, so Europeans had to import it from their colonies.

 NEW YORK STANDARDS

PI **2.5** Students investigate key events and developments and major turning points in world history to identify the factors that brought about change and the long-term effects of these changes.

Transportation Technology

Improvements in transportation technology were key to the growth of the global economy. Giant new steamships could carry more goods more quickly than ever before. These ships sailed along major shipping routes and relied on coaling stations and strategic waterways such as the Suez Canal, shown here. The canal, opened in 1869, dramatically cut the time and cost of shipping goods from Asia to Europe, further increasing global trade.

THE AGE OF IMPERIALISM **755**

Interpreting Maps
Imperialism and a Global Economy

Location Name three raw materials listed on the map, and where they were found. *Asia: rubber, silk, spices; Africa: metals*

Movement What effect did steamships have upon global trade? *steamships could carry more goods, more quickly than ever before*

Activity **Canal Routes** Have students locate the Panama Canal and the Suez Canal on the map. Ask students what routes must have been used before these canals existed. Then, have students write a short paragraph about the importance of key canals to the global economy. **LS** Visual-Spatial, Verbal-Linguistic

---

Differentiating Instruction

Below Level

Learners Having Difficulty

Standard English Mastery

Materials: Outline map showing Asia and Europe

1. Review with students where rubber came from, where it went, and its many uses. Explain to students that rubber is just one example of a raw material found in European colonies that could be used in manufactured goods.

2. On outline maps, have students draw the journey of a rubber plant from Asia to Europe. On their maps, students should label the line, and the continents of Asia and Europe.

3. Have students write a short paragraph describing rubber as an example of imperialism and the global economy. **LS** Visual-Spatial, Verbal-Linguistic

📝 **Alternative Assessment Handbook,** Rubrics 20: Map Creation; and 40: Writing to Describe

Answers

Interpreting Maps 1. *Belgium, Great Britain, France, Germany, Italy, Portugal, Spain; metals;* **2.** *U.S., Europe, Japan*

Getting Started

Use the **Interactive Reader and Study Guide** to familiarize students with the section content.

📄 **Interactive Reader and Study Guide,** Section 3

Academic Vocabulary

Review with students the high-use academic term in this section.

discrimination the act of treating a person differently because of race, gender, or national origin (p. 757)

📄 **CRF: Vocabulary Builder: Section 3**

Taking Notes

New Imperialism in Africa—rapid division of Africa by European powers to obtain manufacturing materials during Industrial Revolution; competition among European nations contributed to imperialism, as did discrimination and Social Darwinism

European Nations in Africa—aided by advanced in medicine, weapons, communication, and transportation; Suez Canal influenced Britain's interest in Egypt; Berlin Conference mediated European disputes; Boer War fought over southern Africa; Belgian king controlled Congo with brutal methods

Resistance to Imperialism—Zulu fought the British; Ethiopians defeated Italians; Malinke people fought against French rule in West Africa; Maji Maji Rebellion was put down by Germans in East Africa

go.hrw.com
Online Resources

KEYWORD: SHL IMP
ACTIVITY: Democratic
Republic of the Congo Today

---

3 The Scramble for Africa

BEFORE YOU READ

MAIN IDEA

In the late 1800s and early 1900s, European powers claimed land in much of Africa.

READING FOCUS

1. What factors led to the new imperialism?

2. How did European powers claim territory in Africa?

3. How did Africans resist European imperialism?

KEY TERMS AND PEOPLE

Social Darwinism
Cecil Rhodes
Suez Canal
Berlin Conference
Leopold II
Shaka
Menelik II

🗽 **NEW YORK**

PI **2.3** Students analyze evidence critically and demonstrate an understanding of how circumstances of time and place influence perspective.

PI **3.1** Students analyze the roles and contributions of individuals and groups.

THE INSIDE STORY

How did Ethiopia remain independent? In 1889 the emperor of Ethiopia, Menelik II, signed a treaty with Italy. This treaty gave control over what is now Eritrea to the Italians in exchange for weapons and a sum of money. An error in the translation of the treaty, however, led both sides to war.

The Italian translation of the treaty led Italy to believe that it not only controlled Eritrea but that it also had a protectorate over Ethiopia. The version of the treaty in Amharic—the official language of Ethiopia—led Menelik to believe he was only giving up Eritrea. Menelik rejected the claim over Ethiopia and denounced the entire treaty, knowing it would lead to war.

Menelik initiated the war, amassing some 100,000 Ethiopian soldiers and advancing upon the Italian forces at Adwa. The Italian force was disorganized, and the Ethiopians quickly defeated it on March 1, 1896, in the Battle of Adwa. About 70 percent of the Italian forces perished in the battle. The Italians retreated through unfamiliar terrain while local peoples harassed them.

The Battle of Adwa marked a high point of African resistance to European imperialism. An African army had crushed a European army in battle and in doing so had ensured the continued independence of Ethiopia. ◼

The Negus Menelik II at Battle of Aduwa, 1896

▲ **Menelik II at the Battle of Adwa**

Teach the Main Idea
At Level

The Scramble for Africa

1. **Teach** Ask students the Reading Focus questions to teach this section.

2. **Apply** Have students work in pairs to make graphic organizers showing which European countries controlled which African colonies, along with the date they established their control.

3. **Review** Review student graphic organizers as a class. Guide students in a discussion of the reasons European nations felt entitled to take control of Africa.

4. **Practice/Homework** Have each student write a letter to the editor about the results of the Berlin Conference from the point of view of an American living at that time. **LS Visual-Spatial, Verbal-Linguistic**

📄 **Alternative Assessment Handbook,** Rubrics 13: Graphic Organizers; and 17: Letters to Editors

The New Imperialism

European countries controlled only a small part of Africa in 1880, but by 1914, only Ethiopia and Liberia remained independent. During the period known as the "Scramble for Africa" European powers rapidly divided Africa.

Historians view the scramble as the most visible example of the new imperialism. Unlike the imperialism of the 1500s and 1600s, the new imperialism was not based on settlement of colonies. Instead, European powers worked to directly govern large areas occupied by non-European peoples. Europeans were driven by economic interests, political competition, and cultural motives.

Economic Interests Before the early 1800s, several European nations profited from the slave trade in Africa. However, after some nations passed laws abolishing the slave trade, Europeans looked to Africa instead as a source for raw materials. During the Industrial Revolution, Europeans needed materials such as coal and metals to manufacture goods. These needs fueled Europeans' desire for land with plentiful natural resources—resources that were available in Africa.

To gather and export these natural resources, European entrepreneurs, or independent businesspeople, developed their own mines, plantations, and trading routes. Sometimes the entrepreneurs would call on their home countries to protect their economic interests from European competitors. In this way, the drive for colonization sometimes came from ambitious individuals, rather than from European governments.

Political Competition Imperialism in Africa reflected struggles for power in Europe, such as the long-term rivalry between France and Britain. As France expanded its control over West and Central Africa, Britain began to expand its colonial empire to block the French. The rise of Germany and Italy as European powers also contributed to the new imperialism. Both nations jumped into the race for colonies to assert their status as great powers.

Nationalism also contributed to the rise of the new imperialism. European leaders believed that controlling colonies would gain them more respect from other leaders.

Cultural Motives In addition to practical matters of economics and politics, the new imperialism was motivated by cultural attitudes. In particular, European imperialists felt they were superior to non-European peoples. These Europeans argued that humanity was divided into distinct peoples, or races, and there were significant biological differences between the races. Most Europeans who held these views believed that people of European descent were biologically superior to people of African or Asian descent.

As a result, some Europeans believed their rule in Africa was justified because they were teaching Africans good government, European customs, and Christian values. Some imperialists even believed their actions in Africa were noble. They saw it as their duty to educate those people they considered inferior. They referred to their influence in Africa as "the white man's burden," after a poem by the English writer Rudyard Kipling.

Defenders of imperialism also often applied Charles Darwin's theory of natural selection to the struggle between nations and races. Darwin argued that species that are more fit for their environment will survive and reproduce. The notion of **Social Darwinism** stated that certain nations or races are more fit than others. Social Darwinists believed these "fit" nations came to rule over the nations that are "less fit," and often showed <u>discrimination</u> against citizens of the ruled nations.

One outspoken advocate of Social Darwinism was Englishman **Cecil Rhodes**. A wealthy businessman, Rhodes once explained how he felt about British influence in Africa:

HISTORY'S VOICES

❝I contend that we are the finest race in the world and that the more of the world we inhabit the better it is for the human race . . . What an alteration there would be if they [Africans] were brought under Anglo-Saxon influence.❞

—Cecil Rhodes, *Confessions of Faith*, 1877

Rhodes believed that a railway linking Britain's Cape Colony in southern Africa to Cairo, Egypt, in the north would bring what he saw as the benefits of civilization to all Africans.

READING CHECK **Find the Main Idea** What were some reasons that European powers scrambled to claim colonies in Africa?

TAKING NOTES

Take notes on new imperialism in Africa, European nations in Africa, and resistance to imperialism.

 NEW YORK
CC Unit 5-H1
Reasons for imperialism

ACADEMIC VOCABULARY

discrimination the act of treating a person differently because of race, gender, or national origin

---

---

2 How did European powers claim territory in Africa? *Britain took control of Egypt, began to compete with France over trade in West Coast of Africa; Belgium began to develop commercial interests; Germany declared protectorates over four African territories*

European Claims in Africa

Recall What was the extent of European control of Africa prior to the 1880s? *They controlled only some parts of the African coast.*

Summarize What developments spurred European expansion in Africa after 1880? *British takeover of Egypt to ensure security of the Suez Canal; British and French competition over trade to the interior of West Coast colonies; development of Belgian commercial interests in the Congo; rise of new powers that sought colonial empires*

📋 **CRF:** Literature: *Heart of Darkness*

READING SKILLS

Identifying Supporting Details What details are given that explain European claims in Africa?

European Claims in Africa

Prior to the 1880s, Europeans controlled some parts of the African coast. In the 1880s, driven by their new economic, political, and cultural motives, Europeans began to compete for additional territory in Africa.

Scientific Advances and Imperialism

In Africa Europeans faced a huge continent with rugged terrain that could make travel and control difficult. In the 1880s, however, several European scientific advances came together to make traveling in and controlling Africa easier. With the discovery of the drug quinine, Europeans protected themselves against one of the biggest threats, malaria. With the development of the first automatic machine gun, they created a strong military advantage, one that enabled them to defeat and subdue African peoples who had no modern weapons. Finally, with the development of telegraphs, railroads, and steamships, Europeans overcame many of the problems of communication and travel.

Suez Canal

In 1869 another technological advancement, the **Suez Canal**, influenced Britain's interest in Egypt. The canal linked the Mediterranean with the Red Sea, drastically shortening the trip from Europe to the Indian Ocean by eliminating the need for ships to sail around the southern tip of Africa.

When the Egyptian government appeared unstable in 1882, the British occupied Egypt to protect British interests in the Suez Canal. Britain later established partial control over Egypt as a protectorate to ensure British access to the canal.

Division of Africa

Meanwhile, European nations continued to compete aggressively for other territories in Africa. To create order and prevent conflict between European nations, European leaders met in Berlin, Germany, in 1884–1885 to divide African territory. Leaders at the **Berlin Conference** agreed that when a European nation claimed a new African territory, it had to notify other European nations and prove that it could control the territory. As they divided Africa, European leaders paid no attention to Africans' traditional ethnic boundaries. This disregard for the African peoples land would later cause conflict.

🗽 **NEW YORK**

CC Unit 5-H4c
African resistance—Zulu Empire

The Boer War

In southern Africa, the British met opposition to land claims. Dutch settlers, known as Boers, had lived in the region since the 1600s. After gold was discovered there in the late 1800s, the Boers refused to grant political rights to foreigners, including the British. Tensions between the two groups heightened as Britain tried to make Boer territory a part of the British Empire. In 1899 war broke out.

During the Boer War, British forces vastly outnumbered Boer forces. Nevertheless, using guerrilla tactics, the Boers quickly gained an advantage over British troops. The British responded by destroying Boer farms and imprisoning women and children in concentration camps. More than 20,000 Boer women and children died of disease in the camps. In the end the British defeated the Boers, and in 1902, Boer territory became the self-governing Union of South Africa under British control.

Belgian Congo

Unlike most of Africa, the Congo Free State in Central Africa was not ruled by a European country. Instead, the king of Belgium, **Leopold II**, claimed the territory for himself. Leopold created a personal fortune by exploiting the Congo's natural resources.

In the 1890s and early 1900s in Europe and the United States, the demand for rubber increased as the need for bicycle and automobile tires increased. To meet this demand, Leopold forced his Congolese subjects to extract rubber from the region's rubber trees. Millions of workers died from overwork and disease. Eventually an international outcry over Leopold's brutal tactics caused the Belgian government to take control of the Congo in 1908.

READING CHECK **Infer** How did the Berlin Conference contribute to the Scramble for Africa?

African Resistance

Africans did not passively accept European claims to rule over them. As European troops advanced on African territory, they often met stiff resistance from local rulers and peoples.

The Zulu

The Zulu people resisted colonialism for more than 50 years. In the early 1800s the Zulu leader **Shaka** built a strong Zulu kingdom by subduing several neighboring peoples.

Skills Focus: Identifying Problem and Solution

At Level

Reading Skill
The Scramble for Africa

1. Tell students they are delegates to the Berlin Conference. Students may choose to represent any of the nations that actually sent delegations to the conference. Have students write a list of their country's goals for the conference and ways in which they hope that their goals will be accomplished.

2. Have volunteers identify the nation they represent and read their goals and solutions.

3. Guide students in a discussion of the Berlin Conference.

4. As an extension, have students prepare scripts and re-enact the Berlin Conference for the class. **LS Verbal-Linguistic, Kinesthetic**

📋 **Alternative Assessment Handbook**, Rubrics 33: Skits and Reader's Theater; and 38: Writing to Classify

---

Answers

Reading Skills *scientific advances—quanine, machine gun, telegraphs, railroads, steamships; Suez Canal—shortened trip from Europe to Indian Ocean; Berlin Conference—agreement to create order and prevent conflict among Europeans; Boer War—Dutch vs. British in southern Africa; Belgian Congo—King Leopold II overworked subjects to extract rubber to sell*

Reading Check *set rules for the division of Africa among the European nations*

IMPERIALISM IN AFRICA

European Colonies
- Belgian
- British
- French
- German
- Italian
- Portuguese
- Spanish
- Independent

1910 Date of colonization

SPANISH MOROCCO 1912
FRENCH MOROCCO 1912
IFNI 1860
RIO DE ORO 1885
TUNISIA 1881
Mediterranean Sea
ALGERIA 1830
LIBYA 1912
EGYPT 1882
Red Sea

GAMBIA 1888
PORTUGUESE GUINEA 1901
SIERRA LEONE 1808
LIBERIA
GOLD COAST 1874
TOGO 1884
RÍO MUNI 1900
FRENCH WEST AFRICA 1874
NIGERIA 1884
FRENCH EQUATORIAL AFRICA 1910
ANGLO-EGYPTIAN SUDAN 1889
ERITREA 1890
FRENCH SOMALILAND 1884
BRITISH SOMALILAND 1889
ETHIOPIA
ITALIAN SOMALILAND 1884

ATLANTIC OCEAN
0° Equator

CAMEROONS 1884
FRENCH EQUATORIAL AFRICA 1910
CABINDA 1886
BELGIAN CONGO 1908
UGANDA 1895
BRITISH EAST AFRICA (KENYA) 1886
GERMAN EAST AFRICA (TANGANYIKA) 1885
ZANZIBAR (British Protectorate) 1886

INDIAN OCEAN

0 500 1,000 Miles
0 500 1,000 Kilometers
Miller cylindrical projection

ANGOLA 1891
NORTHERN RHODESIA 1891
NYASALAND 1891
GERMAN SOUTHWEST AFRICA 1884
SOUTHERN RHODESIA 1890
MOZAMBIQUE 1500
MADAGASCAR 1895
WALVIS BAY (Union of South Africa) 1910
BECHUANALAND 1885
SWAZILAND 1907
BASUTOLAND 1871
UNION OF SOUTH AFRICA 1910

IMPERIALISM IN AFRICA, C. 1880

GEOGRAPHY SKILLS INTERPRETING MAPS

1. **Location** Which nation successfully remained independent during the Scramble for Africa?
2. **Regions** During which decade did European nations seize the greatest amount of land in Africa?

Cetshwayo, king of the Zulu nation, led his army to resist imperial control. Though Zulu resistance was fierce, the British defeated them in 1879.

THE AGE OF IMPERIALISM **759**

Direct Teach

Info to Know

The Berlin Conference In 1884 European leaders met in Germany to resolve potential conflicts over African colonies. With no regard for the boundaries the Africans already had in place (which were often based on the location of ethnic groups), the Europeans carved up Africa among themselves. The decisions made at the Berlin Conference continue to hamper the continent's development.

Activity Africa Today Have students compare the map of Africa on this page with a map of Africa today. Have them list the countries that now exist that were once European colonies. **LS Visual-Spatial**

Map Transparency: Imperialism in Africa

Skills Focus: Analyzing Secondary Sources

At Level

Reading Like a Historian Skill
African Resistance

Research Required

1. Organize students into four groups and assign one of the following nationalities to each group: The Zulu, Ethiopia, French West Africa, and German East Africa

2. Have students use the information about African resistance in the text and from reliable print and online sources to create posters that illustrate the key people and events of the New Imperialism.

3. Have students include several of the following on their posters: pictures, photographs, first-person accounts, contemporary newspaper stories, maps, charts, graphs, and time lines.

4. Have groups present their posters to the class. Display posters in the classroom for students to see. **LS Verbal-Spatial, Kinesthetic**

Alternative Assessment Handbook, Rubrics 1: Acquiring Information; 24: Oral Presentations; and 28: Posters

Answers

Interpreting Maps *1. Ethiopia; 2. the 1880s*

759

❸ How did Africans resist European imperialism? *in battle, sometimes with modern weapons and sometimes without them*

African Resistance

Recall What was the only nation in Africa that was able to retain its independence? *Ethiopia*

Summarize What happened in German East Africa? *In the Maji Maji Rebellion, Africans rebelled, using so-called magic water to protect themselves. Tens of thousands of them died.*

📦 **Quick Facts Transparency:** The New Imperialism in Africa

Close

Have students summarize the events that occurred in the European scramble for Africa.

Review

 Online Quiz, Section 3

Assess

SE Section 3 Assessment

📄 **Progress Assessment**: Section 3 Quiz

📄 **Alternative Assessment Handbook**

Reteach/Intervene

📄 **Interactive Reader and Study Guide**, Section 3

💿 **Interactive Skills Tutor CD-ROM**

Answers

Reading Check *by building a modern army, matching European firepower, and defeating the Italians at the Battle of Adowa*

760

THE NEW IMPERIALISM IN AFRICA
QUICK FACTS

CAUSES
- European nations needed raw materials.
- European leaders wanted power and land.
- Europeans believed in Social Darwinism.

EFFECTS
- Africans lost their land and independence.
- Many Africans died resisting the Europeans.

In 1879 the British invaded Zulu territory. The Zulus, led by Shaka's nephew Cetshwayo (kech-WAH-yoh), won a major victory, but the Zulus could not resist the superior military might of the British for long. In about six months, the British defeated the Zulus and annexed their kingdom as a colony.

Ethiopia Only the African nation of Ethiopia was able to retain its independence by matching European firepower. In 1889 the emperor of Ethiopia, **Menelik II**, undertook a program of modernization that included a modern army.

In 1895 Italian forces invaded Ethiopia over a treaty dispute. Within a year, however,

Menelik's forces—more numerous and better armed than the Italians— defeated the Italians at the Battle of Adwa.

French West Africa Even without modern weapons, other Africans still fiercely resisted European powers. In West Africa, the leader of the Malinke peoples, Samory Touré, formed his own army to fight against French rule. Touré fought the French for 15 years and proclaimed himself king of Guinea. However, in 1898 the French captured Touré and defeated his army. This act ended all resistance to French rule in West Africa.

German East Africa Religious symbolism often played a significant role in African resistance as Africans called on their gods and ancestors for spiritual guidance. For example, in 1905 in the colony of German East Africa, several African peoples united to rebel against the Germans' order to grow cotton for export to Germany. To combat the Germans, a spiritual leader encouraged his followers to sprinkle magic water, or *maji*, all over their bodies to protect themselves from German bullets. The magic water did not work. This Maji Maji Rebellion, as it became known, was quickly put down by the Germans, who killed tens of thousands of Africans.

READING CHECK Draw Conclusions How did Ethiopia resist imperialism?

Reviewing Ideas, Terms and People

1. **a. Define** What is Social Darwinism?
   b. Explain Why did European nations want raw materials from Africa?
   c. Evaluate What drove European leaders to claim African territory?

2. **a. Recall** What advances in technology made European domination of Africa possible?
   b. Explain What was the purpose of the Berlin Conference?
   c. Support a Position Do you think Leopold II should have claimed the Belgian Congo for himself? Why or why not?

3. **a. Identify** Who were the Zulu?
   b. Draw Conclusions How did Ethiopians under Menelik II defeat the Italians?

Critical Thinking

4. **Sequence** Using your notes, make a list of the key events in European imperialism in Africa. Then organize the events on a time line like the one below.

FOCUS ON WRITING

5. **Narration** Write a brief news report on the Battle of Adowa. Use chronological order to tell what happened from the beginning to the end of the battle.

760 CHAPTER 25

Section 3 Assessment Answers

1. **a.** the notion that certain nations or races are more fit than others and that those nations should rule over the "less fit" nations
   b. in order to manufacture goods.
   c. for political reasons, as evidence of power, and economic reasons, as a source of raw materials for factories and a potential market for finished products

2. **a.** quinine, the machine gun, telegraphs, railroads, and steamships
   b. to divide African territory among the European nations

   c. possible answer—no, because he was a brutal leader

3. **a.** an African group who resisted colonialism for more than 50 years
   b. Ethiopia had a modern army that was larger and better armed than the Italian army.

4. 1869, Suez Canal opens; 1879, British vs. Zulu; 1882, British occupy Egypt; 1884, Berlin Conference; 1895, Ethiopia defeats Italy; 1902, Boer territory becomes British

5. Students should explain how the Ethiopians won the battle.

Imperialism in Latin America

BEFORE YOU READ

MAIN IDEA

Imperialism in Latin America involved the United States and European nations seeking to strengthen their political and economic influence over the region.

READING FOCUS

1. How did various groups struggle for power in Mexico before and during the Mexican Revolution?

2. How did growing U.S. influence in Latin America change the region?

KEY TERMS AND PEOPLE

Antonio López de Santa Anna
Porfirio Díaz
Emiliano Zapata
Francisco "Pancho" Villa
Venustiano Carranza
José Martí
Spanish-American War
Emilio Aguinaldo
Roosevelt Corollary

NEW YORK

P1 2.5 Students investigate key events and developments and major turning points in world history to identify the factors that brought about change and the long-term effects of these changes.

REVOLUTION ON THE RUN

◄ Pancho Villa leads other Mexican rebels on horseback.

THE INSIDE STORY

How did a revolutionary win by running? Of all of the leaders of the Mexican Revolution, Francisco "Pancho" Villa fascinated Americans the most. Villa's successes in battle and his colorful personality made him a darling of the American media in 1913 and 1914. He gave interviews to U.S. journalists and allowed a Hollywood film crew to make a movie about his life. Because of Villa's revolutionary battles against wealth and privilege, journalists called him a "Mexican Robin Hood."

But the media adoration began to change in 1916. Villa became angry that the United States had recognized the government of Venustiano Carranza, his rival for power. He launched an attack on Columbus, New Mexico, in which 19 U.S. citizens were killed, and then retreated to Mexico. Villa's goal was to provoke the United States into invading Mexico, an act Villa thought would destroy relations between the United States and Carranza governments.

U.S. president Woodrow Wilson sent General John J. Pershing on an expedition across the Mexican border to capture Villa—dead or alive. For 11 months Pershing pursued Villa through northern Mexico, but he never caught him. The pursuit accomplished Villa's goal, however. It soured relations between Mexico and the United States. ■

Teach the Main Idea

At Level

Imperialism in Latin America

1. **Teach** Ask students the Reading Focus questions to teach this section.

2. **Apply** Have students make a time line showing the major events from this section. Student time lines should begin with Mexican independence in 1821 and end with the Mexican Constitution of 1917.

3. **Review** Review student time lines as a class. Discuss the ways in which European and U.S. imperialism has affected Latin America in the early 19th century.

4. **Practice/Homework** Tell students they are newspaper editors in Mexico City in 1861. Have students write an editorial about the installation of the Austrian archduke Maximilian as emperor of Mexico by the French. Students may take either the liberal or conservative view, but should maintain their selected editorial perspective.

LS Visual-Spatial, Verbal-Linguistic

Alternative Assessment Handbook, Rubrics 36: Time Lines; and 43: Writing to Persuade

---

Preteach

Getting Started

Use the **Interactive Reader and Study Guide** to familiarize students with the section content.

Interactive Reader and Study Guide, Section 4

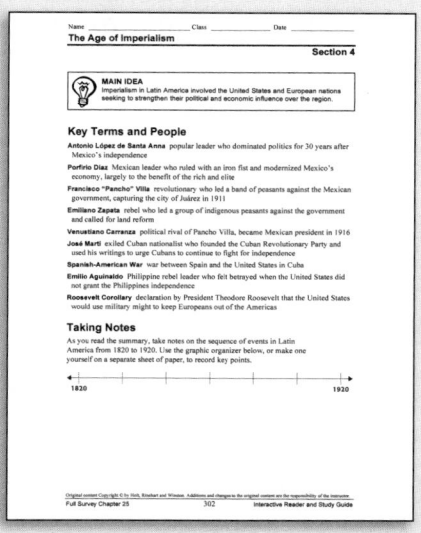

CRF: Vocabulary Builder: Section 4

Taking Notes

1821: Mexico declares independence from Spain; 1855: Mexican president Santa Anna is overthrown; 1861: French emperor Napoleon III overthrows Mexican goverment, installs archduke Maximilian as emperor; 1895: José Marti returned to Cuba to join uprising against the Spanish; 1898: Spanish American War begins; 1904-1914: Panama Canal is built; 1911: Rebels led by Pancho Villa capture Juárez in the Mexican Revolution; 1917: new Mexican constitution goes into effect

go.hrw.com

Online Resources

KEYWORD: SHL IMP
ACTIVITY: Report on Imperialism

❶ How did various groups struggle for power in Mexico before and during the Mexican Revolution? *civil war, jailing opposition, peasant revolt*

Power Struggles in Mexico

Identify Who was Antonio López de Santa Anna? *President of Mexico who dominated Mexican politics in the 30 years after independence*

Analyze Why did Napoleon III send French troops into Mexico in 1861? *He dreamed of restoring a French empire in the Americas.*

📃 CRF: Biography: José Guadalupe Posada

Biography

Mariano Azuela (1873-1952) Mariano Azuela began writing newspaper articles against the regime of Porfirio Díaz in 1896, while working on a degree in medicine. He wrote his most famous novel, *Los de abajo* (The Underdogs), while serving as an army doctor for Pancho Villa's revolutionary forces. After Villa's defeat in 1915, Azuela fled to El Paso, Texas, where he finished the novel. *Los de abajo* follows the career of an imaginary revolutionary leader, Demetrio Macías, as he rises from the leadership of a group of Native Americans to the position of general under Pancho Villa.

Teaching Tip

The sequence of events in Mexico may be confusing for some students. If so, have students create a sequencing chart of the leaders and retain it as a study tool.

Answers

Faces of History *possible answer— because he grew up among people whose land was taken from them*

FACES OF HISTORY

Emiliano ZAPATA 1879–1919

Emiliano Zapata was a Mexican revolutionary who fought for the rights of the rural poor. Orphaned at age 17, Zapata led his neighbors in taking back land that had been seized from them. Later, he helped Francisco Madero overthrow Díaz as president of Mexico but quickly grew dissatisfied with the pace of land reform. He led a campaign that seized land and returned it to peasants. He later helped defeat Victoriano Huerta, occupied Mexico City with Pancho Villa, and implemented land reform. His campaign came to a swift end after he was ambushed and killed by the forces of Venustiano Carranza.

Infer Why do you think the cause of land reform was so important to Emiliano Zapata?

TAKING NOTES

Take notes on the sequence of events in Latin America from 1820 to 1920.

1820 — 1920

NEW YORK

CC Unit 5-E5b
Roles of Porfirio Díaz, Francisco "Pancho" Villa, and Emiliano Zapata in the Mexican Revolution

Power Struggles in Mexico

Although Mexico won its independence from Spain in 1821 and became a republic in 1823, political factions struggled for control of the government. Conflict among political groups caused violence well into the next century.

Early Conflicts In the 30 years after independence, Mexican politics was dominated by **Antonio López de Santa Anna**. His popularity relied on numerous military victories, and he served as president five times between 1833 and 1855. He began his career aligned with liberal reformers, but as his power increased his rule became more conservative. He was exiled from the country several times, only to return to power as his enemies were defeated. Finally, in 1855 a group of reformers overthrew and exiled Santa Anna, and he did not return.

The leader of these reformers, Benito Juárez, put forth a series of major reforms that reduced the power of the Catholic Church and the military. Conservatives were outraged by these efforts. Soon, a civil war erupted. With support from the U.S. government, Juárez and his liberal allies triumphed.

The Second Mexican Empire The conservatives found a powerful ally in Europe. French emperor Napoleon III dreamed of restoring a French empire in the Americas. In 1861 he sent French troops into Mexico, overthrew the Mexican government, and installed Austrian archduke Maximilian as emperor of Mexico.

Mexican conservatives supported Maximilian at first because they believed he would restore the power of the church. But Maximilian ended up alienating both conservatives and liberals. When the French withdrew their troops, Maximilian did not have enough support to stay in power. Forced to surrender, Maximilian was executed by Republican troops.

The Mexican Republic was restored, and Juárez was reelected as president. Because of Juárez's courageous resistance to Maximilian and the French, he became one of Mexico's greatest national heroes.

The Mexican Revolution After the death of Juárez, **Porfirio Díaz** came to power. Ruling with an iron fist, he maintained law and order in Mexico. Díaz imprisoned his opponents and used the army to keep the peace at any cost.

Díaz helped modernize Mexico by encouraging foreign investment. Mexican exports boomed, and railroads expanded quickly. Yet most Mexicans remained extremely poor. Wealth was concentrated in the hands of foreign investors and a small Mexican elite. Half of the population was bound to debt-slavery, and discontent began to grow.

In the election of 1910, Díaz controlled the outcome. He jailed his opponent, the reform-minded Francisco Madero. After being released from jail, however, Madero fled to Texas and declared himself president of Mexico. He called for a revolution against the Díaz government.

When Madero returned to Mexico later that year, he found rebellion spreading across the nation. Two men gathered support from the lowest classes and began attacking government forces. **Francisco "Pancho" Villa** led a band of rebels who supported Madero's ideas. They disgraced Díaz's government by capturing the city of Juárez in 1911. At the same time, a group of indigenous peasants led by **Emiliano Zapata** arose and called for land reforms. Díaz was soon forced to resign.

More Violence Madero was elected president later that year, but turmoil in Mexico continued. Within months, army chief Victoriano Huerta seized power and imprisoned Madero. Former supporters of Madero opposed Huerta. In the north, Pancho Villa's army of small ranchers, unemployed workers, and cowboys also rose up against Huerta. Zapata's peasant

Power Struggles in Mexico

1. Organize students into small groups. Tell half of the groups they represent Mexican conservatives who oppose Benito Juárez. Tell the other groups they represent Mexican liberals led by Benito Juárez. Have each group prepare arguments in support of its position, either for or against Juárez's series of reforms. You might wish to have students conduct additional research to help them prepare their arguments.

2. Hold a classroom debate on reforms in Mexico. At the end of the debate, ask students to identify which side presented the most convincing arguments and to explain why.

3. Guide students in a discussion of the causes and effects of Juárez's series of reforms. Ask students why they think conservatives would prefer to be ruled by a foreign emperor rather than a popularly elected native president.

LS Interpersonal, Verbal-Linguistic

📃 **Alternative Assessment Handbook**, Rubric 10: Debates

Mexican Revolution

This mural by David Siquieros depicts the solidarity of Mexican peasants, led by Emiliano Zapata, in their struggle to regain the land once taken from them.

army revolted against Huerta in the south. Even the United States opposed him after Madero was executed in 1914.

The United States intervened by sending Marines to occupy the city of Veracruz, bringing Mexico and the United States close to war. Huerta struggled to stay in power but resigned in July and fled to Spain.

Carranza as President With Huerta gone, Carranza declared himself president. Zapata and Villa, however, refused to support Carranza, and the nation was plunged into another civil war. But by the end of 1915, Carranza had defeated his rivals.

Villa continued to lead attacks against the Carranza government. Upset that the United States recognized Carranza as president, Villa launched an attack across the U.S. border. U.S. forces pursued Villa back across the Mexican border, but were unable to capture him. In 1920 he finally agreed to halt his attacks.

With his political position now secure, Carranza took on the task of nation building. A new constitution went into effect in 1917, allowing the government to redistribute land, limited the power of the church, and protected the rights of citizens. Despite these improvements, Mexico still struggled with the problem of widespread poverty made worse by the damage done by years of revolution.

READING CHECK **Sequence** What were the major events of the Mexican Revolution?

Growing U.S. Influence

The United States had become a growing economic force in Latin America by the late 1800s. Economic power and political power grew together, and the United States exerted its influence and control in many ways.

Uprising in Cuba One of Spain's colonies in the Americas was the island of Cuba. In the 1860s Cuban nationalists began fighting for independence. Spain's response was to exile the leaders of the nationalist revolts.

One exiled leader managed to continue the struggle for independence from New York City. A poet and journalist, **José Martí**, communicated to Cubans through his writing, urging them to continue to fight for independence. While exiled, he founded the Cuban Revolutionary Party and in 1895 he returned to Cuba to join an uprising against the Spanish.

The Spanish responded brutally to the uprising. Martí was killed, and thousands of Cubans were forced into camps controlled by the Spanish army. The conditions were terrible, and many died from disease or starvation.

THE IMPACT TODAY

A statue of José Martí stands in New York City's Central Park. The statue was a gift of the Cuban government in 1965.

Reading Focus

2 How did growing U.S. influence in Latin America change the region? *Cuba gained independence from Spain; Panama Canal was built; Roosevelt Corollary threatened miliary force to keep Europe out of the Americas*

Growing U.S. Influence

Identify Who was José Martí? *poet and journalist who founded the Cuban Revolutionary Party*

Summarize How did people in the United States respond to the Cuban Revolution? *They sympathized with the Cuban rebels, seeing their struggle as similar to the American Revolution.*

Activity **Yellow Journalism** Explain to students that yellow journalism uses sensationalism to put forth a message. Have students write yellow journalism headlines about the Spanish American War. Display the headlines for all to see. As an extension, have students write a brief article using yellow journalism. **LS Verbal-Linguistic**

Alternative Assessment Handbook, Rubric 23: Newspapers

Primary Source

"… therefore I come to ask your approval that I should use the armed forces of the United States in such ways and to such an extent as may be necessary to obtain from General Huerta…the fullest rights and dignity of the United States…"

–Woodrow Wilson, Address to Congress, April 20, 1914

Answers

Reading Check *President Porforío Diaz jailed his opponent, Francisco Madero; Madero called for a revolution; Francisco "Pancho" Villa led a band of rebels who captured city of Juárez; Emiliano Zapata called for land reforms; Diaz resigned*

Skills Focus: Recognizing Bias in Primary Sources

At Level

Reading Like a Historian Skill
Mexican Leaders of the 1800s

Research Required

1. Organize the class into small groups. Have each group conduct outside research to find pictures of Antonio López de Santa Anna, Benito Juárez, and Emperor Maximilian. Pictures may include paintings, drawings, and cartoons.

2. Have each student choose a picture of one of the three men and write a brief essay analyzing it. Students should answer these questions: How is the leader portrayed, favorably or unfavorably? What can you tell about the leader from his

picture? What is the point of view of the artist or creator of the drawing? How can you tell?

3. Have volunteers share the pictures and their analyses with the rest of the class.

4. Guide the class in a discussion of the three Mexican leaders. How does each man represent his type—the caudillo, the reformer, and the European imperialist? **LS Visual-Spatial**

Alternative Assessment Handbook, Rubrics 3: Artwork; and 38: Writing to Classify

Growing U.S. Influence

Recall What territory did the United States acquire at the end of the Spanish-American War? *Puerto Rico, Guam, the Philippines*

Sequence List the events that led to the Spanish-American War. *The U.S. battleship* Maine *exploded in Havana's harbor; Americans assumed Spain was responsible; Congress declared war*

📰 **CRF: Primary Source:** U.S. Imperialism

🗺 **Map Transparency:** United States Intervention in the Caribbean

---

The Spanish-American War In the United States, many people already felt sympathy for the Cuban rebels. They viewed the Cuban struggle for freedom as similar to their own American Revolution. U.S. newspapers printed scandalous stories and large, shocking illustrations about events in Cuba. Newspapers using this sensationalist style of reporting, known as yellow journalism, urged the United States to enter the war.

In February 1898 the U.S. battleship *Maine* mysteriously exploded in Havana's harbor, and many Americans immediately assumed that Spain was responsible. Congress declared war, and the **Spanish-American War** began.

The war was a disaster for Spain. The Spanish army was defeated in Cuba, and Spanish navy fleets were destroyed in the Philippines and Cuba. Within three months, the United States had won the war. In the treaty ending the war, the United States received Puerto Rico and Guam, and agreed to purchase the Philippines for $20 million.

Even though Spain agreed to give up Cuba, some Americans did not want Cuba to have full independence. Instead the United States made Cuba a protectorate by forcing it to include the Platt Amendment as part of its new constitution. The Platt Amendment allowed the United States to intervene in Cuba, to approve foreign treaties, and to lease land at Guantánamo Bay for a naval base.

Revolt in the Philippines In the Philippines, another Spanish colony, nationalists believed that the Spanish-American War would bring them independence. But rather than grant the Philippines independence, the United States made it an American colony. Rebel leader **Emilio Aguinaldo**, who had cooperated with U.S. forces against the Spanish, felt betrayed.

Filipino rebels revolted against the U.S. occupation. In three years of fighting, more than 200,000 Filipinos died from combat or disease. They did not win independence. The United States ruled the Philippines through a governor appointed by the U.S. president until 1935. The Philippines were not granted full independence until 1946.

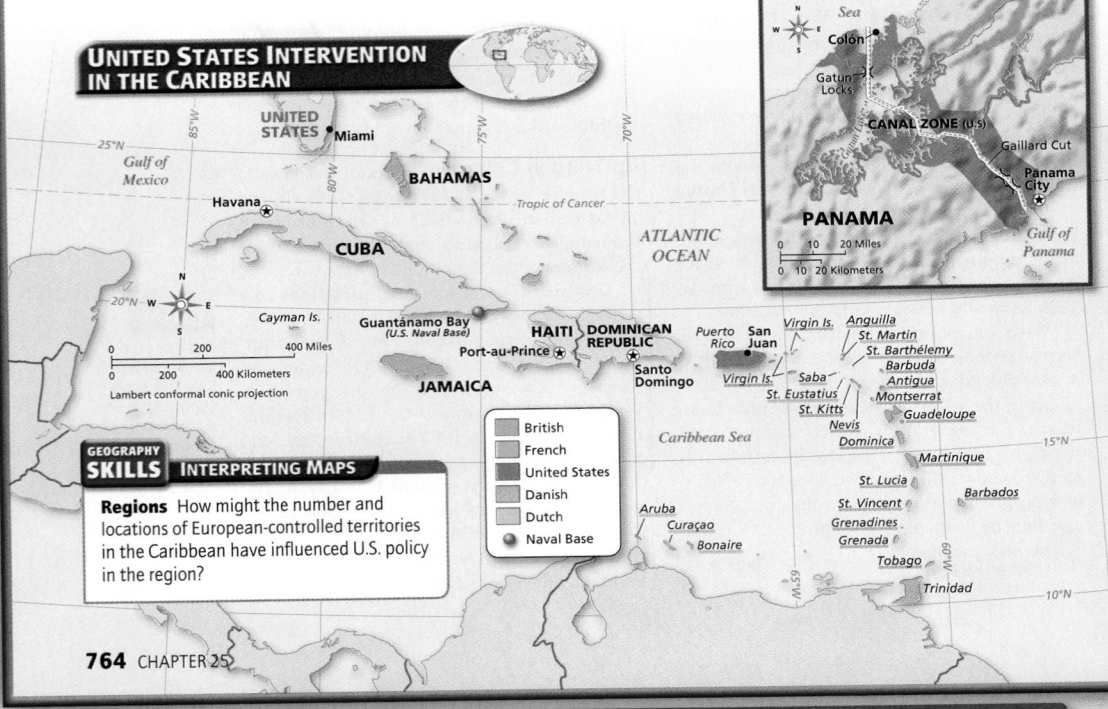

THE PANAMA CANAL

UNITED STATES INTERVENTION IN THE CARIBBEAN

GEOGRAPHY SKILLS | **INTERPRETING MAPS**

Regions How might the number and locations of European-controlled territories in the Caribbean have influenced U.S. policy in the region?

Legend:
- British
- French
- United States
- Danish
- Dutch
- ◉ Naval Base

764 CHAPTER 25

Differentiating Instruction

Below Level

Special Education Students

1. Draw the chart as shown, omitting the italicized answers. Have students copy the charts onto their own paper.

2. Have students use the information in the section to complete the chart, showing the actions of the United States in each area. When students have finished, create a chart for all to see. Have students correct their work and retain the charts as a study tool. **LS Visual-Spatial**

📰 **Alternative Assessment Handbook**, Rubric 7: Charts

Area	Actions
Cuba	*entered Spanish-American War; made Cuba a protectorate*
Philippines	*made Philippines an American colony; granted independence in 1946*
Colombia	*supported uprising against Colombia; ruled Panama Canal Zone*

Answers

Interpreting Maps *possible answer— The United States may have attempted to limit future European colonization.*

The Panama Canal With the building of the Panama Canal, the United States gained control over more territory. A French company had tried unsuccessfully to build a canal across the Isthmus of Panama, then part of Colombia, in the 1880s. In 1903 the United States bought the French property and equipment, but Colombia refused to allow the United States to build the canal.

Determined to build the canal, U.S. president Theodore Roosevelt sent U.S. warships to support an uprising against Colombia. After Panama was declared independent, the new nation quickly signed a treaty granting the United States a strip of land to build the canal. This became the Panama Canal Zone, which was ruled directly by the United States.

The Panama Canal was built between 1904 and 1914. Its construction was a marvel of modern engineering but major medical advances were required to control the effects of yellow fever and malaria upon canal workers. When the Panama Canal opened, it shortened the sea voyage from San Francisco to New York City by about 8,000 miles.

A Warning to Europeans In 1823, with the proclamation of the Monroe Doctrine, the United States declared the Americas off-limits to European imperialism except for colonies that already existed. Until the end of the Spanish-American War, however, the Monroe Doctrine was seen by European powers as no more than an idle threat.

By the late 1800s, Europe and the United States had considerable financial interests in Latin America. Many Latin American nations had become deeply indebted to foreign creditors. In 1904 European creditors threatened to use military force to collect their debts in the Dominican Republic.

To protect U.S. interests and maintain stability in the region, President Roosevelt announced the **Roosevelt Corollary** to the Monroe Doctrine.

HISTORY'S VOICES

❝ Chronic wrongdoing . . . in the Western Hemisphere . . . may force the United States, however reluctantly, . . . to the exercise of an international police power. ❞
—Theodore Roosevelt, Roosevelt Corollary, 1904

The United States vowed to use its military might to keep Europeans out of the Americas.

Increasing U.S. Power The United States sent troops to several nations in the early 1900s. U.S. forces entered Haiti, the Dominican Republic, Nicaragua, and Cuba with the stated goal of restoring civil order. The United States took control of the finances of these countries, claiming a need to prevent financial chaos. In reality, the United States used the Roosevelt Corollary to become even more involved in the political affairs of Latin American countries.

READING CHECK **Find the Main Idea** How did the United States gain control over more territory in the late 1800s and early 1900s?

---

go.hrw.com
Online Quiz
Keyword: SHL IMP HP

Reviewing Ideas, Terms, and People
1. **a. Identify** Who was Porfirio Díaz?
   b. Identify Cause and Effect What was the effect of Victoriano Huerta's seizing power and imprisoning Madero?
   c. Elaborate How successful was **Venustiano Carranza** in quelling the turmoil of the Mexican Revolution?
2. **a. Recall** What event pushed the United States into war with Spain?
   b. Draw Conclusions Why did President Roosevelt develop the **Roosevelt Corollary** to the Monroe Doctrine?
   c. Predict What do you think was the Latin American reaction to increasing U.S. power in the early 1900s?

Critical Thinking
3. **Identify Cause and Effect** Copy this chart and use your notes from the section to explain the causes of the Mexican Revolution.

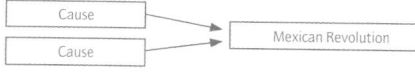

Cause →
Cause → Mexican Revolution

FOCUS ON WRITING
4. **Persuasion** Using details from the section, write an editorial on the growing influence of the United States in Latin America. Take the point of view of a Latin American.

Section 4 Assessment Answers

1. **a.** ruler of Mexico who came to power after the death of Juárez; overthrown in Mexican Revolution
   b. the United States sent Marines to occupy the city of Veracruz
   c. possible answer—he was somewhat successful, but civil war and widespread poverty persisted
2. **a.** the sinking of the U.S. battleship *Maine*
   b. in order to protect U.S. interests and maintain stability in Latin America
   c. possible answer—Latin American nations may have resented the foreign influence.
3. Most Mexicans were poor; wealth was in the hands of foreign investors and the elite; Díaz jailed his opponent Francisco Madero
4. Student editorials should describe the actions of the United States in Latin America, including in Mexico, Cuba, and Colombia, from the point of view of a Latin American.

Answers

Reading Check *gained Guam, Puerto Rico, and the Philippines after the Spanish-American War; ruled the Panama Canal Zone after supporting an uprising against Colombia; added the Roosevelt Corollary to the Monroe Doctrine; sent troops to Haiti, the Dominican Republic, Nicaragua, and Cuba*

Imperialism

Word Help

coerced forced

assimilate to make part of a culture or group

yoke bondage; something that is oppressive and restrictive

Info to Know

Dollar Diplomacy Dollar diplomacy was started in 1909 by President William H. Taft to help Americans make money in other countries. It was used mainly in Central America and the Caribbean. American companies started businesses there. Then the United States used its economic strength to protect the businesses. In this way, the business continued to make money and the United States maintained power in these nations. Over time, many people resisted U.S. efforts to control them through dollar diplomacy. By 1912 President Taft had given up on dollar diplomacy. Today the phrase is used to describe efforts by one country to control another through money.

Imperialism

Historical Context The documents that follow reveal a number of different attitudes concerning the effects of imperialism.

Task Examine the selections and answer the questions that follow. After you have studied the documents, you will be asked to write an essay contrasting the views of people on both sides of the imperialism debate. You will need to use evidence from the selections and from the chapter to support the position you take in your essay.

NEW YORK STANDARDS

PI 2.5 Students investigate key events and developments and major turning points in world history to identify the factors that brought about change and the long-term effects of those changes.

PI 3.2 Students explain the dynamics of cultural change and how interactions between and among cultures have affected various cultural groups throughout the world.

DOCUMENT 1

A Chinese View of Democracy

Sun Yixian, the spokesman of Chinese nationalism, fiercely opposed imperialism. He did not believe that China needed any help from other countries to thrive. In fact, in his *History of the Chinese Revolution*, Sun argued that China was at its best when it remained free from any outside influence.

> Revelations of Chinese history prove that the Chinese as a people are independent in spirit and in conduct. Coerced into touch with other people, they could at times live in peace with them by maintaining friendly relations and at others assimilate them... During the periods when their political and military prowess declined, they could not escape for the time from the fate of a conquered nation, but they could eventually vigorously reassert themselves. Thus the Mongol rule of China, lasting nearly a hundred years was finally overthrown by Tai Tse of the Ming dynasty and his loyal follower. So in our own time was the Manchu yoke thrown off by the Chinese. Nationalistic ideas in China did not come from a foreign source; they were inherited from our remote forefathers.

DOCUMENT 2

Roosevelt in the Caribbean

Under President Theodore Roosevelt, the United States expanded its influence over nations in the Caribbean and the rest of Latin America after the Spanish-American War. In this cartoon, Roosevelt marches through the Caribbean while carrying a club, a reference to a West African proverb that was one of his favorite expressions: "Speak softly and carry a big stick; you will go far."

Differentiating Instruction

Below Level

Learners Having Difficulty

1. Review with students the material in the text about Sun Yixian, Chinese nationalism, and the end of the Qing dynasty.

2. Organize students into mixed-ability groups, and have groups review Document 1. Have each student write answers to the following questions: How does Sun Yixian describe China in the past? What does he say the past indicates about China's future?

3. Have students write newspaper editorials from the point of view of a Chinese nationalist who opposes Western influence. Editorials should use the same logic used by Sun Yixian in Document 1, but students should use their own words. **LS Interpersonal, Verbal-Linguistic**

   Alternative Assessment Handbook, Rubric 17: Letters to Editors

DOCUMENT 3

Kipling's "The White Man's Burden"

British poet Rudyard Kipling was born in India—at the time a British colony—and was a great supporter of imperialism. He believed that the countries of Europe and the United States had a duty to help the people of Africa, Asia, and Latin America, a duty he referred to as the "White Man's Burden" in the 1899 poem of that name, part of which is printed below.

Take up the White Man's burden—
Ye dare not stoop to less—
Nor call too loud on Freedom
To cloke your weariness;
By all ye cry or whisper,
By all ye leave or do,
The silent, sullen peoples
Shall weigh your gods and you.

Take up the White Man's burden—
Have done with childish days—
The lightly proferred laurel,
The easy, ungrudged praise.
Comes now, to search your manhood
Through all the thankless years
Cold, edged with dear-bought wisdom,
The judgments of your peers!

DOCUMENT 4

Letter to the Emperor of Japan

In 1853 U.S. president Millard Fillmore sent Commodore Matthew Perry and four large warships to Japan. His purpose was the request the opening of Japan to trade with the United States. An excerpt from Fillmore's letter to the emperor of Japan appears below.

GREAT AND GOOD FRIEND: I send you this public letter by Commodore Matthew C. Perry, an officer of the highest rank in the navy of the United States, and commander of the squadron now visiting Your imperial majesty's dominions.

I have directed Commodore Perry to assure your imperial majesty that I entertain the kindest feelings toward your majesty's person and government, and that I have no other object in sending him to Japan but to propose to your imperial majesty that the United States and Japan should live in friendship . . . with each other.

These are the only objects for which I have sent Commodore Perry, with a powerful squadron, to pay a visit to your imperial majesty's renowned city of Yedo: friendship, commerce, a supply of coal and provisions, and protection for our shipwrecked people.

Skills FOCUS — READING LIKE A HISTORIAN

DOCUMENT 1
a. **Recall** What does Sun Yixian say are two characteristics of the Chinese people?
b. **Draw Conclusions** Do you think Sun would have welcomed Europeans to China? Why or why not?

DOCUMENT 2
a. **Explain** What does the "big stick" symbolize?
b. **Infer** Do you think this cartoonist approved of American imperialism? Why or why not?

DOCUMENT 3
a. **Describe** What does the "White Man's Burden" mean?
b. **Analyze** Why does Kipling urge European nations to become involved in other societies?

DOCUMENT 4
a. **Identify** Why does President Fillmore say he has sent Perry and his squadron to Japan?
b. **Infer** Why do you think President Fillmore mention that Perry has arrived "with a powerful squadron"?

DOCUMENT-BASED ESSAY QUESTION

How did attitudes toward imperialism differ between the people who were founding colonies and those whose countries were colonized? Using the documents above and information from the chapter, form a thesis that explains your position. Then write a short essay to support it.

See **Skills Handbook**, p. H25

THE AGE OF IMPERIALISM **767**

Skills Focus: Analyzing Primary Sources
At Level

Reading Like a Historian Skill
Reasons for Imperialism

1. Have students review Documents 3 and 4 and identify the reasons given for imperialism. Remind students that these documents are written from an imperialist point of view; people in the colonized countries probably had a different perspective.

2. Organize students into mixed ability groups. Have each group identify the reasons each document presents for Western influence in other parts of the world.

3. Guide a class discussion about Documents 3 and 4. Ask the following questions: In what ways do these documents represent an imperialist point of view? What would people in the colonized countries think of the concept of the "White Man's Burden"? How might the emperor of Japan have responded to Fillmore's letter? **LS Interpersonal**

   Alternative Assessment Handbook, Rubric 11: Discussions

Document-Based Investigation

Word Help

sullen gloomy, repressed

proferred given

Biography

Rudyard Kipling (1865–1936) Rudyard Kipling was a British writer of poems, novels, and short stories. His best known works include the children's books *Just So Stories* and *The Jungle Book* and the novel *Kim*, whose main character is an Irish orphan in India who adopts Indian customs. Like Kim, Kipling was born in India, where he learned the Hindi language at a young age. Unlike his character, however, Kipling began attending school in England at the age of five.

Answers

Reading Like a Historian
Document 1 a. *They are independent both in their thoughts and in their actions.* **b.** *possible answer—No, Sun Yixian believes the Chinese people are meant to be independent and will eventually rebel against outside influence.* **Document 2 a.** *The big stick represents the use of force against enemies.* **b.** *possible answer—No, because it looks as if Roosevelt is using too much influence in too small an area;* **Document 3 a.** *the idea that it is a white person's duty to help the people of Africa, Asia, and Latin America;* **b.** *because they have wisdom; because it is their responsibility;* **Document 4 a.** *to become friends with Japan, to open trade with Japan, to provide coal, provisions, and protection for shipwrecked Americans in Japan;* **b.** *possible answer—because he wished to intimidate Japan.* **Essay** *Student essays should contrast the attitudes of colonized countries with the attitudes of imperialists, using details and examples from the documents and the chapter.*

767

Visual Summary

Review and Inquiry Review the cause-and-effect chart with students. Then, have students work individually or in groups to find an example of each concept. Have volunteers share their examples with the class.

Quick Facts Transparency: Visual Study Guide: The Age of Imperialism

Review Key Terms and People

1. Roosevelt Corollary
2. Raj
3. Menelik II
4. Boxer Rebellion
5. Venustiano Carranza
6. Emperor Meiji
7. Social Darwinism

Comprehension and Critical Thinking

8. a. ruled India in the name of Great Britain
b. British rule led to the rise of Indian nationalism.
c. possible answer—more benefits, because the British modernized the country, and India eventually gained its independence

9. a. the idea that people living in other countries have the right to be tried in the courts of their own home country
b. Chinese nationalists rose up against their Qing leaders because of Western influence.
c. Japan's reforms involved modernization and industrialization, which better prepared it for becoming a world power, rather than simply isolating the nation.

10. a. It set rules for how European nations should divide Africa.
b. to gain new markets and new raw materials; did not want other nations to gain territory in Africa first
c. possible answer—The lines Europeans drew to divide African territory did not take into account Africa's traditional borders, which might lead to ethnic conflict later.

VISUAL STUDY GUIDE

Imperialism in the 1800s

CAUSES

Desire for Resources and Markets
- Western industrializing countries needed raw materials and consumers for manufactured goods.

Political Competition Among Western Nations
- Long-standing rivalries and the rise of nationalism led countries to compete for power.

Western Belief in Cultural Superiority
- Westerners believed it was their duty and their right to rule over and "civilize" other peoples.

Imperialism

EFFECTS

Colonization
- European nations, and to a lesser degree the United States and Japan, exerted their power and influence over much of the globe.

Rise of Nationalism
- The experience of colonial rule, as well as exposure to Western ideas, led to the development of nationalism in parts of Asia and Africa.

Exploitation of Peoples Under Colonial Rule
- Through exploitation of resources and the labor of peoples under colonial rule, imperial nations benefited at the expense of those they ruled.

Key Events of Imperialism

1842 ▪ Opium War and Treaty of Nanjing

1853 ▪ Commodore Perry opens Japan

1857 ▪ Sepoy Mutiny results in British government taking direct control over India

1861 ▪ France installs Austrian archduke Maximilian as the emperor of Mexico

1862 ▪ Treaty of Saigon gives France control over most of Vietnam

1868 ▪ Meiji era begins in Japan

1884 ▪ Berlin Conference sets the rules for European control over Africa

1885 ▪ Indian National Congress founded

1894 ▪ Japan wins the Sino-Japanese War

1898 ▪ U.S. wins the Spanish-American War

1900 ▪ Boxer Rebellion in China

1906 ▪ The Muslim League founded

1911 ▪ Chinese and Mexican revolutions begin

1914 ▪ Panama Canal opens

Review Key Terms and People

Fill in each blank with the name or term that correctly completes the sentence.

1. The _____ declared that the United States would use its military power to prevent Europeans from gaining control in the Americas.

2. The period of British rule in India is often referred to as the _____.

3. _____ successfully resisted Western attempts to conquer Ethiopia.

4. During the _____, Chinese nationalists laid siege to foreign compounds in Beijing for 55 days.

5. _____ declared himself president of Mexico after Huerta was forced to flee in 1914.

6. _____ began an era of modernization in Japan.

7. The notion that certain nations or races are more fit than others is called _____.

---

11. a. a leader of the Mexican Revolution; president of Mexico
b. Madero called for a revolution; rebel groups led by Pancho Villa and Emiliano Zapata staged attacks
c. Napoleon III made Archduke Maximilian of Austria the emperor of Mexico, leading to conflict between Mexicans who supported Maximilian and those who opposed him. The United States supported Benito Juárez in his rebellion against Santa Anna and later, Maximilian.

Reading Skills

12. The Indian National Congress, which was mainly Hindu, led boycotts of British goods to protest a partition. The Muslim League was founded because Muslims believed the Indian National Congress might be preserving the interests of Hindus at the expense of Muslims.

13. information about Western society, military practices, and economics

Comprehension and Critical Thinking

SECTION 1 *(pp. 741–745)*

8. a. Recall What role did the British East India Company have in India until 1857?

b. Identify What effect did British rule have on the development of Indian nationalism?

c. Evaluate Did the British bring more benefits or more harm to India? Explain your answer.

SECTION 2 *(pp. 746–753)*

9. a. Define What was extraterritoriality?

b. Identify Cause In what ways did European imperialism contribute to the downfall of the Qing dynasty in China?

c. Elaborate Why were Japan's reforms more effective at resisting Western imperialism than China's reforms were?

SECTION 3 *(pp. 756–760)*

10. a. Identify What did the Berlin Conference achieve?

b. Draw Conclusions Why were Europeans so eager to gain control over Africa?

c. Predict Given how Europeans gained control over Africa, what might be the long-term effects?

SECTION 4 *(pp. 761–765)*

11. a. Recall Who was Francisco Madero?

b. Sequence What were the major events of the Mexican Revolution?

c. Evaluate How did interference from outside nations contribute to unrest in Mexico in the 1800s and early 1900s?

Reading Skills

Identifying Supporting Details *Use what you know about identifying supporting details to answer the questions below.*

12. As Indian nationalism began to develop in the late 1800s and early 1900s, why were two different organizations created to fight for the rights of Indians?

13. What information did the Iwakura Mission seek on its two-year journey through the United States and Europe?

Analyzing Primary Sources

Reading Like a Historian *This political cartoon below was drawn by American cartoonist Thomas Nast in 1885.*

The World's Plunderers, by Thomas Nast, 1885
The Granger Collection, New York

14. Explain What do the "grab bags" symbolize?

15. Draw Conclusions What do you think the artist thought about European imperialism?

Using the Internet

go.hrw.com
Practice Online
Keyword: SHL IMP

16. The Berlin Conference set the ground rules for the European nations that wanted to divide Africa amongst themselves. Using the Internet, research the decisions made at the Berlin Conference. Then make a list of all provisions contained in the General Act of the Berlin Conference, including a map that shows the territorial decisions.

WRITING ABOUT HISTORY

Exposition: Writing a News Article *In 1853 Commodore Perry and his warships ended two centuries of Japan's isolation from the West.*

17. Assignment: Write a news article in which you explain what happened as a result of Commodore Perry's missions to Japan in 1853 and 1854. Be sure to include the reactions of the Japanese and the Americans to this contact. To provide depth to your story, use specific details from the chapter and from other research.

Answers

Analyzing Primary Sources

14. African territories

14. possible answer—he probably disliked it; the title of the cartoon "The World's Plunderers" gives a negative connotation.

Using the Internet

16. Go to the HRW Web site and enter the keyword shown to access a rubric for this activity.

KEYWORD: SHL IMP

Writing About History

17. Student articles should describe the reasons behind Commodore Perry's visit to Japan, and Japanese reactions to the visit. Articles should use details and examples from the chapter to analyze the effects of the visit upon both Americans and Japanese. A rubric for the activity is provided in **CRF**: Writing for the SAT.

HOLT
History's Impact

► **Video Program: The Age of Imperialism**
Refer to the Video Program Teacher's Guide for the answer to the closing question.

Review and Assessment Resources

Review and Reinforce

 CRF: Chapter Review

 **Quick Facts Transparency**: Visual Study Guide: The Age of Imperialism

 Spanish Chapter Summaries Audio CD Program

OSP **Holt PuzzlePro**: Quiz Show for ExamView

Quiz Game CD-ROM

Assess

PASS: Chapter Test, Forms A and B

Alternative Assessment Handbook

OSP **ExamView Test Generator**, Chapter Test

Differentiated Instruction Modified Worksheets and Tests CD-ROM: Chapter Test

HOAP **Holt Online Assessment Program** (in the Premier Online Edition)

Reteach/Intervene

Interactive Reader and Study Guide

Differentiated Instruction Teacher Management System: Lesson Plans for Differentiated Instruction

Differentiated Instruction Modified Worksheets and Tests CD-ROM: Chapter Test

Interactive Skills Tutor CD-ROM

go.hrw.com
Online Resources
KEYWORD: SHL TEACHER

You can use these pages to have students simultaneously review the unit and practice taking standardized tests.

Answers

1. 4
The Industrial Revolution, Section 1

2. 3
The Industrial Revolution, Section 2

3. 1
The Industrial Revolution, Section 2

4. 4
The Industrial Revolution, Section 3

5. 1
Life in the Industrial Age, Section 1

6. 2
Life in the Industrial Age, Section 2

7. 3
Life in the Industrial Age, Section 3

8. 4
Reforms, Revolutions, and War, Section 1

9. 4
Reforms, Revolutions, and War, Section 2

10. 4
Reforms, Revolutions, and War, Section 3

UNIT 7
Regents Practice

Directions Write your answer for each statement or question on a separate answer sheet. Choose the number of the word or expression that best completes the statement or answers the question.

1 The Industrial Revolution began in Great Britain in part because
1 Britain imported technology from the United States.
2 Britain had laws against the enclosure movement.
3 Britain had a large number of immigrant workers.
4 Britain had key resources like iron and coal.

2 As factories in Great Britain grew,
1 mass production decreased.
2 the textile industry became less important.
3 cottage industries declined.
4 workers moved away from cities.

3 Why did some factory owners prefer to hire women and children to work in their factories?
1 because women and children would work for lower wages
2 because women and children were less likely to get sick
3 because it was illegal for men to work in factories
4 because men preferred to work outdoors

4 Which thinker called for workers around the world to unite and overthrow the capitalist system?
1 Adam Smith
2 Thomas Malthus
3 Thomas Edison
4 Karl Marx

5 Industrialization led to
1 technological advances like railroads and electricity.
2 the decline of the middle class.
3 less leisure time for ordinary people.
4 the decline of capitalist economies.

6 How did medical advances of the 1800s change industrial societies?
1 They enabled governments to provide free health care.
2 They helped to lower infant mortality rates.
3 They caused a decrease in the amount of pollution.
4 They ended the need for vaccinations.

7 Many industrial cities in the 1800s
1 severely restricted the growth of suburbs.
2 had traffic problems as cars became common.
3 started to become more livable as infrastructure improved.
4 lost population as workers moved back to rural areas.

8 How did government reforms in Britain affect women's suffrage?
1 Women lost the right to vote.
2 Women could vote only if they were over 50.
3 Women could only vote in local elections.
4 Women could vote in all elections.

9 Which letter on the map below indicates the country where the Dreyfus affair occurred?

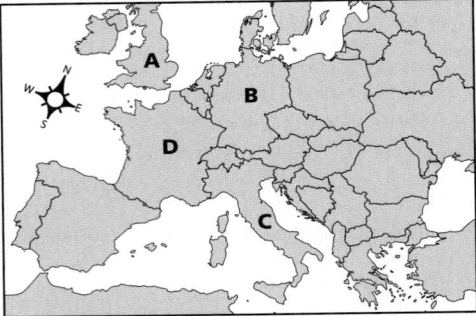

1 A
2 B
3 C
4 D

10 Both Toussaint L'Ouverture and Simón Bolívar
1 served as colonial governors for Spain in the Americas.
2 were priests who argued for better treatment of native peoples.
3 fought against the spread of Enlightenment ideas.
4 led independence movements in the Americas.

11 When was slavery abolished in the United States?

1 at the beginning of the Revolutionary War

2 during the Civil War

3 before the Louisiana Purchase

4 at the end of the French and Indian War

12 Two of the first countries in Europe to unify under nationalist movements were

1 Austria and Poland.

2 Norway and Greece.

3 Spain and Austria.

4 Italy and Germany.

13 Giuseppe Garibaldi is associated with Italian

1 exploration.

2 monarchy.

3 isolationism.

4 nationalism.

14 The quote below by France's minister of foreign affairs in 1883 is an attempt to justify what policy?

"The policy of colonial expansion is a political and economic system . . . One can relate this system to three orders of ideas: economic ideas, ideas of civilization in its highest sense, and ideas of politics and patriotism."

1 industrialization

2 imperialism

3 nationalism

4 reform

15 One reason the British wanted to control India was

1 to encourage Indian nationalism.

2 to buy manufactured goods from India.

3 to get access to India's raw materials.

4 to set up a democracy in India.

16 What caused the Boxer Rebellion in China?

1 military duties that were forced on the Chinese

2 resentment against foreigners

3 resistance to the introduction of modern technology

4 the fear of a Japanese invasion

17 How did the Meiji Restoration affect Japan?

1 Japan's economy became modern and industrialized.

2 Japan became more isolated.

3 China invaded and occupied Japan.

4 Japan moved away from Western ideas

18 What happened at the Berlin Conference?

1 Germany and France signed an agreement to end the Franco-Prussian War.

2 European leaders met to decide how to divide Africa.

3 Great Britain and Germany met to discuss how to prevent the spread of industrial technologies.

4 Austria demanded that Germany renounce claims to its territory.

REVIEWING THE UNIT

Constructed Response Industrialization, nationalism, and imperialism are all related. Recall what you have learned about each topic. Then write a brief essay in which you summarize how industrialization influenced the rise of nationalism in Europe and how nationalism and the growth of industrial economies contributed to the growth of imperialism.

CONNECTING TO THE PREVIOUS UNIT

Constructed Response Basic ideas about science, knowledge, and progress that developed during the Scientific Revolution contributed to the development of the Industrial Revolution. Recall the major changes that occurred during the Scientific Revolution. Then write a brief essay on how those changes set the stage for the beginnings of the Industrial Revolution.

Unit Review

Answers

11. 2

Reforms, Revolutions, and War, Section 4

12. 4

Nationalism in Europe, Sections 1 & 2

13. 4

Nationalism in Europe, Section 1

14. 2

The Age of Imperialism, Section 3

15. 3

The Age of Imperialism, Section 1

16. 2

The Age of Imperialism, Section 2

17. 1

The Age of Imperialism, Section 2

18. 2

The Age of Imperialism, Section 3

Reviewing the Unit

Student essays should mention that industrialized nations sought colonies as a source of raw materials and to provide a market for their manufactured goods.

Connecting to the Previous Unit

Student essays should indicate that the scientific method, which evolved during the Scientific Revolution, helped set the stage for the Industrial Revolution. Observation and experimentation led to many of the developments that made the Industrial Revolution possible. For example, British inventors learned to harness the power of steam. The result was the steam engine that revolutionized both manufacturing and transportation.

Unit Review

Themes & Global Connections

Science and Technology

Interchangeable Parts The idea of using of interchangeable parts dates back to Gutenberg's printing press, which depended on type that was completely interchangeable. Early attempts at interchangeability in manufacturing met with only limited success. As early as 1828, however, interchangeable parts were used in clocks. By the time of the Civil War, rifles and muskets were made with interchangeable parts. After the war, first sewing machines and then typewriters used them. But it took Henry Ford to revolutionize manufacturing by using assembly lines along with interchangeable parts.

Economic Systems

"Gentlemanly Capitalism" In 1995 a pair of books on British imperialism presented the idea of "gentlemanly capitalism" as the driving force in the economic development of Britain and its empire. According to this theory, it was the British upper classes, not the industrialists, that invested around the world and shaped British imperialism; they had the political power to shape imperial policies to fit their investments.

THEME
SCIENCE AND TECHNOLOGY

What new advances in science and technology occurred during the Industrial Revolution?

During the Industrial Revolution, scientists and engineers made major advances in the science and technology of industry. They invented new machines, learned how to harness new sources of power, created a system of factory production, and developed ways to mass produce goods.

TECHNOLOGICAL ADVANCES DURING THE INDUSTRIAL REVOLUTION

New Inventions
New inventions, such as the spinning jenny and steam engine, changed the way people produced goods. Large and complex machines of iron and steel became the main tools of industry.

New Sources of Power
To power their new inventions, people burned fossil fuels like coal. Fossil fuels provided abundant energy to move steam-powered machines and generate electricity.

Creation of Factories
With new machines and new sources of power, the very nature of how work was organized changed. The huge new industrial machines required people to come together in large factories to produce goods like cotton and wool textiles, railroad cars, and iron and steel.

Mass Production of Goods
The scale of industrial production was so enormous that mass production became common, and factories produced more goods than ever before.

THEME
ECONOMIC SYSTEMS

How did the Industrial Revolution change the world's economic systems?

The technological advances made during the Industrial Revolution had far-reaching effects on the world economy. In industrializing countries, production increased and economies boomed as a new urban middle class developed. At the same time, a global economy began to emerge that was dominated by the world's industrial countries.

EFFECTS OF THE INDUSTRIAL REVOLUTION ON ECONOMIC SYSTEMS

- The amount of manufactured goods in industrializing countries increased dramatically, causing prices to fall and standards of living to rise.
- A new middle class of workers developed.
- Cities grew rapidly into industrial centers as people flocked to factories to work.
- Industrial countries worked to secure access to raw materials for their factories and to export their manufactured goods.
- A global economic system dominated by industrial countries began to develop.

772 UNIT 7

Skills Focus: Identifying Cause and Effect   **At Level**

Reading Skill
The Effects of Nationalism

1. Have students come up with examples of nationalism from the last 20 years. As they mention examples, make a list for the class to see. *Examples might include the former Soviet Union, the former Yugoslavia, Rwanda, the Kurds in Iraq and Turkey, etc.*

2. Have each student choose one of the places from the list and conduct research about what the effects of nationalism were in that instance. Students should try to find essays on nationalism from a variety of different places. Have students write a paragraph explaining their research findings.

3. Have volunteers read their paragraphs to the class.

4. Guide the class in a discussion of the effects nationalism continues to have in the modern world. **LS Verbal-Linguistic**

Alternative Assessment Handbook, Rubrics 6: Cause and Effect and 11: Discussions

THEME
GOVERNMENT AND CITIZENSHIP

How did nationalism affect government and citizenship?

In the 1800s, the rise of nationalism, or devotion to one's national group, had major impacts on government and citizenship around the world. Nationalism led to revolutions and the rise of the nation-state as the main form of government.

EFFECTS OF NATIONALISM ON GOVERNMENT AND CITIZENSHIP

- Revolutions in Europe and Latin America led to the creation of new governments based on national groups—people that share a common identity and features such as language, religion, or culture.
- Citizens felt a connection to their government through a shared identity, common history, and national symbols.
- Nonnational states that were imposed by rulers from the top down were challenged, overthrown, and replaced by new governments.
- The nation-state became the dominant form of government.

Skills FOCUS UNDERSTANDING THEMES

How have industrialization and nationalism shaped the world today? Use your textbook and other resources to gather information about what the world was like before the Industrial Revolution and the rise of modern nationalist movements and what it is like now. Then create a chart like the one below and use it to compare how the world has changed.

	Then	Now
Science and Technology		
Economic Systems		
Government and Citizenship		

Global Connections

Making Connections This chart shows basic economic data for three different countries today. What does this data indicate about the different levels of industrialization in each country? How do you think the Industrial Revolution affected these countries differently? Write a short essay explaining how this data relates to the Industrial Revolution and its uneven effects around the world.

	Major Industries	Labor Force	Urban	Per Capita GDP
United Kingdom	Machine tools, electric power equipment, automation equipment, railroad equipment, shipbuilding, aircraft	Agriculture 1.5%, industry 19.1%, services 79.5%	89.1%	$29,600
Nigeria	Crude oil, mining, palm oil, peanuts, cotton, rubber	Agriculture 70%, industry 10%, services 20%	46.7%	$1,000
Thailand	Tourism, textiles and garments, agricultural processing, beverages, tobacco, cement	Agriculture 49%, industry 14%, services 37%	31.9%	$8,100

Source: *The World Almanac and Book of Facts, 2006*

INDUSTRIALIZATION AND NATIONALISM **773**

Unit Review

Government and Citizenship

The Changing Face of Nationalism
Nationalism was originally a liberal cause. Liberals believed that every people had the right to a state of their own. They believed that governments owed their existence to the consent of the governed. After the failure of the revolutions in 1848, conservative monarchs with notions of cultural or racial unity took the lead in nation-building. They used war and diplomacy rather than reforms to build nation-states in Germany and Italy.

Activity Analyzing Primary Sources Write the following quotation from French President Charles De Gaulle for students to see: "Patriotism is when love of your own people comes first; nationalism, when hate for people other than your own comes first." Have students write a paragraph explaining what this means in the context of this unit.

Understanding Themes

Answers will vary. Charts should include details from the unit that depend on which examples students choose. Under "Government and Citizenship" students should indicate that most Western nations were monarchies in which common people had few rights, whereas today most Western nations have democratic governments with universal adult suffrage.

Global Connections

Answers will vary, but student essays should note that the United Kingdom is the most industrialized nation, as well as the most urban. Agricultural workers account for very little of the labor force, compared with Nigeria, where 70% of the labor force is engaged in agriculture, and Thailand, where nearly half the labor force is engaged in agriculture. Major British industries tend to involve more sophisticated technology than those in Thailand, and most of Nigeria's industries are "low tech." These differences probably reflect the fact that Britain was an industrial and colonial power, and Nigeria is a former colony, where there was no incentive to industrialize until after it achieved independence.

Differentiating Instruction

Above Level

Advanced Learners/Gifted and Talented

Research Required

1. Draw a table like the one at the bottom of this page for students to see, but label the first row with the name of your community and the second with the name of your state. The third row should be labeled United States. Leave the cells under the headings empty.

2. Organize students into small groups. Have each group copy the table and conduct research about the local, state, and national economies to fill it in. Students should use reliable and current sources, such as census records, economic development Web sites, etc.

3. Have volunteers provide information to fill in the master chart.

4. Guide the class in a discussion of the economy in your community compared with the state as a whole and the national economy. Then compare those economies with the ones listed in the table on this page. **LS Interpersonal, Visual-Spatial**

📝 **Alternative Assessment Handbook**, Rubrics 7: Charts; 9: Comparing and Contrasting; and 14: Group Activity

Unit Review

Summarizing the Unit

During the period covered in this unit, the world went through many changes. Write the following terms for students to see: *technology, industrialization, urbanization, nationalism,* and *imperialism.* Ask students what effects these things had on the world during this period. *New technology fueled industrialization, which in turn led to urbanization, improvements in education, and growing democracy. Nationalism changed the map of Europe, while imperialism changed the map of the world as European nations scrambled for colonies.*

Answers

Thinking Like a Historian

*possible answers—***A.** *Industrialization led to capitalism and urbanization.* **B.** *Industrialization let to increased nationalism because nations were competing for natural resources to fuel the demands of their growing industries.* **C.** *As nations became industrialized, they sought colonial empires to provide raw materials as well as markets for their manufactured goods.*

UNIT 7
IN BRIEF
Below is a chapter-by-chapter summary of the main ideas in this unit, followed by a summary activity for the unit.

CHAPTER 21 The Industrial Revolution
1700–1900

MAIN IDEA The Industrial Revolution and the factory system changed how goods were made as industry moved from the home and into factories.

SECTION 1 The Industrial Revolution began in Great Britain, which had the necessary factors of production, and later spread to other countries.

SECTION 2 The factory system changed life for workers and created new labor conditions.

SECTION 3 New economic ideas such as Marxism arose in response to industrialization.

CHAPTER 22 Life in the Industrial Age
1800–1900

MAIN IDEA During the Industrial Age, cities grew and changed, new inventions and advances changed life, and people enjoyed new cultural pursuits.

SECTION 1 The telegraph, telephone, and railroad led to a transportation and communication revolution.

SECTION 2 New ideas in the sciences included discoveries in biology, physics, chemistry, and medicine.

SECTION 3 As cities grew larger and became more livable, a growing middle class enjoyed new leisure activities and new movements in the arts.

CHAPTER 23 Reforms, Revolutions, and War
1800–1900

MAIN IDEA In the 1800s, industrialization in Britain led to reform, a new government formed in France, much of Latin America achieved independence, and a costly civil war struck the United States.

SECTION 1 Reforms in Britain increased voting rights, abolished slavery, and improved working conditions.

SECTION 2 After a revolution against the monarchy, France worked to create a democratic government.

SECTION 3 In the Americas, new countries formed after gaining independence from European rule.

SECTION 4 The United States expanded westward in the 1800s and suffered through a bloody civil war.

CHAPTER 24 Nationalism in Europe
1800–1920

MAIN IDEA During the 1800s, nationalist movements spread throughout Europe, and people united to form their own nation-states.

SECTION 1 After years of rebellion against Austrian control, several Italian states unified to form Italy.

SECTION 2 Otto von Bismarck successfully led the German people in two wars against Austria and France, which finally unified German states into one nation.

SECTION 3 In central and eastern Europe, ethnic groups struggled for independence against two powerful empires—the Austrian Empire and the Ottoman Empire.

SECTION 4 In the 1800s and early 1900s, Russians revolted against the absolute power of the czars.

CHAPTER 25 The Age of Imperialism
1800–1920

MAIN IDEA In the 1800s, European nations colonized large areas of Africa, Asia, and Latin America.

SECTION 1 British rule over India supplied British factories with raw materials like cotton and tea.

SECTION 2 While China was controlled by European traders, Japan had limited contact with the West.

SECTION 3 Europe's imperial powers divided up and colonized most of Africa despite African resistance.

SECTION 4 While nations in Latin America gained independence from Spain and Portugal, the United States exerted its influence in the Caribbean.

Thinking like a Historian
Summary and Extension Activity

The Industrial Revolution had dramatic effects on Europe and the rest of the world. Write one paragraph on each of the following topics to describes how industrialization influenced each:

A. Economies and societies

B. Nationalism

C. The rise of imperialism

Unit Resources

Review and Reinforce

- **Global History and Geography Regents Test Prep Workbook**
- **Regents Review Transparencies**
- **CRF:** Chapter Review
- **Spanish Chapter Summaries Audio CD Program**
- OSP **Holt PuzzlePro:** Quiz Show for ExamView
- **Quiz Game CD-ROM**

Assess

- **PASS:** Unit Test, Forms A and B
- **Alternative Assessment Handbook**
- OSP **New York ExamView Test Generator** correlated to NY SS Standards
- **Differentiated Instruction Modified Worksheets and Tests CD-ROM:** Chapter Test
- HOAP **Holt Online Assessment Program** (in the Premier Online Edition)

Reteach/Intervene

- **Interactive Reader and Study Guide**
- **Differentiated Instruction Teacher Management System:** Lesson Plans for Differentiated Instruction
- **Differentiated Instruction Modified Worksheets and Tests CD-ROM:** Chapter Test
- **Interactive Skills Tutor CD-ROM**

go.hrw.com
Online Resources

KEYWORDS: SHL IND, SHL LIF, SHL REF, SHL NAT, SHL IMP

The World at War
1914–1945

CHAPTER 26
World War I
1914–1918

CHAPTER 27
The Interwar Years
1919–1939

CHAPTER 28
World War II
1930–1945

Themes

GOVERNMENT AND CITIZENSHIP
Nationalism in Europe caused government rivalries and alliances that led to devastating world wars and inspired citizens to fight for their countries.

SCIENCE AND TECHNOLOGY
New inventions changed the science and technology of modern warfare, which became more deadly and destructive than ever before.

SOCIETY
Entire countries were mobilized for war, and the global conflicts left millions of soldiers and civilians dead and societies in ruins.

German and British fighter pilots try to outmaneuver each other in this painting of World War I.

Battle between German and British airplanes, artist unknown, 1916

775

Unit Preview

Introducing the Unit
In this unit, students will read about two world wars that shaped relations between nations for the years that followed. Discuss with students the overall causes of war. Have students compare and contrast the causes of World War I and II with the war in Iraq and the war on terrorism.

Connecting to Themes
Activity **New Weaponry** Explain to students that trench warfare gave way to advancements in science and technology as new weaponry was developed. Have students explain how poison gas, tanks, and aircraft gave the Allies and the Axis Powers new advantages in combat. Guide students in a discussion about how the resulting death tolls affected societies across the globe.

Reading Like a Historian
Interpreting Visuals
Fighter Planes At the beginning of World War I, planes were generally unarmed. Aerial combat consisted of pilots shooting at each other with rifles and pistols. Air warfare was revolutionized in May 1915, however, with Germany's introduction of an "interrupter gear" that allowed a machine gun mounted near the front of a plane to fire forward without hitting its own propeller. This invention was quickly copied by the Allies and led directly to the development of specialized "fighter" planes.

Unit Resources

Planning
- **Differentiated Instruction Teacher Management System:** Unit Pacing Guide
- OSP **New York One-Stop Planner CD-ROM:** Teacher Management System
- **Power Presentations with Video CD-ROM**

Standards Mastery
- **Global History and Geography Regents Test Prep Workbook**
- **Regents Review Transparencies**

Differentiating Instruction
- **Differentiated Instruction Teacher Management System:** Lesson Plans for Differentiated Instruction
- **Differentiated Instruction Modified Worksheets and Tests CD-ROM**

Enrichment
- **A World History Teacher's Guide to Analyzing Movies**
- **Document-Based Activities for World History**
- **World History Outline Maps**
- **Reading Like a Historian: World History Toolkit**
- **World History Primary Source Library CD-ROM**

Assessment
- **PASS:** Unit Test, Forms A and B
- **Alternative Assessment Handbook**
- OSP **New York ExamView Test Generator correlated to NY SS Standards**
- HOAP **Holt Online Assessment Program** (in the Premier Online Edition)

Chapter 26 Planning Guide

World War I

Chapter Overview	Reproducible Resources	Technology Resources
CHAPTER 26 pp. 776–803 **Overview: In this chapter, students will learn about the causes, battles, and effects of World War I.** KI 2, 4; PI 2.3, 2.5, 4.1, 4.2, 4.4 See pp. T32–T55 for a detailed correlation to the New York State Core Curriculum for Global History and Geography and the New York Learning Standards.	**Differentiated Instruction Teacher Management System:*** • Pacing Guide • Lesson Plans for Differentiated Instruction **Interactive Reader and Study Guide:** Chapter Summary* **Chapter Resource File*** • Writing for the SAT • Social Studies Skill • Chapter Review **World History Outline Maps**	OSP **New York One-Stop Planner CD-ROM:** Calendar Planner **Live Ink© Online Reading Help** **Student Edition on Audio CD Program** **Differentiated Instruction Modified Worksheets and Tests CD-ROM** **World History Primary Source Library CD-ROM** **Power Presentations with Video CD-ROM** **History's Impact: World History Video Program (VHS/DVD):** World War I
Section 1: **The Great War Begins** **The Main Idea:** Europe in 1914 was on the brink of war. After an assassination, the nations of Europe were drawn one by one into what would be called the Great War, or World War I. PI 2.5, 4.1	**Differentiated Instruction Teacher Management System:** Section 1 Lesson Plan* **Interactive Reader and Study Guide:** Section 1 Summary* **Chapter Resource File*** • Vocabulary Builder: Section 1 • Biography: Sophie, Duchess von Hohenberg • History and Geography: World War I: Early Fighting	**Regents Review Transparency:** Section 1* **Map Transparency:** European Alliances and Military Forces, 1914* **Map Transparency:** World War I Battles, 1914* **Quick Facts Transparency:** Causes of World War I*
Section 2: **A New Kind of War** **The Main Idea:** With the introduction of new types of warfare and new technologies, World War I resulted in destruction on a scale never before imagined. PI 2.5	**Differentiated Instruction Teacher Management System:** Section 2 Lesson Plan* **Interactive Reader and Study Guide:** Section 2 Summary* **Chapter Resource File*** • Vocabulary Builder: Section 2 • Biography: Edith Wharton	**Regents Review Transparency:** Section 2* **Map Transparency:** World War I Battles, 1915–1917* **Internet Activity:** Propaganda Poster
Section 3: **Revolution in Russia** **The Main Idea:** The war and social unrest combined to push Russia to the edge of a revolution. The events that followed led to Russia's exit from the war and became a major turning point in world history. PI 2.5, 4.2	**Differentiated Instruction Teacher Management System:** Section 3 Lesson Plan* **Interactive Reader and Study Guide:** Section 3 Summary* **Chapter Resource File*** • Vocabulary Builder: Section 3 • Biography: Leon Trotsky	**Regents Review Transparency:** Section 3* **Internet Activity:** Treaty of Versailles
Section 4: **The War Ends** **The Main Idea:** After several years of bloody stalemate—and the entry of the United States into the conflict—the Allied Powers finally prevailed. The peace, however, proved difficult to establish. PI 2.3, 4.2, 4.4	**Differentiated Instruction Teacher Management System:** Section 4 Lesson Plan* **Interactive Reader and Study Guide:** Section 4 Summary* **Chapter Resource File*** • Vocabulary Builder: Section 4 • Biography: Arthur Zimmerman • Literature: *The Sun Also Rises* • Primary Source: The Fourteen Points	**Regents Review Transparency:** Section 4* **Map Transparency:** Europe and the Middle East* **Quick Facts Transparency:** Effects of World War I*

HOLT
History's Impact
World History Video Program (VHS/DVD)
World War I

Review, Assessment, Intervention

 Global History and Geography Regents Test Prep Workbook

 Quick Facts Transparency: World War I*

Progress Assessment Support System (PASS): Chapter Test*

Spanish Chapter Summaries Audio CD Program

 Differentiated Instruction Modified Worksheets and Tests CD-ROM: Modified Chapter Test

OSP **New York One-Stop Planner CD-ROM:** ExamView Test Generator (English/Spanish)

HOAP **Holt Online Assessment Program (HOAP),** in the Holt Premier Online Student Edition

 PASS: Section 1 Quiz*

 Online Quiz: Section 1

 Alternative Assessment Handbook

 PASS: Section 2 Quiz*

 Online Quiz: Section 2

 Alternative Assessment Handbook

 PASS: Section 3 Quiz*

 Online Quiz: Section 3

 Alternative Assessment Handbook

 PASS: Section 4 Quiz*

 Online Quiz: Section 4

 Alternative Assessment Handbook

Power Presentation with Video CD-ROM

Power Presentations with Video are visual presentations of each chapter's main ideas. Presentations can be customized by including Quick Facts charts, images and maps from the textbook, and video clips.

Holt Online Learning

go.hrw.com
Teacher Resources
KEYWORD: SHL TEACHER

go.hrw.com
Student Resources
KEYWORD: SHL WWI

- Document-Based Questions
- Interactive Multimedia Activities

- Current Events
- Chapter-Based Internet Activities
- and more!

Holt Premier
Online Student Edition

Complete online support for interactivity, assessment, and reporting
- Interactive Maps and Notebook
- Homework Practice and Research Activities Online

CHAPTER 26 PLANNING GUIDE

The Big Picture

Peter N. Stearns

Perspective Almost any history of anything, that reaches 1914, sees World War I as a watershed. Obviously the war introduced massive changes into European history. It profoundly affected the United States, the emerging British Commonwealth, and the Middle East—putting a final touch to the collapse of the Ottoman Empire. Participation in the war stimulated significant changes in South Asia and Africa, spurring new levels of nationalist frustration, while shifting the balance in East Asia as well, particularly in creating new opportunities but also new concerns for Japan. The war must be evaluated in another sense as well, as the first clearly modern war in terms of the impact of industrial weaponry and forms of organization. Not only new weapons and unprecedented death rates, but also new government controls and propaganda introduced novel, often troubling, innovations into world history. Comparing this war to earlier types of warfare, and looking to the war as cause of major subsequent developments in world history, provides vital analytical opportunities.

Origins Causes of World War I were once hotly debated, as many people sought to place particular blame on one country or another. At this point, historians more commonly agree that the alliance system and rising levels of armament constrained choice, and when a particular crisis emerged—the assassination of the Austrian archduke—the system was too inflexible to avoid major conflict. To what extent the war reflected larger tensions in the industrial economy and society can still be debated: a number of participants may initially have been inclined to see war as an escape hatch from pressing domestic tensions.

The Peace Settlement Fairly obviously, the peace settlement did not work well. It may usefully be compared with other settlements such as Vienna in 1815. Punitive measures toward Germany and the creation of weak states in east-central Europe were at least part of the problem. Efforts to innovate through the League of Nations were well intentioned but inadequate against ongoing tensions. Several major empires were permanently destroyed, and the map both of Europe and the Middle East was redrawn. Victorious European powers hoped to resume attention to empire, though new de facto colonies were now held as League mandates; but the war had created forces—new weaknesses in Europe, new demands outside—that would increasingly jeopardize imperialism.

Recent Scholarship

With *Sites of Memory, Sites of Mourning: The Great War in European Cultural History* (1995), Jay Winter expresses a leading theme in recent history: the way modern wars, and World War I in particular, inspire new kinds of historical memories which in turn mark major disruptions in popular culture. Winter captures the impact of unprecedented bloodshed and the hardships of the domestic front, as they would help form later memories and monuments. He is adept at portraying similarities and distinctions in the major national experiences. The war itself is well treated in John Keegan's *The First World War* (1999).

Differentiating Instruction

 Differentiated Instruction Teacher Management System
- Pacing Guide
- Lesson Plans for Differentiated Instruction

 Interactive Reader and Study Guide

Spanish Chapter Summaries Audio CD Program

Student Edition on Audio CD Program

 Differentiated Instruction Modified Worksheets and Tests CD-ROM
- Vocabulary Flash Cards
- Modified Vocabulary Builder Activities
- Modified Chapter Review Activity
- Modified Chapter Test

OSP One-Stop Planner CD-ROM
- ExamView Test Generator (English/Spanish)
- PuzzlePro
- Quiz Show for ExamView
- Transparencies and Videos

TE Differentiated Activities in the Teacher's Edition
- Geography's Effects on the Course of War, p. 780
- Tanks and Aircraft of World War I, p. 784
- Lenin's Decree, p. 792
- Propaganda Pamphlet, p. 798
- World War I Speeches, p. 801

Reading Like a Historian
Sam Wineburg

The U.S. in Haiti Woodrow Wilson campaigned for re-election on the slogan "He Kept us Out of War," and our chapter describes the former president as reluctant to embroil the United States in "the affairs of other nations." This is true if these "other nations" happened to be located in Europe. When it came to our own hemisphere, Wilson and American forces meddled in the affairs of Cuba, Mexico, Panama, and Nicaragua. Indeed, it was under Wilson's watch that the longest American military intervention—an occupation that lasted 19 years and cost thousands of lives—began in Haiti.

With Haiti experiencing social turmoil and political instability, Wilson feared that Germany might invade the island nation and threaten free access to the Panama Canal. On July 28, 1915, he ordered the U.S. Marines to occupy the island, ostensibly to restore order and protect American financial interests. Before long, the Marines introduced a system of "corveé labor," a kind of indentured servitude in which Haitian peasants were forced to work on public works projects at subsistence wages under conditions resembling a chain gang. In his memoirs, Lieutenant General Lewis B. Puller compared these projects to the "building of the pyramids." Watching peasants collapse from heavy labor under the Haitian heat, Puller's conscience wore thin. "I may go to hell for this," he later disclosed to a confidant.

Revolts In the period between 1915 and 1920, some 2,000 to 3,000 Haitians perished in revolts against American rule, many of them followers of Charlemagne Péralte, the rebel leader who waged a guerrilla war against the American forces. Under the pretense of spreading democracy, Americans "helped" Haitians write a constitution. But the document was a sham. Wilson's Assistant Secretary of the Navy, Franklin Delano Roosevelt, indiscreetly boasted in his 1920 campaign for vice president that he was qualified to run a nation: "You know I have had something to do with the running of a couple of little republics. The facts are that I wrote Haiti's

Constitution myself, and, if I do say it, I think it a pretty good Constitution." Haiti's "new" constitution allowed Americans, among other things, the "right" to buy Haitian land.

Indeed, the "agreements" signed with Haiti under Wilson virtually turned the nation into a vassal state in which American banks held controlling interests in the Haitian treasury, and granted concessions to American companies to build railroads and run agricultural plantations. These developments did not go unnoticed—particularly among black Americans. Writing in the magazine *The Crisis*, the official publication of the NAACP, W.E.B. Dubois conceded that Haiti had suffered from poor government but noted that the Wilson Administration should "help Haiti rid herself of thieves and not try to fasten American thieves on her." Pressure by the NAACP helped lead to two 1920 fact-finding missions, one by the Navy and the other by the Marines. Both commissions admitted individual acts of wrongdoing, but unsurprisingly concluded that these were isolated incidents and not part of general policy. This did not stop the Haiti-Santo Domingo Independence Society from publishing an advertisement in *The Nation* on November 9, 1921, under the banner "Why Should YOU Worry About Haiti?" which told readers that "Your Government killed two or three thousand harmless Haitians—as against thirteen Marines killed; Your Government is still maintaining martial law in Haiti and continuing an 'American' rule which is in effect 'government of, for, and by, the National City Bank'; and Because You, as an American, are responsible."

Wilson's re-election slogan "he kept us out of war" was true only on one condition: that America turn a blind eye to events in its own backyard.

Chapter Main Ideas

Section 1 Europe in 1914 was on the brink of war. After an assassination, the nations of Europe were drawn one by one into what would be called the Great War, or World War I.

Section 2 With the introduction of new types of warfare and new technologies, World War I resulted in destruction on a scale never before imagined.

Section 3 The war and social unrest combined to push Russia to the edge of a revolution. The events that followed led to Russia's exit from the war and became a major turning point in world history.

Section 4 After several years of bloody stalemate—and the entry of the United States into the conflict—the Allied Powers finally prevailed. The peace, however, proved difficult to establish.

🏛 New York Standards

Key Idea 2 Establishing timeframes, exploring different periodizations, examining themes across time and within cultures, and focusing on important turning points in world history help organize the study of world cultures and civilizations.

Key Idea 4 The skills of historical analysis include the ability to investigate differing and competing interpretations of the theories of history, hypothesize about why interpretations change over time, explain the importance of historical evidence, and understand the concepts of change and continuity over time.

Key to Differentiating Instruction

Below Level

Basic-level activities designed for all students encountering new material

At Level

Intermediate-level activities designed for average students

Above Level

Challenging activities designed for honors and gifted and talented students

Standard English Mastery

Activities designed to improve standard English usage

CHAPTER

26 1914–1918

World War I

THE BIG PICTURE A variety of powerful forces—including growing nationalism, a tangle of alliances, and decades of rivalry and competition—created conditions that transformed a single assassination into a worldwide war. After years of unprecedented bloodshed and political upheaval, the warring nations finally reached an uneasy peace.

Theme GOVERNMENT AND CITIZENSHIP
The role of governments and citizens in wartime has varied greatly throughout history. In this chapter you will examine how citizens contributed to the war effort during World War I.

TIME LINE

| CHAPTER EVENTS | **June 28, 1914** Archduke Franz Ferdinand is assassinated in Sarajevo. | **July 28, 1914** Austria-Hungary declares war on Serbia, and World War I begins. | **May 1915** Germany attacks and sinks the *Lusitania*. | **December 1915** The Gallipoli Campaign ends. | **February 1916** The Battle of Verdun begins. |

1914   **1916**

| WORLD EVENTS | | **August 1914** The Panama Canal opens. | | **November 1916** Germany and Austria-Hungary establish the Kingdom of Poland. |

Introduce the Chapter

At Level

World War I, 1914–1918

1. Review with students the definition of *alliance*.

2. Organize students into small groups and have each group make a list of reasons alliances are formed between nations. *trade, shared resources, mutual economic aid, defense*

3. Have students picture what happens when a pebble is thrown into a pond. *Ripples fan out far beyond where the pebble landed.* Explain that World War I began with just one man assassinating another, but this seemingly small event affected the lives of millions of people. Tell students that because of political alliances, many nations became involved in World War I.

4. Have students list the countries that became involved in World War I. Have them decide which countries were allied to one another. Have students work in pencil so they can revise their lists as needed. **LS Interpersonal**

📝 **Alternative Assessment Handbook**, Rubric 14: Group Activity

HOLT
History's Impact
► **Video Program: World War I**
See the Video Teacher's Guide for strategies for using the video segment.

Reading Like a Historian
Analyzing Primary Sources Have students examine the photograph on these pages. Have them observe where the soldiers are, how they are standing, and where they are looking. Have students determine whether or not they think the photographer was in danger.

Reading like a Historian

This photograph shows a British tank and British soldiers during a battle in 1917. World War I marked the first time that tanks were used in combat.

Analyzing Visuals How do you think the use of tanks during World War I would change the nature of warfare? Explain your answer, referring to details from the photograph.

See **Skills Handbook**, p. H26

November 1917
Communists take control of Russia in the Bolshevik Revolution.

November 11, 1918
An armistice ends the war.

1918

June 1917
The first Pulitzer Prizes are awarded.

WORLD WAR I **777**

Explore the Time Line

1. Where was Archduke Ferdinand assassinated? *Sarajevo*
2. What action did Germany take in May of 1915? *attacked and sank the* Lusitania
3. When was the Kingdom of Poland established? *November 1916*
4. When did an armistice end the war? *November 11, 1918*

Info to Know

Inventing the Tank In 1914, Col. E.D. Swinton of Britain suggested mounting armor and firepower on an American Caterpillar Tractor. When the vehicles were sent to France, the shipping label read "water tanks," to disguise the shipment from the Germans. Such vehicles are still called "tanks" today.

Make Inferences Why would armor help a tank in trench warfare? *would protect it from barbed wire and enemy fire*

go.hrw.com
Online Resources

Chapter Resources:
KEYWORD: SHL WW1
Teacher Resources:
KEYWORD: SHL TEACHER

Answers

Reading Like a Historian *help armies cross wide, trenches; better protect soldiers; larger gun more deadly*

Geography Starting Points

The Schlieffen Plan Before the war broke out, Count Alfred von Schlieffen, the chief of the German general staff, developed a planned invasion of France in 1905. From several points along the border, German troops would sweep through Belgium into northeastern France and destroy the French armies at Paris. Schlieffen emphasized the need for a strong right wing of the German army, advancing as far west as possible. The plan was abandoned, however, by the circumstances of the war.

🗺 **Map Transparency:** European Alliances and Military Forces, 1914

📑 **World History Outline Maps**

✳ **Interactive Map:** European Alliances and Military Forces, 1914

✳Interactive EUROPEAN ALLIANCES AND MILITARY FORCES, 1914

Map legend:
- Allied Powers
- Central Powers
- Neutral nations
- 🚢 100,000 troops

0 — 250 — 500 Miles
0 — 250 — 500 Kilometers
Azimuthal equal-area projection

Starting Points In the late 1800s and early 1900s, European nations began a massive military buildup, in part to protect their overseas colonies from rival powers. At the same time, these nations formed a complicated network of alliances to protect themselves from opposing armed forces. By 1914 the uneasy peace was about to end.

1. **Identify** Which nations were members of the Allied Powers in 1914? Which nations made up the Central Powers?

2. **Predict** Given the alliances and the size of the armed forces in Europe in 1914, what might happen if conflict broke out?

🔊 **Listen to History**

Go online to listen to an explanation of the starting points for this chapter.

go.hrw.com
Keyword: SHL WW1

Skills Focus: Analyzing Maps
At Level

Social Studies Skill
Comparing Troop Strengths

1. Draw the chart for students to see. Omit the italicized answers. Have students work in pairs to copy and fill in their charts. Students should list the names of all the Central Powers first, and list all the Allied Powers below them.

2. Have students determine the correct number of troops and have them record the numbers next to each country. **LS** Visual-Spatial

📑 **Alternative Assessment Handbook**, Rubrics 13: Graphic Organizers; and 21: Map Reading

Comparative Troop Strengths	
Countries	**Troops**
Germany	*1,900,000*
Austria-Hungary	*450,000*
United Kingdom	*100,000*
France	*1,300,000*
Serbia	*200,000*
Russia	*1,400,000*

Answers

Geography Starting Points
1. *Allied Powers—France, Montenegro, Russia, Serbia, United Kingdom; Central Powers—Austria, Hungary, Germany;*
2. *possible answer—The Allied Powers have more troops and would likely win, but would face a difficult challenge defeating Germany.*

SECTION 1 The Great War Begins

BEFORE YOU READ

MAIN IDEA

Europe in 1914 was on the brink of war. After an assassination, the nations of Europe were drawn one by one into what would be called the Great War, or World War I.

READING FOCUS

1. Why was Europe on the brink of war in 1914?
2. Why did war break out?
3. What were the results of the fighting in 1914?

KEY TERMS AND PEOPLE

Triple Alliance
Triple Entente
Franz Ferdinand
Gavrilo Princip
neutral
Central Powers
Allied Powers
Western Front

NEW YORK

PI 2.5 Students investigate key events and developments and major turning points in world history to identify the factors that brought about change.

PI 4.1 Students identify historical problems.

THE INSIDE STORY

How did an archduke's trip lead to war? It seemed like a bad idea for Austrian archduke Franz Ferdinand to make a trip to the Bosnian city of Sarajevo (SAR-uh-YAY-voh). After all, Austria had taken over Bosnia and Herzegovina just six years earlier, and many Bosnians were still bitterly opposed to Austrian rule.

Bosnia was also the home of many Serbs and ethnic Slavs who were equally outraged by Austria's actions. Serbian leaders hoped to expand Serbia by uniting the ethnic Slavs in Bosnia, but Austria-Hungary stood in the way. Now the future ruler of the Austro-Hungarian Empire was coming to pay a visit.

Franz Ferdinand's visit to Sarajevo fell on June 28, which was also St. Vitus Day, a holiday that symbolized Serbian unity. Members of a Serbian terrorist group known as the Black Hand plotted to kill Franz Ferdinand.

On the day that the archduke visited Sarajevo, seven members of the Black Hand positioned themselves around the city to watch for him. One would-be assassin, 19-year-old Gavrilo Princip, had just stepped out of a sandwich shop when Franz Ferdinand's car pulled up in front of him. Unable to believe his luck, Princip grabbed his pistol and fired, killing both the archduke and the archduke's wife, Sophie. This assassination started a chain of events that, within weeks, would pull most of Europe into the largest war the world had ever seen. ■

▼ Soldiers arrest Gavrilo Princip after he shoots Archduke Franz Ferdinand.

A MURDER IN BOSNIA

WORLD WAR I **779**

Preteach

Getting Started

Use the **Interactive Reader and Study Guide** to familiarize students with the section content.

📖 **Interactive Reader and Study Guide,** Section 1

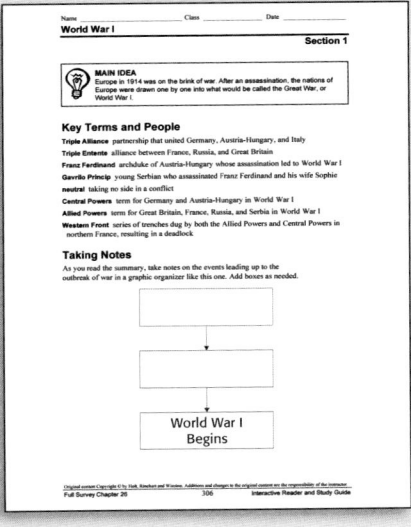

📑 **CRF:** Vocabulary Builder: Section 1

Taking Notes

assassination of Archduke Ferdinand starts a chain of events; militarism, alliances, imperialism, and nationalism cause tensions in Europe

---

Teach the Main Idea

At Level

Events of World War I

Materials: chart paper

1. **Teach** Ask students the Reading Focus questions to teach this section.

2. **Apply** Organize students into small groups. Have each group create a two-column chart listing several causes and effects they identify in each section of this chapter.

3. **Review** Using chart paper, create a large causes-and-effects chart for students to see. For each section, have volunteers from each group record causes and effects they discovered.

4. **Practice/Homework** Have each student write a one-paragraph summary of the major events of the Great War. **LS Verbal-Linguistic, Visual-Spatial**

📑 **Alternative Assessment Handbook**, Rubric 6: Cause and Effect

1 Why was Europe on the brink of war in 1914? *rising tensions resulting from militarism, alliances, imperialism, and nationalism*

Europe on the Brink of War

Recall Why did European nations build up their military forces? *to protect their overseas colonies*

Summarize What did the leaders of alliances in the late 1800s believe? *that their alliances would keep the peace, and that no single nation would attack another*

Predict What do you think will happen between these groups of allies? *possible answer—When one nation is attacked, its allies will join to defend them, resulting in a larger war.*

Info to Know

Heart Surgery Cardiac surgery was first performed during World War I. In 1896 author Stephen Paget wrote the opinion that heart surgery was impossible and should not be attempted by surgeons. In 1917, however, British surgeon George Grey Turner removed a bullet from a soldier's heart. Even though there was no blood bank, no antibiotics, only primitive anesthesia, and poor lighting at the time, the soldier lived through the surgery and was still living in 1940 when the case was finally reported. Nearly half a century after Paget's statement, heart surgery at last became accepted and techniques advanced rapidly.

Causes of World War I

Analyze Which factor listed in the chart most influenced ethnic Serbs to rebel against Austria-Hungary? *nationalism*

📖 **Quick Facts Transparency:** Causes of World War I

Answers

Reading Check *rising tensions as result of militarism, alliances, imperialism, and nationalism*

780

TAKING NOTES

Take notes on the events leading up to the outbreak of war.

World War I Begins

NEW YORK

CC Unit 6-A2
Causes of World War I

Europe on the Brink of War

In 1914, rising tensions in Europe had the continent on the brink of war. These tensions were the result of four factors: militarism, alliances, imperialism, and nationalism.

Militarism Throughout the late 1800s and early 1900s, European countries had undertaken a massive military buildup. This militarism was caused mostly by the desire to protect overseas colonies from other nations. Across Europe, the size of armed forces and navies had risen sharply, particularly in Germany.

The growing power of Europe's armed forces left all sides anxious and ready to act at the first sign of trouble. In this nervous environment, even a minor disagreement had the potential to turn quickly into armed conflict.

Alliances Seeking to protect themselves from opposing armed forces, the nations of Europe formed a series of alliances, or partnerships. For example, in the late 1800s, the so-called **Triple Alliance** united Germany, Austria-Hungary, and Italy. France and Russia feared Germany's growing power and formed their own alliance. Soon Great Britain joined with France and Russia in a less formal promise to cooperate—an entente (ahn-TAHNT). France, Russia, and Great Britain thus became known as the **Triple Entente**. Leaders hoped that these alliances would help keep the peace. They believed that no single nation would attack another, since that action would prompt the attacked nation's allies to join the fight.

Imperialism The quest to build empires in the late 1800s and early 1900s had created much rivalry and ill will among the nations of Europe. Germany, France, Russia, and Great Britain each saw themselves as great imperial nations. They believed they could not afford to stand by while a rival empire gained power.

Nationalism An important part of the rising tensions in Europe was an increase in nationalism beginning in the late 1800s. Nationalism is a strong devotion to one's national group or culture. In Europe, nationalism led to the formation of new countries, including Germany and Italy, and struggles for power.

The most visible of these power struggles was in the Balkan Peninsula, a region of

780 CHAPTER 26

CAUSES OF WORLD WAR I

MILITARISM
- European nations engage in a massive military buildup.

ALLIANCES
- European countries form partnerships to protect themselves.

IMPERIALISM
- Rival empires seek to keep power.

NATIONALISM
- People feel loyalty and devotion to their country or culture.

southeastern Europe that was home to many ethnic groups. In the early 1900s, some of these ethnic groups were trying to break free from the Ottoman Empire, which had ruled the Balkans for hundreds of years but was now nearing collapse.

Some of the strongest nationalist tensions in the Balkans were in Serbia. At the time, Serbia was an independent nation. Many ethnic Serbs, however, lived outside Serbia in other areas of the Balkans. Serbian leaders wanted to expand the nation's borders and unite all their people in a "greater Serbia." But Austria-Hungary, the powerful empire to the north of Serbia, opposed any Serbian expansion, fearing that such growth might encourage ethnic groups within Austria-Hungary to rebel. Tensions between Austria-Hungary and Serbs would continue to rise in the early 1900s.

READING CHECK **Summarize** Why was Europe on the brink of war in 1914?

War Breaks Out

In the midst of the tensions and resentment the Serbs felt toward Austria-Hungary, the archduke of Austria-Hungary, **Franz Ferdinand**, decided to visit the Bosnian city of Sarajevo (SAR-uh-YAY-voh). On June 28, 1914, as Franz Ferdinand's car drove through the Sarajevo

---

Differentiating Instruction

At Level

Special Education Students

Research Required

Materials: chart paper

1. Review with students the locations of countries that became involved in World War I.

2. Organize students into groups of four or five. Assign each group one border area between two non-allied nations.

3. Have each group find and trace a detailed map of its assigned area, including landform details and routes across the borders. Ask each group to select a member to find and print out detailed aerial photos of the border area.

It may take several prints to cover the full border. Have students attach the printouts to the outside of the drawn maps, using arrows to indicate which sections they represent.

4. Based on their observations, have group members write their predictions about how the landforms might affect the course of war at that location. Allow time for groups to share their work. **LS** **Interpersonal, Visual-Spatial**

📖 **Alternative Assessment Handbook**, Rubrics 20: Map Creation; and 30: Research

WORLD WAR I BATTLES, 1914

Legend:
- Allied Powers
- Central Powers
- Neutral nations
- Allied Powers advance
- Central Powers advance
- Front line
- Allied Powers victory
- Central Powers victory

GEOGRAPHY SKILLS INTERPRETING MAPS

1. **Location** Where was the Western Front located at this time? What were the results of the major battles fought there?
2. **Movement** Describe the movements of the Allied Powers and the Central Powers.

streets, a young Serbian man, **Gavrilo Princip,** opened fire with his pistol, killing the archduke and the archduke's wife, Sophie.

The Impact Princip was arrested after the assassination. When he was identified as a Serb, Austria-Hungary decided to use the murder as an excuse to punish Serbia. Austria-Hungary made a series of humiliating demands of Serbia and then declared war on July 28, 1914.

Russia, a country with many people of Slavic ethnicity, had previously promised to support the Serbs if Austria-Hungary attacked. When Russia prepared to fulfill its promise to the Serbs, Austria-Hungary's ally Germany saw the Russian action as a threat. Germany declared war on Russia and then on Russia's ally, France. Thus, Europe's alliances and rivalries turned the action of a single assassin into a major conflict.

Fighting Begins Located in central Europe, Germany faced a war on two fronts—against Russia to the east and France to the west. Years earlier, German military planners had developed the Schlieffen Plan, which called for German troops to quickly defeat France in the west and then head east to fight Russia. German leaders believed this strategy would be effective because Russia's vast size meant that the Russian military would need some time to move toward the German border.

Germany began with a quick strike into Belgium, which was located between Germany and France. Belgium was a **neutral** country, or a country that takes no side in a conflict. Still, Germany planned to sweep through that country and then move on to France. Germany's attack on a neutral country led Great Britain to declare war on Germany.

The main players of what came to be called World War I, or the Great War, were now in place. Germany and Austria-Hungary made up one side, known as the **Central Powers.** Great Britain, France, Russia, and Serbia were known as the **Allied Powers.**

READING CHECK **Sequence** What events led to the outbreak of World War I?

READING SKILLS

Understanding Sequencing In what order did the Allied Powers become involved in the war?

WORLD WAR I **781**

Skills Focus: Interpreting Movement Maps

At Level

Prep Required

Social Studies Skill
Troop Strength

Materials: one black outline map per student, glue, punched holes from two colors of paper

1. Distribute black outline maps of Europe to each student. Review the numbers of troops shown on the Geography Starting Points map, European Alliances and Military Forces, 1914.

2. Have students lightly pencil in the front lines and the arrows representing advances from the map on this page. Distribute piles of two colors of paper punch-outs to each row of students.

3. Using the punch-outs to represent each group of 100,000 troops, have students distribute the appropriate number of troops as they were likely to have been placed by the Allied Powers and the Central Powers. Use different colors to represent each allied group. Display student work. **LS** Visual-Spatial

📋 **Alternative Assessment Handbook,** Rubric 20: Map Creation

---

Direct Teach

Reading Focus

2 Why did war break out? *Austria-Hungary blamed Serbia for the assassination of Archduke Ferdinand, leading to war between both countries' allies.*

War Breaks Out

Recall Which country did Germany attack on its way to invade France? *Belgium*

Explain Why did Germany declare war on Russia? *Germany, an ally of Austria-Hungary, saw Russia's plan to support the Serbs as a threat.*

Activity **Russian Advancement** Have students refer to the map and propose an alternate position for the advance of Russia. Use sticky notes on a wall map, if available, to indicate proposed Russian positions. Have students discuss and explain their ideas. **LS** Visual-Spatial

📋 **Alternative Assessment Handbook,** Rubric 6: Cause and Effect

💾 **Map Transparency:** World War I Battles, 1914

📋 **CRF:** Biography: Sophie, Duchess von Hohenberg

Answers

Reading Skills *Germans attack Belgium, Great Britain declares war on Germany, French and British fight in Battle of the Frontiers, Russia attacks Germany from east*

Interpreting Maps 1. *along the border of Germany and France; refer to map;* **2.** *The Central Powers advanced toward Russia to the east, France to the west, and Serbia to the south; the Allied Powers advanced along the Eastern Front.*

Reading Check *Serbian Gavrilo Princip killed Austrian Archduke Ferdinand and his wife; Germany (an ally of Austria-Hungary) declared war on Russia (an ally of Serbia); Germany attacked Belgium; Great Britain declared war on Germany*

781

❸ What were the results of the fighting in 1914? *Both sides suffered heavy losses; Russia attacked East Prussia; trench warfare began; the war became a bloody stalemate.*

Fighting in 1914

Identify What was the name of the disastrous Russian battle? *The Battle of Tannenberg*

Identify Cause and Effect What effect did the Russian attack on East German territory have on the Western Front? *It distracted the Germans and removed pressure on France.*

📑 **CRF:** History and Geography: World War I: Early Fighting

Close

Have students explain how alliances caused World War I to expand quickly.

Review

📑 **Online Quiz**, Section 1

Assess

SE Section 1 Assessment

📑 **Progress Assessment:** Section 1 Quiz

📑 **Alternative Assessment Handbook**

Reteach/Intervene

📑 **Interactive Reader and Study Guide,** Section 1

💿 **Interactive Skills Tutor CD-ROM**

Answers

Faces of History *was aggressive and tactless, determined to make Germany a world power*

Reading Check *Germany advanced though Belgium to attack France; Russia attacked East Prussia; Russians crushed in Battle of Tannenberg; British and French forces regrouped; millions died or were wounded; trench warfare resulted in a stalemate*

782

FACES OF HISTORY

Kaiser WILHELM II
1859–1941

Friedrich Wilhelm Viktor Albert became emperor of Germany when he was only 29 years old. Wilhelm believed the ideal ruler was someone who would make a nation powerful and respected. He was determined to make Germany a world power.

Under Wilhelm's rule, the German armed forces underwent a massive expansion. Wilhelm believed that his personal relationships with the leaders of Great Britain and Russia would help prevent war, but he was mistaken. His aggressive, tactless actions, combined with his desire to build a powerful German military, helped lead the world into a devastating war.

Find the Main Idea How did Wilhelm help cause World War I?

Fighting in 1914

Germany's plans for a swift victory in France soon failed. By the end of 1914, the Great War had become a bloody stalemate.

Early Battles Beginning in August 1914, German troops fought French and British forces in a series of clashes known as the Battle of the Frontiers. Both sides suffered heavy losses, but the result was a German victory.

While France was struggling to fight off Germany during the Battles of the Frontiers, Russia attacked German territory from the east. The results for the Russians were disastrous. In the Battle of Tannenberg, German forces crushed the Russian invasion.

The Russian attack had failed to defeat the Germans, but it succeeded in distracting German forces from their advance on France. This distraction allowed Allied forces to collect themselves and turn on the German invaders.

Trench Warfare Begins In the Battle of the Marne in early September 1914, the Allied troops succeeded in driving the Germans back. After retreating, German forces dug a series of trenches, or deep ditches, along the Aisne (AYN) River and awaited the Allied attack. One British soldier described the German trenches:

HISTORY'S VOICES

❝ [German] infantry are holding strong lines of trenches among and along the edge of the numerous woods which crown the slopes. These trenches are elaborately constructed and cleverly concealed. In many places there are wire entanglements. ❞
—British colonel Ernest Swinton, September 18, 1914

From their strongly defended trenches on the Aisne, the Germans were able to fight back the Allied forces. But the Allied forces soon dug trenches of their own. As a result, German and Allied positions would change little in the coming months, despite a series of major battles. The deadlocked region in northern France became known as the **Western Front.**

READING CHECK **Summarize** What were the major events of the fighting in 1914?

SECTION 1 ASSESSMENT

go.hrw.com
Online Quiz
Keyword: SHL WW1 HP

Reviewing Ideas, Terms, and People

1. a. Identify What were the **Triple Alliance** and the **Triple Entente**?
b. Explain Why do you think European governments expanded the size of their armed forces?
c. Draw Conclusions How did the increased size and power of military forces make fighting more likely?

2. a. Describe What was the crime that led to the start of World War I?
b. Make Inferences After **Franz Ferdinand** was killed, why do you think that Austria-Hungary chose to take the actions it did?
c. Develop How might Germany have worked to stop the war from beginning?

3. a. Recall What forces fought in the war's first major battle?
b. Analyze How did the construction of trenches affect the war in 1914?

Critical Thinking

4. Identify Cause and Effect Using your notes on the section and a graphic organizer like the one below, explain how the events of the late 1800s and early 1900s led up to the outbreak of World War I.

☐ → ☐ → ☐ → ☐ → ☐

FOCUS ON SPEAKING 🎤

5. Persuasion Write notes for a speech that a European leader trying to prevent the outbreak of war might have given in July 1914. Use details from the chapter in your notes.

Section 1 Assessment Answers

1. a. The Triple Alliance united Germany, Austria-Hungary, and Italy. The Triple Entente included France, Russia, and Great Britain.
b. possible answer—to protect overseas colonies from other nations
c. The growing power of Europe's armed forces left all sides ready for war.

2. a. the assassination of Archduke Franz Ferdinand and his wife by Gavrilo Princip
b. possible answer—Austria-Hungary opposed Serbian expansion, so they used the assassination as an excuse to punish Serbia.

c. possible answer—Germany could have avoided attacking Serbia's allies.

3. a. German troops fought French and British
b. Trench warfare would cause higher casualties.

4. buildup of armed forces in Europe; alliances formed; assassination of Archduke Franz Ferdinand; Germany invaded Belgium and France; Great Britain and Russia join the war

5. possible speech topics—alliances will not prevent war; militarism should be avoided; nationalism and imperialism may lead to war

2 A New Kind of War

BEFORE YOU READ

MAIN IDEA

With the introduction of new types of warfare and new technologies, World War I resulted in destruction on a scale never before imagined.

READING FOCUS

1. How was the World War I battlefield different than those of earlier wars?
2. How did the war affect the home front?
3. What happened on the Western Front?
4. How did the war spread around the world?

KEY TERMS

trench warfare
total war
propaganda
Battle of Verdun
Gallipoli Campaign
genocide

NEW YORK

P1 2.5 Students investigate key events and developments and major turning points in world history to identify the factors that brought about change and the long-term effects of these changes.

POISON FROM THE SKY

THE INSIDE STORY

Can you protect yourself against the air? The exhausted British soldiers were taking a break from the bitter fighting with German forces. In the distance, they could see the other end of their own line of trenches. This section was occupied by British allies, including soldiers from France and from the French colony of Algeria.

The resting British soldiers noticed a curious thing. Floating through the air from the German lines toward the Allied trenches was a slow-moving cloud of yellowish smoke. Soon, from the direction of the strange cloud came a steady stream of running men, throwing away clothing, equipment, and anything else that might slow them down.

The British were at first horrified at what they thought was the cowardly retreat of the French and Algerians. They soon learned, however, that the terrified men had good reason to run. The yellow cloud that had floated into their trenches was chlorine gas, a deadly poison. When inhaled, this gas damages lung tissue and causes victims to cough violently and choke. In some cases, the gas kills.

The poison gas used against the Allied troops was one of many new weapons that first appeared in World War I. Together these weapons produced a horrifying level of death and destruction. ■

▲ Gas masks were vital equipment for soldiers in the World War I trenches.

The World War I Battlefield

Poison gas and the other new weapons developed during World War I were a response to a massive deadlock. By the end of 1914, two systems of trenches stretched for hundreds of miles over western Europe. Across the Western Front, millions of Allied and Central Powers soldiers lived in these trenches, surrounded by flying bullets, bombs, and grenades.

WORLD WAR I **783**

Preteach

Getting Started

Use the **Interactive Reader and Study Guide** to familiarize students with the section content.

📖 **Interactive Reader and Study Guide,** Section 2

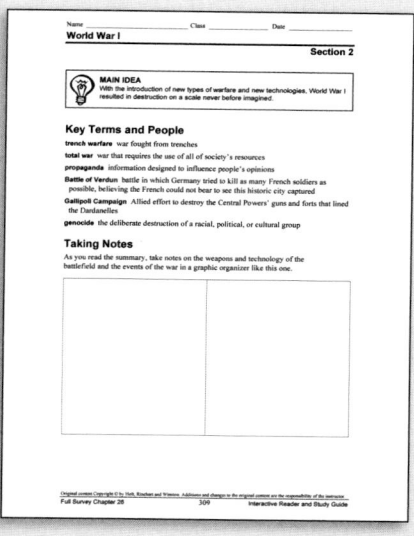

📝 **CRF:** Vocabulary Builder: Section 2

Taking Notes

soldiers on the battlefields face miserable life in the trenches; new weapons such as poison gas, machine guns, tanks, and faster aircraft used; Ottoman Empire joins Central Powers; Italy joins Allied Powers; war spreads to Asia and Africa

go.hrw.com
Online Resources

KEYWORD: SHL WW1
ACTIVITY: Propaganda
Poster

Teach the Main Idea

At Level

A New Kind of War

1. **Teach** Ask students the Reading Focus questions to teach this section.

2. **Apply** Organize students into small groups. Write these topics for all to see: On the Battlefield, At Home, Around the Globe. Have groups write newspaper articles about the changes war brought to these three areas. Group members should write articles about each topic.

3. **Review** Have groups share their newspaper articles with the class. As you review the section, have students revise their articles as needed.

4. **Practice/Homework** Have each student write a list of changes for each of the three locations covered. **LS Interpersonal, Visual-Spatial**

📝 **Alternative Assessment Handbook**, Rubrics 14: Group Activity; and 23: Newspapers

❶ How was the World War I battlefield different than those of earlier wars? *poison gas, new weapons, trench warfare*

The World War I Battlefield

Recall Where does the term "no-man's-land" come from? *from the dangerous open area between trenches*

Compare In what way were the new trenches different from earlier warfare? *Soldiers had long hidden behind mounds of earth for safety, but now systems of trenches stretched for hundreds of miles.*

Identify Cause and Effect What developments resulted from the trench warfare stalemate? *new technology such as gas warfare, tanks, and aircraft*

Recent Scholarship

Historian Hew Strachan takes a less traditional stance in his book *The First World War,* which describes the war as less about soldiers' courage and more about a race for the latest warfare technology. According to Strachan, World War I generals focused mainly on new weapons and tactics rather than on troop strength and bravery. *The First World War* also outlines the far-reaching effects of the war and discusses how it affected soldiers.

The First World War by Hew Strachan. Viking, 2004.

Trench Warfare The idea of **trench warfare**, or fighting from trenches, was not new. Soldiers had long hidden behind mounds of earth for safety. But no one had ever experienced trench warfare on the scale seen in Europe in 1914.

Life in the trenches was often miserable. Rainstorms produced deep puddles and thick mud, and sanitation was a constant problem. Sometimes removing dead bodies from trenches or the surrounding area was impossible. Lice, rats, and other unpleasant creatures were always present.

Occasionally soldiers would be ordered "over the top" of their trench to attack the enemy. They would jump out of their trench and sprint across the area between opposing trenches, called no-man's-land. As they ran, many were cut down by enemy guns. Thousands of soldiers on both sides died in no-man's-land, their bodies left where they fell.

New Weapons Neither the Allies nor the Central Powers were able to make significant advances past the enemy's trenches. As a result, each side turned to new weapons and technology to win the war.

Poison gas was one of the new weapons used in the war. Different types of gas could blind, choke, or burn the victims. Gas killed or injured thousands of people, but its value was limited. A change in wind direction, for example, could blow the gas back toward the troops who had launched it. Also, both sides developed gas masks, which provided some protection.

Other new weapons were far more effective. For example, rapid-fire machine guns came into wide use during the war. Modern industry also produced artillery and high-explosive shells with enormous destructive power.

Tanks and Aircraft Both tanks and aircraft were first used in World War I. Tanks, armored vehicles that could cross rough battlefield terrain, were pioneered by the British. Because reliability was a problem, however, they would not make a contribution until late in the war.

Aircraft, on the other hand, were useful from the beginning. At the start of the war, few

NEW YORK

CC Unit 6-A4
Effects of scientific/technological advances on warfare

TAKING NOTES

Take notes on the weapons and technology of the battlefield and the events of the war.

★ **Interactive**
HISTORY CLOSE-UP

Trench Warfare

It was nearly impossible to capture an enemy trench, protected as it was by machine guns, rows of barbed wire, and armed soldiers. As a result, trench warfare turned into a stalemate. Countless troops died in the trenches, with little real effect on the war.

Soldiers fired artillery shells containing poison gas into enemy trenches.

784 CHAPTER 26

Differentiating Instruction

Above Level

Advanced Learners/Gifted and Talented

Research Required

1. Remind students that tanks and aircraft were developed for battlefield use in World War I.

2. Organize students into groups of four or five. Groups should designate an illustrator, a researcher, and two or more capabilities analysts. Have each group choose either tanks or aircraft of World War I as their subject.

3. Have groups conduct research about the development of their vehicle type. Tell students to focus on new developments and capabilities as well as the appearance of their vehicle type.

4. Ask each group to create a detailed poster illustrating and explaining the capabilities of the vehicles they are researching and their value in the battlefield. Allow time for groups to present their posters. **LS** **Interpersonal, Visual-Spatial**

📝 **Alternative Assessment Handbook**, Rubrics 28: Posters; and 30: Research aircraft existed, and they were used mainly to observe enemy positions. Soon, mechanics began to attach machine guns to airplanes, and pilots began to drop bombs from the air. As the war dragged on, new, faster airplanes proved useful in attacking battlefields and cities.

Despite the new technologies, however, neither side was able to gain an advantage on the battlefield. Trench warfare, with all its miseries, dragged on.

READING CHECK Summarize How did new technology affect the World War I battlefield?

War on the Home Front

The nations fighting in World War I soon realized that winning this new type of war would require the use of all of society's resources. This tactic is called **total war**. Governments began to take stronger control of their citizens' lives.

Government Actions In some countries, new controls resulted in changes to the nation's industries and economy. Factories began to produce military equipment. Civilians conserved food and other goods for military use.

Governments also sought to control public opinion. They censored newspaper reports about the fighting, worried that truthful descriptions of casualties might discourage the public. Governments also created **propaganda**, information designed to influence people's opinions, in order to encourage support of the war effort. Posters, pamphlets, and articles urged people to volunteer or told stories of the enemy's brutal actions.

German zeppelins—large, gas-filled airships—bombed British and French trenches and cities.

Airplanes fought in the skies above the trenches, firing on soldiers below.

Machine guns fired hundreds of bullets each minute and were used to defend trenches against enemy attacks.

Armored tanks could flatten barbed wire and cross enemy trenches.

Skills FOCUS INTERPRETING VISUALS

Analyze What role did new weapons and military tactics play in trench warfare? Use details from the image to support your answer.

Go online for a closer look at survival and this event.

go.hrw.com
COULD YOU HAVE SURVIVED?
Keyword: SHL WW1

WORLD WAR I **785**

Direct Teach

Reading Focus

2 How did the war affect the home front? *Involved nations' governments took control of the lives of their people and women entered the workforce.*

War on the Home Front

Describe What is total war? *the tactic of using all of society's resources to fight a war*

Rate What is your opinion of the use of propaganda and censorship? *possible answer—It would unify people to support the war effort, but it is wrong to keep people from knowing about what is happening.*

Teaching Tip

Some wartime music reflected propaganda's positive spin on the war. Locate some recordings and share them with your class.

About the Illustration
This illustration is an artist's conception based on available sources. Historians, however, are uncertain exactly what this scene looked like.

Skills Focus: Recognizing Bias in Primary Sources | At Level

Reading Like a Historian Skill
Influencing Public Opinion

1. Tell students that governments of nations involved in World War I felt a need to influence public opinion. Tell students that catchy tunes often painted a rosy picture of the war.

2. Organize students into small groups. Have each group conduct research using reliable online or print sources to locate World War I propaganda.

3. Using the propaganda material found in their research as a model, have groups create propaganda by writing new lyrics to a well-

known melody such as "Happy Birthday" or "Clementine." Tell students that their lyrics should represent the positive attitude that the government would have wanted to use in propaganda.

4. Encourage volunteers to sing or recite their songs to the class. **LS** Interpersonal, Auditory-Musical

Alternative Assessment Handbook, Rubrics 14: Group Activity; and 26: Poems and Songs

Answers

History Close-Up *New weapons and tactics made fighting deadlier—zeppelins and airplanes fired from the skies; machine guns fired hundreds of bullets per minute; tanks crossed enemy trenches.*

Reading Check *New technologies such as poison gas and rapid-firing machine guns made the battlefield more dangerous; faster airplanes proved useful in attacking battlefield positions, factories, and cities; neither side was able to gain an advantage.*

785

3 What happened on the Western Front? *France and Germany both suffered enormous casualties in the Battle of Verdun; the Battle of the Somme resulted in enormous casualties for the British and Germans; Germans defeated British in the Third Battle of Ypres; front lines remained unchanged.*

Battles on the Western Front

Recall What made the Verdun location special to the French? *It had been an important fortress since Roman times.*

Explain What did the Germans mean by saying they would "bleed France white"? *Germany intended to kill as many French soldiers as possible.*

Evaluate Was Britain successful in reaching their goal for the Battle of the Somme? *possible answer—Only partly: many Germans were killed, but there was no major breakthrough.*

📄 **CRF:** Biography: Edith Wharton

Info to Know

Women's Roles In addition to working at critical jobs and serving in Europe, American women contributed to the Allies' war effort in another important way by conserving food. Some 20 million homemakers signed pledge cards distributed by the government, promising not to serve meat on Mondays, to conserve other foodstuffs, and to grow their own vegetables in "Victory Gardens." In return, they received stickers to display in the windows of their homes, indicating that they were cooperating with the war effort.

Answers

Linking to Today *Today, women fill many roles in the armed forces, ranging from soldiers on the front lines to support staff on the home front, whereas in World War I women were mostly nurses.*

Reading Check *The government took over factories; civilians conserved food and materials; propaganda was produced; women joined the work force.*

Women in War

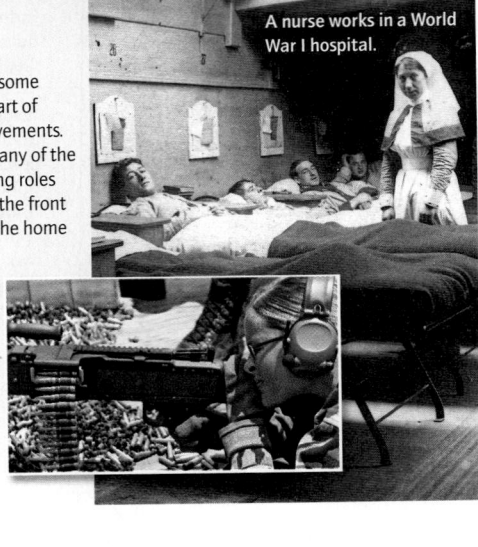

A nurse works in a World War I hospital.

In World War I, only a few hundred women fought as soldiers, nearly all in the Russian army. These soldiers were the exceptions.

Most women who wanted to help the war effort had only two options: assist on the home front or work as nurses for the armed forces. Thousands of women chose to serve as nurses. Many worked in hospitals or medical-aid stations near the war's front lines, where they faced terrible conditions while helping wounded soldiers.

The role of women in the armed forces began to change slowly after the war. In World War II, most women were still limited to non-combat roles, but some fought as soldiers or as part of organized resistance movements. Today, women serve in many of the world's armed forces, filling roles ranging from soldiers on the front lines to support staff on the home front.

Summarize How has the role of women in war changed since World War I?

An American soldier fires a machine gun. ▶

Women and the War With millions of men at battle, much of the work on the home front was done by women. Some worked in factories producing weapons and other war supplies. These women helped send important shipments of food and weapons to the front lines. Others served as nurses to wounded soldiers. The contributions women made during the war helped transform public views of what women could do. In some countries, this change helped women finally win the right to vote.

READING CHECK **Find the Main Idea** In what ways did the war affect the home front?

Battles on the Western Front

While people on the home front supported their troops, the war in Western Europe was going badly for the Allied Powers. In 1915, a series of battles had resulted in many Allied casualties.

The Italian Front In May 1915, Italy entered World War I by joining the Allied Powers. Italy's first move was to send its forces against Austria-Hungary on the Italy-Austria border. In a long series of back-and-forth battles, Italy made little progress.

The Battle of Verdun Meanwhile, the Germans were making plans for an assault on the French fortress of Verdun. Verdun had been an important French fortress since Roman times. German leaders believed that the French, unable to bear seeing the city captured, would defend it at all costs. The **Battle of Verdun** was meant solely to kill or injure as many French soldiers as possible—to "bleed France white," said the German commander.

From the start of the battle in February 1916 to its end that December, France suffered some 400,000 casualties. Germany, however, endured nearly as many. The battle left both sides weakened, and the stalemate continued.

The Battle of the Somme The British launched their own attack, intended partly to pull German troops away from Verdun, in June 1916. This British attack took place in the Somme River area of France.

The Battle of the Somme was the main Allied assault during 1916. On the first day of fighting alone, the British suffered nearly 60,000 casualties. Just as in the Battle of Verdun, by the time fighting ended in December 1916 there had been no major breakthroughs. Both sides lost an enormous number of troops.

Collaborative Learning

At Level

Women of the New Century

Research Required

1. Remind students that prior to World War I, most women worked in their homes. Tell students that there were rare exceptions in which women made history and furthered the cause of women's rights.

2. Organize students into small groups. Have students conduct research about women who made an impact on the early twentieth century, such as Marie Curie, or Amelia Earhart. Each group should select a different person.

3. Have students assign specific tasks to each group member: note taking, compiling research, etc. Presentations should include an illustration or photograph of the person and her most important accomplishments.

4. Have each group prepare a short presentation to share with the class. **LS Verbal-Linguistic**

📄 **Alternative Assessment Handbook**, Rubrics 14: Group Activity; 24: Oral Presentations; and 30: Research

The Third Battle of Ypres The year 1917 went badly for the Allies. That spring, a failed French offensive caused rebellion among some French soldiers. In July, the British began an offensive near Ypres (ee-pruh), Belgium, where two earlier German attacks had taken place. The Third Battle of Ypres was a disaster for the British, who ended the attack in November. After three years of battle in western Europe, the front lines were virtually unchanged.

READING CHECK **Summarize** What was the result of the battles on the Western Front?

War around the World

Much of the early fighting took place in Europe, but the conflict quickly became a true world war as fighting spread around the globe. Over 30 nations officially took sides in the war, and other countries became involved in less formal ways.

The Gallipoli Campaign A new power had entered the battle on the Eastern Front in late 1914, when the Ottoman Empire joined the Central Powers. The vast empire was weakening, but it still had a vital location. The Ottomans controlled an important sea passage called the Dardanelles (dahr-den-ELZ), which was part of the water route between the Black Sea and the Mediterranean. The Allies used the Dardanelles to ship supplies to Russia.

To destroy the guns and forts that lined the Dardanelles, the Allies landed a force on the Gallipoli Peninsula in the spring of 1915. After months of fighting and nearly 200,000 casualties, the Allies gave up. The **Gallipoli Campaign** was a failure.

The Ottoman Empire did suffer a major loss later in the war when its subjects in the Arabian Peninsula rebelled. To take advantage of this revolt, the British sent officer T. E. Lawrence to support the Arabs. With Lawrence's help, the Arabs overthrew Ottoman rule.

WORLD WAR I BATTLES, 1915–1917

Legend:
- Allied Powers
- Central Powers
- Neutral nations
- Farthest Central Powers advance
- Allied Powers victory
- Central Powers victory
- Undecided outcome

Map labels: North Sea, DENMARK, SWEDEN, Baltic Sea, RUSSIA, UNITED KINGDOM, NETHERLANDS, 3rd Ypres July–Nov. 1917, Elbe R., London, Berlin, Oder R., Lutsk June 1916, EASTERN FRONT, BELGIUM, GERMANY, Vimy Ridge April 1917, Cambrai Nov.–Dec. 1917, Somme July–Nov. 1916, LUX., Przemysl Sept. 1914–March 1915, Dnieper R., Paris, Verdun Feb.–Dec. 1916, 2nd Marne July–Aug. 1918, Danube R., Vienna, Budapest, Dniester R., ATLANTIC OCEAN, WESTERN FRONT, SWITZ., Caporetto Oct.–Nov. 1917, AUSTRIA-HUNGARY, Danube R., FRANCE, Po R., ROMANIA, Black Sea, ITALY, Sarajevo, SERBIA, BULGARIA, Rome, MONTENEGRO, ALBANIA, Constantinople, Gallipoli April–Dec. 1915, GREECE, OTTOMAN EMPIRE

GEOGRAPHY SKILLS INTERPRETING MAPS

Location What were the results of the major battles fought on the Western Front during this time?

0   200 Miles
0   200 Kilometers
Azimuthal equal-area projection

WORLD WAR I **787**

787

Direct Teach

Reading Focus

War around the World

Recall What did Turkish leaders claim about the Armenians? *that they were aiding the Russians*

Make Generalizations Why do you think some colonists were reluctant to help colonial rulers? *possible answer— They may have felt that their contribution would make no difference.*

Review & Assess

Close

Review with students the new kinds of technology developed for use in World War I and how war spread quickly around the world.

Review

🔲 **Online Quiz**, Section 2

Assess

SE Section 2 Assessment

📝 **Progress Assessment**: Section 2 Quiz

📝 **Alternative Assessment Handbook**

Reteach/Intervene

📝 **Interactive Reader and Study Guide**, Section 2

💿 **Interactive Skills Tutor CD-ROM**

Answers

Reading Check *Europe, Asia, Africa, and the Pacific*

788

🗽 **NEW YORK**

CC Unit 6-A5
Armenian
Massacre

THE IMPACT TODAY

The Turkish government officially denies that the Armenian deaths should be considered genocide, although most historians disagree.

The Armenian Massacre As the Gallipoli Campaign went on, a different conflict occurred elsewhere in the Ottoman Empire. In late 1914, Russia had launched an attack in the Caucasus (KAW-kuh-suhs), a mountain region that lies between the Black and Caspian seas and borders northeastern Turkey. The area was home to ethnic Armenians. Because most were Christians, Armenians formed a minority group in the largely Muslim Ottoman Empire.

Ottoman leaders claimed that the Armenians were aiding the Russians. In the spring of 1915, Ottoman leaders began forcibly removing Armenians from the Caucasus. Some 600,000 Armenians died from violence and starvation. Ottoman leaders were accused by many of **genocide**—the deliberate destruction of a racial, political, or cultural group.

Other Fighting Battles were also fought elsewhere in Asia and in Africa. Japan, for example, had declared war on Germany in 1914 as part of a military agreement with Great Britain. Far from the battlefields of Europe, Japanese forces captured German colonies in China and the Pacific. British and French troops attacked German colonies in Africa.

Allied colonies scattered around the world made many contributions to the war. For example, soldiers from all parts of the British Empire—India, Australia, Canada, New Zealand—took part in the war. Some of these people worked as laborers to keep the armies supplied. Many others fought and died in battle, such as the Algerians who fought for France.

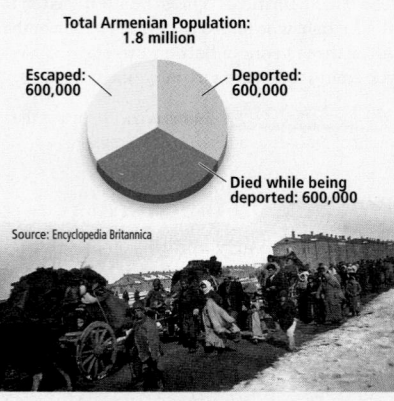

THE ARMENIAN MASSACRE

Nearly 2 million ethnic Armenians were deported to Mesopotamia and what is now Syria during World War I. During this forced relocation, hundreds of thousands starved to death or were killed by Ottoman soldiers and police.

**Total Armenian Population:
1.8 million**

Escaped: 600,000
Deported: 600,000
Died while being deported: 600,000

Source: Encyclopedia Britannica

▲ Armenians who escaped during the relocation arrive in a refugee camp.

Although some colonial peoples were reluctant to help their rulers, others volunteered to fight in the hopes that their service would help win independence. They would soon discover that these hopes were in vain.

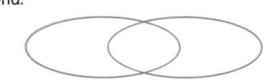 **READING CHECK Summarize** In what areas of the world did the war take place?

SECTION 2 ASSESSMENT

go.hrw.com
Online Quiz
Keyword: SHL WW1 HP

Reviewing Ideas, Terms, and People

1. **a. Describe** How did World War I differ from previous wars?
   b. Identify Cause and Effect How did the technological developments of World War I affect **trench warfare**?

2. **a. Recall** How did civilians help support the war effort?
   b. Infer How do you think **total war** affected life on the home front?

3. **a. Recall** What were the results of the **Battle of Verdun** and the Battle of the Somme?
   b. Explain Why did the Western Front change very little between 1915 and 1917?

4. **a. Recall** What happened in the **Gallipoli Campaign**?
   b. Summarize List the war's events outside of Europe.

Critical Thinking

5. **Compare** Using your notes on the section and a graphic organizer like the one below, explain how the war on the Western Front was different from the war elsewhere in the world.

FOCUS ON WRITING

6. **Description** From the perspective of a World War I soldier, write a letter describing life in the trenches. Use details from the section in your letter.

Section 2 Assessment Answers

1. **a.** new technologies and types of warfare; involved many nations
   b. Tanks, aircraft, and poison gas killed millions.

2. **a.** Civilians conserved food and materials; women joined the work force.
   b. Women joined the work force for the first time; citizens united to help their countries.

3. **a.** Both battles resulted in enormous casualties but the front lines were virtually unchanged.
   b. Both sides were evenly matched, developing technology at the same pace.

4. **a.** Allies suffered nearly 200,000 losses.
   b. The Japanese captured German colonies in China and the Pacific; British and French troops attacked German colonies in Africa.

5. West—German forces attacked first, front lines did not move, trench warfare and new technology used; Both—suffered massive casualties; East—Russian forces attacked first, front lines moved east

6. Answers will vary but should include details about trench warfare.

3 Revolution in Russia

BEFORE YOU READ

MAIN IDEA

The war and social unrest combined to push Russia to the edge of a revolution. The events that followed led to Russia's exit from the war and became a major turning point in world history.

READING FOCUS

1. What was Russia's experience in World War I?
2. What were the main events of the Russian Revolution?
3. What major events took place after the Russian Revolution?

KEY TERMS AND PEOPLE

Bolsheviks
Grigory Rasputin
Marxism-Leninism
Leon Trotsky
New Economic Policy

 NEW YORK

PI 2.5 Students investigate key events and developments in world history.

PI 4.2 Students interpret and analyze documents and artifacts related to significant developments and events in world history.

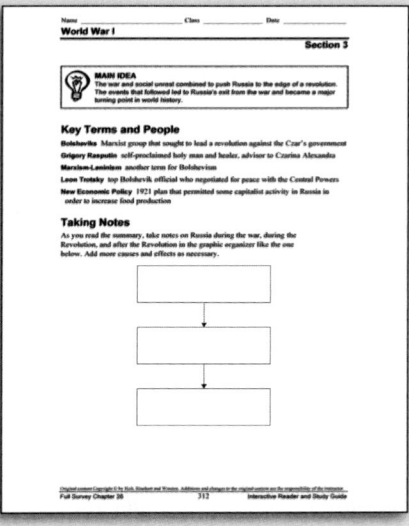

THE INSIDE STORY

How could an illiterate peasant control the Russian Empire?

Grigory Rasputin was filthy, illiterate, and believed by some people to be insane. But he was also a self-proclaimed holy man and healer as well as a trusted adviser to Russia's Czarina Alexandra.

Rasputin's influence on the Russian royal family began in the early 1900s, when he first met Czar Nicholas II and Czarina Alexandra. Their son, Alexis, suffered from hemophilia, a disease in which injuries can result in uncontrolled bleeding. Rasputin had a reputation as a man who could heal the sick, and the royal family was eager to see if he could help their son. Indeed, Rasputin seemed to relieve the boy's suffering. Rasputin soon became a common sight at the royal palace.

In the presence of the royal family, Rasputin was careful to appear as a humble, holy peasant. But his actions were very different outside the palace, where his immoral behavior soon created a scandal. When outraged Russians protested, the czar refused to believe their stories.

After Nicholas went off to lead Russia's armies in World War I, Rasputin became Alexandra's personal adviser. He helped her make decisions on a variety of issues, including political appointments and military actions. Nearly all of the decisions proved disastrous for Russia.

In December 1916, a group of Russian nobles formed a plan to murder Rasputin and save Russia from his influence. The nobles poisoned and shot Rasputin, but he did not die. Finally, they drowned him in an icy Russian river. While Rasputin could do no more harm to Russia, the nation was anything but saved. ◼

◀ **Known as the Mad Monk, Rasputin had great power over Russia.**

WORLD WAR I **789**

Preteach

Getting Started

Use the **Interactive Reader and Study Guide** to familiarize students with the section content.

📖 **Interactive Reader and Study Guide**, Section 3

Academic Vocabulary

Review with students the high-use academic term in this section.

fundamental important or vital (p. 792)

📖 **CRF**: Vocabulary Builder: Section 3

Taking Notes

Russia entered the war unprepared to meet its army's needs; Russia was crushed; Bolsheviks revolted against Czar Nicholas II; Trotsky accepted the Treaty of Brest-Litovsk; ussia had a civil war; the economy improved; the USSR was formed.

go.hrw.com
Online Resources

KEYWORD: SHL WW1
ACTIVITY: Treaty of Versailles

Teach the Main Idea

Revolution in Russia

1. **Teach** Ask students the Reading Focus questions to teach this section.

2. **Apply** Organize students into small groups. Have each group identify and list the major events in this section. Caution students not to rely solely on the time line in the chapter, as many other details are important.

3. **Review** Ask volunteers to share events they identified and write them for students to see. Have students help number the events in order while they write their own lists.

4. **Practice/Homework** Have each student create a flow chart of the major events of the Russian Revolution. **LS Verbal-Linguistic, Visual-Spatial**

📖 **Alternative Assessment Handbook**, Rubric 13: Graphic Organizers

1 What was Russia's experience in World War I? *After the revolution in 1905, there were economic problems, worker strikes, and a Marxist group sought to lead a revolution against the czar's government.*

Russia and World War I

Recall When did Czar Nicholas II promise reform? *after the revolution in 1905*

Evaluate What do you think about the government's hope that the military crisis would cause people to rally around their leadership? *possible answer—Their hopes were unrealistic because people wanted change.*

Make Inferences Why do you think the Bolsheviks gained popularity? *possible answer—the Russian people grew increasingly discontent with the Russian government and wanted reform.*

Info to Know

Russian Weather Notice the Russian soldiers' clothing in the photograph on this page. Most of Russia's extreme climate is best compared to that of Alaska, Antarctica, and Northern Canada. The huge Russian landmass is inland, away from the warming influence of coastal waters. It is also located at high latitudes, where it is cold year-round. The weather is so severe that, even today, water, rail, and road transport are interrupted or stopped entirely during winter.

TAKING NOTES

Take notes on Russia during the war, during the Revolution, and after the Revolution.

Russia and World War I

On the eve of World War I, Russia was a troubled nation. Czar Nicholas II had promised reform after the revolution of 1905, but he delivered little real change. Economic conditions grew worse, and another revolution seemed near.

The Years Before the War A small Marxist group known as the **Bolsheviks** (BOHL-shuh-viks) sought to change life in Russia through revolution. Led by Vladimir Lenin, the Bolsheviks wanted to overthrow the czar so that the proletariat—the industrial workers—could gain the power to rule Russia as a socialist country. This plan was an adaptation of Marxist ideas. Marx had predicted a spontaneous uprising of the proletariat to overthrow capitalism, but Bolsheviks had other plans. They wanted an elite group—themselves—to lead a revolution and keep much of the power over Russia. Although the Bolsheviks had little influence in the early 1900s, they gained followers as Russia's problems grew more serious.

By 1914, economic conditions in Russia were so bad that the arrival of World War I provided some relief for Nicholas and his top government officials. They hoped that the military crisis would help unite the country and cause the people to rally around their leadership.

Russia in World War I At the start of the war, Russia had an enormous army of some 6 million soldiers. As the czar had hoped, the outbreak of fighting did help provide a burst of patriotism. People from across the country rushed to join the military.

In many other ways, however, Russia was ill-prepared for war. Russian factories were not able to produce ammunition and other military supplies quickly enough to meet the army's needs. In addition, the nation's transportation system was weak. As a result, moving troops and equipment to the right places at the right times proved very difficult.

To make matters worse, the Russian military was not prepared to fight a major war. Its equipment was outdated, and many of its leaders were of poor quality. Russian officers commonly advanced on the basis of personal connections rather than actual ability.

Initially, the Russians enjoyed success on the battlefield, but the losses soon outnumbered the victories. In both victory and defeat, however, Russia's costs in human life were great. Millions of Russian soldiers were wounded or killed during the war's early battles.

Conditions Grow Worse In 1915, Czar Nicholas II decided to take personal command of the Russian forces. The move made little sense. As one of Russia's top commanders said, the czar "understood literally nothing about military matters." Nevertheless, it was now clear that the czar's fate was linked with the fate of Russia's armed forces. If they failed, so would he.

TIME LINE

Russia in Turmoil

August 1914 Russia enters World War I on the side of the Allied Powers.

March 1917 Russian citizens revolt and force Czar Nicholas II to give up power. A provisional government is established.

November 1917 In the Bolshevik Revolution, Communists led by Vladimir Lenin take over the Russian government.

790 CHAPTER 26

Skills Focus: Comparing and Contrasting

At Level

Reading Skill
Battle Preparations

1. Have students review sections two and three to recall information about German and Russian preparedness for war. Discuss with students each side's strengths and weaknesses as they went into battle.

2. Have volunteers call out their ideas about these topics as you raise them: ammunition, weapons, leadership, troops, and supplies.

3. Have each student write a paragraph contrasting the two nations' preparedness for war. **LS Verbal-Linguistic**

Alternative Assessment Handbook, Rubrics 9: Comparing and Contrasting; and 37: Writing Assignments

The war had been going badly for Russia, but once the czar took command, the situation for Russia grew even worse. A few months later the Central Powers were able to stop a major Russian offensive. That defeat destroyed the Russian soldiers' faith in their leaders. With little strength and even less confidence, the Russian army seemed doomed.

Conditions in Russia itself were even worse than they were on the battlefield. Food and other goods were growing scarce in Russian cities, and impoverished Russian peasants were growing desperate. The czar had left his wife, the unpopular Czarina Alexandra, in control of the country when he went off with the troops. She relied on the advice of **Grigory Rasputin**, a self-proclaimed holy man and healer whom many Russians viewed as corrupt and immoral. With the government under his influence, the already shaky Russian support for the monarchy dipped even lower.

READING CHECK **Find the Main Idea**
How did World War I affect Russia?

◀ A Bolshevik poster seeks to recruit soldiers during the Russian Civil War.

March 1918 The Bolshevik government signs the Treaty of Brest-Litovsk, which ends Russian involvement in World War I.

November 1920 After three years of fighting, the Russian Civil War ends with a Bolshevik victory.

The Russian Revolution

By the end of 1916, Russia was once again on the edge of a revolution. As the new year began and conditions in Russia continued to worsen, the Russian people clearly wanted change.

Revolution Begins On March 8, 1917, unhappy citizens took to the streets of Petrograd, the Russian capital, to protest the lack of food and fuel. Sympathetic police and soldiers in Petrograd refused to follow orders to shoot the rioters. The government was helpless.

While protests raged in the streets, Czar Nicholas II ordered the Duma, Russia's legislature, to disband. The Duma defied this order. With Russia's citizens, soldiers, and government all refusing to obey Nicholas, it was clear that he had lost control of the nation. On March 15, Nicholas was forced to abdicate, or step down, as czar. The Russian monarchy had come to an end.

The March revolution that forced Nicholas to step down is known as the February Revolution in Russia. At the time of the revolution, Russia used an old type of calendar that was 13 days behind the one used in the rest of Europe and the United States. Russia adopted the new calendar in 1918.

The Provisional Government After the fall of the czar, the Duma established a provisional, or temporary, government. This government was led by Aleksandr Kerensky.

December 1922
The Soviet Union is formed.

Skills Focus **INTERPRETING TIME LINES**

Summarize What actions did the Bolsheviks take in Russia between 1914 and 1922?

READING SKILLS

Understanding Sequencing What events took place in Russia in 1917 before the czar stepped down?

NEW YORK

CC Unit 6-B3
March Revolution and provisional government

Direct Teach

Reading Focus

2 **What were the main events of the Russian Revolution?** *With the Russian citizens, the army, and the Duma against him, Czar Nicholas abdicated; the Duma formed a provisional government; the Russian army collapsed; the Bolsheviks took over*

The Russian Revolution

Identify What were the Russian citizens protesting? *the lack of food and fuel*

Define What was the Duma? *Russia's legislature*

Contrast Explain the difference between Kerensky's leadership and that of Vladimir Lenin. *Kerensky's provisional government called for continued fighting in World War I, an unpopular stance with the Russians, who were tired of the war. Lenin was popular with Russians because he attacked Kerensky's government and represented change.*

Skills Focus: Interpreting Time Lines

At Level

Research Required

Social Studies Skill
A More Detailed Time Line
Materials: tape, lined paper

1. Have students tape three sheets of lined paper together end-to-end.

2. Have students use information from their text and reliable online sources to find other events that occurred in Russia during this period and add them to their time lines. Students should leave the same amount of space for each year and may attach more paper as needed. *Time lines should include some of the following events:*

late 1915: Czar Nicholas II takes command of Russian forces; late 1916: Russia on verge of a revolution; December 1916: Rasputin murdered by Russian nobles; late 1918: Russia adopts calendar used by Europe and the U.S.

3. Have students share their time lines with the class and use them as a study guide.
   LS Visual-Spatial

   Alternative Assessment Handbook, Rubric 36: Time Lines

Answers

Reading Skills *Citizens protested in Petrograd, Czar Nicholas ordered Duma to be disbanded, Duma refused.*

Time Line *took over Russian government; ended Russia's involvement in World War I; claimed victory in Russian Civil War*

Reading Check *poor economic conditions, worker strikes, unpopular czar*

The Russian Revolution

Describe What was Marxism-Leninism? *a political philosophy that called for the abolition of private property and the enforcement of social equality*

Analyze How did events in the war help the Bolsheviks? *Russia's failed military offensive in 1917 collapsed the Russian army and led to support for the Bolsheviks.*

3 What major events took place after the Russian Revolution? *Russia signed peace treaty and lost a huge territory; civil war between Bolsheviks and the White Army; Lenin's New Economic Policy*

After the Revolution

Identify What was the White Army? *a group opposing the Bolsheviks, including army leaders, political opponents, and wealthy Russians who opposed communism*

Make Inferences Why were many Russians upset by the treaty ending the war? *Russia was forced to give up huge chunks of its empire.*

🗎 **CRF:** Biography: Leon Trotsky

Answers

Faces of History *Lenin founded the Bolshevik Party and sought to establish a Communist social system.*

Reading Check *the February Revolution and the Bolshevik Revolution*

792

FACES OF HISTORY

Vladimir LENIN
1870–1924

The son of a teacher, Vladimir Lenin graduated first in his class from high school and seemed destined to be a scholar. Instead, he soon became a Marxist and fought for revolution in Russia.

When Lenin was 17 years old, his older brother was hanged for plotting to kill the Russian czar. Lenin himself soon turned against the Russian government. He founded the Bolshevik Party and sought to establish a Communist social system, in which there would be no economic classes and no private property. Today he is considered the father of the Russian Revolution.

Infer Why is Lenin considered the father of the Russian Revolution?

Many Russians were unhappy with their new leadership. The government planned to continue fighting in World War I, even though most Russians were thoroughly tired of war. Russian peasants, who simply wanted land and food, felt that Kerensky's government was doing too little to help.

Leading the opposition to Kerensky's provisional government were the Bolsheviks, who wanted a <u>fundamental</u> change in Russian government and society—an immediate Marxist revolution. They planned to abolish private property and enforce social equality, and believed that this revolution would soon sweep the world.

Bolshevism later became known as **Marxism-Leninism**, after Bolshevik leader Vladimir Lenin. Lenin had been forced to live outside Russia because of his revolutionary ideas, but he returned to Russia in April 1917. This return was arranged by Germany, which hoped Lenin would stir unrest in Russia and weaken the Russian effort in World War I.

ACADEMIC VOCABULARY
fundamental
basic

🎬 **NEW YORK**
CC Unit 6-B4
Bolshevik Revolution

The Bolshevik Revolution In mid-1917, Kerensky's government ordered a final military offensive against the Central Powers along the Eastern Front. The drive failed. Even worse, it led to widespread rebellion in the Russian army. "I have received word," wrote one officer, "that in some units the officers are being slaughtered by their own men." The weakened Russian army had collapsed.

The conditions were ideal for Lenin to lead a Bolshevik takeover. In November 1917, armed Bolshevik factory workers known as the Red

---

Guard attacked the provisional government. The October Revolution—its name came from the old Russian calendar—was brief. After a nearly bloodless struggle, Kerensky's government collapsed. Russia was now in Bolshevik hands, and Lenin became the nation's leader.

Lenin wasted no time in establishing a radical Communist program. He soon made private ownership of land illegal.

HISTORY'S VOICES

❝All private ownership of land is abolished immediately without compensation [payment to the owners]. All landowners' estates and all land belonging to the Crown, to monasteries, church lands with all their livestock and . . . property . . . are transferred to the disposition [control] of the township Land Committees.❞

—Vladimir Lenin, *Decree on Land*, October 26, 1917

The Bolsheviks gave this land to peasants. Similarly, the Bolsheviks seized Russia's factories and gave control of the factories to workers. With these actions, millions of Russians gained new power over their daily lives, but this power did not ensure that good times lay ahead.

READING CHECK **Summarize** What were the main events of the Russian Revolution?

After the Revolution

After the Bolshevik Revolution, Lenin set about ending Russia's involvement in World War I. He sent **Leon Trotsky**, a top Bolshevik official, to negotiate for peace with the Central Powers. Because Russia's army was virtually powerless, Trotsky had to accept an agreement that was harsh on Russia. Russia had finally gained peace, but was forced to give up huge chunks of its empire.

Civil War The Bolsheviks' acceptance of the treaty upset many Russians deeply. As a result, some of the Bolsheviks' opponents organized into what came to be called the White Army. The Whites included some army leaders, political opponents of the Bolsheviks, and wealthy Russians who opposed Lenin's Communist system. The only thing that united them was their opposition to the Bolsheviks. The Whites received some military help from countries that opposed the Bolsheviks, such as France and the United States.

Differentiating Instruction

Below Level

Struggling Readers

Standard English Mastery

1. Have students read Lenin's decree in the text labeled History's Voices above. Read it aloud to students to facilitate understanding.

2. Have students paraphrase each of the two sentences of Lenin's decree in their own words.

3. Have students add several more sentences to the decree, in which Lenin explains to the people the reason he is taking these drastic steps.

4. Allow time for students to exchange papers and read each other's work. Students should make any necessary revisions to align their work with standard English usage. 🔲 **Verbal-Linguistic**

🗎 **Alternative Assessment Handbook**, Rubric 43: Writing to Persuade

For three years, civil war raged between Lenin's Bolshevik Red Army and the White Army. Millions of Russians died in the fighting and famines that swept across Russia, until the Bolsheviks triumphed in late 1920.

New Economic Policy The civil war pushed Russia's collapsing economy to the edge of total ruin. Especially hard hit were poor peasants and workers, who had been forced to endure terrible sacrifices in order to win the war.

Lenin responded to this crisis in 1921. He introduced the **New Economic Policy**, a plan that permitted some capitalist activity. Peasants, for example, could sell their food at a profit. The plan was meant to encourage more food production, which Russia badly needed.

The Soviet Union By 1922 the Russian economy was beginning to improve. That same year, Russia reunited with several neighboring lands that had been part of the Russian Empire before 1917. The new country was called the Union of Soviet Socialist Republics—also known as the Soviet Union. Russia's Communist leadership dominated the new country.

While the Soviet Union's economy gained strength, Lenin's own health was failing. After a series of strokes, he died in 1924. Lenin had no clear successor, and his death soon led to a struggle for control of the Soviet Union.

READING CHECK **Sequence** What events took place after the Russian Revolution?

Lenin's Call to Power

Lenin issued his "Call to Power" on October 24, 1917—according to the old Russian calendar—urging Russians to rise up and seize power from the provisional government.

"I am writing these lines on the evening of the 24th. The situation is critical in the extreme. In fact it is now absolutely clear that to delay the uprising would be fatal.

"With all my might I urge comrades to realize that everything now hangs by a thread; that we are confronted by problems which are not to be solved by conferences or congresses (even congresses of Soviets), but exclusively by peoples, by the masses, by the struggle of the armed people.

". . . We must not wait. We must at all costs, this very evening, this very night, arrest the government, having first disarmed the officer cadets, and so on.

"We must not wait! We may lose everything! . . .

"All districts, all regiments, all forces must be mobilized at once . . .

"The government is tottering. It must be given the death-blow at all costs."

Skills FOCUS **READING LIKE A HISTORIAN**

1. **Explain** What did Lenin want Russians to do? Why?
2. **Analyzing Primary Sources** What words does Lenin use to try to convince readers to follow his instructions?

See **Skills Handbook**, p. H25

SECTION 3 ASSESSMENT

go.hrw.com
Online Quiz
Keyword: SHL WW1 HP

Reviewing Ideas, Terms, and People

1. **a. Recall** What was the condition of the Russian military at the beginning of World War I?
   b. Summarize How did the **Bolsheviks** plan to change Russian society?
   c. Make Judgments Do you think that Czar Nicholas II's decision to take over as commander in chief of the Russian army was wise? Why or why not?

2. **a. Identify** What role did Vladimir Lenin have in Russia in 1917?
   b. Elaborate Why do you think many Russians were anxious for radical change in 1917?

3. **a. Recall** When did the Russian Civil War begin?
   b. Identify Cause and Effect Why did the Russian economy begin to improve after the civil war?

Critical Thinking

4. **Sequence** Using your notes on the section and a graphic organizer like the one below, identify the causes and effects of the Russian Revolution.

FOCUS ON WRITING

5. **Exposition** In a paragraph, explain why Lenin and the Bolsheviks took the actions they did between 1917 and 1924. Use details from the section to support your explanation. Be sure to include information about Bolshevik political and economic goals.

WORLD WAR I **793**

Section 3 Assessment Answers

1. **a.** big army, but not modernized
   b. by abolishing private property and establishing social equality
   c. possible answer—No, because he understood little about military matters.

2. **a.** Lenin was the Bolshevik leader when conditions were ideal for a takeover of the government.
   b. Most Russians were tired of war, and the peasants wanted land and food.

3. **a.** when the White Army rose up against the Bolsheviks

   b. Allowing the peasants to sell their food for a profit encouraged more food production and improved the economy.

4. Causes—Russia signs peace treaty and loses huge part of its empire; opponents of Bolshevism organize into the White Army; Effects—millions die in fighting and famine; Russia's economy collapses

5. possible details—poor economic conditions; unpopular czar; Bolsheviks believed that Marxism-Leninism would solve Russia's problems

Getting Started

Use the **Interactive Reader and Study Guide** to familiarize students with the section content.

📄 **Interactive Reader and Study Guide,** Section 4

Academic Vocabulary

Review with students the high-use academic terms in this section.

assessed evaluated or determined (p. 797)

generation group of people born and living about the same time (p. 798)

📄 **CRF:** Vocabulary Builder: Section 4

Taking Notes

The United States entered the war; Germany advanced into France; Allied forces combined tank and aircraft use; Central Powers were defeated; peace treaties were negotiated; economies were devastated; many countries experienced political unrest.

SECTION 4 The War Ends

BEFORE YOU READ

 NEW YORK

PI 2.3 Students analyze evidence critically.

PI 4.2 Students interpret and analyze documents and artifacts related to significant developments and events in world history.

MAIN IDEA

After several years of bloody stalemate—and the entry of the United States into the conflict—the Allied Powers finally prevailed. The peace, however, proved difficult to establish.

READING FOCUS

1. Why did the United States enter the war?
2. What events led to the end of the fighting?
3. What issues made the peace process difficult?
4. What were the costs of the war?

KEY TERMS AND PEOPLE

Woodrow Wilson
U-boats
Zimmermann Note
armistice
Fourteen Points
Treaty of Versailles
League of Nations
mandates
Balfour Declaration

THE INSIDE STORY

Why would Germany attack a passenger liner? For passengers packing their bags for the ocean voyage from New York to Great Britain, the advertisement in the newspaper must have been alarming. The notice was from the German government, and it warned that any ship approaching Great Britain was subject to attack.

Still, the *Lusitania* was a passenger liner. It carried nearly 2,000 innocent civilians. Surely German submarines would not attack a helpless, harmless vessel like the *Lusitania*.

The Germans, however, felt that they could not trust passenger ships. The British routinely hid war supplies on civilian ships, using them to transport guns and ammunition across the ocean. Germany couldn't afford to simply ignore passenger ships. Sinking anything that sailed into or out of Great Britain was a safer policy.

In early May 1915, when a German submarine spotted the *Lusitania* off the coast of Ireland in the Atlantic Ocean, the submarine's commander did not hesitate. The submarine fired a single torpedo, which struck the ship squarely. This blast set off another, larger explosion inside the ship. Badly damaged, the *Lusitania* sank in a mere 18 minutes. Nearly 1,200 people lost their lives, including more than 120 U.S. citizens. ◼

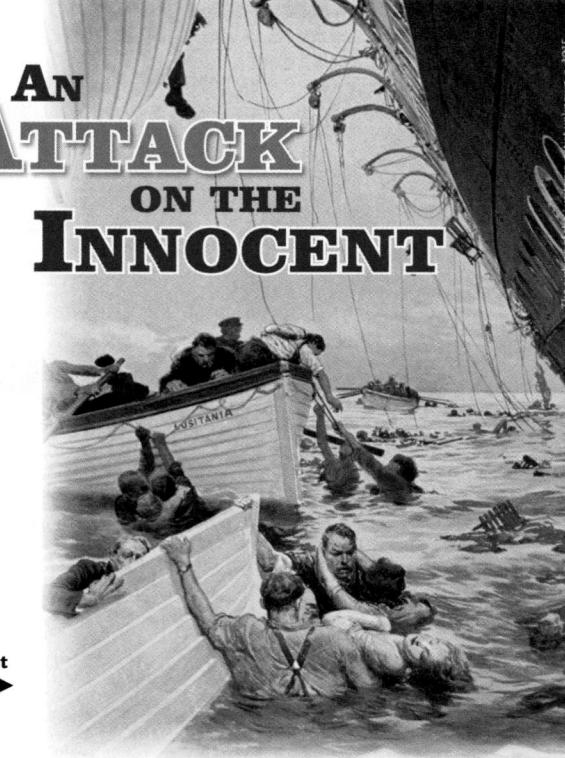

AN ATTACK ON THE INNOCENT

The *Lusitania* sank so quickly that many passengers were drowned. ▶

Teach the Main Idea

At Level

The War Ends

1. **Teach** Ask students the Reading Focus questions to teach this section.

2. **Apply** Have students create a cause-and-effect flow chart listing the main events they identify in each section of this chapter.

3. **Review** For each section, ask volunteers to share the events they discovered. Write the events on a class flow chart for students to see and have them revise the flow charts as necessary. Encourage students to add to

their flow charts as they review the section and to use them as a study guides.

4. **Practice/Homework** Have each student write a one-paragraph summary of the major events of the war's end. 🅻🅂 **Verbal-Linguistic, Visual-Spatial**

📄 **Alternative Assessment Handbook,** Rubric 13: Graphic Organizers

The United States Enters the War

German attacks on ships carrying American passengers angered the American people and their leaders. Those attacks, as well as information about a German plan to have Mexico attack the United States, pushed the United States into World War I.

American Neutrality In the early years of the war the United States was neutral, although the American public generally supported the Allies. Still, most Americans agreed with President **Woodrow Wilson**, who did not want to become involved in the huge conflict on the other side of the Atlantic Ocean. He believed that the United States should stay out of the affairs of other nations. In 1916, in fact, Wilson used the slogan "He kept us out of war" to help win reelection.

Trouble on the Seas Remaining neutral was not easy when Germany attacked civilian ships. These attacks were part of a policy called unrestricted submarine warfare. Under this policy, any ship traveling in the waters around Great Britain was subject to attack by German submarines, or **U-boats**. Germany initially used its U-boats to attack British naval vessels, but then began targeting merchant ships delivering goods to Great Britain. Targeting merchant ships was an effective tactic, since the island of Great Britain depended heavily on supplies shipped on the seas.

The passenger ship *Lusitania* was sunk under the German policy of unrestricted warfare, killing some 1,200 people, including over 120 Americans. The sinking of the *Lusitania* was followed in August and September 1915 by two more sinkings in which more American citizens died.

The U.S. government complained bitterly to Germany about the loss of American lives. Fearing U.S. entry into the war, Germany finally agreed to stop attacking passenger ships.

By 1917, though, German leaders realized that, to defeat the powerful British navy, they would need to return to unrestricted submarine warfare. This act might bring the United States into the war. The German leaders hoped, however, that they could defeat the Allied Powers before U.S. forces could have an impact.

FACES OF HISTORY
Woodrow WILSON
1856–1924

U.S. president Woodrow Wilson is often remembered for his efforts for world peace. During the early years of World War I, Wilson worked tirelessly for peace, winning reelection in 1916 in part by promising to keep the United States out of the war.

By the following year, however, Wilson felt that the war was becoming a serious threat to the world's future. He hoped that a victory by the Allied Powers could help bring about a lasting peace and urged Congress to declare war. His Fourteen Points speech proposed the League of Nations, which would help prevent future wars. For his peacemaking efforts, Wilson earned the Nobel Peace Prize in 1919.

Summarize How did Wilson work for world peace?

The Zimmermann Note The repeated attacks on shipping moved the United States closer to declaring war against Germany. In February of 1917, the discovery of the so-called Zimmermann Note provided the final push. The **Zimmermann Note** was a secret message from German diplomat Arthur Zimmermann to officials in Mexico in which Germany proposed that Mexico attack the United States. In return, Germany promised, Mexico would gain the U.S. states of Texas, Arizona, and New Mexico, all of which had once belonged to Mexico. German leaders hoped that an American war with Mexico would keep the United States out of the war in Europe.

The Zimmermann Note greatly angered the American public, which now began to call for war against Germany. After all, Americans had much in common with the Allied Powers. Many Americans traced their ancestry to Great Britain, for example, and the two nations shared the same language and many cultural traditions. The United States also had strong financial ties to the Allied Powers and was selling millions of dollars' worth of war goods to Britain each week.

By early 1917, the various forces pushing the United States toward war were too strong to resist. In April 1917, the United States entered the war on the side of the Allied Powers.

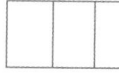

TAKING NOTES

Take notes on the events that led to the war's end, the peace process, and the war's costs.

READING CHECK **Identify Cause and Effect** How did unrestricted submarine warfare affect U.S. entry into the war?

---

❷ What events led to the end of the fighting? *As Germany advanced toward Paris, they lost 900,000 troops. American troops arrived, and the Alllies combined the use of tanks and aircraft.*

The End of the Fighting

Explain Even though the Americans had just declared war, what reasons for hope did the Germans have? *It would be months before American troops would arrive, and Russia was out of the war.*

Identify What did the Russian collapse allow Germany to do? *transfer troops from the Eastern Front back to France*

Evaluate In what ways were the Germans likely unprepared for the Allies' use of tanks and aircraft at the Second Battle of the Marne? *possible answer—They had suffered heavy losses, had young recruits and a poor food supply, and could not compete with the new technology.*

Teaching Tip

Suggest that students read the novel *All Quiet on the Western Front*, which was first published in 1928. Set late in World War I, the book gives a clear picture of the war's impact on both sides.

Answers

Reading Like a Historian 1. *fan— shows it was hot; block of ice—shows that American patience was lessening;*
2. *a supporter, because it appears that the ice will certainly melt; Uncle Sam appears angry or frustrated*

Reading like a Historian

U.S. Neutrality

Interpreting Political Cartoons Many Americans initially thought of World War I as a far-off European conflict that had little effect on the United States. They did not want to become involved in the fighting. However, as the war continued and as Germany attacked neutral ships with American passengers, American feelings slowly changed. This cartoon took a stand on the American position of neutrality.

To interpret what this cartoon says about American involvement in the war, think about

• the text and symbols used in the cartoon
• the artist's message

Melting, by Lute Pease, c. 1917

The figure of Uncle Sam represents the United States.

This block of ice labeled "Patience with Germany" is melting.

PATIENCE WITH GERMANY

Skills FOCUS **READING LIKE A HISTORIAN**

1. **Symbols** Why did the artist use a fan and a block of ice in this cartoon?
2. **Message** Was this cartoon created by a supporter or an opponent of U.S. entry into the war? How can you tell?

See **Skills Handbook, p. H27**

The End of the Fighting

FOCUS ON NEW YORK

New Yorkers made up about 10 percent of all U.S. troops in the war. Among the most celebrated military units to serve was the 369th Infantry, known as the Harlem Hell Fighters. This African American unit served a record 191 days in the trenches.

German leaders knew that the U.S. decision to enter the war would dramatically increase the strength of the Allied Powers. To win the war, Germany and the other Central Powers would have to deal a decisive blow before the United States had time to raise an army, train soldiers, and ship troops and supplies to the front lines.

A New German Offensive Germany's opportunity to win the war before the U.S. military could mobilize came with Russia's withdrawal from the war. Russia had endured revolution and civil war, and by the end of 1917 was out of the war entirely. With German troops no longer needed to fight Russia on the Eastern Front, Germany could launch a new offensive in the west.

Germany transferred troops back to France, and in March 1918, launched a major assault on the Western Front. For a while, German forces made great progress against Allied defenders, advancing to within 40 miles of the French capital of Paris.

The offensive came at a high cost to Germany, however. By the end of June, they had lost 800,000 troops. Also by that time, hundreds of thousands of Americans had arrived in Europe. These soldiers helped on the battlefield, but they also gave the Allies hope—and discouraged the Germans.

German Collapse Slowly, the balance of power shifted. In the Second Battle of the Marne, Allied forces stopped the German assault—just as they had stopped the

---

Skills Focus: Making Oral Presentations   At Level

Reading Like a Historian Skill
A BBC News Report

1. Organize students into groups of six or seven. Tell students they are reporters preparing a radio newscast for the British Broadcasting Corporation (BBC) about the collapse of Germany in 1918.

2. Tell students to organize their groups as follows: one member is the anchor at the news desk who introduces each reporter, another is a reporter describing the retreat of Allied troops; another reporter interviews people on

the streets of London; the remaining students are the people being interviewed.

3. Have groups perform their broadcasts for the class. Encourage students to speak with appropriate accents and use expressions of the period. 🄛 **Verbal-Linguistic, Kinesthetic**

📖 **Alternative Assessment Handbook**, Rubrics 24: Oral Presentations; 33: Skits and Reader's Theater

Germans at the Marne in 1914. Now the Allies went on the offensive. Combining effective use of tanks and aircraft, Allied forces gained huge amounts of territory. Many Germans simply gave up without a fight, knowing that Germany was a defeated force.

HISTORY'S VOICES

"[German] officers in particular inform us of the weakness of their forces, the youth of their recruits, and the influence of the American entry. They are depressed by their heavy losses, by the poor quality of their food . . . They are worried and begin to doubt German power."

—French report on German morale, September 1918

In October Allied forces broke through the heavily fortified Hindenburg Line. Germany's end was near. Soon German leaders approached the Allies seeking an **armistice**, or truce. Peace terms were agreed to on November 11, 1918. By this time, the other Central Powers had admitted defeat. World War I was over.

READING CHECK Summarize How did fighting come to an end?

A Difficult Peace

Although peace had come to the battlefield, the leaders of the war's major countries still had to work out a formal peace agreement. This task would prove to be difficult.

Differing Allied Goals In early 1918, while fighting was still going on, Woodrow Wilson had announced his vision of world peace. This plan for peace was called the **Fourteen Points**. These points included the reduction of weapons and the right of all people to choose their own governments. He also proposed forming an organization in which the world's nations would join to protect one another from aggression.

Not everyone shared Wilson's goals. In fact, the leaders of the four major Allies—Great Britain, France, the United States, and Italy—had very different ideas about a peace treaty. The French, led by Georges Clemenceau, wanted to punish Germany. Clemenceau also wanted Germany to pay for the costs of the war.

Great Britain's David Lloyd George stood somewhere between Clemenceau and Wilson. He also wanted to punish Germany, yet he did not want to see Germany weakened. He was

anxious, for example, that Germany be able to stop the spread of communism from Russia.

Italy's leader Vittorio Orlando hoped to gain territory for his nation. He was disappointed to find himself largely ignored by other leaders during the peace talks.

The Treaty of Versailles After difficult negotiations, the Allies finally compromised on the **Treaty of Versailles**. The treaty was named after the French Palace of Versailles, where the treaty signing took place.

The treaty came much closer to Clemenceau's vision than to Wilson's. Germany was forced to pay an enormous amount of money to the war's victims. The treaty also **assessed** responsibility for the war. Germany was forced to take full responsibility for the conflict.

Other parts of the Treaty of Versailles were designed to weaken Germany. The treaty forced Germany to limit the size of its military. Germany also had to return conquered lands to France and to Russia. Other German lands were taken to form the newly independent nation of Poland, and German colonies around the globe were given to various world powers.

Germans were furious about the humiliating terms of the treaty, but they had no choice but to accept them. Germany signed the treaty on June 28, 1919. The reparations crippled the German economy and the bitterness caused by the Treaty of Versailles would have an effect on German politics in the years to come.

Yet the treaty did contain one victory for Wilson. It established the organization of world governments he had envisioned in his Fourteen Points. This organization was called the **League of Nations**. The League's main goals were to encourage international cooperation and to keep peace between nations. But the League did not represent all the world's nations. Germany, for example, was excluded from the League. In addition, Wilson was unable to convince the U.S. government to ratify the Treaty of Versailles, as some Americans worried that the League of Nations would drag them into another far-off war. The U.S. absence greatly weakened the League.

Other Treaties Allied leaders also created separate agreements with all of the defeated Central Powers. These treaties made important changes to Europe.

ACADEMIC VOCABULARY

assessed evaluated or determined

---

❸ What issues made the peace process difficult? *Each of the four major Allies had different goals, which made it difficult for them to come to an agreement.*

A Difficult Peace

Explain What did France want to do to Germany? Why? *to severely punish Germany and have them pay for the costs of the war; because France had been severely damaged in the war*

Contrast In what way was the goal of Italy's leader different from those of the other negotiators? *He wanted to gain territory for his nation.*

Evaluate What are some possible reasons Allied leaders created separate agreements with all the defeated Central Powers? *possible answer— Many of the nations caused little of the war's destruction and would not likely pose a threat to the Allies in the future.*

📑 **CRF**: Primary Source: The Fourteen Points

Biography

Joan Miró (1893–1983) Spanish oil painter Joan Miró is known for his Surrealist works characterized by bright colors and fanciful shapes. Miró was born in Barcelona, Spain, where he studied art. Many of his works depict a light-hearted fantasy world, and others are somewhat disturbing. Both types were typical of Surrealist work. In 1919 Miró traveled to Paris, where his work was influenced by Dada and Cubism. Though he worked in other media such as ceramics and tapestry, he is known today for his delightful, amusing paintings.

Answers

Reading Check *The Allies used tanks and aircraft at the Marne, then broke through the Hindenburg Line, and Germans sought an armistice.*

Skills Focus: Analyzing Alternative Points of View

At Level

Research Required

Reading Like a Historian Skill
Each Country's Wish

1. Have students list the five Allied Powers. *France, Russia, Great Britain, Italy, the United States*

2. Organize the class into four groups. Assign one group to each of the following: France, Russia, Great Britain, and Italy.

3. Have each group conduct research about its assigned country in World War I and write goals, as Woodrow Wilson did for the peace negotiations, representing their country.

4. Have volunteers share their ideas while their classmates take notes. Ask students to select one idea and write a paragraph supporting it.
   🅛 **Interpersonal, Verbal-Linguistic**

   📑 **Alternative Assessment Handbook**, Rubrics 14: Group Activity; and 43: Writing to Persuade

797

4 What were the costs of the war?
Nearly nine million soldiers died and millions more were wounded or taken prisoner; many national economies were destroyed; some nations and English colonies experienced political unrest.

The Costs of the War

Explain How did influenza spread worldwide? *The disease spread rapidly in crowded military conditions and soldiers carried it home at war's end.*

Contrast How were the economies of the United States and Japan different from those of France and Russia? *The United States and Japan prospered during the war; France and Russia's economies were destroyed.*

🖭 **Map Transparency:** Europe and the Middle East

Interpreting Maps
Europe and the Middle East

Location Name the seven new nations that were formed from formerly Russian land after the war. *Finland, Estonia, Latvia, Lithuania, East Prussia, Poland*

Human/Environment Interaction What are some reasons that Luxembourg became an occupied zone? *It shared a long border with the newly-reduced Germany and needed protection from invasion.*

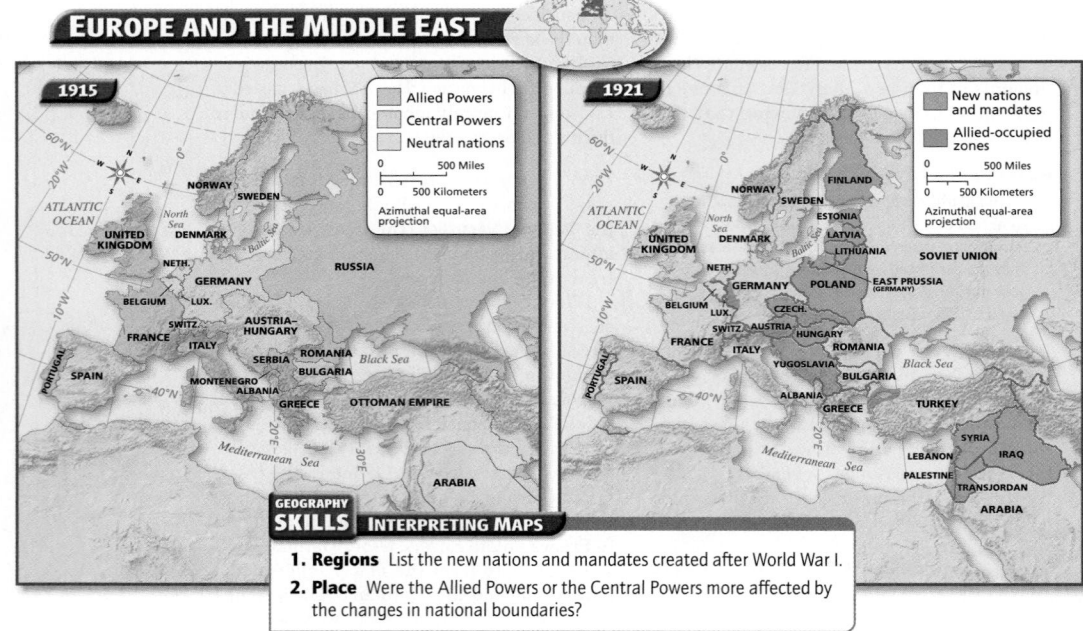

EUROPE AND THE MIDDLE EAST

1915
- Allied Powers
- Central Powers
- Neutral nations

0   500 Miles
0   500 Kilometers
Azimuthal equal-area projection

1921
- New nations and mandates
- Allied-occupied zones

0   500 Miles
0   500 Kilometers
Azimuthal equal-area projection

GEOGRAPHY SKILLS **INTERPRETING MAPS**

1. **Regions** List the new nations and mandates created after World War I.
2. **Place** Were the Allied Powers or the Central Powers more affected by the changes in national boundaries?

ACADEMIC VOCABULARY
generation group of people born and living about the same time

THE IMPACT TODAY
Scientists today are worried that a type of influenza known as avian flu, or bird flu, might turn into another worldwide flu epidemic.

🎬 **NEW YORK**
CC Unit 6-A3
Impacts of World War I

The vast lands of Austria-Hungary and the Ottoman Empire were broken apart, forming the independent nations of Austria, Hungary, Yugoslavia, Czechoslovakia, and Turkey. German territories in Africa and the Pacific Ocean were also given to other countries to control.

In the Middle East, former Ottoman lands were turned into **mandates**, or territories to be ruled by European powers. Syria and Lebanon became French mandates, and Palestine and Iraq became British mandates. Meanwhile in Europe, the Zionist movement to create a Jewish state in the Middle East was growing. In 1917, Britain issued the **Balfour Declaration**, which favored establishing a Jewish state in Palestine, the ancient Jewish homeland. Later, Britain created Transjordan from the Palestine Mandate and named Abdullah as Transjordan's first ruler. European nations were supposed to control the mandates only until those territories were able to govern themselves. In reality, mandates became colonies.

 READING CHECK **Summarize** Why was it so difficult to work out a peace agreement?

The Costs of the War

World War I was the most devastating conflict the world had ever seen. It would take years for the nations involved to recover.

Human Costs Nearly 9 million soldiers were killed in battle. Millions more were wounded or taken prisoner. In nations such as Germany, Russia, and France, almost an entire generation of young men died or were wounded in the war.

In the spring of 1918, the suffering became worse when a deadly outbreak of influenza swept across the globe. The disease spread rapidly in crowded military conditions and as soldiers made their way home at the war's end. Worldwide, perhaps 50 million people or more died in the epidemic.

Economic Costs The war also destroyed national economies. In places such as France, Belgium, and Russia, where much fighting took place, farmland and cities alike were devastated. Economic chaos soon spread misery throughout many parts of Europe.

Differentiating Instruction

Below Level

English-Language Learners

Materials: 8 ½ x 11" unlined paper, colored markers

1. Have students picture how farms in eastern France would have looked after battles were fought. Remind students that most men had been killed or wounded.

2. Tell students they will create uplifting propaganda to inspire people rebuilding their lives after the war. Suggest songs and poems, recipes appropriate for those with limited resources, workshop ideas for repairing homes, instructions for how to reclaim battle-scarred farmland, and so on.

3. Have each student develop one concept to contribute to a class pamphlet. Instruct students to leave a 1" margin on the left side blank for binding

4. Compile the pamphlet ideas into a simple binder and display in the classroom.
LS **Intrapersonal, Visual-Spatial**

📝 **Alternative Assessment Handbook,** Rubrics 3: Artwork; and 40: Writing Assignments

Answers

Interpreting Maps 1. *Finland, Estonia, Latvia, Lithuania, East Prussia, Poland, Austria, Hungary, Czechoslovakia, Yugoslavia, Iraq, Palestine, Lebanon, Syria;* **2.** *Refer to map*

Reading Check *because each of the four major Allies had different goals*

The war also cost Europe its role as the dominant economic region of the world. Countries such as the United States and Japan prospered during the war. In addition, countries that had formerly relied on European imports turned to new sources or developed their own products.

Political Changes World War I caused widespread political unrest, including the Communist revolution in Russia. After the war, the monarchies in Austria-Hungary, Germany, and the Ottoman Empire were all overthrown, and many other countries also experienced political upheaval. This widespread political and social turmoil would help shape the world in the years to come.

Unrest in Colonies The growing unrest affected European colonies as well. Many colonists who had fought in the war had heard the Allied leaders speak noble words about the importance of democracy and freedom. After they shed blood for these ideals on behalf of their colonial rulers, the colonists came to expect these rights for themselves.

Instead, the colonists soon found that their wartime sacrifices had not won them any new freedoms. The powers of Europe simply split up the lands controlled by the German, Austro-Hungarian, and Ottoman empires and distributed them to other colonial powers. Independence would have to wait.

READING CHECK **Find the Main Idea** What were the costs of the war?

EFFECTS OF WORLD WAR I

HUMAN COSTS
- 8.5 million soldiers died.
- 13 million civilians died.
- 21.2 million soldiers were wounded.

ECONOMIC COSTS
- The war cost the world's nations an estimated $332 billion.

POLITICAL CHANGES
- Austria-Hungary and the Ottoman Empire were broken apart.
- Germany was greatly weakened.
- The Russian monarchy was overthrown.
- New countries and colonies formed in Europe and the Middle East.
- European colonies in Africa and Asia changed hands.

▲ The war destroyed large areas of Europe.

SECTION 4 ASSESSMENT

go.hrw.com
Online Quiz
Keyword: SHL WW1 HP

Reviewing Ideas, Terms, and People

1. **a. Describe** What role did **U-boats** have in World War I?
   b. Identify Cause and Effect Why did the United States enter the war in 1917?

2. **a. Recall** What was the outcome of Germany's last offensive?
   b. Explain What effect did U.S. troops have on the war?

3. **a. Describe** How did the **Treaty of Versailles** affect Germany?
   b. Compare and Contrast How did the various Allied goals for peace differ?

4. **a. Recall** What event that began in 1918 added to the suffering caused by the fighting in World War I?
   b. Predict How do you think the political unrest after World War I will affect the world in the years that follow?

Critical Thinking

5. **Identify Cause and Effect** Using your notes on the section and a graphic organizer like the one below, explain what you believe was the most significant effect of World War I.

World War I → [ ]

FOCUS ON WRITING

6. **Description** Choose one of the three types of costs of World War I—human, economic, or political. Write a newspaper article explaining those costs.

WORLD WAR I **799**

Section 4 Assessment Answers

1. **a.** used by Germans to attack ships near Britain, causing U.S. to enter war.
   b. Germany broke its promise to stop attacking passenger ships and attempted to push Mexico to attack the United States.

2. **a.** They lost 800,000 troops.
   b. helped shift the balance of power

3. **a.** Reparations required by the Treaty of Versailles hurt the German economy.
   b. France wanted to punish Germany; Italy wanted territory; U.S. wanted peace; Great Britain wanted to punish Germany without weakening it

4. **a.** a deadly outbreak of influenza
   b. possible answer—Monarchies would be overthrown and new governments formed.

5. possible answer—World War I resulted in the overthrowing of many monarchies and the growth of communism, which would shape the world for many years to come.

6. possible answers—human: millions of lives lost; economic: some nations' economies badly hurt; political: redrawn boundaries

---

799

Causes of World War I

Word Help

sheathe place into a case or covering

commend to entrust for care or preservation

implore to call or pray for earnestly

premeditated deliberately planned; calculated

conciliatory that which will gain goodwill or favor

Info to Know

Wilhelm II When his grandfather died and his father passed soon after, Wilhelm became Kaiser of Germany at age 29. During his thirty-year reign, the indecisive leader lost control of the military and failed to negotiate peace when it was within his grasp. When Germany at last surrendered, Wilhelm gave up the throne and exiled himself in the Netherlands. This ended the monarchy in Germany and soon after, Hitler rose to power.

Activity **Analyzing Primary Sources** Have students volunteer what they know about sound technology of the World War I era. *Examples include victrolas, microphones, the telegraph, and early radios.* Tell students they are news reporters in 1918. Ask them the following questions: How would you make sure the news you report is accurate? What tools are used today that help to ensure accurate reporting?

CHAPTER

26 Document-Based Investigation

Causes of World War I

NEW YORK STANDARDS

PI **4.2** Students interpret and analyze documents and artifacts related to significant developments and events in world history.

PI **4.4** Students analyze different interpretations of important events in world history.

Historical Context The documents below provide information about the causes of World War I.

Task Examine the documents and answer the questions that follow. After you have studied all the documents, you will be asked to write an essay about the causes of World War I. You will need to use evidence from these selections and from the chapter to support the position you take in your essay.

DOCUMENT 1

The German Perspective

Wilhelm II, the ruler of Germany, gave this speech from the balcony of the royal palace in Berlin on July 31, 1914.

> A momentous hour has struck for Germany. Envious rivals everywhere force us to legitimate defense. The sword has been forced into our hands. I hope that in the event that my efforts to the very last moment do not succeed in bringing our opponents to reason and in preserving peace, we may use the sword, with the help of God, so that we may sheathe it again with honor. War will demand enormous sacrifices by the German people, but we shall show the enemy what it means to attack Germany. And so I commend you to God. Go forth into the churches, kneel down before God, and implore his help for our brave army.

DOCUMENT 2

The British Perspective

On January 5, 1918, British prime minister David Lloyd George made this statement about Great Britain's war goals.

> We are not fighting a war of aggression against the German people. Their leaders have persuaded them that they are fighting a war of self-defence against a league of rival nations bent on the destruction of Germany. That is not so. The destruction or disruption of Germany or the German people has never been a war aim with us from the first day of this war to this day. Most reluctantly, and indeed quite unprepared for the dreadful ordeal, we were forced to join in this war in self-defence . . . we had to join in the struggle or stand aside and see Europe go under and brute force triumph over public right and international justice. It was only the realization of that dreadful alternative that forced the British people into war.

DOCUMENT 3

The Allied Powers Perspective

After the war's end, the victorious Allied Powers formed a commission to determine responsibility for the war. Below are the conclusions of the commission, which were issued on May 6, 1919.

> 1. The War was premeditated by the Central Powers together with their Allies, Turkey and Bulgaria, and was the result of acts deliberately committed in order to make it unavoidable.

> 2. Germany, in agreement with Austria-Hungary, deliberately worked to defeat all the many conciliatory proposals made by the Entente Powers and their repeated efforts to avoid war.

Skills Focus: Recognizing Bias in Primary Sources   At Level

Reading Like a Historian Skill
Kaiser Wilhelm II

1. Read Wilhelm II's speech above aloud to the students. Explain that this indecisive leader encouraged his military leaders to make their own decisions. Thus, he lost control of them even when he might have been able to negotiate peace.

2. Have groups identify key words or phrases in Document 1 above that support Kaiser Wilhelm's view of Germany as a peaceful nation that is under attack.

3. Guide students in a discussion of the persuasiveness of Kaiser Wilhelm's speech. If they were Germans living in 1914, would they have believed the speech? Why or why not? **LS** **Interpersonal, Verbal-Linguistic**

   Alternative Assessment Handbook, Rubrics 16: Judging Information; and 40: Writing to Describe

The American Perspective

The cartoon at right was created by American artist Orson Lowell. Published in March 1918, it shows Germany's Kaiser Wilhelm II hanging by a noose attached to a plank of wood marked "Greedy Ambition." Other figures in the cartoon represent Great Britain, the United States, France, and other countries that fought the Central Powers during World War I.

Now Then, All Together!, by Orson Lowell, 1918

DOCUMENT 1
a. Interpret Who does Wilhelm blame for the war?
b. Make Judgments The day after Wilhelm gave this speech, Germany declared war on Russia. Do you think that action supports or contradicts what he said in his speech?

DOCUMENT 2
a. Explain What words does Lloyd George use to suggest that Great Britain did not want war?
b. Evaluate Would Lloyd George agree or disagree with Document 1?

DOCUMENT 3
a. Identify What nation or nations does this document blame for causing the war?
b. Evaluate Do you think the authors of this document were biased about the causes of the war? Why or why not?

DOCUMENT 4
a. Draw Conclusions What are the figures attempting to do to the globe? Why?
b. Interpret Who does the artist blame for the war? Does he believe that others feel the same way?

DOCUMENT-BASED ESSAY QUESTION

Why might the different sides in the war view the causes of the war differently? Using the documents above and information from the chapter, form a thesis that explains your position. Then write a short essay to support your position.

See **Skills Handbook**, pp. H25, H27, H29

Differentiating Instruction

Advanced Learners/Gifted and Talented

Background: Tell students that leaders of free nations often present formal addresses to their countrymen and their allies like the one given by David Lloyd George in Document 2. Sometimes such speeches are written by professionals known as ghost writers.

1. Have a volunteer read George's address aloud dramatically.
2. Organize students into small groups and have each group choose a country that was involved in World War I, and is not represented among the documents. Have students conduct research to identify the country's leader and the reasons that nation became involved in the war.
3. Have groups write a speech as if the leader they chose were addressing his nation about its involvement in World War I.
4. Allow time for presentations of the speeches.
   LS Interpersonal, Verbal-Linguistic

Alternative Assessment Handbook, Rubrics 24: Oral Presentations; and 30: Research

Info to Know

The Allied Powers Commission The Allied Powers Commission was a group formed in January 1919 made up of twenty-five people, two from each main Allied power (the United States, Britain, France, Italy, and Japan), and one each from Belgium, Greece, Poland, Romania, and Serbia. The group's full title was The Commission on the Responsibility of the Authors of the War and on Enforcement of Penalties.

Answers

Reading Like a Historian
Document 1. a. *the nations he claims has attacked Germany;* **b.** *possible answer—contradicts, because he claims that he is trying to preserve peace and that Germany is the victim;*
Document 2. a. *possible answers— "reluctantly, quite unprepared, dreadful ordeal, forced to join this war in self-defence";* **b.** *He would disagree.*
Document 3. a. *The Central Powers and their allies;* **b.** *Yes, because they had recently been fighting the Central Powers in a costly, deadly war.* **Document 4.**
a. *push it from under Kaiser Wilhelm II; would cause him to be hanged;* **b.** *blames the ambition and greed of Kaiser Wilhelm II; believes all those who fought the Central Powers agree.*
Essay *Student essays will vary but should discuss the different viewpoints on the causes of the war.*

Answers

Visual Summary

Review and Inquiry Organize students into small groups. Assign each group one cause or effect from the Visual Study Guide. Have groups write a paragraph to present orally, explaining their item and its importance.

Quick Facts Transparency: Visual Study Guide: World War I

Review Key Terms and People

1. b.
2. f.
3. g.
4. h.
5. c.
6. a.
7. e.
8. d.

Comprehension and Critical Thinking

9. a. the Triple Alliance and the Triple Entente
b. The Austrians blamed Serbia for the assassination, which led to the involvement of both sides' allies.
c. The growing power of European armed forces added to the tension, and the alliances led many more nations to join the war.

10. a. Soldiers lived in and fought from a massive system of trenches that stretched for hundreds of miles.
b. possible answer—It involved new weapons such as gas and machine guns, and technology such as tanks and aircraft, which caused millions of casualties.
c. Without propaganda, fewer people would have supported the war and volunteered to fight.

11. a. Czar Nicholas II became increasingly unpopular and many wanted to overthrow the government.
b. The defeat of Russian troops led to the abdication of the czar and the Bolshevik Revolution.
c. possible answer—It would cause a struggle for control of the Soviet Union.

12. a. It proposed the League of Nations, which intended to keep peace between nations. Some countries were excluded from the League, however, which weakened it.
b. The United States helped on the battlefield, helped shift the balance of power, and influenced peace negotiations.
c. War reparations would cripple Germany's economy.

VISUAL STUDY GUIDE

Causes and Effects of World War I

CAUSES

- Military buildup in Europe
- European countries form alliances
- Rival European empires try to keep and expand their power
- Growing nationalism
- Assassination of Archduke Franz Ferdinand

World War I

EFFECTS

- Tens of millions of people killed or wounded
- Much of Europe destroyed
- Widespread political unrest and economic problems
- New countries formed in Europe
- Mandates established in the Middle East
- League of Nations established

Key Events of World War I

1881	▪ Triple Alliance formed
1907	▪ Triple Entente formed
1914	▪ Archduke Franz Ferdinand murdered ▪ Austria-Hungary declares war on Serbia ▪ Germany declares war on Russia and France and invades Belgium ▪ Trench warfare begins
1915	▪ German U-boat sinks *Lusitania* ▪ Czar Nicholas II takes command of Russian forces ▪ Armenian Massacre takes place
1916	▪ Tanks first used in the war ▪ Battle of Verdun becomes longest battle of the war
1917	▪ Russian Revolution takes place ▪ United States enters the war
1918	▪ Armistice ends the fighting
1919	▪ Treaty of Versailles signed

Review Key Terms and People

Match each numbered definition with the letter of the correct item from the list below.

Column I
- **a.** Grigory Rasputin
- **b.** Central Powers
- **c.** armistice
- **d.** League of Nations
- **e.** Bolshevik
- **f.** total war
- **g.** fundamental
- **h.** U-boat

Column II
1. Germany, Austria-Hungary, Ottoman Empire
2. War using all of society's resources
3. Important or vital
4. German submarine
5. Truce that ended the fighting in World War I
6. Controversial adviser to the czar during World War I
7. Radical Communist group that took over Russia in 1917
8. Organization of countries proposed in Wilson's Fourteen Points

802 CHAPTER 26

Reading Skills

13. before the United States

14. after the war

15. citizens protested lack of food and fuel; police shot rioters; czar ordered Duma to disband; Duma defied the order

History's Impact video program
Review the video to answer the closing question: What impact has modern warfare had on the world today?

Comprehension and Critical Thinking

SECTION 1 *(pp. 779–782)*

9. a. Recall What were the two major alliances in Europe in the years leading up to World War I?

b. Explain How did the assassination of Franz Ferdinand contribute to the start of World War I?

c. Elaborate How did militarism and alliances help cause World War I?

SECTION 2 *(pp. 783–788)*

10. a. Describe What was trench warfare?

b. Make Generalizations What general statement could you make to describe the fighting in World War I?

c. Evaluate How important was the role of propaganda in World War I? Explain your answer.

SECTION 3 *(pp. 789–793)*

11. a. Describe What was the general attitude of the Russian people toward their government in the early 1900s?

b. Identify Cause and Effect How did World War I affect the Russian people and their relationship with their government?

c. Predict How do you think Lenin's death would affect the Soviet Union?

SECTION 4 *(pp. 794–799)*

12. a. Identify How did the Fourteen Points affect the peace agreement at the end of the war?

b. Identify Cause and Effect What was the result of the U.S. entry into the war?

c. Support a Position Which effect of World War I do you think will have the greatest impact on the world? Why?

Reading Skills

Understanding Sequencing *Use what you know about understanding sequencing to answer the questions below.*

13. Did Austria-Hungary enter the war before or after the United States did?

14. Did the creation of mandates in the Middle East take place before or after the war?

15. What events led up to Czar Nicholas II stepping down as leader of Russia?

Interpreting Political Cartoons

Reading Like a Historian *The cartoon below shows a hand carving up a map of the southwestern United States.*

Carving up the United States, by Clifford Berryman, 1917

16. Draw Conclusions The eagle on the glove symbolizes Germany. Whose hands are in the cartoon?

17. Analyze To what event was the cartoonist referring? What do you think the cartoonist thought about this event?

Using the Internet

go.hrw.com
Practice Online
Keyword: SHL WW1

18. The Treaty of Versailles had an enormous effect on Germany and the rest of Europe following World War I. Using the Internet, research the Treaty of Versailles. Then write a detailed report about the treaty, its terms, and its effects on Germany. Be sure to include an evaluation of the treaty's strengths and weaknesses.

WRITING FOR THE SAT ✎

Think about the following issue:

The forces of nationalism and imperialism played a major role in causing World War I. The war was the largest conflict the world had ever seen, and years of battles took place before the armistice and the Treaty of Versailles finally brought an end to the fighting.

19. Assignment: Did World War I resolve the disagreements that had caused the war? Write a short essay in which you develop your position on this issue. Support your point of view with reasoning and examples from your reading and studies.

Interpreting Political Cartoons

16. German Foreign Secretary Arthur Zimmerman

17. the Zimmerman Note; probably blamed Zimmerman for German aggression

Using the Internet

18. Go to the HRW Web site and enter the keyword shown to access a rubric for this activity.

KEYWORD: SHL WWI

Writing for the SAT

19. Student essays might include one of the following ideas—did resolve, by punishing Germany for the invasions; did not resolve, because the Treaty of Versailles did not provide for a lasting peace.
A rubric for this activity is provided in **CRF:** Writing for the SAT.

HOLT

History's Impact

▶ **Video Program: World War I**
See the Video Program Teacher's Guide for the answer to the closing question.

Review and Assessment Resources

Review and Reinforce

 CRF: Chapter Review

 Quick Facts Transparency: Visual Study Guide: World War I

◥ **Spanish Chapter Summaries Audio CD Program**

OSP **Holt PuzzlePro:** Quiz Show for ExamView

 **Quiz Game CD-ROM**

Assess

▤ **PASS:** Chapter Test, Forms A and B

▤ **Alternative Assessment Handbook**

OSP **ExamView Test Generator,** Chapter Test

● **Differentiated Instruction Modified Worksheets and Tests CD-ROM:** Chapter Test

HOAP **Holt Online Assessment Program** (in the Premier Online Edition)

Reteach/Intervene

▤ **Interactive Reader and Study Guide**

▤ **Differentiated Instruction Teacher Management System:** Lesson Plans for Differentiated Instruction

● **Differentiated Instruction Modified Worksheets and Tests CD-ROM:** Chapter Test

● **Interactive Skills Tutor CD-ROM**

go.hrw.com
Online Resources

KEYWORD: SHL TEACHER

Chapter 27 Planning Guide

The Interwar Years

Chapter Overview	Reproducible Resources	Technology Resources

CHAPTER 27
pp. 804–831
Overview: In this chapter, students will learn how different nations' leaders dealt with social, political, and economic chaos during the period between World War I and II.

KI 1, 4; PI 1.1, 1.2, 1.4, 4.2, 4.4
See pp. T32–T55 for a detailed correlation to the New York State Core Curriculum for Global History and Geography and the New York Learning Standards.

 Differentiated Instruction Teacher Management System:
• Pacing Guide
• Lesson Plans for Differentiated Instruction

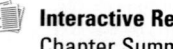 **Interactive Reader and Study Guide:**
Chapter Summary*

 Chapter Resource File*
• Writing for the SAT
• Interdisciplinary Project: The Depression and Photojournalism
• Economics and History: Defense Spending

OSP **New York One-Stop Planner CD-ROM:**
Calendar Planner

Live Ink© Online Reading Help

Student Edition on Audio CD Program

 Differentiated Instruction Modified Worksheets and Tests CD-ROM

Interactive Skills Tutor CD-ROM

World History Primary Source Library CD-ROM

History's Impact: World History Video Program (VHS/DVD): The Interwar Years

---

SECTION 1:

Unrest in Asia and Africa

The Main Idea: During the chaotic years following World War I, nationalist feeling increased in Asia and Africa. The resulting unrest continued into the 1930s.

PI 1.1, 1.4

 Differentiated Instruction Teacher Management System: Section 1 Lesson Plan*

 Interactive Reader and Study Guide: Section 1 Summary*

 Chapter Resource File*
• Vocabulary Builder: Section 1
• Biography: Reza Shah Pahlavi
• Primary Source: British White Paper of June 1922
• Literature: *A Passage to India*

Regents Review Transparency: Section 1*

Map Transparency: Postwar Colonies and Nationalism, 1920s*

Map Transparency: The Long March, 1934–1935*

SECTION 2:

The Depression

The Main Idea: In the late 1920s an economic depression started in the United States and quickly spread around the globe, causing great hardship and creating ideal conditions for political unrest.

PI 1.2, 1.4

 Differentiated Instruction Teacher Management System: Section 2 Lesson Plan*

 Interactive Reader and Study Guide: Section 2 Summary*

 Chapter Resource File*
• Vocabulary Builder: Section 2
• Biography: Bessie Smith
• History and Geography: The Great Depression

 Regents Review Transparency: Section 2*

Quick Facts Transparency: Causes of the 1929 Stock Market Crash*

Quick Facts Transparency: Major U.S. Social Reforms*

Internet Activity: U.S. Economy

SECTION 3:

Japanese Imperialism

The Main Idea: A modernized Japan emerged from World War I as one of the world's leading powers. Dreams of empire, however, led the country in a dangerous direction.

PI 1.1, 4.4

 Differentiated Instruction Teacher Management System: Section 3 Lesson Plan*

Interactive Reader and Study Guide: Section 3 Summary*

 Chapter Resource File*
• Vocabulary Builder: Section 3
• Biography: Sadao Araki

 Regents Review Transparency: Section 3*

Map Transparency: Japanese Aggression, 1931–1937*

Quick Facts Transparency: Major Japanese Events 1920 to 1940*

Section 4:

Dictatorships in Europe

The Main Idea: The political and social unrest that followed World War I helped totalitarian dictators rise to power in Europe.

PI 1.1, 4.2

 Differentiated Instruction Teacher Management System: Section 4 Lesson Plan*

Interactive Reader and Study Guide: Section 4 Summary*

Chapter Resource File*
• Vocabulary Builder: Section 4
• Biography: Haile Selassie

 Regents Review Transparency: Section 4*

Quick Facts Transparency: Common Features of Totalitarian Governments*

HOLT
History's Impact
World History Video Program (VHS/DVD)
The Interwar Years

Review, Assessment, Intervention

 Global History and Geography Regents Test Prep Workbook

 Quick Facts Transparency: The Interwar Years*

 Spanish Chapter Summaries Audio CD Program

 Program Assessment Support System (PASS): Chapter Test*

Differentiated Instruction Modified Worksheets and Tests CD-ROM: Modified Chapter Test

OSP **New York One-Stop Planner CD-ROM:** ExamView Test Generator (English/Spanish)

HOAP **Holt Online Assessment Program (HOAP),** in the Holt Premier Online Student Edition

 PASS: Section 1 Quiz*

 Online Quiz: Section 1

 Alternative Assessment Handbook

 PASS: Section 2 Quiz*

 Online Quiz: Section 2

 Alternative Assessment Handbook

PASS: Section 3 Quiz*

Online Quiz: Section 3

Alternative Assessment Handbook

 PASS: Section 4 Quiz*

Online Quiz: Section 4

Alternative Assessment Handbook

Power Presentation with Video CD-ROM

Power Presentations with Video are visual presentations of each chapter's main ideas. Presentations can be customized by including Quick Facts charts, images and maps from the textbook, and video clips.

Holt Online Learning

go.hrw.com
Teacher Resources
KEYWORD: SHL TEACHER

go.hrw.com
Student Resources
KEYWORD: SHL IWY

- Document-Based Questions
- Interactive Multimedia Activities

- Current Events
- Chapter-Based Internet Activities
- and more!

Holt Premier
Online Student Edition
Complete online support for interactivity, assessment, and reporting
- Interactive Maps and Notebook
- Homework Practice and Research Activities Online

CHAPTER 27 PLANNING GUIDE

The Big Picture

Peter N. Stearns

A Balance Sheet World War I substantially weakened the major European powers, but not, initially, their ambitions. There was every interest in maintaining and even expanding empire, with a slight bow to new commitments to the League of Nations. But the war had accelerated new currents in Africa and Asia. This involved new nationalist agitation, including the emergence of an independent Turkey. It also involved the enhancement of power centers in Asia, in China to an extent, and even more in Japan. Despite these larger developments, European struggles held pride of place, and key nationalist tensions were not resolved during the aftermath of the war. Then, when new economic woes hit Europe through the great Depression, forces of totalitarianism, particularly in Nazi Germany, made European stabilization virtually impossible.

The 1920s and the Depression Various initiatives occurred during the 1920s, including dramatic changes in popular culture; some efforts to resolve diplomatic tensions with Germany; and some signs of renewed economic vitality in the Western world. But basic issues were not resolved, including a number of clear economic weaknesses. This set a context for the dramatic reverberations of the Depression literally around the world. Unemployment increased widely and social tensions grew rapidly. While some societies responded to the Depression successfully, global economic recovery remained incomplete even in 1939.

Collapse of Globalization Developments in the interwar decades called into serious question the network of global economic, political and cultural relationships built up, under Western sponsorship, in the later 19th century. The Soviet Union pulled away, into substantial economic isolation. Japan tried to build its own empire as an alternative to full global involvement, and of course the United States turned away from global alliances as well while still participating in international economic activity. Full globalization would resume only some decades later, after another devastating war.

Recent Scholarship

The Ebbing of European Ascendancy: An International History of the World, 1914-1945 (2002), by Sally Marks, has become the standard treatment of international relations in a busy and troubled period. Marks covers the essential landmarks—including world wars, the frenzied diplomacy of the 1920s, and the failed response to the rise of fascism—but she keeps in mind the bigger picture. European developments are carefully linked to emerging global power centers and challenges. In these three decades, European powers fatally weakened their capacity to retain global dominance by two brutal and wasting internal struggles, while other societies and movements began to see new opportunities for self-assertion. This is a masterful study of a watershed period in contemporary world history.

Differentiating Instruction

  Differentiated Instruction Teacher Management System
- Pacing Guide
- Lesson Plans for Differentiated Instruction

Interactive Reader and Study Guide

 Spanish Chapter Summaries Audio CD Program

 Student Edition on Audio CD Program

 Differentiated Instruction Modified Worksheets and Tests CD-ROM
- Vocabulary Flash Cards
- Modified Vocabulary Builder Activities
- Modified Chapter Review Activity
- Modified Chapter Test

OSP One-Stop Planner CD-ROM
- ExamView Test Generator (English/Spanish)
- PuzzlePro
- Quiz Show for ExamView
- Transparencies and Videos

TE **Differentiated Activities in the Teacher's Edition**
- Comparing Gandhi and Atatürk, p. 809
- Failing Economy Posters, p. 813
- Japan's Economic Problems, p. 819
- Hirohito and the Nanjing Massacre, p. 821

Reading Like a Historian

Sam Wineburg

Maps as Historical Texts Many students regard maps as neutral representations of three-dimensional spaces. But for historians, maps are like any other historical text. They reflect a point of view, are rooted in a particular context, and shed light on one facet of a multi-faceted historical reality.

Consider the map on page 820, whose title heralds its purpose: to convey information about Japan's aggressive seizure of territory in the years before World War II. The map's colored legend paints "Japan and her colonies" in red and the "area invaded by Japan" in orange. Aside from providing the name of the Soviet Union to the north, the countries that do not fall under Japan's sphere go unmarked. We might surmise that the map's purpose is to focus our attention on the issue before us—"Japanese Aggression"—and to show that by seizing Korea and conquering broad swaths of China, Japan's voracious expansionism succeeded in more than doubling its territory.

What would happen if we tinkered with this map and started to label the unmarked countries? We might begin underneath Taiwan by labeling the Philippines and adding to the map's legend "area colonized by the United States" (or, if we were writing from a Philippine perspective, "territory invaded by the United States"). Moving west, we would then label the territory that constitutes present-day Vietnam, Laos, and Cambodia as French Indochina—part of the French colonial venture that was justified by Prime Minister Jules Ferry, who proclaimed "We must say openly that indeed the high races have a right over the lower races."

Examining Scope If we zoomed out to enlarge the map's scope, we would label Indonesia as the Dutch West Indies, except for East Timor, which was Portugal's. And the biggest colonial overlord in this enlarged picture would be Great Britain, whose prizes would include Malaya, Hong Kong, Burma, and the glimmering jewel in the crown, India. Our

new map would show a Far East ringed by the expansionist outposts of European countries and the Johnny-come-lately colonialist, the United States. As the Pulitzer-prize winning historian John Dower observed in *Embracing Defeat: Japan in the Wake of World War II:* "Colonialism and imperialism more generally, defined the twentieth century Asia in which Japan was accused of having conspired to wage an aggressive war. Japan's colonial and neo-colonial domain (Formosa, Korea, and Manchuria) existed alongside the Asian overseas possessions of . . . Britain, France, the Netherlands, and the United States. China itself, nominally sovereign, had been a congeries of Japanese, European, and American 'special rights and interests'."

None of this is to excuse Japanese aggression, which was unqualifiedly brutal. It does, however, put into perspective Japan's behavior prior to World War II, which employed many of the same tactics Western nations used in ravenously gobbling up huge chunks of Africa and Asia. This double standard did not go unnoticed during the 1946 Tokyo war trials. The Indian jurist Radhabinod Pal trenchantly pointed out the hypocrisy of Western nations who, on one hand, condemned Japan's brutal acquisition of Manchuria while, on the other, knew full well that the colonial map of Asia was "acquired by such aggressive measures." Indeed, observed Pal, the "Amau Doctrine" under which Japan claimed "special rights" over China found "obvious precedent in the conduct of the United States in pursuance of the Monroe Doctrine."

Maps, like all historical documents, capture one slice of geographic reality. Every map discloses some facts while remaining mute about others. Our map is no exception.

Chapter Main Ideas

Section 1 During the chaotic years following World War I, nationalist feeling increased in Asia and Africa. The resulting unrest continued into the 1930s.

Section 2 In the late 1920s, an economic depression started in the United States and quickly spread around the globe, causing great hardship and creating ideal conditions for political unrest.

Section 3 A modernized Japan emerged from World War I as one of the world's leading powers. Dreams of empire, however, led the country in a dangerous direction.

Section 4 The political and social unrest that followed World War I helped totalitarian dictators rise to power in Europe.

New York Standards

Key Idea 1 The study of world history requires an understanding of world cultures and civilizations, including an analysis of important ideas, social and cultural values, beliefs, and traditions. This study also examines the human condition and the connections and interactions of people across time and space and the ways different people view the same event or issue from a variety of perspectives.

Key Idea 4 The skills of historical analysis include the ability to investigate differing and competing interpretations of the theories of history, hypothesize about why interpretations change over time, explain the importance of historical evidence, and understand the concepts of change and continuity over time.

Key to Differentiating Instruction

Below Level

Basic-level activities designed for all students encountering new material

At Level

Intermediate-level activities designed for average students

Above Level

Challenging activities designed for honors and gifted and talented students

Standard English Mastery

Activities designed to improve standard English usage

804 CHAPTER 27

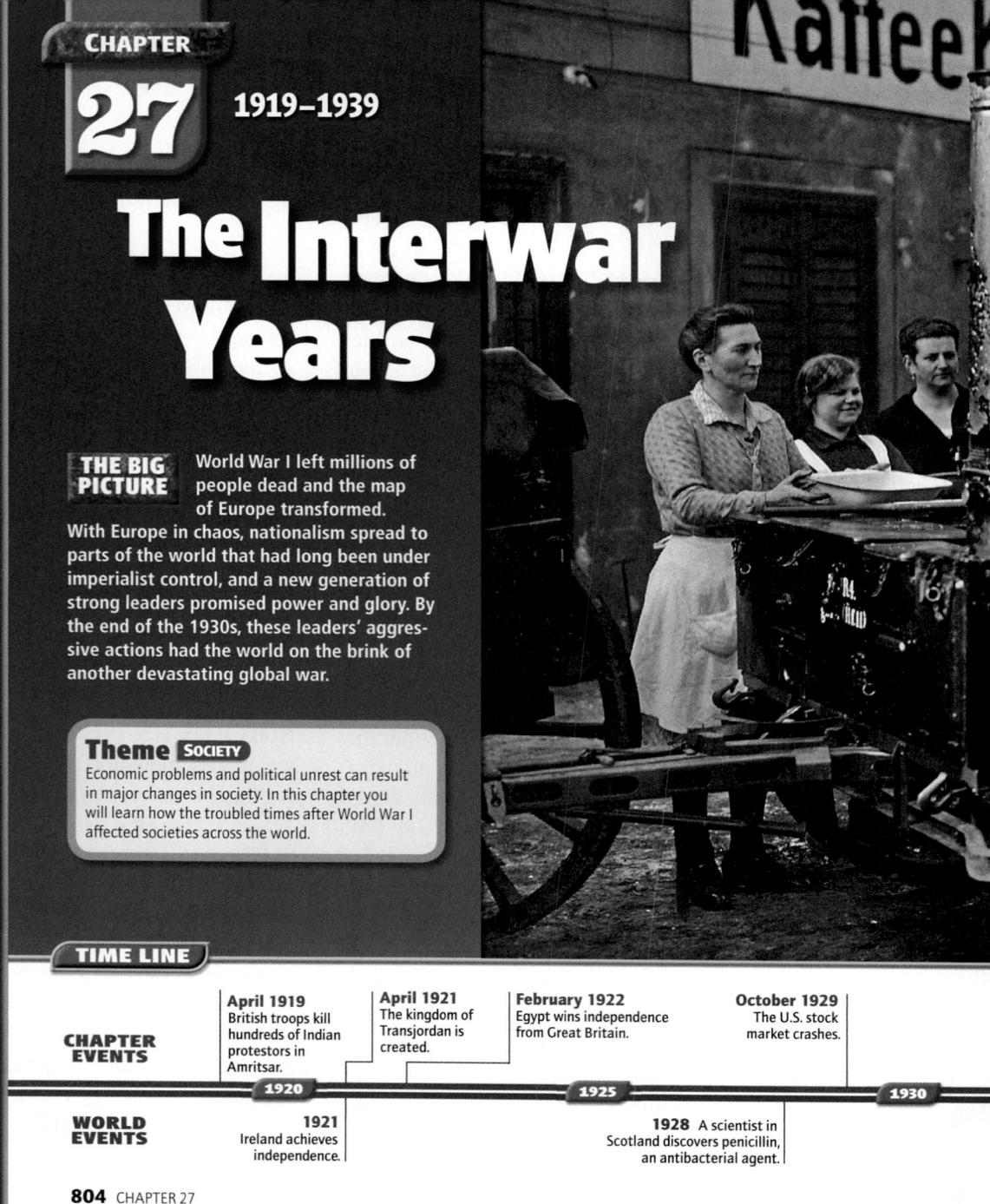

CHAPTER

27 1919–1939

The Interwar Years

THE BIG PICTURE World War I left millions of people dead and the map of Europe transformed. With Europe in chaos, nationalism spread to parts of the world that had long been under imperialist control, and a new generation of strong leaders promised power and glory. By the end of the 1930s, these leaders' aggressive actions had the world on the brink of another devastating global war.

Theme SOCIETY
Economic problems and political unrest can result in major changes in society. In this chapter you will learn how the troubled times after World War I affected societies across the world.

TIME LINE

CHAPTER EVENTS

April 1919 British troops kill hundreds of Indian protestors in Amritsar.

April 1921 The kingdom of Transjordan is created.

February 1922 Egypt wins independence from Great Britain.

October 1929 The U.S. stock market crashes.

1920   1925   1930

WORLD EVENTS

1921 Ireland achieves independence.

1928 A scientist in Scotland discovers penicillin, an antibacterial agent.

804 CHAPTER 27

Introduce the Chapter

At Level

The Interwar Years
Materials: construction paper

1. Tell students that during the period they will be studying, the world had become more interconnected. Students will make posters to represent the content of each section of the chapter.

2. Organize students into four groups (or eight if the class is large). Assign one section of the chapter to each group. Have groups scan the sections they were assigned, listing important facts and events.

3. Distribute paper. Have each group prepare a poster representing the content of its assigned section.

4. Allow time for groups to display and present their finished posters. **LS Interpersonal, Visual-Spatial**

Alternative Assessment Handbook, Rubrics 14: Group Activity; and 28: Posters

September 1931
Japan invades Manchuria.

January 1933
Adolf Hitler becomes chancellor of Germany.

October 1935 Italian forces invade Ethiopia.

November 1938
Anti-Jewish riots sweep Germany.

1935

1939

1933
Prohibition ends in United States.

1935 An earthquake kills 20,000 people in Pakistan.

1939
The Spanish Civil War ends with a Fascist victory.

Reading like a Historian

This photograph shows a soldier distributing food to hungry Germans in 1931 during a severe economic depression. Germany's economic problems soon helped lead to the rise of a powerful dictator.

Analyzing Visuals How do you think these German women felt about the food provided by the army? How might Germany's economic problems have contributed to the rise of a dictator?

See **Skills Handbook**, p. H26

THE INTERWAR YEARS **805**

Explore the Time Line

1. In what year did Ireland achieve independence? *1921*

2. When did the U.S. stock market crash? *October 1929*

3. Name the two countries that invaded other countries during the 1930s. *Japan and Italy*

4. When did anti-Jewish riots sweep Germany? *November 1938*

Info to Know

Globalization of the Depression The Great Depression in the United States spread through Europe and beyond. Though most economies usually recover at the end of a decade-long cycle of business, the worldwide aspect of this depression made it far worse. Germany, already paying reparations after World War I, suffered hyperinflation, making its currency worthless.
Draw Conclusions Why was Germany's economy suffering even before the Great Depression began? *Germany was paying reparations for World War I damages.*

• Chapter Preview •

HOLT
History's Impact
► **Video Program: The Interwar Years** See the Video Teacher's Guide for strategies for using the video segment.

Reading Like a Historian

Analyzing a Photograph Have students examine the photograph on these pages and then explain what is happening. Guide students in a discussion of what this photograph tells us about the people and their living conditions.

go.hrw.com
Online Resources

Chapter Resources:
KEYWORD: SHL IWY
Teacher Resources:
KEYWORD: SHL TEACHER

Answers

Reading Like a Historian *possible answer—The women appear pleased and grateful; because of Germany's economic problems, Germans may have been likely to accept a dictator who promised aid.*

Geography Starting Points

Activity **Analyzing Proverbs** Read the African proverbs below to students, and write them for all to see. Have students explain how the proverbs might have related to African struggles with colonial rule. *possible answers—In British colonies, the British took over the justice systems; African colonies were controlled by Europeans, and conflicts fairly frequent.* As an extension, have students write their own proverbs reflecting the images shown on this page.

🗺 **Map Transparency**: Postwar Colonies and Nationalism, 1920s

📝 **World History Outline Maps**

✳ **Interactive Map:** Postwar Colonies and Nationalism, 1920s

Primary Source
African Proverbs

"Show me your friend and I will show you your character."
—Kwaku Boateng

"Where the leopard is made the judge the goat will never get a fair judgment."
—Makanze Emeka

"Great towns grow with peace but not killing and intimidation."
—Prince Arusi Obi

Answers
Geography Starting Points
1. *Africa;* 2. *possible answer—might cause colonies to rebel; later maps might show fewer colonial possessions*

806

GEOGRAPHY Starting Points

✳ Interactive
POSTWAR COLONIES AND NATIONALISM, 1920s

The destruction of World War I helped lead to the rise of dictators in Europe.

Japanese nationalism led to an increasingly aggressive military.

Indian nationalist leader Subhas Chandra Bose speaks to a crowd in India.

Map legend:
- United Kingdom and possessions
- France and possessions
- Spain and possessions
- Portugal and possessions
- Netherlands and possessions
- Japanese Empire
- Belgium and possessions
- Italy and possessions
- U.S. possessions

Starting Points During the years of political and economic instability that followed World War I, nationalism grew in areas that had long been under the power of other nations. In some places this nationalism led to struggles for independence, while in others it led to the rise of powerful leaders who promised to build new empires—by force.

1. **Analyze** During the 1920s, where were most colonial possessions located?
2. **Predict** How do you think the growth of nationalism might affect the area of the world shown in this map? How might the map be different in the 1940s? In the 1960s?

🔊 **Listen to History**

Go online to listen to an explanation of the starting points for this chapter.

go.hrw.com

Keyword: SHL IWY

806 CHAPTER 27

Skills Focus: Analyzing Maps

At Level

Social Studies Skill
Nationalism's Impact

1. Draw the chart for students to see. Omit the italicized answers. Have students copy the chart, and fill the Impact column with a sentence about each of the areas listed.

2. Have students refer to the map on this page and create a statement explaining its title. Have volunteers share their answers.
   📊 Visual-Spatial, Verbal-Linguistic

📝 **Alternative Assessment Handbook**, Rubrics 13: Graphic Organizers; and 21: Map Reading

Nationalism's Impact	
Area	*Impact*
Western Europe	*People struggle to rebuild after World War I.*
British Colonies	*Nationalism in Asia and Africa causes unrest in the colonies.*
Japan	*Japan modernizes its military, hoping to enlarge its empire.*

Unrest in Asia and Africa

BEFORE YOU READ

MAIN IDEA

During the chaotic years following World War I, nationalist feeling increased in Asia and Africa. The resulting unrest continued into the 1930s.

READING FOCUS

1. What happened in China after World War I?
2. What changes took place in India?
3. How did nationalism affect the Middle East?
4. How did nationalism affect Africa?

KEY TERMS AND PEOPLE

Jiang Jieshi
Mao Zedong
Long March
Amritsar Massacre
Mohandas Gandhi
Kemal Atatürk

 NEW YORK

PI 1.1 Students define culture and civilization, explaining how they developed and changed over time.

PI 1.4 Students understand the broad patterns, relationships, and interactions of cultures and civilizations during particular eras and across eras.

THE LONG MARCH

◀ Mao Zedong led the Chinese Communist troops during the Long March.

THE INSIDE STORY

Would you march 6,000 miles for your beliefs? In 1934 the civil war in China was going poorly for the Chinese Communist army. The Communists were trapped near their base in southeastern China, with some 700,000 nationalist troops, known as Guomindang, waiting to attack. Communist leaders knew they needed to escape to continue their struggle for a Communist China.

That October, the remaining 100,000 Communist troops and supporters broke through Guomindang lines and fled toward northern China. Led by Mao Zedong, they struggled to cross rivers and swamps and to climb over high, snow-covered mountains in their search for safety. During the first three months of their journey, the Communists

faced near-constant attacks from the Guomindang air force and ground troops. Many marchers died as a result.

Finally, after traveling thousands of miles across some of the harshest terrain in China, the Communists arrived at a safe haven. Only 8,000 of the marchers had survived. In the years to come, however, their vision of a Communist China would get closer to reality. ■

China after World War I

World War I had devastated large parts of Europe, and postwar treaties and political unrest had reshaped many nations. Although China's role in the war had been small, it faced unrest during the postwar period.

THE INTERWAR YEARS **807**

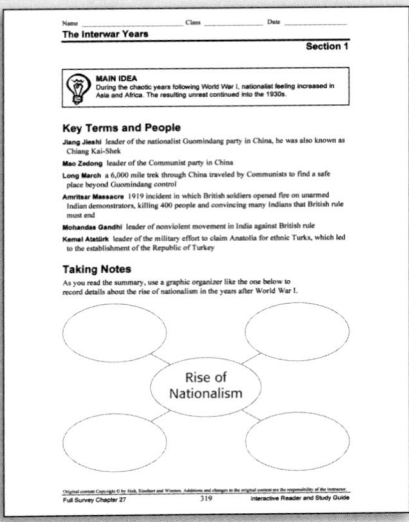

Reading Focus

❶ What happened in China after World War I? *Chinese student protests led to rise in nationalism; Communist Party formed; nationalist Guomindang Party attacked rival Communists; Mao Zedong led Communists on Long March*

China after World War I

Describe What was the May Fourth Movement? *protests and strikes by students demanding change in China*

Evaluate Should Communists have continued fighting Chinese forces or retreated on the Long March? *possible answers—continued fighting, because many thousands of them died on the Long March; retreated, because they were able to regain strength*

Map Transparency: The Long March, 1934–1935

Recent Scholarship

In *The Great Wall: China Against the World, 1000 BC—2000 AD,* author Julia Lovell reveals the many faces of the Great Wall, its reality, image, and how it has shaped its nation with new understanding. Lovell views it in a modern perspective, as she equates it to a "Great Firewall" of the Internet, protecting China from international attack.

The Great Wall: China Against the World, 1000 BC—2000 AD by Julia Lovell. Grove Press, 2006

Answers

Interpreting Maps *They traveled around the city of Zunyi, across the Chang Jiang (Yangzi River), to the city of Luding, then crossed the Jiang Shan mountains, and finally arrived in the northern city of Yan'an.*

Reading Check *1919: strikes and protests; 1921: Communist Party of China formed; 1927: nationalists attack Communists; 1934: Long March*

TAKING NOTES Take notes about the rise of nationalism in China, India, the Middle East, and Africa.

Rise of Nationalism

The May Fourth Movement In 1917 China had declared war on Germany, hoping that after the war the grateful Allied Powers would return German-controlled Chinese territories to China. The Treaty of Versailles, however, gave Germany's Chinese territories to Japan, which had captured this land during the war. To the Chinese, the Versailles treaty was a sign that the world still saw China as a weak nation.

On May 4, 1919, thousands of angry students in Beijing demanded change. Strikes and protests swept the country in what came to be called the May Fourth Movement.

An Uneasy Partnership The Guomindang nationalists still had the support of some Chinese, but many others believed that communism was the best way to strengthen and modernize China. In 1921 the Communist Party of China was formed. The Communists and the Guomindang formed an uneasy partnership, working together to fight the warlords who controlled many areas of China.

This partnership made many gains in the early 1920s. Under the leadership of **Jiang Jieshi** (jee-AHNG jee-ay-SHEE), also known as Chiang Kai-Shek (jee-AHNG ky-SHEK), continued to fight the warlords and foreign imperialism. Soon, the Guomindang controlled much of China.

Jiang eventually turned against his Communist allies. Because the success of the Communist-Guomindang partnership had expanded Communist influence in China, some Guomindang nationalists were upset. They urged Jiang to take action. In 1927 Jiang had his forces attack Communists in several cities, killing thousands of people. This action marked the beginning of the Chinese Civil War.

The Long March A number of Communists survived Jiang's attack, among them a leader named **Mao Zedong**. Mao and his fellow survivors tried to rebuild their organization. By 1934, however, the Guomindang had the Communists under serious military pressure. To escape, Mao led 100,000 Communist supporters on a 6,000-mile trek through China. The purpose of this **Long March** was to find a safe place for the Chinese Communists in a part of China beyond Guomindang control.

Only 8,000 of Mao's followers survived the terrible conditions of the Long March. Eventually, however, they would regain their strength and begin another battle against Jiang.

READING CHECK **Sequence** What happened in China after World War I?

Changes in India

The early 1900s also saw the rise of nationalist feeling in India. This soon led to increasing tension between Indians and their British rulers.

THE LONG MARCH, 1934–1935

Map labels: Beijing, KOREA, Yellow Sea, Yan'an, Yellow River, Shanghai, CHINA, Yangzi River, East China Sea, Jiajin Shan, Luding, Chang Jiang, Zunyi, Ruijin, TAIWAN, Tropic of Cancer, 20°N, South China Sea, 120°E, Hainan

Legend: Communist bases; Nationalist strike against the Communists; Route of Long March

0 200 Miles
0 200 Kilometers
Two-point equidistant projection

808 CHAPTER 27

GEOGRAPHY SKILLS **INTERPRETING MAPS**

Movement Describe the movements of the Chinese Communists during the Long March, including references to cities and major geographic features.

Skills Focus: Interpreting Movement Maps

At Level

Social Studies Skill
The Long March

Research Required

Materials: poster paper

1. Review the route followed by Mao Zedong and his Communist followers to Yan'an. Have students create their own outline maps of China, based on the map on this page.

2. Have students work in pairs or small groups to determine the landforms that would have presented barriers on the Long March and those that would have made the route easier. Have students add these landforms to their maps.

3. Ask students what factors other than landforms might have influenced Mao's route.

4. Have students write a short essay about the challenges posed by the Long March route, and how this rigorous journey might have influenced the determination of Mao's Chinese Communists to preserve their beliefs.

LS **Visual-Spatial, Verbal-Linguistic**

Alternative Assessment Handbook, Rubrics 12: Drawing Conclusions; and 20: Map Creation

India and World War I Some 800,000 Indians had served with the British in World War I, fighting on the Western Front and in the Middle East. After the war's end, the surviving Indian soldiers returned home to find that their wartime sacrifices had not won them any new freedoms. It was clear that Britain planned to keep firm control over India. Anger and unrest among the Indian population grew.

In 1919 the British passed the Rowlatt Acts, which allowed the British to deal harshly with the growing opposition in India. Indians were outraged. At an April 1919 protest in the Indian city of Amritsar (uhm-RIT-suhr), British soldiers opened fire on a large crowd of peaceful, unarmed demonstrators. Nearly 400 people were killed. The **Amritsar Massacre** helped convince many Indians that they must rid themselves of their British rulers.

Gandhi's Protests After the Amritsar Massacre, Indian lawyer **Mohandas Gandhi** started to organize protests against Britain. Gandhi believed in two important concepts. One was ahimsa, or nonviolence toward living things, which was an important value in Gandhi's Hindu religion. The second was civil disobedience, or a refusal to obey unjust laws.

In 1920 Gandhi began his first nonviolent action against British rule. He encouraged Indians to boycott all British products. For example, Gandhi stopped wearing clothes made from British cloth. Many Indians began to make their own thread and cloth, and the spinning wheel became a symbol of Gandhi's peaceful movement for change.

In 1930 Gandhi launched a protest against the British monopoly on salt. The issue seemed minor, but it captured the interest of the public. Soon, thousands of Indians were producing their own salt—and defying British law.

Gandhi's Progress Gandhi inspired millions of Indians to resist British rule. He and his followers were arrested often, but this increased public sympathy for their cause.

Gandhi's efforts did lead to some changes. In 1935 the British Parliament gave Indians a limited degree of self-rule. Still, this was far from the full independence that Gandhi sought, and India's struggle did not end.

READING CHECK **Identify the Main Idea** How did Gandhi work for change in India?

Mohandas Gandhi believed that nonviolent resistance is the best way to achieve change in a society where others hold all the power. This strategy was greatly influenced by his religious beliefs.

Gandhi grew up in a deeply religious home. His mother practiced a form of Hinduism that emphasized nonviolence and held that everything in the universe is eternal. As a result, Gandhi came to believe in the importance of causing no harm to other living beings. This emphasis on nonviolence became an important element of India's struggle for independence from Great Britain, which Gandhi led.

Summarize How did Gandhi's religious beliefs affect the Indian independence movement?

The Middle East

The years after World War I saw nationalist hopes and dreams flourish throughout much of the Middle East too. Some of these nationalist movements achieved their goals—but others did not.

Turkey and Atatürk Under the Treaty of Sèvres after World War I, the Ottoman Empire agreed to give up control of much of its territory, including the homeland of the ethnic Turkish population. The Allied Powers planned to give these lands to Greece and other nations.

But the Turks, led by a World War I hero named Kemal Mustafa, fought these plans. They defeated Greek forces sent to claim Turkish territory, and in October 1923 Kemal Mustafa announced the establishment of the Republic of Turkey. He later came to be known as **Kemal Atatürk**, or "Father of the Turks."

As the first president of Turkey, Atatürk sought to turn it into a modern nation. He believed this modernization required ending the influence of the Muslim religion on government and personal life. Thus, he made Turkey's government completely secular, or nonreligious. Until his death in 1938, Atatürk's leadership in Turkey led to advances in industry, education, and many other fields.

Persia Similar reforms took place in Persia. In 1921 Reza Khan led an overthrow of Persia's shah, or emperor. Khan himself became shah in 1925.

NEW YORK

CC Unit 6-C3 Modernization of a secular Turkey in response to European imperialism

READING SKILLS
Understanding Comparison and Contrast How were reforms in Turkey and Persia alike?

Reading Focus

The Middle East

Recall What did Arab nationalists want at the end of World War I? *an independent Arab state*

Describe What was one result of the Balfour Declaration? *thousands of Jews immigrated to Palestine*

📄 **CRF**, Primary Source: British White Paper of June 1922

Reading Focus

❹ How did nationalism affect Africa? *African colonies wanted independence from Europe; pan-African movement*

Nationalism in Africa

Identify Why did African nationalism grow after World War I? *Many Africans had served in European armies during the war.*

Explain How was the African economy affected by the war? *suffered, trade dried up, European spending almost stopped*

Teaching Tip

Some students may have very strong feelings about issues in the Middle East. If so, review events from the history of the area, presenting a balance of opinions.

Answers

Linking to Today *both wanted states in Palestine; after World War I, France and Great Britain set up mandates in the Middle East; many Arabs and Jews moved to Palestine; a plan to divide Palestine between them failed; state of Israel was created, war broke out*

Reading Check *reforms and independence in Turkey and Persia;*

Linking TO Today

Roots of the Arab-Israeli Conflict

The modern Arab-Israeli conflict over the control of land in the Middle East has long resisted attempts at resolution. The roots of this conflict can be traced back many years.

In the late 1800s Jews from Europe began to establish small colonies in Palestine, their ancient homeland, as part of an effort to rebuild a Jewish state. By the early 1900s, a growing Arab nationalist movement had also developed, which wanted to form an independent Arab state in the Middle East.

When World War I ended, France and Great Britain set up mandates in the Middle East. Both Arabs and Jews were unhappy with this decision. Still, after the war, thousands of foreign-born Arabs and Jews moved to Palestine. Tensions increased, and violence between the two groups broke out.

In an attempt at compromise, the United Nations issued a plan to divide Palestine between Jews and Arabs in 1947. Although the Jews accepted this plan, Arabs felt it was unfair and rejected it. In 1948 Britain pulled out of Palestine and the state of Israel was created. Five Arab states immediately attacked Israel. Although Israel won this war, it was the first of many Arab-Israeli wars that followed. Today, the Arab-Israeli conflict continues.

Summarize What are the origins of the conflict between Arabs and Jews?

▲ Jewish settlers arrive in the newly formed state of Israel.

Khan, who ruled as Reza Shah Pahlavi (ri-ZAH SHAH PA-luh-vee), wanted to make Iran into a modern and fully independent nation. Reza Shah sought to advance industry and to improve education. In 1935 he changed Persia's name to Iran.

French and British Mandates Arab nationalists, supported by the British, had rebelled against the Ottoman Empire in 1916. Led by Husayn bin Ali (hoo-SAYN bin ah-LEE), they wanted to create an independent Arab state stretching from Syria to Yemen.

Meanwhile, another national movement was growing stronger. The Jewish national movement, called Zionism, hoped to rebuild a Jewish state in the ancient Jewish homeland. In the 1917 Balfour Declaration, the British government declared its support for a Jewish homeland in Palestine, while respecting the "rights of existing non-Jewish communities."

Instead of fulfilling these Arab and Jewish nationalist hopes, the postwar peace agreements established French and British mandates in the Middle East. France gained control of Syria and Lebanon, and Britain gained control of Iraq and what was called the Palestine

📺 **NEW YORK**
CC Unit 6-C10
Arabic and Zionist nationalism

Mandate. Both Arabs and Jews were unhappy, believing wartime promises had been broken.

In 1921 the British gave the eastern part of the Palestine Mandate to Husayn's son Abdullah as the kingdom of Transjordan (now Jordan). That same year the British installed Husayn's son Faisal as the king of Iraq, the British mandate on Transjordan's northeastern border. Palestine's population soon expanded greatly as tens of thousands of Jews and Arabs immigrated to the land. Palestinian Arab anger over this Jewish immigration led to conflict in the mid-1930s. Indeed, the conflict in this region continues today.

READING CHECK **Compare** What issues did nations in the Middle East face after World War I?

Nationalism in Africa

During World War I, Africa had been almost entirely under the rule of European colonial powers. Hundreds of thousands of Africans served in European armies during the war, and tens of thousands of them lost their lives. This wartime experience did much to increase nationalist feeling in Africa.

Skills Focus: Analyzing Alternative Points of View | At Level

Reading Like a Historian Skill
African Freedom and Colonialism

1. Have students review the information about Africa in the text, and guide them in a discussion about African colonies after World War I.

2. Organize students into small groups. Remind students that many African songs, poems, and even speeches are written with a refrain throughout the work. Have each group write two songs or poems using this technique. One poem or song should reflect the desire for

freedom in African colonies. The other should reflect the viewpoint of Europeans who stand to lose valuable resources in Africa.

3. Guide students in a discussion of the viewpoints presented. Who lost and gained the most in Africa's quest for independence?
🔲 **Auditory-Musical**

📋 **Alternative Assessment Handbook**, Rubric 26: Poems and Songs

Nationalist Feeling Grows Many Africans believed they had earned independence from European control through their wartime sacrifices. Further, the war had caused great economic hardship in many parts of Africa. Trade with Europe, on which many African colonies depended, dried up, and European spending in African colonies slowed to a trickle. In short, Africans felt that they had suffered a great deal for Europe and had little to show for it.

African anger further increased because of the Treaty of Versailles. No Africans were involved in the negotiations, and the European powers simply gave Germany's African colonies to other countries as mandates rather than granting them independence.

Working for Independence In the years after World War I, Africans' frustrations at the actions of the European powers led them to seek greater independence. For example, a series of meetings known as Pan-African Congresses began in 1919. Organized by people of African heritage living around the world, these conferences led to a series of demands for African independence.

North African Arabs also took action to win independence in British-controlled Egypt. After the war, in which hundreds of thousands of Egyptians had served, a group of Egyptians tried to bring a demand for independence to the British government. When some members of the group were arrested, protests swept the country. Many Egyptians were killed.

Africans United
Speakers gather at the Second Pan-African Congress, held in Belgium in 1921. American W.E.B. Du Bois, one of the organizers of the congress, is second from the right.

The British eventually recognized that they could not maintain full control of Egypt. In February 1922 they formally declared that Egypt was an independent nation.

Egypt's independence was a victory for nationalism in Africa, but it was not the start of a trend in the postwar years. Indeed, the continent remained almost entirely under European control in the 1920s and 1930s. During this time, African desire for reform and independence continued to grow. Yet it would take time—and another world war—before nationalism in Africa would lead to major change on the continent.

READING CHECK **Summarize** How did World War I help inspire feelings of nationalism in Africa?

SECTION 1 ASSESSMENT

go.hrw.com
Online Quiz
Keyword: SHL IWY HP

Reviewing Ideas, Terms, and People

1. **a. Identify** Who were **Jiang Jieshi** and **Mao Zedong**?
   b. Draw Conclusions Why do you think the Guomindang and the Communists worked together in China in the early 1920s?

2. **a. Describe** What two key concepts did **Mohandas Gandhi** use in his protests?
   b. Evaluate Why do you think Gandhi's repeated arrests helped build sympathy for his cause?

3. **a. Recall** Why did many Arabs feel mistreated at the end of World War I?
   b. Elaborate Explain how the Balfour Declaration influenced events in the Middle East following World War I.

4. **a. Describe** How did World War I affect Africa?
   b. Summarize What happened in Egypt after World War I?

Critical Thinking

5. **Sequence** Use your notes on the section to summarize how the growth of nationalism was similar in each region.

CHINA	
INDIA	
MIDDLE EAST	
AFRICA	

FOCUS ON SPEAKING

6. **Exposition** Write a brief speech that might have been given at the First Pan-African Congress in 1919. In a few sentences, summarize the arguments in favor of independence for African colonies.

THE INTERWAR YEARS **811**

Section 1 Assessment Answers

1. **a.** Jiang Jieshi—led Guomindang; Mao Zedong—Chinese Communist leader
   b. shared similar goals

2. **a.** nonviolence and civil disobedience
   b. possible answer—He hurt no one.

3. **a.** expected an independent Arab state
   b. Britain supported the Zionist movement

4. **a.** Africans died fighting; war caused great economic hardship
   b. Egyptians killed in independence protests; Egypt eventually won independence

5. China—May Fourth Movement: Communist Party formed: the Long March; India—Amritsar Massacre: Ghandi's nonviolent protests: India gains partial independence; Middle East—Turks defeat Greek forces and establish Republic of Turkey: Reza Khan overthrows Persia's shah and founds Iran; Africa—Pan-African Congresses: Egyptian independence

6. Speeches might argue that Africans earned their independence by serving in World War I.

811

Preteach

Getting Started

Use the **Interactive Reader and Study Guide** to familiarize students with the section content.

📝 **Interactive Reader and Study Guide,** Section 2

[worksheet illustration]

Academic Vocabulary

Review with students the high-use academic term in this section.

prosperity wealth or success (p. 813)

📝 **CRF:** Vocabulary Builder: Section 2

Taking Notes

The U.S. economy was booming during the 1920s, so many Americans bought stock. Poor consumers could no longer buy products. In 1929, a huge sell-off led to the stock market crash. The Great Depression was caused by many factors. Hoover's minimal governmental response didn't work. Roosevelt fought the crisis with the New Deal, employing people and regulating banking and the stock market. The Depression had a worldwide impact. The Smoot-Hawley Tariff Act slowed world trade, ruining some foreign economies. War recovery and economic problems in Europe led to political unrest, and changes in government.

go.hrw.com
Online Resources
KEYWORD: SHL IWY
ACTIVITY: U.S. Economy

BEFORE YOU READ

MAIN IDEA

In the late 1920s an economic depression started in the United States and quickly spread around the globe, causing great hardship and creating ideal conditions for political unrest.

READING FOCUS

1. What happened to the U.S. economy during the 1920s?

2. How did the Depression spread throughout the United States?

3. How did the Depression affect the world?

KEY TERMS AND PEOPLE

credit
Black Tuesday
Great Depression
Franklin Delano Roosevelt
New Deal
John Maynard Keynes
Smoot-Hawley Tariff Act

 NEW YORK

PI **1.2** Students understand the development and connectedness of Western civilization and other civilizations.

PI **1.4** Students understand the broad patterns, relationships, and interactions of cultures.

THE INSIDE STORY

Could the good times last forever? During the decade known as the Roaring Twenties, times were good for many Americans. The economy was booming, unemployment was low, and the stock market was climbing steadily. It was an exciting time for American popular culture as well. Movies and radio exploded in popularity and artists and writers throughout the country documented the great economic and social changes taking place. It seemed the good times would never end.

▲ **This 1929 magazine cover shows a woman enjoying the good times.**

The growing stock market was one thing that seemed likely to last forever. In fact, many Americans in 1929 believed that the price of stocks would always rise. Who could blame them? In the two years before 1929, the stock market had doubled in value. Investing in stocks seemed like an easy way to wealth.

In the summer of 1929, businessman John J. Raskob wrote a magazine article about investing in the stock market. The article's title sums up what he and many other people felt about buying stocks in the 1920s: "Everybody Ought to Be Rich." In the article, Raskob said that investing in the stock market was a simple matter, and that the average American could—and should—do so. But just two months after "Everybody Ought to Be Rich" was published, many stock investors were not even close to being rich. They were flat broke. ∎

The U.S. Economy in the 1920s

At the end of World War I, the United States was the world's leading economic power. That position grew stronger during the boom times of the 1920s, but by the end of the decade the U.S. economy was crashing.

Economic Growth During World War I, American farms and factories supplied much of the world with the food and supplies needed to fight the war. Although the American economy slowed down briefly when the war ended, it was booming again by 1921. Growth was steady throughout most of the 1920s.

Most of this economic growth occurred in industry, with automobile manufacturing a huge part of the boom. In addition, American factories also busily turned out a wide range of consumer goods—from radios to vacuum cleaners to washing machines.

Teach the Main Idea

At Level

The Great Depression

Materials: construction paper

1. **Teach** Ask students the Reading Focus questions to teach this section.

2. **Apply** Organize students into small groups. Have groups scan the section and list the factors that caused the Great Depression, and the reasons it had a worldwide impact. Distribute construction paper. Have groups use the atlas in their texts to sketch a simple outline map of the world and write their

facts in boxes with arrows pointing to the areas affected.

3. **Review** Display students' labeled maps for all to see.

4. **Practice/Homework** Have each student write a summary paragraph about the causes of the Great Depression and its worldwide impact. **LS** **Verbal-Linguistic, Visual-Spatial**

📝 **Alternative Assessment Handbook**, Rubrics 1: Acquiring Information; and 20: Map Creation

The success of American industry was reflected in the stock market. During the 1920s the overall value of the stocks traded at the nation's stock markets rose an astounding 400 percent. Many Americans rushed to buy stocks, afraid they would miss out on the prosperity. Some borrowed money from stockbrokers in order to buy stocks, in what is known as buying on margin. This increasing investment in the stock market drove stock prices even higher.

Hidden Problems The stock market was booming, but there were hidden problems affecting the American economy. For example, the new wealth being created was not distributed evenly. The richest 1 percent of the population earned 19 percent of the nation's income.

Also, for much of the 1920s, the easy availability of credit allowed Americans to increase their spending on consumer goods. **Credit** is an arrangement in which a purchaser borrows money from a bank or other lender and agrees to pay it back over time. By the end of the decade, many consumers were reaching the limit of their credit and could no longer afford to buy the products that had kept the U.S. economy expanding.

The Stock Market Crash By the fall of 1929, consumer spending had slowed, and sales of some products had suffered badly.

Fears began to grow that stock prices might soon drop. Then, at the end of October, some nervous investors began to sell off their stocks. Others joined in, and a huge sell-off began.

The worst day was October 29, known as **Black Tuesday**. On that single day, investors sold off 16 million shares. With few people wanting to buy the stocks that flooded the market, stock prices collapsed completely. Many investors who had borrowed money to buy stocks were forced to sell at a loss to repay their loans.

The massive stock market crash ruined many investors, but they were not the only ones affected. Banks that had lent money to these investors were in deep financial trouble as well. Furthermore, the crash delivered a devastating blow to American industry, which had already been struggling. Indeed, the effects of the great crash would soon be felt throughout the country—and beyond.

READING CHECK **Sequence** What happened to the U.S. economy during the 1920s?

The Depression Spreads

Following the stock market crash, the American economy took a severe downward dive. This economic downturn became known as the **Great Depression**. The Depression was the result of a number of complex factors.

ACADEMIC VOCABULARY
prosperity wealth or success

Take notes on the causes and spread of the Great Depression.

Causes	Spread

 NEW YORK

CC **Unit 6-C5**
Great Depression —causes and impacts

CAUSES OF THE 1929 STOCK MARKET CRASH

- Increasing speculation in stock market
- Stock prices at unrealistic levels
- Increasing consumer reliance on credit
- Declining consumer spending
- Struggling businesses

Stock Market Crash

During the Depression, many businesses failed and millions of people were unemployed.

THE INTERWAR YEARS **813**

813

Reading Focus

❷ How did the Depression spread throughout the United States? *Industry slowed, people lost jobs, and government response did not work.*

The Depression Spreads

Explain What caused some banks to go out of business? *Businesses and investors failed to pay off loans; anxious depositors withdrew their savings.*

Identify Cause and Effect What effect did joblessness have on Americans? *They could not buy needed goods or food, hurting industry further.*

Make Inferences How do you think Americans felt about Herbert Hoover? *possible answer—frustrated that the president would not take action to help those who lost jobs*

📝 **CRF:** Biography: Bessie Smith

Biography

Langston Hughes (1902–1967) The Harlem Renaissance fueled creative genius, as can be seen in the poetry and novels of Langston Hughes. Hughes was born in Missouri. He was raised by his grandmother in Kansas, and in his teens moved to Illinois and then to Ohio with his mother. He very nearly followed the path of a developing musical sensation, the blues. In his work, Hughes honored the American poor as they struggled through the Depression with determination and strength. Hughes gave some of his poems to the famous critic Vachel Lindsay, whose praise helped him gain recognition.

Industry Slows One cause of the Depression was a slowdown in industry. This slowdown had begun before the crash but worsened quickly after it. As industry slowed, workers lost their jobs. By 1933 one out of every four workers was unemployed. Joblessness and poverty reduced Americans' ability to buy food and goods, which hurt industry even further.

As businesses and investors failed to pay off loans, banks also suffered. At the time, a bank's failure meant that people who had savings in the bank could lose their money. As a result, the rumor that a bank was struggling could cause anxious depositors to withdraw all their savings, driving the bank out of business.

Government Response U.S. president Herbert Hoover believed that the federal government should have a limited role in business affairs. As a result, he favored a minimal government response to the crisis. In fact, some of his advisers believed the Great Depression was a normal, healthy adjustment to an overheated economy. Hoover eventually took some actions to fight the Depression, but many Americans felt that he was doing too little.

Roosevelt Elected In 1932 U.S. voters elected **Franklin Delano Roosevelt** as president. Under Roosevelt, the federal government's role in the lives of Americans greatly increased. Roosevelt pushed forward a program known

---

THE ARTS AROUND THE WORLD

Music
The Blues

What is it? The blues is a simple yet expressive form of music that developed in the American South in the late 1800s. Blues songs evolved in African American communities, combining aspects of spirituals, work songs, and traditional African music. Most blues songs express feelings of sadness, often about problems in love. When southern African Americans moved to northern cities in search of work during World War I and the Great Depression, they took the blues with them. As a result, the music spread throughout the north.

Why is it important?
• Blues is an important African American contribution to modern culture.
• Blues has been a major influence on later forms of music, including jazz, rock, and hip-hop.

Blues musician Robert Johnson is sometimes called the grandfather of rock and roll.

Bessie Smith was one of the most popular blues singers of the 1920s and 1930s.

The deep poverty in the Mississippi Delta influenced the early blues. ▶

"Worry Blues" sung by Jesse Lockett

Everything that I do seem like I do it wrong,
Everything that I do seem like I do it wrong,
Sometimes I regret that I was ever born.

Blues and trouble seem to be my best friend,
Blues and trouble seem to be my best friend,
Even when my blues leave me, then my troubles begin.

Skills FOCUS **INTERPRETING VISUALS**

1. **Summarize** How did blues music spread?
2. **Infer** How did the Great Depression affect blues music?

814 CHAPTER 27

Skills Focus: Analyzing Secondary Sources ┃ At Level

Reading Like a Historian Skill
Opinions of Hoover's Response

┃ **Research Required**

1. Remind students that President Hoover did very little to boost the economy when the stock market crashed because he believed that government should take a limited role in business affairs.

2. Organize students into small groups. Have each group conduct research to find information about Hoover's responses to the stock market crash. Have students examine sources for possible bias.

3. Have groups prepare a display of the articles they found, accompanied by their conclusions about potential bias in each source.

4. Have students form a generalization about President Hoover's response to the crash.
   LS **Verbal-Linguistic, Interpersonal**

   📝 **Alternative Assessment Handbook**, Rubrics 12: Drawing Conclusions; and 30: Research as the **New Deal**, aimed at fighting the Great Depression. Roosevelt and his advisers believed that government spending could help start an economic recovery. The New Deal established public works programs that gave jobs to the unemployed and it provided government money for welfare and other relief programs. The New Deal also created new regulations to reform and protect the stock market and the banking system.

New Economic Theories The increased government spending was supported by the theories of **John Maynard Keynes**, a British economist. Keynes believed that governments could limit or even prevent economic down-

turns. He argued that governments could do this by spending money—even if it meant having an unbalanced budget. In an economic depression, Keynes said, government spending would help increase economic output. Factories would have to hire workers to meet the new demand, providing workers with income. Eventually, the workers would begin spending—and the depression would end.

Indeed, increased government spending seemed to help the U.S. economy, at least initially. But the Great Depression lingered on throughout the 1930s.

READING CHECK **Identify Cause and Effect**
Explain the factors that led to the Great Depression.

The Worldwide Depression

In 1929 American businesses were responsible for much of the world's industrial output. America was also one of the world's leading importers and lenders of money. Thus, events affecting the American economy were sure to have an impact on other countries. The Great Depression that began in the United States soon spread around the world.

Before the Crash Some areas of the world were having economic difficulties even before the American stock market crash. In Europe, most countries were still struggling to recover from the devastating effects of World War I. Many of the former Allied Powers were deeply in debt to the United States. In Great Britain, high interest rates in the late 1920s led to decreased spending and high unemployment. In Germany, the steep reparations the nation had been forced to pay after the war led to severe inflation, making German money virtually worthless and crippling the German economy. In Japan, a severe economic depression in 1927 had forced many banks to close. For these and other countries, the Great Depression was just the latest in a long series of economic crises. The effects of this latest collapse, however, were far worse.

A Slowdown in Trade In 1930 President Hoover signed the **Smoot-Hawley Tariff Act**. This act placed heavy taxes on imported goods in an attempt to encourage Americans to buy goods and products made in the United States.

FOCUS ON NEW YORK

Before becoming president, Franklin Roosevelt worked to end the Depression as governor of New York. Much of Roosevelt's national New Deal legislation had first been passed and tested in New York.

THE SPREAD OF THE BLUES

Detroit
Chicago
New York
St. Louis
Washington, D.C.
Memphis
ORIGIN OF THE BLUES
New Orleans
Gulf of Mexico
ATLANTIC OCEAN

NEW YORK STANDARDS
PI 1.2

THE INTERWAR YEARS **815**

815

Direct Teach

Reading Focus

The Worldwide Depression

Recall Name two countries in which extremists gained strength as economies worsened. *Germany, Italy*

Make Inferences How did the Great Depression contribute to the rise of totalitarian leaders? *Widespread misery led people to trust powerful leaders who promised to fix problems.*

Review & Assess

Close

Review the factors that led to the worldwide Great Depression and its political consequences.

Review

 Online Quiz, Section 2

Assess

SE Section 2 Assessment

📋 **Progress Assessment**: Section 2 Quiz

📋 **Alternative Assessment Handbook**

Reteach/Intervene

📋 **Interactive Reader and Study Guide**, Section 2

💿 **Interactive Skills Tutor CD-ROM**

Answers

Interpreting Graphs *Unemployment rose in the United States, Great Britain, and Germany, and world trade declined.*

Reading Check *World trade slowed, ruining some foreign economies. War recovery and economic problems in Europe led to political unrest and changes in government.*

816

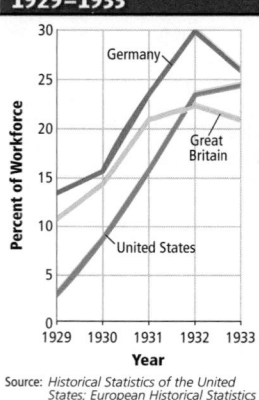

UNEMPLOYMENT, 1929–1933

Germany

Great Britain

United States

Source: Historical Statistics of the United States; European Historical Statistics

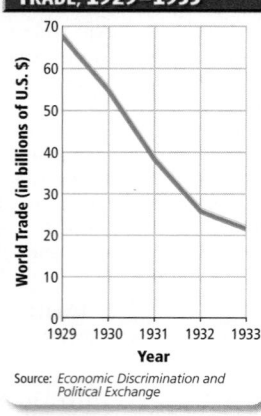

DECLINE OF WORLD TRADE, 1929–1933

Source: Economic Discrimination and Political Exchange

Skills FOCUS INTERPRETING GRAPHS

Summarize How did the Great Depression affect unemployment and world trade?

These American goods would be cheaper than the imported goods which were taxed. The act backfired. The new tariff led countries around the world to increase their own tariffs on American goods. As a result, world trade slowed to a standstill. For many nations, the loss of foreign trade crippled their economies.

As trade slowed, the prices for trade goods collapsed. In Japan, for example, the price of silk dropped sharply. This product was a major export and responsible for nearly 20 percent of Japanese farm income. The decline of Japan's silk industry is just one example of the collapsing markets and economic hardship found all over the world.

Political Impact The postwar era had been challenging for many European governments. The difficult peace process and the formation of new nations out of the ruins of empires had left many countries politically unstable.

As the Depression continued, unrest grew worse. Political instability in Great Britain and France led to the formation of several new governments during the Depression, as desperate citizens looked for leaders who could help them.

In other countries, extremist political groups gained strength as economies worsened. In Germany, for example, the National Socialist (Nazi) Party unfairly blamed Jews for many of the country's problems and promised to rebuild a powerful German empire. Italy had already fallen under the rule of the dictator Benito Mussolini. During the Depression years, Mussolini tightened his control on the nation.

Indeed, the widespread misery and hopelessness created ideal conditions for the rise of powerful leaders who promised to restore their nations to glory. The world was in the midst of troubled times, but a worse crisis lay ahead.

READING CHECK Summarize How did the Depression spread to the rest of the world?

SECTION 2 ASSESSMENT

go.hrw.com
Online Quiz
Keyword: SHL IWY HP

Reviewing Ideas, Terms, and People

1. a. Describe What role did **credit** play in the success of the U.S. economy in the 1920s?
b. Identify Cause and Effect How did the success of the stock market in the 1920s contribute to its collapse?

2. a. Identify How did the slowdown in American industry affect the economy?
b. Compare and Contrast Compare and contrast the policies of Herbert Hoover and **Franklin Delano Roosevelt**.

3. a. Recall Why and how did the **Great Depression** spread from the United States to other countries?
b. Elaborate Why do you think economic and political turmoil in Europe may have made some people more willing to accept a dictator?

Critical Thinking

4. Compare and Contrast Use your notes on the section to compare and contrast the Great Depression in the United States and in the rest of the world.

United States   World

FOCUS ON WRITING ✎

5. Exposition Write a letter that someone who lost his or her job in the Great Depression might have written to a friend.

816 CHAPTER 27

Section 2 Assessment Answers

1. a. People bought goods and stocks on credit, creating jobs and fueling the economy.
b. Investors who borrowed money to buy stocks were forced to sell at a loss.

2. a. workers lost their jobs, could not buy goods, hurting industry even more
b. Hoover—limited government role in business affairs; Roosevelt—increased government spending for jobs program, welfare, relief

3. a. United States was a world leader in lending, importing, and manufacturing; Smoot-Hawley Tariff Act backfired

b. People were desperate for strong leadership to solve the economic crisis.

4. U.S.—stock market crash, eventually New Deal started; both—farmers hit hard, Smoot-Hawley Tariff Act slowed trade, widespread misery and hopelessness; World—still recovering from war, owed U.S. and other nations money, political instability, rise of dictatorships

5. Student letters should include details from the section about life during the Great Depression.

Focus on Themes

Society

During the Great Depression, many people around the world depended on government-administered social welfare programs to provide food and jobs. In the United States, social welfare programs to help poor and unemployed Americans were first established during this time period. Today, many nations have similar programs to aid their citizens.

SOCIAL WELFARE PROGRAMS THEN The first modern social programs were established in Germany in the late 1800s and included health insurance, workers' compensation, and pensions for the elderly and the disabled. By the 1920s similar social welfare programs had become common in Europe and in much of the Western Hemisphere.

In the United States, however, social services were the responsibility of state and local governments, churches, and voluntary organizations. The crippling effects of the Great Depression changed that. Beginning with Franklin Roosevelt's New Deal, the federal government established a variety of national social welfare programs to aid poor, unemployed, and elderly Americans in need of help.

▲ **THEN** Workers at a Chicago soup kitchen serve food to unemployed men during the Great Depression.

SOCIAL WELFARE PROGRAMS NOW Social programs are widespread today but are most common in Western Europe. In many countries, social welfare programs to help those in need are seen as an important government responsibility.

While most countries offer some form of social welfare, there is much disagreement about the services that should be offered as well as the amount of money that should be spent on them. Most programs are funded by a combination of contributions from employers, persons covered by insurance programs, and general government revenue. Some people worry that offering generous welfare programs can cause governments to spend too much money and may discourage the unemployed from finding jobs.

Skills Focus — UNDERSTANDING THEMES

1. **Summarize** How did the Great Depression affect social welfare programs in the United States?
2. **Infer** Why do some people object to welfare programs?
3. **Draw Conclusions** Why do you think national social welfare programs were established later in the United States than in many European countries?

Skills Focus: Making Oral Presentations
At Level

Reading Like a Historian Skill
Town Hall Forum Speaker
Research Required

1. Discuss the Understanding Themes questions with students. Have students explain why the U.S. government agreed to implement the New Deal.

2. Organize students into seven groups. Assign one Social Reform from the Quick Facts list to each group. Have each group discuss and list the benefits and problems associated with its assigned program. Students should

conduct outside research on their assigned project to determine its effects.

3. Have each group prepare two short speeches, one supporting the program, and one opposing the program.

4. Next, have volunteers present their speeches while the rest of the class listens and takes notes. **LS Interpersonal, Verbal-Linguistic**

Alternative Assessment Handbook, Rubrics 18: Listening; and 24: Oral Presentations

---

Focus on Themes

Society

Info to Know

Daily Life To help students understand how the Great Depression affected people's daily lives and changed the very fabric of society, mention the following true events and statistics from the United States during the 1930s: a group of 50 desperate men were seen behind a Chicago restaurant fighting violently over a garbage can; some Americans emigrated to Russia to seek jobs; the suicide rate reached its peak; jurors acquitted two families who shot their landlords to prevent being evicted.

Quick Facts Transparency: Major U.S. Social Reforms

Answers

Understanding Themes 1. *shifted responsibility for social services to federal government (away from state and local governments, churches, and voluntary organizations);* **2.** *Some people worry that programs are too costly and may discourage the unemployed from finding jobs.* **3.** *possible answer—Economic conditions in the United States were generally prosperous before the Great Depression.*

Getting Started

Use the **Interactive Reader and Study Guide** to familiarize students with the section content.

📖 **Interactive Reader and Study Guide**, Section 3

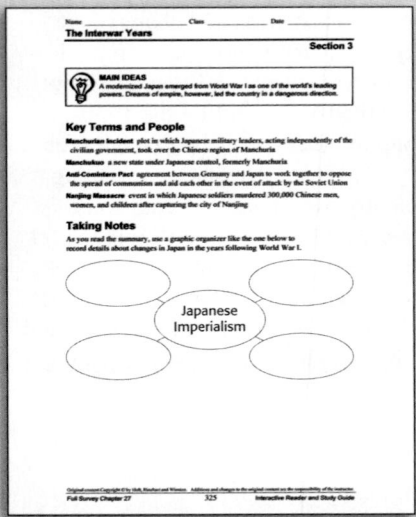

Academic Vocabulary

Review with students the high-use academic term in this section.

subsequent later; following in time (p. 822)

📓 **CRF:** Vocabulary Builder: Section 3

Taking Notes

Japan needed natural resources and raw materials to support its growing industry and population. Japan was quickly becoming an urban, industrialized nation. The military sought and was gaining more power in government. The 1924 American law barring Japanese immigration offended the Japanese, who were becoming increasingly nationalistic.

SECTION 3 Japanese Imperialism

BEFORE YOU READ

MAIN IDEA

A modernized Japan emerged from World War I as one of the world's leading powers. Dreams of empire, however, led the country in a dangerous direction.

READING FOCUS

1. How did Japan change in the 1920s?
2. Why did the Japanese military's influence grow?
3. What were the reasons for Japanese aggression in the 1930s?

KEY TERMS

Manchurian Incident
Manchukuo
Anti-Comintern Pact
Nanjing Massacre

 NEW YORK

PI 1.1 Students define culture and civilization, explaining how they developed and changed.

PI 4.4 Students analyze different interpretations of important events, issues, or developments in world history.

THE INSIDE STORY

Why would an army bomb its own railway? In 1931, a bomb exploded in the Chinese region of Manchuria, damaging a Japanese-controlled railway line. Japanese soldiers stationed in Manchuria immediately blamed the blast on Chinese sabotage. Given Chinese unhappiness with the Japanese presence in China, it was easy to believe that China was responsible for the attack.

However, China had nothing to do with the explosion. The bomb had been planted by Japanese soldiers who wanted to use the excuse of this alleged Chinese attack to quickly take over Manchuria. Japan would then have access to the region's rich natural resources, which were badly needed by Japanese industry.

The Japanese plot worked perfectly, except for one thing: Japan's government did not support the military action. Indeed, Japan's civilian leaders had known nothing about the plot. But when Japanese troops began to move into northern Manchuria three days after the explosion, military leaders refused to obey the government's orders to stop the invasion. The Japanese public supported the army's actions, and the government had little choice but to go along. Soon, the Japanese military dominated Manchuria—and was growing ever more aggressive. ◼

A SECRET PLOT

A Chinese city burns after a devastating Japanese attack. ▼

Teach the Main Idea

At Level

Japanese Imperialism

1. **Teach** Ask students the Reading Focus questions to teach this section.

2. **Apply** Have students work individually or in mixed-ability pairs to create their own two-column charts showing the problems within Japan and the problems Japan was having with other nations during this time period. For problems within Japan, students should include the economy, strikes, and lack of natural resources.

3. **Review** Have students share the information on their charts, and create a class chart for all to see. Have students retain their charts to use as a study tool.

4. **Practice/Homework** Have students use their charts to write an "in-depth" magazine article about the rise of Japanese imperialism.
LS Verbal-Linguistic, Visual-Spatial

📓 **Alternative Assessment Handbook**, Rubrics 7: Charts; and 19: Magazines

Japan in the 1920s

At the end of World War I, Japan stood as one of the world's foremost powers. It was a remarkable accomplishment for a country that just a half-century before had been a relatively weak agricultural nation. Even so, Japan's postwar years were not easy ones.

Economic Challenges Japan's economy had undergone many changes during the Meiji restoration, when the nation's economy first began to industrialize. By the early 1920s this rapid industrialization had begun to create problems. Peasants and rural workers had not shared in the nation's new prosperity, and once World War I ended many industries experienced slowdowns. As a result, businesses began to lay workers off, and unrest grew. Strikes and labor disputes increased sharply in the 1920s.

Japan faced other economic challenges during the 1920s as well. The small island country did not have the natural resources needed to supply modern industry and was forced to import these materials. To pay for them, Japan sold its manufactured goods abroad. But because other countries passed tariffs to protect their own products against foreign competition, Japan had difficulty exporting enough goods to survive economically. To get the natural resources needed to support its growing population, Japanese leaders decided their nation needed to expand.

Social Changes Japan's rapid shift from a feudal agricultural nation to a more urban industrial country affected more than just its economy. The shift, combined with universal education and new ideas from the West, led to changes in Japanese society. Democracy began to flourish, and a vibrant system of political parties emerged. Some young people adopted Western fashions and beliefs and began to question traditional Japanese values, such as obedience and respect for authority. More conservative Japanese, including military leaders, resented these changes and believed that straying from traditional Japanese beliefs and interests had corrupted the country.

> **READING CHECK** **Summarize** What changes took place in Japan during the 1920s?

EVENTS IN JAPAN, 1929–1940

QUICK FACTS

1929 The Great Depression hits Japan.

1931 Japan takes control of Manchuria, China.

1933 Japan withdraws from the League of Nations.

1934 Japan announces it will no longer submit to limits on its navy.

1936 Japan signs agreement with Germany.

1937 Japanese troops kill hundreds of thousands of civilians in Nanjing, China.

1940 Japan attempts to expand its power in Asia by proposing an economic alliance of Asian nations.

▼ Japanese troops invade China.

TAKING NOTES
Take notes on Japanese imperialism in the years following World War I.

(Japanese Imperialism)

Growing Military Influence

A serious economic crisis struck Japan in 1927, followed shortly thereafter by the Great Depression. Many Japanese lost faith in their government, which seemed unable to help them, and began to look to the Japanese military for leadership during this time of crisis.

The Military's Vision Military officers envisioned a united Japan—a society devoted to the emperor and to the glory of the nation ruled by the military leadership. Thus, they began to seek more power over Japan's civilian government.

THE INTERWAR YEARS **819**

819

❸ What were the reasons for Japanese aggression in the 1930s? *Military leaders realized they could not compete with industrialized nations.*

Japanese Aggression

Explain How did Japan's military leaders make up for industrial limitations? *by building a fighting spirit in the Japanese troops and members of the public*

Contrast How was the Japanese military different from that of industrialized nations? *Japan had not yet developed technology and industrial power.*

🗝 **Map Transparency**: Japanese Aggression, 1931–1937

Info to Know

The Great Kanto Earthquake Just as Japan was undergoing significant changes and facing serious economic challenges, a natural disaster hit. In September 1923, a strong earthquake devastated a large area around Yokohama and Tokyo. It destroyed buildings and took the lives of approximately 145,000 people.

Answers

Interpreting Maps *Refer to map.*

Reading Check *People lost faith in their government's leadership and began to look to military leadership to help overcome economic problems.*

820

Foreign Relations The military's influence in Japan grew in part because of public opposition to the Japanese government's foreign policy. After World War I, the civilian leaders of Japan's government had made several treaties with the West to limit the size of the Japanese navy. Military officials were furious over these agreements, which seemed to put an end to Japan's overseas expansion.

In 1924 the United States passed a law barring Japanese immigration. This action by one of Japan's supposed allies deeply offended Japanese pride, and some Japanese began to question their government's policy of cooperation with the West. Increasingly, the Japanese public began to put its faith in the military, drawn to its nationalist vision of a strong Japan that would defer to no other country.

READING CHECK **Analyze** Why did the Japanese military's influence increase in the 1920s?

Japanese Aggression

As the 1920s came to an end, Japan's military gained power, widening the gap between the military and the civilian government. Without civilian controls, Japan's military became more aggressive toward other nations.

Building a Fighting Spirit World War I had shown that modern war would rely on technology and industrial power. Japan's military leaders realized that Japan would have difficulty contending directly with the large industrial nations of the world. First, they did not have the industrial capacity; and, second, they had been forced to limit the size of their navy after the war.

To make up for their nation's industrial limitations, Japan's military leaders focused on a different kind of weapon: the Japanese soldiers. They began to promote the fighting spirit of the Japanese troops. This bravery, many officers claimed, could make up for a lack of modern weaponry. "If against tanks you have no anti-tank guns," said one officer, "it becomes a matter of using human bullets." In the Japanese military's instruction manual, the words *surrender*, *retreat*, and *defense* were removed to encourage the idea that these were no longer possibilities.

Japan's military leaders also tried to inspire a fighting spirit among members of the public. One way they did so was by placing military personnel in the public schools to shape the thinking of Japanese children. One Japanese leader described the military's goals:

HISTORY'S VOICES

❝To impart the belief in ultimate victory to the people and the army . . . I applied education and training to the schools and to the youths, and I planned for soundness of heart and mind among the people. At the same time, by encouraging unity . . . between the people and the army, I worked to secure the position of the army as the pillar of the nation.❞

—Ugaki Kazushige, army minister, 1928

JAPANESE AGGRESSION, 1931–1937

- Japan and colonies
- Areas invaded by Japan
- Japanese advance

GEOGRAPHY SKILLS **INTERPRETING MAPS**

Movement Summarize Japan's actions in East Asia between 1931 and 1937.

820 CHAPTER 27

Skills Focus: Analyzing Primary Sources

Below Level

Standard English Mastery

Reading Like a Historian Skill
Ugaki Kazushige's Goals

1. Remind students that the Japanese military was determined to increase its political power, as well as its military might.

2. Read the quote from Ugaki Kazushige in History's Voices to students. Then have students copy the quote onto their own papers, leaving space between lines. Have students underline their copy of the quote to separate each of Kazushige's thoughts. Have students rewrite each goal as a sentence.

3. Write this goal of Japanese officers for students to see, "...a united Japan—a society devoted to its emperor and to the glory of the nation, under the rule of military leadership." Have students write a paragraph explaining how Kazushige's statement supports this goal.
LS **Verbal-Linguistic**

📝 **Alternative Assessment Handbook**, Rubric 37: Writing Assignments

Reading like a Historian

The Nanjing Massacre

Recognizing Bias in Secondary Sources
In 1937 the Japanese army killed many Chinese civilians and soldiers in Nanjing, China. Historians generally agree that the total number of deaths was at least 100,000, but the events at Nanjing remain controversial. In China, the story of Nanjing is told very differently from in Japan.

Even accounts of historical events that are meant to be neutral can show bias. As you read these excerpts from Chinese and Japanese textbooks, consider these factors:

• the country the textbook came from
• the textbook's point of view
• the words used to describe the Japanese soldiers' actions

> What word does this selection use to describe the Japanese soldiers? What does this suggest?

> Wherever they went, the Japanese aggressors burned, killed, raped, looted, and committed the most heinous crimes imaginable. After the Japanese army occupied Nanjing, they unleashed the bloodiest massacre of the city's residents, and committed monstrous crimes. Some peaceful residents were shot as practice targets, others were butchered as bayonet practice targets, and still others were buried alive.
> —From a Chinese middle school history textbook

> How does this selection describe the ways that Chinese civilians were killed?

> What does this selection imply with the wording "It is said to have killed"?

> The Japanese army encountered fierce resistance everywhere. It is said to have killed 200,000 people after occupying Nanking (Nanjing), and it was censured by various foreign governments. But the Japanese people were not informed of these facts.
> —From a Japanese middle school history textbook

> Look at the last sentence of this selection. Why do you think the textbook included this sentence?

Skills Focus   **READING LIKE A HISTORIAN**

1. **Language** Compare and contrast the words used to describe the Japanese soldiers' actions in Nanjing.
2. **Point of View** How are the two versions of this event similar and different? How can you explain these similarities and differences?

See **Skills Handbook**, p. H31

Taking Over the Government A group of Japanese military leaders plotted to replace the nation's government with a military dictatorship, believing that aggressive nationalist leadership was vital to Japan's future. They wanted to build a Japanese empire. During the 1930s, Japanese soldiers, military leaders, and members of nationalist organizations carried out a series of assassinations of government officials, including prime ministers and cabinet members. Some of these crimes were punished, but Japan's civilian government gradually gave in to the military's demands for power. Slowly, Japan's government grew more dominated by the military.

Conquering Manchuria The Japanese military's aggression soon became clear. In the **Manchurian Incident** in 1931, Japanese military leaders decided to conquer the Manchuria region of northeastern China, which was rich in natural resources such as coal and iron. Many in the army believed that Manchuria's resources would help free Japan from economic reliance on trade with the West and would thus allow Japan to compete with large industrial nations.

Japanese forces moved quickly to gain control of Manchuria. The Japanese public supported this action, and the civilian government was virtually powerless to stop it.

THE INTERWAR YEARS **821**

Differentiating Instruction

Above Level

Advanced Learners/ Gifted and Talented

1. Review the information in the text about the growing strength of the Japanese military. Tell students that Hirohito became emperor of Japan in 1926. The emperor had supreme authority over Japan, but some historians believe that Hirohito simply accepted the advice of the Japanese ministers and military advisers.

2. Have students conduct outside research on the role of Hirohito in Japanese political and military affairs prior to World War II. Students should focus their research on the role Hirohito played, or did not play, in formulating Japan's expansionist policies and in the Nanjing Massacre.

3. Have students prepare a multimedia presentation showing the results of their research. **LS Verbal-Linguistic**

📋 **Alternative Assessment Handbook**, Rubric 22: Multimedia Presentations

---

Reading Focus

Japanese Aggression

Identify List two ways Japan isolated itself from the western powers. *withdrew from the League of Nation; announced it would no longer agree to any limits on its naval forces*

Analyze Why did Japan invade Manchuria? *Manchuria had rich natural resources, which Japan needed.*

Activity **Nanjing Massacre** Have students conduct research to find more sources on the Nanjing Massacre, examining each for possible bias. Have each student write an essay comparing the accounts and giving a possible explanation of what happened in Nanjing in 1937. **LS Verbal-Linguistic**

📋 **Alternative Assessment Handbook**, Rubrics 30: Research; and 37: Writing Assignments

📋 **CRF:** Biography: Sadao Araki

Answers

Reading Like a Historian 1. *Chinese textbook uses emotionally charged words like "heinous," "monstrous;" Japanese textbook describes event more neutrally, states that Japanese people were not informed of the massacre;* **2.** *Chinese version shows strong opinion, because so many Chinese people died in the massacre; Japanese version describes the event in terms of the supposed facts, probably because the Japanese government did not share the facts of the massacre with the people at the time.*

821

• Review & Assess •

Reading Focus

Japanese Aggression

Recall Approximately how many Chinese men, women, and children do historians believe were killed in the Nanjing Massacre? *as many as 300,000*

Develop What do you think the Anti-Comintern Pact nations had in common? *possible answers—anti-Communist, strong military influence in government*

Elaborate What might Southeast Asians have thought of the Japanese proposal to create the Greater East Asia Co-Prosperity Sphere? *possible answer—Many would not have trusted the aggressive Japanese.*

• Review & Assess •

Close

Have students describe the modernization and subsequent militarization of Japan.

Review

Online Quiz, Section 3

Assess

SE Section 3 Assessment

Progress Assessment: Section 3 Quiz

Alternative Assessment Handbook

Reteach/Intervene

Interactive Reader and Study Guide, Section 3

Interactive Skills Tutor CD-ROM

Answers

Reading Check *military dominated the Japanese government; Japan needed more natural resources, wanted to increase the size of its empire*

822

THE IMPACT TODAY

In April 2005, some 20,000 Chinese demonstrators attacked the Japanese embassy in Beijing, China, furious about a new Japanese high school textbook that referred to the Nanjing Massacre only as an "incident."

ACADEMIC VOCABULARY

subsequent later; following in time

NEW YORK

CC Unit 6-C7
Japanese militarism and imperialism

Eventually, Japanese troops set up a government in the region. They announced that Manchuria was a new state under Japanese control called **Manchukuo** (man-CHOO-kwoh).

Forming New Alliances The League of Nations strongly condemned Japan's aggressive actions in Manchuria. In response, Japan simply withdrew from the league in 1933. The following year, Japan further isolated itself from the Western powers by announcing that it would no longer agree to limits on the size of its navy.

While Japan was making its break with much of the West, it was growing closer to Germany. In 1936 the two nations signed an agreement known as the Anti-Comintern Pact. In the **Anti-Comintern Pact**, Japan and Germany agreed to work together to oppose the spread of communism. Each nation promised to come to the aid of the other if that country was attacked by the Soviet Union. The following year, Italy joined the pact.

War in China Conflict between Japan and China had continued ever since the Manchurian Incident, but grew worse as Japan became increasingly aggressive and seized more territory in eastern China. Some in Japan began to worry that the Chinese Communists and Guomindang nationalists might again join forces and turn on Japan, perhaps with the support of Japan's old enemy, the Soviet Union. With tensions rising, a series of violent incidents in the summer of 1937 between Chinese troops and Japanese forces stationed in China led to open warfare between the two nations. This conflict became known as the Second Sino-Japanese War.

One of the war's early battles occurred in Nanjing, also known as Nanking. After capturing the city, Japanese troops went on a murderous rampage, killing Chinese soldiers and civilians alike. At least 100,000 Chinese men, women, and children were killed in the **Nanjing Massacre**. The world reacted in horror to the bloody incident.

A Move toward Wider War Japan had some early victories in China, but subsequent battles did not go Japan's way. China was simply too large for Japan to conquer easily, and the war turned into a long, costly struggle.

In search of natural resources to supply its military needs, Japan looked to Southeast Asia. This region was rich in rubber, oil, and other key resources. In 1940 Japan's foreign minister proposed the creation of what he called the Greater East Asia Co-Prosperity Sphere. This was to be a group of nations whose combined resources would allow independence from Western control. The proposal was presented as an economic benefit for the region, but it was little more than another attempt to build a Japanese empire.

Japan's aggression in Asia was viewed with alarm by other nations. They did not welcome the expansion of a Japanese empire.

READING CHECK **Analyze** Why did Japanese aggression increase in the 1930s?

SECTION 3 ASSESSMENT

go.hrw.com
Online Quiz
Keyword: SHL IWY HP

Reviewing Ideas, Terms, and People

1. a. Describe What were some of the challenges facing the Japanese in the 1920s?
   b. Explain How did Japanese society change after World War I?

2. a. Recall What did Japanese military leaders believe their nation should be like?
   b. Summarize Why did the Japanese people begin to put their faith in the military?

3. a. Identify Identify the following event and its significance to Japan in the 1930s: **Manchurian Incident**
   b. Evaluate Why do you think the people of Japan supported their military's aggressive actions?

Critical Thinking

4. Sequence Copy the time line below and use your notes from the section to identify key events and changes in Japan in the years after World War I.

1920 ———————————————— 1940

FOCUS ON SPEAKING

5. Persuasion Were the Japanese army's actions in Manchuria good or bad for Japan? Write a short conversation from the 1930s in which two Japanese people debate this question.

822 CHAPTER 27

Section 3 Assessment Answers

1. a. poverty, industrial slowdown, unemployment, labor disputes, and reduced exports
b. economic changes, urbanization, universal education, and other social changes

2. a. a society devoted to its emperor and to the glory of the nation, under military rule
b. lost faith in their government

3. a. 1931 invasion to gain Manchuria's natural resources, resulted in condemnation by the League of Nations
b. possible answer—felt they needed strong, military leadership to end the economic crisis

4. 1922—agrees to limit the size of its navy; 1927—serious economic crisis; 1931—takes control of Manchuria; 1933—withdraws from the League of Nations; 1934—announces it will no longer limit its navy's size; 1936—Anti-Comintern Pact; 1937—Nanjing Massacre, Anti-Comintern Pact with Italy; 1940—Greater East Asia Co-Prosperity Sphere proposed

5. possible conversation topics—good, increased natural resources; bad, resulted in split with League of Nations

4 Dictators in Europe

BEFORE YOU READ

MAIN IDEA
The political and social unrest that followed World War I helped totalitarian dictators rise to power in Europe.

READING FOCUS
1. How did Benito Mussolini rule Italy?
2. How did Joseph Stalin rule the Soviet Union?
3. How did Adolf Hitler rule Germany?

KEY TERMS AND PEOPLE
Benito Mussolini
fascism
totalitarianism
Joseph Stalin
Gulag
Adolf Hitler
Nazi Party
anti-Semitism
Nuremberg Laws
Kristallnacht

 NEW YORK

PI **1.1** Students define culture and civilization, explaining how they developed and changed.

PI **4.2** Students interpret and analyze documents and artifacts related to significant developments and events in world history.

THE INSIDE STORY

How could someone take over a nation without a fight? Dreaming of greatness for his beloved Italy, Benito Mussolini plotted to take over the Italian government. His plan called for his followers to capture key buildings in the Italian capital of Rome, while some 30,000 more supporters waited outside the city, ready to march in for support. This show of force was impressive, but it might not be enough to defeat the Italian armed forces.

A POWER GRAB IN ITALY

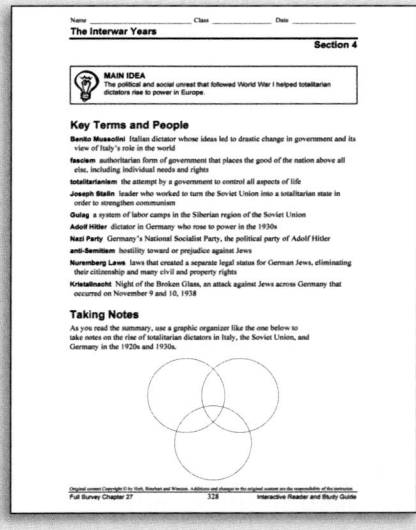

▲ Mussolini (center) and his followers enter Rome in 1922.

Mussolini's plan, however, was a triumph. Italy's king was worried that the Italian armed forces would not remain loyal to him and was unwilling to risk a battle with Mussolini's protestors. Mussolini realized this and rushed by train to Rome. After entering the city he met with the king, who asked Mussolini to form a new Italian government. Only then did Mussolini order his followers into the city for a triumphant "March on Rome." ■

Mussolini's Italy

After the end of World War I, new ideas about government power arose in Italy. Those ideas, promoted by **Benito Mussolini**, led to drastic change in the Italian government and its view of Italy's role in the world.

Fascist Ideology Mussolini, who became known as *Il Duce* (il DOO-chay), or "the leader," wanted to build a great and glorious Italian empire. In 1919 he founded the National Fascist Party. The party took its name from the Latin word *fasces*, which referred to an ancient Roman symbol for the unity and strength of the state.

Fascism is an authoritarian form of government that places the good of the nation above all else, including individual needs and rights. Fascists envision an aggressive state ruled by a dictator, an all-powerful leader who makes all major decisions.

Mussolini in Power By 1922 the Fascists had become a significant force in Italian politics. But that wasn't enough for Mussolini. He wanted to rule Italy. In October he led the so-called March on Rome. This show of force convinced Italy's king to put Mussolini at the head of Italy's government.

THE INTERWAR YEARS **823**

📝 **CRF:** Vocabulary Builder: Section 4

Taking Notes
Italy—1919: Mussolini founds the National Fascist Party, develops totalitarian government; 1935: Italy overtakes Ethiopia; Soviet Union—1924: Stalin leads the Soviet Union; 1927: Stalin introduces first Five Year Plan, Stalin orders collectivization and responds to resistance with violence, 1932: Ukranians starve, Stalin begins the Great Purge, totalitarian rule indoctrinates children, discourages religion, and idealizes Stalin; Germany—Nation suffers postwar turmoil; 1923: Hitler's first attempt to overthrow the government, writes Mein Kampf in jail, supports anti-Semitism; 1933: Hitler becomes Chancellor, 1935: Nuremburg laws established; 1938: Kristallnacht occurs

---

Teach the Main Idea

At Level

Dictators in Europe

1. **Teach** Ask students the Reading Focus questions to teach this section.

2. **Apply** Have students create a Venn diagram in which they show the similarities and differences among the three leaders discussed in this section: Mussolini, Stalin, and Hitler. Have students include a simple sketch of each leader, based on images in the section.

3. **Review** Have volunteers share and discuss their diagrams. Have students compare and correct their own work.

4. **Practice/Homework** Have each student write a one-paragraph summary of the similarities between these three leaders.
   LS **Verbal-Linguistic, Visual-Spatial**

   📝 **Alternative Assessment Handbook**, Rubric 9: Comparing and Contrasting

❶ How did Benito Mussolini rule Italy? *as the all-powerful leader of a totalitarian government*

Mussolini's Italy

Explain Describe the type of government fascists envision. *Under fascism, an authoritarian from of government that places the good of the nation above all else, fascists envision an aggressive state ruled by a dictator.*

Analyze Why did Italy invade Ethiopia? *to show military strength, expand Italy's territories*

📄 **CRF:** Economics and History: Defense Spending in the 1930s

❷ How did Joseph Stalin rule the Soviet Union? *totalitarian rule, with violence, fear, propaganda*

Stalin's Soviet Union

Recall What were the goals of Stalin's Five-Year Plans? *modernize Soviet economy, increase Soviet industrial output*

Contrast How do capitalism and central planning differ? *capitalism: market forces influence production; central planning: government controls production of goods*

🗄 **Quick Facts Transparency**: Common Features of Totalitarian Governments

📄 **CRF:** Biography: Haile Selassie

Answers

Reading Check *with unlimited power; totalitarianism*

Reading Skills *Marx predicted the state would wither away, but Stalin increased government control.*

824

Common Features of Totalitarian Governments

Examples of totalitarian governments include Italy under Mussolini, the Soviet Union under Stalin, and Germany under Hitler. These governments shared many common features.

Political
- The state is more important than individuals.
- The government is controlled by a single political party.
- A powerful dictator unites the people and symbolizes the government.

Social
- The government controls all aspects of daily life.
- Secret police use terror and violence to enforce government policies.
- Citizens are denied basic rights and liberties.

Economic
- The government controls businesses and directs the national economy.
- Labor and business are used to fulfill the objectives of the state.

📝 **TAKING NOTES**

Take notes on the rise of totalitarian dictators in Italy, the Soviet Union, and Germany.

Italy	Soviet Union	Germany

READING SKILLS

Understanding Comparison and Contrast How did Stalin's approach differ from Marx's prediction?

🎬 **NEW YORK**

CC Unit 6-B6 Stalin and the rise of a modern totalitarian state: industrialization, command economy, collectivization

824 CHAPTER 27

Once in power, Mussolini moved to establish a dictatorship. Using threats, violence, and his political skill, he had soon outlawed all opposition and taken unlimited power.

Fascist Italy Mussolini was not satisfied merely with political control. He tried to influence Italians' thoughts, feelings, and behaviors. The attempt by a government to control all aspects of life is called **totalitarianism**.

Mussolini's totalitarian program had many parts. Two of the most effective parts of this program were his use of propaganda to promote Italy's greatness and his establishment of festivals and holidays that reminded modern Italians of their proud Roman heritage.

The Invasion of Ethiopia Mussolini set out to make Italy a strong military power. To that end, he looked around for an easy target and spotted Ethiopia. Ethiopia had two serious disadvantages. It was located between two Italian colonies and its military was ill-equipped. Italian forces crushed the Ethiopians in 1935.

Ethiopian leader Haile Selassie (HY-lee suh-LA-see) appealed to the League of Nations to take action against Italy's aggression. Although much of the world condemned Italy's attack, no nation was willing to get involved and risk another world war. The League placed some economic sanctions on Italy but took no real action.

READING CHECK **Identify the Main Idea**
How did Mussolini rule Italy?

Stalin's Soviet Union

Soviet leader Vladimir Lenin had died in 1924, shortly after the Communist Soviet Union was formed. After a struggle for power, **Joseph Stalin** became the new Soviet leader.

Communism Under Stalin Although Karl Marx had predicted that the state would gradually wither away under communism, Stalin took a very different approach. Instead of reducing the government's power, he worked to turn the Soviet Union into a totalitarian state, intent on controlling every aspect of Soviet life. Stalin believed this was necessary in order to strengthen communism in the Soviet Union.

The Five-Year Plans A major part of Stalin's plan to strengthen Soviet communism was the modernization of the Soviet economy. In 1928 he began the first Five-Year Plan. Other such plans would follow later. Under the Five-Year Plans, each factory and mine had production goals set by the state.

These plans reflected the Soviet system of central planning, in which the government makes major decisions about the production of goods. Central planning differs from a capitalist economic system, such as that of the United States. In capitalism, market forces are the major influence on production.

The Five-Year Plans did, as Stalin had hoped, lead to increases in Soviet industrial output. During the first two Five-Year Plans, for example, Soviet production of oil more

---

Skills Focus: Comparing and Contrasting

At Level

Reading Skill
Comparing Empire Builders

1. Remind students about the empire builders and dictators of other nations and time periods they have studied. Have students create a class list for all to see. Students may wish to refer to their texts to create the list.

2. Organize students into small groups. Have each group pick one leader from this section and one from the past. Have students use their texts to review the ways in which each leader built his empire.

3. Have groups make a list of factual comparisons between the two leaders. Then have each group form a closing generalization statement about the similarities and differences between the two.

4. Have volunteers from each group present their comparisons to the rest of the class.
   LS Interpersonal, Verbal-Linguistic

📄 **Alternative Assessment Handbook**, Rubrics 9: Comparing and Contrasting; and 24: Oral Presentations than doubled, while coal and steel production quadrupled. The demands placed on Soviet workers, however, were high.

Collectivization and Famine Stalin also wanted to increase Soviet farm input. He believed that the millions of small, individually owned Soviet farms would be more productive if they were combined to form larger, mechanized farms. This combining of small farms was called collectivization.

After the Russian Revolution, one of Lenin's first acts had been to give land to Russian peasants. Now Stalin tried to take that land back. When peasants resisted, Stalin responded violently. Stalin's forces executed thousands and sent many more to a remote and frigid region of the Soviet Union called Siberia. In Siberia these Soviets worked—and often died—in a system of labor camps called the **Gulag**.

Still, resistance to collectivization continued. One center of this resistance was the republic of Ukraine (yoo-KRAYN). To punish the Ukrainians, Stalin refused to send food to aid them when a famine struck the region in 1932. Millions of Ukrainians starved to death.

Political Purges By the mid-1930s Stalin had absolute power, but he still feared that people were plotting against him. In response, he began a campaign known as the Great Purge, or the Great Terror. To purge is to get rid of people or things considered undesirable. In a series of purges, Stalin attacked real and imagined opponents of his rule. Thousands of Communist leaders, military officers, and ordinary citizens were executed or sent to the Gulag.

Totalitarian Rule Stalin's regime dominated Soviet life. Children were encouraged to join youth organizations where they were taught the attitudes and beliefs that Soviet leaders wanted them to have. Religion was discouraged, and many churches were closed.

All across Russia, portraits of Stalin decorated public places, creating a heroic and idealized image of the Soviet leader. Streets and towns were renamed in his honor. By promoting this cult of personality and ruthlessly removing any opposition, Stalin gained a stranglehold over Soviet society.

READING CHECK **Summarize** How did Stalin use fear and violence to rule the Soviet Union?

Soviet leader Joseph Stalin delivers a speech at a rally. ▶

THE INTERWAR YEARS **825**

PRIMARY SOURCES

Stalin's Five-Year Plan

In January 1933, Joseph Stalin delivered this report on the results of the first Five-Year Plan.

"What is the five-year plan? . . .

"The fundamental task of the five-year plan was to transfer our country, with its backward . . . technology, on to the lines of new, modern technology.

"The fundamental task of the five-year plan was to convert the U.S.S.R. [Soviet Union] from an agrarian and weak country . . . into an industrial and powerful country.

"The fundamental task of the five-year plan was . . . to ensure the economic basis of socialism in the countryside and thus to eliminate the possibility of the restoration of capitalism in the U.S.S.R.

"Finally, the task of the five-year plan was to create all the necessary technical and economic prerequisites for increasing to the utmost the defensive capacity of the country, enabling it to organize determined resistance to any attempt at military intervention from abroad, to any attempt at military attack from abroad."

Skills FOCUS READING LIKE A HISTORIAN

1. **Summarize** What was the Five-Year Plan?
2. **Analyze Primary Sources** In the last paragraph, what does Stalin seem to be worried about? Why might this be?

See **Skills Handbook**, p. H25

● **Direct Teach** ●

Reading Focus

Stalin's Soviet Union

Explain What led to the starvation of Ukranian peasants in 1932? *They resisted collectivization, so Stalin refused to send food when famine struck the region.*

Contrast How did the farm ownership actions of Lenin and Stalin differ? *Lenin gave land to peasants; Stalin took the land back and placed it under government control.*

Make Inferences Why was Stalin determined to influence the attitudes and behavior of the Russian people? *possible answers—He was obsessed with power. He feared opposition.*

Info to Know

Joseph Stalin When Stalin was only ten years old, his father died, leaving his illiterate mother to raise him alone. He was awarded a scholarship and attended the Orthodox theological seminary from his early teen years until he was expelled five years later, about the time he became involved with a group that spread nationalistic and socialistic ideas in Georgia. Though Stalin eventually turned against his church, his religious background influenced his speeches.

Skills Focus: Analyzing Primary Sources

At Level

Reading Like a Historian Skill
Five-Year Plans

Research Required

1. Have students review the Primary Sources feature, Stalin's Five-Year Plan. Guide students in a discussion of the excerpt to help ensure that all students understand it.

2. Have students conduct outside research using reliable print and Internet sources on the effectiveness of Stalin's Five-Year Plans and their effect on the Soviet economy. Students should try to find one article that defends

the plans and one article that criticizes their effects on the Soviet economy and people.

3. Have students write an essay summarizing the two documents and explaining any bias they believe the authors might have.

📖 **Alternative Assessment Handbook**, Rubrics 30: Research; and 42: Writing to Inform

---

Answers

Primary Sources 1. *a plan to modernize the Soviet Union in terms of its economy and its military;* **2.** *military attack from abroad; because the country had recently faced attack in World War I*

Reading Check *executed those who resisted him; sent opponents to Siberia to work in labor camps*

3 How did Adolf Hitler rule Germany? *used fear, violence, and propaganda to maintain power*

Hitler's Germany

Explain What does *Mein Kampf* reveal about Hitler? *describes his major political ideas and his belief in racial superiority of the German people*

Identify Cause and Effect What led to the growth of the Nazi Party? *The message of restoring German greatness appealed to Germans who wanted a strong leader to help solve Germany's problems.*

Biography

René Magritte (1898–1967) Belgian surrealist painter René Magritte served in the military at the close of World War I. The images left in his mind were likely things he would rather have forgotten, so it isn't surprising to see idealized or otherworldly objects appear in his paintings. Clever compositions, such as one with an eye served on a plate, compel viewers to closely examine his unusual work.

Info to Know

The Weimar Republic The failure of Germany's democratic postwar government was brought on by many complex issues. The average German was unaware of the enormous spending during the war and tended to blame the country's economic condition on its leadership. The Weimar Republic had to triple the taxes it imposed on citizens in order to pay off war debts, to help pay for social services, and to pay the reparations agreed to in the Versailles Treaty.

Answers

Faces of History *possible answer— Germany had suffered a humiliating defeat in World War I, followed by years of economic trouble. Hitler's message of German greatness probably appealed to Germans who were suffering.*

826

Hitler's Germany

Germany underwent great changes after World War I. Like Mussolini and Stalin, Germany's **Adolf Hitler** rose to power during a time of conflict and political instability.

Postwar Germany After World War I, Germany formed a new republican government known as the Weimar (vy-mahr) Republic. This government was extremely unpopular among Germans, who blamed it for the humiliating Versailles treaty and for the economic problems that overwhelmed Germany after the war. Inflation soared in Germany in the early 1920s, and the German mark became virtually worthless. Many Germans saw their savings wiped out. Although an economic recovery began in the late 1920s, the Great Depression soon brought even more political and economic chaos to Germany.

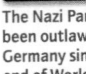

NEW YORK

CC Unit 6-C6
Weimar Republic and the rise of fascism

THE IMPACT TODAY

The Nazi Party has been outlawed in Germany since the end of World War II. Still, extremist Neo-Nazi groups that hold racist or anti-Semitic beliefs exist today in Germany, the United States, and other nations.

Hitler's Early Career Adolf Hitler, born in Austria in 1889, served in the German army during World War I. In the chaos of postwar Germany, he became involved with a group of right-wing extremists and soon joined the Nationalist Socialist Party, or **Nazi Party**.

With the Nazis, Hitler discovered that he had a talent for public speaking and leadership. He soon became a key figure in the party, but he wanted greater power. In October 1923 he led an attempt to overthrow Germany's government. The effort failed, and Hitler received a short prison term. While in prison, he wrote a book titled *Mein Kampf*—German for "My Struggle." The book described Hitler's major political ideas, including nationalism and the racial superiority of the German people, whom he called Aryans.

Hitler Gains Power After Hitler was released from prison, he continued to work to gain power. The economic effects of the Great Depression helped his cause, as the German people were desperate for a strong leader who would improve their lives. Hitler promised to rebuild Germany's military. He spoke of a mighty German empire and said that Germans were the "master race." His claims about German greatness won the Nazi Party many new supporters who wanted to believe that his words were true.

Through Hitler's efforts the Nazis continued to gain strength in the early 1930s. They became the most popular of Germany's many political parties. As a result, in 1933 Hitler was appointed to the position of chancellor, the most powerful post in the German government.

Hitler Controls Germany Once in power, Hitler began to crush his opposition. Many of his opponents were arrested; others were intimidated by Nazi thugs. By these means, Hitler bullied the German legislature into giving him dictatorial powers.

Increasingly, Hitler's rule took the form of a totalitarian regime. Nazi propaganda built up a cult of personality glorifying Hitler as the Führer (FYOOR-uhr), or "leader." Nazi youth organizations shaped the minds of young Germans, who pledged complete loyalty to Hitler and Germany.

Hitler began to rebuild the German military and improve the German economy. Strict wage controls and massive government spending on public works programs helped reduce unemployment. Much of the spending was for the rearmament of the German military, although it also included the construction of new public buildings and roads.

Nazi Anti-Semitism A key component of the Nazi system was strong anti-Semitic beliefs. **Anti-Semitism** is hostility toward or prejudice against Jews. Hitler blamed Jews for many of Germany's problems, including its defeat in World War I.

FACES OF HISTORY

Adolf HITLER
1889–1945

After Germany's humiliating defeat in World War I, a soldier named Adolf Hitler vowed to rebuild a German empire. After the war ended he became active in a small German political party.

A master of propaganda and a stirring public speaker, Hitler soon became known for his attacks on the Treaty of Versailles, Communists, Jews, and anyone or anything else he believed to be a threat to German greatness. Twisting facts to suit his purposes, Hitler used German anger over World War I and the economic effects of the Great Depression to convince Germans that he would restore their nation to glory.

Infer Why do you think so many Germans found Hitler's ideas appealing in the years after World War I?

826 CHAPTER 27

Skills Focus: Making Generalizations

At Level

Prep Required

Reading Skill
The Nuremberg Laws

1. Obtain copies of one or more of the Nuremberg Laws and read the laws to the class. Then review the information in the text about the Nuremberg Laws. Guide students in a discussion of its effects on Jewish citizens of Germany.

2. Have students write letters to the editor of a newspaper protesting the new laws. In their letters students should explain why these laws are unjust and discriminatory.

3. Have students share their letters with the class. **LS Verbal-Linguistic**

Alternative Assessment Handbook, Rubric 17: Letters to Editors

Anti-Semitism had a long history in largely Christian Europe. In fact, Christian hostility toward Jews had existed since the Middle Ages. Nazi anti-Semitism combined this religious hostility with modern—and false—beliefs that Jews were a separate race. Under the Nazis, anti-Semitism combined prejudice based on religion with hatred based on ancestry.

During the 1930s Hitler's Nazi government passed many laws aimed at excluding Jews from mainstream German life. They prohibited Jews from marrying Germans. In 1935 the **Nuremberg Laws** created a separate legal status for German Jews, eliminating their citizenship and many civil and property rights, such as the right to vote. Jews' right to work in certain jobs was limited. The Nuremberg Laws defined a person as Jewish based on the ancestry of grandparents—not religious beliefs.

The Nazis also mounted more direct attacks. On the nights of November 9 and 10, 1938, they encouraged anti-Jewish riots across Germany and Austria. This attack came to be known as **Kristallnacht** (KRIS-tahl-nahkt), or the Night of Broken Glass. During the riots, nearly 100 Jews were killed, and thousands of Jewish businesses and places of worship were damaged and destroyed. Yet as terrifying as this anti-Jewish violence and destruction were, greater horrors were yet to come. Indeed, Hitler's Germany was about to lead the world into history's bloodiest war.

READING CHECK **Analyze** How did Hitler's anti-Semitism affect the way he ruled Germany?

The Nuremberg Rallies

Under Adolf Hitler, the Nazi Party staged enormous public rallies in Nuremberg, Germany, during the 1930s. At the rallies, hundreds of thousands of Germans listened to pro-Nazi speeches and took part in parades and demonstrations.

SECTION 4 ASSESSMENT

go.hrw.com
Online Quiz
Keyword: SHL IWY HP

Reviewing Key Terms and People

1. **a. Describe** How did **Benito Mussolini** use **fascism** and **totalitarianism** to rule Italy?
   b. Sequence Trace the major steps in Mussolini's rise to power in Italy.

2. **a. Recall** What steps did **Joseph Stalin** take to try to modernize the Soviet economy?
   b. Make Generalizations How did Stalin respond to public or internal opposition?

3. **a. Identify** Identify the following: **Nazi Party**, **Nuremberg Laws**, and **Kristallnacht**.
   b. Develop How did economic and political conditions in postwar Germany contribute to **Adolf Hitler's** rise to power?

Critical Thinking

4. **Make Generalizations** Using your notes on the section, compare and contrast the ways that Mussolini, Stalin, and Hitler rose to power and kept power.

	Mussolini	Stalin	Hitler
Rise to power			
Methods used to keep power			

FOCUS ON WRITING

5. **Description** Write a journal entry that a Soviet citizen might have written in the 1930s describing daily life in the Soviet Union under Stalin.

THE INTERWAR YEARS **827**

THE INTERWAR YEARS **827**

Section 4 Assessment Answers

1. **a.** tried to control Italians' thoughts, feelings, and behaviors; used threats and violence
   b. March on Rome; king placed Mussolini at head of Italy's parliamentary government; used violence, political skills to establish a dictatorship

2. **a.** set up Five-Year Plans; set production goals; collectivized farms
   b. with violence; people were exiled to labor camps in Siberia, starved, executed, and imprisoned

3. **a.** Nazi Party—the National Socialist Party that gave Hitler his start; Nuremberg Laws—anti-Semitic laws passed in 1935; Kristallnacht—anti-Jewish riots resulting in the death of nearly 100 Jews and damage to thousands of Jewish businesses and places of worship
   b. possible answer— German people wanted change, end to economic problems, hoped for a strong empire

4. Mussolini—1922; used political skill, threats, violence, and propaganda; outlawed all opposition; Stalin—1924; used fear, violence, propaganda, purged opponents; Hitler—1933; used political skill, fear, violence, crushed his opposition, used propaganda; passed anti-Semitic laws; all came to power in post-war economic depression

5. Student letters should include details from the section about daily life under Stalin.

Reading Focus

Hitler's Germany

Recall What is anti-Semitism? *hostility toward or prejudice against Jews*

Analyze Why is Kristallnacht remembered as a significant event? *signifies the beginning of Nazi violence against Jews*

• Review & Assess •

Close

Have students compare and contrast the totalitarian dictatorships of Mussolini, Stalin, and Hitler.

Review

Online Quiz, Section 4

Assess

SE Section 4 Assessment

Progress Assessment: Section 4 Quiz

Alternative Assessment Handbook

Reteach/Intervene

Interactive Reader and Study Guide, Section 4

Interactive Skills Tutor CD-ROM

Answers

Reading Check *Anti-Semitism led to the Nuremberg Laws, riots, and direct attacks on Jews.*

Document-Based Investigation

Nationalism in India and Germany

Word Help

perpetuate to cause to last indefinitely
diplomacy negotiations between nations

Activity **Analyzing Primary Sources** Have students volunteer information they can infer from the photograph of the Salt March. Ask students what questions they might ask to determine what this photograph represents.

Info to Know

Mohandas Gandhi Gandhi lived in South Africa for a number of years, where he led protests against government discrimination toward Indians, a struggle that lasted for more than seven years. After his return to India, Gandhi began to lead protests there; some critics charged that he was moving too quickly; others said he moved too slowly. Today, most agree that Gandhi was a great mediator who was able to reconcile the interests and beliefs of many different groups.

Nationalism in India and Germany

NEW YORK STANDARDS

PI **4.2** Students interpret and analyze documents and artifacts related to significant developments and events in world history.

Historical Context The documents below provide information about the rise of different forms of nationalism in India and Germany during the early 1900s.

Task Examine the documents and answer the questions that follow. After you have studied all the documents, you will be asked to write an essay about different responses to the rise of nationalism during the early 1900s. You will need to use evidence from these selections and from the chapter to support the position you take in your essay.

DOCUMENT 1

The Salt March

In 1930 Indian nationalist leader Mohandas Gandhi led the so-called Salt March as a peaceful protest against the British rule of India. The British arrested some 60,000 Indians during the protest, which drew worldwide attention and helped advance Indian efforts for independence. In this photograph, Gandhi is the fourth person from the left.

DOCUMENT 2

Gandhi's Philosophy

During a visit to Great Britain in 1931 as part of his efforts to win independence for India, Gandhi gave this speech on an American radio station. The following passage describes the Indian independence movement.

India is by itself almost a continent. It contains one-fifth of the human race. It represents one of the most ancient civilizations. It has traditions handed down from tens of thousands of years, some of which, to the astonishment of the world, remain intact. If India is to perpetuate the glory of her ancient past, it can do so only when it attains freedom. The reason for the struggle having drawn the attention of the world, I know does not lie in the fact that we Indians are fighting for our liberty, but in the fact that the means adopted by us for attaining that liberty are unique and, as far as history shows us, have not been adopted by any other people of whom we have any record. The means adopted are not violence, not bloodshed, not diplomacy as one understands it nowadays, but they are purely and simply truth and non-violence. No wonder that the attention of the world is directed towards this attempt to lead a successful, bloodless revolution.

Skills Focus: Recognizing Bias in Primary Sources   At Level

Reading Like a Historian Skill
The Other View

1. Remind students that historical documents often show clear bias when they are analyzed today. Have students carefully review Documents 2, 3, and 4.

2. Have students identify statements that exhibit bias. Have students write these statements onto their own papers, and then write down their reactions to these statements.

3. Organize students into mixed-ability pairs. Have pairs write an unbiased statement that corresponds to each biased statement on their lists. Have each pair share its biased and unbiased statements, as well as its reaction to the biased statements with the class.
   LS **Interpersonal, Verbal-Linguistic**
   Alternative Assessment Handbook, Rubric 16: Judging Information

DOCUMENT 3

The Nazi Party's Goals

In a speech in 1920, Germany's Adolf Hitler outlined the Twenty Five Points of the Nazi Party, which summarized Nazi goals. Selected points are listed below.

1. We demand the union of all Germans in a Great Germany on the basis of the principle of self-determination of all peoples . . .

3. We demand land and territory (colonies) for the maintenance of our people and the settlement of our surplus population.

4. Only those who are our fellow countrymen can become citizens. Only those who have German blood, regardless of creed, can be our countrymen. Hence no Jew can be a countryman . . .

7. We demand that the State shall above all undertake to ensure that every citizen shall have the possibility of living decently and earning a livelihood. If it should not be possible to feed the whole population, then aliens (noncitizens) must be expelled from the Reich.

8. Any further immigration of non-Germans must be prevented. We demand that all non-Germans who have entered Germany since August 2, 1914, shall be compelled to leave the Reich immediately.

DOCUMENT 4

Nationalism in Germany

Hitler gave this speech at a Nazi rally in Nuremberg, Germany, in 1927.

Our fellow party member . . . began his speech by saying that it is critical for a nation that its territory correspond to its population. As he put it so well: 'The nation needs space' . . . The question confronts us today as insistently as ever: No government, of whatever kind, can long escape dealing with it. Feeding a nation of 62 million means not only maintaining our agricultural productivity, but enlarging it to meet the needs of a growing population . . .

The first way to satisfy this need, the adjustment of territory to population, is the most natural, healthy and long-lasting . . .

If a nation today proclaims the theory that it will find happiness in lasting peace, and attempts to live according to that theory, it will one day inevitably succumb to this most basic form of cowardice. Pacifism is the clearest form of cowardice, possessing no willingness to fight for anything at all . . .

62 million people have an impossible amount of land. There are 20 million 'too many'. This nation cannot survive in the long term. It must find a way out.

Word Help

creed set of beliefs or guiding principles

pacifism nonresistance or nonviolence in settling disputes

succumb give in, yield to an overpowering appeal or desire

Info to Know

The Nuremberg Trials The city of Nuremberg, Germany was the site of many Nazi rallies during the 1930s. After World War II, it also became the site of the historic Nuremberg Trials, in which Allied Powers put Nazi war criminals on trial for killing more than 6 million Jews and 5 million other Europeans during the war. The Nuremberg Trials sentenced many Nazi leaders to death for their actions, showing that military orders from superiors are not a valid reason for committing war crimes. This marked the first war crimes trial in modern history.

Skills Focus: READING LIKE A HISTORIAN

DOCUMENT 1
a. Describe According to this photograph, was the Salt March a peaceful protest or a violent one?
b. Analyze What does this photograph tell you about the type of people on the Salt March and their behavior?

DOCUMENT 2
a. Identify What means does Gandhi say are being used by Indians in their struggle for independence?
b. Contrast How are these means different from those used in other struggles for independence?

DOCUMENT 3
a. Make Generalizations How does this document suggest that non-Germans be treated?
b. Summarize How does this document express an aggressive form of nationalism?

DOCUMENT 4
a. Identify What does Hitler believe that Germany must do in order to survive?
b. Compare and Contrast How does Hitler's opinion about peace differ from the belief that Gandhi expresses in Document 2?

DOCUMENT-BASED ESSAY QUESTION

How and why did expressions of nationalism differ in Gandhi's India and Hitler's Germany? Using the documents above and information from the chapter, form a thesis that supports your position. Then write a short essay to support your position.

See Skills Handbook, pp. H25, H26

Skills Focus: Identifying Problem and Solution

At Level

Reading Like a Historian Skill
Overpopulation Solutions

1. Tell students that in recent years many people have come to believe that the world is becoming crowded and overpopulated, the same problem that brought about the impassioned speeches presented in Documents 3 and 4.

2. Organize students into small groups. Have each group devise a logical plan to address the problem of crowding and then prepare a speech discussing its solution and persuading others that this is the best course of action.

Allow time for students to rehearse their speeches.

3. When students are ready, have the presenters deliver speeches.

4. As an extension, have students write a paragraph expressing support for the solution they feel would work best. **LS Interpersonal, Verbal-Linguistic**

Alternative Assessment Handbook, Rubrics 11: Discussions; and 24: Oral Presentations

Answers

Reading Like a Historian
Document 1. a. *a peaceful protest;* **b.** *they appear patient and nonviolent;* **Document 2. a.** *truth and nonviolence;* **b.** *Other struggles use violence, bloodshed, and diplomacy.* **Document 3. a.** *The document suggests that non-Germans should be denied citizenship, and expelled from the country if there is ever not enough food. Furthermore, it states that non-Germans should not be allowed to enter Germany, and that any non-German who entered after a certain date should be expelled.* **b.** *It bases nationalism on heritage and discriminates against anyone without "German blood."* **Document 4. a.** *fight for more territory;* **b.** *Hitler—believed peace is a form of cowardice, which shows lack of purpose; Gandhi—believed non-violence is the best form of revolution;* **Essay** *Student essays should show an understanding of different views of nationalism and should include information from each of the four documents.*

Answers

Visual Summary

Review and Inquiry Organize students into three groups. Have each group create a poster depicting information about one of the following topics: Causes and Effects of the Great Depression, Japanese Imperialism, and Growing Nationalism and Aggression.

Quick Facts Transparency: Visual Study Guide: The Interwar Years

Review Key Terms and People

1. Kemal Atatürk, or Kemal Mustafa
2. Smoot-Hawley Tariff Act
3. Gulag
4. Manchurian Incident
5. Mohandas Gandhi
6. Joseph Stalin
7. Anti-Comintern Pact
8. Mao Zedong
9. National Socialist Party, also known as the Nazi Party
10. New Deal
11. prosperity

Comprehension and Critical Thinking

12. a. Jiang Jieshi—leader of the Chinese nationalist Guomindang party; Mao Zedong—Chinese Communist party leader who led Communists on the Long March
b. In each area, nationalism led to desire for independence.
c. possible answer—Gandhi's nonviolent actions and acts of civil disobedience required patience, but they increased sympathy for the cause and harmed no one.

13. a. The economy was booming, unemployment was low, and the stock market was climbing steadily.
b. It caused other nations to increase tariffs on American goods, which brought world trade to a standstill.
c. possible answer—Yes, people wanted quick changes, and the democratically elected leaders who were in office often could not make quick, drastic changes so they turned to dictators for help.

VISUAL STUDY GUIDE

QUICK FACTS

CAUSES

- U.S. economic growth in the 1920s hides serious problems in the economy.
- Speculation in the U.S. stock market drives up prices
- U.S. stock market crashes in October 1929.
- Crash devastates U.S. businesses, investors, and banks.
- Economic crisis begins to spread around the world.

Great Depression

EFFECTS

- In Europe, countries still struggling to recover from World War I are hit hard by the Depression.
- World trade slows and national economies are crippled.
- Political unrest grows.
- In some countries, extremist political groups and totalitarian leaders take power.

Growing Japanese Aggression

- Social and economic changes in Japan lead many Japanese people to lose faith in their government.
- Nationalist military leaders gradually take control of Japan's government.
- Japan begins to pursue aggressive, expansionist policies.
- Japan invades Manchuria in 1931.
- War with China begins in 1937, leading to the Nanjing Massacre. Japan looks elsewhere for the natural resources needed to supply its war machine.

Growing Nationalism and Aggression

1917	In the Balfour Declaration, Britain announces its support for a Jewish state
1919	China's nationalist May Fourth Movement begins
1920	Mohandas Gandhi begins boycott of British products
1921	Reza Khan overthrows Persia's shah China's Communist Party formed
1922	Benito Mussolini takes power in Italy Egypt gains independence
1923	Republic of Turkey formed Adolf Hitler tries to overthrow German government
1924	Joseph Stalin begins to take power in the Soviet Union
1927	Stalin announces first Five-Year Plan
1931	Japan takes control of Manchuria
1933	Hitler becomes chancellor of Germany
1935	Italy invades Ethiopia Germany's Nazi government passes anti-Semitic Nuremberg Laws Chinese Communist Party finishes the Long March
1937	Japan begins war with China

Review Key Terms and People

Identify the correct person or term from the chapter that best fits each of the following descriptions.

1. Founder of modern Turkey
2. Action by U.S. government during the Great Depression that led to a drop in world trade
3. Soviet system of prison camps
4. Japanese plot to take over part of China
5. Leader who used nonviolence and civil disobedience in struggle for Indian independence
6. Totalitarian leader of the Soviet Union
7. 1930s agreement between Japan and Germany
8. Leader of Chinese Communists
9. Adolf Hitler's political party
10. Franklin Roosevelt's response to the Depression
11. Wealth or success

830 CHAPTER 27

---

14. a. Japan stood as one of the world's foremost powers, but began to have economic problems.
b. The military grew dissatisfied with the civilian government because of its foreign policy, especially treaties with the west that limited the size of Japan's navy.
c. possible answer—Japan effectively compensated for its lack of industrial power by encouraging a fighting spirit.

15. a. a leader who has complete political control, and also seeks to influence the thoughts, feelings, and behaviors of the people
b. similar—totalitarian dictators who used threats, violence and propaganda to control and influence their people; different— Hitler and Stalin encouraged the cult of personality; Hitler won the appointment of German chancellor; Mussolini used show of force to convince king to place him at head of government
c. possible answer—Citizens are somewhat responsible for the rise of dictators, especially when dictators replace democratic leaders. They might believe a change in leadership, no matter how aggressive, can fix a country's problems.

History's Impact video program

Review the video to answer the closing question: How do changes made after the 1929 stock market crash help protect the American economy today?

Comprehension and Critical Thinking

SECTION 1 *(pp. 807–811)*

12. a. Identify Who were Jiang Jieshi and Mao Zedong?

b. Compare How were China, India, Middle Eastern countries, and African countries similar in their reaction to the aftermath of World War I?

c. Evaluate What were the strengths and weaknesses in Gandhi's methods for seeking independence in India?

SECTION 2 *(pp. 812–816)*

13. a. Describe What was the state of the American economy throughout most of the 1920s?

b. Explain Why did the Smoot-Hawley Tariff Act have such a dramatic effect on trade?

c. Evaluate Do you think the effects of the Great Depression were the main cause of the rise of dictators? Why or why not?

SECTION 3 *(pp. 818–822)*

14. a. Recall What was Japan's position in the world after World War I?

b. Summarize Why was the Japanese military growing increasingly dissatisfied with Japan's civilian government in the 1920s?

c. Make Judgments What do you think of the Japanese military's commitment to the notion of fighting spirit as a key weapon? Why?

SECTION 4 *(pp. 823–827)*

15. a. Describe What is a totalitarian dictator?

b. Compare and Contrast In what ways were Mussolini, Stalin, and Hitler similar and different?

c. Evaluate To what extent were the citizens of Italy, the Soviet Union, and Germany responsible for the rise of Mussolini, Stalin, and Hitler?

Reading Skills

Understanding Comparison and Contrast *Use what you know about understanding comparison and contrast to answer the questions below.*

16. How were Arab and Jewish responses to postwar mandates similar and different?

17. Did the Great Depression affect the United States and Europe in similar ways? Explain your answer.

Recognizing Bias in Secondary Sources

Reading Like a Historian

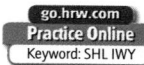 The two lines of Chinese soldiers defended either side of the railroad bridge. Facing hundreds of Japanese attackers, they were not cowed in the least, and they engaged in intense hand-to-hand fights with [the] enemies. Nearly all of them died at the end of the battle of the bridge. Seeing their comrades fall in the battle, other soldiers, without showing too much sorrow, clenched their teeth. They fought forward. Even the wounded who were ordered to retreat were still charging ahead. **"**

—From a Chinese history textbook

18. Explain How does this excerpt demonstrate bias? What words or phrases show bias?

19. Infer How might a Japanese textbook describe this battle differently?

Using the Internet

go.hrw.com
Practice Online
Keyword: SHL IWY

20. Although Adolf Hitler and Joseph Stalin shared some characteristics in the way they ruled their nations, there are also important differences between the two. Using the Internet, research how Hitler and Stalin led their countries. Then write a detailed report that compares and contrasts the two leaders. Be sure to include information about how each person rose to power, as well as how each used that power to control his country. You may wish to discuss each leader's goals for his nation, as well as his use of propaganda, threats, and secret police to maintain power.

WRITING FOR THE SAT

Think about the following issue:

In the 1920s and 1930s the Japanese military gradually took control of Japan's civilian government. The military's aggressive nationalism became increasingly popular with the Japanese public, but expansion in Asia in the early 1930s led to a costly war with China.

21. Assignment: Why did the Japanese people support their military's aggressive actions? Write a short essay in which you develop your position on this issue. Support your point of view with reasoning and examples from your reading and studies.

Answers

Reading Skills

16. both disliked mandates; Jews accepted UN plan, Arabs rejected it

17. No, for Europe, the Great Depression was just the latest in a series of economic crises.

Recognizing Bias in Secondary Sources

18. depicts Chinese soldiers as brave; "not cowed in the least;" "without showing too much sorrow"

19. possible answer—might emphasize bravery of Japanese soldiers

Using the Internet

20. Go to the HRW Web site and enter the keyword shown to access a rubric for this activity.

KEYWORD: SHL IWY

Writing for the SAT

21. Student essays might discuss the need for an improved farming economy, as the United States might become dependent upon other nations for its food supply.

A rubric for the activity is provided in **CRF**: Writing for the SAT..

HOLT

History's Impact

▶ **Video Program: The Interwar Years**

See to the Video Program Teacher's Guide for the answer to the closing question.

Review and Assessment Resources

Review and Reinforce

- **CRF:** Chapter Review
- **Quick Facts Transparency:** Visual Study Guide: The Interwar Years
- **Spanish Chapter Summaries Audio CD Program**
- OSP **Holt PuzzlePro:** Quiz Show for ExamView
- **Quiz Game CD-ROM**

Assess

- **PASS:** Chapter Test, Forms A and B
- **Alternative Assessment Handbook**
- OSP **ExamView Test Generator**, Chapter Test
- **Differentiated Instruction Modified Worksheets and Tests CD-ROM:** Chapter Test
- HOAP **Holt Online Assessment Program** (in the Premier Online Edition)

Reteach/Intervene

- **Interactive Reader and Study Guide**
- **Differentiated Instruction Teacher Management System:** Lesson Plans for Differentiated Instruction
- **Differentiated Instruction Modified Worksheets and Tests CD-ROM:** Chapter Test
- **Interactive Skills Tutor CD-ROM**

go.hrw.com
Online Resources

KEYWORD: SHL TEACHER

Chapter 28 Planning Guide

World War II

Chapter Overview	Reproducible Resources	Technology Resources
CHAPTER 28 pp. 832–867 **Overview:** In this chapter, students will learn about events that led up to World War II, the battles involving the Allies and the Axis Powers, and the war's effects. ■ KI 1, 2; PI 1.3, 1.4, 2.5 See pp. T32–T55 for a detailed correlation to the New York State Core Curriculum for Global History and Geography and the New York Learning Standards.	**Differentiated Instruction Teacher Management System:*** • Pacing Guide • Lesson Plans for Differentiated Instruction **Interactive Reader and Study Guide:** Chapter Summary* **Chapter Resource File*** • Writing for the SAT • Social Studies Skill • Chapter Review **World History Outline Maps**	Live Ink© Online Reading Help Student Edition on Audio CD Program Differentiated Instruction Modified Worksheets and Tests CD-ROM World History Primary Source Library CD-ROM Power Presentations with Video CD-ROM History's Impact: **World History Video Program (VHS/DVD):** World War II
Section 1: **Axis Aggression** **The Main Idea:** While Hitler became increasingly aggressive in the late 1930s, other leaders sought to appease him. The effort backfired and led to the outbreak of World War II. ■ PI 1.4, 2.5	**Differentiated Instruction Teacher Management System:** Section 1 Lesson Plan* **Interactive Reader and Study Guide:** Section 1 Summary* **Chapter Resource File*** • Vocabulary Builder: Section 1 • Biography: Queen Elizabeth • Primary Source: The Atlantic Charter	**Regents Review Transparency:** Section 1* **Map Transparency:** Axis Advances, 1939–1941* **Map Transparency:** The London Blitz, 1940*
Section 2: **The Allied Response** **The Main Idea:** The early years of World War II went poorly for the Allies. But after the United States joined the war, the Allies soon recovered and began making gains against the Axis. ■ PI 1.3, 1.4, 2.5	**Differentiated Instruction Teacher Management System:** Section 2 Lesson Plan* **Interactive Reader and Study Guide:** Section 2 Summary* **Chapter Resource File*** • Vocabulary Builder: Section 2 • Biography: Rosie the Riveter • History and Geography: Japanese Internment Camps	**Regents Review Transparency:** Section 2* **Map Transparency:** World War II in Europe and North Africa, 1941–1943* **Map Transparency:** War in the Pacific, 1942–1944*
Section 3: **The Holocaust** **The Main Idea:** During World War II, Germany's Nazi government murdered some 6 million Jews and 5 million others in Europe. These actions became known as the Holocaust. ■ PI 1.4, 2.5	**Differentiated Instruction Teacher Management System:** Section 3 Lesson Plan* **Interactive Reader and Study Guide:** Section 3 Summary* **Chapter Resource File*** • Vocabulary Builder: Section 3 • Biography: Raoul Wallenberg	**Regents Review Transparency:** Section 3* **Internet Activity:** Report on Anne Frank
Section 4: **The End of the War** **The Main Idea:** In 1945 the Allies finally triumphed over the Axis Powers in Europe and Asia but the war left many nations in ruins. ■ PI 1.3, 1.4, 2.5	**Differentiated Instruction Teacher Management System:** Section 4 Lesson Plan* **Interactive Reader and Study Guide:** Section 4 Summary* **Chapter Resource File*** • Vocabulary Builder: Section 4 • Biography: Harry S Truman	**Regents Review Transparency:** Section 4* **Quick Facts Transparency:** Causes and Effects of World War II* **Map Transparency:** The End of the War, 1944–1945* **Internet Activity:** D-Day

go.hrw.com　　 Print Resource　　 Transparency

LS Learning Styles　　 Audio CD　　💿 CD-ROM

📹 Video　　**SE** Student Edition　　**TE** Teachers Edition

OSP One-Stop Planner CD-ROM　　📹 NY Standards Mastery
*also on One-Stop Planner CD-ROM

Review, Assessment, Intervention

📹 **Global History and Geography Regents Test Prep Workbook**

 Quick Facts Transparency: World War II*

📢 **Spanish Chapter Summaries Audio CD Program**

📄 **Program Assessment Support System (PASS):** Chapter Test*

OSP **New York One-Stop Planner CD-ROM:** ExamView Test Generator (English/Spanish)

HOAP **Holt Online Assessment Program (HOAP),** in the Holt Premier Online Student Edition

---

 PASS: Section 1 Quiz*

 Online Quiz: Section 1

 Alternative Assessment Handbook

 PASS: Section 2 Quiz*

 Online Quiz: Section 2

 Alternative Assessment Handbook

 PASS: Section 3 Quiz*

 Online Quiz: Section 3

 Alternative Assessment Handbook

📄 **PASS:** Section 4 Quiz*

📄 **Online Quiz:** Section 4

📄 **Alternative Assessment Handbook**

HOLT

History's Impact
World History Video Program (VHS/DVD)
World War II

Power Presentation with Video CD-ROM

Power Presentations with Video are visual presentations of each chapter's main ideas. Presentations can be customized by including Quick Facts charts, images and maps from the textbook, and video clips.

Holt ●nline Learning

go.hrw.com
Teacher Resources
KEYWORD: SHL TEACHER

go.hrw.com
Student Resources
KEYWORD: SHL WW2

• Document-Based Questions
• Interactive Multimedia Activities

• Current Events
• Chapter-Based Internet Activities
• and more!

Holt Premier
Online Student Edition

Complete online support for interactivity, assessment, and reporting

• Interactive Maps and Notebook
• Homework Practice and Research Activities Online

CHAPTER 28 PLANNING GUIDE

The Big Picture

Peter N. Stearns

The Course of the War Both in Europe and in Asia, the 1930s saw sequences of events that prepared for World War II, provoking inadequate and divided responses from the Western democracies and the Soviet Union. Not surprisingly, the early years of outright war saw key gains by Germany and Japan and their allies—"their finest hour," as Churchill might have put it. In both cases, however, turning points occurred that reversed the tide and brought steady, if gradual, Allied advances until ultimate victory.

Beneath the Surface World War II continued trends visible in World War I—governments' mobilization of labor, materials, and propaganda along with military developments themselves. This was a pattern that has been called total war. More than the previous world war, however, World War II further blurred the distinction between military and civilians with the massive bombardments of civilian populations by all major participants. The first use of nuclear weapons added further innovation to this category. The Holocaust deserves major attention as a particularly horrible offshoot of the war.

Global Patterns The war's settlement was conclusive in some respects, confirming the defeat of the Axis powers, but inconclusive in others given the emerging disputes between the Soviet Union and the United States-led West. The war also should be reviewed in patterns of impact levels. The war and its immediate consequences recast relationships in East and Southeast Asia, and to an extent India as well, setting conditions for further upheaval in China and for rapid decolonization. The same applies to North Africa. Europe was redefined not only by the new Soviet-Western division but also by the realization that a continent of warring nation-states was a recipe for failure. The war was also decisive in Jewish history and in the growth of the government in the United States as well as in United States global power. Ripple effects also apply to Africa, the Middle East and Latin America, though with descending urgency.

Recent Scholarship

Civilians and the War World War II had devastating effects on civilians. A.C. Grayling's *Among the Dead Cities: The History and Moral Legacy of the WWII Bombing of Civilians in Germany and Japan* (2006) deals with crucial aspects of this feature of the war. The treatment is even-handed: Grayling gives careful attention to the arguments of those who pushed for the bombing of cities, including the precedents set by German and Japanese actions. He ultimately contends, however, that the policies were both misguided and unnecessary. This is a challenging global vantage point that can promote constructive debate.

Differentiating Instruction

 Differentiated Instruction Teacher Management System
- Pacing Guide
- Lesson Plans for Differentiated Instruction

 Interactive Reader and Study Guide

Spanish Chapter Summaries Audio CD Program

Student Edition on Audio CD Program

 Differentiated Instruction Modified Worksheets and Tests CD-ROM
- Vocabulary Flash Cards
- Modified Vocabulary Builder Activities
- Modified Chapter Review Activity
- Modified Chapter Test

OSP One-Stop Planner CD-ROM
- ExamView Test Generator (English /Spanish)
- PuzzlePro
- Quiz Show for ExamView
- Transparencies and Videos

TE Differentiated Activities in the Teacher's Edition
- The Munich Conference, p. 837
- Attack Pearl Harbor, p. 841
- Battles in North Africa, p. 846
- German Invasion of the Soviet Union, p. 848
- The Allied Advance in the Pacific, p. 849
- Illustrating Poetic Images, p. 851
- "Hatred" Essays, p. 851
- Battle of the Bulge, p. 860

Reading Like a Historian

Sam Wineburg

Exhibition Controversy During Fall, 1994, opinion pages of major newspapers raged with arguments for and against a proposed exhibition at the Smithsonian Institution commemorating the fiftieth anniversary of the dropping of the atomic bomb and the end of World War II. The fury unleashed by the proposed exhibit made one thing absolutely clear: while the war might have ended fifty years before, the battle over its meaning continued to rage.

Veterans' groups took offense at the thought that there might be other reasons for dropping the bomb besides bringing the Japanese to a speedy surrender. The mere suggestion, they claimed, disrespected the memory of their fallen comrades. After the museum made some changes in response, a group of professional historians and authors accused the museum of "intellectual corruption" and "historical cleansing," with one author claiming that the Smithsonian had traded historical integrity for "feel-good national myths."

By January 1995, the exhibit was pronounced dead on arrival, gasping its last breath before a single person passed through the turnstiles. Smithsonian secretary I. Michael Heyman, a man who months before spoke about the museum's need to "explore and present the complexities of our subjects," wondered whether the very idea was conceived in error. It had been a mistake, he concluded, to have tried "to couple an historical treatment of the use of atomic weapons with the 50th anniversary commemoration of the end of the war."

Rethinking the Past Can celebration of history be reconciled with its critical evaluation? In his post-mortem on the Smithsonian affair, Pulitzer-prize winning MIT historian John Dower was pessimistic. We celebrate the past in order to cultivate pride in the rightness of "our side" and to deepen the attachment we feel to our cause. On the other hand, according to Dower, to examine the past historically means that we must "use the perspective of time, together with access to previously unavailable materials, to rethink the past." This "rethinking" yields questions and ambiguity. For example, thinking historically pits the commonly accepted belief that the US used the bomb to defeat Japan quickly against interpretations that draw on little-known documents. A government report, first released in 1946, estimated that even without dropping the bomb Japan was ready to capitulate to Allied forces by the end of 1945. Other documents reveal that before the bomb was dropped, military brass already anticipated a post-war power struggle with the USSR. They saw the bomb as a powerful way to warn the Soviets about what awaited them should they fall out of line.

Adding to these factors were domestic pressures on the Truman administration, which had inherited a top-secret and pricey Manhattan Project and needed something to show for it.

Other declassified government documents reveal that the president and his advisors drew on reports drafted by America's top scientists. In a 1945 report, Arthur Compton sounded an argument for using the bomb in order to teach the world a lesson. "If the bomb were not used in the present war the world would have no adequate warning as to what was to be expected if war should break out again."

None of these factors—flexing our muscles before the Soviets, justifying the expenses of the Manhattan Project, or acting as a deterrent for the nations of the world—were immediately tied to bringing the Japanese to a hasty surrender. Neither do they cancel out that reason. All told, we must contend with the thorny fact that complex decisions often have sets of complex causes.

Thinking historically means embracing this complexity, not shrinking from it.

Chapter Main Ideas

Section 1 While Hitler became increasingly aggressive in the late 1930s, other leaders sought to appease him. The effort backfired and led to the outbreak of World War II.

Section 2 The early years of World War II went poorly for the Allies. But after the United States joined the war, the Allies soon recovered and began making gains against the Axis.

Section 3 During World War II, Germany's Nazi government deliberately murdered some 6 million Jews and 5 million others in Europe. These actions became known as the Holocaust.

Section 4 In 1945 the Allies finally triumphed over the Axis Powers in Europe and Asia, but the war left many nations in ruins.

New York Standards

Key Idea 1 The study of world history requires an understanding of world cultures and civilizations, including an analysis of important ideas, social and cultural values, beliefs, and traditions. This study also examines the human condition and the connections and interactions of people across time and space and the ways different people view the same event or issue from a variety of perspectives.

Key Idea 2 Establishing timeframes, exploring different periodizations, examining themes across time and within cultures, and focusing on important turning points in world history help organize the study of world cultures and civilizations.

Key to Differentiating Instruction

Below Level

Basic-level activities designed for all students encountering new material

At Level

Intermediate-level activities designed for average students

Above Level

Challenging activities designed for honors and gifted and talented students

Standard English Mastery

Activities designed to improve standard English usage

CHAPTER 28 1930–1945
World War II

THE BIG PICTURE The aggression of tyrants in Europe and Asia exploded in another world war in 1939. At first, the Axis armies of Germany, Japan, and Italy gained territory and inflicted great suffering. But after years of conflict, the Allies, led by Great Britain, the United States, and the Soviet Union, prevailed.

Theme SCIENCE AND TECHNOLOGY
The needs of wartime have often resulted in the creation of new weapons, with sometimes terrifying consequences. In this chapter you will learn how the Allies and the Axis Powers used science and technology in their efforts to win World War II.

Invasion of Italy, by William G. Lawrence, 1943

TIME LINE

CHAPTER EVENTS

September 1939 German forces invade Poland, beginning World War II.

May 1940 Germany invades France.

December 7, 1941 Japan attacks Pearl Harbor, drawing the United States into World War II.

The Battle of Stalingrad August 1942– February 1943

June 6, 1944 The Allies storm ashore at Normandy, France, on D-Day.

1939 · 1941 · 1943

WORLD EVENTS

August 1940 Former Soviet revolutionary Leon Trotsky is killed in Mexico.

August 1942 Gandhi is arrested after calling for Britain to leave India.

1943 Penicillin comes into wide use as an antibiotic.

832 CHAPTER 28

Introduce the Chapter

At Level

World War II

1. Write the following scenario for students to see: You are an American living in Europe in 1939, at the outbreak of war in Poland. Should you stay and fight, or return home as soon as possible? If you decide to return home, would you try to encourage the United States to enter the war?

2. Give students time to consider the question and lead a class discussion of the scenario and questions. List students' answers for the class to see. Encourage students to explain their reasoning and opinions.

3. Tell students that in this chapter they will learn how the aggression of dictators in Europe and Asia after World War I led to a second world war starting in 1939. **LS Verbal-Linguistic**

Alternative Assessment Handbook, Rubric 11: Discussions

• **Chapter Preview** •

HOLT
History's Impact
▶ **Video Program: World War II**
See the Video Teacher's Guide for strategies for using the video segment.

Reading Like a Historian
Analyzing Visuals Have students look closely at the image on these pages. Explain to students that there were many bloody battles in World War II, both in Europe and in the Pacific. Ask students what type of warfare this painting captures. *attacks from the air with bombers, by sea with naval warfare, and ground warfare with tanks*

Reading like a Historian

This painting shows the Allied invasion of Italy in 1943—the first major Allied advance into Europe since the beginning of the war.

Analyzing Visuals The man who created this painting was an artist with the United States Coast Guard. What do you think he tried to show in this painting? Explain your answer.

See **Skills Handbook**, p. H26

| **July 1944** Soviet troops discover an abandoned Nazi death camp. | **May 7, 1945** Germany formally surrenders. | **August 15, 1945** Japan surrenders after atomic bombs are dropped on Hiroshima and Nagasaki. |

1945

1944 The first large automatic computer is developed.

WORLD WAR II **833**

Explore the Time Line

1. What event caused the United States to enter World War II? *Japan attacked Pearl Harbor.*

2. How long did World War II last? *nearly six years*

3. What event occurred on June 6, 1944? *D-Day—Allies stormed ashore at Normandy, France*

Info to Know

Admiral Chester W. Nimitz Late in 1941, U.S. Admiral Chester W. Nimitz was appointed to command the U.S. Pacific fleet. Nimitz was the mastermind behind the complex strategy used in the Pacific known as island hopping, in which U.S. naval and land forces seized one Pacific island after another, advancing closer to Japan.

Make Inferences Why do you think Nimitz planned to seize islands closer and closer to Japan? *possible answer—He wanted islands near Japan as bases for bombing and ultimately invading Japan.*

go.hrw.com
Online Resources

Chapter Resources:
KEYWORD: SHL WW2
Teacher Resources:
KEYWORD: SHL TEACHER

Answers

Reading Like a Historian *possible answer—people storming the beaches, the role of amphibious landing craft and airplanes, the dangerous landing conditions*

Geography Starting Points

Roots of Facism The word facism comes from the Italian word *fascio*, which refers to peasant organizations and labor unions. The word is derived from the Latin word *fasces*, which are bundles of wooden rods tightly bound together and used to hold an axe blade. Fasces were used by ancient Roman bodyguards and became a symbol of strength and unity, which is one reason Italian dictator Benito Mussolini chose it as a symbol for the Fascist Party. The fasces symbol has even appeared on some American coins.

Map Transparency: Europe, 1930s

World History Outline Maps

Answers

Geography Starting Points
1. *possible answer—Nations might attack other nations or form an alliance.*
2. *possible answer—They might try to wage war or make deals with other dictators.*

834

GEOGRAPHY Starting Points

✷ Interactive
EUROPE, 1930s

Adolf Hitler dreamed of a mighty German empire. He began to secretly build up the German military.

Communist dictator Joseph Stalin crushed his political opponents and dominated all aspects of Soviet life.

Fascist dictator Francisco Franco held power in Spain after the Spanish Civil War ended in the 1930s.

0   150   300 Miles
0   150   300 Kilometers
Azimuthal equal-area projection

Fascist Benito Mussolini promised to restore Italy's greatness. He had a vision of a strong, powerful Italian military.

Starting Points As Europe struggled to recover and rebuild following World War I, many citizens looked for strong leaders. By the mid-1930s, some countries had fallen under the rule of dictators who promised power and glory for their nations. As the decade continued, their aggressive actions would lead the world closer to another devastating war.

1. **Analyze** What do you think happened in Europe as dictators tried to make their nations more powerful?

2. **Predict** How do you think other countries in Europe reacted to the rise of aggressive dictators?

◄)) Listen to History

Go online to listen to an explanation of the starting points for this chapter.

go.hrw.com
Keyword: SHL WW2

834 CHAPTER 28

Skills Focus: Analyzing Maps

At Level

Social Studies Skill
World Leaders, 1930s

Research Required

1. Draw the chart as shown for students to see. Omit the italicized answers. Have students copy the chart onto their own papers.

2. Have students scan the chapter and use information from the map on this page to fill in the chart. Suggest to students that they add a Notes column to add information about each leader as they study the chapter and use their charts as a study guide. **LS** **Visual-Spatial, Logical-Mathematical**

 Alternative Assessment Handbook, Rubric 7: Charts

Country	Leader in 1930s
Spain	*Francisco Franco*
France	*Edouard Daladier*
England	*Neville Chamberlain*
Germany	*Adolf Hitler*
Italy	*Benito Mussolini*
U.S.S.R.	*Joseph Stalin*

1 Axis Aggression

BEFORE YOU READ

MAIN IDEA
In the late 1930s Germany and Japan used military force to build empires. Their aggressive actions led to the outbreak of World War II.

READING FOCUS
1. In what ways did Germany expand in the late 1930s?
2. What alliances did Axis nations make in the 1930s?
3. How did the war begin?
4. What were the causes and effects of Japan's attack on the United States?

KEY TERMS AND PEOPLE
appeasement
Winston Churchill
Axis Powers
nonaggression pact
blitzkrieg
Allies
Battle of Britain
Hideki Tojo
isolationism

NEW YORK

PI 1.4 Students understand the broad patterns, relationships, and interactions of cultures and civilizations.

PI 2.5 Students investigate key events and developments and major turning points in world history.

Adolf Hitler meets with German military leaders.

A **FATEFUL** MEETING

THE INSIDE STORY

How did a secret meeting outline Hitler's plan for world war? A secret meeting took place deep in the heart of Nazi Germany on November 5, 1937. Present were German leader Adolf Hitler and a few of his top military and government advisers. One of those advisers, Colonel Friedrich Hossbach, took notes. These notes give a chilling description of Hitler's vision for the future of Germany.

Earlier in the day, Hitler had assured the Polish ambassador that Germany would respect Poland's territory on its eastern border. He also had stated that Germany had no intention of taking any Polish land. But at this secret meeting, Hitler said something very different.

Hitler began by swearing those present to secrecy. The subject that he was about to discuss was of vital importance. Germany, he said, faced a bleak future unless it could solve the problem of its limited territory. Simply put, Germany in its present form was too small to be self-sufficient.

According to Hossbach's notes, Hitler believed there was just one possible answer. "Germany's problem," Hossbach wrote, "could only be solved by means of force." Germany needed to act quickly. Within a few years, the powerful German military, newly rebuilt after its post–World War I destruction, would become outdated while other nations grew stronger. Hitler argued that Germany must soon seize Eastern Europe and prepare for conflict with Great Britain and France. The time to strike was coming soon.

Hossbach compiled his report several days after hearing Hitler's words. They provide a clear picture of the threat growing in Europe in the late 1930s as Germany headed down the road to war. ◼

WORLD WAR II **835**

Getting Started

Use the **Interactive Reader and Study Guide** to familiarize students with the section content.

📝 **Interactive Reader and Study Guide**, Section 1

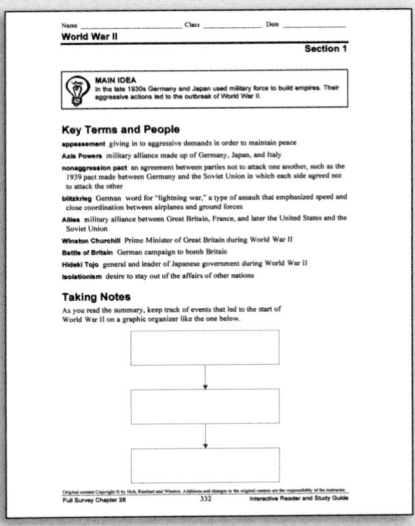

Academic Vocabulary

Review with students the high-use academic terms in this section.

violate break or ignore (p. 836)

hypothesis assumption or theory (p. 836)

📝 **CRF: Vocabulary Builder: Section 1**

Taking Notes

Germany rebuilds military, militarizes the Rhineland, annexes Austria and the Sudetenland, and invades Poland.

Teach the Main Idea

At Level

Axis Aggression

1. **Teach** Ask students the Reading Focus questions to teach this section.

2. **Apply** Draw a blank time line for students to see with the years 1938 through 1942. Have students copy the time line onto their own papers and work in pairs to place events and dates discussed in this section in the proper order. *Anschluss (March, 1938); Annexation of Sudetenland (Sept. 1938); Attack on Poland (Sept. 1939); Attack on France (May 1940); Battle of Britain (Aug.–Oct. 1940);*

Invasion of the Soviet Union (June 1941); Attack on Pearl Harbor (Dec. 7, 1941); U.S. enters the war (Dec. 8, 1941)

3. **Review** Review student time lines as a class. Add events as students name them.

4. **Practice/Homework** Have each student write a newspaper article describing the attack on Pearl Harbor. **LS Visual-Spatial, Verbal-Linguistic**

📝 **Alternative Assessment Handbook**, Rubrics 36: Time Lines; and 40: Writing to Describe

Reading Focus

1 In what ways did Germany expand in the late 1930s? *It took over German-speaking Austria and the Czech Sudetenland, which had large German-speaking populations.*

Germany Expands

Recall What was the reason Hitler gave for building submarines and warships? *to resist the spread of communism*

Predict What do you think would have happened if the British and French had stood up to Hitler when he threatened to annex the Sudetenland? *possible answer—Hitler might have stopped annexing land and been satisfied with Austria.*

📄 **CRF:** Writing for the SAT

Info to Know

English Roots of Nazi Geopolitics
Hitler's plans for German expansion owed much to theories of geopolitics, or the relationship between land and foreign policy. In the early 1900s English geopolitician Sir Halford Mackinder argued that a nation's power depended on its control of large areas of land. Mackinder believed the most important area was Eurasia and Africa, a vast connected landmass that he called the World Island. Whoever controlled the central regions of Eurasia that included Germany and Russia could control the rest of the World Island as well. His ideas received little attention in Great Britain before World War II, but they were used in Germany to support the Nazis' geopolitical ideas.

Answers

Reading Skills *He wanted Germany to have more territory.*

Reading Check *followed a policy of appeasement, giving in to Hitler's demands to maintain peace*

836

READING SKILLS

Understanding Causes and Effects Why did Hitler want Germany to expand?

TAKING NOTES

Take notes on the events leading up to the start of World War II.

☐
↓
☐
↓
☐

ACADEMIC VOCABULARY

violate break or ignore

Germany Expands

The Treaty of Versailles, which ended World War I, had seriously damaged the German economy. The terms of the treaty left Germans feeling humiliated. Adolf Hitler came to power in 1933 with a promise to restore German greatness. He wanted the nation to have lebensraum (LAY-buhnz-rowm), or "living space," in which the German people could grow and prosper. In other words, Hitler wanted Germany to have more territory. Germany's neighbors were well aware of the threat of German expansion. But with memories of the devastation of World War I still fresh, no one was willing to fight over Hitler's words.

Rebuilding the German Military Hitler soon realized that European leaders were no more willing to fight over his actions than over his words. After gaining control of the government when he became chancellor in 1933, Hitler secretly began to rebuild the German military, which had been greatly weakened after World War I. Before long, however, he was openly stating his plan to re-arm Germany. Even though this action would violate the Treaty of Versailles, it went virtually unchallenged. In 1935, for example, Britain agreed to a new treaty allowing Germany to build submarines and other warships—again, in violation of the Treaty of Versailles. Hitler claimed that he was building German military strength to resist the spread of communism. Hitler's claim was a diversion, though. He was actually planning to make war to build a mighty German empire.

Militarizing the Rhineland By 1936 Hitler was ready to take more direct action. In March he sent a small armed force into the Rhineland. This was German territory that bordered France. Hitler claimed to be reacting to a recent French-Soviet military agreement, which he said threatened Germany. The militarization of the Rhineland was another violation of the Treaty of Versailles, which required that German troops stay out of the region.

The French, along with the British, complained about Germany's treaty violations. They took no direct action, however. German troops remained in the Rhineland, and Hitler grew bolder.

Annexing Austria Hitler knew that his opponents in Europe hoped to avoid war. Therefore, he began to plot more aggressive moves.

His next target was Austria, a German-speaking country that bordered Germany and was Hitler's birthplace. He had long dreamed of uniting all the German-speaking people in Europe. In fact, Hitler's Nazi party already had many supporters in Austria.

In early 1938 Hitler began to demand that Austrian officials accept annexation by Germany. Annexation is the formal joining of one country to another. The German term for this annexation with Austria was *Anschluss* (AHN-shloos). When it became clear that Hitler would conquer Austria by force and that many of the Austrian people supported unification with Germany, the Austrian government gave in. In March 1938 German forces marched into Austria without opposition. The independent country of Austria was no more.

A Growing Crisis After the takeover of Austria, Hitler was convinced that no one dared to stop him. Next he turned to Czechoslovakia. It had a large German-speaking population, many of whom lived in a region known as the Sudetenland (soo-DAY-tuhn-land). These people were eager to join Germany. Hitler began to threaten the Czech government. The Czechs, in turn, prepared for war. The Czechs believed that if fighting began they could count on the support of France.

Though the growing crisis alarmed the French and British, they were still more interested in avoiding conflict than in confronting Hitler. At a meeting in September 1938 in Munich, Germany, British prime minister Neville Chamberlain and French leader Edouard Daladier agreed not to block Hitler's way. Czechoslovakia was told that if it fought Germany, it would do so alone.

Chamberlain returned to Great Britain believing that his policy of **appeasement**, or giving in to aggressive demands in order to maintain peace, had prevented an unnecessary war. However, others were convinced that this was wrong, and that Hitler would not stop after annexing the Sudetenland. In Britain's Parliament, **Winston Churchill** had spoken out against Chamberlain's plans. "Why not make a stand [against Hitler] while there is still a good company of united, very

---

Skills Focus: Making Inferences

Reading Skill
Czechoslovakia's Fate

Background: Remind students that Czechoslovakia was one of the new nations formed from the former Austro-Hungarian Empire in 1918 after World War I.

1. Guide the class in a discussion of Hitler's early actions that violated the terms of the Treaty of Versailles, including rebuilding the German military, moving troops into the Rhineland and the Anschluss with Austria.

2. Tell students that it is September 1938 and they are students in Czechoslovakia. Have them write a letter to a relative in the United States explaining how they feel about having the rest of Europe stand by as the Sudetenland—a part of Czechoslovakia—is taken over by Germany.

3. Ask volunteers to read their letters to the class. **LS** **Verbal-Linguistic, Intrapersonal**

📄 **Alternative Assessment Handbook,** Rubric 25: Personal Letters

Allied-controlled territory (1941)
Axis-controlled territory (1941)
Neutral (1941)
← Axis advance

0   200   400 Miles
0   200   400 Kilometers
Azimuthal equal-area projection

GEOGRAPHY SKILLS | **INTERPRETING MAPS**

go.hrw.com
Interactive Map
Keyword: SHL WW2

1. **Movement** Describe the major Axis advances in Europe.
2. **Location** How much European territory did the Axis Powers control by 1941?

---

powerful countries?" Churchill asked. Few listened to his hypothesis. In Great Britain, Chamberlain was greeted as a hero. "I believe it is peace for our time," he told an audience. "Go home and get a nice quiet sleep."

READING CHECK Make Generalizations
How did the British and French respond to Germany's expansion and aggression?

Alliances and Civil War

While Hitler was threatening Europe in the 1930s, he was also busy building alliances with other totalitarian governments. These alliances put him in league with some of the world's other major aggressors.

The Axis Forms Aggressive and totalitarian regimes had also emerged in Italy and Japan in the years after World War I. These countries demonstrated a willingness to use military force to achieve their goals. They also showed a disregard for the opinions of other nations.

Not surprisingly, perhaps, the similarities between Germany, Italy, and Japan led to a series of agreements that joined them together in a military alliance. These countries later came to be known as the **Axis Powers**.

One important agreement came in 1936, when Germany and Japan agreed to the Anti-Comintern Pact. This agreement united the two countries in an effort to prevent the spread of communism and to oppose the Soviet Union. The next year, Italy joined in the agreement. Later, in 1939, Italy and Germany signed a military alliance in which each side pledged to aid the other in the event of war.

The Spanish Civil War Italy and Germany also worked for an alliance with Spain. In 1936 fierce political conflict there had led to the outbreak of the Spanish Civil War. On one side were the Nationalists, a Fascist group.

ACADEMIC VOCABULARY
hypothesis assumption or theory

WORLD WAR II **837**

Alliances and Civil War

Analyze What was the international impact of the Spanish Civil War? *Italy and Germany supported the Nationalists. The Soviet Union supported the Republicans. The victory of the Nationalists further strengthened the positions of Italy and Germany.*

Make Inferences What might be an effect of Hitler's alliances and the rise of dictatorships after the Spanish Civil War? *possible answer—Hitler would have little to stop his expansion in Europe.*

Biography

Pablo Picasso (1881–1973) Pablo Picasso is regarded as one of the most important artists of the 20th century. He was born in Málaga, Spain, where his father taught art. After 1900 Picasso spent most of his time in France, where he became one of the pioneers in the modern art movement known as cubism.

Picasso was a strong supporter of the Republican cause during the Spanish Civil War. In 1937 Picasso created a mural for Spain's pavilion at an international exposition in Paris. Soon afterward he heard that the Spanish town of Guernica had been bombed by the Nazis in support of General Francisco Franco's attempt to overthrow the Spanish republic. His painting "Guernica" expresses his outrage over the bombing. Picasso created the painting in black and white to reflect the seriousness of the subject. Picasso asked that "Guernica" be kept in the United States until democracy returned to Spain. In 1981, after Franco's death, the painting was placed in a museum in Madrid.

Answers

Reading Check *Japan and Italy; he also signed a nonaggression pact with the Soviet Union*

Italy and Germany gave military support to the Nationalists, who were led by Spanish general Francisco Franco. On the other side were the Republicans, who were supported by the Soviet Union. After years of bloody fighting, Franco's Nationalists defeated the Republicans. Franco's victory added Spain to the list of European nations under the control of a Fascist dictator.

A Secret Deal with Stalin During the late 1930s Fascist Germany and Italy strongly opposed the Communist Soviet Union. This was in part because fascism and communism were very different. Fascism was based in extreme nationalism and loyalty to the state, while communism sought international change and a classless society. As a result, Soviet leader Joseph Stalin felt that the German military expansion threatened his nation.

In the summer of 1939 British and French officials, concerned about Hitler's aggressive actions, were discussing a possible alliance with the Soviets. But Stalin had lost confidence that the British and French would help protect his country from Germany's growing armies. As a result, Stalin was secretly negotiating a separate agreement with the Germans.

That agreement, the Nazi-Soviet Non-Aggression Pact, was revealed in August 1939. A **nonaggression pact** is an agreement in which each side promises not to attack the other. This pact was designed to allow further German aggression in Europe. A secret section of the pact also recognized each side's right to take territory in Eastern Europe, including dividing Poland into Soviet and German areas.

News of the pact shocked the British and French, who had hoped that the Soviets would support them in the event of a German attack. But it was now clear that Hitler was on the march. Only force would stop him.

READING CHECK **Identify Supporting Details** With whom did Hitler seek alliances in the late 1930s?

The War Begins

Just days after reaching his agreement with the Soviets, Hitler was ready for all-out war. On September 1, 1939, Germany launched an attack on Poland. This assault marked the start of World War II.

Lightning Attacks German forces used a new tactic in their assault on Poland. Known as **blitzkrieg**, German for "lightning war," it emphasized speed and close coordination between planes in the air and fast-moving forces on the ground. A blitzkrieg began with air attacks that damaged defenses and caused panic among civilians. Meanwhile, fast-moving columns of tanks and mobile artillery struck deep into the countryside. Behind them came foot soldiers, who swept through the area looking for any remaining areas of resistance.

The German attack on Poland had a devastating effect. The Polish air force was quickly destroyed. On land, Polish soldiers fought bravely, but they were nearly powerless to stop the German forces. In addition, the Polish countryside offered few natural barriers to slow the blitzkrieg.

One thing Poland did have was the support of Great Britain and France. Both had promised to help if Poland was attacked. On September 3, Britain and France declared war on Germany. They became known as the **Allies**. Neither country, however, gave any significant help to Poland. The collapse of the Polish defenses was so fast that little could be done to stop Poland's defeat. In just weeks, Poland was in German hands.

Even before the conquest of Poland was complete, German troops began to move into position on Germany's western border. Hitler wanted to destroy his major enemies in Europe, and he was eager to begin an assault on France. Throughout the winter of 1939–1940, German leaders made their plans for an invasion.

The Attack on France The German assault began in the spring of 1940. First came a quick, well-planned invasion of lightly defended Denmark and Norway. Capturing these countries helped improve Germany's access to the Atlantic Ocean. Then, on May 10, the long-expected attack on France began.

The German assault slammed first into the Netherlands and Belgium, countries that lay between Germany and France. Allied forces rushed to meet the invasion, but they were no match for the German attack.

At the same time, another German force was attacking farther to the south, in the Ardennes (ahr-DEN); a dense forest region along the border between France and Belgium.

Social Studies Skill
The Soviet Factor

1. Organize the class into four groups to represent the military high commands of Germany, Great Britain, France, and Poland. Have each group discuss what course a war in Europe might take and how the Soviet Union might be a factor.

2. Have each group draft a memorandum detailing a recommended plan of action for its national leaders. Each plan should include two alternatives—one that assumes the Soviet Union will continue to cooperate with Germany and another that assumes that the Soviet Union will enter the war on the side of the Allies.

3. Have volunteers from each group present their plans of action to the class.

4. Guide the class in a discussion of each group's plans of action. **LS** **Interpersonal, Verbal-Linguistic**

📝 **Alternative Assessment Handbook**, Rubrics 14: Group Activity; and 24: Oral Presentations

The London Blitz

The London Blitz began in September 1940, when Germany bombed London, the British capital. The German goal was to terrorize the British people so that they would lose the will to fight. For 57 straight nights, German bombs pounded London. They destroyed huge areas of the city and killed tens of thousands of people. Despite the destruction, the British people refused to surrender.

Some 200 German bombers attacked London each night. British fighters shot them down faster than German factories could replace them.

Searchlights targeted German aircraft for British anti-aircraft guns.

Fires raged throughout London, and many of the city's buildings lay in ruins.

Many Londoners found shelter from German bombs in the city's subway system—the Underground.

THE LONDON BLITZ, 1940–1941

0   50   100 Miles
0 50 100 Kilometers

German-controlled territory

← German bombing route

North Sea

UNITED KINGDOM   **NETHERLANDS**
London

Thames

BELGIUM

English Channel

Paris ✶
FRANCE

Skills FOCUS   **INTERPRETING VISUALS**

Draw Conclusions If British fighters could shoot down German planes faster than Germany could produce them, what do you think would be the eventual result of the Blitz?

go.hrw.com
COULD YOU HAVE SURVIVED?
Go online for a closer look at survival and this event.   Keyword: SHL WW2

WORLD WAR II **839**

Collaborative Learning

At Level

Research Required

The Blitz

1. Organize students into small groups. Have each group conduct outside research on the London Blitz, including at least one eyewitness account of the Blitz.

2. Have each group write a short scene from a play or film about the London Blitz using research and information on this page. Scripts should provide roles for each of the group's members. Students can focus on the Blitz from the point of view of the Royal Air

Force pilots who defended Britain, London civilians, or German pilots.

3. Have groups present their scenes for the class as reader's theater.

4. Guide the class in a discussion of the scenes. What did they all have in common? What aspects were unique? What do students think it would have been like to live in London during the Blitz? **LS** **Interpersonal, Kinesthetic**

 Alternative Assessment Handbook, Rubrics 30: Research; and 33: Skits and Reader's Theater

Reading Focus

3 How did the war begin? *the invasion of Poland, followed by the massing of German troops on its western border*

The War Begins

Explain How did the blitzkrieg get its name? *from the German words for "lightning war"*

Contrast How did the reaction of Great Britain and France to the invasion of Poland differ from reaction to previous German expansion? *When Germany invaded Poland, Great Briain and France declared war on Germany. Previously, they stood by, allowing Hitler to have his way.*

History Close-Up

Blackouts During the Blitz, Londoners were subject to blackout restrictions and had to cover their windows at night with black material. Streetlights were not lit, and drivers were not permitted to turn on their headlights. These precautions were taken to make it harder for German bombers to find their target, but all the bombers had to do was follow the River Thames to the docks on London's East End.

🖐 **Map Transparency:** The London Blitz, 1940

Info to Know

Saving Children As early as September 1939, fearing potential air attacks, British authorities prepared to evacuate children from London. Thousands of children relocated from the city to temporary homes in the countryside beyond the reach of German bombers. Although relocating children separated families, it saved many lives as Germans persistently bombed London during the Blitz.

Answers

Interpreting Visuals *possible answer—Germany would stop the attacks; they would run out of airplanes.*

The War Begins

Recall Why was the Soviet Red Army, with millions of soldiers, unable to withstand the German blitzkrieg? *because its troops were poorly trained and equipped, and Germany's attack was unexpected*

Contrast How did Hitler's attack on Great Britain differ from his attack on France? *He used armies with tanks to invade France, but he used aircraft to attack Britain.*

Predict How do you think the rescue of the Allied troops from Dunkirk affected the outcome of the war? *possible answer—If it hadn't taken place, the Allies would have been weakened and the Germans might have won the war.*

 CRF: Biography: Queen Elizabeth

CRF: Primary Source: The Atlantic Charter

Info to Know

The Maginot Line After World War I, the French spent millions of francs building a defensive structure known as the Maginot Line. It consisted of a vast series of underground bunkers and fortresses, which were connected by underground tunnels and underground railways. This system could be used to defend the entire border with Germany against attack. What the builders did not anticipate, however, was that the Germans would overrun the Netherlands and Belgium and invade France through them. The Maginot Line proved virtually useless against the German attack in 1940.

Answers

Faces of History *gift for words to rally British people; faced danger posed by Germany*

Reading Check *invasion of Poland, followed by the massing of German troops on its western border*

Winston CHURCHILL 1874–1965

One of the great leaders of World War II was Winston Churchill. The prime minister of Great Britain, Churchill used his gift for words to rally the British people to victory during the early years of the war, when all hope seemed lost.

Churchill had been active in British politics since 1900, but it was the growing danger posed by Germany in the 1930s that brought out his finest qualities as a leader and speaker. He became prime minister after war broke out. In that role, he led the British people throughout the war, urging them to remain strong in their opposition to Nazi Germany. His refusal to consider surrendering helped preserve Britain as a base from which the Allies could eventually attack Hitler's armies.

Find the Main Idea What qualities of leadership did Churchill display?

French leaders believed that the thick forest was impossible for an army to pass through and had left it virtually undefended. Consequently, when German tanks emerged from the Ardennes, they quickly overwhelmed the light resistance they met there.

From the Ardennes the German tanks rumbled northwest toward the French coast. The Germans trapped hundreds of thousands of Allied troops, who retreated to the coastal city of Dunkirk. There, in a heroic rescue, Allied military and civilian ships saved over 300,000 soldiers and brought them to Great Britain.

Although disaster had been avoided at Dunkirk, France was doomed. The remaining Allied forces were unable to slow the Germans' steady march toward Paris. On June 22, 1940, France surrendered to Germany.

Germany occupied much of France, but placed part of the country under the control of French officials who cooperated with Hitler. This area was known as Vichy (VEE-shee) France. Some French leaders, including Charles de Gaulle, escaped to Britain. There they organized resistance to German and Vichy control of France. Within France, resistance fighters fought to liberate their country.

The Battle for Britain Despite the French resistance effort, Great Britain now stood alone against what appeared to be an unstoppable German war machine. But conquering Britain would prove to be far more difficult for Hitler

than taking the rest of Europe had been. Britain was now led by Winston Churchill, who had replaced Neville Chamberlain as prime minister in May 1940. Churchill's fighting spirit inspired confidence among the British people.

HISTORY'S VOICES

❝We shall fight on the beaches, we shall fight on the landing grounds, we shall fight in the fields and in the streets, we shall fight in the hills. We shall never surrender.❞
—Winston Churchill, June 4, 1940

Between August and October of 1940 Germany sent thousands of aircraft over the English Channel to attack British targets in what became known as the **Battle of Britain**. Hitler's plan was to destroy the British Royal Air Force and thus make it possible to invade Britain. For the first time in the war, the Germans failed. The British were aided by a new technology called radar. Radar uses radio signals to locate and create an image of distant objects. In the Battle of Britain, radar allowed the British to detect incoming German air attacks before the German planes were visible. This made British air defenses much more effective.

As the battle continued into the fall of 1940, German planes began to bomb British ports and cities, including London. This assault became known as the London Blitz. Hitler's goal in attacking civilians was to terrorize the British public and break their will to fight. German bombs killed thousands of civilians and destroyed large areas of London and other major cities, but the British refused to give in.

Bombing continued into early 1941, but German losses increased. Finally, Hitler was forced to call off his plans to invade Britain.

The Invasion of the Soviet Union The German failure in Great Britain may have frustrated Hitler, but it did not stop him. He quickly shifted his attention back to the east. In June 1941 Hitler broke his nonaggression pact with Stalin and sent some 3 million German troops pouring into the Soviet Union. At first the German blitzkrieg was highly effective against the Soviets. Just as they had in Poland and France, German tanks and soldiers raced across the Soviet countryside. The Soviet Red Army had millions of soldiers, but its poorly trained and equipped troops were no match for the overwhelming German forces.

Skills Focus: Making Inferences

At Level

Reading Skill
The Battle of Britain

1. Guide the class in a discussion of the Battle of Britain using the following questions as a guide: What factors helped Britain resist German attacks? *it is an island; Churchill's inspiration; radar* What was Great Britain's strategic importance to the Germans? *could help them protect rest of Western Europe if U.S. entered war* What was Great Britain's strategic importance to the Allies? *could provide a base to stage an Allied attack on Europe's mainland*

2. Have each student write a journal entry describing life in Great Britain if the Germans had won the Battle of Britain.

3. Have volunteers read their entries to the class.
   LS **Verbal-Linguistic, Intrapersonal**

   Alternative Assessment Handbook, Rubrics 11: Discussions; and 15: Journals

Despite the steep losses suffered by the Soviet army, the Soviet Union did not collapse. By autumn the Germans had pushed deep into Soviet territory, but they had not managed to reach their major goals of Leningrad and Moscow, the Soviet capital. Further, they had not prepared for the extremely harsh temperatures of the Soviet winter. German troops lacked warm clothing, and their vehicles and equipment worked poorly in the frigid conditions. As winter set in, their progress slowed, then stopped.

At the same time, the Soviets were beginning to recover from the huge number of casualties they had suffered in the early fighting. The vast population of the Soviet Union allowed the Soviet armies to rebuild quickly. The Soviets had survived the mighty German onslaught, and for the first time they were beginning to fight back.

READING CHECK **Sequence** With what events did the war begin?

Japan Attacks

While war spread across Europe, another threat to peace was taking shape halfway around the world. Recall that Japan's military expansion and aggression in Asia during the 1930s had concerned many observers, including American leaders. Most Americans, however, wanted to stay out of the growing conflict overseas.

In 1941 Japan moved its forces into French Indochina, a French colony in Southeast Asia. This region was rich in oil, rubber, and other natural resources that Japan would need to supply its military. In response, nervous American leaders banned the sale of oil to Japan, a move that was designed to slow the Japanese war machine. This was a serious threat to Japan's future plans.

The Japanese government continued to hold peace talks with the United States. Meanwhile, Japan secretly planned for war.

Pearl Harbor For months, Japanese military leaders under General **Hideki Tojo** had been developing plans for a surprise attack on the American naval base at Pearl Harbor, Hawaii. This base was home to the U.S. Navy's Pacific Fleet. As the sun rose on Sunday morning, December 7, 1941, the Japanese attack began.

The Attack on Pearl Harbor

The day after the attack on Pearl Harbor, President Franklin D. Roosevelt asked Congress to declare war on Japan.

"Yesterday, December 7th, 1941—a date which will live in infamy—the United States of America was suddenly and deliberately attacked by naval and air forces of the Empire of Japan . . .

"As commander in chief of the Army and Navy, I have directed that all measures be taken for our defense. But always will our whole nation remember the character of the onslaught against us.

"No matter how long it may take us to overcome this premeditated invasion, the American people in their righteous might will win through to absolute victory . . .

"Hostilities exist . . . our people, our territory, and our interests are in grave danger.

"With confidence in our armed forces, with the unbounding determination of our people, we will gain the inevitable triumph—so help us God."

Skills FOCUS **READING LIKE A HISTORIAN**

1. **Analyze Primary Sources** How does President Roosevelt describe Japan's actions?

2. **Infer** In what way do you think the American public would have responded to Roosevelt's speech?

See **Skills Handbook**, p. H25

▼ American soldiers abandon the burning USS *California* during the attack on Pearl Harbor.

WORLD WAR II **841**

Reading Focus

4 What were the causes and effects of Japan's attack on the United States? *Causes—Japan's military expansion and aggression; alliance with Germany and Italy; response to America's ban on the sale of oil; Effects—U.S. declared war on Japan.*

Japan Attacks

Identify Who was General Hideki Tojo? *the head of the Japanese government*

Cause and Effect Why did American leaders ban oil sales to Japan? *in response to the Japanese invasion of French Indochina*

Primary Source

In an excerpt from his book *At Dawn We Slept,* historian Gordon Prange relates an eyewitness account of the attack on Pearl Harbor:

"When the attack began, ... the explosion of bombs, the whine of bullets, the roar of planes, the belching guns of aroused defenders, the acrid smell of fire and smoke—all blended into a nerve-racking cacophony [sound] of chaos. ... Bombardiers still dropped their torpedoes, while dive bombers pounced like hawks. ... Far above, high-level bombers rained their deadly missiles as fighters shuttled in and out, weaving together the fearful tapestry of destruction."

Differentiating Instruction

Below Level

Learners Having Difficulty

Materials: butcher paper, paints or colored markers

1. Guide the class in a discussion of the attack on Pearl Harbor using the following questions:

• Describe the attack. *Hundreds of Japanese fighters and bombers dropped bombs on the American base.*

• What was the result of the attack? *2,400 Americans dead, nearly 200 aircraft destroyed, eight battleships sunk or damaged*

• What good news was there? *Three aircraft carriers were out to sea and therefore spared.*

• How did the attack affect Americans? *Isolationism disappeared as news of attack spread. Congress declared war on Japan.*

2. Organize the class into small groups. Have groups create murals of the Pearl Harbor attack.

3. Display students' murals in a classroom exhibit. **LS** **Interpersonal, Visual-Spatial**

Alternative Assessment Handbook, Rubrics 3: Artwork; 11: Discussions; and 14: Group Activity

Answers

Reading Like a Historian
1. *shameful, sudden, deliberate;*
2. *possible answer—They would feel encouraged, determined, and patriotic.*

Close

Have students summarize the Axis aggression that led up to the entry of the United States into the war.

Review

Online Quiz, Section 1

Assess

SE Section 1 Assessment

Progress Assessment: Section 1 Quiz

Alternative Assessment Handbook

Reteach/ Intervene

Interactive Reader and Study Guide, Section 1

Interactive Skills Tutor CD-ROM

Answers

Reading Check *American leaders banned the sale of oil to Japan, which threatened Japan's future plans in French Indochina.*

NEW YORK

CC Unit 6-D7
Japan's role in
World War II

For nearly two weeks Japanese aircraft carriers had been approaching Pearl Harbor from the north, undetected by the American military. When the attack started, hundreds of Japanese fighters and bombers launched from the carriers and sped over Pearl Harbor, dropping bombs and torpedos on the American base below. The raid was a complete surprise.

American Eddie Jones was onboard the USS *California* in Pearl Harbor when the attack began.

HISTORY'S VOICES

❝You couldn't believe it was happening. You could see it in front of your eyes, but you couldn't believe it. Here it was, a beautiful morning—a beautiful Sunday morning—and you see everything blowing up and ships sinking and men in the water. And you think, we're at peace with the world. This can't be happening.❞

—Seaman Second Class Eddie Jones, in *War Stories: Remembering World War II*

Although American military planners had long believed that an attack on Pearl Harbor was a possibility, the base was lightly defended. Most American planes never had the chance to leave the ground.

The attack lasted less than two hours, but the destruction was enormous. Some 2,400 Americans were dead. Nearly 200 aircraft were destroyed, and all eight battleships in the harbor were sunk or damaged. Perhaps the only good news for the Americans was that the three aircraft carriers normally stationed at Pearl Harbor were out to sea during the attack and were unharmed.

The American Response The attack on Pearl Harbor had a profound effect on the American public. Until then, many Americans had believed that the United States should stay out of Europe's war and protect its own interests. This desire to avoid involvement in the affairs of other nations is known as **isolationism**. Isolationism was common in the United States after World War I, when many Americans questioned what the costly Allied victory in that war had actually accomplished. But as news of the attack on Pearl Harbor spread, most isolationism quickly disappeared. On December 8 the U.S. Congress declared war on Japan. Three days later, Germany and Italy declared war on the United States. With these actions, the United States joined the Allies in the global fight against the Axis Powers.

READING CHECK Find the Main Idea Why did Japan attack the United States?

SECTION 1 ASSESSMENT

go.hrw.com
Online Quiz
Keyword: SHL WW2 HP

Reviewing Ideas, Terms, and People

1. **a. Identify** What are some examples of Hitler's growing military aggression in the late 1930s?
   b. Compare and Contrast Compare and contrast Germany's actions in the Rhineland, Austria, and Czechoslovakia.
   c. Evaluate How would you describe Neville Chamberlain's policy toward Hitler in the late 1930s?

2. **a. Recall** Who were the Axis Powers?
   b. Make Inferences Why do you think Hitler sought allies in the late 1930s?
   c. Evaluate What do you think about Stalin's decision to make a deal with Hitler rather than trust the British and French to help stop the Germans? Explain.

3. **a. Recall** What event marked the start of World War II?
   b. Compare and Contrast Describe Germany's successes and failures in France, Great Britain, and the Soviet Union.

4. **a. Recall** What events led up to the Japanese attack on Pearl Harbor?

b. Identify Cause and Effect What was the significance of the attack on Pearl Harbor in terms of American public opinion?

Critical Thinking

5. **Sequence** Use your notes and a graphic organizer like this one to explain how events of the 1930s led to the outbreak of World War II. How did the world react to each event.

[ ] → [ ] → [ ] → [ ] → [ ]

FOCUS ON SPEAKING

6. **Persuasion** Write a brief conversation between Neville Chamberlain and Winston Churchill. In your conversation, have the speakers discuss what Great Britain should do about Germany's increasingly aggressive actions.

Section 1 Assessment Answers

1. **a.** rebuilding the German military, militarizing the Rhineland, annexing Austria
   b. possible answer—hoped to avoid or delay war by giving Hitler what he wanted
   c. possible answer—He believed that appeasement would prevent war.

2. **a.** Germany, Italy, and Japan
   b. possible answer—He knew he needed allies to get what he wanted.
   c. possible answer—Stalin should have known that Hitler would act aggressively because Germans had been untrustworthy.

3. **a.** Germany's invasion of Poland
   b. Success—forced French surrender in 1940; destroyed much of London in Blitz; blitzkrieg effective against Soviets; Failures—French resistance in Vichy; British refuse to surrender, German troops ill-equipped for winter, Soviet army rebuilds.

4. **a.** Japan had moved into French Indochina. In response, American leaders banned the sale of oil to Japan. Japan held peace talks with the U.S. while secretly planning for war.

b. Many Americans no longer felt U.S. should stay out of the war.

5. Germany rebuilds military, militarizes the Rhineland, annexes Austria and the Sudetenland, invades Poland.

6. Student conversations should show an understanding of the viewpoints of both Chamberlain and Churchill.

The Allied Response

BEFORE YOU READ

MAIN IDEA

The early years of World War II went poorly for the Allies. But after the United States joined the war, the Allies soon recovered and began making gains against the Axis.

READING FOCUS

1. In what ways were Americans involved in the early years of the war?
2. How did the war in North Africa and Italy progress?
3. What was the turning point in the Soviet Union?
4. What was the turning point in the Pacific?

KEY TERMS AND PEOPLE

Erwin Rommel
Battle of El Alamein
Dwight D. Eisenhower
Siege of Leningrad
Battle of Stalingrad
Douglas MacArthur
Bataan Death March
Battle of Midway
Battle of Guadalcanal
kamikazes

 NEW YORK

PI 1.4 Students understand the broad patterns, relationships, and interactions of cultures and civilizations.

PI 2.5 Students investigate key events and developments and major turning points in world history.

THE INSIDE STORY

Could old newspapers help win a war? Defeating the Axis armies required a huge effort from the Allies. In the Allied nations, millions of people volunteered to fight. Others found different ways to help.

The war effort required enormous amounts of raw materials to make the supplies needed to win the war, from airplanes to ammunition to food. In Great Britain and the United States, civilians took part in efforts to save these precious resources for the soldiers fighting overseas.

Rationing and recycling were two ways the average British or American civilian helped the war effort. The federal government rationed, or limited, many products during the war, including certain foods, clothing, and gasoline. Rationing meant sacrifices for all. Civilians received a

certain number of ration stamps, which could be used to buy rationed products such as meats, butter, and canned vegetables. Many people planted "victory gardens" to grow extra food.

Recycling was another way people on the home front contributed to the war effort. They collected metal, rubber, newspapers, even kitchen fat, all of which could be used in the war effort. For example, metal cans could be turned into ammunition or guns, while kitchen fat was used to make glycerin, an ingredient in explosives and medicines.

These scrap drives provided scarce materials for the war effort and they also brought civilians together to support the Allied struggle. They helped people at home stay strong during the uncertain days of the bloodiest war the world had ever seen. ■

RECYCLING FOR VICTORY

► American children collect old paper for the Allied war effort.

WORLD WAR II **843**

The Allied Response

1. **Teach** Ask students the Reading Focus questions to teach this section.

2. **Apply** Have students create four-column charts about the information in this chapter. Each chart should have the following headings: Atlantic, North Africa/Italy, Europe, and Pacific. Students should list significant battles and events under each heading.

3. **Review** Review students' charts as a class. Ask students which event covered in this

chapter is the most important. Write their responses for the class to see.

4. **Practice/Homework** Ask students to write a short essay comparing the treatment of the Japanese during World War II with the treatment of people of Middle Eastern or Islamic background following the terrorist attacks of September 11, 2001. **LS Visual-Spatial, Verbal-Linguistic**

   Alternative Assessment Handbook, Rubrics 7: Charts; and 37: Writing Assignments

---

Getting Started

Use the **Interactive Reader and Study Guide** to give students a quick preview of the section.

📓 **Interactive Reader and Study Guide**, Section 2

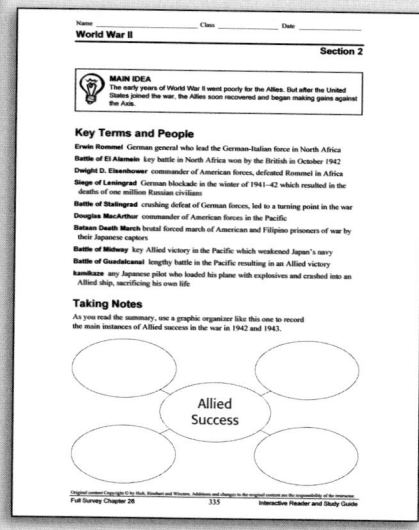

📄 **CRF:** Vocabulary Builder: Section 2

Taking Notes

better equipment and breaking of a key German code help Allies gain control of the Atlantic; Allies win control of North Africa, move north through Italy; German forces defeated at Stalingrad; Japan's navy suffers terrible blow in Battle of Midway

Reading Focus

1 In what ways were Americans involved in the early years of the war? *The U.S. gave military aid to Great Britain, which led to shooting between American vessels and German craft and the sinking of an American escort ship by a German U-boat.*

Early American Involvement

Recall Before declaring war on Japan, how did the United States help the Allies? *by offering military aid to Great Britain in the form of ships and military escorts for convoys*

Summarize How did the United States mobilize for war? *Men volunteered to fight or were drafted, women filled non-combat roles, factories converted to producing weapons and supplies.*

📄 CRF: Biography: Rosie the Riveter

Info to Know

U.S. Neutrality In 1940 the United States was officially neutral. Congress had passed Neutrality Acts in 1937 and 1939 to keep the United States from being drawn into European wars. Nevertheless, President Roosevelt believed that the United States should serve as a "great arsenal of democracy." After his reelection that year, he presented a military aid bill to Congress. His proposal would "lend-lease" or otherwise provide supplies needed by any country whose security was considered vital to the defense of the United States. Congress passed the Lend-Lease Act, providing much-needed assistance to Great Britain while buying time for the United States to prepare for war.

Answers

Reading Check *Many factories converted to produce weapons and supplies; Americans made do with less food, fuel, and other items; people planted "victory gardens."*

844

TAKING NOTES
List the main instances of Allied success in the war in 1942 and 1943.

Allied Success

THE IMPACT TODAY
The Manzanar internment camp in California is now a national historic site operated by the National Park Service.

FOCUS ON NEW YORK
Because of the demand for labor, the U.S. government established the Bracero Program in 1942. This program allowed some Mexican workers to take temporary jobs in the United States. Hundreds came to upstate New York to perform vital jobs for the war effort.

Early American Involvement

The Japanese attack on Pearl Harbor ended most American resistance to entering the war. But even before the United States declared war on Japan, the country had been helping the Allies by shipping supplies across the Atlantic Ocean.

The Battle of the Atlantic Control of the Atlantic Ocean was a critical factor in World War II. Great Britain and the Soviet Union depended heavily on supplies shipped by sea to their ports. If Germany gained control of the seas and cut off Allied access to food and equipment, the war would soon be lost.

Germany's navy was powerful, but it did not have enough ships to match the battleships of Great Britain. As a result, the Germans came to rely on the same weapon they had used in World War I—the U-boat, or submarine. U-boats inflicted enormous damage on the Allies, sinking hundreds of merchant supply ships in the early years of the war.

Before entering the war, the United States offered military aid to Great Britain in the form of ships and military escorts for convoys. Convoys were groups of many ships that offered safety in numbers. This aid led to shooting between American and German vessels. In October 1941 a U-boat sank the American escort ship USS *Reuben James*, killing most of its crew. It was the first U.S. Navy ship sunk by Germany during the war.

The American Home Front Less than two months after the *Reuben James* went down, Japan attacked Pearl Harbor. After the United States entered the war, the nation had to mobilize, or bring its military forces into readiness. This was an enormous task. To defeat the powerful Axis armies, the United States would need soldiers, sailors, and pilots, as well as a great deal of military equipment and supplies.

Millions of American men volunteered to fight for their country, and still more were drafted, or required to serve. While women were not permitted to take part in combat, they filled other roles in the military, working as pilots, clerks, and in other positions. The nation also responded quickly to the need for war supplies. For example, many factories that made consumer goods were converted to produce

weapons and supplies. The enormous demand for workers gave new employment opportunities to many women and African Americans.

Americans at home found other ways to help their country. They made do with less food, fuel, and other items, all of which were needed by the armed forces. They participated in scrap drives to collect materials such as iron and rubber, which could be recycled for military purposes.

But wartime patriotism had negative effects too. Some government officials worried that Americans of German, Italian, and Japanese descent would help the enemy. German Americans and Italian Americans faced certain restrictions during the war, but Japanese Americans were treated most harshly.

More than 100,000 Japanese Americans on the West Coast were forced to leave their homes and businesses and travel to internment camps. Most were American citizens, but the government was concerned only with their racial background. Life in the camps was hard. Many were located in desert areas with a harsh climate and were surrounded by guards and barbed wire fences. Families lived in small facilities, and the quality of education and health care was poor. It was not until later in the war that they were released.

Winning the Atlantic After the United States was officially at war, Germany sent its U-boats into American waters. They hoped to destroy American merchant ships. Indeed, hundreds of American ships went down.

By 1943, however, the Allies had made a number of adjustments in the war for the Atlantic. For one thing, Allied factories finally began producing ships and planes in large numbers. This meant better equipped convoys, which had more firepower to find and destroy U-boats. The Allies had also broken a key German code system used to transmit information about German plans. This helped the Allies learn the locations of German U-boats.

Thanks to these improvements, losses to U-boats dropped sharply. The vital supply line to Great Britain and the Soviet Union was kept open, and the Atlantic belonged to the Allies.

READING CHECK **Find the Main Idea** How were Americans on the home front involved in the war?

Skills Focus: Analyzing Alternative Points of View · **At Level**

Reading Like a Historian Skill
America's Role in World War II

1. Organize students into five groups. Tell them that they are members of Congress in 1939, planning U.S. response to events in Europe including the German invasion of Poland.

2. Have each group split into two teams. One student in each group should serve as moderator. One team should support entering the war on the side of the Allies to prevent further German aggression. The other team should favor isolationism.

3. Have each group conduct a debate. Students may use information from their textbooks and may conduct additional research to support their arguments.

4. Have moderators announce the winners based on the most convincing argument.
   LS Interpersonal, Verbal-Linguistic

📄 **Alternative Assessment Handbook**, Rubrics 10: Debates; and 14: Group Activity

WORLD WAR II IN EUROPE AND NORTH AFRICA, 1941–1943

Interactive

Legend:
- Allied-controlled territory (1942)
- Allied advance
- Axis-controlled territory (1942)
- Axis advance
- Neutral (1942)
- Major battle

0   300   600 Miles
0   300   600 Kilometers
Azimuthal equal-area projection

GEOGRAPHY SKILLS | **INTERPRETING MAPS**

go.hrw.com
Interactive Map
Keyword: SHL WW2

1. **Movement** Describe the major Allied advances in North Africa and Italy.
2. **Location** What areas of Europe and North Africa did the Allies control in 1942?

War in North Africa and Italy

While the fighting for the Atlantic was still raging, Italian and British forces began a battle for the control of North Africa. This territory was vital for the Allies. If the British could control North Africa, they would be able to protect the Suez Canal, the shipping route that linked the Mediterranean Sea with the oil fields of the Middle East. Keeping this oil supply flowing was essential to the British war effort.

In the fall of 1940, Italian forces based in Libya attacked British-controlled Egypt. This attack was a failure. British forces not only eliminated the Italian threat to Egypt, they soon drove into Libya and threatened to gain control of all of North Africa. Hitler was forced to send German forces to support the Italians.

Back-and-Forth Fighting The new German and Italian force in Africa—called the Afrika Korps—was led by German general **Erwin Rommel**. He quickly earned his nickname, the Desert Fox, by skillfully pushing British out of Libya and back into Egypt.

The Afrika Korps, however, had trouble supplying its forces, and this limited its effectiveness. Throughout 1941 and into 1942, the British and the Afrika Korps traded blows.

A key battle took place in October 1942, at El Alamein (el a-luh-MAYN) in Egypt. British troops under General Bernard Montgomery took advantage of Rommel's supply problems.

WORLD WAR II **845**

War in North Africa and Italy

Recall Recall How did German general Erwin Rommel earn his nickname, the Desert Fox? *by skillfully pushing the British out of Libya and back into Egypt*

Summarize How did the Germans respond to the Allied invasion of Italy? *The Germans fought to keep the Allies from moving north.*

Recent Scholarship

The women of Leningrad share their perspective in *Writing the Siege of Leningrad: Women's Diaries, Memoirs and Documentary Prose,* by Cynthia Simmons and Nina Perlina. Because the men were at the front, women were forced to run the city and defend their homes. Industry continued to operate and schools were open, even though the city was being constantly bombed, supplies were cut off, and people were dying of starvation. Stories of Leningrad's inhabitants have more in common with those of concentration camp prisoners than with typical war stories. Recently scholars have begun to focus on the writings of the women of Leningrad, which often differ from official Soviet depictions of the siege.

Writing the Siege of Leningrad: Women's Diaries, Memoirs and Documentary Prose by Cynthia Simmons and Nina Perlina. Greta Bucher, 2004.

Answers

Faces of History *He was patient, diplomatic, and a skilled military planner.*

Reading Check *They drove the Axis out of North Africa and used it as a base for launching an invasion of Europe through Italy.*

Using information gained from secret German codes, the British won a smashing victory. As a result of the **Battle of El Alamein**, Axis power in North Africa was severely weakened.

The Americans Join the Battle As the British and the Afrika Korps fought in Libya and Egypt, Allied leaders were planning to bring American troops to the European battlefield. The Soviets wanted the Allies to invade Europe, creating a second front that would force Hitler to pull troops away from Soviet territory. British and American leaders insisted that planning for such a huge action would take time. They decided to invade the western part of North Africa first, in the French colonies of Morocco, Algeria, and Tunisia.

In November 1942 a combined American and British force landed in North Africa. It was led by American general **Dwight D. Eisenhower**. The Allies faced little resistance after landing, and French forces soon joined them.

The landing put Rommel in a difficult spot, with strong Allied forces both to the east and west. His supply problems also continued to worsen. After several battles, during which the Americans first experienced combat in the war, the Germans and Italians were finally trapped. In May 1943, they surrendered. Nearly 250,000 Axis soldiers were taken prisoner. All of North Africa was now in Allied hands.

Fighting in Italy The next goal for the Allies was Italy itself. In July 1943 Allied soldiers moved north from Africa and landed on the

NEW YORK
CC Unit 6-D4
Key events of World War II

Italian island of Sicily. Italian resistance was weakening, and by the end of the month the Italian government had forced dictator Benito Mussolini from power. The Allies captured the island a few weeks later and made plans to invade mainland Italy.

But Hitler was not going to allow the Allies to simply march through Italy into the center of Europe. After the Allies moved into southern Italy in September 1943, the invasion was slowed by German resistance as troops moved north. Bloody fighting there would continue for months to come.

READING CHECK **Summarize** What did Allied troops accomplish in the war in North Africa and Italy?

A Turning Point in the Soviet Union

The 1941 German invasion of the Soviet Union had sputtered to a halt when the Soviet winter set in. German equipment failed in the brutally cold conditions, and Hitler's poorly equipped troops suffered greatly.

Their suffering, however, was mild compared to that of the citizens of Leningrad. After German troops failed to capture the city in 1941, Hitler ordered a siege, or a military blockade designed to force the city to surrender. "In this war for existence," he said, "we have no interest in keeping even part of this great city's population." In the winter of 1941–1942, Soviet civilians starved to death at a rate of 3,000–4,000 a day. Eventually, as many as 1 million civilians would perish in the **Siege of Leningrad**.

The Battle of Stalingrad As the weather warmed in the spring of 1942, Hitler ordered renewed assaults on the Soviet Union. To aid in the attack, he assembled a large force, including troops drawn from Italy, Romania, and Hungary.

At first, Axis forces fought well, though shortages of fuel slowed their advance. By the end of the summer, a large Axis force was poised to take the industrial city of Stalingrad on the Volga River. Stalingrad was one of the largest cities in the Soviet Union. Its factories produced tanks, guns, and other military equipment for the Soviet armies. Stalingrad's ports on the Volga shipped grain, oil, and other products throughout the Soviet Union.

FACES OF HISTORY

Dwight D. EISENHOWER
1890–1969

Dwight D. Eisenhower was known for being patient, diplomatic, and a skilled planner. With these character traits, he proved to be the ideal person to lead the Allied armies in World War II.

Born in Texas and raised in the small farm town of Abilene, Kansas, Eisenhower attended the U.S. Military Academy and rose steadily through the ranks of the Army. During World War II, he was named supreme commander of the Allied forces in Europe. In this role Eisenhower planned and commanded D-Day, the invasion of France. After the war, Eisenhower served two terms as president.

Draw Conclusions In what ways did Eisenhower's character traits help make him a good leader?

846 CHAPTER 28

Differentiating Instruction

At Level

Research Required

Struggling Readers

Materials: outline maps of North Africa and the Mediterranean

1. Organize students into groups of four or five. Have each group conduct research to follow the progress of the battles in North Africa from 1941 to 1943. Have each group make a chart listing the battles, their locations, the major participants, and their outcomes.

2. Give each group an outline map of North Africa and the Mediterranean. Have each group work together to map the battles in

North Africa, labeling them with their names and dates.

3. Conduct a discussion of the war in North Africa. Point out that much of North Africa is desert, and ask students to explain North Africa's strategic importance. *controlled the Suez Canal; provided a launching pad for the invasion of Italy* **LS** Visual-Spatial, Interpersonal

Alternative Assessment Handbook, Rubrics 14: Group Activity; 20: Map Creation; and 30: Research

Reading like a Historian

Propaganda Posters

Analyzing Visuals Many countries used propaganda during World War II to try to influence the way people thought. Propaganda is information and ideas designed to promote a certain cause. In World War II, governments would create propaganda posters to encourage citizens to support the war effort. Some posters urged people to join the armed forces or to conserve food and gasoline for soldiers. Others warned about the evil intentions of the enemy.

To analyze what these posters suggest about World War II, think about

- the words in the poster
- the similarities and differences in the two posters

This German poster was created in 1942. It shows a German soldier on the battlefield.

The German text means "This is how we fight. You, too, must work for victory."

This American poster was created in 1942. It shows a German airplane in flames.

"Scrap" refers to the products Americans recycled to help the war effort. "Scrapping" also means "fighting."

Skills Focus — READING LIKE A HISTORIAN

1. Words What does the German poster mean by "You, too, must work for victory"?

2. Message Are the messages of the two posters similar or different? Why do you think that is?

See **Skills Handbook**, p. H26

Reading Focus

3 What was the turning point in the Soviet Union? *the Battle of Stalingrad*

A Turning Point in the Soviet Union

Recall What were the results of the Siege of Leningrad? *During the winter of 1941–1942, 3,000 to 4,000 civilians starved to death each day. In all, as many as one million civilians perished.*

Summarize Why did Axis forces want to take Stalingrad? *It was one of the largest cities in the Soviet Union, a major industrial center, and a center for shipping.*

CRF: Social Studies Skills: Interpreting Infographics

Reading Like a Historian
Propaganda Posters

Compare and Contrast Compare and contrast the two posters shown on this page. How are they similar? How are they different? *possible answer—Similar: both motivate intended audience to action to help a nation; Different: German poster promotes helping Germany, American poster promotes fighting Germany.*

Skills Focus: Analyzing Visuals

At Level

Reading Like a Historian Skill
Propaganda Posters

Materials: poster board, colored pencils, markers

1. Guide the class in a discussion of the propaganda posters on this page. Remind students that propaganda is information about an organization to promote a policy or idea. Ask students what these posters have in common. Point out that propaganda can take many forms, such as articles, books, and movies.

2. Have students use reliable online or print sources to find other examples of propaganda posters. Students may find posters from other periods, such as World War I and World War II.

3. Display posters for the class to see. Guide the class in a discussion about why each poster classifies as propaganda.

4. Have students create their own propaganda posters. Display student posters in a classroom exhibit. **LS** Visual-Spatial

Alternative Assessment Handbook, Rubrics 11: Discussions; and 28: Posters

Answers

Reading Like a Historian 1. *It is encouraging German citizens to help their country.* **2.** *possible answer—The posters' messages are similar because they are both encouraging citizens to support the war effort.*

Reading Focus

A Turning Point in the Soviet Union

Explain Why was Stalin so determined to hold Stalingrad? *The city was named for him.*

Summarize What was the outcome of the Battle of Stalingrad? *Over a million Soviet soldiers died, but Hitler suffered a crushing defeat; German army was forced to retreat to the west, — a turning point in the war.*

Make Judgements Why do you think Hitler stated "Surrender is forbidden"? *possible answer—He was probably blinded by his own ambition and refused to admit defeat.*

Info to Know

MacArthur and the Philippines Ten hours after attacking Pearl Harbor, the Japanese attacked Clark Air Force Base in the Philippines, which at that time was a U.S. possession. American General Douglas MacArthur had been put in charge of building a Philippine army. After the Japanese attack, MacArthur took his forces to the island fortress of Corregidor in Manila Bay and to the nearby Bataan Peninsula. The United States was concentrating its forces in Europe, and ordered MacArthur to evacuate members of the Philippine government and lead the war against Japan from Australia. Although it went against his belief in an officer's duty, MacArthur left his men, promising them, "I shall return." He fulfilled his promise in October 1944, when he waded ashore at Leyte Gulf and drove the Japanese out of the Philippines.

Answers

Reading Skills *It showed the Allies that the German army was no longer invincible.*

Reading Check *The German army had seemed invincible, but after failing to take Stalingrad, it was now retreating to the west.*

848

NEW YORK

CC Unit 6-D7
Japan's role in World War II

The **Battle of Stalingrad** was one of the most brutal of the war. After having bombed the city into rubble with air and artillery attacks, German troops moved into the ruins to wipe out the surviving Soviets. The Soviet defenders, pinned between the Germans and the Volga River, fought furiously for each bombed-out building and cellar hole. Soviet leader Joseph Stalin wanted to save the city that was named after him and insisted on holding it at all costs. Those costs were high. Estimates vary, but many tens of thousands of soldiers on each side died in this phase of the battle alone.

While somehow managing to hold off the German attack through the fall of 1942, Soviet marshal Georgy Zhukov (zoo-kov) gathered his remaining forces for a counterattack. By November, the Soviets were ready to strike. A strong force broke through the Axis defenses, quickly surrounding some 250,000 men.

There was still a chance for the trapped Axis soldiers to retreat to the west and try to break through the trap, but Hitler refused to allow it. Instead, he insisted that they stand and fight, promising to supply the force by air. This effort fell far short. Hunger, cold, and Soviet attacks soon took a dreadful toll. One German soldier recorded the scene in the overflowing field hospital.

HISTORY'S VOICES

❝Here was the greatest misery that I have seen in my whole life. An endless wailing of wounded and dying men . . . most of them had received nothing to eat for days.❞
—Alois Dorner, German soldier, January 1943

In late January, the German commander told Hitler that his troops had no ammunition, food, or medicine. "Surrender is forbidden," was Hitler's reply. Within days, 90,000 half-dead Axis survivors were finally captured. Many of them would soon die in Soviet prison camps.

Over 1 million Soviet soldiers had died in the defense of Stalingrad, but the result was a crushing defeat for Hitler. The seemingly invincible German army was now retreating to the west. This, along with the Allied victories in North Africa and Italy, marked a turning point in the war.

READING
SKILLS

Understanding Causes and Effects What was the effect of Germany's loss at Stalingrad?

READING CHECK **Summarize** Why was the Battle of Stalingrad a turning point?

848 CHAPTER 28

A Turning Point in the Pacific

Meanwhile in the Pacific, the attack on Pearl Harbor had been an enormous success for Japan. The damage to the U.S. Navy's Pacific Fleet took time to overcome and limited the American ability to strike back at Japan. In addition, in the early years of the war the Allies chose to focus on the fighting in Europe.

The Allies Fight Back Fortunately for the Allies, the Pacific Fleet's three aircraft carriers were not damaged in the attack on Pearl Harbor. Without the air power that aircraft carriers provided, Allied ground and naval forces would have been at the mercy of Japanese bombers. Still, following the devastation of Pearl Harbor, the Japanese navy ruled the seas.

The early months in the Pacific were difficult for the Allies. The Japanese forces were better equipped and fighting closer to home. They moved almost at will, conquering vital territory—Singapore, Hong Kong, Burma, and many strategic islands in the Pacific.

Another target was the American-held Philippines. There General **Douglas MacArthur** led a small number of American soldiers and poorly equipped Filipino troops in a doomed defense. Following the American surrender of the Philippines in April 1942, the Japanese forced 70,000 prisoners to march up the Bataan Peninsula to a distant prison camp. During this **Bataan Death March**, tropical heat, lack of food and water, and brutal violence from their captors killed 600 American and up to 10,000 Filipino prisoners. Thousands more of the survivors later perished in the inhumane prison camp.

The Battle of Coral Sea Japan was at the height of its power in May 1942 when Japanese and American aircraft carriers first came together in battle. The location was the Coral Sea, a body of water off the northeast coast of Australia. The battle took place as Japanese forces were preparing to invade the British-controlled Port Moresby on the island of New Guinea. A group of Allied vessels tried to block the attack. Both sides lost an aircraft carrier in the Battle of Coral Sea. This hurt the Americans more than it hurt the Japanese. Yet the battle marked the first time that the relentless Japanese advance had been stopped.

Differentiating Instruction

Below Level

Learners Having Difficulty

1. Have students create a short story, journal entry, or political cartoon about the German invasion of the Soviet Union.

   • A short story might tell of an invasion-related event through the eyes of a German or Soviet soldier, a guerilla fighter, or a Russian civilian.

   • A journal entry might express the feelings of a German soldier, a Soviet soldier defending his homeland, a woman left behind during the Siege of Leningrad, or a teenage survivor of the Battle of Stalingrad.

   • A cartoon might portray the changing relationship between Hitler and Stalin.

2. Have volunteers share their creations with the rest of the class.

3. Guide the class in a discussion of students' creations. How accurate or believable is each student's work? How well do students reflect their chosen point of view? **LS Verbal-Linguistic, Intrapersonal**

Alternative Assessment Handbook, Rubrics 27: Political Cartoons; and 37: Writing Assignments

The Battle of Midway A month later, in June 1942, Japanese and American carriers again fought on the high seas in the **Battle of Midway**. The Japanese had planned to capture the strategic island of Midway in the middle of the Pacific Ocean, home to a key American military base. Japanese leaders wanted the island, but they also wanted to lure the American fleet into a naval battle in which the Americans would be outnumbered and destroyed.

The Japanese had the advantage in the number of ships and aircraft carriers they could bring to Midway. But the Americans had a more important advantage: they had bro-

ken the secret Japanese code used to transmit messages. As a result, the Americans knew the date and location of the planned Japanese attack. American admiral Chester Nimitz was therefore able to plan an effective defense that overcame the Japanese superiority in firepower. Nimitz's plan worked perfectly. In the battle that followed, the Americans destroyed four Japanese carriers with a loss of only one of their own. The Allies had won a great victory, and Japan's navy had suffered a terrible blow.

The aircraft carrier USS *Yorktown* burns after being hit by Japanese torpedoes during the Battle of Midway.

Interactive

WAR IN THE PACIFIC, 1942–1944

OUTER MONGOLIA
MANCHURIA
CHINA
Beijing
KOREA
JAPAN
Tokyo
INDIA
BURMA
Hong Kong Dec. 1941
SIAM
INDOCHINA
PHILIPPINES
Manila
Bataan & Corregidor Jan.–May 1942
Leyte Gulf Oct. 1944
MALAY STATES
Singapore Feb. 1942
Borneo
DUTCH EAST INDIES
INDIAN OCEAN
New Guinea
Buna-Gona Nov. 1942–Jan. 1943
Caroline Islands
Peleliu Sep.–Nov. 1944
Guam July–Aug. 1944
Saipan June–July 1944
Mariana Islands
Enewetak Feb. 1944
Marshall Islands
Kwajalein Jan.–Feb. 1944
Midway June 1942
Tropic of Cancer
Pearl Harbor
20°N
Hawaii (U.S.)
PACIFIC OCEAN
0° Equator
Tarawa Nov. 1943
Gilbert Islands
Bougainville Oct. 1943–Mar. 1944
Solomon Islands
Guadalcanal Aug. 1942–Feb. 1943
Coral Sea May 1942
0   600   1,200 Miles
0   600   1,200 Kilometers
Miller cylindrical projection
100°E   120°E
20°S
Tropic of Capricorn
160°E   180°   160°W

go.hrw.com
Interactive Map
Keyword: SHL WW2

Controlled by Japan (1942)
Allied advance
Major battle

GEOGRAPHY SKILLS **INTERPRETING MAPS**

1. **Movement** Using the map, describe the Allied strategy in the Pacific region.
2. **Location** Why do you think the Allies attacked so many small islands rather than Japan itself?

WORLD WAR II **849**

Direct Teach

Reading Focus

4 What was the turning point in the Pacific? *the Battle of Midway*

A Turning Point in the Pacific

Recall What part of the U.S. Pacific fleet had not been damaged in the attack on Pearl Harbor? *aircraft carriers*

Summarize What advantage did the U.S. military have that helped overcome the Japanese forces in the Battle of Midway? *Americans had broken the secret Japanese code used to transmit messages and knew the date and location of the planned attack.*

Evaluate Why do you think that there was only a small force of Americans in the Philippines when the Japanese attacked in December 1941? *possible answer—The U.S. had just entered the war, and hadn't had a chance to station more troops there.*

Map Transparency: War in the Pacific, 1942–1944

Interactive Map: War in the Pacific

Answers

Interpreting Maps 1. *The Allies moved from one island to another, making their way to the Philippines.*
2. *possible answer—The Allies skipped Japanese strongholds, capturing weaker targets to use as bases to move closer to Japan.*

Differentiating Instruction

Above Level

English-Language Learners

1. Have students look at the map on this page. Ask them what is significant about the Allied advance in the Pacific. *There are two lines of Allied advance.* Draw the graphic organizer for students to see, leaving space for several boxes and arrows on each side. Omit the sample italicized answers.

2. Have students copy the graphic onto their own papers and tell them to add boxes as needed to show the principle Allied lines of advance in the Pacific and the dates

and locations of individual battles. Have students work in pairs to fill in the graphic organizer showing how the two lines of advance come together. Add boxes to the class graphic organizer as volunteers call out the correct answers. **LS Interpersonal, Visual-Spatial**

Alternative Assessment Handbook, Rubric 13: Graphic Organizers

Midway, June 1942 → Tarawa, Nov. 1943

Coral Sea, May 1942 → Bougainville, Oct. 1943–March 1944

Tarawa → Philippines ← Bougainville

Reading Focus

A Turning Point in the Pacific

Describe Describe the Allied island-hopping strategy. *The Allies skipped over Japanese strongholds and captured weaker targets, which were then used as bases for the next attacks, moving ever closer to Japan. This cut Japanese strongholds off from outside supplies, eventually weakening them.*

Evaluate What effect did Japanese kamikaze attacks have? *They didn't change the outcome of the Battle of Leyte Gulf, although they did sink dozens of Allied ships during the closing years of the war.*

📑 **CRF:** History and Geography: Japanese Internment Camps

● Review & Assess ●

Close

Guide the class in a discussion of this question: What difference do you think U.S entry into World War II made?

Review

 Online Quiz, Section 2

Assess

SE Section 2 Assessment

📑 **Progress Assessment:** Section 2 Quiz

📑 **Alternative Assessment Handbook**

Reteach/Intervene

📑 **Interactive Reader and Study Guide,** Section 2

💿 **Interactive Skills Tutor CD-ROM**

Answers

Reading Check *It changed the balance of power in the Pacific, eliminating the once great Japanese advantage on the seas, and allowing the Allies to go on the offensive.*

850

Island Hopping The Battle of Midway had changed the balance of power in the Pacific. The once great Japanese advantage on the seas no longer existed, and the Allies could finally go on the offensive.

In the Pacific, the Allies pursued a strategy that became known as island hopping. This involved skipping over Japanese strongholds and capturing weaker targets. These captured islands were then used as bases for the next attacks, which moved ever closer to Japan. The bypassed Japanese strongholds, meanwhile, were cut off from outside supplies and would eventually weaken.

This was not always an easy task. For example, the Allied invasion of the island of Guadalcanal, near Australia, led to a series of brutal battles in late 1942 and early 1943. For six months, American forces fought Japanese troops on the swamp- and jungle-covered island in the **Battle of Guadalcanal**. Each side won small victories until the Japanese troops finally fled the island in February 1943.

Many other bloody battles followed. During the fighting, the Japanese demonstrated a willingness to fight to the death that amazed and terrified the Allied soldiers. Still, the Allies made steady progress in the South Pacific.

From 1942 through 1944, the Allies captured locations in the Solomon, Gilbert, Marshall, Caroline, and Mariana islands. By the middle of 1944, Allied forces had fought to within striking distance of the Philippines. General MacArthur, who had surrendered the Philippines in 1942, led the Allied troops.

The first major battle in the Philippines was the Battle of Leyte (LAY-tee) Gulf, which took place in October 1944. It was the largest naval battle ever fought. Leyte Gulf saw the first major use of a new Japanese weapon—the kamikaze attack. The **kamikazes** were Japanese pilots who loaded their planes with explosives and deliberately crashed into Allied ships, sacrificing their own lives in the process. Kamikaze attacks did not change the outcome of Leyte Gulf, but they did sink dozens of Allied ships during the closing years of the war.

The Battle of Leyte Gulf ended in an Allied victory. It would take months more of fighting for the Allies to take control of the Philippines, but Japan's once-mighty naval power was virtually destroyed.

READING CHECK **Find the Main Idea** How was the Battle of Midway a turning point in the war in the Pacific?

SECTION 2 ASSESSMENT

go.hrw.com
Online Quiz
Keyword: SHL WW2 HP

Reviewing Ideas, Terms, and People

1. a. Recall What was the key German weapon in the battle for the Atlantic?

b. Identify Cause and Effect What helped lead to the increasing Allied success in the battle for control of the Atlantic?

2. a. Identify What was the significance of the **Battle of El Alamein**?

b. Sequence What were the main events leading up to the Allied invasion of Italy?

3. a. Identify What was the significance of the **Battle of Stalingrad**?

b. Evaluate How did the stubbornness of both Hitler and Stalin affect the outcome of the Battle of Stalingrad?

4. a. Identify What was the first major battle in World War II that stopped the Japanese advance?

b. Elaborate Why was the outcome of the **Battle of Midway** so important to the Allies?

Critical Thinking

5. Identify Cause and Effect Use your notes for this section and a chart like the one below to identify the main turning points of the war in 1942–1943.

FOCUS ON WRITING

6. Description Write a one-paragraph letter home from the viewpoint of a civilian in Stalingrad during the Battle of Stalingrad. In your letter, describe the battle and its outcome.

850 CHAPTER 28

Section 2 Assessment Answers

1 a. U-boats

b. better equipped Allied convoys and the breaking of a key German code system

2. a. It was a smashing victory for the British, and severely weakened Axis power in North Africa.

b. the defeat of Axis forces in North Africa; the move of Allied soldiers from Africa to Sicily; weakened resistance among the Italians; Mussolini's fall from power

3. a. It was one of the turning points of the war, as Soviet forces broke through Axis defenses

and forced them to retreat to the west.

b. Stalin held the city at all costs; Hitler refused to allow his troops to retreat; over a million Soviet soldiers died; Hitler suffered a crushing defeat.

4. a. Battle of Coral Sea

b. changed balance of power in Pacific

5. Answers should include three of the following: Battle of El Alamein; Battle of Stalingrad; Battle of Coral Sea; Battle of Midway

6. Student letters will vary but should show an understanding of the Battle of Stalingrad.

World Literature

Wislawa Szymborska (1923–)

NEW YORK STANDARDS

P1 1.3 Students analyze historic events from around the world by examining accounts written from different perspectives.

About the Reading Poet Wislawa Szymborska was born in western Poland in 1923. She studied Polish literature and sociology in college and published her first poem in 1945. Many of her poems are less than a page in length, but they are powerful reflections on subjects such as war, love, and human suffering. Szymborska was awarded the Nobel Prize for Literature in 1996.

AS YOU READ Think about what this poem might have to do with World War II.

Excerpt from

Hatred

by Wislawa Szymborska

Nazi soldiers round up Polish Jews in Warsaw in 1942.

See how efficient it still is,
how it keeps itself in shape—
our century's hatred.
How easily it vaults the tallest obstacles.
How rapidly it pounces, tracks us down.

It's not like other feelings.
At once both older and younger.
It gives birth itself to the reasons
that give it life.
When it sleeps, it's never eternal rest.
And sleeplessness won't sap its strength; it feeds it.

One religion or another—
whatever gets it ready, in position.
One fatherland or another—
whatever helps it get a running start.
Justice also works well at the outset
until hate gets its own momentum going.
Hatred. Hatred.
Its face twisted in a grimace
of erotic ecstasy . . .

Hatred is a master of contrast—
between explosions and dead quiet,
red blood and white snow.
Above all, it never tires
of its leitmotif—the impeccable executioner
towering over its soiled victim.

It's always ready for new challenges.
If it has to wait awhile, it will.
They say it's blind. Blind?
It has a sniper's keen sight
and gazes unflinchingly at the future
as only it can.

Skills FOCUS **READING LIKE A HISTORIAN**

go.hrw.com
World Literature
Keyword: SHL WRLIT

1. **Analyze** What words does Szymborska use to suggest that hatred is a living thing?

2. **Interpret Literature as a Source** How do you think Szymborska's Polish background may have affected this poem?

See **Skills Handbook**, p. H28

WORLD WAR II **851**

"Hatred"

Word Help

vault to jump or leap over

outset begining

momentum the force a moving object has as a result of its motion

grimace twisted or distorted facial expression

impeccable flawless; incapable of wrongdoing

Meet the Writer

Wislawa Szymborska (1923-) Wislawa Szymborska did not have to look far for the subject of her poem "Hatred." The twentieth century was a very difficult one for her native country. Poland was one of the new nations on the map of Europe in 1918, following World War I. Just 21 years later it was overrun by Germany and the Soviet Union and became a Soviet satellite after World War II.

Szymborska's first collection of poems was published in 1952, when Poland was under Communist control. In that book and her next, she tried to conform to Socialist Realism, the Communist government's officially approved literary style. She now disowns these, saying that Socialist Realism did not represent her poetic intentions.

When Szymborska won the Nobel Prize in 1996 she had published 16 volumes of poetry. In Poland, many people memorize and recite her poems. Instead of seeking publicity, however, she does her best to stay out of the spotlight.

Differentiating Instruction

Learners Having Difficulty
Below Level

Tell students that poetry often presents very powerful images. In her poem "Hatred," Witislawa Szymborska has used words to paint a vivid image of that emotion. Have students work in pairs to create pictures that illustrate Szymborska's images. Display students' pictures for the class to see. Guide the class in a discussion of the pictures. **LS** **Interpersonal, Visual-Spatial**

Alternative Assessment Handbook, Rubric 3: Artwork

Advanced Learners/ Gifted and Talented
Above Level

Have students write an essay about an event of the past century that could have been inspired by hatred. Students' essays should answer the following questions: What violent act(s) did it inspire? What, if anything, could be done to change that hatred to acceptance? Ask volunteers to read their essays to the rest of the class. **LS** **Verbal-Linguistic**

Alternative Assessment Handbook, Rubrics 35: Solving Problems; and 41: Writing to Express

Answers

Reading Like a Historian 1. *vaults, pounces, sleeps;* **2.** *possible answer— Szymborska's poem may describe the "hatred" with which German forces devastated Poland in the blitzkrieg.*

The Battle of Stalingrad

Activity **Victory and Defeat** Have students write two short newspaper articles and headlines—one announcing the victory at Stalingrad for an American newspaper, the other announcing the defeat for a German newspaper.

Info to Know

What's in a Name? Some historians have argued that Hitler was determined to take Stalingrad because of his deep-seated hatred for Russian leader, Joseph Stalin. It has also been argued that the Russians put up an incredible defense because the city was named for their Russian leader. In 1961, Stalingrad was renamed Volgograd, "the town on the Volga."

Primary Source

"Surrender is forbidden. 6 Army will hold their positions to the last man and last round and by their heroic endurance will make an unforgettable contribution towards the establishment of a defensive front and the salvation of the Western world."

—Supreme Commander (Hitler) to 6 Army, January 24, 1943

Info to Know

General Friedrich von Paulus Friedrich von Paulus served as commander of the German Sixth Army and was ordered by Hitler to take Stalingrad. When it became clear that the German Army might become trapped, he requested that the army be allowed to withdraw his troops from Stalingrad. Hitler refused. The surrender of the German Army in February 1943 infuriated Hitler, who ordered a day of national mourning for the men who had been killed and to recognize the shame of the defeat. Von Paulus was imprisoned by the Russians and then later testified at the Nuremberg Trials.

HISTORY & Geography

The Battle of Stalingrad

Battles and wars are fought to control territory. For Germany, capturing the city of Stalingrad was a key goal—it would help the Germans take the rich oil fields and industrial areas of the southern Soviet Union.

But geography helped the Soviets win the Battle of Stalingrad. First, Stalingrad was located far from Germany, which made it hard for the Germans to supply and reinforce their troops. Second, the Soviets used the city's environment to their advantage, fighting a deadly urban war. Finally, the Soviet winter killed German soldiers and ruined equipment. In the end, Germany suffered a major defeat.

The Factory District

Some of the most intense fighting took place in the ruins of the factories in northern Stalingrad. Soviet defenders hid in the wreckage to ambush German attackers.

THE INVASION OF THE SOVIET UNION, 1941–1943

FINLAND

ESTONIA Leningrad 1941

LATVIA

North Sea

Baltic Sea

LITHUANIA

EAST PRUSSIA

SOVIET UNION

Warsaw

POLAND

Stalingrad 1942–1943

1942

1942

CZECHOSLOVAKIA

1942

1942

HUNGARY

ROMANIA

YUGOSLAVIA

Black Sea

BULGARIA

30°E

ALBANIA

40°N

GREECE

TURKEY

Allied-controlled territory (1942)

Axis-controlled territory (1942)

Axis advance

Neutral (1942)

Major battle

0 200 400 Miles
0 200 400 Kilometers

▲ German tanks and equipment lay in ruins after a Soviet attack outside Stalingrad.

Differentiating Instruction

Below Level

Learners Having Difficulty

Materials: colored markers, drawing paper, map of Europe showing the Soviet Union

1. Organize the class into mixed-ability pairs. Have each pair create its own map of the Soviet Union. Maps should show the city of Stalingrad.

2. Have each pair draw the German advance across the Soviet Union on their maps. Maps should also include a key showing the dates of the German siege of Stalingrad.

3. Have students include the length of the siege on their map keys.

4. Have volunteers share their maps with the class. Have students keep the maps as a study tool. **LS** **Interpersonal, Logical-Mathematical**

📝 **Alternative Assessment Handbook**, Rubric 20: Map Creation

NEW YORK STANDARDS

PI 2.5 Students investigate key events and developments and major turning points in world history to identify the factors that brought about change and the long-term effects of these changes.

The Volga River

The wide river helped protect the Soviets from a German attack from the rear, but it also meant that getting supplies and reinforcements was difficult.

▲ Soviet troops engaged in house-to-house fighting during the battle.

GEOGRAPHY
SKILLS | **INTERPRETING MAPS**

1. **Location** How did Stalingrad's location on the Volga River both help and hurt the Soviet defenders?

2. **Human-Environment Interaction** How was the Battle of Stalingrad affected by geography?

WORLD WAR II **853**

History and Geography

Info to Know

Combat in Stalingrad Over one million soldiers were killed in the fighting in Stalingrad. It has been reported that the average life-expectancy of Soviet soldiers during the fighting was about one day, 24 hours. German troops, who had experienced easier victories during the Blitzkrieg, were suddenly involved in hand-to-hand, door-to-door combat. They suffered from lack of fuel, ammunition, and clothing. Many died from exposure to the cold winter weather, disease, and hunger.

Primary Source

"The Red Army and Navy and the whole of the Soviet people must fight for every inch of Soviet soil, fight to the last drop of blood for our towns and villages…onward to victory!"

—Joseph Stalin, July 1941

Primary Source

"The disaster of Stalingrad profoundly shocked the German people and armed forces alike…Never before in Germany's history had so large a body of troops come to so dreadful an end."

—General Siegfried von Westphal, 1943

Skills Focus: Identifying Main Idea and Details

At Level

Reading Skill
Military Decisions

1. Review the information in the feature and in the text about the Battle of Stalingrad. Remind students that the German army was ordered to stay in the city and continue the battle despite the difficult conditions.

2. Have students write a petition to Hitler and military leaders in Berlin asking permission to withdraw the German troops from the city.

Students should focus on the bitter cold, lack of supplies, and hopeless fighting conditions faced by the army.

3. Have volunteers share their letters with the class. **LS** **Verbal-Linguistic**

📝 **Alternative Assessment Handbook**, Rubric 43: Writing to Persuade

Answers

Interpreting Maps 1. *The Volga was used to transport goods and soldiers into Stalingrad, for either Russia or Germany.* **2.** *Stalingrad was far from Germany, which made it difficult for Germans to supply and reinforce their troops; Soviets used the urban environment to their advantage; harsh Soviet winter killed many ill-equipped German troops.*

853

Preteach

Preteach

Getting Started

Use the **Interactive Reader and Study Guide** to give students a quick preview of the section.

📝 **Interactive Reader and Study Guide**, Section 3

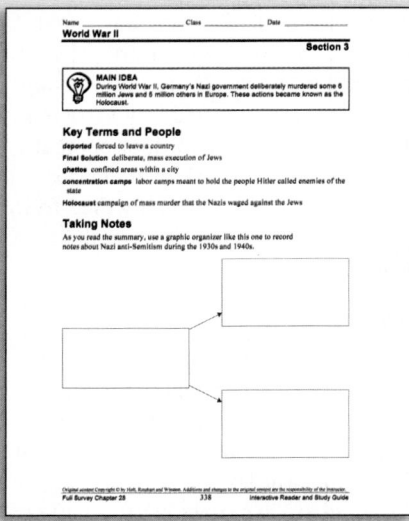

🗒 **CRF:** Vocabulary Builder: Section 3

Taking Notes

Nazi Anti-Semitism—Nazi government passes a variety of restrictive laws targeting German Jews; thousands of Jews are deported or flee Germany; Nazi leaders implement the "Final Solution;" Jews are forced into ghettos and sent to concentration camps; six million Jews are killed.

Online Resources

go.hrw.com

KEYWORD: SHL WW2
ACTIVITY: Report on Anne Frank

SECTION 3 The Holocaust

BEFORE YOU READ

MAIN IDEA

During World War II, Germany's Nazi government deliberately murdered some 6 million Jews and 5 million others in Europe. These actions became known as the Holocaust.

READING FOCUS

1. What was the history of Nazi anti-Semitism during the 1930s?
2. What was the Nazi government's "Final Solution"?
3. How did the world react to Hitler's efforts to destroy European Jews?

KEY TERMS AND PEOPLE

deported
Final Solution
ghetto
concentration camps
Holocaust

TAKING NOTES Take notes about Nazi anti-Semitism during the 1930s and 1940s.

THE INSIDE STORY

Can music keep you alive? As a young musician played Chopin's Nocturne in C-sharp Minor for a radio broadcast, a German attack knocked the radio station off the air. That was the last broadcast of Polish Radio until the end of World War II. The year was 1939, and the young musician was Wladyslaw Szpilman (SPEEL-man), a Jewish pianist.

After German forces stormed through Poland, Szpilman—with his family and thousands of other Jews—was forced into a small, confined area of the city of Warsaw. When other Warsaw Jews were shipped off to Nazi labor camps, Szpilman managed to escape. He survived by hiding in the ruins of Warsaw, living in the rubble of bombed out buildings. Somehow, he managed to find enough food to stay alive. He kept his sanity by playing musical pieces in his head, mentally performing everything he had ever played or composed.

Near the end of the war, Szpilman was discovered by a German soldier, Wilm Hosenfeld. When Hosenfeld found out that Szpilman was a pianist, he demanded that Szpilman prove this by playing an abandoned piano. Szpilman had not touched a piano in over two years, but his fingers slowly remembered what to do. Soon, the sounds of Chopin echoed through the ruined building. Hosenfeld had grown to hate his government's murderous policies toward Jews and decided to protect the pianist. In the closing days of the war, Hosenfeld helped Szpilman survive by bringing him food and keeping his hiding place a secret.

When Polish radio returned to the air after the end of the war in 1945, its first broadcast was performed by Wladyslaw Szpilman—playing the same Chopin piece that had been interrupted by Nazi bombs six years earlier. ◼

Nazi Anti-Semitism

At the time of Hitler's rise to power in Germany, there were about 9 million Jews in Europe. Most lived outside Germany, but Hitler still blamed Jews for many of Germany's problems. He also promoted a belief in the racial superiority of the German people. There was no factual basis for Hitler's anti-Semitism or for his claims about the German "master race." However, for many Germans who had suffered through World War I, the humiliation of the Treaty of Versailles, and the economic crises of the 1920s and 1930s, there was something appealing in Hitler's twisted vision. Jews were a convenient scapegoat—a group to blame for Germany's problems.

A Musician's Survival

◀ Wladyslaw Szpilman at his piano

Teach the Main Idea

At Level

The Holocaust

1. **Teach** Ask students the Reading Focus questions to teach this section.

2. **Apply** Organize students into small groups. Have groups discuss the Holocaust and then list factors that allowed it to happen. *The Holocaust was Hitler's genocidal campaign against the Jews. Factors: anti-Semitism; Hitler's ideas of a "master race;" countries' limited immigration; many of the countries Hitler's armies conquered had large Jewish populations*

3. **Review** Ask volunteers from each group to read their definitions and lists to the class. Guide the class in a discussion of the Holocaust.

4. **Practice/Homework** Have each student write a one-page essay about whether the Holocaust, or something similar to it, could happen today. 🅛🅢 **Interpersonal, Verbal-Linguistic**

🗒 **Alternative Assessment Handbook**, Rubrics 11: Discussions; and 14: Group Activity

Hitler's anti-Semitism was not new. As you read in the previous chapter, there was a long history of anti-Semitism in Europe. But in Nazi Germany this hostility based on religion changed into hatred based on race. During the 1930s, Hitler's Nazi government passed the Nuremberg Laws, creating a separate legal status for German Jews. Thousands of Jews were deported from Germany. To be **deported** is to be forced to leave a country. Many thousands of others left Germany on their own.

Emigration, however, was not an option for all German Jews. Nazi laws had left many without money or property, and countries were often unwilling to take in poor immigrants. The United States and many European nations were still recovering from the Great Depression and would not accept newcomers who would compete for scarce jobs. Furthermore, some countries, including the United States, had strict limits on the number of Germans who could enter the country.

As a result, at the start of World War II, about 250,000 Jews still lived in Germany and Austria. With the outbreak of war, emigration became even more difficult, and Germany finally outlawed it in late 1941. The remaining Jews under German rule were trapped.

READING CHECK **Summarize** Describe Nazi anti-Semitism in the 1930s.

The "Final Solution"

As Hitler's powerful armies conquered large areas of Europe during the early years of World War II, millions of Jews came under Nazi control. As a result, Nazi leaders eventually adopted a plan they called the **Final Solution**: the deliberate mass execution of Jews.

The Killing Begins The Nazis used several brutal methods to deal with the Jewish civilians who came under German control. At first, some Jews were forced into a **ghetto**, or a confined area within a city. Often, walls or barbed wire fences prevented the Jews from leaving, and armed guards shot those trying to escape. The most notorious ghetto was in the Polish city of Warsaw, which housed 400,000 people. Most of these people eventually died of starvation or were murdered by the Nazis.

Other Jews were sent to labor camps called **concentration camps**, which were meant to hold the people Hitler called enemies of the state. At the camps, Jews and other prisoners were forced to work as slave laborers. Some were subjected to cruel medical experiments. All endured severe hunger, which killed many.

Hitler's forces also carried out large-scale executions of Jews and other civilians in villages across Poland. German soldiers gunned down men, women, and children without mercy.

During Germany's invasion of the Soviet Union in 1941, the Nazis established mobile killing units to destroy the Jews who lived in Soviet territory. These mobile killing units carried out executions on a massive scale, often aided by local people and police, known as collaborators. For example, in one two-day period in September 1941, nearly 35,000 Jews were murdered at a place called Babi Yar, near the Soviet city of Kiev.

Yet as bloody as this work was, Nazi leaders were not satisfied. The killing was simply leaving behind too much evidence of Nazi crimes. Therefore, the Germans established a number of special concentration camps in Poland for the main purpose of killing large numbers of Jews and destroying their bodies. These death camps, such as Auschwitz, had specially designed gas chambers in which thousands of people were killed every day. The camps also had furnaces for the disposal of bodies.

READING SKILLS **Understanding Causes and Effects** Why did the Nazis establish death camps?

3 How did the world react to Hitler's efforts to destroy European Jews? *with disbelief; when reports were confirmed, U.S. and Great Britian officials met to discuss possible responses*

The World Reacts

Recall What evidence of German atrocities did the Allies find at Bergen-Belsen? *35,000 bodies and 60,000 survivors, many too starved or ill to be saved*

Make Inferences Why do you think it took so long to respond to the reports of Germany's widespread killing of Jews in Europe? *possible answer—The reports seemed too horrific to believe, so there was little incentive to come up with a response.*

📑 CRF: Biography: Raoul Wallenburg

Info to Know

Efficient Murder Soon after invading the Soviet Union, the Nazis began to experiment on Russian Jews and other Soviet prisoners to determine the most efficient way to kill large numbers of people. The first method tried—machine-gunning massed groups of prisoners—was rejected as labor-intensive, inefficient, and hard to keep secret. The first experiment with gas—confining prisoners in trucks with altered exhaust systems until they were overcome by carbon monoxide fumes—was also rejected as too slow. In September 1941, some 600 Soviet POWs were placed in a sealed area with crystals of Zyklon B, a commercial pesticide. The victims quickly died of asphyxiation. The Germans later used this method to kill millions of Jews.

Answers

Forensics in History *possible answer—to prove that he was dead so that attempts to find him and bring him to justice could end*

Reading Check *Nazi plan for the mass execution of Jews—by gathering Jews into ghettos and concentration camps and killing them*

FORENSICS in History

Was It the Angel of Death?

The body of Wolfgang Gerhard, dug up in Embu, Brazil, in 1985 was little more than rotting bones. But Nazi hunters believed Gerhard was actually the Nazi war criminal Josef Mengele—known as the Angel of Death for his cruel medical experiments on concentration camp prisoners. Could modern science find out once and for all?

How could he be identified? All the cells in the human body contain DNA. DNA directs the formation, growth, and reproduction of cells. Sections of DNA called genes can be used to tell one human being apart from another through a process called genetic fingerprinting. Genes can also be used to establish whether people are related.

In 1985, documents were discovered that connected Mengele to Gerhard, and a team of forensics scientists set out to determine whether the bones in Brazil were those of the Angel of Death.

The scientists used genetic fingerprinting to find the answer. They took DNA samples from the remains of Gerhard's body and compared them to DNA from Mengele's son, who still lived in Germany. The results? The odds were 1,800 to 1 that the remains were from anyone other than Mengele. Later, dental records and other DNA tests found the same results. In other words, the man who had been calling himself Wolfgang Gerhard was indeed Josef Mengele, the Angel of Death.

▲ Josef Mengele in 1945

Draw Conclusions Why do you think it was important to determine the identity of Josef Mengele?

The Victims Jews were not the only victims of Nazi concentration and death camps. The Nazis also imprisoned other groups they viewed as inferior, including Poles, Slavs, homosexuals, people with disabilities, and the Romany, an ethnic group also known as Gypsies. By the end of the war, some 5 million people from these groups had died in Nazi camps.

It was Jews, however, who suffered the most under the Nazis. During the war, 6 million Jews—two of every three in Europe—died at Nazi hands. Entire families were killed. Today we refer to this mass murder of Jews as the **Holocaust**.

FOCUS ON NEW YORK

The only formal refugee camp established by the U.S. government during the war was located at Fort Ontario in Oswego, New York. The camp held 982 refugees, mostly Jewish Holocaust survivors.

> **READING CHECK** **Find the Main Idea** What was the Final Solution, and how did the Nazis attempt to carry out this plan?

The World Reacts

Other countries were aware of the Nazi government's anti-Semitism in the 1930s. After the outbreak of war, however, the full extent of Hitler's brutality was shielded from the outside world.

In 1942 people in the United States and Europe began to hear disturbing reports of widespread killing of Jews in Europe. At first, these reports seemed too horrific to believe. But as the reports were investigated and confirmed, officials in the United States and Great Britain met to discuss possible responses. No concrete action was taken, however.

Finally, in January 1944, after millions of Jews had already died, the United States established the War Refugee Board to help rescue European Jews. The board helped save some 200,000 Jews. But Allied leaders were unwilling to take actions such as bombing the railroad lines that led to the death camps. This government inaction was in part because Allied leaders did not want to do anything that might interfere with the war effort. Apathy and anti-Semitism also contributed to this inaction.

As Allied forces in Europe started to push back the Germans, they came upon Nazi camps. In the summer of 1944, Soviet troops made one of the first discoveries, an abandoned death camp in Poland. The Germans had tried to cover up evidence of their crimes before leaving—including removing or killing the prisoners.

Collaborative Learning

At Level

Saving the Jews

1. Organize students into groups of four or five. Tell them that it is 1942 and they have just heard about Hitler's widespread killing of Jews in Europe.

2. Have each group develop a campaign to convince the U.S. government to take action to save European Jews. Campaigns may include letters to editors or elected officials, speeches, posters, or other materials they think would help convince people to stop Hitler's widespread killing of Jews.

3. Have each group present its campaign to the rest of the class.

4. Lead the class in a discussion of student campaign materials. 🖪 **Interpersonal**

📑 **Alternative Assessment Handbook**, Rubric 14: Group Activity

Eventually, though, the Germans were unable to hide their actions. When the Soviets liberated the Auschwitz death camp in January of 1945, they found about 7,000 starving survivors. They also found hundreds of thousand of pieces of clothing—a strong indication that many more people had been held there.

In April 1945, American forces reached the Buchenwald camp. There they found thousands of corpses as well as many inmates who were nearly dead. Around the same time, the British reached the Bergen-Belsen camp, where tens of thousands had been murdered.

The soldiers who discovered the death camps were shocked at what they found. American soldier Reid Draffen visited the Dachau camp after it had been liberated by the Allies, and remembered the horrible scene:

HISTORY'S VOICES

"I thought I had seen everything. I was a hardened soldier. I had been in combat since October 1944, and I had seen death and destruction that was unparalleled in modern times. But this—there are no words to describe this."

—Captain Reid Draffen, in *War Stories: Remembering World War II*

The scenes of horror at the death camps gave the world a clear picture of what a world controlled by Adolf Hitler might have been like. But Nazi hopes of world domination were about to come to an end.

READING CHECK Summarize How did the world react to Nazi killing of Jews and other prisoners?

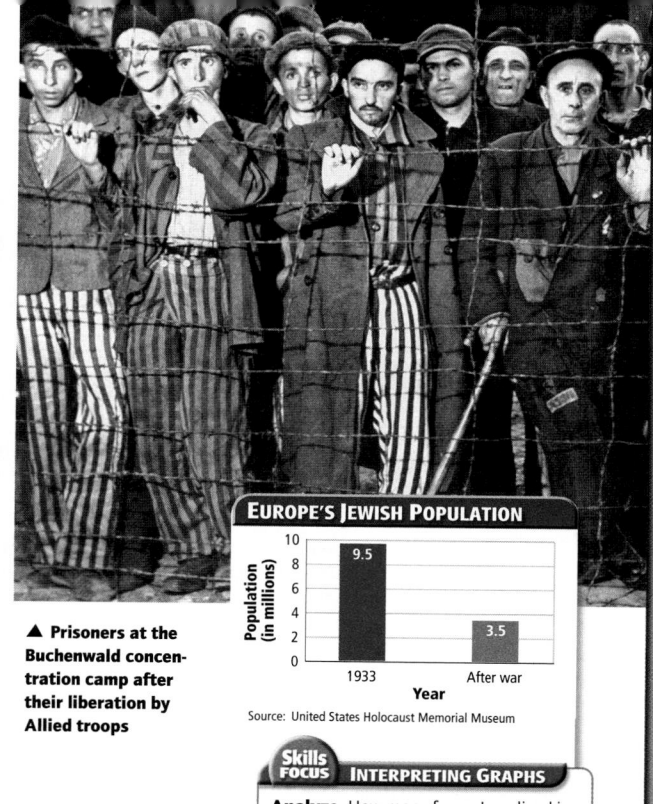

▲ **Prisoners at the Buchenwald concentration camp after their liberation by Allied troops**

EUROPE'S JEWISH POPULATION

Population (in millions) — 1933: 9.5, After war: 3.5

Source: United States Holocaust Memorial Museum

INTERPRETING GRAPHS

Analyze How many fewer Jews lived in Europe in 1950 than had lived there in 1933, before World War II began?

---

go.hrw.com
Online Quiz
Keyword: SHL WW2 HP

SECTION 3 ASSESSMENT

Reviewing Ideas, Terms, and People

1. a. Describe What was the official Nazi policy toward Jews prior to World War II?

b. Identify Cause and Effect What were the effects of Nazi anti-Jewish policies on Germany's Jewish population?

2. a. Identify What was the Nazi government's **Final Solution**?

b. Contrast Contrast Nazi policies toward Jews before and after the start of the war.

c. Elaborate Why did the Germans build death camps?

3. a. Identify What was the significance of the War Refugee Board?

b. Analyze Why did the Allies fail to take more actions to stop the Nazi killing of Jews?

c. Predict What might have happened if the Allies had made liberating the Jews a priority early in the war?

Critical Thinking

4. Sequence Copy the chart below and use your notes from the section to describe the main events of the Holocaust.

[ ] → [ ] → [ ]

FOCUS ON WRITING

5. Persuasion Could the Allies have done more to lessen the loss of life during the Holocaust? If so, what actions should the Allies have taken? Using information from the section, write a newspaper editorial that presents your views.

WORLD WAR II **857**

Section 3 Assessment Answers

1. a. Germany passed a variety of restrictive laws creating a separate legal status for Jews, denying them citizenship and the right to hold government jobs, and severely limiting their right to work and own property. Thousands of Jews were deported.
b. Many fled Germany, but Nazi laws left many German Jews without money or property. Also, some countries were unwilling to take in poor immigrants.

2. a. deliberate, mass execution of Jewish prisoners

b. Before the war, the Nazis just stripped the Jews of their rights and property. After the start of the war, they decided to kill them all.
c. to efficiently kill large numbers of Jews and dispose of their bodies

3. a. It helped save some 200,000 Jews.
b. They were focused on defeating the Axis Powers.
c. possible answer—It probably would have been difficult, since the concentration camps were behind enemy lines. It could have shifted the focus of the war and allowed Hitler to concentrate on defending the German homeland, prolonging the war.

4. German Jews stripped of rights and property; Jews forced into ghettos, sent to concentration camps; Einsatzgruppen carry out mass executions; Germans set up death camps; Allies free concentration camps

5. Editorials will vary but should present convincing ideas about lessening the loss of life during the Holocaust.

WORLD WAR II **857**

BEFORE YOU READ

MAIN IDEA
In 1945 the Allies finally triumphed over the Axis Powers in Europe and the Pacific, but the war left many nations in ruins.

READING FOCUS
1. How did the war end in Europe?
2. How did the war end in the Pacific?
3. What were the Allied plans for the postwar world?

KEY TERMS AND PEOPLE
D-Day
V-E Day
Battle of Iwo Jima
Battle of Okinawa
Harry S Truman
Hirohito
V-J Day
Yalta Conference
United Nations
Potsdam Conference

 NEW YORK

PI 1.4 Students understand the broad patterns, relationships, and interactions of cultures and civilizations.

PI 2.5 Students investigate key events and developments and major turning points in world history.

THE INSIDE STORY

How do you take back an entire continent? Packed tightly onto thousands of landing craft, more than 150,000 Allied troops set out for the beaches of German-held France. It was D-Day—June 6, 1944. When the ships neared shore, each landing craft's gate went down, and the soldiers had to plow through waist-deep water directly into German gunfire. Some were killed before they reached land. Those who made it to shore had to race past mines, ruined equipment, and their dead and wounded friends to find temporary shelter from the deadly fire.

Still, the invaders pushed on. As thousands of soldiers fell, thousands more fought their way up the bluffs that overlooked the beaches. One by one, they captured the German positions. By the end of the day, the Allies had taken all five beaches they had attacked. With over 10,000 Allied casualties, the price was high.

The first battle in the invasion of Europe was successful. The Allies had taken more than a year to plan the massive invasion, but it was worth the time it took. Germany now had to contend with a major Allied force in Western Europe and with the Soviets in the east. It was the beginning of the end for Germany. ■

STORMING THE BEACHES

◀ Allied troops land at Normandy on D-Day.

Teach the Main Idea

At Level

The End of the War

1. **Teach** Ask students the Reading Focus questions to teach this section.

2. **Apply** Have students create an outline of the section using the heads as main points. Have them identify at least two main ideas under each of the subheadings.

3. **Review** Review students' outlines as a class. Have students identify the points in their outlines that they feel are most important or most interesting. Guide students in a discussion of the Tehran, Yalta,

and Potsdam conferences, at which the Allies made plans for the future.

4. **Practice/Homework** Tell students that they are newspaper reporters covering the Yalta Conference. Have each student write a news story explaining what took place and the results of the conference. **LS Logical-Mathematical, Verbal-Linguistic**

Alternative Assessment Handbook, Rubrics 36: Time Lines; and 37: Writing Assignments

---

Preteach

Getting Started

Use the **Interactive Reader and Study Guide** to give students a quick preview of the section.

Interactive Reader and Study Guide, Section 4

Name _____ Class _____ Date _____
World War II
Section 4

MAIN IDEA
In 1945 the Allies finally triumphed over the Axis Powers in Europe and the Pacific, but the war left many nations in ruins.

Key Terms and People
D-Day June 6, 1944, the day Allied forces invaded France on the beaches of Normandy
V-E Day Victory in Europe Day, May 8, 1945, the day Allied victory was declared
Battle of Iwo Jima brutal battle in which the Allies captured a strategic island close to Japan
Battle of Okinawa Pacific battle that claimed 12,000 American lives for an Allied victory
Harry S Truman U.S. President who made the decision to use the atomic bomb
Hirohito Japanese emperor who surrendered to Allies
V-J Day August 15, 1945, the day Japan surrendered to the Allies, ending World War II
Yalta Conference meeting held by the Allied nations to plan postwar Europe
Potsdam Conference meeting of Allied leaders in which tension between the Soviet Union and the other Allies surfaced
United Nations world organization meant to encourage international cooperation and the prevention of war

Taking Notes
As you read the summary, take notes about the end of the war, using a graphic organizer like the one below.

Europe	Pacific

Full Survey Chapter 28   341   Interactive Reader and Study Guide

---

Academic Vocabulary

Review with students the high-use academic term in this section.

sufficient enough of what is needed (p. 859)

CRF: Vocabulary Builder: Section 4

Taking Notes

Europe—Allies fight strong German defenses on D-Day, quickly recover most of France; Germany defeated at Battle of the Bulge; Hitler commits suicide; Germany surrenders; Pacific—Battle of Iwo Jima and Battle of Okinawa claim thousands of lives; atomic bombs dropped on Hiroshima and Nagasaki; Japanese emperor Hirohito surrenders

---

go.hrw.com
Online Resources
KEYWORD:SHL WW2
ACTIVITY: D-Day

War Ends in Europe

While American and British military leaders were planning the invasion of France, German soldiers were busy fighting the Soviet armies in the east. After the Soviet triumph at Stalingrad in early 1943, the Soviets eventually pushed the Germans backward. By the end of the year, Axis forces had suffered 2 million casualties. Outnumbered, they were unable to stop the relentless Soviet advance.

Soviet Victories In early 1944 the Soviets finally ended the Siege of Leningrad. A major offensive in the summer achieved great success for the Soviets, leading to another 800,000 German casualties. Other important victories followed, driving Axis forces out of the Soviet Union and back into central Europe. By the end of January 1945 Soviet forces were within 40 miles of the German capital of Berlin.

D-Day As the Soviets forced the Axis armies back toward Germany, the other Allies were finalizing their plans for a massive invasion of Western Europe.

An effective invasion of Europe would be difficult. For one thing, the assault would have to come by sea. It would also have to be made directly against strong German positions.

The Allied preparations were led by American generals George Marshall and Dwight Eisenhower. In addition to assembling and training <u>sufficient</u> troops, the Allies needed to develop specialized equipment for transporting tanks and troops across open water. They also staged a complex plan to mislead Hitler about where the invasion would take place.

On June 6, 1944—**D-Day**—Allied forces invaded France. Over 150,000 troops landed on the beaches of Normandy that first day, forcing through the strong German defenses. Casualties were high, but D-Day was a huge victory for the Allies. With the beaches secured, more Allied forces poured into France. By July nearly 1 million soldiers had come ashore.

After some bloody fighting in the first few weeks following the landing, the Allied forces broke through German defenses in July. The Allies quickly reconquered much of France. By the end of August, the Germans had surrendered Paris. Eisenhower reported that "the enemy is routed [defeated] and running."

The Battle of the Bulge But Hitler was not yet finished. In December 1944 he ordered one last, massive counterattack in Belgium. At first the Germans made solid advances, producing a bulge in the Allied battle lines. Thus, the battle became known as the Battle of the Bulge.

ACADEMIC VOCABULARY
sufficient enough of what is needed

TAKING NOTES
As you read, compare the end of the war in Europe and in the Pacific.

Europe	Pacific

THE END OF THE WAR, 1944–1945

NORWAY · SWEDEN · FINLAND
North Sea
IRELAND · DENMARK · Baltic Sea
UNITED KINGDOM · NETH. · 1945 · Berlin 1945 · SOVIET UNION
BELGIUM · 1945 · GERMANY 1943–1945
Normandy 1944 · Battle of the Bulge 1944–1945
ATLANTIC OCEAN · FRANCE
SWITZ. · SLOVAKIA · HUNGARY
VICHY FRANCE · ITALY · ROMANIA
SPAIN · CROATIA · 1943–1944
MONTENEGRO · SERBIA · BULGARIA

0   200   400 Miles
0   200   400 Kilometers
Azimuthal equal-area projection

- Allied-controlled territory (1944)
- Allied advance
- Axis-controlled territory (1944)
- Neutral (1944)
- ✪ Major battle

GEOGRAPHY SKILLS INTERPRETING MAPS

Movement Describe the Allied advances in 1944 and 1945.

Direct Teach

Reading Focus

1. **How did the war end in Europe?**
Soviets pushed Hitler's troops backward in the east and Allies launched D-Day invasion of France in the west, pushing toward Germany.

War Ends in Europe

Recall When did the Siege of Leningrad end? *early 1944*

Analyze Why was it so difficult to open a second front in the war in Europe? *It had to come by sea, and had to be made against strong German positions.*

Evaluate Why do you think Hitler ordered the massive counterattack that led to the Battle of the Bulge? *possible answer—He wanted to make one last-ditch effort to turn back the Allies.*

Map Transparency: The End of the War, 1944–1945

MISCONCEPTION ALERT

You won't find it in many encyclopedias, but the largest Allied offensive operation of World War II took place in the Soviet Union, not on the shores of Normandy. In the summer of 1944, a Soviet offensive called Operation Bagration inflicted far more damage to the Germans than the D-Day landings. Stalin's campaign wiped out three Axis armies to support the Allied invasion of France, free Soviet territory from the Germans, and break the German war machine.

Skill Focus: Making Inferences

At Level

Reading Skill
What If D-Day Had Failed?

Background: Remind students that Allied casualties were high during the D-Day invasion because the attack came by sea and the Germans had strong coastal defenses.

1. Guide a discussion with students about what might have happened if the Allies' D-Day invasion of France had failed. How might it have affected the outcome of the war?

2. Have students write a scenario about what could have happened if the Germans had been

expecting the attack to come from where it did and had been able to turn back the invasion.

3. Have volunteers read their scenarios to the class.

4. Guide the class in a discussion of students' scenarios. **LS Verbal-Linguistic**

Alternative Assessment Handbook, Rubric 37: Writing Assignments

---

Answers

Interpreting Maps *Allies advanced west from Soviet Union through Eastern Europe toward Germany; moved from United Kingdom to Normandy, France, and then to Germany; advanced north from Italy and southern France*

859

2 How did the war end in the Pacific? *The Allies continued their island-hopping strategy and attacked the major islands of Japan from the air; then the U.S. dropped two atomic bombs on Japanese cities.*

War Ends in the Pacific

Explain Why did the Allies dread the idea of invading the major islands of Japan? *Japanese defenders' willingness to fight to the death led Allied military leaders to believe that an invasion could cost up to one million Allied killed and wounded.*

Elaborate Do you think that the United States was justified in dropping atomic bombs on civilian targets in Japan? Why or why not? *possible answer—No, civilized nations don't kill civilians.*

Info to Know

Iwo Jima The famous photograph on this page shows U.S. servicemen raising the American flag on Iwo Jima after winning one of the bloodiest battles of the war. The tiny island was honeycombed with caves and tunnels, protecting many guns. After attacking the island for more than two months with shells and bombs, some 30,000 U.S. marines stormed ashore in February of 1945. Japanese resistance was so fierce that after three days of combat, the marines had advanced only about 700 yards inland.

Answers

Reading Like a Historian *possible answer—It is a powerful image that portrays U.S. Marines' determination and strength against a persistent enemy.*

Reading Check *The Allies quickly reconquered much of France and started to push into Germany from the west.*

By January 1945, the Allies had crushed the German offensive at the Battle of the Bulge. Germany's defeat marked the end of major German resistance. Within two months, Allied forces had crossed the Rhine River into Germany and were racing toward Berlin. At the same time, Soviet troops were advancing through Germany from the east.

The Germans Surrender The Soviets were the first to reach Berlin, surrounding the city in late April 1945. On May 2 they found the body of Adolf Hitler near his Berlin bunker. He had taken his own life. Berlin surrendered that same day.

With Hitler dead and Berlin in Allied hands, the war in Europe was all but over. Germany surrendered on May 7. The next day was proclaimed **V-E Day**—Victory in Europe Day. After nearly six years of bloody battle, the war in Europe was over.

> **READING CHECK** **Draw Conclusions** What effect did D-Day have on the war in Europe?

War Ends in the Pacific

Although the Allies had achieved victory in Europe, war was still raging in the Pacific. The Allied island-hopping strategy continued to push back the Japanese, but there were several battles yet to come.

Final Battles By mid-1944 American bombers had begun making regular bombing raids on Japanese cities, including the capital, Tokyo. The attacks did severe damage, but the great distance American pilots had to travel from their bases to Japan made the raids risky.

To reduce these risks, the Americans needed bases closer to Japan. In February 1945 Allied troops landed on the Japanese island of Iwo Jima (EE-woh JEE-muh), some 750 miles south of Tokyo. During the month-long **Battle of Iwo Jima**, nearly 7,000 Americans died to capture the tiny island. More than 20,000 Japanese defenders had been on the island when the Americans attacked. All but a thousand of them fought to the death.

Iwo Jima

The Marine Corps War Memorial is located at Arlington National Cemetery in Virginia.

Skills Focus **READING LIKE A HISTORIAN**

The photograph at left was taken on the top of Iwo Jima's Mount Suribachi on February 23, 1945, during the Battle of Iwo Jima. The image was immediately popular in the United States and was used by the U.S. government as part of a campaign to help raise money for the war effort. It later won the Pulitzer Prize for photography.

Analyzing Visuals Why do you think the Marine Corps memorial statue was modeled on the photo of the flag raising at Iwo Jima?

See **Skills Handbook**, p. H26

Differentiating Instruction

Above Level

Research Required

Advanced Learners/Gifted and Talented

1. Have students conduct research on the Battle of the Bulge, making a list of facts about the battle, including the following:
   - When and where it took place
   - How long it lasted
   - Who was involved in it
   - Why it was important
   - Number of casualties

2. Have students find and read at least one eyewitness account of the Battle of the Bulge.

3. Have students write a brief essay explaining which material made the battle more interesting—the "cold facts" or the personal account. Students should reinforce their opinions with examples.

4. Have volunteers read their essays to the class.
   LS **Verbal-Linguistic**

Alternative Assessment Handbook, Rubrics 30: Research; and 37: Writing Assignments

After Iwo Jima, the Americans invaded Okinawa (OH-kee-NAH-wah), an island barely 350 miles from Japan. The **Battle of Okinawa**, which lasted nearly three months, claimed 12,000 American lives. The Japanese lost the battle along with nearly all of the more than 100,000 defenders.

The Atomic Bomb After Okinawa, the next step for the Allies was to take Japan itself. But the experiences of Iwo Jima and Okinawa made the Allies dread the idea of invading the major islands of Japan. The Japanese defenders' willingness to fight to the death led American military leaders to conclude that an invasion of Japan would be too costly. They calculated that an invasion could cost up to 1 million killed or wounded Allied soldiers.

As a result, American leaders considered another option: the atomic bomb. This weapon used the energy released by the splitting of atoms and was far more powerful than ordinary bombs. A program to develop the bomb had begun in 1939, and a bomb had been successfully tested in July 1945.

Harry S Truman, who had become president when Franklin Roosevelt died in May 1945, was forced to make a difficult decision. Should the United States use the atomic bomb? Many of Truman's advisers believed that using the atomic bomb would help bring the war to a quick end and save American lives. Others believed that such a powerful weapon should be used only as a last resort. In the end, Truman decided to drop the bomb on a Japanese city in the hopes that the mighty new weapon would cause Japan to surrender.

On July 26, 1945, the Allies issued a demand for Japan's surrender. When the Japanese did not respond, plans to use the bomb went forward. On August 6, an American plane dropped an atomic bomb on the Japanese city of Hiroshima. The devastation was extreme. More than 70,000 people were killed instantly, and thousands of buildings were destroyed. Yet even this horror was not enough to bring a quick Japanese surrender. On August 9, the Americans dropped a second bomb, this time over the city of Nagasaki. Another 75,000 people died. Tens of thousands of residents of both cities would later die from radiation poisoning, an effect of their exposure to the bombs' radioactive materials.

A mushroom cloud rises over Nagasaki after the explosion of the atomic bomb.

PRIMARY SOURCES

Hiroshima

Father John A. Siemes, a German priest, was in Hiroshima when the atomic bomb was dropped on August 6, 1945. He later described the explosion:

"Suddenly . . . the whole valley is filled by a garish light which resembles the magnesium light used in photography, and I am conscious of a wave of heat. I jump to the window to find out the cause of this remarkable phenomenon, but I see nothing more than that brilliant yellow light . . . I realize now that a bomb has burst . . .

"The bright day now reveals the frightful picture ... Where the city stood everything, as far as the eye could reach, is a waste of ashes and ruin. Only several skeletons of buildings completely burned out in the interior remain. The banks of the river are covered with dead and wounded, and the rising waters have here and there covered some of the corpses . . .

"As a result of the explosion of the bomb ... almost the entire city was destroyed at a single blow."

Skills FOCUS READING LIKE A HISTORIAN

1. **Make Generalizations** What does this source tell you about the power of the atomic bomb?
2. **Analyze Primary Sources** How would you expect the Japanese government to respond to the bombing of Hiroshima?

See **Skills Handbook**, p. H25

Primary Sources

Hiroshima

Analyze Was it really necessary to use atomic weapons against Japan? Many of the top U.S. military leaders did not think so. Dwight D. Eisenhower, supreme commander of the Allies in Europe during World War II and later President of the United States, was one of them. In his 1963 book *Mandate for Change, 1953–1956,* Eisenhower wrote of being told by Secretary of War Henry L. Stimson that an atomic bomb was about to be dropped on a Japanese city:

"During his recitation of the relevant facts, I had been conscious of a feeling of depression and so I voiced to him my grave misgivings, first on the basis of my belief that Japan was already defeated and that dropping the bomb was completely unnecessary, and secondly because I thought that our country should avoid shocking world opinion by the use of a weapon whose employment was, I thought, no longer mandatory as a measure to save American lives."

Other World War II military leaders who felt that the bombing was unnecessary included President Truman's chief of staff, Admiral William D. Leahy; General Douglas MacArthur, who served as supreme commander in the Pacific during the war; and Admiral Chester W. Nimitz, commander in chief of the Pacific Fleet.

CRF: Biography: Harry S Truman

Skills Focus: Identifying Problem and Solution   At Level

Reading Skill
Defeating Japan

1. Tell students that it is 1945 and they are advisers to President Truman. The Allies have captured Okinawa, and they plan to invade the major islands of Japan. Have each student write a memorandum recommending an action to bring the war to an end. Students should weigh the feasibility of using traditional methods, such as strategic air strikes backed up by marines on shore, as opposed to more radical options, such as dropping an atomic bomb. Students should also look at the ethical and long-term consequences of their recommendations. Have them list the pros and cons of each in their memorandums and make a recommendation based on their lists.

2. Have volunteers read their memorandums to the class. Guide the class in a discussion of students' memorandums. **LS Verbal-Linguistic**

   Alternative Assessment Handbook, Rubric 43: Writing to Persuade

Answers

Reading Like a Historian 1. *It is extremely powerful and devastating.* **2.** *possible answer—Japan would immediately surrender.*

Reading Check *the dropping of atomic bombs on the Japanese cities of Hiroshima and Nagasaki*

3 What were the Allied plans for the postwar world? *Roosevelt and Churchill wanted no territorial gain and wanted a peaceful world in which nations chose their own governments and worked together for mutual prosperity. Stalin joined the two leaders at a conference, and agreed to work toward peace, but wanted former Polish territory.*

The Postwar World

Identify What was the Atlantic Charter? *a joint declaration by Franklin Roosevelt and Winston Churchill outlining what the two men saw as the purpose of the war*

Summarize What were some of the challenges that faced the postwar world? *Much of Europe and Asia lay in ruins, national economies were near collapse, millions of displaced people had to rebuild their lives, and concerns increased about the spread of communism and Soviet influence.*

 Quick Facts Transparency: World War II Casualties

Primary Source

The eighth point of the Atlantic Charter stated that "all of the nations of the world, for realistic as well as spiritual reasons, must come to the abandonment of the use of force. Since no future peace can be maintained if land, sea or air armaments continue to be employed by nations which threaten, or may threaten, aggression outside of their frontiers, they believe… that the disarmament of such nations is essential. They will likewise aid and encourage all other practicable measures which will lighten for peace-loving peoples the crushing burden of armaments."

WORLD WAR II CASUALTIES

QUICK FACTS

		MILITARY DEAD	MILITARY WOUNDED	CIVILIAN DEAD
ALLIES	China	1,310,000	1,753,000	1,000,000+
	France	213,000	4,000,000	350,000
	Great Britain	264,000	277,000	93,000
	Soviet Union	11,000,000	unknown	7,000,000+
	United States	292,000	672,000	6,000
AXIS	Germany	3,500,000	5,000,000	780,000
	Italy	242,000	66,000	153,000
	Japan	1,300,000	4,000,000	672,000

Source: Encyclopedia Britannica

NEW YORK

CC Unit 6-D12 Post-World War II world

Finally acknowledging Japan's utter defeat, Japanese emperor **Hirohito** surrendered on August 15, 1945, the date now known as **V-J Day**. World War II was finally over.

READING CHECK **Find the Main Idea** What brought an end to the war in the Pacific?

The Postwar World

At the end of the war, much of Europe and Asia lay in ruins. Tens of millions of people had died in the war, many of them civilians. The heaviest losses were in the nations of Eastern Europe, including Poland, Yugoslavia, and the Soviet Union, but Germany, Japan, and China had also suffered greatly. In these areas the physical devastation was nearly complete. Entire cities, villages, and farms had been destroyed or damaged heavily, and national economies were near collapse. Food, shelter, and medicine were scarce.

The war also uprooted millions of people in Europe and Asia. These displaced persons included former prisoners of war, survivors of Nazi concentration camps, people who had fled their homes when fighting grew near, and even people who had been forced out when national borders changed after the war. These millions of people had to begin to rebuild their lives. Tragically, this was made even more difficult for some Polish Jews, who returned to their homes to find that their property had been taken. Dozens of these Holocaust survivors were murdered by hostile neighbors.

Planning for the Future For years, Allied leaders had been planning for the day the war would finally end. For example, in July 1941, even before the United States entered the war, President Franklin Roosevelt met with Winston Churchill. They issued a joint declaration called the Atlantic Charter. The charter outlined what the two leaders saw as the purpose of the war. Together they proclaimed that they sought no territorial gain, and they looked forward to a peaceful world in which all nations chose their own governments and worked together for mutual prosperity.

In late November 1943 Roosevelt and Churchill were joined by Joseph Stalin at a conference in Tehran, Iran. There the three leaders agreed on a schedule for the D-Day invasion. They also agreed to work together in the peace that would follow the war.

HISTORY'S VOICES

❝We shall seek the cooperation and active participation of all nations, large and small, whose peoples in heart and mind are dedicated … to the elimination of tyranny and slavery, oppression and intolerance. We will welcome them … into a world family of Democratic Nations.❞

—Declaration of the Three Powers, December 1, 1943, Tehran

Yalta and Potsdam In early 1945, when the Allies were on the brink of victory, they were having difficulties agreeing on the plans for peace. These difficulties came to the surface at the **Yalta Conference**, held in Soviet territory.

The primary goal of the conference was to reach agreement on what to do with postwar Europe. Roosevelt, Stalin, and Churchill agreed on plans for governing the soon-to-be conquered

862 CHAPTER 28

Skills Focus: Analyzing Visuals

At Level

Reading Like a Historian Skill
After the War

Research Required

1. Have students conduct research to find photographs depicting war damage. If possible, students should find photographs that show the same locations before and after the war. *Possible locations—Hiroshima and Nagasaki, Japan; Dresden, Germany; London, England; Berlin, Germany; Warsaw, Poland; Manila, the Philippines; and Stalingrad, USSR.*

2. Have students make copies of their photographs and conduct research on the

location using the following questions as guidelines: How extensive was the damage? What happened to the people who lived in the vicinity where damage occurred? How long did it take to rebuild afterward?

3. Have students present their photos and describe the war's damage. **LS Interpersonal, Visual-Spatial**

Alternative Assessment Handbook, Rubrics 24: Oral Presentations; and 30: Research

Germany. Stalin, however, was able to get his way on other key points, such as keeping territory that had formerly been part of Poland. In return, he promised to respect democratic ideals in the Eastern European countries his armies now occupied. President Roosevelt also managed to win some points. For example, he persuaded Stalin to join the fight against Japan soon after the war in Europe ended.

Roosevelt also convinced Stalin to agree to join a new world organization proposed by the Allies—the **United Nations**. Like the earlier League of Nations, the United Nations (UN) was designed to encourage international cooperation and prevent war. In June 1945 representatives of many of the world's nations signed the UN charter. The United States, Great Britain, France, the Soviet Union, and China formed the UN Security Council and had more power than other member nations.

In July 1945, Allied leaders met again, this time in the German city of Potsdam. The **Potsdam Conference** took place amid growing ill will between the Soviet Union and the other Allies. The Allies discussed many issues concerning postwar Europe, but often had difficulty reaching agreement.

Soviet Plans In the closing months of the war, American and British leaders were concerned about Stalin's intentions in Eastern Europe. They worried that communism and

Soviet influence would spread in the postwar world. As you will learn, they were correct: Stalin would soon break his promises about respecting democracy in Eastern Europe. World War II had ended, but another struggle was about to begin.

READING CHECK **Summarize** What major decisions did Allied leaders make at Yalta and Potsdam?

CAUSES AND EFFECTS OF WORLD WAR II

CAUSES
- Economic hardship and political unrest following World War I
- Aggressive leaders in Germany, Italy, and Japan wanted to expand their nations.
- Germany invaded Poland, and Japan attacked the United States.

EFFECTS
- Millions of people were killed, and large areas of Europe and Asia were damaged or destroyed.
- The Allies occupied Japan and parts of Europe.
- The United Nations was created to help prevent future wars.
- Conflict began between the Soviet Union and the other Allies over the fate of Eastern Europe.
- The United States and the Soviet Union emerged as the world's two major powers.

SECTION 4 ASSESSMENT

go.hrw.com
Online Quiz
Keyword: SHL WW2 HP

Reviewing Ideas, Terms, and People

1. a. Identify What was the significance of **D-Day** in the war in Europe?

b. Identify Cause and Effect How did the Allies' careful planning pay off in the D-Day invasion?

c. Predict If the D-Day invasion had failed, how might the outcome of the war have been different?

2. a. Describe What enabled the Americans to go on the offensive in the Pacific?

b. Make Inferences How did the experiences of Iwo Jima and Okinawa affect the Allied decision to drop the atomic bomb?

c. Predict How do you think the American development of the atomic bomb would affect the world in the years after the war?

3. a. Identify Identify one of the conferences attended by the leaders of the Allied nations.

b. Evaluate How do you think the coordination of military efforts may have helped the Allies in World War II?

Critical Thinking

4. Explain Copy the chart below and use your notes from the section to explain what led to the end of the war.

End of War

FOCUS ON SPEAKING

5. Narration Using details from the section, write a speech that an Allied leader might have given about the Allied plans for the postwar world.

WORLD WAR II **863**

The Holocaust

Word Help

crematorium a building containing an oven for cremating, or burning, dead bodies

cordwood wood stacked in cords, or piles

Recent Scholarship

In 1994, a book titled *"The Good Old Days": The Holocaust as Seen by Its Perpetrators and Bystanders* gave a chilling picture of what really happened during the Holocaust. It shows that thousands of people in Germany and eastern Europe went along with the "Final Solution." Maximilian Grabner tried to excuse his participation by saying that he did it out of consideration for his family. Grabner was investigated by the Nazis for killing 2,000 prisoners and was sentenced to death.

"The Good Old Days": The Holocaust as Seen by Its Prepetrators and Bystandars edited by Ernst Klee, Willi Dressen, and Volker Reiss. Free Press, 1994.

Info to Know

The Shanghai Ghetto When many countries, including the United States, were turning back Jewish refugees, China welcomed them. About 30,000 mostly German Jews managed to make their way to the Chinese port of Shanghai. During World War II, Shanghai was occupied by Japan. As a German ally, Japan imprisoned Jews and set up a ghetto. After Shanghai was liberated at the end of the war, most of the Jewish refugees left to try to rebuild their lives in elsewhere.

The Holocaust

Historical Context The documents below provide information about the Holocaust.

Task Examine the selections and answer the questions that follow. After you have studied the documents, you will be asked to write an essay about how an event like the Holocaust could have taken place. You will need to use evidence from these selections and from the chapter to support the position you take in your essay.

NEW YORK STANDARDS

P1 1.3 Students analyze historic events from around the world by examining accounts written from different perspectives.

DOCUMENT 1

An American Soldier's Reaction

Leon Bass was an African American soldier who visited the Buchenwald camp in April 1945, shortly after it had been liberated by the Allies.

Then we saw the crematorium where the dead bodies were outside, stacked up like cordwood, and we went into the crematorium and you could see the residue in the ovens—the rib cages, the skulls. And it was so hard to believe—to understand why. What did these people do that merited this kind of treatment? And it boggles the mind when you think that it had gone on for almost ten years before we got into the war! Why wasn't it dealt with? Why did nobody scream and shout, 'Stop!' They never did.

DOCUMENT 2

A Gestapo Officer's Justification

Maximilian Grabner was the head of the Gestapo, or secret police, at the Auschwitz-Birkenau death camp. After the war's end, he tried to explain his actions.

To kill three million people is in my view the greatest crime of all. I only took part in this crime because there was nothing I could do to change anything. The blame for this crime lay with National Socialism [the Nazi Party]. I myself was never a National Socialist. Nevertheless, I still had to join the Party.

. . . I only took part in the murder of some three million people out of consideration for my family.

DOCUMENT 3

Nazi Camp Locations

Nazi prison camps spread throughout Europe as military victories brought more Jews under German control. Death camps were designed mainly to kill large numbers of Jews, while mobile killing units were Nazi police forces that traveled throughout Europe to execute Jews. Many of the Nazi camps were located near towns or cities in areas that had large Jewish populations.

NAZI CAMP LOCATIONS

Death camp
Labor camp
Mobile killing unit

0 100 200 Miles
0 100 200 Kilometers

Skills Focus: Making Oral Presentations   At Level

Reading Like a Historian Skill
Genocide

Background: Remind students that *genocide* means the systematic killing of a group of people. Tell the class that, although the word was first used in connection with Hitler's "Final Solution," genocide has taken place throughout history.

1. Guide the class in a discussion of genocide. What other examples of genocide can they think of in the last century? *Cambodia, Rwanda, Iraq, Bosnia, Sri Lanka, Guatemala, East Timor, etc.*

2. Organize students into small groups. Have each group research one of the other examples of genocide and write a report about its causes and how (or if) it was stopped.

3. Ask each group to present its report to the class.

4. Guide the class in a discussion of genocide based on student reports. **LS Interpersonal, Verbal-Linguistic**

Alternative Assessment Handbook, Rubrics 14: Group Activity; and 30: Research

DOCUMENT 4

A German Witness

Herman Graebe was a German engineer working in the Ukraine. On October 5, 1942, he accidentally discovered a Nazi mobile killing unit executing Ukrainian Jews. He later described what he saw.

> I heard rifle shots in quick succession from behind one of the earth mounds . . . I walked around the mound and found myself confronted by a tremendous grave. People were closely wedged together and lying on top of each other so that only their heads were visible. Nearly all had blood running over their shoulders from their heads. Some of the people shot were still moving. Some were lifting their arms and turning their heads to show that they were still alive. The pit was nearly two-thirds full. I estimated that it already contained about a thousand people. I looked for the man who did the shooting. He was an SS [Nazi military police] man, who sat at the edge of the narrow end of the pit, his feet dangling into the pit. He had a tommy-gun on his knees and was smoking a cigarette.

DOCUMENT 5

An American Learns about Hitler's Plan

Howard Elting, Jr., was an American official stationed in Switzerland. The document below is from a letter he wrote to the U.S. secretary of state on August 10, 1942.

> This morning Mr. Gerhart M. RIEGNER, Secretary of the World Jewish Congress in Geneva, called in great agitation. He stated that he had just received a report from a German business man of considerable prominence, who is said to have excellent political and military connections in Germany and from whom reliable and important political information has been obtained on two previous occasions, to the effect that there has been and is being considered in Hitler's headquarters a plan to exterminate all Jews from Germany and German controlled areas in Europe after they have been concentrated in the east (presumably Poland). The number involved is said to be between three-and-a-half and four millions and the object is to permanently settle the Jewish question in Europe. The mass execution if decided upon would allegedly take place this fall.

Skills FOCUS — READING LIKE A HISTORIAN

DOCUMENT 1
a. **Recall** What did Bass see at the camp?
b. **Infer** Do you think Bass believed that the Allies should have done more to stop the Holocaust? Why or why not?

DOCUMENT 2
a. **Explain** How does Grabner try to justify his actions?
b. **Analyze** What does Grabner mean by saying he took part in the murder "out of consideration for my family"?

DOCUMENT 3
a. **Identify** Which large cities were Nazi camps near?
b. **Draw Conclusions** Where were most Nazi camps and killing units located? Why?

DOCUMENT 4
a. **Recall** How many bodies does Graebe say were in the mass grave?

b. **Infer** What was the executioner's attitude toward the mass murder? How can you tell?

DOCUMENT 5
a. **Identify** What did Gerhart Riegner believe was going to happen to European Jews?
b. **Infer** Compare the date of Elting's letter to the date of the War Refugee Board's establishment. What do these dates suggest about the U.S. response to the Holocaust?

DOCUMENT-BASED ESSAY QUESTION

How could an event as large and as terrible as the Holocaust have taken place? Using the documents above and information from the chapter, form a thesis that explains your position. Then write a short essay to support it.

See **Skills Handbook**, p. H25

Info to Know

Stopping Racism Leon Bass was only 19 years old when he witnessed the liberation of Buchenwald in 1945. As an African American, he was a member of a segregated army unit. After Buchenwald, he realized that human suffering is universal, and that the Nazis had practiced the ultimate racism in their death camps. In the 1960s Bass became involved in the American civil rights movement. He continued to work in the field of Holocaust education and to promote understanding between African Americans and Jews.

Answers

Reading Like a Historian
Document 1. a. *describes horrific conditions at Buchenwald, such as seeing bodies "stacked up like cordwood;"* **b.** *possible answer— Yes, because no one did anything to stop it.* **Document 2. a.** *He says there was nothing he could do to change anything, and that he only did it out of consideration for his family.* **b.** *possible answer—that his family might have come to some harm if he had refused.* **Document 3. a.** *Poland, Warsaw;* **b.** *in areas with a large Jewish population; eliminated transportation issues for Germans;* **Document 4. a.** *about a thousand;* **b.** *indifference; casually smoking, dangling his feet;* **Document 5. a.** *they would be exterminated;* **b.** *Elting's letter is dated about a year and a half before the War Refugee Board was established, which shows that U.S. response was slow;* **Essay Question 6.** *Students' essays should show an understanding of the fact that Germans did little to stop the crimes. If the people of Germany had refused to allow Hitler to carry out his "Final Solution," they could have stopped it.*

Skills Focus: Analyzing Primary Sources

Below Level

Reading Like a Historian Skill
Speaking Out

Materials: poster paper, colored markers

1. Guide the class in a discussion of Documents 1, 4, and 5. Ask students to think about the graphic atrocities described in Documents 1 and 4 and contrast them with the information in Document 5.

2. Have students work in pairs to create posters against the persecution of European Jews.

3. Ask volunteers to share their posters with the class, explaining them as they show them.

4. Guide the class in a discussion of students' posters. **LS** **Interpersonal, Visual-Spatial**

   Alternative Assessment Handbook, Rubrics 11: Discussions; and 28: Posters

Answers

Visual Summary

Review and Inquiry Organize students into four groups, and assign each group one of the topics in the quick facts chart: German aggression leads to war, Axis Powers make early gains, The Allies fight back, and The War ends. Have each group write a short summary of its assigned topic.

Quick Facts Transparency: Visual Study Guide: World War II: 1939–1945

Review Key Terms and People

1. appeasement
2. Axis
3. radar
4. Holocaust
5. violate
6. Battle of Stalingrad
7. ghettos
8. Final Solution
9. D-Day
10. Battle of Okinawa

Comprehension and Critical Thinking

11. a. They took no direct action, hoping to avoid war.
b. Britain's use of radar in the Battle of Britain made their air defences more effective when German planes flew over the English Channel, whereas the German assault on France was quick and well planned.
c. possible answer—The attack on Pearl Harbor caused many Americans to rethink isolationism; as a result, American forces became a determined enemy of Japan.

12. a. the Allies
b. It changed the balance of power in the Pacific, allowing Allies to go on the offensive.
c. He failed to plan for the harsh Soviet winter. By refusing to allow his troops to retreat, many of them ran out of ammunition, food, and medicine.

VISUAL STUDY GUIDE

QUICK FACTS

World War II: 1939–1945

German aggression leads to war
- Rhineland militarized
- Austria and parts of Czechoslovakia annexed
- Poland invaded

Axis Powers make early gains
- Germany conquers Denmark, Norway, France, invades Soviet Union
- Nazis adopt the Final Solution and establish death camps
- Japan attacks Pearl Harbor, rules the Pacific

The Allies fight back
- British and Americans win in North Africa, Italy
- Soviets win at Stalingrad
- Americans win at Midway, begin island hopping

The war ends
- Soviets push back Germans from the east
- After D-Day, other Allies push toward Germany from the west
- Americans win in Pacific; atomic bomb ends war

Major Events of World War II

1939
- Nazi-Soviet nonaggression pact
- German troops invade Poland and the war begins

1940
- Germany conquers France
- Battle of Britain begins

1941
- Germany invades the Soviet Union
- Japan attacks Pearl Harbor
- United States enters the war

1942
- Allies win the Battle of Midway
- Allied victory at El Alamein
- Allies begin to hear reports of widespread killings of Jews in Europe

1943
- Soviets win the Battle of Stalingrad
- Allies invade Italy

1944
- Allies invade France in D-Day
- Allies begin to discover death camps

1945
- Allies meet at Yalta and Potsdam
- Germany surrenders
- Allies win battles of Iwo Jima and Okinawa
- Allies drop atomic bombs on Hiroshima and Nagasaki
- Japan surrenders and the war ends

Review Key Terms and People

Complete each sentence by filling the blank with the correct term or person.

1. Neville Chamberlain pursued a policy known as _____ in dealing with the Germans.

2. Germany, Italy, and Japan formed an alliance known as the _____.

3. The British used the technology of _____ to help them win the Battle of Britain.

4. In 1941, Hitler's forces began the widespread, systematic killing that marked the start of the _____.

5. Hitler's plan to rearm Germany was an action that would _____ the Treaty of Versailles.

6. The Germans lost the _____ after being surrounded by Soviet troops.

7. In some cities the Nazis forced Jews to live in a _____, or confined area.

8. The _____ was the Nazi plan for the deliberate, mass execution of Jews.

9. On _____, the Allies launched a major, long-planned invasion of Europe.

10. The _____ was formed after the war to encourage international cooperation and prevent war.

---

13. a. They tried to get rid of German Jews by deporting them or forcing them to leave by stripping them of their citizenship and property rights.
b. As the Germans moved into new areas of Europe, millions of Jews came under their power. Nazi leaders came up with the "Final Solution"—the deliberate, mass execution of Jewish prisoners.
c. possible answer—Only after the Allies had forced the Germans to retreat were they able to liberate the prisoners.

14. a. Hitler ordered one last, massive counter-attack in Belgium in December 1944, but the D-Day attack let to Germany's surrender on May 7, 1945.
b. President Truman's decision to drop two atomic bombs in Japan—one on Hiroshima, and one on Nagasaki
c. millions killed; much of Europe and Asia destroyed; Allies occupied Japan and parts of Europe; United Nations created; U.S. and Soviet Union become world's two major powers

History's Impact video program
Review the video to answer the closing question:
How did events after World War II lead to the
beginning of the Cold War?

Comprehension and Critical Thinking

SECTION 1 *(pp. 835–842)*

11. a. Recall How did Great Britain and France respond to Hitler's aggression in the late 1930s?

b. Explain Why were the results of German attacks on France and Britain so different?

c. Predict How might the Japanese success at Pearl Harbor have later hurt their cause?

SECTION 2 *(pp. 843–850)*

12. a. Identify Who won the battle to control the Atlantic?

b. Explain In what ways did the Allied victory at Midway affect the war in the Pacific?

c. Make Judgments How did the Battle of Stalingrad demonstrate Hitler's poor judgment?

SECTION 3 *(pp. 854–857)*

13. a. Describe How did the Nazi government treat German Jews before World War II began?

b. Identify Cause and Effect How did German military victories lead to the Nazi's Final Solution?

c. Evaluate What do you think of the Allies' decision to focus on winning the war rather than immediately trying to save the people in Nazi death camps?

SECTION 4 *(pp. 858–863)*

14. a. Recall What effect did D-Day have on the war in Europe?

b. Cause and Effect What events helped bring about an end to the war in the Pacific?

c. Elaborate In what ways did World War II affect the world?

Reading Skills

Understanding Causes and Effects *Use what you know about understanding causes and effects to answer the questions below.*

15. Why did Germany begin to threaten much of Europe in the 1930s?

16. What effects did Japan's attack on Pearl Harbor have on the war?

17. List the causes and effects of Nazi anti-Semitism during the 1930s and 1940s.

Analyzing Visuals

Reading Like a Historian *The American propaganda poster below shows a man being urged to be quiet by Uncle Sam, a symbol of the United States.*

Quiet! Loose Talk Can Cost Lives, Dal Holcomb, 1942

18. Explain Why is the man—and the viewer—being told to be quiet? How can talk "cost lives"?

19. Draw Conclusions Why do you think the artist used the symbol of Uncle Sam?

Using the Internet

go.hrw.com
Practice Online
Keyword: SHL WW2

20. The Allied invasion of France, or D-Day, began on June 6, 1944, when 150,000 soldiers landed on the beaches of Normandy. Using the Internet, research what happened in Normandy on D-Day. Then write a report about the first 24 hours after the landing, using eyewitness accounts and other documents to support your work.

WRITING ABOUT HISTORY

Persuasion: Writing an Evaluation *In the late 1930s, many Americans did not want to become involved in conflict in Europe, believing that the United States should stay out of troubles overseas. Others thought it was dangerous to ignore the aggressive actions of dictators in Europe and Asia.*

21. Assignment: In an essay, evaluate the wisdom of American isolationism. To provide support for your evaluation, use specific reasons and examples from the chapter and from other research.

WORLD WAR II **867**

WORLD WAR II **867**

You can use these pages to have students simultaneously review the unit and practice taking standardized tests.

Answers

1. 4
World War I, Section 1

2. 4
World War I, Section 1

3. 1
World War I, Section 1

4. 3
World War I, Section 3

5. 4
World War I, Section 2

6. 4
World War II, Section 1

7. 3
World War I, Section 4

8. 4
The Interwar Years, Section 2

9. 1
*The Interwar Years,
Sections 3 and 4*

10. 2
The Interwar Years, Section 3

11. 1
The Interwar Years, Section 4

UNIT 8
Regents Practice

Directions Write your answer for each statement or question on a separate answer sheet. Choose the number of the word or expression that best completes the statement or answers the question.

1 **In 1914 many European leaders believed that alliances would**
1 improve world trade.
2 support the League of Nations.
3 lead to war.
4 help prevent war.

2 **What event triggered the outbreak of World War I?**
1 the Russian Revolution
2 Germany's invasion of Poland
3 the assassination of Archduke Franz Ferdinand
4 French aggression toward Italy

3 **During World War I trench warfare led to**
1 a military stalemate.
2 very few casualties.
3 a quick end to the war.
4 war in the Pacific.

4 **Who led the Bolsheviks during their October Revolution against the Russian czar?**
1 Joseph Stalin
2 Karl Marx
3 Vladimir Lenin
4 Alexander Kerensky

5 **During World War I, more than 1 million Armenians were deported or killed in**
1 Germany.
2 Russia.
3 France.
4 the Ottoman Empire.

6 **The terms of the Treaty of Versailles are often blamed for contributing to**
1 the Russian Revolution.
2 the rise of Nazism in Germany.
3 Japanese aggression in China.
4 U.S. isolationism.

7 **Which of the following was one political outcome of World War I?**
1 The Bolsheviks in Russia were overthrown.
2 Tensions in European colonies decreased.
3 The Ottoman Empire broke apart.
4 The United Nations was formed.

8 **The Great Depression helped lead to**
1 World War I.
2 a rise in world trade.
3 the growth of free trade associations.
4 the rise of dictators in Europe.

9 **In the 1930s, Germany, Italy, and Japan**
1 worked to build empires around the globe.
2 became more democratic.
3 reduced the size of their militaries.
4 pursued isolationist policies.

10 **Why did Japan invade Manchuria?**
1 in response to a Manchurian attack on Japan
2 to gain control of Manchuria's natural resources
3 the people of Manchuria wanted to join Japan
4 Japan had an alliance with China

11 **What was a common feature of the totalitarian dictators who rose to power after World War I?**
1 They used violence and fear to maintain power.
2 They were elected democratically.
3 They were Communist.
4 They were Fascist.

12 The quotation below by British prime minister Neville Chamberlain in 1938 is an example of what policy? Base your answer on the passage and on your knowledge of history.

"We should seek by all means in our power to avoid war, by analysing possible causes, by trying to remove them, by discussion in a spirit of collaboration and good will. I cannot believe that such a programme would be rejected by the people of this country, even if it does mean the establishment of personal contact with the dictators."

1 isolationism
2 appeasement
3 aggression
4 containment

13 France and Great Britain declared war on Germany in 1939 as a direct result of

1 Germany's annexation of Austria.
2 Germany's attack on France.
3 Germany's invasion of Poland.
4 Germany's militarization of the Rhineland.

14 Which of the following was a key turning point in Germany's invasion of the Soviet Union?

1 the Blitz
2 the Battle of the Bulge
3 the Battle of Midway
4 the Battle of Stalingrad

15 Why did Japan attack Pearl Harbor?

1 Japan saw the United States as a threat to Japanese expansion in Asia.
2 Japan's leaders had promised Germany they would attack the United States.
3 Japan wanted Pearl Harbor's natural resources.
4 Japan wanted to oust the U.S. military from China.

16 What was the goal of the Nazis' Final Solution?

1 to take control of the Soviet Union
2 to murder all European Jews
3 to drop atomic bombs on Great Britain
4 to invade the United States

17 What best explains the data on the chart below? Base your answer on the data and on your knowledge of history.

World War II Casualties

■ Military deaths ■ Civilian deaths

Source: Encyclopedia Britannica

1 new military technologies and total war
2 trench warfare and poison gas
3 atomic weapons
4 U-boats and torpedoes

18 The main purpose of the Yalta Conference was to decide

1 how to destroy Nazi concentration camps.
2 what to do with postwar Europe.
3 how to stop the spread of communism.
4 when to invade Germany.

REVIEWING THE UNIT

Constructed Response World leaders played key roles in the events of World Wars I and II. These leaders included Kaiser Wilhelm II, Woodrow Wilson, Winston Churchill, Franklin Roosevelt, Adolf Hitler, Joseph Stalin, Emperor Hirohito, and Dwight Eisenhower. Recall the roles that two world leaders played in these world wars. Then write a brief essay in which you summarize how each was involved in and influenced the course of these wars and history.

CONNECTING TO THE PREVIOUS UNIT

Constructed Response Industrialization, nationalism, and imperialism all helped to set the stage for World Wars I and II. Choose one of these topics to explore. Write a brief essay in which you explain how your topic affected key countries in Europe and was one of the causes of the world wars.

THE WORLD AT WAR **869**

12. 2
World War II, Section 1

13. 3
World War II, Section 1

14. 4
World War II, Section 2

15. 1
World War II, Section 1

16. 2
World War II, Section 3

17. 1
World War II, Section 4

18. 2
World War II, Section 4

Reviewing the Unit

Essays should discuss two world leaders who were involved in World War I or World War II and should summarize the involvement and influence of the leaders in the war and in history.
possible brief essay—
Dwight Eisenhower and Emperor Hirohito both played important roles in history and in World War II. Eisenhower was supreme commander of the Allies in Europe and the commander on D-Day. An integral part of the Allies' success, Eisenhower became president of the United States after the war, continuing his leadership. Japanese Emperor Hirohito also played an important, if less valiant, role. Following the dropping of the atomic bomb, Hirohito surrendered, ending World War II.

Connecting to the Previous Unit

Student essays should explain how industrialization, nationalism, or imperialism affected key European countries and helped cause the world wars.
possible essay topic—
Industrialism and its inception and impact on Great Britain's economy and society

Government and Citizenship

Rise of Fascism Following World War I, many Europeans were looking for new leadership to restore pride in their countries. As a result, ambitious militant leaders had the opportunity to take control of a vulnerable public. In Italy, Benito Mussolini led the Fascist Party, which was formed in 1919. The Fascists gained the nickname the Blackshirts for the black shirts they wore as part of their uniform. They fought against trade unionists, Communists, farm organizations, and Socialists, which was ironic, as Mussolini was a former Socialist.

Science and Technology

Gases in World War I Gas warfare was first used by German troops in 1915. Chlorine gas, a lung irritant, was released by soldiers from a cylinder. The wind spread the gas to enemy trenches. Other gases used during this time caused tearing, sneezing, vomiting, and skin irritation and burning. At the time, soldiers had little or no protection from such attacks.

Recent Scholarship

According to British Scholar Martin Pugh, fascism may not have gained popularity in other parts of Europe, but its ideas were widely adopted in Great Britain during the interwar years. In his book *Hurrah for the Blackshirts: Fascists and Fascism in Britain Between the Wars,* Pugh states that England's leadership during this time reflected fascism's influence.

Hurrah for the Blackshirts: Fascists and Fascism in Britain Between the Wars by Martin Pugh. Pimlico, 2006.

THEME
GOVERNMENT AND CITIZENSHIP

How did nationalism affect government and citizenship in World Wars I and II?

Nationalism, which was a driving force behind the world wars of the 1900s, had many significant effects on government and citizenship in Europe. Nationalism led to government rivalries and alliances, opened the door to new forms of government, and inspired citizens to fight for and defend their countries.

EFFECTS OF NATIONALISM ON GOVERNMENT AND CITIZENSHIP IN EUROPE, 1914–1945

Government Rivalries and Alliances
- Europe's countries competed for power, resources, and influence.
- National rivalries led governments to build strong militaries and form alliances for security and protection.
- When conflict broke out, government leaders were committed to supporting their allies, which led to world wars.

New Forms of Government
- After World War I, some citizens wanted new leaders to rebuild their countries and restore national pride.
- As a result, fascist leaders rose to power and formed new governments in Germany and Italy.

Citizens Defend Their Government
- In warring countries, feelings of national pride and duty led many citizens to volunteer for military service.
- These citizens responded to their governments' calls to defend and protect their homeland from enemy armies.

THEME
SCIENCE AND TECHNOLOGY

How did industrialization change the science and technology of warfare?

The advances made during the Industrial Revolution enabled scientists and engineers to invent many new military technologies. As new weapons and equipment became a key part of battles, the nature of warfare changed. Industrial facilities became key components of a country's ability to wage war—and key targets for its enemies.

CAUSES AND EFFECTS OF MODERN WARFARE TECHNOLOGIES

CAUSES
- Military engineers developed new technologies like machine guns, tanks, submarines, artillery, poison gas, and atomic weapons.
- Existing technologies, like airplanes and steamships, were modified for war.

EFFECTS
- Battle zones became scenes of enormous death and destruction.
- War became an industrial competition as countries produced huge amounts of weapons and supplies to keep up with their enemies.
- Factories and industries became military targets and were attacked to weaken an opponent's ability to wage war.

870 UNIT 8

Differentiating Instruction

Learners Having Difficulty

1. Review with students the technological advancements that contributed to new weapons used in the world wars.

2. Tell students they are soldiers fighting in Europe during World War I or World War II. Have each student write a letter home to a friend or family member. The letter should describe what war is like with the new technology. For example, a soldier might be stationed on a submarine or be living in a World War I trench.

3. Tell students to use descriptive words and active verbs in their letters so the recipient will get a vivid picture of what the fighting was like.

4. Have volunteers read their letters to the class. Discuss what life must have been like for soldiers who served in one of the world wars.
   LS Verbal-Linguistic

   Alternative Assessment Handbook, Rubric 25: Personal Letters

THEME
SOCIETY

In what ways did the world wars affect society in Europe?

World Wars I and II affected society like never before. As entire countries mobilized for war, governments placed new controls on society to help achieve victory. But in the end, the massive scale of the wars left societies devastated.

Mobilizing Society
Countries mobilized for total war and devoted all resources to it. Soldiers went off to fight, and men and women worked in factories to produce weapons, vehicles, and other war-related goods.

World Wars

Controlling Society
Governments controlled information to shape public opinion and keep morale high. They also set up rationing systems and restricted the rights of groups they mistrusted.

Societies in Ruins
The wars caused millions of military and civilian casualties. Huge areas were reduced to rubble, leaving towns, farms, and economies ruined.

Skills FOCUS UNDERSTANDING THEMES

How did World Wars I and II affect government and citizenship, science and technology, and society in one country? Choose a country in Europe that fought in both World War I and II. Use your textbook and other resources to gather information about how each war affected that country. Then create a chart like the one below that compares and contrasts the effects of the two wars.

	World War I	World War II
Effects on Government and Citizenship		
Effects on Science and Technology		
Effects on Society		

Global Connections

World Wars I and II affected the entire world. Even places far away from the battle zones were affected as fighting interrupted trade routes, used valuable resources, and forced countries to choose sides.

Making Connections This map shows German U-boat attacks during World War II. How do you think these attacks affected places far away from the fighting? Which areas were affected? Use the map to write a short paragraph explaining how U-boat attacks are one example of the worldwide effects of World War II.

U-BOAT ATTACKS, 1939–1945

NORTH AMERICA

EUROPE

ATLANTIC OCEAN

PACIFIC OCEAN

AFRICA

SOUTH AMERICA

INDIAN OCEAN

- Allied territory (Nov. 1942)
- Axis territory (Nov. 1942)
- Neutral
- • U-Boat sinkings Sep. 3, 1939–Dec. 6, 1941
- · U-Boat sinkings Dec. 7, 1941–May 8, 1945

0 1,000 2,000 Miles
0 1,000 2,000 Kilometers
Miller projection

THE WORLD AT WAR **871**

Society

Women's War Efforts Many women in Europe had suspended their efforts for women's rights and suffrage to help with the war effort. After World War I women demanded recognition for their wartime contributions. They gained voting rights in many countries, including Germany, Sweden, Spain, Austria, Poland, and Canada. Women gained a stronger legal position in Great Britain. Although many women stopped working outside the home after the war, they were presented with a greater variety of job opportunities.

Understanding Themes

Student charts should compare how the world wars affected the country's government and citizenship, science and technology, and society.

Global Connections

Student paragraphs should explain how U-boat attacks during World War II affected countries throughout the world. possible short paragraph—
As the map shows, most countries chose sides in the war, while only a few were neutral. Even countries far away from the most devastating fighting chose sides. The map also shows that there were U-Boat sinkings far from the main battles—in the Caribbean, around South America, and as far south as the tip of Africa.

Collaborative Learning

At Level

War Effort Slogans

Research Required

Materials: poster board, colored markers

1. Organize students into small groups. Have each group conduct research using reliable online sources to locate information about the U.S. war effort at home during World War I or World War II.

2. Have students choose one particular program associated with the war effort, such as liberty bonds or victory gardens. Have students use the information found in their research to brainstorm a slogan for their chosen program.

3. Have each group create a poster that illustrates its chosen slogan.

4. Have volunteers present their posters to the class. **LS Visual-Spatial, Verbal-Linguistic**

Alternative Assessment Handbook, Rubrics 14: Group Activity; and 34: Slogans and Banners

Unit Review

Summarizing the Unit

In this unit, students learned that Europe endured drastic changes—geographically, economically, and politically. For example, Austria and Poland were new nations created by treaty. While established nations such as France had to rebuild, the new nations of eastern Europe had to start from scratch. Have students name some of the challenges these new countries faced. *New nations lacked democratic traditions and had to establish new governments, choose new leaders, and deal with unfamiliar political conflicts.*

Answers

Thinking Like a Historian

Student charts, graphs, or graphic organizers should show how the world wars affected the economy and government of either Germany or Japan. possible responses—
A. *Reparations crippled the German economy; after World War II, the economy was again devastated; many cities, villages, and farms were destroyed or damaged.*
B. *Germany forced to pay reparations and limit the size of its military; German land was lost; Weimar Republic was founded; political unrest; Hitler gained power; after World War II, Germany lost lands and eventually developed a democratic government*
C. *Much of Europe and Asia were left in ruins; United States and Soviet Union emerge as world's two major powers.*

UNIT 8
IN BRIEF
Below is a chapter-by-chapter summary of the main ideas in this unit, followed by a summary activity for the unit.

CHAPTER 26 — World War I
1914–1918

MAIN IDEA A host of powerful factors, including growing nationalism, military alliances, and European rivalries, created conditions that quickly transformed a single assassination into a bloody worldwide war.

SECTION 1 Europe in 1914 was on the brink of war. The assassination of Archduke Franz Ferdinand quickly led to the outbreak of what came to be called the Great War, or World War I.

SECTION 2 The development of new technologies and new types of warfare during World War I caused destruction on a scale never before imagined.

SECTION 3 Russia's losses in the war and widespread social unrest led to the Russian Revolution, which was led by Vladimir Lenin and the Bolsheviks.

SECTION 4 After several years of stalemate—and the U.S. entry into the war—the Allied Powers finally prevailed. The war was over, but the peace proved difficult to establish.

CHAPTER 27 — The Interwar Years
1919–1939

MAIN IDEA Following the destruction and chaos of World War I, the postwar world suffered from instability and serious economic and social problems. Under these conditions, nationalism spread, and a new generation of strong leaders promised a return to power and glory.

SECTION 1 During the chaotic years after World War I nationalist feelings grew in Asia, Africa, and the Middle East, leading to widespread unrest.

SECTION 2 Beginning in the late 1920s, an economic depression quickly spread around the globe, creating ideal conditions for political change.

SECTION 3 Economic and social changes in Japan led to growing tensions in society. Japan's military gradually took control of the nation's government and attacked China.

SECTION 4 The social and political turmoil that followed the war allowed totalitarian dictators to take power in Italy, Russia, and Germany.

CHAPTER 28 — World War II
1930–1945

MAIN IDEA The aggressive actions of Germany, Italy, and Japan led to the outbreak of World War II in 1939. At first the Axis armies won many battles, but after years of conflict the Allies triumphed.

SECTION 1 In the late 1930s, Germany, Italy, and Japan used military force to build growing empires. Their aggressive actions led to the start of World War II.

SECTION 2 The early years of World War II went poorly for the Allies. After the United States joined the war, however, the Allies recovered and began making gains against the Axis armies.

SECTION 3 During World War II Germany's Nazi government deliberately murdered some 6 million Jews and 5 million others in Europe. These actions became known as the Holocaust.

SECTION 4 In 1945 the Allies finally defeated the Axis Powers. But the war had disastrous consequences for many countries around the world. It left millions of people dead, millions uprooted, and many lives destroyed. Some entire nations were in ruins.

Thinking like a Historian
Summary and Extension Activity

The two world wars of the 1900s had dramatic effects on many countries' economies, governments, and relations with other nations. Perhaps no two countries were affected more than Germany and Japan. Choose one of these countries and create a chart, graph, or graphic organizer to show how world wars affected its:

A. Economy
B. Government
C. International Relations

Unit Resources

Review and Reinforce

- **Global History and Geography Regents Test Prep Workbook**
- **Regents Review Transparencies**
- **CRF:** Chapter Review
- **Spanish Chapter Summaries Audio CD Program**
- OSP **Holt PuzzlePro:** Quiz Show for ExamView
- **Quiz Game CD-ROM**

Assess

- **PASS:** Unit Test, Forms A and B
- **Alternative Assessment Handbook**
- OSP **New York ExamView Test Generator correlated to NY SS Standards**
- **Differentiated Instruction Modified Worksheets and Tests CD-ROM:** Chapter Tests
- HOAP **Holt Online Assessment Program** (in the Premier Online Edition)

Reteach/Intervene

- **Interactive Reader and Study Guide**
- **Differentiated Instruction Teacher Management System:** Lesson Plans for Differentiated Instruction
- **Differentiated Instruction Modified Worksheets and Tests CD-ROM:** Chapter Tests
- **Interactive Skills Tutor CD-ROM**

go.hrw.com
Online Resources

KEYWORDS: SHL WW1, SHL IWY, SHL WW2

UNIT 9

The Contemporary World

1945–Present

The Petronas Towers rise above the city of Kuala Lumpur, Malaysia.

CHAPTER 29
Europe and North America
1945–Present

CHAPTER 30
Asia
1945–Present

CHAPTER 31
Africa and the Middle East
1945–Present

CHAPTER 32
Latin America
1945–Present

CHAPTER 33
Today's World

Themes

ECONOMIC SYSTEMS
Regional trade agreements and globalization are two key factors that affect the world's economic systems today.

GEOGRAPHY AND ENVIRONMENT
Issues such as land and resource use, global warming, environmental protection, and population shifts shape the world's people and places.

SOCIETY
Terrorism, human rights, and civil rights are just some of the important concerns for people in societies around the world.

873

● **Unit Preview** ●

Introducing the Unit
Have students name the most significant historical events since the end of World War II. As they name them, make a list of the events for the class to see. Then have students to help rank the events in order of importance, from most important to least important. Which event did students choose as the most significant? Why?

Connecting to Themes
Activity **Globalization** Tell students that globalization is the process in which trade and culture link together countries around the world. Guide students in a discussion of the ways in which globalization affects them and their community.
LS **Verbal-Linguistic**

Reading Like a Historian
Interpreting Visuals
The Petronas Towers At 1,483 feet (452 meters), the Petronas Towers are the tallest buildings in the world. The buildings' developers wanted to create a monument that would commemorate Kuala Lumpur's position as a commercial and cultural capital. The basic design is meant to evoke Malaysia's Islamic heritage while embracing the nation's future.

Unit Resources

Planning
- **Differentiated Instruction Teacher Management System:** Unit Pacing Guide
- OSP **New York One-Stop Planner CD-ROM:** Teacher Management System
- **Power Presentations with Video CD-ROM**

Standards Mastery
- **Global History and Geography Regents Test Prep Workbook**
- **Regents Review Transparencies**

Differentiating Instruction
- **Differentiated Instruction Teacher Management System:** Lesson Plans for Differentiated Instruction
- **Differentiated Instruction Modified Worksheets and Tests CD-ROM**

Enrichment
- **A World History Teacher's Guide to Analyzing Movies**
- **Document-Based Activities for World History**
- **World History Outline Maps**
- **Reading Like a Historian: World History Toolkit**
- **World History Primary Source Library CD-ROM**

Assessment
- **PASS:** Unit Test, Forms A and B
- **Alternative Assessment Handbook**
- OSP **New York ExamView Test Generator correlated to NY SS Standards**
- HOAP **Holt Online Assessment Program** (in the Premier Online Edition)

Chapter 29 Planning Guide

Europe and North America

Chapter Overview	Reproducible Resources	Technology Resources

CHAPTER 29
pp. 874–905

Overview: In this chapter, students will learn how World War gave way to new alliances, but also to a new war, resulting in a rivalry between two superpowers: the United States and the Soviet Union.

KI 3, 4; PI 3.1, 3.2, 3.3, 4.1, 4.2
See pp. T32–T55 for a detailed correlation to the New York State Core Curriculum for Global History and Geography and the New York Learning Standards.

Differentiated Instruction Teacher Management System:
• Pacing Guide
• Lesson Plans for Differentiated Instruction

Interactive Reader and Study Guide:
Chapter Summary*

**Chapter Resource File*
• Writing About History
• Social Studies Skill
• Chapter Review

OSP New York One-Stop Planner CD-ROM:
Calander Planner

Live Ink© Online Reading Help

Student Edition on Audio CD Program

Differentiated Instruction Modified Worksheets and Tests CD-ROM

World History Primary Source Library CD-ROM

History's Impact: World History Video Program (VHS/DVD): Europe and North America

---

Section 1:
Beginnings of the Cold War

The Main Idea: Once partners in war, the Soviet Union and the other former Allies found it much more difficult to cooperate in peace. The result was an era of conflict and confrontation called the Cold War.

PI 3.3

Differentiated Instruction Teacher Management System: Section 1 Lesson Plan*

Interactive Reader and Study Guide: Section 1 Summary*

**Chapter Resource File*
• Vocabulary Builder: Section 1
• Biography: George Marshall
• History and Geography: Berlin Crisis
• Primary Source: The North Atlantic Treaty

Regents Review Transarency: Section 1*

Map Transparencies: Communist and NATO Countries, 1949; The Iron Curtain, 1949; The Korean War, 1950–1951*

Quick Facts Transparency: Causes and Effects of the Cold War*

Section 2:
Superpower Rivalries

The Main Idea: As the Cold War continued, the world's two superpowers—the Soviet Union and the United States—competed for power and influence around the world.

PI 4.1, 4.2

Differentiated Instruction Teacher Management System: Section 2 Lesson Plan*

Interactive Reader and Study Guide: Section 2 Summary*

**Chapter Resource File*
• Vocabulary Builder: Section 2
• Biography: Willy Brandt

Regents Review Transparency: Section 2*

Map Transparencies: The Cuban Missile Crisis; Cold War Hot Spots*

Internet Activity: The Cold War*

Section 3:
Changing Societies

The Main Idea: The Cold War brought tremendous economic and social change to North America, Western Europe, and Eastern Europe and the Soviet Union.

PI 3.1, 3.2

Differentiated Instruction Teacher Management System: Section 3 Lesson Plan*

Interactive Reader and Study Guide: Section 3 Summary*

**Chapter Resource File*
• Vocabulary Builder: Section 3
• Biography: Rosa Parks
• Literature: *Invisible Man*

Regents Review Transparency: Section 3*

Quick Facts Transparency: Contrasting Economic Systems*

Internet Activity: Report on Europe and North America in the Postwar Years

---

Section 4:
After the Cold War

The Main Idea: The Soviet Union collapsed in 1991 and the Cold War came to an end, bringing changes to Europe and leaving the United States as the world's only superpower.

PI 3.1, 3.2, 4.1, 4.2

Differentiated Instruction Teacher Management System: Section 4 Lesson Plan*

Interactive Reader and Study Guide: Section 4 Summary*

**Chapter Resource File*
• Vocabulary Builder: Section 4
• Biography: Condoleezza Rice

Regents Review Transparency: Section 4*

Map Transparencies: The Breakup of the Soviet Union, 1991; The European Union, 2006*

Quick Facts Transparency: Recent U.S. Military Involvement, 2001–Present*

TEACHER'S EDITION

Review, Assessment, Intervention

- **Global History and Geography Regents Test Prep Workbook**

- **Quick Facts Transparency:** Europe and North America*

- **Progress Assessment Support System (PASS):** Chapter Test*

- **Differentiated Instruction Modified Worksheets and Tests CD-ROM:** Modified Chapter Test

- **OSP New York One-Stop Planner CD-ROM:** ExamView Test Generator (English/Spanish)

- **HOAP Holt Online Assessment Program (HOAP),** in the Holt Premier Online Student Edition

---

- **PASS:** Section 1 Quiz*
- **Online Quiz:** Section 1
- **Alternative Assessment Handbook**

- **PASS:** Section 2 Quiz*
- **Online Quiz:** Section 2
- **Alternative Assessment Handbook**

- **PASS:** Section 3 Quiz*
- **Online Quiz:** Section 3
- **Alternative Assessment Handbook**

- **PASS:** Section 4 Quiz*
- **Online Quiz:** Section 4
- **Alternative Assessment Handbook**

Power Presentation with Video CD-ROM

Power Presentations with Video are visual presentations of each chapter's main ideas. Presentations can be customized by including Quick Facts charts, images and maps from the textbook, and video clips.

Holt Online Learning

go.hrw.com
Teacher Resources
KEYWORD: SHL TEACHER

go.hrw.com
Student Resources
KEYWORD: SHL ENA

- Document-Based Questions
- Interactive Multimedia Activities

- Current Events
- Chapter-Based Internet Activities
- and more!

Holt Premier
Online Student Edition

Complete online support for interactivity, assessment, and reporting

- Interactive Maps and Notebook
- Homework Practice and Research Activities Online

Before You Teach

The Big Picture

Peter N. Stearns

Postwar Trends After World War II, in Europe and North America, a Cold War and an arms race led to dramatic social and economic change and, in the case of Western Europe, dramatic political innovation as well. The United States replaced Western Europe as the dominant global power, taking the lead in many of the conflicts that developed during and after the Cold War.

The Cold War Tensions between the United States and the Soviet Union emerged quickly after World War II. Soviet desire for a protective belt against Germany combined with the opportunity to force-feed communist states in Eastern Europe. The West responded with rapid rearmament and an anti-Soviet alliance system. Specific crises in Germany, Korea, Vietnam, Cuba, and elsewhere dotted the Cold War. Equally ominous was the steady buildup of nuclear weapons. Negotiations led to arms control measures from the 1960s onward. The Cold War finally ended with the collapse of the Soviet Union, amid severe economic pressure, between 1985 and 1991.

Social and Political Change Economic growth after World War II created many social changes. Consumerism advanced. Class differentiation receded. Racial tensions led to new civil rights movements, but new patterns of immigration created further divisions. The women's movement and dramatic new work patterns ushered in major changes in gender relations and family life. Some of these currents touched Eastern Europe, but economic and social developments there lagged despite rapid economic recovery from World War II. Democracy spread widely, first in Western Europe and then after 1989 in most of Eastern Europe. The most dramatic international relations initiative in the region was Europe's Common Market, now the European Union. This reduced centuries-old national tensions, spreading after 2000 to much of East-Central Europe. The end of the Cold War was disrupted by new conflicts, particularly with terrorist movements, and growing United States involvement in the Middle East.

Recent Scholarship

In *Europe Recast: A History of the European Union* (2004), Desmond Dinan offers a balanced study of one of the most striking developments in contemporary world history. Dinan discusses the factors that led to this dramatic innovation and probes the tensions and issues that have plagued the experiment since its founding. The gains and strains of recurrent expansion are given careful attention. Overall, the book makes it clear how much Europe has changed, while allowing discussion of continuing issues and constraints. Europe has both declined as a world player and has addressed some key problems with imaginative vigor. This study encourages discussion about what the future holds, as new power centers arise in other parts of the world.

Differentiating Instruction

 Differentiated Instruction Teacher Management System
- Pacing Guide
- Lesson Plans for Differentiated Instruction

 Interactive Reader and Study Guide

Spanish Chapter Summaries Audio CD Program

Student Edition on Audio CD Program

 Differentiated Instruction Modified Worksheets and Tests CD-ROM
- Vocabulary Flash Cards
- Modified Vocabulary Builder Activities
- Modified Chapter Review Activity
- Modified Chapter Test

OSP One-Stop Planner CD-ROM
- ExamView Test Generator (English/Spanish)
- PuzzlePro
- Quiz Show for ExamView
- Transparencies and Videos

TE Differentiated Activities in the Teacher's Edition
- The Bay of Pigs, p. 884
- The European Union, p. 890
- Conflicts in Yugoslavia's Republics, p. 896
- Creating a Political Cartoon, p. 902

Reading Like a Historian
Sam Wineburg

On October 4, 1957, the USSR successfully launched an R-7 intercontinental ballistic missile that carried a 58-centimeter steel globe dubbed "Sputnik." This metal ball, weighing 184 pounds, orbited the earth and punctured American pride.

The Space Race As our chapter describes, American reaction was swift, bordering on panic. A new government agency, the National Aeronautics and Space Administration (NASA) was hastily formed, signaling a major new commitment in government support for research and development in science. Americans read commentaries like those in the Chicago Daily News, which warned that if the Russians could hurl a metal ball around the earth it wouldn't be long before a larger object, carrying a nuclear payload, had our address on it. Private citizens rushed to construct backyard bomb shelters and schools conducted air raid drills in which schoolchildren were taught to cover their eyes to protect them from the flash of a nuclear explosion.

Predictable reactions, we might say. But ask your students if they can imagine other reactions. Students may be able to come up with other ideas, but I doubt that they will chance on this one: Americans interpreted Sputnik as a crushing indictment of their schools.

The Birth of a Crisis The March 24, 1958 cover of Life Magazine declared that there was a "Crisis in Education." Life offered a damning comparison of the rigors of the Soviet system versus the Mickey Mouse, happy-go-lucky atmosphere of American schooling. The magazine profiled two students, Chicago's Stephen Lapekas and Moscow's Alexei Kutzhov. Stephen boasted that he was reading Robert Louis Stevenson's *Kidnapped*, while Alexei had already mastered English as a second language, the complete works of Shakespeare, and George Bernard Shaw.

Accompanying the main article was an essay by Sloan Wilson, author of *The Man in the Grey Flannel Suit,* itself a critique of American conformism. Wilson's piece, entitled "It's Time to Close our Carnival," pulled no punches: "The facts of the school crisis are out and in plain sight …A surprisingly small percentage of high school students is studying what used to be considered basic subjects…It is hard to deny that America's schools, which were supposed to reflect one of history's noblest dreams and to cultivate the nation's youthful minds, have degenerated into a system for coddling and entertaining the mediocre."

On the heals of this "crisis" Congress passed the one billion "National Defense Education Act" (NDEA) making education an issue of national security. Pouring money into math, science, and language instruction—recall the "New Math"—the NDEA represented a major shift in Federal education policy, which to that point had largely been an issue at the local and state level. At the initiative of President Eisenhower, the nation's top scientists, such as Glenn T. Seaborg, the 1951 Nobel laureate in chemistry and the discoverer of plutonium, occupied their time writing high school curriculum—this was after all an issue of national security. Overnight American schools went from being hunky-dory to being "in crisis."

Continuity and change is a major theme running throughout all of history. Much has changed since the Soviets launched Sputnik and the fallout landed on American schools. But the notion that the "schools are to blame," that they are "in crisis," perpetual crisis, remains a fixture in American rhetoric and culture—displaying a wondrous staying power that seemingly knows no time.

Chapter Main Ideas

Section 1 Once partners in war, the Soviet Union and the other former Allies found it much more difficult to cooperate in peace. The result was an era of conflict and confrontation called the Cold War.

Section 2 As the Cold War continued, the world's two superpowers—the Soviet Union and the United States—competed for power and influence around the world.

Section 3 The Cold War brought tremendous economic and social change to North America, Western Europe, and Eastern Europe and the Soviet Union.

Section 4 The Soviet Union collapsed in 1991 and the Cold War came to an end, bringing changes to Europe and leaving the United States as the world's only superpower.

🗽 New York Standards

Key Idea 3 Study of the major social, political, cultural, and religious developments in world history involves learning about the important roles and contributions of individuals and groups.

Key Idea 4 The skills of historical analysis include the ability to investigate differing and competing interpretations of the theories of history, hypothesize about why interpretations change over time, explain the importance of historical evidence, and understand the concepts of change and continuity over time.

Key to Differentiating Instruction

Below Level

Basic-level activities designed for all students encountering new material

At Level

Intermediate-level activities designed for average students

Above Level

Challenging activities designed for honors and gifted and talented students

Standard English Mastery

Activities designed to improve standard English usage

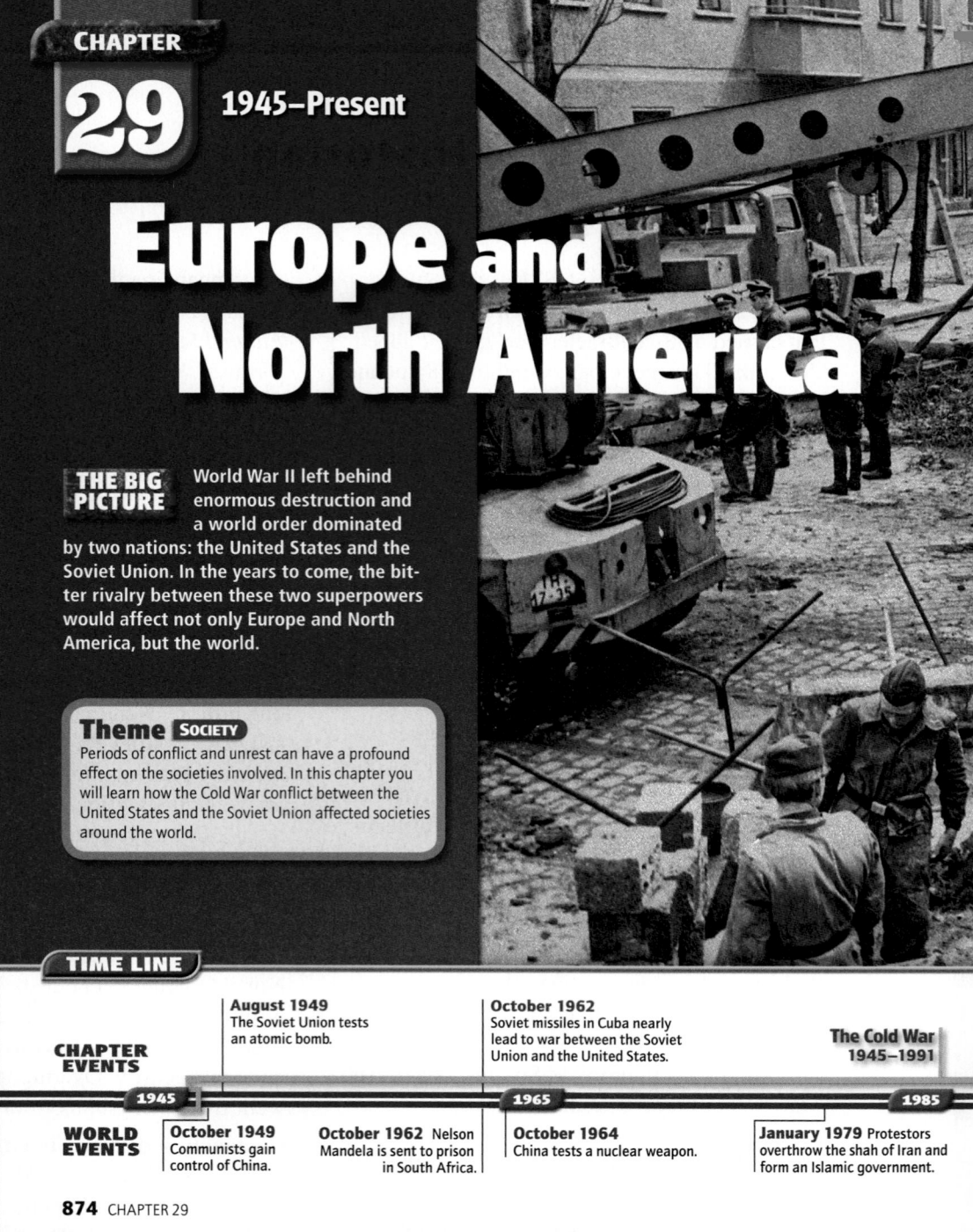

CHAPTER

29   1945–Present

Europe and North America

THE BIG PICTURE World War II left behind enormous destruction and a world order dominated by two nations: the United States and the Soviet Union. In the years to come, the bitter rivalry between these two superpowers would affect not only Europe and North America, but the world.

Theme SOCIETY
Periods of conflict and unrest can have a profound effect on the societies involved. In this chapter you will learn how the Cold War conflict between the United States and the Soviet Union affected societies around the world.

TIME LINE

CHAPTER EVENTS

August 1949 The Soviet Union tests an atomic bomb.

October 1962 Soviet missiles in Cuba nearly lead to war between the Soviet Union and the United States.

The Cold War 1945–1991

1945 — 1965 — 1985

WORLD EVENTS

October 1949 Communists gain control of China.

October 1962 Nelson Mandela is sent to prison in South Africa.

October 1964 China tests a nuclear weapon.

January 1979 Protestors overthrow the shah of Iran and form an Islamic government.

874 CHAPTER 29

Introduce the Chapter [At Level]

Europe and North America

1. Explain the following scenario to students: World War II, a long, devastating conflict that involved almost every country in the world, has ended. New conflicts over government, land, and control of people, have begun to emerge between two large, dominant countries. Have students answer the following questions: How would you reduce the conflict and solve the dispute between the nations? What steps would you take to prevent another war?

2. List student answers for the class to see. Review with students what they learned in the last chapter about World War II and the "Big Three," the United States, Great Britain, and the Soviet Union.

3. Tell students that in this chapter they will learn about a period of hostility and tension between the Soviet Union and the United States called the Cold War. **LS** **Verbal-Linguistic**

📝 **Alternative Assessment Handbook**, Rubric 11: Discussions

Elsenstr.

Reading
like a Historian

This 1963 photograph shows the Berlin Wall, which divided Communist East Berlin from democratic West Berlin. In the photo, East Berlin police rebuild a section of the wall that was damaged when an East German teenager rammed a truck through it and escaped to the West.

Analyzing Visuals What does this image suggest about the way some Communist leaders treated citizens?

See **Skills Handbook**, p. H26

November 1989
The Berlin Wall falls.

December 1991 The Soviet Union collapses.

March 2003 The U.S.-led invasion of Iraq begins.

November 1995 Israeli leader Yitzhak Rabin is assassinated.

1985

2005

EUROPE AND NORTH AMERICA **875**

Chapter Preview

HOLT
History's Impact
► Video Program:
Europe and North America
See the Video Teacher's Guide for strategies for using the video segment.

Reading Like a Historian

The Berlin Wall Approximately 2.5 million people from East Germany fled to the west between 1949 and 1961. Many of those who left were skilled and well educated. To prevent further loss of its skilled workforce, East Germany decided to erect a wall, and on the night of August 12-13, 1961, the first Berlin Wall, which was built with cinder blocks and barbed wire, went up.

Explore the Time Line

1. When did the Communists take control of China? *October 1949*

2. What events occurred in 1962? *Cuban Missile Crisis, Nelson Mandela imprisoned in South Africa*

3. How many years after the Soviet Union test of an atomic bomb did China test a nuclear bomb? *15 years*

4. How long did the Cold War last? *46 years*

Info to Know

The Wall Comes Down The following is an eyewitness account of the night the Berlin Wall was torn down in 1989: "…people cheered and clapped. East Germans drove through the applause, grinning, dazed, as thousands of flashbulbs went off. …streams of people were walking, talking together. Despite the brilliantly cold night, car windows were open and everyone talked to each other."

Make Inferences What do you think the fall of the Berlin Wall symbolized? *possible answer— hope, unity among Germans, freedom*

go.hrw.com
Online Resources

Chapter Resources:
KEYWORD: SHL ENA
Teacher Resources:
KEYWORD: SHL TEACHER

Answers

Reading Like a Historian *lack of trust, felt a wall was needed to keep citizens inside East Germany*

Geography Starting Points

NATO NATO was formed in April 1949 and had 12 members; by 2006, there were 26 member nations from North America and Europe. The goal and role of NATO is to protect the freedom and security of member nations through political and military means. Russia is not a member, but is considered a partner country, and in May 2002, a NATO-Russia Council was established, strengthening the partnership between NATO and Russia.

Primary Source

"It was, frankly, very gratifying to sit at this table with the members of this NATO alliance to remember its extraordinary past, which, ... managed to, through common values and resoluteness, face down imperial communism on this continent and to see the emergence of a Europe whole, free and at peace with itself."
—Remarks by Secretary of State Condoleezza Rice at NATO Headquarters, Brussels, February 9, 2005

📇 **Map Transparency:** Communist and NATO Countries, 1949

🗺 **World History Outline Maps**

✳ **Interactive Map:** Communist and NATO Countries, 1949

GEOGRAPHY Starting Points

Interactive
COMMUNIST AND NATO COUNTRIES, 1949

Communism and Soviet influence spread quickly across much of Asia and Eastern Europe after World War II.

The NATO alliance was formed in 1949 to counter Soviet power in Eastern Europe.

■ Communist countries
■ NATO countries

Starting Points While communism spread across Asia and Eastern Europe after World War II, the United States and other democratic nations worried about the possibility of another world war. As conflict between the two sides grew, a new era of competition for power and influence began.

1. **Identify** Which nations were members of NATO in 1949? Which countries were Communist?

2. **Predict** How might the increasing competition between NATO countries and Communist countries affect the world?

🔊 **Listen to History**

Go online to listen to an explanation of the starting points for this chapter.

go.hrw.com
Keyword: SHL ENA

876 CHAPTER 29

Skills Focus: Drawing Conclusions

At Level

Reading Skill
NATO Countries

1. Have students use the map on this page to locate the 12 founding members of NATO: Belgium, Canada, Denmark, France, Iceland, Italy, Luxembourg, Netherlands, Norway, Portugal, the United Kingdom, and the United States.

2. Have students write a list of reasons why they think Germany and Spain were not among the original members.

3. Have volunteers read their lists to the class.

4. Guide students in a class discussion about the founding of NATO. Do they think a military alliance such as NATO is an effective way to counter Communist powers? 🛅 **Verbal-Linguistic**

🗒 **Alternative Assessment Handbook**, Rubrics 11: Discussions; and 21: Map Reading

Answers

Geography Starting Points

1. *NATO—U.S., Canada, Iceland, Norway, U.K., Denmark, Netherlands, Belgium, Luxembourg, France, Portugal, Italy; Communist—N. Korea, China, Soviet Union, Poland, E. Germany, Czechoslovakia, Romania, Hungary, Yugoslavia, Bulgaria, Albania* **2.** *possible answer—increased tension, desire for power and control*

1 Beginnings of the Cold War

BEFORE YOU READ

MAIN IDEA

Once partners in war, the Soviet Union and the other former Allies found it much more difficult to cooperate in peace. The result was an era of conflict and confrontation called the Cold War.

READING FOCUS

1. How did peace create problems for the Allies?
2. How did the Cold War conflict worsen in the late 1940s?
3. What were some of the early Cold War confrontations?

KEY TERMS

Nuremberg trials
Cold War
iron curtain
Truman Doctrine
Marshall Plan
containment
Berlin airlift
NATO
Warsaw Pact

NEW YORK

PI 3.3 Students examine the social/cultural, political, economic, and religious norms and values of Western and other world cultures.

Joseph Stalin and Harry Truman pose for the camera at the Potsdam Conference.

TROUBLE AT POTSDAM

THE INSIDE STORY

How did a hot war turn cold? On the final day of the Potsdam Conference in 1945, U.S. president Harry S Truman was worried. He thought that Soviet leader Joseph Stalin had been stubborn and difficult to deal with and was concerned about Soviet plans for postwar Eastern Europe.

Truman made an appeal to Stalin on a minor issue, hoping that Stalin would demonstrate his goodwill and agree to compromise. Before Truman could even complete his request, Stalin interrupted him. "No!" shouted the Soviet leader.

It was an awkward moment, and Truman felt insulted by Stalin's manner. Little did he know that this difficult exchange was just a taste of what was to come in the increasingly tense U.S.-Soviet relationship. ◼

The Problems of Peace

In World War II the Allies had worked together to defeat the Axis armies. With the war over, the Allies had to decide what to do with the shattered nations of Europe. This task placed a great strain on the alliance.

Occupying Germany When the war in Europe ended in May 1945, much of Germany was in ruins and it had no functioning government. The victorious Allies needed to establish a system to govern Germany and rebuild the nation. The Allies had thought ahead to the end of the war and had begun to plan for Germany's future even before fighting ceased. At the Potsdam Conference, they agreed on several major issues.

EUROPE AND NORTH AMERICA **877**

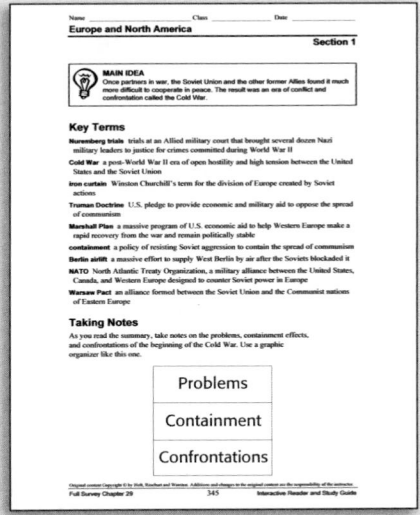

Teach the Main Idea

At Level

Beginnings of the Cold War

1. **Teach** Ask students the Reading Focus questions to teach this section.

2. **Apply** Have students work in mixed-ability pairs to make a list of the maps and other visuals in the chapter. Then have students scan the section and write a brief explanation about the significance of each visual and how it relates to the section title, Beginnings of the Cold War.

3. **Review** Have volunteers share their explanations with the class. Then guide

students in a discussion about the significance of the iron curtain and the Korean War in the Cold War.

4. **Practice/Homework** Have students write a short essay explaining the reasons for the Cold War and whether or not they think it could have been prevented. **LS Visual-Spatial, Verbal-Linguistic**

📘 **Alternative Assessment Handbook**, Rubric 37: Writing Assignments

Direct Teach

Reading Focus

1 How did peace create problems for the Allies? *Allies disagreed on what to do with Eastern Europe and how governments of these countries should be organized.*

The Problems of Peace

Describe How did the Allies solve the issue of reparations with Germany? *They decided that Germany would pay with equipment in addition to currency.*

Summarize Why did the Soviet Union want more power over Eastern Europe? *Stalin wanted to make sure that the Soviet Union had friendly, Communist governments as neighbors.*

📦 **Map Transparency:** The Iron Curtain, 1949

Primary Source

"A shadow has fallen upon the scenes so lately lighted by the Allied victory. Nobody knows what Soviet Russia and its Communist international organization intends to do in the immediate future, or what are the limits, if any, to their expansive… tendencies… It is my duty to place before you certain facts about the present position of Europe. From Stettin in the Baltic to Trieste in the Adriatic an iron curtain has descended across the Continent."

—Winston Churchill, speech at Westminster College, March 5, 1946

✳️ **Interactive Map:** The Iron Curtain, 1949

THE IRON CURTAIN, 1949

Non-Communist
Communist
— Iron curtain
‑ ‑ Administrative zones

DIVIDED BERLIN, 1949

▲ In a famous speech, Winston Churchill described a Communist "iron curtain" descending on Europe.

GEOGRAPHY SKILLS — **INTERPRETING MAPS**

go.hrw.com
Interactive Map
Keyword: SHL ENA

1. **Location** What countries were on the eastern side of the iron curtain?
2. **Place** How were Germany and Berlin divided?

TAKING NOTES

Take notes on the problems, containment effects, and confrontations of the beginning of the Cold War.

| Problems |
| Containment |
| Confrontations |

ACADEMIC VOCABULARY

currency money

First, the Allies agreed to temporarily divide Germany into four zones of occupation. The Soviet Union would control about one-third of the country. The remaining two-thirds would be divided into three zones, to be controlled by the United States, France, and Great Britain.

Second, the Allies also divided the German capital, Berlin. Though this city lay deep within the Soviet-controlled region of Germany, it was divided into four zones of occupation.

Third, the Allies worked together to establish a plan to rid Germany of any remnants of the Nazi Party and Nazi beliefs, in part by bringing former Nazi and military leaders to justice for crimes committed during the war. At the **Nuremberg trials**, which were held in Nuremberg, Germany, between 1945 and 1949, Allied military courts tried more than two hundred Nazi and military officials. Several dozen were sentenced to death for their roles in the Holocaust and in other war crimes.

Finally, the Allies agreed on a plan for Germany to pay reparations for the destruction caused by the war. These reparations were in the form of German currency and German industrial equipment. The Soviet Union received the largest share, since that country had suffered the greatest destruction.

Eastern Europe While the Allies were able to agree on postwar Germany, deciding what to do with the rest of Europe proved more difficult. Even before the war ended, the major Allied powers were in conflict. American and British leaders argued with each other, and the Soviets often disagreed with both.

At the Potsdam Conference in the summer of 1945, the two sides argued over Eastern Europe, which bordered the Soviet Union and was occupied by Soviet forces. The Soviet Union had been invaded by Germany during both world wars, and Soviet leaders believed that they needed a buffer zone of friendly governments in Eastern Europe to guard against another such attack.

Soviet dictator Joseph Stalin promised to respect the rights of people in Eastern Europe to choose their own governments. American and British leaders, however, believed that Stalin planned to establish pro-Soviet Communist governments throughout Eastern Europe and beyond. Although the war in Europe had ended, growing tensions between the Allies were about to lead to another conflict.

READING CHECK **Identify Supporting Details** What problems did peace bring for the Allies?

878 CHAPTER 29

Skills Focus: Analyzing Maps

At Level

Prep Required

Social Studies Skill
Potsdam Conference

1. Display political maps of Europe before and after World War I, after World War II, and Europe as it is today.

2. Distribute blank outline maps of Europe. Have students show and compare the national boundaries of individual countries after the two wars. Point out that after World War II, Poland, Czechoslovakia, Hungary, Romania, Bulgaria, Albania, and East Germany came under Soviet control. Estonia, Latvia, and Lithuania became

part of the USSR. Yugoslavia also had a Communist government.

3. Have students compare the map of Europe after World War II with the map of the iron curtain on this page. Then have volunteers explain why the iron curtain appeared where it did. **LS** **Visual-Spatial**

📖 **Alternative Assessment Handbook**, Rubrics 20: Map Creation; and 21: Map Reading

---

Answers

Interpreting Maps 1. *Soviet Union, East Germany, Poland, Czechoslovakia, Romania, Hungary, Yugoslavia, Bulgaria, Albania, Greece* **2.** *Both were divided into east and west sections.*

Reading Check *how to treat defeated countries, disagreements on what to do with Eastern Europe*

The Conflict Worsens

The relationship between the Soviet Union and the Western nations continued to worsen after the war. Soon the United States and the Soviet Union entered an era of tension and hostility, which became known as the **Cold War**.

The Struggle Begins The Cold War was more than a military rivalry. It was a struggle for power and control between two nations with very different forms of government, economic systems, and ways of life. In short, the Cold War was a conflict between communism and capitalist democracy.

With the backing of Soviet troops, pro-Soviet Communist governments were soon established throughout Eastern Europe. Only Yugoslavia avoided Soviet domination, although that nation was also led by a Communist dictator. As communism spread throughout Eastern Europe, tension between the Soviet Union and the western democracies continued to grow. This tension was worsened by the Soviet failure to remove troops from northern Iran, which the Soviet Union had occupied during the war. In January 1946, President Truman warned his secretary of state, "Another war is in the making."

In February 1946 Stalin stated publicly that he believed war between the East and West was bound to happen in the future. The next month, former British leader Winston Churchill gave a speech in the United States. Churchill used the image of an **iron curtain** to describe the sharp division of Europe that was the result of Soviet actions. This division, he said, was a serious threat to peace.

HISTORY'S VOICES

❝Our difficulties and dangers will not be removed by closing our eyes to them. They will not be removed by mere waiting to see what happens; nor will they be removed by a policy of appeasement.❞

—Winston Churchill, speech, March 5, 1946

The West Resists The democratic nations of the West soon faced a test of their resolve to contain the Communist East. In early 1947 Soviet-backed Communists were threatening the governments of Greece and Turkey. President Truman used the opportunity to announce what became known as the Truman

---

PRIMARY SOURCES

The Marshall Plan

In a speech at Harvard University on June 15, 1947, U.S. secretary of state George C. Marshall outlined his plan to help rebuild the postwar European economy.

"The truth of the matter is that Europe's requirements for the next three or four years of foreign food and other essential products—principally from America—are so much greater than her present ability to pay that she must have substantial additional help or face economic, social, and political deterioration of a very grave character . . .

"It is logical that the United States should do whatever it is able to do to assist in the return of normal economic health in the world, without which there can be no political stability and no assured peace. Our policy is directed not against any country or doctrine but against hunger, poverty, desperation, and chaos."

Skills Focus — READING LIKE A HISTORIAN

1. **Summarize** Why does Marshall say that the United States needs to help Europe?
2. **Analyze Primary Sources** Is Marshall worried about the spread of communism? Explain your answer.

See **Skills Handbook**, p. H25

Doctrine. The **Truman Doctrine** was a pledge to provide economic and military aid to oppose the spread of communism. The United States was committed, Truman said, to helping free peoples resist takeover by "armed minorities or outside pressures." The U.S. Congress agreed to send hundreds of millions of dollars in aid to Greece and Turkey.

Similar war-related economic problems existed throughout much of Europe. Truman believed that if conditions grew worse, more Europeans might turn to communism. So in mid-1947, the U.S. government launched a massive program of economic aid. The **Marshall Plan**, named after U.S. secretary of state George Marshall, provided $13 billion for rebuilding Europe. The plan helped Western Europe make a rapid recovery from the war, and it also helped preserve political stability.

READING CHECK **Summarize** How did conflict between East and West worsen after World War II?

NEW YORK

**CC Unit 7-A5a;
7-A5b** Marshall Plan; Truman Doctrine

Reading Focus

2 How did the Cold War conflict worsen in the late 1940s? *establishment of Communist governments in Europe, Soviet Union did not remove troops from Iran, U.S. commitment to provide economic and military aid to countries threatened by spread of communism*

The Conflict Worsens

Explain Why did President Truman issue the Truman Doctrine? *to show of force against Communist aggression and to prevent spread of communism; to help countries struggling to fight communism*

Evaluate Do you think the Marshall Plan was a success in establishing peace in Europe? *possible answers— yes, made rebuilding possible, increased support for democracy; no, may have increased tensions between Eastern Europe and the West*

📄 **CRF:** Biography: George Marshall

Primary Source

"I believe that our help should be primarily through economic and financial aid which is essential to economic stability and orderly political processes."
—Harry S Truman, speech to joint session of Congress, March 12, 1947

Skills Focus: Analyzing Costs and Benefits

Above Level

Research Required

Social Studies Skill
The Marshall Plan

1. Have students conduct outside research using both print and Internet sources to learn more about the Marshall Plan, what it entailed, and its consequences in Europe and within the United States.

2. Have students write an economic and political analysis about the ways in which the Marshall Plan helped make the United States a superpower. Students should include charts

and graphs with economic data to support the arguments in their analyses.

3. Have volunteers present their research papers to the class. Then guide students in a discussion of the importance and effectiveness of the Marshall Plan.

LS **Logical-Mathematical, Verbal-Linguistic**

📄 **Alternative Assessment Handbook**, Rubrics 1: Acquiring Information; and 42: Writing to Inform

---

Answers

Primary Sources 1. *believed that if Europe didn't receive U.S. aid, it would face "economic, social, and political deterioration;"* **2.** *possible answers—no, because he says his policy isn't directed at "any country or doctrine;" yes, because he wanted to preserve political stability*

Reading Check *communism spread to most of Eastern Europe, the Soviet Union would not withdraw troops from Iran, the West resists with Truman Doctrine, aid to Turkey and Greece*

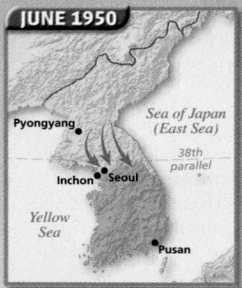

JUNE 1950

Pyongyang
Inchon• •Seoul
Sea of Japan (East Sea)
38th parallel
Yellow Sea
•Pusan

❶ In a surprise attack, North Korean troops invade the South.

SEPT. 1950

Pyongyang
Seoul
Inchon
Sea of Japan (East Sea)
38th parallel
Yellow Sea
•Pusan

❷ UN forces land at Inchon, attacking behind North Korean lines.

SEPT.–OCT. 1950

Pyongyang
•Seoul
Inchon
Sea of Japan (East Sea)
38th parallel
Yellow Sea
•Pusan

❸ UN forces quickly push north from Pusan and Inchon.

NOV. 1950–JAN. 1951

Pyongyang•
Seoul•
Inchon
Sea of Japan (East Sea)
38th parallel
Yellow Sea
•Pusan

❹ China enters the war on the side of North Korea.

☐ Controlled by North Korea
☐ Controlled by South Korea
◄━ North Korean forces
◄━ UN forces

0   150   300 Miles
0   150   300 Kilometers
Lambert conformal conic projection

GEOGRAPHY SKILLS INTERPRETING MAPS

go.hrw.com
Interactive Map
Keyword: SHL ENA

Territory changed hands frequently during the Korean War as troops moved over an area smaller than the state of California.

Movement Describe North Korean movements during the war.

Reading Focus

❸ What were some of the early Cold War confrontations? *Berlin blockade and Airlift, Korean War*

Cold War Confrontations

Explain Were the UN efforts in Korea effective? How can you tell? *possible answer—The UN did not achieve all its military goals, but neither did North Korean forces; the border remained where it was before the conflict.*

Make Predictions What might have happened if the Berlin airlift had been unsuccessful? *possible answer— Soviet Union would have taken control of Berlin; might have led to Soviet control of Germany, possibly war*

🗄 **Map Transparency:** The Korean War, 1950–1951

📑 **CRF:** History and Geography: Berlin Crisis Forges New Alliances

📑 **CRF:** Primary Source: The North Atlantic Treaty

✳ **Interactive Map:** The Korean War, 1950–1951

Recent Scholarship

John Lewis Gaddis provides a comprehensive history of the Cold War from beginnings to aftermath in *The Cold War: A New History*. While Gaddis provides a complete analysis of the beginnings of the Cold War, he focuses on the failed ideologies, class struggles, and economic woes that led to the downfall of the Soviet Union.

The Cold War: A New History by John Lewis Gaddis. Penguin Press, 2005.

FOCUS ON NEW YORK

The New York State Korean War Veterans Memorial in Albany honors the 482,000 New Yorkers who served in the armed forces during the Korean War.

NEW YORK

CC **Unit 7-A5; 7-A6** Political climate of the Cold War; Korean War

ACADEMIC VOCABULARY

import bring goods into a place

Cold War Confrontations

The Truman Doctrine and the Marshall Plan demonstrated the West's Cold War policy of **containment**, which involved resisting Soviet aggression in order to contain the spread of communism. The confrontations between East and West soon became increasingly severe.

Crisis in Berlin The division of Germany and of Berlin was originally meant to be temporary. In 1947, however, Western leaders began planning for the creation of an independent democratic German nation, to be formed from the three western zones of occupation. They also planned to establish a democratic government in West Berlin, deep inside the Soviet zone. The Soviets opposed this plan.

In June 1948, the Soviets blocked off all land, rail, and water routes into West Berlin. As a result, Berlin's 2 million residents were no longer able to import food, coal, and other vital supplies. The Soviets hoped these measures would force the West to leave Berlin.

Western leaders refused to give in. They organized the **Berlin airlift**, a massive effort to supply West Berlin by air. At one point, a cargo plane was taking off from or landing in Berlin

every 30 seconds. The Berlin airlift was a success, and the Soviets called off the blockade of Berlin in May 1949.

New Nations and Alliances Within days of the end of this crisis, the western zones of Germany formed the Federal Republic of Germany, or West Germany. A few months later, the Soviet zone became the German Democratic Republic, or East Germany.

Also in the aftermath of the airlift, the United States, Canada, and most Western European countries joined together in a military alliance. The alliance, called the North Atlantic Treaty Organization, or **NATO**, was designed to counter Soviet power in Europe. In 1955, the Soviet Union and the Communist nations of Eastern Europe formed their own alliance, known as the **Warsaw Pact**.

War in Korea After Japan's surrender in World War II, the Allies had gained control of the Korean Peninsula. The Soviet Union and the United States agreed to temporarily divide the country in half. The Soviets quickly established a Communist government in the northern half of Korea. In the South, the United States supported a non-Communist regime.

880 CHAPTER 29

Answers

Interpreting Maps *invades the south, June 1950; pushed back by UN forces, Sept.–Oct. 1950; China helps North Korea advance south again, November 1950– January 1951*

Skills Focus: Sequencing

Below Level

Reading Skill
The Korean War

1. Draw the chart for students to see. Omit the italicized answers.

2. Have students work in mixed-ability pairs to copy and complete the chart with the events that led up to UN involvement in the Korean War. **LS** **Visual-Spatial**

📑 **Alternative Assessment Handbook,** Rubric 13 Graphic Organizers

> Allies agree at Yalta that Korea should be free, but temporarily divided, following the war.
> ↓
> Japan surrenders.
> ↓
> *Soviet Union establishes Communist government in North Korea, United States promotes democratic system in South Korea.*
> ↓
> *North Korea builds up forces along the 38th parallel.*
> ↓
> *United States and Soviet Union withdraw troops from South and North Korea, respectively.*
> ↓
> *North Korea invades South Korea, captures Seoul*
> ↓
> Truman commits U.S. troops and asks the UN to approve use of force to stop North Korean invasion.

In June 1950 the North Koreans attacked South Korea. Their goal was to unite the country under a Communist government. Believing that a failure to defend South Korea might lead to other attempts at Communist expansion, the United States asked the United Nations to approve the use of force to stop the invasion. U.S. Army general Dwight Eisenhower warned, "We'll have a dozen Koreas soon if we don't take a firm stand." The United Nations soon formed a military force with troops from 17 nations and sent these soldiers to Korea. Most of the soldiers were Americans.

In spite of the UN involvement, the North Koreans nearly conquered the South within a matter of months. Then, UN forces led by American general Douglas MacArthur carried out a daring invasion at Inchon, behind enemy lines. The Inchon landing tipped the balance back in favor of the UN forces. Soon, they had pushed the North Koreans out of South Korea and driven deep into North Korea, near the Chinese border.

The war shifted once more when Communist Chinese forces poured into Korea to aid the North Koreans. With overwhelming numbers, they drove the UN forces back out of North Korea.

During 1951, the war settled into a stalemate. The battle lines lay just about where they had been before North Korea's initial invasion. In 1953 both sides agreed to an armistice.

CAUSES AND EFFECTS OF THE COLD WAR

CAUSES
- Disagreements between the Allies during World War II
- Differing U.S. and Soviet political and economic systems
- Differing goals for postwar Germany and Eastern Europe
- Soviet expansion of communism in Eastern Europe
- Resistance to Soviet aggression by United States

EFFECTS
- Political and military struggles around the world
- Increased military spending, leading to an arms race
- The ever-present danger of nuclear war

After three years of fighting and some 4 million casualties, the Korean War was over. But little had changed since the war began. North Korea remained a Communist state, and South Korea was an ally of the West.

THE IMPACT TODAY
The tension between North and South Korea is still a major regional and international problem.

 READING CHECK **Summarize** What were some Cold War confrontations of the 1940s and 1950s?

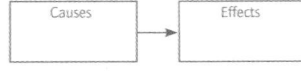

SECTION 1 ASSESSMENT

go.hrw.com
Online Quiz
Keyword: SHL ENA HP

Reviewing Ideas, Terms, and People

1. a. Describe What questions about postwar Europe did the Allies face?
b. Infer Why do you think the Allies decided to divide Germany into four zones of occupation?
c. Evaluate How did Soviet plans for Eastern Europe differ from those of the other Allies?

2. a. Identify Identify the following: **iron curtain**, **Truman Doctrine**, **Marshall Plan**
b. Make Inferences Why do you think President Truman believed that poverty and suffering created conditions in which communism might spread?

3. a. Recall What were two major conflicts between the East and the West in the late 1940s and early 1950s?
b. Evaluate Was the Korean War a success for the United States? Explain your answer.

Critical Thinking

4. Identify Supporting Details Using your notes on the section, identify the causes of the Cold War and its effects during these early years.

Causes	→	Effects

FOCUS ON WRITING

5. Exposition Write a paragraph that summarizes Soviet actions in Europe after World War II. Be sure to include details from the section.

EUROPE AND NORTH AMERICA **881**

881

Preteach

Getting Started

Use the **Interactive Reader and Study Guide** to familiarize students with the section content.

📝 **Interactive Reader and Study Guide,** Section 2

📝 **CRF:** Vocabulary Builder: Section 2

Taking Notes

Cuban Missile Crisis, arms race, Sputnik, Vietnam War, Berlin Wall, Bay of Pigs invasion, battle over the Suez Canal, battle over Angola, SALT I and II, ABM Treaty

go.hrw.com
Online Resources
KEYWORD: SHL ENA
ACTIVITY: The Cold War

---

2 Superpower Rivalries

BEFORE YOU READ

MAIN IDEA
As the Cold War continued, the world's two super-powers—the Soviet Union and the United States—competed for power and influence around the world.

READING FOCUS
1. How did the arms race begin in the 1950s and early 1960s?
2. How did the Cold War contribute to conflict around the world?
3. How did the superpowers attempt to achieve arms control during the Cold War?

KEY TERMS
hydrogen bomb
deterrence
arms race
Sputnik
Bay of Pigs invasion
Cuban missile crisis
nonaligned nations
détente

NEW YORK

PI 4.1 Students identify historical problems, pose analytical questions or hypotheses, research analytical questions or test hypotheses, formulate conclusions or generalizations.

PI 4.2 Students interpret and analyze documents and artifacts.

THE INSIDE STORY

Was nuclear war at hand? President John F. Kennedy was in his White House bedroom eating breakfast when he heard about a startling discovery—an American spy plane had photographed several Soviet nuclear missiles on a launching pad on the island of Cuba, just 90 miles from American territory. A missile fired from Cuba could potentially hit targets in the eastern United States within a few minutes. Was nuclear war at hand?

During the first frantic days after this discovery, U.S. officials tried to decide what actions to take. Should the United States invade Cuba? Bomb the missile sites? Attack the Soviet Union?

The Soviets claimed that the missiles were only intended to protect Cuba from an American attack, not to attack the United States. Still, President Kennedy demanded that the Soviets remove the missiles. He also considered military options—options he knew might trigger a nuclear war.

The tense standoff lasted for nearly two weeks. Finally, after much negotiation, the Soviets removed the missiles. In exchange, the United States agreed to remove U.S. missiles from Turkey and promised not to attack Cuba. Nuclear disaster had been avoided—at least for a while. ◼

A U.S. surveillance photograph shows eight missiles carried by a Soviet cargo ship. ▶

The Arms Race Begins

During the 1950s and early 1960s nuclear war seemed to draw ever closer as the Soviet Union and the United States raced to develop powerful new weapons. This rivalry between the world's two superpowers became increasingly tense—and dangerous.

The Nuclear Arms Race In 1949 the West was deeply shaken by news of a successful Soviet test of an atomic bomb. Suddenly, the great military advantage the United States had enjoyed over the Soviet Union was gone.

Immediately, the United States sought to develop even more powerful weapons. Atomic bombs used energy created by splitting apart atoms; but using nuclear fusion, or the fusing together of atoms, could produce a much larger explosion. Fusion is the process that creates the enormous energy of the sun and stars.

Crisis in CUBA

882

Teach the Main Idea

At Level

Superpower Rivalries

1. **Teach** Ask students the Reading Focus questions to teach this section.

2. **Apply** Organize students into groups of three. Assign one Reading Focus question to each student in the group and have students scan the section to answer the question. Have each member of the group teach the others in the group the answer to the question.

3. **Review** Make a class list of all the regions mentioned in the section and guide students in a discussion of their significance to the

Cold War and the rivalries between the superpowers.

4. **Practice/Homework** Have students identify one conflict involving the United States and the Soviet Union. Have students write letters to the editor describing the conflict and expressing their opinions about whether the conflict was justified or not.
LS Verbal-Linguistic

📝 **Alternative Assessment Handbook,** Rubric 17: Letters to Editors

In the fall of 1952 the United States tested the first fusion-powered **hydrogen bomb** with spectacular results, completely vaporizing the island on which the bomb was tested. As with the atomic bomb, the U.S. technological advantage was short-lived. Less than one year later the Soviets tested their own hydrogen bomb.

This development of nuclear weapons forced both sides to change their military tactics. Instead of relying upon conventional forces, such as troops and tanks, U.S. and Soviet leaders increased their stockpiles of nuclear weapons. These weapons soon became central to each side's defense strategy, a strategy based on the principle of deterrence. **Deterrence** is the development of or maintenance of military power to deter, or prevent, an attack.

The two superpowers were locked in an **arms race**, a struggle between nations to gain an advantage in weapons. The United States soon had far more nuclear weapons than the Soviet Union, and it was clear that a nuclear attack by either side would lead to terrible destruction.

TAKING NOTES

Take notes on the major events of the Cold War from the 1940s through the 1980s.

HISTORY CLOSE-UP

The Cuban Missile Crisis

During October 1962, the U.S.-Soviet confrontation over Soviet missiles in Cuba brought the world close to a nuclear war. This map—which is based on a map created for President John F. Kennedy by a U.S. intelligence agency—shows major U.S. cities within the 1,200-mile range of Soviet medium-range missiles fired from Cuba. Long-range missiles could hit targets as far as 4,000 miles away.

Skills FOCUS — INTERPRETING VISUALS

Explain How did U.S. officials react to the discovery of Soviet nuclear missiles on Cuba? Why did they view the missiles as such a threat?

October 14, 1962 A U.S. spy plane first photographs a missile on a launching site. Other sites are soon identified.

October 23, 1962 A Soviet nuclear warhead bunker is under construction at San Cristobal, Cuba.

October 25, 1962 The U.S. ambassador to the United Nations confronts the Soviet ambassador, displaying photos of the Soviet missiles.

EUROPE AND NORTH AMERICA **883**

Skills Focus: Comparing and Contrasting

At Level

Reading Skill
The Cuban Missile Crisis

1. Review with students the information about the Cuban Missile Crisis. Then have students create two political cartoons. One cartoon should show the Soviets removing their missiles from Cuba. The other cartoon should show Kennedy winning a fight against Khrushchev in the crisis.

2. Have volunteers share their cartoons with the class.

3. Guide students in a discussion of the cartoons and the role that the Cuban Missile Crisis may have played in the Strategic Arms Limitations Talks. **LS Visual-Spatial**

   Alternative Assessment Handbook, Rubric 27: Political Cartoons

Reading Focus

1. How did the arms race begin in the 1950s and early 1960s? *Soviets developed and tested atomic bomb; U.S. followed and countered with hydrogen bomb; both countries developed ICBMs*

The Arms Race Begins

Identify What did the United States test in 1952? *the first fusion-powered hydrogen bomb*

Make Judgments Do you agree with the U.S. response to the Soviet testing of an atomic bomb? Why or why not? *possible answer—No, it intensified already strained relations.*

History Close-up
The Cuban Missile Crisis

Kennedy's Reaction President Kennedy's reaction to the Cuban Missile crisis was not one of diplomatic negotiation. His plan was to isolate Cuba in order to prevent any more military shipments from the Soviet Union. His next move was to address the Soviets in a televised statement on the evening of October 22, 1962; a few days later the Soviets agreed to remove the missiles.

Map Transparency: The Cuban Missile Crisis

Primary Source

"I call upon Chairman Khrushchev to halt and eliminate this clandestine, reckless, and provocative threat to world peace and to stable relations between our two nations. I call upon him further to abandon this course of world domination and to join in an historic effort to end the perilous arms race and transform the history of man.
—John F. Kennedy, Address on the Cuban Crisis, October 22, 1962

Answers

History Close-Up *wanted immediate removal of the missiles; could have destroyed a number of U.S. cities*

❷ How did the Cold War contribute to conflict around the world? *Directly and indirectly, the United States and the Soviet Union entered into military battles in an effort to stop or assist in the spread of communism.*

Cold War Around the World

Explain What were the causes of the Vietnam War? *Vietnam had been partitioned into Communist-controlled North and anti-Communist South. When the North began fighting to unify the country, the United States intervened.*

Analyze Do you think the United States should have prevented Castro's forces from taking over Cuba's government? Explian your answer. *possible answer—yes, would have prevented installation of Communist government; no, was not clear that Castro would create a Communist dictatorship and Cuba's previous government was corrupt*

📋 **CRF:** Biography: Willy Brandt

Soviet Union Launches *Sputnik* In October 1957 the arms race took another leap forward with the Soviet Union's successful launch of *Sputnik*. *Sputnik* was history's first artificial satellite—an object that orbits the earth.

Americans had always believed they had a technological advantage over the Soviets. With the launch of *Sputnik*, Americans feared that Soviet military technology had leaped ahead of their own. In response, the U.S. government established the National Aeronautics and Space Administration, or NASA, in 1958. This agency would eventually return the United States to the forefront of space research.

Public Fears The growing threat of nuclear war had a significant impact on people in the United States and other nations. Many people built bomb shelters in hopes that these structures would help protect them from a nuclear explosion. American schools led air-raid drills to prepare students for a possible Soviet attack; and a number of movies, books, and comic books had plots centered on the dangers of radiation and nuclear war.

READING SKILLS
Making Inferences Why do you think that so many Americans feared Communists in the United States?

Most significantly, the Cold War led to a so-called Red Scare in the United States as many Americans feared possible Communist influence in the U.S. government. In the late 1940s and early 1950s Senator Joseph McCarthy and a congressional committee led the effort to expose Communists in the American film industry and government, accusing many innocent people of Communist activities.

READING CHECK **Identify Supporting Details** How did the arms race begin?

Cold War Around the World

THE IMPACT TODAY
The United States enforces a trade embargo against Cuba that was first enacted in 1962, after Fidel Castro's government confiscated hundreds of millions of dollars worth of U.S. property and businesses.

The Korean War had shown that Cold War rivalry could lead to conflict far from the United States or the Soviet Union. During the Cold War, this rivalry led to struggles for influence in countries around the world.

War in Southeast Asia At the end of World War II, France sought to reestablish its former colonial control over Southeast Asia. In one Southeast Asian country, Vietnam, Communist rebels fought back, forcing the French to give up control of Vietnam. In the resulting peace agreement, Vietnam was temporarily divided into

northern and southern halves. Communists controlled the North and an anti-Communist regime ruled the South.

American officials were concerned about the spread of communism in Vietnam. They had supported the French struggle against the Communists; and after Vietnam's division, they supported the non-Communist government of the South. When a revolution began in the South, the United States sent military aid to fight the rebels. Eventually, the North Vietnamese began to fight alongside the rebels in an effort to reunite Vietnam.

Although the American military commitment grew, the Vietnam War dragged on until the mid-1970s. You will read more about this war in the next chapter.

Another Crisis in Berlin After Communist East Germany and democratic West Germany formed in 1949, tens of thousands of East Germans left their country by crossing from East Berlin into West Berlin. Some wanted to live in a free, democratic nation, while others simply crossed the border in search of work. By 1961 as many as 1,000 people a day were making the daily trip between their homes in East Germany and jobs in West Berlin. To stop this exodus, East Germany began erecting a tall barrier between the two halves of the city. This barrier, known as the Berlin Wall, was heavily guarded. Anyone attempting to cross it risked being shot by East German guards.

The Berlin Wall succeeded in slowing the flight of East Germans to West Germany. It also came to symbolize the brutality of the Communist system.

Communism in Cuba In 1959 rebels under the leadership of Fidel Castro overthrew Cuba's dictator and installed a Communist government. Once in power, Castro established a centrally planned economy and forged close ties with the Soviet Union. Castro's actions worried the United States. Cuba is located only 90 miles south of Florida, and its alliance with the Soviet Union brought the Cold War alarmingly close to American territory.

The U.S. government, seeking to overthrow Castro, secretly trained an invasion force of approximately 1,500 Cubans who had fled Castro's regime. In April 1961 this force came ashore at Cuba's Bay of Pigs. American

Differentiating Instruction

Learners Having Difficulty

1. Write the following questions for students to see: What was the Bay of Pigs? Why did the administration support the invasion? What were some consequences of the failed invasion?

2. Have students work in mixed-ability pairs to copy and answer the questions. Then have students develop five questions that President Kennedy might have asked about the plans for the invasion. Have students exchange papers and answer each other's questions.

3. Have volunteers share their questions and answers.

4. Guide students in a discussion of the Bay of Pigs. **LS** **Verbal-Linguistic**

📋 **Alternative Assessment Handbook,** Rubrics 11: Discussions; and 12: Drawing Conclusions

Answers

Reading Skills *possible answer—Heightened tensions in U.S.-Soviet relations coupled with the threat of nuclear war caused many American to fear Communists in the United States.*

Reading Check *development of atomic and hydrogen bombs*

COLD WAR HOT SPOTS

EAST GERMANY
SOVIET UNION
UNITED STATES
ATLANTIC OCEAN
GREECE
TURKEY
LEBANON
IRAQ
AFGHANISTAN
KOREA
EGYPT
IRAN
CUBA
LAOS
VIETNAM
PACIFIC OCEAN
EL SALVADOR
CAMBODIA
MALAYSIA
NICARAGUA
CONGO
INDONESIA
PACIFIC OCEAN
ANGOLA
INDIAN OCEAN
CHILE

Robinson projection

0   1,500   3,000 Miles
0   1,500   3,000 Kilometers

Areas of conflict

Built by Communist East Germany, the Berlin Wall divides Berlin.

Refugees search for safety during the Angolan civil war.

U.S. troops fight Communist rebels in Vietnam.

officials had believed the **Bay of Pigs invasion** would start a massive Cuban uprising against Castro. Instead, the invaders were quickly defeated.

In 1962 came the **Cuban missile crisis**, a confrontation between the United States and the Soviet Union over the installation of Soviet nuclear missiles in Cuba. After a two-week standoff, Soviet leaders removed the missiles when the United States agreed to remove U.S. missiles from Turkey and promised not to attack Cuba.

Other Cold War Conflicts The Cold War rivalry also played out in the Middle East, Africa, and Central and South America.

In 1956 Egypt angered the West by taking over the Suez Canal, which had been controlled primarily by Great Britain and France. After Britain, France, and Israel attacked Egypt, the Soviet Union threatened to fight on Egypt's side. Afraid of a larger war, the United States quickly demanded that its Western allies halt their attack; and the conflict came to an end.

GEOGRAPHY SKILLS **INTERPRETING MAPS**

1. **Regions** Where did Cold War conflicts take place?
2. **Location** Why do you think there were no conflicts in the United States or the Soviet Union?

In Africa, the final years of European colonial rule created numerous power struggles, as well as much involvement by the superpowers. In 1960, for example, Belgium ended its colonial control of the Congo (now the Democratic Republic of the Congo). After the Belgians left the Congo, military leader Joseph Mobutu gradually took control. The United States and other Western countries supported his dictatorship because they believed he would be a good ally against the Soviet Union.

The African country of Angola won independence from Portugal in 1975, but years of civil war followed. The United States and the Soviet Union supported opposing sides in this conflict, which lasted until 1991.

NEW YORK

CC Unit 7-A5h
Surrogate superpower rivalries

EUROPE AND NORTH AMERICA **885**

Cold War Around the World

Identify Cause and Effect What caused Chile's military to overthrow Allende and what was the result? *The United States had secretly supported opposition to Allende; the Communist regime was ousted.*

Make Inferences Why do you think non-aligned countries refused to take sides? *possible answer—They wanted to avoid conflict and keep peace in their own countries.*

Reading Focus

❸ How did the superpowers attempt to achieve arms control during the Cold War? *United States tried open skies treaty, signed Test Ban Treaty, SALT I, ABM Treaty, SALT II, Intermediate-Range Nuclear Forces Treaty*

Attempts at Arms Control

Identify What was the ABM Treaty? *Anti-Ballistic-Missile Treaty; prevented development of weapon that would shoot down nuclear missiles*

Contrast What were the differences between SALT I and SALT II? *SALT I led to signed ABM Treaty; SALT II produced treaty that was never ratified.*

Reading like a Historian

A Soviet Military Parade

Analyzing Visuals The Cold War strategy of deterrence relied upon the threat of nuclear war. As a result, the enemy's perception of a nation's military power could be nearly as important as the military power itself. In this 1986 photograph, a Soviet military parade travels through Moscow's Red Square in celebration of the anniversary of the 1917 Bolshevik Revolution.

To interpret what this photograph suggests about the use of military force in the Cold War, think about

- the subject of the photo
- the details of the photo
- the reasons why this parade might have been held

This banner shows Vladimir Lenin, the leader of the Bolshevik Revolution, and the socialists Friedrich Engels and Karl Marx.

Thousands of Soviet citizens watch the parade.

These Soviet military vehicles are SCUD nuclear missile launchers.

Skills FOCUS READING LIKE A HISTORIAN

1. **Subject** Why do you think banners showing Soviet slogans and figures were displayed?
2. **Details** Why might there be so many people watching the parade?
3. **Reasons** Why might this parade of military equipment have taken place?

See **Skills Handbook**, p. H26

Superpower rivalries also affected Central and South America, where the United States supported efforts to overthrow regimes allied with the Soviet Union. In the early 1970s the United States secretly supported opposition to Chile's democratically elected leader, Salvador Allende, a socialist. As a result, Chile's military overthrew Allende in 1973. In 1983 U.S. forces ousted a Communist regime that had seized power on the island of Grenada.

Many countries sought to avoid being caught up in this worldwide rivalry between superpowers. Starting in the 1950s a number of nations refused to support either side. Instead, these so-called **nonaligned nations** sought to use their combined strength to promote the interests of poorer countries.

READING CHECK Find the Main Idea How did the Cold War play out around the world?

Skills Focus: Drawing Conclusions

Below Level

Standard English Mastery

Reading Skill
Arms Control Treaties

1. Review with students the information in the text about SALT I and II. Have students work in mixed-ability pairs to write brief summaries of the information in the text about the talks.

2. Guide students in a discussion of the importance, effectiveness, and limitations of treaties that prevent or limit development of weapons and missiles. Have students take notes during the discussion.

3. Have students use the information in their written summaries and class discussion notes to write a paragraph supporting or opposing arms control treaties. Have students work in pairs to review their first-draft paragraphs. Have students incorporate corrections into their final drafts. **LS Verbal-Linguistic**

Alternative Assessment Handbook, Rubrics 11: Discussions; and 37: Writing Assignments

Answers

Reading Like a Historian 1. *possible answer—to show its enemies that it was strong and united;* **2.** *possible answers—They wanted to show pride in their country; they were curious about the actions of their leader.* **3.** *possible answer—It was a show of military force to both citizens and enemies.*

Reading Check *Communism was spreading to many other countries, and the United States became involved in an attempt to stop its spread around the world.*

Attempts at Arms Control

While relations between East and West were largely hostile throughout the Cold War, some attempts at cooperation were made. Both sides worked to limit the spread of nuclear weapons and avoid the threat of nuclear war.

Early Arms Control In 1955 President Eisenhower proposed a so-called open skies treaty with the Soviet Union. This agreement would allow each side to fly over the other's territory and gather accurate information about its weapons. With accurate information, Eisenhower argued, neither side would have to imagine the worst about their enemy. Soviet leaders rejected this idea but proposed arms control measures of their own, periodically suggesting total nuclear disarmament. The United States rejected the Soviet proposals.

Eisenhower was followed in office by President John F. Kennedy. Kennedy favored limiting nuclear weapons tests as a means of slowing the development of new and more deadly technologies. The Cuban missile crisis helped convince both sides that it was important to make some progress on arms control; and in 1963 the United States and the Soviet Union agreed on a Test Ban Treaty. This treaty outlawed nuclear testing in the atmosphere, in outer space, and underwater.

SALT I and II In 1968 Richard Nixon was elected U.S. president. He sought what he called **détente** (day-TAHNT), or reduced tension between the superpowers. One result of his efforts was the start of negotiations known as the Strategic Arms Limitations Talks, or SALT I. The talks led to agreements limiting the number of nuclear weapons held by each side. SALT I also led to the Anti-Ballistic Missile (ABM) Treaty, which prevented the development of weapons designed to shoot down nuclear missiles. The ABM Treaty was meant to ensure that each side remained vulnerable to the other's nuclear weapons. This vulnerability was an important element of the principle of deterrence, which many people felt had been a key factor in the prevention of nuclear war.

The two sides then began a new round of talks, called SALT II. These talks resulted in an arms control treaty in 1979, although it was never ratified by the U.S. Senate.

The 1980s Ronald Reagan was elected U.S. president in 1980. He took an aggressive position against the Soviet Union and spoke of developing a missile defense system, an idea that seemed to violate the spirit of the ABM Treaty. But President Reagan also began arms reduction talks with Soviet leader Mikhail Gorbachev. In 1988 the two countries ratified the Intermediate-Range Nuclear Forces (INF) Treaty, which called for the elimination of certain types of missiles. After many years of conflict, the relationship between the Soviet Union and the United States was finally beginning to improve.

> **READING CHECK** **Sequence** What were the major arms control agreements negotiated by the Soviet Union and the United States?

SECTION 2 ASSESSMENT

go.hrw.com
Online Quiz
Keyword: SHL ENA HP

Reviewing Ideas, Terms, and People

1. **a. Recall** What were some of the key technological developments affecting the Cold War in the 1950s?
   b. Explain How did an **arms race** develop between the Soviet Union and the United States?
   c. Evaluate Do you believe that **deterrence** was the best strategy to prevent nuclear war?

2. **a. Identify** What was the significance of the **Cuban missile crisis**?
   b. Explain Why did the Cold War spread around the world?
   c. Make Judgments Do you think the United States was justified in supporting the overthrow of Communist governments during the Cold War?

3. **a. Recall** What were some of the arms control agreements reached during the Cold War?
   b. Evaluate What do you think of the reasoning behind the Anti-Ballistic Missile Treaty?

Critical Thinking

4. **Evaluate** Using your notes on the section and a graphic organizer like the one below, identify the five most important events of the Cold War and rank them in their order of importance.

☐ → ☐ → ☐ → ☐ → ☐

FOCUS ON SPEAKING

5. **Exposition** Write a brief conversation that two U.S. officials might have had during the Cuban missile crisis. The topic of the conversation should be possible ways to resolve the crisis.

Section 2 Assessment Answers

1. **a.** hydrogen bombs, ICBMs, satellites
   b. Each side was trying to develop more advanced weaponry than the other.
   c. possible answers—Yes, it showed other nations that nuclear war was not an acceptable option; no, it provoked the enemy.

2. **a.** It showed the world that both the United States and the Soviet Union could decrease their nuclear weaponry, and ultimately led to a reduction of weaponry in the arms race.

   b. The U.S.-Soviet rivalry for control led to conflicts in other parts of the world.
   c. possible answer—No, ultimately these efforts were not successful in establishing democracies and respecting human rights.

3. **a.** Test Ban Treaty, SALT I agreements, ABM Treaty
   b. possible answer—did not stop the development or production of nuclear missiles; was an attempt to end the arms race

4. Answers should include five of the following: arms race, *Sputnik*, Cuban Missile Crisis, Vietnam War, Berlin Wall, Bay of Pigs invasion, battle over the Suez Canal, battle over Angola, SALT I and II, ABM Treaty

5. Conversations should demonstrate an understanding of the Cuban Missile Crisis and its ramifications.

888 CHAPTER 29

Getting Started

Use the **Interactive Reader and Study Guide** to familiarize students with the section content.

📝 **Interactive Reader and Study Guide,** Section 3

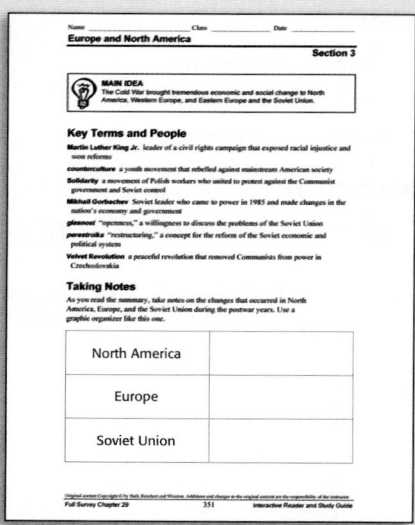

📝 **CRF:** Vocabulary Builder: Section 3

Taking Notes

North America—boom immediately followed war, social movements; Europe— economic unity, overall prosperity, many immigrants look for jobs, Common Market; Soviet Union—recovery, de-Stalinization, communism continues, anti-Communist revolts in Eastern Europe, Gorbachev implements glasnost and perestroika

go.hrw.com
Online Resources

KEYWORD: SHL ENA
ACTIVITY: Report on Europe and North America in the Postwar Years

---

SECTION 3 Changing Societies

BEFORE YOU READ

MAIN IDEA

The Cold War brought tremendous economic and social change to North America, Western Europe, and Eastern Europe and the Soviet Union.

READING FOCUS

1. What were the major social changes taking place in North America after World War II?

2. How did Western Europe recover economically in the postwar era?

3. How did Eastern Europe and the Soviet Union change after World War II?

KEY TERMS AND PEOPLE

Martin Luther King Jr.
counterculture
Solidarity
Mikhail Gorbachev
glasnost
perestroika
Velvet Revolution

 NEW YORK

PI 3.1 Students analyze the roles and contributions of individuals and groups to social, political, economic, cultural, and religious practices and activities.

PI 3.2 Students explain the dynamics of cultural change.

 THE INSIDE STORY

Were kids and cars everywhere in postwar America? It seemed that children were everywhere in 1950s America. Millions of American veterans started families when they returned home after World War II, and the number of babies born each year soared. At the same time the nation entered this so-called baby boom, it also entered an economic boom.

In the 1950s the American economy was red hot. Jobs were plentiful, wages were increasing, and Americans were eagerly spending their paychecks on cars, homes, and other consumer goods. Car manufacturers spurred demand with exciting new features, such as aircraft-inspired tailfins, and designs that changed each year. Meanwhile, American builders were putting up countless houses and suburban developments throughout the country. These new homes were filled with a variety of shiny new products: refrigerators, stoves, radios, television sets. While the 1950s was a time of peace and prosperity for many Americans, great social changes lay ahead. ■

THE POSTWAR BOOM

Enjoying their new car, an American family poses for a photograph. ▼

Teach the Main Idea

At Level

Changing Societies

1. **Teach** Ask students the Reading Focus questions to teach this section.

2. **Apply** Have students create an outline of the section using the heads as main points. Have students list at least two main ideas under each of the blue subheadings.

3. **Review** Review student outlines as a class. Have students identify the points in their outlines that they feel best reflect the section title, Changing Societies.

4. **Practice/Homework** Have students create a "Before and After" poster showing how society in Eastern Europe changed during the postwar era. **LS Verbal-Linguistic, Visual-Spatial**

📝 **Alternative Assessment Handbook,** Rubrics 28: Posters; and 42: Writing to Inform

North America

The postwar United States was a land of tremendous prosperity. At the same time, the country was undergoing rapid social change.

The U.S. Economy Overall, the U.S. economy—already the most powerful in the world—enjoyed great success in the years after World War II. By 1960 the total value of all U.S. goods and services was two-and-a-half times greater than it had been in 1940. Much of this economic growth was driven by consumer spending. After years of economic depression and war, Americans were ready to buy consumer goods.

By the early 1970s, however, rapid inflation and high unemployment had slowed the U.S. economy dramatically. At the same time, events in the Middle East disrupted the distribution of the world's oil supply. This disruption led to a steep spike in the cost of energy, which drove the prices of other goods higher. The nation's economic problems lasted into the early 1980s before unemployment dropped and the economy began another period of sustained growth. At the same time, however, the nation's debts grew sharply as the federal government increasingly spent more money than it received in taxes.

The postwar decades also brought major structural changes to the economy. The nation's heavy industry suffered during the 1970s and 1980s, as American shipbuilders, automakers, and steel companies found it more difficult to compete with companies in other countries. Many Americans lost their jobs when U.S. companies closed their factories. American companies in other industries still proved successful, creating many new jobs in advanced technology and in service industries such as banking, health care, and sales.

Social Changes During the 1950s, the booming U.S. economy helped raise the living standard of millions of Americans. So, too, did the so-called G.I. Bill of Rights, a law that helped millions of American veterans attend college—a choice that used to be available mainly to the wealthy. Also during this time, many World War II veterans married and started families. Birthrates rose, and the nation entered a so-called baby boom.

FACES OF HISTORY

Martin Luther KING Jr.
1929–1968

A Baptist minister and social activist, Martin Luther King Jr. was a leader of the African American civil rights movement. King was known for his powerful speaking ability as well as his reliance on nonviolence and civil disobedience in his protests against racial injustice.

King first came to national attention in 1955, when he led a boycott of the segregated bus system in Montgomery, Alabama. He and other leaders soon organized marches and protests throughout the United States, which eventually led to sweeping civil rights reform. King received the Nobel Peace Prize in 1964, but four years later, he was assassinated by an opponent of civil rights.

Summarize How did King work for civil rights for African Americans?

African Americans made major advances in the postwar era. During the war they had served bravely—but in units segregated from whites. Recognizing this injustice, in 1948 President Truman issued an executive order ending segregation in the armed forces.

The desegregation of the military was just the first in a series of victories for African Americans. In 1954 the U.S. Supreme Court ruled in *Brown* v. *Board of Education* that the segregation of public schools had to end. This decision was followed by a civil rights campaign led by **Martin Luther King Jr.**, James Farmer, Malcolm X, and many other activists and organizations. After years of struggle against racial injustice, the civil rights movement achieved some major reforms. In 1964 the U.S. Congress passed the Civil Rights Act, and the following year the Voting Rights Act. These laws knocked down longstanding barriers to equality for African Americans. The laws did not end racism, but they laid the groundwork for future progress.

The civil rights movement helped inspire a renewed women's rights movement in the 1960s and 1970s. The core belief of this movement was that women and men should be socially, politically, and economically equal. Some women also wanted to change traditional ideas about women's roles, including the idea that women would be happiest as wives, mothers, and homemakers. This effort met with opposition from others—including some women—who believed in the importance of maintaining traditional family roles.

TAKING NOTES

Take notes on the changes that occurred in North America, Europe, and the Soviet Union during the postwar years.

N. America	
Europe	
Soviet Union	

Skills Focus: Analyzing Primary Sources

At Level

Reading Like a Historian Skill
Martin Luther King, Jr. and Mohandas Gandhi

Research Required

Materials: construction paper, colored markers

1. Have students use reliable print and online sources to conduct research about the lives of Martin Luther King, Jr. and Mohandas Gandhi, focusing on the nonviolent protests they both organized. In their research, students should find three quotes from each leader about his quest for freedom and civil rights.

2. Have students create posters about their quotes. Students should choose one quote from each leader and create a visual to illustrate the chosen quotes.

3. Have students share their posters with the class and explain why they selected the quotes shown on the poster.

📋 **Alternative Assessment Handbook**, Rubrics 28: Posters; and 30: Research

---

Reading Focus

❶ What were the major social changes taking place in North America after World War II? *civil rights movement, feminism, counterculture movement, returning soldiers buying homes and attending college, baby boom*

North America

Recall What was the main driving factor for economic growth in the United States after the war? *consumer spending*

Analyze What were the long-term results of *Brown* v. *Board of Education*? *ended segregation in public schools, paved the way for broader civil rights reforms for minorities and for women*

📋 **CRF:** Biography: Rosa Parks
📋 **CRF:** Literature: *Invisible Man*

Biography

Betty Friedan (1921–2006) Betty Friedan graduated from Smith College in 1942, settled in New York, became a journalist, married, and continued to work as a freelance writer for a variety of magazines. In 1957, in response to a college questionnaire, Friedan discovered that many of her friends were unhappy with their traditional roles as housewives. She began to conduct extensive research, which she published in her book *The Feminine Mystique*. This bestseller challenged the established, restricted role of women as mothers and wives. In 1966 Friedan help found the National Organization for Women and throughout her life, she helped shape society's attitudes toward women and women's views of themselves.

Answers

Faces of History *powerful speaker, promoted nonviolence, protested racial injustice, organized marches to fight for civil rights reform*

North America

Identify Cause and Effect What caused the counterculture in the 1960s? *civil rights movement inspired many teenagers and young adults to rebel against social norms*

Explain How did Canadian military veterans receive help? *Government programs helped them attend college, establish businesses, and buy homes.*

CRF: Interdisciplinary Project: The Youth Market Emerges

② How did Western Europe recover economically in the postwar era? *slowly at first, but with the help of the Marshall Plan, most of Western Europe recovered better than before the war*

Western Europe

Recall Why were immigrants attracted to Europe following World War II? *availability of jobs*

Draw Conclusions Why do you think European farms produced more after the war than before? *possible answer—With help from the Marshall Plan, farmers bought more advanced machinery, and farms became more mechanized, leading to higher yields.*

Summarize What were the goals of the Common Market? *to eliminate trade barriers in Europe and create unified economic policies and a market that would rival the U.S*

Answers

Reading Skills *possible answer— Canada had similar economic and social issues as the United States, such as civil rights and women's movements.*

Reading Check *economic boom; veterans bought homes and consumer goods, went to college; the civil rights, feminist, and counterculture movements*

Women were not alone in questioning social norms. In the 1960s the **counterculture**—a rebellion of teenagers and young adults against mainstream American society—spread across the country. Many young people adopted unconventional values, clothing, and behavior, which shocked some mainstream Americans. Some young Americans questioned the government's actions in the Vietnam War.

READING SKILLS

Making Inferences Why do you think Canada underwent many of the same changes as the United States?

Changes in Canada Canada underwent many of the same economic and social changes. Government programs helped military veterans go to college, establish a business, or buy a home. The economy provided many jobs, and birthrates rose. Canada also had an active civil rights movement, women's movement, and counterculture. During the Vietnam War, Canada sheltered many American men who fled the military draft in the United States.

During the 1960s the province of Quebec experienced what was called the Quiet Revolution. This movement featured a growing nationalism among French-speaking residents of Quebec as well as a call for the separation of Quebec from the rest of Canada. It remains a significant force in Canadian politics today.

READING CHECK **Summarize** What postwar changes took place in North America?

Western Europe

Western Europe faced a challenging future after World War II. But, in spite of the devastation left by the war, the region made a remarkable recovery.

Postwar Recovery At the end of World War II, much of Western Europe lay in ruins. Vast amounts of property and farmland had been destroyed, national economies had collapsed, and millions of people had been displaced from their homes.

Western Europe seemed to be on the brink of chaos. Nevertheless, chaos did not come, thanks in large part to the Marshall Plan. With American aid, Western Europe's factories and farms were producing more by the early 1950s than they had before the war. West Germany grew into a major economic power, and growth was strong in most other countries.

Prosperity did not eliminate poverty, however. Certain countries enjoyed more success than others, and the region endured some difficult economic times. When the availability of jobs attracted many immigrants from European nations' former colonies, the influx of people from different cultures caused strain in some places as Europeans struggled to adapt to the newcomers. The overall story of postwar

▲ Allied troops move toward the Reichstag after Germany's surrender in May 1945.

Rebuilding Europe
Much of Europe lay in ruins after World War II, but the region was quickly rebuilt. In Berlin, the Reichstag—home to Germany's parliament—was reconstructed in the early 1960s.

Advanced Learners/Gifted and Talented

1. Have students read the information under the heading Alliances and Economic Unity about the European Economic Community and the European Free Trade Association. Then have students conduct outside research to learn more about these organizations, how they function, and what problems they encountered. In their research students should investigate how the European Union came into being, what its functions are, and how successful it has been in meeting its economic

and political goals. Students should support their findings with appropriate analytical data showing the growth of the European Union.

2. Have students prepare multimedia presentations of their research findings and present them to the class. **LS Visual-Spatial, Logical-Mathematical**

Alternative Assessment Handbook, Rubrics 22: Multimedia Presentations; and 30: Research

Western Europe, however, is one of remarkable success.

Alliances and Economic Unity World War II had changed Europe's place in the world. The continent was no longer the center of world power; instead, the United States and the Soviet Union were the centers of power. During the postwar years, European nations began to end longstanding rivalries with one another and work together for their common good. The formation of NATO in 1949 helped unify many European nations in a strong military alliance with the United States and Canada. Through NATO, countries that had warred for centuries now relied on each other for security. Despite ongoing tension with the Soviet Union and Eastern Europe, Western Europe remained at peace during the Cold War.

Many nations in Western Europe also moved toward economic unity. Early efforts led to cooperation in the coal and steel industries and in the development of atomic energy. Over time, Western European countries undertook broader efforts to develop a single regional market free of trade barriers and with unified economic policies. The goal was to create a single market that might rival that of the United States.

In 1957 six European nations founded the European Economic Community, also known as the Common Market. In 1960, seven other European countries formed the rival European Free Trade Association. True economic unity in Europe, however, was still years in the future.

READING CHECK Find the Main Idea
Describe the economic recovery in Western Europe after World War II.

Eastern Europe and the Soviet Union

The challenges facing the Soviet Union and the Eastern European nations under its control were even more overwhelming than those facing Western Europe. Like Western Europe, however, the region soon began to recover.

The Postwar Soviet Union Tens of millions of Soviet citizens had been killed in World War II, and the nation's cities, farms, and industries had suffered heavy damage. Soviet

dictator Joseph Stalin was determined to rebuild quickly. Remember that the Soviet Union had a centrally planned economy, or a command economy. In a command economy the government controls all economic decisions. Under strict government controls, the country was producing goods at prewar levels by 1953.

Nikita Khrushchev eventually became the leader of the Soviet Union and undertook an effort to "de-Stalinize" the Soviet Union, tearing down statues of Stalin and renaming streets and towns named after Stalin. Khrushchev also loosened some of the more drastic Stalin-era economic and political restrictions.

Despite these changes, Khrushchev and his successors remained committed Communists. They continued to limit the individual freedoms of Soviet citizens, and they maintained a generally hostile stance against the West.

Revolts in Eastern Europe The changes in the Soviet Union after Stalin's death led some in Eastern Europe to hope that the Soviets might end their domination of the region. Soviet leaders, however, made it clear that the reforms were limited. The Soviets used—or threatened—force to crush public protests in many countries and to assert their control. Soviet troops put down revolts in East Germany (1953), Poland (1956), Hungary (1956), and Czechoslovakia (1968).

EUROPE AND NORTH AMERICA **891**

CONTRASTING ECONOMIC SYSTEMS

COMMAND ECONOMIES (such as the Soviet Union)	MARKET ECONOMIES (such as the United States)
The government makes all economic decisions.	The government has minimal involvement in the economy.
The government decides what goods and products to make and how much to produce.	Market forces such as supply and demand determine the type and quantity of goods and products.
The government decides what wages to pay and what prices to charge for goods.	Wages and prices are set largely by market forces.
The government owns most property.	Private citizens and businesses own most property.

NEW YORK
CC Unit 7-C2
A comparison of market versus command economies

Eastern Europe and the Soviet Union

Recall How did glasnost affect the people of the Soviet Union? *was a beginning of free speech; people were able to discuss national problems*

Explain Why did Gorbachev want to reduce spending on weapons? *needed to reform the economy, spend more on consumer products*

Analyze Were the uprisings in Poland, Hungary, and Czechoslovakia successful? Explain your answer. *in the short-term, no; in the long-term, yes, because they paved the way for further protest and end of Soviet control*

Info to Know

Velvet Revolution The Velvet Revolution was a six-week long student demonstration that led to the end of the Czechoslovakian Communist regime without any violence. It began on November 17, 1989, exactly 50 years to the day after a famous student protest against the Nazi occupation. It was a peaceful transition that split the country in two, the Czech Republic and Slovakia.

Answers

Uprisings in Eastern Europe *led protests before waiting for Gorbachev's reforms were in place*

Faces of History *installed major reforms to Soviet's economic and political systems, fostered improved relations with the United States and the West, introduced glasnost and perestroika*

Uprisings in Eastern Europe

Revolutions swept across Eastern Europe in 1989 after Mikhail Gorbachev loosened Soviet controls on the region. *How did Eastern Europeans react to Gorbachev's reforms?*

POLAND
CZECHOSLOVAKIA
HUNGARY
ROMANIA

① Polish demonstrators march in support of the democratic Solidarity movement.

 NEW YORK

CC Unit 7-G4; 7-G5 Mikhail Gorbachev (perestroika and glasnost); Fall of the Berlin Wall

The Soviet crackdowns did not end the protests in Eastern Europe. For example, in 1980 Polish electrician Lech Walesa led hundreds of thousands of workers in an anti-government protest movement known as **Solidarity**. Poland's Communist government used martial law to suppress this anti-Communist movement but could not destroy it.

Glasnost and Perestroika The Soviet economy that had performed so well after the war began to falter in the 1960s. By the 1980s the Soviet Union faced a crisis. The command economy system had worked when the country was establishing its basic industries; but as these industries expanded, central plan-

ning proved inefficient. Government planners set production goals with little regard for the wants and needs of the marketplace. These goals stressed heavy industry, neglecting the goods that consumers needed. As a result, most sectors of the Soviet economy ceased to grow.

When **Mikhail Gorbachev** came to power in the Soviet Union in 1985, he saw the need for change. Gorbachev proposed two radical concepts: **glasnost** and **perestroika**. Glasnost means "openness," and it meant a willingness to discuss openly the Soviet Union's problems. Perestroika means "restructuring" and referred to the reform of the Soviet economic and political system.

HISTORY'S VOICES

❝*Perestroika* is an urgent necessity . . . This society is ripe for change. It has long been yearning for it. Any delay in beginning perestroika could [lead] to . . . serious social, economic and political crises.❞
—Mikhail Gorbachev, *Perestroika: New Thinking for Our Country and the World,* 1987

Gorbachev pushed through a number of major reforms. Hoping to reduce Soviet spending on weapons programs, he aggressively pursued arms control agreements with the United States. Gorbachev also reduced central planning of the Soviet economy and introduced some free-market mechanisms.

Knowing that the Soviet Union could no longer afford to prop up the Communist governments of Eastern Europe, Gorbachev began to pull Soviet troops out of the region, urging local leaders to adopt reforms. His actions reversed decades of Soviet policy in Eastern Europe.

FACES OF HISTORY

Mikhail GORBACHEV 1931–

Mikhail Gorbachev was the leader of the Soviet Union from 1985 to 1991. The son of Russian peasants, he joined the Soviet Communist Party in the 1950s and rose steadily through the party's ranks.

As Soviet leader, Gorbachev's primary goal was to rebuild the nation's stagnant economy. He called for major reforms of the Soviet economic and political system. Under his leadership the Soviet Union began to end its domination of Eastern Europe. Gorbachev also worked to build better relations with the United States and the West and is credited with helping bring an end to the Cold War. For his efforts to improve international relations, Gorbachev received the Nobel Peace Prize in 1990.

Summarize How did Gorbachev work to change the Soviet Union, and how did Soviet relations with the West change under his leadership?

Skills Focus: Comparing and Contrasting [At Level]

Reading Skill
Uprisings in Eastern Europe

1. Have students examine the images in the feature Uprising in Eastern Europe, and review the captions for each image.

2. Have students select one of the three locations and write a newspaper article about the uprising in their chosen location. Students should create first-hand observations of the scene portrayed in the image, provide a historical background, and context for their

articles. Articles should also include a map, based on the map in the feature.

3. Have volunteers share their newspaper articles with the class. **LS Verbal-Linguistic, Visual-Spatial**

📄 **Alternative Assessment Handbook,** Rubric 23: Newspapers

② The struggle for democracy turns violent in Romania, where tanks operated by pro-democracy troops fire on government supporters.

③ Thousands of Czechoslovakians protest against the nation's Communist regime.

Revolutions in Eastern Europe The citizens of Eastern Europe, longing for freedom, did not wait for reform. In 1989 revolution quickly spread across the region as citizens rose up and overthrew their Soviet-backed leaders. Gorbachev, no longer willing to keep Eastern Europe under control, did nothing to interfere.

In most cases, the revolutions were peaceful. In Czechoslovakia the **Velvet Revolution**—so called because it was peaceful—pushed the Communists out of power. In Poland the Solidarity movement forced free elections, and in 1990 Lech Walesa was elected president. Only in Romania, where some military forces remained loyal to the Communist dictator, was there significant bloodshed.

Perhaps the most dramatic changes took place in East Germany. The changes began when Hungary opened its border with Austria in August 1989. By the thousands, East Germans traveled to Hungary to cross this now-open border to the West. Powerless to stop the flood of its citizens streaming into West Germany, the East German government opened the gates of the Berlin Wall in November 1989. Overjoyed Berliners spontaneously began tearing down the wall. The strongest symbol of Soviet repression—and of the Cold War itself—had finally fallen. Less than one year later, East Germany and West Germany were reunified as a single nation.

READING CHECK **Summarize** What changes took place in the Soviet Union and Eastern Europe after World War II?

SECTION 3 ASSESSMENT

go.hrw.com
Online Quiz
Keyword: SHL ENA HP

Reviewing Ideas, Terms, and People

1. **a. Describe** How has the U.S. economy changed since World War II?
   b. Identify Cause and Effect What social changes did the United States experience in the postwar years?

2. **a. Describe** What were the major problems facing Western Europe after the war?
   b. Explain What was the significance of NATO and of the formation of organizations such as the European Economic Community?
   c. Elaborate How might economic unity have contributed to peace in Western Europe in the postwar years?

3. **a. Recall** What were glasnost and perestroika?
   b. Compare How did Stalin's death affect both the Soviet Union and Eastern Europe?
   c. Evaluate What effect did glasnost and perestroika have on Eastern Europe?

Critical Thinking

4. **Identify Supporting Details** Using your notes on the section and a graphic organizer like the one below, identify 10 important events that took place during the postwar years in North America, Western Europe, and Eastern Europe and the Soviet Union, and put the events in chronological order.

1945   1990

FOCUS ON SPEAKING

5. **Persuasion** Write an outline for a speech that Mikhail Gorbachev might have given to persuade the Soviet people to support his policies of glasnost and perestroika. Support your outline with details from the section.

Getting Started

Use the **Interactive Reader and Study Guide** to familiarize students with the section content.

📝 **Interactive Reader and Study Guide,** Section 4

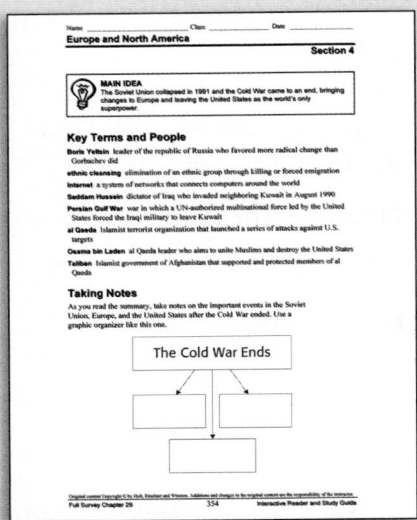

📝 **CRF:** Vocabulary Builder: Section 4

Taking Notes

development of the European Union in Europe, former Soviet Union is still trying to recover and transition from command economy to market economy and different government systems; United States had economic growth, low unemployment, but involved in new conflicts

BEFORE YOU READ

MAIN IDEA

The Soviet Union collapsed in 1991 and the Cold War came to an end, bringing changes to Europe and leaving the United States as the world's only superpower.

READING FOCUS

1. How did the Soviet Union break up?

2. What changes occurred in Europe after communism ended?

3. What challenges does the United States face today?

KEY TERMS AND PEOPLE

Boris Yeltsin
ethnic cleansing
Internet
Saddam Hussein
Persian Gulf War
al Qaeda
Osama bin Laden
Taliban

NEW YORK

PI 3.1 Students analyze the roles and contributions of individuals and groups to social, political, economic, cultural, and religious practices and activities.

PI 3.2 Students explain the dynamics of cultural change.

THE INSIDE STORY

How long can the desire for freedom be held down? The crackdown began one cold Friday in January 1991, as Soviet Red Army tanks rumbled into Vilnius, the capital of Lithuania. Lithuania was a Soviet republic that had declared independence the previous spring. Soviet leaders had rejected this claim of independence but had taken little action to punish Lithuania—until this moment.

The Soviets quickly seized government buildings in Vilnius. But as Soviet tanks pushed toward the Vilnius radio and television broadcasting facilities, a crowd of 1,000 Lithuanian protestors met them. The protestors aimed to stop the Soviets from taking over the broadcast stations. In a violent response the Soviets opened fire on the unarmed protestors, driving the tanks through the crowd. Fourteen Lithuanians died during the brief, one-sided attack, and dozens more were injured.

Even as they faced the Soviet assault, the protestors did not give up. Inside the radio station one last defiant message was sent over the airwaves before the Soviets broke into the building: "It is possible that [the army] can break us with force," the broadcast declared, "but no one will make us renounce freedom and independence." Indeed, although the Soviets soon gained control of Vilnius, tens of thousands of protestors gathered in the city's center to march for independence. Lithuanians had died in the Soviet crackdown, but the desire for freedom could not be put down. ■

894 CHAPTER 29

The Breakup of the Soviet Union

The 1989 fall of the Berlin Wall and the collapse of Soviet-backed regimes in Eastern Europe showed the dramatic crumbling of Soviet power. Soon the Soviet Union itself was falling apart.

The Soviet Union Collapses The Soviet Union consisted of 15 separate republics. Some, such as the Baltic republics of Lithuania, Latvia, and Estonia, which had been independent nations before World War II, had

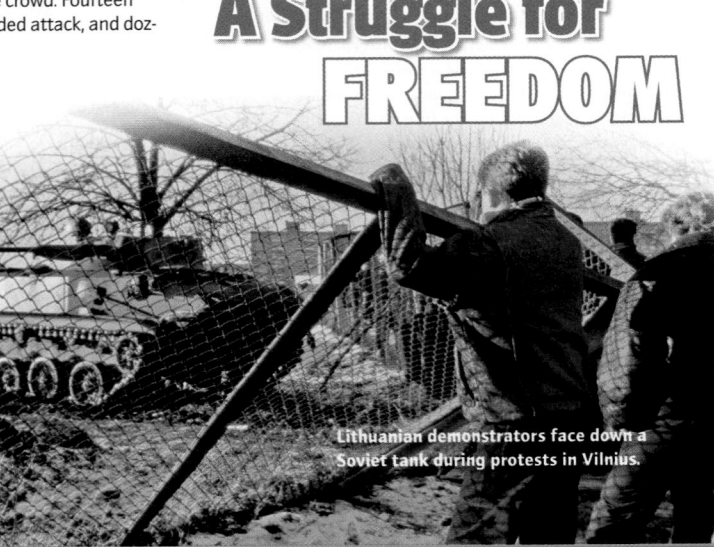

A Struggle for FREEDOM

Lithuanian demonstrators face down a Soviet tank during protests in Vilnius.

Teach the Main Idea

At Level

After the Cold War

1. **Teach** Ask students the Reading Focus questions to teach this section.

2. **Apply** Have students scan the section and make a time line of the events discussed. You might wish to have students work in small groups or mixed-ability pairs for this activity.

3. **Review** Review student time lines as a class, and create a class time line for all to see. Have students correct their work as needed as you fill in the class time line. Have students

identify the events on the class time line they believe contributed most to the end of the Soviet Union.

4. **Practice/Homework** Have students write a paragraph or one-page essay in which they answer this question: Is the world is safer now that the Cold War is over? Why or why not? **LS Verbal-Linguistic, Visual-Spatial**

📝 **Alternative Assessment Handbook,** Rubrics 36: Time Lines; and 43: Writing to Persuade long wanted their freedom. When Lithuania declared independence in 1990, it appeared that other republics planned to do the same. Soviet troops occupied Lithuania, but it was far from certain that the Soviet government had the will—or the power—to stop the independence movement.

In fact, the Soviet government was in crisis. In August 1991 hard-line Communist Party leaders sought to end Mikhail Gorbachev's reforms and preserve the Soviet Union by taking over the Soviet government in a coup d'état. The effort failed, largely because of the opposition of **Boris Yeltsin**, the leader of the republic of Russia. Yeltsin favored even more radical changes for the Soviet Union than Gorbachev had proposed and did not want to see hard-liners take over the Soviet Union.

Although the coup had failed, Gorbachev's power was largely gone. Republic after republic declared independence; and by the end of 1991, the Soviet government had ceased to function. Twelve of the republics eventually united in a loose confederation known as the Commonwealth of Independent States; but the mighty Soviet Union, once one of the two most powerful countries on the globe, no longer existed. After more than 40 years of tension and conflict, the Cold War was finally over.

Economic Change With the fall of the Soviet Union came the end of communism in the former Soviet republics. In Russia, the largest republic, Boris Yeltsin began a massive campaign to alter the economy's basic structure. His goal was to make the economy function more like a capitalist system.

Under the new market reforms, Yeltsin began to allow private ownership of businesses and land. Business owners and workers received more freedom to take advantage of economic opportunity. In return, however, they lost the guarantee of a government-backed job and other government supports.

Early results of Russia's reforms were mixed. A few entrepreneurs prospered, but most ordinary Russians did not. Meanwhile, prices rose sharply, and many Russians could not afford to buy goods in stores. Some began to question the benefits of market reform.

By the early 2000s Russia had rebounded somewhat from the economic crises that came with market reform. Still, the path from communism to capitalism was not an easy one.

Other Issues After the Soviet Union fell, underlying issues in the region bubbled to the top. Two of these issues were ethnic unrest and the need for new governments.

TAKING NOTES

Take notes on the important events in the Soviet Union, Europe, and the United States after the Cold War ended.

The Cold War Ends

NEW YORK

CC Unit 7-G7; 7-G8 Changing political boundaries; Challenges faced by post-communist Russia

THE BREAKUP OF THE SOVIET UNION, 1991

ARCTIC OCEAN

Arctic Circle

North Sea

PACIFIC OCEAN

Bering Sea

Barents Sea

RUSSIA (Kaliningrad)

LATVIA

ESTONIA

LITHUANIA

BELARUS

MOLDOVA

Moscow

UKRAINE

Black Sea

GEORGIA

ARMENIA

AZERBAIJAN

Caspian Sea

KAZAKHSTAN

RUSSIA

Sea of Okhotsk

Sea of Japan (East Sea)

UZBEKISTAN

TURKMENISTAN

KYRGYZSTAN

TAJIKISTAN

GEOGRAPHY SKILLS | **INTERPRETING MAPS**

1. **Place** What are the 15 republics that made up the Soviet Union? Which republic is the largest?

2. **Regions** How might the large number of Soviet republics have contributed to the breakup of the Soviet Union?

EUROPE AND NORTH AMERICA **895**

Direct Teach

Reading Focus

1 How did the Soviet Union break up? *Gorbachev's power reduced, republics within the Soviet Union declared independence, Soviets unable to quell the unrest*

The Breakup of the Soviet Union

Explain Why did the coup d'état in the Soviet Union fail? *Boris Yeltsin, leader of the Russian republic, opposed the coup.*

Analyze Why did Russia's first attempt at market reform result in an economic crisis? *people had never lived in a market economy, difficult adjustment for all*

CRF: Biography: Condoleezza Rice

Info to Know

Boris Yeltsin In 1985 Boris Yeltsin was chosen by Gorbachev to investigate and reform the Moscow Party organization, which was at the time very corrupt. In 1986 Yeltsin was made a nonvoting member of the Politburo, but he had to resign in 1988. In 1990 he quit the Communist Party, and in 1991 he became the first popularly elected leader in Russia's history.

Collaborative Learning

At Level

Impact of Soviet Union's Breakup

Research Required

1. Organize students into small groups.

2. Assign each group a country that emerged after the fall of the Soviet Union.

3. Have groups research their countries focusing on how the country gained independence, conflicts that may have developed, and the current status of the country today.

4. Have each group create a multimedia presentation, and present a culmination of its research to the class. **LS Verbal-Linguistic, Visual-Spatial**

Alternative Assessment Handbook, Rubrics 14: Group Activity; and 22: Multimedia Presentations

Answers

Interpreting Maps 1. *Lativa, Kaliningrad, Estonia, Lithuania, Belarus, Moldova, Ukraine, Georgia, Armenia, Azerbaijan, Turkmenistan, Uzbekistan, Kyrgyzstan, Tejikistan, Kazakhstan, Russia.* **2.** *possible answer—As each declared its independence, the republics united, limiting Soviet's power.*

Reading Focus

❷ What changes occured in Europe after communism ended? *conflict in Yugoslavia, unemployment, migration from east to west, European Union*

Europe after Communism

Identify In which of Yugoslavia's republics did the most violent conflict occur? *Bosnia and Herzegovina*

Summarize What happened in Yugoslavia after communism ended? *conflict between ethnic and religious groups, violence in Serbia and Bosnia and Herzegovina, bloodshed between ethnic Serbs and Muslims in Bosnia, fighting in Serbia, NATO peacekeepers help maintain order*

Activity **Compare** Review with students the information about genocide in the World War II chapter of the text, and have students compare the two situations.

Forensics in History
Identifying the Dead

Genocide Bosnia is a very diverse country with three main populations Serbs—make up about 37 percent, Muslims (Bosniaks) 48 percent, and Croatians 14 percent. Because of this diversity, conflicts between the ethnic groups occurred, resulting in the mass murder of thousandsof people.

Answers

Forensics in History *possible answer—to provide closure and solace to families*

Reading Check *Republics fought for freedom and independence, Communist Party leaders tried to overthrow the government and end Gorbachev's reforms, and republics gained independence.*

One example of ethnic unrest took place in Chechnya (CHECH-nya), an area in the Caucasus region of southwestern Russia. Unlike the republics that had broken away from the Soviet Union, Chechnya was considered part of Russia. When the Chechens tried to gain their independence from Russia, the dispute eventually led to bloody fighting and to an insurgency that still affects the region today. Another example of ethnic conflict occurred in a former Soviet republic in the early 1990s when the ethnic Armenian minority sought to break away from the country of Azerbaijan. Tens of thousands died in the fighting that followed.

NEW YORK

CC Unit 7-G6
Ethnic conflict in former satellite states, e.g., Kosovo, Bosnia

For some of the former republics, the transition from communism to a new government has been challenging. For example, Ukraine held an election in 2004. Among widespread charges of fraud, the election had to be repeated. Still controversial, the results of the elections left Ukraine deeply divided. Such transitions continue to trouble the region.

READING CHECK **Summarize** How and why did the Soviet Union break up?

Europe after Communism

The collapse of the iron curtain brought new opportunities and new challenges to Europe. The end of communism brought much economic change as well as new threats to peace.

Conflict in Yugoslavia In Eastern Europe, Communist governments had maintained strict control over their people. In Yugoslavia this control had helped suppress tensions between the many different ethnic and religious groups that lived in that country's six republics. But as communism slowly collapsed, those tensions began to come to the surface.

Feelings of nationalism in Yugoslavia's republics grew as ethnic and religious tensions increased. Some republics declared independence. Serbia—and ethnic Serbs living in other republics—tried to prevent the breakup of Yugoslavia, and conflict soon broke out in several republics.

The most violent of these wars took place in the republic of Bosnia and Herzegovina, which

FORENSICS in History

Identifying the Dead

Thousands of Bosnian Muslims were executed by Serb forces during the war in Bosnia, their bodies buried in mass graves. As a result, the human remains have become mixed together. Can such remains be identified?

What facts do we have? Scientists and human rights groups have created databases with data about the victims. One database collects information from close relatives of missing persons, including a description of the person's height, hair color, and other identifying features. This database also collects information about the clothing and personal items the person might have had on him or her at the time of death, such as eyeglasses, jewelry, or personal documents. This data is then compared to the corpses in the mass graves, while photographs of jewelry or clothing found on exhumed bodies are shown to relatives. One woman, for example, identified her husband by the socks found on his body.

▲ Scientists gather remains from a mass grave in Bosnia.

Another database is a DNA database. The International Commission for Missing Persons has collected DNA samples from the bodies and from the relatives of missing people. Scientists then compare these DNA samples in order to match family members. By 2006 nearly 10,500 bodies had been identified through DNA testing.

Draw Conclusions Why do you think it is important for people to identify the remains of their loved ones?

Differentiating Instruction

Below Level

Learners Having Difficulty

1. Have students read the Forensics in History feature and review the information in the text about the division of Yugoslavia and the conflicts that followed.

2. Have students work in mixed-ability pairs to develop a written summary and a sequencing chart of the information.

3. Have volunteers share their summaries and charts with the class. Have students review and correct their work as needed.

4. As an extension for more advanced learners, have students write an essay suggesting ways that the bloodshed in Bosnia could have been prevented. **LS Visual-Spatial, Verbal-Linguistic**

Alternative Assessment Handbook, Rubrics 7: Charts; and 37: Writing Assignments

THE EUROPEAN UNION, 2006

Legend: European Union (EU) members

ATLANTIC OCEAN

FINLAND, SWEDEN, ESTONIA, LATVIA, LITHUANIA, IRELAND, UNITED KINGDOM, DENMARK, NETHERLANDS, BELGIUM, GERMANY, POLAND, LUXEMBOURG, CZECH REP., SLOVAKIA, FRANCE, AUSTRIA, HUNGARY, SLOVENIA, PORTUGAL, SPAIN, ITALY, GREECE, MALTA, CYPRUS

North Sea, Baltic Sea, Black Sea, Mediterranean Sea

0   500   500 Miles
0   500   500 Kilometers
Azimuthal equal-area projection

GEOGRAPHY SKILLS INTERPRETING MAPS

Place How many nations made up the European Union in 2006? What countries are European Union members?

declared its independence from Yugoslavia in 1992. Many Bosnian Serbs wanted to remain part of Yugoslavia, and they began a war to prevent Bosnian independence. During this war, Serbs used a policy of ethnic cleansing against Bosnian Muslims. **Ethnic cleansing** is the elimination of an ethnic group from society through killing or forced emigration. After much bloodshed a U.S.-led diplomatic effort finally ended the violence in Bosnia in 1995.

Soon after, another conflict began in the region. This time, fighting was located in the Serbian province of Kosovo, where Serbs and ethnic Albanians fought over control of the area. In the spring of 1999, after peace negotiations had failed, NATO airplanes bombed Serbian targets in an attempt to stop the conflict. NATO peacekeepers eventually took up positions in the region to help maintain order, although Kosovo remains a Serbian province today.

Economic Change The end of communism brought mixed results for the economies of Eastern Europe. The introduction of market reforms created new opportunities for many people. Some started new businesses. The highly skilled got well-paying management or technical jobs in newly private enterprises.

Others in Eastern Europe have fared less well. Earnings have not risen for all workers, and many state-supported factories have closed, leading to high unemployment in some areas. These economic problems have led many Eastern Europeans to move to Western Europe, hoping to take advantage of opportunities there. This has led to strain in some parts of Western Europe, as newcomers compete with longtime residents for jobs and other resources.

The European Union Ongoing efforts to build an economic and political union among the nations of Europe resulted in the establishment of the European Union (EU) in 1992. In recent years a number of Eastern European nations and former Soviet republics have joined the EU, and others are scheduled to join in 2007. These steps have created a single economic unit that is large enough to compete with the United States. Many of the newer members, however, are far poorer than the older Western Europe members. As a result, some people in the wealthier nations worry that their own economies will suffer.

THE IMPACT TODAY

A proposed European Constitution would further unify the members of the EU. All member states need to ratify the treaty for it to take effect; by mid-2006, 15 of the 25 members had ratified it.

READING CHECK **Summarize** How has Europe changed since the end of communism?

Reading Focus

Europe after Communism

Explain How successful were the economic reforms in Eastern Europe? Explain your answer. *possible answers —very successful, created new opportunities; unsuccessful, led to high unemployment, wage discrepancies between those with high paying jobs and those in low-paying jobs*

Predict How might the European Union help ensure peace within Europe? *Nations depend on each other for economic development, which creates unity and a means for resolving conflicts.*

Map Transparency: The European Union, 2006

Info to Know

The European Union The European Union consists of 25 members and almost half a billion people, and its accomplishments are notable. For example, there have been no wars between member countries in the past 60 years. In order for a country to join the European Union it must apply and meet certain criteria. Countries must have a stable democratic government with a competitive market economy.

Skills Focus: Analyzing Visuals

Below Level

Reading Like a Historian Skill

Prep Required

The European Union

1. Before class, visit the Web site for the European Union and prepare a list of member nations and candidate countries. Distribute the list to students or create a class list for all students to see.

2. Have students use the map on this page to create their own maps of Europe showing the countries that belong to the European Union and those that do not.

3. Guide students in a discussion of the goals of the European Union and how effective it has been in achieving those goals and in unifying Europe. **LS Visual-Spatial**

Alternative Assessment Handbook, Rubrics 11: Discussions; and 20: Map Creation

Answers

Interpreting Maps *Refer to map.*
Reading Check *High unemployment has led many Eastern Europeans to move to Western Europe for jobs and opportunites.*

897

❸ What challenges does the United States face today? *The U.S. economy did well in the 1990s with the beginning of the information age, but conflicts continue in the Middle East, as does war on terror*

The United States Today

Recall What fueled the U.S. economy during the 1990s? *developments in computer technology, jobs in information technology, Internet-related companies*

Identify Cause and Effect What led to the Persian Gulf War and how did it end? *Iraq attacked and invaded Kuwait; UN forces moved in, liberated Kuwait, and pushed Iraq back into its own borders.*

 Quick Facts Transparency: Recent U.S. Military Involvement, 2001–Present

Explain and emphasize the differences among the Taliban, Afghanistan, Osama bin Laden, Iraq, and Saddam Hussein.

The United States Today

The end of the Cold War affected the economic, political, and military situation facing the United States. In the 1990s and 2000s the nation adjusted to this new reality.

The Economy For the United States the 1990s was a time of economic success. Economic growth was strong and unemployment was low. Even the budget deficits that had

RECENT U.S. MILITARY INVOLVEMENT, 2001–PRESENT
QUICK FACTS

Afghanistan, 2001–present
• Invasion to overthrow the Taliban government and fight al Qaeda

Iraq, 2003–present
• Invasion to overthrow Saddam Hussein and establish democratic government

Haiti, 2004
• Peacekeeping efforts after Haiti's leader was overthrown

South Asia, 2004–2005
• Humanitarian aid following a devastating tsunami

Pakistan, 2005–2006
• Relief and rebuilding efforts following a major earthquake

In Sri Lanka U.S. soldiers and aid workers deliver food supplies to the victims of a 2004 tsunami.

grown so alarmingly in the 1980s shrank and disappeared by the end of the decade.

Much of the success of the 1990s came from developments in computer technology. The growing availability of powerful, inexpensive computers helped businesses more efficiently store, manage, and use information. Computer software, equipment, and knowledge—known as information technology, or IT—improved rapidly, helping workers in many industries become more productive.

The 1990s also saw the emergence and rapid growth of the **Internet**, a system of networks that connects computers around the world. The development of Internet technology seemed to create tremendous opportunities for commerce. Entrepreneurs started hundreds of Internet-related companies known as dotcoms, after the ".com" that appears in many Internet addresses. Investors eagerly bought billions of dollars worth of stock in dot-coms, but many had gone out of business by the end of the decade, contributing to a slowdown of the U.S. economy.

Although the economy began to improve in the early 2000s, high energy costs, increased government spending, and a rising national debt remained areas of economic concern. At the same time, the gap between the incomes of the richest and poorest Americans continued to widen. The U.S. poverty rate also increased during the early 2000s, leading to a higher rate than in most other industrialized nations.

New Conflicts Even as the Cold War was coming to an end, the United States faced a new conflict in the Middle East. Iraq, led by dictator **Saddam Hussein**, attacked neighboring Kuwait in August 1990. The invasion troubled the United States in part because Iraq seemed to threaten the oil supplies produced by Kuwait and nearby Saudi Arabia.

After negotiations failed to convince Iraq to leave Kuwait, the United States led a multinational force into battle in the **Persian Gulf War**. The coalition troops quickly freed Kuwait, and Saddam agreed to obey firm new limits on his military forces and weapons.

U.S. forces also took part in peacekeeping missions around the globe, including the NATO operations in Kosovo. In the early 1990s, 43 American soldiers died in the African country of Somalia when the UN famine relief program

---

Skills Focus: Recognizing Bias in Primary Sources | **At Level**

Reading Like a Historian Skill
Current Events

Research Required

Materials: construction paper

1. Review the information in the Quick Facts chart with students. Have students select one event that they wish to know more about.

2. Have students find at least three newspaper, magazine, or Internet features on their chosen event. Have students read the articles carefully and write a summary of each. Have students post their summaries on a single sheet of construction paper. At the end of each

summary, have students write a few sentences describing the bias in each article that they found and reasons why they believe that the authors may have taken the position they did.

3. Have volunteers share and explain their posters. Create a class display of student work. **LS Verbal-Linguistic, Visual-Spatial**

📝 **Alternative Assessment Handbook**, Rubrics 16: Judging Information; and 30: Research they were assisting became involved in conflict. In 1994 U.S. forces helped restore Haiti's elected government after a coup.

U.S. leaders also continued to work toward a solution to the conflict between Israel and the Palestinians. There were some bright spots, including the 1993 Oslo Accords, in which the Palestine Liberation Organization (PLO) recognized Israel's right to exist and Israel recognized the PLO as the representative of the Palestinian people. Overall, however, the conflict continued to defy a peaceful resolution.

The War on Terror The 1990s also saw the beginning of a series of terrorist attacks on American targets within the United States and overseas, including bombings of the World Trade Center, in New York City, in 1993 and the U.S. embassies in Kenya and Tanzania in 1998. Over time, U.S. officials began to see that these and other attacks were planned and carried out by the Islamist terrorist organization **al Qaeda**, which was led by **Osama bin Laden**. Bin Laden saw the United States as an enemy of Islam and claimed that his goal of a worldwide Islamic revolution required the destruction of the United States.

Al Qaeda launched its deadliest attack on September 11, 2001. On that day, terrorists hijacked four passenger airplanes and crashed them into the World Trade Center and the Pentagon, outside Washington, D.C. One plane crashed in rural Pennsylvania. Nearly 3,000 people died in the attacks.

In what soon became known as the war on terror or the war on terrorism, U.S. officials responded quickly to the attacks, targeting al Qaeda and the Taliban. The **Taliban** was a group that was then governing Afghanistan according to a strict interpretation of Islamic law. The Taliban supported and protected members of al Qaeda. In the fall of 2001, a U.S.-led military campaign invaded Afghanistan and forced out the Taliban.

President George W. Bush then focused on Iraq. Saddam Hussein had used chemical weapons against Iran in the 1980s, and some U.S. officials claimed that he still possessed such weapons and that he supported anti-American terrorist organizations.

A U.S.-led invasion attacked Iraq in March 2003 and quickly toppled the Iraqi government. American weapons inspectors, however,

failed to find stockpiles of biological or chemical weapons or any evidence proving Saddam had a role in the September 11 attacks.

After the invasion U.S. and coalition forces occupied Iraq and began a massive rebuilding program. Iraqis elected a new government and approved a new constitution, but the nation faced ongoing violence as religious extremists and former Saddam loyalists attacked non-Iraqis as well as Iraqis who cooperated with foreign troops. As U.S. and Iraqi casualties increased, it became clear that rebuilding a stable Iraq would take years.

READING CHECK **Summarize** What threats does the United States face today?

SECTION 4 ASSESSMENT
go.hrw.com
Online Quiz
Keyword: SHL ENA HP

Reviewing Ideas, Terms, and People

1. **a. Recall** What events led to the breakup of the Soviet Union?
   b. Identify Cause and Effect How did the breakup of the Soviet Union affect Russia and the other former Soviet republics?
   c. Make Judgments Was the end of communism in the Soviet Union positive or negative for the former Soviet republics? Explain your answer.

2. **a. Recall** Which country experienced widespread ethnic conflict following the collapse of its Communist regime?
   b. Make Generalizations What effect did the fall of communism have on European economies?

3. **a. Identify** How have **al Qaeda** and **Osama bin Laden** affected U.S. policy in the post–Cold War era?
   b. Summarize How has the U.S. economy changed in the years following the end of the Cold War?
   c. Evaluate Do you think the United States has become safer and more secure since the end of the Cold War, or less so? Explain.

Critical Thinking

4. **Identify Supporting Details** Use your notes on the section and a graphic organizer like this one to describe the similarities and differences among the former Soviet Union, other parts of Europe, and the United States during the years after the Cold War.

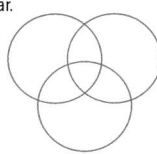

FOCUS ON SPEAKING

5. **Description** Write an outline for a three-minute story for a radio report describing life in Eastern Europe and the former Soviet Union after the collapse of the Soviet Union. Be sure to use details from the section in your news story.

Reading Focus

The United States Today

Identify What is al Qaeda? *an Islamic terrorist organization led by Osama bin Laden*

Explain What is the relationship among the Taliban, Afghanistan, and Osama bin Laden? *The Taliban ruled Afghanistan and supported and protected members of al Qaeda, including Osama bin Laden.*

Review & Assess

Close
Guide students in a discussion of the events around the world that followed the Cold War.

Review
Online Quiz, Section 4

Assess
SE Section 4 Assessment
Progress Assessment: Section 4 Quiz
Alternative Assessment Handbook

Reteach/Intervene
Interactive Reader and Study Guide, Section 4
Interactive Skills Tutor CD-ROM

Section 4 Assessment Answers

1. **a.** Communist leaders tried to overthrow the government; Gorbachev lost power, and republics gained independence.
   b. some prospered, others failed, bloody fighting in Chechnya, ethnic conflicts
   c. possible answers—positive: it allowed republics to become independent; negative: ethnic unrest still exists

2. **a.** Yugoslavia
   b. mixed results: market reforms created businesses, but low earnings, high unemployment, competitive job market

3. **a.** resulted in war on terror, U.S. military responses in Afghanistan and Iraq
   b. Internet, technology created economic success
   c. possible answer—safer, threat of large-scale attacks by Soviet Union gone

4. **a.** Charts should show the economic, political, and social similarities and differences in countries following the Cold War.

5. Outlines should demonstrate an understanding of the conditions in Eastern Europe following the Soviet Union collapse.

Answers

Reading Check *conflicts in the Middle East and the war on terror*

899

The Nuclear Age

Info to Know

Anti-Ballistic Missile Treaty In 2001 the United States withdrew themselves from the Anti-Ballistic Treaty with Russia. President George W. Bush declared that the ABM Treaty hindered the United States from properly defending the country from terrorism. President Bush also declared that the Cold War was "long gone" and that Russia and the world have no need to worry about the U.S. withdrawal from the treaty.

Nuclear Power There are just over 100 licensed, commercial nuclear reactors in the United States, which generate about 20 percent of the electricity produced in the country. About 400 commercial nuclear reactors exist in the world today.

Info to Know

Star Wars The Strategic Defense Initiative (SDI) was referred to as Star Wars. President Ronald Reagan believed that the nation needed to develop new ways to defend itself against nuclear weapons. In response to critics of SDI, the U.S. Department of Defense argued that in pursuing strategic defenses, the U.S. goal was not to eliminate or replace the policy of deterrence, but to enhance it.

HISTORY & Geography

The Nuclear Age

Today nuclear weapons and other nuclear materials are found around the world. Although nuclear materials can be used for peaceful purposes, the spread of nuclear weapons poses a serious threat to the world's safety. Mounted on long-range missiles, these weapons can travel thousands of miles in minutes and in the hands of terrorists or aggressive governments could cause widespread devastation.

As fears of nuclear war grew during the Cold War, so did international efforts to limit nuclear weapons. By 2006 nearly all the world's nations had signed an agreement pledging to prevent the further spread of nuclear weapons. Still, at least nine nations possess nuclear weapons today and others are believed to be secretly developing such weapons.

UNITED STATES
10,000

United States
Despite the end of the Cold War and the collapse of the Soviet Union, the United States still has more nuclear weapons than any other nation.

GLOBAL NUCLEAR WEAPONS, 1945–2005

Nuclear Weapons (in thousands): 10, 20, 30, 40, 50, 60, 70
Year: 1945, 1955, 1965, 1975, 1985, 1995, 2005

Sources: *Bulletin of the Atomic Scientists;* Global Security Newswire

TIME LINE

Nuclear Weapons

July 16, 1945 In New Mexico, the United States tests the world's first atomic bomb.

EXTRA
TRUMAN GETS EVIDENCE RUSSIANS HAVE A-BOMB
"Explosion Occurred in U.S.S.R. Within Recent Weeks," President Tells Cabinet—Stresses Need for Control

August 29, 1949 The Soviet Union tests its first atomic bomb, years earlier than most U.S. experts had predicted.

1972 Soviet leader Leonid Brezhnev and U.S. president Richard Nixon sign the Anti-Ballistic Missile Treaty.

900 CHAPTER 29

Skills Focus: Making Oral Presentations

At Level

Reading Like a Historian Skill
Strategic Defense Initiative

1. Remind students that President Ronald Reagan was known as the "Great Communicator" partly because of his clear, simple way of explaining policy. Remind students, too, that the Strategic Defense Initiative was not without its critics.

2. Have students prepare a persuasive speech that President Reagan could have delivered to the American people explaining why he believes that the United States must invest in the SDI. Students should include reasons why Reagan believes that the program will successfully defend the United States and ensure that the nation is not attacked by nuclear weapons.

3. Have students practice their speeches. Choose volunteers to deliver their speeches to the class. **LS** **Verbal-Linguistic, Auditory-Musical**

Alternative Assessment Handbook, Rubric 24: Oral Presentations

Map

200 Number of nuclear warheads
◈ Selected nuclear facility (production, research, or weapons-related material)
▢ Nuclear weapons nation

UNITED KINGDOM 200

FRANCE 350

RUSSIA 7,300

NORTH KOREA 6-8 ?

CHINA 400

ISRAEL 100-200

PAKISTAN 30-50

INDIA 40-90

Pakistan
In 2004, Pakistani engineer A.Q. Khan confessed to selling nuclear weapons technology to Libya, Iran, and North Korea.

Israel
The Israeli government has never officially confirmed Israel's possession of nuclear weapons, but most experts believe that Israel had become a nuclear power by the early 1970s.

NEW YORK STANDARDS

PI 4.1 Students identify historical problems, pose analytical questions or hypotheses, research analytical questions or test hypotheses, formulate conclusions or generalizations, raise new questions or issues for further investigation.

1983 U.S. president Ronald Reagan proposes the Strategic Defense Initiative (SDI), a missile defense system in space.

2006 North Korea continues to develop nuclear weapons at its Yongbyon nuclear facility.

GEOGRAPHY SKILLS | INTERPRETING MAPS

1. **Place** Which countries have nuclear weapons?
2. **Regions** Which areas of the world have the greatest number of nuclear facilities? Do all countries with nuclear facilities have nuclear weapons?

EUROPE AND NORTH AMERICA **901**

History and Geography

Info to Know
Nuclear Technology in Asia In 2006, the United States signed an agreement with India to allow the transfer of U.S. nuclear technology, for civilian and military purposes. India agreed to accept the conditions of the Non-Proliferation Treaty, and to continue its moratorium on the testing of nuclear weapons.
North Korea In early October 2006, North Korean officials announced that the country had successfully tested a nuclear weapon in the capital city of Pyongyang. The announcement received immediate condemnation from the United States, China, and other nations.

Primary Source
"The transfer of nuclear weapons... would be considered a grave threat to the United States. And we would hold North Korea fully accountable for the consequences of such action."
—President George W. Bush, October 10, 2006

Skills Focus: Drawing Conclusions   At Level

Reading Skill
Nuclear Power Debate

1. Organize students into small groups.

2. Have groups conduct research using reliable Internet sources to locate current information about the status of using nuclear energy for power, and nuclear materials in the world's nations.

3. Have groups take notes on their findings. Each group should come to a consensus about the benefits and potential negative impact of the use of nuclear energy.

4. When groups have had enough time to prepare their arguments, conduct a class debate about the pros and cons of nuclear power. **LS Verbal-Linguistic**

📝 **Alternative Assessment Handbook**, Rubrics 10: Debates; and 30: Research

Answers

Interpreting Maps 1. *United States, U.K., France, Israel, Russia, China, Pakistan, India, North Korea;* **2.** *Europe and Russia, no*

Document-Based Investigation

The Collapse of the Soviet Union

Word Help

accelerating faster

anew for an additional time

Info to Know

Russian Economy Between 1998 and 2005, the Russian economy grew on average 6.4 percent each year. Poverty continues to decline today, and the middle class continues to grow. Russia's foreign debt has also been decreasing in recent years.

Teaching Tip

Make sure that students understand what the phrase "Mayday" means." The term is the voice radio signal for ships and people in serious trouble at sea. It is officially recognized around the world. Mayday comes from the French term *m'aidez*, or "help me."

The Collapse of the Soviet Union

Historical Context The documents below provide information about the final years of the Soviet Union.

Task Study the selections and answer the questions that follow. After you have studied all the documents, you will be asked to write an essay about the collapse of the Soviet Union. You will need to use evidence from these selections and from the chapter to support the position you take in your essay.

DOCUMENT 1

A Cartoonist's View

The cartoon at right, created by the American artist Dick Adair, shows a crowd of angry Soviet citizens protesting conditions in their country. The men looking down at the crowd represent Soviet government officials and military leaders.

Mayday! Mayday! by Dick Adair, c. 1991

DOCUMENT 2

A U.S. Intelligence Report

The following document is an excerpt from a June 1991 Central Intelligence Agency report to the U.S. Congress.

> Six years after Mikhail Gorbachev launched the policies and reforms that have come to be known as *perestroyka*, the Soviet economy is in crisis. Output is declining at an accelerating rate, inflation threatens to rage out of control, interregional trade has broken down, and the center and the republics are engaged in a fierce political struggle over the future of the multinational state . . . Even if reform proceeds anew, tough economic times are in store for the Soviets.

DOCUMENT 3

The Soviet Premier's Complaint

At a government meeting in October 1990, the premier of the Soviet Union, Nikolai Ryzhkov, complained about the country's deteriorating situation.

> How long can we take this?! The government has turned into whipping boys! No one listens to us! You summon someone and they don't even show up! No one follows directions! The country is out of control! We're in the midst of a complete collapse! All the media are against us . . . We have to get back the support of [Soviet newspapers] . . . And get rid of, fire, half of those in television.

902 CHAPTER 29

Differentiating Instruction

At Level

English-Language Learners

1. Have students examine the political cartoon on this page. Then read Document 2 aloud, explaining what each sentence means.

2. Have students create their own political cartoon reflecting the same idea as shown in Document 1. Student cartoons should have a caption and carry a clear message.

3. Have volunteers share their cartoons with the class. Then guide students in a discussion of the problems facing the Soviet Union just before its collapse. **LS Visual-Spatial**

📝 **Alternative Assessment Handbook**, Rubric 27: Political Cartoons

DOCUMENT 4

Mikhail Gorbachev's Opinion

Former Soviet leader Mikhail Gorbachev wrote about the causes of the nation's collapse in his 2000 book, *On My Country and the World*.

Were there problems in the Soviet Union, including ethnic problems? Yes, there were political, economic, and social problems—and problems between nationalities . . .

[Under Stalin's rule the Soviet Union's] borders were carved out arbitrarily, the rights of one or another nationality were flagrantly violated, and during and immediately after World War II many nationalities were subjected to wholesale repression. They were deported from their ancient homelands and resettled in remote parts of the country. Tens of thousands of people perished in the process. Even under these conditions, however, closer ties and joint efforts among the various nationalities in the Soviet Union allowed all of them to accelerate their development sharply . . . The different nations and nationalities grew stronger, and each acquired an increasingly profound sense of its own identity.

In other words, contradictory processes were at work . . . Severe problems accumulated and were not resolved. Why did this happen? The official conception was that relations among the nationalities . . . were in sufficiently good shape, that in general there were no serious problems.

DOCUMENT 5

Ronald Reagan's View

During a January 1989 speech, U.S. president Ronald Reagan remembered a visit to the Soviet Union.

Once, during the heady days of the Moscow summit, Nancy [Reagan] and I decided to . . . visit the shops on Arbat Street—that's a little street just off Moscow's main shopping area. Even though our visit was a surprise, every Russian there immediately recognized us and called out our names and reached for our hands. We were just about swept away by the warmth. You could almost feel the possibilities in all that joy. But within seconds, [Soviet secret police] pushed their way toward us and began pushing and shoving the people in the crowd. It was an interesting moment. It reminded me that while the man on the street in the Soviet Union yearns for peace, the government is Communist. And those who run it are Communists, and that means we and they view such issues as freedom and human rights very differently.

We must keep up our guard, but we must also continue to work together to lessen and eliminate tension and mistrust. My view is that President Gorbachev is different from previous Soviet leaders. I think he knows some of the things wrong with his society and is trying to fix them. We wish him well.

Skills FOCUS: READING LIKE A HISTORIAN

DOCUMENT 1
a. Describe What are Soviet citizens complaining about?
b. Analyze According to the cartoonist, how are Soviet officials reacting to these problems?

DOCUMENT 2
a. Recall What does the report say about the Soviet Union?
b. Evaluate Would the authors of this document agree or disagree with Document 1?

DOCUMENT 3
a. Identify What is Ryzhkov complaining about?
b. Interpret Does he believe the government is responsible for the country's problems? Explain your answer.

DOCUMENT 4
a. Summarize What problems does Gorbachev say the Soviet Union had?

b. Interpret Does he blame Soviet officials for contributing to this problem?

DOCUMENT 5
a. Recall What does Reagan believe his experience showed about the nature of the Communist Soviet Union?
b. Interpret Do you think he was biased about the Soviet system? Why or why not?

DOCUMENT-BASED ESSAY QUESTION

What events or causes helped bring about the collapse of the Soviet Union? Using the documents above and information from the chapter, form a thesis that explains your position. Then write a short essay to support your position.

See **Skills Handbook**, pp. H25, H27, H33

Skills Focus: Analyzing Primary Sources

[**At Level**]

The Collapse of the Soviet Union

1. Have students review Documents 3 and 4 carefully, focusing on the tone and visual elements in each.

2. Have students choose one of the documents and then use the information in the documents to create a "live" television report of the incident reported.

3. If possible, have students record their report and present the videotape to the class, or have students present their "live" reports to the class.

4. When all reports have been delivered, guide students in a discussion of the causes that resulted in the collapse of the Soviet Union.
   LS **Kinesthetic, Verbal-Linguistic**

   Alternative Assessment Handbook, Rubric 24: Oral Presentations

Answers

Visual Summary

Review and Inquiry Have students list one detail from the text that explains or supports each date on the time line in the Visual Study Guide.

Quick Facts Transparency: Visual Study Guide: Europe and North America

Review Key Terms and People

1. Containment was a policy that involved resisting Soviet aggression to contain the spread of communism.

2. Perestroika was a reform of the Soviet economic and political system.

3. Saddam Hussein was an Iraqi dictator who began the Persian Gulf War after invading Kuwait.

4. The world's first successfully launched satellite was *Sputnik*, created by the Soviet.

5. The iron curtain refers to the division betwwn Communist Eastern Europe and democratic Western Europe.

6. Détente is the reduction of U.S.-Soviet tensions.

7. The development of the hydrogen bomb fueled the arms race.

8. The Marshall Plan provided $13 billion in U.S. aid to rebuild Europe.

9. Al Qaeda is an Islamic terrorist group, responsible for the September 11, 2001 terrorists attacks.

10. The effects of the Cold War included ongoing military struggles and increased military spending.

Comprehension and Critical Thinking

11. a. during the 1945 Potsdam Conference; conflict over the establishment of governments in Eastern Europe
b. The Soviet Union wanted control over Eastern Europe; Allies wanted them to establish their own governments.
c. possible answer—No, it increased East/West conflicts.

12. a. arms race, space race, Korean War, Cuba, Vietnam War
b. causes—Soviet missiles in Cuba, close to the U.S. mainland; effects—

VISUAL STUDY GUIDE

Causes and Effects of the Cold War

CAUSES

Systems of Government
- Soviet Union was a Communist dictatorship.
- United States is a democratic republic.

Postwar Conflict
- Both sides disagreed over Eastern Europe.
- Soviet Union established Communist governments throughout Eastern Europe.
- United States resisted Soviet expansion and aided countries seeking to resist communism.

Cold War

EFFECTS

Military
- Arms race between Soviet Union and United States led to the threat of nuclear war.
- Confrontations took place around the world, including Germany, Cuba, Korea, and many other locations.

Political
- Both sides formed a variety of alliances.
- Soviet Union eventually collapsed, and United States became the world's sole superpower.

Major Events in Europe and North America since 1945

1948	Berlin airlift begins
1949	NATO forms
1950	Korean War starts
1952	United States tests hydrogen bomb
1955	Warsaw Pact forms
1957	Soviets launch *Sputnik*
1961	Construction begins on Berlin Wall
1962	Cuban missile crisis takes place
1972	SALT I agreement is signed
1985	Mikhail Gorbachev comes to power
1988	Major arms control agreement is reached
1989	Iron curtain begins to crumble in Eastern Europe
1991	Soviet Union collapses
1992	European Union established
2001	Al Qaeda attacks the United States
2003	United States invades Iraq

Review Key Terms and People

For each term or name below, write a sentence explaining its significance to Europe or North America between 1945 and the present.

1. containment

2. perestroika

3. Saddam Hussein

4. *Sputnik*

5. iron curtain

6. détente

7. hydrogen bomb

8. Marshall Plan

9. al Qaeda

10. Cold War

904 CHAPTER 29

---

missiles removed, Soviet Union and U.S. remained enemies
c. possible answer—Soviet Union wanted to spread communism; U.S. opposed communism; these regions have significant natural resources and economic opportunities

13. a. postwar economic boom, unemployment dropped but national debt grew, civil rights and women's movement inspired fight for individual freedom, counterculture
b. to reform poor economy
c. possible answer—very effective until the late 1980s; when people could voice dissent, countries began declaring independence

14. a. collapse of Soviet-back regimes in Eastern Europe, fall of Berlin Wall
b. conflict in Middle East, terrorist attacks
c. possible answer—yes, because the Soviet economy was failing, consumers not provided for, economic structure had to change completely for improvements to occur

Comprehension and Critical Thinking

SECTION 1 *(pp. 877–881)*

11. a. Recall When and why did Cold War tensions begin to appear?

b. Contrast How did Allied plans for Eastern Europe differ?

c. Make Judgments Was the U.S. policy of containment effective at preventing the spread of communism? Why or why not?

SECTION 2 *(pp. 882–887)*

12. a. Describe How did the United States and Soviet Union compete during the Cold War?

b. Identify Cause and Effect What were the causes and effects of the Cuban missile crisis?

c. Elaborate Why do you think the United States and the Soviet Union cared about having influence in countries around the world?

SECTION 3 *(pp. 888–893)*

13. a. Identify How did cultural changes affect the United States in the years after World War II?

b. Identify Cause and Effect Why did Mikhail Gorbachev propose glasnost and perestroika?

c. Make Judgments How effective do you think the Soviet system was at controlling public dissent? Explain your answer.

SECTION 4 *(pp. 894–899)*

14. a. Describe What events brought about the breakup of the Soviet Union?

b. Summarize What threats has the United States faced since the end of the Cold War?

c. Evaluate Was the end of communism in Eastern Europe completely positive for those nations? Why or why not?

Reading Skills

Making Inferences *Use what you know about making inferences to answer the questions below.*

15. Given what you know about the Cold War, how do you think Americans reacted to the Soviet test of a hydrogen bomb in 1953?

16. How do you think Soviet citizens responded to Mikhail Gorbachev's policies of glasnost and perestroika?

Analyzing Primary Sources

Reading Like a Historian *This photograph shows demonstrators in the Soviet republic of Lithuania in 1991, protesting the Soviet military crackdown after Lithuania declared its independence.*

17. Describe How would you describe the people taking part in this protest?

18. Infer Why do you think the protest march was a peaceful march instead of a violent uprising?

Using the Internet

go.hrw.com
Practice Online
Keyword: SHL ENA

19. The Cold War and the fear of nuclear war had a profound effect on people in the United States, the Soviet Union, and around the world. Using the Internet, research the effects of Cold War anxieties on movies, books, and other aspects of popular culture. Then write an illustrated report about your findings.

WRITING ABOUT HISTORY

Persuasion: Writing an Evaluation *During the Cold War, each side developed weapons that were capable of completely destroying the enemy. Defense strategies centered on the idea that the threat of massive nuclear retaliation would deter the enemy from starting a conflict.*

20. Assignment: In an essay, evaluate the wisdom of a war strategy that involved the assured destruction of both sides. To provide support for your evaluation, use information from this chapter and from other research as needed.

Answers

Reading Skills

15. possible answer—people probably feared Soviet attacks

16. possible answer—probably embraced them because of frustration with the old system

Analyzing Primary Sources

17. possible answer—calm, but determined

18. possible answer—because people had faith that their government would address their concerns

Using the Internet

19. Go to the HRW Web site and enter the keyword shown to access a rubric for this activity.

KEYWORD: SHL ENA

Writing About History

20. Students should recognize the benefits and disadvantages of deterrents, and the power of the weapons developed during the Cold War. A rubric for this activity is provided in **CRF**: Writing for the SAT.

HOLT

History's Impact
▶ Video Program:
Europe and North America
Refer to the Video Program Teacher's Guide for the answer to the closing question.

Review and Assessment Resources

Review and Reinforce

 CRF: Chapter Review

Quick Facts Transparency: Visual Study Guide: Europe and North America

Spanish Chapter Summaries Audio CD Program

OSP **Holt PuzzlePro**: Quiz Show for ExamView

Quiz Game CD-ROM

Assess

PASS: Chapter Test, Forms A and B

Alternative Assessment Handbook

OSP **ExamView Test Generator**, Chapter Test

Differentiated Instruction Modified Worksheets and Tests CD-ROM: Chapter Test

HOAP **Holt Online Assessment Program** (in the Premier Online Edition)

Reteach/Intervene

 Interactive Reader and Study Guide

Differentiated Instruction Teacher Management System: Lesson Plans for Differentiated Instruction

Differentiated Instruction Modified Worksheets and Tests CD-ROM: Chapter Test

Interactive Skills Tutor CD-ROM

go.hrw.com
Online Resources

KEYWORD: SHL TEACHER

Chapter 30 Planning Guide

Asia

Chapter Overview	Reproducible Resources	Technology Resources
CHAPTER 30 pp. 906–933 **Overview: In this chapter, students will learn about the challenges and economic growth in India, Southeast Asia, China and the Pacific Rim following World War II.** KI 1, 3; PI 1.3, 1.4, 3.1, 3.2, 3.3 See pp. T32–T55 for a detailed correlation to the New York State Core Curriculum for Global History and Geography and the New York Learning Standards.	**Differentiated Instruction Teacher Management System:** • Pacing Guide • Lesson Plans for Universal Access **Interactive Reader and Study Guide:** Chapter Summary* **Chapter Resource File*** • Writing for the SAT • Social Studies Skill • Economics and History • Chapter Review **World History Outline Maps**	OSP **New York One-Stop Planner CD-ROM:** Calander Planner **Live Ink© Online Reading Help** **Student Edition on Audio CD Program** **Differentiated Instruction Modified Worksheets and Tests CD-ROM** **Interactive Skills Tutor CD-ROM** **World History Primary Source Library CD-ROM** **Power Presentations with Video CD-ROM** **History's Impact: World History Video Program (VHS/DVD):** Asia
Section 1: **South Asia after Empire** **The Main Idea:** India gained its independence from Great Britain, but the region entered an era of conflict and challenges. PI 1.4, 3.1	**Interactive Reader and Study Guide:** Section 1 Summary* **Chapter Resource File*** • Vocabulary Builder: Section 1 • Biography: Mohandas Gandhi • History and Geography: The Partition of India	**Regents Review Transparency:** Section 1* **Map Transparency:** Asia, 1945* **Map Transparency:** Religious Groups in India and Pakistan, 1947*
Section 2: **Independence Struggles in Southeast Asia** **The Main Idea:** Long under colonial domination, many Southeast Asian nations achieved independence in the postwar years. The transition, however, was not always a smooth one. PI 1.4, 3.3	**Differentiated Instruction Teacher Management System:** Section 2 Lesson Plan* **Interactive Reader and Study Guide:** Section 2 Summary* **Chapter Resource File*** • Vocabulary Builder: Section 2 • Biography: Loung Ung	**Regents Review Transparency:** Section 2* **Map Transparency:** Southeast Asia, 1965* **Map Transparency:** The Vietnam War, 1964–1975*
Section 3: **Communist China** **The Main Idea:** China has undergone many changes since becoming a Communist nation in 1949. Today, after making many market reforms, China has a rapidly growing economy. PI 3.1, 3.3	**Interactive Reader and Study Guide:** Section 3 Summary* **Chapter Resource File*** • Vocabulary Builder: Section 3 • Biography: Zhang Yimou • Primary Source: A Red Guard Describes the Cultural Revolution	**Regents Review Transparency:** Section 3* **Internet Activity:** Biography of an Asian Leader
Section 4: **The Rise of Pacific Rim Economies** **The Main Idea:** The nations of the Asian Pacific Rime underwent remarkable economic growth in the years after World War II, but significant challenges remain. PI 1.3, 3.1, 3.2, 3.3	**Differentiating Instruction Teacher Management System:** Section 4 Lesson Plan* **Interactive Reader and Study Guide:** Section 4 Summary* **Chapter Resource File*** • Vocabulary Builder: Section 4 • Biography: Soichiro Honda • Literature: *Hiroshima Notes*	**Regents Review Transparency:** Section 4*

TEACHER'S EDITION

CHAPTER 30 PLANNING GUIDE

HOLT
History's Impact
World History Video Program (VHS/DVD)
Asia

Review, Assessment, Intervention

- **Global History and Geography Regents Test Prep Workbook**
- **Quick Facts Transparency:** Asia*
- **Progress Assessment Support System (PASS):** Chapter Test*
- **Differentiated Instruction Modified Worksheets and Tests CD-ROM:** Modified Chapter Test
- OSP **New York One-Stop Planner CD-ROM:** ExamView Test Generator (English/Spanish)
- HOAP **Holt Online Assessment Program (HOAP),** in the Holt Premier Online Student Edition

---

- **PASS:** Section 1 Quiz*
- **Online Quiz:** Section 1
- **Alternative Assessment Handbook**

- **PASS:** Section 2 Quiz*
- **Online Quiz:** Section 2
- **Alternative Assessment Handbook**

- **PASS:** Section 3 Quiz*
- **Online Quiz:** Section 3
- **Alternative Assessment Handbook**

- **PASS:** Section 4 Quiz*
- **Online Quiz:** Section 4
- **Alternative Assessment Handbook**

Power Presentation with Video CD-ROM

Power Presentations with Video are visual presentations of each chapter's main ideas. Presentations can be customized by including Quick Facts charts, images and maps from the textbook, and video clips.

Holt Online Learning

go.hrw.com
Teacher Resources
KEYWORD: SHL TEACHER

go.hrw.com
Student Resources
KEYWORD: SHL ASA

- Document-Based Questions
- Interactive Multimedia Activities

- Current Events
- Chapter-Based Internet Activities
- and more!

Holt Premier
Online Student Edition
Complete online support for interactivity, assessment, and reporting

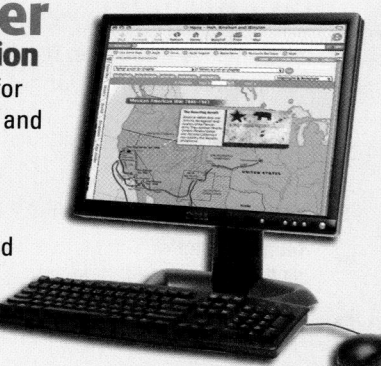

- Interactive Maps and Notebook
- Homework Practice and Research Activities Online

Before You Teach

The Big Picture

Peter N. Stearns

South Asia Asia is a huge continent, with many separate cultures and traditions. This makes comparison a vital analytical tool. In India, decolonization began in the 1940s. National unity could not be retained in the face of religious disputes, some of which had been encouraged by the British. Three separate nations resulted amid diplomatic and military tensions. India itself developed a vigorous and durable democracy. The new nation struggled with economic change, population growth, and rural conservatism. Still agricultural productivity was strong and, from the 1990s, industrial growth surged forward as well.

Southeast Asia Decolonization in Vietnam, Laos, and Cambodia involved massive conflict, first with the French and later against American military intervention. A communist revolutionary effort accompanied the struggle. Vietnamese independence and unification introduced greater flexibility into the communist system, allowing for some market-based economic development. Indonesia, the largest nation in the region, gained independence more peacefully, but then faced a long period of authoritarian rule that later yielded to democratic political forms and new regional strife.

China The big news here was the communist triumph by 1949, and the successive Maoist experiments in economic and political control. Systematic changes involved educational reforms and new public health measures that dramatically reduced infant mortality. In 1978 the regime shifted gears, allowing more market capitalism that generated intense industrial growth and a new global economic role. Still, China continued its authoritarian political controls against democratic movements.

Japan and the Pacific Rim This region featured dramatic economic growth, after a brief post-World War II recovery period. Japan led the way, developing new political institutions and a new level of economic development. Other Pacific Rim nations, notably South Korea and Taiwan, also produced latter day industrial revolutions.

Recent Scholarship

Alan T. Wood's *Asian Democracy in World History* (2004) takes up one of the more interesting and complex trends in South and East Asia. Wood carefully defines democracy and notes European precedents. He explores early post-World War II democracies in India, Japan, and the Philippines, noting reasons for their emergence amidst a regional climate of communist and authoritarian rule. Later democratic developments include South Korea, Taiwan, and the abortive surge in China. A third major section treats the flowering of democracy in Southeast Asia, including Indonesia. Overall, this is a carefully comparative book, combining clear description with lucid, explanatory analysis.

Differentiating Instruction

 Differentiated Instruction Teacher Management System
- Pacing Guide
- Lesson Plans for Differentiated Instruction

Interactive Reader and Study Guide

Spanish Chapter Summaries Audio CD Program

Student Edition on Audio CD Program

 Differentiated Instruction Modified Worksheets and Tests CD-ROM
- Vocabulary Flash Cards
- Modified Vocabulary Builder Activities
- Modified Chapter Review Activity
- Modified Chapter Test

OSP One-Stop Planner CD-ROM
- ExamView Test Generator (English/Spanish)
- PuzzlePro
- Quiz Show for ExamView
- Transparencies and Videos

TE Differentiated Activities in the Teacher's Edition
- Religions in India Poster, p. 910
- Colonial Independence Maps, p. 915
- The Tet Offensive, p. 917
- Political Cartoon: Mao's Programs, p. 922
- Japanese Postwar Recovery, p. 927
- Asian Imports and Exports, p. 928
- Cultural Revolution Posters, p. 931

Reading Like a Historian

Sam Wineburg

"Once upon a time ..." begins our children's stories, but how should we begin a historical story? This is not a trick question. A narrative's opening reflects a historian's choices and assumptions. A different historian coming to the same event may locate its beginning in another place entirely.

In narrating the struggles for independence in Southeast Asia, our chapter first notes American involvement with its participation at the 1954 Geneva Peace Conference on the future status of Vietnam. Until then, our chapter seems to suggest, Vietnamese independence was a French affair, with the "Viet Minh fighting France to win independence." The United States, we are told, only becomes actively involved in 1956, when President Eisenhower becomes convinced that Vietnam would be the next domino to fall in the communist struggle for world domination.

Once Upon a Time in Vietnam How else might we begin the story of America's tangled involvement in Vietnam? Consider these different possibilities:

Scenario One: Our story would begin in the waning days of World War II with President Roosevelt's antipathy for European colonial policy, particularly the venality of the French. In a note to Secretary of State Cordell Hall, Roosevelt wrote, "Indochina should not go back to France but [should] be administered by an international trusteeship ... France has milked it for one hundred years. The people of Indochina are entitled to something better than that." In this beginning, the US opposes the return of corrupt French rule and supports the aspirations of the Vietnamese for self-determination.

Scenario Two: This story begins with Ho Chi Minh, the leader of the Viet Minh, long before he became the archenemy of the US. We find Ho in the foggy days of 1945-46, before American policy has crystallized, a period in which Ho wrote eight different letters to President Truman, including one in which he requested that "the United States as guardians and champions of World Justice ... take a decisive step in support of our independence ... Like the Philippines, our goal is full independence and full cooperation with the United States. We will do our best to make this independence profitable to the whole world." We might try to explain why, on the record at least, Ho's appeals to President Truman went unanswered. (This letter was dated February 16, 1945, but not declassified until 1972).

Scenario Three: This story begins with a seven-hour meeting between President Truman and Charles de Gaulle on August 21, 1945, on the fate of French Indochina. It then moves to the collapse of the Chinese Nationalists and Mao's declaration in 1949 of a "People's Republic of China." Viewing all of Southeast Asia as a battleground against communism, President Truman on July 26, 1950, authorized 15 million dollars of military aid to the French, still holding, albeit precariously, onto power in Vietnam. If we started here, we would have to rewrite the French collapse at Dien Bien Phu in 1954 as the defeat of a regime propped up by American military aid and American military advisers in a nation that had already become a Cold War chessboard.

The beginnings of stories do not innocently present themselves to the storyteller. They are matters of choice and judgment—as well as political leaning. Often the key to discerning historical interpretation is by engaging in an intellectual experiment in alternative beginnings.

Indeed, the more we learn about the tangled web of Vietnam—and the role the United States played in it—the more alternative beginnings start to multiply.

Chapter Main Ideas

Section 1 India gained its independence from Great Britain, but the region entered an era of conflict and challenges.

Section 2 Long under colonial domination, many Southeast Asian nations achieved independence in the postwar years. The transition, however, was not always a smooth one.

Section 3 China has undergone many changes since becoming a Communist nation in 1949. Today, after making many market reforms, China has a rapidly growing economy.

Section 4 The nations of the Asian Pacific Rim underwent remarkable economic growth in the years after World War II, but significant challenges remain.

🐘 New York Standards

Key Idea 1 The study of world history requires an understanding of world cultures and civilizations, including an analysis of important ideas, social and cultural values, beliefs, and traditions. This study also examines the human condition and the connections and interactions of people across time and space and the ways different people view the same event or issue from a variety of perspectives.

Key Idea 3 Study of the major social, political, cultural, and religious developments in world history involves learning about the important roles and contributions of individuals and groups.

Key to Differentiating Instruction

Below Level

Basic-level activities designed for all students encountering new material

At Level

Intermediate-level activities designed for average students

Above Level

Challenging activities designed for honors and gifted and talented students

Standard English Mastery

Activities designed to improve standard English usage

CHAPTER

30   1945–Present

Asia

THE BIG PICTURE Following World War II, the nations of Asia worked to win political and economic independence. Their efforts were complicated by Cold War tensions, religious and ethnic conflicts, and struggles for political power. Despite these obstacles, some nations achieved great success in building strong, vibrant economies, and improved the lives of people throughout the region.

Theme ECONOMIC SYSTEMS

In the years after World War II, many Asian nations looked for ways to build their economic and political strength. In this chapter you will examine how these nations worked toward economic development and how some achieved economic success.

TIME LINE

CHAPTER EVENTS

August 1947 India is partitioned.

May 1954 Vietminh defeat French at Dien Bien Phu.

Mao Zedong leads China 1949–1976

April 1975 North Vietnam wins the Vietnam War.

1945 — 1965 — 1985

WORLD EVENTS

May 14, 1948 Israel declares its statehood.

1954 Gamal Abdel Nasser seizes power in Egypt.

1961 The Soviet Union sends the first human into outer space.

1979 Sandinista rebels win control of Nicaragua.

906 CHAPTER 30

Introduce the Chapter

At Level

Asia

Materials: 12" x 18" construction paper

1. Organize students into four groups. Assign a section to each group and give each group a sheet of construction paper.

2. Have groups copy their section number and Main Idea paragraph in the center of their papers. Have groups work together to write subheads and important details beneath each subhead. Have students add appropriate illustrations to their posters.

3. When groups have finished, have them display their work and present it to the class.

4. As homework, ask students to write a short paragraph about why the information in this chapter might be important. **LS** **Interpersonal, Visual-Spatial**

📄 **Alternative Assessment Handbook**, Rubrics 14: Group Activity; and 28: Posters

History's Impact video program
Watch the video to understand the impact of Vietnam's location.

阶级文化大革命万岁

Reading like a Historian

This photograph was taken during China's Cultural Revolution of the late 1960s, an effort by Chinese leaders to rid the nation of its old ways. The Chinese characters on the large signs translate as "Long live the proletariat's [workers'] great cultural revolution."

Analyzing Visuals How do you think a large public rally like this might have helped the Chinese government maintain power and minimize dissent?

See Skills Handbook, p. H26

June 1989
Chinese troops attack pro-democracy demonstrators in Tiananmen Square.

1997
A financial crisis slows growth in the Pacific Rim.

2005

1993 Apartheid officially ends in South Africa.

March 2003
A U.S.-led force invades Iraq.

ASIA **907**

Explore the Time Line

1. What major world event occurred in 1961? *The Soviet Union sent the first human being into outer space.*

2. How long did Mao Zedong lead China? *27 years*

3. When was Iraq invaded by U.S.-led forces? *2003*

4. When did a financial crisis slow growth in the Pacific Rim? *1997*

Info to Know

The Red Guard The Red Guard was formed to carry out Mao's goals for the Cultural Revolution. They were mostly urban youths, mobilized as their schools were shut down. They were told to attack all traditional values and "bourgeois things" and to publicly criticize party officials. **Predict** How might people respond to the Red Guard? *possible answer—Some people might begin to question communism; others might avoid dissent for fear of being harmed.*

• Chapter Preview •

HOLT
History's Impact
▶ **Video Program: Asia**
See the Video Teacher's Guide for strategies for using the video segment.

Reading Like a Historian

Analyzing Visuals Have students examine the photograph on these pages. Tell them that the portrait hanging on the wall depicts Mao Zedong, leader of the Chinese Communist Party. Ask students what they think might happen to a person who did not attend the rally, or who questioned its message.

go.hrw.com
Online Resources

Chapter Resources:
KEYWORD: SHL ASA
Teacher Resources:
KEYWORD: SHL TEACHER

Answers

Reading Like a Historian *possible answer—People would be less likely to dissent when they saw how many others supported the government.*

Geography Starting Points

Himalayan Ascents Nepalese sherpa Tenzing Norgay climbed Mt. Everest over 50 years ago with Britain's Sir Edmund Hillary. It was the first time that the daunting 29,035 foot high summit had been touched by man. Hillary has since made it his mission to help with another ascent, the rise of the sherpa standard of living. Hillary's Himalayan Trust has built twenty-seven schools, a dozen medical clinics, two hospitals, two airfields, and several bridges under "Sir Ed's" watchful care.

Interpreting Maps
Asia, 1945

Location Which four countries were under British rule in 1945? *India, Burma, Malaysia, Brunei*

Human/Environment Interaction What geographic feature may have served to protect Nepal and Bhutan from British control? *The Himalayas* What are some possible advantages to controlling western Malaysia? *possible answer—Malaysia lies along the logical shipping routes between the Far East and India and Africa, so Singapore could be a major trade center and shipping port.*

📦 **Map Transparency:** Asia, 1945

📜 **World History Outline Maps**

✴ **Interactive Map:** Asia, 1945

GEOGRAPHY **Starting Points**

Interactive ASIA, 1945

- British colony
- French colony
- Dutch colony
- Portuguese colony
- U.S.-controlled
- Soviet-controlled

In India, Mohandas Gandhi led the struggle for independence from Great Britain.

China was an independent nation in the midst of a civil war. The Communists were led by Mao Zedong.

In French Indochina, Ho Chi Minh led the fight for independence from France.

SOVIET UNION

MONGOLIA

IRAN   AFGHANISTAN

JAPAN

KOREA

CHINA

East China Sea

NEPAL   BHUTAN

INDIA

TAIWAN

PACIFIC OCEAN

BURMA

South China Sea

PHILIPPINES

INDIAN OCEAN

THAILAND   FRENCH INDOCHINA

CEYLON

BRUNEI

MALAYSIA

SINGAPORE   INDONESIA

EAST TIMOR (PORTUGAL)

0   500   1,000 Miles
0   500   1,000 Kilometers
Two-point equidistant projection

Starting Points After World War II, independence movements grew stronger in the European colonies scattered throughout Asia. In the years to come, these colonies would win their independence and face the challenge of building stable governments, economies, and societies.

1. **Identify** Which Asian nations were controlled by other countries in 1945?

2. **Predict** What might happen to these nations after they gain independence?

🔊 **Listen to History**

Go online to listen to an explanation of the starting points for this chapter.

go.hrw.com
Keyword: SHL ASA

Skills Focus: Analyzing Maps

At Level

Social Studies Skill
Factors Influencing Economic Independence

1. Remind students that various factors influenced whether nations' economies could survive on their own. Tell students they will determine the economic advantages of different areas of Asia in 1945.

2. Organize students into small groups. Assign each group one country from the map on this page. Write the following headings for students to see: Location, Climate, Products, and Political Climate for Trade. Have groups

conduct research and record observations about their assigned country. Have groups make a prediction about the country's potential economic success. Have groups share their observations and prediction with the class.

3. As homework, have students list factors that might indicate potential economic success of a country. 🔲 **Interpersonal, Verbal-Linguistic**

📝 **Alternative Assessment Handbook**, Rubrics 12: Drawing Conclusions; and 21: Map Reading

Answers

Geography Starting Points
1. *India, Burma, Ceylon, French Indochina, Malaysia, Brunei, Phillippines, East Timor, Korea;* 2. *possible answer— They would have to form their own governments and maintain stability.*

1 South Asia after Empire

BEFORE YOU READ

MAIN IDEA
India gained its independence from Great Britain, but the region entered an era of conflict and challenges.

READING FOCUS
1. What events led to independence and conflict in India?
2. What happened to India after the nation won its independence?
3. What challenges face the countries of South Asia?

KEY TERMS AND PEOPLE
Muhammad Ali Jinnah
partition
Jawaharlal Nehru
Indira Gandhi
Pervez Musharraf

THE INSIDE STORY

What is the price of independence? It is the summer of 1947, and more than 10 million Indians are on the move across the British colony of India. The British Parliament has just passed an act dividing India into two independent nations—Hindu India and Islamic Pakistan. People have one month to decide which country to live in and to travel to their new home.

People are scrambling for trains or trying to find other forms of transportation. They're deciding what personal belongings they can take to their new country and what they must leave behind. Most Hindus and Sikhs opt for India, while most Muslims choose Pakistan. As their paths cross, violence erupts—hundreds of thousands of people are dying.

Indians have finally won their independence from Great Britain. But peace will have to wait. ◾

A Nation Torn Apart

▼ Millions traveled across the Indian subcontinent on overcrowded trains.

ASIA **909**

Teach the Main Idea

At Level

South Asia after Empire

1. **Teach** Ask students the Reading Focus questions to teach this section.

2. **Apply** Organize students into small groups. Assign one part of this section to each group: Independence and Conflict, India after Independence, and Challenges in South Asia. Have groups create news headlines about their topic that might appear in various Asian newspapers.

3. **Review** Have groups share their headlines with the class. Guide the class in a discussion about the accuracy of the headlines.

4. **Practice/Homework** Have each student write a newspaper article about the main topics in this section. **LS Interpersonal, Verbal-Linguistic**

📰 **Alternative Assessment Handbook**, Rubrics 14: Group Activity; and 23: Newspapers

---

Reading Focus

1 What events led to independence and conflict in India? *"Quit India" campaign; Gandhi's imprisonment, and riots; Muslims call for partition; Britain believed partition would ensure stability; they ended rule of India, formed two separate nations*

Independence and Conflict

Recall Who led the Muslim League at this time? *Muhammad Ali Jinnah*

Sequence Place the following in order: a. India becomes independent, b. World War II begins, c. Gandhi is imprisoned. *b, c, a*

Evaluate Do you think partition helps people of different faiths get along? *possible answer—No, they will still fight over the borders. Learning about other faiths and practicing tolerance is a better solution.*

📄 **CRF:** Biography: Mohandas Gandhi

📄 **CRF:** History and Geography: The Partition of India

Interpreting Maps
Religious Groups in India and Pakistan, 1947

Human/Environment Interaction How might Kashmir and Ceylon have become Buddhist? *possible answer— Chinese Buddhists must have traveled over the mountains to reach Kashmir, and Chinese ships probably brought sailors to Ceylon.*

Movement Why do you suppose partition created two distant lands for Pakistan? *possible answer—Large populations of Muslims must have been in both areas and it would have been a great hardship for those in the east to move to the far western half.*

🗺️ **Map Transparency:** Religious Groups in India and Pakistan, 1947

Answers

Interpreting Maps 1. *Muslim;* **2.** *India*

910

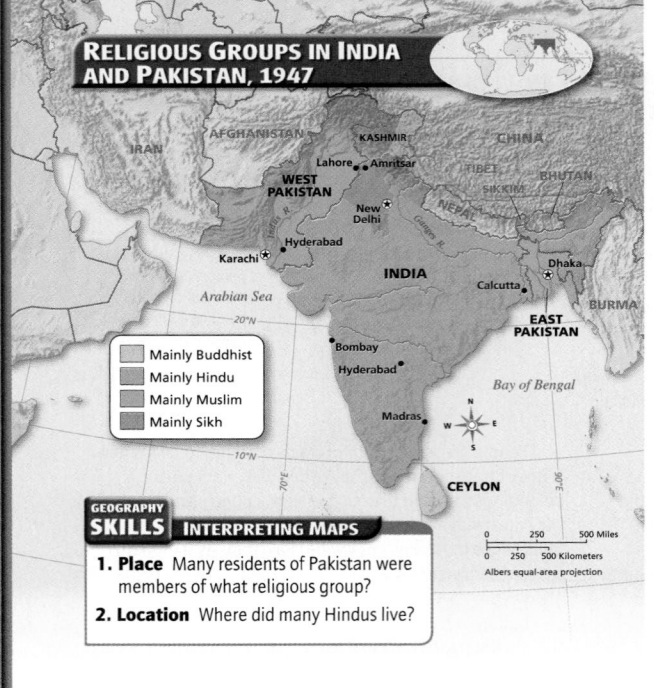

RELIGIOUS GROUPS IN INDIA AND PAKISTAN, 1947

- Mainly Buddhist
- Mainly Hindu
- Mainly Muslim
- Mainly Sikh

GEOGRAPHY SKILLS | **INTERPRETING MAPS**

1. Place Many residents of Pakistan were members of what religious group?

2. Location Where did many Hindus live?

TAKING NOTES

Take notes about the events in India and Pakistan that followed partition.

NEW YORK

CC Unit 7-E2
India—independence and partition

Independence and Conflict

Great Britain had controlled India for nearly two hundred years, but by the early 1900s the British control of the region was starting to weaken. At the same time, religious tensions were pulling India apart.

Indian Nationalism Grows A movement for independence in India gained strength throughout the early 1900s. By the mid-1930s the Indian National Congress and Mohandas Gandhi had won some self-rule for Indians.

When World War II began, the British informed India that Indians would have to fight for the Allies. Furious at being forced to participate in a war for democracy while being denied their own independence, the Indian National Congress refused to support the war effort. Instead, Gandhi began the so-called "Quit India" campaign. This effort was a nonviolent protest that aimed to drive the British from India.

The British immediately imprisoned Gandhi and thousands of Congress officials. These actions increased anti-British feelings, and riots erupted throughout India. The violence

910 CHAPTER 30

and increasing Indian nationalism helped convince the British that maintaining control of India was too costly. When the war ended, the British began making plans to leave India.

Religious Conflict and Partition India had long had two main religious groups: Hindus and Muslims. In 1940 India was home to about 255 million Hindus and 92 million Muslims. Smaller numbers of Indians were Sikhs (SEEKS), Christians, or Buddhists. As hopes for Indian independence rose, so did religious tensions. Some Muslims, fearing that an independent democratic India would be dominated by India's large Hindu population, believed that Indian Muslims needed a separate nation in order to protect their rights.

Muhammad Ali Jinnah led the Muslim League, an organization that worked for the interests of India's Muslims. In 1940 the Muslim League formally called for a **partition**, or division, of India and the creation of separate Muslim and Hindu countries. Gandhi strongly opposed the division of India, but there was little he could do to prevent it.

As violence between Muslims and Hindus increased during the early 1940s, British leaders came to believe that partition was the best way to ensure a safe and stable region. They decided to divide India into separate Hindu and Muslim nations.

Great Britain formally ended its colonial rule of India in August 1947 and two new nations were created: Muslim East and West Pakistan and Hindu India. **Jawaharlal Nehru** (juh-WAH-huhr-lahl NAY-roo), who would be India's first prime minister, spoke on the eve of independence.

HISTORY'S VOICES

❝It is a fateful moment for us in India, for all Asia and for the world. A new star rises, the star of freedom in the East, a new hope comes into being, a vision long cherished materializes.❞

—Jawaharlal Nehru, speech, August 14, 1947

Violence after Partition The division of India into two nations also divided the religious groups that lived in India. Most of the residents of Pakistan were Muslims and many in India were Hindu, but followers of other religions lived in each new country as well. As a result, millions of people on each side of the bor-

Differentiating Instruction

Advanced Learners/ Gifted and Talented

Research Required

Materials: 12" x 18" construction paper

1. Point out to students that religious differences contributed to much conflict in mid-20th century India. Tell students they will create posters representing basic facts about the four main faiths of 1947 India.

2. Organize students into four groups. Assign one of the following to each group: Buddhism, Hinduism, Islam, and Sikhism.

3. Have groups research the development of their assigned religion, and create a Basic Facts poster for display. Encourage students to investigate customs, holy cities, famous people, and nations with large populations of each religion's followers.

4. When groups have finished their posters, have groups share them with the class.

LS Interpersonal, Visual-Spatial

📄 **Alternative Assessment Handbook**, Rubrics 14: Group Activity; 28: Posters; and 30: Research der decided to move. Muslims in India moved to Pakistan. Hindus and Sikhs in Pakistan left for India. As millions of people crossed the subcontinent, violence between different religious groups flared. Over a million people died.

Gandhi himself was a victim of the bloodshed. In January 1948 he was shot and killed by a fellow Hindu who blamed Gandhi for the partition of India and believed that Gandhi had sacrificed Hindu interests to protect Muslims.

War over Kashmir Complicating relations between India and Pakistan was the fact that not all border issues had been settled at partition. One major point of conflict was the region of Kashmir, near the northern border of India and Pakistan. Soon after partition, India and Pakistan began to fight over control of Kashmir. This continued until a cease-fire in 1949 divided the region into two parts, one controlled by India and the other by Pakistan. Later, China claimed control of part of Kashmir as well. Kashmir was the site of frequent conflicts between India and Pakistan in the years after partition.

READING CHECK Identify Cause and Effect
How did India's independence lead to conflict?

India after Independence

India became the world's largest democracy when the nation won its independence in 1947. In the years after independence, India faced many challenges.

India under Nehru Prime Minister Jawaharlal Nehru led India through the difficult early years of independence. Nehru emphasized the need for unity and economic and social reforms, as well as a respect for democratic ideals. He worked to increase the legal rights of women, to improve the lives of the poor, and to prevent discrimination based on caste, or inherited status. Under Nehru's leadership, India utilized modern science and technology to improve its industry and agriculture. During the Cold War, India played an important role in the formation of the nonaligned movement when it chose to focus on economic development instead of taking sides in the conflict.

ACADEMIC VOCABULARY
utilize to make use of

After Nehru Nehru died in 1964. Two years later his daughter, **Indira Gandhi**, was elected prime minister. Her rise to power showed that the role of women in Indian society had improved in the years after independence.

Linking TO Today

The Conflict in Kashmir

On top of the frigid Siachen Glacier, some 20,000 feet above sea level, Indian and Pakistani troops struggle to control the region of Kashmir. This conflict on the world's highest battlefield has its roots in India's 1947 partition.

When Great Britain partitioned India, the Hindu ruler of Kashmir agreed to join India. This decision left Kashmir's largely Muslim population furious. Pakistan soon sent forces into the region to take control of Kashmir, which it considered a part of its territory, and India immediately followed suit. War broke out.

The war in Kashmir lasted until a UN-brokered cease-fire took effect at the start of 1949 and temporarily divided Kashmir at the battle line. In the cease-fire, both sides agreed to hold a vote to determine the preference of the people of Kashmir. That vote was never held.

Today, Kashmir is still disputed territory. Much of the region's Muslim population lives in the Indian-controlled area, and militants there fight this Indian control. India claims that these fighters are terrorists supported by Pakistan, but Pakistan claims that the fighters are Kashmir residents rising up in an independence movement. Thousands of people have died in the fighting in Kashmir.

Summarize Why is Kashmir disputed territory?

| Kashmir region |
| Controlled by India |
| Controlled by Pakistan |
| Controlled by China |

0   200 Miles
0   200 Kilometers

CHINA
PAKISTAN
INDIA

A Pakistani soldier guards the Pakistan-controlled section of Kashmir.

ASIA **911**

Skills Focus: Comparing and Contrasting

At Level

Reading Skill
Disputes Involving New Nations

1. Remind students that the formation of new nations often involves violent conflict.

2. Draw the chart for students to see, omitting the italicized answers. Have students copy the chart and fill in the answers. When students have completed their charts, have them write a short essay comparing the two disputes. **LS** **Visual-Spatial, Verbal-Linguistic**

✍ **Alternative Assessment Handbook**, Rubrics 6: Cause and Effect; and 13: Graphic Organizers

	Kashmir	East Pakistan
Date	*1949; 1964*	*1971*
Cause	*unresolved border dispute*	*distance from West Pakistan, ethnic differences, government policies*
Goal	*to gain territory*	*independence*
Action	*wars*	*civil war*
Result	*division of Kashmir; still unresolved*	*formation of independent Bangladesh*

Direct Teach

Reading Focus

❷ What happened to India after the nation won its independence? *Jawaharial Nehru and Indira Gandhi each served as prime minister, reforms, Sikh independence movement, Indira Gandhi assassinated*

India after Independence

Recall What were some reforms Nehru made? *increased legal rights of women, improved life for poor, prevented discrimination based on caste, emphasized need for unity and economic development*

Describe What happened in 1984 in the Indian state of Punjab? *small group of militant Sikhs occupied the Golden Temple; Indira Gandhi orders them driven out; hundreds killed at the temple and sacred items destroyed; Gandhi assassinated, touching off a wave of anti-Sikh violence in India*

Info to Know

Mahatma In references to Mohandas Gandhi, the names Mohandas and Mahatma seem to be used interchangeably. However, his given name was Mohandas, but Mahatma is a term bestowed upon him by the people of India to honor him. This title is given only to people of exceptional merit. It comes from maha-atman, which means great self. In Gandhi's case, "great soul" might be the best translation.

MISCONCEPTION ALERT

Indira Gandhi is no relation to Mohandas Gandhi. She is the daughter of Jawaharlal Nehru.

Answers

Linking to Today *because both India and Pakistan claim the territory*

Reading Check *When India gained independence, new nations were formed along religious lines, leading to conflicts between the groups.*

India after Independence

Describe What problem does India continue to face today? *Millions of Indians live in poverty in crowded cities such as Mumbai and Kolkata.*

Identify Cause and Effect What actions did India take in the 1990s, leading to significant economic gains? *loosened control of many industries, reduced trade barriers*

Info to Know

Henotheism It is difficult and confusing to assign an "-ism" to the Hindu faith. It has been called Trinitarian, because Brahman is viewed as three persons: Brahma the Creator, Vishnu the Preserver, and Shiva the Destroyer. However, Hinduism is more accurately described as henotheism. While Hindus believe in one supreme God, they also worship multiple deities, though each is considered a form or facet of the supreme God. Especially important to an area where religious tension has often led to violence is Hinduism's accepting attitude toward other faiths, expressed by this saying: "The truth is One, but different Sages call it by Different Names."

Answers

World Religions *that everything in the world is a reflection of Brahman, the universal spirit; that there is a continual pattern of birth, death, and rebirth*

Reading Check *focused on economic development; increased rights for women and the poor; became the world's largest democracy*

World Religions

Hinduism

Hinduism is one of the world's oldest religions. It is the largest religion in India today and the third largest in the world.

Origins of Hinduism Unlike other religions, Hinduism has no single founder. Instead, it evolved gradually over thousands of years and was influenced by the cultures and traditions of many peoples.

Hinduism teaches that everything in the world is a reflection of Brahman, a single universal spirit. Most Hindus believe that various aspects of Brahman, called *devas*, are active in the world and help keep order in nature.

Hindus believe that the universe and everyone in it are part of a continual pattern of birth, death, and rebirth. After death, they believe that the *atman*, or soul, will be released from the body and later reborn in another body through a process called reincarnation. The nature of the person's new life will be shaped by his or her karma, the sum effect of his or her deeds and actions during the past life. For Hindus, the ultimate goal of existence is *moksha*, or escape from the cycle of death and rebirth and a reunion with Brahman.

Hinduism Today Hinduism is practiced primarily in India, where it originated. Based on many sacred texts and practices, Hinduism often combines new ideas with existing practices. In part because of the religion's many influences, the practice of Hinduism varies widely, with certain beliefs and customs more common in some regions than others. Hinduism is composed of countless sects, with no governing organization.

Summarize What are the major beliefs of Hinduism?

Some Hindu temples are covered with intricate carvings.

HINDUS BY COUNTRY, 2005

Other
50 million

India
882 million

Source: *The World Factbook, 2006*

Indira Gandhi served four terms as prime minister. One challenge she faced was from a Sikh independence movement in the Indian state of Punjab. In 1984 a small group of militant Sikhs occupied the Golden Temple, the holiest shrine of the Sikh religion, in Amritsar, India. Gandhi ordered Indian troops to drive the militants out of the temple. When the troops attacked the shrine, hundreds of people were killed, including many who had nothing to do with the temple's occupation. The attack damaged the temple and Sikh holy scriptures.

The violent attack on the temple outraged many Sikhs—including Sikhs who had not supported the militants. In October 1984 Indira Gandhi's Sikh bodyguards assassinated her. This killing touched off a wave of anti-Sikh violence in India that left thousands dead.

The events of 1984 remain a bitter subject today. The incidents greatly harmed relations between India's Sikh minority and the Indian government.

Modern India In the 1990s India undertook some reforms that have led to significant economic gains. For example, the government loosened its controls on many industries and reduced its trade barriers, which helped encourage the growth of new businesses. Although most Indians still work in agriculture, service industries, particularly information technology and the customer-service industry, have expanded rapidly. In recent years, the Indian economy has grown at a remarkable rate.

The strong economy has brought prosperity to only a minority of the country's 1.1 billion people. Millions of Indians live in poverty in crowded cities such as Mumbai and Kolkata. A variety of charity groups work to provide food, clothing, and medical aid to India's poor. One of the best-known groups is the Missionaries of Charity, founded in Kolkata by Roman Catholic nun Mother Teresa.

READING CHECK **Summarize** How did India change after winning its independence?

Skills Focus: Analyzing Primary Sources

Reading Like a Historian Skill
The Functions of the Vedas

Materials: copies of several Yajur Vedas, printed out from the Internet or other sources

1. Remind students that the Vedas are rituals, hymns, incantations, and sacrifices meant to aid people in the practice of Hinduism.

2. Organize students into small groups. Distribute one veda per group. Have groups read their assigned veda and discuss how its words would relate to the lives of poor, agrarian Hindus. Groups should explain the purpose of the veda. Was it written to teach a lesson, guide a worship ritual, or offer praise to a deity? Have groups share their findings with the class.

3. As homework, have students write a short essay on the function of the veda in the lives of Hindus. Essays should draw parallels to other religious practices. **LS Interpersonal, Verbal-Linguistic**

Alternative Assessment Handbook, Rubrics 12: Drawing Conclusions; and 14: Group Activity

Challenges in South Asia

The history of other nations in South Asia has been as turbulent as that of India. Today, those nations face a range of challenges.

Civil War in Pakistan When Pakistan was created in 1947 it had two parts—West Pakistan and East Pakistan. The areas were separated by over 1,000 miles and by deep differences in language, religion, and culture. In addition, the west, though smaller in population, controlled the country's government. Government policies and spending favored the west while the east remained desperately poor.

In 1971 East Pakistan decided to seek independence. The Pakistani government responded with armed force, and in the civil war that followed, many thousands of people died. After India sent troops to support East Pakistan, Pakistan was forced to accept the independence of the East—now called Bangladesh.

Troubles in Bangladesh Bangladesh faced very difficult times after the civil war. The nation is one of the poorest and most densely populated countries in the world. Much of Bangladesh is just a few feet above sea level, and devastating floods and storms have often swept across the country, killing many people and leading to widespread famine. The nation has seen a series of governments since independence, but in recent years Bangladesh has attempted to build a stable democracy.

Instability in Pakistan Pakistan has also faced instability in the years since the civil war. Ethnic and religious conflicts have been common, including disagreements about the role of Islam in government. A series of leaders have taken power, some through election and some through military coups, as when General **Pervez Musharraf** took power in 1999 by overthrowing the elected government. Musharraf's government has worked with the United States to fight al Qaeda and the Taliban in neighboring Afghanistan.

Nuclear Weapons Even in the best of times, relations between India and Pakistan have been tense, with war a near-constant threat. This tension is one reason that India's testing of a nuclear weapon in 1974 caused alarm around the world. In 1998, after another Indian test, Pakistan tested its own nuclear bomb. The threat of nuclear war has kept tensions high.

Ethnic and Religious Tensions The region continues to experience powerful divisions and conflict based on religious and ethnic differences. Much of this stems from the long-standing hostility between Hindus and Muslims, which continues to cause conflict between India and Pakistan.

Ethnic fighting also plagues India's neighbor, Sri Lanka. This island nation, formerly known as Ceylon, was a British colony until winning independence in the late 1940s. Since the 1980s, fighting between the Buddhist Sinhalese majority, which holds most political power, and the Hindu Tamil minority has killed tens of thousands. Religious tension has intensified this struggle between ethnic groups.

READING SKILLS

Identifying Problems and Solutions What problem does Sri Lanka face?

READING CHECK **Identify Supporting Details** What challenges do the nations of South Asia face today?

SECTION 1 ASSESSMENT

go.hrw.com
Online Quiz
Keyword: SHL ASA HP

Reviewing Key Terms and People

1. a. Recall Why did the Muslim League propose the **partition** of India?
b. Explain How has the dispute over Kashmir affected the relationship between India and Pakistan?
c. Make Judgments Do you believe that the partition was the best way to ensure a safe and stable region, given the events that followed?

2. a. Recall What important events took place in India in 1984?
b. Summarize What political, economic, and social changes took place in India after independence?

3. a. Describe Why did East Pakistan seek independence in 1971?
b. Explain How have ethnic and religious tensions affected South Asia?

Critical Thinking

4. Identify Supporting Details Use your notes on the section and a graphic organizer like the one below to compare and contrast the events that followed partition in India and Pakistan.

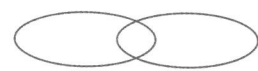

FOCUS ON SPEAKING

5. Exposition Write an outline for a brief television news report on the history of India and Pakistan since the partition in 1947. Be sure to include details from the section in your outline.

ASIA **913**

Section 1 Assessment Answers

1. a. partition to separate India by faiths
b. increased tensions
c. possible answer—No, the partition probably increased religious tensions.

2. a. Sikh independence movement in Punjab, assassination of Indira Gandhi
b. economic development, reforms increasing rights of women and the poor, limiting discrimination based on caste, nonaligned in the Cold War

3. a. because of differences in religion, poverty in the east

b. resulted in civil war in Bangladesh, tension between India and Pakistan, ethnic fighting in Sri Lanka

4. India—economic and social reforms, democracy, Sikh independence movement, assassination of Indira Gandhi; Pakistan—Bangladesh independence movement, civil war, instability, Musharraf overthrows elected government in 1999; Both—independence movements, nuclear weapons

5. Student outlines should include events from the graphic organizer in question 4.

Reading Focus

3 What challenges face the countries of South Asia? *nuclear weapons, religious and ethnic tensions, extreme poverty, political upheaval*

Challenges in South Asia

Recall Which two groups continue fighting in Sri Lanka? *the Sinhalese and the Tamils*

Sequence What events led to the independence of Bangladesh? *East Pakistan decided to seek independence in 1971; government responded with force; thousands died in civil war; India sent troops to support East Pakistan, which became Bangladesh*

• **Review & Assess** •

Close

Review with students the independence and partition of India, the major challenges facing the new nation, and the ongoing challenges facing South Asia.

Review

Online Quiz, Section 1

Assess

SE Section 1 Assessment
Progress Assessment: Section 1 Quiz
Alternative Assessment Handbook

Reteach/Intervene

Interactive Reader and Study Guide, Section 1
Interactive Skills Tutor CD-ROM

Answers

Reading Skills *ethnic fighting between Buddhist Sinhalese majority and Hindi Tamil minority*

Reading Check *poverty, religious and ethnic tensions, nuclear weapons, famine, political upheaval*

913

Independence Struggles in Southeast Asia

Preteach

Getting Started

Use the **Interactive Reader and Study Guide** to familiarize students with the section content.

📘 **Interactive Reader and Study Guide, Section 2**

[Worksheet image: "Asia" Section 2 — MAIN IDEA, Key Terms and People, Taking Notes graphic organizer with rows for Vietnam, Indonesia, Cambodia, Other Nations]

📝 **CRF:** Vocabulary Builder: Section 2

Taking Notes

Vietnam—Vietminh fight French for Vietnamese independence; Ho Chi Minh leads resistance; French surrender; country divided; U.S. leaders want South Vietnam independent; Gulf of Tonkin Resolution increases American presence; North's Tet Offensive atrocities weaken U.S. public support; U.S. fighting spreads north; U.S. and North Vietnam peace agreement reached in 1973; Vietnam unified in 1976; Indonesia—a military dictatorship, but has returned to democracy; Cambodia— Pol Pot leads Khmer Rouge to gain control of Cambodia in 1975; brutal Khmer Rouge regime fights Vietnam; Pol Pot forced from power; UN helps Cambodia become democratic; Myanmar— a military dictatorship since 1960s, has resisted democracy;

BEFORE YOU READ

MAIN IDEA

Long under colonial domination, many Southeast Asian nations achieved independence in the postwar years. The transition, however, was not always a smooth one.

READING FOCUS

1. How did independence come to Southeast Asia?
2. What were the main causes of the Vietnam War?
3. How has Southeast Asia changed in recent decades?

KEY TERMS AND PEOPLE

Vietminh
Ho Chi Minh
domino theory
Vietcong
Sukarno
Suharto
Khmer Rouge
Pol Pot
Aung San Suu Kyi

 NEW YORK

PI 1.4 Students understand the broad patterns, relationships, and interactions of cultures and civilizations.

PI 3.3 Students examine the social/cultural, political, economic, and religious norms and values of Western and other world cultures.

A TERRIBLE DECISION

 THE INSIDE STORY

How did the French lose a war with one bad decision? After World War II the French struggled to regain control of their colonies in Southeast Asia. In Vietnam, French troops fought a guerrilla group, known as the Vietminh, that sought to win Vietnam's independence. French leaders decided to build a new military base at Dien Bien Phu (DYEN BYEN FOO) to help defeat the Vietminh. It was a terrible decision.

The French base was located at the bottom of a bowl-shaped valley. When the Vietminh cut off all the roads leading to the area, the fort could be supplied only from the air. Still, French leaders were unconcerned, believing the Vietminh were too weak to defeat them.

When the Vietminh attacked Dien Bien Phu in March 1954, they quickly overwhelmed the French defenses above the valley. Then the Vietminh began to pound the French base below with powerful artillery fire. Under constant bombardment, the French were unable to fly supply aircraft in or out of Dien Bien Phu. Heavy monsoon rains added to their misery. By early May, the French were completely defeated and were forced to surrender to the Vietminh. French control of Southeast Asia had come to an end. ■

◄ **French troops parachute into Dien Bien Phu.**

914 CHAPTER 30

Teach the Main Idea

At Level

Independence Struggles in Southeast Asia

1. **Teach** Ask students the Reading Focus questions to teach this section.

2. **Apply** Organize students into three groups. Assign one part of this section to each group. Have groups create a list of important events from their assigned part of this section.

3. **Review** When groups have completed their lists, have them present their work. Have students use sticky notes to indicate the location of important events.

4. **Practice/Homework** Have each student write a one paragraph summary about the struggles for independence in Southeast Asia.

   LS Interpersonal, Visual-Spatial

   📝 **Alternative Assessment Handbook,** Rubrics 1: Acquiring Information; and 14: Group Activity

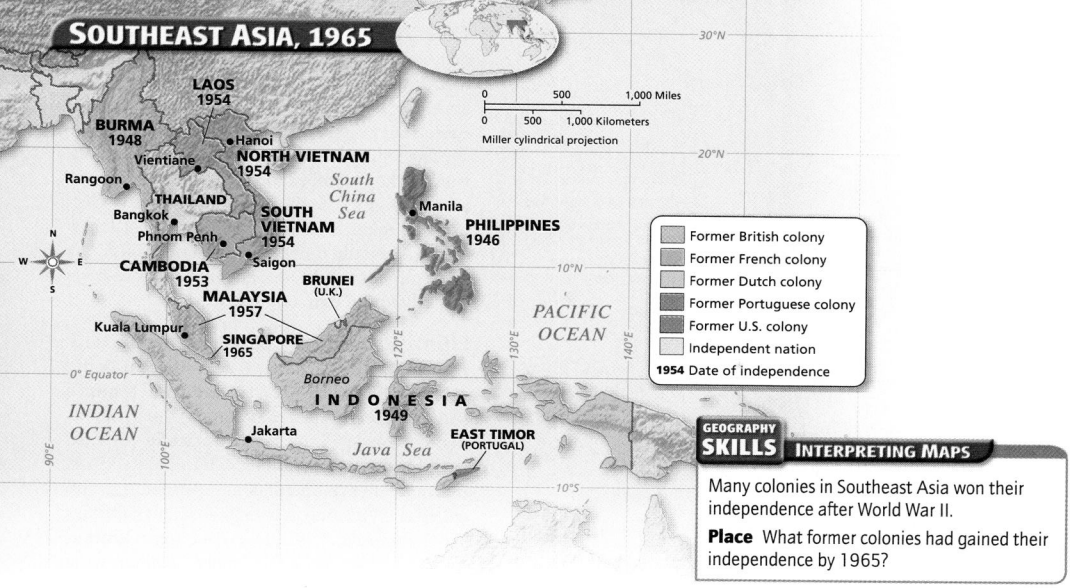

SOUTHEAST ASIA, 1965

LAOS 1954
BURMA 1948
Hanoi
Vientiane
NORTH VIETNAM 1954
Rangoon
THAILAND
Bangkok
SOUTH VIETNAM 1954
Phnom Penh
Saigon
South China Sea
Manila
PHILIPPINES 1946
CAMBODIA 1953
BRUNEI (U.K.)
MALAYSIA 1957
PACIFIC OCEAN
Kuala Lumpur
SINGAPORE 1965
Borneo
INDIAN OCEAN
Jakarta
INDONESIA 1949
Java Sea
EAST TIMOR (PORTUGAL)

0 500 1,000 Miles
0 500 1,000 Kilometers
Miller cylindrical projection

Former British colony
Former French colony
Former Dutch colony
Former Portuguese colony
Former U.S. colony
Independent nation
1954 Date of independence

GEOGRAPHY SKILLS INTERPRETING MAPS

Many colonies in Southeast Asia won their independence after World War II.

Place What former colonies had gained their independence by 1965?

Independence in Southeast Asia

Before World War II much of Southeast Asia was controlled by major colonial powers. For example, Burma (now known as Myanmar) and Malaya (now Malaysia) were controlled by the British. The Philippines was under the control of the United States, while the country now known as Indonesia was a Dutch colony. The modern-day countries of Vietnam, Laos, and Cambodia were part of a French colony known as French Indochina.

During the war, the Japanese occupied these Southeast Asian colonies. This occupation helped weaken the grip of the European and American powers. When World War II ended, some nations decided to end their colonial presence in the region. The United States, for example, granted independence to the Philippines in 1946, while the British gave up control of Burma in 1948.

In other cases, however, independence came only with struggle. Communist rebels in Malaya, for example, fought the British before they achieved independence. In Indochina, a group known as the **Vietminh** fought French troops to win Vietnamese independence. The

leader of the Vietminh, **Ho Chi Minh**, was a Communist. He received assistance in his effort from China and the Soviet Union. His major goal, however, was independence for Vietnam, not the expansion of communism. After years of fighting, the Vietminh finally defeated France, and French control of Indochina came to an end.

READING CHECK Make Generalizations How did Southeast Asian nations achieve independence?

The Vietnam War

The fighting with France had ended, but the conflict in Vietnam was far from over. Ho Chi Minh's dream of a united, independent Vietnam would only be achieved after years of war.

Planning Vietnam's Future In 1954 representatives from France, Vietnam, the United States, the Soviet Union, and other nations met in Switzerland to establish a peace agreement for Vietnam. The talks reflected the Cold War tensions of the mid-1950s. Worried about the spread of communism, the Western powers did not want to give Ho Chi Minh and the Communists complete control of Vietnam.

TAKING NOTES

Take notes about the struggles for independence and the political changes in Southeast Asia after World War II.

Vietnam	
Indonesia	
Cambodia	
Other Nations	

 NEW YORK

CC **Unit 7-E4a**
Vietnam/Ho Chi Minh

ASIA **915**

Direct Teach

Reading Focus

1 How did independence come to Southeast Asia? *many struggles for independence from foreign colonial rule*

Independence in Southeast Asia

Identify Before World War II, which parts of Southeast Asia were controlled by Great Britain? *Burma (now known as Myanmar) and Malaya (now Malaysia)*

Predict Given that the French had western allies from past world wars, what do you think might happen in the conflict with the Vietminh? *possible answer— Allies of the French might come to their aid.*

Map Transparency: Southeast Asia, 1965

Reading Focus

2 What were the main causes of the Vietnam War? *Vietnam divided after defeat of French; U.S fears spread of communism; Vietcong joined by North Vietnamese to defeat South Vietnamese fighters.*

The Vietnam War

Recall What worried Western leaders at the conference in Switzerland? *the spread of communism*

Explain What was the domino theory? *the belief that if Vietnam fell to communism, other Southeast Asian countries would quickly follow*

Differentiating Instruction

Below Level

Learners Having Difficulty

Materials: black outline masters of Southeast Asia, colored pencils

1. Remind students that between the end of World War II and 1975, many colonies in Southeast Asia gained independence. Tell students they will create maps to show which colonies did so peacefully, and which ones had to fight for independence.

2. Distribute maps and have students copy the country names and dates of independence from the map on this page.

3. Have students refer to this page to find how some former colonies achieved independence. If war was involved, students should color the country red. If the transition was peaceful, they should color it blue.

4. As homework, ask students to write a short paragraph, reviewing how these countries achieved independence. **LS** **Visual-Spatial, Verbal-Linguistic**

Alternative Assessment Handbook, Rubrics 1: Acquiring Information; and 20: Map Creation

Answers

Interpreting Maps *Burma, Laos, Cambodia, North Vietnam, South Vietnam, Malaysia, Singapore, Indonesia, Philippines*

Reading Check *In some areas, Japanese occupation during World War II helped weaken the grip of the European and American powers in the region. In others, independence came with struggle.*

915

The Vietnam War

Identify What resolution served to escalate the United States' involvement? *the Gulf of Tonkin Resolution*

Explain Why did the United States support South Vietnam? *to keep it from being taken over by the North, and therefore becoming Communist*

Analyze In what way did the U.S. involvement cause North Vietnam and the Vietcong to change their strategy? *Instead of pressing for a quick victory, the Vietcong focused on outlasting their enemies.*

Map Transparency: The Vietnam War, 1964–1975

Interactive Map: The Vietnam War, 1964–1975

Info to Know

Diem's Values When the Viet Minh first took over in 1945, Ngo Dinh Diem was offered a job in the Ho Chi Minh government. Diem, who felt that Communists posed a threat to his Catholic values and to Vietnamese independence, turned down the job. A few years later, Diem exiled himself and came to live in the United States. It was then that the Eisenhower administration chose him to serve as first prime minister of South Vietnam. Diem's "values" did not include religious tolerance, however. His nepotism, corruption, and cruelty moved several Buddhist monks to set fire to themselves in public protest. News and photos of this shocked the American people and led to the end of U.S. support for Diem.

Answers

Interpreting Maps *The Vietcong controlled most of South Vietnam, excluding some small areas.*

Faces of History *inspired him to demand independence for Vietnam*

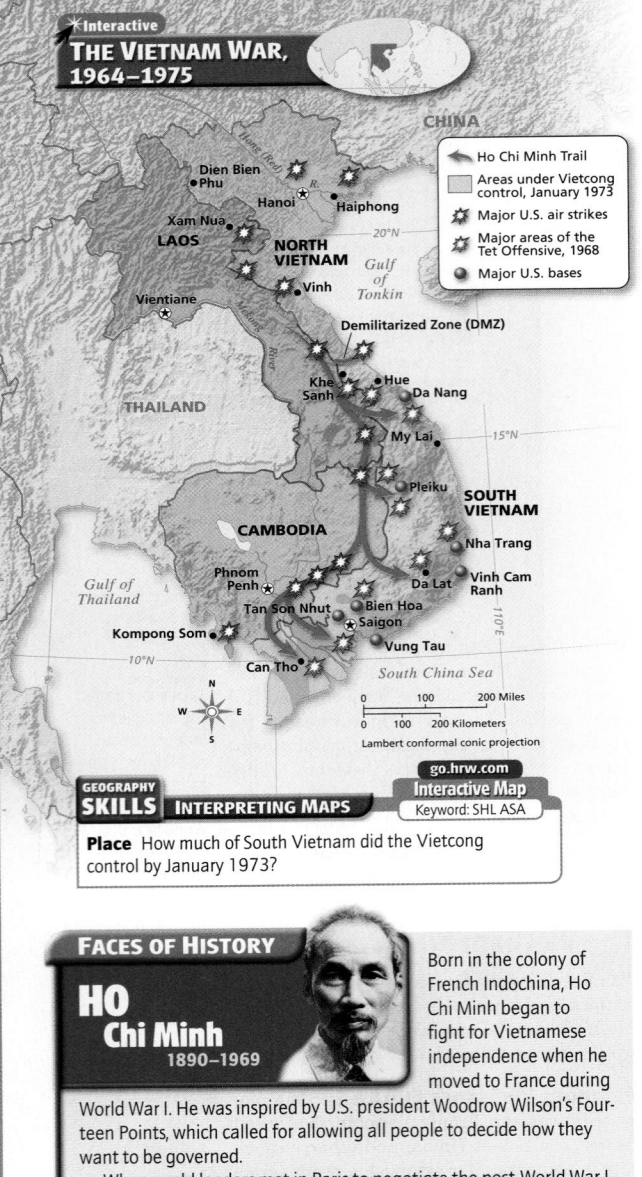

*Interactive
THE VIETNAM WAR, 1964–1975

Ho Chi Minh Trail
Areas under Vietcong control, January 1973
Major U.S. air strikes
Major areas of the Tet Offensive, 1968
Major U.S. bases

CHINA

Dien Bien Phu
Hanoi
Haiphong
Xam Nua
LAOS
NORTH VIETNAM
20°N
Gulf of Tonkin
Vientiane
Vinh
Demilitarized Zone (DMZ)
Khe Sanh
Hue
Da Nang
THAILAND
My Lai
15°N
Pleiku
SOUTH VIETNAM
CAMBODIA
Nha Trang
Gulf of Thailand
Phnom Penh
Da Lat
Vinh Cam Ranh
Tan Son Nhut
Bien Hoa
Saigon
Kompong Som
Vung Tau
10°N
Can Tho
South China Sea
110°E

0   100   200 Miles
0   100   200 Kilometers
Lambert conformal conic projection

GEOGRAPHY SKILLS INTERPRETING MAPS

go.hrw.com
Interactive Map
Keyword: SHL ASA

Place How much of South Vietnam did the Vietcong control by January 1973?

FACES OF HISTORY

HO Chi Minh
1890–1969

Born in the colony of French Indochina, Ho Chi Minh began to fight for Vietnamese independence when he moved to France during World War I. He was inspired by U.S. president Woodrow Wilson's Fourteen Points, which called for allowing all people to decide how they want to be governed.

When world leaders met in Paris to negotiate the post-World War I peace treaty, Ho Chi Minh sent them a petition demanding Vietnam's independence, but received no response. He soon began to use Communist ideas in his struggle for independence, believing that peasants would play a key role in the fight for an independent Vietnam.

Find the Main Idea How did the Fourteen Points affect Ho Chi Minh?

916 CHAPTER 30

Thus, Vietnam was divided temporarily into northern and southern halves. The Communists would control the north. According to the agreement, in 1956 Vietnamese voters would choose a government for a reunited Vietnam.

The United States feared that Communists would take control of South Vietnam. U.S. president Dwight Eisenhower warned that if Vietnam fell to communism, other Southeast Asian countries would quickly follow. This belief that communism would spread to other countries was called the **domino theory**.

Fighting Begins The United States supported South Vietnam to keep it from being taken over by the North. South Vietnam's leader, Ngo Dinh Diem (NGOH DIN dee-EM), prevented the 1956 election and made enemies with his corrupt, brutal rule. By the late 1950s many of Diem's enemies had formed a group called the **Vietcong**, a term meaning "Vietnamese Communist." Not all Vietcong were Communists, but they shared the goal of overthrowing Diem's government and reuniting Vietnam. Soon, North Vietnamese forces entered South Vietnam to fight alongside the Vietcong.

Fighting Escalates As Vietcong influence spread, the United States increased its aid to South Vietnam. The United States also sent thousands of military advisers to help South Vietnamese forces.

In August 1964 U.S. president Lyndon B. Johnson informed Congress that two U.S. Navy ships sailing off North Vietnam's coast had been the victims of an unprovoked attack by North Vietnamese gunboats. It was true that one U.S. ship had been fired upon by North Vietnamese who believed the ship had attacked them the previous day, but the second attack seems to have been a misunderstanding. Johnson did not mention the full facts, and Congress passed the Gulf of Tonkin Resolution. This resolution gave Johnson the power to expand U.S. involvement without a formal declaration of war. As a result, the American military presence in Vietnam grew quickly, with hundreds of thousands of combat troops sent to the region.

The increased U.S. involvement forced North Vietnam and the Vietcong to change their military strategy in South Vietnam. Rather than pressing for a quick victory, they focused on outlasting their enemies.

Skill Focus: Analyzing Primary Sources

At Level

Reading Like a Historian Skill
Letters From Vietnam

Research Required

1. Remind students that when people were sent to war in Vietnam, the letters they sent home often revealed the reality of war that was not reported in the news.

2. Organize students into small groups. Have students conduct online research to locate letters written by soldiers and medical personnel who served in Vietnam. Have students print out one or more letters to analyze.

3. Have groups discuss the letters and highlight areas that might be of particular interest to historians, and explain their highlighted choices.

4. As homework, have students write a short paragraph explaining the value of letters as primary sources. **LS** **Interpersonal, Verbal-Linguistic**

Alternative Assessment Handbook, Rubrics 16: Judging Information; and 30: Research

Two Views on
The Domino Theory

President Dwight Eisenhower and many other U.S. leaders believed that if one nation fell to communism, others might quickly follow.

❝You have a row of dominoes set up, you knock over the first one, and what will happen to the last one is the certainty that it will go over very quickly. So you could have the beginning of a disintegration that would have the most profound influences . . . Asia, after all, has already lost some 450 millions of her peoples to the Communist dictatorship, and we simply can't afford greater losses.**❞**

Dwight Eisenhower
—April 7, 1954

Robert McNamara was the U.S. secretary of defense during the first part of the Vietnam War. At the time, he believed in the domino theory, but he later came to regret the U.S. actions in Southeast Asia.

❝I am certain we exaggerated the threat. Had we never intervened, I now doubt that the dominoes would have fallen; I doubt that all of Asia would have fallen under Communist control. I doubt that the security of the West would have been materially and adversely affected had we not intervened . . . That was our major error.**❞**

Robert McNamara
—April 16, 1996

Skills FOCUS INVESTIGATING HISTORY

Infer Do you think world events that took place after Eisenhower spoke had any effect on McNamara's opinion? Why or why not?

Tet: A Turning Point In 1968 the North Vietnamese army and the Vietcong carried out a daring strike against cities and other targets across South Vietnam. Because the attack began on the Vietnamese New Year, called *Tet*, it came to be called the Tet Offensive.

The offensive was a military setback for the Vietcong, but it still delivered a heavy political blow to the U.S. and South Vietnamese effort. American leaders had claimed that victory in Vietnam was close at hand, but the Tet Offensive dramatically showed this was not the case. Thus, the attacks greatly weakened American public support for the war.

After the Tet Offensive, the war expanded into Laos and Cambodia, Vietnam's neighbors, where the North Vietnamese had built a supply network known as the Ho Chi Minh Trail. U.S. efforts to destroy the trail largely failed.

As more American soldiers were killed or wounded in the conflict, the American public's opposition to the war grew. After long negotiations, the United States reached a peace agreement with North Vietnam in 1973 and withdrew its military support. Without that support, the South quickly lost ground. In April 1975 North Vietnamese tanks rolled into Saigon, South Vietnam's capital, ending the war.

After the War Vietnam was reunited officially in 1976, but the nation faced major problems. Millions of Vietnamese had died or been made homeless during the war, and the Vietnamese economy was severely crippled.

Vietnam abandoned its Soviet-style planned economy in the mid-1980s and adopted economic reforms, which resulted in slow but largely steady economic growth. In 1995 the United States formally recognized the united Vietnam, and soon after, the two nations agreed to improve their trade relationship. Although Vietnam has undergone many economic reforms since the war ended, political reforms have been slower to arrive. Today, Vietnam remains a Communist nation.

READING CHECK **Summarize** Summarize the course of the Vietnam War.

FOCUS ON NEW YORK
Over 4,000 New Yorkers died while serving in the Vietnam War. The New York State Vietnam Memorial in Albany honors their service.

THE IMPACT TODAY
In the fall of 2006 Vietnam was working to join the World Trade Organization, an act that would open up the country to more foreign trade and investment.

Reading Focus

The Vietnam War

Recall Why was the 1968 offensive known as the Tet Offensive? *because it took place on the Vietnamese New Year, called Tet*

Evaluate Which side benefited most from the Tet Offensive? *possible answer—The Vietcong showed they were capable of effective attacks against American forces; they also benefited from the secondary effect of weakened American public support.*

Describe Describe the political situation in Vietnam today. *It is a Communist nation. The united Vietnam is formally recognized by the United States.*

Info to Know

Lunar New Year The celebration of the Tet is significant to the Vietnamese, providing three days of celebration that emphasize their cultural identity. The Tet festival dates back to the Bronze Age and emphasizes the cultural identity of the Vietnamese. Though there are several Tet festivals per year, the most significant one marks the lunar new year. Entire villages celebrate together, expressing the unities of man and nature, of people with their ancestors, of families with faraway members, and of people with their neighbors.

Differentiating Instruction

Below Level

Learners Having Difficulty

1. Remind students that the Tet Offensive resulted in a major decline in the American public's support for the war.

2. Have students read each view presented in the Counterpoints feature on this page. When students have a clear understanding of each quote, have them paraphrase each point of view in their own words.

3. Have volunteers read their paraphrases aloud to the class.

4. Guide students in a class discussion about each point of view, and the tense atmosphere in the United States during this time.
   LS **Intrapersonal, Verbal-Linguistic**

   Alternative Assessment Handbook, Rubrics 11: Discussions; and 37: Writing Assignments

Answers

Counterpoints *Since all of Asia did not fall to the communists, it is likely McNamara based his conclusion on world events.*

Reading Check *United States feared Communists would take control of South Vietnam; war began and U.S. involvement increased American public opposition to the war grew; United States removed troops; North Vietnamese took control of South Vietnam.*

3 How has Southeast Asia changed in recent decades? *Many nations have gained independence from colonial rule and have struggled to build stable, independent countries.*

Changes in Southeast Asia

Identify When did Indonesia win its independence? *1949*

Describe How did the Cold War affect Indonesia? *Sukarno, Indonesia's first president, adopted policies that supported communism.*

Evaluate What was positive and what was negative about Suharto's rule? *positive—Indonesian economy revived temporarily; negative—authoritarian regime was corrupt*

CRF: Biography: Loung Ung

World Religions
Buddhism

Describe What are Buddhists to do while they seek enlightenment? *lead virtuous, moral lives, and attempt to purify their minds in order to reach nirvana*

Analyze Rounding to the nearest hundred years, how long has it been since the death of Siddhartha Gautama, the Buddha? *2,500 years*

Info to Know

Buddhism's Growth The American Buddhist population has increased dramatically in the last decade. Buddhism is now listed among the top ten organized religions in the United States.

Answers

World Religions *Siddharta Gautama became known as the Buddha and traveled across India teaching his ideas.*

Buddhism

Buddhism is one of the most common religions in Southeast Asia. Many of the people of Vietnam, Cambodia, and Laos are Buddhists.

Origins of Buddhism The religion and philosophy of Buddhism developed from the teachings of a man named Siddhartha Gautama, a Hindu who was born in India around 563 BC. As a young man, Siddhartha spent years wandering throughout India, searching for answers to his questions about the meaning of human life. After much meditation he found the answers he had been looking for. From that point on, he was known as the Buddha, or the "Enlightened One." The Buddha spent the rest of his life traveling across northern India, teaching people his ideas. By the time of his death around 483 BC, the Buddha's teachings were spreading rapidly.

Buddhism is based on the teachings of the Buddha. A key aspect of Buddhism is the search for enlightenment, or the understanding of the true nature of reality. Buddhists seek to lead virtuous, moral lives, and attempt to purify their minds in order to reach nirvana, or a state of perfect peace.

Buddhism Today Some 350–400 million people in the world are Buddhists. Buddhists live on every continent, but the majority of the religion's followers are in Asia. Buddhism is a powerful religious, political, and cultural force in many parts of the world today.

Today, two major branches of Buddhism exist: Theraveda and Mahayana. Mahayana is the larger branch.

Summarize How did Buddhism develop?

This large bronze statue of the Buddha in Hong Kong attracts many visitors.

BUDDHISTS BY COUNTRY, 2005

Country	Buddhist Population (in millions)
China	104 million
Japan	94.1 million
Thailand	60.1 million
Myanmar (Burma)	46.8 million
Vietnam	41.5 million

Source: U.S. Department of State

NEW YORK
CC Unit 7-E4
Southeast Asia

Changes in Southeast Asia

Some of the political and social forces that tore apart Vietnam were also at work elsewhere in the region. During the years after World War II, other nations in Southeast Asia struggled to build stable, independent countries.

Indonesia The nation now known as Indonesia consists of over 13,000 islands spread across the Indian and Pacific oceans. Before being taken over by Japan in World War II, Indonesia had been a Dutch colony known as the Dutch East Indies. When the Dutch tried to regain control after the war, they faced an independence movement led by **Sukarno**. After several years of fighting, Indonesia won its independence in 1949.

Sukarno became Indonesia's first president and eventually moved to take greater control of the government, replacing the elected parliament with his supporters. Although

Sukarno initially tried to stay out of the Cold War, he later adopted policies that allied Indonesia with the Soviet Union and supported the growth of Indonesia's Communist party. At the same time, Sukarno's economic policies pushed the nation close to bankruptcy.

In 1965 a group of army officers and Communists tried to seize power in a coup d'état. The head of the army, General **Suharto**, fought back. In the struggle for power that followed the attempted coup, hundreds of thousands of Communists and alleged Communists were murdered. When the struggle ended, Suharto took control of the country.

Suharto ruled Indonesia for many years. His authoritarian regime was corrupt, but under his rule the Indonesian economy revived. By the 1980s, however, some Indonesians had started to turn against him, resenting his corruption and his use of power. When the Indonesian economy collapsed in 1997, protests and riots broke out; and Suharto stepped down the

---

Skills Focus: Making Written Presentations

At Level

Reading Like a Historian Skill
Sukarno and Suharto

Research Required

1. Explain to students that Sukarno and Suharto were two early leaders in Indonesia.

2. Refer students to the Faces of History biography of Ho Chi Minh in this section. Have students conduct independent research to create their own Faces of History biography of either Sukarno or Suharto. Biographies should include years lived, interesting facts about the person, and a question at the end.

3. Collect the biographies and redistribute them. Each student should have a biography written by another student. Tell students to read the biographies and answer the questions.

LS Verbal-Linguistic

Alternative Assessment Handbook, Rubrics 4: Biographies; 30: Research; and 42: Writing to Inform following year. In subsequent years, a series of democratic governments worked to rebuild the nation's economy.

Today, Indonesia has the fourth-largest population in the world and is home to over 300 ethnic groups. Most Indonesians are Muslims, but a large Christian minority exists, as well as Hindus and Buddhists. At times, this diversity has led to conflict. On the island of Sulawesi, for example, thousands of Indonesians died in fighting between Christians and Muslims. In the early 2000s, Muslim radicals were linked to several terrorist attacks in Indonesia.

The nation was faced with a new challenge in 2004 when a devastating tsunami struck Indonesia and other parts of Southeast Asia, killing over 225,000 people and causing widespread destruction.

East Timor In 1975 Indonesia seized control of East Timor, a former Portuguese colony that had declared its independence just days before. For nearly three decades, East Timorese fought against the Indonesian invasion. Over 100,000 people died. In 2002 East Timor finally won its independence.

Cambodia Cambodia endured years of struggle after it won independence from France in 1953. In 1975 a Communist group called the **Khmer Rouge** (kuh-MER roozh) gained control of the country. Led by **Pol Pot**, the Khmer Rouge established a Communist government and renamed the country Democratic Kampuchea (cam-pooh-CHEE-uh).

The Khmer Rouge also began a radical program to rebuild Cambodian society. The goal was to create a country in which nearly everyone would work as a simple peasant. The Khmer Rouge believed that in order to achieve this goal, all the influences of urban life and modern civilization had to be destroyed.

The Khmer Rouge set about their task with tremendous brutality. All opposition—real or imagined—was destroyed. Anyone who showed any sign of having been educated was killed, and many others were worked or starved to death. At least 1.5 million Cambodians died—out of a population of 7 million.

Growing conflict between the Khmer Rouge and Vietnam soon turned into war. Vietnam invaded Cambodia, forcing Pol Pot from power in 1979. Peace did not come quickly, however,

as Pol Pot led Khmer Rouge guerrillas in a civil war that raged in Cambodia throughout the 1980s. In 1993 the United Nations helped organize an election, and today Cambodia is a constitutional monarchy with a democratically elected parliament. The nation is slowly rebuilding itself after many years of war.

Myanmar Burma, which is now known as Myanmar, won independence from Great Britain in 1948. The new nation faced many difficulties, including a weak central government and severe ethnic tensions. A military dictatorship seized power in the 1960s, and the military still controls Myanmar today. An opponent of the government, **Aung San Suu Kyi** (AWNG SAHN SOO CHEE), won the Nobel Peace Prize in 1991 for her efforts to promote democracy in Myanmar. Yet the government has held her in prison or under house arrest for much of the time since the late 1980s.

READING CHECK **Make Generalizations** How have nations in Southeast Asia changed?

THE IMPACT TODAY

In 2006 Cambodia approved the selection of 30 judges to preside over genocide trials for surviving Khmer Rouge leaders.

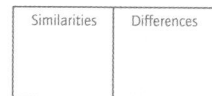

SECTION 2 ASSESSMENT

go.hrw.com
Online Quiz
Keyword: SHL ASA HP

Reviewing Key Terms and People

1. **a. Identify** Who were the **Vietminh** and **Ho Chi Minh**?
   b. Contrast How did colonies in Southeast Asia achieve independence in different ways?

2. **a. Define** Define the following terms: **domino theory, Vietcong**
   b. Analyze How did the Tet Offensive affect the Vietnam War?
   c. Evaluate How do you think U.S. belief in the domino theory affected American involvement in the Vietnam War?

3. **a. Recall** What did the **Khmer Rouge** do in Cambodia?
   b. Summarize Summarize the events in Indonesia after World War II.

Critical Thinking

4. **Compare and Contrast** Use your notes and a graphic organizer like the one below to answer the following questions: In what ways were postwar events in Vietnam similar to events in other nations in Southeast Asia? How were they different?

Similarities	Differences

FOCUS ON WRITING

5. **Narration** Write a one-paragraph encyclopedia entry on the life of Ho Chi Minh. Include the main events of his life in chronological order.

ASIA **919**

Review & Assess

Close
Review with students the changes in Southeast Asia in the postwar years, the effects of the Vietnam War, and the recent changes in Southeast Asia.

Review
Online Quiz, Section 2

Assess
SE Section 2 Assessment
Progress Assessment: Section 2 Quiz
Alternative Assessment Handbook

Reteach/Intervene
Interactive Reader and Study Guide, Section 2
Interactive Skills Tutor CD-ROM

Answers

Reading Check *Many of its natioons have gained independence from colonial rule, but have struggled to build stable, independent governments.*

Section 2 Assessment Answers

1. **a.** Vietminh—guerrilla group that fought for Vietnamese independence; Ho Chi Minh—Communist leader of the Vietminh
   b. Some granted independence; others struggled for independence.

2. **a.** domino theory: the belief that if Vietnam fell to communism, other Southeast Asian countries would quickly follow; Vietcong: Vietnamese Communists
   b. heavy blow to American forces proved victory was not close at hand, and weakened public's support for the war.

   c. possible answer—Without this belief, the United States might never have become involved in the Vietnam War.

3. **a.** began radical program to rebuild Cambodian society; killed 1.5 million people suspected of opposition
   b. won independence; Sukarno adopted Communist policies; General Suharto fought back against coup; Suharto took control of government, stepped down in 1997; democratic governments worked to rebuild economy

4. all endured years of struggle; Vietminh fought for independence; North became Communist; South backed by United States; after Vietnam War North takes control of Vietnam; Other Countries—Khmer Rouge begins radical program, kills 1.5 million in Cambodia; Indonesia seizes East Timor in 1975, and East Timor finally wins independence in 2002; military dicatorship in Myanmar

5. Student entries should include details and events from the life of Ho Chi Minh.

920 CHAPTER 30

Preteach

Preteach

Getting Started

Use the **Interactive Reader and Study Guide** to familiarize students with the section content.

📑 **Interactive Reader and Study Guide,** Section 3

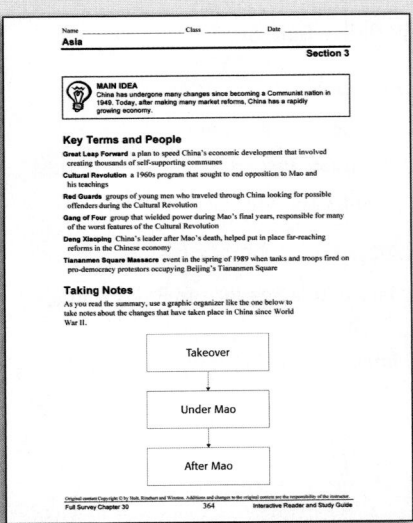

Academic Vocabulary

Review with students the high-use academic terms in this section.

ideology a system of ideas, often political (p. 921)

initiate to begin (p. 922)

📑 **CRF:** Vocabulary Builder: Section 3

Taking Notes

Takeover—civil war resumed between nationalist Guomindang and Chinese Communists; China became Communist in 1949; Under Mao—many so-called opponents killed or sent to labor camps; Great Leap Forward; Cultural Revolution; After Mao—reforms began, Gang of Four imprisoned, Deng Xiaoping made market reforms known as the Four Modernizations; protests lead to Tiananmen Square Massacre in 1989; today China's economy is second largest in the world

go.hrw.com
Online Resources

KEYWORD: SHL ASA
ACTIVITY: Biography of an Asian Leader

---

3 Communist China

BEFORE YOU READ

MAIN IDEA
China has undergone many changes since becoming a Communist nation in 1949. Today, after making many market reforms, China has a rapidly growing economy.

READING FOCUS
1. How did the Communists take over China?
2. What were the main events that took place in China under Mao's leadership?
3. How did China change in the years after Mao's death?

KEY TERMS AND PEOPLE
Great Leap Forward
Cultural Revolution
Red Guards
Gang of Four
Deng Xiaoping
Tiananmen Square Massacre

 NEW YORK

PI 3.1 Students analyze the roles and contributions of individuals and groups.

PI 3.3 Students examine the social/cultural, political, economic, and religious norms and values of Western and other world cultures.

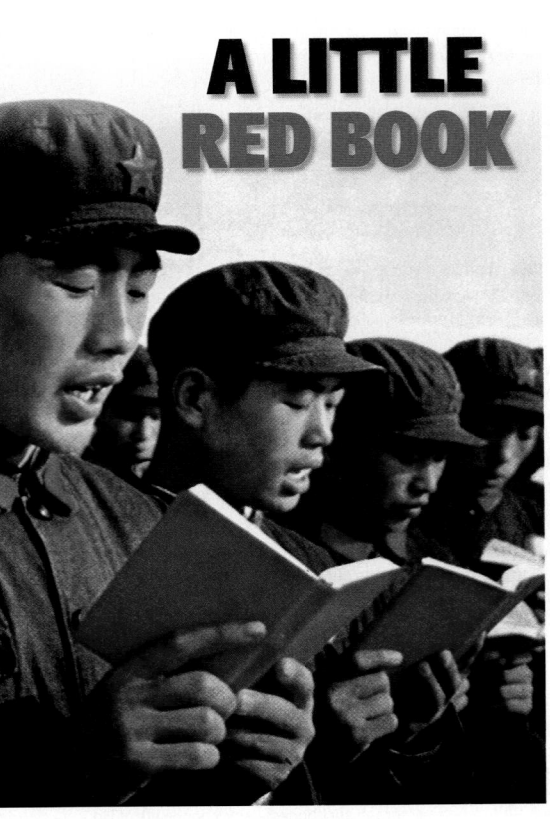

▲ **Chinese soldiers recite passages from Mao's writings.**

THE INSIDE STORY *Did everyone in China have a little red book?* In 1960s-era Communist China, the color red symbolized the Communist revolution that had swept over the nation two decades earlier. Red was everywhere in China—on posters, banners, and flags—but it may have been most visible on the pocket-sized red books that nearly all Chinese people carried with them. This so-called "Little Red Book," or *Quotations From Chairman Mao*, was a collection of Mao Zedong's writings and political ideas. Originally published to shape Chinese soldiers' political beliefs, by the late 1960s the book was enormously popular among the public.

The adoration of Mao's words extended to Mao himself. In newspapers, photographs, and propaganda posters, the Chinese government actively encouraged virtual worship of Mao, showing him as a larger-than-life, godlike figure. It was expected that a Chinese home would have an official portrait or bust of Mao displayed in a prominent location. In fact, the failure to possess a book of Mao's writings or a portrait of the leader was often interpreted as a sign that a person was anti-Mao or anti-Communist and could lead to punishment. In one case, a man was jailed for seven years for accidentally breaking a bust of Mao. Having a "Little Red Book," then, was a way to demonstrate loyalty to the Communist leader—and to provide protection against being accused of disloyalty. ■

Communists Take Over China

During World War II the Chinese Communists and the nationalist Guomindang had agreed to put aside their differences in order to fight the Japanese invaders. Once the war ended with Japan's defeat, however, the civil war resumed.

Teach the Main Idea
At Level

Communist China

Materials: 3 sheets of chart paper

1. **Teach** Ask students the Reading Focus questions to teach this section.

2. **Apply** Organize students into three groups. Assign one of the following topics to each group: Communists Take Over China, China under Mao, and China After Mao. Distribute chart paper and have groups design and assemble collages made up of notes and drawings representing the information presented in their assigned part of this section.

3. **Review** Allow time for groups to share their work with the class.

4. **Practice/Homework** Have each student write a short paragraph about China from 1934 to the present. 🔳 **Visual-Spatial, Verbal-Linguistic**

📑 **Alternative Assessment Handbook,** Rubrics 1: Acquiring Information; 14: Group Activity; and 8: Collages

Although the Guomindang forces outnumbered Mao's Communists, the Communists had wide support among China's peasants, who made up the vast majority of the nation's population. Rural Chinese peasants had long been oppressed by brutal landlords and high taxes, as well as by the policies of Jiang Jieshi's corrupt government. Because the Communists promised to take land from the landlords and distribute it to the peasants, public support for the Communists was widespread.

By 1949 the Communists had driven the Guomindang almost entirely from China, with Guomindang control limited to a few small areas on the mainland and several islands, including Taiwan. On October 1 Mao Zedong stood before a huge crowd in Beijing and announced the formation of the People's Republic of China.

China faced many difficulties, including a crippled economy and the lack of a functional government. Some countries that opposed communism, such as the United States, refused to recognize Mao, claiming that Jiang's government on Taiwan was China's true government. But Mao was in power to stay.

READING CHECK Summarize Why did peasants support the Communist takeover of China?

China under Mao

Having defeated the Guomindang, Mao set about building a Communist China. His first concern was rebuilding a country that had been torn apart by years of civil war.

Rebuilding China Communist ideology shaped the new government's efforts to change China's political and economic systems. The government discouraged the practice of religion and, as Communist leaders had promised peasants during the civil war, seized the property of rural landowners and redistributed it among the peasants. China soon put in place Soviet-style five-year plans for industrial development. The first plan, completed in 1957, succeeded in doubling China's small industrial output. Indeed, the early efforts to build the Chinese economy were remarkably successful at improving the economy and reducing rural poverty, and they had much public support. Mao's policies led to improvements in lit-

eracy rates and public health, and Chinese life expectancy increased sharply over the next few decades.

These improvements came at a cost, however. To consolidate Communist control over China, the government soon began to eliminate the so-called "enemies of the state" who had spoken out against the government's policies. Many thousands of Chinese—including public officials, business leaders, artists, and writers—were killed or sent to labor camps in the early years of Communist rule.

The Great Leap Forward The Soviet Union provided much financial support and other aid to China in its first years as a Communist nation. China modeled many of its new political, economic, and military policies on the Soviet system. During the 1950s, however, territorial disputes and differences in ideology slowly pushed China away from its Soviet ally. In a break from Soviet-style economic planning, in 1958 Mao announced a program, the **Great Leap Forward**, designed to increase China's industrial and agricultural output. The plan created thousands of communes, or collectively owned farms, of about 20,000 people each. Each commune was to produce food and to have its own small-scale industry.

The plan was a disaster. The small commune factories failed to produce the quantity or quality of goods that China needed, and a combination of poor weather and farmers' neglect led to sharp drops in agricultural production.

TAKING NOTES

Take notes about the changes that have taken place in China since World War II.

Takeover

↓

Under Mao

↓

After Mao

ACADEMIC VOCABULARY

ideology a system of ideas, often political

NEW YORK

CC **Unit 7-D3** Communism under Mao Zedong

Skills Focus: Recognizing Bias in Primary Sources   At Level

Reading Like a Historian Skill   Prep Required
Mao's Little Red Book

Materials: copies of various pages from *Quotations from Chairman Mao*, available in English on the Internet.

Background: Tell students that many Chinese citizens had a copy of *Quotations from Chairman Mao* during his rule. The "Little Red Book" was a guide to life as a loyal Communist.

1. Organize students into small groups. Distribute copies of several quotations to each group. Ask groups to discuss their assigned

quotations, marking wording that reflects any sort of bias. Have students record the observations and opinions expressed by group members about each quotation.

2. Have groups share their results with the class.

3. As homework, have students write a paragraph summarizing Mao Zedong's ideas.
LS Interpersonal, Verbal-Linguistic

Alternative Assessment Handbook, Rubrics 14: Group Activity; and 16: Judging Information

• **Direct Teach** •

Reading Focus

1 How did the Communists take over China? *The Guomindang and the Communists fought the Japanese invasion. Afterwards, with wide support from peasants, the Communists drove the Guomindang out of China.*

Communists Take Over China

Recall How did the United States feel about the People's Republic of China? *They refused to recognize it and claimed that Jiang's government was the true Chinese government.*

Rate What is your opinion of a leader who can raise an army of one million within a few years? *possible answer— He must have had great charisma and persuasive powers to do so.*

Reading Focus

2 What were the main events that took place in China under Mao's leadership? *the Great Leap Forward, the Cultural Revolution*

China under Mao

Explain Why did Mao institute the Great Leap Forward? *to increase China's agricultural and industrial output*

Make Inferences From your knowledge of Mao's ordered executions of hundreds of thousands, what sort of person do you think he was? *possible answer—He feared opposition, and may have been paranoid.*

Answers

Faces of History *Mao believed that, the peasants would be the revolutionaries.*

Reading Check *because the Communists promised them land*

China under Mao

Describe What were the early results of the Great Leap Forward? *Factories and farms failed to produce well and there was widespread famine.*

Explain What was the purpose of the Cultural Revolution? *Mao tried to regain some of the power and prestige he had lost under the Great Leap Forward.*

Identify Cause and Effect What caused China's complete isolation? *Mao's harsh treatment of his citizens and the failure of the Great Leap Forward led other nations, including the Soviet Union, to criticize him. Relations between the two countries broke down completely by the 1960s.*

📄 **CRF:** A Red Guard Describes the Cultural Revolution

Biography

Qi Shu Fang (c.1943—) Qi Shu Fang is a significant contributor in the history of Chinese opera. She began her studies of opera in 1947 when she was only 4 years old. By the 1960s, she was performing nationally, but the Cultural Revolution (1966-1976) limited performances to only a few patriotic plays. At 22, she was among those selected to perform in one of them. Millions saw her play the part of a courageous peasant girl, Chang Bao, or "Constant Treasure." Later, political change reopened the traditional repertory, and she performed in other countries as well. In 1987 Qi Shu Fang immigrated to the United States, where she established her own Chinese opera troupe.

Answers

History Close-Up *possible answer— The protest grew larger, and the Chinese government did not agree with its pro-democracy message.*

Reading Check *The failure of the Great Leap Forward and the isolation of China triggered the Cultural Revolution.*

922

As a result, famine spread throughout rural China. Tens of millions of Chinese starved to death between 1959 and 1961.

The failure of the Great Leap Forward led to criticism of Mao by many people, including Soviet leaders. The Soviet criticism, and the withdrawal of Soviet industrial aid in 1960, helped widen the rift between the two Communist nations. By the early 1960s relations between the two countries had broken down completely. Communist China found itself virtually isolated in the world community.

The Cultural Revolution In the mid-1960s Mao tried to regain some of the power and prestige he had lost after the Great Leap Forward. He <u>initiated</u> a new movement called the **Cultural Revolution**, which sought to rid China of its old ways and create a society in which peasants and physical labor were the ideal. This campaign of social change meant eliminating intellectuals such as teachers, skilled workers, and artists, who Mao feared wanted

ACADEMIC VOCABULARY
initiate to begin

to end communism and bring back China's old ways.

Mao shut down China's schools and encouraged militant high school and college students known as **Red Guards** to carry out the work of the Cultural Revolution by criticizing intellectuals and traditional values. But Mao soon lost control of the movement. The Red Guards traveled through China's cities and villages, looking for possible offenders and torturing or killing people they believed to be politically corrupt. They murdered hundreds of thousands of people. By the late 1960s China was on the verge of civil war before Mao managed to regain control and break up the Red Guards.

Although the Cultural Revolution reestablished Mao's dominance in China, it caused terrible destruction in Chinese society. In many areas, civil authority collapsed, while economic activity fell off sharply.

READING CHECK **Analyze** How did life in China change under Mao?

HISTORY CLOSE-UP

Tiananmen Square, 1989

More than 1 million pro-democracy protestors occupied Beijing's Tiananmen Square in the spring of 1989. At first, Chinese leaders tolerated the demonstration, but as the protest grew larger they decided to crack down. In the evening hours of June 3, the government sent tanks and troops into the square to crush the protestors, killing hundreds.

TIANANMEN SQUARE

- Zhongshan Park
- Tiananmen Gate
- Great Hall of the People
- TIANANMEN SQUARE
- Monument to the People's Heroes
- Chinese National Museum
- Mao Zedong Mausoleum

Skills Focus **INTERPRETING VISUALS**

Infer Why did Chinese leaders crack down on the demonstrations in Tiananmen Square?

922 企业物资...

DAY 1

April 15 After the death of a reformist Chinese political leader, students gather in Tiananmen Square to call for democratic reform.

Differentiating Instruction

Below Level

Struggling Readers; Learners Having Difficulty

1. Copy the chart for students to see, omitting the italicized words. Have students copy and fill in the chart alone, or in pairs.

2. When students have had adequate time to fill in their charts, allow them to compare and complete their work. Have students draw a political cartoon that relates to one of Mao's programs. 🄻 **Verbal-Linguistic, Visual-Spatial**

📄 **Alternative Assessment Handbook,** Rubrics 7: Charts; and 27: Political Cartoons

	Great Leap Forward	Cultural Revolution
Date	*1958*	*mid-1960s*
Goal	*to speed China's development*	*create a society where peasants and physical labor were the ideal*
Actions	*formed communes, set production goals*	*Red Guard tortured or killed suspected offenders*
Result	*famine, China's isolation*	*destruction in Chinese society*

China After Mao

Mao Zedong died in 1976. Though Mao was a revered figure in China, his death was followed by a retreat from many of his policies.

Reforms Begin China began to end its isolation from the rest of the world in the early 1970s. U.S. president Richard Nixon ended decades of U.S. hostility toward the nation by visiting China in 1972 and meeting with Mao, who by that time was in poor health.

During the last years of Mao's life, much of the power in China was wielded by a group of four people known as the **Gang of Four**. This group, which included Mao's wife, Jiang Qing (jee-AHNG ching), was responsible for many of the worst features of the Cultural Revolution. After Mao's death, more moderate leaders imprisoned the Gang of Four.

Deng Xiaoping (DUHNG SHOW-ping) eventually became China's leader and helped put in place far-reaching market reforms in the Chinese economy. Deng's reform plan was called the Four Modernizations after the four economic areas it sought to modernize: agriculture, industry, science and technology, and national defense. The plan gave businesses new freedom to make economic decisions.

Tiananmen Square Inspired by the movement toward economic freedom, many Chinese demanded more political freedom. In the spring of 1989, as democratic reforms were sweeping through Eastern Europe, more than 1 million pro-democracy protestors occupied Beijing's Tiananmen (tee-AN-uhn-men) Square.

China's leaders became increasingly impatient with the protests. After repeatedly asking the protestors to leave the square, they finally responded with force. Tanks and troops moved into the square in June 1989, killing many protestors in the **Tiananmen Square Massacre**. True freedom had not yet arrived in China.

China Today China's economy has grown rapidly as market reforms have continued.

READING SKILLS
Identifying Problems and Solutions How did Deng try to solve China's economic problems?

 NEW YORK
CC Unit 7-D4 Communism under Deng Xiaoping

May 30 Near the official portrait of Mao Zedong, students build a large statue that comes to be known as the "Goddess of Democracy."

DAY 16

June 3 Chinese soldiers move into Tiananmen Square to force out the protestors. Hundreds of protestors are killed.

DAY 19

June 5 In this famous image from the events at Tiananmen Square, an unarmed man faces down a line of Chinese tanks.

DAY 21

923

Direct Teach

Reading Focus

3 How did China change in the years since Mao's death? *New reforms have dramatically improved the economy and the standard of living for the Chinese, and increased China's participation in the world economy.*

China After Mao

Recall When did Mao Zedong die? *1976*

Explain What happened to the Gang of Four after Mao's death? *They were arrested and imprisoned.*

Develop What are some possible reasons so many people were killed in Tiananmen Square? *possible answer— Frustration caused leaders to call for force, and the military did not issue a warning, or fire a few shots, but they responded with the full force of tanks and troops.*

CRF: Biography: Zhang Yimon

Teaching Tip

Remind students that Mao Zedong led a popular revolution to save his people from what many people felt was a corrupt regime. Guide a discussion about the positive and negative effects of his leadership.

Skills Focus: Comparing and Contrasting

At Level

Reading Skill
Mao Zedong and Deng Xiaoping

1. Copy the chart for all to see. Omit the italicized answers. Have students copy and complete the chart.

2. Guide a class discussion comparing and contrasting Mao's Great Leap Forward and Deng's Four Modernizations. Which plan succeeded and which plan failed? Why? **LS Verbal-Linguistic**

Alternative Assessment Handbook, Rubrics 7; Charts; and 9: Comparing and Contrasting

Great Leap Forward (Mao Zedong)	Four Modernizations (Deng Xiaoping)
20,000 communes, or collectively owned farms	*economic reforms in four areas: agriculture, industry, science and technology, and national defense*
resulted in famine, starvation of millions of Chinese people	*businesses had freedom to make economic decisions*
Soviet Union criticized Mao	*Chinese economy grew rapidly*

Answers

Reading Skills *made market reforms to modernize the economy*

Close

Review with students how the Communists took control, Mao's leadership, and the changes in China since Mao's death.

Review

Online Quiz, Section 3

Assess

SE Section 3 Assessment

Progress Assessment: Section 3 Quiz

Alternative Assessment Handbook

Reteach/Intervene

Interactive Reader and Study Guide, Section 3

Interactive Skills Tutor CD-ROM

Answers

Primary Sources 1. *combining elements of a planned economy with elements of a market economy;* **2.** *"no alternative," "only road to prosperity"*

Reading Check *isolation lessened, more moderate leaders took power, new economic freedom led to call for political freedom, improved standard of living*

Economic Reforms in China

In 1985 Chinese leader Deng Xiaoping spoke about the economic reforms that China was undergoing.

"There is no fundamental contradiction between socialism and a market economy . . . If we combine a planned economy with a market economy, we shall be in a better position to liberate the productive forces and speed up economic growth . . .

"It is clear now that the right approach is to open to the outside world, combine a planned economy with a market economy and introduce structural reforms . . .

"In short, the overriding task in China today is to throw ourselves heart and soul into the modernization drive. While giving play to the advantages inherent in socialism, we are also employing some capitalist methods—but only as methods of accelerating the growth of the productive forces . . . China has no alternative but to follow this road. It is the only road to prosperity."

Skills Focus **READING LIKE A HISTORIAN**

1. **Summarize** What economic changes was Deng advocating?
2. **Analyze Primary Sources** What words does Deng use to justify the economic reforms?

See **Skills Handbook**, p. H25

Today, China's economy is the second largest in the world, behind only the United States. As the economy has improved, so has the standard of living for many Chinese. Still, economic growth has not reached all of China's 1.3 billion people. To prevent further population growth from harming economic development, the Chinese government encourages families to have only one child.

China faces other challenges as its large population and rapidly expanding industries place high demands on the nation's resources and environment. The country has been forced to import enormous quantities of coal, iron ore, oil, and natural gas to meet its energy and resource needs, leading to shortages—and higher costs—of these resources on the global market. Furthermore, the rapid industrial expansion has led to widespread air and water pollution within China.

Human rights abuses are another concern for many critics of China. The Chinese government continues to limit free speech and religious freedoms, and it exercises strict control over the media. Political protestors can be jailed, and the nation's courts are accused of failing to provide fair trials. Critics increased their calls for reforms after Beijing was chosen to host the 2008 Olympic Games.

READING CHECK **Make Generalizations** How did China change in the years after Mao's death?

SECTION 3 ASSESSMENT

go.hrw.com
Online Quiz
Keyword: SHL ASA HP

Reviewing Key Terms and People

1. **a. Describe** What happened in China after the end of World War II?
   b. Explain Why did most Chinese peasants support the Communists?
2. **a. Identify** Summarize the following events: **Great Leap Forward, Cultural Revolution**
   b. Explain Why did the Cultural Revolution lead to such chaos and disorder in China?
   c. Evaluate Evaluate the successes and failures of Communist China under Mao Zedong.
3. **a. Recall** Summarize the challenges that China faces today.
   b. Contrast Contrast Chinese leaders' willingness to make economic reforms with their willingness to make democratic reforms.

Critical Thinking

4. **Identify Cause and Effect** Use your notes on the section and a graphic organizer like the one below to describe the effects of the events listed.

Mao Takes Power	→	
Great Leap Forward	→	
Cultural Revolution	→	
Mao Dies	→	

FOCUS ON SPEAKING

5. **Persuasion** Write a brief speech that a protestor might have given in Tiananmen Square in May 1989 about the need for democratic reform in China.

924 CHAPTER 30

Section 3 Assessment Answers

1. **a.** Mao Communists drove the Guomindong out of China; people's Republic of China is formed; Mao is in power
   b. because the Communists promised to take land from landlords and give it to the peasants

2. **a.** Great Leap Forward—an economic plan that created thousands of communes and assigned food and industrial production quotas but resulted in famine; Cultural Revolution—a plan for Mao to regain some of his former power and prestige

   b. Civil authority collapsed, economic activity fell off sharply.
   c. possible answer—Mao had some early successes, but his later plans and brutality were a disaster for China.

3. **a.** economic growth has not reached all people; pollution; human rights abuses
   b. possible answer—Deng Xiaoping was willing to introduce some capitalist elements into the economy, but today, Chinese people still lack basic rights.

4. Mao Takes Power—a campaign to strengthen his control and transform the Chinese economy and culture; Great Leap Forward—factory and farm failures and famine led to the isolation of China from the rest of the world; Cultural Revolution—the killing of thousands, collapse of civil authority, fall off of economic activity; Mao Dies—retreat from many of his policies

5. Student speeches should point out that political freedoms should accompany economic freedoms.

The Rise of Pacific Rim Economies

BEFORE YOU READ

MAIN IDEA
The nations of the Asian Pacific Rim underwent remarkable economic growth in the years after World War II, but significant challenges remain.

READING FOCUS
1. How did Japan change during the postwar years?
2. How did the nations of the Pacific Rim change after World War II?
3. How did the Asian Tigers develop?

KEY TERMS AND PEOPLE
Ferdinand Marcos
Corazon Aquino
Kim Il Sung
Kim Jong Il
Asian Tigers

NEW YORK

PI 3.2 Students explain the dynamics of cultural change and how interactions between and among cultures have affected various cultural groups throughout the world.

PI 3.3 Students examine the social/ cultural, political, economic, and religious norms and values of Western and other world cultures.

AN EMPEROR SURRENDERS

◀ **Three weeping Japanese girls react to Emperor Hirohito's announcement that Japan had surrendered to end World War II.**

THE INSIDE STORY

What happens after an emperor surrenders? To the Japanese people, Emperor Hirohito was more than an emperor. To them, he was a living god and the latest in a line of divine rulers that stretched back hundreds of years.

Japanese citizens had never heard Hirohito's voice—until August 14, 1945. Speaking over the radio following the devastating atomic bomb attacks on Hiroshima and Nagasaki, Hirohito informed his stunned subjects that World War II was over. "The hardships and sufferings to which our nation is to be subjected hereafter will be certainly great," he warned.

Indeed, much would change in Japan in the years after the war. Emperor Hirohito would remain on his throne, but he would lose his authority and his divine status as a living god. Japan's economy, government, and many of its basic institutions would be rebuilt under U.S. occupation and control, and Japanese society would undergo many changes.

Yet while the changes ahead, as Hirohito had predicted, would be difficult and painful, Japan's rapid recovery from the war would become one of history's great success stories. The nation had lost the war, but in the space of a few short years, Japan would become one of the world's leading economic powers. ∎

ASIA **925**

Preteach

Getting Started
Use the **Interactive Reader and Study Guide** to familiarize students with the section content.

📝 **Interactive Reader and Study Guide,** Section 4

Name _____ Class _____ Date _____
Asia
Section 4

MAIN IDEA
The nations of the Asian Pacific Rim underwent remarkable economic growth in the years after World War II, but significant challenges remain.

Key Terms and People
Ferdinand Marcos Philippine president who became an authoritarian dictator in the 1970s
Corazon Aquino president of the Philippines, elected in 1986 after her husband, a rival of Marcos, was assassinated
Kim Il Sung Communist dictator who ruled North Korea after the end of the Korean War
Kim Jong Il son of Kim Il Sung, became ruler of North Korea after his father's death
Asian Tigers Asian nations that made great economic gains by following Japan's example

Taking Notes
As you read the summary, use a graphic organizer like the one below to take notes on the causes and effects of Asian economic growth.

Causes
↓
Growth
↓
Effects

Full Survey Chapter 30   367   Interactive Reader and Study Guide

📝 **CRF:** Vocabulary Builder: Section 4

Taking Notes
Causes—economic and military aid, Japan provided supplies to U.S. and U.N. forces during Korean War; work ethic, skilled workforce, increased exports; Effects—population growth; Japan has become a major economic power, improved standard of living

---

Teach the Main Idea

At Level

The Rise of Pacific Rim Economies

Materials: 4 ½" x 12" construction paper in a variety of colors, tape

1. **Teach** Ask students the Reading Focus questions to teach this section.

2. **Apply** Organize students into three groups. Assign a heading from this section to each group: Postwar Japan, The Pacific Rim, and The Asian Tigers. Have groups record causes and effects for their assigned heading, neatly copy each pair onto a strip of construction paper, and tape each pair together.

3. **Review** Display and discuss the cause-and-effect chains.

4. **Practice/Homework** Have each student write a short paragraph about the economies of the Pacific Rim countries. **LS** Verbal-Linguistic, Visual-Spatial

📝 **Alternative Assessment Handbook**, Rubrics 6: Cause and Effect; and 13: Graphic Organizers

❶ **How did Japan change during the postwar years?** *Japan's citizens gained new civil rights, a democratic government was established, new political parties formed, the economy grew, the standard of living improved*

Postwar Japan

Identify Which American was given control of occupied Japan? *General Douglas MacArthur*

Recall How did the building of a democratic government begin? *a new constitution went into effect in 1947.*

📄 **CRF:** Literature: *Hiroshima Notes*

Recent Scholarship

In *America and the Japanese Miracle: The Cold War Context of Japan's Postwar Economic Revival, 1950-1960*, Aaron Forsberg describes how the Cold War fears of the United States and its allies governed many aspects of foreign relations in Asia. The American government became deeply involved in the recovery of Japan after that country's surrender at the end of World War II. This unusually deep involvement influenced America's international relations for many years, which is outlined in Forsberg's book.

America and the Japanese Miracle: The Cold War Context of Japan's Postwar Economic Revival, 1950-1960 by Aaron Forsberg. The University of North Carolina Press, 2000.

Answers

Reading Like a Historian 1. *Japan;* **2.** *as a threat; Japan is the child and the United Nations is the parent*

926

TAKING NOTES

Take notes on the causes and effects of Asian economic growth.

Causes
↓
Growth
↓
Effects

THE IMPACT TODAY

Nationalist Japanese leaders have expressed a desire to revise the constitution to give the military more power.

Postwar Japan

Japan suffered terrible destruction during World War II. After the war, the nation needed to rebuild its government and economy.

American Occupation After World War II, U.S. troops occupied Japan, and American general Douglas MacArthur took control of the Allied efforts to rebuild the nation. The rebuilding process had three basic steps: demilitarizing Japan, building a democratic government, and establishing an economy that could support a peaceful and democratic Japan.

MacArthur's first job was to demilitarize Japan. He removed all wartime political, military, and business leaders from power. Many were tried as war criminals. MacArthur also dismantled the armed forces and shut down Japan's military industries.

The second step, building a democratic government, began with a new constitution for Japan, which went into effect in 1947. The new constitution gave far more power to the Japanese people than the previous constitution had, establishing a parliamentary democracy and giving all Japanese adults the right to vote for Japan's Diet, or parliament. The emperor was no longer a sacred being but was now simply a symbol of the state. The constitution placed great emphasis on the importance of human rights and greatly expanded Japanese citizens' civil rights, including the rights of freedom of speech, assembly, and religion. The constitution forbade Japan from building a military capable of attacking other countries.

The new constitution also guaranteed the right to organize political parties, which led to the formation of countless new parties, both small and large. The most important new party was the Liberal Democratic Party (LDP), a generally conservative party with a pro-U.S. foreign policy that dominated Japanese politics after the party's formation in 1955.

Reading like a Historian

Occupation of Japan

Analyzing Primary Sources After World War II, American troops occupied Japan under the command of General Douglas MacArthur. MacArthur's main tasks were to demilitarize Japan, to establish a new, democratic national government, and to create a successful economy. This document is an excerpt from the official orders given to MacArthur concerning the occupation of Japan.

As you read the selection, consider these factors:

- the point of view of the authors
- the words used to describe Japan, and what the choice of words suggests about Allied views of Japan

Skills FOCUS **READING LIKE A HISTORIAN**

1. **Point of View** Who or what do the authors blame for the war?
2. **Words** What does the "family of nations" metaphor suggest about how the authors viewed Japan's role in the world? In this "family," who is the child and who is the parent?

See **Skills Handbook**, p. H25

> The ultimate objective of the United Nations [in] Japan is to foster conditions which will give the greatest possible assurance that Japan will not again become a menace to the peace and security of the world and will permit her eventual admission as a responsible and peaceful member of the family of nations . . .
>
> By appropriate means you will make clear to all levels of the Japanese population the fact of their defeat. They must be made to realize that their suffering and defeat have been brought upon them by the lawless and irresponsible aggression of Japan, and that only when militarism has been eliminated . . . will Japan be admitted to the family of nations.
>
> —Joint Chiefs of Staff Instructions to General Douglas MacArthur, 1945

926 CHAPTER 30

Skill Focus: Analyzing Alternative Points of View | At Level

Reading Like a Historian Skill
Two Views of Occupation

1. Tell students that films of American life were shown to people in occupied Japan. Some had never seen a color movie or used electricity.

2. Have students choose the viewpoint of one of the following Japanese people: a peasant farmer, an industrial worker, an urban survivor of the Allied bombing, or a suburban housewife.

3. Have each student write a letter to the American head of the Occupation Forces Educational Services. Letters should be written from the assigned viewpoints, expressing their reaction to the educational films they have seen, and their needs during their nation's recovery.

4. Have volunteers read their letters to the class.
   LS **Verbal-Linguistic, Intrapersonal**

   📄 **Alternative Assessment Handbook**, Rubrics 25: Personal Letters; 41: Writing to Express

The third step, rebuilding the Japanese economy, led MacArthur to make many economic changes. For example, he sought to break up the large organizations known as zaibatsu that had dominated Japanese industry. He also established a land reform program that gave farmland to farmers who had previously rented their land.

Economic Recovery U.S. economic aid flowed freely, but perhaps the biggest boost to the Japanese economy came with the outbreak of the Korean War in 1950. During the conflict, Japan served as a key source of supplies for the U.S. and UN forces fighting in nearby Korea.

After the Korean War, Japan built its economy around foreign trade and the production of consumer goods. Japan constructed modern factories and quickly rebuilt its heavy industry, including steel and automobile manufacturing. The strong Japanese work ethic and good relations between management and labor contributed to the industrial growth, and exports rose quickly. In the 1970s Japan began to focus on electronics and computer technology and soon became a world leader in those areas.

Even compared to the postwar growth of most western democracies, Japan's success was stunning. The U.S. occupation of Japan ended in 1952; by 1968, Japan had the world's second-largest economy. Despite some problems in recent years, including a recession in the 1980s, Japan is still a major economic power.

Social Changes The postwar economic growth led to an improved standard of living for Japanese workers and brought many other social changes to Japan. The new urban industries attracted workers from agriculture and small businesses, and the population of Japan's cities grew rapidly. In the late 1800s only 15 percent of all Japanese lived in urban areas; by 1970, more than 80 percent did so.

Japanese culture and family life changed as well. In the postwar years, many Japanese young people adopted American customs, music, movies, and food. Gender roles changed as more women began attending high school and college and won new social and legal freedoms. At the same time, the importance of the extended family began to decline.

READING CHECK **Summarize** How did Japan change in the postwar years?

After World War II, the Japanese economy came to rely heavily on automobile production and electronics and computer technology.

The Pacific Rim

The Pacific Rim refers to the countries that border or are located in the Pacific Ocean. Like Japan, other nations in the Asian Pacific Rim worked to build their economies and support the growth of democracy after World War II.

The Philippines The Philippines, a group of islands in Southeast Asia, won independence from U.S. control in 1946. The nation established a democratic government and kept close ties to the United States. By the early 1970s, however, President **Ferdinand Marcos** had become an authoritarian dictator. Marcos imposed martial law, arrested his opponents, and stole millions of dollars from the nation.

As public opposition to Marcos increased in the early 1980s, one of his chief rivals, Benigno Aquino, was assassinated. This killing, which many thought Marcos had ordered, led to antigovernment riots across the Philippines. Facing international pressure, Marcos allowed elections in 1986. Voters elected **Corazon Aquino**, Aquino's widow, as the nation's new president.

Under Corazon Aquino and later leaders, the Philippines struggled to return to democracy, as well as to build the nation's economy. Although the economy began to improve in the 1990s, many Filipinos still live in poverty. Other challenges include groups of separatist Communist and Muslim rebels who have used guerrilla warfare and terrorist attacks in their fights to establish independent states.

NEW YORK

CC Unit 7-A3; 7-C3c United States occupation of Japan; Japan becomes an economic superpower

ASIA **927**

Direct Teach

Reading Focus

Postwar Japan

Explain How did the attitude of Japanese people contribute to their own recovery? *Their work ethic contributed to strong economic performance.*

Contrast How did Japanese industry change from prewar to postwar? *The prewar economy had more light industry, but postwar efforts focused on rebuilding heavy industries.*

📄 **CRF:** Biography: Soichiro Honda

📄 **CRF:** Economics and History: Exports of East Asian Nations Since 1950

Reading Focus

2 How did the nations of the Pacific Rim change after World War II? *worked to build their economies and support the growth of democracy*

The Pacific Rim

Recall When did the Philippines gain independence from the United States? *1946*

Contrast How did the presidencies of Ferdinand Marcos and Corazon Aquino differ? *Marco was an authoritarian dictator, and Aquino struggled to return to democracy.*

Differentiating Instruction

Below Level

Special Education Students

Materials: 12" x 4" construction paper strips

1. Remind students that after the war, Americans and the Japanese worked to help Japan recover from the war's effects.

2. Review with students the information that follows the heading, Postwar Japan, starting on the previous page. Read aloud one paragraph at a time, asking volunteers to name specific aids to recovery. When volunteers call one out, give them paper strips on which to record their ideas in bold letters.

3. When you have reviewed all of Postwar Japan, ask students to arrange the "aids to recovery" strips for display.

4. As homework, have students write about what one example most helped the recovery of Japan. **LS** **Verbal-Linguistic, Visual-Spatial**

📄 **Alternative Assessment Handbook**, Rubric 1: Acquiring Information

Answers

Reading Check *standard of living improved; economy grew; culture adopted some American elements; gender roles changed*

927

Reading Focus

The Pacific Rim

Identify Who is Kim Jong Il and how is he related to Kim Il Sung? *the ruler of North Korea; Kim Jong Il is the son of Kim Il Sung*

Contrast How has the economy of North Korea differed from the economy of South Korea? *The Communist North Korean economy has deteriorated; the South Korean economy has improved, with U.S. economic aid.*

Info to Know

World's Tallest Buildings As of 2006, 47 of the 100 tallest buildings in the world are located in Asia. Eight of the top ten are in Asian countries. Though the Sears Tower and the Empire State Building each have more stories, (110 and 102 respectively), the Taipei 101 rises 1,667 feet from ground level. Its base is topped by eight tiers of eight pagoda-like structures.

Singapore
A former British colony, this small city-state is the busiest port in Southeast Asia and is a world leader in trade, industry, and banking.

ECONOMIC GROWTH IN ASIA, 1986–2004

Skills Focus — **INTERPRETING GRAPHS**

Compare and Contrast How did the economies of South Korea, Taiwan, and Singapore change between 1986 and 2004? Was this a time of constant economic growth for all three countries?

North Korea and South Korea Korea, on China's northeastern border, remained a divided nation after the end of the Korean War in 1953. In North Korea, Communist dictator **Kim Il Sung** formed a government based on the Soviet model, with the state controlling much of the economy and most spending devoted to heavy industry and the military. With Soviet and Chinese aid, North Korea made significant gains; but poverty and food shortages spread across the nation as foreign aid decreased.

When Kim Il Sung died in 1994, his son, **Kim Jong Il**, took power. Under Kim Jong Il's rule, the North Korean economy has continued to deteriorate. Despite its economic problems, the North has funded an expansion of its military programs. In 2006 North Korea tested a nuclear weapon for the first time.

South Korea followed a different path. With the help of heavy U.S. economic aid, Syngman Rhee and other leaders built up the nation's industries, emphasizing foreign trade and the production of consumer goods. Despite much economic success, South Koreans had little freedom or political stability, and repeated uprisings and military coups replaced one authoritarian government with another. Reform finally began in the late 1980s with the adoption of a more democratic constitution. South Korea has tried to improve its relationship with the North in recent years, but North Korea's possession and testing of nuclear weapons has led to more tension in the region.

Taiwan The Guomindang nationalists settled on the island of Taiwan after they were driven from mainland China by the Communists in 1949. With economic and military aid from the United States, Taiwan was able to build a successful economy based on international trade and the production of consumer goods. The Guomindang ruled Taiwan under martial law until the 1980s, when they ended martial law and allowed other political parties to form. This movement toward democracy continued in later years. Today, China views Taiwan as an integral part of China and insists that the two areas will eventually be reunited. Taiwan, however, resists this pressure from China.

READING CHECK **Summarize** How did most of the Pacific Rim nations move toward democracy?

Differentiating Instruction

Above Level

Advanced Learners/Gifted and Talented

Research Required

1. Organize students into small groups. Tell students that the U.S. Census bureau keeps extensive records about trade.

2. Have each group conduct online research to determine which Asian nations have been top trading partners with the United States over the last year. Remind students to record information for imports as well as exports.

3. Next, have groups discuss their data, whether or not is it is complete, what precisely it represents, and what they can conclude from it. Have each group record its conclusions.

4. Allow class time for groups to share their discoveries with the class. **LS Interpersonal, Logical-Mathematical**

📄 **Alternative Assessment Handbook**, Rubrics 12: Drawing Conclusions; 14: Group Activity; and 30: Research

Answers

Interpreting Graphs *GDP increased; No, South Korea saw a sharp decline in GDP in 1998, but continued to grow after that.*

Reading Check *with U.S. economic aid*

The Asian Tigers

While Japan was building one of the world's strongest economies in the years after World War II, other Asian nations were also making great economic gains. Because of their economic success, South Korea, Hong Kong, Taiwan, and Singapore became known as the **Asian Tigers**.

Spectacular Growth The Asian Pacific Rim entered the 1960s as a largely poor and under-developed region. Over the next few decades, however, the Asian Tiger economies performed spectacularly, with average growth far higher than that of similar economies in Latin America or Africa.

To achieve these results, these countries followed a pattern similar to the one used by postwar Japan. For example, they generally provided ample education and training for their citizens, which helped produce the skilled workforce necessary for industrial expansion. The nations also received large amounts of economic aid from the United States during the early stages of the Cold War and further benefited from their access to the major shipping routes of the Pacific Ocean.

As in Japan, the Asian Tigers focused on growth through exports of consumer goods, primarily to the United States. Low costs for labor and production, as well as a loyal, dedicated workforce, allowed them to make low-cost products that could sell in the United States.

An Economic Crisis The economies of Japan and the Asian Tigers suffered a shock when a severe financial crisis hit the region in 1997. The crisis was in many ways a result of the region's great success. The decades of superior performance had led many foreign companies to invest heavily in the region's economies, and a lack of government regulation allowed Asian Tiger banks to borrow far more money than they needed.

The crisis began when banks began to fail in Thailand. The financial panic quickly spread through the region: foreign investors sold their holdings, stock and real estate prices collapsed, currencies lost value, and the region was overwhelmed by debts that it could not pay. The collapse undid years of progress.

An Asian Century Over the following decade, the region began to recover from the economic disaster, and nations like Indonesia, Malaysia, Thailand, and the Philippines began to emerge as economic powers. The great success of many Asian economies had many observers celebrating a so-called Asian miracle. Some predicted that the 2000s would be an "Asian century" in which Asia would surpass Europe and North America as the dominant economic region in the world.

READING SKILLS

Identifying Problems and Solutions What problem did the Asian Tigers face in 1997?

 NEW YORK

CC Unit 7-C5
Pacific Rim economies/ economic crisis

READING CHECK **Find the Main Idea** How did the Asian Tigers follow Japan's model of economic growth?

---

go.hrw.com
Online Quiz
Keyword: SHL ASA HP

Reviewing Key Terms and People

1. **a. Recall** What role did the United States play in postwar Japan?
   b. Summarize Why did Japan make such an impressive economic recovery after World War II?
   c. Make Judgments In your opinion, did Japan's government, economy, or society change the most in the years after World War II? Why do you think so?

2. **a. Recall** Summarize the political changes in the Philippines after the nation won its independence.
   b. Compare and Contrast Compare and contrast the development of North Korea and South Korea after the Korean War.

3. **a. Identify** What are the **Asian Tigers**?
   b. Make Generalizations Describe the basic features of the Asian Tigers and their approach to economic growth.

Critical Thinking

4. **Compare** Use your notes on the section and a graphic organizer like the one below to compare economic changes in Japan and the Asian Tigers.

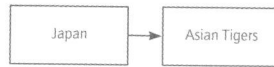

FOCUS ON WRITING

5. **Exposition** Write a brief paragraph that explains how and why Japan changed in the years after World War II. Be sure to mention changes in Japan's government, economy, and society. Use details from the section to support your conclusions.

ASIA **929**

Section 4 Assessment Answers

1. **a.** occupied Japan; provided economic aid
   b. Japan focused rebuilding efforts on heavy industry and exports rose. The people's work ethic also contributed.
   c. possible answer—society, because it adopted parts of American culture

2. **a.** first was an authoritarian dictatorship, then became more democratic
   b. North Korea's economy declined, while South Korea's improved dramatically.

3. **a.** Pacific Rim nations who experienced great economic gains after World War II

   b. provided education and training to create a skilled workforce; received U.S. economic aid; focused on growth through exports

4. Changes—economic aid, work ethic, education and training to create skilled workforce, increased exports

5. Student paragraphs should describe the American occupation, as well as Japan's economic recovery and social changes, using details from the section.

Direct Teach

Reading Focus

❸ How did the Asian Tigers develop? *They provided their citizens with education and training, took advantage of economic aid from the United States, and focused on producing goods for export.*

The Asian Tigers

Identify Which Asian countries are known as Asian Tigers? Why? *South Korea, Hong Kong, Taiwan, and Singapore; because they made great economic gains in the years after World War II*

Identify Cause and Effect What led to the financial crisis of 1997? *Foreign companies invested heavily in Asian Tiger economies, and lack of government regulations led to problems, so banks began to fail.*

Review & Assess

Close

Review the effects of changes made in Japan following World War II, and the reasons behind economic growth in the Pacific Rim.

Review

Online Quiz, Section 4

Assess

SE Section 4 Assessment

Progress Assessment: Section 4 Quiz

Alternative Assessment Handbook

Reteach/Intervene

Interactive Reader and Study Guide, Section 4

Interactive Skills Tutor CD-ROM

Answers

Reading Skills *severe financial crisis*
Reading Check *provided education and training for workers; focused on exports*

Info to Know

Four Goals In his last decade of leadership, Chairman Mao worried that his country would develop problems similar to those in the Soviet Union. He also wanted to renew the revolutionary spirit of his people. He set four goals for the Cultural Revolution: to replace his designated successors with leaders more faithful to his current thinking; to rectify the Chinese Communist Party; to provide China's youths with a revolutionary experience; and to achieve some specific policy changes to make the educational, health care, and cultural systems less elitist.

The Cultural Revolution

Historical Context The documents below provide information about China's Cultural Revolution, the movement during the 1960s that sought to rid China of its old ways and create a society in which peasants and physical labor were the ideal.

Task Examine the selections and answer the questions that follow. After you have studied the documents, you will be asked to write an essay about the Cultural Revolution. You will need to use evidence from these selections and from the chapter to support the position you take in your essay.

NEW YORK STANDARDS

PI 1.3 Students analyze historic events from around the world by examining accounts written from different perspectives.

PI 3.1 Students analyze the roles and contributions of individuals and groups to social, political, economic, cultural, and religious practices and activities.

DOCUMENT 1

Mao and the Army

The poster at right was created during 1969, at the height of the Cultural Revolution. It shows Mao watching over a group of Chinese soldiers, most of whom are holding a copy of the so-called "Little Red Book"—a collection of Mao's writings and political ideas. The Chinese characters at the bottom of the poster translate as "The Chinese People's Liberation Army is the great school of Mao Zedong thought."

中国人民解放军是毛泽东思想大学校

The Chinese People's Liberation Army is the Great School of Mao Zedong Thought, artist unknown, 1969

DOCUMENT 2

The Song of Ox-Ghosts and Snake-Demons

This song was composed by a Chinese student and quickly spread throughout the country during the Cultural Revolution. The Red Guards punished certain teachers in part by forcing the teachers to sing this song several times a day. If the singing was unsatisfactory, the teachers would be beaten or otherwise punished.

I am an ox-ghost and snake-demon.
I am an ox-ghost and snake-demon.
I am guilty. I am guilty.
I committed crimes against the people,
So the people take me as the object of the dictatorship.
I have to lower my head and admit to my guilt.
I must be obedient. I am not allowed to speak or act incorrectly.
If I speak or act incorrectly,
May you beat me and smash me,
Beat me and smash me.

Skills Focus: Analyzing Visuals

At Level

Reading Like a Historian Skill
Analyzing Posters

1. Remind students that posters have long communicated ideas to the masses. In China, they were particularly effective in reaching uneducated peasants who could not read. Tell students they will conduct research and analyze a specific poster from the Cultural Revolution.

2. Organize students into small groups. Have each group conduct online research to locate Chinese propaganda posters online. Have students select one poster and print it out.

3. Write the following questions for students to see and have students answer them on their own papers: Do any objects shown symbolize something? What message do you think the poster is trying to convey?

4. Have students write a short paragraph about the objectives of propaganda posters.
   LS Verbal-Linguistic, Interpersonal

   Alternative Assessment Handbook, Rubrics 14: Group Activity; and 30: Research

DOCUMENT 3

Violence Against Teachers

This excerpt from a 1996 paper written by historian Youqin Wang describes the violence against teachers that was common during the Cultural Revolution.

In the afternoon of August 5, 1966, some tenth grade students at the Girls Middle School attached to Beijing Teachers University started [beating] . . . a group comprised of three vice principals and two deans . . . Many students came to join them. The students . . . forced them to kneel on the ground, hit them with nail-spiked clubs, scalded them with boiling water, and so on. After three hours of torture, the first vice principal, Bian Zhongyun, lost consciousness and was put into a garbage cart. Two hours later she was sent to the hospital across the street. There, she was later found to have been dead for some time . . .

In most cases, beatings were a collective activity, conducted not by single students but by a group of Red Guards. A group of Red Guards acted together, inciting each other and encouraging hostilities. Sometimes, a beating happened in front of hundreds of people . . . Bian Zhongyun, the first victim of the violence of 1966, died after being beaten by many students. During the several hours of torture, no one at this school of more than 1,600 students tried to dissuade the beaters from these inhuman actions . . . There was no sense of guilt, but rather an excited, giddy atmosphere.

DOCUMENT 4

The Cultural Revolution's Goals

The document below is from a June 7, 1966, editorial in the *People's Liberation Army Daily*, the official newspaper of the Chinese military.

The current great socialist cultural revolution is a great revolution to sweep away all monsters and a great revolution that remoulds the ideology of people and touches their souls. What weapon should be used to sweep away all monsters? What ideology should be applied to arm people's minds and remould their souls? The most powerful ideological weapon, the only one, is the great Mao Tse-tung's thought . . .

In this great, stormy cultural revolution, the masses of workers, peasants and soldiers are playing the role of the main force—this is the result of their efforts in creatively studying and applying Mao Tse-tung's thought and arming their ideology with it . . .

Chairman Mao is the radiant sun lighting our minds. Mao Tse-tung's thought is our lifeline. Those who oppose Mao Tse-tung's thought, no matter when they do so and what kind of "authorities" they are, will be denounced by the entire Party and the whole nation.

Skills FOCUS — READING LIKE A HISTORIAN

DOCUMENT 1
a. **Describe** How is Mao depicted in this poster?
b. **Infer** According to this poster, what is the military's role during the Cultural Revolution?

DOCUMENT 2
a. **Recall** What are singers of this song allegedly guilty of?
b. **Explain** Why did Red Guards believe that the singers were guilty of these actions?

DOCUMENT 3
a. **Identify Main Ideas** What does the author of this document say that Red Guards did to teachers?
b. **Compare and Contrast** How does this description of the Cultural Revolution differ from that shown in Document 1?

DOCUMENT 4
a. **Identify** What are the goals of the Cultural Revolution?
b. **Interpret** How will the "weapon" described here help win the Revolution?

DOCUMENT-BASED ESSAY QUESTION

How did the reality of the Cultural Revolution differ from the government's claims about the Revolution? Using the documents above and information from the chapter, form a thesis that explains your position. Then write a short essay to support your position.

See *Skills Handbook*, pp. H25, H26, H33

ASIA **931**

Document-Based Investigation

Info to Know

Four Rights Mao's ideological "Little Red Book" (*Quotations from Chairman Mao*) included four ideas that were so important that they eventually became part of the state constitution. These rights were: "speaking out freely, airing views fully, holding great debates, and writing big-character posters." Many Chinese youths enthusiastically followed Mao's guidelines. As the army and party authorities were told not to suppress the Red Guards, their actions finally led to widespread disorder in the nation.

Answers

Reading Like a Historian
Document 1 a. *he is depicted as large, watchful, content;* **b.** *to further Mao's ideas;* **Document 2 a.** *speaking and acting incorrectly, which is considered a crime against the people;* **b.** *possible answer—They assumed the words were an admission of guilt.* **Document 3 a.** *The Red Guards beat groups of teachers.* **b.** *This description claims that the Red Guards were ruthless and lacked guilt, whereas in Document 1 the Red Guards simply look happy;* **Document 4 a.** *to "sweep away" thoughts of the past and old ideologies;* **b.** *possible answer—Mao Zedong's teachings will help rid China of past ways of thinking.* **Essay** *Student essays should point out that although the Chinese government claimed that the Cultural Revolution was a glorious thing, in reality, the revolution was often brutally violent. Essays should support this position with details from the documents and from Section 3 of this chapter.*

Differentiating Instruction

At Level

Learners Having Difficulty

Materials: 12" x 18" construction paper, colored markers

1. Tell students they are members of the Red Guards who want to spread Mao's ideology. Remind students that at the outset, these young people were enthusiastic, not destructive.

2. Have students refer to information in this chapter to choose an idea to express in their poster. Student work should show Chinese people participating in an activity that reflects the ideals of the Cultural Revolution. A brief slogan should also be added.

3. Allow adequate time for students to plan their posters. They may need homework time to complete their work.

4. Display the posters and guide a class discussion about the ideals of Mao Zedong's followers. **LS Visual-Spatial**

Alternative Assessment Handbook, Rubrics 28: Posters; and 34: Slogans and Banners

Answers

Visual Summary

Review and Inquiry Organize students into three groups. Assign each group one section from the Visual Study Guide. Have groups plan a set of political cartoons to express the main concepts taught in their assigned section. Distribute 8 ½" x 11" unlined paper and have students draw their ideas. Display cartoons grouped by the subjects South Asia, Southeast Asia, China, and Pacific Rim Economies.

Quick Facts Transparency: Visual Study Guide: Asia

Review Key Terms and People

1. Ho Chi Minh
2. Great Leap Forward
3. Suharto
4. Jawaharlal Nehru
5. Deng Xiaoping
6. Khmer Rouge
7. Ferdinand Marcos
8. partition
9. Asian Tigers
10. ideology
11. domino theory

Comprehension and Critical Thinking

12. a. After Gandhi was imprisoned, riots erupted throughout India, convincing the British that maintaining control of India was too costly.
b. Following independence from Great Britain, the main basis for partition was border issues.
c. possible answer—No, because the violence after partition created even more tension.

13. a. American leaders wanted to prevent the spread of communism.
b. Indonesia—ruled by military leader; Suharto stepped down in 1997 and subsequent democratic governments worked to rebuild economy; Cambodia—Khmer Rouge instituted brutal program to root out opposition, killing at least 1.5 million people; war with Vietnam; Both—were Communist, now are democratic

c. because they have struggled with political tensions and war; have not received aid

14. a. Great Leap Forward—Mao's 1958 plan to speed economic development; was a horrible disaster, resulting in famine, and the isolation of China; Cultural Revolution—Mao's plan to regain power and prestige
b. China saw a retreat from many of Mao's policies.
c. possible answer—Mao made some achievements in his early years. However, in carrying out his plans during his last years, he lost control and there was terrible

destruction in China. The negative aspects of his rule outweigh the positive ones.

15. a. After Japan's defeat, U.S. forces occupied the country and MacArthur took control of the country. Japan's economy grew.
b. began as an authoritarian dictatorship but slowly became more democratic
c. Some nations of the Pacific Rim, known as Asian Tigers, have achieved great economic gains since World War II. Others have struggled with political problems that have harmed their economies.

Independence in Asia

- The postwar years saw many struggles for independence in Asia. Some were peaceful, but others were violent conflicts.
- The Philippines gains independence from the United States in 1946.
- India and Pakistan gain independence from Great Britain after the 1947 partition of India.
- Burma (Myanmar) gains independence from Great Britain in 1948.
- Indonesia wins independence from the Netherlands in 1949 after years of fighting.
- France is forced out of Indochina in the early 1950s, leading to independence for Cambodia, Laos, and Vietnam.
- Bangladesh wins independence after a civil war with Pakistan in 1971.
- East Timor wins independence from Indonesia in 2002.

Pacific Rim Economies

- Japan builds its postwar economy around foreign trade and the production of consumer goods, becoming one of the world's leading economies.
- Other Pacific Rim nations follow Japan's model to achieve great economic growth.
- An economic crisis in 1997 sets the region back, but economic growth continues today.
- Some predict that the 2000s will be a century dominated by Asian nations.

The Rise of Modern China

- Communists led by Mao Zedong defeat the nationalist Guomindang and take power in China in 1949.

⬇

- China's government puts in place Soviet-style five year plans for industrial development, successfully improving the economy and reducing rural poverty.

⬇

- Mao announces the Great Leap Forward, a plan designed to increase China's agricultural and industrial output. The plan fails, and tens of millions starve.

⬇

- Mao launches the Cultural Revolution to rid China of its old ways, eliminating intellectuals. Red Guards attack people they believe to be politically corrupt.

⬇

- After Mao's death, Deng Xiaoping puts in place market reforms in the Chinese economy. Troops attack pro-democracy protestors at Tiananmen Square.

⬇

- China's economy grows rapidly in recent years, but population growth, environmental problems, and human rights abuses remain areas of concern.

Review Key Terms and People

Identify the correct term or person from the chapter that best fits each of the following descriptions.

1. leader of the Vietminh in the Vietnam War
2. disastrous plan to increase China's industrial and agricultural output
3. authoritarian general who ruled Indonesia for many years
4. first prime minister of India
5. Chinese leader who put in place market reforms
6. group that used violence to destroy the influences of modern civilization in Cambodia
7. authoritarian dictator of the Philippines
8. division of India into two independent nations
9. Pacific Rim nations with great economic success
10. a system of ideas, often political
11. belief that communism would quickly spread to other countries

History's Impact video program

Review the video to answer the closing question: What role did North and South Vietnam's location have on the domino theory?

Comprehension and Critical Thinking

SECTION 1 *(pp. 909–913)*

12. a. Recall How did India and Pakistan gain their independence?

b. Summarize Summarize the changes in India and Pakistan after partition.

c. Make Judgments Given the events that followed, do you believe Great Britain's decision to partition India was wise? Why or why not?

SECTION 2 *(pp. 914–919)*

13. a. Recall Why did the United States become involved in the Vietnam War?

b. Compare and Contrast Compare and contrast the political changes in Indonesia and Cambodia in the years after World War II.

c. Make Judgments Why do you think some countries in Southeast Asia had difficulty building stable, independent nations?

SECTION 3 *(pp. 920–924)*

14. a. Identify What were the Great Leap Forward and the Cultural Revolution?

b. Make Generalizations In what ways did China change after Mao Zedong's death?

c. Evaluate Do Mao's positive contributions to China's development outweigh the negative aspects of his years in power? Why or why not?

SECTION 4 *(pp. 925–929)*

15. a. Describe How did Japan's government and economy change after World War II?

b. Summarize Summarize the history of the Philippines after the nation gained its independence.

c. Evaluate Evaluate the economic successes and failures of Pacific Rim nations.

Reading Skills

Identifying Problems and Solutions *Read the passage below, which comes from Section 1 of this chapter. Then answer the question that follows.*

❝The violence and increasing Indian nationalism helped convince the British that maintaining control of India was too costly. When the war ended, the British began making plans to leave India.❞

16. What problem did British leaders face in India? What was their solution to this problem?

Analyzing Primary Sources

Reading Like a Historian *The passage below is an excerpt from an editorial in a Chinese newspaper written during the Cultural Revolution.*

❝Every sentence by Chairman Mao is the truth, and carries more weight than ten thousand ordinary sentences. As the Chinese people master Mao Tse-Tung's thought, China will be prosperous and ever-victorious.❞

–*People's Liberation Army Daily* Editorial, June 7, 1966

17. Explain How does the writer feel about Mao Zedong?

18. Draw Conclusions How did beliefs like that expressed in this document lead to violence during the Cultural Revolution?

Using the Internet

go.hrw.com
Practice Online
Keyword: SHL ASA

19. China and India are the world's two most populous countries, and both have an enormous—and growing—influence on the world economy. Using the keyword above, research how the Chinese and Indian economies have developed over the past several decades. Then write a report about these economies and their influence on the world. Include details about how the economies have developed and how government leaders are trying to shape the economies in the future.

WRITING FOR THE SAT

Think about the following issue:

The years after World War II saw independence movements spread across Asia. Many former colonies gained their independence—some peacefully, but others through armed conflict. After independence, some nations turned toward democracy, but others were led by authoritarian regimes or Communist governments.

20. Assignment: Why did some Asian nations become democratic while others were led by dictators or Communist governments? Write a short essay in which you develop a position on this issue. Support your point of view with reasoning and examples from your reading.

Answers

Reading Skills

16. violence and nationalism; left India

Analyzing Primary Sources

17. The writer greatly admires Mao.

18. possible answer—Such admiration for Mao Zedong led to violence against those who opposed him or were suspected of opposing him.

Using the Internet

19. Go to the HRW Web site and enter the keyword shown to access a rubric for this activity.

KEYWORD: SHL ASA

Writing for the SAT

20. Student responses should include a clear position statement and supporting details. Examples of former Asian colonies might include Cambodia and Indonesia, which eventually became democratic, and Vietnam, which became Communist.

A rubric for the activity is provided in **CRF**: Writing for the SAT.

HOLT

History's Impact
▶ **Video Program: Asia**
Refer to the Video Program Teacher's Guide for the answer to the closing question.

Review and Assessment Resources

Review and Reinforce

- **CRF:** Chapter Review
- **Quick Facts Transparency:** Visual Study Guide: Asia
- **Spanish Chapter Summaries Audio CD Program**
- **OSP Holt PuzzlePro:** Quiz Show for ExamView
- **Quiz Game CD-ROM**

Assess

- **PASS:** Chapter Test, Forms A and B
- **Alternative Assessment Handbook**
- **OSP ExamView Test Generator,** Chapter Test
- **Differentiated Instruction Modified Worksheets and Tests CD-ROM:** Chapter Test
- **HOAP Holt Online Assessment Program** (in the Premier Online Edition)

Reteach/Intervene

- **Interactive Reader and Study Guide**
- **Differentiated Instruction Teacher Management System:** Lesson Plans for Differentiated Instruction
- **Differentiated Instruction Modified Worksheets and Tests CD-ROM:** Chapter Test
- **Interactive Skills Tutor CD-ROM**

go.hrw.com
Online Resources
KEYWORD: SHL TEACHER

Chapter 31 Planning Guide

Africa and the Middle East

Chapter Overview	Reproducible Resources	Technology Resources
CHAPTER 31 pp. 934–963 **Overview:** In this chapter, students will learn how many countries in Africa and the Middle East struggled to gain their independence after World War II, and the political, religious, and economic issues that followed. KI 2, 4; PI 2.3, 2.4, 2.5, 4.2, 4.4 See pp. T32–T55 for a detailed correlation to the New York State Core Curriculum for Global History and Geography and the New York Learning Standards.	**Differentiated Instruction Teacher Management System:*** • Pacing Guide • Lesson Plans for Differentiated Instruction **Interactive Reader and Study Guide:** Chapter Summary* **Chapter Resource File*** • Writing About History • Social Studies Skill • Chapter Review **World History Outline Maps**	OSP **New York One-Stop Planner CD-ROM:** Calendar Planner **Live Ink© Online Reading Help** **Student Edition on Audio CD Program** **Differentiated Instruction Modified Worksheets and Tests CD-ROM** **World History Primary Source Library CD-ROM** **Power Presentations with Video CD-ROM** **History's Impact: World History Video Program (VHS/DVD):** Africa and the Middle East
Section 1: **African Nations Gain Independence** **The Main Idea:** After World War II, almost all countries in Africa gained independence from ruling European powers. PI 2.5, 4.2	**Differentiated Instruction Teacher Management System:** Section 1 Lesson Plan* **Interactive Reader and Study Guide:** Section 1 Summary* **Chapter Resource File*** • Vocabulary Builder: Section 1 • Biography: Léopold Senghor • Primary Source: Independence in Kenya	**Regents Review Transparency:** Section 1* **Map Transparency:** Africa and the Middle East, 1950* **Map Transparency:** Independence in Africa*
Section 2: **Post-Colonial Africa** **The Main Idea:** Newly independent African nations struggled with poverty, conflict, and ineffective governments. In recent years some countries sought better government by holding democratic elections. PI 2.4, 2.5	**Differentiated Instruction Teacher Management System:** Section 2 Lesson Plan* **Interactive Reader and Study Guide:** Section 2 Summary* **Chapter Resource File*** • Vocabulary Builder: Section 2 • Biography: Nelson Mandela • Literature: *Things Fall Apart*	**Regents Review Transparency:** Section 2* **Quick Facts Transparency:** Political Trends in Post-Colonial Africa* **Internet Activity:** Desmond Tutu
Section 3: **Nationalism in North Africa and the Middle East** **The Main Idea:** The rise of nationalism in North Africa and the Middle East led to independence for some countries and to conflicts with the West. PI 2.3	**Differentiated Instruction Teacher Management System:** Section 3 Lesson Plan* **Interactive Reader and Study Guide:** Section 3 Summary* **Chapter Resource File*** • Vocabulary Builder: Section 3 • Biography: Danièle Djamila Amrane-Minne	**Regents Review Transparency:** Section 3* **Quick Facts Transparency:** Causes and Effects of the Suez Canal Crisis*
Section 4: **Conflicts in the Middle East** **The Main Idea:** Regional issues in the Middle East have led to conflicts between Israel and its neighbors and to conflicts in and between Iran and Iraq. PI 2.5, 4.4	**Interactive Reader and Study Guide:** Section 4 Summary **Chapter Resource File*** • Vocabulary Builder: Section 4 • Biography: Hanan Ashrawi • History and Geography: Conflicts in the Persian Gulf	**Regents Review Transparency:** Section 4* **Map Transparency:** Creation of Israel, 1947–2006*

go.hrw.com	Print Resource	Transparency
LS Learning Styles	Audio CD	CD-ROM
Video	**SE** Student Edition	**TE** Teacher's Edition

OSP One-Stop Planner CD-ROM   NY Standards Mastery
*also on One-Stop Planner CD-ROM

Review, Assessment, Intervention

- **Global History and Geography Regents Test Prep Workbook**

- **Quick Facts Transparency:** Africa and the Middle East*

- **Progress Assessment Support System (PASS):** Chapter Test*

- **Differentiated Instruction Modified Worksheets and Tests CD-ROM:** Modified Chapter Test

- **OSP New York One-Stop Planner CD-ROM:** Exam View Test Generator (English/Spanish)

- **HOAP Holt Online Assessment Program (HOAP),** in the Holt Premier Online Student Edition

---

- **PASS:** Section 1 Quiz*
- **Online Quiz:** Section 1
- **Alternative Assessment Handbook**

- **PASS:** Section 2 Quiz*
- **Online Quiz:** Section 2
- **Alternative Assessment Handbook**

- **PASS:** Section 3 Quiz*
- **Online Quiz:** Section 3
- **Alternative Assessment Handbook**

- **PASS:** Section 4 Quiz*
- **Online Quiz:** Section 4
- **Alternative Assessment Handbook**

Power Presentation with Video CD-ROM

Power Presentations with Video are visual presentations of each chapter's main ideas. Presentations can be customized by including Quick Facts charts, images from the text, and video clips.

Holt Online Learning

go.hrw.com
Teacher Resources
KEYWORD: SHL TEACHER

go.hrw.com
Student Resources
KEYWORD: SHL AFR

- Document-Based Questions
- Interactive Multimedia Activities

- Current Events
- Chapter-Based Internet Activities
- and more!

Holt Premier
Online Student Edition

Complete online support for interactivity, assessment, and reporting
- Interactive Maps and Notebook
- Homework Practice and Research Activities Online

Before You Teach

BEFORE YOU TEACH

The Big Picture

Peter N. Stearns

Patterns in Africa Decolonization in sub-Saharan Africa began in the 1950s. In many cases it was relatively peaceful, but there were sharp conflicts in a few regions. The South African struggle against the apartheid system was both distinctive and significant. Most new nations in Africa began with democratic intentions, but quickly turned to authoritarian rule. Various internal ethnic conflicts occurred, and some trouble spots expanded in the 1990s and 2000s. Massive bloodshed resulted in several tragic cases. Many African regions also suffered from low levels of economic development and continued exploitation by industrial nations eager to acquire resources. In some regions environmental degradation, famine, and disease produced even greater hardship. By the 1990s a new democratic current gained strength, producing new regimes in several African countries. Cultural developments included a strong focus on adapting traditional arts, adjusting to the growing importance of Islam and Christianity, and the expansion of urban consumerism.

Patterns in North Africa and the Middle East Violent independence struggles were acute in Algeria, but new nations emerged more peacefully in most of North Africa and the Middle East. A brief dispute accompanied Egypt's takeover of the Suez Canal. The establishment of the state of Israel and ensuing conflicts, both with neighboring Arab states and with the large Palestinian minority, created ongoing tensions in much of the region. Monarchies or one-party rule were common. Secular interests predominated in many states, despite the ongoing importance of Islam. Along with independence, several Middle Eastern states gained greater control over oil reserves and generated considerable wealth. At the same time, poverty in cities, resentment against widespread Western diplomatic influence, and reactions to authoritarian states helped generate a growing fundamentalist movement within Islam, which would exert important political strength in the region from the late 1970s onward. While dramatic conflicts punctuated much of contemporary Middle Eastern history, other important developments involved significant new opportunities for many women, expansion of education, and the emergence of industrial sectors in several regions.

Recent Scholarship

Analyzing the rise of religious fundamentalism is one of the most important and most challenging tasks for world historians. *In Understanding Fundamentalism: Christian, Islamic, and Jewish Movements* (2001), Richard Antoun offers a useful comparative framework for dealing with all three of the "religions of Abraham." He looks at the scriptural arguments and bases for fundamentalism, in terms of their shared impulses and different interpretations. He sees three different strategies emerging, one per religion, for seeking new levels of purity. He also deals with fundamentalism as a common experience in terms of total involvement and high levels of activism.

Differentiating Instruction

 Differentiated Instruction Teacher Management System
- Pacing Guide
- Lesson Plans for Differentiated Instruction

 Interactive Reader and Study Guide

Spanish Chapter Summaries Audio CD Program

Student Edition on Audio CD Program

 Differentiated Instruction Modified Worksheets and Tests CD-ROM
- Vocabulary Flash Cards
- Modified Vocabulary Builder Activities
- Modified Chapter Review Activity
- Modified Chapter Test

OSP One-Stop Planner CD-ROM
- ExamView Test Generator (English/Spanish)
- PuzzlePro
- Quiz Show for ExamView
- Transparencies and Videos

TE Differentiated Activities in the Teacher's Edition
- Comparing Independence in Ghana and Kenya, p. 939
- African Sculpture, p. 942
- History of the Congo, p. 945
- "After the Deluge" Poetry, p. 948
- Suez Canal Location, p. 952

Reading Like a Historian
Sam Wineburg

Let's imagine that a reader comes to our chapter knowing little about Ghana—indeed, nothing more than what's on page 938: that Kwame Nkrumah was a leader in Ghana's nationalist movement, that he organized demonstrations against the British and became Ghana's first prime minister. Armed with this scanty information, the reader, who in this case also happens to be a historian—but not a specialist on Africa—turns to the "Reading Like a Historian" feature at the page's bottom. How might a historian with only the barest knowledge of Africa—a specialist in, say, Medieval France, approach this document?

Facing a new document, the first thing a historian does is to scan its attribution—a process known as sourcing. What is the document: a letter? A book? A speech? What do we know about its author? When was it written and what else was going on at the same time? What clues about the author are revealed in the document's title? In other words, before examining a text's substance, its attribution is carefully interrogated. The clues it yields generate questions the historian then brings to the reading of the actual text.

Our document's title seems straightforward with one exception: the charged word "ideology." Ideology emits negative connotations, tainted by foiled grand plans and failed social visions. But these are today's associations, formed in history's hindsight: we've seen with our own eyes the dissolution of Soviet ideologies and witnessed the disintegration of the Iron Curtain. Back in 1961, however, "ideology" still carried high hopes. Used as a title as it is here—"A Statement of African Ideology"—the word typically signaled a socialist project influenced by the Marxist-Leninist tradition.

A historian would also note the document's date, 1961, and situate it as two years after the Cuban revolution, when socialism was on the rise among developing nations. With these hunches, the historian would move to the text itself, noting that Nkrumah champions "economic development"

that "must be planned and pursued as a whole." Knowing little about Nkrumah, our historian would develop a strong hunch that the document's author was, himself, a socialist.

A little digging on the Web shows this to be correct. Nkrumah was heavily influenced by the Pan-Africanist ideas of Marcus Garvey and the classic communist writings of Vladimir Lenin. At Ghana's helm in the early sixties, he embraced socialist ideas of a planned, state-directed economy that, in Ghana's case, took a lucrative cacao industry and by fixing state prices (often set below the world market, which led to widespread smuggling) brought it to ruin.

In 1961, Nkrumah visited the Soviet Union and returned home entranced by mammoth public works projects and multi-year development plans. In short order, he unveiled his own Seven-Year plan—that because of inflexible economic assumptions and widespread corruption—failed to realize even a fraction of its inflated hopes.

Clearly this information fills in the initial hunches of our historian. But the general contours of this direction were evident—in skeletal form—just from the document's attribution. By the time students reach Chapter 31, they will have encountered many of these ideas—communism, capitalism, ideology, the Cold War, the Five Year Plans of the USSR and state-sponsored central planning. Some students will in fact possess the background knowledge they need to form similar hunches, but will not know how to draw on this knowledge to move beyond the document's literal meaning.

It is our job to model for them how to do just that.

Chapter Main Ideas

Section 1 After World War II, almost all countries in Africa gained independence from ruling European powers.

Section 2 Newly independent African nations struggled with poverty, conflict, and ineffective governments. In recent years some countries sought better government by holding democratic elections.

Section 3 The rise of nationalism in North Africa and the Middle East led to independence for some countries and to conflicts with the West.

Section 4 Regional issues in the Middle East have led to conflicts between Israel and its neighbors and to conflicts in and between Iran and Iraq.

New York Standards

Key Idea 2 Establishing timeframes, exploring different periodizations, examining themes across time and within cultures, and focusing on important turning points in world history help organize the study of world cultures and civilizations.

Key Idea 4 The skills of historical analysis include the ability to investigate differing and competing interpretations of the theories of history, hypothesize about why interpretations change over time, explain the importance of historical evidence, and understand the concepts of change and continuity over time.

Key to Differentiating Instruction

Below Level

Basic-level activities designed for all students encountering new material

At Level

Intermediate-level activities designed for average students

Above Level

Challenging activities designed for honors and gifted and talented students

Standard English Mastery

Activities designed to improve standard English usage

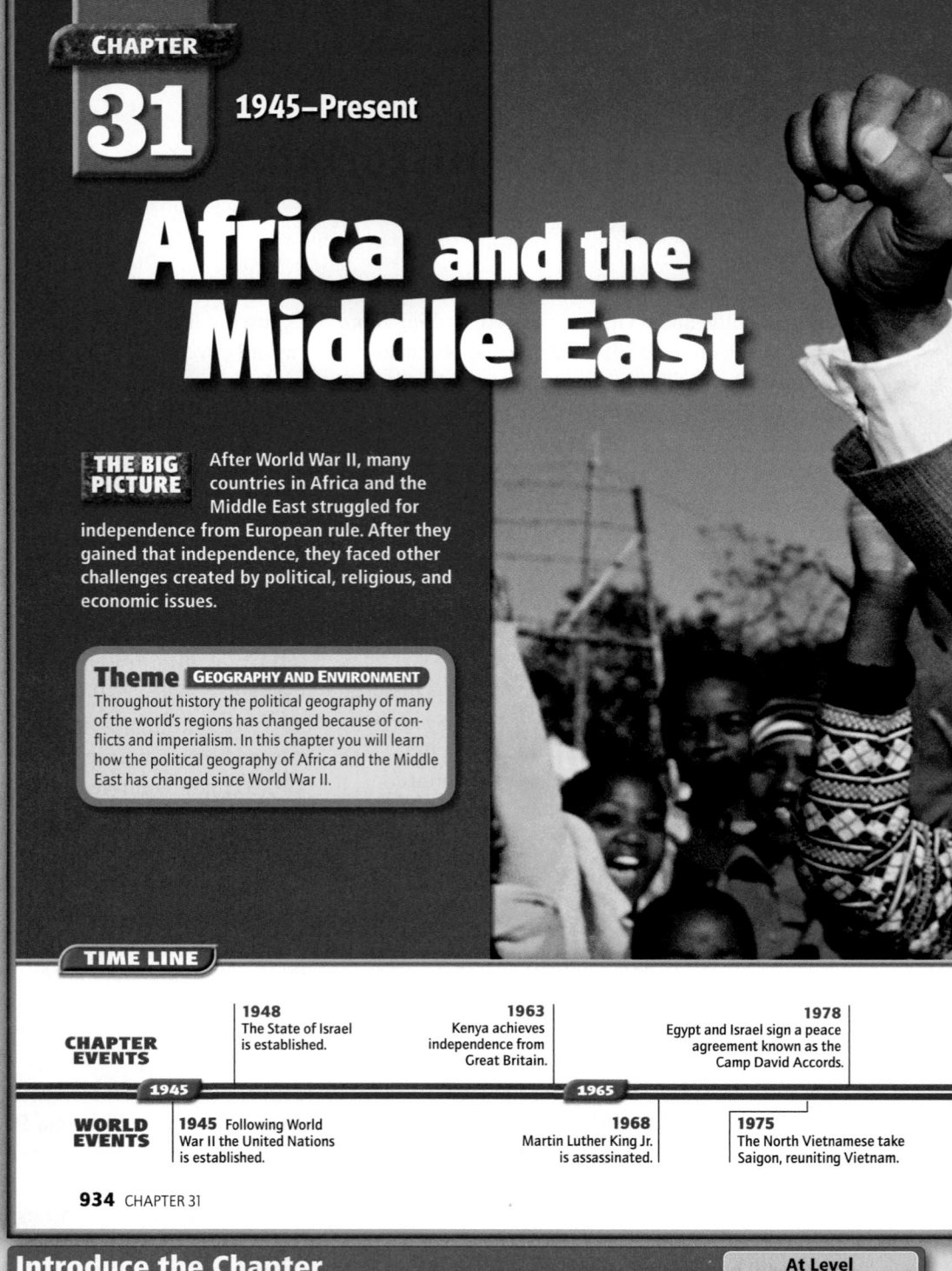

CHAPTER 31 1945–Present

Africa and the Middle East

THE BIG PICTURE After World War II, many countries in Africa and the Middle East struggled for independence from European rule. After they gained that independence, they faced other challenges created by political, religious, and economic issues.

Theme GEOGRAPHY AND ENVIRONMENT
Throughout history the political geography of many of the world's regions has changed because of conflicts and imperialism. In this chapter you will learn how the political geography of Africa and the Middle East has changed since World War II.

TIME LINE

CHAPTER EVENTS

1948 The State of Israel is established.

1963 Kenya achieves independence from Great Britain.

1978 Egypt and Israel sign a peace agreement known as the Camp David Accords.

1945

1965

WORLD EVENTS

1945 Following World War II the United Nations is established.

1968 Martin Luther King Jr. is assassinated.

1975 The North Vietnamese take Saigon, reuniting Vietnam.

Introduce the Chapter

At Level

Africa and the Middle East

1. Have students create a list of what they already know about Africa and the Middle East. Have volunteers share their statements with the class.

2. Write down student statements for all to see.

3. Guide students in a discussion of these statements about Africa and the Middle East. As a class, sort out assumptions, stereotypes, and statements that are factual.

4. Guide students in a discussion of present-day economic, political, and social conditions in Africa and the Middle East. Remind students that Africa is a vast continent, and that conditions vary from country to country. Also remind students that the Middle East consists of a number of countries, cultures, religions, and government styles. **LS Verbal-Linguistic**

Alternative Assessment Handbook, Rubric 11: Discussions

Reading like a Historian

After spending 27 years in prison for his activities against South Africa's apartheid government, Nelson Mandela was released in 1990 and became South Africa's president four years later. In this photo, Mandela visits a school in Johannesburg.

Analyzing Visuals How does this photograph show Nelson Mandela's importance as a leader to black South Africans?

See **Skills Handbook**, p. H26

1982 Great Britain and Argentina go to war over the Falkland Islands.

1985

1994 Nelson Mandela is elected president of South Africa.

1997 Hong Kong reverts to Chinese control.

1999 The United States and NATO stop "ethnic cleansing" in Kosovo.

2005 Iraq holds democratic elections.

2005

AFRICA AND THE MIDDLE EAST **935**

• **Chapter Preview** •

HOLT
History's Impact
▶ **Video Program: Africa and the Middle East**
See the Video Teacher's Guide for strategies for using the video segment.

Reading Like a Historian

Analyzing Visuals Nelson Mandela was chosen to be president by South Africa's National Assembly, after the first election in which black people were allowed to vote. The election represented a turning point in the history of South Africa.

go.hrw.com
Online Resources

Chapter Resources:
KEYWORD: SHL AFR
Teacher Resources:
KEYWORD: SHL TEACHER

Explore the Time Line

1. In what year was the state of Israel established? *1948*

2. What were the Camp David Accords? *a peace agreement between Israel and Egypt, signed in 1978*

3. What nation declared independence from Great Britain in 1963? *Kenya*

4. Who worked together to stop "ethnic cleansing" in Kosovo in 1999? *NATO and the United States*

Info to Know

South Africa and Russia South Africa and Russia have pledged to become closer partners. As the world's mineral and diamond superpowers, an alliance might give them a monopoly over the world's mineral and diamond market. Between diamond firms in South Africa and Russia, the two nations hold 75 percent of the world's diamond mining.
Predict How might this alliance affect both the South African and Russian economy? *possible answer—The price of diamonds would probably increase, which might help both countries in producing revenue and jobs.*

Answers

Reading Like a Historian *possible answer—The crowd seems to be cheering for Mandela, suggesting that he is a popular leader in South Africa.*

935

Geography Starting Points

1948 Election in South Africa The 1948 elections in South Africa marked a turning point for the nation. The two political parties, the United Party and the HNP, or Reunited National Party, had very different ideas about segregation. The United Party argued that segregation was impossible especially because many Africans and people of African descent had moved into the cities. The United Party also had members of mixed ancestry. The HNP argued for complete segregation and for no representation for Africans in South Africa's parliament. The HNP proposed that African laborers in the cities should be considered a temporary solution to labor problems, and that these laborers should be moved back into countryside whenever needed to meet the country's agricultural needs. The HNP also called on a ban of interracial marriages, the creation of black trade unions, and stricter enforcement of job reservation. The HNP won the 1948 election, began apartheid, and ruled South Africa until 1994.

🖼 **Map Transparency:** Africa and the Middle East, 1950

📄 **World History Outline Maps**

✳ Interactive Map: Africa and the Middle East, 1950

Teaching Tip

Show students a large map of Africa and the Middle East to make sure that they have an overall understanding of the geography of the areas they will be studying this chapter.

Answers

Geography Starting Points
1. *possible answer—Africans did not have equal rights, were not treated with dignity or respect by their colonial rulers and had no say in their own county's affairs;* **2.** *possible answer—through protest and rebellion*

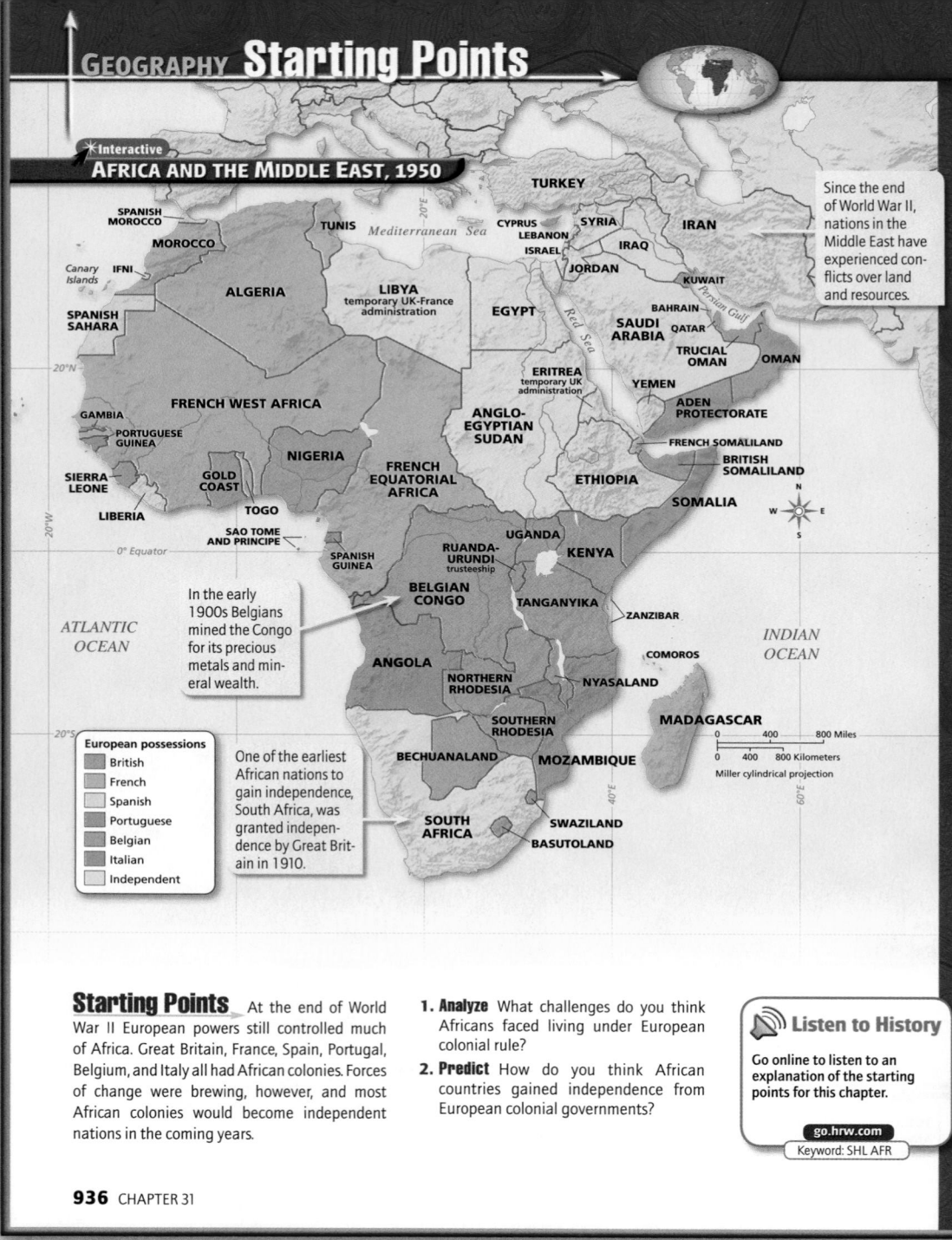

GEOGRAPHY Starting Points

*Interactive
AFRICA AND THE MIDDLE EAST, 1950

Since the end of World War II, nations in the Middle East have experienced conflicts over land and resources.

In the early 1900s Belgians mined the Congo for its precious metals and mineral wealth.

One of the earliest African nations to gain independence, South Africa, was granted independence by Great Britain in 1910.

European possessions
- British
- French
- Spanish
- Portuguese
- Belgian
- Italian
- Independent

0   400   800 Miles
0 400 800 Kilometers
Miller cylindrical projection

Starting Points At the end of World War II European powers still controlled much of Africa. Great Britain, France, Spain, Portugal, Belgium, and Italy all had African colonies. Forces of change were brewing, however, and most African colonies would become independent nations in the coming years.

1. **Analyze** What challenges do you think Africans faced living under European colonial rule?

2. **Predict** How do you think African countries gained independence from European colonial governments?

🔊 **Listen to History**

Go online to listen to an explanation of the starting points for this chapter.

go.hrw.com
Keyword: SHL AFR

936 CHAPTER 31

Skills Focus: Analyzing Maps

At Level

Social Studies Skills
Africa and the Middle East, 1950

1. Have students study the map on this page, paying close attention to the different regions of Africa and the Middle East and the countries that colonized them.

2. Have students identify regions where colonization might have created the most difficulties. For example, French West Africa was a gigantic area; its size could have presented many difficulties in governing, transportation, building infrastructures, etc.

3. Have students compare this map with a current map of Africa. Have students identify and list the countries that emerged from the colonial holdings shown on this map.

4. Guide students in a discussion about the colonization of Africa and how it continues to affect the continent today. 🖥 **Verbal-Linguistic, Visual-Spatial**

📄 **Alternative Assessment Handbook**, Rubrics 12: Drawing Conclusions; and 21: Map Reading

African Nations Gain Independence

BEFORE YOU READ

MAIN IDEA

After World War II, almost all countries in Africa gained independence from ruling European powers.

READING FOCUS

1. What ideas and actions led to independence for British and French colonies?

2. Why did Portuguese and Belgian colonies have difficulty achieving independence?

3. What effect did apartheid have on the lives of black South Africans?

KEY TERMS AND PEOPLE

Kwame Nkrumah
Jomo Kenyatta
Mau Mau
apartheid

 NEW YORK

P1 2.5 Students investigate key events and developments and major turning points in world history to identify the factors that brought about change and the long-term effects of these changes.

From **PRISONER** to **PRIME MINISTER**

◄ **Kwame Nkrumah speaks to a crowd of supporters.**

THE INSIDE STORY

How did a jailed radical become leader of an African nation? In 1951 Kwame Nkrumah sat in jail in the Gold Coast, a British colony, serving a three-year jail sentence for subversive activities. Nkrumah was the head of the Convention People's Party (CPP), and the British saw him as a dangerous radical.

At the same time, the British were holding elections in the Gold Coast. Assuming that these elections would be the first step toward self-government in the colony, the British hoped moderates would win the elections. The moderates did not win. Instead, the Convention People's Party won a majority of the seats.

The British governor of the Gold Coast now faced a dilemma. He could ignore the election results and keep Nkrumah in jail, or he could release Nkrumah and ask him to form a government. On November 12, 1951, the governor released Nkrumah from prison and asked him to form a government, which he did. In 1952 Nkrumah became the prime minister of the Gold Coast, and when the country achieved independence from Britain in 1957, he became the prime minister of the new nation—Ghana. ■

AFRICA AND THE MIDDLE EAST **937**

---

1 What ideas and actions led to independence for British and French colonies? *desire for self-government, nationalism; Ghana—Britain tried experiment of self-government, elected leader pushed for full independence; Kenya—rebel insurgency against white settlers; French colonies—given choices, granted independence*

British and French Colonies

Define What is decolonization? *the withdrawal of colonial powers from their colonies and areas of influence*

Recall What was the first British colony to achieve independence? *the Gold Coast, which was renamed Ghana*

Summarize How did Ghana achieve independence? *Britain decided to hold elections for a national assembly; Nkrumah's party won majority, embarked on a campaign for self-government and independence; Britain granted colony full independence*

📋 **CRF:** Biography: Léopold Senghor

📋 **CRF:** Primary Source: The Independence Movement in Kenya

---

Reading Like a Historian

Kwame Nkrumah's *I Speak of Freedom*

(Activity) **Powerful Words** Have students identify words and phrases in the speech that show pride and invite action. **LS Verbal-Linguistic**

Primary Source

"It is far better to be free to govern or misgovern yourself than to be governed by anybody else."
—Kwame Nkrumah

Answers

Reading Like a Historian **1.** *that he believes African nations should unite* **2.** *He thinks economic development is within Africa's grasp.*

938

TAKING NOTES
Take notes on African independence movements.

British and French	
Portuguese and Belgian	
South Africa	

NEW YORK

CC Unit 5-E2a African independence movements (Ghana and Kenya)

CC Unit 5-E3b Role of Kwame Nkrumah

British and French Colonies

After 1945 European colonial powers began a process of decolonization—the withdrawal of colonial powers from their colonies and areas of influence. Great Britain and France led the way by gradually leaving their colonies and granting them independence.

Ghana After World War II the British colony of the Gold Coast in West Africa was the first British colony to achieve independence. To gain independence, some African leaders in the Gold Coast established a convention to demand greater participation in government. The goal of the convention was to cooperate with the British and gain influence as peacefully as possible.

However, a less cooperative nationalist movement was brewing in the Gold Coast. In 1947 **Kwame Nkrumah** became the leader of the Gold Coast nationalist movement and established the Convention People's Party (CPP). As leader of the CPP, Nkrumah led strikes and demonstrations. The British responded by jailing him. Yet, even while in jail, Nkrumah transformed the CPP into a major political party with considerable popular support. Faced with this kind of pressure, the British eventually agreed to allow national elections in the Gold Coast in 1951. The CPP swept the national elections.

In part because Nkrumah continued to press for independence, Britain granted the Gold Coast full self-government in 1957. Nkrumah became the first prime minister of the new nation, which he named Ghana.

Kenya In Kenya in the 1950s, the path to independence did not go as smoothly as it did in Ghana. The ownership of land and the possibility of independence led to conflict between white Kenyan farmers and the native Kikuyu people. The farmers feared independence would cause them to lose large tracts of valuable cash crops, such as coffee, which they grew in the Kenyan highlands. The Kikuyu considered the highlands their ancestral homeland, and they wanted the land back.

A leader of Kenya's nationalist movement, **Jomo Kenyatta**, argued for the Kikuyu's right to the land and its importance.

Reading like a Historian

Kwame Nkrumah's *I Speak of Freedom*

Analyzing Primary Sources One way we can learn about the past is by carefully analyzing primary sources. Primary sources are valuable to historians because these sources provide critical information about an event or time period.

In this excerpt, Kwame Nkrumah writes about the need for African nations to unite. He describes the value of Africa's natural resources and the need for African nations to come together to profit from these resources. When analyzing this primary source, think about

- the author of the source
- the point of view of the author

Skills FOCUS **READING LIKE A HISTORIAN**

1. Author What can you learn about Kwame Nkrumah by reading this excerpt?

2. Point of View How does Nkrumah view Africa's future?

See **Skills Handbook**, p. H25

> Never before have a people had within their grasp so great an opportunity for developing a continent endowed with so much wealth. Individually, the independent states of Africa, some of them potentially rich, others poor, can do little for their people. Together, by mutual help, they can achieve much. But the economic development of the continent must be planned and pursued as a whole . . . Only a strong political union can bring about full and effective development of our natural resources for the benefit of our people.
>
> —Kwame Nkrumah, *I Speak of Freedom: A Statement of African Ideology,* 1961

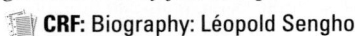

Skills Focus: Analyzing Primary Sources

Above Level

Reading Like a Historian Skill
I Speak of Freedom

1. Have students review the excerpt from Nkrumah's speech on this page. Guide students in a discussion of the points Nkrumah makes, and ensure that students understand the vocabulary, tone, message, and the audience for whom this speech was intended. Have students take notes during the discussion.

2. Then have students write another speech with the same tone that Nkrumah might have written to make the same point he makes in this speech.

3. Have students practice their speeches. Choose volunteers to deliver their speeches to the class. **LS Verbal-Linguistic, Auditory-Musical**

📋 **Alternative Assessment Handbook,** Rubric 24: Oral Presentations

"It is the key to the people's life; it secures them that peaceful tillage [cultivation] of the soil which supplies their material needs and enables them to perform their magic and traditional ceremonies in undisturbed serenity."

—Jomo Kenyatta, *Facing Mount Kenya*

To rid Kenya of the white farmers and gain their land back, many Kikuyu farmers formed a violent movement called the **Mau Mau**. For several years the group terrorized the highlands of Kenya. They murdered anyone who opposed them, including other Africans who cooperated with the white settlers.

The British eventually regained control of the colony by murdering and torturing some members of the Mau Mau movement. Nevertheless, by the late 1950s the British were convinced that they must accept decolonization. A few years later, in 1963, Kenya became an independent nation with Jomo Kenyatta as the nation's first prime minister.

French Africa Whereas the British colonies followed one path toward independence, France's African colonies followed another path. Unlike the British, the French had always insisted that their goal was to incorporate their African colonies into France itself. After World War II, France's prime minister, Charles de Gaulle, tried to pursue that goal. At the same time, he tried to respond to calls for greater African participation in France's colonial government.

Some African leaders in France's colonies believed they should have greater opportunities for self-rule, but rejected a final break with France. These leaders believed Africans could attain economic and cultural benefits from a continuing relationship with France. In 1958, de Gaulle called for a referendum on the continuing union between France and its African colonies. He gave African leaders the choice between remaining tied to France through a new organization of colonies known as the French Community and becoming completely independent. Most colonies voted to become part of the French Community. A few years later France granted most of the colonies of the French Community independence.

READING CHECK **Find the Main Idea** How did Britain grant independence to its African colonies?

FACES OF HISTORY

Jomo KENYATTA
1894–1978

As a young man in the 1920s, Kenyatta joined a group that protested against Kenya's white-minority government. As a member of the Kikuyu tribe of Kenya, Jomo Kenyatta spent most of his life fighting to gain more rights for the Kikuyu.

In 1952 the Kenyan government arrested and jailed Kenyatta for leading a movement—called the Mau Mau—against European settlers in Kenya. Although, Kenyatta denied he had any involvement in the movement, he remained in jail for seven years. In 1963, several years after Kenyatta's release from prison, Kenyans celebrated their independence and elected Kenyatta as their prime minister.

Infer Why do you think Kenyans elected Kenyatta as prime minister?

Portuguese and Belgian Colonies

For the Belgian and Portuguese colonies in Africa, the transition to independence was more difficult than for the British and French colonies. The Belgians and the Portuguese held on to their African colonies longer than any other European nations until violence forced them to decolonize.

After World War II, the Belgian government agreed that it should prepare the people of the Belgian Congo for self-government. In the 1950s, African nationalists in the Congo demanded immediate self-government. In 1960 the Belgians suddenly announced that they would withdraw completely from the Congo. Soon violence toward Belgian settlers and a civil war in the Congo erupted.

As Portugal continued to hold on to its colonies, African leaders emerged in the colonies of Angola, Portuguese Guinea, and Mozambique. These leaders organized their own armies to fight for independence. As a result, long years of bloody warfare between the Africans and the Portuguese marked the last decades of Portuguese rule. Years of war and a military coup in Portugal drained Portugal's economy, making it impossible for the Portuguese to support their colonies. In 1974 Portugal withdrew completely from Africa.

READING CHECK **Summarize** How did Africans in the Portuguese colonies achieve independence?

NEW YORK

CC Unit 5-E3b
Role of Jomo Kenyatta

AFRICA AND THE MIDDLE EAST **939**

Direct Teach

Reading Focus

2 Why did Portuguese and Belgian colonies have difficulty achieving independence? *Portugal and Belgium hung on to their colonies until violence forced them to decolonize.*

Portuguese and Belgian Colonies

Recall Where did Portugal have colonies in Africa? Where did Belgium have a colony? *Portugal—Angola, Portuguese Guinea, and Mozambique; Belgium—Belgian Congo*

Analyze Why did Portugal ultimately withdraw from Africa? *War and a military coup drained Portugal's economy.*

Info to Know

Early History of Kenya Before the Europeans came to Kenya, the economy was simple. Wealth was determined by land and livestock. The British introduced money and taxation, and they claimed land for themselves. In order to provide for themselves and their families, African men had to serve the British. The Kenyans received one-fifth the amount whites received for doing the same work, so it's not surprising that revolt and rebellion occurred.

Answers

Faces of History *possible answer—Kenyatta was a hero to Kenyans because of his involvement in the independence movement.*

Reading Check (left) *Britain granted independence to its colonies after they began nationalist movements.* **(right)** *African leaders organized armies to fight for independence; years of bloody warfare ended Portuguese rule.*

Differentiating Instruction

Above Level

Advanced Learners/Gifted and Talented

1. Have students read the information in the text on the quest for independence in both Ghana and Kenya.

2. Then read this quote from Kwame Nkrumah to students: "Freedom is not something that one people can bestow on another as a gift. They claim it as their own and none can keep it from them."

3. Have students write an essay in which they discuss how this quotation can be applied to both Ghana and Kenya as they fought to achieve independence from the British.
   LS **Verbal-Linguistic**

   Alternative Assessment Handbook, Rubric 37: Writing Assignments

Interpreting Maps

Independence in Africa

Activity Sequence Have students list the countries shown on the map in order of when each achieved its independence. **LS** **Logical-Mathematical**

Map Transparency: Independence in Africa

Info to Know

Sub-Saharan Africa While conditions vary from country to country, poverty and lack of education are widespread in sub-Saharan Africa. About 700 million people live in 47 countries, and 34 of the world's poorest countries are in Africa. The country's gross national income ranges from under $100 per person in Burundi to over $7,000 in the Seychelles. In 2001, the number of Africans living in poverty was about 314 million—just under half of the population.

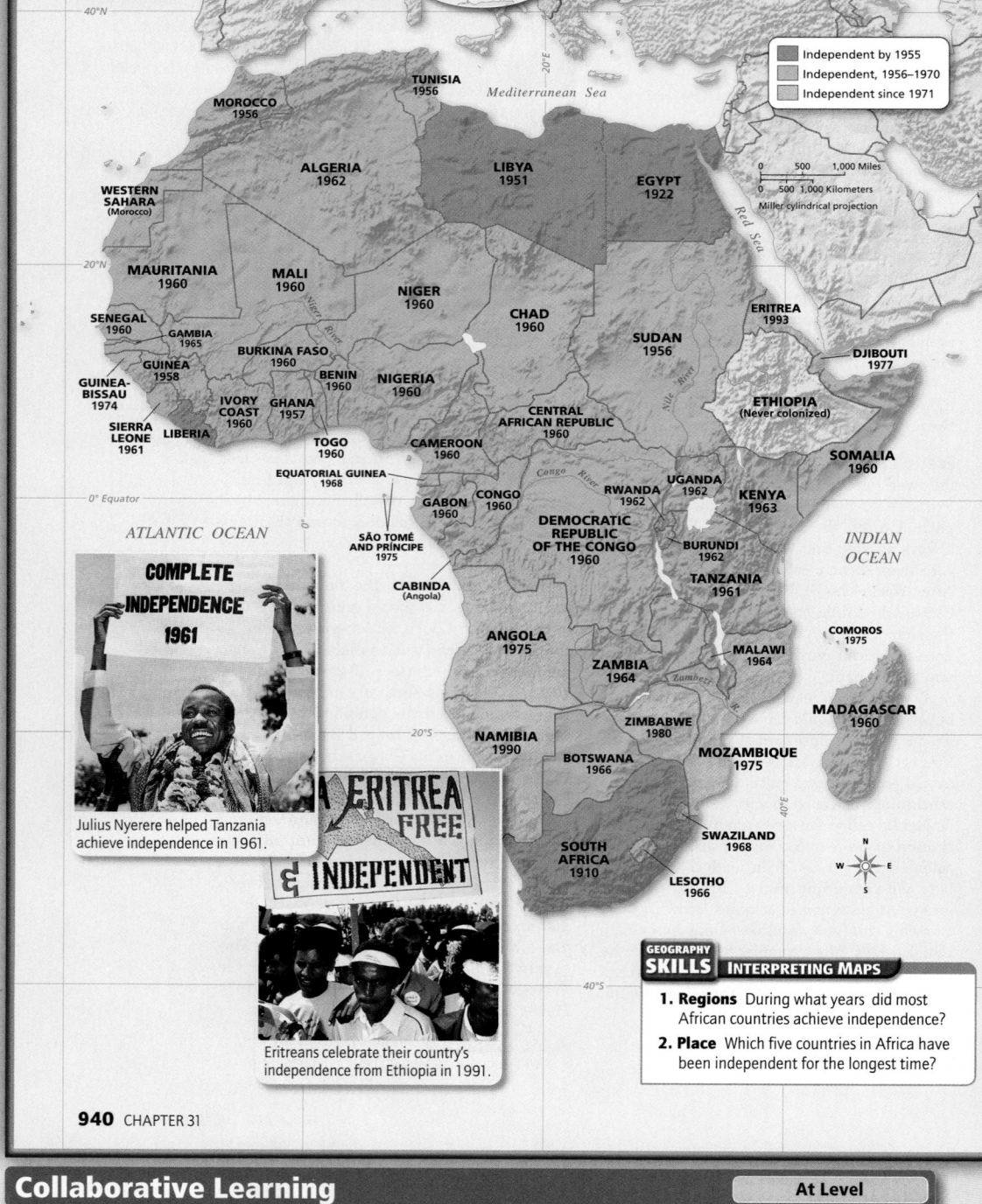

INDEPENDENCE IN AFRICA

Legend:
- Independent by 1955
- Independent, 1956–1970
- Independent since 1971

MOROCCO 1956
TUNISIA 1956
ALGERIA 1962
LIBYA 1951
EGYPT 1922
WESTERN SAHARA (Morocco)
MAURITANIA 1960
MALI 1960
NIGER 1960
CHAD 1960
SUDAN 1956
ERITREA 1993
SENEGAL 1960
GAMBIA 1965
BURKINA FASO 1960
GUINEA 1958
BENIN 1960
NIGERIA 1960
DJIBOUTI 1977
GUINEA-BISSAU 1974
IVORY COAST 1960
GHANA 1957
CENTRAL AFRICAN REPUBLIC 1960
ETHIOPIA (Never colonized)
SIERRA LEONE 1961
LIBERIA
TOGO 1960
CAMEROON 1960
SOMALIA 1960
EQUATORIAL GUINEA 1968
GABON 1960
CONGO 1960
UGANDA 1962
KENYA 1963
SÃO TOMÉ AND PRÍNCIPE 1975
CABINDA (Angola)
DEMOCRATIC REPUBLIC OF THE CONGO 1960
RWANDA 1962
BURUNDI 1962
TANZANIA 1961
ANGOLA 1975
ZAMBIA 1964
MALAWI 1964
COMOROS 1975
NAMIBIA 1990
ZIMBABWE 1980
MADAGASCAR 1960
BOTSWANA 1966
MOZAMBIQUE 1975
SOUTH AFRICA 1910
SWAZILAND 1968
LESOTHO 1966

ATLANTIC OCEAN
INDIAN OCEAN
Mediterranean Sea
Red Sea

COMPLETE INDEPENDENCE 1961
Julius Nyerere helped Tanzania achieve independence in 1961.

ERITREA FREE & INDEPENDENT
Eritreans celebrate their country's independence from Ethiopia in 1991.

GEOGRAPHY SKILLS **INTERPRETING MAPS**

1. **Regions** During what years did most African countries achieve independence?
2. **Place** Which five countries in Africa have been independent for the longest time?

940 CHAPTER 31

Collaborative Learning

At Level

Independence in Africa

Research Required

1. Organize students into small groups, and have each group list three or four African countries that students want to learn more about.

2. Have each group vote to select one country. Create a class list of each group's country. Try to avoid duplication of countries on the list. Some groups may have to vote again to choose another country.

3. Have groups conduct outside research about their chosen country. Research should focus on current events, problems, challenges, advantages, and resources the country possesses. Remind students to use reliable sources.

4. Have groups prepare multimedia presentations for the class about their chosen countries. Reports should include maps, charts, and graphs as a means of telling the country's story. **LS** **Verbal-Linguistic, Visual-Spatial**

Alternative Assessment Handbook, Rubrics 14: Group Activity; and 22: Multimedia Presentations

Answers

Interpreting Maps 1. *1950s and 1960s;* **2.** *Ethiopia, Liberia, Libya, Egypt, South Africa*

South Africa

In the early 1900s South Africa was run by white Afrikaners—descendants of the original Dutch settlers. Even though South Africa had received its official independence from Great Britain in 1910, nonwhites in South Africa were not free under the Afrikaner government of South Africa. The government passed restrictive laws meant to limit the freedom of nonwhites in South Africa.

Apartheid In 1948 racial discrimination heightened when the Afrikaner-dominated National Party came to run the South African government. The National Party <u>instituted</u> a policy of **apartheid**, which means "apartness" in the Afrikaans language. This policy divided people into four racial groups: White, Black, Colored (mixed ancestry), and Asian.

Apartheid attempted to create a greater separation between nonwhites and whites and impose harsh controls over nonwhites. Apartheid laws banned interracial marriages, and placed further restrictions on African ownership of land and businesses.

Apartheid laws were especially harsh on blacks in South Africa. They were required to carry passes or identity books, which indicated where they lived and worked. Further restrictions blacks faced included imprisonment if the police found them in an area for more than 72 hours without a pass.

Under apartheid, only white South Africans could vote or hold political office. Blacks, who made up nearly 75 percent of the population, were denied South African citizenship and were restricted to certain occupations with very little pay.

Homelands Apartheid laws also placed strict limits on where blacks could live. In cities, blacks were required to live in impoverished areas called townships. Government laws restricted the types of businesses allowed in townships, ensuring that the people would stay poor. Starting in the 1950s, the government created rural "homelands" for different African tribes or groups. Most of these areas did not include good farmland or resources.

The South African government used these homelands as an excuse for depriving millions of black South Africans of citizenship. In addition, millions of black men were forced to migrate miles from the homelands to work in mines, factories, and farms. These men were not permitted to bring their families with them. As a result, the homeland policy made millions of black South Africans resident aliens in their own country.

READING CHECK **Find the Main Idea** What was apartheid, and how did it function?

 NEW YORK

CC Unit 5-E3e Apartheid— policy of racial separation and segregation

ACADEMIC VOCABULARY

institute to originate and establish

READING SKILLS

Drawing Conclusions What can you conclude about the effects of South Africa's independence?

SECTION 1 ASSESSMENT

go.hrw.com
Online Quiz
Keyword: SHL AFR HP

Reviewing Ideas, Terms, and People

1. **a. Identify** Who was **Kwame Nkrumah**?
   b. Compare and Contrast How did the process of gaining independence differ for British and French colonies in Africa?
   c. Evaluate Do you think the Kikuyu people had a right to the land the white farmers owned? Why or why not?
2. **a. Recall** What happened in the Belgian Congo after independence?
   b. Identify Cause and Effect What caused Portugal to finally withdraw from its African colonies?
3. **a. Define** What was **apartheid**?
   b. Explain How were the lives of blacks in South Africa restricted by apartheid laws?
   c. Elaborate How did homelands deny citizenship to blacks in South Africa?

Critical Thinking

4. **Identify Cause and Effect** Copy the graphic organizer here and use it and your notes from this section to list the causes of African independence movements and their effects.

| Causes | → | African Independence Movements | → | Effects |

FOCUS ON WRITING

5. **Exposition** In a brief paragraph, compare and contrast the nationalist movements in Ghana and Kenya. Be sure to use supporting details from the section.

Section 1 Assessment Answers

1. **a.** leader of the Convention People's Party; first prime minister and president of Ghana
   b. British colonies rebelled; French colonies granted independence without fighting
   c. possible answer—Yes, it was their ancestral homeland.
2. **a.** Civil war erupted.
   b. War and a military coup drained Portugal's economy.
3. **a.** a policy in South Africa that divided whites and nonwhites into four groups, separating them and placing harsh controls on nonwhites

   b. interracial marriages banned, land and business ownership restricted, blacks had to carry identification, could not vote, hold political office or certain jobs, had to live in certain places
   c. made millions of black South Africans resident aliens in their own country
4. Causes—nationalism, desire for self-government; Effects—civil wars, violence, independence, formation of new nations
5. Students should cite the desire for self-government, and the unfair colonial system.

● **Direct Teach** ●

Reading Focus

❸ What effect did apartheid have on the lives of black South Africans? *had to carry passes or identity books; could not vote, hold political office, or work in certain jobs; were not considered citizens; were required to live in impoverished areas*

South Africa

Identify Who were the Afrikaners? *white descendants of the original Dutch settlers of South Africa*

Interpret How does the meaning of the word apartheid relate to its policies? *means "apartness;" apartheid separated nonwhites and whites, discriminating against nonwhites*

● **Review & Assess** ●

Close

Have students compare and contrast the African countries that struggled the most to gain independence with countries struggled the least.

Review

Online Quiz, Section 1

Assess

SE Section 1 Assessment

Progress Assessment: Section 1 Quiz

Alternative Assessment Handbook

Reteach/Intervene

Interactive Reader and Study Guide, Section 1

Interactive Skills Tutor CD-ROM

Answers

Reading Skills *possible answer—Even after independence, nonwhites in South Africa did not have freedom.*

Reading Check *policy of separating whites and nonwhites and placing restrictions upon nonwhites; enforced by police, laws*

941

The Arts Around the World

African Sculpture

Info to Know

African Sculpture African sculpture was not created for beauty or to be sold but to recall important events or feelings. The most common types of African sculpture are of the human form, and wood is the most commonly used material. African art is designed to show laws and history, and to teach these to young people. Another purpose of African art is to serve as a transmitter between human and supernatural happenings; it also shows the wealth and status of those who possess it.

Sculpture

African Sculpture

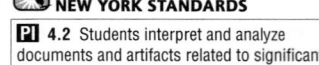

NEW YORK STANDARDS

P1 4.2 Students interpret and analyze documents and artifacts related to significant developments and events in world history.

What is it? African sculpture includes many different forms such as masks, statues, and carvings. In Africa, peoples of different regions and cultures create styles of sculpture that reflect their unique cultures. Many of these styles use the human form as a subject. One of the highest compliments an African artist can receive is someone praising their work by saying it "looks like a human being."

Key characteristics:
- Highly skilled artists learn to sculpt at an early age from a master sculptor.
- Sculptures usually represent royalty, ancestors, animals, or spirits.
- Traditional materials used to create sculptures include wood, metals, and clay.

Why is it important?
- Sculpture shows us the rich diversity of cultures throughout Africa.
- African sculpture is a significant art form that is passed on from generation to generation to keep African history and cultures alive.

These masks from South Africa represent the diversity of styles among African artists who created them.

This Yoruba artist is from Nigeria. Over the past 700 years the Yoruba have been known for their skilled craftsmanship and the bronze sculptures they produce like the one pictured above.

Skills FOCUS **INTERPRETING VISUALS**

Compare What characteristics do these three forms of African sculpture have in common?

Differentiating Instruction

Below Level

Special Education Students

Materials: modeling clay, paper, colored markers

1. Read the information in the feature to students and explain any words that might be unfamiliar to them. Help students understand the information, and have them examine the artwork on the page.

2. Have students draw a sculpture that they would like to make. Student sculptures should reflect the information in the text.

3. Have students use the clay to create their own African sculpture. Display the sculptures in a classroom exhibit. You might wish to hold an exhibit "opening" by inviting other classes to view the artwork. Encourage students to create invitations to the classroom exhibit.
LS Visual-Spatial, Kinesthetic

📖 **Alternative Assessment Handbook**, Rubric 3: Artwork

Answers

Interpreting Visuals *All of the sculptures depict human faces, appear to be made of wood*

942

SECTION 2
Post-Colonial Africa

BEFORE YOU READ

MAIN IDEA
Newly independent African nations struggled with poverty, conflict, and ineffective governments. In recent years some countries sought better government by holding democratic elections.

READING FOCUS
1. What political challenges did Africans face after independence?
2. What economic and environmental challenges did Africans face after independence?
3. How did Africans revive their culture after independence?

KEY TERMS AND PEOPLE
African National Congress
Nelson Mandela
Sharpeville Massacre
Soweto Uprising
F. W. de Klerk
one-party system
patronage
Mobutu Sese Seko
desertification
negritude movement

NEW YORK
PI 2.5 Students investigate key events and developments and major turning points in world history to identify the factors that brought about change and the long-term effects of these changes.

THE INSIDE STORY

How did black South Africans end 300 years of white rule in only four days? First the elderly and the ill came to vote. Some came in wheelchairs and some with canes to cast their ballots in South Africa's first democratic election. On the following day, April 27, 1994, South Africa's general population began to vote. In some black areas voters waited in line for more than 10 hours. In rural areas, some voters had to cast their ballots by candlelight.

In some cases, black voters went to cast ballots in white areas where the lines were shorter. The racial hostility that had dominated South Africa for so long seemed to have disappeared. Black and white voters shared a sense of elation as they participated in the rebirth of their nation—the new, democratic South Africa.

For older black voters, the chance to vote was empowering. Many thought that it would never be possible for them to choose their own government. "My parents never saw this day. My husband never saw this day," said Mildred Motsuenane. "I can tell you dawn is breaking and the dark light is gone." For voters like Mildred, this was not merely an election, but was a chance for people to get their dignity back. ■

Dawn of a New Day

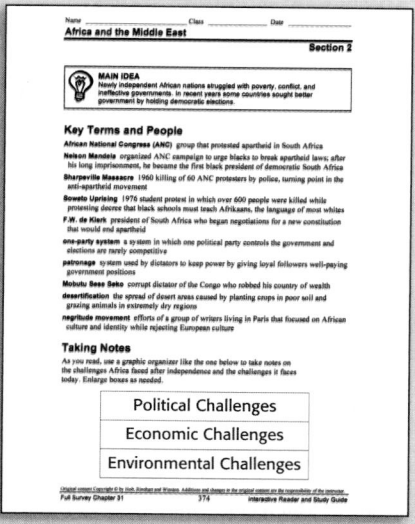

South Africans line up to cast their votes in the country's democratic elections. ▶

AFRICA AND THE MIDDLE EAST **943**

Teach the Main Idea

At Level

Post-Colonial Africa

1. **Teach** Ask students the Reading Focus questions to teach this section.

2. **Apply** Have students create an outline of the section using the heads as main points. Have students identify at least two main ideas under each of the red subheadings.

3. **Review** Review student outlines as a class. Have students identify the points in their outlines that they feel are most important in the development of post-colonial Africa.

4. **Practice/Homework** Have students make generalizations to answer this question: Why did African countries turn to dictatorships and one-party governments instead of pursuing democracy and free elections? Have students write a brief essay explaining their answers. **LS Verbal-Linguistic, Visual-Spatial**

📋 **Alternative Assessment Handbook**, Rubric 37: Writing Assignments

---

Preteach

Getting Started
Use the **Interactive Reader and Study Guide** to familiarize students with the section content.

📖 **Interactive Reader and Study Guide**, Section 2

[Interactive Reader and Study Guide worksheet preview]

Name _____ Class _____ Date _____
Africa and the Middle East
Section 2

MAIN IDEA
Newly independent African nations struggled with poverty, conflict, and ineffective governments. In recent years some countries sought better government by holding democratic elections.

Key Terms and People
African National Congress (ANC) group that protested apartheid in South Africa
Nelson Mandela organized ANC campaign to urge blacks to break apartheid laws; after his long imprisonment, he became the first black president of democratic South Africa
Sharpeville Massacre 1960 killing of 60 ANC protesters by police, turning point in the anti-apartheid movement
Soweto Uprising 1976 student protest in which over 600 people were killed while protesting decree that black schools must teach Afrikaans, the language of most whites
F.W. de Klerk president of South Africa who began negotiations for a new constitution that would end apartheid
one-party system a system in which one political party controls the government and elections are rarely competitive
patronage system used by dictators to keep power by giving loyal followers well-paying government positions
Mobutu Sese Seko corrupt dictator of the Congo who robbed his country of wealth
desertification the spread of desert areas caused by planting crops in poor soil and grazing animals in extremely dry regions
negritude movement efforts of a group of writers living in Paris that focused on African culture and identity while rejecting European culture

Taking Notes
As you read, use a graphic organizer like the one below to take notes on the challenges Africa faced after independence and the challenges it faces today. Enlarge boxes as needed.

| Political Challenges |
| Economic Challenges |
| Environmental Challenges |

Full Survey Chapter 31 · 374 · Interactive Reader and Study Guide

Academic Vocabulary

Review with students the high-use academic term in this section.

infrastructure public works, such as buildings and roads, that are needed to support a population (p. 946)

📋 **CRF:** Vocabulary Builder: Section 2

Taking Notes

Political—apartheid, Sharpeville Massacre, Soweto Uprising; military dictatorships, ethnic conflicts, civil war

Economic—many nations not industrialized at time of independence, turned to international organizations like the World Bank for loans

Environmental—diseases like malaria and AIDS, desertification

---

go.hrw.com
Online Resources

KEYWORD: SHL AFR
ACTIVITY: Apartheid in South Africa

Reading Focus

1 What political challenges did Africans face after independence? *dictatorships; ethnic conflict and civil war; protests against apartheid*

Political Challenges

Recall What caused the Soweto Uprising? *a new policy that black students be taught Afrikaans*

Explain How did F.W. de Klerk's actions help with the end of apartheid? *released Nelson Mandela from prison, reinstated the African National Congress, allowed the first non-racial elections*

Activity **Soweto Poems** Have students write a poem or song commemorating the Soweto Uprising.

LS Auditory-Musical

Alternative Assessment Handbook, Rubric 26: Poems and Songs

CRF: Biography: Nelson Mandela

Recent Scholarship

In His Own Words, by Nelson Mandela, is a collection of the prolific leader's speeches covering a wide variety of topics. Whether discussing politics, education, or culture, Mandela offers compelling thoughts about his experiences as a leader dedicated to preserving freedom.

In His Own Words by Nelson Mandela. Little Brown & Co., 2004.

Answers

Primary Sources 1. *a democratic and free society in which people of all races have equal oppor-tunities;* **2.** *possible answer—He probably inspired followers with his dedication.*

944

Take notes on the challenges Africa faced after independence and the challenges it faces today.

| Political Challenges |
| Economic Challenges |
| Environmental Challenges |

NEW YORK

CC Unit 7-E3e
African National Congress, Nelson Mandela, and F. W. de Klerk

Political Challenges

In the 1950s and 1960s many former European colonies in Africa were ruled by dictators and some nations fell into civil war. However, the 1990s brought renewed hope with the return of democracy in many African countries and the end of the apartheid system in South Africa.

Protesting South Africa's Apartheid In the early 1900s a group of blacks in South African had formed the **African National Congress (ANC)**. The ANC petitioned the government and held peaceful protests against apartheid. In the 1940s, however, younger and more radical members joined the organization, including a young lawyer named **Nelson Mandela**. In 1952 Mandela helped organize a campaign that urged blacks in South Africa to break apartheid laws. The ANC gained a mass following from this campaign.

In 1960 the ANC drastically changed its peaceful philosophy after police fired on demonstrators in the township of Sharpeville,

---

PRIMARY SOURCES

Mandela's Trial Speech

In 1964 Nelson Mandela gave a speech at the Rivona Trial, in which 10 ANC leaders were accused of promoting acts of sabotage and violent revolution. In the speech, Mandela explained why ANC leaders felt they had no choice but to use violence to resist the government. He also eloquently expressed his commitment to his principles.

"During my lifetime I have dedicated myself to this struggle of the African people. I have fought against white domination, and I have fought against black domination. I have cherished the ideal of a democratic and free society in which all persons live together in harmony and with equal opportunities. It is an ideal which I hope to live for and to achieve. But if needs be, it is an ideal for which I am prepared to die."

—Nelson Mandela, April 20, 1964

Skills FOCUS READING LIKE A HISTORIAN

1. Explain To what cause does Mandela say he is committed?

2. Analyze Primary Sources What impact do you think Mandela's speech had on his cause?

See **Skills Handbook**, p. H25

944 CHAPTER 31

---

killing more than 60 people. The **Sharpeville Massacre** was a turning point in the anti-apartheid movement. Some ANC leaders, including Mandela, decided that they would have to meet violence with violence. In response to this decision, the government banned the ANC and jailed Mandela.

In 1976, a major student protest movement took place in the township of Soweto. The **Soweto Uprising** was set off by a government decree that black schools teach their students Afrikaans—the language spoken by the majority of white South Africans. When police killed a protesting student, the peaceful march developed into a revolt. The police crushed the uprising, but more than 600 people were killed and 4,000 wounded.

After the uprising, violence erupted in many black townships, while the ANC fought to end apartheid. At the same time, much of the international community imposed trade sanctions, or restrictions, on South Africa in an attempt to force the nation to abandon apartheid.

Democracy in South Africa In 1990 under President **F.W. de Klerk**, South Africa legalized the ANC and began negotiations to enact a new constitution that would end apartheid. De Klerk released Mandela from prison and lifted the long-standing ban on the African National Congress. De Klerk also abolished the homelands and held South Africa's first democratic elections. The ANC swept the elections, and

Nelson Mandela in Johannesburg in the early 1960s.

Skills Focus: Making Generalizations

Below Level

Reading Skill
Apartheid

Standard English Mastery

1. Review the information in the text about apartheid, the Soweto Uprising, and the imprisonment of Nelson Mandela. Have students work in mixed-ability pairs to create a graphic organizer that summarizes the information.

2. Guide students in a discussion of the anti-apartheid movement, and have students take notes during the class discussion. Focus

student attention on the embargoes and divestments in businesses that occurred.

3. Have students use their notes and graphic organizers to write a letter to the editor of a South African newspaper encouraging an end to apartheid. Have students review their drafts in mixed-ability pairs, correct their work, and turn in the final letter. **LS** Verbal-Linguistic

Alternative Assessment Handbook, Rubrics 11: Discussions; and 17: Letters to Editors

Nelson Mandela became the first black president of a democratic South Africa.

Military Dictatorships By the end of the 1960s almost all of the newly independent African nations had adopted a **one-party system**. In this system, a single political party controls the government and elections are rarely competitive. In many countries opposition parties were outlawed.

Dictators ruled many of these African nations by maintaining their power through **patronage**, giving their loyal followers well-paying positions in the government. Some corrupt officials required bribes for government contracts or licenses. These officials also ran government enterprises for their own personal profit, and sometimes stole money from the public treasury.

This new generation of African dictators robbed their countries of their wealth. For example, **Mobutu Sese Seko**, dictator of the Congo, amassed a personal fortune of about $5 billion and built a $100 million palace. While Mobutu enriched himself, his nation's people fell into poverty. Other dictators committed similar offenses.

Ethnic Conflicts and Civil War When the European powers divided Africa into colonies, preexisting political units were not maintained. After independence, rival ethnic groups competed for control.

Some of these conflicts led to destructive civil wars. In 1967 in Nigeria people of the Igbo-speaking ethnic group of eastern Nigeria proclaimed their own independent state of Biafra. As a result, a bloody civil war erupted. About 2 million Nigerians died from fighting, and just as many died of starvation. After Biafra collapsed, the territory rejoined Nigeria.

Similarly, a civil war and a severe drought led to enormous suffering in Somalia in 1992. Hundreds of thousands of Somalis died when warring militias stole food sent to Somalia from international relief agencies. The United States and the United Nations tried to help but were unsuccessful.

In the 1990s tensions between two ethnic groups, the Hutu and the Tutsi, in Rwanda erupted in widespread violence. In 1994 the Hutu-led government encouraged a genocide of Tutsi and moderate Hutu civilians, which

resulted in the massacre of about 1 million Tutsi and moderate Hutus. Many more civilians fled to refugee camps in the neighboring countries of Burundi, Uganda, and the Democratic Republic of the Congo.

Democracy for Some Despite conflicts and war throughout the late 1900s, many African countries were still dictatorships. During the Cold War, the United States and the Soviet Union had each provided large amounts of money to dictators who were friendly to their side. But when the Cold War ended in 1989, most of that money dried up. The lack of funding began to weaken some of the dictators' governments. Many Africans saw this weakness as an opportunity to create democratic governments and they demanded elections.

By 2005, more than 30 African countries had abandoned one-party systems and held elections. Results of these elections were mixed, however. Some former dictators resorted to fraud and intimidation to win elections. Others were elected because the people preferred them to other alternatives.

READING CHECK **Draw Conclusions** Why did most African states adopt a one-party system?

POLITICAL TRENDS IN POST-COLONIAL AFRICA

Since gaining independence, many African countries have struggled to build stable governments.

ONE-PARTY RULE AND MILITARY DICTATORSHIPS

After many African countries gained independence following World War II, strong leaders seized power and set up one-party rule or military dictatorships. Although some of these regimes lasted for many years, others were toppled and replaced in military coups, which were common.

ETHNIC CONFLICTS AND CIVIL WAR

Africa's ethnic diversity and rivalries, combined with country borders that were drawn without consideration of ethnic homelands, led to conflicts and civil wars in many countries.

STRUGGLES WITH DEMOCRACY

Beginning in the early 1990s many African countries began to make progress toward democracy and overcome their history of dictatorship and conflict. However, most countries still struggled to hold free and fair elections and maintain stability.

NEW YORK

CC Unit 7-E3d
Nigeria and civil war

CC Unit 7-E3g
Ethnic tensions in Rwanda

Differentiating Instruction

Above Level

Advanced Learners/Gifted and Talented

Research Required

1. Have students review the information about Mobutu Sese Seko and the Congo. Tell students that the history of the Congo, a country rich in natural resources, is one of tragedy, bloodshed, and wasted wealth.

2. Have students research the history of the Congo from the time of Patrice Lumumba to the current day. Students should follow the events that occurred when Mobutu was dictator. Student research should include Mobutu's replacement by both Laurent

Kabila and his son Joseph Kabila, and the presidential elections held since that time.

3. Have students prepare a multimedia presentation of their research with maps, charts, and statistics supporting their findings. In their conclusions students should predict what lies ahead for the Congo. **LS Verbal-Linguistic, Visual-Spatial**

Alternative Assessment Handbook, Rubrics 22: Mulitimedia Presentations; and 30: Research

---

Economic and Environmental Challenges

Define What is desertification? *the spread of desertlike conditions, contributing to drought and famine*

Make Inferences Why do you think such a small percentage of Africans with AIDS are receiving treatment? *possible answers—lack of education, lack of infrastructure to deliver treatment, lack of money to pay for expensive treatments*

Interpreting Graphs
Challenges in Post-Colonial Africa

Make Generalizations Why has the number of people with HIV risen so rapidly since 1992? *possible answer— Resources to help the people with HIV are lacking; people are not being educated about the disease.*

Info to Know

Facts about AIDS in Sub-Saharan Africa AIDS is the leading cause of death in Africa; 70 percent of all people infected with HIV live in sub-Saharan Africa. In 2004, 3.1 million people in sub-Saharan Africa were newly infected with HIV. Because of HIV and AIDS, schools are being closed due to the deaths of teachers.

Answers

HIV in Sub-Saharan Africa *possible answers—results in many deaths, leaves many children orphans, makes people fearful*

Reading Check *planting crops in poor soil and grazing animals in dry areas, causing soil to dry out even more*

946

CHALLENGES IN POST-COLONIAL AFRICA

Poverty and health issues like HIV are two of the main challenges in Africa today. Many poor Africans live in makeshift housing in shantytowns like this one in Soweto, South Africa.

HIV IN SUB-SAHARAN AFRICA

Source: World Health Organization

Skills Focus INTERPRETING GRAPHS

Analyze In what ways do you think the growth of HIV in sub-Saharan Africa affects society?

Economic and Environmental Challenges

NEW YORK

CC Unit 8-A2d Cycles of poverty and disease

CC Unit 8-C3 Desertification

After achieving independence, many African nations faced economic challenges that came with their new status. In addition, Africans had to combat the spread of disease and environmental problems.

Struggling Economies After independence, the economies of most African nations were fragile because they depended on only one or two exports for their support. African nations were not yet industrialized and depended on farming or the mining of raw materials. For example, Ghana depended on cocoa, and Nigeria, on oil.

To support themselves, many African nations turned to international organizations, such as the World Bank, for development loans. However, even with economic help, bad planning and corrupt leaders left these nations with huge debts and no <u>infrastructure</u>.

ACADEMIC VOCABULARY
infrastructure
public works, such as buildings and roads, that are needed to support a population

Disease African nations have also been challenged by the management of deadly diseases. Malaria, a disease that is spread by mosquitoes, continues to be one of the most common causes of death in much of Africa today.

In the 1980s a new disease, acquired immune deficiency syndrome (AIDS), spread rapidly through Africa. The HIV virus that causes AIDS weakens the body's immune system and results in death. The social costs of HIV/AIDS in sub-Saharan Africa are staggering. Millions of children are orphans because their parents died from AIDS. A small percentage of infected Africans are receiving AIDS treatment, but prevention programs continue to be somewhat effective in several countries.

Desertification The scarcity of fertile farmland and pastures for livestock is a challenge for many Africans today. Farmers must plant crops in poor soil, and herders have to graze their animals in extremely dry regions. As a result, the soil in these areas dries out, and the natural grasses cannot grow. The Sahara and the Sahel in North Africa are expanding today due to **desertification**, the spread of desertlike conditions. Desertification threatens the future of Africa by contributing to the cycles of drought and famine that plague many African countries today.

READING CHECK Identify Cause and Effect
What causes desertification in Africa?

Skills Focus: Identify Problem and Solution
Above Level

Reading Skill
Fighting AIDS in Africa

1. Have students review the information in the text about HIV/AIDS in sub-Saharan Africa.

2. Have students conduct independent research using reliable online resources to learn about organizations working to reduce the spread of AIDS in Africa, and to treat those who already have the disease.

3. Have students choose one organization about which to write a report. Have students write a few paragraphs describing the organization's goals, and evaluating how successful the organization has been to date. Students might wish to include graphs or charts in their reports. Each report should include a bibliography of sources. **LS Verbal-Linguistic**

Alternative Assessment Handbook, Rubrics 30: Research; and 37: Writing Assignments

Revival of African Culture

In spite of the challenges African countries have faced since independence, Africans have experienced a cultural revival. Many Africans lost faith in their own culture during the colonial era, but a new generation of African writers, artists, and musicians has emerged to establish a powerful African identity.

Language and Literature During colonial rule Africans preserved their culture and used it as a means of expressing dissatisfaction with colonial rule. For example, many Africans in East Africa continued to study Swahili, an African language. After independence in the early 1960s, Swahili became the national language in both Kenya and Tanzania. Swahili writers maintained a strong tradition of poetry, plays, and novels.

A new type of African literature developed in the French-speaking colonies of West Africa. A group of African and Caribbean students living in Paris in the 1930s founded the **negritude movement**. Their writings rejected European culture and focused on African culture and identity.

In the years after independence, African writers shifted their focus from a criticism of European colonialism to a criticism of African leaders. However, many of these writers faced censorship and harassment by the African governments they ridiculed. Writers such as Wole Soyinka spent time in prison for opposing the Nigerian government through his writings. Other African writers fled Africa to escape possible imprisonment.

Art, Music, and Dance Just as literature became a new means of expressing African identity, so did the traditional arts such as sculpture, music, and dance. African artists began to produce traditional pieces, such as ceremonial masks, African musical instruments, and sculptures carved from wood or cast in bronze. These African artists incorporated new ideas and materials into their work, giving the revival of African art a new vitality and creativity. As a result, African art is highly valued on the world market today.

Music and dance are also an important art form in many African societies. African musicians have traditionally played music to honor their history and mark special occasions. Traditional dances are also performed in many African cultures to celebrate specific events or special ceremonies.

In the 1960s African musicians began to blend traditional African styles with Western musical styles. To create this new music, African musicians used common Western instruments in addition to traditional African instruments. Later, in the 1980s, African popular music, or Afro-Pop, became popular in Europe and throughout the world. As a result, many African musicians are internationally known today.

READING CHECK **Find the Main Idea** What subject did many African writers focus on after independence?

SECTION 2 ASSESSMENT

go.hrw.com
Online Quiz
Keyword: SHL AFR HP

Reviewing Ideas, Terms, and People
1. **a. Define** What are **one-party systems**?
   b. Draw Conclusions Why were civil wars common in post-colonial Africa?
   c. Elaborate How important was the end of apartheid?
2. **a. Recall** What caused African economies to struggle and depend on outside aid?
   b. Explain Why has economic development been so difficult in Africa?
   c. Develop What do you think African leaders should do to improve economic conditions in their countries?
3. **a. Define** What was the **negritude movement**?
   b. Analyze In what ways have Africans preserved their traditional culture?

Critical Thinking
4. **Summarize** Copy the graphic organizer below and use it to list the key people or events that are related to Africa's challenges.

	Key People or Event
Apartheid	
Dictatorship and War	
Struggling economies	
Disease	
Desertification	

FOCUS ON WRITING

5. **Narration** Write a brief radio report that might have been broadcast after Nelson Mandela was elected president of South Africa in 1994. In your report, relate the sequence of events that ended apartheid in South Africa.

Direct Teach

Reading Focus

③ How did Africans revive their culture after independence? *through literature, art, music, and dance*

Revival of African Culture

Identify Who is Wole Soyinka? *a writer who spent time in prison for criticizing the Nigerian government*

Explain How was the Swahili language significant in post-colonial Africa? *possible answer—represented African culture, became national language in some places, used in African literature*

CRF: Literature: *Things Fall Apart*

Review & Assess

Close
Guide students in a discussion about post-colonial Africa and why some countries continue to struggle.

Review
Online Quiz, Section 2

Assess
SE Section 2 Assessment
Progress Assessment: Section 2 Quiz
Alternative Assessment Handbook

Reteach/Intervene
Interactive Reader and Study Guide, Section 2
Interactive Skills Tutor CD-ROM

Section 2 Assessment Answers

1. **a.** single political party controls the government
   b. Colonies had been divided without regard to cultures or ethnic groups.
   c. very important; ended white domination, led to democracy and increased liberties
2. **a.** Few exports supported their economies.
   b. bad planning, corrupt leaders resulted in debt, lack of infrastructure
   c. possible answers—work to prevent desertification, end spread of disease, and place good leaders in power

3. **a.** a literary movement rejecting European culture and focusing on African identity
   b. through language and the arts
4. Apartheid—ANC, Mandela, de Klerk, Sharpeville Massacre, Soweto Uprising, Mandela's election; Dictatorship and War—Mobutu Sese Seko, civil war, genocide; Struggling economies: many depend on loans; Disease: malaria, AIDS; Desertification: creates drought, famine
5. Reports should discuss apartheid and the actions of President F.W. de Klerk.

Answers

Reading Check *criticism of African leaders*

947

World Literature

Wole Soyinka (1934–)

"After the Deluge"

Word Help

denomination value (as of money)

bullion uncoined gold or silver in bars

Meet the Writer

Wole Soyinka (1934–) Wole Soyinka was born in 1934 in western Nigeria. In 1960 he formed a theater group called "The 1960 Masks" and then in 1964, he formed the "Orison Theatre Company" that served as a way for him to produce and act in his own plays. During the civil war in Nigeria, he asked for a cease fire in a 1967 article. In response, he was arrested and accused of conspiring with the Biafra rebels. He was detained for 22 months. In 1986 Soyinka became the first African to win the Nobel Prize for Literature.

About the Reading In 1967 the Nigerian government arrested Wole Soyinka for his outspoken criticism of the military dictator who had forcibly seized power of the government. The subject of this poem is a nameless dictator who, like many corrupt African leaders, took money from his nation's fortune while people in his country were suffering from poverty.

AS YOU READ Think about how the dictator's lifestyle led to his demise.

"After the Deluge"
by Wole Soyinka

Once, for a dare,
He filled his heart-shaped swimming pool
With bank notes, high denomination
And fed a pound of caviar to his dog.
The dog was sick; a chartered plane
Flew in replacement for the Persian rug.

He made a billion yen
Leap from Tokyo to Buenos Aires,
Turn somersaults through Brussels,
New York, Sofia and Johannesburg.
It cracked the bullion market open wide.
Governments fell, coalitions cracked
Insurrection raised its bloody flag
From north to south.

He knew his native land through iron gates,
His sight was radar bowls, his hearing
Electronic beams. For flesh and blood,
Kept company with a brace of Dobermans.
But—yes—the worthy causes never lacked
His widow's mite, discreetly publicized.

He escaped the lynch days. He survives.
I dreamt I saw him on a village
Water line, a parched land where
Water is a god
That doles its favors by the drop,
And waiting is a way of life.
Rebellion gleamed yet faintly in his eye

Traversing chrome-and-platinum retreats. There,
Hubs of commerce smoothly turn without
His bidding, and cities where he lately roosted
Have forgotten him, the preying bird
Of passage.

They let him live, but not from pity
Or human sufferance. He scratches life
From earth, no worse a mortal man than the rest.
Far, far away in dreamland splendor,
Creepers twine his gates of bronze relief.
The jade-lined pool is home
To snakes and lizards; they hunt and mate
On crusted algae.

In 1997 the Central African Republic crowned an emperor.

Skills FOCUS **READING LIKE A HISTORIAN**

1. **Explain** How did the dictator live?
2. **Interpret Literature as a Source** What bias does Soyinka show in this poem? How do you think Soyinka's experiences shaped his point of view?

See **Skills Handbook**, p. H28

Differentiating Instruction

English-Language Learners; Special Education Students

Below Level

Read the excerpt from the poem "After the Deluge" to students. Have students visualize what Soyinka is referring to in the poem as you read it. Have students draw their visualizations.

LS Visual-Spatial

Alternative Assessment Handbook, Rubric 3: Artwork

Advanced Learners/Gifted and Talented

Above Level

Have students read the excerpt of the poem "After the Deluge." Then, have students write their own poems using similar language, tone, and ideas. **LS** Auditory-Musical

Alternative Assessment Handbook, Rubric 26: Poems and Songs

Answers

Reading Like a Historian 1. *He lived in extreme luxury, protecting himself from rebellion behind iron gates.* **2.** *writes from the people's point of view; biased against the dictator*

Nationalism in North Africa and the Middle East

BEFORE YOU READ

MAIN IDEA

The rise of nationalism in North Africa and the Middle East led to independence for some countries and to conflicts with the West.

READING FOCUS

1. How did independence come to French North Africa?
2. What events led to the creation of Israel?
3. How did nationalism cause changes in Egypt and Iran?

KEY TERMS AND PEOPLE

David Ben-Gurion
Gamal Abdel Nasser
Suez Crisis
Baghdad Pact
Pan-Arabism
Mohammad Reza Pahlavi

NEW YORK

PI **2.3** Students analyze evidence critically and demonstrate an understanding of how circumstances of time and place influence perspective.

▲ French troops patrol the streets of Algiers.

BATTLE of ALGIERS

THE INSIDE STORY

How did Algerians win their independence? Bombs explode in crowded cafes, restaurants, and markets in the French section of Algiers. In response, government troops close off the Casbah, the old section of the city. They search houses and arrest thousands of people. Many of those arrested are tortured.

This was the scene in Algiers in 1956 when an Algerian nationalist group, the National Liberation Front (FLN), decided to take its war for independence against Algeria's French rulers to the cities. The FLN launched a campaign of bombings and assassinations aimed at both police and civilians. The French responded with a harsh crackdown on Arab residents.

Through tough interrogations of the people they had arrested, the French were able to track down most of the leadership of the FLN. The leaders were killed or thrown into prison, effectively shutting down the FLN's terror campaign.

Even though the French won the Battle of Algiers, they lost Algeria. The harsh tactics the French used increased popular support for the FLN, and six years later Algeria won its independence.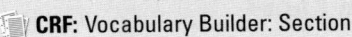

AFRICA AND THE MIDDLE EAST **949**

Teach the Main Idea

At Level

Nationalism in North Africa and the Middle East

1. **Teach** Ask students the Reading Focus questions to teach this section.

2. **Apply** Have each student draw a map of North Africa and the Middle East. Then organize students into groups of three, and assign each student one of the topics discussed in the section. Have students use their maps to locate the countries discussed in their assigned section and record one pertinent fact about the country on the map.

3. **Review** Create or show a large class map for all to see. Have volunteers identify the countries and facts about each. Have students add to or correct their own work as needed.

4. **Practice/Homework** Have students select one country in the section and write a summary of its independence movement.

   LS **Visual-Spatial, Verbal-Linguistic**

   Alternative Assessment Handbook, Rubrics 20: Map Creation; and 37: Writing Assignments

---

Direct Teach

Reading Focus

1 How did independence come to French North Africa? *North Africans resisted colonialism by force.*

French North Africa

Recall Why did France give up its protectorates in Morocco and Tunisia? *decided it could not fight guerrilla wars in Morocco, Tunisia, and Algeria at the same time*

Make Inferences Why did France launch such a violent counterattack in Algeria? *possible answer—believed that if they reacted with force the FLN would stop its attacks*

Draw Conclusions Why did France decide that Algeria was more important to fight for than Morocco and Tunisia? *possible answer—Algeria had more resources, wealth, and a large European population.*

📝 **CRF:** Biography: Danièle Djamila Amrane-Minne

Info to Know

Pied Noir The French words *pied noir* mean "black foot" and refer to the French settlers in Algeria prior to 1962. In 1962 roughly 900,000 pied noirs fled Algeria. They took the motto, "suitcase or coffin" on justifying their mass exodus.

Answers

Reading Check *The French government negotiated with nationalist leaders in Morocco and Tunisia and allowed them independence, but fought the FLN to keep control of Algeria.*

950

TAKING NOTES Take notes on key events and dates in the history of North Africa and the Middle East.

French North Africa	
Israel	
Egypt	
Iran	

🖥️ **NEW YORK**
CC Unit 7-F2
Creation of Israel

French North Africa

After World War II, France faced growing nationalist movements in its North African protectorates of Morocco, Tunisia, and Algeria. In all three places, resistance to colonialism had a strong influence on national identity.

Morocco and Tunisia In both Morocco and Tunisia, nationalist campaigns for independence began to grow in the early and mid-1900s. Attempts by France to crack down on these growing movements eventually led to increasing unrest, demonstrations, and guerrilla wars.

Meanwhile, Algeria was also struggling for independence. Algeria was far more important to the French because it was home to a large French settler population. Eventually, the French government concluded that it could not fight guerrilla wars in Algeria, Morocco, and Tunisia at the same time. As a result, France decided to negotiate with nationalist leaders in Morocco and Tunisia. Both countries were granted independence in 1956.

Algeria France had been involved in Algeria since 1830, when it first took control of some areas there. Later, France began to encourage large-scale European settlement in Algeria. By the 1950s there were more than 1 million European settlers in the area. These settlers owned the best land, dominated the economy, and had a grip on political power.

In 1954 a group of Algerian nationalist leaders formed the National Liberation Front (FLN). When the FLN began a campaign of armed attacks against French targets in November 1954, the French responded with mass arrests and raids on Muslim towns.

The next year the FLN decided to directly target French settlers. In one city, attacks killed more than 100 people. French forces and groups of settlers responded by attacking Muslims. Between 1,200 and 12,000 Muslims were killed in these reprisal attacks. These attacks set the pattern for the deadly war in Algeria—the FLN targeted French civilians, and the French responded by attacking the Muslim population.

In Algiers, the Algerian capital, the FLN launched a campaign of bombings and assassinations directed at both civilians and the

950 CHAPTER 31

military. The French responded with a harsh counterterrorism campaign that included torture of suspected FLN members. By the summer of 1957, the FLN had been largely defeated in Algiers. But the war was far from over.

French settlers in Algeria became increasingly angry over a perceived lack of support from the French government. In May 1958 French troops and a mob of settlers seized power in Algiers, demanding a change in government in Paris. Their demands were met when Charles de Gaulle was appointed prime minister in June 1958. De Gaulle was seen as a strong supporter of the settler population of Algeria.

De Gaulle hoped to satisfy both the French settlers and the Algerian nationalists by giving Algeria a limited degree of self-government. But he faced a violent reaction from the French settlers, who did not want France to give up any degree of control over Algeria, and the nationalists, who wanted full independence for Algeria.

De Gaulle finally decided that French rule in Algeria could not be maintained. He opened peace talks with the FLN in February 1961 and signed an agreement granting Algeria independence in 1962.

READING CHECK **Contrast** How was the struggle for independence in Algeria different from the struggle in Morocco and Tunisia?

The Creation of Israel

Nationalism also led to the creation of Israel. Since the late 1800s the Jewish nationalist movement known as Zionism had been growing, and Jews had been calling for an independent state in their ancient homeland. After World War II, Jewish dreams of an independent Jewish state were finally realized.

End of the British Mandate After World War I, the League of Nations gave Britain control over the mandate of Palestine and required Britain to make preparations for a Jewish homeland there. Following World War II, Jewish leaders in Palestine pressed the British to create a Jewish state. With the horrors of the Holocaust revealed to the world, the international community was sympathetic to the Zionist cause.

Skills Focus: Comparing and Contrasting
At Level

Reading Skill
Middle East Conflicts

1. Organize students into small, mixed-ability groups. Have each group copy and complete the chart as shown.

2. When groups have finished, create a large class chart for all to see, and post it in the classroom. Have students copy the chart and retain it as a study tool. 👁️ **Visual-Spatial**

📝 **Alternative Assessment Handbook**, Rubrics 6: Cause and Effect, and 7: Charts

Conflicts in the Middle East		
Location	**Causes**	**Effects**

Judaism

The country of Israel sits in the heart of the Middle East. Israel is also the heart of Judaism, serving as a homeland and spiritual center for followers of one of the world's most ancient religions.

Origins of Judaism Before 1200 BC, nomadic Hebrew tribes settled in Canaan, a region on the eastern Mediterranean Sea. Over time, their beliefs developed into Judaism, the earliest monotheistic religion still in existence.

Jews believe that their religion was revealed by God to Moses, an early prophet who according to Jewish belief led the Israelites out of slavery from Egypt. These events are outlined in the Torah, the most sacred text of Judaism. The Torah is the first part of the Hebrew Bible, or Tanach.

By about 930 BC, kings had united the different tribes of the Israelites, and the Temple in Jerusalem became the Israelites' major religious center. By the 500s BC, invaders from outside conquered the region. As a result, many Jews were forced out. They later returned and established the Kingdom of Judea.

Judaism Today Today about 15 million Jews live around the world. The majority live in Israel and the United States, but many other countries have Jewish minorities.

Jews are a very diverse group. They have different beliefs and follow many different customs. They are united by common beliefs, a shared history, and a shared language—Hebrew. It is the language of the Hebrew Bible, of prayer, and is the everyday language of the State of Israel.

Infer How do you think common beliefs and history unite the Jewish people?

WORLD JEWISH POPULATION BY COUNTRY, 2005

- Russia 5%
- France 4%
- Argentina 3%
- Canada 3%
- United Kingdom 2%
- Other 9%
- Israel 34%
- United States 40%

Source: Jewish Virtual Library

Jews pray at the Western Wall in Jerusalem.

In 1947 Britain announced that it was giving up control of the mandate and turning the matter over to the United Nations. The UN proposed to partition, or divide, Palestine into a Jewish state and an Arab state with Jerusalem under international control. Jewish leaders accepted the proposal, but Arab leaders rejected it. Despite Arab objections, the UN General Assembly passed a resolution supporting the partition as <u>valid</u>.

Independence and War As the British left Palestine, **David Ben-Gurion** and other Jewish leaders declared the birth of the democratic State of Israel on May 14, 1948. Ben-Gurion later became Israel's first prime minister.

The day after Israel declared its independence, armies from the Arab countries of Egypt, Syria, Lebanon, Transjordan, and Iraq invaded Israel, launching the first Arab-Israeli war. The war lasted from May to December 1948. In the end, the Arab armies were soundly defeated.

Arab states negotiated cease-fire agreements with Israel, but they would not sign permanent peace treaties.

One result of this first Arab-Israeli war was that the Arab state proposed by the UN did not come into existence. Instead, during the fighting both Israel and neighboring Arab countries seized and held the land that had been planned for the new state. At the end of the war, Egypt controlled the Gaza Strip, and Transjordan controlled the territory west of the Jordan River known as the West Bank.

The war also caused massive refugee problems. By the end of the fighting, around 700,000 Palestinian Arabs had become refugees. They fled or were expelled from areas that Israel took control of as well as from the general war and chaos. Meanwhile, many Jewish refugees fled or were expelled from Arab countries and resettled in Israel.

ACADEMIC VOCABULARY

valid correct or justified

READING CHECK **Summarize** What events led to the creation of Israel as an independent state?

Reading Focus

❷ **What events led to the creation of Israel?** *1947: Britain announced it was giving up control of the mandate; UN proposed to partition Palestine into a Jewish state and an Arab state; 1948: Jewish leaders declared birth of the State of Israel*

The Creation of Israel

Describe What was the UN's plan for Palestine? *to divide Palestine into Jewish and Arab states*

Make Inferences What role did World War II play in the establishment of Israel? *The Holocaust created great sympathy for Jews who survived and created support for a separate Jewish state.*

Identify Cause and Effect What were some effects of the first Arab-Israeli war? *proposed Arab state did not come into existence; 700,000 Palestinian Arabs became refugees*

World Religions

Judaism

Analyzing Graphs Which country has the largest population of Jewish people? *the United States*

Answers

World Religions *possible answer—by providing them with a shared history*

Reading Check *1947: Britain announced it was giving up control of the mandate; UN proposed to partition Palestine into a Jewish state and and Arab state; 1948: Jewish leaders declared birth of the State of Israel*

Skills Focus: Analyzing Alternative Points of View | Above Level

Reading Like a Historian Skill
Palestine and Israel

1. Review the information about the creation of Israel with students, and remind students that both Palestine and Israel have legitimate claims to land in the Middle East. Have students conduct outside research to find several articles about the creation of Israel from both the Arab and Israeli points of view. Tell students to look for scholarly, historical articles that are sensitive to the needs and claims of both.

2. Have students answer the questions who, what, why, when and how about each of their articles. Then have students analyze the articles for language that shows bias.

3. Have students present their research findings to the class. **LS Verbal-Linguistic**

📝 **Alternative Assessment Handbook**, Rubrics 24: Oral Presentations; and 30: Research

3 How did nationalism cause changes in Egypt and Iran? *The two countries began to reclaim land, and nationalize industries and resources.*

Changes in Egypt and Iran

Explain Why were Egyptians dissatisfied with King Farouk? *corruption, loss in First Arab-Israeli War, growing gap between rich and poor*

Sequence What led to the Suez Canal crisis? *Egypt signed arms deal with Czechoslovakia; U.S. refused to lend Egypt money to build Aswan Dam; Nasser nationalized Suez Canal; Britain, France, Israel attacked Egypt*

Quick Facts Transparency: Causes and Effects of the Suez Canal Crisis

Changes in Egypt and Iran

Israel's victory in the first Arab-Israeli war had effects throughout the Arab world. The victory discredited many of the region's leaders. As the pro-Western leaders lost popular support, a group of young nationalist leaders came to power in places such as Egypt and Iran. These new nationalist leaders soon came into conflict with the West.

A New Government in Egypt Egypt had gained its formal independence from Great Britain in 1922. But in many ways Egypt was not a fully independent country. British troops occupied the Suez Canal Zone, and a 1936 treaty allowed Britain to defend Egypt if it was attacked. The Egyptian monarch, King Farouk I, was strongly pro-British and seen as dependent on the British for his power.

Egypt's loss in the first Arab-Israeli war discredited King Farouk I and the leaders of Egypt's parliament. Many Egyptians believed that corruption in the palace, the parliament, and the army contributed to the defeat. The growing gap between rich and poor under the post-independence government also angered many Egyptians.

Out of this dissatisfaction came a 1952 military coup led by a 34-year-old colonel named **Gamal Abdel Nasser**. A group of young nationalist army officers staged the coup. Nasser and his co-conspirators moved quickly to consolidate power. They forced King Farouk out of power, abolished the monarchy, banned existing political parties, and created a single government party. Nasser also undertook an ambitious program of land reform to gain support among the poor.

The Suez Crisis Nasser became the most important figure in the Arab world after his confrontation with Britain, France, and Israel over the Suez Canal. This confrontation, known as the **Suez Crisis**, had its roots in the politics of the Cold War.

After Nasser came to power, he refused to join the **Baghdad Pact**, the U.S.-led alliance against communism in the Middle East. Then, when Nasser requested that western countries sell him arms, they refused. As a result, Nasser turned to Czechoslovakia, which was controlled by the Soviet Union, and signed an arms deal. The United States and Britain responded by refusing to loan Egypt money to build a dam on the Nile River at Aswan.

Nationalism in Egypt

Gamal Abdel Nasser led Egypt from the mid-1950s until 1970. A popular leader, he promoted nationalism in Egypt and the Arab world.

CAUSES AND EFFECTS OF THE SUEZ CANAL CRISIS
QUICK FACTS

Causes

- Egypt signs an arms deal with Czechoslovakia.
- The United States and Great Britain decide not to help Egypt fund the Aswan High Dam.
- Egypt blocks Israeli shipping and supports raids against Israel.
- Egypt takes over control of the Suez Canal.
- Great Britain, France, and Israel secretly agree to attack Egypt and take the canal back.

Effects

- Egypt is defeated militarily, but Nasser emerges as a hero for standing up to the West.
- A desire for Arab unity, or Pan-Arabism, increases.
- Hostility between Egypt and Israel increases.

Differentiating Instruction

Below Level

Learners Having Difficulty

Materials: blank outline maps of the Middle East, colored pencils or markers

1. Review the information in the text about the Suez Canal crisis. Have students locate the Suez Canal in the atlas of their textbooks. Tell students that the Suez was an important waterway because it shortened the sea voyage to Asia.

2. Distribute outline maps to students. Have students label Egypt, the Mediterranean Sea, the Red Sea, and the Suez Canal.

3. Have students draw a sea route from the Mediterranean to the Red Sea, using one color. Then, in another color, have students draw the sea route that European ships would have to take if Egypt closed the Suez Canal.

LS Visual-Spatial

Alternative Assessment Handbook, Rubric 20: Map Creation

Nasser was enraged that the United States and Britain denied him the funding necessary to build the dam. In response, he decided to nationalize, or take control of, the Suez Canal, which was owned by an international company controlled by Britain and France.

For many people in the Arab world, Nasser's action was celebrated as an act of defiance against European imperialism. But the British and French were outraged by this seizure of property. Hostility between Egypt and Israel was also growing.

In October 1956 Britain, France, and Israel launched a coordinated attack on Egypt. Israel invaded the Sinai Peninsula, and British and French troops occupied the Suez Canal Zone. Militarily, they defeated the Egyptian forces.

The United States did not support these actions, which created tensions with the Soviet Union. The U.S. government pressured Britain, France, and Israel to withdraw, which they did. When these countries withdrew and Egypt was left in control of the Suez Canal, the Suez Crisis became a great victory for Nasser. He became a hero in the Arab world.

Nasser promoted **Pan-Arabism**, or Arab unity, hoping to unite the Arab world. He brought Egypt and Syria together in 1958 as the United Arab Republic, but Syria withdrew two years later. Despite this failure, Nasser remained very popular in the Arab world.

Conflict in Iran When **Mohammad Reza Pahlavi** became shah of Iran in 1941, British and Russian troops occupied parts of the country. A British-run company also controlled Iran's highly profitable oil industry and kept most of the profits.

Iranian nationalists were determined to take control of the country's oil resources, reduce the power of the shah, and establish a constitutional monarchy. These nationalists were led by Mohammad Mosaddeq, an opponent of foreign influence in Iran.

In 1951 the Iranian parliament named Mosaddeq prime minister and voted to nationalize the Iranian oil industry. In response, Britain and the United States called for a boycott of Iranian oil, preventing Iran from selling much of its oil on the world market.

Meanwhile, Mosaddeq worked to reduce the power of the monarchy. He placed army forces under the control of the government, not

the shah. He reduced the size of the army and forced officers loyal to the shah to leave.

Many military officers were upset with these reforms, and some joined a coup to replace Mosaddeq that was supported by the United States and Britain. When the coup was successful, Mosaddeq was overthrown and the shah returned to power.

After returning to power, the shah began an ambitious program of reforms, including land reform and a campaign to increase literacy. Iran's industry, education, and health care improved. Education and employment opportunities for women also improved.

The shah continued to rule with an iron hand, however. He used his secret police to spy on, intimidate, and torture the opposition. The shah's reforms were also opposed by conservatives who viewed them as moving Iran away from traditional Islamic values.

READING CHECK **Find the Main Idea** What changes occurred in Egypt and Iran, and how were they related to nationalism?

SECTION 3 ASSESSMENT

go.hrw.com
Online Quiz
Keyword: SHL AFR HP

Reviewing Ideas, Terms, and People

1. **a. Recall** How did the large population of French settlers in Algeria affect Algeria's history?
   b. Compare and Contrast What tactics were used by the FLN and by the French in the struggle in Algeria?
2. **a. Describe** What was the UN plan for the partition of Palestine?
   b. Sequence What happened after **David Ben-Gurion** and other Jewish leaders announced the creation of the State of Israel in 1948?
   c. Predict How might the events of 1947 and 1948 have set the stage for more conflicts between Israel and Arab states in the Middle East?
3. **a. Describe** Who was **Gamal Abdel Nasser**, and how did he promote Pan-Arabism?
   b. Summarize What events led to the **Suez Crisis**?
   c. Develop How did the policies of **Mohammad Reza Pahlavi** both help and hurt Iran?

Critical Thinking

4. **Sequence** Use your notes from this section and a graphic organizer like this one to create a time line of the key events in North Africa and the Middle East.

1945 ————————————— 1965

FOCUS ON WRITING

5. **Exposition** Write a brief newspaper article that describes the crisis over the Suez Canal.

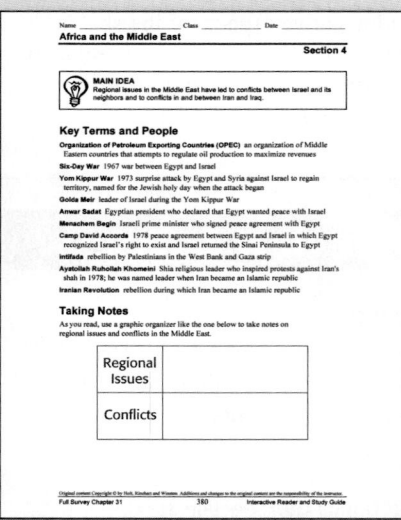
BEFORE YOU READ

MAIN IDEA

Regional issues in the Middle East have led to conflicts between Israel and its neighbors and to conflicts in and between Iran and Iraq.

READING FOCUS

1. How have regional issues contributed to conflicts in the Middle East?
2. What were some key events in the Arab-Israeli conflict?
3. What caused a revolution in Iran?
4. How have conflicts in Iraq affected that country?

KEY TERMS AND PEOPLE

Organization of Petroleum Exporting Countries (OPEC)
Six-Day War
Yom Kippur War
Golda Meir
Anwar Sadat
Menachem Begin
Camp David Accords
intifada
Ayatollah Ruhollah Khomeini
Iranian Revolution

 NEW YORK

PI 2.5 Students investigate key events and developments and major turning points in world history to identify the factors that brought about change and the long-term effects of these changes.

A DIFFICULT PEACE

THE INSIDE STORY
How did a meeting in Maryland lead to peace between Egypt and Israel? In the summer of 1978 Egypt and Israel were holding peace talks after decades of conflict. U.S. president Jimmy Carter decided to bring together Egyptian and Israeli leaders for face-to-face negotiations. Carter invited Egyptian president Anwar Sadat and Israeli prime minister Menachem Begin to a meeting at Camp David, the U.S. presidential retreat in northern Maryland.

At first, the meetings went poorly. Israeli and Egyptian delegates sat in different sections of the dining room. On the third day of talks, discussions between Begin and Sadat broke down into heated arguments. One of Begin's advisers suggested that Begin and Sadat be kept apart for the remainder of the negotiations.

President Carter and his staff kept working for an agreement. The U.S. team went back and forth between the Egyptians and the Israelis, gathering comments and suggested changes to a proposed peace agreement. U.S negotiators wrote 23 drafts of an agreement before coming up with a version that both sides would accept. After 13 days of intense negotiations, Begin and Sadat finally signed the agreement—the first peace treaty between Israel and one of its Arab neighbors. ■

Regional Issues

Over the last few decades, major conflicts have erupted in the Middle East. Although the circumstances surrounding each of these conflicts were unique, some general regional issues have contributed to the conflicts. These regional issues include the presence of huge oil reserves, the growth of Islamism, and the conflict between Israel and its neighbors.

Oil in the Middle East About two-thirds of the world's known oil reserves are located in the Middle East. These vast oil reserves have been a great source of wealth for Saudi Arabia, Iran, Iraq, Kuwait, and other countries. Most of the region's oil-rich countries

▲ **Anwar Sadat (left), Jimmy Carter (middle), and Menachem Begin (right) in 1978**

954 CHAPTER 31

are members of the **Organization of Petroleum Exporting Countries (OPEC)**, which attempts to regulate the production of oil exports to maximize revenues.

Oil revenues have allowed governments in the Middle East to modernize their countries and promote industrialization, economic development, and social programs. However, oil has also been a source of conflict. Some governments have used oil revenues to build up their military, maintain power, and even threaten their neighbors. Oil wealth has also caused internal clashes within countries and societies. In addition, the region's strategic importance as a source of oil has led outside nations to become involved in Middle Eastern affairs and politics.

Growth of Islamism Another regional issue that has led to conflict is the growth of Islamism, or Islamic fundamentalism, a movement to reorder government and society according to Islamic laws. Islamists believe that Muslim countries have strayed from the path of true Islam by following Western models of political and economic development. Over the last decades, countries such as Egypt, Iran, and Iraq have seen a growth in Islamism, which has led to conflicts within society and government. Furthermore, some Islamic extremists have used violence to try to bring about the changes they want. These radical extremists have attacked regional governments, their allies, and innocent civilians.

Conflicts with Israel A third regional issue that has been a source of conflict in the Middle East involves Israel. Since Israel was established in 1948, most Middle Eastern countries have refused to recognize its right to exist. Some countries have repeatedly attacked Israel and funded militant groups that conduct raids and terrorist attacks against Israelis. A series of wars between Israel and its neighbors has led to the expansion of Israel, which controls more land now than it did in 1948. As a result, many Palestinian Arabs live under Israeli control, another source of tension and conflict in the region.

READING CHECK Summarize What regional issues have led to conflicts in the Middle East?

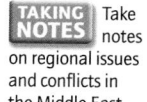 **TAKING NOTES** Take notes on regional issues and conflicts in the Middle East.

Regional Issues
Conflicts

 NEW YORK
CC Unit 7-F9
Islamic fundamentalism

Reading Focus

1 How have regional issues contributed to conflicts in the Middle East? *Oil revenues have been used to build up military power, growth of Islamism has led to conflict, and most Middle Eastern countries do not recognize Israel's right to exist.*

Regional Issues

Recall How have Middle Eastern nations used their profits from oil? *industrialization, health care, education, military*

Make Generalizations How has political Islam hindered the relationship between the Middle East and the Western world? *Radical extremists have used violence to try to bring about the changes they want.*

Interpreting Maps
Creation of Israel, 1947–2006
Activity Summarizing Events
Have students examine each of the maps and summarize what happened in Israel between the two time periods.
LS Visual-Spatial

Map Transparency: Creation of Israel, 1947–2006

CREATION OF ISRAEL, 1947–2006

1947

Mediterranean Sea
LEBANON
SYRIA
Haifa
Sea of Galilee
Nablus
Tel Aviv
Jerusalem (International city)
Ramallah
Gaza
Hebron
Dead Sea
TRANS-JORDAN
EGYPT

UN-proposed Jewish state
UN-proposed Arab state

0   50   100 Miles
0   50   100 Kilometers
Cassini-Soldner transverse cylindrical projection

ISRAEL AFTER THE SIX-DAY WAR, 1967

LEBANON
GOLAN HEIGHTS
SYRIA
Mediterranean Sea
Jerusalem
WEST BANK
GAZA STRIP
ISRAEL
JORDAN
Sinai Peninsula
EGYPT
SAUDI ARABIA

ISRAEL TODAY, 2006

LEBANON
SYRIA
GOLAN HEIGHTS
Mediterranean Sea
GAZA STRIP
Jerusalem
WEST BANK
ISRAEL
JORDAN
EGYPT

Israeli-occupied
Some areas controlled by the Palestinian Authority

GEOGRAPHY SKILLS INTERPRETING MAPS
1. Location What countries border Israel?
2. Place How has the territory under Israel's control changed since 1967?

AFRICA AND THE MIDDLE EAST **955**

Skills Focus: Sequencing

Below Level

Reading Skill
Creation of Israel

1. Organize students into mixed-ability pairs or small groups. Have students review the maps on this page showing Israel in 1947, 1967, and 2006. Then have students create a time line of events discussed in the section. Students should include the consequences or results of each event.

2. Have volunteers share their time lines and create a class time line for all to see. Have students add to or correct their work as needed.

3. As an extension, have students create a visual to illustrate each event on their time lines. Visuals could include charts, graphs, or small maps. **LS** Visual-Spatial, Interpersonal

Alternative Assessment Handbook, Rubric 36: Time Lines

Answers

Interpreting Maps 1. *Egypt, Jordan, Syria, Lebanon;* **2.** *in 2006, Sinai Peninsula under Egypt's control, some areas of Jerusalem controlled by Palestinian Authority, Golan Heights no longer just occupied by Israel*

Reading Check *use of oil revenues; growth of Islamism; conflicts with Israel*

955

2 What were some key events in the Arab-Israeli conflict? *Six-Day War, Yom-Kippur War, Camp David Accords, intifada, Oslo Accords, second intifada, Israel withdraws from Gaza*

The Arab-Israeli Conflict

Sequence How did the Six-Day War lead to the Yom Kippur War? *At the end of the Six-Day War in 1967, Israel controlled territory in the West Bank and Gaza; Egypt and Syria launched the Yom Kippur War in 1973 in an attempt to win the territory back.*

Explain Why did Israel invade Lebanon in 1978 and 1982? *to stop PLO guerrilla attacks against Israel*

Info to Know

Golda Meir Golda Meir moved from Ukraine to Milwaukee, Wisconsin in 1906. Meir joined the Labor Zionist Party in 1915 and in 1939, Meir attended the Zionist Congress in Geneva to ensure the safety of European Jews. She became part of the People's Council that signed the proclamation starting the State of Israel in 1948. From 1969 to 1974 she served as the Prime Minister of Israel.

Primary Source

"The Egyptians could run to Egypt, the Syrians into Syria. The only place we could run was into the sea, and before we did that we might as well fight."
—Golda Meir

Answers

Faces of History *was active in Zionist movement, signed document declaring the establishment of Israel*

The Arab-Israeli Conflict

The Arab-Israeli conflict that began in 1948 has continued through the years. In 1967 and again in 1973, war erupted. Six years after the 1973 war, Egypt and Israel signed a peace agreement, but unrest among Palestinian Arabs in Israel remained a major problem.

War in 1967 and 1973 In 1967 Egypt demanded that the UN remove its troops from Gaza and the Sinai Peninsula. Egyptian troops then moved into the Sinai, and Egypt began to close off the Gulf of Aqaba, Israel's route to the Red Sea. Expecting a large-scale Arab attack, Israel decided to strike first.

Israel launched air strikes against Egypt, Syria, and Jordan, destroying most of their airplanes on the ground. Israeli ground troops then moved in and rapidly defeated Arab forces. In this war, called the **Six-Day War**, Israel took control of the Golan Heights, Sinai Peninsula, Gaza Strip, West Bank, and East Jerusalem. Israel gained control of land in the West Bank and Gaza with a large Palestinian population.

Determined to win their territory back, Egypt and Syria launched the **Yom Kippur War**, a surprise attack against Israel in 1973. The war takes its name from the Jewish holy day

NEW YORK
CC Unit 7-F3b
Middle East peace treaties

FACES OF HISTORY

Golda MEIR
1898–1978

Golda Meir was one of the founders of the State of Israel and one of the first women to lead a national government in the modern era. She spent much of her life working toward the creation of Israel and helping build the foundation of the new country after it achieved independence in 1948.

Golda Meir was born in Ukraine. In 1906 her family immigrated to the United States, where Meir went to school and became active in the Zionist movement. In 1921 she moved to the British Mandate of Palestine and eventually became very influential there. When Israel declared its establishment in 1948, she was one of 24 people to sign the document. She later served in Israel's government as ambassador to the Soviet Union, minister of labor, foreign minister, and finally prime minister. In all of these positions, Golda Meir worked to build a strong government, make sure that the country was secure, and see to it that Israel's citizens had the resources they needed.

Summarize How did Golda Meir help establish the State of Israel?

when the attack began. At first, Arab troops made gains in the war. Israel's government, led by **Golda Meir**, was not fully prepared for the attack and needed military support from the United States. With U.S. support, Israeli forces regrouped and pushed back the Egyptian and Syrian armies. After weeks of fighting, both sides agreed to a cease-fire.

During the war, Arab members of OPEC declared an oil embargo, or a refusal to sell oil, to countries supporting Israel, including the United States. The price of oil around the world rose dramatically as a result.

A Peace Agreement Until the late 1970s no Arab nation had recognized Israel's right to exist. Then, in 1977, Egyptian president **Anwar Sadat** made a momentous declaration: Egypt wanted peace with Israel. To help facilitate this historic peace, U.S. president Jimmy Carter invited Sadat and Israeli prime minister **Menachem Begin** to Camp David, the presidential retreat in Maryland. There, in 1978, Sadat and Begin reached an agreement known as the **Camp David Accords**. Egypt recognized Israel, and Israel returned the Sinai Peninsula to Egypt. The treaty ended 30 years of hostility between Egypt and Israel.

Palestinian Unrest As Egypt and Israel made peace, Palestinian Arabs continued their struggle for nationhood. Under the UN partition plan of 1947, there were supposed to be two states in Palestine—a Jewish state and an Arab state. After the Arab-Israeli war of 1948, however, the land set aside for the Arab state was occupied by Israel, Egypt, and Jordan.

Palestinian nationalism was strong, and in 1964 the Palestine Liberation Organization (PLO) formed with a pledge to destroy Israel and replace it with a Palestinian state. After Yasser Arafat became leader in 1969, the PLO launched a campaign of guerrilla attacks against Israel, first from Jordan and later from Lebanon. In an effort to stop the PLO attacks, Israel invaded Lebanon in 1978 and again in 1982.

Meanwhile, tensions were building in the West Bank and Gaza, where Israel had begun building settlements. In 1987 Palestinian resentment of Israeli occupation boiled over into a rebellion called the **intifada**. During the intifada, Palestinian youths battled Israeli troops

Skills Focus: Analyzing Maps

At Level

Israel and Its Neighbors

Materials: construction paper, colored pencils

1. Have students examine the maps in this section and then create their own maps of Israel and neighboring countries. Have students use the atlas in their text to add capitals, major cities, and physical features.

2. Have students trace the events in the section about Arab-Israel conflicts on their maps. Students should show land lost and gained, areas of disputes, and where wars took place.

3. When students have finished their maps, guide students in a discussion of the role of geography in Middle East conflicts, and remind them of the size of the region.

LS Visual-Spatial

Alternative Assessment Handbook, Rubrics 11: Discussions; and 20: Map Creation

Islam

Islam, one of the world's largest religions, has its roots in the Middle East. For more than 1,300 years, Islam has provided the rhythm for daily life in much of the region.

Origins of Islam The center of Islam is in Mecca, Saudi Arabia. Muslims believe that Muhammad received his first message from God in Mecca in about 610. Soon, Muhammad began to tell others about these messages, which form the basis of Islamic beliefs.

The sacred text of Islam is the Qur'an, which contains the messages Muhammad is said to have received from God. Muslims believe that the words in the Qur'an are the direct word of God. Believers around the world memorize the Qur'an and recite its teachings. As a result, the Qur'an is one of the most widely read texts in the world.

After Muhammad died in 632, his followers spread Islam rapidly across much of the Middle East and North Africa. In the following centuries, Islam continued to spread even more, eventually reaching farther into Africa, Asia, and Europe.

Islam Today About 1.3 billion Muslims live in the world today. The majority live in the Middle East, Africa, and Asia. Millions of Muslims also live in major cities throughout the world. Every year, as many as 3 million Muslims make a religious pilgrimage, or hajj, to Mecca.

Summarize How is Islam rooted in the Middle East?

The Blue Mosque in Istanbul, Turkey

MUSLIM POPULATION BY COUNTRY, 2006

COUNTRY	TOTAL NUMBER OF MUSLIMS (Percentage of total population)
Indonesia	212,937,000 (88%)
Pakistan	157,547,000 (97%)
India	140,434,000 (13%)
Bangladesh	119,785,000 (83%)
Egypt	72,855,000 (94%)
Turkey	69,660,000 (99.8%)
Iran	67,338,000 (99%)
Nigeria	64,383,000 (50%)
Ethiopia	34,700,000 (47.5%)
Algeria	32,207,000 (99%)

Source: The World Almanac and Book of Facts, 2006

---

in widespread street violence. Israel responded with strong military and police resistance, but the fighting continued until the early 1990s.

In 1993 PLO leader Yasser Arafat and Israeli prime minister Yitzhak Rabin negotiated the Oslo Accords to end the violence. The agreement called for the Palestinians to gradually gain control over the governing of the West Bank and Gaza. Israel and the PLO were supposed to sign a permanent agreement by 1998.

Extremists on both sides worked hard to undermine the peace process. The militant group Hamas launched suicide bombings in Israel. An Israeli religious fanatic assassinated Rabin in 1995. Eventually, relations between the Israeli and Palestinian leadership soured.

In 2000 a second intifada began. This time, Palestinian youths were joined by Palestinian security forces with guns. Hamas sent suicide bombers into Israel to attack civilians. The Israelis countered by sending troops backed by tanks, fighter jets, and helicopter gunships into cities in the West Bank and Gaza.

In 2004 Yasser Arafat died and was succeeded by Mahmoud Abbas. That same year, Israeli prime minister Ariel Sharon decided that Israel would withdraw from Gaza and parts of the West Bank. Israeli troops compelled Israeli settlers to leave Gaza and turned it over to the Palestinians in 2005. But tensions grew once more when Hamas, which many countries consider a terrorist organization, won control of the Palestinian parliament in 2006.

Also in 2006, armed conflict erupted after militants kidnapped several Israeli soldiers along the borders with Gaza and Lebanon. Israel launched massive air strikes and ground offensives in Gaza and southern Lebanon to root out extremists and secure its borders.

READING CHECK **Sequence** Describe the sequence of events in the Arab-Israeli conflict.

Reading Focus

The Arab-Israeli Conflict

Identify Name the two leaders who participated in the Oslo Accords. *PLO leader Yasser Arafat and Israeli Prime Minister Yitzhak Rabin*

Sequence What are some developments of the Arab-Israeli conflict in the 2000s? *2000: second intifada began; 2005: Israeli settlers leave Gaza and turn it over to Palestinians; 2006: Hamas won control of Palestinian parliament; 2006: militants kidnapped several Israeli soldiers along the border of Gaza and Lebanon, Israel launched air strikes*

CRF: Biography: Hanan Ashrawi

Primary Source

"Peace for us means the destruction of Israel. We are preparing for an all-out war, a war which will last for generations."

"I come bearing an olive branch in one hand, and the freedom fighter's gun in the other. Do not let the olive branch fall from my hand."

—Yasser Arafat

Activity **Analyzing Primary Sources** Have students contrast these two quotes by Yasser Arafat and suggest reasons Arafat changed his position so dramatically. Remind students that Arafat won the Nobel Peace Prize in 1994.

LS Verbal-Linguistic

Skills Focus: Comparing and Contrasting

At Level

Reading Skill
Islam and Judaism

Research Required

1. Have students review the features on Islam and Judaism in this chapter. Then have students conduct outside research using reliable print and online sources to learn more about the two religions.

2. Have student show the results of their research in a chart in which they compare and contrast the two religions. Students should show similarities as well as the differences between the two.

3. Have volunteers share their charts with the class. **LS** Verbal-Linguistic, Visual-Spatial

Alternative Assessment Handbook, Rubrics 7: Charts; 9: Comparing and Contrasting; and 30: Research

Answers

World Religions *Islam was founded in the Middle East, and the religion has been a major influence on the region for 1,300 years. A majority of Middle Easterners are Muslims.*

Reading Check *1967: Six-Day War; 1973: Yom Kippur War; 1978: Camp David Accords; 1987: intifada; 1993: Oslo Accords; 2000: second intifada; 2005: Israel withdraws from Gaza*

957

③ What caused a revolution in Iran? *protests against the rule of the shah*

Revolution in Iran

Identify Who is Ayatollah Ruhollah Khomeini? *Shia religious leader, coordinated rebellion against shah, became Iran's leader in 1979*

Make Inferences Why were Khomeini's policies so strongly anti-Western? *The shah had been ousted because of his ties to Western governments and oil companies; Islamists opposed such ties to the west.*

④ How have conflicts in Iraq affected that country? *Wars, economic sanctions, and insurgency have created the potential for civil war; ongoing violence has devestated much of the country.*

Conflict in Iraq

Identify Cause and Effect What was the cause of the Iran-Iraq War? *border disputes, Iran called for revolution among Iraq's Shiite population*

Evaluate Do you think Iraq could have been successful in taking control of Kuwait if the UN had not intervened? *possible answer—Yes, Iraq had the largest army in Arab world, Kuwait is much smaller*

📄 **CRF:** History and Geography: Conflicts in the Persian Gulf

---

Conflict in Iraq

1958 Army officers overthrow Iraq's monarchy and kill King Faisal II.

1979 Saddam Hussein, a leader of the Baath Party, becomes president of Iraq.

1968 The nationalist Baath Party takes power in Iraq.

1980 Iraq invades Iran, sparking the deadly Iran-Iraq War (1980–1988).

NEW YORK

 Unit 7-F7 Revolution in Iran

Revolution in Iran

A different kind of conflict erupted in Iran, where a revolution ousted the shah, Mohammad Reza Pahlavi. The shah had close ties to Western governments and oil companies. With their support, Iran westernized, and foreign influence grew. By the 1970s, Iran had changed from a traditional rural society to a more industrialized and urban one. Many Iranians felt threatened by this rapid change, while others felt betrayed by a government they viewed as corrupt. Islamists, in particular, opposed the shah because of his ties to the West.

In 1978 Iranians began to protest against the shah's rule. These protests were inspired by **Ayatollah Ruhollah Khomeini** (koh-MAY-nee), a Shia religious leader. Unable to calm the unrest, the shah fled Iran in 1979. During the **Iranian Revolution** Iran became an Islamic republic with Khomeini as its leader.

Under Khomeini's regime, the government suppressed political opposition and enforced strict social and religious values. Iran's foreign policy became strongly anti-Western, especially after the shah went to the United States for medical treatment.

THE IMPACT TODAY

Since the hostage crisis, the United States Government has not reestablished an embassy in Tehran or any diplomatic relations with the Iranian government.

In 1979 Iranian revolutionaries seized the U.S. embassy in Tehran and took 66 Americans hostage. The Iranians demanded that the shah be returned to Iran to stand trial. Although the shah left the United States shortly thereafter, the Iranians continued to hold the hostages until January 1981.

READING CHECK **Sequence** What was the sequence of events that led to the Iranian Revolution?

Conflict in Iraq

As Iran's new government was dealing with the hostage crisis, it soon found itself at war with its neighbor, Iraq. Later, Iraq fought two wars against U.S.-led coalitions before the government of Saddam Hussein was overthrown.

The Iran-Iraq War In 1980 Iraq attacked Iran because of border disputes and because Iran's new government called for revolution among Iraq's Shiite population. The war was long and costly, with as many as 500,000 dead on both sides. During the war, Iraq used chemical weapons against Iranian troops as well as Kurdish Iraqis who supported Iran. In 1988, after years of stalemate, Iran and Iraq agreed to a cease-fire.

The Persian Gulf War After the cease-fire, Saddam Hussein continued to build up Iraq's military, even though Iraq already had the largest army in the Arab world. In 1990 Iraq accused neighboring Kuwait of drilling into an Iraqi oil field and stealing oil. Hussein used this excuse to invade Kuwait.

In an effort to end the Iraqi occupation of Kuwait, the UN passed economic sanctions against Iraq. Those sanctions failed. As a result, a U.S.-led coalition launched the Persian Gulf War, attacking the Iraqi forces in Kuwait. In weeks, Kuwait was freed.

After the war, the UN continued its economic sanctions, insisted that Iraq destroy its chemical and biological weapons and agree not to develop nuclear weapons. But Iraq failed to fully cooperate with UN weapons inspectors

---

Skills Focus: Identifying Main Ideas and Details   `At Level`

Reading Skill   `Research Required`
Reporting on Iraq

1. Organize students into nine groups. Assign one of the events from the Conflict in Iraq time line to each group.

2. Tell students they are newspaper reporters covering their assigned event. Have students conduct research on the event, using reliable online sources.

3. When students have had enough time to gather research, have them create the front page of a newspaper about the event,

including a headline, at least two articles, and a map or graphic. Articles should convey details about the event using the five Ws and one H of journalism (who, what, where, when, why, and how.)

4. Have each group present its newspaper page to the class **LS** **Verbal-Linguistic, Visual-Spatial**

📄 **Alternative Assessment Handbook**, Rubrics 14: Group Activity; 23: Newspapers; and 30: Research

---

Answers

Reading Check *Protests began against the shah; the shah fled Iran in 1979; Iran became an Islamic republic with Khomeini as its leader.*

1991 A U.S.-led coalition forces Iraq out of Kuwait in the Persian Gulf War.

2005 Millions of Iraqis vote for a transitional national assembly.

1988 Iraq uses poison gas against its Kurdish minority for supporting Iran in the war.

1990 Iraq invades Kuwait.

2003 In the Iraq War, a U.S.-led coalition overthrows Hussein's government and occupies Iraq.

Skills FOCUS | **INTERPRETING TIME LINES**

Identify What major wars did Iraq fight under Saddam Hussein?

who had been sent to verify that Iraq's weapons had been destroyed.

The Iraq War Following the attacks of September 11, 2001, some U.S. leaders believed that Saddam Hussein posed a greater threat to the United States than before. They worried that Hussein might have deadly weapons that he could give to terrorists. A new round of UN weapons inspections did not find any stockpiles of chemical, biological, or nuclear weapons; but again, Iraq did not fully cooperate with the inspections. Some U.S. officials were convinced that Hussein was hiding weapons. As a result, in 2003 another U.S.-led coalition invaded Iraq, quickly forcing Hussein out of power.

The coalition then moved to bring order to the nation, but efforts to restore peace were thwarted. A growing insurgency, or armed rebellion, by different groups from both inside and outside Iraq targeted coalition forces, their Iraqi allies, and innocent civilians. Insurgent attacks grew more and more deadly.

Meanwhile, the coalition worked to create a new, democratic government in Iraq. In 2004 political power was transferred to the Iraqis. In 2005 Iraqis voted in the country's first multiparty election in 50 years and later approved a new constitution that would make Iraq an Islamic federal democracy. But even as Iraq made progress toward a new government, continuing violence and the potential for civil war made the country's future highly uncertain.

READING CHECK **Infer** What are the main problems Iraq has faced in recent years?

SECTION 4 ASSESSMENT

go.hrw.com
Online Quiz
Keyword: SHL AFR HP

Reviewing Ideas, Terms, and People

1. a. Recall How has oil affected conflicts in the Middle East?
b. Summarize What is Islamism?

2. a. Describe Describe the wars of 1967 and 1973.
b. Support a Position What key steps do you think must be taken to begin to resolve the Arab-Israeli conflict?

3. a. Describe What was **Ayatollah Ruhollah Khomeini's** role in the **Iranian Revolution**?
b. Analyze How do you think Iran's seizure of the U.S. embassy affected its relations with the West?

4. a. Recall Why did Iraq invade Kuwait, and what resulted from this action?
b. Predict What challenges do you think Iraq will face in the coming years?

Critical Thinking

5. Identify Cause and Effect Using your notes, fill in a graphic organizer like the one below to identify causes and effects of the Arab-Israeli conflict, Iranian Revolution, and wars in Iraq.

Causes	Effects

FOCUS ON WRITING

6. Description For a library display on the Camp David Accords, write a paragraph describing the scene at Camp David when the agreement was reached.

AFRICA AND THE MIDDLE EAST **959**

Section 4 Assessment Answers

1. a. Oil revenues have been used for military buildup.
b. a movement to reorder government and society according to Islamic laws

2. a. 1967: Israel takes control of territory, including land in the West Bank and Gaza, in Six-Day War; 1973: Egypt and Syria launch Yom Kippur War to regain territory
b. possible answer—A peace agreement needs to be created that will be acceptable to both Arabs and Israelis.

3. a. inspired protests against shah, became Iran's leader after the shah fled Iran
b. possible answer—probably made the West distrust Iran even more

4. a. accused Kuwait of drilling into an Iraqi oil field and stealing oil; UN passed economic sanctions; U.S.-led coalition launched the Persian Gulf War
b. possible answer—to continue to hold elections and develop its new, democratic government; to stop violence and the insurgency

5. Arab-Israeli Conflict—Causes: dispute beween Arabs and Israelis over territory; Effects: wars, continuing violence; Iranian Revolution—Causes: protests against shah; shah's ties to West; Effects: new Islamic republic formed; Wars in Iraq—Causes: disputes over oil; Iraq's occupation of Kuwait; Iraq's failure to fully cooperate with UN inspections; Effects—growing insurgency; new, democratic government in Iraq

6. Students should draw upon information in this section to create detailed descriptions.

Document-Based Investigation

The Iranian Revolution

Info to Know

Khomeini and Technology Despite his rejection of Western values and his call for a return to strict Shia customs, Khomeini did not oppose the use of modern Western technology. After being exiled from Iran, he eventually settled in Paris where he coordinated the opposition movement against the shah of Iran through telecommunications. He used tape-recorded messages to express his revolutionary ideas. With the help of supporters in Paris, the messages were relayed to the people of Iran by telephone. Protests and demonstrations in Iran became more radical, and in 1979 Khomeini replaced the shah as the new ruler.

The Iranian Revolution

Historical Context The four documents below present opinions from both sides of the Iranian Revolution of 1979.

Task Study the selections and answer the questions that follow. After you have studied all the documents, you will be asked to write an essay explaining why the Iranian Revolution occurred. You will need to use evidence from these selections and from the chapter to support the position you take in your essay.

NEW YORK STANDARDS

PI 4.4 Students analyze different interpretations of important events, issues, or developments in world history by studying the social, political, and economic context in which they were developed; by testing the data source for reliability and validity, credibility, authority, authenticity, and completeness; and by detecting bias, distortion of the facts, and propaganda by omission, suppression, or invention of facts.

DOCUMENT 1

Iran before the Revolution

Before the Revolution of 1979, Iran was ruled by Mohammad Reza Pahlavi, who worked to modernize and Westernize the country. As part of his effort to change Iran—a goal not shared by all Iranians—the shah wanted closer ties with the United States, a desire he expressed in a toast delivered to U. S. president Richard Nixon at a state dinner in 1972.

> Depending upon 25 centuries of national heritage and sovereignty, we today have started a new period of renewing our past glories, based on the eternal values of our culture and civilization, and hope that the pages of our future history will also be thumbed through with the same national pride based on honor, righteousness, peace, and justice.
>
> We have based our independent national policy on international understanding in the path of national reconstruction and the strengthening of world peace, coexistence, and, above all, cooperation. It is to be noted that we shall not tolerate any inequality from any quarter in our relations with other countries. Certainly under no circumstances will we allow any violation of our land or of our rights.

DOCUMENT 2

Leader of the Revolution

The Iranian Revolution was led by Ayatollah Ruhollah Khomeini, a Muslim leader who had been exiled from Iran for making derogatory comments against both the shah and the United States. Though the ayatollah died in 1989, images of him, such as this mural in a busy Tehran street, can still be seen all over Iran.

Skills Focus: Analyzing Visuals

At Level

Reading Like a Historian Skill
A Tehran Mural

Standard English Mastery

1. Have students review Document 2. Tell students that the image is a photograph of a mural in Tehran that depicts Ayatollah Khomeini.

2. Guide a class discussion about the mural. What might its purpose have been? Does the ayatollah look like someone to be feared, or someone to be loved? Why was the mural painted in this style? Why might it still exist in Tehran today, even though the ayatollah died in 1989, and Iran is now led by different people?

3. Have students write a paragraph explaining why they think the mural showing the ayatollah is significant, and why similar murals can still be seen all over Iran today.

LS Verbal-Linguistic,

Alternative Assessment Handbook, Rubric 37: Writing Assignments

DOCUMENT 3

The Ayatollah Speaks

Shortly after the overthrow of the shah, Ayatollah Khomeini addressed the people of Iran about the events that inspired the revolution.

Your opponents, oppressed people, have never suffered. In the time of the *taghut* [impurity], they never suffered because either they were in agreement with the regime and loyal to it, or they kept silent. Now you have spread the banquet of freedom in from of them and they have sat down to eat. Xenomaniacs, people infatuated with the West, empty people, people with no content! Come to your senses; do not try to westernize everything you have! Look at the West, and see who the people are in the West that present themselves as champions of human rights and what their aims are. Is it human rights they really care about, or the rights of the superpowers? What they really want to secure are the rights of the superpowers. Our jurists should not follow or imitate them. You should implement human rights as the working classes of our society understand them. Yes, they are the real Society for the Defense of Human Rights. They are the ones who secure the well-being of humanity; they work while you talk; for they are Muslims and Islam cares about humanity.

DOCUMENT 4

An American View of the Revolution

The revolution in Iran drew attention around the world. Scholars tried to explain its causes. One such scholar was Lewis Ware, who published this passage in the *Air University Review* in 1980. In his article, Ware points out that many Iranians did not consider the shah to be their legitimate ruler. He had already been overthrown once before, in 1953, and only regained his position through the intervention of the CIA. As a result, many Iranians considered him a puppet of the U. S. government.

The Shah was the great modernizer of Iran. To further his goals he chose an autocratic model of nation-building bequeathed to him by his father, Reza Shah. During his reign a need for independence informed Muhammad Reza Pahlavi's vision of Iranian grandeur from which he never wavered and to which he applied the limitless resources of absolute monarchy. He failed to unite Iran under his person and destroyed in the process any possibility for Iran to act in an unrestrained environment . . . The Shah's debacle came about because there had never been, nor could there ever be under the circumstances, a general agreement on the meaning of progress. As a consequence, the Shah was denied the very security and legitimacy his regime needed to exist.

Skills FOCUS: READING LIKE A HISTORIAN

DOCUMENT 1
a. **Identify** What values does the shah say he wants Iran to be known for?
b. **Elaborate** How do you think the shahs' opinions would have been received by those who did not share his goals?

DOCUMENT 2
a. **Explain** Why do you think the ayatollah's image can still be seen throughout Iran?
b. **Develop** What does the popularity of the ayatollah's image suggest about people's views of his ideas?

DOCUMENT 3
a. **Describe** What does the ayatollah say is Westerners' real motivation for their involvement in Iran?
b. **Contrast** How did the ayatollah's views differ from the shah's? Which do you think were shared by more Iranians?

DOCUMENT 4
a. **Analyze** How does Ware characterize the shah's reign?
b. **Interpret** Why does Ware think the shah's government was overthrown?

DOCUMENT-BASED ESSAY QUESTION

The Iranian Revolution of 1979 was led by Ayatollah Khomeini, but he did not fight alone. Khomeini was supported by a huge segment of Iran's population. Could the revolution have been successful without the people's support? Using the documents above and information from the chapter, form a thesis about the role of the Iranian people in the revolution. Then write a short essay to support your position.

See **Skills Handbook**, pp. H25–H26, H30

Skills Focus: Analyzing Alternative Points of View   `At Level`

Reading Like a Historian Skill
Two Speeches

1. Tell students that Document 1 was a toast delivered to the U.S. president several years before the Iranian Revolution. Have a volunteer read it aloud. Which words in the speech emphasize the ties between Iran and the United States?

2. Tell students that Document 3 was a speech meant to support the new leadership of Ayatollah Khomeini. Have a volunteer read the speech aloud. Have students identify the words and phrases that emphasize the ayatollah's message.

3. Guide a class discussion about the two speeches. How is Iran's relationship with the West different after the Iranian Revolution?

4. Have students write a brief description of how Iran's relationship to the West changed after the Iranian Revolution. **LS Verbal-Linguistic**

Alternative Assessment Handbook, Rubric 40: Writing to Describe

Answers

Visual Summary

Review and Inquiry Have students write a summary of the key events in Africa and the Middle East listed on this page.

📖 **Quick Facts Transparency:** Visual Study Guide: Africa and the Middle East

Review Key Terms and People

1. Jomo Kenyatta
2. apartheid
3. one-party system
4. negritude movement
5. Gamal Abdel Nasser
6. David Ben-Gurion
7. Pan-Arabism
8. Camp David Accords
9. intifada
10. Ayatollah Ruhollah Khomeini
11. Organization of Petroleum Exporting Countries (OPEC)
12. institute

Comprehension and Critical Thinking

13. a. a leader of Kenya's nationalist movement
b. by establishing the Convention People's Party (CPP) and leading strikes and demonstrations
c. possible answer—The establishment of homelands implied that black people were not citizens of South Africa.

14. a. helped organize a campaign that encouraged blacks in South Africa to break apartheid laws
b. about 1 million Tutsi and moderate Hutus massacred; many more became refugees
c. possible answer—by removing corrupt leaders from power

VISUAL STUDY GUIDE

Conflicts in the Middle East

- The region's oil wealth has led to the build up of military forces, internal clashes within countries and societies, and outside influence by the world powers.
- The growth of Islamism in countries such as Egypt, Iran, and Iraq has led to conflicts within societies and governments.
- Since the State of Israel was established in 1948, a conflict between Arabs and Israelis has existed.
- During the Iranian Revolution in 1979, Islamists ousted the shah and Iran became an Islamic republic.
- In the late 1900s and early 2000s, Iraq was involved in three wars: the Iran-Iraq War, the Persian Gulf War, and the Iraq War.

Challenges in Africa

- Decades of protest against apartheid led to its end, and South Africans elected the country's first black president—Nelson Mandela.
- Dictators led governments with one-party systems in many newly independent countries.
- After independence, ethnic conflicts and civil war broke out in some African countries.
- Many countries struggled to establish democratic governments, while some countries were ruled by corrupt leaders.
- Today Africa faces many economic and environmental challenges, such as struggling economies, disease, and desertification.

Key Events in Africa and the Middle East, 1945–Present

1948 ▪ The State of Israel is established, and the first Arab-Israeli war begins.

1956 ▪ Morocco and Tunisia gain independence from France.

1956 ▪ Egypt seizes the Suez Canal, sparking the Suez Crisis.

1957 ▪ Ghana gains independence.

1960 ▪ Belgium withdraws from the Belgian Congo.

1963 ▪ Britain grants independence to Kenya, and Jomo Kenyatta becomes prime minister.

1967 ▪ Israel fights Egypt, Syria, and Jordan in the Six-Day War.

1973 ▪ Egypt and Syria attack Israel in the Yom Kippur War.

1974 ▪ Portugal withdraws from its African colonies after years of war.

1978 ▪ Egypt and Israel sign the Camp David Accords.

1991 ▪ A U.S.-led coalition forces Iraq out of Kuwait in the Persian Gulf War.

1994 ▪ South Africans elect Nelson Mandela as president.

2003 ▪ A U.S.-led coalition invades Iraq and forces Saddam Hussein from power.

Review Key Terms and People

Identify the term or person from the chapter that best fits each of the following descriptions.

1. leader of Kenya's independence movement
2. policy of racial segregation in South Africa
3. system in which a single political party controls the government
4. a literature movement focused on African identity
5. Egyptian nationalist leader
6. first Israeli prime minister
7. Arab unity
8. peace agreement between Egypt and Israel
9. Palestinian rebellion
10. leader of the Iranian Revolution
11. organization of oil-rich countries
12. to originate and establish

15. a. A nationalist movement known as Zionism called for an independent Jewish state.
b. In Egypt, the rise of a nationalist leader led to the Suez crisis; in Iran, nationalism led to opposition to foreign influence.
c. possible answer—a stronger claim, because the prime minister felt obligated to support the French settlers in Algeria

16. a. oil and the growth of Islamism
b. the Six-Day War, the Yom Kippur War, the Camp David Accords, intifada, the Oslo Accords
c. possible answer—There has been continuing violence and a growing insurgency.

History's Impact video program

Watch the video to answer the closing question: How has oil impacted the Arabian Peninsula and the rest of the world?

Comprehension and Critical Thinking

SECTION 1 *(pp. 936–941)*

13. a. Recall Who was Jomo Kenyatta?

b. Explain How did Kwame Nkrumah help gain independence for the Gold Coast?

c. Evaluate How do you think the establishment of homelands prevented black South Africans from gaining equal rights in South Africa?

SECTION 2 *(pp. 943–947)*

14. a. Describe What role did Nelson Mandela play in the ANC in the 1950s and 1960s?

b. Summarize How did ethnic conflict affect the peoples of Rwanda in the 1990s?

c. Predict How do you think Africans should work to overcome economic and environmental challenges such as disease and desertification?

SECTION 3 *(pp. 949–953)*

15. a. Recall How did nationalism lead to the creation of the State of Israel?

b. Contrast How did the rise of nationalist leaders in both Egypt and Iran affect those countries differently?

c. Support a Position Do you think the French settler population in Algeria gave France a stronger or weaker claim to Algeria? Explain.

SECTION 4 *(pp. 954–959)*

16. a. Describe Describe two regional issues that have contributed to conflicts in the Middle East.

b. Summarize What were the key events of the Arab-Israeli conflict since the 1960s?

c. Elaborate How have events in Iraq made it difficult for Iraqis to establish a stable democracy?

Reading Skills

Drawing Conclusions *Use what you know about drawing conclusions to answer the questions below.*

17. If you know that South Africa's apartheid system was abolished, what can you conclude about how life for black South Africans changed?

18. If you know that most of world's countries depend on oil and the Middle East has most of the world's oil, what can you conclude about the future of the Middle East?

Analyzing Primary Sources

Reading Like a Historian *The excerpt below is from a speech that Nelson Mandela gave in 1994 after he was inaugurated as the president of South Africa.*

❝We have triumphed in the effort to implant hope in . . . our people. We enter into a covenant that we shall build the society in which all South Africans, both black and white, will be able to walk tall, without any fear in their hearts, assured of their inalienable right to human dignity—a rainbow nation at peace with itself and the world.❞

—Nelson Mandela, Inaugural Address, May 10, 1994

19. Infer What former South African policy might have affected what Mandela says in his speech?

20. Interpret What do you think Mandela means by the phrase "a rainbow nation at peace with itself and the world"?

go.hrw.com
Practice Online
Keyword: SHL AFR

Using the Internet

21. In 1947 the United Nations proposed a plan to divide Palestine into separate Jewish and Arab states. Using the Internet, research the proposal and the reaction it received. Then write a report about the UN plan, using maps and other documents to support your work. Be sure to include information about how people living in Palestine reacted to the proposal.

WRITING ABOUT HISTORY

Exposition: Comparing and Contrasting *After World War II, nationalist movements grew in many areas European powers controlled in Africa and the Middle East. In some countries, the transition to independence took very different forms.*

22. Assignment: In an essay, compare and contrast nationalist movements in two nations discussed in this chapter. To provide support for your essay, use information from this chapter and from other research as needed. Be sure to collect facts and examples to clearly illustrate the points you are making about how the struggles for independence in these nations were similar and different.

Answers

Reading Skills

17. that black South Africans gained more rights and freedoms

18. that the future of the Middle East will vcontinue to be important to the world

Analyzing Primary Sources

19. apartheid

20. possible answer—a nation in which people of all races live in harmony with each other and the rest of the world

Using the Internet

21. Go to the HRW Web site and enter the keyword shown to access a rubric for this activity.

KEYWORD: SHL AFR

Writing About History

22. Student essays should compare and contrast two nationalist movements covered in this chapter, using details and examples to strengthen the comparison.

A rubric for the activity is provided in **CRF**: Writing for the SAT.

HOLT

History's Impact

▶ **Video Program: Africa and the Middle East**

Refer to the Video Teacher's Guide for the answer to the closing question.

Review and Assessment Resources

Review and Reinforce

 CRF: Chapter Review

Quick Facts Transparency: Visual Study Guide: Africa and the Middle East

Spanish Chapter Summaries Audio CD Program

OSP **Holt PuzzlePro**: Quiz Show for ExamView

Quiz Game CD-ROM

Assess

PASS: Chapter Test, Forms A and B

Alternative Assessment Handbook

OSP **ExamView Test Generator**, Chapter Test

Differentiated Instruction Modified Worksheets and Tests CD-ROM: Chapter Test

HOAP **Holt Online Assessment Program** (in the Premier Online Edition)

Reteach/Intervene

Interactive Reader and Study Guide

Differentiated Instruction Teacher Management System: Lesson Plans for Differentiated Instruction

Differentiated Instruction Modified Worksheets and Tests CD-ROM: Chapter Test

Interactive Skills Tutor CD-ROM

go.hrw.com
Online Resources

KEYWORD: SHL TEACHER

Chapter 32 Planning Guide

Latin America

Chapter Overview	Reproducible Resources	Technology Resources
CHAPTER 32 pp. 964–987 **Overview: In this chapter, students will learn about the political and economic problems in Latin America from 1945 to the present.** KI 1, 3; PI 1.3, 1.4, 3.1, 3.3 See pp. T32–T55 for a detailed correlation to the New York State Core Curriculum for Global History and Geography and the New York Learning Standards.	**Differentiated Instruction Teacher Management System:*** • Pacing Guide • Lesson Plans for Differentiated Instruction **Interactive Reader and Study Guide:** Chapter Summary* **Chapter Resource File*** • Writing for the SAT • Social Studies Skill • Chapter Review **World History Outline Maps**	**OSP** **New York One-Stop Planner CD-ROM:** Calendar Planner **Live Ink© Online Reading Help** **Student Edition on Audio CD Program** **Differentiated Instruction Modified Worksheets and Tests CD-ROM** **Interactive Skills Tutor CD-ROM** **World History Primary Source Library CD-ROM** **Power Presentations with Video CD-ROM** **History's Impact: World History Video Program (VHS/DVD):** Latin America
Section 1: **Revolution and Intervention** **The Main Idea:** In reaction to economic and social conditions in Latin America after World War II, many Central American countries experienced revolutions that involved intervention by the United States. PI 1.2, 1.4	**Differentiated Instruction Teacher Management System:** Section 1 Lesson Plan* **Interactive Reader and Study Guide:** Section 1 Summary* **Chapter Resource File*** • Vocabulary Builder: Section 1 • Biography: Juan José Arévalo • Primary Source: Nicaraguans Protest U.S. Support of the Contras • History and Geography: Superpower Showdown	**Regents Review Transparency:** Section 1* **Map Transparency:** Turmoil in Latin America, 1945–Present* **Internet Activity:** Latin America
Section 2: **The Rise of Dictatorships** **The Main Idea:** Spiraling economic and social problems and political turmoil in Latin America led military leaders to seize power and install repressive regimes. PI 1.2, 3.1	**Differentiated Instruction Teacher Management System:** Section 2 Lesson Plan* **Interactive Reader and Study Guide:** Section 2 Summary* **Chapter Resource File*** • Vocabulary Builder: Section 2 • Biography: Enriqueta Barnes de Carlotto • Literature: *My Invented Country*	**Regents Review Transparency:** Section 2*
Section 3: **Democratic and Economic Reforms** **The Main Idea:** In the 1980s, repressive regimes in Latin America fell, and more moderate elected leaders brought some measure of political and economic progress. PI 1.3, 1.4, 3.3	**Differentiated Instruction Teacher Management System:** Section 3 Lesson Plan* **Interactive Reader and Study Guide:** Section 3 Summary* **Chapter Resource File*** • Vocabulary Builder: Section 3 • Biography: Luiz Inácio Lula da Silva	**Regents Review Transparency:** Section 3* **Map Transparency:** Poverty in Latin America, 2006* **Quick Facts Transparency:** Mexico Then; Mexico Now* **Internet Activity:** Current Events in Latin America

Review, Assessment, Intervention

Global History and Geography Regents Test Prep Workbook

Quick Facts Transparency: Latin America*

Spanish Chapter Summaries Audio CD Program

Progress Assessment Support System (PASS): Chapter Test*

Differentiated Instruction Modified Worksheets and Tests CD-ROM: Modified Chapter Test

OSP **New York One-Stop Planner CD-ROM:** ExamView Test Generator (English/Spanish)

HOAP **Holt Online Assessment Program (HOAP),** in the Holt Premier Online Student Edition

---

PASS: Section 1 Quiz*

Online Quiz: Section 1

Alternative Assessment Handbook

PASS: Section 2 Quiz*

Online Quiz: Section 2

Alternative Assessment Handbook

PASS: Section 3 Quiz*

Online Quiz: Section 3

Alternative Assessment Handbook

Power Presentation with Video CD-ROM

Power Presentations with Video are visual presentations of each chapter's main ideas. Presentations can be customized by including Quick Facts charts, images and maps from the textbook, and video clips.

Holt Online Learning

go.hrw.com
Teacher Resources
KEYWORD: SHL TEACHER

go.hrw.com
Student Resources
KEYWORD: SHL LAT

- Document-Based Questions
- Interactive Multimedia Activities

- Current Events
- Chapter-Based Internet Activities
- and more!

Holt Premier
Online Student Edition

Complete online support for interactivity, assessment, and reporting

- Interactive Maps and Notebook
- Homework Practice and Research Activities Online

The Big Picture

Peter N. Stearns

Inequality The division between rich and poor is a long-standing problem in Latin America. The elite's control of natural resources, such as land, coupled with their control over economic and political institutions has severely limited the opportunities open to less powerful members of society. Extreme poverty and inadequate political representation have led to social and political instability. These circumstances have also led to a crisis of confidence among investors that has undermined economic growth in many nations.

Dictatorship The long-term rule of one man or one party (like the PRI of Mexico) characterized the governments of many Latin American countries in the second half of the twentieth century. The populace supported or endured heavy-handed leaders who promised to maintain order. But, continued and increasingly violent repression, sometimes exacerbated by corruption, brought resistance by ordinary folk into the open. In time, such protests precipitated the downfall of oppressive and corrupt regimes in Latin America.

Open Societies Recently, many governments in Latin America have returned to democratic rule. More responsive political and economic institutions have not solved new problems, such as those associated with the North American Free Trade Association (NAFTA). More open political structures do, however, give voice to the masses. In recent years, voters in many Latin American countires have excercised their right to vote by electing populist political leaders who promise to improve their standard of living.

Recent Scholarship

One of the best and most readable accounts of the modern era in Latin America is a text entitled *Born in Blood and Fire: A Concise History of Latin America* (2001), by John C. Chasteen. In addition to providing an excellent overview of this region's complicated history, the author analyzes political cartoons, paintings and murals, as well as movies that portray historical events. Special attention should be paid to the author's short essays called "Countercurrents." These essays highlight special dimensions of the broader themes covered in the chapters.

Differentiating Instruction

 Differentiated Instruction Teacher Management System
- Pacing Guide
- Lesson Plans for Differentiated Instruction

 Interactive Reader and Study Guide

 Spanish Chapter Summaries Audio CD Program

Student Edition on Audio CD Program

 Differentiated Instruction Modified Worksheets and Tests CD-ROM
- Vocabulary Flash Cards
- Modified Vocabulary Builder Activities
- Modified Chapter Review Activity
- Modified Chapter Test

OSP **One-Stop Planner CD-ROM**
- ExamView Test Generator (English and Spanish)
- PuzzlePro
- Quiz Show for ExamView
- Transparencies and Videos

TE **Differentiated Activities in the Teacher's Edition**
- Brazilian Lifestyles, p. 968
- Castro's Agrarian Reform Law, p. 969
- Victims of the "Dirty War", p. 974
- Economic Conditions and Changes, p. 981
- Analyzing Primary Sources, p. 985
- Higher Trade and Lower Employment, p 985

Reading Like a Historian
Sam Wineburg

Exploring Context How might historians approach the photo essay on Cuba that appears on page 972? Even before viewing this essay, they would note the context in which these photos appear: a textbook produced in the United States. Why would it matter that it was an American textbook rather than, say, a Canadian one? Because the United States has imposed a travel and trade embargo on Cuba for the last 45 years and maintains no diplomatic relations with this island nation. Canada, on the other hand, is Cuba's largest trading partner and more Canadians visit Cuba per year than tourists from any other nation. Just knowing where our book was published leads to certain expectations over others.

Have your students examine the five images and captions under the title "Communism in Cuba." The caption at the top of the essay announces that "Castro's policies have had mixed results." From this, we might indeed expect something mixed, a balance of good and bad attributes. But three of the four titles—"Stalled Economy," "Lack of Political Freedom," and "Scarcity of Food"—are decidedly in one direction.

Point of View The image that accompanies the Cuba's "stalled economy" is a close up of a vintage American car. "Because Cuba's communist policies have led to trade embargos . . . most cars in Cuba are from the 1950s." Have your students think about agency in this caption. Ask them how they might rewrite it if they wanted the reader to form a different impression. Compare the book's caption to this rewritten one: "Because the American government does not allow Ford, GE, and Chrysler to sell new cars to Cuba, many people, especially the poor, are forced to drive American automobiles dating back to the 1950s." How does each caption make us feel about the image before us?

We could use the same picture and, by writing a different caption, give it a different spin. We could turn the image/caption pairing into something positive, accentuating the ingenuity of the Cuban people, who have created cottage industries to make parts that keep classic cars running.

Farfetched? This is exactly what National Geographic photographer David Allen Harvey did in a 2006 photo essay. Accompanying an image of a vintage American car driving by a boxy Russian Lada on the sandy roadway alongside Havana's Malecón seaside avenue, Harvey wrote: "I think that the steel they made cars from in the 1950s must be tougher than today's materials. People drive those old cars in salt air and even drive them in flooded areas where the ocean comes over the [seawall]. But they don't seem to rust out and those guys keep them up somehow, they're able to just keep them going."

If we were to go to Cuba we might certainly see many cars like the one depicted in our textbook. But camera in hand, we could choose to shoot pictures of different scenes. In a six-part investigative report published in the *Bangor Daily News* in 2000, Gordon Bonin also observed fleets of vintage autos cruising Havana's streets. But he also noted "the roads swarm with new Hyundais, Daewoos, Citroens, Peugeots and Toyotas. Fewer in number, but more prominent by their rarity, are the black Mercedes and Audis." A photo of 'swarming' Asian imports would give a different impression of Cuba still.

The process of connecting a photograph to its caption is so spontaneous that many students don't even realize that their eye has been directed. To the question students are asked at the bottom of 972—"What can you say about life in Cuba based on these photographs?"—historians would ask, "What do the caption writers of this essay want us to say about life Cuba based on these photographs and captions?"

Chapter Main Ideas

Section 1 In reaction to economic and social conditions in Latin America after World War II, many Central American countries experienced revolutions that involved intervention by the United States.

Section 2 Spiraling economic and social problems and political turmoil in Latin America led military leaders to seize power and install repressive regimes.

Section 3 In the 1980s, repressive regimes in Latin America fell, and more moderate elected leaders brought some measure of political and economic progress.

New York Standards

Key Idea 1 The study of world history requires an understanding of world cultures and civilizations, including an analysis of important ideas, social and cultural values, beliefs, and traditions. This study also examines the human condition and the connections and interactions of people across time and space and the ways different people view the same event or issue from a variety of perspectives.

Key Idea 3 Study of the major social, political, cultural, and religious developments in world history involves learning about the important roles and contributions of individuals and groups.

Key to Differentiating Instruction

Below Level

Basic-level activities designed for all students encountering new material

At Level

Intermediate-level activities designed for average students

Above Level

Challenging activities designed for honors and gifted and talented students

Standard English Mastery

Activities designed to improve standard English usage

CHAPTER

32 1945–Present

Latin America

THE BIG PICTURE Latin America has experienced many political and economic shifts since 1945. Revolutions and repressive governments have coincided with shifts toward government-controlled economies or more open market economies. In recent years, Latin America has made great strides toward democracy but still faces many economic and political challenges.

Theme ECONOMIC SYSTEMS
A common theme in Latin American history has been how to develop strong, diverse economies that meet the needs of the people. In this chapter you will learn about Latin America's struggles to create modern and productive economic systems.

TIME LINE

CHAPTER EVENTS	**1959** The Cuban Revolution brings Fidel Castro to power.	**1973** Augusto Pinochet takes power in Chile in a military coup.	**Argentina's "dirty war" 1976–1983**

1945 ———————————————— **1965** ————————————————

WORLD EVENTS	**1949** The Chinese Communist Party takes full control of China.	**1967** The Six-Day War takes place between Israel and Arab nations.	**1980** Zimbabwe wins independence from Great Britain.

964 CHAPTER 32

Introduce the Chapter

At Level

Latin America

1. Have students make a list of all the material things people need in order to survive. Then have students make a list of basic rights and freedoms that people need in order to live in a just and fair society.

2. Have volunteers share their ideas and create a class list for all to see. You may wish to add several amendments from the Bill of Rights to the class list if students do not include them.

3. Have students name common traits of dictatorships, such as lack of security, little freedom, poor economy, and poor standard of living.

4. Guide students in a discussion of conditions in countries run by dictators. Why do people in these countries often lack material necessities and basic human rights?
LS Verbal-Linguistic

Alternative Assessment Handbook, Rubrics 11: Discussions; and 12: Drawing Conclusions

Reading like a Historian

Thousands of supporters attend a political rally for a presidential candidate in Uruguay. Rallies like this one are common in Latin America, as people express their support for or opposition to their government.

Analyzing Visuals What does this scene tell you about politics in modern Latin America?

See **Skills Handbook**, p. H26

1992
Mexico, the United States, and Canada sign the North American Free Trade Agreement (NAFTA).

2006
In reaction to failed economic reforms, Bolivians elect a leftist president.

1985 ——————————————— 2005

1992 A treaty to establish the European Union is signed.

2001 Terrorists attack the World Trade Center and the Pentagon in the United States.

LATIN AMERICA **965**

• Chapter Preview •

HOLT
History's Impact
► **Video Program: Latin America**
See the Video Teacher's Guide for strategies for using the video segment.

Reading Like a Historian

Analyzing Visuals Uruguay is a small coastal country in southeast South America. Like many countries in South America, it faced political problems starting in the 1950s and 1960s, including a period of military rule. Since 1985, however, Uruguay has been ruled by democratically elected presidents. Have students take a moment to examine the photograph on this page. Ask students why a presidential rally might be so popular in Uruguay, considering the country's recent history.

Explore the Time Line

1. When did Castro come to power in Cuba?
   1959
2. How long was the "dirty war" in Argentina?
   about 7 years
3. What two significant events occurred in 1992? *NAFTA was signed; treaty to establish European Union was signed*

Info to Know

NAFTA and Mexico The North American Free Trade Agreement has not yet achieved all of its goals. Mexico has experienced some economic success and growth, but not as much as the United States and Canada. Mexico's northern states are seeing more benefits from NAFTA, while the southern states continue to lag behind. Overall, Mexico is benefiting, but not as much as proponents of NAFTA had hoped.

Draw Conclusions Why do you think Mexico has not benefited as much from NAFTA as the United States and Canada? *possible answer— lack of infrastructure, skilled workforce*

go.hrw.com
Online Resources

Chapter Resources:
KEYWORD: SHL LAT
Teacher Resources:
KEYWORD: SHL TEACHER

Answers

Reading Like a Historian *People in some Latin American countries have the right to gather and demonstrate their political beliefs.*

965

Geography Starting Points

Response to Argentina's "dirty war"
In 1983 Argentina's new democratic government began to prosecute members of its former military government. Hundreds of military personnel and five members of the military junta were prosecuted and convicted of human rights violations.

Biography

Tomás Eloy Martínez (1934–) Tomás Eloy Martínez was born in Argentina in 1934 and wrote for a number of newspapers and publications. From 1972 to 1975 he wrote opinion columns that were staples in the dissent against Argentina's military dictatorship. In response, the government forced Martínez into exile. He moved to Venezuela, where he began to work for a newspaper called *El Nacional*. In 1979 he founded his own daily publication, *El Diario,* which is still in circulation today. In addition to his work as a newspaper journalist, Martínez as written several screenplays and books and is the recipient of seven honorary doctorates. Referring to the journalism profession, Martínez once stated, "To query, to learn, and to doubt a hundred times over before reporting about something: these are the most important verbs in the most risky, passionate profession of the world."

- **Map Transparency**: Turmoil in Latin America, 1945–Present
- **World History Outline Maps**
- **Interactive Map**: Turmoil in Latin America, 1945–Present

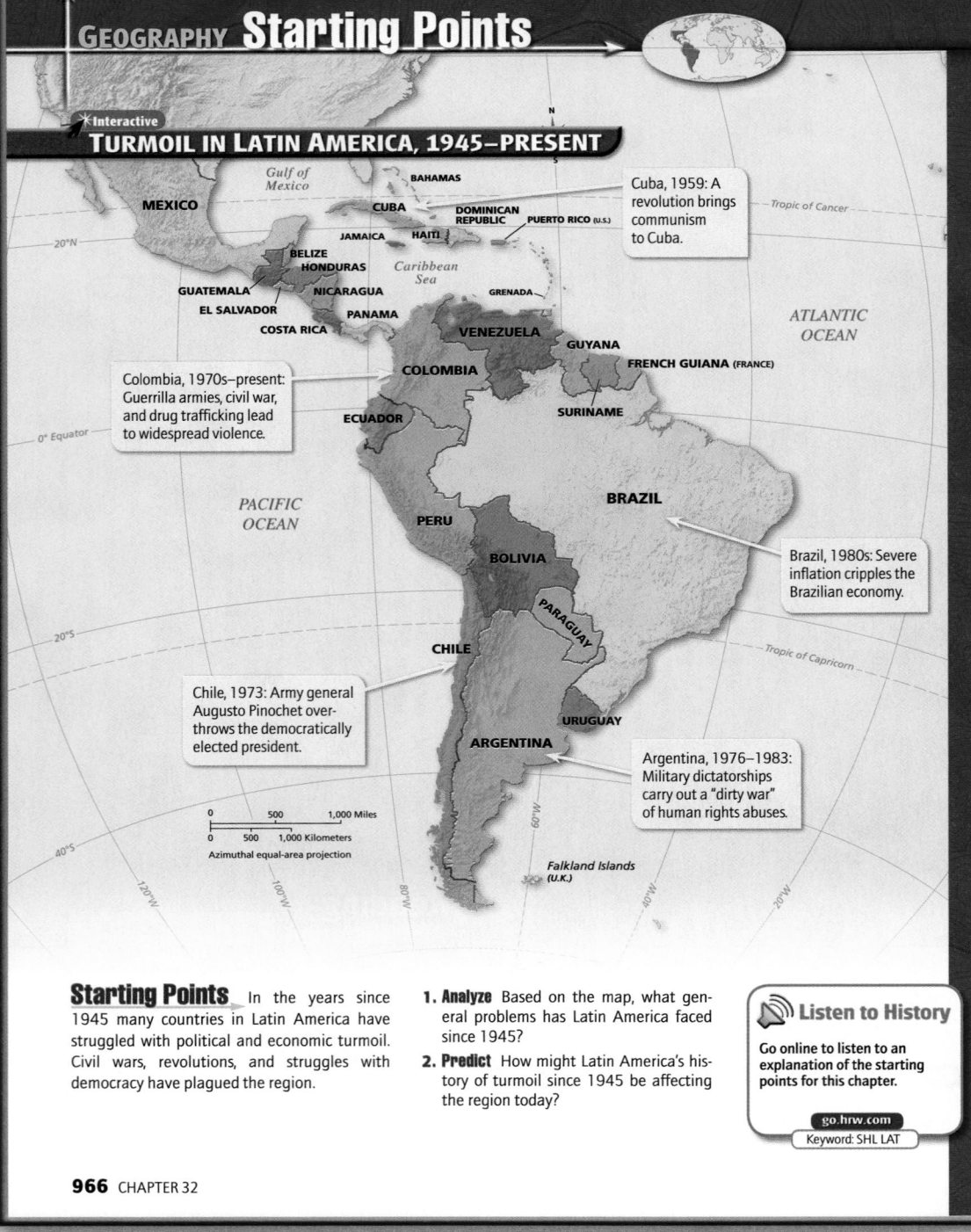

GEOGRAPHY Starting Points

TURMOIL IN LATIN AMERICA, 1945–PRESENT

Cuba, 1959: A revolution brings communism to Cuba.

Colombia, 1970s–present: Guerrilla armies, civil war, and drug trafficking lead to widespread violence.

Brazil, 1980s: Severe inflation cripples the Brazilian economy.

Chile, 1973: Army general Augusto Pinochet overthrows the democratically elected president.

Argentina, 1976–1983: Military dictatorships carry out a "dirty war" of human rights abuses.

Starting Points In the years since 1945 many countries in Latin America have struggled with political and economic turmoil. Civil wars, revolutions, and struggles with democracy have plagued the region.

1. **Analyze** Based on the map, what general problems has Latin America faced since 1945?

2. **Predict** How might Latin America's history of turmoil since 1945 be affecting the region today?

Listen to History

Go online to listen to an explanation of the starting points for this chapter.

go.hrw.com
Keyword: SHL LAT

966 CHAPTER 32

Skills Focus: Analyzing Maps

`At Level`

Social Studies Skill
Latin America Time Lines

1. To help students understand the information on the map, have them create their own time lines of Latin American events, using the information in the text boxes.

2. Organize students into small groups, and assign each group one of the five countries discussed: Argentina, Brazil, Chile, Columbia, and Cuba.

3. Have students use information from their texts to add information to their time lines about their assigned country and its political and economic problems.

4. Have volunteers from each group present their time lines to the class. **LS Visual-Spatial, Verbal-Linguistic**

- **Alternative Assessment Handbook**, Rubrics 14: Group Activity; and 36: Time Lines

Answers

Geography Starting Points
1. *revolutions, economic hardships, social changes, dictatorships, wars*
2. *possible answer—Countries are still recovering from economic hardships and trying to establish stable, democratic governments.*

966

SECTION 1
Revolution and Intervention

BEFORE YOU READ

MAIN IDEA
In reaction to economic and social conditions in Latin America after World War II, many Central American countries experienced conflicts that involved intervention by the United States.

READING FOCUS
1. What were some key economic and social trends in postwar Latin America?
2. How did the Cuban Revolution come about and what changes did it bring?
3. What other conflicts arose in Central America?

KEY TERMS AND PEOPLE
import-substitution led industrialization
Liberation Theology
Fidel Castro
Che Guevara
Sandinistas
junta
Contras

LAND FOR THE LANDLESS

◄ Members of Brazil's Landless Workers' Movement march to the capital.

THE INSIDE STORY

Who has a right to a country's land? In Brazil, less than 3 percent of the population owns about two-thirds of the country's farmland. As a result, more than 1.5 million landless workers have joined together to try to get land for Brazil's poor citizens.

Brazil's huge Landless Workers' Movement, known as the MST for its initials in Portuguese, was founded in 1984. The MST organizes groups of landless farmers to invade and build camps on large, unused private lands. One MST leader explained the reasons for these land invasions: "You have a right to land. There are unused properties in the region.

There is only one way to force the government to expropriate [take] them. You think they'll do it if we write them a letter? Asking the mayor is a waste of time, especially if he's a landowner. You could talk to the priest, but if he's not interested, what's the point? We have to organize and take over that land ourselves."

Over the years, the MST has gained legal rights to much land. About 350,000 families have acquired land through land invasions and takeovers. However, these invasions naturally anger Brazil's large landowners. As a result, the MST is regularly in conflict with the police and other government officials. ■

LATIN AMERICA **967**

968

TAKING NOTES
Take notes on trends in Latin America and on the conflicts in this section.

Trends	Conflicts

Trends in Latin America

Latin America includes the countries south of the United States, from Mexico and the Caribbean to South America. After World War II, many countries in the region struggled to address problems of poverty and inequality. The roots of these problems go back to Latin America's long history of colonialism. Under colonialism, most land and wealth were concentrated in the hands of the elite, and economies were based mainly on agricultural exports.

Economic Trends One main economic trend in Latin America was industrialization. Economies in the region had long been based on the export of cash crops and raw materials and the import of manufactured goods. To decrease dependence on foreign countries, many countries adopted a policy of **import-substitution led industrialization**. Under this policy, local industries are developed to replace the need to import manufactured goods. However, even as industry grew, Latin America still depended on foreign countries for investment, technology, loans, and military aid.

As Latin America's countries industrialized, rural land use remained a major issue. A small group of elites, many tied to U.S. business interests, owned much of the land in Latin America, while many peasants struggled to find land to farm. Some countries tried to address this issue by taking land from large landholders and giving it to landless peasants. Although this policy had mixed results, it became another major economic trend in the region.

Social Trends The large gap between rich and poor in Latin America was also a major social issue. Some groups, including the church, tried to address this issue. Many priests began to promote **Liberation Theology**, the belief that the church should be active in the struggle for economic and social equality. Although it was criticized by the Catholic Church, the Liberation Theology movement became popular in heavily Catholic Latin America.

While some people looked to the church for help with their problems, others looked to the cities. Unable to make a living in rural areas, people flocked to the region's cities. This movement caused rapid urbanization. But many people found that life was no easier in the cities. Shortages of food, housing, and safe drinking water continued to present challenges for many in Latin America.

READING CHECK **Summarize** How did people in Latin America try to deal with some of the region's economic and social problems?

Urbanization in Latin America

Huge, rapidly growing cities are a common feature in Latin America. In many cities, such as Fortaleza, Brazil, upscale apartment buildings and offices are concentrated downtown and are surrounded by massive slums on the city's outskirts. *How might the gap between rich and poor people affect life in the cities?*

968 CHAPTER 32

The Cuban Revolution

In Cuba, social and economic trends led to a revolution. There, social inequality and heavy U.S. influence led to a revolt that brought communism to this large Caribbean island.

Reasons for Revolt Like much of Latin America, Cuba was very dependent on the United States. By the 1950s Cuba's modern hotels and gambling casinos were owned by wealthy Americans and Cuba's elite. U.S. businesses also owned huge sugar and tobacco plantations. These plantations produced valuable exports, but little land was left for average people to grow food. Cuba was one of the richest, most developed countries in Latin America. Yet most Cubans struggled to get by and earn a decent living.

Business interests encouraged the U.S. government to support a string of corrupt dictators in Cuba. The last of these dictators was Fulgencio Batista, an anticommunist who seized power in a 1952 military coup. Batista's Cuba was "a rich country with too many poor people," critics charged. Batista's coup stirred a wave of discontent and nationalism among the poor.

In 1953 a young lawyer named **Fidel Castro** led an unsuccessful attack on a Cuban army barracks. Castro was arrested and imprisoned. But two years later, he returned with a group of revolutionaries and launched a guerrilla war that became a full-scale revolution. When Batista fled the country on January 1, 1959, Cuba was left in the control of Castro, a brash leader who would outlast at least 10 U.S. presidents and the rest of the Cold War.

Goals of the Revolution Although there was broad public support for the revolution to remove Batista, most people did not know exactly what kind of revolution Castro would lead. Many middle-class Cubans supported moderate democratic reforms. But many of Castro's revolutionaries, including his brother Raul and the fiery leader **Che Guevara**, wanted to set up a Marxist regime. Castro was mainly focused on ending U.S. dominance, redistributing wealth, and reforming society.

To achieve these goals, Castro threw his energies into restructuring Cuba's economy, society, government, and foreign policy. In 1961 he launched a program that virtually ended

illiteracy within one year. He also created a system of free, nationwide medical care that helped raise life expectancy to near-U.S. levels. To reduce economic inequality, Castro limited the size of landholdings and nationalized all private property and businesses in Cuba.

To ensure that he had the power to make such radical changes, Castro took full control over the government. Then he took away freedom of the press. These radical actions led Cuba more and more toward communism and a confrontation with the United States, which saw communism anywhere in the Americas as a threat to U.S. security.

NEW YORK

CC Unit 7-H3
Causes and impact of the Cuban Revolution

PRIMARY SOURCES

Fidel Castro Speech

In the early years of the Cuban Revolution, Fidel Castro felt he needed to defend the policies of Cuba's new government. He did so in this speech to the UN General Assembly on September 26, 1960.

"Then followed the next law, an essential and inevitable law for our country, and a law which sooner or later will have to be adopted by all countries of the world, at least by those which have not yet adopted it: the Agrarian Reform Law. Of course, in theory everybody agrees with the Agrarian Reform Law. Nobody will deny the need for it unless he is a fool. No one can deny that agrarian reform is one of the essential conditions for the economic development of the country . . . In my country it was absolutely necessary: more than 200,000 peasant families lived in the countryside without land on which to grow essential food crops.

". . . Was it a radical agrarian reform? We think not. It was a reform adjusted to the needs of our development, and in keeping with our own possibilities of agricultural development. In other words, [it] was an agrarian reform which was to solve the problems of the landless peasants, the problem of supplying basic foodstuffs, the problem of rural unemployment, and which was to end, once and for all, the ghastly poverty which existed in the countryside of our native land."

Skills FOCUS READING LIKE A HISTORIAN

1. **Explain** Why did Castro think it was necessary to pass the Agrarian Reform Law?

2. **Analyze Primary Sources** Against what criticisms do you think Castro felt he needed to defend his policies?

See **Skills Handbook**, p. H25

LATIN AMERICA **969**

Direct Teach

Reading Focus

2 How did the Cuban Revolution come about and what changes did it bring? *discrepancy between rich and poor, corrupt dictator, Fidel Castro led revolt; virtually ended illiteracy, provided free healthcare, nationalized properties and businesses, communism, loss of civil liberties*

The Cuban Revolution

Describe What changes did Castro and Che Guevara want for Cuba? *a Marxist regime; end to U.S. dominance, wealth redistribution, reformed society*

Summarize What were Castro's first actions after seizing power? *virtually ended illiteracy, established free medical care, limited size of landholdings, nationalized private properties and businesses*

Activity Cuba Time Line Have students make a time line focusing on important events and dates in Cuban history from the 1950s to the present day.
LS Visual-Spatial
Alternative Assessment Handbook, Rubric 36: Time Lines

Primary Source

Fidel Castro Speech

Analyze Why did Castro defend his actions before the United Nations? *possible answer—concerned about international reaction to seizing land from its owners and giving it to the poor*

Differentiating Instruction

Above Level

Advanced Learners/ Gifted and Talented

Research Required

1. Have students read the excerpt on this page from the speech Fidel Castro gave to the United Nations on his Agrarian Reform Law.

2. Then have students conduct outside research on Castro's Agrarian Reform Law and its effects. Have students focus their research on both the negative and positive outcomes of the law.

3. Have students use their research to write a two-page petition to the United Nations persuading it to support Cuba's Agrarian Reform Law and to insist that other countries adopt this land reform measure. **LS** Verbal-Linguistic

Alternative Assessment Handbook, Rubrics 5: Business Letters; and 43: Writing to Persuade

Answers

Primary Sources 1. *to improve the economy, supply basic food for peasants, help end rural unemployment and poverty;* **2.** *possible answer—that it was unfair, radical*

History Close-Up

Info to Know

Communism in Cuba Fidel Castro took power of Cuba in 1959. In 1962, 78,000 Cubans fled Cuba and migrated to the United States. Castro then restricted travel between the United States and Cuba until 1965 when the government decided to permit air travel to Miami. During the next eight years, approximately 50,000 Cubans left their country and moved to the United States. Then in 1980, in what is known as the Mariel immigration, about 125,000 people fled Cuba in boats. In 1994 and 1995, the United States and Cuba signed agreements that allowed 20,000 Cubans to immigrate each year.

Fidel Castro Fidel Castro graduated from the School of Law at the University of Havana in 1950 and became involved in politics. He was imprisoned in Cuba after leading a rebel attack against Batista. Both he and his brother Raul were granted political amnesty in 1955 and moved to Mexico. They returned to Buba in 1956, and in 1959, Castro and his group of 800 guerrillas had forced Batista to flee, winning against the Cuban army of 30,000. One U.S. diplomat, Wayne Smith, has said that Fidel Castro will be remembered because "he stood up to the United States and survived." In August 2006, Fidel Castro was hospitalized and turned power over, at least temporarily, to his brother, Raul.

Teaching Tip

Remind students that Fidel Castro has ruled Cuba since 1959. Many Cubans have only known one leader for their entire lifetime.

Answers

Interpreting Visuals *possible answers—Cubans have access to free education and health care; they must support the government; scarcity of food and goods continues; U.S. embargo has affected available products*

HISTORY CLOSE-UP

Communism in Cuba

The Cuban Revolution affected many aspects of life in Cuba. Today the government controls the press, the economy, and social services. But Castro's communist policies have had mixed effects on the island and its people.

A Stalled Economy
A U.S. embargo on trade with Cuba has been in place since the 1960s. As a result, most cars in Cuba date from the 1950s, and many old buildings are in disrepair.

Lack of Political Freedoms While many Cubans support Castro and his policies, those who oppose the government are not free to express their opinions openly.

Scarcity of Food and Goods The Cuban government regulates the distribution of food and other goods, and scarcity is a major problem.

Free Education and Health Care Everyone is Cuba, such as these children, has access to free education and health care through government-run schools and clinics.

Skills FOCUS **INTERPRETING VISUALS**
Infer What can you say about life in Cuba based on these photographs?

970 CHAPTER 32

Skills Focus: Comparing and Contrasting

Above Level

Reading Skill
Revolutions in History

1. Have students read the information about the revolution that took place in Cuba and the effects it had on the country.

2. Have students use the information in their texts to compare and contrast the revolution in Cuba that led to communism with other revolutions they have studied including the U.S. fight for freedom from Great Britain, the French Revolution, the revolutions of 1848, and the rise of communism in China and Russia.

3. Have students write an essay or create a multimedia presentation in which they explain why some revolutions have led to democracy, freedom, and civil rights, and others have led to dictatorships and communism. **LS Verbal-Linguistic, Visual-Spatial**

Alternative Assessment Handbook, Rubric 42: Writing to Inform

U.S. Involvement Cuba's move toward communism during the Cold War troubled U.S. leaders. They viewed Latin America as part of a U.S. sphere of influence and wanted to keep communism out of the region. Shortly after World War II, the United States helped set up the Organization of American States (OAS), an organization of countries in the Americas that promotes economic and military cooperation. The OAS was strongly anticommunist.

Repeated U.S. attempts to oust Cuba's communist leaders failed. In 1961 a U.S.-trained invasion force of Cuban exiles landed in the Bay of Pigs, along Cuba's southern coast. Their mission was designed to spark a nationwide uprising against Castro. But it was a disaster. Cuban troops easily defeated the invaders.

Still stinging from this defeat, U.S. president John F. Kennedy soon found himself in a far more serious crisis with Cuba and the Soviet Union. In 1962 the CIA learned that the Soviet Union was building nuclear missile sites in Cuba. Missiles from these sites would be able to easily hit targets in America. Kennedy ordered a naval blockade to intercept Soviet ships loaded with missiles for Cuba. This tense confrontation, known as the Cuban missile crisis, brought the world as close to nuclear war as it had ever been. In the end, however, a compromise was reached, and the Soviet Union removed the missile sites.

Results of the Revolution In the years since these Cold War conflicts, the Cuban Revolution has had mixed results. For example, Cubans have good access to health care and education. However, people's civil liberties are restricted under a one-party system. The government jails opponents and watches citizens through a network of neighborhood spies.

Economic effects have also been mixed. Castro's policies led many Cubans to leave the country. Most went to the United States, and Cuba's economy struggled as a result. Castro relied on the Soviet Union for economic support. But when the Soviet Union collapsed in 1991, Cuba's economy suffered. Cuba has also suffered for decades because of a U.S. economic embargo.

READING CHECK Identify Cause and Effect What were some of the causes and effects of the Cuban Revolution?

Other Conflicts

As in Cuba, economic inequality was a serious problem in other Central American countries. Yet economic conditions were not the only cause of conflicts. Political corruption and repression affected many places as well. In addition, U.S. support for anticommunist but corrupt governments stirred nationalist passions in Guatemala, El Salvador, and Nicaragua.

Guatemala In 1952 Guatemala's president, Jacobo Arbenz, used land reform to take over large landholdings and distribute the land to peasants. This policy hurt the United Fruit Company, an American company that owned huge amounts of mostly uncultivated land in Guatemala.

Pressure from the United Fruit Company, along with concerns that Arbenz was a leftist, or radical, persuaded the U.S. government that Guatemala's president must be removed from power. The CIA <u>intervened</u> in a coup that toppled Arbenz in 1954 and replaced him with a military dictator. The coup was the start of nearly a half century of repressive dictatorships in Guatemala.

The harshness of the government and the end of social reforms upset many peasants. Some joined rural guerrilla forces, and civil war raged from the 1970s to the 1990s between the guerrillas and government troops. Finally, in 1996, a peace accord brought an end to the fighting.

El Salvador Civil war also struck El Salvador, where military dictatorships kept power through unfair elections and repression. In 1980 government assassins gunned down Archbishop Oscar Romero, an outspoken government critic, as he was leading mass. Romero was one of many priests in Latin America who supported Liberation Theology.

Romero's murder sparked a bloody civil war between Communist-supported guerrilla groups and the army. Peasant villagers were often caught in the middle as government-sponsored "death squads" roamed the countryside killing civilians suspected of aiding the opposition. The Reagan administration supported the Salvadoran government and the army by providing money and military aid. Violence continued into the 1990s.

ACADEMIC VOCABULARY
intervene to enter into an event to affect its outcome

---

❸ **What other revolutions arose in Central America?** *Guatemala—civil war between guerilla fighters and military; El Salvador—civil war between Communist-supported guerrillas and the army; Nicaragua—Sandinistas came to power, Contras, a rebel group, continued violent attacks on the country*

Other Revolutions

Explain What event sparked the civil war in El Salvador? *murder of Archbishop Oscar Romero, who supported Liberation Theology*

Analyze Why did the United States support the Somoza family and the Contras in Nicaragua? *Somozas opposed communism and the Contras opposed socialism.*

 CRF: Biography: Juan José Arévalo
 CRF: Primary Source: Nicaraguans Protest U.S. Support of the Contras
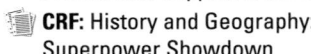 **CRF:** History and Geography: Superpower Showdown

---

Skills Focus: Drawing Conclusions
At Level

Reading Skill
Castro in Cuba

1. Have students review the information on this page about Cuba's relationship with the United States, focusing on the Cuban economy.

2. Have students use the information to create a political cartoon showing the problems in Cuba that resulted from the U.S. trade embargo and from Castro's economic policies. Students should create a cartoon and an appropriate caption.

3. Have students share their cartoons in small groups and then post the cartoons for all to see. **LS Visual-Spatial**

Alternative Assessment Handbook, Rubric 27: Political Cartoons

Answers

Reading Skills *economic inequality, political corruption, repression, and U.S. support for anticommunist but corrupt governments stirred nationalist passions in Central American countries*

Reading Check *Causes—social inequality, U.S. influence, revolts; Effects—access to health care and education, but restricted freedom, economy still suffers*

971

Close

Have students name the countries discussed in the section, and discuss the economic and political problems facing each country.

Review

Online Quiz, Section 1

Assess

SE Section 1 Assessment

Progress Assessment: Section 1 Quiz

Alternative Assessment Handbook

Reteach/Intervene

Interactive Reader and Study Guide, Section 1

Interactive Skills Tutor CD-ROM

Civil War

In 1979 leftist guerrillas in El Salvador launched a civil war against the country's military government. Here, a guerrilla fighter guards a roadblock in the country's rural interior, where much of the fighting took place.

 NEW YORK

CC Unit 7-H4 Nicaragua and the Sandinistas

Nicaragua Nicaragua also struggled with instability. Nicaragua had been ruled for four decades by members of the Somoza family. This wealthy family controlled about a quarter of the country's farmland. The Somozas' anti-communist views kept them in favor with the United States, but their corruption and violent repressive tactics alarmed many Nicaraguans. An anti-Somoza movement gained strength. In 1979 Somoza was forced to flee after a revolutionary group known as the **Sandinistas** took over the capital.

The Sandinistas ruled as a **junta** (HOON-tuh), a group of leaders who rule jointly. To deal with the country's many problems, they launched a program of economic and social reform. They set up some state-owned collective farms but also allowed private ownership of land. The Sandinistas also passed laws to protect workers' rights and began a Castro-style campaign to increase literacy. Unlike Castro, however, they allowed political opposition, both in the media and in elections.

Eventually, several factors pushed the Sandinistas to become more radical. The Reagan administration cut off financial aid to Nicaragua, leaving the Sandinistas to look to socialist countries for financial aid. In addition, a U.S.-trained and funded rebel group, the **Contras**, carried out a campaign of violence in Nicaragua that made it harder and harder for the junta to govern.

Eager to prove their government was still democratic in spite of its socialist leanings, the Sandinistas held an election in 1984. They were easily reelected. However, increasing economic troubles and violence continued throughout the 1980s.

READING CHECK **Make Generalizations** How did U.S. influence affect conflicts in Guatemala, El Salvador, and Nicaragua?

SECTION 1 ASSESSMENT

go.hrw.com
Online Quiz
Keyword: SHL LAT HP

Reviewing Ideas, Terms, and People

1. **a. Describe** What conditions in postwar Latin America made many countries politically unstable?
   b. Infer Why did **Liberation Theology** become popular in Latin America?
   c. Evaluate What was one benefit and one drawback of **import-substitution led industrialization**?

2. **a. Identify** Who is **Fidel Castro**? How did he come to power?
   b. Summarize How has the Cuban Revolution affected life for people in Cuba?
   c. Predict What challenges might Cuba's government face after Castro's rule has ended? Explain your answer.

3. **a. Recall** Why did the United States get involved in Guatemalan politics in the 1950s?
   b. Analyze What factors led to the failure of the **Sandinista** government?
   c. Support a Position Do you think the United States should have become involved in civil wars in Central America? Why or why not?

Critical Thinking

4. **Identify Cause and Effect** Using your notes, identify major causes and effects of revolutions and civil wars in Central America. How were these causes and effects similar and different from country to country?

	Cause	Effect
Cuba		
Guatemala		
El Salvador		
Nicaragua		

FOCUS ON WRITING

5. **Exposition** Imagine you are a citizen of Cuba, El Salvador, or Nicaragua. Write a short letter to a friend explaining the conflict in your country, identifying who is fighting, and analyzing what people are fighting for.

Answers

Reading Check *civil war, violence, some corrupt leaders overthrown, economic problems, some financial and military aid*

Section 1 Assessment Answers

1. **a.** poverty and inequality
   b. People hoped the Church would help solve economic and political problems.
   c. helped countries become more self-sufficient; countries relied on U.S. and other countries for investments, led to high debt

2. **a.** Cuba's leader; led revolt that forced Batista to flee, seized control of government
   b. virtually ended illiteracy, provided free health care; became Communist; restricted civil liberties; caused economic problems

c. possible answers—a democratic revolt; U.S. aid; end to trade embargo

3. **a.** A U.S. company risked losing land in a land reform movement.
   b. The U.S. cut off financial aid to Nicaragua, funded the Contras
   c. possible answers—Yes, the United States should support democracy and its own interests in Latin America; no, many Latin American leaders are elected and are trying to solve various problems.

4. Cuba—inequality, heavy U.S. influence; Communist dictator; Guatemala—U.S. helped overthrow president; military dictator, civil war; El Salvador—murder of archbishop; civil war; Nicaragua— Sandinistas seized power, war between the Sandinistas and Contras

5. Student letters should address the issues that faced Nicaragua, Cuba, or El Salvador.

2 The Rise of Dictatorships

BEFORE YOU READ

MAIN IDEA

Spiraling economic and social problems and political turmoil in Latin America led military leaders to seize power and install repressive regimes.

READING FOCUS

1. How did life change under dictatorships in Argentina?
2. What changes occurred during the dictatorship in Brazil?
3. What was life like in Chile during Pinochet's dictatorship?
4. How did dictatorships affect life in other countries?

KEY TERMS AND PEOPLE

Juan Perón
populist
hyperinflation
Augusto Pinochet
Manuel Noriega
Shining Path

 NEW YORK

PI 1.2 Students understand the development and connectedness of Western civilization and other civilizations and cultures in many areas of the world over time.

PI 3.1 Students analyze the roles and contributions of individuals and groups to social, political, economic, cultural, and religious practices and activities.

VOICE OF THE PEOPLE

▲ Evita waves to her admirers.

THE INSIDE STORY *Why was a dictator's wife so loved by her people?* To her admirers, Eva Perón was the voice of Argentina's poor working class. As her husband, Argentine president Juan Perón, became more and more powerful, Evita ("little Eva") never let him forget the workers—the people whose support had helped him rise to power.

Although she never held any official posts during her husband's presidency, Evita essentially ran the government's health and labor departments. Focusing on charity work, she created the Eva Perón foundation to help the poor. This foundation built hospitals, schools, orphanages, and other institutions to help Argentina's poor and needy citizens. In addition, Evita championed the rights of women.

In 1952 Evita died tragically from cancer at the age of 33. The nation was devastated. Massive crowds of mourners lined up for miles to attend her funeral. Even today Evita's popularity lives on in books, films, and a Broadway musical. ▪

Argentina

After World War II, when many countries around the world got rid of dictators, Argentina and other Latin American countries saw a rise of dictatorships. Many of these rulers did not come to power with the intent to rule as dictators. But social and economic conditions allowed them to take tremendous power at the expense of people's personal freedoms.

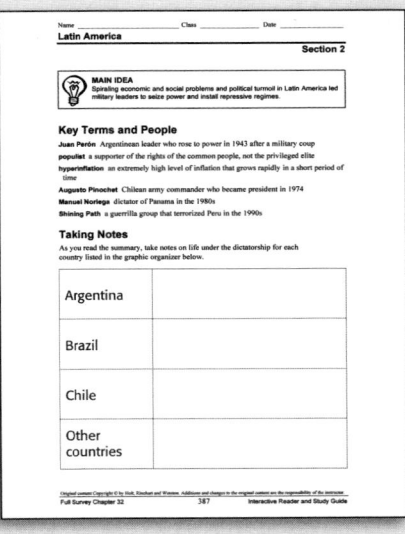

Teach the Main Idea

At Level

The Rise of Dictatorships

1. **Teach** Ask students the Reading Focus questions to teach this section.

2. **Apply** Organize the students into groups of four. Have each student scan one of the topics covered in the section and write down the main points. Have students share their notes and add the information about each topic covered in the section.

3. **Review** Have volunteers share the information and create a class outline of the section. Have students correct their own work and retain the notes and the outline as a study tool.

4. **Practice/Homework** Have students create an illustrated time line chronicling the important events discussed in the section.
   LS Verbal-Linguistic, Visual-Spatial

   📝 **Alternative Assessment Handbook,** Rubrics 14: Group Activity; and 36: Time Lines

① How did life change under dictatorships in Argentina? *the economy took a downturn, personal freedoms were denied, "dirty war" of violence and fear*

Argentina

Summarize How did the Peróns reform Argentina? *established minimum wage, eight-hour workday, paid vacations; built schools, hospitals, homeless shelters*

Draw Conclusions Why did the Argentinean government carry out the "dirty war"? *to eliminate opposition, maintain complete control over Argentina through fear and repression.*

📄 **CRF:** Biography: Enriqueta Barnes de Carlotto

Reading Like a Historian

Mothers of Plaza de Mayo The Mothers of Plaza de Mayo are still protesting. They are still on a mission to bring justice for their disappeared loved ones and they are tackling current events as well. This group of politically minded women continues to be a source of active resistance, whose movement is based on respect for human dignity and human life.

Answers

Reading Like a Historian 1. *less biased; written by outsider; perhaps favoring the point of view of those she interviewed;* **2.** *benefits—fresh in memory; disadvantages—can be emotionally charged, not placed within historical context;* **3.** *possible answer— might be a little biased in support of mothers who were hoping to find their children*

Take notes on life during the dictatorships in these countries.

Argentina
Brazil
Chile
Other countries

📺 **NEW YORK**

CC **Unit 7-H2a**
Perón in Argentina

CC **Unit 7-H2b**
Mothers of the Plaza de Mayo

Perónism Beginning in 1943, **Juan Perón** rose to power following a military coup. With the help of his wife, Eva, Perón quickly proved himself to be a **populist**, a supporter of the rights of the common people as opposed to the privileged elite. With Eva in charge of labor and social programs, Perón made radical changes. He created a minimum wage, an eight-hour workday, and paid vacations. He built schools, hospitals, and homeless shelters. A booming postwar economy helped pay for these benefits.

However, there was a downside to Perón's rule. He tried to boost industrialization, but the effort failed because of a lack of resources. He also placed the cattle and wheat industries under government control. Farm production plunged as a result, damaging the nation's economy. In addition, Perón ruled with an iron fist. He turned Argentina into a one-party state and suppressed opposition and freedom of speech. Perón had become a dictator.

Military Dictatorships Perón's eventual downfall in 1955 was followed by decades of economic and political turmoil. For many years, right-wing military dictatorships ruled Argentina. They struggled with declining industry and rising unemployment, inflation, and foreign debt. Meanwhile, they cracked down on dissent by severely limiting people's personal freedoms.

Argentina entered a particularly ugly period in history from 1976 to 1983. During those years, the government carried out a "dirty war," as it was known, against suspected dissidents. It was a secret war carried out in the middle of the night. Soldiers seized people from their homes and took them to detention centers, where they were tortured and often killed. Some 10,000 to 30,000 people vanished during this time. The victims included both critics of the government and those falsely accused of being critics.

Reading like a Historian

Mothers of Plaza de Mayo

Evaluating Historical Interpretation When historians interpret the past, they build on and add to the knowledge, information, and sources of other scholars who have come before them. Through this process, historians arrive at their own interpretation of events based on their sources and their personal background and experiences.

The selection here is one historian's interpretation of the role of the Mothers of Plaza de Mayo. To evaluate this historical interpretation, think about

- the author of the source
- the date the source was created
- the author's background or perspective

Skills FOCUS **READING LIKE A HISTORIAN**

1. **Author** Jo Fisher based her book on interviews with more than 40 mothers and grandmothers in Argentina. How does that affect the author's credibility?

2. **Date** What benefits and drawbacks are there for historical interpretation when it occurs soon after an event takes place?

3. **Background** The author developed a close connection with the mothers and their cause. How might that affect her interpretation?

See **Skills Handbook, p. H32**

> The decision to install a permanent weekly presence in Plaza de Mayo was an act of desperation rather than one of calculated political resistance. It was a sense of desperation which the women believed only other mothers who had lost their children would share. . . . The Mothers, however, who had no legal or political expertise, recognized that their only weapon was direct action. They were committed to their illegal meetings in the square. Only by demonstrating their collective strength would they have any chance of breaking through the wall of silence erected by the authorities . . .
>
> —Jo Fisher, from *Mothers of the Disappeared,* 1989

This book was published in 1989, soon after the events it describes had taken place.

Differentiating Instruction

Below Level

Special Education Students

Materials: plain paper, pencils

1. Review the information in the text about the "dirty war" and the efforts of the Mothers of Plaza de Mayo.

2. Have students create a "Child Missing" poster for a young Argentine man or woman who became a victim of the "dirty war."

3. As an extension or for more advanced students, have students write an obituary for the person they have drawn in the poster.

4. Have students share their posters and obituaries with the class. **LS Visual-Spatial**

📄 **Alternative Assessment Handbook**, Rubrics 3: Artwork; and 28: Posters

Desperate relatives tried to find out what happened to their loved ones. A group of mothers of the disappeared marched every week in the Plaza de Mayo, a square outside government buildings in Buenos Aires. Although they did not get the answers they wanted from the government, they did manage to bring national and international attention to the tactics of Argentina's military dictatorship.

READING CHECK **Find the Main Idea** How did dictatorships affect society in Argentina?

Brazil

Brazil followed a path similar to Argentina's. For a while, however, it seemed like Brazil would take a more stable and democratic route. With the death of a dictator in 1954, Juscelino Kubitschek (zhoo-se-LEE-noh KOO-bih-shek) came to power in a free election. Kubitschek promised "fifty years of progress in five." Foreign investment flowed into Brazil and helped the president achieve his goal. The results of this economic progress can be seen in the capital city of Brasília. The city, built in just three years at a cost of about $2 billion, became a symbol of pride and modernity.

The modernization effort, however, bankrupted Brazil's economy. As a result, military rulers seized control in 1964. For a time, they achieved success, creating the "Brazilian miracle" of 1968 to 1973. Industrial exports, farming, and mining grew. In fact, during this time Brazil's economy grew faster than any other in the world.

To achieve such rapid growth, Brazil's military dictatorship froze wages. Living standards declined sharply as a result. If people complained about the government, they risked becoming victims of government death squads that kidnapped, tortured, and killed.

As opposition to the military dictatorship grew, the economy crashed again. When oil prices rose in the 1970s, the economy spiraled into debt and **hyperinflation**, an extremely high level of inflation that grows rapidly in a short period of time. By 1990 the inflation rate was more than 2,500 percent.

READING CHECK **Identify Cause and Effect** What caused Brazil's economic problems?

HISTORY and Economics

Budgeting Money and Preventing Debt

Money is a limited resource, and using it wisely requires a plan for spending called a budget. A budget that is carefully planned and followed can help ensure that needs and wants are provided for appropriately. Responsible budgeting can also help prevent debt.

Budgeting and Debt in History In the 1960s and 1970s Brazil's leaders decided to borrow money to pay for the development of the nation's industries. They believed accumulating this debt was justified because future economic growth would create trade surpluses that the country could use to repay its loans. But that did not happen. Instead, the cost of oil skyrocketed in 1973 and 1979. Higher oil prices made industrialization dramatically more expensive than Brazil's leader had planned on when making the country's budget. As a result, Brazil's national and foreign debt spiraled out of control.

BRAZIL'S FOREIGN DEBT, 1965–1985

Sources: *The Brazilian Economy: Growth and Development;*
A Dívida Externa Brasileira 1964–1982: Evolução e Crise

Budgeting and Debt in Your Life In your life, you will also need to budget to pay the bills and stay out of debt. For example, will you take out loans to pay for college? How much debt should you take on to buy a car or a house? Answering questions like these will require you to carefully budget your earnings and expenses. Of course, you will not be able to anticipate all the factors that may affect your personal finances in the future. As a result, you may decide that the best approach will be to keep your budget balanced, take on as little debt as possible, and have enough savings to cover any emergencies.

Draw Conclusions Why is it important for people to budget their money?

Reading Focus

❷ What changes occurred during the dictatorship in Brazil? *incurred great debt, living standards declined; death squads; economy crashed, inflation skyrocketed*

Brazil

Explain Why did military leaders seize control of the government? *Modernization had crippled the economy; military leaders thought they could fix the problem.*

Evaluate Do you think Brazil's phenomenal economic growth hurt or helped the country? *possible answers— helped: exports, farming, mining expanded; hurt: with wage freezes, living standards declined*

History and Economics
Budgeting Money and Preventing Debt

The Cruzado Plan In 1982, Brazil could no longer borrow money internationally and so it started to borrow domestically. By 1986 Brazil's domestic and international debt had risen to the same level. To help reduce inflation and to solve its economic woes, Brazil began the Cruzado Plan and froze prices and wages. The results were that inflation was brought down dramatically, but Brazil's currency was overvalued, which led to new economic problems.

Skills Focus: Identifying Main Idea and Details   **Below Level**

Reading Skill   **Standard English Mastery**
Current Events in Brazil

Materials: newspapers, magazines, scissors

1. Have the students review the information about Brazil's economy.

2. Have students find an article about Brazil in magazines, newspapers, or from reliable online sources.

3. Have students answer the following questions about their articles on a separate piece of paper: Who was involved? What happened?

Where did it happen? When did it happen? Why is it important?

4. Have students use the information from their answers to these questions to write a summary of their articles.

5. Have volunteers share their summaries and discuss as a class. **LS** **Verbal-Linguistic**

📃 **Alternative Assessment Handbook**, Rubric 42: Writing to Inform

Answers

History and Economics *possible answer—so they can keep debt at a minimum and become less dependent upon others*

Reading Check *(top) people lived in fear; economy suffered; (bottom) foreign investment, excessive domestic spending, dependence on imported petroleum products*

975

3 What was life like in Chile during Pinochet's dictatorship? *civil rights restricted, no free speech, no opposition tolerated*

Chile

Describe What changes did Allende make in Chile? *improvements in housing, education, health care, land reform*

Compare How was repression in Chile similar to repression in Argentina and Brazil? *government used violence as a tool to keep power; thousands of people were arrested and disappeared*

 CRF: Literature: *My Invented Country*

4 How did dictatorships affect life in other countries? *caused turmoil, economic disasters, and instability, raised international concern*

Other Dictatorships

Explain Why was President Aristide unsuccessful? *was unable to solve Haiti's economic problems*

Summarize Why did the United States intervene in Panama? *believed that Manuel Noreiga, a drug smuggler, would abuse his power over the Panama Canal*

Answers

The Pinochet Regime *displaying images of loved ones*

Reading Skills *cause—socialist-style policies; effect—Pinochet became dictator*

Reading Check *economic problems, socialist-style policies, CIA provided funding and training to opposition, a coup took place*

The Pinochet Regime

Augusto Pinochet led a military coup in Chile in 1973.

During Pinochet's regime, thousands of people disappeared. Their relatives continue to protest against the government, demanding to know what happened. *What tactics are the protesters using?*

Chile

As in Argentina and Brazil, economic problems led to drastic changes in Chile's government. Like so many other Latin American countries, Chile spent a period of time under the rule of a dictator.

Allende's Presidency In 1970 Chileans elected the leftist Salvador Allende president. Allende tried to improve the lives of the working class and stimulate the economy. He spent huge amounts of money on housing, education, and health care. The government broke up large estates and distributed the land to peasants. It also nationalized foreign-owned companies. For a time, Allende's measures were successful and widely popular.

However, Allende soon ran into trouble. Industrial and farm production fell, prices rose, and food shortages spread. In addition, Allende's leftist policies alienated business owners and worried the U.S. government. The CIA began providing secret funding and military training to opposition groups in hopes of triggering a coup.

As the economy failed and more people turned against Allende, the military rebelled. On September 11, 1973, fighter planes bombed the presidential palace. Allende and more than 3,000 others died in the coup.

READING SKILLS

Understanding Causes and Effects What was one cause and one effect of the 1973 coup?

The Pinochet Regime Several weeks before the coup, Allende had appointed a new commander in chief of the army, **Augusto Pinochet** (peen-oh-SHAY). General Pinochet was closely involved in the coup. He took command of the new military junta and became president in 1974.

Pinochet moved quickly to destroy the opposition. He disbanded congress, suspended the constitution, and banned opposition parties. He also censored the media. Within three years, an estimated 130,000 people were arrested for opposing the government. As in Argentina and Brazil, the government used violence as a tool to keep power. Thousands of people disappeared, were tortured, or fled into exile.

Despite the political crackdown, during this period the economy experienced several periods of rapid growth. Pinochet's government promoted capitalism, and exports grew.

READING CHECK **Summarize** How did events in Chile lead to a dictatorship?

Other Dictatorships

Military coups and elections brought other dictators to power throughout Latin America from the 1960s to the 1980s. These dictators had negative effects on their countries and caused serious international concern.

Skills Focus: Making Generalizations

Below Level

Reading Skill
Art as Protest

Materials: construction paper, art supplies, photographs of *arpilleras*, (a type of Latin American tapestry)

1. Display the sample arpilleras for all to see. Tell students that arpilleras are tapestries created to show daily life, and that they were first used as a form of protest in Chile.

2. Have students make their own arpillera depicting the daily life of a person living in Chile during the military dictatorship.

3. Have students share their work in small groups or with the entire class. **LS Visual-Spatial**

Alternative Assessment Handbook, Rubric 3: Artwork

Haiti In Haiti, one family headed a dictatorship for 28 years. In 1957 François Duvalier was elected president, but he quickly began to repress any opposition. When he died, his son carried on the dictatorship.

The corruption of the Duvaliers made Haiti's bad economy even worse. In 1986 riots broke out in protest, and Duvalier was forced to flee. After several years of turmoil, Haitians elected Jean-Bertrand Aristide president in 1990. He had a plan to improve living standards for the poor. However, his presidency lasted just seven months before he was pushed from power by a military coup.

Aristide returned to power in 1994 when, faced with an invasion by U.S. troops, the Haitian military stepped down. But although he was popular with the poor, he was unable to solve the country's economic problems and was eventually pushed from power again.

Panama During the 1980s Panama came under the control of a dictator, **Manuel Noriega**. Noriega brutally crushed his enemies and used the country as a base for drug smuggling.

Noriega caused international concern. The Panama Canal, which had been under the control of the United States since its construction, was scheduled to be handed over to Panama in 1999. Because of the economic importance of the canal to worldwide shipping, Noriega's misrule posed a threat to worldwide economic interests.

In 1989 the United States sent troops to Panama City to arrest Noriega. Noriega surrendered and was sent to a prison in Florida on charges of drug trafficking. Democratic elections in Panama followed in 1994, and transfer of the canal occurred smoothly in 1999.

Peru In 1990 Peru faced the challenges of a poor economy and a guerrilla group known as the **Shining Path** that was terrorizing the countryside. In these conditions, Alberto Fujimori won the presidential election. Fujimori took drastic measures to improve the economy and stop the Shining Path. When congress complained that he had abused his power as president, Fujimori disbanded congress and suspended the constitution.

Although Fujimori had essentially become a dictator, Peru held elections in 1995. With the economy booming and significant progress being made against guerrilla activity, Fujimori won again. However, scandals and fraud eventually forced him to resign after the election of 2000.

READING CHECK Compare What did the dictators in Haiti, Panama, and Peru have in common?

NEW YORK

CC Unit 7-H8
Return of the Panama Canal

SECTION 2 ASSESSMENT

go.hrw.com
Online Quiz
Keyword: SHL LAT HP

Reviewing Ideas, Terms, and People

1. a. Define What is a **populist**?
   b. Infer Why do you think Argentina's military dictatorships cracked down on dissent?
   c. Make Judgments Do you think the results achieved by the mothers of the disappeared were worth the risk of protesting against the government? Explain your answer.

2. a. Describe What was life like in Brazil during the military dictatorships?
   b. Analyze What led to **hyperinflation** in Brazil?
   c. Elaborate How might Brazil have avoided its economic troubles?

3. a. Identify Who became dictator of Chile after the coup that ended Allende's rule?
   b. Sequence What events led to a military coup in Chile?
   c. Support a Position What is your reaction to the argument that strong, repressive leadership was needed to achieve economic progress in Chile?

4. a. Identify Who was **Manuel Noriega**?

   b. Infer What role did the **Shining Path** play in allowing Fujimori to essentially become a dictator?
   c. Elaborate How might the situation in Panama have been different if the Panama Canal were not at stake?

Critical Thinking

5. Compare and Contrast Choose two countries from this section. Using your notes and a graphic organizer like this one, describe similarities and differences between those countries.

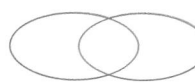

FOCUS ON WRITING

6. Description Imagine you live in Chile in 1974. Write a short journal entry describing the recent changes in your government and how those changes might affect Chile's future.

LATIN AMERICA **977**

977

3 Democratic and Economic Reforms

BEFORE YOU READ

 NEW YORK

MAIN IDEA

In the 1980s, repressive regimes in Latin America fell, and more moderate elected leaders brought some measure of political and economic progress.

READING FOCUS

1. How did democracy return to Latin America?

2. How has democracy in Mexico changed in recent years?

3. What have been the results of market reforms in Latin America?

KEY TERMS AND PEOPLE

Violeta Chamorro
North American Free Trade Agreement (NAFTA)
Vicente Fox
Hugo Chávez

PI 3.3 Students examine the social/cultural, political, economic, and religious norms and values of Western and other world cultures.

THE INSIDE STORY

How did a dictator's attempt to distract his people lead to war?

In early 1982 Argentina's military government was faced with a weakening economy and public outcry over the mysterious disappearances of government critics. Argentina's government, led by General Leopoldo Galtieri, wanted to distract the country from its problems. So Galtieri started a war. On April 2, about 9,000 Argentine troops invaded the British-controlled Falkland Islands in the South Atlantic, about 300 miles off Argentina's coast.

The Falklands—known as the Malvinas in Argentina—consist of two main islands and hundreds of tiny ones. The 2,000 or so Falklands residents were mainly sheep-farming British citizens. Great Britain and Argentina had both claimed these small islands for about 150 years. But Galtieri wanted to take them from the British once and for all.

Galtieri's political gamble failed. First, Galtieri did not expect the British to fight back, but they did. Second, he did not count on the role the United States would play in the conflict. Argentina and the United States had recently enjoyed good relations, and Galtieri thought the United States would remain neutral. Instead, the United States supported Great Britain.

In addition to these political miscalculations, Argentina's armed forces suffered a major defeat. The country's poorly trained troops were no match for the British army. The situation quickly got so bad that some Argentine commanders abandoned their soldiers. The British easily

recaptured the islands and took many Argentine soldiers prisoner. About 700 Argentines and some 250 British troops lost their lives in the fighting.

To make things worse, military leaders lied to the public about the war by giving them false reports of victory. When the truth was discovered, the ruling military was humiliated and discredited. Although the war lasted just 74 days, it helped bring down the dictatorship. ◼

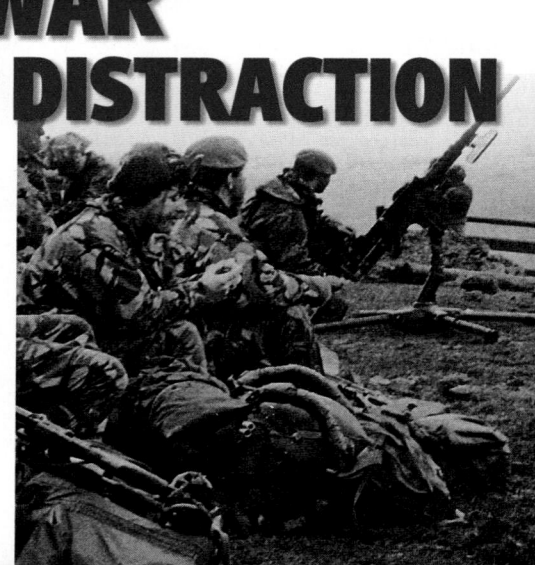

A WAR OF DISTRACTION

Return of Democracy

After decades of struggling through civil wars and conflicts, dictatorships across Latin America started falling in the 1980s and 1990s. Voters were finally able to elect leaders who put an end to military rule, and moderate civilian politicians began a series of political and economic reforms.

The Failures of Dictatorships Latin America's military governments fell for a number of reasons. One major reason was that many had failed to achieve social and economic reforms. Poverty, malnutrition, and infant mortality remained high throughout most of the region. As a result, poor, landless peasants continued to stream into cities and settled in giant shantytowns in search of work. Even the "Brazilian miracle" had gone sour. It turned out to be a miracle for the few—the military, large landowners, and wealthy businesspeople.

In addition to failing to improve people's economic lives, the dictatorships did not manage to bring about stability and security. In Central America, death squads roamed cities and the countryside while civil wars raged. In South America, civil rights were severely repressed. Governments in Argentina, Brazil, and Chile dealt with opposition through mysterious disappearances, torture, and killings carried out by the military dictatorships. Some people began to demand a change.

British soldiers fight Argentine forces in the Falkland Islands. ▼

FACES OF HISTORY

Violeta CHAMORRO
1929–

Violeta Chamorro began her political career as a member of Nicaragua's Sandinista government. However, she soon became an outspoken critic of the Marxist policies of the Sandinistas.

In 1990 the Sandinistas allowed a presidential election, and Chamorro defeated the Sandinista candidate, Daniel Ortega, to become the first female president in Central America. During her presidency, she worked to unify the country, which had been deeply divided by civil war. She brought the war to an end and reversed many Sandinista policies, such as Sandinista control of the military and restrictions on freedom of the press.

Summarize How did Violeta Chamorro change politics in Nicaragua?

A Peaceful Transition Despite this history of violence and repression, the return of democracy in Latin America was actually fairly peaceful. The change came when a combination of internal and external forces began to apply pressure for reform. International lenders, including the International Monetary Fund (IMF), the World Bank, and large corporate banks, began to demand changes in the way countries were governed as a condition for receiving loans. Also, pro-democracy groups inside and outside the region, such as the Organization of American States, began calling for countries to restore voting rights and allow political opposition. Military leaders began to realize that they needed to relax some of the restrictions on society and integrate some limited freedoms into their policies.

Given a chance to vote, people did. Countries across the region voted out the military and voted in new civilian governments.

Democracy in Brazil returned in the early 1970s. Argentina followed after the Falklands War in 1982. Central American countries returned to relative calm in the 1980s and 1990s with the election of moderate governments, such as that of **Violeta Chamorro** in Nicaragua. In Chile, which enjoyed more economic success than most of the region, the Pinochet regime fell in 1990.

TAKING NOTES

Take notes on the chain of events that brought democratic and economic reforms to Latin America.

ACADEMIC VOCABULARY

integrate to blend or join together

READING CHECK **Identify Cause and Effect** What factors brought about the return of democracy in Latin America?

LATIN AMERICA **979**

② How has democracy in Mexico changed in recent years? *A non-PRI president in office; signing of NAFTA*

Democracy in Mexico

Describe What is the purpose of NAFTA? *improve economies of Canada, U.S., and Mexico by eliminating tariffs among the three nations*

Analyze How did PRI retain its control over the Mexican government? *fraudulent elections, use of force, bought votes*

Two timely issues are examined in *Free Trade and the Environment: Mexico, NAFTA, and Beyond*. Author Kevin Gallagher argues that Mexico's free trade policies have had environmental benefits and have not resulted in lax environmental standards nor in incentives for polluting industries, as others have suggested would happen.

Free Trade and the Environment: Mexico, NAFTA, and Beyond by Kevin Gallagher. Stanford University Press, 2004.

Democracy in Mexico

Mexico's path to democracy was different from other countries in the region. Unlike most other Latin American countries, Mexico experienced relative political stability in the second half of the 1900s. Although Mexico was never really a dictatorship, it was not very democratic either.

One-Party Rule For more than 70 years, the Institutional Revolutionary Party, or PRI, ruled Mexico with almost no opposition. It controlled congress, and PRI candidates won every presidential election. Often these political victories were achieved through fraud and force. At election time, candidates gave gifts of food and other goods to poor people to win their votes.

In spite of the political situation, Mexico's economy remained quite strong. Boosted by Mexico's rich oil reserves, industry grew for many years. However, because of the PRI economic policies, Mexican industry became increasingly dominated by foreign companies. As these companies' profits increased, more money went to foreign countries. Mexico's foreign debt grew tremendously, and poverty and inequality remained.

Demands for Reform Worsening economic conditions and growing frustration with political corruption left the ruling party open to take all the blame. In addition, a number of crises struck Mexico that caused more dissatisfaction with the PRI.

The first crisis occurred in 1968 when police and military forces opened fire on a group of peaceful student protesters. The event left hundreds dead and wounded. To make matters worse, the government tried to cover up the extent of the tragedy. A Mexican teacher explained how the massacre affected people's views of the government:

HISTORY'S VOICES

❝The . . . incident led those who sincerely believed that great improvements had been made in our democratic institutions, and that the political and social system of our country was basically sound except for certain minor failings and mistakes, to re-examine all their most cherished beliefs.❞

—Elena Quijano de Rendón, quoted in *Massacre in Mexico*, by Elena Poniatowska

Another crisis occurred in the 1980s when

NEW YORK

CC Unit 7-C6
North American Free Trade Agreement (NAFTA)

Changes in Mexico

Mexico has made much progress toward a fairer and more inclusive political system in recent years. No longer dominated by one party, Mexico's government is more democratic today and is working to improve the country's economy.

▲ Mexican riot police arrest student protesters in 1968 following violent clashes that killed as many as 300 people.

world oil prices fell. Mexico's economy relied heavily on oil production and exports, and the fall in prices caused oil revenues to be cut in half. The country fell into a severe economic decline. High inflation and unemployment meant that many people struggled to support themselves. When a major earthquake destroyed large parts of Mexico City in 1985, the huge cost of rebuilding created more problems for the government and the economy. Public dissatisfaction with the PRI increased.

Events of the 1990s brought even more concern to Mexicans. In 1992 Mexico, the United States, and Canada signed the **North American Free Trade Agreement (NAFTA)**, a free-trade agreement that eliminated tariffs on trade between the three countries. NAFTA was designed to improve the countries' economies, but many Mexicans feared the economic effects of increased competition from foreign imports.

In 1994 a peasant uprising in the Mexican state of Chiapas and the government's decision to devalue the Mexican currency again shook the public's confidence. As more Mexicans faced new hardships in their daily lives, something had to change.

Skills Focus: Analyzing Primary Sources

At Level

Reading Like a Historian Skill
Mexico's Elections, 2006

Research Required

Materials: plain paper, colored markers

1. Have students conduct outside research using reliable print and online sources to learn more about the 2006 presidential candidates in Mexico, their parties, and their platforms.

2. Have students use the information from their research to prepare a campaign slogan for one of the principal candidates.

3. Organize students into small groups, based on the candidate they selected, and have groups create a campaign poster for each candidate using their slogans.

4. Have volunteers share their posters, and put them on display in the classroom.
   LS Visual-Spatial

📖 **Alternative Assessment Handbook**, Rubrics 28: Posters; and 34: Slogans and Banners

Mexico Then	Mexico Now
One political party, the PRI, controlled congress.	The PRI is just one of many political parties to have representation in congress.
The PRI candidate won every presidential election.	Mexicans have elected presidents from opposition parties.
Elections were characterized by corruption and fraud.	Elections are much more open and are closely monitored for fraud.
The government crushed dissent, sometimes violently.	People can openly criticize the government.
Mexico had tremendous foreign debt, inflation, and unemployment.	Economic problems remain, but foreign debt, inflation, and unemployment are down.
Many industries were nationalized, and imports and exports were limited.	Imports and exports are up, and Mexicans have access to more goods.

Felipe Calderón won Mexico's closely contested presidential election in 2006. ▶

A New Era Change began in 1997 when opposition parties won a number of seats in congress. In 2000, voters ended 71 years of PRI rule when they elected as president **Vicente Fox**, a member of the conservative PAN party.

Fox faced the challenge of creating a functioning government and stable economy. In addition, he worked to end the uprising in Chiapas, end corruption, and improve relations with the United States. Fox made progress on most of his goals. However, relations between the two countries were strained in 2006 when political leaders in the United States worked to reform immigration laws and improve border security. Fox argued that both countries needed to address the economic disparities that encouraged illegal immigration and to recognize the status of immigrant workers in the United States.

Mexico maintained its commitment to democracy with elections in 2006. Felipe Calderón, of the conservative PAN party, won an extremely close race. He faced the recurring challenge of improving Mexico's economy.

READING CHECK **Find the Main Idea** In what way was Mexico not very democratic until 2000?

Market Reforms

The shift to democracy that swept through countries from Mexico to Argentina brought economic changes as well. Under pressure from Western banks, deeply indebted Latin American countries began a series of reform measures in the 1990s. These measures were difficult, but they held out the promise of economic progress and stability. The reforms included

- drastically cutting government spending, including funding for social programs
- ending some government subsidies of businesses
- selling government services to private enterprise
- returning inefficient, government-controlled businesses to private ownership
- strengthening regional trade agreements and establishing new ones.

These cost-cutting, free-market measures were intended to stabilize shaky economies by reducing inflation and expanding exports. They were also expected to enable countries to pay their debts.

ACADEMIC VOCABULARY

security freedom from danger or fear

LATIN AMERICA **981**

Market Reforms

Recall How has the gap between rich and poor changed? *It has gotten worse.*
Draw Conclusions What led to the elections of leftist-leaning leaders in the early 2000s? *inability of existing governments to solve economic problems*

Info to Know

Latin American Poverty Though poverty levels are still high, Latin America is making progress. In 2003 the total number of people living in poverty was about 44 percent, but by 2005 it had dropped to about 40 percent. Latin American economies have been growing; in 2004, economies grew 5.6 percent, the largest increase in 25 years. The infant mortality rate has dropped from 43 deaths per 1000 in 1990 to 25 death per 1000 in 2003.

🔲 **Map Transparency**: Poverty in Latin America

Primary Source

"Brazil has rediscovered itself, and this coming together is visible in the enthusiasm felt throughout society and in the mobilization of the country to deal with the enormous problems ahead."
—Luis Inácio Lula da Silva, in a speech at the World Economic Forum, Davos, Switzerland, 2003

"We have to reinvent socialism. It can't be the kind of socialism that we saw in the Soviet Union, but it will emerge as we develop new systems that are built on cooperation, not competition."
—Hugo Chávez, in a speech at the World Social Forum, Porto Alegre, Brazil, 2005

Answers

Interpreting Maps *Lowest—Brazil; Chile; Dominican Republic; Highest— Bolivia, Guatemala, Suriname*

Reading Check *by electing leftist- leaning governments or those who are sympathetic to the plight of the poor*

982

Results of Market Reforms The free-market reforms of the 1990s had mixed results. Many countries experienced economic growth and stability as private enterprise became stronger, but others suffered.

Some successes occurred in Brazil and Chile. Brazil's inflation fell from quadruple digits in 1994 to less than 7 percent in 2006. In Chile, reforms cut the poverty rate in half between 1990 and 2003. In addition, fruit exports soared as new markets opened. Business owners celebrated the economic changes. Reassured bankers, as well as international lenders such as the International Monetary Fund and the World Bank, loaned billions of dollars for increased economic development in Latin America.

Struggles continued in other parts of Latin America. Overall, exports from the region generally remained sluggish, as many countries were dependent on single commodities.

NEW YORK

CC **Unit 7-H7**
Latin American immigration to the United States

THE IMPACT TODAY

Many people from Latin America migrate to the United States hoping for economic opportunities they do not have at home.

In addition, the many reform measures caused hardships in some countries.

One country that suffered from these reform measures was Argentina. Once viewed as a model for economic growth and stability, Argentina experienced a deep recession in 2001 and 2002. When the country could not pay its multi-billion-dollar debt, the president responded by devaluing Argentina's currency. Therefore, people's money was suddenly worth less than it was before. As a result, banks failed, and the unemployment rate reached more than 20 percent. Many middle-class people who had held good jobs suddenly found themselves struggling to buy basic necessities. By the end of 2003, however, the economy had mostly stabilized once more.

Even where market reforms have benefited national economies, many people have not felt the positive effects. For example, poverty is still widespread in Latin America. Nearly one-third of the population lives on less than two dollars a day. In addition, the gap between rich and poor has widened. In 2003 about 10 percent of the region's population earned nearly half of all income.

Still, supporters of market reforms insist that the reforms simply have not gone far enough or had enough time to make an impact. They argue that key elements of reform, such as laws to protect property rights and business contracts, have not been made. Also, political corruption cripples businesses in much of Latin America.

Reactions to Market Reforms Latin Americans' dissatisfaction with economic problems and with their governments' seeming inability to solve them has led to more political and economic shifts in the region. Starting in the late 1990s elections brought populist, left-leaning leaders to power in some countries.

In 1998 Venezuelans elected **Hugo Chávez** president. Popular among the poor, Chávez set out to eliminate poverty. To do so, however, he rejected certain aspects of capitalism. Chávez's policies appear to have had limited success, but problems remain. Also, critics both within and outside Venezuela are concerned that he has turned the country away from democracy and toward dictatorship.

Another dramatic shift occurred in Bolivia. There, indigenous leader Evo Morales defeated

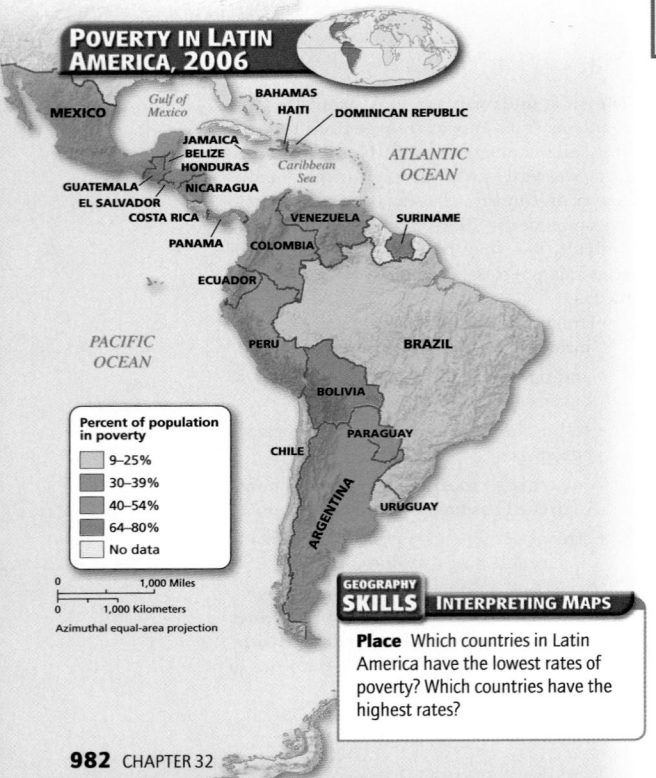

POVERTY IN LATIN AMERICA, 2006

Percent of population in poverty
- 9–25%
- 30–39%
- 40–54%
- 64–80%
- No data

0   1,000 Miles
0   1,000 Kilometers
Azimuthal equal-area projection

GEOGRAPHY SKILLS **INTERPRETING MAPS**

Place Which countries in Latin America have the lowest rates of poverty? Which countries have the highest rates?

982 CHAPTER 32

Skills Focus: Analyzing Maps

Below Level

Social Studies Skill
Poverty in Latin America

1. To help students understand the map on this page, ask: Which country or countries have the highest percentage of poverty? Which country or countries have the lowest percentage?

2. Have students create a chart like the one shown to record poverty levels in each country. **LS** **Visual-Spatial**

📖 **Alternative Assessment Handbook,** Rubrics 7: Charts; and 21: Map Reading

Country	% of population living in poverty
Argentina	*30–39%*
Brazil	*5-25%*
Chile	*5-25%*

Latin American Economies Today

Economies are growing in most Latin American countries today. As industries become more competitive and exports and imports grow, the middle class is expanding and people are gaining more access to consumer goods. Still, not everyone benefits from these changes. *Why do you think an improved national economy might not benefit everyone?*

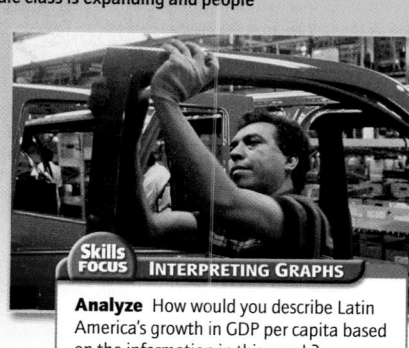

◀ An autoworker assembles trucks in Mexico.

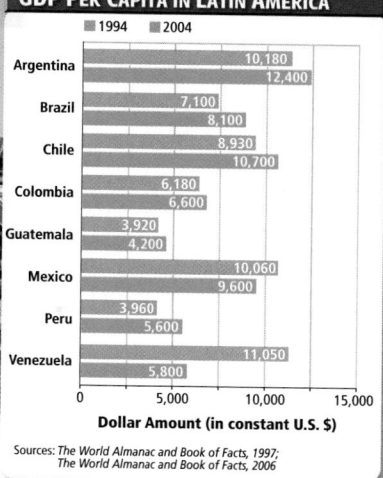

GDP PER CAPITA IN LATIN AMERICA

■ 1994 ■ 2004

Country	1994	2004
Argentina	10,180	12,400
Brazil	7,100	8,100
Chile	8,930	10,700
Colombia	6,180	6,600
Guatemala	3,920	4,200
Mexico	10,060	9,600
Peru	3,960	5,600
Venezuela	11,050	5,800

Dollar Amount (in constant U.S. $)

Skills FOCUS INTERPRETING GRAPHS

Analyze How would you describe Latin America's growth in GDP per capita based on the information in this graph?

Sources: *The World Almanac and Book of Facts, 1997; The World Almanac and Book of Facts, 2006*

a former IMF official in a 2005 election. Morales nationalized the natural gas industry in an effort to enable all Bolivians to benefit from their resources. He also supported farmers who grew coca leaves, which have traditional uses but can also be used to make cocaine.

In Brazil voters turned to a leftist president when they elected Luiz Inácio Lula da Silva in 2002. They hoped that Lula, a former union leader, would be sympathetic to the problems of the poor. Although people were concerned that Lula's former ties to the Communist Party would lead Brazil in the wrong direction, Lula managed to balance the interests of social reformers and businesses.

READING CHECK Make Generalizations
How have people in Latin America reacted to market reforms in recent years?

SECTION 3 ASSESSMENT

go.hrw.com
Online Quiz
Keyword: SHL LAT HP

Reviewing Ideas, Terms, and People

1. a. Describe What failures caused the fall of dictators in Latin America?
b. Analyze What factors made possible a peaceful transition to democracy?
c. Make Judgments Did foreign countries have a right to push for political changes in Latin America? Explain your answer.

2. a. Describe Why was the election of **Vicente Fox** significant for Mexico?
b. Sequence What were the major crises facing Mexico, in chronological order, that led to the end of one-party rule?
c. Make Judgments Several crises helped bring about the end of PRI rule. Were Mexicans right to blame their government for the situation in their country? Explain your answer.

3. a. Describe Describe two market reforms that took place in Latin America.

b. Analyze What were the positive and negative effects of the economic reforms of the 1990s?
c. Predict How do you think the move toward leftist leaders might affect Latin America in the future?

Critical Thinking
4. Identify Cause and Effect Using your notes, fill in a graphic organizer like the one below with at least two main causes of democratic and economic reform in Latin America.

Cause	
Cause	→ Democratic and Economic Reform

FOCUS ON SPEAKING

5. Persuasion Imagine you are a citizen of a Latin American country in the 1970s or 1980s. Write a short speech explaining why there is a need for political or economic reform in your country.

LATIN AMERICA **983**

Section 3 Assessment Answers

1. a. did not solve economic and social problems, death squads, repression of civil rights
b. internal and external pressure; new requirements for loans; pro-democracy groups
c. possible answer—Yes, they forced governments to institute basic human rights and civil liberties.

2. a. he was the first non-PRI president in 71 years; fair election
b. 1968, police attack student protesters; 1980s, oil prices fell, severe economic

decline; 1985, devastating earthquake in Mexico City; 1992, NAFTA; 1994, peasant uprising in Chiapas, devaluation of currency
c. possible answer—Not entirely, the drop in oil prices and the earthquake created severe economic hardships.

3. a. cost-cutting, free-market measures; turning government enterprises to private ownership; ending some government subsidies of businesses
b. positive—inflation slowed; money flowed in from outside sources; negative—wide-

spread poverty; gap between rich and poor widened
c. possible answers—curtailment of human rights, political instability

4. pressure from IMF and World Bank; pro-democracy groups; military leaders began to relax restrictions

5. Speeches should include government-sponsored violence, repression of civil rights, and growing poverty.

983

Info to Know

NAFTA NAFTA has not been a complete success in all of Mexico. Guillermo Perry, World Bank Chief Economist for Latin America and the Caribbean has said the following: "NAFTA definitely further plugged Mexico into the most dynamic economy in the world, but the country's development across the 1990s, including the NAFTA period, was unequal … The most developed and competitive regions and sectors have clearly benefited from the trade liberalization, while those lagging behind have not. Extending the benefits of greater integration [to] all society remains the challenge."

NAFTA

Historical Context The four documents below represent different views of the effect the North American Free Trade Agreement (NAFTA) has had on Mexico.

Task Study the selections and answer the questions that follow. After you have studied all the documents, you will be asked to write an essay explaining whether NAFTA has been good or bad for Mexico. You will need to use evidence from these selections and from the chapter to support the position you take.

NEW YORK STANDARDS

PI 1.3 Students analyze historic events from around the world by examining accounts written from different perspectives.

PI 1.4 Students understand the broad patterns, relationships, and interactions of cultures and civilizations during particular eras and across eras.

DOCUMENT 1

Mexico's Balance of Trade

This table shows Mexico's trade balance with the United States and Canada from 1993 to 2003. Negative numbers mean that Mexico imported more than it exported. Positive numbers mean that Mexico exported more than it imported.

MEXICO'S TRADE BALANCE, 1993–2003		
YEAR	WITH THE UNITED STATES	WITH CANADA
1993	−1,164*	1,723*
1994	−1,350	1,713
1995	15,393	2,527
1996	17,506	2,677
1997	14,549	3,081
1998	15,857	2,863
1999	22,812	3,474
2000	24,577	4,109
2001	30,3041	3,587
2002	37,146	3,609
2003	40,648	4,588
*in millions of U.S. dollars		

Sources: *The World Almanac and Book of Facts, 2006;*
The Canadian Trade Commissioner Service

DOCUMENT 2

A Political Cartoon

This cartoon ran in a Mexico City newspaper in 2004. It shows one artist's opinion of NAFTA's effects.

Mr. Dumping, published in *El Universal,* October 13, 2004

caglecartoons.com/espanol

Skills Focus: Interpreting

At Level

Reading Like a Historian Skill
NAFTA Cartoons

1. Have students examine the political cartoon shown in Document 2.

2. Have students work in mixed-ability pairs to write a few sentences describing what the cartoon represents and the cartoonist's point of view. Have volunteers share their work.

3. Have students create two political cartoons, one supporting NAFTA and the other opposing it.

4. Have students share their cartoons with the class. **LS Visual-Spatial**

Alternative Assessment Handbook, Rubric 27: Political Cartoons

DOCUMENT 3

Report of the World Bank

Economists studied NAFTA's effects on Mexico for a report published by the World Bank in 2003. The excerpt below contains some of their findings.

The report's main conclusion regarding NAFTA is that the treaty has helped Mexico get closer to the levels of development of its NAFTA partners. The research suggests, for example, that Mexico's global exports would have been about 25% lower without NAFTA, and foreign direct investment (FDI) would have been about 40% less without NAFTA. Also, the amount of time required for Mexican manufacturers to adopt U.S. technological innovations was cut in half. Trade can probably take some credit for moderate declines in poverty, and has likely had positive impacts on the number and quality of jobs. However, NAFTA is not enough to ensure economic convergence among North American countries and regions. This reflects both limitations of NAFTA's design and, more importantly, pending domestic reforms.

DOCUMENT 4

An Economic Report

Researchers Timothy A. Wise and Kevin P. Gallagher published their analysis of NAFTA's effects on the Mexican economy in 2002 through an organization called Foreign Policy in Focus.

Official figures from both the World Bank and the Mexican government show that trade liberalization has succeeded in stimulating both trade and investment, and it has brought inflation under control. Mexico's exports have grown at a rapid annual rate of 10.6% in real terms since 1985, and foreign direct investment (FDI) has nearly tripled, posting a real 21% annual growth rate. Inflation has been significantly tamed.

Unfortunately, these figures have not translated into benefits for the Mexican population as a whole. The same official sources show that:

• ... There has been little job creation, falling far short of the demand in Mexico from new entrants into the labor force. Even the manufacturing sector, one of the few sectors to show significant economic growth, has seen a net loss in jobs since NAFTA took effect.

• Wages have declined nationally, with real wages down significantly. The real minimum wage is down 60% since 1982, 23% under NAFTA.

Skills FOCUS — READING LIKE A HISTORIAN

DOCUMENT 1
a. **Describe** What has happened to Mexico's balance of trade with the United States since NAFTA took effect?
b. **Analyze** How do you think the change in balance of trade has affected Mexico's economy?

DOCUMENT 2
a. **Describe** What is happening in the political cartoon?
b. **Infer** What does the artist think about NAFTA's effects on Mexico?

DOCUMENT 3
a. **Identify Main Ideas** What is the main idea of the World Bank's report?
b. **Analyze** How can you tell that the writers are confident about some of their conclusions and less confident about others? Which conclusions are they less confident about? Which words indicate they are more or less confident?

DOCUMENT 4
a. **Identify Main Ideas** What is the main idea of the researchers' report?
b. **Interpret** Does the report give a mostly positive or mostly negative evaluation of NAFTA? Explain your answer.

DOCUMENT-BASED ESSAY QUESTION

Opinions about NAFTA's effect on Mexico range from very positive to very negative. How has NAFTA affected the different segments of Mexican society in different ways? Using the documents above and information from the chapter, form a thesis that expresses your opinion. Then write a short essay to support your opinion.

See **Skills Handbook**, pp. H25, H27

Word Help

exports goods shipped to another country
innovation modernization, new ways of doing something
convergence merging into a unified whole

MISCONCEPTION ALERT

NAFTA has not led to an increase in U.S. agricultural imports. Instead, it has led to an increase in exports. Between 1994 and 2005, U.S. agricultural exports increased to Mexico and Canada jumped from $9.5 billion to about $19 billion. Mexico accounted for $4.5 billion of that increase.

Answers

Reading Like a Historian
Document 1. a. *It increased dramatically; exports exceeded imports.*
b. *strengthened it;* **Document 2. a.** *The supply of American-made goods in Mexico is hurting Mexican industry.*
b. *The artist thinks NAFTA has negatively impacted Mexico.* **Document 3. a.** *that NAFTA is helping Mexico's economy; Mexico's exports have increased;*
b. *Confidence is shown by the use of specific numbers and statistics; words such as "probably" and "likely" indicate areas where the authors are less confident.* **Document 4. a.** *Most Mexicans are not benefiting from NAFTA.* **b.** *negative, focuses more on the problems.* **Essay** *Student essays should recognize that NAFTA had mixed results in Mexico. Exports and productivity have increased, but not everyone has benefited.*

Differentiating Instruction

Learners Having Difficulty — Below Level

Have students work in mixed-ability pairs and reread Documents 3 and 4. Then have students work individually to write a paraphrase of the two documents. Have pairs share their paraphrases. **LS Verbal-Linguistic**

Alternative Assessment Handbook, Rubric 37: Writing Assignments

Advanced Learners/ Gifted and Talented — Above Level

Have students examine Documents 3 and 4. Then have students explain or theorize why the balance of trade has increased so dramatically, while real wages have declined and job creation has stalled. **LS Verbal-Linguistic**

Alternative Assessment Handbook, Rubric 37: Writing Assignments

Visual Summary

Review and Inquiry Have students match the political trends on the left with the events on the time line.

Quick Facts Transparency: Visual Study Guide: Latin America

Review Key Terms and People

1. junta
2. Fidel Castro
3. NAFTA
4. Augusto Pinochet
5. Juan Perón
6. Contras
7. intervene

Comprehension and Critical Thinking

8. a. Church became active in social and economic struggles.
   b. similarities—the U.S. intervened, between guerilla and military armies; differences—led to dictatorship in Guatemala; Sandinistas instituted some reforms
   c. positive—established free health care, virtually ended illiteracy; reduced economic inequality; negative—civil liberties are restricted; there is a one-party system

9. a. supported the poor and working class; established minimum wage, eight-hour working day; built schools, hospitals, and homeless shelters
   b. similar—absolute dictatorships, controlled people with violence; economies suffered; different—mothers protested in Argentina; Brazil, opposition grew, Chile, not everyone suffered
   c. possible answer—Yes, the U.S. helped establish less corrupt governments and institute democratic reforms.

10. a. It was a one party rule; won victories through corruption and fraud.
   b. mixed results; rate of inflation has decreased, poverty rate has decreased, increase in some exports; poverty gap has widened

---

VISUAL STUDY GUIDE

Political Trends in Latin America

Dictatorships
- Argentina under Perón and the military
- Brazil under the military
- Chile under Pinochet
- Haiti under the Duvaliers
- Panama under Noriega

⬇

Moderate Reforms
- Argentina after the Falklands War
- Brazil with the end of the military dictatorship
- Chile after Pinochet
- Nicaragua under Chamorro
- Mexico with the election of Fox

⬇

Leftist Movements
- Cuban Revolution under Castro
- Sandinistas in Nicaragua
- Shining Path in Peru
- Chávez in Venezuela
- Morales in Bolivia
- Lula in Brazil

Key Events in Latin America

1954 ■ Jacobo Arbenz, an elected leftist, is overthrown in Guatemala.

1959 ■ The Cuban Revolution brings Fidel Castro to power.

1968 ■ The Mexican army kills hundreds of unarmed student protesters.

Early 1970s ■ Oil prices surge, which benefits Mexico and Venezuela but hurts Brazil.

1973 ■ President Salvador Allende is killed in a coup in Chile, and Augusto Pinochet takes power the next year.

1976 ■ Argentina's "dirty war" begins.

1979 ■ Nicaraguan revolution brings leftist Sandinistas to power.

1980 ■ Archbishop Oscar Romero is assassinated in El Salvador, which worsens that country's civil war.

1980s ■ Debt and hyperinflation bring Latin American countries to the brink of economic collapse.

1982 ■ The Falklands War helps bring down Argentina's dictatorship.

2000 ■ One-party rule ends in Mexico with the election of Vicente Fox.

Review Key Terms and People

Identify the term or person from the chapter that best fits each of the following descriptions.

1. a group of leaders who rule jointly

2. dictator who brought a communist revolution to Cuba

3. agreement to eliminate tariffs on trade between Mexico, the United States, and Canada

4. dictator in Chile who improved the economy but severely repressed personal freedoms

5. leader who supports the rights of the common people as opposed to the privileged elite

6. U.S.-trained and funded rebel group in the Nicaraguan civil war

7. to enter into an event to affect its outcome

986 CHAPTER 32

---

c. possible answer—They hope for solutions to their economic problems and want a better standard of living.

Reading Skills

11. pressure from pro-democracy groups; new requirements from the IMF and World Bank

12. positive—drop in the rate of inflation, some stability; negative—unemployment high, high poverty rates, gap between rich and poor grew, not equal benefits to all countries

13. economy was failing; dictator took power, limited civil rights

14. discredited and brought down the military dictatorship

15. too much debt, excessive dependence on imported oil

Evaluating Historical Interpretation

16. leftist, holy crusade, campaign of public misinformation, covert terrorist operations

17. He does not agree with U.S. involvement.

History's Impact video program
Review the video to answer the closing question:
What impact does NAFTA have on Mexico?

Comprehension and Critical Thinking

SECTION 1 *(pp. 967–972)*

8. a. Recall What influence did Liberation Theology have on Latin American politics?

b. Compare and Contrast What were two similarities and two differences between the civil wars in Guatemala and Nicaragua?

c. Evaluate How did Fidel Castro's policies change Cuba in both positive and negative ways?

SECTION 2 *(pp. 973–977)*

9. a. Describe What aspects of Juan Perón's rule show that he was a populist?

b. Compare and Contrast How were the military dictatorships in Argentina, Brazil, and Chile both similar and different?

c. Make Judgments The United States played a role in the politics of Chile, Haiti, and Panama. Was intervention by the United States justified in each of these cases? Explain your answer.

SECTION 3 *(pp. 978–983)*

10. a. Describe In what ways was the PRI like a dictatorship?

b. Make Generalizations How have market reforms changed Latin American economies in recent years?

c. Elaborate Why do you think people in many Latin American countries have been looking to populist, left-leaning leaders in recent years?

Reading Skills

Understanding Causes and Effects *Use what you know about understanding causes and effects to answer the questions below.*

11. What were two causes of the end of dictatorships in Latin America?

12. What have been the positive and negative effects of market reforms in Latin America?

13. What was one cause and one effect of the 1973 coup in Chile?

14. What major effect did the Falklands War have on Argentina?

15. What were two causes of economic trouble in Brazil during the military dictatorship?

Evaluating Historical Interpretation

Reading Like a Historian *The selection below is one historian's interpretation of U.S. influence in Central American civil wars.*

❝Ronald Reagan's campaigns against the leftist Sandinista regime in Nicaragua and the leftist . . . guerrillas in El Salvador took on all the characteristics of a holy crusade against communist forces in Central America. From the beginning of his first term, President Reagan sought to overthrow the Sandinistas, employing tactics that included economic sanctions, a campaign of public misinformation, support of rightist counterrevolutionary armies (the contras), and covert terrorist operations aided by the CIA.❞

—Benjamin Keen, *A History of Latin America*, 1996

16. Analyze Which words or phrases suggest the writer might have a bias one way or another?

17. Infer What do you think the writer thinks of U.S. involvement in Nicaragua and El Salvador?

Using the Internet

go.hrw.com
Practice Online
Keyword: SHL LAT

18. Latin America faces many political and economic challenges today. Using the keyword above, research current events in Latin America that relate to some of these challenges. Then write a one-paragraph summary of two of the articles that you find.

WRITING FOR THE SAT

Think about the following issue:

Countries in Latin America have experimented with different types of governments. Leftist leaders believed that the way to achieve economic progress in societies where few people held most of the wealth was for the common people to take over the government. Rightist leaders believed that only a leader who ruled with an iron fist could force a country to take the painful steps required to reform an inefficient economy.

19. Assignment: Is either of these theories valid in Latin America? Is neither valid? Is either partly valid? Write a short essay in which you develop your position on this issue. Support your point of view with reasoning and examples from your reading and studies.

Answers

Using the Internet

18. Go to the HRW Web site and enter the keyword shown to access a rubric for this activity.

KEYWORD: SHL LAT

Writing for the SAT

19. Student essays should mention that rebellions can have unexpected consequences, as their study of this chapter shows. Essays should also discuss that while dictatorships can solve problems in the short-run, human rights usually suffer.
A rubric for this activity is provided in **CRF**: Writing for the SAT.

HOLT

History's Impact

▶ **Video Program**
See the Video Program Teacher's Guide for the answer to the closing question.

Review and Assessment Resources

Review and Reinforce

- **CRF**: Chapter Review
- **Quick Facts Transparency**: Visual Study Guide: Latin America
-  **Spanish Chapter Summaries Audio CD Program**
- OSP **Holt PuzzlePro**: Quiz Show for ExamView
- **Quiz Game CD-ROM**

Assess

- **PASS**: Chapter Test, Forms A and B
- **Alternative Assessment Handbook**
- OSP **ExamView Test Generator**, Chapter Test
- **Differentiated Instruction Modified Worksheets and Tests CD-ROM**: Chapter Test
- HOAP **Holt Online Assessment Program** (in the Premier Online Edition)

Reteach/Intervene

- **Interactive Reader and Study Guide**
- **Differentiated Instruction Teacher Management System**: Lesson Plans for Differentiated Instruction
- **Differentiated Instruction Modified Worksheets and Tests CD-ROM**: Chapter Test
- **Interactive Skills Tutor CD-ROM**

go.hrw.com
Online Resources
KEYWORD: SHL TEACHER

Chapter 33 Planning Guide

Today's World

Chapter Overview	Reproducible Resources	Technology Resources
CHAPTER 33 pp. 988–1013 **Overview:** In this chapter, students will learn about the economic, environmental, and technological changes and challenges in the world today. **KI 1, 3; PI .1, 1.3, 1.4, 3.1, 3.2, 3.3** See pp. T32–T55 for a detailed correlation to the New York State Core Curriculum for Global History and Geography and the New York Learning Standards.	**Differentiated Instruction Teacher Management System:** • Pacing Guides • Lesson Plans for Universal Access **Interactive Reader and Study Guide:** Chapter Summary* **Chapter Resource File*** • Writing About History • Social Studies Skill • Chapter Review **World History Outline Maps**	**OSP New York One-Stop Planner CD-ROM:** Calendar Planner **Live Ink© Online Reading Help** **Student Edition on Audio CD Program** **Differentiated Instruction Modified Worksheets and Tests CD-ROM** **World History Primary Source Library CD-ROM** **Power Presentations with Video CD-ROM** **History's Impact: World History Video Program (VHS/DVD):** Today's World
Section 1: **Globalization** **The Main Idea:** Globalization affects economies and lives around the world. **PI 1.1, 3.2**	**Interactive Reader and Study Guide:** Section 1 Summary* **Chapter Resource File*** • Vocabulary Builder: Section 1 • Biography: Amadou and Mariam • History and Geography: Economic Independence • Primary Source: The Impact of Globalization	**Regents Review Transparency:** Section 1* **Map Transparency:** World per Capita GDP, 2006* **Quick Facts Transparency:** Major Trade Organizations and Agreements* **Internet Activity:** Television: Its History
Section 2: **Society and Human Rights** **The Main Idea:** People and countries are working together to help solve problems such as poverty and disease, adjust to new patterns of migration, and to protect human rights in societies around the world. **PI 3.3**	**Differentiated Instruction Teacher Management System:** Section 2 Lesson Plan* **Interactive Reader and Study Guide:** Section 2 Summary* **Chapter Resource File*** • Vocabulary Builder: Section 2 • Biography: Louise Arbour • Literature: *Cry, the Beloved Country*	**Regents Review Transarency:** Section 2* **Map Transparency:** Worldwide Average Life Expectancy*
Section 3: **Security and Terrorism** **The Main Idea:** Terrorism, the potential use of weapons of mass destruction, and ethnic and religious tensions threatens security around the world. **PI 1.4, 3.2**	**Differentiated Instruction Teacher Management System:** Section 3 Lesson Plan* **Interactive Reader and Study Guide:** Section 3 Summary* **Chapter Resource File*** • Vocabulary Builder: Section 3 • Biography: Rose Riso	**Regents Review Transarency:** Section 3* **Map Transparency:** Worldwide Terrorism Incidents*
Section 4: **The Environment, Science, and Technology** **The Main Idea:** People are working together to protect the environment and using science and technology to improve living conditions around the world. **PI 1.3, 1.4, 3.1**	**Differentiated Instruction Teacher Management System:** Section 4 Lesson Plan* **Interactive Reader and Study Guide:** Section 4 Summary* **Chapter Resource File*** • Vocabulary Builder: Section 4 • Biography: Yuet Wai Kan	**Regents Review Transarency:** Section 4* **Quick Facts Transparency:** Worldwide Internet Access, 2006* **Internet Activity:** Investigate Global Warming

HOLT
History's Impact
World History Video Program (VHS/DVD)
Today's World

Review, Assessment, Intervention

Global History and Geography Regents Test Prep Workbook

Quick Facts Transparency: Today's World*

Spanish Chapter Summaries Audio CD Program

Differentiated Instruction Modified Worksheets and Tests CD-ROM: Modified Chapter Test

OSP   **New York One-Stop Planner CD-ROM:** ExamView Test Generator (English/Spanish)

HOAP   **Holt Online Assessment Program (HOAP),** in the Holt Premier Online Student Edition

---

PASS: Section 1 Quiz*

Online Quiz: Section 1

Alternative Assessment Handbook

PASS: Section 2 Quiz*

Online Quiz: Section 2

Alternative Assessment Handbook

PASS: Section 3 Quiz*

Online Quiz: Section 3

Alternative Assessment Handbook

PASS: Section 4 Quiz*

Online Quiz: Section 4

Alternative Assessment Handbook

Power Presentation with Video CD-ROM

Power Presentations with Video are visual presentations of each chapter's main ideas. Presentations can be customized by including Quick Facts charts, images and maps from the textbook, and video clips.

Holt Online Learning

go.hrw.com
Teacher Resources
KEYWORD: SHL/TEACHER

go.hrw.com
Student Resources
KEYWORD: SHL TOD

- Document-Based Questions
- Interactive Multimedia Activities

- Current Events
- Chapter-Based Internet Activities
- and more!

Holt Premier
Online Student Edition
Complete online support for interactivity, assessment, and reporting
- Interactive Maps and Notebook
- Homework Practice and Research Activities Online

CHAPTER 33 PLANNING GUIDE

The Big Picture

Peter N. Stearns

Globalization The big news, after the end of the cold war, was the process of globalization and resistance to it. Globalization involves an intensification of international contacts and the consequences of those contacts, in areas of human endeavor from economics through politics to culture. Today, economic globalization involves multinationals and movements toward free trade, but also debate and resistance. Globalization has differential economic results for advanced industrial countries and those countries that are still largely agricultural. Still, a key development of the early 21st century has been the rapid economic growth of countries like China and India.

Cultural and Political Aspects Cultural influences have spread widely thanks to the activities of multinational organizations and information technologies. The consumer styles of the United States, Western Europe, and Japan have had a global impact that has sparked resistance in the name of traditional and regional identities. Organizations, including international NGOs, have worked for adherence to human rights standards with mixed results. Global contacts have increased the potential for the rapid dissemination of disease. Today. new patterns of migration involve longer distances and lead to greater cultural diversity. Resistance to migration has developed as well.

Terrorism and Conflict Terrorism has a long human history. Over the past few decades terrorist methods and effects have become more sophisticated. Contemporary terrorism reflects many problems and tensions, particularly in the Middle East. Some observers point to government-sponsored attacks on civilians as another component of today's terrorism. Many societies have taken increasing measures against terrorism, and terrorists rarely win significant political results. Other international tensions have involved concern about the spread of new types of weapons, particularly nuclear weaponry.

Environmental Change Increased pollution levels caused growing concern around 2000. Environmental globalization involves all the human activities that cause global environmental deterioration. Population growth and advancing consumerism has underwritten environmental change, with particular involvement from the United States. Global technologies and the rapid spread of scientific research rounded out the world's agenda by the early 21st century.

Recent Scholarship

Historians have fruitfully explored globalization around two themes: first, the different patterns of regional adjustment and resistance to globalization in historical perspective, and second the more fundamental issue of how new globalization is compared to previous surges in global contacts. *The New Global History* (2006) by Bruce Mazlish takes the lead in arguing for dramatic novelty, as against earlier passages in world history. His new book makes the case strongly, while also illustrating different facets of globalization and regional-global interactions. His approach should stimulate serious discussion, as its contentions are central to the challenge of relating contemporary changes to past patterns.

Differentiating Instruction

 Differentiated Instruction Teacher Management System
- Pacing Guide
- Lesson Plans for Differentiated Instruction

 Interactive Reader and Study Guide

Spanish Chapter Summaries Audio CD Program

Student Edition on Audio CD Program

 Differentiated Instruction Modified Worksheets and Tests CD-ROM
- Vocabulary Flash Cards
- Modified Vocabulary Builder Activities
- Modified Chapter Review Activity
- Modified Chapter Test

OSP One-Stop Planner CD-ROM
- ExamView Test Generator (English/Spanish)
- PuzzlePro
- Quiz Show for ExamView
- Transparencies and Videos

TE Differentiated Activities in the Teacher's Edition
- Global Automobile Production, p. 993
- Terrorist Attacks, p. 1001
- Terrorism in Recent Years, p. 1002
- Global Warming, p. 1009

Reading Like a Historian
Sam Wineburg

"Fair Trade" It has been called "the book that killed colonialism" but few Americans know its name. Published in 1860 by Eduard Douwes Dekker, the semi-autobiographical *Max Havelaar* chronicles the exploits of a colonial official in the Dutch East Indies. *Max Havelaar* leaves no doubt as to the brutality of a regime that ordered the Javanese to cultivate coffee and tea under a system ("cultuurstelsel") that required them to turn over a proportion of their crop to the government. When crops failed or a drought hit, farmers were left with nothing to fall back on. Starvation and malnutrition raged in the Indonesian countryside.

On publication, *Max Havelaar* caused only a minor stir. But after a few years, its message sparked reformist efforts all over Europe. The book led to changes in Dutch colonial policy—especially the repeal of cultuurstelsel—and helped initiate a program of building schools and hospitals.

We can assess the influence of *Max Havelaar* because we have the distance and perspective from which to view it. However, if we were trying to write about the book's impact in 1862, we would have little idea of its ultimate fate. Such is the problem of writing contemporary history.

The Impact Today A similar problem confronts us in trying to assess the impact of the contemporary movement known as "fair trade," which our chapter describes as a counterbalance to "free trade." After petroleum, coffee is the largest commodity on the world market, and the US is world's largest consumer—accounting for 40 percent of international consumption.

When Americans go to their specialty roaster and spend $10.00/lb for their fragrant "Breakfast Blend," the farmer who grew these beans gets as little as twenty cents—a measly 2 percent—of this sum. Those who benefit most in this web of financial excess are the middlemen who stand between us and the grower: throngs of buyers, exporters, importers, wholesalers, roasters, and retailers, each inflating the price before they pass on the beans to the next link in the chain.

In 1992 the inequities built into this system led a group of European reformers to create the first "fair trade" coffee organization, appropriately named "Max Havelaar" (http://www.maxhavelaar.ch/en/) and headquartered in Basel, Switzerland. Its goal was to eliminate the middlemen from this system—or at least some of them—so that the growers could earn a decent wage for their beans. Today, the going price paid to farmers is stabilized at $1.26, far higher than the open market but one that is ultimately passed on to consumers in higher prices.

Will coffee aficionados put their money where their conscience is? In Western Europe at least, the answer seems to be yes. Fair trade coffee now accounts for 3 percent of all sales in countries like the Netherlands, Switzerland, and Luxembourg. In contrast, as of 2001, fair trade accounted for a minuscule fraction of the American coffee market—a mere 0.2 percent.

A 2003 study by political scientists Margaret Levi and April Linton and published in the journal *Politics & Society*, found that in Seattle, America's coffee capital, when the choice came down to caffeine scruples or a tasty brew, consumers leaned decidedly toward the latter: "Store buyers report that their decisions to stock Fair Trade coffees and customers' decisions to buy them are based as much on good taste in the cup as on a desire to help coffee farmers."

It is impossible know whether Fair Trade will become more than a flash in the cup, or whether it will alter how we think not only about coffee— but about the ethics of all kinds of foodstuffs.

Trying to answer this question remains little more than a guess. This is why historians stick to writing about the past.

Chapter Main Ideas

Section 1 Trade and culture link economies and lives around the world.

Section 2 People and countries are working together to protect human rights, help solve problems such as poverty and disease, and adjust to new patterns of migration.

Section 3 Terrorism, the potential use of weapons of mass destruction, and ethnic and religious tensions threaten security around the world.

Section 4 People are working together to protect the environment and using science and technology to improve living conditions around the world.

New York Standards

Key Idea 1 The study of world history requires an understanding of world cultures and civilizations, including an analysis of important ideas, social and cultural values, beliefs, and traditions. This study also examines the human condition and the connections and interactions of people across time and space and the ways different people view the same event or issue from a variety of perspectives.

Key Idea 3 Study of the major social, political, cultural, and religious developments in world history involves learning about the important roles and contributions of individuals and groups.

Key to Differentiating Instruction

Below Level

Basic-level activities designed for all students encountering new material

At Level

Intermediate-level activities designed for average students

Above Level

Challenging activities designed for honors and gifted and talented students

Standard English Mastery

Activities designed to improve standard English usage

CHAPTER

33

Today's World

THE BIG PICTURE The world today is changing at a rapid rate. People are working together to promote economic development, eliminate threats to global security, protect the environment, and advance science and technology.

Theme GEOGRAPHY AND ENVIRONMENT
Balancing economic growth and development with resource use can be challenging. In this chapter you will learn how people are working together to protect the environment while supporting the needs of businesses and economies.

TIME LINE

CHAPTER EVENTS

September 11, 2001 Terrorists hijack four passenger airplanes and attack the United States.

February 2003 An ethnic conflict begins in the Darfur region of western Sudan.

March 2003 A U.S.-led military coalition invades Iraq to remove Saddam Hussein from power.

2001 — 2003

WORLD EVENTS

January 2002 The euro becomes the common currency for most of Western Europe.

April 2003 Scientists with the Human Genome Project announce they have mapped the human genetic code.

988 CHAPTER 33

Introduce the Chapter

At Level

Today's World

1. Have students name important events in the United States and the world that have happened during their lifetimes. Remind students not to focus solely on wars or conflicts, but to name positive changes that have occurred in the world as well.

2. Create a class list for all to see and broadly categorize them, using such heads as medicine, science and technology, global conflicts, etc.

3. Review the list of events with students, and have volunteers explain the importance and possible consequences of each event.

4. Tell students that in this chapter they will learn about the important issues facing today's world, including terrorism, security, the environment, technology, human rights, trade, and globalization.
   LS Verbal-Linguistic

   Alternative Assessment Handbook, Rubric 11: Discussions

History's Impact video program
Watch the video to understand the impact of September 11, 2001.

Reading like a Historian

This photograph shows a busy nighttime scene in the Shinjuku area of Tokyo, Japan. Shinjuku is a major commercial center and is home to the world's busiest train station as well as to a large number of successful stores, restaurants, and night clubs.

Analyzing Visuals What does this photograph tell you about life in Japan? What does it indicate about Japan's level of technology and resource use?

See **Skills Handbook**, p. H26

December 2004 A tsunami strikes Southeast Asia, killing more than 225,000 people.

August 2005 Hurricane Katrina hits New Orleans and the Gulf Coast of the United States.

2005

2007

August 2005 South Korean scientists announce the first successful cloning of a dog.

March 2006 CAFTA, a free trade agreement between the United States and several Caribbean countries, goes into effect.

TODAY'S WORLD **989**

• Chapter Preview •

HOLT

History's Impact
► **Video Program: Today's World**
See the Video Teacher's Guide for strategies for using the video segment.

Reading Like a Historian

Shinjuku, Japan Shinjuku makes up one of the 23 wards, or districts, of Tokyo, but is a thriving metropolis in its own right. Its train station, for example, accommodates more than two million passengers each day. The Shinjuku business district contains some of Tokyo's tallest skyscrapers.

go.hrw.com
Online Resources

Chapter Resources:
KEYWORD: SHL TOD
Teacher Resources:
KEYWORD: SHL TEACHER

Explore the Time Line

1. What two natural disasters occurred within a year of each other? *tsunami in Southeast Asia; Hurricane Katrina in the United States*

2. When did two major scientific achievements involving DNA occur, and what were they? *April 2003, scientists announce they have mapped the human genetic code; August 2005, South Korean scientists announce the successful cloning of a dog*

3. How long after September 11, 2001, did the U.S. invade Iraq? *18 months*

Info to Know

Human Genome Project Scientists have discovered that genetics may play an important role in health. It is thought that a person's DNA can determine how susceptible or resistant a person is to certain diseases. Some scientists believe that in the future, doctors will be able to look at a newborn's DNA to determine the diseases and illnesses to which the child might be susceptible. **Predict** How would this new research help? *possible answer—Doctors could use the information to treat children before they become seriously ill, perhaps reducing infant mortality rates.*

Answers

Reading Like a Historian *possible answer—Japan's economy has thrived, as shown by its modern cities with bustling business districts.*

Geography Starting Points

Per capita Income in the United States
Per capita income in the United States has risen dramatically in the last half century. In 1935, per capita income was $474; in 1945, $1,235. In 1965, it was approximately $2,800, in 1985, $14,758, and in 2005, it was $34,586.

Activity Per capita Income Have students calculate the percentage increase in the United States' per capita income from 1985 to 2006. **LS Logical-Mathematical**

🗺 **Map Transparency:** World Per Capita GDP, 2006

📝 **World History Outline Maps**

✳ **Interactive Map:** World Per Capita GDP, 2006

Teaching Tip

Remind students that two very reliable sources of current economic data on foreign countries are available online through the World Bank and the CIA World Factbook. Have students explain why the World Bank tracks GDP and per capita income of individual countries.

GEOGRAPHY Starting Points

✳Interactive WORLD PER CAPITA GDP, 2006

- less than $5,000
- $5,000–9,999
- $10,000–19,999
- $20,000–29,999
- more than $30,000

All figures in U.S. $

Robinson projection

Senegal Developing countries like Senegal have low per capita GDPs, slow economic growth, and a low standard of living.

Australia Developed countries like Australia have high per capita GDPs, modern and industrial economies, and a high standard of living.

Starting Points In recent years, the world has changed rapidly as a global economy develops. New methods of transportation and communication continue to bring nations and cultures closer together. Despite economic growth in some areas, however, many countries are still working hard to build strong economies and provide opportunities for their citizens.

1. Analyze Which parts of the world have the lowest and highest per capita GDPs? What might explain this regional difference?

2. Predict How do you think the continued growth of global trade might affect this map? Do you think the map will look the same in 2020? in 2040?

 **Listen to History**

Go online to listen to an explanation of the starting points for this chapter.

go.hrw.com
Keyword: SHL TOD

990 CHAPTER 33

Skills Focus: Interpreting Cartograms   At Level

Social Studies Skill
World Economy

1. Review with students what cartograms are, how they differ from normal maps, and the types of information they show. Have students explain why economic data is often showed in cartogram form. You might wish to show students examples of cartograms.

2. Have students work in pairs to create a cartogram showing the data represented on the world map in the feature.

3. Have volunteers share their cartograms with the class and explain how they converted the data into this format. **LS Logical-Mathematical, Visual-Spatial**

📝 **Alternative Assessment Handbook**, Rubric 20: Map Creation

Answers

Geography Starting Points
1. *Lowest—South America and parts of Central America, much of Asia, Eastern Europe, Africa; Highest—Western Europe, United States, Canada, Australia; areas with lower GDPs are poorer, many are not yet industrialized;* **2.** *possible answer—As global trade increases, the map might show less difference in GDP between countries.*

1 Trade and Globalization

BEFORE YOU READ

MAIN IDEA

Trade and culture link economies and lives around the world.

READING FOCUS

1. How does economic inter-dependence affect countries around the world?
2. What are some patterns and effects of global trade?
3. How does globalization lead to cultural exchange?

KEY TERMS

globalization
interdependence
multinational corporations
outsourcing
free trade
popular culture
cultural diffusion

NEW YORK

PI 1.1 Investigate the various compo-nents of cultures and civilizations including economic systems.

PI 3.2 Students explain the dynamics of cultural change.

CHOPPING DOWN THE FUTURE

◄ A pile of logs in Naren awaits the construction of more new homes.

THE INSIDE STORY

Does prosperity have its own risks? People living in the small Chinese village of Naren were once among the poorest people in the world. Now, however, they are relatively rich—and all because of a wild mushroom.

The mushrooms that grow beneath the oak and pine trees of Naren can bring high prices in Japan, where they are considered a rare delicacy. Beginning in the 1980s, Naren villagers began to gather these mushrooms to sell to Japanese consumers. It is possible for a villager to earn more than one thousand dollars in a single summer by harvesting mushrooms—an enormous amount of money in Naren.

The money from mushrooms has changed life in Naren. People who used to live in small shacks have been able to build huge wooden houses and fill them with modern luxu-ries, including TVs, CD players, and satellite dishes.

However, this increased prosperity has brought problems as well. As villagers chop down trees to build their new wooden houses, the forests of Naren are slowly shrinking. Without forests to absorb rainfall, disastrous floods are becoming more common. Some villagers worry that even more tree cutting could mean the end of the valuable mushrooms that grow under those trees—and of their new modern lifestyle. ■

TODAY'S WORLD **991**

Preteach

Getting Started

Use the **Interactive Reader and Study Guide** to familiarize students with the section content.

📖 **Interactive Reader and Study Guide**, Section 1

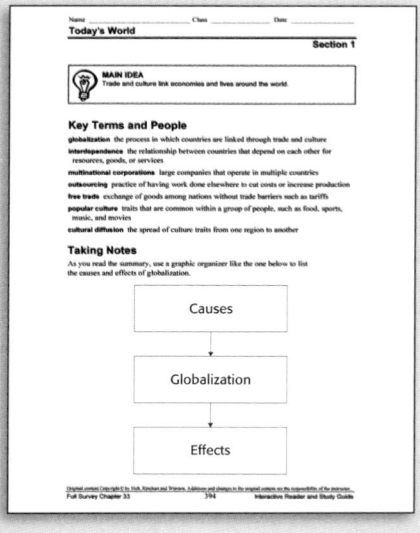

📄 **CRF:** Vocabulary Builder: Section 1

Taking Notes

Causes—the need to have closer relationships between the world's nations; easier, faster global trade; Effects—economic interdependence; links between developed and developing countries; outsourcing with multinational countries; free trade; cultural exchange; changes in popular culture

go.hrw.com
Online Resources

KEYWORD: SHL TOD
ACTIVITY: Television: Its History and Impact

Teach the Main Idea

At Level

Trade and Globalization

1. **Teach** Ask students the Reading Focus questions to teach this section.

2. **Apply** Have students create an outline of the section using the heads as main points. Have students identify at least two main ideas under each of the blue subheadings.

3. **Review** Review student outlines as a class. Have students identify the points in their outlines that they feel are most important or most interesting and have them explain their reasoning to the class. Guide students in a

discussion about the ways their everyday lives are affected by international trade and globalization.

4. **Practice/Homework** Have students think about what they wear, what they do for fun, where they work, and what transportation their families use. Have students write a short essay explaining how globalization affects them personally. **LS Verbal-Linguistic**

📄 **Alternative Assessment Handbook**, Rubrics 11: Discussions; and 42: Writing to Inform

❶ How does economic interdependence affect countries around the world? *Countries are linked through trade and culture; developing and developed countries depend upon one another for goods and services.*

Economic Interdependence

Define What is economic interdependence? *relationship between countries in which they depend one another for a variety of resources, goods, or services*

Predict How do you think outsourcing will affect developed countries in the future? *possible answer—It could lead to higher unemployment in the developed countries, help lower the cost of goods, and increase prosperity and employment rates around the world.*

📄 **CRF:** History and Geography: Economic Interdependence

Info to Know

Outsourcing to India In the early 2000s, India was the leader in outsourcing. India was receiving about 80 to 90 percent of the outsourcing jobs in the world. This is helping to raise the standard of living in India and is providing much needed jobs in the country. India has equipped itself with the technology and resources to manage international contracts and to provide services to other developed countries.

Answers

Reading Skills *possible answer— Japan is an industrialized nation with advanced technology and a strong economy.*

Reading Check *helps to provide jobs in developing countries, increases production and decreases cost for multinational companies*

TAKING NOTES Take notes on the causes and effects of globalization.

Causes
↓
Globalization
↓
Effects

NEW YORK

CC **Unit 8-B3** Economic interdependence

READING SKILLS

Making Generalizations Combine what you already know about Japan with the information in this paragraph. Form a generalization about Japan's economy.

Economic Interdependence

At the beginning of the twenty-first century, the world was divided over a number of political, cultural, and economic issues. At the same time, however, countries around the world found themselves tied together like never before.

Globalization The force behind the new, closer relationships among the world's nations is globalization. **Globalization** is the process in which trade and culture link together countries around the world. Trade between nations is not new, but improvements in transportation and communication in recent years have made global trade much easier.

One major effect of global trade is increased economic interdependence among the world's countries. **Interdependence** is a relationship among countries in which they depend on one another for resources, goods, and services. Economic interdependence occurs because countries vary greatly in the types of goods and services they need and can provide.

Developed and Developing Countries
The goods and services a nation can provide, and those it needs, depend on the level of economic development in that country. The world's countries are often grouped into two basic categories—developed and developing countries—based on their level of economic development.

Developed countries are industrialized nations with strong economies and a high standard of living. The world's wealthiest and most powerful nations, such as the United States and Japan, are developed countries. People in developed countries generally have access to good health care, education, and technology.

About 20 percent of the world's nations are considered to be developed, while the remainder are known as developing countries. Developing countries are those with less productive economies and a lower standard of living, such as Guatemala and the Philippines. Many people in these countries lack adequate education and health care.

Not all developing countries are in similar economic situations. The world's poorest nations making the least economic progress are known as least-developed countries. Most of the least-developed countries are located in Africa and southern Asia. These nations suffer

992 CHAPTER 33

---

from great poverty, a lack of political and social stability, and ongoing war or other conflict.

Multinational Corporations The increasing interdependence of the world's countries has been accompanied by the dramatic growth of multinational corporations. **Multinational corporations** are large companies that operate in multiple countries.

One benefit to multinational corporations from their international operations comes from **outsourcing**, the practice of having work done elsewhere to cut costs or increase production. For example, multinational corporations often build manufacturing facilities in developing countries, where materials and labor are relatively inexpensive.

Advocates of multinational corporations believe they create jobs and wealth in the developing countries they operate in. Critics say that they fail to improve the standard of living in developing countries and that outsourcing causes job loss in the company's home country.

Global Economic Ties One effect of economic interdependence is that certain events or actions can affect the economies of many nations. This global interdependence is particularly evident in times of uncertainty.

In the early 2000s, for example, the price of crude oil rose dramatically, nearly tripling in just two years. One factor in this increase was the rising world demand for oil, especially in rapidly industrializing countries like China and India. Another factor was growing concern about the available supply of oil in the world, both because of fears about dwindling oil reserves and because of unrest in some of the oil-producing regions of the Middle East.

Since all countries depend on oil for energy in some way, the rise in oil prices was felt around the world. Developed countries such as the United States that rely heavily on oil for shipping, transportation, and energy were faced with dramatically higher costs. Some poor nations in Africa could not afford to import oil at the higher prices and faced shortages. The rise in oil prices led to increased demand for alternative energy sources as well as attempts to reduce oil consumption.

READING CHECK **Summarize** How does economic interdependence affect the world?

Collaborative Learning

At Level

Outsourcing

Research Required

1. Review the information in the text about multinational corporations and outsourcing. Then organize the students into two groups. Have one group represent members of a multinational corporation that believes that outsourcing has a positive worldwide effect; the other group should represent those who oppose outsourcing to foreign countries.

2. Have students use reliable Internet or current print sources to acquire information about both sides of this issue.

3. Have each group prepare its arguments and then debate the effects and consequences of outsourcing. Have all students take notes during the debate.

4. Have students use the information from their notes to write a letter to the editor stating and supporting their own position on this topic.

LS **Verbal-Linguistic**

📄 **Alternative Assessment Handbook**, Rubrics 10: Debates; and 17: Letters to Editors

Global Trade

Globalization often leads to or promotes free trade. **Free trade** is the exchange of goods among nations without trade barriers such as tariffs. Supporters of free trade believe that it gives producers more markets in which to sell goods and allows consumers to purchase higher-quality goods at lower prices.

International Trade Organizations A variety of international trade organizations exist today, many of which work to promote and regulate free trade. The first major international agreement on free trade came in 1948, when the General Agreement on Tariffs and Trade (GATT) was signed. Member countries worked to limit trade barriers and settle trade disputes. In 1995, GATT was replaced by the World Trade Organization (WTO). Some 150 countries are members of the WTO, which monitors national trade policies and helps resolve trade disputes.

Another group that has a major effect on international trade today is the Organization of Petroleum Exporting Countries, or OPEC. A group of oil-rich nations, OPEC works to control the production and price of oil.

HISTORY CLOSE-UP

A Global Economy

It takes about 15,000 parts to make a typical modern automobile. The growth of the global economy means that automakers can buy these parts from countries all over the world, depending on where they can get the best prices and the highest-quality parts.

Many engines are manufactured in the United States and Canada.

Bumpers are often designed and produced in France, Germany, and the United States.

Tires are made in a variety of countries, including South Korea, China, and Mexico.

Seats are sometimes assembled in Japan from covers sewn in Mexico.

MOTOR VEHICLE PRODUCTION, 1950–2000

— United States — Japan — Western Europe

Source: *The World Almanac and Book of Facts, 2006*

Skills FOCUS INTERPRETING GRAPHS

Analyze How has the global production of motor vehicles changed between 1950 and 2000?

Skills FOCUS INTERPRETING VISUALS

Find the Main Idea How has globalization affected the nature of automobile production?

TODAY'S WORLD **993**

Differentiating Instruction

Below Level

Special Education Students

1. Remind students that cars are not made in just one factory in a single country. Have students work in mixed-ability pairs to list the countries mentioned in the History Close-Up feature. Make a class list for all to see.

2. Use a large world map to show students where these countries are located. Then have students create their own world maps highlighting the countries mentioned in the feature.

3. As a class, calculate the distances between the countries discussed in the feature. **LS Visual-Spatial, Logical-Mathematical**

   Alternative Assessment Handbook, Rubric 20: Map Creation

Reading Focus

❷ **What are some patterns and effects of global trade?** *free trade, international trade organizations, developing countries provide new markets for goods and services, developed countries provide technology and money to raise standard of living in the developing countries*

Global Trade

Explain What do supporters of free trade believe? *that free trade gives producers more markets to sell their goods and allows for high-quality, low cost goods*

Summarize What was the purpose of GATT, and what was its successor? *General Agreement on Tariffs and Trade worked to limit trade barriers, settle trade disputes; replaced in 1995 by the World Trade Organization*

📄 **CRF:** Primary Source: The Impact of Globalization on World Cultures

Info to Know

Car Manufacturing Remind students that many cars, including luxury cars, are the result of outsourcing. For example, in 2005, about 80 percent of Porsche production was outsourced. According to an October 2005 article in *Business Week*, "Buyers of the highly successful Porsche Cayenne sport-utility vehicle, which starts at $41,000, are probably unaware that VW workers produce more than 85 percent of the wholesale value of every Cayenne, and that the Cayenne shares 65 percent of its parts and modules with VW's Touareg."

Answers

Interpreting Graphs *In 1950, the United States produced the most cars; in 2000, Western Europe, Japan, and the United States each produced roughly the same percentage of cars.*

Interpreting Visuals *allows one car to be manufactured with parts made in many different countries*

❸ How does globalization lead to cultural exchange? *cultural diffusion, increased travel to other countries for work or vacation, goods from other countries available*

Cultural Exchange

Analyze What benefits of globalization do you see in your life? *possible answers—video games, different foods, electronics, books, new cultures*

Evaluate What steps can countries take to ensure that their own cultural heritage is not lost? *possible answers— celebrate national holidays, emphasize cultural pride, patriotism, and family values*

 CRF: Biography: Amadou and Mariam

 **Quick Facts Transparency:** Major Trade Organizations and Agreements

Info to Know

Globalization Developing countries have increased their trade overall, from 19 percent in 1971 to 29 percent in 1999. Some developing countries have benefited more than others. For example, countries in Asia are profiting, while African nations struggle. Successfully increasing trade and raising the standard of living in developing countries means that the need for international aid is decreasing.

Answers

Reading Like a Historian 1. *Sklair believes globalization hurts the poor; Desai believes globalization has caused poverty to go down.* **2.** *Sklair uses repetition for emotional effect; Desai cites factual information, such as the percentage of people living in poverty.*

Reading Check *can provide opportunities for developing countries; opponents believe global trade exploits developing nations, supporters believe it provides for the production and sale of high-quality, low cost goods*

Reading like a Historian

Globalization

Analyzing Points of View There are a variety of opinions about the effects of globalization on the world. In these excerpts from a discussion about globalization, two experts debate the subject. To analyze these views on globalization, consider:

- the main points in each argument
- the emotional or factual language used

> And you see it in the streets of every city in the world . . . The rich are getting richer . . . and then the poor, the people at the bottom of the barrel . . . seem to be getting poorer . . . I suggest we get realistic and we acknowledge the undoubted fact that globalization is very good for the rich and very bad for the poor.
>
> —Leslie Sklair, sociologist, 2001

> Inequality is growing, but poverty is going down . . . The whole level [of wealth] moves such that people who used to be classified as poor are no longer poor . . . The last 20 years of growth has made more people get out of poverty than at any time in history. Today . . . the maximum amount of people in poverty is about 20 percent. . . . In 1800, it would be 80 percent.
>
> —Meghnad Desai, economist, 2001

Skills Focus — READING LIKE A HISTORIAN

1. **Point of View** How do these opinions on globalization vary?
2. **Language** How do the authors use emotional and factual language in support of their points of view?

See **Skills Handbook**, p. H33

Regional Trade Many countries belong to at least one regional trade bloc, or group, which they form to promote free trade and to deal with economic issues with neighboring nations. The largest regional trade bloc is the European Union (EU), with 25 member countries. Other regional trade blocs include the North American Free Trade Agreement (NAFTA), the Association of Southeast Asian Nations (ASEAN), and the Southern African Development Community (SADC).

Effects of Global Trade Global trade has some clear benefits. Developing countries can provide new and valuable markets for goods and services produced by developed countries. In return, the technology, services, and money provided by developed countries can improve public services and raise the standard of living in developing countries.

On the other hand, opponents of globalization argue that the process benefits wealthy developed nations at the expense of developing nations. For example, they say that free trade encourages practices that exploit workers and destroy the environment in developing coun-

tries. Anti-globalization activists sometimes take part in protests against the World Trade Organization, the International Monetary Fund, the World Bank, and other organizations that seek to regulate the global economy.

Other people who oppose free trade work to promote what they call fair trade. One example is the fair trade coffee movement, which guarantees that fair prices are paid to the farmers who grow coffee beans in an effort to improve farmers' standard of living. Companies involved in fair trade see it as a way of promoting social responsibility.

READING CHECK **Find the Main Idea** How does global trade affect the world?

Cultural Exchange

With globalization, countries are linked not only through trade but also through culture. While people have had cultural exchanges for thousands of years, modern methods of transportation and communication allow these exchanges of ideas and customs to happen faster than ever before.

Collaborative Learning

At Level

Cultural Diffusion

1. Organize students into small groups. Have students in each group develop a list of their favorite foods, communication and music items, sports, and entertainment.

2. Have students use the information in their texts or outside sources to research the origin of their favorite items.

3. Have students present their findings to the class and explain how these items came to be a part of American culture and daily life. Then guide students in a discussion about cultural diffusion and globalization.

LS Verbal-Linguistic

 Alternative Assessment Handbook, Rubrics 11: Discussions; and 14: Group Activity

Culture Traits Spread Globalization leads to changes in popular culture. **Popular culture** refers to culture traits such as food, sports, and music, that are common within a group of people. Although popular cultures vary from one country to another, globalization is causing **cultural diffusion**, or the spread of culture traits from one region to another. Rapid modern transportation systems permit many people to travel to different countries for work or vacation. When people travel, they see new styles of clothing, try other foods, and hear different types of music. Other people move permanently from one country to another, bringing with them elements of their own culture to their new homes.

Television, movies, music, and other forms of mass media are the most powerful methods of cultural diffusion. For example, people around the world can readily watch satellite news channels and movies from the United States and Europe, while people in Western nations can listen to traditional African or Asian music on the radio. The Internet is another means for the exchange of images and ideas. In this way, mass media plays a huge role in cultural changes.

Effects of Cultural Changes Some people believe that these changes are largely negative. They argue that mass media and advertising encourage the growth of consumerism, or a preoccupation with the buying of consumer goods. For example, as people in developing countries become wealthier, many begin to spend their new money on consumer goods from toothpaste to clothing to automobiles. This market for consumer goods, opponents say, is shaped by the media and advertising rather than by actual needs. Thus, they worry that globalization is beginning to create a common world culture and is encouraging traditional cultures to lose some of their uniqueness.

Globalization is creating a world community where people are linked together through economics and culture. One of the biggest challenges of globalization may be to preserve valuable traditional cultures and at the same time provide enrichment from other places around the world.

READING CHECK Summarize How is cultural exchange a part of globalization?

MAJOR TRADE ORGANIZATIONS AND AGREEMENTS

ORGANIZATION (date formed)	Current Members and Goals
General Agreement on Tariffs and Trade (GATT) (1948)	125 members (in 1995); worked to reduce tariffs and other international trade barriers; replaced by WTO
World Trade Organization (WTO) (1995)	Nearly 150 members; promotes lower trade barriers
Group of Eight (G-8) (1975, as G-6)	8 major industrial democracies; discuss international economic, environmental, and other issues
Organization of Petroleum Exporting Countries (OPEC) (1960)	11 major oil-exporting countries, most in Middle East; coordinate oil policies of members
European Union (EU) (1993)	25 European nations; work for European economic and political integration

---

SECTION 1 ASSESSMENT

go.hrw.com
Online Quiz
Keyword: SHL TOD HP

Reviewing Ideas, Terms, and People

1. **a. Define** What is **globalization**?
   b. Explain How are **multinational corporations** an example of economic **interdependence** between developed and developing countries?
   c. Evaluate What are some benefits and drawbacks of **outsourcing**?

2. **a. Identify** What is the World Trade Organization?
   b. Compare and Contrast How do supporters and opponents of global free trade differ in their views of it?
   c. Elaborate Why do you think countries may want to join multiple regional trade blocs?

3. **a. Recall** What types of culture traits make up **popular culture**?
   b. Explain How do mass media affect **cultural diffusion**?
   c. Evaluate What recent change do you think has been the biggest cause of global diffusion?

Critical Thinking

4. **Make Judgments** Do you think globalization has had a greater effect on developed countries or developing countries? Use your notes on the section to explain your answer.

Globalization	→	Greater Effects

FOCUS ON SPEAKING

5. **Persuasion** Prepare a list of points that a government official in a developing country might use in a speech to convince other government and business leaders that the country should sign a free trade agreement.

Recent Scholarship

Though many people believed the world was flat before explorations in the 1400s proved them wrong, author Thomas L. Friedman says the world today actually is flat, at least in a metaphorical sense. In his book *The World Is Flat*, Friedman analyzes patterns of globalization in recent years and how electronic communication has enabled the world to become interconnected. Providing an example of just how progressive technology has become, Friedman issued an update of his book a year after the hardcover was published, adding revised content.

The World Is Flat by Thomas Friedman. Farrar, Straus and Giroux, 2005. (Updated edition, 2006)

Review & Assess

Close

Have students explain what globalization is and summarize its possible positive and negative effects.

Review

go.hrw.com **Online Quiz**, Section 1

Assess

SE Section 1 Assessment

Progress Assessment: Section 1 Quiz

Alternative Assessment Handbook

Reteach/Intervene

Interactive Reader and Study Guide, Section 1

Interactive Skills Tutor CD-ROM

Answers

Reading Check *leads to cultural diffusion, more travel to other countries for work or vacation, exotic goods from other countries available*

Section 1 Assessment Answers

1. **a.** process in which countries are linked to each other through trade and culture
   b. Multinational companies sometimes outsource work to developing countries.
   c. benefits—goods and services at lower cost, jobs in developing countries; drawbacks—developed countries lose some jobs, become more dependent on corporations

2. **a.** international organization that monitors trade policies and helps solve disputes
   b. supporters—both developing and developed countries benefit; opponents—helps developed nations more, exploits developing nations
   c. possible answer—for resources and labor

3. **a.** food, sports, music, and movies
   b. allows sharing and exchange of cultures
   c. possible answers—ease of transportation and communication, the Internet

4. possible answer—developing countries; they are provided with jobs and resources

5. Lists should include free tariffs, more resources, and an increase in jobs.

Getting Started

Use the **Interactive Reader and Study Guide** to familiarize students with the section content.

📖 **Interactive Reader and Study Guide**, Section 2

Academic Vocabulary

Review with students the high-use academic terms in this section.

welfare displace to force to leave home or homeland (p. 997)

displace to force to leave home or homeland (p. 998)

📝 **CRF: Vocabulary Builder: Section 2**

Taking Notes

Human Rights—problems include torture, slavery, killing; United Nations and NGOs work to improve and protect human rights; human rights usually better protected in democratic countries; Poverty and Disease—more than 20 percent of people in the world live on less than $1 per day; poverty more common in developing countries; international health organizations seek to control diseases; Population Movement—movement has increased dramatically in recent years; globalization makes movement easier; wealthy developed nations in North America and Europe are traditional destinations for migrants; fastest growing cities are in developing countries

---

SECTION 2 — Social Challenges

BEFORE YOU READ

MAIN IDEA

People and countries are working together to protect human rights, help solve problems such as poverty and disease, and adjust to new patterns of migration.

READING FOCUS

1. How are individuals, groups, and nations working to protect human rights?
2. What global challenges do people around the world face?
3. What are the causes and effects of population movement?

KEY TERMS

NGO
famine
epidemic
refugees

🗽 **NEW YORK**

PI 3.3 Students examine the social/cultural, political, economic, and religious norms and values of Western and other world cultures.

RUNNING FOR FREEDOM

THE INSIDE STORY

Can running keep you alive?
During his final year of high school in the Central African nation of Burundi, champion runner Gilbert Tuhabonye dreamed of attending college in the United States. Instead, an outbreak of ethnic violence nearly killed him.

Tuhabonye is a Tutsi, one of the two main ethnic groups in Burundi. The other group is the Hutu. In October 1993, a mob of Hutus attacked Tuhabonye's village and forced the Tutsis into the school building, which they set on fire. For hours, Tuhabonye lay trapped in the flames, protected only by the bodies of his dead classmates.

Finally, he gathered the strength to break free. With his back on fire, he broke through a window and escaped into the nearby woods. His legs were so badly burned that they barely functioned, but he refused to give up. Tuhabonye made his way to a hospital for treatment, where he had to learn again how to walk and, eventually, to run.

Less than three years after Tuhabonye nearly died, he was a member of Burundi's Olympic team. Soon after, he enrolled in college in the United States—where he was given a running scholarship. Today, Gilbert Tuhabonye lives in the United States, where he trains runners and tells his story of how running helped him survive. ◾

◀ **Runner Gilbert Tuhabonye trains in Texas.**

996 CHAPTER 33

Teach the Main Idea

At Level

Social Challenges

1. **Teach** Ask students the Reading Focus questions to teach this section.

2. **Apply** Organize students into groups of three. Assign one of the three topics in the section, Human Rights, Global Challenges, and Population Movement, to each student in a group. Have students write a summary of the information about their topic, and read them to the rest of the group. Have students ask and answer questions about the summaries.

3. **Review** Guide students in a discussion of the importance of human rights, and develop a class list of the rights students believe to be most important in a democratic society.

4. **Practice/Homework** Have students select one of the global challenges discussed in the section and write a proposal containing workable solutions to their chosen problem.
   LS Interpersonal, Verbal-Linguistic

📝 **Alternative Assessment Handbook**, Rubrics 14: Group Activity; and 37: Writing Assignments

Human Rights

Violence and human rights abuses are not new, but globalization has made the world more aware of such events. In recent years, many nations have pledged to respect human rights.

Statements on Human Rights In 1948 the United Nations issued the Universal Declaration of Human Rights. It states that all people deserve basic rights "without distinction of any kind, such as race, color, sex, language, religion, political or other opinion, national or social origin, property, birth or other status." Countries that signed the Helsinki Accords in 1975 agreed to respect human rights.

Human Rights Abuses In spite of these agreements, torture, slavery, killing, and other human rights abuses are daily occurrences in some countries. These abuses are most common in countries that are not democracies or are in the process of establishing democracy.

Some groups of people are at a greater risk of human rights abuses than others. People who disagree with their government or people who are members of a religious or ethnic minority are more likely to be victims of human rights abuses. Women and children are also at increased risk for violence and abuse.

Working for Rights Many individuals and groups are working to improve and protect human rights around the world. The United Nations investigates human rights abuses and works with national governments to protect rights. In addition, some groups called NGOs work to protect the rights of particularly threatened groups. An **NGO** is a nongovernmental organization that is formed to provide services or to promote certain public policies. NGOs such as the International Red Cross work to improve the welfare of groups such as women, children, and indigenous peoples and have played key roles in the fights against slavery, violence against women, and apartheid.

Other changes in the world have also led to improved human rights. Human rights are usually better protected in democratic countries, and the spread of democracy has led to the spread of human rights.

> **READING CHECK** **Make Generalizations** How are human rights threatened and protected?

FACES OF HISTORY

Aung San SUU KYI
1945–

An activist for democracy in her native Myanmar (Burma), Aung San Suu Kyi has long been an opponent of her country's harsh military government. In 1990 her political party won a large majority of the seats in Myanmar's parliament, but the military rulers refused to give up power. Instead, they placed Aung San and other democratic leaders under house arrest.

Despite her imprisonment, she continued to fight for democratic reform and free elections in Myanmar. For her nonviolent struggle for democracy, Aung San was awarded the Nobel Peace Prize in 1991. As of 2006 she remained under house arrest.

Summarize What does Aung San hope to achieve in Myanmar?

Global Challenges

Although globalization is improving the lives of some people, many still face major challenges, including poverty, disease, and natural disasters. These challenges greatly affect worldwide life expectancy.

Poverty Poverty is a major problem in many countries. More than 20 percent of the world's people live on less than $1 per day and do not have access to basic services such as education and health care. Poverty can have many causes, including a lack of natural resources, wars, poor government planning, and rapid population growth. One result of poverty can be a **famine**, or an extreme shortage of food.

Although poverty is found in even the world's wealthiest countries, it is more common in developing countries. In an attempt to reduce poverty, developed countries give or loan billions of dollars every year to poor countries. When used carefully, this foreign aid can make a vital contribution to reducing poverty.

Disease Although many diseases have their largest impact on a local or regional level, globalization has made controlling disease a challenge for the entire world. International air travel allows diseases to spread rapidly as infected people move from place to place. For example, in November 2002 a type of pneumonia known as SARS appeared in China. Over the next few months, SARS spread to other countries in Asia, Europe, and the Americas.

TAKING NOTES
Take notes on the social challenges of human rights, poverty and disease, and population movement.

Social Challenges
1.
2.
3.

ACADEMIC VOCABULARY
welfare well-being

NEW YORK
CC Unit 8-A2
Population pressures and poverty

CC Unit 8-B4
World hunger

997

Global Challenges

Explain Why do diseases spread more quickly today? *air travel and the number of people traveling*

Make Generalizations How does disease affect population and life expectancy? *possible answer—many diseases that plague the world are deadly, and others can be deadly if left untreated; reduce population*

Map Transparency: World Average Life Expectancy, 2002

3 What are the causes and effects of population movement? *causes—war, persecution, poverty, jobs, education; effects—urbanization, crowded cities, lack of jobs for newcomers*

Population Movement

Explain What are migration push-pull factors? *reasons people leave their home country, such as war, persecution, or poverty; reasons people move to a new country, for jobs and better life*

Make Inferences What makes people in developing countries move from the rural to urban areas? *possible answer—search for a better life, higher-paying jobs*

Answers

Interpreting Maps *much of Africa and parts of Asia; more poverty and exposure to deadly diseases, inadequate health care*

Reading Skills *possible answer— Natural disasters can have devastating effects on a community's economy and on people's lives.*

Reading Check *poverty, disease, natural disasters*

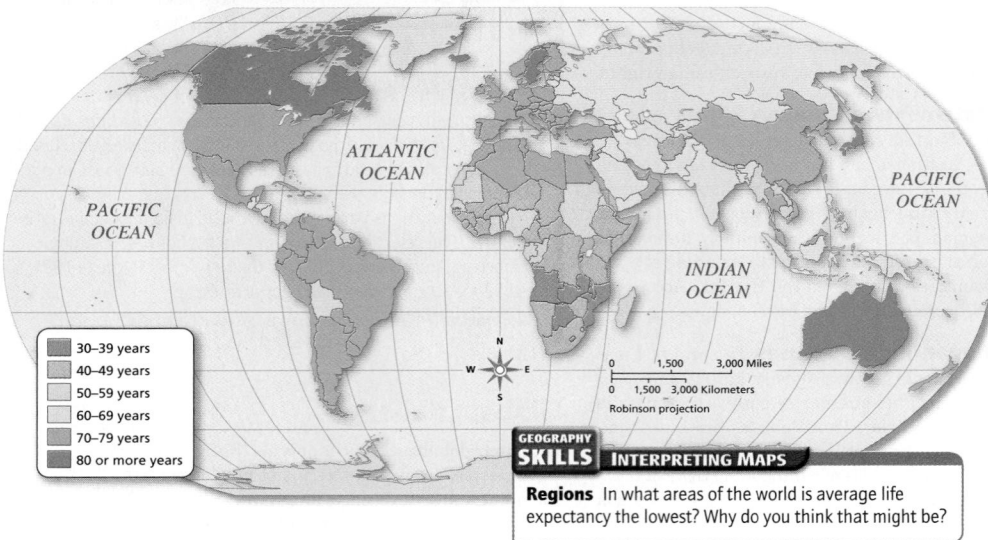

WORLD AVERAGE LIFE EXPECTANCY, 2002

- 30–39 years
- 40–49 years
- 50–59 years
- 60–69 years
- 70–79 years
- 80 or more years

0   1,500   3,000 Miles
0   1,500 3,000 Kilometers
Robinson projection

GEOGRAPHY SKILLS **INTERPRETING MAPS**

Regions In what areas of the world is average life expectancy the lowest? Why do you think that might be?

NEW YORK

CC Unit 8-A3 Migration

ACADEMIC VOCABULARY

displace to force to leave home or homeland

READING SKILLS

Making Generalizations Combine what you already know with what you have learned in this paragraph. Form a generalization about natural disasters.

Hundreds of people were killed in the epidemic. An **epidemic** is an outbreak of contagious disease that spreads quickly and affects many people. HIV/AIDS is another recent epidemic. Over 25 million people have died from AIDS since 1981, and millions more are infected by the disease.

International health organizations and local governments have had some success controlling the spread of certain diseases. Much of the success has come from educating people about the prevention of disease, as well as making medicines cheaper and more available.

Natural Disasters Natural disasters such as hurricanes, earthquakes, and floods also affect many areas of the world, often causing deaths and destroying homes and businesses. In December 2004, for example, a tsunami devastated large areas of Southeast Asia, killing over 225,000 people. Fortunately, many individuals, governments, and humanitarian organizations provide aid to regions suffering from natural disasters.

READING CHECK **Summarize** What are some of the challenges facing people around the world?

998 CHAPTER 33

Population Movement

The movement of people around the world has increased dramatically in recent years. Some people choose to move in search of better opportunities in new places, while others are **refugees**, people who flee violence in their home country to seek safety in another nation.

Migration Many factors can cause people to leave their homes and migrate to a new place. Some of these factors "push" people to leave their homeland, while others "pull" people to a new place. Typical push factors that displace people include war, persecution, and poverty. Pull factors include opportunities in a particular country for jobs and a better life.

Migration has been changed significantly by globalization. With modern air transportation, migrants today can quickly travel far from their home countries. As a result, they can settle in places that are very different from their former homes, and the mixing of cultures can be dramatic. Furthermore, migrants are often able to return to their native countries to visit, which makes it easier to retain their own cultures, languages, and habits.

Skills Focus: Making Generalizations

At Level

Reading Skill
Natural Disasters

1. Review with students some of the natural disasters that have occurred recently. Students might mention Hurricane Katrina, recent tsunamis, earthquakes, etc. Make a class list for all to see. Then review the ways in which the national and international community responded to each disaster on the list.

2. Have students write a song or poem commemorating one of the events on the class list. Student work should be sensitive to the loss of life, property, and way of life that occurs during a severe natural disaster.

LS Auditory-Musical

Alternative Assessment Handbook, Rubric 26: Poems and Songs

The countries that have traditionally been the destinations of most migrants are wealthy developed nations in North America and Europe. Often, migrants do manage to find work and provide a better life for themselves and their families. Sometimes, however, they fail to find jobs or they face discrimination in their new countries. Some people want to limit the number of migrants allowed into their countries because they think the newcomers take away jobs and services from native citizens. Others worry that the traditions and languages of the migrants will change the culture of the country.

Urbanization Another type of migration happens within countries. In many parts of the world, people in search of jobs or better opportunities are moving in large numbers to urban areas from rural areas. This increase in the percentage of people who live in cities is called urbanization.

The world's fastest-growing cities are located in developing countries. As the populations of these countries grow, more of their people move to the cities looking for work. The vast urban areas of Mumbai, India, and São Paulo, Brazil, are examples of rapidly growing cities. Urban growth in developed countries is much slower, but rapid urbanization is a main factor in worldwide population movement.

READING CHECK Find the Main Idea What are some main reasons for population movement?

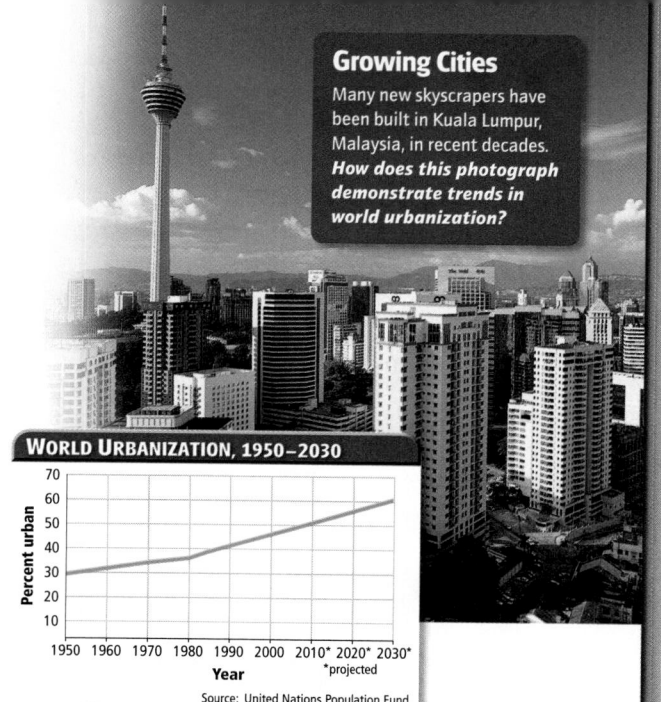

Growing Cities
Many new skyscrapers have been built in Kuala Lumpur, Malaysia, in recent decades. *How does this photograph demonstrate trends in world urbanization?*

WORLD URBANIZATION, 1950–2030

Source: United Nations Population Fund

Skills FOCUS INTERPRETING GRAPHS

Summarize How has world urbanization changed since 1950? How is it projected to change in the future?

SECTION 2 ASSESSMENT

go.hrw.com
Online Quiz
Keyword: SHL TOD HP

Reviewing Ideas, Terms, and People

1. **a. Identify** What is the purpose of the Universal Declaration of Human Rights?
   b. Explain What role do NGOs play in protecting human rights?
   c. Predict How do you think the spread of democracy might affect human rights around the world? Explain your answer.

2. **a. Identify** What are some of the main challenges facing certain people and countries around the world today?
   b. Explain How can an epidemic of a disease affect a country's economy?
   c. Elaborate Why is it so difficult to reduce poverty?

3. **a. Identify** What are some push and pull factors of migration?
   b. Make Inferences Why are the world's fastest-growing cities found in developing countries?

Critical Thinking

4. **Elaborate** Use your notes on the section and a graphic organizer like the one below to explain how social challenges affect the world today.

Social challenges

FOCUS ON WRITING

5. **Exposition** Write a letter from a person who has migrated to a new country to a friend back home. Tell the friend what you like and do not like about the new country.

TODAY'S WORLD **999**

Section 2 Assessment Answers

1. **a.** to assert the basic rights of all people
   b. provide services or promote public policies
   c. possible answer—will probably improve human rights, because democratically elected leaders are held accountable for their actions by the voters

2. **a.** poverty, disease, natural disasters
   b. possible answer—can hurt economy by decreasing workers and consumers
   c. possible answer—it is widespread; some causes are difficult to prevent

3. **a.** war, persecution, poverty; jobs, education, opportunities
   b. Rapid population growth leads people to move to cities looking for work.

4. Social challenges—poverty, disease, human rights abuses; Effects—increased urbanization, migration, globalization

5. Student letters should demonstrate an understanding of the causes and effects of migration.

• Review & Assess •

Close

Have students list human rights violations, problems associated with worldwide poverty and disease, and the effects of population movement.

Review

Online Quiz, Section 2

Assess

SE Section 2 Assessment

Progress Assessment: Section 2 Quiz

Alternative Assessment Handbook

Reteach/Intervene

Interactive Reader and Study Guide, Section 2

Interactive Skills Tutor CD-ROM

Answers

Growing Cities *shows increase in urbanization because large, modern skyscrapers indicate population growth in the city*

Interpreting Graphs *The percentage of people living in urban areas has increased, and it is projected to continue increasing.*

Reading Check *to escape war, persecution, poverty; search for better jobs, education, better life*

999

Preteach

Getting Started

Use the **Interactive Reader and Study Guide** to familiarize students with the section content.

📋 **Interactive Reader and Study Guide**, Section 3

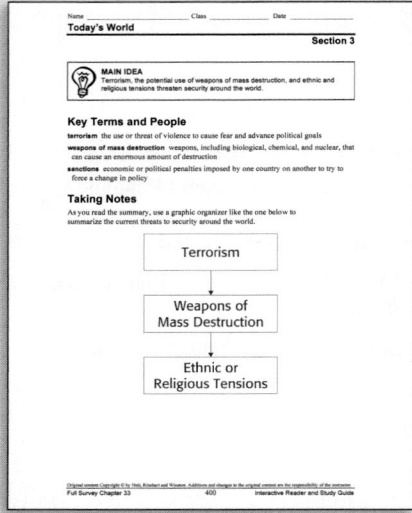

Academic Vocabulary

Review with students the high-use academic term in this section.

legislation laws or rules passed by a governing body (p. 1002)

📋 **CRF: Vocabulary Builder: Section 3**

Taking Notes

Terrorism—unlawful use or threat of violence to cause fear and to advance political, religious, or ideological goals; Weapons of Mass Destruction—weapons that can cause enormous destruction; Ethnic or Religious Tensions—create willingness to destroy or kill; can cause civil war within countries or regions, genocide

---

BEFORE YOU READ

MAIN IDEA

Terrorism, the potential use of weapons of mass destruction, and ethnic and religious tensions threaten security around the world.

READING FOCUS

1. How does the threat of terrorism affect today's world?
2. What other threats to world security exist today?

KEY TERMS

terrorism
weapons of mass destruction (WMD)
sanctions

NEW YORK

PI 1.4 Students understand the broad patterns, relationships, and interactions of cultures and civilizations.

PI 3.2 Students explain how interactions between and among cultures have affected various cultural groups.

PREPARING FOR AN ATTACK

During a terrorism preparedness drill, emergency response workers aid a "victim" of a simulated attack.

THE INSIDE STORY

How do you prepare for the worst? One November day, three people dressed as maintenance workers walked into a crowded Oklahoma mall. They calmly went about their business tending the mall's plants and then left. But the plant sprayers they used actually contained a deadly contagious disease—smallpox. Soon, dozens of people in Oklahoma had come down with smallpox, and the disease continued to spread.

Fortunately, this incident was only a test. The "smallpox" outbreak was a simulated crisis planned by the federal government and carried out at an Air Force base near Washington, D.C. The goal was to see how prepared the nation was to deal with a possible terrorist attack and to learn how the government's response to an attack could be improved. Indeed, the government learned valuable lessons from the exercise. Exercises like this have become increasingly common in the world today as governments work to protect their citizens from the threat of terrorist attacks. ◼

The Threat of Terrorism

A major threat to global security today is terrorism. **Terrorism** is the unlawful use or threat of violence to cause fear and to advance political, religious, or ideological goals. Terrorists often intentionally target unarmed and unsuspecting civilians during their attacks.

Teach the Main Idea

Threats to World Security

1. **Teach** Ask students the Reading Focus questions to teach this section.

2. **Apply** Have students review the terrorism time line that appears in this section. Then have students draw a world map using the atlas in their text book as a reference. Have students locate and show the site of each event on the time line on their maps. Student maps should also contain a key to the events.

3. **Review** Review student maps as a class. Have volunteers explain what happened in each country that was targeted by terrorist groups.

4. **Practice/Homework** Have students write a one-page memo describing how life in the United States, and in other countries, changed following the September 11, 2001, attacks on the World Trade Center.

   LS Visual-Spatial, Verbal-Linguistic

   📋 **Alternative Assessment Handbook**, Rubrics 20: Map Creation; and 40: Writing to Describe

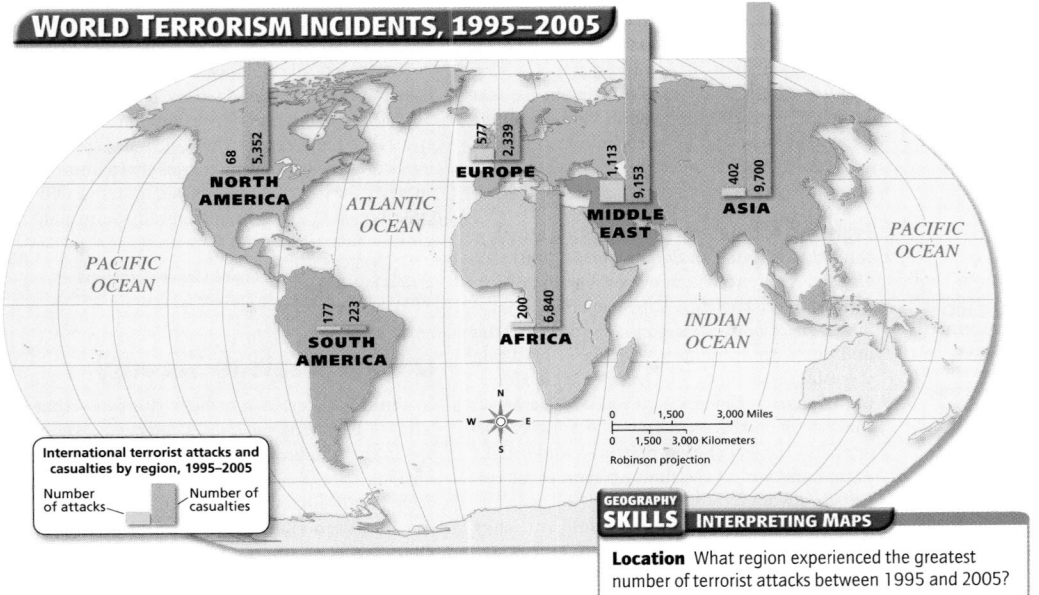

WORLD TERRORISM INCIDENTS, 1995–2005

International terrorist attacks and casualties by region, 1995–2005

Number of attacks — Number of casualties

NORTH AMERICA — 68 / 5,352
SOUTH AMERICA — 177 / 223
EUROPE — 577 / 2,339
MIDDLE EAST — 1,113 / 9,153
AFRICA — 200 / 6,840
ASIA — 402 / 9,700

0 — 1,500 — 3,000 Miles
0 — 1,500 — 3,000 Kilometers
Robinson projection

GEOGRAPHY SKILLS INTERPRETING MAPS

Location What region experienced the greatest number of terrorist attacks between 1995 and 2005?

Terrorism in History Terrorism is not a modern phenomenon, but over the last 200 years acts of terrorism have become far more common. Traditionally, terrorist groups have used terrorism to overthrow governments, fight for independence, or change society. In the late 1800s and early 1900s, for example, different terrorist groups around the world killed a number of kings, presidents, and other political leaders. Other terrorists attacked ordinary citizens in order to further their goals.

Terrorist Attacks Over the past few decades, the number of worldwide terrorist attacks has increased, as has the violence of these attacks. Few regions of the world have been spared from terrorism. In Latin America, terrorism connected to the illegal drug trade is a major problem in Colombia and Peru. In Great Britain, the Irish Republican Army (IRA) for many years engaged in terrorist attacks on British targets in an attempt to end British control of Northern Ireland. In South Asia, the Tamil Tigers in Sri Lanka have used suicide bombings and other terrorist tactics in their fight for an independent state.

Terrorism in the Middle East Increasingly, the Middle East has become a focus of efforts against international terrorist groups. In part this is because of the ongoing Arab-Israeli conflict as well as the region's history of Western colonial domination, which have led to resentment of the West among some Arabs. The region is home to some radical Muslim organizations that claim that Islam justifies terrorist attacks against innocent civilians. These terrorist actions, however, are contrary to Islamic law, and are condemned by most Muslims.

In the 1980s, Islamist groups such as Hamas, Hezbollah, and al Qaeda increasingly used terrorist tactics against Israel and some Western nations. Some of these groups, such as Hamas, seek to destroy Israel and create an independent Palestinian state, while others want to rid the Middle East of Western influences. In some cases, these groups are funded or otherwise aided by certain governments in what is known as state-sponsored terrorism.

The Lebanese group Hezbollah, for example, is supported by Iran. Hezbollah formed after the 1982 Israeli invasion of Lebanon and has the primary goal of the destruction of Israel.

NEW YORK

CC Unit 7-F4
Role of terrorism in the Middle East

TAKING NOTES

Use this graphic organizer to take notes on the threats to world security.

Terrorism

Weapons of Mass Destruction

Ethnic or Religious Tensions

TODAY'S WORLD **1001**

1001

2 What other threats to world security exist today? *weapons of mass destruction, ethnic and religious conflicts*

Other Threats to Security

Identify What is a biological weapon? *weapon made from organisms or toxins found in nature that are deadly to humans, also diseases and poisons*

Recall How many nations signed a treaty prohibiting biological weapons, and in what year was the treaty signed? *more than 70 nations; 1972*

Themes Through Time
Terrorism

Identify How many people were killed in the Pan Am Flight 103 attack? *270*

Sequence What two events happened in 1995, and how long was the period between the events? *attack on Tokyo subway system, Oklahoma City bombing; about 1 month*

ACADEMIC VOCABULARY
legislation laws or rules passed by a governing body

FOCUS ON NEW YORK
A memorial garden and museum will commemorate the September 11th attacks in New York City. New shops and offices will be built to restore the vibrant street life of lower Manhattan.

Although Israel, the United States, and several other nations consider Hezbollah to be a terrorist organization, in some nations it is seen as a legitimate resistance movement against Israel. In July 2006 Hezbollah kidnapped two Israeli soldiers and fired rockets into Israeli, triggering a month-long conflict between Israel and Lebanon.

Fighting Terrorism After al Qaeda attacked the United States on September 11, 2001, the U.S. government took many actions to prevent future terrorist attacks. The government passed new legislation to strengthen its international and domestic intelligence services, including the establishment of the Department of Homeland Security. Government leaders increased their focus on the security of the nation's borders and transportation networks and sought to find and cut off the funding sources for terrorist networks.

The government also used military action—or the threat of action—to pressure countries it suspected of supporting terrorists. In 2001, for example, a U.S.-led military campaign invaded Afghanistan and forced out the Taliban government, which had supported and protected members of al Qaeda. In 2003, another U.S.-led invasion targeted Iraq and its dictator Saddam Hussein. Some American officials claimed that Saddam possessed dangerous biological and chemical weapons and supported anti-American terrorist groups. This was later found not to be the case.

Other countries faced similar security issues. Bomb attacks on trains and buses in Madrid, London, and Jerusalem, for example, spurred Spain, Great Britain, and Israel to investigate ways to use technology to improve security for their transportation systems. Officials hoped that these measures would help prevent future terrorist attacks.

READING CHECK Make Generalizations How are countries working to prevent terrorism?

Other Threats to Security

In addition to terrorist attacks, there are other threats to global security. Dangerous weapons in the hands of terrorist groups or certain nations threaten public safety. In addition, ethnic and religious tensions in some areas of the world contribute to a lack of security for many people.

Dangerous Weapons Countries around the world possess weapons of mass destruction. **Weapons of mass destruction (WMD)** are weapons, including biological, chemical, and nuclear weapons, that can cause an enormous amount of destruction. Terrorist groups or governments may seek to use these weapons for their own purposes.

Themes Through Time

TERRORISM

SOCIETY Acts of terrorism go back thousands of year—at least as far as the times of ancient Greece and Rome. Over the last four decades, however, terrorism has grown far more common—and more violent. Today, terrorism is a major threat to the world's security.

September 1972 Palestinian terrorists take hostage and kill 11 Israeli athletes at the 1972 Olympic Games in Munich, Germany.

December 1988 Pan Am Flight 103 explodes over Scotland, killing 270 people. A Libyan man is later convicted for his role in the bombing.

1975   1985

April 1983 A suicide bomber attacks the U.S. embassy in Beirut, Lebanon, killing 63 people. The group Hezbollah is believed to be responsible.

■115

Differentiating Instruction
Above Level

Advanced Learners/Gifted and Talented
Research Required

1. Have students study the terrorism time line.
2. Have students select one event on the time line that they would like to research.
3. Have students conduct research about the terrorist event they have chosen. Students should investigate the causes, the event itself, and the consequences, both international and within the country where the attack took place.

4. Have students develop a multimedia presentation describing the attack, what might have led to the attack, the implications of the attack, and the effect that it had on its country.
LS **Verbal-Linguistic, Visual-Spatial**

Alternative Assessment Handbook, Rubrics 6: Cause and Effect; and 22: Multimedia Presentations

---

Answers

Reading Check *strengthened intelligence services, increased security, military actions*

Biological weapons are made with organisms or toxins found in nature, including diseases and poisons such as anthrax, plague, and smallpox. In 1972 more than 70 nations signed a treaty prohibiting the production or possession of biological weapons. Nevertheless, officials have begun to worry about biological attacks by terrorist groups, in part because biological weapons are relatively easy and inexpensive to develop. In 2001, for example, anthrax sent through the mail killed five Americans.

Chemical weapons such as mustard gas and nerve gas use chemical toxins to kill or injure. Like biological weapons, chemical weapons can do much damage. Chemical weapons were used during both world wars, and in the 1980s Saddam Hussein used them in the Iran-Iraq War and against Iraqi Kurds. In 1995 a Japanese religious group used the nerve gas sarin in an attack on the Tokyo subway system.

Nuclear weapons are the biggest threat to the world in the twenty-first century. Experts fear that such weapons will fall into the hands of terrorists. During the Cold War, the United States, the Soviet Union, and 60 other nations signed the Nuclear Non-proliferation Treaty, an arms control agreement meant to stop the spread of nuclear weapons. Today, nearly every nation in the world has agreed to this treaty. Still, at least nine countries are known to possess nuclear weapons, while others are believed to be trying to develop them.

One difficulty in controlling nuclear weapons is that nuclear technology can be used for legitimate purposes, such as generating energy. Because of the international concern over the development of nuclear weapons, many countries and international organizations are making efforts to ensure that nuclear technology is used safely. For example, the International Atomic Energy Agency (IAEA) routinely monitors countries suspected of developing nuclear weapons. In addition, countries have also placed sanctions on other nations they consider nuclear threats. **Sanctions** are economic or political penalties imposed by one country on another to try to force a change in policy.

Ethnic and Religious Conflicts High-tech weapons are a threat to world security because of their power to destroy and kill. Ethnic and religious conflicts are a threat because they create a willingness to destroy or kill. These conflicts have led to suicide bombings, mass killings, and other abuses.

September 2001 Al Qaeda terrorists use four hijacked airplanes to attack U.S. targets, killing some 3,000 people.

September 2004 Some 330 people taken hostage by Chechen terrorists are killed in a battle between the terrorists and Russian soldiers.

1995

2005

March 1995 A Japanese religious group releases poisonous sarin gas in the Tokyo subway system, killing 12 and injuring hundreds.

April 1995 American anti-government radicals bomb a government building in Oklahoma City, Oklahoma, killing 168 people.

Skills FOCUS **UNDERSTANDING THEMES**

Summarize How have acts of terrorism affected the world since the early 1970s?

TODAY'S WORLD **1003**

Direct Teach

Primary Sources

Ethnic Conflict in Darfur

Activity Interpreting Maps Have students locate the Darfur region, Sudan, and Chad on a map of Africa.
LS Visual-Spatial

Review & Assess

Close

Have students review threats to world security and identify what actions governments have taken to confront those threats.

Review

Online Quiz, Section 3

Assess

SE Section 3 Assessment
Progress Assessment: Section 3 Quiz
Alternative Assessment Handbook

Reteach/Intervene

Interactive Reader and Study Guide, Section 3
Interactive Skills Tutor CD-ROM

Ethnic Conflict in Darfur

The conflict in the Darfur region of Sudan between rebel forces and government-supported Janjaweed fighters had spread to the Sudan-Chad border by 2006. In this interview, a 48-year-old man from Djawara, Chad, describes a Janjaweed attack on his village. The Janjaweed killed some 75 villagers within a few hours.

> Hijab generally refers to a headscarf worn by some Muslim women, but here means an amulet that is filled with printed verses from the Qur'an.

"I ran away but I was caught with others by a group of Janjaweed at 500 meters from the village. They took off my hijab. We were surrounded by Janjaweed, more than fifty I would say, maybe one hundred. They tried to kill us with machetes and knives. I was hit on the head. At some point, the Janjaweed decided to finish us off and asked someone in the group to shoot us. The guy took his Kalashnikov and shot. Everybody collapsed. I felt that I had been shot in the arm, and I fell down."

> A Kalashnikov is an assault rifle.

Skills FOCUS **READING LIKE A HISTORIAN**

1. **Describe** What is the speaker describing?
2. **Analyze Primary Sources** According to the speaker, how did his fellow villagers die?

See **Skills Handbook**, p. H25

For example, in 1994 in the African nation of Rwanda, tensions between Tutsi and Hutu ethnic groups led to massacres in which some 1 million people were killed. Most of the victims were Tutsis, killed by Hutu militias. Another 2 million Tutsi and Hutu refugees fled to neighboring countries, where food shortages and disease killed thousands, despite international humanitarian aid. French and UN troops worked to maintain a ceasefire in Rwanda until a new government could establish order and end the violence. In 1998, some of the people involved in the genocide were convicted and executed for their crimes.

A similar situation occurred in the early 2000s in the Darfur region of Sudan. There, Arab militias, supported by the government, attacked African villagers and looted and destroyed their homes. The African Union sent a peacekeeping force to Sudan to try to end the conflict, but the violence continues. By 2006 some 400,000 people had been killed in Darfur, and more than 2 million others had fled to refugee camps.

Violence caused by ethnic and religious hatred is a significant threat to people in many places around the world. As nations face the risk of terrorist attacks, the use of weapons of mass destruction, and ethnic and religious conflict, people around the world are working hard to protect public safety.

READING CHECK **Identify Problem and Solution** How are countries and international groups dealing with threats to world security?

go.hrw.com
Online Quiz
Keyword: SHL TOD HP

SECTION 3 ASSESSMENT

Reviewing Ideas, Terms, and People

1. **a. Define** What is **terrorism**?
   b. Explain How did the United States seek to prevent future terrorist attacks after September 11, 2001?
   c. Evaluate Do you think the measures being taken in Europe, Israel, and the United States to prevent future terrorist attacks will be successful? Why or why not?

2. **a. Recall** What are three main types of **weapons of mass destruction (WMD)**?
   b. Make Inferences How have ethnic and religious tensions affected the world?
   c. Predict How do you think countries involved in threatening activities might respond to **sanctions**?

Critical Thinking

3. **Evaluate** Identify three threats to national security and rank them from least threatening to most threatening. Use your notes from the section and a graphic organizer like the one below to support your answer.

> Most
>
> Least

FOCUS ON WRITING

4. **Persuasion** Write a letter to the editor. Propose one way to eliminate or reduce a threat to society. Identify two reasons why your proposal would work.

1004 CHAPTER 33

Section 3 Assessment Answers

1. **a.** the unlawful use or threat of violence to cause fear and advance political, religious, or ideological goals
   b. strengthened domestic and international intelligence, increased security, military action in Afghanistan to remove Taliban government
   c. possible answer—Yes, nations will work together to eradicate terrorism, but there is always new technology, new ways to attack, and terrorist groups determined to cause havoc and fear.

2. **a.** biological, chemical, nuclear
   b. have caused a significant threat of violence in many parts of the world
   c. possible answer—They might choose to change their policies.

3. possible answer—from least to most: WMDs, terrorism, ethnic and religious conflict

4. Student letters should identify a realistic threat, a reasonable solution, and two reasons supporting the solution.

Answers

Primary Sources **1.** *an ethnic attack;* **2.** *They were attacked with machetes, knives, and guns.*

Reading Check *peacekeeping missions, imposing sanctions*

Environment and Technology

BEFORE YOU READ

MAIN IDEA

People are working together to protect the environment and using science and technology to improve living conditions around the world.

READING FOCUS

1. What are people doing to protect the environment?
2. What changes are recent advances in science and technology bringing to the world?

KEY TERMS AND PEOPLE

sustainable development
deforestation
global warming
biotechnology
genetic engineering
green revolution
cloning

NEW YORK

PI 1.4 Students analyze changing and competing interpretations of issues.

PI 3.1 Students analyze the roles and contributions of individuals and groups.

THINKING GLOBALLY, ACTING LOCALLY

THE INSIDE STORY

Can planting a tree improve people's lives? Wangari Maathai was born in Kenya in 1940. It was rare in those days for girls in Kenya to receive an education, but Maathai studied biology and eventually earned a doctoral degree. She was the first woman in all of East and Central Africa to do so.

Maathai saw that environmental problems were harming Kenya. Soil erosion meant that grazing lands for livestock were disappearing. Also, Kenyans had to travel farther and farther from home to find wood for their cooking fires. These problems were leading to poverty. In 1977, Maathai decided to take action and founded the Green Belt Movement to restore Africa's forests.

Since then, the Green Belt Movement has planted 30 million trees across Africa. It has also worked to fight poverty, hunger, and political corruption. In 2004, Maathai was awarded the Nobel Peace Prize for her work. ▪

TODAY'S WORLD **1005**

Teach the Main Idea

Environment and Technology

1. **Teach** Ask students the Reading Focus questions to teach this section.

2. **Apply** Have students scan the section and make a list of the visuals, including charts. Then organize the class into small groups and have each group explain how the image relates to the section title. Have volunteers share their explanations with the class.

3. **Review** Guide students in a discussion of the growing importance of technology and of protecting the environment.

4. **Practice/Homework** Have students select one scientific or technological breakthrough discussed in the section and write a paragraph explaining how that breakthrough has affected their own lives. **LS** **Verbal-Linguistic**

Alternative Assessment Handbook, Rubrics 11: Discussions; and 37: Writing Assignments

---

1 What are people doing to protect the environment? *improving resource use, reducing pollution*

Protecting the Environment

Recall What has caused the world's population to increase over the past 200 years? *improved nutrition and medical treatment*

Summarize Explain the negative impact of deforestation. *After trees are cleared from forest areas, animals and plants that lived there can become extinct.*

Info to Know

Green Buildings Green buildings are designed to reduce the negative impact the building has on the environment. These buildings use less energy and water, and are usually built near public transportation to reduce the need to drive cars. To promote land recycling, the green buildings are built on already developed land.

Desertification The desertification in the Sahel region of West Africa began in about 1968. It has led to the deaths of over 100,000 people, and desertification and overgrazing has led to the deaths of over 12 million cattle.

TAKING NOTES

Take notes on the effects of recent advances in science and technology.

Advance
Science   Technology

NEW YORK

CC Unit 8-C
The environment and sustainability

Protecting the Environment

As globalization increases and the world's population continues to grow, so do our demands on the environment. The challenge we face today is how to balance growth and development with practices that will help protect the resources and environments we all count on.

Resource Use Over the past 200 years, improved nutrition and medical treatment have led to a dramatic increase in the world's population. Since 1800 the earth's population has grown from 1 billion to well over 6 billion. As the population has increased, industrialization and development have placed great strain on the world's resources and environment.

Development can improve lives and strengthen a nation's economy, but achieving sustainable development is a major challenge. **Sustainable development** is economic development that does not permanently damage resources. With sustainable development, people try to balance the need for development with protection of the environment. In some parts of the world, for example, people seek to protect resources by limiting their use or by setting aside areas where no development is allowed. In other parts of the world, however, the environment receives little protection.

In areas of Africa, Asia, and Latin America, particularly in the Amazon region of Brazil, **deforestation**, or the clearing of trees, is taking place at a rapid rate. In these places, trees are burned or cut down in order to dig mines or to clear land for farming or cattle ranching. As a result, some species of animals and plants that live in these forests have become extinct because of deforestation.

In the Sahel region of West Africa, people are struggling with desertification, or the spread of desert-like land conditions. Desertification is caused partly by drought and partly by human activity. People cut trees for firewood and allow livestock to overgraze the land. Without plants to anchor the soil, wind blows rich soil away, and the land becomes useless.

Pollution The global environment has been seriously affected by pollution. Human beings have always polluted their environments, but pollution did not become a serious issue until the Industrial Revolution. That revolution brought new industrial processes, which created waste products that harmed the air, water, and land. By the 1960s, pollution had increased so much that some scientists had begun to see it as a growing threat to human survival.

Green Buildings
So-called green buildings are designed to reduce the building's use of resources and its impact on the environment.

The roof of Chicago's City Hall is largely covered with plants, which reduces energy use and filters rainwater.

Insulation and construction techniques, such as solar panels, help reduce this home's energy consumption.

1006 CHAPTER 33

Skills Focus: Making Oral Presentations

At Level

Reading Like a Historian Skill
Public Service Announcement

1. Have students review the information on environmental issues in this section.

2. Have students pick one environmental issue and conduct research about it using reliable online sources.

3. Have students prepare a public service announcement about their chosen issue. The announcement should inform people about

the environmental problem, its consequences, and ways to help solve the problem. Students might wish to make a multimedia presentation with both video and audio components.
LS Kinesthetic

Alternative Assessment Handbook, Rubric 24: Oral Presentations

Countries around the world find it hard to agree on how best to fight pollution. One debate surrounds the issue of **global warming**, or the rise in the surface temperature of the earth over time. This rise could bring about disastrous changes in the earth's climate. Scientists agree that the earth's temperature has increased slightly over the past 100 years, and many believe that air pollution caused by human activity has brought about this rise.

Although some governments have taken action against pollution and global warming by passing laws to protect the world's air and water, many nations do not have strict pollution controls in place. The United States, for example, has passed many environmental laws but is one of the world's largest polluters. Some nations fear that placing strict limits on the emissions of carbon dioxide and other gases that contribute to global warming might harm economic development. Preventing and reducing pollution while protecting businesses and economies is a major international challenge.

Even when environmental laws are in place, pollution and toxic waste can be released because of accidents at industrial facilities. In 1984, for example, a leak of toxic gas from an Indian factory killed over 15,000 people and injured a half-million more. Two years later, the meltdown of the Soviet Union's Chernobyl nuclear plant sent deadly radiation into the air over parts of Europe.

READING CHECK **Find the Main Idea** What environmental issues face the world today?

Science and Technology

Advances in science and technology have greatly changed the world in recent years. While new discoveries have brought great benefits, they have also raised new questions and challenges.

Space Exploration Some of the greatest discoveries and scientific advances in recent years have come from space exploration. Data collected from satellites and during space shuttle missions have given scientists new information about the origins and development of stars, galaxies, and planets. Other data is helping scientists understand climate change on the earth.

WORLD INTERNET ACCESS, 2006

REGION	POPULATION	INTERNET ACCESS
North America	331 million	68.6%
Oceania	34 million	54.1%
Europe	807 million	38.2%
South and Central America	554 million	15.1%
Middle East	190 million	10.0%
Asia	3,668 million	9.9%
Africa	915 million	3.6%

Source: Internet World Stats

Space exploration has also led to the development of technologies that are widely used today. Consumer products ranging from scratch-resistant eyeglass lenses to farther-flying golf balls are the results of experiments performed by scientists for the world's space programs.

The Information Age Other advances in science and technology have led to great changes in the way we transmit and receive information. In fact, the exchange of information is such an important part of modern life that some people say we are living in the Information Age.

Today, space satellites transmit the signals for cell phones and satellite television, both of which have become increasingly common around the world. Personal computers and the Internet link people, educational institutions, businesses, and governments around the world, allowing instant communication. More and more people are working, shopping, and maintaining friendships online.

Not all areas of the world have joined the Information Age, however. This difference in access to the Internet and other information and communications technologies is called the digital divide. Given the importance of information technology in aiding economic development, the digital divide is an obstacle that many people are trying to overcome.

Direct Teach

Reading Focus

2 What changes are recent advances in science and technology bringing to the world? *new products, increased knowledge, better and faster access to information, better medical care, larger crops*

Science and Technology

Recall What advances in consumer products have come from space exploration? *scratch-resistant eyeglass lenses, farther-flying golf balls*

Describe What is the digital divide? *difference in access to the Internet and other information and communications technologies*

Predict How will genetic engineering affect the world in ten years? *possible answer—new crops, larger crop production, less hunger*

🖫 **Quick Facts Transparency:** World Internet Access, 2006

🗒 **CRF:** Biography: Yuet Wai Kan

Skills Focus: Comparing and Contrasting

At Level

Reading Skill
Genetically Engineered Crops

Materials: construction paper, colored markers

1. Have students review the information about the green revolution and genetically engineered crops. Discuss the advantages of and concerns about genetic engineering, and have students take notes during the discussion.

2. Have students create a print advertisement to promote or discredit genetically engineered crops. Ads should carry a distinct message, a slogan, and a brief argument or comment supporting the position stated in the ad.

3. Have students present their advertisements to the class.
   LS **Verbal-Linguistic**
   🗒 **Alternative Assessment Handbook**, Rubric 2: Advertisements

Answers

Reading Check *pollution, global warming, deforestation, desertification*

1007

FACES OF HISTORY

James D. WATSON
1928–

An American scientist, James D. Watson was one of the discoverers of the structure of DNA, the material that carries genetic information in all forms of life. This discovery in the 1950s played a crucial role in the later study of genetics and in genetic engineering.

In later years, Watson continued to research human biology and genetics and led the Human Genome Project, a scientific project to determine the chemical structure of every human gene. Watson is a strong supporter of genetically modified crops and other genetic engineering, believing that the benefits outweigh any possible risks.

Infer Given Watson's scientific background, why might he support genetic engineering?

Medicine and Genetic Engineering The world has greatly benefited from the medical advances that took place in the years after World War II. Scientists and doctors developed many medicines and vaccines that prevent the spread of contagious diseases and treat physical and mental illnesses, as well as techniques that allow surgeons to transplant human organs. Advances in medical technology, including ultrasound, laser, and computer technology, have allowed doctors to more easily treat the human body.

Developments in genetics—the study of genes and heredity—have led to the rapid growth of the field of **biotechnology**, or the use of biological research in industry. Some biotechnology companies manufacture vaccines to treat diseases, while other compa-

nies have genetically modified types of food plants—grains, fruits, and vegetables. Altering the genetic makeup of a plant or animal is called **genetic engineering**. Genetically modified plants can be hardier and more productive than conventional ones and are often grown in areas of the world where other crops struggle.

Genetically modified plants are one part of the green revolution. The **green revolution** is an ongoing attempt by agricultural scientists to increase the world's food production by developing new types of wheat, rice, and other food crops. With enough water, fertilizer, and pesticides, the genetically modified crops can produce much more food than unmodified crops. Advocates believe that genetically modified crops can reduce pesticide use and bring higher profits for farmers. Others, however, are concerned about the crops' unknown effects on humans and the environment as well as a possible reduction of genetic diversity.

Another use of genetic engineering that has brought debate is cloning. **Cloning** is the process of creating identical organisms from a cell of an original organism. Although cloning offers possibilities for improving livestock and for medical research, it also presents serious moral, ethical, and legal questions. As we go forward into the twenty-first century, we will continue to use science and technology to solve problems and improve lives, while dealing with the important ethical questions these new technologies may raise.

READING CHECK **Make Generalizations** How have recent advances in science and technology brought both great benefits and new challenges?

 SECTION 4 ASSESSMENT

go.hrw.com
Online Quiz
Keyword: SHL TOD HP

Reviewing Ideas, Terms, and People

1. **a. Define** What is **deforestation**?
   b. Make Inferences Why might some people not want to limit pollution?
   c. Elaborate How might politics and economics interfere with achieving **sustainable development**?

2. **a. Describe** How have improvements in information and communication technologies affected the world?
   b. Identify Cause and Effect What have been some results of the **green revolution**?
   c. Elaborate What moral, ethical, and legal questions do you think **cloning** presents?

Critical Thinking

3. **Make Judgments** Using your notes, explain what recent scientific or technological achievement you believe has had the biggest impact on the world today.

Achievement	→	Impact

 **FOCUS ON WRITING**

4. **Exposition** Write a short paragraph in which you explain the benefits and drawbacks of genetic engineering.

1008 CHAPTER 33

Focus on Themes

Geography and Environment

Many factors shape the earth's climate. Some are natural, such as volcanic eruptions, ocean circulation, and changes in the earth's orbit. In recent years, however, scientists have begun to understand that human activities have also contributed to climate change. Climate change can take many forms, including higher ocean levels, decreased precipitation, and increased surface temperatures. These changes are commonly known as global warming.

CLIMATE CHANGE THEN The global climate is constantly changing. By the end of the 1800s, most scientists had come to understand that global temperatures have warmed and cooled repeatedly over millions of years, leading to ice ages and periods of tropical weather.

In 1896 a Swedish chemist proposed that increases in carbon dioxide and other so-called greenhouse gases—those produced by burning fossil fuels such as coal and oil—might lead to an increase in the earth's temperature by trapping heat from the sun's rays. At first, few scientists took the idea seriously, but by the 1970s, some scientists had begun to explore the possibility that human actions can contribute to climate change.

Since 1979 more than 20% of the Polar Ice Cap has melted away.

NORTH POLE

ARCTIC SEA ICE BOUNDARY IN 1979

▲ **NOW** The frozen Arctic region has gradually melted as the earth's temperature has increased.

CLIMATE CHANGE NOW The rise of the environmentalist movement in the 1960s and 1970s brought new public attention to the idea that human activity could affect the planet, and scientific research on climate change increased. Studies have shown that carbon dioxide can indeed build up in the atmosphere and has done so steadily since the mid-1800s, when fossil fuels began to be burned in large amounts during the Second Industrial Revolution.

Decades of scientific research have made it clear that the world's climate is changing. The human effect on that change, however, is less clear. Some scientists and government officials argue that the recent global warming is due to natural changes in the earth's climate rather than to human actions. By the late 1980s, however, many countries were attempting to limit their production of greenhouse gases. There is disagreement about the appropriate actions to take, but climate change is an issue that will continue to affect the world in coming years.

▲ **THEN** Glaciers began to melt and retreat around 1850 as the world's climate warmed.

 Skills FOCUS **UNDERSTANDING THEMES**

1. **Summarize** How has the world's climate changed over time?
2. **Find the Main Idea** Why do many scientists believe that humans have contributed to climate change?
3. **Infer** Why might people have different opinions about the causes of climate change?

TODAY'S WORLD **1009**

Differentiating Instruction

At Level

English-Language Learners

Standard English Mastery

1. Have students review the information in the text about global warming. Guide students in a discussion about the ways in which scientists believe the problem could be alleviated or perhaps solved. Have students take notes during the discussion and then review their notes in small groups.

2. Have volunteers propose solutions that might work in their own community to solve the problems of global warming. Create a class list for all to see and have students copy the list.

3. Have students use their notes from the class discussion and the class list of solutions to write a letter to the editor describing a solution and steps the community could take to implement it.

4. Have students use proper grammar, style, and a dictionary to help them as they write their letters. **LS Verbal-Linguistic**

📖 **Alternative Assessment Handbook**, Rubric 17: Letters to Editors

Focus on Themes

Geography and Environment

Info to Know

Facts about Global Warming Spring ice thaw and fall freezing happens 9 days earlier and 10 days later, respectively, than it did 150 years ago. Alaska, western Canada, and eastern Russia's average temperature has risen 5 to 7 degrees over what it was 50 years ago. In 1910, there were approximately 150 glaciers in Montana's Glacier Park; now only 30 glaciers are left. Average global sea level has risen 4 to 8 inches, and since the 1860s, the atmosphere's carbon dioxide level has risen almost 100 parts per million.

Answers

Understanding Themes 1. *warmed and cooled repeatedly;* **2.** *because studies have shown that carbon dioxide can build up in the atmosphere, and has done so steadily since humans began to burn fossil fuels in large amounts;* **3.** *because many factors shape the earth's climate*

1009

Document-Based Investigation

Genetically Modified Crops

Word Help

biotechnology biological sciences applied to genetic engineering and some DNA techniques

erosion gradually worn away

biodiversity variety of organisms found within a specified geographic region

Info to Know

Norman Borlaug Norman Borlaug spent 27 years of his career working with Mexican scientists to improve their wheat production. He also began working with scientists all around the world helping them with their production of wheat. He won the Nobel Peace Prize in 1970 for his work with the green revolution and genetically engineered crops.

Teaching Tip

Make sure that students understand the abbreviations used in the cartoon. B.G.H. is Bovine Growth Hormone, which increases milk production in cows. D.D.T., dichloro-diphenyl-trichloroethane, is a toxic pesticide, once widely used, no longer legal in the United States. P.C.Bs, Polychlorinated Biphenyls, are mixtures of man-made chemicals that were widely used in plastics, rubber products, and numerous other industrial ways, are toxic. Their manufacture, processing and distribution are now prohibited under the 1976 Toxic Substances Control Act.

Genetically Modified Crops

NEW YORK STANDARDS

PI 1.3 Students analyze historic events from around the world by examining accounts written from different perspectives.

Historical Context The documents below provide information about the debate over genetically modified crops.

Task Examine the documents and answer the questions that follow. After you have studied all the documents, you will be asked to write an essay about genetically modified crops. You will need to use evidence from these selections and from the chapter to support the position you take in your essay.

DOCUMENT 1

A Cartoonist's View

The cartoon at right was created by American cartoonist Andy Singer. Published in 2002, it shows a farmer singing about farm life while spraying crops, using the children's song "Old MacDonald Had a Farm" as a basis for the song's lyrics.

Old MacDonald's Agribusiness Farm, by Andy Singer, 2002

DOCUMENT 2

Norman Borlaug's Opinion

A scientist and crop researcher, American Norman Borlaug received the Nobel Peace Prize in 1970 for his work to end world hunger. In this 2002 interview, he speaks about the use of biotechnology and the development of genetically modified crops.

> Biotechnology will help these [developing] countries accomplish things that they could never do with conventional plant breeding. The technology is more precise and farming becomes less time consuming. The public needs to be better informed about the importance of biotechnology in food production so it won't be so critical . . .

You can philosophize about this but I've been in the field for a long time and I believe genetically modified food crops will stop world hunger . . .

If we had continued practicing conventional farming, we would have cut down millions of acres of forest, thereby destroying wildlife habitat, in order to increase cropland to produce enough food for an escalating population. And we would have to use more herbicides in more fields, which would damage the environment even more. Technology allows us to have less impact on soil erosion, biodiversity, wildlife, forests, and grasslands.

1010 CHAPTER 33

Skills Focus: Analyzing Alternative Points of View | Below Level

Reading Like a Historian Skill
Debating Genetically Modified Crops

1. Have students review the information in the chapter regarding genetically modified crops. Then have students write a paraphrase of each of the documents, using simpler vocabulary. Students should be sure to note whether each document is in favor of genetic modification, or against it.

2. Organize students into two groups for a class debate on genetic engineering. Students should use arguments presented in the documents during the debate.

3. After the debate, have students make their own political cartoons reflecting one viewpoint or the other. **LS** Interpersonal, Visual-Spatial

   Alternative Assessment Handbook, Rubrics 10: Debates; and 27: Political Cartoons

DOCUMENT 3

A Concern about Food Safety

The excerpt below is from *Fatal Harvest: The Tragedy of Industrial Agriculture*, a 2002 collection of essays edited by Andrew Kimbrell, the director of the Center for Food Safety. The Center opposes genetically modified crops.

> The myths of industrial agriculture share one underlying and interwoven concept—they demand that we accept that technology always equals progress. This blind belief has often shielded us from the consequences of many farming technologies. Now, however, many are asking the logical questions of technology: A given technology may be progress, but progress toward what? What future will that technology bring us?... As a growing portion of society realizes that pesticides, fertilizers, monoculturing, and factory farming are little more than a fatal harvest, even the major agribusiness corporations are starting to admit that some problems exist. Their solution to the damage caused by the previous generation of agricultural technologies is—you guessed it—more technology. "Better" technology, biotechnology, a technology that will fix the problems caused by chemically intensive agriculture. In short, the mythmakers are back at work.

DOCUMENT 4

The History of Genetic Modification

In this October 2000 essay in the plant biology journal *Plant Physiology*, Norman Borlaug writes about genetically modified crops.

> The fact is that genetic modification started long before humankind starting altering crops by artificial selection. Mother Nature did it, and often in a big way. For example, the wheat groups we rely on for much of our food supply are the result of unusual (but natural) crosses between different species of grasses... Neolithic humans domesticated virtually all of our food and livestock species over a relatively short period 10,000 to 15,000 years ago. Several hundred generations of farmer descendants were subsequently responsible for making enormous genetic modifications in all of our major crop and animal species... Thanks to the development of science over the past 150 years, we now have the insights into plant genetics and breeding to do purposefully what Mother Nature did herself in the past by chance.

> Genetic modification of crops is not some kind of witchcraft; rather, it is the progressive harnessing of the forces of nature to the benefit of feeding the human race.

Word Help

monoculture cultivation of a single crop on a farm or in a region or country

agribusiness farm industry

Info to Know

Green Revolution and the World

The green revolution set out to eliminate hunger and famine by developing heartier or productive varieties of crops. By the 1990s, 75 percent of Asian rice had new varieties, and almost 50 percent of the wheat in Africa also had new varieties.

Skills FOCUS — READING LIKE A HISTORIAN

DOCUMENT 1
a. **Identify** What is the cartoonist's opinion about genetically modified crops?
b. **Make Judgments** Do you think the cartoonist's use of humor to support his opinion is effective? Why or why not?

DOCUMENT 2
a. **Identify** What is Borlaug's opinion about genetically modified crops? What words or phrases support your answer?
b. **Explain** What arguments does Borlaug use to support his opinion?

DOCUMENT 3
a. **Identify** What is the author's opinion about genetically modified crops?
b. **Analyze** How does the author use factual and emotional language to support this view?

DOCUMENT 4
a. **Compare and Contrast** Does the author agree or disagree with the writer of Document 3? What words or phrases support your answer?
b. **Make Judgments** How does the author support his position? Do you think his arguments are valid?

DOCUMENT-BASED ESSAY QUESTION

Why might people view genetically modified crops differently? Using the documents above and information from the chapter, form a thesis that explains your position. Then write a short essay to support your position.

See **Skills Handbook**, pp. H25, H27, H29

Collaborative Learning   [At Level]

Choosing the Best Argument

1. Organize students into groups of four. Assign each student in each group one document, and have the students write a paraphrase or summary of the assigned document. Have students share the information within their groups, so that all four documents are reviewed by the groups.

2. Have groups decide which document they think makes the best argument. Tell groups they should consider the following questions when making their choice: Does the document use facts or emotional language? Is the argument persuasive? Why or why not?

3. Have groups list specific reasons to support their choice.

4. Have volunteers present their group's chosen document and cite specific examples and information that support their choice.
   LS Verbal-Linguistic

   Alternative Assessment Handbook, Rubrics 14: Group Activity; and 24: Oral Presentations

Answers

Reading Like a Historian
Document 1. a. *that they are harmful;* **b.** *possible answers—no, because if the plants hurt people it would be a serious matter; yes, humor gets his message across;* **Document 2. a.** *that they will end world hunger and help the environment; "genetically modified food crops will stop world hunger;" "would have cut down millions of acres of forest;"* **b.** *argues that his opinion is more valid because he has been in the field for a long time, and that others are merely philosophizing;* **Document 3. a.** *that these crops may have unintended negative consequences; that technology does not necessarily mean progress;* **b.** *asks rhetorical questions, labels supporters of genetic modification as "blind" and "mythmakers;"* **Document 4. a.** *disagrees; "not some kind of witchcraft," "progressive;"* **b.** *states that nature and many earlier farmers also genetically modified crops; possible answers—no, because the outcome of the earlier modifications has no bearing on the outcome of today's genetic engineering; yes, his argument gives good examples for why people should not fear the new technology;* **Essay** *Student essays should explore both sides of the debate over genetically modified crops, using details from the documents and the chapter to explain the differing opinions.*

VISUAL STUDY GUIDE

Globalization

Effects of Globalization

Economic Effects
- Increased economic interdependence among the world's nations
- Growth of the free trade movement
- Establishment of international trade organizations and agreements
- Rise of multinational corporations

Social Effects
- Population movement around the world through migration and urbanization
- Spread of culture traits from one region to another
- International efforts to fight poverty and disease and provide aid to regions suffering from national disasters
- Efforts to protect human rights by NGOs and other groups

Environmental Issues
- Population growth strains the world's resources and the environment
- Achieving sustainable development is a major challenge
- Limiting pollution and fighting global warming while protecting businesses and economies is an important international issue

Threats to World Security
- Acts of terrorism
- Terrorist groups or dangerous nations using biological, chemical, or nuclear weapons
- Ethnic and religious hatred and violence

Review Key Terms

Identify the correct term or person from the chapter that best fits each of the following descriptions.

1. laws or rules passed by a governing body
2. the rise in the surface temperature of the earth over time
3. biological, chemical, and nuclear weapons
4. changing the genetic makeup of a plant or animal to create a new type
5. a relationship between countries in which they rely on one another for resources, goods, and services
6. economic development that does not permanently damage resources
7. the process in which countries are linked to each other through trade and culture

Reading Skills

12. possible answer—The growth of the global economy allows for increased economic interdependence.

13. possible answer—Due to advances in technology, in addition to globalization, people are able to travel quickly, and communicate easily around the world.

14. possible answer—Migration effects globalization, because people move into new areas, bringing their cultures with them.

Comprehension and Critical Thinking

SECTION 1 *(pp. 991–995)*

8. a. Describe What are some main differences between developed and developing countries?

b. Explain How do multinational corporations benefit from global economic interdependence?

c. Make Judgments Do you think cultural diffusion has mostly positive or negative effects? Explain your answer.

SECTION 2 *(pp. 996–999)*

9. a. Recall What are some factors that can contribute to poverty?

b. Make Inferences Why do you think threats to human rights have occurred particularly in countries that are not democracies or are just trying to establish democracy?

c. Predict How might increasing migration and urbanization affect the world?

SECTION 3 *(pp. 1000–1004)*

10. a. Describe Name four examples of recent terrorism and list where they occurred.

b. Summarize Summarize the threats posed to the world's security by terrorism and weapons of mass destruction.

c. Elaborate What issues are involved in trying to stop the spread of nuclear weapons?

SECTION 4 *(pp. 1005–1008)*

11. a. Recall What kinds of improvements in living conditions have recent advances in biology brought about?

b. Identify Cause and Effect What are some causes and effects of desertification?

c. Evaluate Do you think protecting the environment or encouraging development is more important? Explain your answer.

Reading Skills

Making Generalizations *Use what you have learned in this chapter to make a generalization about each topic below.*

12. the global economy

13. technology and globalization

14. migration and globalization

Analyzing Points of View

Reading Like a Historian *The two selections below show alternative points of view on the use of genetic engineering in corn production.*

❝There are a number of Oaxacans, especially campesinos [farmers], who consider the presence of any transgenes in maize [corn] as an unacceptable risk to their traditional farming practices, and the cultural, symbolic, and spiritual value of maize. That sense of harm is independent of its scientifically studied potential or actual impact upon human health, genetic diversity, and the environment.❞

—Report of the Commission for Environmental Cooperation, a division of NAFTA, 2004

❝The report also fails to consider the potential benefits of biotechnology . . . Biotechnology offers the world . . . opportunities to combat hunger and protect the environment.❞

—Joint statement of the Environmental Protection Agency and the U.S. Trade Representative on the NAFTA report, 2004

15. Explain On what basis does the NAFTA report claim that genetically modified corn is bad for Mexico?

16. Interpret What differences are at the root of the disagreement between the two sources?

Using the Internet

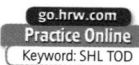
go.hrw.com
Practice Online
Keyword: SHL TOD

17. Global warming is an important—and controversial—issue. Using the Internet, research the ongoing debate about the causes and impact of global warming. Then write a report that summarizes and evaluates the major positions and arguments about climate change.

WRITING ABOUT HISTORY

Exposition: Writing and Explanation *Advances in science and technology have encouraged economic growth and population growth. These results have, in turn, threatened the environment in many places around the world.*

18. Assignment: In an essay, explain how societies balance their need for economic development with the pressures development places on the environment. To support your explanation, use information from this chapter and from other research as needed. Be sure to collect facts and examples that clearly illustrate the points you are making.

You can use these pages to have students simultaneously review the unit and practice taking standardized tests.

Answers

1. 4
   Europe and North America, Section 1

2. 2
   Europe and North America, Section 1

3. 1
   Europe and North America, Section 2

4. 3
   Europe and North America, Section 2

5. 4
   Europe and North America, Section 4

6. 2
   Asia, Section 1

7. 3
   Asia, Section 2

8. 2
   Asia, Section 3

Directions Write your answer for each statement or question on a separate answer sheet. Choose the number of the word or expression that best completes the statement or answers the question.

1 The U.S. effort to rebuild Europe after World War II was known as
1 the Truman Doctrine.
2 the Monroe Doctrine.
3 the domino theory.
4 the Marshall Plan.

2 The quote below from Winston Churchill in 1946 came at the beginning of what conflict?

"From Stettin in the Baltic to Trieste in the Adriatic, an iron curtain has descended across the Continent . . . All these famous cities and the populations around them lie in the Soviet sphere and are subject, in one form or another, not only to Soviet influence, but to a very high degree and increasing measure of control from Moscow."

1 World War II
2 the Cold War
3 the Korean War
4 the Vietnam War

3 What caused the Cuban missile crisis?
1 The Soviet Union began transporting nuclear missiles to Cuba.
2 The Cuban government sold nuclear missiles to Venezuela.
3 The United States aimed nuclear missiles at Cuba.
4 The Soviet Union agreed to buy nuclear missiles from Cuba.

4 In what ways did the Cold War conflict between the Soviet Union and the United States affect the rest of the world?
1 The United States set up satellite states in Eastern Europe.
2 The Soviet Union formed NATO to guard against a possible attack by Western powers.
3 The United States and the Soviet Union competed to gain influence and control around the world.
4 Soviet and U.S. troops fought each other directly in many countries.

5 Which event led to the end of the Cold War?
1 The United States and the Soviet Union signed a truce to end the war after the Cuban missile crisis.
2 The United States and the Soviet Union both decided to reduce military spending.
3 The United States developed a missile defense system that neutralized the threat of nuclear weapons.
4 The Soviet Union suffered from serious economic problems and collapsed.

6 India was partitioned in 1947 largely because
1 India's neighbors feared a unified India would dominate the region.
2 differences between Hindus and Muslims created religious conflict.
3 the Soviet Union was trying to set up a Communist government in eastern India.
4 Great Britain and the United States feared that India had nuclear weapons.

7 How was the Vietnam War related to the domino theory?
1 Vietnam had built up its military and planned to invade Cambodia and Thailand.
2 The Soviet Union invaded China to prevent it from attacking Vietnam.
3 The United States did not want a Communist government to take control of Vietnam.
4 France agreed to allow Vietnam to set up a democracy to stop the spread of communism.

8 Under Deng Xiaoping, China
1 became a Communist country.
2 began economic reforms.
3 launched the Cultural Revolution.
4 battled the nationalist Guomindang forces.

9 What event in China's history does this photo represent?

1 the Communist takeover of China
2 China's long conflict with Taiwan
3 the Cultural Revolution
4 the protests at Tiananmen Square

10 The term Asian Tigers refers to
1 countries in Asia that experienced tremendous economic growth in the 1980s.
2 countries in Asia that have used their strong militaries to threaten their neighbors.
3 the Communist countries of Asia.
4 countries in Asia that have nuclear weapons.

11 Both Kwame Nkrumah and Jomo Kenyatta
1 were imprisoned in South Africa during apartheid.
2 were Arab nationalists.
3 led independence movements in Africa.
4 were African dictators in the 1980s.

12 What was a key result of the Camp David Accords?
1 Israel agreed to return to its 1948 boundaries.
2 Syria and Lebanon agreed to a common border.
3 Iran and Iraq ended their long war.
4 Egypt and Israel settled their conflict peacefully.

13 How did the Iranian Revolution change Iran?
1 A conservative religious government came to power.
2 Iran established better relations with the West.
3 Iran became a Communist country.
4 Freedom of religion and speech were allowed.

14 How has the United States been involved in Central America in the postwar era?
1 The United States invaded Nicaragua and El Salvador in the 1980s.
2 The United States has repeatedly blockaded the Panama Canal.
3 The United States has supported anticommunist governments and insurgent groups.
4 The United States has worked to end free trade agreements in the region.

15 One thing that Juan Perón and Augusto Pinochet have in common is that both
1 led military dictatorships in Latin America.
2 served as president of Argentina.
3 led Communist uprisings in Central America.
4 refused to join NAFTA.

16 How is globalization changing the world?
1 It is eliminating poverty in many countries.
2 It is linking countries through trade and culture.
3 It is reducing economic interdependence.
4 It is eliminating free trade.

17 Which international agency works to resolve international conflicts and humanitarian crises?
1 GATT
2 NAFTA
3 UN
4 G-8

REVIEWING THE UNIT

Constructed Response The superpower rivalry between the United States and the Soviet Union affected the whole world. Pick two world regions from this unit and write a brief essay on how superpower conflicts affected their history since 1945. What conflicts occurred, and how were superpowers involved?

CONNECTING TO THE PREVIOUS UNIT

Constructed Response The roots of the Cold War can be traced back to events at the end of World War II. What were some of these events, and how did they set the stage for postwar conflict? Write a brief essay outlining how two events at the end of World War II laid the foundation for Cold War conflicts.

Answers

9. 4
Asia, Section 3

10. 1
Asia, Section 4

11. 3
Africa and the Middle East, Section 1

12. 4
Africa and the Middle East, Section 4

13. 1
Africa and the Middle East, Section 4

14. 3
Latin America, Section 1

15. 1
Latin America, Section 2

16. 2
Today's World, Section 1

17. 3
Africa and the Middle East, Sections 2–4; Today's World, Sections 2–3

Reviewing the Unit

Student essays will vary, but might mention the Soviet blockade of Berlin and the Cuban missile crisis. In the first case, the Soviet Union hoped to force the Western nations to abandon Berlin. The Soviets were forced to lift their blockade after the Western allies used an airlift to deliver food and other supplies to West Berlin. In the second instance, after the failed Bay of Pigs invasion, the Soviet Union installed missiles in Cuba, 90 miles from the United States. After the United States threatened to take military action—which could have resulted in a nuclear war—the Soviets removed the missiles.

Connecting to the Previous Unit

Student essays should discuss two critical events that occured at the end of World War II and their connection to later Cold War conflicts.

Unit Review

Economic Systems

Cultural Protection In 2005 the UN Educational, Scientific and Cultural Organization (UNESCO) approved the first international treaty designed to protect cultures from foreign competition. The measure was a response to increasing globalization, which threatens to diminish local cultures. U.S. officials objected to the measure, saying that it could be used to block the flow of ideas, goods, and services. The measure was supported by Canada and Britain, normally among America's closest allies. Only Israel joined the United States in voting against the measure.

Society

Globalization and Terrorism

A connection can be made between globalization and terrorism. Computers, jets, and other technology have sped up globalization and broken down traditional ideas of sovereign nation-states. At the same time, tools of globalization can be used to spread terror.

Primary Source

"Analyzing terrorism as something separate from globalization is misleading and potentially dangerous. Indeed globalization and terrorism are intricately intertwined forces characterizing international security in the twenty-first century."
—Audrey Kurth Cronin, Specialist in International Terrorism at the Congressional Research Service at the Library of Congress

Activity **Analyzing Primary Sources** Write the quote by Audrey Kurth Cronin above for students to see. Have students write two or three paragraphs explaining what the quote means, whether they agree or not, and why. **LS Verbal-Linguistic**

Themes & Global Connections

THEME
ECONOMIC SYSTEMS

How is globalization changing the world's economic systems?

Globalization is the process by which countries are linked through trade and culture. Improvements in mass communication and modern transportation technologies have allowed people, goods, and information to spread around the globe faster than ever before. As a result, global and regional trade are growing, and countries are increasingly linked economically and culturally.

Global Culture
A global culture is developing as people have more access to the same information and products.

Free Trade
Regional trade organizations that seek to lower trade barriers and increase trade among countries are growing.

Growth of Trade
Global and regional trade are growing as the world economy expands.

Effects of Globalization

Outsourcing
Companies are sending more work overseas, creating jobs in some places but eliminating them in others.

Interdependence
Countries are relying on each other more than ever for goods and services.

Multinational Corporations
Large companies that operate around the world are growing in size and influence.

THEME
SOCIETY

What challenges do societies around the world face today?

In both developed and developing countries, people face many difficult issues that affect their societies. These include safeguarding human rights, fighting poverty and health problems, providing services and economic opportunities to migrants and immigrants, and protecting societies from the threats of terrorism and conflict.

CHALLENGES FACING SOCIETIES TODAY

Human Rights Despite government commitments to protect human rights, people around the world are still victims of human rights abuses.

Poverty Poverty is a major problem in both developed and developing countries, despite global efforts to reduce it.

Health Fighting disease and hunger, making quality health care available, and educating people about health issues are worldwide challenges.

Migration and Urbanization As cities grow and people migrate to new places, providing them with jobs and services is a challenge.

Terrorism and Security Societies around the world face increasing threats from terrorism and regional conflicts.

1016 UNIT 9

Differentiating Instruction

Below Level

English-Language Learners

Materials: poster paper, colored pencils or markers

1. Organize students into mixed-ability pairs. Ask students what they think is the biggest challenge facing societies today. Have each pair decide on a challenge and write it on a sheet of paper. (Students may choose one of those listed in the chart at the bottom of this page, or another challenge, such as an aging population.)

2. Have pairs create a poster to build awareness of the challenge they identified.

3. Display student posters for the class to see.

4. Guide students in a discussion of the challenges they illustrated. What are some possible ways of dealing with these challenges? **LS Visual-Spatial**

   Alternative Assessment Handbook, Rubrics 11: Discussions; 28: Posters; and 35: Solving Problems

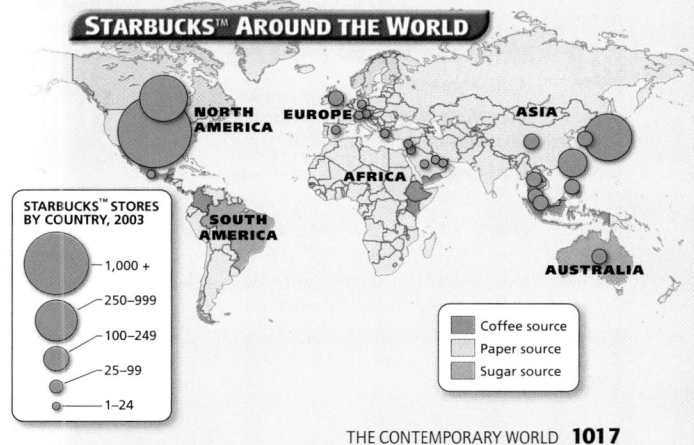

GEOGRAPHY AND ENVIRONMENT

What environmental challenges are affecting the world's people and places?

As populations and economies grow, so too does the need for resources and the demands on the environment. The challenge that people face around the globe is how to balance growth and development with practices that will help preserve and protect the natural resources and environments that we depend on.

ENVIRONMENTAL CHALLENGES TODAY

Using Resources Wisely People need to use resources to survive, and using them in a sustainable way can be a major challenge.

Protecting the Environment Living in and using the earth's environments while protecting them is a challenge as populations grow and developments spread.

Reducing Pollution Preventing and cleaning up pollution of the land, water, and air is a challenge in many places.

Fighting Global Warming Reducing greenhouse gases without disrupting economies is an international challenge.

Skills FOCUS UNDERSTANDING THEMES

How have globalization, challenges facing society, and environmental issues affected the community you live in? Read a local newspaper to gather information about current events in your community. Then create a chart like this one and use it to describe how these global themes are affecting the area where you live.

	Effects on My Community
Globalization	
Societal Challenges	
Environmental Challenges	

Global Connections

With globalization, places around the world are connected more than ever before. The people, culture, and businesses in one place can affect those of other places far away.

Making Connections This map shows the store locations and major resource locations of a multinational coffee company. How does the information on this map show some of the effects of globalization around the world? Write a short essay identifying three effects of globalization based on this map.

Sources: starbucks.com; U.S. Department of Agriculture; *Fortune Magazine*
Starbucks is a registered trademark of Starbucks U.S. Brands, LLC Ltd.

STARBUCKS™ AROUND THE WORLD

NORTH AMERICA
EUROPE
ASIA
AFRICA
SOUTH AMERICA
AUSTRALIA

STARBUCKS™ STORES BY COUNTRY, 2003
- 1,000 +
- 250–999
- 100–249
- 25–99
- 1–24

Coffee source
Paper source
Sugar source

Geography and Environment

The Kyoto Accord In February 2005 the Kyoto Accord went into effect. This is an international agreement to reduce emissions of carbon dioxide and other greenhouse gasses that have been blamed for global warming. The treaty became legally binding after Russia ratified it in November 2004. However, the world's top polluter, the United States, has not ratified the treaty, saying the changes would be too costly. In one of his first acts upon taking office in 2001, President George W. Bush took the United States out of the Kyoto negotiations. He objected to the fact that large developing countries such as China and India are exempted from its requirements.

Understanding Themes

Answers will vary but might include the loss of jobs due to outsourcing, coping with an aging population, and challenges such as pollution or urban sprawl.

Global Connections

One effect of globalization is that Starbucks depends on raw materials from nations around the world for coffee beans, sugar, and paper. A second effect is that Starbucks is an American-based company that has stores in many nations. A third effect is the spreading of American culture to places like Japan and China. Still another effect is that around the world, Starbucks stores may drive locally owned cafés out of business.

Collaborative Learning

At Level

Reducing Pollution to Fight Global Warming

1. Tell students about the Kyoto Accord (see "Geography and Environment: The Kyoto Accord" in the side margin on this page).

2. Organize students into two groups for a class debate. Tell one group that it will argue in favor of U.S. participation in the Kyoto Accord. Tell the other group that it will argue against U.S. participation in the Kyoto Accord. Give students time to prepare arguments and conduct additional research, if necessary.

3. Moderate a class debate on the desirability of U.S. participation in the Kyoto Accord to reduce pollution and slow global warming.

4. Guide students in a discussion of the Kyoto Accord. What alternatives are there to such an international agreement? **LS** **Interpersonal**

   Alternative Assessment Handbook, Rubrics 10: Debates; 11: Discussions; and 14: Group Activity

Unit Review

Summarizing the Unit

The decades following World War II have been marked by dramatic technological and social changes. At the beginning of the period, there was an ideological Cold War between two superpowers—the United States and the Soviet Union. At the beginning of the new millennium, only one superpower remained, and American culture was spreading throughout the world. Have students create a class chart showing the current state of each of the areas covered in this unit: Europe and North America, Asia, Africa and the Middle East, and Latin America.

Answers

Thinking Like a Historian *Student maps and challenges will vary. possible answers—**A.** the precarious democracies of the former Soviet Union, the rise of fundamental Islamic republics in the Middle East;* **B.** *the effects of globalization, the effects of regional trade blocs;* **C.** *aging populations, epidemics such as avian flu.*

UNIT 9
IN BRIEF
Below is a chapter-by-chapter summary of the main ideas in this unit, followed by a summary activity for the unit.

CHAPTER 29 — Europe and North America
1945–Present

MAIN IDEA The end of World War II left two superpowers: the United States and the Soviet Union. For decades, their rivalry shaped world politics.

SECTION 1 The Soviet Union and the other former Allies found it difficult to cooperate during peacetime.

SECTION 2 During the Cold War, the Soviet Union and the United States competed for power and influence.

SECTION 3 The postwar boom and the Cold War caused social changes in Europe and North America.

SECTION 4 The Soviet Union collapsed in 1991, leaving the United States as the world's only superpower.

CHAPTER 30 — Asia
1945–Present

MAIN IDEA After World War II, the nations of Asia continued their quest for political and economic independence.

SECTION 1 India, a former British colony, achieved independence but also suffered from conflicts.

SECTION 2 Many countries in Southeast Asia achieved independence in the postwar years.

SECTION 3 Communist forces led by Mao Zedong took control of China in 1949 and reshaped the country.

SECTION 4 In East Asia, the postwar era has been a time of great economic growth in countries like Japan, South Korea, and Singapore.

CHAPTER 31 — Africa and the Middle East
1945–Present

MAIN IDEA After World War II, Africa and the Middle East struggled with independence and conflict.

SECTION 1 Most African nations gained independence after 1950.

SECTION 2 African nations faced many challenges that included poverty and corrupt governments.

SECTION 3 In the 1950s and 1960s, nationalism spread across North Africa and the Middle East.

SECTION 4 Conflicts in the Middle East have included the Arab-Israeli conflict, the Iranian Revolution, and two wars in Iraq.

1018 UNIT 9

CHAPTER 32 — Latin America
1945–Present

MAIN IDEA Latin America has experienced a transition from repressive military dictatorships to more open democratic societies. The region's economies have suffered from many problems but have been improving.

SECTION 1 After World War II, revolutions, civil war, and U.S. intervention affected many countries in Central America.

SECTION 2 Economic and social problems allowed dictators to seize control in Argentina, Brazil, Chile, and other countries.

SECTION 3 In the 1980s, dictatorships fell, and moderate governments began political and economic reforms.

CHAPTER 33 — Today's World

MAIN IDEA The world is changing rapidly today as people face issues like globalization, human rights, terrorism and conflict, and changes in science and technology.

SECTION 1 Global trade and cultural exchange are affecting people around the world.

SECTION 2 Fighting poverty, protecting human rights, and preventing disease are major societal challenges.

SECTION 3 Terrorism and ethnic and religious tensions threaten regional and global security.

SECTION 4 People are working together to protect the environment and use resources wisely. At the same time, new developments in science and technology are improving living conditions around the world.

Thinking like a Historian
Summary and Extension Activity

People around the world face many difficult challenges today. What are some of these challenges, and how do they affect the world's major regions? Draw a simple map of the world that includes Europe, North America, Asia, Africa, and Latin America. On each continent, identify key challenges that affect:

A. Government and politics

B. Economies

C. Societies

Unit Resources

Review and Reinforce

- **Global History and Geography Regents Test Prep Workbook**
- **Regents Review Transparencies**
- **CRF:** Chapter Review
- **Spanish Chapter Summaries Audio CD Program**
- OSP **Holt PuzzlePro:** Quiz Show for ExamView
- **Quiz Game CD-ROM**

Assess

- **PASS:** Unit Test, Forms A and B
- **Alternative Assessment Handbook**
- OSP **New York ExamView Test Generator** correlated to NY SS Standards
- **Differentiated Instruction Modified Worksheets and Tests CD-ROM:** Chapter Test
- HOAP **Holt Online Assessment Program** (in the Premier Online Edition)

Reteach/Intervene

- **Interactive Reader and Study Guide**
- **Differentiated Instruction Teacher Management System:** Lesson Plans for Differentiated Instruction
- **Differentiated Instruction Modified Worksheets and Tests CD-ROM:** Chapter Test
- **Interactive Skills Tutor CD-ROM**

go.hrw.com
Online Resources

KEYWORDS: SHL ENA, SHL ASA, SHL AFR, SHL LAT, SHL TOD

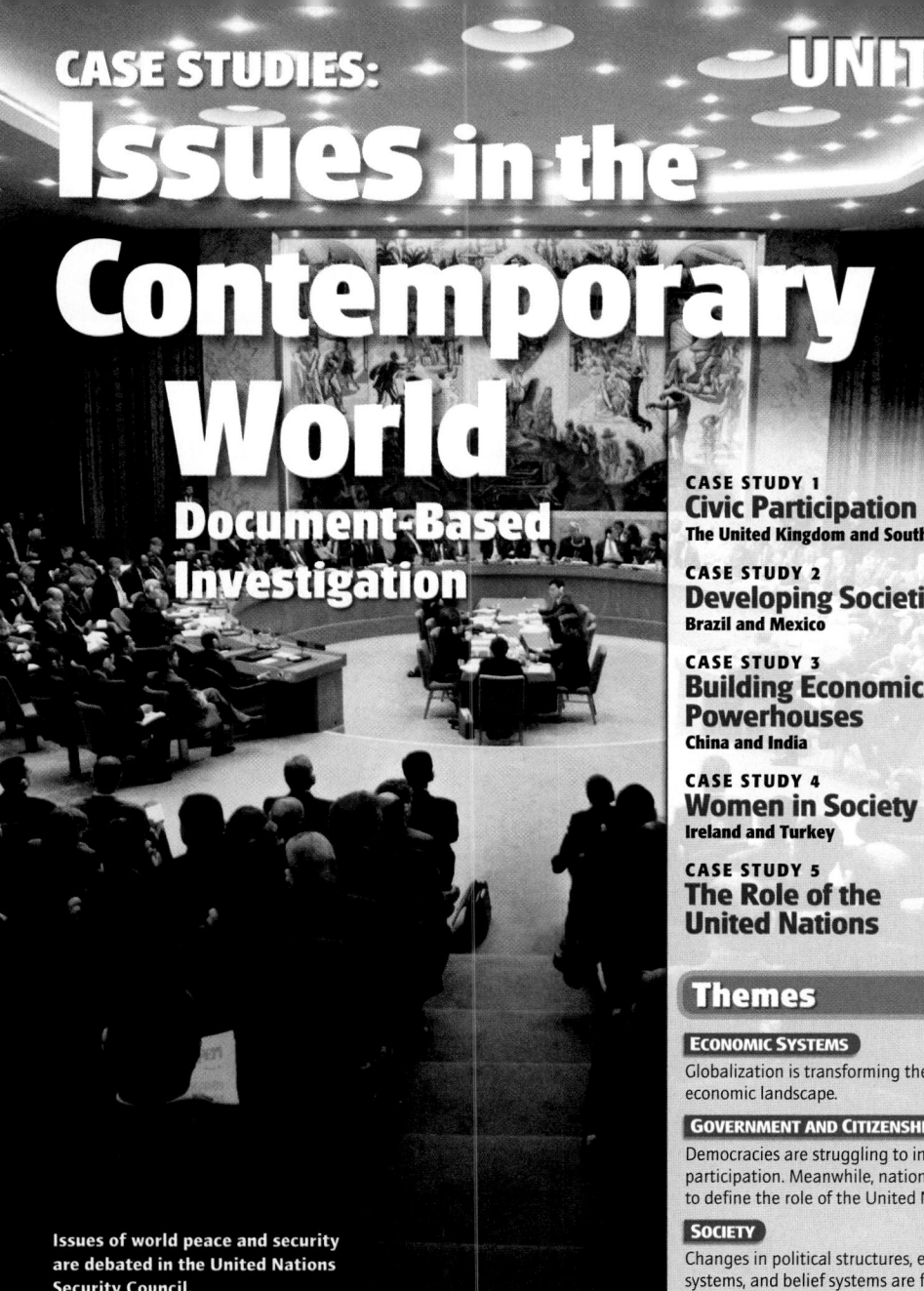

CASE STUDIES:
Issues in the Contemporary World

UNIT 10

Document-Based Investigation

CASE STUDY 1
Civic Participation
The United Kingdom and South Africa

CASE STUDY 2
Developing Societies
Brazil and Mexico

CASE STUDY 3
Building Economic Powerhouses
China and India

CASE STUDY 4
Women in Society
Ireland and Turkey

CASE STUDY 5
The Role of the United Nations

Themes

ECONOMIC SYSTEMS
Globalization is transforming the world's economic landscape.

GOVERNMENT AND CITIZENSHIP
Democracies are struggling to increase citizen participation. Meanwhile, nations are trying to define the role of the United Nations.

SOCIETY
Changes in political structures, economic systems, and belief systems are fundamentally reshaping societies.

Issues of world peace and security are debated in the United Nations Security Council.

1019

Unit Preview

Introducing the Unit

Have students list what they believe are the major global issues of today. Write several of their ideas on the board. Have students review the issues discussed in this unit. For each issue, have students write a sentence explaining how they think the issue could affect them personally. Have students read their sentences to the class.

Connecting to Themes

Activity A Global Economy Have students consider the issue of globalization. Have students write a definition of the term in their own words. Then have students list ways that globalization has impacted their lives. Explain that events and trends in nations such as China and India can have a major effect on the economies of nations around the world. Guide a class discussion about the positives and negatives of globalization.

Reading Like a Historian
Analyzing Visuals

The United Nations Have students take a moment to examine the photograph on this page. Ask students how the arrangement of participants might affect debates of the United Nations Security Council. *possible answer— People are seated in a circular shape, so it is a non-confrontational setting that might foster peaceful debate.*

Unit Resources

Planning
- **Differentiated Instruction Teacher Management System:** Pacing Guide
- **OSP One-Stop Planner CD-ROM:** Teacher Management System

Differentiating Instruction
- **Differentiated Instruction Teacher Management System:** Lesson Plans for Differentiated Instruction
- **Differentiated Instruction Modified Worksheets and Tests CD-ROM**

Enrichment
- **Civic Participation Activities Guide**
- **World History Primary Source Library CD-ROM**

Assessment
- **PASS:** Unit Test A and B
- **Alternative Assessment Handbook**

Issues in the Contemporary World

Chapter Overview	Reproducible Resources	Technology Resources
UNIT 10 pp. 1019–1044 **Overview: Issues in the Contemporary World: In this unit, students will learn about some important issues facing the world today. Students will analyze these contemporary issues and how they affect the United States and its relations with other countries.** KI 1, 3, 4; PI 1.3, 3.2, 3.3, 4.2, 4.3 See pp. T32–T55 for a detailed correlation to the New York State Core Curriculum for Global History and Geography and the New York Learning Standards.	**Differentiated Instruction Teacher Management System:** • Pacing Guide • Lesson Plans for Differentiated Instruction **Interactive Reader and Study Guide:** Unit Summary* **World History Outline Maps**	OSP **New York One-Stop Planner CD-ROM:** Calander Planner **Live Ink© Online Reading Help** **Student Edition on Audio CD Program** **Differentiated Instruction Modified Worksheets and Tests CD-ROM** **Interactive Skills Tutor CD-ROM** **World History Primary Source Library CD-ROM** **Power Presentations with Video CD-ROM** **History's Impact: World History Video Program (VHS/DVD):** Issues in the Contemporary World
Issue 1: **Civic Participation** **The Main Idea:** The United Kingdom, an old democracy, and South Africa, a new democracy, are both experiencing significant declines in voter turnout. PI 1.3, 4.2	**Differentiated Instruction Teacher Management System:** Issue 1 Lesson Plan* **Interactive Reader and Study Guide:** Issue 1 Summary*	**Differentiated Instruction Modified Worksheets and Tests CD-ROM**
Issue 2: **Developing Societies** **The Main Idea:** To build national prosperity, the countries of Latin America seek to establish political, economic, and social stability. PI 4.2, 4.3	**Differentiated Instruction Teacher Management System:** Issue 2 Lesson Plan* **Interactive Reader and Study Guide:** Issue 2 Summary*	**Differentiated Instruction Modified Worksheets and Tests CD-ROM**

UNIT 10 PLANNING GUIDE

go.hrw.com **go.hrw.com**   Print Resource **Print Resource**   Transparency **Transparency**

LS Learning Styles   Audio CD **Audio CD**   CD-ROM **CD-ROM**

Video Video   **SE** Student Edition   **TE** Teacher's Edition

OSP One-Stop Planner CD-ROM   NY Standards Mastery
*also on One-Stop Planner CD-ROM

HOLT
History's Impact
World History Video Program (VHS/DVD)
Issues in the Contemporary World

Review, Assessment, Intervention

- **Global History and Geography Regents Test Prep Workbook**

- **Spanish Chapter Summaries Audio CD Program**

- **Progress Assessment Support System (PASS):**
  Unit Test A and B*

- **Differentiated Instruction Modified Worksheets and Tests CD-ROM:** Modified Chapter Test

- **OSP** **New York One-Stop Planner CD-ROM:** ExamView Test Generator (English/Spanish)

- **HOAP** **Holt Online Assessment Program (HOAP),** in the Holt Premier Online Student Edition

- **Alternative Assessment Handbook**

- **Alternative Assessment Handbook**

Power Presentation with Video CD-ROM

Power Presentations with Video are visual presentations of each chapter's main ideas. Presentations can be customized by including Quick Facts charts, images and maps from the textbook, and video clips.

Holt Online Learning

go.hrw.com
Teacher Resources
KEYWORD: SHL TEACHER

go.hrw.com
Student Resources
KEYWORD: SHL ISSUES

- Document-Based Questions
- Interactive Multimedia Activities

- Current Events
- Chapter-Based Internet Activities
- and more!

Holt Premier
Online Student Edition
Complete online support for interactivity, assessment, and reporting

- Interactive Maps and Notebook
- Homework Practice and Research Activities Online

UNIT 10 PLANNING GUIDE

Unit 10 Planning Guide

Issues in the Contemporary World

Chapter Overview	Reproducible Resources	Technology Resources
Issue 3: **Building Economic Power Houses** **The Main Idea:** China and India have produced massive economic growth in recent decades. PI 1.3, 4.2	**Differentiated Instruction Teacher Management System:** Issue 3 Lesson Plan* **Interactive Reader and Study Guide:** Issue 3 Summary*	**Differentiated Instruction Modified Worksheets and Tests CD-ROM**
Issue 4: **Women in Society** **The Main Idea:** Though world governments have recently pledged to promote gender equality, women in many countries still face discrimination and limited opportunities. PI 3.2, 3.3	**Differentiated Instruction Teacher Management System:** Issue 4 Lesson Plan* **Interactive Reader and Study Guide:** Issue 4 Summary*	**Differentiated Instruction Modified Worksheets and Tests CD-ROM**
Issue 5: **The Role of the United Nations** **The Main Idea:** The mission and size of the United Nations have grown in the six decades since it was founded, but so too have the problems the organization faces. PI 1.3, 4.2	**Differentiated Instruction Teacher Management System:** Issue 5 Lesson Plan* **Interactive Reader and Study Guide:** Issue 5 Summary*	**Differentiated Instruction Modified Worksheets and Tests CD-ROM**

HOLT

History's Impact
World History Video Program (VHS/DVD)
Issues in the Contemporary World

Review, Assessment, Intervention

Alternative Assessment Handbook

Alternative Assessment Handbook

Alternative Assessment Handbook

Differentiating Instruction

Differentiated Instruction Teacher Management System

- Lesson Plans for Differentiated Instruction
- Pacing Guide
- Interactive Reader and Study Guide

Spanish Chapter Summaries Audio CD Program

Student Edition on Audio CD Program

Differentiated Instruction Modified Worksheets and Tests CD-ROM
- Vocabulary Flash Cards
- Modified Vocabulary Builder Activities
- Modified Chapter Review Activity
- Modified Chapter Test

OSP **One-Stop Planner CD-ROM**
- ExamView Test Generator (English/Spanish)
- PuzzlePro
- Quiz Show for ExamView
- Transparencies and Videos

TE **Differentiated Activities in the Teacher's Edition**
- Poster: Civic Participation in the UK and South Africa, p. 1025
- Collage: Successes and Challenges in Daily Life, p. 1027
- Multimedia Presentation: China's Economic Growth, p. 1031
- Political Cartoon: India's/China's Economic Growth, p. 1034
- Poem/Song: Women's Issues in Turkey and Ireland, p. 1039
- Diorama: The UN'S Activities, p. 1041

UNIT 10 PLANNING GUIDE

Issues in the Contemporary World

By now you've read about many issues in world history. What issues do people around the world continue to face today? In the following five sections you will read about some important contemporary issues in today's world.

Issue 1

**Civic Participation
(pp. 1022–1025)**

The United Kingdom, an old democracy, and South Africa, a new democracy, are both experiencing significant declines in voter turnout. What challenges do old and new democracies face in promoting civic participation?

Issue 2

**Developing Societies
(pp. 1026–1029)**

To build national prosperity, the countries of Latin America seek to establish political, economic, and social stability. How are developing countries such as Brazil and Mexico trying to meet the needs of their peoples?

Issue 3

**Building Economic Power-
houses (pp. 1030–1035)**

China and India have produced massive economic growth in recent decades. How are the giant emerging economies of India and China affecting the world?

CASE STUDIES: Issues in the Contemporary World

THE BIG PICTURE The world today is a rapidly changing place. New technologies are reshaping the way economies operate and people interact. But how people and nations react to change is often rooted in the past. That's why studying the past can give you the tools you need to understand the present. The following case studies look at some key issues facing the world today. Use what you have learned to form opinions about these key issues.

Voters in Cape Town line up in the early morning hours to vote in a South Africa election ▶

1020 CASE STUDIES: CONTEMPORARY ISSUES

History's Impact video program
Watch the video to learn more about the role of the United Nations.

Case Study 1   Civic Participation
What challenges do old and new democracies face in promoting civic participation?

Case Study 2   Developing Societies
How are developing nations such as Brazil and Mexico trying to meet the needs of their peoples?

Case Study 3   Building Economic Powerhouses
How are the giant emerging economies of India and China affecting the world?

Case Study 4   Women in Society
How do political and social trends affect the roles of women?

Case Study 5   The Role of the United Nations
What should the role of the United Nations be in international affairs?

1021

HOLT

History's Impact
► **Video Program: Issues in the Contemporary World**
See the Video Teacher's Guide for strategies for using the video segment.

Issue 4
Women in Society (pp. 1036–1039)
Though world governments have recently pledged to promote gender equality, women in many countries still face discrimination and limited opportunities. How do historical and cultural trends affect women's status?

Issue 5
The Role of the United Nations (pp. 1040–1044)
The mission and size of the United Nations have grown in the six decades since it was founded, but so too have the problems the organization faces. What should the role of the United Nations be in international affairs?

Focusing on the Issue

What challenges do old and new democracies face in promoting civic participation? *possible answer—a declining voter turnout and little civic participation in democratic processes*

Key Terms

Preteach the following term:
devolution the redistribution of power from the central government to local governments (p. 1023)

Case Study 1

Document-Based Investigation

Civic Participation
The United Kingdom and South Africa

FOCUSING ON THE ISSUE

What challenges do old and new democracies face in promoting civic participation?

KEY TERMS
devolution

New York Standards

PI 1.3 Analyze historic events from around the world by examining accounts written from different perspectives.
PI 4.2 Interpret and analyze documents and artifacts related to significant developments and events in world history.

South African president Thabo Mbeki greets enthusiastic residents of Manelodi during his successful reelection campaign in 2004.

In a 2005 survey, "Voice of the People," about two-thirds of the respondents in 68 countries said they were generally satisfied with democracy. Yet only one-third said that their own countries were ruled by the will of the people. Citizens may respect the idea of rule by the people, but many do not see it as a reality in their countries.

When people feel they have little voice in their government or that their votes do not count, they may become discouraged about participating in their democratic institutions. In recent years, voter turnout has declined in many countries. Some observers fear that this decline suggests a more general disinterest in civic participation.

Civic participation involves more than voting, of course. There is a range of political activities aimed at influencing government policies, structures, laws, and the use of public resources. Contacting elected representatives, staging protests, and building coalitions to have a louder voice on issues—these are just some of the ways people participate. In addition, factors such as fair elections, honest government, a lively opposition, and free speech help keep citizens engaged.

Participation in a democracy extends beyond politics as well. Nongovernmental organizations (NGOs) have a strong role in many countries, tackling issues from hunger to election monitoring. Local charities and other volunteer organizations also provide crucial support for communities.

The United Kingdom has over a century of democratic tradition. South Africa began its great experiment in rule by the people in 1994, with its first-ever multiethnic elections. Yet both countries are undergoing political changes that will affect the future of their democracies.

1022

Teach the Main Idea

At Level

Civic Participation

1. **Teach** Ask students the Focusing on the Issue question to teach this section.

2. **Apply** Have students work in groups of three to compile a list of five problems they believe are common in contemporary democracies. Have groups rank their lists in order of most serious to least serious.

3. **Review** Have groups share their lists with the class. Using a point system (each group's top-ranked problem = 5 pts; 2nd problem = 4 pts; 3rd problem = 3 pts; 4th problem = 4 pts;

5th problem = 1 pt) tally the different problems each group listed. Using the overall point totals, compile a list of the top five problems the class believes face democracies today.

4. **Practice/Homework** For each item on the class top five list, have students write a paragraph suggesting ways that democracies should try to overcome the problem.
   LS Interpersonal, Verbal-Linguistic

   Alternative Assessment Handbook, Rubrics 35: Solving Problems; and 37: Writing Assignments

Old and new democracies each have their own advantages and problems. The United Kingdom has a stable society, respect for long-established laws and democratic institutions, and a healthy culture of civic volunteerism. In recent years, however, it has been troubled by a declining level of voter turnout in elections. South Africa's young democracy has seen its initially high level of voter turnout drop rapidly. It is struggling to create trustworthy institutions amid social and political unrest. Increasingly, South Africans are participating in civic life through informal organizations.

Democracy in the UK The United Kingdom's parliamentary traditions stretch back at least 700 years. Over the centuries, political change has come slowly. It was not until the twentieth century that the country became fully democratic, extending voting rights to all adult citizens.

Since it was elected in 1997, Britain's Labor government has sought to reform the country's democratic institutions. In part, these efforts are a response to declining voter participation, especially among poor and young voters. "The turnout freefall has triggered a national debate about the public's loss of interest in politics and what to do about it," one university study noted.

One of the Labor government's key reforms has been **devolution**. Devolution is the redistribution of power from the central government to local governments. Devolution of authority to the UK countries of Wales and Scotland took place in the late 1990s. At the time, devolution was hailed as a victory for democratic reform. However, it has not fulfilled the hopes of some of its proponents. They are disappointed because major areas of power remain in the hands of the central government.

Democracy in South Africa In the 2005 "Voice of the People" survey, South Africa topped the charts for optimism. Nearly two-thirds of South Africans said their country was governed by the will of the people—the highest ranking of any country.

In the first few years of independence, South Africans demonstrated their support for democracy by going to the polls in impressive

UK Conservative Party leader David Cameron faces a group of reporters at his party's conference in April 2006.

numbers. High voter turnout in 1994 brought President Nelson Mandela to power. Since then, however, election turnout among the voting-age population has begun to drop sharply.

The main beneficiary of voter participation in South Africa has been the ruling African National Congress (ANC). The ANC has seen its majorities rise in each of the three national elections since the end of apartheid. Voters continue to reward the party for its role in the anti-apartheid struggle. But without an opposition party to challenge and monitor it, the ANC has been troubled by corruption and inefficiency.

Despite a lack of reliable institutions of governance, South Africans' commitment to civic participation remains strong. Membership in informal institutions, such as anti-crime organizations, women's organizations, and trade unions, has soared. Social scientists believe that societies that have a dense network of informal institutions are healthier ones.

Informal institutions strengthen a society. They offer flexible, creative options for solving a society's problems. Albert Oupamoloto is a resident of Soweto, one of South Africa's poorest cities yet one known for its vibrant political life. He describes the optimism that drives much civic participation in South Africa; "Many people think their lives are better because they are free citizens," Oupamoloto says, "and I agree with them."

CIVIC PARTICIPATION **1023**

Direct Teach

Reading Focus

Exploring the Issue

Identify Who was elected president of South Africa in 1994? *Nelson Mandela*

Explain Why was the United Kingdom not considered a fully democratic nation until the twentieth century? *All adult citizens in the nation did not have voting rights until the twentieth century.*

Compare and Contrast How are the democracies of the United Kingdom and South Africa similar and different? *possible answer—similarities: Both nations hold elections for governmental offices; civic participation in both countries has declined in recent years; differences: Britain has a long democratic tradition, while South Africa is a new democracy; the United Kingdom has faced challenges relating to the power balance between central and local governments, while South Africa is still experiencing the impact of its long anti-apartheid struggle.*

Biography

Desmond Tutu (1931–) Desmond Tutu has long been one of South Africa's leading champions for democracy and human rights. A high school teacher as a young adult, Tutu studied religion and became an Anglican priest in 1960. Soon after, he emerged as a major spiritual leader and a vocal critic of apartheid. Questioning the morals of his nation's white-dominated government, Tutu supported economic sanctions against South Africa. In 1984 Tutu won the Nobel Peace Prize for his anti-apartheid work. After his country ended apartheid and became a true democracy, Tutu headed a commission investigating the human rights abuses of the previous regime.

Skills Focus: Making Generalizations

At Level

Reading Skill
The United Kingdom and South Africa Today

1. Have students examine recent newspapers and magazines to find an article about democracy in the United Kingdom or South Africa.

2. Have students write a report about the article they selected. In their reports students should generalize about the status of democracy in the country described in the article.

3. Have students present their reports to the class. Guide students in a discussion about the current political situation in the United Kingdom and South Africa today. **LS Verbal-Linguistic**

Alternative Assessment Handbook, Rubrics 23: Newspapers; and 37: Writing Assignments

Word Help

persistent continuing (p. 1025)
profoundly completely (p. 1025)
apathy lack of interest (p. 1025)

Investigating the Issue

Recall What percentage of voting-age South Africans voted in the 1999 elections? *71.8%*

Make Inferences What does the information in Document 1 and Document 2 suggest about how the number of people who voted for the African National Congress changed between 1994 and 2004? *possible answer—fewer South Africans voted in 2004, though the ANC won more provinces that year; thus, the number of people who voted for the ANC might have stayed about the same in actual number.*

Info to Know

Capitals of South Africa Unlike most other nations, South Africa has three capital cities. Each capital is home to a branch of government. Cape Town, the legislative capital, is the site of the South African Parliament. Pretoria (or Tshwane), the administrative capital, is where South Africa's president and cabinet members meet. Bloemfontein, the judicial capital, is home to South Africa's Supreme Court of Appeal, the nation's highest court.

Answers

Analyzing the Document (left)
possible answers—Both countries experienced a drop in voter turnout; the decline was sharper in South Africa; the decline in the UK may be related to long-term voter apathy while the decline in South Africa may be related to the problems of building a new democracy.
(right) *The ANC gained political strength, dominating the 2004 elections; possible consequences include decline of voter interest in uncontested elections.*

INVESTIGATING THE ISSUE

Democracy in the United Kingdom and in South Africa presents strong comparisons and contrasts. The documents that follow explore these issues by presenting different points of view and arguments. Examine the documents, keeping in mind what you have read about these democracies, and answer the questions that follow.

DOCUMENT 1

The United Kingdom and South Africa—an old democracy and a new one—both have experienced declines in voter turnout in recent years. Both are trying to identify possible causes for the decline and to inspire citizens to participate in the democratic process. This graph shows the election trends in the two countries.

ELECTION TURNOUT, UNITED KINGDOM

Year	Percentage
1987	75.33
1992	77.67
1997	71.46
2001	59.38
2005	61.3

Source: http://www.election.demon.co.uk

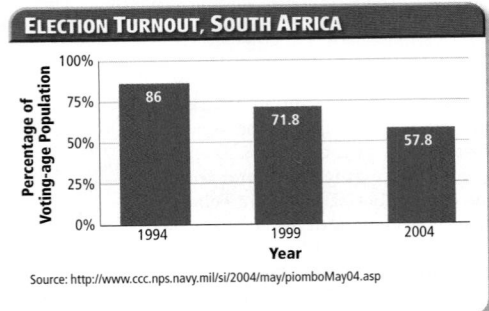

ELECTION TURNOUT, SOUTH AFRICA

Year	Percentage
1994	86
1999	71.8
2004	57.8

Source: http://www.ccc.nps.navy.mil/si/2004/may/piomboMay04.asp

Analyzing the Document
Describe the changes in voter turnout in the two countries during the time period shown here. Compare and contrast the two countries' turnout results. Which country experienced the sharpest decline?

1024 CASE STUDIES: CONTEMPORARY ISSUES

DOCUMENT 2

This series of maps shows the results of South African national elections from 1994, when apartheid ended and the country held its first multiethnic vote.

AFRICAN NATIONAL ELECTIONS, 1994–2004

Election results by province
- African National Congress
- National Party
- Inkatha Freedom Party

1994

1997

2004

Analyzing the Document
What political change does this series of maps show? What are some possible consequences of this change?

Skills Focus: Interpreting Pie and Bar Graphs **Above Level**

Social Studies Skill
Voter Turnout

1. Have students examine the bar graphs on this page. Guide students in a discussion about recent voting trends in the United Kingdom and South Africa.

2. Have students conduct research to find comparable voter turnout percentages in elections in the United States since 1990.

3. Using the data from their research, have students prepare a bar graph of U.S. voter turnout.

4. Have students compare the bar graph they created with the ones on this page. Discuss with the class how American voter participation trends compare with those of the United Kingdom and South Africa. **LS** Visual-Spatial, Logical-Mathematical

Alternative Assessment Handbook, Rubrics 7: Charts; and 30: Research

In 2006 the British government released a study of declining voter turnout. A British magazine examined the report.

> "The real problem . . . lies not with the political system at all, but with changes in society itself. As [the report] observes, two contrasting groups have emerged to whom conventional politics has little appeal.
>
> On one hand there are the relatively well-educated, relatively well-informed, relatively young who expect to make their own decisions, find self-expression in buying what they want when they want it, and see themselves as individuals free of geographic, institutional or social bonds.
>
> On the other are the casualties of de-industrialisation who suffer from persistent poverty and social exclusion. The former are cynical about political leaders and irritated that voting is not more like shopping, while the latter feel bullied and let down by the institutions they rely on for their survival.
>
> Constitutional reform . . . is well worth doing for its own sake. But whether it will make much difference to people who are already profoundly detached from the habits and modes of representative democracy is another matter."
>
> —*The Economist*, March 4, 2006

Analyzing the Document
What two groups does the report describe?

Analyzing the factors underlying the decline in voter turnout has been a source of heated debate in South Africa. This writer remains hopeful that the trend signals a "normalizing" of politics in South Africa.

> "[T]he fact that the major worries of political leaders and analysts was about potential apathy, rather than electoral violence, signifies the politics are becoming increasingly routine, a sign of the institutionalization of democracy in South Africa. . . .
>
> The election process and results demonstrated that politics are normalizing in South Africa, while at the same time pointing to areas that need to be monitored. For now, democracy is stable, institutionalizing itself and performing well. If the country can avoid the pitfalls of permanent party dominance and the slow erosion of democratic freedoms (as occurred in neighboring Zimbabwe after 1980), the second ten years of democracy will be worth celebrating."
>
> —Jessica Piombo, "Politics in a Stabilizing Democracy: South Africa's 2004 Elections," *Strategic Insights*, May 2004

Analyzing the Document
Why does this writer think dropping voter turnout signals a "normalizing" of South African politics? What does she believe needs to be monitored if democracy in South Africa is to grow stronger?

ANALYZING THE ISSUE

go.hrw.com
Research Online
SD7 Case Study

1. Review the documents presented on this issue. What similarities and what differences do they reveal about the challenges to democratic participation in the United Kingdom and in South Africa? What effect, if any, does the age of these democracies have on citizen participation?

2. Review the graph showing South African voter turnout and the map showing election results. What possible connection is there between declining voter turnout and the increased election success of the ANC?

3. Do library or online research to learn more about another democratic reform proposed in the United Kingdom—the elimination of hereditary lordships in Parliament's House of Lords. What effect might the change have on democracy and representation in the United Kingdom?

4. What sort of informal organizations are there in your community? in the United States? Do research to learn about one such organization. Write a one-page paper describing the organization, including its purpose, goals, and membership.

CIVIC PARTICIPATION **1025**

Differentiating Instruction

Below Level

English-Language Learners

1. Organize the class into mixed-ability pairs. Have students review each of the documents included in this case study so they understand the main issues.

2. Have each pair of students create a poster promoting civic participation in government in either the United Kingdom or South Africa.

3. Encourage students to include photographs, charts, newspaper headlines, and cartoons, as well as their own original drawings in their posters.

4. Display the posters for students to see. Allow class time for each pair to explain the concepts included in their posters. **LS Visual-Spatial, Verbal-Linguistic**

Alternative Assessment Handbook, Rubric 28: Posters

● Direct Teach ●

Reading Focus

Investigating the Issue

Describe What does Jessica Piombo not want to see happen in South Africa? *permanent dominance of one political party; loss of democratic freedoms*

Make Inferences What do you think are the goals of the British government commission that issued the report in Document 3? *possible answer—to increase civic participation and democracy in the United Kingdom*

Predict What seems likely to happen in Great Britain if the government adopts the proposed constitutional reforms? *possible answer—little will change; the two major social groups that are currently removed from politics will continue to refrain from participating in democratic processes*

Answers

Analyzing the Document (left) *"well-educated, well-informed, relatively young" and the poor, socially excluded* **(right)** *possible answer—believes the decline is due to apathy and the institutionalizing of politics in South Africa; party dominance and democratic freedoms of citizens*

Analyzing the Issue 1. *possible answers—both nations face challenges in inspiring citizens to vote and participate in politics; differences: voter turnout declined more sharply in South Africa; effect—the newness of democracy in South Africa may account for the sharp drop in voter turnout there since people likely lost interest as one party gained dominance.* **2.** *possible answer—The growing political strength of the ANC has caused citizens to lose interest in voting since the party's candidates face little competition in many districts.* **3.** *Answers should reflect knowledge of British public opinion about hereditary lordships in the House of Lords.* **4.** *Answers should accurately describe an informal organization in your community.*

1025

Focusing on the Issue

How are developing countries such as Brazil and Mexico trying to meet the needs of their peoples? *possible answer—expanding sources of trade; attracting more foreign investment; improving management of government finances*

Key Terms

Preteach the following terms:

indigenous native (p. 1026)

megacity city with a population of 10 million or more (p. 1027)

maquiladora large industrial assembly plant in a Mexican border town that produces finished goods for export to the United States (p. 1027)

Case Study

2

Document-Based Investigation

Developing Societies Brazil and Mexico

FOCUSING ON THE ISSUE

How are developing nations such as Brazil and Mexico trying to meet the needs of their peoples?

KEY TERMS
megacity, maquiladora

New York Standards

PI 4.2 Interpret and analyze documents and artifacts related to significant developments and events in world history.
PI 4.3 Plan and organize historical research projects related to regional or global interdependence.

In order to become more prosperous, developing countries strive to create political, economic, and social stability. The three elements are interconnected. Political stability is one factor that helps businesses take root and thrive. It attracts much-needed foreign investment that strengthens the economy. A strong economy creates jobs, wealth, and consumer markets, helping to build a middle class—the backbone of a stable society. Finally, a contented, stable society promotes political order and helps democracy take root.

Like many developing regions, Latin America has had its share of instability in all three categories. For more than a century, political revolutions have stemmed in part from severe economic gaps between rich and poor. Economically, a reliance on exporting cash crops has kept the region trapped in boom-and-bust cycles; a drop in world prices for commodities can send developing economies into a tailspin. Socially, large migrations have unsettled societies in recent decades, as poor and landless peoples move to urban areas seeking work. Further upheaval has come from the efforts of indigenous peoples in Mexico and elsewhere to gain recognition and equality.

In recent years, however, the region's two most populous countries, Brazil and Mexico, have undergone remarkable political transformations. Brazil emerged from a string of repressive military dictatorships in the 1960s and 1970s to form a modern democracy. In 2000 Mexico set aside more than seven decades of one-party rule and held its first true two-party election.

Economic security, however, has proved more difficult to achieve. Globalization is pitting the two countries against new economic competitors such as India and China. Still, leaders in the both countries are seeking dynamic solutions to produce long-term stability and make use of one of their greatest assets: the enormous human resources they possess in their large populations.

Maquiladora factories, like the one shown above, have fueled much of Mexico's growth but are vulnerable to swings in the world economy.

1026

Teach the Main Idea

At Level

Developing Societies

1. **Teach** Ask students the Focusing on the Issue question to teach this section.

2. **Apply** Organize students into two groups. One group will represent Brazil, the other will represent Mexico. Have each group brainstorm strategies for improving political, economic, and social conditions in its country. Have each group present its top five strategies.

3. **Review** Discuss the lists as a class. Have each group evaluate the potential

effectiveness of the strategies listed by the other group.

4. **Practice/Homework** Have students write a paragraph explaining how "their country" will be different in 10 years after implementing the proposed strategies.

LS Verbal-Linguistic, Interpersonal

Alternative Assessment Handbook, Rubric 37: Writing Assignments

Economically and socially, Brazil and Mexico face many of the same challenges. Both are attempting to broaden their economic bases by expanding their sources of trade and foreign investment. Both are also seeking new solutions to the chronic problem of poverty and inequity in society.

Progress and Problems in Brazil Latin America's largest country, Brazil also has the region's largest economy. The nation made considerable economic progress starting in the mid-1990s despite some severe downturns. It expanded its presence in global markets for agricultural, mining, and manufactured goods. Exports surged, the economy grew, infant mortality dropped, and school enrollment increased. Laws requiring better management of government finances have been praised.

Yet Brazil also has some of the world's most desperate poverty, especially in the **megacities** of São Paulo and Rio de Janeiro. Megacities are those with populations of 10 million or more. Most of Brazil's urban poor live on the fringes of its two megacities. In Rio the *favelas*, or shantytowns, that climb the hillsides are so dangerous the police won't go there. São Paulo is one of the world's most murderous cities, wracked by gang violence. The streets are so dangerous that many wealthy people travel by helicopter, hopping among the city's 240 heliports.

To ease the population pressure on the cities, since the 1970s Brazil has turned to one of its most valuable resources: space. Brazil opened up its vast interior for resettlement and large-scale development. The resulting destruction of rain forests, however, has produced an international outcry and spurred calls for Brazil to limit rural overdevelopment.

Mexico Seeks Solutions Mexico has the second-largest economy in Latin America, now exceeding a trillion dollars. It has large petroleum reserves and a thriving tourism industry. Its location next to the United States has made it possible to expand trade under the North American Free Trade Agreement (NAFTA). Mexico benefits from its **maquiladoras**, the large industrial assembly plants throughout its border towns that produce finished goods for export to the United States.

In its drive to develop, Brazil has become a leader in the production of alternate fuels such as ethanol, refined here in São Tomé.

Mexicans enjoy the highest per-capita income in Latin America. But such averages mask the huge gaps between rich and poor. In 2005 the richest 10 percent of Mexicans earned 25 times what the poorest 10 percent earned—just as they had two decades before. The government estimated extreme poverty at 17.3 percent in 2004.

Efforts to address rural poverty are limited by the fact that only 15 percent of Mexico's large, dry land mass is arable. The lack of land continues to draw peasants from the countryside to the nation's megacity, Mexico City, where nearly one-fifth of the nation's population lives. Not surprisingly, Mexican government policies now focus on urban poverty, because of the massive spinoff problems it creates: violence, political instability, and environmental destruction.

Despite protests from some U.S. leaders, the Mexican government encourages migration to the United States. Migrants, legal and illegal, send much-needed dollars back home to support their families.

Meanwhile, Mexico is focusing on creating a more highly educated work force, a priority the era of globalization. The government pays parents to keep their children in school instead of pulling them out to work in the fields and family businesses.

Direct Teach

Reading Focus

Exploring the Issue

Explain Why do wealthy residents of Sao Paulo travel by helicopter? *to avoid the city's violent streets*

Analyze What economic advantages does Mexico possess? *location next to the United States; large petroleum reserves; attractive to tourists; maquiladoras*

Compare What challenges do both Mexico and Brazil face? *poverty; huge gaps between rich and poor; crime*

MISCONCEPTION ALERT

Many Americans believe that the largest suppliers of oil to the United States are Arab nations in the Middle East. Since 2003, however, Mexico has been America's top supplier of crude oil. In 2005 the United States imported 1,568 thousand barrels of oil *each day* from its neighbor to the south.

Differentiating Instruction

Below Level

Learners Having Difficulty

1. Have students choose one of the two nations described in this case study. Have students create a collage depicting political, economic, and social life in the country they selected.

2. Students may use photographs from newspapers, magazines, or printouts of pictures they find on the Internet for their collages. Instruct students to find images reflecting both successes and challenges in their chosen country.

3. Display collages in a classroom exhibit. Have volunteers share their collages with the class. Volunteers should explain what the images they selected represent. **LS Visual-Spatial, Intrapersonal**

Alternative Assessment Handbook, Rubric 8: Collages

Word Help

infrastructure transportation, communication, and public works systems of a country (p. 1028)

Reading Focus

Investigating the Issue

Identify According to Luiz Ignácio Lula da Silva, what is the combined total of Brazil's exports to Latin America, the European Union, and the United States? *$78 billion*

Predict How do you think auto production in Brazil will change in the coming years? *possible answer—Production of alternate fuel vehicles will continue to rise sharply.*

Info to Know

Brazilian Trade In 2004 Brazil's total exports were $95 billion. The nation's imports for that year totaled $61 billion, creating a trade surplus of $34 billion. The United States accounts for more than one-fifth of Brazil's total exports and imports.

INVESTIGATING THE ISSUE

Over the years Brazil and Mexico have adopted a number of strategies to boost economic development—and to lessen its potential negative effects. The documents that follow explore the issue of development in Brazil and Mexico. Examine the documents, keeping in mind what you have just read about economic development efforts in the two countries.

DOCUMENT 1

Brazil has taken a lead in forming regional trade agreements in Latin America and trade ties outside the region, as a way of broadening and stabilizing its economy. President Luiz Ignácio Lula da Silva explained the philosophy behind this course of action.

> "I think Latin America is going through an important moment in its history.... [O]ur way forward is to consolidate the process of integration, ... physical integration, with infrastructure, with roads, with railways, with communications, with energy. Based on this Brazil has decided to make some investments in other countries. Brazil today has some $3bn of investments in other South American countries, so that we can give South America more infrastructure.
>
> We believe that it is necessary to do much more, because only infrastructure is going to make more circulation possible. Not just goods but people as well. And we have had some results in the period in which we have been in government. Today, Latin America is Brazil's biggest market. We export almost $28bn to the rest of Latin America.... With the European Union we have $27bn and with the US $23bn. This is an extremely important thing. We are showing that it is possible through partnership and with seriousness, that we can help each other, we can help ourselves to grow...."
>
> —Brazilian President Luiz Ignácio Lula da Silva, interview, *Financial Times*, July 2006

Analyzing the Document
Why, according to Lula da Silva, does it make sense for a Brazil to invest money in other countries in the region?

DOCUMENT 2

In 1979 Brazil launched a national program to develop alternate fuels. Ethanol, a type of alcohol produced from refined sugar cane, is the leading alternate fuel. Today, 34,000 gas stations in Brazil have at least one pump dedicated to alternate fuel. The program has drastically reduced Brazil's need for oil and has cut down on auto pollution. But the vast acreage devoted to sugar cane production is causing worry among environmentalists, who fear a loss of biodiversity.

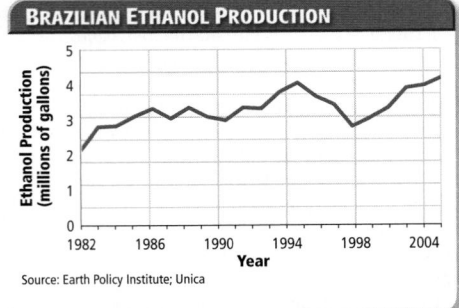

BRAZILIAN ETHANOL PRODUCTION

Source: Earth Policy Institute; Unica

BRAZILIAN ALTERNATE FUEL VEHICLES

Source: Unica

Analyzing the Document
What is the trend in ethanol production? How does the trend correspond to trends in auto manufacturing?

Skills Focus: Interpreting Line Graphs

Social Studies Skill
Population Growth

1. Have students study the graphs titled Brazilian Ethanol Production and Brazilian Alternate Fuel Vehicles on th,is page.

2. Have students conduct research about ethanol production and alternate fuel vehicle production in the United States between the years 1982 and 2004.

3. Have students prepare a graph, similar to the ones on this page, based on the information they found.

4. Have students compare the graphs they created with the Brazil graphs. Discuss with the class how ethanol and alternate fuel vehicle production in the United States and Brazil are similar and different. **LS Visual-Spatial, Logical-Mathematical**

Alternative Assessment Handbook, Rubrics 9: Comparing and Contrasting; and 11: Discussions

Answers

Analyzing the Document (left)
By investing in other Latin American countries, Brazil is strengthening the infrastructure and economies of its major trading partners—this in turn will help increase Brazil's trade income; **(right)** *Ethanol production has mostly increased since 1982; after a decline in the late 1980s and early 1990s, production of alternative fuel vehicles has increased sharply since 1998.*

DOCUMENT 3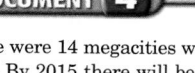

About a third of the people in the Mexican state of Chiapas are descended from the Maya, or "people of the corn," as they call themselves. Since 1994 the indigenous people of Chiapas have waged a battle to end political and cultural repression by the government and bring decent living conditions to the extremely impoverished region. The woman in this photograph participated in a protest by the Zapatista rebels of Chiapas that was held in Mexico City. Such demonstrations drew worldwide support to their cause.

Analyzing the Document
What does this photograph suggest about the cultural identity of the people of Chiapas?

DOCUMENT 4

There were 14 megacities worldwide in 1995. By 2015 there will be 21. Mexico and Brazil have some of the world's largest megacities. These statistics provide a snapshot of population growth in some of the world's megacities.

City/Metropolitan Areas (rank)	Population* (2000)	Percentage of Population (2000)	Projected Population Growth (2000–2015)
Tokyo, Japan (1)	34,450	27.1%	5.1%
Mexico City, Mexico (2)	18,066	18.3%	14.3%
New York City, USA (3)	17,846	6.3%	10.5%
São Paolo, Brazil (4)	17,099	10.0%	16.7%
Mumbai, India (5)	16,086	1.6%	40.8%
Rio de Janeiro, Brazil (14)	10,803	6.3%	14.4%

*All population figures in thousands.

Source: World Almanac Book of Facts, 2005

Analyzing the Document
Compare and contrast the statistics for the Mexican and Brazilian cities listed in the table. Which city has a higher percentage of its country's population? Which city is projected to grow the fastest?

ANALYZING THE ISSUE

go.hrw.com
Research Online
SD7 Case Study

1. Review the documents presented on this issue. What evidence do they present to suggest that development in Brazil and Mexico is a complex challenge?

2. What goals do Brazil and Mexico share in terms of economic development? What are some problems unique to each country?

3. Do online research to learn more about life in the Chiapas region of Mexico. How has life there changed, or not changed, since the Zapatista rebellion in 1994? Why did the rebellion evoke sympathy throughout Mexico and the world? Do you think economic development in Mexico would benefit Chiapas? Why or why not?

4. Research Brazil's policy of alternative fuel development. Compare the positive and negative effects. Do you think the government is justified in pursuing this policy? Explain your reasoning.

DEVELOPING SOCIETIES **1029**

Collaborative Learning
At Level

The Chiapas Conflict

1. Organize students into small groups. Have each group use reliable Internet or print sources to conduct research about the major issues of Mexican government's conflict with the indigenous peoples of Chiapas.

2. Have each group write a skit about the Chiapas conflict. In their skits, students should cover the origins of the controversy, the lives of the Maya people in Chiapas, the role of Zapatista rebels, and the responses of the government.

3. Have students rehearse and perform their skits for the class. **LS Kinesthetic, Interpersonal**

Alternative Assessment Handbook, Rubrics 30: Research; and 33: Skits and Reader's Theater

---

1029

Focusing on the Issue

How are the giant emerging economies of India and China affecting the world?
possible answers—Export goods have flooded global markets, lowering prices; enterprises in other nations have made profits investing in China and India; enterprises in other nations have moved their factories to China; Indian employees provide a host of services at low wages, taking some jobs away from people in other nations.

Key Terms

Preteach the following terms:

offshoring moving an entire factory or other business enterprise abroad (p. 1031)

privatization the private ownership of industries as opposed to government control (p. 1032)

joint ventures business partnerships and co-ownership (p. 1032)

Document-Based Investigation
Building Economic Powerhouses China and India

FOCUSING ON THE ISSUE

How are the giant emerging economies of India and China affecting the world?

KEY TERMS
offshoring, privatization, joint ventures

New York Standards

PI 1.3 Analyze historic events from around the world by examining accounts written from different perspectives.
PI 4.2 Interpret and analyze documents and artifacts related to significant developments and events in world history.

To many observers the question is not whether India and China will bump the United States from its position as the world's largest economy. The question is when, and which country will get there first.

The world's two most populous nations have embarked on ambitious programs to move from failed planned or semi-planned economies to vibrant market economies. Their pathways to success have differed, and each faces challenges that could derail them. China is still a one-party Communist dictatorship, and India's thriving democracy struggles to contain explosive religious conflict. Yet few experts dispute that the changes underway in these two countries are shaking up the world's economies.

The economic successes of India and China are no accident. China began limited economic reforms in the late 1970s and then threw open its doors to private enterprise 20 years later, determined to become the manufacturing capital of the world. India opened its economy later, in the 1990s, but quickly and seized the opportunities of the telecommunications revolution. High-speed Internet connections opened up sudden opportunities for these countries to connect their large labor pools with potential employers and customers around the globe.

The vigorous moves of India and China onto the world stage are affecting economic planning, markets, and wages in other countries. No one is quite sure how this scenario will play out either for India and China—potential competitors who also happen to share a disputed border—or for the Western and Asian industrial giants of the twentieth century. One thing we is for certain: the twenty-first century is truly a new era of global economic interdependence.

China's heavy industry manufacturers, like this tractor factory in the city of Luoyang, have grown increasingly competitive in world markets.

1030

Teach the Main Idea

At Level

Emerging Economic Giants

1. **Teach** Ask students the Focusing on the Issue question to teach this section.

2. **Apply** Have students list the different ways that India and China have changed in recent decades. Have students write a sentence assessing how each change affected the home country (India or China) and how it affected the other nations of the world.

3. **Review** Have students meet in small groups to discuss their lists. Guide a class discussion about whether India and China

should continue on their current paths in the coming years.

4. **Practice/Homework** Have students write a brief essay about how they think China and India will be impacting the global economy in 10 years. **LS Verbal-Linguistic, Interpersonal**

   Alternative Assessment Handbook, Rubrics 11: Discussions; and 37: Writing Assignments

The rise of Asian economies began in the 1960s, when Japan, South Korea, and the other so-called "Asian tigers" began to industrialize at a breathtaking rate. These countries developed efficient, streamlined manufacturing processes that flooded the global market with inexpensive export goods.

Today's "Asian tigers," India and China, may not yet match Japan's GDP, but their rapid economic growth makes for a promising future. Up until now, China has emphasized traditional manufacturing industries. India has focused on new service industries provided via the Internet, from tax preparation to computer technical support.

China's Communist Economy
Under Maoist Communism, China's government tightly controlled all aspects of the nation's economy. Communist leaders tried to move the ancient agricultural society into the modern age. But massive industrialization efforts eventually stalled. The government allowed virtually no private enterprise. The lack of free-market incentives produced low productivity and inefficiency. While Japan and other "Asian tigers" were roaring, China's living standards remained relatively low.

Chinese Capitalism Takes Hold
With the rise to power of Deng Xiaoping in 1978, China cautiously started down a new economic path. Since then, agricultural, industrial, and market reforms have come slowly but steadily.

In the agricultural sector, the government began to allow farmers to sell some of their crops on the free market. Centralized economic planning was relaxed. That allowed regional officials to make free-market decisions on some issues, including trade.

The government also began to encourage foreign investment, although not on the scale that India later embraced. Initially, economic liberalization was confined to the creation of a few "special economic zones," such as the

Factories, like this textile plant in Hubei province, have sprouted up in China's interior.

city of Shenzen. These areas served as testing grounds for China's limited capitalism.

The results were impressive. Farm output doubled during the 1980s. Industrial growth and investment in the special economic zones blossomed. Another round of market reforms was launched in the 1990s, creating what the government called "a socialist market economy." At the same time, China placed strict curbs on its population growth, holding it to a rate of about 13 per 1,000 people. This helped to ease poverty, but it created controversy at home and abroad.

Economic growth surged. By 2005 China had become the second-largest economy in the world, although still far behind the United States in terms of production. Since 1980 China has doubled its share of world trade every five years. It now supplies one-fifth of the world's clothing and one-third of all mobile phones.

In 2001 China's entered the World Trade Organization (WTO). In joining the WTO, China agreed to follow its laws and standards of competitive business and trade practices. The move made China an even more attractive place for foreign investment and for **offshoring**. Unlike outsourcing, which involves moving a part of a business operation, like computer tech support, to another country, the offshoring involves moving an entire factory or other business enterprise abroad.

BUILDING ECONOMIC POWERHOUSES **1031**

Direct Teach

Reading Focus

Exploring the Issue

Recall How did the economies of Japan, Korea, and the other "Asian tigers" change in the late twentieth century? *They rapidly industrialized and dramatically increased their manufacturing output.*

Explain Why did China depart from strict Communist economic policies to adopt market reforms? *Under communism, China's economy stagnated in low production and inefficiency.*

Evaluate How has the shift to limited capitalism affected China's economy? *possible answer—massive economic growth, greater industrial and agricultural output; increased world trade; large amounts of foreign investment; rise in economic crimes and pollution, widespread inequality*

Primary Source

Lester R. Brown, the founder and president of the Earth Policy Institute made the following comments about China's economic power in a 2005 article: "The United States, the world's largest debtor nation, is not heavily dependent on Chinese capital to underwrite its fast-growing debt. If China ever decides to divert this capital surplus elsewhere, either to internal development or to the development of oil, gas, and mineral resources elsewhere in the world, the U.S. economy will be in trouble. China is no longer just a developing country. It is an emerging economic superpower, one that is writing economic history. If this last century was the American century, this one looks to be the Chinese century."

Differentiating Instruction

Above Level

Advanced Learners/Gifted and Talented

1. Organize students into small groups.

2. Have students conduct research on China's recent economic growth using reliable print or online sources. Students should focus their research on foreign investment, trade, and/or other aspects of China's economic interactions with other nations.

3. Have students prepare a multimedia presentation based on their research findings. Allow enough time for groups to gather

research, organize their notes, and prepare their presentations.

4. Have groups make their presentations to the class. **LS Visual-Spatial, Verbal-Linguistic**

Alternative Assessment Handbook, Rubrics 22: Multimedia Presentations; and 30: Research

Exploring the Issue

Identify Which American company announced in 2006 that it would invest $6 billion in India over the following three years? *IBM*

Explain How does the legacy of British colonial rule continue to affect India's economy? *As English speakers, Indians can provide services to other English-speaking nations, including the United States*

Predict Which nation do you believe will have the stronger economy in 20 years, China or India? Explain your answer. *possible answers—India, because of its ties to the West and its capacity to provide services to the English-speaking world; China, because its socialist-capitalist economy combines the strengths of both systems to create massive production.*

Teaching Tip

The World Trade Organization website includes a wealth of information about the trading activities of the nations of the world. Have students access the WTO website and then navigate to find trade statistics relating to India and China. *Trade statistics can be accessed by clicking the Resources link at the top of the WTO homepage (www.wto.org).*

High-tech business parks (left) are sprouting up around Bangalore and other Indian cities. The Internet allows Indian software engineers (right) to serve world customers.

China has struggled to decide how far and how fast to implement reforms. Corruption and slow government decision-making hamper progress. The easing of restrictions on business has produced a rise in economic crimes, widespread inequality, and worrisome levels of pollution. Nevertheless, China is clearly on a path from which it does not intend to turn back.

India's Closed Economy Since it achieved independence from Great Britain in 1948, India has struggled to overcome desperate, grinding poverty. Inspired by the philosophy of independence leader Mohandas K. Gandhi, India adopted a socialist economy. It strove for economic self-sufficiency, with limits on imports and foreign investment. For more than four decades, India's economy was largely closed.

The government embarked on large-scale industrialization in order to meet its own needs and to limit dependence on foreign investment and imports. However, heavy government regulation resulted in decades of inefficiency, over-regulation, poor output, and quality goods.

India Opens Its Doors In the 1990s a democratic India embraced capitalism and began to move to a market economy. The government allowed increasing **privatization**, the private ownership of industries as opposed to government control. It opened the door to limited private investment in some industries. Over time, more and more foreign companies were allowed to operate in India. At first they formed **joint ventures**—business partnerships and co-ownership—with Indian companies.

In the early 2000s, direct foreign investment in India, particularly in telecommunications, took hold. In 2006 the American computer giant IBM announced that it would triple its investment in India over the following three years, to $6 billion.

Government efforts to revamp India's ways of doing business have helped the economy grow at an impressive rate of 7 percent a year since 1991. In addition to a more open business climate, two factors have contributed to making India a world leader in providing high-tech services to businesses worldwide. An emphasis on higher education over the last fifteen years has given India a large pool of highly skilled workers. There are also a large number of English speakers—the legacy of British colonial rule. Looking to the future, many observers believe India's democratic government will give it the flexibility it needs to meet the challenges ahead.

Barriers to Success India still faces formidable obstacles to economic success. High import tariffs and restrictions on direct foreign investment have remained, sparking a national debate on how far to liberalize, or open up, the economy. India's huge population, most of whom still work on farms and in small, traditional businesses, can be an economic asset. Already home to one-sixth of the world's people, the country is expected to become the most populous nation within the 50 years. But the rapid creation of vast wealth has further highlighted the "two Indias": one largely rural and poor; the other urban and prosperous.

Skills Focus: Comparing and Contrasting [At Level]

Reading Skill
The Two Indias

1. Review with students the information in the text about the "two Indias."

2. Have students conduct research about India to learn more about the dual nature of its economy.

3. Based on their research, have students write two paragraphs: one describing a rural Indian, the other describing an urban Indian.

4. Have volunteers share their paragraphs with the class. Guide a class discussion about how the daily life of people in rural India is similar to and different from the daily lives of urban Indians. **LS** **Verbal-Linguistic**

📝 **Alternative Assessment Handbook**, Rubrics 30: Research; and 38: Writing to Classify

Today, university graduates in cities like Bangalore, India, are preparing the tax returns of millions of Americans—overnight, half a world away, via the Internet—for far lower wages than tax preparers get in the United States. China is promoting a balance of high-technology "knowledge jobs" as well, while also boosting manufacturing to become a giant exporter. The opening of these economies poses both challenges and opportunities for the rest of the world.

DOCUMENT 1

In his influential book *The World Is Flat*, Thomas Friedman argued that India and China are leveling, or flattening, the economic playing field. Western industrialized countries are losing their advantages, and other developing countries risk falling farther behind.

> "Because China can amass so many low-wage workers at the unskilled, semiskilled, and skilled levels, because it has such a voracious [huge] appetite for factory, equipment, and knowledge jobs to keep its people employed, and because it has such a massive and burgeoning [growing] consumer market, it has become an unparalleled zone for offshoring. . . .
>
> The more attractive China makes itself as a base for offshoring, the more attractive other developed and developing countries competing with it, like Malaysia, Thailand, Ireland, Mexico, Brazil, and Vietnam, have to make themselves. . . . This has created a process . . . in which countries scramble to see who can give companies the best tax breaks, education incentives, and subsidies, on top of their cheap labor, to encourage offshoring to their shores. . . .
>
> In Cairo, the skyline seems forever the same. In China, if you miss visiting a city for a year, it's like you haven't been there in forever. And in Mexico City, just when Mexicans thought they had turned the corner forever, they ran smack into China, coming the other way and running much faster. . . ."
>
> —Thomas Friedman, *The World Is Flat*, 2005

Analyzing the Document
Why, according to Friedman, does China pose a problem for developing countries like Mexico and Brazil?

DOCUMENT 2

As China industrializes and modernizes, its demand for energy is soaring, as shown in this graph. The increasing need causes concern about the possible effect on global energy prices and supplies.

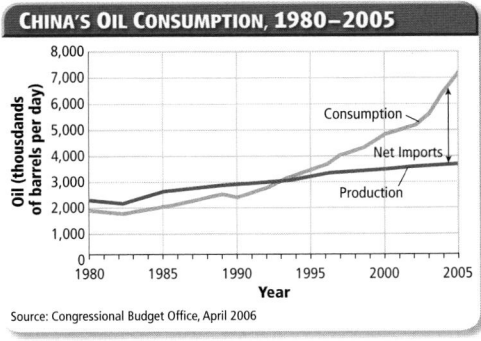

CHINA'S OIL CONSUMPTION, 1980–2005

Source: Congressional Budget Office, April 2006

Analyzing the Document
By roughly how much did China's energy consumption increase between 1980 and 2005? Explain the gap between the two lines since about 1995. What effect could that have on the rest of the world?

BUILDING ECONOMIC POWERHOUSES **1033**

Skills Focus: Interpreting Line Graphs

Social Studies Skill
U.S. Oil Consumption and Production

1. Have students review the line graph on this page and write down the trend(s) it reveals.

2. Have students create a similar line graph based on United States oil production and consumption between 1980 and 2005. This information is available at the Energy Information Administration's Web site.

3. Have students compare the line graph they create with the one on this page.

4. Have students write a paragraph describing the possible conclusions they could draw from their comparisons of the line graphs. Have students discuss their conclusions with the class. **LS Visual-Spatial, Logical-Mathematical**

   Alternative Assessment Handbook, Rubrics 7: Charts; and 9: Comparing and Contrasting

---

Direct Teach

Word Help

lucrative profitable (p. 1034)

geopolitical relating to the political and geographic factors that influence a nation's foreign policy (p. 1035)

adage traditional saying that expresses a common observation (p. 1035)

Reading Focus

Investigating the Issue

Identify What was China's oil production rate in 1990? *3,000,000 barrels per day*

Explain According to Friedman, how is China affecting the developing nations of the world? *possible answer—To compete with China economically, developing countries are scrambling to offer better incentives to attract offshoring.*

Info to Know

World Energy As of 2003, the United States, Russia, and China were the top three producers of energy, accounting for 39% of the world's total production. The three nations were also the top consumers of energy, accounting for 41% of the world's total consumption. The United States was the leader in both categories by wide margins. The United States alone accounted for nearly one quarter of the planet's energy consumption. Americans consumed 40% more energy than they produced.

Answers

Analyzing the Document (left) *possible answer—China, with its large workforce, strong industrial base, and huge consumer market, is able to draw foreign business enterprises away from developing nations.* **(right)** *approximately 5,000,000 barrels a day; possible answers—China's consumption of oil has increased at a much faster rate than its production of oil since 1995; because of this gap, China will have to import more oil, increasing demand, which may cause oil prices to rise for all nations.*

Investigating the Issue

Draw Conclusions What does Aravind Adiga suggest about the impact of remittances on the economy of India? *possible answer—Remittances have had a major impact; the flow of money has transformed cities and towns and helped many Indians rise in economic class.*

Draw Conclusions Do you think India should continue to promote outsourcing and the sending of its young people to work abroad? *possible answer—Yes, outsourcing and remittances have stimulated economic growth and brought new wealth to many Indians; no, India is too dependent upon foreign countries—the nation's economy could crash if trends change overseas.*

Info to Know

Outsourcing in India In 2006 exports of computer software and outsourced services such as call centers and back office operations generated over $23 billion in annual income for India. These sources of revenue continue to grow rapidly each year. By 2010 the country's software and services sector are projected to generate $60 billion in annual revenue.

Answers

Analyzing the Document (left) *Lady Liberty, Uncle Sam, the country of China; how free trade and capitalism will affect budgets; China depicted as wealthy because it benefited from free trade;* **(right)** *greater emphasis on education, more schools and colleges, more wealth in the city; possible answer—The writer is, for the most part, pleased with the changes though he is concerned that his hometown is so dependent upon foreign countries.*

1034

DOCUMENT 3

For decades, the United States has promoted free trade and capitalism around the world. It continues to do so today. In the early years of the twenty-first century, however, the United States ran up large budget and trade deficits.

Analyzing the Document

Who are the characters in this cartoon? What are they concerned about? How does the cartoonist depict China, and why?

DOCUMENT 4

Economic change is transforming India and China. In this article, the writer, who lives in the United States, talks about the cultural changes he observed when returned to visit his hometown of Mangalore, India.

"Back in 1991, when I left, about 300,000 people lived there. Since then its population has doubled But that doesn't begin to describe its transformation. . . .

[The] past decade has seen extraordinary change—and extraordinary excess—in Mangalore. The fastest-growing industry is education. During the 1980s, higher education became the only way out of a broken system for many frustrated young Indians. The best doctors and computer engineers had a fighting chance of nabbing a lucrative job offer from Silicon Valley [California] or Manhattan. So boys and girls throughout India streamed into colleges and institutes, where they studied calculus and organic chemistry with a passion that was probably unrivaled anywhere in the world. In recent years, the trend has accelerated. Mangalore had one medical college when I left; it now has five as well as at least four dental schools and 14 physiotherapy colleges. Some 350 schools, colleges and polytechnics are listed in its yellow pages.

. . . A flood of new money has arrived, thanks to outsourcing jobs, surging real estate prices and expatriate remittances [money that Indians who leave send back to support their families at home]. As a result, many locals have become middle-class, upper-middle-class or even rich. . . .

For better or worse, Mangalore's fate is in the hands of outsiders."

—Aravind Adiga, "My Lost World", *Time*, June 26, 2006

Analyzing the Document

What kinds of changes does the writer identify in his booming hometown? How do you think he feels about the changes?

Differentiating Instruction

Below Level

Learners Having Difficulty

1. Have students review the cartoon on this page. Discuss with the class the issues addressed in the cartoon.

2. Organize students into mixed-ability pairs.

3. Have each pair create a political cartoon that addresses an issue or issues relating to India's or China's economic growth. Cartoons may address the economic relationship of one or both of those nations to the United States.

4. Have students present their cartoons to the class. **LS Visual-Spatial**

   Alternative Assessment Handbook, Rubric 27: Political Cartoons

DOCUMENT 5

Today, a relatively small segment of India's labor force generates the largest share of its income, as measured in gross domestic product (GDP). These pie graphs illustrate that fact.

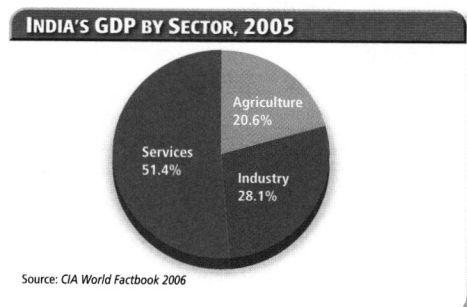

INDIA'S GDP BY SECTOR, 2005

Agriculture 20.6%
Services 51.4%
Industry 28.1%

Source: CIA World Factbook 2006

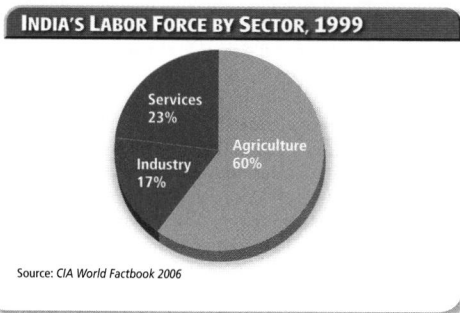

INDIA'S LABOR FORCE BY SECTOR, 1999

Services 23%
Agriculture 60%
Industry 17%

Source: CIA World Factbook 2006

Analyzing the Document
What proportion of India's labor force produces the largest share of its wealth, as measured in GDP? What do you think accounts for this fact?

DOCUMENT 6

The writer is a former governor of Hong Kong and former European Commissioner for External Relations. He notes the high stakes in the India-China competition.

> "India now trains a million engineering graduates a year (against 100,000 each in America and Europe) and stands third in technical and scientific capacity —behind America and Japan but ahead of China. Now when we play the geopolitical game of who will dominate the century to come, we add India to the stand-off between America and China.
>
> . . . I recognise the growing interest in whether we should—businessmen and politicians—place our bets on China's authoritarian model of development or India's democratic approach. The question is given more edge if you accept (which I don't) the old Chinese adage, "No mountain can accommodate two tigers."
>
> —Chris Patten, "Mystery Candidate," *Financial Times*, August 4, 2006

Analyzing the Document
According to Patten, in what way is the competition more than an economic one? Rewrite the last sentence in your own words. What is Patten's view of the issue?

ANALYZING THE ISSUE

go.hrw.com
Research Online
SD7 Case Study

1. Review the documents presented on this issue. What are some ways the economic rise of India and China are affecting the world?

2. What do the documents suggest about the advantages and disadvantages India and China each possess in their effort to become the world's biggest economic power?

3. Read excerpts and reviews of Thomas Friedman's book, *The World is Flat*. What does the title of his book mean? What effect does he think India and China are having on the world economy?

4. What steps do you think the United States could take to meet the challenge of global competition? Consider possibilities relating to education and business growth.

BUILDING ECONOMIC POWERHOUSES **1035**

Document-Based Investigation

Women in Society Ireland and Turkey

FOCUSING ON THE ISSUE

How do historical and cultural trends affect the status of women?

KEY TERMS
secular

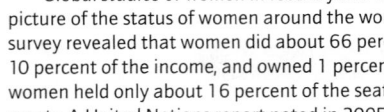

New York Standards

PI 3.2 Explain the dynamics of cultural change and how interactions among and between cultures has affected various cultural groups around the world.
PI 3.3 Examine the social/cultural, political, economic, and religious norms and values of Western and other world cultures.

Global studies of women in recent years have painted a bleak picture of the status of women around the world. For example, a 1999 survey revealed that women did about 66 percent of the work, earned 10 percent of the income, and owned 1 percent of the land. Moreover, women held only about 16 percent of the seats in the world's parliaments. A United Nations report noted in 2005, "Gender is one of the world's strongest markers for disadvantage."

The world's governments have pledged themselves to improve conditions for women. The United Nations Millennium Development Goals set a timetable of 2015 for increasing standards for women. It calls for improvements in the areas of educational opportunities, literacy, employment in non-farm jobs, and participation in national parliaments.

Globalization has helped produce a gradual shift in attitudes in some societies. Globalization emphasizes that countries need to value women as a human resource in order to become economically competitive. Studies show that countries that hold women back from participating in society consistently lag behind in development. In addition, as globalization helps women throughout the world gain greater access to new role models, information, and opportunities, their expectations grow.

Yet as governments try to improve the lives of women, they often must struggle to balance competing demands. Empowerment for women can clash with traditional cultural and religious beliefs. Even some women wonder if too much is lost in the rush for change. Ireland and Turkey are two nations that have faced and continue to face these challenges. The paths they have followed have taken some surprising twists.

Tansu Ciller (left) of Turkey and Mary McAleese (right) of Ireland have risen to the top ranks of government in their respective countries in recent years.

1036

Teach the Main Idea

At Level

The Status of Women

1. **Teach** Ask students the Focusing on the Issue question to teach this section.

2. **Apply** Organize students into two large groups. Have one group list examples of the progress Irish women have made and give examples of inequality Irish women still face. Have the second group do the same for Turkish women.

3. **Review** Have the two groups share their lists. Discuss as a class how the status of

women in Ireland and Turkey is similar and different.

4. **Practice/Homework** Have students write an essay describing opportunities and challenges for a woman living in either Ireland or Turkey today. **LS Verbal-Linguistic, Interpersonal**

Alternative Assessment Handbook, Rubrics 14: Group Activity; and 40: Writing to Describe

Ireland is a predominantly Roman Catholic country, and Turkey is a predominantly Muslim country. In each, religious tradition and, in some cases, religious doctrine, have played a role in shaping the roles of women in society.

Ireland in Transition As recently as the 1970s, an Irish woman who got married could be forced to quit her job. In a largely Roman Catholic country opposed to abortion and birth control, the majority of women stayed home and raised families.

Starting in the 1970s, however, and gathering force in the 1990s, a number of changes began to reshape Irish society. In 1973, Ireland joined the European Economic Community, forerunner to the European Union (EU). As a member of the EU, Ireland has gradually conformed to EU standards on the treatment of women. Also, EU membership has opened Ireland to the world, helping to change attitudes on a number of social issues.

While EU influence has grown, the influence of the Roman Catholic Church has begun to diminish. In 1972 a clause recognizing the "special position" of the Catholic Church in Irish society was removed from the constitution. Since then, the Church has continued to play a large role in politics, but not always successfully. So far, it has convinced Irish voters to uphold restrictions on abortion, but it failed in its efforts to keep divorce illegal.

Social, political, economic, and cultural changes have combined to open up opportunities for women. After a long struggle, the right of married women to work outside the home was guaranteed. The employment of women has risen steadily, from roughly 36 percent of the workforce in 1994 to about 47 percent in 2004. Much of that increase came during the 1990s, when an Irish economic boom produced a need for more workers.

Yet women in Ireland still face inequities. Men earn more than women do, and they have greater access both to living-wage jobs and to high-paying management jobs. Despite success at the top of the political ranks, overall participation of women in public office is low. Ireland ranks 77th out of 188 nations in terms of the proportion of women members of Parliament.

Modern Turkish women express themselves in different ways. Some adopt Western dress and others wear traditional headscarves.

Diverging Trends in Turkey When the modern nation of Turkey was founded in 1923, its leaders built a **secular**, or nonreligious, state in which government and religion are strictly separated by law. Women's rights were written into laws regarding property ownership, inheritance, and suffrage.

Turkey is trying to join the European Union. To further that effort, it has taken numerous steps to bring its laws closer in line with EU requirements and to promote women's rights generally. Yet the reality of equal opportunity has been more difficult to achieve. Women have trouble rising to managerial levels in the workplace. Although Turkish law mandates equal pay, estimates of inequities between women and men range from 10 percent to 40 percent. (In the United States, pay inequities range from 8 to 25 percent.)

In 2002 Turkey took what many saw as a turn away from secular politics. That year, they elected a party with Islamic ties. Commentators were quick to point out, however, that the shift was partly a reaction to corruption in the secular governments of the 1990s.

Recently, a generational divide has opened up among some Turkish women. To older generations, being a "modern" women meant being secular—seeing yourself as a Turkish citizen first and as a Muslim second. Among the new generation, however, some women seek to redefine women's rights and feminism in accordance with their religious beliefs.

WOMEN IN SOCIETY **1037**

Skills Focus: Making Oral Presentations

At Level

Reading Like a Historian Skill
Women Leaders

1. Have students compile a list of interview questions to ask a woman who is in a leadership position. Questions should focus on the challenges and professional experiences of this person.

2. Have students select a woman to interview. This person could be in politics, the business world, organized religion, academia, etc.

3. Have students conduct the interviews and then prepare an oral report based on the interviewees' answers.

4. Have students present their reports to the class. **LS Interpersonal, Verbal-Linguistic**

Alternative Assessment Handbook, Rubrics 18: Listening; and 24: Oral Presentations

---

Reading Focus

Exploring the Issue

Explain In Ireland, how has the influence of the European Union and the influence of the Roman Catholic Church changed in recent years? *the influence of the European Union has grown; the influence of the Roman Catholic Church has declined*

Make Judgments In which nation, Ireland or Turkey, do you think women will make greater progress in achieving equality in the coming years? *possible answers—Ireland: religious restrictions against equality are weakening; as a member of the EU, Ireland's economy will produce more opportunities for women; women in high-ranking offices will inspire more women to participate in politics; Turkey: because it has a long legal tradition mandating equal pay, it seeks to gain EU membership and is motivated to demonstrate the gender equality in its nation to the rest of Europe; women's rights and feminism are becoming more compatible with the nation's Islamic religious beliefs*

Primary Source

"New opportunities in education, employment, business, politics and religion have been seized with enthusiasm by women, transforming their expectations and self-confidence as individuals but also, and crucially, radically transforming the potential of family, of community and of country. Their genius, their energy has flowed much more freely than ever before into the human energy grid and we in Ireland have seen first-hand the manifest resulting uplift in economic, social and political fortunes."
—Mary McAleese, president of Ireland, in a speech at the Cornerstone Conference of the International Women's Forum, May 22, 2003

Word Help

fundamentally radically (p. 1038)

particularistic unique to oneself or one's own group (p. 1039)

Investigating the Issue

Compare A higher percentage of which country's citizens can read and write: Ireland or Turkey? *Ireland*

Interpret What do you think is Mary Robinson's primary goal for giving the speech in Document 2? *possible answer—to encourage the citizens of her country to use new strategies to address women's issues and help bring about gender equality*

Make Inferences How do you think Document 1 influenced Document 2? *possible answer—Ireland's low rank in women's legislative office-holding likely helped inspire Robinson's call for a fundamental reappraisal of women's issues in her country.*

Info to Know

The Supreme Court of Ireland The highest court in Ireland is the Supreme Court. It consists of a Chief Justice and seven regular judges. As of 2006, three of the eight judges on the Supreme Court were women: Susan Denham, Catherine McGuinness, and Fidelma Macken.

Answers

Analyzing the Document (top)
similarities: men have a high literacy rate, religion is important, low rank in terms of the proportion of women MPs; differences: Ireland is primarily Catholic, Turkey is primarily Muslim, Turkey has a much larger population than Ireland, Irish women have a much higher literacy rate than Turkish women; **(bottom)** *legislative and economic inequalities, lack of understanding of women's issues, prejudices against women*

1038

INVESTIGATING THE ISSUE

The changing role of women in societies around the world raises many questions. The documents that follow present data and opinions about how two countries—Ireland and Turkey—are addressing some of these questions. Examine the documents, keeping in mind what you have read about how women's roles are changing in each country. Then answer the questions that follow.

DOCUMENT 1

This chart compares key facts about the populations of Ireland and Turkey. Note that while both countries have had female heads of state, neither is a leader when it comes to electing women to the national legislature.

IRELAND AND TURKEY COMPARISON, 2005	IRELAND	TURKEY
Population	4.1 million	70.5 million
Religion	88.4% Roman Catholic	99.8% Muslim
Adult Literacy Rate	Men 99%, Women 99%	Men 94.3%, Women 78.7%
Women in Parliament, world ranking*	Ranked 77 out of 188	Ranked 126 out of 188

*USA Ranking = 66 out of 188
Source: CIA; International Parliamentary Union

Analyzing the Document
In what way are Ireland and Turkey fairly similar, according to this data? How are they different?

DOCUMENT 2

The election of Ireland's first woman president, Mary Robertson, focused more attention on women's issues. In this speech, Robertson called for new thinking about roles for women in Irish society.

"If the imbalances of the past came, and I believe they did, not simply from legislative and economic inequality but from profound resistances and failures of perception, then it follows that to right that balance we must do more than review our legislation and re-state our economic structures. We must also fundamentally re-appraise our view of who and what is valuable in our society. We must look with fresh and unprejudiced eyes at the work of women, the views of women, their way of organising and their interpretation of social priorities. To achieve this, we must, I believe, begin at the beginning and alter our way of thinking."

—Speech by Mary Robinson, president of Ireland, 1992

Analyzing the Document
According to Robinson, what combination of factors produced inequalities in Irish society?

Collaborative Learning

At Level

Female Heads of State

1. Organize students into five groups. Assign one of the following continents to each group: North America, South America, Europe, Asia, and Africa.

2. Have each group compile a list of all past and current female heads of state in the countries on their continent since 1900.

3. Have groups share their lists with the class. Note the differences in the total number of names on the lists.

4. Guide students in a discussion about possible reasons for the different total numbers on the lists. **LS** Visual-Spatial, Logical-Mathematical

📝 **Alternative Assessment Handbook**, Rubrics 11: Discussions; and 14: Group Activity

Like many countries, Turkey is struggling to live up to its promises of gender equality. This table shows the education gender gap.

EDUCATION RATES IN TURKEY, 2004

	GIRLS	BOYS	GENDER GAP
Primary school	93	100	7.8
Secondary school	57.2	74.3	17.1
College	18.7	24.3	8.3
Adult literacy	78.5	94.4	15.9
Adult literacy, rural	69.2	91	21.8
Adult literacy, urban	83.4	96.1	12.7

Analyzing the Document
Where is the gender gap greatest? Where is it lowest? What do you think accounts for the differences in urban and rural literacy rates?

The controversy over the Muslim head scarf symbolizes the current tensions in Turkey over the role of women. This writer, a Turkish professor of sociology, has studied the attitudes of young Turkish women who are rebelling against secularism and wearing the head scarf.

"What really distinguishes the contemporary Islamic movement [in Turkey] is this presence of women in these movements, so they are the motor of change....

But what happens is that each time these Muslim girls—or women, now—go to public life, pursue their professional career, for instance, they go from home to outside, from private to public life. Each time there is a tension within the [Islamic] movement and, therefore, there is a kind of debate among Islamic women who want to go even more public and Islamic men who remind them that, first of all, they have to be wives and mothers—their sacred roles....

... [A]lthough we are in a country where the majority of the population is Muslim, nevertheless we define the republic as a secular republic. And secularism meant this neutral space where you are not allowed to bring your religious, ethnic, particularistic [individual] identities. So there is this debate now ongoing to what extent we are going to enlarge democratic rights to include this kind of new demands of difference.

—Nilufer Gole, online interview, *Frontline*, PBS, June 2001

Analyzing the Document
How are attitudes toward women's participation in Turkish society changing?

ANALYZING THE ISSUE

go.hrw.com
Research Online
SD7 Case Study

1. How has religious tradition played a role in the shaping women's roles in Ireland and in Turkey? What similarities and differences exist between the two countries on this issue?

2. In what ways is there a gap between the laws and the realities of life for women in both countries? Provide specific examples.

3. Research the role of the president in Ireland. Do you think the function of that position made it easier for women to reach that post? Why or why not?

4. Do research to create a time line of major events in history of women's rights in Ireland, Turkey, and the United States from the 1900s to the present.

Differentiating Instruction

Above Level

Advanced Learners/Gifted and Talented

1. Have students select a topic relating to women's issues in either Ireland or Turkey. Possible topics include individuals (e.g. Tansu Ciller), groups (e.g. textile workers), or conditions (e.g. unequal wages).

2. Have students write a poem or song about the issue they selected. Students having difficulty writing lyrics may choose a popular song and write new words for their topic.

3. Have student present their songs or poems to the class. Students who wrote songs may wish to include music as part of their presentation.

4. Discuss with the class how music and poetry can inspire social change. **LS Auditory-Musical, Verbal-Linguistic**

Alternative Assessment Handbook, Rubrics 11: Discussions; and 26: Poems and Songs

---

Direct Teach

Reading Focus

Investigating the Issue

Recall What portion of Turkish boys is college educated? *about one fourth, or 24.3%*

Make Inferences Why does Gole believe that young Turkish women are "motors of change"? *possible answer—Young Turkish women are participating in a public movement that creates tension among much of the Muslim population. This tension sparks debates that can lead to social change.*

Answers

Analyzing the Document (left)
greatest: adult literacy in rural areas; lowest: primary school education; possible answer—Modern secular values are likely stronger in urban areas, resulting in more educational opportunities for girls; in rural areas, where traditional religious beliefs are stronger, education for girls is less emphasized. **(right)** *women want increased role in public life, debate about increasing democratic rights*

Analyzing the Issue 1. *Religious tradition has generally limited women's rights in Ireland and Turkey; similar—young women in both countries are seeking greater equality and professional opportunities while still honoring the values of their religion. differences—Turkish women seem more at odds with Muslim faith, which emphasizes "sacred" roles of wives and mothers.* **2.** *possible answers—Though Ireland and Turkey legislate equality, women in both nations still face inequalities. In both Ireland and Turkey women are not paid as much as men and have less access to management-level jobs.* **3.** *Answers will vary, but students should support their arguments with specific examples from their research about the Irish president.* **4.** *Answers will vary, but should include relevant events such as gaining the right to vote, passage of laws guaranteeing women's rights and dates woman attained high offices.*

Focusing on the Issue

What should the role of the United Nations be in international affairs? *possible answer—to debate and settle disputes among nations, to preserve human rights, and to foster peaceful relations among nations*

Key Terms

Preteach the following terms:

charter the document that created the United Nations (p. 1040)

General Assembly entity of the United Nations consisting of all member nations (p. 1041)

Security Council entity of the United Nations consisting of 15 member nations that serve as peacekeepers (p. 1041)

Secretariat entity of the United Nations that carries out the organization's administrative tasks (p. 1041)

peacekeeping sending multinational forces into countries to enforce ceasefires or truces among warring countries or warring groups within a single country (p. 1041)

Document-Based Investigation

The Role of the United Nations

FOCUSING ON THE ISSUE

What should the role of the United Nations be in international affairs?

KEY TERMS
charter, General Assembly, Security Council, Secretariat, peacekeeping

New York Standards

PI 1.3 Analyze historic events from around the world by examining accounts written from different perspectives.
PI 4.2 Interpret and analyze documents and artifacts related to significant developments and events in world history.

United Nations Secretary-General Kofi Annan addressing the General Assembly at the opening ceremonies of the sixtieth session of the UN in 2005.

1040

It was an ambitious idea: Create an organization to settle disputes among nations and solve tough global problems. Since its founding in 1945—the outcome of efforts by the United States and its World War II allies—the United Nations has struggled to live up to those high ideals.

The United Nations **charter**, the document that created the organization, lays out four major goals. It aims "to maintain international peace and security; to develop friendly relations among nations; to cooperate in solving international problems and in promoting respect for human rights; and to be a centre for harmonizing the actions of nations." Security, human rights, economic development, healthcare, disaster relief, and refugee aid are among its top concerns today.

From the start, the UN's mission was a delicate balancing act. The charter establishes the principle of equality among nations; yet it assigns an unequal role to the world's powerful nations in maintaining global security—often to the frustration of smaller countries. The United Nations consists of a diversity of shifting alliances, values, voices, interests, and goals. Even within the host country itself, the United States, debate over the very existence of the UN has raged for years.

Since 1945 UN membership has grown from 51 to 191 nations. As the organization has grown, so has its mission. Indeed, the modern-day rise of globalization, terrorism, and nuclear proliferation has challenged the UN in ways its founders never could have imagined. With expansion have come problems: waste, corruption, scandals. Failures to prevent or resolve wars and genocides in various parts of the world during the 1990s and beyond further damaged the UN's image and credibility.

Starting around 2005, the UN launched reforms aimed at dealing with these acknowledged problems. Leaders vowed to retool the organization to effectively meet twenty-first century needs. Critics remained skeptical about whether the UN could succeed in reforming itself.

The Role of the United Nations

1. **Teach** Ask students the Focusing on the Issue question to teach this section.

2. **Apply** Organize students into two groups. Have one group compile a list of general functions and goals of the United Nations. Have the second group make a list of specific operations or policies the United Nations is currently pursuing.

3. **Review** Have volunteers write each list on the board. Have students match the general function or goal to each specific operation

or policy with which it corresponds. Guide a discussion about how the United Nations is currently working to achieve its goals.

4. **Practice/Homework** Have each student write an essay evaluating the success of the United Nations, suggesting future directions the organization should take. **LS Verbal-Linguistic, Intrapersonal**

Alternative Assessment Handbook, Rubrics 14: Group Activity; and 37: Writing Assignments

The UN consists of six main entities: the General Assembly, the Security Council, the Secretariat, the Economic and Social Council, the Trusteeship Council, and the International Court of Justice. The court is held at The Hague, in the Netherlands, while the rest of the operations are based at the UN's global headquarters in New York City.

The **General Assembly** includes all the member nations, and each nation gets one vote on matters before the assembly. The votes are not binding, but they carry weight as a statement of world opinion.

The role of the **Security Council** is to be the guardian of peace. It sends armies to trouble spots to keep the peace, arranges cease-fires, and brokers peace agreements. If countries violate agreements, the Council may impose sanctions. It can even order military action against the offenders. Of the 15 Security Council members, five are permanent—China, France, Russia, the United Kingdom, and the United States. The others serve two-year terms. Each of the permanent members has veto power over Security Council decisions. This arrangement guarantees that the interests of the powerful nations are protected. Recently, there have been discussions about expanding the Security Council to include other powerful nations, such as Japan and Germany.

The **Secretariat** carries out the administrative tasks of the UN, from conducting studies to providing services around the globe. The head of the UN, the secretary-general, is elected for up to two five-year terms.

An Expanding Role Since the end of the Cold War, the UN's mission has expanded. UN workers are now dispersed throughout the world. More than half of the UN's 30,000 non-military employees serve in the field. Civilian field operations include humanitarian relief operations, human rights monitoring, election monitoring, and efforts to combat the drug trade and other global criminal activity.

The major field operation of the UN is **peacekeeping**, or the sending multinational forces into countries to enforce ceasefires or truces among warring countries or warring groups within a single country. In 2006, approximately 80,000 troops from member nations served in

UN peacekeeping troops on patrol in Sudan in 2006. In 1998, the UN received the Nobel Peace Prize for its peacekeeping operations.

UN peacekeeping forces around the globe. In 2006 roughly 70 percent of the UN's budget was dedicated to field operations, up from 50 percent 10 years earlier.

Criticism and Scandal Critics of the UN fault it for reacting slowly to the ethnic genocides in Rwanda and Bosnia in the 1990s. They say the UN is ineffective in combating terrorism and in preventing the spread of nuclear technology to countries such as Iran and North Korea. Some fault the UN for not taking stronger action against the dictatorship of Saddam Hussein in Iraq prior to the U.S. invasion of the country in 2003.

The worst blow to the UN's image in recent times was the Oil-for-Food scandal that broke in 2004. The UN Oil for Food program allowed Iraq to sell its oil to buy humanitarian supplies for its people. Instead of using the oil money to buy food and medicine for suffering Iraqis, Saddam Hussein skimmed billions from the program. UN officials were implicated in profiting from the theft as well.

THE ROLE OF THE UNITED NATIONS **1041**

Reading Focus

Investigating the Issue

Recall What are the three primary categories of UN expenses? *extra-budgetary, peacekeeping, regular*

Describe How does the UN pursue its health care agenda? *through the World Health Organization, a UN branch that coordinates disease-prevention efforts; by including health care issues among its Millennium Development Goals*

Make Generalizations Summarize the information in the three documents on this page in a single statement. *possible answer—The UN has recently achieved notable successes as its vast agenda has continued to expand.*

INVESTIGATING THE ISSUE

Controversy continues to rage around the United Nations. The documents that follow explore these issues by presenting different points of view and arguments. Examine the documents, keeping in mind what you have read about the organization's history, mission, and challenges.

DOCUMENT 1

Reflecting the scope of the UN's mission, in 2005 all 191 UN member countries pledged to achieve the following list of ambitious goals, called the Millennium Development Goals, by 2015.

UN MILLENNIUM DEVELOPMENT GOALS

1. Eradicate extreme poverty and hunger
2. Achieve universal primary education
3. Promote gender equality and empower women
4. Reduce child mortality
5. Improve maternal health
6. Combat HIV/AIDS, malaria and other diseases
7. Ensure environmental sustainability
8. Develop a global partnership for development

Analyzing the Document

How would you characterize the type of goals listed here? Do you think the goals are realistic in the time frame established? Why or why not?

DOCUMENT 2

The World Health Organization, a branch of the UN, has spearheaded efforts to combat disease worldwide. With funding from member states and private groups, the WTO coordinates disease-prevention efforts, such as the drive to eliminate smallpox, which achieved success in 1977. Currently, the WTO is conducting a drive to wipe out polio. The graph below shows the progress of the effort.

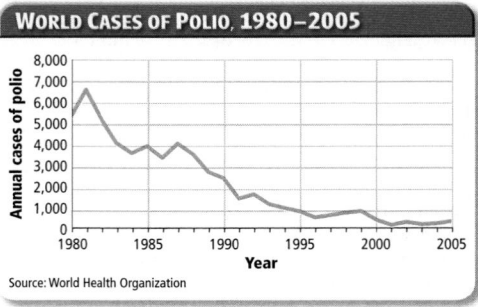

WORLD CASES OF POLIO, 1980–2005

Source: World Health Organization

Analyzing the Document

What is the trend in world cases of polio? What happened between 2000 and 2005?

DOCUMENT 3

The UN's expenses have grown as its mission has expanded. The budget for peacekeeping alone in 2004-2005 was greater than the UN's entire budget in 1996-1997.

Analyzing the Document

During the decade shown here, what portion of UN expenses grew the most? What do you think accounts for that dramatic increase?

UN BUDGETS, 1996–2005

Legend: Extra-budgetary, Peacekeeping, Regular

Budgets (in billions of dollars)

Year	Total	Extra-budgetary	Peacekeeping	Regular
1996-97	(9,324)	4,511	2,210	2,603
1998-99	(8,768)	3,609	2,629	2,530
2000-01	(11,873)	3,931	5,409	2,533
2002-03	(12,854)	4,396	5,567	2,891
2004-05	(18,503)	4,446	9,449	3,608

Source: UN Fact Sheet, March 2006

Skills Focus: Analyzing

At Level

Social Studies Skill
United Nations Peacekeeping Missions

1. Have students visit the UN cartography webpage (http://www.un.org/Depts/Cartographic/english/htmain.htm). Have students select one of the peacekeeping maps listed.

2. Have students research the operation(s) depicted on their chosen map.

3. Have students prepare an informational essay describing the operations shown on their map. For example, students could explain why various troop units are deployed in certain locations.

4. Have students print out their maps and present their essays to the class. **LS Visual-Spatial, Verbal-Linguistic**

Alternative Assessment Handbook, Rubrics 21: Map Reading; and 42: Writing to Inform

---

Answers

Analyzing the Document (top left) *possible answers—ambitious, optimistic; no, too much opposition and conflict in the world; yes, with an increasing budget and resources, UN can match success it had with polio with these goals;* **(top right)** *rise in polio cases in early 1980s, then decline in cases; polio almost completely eliminated;* **(bottom)** *peacekeeping; possible answer—The UN has committed more resources to field operations in recent years.*

American conservatives have been particularly critical of the United Nations over the years. At times they have called for the United States to withdraw from the UN, and they have successfully worked to withhold US funding from the UN.

In this piece from *Commentary* magazine, one of the leading conservative journals in the United States, the writer finds fault with the very structure of the UN. As UN responsibilities grow, the writer argues, so do opportunities for inefficiencies and corruption.

Analyzing the Document
From what you read, do you believe that Rosett believes the United Nations can ever be reformed?

"Since its founding, the institution has added untold numbers of agencies, funds, commissions, programs, "ad-hoc bodies," and "other entities," to the point where most of the UN's own personnel do not know who reports to whom, or how. . . .

There is almost no way to hold the UN accountable for most of what goes on in this growing empire. . . . In fact, there is no procedure at the UN for impeaching or firing the Secretary-General. . . .

The founding purpose of the UN was to bring peace and prosperity to the globe. As to the former, the UN in the age of terror has been in most ways useless and in some ways positively dangerous. The lesson that Saddam Hussein quickly grasped was that the UN lends itself to money-laundering [illegally hiding the transfer of funds]. . . .

Like the Soviet Union of old, the UN is unwieldy, gross, inefficient, and incompetent. . . ."

—"How Corrupt Is the United Nations?"
Claudia Rosett, *Commentary* magazine, April 2006

As of late 2006, the United Nations had sponsored 59 peacekeeping operations since its founding. Sixteen were ongoing. UN peacekeeping has had some notable successes, such as El Salvador and Mozambique in the early 1990s and East Timor in the early 2000s.

In the case of the Arab-Israeli conflict, success has been more elusive. Indeed, over the years there have been seven separate UN peacekeeping missions triggered by the Arab-Israeli conflict. UN peacekeepers have successfully monitored truces or agreements between Israel and its neighbors Syria and Egypt. But a lasting regional peace has remained out of reach. A UN monitoring force in Lebanon since 1978 has been powerless to stop repeated attacks against Israel or two full-scale invasions of Lebanon by Israel. The cartoonist, a supporter of Israel, reflects the frustration that many felt during the Israel-Lebanon War of 2006.

Michael Ramirez, *Investor's Business Daily*, July 24, 2006

Analyzing the Document
How does the cartoonist characterize the UN's response to Middle East conflict?

THE ROLE OF THE UNITED NATIONS **1043**

Exploring the Issue

Recall To what does Claudia Rosett compare the United Nations? *the Soviet Union*

Make Connections What connections can you identify between the two documents on this page? *possible answer—The lack of success of the UN in dealing with the Israel-Lebanon War of 2006 likely caused people to criticize the organization using arguments similar to those of Claudia Rosett.*

Info to Know

UN Relief Efforts Relief to nations across the globe is one of the United Nations' primary missions: the UN carries out this work primarily through four organizations: the World Food Program (provides food to victims of disaster, long-term refugees, and displaced persons), the Office of the UN High Commissioner for Refugees (helps and protects refugees), the UN Children's Fund (addresses the needs of children in developing countries), and the UN Relief and Works Agency for Palestinian Refugees in the Near East (provides health, education, and social services to Palestinian refugees).

Answers

Analyzing the Document (top)
possible answer—No, Rosett believes the problems with the UN are deep-seated and structural—she believes that the UN, like the Soviet Union, is inefficient dissolved. **(bottom)** *unreliable; asleep at the wheel, inferring that the UN could do more to keep peace in the region*

1043

Recall According to Florini, how many nations are equally represented in the General Assembly? *191*

Explain How does Florini believe that the United States has hindered reform in the UN? *inconsistent diplomatic efforts to build consensus for meaningful change, withholding dues*

Make Inferences Why do you think the nations listed by Florini as opponents of reform are actively working against the UN? *possible answers— Those nations do not want outsiders interfering in their domestic business; their governments pursue policies that conflict with the UN's mission.*

Answers

Analyzing the Document *yes; structural flaws ("a fundamentally unsound institutional base"), inefficiency ("mess of largely pointless debates"), overt opposition from several nations ("actively subvert attempts to make the UN function efficiently"), and inconsistent U.S. policies ("only fitfully invested in the long-term, patient diplomacy needed to build consensus for meaningful change")*

Analyzing the Issue 1. *possible answers—The UN has ambitious goals that will present many challenges; the UN needs a lot of money to carry out its agenda; the UN has many opponents.* **2.** *possible answer—A conservative author is more likely to oppose the UN for not supporting recent U.S. foreign policy; a liberal author is more likely to support the UN's humanitarian and peacekeeping missions.* **3.** *possible answers—Several countries on the commission were criticized for human rights abuses; Americans criticized the commission's lack of discussion about human rights issues; the U.S. criticized the addition of Sudan to the commission.* **4.** *Letters will vary, but should discuss specific UN policies, and possible reform strategies.*

1044

DOCUMENT 6

Ann Florini is an analyst for the Brookings Institution, a nonpartisan think tank that often takes positions perceived as liberal. Like Claudia Rosett, she believes that the UN as currently organized is fundamentally flawed. Still, she believes the UN can be reformed.

"But all this [UN] activity depends on a fundamentally unsound institutional base. The UN's fifteen-country Security Council, the only UN body with teeth, gives lopsided power to the victors of World War II. The General Assembly, where all 191 nations theoretically have equal voice, has degenerated [fallen] into a . . . mess of largely pointless debates on a mind-numbing agenda covering every conceivable issue. The fifty-three-member Economic and Social Council is essentially worthless. The Secretariat suffers from a deadwood-ridden staff, extreme micro-management by member states, and an inadequate oversight system that allows plenty of waste, fraud, and abuse . . .

Step one [in reform] is to assign responsibility where it belongs: overwhelmingly with the member countries. . . .

The member countries have never invested the financial and human resources needed to make the UN work well. . . . A few hard-core opponents of reform—insiders point to Syria, Pakistan, Venezuela, Cuba, Egypt, and Iran—actively subvert [undermine] attempts to make the UN function efficiently and effectively. The U.S., where Congress goes into periodic fits of rage over revelations of misdeeds such as the oil-for-food scandal, has only fitfully invested in the long-term, patient diplomacy needed to build consensus [agreement] for meaningful change, and has sometimes shot itself in the foot with bullying tactics like withholding of dues. . . .

The small reforms agreed upon to date may still prove the spark for a real UN renaissance—if a whole lot of people act quickly. . . .

[The United States] must engage effectively but, given the realities of anti-Americanism, quietly with pro-reform forces in New York. . . . And the member states need to regain control of their own delegations in New York, who too often serve personal interests at the expense of national ones.

If all this is done, the UN may be reborn.

—Ann Florini, "The UN at 60: Senescence or Renaissance?"
The Brookings Institution, 2005

Analyzing the Document

Does the writer support the existence of the United Nations? What does she see as the key challenges to its success? Use passages from the excerpt to support your answers.

ANALYZING THE ISSUE

go.hrw.com
Research Online
SD7 Case Study

1. Review the documents presented on this issue. What do they tell you about the difficulties of carrying out the UN's mission?

2. Review the descriptions of the authors of the passages excerpted here. How might their backgrounds affect their point of view about the UN?

3. Research viewpoints about the UN Human Rights Commission. What controversies have surrounded its membership? Why has the United States objected to some of its activities?

4. Considering all the challenges involved in getting UN members to agree on actions and respond quickly to crises, do you think the UN has outlived its usefulness? Do you think it should be strengthened? Do you have another viewpoint? Write a letter to the editor explaining your position and offering reasons to support it.

1044 CASE STUDIES: CONTEMPORARY ISSUES

Skills Focus: Analyzing Alternative Points of View   At Level

Reading Like a Historian Skill
Opinions About the United Nations

1. Have students examine recent newspapers, magazines, or online sources to find two opinion pieces about the United Nations. One article should be pro-UN, and the other should be critical of the UN.

2. Have students write an essay assessing the two articles they selected. Students should recognize if the authors supported their arguments with facts or if their writing is excessively biased to advance an agenda.

3. Have students present their conclusions about the articles they selected to the class.
   LS Verbal-Linguistic

   Alternative Assessment Handbook, Rubric 16: Judging Information

REFERENCE SECTION

Regents Review of World History

The World Almanac Key Events in World History is a brief summary of important turning points in world history. It provides capsule descriptions of events or movements along with brief accounts of their significance. Use this section to review the content in *Human Legacy*.

Millions of years ago First Hominids

About 5–7 million years ago several species of "hominids," or upright walking, human-like primates, were roaming the African continent. By about 2–3 million years ago, early hominids lived in groups, made tools, and gathered food.

Significance These first hominids are the most distant ancestors of modern humans. Fossil records are gradually filling in a still murky picture of these early hominid ancestors.

200,000–100,000 years ago First Modern Humans

Homo sapiens, the species to which all modern humans belong, first lived in East Africa about 200,000 years ago. By 100,000 years ago humans had reached Southwest Asia, and by 35,000 years ago they had reached Europe.

Significance *H. sapiens* spread and thrived. They soon became the sole hominid species, supplanting Neanderthals among others.

14,000 years ago End of the Last Ice Age

Approximately 2 million years ago Earth's atmosphere cooled. Large sheets of ice formed and eventually covered vast portions of the planet's surface. This period, which lasted until about 12,000 BC, is called the Pleistocene epoch, or the last Ice Age. The end of the Pleistocene was marked by a gradual increase in Earth's temperatures. Land that had been covered by ice for millennia gradually became exposed to the sun once again.

Significance As the ice sheets receded, Earth became a more hospitable place. New plant and animal species developed. The Bering Land Bridge, which had connected Asia and the Americas, receded under the ocean, isolating the Americas and their inhabitants.

12,000–10,000 years ago Invention of Agriculture

For thousands of years humans had survived by hunting wild animals and gathering wild plants. Around 10,000 BC, with the climate warmer and drier, some humans discovered that animals and plants could be domesticated, or made to serve their needs directly. Domestication is one of the signs of the transition to the Neolithic Era, or New Stone Age. This happened around the same time in many parts of the world.

Significance Agriculture freed humans from the need to migrate in search of animals and plants for food. This allowed for permanent settlements, labor specialization and, eventually, civilization.

c. 4000 BC Rise of Mesopotamian Cultures

The Sumerians, a people who lived in the area between the Tigris and Euphrates rivers in what is now Iraq, developed what many consider the world's first civilization. Sumerian society was centered on large cities that were supported by irrigated farms in the countryside. Sumerians made use of the first known system of writing, which developed into the wedge-shaped script called cuneiform.

Significance As the world's first civilization, with the first developed system of writing, the Sumerians stand at the beginning of recorded history.

c. 4000–3500 BC Invention of the Wheel

Evidence suggests that people in the Mesopotamian cultures of the Near East had invented wheeled vehicles by as early as the fourth millennium BC. The concept spread rapidly to other civilizations. Remains of an early wooden disk wheel dating to around 3500 BC have been found at a site in what is now the Netherlands.

Significance The wheel was a milestone technological achievement. It made many tasks, from transporting people and goods to making pottery, far easier to accomplish.

c. 3100 BC Upper and Lower Egypt Unite

In ancient times the abundance of the Nile River valley gave rise to the two kingdoms of Upper and Lower Egypt. Around 3100 BC, according to tradition, Menes, an Upper Egyptian king, marched his army north to invade Lower Egypt. His efforts resulted in unification of the civilizations along the Nile into one Egypt. Menes established Egypt's first dynasty, and is considered to be Egypt's first pharaoh.

Significance The unification of Egypt by Menes represents the beginning of a great ancient civilization that lasted nearly 3,000 years.

3000–1500 BC Indus Valley Civilization

Around 3000 BC the Indus Valley civilization developed along the Indus River, in the northwest of the Indian subcontinent. Ruins from the cities of Harappa and Mohenjo Daro show that the Indus Valley civilization possessed strong governments and an economy based on agriculture. The Indus Valley civilization also developed a written language.

Significance The story of civilization in one of the world's most historically rich regions, the Indian subcontinent, began with this first Indus River valley culture.

c. 2700–2300 BC Egyptian Pyramids Built

Egyptians began constructing pyramids to serve as tombs for their pharaohs during the Old Kingdom, in the 2700s BC. The largest of the pyramids, the Great Pyramid of Khufu near Giza, was built during this time. The pyramids are evidence of the Egyptian belief in an afterlife and in the godly stature of their pharaohs.

Significance With nearly 80 pyramids still standing along the west bank of the Nile, the pyramids of Egypt serve as a testament to the strength, material wealth, and ability to mobilize vast resources characteristic of ancient Egypt under the pharaohs.

c. 1750 BC Code of Hammurabi

The Babylonian king Hammurabi rose to power around 1792 BC. By the end of his reign the Babylonian Empire extended through much of the Tigris-Euphrates Valley—a testament to his prowess as a military leader. But Hammurabi is best known for the code of written laws that survives from his reign. The laws, which were written down for all to see, dealt with matters ranging from trade and business to crimes and personal injuries.

Significance The Code of Hammurabi is the earliest known collection of written laws. Combining Sumerian and Semitic traditions, the code represented an advance beyond tribal codes.

c. 1700 BC Hyksos Invasion of Egypt

As the Middle Kingdom in Egypt weakened, a people known as the Hyksos migrated into Egypt from the east. With superior military technology, such as the horse-drawn chariot and the compound bow, the Hyksos were eventually able to establish their power. They ruled Egypt for more than a century, extending the kingdom's boundaries as far as Syria and Palestine, and maintaining peace and prosperity throughout their lands.

Significance The Hyksos kings ushered in a new phase in ancient Egyptian history. They introduced the horse-drawn chariot, which pharaohs of the New Kingdom period would use to build strong armies and expand their territory.

c. 1540–1075 BC New Kingdom in Egypt

Around 1540 BC an Egyptian named Ahmose declared himself pharaoh and drove the Hyksos from Egypt. This was the beginning of the New Kingdom, the period that would see Egypt rise to the peak of its power and glory. Fearful of invasion, future Egyptian pharaohs succeeded in establishing control over possible invasion routes. In the process, they overtook foreign lands and established an empire. Military conquests also expanded Egyptian trade and made the kingdom wealthy. The most famous New Kingdom pharaoh is Ramses II (died c. 1235 BC), who left behind numerous monuments.

Significance The New Kingdom period was the last great flourish of Egyptian power and culture before the empire's long, slow decline.

c. 1500 BC India's Vedic Period Begins

By around 1500 BC a new element became apparent in the Indus Valley region. Many scholars believe that a nomadic people known as the Aryans, originating from the area near the Black Sea, entered the Indus Valley in search of pastureland for their livestock. The synthesis between these new peoples and the indigenous population produced a rich culture, which we can glimpse today through the *Vedas*, one of the great religious texts of Hinduism.

Significance The languages of classical Sanskrit, in which the *Vedas* are written, and modern Bengali and Hindi derive from the Indo-Aryan language.

c. 1766–1100 BC Shang Dynasty in China

The Shang dynasty, the first Chinese dynasty for which solid historical evidence exists, created the first strong state in China, in the Huang River valley. Far-flung irrigation and flood-control systems spurred the Shang to develop a complex bureaucracy. Over time, the Shang expanded their lands. They are known for their outstanding bronzework.

Significance The Shang bureaucracy became a model for later Chinese dynasties. The earliest Chinese system of writing dates from the Shang period.

1200 BC Olmec Civilization in Mexico

Settlements dating from around 1500 BC along the southern Gulf of Mexico coast developed into the Olmec civilization by around 1200 BC. Remains of ceremonial cities that included temples and large stone statues date from this time. Olmec society was supported primarily by agriculture. The Olmec developed a calendar and a writing system. They worshipped a jaguar-like god.

Significance The Olmec developed the first historically known civilization in the Americas. Elements of Olmec civilization can be seen in many later Mesoamerican cultures.

c. 1200 BC Phoenicians Dominate Trade in the Mediterranean Sea

Having settled along the eastern Mediterranean coast by around 2800 BC, the Phoenicians developed a loose union of city-states supported by sea trade with the other Mediterranean cultures of Egypt and Greece. By 1200 BC the Phoenicians were the leading Mediterranean trading power. They established colonies throughout the Mediterranean, including Carthage in North Africa.

Significance As a trading people, the Phoenicians mingled the cultures of Egypt, Mesopotamia, and Greece. Their alphabet was adopted, with some modifications, by the Greeks and later the Romans, becoming the basis of our own.

960 BC Solomon Builds the Temple

King Solomon built the Temple to God in Jerusalem, the center of Israelite worship, in which the Ark of the Covenant containing the Ten Commandments was kept. Religion was the foundation upon which the Israelites, and later the Jews, based their society. Belief in one God and a strong code of ethics are central beliefs of Judaism. The standards of fairness, justice, and righteousness central to Judaism have sustained the Jewish people and their religion for more than 3,000 years. Even though the Temple was destroyed in 586 BC, rebuilt, and destroyed again in AD 70, the Jewish religion and people still thrive.

Significance One of the earliest monotheistic faiths, Judaism has had a major influence on Western society and is one of the world's major religions. The Jewish ethical tradition was later carried forward into Christianity and became known as Judeo-Christian ethics.

c. 700 BC Kushite Dynasty Rules Egypt

As neighbors in the Nile River valley, Kush and Egypt had a long history of relations, including a 500-year period of Egyptian rule of Kush. Following the decline of the New Kingdom in Egypt, Kushite kings launched military attacks against Egypt. Around 716 BC a Kushite king named Piankhi rose to power and declared himself pharaoh. This marked the beginning of the Kushite dynasty in Egypt.

Significance Kushite rulers of Egypt sought to restore Egyptian cultural traditions. They built new temples and pyramids and made efforts to preserve Egyptian writings.

509 BC Founding of the Roman Republic

According to tradition, Rome was founded in 753 BC and ruled by a succession of kings. The last of these was overthrown by nobles in 509 BC, and the Roman Republic was born. Over the next 500 years the Republic greatly expanded in size and power and evolved politically to include democratic elements.

Significance As the Republic expanded, it proved unable to reconcile rule of vast territories with the traditions of self-governance conceived for a city-state. Its example—good, bad, and idealized—nonetheless inspired the efforts of later ages to found republican governments.

500 BC Confucius in China

A Chinese philosopher who lived from 551 to 479 BC during the Zhou dynasty, Confucius urged a system of morality that stressed the importance of family, respect for elders, reverence for ancestors, and honest and just government. His teachings were compiled by his followers in the *Analects*.

Significance The body of thought derived from Confucius's teachings, Confucianism, exerted a profound influence on China and other East Asian culture.

500 BC Buddhism Develops in India

Siddhartha Gautama of India lived from around 563 to 483 BC. Revered for having found true wisdom, he came to be called the Buddha, or Enlightened One. For the remainder of his life the Buddha taught others the way to achieve an enlightened state.

Significance From the Buddha's life and experience arose one of the world's great religions, Buddhism. In the centuries following the Buddha's death, his teachings gained wide acceptance in Asia, shaping the cultural life of the region. In recent times Buddhism's influence has spread to non-Asian cultures.

500 BC Persian Empire under Darius

The largest empire to date at that time, stretching from Asia Minor and Egypt to India, the Persian Empire reached its peak under the emperor Darius, who ruled from 522 to 486 BC. Darius reorganized the administration of the empire and recognized a diversity of religions. His efforts to extend Persian rule to Greece, however, met with defeat.

Significance Darius's reforms helped solidify the power of his dynasty, the Achaemenids. Despite defeat in Greece, the Persian Empire remained the dominant power in the Near East for more than a century.

c. 500–479 BC Persian Wars

When Athens aided Greek city-states in Asia Minor in rebelling against the Persian Empire, a conflict began that became known as the Persian Wars. The Persian leader Darius, and later his son Xerxes, sought to punish Athens by launching invasions of Greece. The Persians captured and burned Athens, but in the end the Greek forces, though fewer in number, defeated the Persians in a great sea battle at Salamis and saved their homeland.

Significance Victory in the Persian Wars led to an expansion of Greek power in the eastern Mediterranean and a flowering of ancient Greek culture and artistic achievement.

c. 480–404 BC Golden Age of Athens

Athens reached the peak of its cultural development during the time of the statesman Pericles (around 460–429 BC) and after. Thanks to the reforms of Pericles, Athenian democracy was at its strongest. Greek art, architecture, poetry, drama, and philosophy flourished at this time.

Significance The cultural legacy of Athens is one of the great sources of Western civilization, serving to influence later art, governments, and philosophy.

431–404 BC Peloponnesian War

Following the Persian Wars, Athens transformed a mutual defense league into an empire, earning enemies and starting it on a collision course with Sparta, its rival for dominance in the Greek world. In 31 BC the rivalry between Athens and Sparta erupted into war, which lasted for 27 years. Ultimately Sparta, with assistance from Persia, was able to cut off food supplies to Athens. This forced Athens to surrender to Sparta in 404 BC.

Significance The Peloponnesian War was the watershed moment in the struggle for power in ancient Greece. Weakened, the Greek city-states declined and were eventually conquered by Philip II of Macedon.

330 BC Alexander the Great's Conquests

After inheriting a united Greece following the assassination in 336 BC of his father, Philip II of Mace-don, Alexander set out to conquer the known world. By 331 BC Alexander and his armies had conquered Asia Minor, Syria, Egypt, Mesopotamia, and all of the lands of the Persian Empire east to the Indus River. For his political and military successes he was called Alexander the Great. He ruled over his vast empire until his death in 323 BC.

Significance Alexander's conquests spread Greek culture from the Mediterranean Sea to India. This Hellenistic, or Greek-like, culture thrived between the time of Alexander's death and the Roman conquest of Greece in 146 BC.

218–201 BC Second Punic War

Rome's expanding borders and increased influence in the western Mediterranean brought the Republic into conflict with Carthage, a powerful commercial city in North Africa. In 218 BC the second of three major wars between the two powers began when the Carthaginian general Hannibal invaded Roman territory. Rome countered by invading North Africa and forcing Hannibal to return to his city. In 202 BC the Romans, led by Scipio, defeated Hannibal and his army at Zama, near Carthage.

Significance The Second Punic War established Rome as the most powerful force in the western Mediterranean. Within 100 years Rome brought the rest of the Mediterranean region under its control.

27 BC Augustus Becomes Rome's Emperor

When the Roman leader Julius Caesar was assassinated in 44 BC, Octavian, his grandnephew and chosen heir, struggled initially to consolidate his own rule. By 31 BC Octavian had quelled unrest in the Roman territories and defeated both his rivals for power. In 27 BC the Roman Senate officially conferred on him the title Augustus, which means "the revered one." Under Augustus the Roman Republic became the Roman Empire.

Significance The roughly 200-year period of political stability in the Roman Empire known as the Pax Romana began with the reign of Augustus.

c. AD 30 Jesus of Nazareth Preaches

Around AD 30, in the Roman province of Judea, Jesus of Nazareth, a Jewish teacher and prophet, began attracting followers. According to the Gospels of the New Testament, he preached a message of repentance and love of God and neighbor. A few years after he began teaching, Jesus was put to death by the Romans.

Significance The story of Jesus and his teachings are the basis for one of the world's great religions. Today over 2 billion people are Christians.

c. AD 47–62 Paul Spreads Christianity

Saul, a Jewish religious official from Tarsus in Asia Minor, at first opposed the spread of Christian beliefs. Better known by his Greek name Paul, he converted to Christianity and devoted his life to preaching and helped establish Christian churches throughout the eastern Mediterranean. Paul also wrote many of the letters that are part of the New Testament. He was imprisoned, and likely executed, by the Romans around 62.

Significance Through his journeys and writings, Paul played a key role in the development of Christian thought and the spread of Christianity in parts of the Roman empire.

250–900 Maya Classic Age

Early Maya villages on the Yucatán Peninsula of Mesoamerica gave rise, though increased trade, to larger towns and cities. During the Maya Classic Age, which lasted from 250 to 900, there were as many as 40 Maya cities with 5,000 to 50,000 inhabitants each. The cities had stone pyramids, temples, palaces, and plazas for public gatherings. Canals controlled the flow of water. Mayans developed systems of astronomy and mathematics to aid in their religious practices. By 900, for uncertain reasons, the Maya civilization rapidly declined.

Significance The Maya were one of the great ancient civilizations of the Western Hemisphere. Today their descendants in Mexico, Belize, and Guatemala still speak variants of the Maya language.

312 Constantine Converts to Christianity

In 284 the Roman Empire was divided in two. Following the death of his father in 306, Constantine became emperor of the Western Roman Empire. The eastern emperor, however, refused to recognize his status and he was forced to contend with a series of rivals. Constantine met one such rival in battle in 312. Before the battle he is said to have had a vision that would later lead him to convert to Christianity. He triumphed and the following year issued the Edict of Milan declaring Christianity to be a legal religion within the empire.

Significance With legal status and support in Rome, the Christian religion, once persecuted and suppressed, was able to grow and flourish. By the end of the fourth century it was the official religion of the Roman Empire.

476 Fall of the Western Roman Empire

Nearly a century of invasions by peoples expanding their territory left the Western Roman Empire in a severely weakened state. In 410 a Germanic people known as the Visigoths captured the city of Rome. The Western Empire continued to be plagued by invaders through 476. In that year a Germanic commander overthrew Romulus Augustulus, the last Roman emperor in the West.

Significance The fall of the Western Roman Empire fractured the unity of the Roman world and marked the beginning of a period in Europe when there were no strong central governments.

529–535 Justinian Preserves Roman Laws

The Eastern Roman Empire, called the Byzantine Empire, carried on after the fall of the Western Roman Empire. Its leaders sought to preserve the power and glory of Rome in the east. In about 529 the emperor Justinian had his scholars begin compiling the laws of the Roman Empire. The result was Justinian's Code. The collection of older laws was issued in Latin; newer ones were issued in Greek, the language of the Byzantines. Central to the code was the idea that established laws prevent people from being subject to the whims of their leaders.

Significance By establishing a clear reference for judicial decisions, Justinian's Code enhanced the stability of the Byzantine Empire. It later influenced legal systems throughout Europe.

622 Muhammad Leaves Mecca

According to Islamic tradition, around 610 an Arab merchant named Muhammad received a calling from God. He began preaching a monotheistic faith to the people of his home city of Mecca, on the Arabian Peninsula. The pagan rulers of Mecca were not receptive to his teachings and harassed Muhammad and his followers, who were called Muslims. In 622 Muhammad left Mecca for the town of Medina, where Islam gained a larger following.

Significance The journey of Muhammad from Mecca to Medina is known as the hegira. Later, Muslims marked the year in which the hegira took place as the first year of the Islamic calendar.

634–711 Spread of Islam

Following Muhammad's death, his successors, known as caliphs, led Arab armies in a rapid conquest of much of the Byzantine Empire, including North Africa, and the Persian Empire. The new Muslim empire stretched as far east as India and as far west as the Atlantic Ocean. In 711 Muslim forces conquered Spain, leading to the development of Muslim civilization in southern Europe.

Significance As Arabic language and Muslim patterns of life became prominent, the conquered peoples slowly converted to Islam. In many of those lands, Islam remains the majority religion today and provides a basis for shared cultural identity.

c. 661–680 Sunni-Shia Split

Disputes over the succession as caliph eventually led to the division of Muslims into several groups. Sunni Muslims accepted the legitimacy of the first four caliphs; Shia Muslims, who considered only Ali a rightful leader, did not. The deaths of Ali (661) and his son Husayn (680) widened the rift. Differing opinions among early Muslims regarding proper theological and religious ideas solidified the differences between Sunni and Shia groups.

Significance Today Sunnis and Shias continue to be the main groups of Muslims, with Sunni Muslims accounting for about 90 percent of Muslims. Shia Muslims live mainly in Iran, Iraq, Lebanon, the Arabian Peninsula, India, and Pakistan.

750–1258 Abbasid Caliphate

The first dynasty of caliphs, the Umayyads, oversaw the initial expansion of the caliphate. In 747 a competing family, the Abbasids, with the support of the Shia, began a rebellion against the Umayyads. By 750 the head of the Abbasid family had become caliph over the Muslim empire, with the Umayyads surviving only in Spain. The Abbasids moved the capital of the caliphate from Damascus to the new city of Baghdad. The Abbasids remained in power, which progressively diminished, until 1258, when Baghdad was overrun by Mongol invaders.

Significance The Abbasid Caliphate ushered in a golden age for the Muslim Empire. Art, literature, music, and scholarship thrived in the caliphate.

800 Charlemagne Crowned Emperor

Charlemagne inherited the Frankish throne from his father in 768. After gaining greater power upon his brother's death, he sought to carry out his vision of building a new Rome. He conquered the Lombards, Saxons, and Avars before finally being repelled by the Moors in Spain. In 799 a new pope, Leo III, asked Charlemagne for help in fighting off opposition to his papacy. Charlemagne obliged, the next year the pope crowned him Emperor of the Romans.

Significance Charlemagne's coronation by the pope granted legitimacy to his conquests and solidified his rule. Charlemagne's realm was the basis of what became known as the Holy Roman Empire, which lasted in various guises until 1806.

c. 800–1591 West African Trading States

In West Africa, along the gold-rich banks of the Niger River, a succession of three powerful kingdoms arose: Ghana, Mali, and Songhai. Control of trans-Saharan trade gave all three their power. Ghana reached its peak under Tunka Manin in about 1067. Early in the 13th century Ghana was overtaken by Mali's empire; its greatest ruler was Mansa Musa, who made a notable pilgrimage to Mecca. In 1468 Mali gave way to Songhai after Sonni Ali captured the important commercial city of Timbuktu. Songhai controlled the trade routes of West Africa until 1591, when a Moroccan force defeated the empire.

Significance Links between West African and Arab traders helped bring Islam into sub-Saharan Africa. The West African trading states developed a rich oral history.

850–1150 Viking Invasions

The Vikings were Scandinavian warriors who, beginning about 850, began a series of invasions of Europe. Many Viking raids were hit-and-run attacks, but sometimes Vikings settled where they raided, as in England and Normandy, France. A Viking leader named Rurik and his clan, the Rus, took control of a town in Eastern Europe. The Rus remained and expanded their domain. From these invasions, the history of Russia began.

Significance The Viking raids destabilized Europe for 200 years. Where the Vikings settled, however, they melded with the local population, contributing customs and language.

850–1250 Manorial and Feudal Systems in Europe

Two related systems governed social relations in medieval Europe. The feudal system, or feudalism, began as a means of mutual defense in the chaos of invasions by Vikings, Magyars, and Muslims. Lords enlisted trained warriors known as knights to defend their lands in return for a fief, a portion of those lands. Lords and vassals, those who accepted fiefs, owed each other service and protection. The manorial system was an economic arrangement that tied serfs, or peasants, to a lord's land. The serfs farmed the lord's land in return for a plot of the lord's land to farm for themselves, the lord's protection, and other services.

Significance The feudal and manorial systems provided the social, economic, and political structures for European society for about 400 years.

c. 1000 Toltecs Dominate Central Mexico

A semi-nomadic people, the Toltec settled in the region around present-day Mexico City around 900. By about 1000 they dominated the region and had spread southward, into the lands of the Maya.

Fierce warriors, the Toltec established three military orders—the Coyote, the Jaguar, and the Eagle—and incorporated military imagery into their art and architecture. They were the dominant power in the region until the mid-1200s.

Significance The Toltec's militaristic culture influenced the late Maya and the emergent Aztec, who eventually established themselves as the dominant power in Mesoamerica in the early 1400s.

1066 Norman Conquest of England

When Edward the Confessor, the king of England, died in 1066 without leaving an heir, Duke William of Normandy, France, a distant relative of Edward's, claimed the English throne. The English selected another man to be their king and William launched an invasion of the island. Backed by a powerful force of Norman knights, he was victorious in the Battle of Hastings in 1066. Shortly thereafter he was crowned King William I of England.

Significance The Norman Conquest ended Anglo-Saxon rule in England. William introduced military feudalism. Over time, a blending of Anglo-Saxon and Norman laws, customs, and language occurred.

1071 Seljuk Turks Conquer Asia Minor

Around 1000 the Seljuk Turks, a Muslim people from Central Asia, began conquering territory in the Middle East. In 1055 they conquered Baghdad, and from there, under the nominal authority of the Abbasid caliph, they ruled Iran, Iraq, and Syria. In 1071 the Seljuk Turks conquered most of the Byzantine territory in Asia Minor. When their power receded elsewhere, Asia Minor, today called Turkey, became the last Seljuk stronghold.

Significance The Seljuks established a system of Islamic schools (called the madrasa) throughout their domain. In Persia their rule led to a revival of Persian as a literary language. Their defeat of the Byzantines was one factor that led to the Crusades.

1095–1291 Crusades

A series of military expeditions from Europe to the Holy Land between 1095 and 1291, the Crusades began when the hard-pressed Byzantine emperor turned to his fellow Christians in Western Europe for help in fending off the Muslim Seljuks. In 1095 Pope Urban II called on Europe's feudal lords to supply soldiers for a war to defend the Byzantine Empire and to take Jerusalem and the area around it, known as the Holy Land, from the Muslims. The First Crusade (1096–1099) succeeded in taking Antioch and Jerusalem. Over the next 200 years at least ten expeditions were undertaken, with varied leadership and diverse purposes. The Crusades ended in 1291, when Muslims captured the city of Acre, the last Christian stronghold in the Holy Land.

Significance The Crusades led to increased trade between Europe and the East. They also spurred political change in Europe, as nobles gained power at the expense of kings.

c. 1200–1294 Mongol Invasions

The Mongol invasions began in the early 1200s, when Genghis Khan and his army began taking territory in China. From there they conquered Central Asia and most of Persia. Other Mongol armies, led by relatives of Genghis Khan, continued the conquests. Kublai Khan finished conquering China, and also captured Tibet and parts of Southeast Asia. Meanwhile Batu, another relative, invaded Europe. He succeeded in bringing Kievan Russia and parts of Poland and Hungary into the Mongol Empire.

Significance By 1294 the Mongols controlled the largest land empire in history. In China, Kublai Khan founded the Yuan dynasty. Kievan Russia remained under Mongol control for nearly 200 years.

c. 1200 Rise of European Trading Cities

Trade in Europe, which had declined following the collapse of the Roman Empire, began to revive following the Crusades. Merchants in Italian city-states like Venice and Genoa controlled the transfer of goods from ships to overland routes; as a result they grew wealthy from trade. In northern Europe, German cities along the Baltic and North Seas created the Hanseatic League to regulate and profit from trade in their region. At its peak the Hanseatic League had 100 member cities.

Significance The revival of trade increased European wealth and power, and brought Europeans into closer contact with the world.

1215 Magna Carta

Frustrated by the demands of King John II, English nobles forced him in 1215 to consent to the provisions in the document known as Magna Carta. The original charter contained 63 clauses, many of which were intended to ensure the feudal rights of nobles. Other clauses, though, sought to protect the rights of all the king's subjects.

Significance In time Magna Carta came to be seen as the foundation of constitutional government in England. The document established that everyone, including monarchs, was subject to the rule of law.

1347–1351 Black Death

Increased trade between Europe and Asia had unintended consequences. One such consequence was the ease with which diseases could spread. The Black Death probably traveled to Europe from China along sea and overland trade routes. The outbreak of this epidemic in the mid-1300s decimated the populations of both continents.

Significance The Black Death severed some of the bonds that held the manorial system together. The shortage of labor gave peasants more bargaining power. Europe's population did not completely rebound until the 1500s.

1350–1600 Renaissance

Literally "rebirth," the Renaissance was a period of cultural renewal starting first in Italy and spreading to all of Europe. Based on the rediscovery of Greek and Roman writings and new appreciation for secular culture and individual achievement, or humanism, the Renaissance inspired advances in the arts and sciences.

Significance The Renaissance profoundly changed how Europeans viewed themselves and their world. The movement's onset represents the close of the Middle Ages, a term invented during the Renaissance to mark its separation from the earlier time.

1400–1500 Inca Empire Flourishes

Having begun as an isolated tribe near Cuzco, in what is now Peru, the Inca, through conquest of neighboring tribes, rose to become a mighty empire. By the mid-1400s the Inca presided over a territory that stretched nearly 2,000 miles along the Andes Mountains from present-day Ecuador to Chile. The Inca are known in history for the strength of their central government, the complexity of their system of roads, and their building skills, shown most dramatically at Machu Picchu.

Significance The Inca Empire ruled 12 million people at its peak, which occurred at the brink of European contact. Ironically, their sophisticated road system sped the Spaniards along on their conquest.

c. 1415–1650 Age of Exploration

Seeking new ways to trade with the civilizations of the Far East, Europeans at the beginning of the 1400s began exploring possible sea routes to Asia. On his 1486–1487 voyage Bartolomeu Dias rounded Africa's southern tip. Later missions led Europeans to America, and ultimately, with Ferdinand Magellan's 1519–1522 voyage, around the world. The Age of Exploration continued through the 1600s with the search for a Northwest Passage that led to the opening of the interior of North America.

Significance The Age of Exploration expanded knowledge of the world and made possible the European colonization of Asia, Africa, and the Americas.

1453 Ottoman Turks Take Constantinople

Toward the end of the 1200s, a new power, the Ottoman Turks, arose in Asia Minor. In the 1300s the Ottomans began to threaten the remaining territory of the Byzantine Empire. They conquered the Balkans and took Adrianople, a Byzantine city, in 1361. In 1453 the Ottomans succeeded in capturing Constantinople, which they renamed Istanbul and made the capital of their empire.

Significance The fall of Constantinople marked the end of the Byzantine Empire. The Ottoman Turks would build a vast empire embracing Egypt, Syria, and much of North Africa that lasted until 1922.

1455 Gutenberg's Printing Press

Though the Chinese developed a printing process in the 100s, printing in Europe exploded after Johannes Gutenberg pioneered the use of movable type in the mid-1400s. Using metal block letters individually laid onto a plate that was then rolled with ink and pressed over paper, Gutenberg began printing copies of the Bible around 1455. The new technology spread quickly. By 1475 printing presses were operating in nations throughout Europe.

Significance The printing press helped make literacy common, spread the ideas of the Renaissance, and introduced a new method of mass communication.

1492 Spanish Unification and Expansion

Ferdinand of Aragon and Isabella of Castile married in 1469 and joined their kingdoms in 1479 to form a united Spain. They used the Inquisition, an investigative body of the Roman Catholic Church, to enforce religious conformity. In 1492 they conquered Granada, the last remaining Muslim kingdom on the Iberian Peninsula. In that year they ordered all Jews and Muslims (whom they called Moors) to become Christians or leave Spain and sponsored Christopher Columbus's voyage across the Atlantic.

Significance United Spain became Europe's dominant power for 100 years. Columbus's voyage led to a Spanish empire in the Americas. The expulsion of non-Christians, however, robbed Spain of much of its commercial and intellectual talent.

1494 Treaty of Tordesillas

Voyages of exploration created conflict as Spain and Portugal staked competing claims over newly discovered lands. In 1493 Pope Alexander VI sought to resolve the disputes by drawing an imaginary line through the Atlantic Ocean. Spain was given rights to all non-Christian lands claimed west of the line, while Portugal was given rights to new claims in the east. The following year, Spain and Portugal agreed to the Treaty of Tordesillas, which moved the demarcation line farther west.

Significance Other European powers largely ignored the line. However, because of the agreement, Portugal was able to establish a colony in Brazil, which is why today Brazilians speak Portuguese, while the rest of Latin America speaks Spanish.

c. 1500–1865 Atlantic Slave Trade

The economies of the European colonies in the Americas were based on plantation agriculture and the extraction of raw materials. Such labor-intensive enterprises required large numbers of workers. To meet these labor needs the colonial powers began transporting Africans across the Atlantic to serve as slaves. In time the slave trade solidified into a system of triangular trade. The journey of Africans from their homelands to the Americas was called the Middle Passage. Conditions for Africans on the journey were brutal, and many died along the way. By the time the slave trade ended in the mid-1800s, some 10 million Africans had been transported to slavery in the Americas.

Significance The slave trade devastated the lives of those who were enslaved and ravaged the countries from which they were taken. In the Americas, slavery contributed to economic development but left lingering social scars.

1502–1722 Persia's Safavid Dynasty

As the 1500s began, a Muslim religious leader named Ismail rose to power over the Safavids, a Shia Muslim clan that had lived in Persia for generations. By 1512 Ismail had succeeded in establishing a Safavid dynasty in Persia. Most Persians were Sunni Muslims, but Ismail proclaimed Shi'ism the empire's official religion. Under Abbas the Great, who reigned from 1578 to 1629, the Safavid Empire reached its peak, with successful wars against the Ottoman Turks. Following Abbas's death in 1629 the empire began a slow decline.

Significance Safavid culture represented a blending of Arab, Persian, and Chinese styles. Safavid adherence to Shia Islam made Persia distinct among Muslim states.

1517 Luther's Ninety-Five Theses

In 1517 Martin Luther, then a 34-year-old Catholic clergyman, posted a list of 95 theses, or statements, critical of the Roman Catholic Church's practice of selling letters of forgiveness, called indulgences. Luther's intent in posting these statements was to spark reform within the church. By 1521, however, Luther's ideas had led to his expulsion from the Roman Catholic Church and sparked the Protestant Reformation. With the break from Rome official, Luther went on to establish a religious movement that became known as the Lutheran Church. Other Protestant movements quickly developed.

Significance With its emphasis on a personal interpretation of scripture, the Protestant Reformation contributed to the growth of individualism. The passions it aroused, however, sparked religious wars that roiled Europe for the next century and a half.

1519–1533 Spanish Conquests in the Americas

In less than fifteen years, Spain overthrew the two most powerful empires in the Americas, the Aztec and the Inca, and established an empire of their own. In 1519 Hernán Cortés landed in Mexico with 600 men. Within two years Cortés succeeded in capturing and destroying the Aztec capital of Tenochtitlán. In 1530 Francisco Pizarro led an expedition to conquer the Inca of South America. By 1533 Pizarro had won the Inca territories from present-day Ecuador to Chile for Spain. Superior weapons, Native American allies, and European diseases that weakened the Indians contributed to Spanish victory.

Significance Wealth from Spain's empire in the Americas fueled Spain's military and political efforts in Europe for 100 years. Disease and exploitation decimated native populations. Over time, a new culture, mixing Spanish and native elements, developed in Central and much of South America.

1526 Mughal Empires of India

Muslim armies entered the Indus River valley as early as the 700s. By the early 1200s the Delhi sultanate extended Muslim rule into the Ganges River valley. In 1526 a Muslim chieftain named Babur led a combined Turk and Mongol army into India from the north. Babur defeated the Delhi sultanate and established the Mughal Empire. Babur's grandson Akbar, greatest of the Mughal rulers, expanded the empire, sponsored inter-religious discussions, and encouraged a blending of Hindu and Muslim cultures. By the early 1700s the Mughals controlled most of the Indian subcontinent, but England's increasing economic and military power was already undermining their rule.

Significance At its height the Mughal Empire ruled as many as 100 million people, making it one of the world's most powerful states. Art, architecture, and literature flourished under the Mughals.

c. 1540–1725 Scientific Revolution

A movement in Europe during the 1500s and 1600s, the Scientific Revolution rejected medieval scholasticism in favor of direct observation of nature and a program of hypothesis tested by experiment (i.e., the scientific method). In 1543 Nicolaus Copernicus (1473–1543) published *On the Revolution of Celestial Spheres,* in which he argued that the sun rather than the Earth was the center of the universe, marks the symbolic birth of the Scientific Revolution. Other notable contributors included Galileo Galilei (1564–1642), who developed the telescope and used experiments to test theories; and Sir Isaac Newton (1642–1727), who invented calculus and codified the laws of motion and gravity.

Significance The Scientific Revolution transformed Europeans' view of the universe, weakened the authority of religion, and, by establishing the scientific method, started an ongoing expansion of human knowledge and technological innovation.

1545–1563 Council of Trent

The Roman Catholic Church responded to the Protestant Reformation with its own reforms. The Catholic, or Counter-, Reformation began under Pope Paul III, who convened the Council of Trent in 1545. The Council acted to correct some of the abuses most criticized by Protestants, such as the sale of indulgences. At the same time, the Council reaffirmed other church doctrines and traditions.

Significance The Council of Trent largely satisfied Catholics' demand for reform. A newly reinvigorated church began to reassert its power.

1588 Defeat of the Spanish Armada

King Phillip II of Spain saw himself as Roman Catholicism's defender. Hoping to depose Queen Elizabeth I, a Protestant, from the English throne, Phillip assembled a fleet of 130 ships known as the Spanish Armada. In August 1588 the English fleet attacked the Armada, causing severe damage. Less than half the Armada returned home to Spain.

Significance The Armada's defeat spared England from invasion, aided its ally, the Netherlands, which was at war with Spain, and began to shift the balance of power in the Atlantic from Spain to England.

1600–1800 Absolute Monarchs in Europe

In the 1600s, as the feudal structure broke down, European monarchs began to assert their right to rule absolutely, without consulting nobles, common

people, or their representative bodies. The archetype of an absolute monarch was Louis XIV of France who once famously uttered, "I am the state." Other notable absolute monarchs included Peter the Great (1672–1725) and Catherine the Great (1729–1796), who "westernized" Russia.

Significance By consolidating fiefs into larger kingdoms, breaking down the feudal system, and centralizing authority, absolute monarchs hastened the development of European nation-states.

1603–1868 Japan's Tokugawa Shogunate

In the Japanese feudal system, the shogun was the emperor's military commander and the actual ruler of the country. From the late 1400s, however, no shogun was able to assert authority over rival, warring factions. In 1603 Tokugawa Ieyasu won a struggle for supremacy and declared himself shogun. He introduced changes to the feudal system that tied peasants to the land, outlawed social mobility, and centralized power in his hands.

Significance The Tokugawa shoguns brought Japan about 200 years of relative calm. However, in the 1630s, fearing destabilization that Christian missionaries might cause, they also closed the country to the outside world.

1618–1648 Thirty Years' War

Tensions between Roman Catholics and Protestants frequently erupted into warfare. When Ferdinand II, King of Bohemia and later Holy Roman Emperor, attempted to impose Catholicism on his subjects, Protestants rebelled. Religion was used to further territorial ambitions, as other European nations, including Denmark, Sweden, and France, involved themselves in the fighting. In the ensuing years a series of devastating wars were fought, mainly on German territory. The fighting came to end with the signing of the Treaty of Westphalia in 1648.

Significance The Thirty Years' War devastated the German territories. The power of the Holy Roman Empire was greatly reduced. Its territories were granted sovereignty, forming the foundation for the modern system of European nation-states.

1688 England's Glorious Revolution

During the 1600s the Stuart monarchs of England tried to assert absolute authority over Parliament. The efforts of Charles I triggered the English Civil War (1641–1649), which resulted in his execution. Oliver Cromwell ruled England as a Commonwealth for eleven years, until the Stuarts were restored in 1660. Conflict between king and Parliament erupted anew in 1685 when James II became king of England. Though most English were Protestant, James was Roman Catholic. Fearing a line of Catholic kings, Parliament asked James to surrender the throne and invited his daughter Mary and her husband William to serve as joint rulers. James fled to exile in France, and William and Mary were crowned after signing the English Bill of Rights.

Significance The bloodless transfer of power, known as the Glorious Revolution, ratified Parliament's power over the monarch.

1700–1800 Age of Enlightenment

A period in European history in which belief in rationalism, natural law and natural rights, secularism, and progress held sway, the Enlightenment is also known as the Age of Reason. Enlightenment thinkers, known in France as *philosophes*, included John Locke, Baron de Montesquieu, and Voltaire.

Significance Enlightenment thinkers advocated reforms in government. The influence of these ideas can be seen in the American and French revolutions and in the governments they produced.

c. 1750–1850 Industrial Revolution

An era in Europe and the United States that saw a rapid expansion of industry and machine-driven production of goods at the expense of farming and handicraft production, the Industrial Revolution began first in Great Britain. New technologies such as the steam engine and iron smelting led to advances in textile manufacturing and transportation (railroads and steamboats).

Significance The Industrial Revolution transformed nations like few events before it. Cities grew quickly, and became crowded and unhealthy, as workers relocated in search of factory jobs. Goods became cheaper for a swelling middle class, but workers suffered terrible exploitation.

1754–1763 Seven Years' War and French and Indian War

The rivalry between Great Britain and France for status as colonial powers and the struggle between Austria and Prussia for dominance over the German states erupted into nine years of warfare. In the French and Indian War, which lasted from 1754 to 1763, France and Great Britain fought for control of North America. In Europe the two nations were also involved in the Seven Years' War. Between 1756 and 1763 a British-Prussian alliance fought a French-Austrian alliance for control of the German states of Saxony and Silesia.

Significance In Europe, no clear victor emerged from the Seven Years' War. Prussia held onto the region of Silesia, but Austria made gains elsewhere. However, Great Britain's victory in the French and Indian War brought it control of France's North American territory.

1775–1781 American Revolution

The American Revolution began in April 1775 with the battles of Lexington and Concord. Initially the Americans' undermanned and poorly equipped Continental Army faced numerous setbacks and almost certain defeat. The first official call for American independence came in 1775, leading to the adoption of the Declaration of Independence on July 4, 1776. An American military victory at Saratoga in 1777 proved a turning point, as it convinced the French to enter the war on the American side. Britain's decision to challenge the Americans in the South ultimately proved fatal. It led to the defeat of the British army at Yorktown, Virginia, in 1781.

Significance The American Revolution was the first successful struggle of a colony for independence from its ruler. The United States of America was established as a democratic republic.

1789 United States Constitution Adopted

Seeking to address some of the problems it faced under the Articles of Confederation, the United States drafted a new Constitution in 1787. Ratified in 1788 and officially adopted in 1789, the United States Constitution established a federal system of shared power between the national and state governments. It created a system of three branches of federal government, with the power of each countered by checks and balances. The Bill of Rights, added in 1791, guaranteed key rights.

Significance The United States Constitution ushered in a new era of constitutional democracy. However, this democracy was incomplete. Most white males and all white females could not vote, and slavery was still legal.

1789 French Revolution Begins

French society evolved through the 1700s, but its political institutions remained static. By 1789 the situation proved unsustainable. At the meeting called by King Louis XVI of the Estates General, France's parliament, representatives of the Third Estate rebelled, declaring themselves to be the National Assembly. In July the citizens of Paris looted and destroyed the Bastille prison. In August, the National Assembly adopted The Declaration of the Rights of Man and of the Citizen, which expressed the revolutionary principles of liberty, equality, and fraternity. A series of constitutions transformed

France into a republic. In 1793 the King was executed, and a Reign of Terror against internal opponents of the revolution began.

Significance The French Revolution completely transformed French government and society. Its successes served as a beacon and its excesses as a caution for later revolutionary movements.

1791–1824 Independence Movements in the Americas

From the atmosphere of liberty inspired by the American and French revolutions arose the Latin American independence movements. The first blow came on the island of Santo Domingo, where Toussaint L'Ouverture led a revolt of African slaves that eventually established an independent Haiti. Mexico achieved independence from Spain in 1821, following a ten-year struggle. In South America, charismatic leaders Simón Bolívar and José de San Martín helped push the Spanish entirely off the continent by 1824. Brazil declared its independence from Portugal in 1822.

Significance Latin American independence brought to an end 300 years of colonial rule in the region.

1796–1815 Napoleonic Wars

Out of the chaos of the French Revolution arose the dramatic personality of General Napoleon Bonaparte. Napoleon used his popularity as a military leader to establish political authority in France in 1799. As emperor, Napoleon reorganized the French state and launched a series of wars to gain control of Europe. Great Britain remained his implacable foe, checking his ambitions at sea and supporting a shifting coalition of allies in Europe. The failure of Napoleon's invasion of Russia in 1812 assured his fall. He made one last bid for power in 1815 but met defeat in the Battle of Waterloo.

Significance The Napoleonic Wars hastened the growth of nationalism and of mass armies, as well as the spread of democratic ideals. The Congress of Vienna, a meeting of European Powers in 1815 to establish a balance of power, ushered in a period of peace and political reaction.

1828–1832 Growth of Democracy in the United States and Great Britain

In the United States the elimination of property ownership requirements for voting increased political participation and ushered in the era of Jacksonian Democracy. The period is named after Andrew Jackson, whose election to the presidency in 1828 symbolized the shift in political power in the United States from the elite to the common citizen. In Great

Britain, years of agitation led to the passage of the Reform Bill of 1832, which redistributed seats in the House of Commons to provide more balanced representation for the country's urban districts. Expansion of the right to vote in Great Britain came later, in stages, starting in 1867.

Significance While full democracy in Great Britain and the United States would have to wait until the 20th century, the period from 1828 to 1832 represented a shift to more representative governments.

1845–1849 Irish Potato Famine

From 1845 to 1849 a fungus devastated Ireland's potato crop. With much of the Irish population living in poverty and dependent on potatoes as a main food source, a severe famine resulted. Great Britain, of which Ireland was a part at that time, did little to provide assistance to the Irish people. Other food products grown in Ireland were not affected by the fungus but were exported because the Irish people could not afford them.

Significance Of the 8.4 million Irish before the famine, 1.1 million are believed to have died of starvation and malnutrition, while another 1.5 million emigrated to the United States or Great Britain.

1848 Revolutions Sweep Europe

In 1848 the monarchies restored by the Congress of Vienna in 1815 began to unravel. Beginning with the February Revolution in France, a series of republican revolutions swept through Europe. One by one, governments fell and monarchs fled. In Paris, Berlin, and Vienna, the urban poor turned radical. Moderates drew back from social revolution. By August of 1849 most of the old governments had been restored. Austria defeated nationalist uprisings in Italy and Hungary, though it was forced to grant Hungary autonomy and abolish serfdom.

Significance Following the failure of the revolutions, many liberals felt disillusioned. Tens of thousands of people from German lands emigrated to the United States to escape political repression at home. Karl Marx's *Communist Manifesto*, published in February of 1848, foretold a new round of more radical revolutions to come.

1859–1871 German and Italian Unification

In the German states and the Italian states—38 and 9 of them respectively—the revolutions of 1848 had been as much about national unification as democratic change. Through warfare, an uprising led by Giuseppe Garibaldi in the south, and by direct vote, a unified Italian kingdom with its capital in

Rome was established by 1870. German unification was accomplished largely through warfare. Led by Otto von Bismarck, Prussia fought the Danish War (1863–64), the Austro-Prussian War (1866), and the Franco-Prussian War (1870–71). Out of these wars arose a united German Empire in 1871 with its capital in Berlin.

Significance Italian and German unification showed the power of nationalism in the late 1900s. A united Germany became the most powerful country in Europe, triggering rivalries that ultimately led to the outbreak of World War I in the 20th century.

1850–1864 Taiping Rebellion in China

By the 1840s China's Qing dynasty, which began in 1644, had grown weak and corrupt. European powers were able to extract valuable trade concessions, which only made the Qing's weakness more apparent. A large increase in population and poverty produced social unrest. In 1850 a Christian convert who believed himself the brother of Jesus of Nazareth started a rebellion that soon gathered wide-spread support. Fearing the loss of trade that the collapse of the Qing dynasty might bring, Western powers eventually stepped in and helped put down the rebellion in 1864.

Significance The Taiping Rebellion lasted for 14 years, caused terrible destruction, and cost millions of lives. The Qing dynasty never recovered control of the country. Western influence grew. Some of the ideas of the Taiping rebels—for instance, common ownership of property—inspired the Chinese Communists in the 20th century.

1854 End of Japanese Isolation

In 1853 United States president Millard Fillmore dispatched Commodore Matthew Perry to Japan with the intention of opening the country to foreign trade. Fearing the use of force, the Japanese reluctantly agreed to the Treaty of Kanagawa in 1854, which opened two Japanese ports to American vessels for obtaining fuel, shelter, and supplies.

Significance The opening of the two ports allowed trade between Japan and the United States. Within two years Japan signed similar treaties with Great Britain, the Netherlands, and Russia. Japan's isolationism was effectively ended.

1861–1865 American Civil War

The election of Abraham Lincoln as United States president in 1860 led to secession of the slaveholding southern states and the formation of the Confederacy. The Civil War began in April 1861 with the Confederate attack on Fort Sumter. The Confederacy

won key early battles, thanks largely to the superior military skill of its general. Northern victories at Vicksburg and Gettysburg in 1863 helped turn the tide of the war. Fighting ended in April 1865, with the surrender of Confederate commander Robert E. Lee to Union commander Ulysses S. Grant at Appomattox Court House in Virginia.

Significance More than 600,000 Americans died in the Civil War, making it the nation's costliest war. Northern victory ensured the preservation of the United States and led to the end of slavery.

1868 Meiji Restoration in Japan

Believing the shogun had failed to stand up to the Western powers, a group of samurai forced the shogun to step down and restore authority to the emperor in 1868. The leaders of the Meiji Restoration wanted to make Japan powerful enough to rival the West. They encouraged the Meiji emperor to implement policies that would enrich the country and strengthen the military.

Significance The Meiji Restoration triggered a rapid transformation of Japanese society. The feudal system ended, educational opportunities improved, and the country industrialized. By the turn of the 20th century Japan had become a world power.

1880–1920 Age of Imperialism

Heightened nationalism, a desire for raw materials and new markets, and a paternalistic missionary zeal all contributed to the rise of Western imperialism. By 1914 the major European powers had divided nearly all of Africa among themselves. Parts of Asia were similarly divided, though many countries, including China, managed to maintain their independence. The United States also became involved in the imperial age by acquiring territories in the Pacific and the Caribbean.

Significance Imperialism drew Africa and Asia into a world economic system whose hubs were Europe and the United States. The relationship between colonizer and colonized, however, was often exploitative and dehumanizing.

1903 Wright Brothers Flight

Orville and Wilbur Wright, two bicycle mechanics from Dayton, Ohio, built the first successful powered airplane. On December 17, 1903, at Kitty Hawk, North Carolina, the Wright brothers made four successful tests of their design.

Significance The Wright brothers and others soon began manufacturing airplanes. Improved designs revolutionized transportation, increased demand for oil, and affected the conduct of warfare.

1914–1918 World War I

Increasingly intense rivalries in Europe, along with heightened feelings of nationalism and a system of military alliances, led to the start of World War I in 1914. The primary opponents were the Central Powers (Germany, Austria-Hungary, and Turkey) and the Allied Powers (Great Britain, France, and Russia). New technologies such as machine guns and four years of stalemated trench warfare made World War I the deadliest war—14 million killed—the world had seen to that point. The U.S. entry into the war in 1917 helped the Allies win.

Significance World War I led to the end of monarchies in Russia, Austria-Hungary, Germany, and Turkey. The horrific number of casualties produced widespread disillusionment. The Treaty of Versailles imposed harsh penalties on Germany, contributing to the outbreak of World War II.

1917 Russian Revolution

Defeats and high casualties in World War I led to revolution in Russia. In the February Revolution of 1917 Czar Nicholas II was forced from power. An interim government was established, but it was ineffectual. In the October Revolution of 1917 the Bolsheviks, a Communist revolutionary group led by Vladimir Lenin, overthrew the interim government and established power. In 1918 a civil war broke out, in which the Bolsheviks prevailed. Collectively the two 1917 revolutions and the years of civil war that followed are known as the Russian Revolution.

Significance The Russian Revolution led to the establishment of the Soviet Union in 1922. The Soviets eventually succeeded in creating a world power, but at a steep cost for some Soviet citizens.

1914–1939 Women Win Voting Rights

As early as 1792, British writer Mary Wollstonecraft called for women's voting rights in *A Vindication of the Rights of Women*. In the United States, the Seneca Falls Convention of 1848 issued a similar call for United States women. However, the first country to grant women voting rights was New Zealand, then still a British colony, in 1893. Between 1914 and 1939, however, 28 nations, including the United States (1920), granted women voting rights.

Significance The extension of voting rights to women placed many societies on a firmer democratic footing. In 1952 the United Nations adopted a resolution calling on all member states to grant women the right to vote on an equal basis with men. Not every nation has complied.

1929–1939 Great Depression

A variety of factors, including reckless investments in stocks, an overreliance by consumers on credit, and a radically uneven distribution of wealth, contributed to the collapse of the United States economy in 1929. The U.S. downturn soon affected other countries, and protectionist trade policies made the situation worse. Countries experienced crushing unemployment and sharply reduced economic output. World trade fell by more than two thirds. For its unprecedented duration and severity, the event came to be called the Great Depression.

Significance In addition to its economic effects, the Great Depression caused political instability in Europe. In Germany, it was one factor in the rise of Nazism and Adolph Hitler. In the United States, the New Deal of President Franklin Roosevelt helped the country avoid serious unrest.

1933–1945 Holocaust

Soon after gaining power in Germany in 1933, Adolf Hitler and his Nazi Party began using the power of the government to persecute German Jews. German conquests early in World War II brought nearly all of Europe's 9 million Jews under Nazi control. In the largest genocide in world history the Nazis attempted to exterminate the entire Jewish population of Europe. This became known as the Holocaust.

Significance The Nazis murdered 6 million Jews in the Holocaust, decimating the Jewish population of Europe. Nazis also killed about 5 million other people from groups they considered undesirable. After the war, many Nazi leaders were convicted of war crimes by an international court.

1939–1945 World War II

Aggressive, militaristic regimes in Italy, Germany, and Japan threatened the uneasy peace that followed World War I. With the German invasion of Poland on September 1, 1939, World War II began. The main participants in the war were the Axis Powers (Germany, Italy and Japan), and the Allied Powers (Great Britain, France, and the Soviet Union). After the Japanese bombed Pearl Harbor on December 7, 1941, the United States entered the war on the Allied side. Initial Axis gains began to erode by 1943. The Allied invasion of France on D-Day (June 6, 1944) and the simultaneous push from the Soviet Union in the east led to victory in Europe in May of 1945. The United States dropped atomic bombs on Hiroshima and Nagasaki, Japan, in August 1945, bringing an end to the Pacific war in September.

Significance With the deaths of 40 to 50 million soldiers and civilians, World War II was by far the most destructive conflict in world history. The United States and the Soviet Union emerged as the world's two superpowers, but competing political systems soon made enemies of the former allies.

1939–1945 Manhattan Project

The Manhattan Project was a top-secret U.S. government program to develop an atomic bomb during World War II. It was motivated by the danger that Germany might be the first to develop atomic weapons. Manhattan Project scientists worked in Los Alamos, New Mexico. They successfully tested the first atomic bomb near Alamogordo, New Mexico, on July 16, 1945.

Significance The creation of the atomic bomb began the age of nuclear weapons. During the Cold War that followed World War II, the United States and the Soviet Union competed in a nuclear-arms race.

1945 United Nations Founded

The failure of the League of Nations to prevent World War II led to calls for a new, stronger international organization. All countries that had declared war on the Axis Powers by March 1, 1945, were invited to the founding conference of the new organization, which was held in San Francisco from April to June of 1945. Conference members drafted a charter declaring the new organization's goals: to maintain international peace and security, promote cordial relations among countries, and develop systems of cooperation for solving a wide range of international problems. The charter was ratified on October 24, 1945, marking the official founding of the United Nations (UN).

Significance The development of Cold War tensions between the United States and Soviet Union meant that the UN never quite functioned as it was intended to. Despite this, the organization has played, and continues to play, a major role in international affairs.

1947–1975 Asia and Africa Decolonized

Following World War II, the economically strained and war-weary European countries had little ability to resist independence movements in their colonies. A wave of decolonization began. British India was one of the first to be decolonized, with its partition into the independent countries of India and Pakistan in 1947. Independence for other Asian nations soon followed. The French were slower to withdraw, fighting losing battles in Vietnam, Algeria, and elsewhere. Decolonization also occurred throughout Africa. By the mid-1960s, most of the continent had achieved independence.

Significance The large number of newly independent countries changed the face of international organizations like the UN. The legacy of colonialism, however, often left the newly formed nations economically dependent and politically ill-prepared for self-government. Violent ethnic disputes and dictatorships were the result.

1947–1989 Cold War

Efforts by the Soviet Union to extend its influence in Eastern Europe and elsewhere led U.S. president Harry Truman to declare the spread of communism a threat to democracy that the United States would resist (the Truman Doctrine, 1947). He also endorsed the Marshall Plan for rebuilding the economies of Europe. The ensuing Cold War was a decades-long rivalry of the United States and its democratic allies against the Soviet Union and its Communist allies. The Cold War led to the formation of new political and military alliances. In April 1949, Western nations formed the North Atlantic Treaty Organization (NATO). The Soviet Union and its allies formed the Warsaw Pact in May 1955.

Significance The Cold War shaped international affairs for decades. The creation of NATO checked Soviet expansion in Europe. The main antagonists avoided a direct confrontation elsewhere, but numerous wars were fought in developing countries as a direct result of the Cold War rivalry.

1948–Present Arab-Israeli Conflicts

Faced with mounting opposition and unrest in Palestine, Great Britain gave up its mandate over the region in 1947. Later that year, the UN voted to partition Palestine into separate Jewish and Arab states. In May 1948 Israel declared itself an independent country. Arab states refused to recognize the new nation. In a series of wars, Israel prevailed over neighboring Arab countries and gained more territory. Large numbers of Palestinian Arabs and Jewish refugees from Arab countries were displaced by the wars. Alternating periods of open warfare and tense quiet have continued to the present day.

Significance Despite peace treaties between Israel and two of its neighbors, Egypt and Jordan, as well as various peace proposals, the region remains unstable. The unsettled matter of Palestinian statehood, the Israeli presence in the West Bank, Palestinian attacks, and hostility from many of Israel's neighbors contribute to the situation's volatility.

1949 Communists Seize Control of China

During World War II, Chinese Nationalists and Chinese Communists ceased their civil war in order to combat Japanese aggression. With the defeat of Japan in 1945, the civil war resumed. In 1949 the Communists under the leadership of Mao Zedong finally succeeded in driving the Nationalists from power. Nationalist leaders and their supporters fled to Taiwan. On the Chinese mainland Mao Zedong's Communists formed the People's Republic of China on October 1, 1949.

Significance Nearly 1 million people died in the Communist takeover of China. Communist efforts to modernize China caused millions more deaths through famine and political persecution. Taiwan grew a vibrant economy but only slowly embraced democracy. The emergence of another Communist state further heightened Cold War tensions.

1950–1953 Korean War

The conflict between the Democratic People's Republic of Korea (North Korea) and the Republic of Korea (South Korea) began when North Korean forces invaded the South. A UN force, made up mostly of U.S. troops, entered the war to block the North Korean invasion. Chinese troops fought alongside the North Koreans. The war ended with North and South Korea divided along almost the same border as before the war. At least 2.5 million people lost their lives in the war.

Significance The Korean War was the first "shooting war" in the Cold War between Communists and U.S. forces. The United States defended South Korea to show that it would protect nations from Communist attack. Following the war, South Korea built a strong economy and a democratic political structure. North Korea remains a Communist dictatorship whose people are impoverished.

1954–1975 Vietnam War

When French colonial rule ended in Vietnam in 1954, the country was divided into North and South Vietnam. The North's government was Communist, while the South's government allied with the West. When South Vietnam's president cancelled elections in 1956 that would have benefited Communists allied with the North, a civil war began. South Vietnam sought and was granted assistance from the United States. U.S. troops began arriving in 1961. By 1968, some 500,000 U.S. troops were on the ground. With victory nowhere in sight and public opinion turning against the war, the United States began withdrawing troops. The last U.S. soldiers left in 1973. Vietnam unified as a Communist state in 1975.

Significance More than 3 million Vietnamese and 58,000 Americans died in the Vietnam War, which also spilled into the neighboring countries of Laos and Cambodia, resulting in the deaths of at least 1 million more people. Vietnam remains a Communist country, but in the late 1980s it began to introduce free market elements into its economy.

1957 European Economic Community Founded

In 1957 Belgium, France, Italy, Luxembourg, the Netherlands, and West Germany established the European Economic Community (EEC). The six members sought economic growth through common policies on tariffs and production quotas. The organization has expanded in scope and ambition over the years. In 1993 it became the European Union (EU), a block of 25 nations with a common currency and common citizenship rights.

Significance The formation of the EEC signaled the beginning of a new era of cooperation among the nations of Europe. As the predecessor to the EU of today, the EEC was important to the formation of modern Europe.

1978–Present Capitalist Reforms in China

Under leader Deng Xiaoping, China began to move toward a market economy by implementing a reform plan called the Four Modernizations. The goal of the plan was to improve agriculture, industry, science and technology, and national defense. Pursuit of these goals led Deng Xiaoping to seek closer ties with the West, including the United States.

Significance China's embrace of market reforms has powered an impressive economic rise, increasing its stature on the world stage. A parallel movement for political reform, however, was cut short by a government crackdown (the Tiananmen Square Massacre) in 1989.

1989–1991 Fall of Communism in Europe

In the 1980s Soviet leader Mikhail Gorbachev attempted to reform the Soviet economy and political system (perestroika and glasnost). The move led to calls for greater freedom in the Soviet Union and Eastern Europe. Under pressure from their people, Communist governments in Eastern Europe began collapsing in 1989. Gorbachev refused to prop them up. The Berlin Wall, one of the most potent symbols of Communist oppression, was dismantled in late 1989. In 1991 the Soviet Union collapsed, as former Soviet republics declared their independence.

Significance The fall of the Soviet Union marked the end of the Cold War. Millions of people in Eastern Europe and the former Soviet Union gained freedom from Communist dictatorships. The United States was left as the world's only superpower.

1994 Genocide in Rwanda

One legacy of European colonial rule in Africa was the establishment of national borders that did not reflect the divisions of African ethnic groups. As a result, ethnically based warfare has been common in postcolonial Africa. The worst case occurred in 1994, when long-simmering hostilities between Hutus and Tutsis in Rwanda erupted. Between 500,000 and 1 million people, mostly Tutsis and moderate Hutus, were killed before the violence ended. Another 2 million people fled the country as refugees.

Significance Civil strife continues to plague Rwanda and its neighbors. The lack of an effective international response to the Rwandan genocide led many to criticize the UN and the major world powers.

1994 Apartheid Ends in South Africa

Apartheid, or legalized racial segregation, became official South African government policy in 1948. A series of laws culminating in the Bantu Homelands Citizenship Act (1970), which stripped black South Africans of voting rights, extended the reach of apartheid into virtually every area of South African life. Opponents of apartheid were treated harshly. Nelson Mandela, leader of the African National Congress, spent 28 years in prison. From 1990 to 1991, South African president F. W. de Klerk's government repealed most apartheid laws. In 1994 Nelson Mandela became president after South Africa's first multiracial election.

Significance The end of apartheid removed the last vestige of white European rule in Africa. The relatively nonviolent transition provided a hopeful sign that other long-standing disputes might one day be resolved peacefully.

1995 World Trade Organization Created

Globalization—the process by which trade and culture link the nations of the world—has been an increasingly prominent part of the post–World War II world. In 1947, efforts to promote free trade and to regulate international trade resulted in the General Agreement on Tariffs and Trade (GATT). The GATT was replaced in 1995 by the World Trade Organization (WTO). The WTO's mandate includes monitoring national trading policies, mediating trade disputes, and enforcing the GATT's provisions.

Significance Globalization is transforming the world, making nations more interdependent and standardizing cultures, and the WTO is a powerful contributor to the process. Critics, however, charge that the WTO provides inadequate protections for labor and the environment and that globalization erodes national sovereignty.

1999 World Population Exceeds 6 Billion

World population has been growing at a startling rate in modern times. It took over 120 years to grow from 1 to 2 billion, but only 33 years to add another billion. In 40 years, from 1959 to 1999, world population doubled to 6 billion—and it continues to grow.

Significance The rate at which world population is increasing has raised concerns about our ability to feed such a large population and the negative effects humans are having on the earth's environment.

2001 Terrorist Attacks of 9/11

On September 11, 2001, terrorists hijacked four American commercial passenger planes. Two planes were crashed into the towers of the World Trade Center in New York City. Another plane was crashed into the Pentagon, near Washington, D.C. The fourth plane went down in a field in Pennsylvania after passengers attempted to take back the aircraft from the terrorists. Approximately 3,000 people, mostly from the United States but from numerous other countries as well, were killed in the attacks.

Significance After the attacks, U.S. president George W. Bush declared a "war on terror." The hijackers were identified as members of al Qaeda, an Islamist terrorist group led by Osama bin Laden and based at the time in Afghanistan. In October 2001, U.S. forces invaded Afghanistan after its government refused to turn over bin Laden and other al Qaeda figures. The invasion toppled the government but failed to capture bin Laden.

2003–Present Iraq War

In 1991 the United States had led an international military coalition that ousted an Iraqi occupying force from Kuwait. A decade later, with Iraq still under UN sanctions for failing to comply with demands to disarm, U.S. president George W. Bush accused Iraqi leader Saddam Hussein of building weapons of mass destruction that could be used against the United States or its allies. Saddam insisted that Iraq had no such weapons but failed to cooperate fully with UN weapons inspectors. Although many nations argued against going to war, the United States insisted that the Iraqi threat be countered. With the support of Great Britain and other allies, U.S. forces invaded Iraq in 2003 and quickly toppled Saddam's government. No weapons of mass destruction were found.

Significance In June 2004, the United States handed control over to an Iraqi government. Over 130,000 U.S. troops remained in Iraq, though, as violence continued. Insurgents carried out frequent attacks against U.S. troops and Iraqi civilians. By 2006, the threat loomed of a prolonged Iraqi civil war.

Using Maps to Understand History

by Dr. Peter Stearns

History is most obviously about time—about when things happen and how change occurs over time. But history makes no sense without place as well as time, since events happen in place as well as in time. This is where maps come in. Maps make place—geographic locations—visible and visual.

Maps are essential in the study of history. They can be used to show specific events, such as battles or wars. They can trace routes of trade, migration, or the diffusion of culture or diseases. They can show change in political alignments, territories, and boundaries. Maps show spatial relationships—where things are in relation to other things. If you want to know if one society is likely to be influenced by another, like Mexico by the United States, look at a map. Much of world history revolves around patterns of connection among regions, and maps help both to illustrate and explain these patterns.

A study of maps can also suggest the possibilities for development that a society might have. Is a region well supplied with easily navigable rivers? Its history will surely be different from a region with fewer or less open rivers. Some geographers argue, in fact, that much of the character of a given society is determined by its geography—whether it will be rich or poor, populous or sparse, centralized or localized. Figuring how far geography defines a region, and for how long in its history, is a key analytical challenge for the historian, and it starts with maps.

Indeed, take a risk, particularly early in your study of world history: try to predict what a society will be like from looking at its features on a map. See how well your effort at geographic determinism works, as you learn about the region's actual history. When you study more recent periods, see if major regions have been able to break through their geographic limits by new forms of technology and organization—or whether, in fact, their patterns can still be pretty well read from their maps.

In the following pages, you will find a refresher on some map and geography basics. Review these concepts. They will help you understand maps—and understand history.

Comparing maps of Europe at two different times can reveal how boundaries shift over time, in this case as a result of World War I.

Mapping the Earth
Using Latitude and Longitude

A **globe** is a scale model of the earth. It is useful for showing the entire earth or studying large areas of the earth's surface.

A pattern of lines circles the globe in east-west and north-south directions. It is called a **grid.** The intersection of these imaginary lines helps us find places on the earth.

The east-west lines in the grid are lines of **latitude.** Lines of latitude are called **parallels** because they are always parallel to each other. These imaginary lines measure distance north and south of the **equator.** The equator is an imaginary line that circles the globe halfway between the North and South Poles. Parallels measure distance from the equator in **degrees.** The symbol for degrees is °. Degrees are further divided into **minutes.** The symbol for minutes is ´. There are 60 minutes in a degree. Parallels north of the equator are labeled with an N. Those south of the equator are labeled with an S.

The north-south lines are lines of **longitude.** Lines of longitude are called **meridians.** These imaginary lines pass through the Poles. They measure distance east and west of the **prime meridian.** The prime meridian is an imaginary line that runs through Greenwich, England. It represents 0° longitude.

Lines of latitude range from 0°, for locations on the equator, to 90°N or 90°S, for locations at the Poles. Lines of longitude range from 0° on the prime meridian to 180° on a meridian in the mid-Pacific Ocean. Meridians west of the prime meridian to 180° are labeled with a W. Those east of the prime meridian to 180° are labeled with an E.

Lines of Latitude

Lines of Longitude

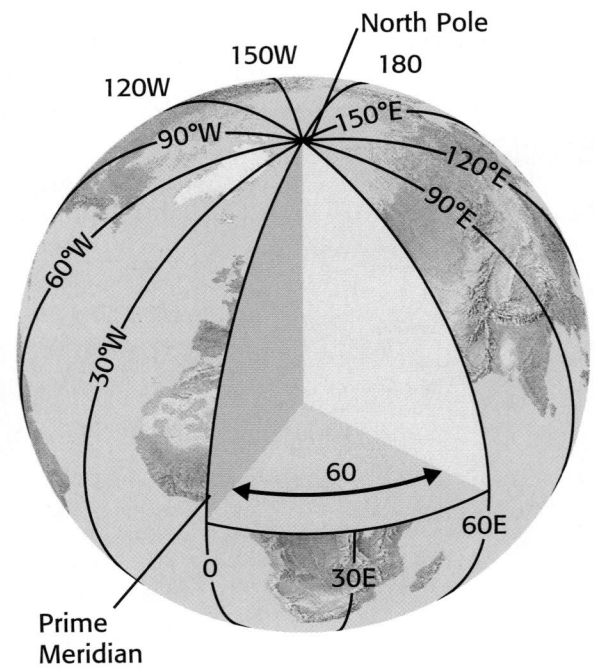

The equator divides the globe into two halves, called **hemispheres**. The half north of the equator is the Northern Hemisphere. The southern half is the Southern Hemisphere. The prime meridian and the 180° meridian divide the world into the Eastern Hemisphere and the Western Hemisphere. However, the prime meridian runs right through Europe and Africa. To avoid dividing these continents between two hemispheres, some mapmakers divide the Eastern and Western hemispheres at 20°W. This places all of Europe and Africa in the Eastern Hemisphere.

Our planet's land surface is divided into seven large landmasses, called **continents**. They are identified in the maps on this page. Landmasses smaller than continents and completely surrounded by water are called **islands**.

Geographers also organize Earth's water surface into parts. The largest is the world ocean. Geographers divide the world ocean into the Pacific Ocean, the Atlantic Ocean, the Indian Ocean, and the Arctic Ocean. Lakes and seas are smaller bodies of water.

Northern Hemisphere

Southern Hemisphere

Western Hemisphere

Eastern Hemisphere

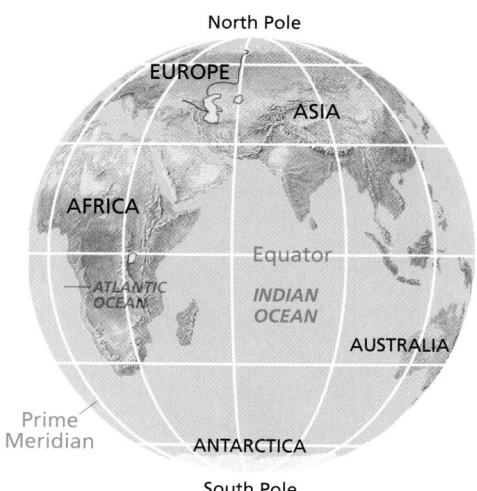

Mapmaking
Understanding Map Projections

A **map** is a flat diagram of all or part of the earth's surface. Mapmakers have created different ways of showing our round planet on flat maps. These different ways are called **map projections**. Because the earth is round, there is no way to show it accurately in a flat map. All flat maps are distorted in some way. Mapmakers must choose the type of map projection that is best for their purposes. Many map projections are one of three kinds: cylindrical, conic, or flat-plane.

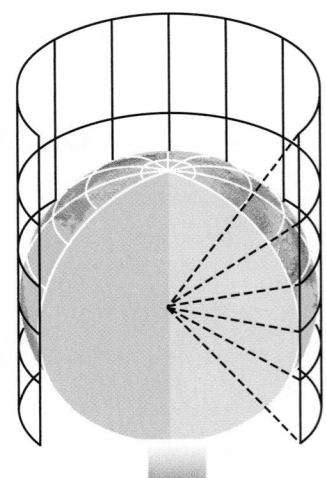

Paper cylinder

Cylindrical Projections

Cylindrical projections are based on a cylinder wrapped around the globe. The cylinder touches the globe only at the equator. The meridians are pulled apart and run parallel to each other instead of meeting at the Poles. This causes landmasses near the Poles to appear larger than they really are. The map below is a Mercator projection, one type of cylindrical projection. Navigators use the Mercator projection because it shows true direction and shape. However, it distorts the size of land areas near the Poles.

Mercator projection

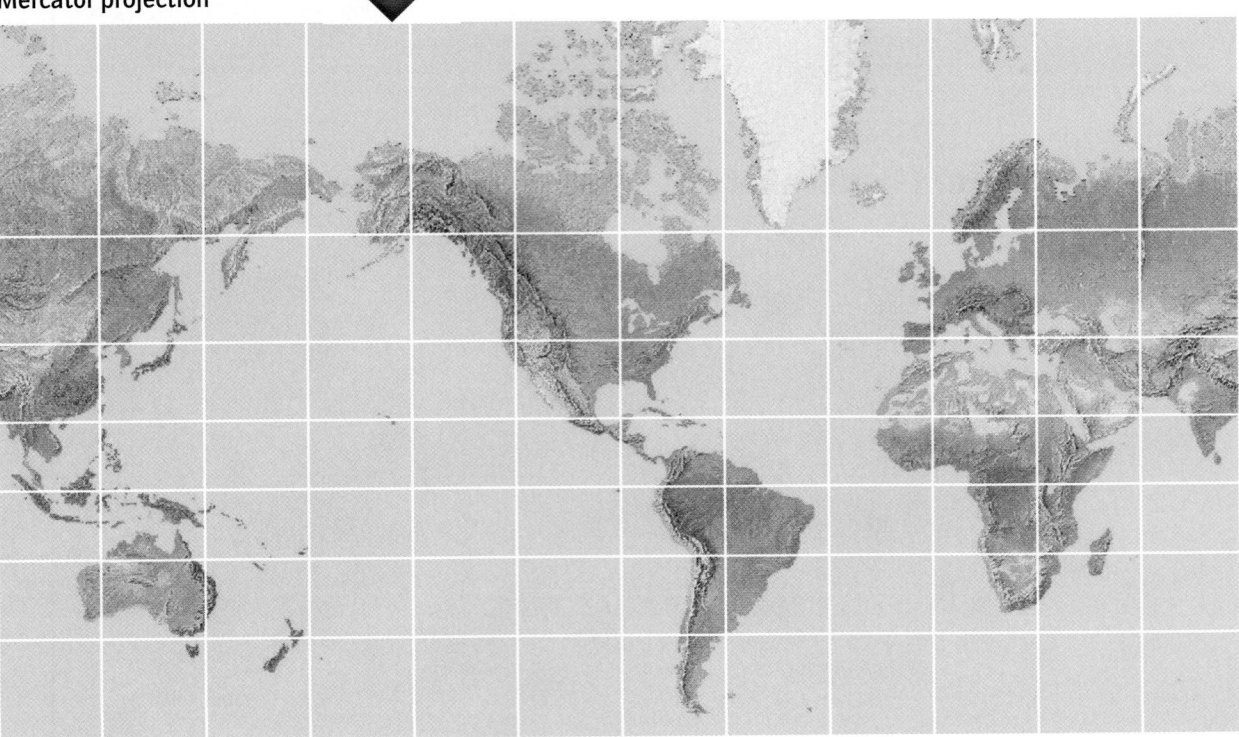

Conic Projections

Conic projections are based on a cone placed over the globe. A conic projection is most accurate along the lines of latitude where it touches the globe. It retains almost true shape and size. Conic projections are most useful for showing areas that have long east-west dimensions, such as the United States.

Paper cone

Conic projection

Flat-plane Projections

Flat-plane projections are based on a plane touching the globe at one point, such as at the North Pole or South Pole. A flat-plane projection is useful for showing true direction for airplane pilots and ship navigators. It also shows true area. However, it distorts the true shapes of land masses.

Flat plane

Flat-plane projection

Map Essentials
How to Read a Map

Maps are like messages sent out in code. Mapmakers provide certain elements that help us translate these codes. These elements help us understand the message they are presenting about a particular part of the world. Of these elements, almost all maps have titles, directional indicators, scales, and legends. The map below has all four of these elements, plus two more—a locator map and an interactive keyword.

1 Title

A map's **title** shows what the subject of the map is. The map title is usually the first thing you should look at when studying a map, because it tells you what the map is trying to show.

Interactive

① EUROPE AFTER THE CONGRESS OF VIENNA, 1815

②

— Boundary of the German Confederation **③**

NAPOLEON'S EMPIRE, 1812

KINGDOM OF SWEDEN AND NORWAY

North Sea

DENMARK

Baltic Sea

UNITED KINGDOM

London — NETHERLANDS

PRUSSIA

④

Paris

LESSER GERMAN STATES

AUSTRIAN EMPIRE

OTTOMAN EMPIRE

0   150   300 Miles
0   150   300 Kilometers
Azimuthal equal-area projection

Vienna

SWITZERLAND

FRANCE

Black Sea

⑤

PARMA   MODENA

LUCCA

40°N

TUSCANY

PORTUGAL

Madrid

Corsica (FRANCE)

PAPAL STATES

Adriatic Sea

Lisbon

KINGDOM OF SARDINIA

Rome

ATLANTIC OCEAN

SPAIN

Sardinia

KINGDOM OF THE TWO SICILIES

10°W

0°

Mediterranean Sea

go.hrw.com

Interactive Map
Keyword: SHL NAP **⑥**

10°E

20°E

30°E

Paris

Vienna

Madrid   Rome

GEOGRAPHY SKILLS INTERPRETING MAPS

1. **Location** What countries surrounded France after the Congress of Vienna?

2. **Regions** Which regions were broken up into small states?

② Locator Map

A **locator** map shows where in the world the area on the map is located. The area shown on the main map is shown in red on the locator map. The locator map also shows surrounding areas so the map reader can see how the information on the map relates to neighboring lands.

③ Legend

The **legend**, or key, explains what the symbols on the map represent. Point symbols are used to specify the location of things, such as cities, that do not take up much space on the map. Some legends show colors that represent elevations. Other maps might have legends with symbols or colors that represent things such as roads, the movement of military forces and battles. Legends can also show political divisions, economic resources, land use, population density, and climate.

— Boundary of the German Confederation

④ Scale

Mapmakers use scales to represent show the distances between points on a map. Scales may appear on maps in several different forms. The maps in this textbook provide a bar **scale**. Scales give distances in miles and kilometers. The scale is often found in the legend. In this textbook, the type of projection used to make the map is shown below the scale bar.

To find the distance between two points on the map, place a piece of paper so that the edge connects the two points. Mark the location of each point on the paper with a line or dot. Then compare the distance between the two dots with the map's bar scale. Because distances on a scale are given in large intervals, you may have to approximate the actual distance.

0   150   300 Miles
0   150   300 Kilometers
Azimuthal equal-area projection

⑤ Compass Rose

A directional indicator shows which way north, south, east, and west lie on the map. Some mapmakers use a "north arrow," which points toward the North Pole. Remember, "north" is not always at the top of a map. The way a map is drawn and the location of directions on that map depend on the perspective of the mapmaker. Most maps in this textbook indicate direction by using a compass rose. A **compass rose** has arrows that point to all four principal directions, as shown.

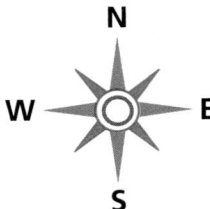

⑥ Interactive Keyword

Some maps in this textbook are interactive. If you go online to the Holt website and type in the map's keyword, you can learn more about the places and events shown on the map.

go.hrw.com
Interactive Map
Keyword: SHL NAP

Working with Maps
Using Different Kinds of Maps

The Atlas in this textbook includes both physical and political maps. **Physical maps** show the major physical features in a region. These features include things like mountain ranges, rivers, oceans, islands, deserts, and plains. **Political maps** show the major political features of a region, such as countries and their borders, capitals, and other important cities.

Historical Map

In this textbook most of the maps you will study are historical maps. Historical maps, such as the one below, show information about the past. This information might include which lands a country controlled, where a certain group of people lived, what large cities were located in a region, or how a place changed over time. Often colors are used to indicate the different things on the map. Be sure to look at the map title and map legend first to see what the map is showing. What does this map show?

THE PERSIAN EMPIRE

Persia under Cyrus, 559 BC
Conquered by Cyrus, 559–530 BC
Conquered by Cambyses, 530–522 BC
Conquered by Darius, 521–486 BC
Royal Road
Capital city

GEOGRAPHY SKILLS | **INTERPRETING MAPS**

1. **Place** What geographic features marked the Persian Empire's northern boundary?

2. **Regions** Which Persian ruler added the most territory to the empire?

THE SILK ROADS

EUROPE

Rome

Black Sea

Mediterranean Sea

Euphrates R.

Antioch

Tyre

Alexandria
EGYPT

AFRICA

Cloth, Spices,
Ivory, Metal, Slaves,
Tortoise shell

Nile R.

Red Sea

Caspian Sea

Tigris R.

Bukhara

Samarkand

PERSIA

Hindu Kush

Indus R.

ARABIA

Cloth, Spices, Ivory, Metal,
Slaves, Tortoise shell,
Precious stones

Arabian Sea

Thar Desert

INDIA

Cloth, Ivory,
Timber, Tortoise shell,
Precious stones

Ganges R.

Bay of Bengal

TIAN SHAN

Kashgar
Taklimakan Desert

Khotan

HIMALAYAS

TIBET

ASIA

GOBI

Dunhuang

Huang He (Yellow R.)

Chang'an (Xian)

Luoyang

CHINA

Chang Jiang (Yangzi R.)

Cloth, Silk, Spices

Guangzhou

Mekong R.

SOUTHEAST ASIA

Yellow Sea

East China Sea

PACIFIC OCEAN

South China Sea

40°N

20°N

60°E

80°E

100°E

120°E

INDIAN OCEAN

N W E S

0   400   800 Miles
0   400   800 Kilometers
Miller cylindrical projection

Legend:
- ● Trade center
- Cloth Trade goods
- ▬ Silk Road routes
- ▬ Other trade routes
- ▨ Han China, c. AD 150
- ▨ Gupta Empire, c. AD 400

GEOGRAPHY SKILLS INTERPRETING MAPS

1. **Place** Why do you think the Silk Roads divided to the west of China?

2. **Movement** What goods moved west from China over the Silk Roads?

Route Map

One special type of historical map is called a route map. A route map, like the one above, shows the route, or path, that someone or something followed. Route maps can show things like trade routes, invasion routes, or the journeys and travels of people. The routes on the map are usually shown with an arrow. If more than one route is shown, several arrows of different colors may be used. What does this route map show?

The maps in this textbook will help you study and understand history. By working with these maps, you will see where important events happened, where empires rose and fell, and where people moved. In studying these maps, you will learn how geography has influenced history.

Geographic Dictionary

OCEAN
a large body of water

CORAL REEF
an ocean ridge made up of skeletal remains of tiny sea animals

GULF
a large part of the ocean that extends into land

PENINSULA
an area of land that sticks out into a lake or ocean

ISTHMUS
a narrow piece of land connecting two larger land areas

BAY
part of a large body of water that is smaller than a gulf

ISLAND
an area of land surrounded entirely by water

DELTA
an area where a river deposits soil into the ocean

STRAIT
a narrow body of water connecting two larger bodies of water

SINKHOLE
a circular depression formed when the roof of a cave collapses

WETLAND
an area of land covered by shallow water

RIVER
a natural flow of water that runs through the land

LAKE
an inland body of water

FOREST
an area of densely wooded land

COAST
an area of land near the ocean

MOUNTAIN
an area of rugged land that generally rises higher than 2,000 feet

VALLEY
an area of low land between hills or mountains

GLACIER
a large area of slow-moving ice

VOLCANO
an opening in Earth's crust where lava, ash, and gases erupt

CANYON
a deep, narrow valley with steep walls

HILL
a rounded, elevated area of land smaller than a mountain

PLAIN
a nearly flat area

DUNE
a hill of sand shaped by wind

OASIS
an area in the desert with a water source

DESERT
an extremely dry area with little water and few plants

PLATEAU
a large, flat, elevated area of land

Themes and Essential Elements of Geography

by Dr. Christopher L. Salter

To study the world, geographers have identified 5 key themes, 6 essential elements, and 18 geography standards.

"How should we teach and learn about geography?" Professional geographers have worked hard over the years to answer this important question.

In 1984 a group of geographers identified the 5 Themes of Geography. These themes did a wonderful job of laying the groundwork for good classroom geography instruction. Teachers used the 5 Themes in classrooms, and geographers taught workshops on how to apply the 5 themes in everyday life.

By the early 1990s, however, some geographers felt the 5 Themes were too broad. They created the 18 Geography Standards and the 6 Essential Elements. The 18 Geography Standards include more detailed information about what geography is, and the 6 Essential Elements are like a bridge between the 5 Themes and 18 Standards.

Look at the chart to the right. It shows how each of the 5 Themes connects to the 6 Essential Elements and 18 Geography Standards. For example, the theme of Location is related to The World in Spatial Terms and, through it, to the first three Standards. Study the chart carefully to see how the other Themes, Elements, and Standards are related.

The last Essential Element and the last two Standards cover The Uses of Geography. These key parts of geography were not covered by the 5 Themes. They emphasize how geographical knowledge can be applied to the study of history and current events and also be used to plan for the future.

5 Themes of Geography

Location The theme of location describes where something is.

Place Place describes the features that make a site unique.

Regions Regions are areas that share common characteristics.

Movement This theme looks at how and why people and things move.

Human-Environment Interaction People interact with their environment in many ways.

6 Essential Elements

18 Geography Standards

1. How to use maps and other tools
2. How to use mental maps to organize information
3. How to analyze the spatial organization of people, places, and environments

I. The World in Spatial Terms

4. The physical and human characteristics of places
5. How people create regions to interpret Earth
6. How culture and experience influence people's perceptions of places and regions

II. Places and Regions

7. The physical processes that shape Earth's surface
8. The distribution of ecosystems on Earth

9. The characteristics, distribution, and migration of human populations
10. The complexity of Earth's cultural mosaics
11. The patterns and networks of economic interdependence on Earth
12. The patterns of human settlement
13. The forces of cooperation and conflict

III. Physical Systems

IV. Human Systems

14. How human actions modify the physical environment
15. How physical systems affect human systems
16. The distribution and meaning of resources

V. Environment and Society

17. How to apply geography to interpret the past
18. How to apply geography to interpret the present and plan for the future

VI. The Uses of Geography

GEOGRAPHY AND MAP SKILLS HANDBOOK

World: Political

Legend:
- ⊛ National capital
- ● Other city

0 500 1,000 Miles
0 500 1,000 Kilometers
Projection: Mollweide

0 200 400 Miles
0 200 400 Kilometers
Projection: Mercator

COUNTRY	CAPITAL
1 Antigua and Barbuda	St. Johns
2 St. Kitts and Nevis	Basseterre
3 Dominica	Roseau
4 St. Lucia	Castries
5 St. Vincent and the Grenadines	Kingstown
6 Barbados	Bridgetown
7 Grenada	St. George's

ARCTIC OCEAN

RUSSIA

EUROPE

Moscow

KAZAKHSTAN

Astana

GEORGIA

UZBEKISTAN

Istanbul

Ankara ARMENIA

TURKEY

AZERBAIJAN

Baku

TURKMENISTAN

Tashkent

Almaty

KYRGYZSTAN

Ulaanbaatar

MONGOLIA

ASIA

Harbin

NORTH
KOREA

Beijing

Pyongyang

JAPAN

Tokyo

Nicosia

CYPRUS

SYRIA

Tehran

Ashgabat

TAJIKISTAN

Tianjin

Seoul

Nagoya

Yokohama

TUNISIA

Tripoli

LEBANON

Beirut

Damascus

Baghdad

IRAN

AFGHANISTAN

Islamabad

Kabul

CHINA

Wuhan

SOUTH
KOREA

Osaka

Jerusalem

ISRAEL

Amman

JORDAN

IRAQ

KUWAIT

BAHRAIN

PAKISTAN

Delhi

NEPAL

Kathmandu

Chongqing

Shanghai

LIBYA

EGYPT

SAUDI
ARABIA

QATAR

OMAN

Riyadh

New
Delhi

Karachi

BHUTAN

BANGLADESH

Guangzhou

Taipei

Tropic of Cancer

AFRICA

NIGER

CHAD

Khartoum

UNITED ARAB
EMIRATES

Muscat

ERITREA

Asmara

OMAN

INDIA

Mumbai
(Bombay)

Calcutta

Dhaka

MYANMAR
(BURMA)

LAOS

Hanoi

Hong
Kong

TAIWAN

Northern
Mariana
(U.S.)

PACIFIC
OCEAN

20°N

N'Djamena

NIGERIA

Abuja

SUDAN

YEMEN

Sanaa

DJIBOUTI

Yangon
(Rangoon)

THAILAND

VIETNAM

Manila

Guam (U.S.)

MARSHALL
ISLANDS

Lagos

CENTRAL
AFRICAN
REPUBLIC

CAMEROON

Addis Ababa

ETHIOPIA

Chennai
(Madras)

Bangkok

CAMBODIA

Phnom Penh

Ho Chi
Minh City

PHILIPPINES

PALAU

SRI
LANKA

Colombo

BRUNEI

FEDERATED STATES
OF MICRONESIA

0° Equator

EQUATORIAL

GABON

SÃO
TOMÉ
AND
PRÍNCIPE

DEMOCRATIC
REPUBLIC
OF THE
CONGO

REP.
OF THE
CONGO

UGANDA

KENYA

Nairobi

SOMALIA

RWANDA

BURUNDI

MALDIVES

Kuala
Lumpur

MALAYSIA

Singapore

SINGAPORE

INDONESIA

NAURU

KIRIBATI

Cabinda
(ANGOLA)

Kinshasa

Luanda

TANZANIA

Dodoma

Dar es Salaam

SEYCHELLES

Jakarta

Surabaya

PAPUA
NEW
GUINEA

Port Moresby

SOLOMON
ISLANDS

TUVALU

ANGOLA

ZAMBIA

Lusaka

MALAWI

COMOROS

MOZAMBIQUE

MADAGASCAR

Antananarivo

INDIAN OCEAN

EAST TIMOR

NAMIBIA

Harare

ZIMBABWE

MAURITIUS

VANUATU

New Caledonia
(FRANCE)

FIJI

Windhoek

BOTSWANA

Gaborone

Pretoria

Maputo

Réunion
(FRANCE)

AUSTRALIA

20°S

Tropic of Capricorn

Johannesburg

Bloemfontein

SWAZILAND

LESOTHO

SOUTH
AFRICA

Cape Town

Sydney

Canberra

Melbourne

NEW
ZEALAND

Wellington

Tasmania

20°E 40°E 60°E 80°E 100°E 120°E 140°E 160°E 60°S

ANTARCTICA

	COUNTRY	CAPITAL
1	Czech Republic	Prague
2	Slovakia	Bratislava
3	Slovenia	Ljubljana
4	Croatia	Zagreb
5	Bosnia and Herzegovina	Sarajevo
6	Macedonia	Skopje
7	Serbia	Belgrade
8	Montenegro	Podgorica
9	Lithuania	Vilnius
10	Latvia	Riga
11	Estonia	Tallinn

ICELAND

Reykjavik

Arctic
Circle

N
W E
S

NORWAY

SWEDEN

FINLAND

0   250   500 Miles
0   250   500 Kilometers

Projection: Mollweide

RUSSIA

St. Petersburg

Oslo

Stockholm

Helsinki

11

10

9

Minsk

Moscow

UNITED
KINGDOM

North
Sea

DENMARK

Copenhagen

Dublin

IRELAND

London

NETHERLANDS

Amsterdam

Berlin

Warsaw

BELARUS

Brussels

BELGIUM

GERMANY

POLAND

Kiev

ATLANTIC
OCEAN

Paris

LUXEMBOURG

1

Vienna

Bratislava

UKRAINE

MOLDOVA

Chisinau

SWITZERLAND

AUSTRIA

2

Budapest

Bern

LIECHTENSTEIN

FRANCE

3

4

HUNGARY

ROMANIA

MONACO

Corsica
(FRANCE)

SAN MARINO

Rome

5

7

Bucharest

BULGARIA

Black Sea

PORTUGAL

ANDORRA

ITALY

VATICAN CITY

8

6

Sofia

Lisbon

Madrid

Balearic
Js. (SPAIN)

Sardinia
(ITALY)

Tirane

ALBANIA

GREECE

SPAIN

Mediterranean
Sea

Athens

Gibraltar (U.K.)

Sicily

MALTA

Crete

ATLAS **R33**

World: Physical

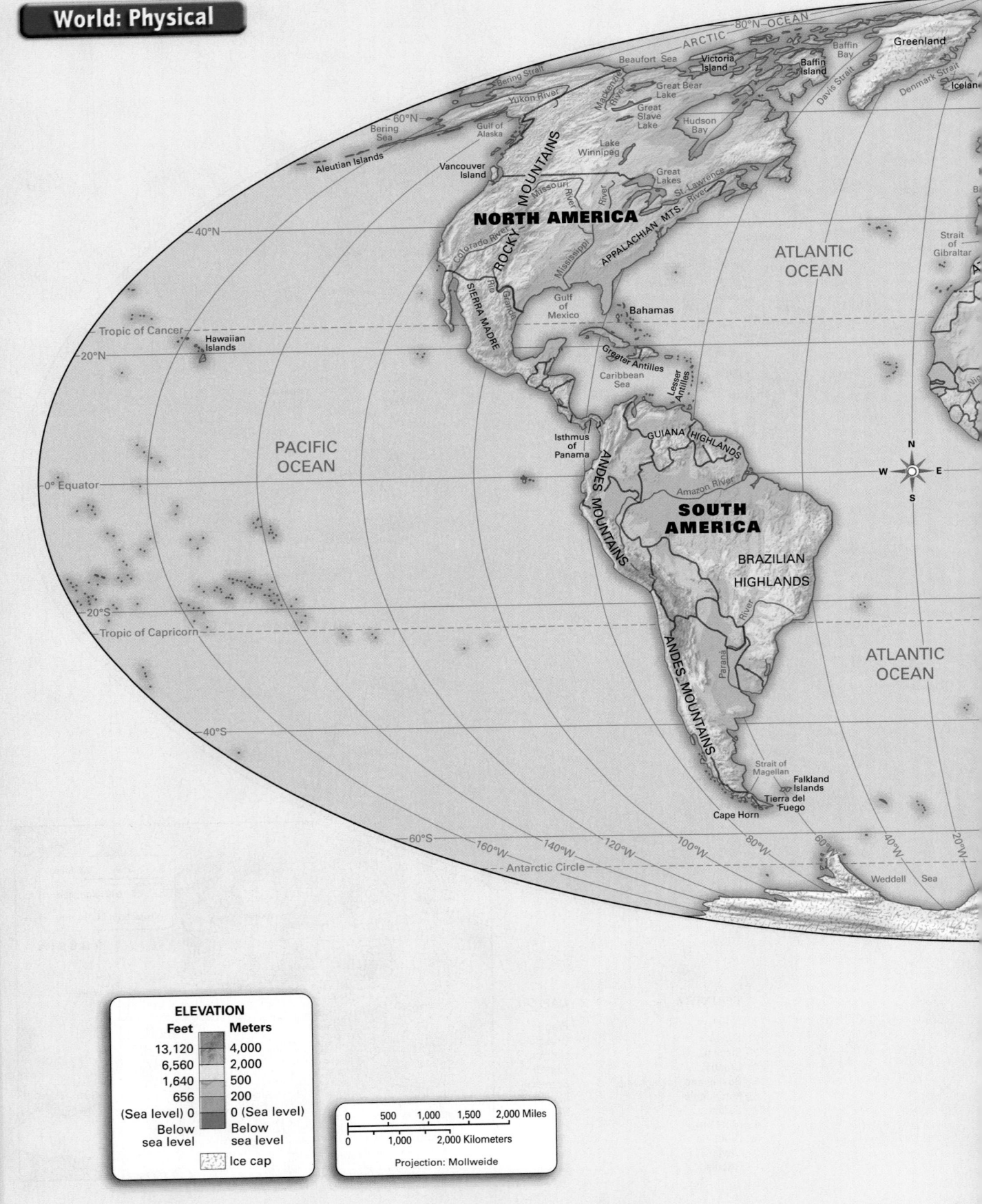

ELEVATION

Feet		Meters
13,120		4,000
6,560		2,000
1,640		500
656		200
(Sea level) 0		0 (Sea level)
Below sea level		Below sea level

Ice cap

| 0 | 500 | 1,000 | 1,500 | 2,000 Miles |
| 0 | 1,000 | 2,000 Kilometers |

Projection: Mollweide

EUROPE

ASIA

AFRICA

SAHARA

ARABIAN PENINSULA

ALPS

U.S.

Mediterranean Sea

Black Sea

URAL MOUNTAINS

Volga River

Ob River

Yenisei River

Lena River

Kolyma River

Aral Sea

Balqash Lake

Lake Baikal

ALTAY MOUNTAINS

GOBI

HIMALAYAS

Caspian Sea

Tigris River

Euphrates River

Nile River

Congo River

Niger River

Persian Gulf

Indus River

Thar Desert

Ganges River

Arabian Sea

Bay of Bengal

Sri Lanka

Strait of Malacca

MALAY PENINSULA

Sumatra

Java

Borneo

Celebes

Chang Jiang (Yangzi) River

Huang He (Yellow River)

Mekong River

South China Sea

Philippine Islands

Taiwan

East China Sea

Kyushu

Shikoku

Honshu

Hokkaido

Sakhalin Island

Sea of Okhotsk

KAMCHATKA PENINSULA

Amur River

60°N

40°N

Tropic of Cancer

20°N

0° Equator

PACIFIC OCEAN

New Guinea

Solomon Islands

Coral Sea

New Hebrides

New Caledonia

Fiji Islands

20°S

Tropic of Capricorn

INDIAN OCEAN

Madagascar

Mozambique Channel

Lake Tanganyika

Lake Victoria

KALAHARI DESERT

Cape of Good Hope

AUSTRALIA

GREAT SANDY DESERT

GREAT VICTORIA DESERT

Darling River

GREAT DIVIDING RANGE

Tasman Sea

Tasmania

NEW ZEALAND

North Island

South Island

ANTARCTICA

ARCTIC 80°N OCEAN

North Cape

Barents Sea

Kara Sea

Laptev Sea

East Siberian Sea

Baltic Sea

20°E 40°E 60°E 80°E 100°E 120°E 140°E 160°E

60°S

0 250 500 Miles
0 250 500 Kilometers

Projection: Mollweide

Denmark Strait

Iceland

British Isles

North Cape

Barents Sea

Kara Sea

KJÖLEN MTS.

Baltic Sea

URAL MTS.

Volga River

NORTHERN EUROPEAN PLAIN

Rhine

Danube

North Sea

Bay of Biscay

ALPS

IBERIAN PENINSULA

Strait of Gibraltar

Mediterranean Sea

Black Sea

Crete

Tigris River

Euphrates River

ATLANTIC OCEAN

60°N

50°N

40°N

10°W 0° 10°E 20°E 30°E 40°E

N
W E
S

Africa: Political

EUROPE

SOUTHWEST ASIA

Azores (PORTUGAL)

Madeira (PORTUGAL)

Strait of Gibraltar

Mediterranean Sea

MOROCCO
Casablanca • Rabat ✪
Algiers ✪
Tunis ✪
TUNISIA
Tripoli ✪

Canary Islands (SPAIN)

El Aaiún

WESTERN SAHARA (Claimed by Morocco)

ALGERIA

LIBYA

Alexandria •
Giza • Cairo ✪
EGYPT

Tropic of Cancer

MAURITANIA
Nouakchott ✪

MALI

NIGER

CHAD

Khartoum ✪

ERITREA
Asmara ✪

Red Sea

Gulf of Aden

CAPE VERDE
Praia ✪

SENEGAL
Dakar •
GAMBIA
Banjul ✪
Bissau ✪
GUINEA-BISSAU
Conakry ✪
Freetown ✪
SIERRA LEONE
Monrovia ✪
LIBERIA

Bamako •
BURKINA FASO
Ouagadougou ✪
GUINEA
CÔTE D'IVOIRE
Yamoussoukro ✪
Abidjan •

Niamey ✪

BENIN
TOGO
GHANA
Lomé ✪
Accra ✪
Porto-Novo ✪

N'Djamena ✪

Lake Chad

NIGERIA
Abuja ✪
Lagos •

SUDAN

DJIBOUTI
Djibouti ✪

ETHIOPIA
Addis Ababa •

CENTRAL AFRICAN REPUBLIC
Bangui ✪

SOMALIA

Mogadishu •

CAMEROON

Gulf of Guinea

Malabo ✪
EQUATORIAL GUINEA
SÃO TOMÉ AND PRÍNCIPE
São Tomé ✪

Yaoundé ✪

REPUBLIC OF THE CONGO
Libreville ✪
GABON

Kisangani •

UGANDA
Kampala ✪

KENYA
Nairobi ✪

Lake Victoria

INDIAN OCEAN

ATLANTIC OCEAN

Brazzaville ✪
CABINDA (ANGOLA)
Kinshasa ✪

DEMOCRATIC REPUBLIC OF THE CONGO
Bujumbura ✪
RWANDA
Kigali ✪
BURUNDI

Dodoma ✪
TANZANIA
Lake Tanganyika

Mombasa •
Pemba •
Zanzibar •
Dar es Salaam •

Victoria ✪
SEYCHELLES

Lake Malawi (Nyasa)

Luanda ✪

Lubumbashi •

COMOROS
Moroni ✪

St. Helena (U.K.)

ANGOLA

ZAMBIA
Lusaka ✪

MALAWI
Lilongwe ✪

Harare ✪
ZIMBABWE
Bulawayo •

MOZAMBIQUE

Antananarivo ✪
MAURITIUS
Port Louis ✪
Réunion (FRANCE)

MADAGASCAR

NAMIBIA
Windhoek ✪

BOTSWANA
Gaborone ✪

Pretoria ✪
Maputo ✪
Mbabane ✪
SWAZILAND

Johannesburg •
Bloemfontein ✪
Maseru ✪
LESOTHO

SOUTH AFRICA

Cape Town ✪

Tropic of Capricorn

✪ National capital
• Other city

0 — 250 — 500 Miles
0 — 250 — 500 Kilometers

Projection: Azimuthal Equal-Area

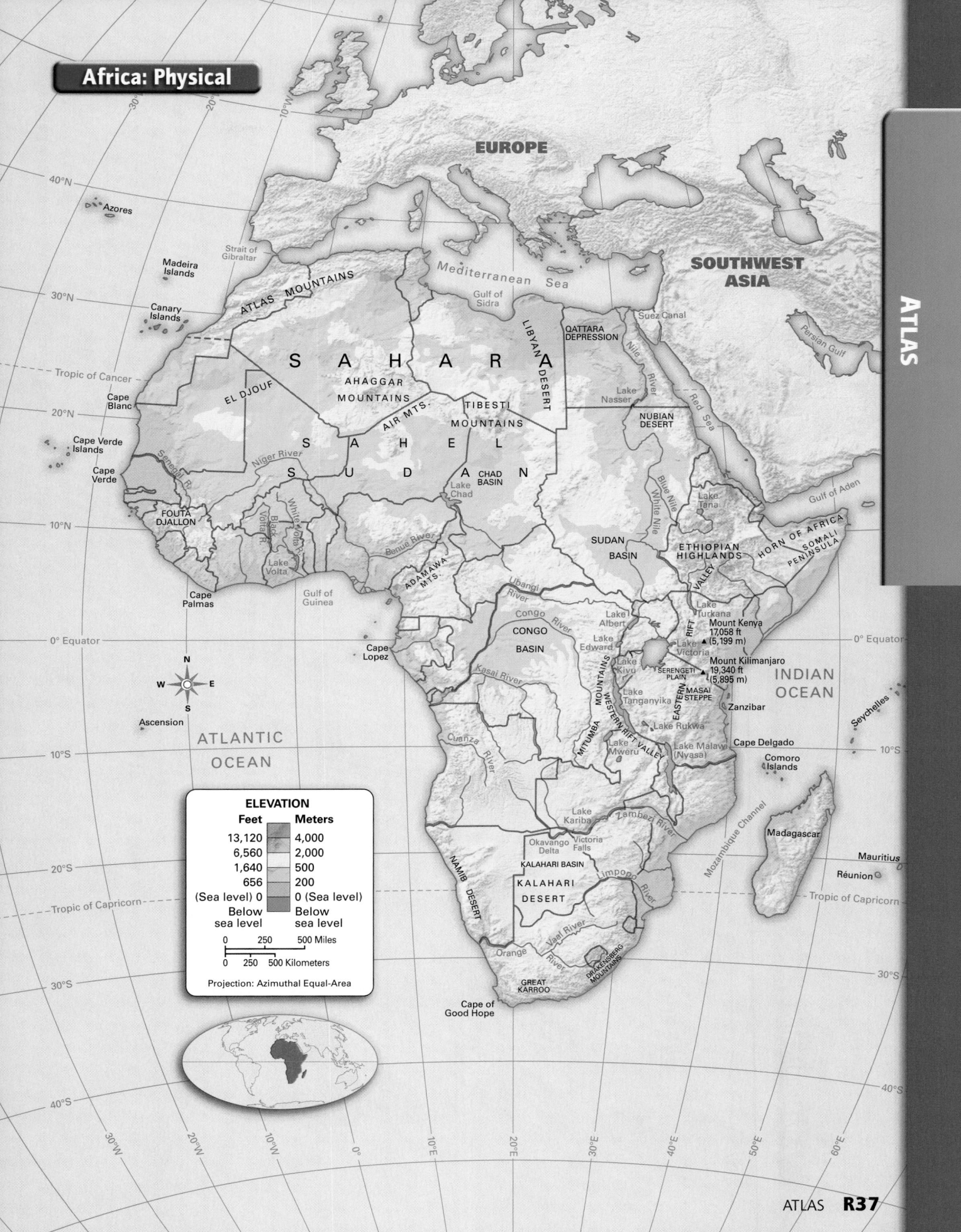

Africa: Physical

EUROPE

SOUTHWEST ASIA

Azores

Madeira Islands

Strait of Gibraltar

ATLAS MOUNTAINS

Mediterranean Sea

Gulf of Sidra

Canary Islands

Tropic of Cancer

Cape Blanc

EL DJOUF

S A H A R A

AHAGGAR MOUNTAINS

AIR MTS.

TIBESTI MOUNTAINS

LIBYAN DESERT

QATTARA DEPRESSION

Suez Canal

Nile River

Lake Nasser

NUBIAN DESERT

Red Sea

Persian Gulf

Cape Verde Islands

Senegal R.

Niger River

S A H E L

S U D A N

White Volta R.

Black Volta R.

Lake Chad

CHAD BASIN

Lake Tana

Blue Nile

White Nile

Lake Turkana

Gulf of Aden

Cape Verde

FOUTA DJALLON

Benue River

Lake Volta

SUDAN BASIN

ETHIOPIAN HIGHLANDS

HORN OF AFRICA

SOMALI PENINSULA

Cape Palmas

Gulf of Guinea

ADAMAWA MTS.

Ubangi River

Congo River

CONGO BASIN

Lake Albert

Lake Edward

RIFT VALLEY

Mount Kenya 17,058 ft (5,199 m)

Cape Lopez

0° Equator

Kasai River

Lake Kivu

Lake Victoria

SERENGETI PLAIN

Mount Kilimanjaro 19,340 ft (5,895 m)

MASAI STEPPE

INDIAN OCEAN

0° Equator

Ascension

ATLANTIC OCEAN

MITUMBA MOUNTAINS

WESTERN RIFT VALLEY

EASTERN

Lake Tanganyika

Zanzibar

Seychelles

Lake Rukwa

Cuanza River

Cape Delgado

10°S

Lake Mweru

Lake Malawi (Nyasa)

Comoro Islands

10°S

Zambezi River

Lake Kariba

Mozambique Channel

Madagascar

ELEVATION

Feet	Meters
13,120	4,000
6,560	2,000
1,640	500
656	200
(Sea level) 0	0 (Sea level)
Below sea level	Below sea level

Okavango Delta

Victoria Falls

KALAHARI BASIN

Limpopo River

Mauritius

Réunion

0 250 500 Miles

0 250 500 Kilometers

Projection: Azimuthal Equal-Area

NAMIB DESERT

KALAHARI DESERT

Tropic of Capricorn

Orange River

Vaal River

DRAKENSBERG MOUNTAINS

GREAT KARROO

Cape of Good Hope

Tropic of Capricorn

Asia: Political

Legend:
- National capitals
- Other cities

750 Miles
500
250
0

750 Kilometers
500
250
0

Projection: Two-Point Equidistant

Countries and regions:

EUROPE

RUSSIA

RUSSIA

KAZAKHSTAN

UZBEKISTAN

TURKMENISTAN

KYRGYZSTAN

TAJIKISTAN

AFGHANISTAN

PAKISTAN

GEORGIA

ARMENIA

AZERBAIJAN

TURKEY

CYPRUS

SYRIA

LEBANON

ISRAEL

JORDAN

IRAQ

IRAN

KUWAIT

BAHRAIN

QATAR

UNITED ARAB EMIRATES

OMAN

SAUDI ARABIA

YEMEN

MONGOLIA

CHINA

NEPAL

BHUTAN

BANGLADESH

INDIA

MYANMAR (BURMA)

LAOS

THAILAND

CAMBODIA

VIETNAM

SRI LANKA

MALDIVES

NORTH KOREA

SOUTH KOREA

JAPAN

TAIWAN

PHILIPPINES

MALAYSIA

SINGAPORE

BRUNEI

INDONESIA

EAST TIMOR

AUSTRALIA

AFRICA

Cities:

Moscow, Yekaterinburg, Chelyabinsk, Omsk, Novosibirsk, Yakutsk, Irkutsk, Vladivostok, Harbin, Fushun, Dalian, Beijing, Qingdao, Nanjing, Shanghai, Wuhan, Chongqing, Chengdu, Guangzhou, Hong Kong, Macao, Ulaanbaatar, Astana, Almaty, Bishkek, Tashkent, Ashgabat, Dushanbe, Islamabad, Kabul, Lahore, Karachi, New Delhi, Delhi, Jaipur, Ahmadabad, Mumbai (Bombay), Bangalore, Chennai (Madras), Kolkata (Calcutta), Kathmandu, Thimphu, Dhaka, Yangon (Rangoon), Mandalay, Bangkok, Vientiane, Phnom Penh, Hanoi, Ho Chi Minh City, Bandar Seri Begawan, Kuala Lumpur, Singapore, Medan, Jakarta, Surabaya, Bandung, Ujung Pandang, Dili, Manila, Colombo, Male

Seoul, Pyongyang, Pusan, Nagasaki, Hiroshima, Kyoto, Osaka, Tokyo, Yokohama, Sapporo, Taipei

Tbilisi, Yerevan, Baku, Tehran, Shiraz, Mosul, Baghdad, Basra, Kuwait City, Manama, Doha, Abu Dhabi, Masqat (Muscat), Riyadh, Mecca, Jidda, Sanaa, Ankara, Istanbul, Izmir, Nicosia, Beirut, Damascus, Tel Aviv, Jerusalem, Amman

Physical features:

Bering Sea, Aleutian Islands (RUSSIA), Sea of Okhotsk, Sakhalin Island, Kuril Islands (RUSSIA), North Pole, Arctic Circle, Barents Sea, Kara Sea, Laptev Sea, Lake Baikal, Lake Balkhash, Aral Sea, Caspian Sea, Black Sea, Mediterranean Sea, Red Sea, Gulf of Aden, Arabian Sea, Persian Gulf, Gulf of Thailand, Bay of Bengal, Andaman Sea, Lakshadweep Islands (INDIA), Nicobar Islands (INDIA), Andaman Islands (INDIA), INDIAN OCEAN, PACIFIC OCEAN, South China Sea, East China Sea, Yellow Sea, Celebes Sea, Java Sea, Arafura Sea, Luzon Strait, Ryukyu Islands (JAPAN), Hainan (CHINA), Socotra (YEMEN), New Guinea, URAL MOUNTAINS, Tropic of Cancer, Equator

Asia: Physical

ELEVATION

Feet	Meters
13,120	4,000
6,560	2,000
1,640	500
656	200
(Sea level) 0	0 (Sea level)
Below sea level	Below sea level

Ice cap

0   250   500   750 Miles
0   250   500   750 Kilometers

Projection: Two-Point Equidistant

EUROPE

AFRICA

AUSTRALIA

PACIFIC OCEAN

INDIAN OCEAN

North Pole

Arctic Circle

Equator

Tropic of Cancer

Bering Sea
Aleutian Islands
KAMCHATKA PENINSULA
CENTRAL RANGE
Sea of Okhotsk
Sakhalin Island
Kuril Islands
Hokkaido
KOLYMA MTS.
CHERSKIY RANGE
VERKHOYANSKY RANGE
STANOVOY MOUNTAINS
Aldan River
Lena River
Shilka River
Amur River
GREATER KHINGAN RANGE
Honshu
Sea of Japan (East Sea)
Korea Strait
Shikoku
Kyushu
Ryukyu Islands
Okinawa
East China Sea
Yellow Sea
NORTH CHINA PLAIN
BOHEA HILLS
QIN LING
Huang He (Yellow River)
Chang Jiang (Yangtze) River
Hong River
Taiwan
Luzon Strait
Hainan
South China Sea
Gulf of Tonkin
Mekong River
INDOCHINA PENINSULA
Chao Phraya River
Gulf of Thailand
MALAY PENINSULA
Philippines
Luzon
Mindanao
Celebes Sea
Celebes
Molucca Sea
Banda Sea
Borneo
Java Sea
Bangka
Java
Sumatra
Mentawai Islands
MADKE MOUNTAINS
New Guinea
Arafura Sea

New Siberian Islands
Wrangel Island
North Land
TAYMYR PENINSULA
CENTRAL SIBERIAN PLATEAU
Tunguska River
Angara River
Lake Baikal
YABLONOVY RANGE
SAYAN MOUNTAINS
ALTAY MOUNTAINS
MONGOLIAN PLATEAU
GOBI
S I B E R I A
Yenisey River
Lower Tunguska River
Ob River
Irtysh River
WEST SIBERIAN PLAIN
KAZAKH UPLANDS
Balqash Lake
TIAN SHAN
TARIM BASIN
TAKLIMAKAN DESERT
KUNLUN MOUNTAINS
PLATEAU OF TIBET
Mount Everest 29,035 ft (8,850 m)
H I M A L A Y A S
INDO-GANGETIC PLAIN
Brahmaputra River
Ganges River
DECCAN PLATEAU
Godavari River
WESTERN GHATS
EASTERN GHATS
THAR DESERT
HINDU KUSH
PAMIRS
TURAN LOWLAND
Syr Darya
Amu Darya
KYZYL KUM
KARA KUM
Aral Sea
Ishim River
Tobol River
Ural River
USTYURT PLATEAU
Caspian Sea
GREAT SALT DESERT
ZAGROS MTS.
Persian Gulf
Gulf of Oman
RUB' AL-KHALI
Socotra Island
Gulf of Aden
AN-NAFUD
SYRIAN DESERT
Tigris River
Euphrates River
CAUCASUS MTS.
Mount Ararat 16,945 ft (5,165 m)
ANATOLIAN PLATEAU
Cyprus
SINAI PENINSULA
Red Sea
Mediterranean Sea
Bosporus
Black Sea
URAL MOUNTAINS
Franz Josef Land
Novaya Zemlya
Kara Sea
Barents Sea

Bay of Bengal
Andaman Islands
Nicobar Islands
Andaman Sea
Sri Lanka
Lakshadweep Islands
Maldives
Arabian Sea

Europe: Political

ASIA

URAL MOUNTAINS

RUSSIA

Nizhny Novgorod

Caspian Sea

Barents Sea

White Sea

Moscow

St. Petersburg

North Cape

ARCTIC OCEAN

Black Sea

30°E

UKRAINE

Kiev

MOLDOVA

Chişinău

Minsk

BELARUS

FINLAND

Gulf of Finland

Tallinn

ESTONIA

LATVIA

Riga

Helsinki

LITHUANIA

Vilnius

RUSSIA

POLAND

Warsaw

Krakow

ROMANIA

Bucharest

Sofia

BULGARIA

Skopje

MACEDONIA

Tirana

ALBANIA

GREECE

Athens

Aegean Sea

Rhodes

Crete

SWEDEN

Baltic Sea

Stockholm

Göteborg

Gulf of Bothnia

SLOVAKIA

Bratislava

Budapest

HUNGARY

Belgrade

SERBIA

Zagreb

CROATIA

BOSNIA AND HERZEGOVINA

Sarajevo

MONTENEGRO

Podgorica

Adriatic Sea

NORWAY

Oslo

Bergen

DENMARK

Copenhagen

Hamburg

Berlin

Dresden

GERMANY

Prague

CZECH REPUBLIC

Vienna

AUSTRIA

SLOVENIA

Ljubljana

Milan

SAN MARINO

San Marino

ITALY

Rome

VATICAN CITY

Naples

Sicily

MALTA

Valletta

Tyrrhenian Sea

North Sea

THE NETHERLANDS

Amsterdam

Cologne

Bonn

Luxembourg

Munich

LIECHTENSTEIN

Vaduz

SWITZERLAND

Bern

Lake Geneva

MONACO

Monaco

Corsica (FRANCE)

Sardinia (ITALY)

Mediterranean Sea

ICELAND

Reykjavík

Faeroe Islands (DENMARK)

Shetland Islands

SCOTLAND

Edinburgh

UNITED KINGDOM

Belfast

NORTHERN IRELAND

Dublin

IRELAND

Liverpool

ENGLAND

London

WALES

British Isles

English Channel

Channel Islands (U.K.)

BELGIUM

Brussels

LUXEMBOURG

Paris

FRANCE

Lyon

Marseille

Bay of Biscay

PYRENEES

Andorra la Vella

ANDORRA

Barcelona

Balearic Islands (SPAIN)

AFRICA

SPAIN

Madrid

Valencia

Seville

Gibraltar (U.K.)

Strait of Gibraltar

PORTUGAL

Lisbon

ATLANTIC OCEAN

70°N

60°N

50°N

40°N

Arctic Circle

30°W

20°W

10°W

0°

10°E

20°E

30°E

40°E

50°E

70°E

N
S
E
W

Europe: Political

National capital
Other city

0   150   300 Miles
0   150   300 Kilometers

Projection: Azimuthal Equal-Area

ATLAS

Europe: Physical

ELEVATION

Feet	Meters
13,120	4,000
6,560	2,000
1,640	500
656	200
(Sea level) 0	0 (Sea level)
Below sea level	Below sea level

Ice cap

| 0 | 150 | 300 Miles |
| 0 | 150 | 300 Kilometers |

Projection: Azimuthal Equal Area

ASIA

URAL MOUNTAINS

Pechora River

Dvina River

North River

KOLA PENINSULA

White Sea

Kama River

Ural River

NORTHERN EUROPEAN PLAIN

Lake Onega

Lake Ladoga

Rybinsk Reservoir

Volga River

Don River

Dnipro River

Sea of Azov

Caspian Sea

Mt. Elbrus 18,510 ft (5,642 m)

CAUCASUS MTS.

CRIMEAN PENINSULA

Black Sea

BALTIC PLAINS

Daugava R.

Dvina River

Gulf of Finland

Gulf of Bothnia

Baltic Sea

Vistula River

Oder River

Elbe River

Dniester River

Prut River

CARPATHIAN MTS.

TRANSYLVANIAN ALPS

Danube River

BALKAN PENINSULA

Sea of Marmara

Aegean Sea

Rhodes

Crete

DINARIC ALPS

Adriatic Sea

APENNINES

Tiber River

Po River

Tyrrhenian Sea

Sicily

Malta

Mediterranean Sea

KJØLEN MOUNTAINS

North Cape

Lake Vänern

Lake Vättern

Kattegat

Skagerrak

Rhine River

Danube River

ALPS

Mont Blanc 15,781 ft (4,810 m)

Lake Geneva

Rhône River

Corsica

Sardinia

Balearic Islands

ARCTIC OCEAN

Barents Sea

Norwegian Sea

North Sea

PENNINES

Thames River

English Channel

Seine River

Loire River

Garonne River

PYRENEES

Bay of Biscay

Ebro River

IBERIAN PENINSULA

Duero River

Tagus River

Guadiana River

Guadalquivir River

Cape Finisterre

Strait of Gibraltar

ATLANTIC OCEAN

AFRICA

Iceland

Faeroe Islands

Shetland Islands

Orkney Islands

Hebrides

British Isles

Irish Sea

Arctic Circle

North America: Political

ARCTIC OCEAN

ASIA

EUROPE

North Pole

Arctic Circle

ICELAND

St. Lawrence Island

Bering Sea

Bering Strait

Nunivak Island

Point Barrow

Beaufort Sea

Queen Elizabeth Islands

Ellesmere Island

Greenland (DENMARK)

Denmark Strait

ALASKA (U.S.)

Banks Island

Victoria Island

Baffin Island

Baffin Bay

Anchorage

Kodiak Island

Gulf of Alaska

Juneau

Alexander Archipelago

Queen Charlotte Islands

Great Bear Lake

Great Slave Lake

Southampton Island

Coats Island

Mansel Island

Hudson Strait

Davis Strait

Cape Farewell

Labrador Sea

Hudson Bay

Anticosti Island

Newfoundland

PACIFIC OCEAN

Edmonton

CANADA

Lake Winnipeg

Calgary

Vancouver Island

Vancouver

Seattle

Portland

Winnipeg

Lake Superior

Lake Michigan

Lake Huron

Prince Edward Island

Cape Breton Island

St. Pierre and Miquelon (FRANCE)

Gulf of St. Lawrence

Quebec

Montreal

Ottawa

Toronto

Lake Ontario

Lake Erie

Boston

Cape Cod

New York City

Philadelphia

Baltimore

Washington, D.C.

ATLANTIC OCEAN

San Francisco

San Jose

Minneapolis

Milwaukee

Chicago

Detroit

Cleveland

Columbus

Indianapolis

St. Louis

Norfolk

Salt Lake City

Great Salt Lake

UNITED STATES

Denver

Kansas City

Los Angeles

San Diego

Tijuana

Phoenix

Memphis

Atlanta

Birmingham

Dallas

Jacksonville

Bermuda (U.K.)

Austin

San Antonio

Houston

New Orleans

Miami

BAHAMAS

Nassau

Turks and Caicos Islands (U.K.)

Tropic of Cancer

Gulf of California

MEXICO

Monterrey

Gulf of Mexico

Florida Keys

Straits of Florida

Havana

CUBA

DOMINICAN REPUBLIC

Puerto Rico (U.S.)

San Juan

ST. KITTS & NEVIS

ANTIGUA & BARBUDA

Guadeloupe (FRANCE)

Guadalajara

Mexico City

Puebla

Mérida

Cayman Is. (U.K.)

Kingston

JAMAICA

HAITI

Port-au-Prince

Santo Domingo

Virgin Is. (U.S., U.K.)

Martinique (FRANCE)

DOMINICA

ST. LUCIA

BARBADOS

ST. VINCENT AND THE GRENADINES

Netherlands Antilles (NETHERLANDS)

GRENADA

Caribbean Sea

Belmopan

BELIZE

GUATEMALA

Guatemala City

HONDURAS

Tegucigalpa

San Salvador

EL SALVADOR

NICARAGUA

Managua

Aruba (NETHERLANDS)

TRINIDAD AND TOBAGO

San José

COSTA RICA

Panama Canal

Panama City

PANAMA

Legend

⊕ National capital

● Other city

| 0 | 300 | 600 Miles |
| 0 | 300 | 600 Kilometers |

Projection: Azimuthal Equal-Area

0° Equator

SOUTH AMERICA

North America: Physical

ASIA

ARCTIC OCEAN
+ North Pole
POLAR ICE PACK

EUROPE

St. Lawrence Island
Bering Sea
Nunivak Island
Bering Strait

BROOKS RANGE
Mt. McKinley 20,320 ft (6,194 m)
ALASKA RANGE
Yukon River
Beaufort Sea

Banks Island
Victoria Island

Queen Elizabeth Islands
Ellesmere Island

Baffin Bay
Greenland

Denmark Strait

Kodiak Island
Gulf of Alaska
Alexander Archipelago
Queen Charlotte Islands
YUKON PLATEAU

Great Bear Lake
Mackenzie River
Great Slave Lake

Baffin Island

Davis Strait

Cape Farewell

Arctic Circle

PACIFIC OCEAN

Vancouver Island
Mount Rainier 14,410 ft (4,392 m)
COAST RANGE
CASCADE RANGE
Columbia

ROCKY

Peace River
Lake Athabasca
Athabasca River

Saskatchewan River
Nelson River

CANADIAN

Southampton Island
Coats Island
Mansel Island
Hudson Bay

Hudson Strait

Labrador Sea

Newfoundland
Anticosti Island

Cape Mendocino

Snake River
SIERRA NEVADA
CENTRAL VALLEY
GREAT BASIN
DEATH VALLEY
Mount Whitney 14,494 ft (4,419 m)
Colorado
COLORADO PLATEAU
Great Salt Lake

GREAT

MOUNTAINS

PLAINS

Lake Winnipeg

Missouri River

BLACK HILLS

Platte River

Arkansas River
OZARK PLATEAU
Red River

SHIELD

Superior
Michigan
Huron
Ontario
Erie

INTERIOR PLAINS

Ohio
Cumberland R.
Tennessee River

St. Lawrence River
Gulf of St. Lawrence
Prince Edward Island
Cape Breton Island

APPALACHIAN MOUNTAINS

Long Island
Cape Cod

ATLANTIC OCEAN

Mississippi River

PIEDMONT
ATLANTIC COASTAL PLAIN

Cape Hatteras

Bermuda

Guadalupe Island
BAJA CALIFORNIA
Gulf of California
Rio Grande
Brazos River
SIERRA MADRE OCCIDENTAL
SIERRA MADRE ORIENTAL

GULF COASTAL PLAIN
Gulf of Mexico

Popocatépetl 17,887 ft (5,452 m)
YUCATÁN PENINSULA
SIERRA MADRE DEL SUR

CENTRAL AMERICA

Florida Keys
FLORIDA PENINSULA
Cape Canaveral

Bahamas

Cuba
Straits of Florida
Greater Antilles
Jamaica

Caribbean Sea
Lake Nicaragua
ISTHMUS OF PANAMA

Hispaniola
Puerto Rico
Lesser Antilles

Trinidad

Tropic of Cancer

SOUTH AMERICA

0° Equator

ELEVATION

Feet	Meters
13,120	4,000
6,560	2,000
1,640	500
656	200
(Sea level) 0	0 (Sea level)
Below sea level	Below sea level

Ice cap

0   300   600 Miles
0   300   600 Kilometers

Projection: Azimuthal Equal Area

South America: Political

Caribbean Sea

CENTRAL AMERICA

VENEZUELA
Barranquilla
Cartagena
Caracas
Lake Maracaibo

Medellín
Bogotá
COLOMBIA
Cali
Malpelo Island (COLOMBIA)

Georgetown
Paramaribo
GUYANA
Cayenne
SURINAME
French Guiana (FRANCE)

ATLANTIC OCEAN

Quito
ECUADOR
Guayaquil
Galápagos Islands (ECUADOR)

Belém

PERU
Trujillo

BRAZIL
Recife

Callao
Lima

PACIFIC OCEAN

Lake Titicaca
La Paz
Arequipa
Lake Poopó
BOLIVIA
Sucre

Brasília

Salvador

Belo Horizonte

Campinas
São Paulo
PARAGUAY
Asunción
Rio de Janeiro

San Ambrosio Island (CHILE)
San Félix Island (CHILE)

Curitiba

CHILE

Pôrto Alegre

Juan Fernández Islands (CHILE)

Córdoba
Rosario
URUGUAY

Valparaíso
Santiago
Buenos Aires
Montevideo

ATLANTIC OCEAN

ARGENTINA

Strait of Magellan
Falkland Islands (U.K.)

Tierra del Fuego
South Georgia Island (U.K.)

Tropic of Capricorn

Equator

⊕ National capital
● Other city

0   250   500 Miles
0   250   500 Kilometers

Projection: Azimuthal Equal-Area

South America: Physical

CENTRAL AMERICA

Caribbean Sea

Panama Canal

Gulf of Panama

Malpelo Island

Galápagos Islands

Gulf of Guayaquil

PACIFIC OCEAN

Margarita Island   Tobago
Trinidad
Lake Maracaibo
Orinoco River Delta

LLANOS
Meta River
Cauca River
Magdalena River

Mount Tolima
18,425 ft
(5,616 m)

Mount Chimborazo
20,561 ft
(6,267 m)

Marañón River

Mount Huascarán
22,205 ft
(6,768 m)

ANDES

Orinoco River

Orinoco River

Angel Falls

GUIANA HIGHLANDS

Devil's Island
Cape Orange

ATLANTIC OCEAN

Amazon River Delta

Río Negro

Japurá River

Caqueta River

Juruá River

Purus River

AMAZON BASIN

Amazon River

Madeira River

Tapajós River

Xingu River

Araguaia River

Tocantins River

Parnaiba River

São Francisco River

BRAZILIAN HIGHLANDS

0° Equator

Beni River

Mamoré River

Ancohuma Peak
20,958 ft
(6,388 m)

Lake Titicaca

Lake Poopó

MATO GROSSO PLATEAU

CHACO

BRAZILIAN PLATEAU

ATACAMA DESERT

Pilcomayo River

Paraguay River

Salado River

Paraná River

Uruguay River

San Ambrosio Island
San Félix Island

ANDES

Mount Aconcagua
22,834 ft
(6,960 m)

Salado River

Juan Fernández Islands

PAMPAS

Colorado River

Rio de la Plata

Tropic of Capricorn

ATLANTIC OCEAN

Chiloé Island

Chonos Archipelago

PATAGONIA

Gulf of San Matías

Gulf of San Jorge
Cape Tres Puntas

Bahía Grande
Strait of Magellan

Tierra del Fuego

Cape Horn

Falkland Islands

South Georgia Islands

ELEVATION

Feet		Meters
13,120		4,000
6,560		2,000
1,640		500
656		200
(Sea level) 0		0 (Sea level)
Below sea level		Below sea level

0   250   500 Miles

0   250   500 Kilometers

Projection: Azimuthal Equal Area

Oceania: Political

Legend
- ⊛ National capital
- ● Other city

1,000 Miles
1,000 Kilometers
500
500
0
0

Projection: Azimuthal Equal-Area

NORTH AMERICA

NORTH PACIFIC OCEAN

SOUTH PACIFIC OCEAN

Tropic of Capricorn

0° Equator

International Date Line

ASIA

Philippine Sea

South China Sea

PALAU
Koror

MICRONESIA

Bonin Islands (JAPAN)
Volcano Islands (JAPAN)
Northern Marianas (U.S.)
Guam (U.S.) • Agana

FEDERATED STATES OF MICRONESIA
Palikir
Truk Is.

MARSHALL ISLANDS
Eniwetok I.
Kwajalein Island
Majuro

Wake Island (U.S.)

NAURU

Tarawa
Gilbert Islands

SOLOMON ISLANDS
Honiara
Guadalcanal I.
Bougainville

PAPUA NEW GUINEA
Port Moresby
New Guinea
Bismarck Archipelago

MELANESIA

TUVALU
Funafuti

VANUATU
Espiritu Santo I.
Malekula I.
Port-Vila
New Caledonia (FRANCE)
Noumea
Loyalty Islands (FRANCE)

FIJI
Suva

Wallis & Futuna (FR.)

SAMOA
Apia
American Samoa
Pago Pago

TONGA
Nuku'alofa

Niue (N.Z.)

TOKELAU (N.Z.)

KIRIBATI

MICRONESIA

Howland I. (U.S.)
Baker I. (U.S.)
McKean I.
Gardner I.
Phoenix Islands

Kingman Reef (U.S.)
Palmyra Island (U.S.)
Washington Island
Fanning Island
Jarvis I. (U.S.)

Starbuck Island

Manihiki Island
Cook Islands (NEW ZEALAND)
Rarotonga Island

Society Islands (FRANCE)
Papeete
Tahiti (FRANCE)

French Polynesia

Marquesas Islands (FRANCE)
Tuamotu Archipelago (FRANCE)
Tubuai Islands (FRANCE)
Rapa Island (FRANCE)

POLYNESIA

Easter Island (CHILE)
Pitcairn (U.K.)
Ducie Island

Midway Island (U.S.)
Johnston Island (U.S.)
Hawaiian Islands
Hawaii (U.S.)

NEW ZEALAND
North Island
Auckland
Wellington
South Island
Christchurch
Chatham Islands (N.Z.)
Kermadec Islands (N.Z.)
Bounty Islands (N.Z.)
Auckland Islands (NEW ZEALAND)
Norfolk Island (AUSTRALIA)

AUSTRALIA
Brisbane
Sydney
Canberra
Melbourne
Hobart
Adelaide
Perth
Darwin
Tasman Sea
Coral Sea
Arafura Sea
Timor Sea
Christmas Island (AUSTRALIA)
INDIAN OCEAN

N E W S

Polar Regions

Arctic (top map)

EUROPE

Kara Sea

Barents Sea

Norwegian Sea

Laptev Sea

ASIA

ARCTIC OCEAN

North Pole

Greenland Sea

Greenland (DENMARK)

ATLANTIC OCEAN

POLAR ICE PACK

International Date Line

North Magnetic Pole

Baffin Bay

Beaufort Sea

Bering Sea

NORTH AMERICA

Arctic Circle

90°E

120°E

60°E

150°E

30°E

180°

90°W

120°W

150°W

30°W

60°W

80°N

60°N

50°N

0   200   400 Miles
0   200   400 Kilometers
Projection:
Polar Azimuthal Equidistant

ATLAS

Antarctic (bottom map)

SOUTH AMERICA

PACIFIC OCEAN

Amundsen Sea

Bellingshausen Sea

Antarctic Peninsula

POLAR ICE PACK

Ross Sea

Marie Byrd Land

Vinson Massif 16,067 ft (4,897 m)

Ellsworth Land

POLAR ICE PACK

International Date Line

Ross Ice Shelf

Ronne Ice Shelf

Weddell Sea

Edith Ronne Land

Filchner Ice Shelf

▲ Mount Markham over 14,275 ft (over 4,351 m)

South Pole

Coats Land

ATLANTIC OCEAN

Adelie Land

South Magnetic Pole

WILKES LAND

ANTARCTICA

ICE CAP

QUEEN MAUD LAND

Shackleton Ice Shelf

American Highland

Enderby Land

INDIAN OCEAN

Antarctic Circle

180°

150°W

120°W

90°W

60°W

30°W

0°

30°E

60°E

90°E

120°E

150°E

50°S

60°S

70°S

80°S

0   250   500 Miles
0   250   500 Kilometers
Projection:
Polar Azimuthal Equidistant

Economics Handbook

What Is Economics?

We can think of economics as a study of the choices people make to satisfy their needs or their wants. Which pair of shoes do you buy—the ones on sale or the ones you really like? Economics may sound dull, but it touches almost every part of your life.

Economics is also one of the major forces in world history. Societies with healthy economies tend to perform better than those with weaker economies. When a civilization decays, a weakened economy is often a leading factor. Learning a little about economics can help in your study of world history.

Glossary of Economic Terms

Here are some of the terms we use to talk about economics:

ECONOMIC SYSTEMS

Countries have developed different economic systems to help them make choices, such as what goods and services to produce, how to produce them, and for whom to produce them. The most common economic systems in the world today are market economies and mixed economies. Market economies generally perform better in terms of worker productivity and consumer choice.

capitalism See market economy.

command economy an economic system in which the central government makes all economic decisions; in theory, the means of production—industrial and agricultural—are "owned" by the people, but since the government makes all economic decisions, it is the true owner; also known as "centrally planned"; the countries of Cuba and North Korea are examples of command economies

communism a political system in which the government owns all property and runs a command economy

free enterprise a system in which businesses operate with little government involvement, such as in a country with a market economy

market economy an economic system based on private ownership, free trade, and competition; the government has little to say about what, how, or

Economic Systems	What to Produce	How to Produce	For Whom to Produce	Examples
Traditional	determined by tradition; economic roles often passed from generation to generation	determined by custom	usually centered around traditional family and social units such as a tribe	Prehistoric hunter-gatherers Aborigines of Australia
Command	determined by government officials	determined by government officials	determined by government officials	Old Kingdom Egypt Middle Ages in Europe Zhou Dynasty in China
Market	determined by individuals	determined by individuals	determined by individuals	United States Canada Australia

for whom goods and services are produced; these decisions are made by individual buyers and sellers in the marketplace; examples include Germany and the United States

mixed economy an economy that is a combination of command, market, and traditional economies; private ownership is allowed

scarcity a condition of limited resources and unlimited wants by people; a fundamental concept in economics

traditional economy an economy in which production is based on customs and tradition, and in which people often grow their own food, make their own goods, and use barter to trade

THE ECONOMY AND MONEY

People, businesses, and countries obtain the items they need and want through economic activities such as producing, selling, and buying goods or services. Countries differ in the amount of economic activity that they have and in the strength of their economies.

balance of payments the accounting record of what a nation owes to and is owed by foreign countries and international organizations

boom and bust a period of rapid economic growth followed by rapid economic contraction; see business cycle

business any commercial enterprise or establishment

business cycle the periodic fluctuation in economic activity, usually reflected in levels of employment, prices, and production or gross domestic product (GDP); there are four phases: expansion, peak, contraction, trough

THE BUSINESS CYCLE

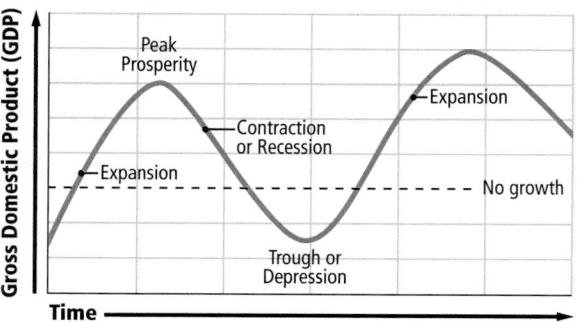

consumer a person who buys goods or services for personal use

consumer good a finished product sold to consumers for personal or home use

corporation a business in which a group of owners share in the profits and losses; as a legal entity separate from its owners, a corporation provides some protection to its owners, who are liable for the corporation's debts and losses only to the extent of their ownership investment in that corporation

currency paper or coins that a country uses for its money supply

demand the amount of goods and services that consumers are willing and able to buy at a given time; see supply and demand

devaluation a reduction in the value of a nation's currency

depression a severe drop, or contraction, in overall business activity over a long period of time; the most severe depression in modern history occurred between 1929–1939, affected nearly every country on Earth, and is known as the Great Depression

developed countries nations with strong economies and a high quality of life; often have high per capita GDPs and high levels of industrialization and technology

developing countries nations with less productive economies and a lower quality of life; often have less industrialization and technology

economic development the level of a country's economic activity, growth, and quality of life

economy the structure of economic life in a country; the total of all economic activity in a given country

entrepreneur someone who undertakes and develops a new business or develops a new product, risking failure or loss for the possibility of financial gain

foreign exchange rate the rate at which one nation's currency can get exchanged for another's

goods objects or materials that humans can purchase to satisfy their wants and needs

gross domestic product (GDP) total market value of all goods and services produced in a country in a given year; *per capita GDP* is the average value of goods and services produced per person in a country in a given year

industrialization the process of using machinery for all major forms of production

inflation an increase in overall prices

investment the purchase of something with the expectation that it will gain in value; usually property, stocks, etc.

leading indicators a set of economic factors, such as GDP and new housing construction starts, that economists use to predict a new phase of the business cycle

money any item, usually coins or paper currency, that is used in payment for goods or services

private property property that is owned by individuals and businesses, rather than the government

producer a person or group that makes goods or provides services to satisfy consumers' wants and needs

productivity the amount of goods or services that a worker or workers can produce within a given amount of time

profit the gain or excess made by selling goods or services over their costs

profit motive the desire to make profits

purchasing power the amount of income that people have available to spend on goods and services

recession a period in which economic activity drops a moderate amount; technically defined as two consecutive quarters of negative growth in GDP

scarcity a condition of limited resources and unlimited wants by people; a fundamental concept in economics

services any activities that are performed for a fee

specie coined money

standard of living how well people are living; determined by the amount of goods and services they can afford

stock a share of ownership in a corporation

stock market an organized market for the sale, purchase, or exchange of shares or stocks in corporations; also known as a "stock exchange;" the origins of stock exchanges date to the Middle Ages

supply the amount of goods and services that are available at a given time; see supply and demand

supply and demand a theory describing how prices vary according to the supply of an item available and the demand for that item: when supply exceeds demand, prices drop; when demand exceeds supply, prices rise.

SUPPLY AND DEMAND

INTERNATIONAL TRADE

Countries trade with each other to obtain resources, goods, and services. Networks of trade in the ancient world, for instance, linked the Roman Empire and China. Beginning in the Age of Exploration, growing global trade led to the development of a global economy.

absolute advantage the ability of a nation, region, or company to produce a certain good or service more efficiently and cheaply than any other nation, region, or company

balance of payments the difference between the value of a country's exports and imports

balance of trade the difference between the value of a country's exports and imports

barter the exchange of one good or service for another

black market the illegal buying and selling of goods, often at high prices

commodity a product that is the same no matter who produces it

comparative advantage the ability of a company or country to produce something at a lower cost than other companies or countries

competition rivalry between businesses selling similar goods or services; a condition that often leads to lower prices or improved products

e-commerce the electronic trading of goods and services, such as over the Internet

exports goods or services that a country sells and sends to other countries

fair trade trade between a company in a developed nation and producers in less-developed nations that aims to make sure that producers receive fair prices for their goods

free trade trade among nations that is not affected by financial or legal barriers; trade without barriers

globalization the process of rapid economic integration among countries, characterized by the free flow of capital, goods, services, and labor

imports goods or services that a country brings in or purchases from another country

interdependence a relationship between countries in which they rely on one another for resources, goods, or services

market the free exchange of goods and services; also called the market place

market clearing price the price of a good or service at which supply equals demand

mercantilism an economic theory that defined a nation's power in terms of specie; used to direct most European economies from 1500 to 1800

multinational corporation a business that is based in one nation but operates divisions or subsidiaries in other nations

one-crop economy an economy that is dominated by the production of a single product

opportunity cost the value of the next-best alternative that is sacrificed when choosing to consume or produce another good or service

outsourcing the practice of using workers from outside of a company

protectionism the use of trade barriers to protect a nation's industries against foreign competition

specialization a focus on only one or two aspects of production in order to produce a product more quickly and cheaply; for example, one worker washes the wheels of the car, another cleans the interior, and another washes the body

tariff a tax charged by a government on imported goods, usually designed to make the imported goods more expensive relative to domestic goods

trade barriers financial or legal limitations to trade; prevention of free trade; see also tariff

trade deficit a condition in international trade in which the value of a nation's imports from another country exceeds the value of its exports to that country

trade-offs the goods or services sacrificed in order to consume or produce another good or service

trade surplus a condition in international trade in which the value of a nation's exports to a particular country exceeds the value of its imports from that country

underground economy illegal economic activities and unreported legal economic activities

PERSONAL ECONOMICS

Individuals make personal choices in how they manage and use their money to satisfy their needs and desires. Individuals have the choice to spend, save, or invest their money.

asset anything of value that is owned by an individual

budget a plan listing the expenses and income of an individual or organization

bankruptcy a legal process in which an individual or business whose debts exceed the value of their assets is forgiven those debts in excess of their assets

credit a system that allows consumers to pay for goods and services over time

credit bureau a company that collects and reports to its clients information about a person's financial condition and past record in meeting his or her financial obligations

credit rating an evaluation of a person's or a company's financial condition and reliability, especially concerning its record of meeting financial obligations

debt an amount of money that is owed

disposable income money that remains after all taxes have been paid

financial institutions businesses that keep and invest people's money and loan money to people; include banks or credit unions

income a gain of money that comes typically from labor or capital

interest the money that a borrower pays to a lender in return for a loan

investment the purchase of something of value with the expectation that over time it will increase in value and produce a profit

loan money given on the condition that it will be paid back, often with interest

need an economic good or service that is basic to survival, such as food, clothing, and shelter

purchasing power the amount of income that people have available to spend on goods and services

savings money or income that is not used to purchase goods or services

stock a share of ownership in a corporation

tax a required payment to a local, state, or national government; different kinds of taxes include sales taxes, income taxes, and property taxes

wage the payment a worker receives for his or her labor

want a desire for goods and services, not necessarily accompanied by the power to satisfy them

value the worth of a good or service for the purposes of exchange, usually expressed as the amount of money a consumer is willing to pay for that good or service

RESOURCES

People and businesses need resources—such as land, labor, and money—to produce goods and services.

capital generally refers to wealth, in particular wealth that can be used to finance the production of goods or services

human capital sometimes used to refer to human skills and education that affect the production of goods and services in a company or country

labor force all people who are legally old enough to work and are either working or looking for work

natural resource any material in nature that people use and value

nonrenewable resource a resource that cannot be replaced naturally, such as coal or petroleum

raw material a natural resource used to make a product or good

renewable resource a resource that Earth replaces naturally, such as water, soil, and trees

INTERNATIONAL ORGANIZATIONS AND TRADE AGREEMENTS

Countries have formed many organizations to promote economic cooperation, growth, and trade. These organizations are important in today's global economy.

European Union (EU) an organization that promotes political and economic cooperation in Europe

International Monetary Fund (IMF) a UN agency that promotes cooperation in international trade and that works to maintain stability in the exchange of countries' currencies

North American Free Trade Agreement (NAFTA) a 1993 agreement in which Canada, Mexico, and the United became one large free-trade zone, meaning that most products could be sold across borders without any sort of tariffs or trade barriers.

Organization of Petroleum Exporting Countries (OPEC) an organization that coordinates the petroleum policies of major oil producing countries

Organization of Economic Cooperation and Development (OECD) an organization of countries that promotes democracy and market economies

United Nations (UN) an organization of countries that promotes peace and security around the globe

World Bank a UN agency that provides loans to countries for development and recovery

World Trade Organization (WTO) an international organization dealing with trade between nations

Economic Handbook Review

REVIEWING VOCABULARY AND TERMS

On a separate sheet of paper, fill in the blanks in the following sentences:

ECONOMIC SYSTEMS

1. **A.** Businesses are able to operate with little government involvement in a _____ system.
   B. In a _____, a central government makes all economic decisions.
   C. _____ is a political system in which the government owns all property and runs a command economy.
   D. Economies that combine parts of command, market, or traditional economies are called _____.
   E. _____ is another name for a market economy, which is based on private ownership, free trade, and competition.

THE ECONOMY AND MONEY

2. **A.** _____ are objects or materials that people can buy to satisfy their needs and wants.
   B. A _____ is any activity that is performed for a fee.
   C. A person who buys goods or services is a _____, and a person or group that makes goods or provides services is a _____.
   D. The amount of goods and services that consumers are willing and able to buy at any given time is known as _____.
   E. The total value of all the goods and services produced in the United States in one year is its _____.

INTERNATIONAL TRADE

3. **A.** If we have an unlimited demand for a natural resource, such as oil, and there is only so much oil in the ground, we have a condition called _____.
   B. The practice of using workers from outside of a company is called _____.
   C. The process of rapid economic integration among countries is called _____.
   D. If a country is able to produce a good or service at a lower cost than other countries, it is said to have a _____.
   E. Trade among nations that is not limited by legal or economic barriers is called _____.

PERSONAL ECONOMICS

4. **A.** A _____ is a required payment to a local, state, or national government that is used to support public services such as education, road construction, and government aid.
   B. The money we do not spend on goods or services is our _____.
   C. You can use _____ to pay for goods and services over time.
   D. The payment that a worker receives for his or her labor is called a _____.
   E. The amount of income that people have available to spend on goods and services is known as their _____.

RESOURCES

5. **A.** Diamonds and gold are examples of _____, which are any materials in nature that people use and value.
   B. The _____ consists of all people who are legally able to work and are working or looking for work.
   C. Wealth that can be used to finance the production of goods and services is called _____.
   D. Oil is an example of a _____, which is a resource that cannot be replaced naturally.
   E. Water and trees are examples of _____, resources that Earth replaces naturally.

ORGANIZATIONS

6. **A.** Many European countries have joined the _____ to help promote political and economic cooperation across Europe.
   B. The _____ consists of many agencies that promote peace and security around the world.
   C. The _____ is a UN agency that provides loans to countries to help them develop their economies.
   D. The _____ is a UN agency that helps protect the stability of countries' currencies.
   E. Many democratic countries promote market economies through the _____.

Answers

Economic Systems

1. A. *free enterprise*

B. *command economy*

C. *Communism*

D. *mixed economies*

E. *Capitalism*

The Economy and Money

2. A. *Goods*

B. *service*

C. *consumer; producer*

D. *demand*

E. *gross domestic product (GDP)*

International Trade

3. A. *scarcity*

B. *outsourcing*

C. *globalization*

D. *comparative advantage*

E. *free trade*

Personal Economics

4. A. *tax*

B. *savings*

C. *credit*

D. *wage*

E. *purchasing power*

Resources

5. A. *natural resources*

B. *labor force*

C. *capital*

D. *nonrenewable resource*

E. *renewable resources*

Organizations

6. A. *European Union (EU)*

B. *United Nations (UN)*

C. *World Bank*

D. *International Monetary Fund (IMF)*

E. *Organization of Economic Cooperation and Development (OECD)*

1. With a partner, compare prices in two grocery stores. Create a chart showing the price of five items in the two stores. Also, figure the average price of the items in each store. How do you think the fact that the stores are near each other affects prices? How might prices be different if one store went out of business? How might the prices be different or similar if the United States had a command economy?

2. With a group, choose four countries from the last unit of your textbook to research. Use your library or the Internet to find out what kind of economic system each country currently has—traditional, command, or market. Do library or Internet research to find the per capita GDP, life expectancy rate, literacy rate, and the number of TVs per 1,000 people for each country. Organize this information in a five-column table. Study the information to see if you can find any patterns. Do countries with higher per capita GDPs have higher life expectancy rates, for example?

3. Work with a partner to identify some of the many types of currency used in either Latin America, Africa, Europe, or Asia. Then imagine that you are the owners of a business in the United States. You have created a new product that you want to sell in the region you selected, but people

there do not use the same currency as you do. To sell your product, you will need to be able to exchange one type of currency for another. Search the Internet or look in a newspaper to find a list of currency exchange rates. For example, if your product sells for 1,000 dollars, what should the cost be in euros? In South African rand? In Japanese yen?

4. With three or four partners, create a skit that illustrates one of the following basic economic concepts: scarcity and limited resources, supply and demand, or opportunity costs and trade-offs. For example, a skit might illustrate supply and demand by showing how the high demand for the best seats at a concert increases the prices for those seats. Perform your skit for the class.

5. You can increase your purchasing power by saving money. One effective way to do this is to deposit savings in a bank account that earns you interest. Suppose you want to save $3,000 for a new computer. You decide to put $300 each month in a savings account that earns three percent interest compounded each month. If the interest is compounded, that means you earn interest on the money you deposit plus on the interest itself. Copy the chart below. Then complete it to show the value of savings at the end of six months.

Month	Monthly Deposit	Compounded Interest Earned (at 3%)	Value of Savings
1	$300	$9	$309.00
2	$300	$18.27	$627.27
3	$300		
4	$300		
5	$300		
6	$300		

Economics Handbook

Answers

1. *Students should recognize that competition keeps prices in the two stores close. If one store went out of business, the closing store might lower prices to sell remaining stock; with no competition, the other store might raise its prices. Student answers will vary but should be logical.*

2. *While answers will vary depending upon countries and factors chosen for comparison, higher GDP is usually correlated to higher life expectancies.*

3. *Answers will vary depending upon chosen currency and exchange rates.*

4. *See Alternative Assessment Handbook, Rubric 33: Skits and Reader's Theater.*

5. *Month 3: Interest: $27.82, Value of Savings: $955.09; Month 4: Interest: $37.65, Value of Savings: $1,292.74; Month 5: Interest: $47.78, Value of Savings: $1,640.52; Month 6: Interest: $58.21, Value of Savings: $1,998.73*

PRIMARY SOURCE LIBRARY

Excerpt from

The Dao De Jing

by Laozi

▲**The Chinese character for Dao**

About the Reading *The Dao De Jing was written about 2,500 years ago. It forms the basis of Daoism, an ancient Chinese belief system that influenced many Asian cultures. Daoism holds that all things in nature are part of a unified whole. Light balances dark, hot balances cold, yin balances yang, to produce a harmony. The word "Dao" is usually translated as "the path" or "the way." The Daoist way counsels retreat from the everyday world. By accepting and living in harmony with the laws of nature, a person can find peace.*

Chapter Two

All under heaven see beauty as beauty only
    because they also see ugliness.
All announce that good is good only because
    they also denounce what is bad.
Therefore, something and nothing give birth to
    one another
Difficult and easy complete one another.
Long and short fashion one another.
High and low arise from one another.
Notes and tones harmonize with one another.
Front and back follow one another.
Thus, the True Person acts without striving
    and teaches without words.
Deny nothing to the ten thousand things.
Nourish them without claiming authority,
Benefit them without demanding gratitude,
Do the work, then move on.
And, the fruits of your labor will last forever.

Chapter Fifteen

The ancient followers of the Dao were subtle,
    mysterious, and penetrating.
They were too deep to be <u>fathomed</u>.
All we can do is describe their appearance.
Hesitant, as if crossing a winter stream.
Watchful, as if aware of neighbors on all sides.
Respectful, like a visiting guest.
Yielding, like ice beginning to melt.
Simple, like an uncarved block.
Open, like a valley.
<u>Obscure</u>, like muddy water.
Who else can be still and let the muddy water
    slowly become clear?
Who else can remain at rest and slowly come
    to life?
Those who hold fast to the Dao do not try to
    fill themselves to the brim.
Because they do not try to be full they can be
    worn out and yet ever new.

---

fathomed understood
obscure unclear, hidden from view

 Skills FOCUS **READING LIKE A HISTORIAN**

1. **Identify** In your own words, state the main idea of Chapter Two.
2. **Elaborate** Daoism arose at a time of political instability in China. How would the ideas expressed in Daoism be appealing in a time of unrest?

Answers

Reading Like a Historian

1. *Students should recognize that the chapter discusses the balance in nature. Students should also recognize the significance of the last sentence, "…the fruits of your labor will last forever."*

2. *Students should discuss the Dao idea of retreating from everyday conflicts and strife. In their responses, students should mention the significant passages and words supporting this idea, including watchful, respectful, yielding.*

Excerpt from

The Apology

from the *Dialogues* of Plato

About the Reading *The Greek philosopher Plato (c. 429–c. 347 BC) was a student of Socrates. Socrates was known for his relentless pursuit of truth and his questioning of authority. In 399 BC, in a time of unrest following Athens' defeat in the Peloponnesian War, Socrates was brought to trial on charges of corrupting the minds of his young students. He was sentenced to death. "The Apology" is Plato's version of Socrates' defense at his trial. As used here, "apology" means a formal defense of one's beliefs or actions.*

A bust of Plato ▲

Let us reflect in another way, and we shall see that there is great reason to hope that death is a good, for one of two things: either death is a state of nothingness and utter unconsciousness, or, as men say, there is a change and migration of the soul from this world to another.

Now if you suppose that there is no consciousness, but a sleep like the sleep of him who is undisturbed even by the sight of dreams, death will be an unspeakable gain. For if a person were to select the night in which his sleep was undisturbed even by dreams, and were to compare with this the other days and nights of his life, and then were to tell us how many days and nights he had passed in the course of his life better and more pleasantly than this one, I think that any man, . . . will not find many such days or nights, when compared with the others. Now if death is like this, I say that to die is gain; for eternity is then only a single night.

But if death is the journey to another place, and there, as men say, all the dead are, what good, O my friends and judges, can be greater than this? If indeed when the pilgrim arrives in the world below, he is delivered from the professors of justice in this world, and finds the true judges who are said to give judgment there, . . . that pilgrimage will be worth making. . . . Nay, if this be true, let me die again and again. . . . Above all, I shall be able to continue my search into true and false knowledge; as in this world, so also in that; I shall find out who is wise, and who pretends to be wise, and is not. What would not a man give, O judges, to be able to examine the leader of the great Trojan expedition; . . . What infinite delight would there be in conversing with them and asking them questions! For in that world they do not put a man to death for this; certainly not. For besides being happier in that world than in this, they will be immortal, if what is said is true.

Wherefore, O judges, be of good cheer about death, and know this of a truth—that no evil can happen to a good man, either in life or after death. . . .

The hour of departure has arrived, and we go our ways—I to die, and you to live. Which is better God only knows.

Skills Focus · READING LIKE A HISTORIAN

1. **Describe** Describe how Socrates feels about death. Does he believe in an afterlife?

2. **Analyze** What does Socrates mean when he says that "in that world they do not put a man to death for this"?

3. **Elaborate** Why might Athenians turn against their tradition of free speech in a time of uncertainty?

PRIMARY SOURCE LIBRARY **R55**

Answers

Reading Like a Historian

1. *Socrates does not fear death; he states that no evil can happen to a good man, in life or after death. He does not know if the afterlife exists or not.*

2. *In the afterlife, Socrates would be able to ask questions freely; he could continue his pursuit of knowledge and not be put to death for these actions.*

3. *Free speech means that people have the right to question policies, practices, and their leaders. During times of unrest, government leaders may feel this right adds to unrest.*

Excerpt from

Politics

by Aristotle

About the Reading *One of the most influential ancient Greek philosophers, Aristotle (384–322 BC) wrote about many subjects, including biology, government, physics, and poetry. Aristotle's* Politics *is one of the most important works of political philosophy. After more than 2,000 years, it is still discussed by political scholars. In this excerpt, Aristotle describes the characteristics of a democracy.*

A bust of Aristotle ▲

The basis of a democratic state is liberty; which, according to the common opinion of men, can only be enjoyed in such a state; this they affirm to be the great end of every democracy. One principle of liberty is for all to rule and be ruled in turn, . . . whence it follows that the majority must be supreme, and that whatever the majority approve must be the end and the just. Every citizen, it is said, must have equality, and therefore in a democracy the poor have more power than the rich, because there are more of them, and the will of the majority is supreme. This, then, is one note of liberty, which all democrats affirm to be the principle of their state. Another is that a man should live as he likes. This, they say, is the privilege of a freeman, since, on the other hand, not to live as a man likes is the mark of a slave. This is the second characteristic of democracy, whence has arisen the claim of men to be ruled by none, if possible, or, if this is impossible, to rule and be ruled in turns; and so it contributes to the freedom based upon equality.

. . . [T]he characteristics of democracy are as follows: the election of officers by all out of all; and that all should rule over each, and each in his turn over all; that the appointment to all offices, or to all but those which require experience and skill, should be made by lot; that no property qualification should be required for offices, or only a very low one; that a man should not hold the same office twice, or not often, or in the case of few except military offices: that the tenure of all offices, or of as many as possible, should be brief, that all men should sit in judgment, or that judges selected out of all should judge, in all matters, or in most and in the greatest and most important . . . ; that the assembly should be supreme over all causes, or at any rate over the most important, and the <u>magistrates</u> over none or only over a very few. . . .

These are the points common to all democracies; but democracy and <u>demos</u> in their truest form are based upon the recognized principle of democratic justice, that all should count equally; for equality implies that the poor should have no more share in the government than the rich, and should not be the only rulers, but that all should rule equally according to their numbers.

---

magistrates government officials
demos democratic populace or citizenry

Skills FOCUS **READING LIKE A HISTORIAN**

1. **Identify** According to Aristotle, what are two principles of liberty? How are they related?

2. **Evaluate** Aristotle asserts that "the majority must be supreme." Do you agree or disagree? Explain your answer.

Answers

Reading Like a Historian

1. *for all to rule and be ruled in turn; man should live as he likes, freedom is based upon equality*

2. *Student answers will vary, but students should discuss the importance of "one person, one vote" in a democracy.*

PRIMARY SOURCE LIBRARY

Excerpt from

The Gallic Wars

by Julius Caesar

A statue of Julius Caesar ▲

About the Reading *Soldier and statesman, Julius Caesar helped transform ancient Rome from a republic to an empire. From 58 to 50 BC, he led a Roman army that conquered Gaul, a land that included modern-day France, Belgium, and parts of Switzerland. He published an account of his campaign in* The Gallic Wars *(50 BC). In this excerpt, Caesar describes the role of the Druids, or priests, in the lives of the Gauls.*

Throughout all Gaul there are two orders of those men who are of any rank and dignity. . . . But of these two orders, one is that of the Druids, the other that of the knights. The former are engaged in things sacred, conduct the public and the private sacrifices, and interpret all matters of religion. To these a large number of the young men <u>resort</u> for the purpose of instruction, and they [the Druids] are in great honor among them. For they determine [judge] respecting almost all controversies, public and private; and if any crime has been perpetrated, if murder has been committed, if there be any dispute about an inheritance, if any about boundaries, these same persons decide it; they decree rewards and punishments; if any one, either in a private or public capacity, has not submitted to their decision, they <u>interdict</u> him from the sacrifices. This among them is the most heavy punishment. Those who have been thus interdicted are esteemed in the number of the impious and the criminal: all shun them, and avoid their society and conversation, lest they receive some evil from their contact; nor is justice administered to them when seeking it, nor is any dignity bestowed on them. Over all these Druids one presides, who possesses supreme authority among them. Upon his death, if any individual among the rest is pre-eminent in dignity, he succeeds; but, if there are many equal, the election is made by the suffrages [votes] of the Druids; sometimes they even contend for the presidency with arms. These assemble at a fixed period of the year in a consecrated [holy] place in the territories of the Carnutes, which is reckoned the central region of the whole of Gaul. Hither all, who have disputes, assemble from every part, and submit to their decrees and determinations. This institution is supposed to have been devised in Britain, and to have been brought over from it into Gaul; and now those who desire to gain a more accurate knowledge of that system generally proceed thither [Britain] for the purpose of studying it.

resort turn to, make use of

interdict prohibit, forbid, ban

Skills FOCUS READING LIKE A HISTORIAN

1. **Describe** Are Druids religious leaders or political leaders? Explain your answer. What does this say about the Gauls?
2. **Draw Conclusions** Why might Julius Caesar want to give an account of his military triumphs in Gaul on the eve of his own war with Pompey?

PRIMARY SOURCE LIBRARY **R57**

Answers

Reading Like a Historian

1. Druids were religious leaders, but since they also served as judges and their leaders were elected, they were also political leaders.

2. to make people aware of his triumphs and to call attention to the importance of knights; remind everyone that he is a strong, victorious military leader

Excerpt from

Beowulf

by Anonymous (translated by Burton Raffel)

About the Reading *The epic poem* Beowulf *is the first great work of English literature. It tells of Beowulf, a warrior from Sweden who sails to Denmark to rid King Hrothgar's people from the monster Grendel. Much of the story is based on early Celtic and Scandinavian folk legends. In this excerpt, Beowulf and Grendel are fighting. Beowulf has seized Grendel's arm. Shrieking with pain and defeat, Grendel tries to flee. But he cannot break Beowulf's powerful grip.*

Viking carving, c. 1100s ▲

That mighty protector of men
Meant to hold the monster till its life
Leaped out, knowing the fiend was no use
To anyone in Denmark. All of Beowulf's
Band had jumped from their beds, ancestral
Swords raised and ready, determined
To protect their prince if they could. Their
    courage
Was great but all wasted: they could hack at
    Grendel
From every side, trying to open
A path for his evil soul, but their points
Could not hurt him, the sharpest and hardest
    iron
Could not scratch at his skin, for that sin-
    stained demon
Had bewitched all men's weapons, laid spells
That blunted every mortal man's blade.
And yet his time had come, his days
Were over, his death near; down
To hell he would go, swept groaning and
    helpless
To the waiting hands of still worse
    fiends.

Now he discovered—once the afflictor
Of men, tormentor of their days—what it
    meant
To feud with Almighty God: Grendel
Saw that his strength was deserting him, his
    claws
Bound fast, <u>Higlac's brave follower</u> tearing at
His hands. The monster's hatred rose higher,
But his power had gone. He twisted in pain,
And the bleeding sinews deep in his shoulder
Snapped, muscle and bone split
And broke. The battle was over, Beowulf
Had been granted new glory; Grendel escaped,
But wounded as he was could flee to his den,
His miserable hole at the bottom of the marsh,
Only to die, to wait for the end
Of all his days.

Higlac's brave follower meaning Beowulf; Higlac is Beowulf's uncle and feudal lord

Skills FOCUS   **READING LIKE A HISTORIAN**

1. **Recall** According to this excerpt, why can Beowulf's men not harm Grendel?
2. **Draw Conclusions** In what way is the poem's blending of Christian belief with ancient mythology characteristic of the Middle Ages?

Answers

Reading Like a Historian

1. *Grendel had bewitched the weapons of Beowulf's men, and his spells had blunted their sword blades.*

2. *Student answers will vary. Students should recognize that Grendel is a mythical being with mythical powers; now he is fighting against Christian forces who will overcome him. Like other stories from the Middle Ages, it is a tale of good and evil.*

Excerpt from

Magna Carta

About the Reading *Magna Carta, or Great Charter, is an agreement between King John of England and a group of English nobles. The nobles forced the king to sign the agreement in 1215. It required the king to give up certain rights, follow certain basic legal procedures, and accept that his power was subject to law. Magna Carta is one of the earliest documents limiting the powers of a ruler and listing the rights of the ruled. The "we" and "us" in* Magna Carta *refer to the king.*

Presenting Magna Carta to King John ▲

[1] In the first place we have granted to God, and by this our present charter confirmed for us and our heirs forever that the English Church shall be free, and shall have her rights entire, and her liberties inviolate; . . . We have also granted to all freemen of our kingdom, for us and our heirs forever, all the underwritten liberties, to be had and held by them and their heirs, of us and our heirs forever.

[7] A widow, after the death of her husband, shall forthwith and without difficulty have her marriage portion and inheritance; nor shall she give anything for her dower, or for her marriage portion, or for the inheritance which her husband and she held on the day of the death of that husband; and she may remain in the house of her husband for forty days after his death, within which time her dower shall be assigned to her.

[8] No widow shall be compelled to marry, so long as she prefers to live without a husband; provided always that she gives security not to marry without our consent, if she holds of us, or without the consent of the lord of whom she holds, if she holds of another.

[38] No <u>bailiff</u> for the future shall, upon his own unsupported complaint, put anyone to his "law," without credible witnesses brought for this purposes.

[39] No freemen shall be taken or imprisoned or <u>disseised</u> or exiled or in any way destroyed, nor will we go upon him nor send upon him, except by the lawful judgment of his peers or by the law of the land.

[40] To no one will we sell, to no one will we refuse or delay right or justice.

[45] We will appoint as justices, constables, sheriffs, or bailiffs only such as know the law of the realm and mean to observe it well.

---

bailiff official employed by an English sheriff to make arrests and executions

disseised deprived of legal possession of property

Skills FOCUS READING LIKE A HISTORIAN

1. **Identify Main Ideas** What are the main ideas in the first paragraph?
2. **Analyze** Paragraphs 38–40 and 45 discuss how justice should be carried out. What do they suggest about justice under King John?
3. **Make Judgments** What does *Magna Carta* tell you about the relationship between kings and nobles under the feudal system?

PRIMARY SOURCE LIBRARY

Answers

Reading Like a Historian

1. Paragraph 1: The Church shall be free, not subject to control by the king, and that the rights and liberties granted in the charter would be granted to English citizens forever.

2. King John may not have carried out laws fairly or justly. People may have been imprisoned capriciously, without a fair trial, or without any trial. Judges may have served the king, not the law, and they may not have understood the law.

3. Students should recognize that under the feudal system, kings had the power to accuse people of crimes, imprison and execute people, and that people had no recourse against a king.

R59

Excerpt from

Summa Theologica

by Thomas Aquinas

About the Reading *Thomas Aquinas (c.1225–1274) was a Roman Catholic philosopher and theologian. Many Catholics consider Aquinas to be the church's greatest theologian. The excerpt below is from Aquinas's most famous work, the* Summa Theologica, *a systematic description of Roman Catholic theology. Aquinas's method is to pose questions and then answer them. In this excerpt, he discusses who may make laws, the purpose of laws, and the limits of laws.*

Thomas Aquinas, from a 1442 book ▲

Whether the reason of any man is competent to make laws?

. . . A law, properly speaking, regards first and foremost the order to the common good. Now to order anything to the common good, belongs either to the whole people, or to someone who is the <u>viceregent</u> of the whole people. And therefore the making of a law belongs either to the whole people or to a public personage who has care of the whole people: since in all other matters the directing of anything to the end concerns him to whom the end belongs. . . .

Whether it belongs to the human law to <u>repress</u> all vices?

. . . Human law is framed for a number of human beings, the majority of whom are not perfect in virtue. Wherefore human laws do not forbid all vices, from which the virtuous <u>abstain</u>, but only the more <u>grievous</u> vices, from which it is possible for the majority to abstain; and chiefly those that are to the hurt of others, without the prohibition of which human society could not be maintained: thus human law prohibits murder, theft and such like.

. . . The purpose of human law is to lead men to virtue, not suddenly, but gradually. Wherefore it does not lay upon the multitude of imperfect men the burdens of those who are already virtuous, viz. that they should abstain from all evil. Otherwise these imperfect ones, being unable to bear such precepts, would break out into yet greater evils: thus it is written . . . (<u>Mt. 9:17</u>) that if "new wine," i.e. precepts of a perfect life, "is put into old bottles," i.e. into imperfect men, "the bottles break, and the wine runneth out."

---

viceregent assistant to a regent or ruler

repress to check, put down, or prevent

abstain refrain, keep from doing

grievous serious, grave

Mt. 9:17 A passage from the Gospel of Matthew in the Christian Bible. Aquinas frequently cites the Bible.

Skills FOCUS **READING LIKE A HISTORIAN**

1. Identify According to Aquinas, who can make laws?

2. Make Inferences What is the purpose of human law? Does Aquinas believe that governments should exercise unlimited powers when it comes to making laws?

Answers

Reading Like a Historian

1. *The people or the ruler who takes care of all the people should make laws.*

2. *to promote the common good, to take care of people; to prevent horrible deeds; to lead men to virtue*

R60

Excerpt from

Travels in Asia and Africa, 1325–1345

by Ibn Battutah

About the Reading *Ibn Battutah (1304–1369?) was one of the greatest travelers of all time. A scholar, judge, and explorer, Battutah traveled throughout the Muslim world for nearly 30 years, covering some 75,000 miles. He visited Turkey, Iran, China, Sri Lanka, Southeast Asia, India, East Africa, and North Africa. Battutah dictated the stories of his journeys to a scholar named Ibn Juzay al-Kalbi. This record of his travels was published as his book* Travels in Asia and Africa, 1325–1345. *This excerpt describes Battutah's visit to Baghdad in 1327, when it was ruled by the Mongols.*

Baghdad garden, 1396 ▲

Thence we travelled to Baghdad, the <u>Abode</u> of Peace and Capital of Islam. Here there are two bridges . . . on which the people promenade night and day, both men and women. The town has eleven cathedral mosques, eight on the right bank and three on the left, together with very many other mosques and <u>madrasas</u>, only the latter are all in ruins.

The baths at Baghdad are numerous and excellently constructed, most of them being painted with <u>pitch</u>, which has the appearance of black marble. This pitch is brought from a spring between Kufa and Basra, from which it flows continually. It gathers at the sides of the spring like clay and is shovelled up and brought to Baghdad. Each establishment has a large number of private bathrooms, every one of which has also a wash-basin in the corner, with two taps supplying hot and cold water. Every bather is given three towels, one to wear round his waist when he goes in, another to wear round his waist when he comes out, and the third to dry himself with. In no town other than Baghdad have I seen all this

elaborate arrangement, though some other towns approach it in this respect.

The western part of Baghdad was the earliest to be built, but it is now for the most part in ruins. In spite of that there remain in it still thirteen quarters, each like a city in itself and possessing two or three baths. The hospital [*maristan*] is a vast ruined edifice, of which only vestiges remain.

The eastern part has an abundance of bazaars, the largest of which is called the Tuesday bazaar. On this side there are no fruit trees, but all the fruit is brought from the western side, where there are orchards and gardens.

Abode home
madrasa (Arabic) school, often associated with a mosque
pitch sticky, oil-based substance used for waterproofing

Skills Focus — READING LIKE A HISTORIAN

1. **Interpret** Why do you think Battutah found the baths in Baghdad worth highlighting in his account? Explain your answer.
2. **Draw Conclusions** What did it say about Muslim civilization at the time that someone like Ibn Battutah could travel so widely in many different lands ?

Answers

Reading Like a Historian

1. Students should recognize that Battutah was surprised by the extensive number and the careful construction of the baths, at a time when many people did not bathe regularly.

2. Students should note that foreigners were welcome; although the logistics were probably difficult, it was possible to travel from country to country.

R61

Excerpt from

The Chronicle

by Jean de Venette

About the Reading *Jean de Venette (c. 1307–c. 1370) was a Roman Catholic monk in Paris. His* Chronicle *covers 1340 to 1368, the years when the Black Death appeared in Europe. De Venette's eyewitness account of the plague and other events provides valuable information about social, religious, and political life of the fourteenth century.*

Burying plague victims in France, 1349 ▲

In the month of August, 1348, after Vespers when the sun was beginning to set, a big and very bright star appeared above Paris, toward the west. . . . It is . . . possible that it was a <u>presage</u> of the amazing pestilence to come, which, in fact, followed very shortly. . . .

This plague, it is said, began among the unbelievers, came to Italy, and then crossing the Alps reached Avignon, where it attacked several cardinals and took from them their whole household. Then it spread, unforeseen, to France, through Gascony and Spain, little by little, from town to town, from village to village, from house to house, and finally from person to person. It even crossed over to Germany, though it was not so bad there as with us. . . .

Some said that this pestilence was caused by infection of the air and waters, since there was at this time no famine nor lack of food supplies, but on the contrary great abundance. As a result of this theory of infected water and air as the source of the plague the Jews were suddenly and violently charged with infecting wells and water and corrupting the air. The whole world rose up against them cruelly on this account. In Germany and other parts of the world where Jews lived, they were massacred and slaughtered by Christians, and many thousands were burned everywhere, indiscriminately. The unshaken, if <u>fatuous</u>, <u>constancy</u> of the men and their wives was remarkable. For mothers hurled their children first into the fire that they might not be baptized and then leaped in after them to burn with their husbands and children. It is said that many bad Christians were found who in like manner put poison into wells. But in truth, such poisonings, granted that they actually were perpetrated, could not have caused so great a plague nor have infected so many people. There were other causes; for example, the will of God and the corrupt <u>humors</u> and evil inherent in air and earth. Perhaps the poisonings, if they actually took place in some localities, reinforced these causes. The plague lasted in France for the greater part of the years 1348 and 1349 and then ceased. Many country villages and many houses in good towns remained empty and deserted. Many houses, including some splendid dwellings, very soon fell into ruins. Even in Paris several houses were thus ruined, though fewer here than elsewhere.

presage sign
fatuous silly and pointless
constancy faithfulness
humors bodily fluids whose balance was thought to be essential to well-being

Skills FOCUS **READING LIKE A HISTORIAN**

1. **Describe** What does Venette think about some of the explanations for the causes of the plague?
2. **Analyze** What do the words "fatuous" and "constancy" used to describe those Jews who chose death rather than abandon their religious faith indicate about the author's point of view?

Answers

Reading Like a Historian

1. *He does not believe that some explanations could be true, for example, poisoning could not have caused so many deaths. Venette does state that the plague could have been the will of God or problems in the air or earth.*

2. *Although Venette's words imply that he believes Jews should have chosen to convert to Christianity and live rather than die, he is impressed with the commitment of the Jewish people to their religion.*

Excerpt from
The Canterbury Tales
by Geoffrey Chaucer

About the Reading *The* Canterbury Tales *are a collection of stories that give us a picture of life in the Middle Ages. By placing travelers together on a pilgrimage, or religious journey, Chaucer (1343–1400) was able to include the entire range of English medieval society in his story. The excerpt, from the Prologue to the poem, introduces a handful of Chaucer's large cast of characters.*

Pilgrims leaving Canterbury, early 1500s ▲

It happened in that season that one day
In Southwark, at The Tabard, as I lay
Ready to go on pilgrimage and start
For Canterbury, most devout at heart,
At night there came into that <u>hostelry</u>
Some nine and twenty in a company
Of sundry folk happening then to fall
In fellowship, and they were pilgrims all
That towards Canterbury meant to ride. . .
    There was a *Knight*, a most distinguished
      man,
Who from the day on which he first began
To ride abroad had followed chivalry,
Truth, honor, generousness, and courtesy.
He had done nobly in his sovereign's war
And ridden into battle, no man more,
As well in Christian as in <u>heathen</u> places,
And ever honored for his noble graces. . .
    A *Monk* there was, one of the finest sort
Who rode the country; hunting was his sport.
A manly man, to be an Abbot able;
Many a dainty horse he had in stable. . .
He did not rate that text at a plucked hen
Which says that hunters are not holy men. . .
    There was a *Merchant* with a forking
      beard
And <u>motley</u> dress; high on his horse he sat,
Upon his head a Flemish beaver hat
And on his feet daintily buckled boots. . .
This estimable Merchant so had set
His wits to work, none knew he was in
    debt. . .

    An *Oxford Cleric*, still a student though,
One who had taken logic long ago
Was there; his horse was thinner than a rake,
And he was not too fat, I undertake,
But had a hollow look, a sober stare;
The thread upon his overcoat was bare. . .
    A worthy *woman* from beside *Bath* city
Was with us, somewhat deaf, which was a pity.
In making cloth she showed so great a bent
She bettered those of Ypres and of Ghent. . . .
A worthy woman all her life, what's more
She'd had five husbands, all at the church door,
Apart from other company in youth;
No need just now to speak of that, forsooth. . .
    There was a *Plowman* with him there. . .
Many a load of dung one time or other
He must have carted through the morning
    dew.
He was an honest worker, good and true.

---

hostelry inn; The Tabard is a lodging place
heathen pagan; for Chaucer, a non-Christian
motley multi-colored
cleric clergyman; Oxford University trained clergymen

Skills Focus — READING LIKE A HISTORIAN

1. Identify Who are some of the people on the pilgrimage?

2. Analyze How does Chaucer's cast of characters represent the changes that were taking place during the High Middle Ages?

Answers

Reading Like a Historian

1. *a variety of people, including a knight, a monk, a merchant, a student from Oxford, a clothmaker from Bath, and a plowman*

2. *People from different backgrounds and classes mixed and traveled together. They were all making a religious pilgrimage.*

PRIMARY SOURCE LIBRARY

Excerpt from

Refusal at the Diet of Worms

by Martin Luther

About the Reading *After being excommunicated by Pope Leo X, Martin Luther (1483–1546) was summoned by Emperor Charles V to appear before the Diet of Worms in 1521. He was given an opportunity to renounce his writings. Luther asked for a day to consider his response. His speech the following day became a ringing defense of individual conscience.*

Martin Luther, c. 1521 ▶

"Your Imperial Majesty and Your Lordships: I ask you to observe that my books are not all of the same kind.

"There are some in which I have dealt with piety in faith and morals with such simplicity and so agreeably with the Gospels that my adversaries themselves are compelled to admit them useful, harmless, and clearly worth reading by a Christian . . .

"The second kind consists in those writings leveled against the papacy and the doctrine of the papists, as against those who by their wicked doctrines and precedents have laid waste Christendom by doing harm to the souls and the bodies of men . . . Through the Pope's laws and through man-made teachings the consciences of the faithful . . . have been devoured . . . by unbelievable tyranny, . . . If then I <u>recant</u> these, the only effect will be to add strength to such tyranny, to open not the windows but the main doors to such blasphemy . . .

"The third kind consists of those books which I have written against private individuals, . . . who have exerted themselves in defense of the Roman tyranny and to the overthrow of that piety which I have taught. I confess that I have been more harsh against them than befits my religious vows and my profession . . .

But it is not in my power to recant them, because that recantation would give that tyranny and blasphemy an occasion to lord it over those whom I defend and to rage against God's people more violently than ever . . .

"And so, through the mercy of God, I ask Your Imperial Majesty, and Your Illustrious Lordships, or anyone of any degree, to defeat them [Luther's books] by the writings of the Prophets or by the Gospels; for I shall be most ready, if I be better instructed, to recant any error, and I shall be the first in casting my writings in the fire . . . "

Thereupon the Orator of the Empire, in a tone of <u>upbraiding</u> . . . asked for a plain reply . . . Was he prepared to recant, or no?

Luther then replied: . . . "Unless I am convicted [convinced] of error by the testimony of Scripture, . . . I cannot and will not recant anything, for to act against our conscience is neither safe for us, nor open to us. On this I take my stand. I can do no other. God help me. Amen."

---

recant withdraw and renounce
upbraiding disapproval

 Skills FOCUS **READING LIKE A HISTORIAN**

1. **Identify** What are the three categories into which Luther places his books? Why does he say that he cannot recant the second kind?
2. **Explain** Why would Luther's position have posed a threat to the authority both of the pope and of the emperor?

Answers

Reading Like a Historian

1. *One group deals with piety in faith and morals; the second group consists of writings critical of the papacy and the ways in which Church doctrines have been interpreted and applied; the third group consists of criticisms of various individuals.*

2. *Students should recognize that Luther's refusal to recant opened the door to strong challenges to the pope and emperor.*

Excerpt from
Don Quixote
by Miguel de Cervantes

About the Reading *Miguel de Cervantes (1547–1616) lived during the peak and decline of Spain's Golden Age. His masterpiece* Don Quixote *(1606; 1615) is a parody of medieval stories of knights and chivalry, which were extremely popular in Cervantes's time. It reflects the disillusionment that began to affect Spanish society as the country declined in power.*

Picasso's drawing of Don Quixote and the windmill ▲

At this point they caught sight of thirty or forty windmills which were standing on the plain there, and no sooner had Don Quixote laid eyes upon them than he turned to his <u>squire</u> and said, "Fortune is guiding our affairs better than we could have wished; for you see there before you, friend Sancho Panza, some thirty or more lawless giants with whom I mean to do battle. I shall deprive them of their lives, and with the spoils from this encounter we shall begin to enrich ourselves; for this is righteous warfare, and it is a great service to God to remove so accursed a breed from the face of the earth."

"What giants?" said Sancho Panza.

"Those that you see there," replied his master, "those with the long arms, some of which are as much as two leagues in length."

"But look, your Grace, those are not giants but windmills, and what appear to be arms are their wings which, when whirled in the breeze, cause the <u>millstone</u> to go."

"It is plain to be seen," said Don Quixote, "that you have had little experience in this matter of adventures. If you are afraid, go off to one side and say your prayers while I am engaging them in fierce, unequal combat."

Saying this, he gave spurs to his steed Rocinante, without pay-ing any heed to Sancho's warning that these were truly windmills and not giants that he was riding forth to attack. Nor even when he was close upon them did he perceive what they really were, but shouted at the top of his lungs, "Do not seek to flee, cowards and vile creatures that you are, for it is but a single knight with whom you have to deal!"

At that moment a little wind came up and the big wings began turning.

He thereupon commended himself with all his heart to his lady Dulcinea, beseeching her to <u>succor</u> him in this peril; and, being well covered with his shield and with his lance at rest, he bore down upon them at a full gallop and fell upon the first mill that stood in his way, giving a thrust at the wing, which was whirling at such a speed that his lance was broken into bits and both horse and horseman went rolling over the plain, very much battered indeed.

---

squire a young nobleman who attends a knight

millstone large stone used for grinding

succor help

 Skills Focus **READING LIKE A HISTORIAN**

1. Describe Use examples from this excerpt to show how Cervantes portrays Don Quixote as both noble and foolish.

2. Analyze In your opinion, is Don Quixote a crazy person who refuses to see things as they really are, or is he more like a person who refuses to compromise his ideals so he can achieve a greater good?

Answers

Reading Like a Historian

1. *noble—fighting for the lady Dulcinea, unafraid, courageous; foolish—fights windmills, does not listen to his friend, gets hurt*

2. *Answers will vary, but based on the excerpt, most students will probably conclude that Don Quixote was a bit crazy.*

Excerpt from

Leviathan

by Thomas Hobbes

About the Reading *Thomas Hobbes (1588–1679) wrote* Leviathan *in 1651, while in exile in France. At the time England was ruled by Parliament, making it unsafe for Royalists like Hobbes. In* Leviathan, *Hobbes argues that in their natural state people are selfish and constantly at war. The only way society can be established is if people surrender some rights to an authority that offers safety. In this excerpt, Hobbes discusses the possible forms of sovereign governments.*

Cover page of *Leviathan* ▲

The difference of <u>Commonwealths</u> consisteth in the difference of the sovereign, or the person representative of all and every one of the multitude. And because the sovereignty is either in one man, or in an assembly of more than one; and into that assembly either every man hath right to enter, or not every one, but certain men distinguished from the rest; it is <u>manifest</u> there can be but three kinds of Commonwealth. For the representative must needs be one man, or more; and if more, then it is the assembly of all, or but of a part. When the representative is one man, then is the Commonwealth a monarchy; when an assembly of all that will come together, then it is a democracy, or popular Commonwealth; when an assembly of a part only, then it is called an aristocracy. Other kind of Commonwealth there can be none: for either one, or more, or all, must have the sovereign power (which I have shown to be indivisible) entire.

There be other names of government in the histories and books of policy; as tyranny and oligarchy; but they are not the names of other forms of government, but of the same forms misliked [misnamed]. For they that are discontented under monarchy call it tyranny; and they that are displeased with aristocracy call it oligarchy: so also, they which find themselves grieved under a democracy call it anarchy, which signifies <u>want</u> of government; and yet I think no man believes that want of government is any new kind of government: nor by the same reason ought they to believe that the government is of one kind when they like it, and another when they mislike it or are oppressed by the governors.

---

commonwealth an independent state or community
manifest clear, plain, apparent
want lack, absence

 Skills FOCUS **READING LIKE A HISTORIAN**

1. **Describe** In your own words, describe Hobbes's three basic forms of commonwealth. What do they have in common?
2. **Draw a Conclusion** What does Hobbes mean when he says that "sovereign power" is "indivisible"? Does that leave any room for compromise in the struggle between king and Parliament?

Answers

Reading Like a Historian

1. *monarchy, one man; democracy, when all come together; aristocracy, assembly of one part; each is a recognized form of government with an accepted sovereign*

2. *Only one person or group can serve as a government; students should support their answers with reason and logic.*

Excerpt from
The Spirit of Laws
by Charles de Secondat, Baron de Montesquieu

About the Reading *Charles de Secondat, Baron de Montesquieu (1689–1755), was a French jurist and influential political thinker during the Enlightenment. He drew on the classical past of ancient Greece and Rome and the contemporary government of Great Britain for some of his ideas. His best-known work, The Spirit of Laws (1748), contains his theories of separation of governing powers and checks and balances, two ideas that strongly influenced the United States Constitution.*

Baron de Montesquieu ▲

In every government there are three sorts of power: the legislative; the executive, in respect to things dependent on the law of nations; and the executive, in regard to things that depend on the civil law.

By virtue of the first, the prince or magistrate enacts temporary or perpetual laws, and amends or <u>abrogates</u> those that have been already enacted. By the second, he makes peace or war, sends or receives embassies; establishes the public security, and provides against invasions. By the third, he punishes criminals, or determines the disputes that arise between individuals. The latter we shall call the judiciary power, and the other simply the executive power of the state.

The political liberty of the subject is a tranquility of mind, arising from the opinion each person has of his safety. In order to have this liberty, it is requisite the government be so constituted as one man need not be afraid of another.

When the legislative and executive powers are united in the same person, or in the same body of magistrates, there can be no liberty; because apprehensions may arise, lest the same monarch or senate should enact tyrannical laws, to execute them in a tyrannical manner.

Again, there is no liberty, if the power of judging be not separated from the legislative and executive powers. Were it joined with the legislative, the life and liberty of the subject would be exposed to <u>arbitrary</u> control, for the judge would then be the legislator. Were it joined to the executive power, the judge might behave with all the violence of an oppressor.

There would be an end of every thing were the same man, or the same body, whether of the nobles or of the people to exercise those three powers that of enacting laws, that of executing the public resolutions, and that of judging the crimes or differences of individuals.

What a situation must the poor subject be in, under those republics! The same body of magistrates are possessed, as executors of the laws, of the whole power they have given themselves in quality of legislators. They may plunder the state by their general determinations; and as they have likewise the judiciary power in their hands, every private citizen may be ruined by their particular decisions.

---

abrogates abolishes
arbitrary unrestrained; based on individual whim

Skills Focus   READING LIKE A HISTORIAN

1. **Analyze** Why does Montesquieu say it is a bad idea to combine legislative and executive powers in one person?

2. **Make Judgments** Review the excerpt from Hobbes on R66. How do his ideas and Montesquieu's differ?

Answers

Reading Like a Historian

1. If legislative and executive functions are carried out by the same person, the laws may be tyrannical and carried out in a tyrannical manner, creating fear among the people; if judges are also legislators, then judges might behave as oppressors.

2. Hobbes discusses three forms of government, monarchy, democracy, and aristocracy. Montesquieu discusses the importance of separating legislative, executive, and judicial functions within a government or governing body.

Excerpt from

The Declaration of Independence

by Thomas Jefferson

Thomas Jefferson ▲

About the Reading *In April 1775, American colonists fought English soldiers at Lexington and Concord. By the summer of 1776, events had advanced far enough that the Continental Congress voted for independence. The job of writing a formal declaration of that independence fell to Thomas Jefferson. Only 33 years old at the time, Jefferson was respected by his colleagues for his writing ability. Still, Congress revised about one-fifth of his draft. The passage that begins "We hold these truths to be self-evident," however, they left untouched. It has become a lasting statement of America's founding ideals.*

In Congress, July 4, 1776

The unanimous Declaration of the thirteen united States of America,

When in the Course of human events it becomes necessary for one people to dissolve the political bands which have connected them with another and to assume among the powers of the earth, the separate and equal station to which the Laws of Nature and of Nature's God entitle them, a decent respect to the opinions of mankind requires that they should declare the causes which <u>impel</u> them to the separation.

We hold these truths to be self-evident, that all men are created equal, that they are <u>endowed</u> by their Creator with certain <u>unalienable</u> Rights, that among these are Life, Liberty and the pursuit of Happiness. — That to secure these rights, Governments are instituted among Men, deriving their just powers from the consent of the governed, — That whenever any Form of Government becomes destructive of these ends, it is the Right of the People to alter or to abolish it, and to institute new Government, laying its foundation on such principles and organizing its powers in such form, as to them shall seem most likely to effect their Safety and Happiness.

impel force
endowed provided, given
unalienable cannot be taken away, given away, or transferred

Skills FOCUS — READING LIKE A HISTORIAN

1. **Identify Main Ideas** What is the main idea in the first paragraph of this excerpt?
2. **Interpret** How are Jefferson's words consistent with the Enlightenment's ideas of John Locke and Jean-Jacques Rousseau?
3. **Support a Position** Is it the right of the people to alter or abolish a government if they wish to? Give reasons that support your position.

Answers

Reading Like a Historian

1. *When a political relationship between peoples is dissolved, the reasons or causes should be publicly stated.*

2. *Each individual has rights that cannot be denied; these are basic human rights to which each of us is entitled. This is one of the Enlightenment ideals.*

3. *Students should recognize that throughout history, oppressed people have sought and won independence, the right to self-govern. Students should support their answers with concrete examples and logic.*

Excerpt from

The Wealth of Nations

by Adam Smith

Adam Smith ▲

About the Reading *Adam Smith (1723–1790) was a Scottish philosopher and economist. In his best-known work,* The Wealth of Nations *(1776), Smith asserted the value of free trade and few, if any, governmental regulations or restraints on trade. Smith's arguments exerted a tremendous force in shaping an era of free trade in the 1800s. In this excerpt, Smith describes how a person's self-interest guides him or her to buy and sell things in order to have the "necessaries of life."*

In civilized society he [man] stands at all times in need of the cooperation and assistance of great multitudes, while his whole life is scarce sufficient to gain the friendship of a few persons. In almost every other race of animals each individual, when it is grown up to maturity, is entirely independent, and in its natural state has occasion for the assistance of no other living creature. . . But man has almost constant occasion for the help of his <u>brethren</u>, and it is in vain for him to expect it from their <u>benevolence</u> only. He will be more likely to prevail if he can interest their self-love in his favour, and show them that it is for their own advantage to do for him what he requires of them. Whoever offers to another a bargain of any kind, proposes to do this. Give me that which I want, and you shall have this which you want, is the meaning of every such offer; and it is in this manner that we obtain from one another the far greater part of those <u>good offices</u> which we stand in need of. It is not from the benevolence of the butcher, the brewer, or the baker, that we expect our dinner, but from their regard to their own interest. We address ourselves, not to their humanity but to their self-love, and never talk to them of our own necessities but of their advantages. Nobody but a

beggar chuses [chooses] to depend chiefly upon the benevolence of his fellow-citizens. Even a beggar does not depend upon it entirely. The charity of well-disposed people, indeed, supplies him with the whole fund of his subsistence. But though this principle ultimately provides him with all the necessaries of life which he has occasion for, it neither does nor can provide him with them as he has occasion for them. The greater part of his occasional wants are supplied in the same manner as those of other people, by treaty, by barter, and by purchase. With the money which one man gives him he purchases food. The old cloaths [clothes] which another bestows upon him he exchanges for other old cloaths which suit him better, or for lodging, or for food, or for money, with which he can buy either food, cloaths, or lodging, as he has occasion.

---

brethren literally brothers; here, fellow men
benevolence kindness
good offices goods and services

 Skills Focus **READING LIKE A HISTORIAN**

1. **Recall** According to Smith, how does man in civilized society differ from "almost every other race of animals"?
2. **Analyze** Why is it necessary for a person to obtain goods by treaty, barter, or purchase?
3. **Predict** Based on this excerpt, why do you think that Smith was an advocate of liberal free trade among nations?

Answers

Reading Like a Historian

1. We need to cooperate and work together to satisfy our needs, we cannot survive alone.

2. By appealing to the needs and wants of another person, we can satisfy our own needs; people do not respond or give out of kindness, but want to get something in return.

3. Students should recognize that Smith is advocating trading what you have for what you want with no barriers to the trade.

Excerpt from the Introduction to

A Vindication of the Rights of Woman

by Mary Wollstonecraft

About the Reading *In 1789 the French Revolution erupted and, with its stirring slogan of "liberty, equality, fraternity," shook European society. Inspired by the ideas of the revolution in France, in 1792 Wollstonecraft wrote* A Vindication of the Rights of Woman. *It is a strong and passionate criticism of the social and economic institutions that lead to inequality for women.*

Mary Wollstonecraft ▲

I have sighed when obliged to confess, that either nature has made a great difference between man and man, or that civilization . . . has been very <u>partial</u>. I have . . . a profound conviction, that the neglected education of my fellow creatures is the grand source of the misery I deplore; and that women in particular, are rendered weak and wretched by a variety of concurring causes. . . . The conduct and manners of women, in fact, evidently prove, that their minds are not in a healthy state; for, like the flowers that are planted in too rich a soil, strength and usefulness are sacrificed to beauty; and the flaunting leaves, after having pleased a <u>fastidious</u> eye, fade, disregarded on the stalk, long before the season when they ought to have arrived at maturity. One cause of this barren blooming I attribute to a false system of education, gathered from the books written on this subject by men, who, considering females rather as women than human creatures, have been more anxious to make them alluring mistresses than rational wives; and the understanding of the sex has been so bubbled by this <u>specious</u> homage, that the civilized women of the present century, with a few exceptions, are only anxious to inspire love, when they ought to cherish a nobler ambition, and by their abilities and virtues exact respect. . . .

Yet, because I am a woman, I would not lead my readers to suppose, that I mean violently to agitate the contested question respecting the equality and inferiority of the sex; but . . . I shall stop a moment to deliver, in a few words, my opinion. In the government of the physical world, it is observable that the female, in general, is inferior to the male. The male pursues, the female yields—this is the law of nature; and it does not appear to be suspended or <u>abrogated</u> in favor of woman. This physical superiority cannot be denied—and it is a noble prerogative! But not content with this natural pre-eminence, men endeavor to sink us still lower, merely to render us alluring objects for a moment; and women, intoxicated by the adoration which men, under the influence of their senses, pay them, do not seek to obtain a durable interest in their hearts, or to become the friends of the fellow creatures who find amusement in their society. . . .

partial biased
fastidious overly fussy; picky
specious showy but false; lacking genuineness
abrogated abolished; repealed

Skills FOCUS   **READING LIKE A HISTORIAN**

1. **Identify Main Ideas** What is the main idea of this excerpt?
2. **Explain** In your own words, explain how Wollstonecraft responds to the issue of the equality of the sexes.
3. **Elaborate** How did Wollstonecraft's ideas differ from those of other Enlightenment thinkers? Explain.

Answers

Reading Like a Historian

1. *that men consider and treat women as inferior; women are denied education, which makes them inferior; that women should not consider themselves objects of adoration, but aspire to a larger role*

2. *She argues that women should not accept their roles as inferior beings.*

3. *Students should support their positions with logic and refer to specific arguments from the excerpt.*

Excerpt from

The Communist Manifesto

by Karl Marx and Friedrich Engels

About the Reading *In the 1840s, a new philosophy of history and the nature of human beings—communism—appeared. Communism views humans as historical beings whose lives and work are determined by the material conditions of the society in which they live. Communism also envisions a society in which there is no private property and in which workers will not be exploited and forced to live in poverty and misery. Marx and Engels wrote* The Communist Manifesto *(1848) as an explanation of the doctrines and theories of communism.*

Karl Marx ▲

The history of all hitherto existing society is the history of class struggles. . . .

Freeman and slave, patrician and plebian, lord and serf, guild-master and journeyman, in a word, oppressor and oppressed, stood in constant opposition to one another, carried on an uninterrupted, now hidden, now open fight, a fight that each time ended, either in a revolutionary reconstitution of society at large, or in the common ruin of the contending classes. . . .

We have seen above that the first step in the revolution by the working class is to raise the proletariat to the position of ruling class to win the battle of democracy.

The proletariat will use its political supremacy to wrest, by degree, all capital from the bourgeoisie, to centralize all instruments of production in the hands of the state, i.e., of the proletariat organized as the ruling class; and to increase the total productive forces as rapidly as possible. . . .

When, in the course of development, class distinctions have disappeared, and all production has been concentrated in the hands of a vast association of the whole nation, the public power will lose its political character. Political power, properly so called, is merely the organized power of one class for oppressing another. If the proletariat during its contest with the bourgeoisie is compelled, by the force of circumstances, to organize itself as a class; if, by means of a revolution, it makes itself the ruling class, and, as such, sweeps away by force the old conditions of production, then it will, along with these conditions, have swept away the conditions for the existence of class antagonisms and of classes generally, and will thereby have abolished its own supremacy as a class.

In place of the old bourgeois society, with its classes and class antagonisms, we shall have an association in which the free development of each is the condition for the free development of all.

The Communists disdain to conceal their views and aims. They openly declare that their ends can be attained only by the forcible overthrow of all existing social conditions. Let the ruling classes tremble at a communist revolution. The proletarians have nothing to lose but their chains. They have a world to win.

Proletarians of all countries, unite!

---

proletariat workers or working-class people
bourgeoisie the wealthy middle class; capitalists

Skills FOCUS **READING LIKE A HISTORIAN**

1. Recall How have all previous "class struggles" ended?

2. Analyze According to Marx, how and why will a communist revolution take place? Is his prediction realistic?

Answers

Reading Like a Historian

1. *either in a revolutionary change in society or in the ruin of the classes (rulers and subjects, oppressors and oppressed) that were fighting each other*

2. *A Communist revolution will occur as an open fight; it will occur because oppressed and oppressors are in constant opposition. Students should show an understanding of the failure of communism in Russia and the Soviet Union.*

PRIMARY SOURCE LIBRARY

Excerpt from

All Quiet on the Western Front

by Erich Maria Remarque

Trench in World War I ▲

About the Reading *Erich Maria Remarque (1898–1970) was born in Germany and served in the German army during World War I. His novel* All Quiet on the Western Front *(1929) describes the routine horrors of war that soldiers faced in the trenches that spread across Western Europe.*

There are so many airmen here, and they are so sure of themselves that they give chase to single individuals, just as though they were hares. For every one German plane there come at least five English and American. For one hungry, wretched German soldier come five of the enemy, fresh and fit. For one German army loaf there are fifty tins of canned beef over there. We are not beaten, for as soldiers we are better and more experienced; we are simply crushed and driven back by overwhelming superior forces.

Behind us lay rainy weeks—grey sky, grey fluid earth, grey dying. If we got out, the rain at once soaks through our overcoat and clothing;—and we remain wet all the time we are in the line. We never get dry. Those who will wear high boots tie sand bags round the tops so that the mud does not pour in so fast. The rifles are caked, the uniforms caked, everything is fluid and dissolved, the earth one dripping, soaked, oily mass in which lie yellow pools with red spiral streams of blood and into which the dead, wounded, and survivors slowly sink down.

The storm lashes us, out of the confusion of grey and yellow the hail of splinters whips forth the child-like cries of the wounded, and in the night shattered life groans painfully into silence.

Our hands are earth, our bodies clay and our eyes pools of rain. We do not know whether we still live.

Then the heat sinks heavily into our shell-holes like a jelly fish, moist and oppressive and on one of those late summer days, while bringing food, Kat falls. We two are alone. I bind up his wound; his shin seems to be smashed. It has got the bone, and Kat groans desperately: "At last—just at the last—"

I comfort him. "Who knows how long this mess will go on yet! Now you are saved—"

The wound begins to bleed fast. Kat cannot be left by himself while I try to find a stretcher. Anyway, I don't know of a stretcher-bearer's post in the neighborhood.

Kat is not very heavy; so I take him up on my back and start off to the dressing station with him.

Twice we rest. He suffers acutely on the way. We do not speak much. I have opened the collar of my tunic and breathe heavily, I sweat and my face is swollen with the strain of carrying. All the same I urge him to let us go on, for the place is dangerous.

Skills FOCUS — READING LIKE A HISTORIAN

1. **Describe** How does the narrator describe the conditions on the battlefield?

2. **Infer** After Kat is wounded, why do you think the narrator tells him "Now you are saved"?

Answers

Reading Like a Historian

1. *The narrator paints a grim picture of the battlefield, wet, grey, muddy, lack of food and supplies, wounded and dying soldiers.*

2. *Students should recognize that Kat will be removed from the battlefield.*

PRIMARY SOURCE LIBRARY

Excerpt from

On Nonviolent Resistance

by Mohandas K. Gandhi

About the Reading *Mohandas K. Gandhi (1869–1948) was the leader of India's fight for independence from British rule. Though Gandhi was often arrested and imprisoned for his actions, he urged his followers to adhere to the principles of nonviolence. The following excerpt is from a 1916 speech made to Gandhi's Hindu supporters at Kochrab Ashram in India. It was collected with other of Gandhi's writings and published in 1922.*

Mohandas K. Gandhi ▶

There are two ways of countering injustice. One way is to smash the head of the man who perpetrates injustice and to get your own head smashed in the process. All strong people in the world adopt this course. Everywhere wars are fought and millions of people are killed. . . . Pride makes a victorious nation bad-tempered. It falls into luxurious ways of living. Then for a time, it may be conceded, peace prevails. But after a short while, it comes more and more to be realised that the seeds of war have not been destroyed but have become a thousand times more nourished and mighty. No country has ever become, or will ever become, happy through victory in war. A nation does not rise that way, it only falls further. In fact, what comes to it is defeat, not victory. And if, perchance, either our act or our purpose was ill-conceived, it brings disaster to both belligerents.

But through the other method of combating injustice, we alone suffer the consequences of our mistakes, and the other side is wholly spared. This other method is <u>satyagraha</u>. One who resorts to it does not have to break another's head; he may merely have his own head broken. He has to be prepared to die himself suffering all the pain. . . . [N]o State is possible without two entities (the rulers and the ruled). You are

our sovereign, our Government, only so long as we consider ourselves your subjects. When we are not subjects, you are not the sovereign either. So long as it is your endeavour to control us with justice and love, we will let you do so. But if you wish to strike at us from behind, we cannot permit it. Whatever you do in other matters, you will have to ask our opinion about the laws that concern us. If you make laws to keep us suppressed in a wrongful manner and without taking us into confidence, these laws will merely adorn the statute-books. We will never obey them. Award us for it what punishment you like, we will put up with it. Send us to prison and we will live there as in a paradise. Ask us to mount the <u>scaffold</u> and we will do so laughing. Shower what sufferings you like upon us, we will calmly endure all and not hurt a hair of your body. We will gladly die and will not so much as touch you. But so long as there is yet life in these our bones, we will never comply with your arbitrary laws.

---

satyagraha power of truth without force or violence to change political and other circumstances; insistence on truth

scaffold raised wooden platform used for public executions

Skills FOCUS READING LIKE A HISTORIAN

1. Identify Main Ideas What are the two ways to counter injustice to which Gandhi refers?

2. Explain How did Gandhi use nonviolent resistance in the struggle for Indian independence?

Answers

Reading Like a Historian

1. *react violently and then be treated with violence;* satyagraha, *nonviolent protest and response*

2. *refusal to obey laws that suppress the people; accept prison sentences; endure suffering, punishment, and if necessary, death*

R73

Guernica

by Pablo Picasso

About the Artist *Pablo Picasso (1881–1973) was one of the most famous artists of the twentieth century, restlessly pioneering bold, new styles. Born in Barcelona, Spain, Picasso spent much of his career in Paris, then the art capital of the world. Picasso mostly avoided politics, but during the Spanish Civil War (1936–1939), he sided with the Republican government, which commissioned a painting to commemorate the bombing of the small town of Guernica by Fascist forces in 1937.*

About the Painting Mondays were market days in Guernica, a town of about 5,000 people with no military significance. On Monday, April 27th, 1937, Nazi bombers dumped 100,000 pounds of bombs on the town, reducing it to rubble. The Nazis, who were allies of the Spanish Nationalists, later admitted that the purpose of this unprecedented attack was to test a new military tactic—carpet-bombing civilians to kill them and break their morale.

Guernica is a large oil-on-canvas painting measuring 11.5 feet high by 25.5 feet wide. It is done in Cubist style, which uses interlocking geometric shapes to portray the world in a nonrealistic fashion. Picasso restricted his palette of colors to back, white, and shades of gray. He set the scene inside a room open at the left. A bull stands over a woman grieving over a dead child in her arms. Other images in the painting include a horse, wounded by a spear or lance; a dead soldier; a female figure floating into the room (above and to the right of the horse), carrying a lamp; and another female figure (at the far right) falling through a burning building. Interpretations of the painting and the individual images in it vary widely. Picasso said, "If you give a meaning to certain things in my paintings it may be very true, but it is not my idea to give this meaning. . . . I make the painting for the painting. I paint the objects for what they are."

Skills FOCUS READING LIKE A HISTORIAN

1. **Describe** How does Picasso show the bombing of Guernica in his painting?

2. **Interpret** Why do you think Picasso chose to create such a large painting in the Cubist style and in such stark colors? Select one part of the painting and interpret its meaning.

3. **Evaluate** Would you say that Picasso's painting is as effective a statement about the horror and destruction of war today as it was in 1937? Why or why not? Refer to images in the painting to support your answer.

Answers

Reading Like a Historian

1. *Students should recognize that people and animals have been killed, dismembered, and that this is a scene of total destruction.*

2. *Students should recognize that Picasso was a Cubist and that in the fragmentation, he was able to capture the destructive forces of the bombs. Student answers will vary depending upon the image chosen.*

3. *Student answers will vary but should show an understanding of the painting.*

Never Shall I Forget

by Elie Wiesel

Elie Wiesel ▲

About the Reading *Elie Wiesel (1928–) was fifteen years old when he and all the other Jews in his Romanian village were shipped to Nazi concentration camps in Poland and Germany during World War II. In 1955 Wiesel wrote a nine-hundred-page memoir, which was later condensed and republished under the title* Night. *The following excerpt originally appeared as a prose passage in* Night.

Never Shall I Forget

Never shall I forget that night, the first night in camp, that turned my
　　life into one long night seven times sealed.

Never shall I forget that smoke.

Never shall I forget the small faces of the children whose bodies I saw
　　transformed into smoke under a silent sky.

Never shall I forget those flames that consumed my faith for ever.

Never shall I forget the nocturnal silence that deprived me for all
　　eternity of the desire to live.

Never shall I forget those moments that murdered my God and my soul
　　and turned my dreams to ashes.

Never shall I forget those things, even were I condemned to live as long
　　as God Himself.

Never.

Skills FOCUS **READING LIKE A HISTORIAN**

1. **Describe** What is the effect on the reader of Wiesel's repeated use of the word "never"?

2. **Interpret** What does Wiesel mean by "bodies . . . transformed into smoke"?

3. **Elaborate** How did Wiesel's time in the concentration camp affect him?

Answers

Reading Like a Historian

1. Students should recognize the force of the repetition of the word "never;" these are memories that Wiesel will never forget.

2. Students should remember that during the Holocaust, Jewish people were murdered in a variety of ways, including in crematoriums.

3. It deprived him of the desire to live, filled him with horrific memories that he will never forget.

PRIMARY SOURCE LIBRARY

Excerpt from

Address to the United Nations

by Eleanor Roosevelt

Eleanor Roosevelt ▲

About the Reading *As the world learned of the atrocities committed by Nazi Germany, members of the United Nations saw the need to clarify fundamental human rights. A UN commission drafted the Universal Declaration of Human Rights. Former First Lady Eleanor Roosevelt (1884–1962) represented the United States when the UN General Assembly adopted the document on December 10, 1948. The excerpt below is taken from her speech to the General Assembly.*

In giving our approval to the Declaration today it is of primary importance that we keep clearly in mind the basic character of the document . . . It is a Declaration of basic principles of human rights and freedoms . . . to serve as a common standard of achievement for all peoples of all nations.

We stand today at the threshold of a great event both in the life of the United Nations and in the life of mankind. This Universal Declaration of Human Rights may well become the international Magna Carta of all men everywhere[,] . . . an event comparable to the proclamation of the Declaration of the Rights of Man by the French people in 1789, the adoption of the Bill of Rights by the people of the United States, and the adoption of comparable declarations at different times in other countries.

. . . This must be taken as testimony of our common aspiration first voiced in the Charter of the United Nations to lift men everywhere to a higher standard of life and to a greater enjoyment of freedom. Man's desire for peace lies behind this Declaration. The realization that the flagrant violation of human rights by Nazi and Fascist countries sowed the seeds of the last world war has

supplied the impetus for the work which brings us to the moment of achievement here today.

In a recent speech in Canada, Gladstone Murray said:

The central fact is that man is fundamentally a moral being. That the light we have is imperfect does not matter so long as we are always trying to improve it. . . . We are equal in sharing the moral freedom that distinguishes us as free men. Man's status makes each individual an end in himself. No man is by nature simply the servant of the state, or of another man . . . the ideal and fact of freedom—and not technology—are the true distinguishing marks of our civilization.

This Declaration is based upon the spiritual fact that man must have freedom in which to develop his full stature and through common effort to raise the level of human dignity. We have much to do to fully achieve and to assure the rights set forth in this Declaration.

Skills FOCUS   **READING LIKE A HISTORIAN**

1. **Recall** To what other documents does Roosevelt compare this Declaration?

2. **Explain** How were the events of World War II important in spurring the adoption of the Universal Declaration of Human Rights?

Answers

Reading Like a Historian

1. *Magna Carta, 1789 French Declaration of the Rights of Man, U.S. Constitutional Bill of Rights*

2. *The loss of life during battles, the genocide that occurred in the Holocaust, and the loss of freedom that occurred in Nazi and Fascist countries all helped spur this declaration.*

Excerpt from
Inaugural Address
by Nelson Mandela

Nelson Mandela ▲

About the Reading *After years of imprisonment for opposing white rule in South Africa, Nelson Mandela (1918–) was freed in 1990. He led his party, the African National Congress, in negotiations with the government of President F. W. de Klerk. The two leaders agreed to a timetable for the end of apartheid and a date for South Africa's first democratic elections. In that election, held in 1994, Mandela was elected president.*

Today, all of us do, by our presence here, and by our celebrations in other parts of our country and the world, confer glory and hope to newborn liberty . . .

Our daily deeds as ordinary South Africans must produce an actual South African reality that will reinforce humanity's belief in justice, strengthen its confidence in the nobility of the human soul and sustain all our hopes for a glorious life for all . . .

To my compatriots, I have no hesitation in saying that each one of us is as intimately attached to the soil of this beautiful country as are the famous jacaranda trees of Pretoria and the mimosa trees of the bushveld . . . .

That spiritual and physical oneness we all share with this common homeland explains the depth of the pain we all carried in our hearts as we saw our country tear itself apart in a terrible conflict, and as we saw it spurned, outlawed and isolated by the peoples of the world. . . .

The time for the healing of the wounds has come.

The moment to bridge the chasms that divide us has come.

The time to build is upon us.

We have, at last, achieved our political emancipation. We pledge ourselves to liberate all our people from the continuing bondage of poverty, deprivation, suffering, gender and other discrimination. . . .

We have triumphed in the effort to implant hope in the breasts of the millions of our people. We enter into a covenant that we shall build the society in which all South Africans, both black and white, will be able to walk tall, without any fear in their hearts, assured of their inalienable right to human dignity—a rainbow nation at peace with itself and the world. . . .

We understand it still that there is no easy road to freedom.

We know it well that none of us acting alone can achieve success.

We must therefore act together as a united people, for national reconciliation, for nation building, for the birth of a new world. . . .

Never, never and never again shall it be that this beautiful land will again experience the oppression of one by another and suffer the indignity of being the skunk of the world.

Let freedom reign.

Skills FOCUS — READING LIKE A HISTORIAN

1. **Identify** What does Mandela want South Africans to do—for themselves and for the people of the world?

2. **Explain** What goals does Mandela set out for South Africa's future?

Answers

Reading Like a Historian

1. *liberate people from poverty, deprivation, suffering, all types of discrimination; build a society where all people are respected*

2. *national reconciliation, nation building, end oppression*

Excerpt from

Nobel Peace Prize Acceptance Speech

by Aung San Suu Kyi

Aung San Suu Kyi ▲

About the Reading *Aung San Suu Kyi (1945–), a pro-democracy activist in Myanmar (Burma), has repeatedly been arrested by Myanmar's military dictatorship. In 1991 she was awarded the Nobel Peace Prize. Her son delivered her acceptance speech, as she was under house arrest.*

I stand before you here today to accept on behalf of my mother, Aung San Suu Kyi, this greatest of prizes, the Nobel Prize for Peace. Because circumstances do not permit my mother to be here in person, I will do my best to convey the sentiments I believe she would express.

Firstly, I know that she would begin by saying that she accepts the Nobel Prize for Peace not in her own name but in the name of all the people of Burma. She would say that this prize belongs not to her but to all those men, women and children who, even as I speak, continue to sacrifice their wellbeing, their freedom and their lives in pursuit of a democratic Burma. . . .

I know that if she were free today my mother would, in thanking you, also ask you to pray that the oppressors and the oppressed should throw down their weapons and join together to build a nation founded on humanity in the spirit of peace.

Although my mother is often described as a political dissident who strives by peaceful means for democratic change, we should remember that her quest is basically spiritual. As she has said, "The quintessential revolution is that of the spirit," and she has written of the "essential spiritual aims" of the struggle. The realization of this depends solely on human responsibility. At the root of that responsibility lies, and I quote, "the concept of perfection, the urge to achieve it, the intelligence to find a path towards it, and the will to follow that path if not to the end, at least the distance needed to rise above individual limitation . . . To live the full life," she says, "one must have the courage to bear the responsibility of the needs of others. . . ." And she links this firmly to her faith when she writes, ". . . Buddhism . . . places the greatest value on man, who alone of all beings can achieve the supreme state of <u>Buddhahood</u>. Each man has in him the potential to realize the truth through his own will and endeavor and to help others to realize it." Finally she says, "The quest for democracy in Burma is the struggle of a people to live whole, meaningful lives as free and equal members of the world community. It is part of the unceasing human endeavor to prove that the spirit of man can transcend the flaws of his nature."

Buddhahood in Buddhism, a peaceful and gentle state

Skills FOCUS   **READING LIKE A HISTORIAN**

1. **Identify** To whom would Aung San Suu Kyi say that the Nobel Peace Prize belongs?
2. **Analyze** For Suu Kyi, what is the nature of the struggle for democratic change, and how will success in that struggle be realized?

Answers

Reading Like a Historian

1. *all of the people of Burma, especially those who are working for democracy*

2. *struggle—for people to "join together to build a nation founded on humanity in the spirit of peace," for people to be able "to live whole, meaningful lives as free and equal members of the world community"; success—when Burma has a democratic government and people accept their human responsibilities*

Biographical Dictionary

A

'Abbas (1571–1629) Shah of the Safavid Empire in Persia from 1588 to 1629; his military victories against the Ottomans and skilled administration brought about a golden age in Safavid history. (p. 503)

Abraham According to the Bible, the originator of the Jewish line of descent; according to the Qu'ran, the ancestor of the Arabs; he held a deep devotion to and a great trust in the will of God. (p. 46)

Abu Bakr (c. 573–634) First Muslim caliph; as a close companion and successor to Muhammad, he unified the restive Bedouin tribes of central Arabia into a strong fighting force that he led into Iraq and Syria. (p. 263)

Aguinaldo, Emiliano (1869–1964) Self-proclaimed president of the new Philippine Republic in 1899; he fought for Filipino independence from the United States. (p. 764)

Akbar the Great (1542–1605) Mughal emperor of India; he ruled from 1556 until 1605 and continued the policy of conquest put in place under regent Bairim Khan, enlarging his empire to include nearly all of the Indian peninsula north of the Godavari River. (p. 505)

Alexander the Great (356–323 BC) King of Macedon and conqueror of much of Asia; he is considered one of the greatest generals of all time. (p. 151)

Alexander I (1777–1825) Czar of Russia from 1801 to 1825; after the defeat of the Napoleon's army in 1812, he became one of the most powerful leaders in Europe, supporting the suppression of all revolutionary movements in Russia and Europe. (p. 615)

Alexander II (1818–1881) Czar of Russia from 1855 to 1851; he freed the Russian serfs and passed other liberal reforms in Russia. (p. 730)

Alexander Nevsky (c. 1220–1263) Russian hero; he defeated the Swedes and the Teutonic knights. As grand duke of Kiev, he was vassal of the Mongols, who controlled much of Russia at the time. (p. 360)

Alfred the Great (849–899) King of Wessex from 871 to 899; he defeated Danish invaders and united Anglo-Saxon England under his control. He compiled a code of laws and promoted learning. (p. 362)

Ali, Sunni (died 1492) First great leader of Africa's Songhai Empire; he organized an uprising against Malian rule and established a new empire in Songhai. (p. 299)

Alighieri, Dante (1264–1321) Italian poet and humanist; he was the author of *The Divine Comedy*, one of the greatest literary classics. (p. 416)

Anawratha (died 1077) First king of Pagan from 1044 to 1077; he united a territory that included much of modern day Myanmar (Burma); a devout Buddhist, he built thousands of Buddhist temples. (p. 331)

Aquino, Corazon (1933–) Philippine politician and president of the Philippines from 1986 to 1992; she struggled to restore political stability, return to democracy, and rebuild the nation's economy. (p. 927)

Archimedes (287–212 BC) Greek mathematician and inventor; he was known for his work in geometry, physics, and mechanics. (p. 155)

Aristotle (384–322 BC) Greek philosopher and student of Plato; he taught that logic was the tool for any necessary inquiry; his work later became the basis for medieval scholasticism. (p. 143)

Arkwright, Richard (1732–1792) English inventor; in 1769 he patented the spinning frame, which spun stronger, thinner, thread. (p. 636)

Aryabhata (476–c. 550) Gupta mathematician and astronomer; he argued that the earth revolves around the sun and correctly explained the causes of eclipses. (p. 241)

Ashoka (died c. 232 BC) Mauryan emperor from c. 273–c. 232 BC; one of the greatest rulers of ancient India, he brought nearly all of India under one authority for the first time in history. He also promoted the spread of Buddhism. (p. 235)

Atahualpa (c. 1502–1533) Last Inca king; he was taken prisoner by Pizarro and his army after refusing to accept Christianity and surrender his empire to Spanish conquistadors. He was killed by the Spanish and his empire was taken over. (p. 478)

Atatürk, Kemal (1881–1938) Turkish leader and founder of modern Turkey; he sought to transform Turkey into a modern, secular state with separation between religion (Islam) and government. (p. 809)

Attila (c. AD 406–453) King of the Huns from 434 to 453; he invaded parts of the Roman Empire, devastating the Balkan countries and northern Greece when promised tribute was not paid. Plague and famine helped forestall his invasion of Italy. (p. 191)

Augustine of Hippo (354–430) Early Christian church father and philosopher; his writings helped shape Christian doctrine for centuries. (p. 363)

BIOGRAPHICAL DICTIONARY

Augustus (63 BC–AD 14) First emperor of Rome; he established the Second Triumvirate with Mark Antony and Lepidus. He created the imperial system of administration, established new coinages, and encouraged trade. (p. 174)

Aung San Suu Kyi (1945–) Burmese political leader; she won the Nobel Peace Prize in 1991 for her efforts to promote democracy in the country of Myanmar (Burma). (p. 919)

Aurangzeb (1618–1707) Mughal emperor of India (1658-1707); he expanded Mughal power to its greatest extant. However, his efforts to impose his strict religious views helped undermine Mughal rule. (p. 507)

Babur (1483–1530) Founder of the Mughal empire of India; he invaded Afghanistan and India and established an empire there. (p. 505)

Ban Zhao (AD 45–c. 115) Confucian scholar of the Han period; she wrote a classic Confucian text on the role of women, *Lessons for Women*, in which she argues that women should show humility and obedience toward their husbands and families. (p. 229)

Begin, Menachem (1913–1992) Israeli politician and prime minister; he signed a peace treaty with Anwar Sadat that ended thirty years of conflict between Israel and Egypt. (p. 956)

Beethoven, Ludwig van (1770–1827) German composer who spanned the Classical and Romantic periods; often considered the greatest composer; wrote symphonies, quartets, and sonatas. (p. 676)

Belisarius (c. 505–565) Byzantine general under Justinian I; he led expeditions to overthrow the Vandal kingdom in North Africa and occupied parts of Italy for Justinian. (p. 348)

Bell, Alexander Graham (1847–1922) American inventor and educator; his interest in electrical and mechanical devices to aid people with hearing impairments led to the development and patent of the telephone. (p. 664)

Ben-Gurion, David (1886–1973) Israeli statesman; he founded the Histadrut labor organization and was head of the Mapai Labor Party from 1930 to 1965. (p. 951)

bin Laden, Osama (1957–) Founder of al Qaeda, the terrorist network responsible for the attacks of September 11, 2001, and other attacks. (p. 899)

Bismarck, Otto von (1815–1898) German statesman; he became the leading force behind German unification. His main political goal was for Prussia to gain power over Austria. (p. 719)

Bolívar, Simón (1783–1830) South American revolutionary who led independence wars in the present nations of Venezuela, Colombia, Panama, Ecuador, Peru, and Bolivia. (p. 699)

Bonaparte, Napoleon (1769–1821) general; Emperor of France; he seized power in a coup d'état in 1799; he led French armies in conquering much of Europe, placing his relatives in positions of power. Defeated at the Battle of Waterloo, he was exiled on the island of Elba. (p. 609)

Borromeo, Charles (1538–1584) Archbishop of Milan from 1560 to 1584; he took steps to implement the reforms ordered by the Council of Trent. (p. 457)

Buddha (c. 563–483 BC) Founder of Buddhism, also known as Siddhartha Gautama; he gave up princely life to search for truth and enlightenment. He established the Buddhist religion based on the Four Noble Truths and the Eightfold Path. (p. 104)

Buonarroti, Michelangelo (1475–1564) Italian Renaissance sculptor, architect, painter, and poet; he sculpted the *Pieta* and the *David*, and he painted the ceiling of the Sistine Chapel. (p. 443)

Caesar, Julius (100–47 BC) Roman general and one of the greatest military leaders in history; he conquered most of Gaul and was named dictator for life in Rome. He was later murdered by a group of senators who opposed his enlarged powers. (p. 173)

Calvin, John (1509–1564) French Protestant theologian of the Reformation; he founded Calvinism, which was associated with the doctrine of predestination. (p. 452)

Carnegie, Andrew (1835–1919) American industrialist and humanitarian; he led the expansion of the U. S. steel industry in the late 1800s and early 1900s. (p. 647)

Carranza, Venustiano (1859–1920) Mexican revolutionist and politician; he led forces against Vitoriano Huerta during the Mexican Revolution (1910-1920). (p. 763)

Castiglione, Baldassare (1479–1529) Italian diplomat and writer; he wrote *The Courtier*, one of the most important books of the Renaissance, in which he delineates the rules and correct behaviors for a courtier to adopt in order to win favor from a ruler. (p. 440)

Castro, Fidel (1926–) Communist political leader of Cuba; he helped overthrow the Cuban government in 1959 and seized control of the country, exercising total control of the government and economy. (p. 969)

Catherine the Great (1729–1796) Czarina of Russia from 1762 to 1796; ruling with absolute power, she introduced a number of reforms that extended Peter the Great's policy of "westernization." (p. 555)

Cavour, Camillo di (1810–1861) Italian statesman and premier of the kingdom of Sardinia; architect of the Italian unification movement in the late 1800s. (p. 715)

Cervantes, Miguel de (1547–1616) Spanish novelist, dramatist, and poet; he wrote *Don Quixote de la Mancha*. (p. 537)

Chamorro, Violetta (1929–) President of Nicaragua from 1990 to 1997; she was the first woman to govern a Central American nation. (p. 979)

Chandragupta Maurya (c. 321–c. 298 BC) Founder of the Mauryan Empire in India; he conquered much of northern India and ruled over parts of Pakistan. (p. 233)

Chandra Gupta II (300s–400s) Emperor of the Gupta; during his reign the Gupta Empire reached its peak. He extended the territory of the empire. His regime was a time of prosperity and cultural flourishing for much of India. (p. 237)

Charlemagne (c. 742–814) King of the Franks from 768 to 814; he united much of France, Germany and northern Italy in on Frankish empire; crowned Emperor of the e Roman people in 800. (p. 373)

Charles I (1600–1649) King of England, Scotland, and Ireland from 1625 to 1649; his conflict with Parliament started the English Civil War. He was beheaded in 1649. (p. 547)

Charles II (1630–1685) King of England, Scotland, and Ireland from 1660 to 1685 and eldest son of King Charles I; he was asked by Parliament to rule England after the death of Oliver Cromwell. (p. 549)

Charles V (1500–1558) King of Spain (as Charles I); Holy Roman Emperor (as Charles V) from 1519 to 1558; his opposition to the Protestant Reformation embroiled Spain in a series of wars throughout his reign. (p. 536)

Chaucer, Geoffrey (c. 1340–1400) English poet; he wrote *The Canterbury Tales*, 23 stories of pilgrims assembled at the Tabard Inn in Southwark. (p. 416)

Chávez, Hugo (1954–) Venezuelan political leader and president; he set out to eliminate poverty in his country, but his methods of doing so tended to turn his country away from democracy and toward a dictatorship. (p. 982)

Churchill, Winston (1874–1965) British prime minister; he opposed the policy of appeasement and led Great Britain through World War II. (p. 836)

Cleisthenes (died c. 570 BC) Ancient Greek ruler often called the "father of democracy." He increased the size of the council that governed Athens to 500, and he reorganized Athenian tribes on a geographical rather than familial basis. (p. 135)

Clovis (c. 466–511) King of the Franks from 481 to 511; he established the kingdom of the Franks in the late 400s; according to legend, his victories convinced him to convert to Christianity. (p. 362)

Columbus, Christopher (1451–1506) Italian explorer, sailing for Spain, who reached the Americas in 1492 while searching for a western sea route from Europe to Asia. (p. 473)

Copernicus, Nicolaus (1473–1543) Polish astronomer; he proposed the heliocentric, or sun-centered, theory of the universe. (p. 569)

Cortés, Hernan (1485–1547) Spanish conquistador; from 1519 to 1521, he defeated the Aztec Empire, conquering Mexico for Spain. (p. 477)

Cromwell, Oliver (1599–1658) Lord Protector of England; in 1642 he led Parliament's forces in deposing King Charles I; he became ruler of England in 1653. (p. 547)

Cruz, Sister Juana Ines de la (1651–1695) Mexican nun and poet; she wrote poetry, prose, and plays. (p. 537)

Curie, Marie (1867–1934) and **Pierre** (1859–1906) European chemists and physicists; they discovered radium and polonium in 1898. (p. 667)

Cyril (c. 827–869) and **Methodius** (c. 825–884) Brothers and Christian missionaries; their use of the Slavonic language helped convert many Moravians to Christianity. They developed a written alphabet for the Slavonic language that became known as the Cyrillic alphabet. (p. 358)

Cyrus the Great (died 529 BC) King of Persia and founder of the Persian Empire; he defeated the Median army and united the Persians and Medians under his rule. (p. 51)

Darius I (550–486 BC) King of Persia from 522 to 486 BC; he reorganized and strengthened the Persian Empire by reforming the army and the government. (p. 52)

Darwin, Charles (1809–1882) English scientist; he proposed the theory of evolution through natural selection, which came to be known as Darwinism. (p. 667)

Deng Xiaoping (1904–1997) Chinese revolutionary and government leader; after a struggle for power following Mao's death, Deng took power in 1981; he made far-reaching market reforms in the Chinese economy. (p. 923)

Descartes, René (1596–1650) French philosopher, mathematician, and scientist; his belief that all things should be doubted until they could be proved by reason became one of the underpinnings of the scientific method. (p. 569)

Díaz, Porfirio (1830–1915) Mexican general and politician; president and dictator of Mexico for 30 years, he sought foreign investment but ruled harshly. (p. 762)

Dickens, Charles (1812–1870) English author during the Victorian era; he wrote *Great Expectations, A Christmas Carol, Oliver Twist,* and *A Tale of Two Cities,* among many other works. (p. 676)

Diocletian (245–313) Roman emperor from 284 to 305; he divided the Roman Empire into eastern and western halves. (p. 189)

Disraeli, Benjamin (1804–1881) British statesman; as prime minister, he oversaw the passage of key reforms, including an extension of male suffrage. (p. 688)

Drake, Sir Francis (c. 1540–1596) English admiral; he rounded the tip of South America and explored the west coast. He ended up heading west to return to England, thus becoming the second man to circumnavigate the globe. (p. 474)

Dürer, Albrecht (1471–1528) German painter, engraver, and theoretician; he combined Italian Renaissance techniques of realism and perspective with elements unique to the northern Renaissance, such as the use of oils in his painting. (p. 447)

Edison, Thomas (1847–1931) American inventor of over 1,000 patents, including the light bulb; he established a power plant that supplied electricity to parts of New York City. (p. 660)

Einstein, Albert (1879–1955) American theoretical physicist; he developed the theory of relativity among his many scientific theories and was awarded the Nobel Prize for physics in 1921. (p. 668)

Eisenhower, Dwight D. (1890–1969) General; thirty-fourth president of the United States; as Supreme Allied Commander in Europe during World War II, he led the Allied invasions of North Africa and of France (D-Day). (p. 846)

El Greco (c. 1541–1614) Greek painter in Spain; chiefly religious in nature, his works express the spirit of the Counter, or Catholic, Reformation. (p. 537)

Eleanor of Aquitaine (c. 1122–1204) Queen of France and England; she was one of the most powerful women in Europe during the Middle Ages. (p. 388)

Elizabeth I (1533–1603) Queen of England from 1558 to 1603; a skillful politician and diplomat, she reasserted Protestant supremacy in England. (p. 454)

Equiano, Olaudah (c. 1750–1797) African American abolitionist; he was an enslaved African who was eventually freed, became a leader of the abolitionist movement, and wrote *The Interesting Narrative of the Life of Olaudah Equiano.* (p. 489)

Erasmus, Desiderius (1466–1536) Dutch priest and humanist; he wrote on the need for a pure and simple Christian life. To his regret, his writings fanned the flames of discontent with the Roman Catholic Church. (p. 445)

Erastosthenes (c. 276–c. 194 BC) Greek astronomer and geographer; he calculated the circumference of the globe using careful observations and simple geometry. (p. 155)

Eriksson, Leif (died c. 1020) Norwegian explorer; he led a group of Vikings to North America and settled on the eastern shore of modern-day Canada. (p. 380)

Euclid (died c. 275 BC) Greek geometer; he created practical books on geometric forms and mathematics. His work formed the basis for later European studies in geometry. (p. 155)

Eyck, Jan van (c. 1390–1441) Flemish painter; his paintings focused on landscapes and domestic life and fused the everyday with the religious. (p. 447)

Ezana (c. AD 300s) Aksumite ruler; he destroyed the Kush capital of Meroë and took over the kingdom of Kush around AD 320. (p. 289)

Faraday, Michael (1791–1867) English scientist; he invented the dynamo—a machine that generated electricity. His invention eventually led to today's electrical generators. (p. 660)

Ford, Henry (1863–1947) American business leader; he revolutionized factory production through use of the assembly line and popularized the affordable automobile (Model T). (p. 662)

Fox, Vicente (1942–) Mexican political leader and president of Mexico; he was the first democratically elected opposition candidate in Mexico's history. (p. 981)

Francis of Sales (1567–1622) French Roman Catholic leader and preacher; he worked to win back the district of Savoy, in France, from Calvinism. (p. 457)

Franklin, Benjamin (1706–1790) American statesman; he was a philosopher, scientist, inventor, writer, publisher, first U. S. postmaster, and member of the committee to draft the Declaration of Independence. (p. 582)

Franz Ferdinand (1863–1914) Heir to the throne of Austria-Hungary whose assassination by a Serb nationalist started World War I. (p. 780)

Franz Josef I (1830–1916) Emperor of Austria-Hungary from 1848 to 1916; during his long reign he took small steps to address the democratic and nationalist aspirations of his people. (p. 724)

Frederick the Great (1712–1786) King of Prussia from 1740 to 1786; through victories in a series of wars with Austria, Prussia's main rival for dominance among the German states, Frederick made Prussia a major European power in the late 1700s. (p. 557)

Frederick Wilhelm IV (1795–1861) King of Prussia from 1840 to 1861; when revolution broke out in Prussia in 1848, Frederick Wilhelm promised a constitution and other reforms, which he later disavowed. (p. 719)

Freud, Sigmund (1856–1939) Austrian psychiatrist and founder of psychoanalysis; he treated hysteria using hypnosis and believed that complexes of repressed and forgotten impressions underlie all abnormal mental states. (p. 670)

Fulton, Robert (1765–1815) American engineer and inventor; he built the first commercially successful, full-sized steamboat, the *Clermont*, which led to the development of commercial steamboat ferry services for goods and people. (p. 637)

Galen (129–c. 199) Greek physician; he wrote several volumes that summarized all the medical knowledge of his day. (p. 180)

Galilei, Galileo (1564–1642) Italian astronomer, mathematician, and physicist; he discovered the law of motion of falling objects and invented the first working telescope; his discoveries put him into conflict with the Roman Catholic Church. (p. 570)

Gama, Vasco da (c. 1469-1524) Portuguese navigator; in 1497-1499, he became the first European to sail around Africa and reach India by sea. (p. 472)

Gandhi, Indira (1917–1984) Indian politician; daughter and mother of Indian prime ministers, she was India's first female prime minister; her term was marred by sectarian violence involving India's Sikh minority. (p. 911)

Gandhi, Mohandas (1869–1948) Leader of India's struggle for independence from Great Britain; he organized the population for protest through the methods of nonviolent resistance and civil disobedience. (p. 809)

Garibaldi, Giuseppe (1807–1882) Italian military and nationalist leader; he unified the southern states of Italy and joined them to the north to form the united Kingdom of Italy. (p. 716)

Genghis Khan (c. 1162–1227) Mongol warrior and ruler; he forged the Mongol tribes into a fighting force that conquered much of Asia, including parts of China. (p. 317)

Gorbachev, Mikhail (1931–) Russian politician; he was the last president of the Soviet Union before the country's collapse in 1991. (p. 892)

Gracchi Tiberius Sempornius Gracchus (163–133) and his brother Gaius Sempronius Gracchus (153–121); Roman statesmen; they tried to help ex-soldiers in Rome by redistributing public land to small farmers. The Roman elite reacted violently to these actions and led mobs that killed the brothers. (p. 172)

Gregory VII (c. 1020–1085) Roman Catholic pope; his assertion of church power to appoint bishops led him into conflict with Holy Roman Emperor Henry IV, who claimed the powers for himself. Gregory excommunicated Henry, who relented. (p. 394)

Gregory the Great (c. 540–604) Roman Catholic pope from 590 to 604; he restored monastic discipline and was zealous in propagating Christianity. (p. 363)

Guevara, Che (1928–1967) Argentinean revolutionary leader; he was an aide to Fidel Castro during the Cuban revolution. (p. 969)

Gutenberg, Johannes (c. 1397–1468) German inventor and printer; he invented movable type. His first printed publication was a 1,282-page Bible. (p. 445)

Hammurabi (ruled c. 1792–1750 BC) King of Babylonia; he was a brilliant military leader who brought all of Mesopotamia into the Babylonian Empire. He is known for his uniform code of 282 laws, the earliest known set of written laws. (p. 37)

Harun al-Rashid (c. 766–809) Fifth Abbasid caliph (ruled 786 to 809); under his rule, the Abbasid dynasty reached its height and Islamic culture experienced a flowering. (p. 266)

Hatshepsut (died 1468 BC) Queen of ancient Egypt; she took the throne in place of her stepson, Thutmose III, and during her reign, focused on temple-building projects and trade. (p. 68)

Henry IV (1050–1106) King of Germany from 1056 to 1106 and Holy Roman Emperor from 1056 to 1106; he was excommunicated by Pope Gregory VII over bishop appointments; he acknowledged the pope's authority and was readmitted to the church. (p. 394)

Henry IV (1553–1610) King of France from 1589 to 1610; he issued the Edict of Nantes (1598), which permitted Protestant worship, in order to restore peace to France. (p. 541)

Henry VII (1457–1509) King of England; he was the first king from the house of Tudor; his defeat of Richard III and his assumption of the throne marked the end of the Wars of the Roses and the beginning of a new era in England's history. (p. 422)

Henry VIII (1491–1547) King of England from 1509 to 1547; his desire to annul his marriage led to a conflict with the pope, England's break with the Roman Catholic Church, and its embrace of Protestantism. Henry established the Church of England in 1532. (p. 453)

Henry the Navigator (1394–1460) Prince of Portugal and patron of exploration; he made no voyages himself but spent his life directing voyages of discovery along the African coast. (p. 471)

Herodotus (c. 484–c. 425 BC) Greek historian; his most famous work is *The Histories*, which describes major events of the Persian Wars. (p. 145)

Herzl, Theodor (1860–1904) Hungarian Zionist leader; in 1896 he wrote *The Jewish State*, which outlined plans for an independent Jewish country. (p. 694)

Hidalgo, Miguel (1753–1811) Mexican priest and revolutionary; he made the first public call for Mexican independence. In 1810 he rang a bell in his hometown calling the peasants to fight for their independence from Spain. He was captured and executed. (p. 696)

Hildegard of Bingen (1098–1179) Medieval nun and author; she wrote dozens of poems and music to accompany them. (p. 415)

Hirohito (1901–1989) Emperor of Japan from 1926 to 1989; he led Japan during World War II and was forced into unconditional surrender following the atomic-bomb attacks on Hiroshima and Nagasaki. (p. 861)

Hitler, Adolf (1889–1945) Totalitarian dictator of Germany; his invasion of European countries led to World War II. He espoused notions of racial superiority and was responsible for the mass murder of millions of Jews and others in the Holocaust. (p. 826)

Ho Chi Minh (1890–1969) Vietnamese nationalist and revolutionary leader; president of the Democratic Republic of Vietnam (North Vietnam) from 1945 to 1969; he wanted to bring communism to South Vietnam. (p. 915)

Homer (800s–700s BC) Greek poet, he wrote the epic poems the *Iliad* and the *Odyssey*, which tell stories set during and after the Trojan War. (p. 144)

Hongwu (1328–1398) First emperor of the Ming dynasty in China; he drove the Mongols out of China, Korea, and Manchuria. He concentrated all power in his own hands. (p. 510)

Hudson, Henry (died 1611) English navigator; he sailed for the Dutch East India Company and discovered the Hudson River in present-day New York. (p. 474)

Hugh Capet (c. 938–996) King of France from 987 to 996; elected by Frankish nobles to succeed King Louis V, he founded the Capetian dynasty, which ruled France for 300 years. (p. 390)

Hussein, Saddam (1937–) President of Iraq from 1979 to 2003; he established a brutal dictatorship, suppressed all dissent, and led Iraq into wars with Iran (1980–1990) and Kuwait (1991). He was removed from power in 2003 by U. S. -led forces. (p. 898)

Ibn Khaldun (1211–1282) Muslim writer; he wrote the *Muqaddimah*, which traced the history of the Muslim world. (p. 272)

Ibn Rushd (1126–1198) Spanish-Arab philosopher; also known as Averroes; influenced by Aristotle, his best-known writings explore the relationship between reason and faith. (p. 272)

Ibn Sina (980–1037) Persian philosopher and physician; also known as Avicenna; noted as a medical scholar, he contributed to many other fields of study. (p. 272)

Ibsen, Henrik (1828–1906) Norwegian poet and dramatist; he wrote *A Doll's House*, which revealed the unfair treatment of women in the home. (p. 676)

Ignatius of Loyola (1491–1556) Spanish churchman and founder of the Jesuits (1534); this order of Roman Catholic priests proved an effective force for reviving Catholicism during the Catholic Reformation. (p. 456)

Ivan IV (1530–1584) Grand duke of Russia and the first Russian ruler to assume to title of czar; also known as Ivan the Terrible. He instituted a campaign of terror against disfavored boyars. He killed his son, leaving no heir to the throne. (p. 553)

Jefferson, Thomas (1743–1826) American statesman; third president of the United States; he was a member of two Continental Congresses, chairman of the committee to draft the Declaration of Independence, the Declaration's main author and one of its signers. (p. 582)

Jesus of Nazareth (AD 1–30) First-century Jewish teacher and prophet; he founded Christianity and taught about kindness and love of God. His teachings spread through the Roman Empire and, eventually, the rest of the world. (p. 184)

Jiang Jieshi (1887–1975) Chinese general and politician; he succeeded Sun Yixian as leader of the Nationalist Party in China and led attacks against Communists in China in the 1920s. (p. 808)

Jinnah, Muhammad Ali (1876–1948) Indian politician and founder of Pakistan; as leader of the Muslim League, he believed that Indian Muslims needed a separate nation and called for a partition in 1940. (p. 910)

Joan of Arc (c. 1412–1431) French soldier and national heroine; she rallied the French troops during the Hundred Years' War and was burned at the stake for heresy. (p. 421)

Johanson, Donald (1943–) American anthropologist; he discovered a partial Australopithecine skeleton in Ethiopia, which he named Lucy. (p. 6)

Justinian I (483–565) Byzantine emperor from 527 to 565; he reunited the parts of the Roman Empire, simplified Roman laws with Justinian's Code, and ordered Hagia Sophia built. (p. 348)

Kalidasa (c. AD 600s) Indian dramatist and poet, often called the "Indian Shakespeare;" his poems and plays were written on historical, mythological, and romantic subjects. (p. 240)

Kangxi (1654–1722) Chinese emperor of the Qing dynasty from 1661 to 1722; his reign was one of relative internal peace. He constructed many public works and was a patron of the arts. (p. 512)

Kautilya (c. 300 BC) Indian philosopher and politician and advisor to Chandragupta; he wrote *Arthashastra*, a great work on how rulers seize and maintain power. (p. 234)

Kenyatta, Jomo (c. 1893–1978) African political leader and first president of Kenya from 1964 to 1978; he was a leader of the African nationalist movement. (p. 938)

Keynes, John Maynard (1883–1946) British economist; his revolutionary economic theory, which stated that governments could prevent economic downturns by deficit spending, provided the basis for some of Franklin D. Roosevelt's New Deal policies. (p. 815)

Khomeini, Ayatollah Ruhollah (c. 1900–1989) Iranian political and religious leader; he led a revolution to overthrow the Shah of Iran's government in 1979; he ruled the country for the next ten years. (p. 958)

Kim Il Sung (1912–1994) North Korean political leader and chief of state of the Democratic People's Republic of Korea from 1948 to 1994; he established a government party based on the Soviet model, with the state controlling much of the economy, financing heavy industry and the military. (p. 928)

Kim Jung Il (1941–) Dictatorial leader of North Korea; under his rule the North Korean economy has continued to deteriorate. (p. 928)

King, Martin Luther Jr. (1929–1968) American civil rights leader; he was a celebrated and charismatic advocate of civil rights for African Americans in the 1950s and 1960s. He was assassinated in 1968. (p. 889)

Klerk, F. W. de (1936–) South African statesman and president of South Africa from 1989 to 1994; he began the process of ending apartheid in South Africa by lifting the ban on antiapartheid parties and releasing Nelson Mandela from prison. (p. 944)

Kublai Khan (1215–1294) Mongol emperor and founder of the Yüan Dynasty, grandson of Genghis Khan; he continued his grandfather's wars of conquest in China. He moved the Mongol capital to China and expanded his empire beyond China. (p. 318)

Lalibela (c. 1180–c. 1250) Ethiopian ruler from about 1200 to 1250; he is known for building large stone Christian churches, many of which are still standing today. (p. 290)

Las Casas, Bartolomé de (1474–1566) Spanish missionary and historian; he sought to protect Native Americans from Spanish mistreatment by replacing them as laborers with imported African slaves. (p. 479)

Leakey, Louis (1903–1972) British archaeologist and anthropologist of East Africa; he was convinced that Africa was the best place to search for human origins and made many important archaeological discoveries there. (p. 7)

Leakey, Mary (1913–1996) British archaeologist; along with her husband, Louis, she made great discoveries of early hominids in East Africa. (p. 6)

Lenin, Vladimir (1870–1924) Russian revolutionary and founder of Bolshevism; he rose to power in Russia following the Russian Revolution in 1917. (p. 730)

Leonardo da Vinci (1452–1519) Italian painter, sculptor, architect, musician, engineer, and scientist; his interests and talents spanned numerous disciplines. He painted the *Mona Lisa*. (p. 443)

Leopold II (1835–1909) King of Belgium from 1865 to 1909; he financed an expedition to the Congo and assumed the title of sovereign of the Congo Free State. His armies treated the Congolese brutally and exploited them as workers. (p. 758)

Lincoln, Abraham (1809–1865) Sixteenth president of the United States; his election led to the secession of the Southern states and the Civil War; Lincoln successfully preserved the Union and issued the Emancipation Proclamation. He was assassinated in 1865. (p. 703)

Liu Bang (c. 250–195 BC) First emperor of the Han dynasty in China; he did away with the Legalist policies of the Qin and appointed Confucian scholars as his advisors. (p. 224)

Locke, John (1632–1704) English philosopher and founder of British empiricism; he developed political and economic theories during the Enlightenment. He wrote *Two Treatises on Government* in which he declared that people have a right to rebel against governments that do not protect their rights. (p. 575)

Louis XIII (1601–1643) King of France from 1610 to 1643; a relatively weak ruler, he let Cardinal Richelieu, his chief minister, hold great sway during his reign. (p. 541)

Louis XIV (1638–1715) King of France from 1643 to 1715; known as the Sun King, he built the palace at Versailles as a means to consolidate absolute power; a series of wars at the end of his long reign drained France's wealth. (p. 542)

Louis XVI (1754–1793) King of France from 1774 to 1792; his unpopular policies helped trigger the French Revolution. Deposed by the National Convention, he was executed by guillotine. (p. 594)

Louis Philippe (1773–1850) King of France from 1830 to 1848; he came to power after the July Revolution and he was known as the "citizen king" for showing an interest in the working class and having much in common with the middle class. (p. 692)

Louis Napoleon (1808–1873) Emperor of France from 1852 to 1870; after winning the presidential election in 1848, he staged a coup d'état and took absolute power. A nephew of Napoleon I, he ruled during a time of economic prosperity in France. (p. 692)

Luther, Martin (1483–1546) German monk whose protests against the Catholic Church in 1517 (the Ninety-Five Theses) led to calls for reform and to the movement known as the Reformation. (p. 450)

Macartney, Lord George (1737–1806) British diplomat; he visited China in 1793 to discuss expanding trade. He was sent away after his goods were found to be inferior and he refused to kowtow to the emperor. (p. 513)

MacArthur, Douglas (1880–1964) American general, he commanded U. S. troops in the southwest Pacific during World War II and administered Japan after the war ended. He later commanded UN forces at the beginning of the Korean War, until he was removed by President Truman. (p. 848)

Machiavelli, Niccolo (1469–1527) Italian political philosopher and statesman; he wrote *The Prince*, which advised rulers to separate morals from politics. He insisted that a ruler do whatever is necessary to succeed and that the ends would justify the means. (p. 440)

Madison, James (1751–1836) American statesman; he was a delegate to the Constitutional Convention and the. He is known as the "father of the Constitution." (p. 584)

Magellan, Ferdinand (c. 1480–1521) Portuguese navigator; his ships were the first to circumnavigate the globe, though he died on the journey. (p. 474)

Malthus, Thomas (1766–1834) English economist and sociologist; his theory that population growth would exceed the growth of food production and that poverty would always exist was used to justify low wages and laws restricting charity to the poor. (p. 647)

Mandela, Nelson (1918–) Former guerrilla fighter; statesman; he helped end apartheid and became the first black president of South Africa. (p. 944)

Mansa Musa (died 1332) Leader of Mali who held power from 1307 to 1332; he conquered the Kingdom of Songhai. He expanded trade, supported the arts, and promoted Islam. (p. 298)

Mao Zedong (1893–1976) Leader of the Chinese Communists; he led a successful revolution and established a Communist government in China in 1949. (p. 808)

Marconi, Guglielmo (1874–1937) Italian physicist; he experimented with wireless telegraphy and established communication across the English Channel between France and England. (p. 664)

Marcos, Ferdinand (1917–1989) Philippine politician; he was elected president of the Philippines in 1965, but soon became an authoritarian dictator. He imposed martial law, arrested his political opponents, and stole millions from his country's treasury. (p. 927)

Maria Theresa (1717–1780) Austrian archduchess, queen of Bohemia and Hungary from 1740 to 1780; she took the throne after the War of the Austrian Succession. She was on of the most beloved monarchs in the history of Austria. (p. 556)

Marie-Antoinette (1755–1793) Queen of France, wife of King Louis XVI; she was queen during the French Revolution and disliked by many French citizens. She was found guilty of treason and guillotined. (p. 594)

Marius, Gaius (c. 157–86 BC) Roman general and politician; he eliminated property restrictions for acceptance into the army and began to accept anyone who wished to join the Roman army. He made armies into private forces that became devoted to their generals. (p. 172)

Martí, José (1853–1895) Cuban writer and independence fighter; he was killed in battle but became a symbol of Cuba's fight for freedom. (p. 763)

Marx, Karl (1818–1883) German social philosopher and chief theorist of modern socialism and communism; he declared that as capitalism grew, more and more workers would become impoverished and miserable. He advocated for a state in which the workers own the means of production and govern themselves. Along with Friedrich Engels, he wrote the *Communist Manifesto* in 1848, explaining their philosophy. (p. 649)

Mazzini, Giuseppe (1805–1872) Italian patriot; he formed the nationalist group called Young Italy to fight for the unification of the separate Italian states into one nation. (p. 714)

Medici, Lorenzo de (1449–1492) Florentine ruler; he supported some of the most talented Renaissance artists. He was known for his patronage and liberal mind. (p. 442)

Mehmed II (1432–1481) Sultan of the Ottoman Empire from 1444 to 1446 and again from 1451 to 1481; he was a strong military leader who conquered the Byzantine capital of Constantinople. (p. 501)

Meiji, Emperor (1852–1912) Emperor of Japan from 1867 to 1912; he restored imperial rule to Japan and, with the help of samurais, pushed for many reforms in Japan. (p. 750)

Meir, Golda (1898–1978) Israeli politician; she was the prime minister of Israel during the Yom Kippur War and sought assistance and supplies from the United States. (p. 956)

Menelik II (1844–1913) Emperor of Ethiopia after 1889; he gained Ethiopian independence from Italy in 1896. (p. 760)

Menes (fl. 3100 BC) First pharaoh of Egypt; he is credited with uniting Upper and Lower Egypt and is said to have founded the city of Memphis, the capital of unified Egypt. (p. 64)

Metternich, Prince Klemens von (1773–1859) Austrian statesman and diplomat; he was the Austrian representative at the Congress of Vienna. (p. 617)

Mobutu Sese Seko (1930–1997) President of Zaire; he made himself dictator and, over the course of his rule, amassed great wealth for himself at the expense of his people, who remained poor. (p. 945)

Moctezuma II (1466–1520) Aztec ruler from 1502 to 1520; he was the emperor of the Aztecs when Cortés and his army conquered the empire. He was taken prisoner and killed during battle with the Spanish army. (p. 477)

Montesquieu, Baron de (1689–1755) French jurist and political philosopher; he explored democratic theories of government. He proposed a government divided into three branches and greatly influenced the United States Constitution. (p. 576)

More, Sir Thomas (1478–1535) English statesman and author; he wrote *Utopia*, which describes an ideal society. (p. 446)

Morelos, José María (1765–1815) Creole priest; he became the leader of the revolutionary movement in Mexico after Miguel Hidalgo's death. (p. 698)

Morse, Samuel (1791–1872) American artist and inventor; he applied scientists' discoveries of electricity and magnetism to develop the telegraph. (p. 663)

Moses (1500s–1400s BC) Hebrew prophet and lawgiver; according to the Bible, he led the Hebrew people out of Egypt and back to Canaan in the Exodus. According to the Bible, it was during this journey that he received the Ten Commandments from God. (p. 46)

Muhammad (c. 570–632) Prophet of Islam whom Muslim recognize as Allah's messenger to all humankind. His teachings form the basis of Islam. (p. 258)

Muhammad, Askia (died 1538) King of Songhai from 1493 to 1598; he was known for encouraging a revival of Muslim learning in the West African kingdom during his rule. (p. 300)

Murasaki, Lady Shikibu (c. 978–c. 1026) Japanese courtier and writer; she wrote *The Tale of Genji*, a masterpiece of Japanese literature widely considered to be the world's first novel. (p. 326)

Musharraf, Pervez (1943–) Pakistani general; he overthrew the elected government of Pakistan in 1999 and became president. (p. 913)

Mussolini, Benito (1883–1945) Italian Fascist leader; he ruled as Italy's dictator for more than 20 years beginning in 1922. His alliance with Hitler brought Italy into World War II. (p. 823)

Nasser, Gamal Abdal (1918–1970) Egyptian army officer, political leader, and first president of the republic of Egypt; he helped lead a military coup that forced King Faruq to abdicate. He banned existing political parties and undertook an ambitious land reform program to gain support for his regime among the poor. (p. 952)

Nebuchadnezzar II (c. 630–562 BC) Chaldean king of Babylon from 605 to 562 BC; he rebuilt Babylon into a beautiful city noted for its famed Hanging Gardens. (p. 43)

Nehru, Jawaharlal (1889–1964) Indian statesman; he was the first prime minister of an independent India at the end of British colonial rule. (p. 910)

Nelson, Admiral Horatio (1758–1805) British admiral; he defeated Napoleon's navy in Egypt and again at the Battle of Trafalgar (1805). (p. 609)

Newton, Isaac (1642–1727) English mathematician and natural philosopher; he discovered the law of gravity as well as laws on the physics of objects. (p. 570)

Nkrumah, Kwame (1909–1972) Ghanaian nationalist leader and statesman; he pushed for Ghanaian independence from Great Britain and was elected Ghana's first president in 1957. (p. 938)

Noriega, Manuel (1938–) Panamanian general and dictator; he brutally crushed his enemies and used the country as a base for drug smuggling. (p. 977)

Omar Khayyam (c. 1048–c. 1131) Persian poet, mathematician, astronomer, and philosopher; author of *The Rubaiyat*, a collection of poems about a man who celebrates the simple pleasures in life. (p. 274)

Otto the Great (912–973) King of Germany (936–973) and Holy Roman Emperor (962–973); he defeated the Magyar army, which ended the Magyar raids in the mid-900s. (p. 390)

Pachacuti (died 1471) Inca leader from 1438 to 1471; with the help of his son, Topa Inca, he extended the Incan empire through the use of military force and political alliances. (p. 213)

Pahlavi, Mohammad Reza (1919–1980) Shah of Iran from 1941 to 1979; during his reign, Iran's oil industry was controlled by foreign interests. He was overthrown in a revolution led by the Ayatollah Khomeini. (p. 953)

Pankhurst, Emmeline (1858–1928) British woman suffragist; she founded the Women's Social and Political Union in 1903. In support of women's suffrage, she led hunger strikes and was arrested often for her actions. (p. 688)

Pasteur, Louis (1822–1895) French chemist; his experiments with bacteria disproved the theory of spontaneous generation and led to the germ theory of infection. He also developed vaccines for anthrax and rabies. (p. 668)

Paul (c. AD 10–67) Apostle to the Gentiles; he worked to spread Jesus' teachings and wrote letters that explained key ideas of Christianity. (p. 185)

Pavlov, Ivan (1849–1936) Russian physiologist and experimental psychologist; he researched the physiology of the heart, the digestive system, the brain, and the higher nervous system. He conducted a famous experiment with dogs demonstrating conditioned reflex. (p. 669)

Pedro I (1798–1834) First emperor of Brazil (1822–1831); he declared Brazil's independence from Portugal, where Pedro's father was king. (p. 700)

Pericles (c. 495–429 BC) Athenian statesman; he encouraged the spread of democracy in Athens and the growth of the city-state's power. (p. 139)

Perón, Juan (1895–1974) President of Argentina from 1946 to 1955 and again from 1973 to 1974; he rose to power following a military coup d'état and was a supporter of the rights of the people. (p. 974)

Peter the Great (1672–1725) Czar of Russia from 1682 to 1725; he transformed Russia into a modern state. He was an absolute monarch who brought the ways of Western Europe to Russia and made various reforms. (p. 553)

Philip II (1527–1598) King of Spain (1556–1598), Naples from (554–1598), and Portugal (1580–1598); he led Roman Catholic efforts to recover parts of Europe from Protestantism. He was defeated by England and the Netherlands. (p. 536)

Piankhi (c. 751–716 BC) King of ancient Kush; he led the Kushites north into Egypt, conquering all of Egypt and making himself pharaoh. (p. 83)

Pinochet, Augusto (1915–) President and dictator of Chile from 1973 to 1990; he planned and carried out a coup of Salvador Allende's government in Chile. (p. 976)

Pisan, Christine de (1364–c. 1430) French poet and author; her work *The City of Women* discusses the role of women in society. She championed the causes of equality and education for women. (p. 446)

Pizarro, Francisco (c. 1476–1541) Spanish conquistador, conqueror of Peru; founder of Lima, Peru. From 1530 to 1533, he conquered the Inca Empire. (p. 478)

Plato (c. 427–347 BC) Greek philosopher; a student of Socrates, he started a school in Athens called the Academy. In *The Republic* he describes an ideal society run by philosopher-kings. (p. 143)

Pol Pot (1925–1998) Cambodian political leader; he led the Khmer Rouge guerillas in establishing a Communist government in Cambodia. Once in power, the Communists' brutal efforts to restructure Cambodian society left 1. 5 million people dead. (p. 919)

Polo, Marco (1254–1324) Venetian traveler in China; he worked for Kublai Khan and was sent on missions throughout the Mongol empire and in India. (p. 320)

Princip, Gavrilo (1894–1918) Serbian nationalist; he assassinated Archduke Franz Ferdinand of Austria- Hungary, which started World War I. (p. 781)

Ptolemy (c. 367–c. 282 BC) One of Alexander the Great's generals, he founded a dynasty that ruled Egypt for nearly 300 years. (p. 180)

Qianlong (1711–1799) Emperor of the Qing dynasty from 1735 to 1796; he was the grandson of Kangxi. During his reign, China expanded to its greatest size. He limited foreign contacts and ordered traders to conduct business with the Chinese government, not with private merchants. (p. 512)

Ramses the Great (died c. 1237 BC) Pharaoh of Egypt; he led an army against Hittite invaders of Egypt. He ruled Egypt with extravagance and built more temples and monuments than any other Egyptian pharaoh. (p. 69)

Raphael (1483–1520) Italian Renaissance painter; he painted frescos, his most famous being *The School of Athens*. (p. 443)

Rasputin, Grigory (1872–1916) A self-proclaimed Russian holy man and prominent figure at the court of Czar Nicholas II. He was viewed as corrupt, and support for czarist Russia deteriorated because of him. (p. 791)

Rhodes, Cecil (1853–1902) British imperialist and business magnate; he was one of the foremost advocates of expanding the British Empire and was a strong believer in the superiority of the "Anglo-Saxon" race. (p. 757)

Ricci, Matteo (1552–1610) Italian missionary; he traveled to China in 1583. He learned the language and adopted many Chinese customs, which gained him entry to the Ming court. He introduced China to European learning in mathematics, science, and technology. (p. 511)

Richard the Lion-Hearted (1157–1199) King of England from 1189 to 1199; he fought in the Holy Land against Saladin during the Third Crusade. He eventually ceased fighting and returned to England. (p. 406)

Richelieu, Cardinal (1585–1642) French minister and chief minister of King Louis XIII; he wanted to strengthen the monarchy and fought against Huguenot resistance to the Catholic monarchy. (p. 541)

Robespierre, Maximilien (1758–1794) Leading figure of the French Revolution; he was known for his intense dedication to the Revolution. He became increasingly radical and led the National Convention during its most bloodthirsty time. (p. 602)

Rommel, Erwin (1891–1944) German general during World War II; he commanded the Afrika Korps and was nicknamed the Desert Fox for his leadership. (p. 845)

Roosevelt, Franklin Delano (1882–1945) Thirty-second president of the United States; he was elected president four times. He led the United States during the major crises of the Great Depression and World War II. (p. 814)

Rousseau, Jean-Jacques (1712–1778) Swiss-French political philosopher; he valued the social contract and addressed the nature of man in his work *On the Origin of Inequality*. (p. 575)

Rumi (c. 1207–1273) Persian poet; he was a Sufi mystic and founded a Sufi order whose members use music and dancing in their rituals. His poems are still read by many today. (p. 274)

S

Sadat, Anwar (1918–1981) Egyptian soldier and statesman; he launched the Yom Kippur War against Israel. (p. 956)

Saladin (1138–1193) Muslim sultan and hero; he campaigned to drive the Christians from the Holy Land. He stopped an army of crusaders under Richard the Lion-Hearted of England. (p. 405)

San Martín, José de (1778–1850) South American revolutionary; he led troops in Argentina, Chile, and Peru and gained independence for these nations. (p. 699)

Santa Anna, Antonio López de (1794–1876) Mexican general, president, and dictator; he fought in the Texas Revolution and seized the Alamo but was defeated and captured by Sam Houston at San Jacinto. (p. 762)

Sargon I (died c. 2300 BC) King of Akkad in Mesopotamia; he is considered the founder of Mesopotamia and conquered many cities along the middle Euphrates to northern Syria. He established trade routes with the Indus Valley, the coast of the Oman islands, and the shores of the Persian Gulf. (p. 36)

Shah Jahan (1592–1666) Mughal emperor of India from 1628 to 1658; under his rule, Mughal power reached its height and his age was the golden period of Muslim art and architecture. (p. 507)

Shaka (died 1828) Founder of the Zulu Empire; he reorganized the army and introduced new fighting tactics. He subdued neighboring peoples, consolidating an empire that encompassed most of southern Africa. (p. 758)

Shakespeare, William (1564–1616) English dramatist and poet; he is considered one of the greatest dramatists of all time and wrote such works as *Romeo and Juliet, Hamlet,* and *A Midsummer Night's Dream*. (p. 446)

Shi Huangdi (259–210 BC) First Qin ruler of China; he built institutions that helped China remain unified for almost 2,000 years. (p. 224)

Shotoku, Prince (573–622) Regent of Japan from 593 until 622; he used the Chinese model of government to increase the power of the emperor. He weakened the power of the clan to oppose the emperor. (p. 324)

Sima Qian (c. 145–90 BC) Chinese historian, sometimes called the "father of Chinese history;" he wrote the *Historical Records*, or *Shiji*, in which he attempts to provide a complete history of China from the Yellow Emperor to the reign of Wudi. (p. 232)

Smith, Adam (1723–1790) Scottish economist; he became the leading advocate of laissez faire economics and is considered by some to be the "father of modern economics." He wrote the first true text on economics, *The Wealth of Nations*, in 1776. (p. 647)

Socrates (469–399 BC) Greek philosopher of Athens; his teaching style was based on asking questions. He wanted people to question their own beliefs. He was arrested and condemned to death for challenging authority. (p. 143)

Solon (c. 630–c. 560 BC) Athenian statesman; he introduced the first civil democracy in Greece and created the Boule. (p. 135)

Stalin, Joseph (1879–1953) Totalitarian dictator of the Soviet Union; he led the Soviet Union through World War II and created a powerful Soviet sphere of influence in Eastern Europe after the war. (p. 824)

Suharto (1921–) President of Indonesia from 1967 to 1998; he seized power in Indonesia from Sukarno in a coup d'état. His authoritarian and corrupt rule eventually led to his ouster. (p. 918)

Sukarno (1901–1970) Indonesian politician; he became Indonesia's first president after he led an independence movement there. A strong anti-communist, whose policies resulted in the deaths of hundreds, he was deposed in a coup led by Suharto. (p. 918)

Sulla, Lucius Cornelius (138–78 BC) Roman general and politician; he became consul in 88 BC, led a civil war against Marius and his followers, emerged victorious, and became dictator. (p. 172)

Suleyman I (1495–1566) Sultan of the Ottoman Empire from 1520 to 1566; he expanded the empire and took on a large economic and political role in the affairs of Europe and the Mediterranean. (p. 501)

Sun Yixian (1866–1925) Chinese statesman and revolutionary leader; he believed that China should be a democracy but that it first needed to replace the Qing dynasty with a ruling nationalist party. He founded the Revolutionary Alliance in 1905. (p. 750)

Sundiata (died 1255) Founder and ruler of Mali; he organized an army and defeated the other kingdoms of West Africa. (p. 297)

Talleyrand, Charles Maurice de (1754–1838) French states-man and diplomat; he was one of the negotiators at the Congress of Vienna. He represented France on behalf of Louis XVIII. (p. 617)

Taizong (599–649) Second emperor of the Tang dynasty from 626 to 649; he secured his throne by having his two brothers and their ten sons executed. He estab-lished schools to train candidates to take civil service exams. (p. 310)

Teresa of Avila (1515–1582) Spanish Carmelite nun and one of the principal saints of the Roman Catholic Church; she reformed the Carmelite order. Her fervor for the Catholic Church proved inspiring for many people during the Reformation period. (p. 458)

Theodora (died 548) Byzantine empress; she was mar-ried to Justinian and exerted a great influence over him and over the political and religious events of the empire. (p. 348)

Thomas Aquinas (1225–1274) Italian philosopher and theologian; he argued that rational thought could be used to support Roman Catholic belief. (p. 417)

Thucydides (c. 460–400 BC) Greek historian of Athens; he wrote *The History of the Peloponnesian War*. He is regarded as the first critical historian and is often ranked as the greatest historian of antiquity. (p. 145)

Tokugawa Ieyasu (1542–1616) Japanese warrior and dictator; he was appointed shogun by the emperor, thus assuming complete control of the government and establishing the Tokugawa shogunate. (p. 519)

Tojo, Hideki (1884–1948) Japanese nationalist and gen-eral; he took control of Japan during World War II. He was later tried and executed for war crimes. (p. 841)

Tolstoy, Leo (1828–1910) Russian novelist; his novel *War and Peace* portrayed war as confusing and horrible. (p. 676)

Toussaint L'Ouverture (c. 1744–1803) Haitian patriot and martyr; he took control of Hispaniola for the French and was a hero of the people. Napoleon felt threatened by his growing popularity and had him captured and killed in 1803. (p. 696)

Trotsky, Leon (1879–1940) Russian Communist revolu-tionary; he negotiated the peace between Russia and the Central Powers to end Russian involvement in World War I. (p. 792)

Truman, Harry S (1884–1972) Thirty-third president of the United States; he became president upon the death of Franklin D. Roosevelt. He led the United States through the end of World War II and the beginning of the Cold War. (p. 861)

Trung Nhi (died 43 AD) Vietnamese nationalist and hero; along with her sister Trung Trac, she raised an army that drove the Chinese out of Vietnam for a short period. (p. 333)

Trung Trac (died 43 AD) Vietnamese nationalist and hero; along with her sister Trung Nhi, she raised an army that drove the Chinese out of Vietnam for a short period. (p. 333)

Tull, Jethro (1674–1741) British inventor; he invented the seed drill. (p. 634)

Urban II (c. 1042–1099) Roman Catholic pope from 1088 to 1099; he called on Christians to launch the First Crusade. (p. 404)

Velázquez, Diego (1465–1524) Spanish painter; he painted in a realistic style but also worked in impressionism towards the end of his career. (p. 537)

Victor Emmanuel (1820–1878) King of Sardinia-Piedmont from 1849 to 1861 and king of Italy from 1861 to 1878; he was the first king of a united Italy. (p. 716)

Victoria, Queen (1819–1901) Queen of Great Britain and Ireland from 1837 to 1901 and empress of India from 1876 to 1901; she had the longest reign in all of British history and she allowed Parliament to become more involved in running the government. (p. 688)

Villa, Francisco "Pancho" (1878–1923) Mexican bandit and revolutionary leader; he led revolts against Carranza and Huerta. He was pursued by the United States but evaded General Pershing. (p. 762)

Vladimir I (c. 965–1015) Grand prince of Kiev; he con-verted to Orthodox Christianity in the 980s and made it the state religion. (p. 358)

Voltaire (1694–1778) French philosopher and author; he was a supporter of Deism, the idea that God was no longer involved with the universe after creating it. He also advocated a tolerant approach to religion. (p. 576)

BIOGRAPHICAL DICTIONARY

W

Washington, George (1732–1799) First president of the United States; he commanded the Continental Army during the Revolutionary War and served as a representative to the Continental Congress. (p. 583)

Watt, James (1736–1819) Scottish inventor; he developed crucial innovations to make the steam engine efficient, fast, and better able to power machinery. (p. 637)

Wellington, Duke of (1769–1852) British soldier and statesman; he led the British troops against Napoleon at the Battle of Waterloo. (p. 616)

Wendi (541–604) Emperor of China; he founded the Sui dynasty and worked to build a centralized government. He also began the construction of the Grand Canal. (p. 310)

Wilhelm I (1797–1888) King of Prussia from 1861 to 1888 and emperor of Germany from 1871 to 1888; he chose Otto von Bismarck as Prussia's prime minister, and together they unified Germany. (p. 719)

William and Mary King William III (1650–1702) and Queen Mary II (1662–1694), rulers of Great Britain who replaced King James II as a result of the Glorious Revolution. (p. 550)

William the Conqueror (c. 1027–1087) King of England from 1060 to 1087; he was a powerful French noble who conquered England and brought feudalism to England. (p. 388)

Wilson, Woodrow (1856–1924) Twenty-eighth president of the United States; he proposed the League of Nations after World War I as a part of his Fourteen Points. (p. 795)

Wordsworth, William (1770–1850) English Romantic poet; his works include *The Evening Walk, Descriptive Sketches, The Prelude,* and *The Excursion.* (p. 676)

Wright, Orville (1871–1948) and **Wilbur** (1867–1912) American pioneers of aviation; they went from experiments with kites and gliders to piloting the first successful gas-powered airplane flight. (p. 663)

Wu Zhao (625–705) Empress of China from 690 to 705; she was the only woman to hold the title of emperor and was very powerful. (p. 310)

Wudi (141–87 BC) Fifth emperor of the Han dynasty in China; he led the Han dynasty during its peak and substantially increased Chinese territory. (p. 226)

X

Xerxes (c. 519–465 BC) King of Persia; his armies invaded Greece but were eventually defeated by the Greeks. (p. 53)

Y

Yaroslav the Wise (978–1054) Grand duke of Kiev from 1019 to 1054; he promoted Christianity and civilization in Russia and began a codification of the law. (p. 357)

Yeltsin, Boris (1931–) Russian politician and president of Russia in the 1990s; he was the first popularly elected leader of the country. (p. 895)

Yi Song-gye (1335–1408) Founder of the Korean Choson dynasty; his dynasty became one of the longest continuous dynasties in history. (p. 521)

Yonglo (1360–1424) Third emperor of the Ming dynasty in China; he ordered the reconstruction of Beijing and made it the new capital of China. He also commissioned an encyclopedia that covered history, philosophy, literature, astronomy, medicine, and numerous other topics. (p. 510)

Z

Zapata, Emiliano (1879–1919) Mexican revolutionary; he led the revolt against Porfirio Díaz in the south of Mexico during the Mexican Revolution. (p. 762)

Zhang Qian (died 113 BC) Chinese official under Emperor Wudi; he was sent on a journey through China to form an alliance with the Xiongu tribe to the west. His travels led to a vast increase in trade and the establishment of the Silk Road. (p. 231)

Zheng He (1371–c. 1433) Admiral, diplomat, and explorer during China's Ming dynasty; his Chinese fleet visited more than 30 countries. (p. 510)

Zoroaster (c. 628–c. 551 BC) Religious teacher and prophet of ancient Persia; he founded a religion known as Zoroastrianism based on the idea that people have free will and can act as they choose. (p. 53)

English and Spanish Glossary

MARK	AS IN	RESPELLING	EXAMPLE
a	alphabet	a	*AL-fuh-bet
ā	Asia	ay	AY-zhuh
ä	cart, top	ah	KAHRT, TAHP
e	let, ten	e	LET, TEN
ē	even, leaf	ee	EE-vuhn, LEEF
i	it, tip, British	i	IT, TIP, BRIT-ish
ī	site, buy, Ohio	y	SYT, BY, oh-HY-oh
	iris	eye	EYE-ris
k	card	k	KAHRD
ō	over, rainbow	oh	OH-vuhr, RAYN-boh
u̇	book, wood	ooh	BOOHK, WOOHD
ȯ	all, orchid	aw	AWL, AWR-kid
ȯi	foil, coin	oy	FOYL, KOYN
au̇	out	ow	OWT
	cup, butter	uh	KUHP, BUHT-uhr
ü	rule, food	oo	ROOL, FOOD
yü	few	yoo	FYOO
zh	vision	zh	VIZH-uhn

*A syllable printed in small capital letters receives heavier emphasis than the other syllable(s) in a word.

Phonetic Respelling and Pronunciation Guide

Many of the key terms in this textbook have been respelled to help you pronounce them. The letter combinations used in the respelling throughout the narrative are explained in the following phonetic respelling and pronunciation guide. The guide is adapted from **Webster's Tenth New College Dictionary, Merriam-Webster's New Geographical Dictionary, and Merriam-Webster's New Biographical Dictionary.**

A

Abbasid dynasty that overthrew the Umayyad dynasty to rule the Muslim caliphate from 750 to 1258; for 150 years the Abbasids maintained the unity of the caliphate and Islamic culture and civilization flourished. (p. 265)
Abasida gobernantes del Imperio musulmán que derrocaron a la familia Umayyad y establecieron un régimen que contribuyó a fortalecer el imperio, lo cual brindó gran prosperidad y crecimiento cultural a la cultura islámica (pág. 265)

abbot the elected head of a monastery (p. 364)
abad autoridad elegida de un monasterio (pág. 364)

abolition abolishment of slavery (p. 703)
abolición eliminación de la esclavitud (pág. 703)

absolute monarch a ruler that has unlimited power and authority over his or her people (p. 535)
monarca absoluto gobernante con poder y autoridad ilimitados sobre su pueblo (pág. 535)

acropolis a walled, high area surrounding a polis (p. 129)
acrópolis área elevada y defendida por muros que rodea a una polis (pág. 129)

acupuncture Chinese medical practice that involves inserting needles into the skin in order to relieve pain (p. 232)
acupuntura práctica médica china que consiste en insertar agujas en la piel para aliviar el dolor (pág. 232)

adobe sun-dried brick used by the Pueblo Indians for building (p. 200)
adobe ladrillos secados al sol que los indios Pueblo usaban para construir (pág. 200)

African Diaspora the dispersal of people of African descent throughout the Americas and Western Europe due to the slave trade (p. 491)
diáspora africana resultado del comercio de esclavos, cuando muchos africanos y sus descendientes fueron llevados a la Américas y a Europa Occidental (pág. 491)

African National Congress political organization in South Africa; founded in 1912, it developed into the main opposition force to apartheid (p. 944)
Congreso Nacional Africano organización política de Sudáfrica; fundada en 1912, comenzó como una agrupación pacífica que luchaba por los derechos civiles y se oponía al apartheid (pág. 944)

agora an open area that served as a meeting place and market in early Greek city-states (p. 129)
ágora área abierta que servía como lugar de encuentro y mercado en las primeras ciudades estado griegas (pág. 129)

ahimsa in Jainism, nonviolence and respect for all living things (p. 102)
ahimsa en el jainismo, pacifismo y respeto por todos los seres vivos (pág. 102)

al Qaeda "the base"; Islamist terrorist organization responsible for the September 11 attacks (p. 899)
al Qaeda literalmente significa "la base"; grupo fundamentalista islámico (pág. 899)

alliance a formal agreement between two or more nations entered into to advance common interests or causes (p. 208)
alianza acuerdo formal entre dos o más naciones; promover causas o intereses comunes (pág. 208)

Allied Powers the alliance formed between Britain, France, and Russia during World War I (p. 781)
Potencias Aliadas alianza que formaron Gran Bretaña, Francia y Rusia durante la Primera Guerra Mundial (pág. 781)

Allies the alliance of Britain, France, and Russia in World War II; joined by the United States after the Japanese bombing of Pearl Harbor in 1941 (p. 838)
Aliados alianza de Gran Bretaña, Francia y Rusia durante la Segunda Guerra Mundial; Estados Unidos se unió tras el bombardeo de Pearl Harbor en 1941 (pág. 838)

Amritsar Massacre (1919) an event in which British troops fired on a large crowd of peaceful, unarmed Indian protestors, killing some 400 people; it led to a campaign of protest led by Gandhi (p. 809)
masacre de Amritsar (1919) suceso ocurrido en la India en el cual los soldados británicos dispararon contra una multitud de manifestantes pacíficos que no llevaban armas; murieron aproximadamente 400 personas (pág. 809)

anesthetic a drug that inhibits pain during surgery (p. 668)
anestesia droga que inhibe el dolor durante una cirugía (pág. 668)

Angkor Wat Hindu temple complex built by the Khmer rulers of Cambodia in the 1100s (p. 332)
Angkor Wat templo construido por los gobernantes Khmer de Camboya (pág. 332)

animism the belief that all things in nature have spirits (p. 11)
animismo creencia de que todas las cosas en la naturaleza tienen espíritu (pág. 11)

Anti-Comintern Pact (1936) agreement signed between Germany and Japan in which they established their opposition to the Comintern, a Soviet-sponsored international organization aimed at spreading communism (p. 822)
Pacto Anti-Comintern (1936) acuerdo firmado entre Alemania y Japón para establecer su oposición al Comintern, una organización internacional promovida por la Unión Soviética que se dedicaba a difundir el comunismo (pág. 822)

anti-Semitism hostility or prejudice towards Jews (pp. 694, 826)
antisemitismo creencias en contra de los judíos (pág. 694, 826)

annulled declared invalid based on church laws (p. 453)
anular declarar inválido según las leyes de la Iglesia (pág. 453)

apartheid the South African government's official policy of legalized racial segregation throughout the society (p. 941)
apartheid política oficial del gobierno sudafricano que consiste en la segregación racial legalizada en toda la sociedad (pág. 941)

appeasement giving in to aggressive demands in order to avoid war (p. 836)
pacificación ceder a las demandas de potencias intransigentes para evitar una guerra (pág. 836)

Apostles the 12 chosen disciples of Jesus; they were the first Christian missionaries (p. 185)
apóstles los 12 discípulos elegidos por Jesús; fueron los primeros misioneros cristianos (pág. 185)

apprentice a person who learns a skill under a master of the trade (p. 412)
aprendiz persona que aprende una destreza con un maestro del oficio (pág. 412)

aqueducts manmade channels used to transport water; ancient Romans built impressive aqueducts (p. 180)
acueductos canales hechos por el hombre para llevar agua a las ciudades de la antigua Roma (pág. 180)

archipelago a large group or chain of islands (p. 323)
archipiélago gran grupo o cadena de islas (pág. 323)

archon a chief of state of ancient Athens (p. 136)
arconte jefe de gobierno en Atenas (pág. 136)

armistice an agreement to cease fighting, usually in a war (p. 797)
armisticio acuerdo para cesar una lucha, generalmente en una guerra (pág. 797)

arms race competition between nations to gain an advantage in weapons (p. 883)
carrera armamentística competencia entre naciones para tener ventaja en cuanto a la cantidad de armas (pág. 883)

artifacts objects that people in the past made or used, such as coins, pottery, and tools. (p. 6)
artefactos objetos hecho por los primeros humanos, como una herramienta, una pieza de cerámica o un arma (pág. 6)

artisans skilled craftspeople who make goods, such as pottery or baskets, by hand (p. 21)
artesanos trabajadores que hacen productos a mano, como piezas de cerámica o canastas (pág. 21)

Asian Tigers term referring to South Korea, Hong Kong, Taiwan, and Singapore, which built strong export-driven economies in the late 1900s (p. 929)
tigres asiáticos países de Asia que siguen un modelo de desarrollo económico similar al japonés (pág. 929)

assembly line a mass-production process in which a product is moved forward through many work stations where workers perform specific tasks (p. 645)
línea de montaje proceso de producción en masa en el que un producto pasa por varias etapas en las que los trabajadores hacen tareas específicas (pág. 645)

astrolabe an instrument for determining the positions and movements of heavenly bodies (p. 272)
astrolabio instrumento usado para determinar la posición y el movimiento de los cuerpos celestes (pág. 72)

augurs priests in ancient Rome who specialized in interpretation of the natural phenomena sent by the gods (p. 179)
augures sacerdotes de la antigua Roma que se especia- lizaban en la interpretación de los fenómenos naturales enviados por los dioses (pág. 179)

Austro-Prussian War (1866) war fought between Prussia and Austria lasting seven weeks; Prussian victory dissolved the German Confederation and led to the exclusion of Austria from German affairs (p. 720)
Guerra austro-prusiana (1866) guerra entre Prusia y Austria; la victoria prusiana provocó la exclusión de Austria de Alemania (pág. 720)

autocracy a government in which the ruler holds absolute power (p. 729)
autocracia forma de gobierno en la que el gobernante tiene poder absoluto (pág. 729)

Axis Powers the alliance of Germany, Italy, and Japan in World War II (p. 837)
Potencias del Eje alianza de Alemania, Italia y Japón durante la Segunda Guerra Mundial (pág. 837)

Baghdad Pact during the Cold War, a U.S.-led alliance against communism in the Middle East (p. 952)
Pacto de Bagdad alianza dirigida por Estados Unidos contra el comunismo en Medio Oriente (pág. 952)

balance of trade the difference in value between what a nation imports and exports over a period of time (p. 484)
balance comercial la diferencia en valor entre lo que una nación importa y lo que exporta a lo largo de un período de tiempo (pág. 484)

Balfour Declaration (1917) a statement issued by the British foreign secretary in favor of establishing a Jewish homeland in Palestine (p. 798)
Declaración de Balfour declaración escrita por el Ministro de Asuntos Exteriores británico a un líder sionista de Palestina (pág. 798)

Balkan Wars (1912–1913) two wars that cost the Otto-man Empire all of its European territories except the area around Constantinople (Istanbul) (p. 727)
Guerras de los Balcanes (1912–1913) dos guerras que se libraron por el último de los territorios europeos del Imperio otomano; a causa de ellas, el área que rodea a Constantinopla (Estambul) quedó como el único ter-ritorio otomano en Europa (pág. 727)

Bantu a family of closely related African languages; one of any of the African peoples who speak that language (p. 287)
Bantú familia de lenguas africanas estrechamente relacionadas; miembro de cualquiera de los pueblos africanos que hablan estas lenguas (pág. 287)

Bataan Death March (1942) a forced march of American and Filipino prisoners of war captured by the Japa-nese in the Philippines in World War II (p. 848)
marcha de la muerte de Bataan (1942) marcha forzada de los prisioneros de guerra estadounidenses y filipi-nos capturados por los japoneses en Filipinas durante la Segunda Guerra Mundial (pág. 848)

Battle of Britain (1940) three month air battle between Germany and Great Britain fought over Great Britain during World War II; Britain's victory forestalled a German invasion (p. 840)
batalla de Inglaterra (1940) serie de batallas aéreas entre Alemania y Gran Bretaña que se libraron en Gran Bretaña durante la Segunda Guerra Mundial (pág. 840)

Battle of El Alamein (1942) World War II battle in which the Britain won a decisive victory over Germany in Egypt, securing the Suez Canal (p. 846)
batalla de El Alamein (1942) batalla clave de la Segunda Guerra Mundial donde los británicos obtu-vieron una victoria aplastante sobre los alemanes en Egipto (pág. 846)

Battle of Guadalcanal (1942-1943) World War II battle in the Pacific; it represented the first Allied counter-attack against Japanese forces; Allied victory forced Japanese forces to abandon the island (p. 850)
batalla de Guadalcanal (1942-1943) batalla de la Segunda Guerra Mundial que se libró en el Pacífico por tierra, mar y aire; la victoria aliada obligó a las fuerzas japonesas a abandonar la isla (pág. 850)

Battle of Iwo Jima (1945) World War II battle between Japanese forces and invading U.S. troops (p. 860)
batalla de Iwo Jima (1945) batalla de la Segunda Guerra Mundial entre las fuerzas japonesas y el ejército invasor estadounidense (pág. 860)

Battle of Midway (1942) World War II naval battle fought in the Pacific; the Americans broke the Japanese code and knew the date and location of the attack, setting the stage for a major American victory (p. 849)
batalla de Midway (1942) batalla de la Segunda Guerra Mundial librada en el Pacífico; los estadounidenses descifraron el código japonés y averiguaron dónde y cuándo atacarían los japoneses, lo que les permitió obtener una victoria importante (pág. 849)

Battle of Okinawa (1945) World War II victory for the Allied troops that resulted in the deaths of almost all of the 100,000 Japanese defenders; the battle claimed 12,000 American lives (p. 860)
batalla de Okinawa (1945) victoria de los Aliados en la Segunda Guerra Mundial que tuvo como consecuencia la muerte de los casi 100,000 defensores japoneses; los estadounidenses perdieron 12,000 soldados en la batalla (pág. 860)

Battle of Stalingrad (1942) World War II battle between invading German forces and Soviet defenders for control of Stalingrad, a city on the Volga River; each side sustained hundreds of thousands of casualties; Germany's defeat marked turning point in the war (p. 848)
batalla de Stalingrado (1942) una de las batallas más sangrientas de la Segunda Guerra Mundial, en la que los soviéticos defendieron la ciudad, a costa de decenas de miles de vidas, y lograron echar a los alemanes de la ciudad (pág. 848)

Battle of Verdun (1916) the longest battle of World War I; it ended in stalemate, with both sides suffering hundreds of thousands of casualties (p. 786)
batalla de Verdún (1916) la batalla más larga de la Primera Guerra Mundial; ambos bandos quedaron muy debilitados tras perder decenas de miles de vidas (pág. 786)

Bay of Pigs invasion (1961) the failed attempt of Cuban exiles backed by the U.S. to overthrow the Cuban socialist government of Fidel Castro (p. 885)
invasión de la Bahía de Cochinos (1961) intento frustrado de los exiliados cubanos, apoyados por Estados Unidos, de derrocar al gobierno socialista de Fidel Castro (pág. 885)

bedouins small groups of nomadic people in Arabia (p. 257)
beduinos pequeños grupos de pueblos nómadas de Arabia (pág. 257)

Benedictine Rule a collection of rules or guidelines for monks and monasteries; named for Benedict of Nursia; widely used in Europe in the Middle Ages (p. 364)
regla benedictina serie de 73 capítulos que detallaban cómo debían organizarse los monjes y los monasterios (pág. 364)

Berlin airlift (1948–1949) a program in which the United States and Britain shipped supplies by air to West Berlin during the Soviet blockade of all routes to the city (p. 880)
puente aéreo de Berlín (1948–1949) programa de envío de suministros a Berlín occidental por parte de Estados Unidos y Gran Bretaña durante el bloqueo soviético de todas las vías de acceso a la ciudad (pág. 880)

Berlin Conference (1884–1885) a meeting at which representatives from European nations agreed upon rules for the European colonization of Africa (p. 758)
Conferencia de Berlín (1884–1885) encuentro en el que representantes de países europeos acordaron reglas para la colonización europea de África (pág. 758)

Bessemer process a process developed in the 1850s that led to faster, cheaper steel production (p. 661)
proceso de Bessemer proceso desarrollado en la década de 1850 que permitió producir acero de forma más rápida y económica (pág. 661)

biotechnology the use of biological research in industry (p. 1008)
biotecnología usa de la investigación biológica en la industria (pág. 1008)

bishop a high-ranking official of the Roman Catholic Church who oversees a group of churches in a particular region or city (p. 187)
obispo funcionario de alto rango de la Iglesia católica que supervisa un grupo de iglesias de una región o ciudad en particular (pág. 187)

Black Death a terrible outbreak of bubonic plague that swept through Europe, beginning in 1347 (p. 422)
Peste Negra terrible plaga de peste bubónica que comenzó en 1347 y arrasó Europa (pág. 422)

Black Tuesday October 29, 1929, the day that the United States stock market crashed (p. 813)
martes negro 29 de octubre de 1929, día en que el mercado de valores de Estados Unidos colapsó (pág. 813)

blitzkrieg a German word meaning "lightning war"; a fast, forceful style of fighting used by Germans in World War II (p. 838)
blitzkrieg palabra alemana que significa "guerra relámpago"; estilo de combate rápido y contundente que usaron los alemanes en la Segunda Guerra Mundial (pág. 838)

Bloody Sunday January 22, 1905, the day that czarist troops fired on protestors at the Winter Palace, igniting the Russian Revolution of 1905 (p. 732)
Domingo sangriento 22 de enero de 1905 acontecimiento inspirador de la Revolución rusa de 1905, cuando el ejército disparó contra unos manifestantes frente al Palacio de Invierno (pág. 732)

Bolsheviks Marxists whose goal was to seize state power and establish a dictatorship of the proletariat; Soviet Communists (p. 790)
bolcheviques seguidores de Marx cuyo objetivo era apropiarse del poder estatal y establecer una dictadura del proletariado; comunistas soviéticos (pág. 790)

bourgeoisie the urban middle class; merchants, professionals, and manufacturers (p. 595)
burguesía la clase media urbana; mercaderes, profesionales y fabricantes (pág. 595)

Boxer Rebellion (1900) a siege of a foreign settlement in Beijing by Chinese nationalists who were angry at foreign involvement in China (p. 749)
rebelión de los boxers (1900) asedio a un asentamiento extranjero en Beijing por parte de nacionalistas chinos que estaban en desacuerdo con la intervención extranjera en China (pág. 749)

boyars wealthy Russian landowners (p. 552)
boyars ricos terratenientes ruso (pág. 552)

British East India Company a joint-stock company granted a royal charter by Elizabeth I in 1600 for the purpose of controlling trade in India (p. 742)
British East India Company sociedad por acciones a la que Isabel I otorgó un cédula real en 1600 para controlar el comercio en la India (pág. 742)

Bronze Age (c. 3000 BC) the period after the Stone Age, when people began to make items out of bronze (p. 17)
Edad de Bronce (circa 3000 a.C.) perído posterior a la Edad de Piedra en el que las personas comenzaron a fabricar objetos de bronce (pág. 17)

Buddhism the religion founded by Siddhartha Gautama, which teaches the Four Noble Truths and following the Eightfold Path (p. 104)
budismo religión fundada por Siddhartha Gautama que enseña las Cuatro Nobles Verdades y a seguir el sendero óctuple (pág. 104)

bureaucracy a highly structured organization, often governmental, managed by officials (p. 66)
burocracia departamentos y agencias dirigidos por funcionarios no electos cuyo propósito es dirigir el gobierno (pág. 66)

Bushido "way of the warrior;" code of behavior of Japanese samurai warriors, stressing bravery, loyalty, and honor (p. 517)
bushido "vía del guerrero"; código de conducta de los guerreros samuráis japoneses que destacaba la valentía, la lealtad y el honor (pág. 517)

Byzantine Empire (395–1453) name historians give to the Eastern Roman Empire; it refers to Byzantium, the name of the capital city before it was changed to Constantinople (p. 347)
Imperio bizantino (395–1453) parte oriental del anterior Imperio romano, que data del año 330 d.C., cuando Constantino I reconstruyó Bizancio y la transformó en su capital (pág. 347)

caliph "successor to the Prophet"; title given to the political and religious leader of Muslims (p. 263)
califa "sucesor del Profeta"; título dado al líder político y religioso de los musulmanes (pág. 263)

caliphate area ruled by a caliph (p. 263)
califato área gobernada por un califa (pág. 263)

calligraphy the art of fine handwriting (p. 273)
caligrafía arte de escribir a mano con destreza (pág. 273)

Camp David Accords (1978) a peace agreement mediated by U.S. President Carter between Egyptian President Anwar Sadat and Israeli Prime Minister Menachem Begin (p. 956)
Acuerdos de Camp David (1978) acuerdos de paz entre el presidente egipcio Anwar Sadat y el primer ministro israelí Menachem Begin en los que el presidente Estados Unidos Carter actuó como mediador (pág. 956)

capitalism economic system in which most businesses are privately owned (p. 487)
capitalismo sistema económico donde la mayoría de las empresas son de propiedad privada (pág. 487)

caravel a sailing vessel that uses square and triangular sails to help it sail against the wind (p. 471)
carabela barco de velas triangulares y cuadradas que permiten navegar con el viento en contra (pág. 471)

castes social classes in the ancient Indian class system; see also *varnas* (p. 97)
castas sistema de clases de la sociedad tradicional de la India (pág. 97)

cataracts rocky stretches in a river marked by rapid currents or waterfalls (p. 64)
rápidos parte rocosa del curso de un río donde la corriente es rápida y abundan las cascadas (pág. 64)

census a population count that includes other demographic data (p. 213)
censo recuento de la población que incluye otros datos demográficos (pág. 213)

Central Powers the alliance between Germany, Austria-Hungary, and the Ottoman Empire during World War I (p. 781)
Potencias Centrales alianza entre Alemania, el Imperio austrohúngaro y el Imperio otomano durante la Primera Guerra Mundial (pág. 781)

charter a founding document or agreement, such as the one that created the United Nations (p. 1040)
carta de constitución documento que crea organizaciones, como Naciones Unidas (pág. 1040)

Christendom term historians use to denote the society, concentrated in Western Europe, that developed in the Middle Ages in which people were linked by common customs and the Christian religion (p. 363)
cristiandad la sociedad cristiana, formada en el siglo V; unió a la mayoría de los europeos occidentales a través de una religión y costumbres comunes (pág. 363)

Christianity a religion based on the teaching of Jesus of Nazareth (p. 183)
cristianismo religión basada en las enseñanzas de Jesús de Nazaret (pág. 183)

circumnavigate to proceed completely around (p. 474)
circunnavegar dar una vuelta completa alrededor de algo (pág. 474)

circus the site of chariot races in ancient Rome (p. 178)
circo pista de carreras de cuadrigas de la antigua Roma (pág. 178)

citadel a fortress (p. 95)
ciudadela fortaleza (pág. 95)

city-state a political unit that includes a town or a city and the surrounding land controlled by it (p. 34)
ciudad estado unidad política que incluye un pueblo o una ciudad y las tierras vecinas que están bajo su control (pág. 34)

civil law a form of law based on a written code of laws (p. 182)
derecho civil forma de derecho basada en un código de leyes escrito (pág. 182)

civil service a centralized administrative system that runs the day-to-day business of government (p. 226)
administración pública sistema administrativo centralizado que se encarga de los asuntos cotidianos del gobierno (pág. 226)

civilization a complex, organized society that has advanced cities, a government, religion, record keeping and writing, job specialization, social classes, and arts and architecture (p. 19)
civilización sociedad compleja y organizada que tiene ciudades desarrolladas, un gobierno, una religión, registros escritos, especialización laboral, clases sociales y arte y arquitectura (pág. 19)

clergy church leaders (p. 350)
clero líderes de la iglesia (pág. 350)

cloning the process of making a genetically identical copy of an animal's cell (p. 1008)
clonación proceso de hacer una copia genéticamente idéntica de la célula de un animal (pág. 1008)

codex books made by Mayans out of the inner bark of wild fig trees (p. 206)
códices libros hechos por los mayas con la corteza interna de higueras silvestres (pág. 206)

Cold War an era of high tension and bitter rivalry between the United States and the Soviet Union in the decades following World War II (p. 879)
Guerra Fría época de mucha tensión y rivalidad implacable entre Estados Unidos y la Unión Soviética tras el fin de la Segunda Guerra Mundial (pág. 879)

Columbian Exchange the transfer of plants, animals, and diseases between the Americas and Europe, Asia, and Africa beginning with the voyages of Columbus (p. 483)
intercambio colombino intercambio de plantas, animales y enfermedades entre las Américas, Europa, Asia y África (pág. 483)

commonwealth a republican government based on the common good of all the people (p. 548)
commonwealth gobierno democrático basado en el bien común de todos los ciudadanos (pág. 548)

communism economic and political system in which government owns the means of production and controls economic planning (p. 649)
comunismo sistema político y económico en que el gobierno posee los medios de producción y controla la planificación económica (pág. 649)

concentration camps detention sites created for military or political purposes to confine, terrorize, and, in some cases, kill civilians (p. 855)
campos de concentración lugares de detención creados con fines militares o políticos para confinar, intimidar y, en algunos casos, matar a civiles (pág. 855)

Confucianism a belief system based on the teachings of Chinese philosopher Confucius (551–479 BC) that stressed treating one another humanely and honoring one's family (p. 112)
confucianismo filosofía basada en las enseñanzas de Confucio (551–479 B.C.) que hace hincapié en comportarse bien con el prójimo y en respetar y honrar a la propia familia (pág. 112)

conquistador a Spanish soldier and explorer who led military expeditions in the Americas and captured land for Spain (p. 477)
conquistador soldados y exploradores español que encabezó expediciones militares en América y capturó territorios en nombre de España (pág. 477)

constitution a political structure (p. 166)
constitución una estructura política (pág. 166)

constitutional monarchy a monarchy limited by certain laws (p. 550)
monarquía constitucional monarquía limitada por ciertas leyes (pág. 550)

consuls the chief executives elected to run the government in ancient Rome (p. 166)
cónsules autoridades ejecutivas elegidas para gobernar en la antigua Roma (pág. 166)

containment the United States policy adopted in the 1940s to stop the spread of communism by providing economic and military aid to countries opposing the Soviets (p. 880)
contención política estadounidense adoptada en la década de 1940 para detener la difusión del comunismo; se proporcionó ayuda económica y militar a los países que se oponían a los soviéticos (pág. 880)

Continental System the system of commercial blockades of Britain and continental Europe set in place by Napoleon with the intent of destroying Britain's economy (p. 610)
Sistema Continental sistema de bloqueos comerciales a Gran Bretaña y Europa continental impuestos por Napoleón para intentar destruir la economía británica (pág. 610)

Contras rebels seeking to overthrow Nicaragua's Sandinista government in the 1980s; financed by the United States (p. 972)
contras rebeldes que intentaban derrocar el gobierno sandinista de Nicaragua; financiados por Estados Unidos (pág. 972)

cottage industry a usually small-scale industry carried on at home by family members using their own equipment (p. 635)
industria casera industria que los miembros de una familia desarrollan en el hogar, generalmente a pequeña escala y con sus propias herramientas (pág. 635)

Council of Trent a meeting of church leaders in the 1500s whose purpose was to clearly define Catholic doctrines for the Catholic Reformation (p. 456)
Concilio de Trento encuentro de los líderes de la Iglesia en el siglo XVI con el fin de definir claramente las doctrinas católicas para la Reforma católica (pág. 456)

counterculture a rebellion of teens and young adults against mainstream American culture in the 1960s (p. 890)
contracultura rebelión de adolescentes y adultos jóvenes contra la cultura masiva estadounidense en la década de 1960 (pág. 890)

Counter-Reformation the Catholic Church's series of reforms in response to the spread of Protestantism in the mid-1500s to the early 1600s (p. 456)
Contrarreforma serie de reformas que emprendió la Iglesia católica como respuesta a la difusión de las iglesias protestantes (pág. 456)

counterrevolution a revolution against a government established by a revolution (p. 604)
contrarrevolución revolución contra un gobierno establecido por una revolución (pág. 604)

counts title of nobility; in Charlemagne's empire, chosen officials who ruled parts of the empire in his name (p. 375)
condes funcionarios elegidos por Carlomagno que administraban las distintas partes de su imperio (pág. 375)

coup d'état "stroke of state"; the sudden overthrow of a government by force (p. 609)
golpe de estado derrocamiento súbito de un gobierno por la fuerza (pág. 609)

court a gathering of nobles around a monarch (p. 109)
corte reunión de nobles (pág. 109)

covenant a binding agreement (p. 46)
pacto acuerdo vinculante (pág. 46)

credit an arrangement by which a purchaser borrows money from a bank or other lender and agrees to pay it back over time (pp. 410, 813)
crédito acuerdo por el cual un comprador pide dinero a un banco o a otro prestamista para hacer una compra y se compromete a devolverlo en determinado tiempo (pág. 410, 813)

creoles people of Spanish or Portuguese descent born in the Americas (p. 696)
criollos nativos de las Américas descendientes de españoles o portugueses (pág. 696)

Crimean War (1853–1856) war between the Ottoman Empire and Russia, ostensibly over access for Eastern Orthodox Christians to the Holy Land, controlled by the Ottomans; Britain and France allied with the Ottomans to check Russian expansion (p. 726)
Guerra de Crimea (1853–1856) guerra entre Gran Bretaña, Francia y los turcos otomanos por un lado y Rusia por el otro, causada por disputas religiosas entre los cristianos católicos y los cristianos ortodoxos en Palestina (pág. 726)

Crusades (1096–1204) a series of wars carried out by European Christians to gain control of the Holy Land from their Muslim rulers (p. 404)
Cruzadas (1096–1204) serie de guerras santas encabezadas por los católicos para recuperar partes de Medio Oriente, en posesión de los musulmanes (pág. 404)

Cuban Missile Crisis (1962) confrontation between the United States and the Soviet Union over Soviet missiles in Cuba (p. 885)
   crisis de los misiles en Cuba (1962) confrontación entre Estados Unidos y la Unión Soviética acerca de los misiles soviéticos en Cuba (pág. 885)

cultural diffusion the spreading of culture from one society to another (p. 23, 995)
   difusión cultural transmisión cultural de una sociedad a otra (pág. 23, 995)

Cultural Revolution the violent attempt at social change in China launched by Mao Zedong in 1966 (p. 922)
   Revolución cultural intento violento de cambiar la sociedad china, ideado por Mao Tsé-Tung en 1966 (pág. 922)

culture a group's knowledge, beliefs, values, and customs (p. 6)
   cultura conocimientos, valores, creencias y costumbres de un grupo (pág. 6)

cuneiform Sumerian writing (p. 35)
   cuneiforme tipo de escritura que usaban los sumerios (pág. 35)

Cyrillic alphabet an alphabet derived from the Greek alphabet and used for writing Slavic languages (p. 358)
   alfabeto cirílico alfabeto derivado del alfabeto griego y usado en las lenguas eslavas (pág. 358)

czar "caesar"; title taken by the ruler of Russia (p. 552)
   zar "césar"; título que llevaba el gobernante del ruso (pág. 552)

daimyo a warrior lord in feudal Japan who controlled vast amounts of land and commanded a private army of samurai (p. 519)
   daimyo señor guerrero del Japón feudal que controlaba grandes extensiones de tierra y lideraba un ejército privado de samuráis (pág. 519)

Daoism a system of ideas and beliefs based on the teachings of Chinese thinker Laozi, who believed that people should live a simple, honest life and not interfere with the course of natural events (p. 112)
   taoísmo sistema de ideas y creencias basadas en las enseñanzas del pensador chino Laozi, quien creía que se debe vivir una vida sencilla y honesta sin interferir con el desarrollo natural de los acontecimientos (pág. 112)

D-Day June 6, 1944; the first day of the Allied invasion of Normandy in World War II (p. 859)
   Día D 6 de junio de 1944; el primer día de la invasión de los Aliados a Normandía durante la Segunda Guerra Mundial (pág. 859)

Declaration of the Rights of Man and of the Citizen a document that laid out the basic principles of the French Revolution—liberty, equality, and fraternity (p. 598)
   Declaración de los Derechos del Hombre y del Ciudadano documento que estableció los principios básicos de la Revolución francesa: libertad, igualdad y fraternidad (pág. 598)

deforestation the clearing of forests (p. 1006)
   deforestación tala de árboles (pág. 1006)

delta a triangular region formed at the mouth of a river by deposits of silt (p. 64)
   delta región triangular formada en la desembocadura de un río por depósitos de cieno (pág. 64)

democracy a government run by the people (p. 135)
   democracia gobierno del pueblo (pág. 135)

deported forced to leave a country (p. 855)
   deportado obligado a dejar un país (pág. 855)

desertification the transformation of habitable land to desert through a change in climate or destructive land use (p. 946)
   desertificación transformación de una región habitable en un desierto, a través de un cambio en el clima o el uso destructivo de la tierra (pág. 946)

détente efforts taken by U.S. president Nixon in the late 1960s and early 1970s to lower Cold War tensions (p. 887)
   détente intento que hizo el presidente Nixon a finales de la década de 1960 y comienzos de la década de 1970 para reducir la tensión de la Guerra Fría (pág. 887)

deterrence the development of or maintenance of military power to deter, or prevent, an attack (p. 883)
   disuasión desarrollo o mantenimiento de un poder militar para disuadir, o impedir, un ataque (pág. 883)

devolution the redistribution of power from the central government to local governments (p. 1023)
   devolución redistribución del poder del gobierno central a los gobiernos locales (pág. 1023)

dharma in Hinduism, the religious and moral duties of an individual (p. 100)
   dharma en el hinduismo, las obligaciones religiosas y morales de un individuo (pág. 100)

Diaspora the dispersal of the Jews from their homeland in Palestine during the 2,600 years that followed the destruction of the Solomon's Temple in Jerusalem in 586 BC by the Chaldeans (p. 48)
   diáspora dispersión de los judíos desde su tierra natal en Palestina durante los 2,600 años que siguieron a la destrucción del Templo de Jerusalén, en el año 586 b.C. (pág. 48)

dictator a political leader holding unlimited power (p. 167)
   dictador cargo político en el cual, quien lo ocupa, tiene poder ilimitado (pág. 167)

direct democracy the type of governing system where all people vote directly on an issue (p. 136)
democracia directa sistema de gobierno donde todos los ciudadanos votan directamente sobre una cuestión (pág. 136)

disciples followers of Jesus (p. 184)
discípulos seguidores de Jesús (pág. 184)

divine right the belief that a ruler's authority comes directly from God (p. 535)
derecho divino creencia de que la autoridad de un gobernante viene directamente de Dios (pág. 535)

division of labor when certain people do a specific task or type of work (p. 19)
división del trabajo cuando ciertas personas hacen una tarea o trabajo específicos (pág. 19)

Domesday Book the written record of English land-owners and their property made by order of William the Conqueror in 1085–1086 (p. 388)
Domesday Book registro escrito de las propiedades de los terratenientes ingleses hecho por orden de Guill-ermo el Conquistador entre 1085 y 1086 (pág. 388)

domestication taming animals and adapting crops for human use (p. 13)
domesticación adaptar animales y cultivos para el uso humano (pág. 13)

domino theory the belief during the Cold War that the fall of one non-communist country to communism would cause neighboring non-communist countries also to fall to communists (p. 916)
teoría del dominó creencia de que el comunismo se difundiría a otros países durante de la Guerra Fría (pág. 916)

Dreyfus affair a political scandal that divided France in the 1890s, involving the wrongful conviction of Jewish army officer Alfred Dreyfus for treason (p. 694)
caso Dreyfus escándalo político que dividió a Francia en la década de 1890 y que se inició cuando el militar judío Alfred Dreyfus fue condenado erróneamente por traición (pág. 694)

Dual Monarchy Austria-Hungary (1867–1918), two sepa-rate, equal states ruled by one monarch (p. 724)
monarquía dual sistema de gobierno donde un mismo rey gobierna a dos estados (pág. 724)

dualism the belief that the world is controlled by two opposing forces, good and evil (p. 53)
dualismo creencia de que el mundo está controlado por dos fuerzas opuestas: el bien y el mal (pág. 53)

Duma the Russian legislative assembly, formed after the Revolution of 1905 (p. 732)
Duma asamblea rusa formada después de la Revolu-ción de 1905 que aprobaba todas las leyes (pág. 732)

dynastic cycle the rise and fall of the Chinese dynasties (p. 111)
ciclo dinástico el ascenso y la caída de las dinastías chinas (pág. 111)

dynasty a family of rulers whose right to rule is hereditary (p. 35)
dinastía familia de gobernantes cuyo derecho a gobenar es herditario (pág. 35)

Edict of Nantes (1598) a declaration of French king Hen-ry IV in which he promised that Protestants could live peacefully in France and were free to establish houses of worship in selected French cities (p. 541)
Edicto de Nantes (1598) declaración del rey francés Enrique IV, donde prometía que los protestantes podrían vivir en paz en Francia y eran libres de establecer sus lugares de culto en ciertas ciudades francesas (pág. 541)

Eightfold Path the Middle Way and part of the Four Noble Truths that the Buddha taught as the means to nirvana or enlightenment (p. 104)
sendero óctuple el Camino Medio y parte de las Cuatro Nobles Verdades que Buda enseñaba como sendero hacia el nirvana o la iluminación (pág. 104)

elite a group of persons, or a member of such a group, enjoying superior intellectual, social, or economic status (p. 204)
élite grupo de personas o miembros de ese grupo que gozan de una posición intelectual, social o económica superior (pág. 204)

Emancipation Proclamation (1862) an order issued by President Abraham Lincoln freeing the enslaved people in areas rebelling against the Union (p. 704)
Proclamación de Emancipación (1862) decreto emitido por el presidente Abraham Lincoln para liberar a los esclavos en las áreas que se rebelaban contra la Unión (pág. 704)

enclosure movement a process in Europe from 1700s to the mid-1800s where landowners fenced small fields to create large farms, allowing for more efficient farm-ing methods and increased the food supply (p. 635)
movimiento de cercamiento proceso por el cual los terratenientes cercaban pequeños campos para crear grandes granjas; esto permitía aplicar métodos agrícolas más rentables y aumentó el suministro de alimentos (pág. 635)

encomienda Spanish colonial system in which a colonist was given a certain amount of land and a number of Native Americans to work the land in exchange for teaching the Native Americans Christianity (p. 477)
encomienda sistema por el cual un colono recibía una porción de tierra y un grupo de indígenas norteam-ericanos lo cultivaban a cambio de recibir enseñanzas cristianas (pág. 477)

ENGLISH AND SPANISH GLOSSARY

enlightened despots the absolute monarchs in 18th- century Europe who ruled according to the principles of the Enlightenment (p. 578)
déspotas ilustrados los monarcas absolutos europeos del siglo XVIII, que gobernaban según los principios de la Ilustración (pág. 578)

Enlightenment a time of optimism and possibility from the late 1600s to the late 1700s; also called the Age of Reason (p. 574)
Ilustración época de optimismo y nuevas posibilidades que comenzó en Europa en el siglo XVII; también llamada Edad de la Razón (pág. 574)

entrepreneur a risk taker who starts a new business within the economic system of capitalism (p. 647)
empresario persona que corre un riesgo para emprender un negocio dentro del sistema económico capitalista (pág. 647)

epidemic an outbreak of a contagious disease that spreads rapidly and affects many people (p. 998)
epidemia algo que afecta a muchas personas y se propaga o extiende rápidamente (pág. 998)

ethnic cleansing the elimination of an ethnic group from society through killing or forced migration (p. 897)
limpieza éthnica eliminación de un grupo éthnico de una sociedad, ya sea asesinando o expulsando del área a los miembros de dicho grupo (pág. 897)

Eucharist a ceremony of some Christian denominations that commemorates Jesus' last supper with his disciples (p. 187)
Eucaristía ceremonia especial del cristianismo que conmemora la última cena de Jesús y sus discípulos (pág. 187)

Exodus the escape of the Hebrews from Egypt (p. 46)
Éxodo huida de los hebreos de Egipto (pág. 46)

extraterritoriality the right of citizens to be tried in the courts of their native country rather than in the courts of the country that they are living in (p. 747)
extraterritorialidad derecho de un ciudadano a ser juzgado por una corte de su país natal y no del país donde vive (pág. 747)

F

factors of production the basic resources for industrialization, such as land, labor, and capital (p. 635)
factores de producción recursos básicos para la indus- trialización, como la tierra, la mano de obra y el capital (pág. 635)

factory a place where goods are manufactured in mass quantity (p. 636)
fábrica lugar de producción masiva de bienes (pág. 636)

famine an extreme shortage of food (p. 997)
hambruna escasez extrema de alimentos (pág. 997)

fascism a totalitarian system of government that focuses on the good of the state rather than on the good of the individual citizens (p. 823)
fascismo sistema totalitario de gobierno que se centra en el bien del estado y no en el bienestar de los ciudadanos individuales (pág. 823)

fealty the loyalty owed by a vassal to his feudal lord (p. 383)
fidelidad lealtad que un vasallo le debe a su señor feudal (pág. 383)

federal system a system of government in which power is divided between a central, or a federal, government and individual states (p. 584)
sistema federal sistema de gobierno donde el poder se divide entre un gobierno central o federal, y estados individuales (pág. 584)

Fertile Crescent a region of rich farmland that curves from the Mediterranean Sea to the Persian Gulf centered on the area between the Tigris and Euphrates rivers (p. 33)
Media Luna de las tierras fértiles región de ricas tierras de cultivo en Medio Oriente, que se extiende desde el valle del Nilo hasta los ríos Tigris y Éufrates (pág. 33)

feudal system a political and social system based on the granting of land in exchange for loyalty, military assistance, and other services (p. 383)
sistema feudal sistema político y social basado en la cesión de tierras a cambio de lealtad, protección militar y otros servicios (pág. 383)

fief a grant of land from a lord to a vassal (p. 383)
feudo cesión de tierras por parte de un señor a un vasallo (pág. 383)

filial piety a love and respect for one's parents and ancestors (p. 229)
piedad filial amor y respeto por los propios padres y antepasados (pág. 229)

Final Solution the Nazi Party's plan to murder the entire Jewish population of Europe and the Soviet Union (p. 855)
Solución Final plan del Partido Nazi para asesinar a toda la población judía de Europa y la Unión Soviética (pág. 855)

First Estate in pre-Revolution France, the clergy (p. 594)
primer estado en la Francia prerrevolucionaria, el clero (pág. 594)

Five Pillars of Islam behaviors and obligations that are common to all Muslims, which include the profession of faith, the performance of five daily prayers, the giving of alms, the requirement to fast, and the journey to Mecca, or Hajj (p. 259)
cinco pilares del Islam prácticas y obligaciones comunes a todos los musulmanes, que incluyen la profesión de la fe, rezar cinco plegarias diarias, dar limosnas, ayunar y peregrinar a la Meca, o hajj (pág. 259)

flying buttress an arched stone support on the outside of buildings, which allows builders to construct higher walls (p. 414)
arbotante estructura de piedra en forma de arco que sirve de apoyo para el exterior de un edificio, lo que permite construir muros más altos (pág. 414)

forum the assembly place of an ancient Roman city (p. 165)
foro lugar de asamblea en una antigua ciudad romana (pág. 165)

Four Noble Truths in Buddhism, the guidelines that are the essence of the Buddha's teaching: that life is suffering, that desires cause suffering, that the annihilation of desires can relieve suffering, and that the way to relieve suffering is to follow the Eightfold Path (p. 104)
Cuatro Nobles Verdades en el budismo, pautas esenciales de las enseñanzas de Buda: que la vida es sufrimiento, que los deseos causan sufrimiento, que la anulación de los deseos puede aliviar el sufrimiento, que para lograr esto se debe seguir el sendero óctuple (pág. 104)

Fourteen Points President Woodrow Wilson's plan for organizing post–World War I Europe and for avoiding future wars (p. 797)
Catorce Puntos plan del presidente Woodrow Wilson para organizar Europa después de la Primera Guerra Mundial y evitar futuras guerras (pág. 797)

Franco-Prussian War (1870–1871) a war fought between France and Prussia that ended in the defeat of France and the unification of Germany (p. 720)
Guerra franco-prusiana (1870–1871) guerra entre Francia y Prusia que terminó con la derrota de Francia y la fundación de Alemania (pág. 720)

free trade the exchange of goods among nations without barriers such as tariffs, or taxes (p. 993)
libre comercio intercambio de bienes entre naciones sin barreras como aranceles o impuestos (pág. 993)

friars members of certain Roman Catholic religious orders; first prominent in the Europe of the late Middle Ages; unlike monks, friars preached in towns (p. 420)
frailes monjes que predicaban para los pobres en las ciudades europeas en desarrollo (pág. 420)

G

Gallipoli Campaign (1915) failed attempt by the Allies in World War I to take control of the Dardanelles (p. 787)
campaña de Gallipoli (1915) intento de los Aliados en la Primera Guerra Mundial de tomar el control de los Dardanelos; terminó en un fracaso (pág. 787)

Gang of Four powerful group of radicals, including Madame Mao, responsible for many of the excesses of China's Cultural Revolution in the 1960s and 1970s; they lost power after Mao's death in the 1976 (p. 923)
Banda de los Cuatro grupo comunista radical de la señora Mao, que quería continuar la Revolución cultural en China (pág. 923)

Ge'ez an ancient Afro-Asiatic language; it is still used today as a liturgical language in the Ethiopian Coptic Church (p. 289)
ge'ez antigua lengua afroasiática; todavía tiene un uso litúrgico en la Iglesia copta de Etiopía (pág. 289)

General Assembly a United Nations body consisting of all the member nations (p. 1041)
Asamblea General de Naciones Unidas; está formada por todas las naciones miembro (pág. 1041)

genetic engineering changing the genetic makeup of a plant or animal to create a new type (p. 1008)
ingeniería genética cambio de la estructura genética de una planta o un animal para crear un nuevo tipo (pág. 1008)

genocide the killing of an entire people (p. 788)
genocidio asesinato de todo un pueblo (pág. 788)

gentry wealthy landowners involved in commercial activities, such as trade, who have political power (p. 315)
pequeña nobleza terratenientes ricos que participaban en actividades comerciales y tenían poder político (pág. 315)

geocentric theory scientific theory that has the earth as the center of the universe with the sun and stars revolving around it (p. 568)
teoría geocéntrica teoría científica que afirma que la Tierra es el centro del universo y el Sol y las estrellas giran a su alrededor (pág. 568)

ghazis warriors for the Islamic faith (p. 500)
gazis guerreros de la fe islámica (pág. 500)

ghetto an area where minority groups live (p. 855)
gueto área donde vive un grupo de personas de un determinado origen étnico (pág. 855)

glasnost "openness"; refers to a new era of media freedom in the Soviet Union under Mikhail Gorbachev in the 1980s (p. 892)
glasnost "apertura": se refiere a una nueva era de libertad de los medios de comunicación en la Unión Soviética bajo el gobierno de Mikhail Gorbachev (pág. 892)

ENGLISH AND SPANISH GLOSSARY

global warming an increase in the average temperature of the earth's atmosphere (p. 1007)
calentamiento global aumento de la temperatura promedio de la atmósfera terrestre (pág. 1007)

globalization the process in which trade and culture link together countries around the world (p. 992)
globalización hacer global o universal el alcance o la aplicación de algo (pág. 992)

Glorious Revolution (1688) a nonviolent revolution in which leaders of Britain's Parliament invited Mary, daughter of King James II, and her husband, the Dutch ruler William of Orange, to replace King James II (p. 550)
Revolución gloriosa (1688) revolución pacífica en que los líderes del Parlamento británico invitaron a María, hija del rey Jacobo II, y a su marido, el gobernante holandés Guillermo de Orange, a sustituir al rey Jacobo II (pág. 550)

glyphs a symbolic picture carved onto a surface (p. 206)
glifos dibujo simbólico grabado en una superficie (pág. 206)

Gothic a style of church architecture developed during the 1100s characterized by tall spires and flying buttresses (p. 414)
gótica estilo de arquitectura religiosa caracterizado por chapiteles altos y arbotantes que se desarrolló en el siglo XII (pág. 414)

Great Depression (1929–1930s) a severe worldwide depression that followed the collapse of the United States stock market; prices and wages fell, business activity slowed, and unemployment rose (p. 813)
Gran Depresión (1929–década de 1930) grave crisis económica mundial que siguió al colapso del mercado de valores de Estados Unidos; los precios y los salarios bajaron, la actividad comercial disminuyó y aumentó el desempleo (pág. 813)

Great Leap Forward (1958) Mao Zedong's second Five-Year Plan for China; its goal was to speed progress (p. 921)
Gran Salto Adelante (1958) segundo plan de cinco años para China de Mao Tsé-Tung, cuyo fin era acelerar el progreso (pág. 921)

green revolution a significant increase in agricultural productivity resulting from the introduction of high-yield varieties of grains, the use of pesticides, and improved management techniques (p. 1008)
revolución verde aumento significativo de la productividad agrícola debido a la introducción de variedades de cereales de alto rendimiento, el uso de pesticidas y la mejora de las técnicas de administración (pág. 1008)

griots professional West African storytellers (p. 286)
griots contadores de cuentos profesional de África occidental (pág. 286)

guilds associations of people who worked at the same craft or trade during the Middle Ages (p. 411)
gremios asociaciones de personas que trabajaban en el mismo oficio o comercio en la Edad Media (pág. 411)

guillotine a device used during the French Revolution for beheading people (p. 602)
guillotina aparato usado durante la Revolución francesa para decapitar a las personas (pág. 602)

Gulag a Soviet forced labor camp or prison, used especially for political dissidents (p. 825)
gulag campo de trabajos forzados de la Unión Soviética, destinado especialmente para los prisioneros políticos (pág. 825)

haiku a Japanese poem that consists of 17 syllables set in three lines (p. 521)
haiku poema japonés que consiste en 17 sílabas dispuestas en tres versos (pág. 521)

Hanseatic League an organization of north-German cities and towns that organized and controlled trade throughout northern Europe from the 1200s through the 1400s (p. 409)
Liga hanseática organización del norte de Alemania que se encargaba de organizar y controlar el comercio de todo el norte de Europa durante los siglos XIII, XIV y XV (pág. 409)

hegira Mohammad's journey from Mecca to Medina (p. 258)
hégira viaje de Mohamed de la Meca a Medina (pág. 258)

heliocentric theory scientific theory that has the sun as the center of the universe with the earth rotating around the sun (p. 569)
teoría heliocéntrica teoría científica que afirma que el Sol es el centro del universo y la Tierra gira a su alrededor (pág. 569)

Hellenistic the blending of Greek cultures with those of Persia, Egypt, and Central Asia following the conquests of Alexander the Great (p. 153)
helenístico mezcla de las culturas griegas con las culturas de Persia, Egipto y Asia Central (pág. 153)

helots in ancient Greece, state slaves (p. 130)
ilotas en la antigua Grecia, esclavos del estado (pág. 130)

heresy an opinion that goes against the teachings of a church (p. 419)
herejía opinión que va en contra de las enseñanzas de una iglesia (pág. 419)

hieroglyphics a form of ancient writing in which picture symbols represent sounds (p. 78)

jeroglíficos forma de escritura antigua en la que los sonidos se representan con dibujos (pág. 78)

Hindu-Arabic numerals the number system that we use today, created by Indian scholars and brought to Europe by Arabs (p. 241)

números indoarábigos sistema numérico que usamos hoy en día; fue creado por estudiosos de la India y traído a Europa por los árabes (pág. 241)

Hinduism the largest religion in India; Hindus believe that everything in the world is a power of Brahman, the single great universal being; they also believe in reincarnation and strive to break free from the cycle of rebirth. (p. 99)

hinduismo la religión más importante de la India; los hindúes creen en la reencarnación y se esfuerzan por liberarse del ciclo de renacimiento (pág. 99)

Holocaust the killing of millions of Jews and others by the Nazis during World War II (p. 856)

Holocausto asesinato de millones de judíos y otras personas por los nazis durante la Segunda Guerra Mundial (pág. 856)

Holy Land region that included Jerusalem and the are around it, considered holy by Jews, Christians, and Muslims (p. 404)

Tierra Santa la región donde Jesús fue crucificado y enterrado (pág. 404)

hominid an early humanlike creature that is believed to be the ancestor of humans (p. 6)

homínido criatura primitiva parecida a los humanos, de quien se cree que descienden los humanos (pág. 6)

hoplites foot soldiers in ancient Greece (p. 130)

hoplitas soldados de infantería de la antigua Grecia (pág. 130)

hubris great pride (p. 132)

hibris orgullo desmesurado (pág. 132)

Huguenot a French Protestant (p. 541)

hugonote protestante francés (pág. 541)

humanism an intellectual movement during the Renaissance that focused on the study of worldly subjects, such as poetry and philosophy, and on human potential and achievements (p. 439)

humanismo movimiento intelectual del Renacimiento que se centró en el estudio de temas terrenales como la poesía y la filosofía, y en el potencial humano y sus logros (pág. 439)

Hundred Days (1815) period that marks the time between Napoleon's return to Paris from Elba (March 20), his final defeat at Waterloo (June 18), and the restoration of King Louis XVIII (June 28) (p. 616)

Cien Días (1815) período que marca la época entre el regreso de Napoleón a París desde Elba (20 de marzo) y la restauración del rey Luis XVIII (28 de junio) (pág. 616)

Hundred Years' War (1337–1453) war fought between France and England for control of the French throne (p. 421)

Guerra de los Cien Años (1337–1453) guerra entre Francia e Inglaterra por el control del trono francés (pág. 421)

hunter-gatherers people who hunt animals and gather wild plants to provide for their needs (p. 10)

cazadores y recolectores personas que cazan animales y recolectan plantas silvestres para satisfacer sus necesidades (pág. 10)

hydrogen bomb a nuclear weapon that gets its power from the fusing together of hydrogen atoms (p. 883)

bomba de hidrógeno arma nuclear que debe su potencia a la fusión de átomos de hidrógeno (pág. 883)

hyperinflation an extremely high level of inflation that grows rapidly in a short period of time (p. 975)

hiperinflación nivel de inflación extremadamente alto que aumenta con rapidez en un corto período de tiempo (pág. 975)

icon a painting or carving of Jesus, the Virgin Mary, or a saint (p. 350)

icono pintura o grabado de Jesús, la Virgen María o un santo (pág. 350)

illumination the process of decorating a written manuscript with pictures or designs (p. 415)

ilustración proceso de decorar un manuscrito con dibujos o diseños (pág. 415)

import-substitution led industrialization an economic policy of replacing certain imported goods with a country's own manufactured goods (p. 968)

industrialización de sustitución de importaciones política económica que consiste en reemplazar ciertos bienes importados por bienes producidos en el país (pág. 968)

impressionism a new style of painting that began in France in the 1860s in which artists used light, vivid color, and seeming motion to capture an impression of a scene (p. 676)

impresionismo novedoso estilo de pintura que comenzó en Francia en la década de 1860 en la que los artistas usaban juegos con la luz, el movimiento y el uso de colores vivos (pág. 676)

indemnity compensation that is paid to a nation for the damage inflicted upon it in a war (p. 618)

indemnización compensación que se paga a una nación por los daños causados a dicha nación (pág. 618)

Indian National Congress a major political party in India; founded in 1885 to press for greater rights for Indians under British rule, it later became one of the main forces calling for Indian independence (p. 744)

Congreso Nacional de la India importante partido político de la India, fundado en 1885 con el fin de organizar a los ciudadanos en la lucha contra el Imperio británico (pág. 744)

Indo-Europeans a group of semi-nomadic people who migrated from southern Russia to the Indian subcontinent around 1700 BC (p. 40)

indoeuropeos grupo de pueblos seminómadas que migraron desde el sur de Rusia hasta el subcontinente indio hacia el año 1700 a.C. (pág. 40)

indulgences pardons issued by the pope of the Roman Catholic Church that could reduce a soul's time in purgatory; from the 1100s to the 1500s, indulgences could be purchased, which led to corruption (p. 450)

indulgencias perdones comprados a la Iglesia católica con el fin de evitar un castigo por un pecado (pág. 450)

Industrial Revolution a period of rapid growth in the use of machines in manufacturing and production that began in the mid-1700s (p. 633)

revolución industrial período de rápido crecimiento del uso de las máquinas para la producción; comenzó a mediados del siglo XVIII (pág. 633)

industrialization developing industries for the production of goods (p. 635)

industrialización desarrollo de las industrias que producen bienes (pág. 635)

inflation increased prices for goods and services combined with the reduced value of money (p. 189)

inflación aumento del precio de los bienes y servicios combinado con la reducción del valor del dinero (pág. 189)

Inquisition institution of the Roman Catholic Church that sought to eliminate heresy by seeking out and punishing heretics; especially active in Spain in the later 1400s and 1500s (p. 420)

Inquisición institución de la Iglesia católica romana que intentaba eliminar la herejía persiguiendo y castigando a los herejes; fue particularmente activa en España en el siglo XV (pág. 420)

interchangeable parts identical machine-made parts that can be substituted for each other in manufacturing (p. 645)

piezas intercambiables partes idénticas que se pueden reemplazar entre sí (pág. 645)

interdependence a relationship between countries in which they rely on one another for resources, goods, or services (p. 992)

interdependencia relación entre países que se produce cuando dependen mutuamente para poder obtener recursos, bienes o servicios (pág. 992)

Internet an electronic system that allows the linking of millions of individual computers around the world (p. 898)

Internet sistema electrónico que conecta a millones de computadoras individuales de todo el mundo (pág. 898)

intifada a violent uprising by Palestinians against the Israeli occupation of the West Bank and Gaza Strip in the late 1980s (p. 956)

intifada levantamiento violento de los palestinos contra la ocupación israelí de Cisjordania y la franja de Gaza a finales de la década de 1980 (pág. 956)

Iranian Revolution (1978–1979) a revolution against the shah of Iran led by the Ayatollah Ruhollah Khomeini, which resulted in Iran becoming an Islamic republic with Khomeini as its leader (p. 958)

Revolución iraní (1978–1979) revolución contra el sha de Irán dirigida por el ayatolá Ruhollah Khomeini, cuyo resultado fue que Irán se transformó en una república islámica dirigida por Khomeini (pág. 958)

iron curtain term coined by Winston Churchill in 1946 to describe an imaginary line dividing Communist countries in the Soviet bloc from countries in Western Europe during the Cold War (p. 879)

cortina de hierro término creado por Winston Churchill en 1946 para describir una línea imaginaria que separaba a los países comunistas del bloque soviético de los países de Europa occidental durante la Guerra Fría (pág. 879)

Iroquois League an alliance of five (later, six) Native American tribes formed in the 1500s for defense and self-governance (p. 202)

Liga de Iroqueses alianza de indígenas estadounidenses, formada para gobernarse a sí mismos (pág. 202)

Islam a monotheistic religion whose prophet is Muhammad and whose holy book is the Qur'an; the term means "achieving peace through surrender to God" (p. 258)

Islam religión enseñada por Mahoma; el término significa literalmente "entregarse" o "someterse" (pág. 258)

isolationism staying out of the affairs and wars of other nations; the position initially held by the United States at the beginning of World War II (p. 842)
aislacionismo permanecer al margen de los asuntos y los conflictos bélicos de otras naciones; postura que mantenía Estados Unidos al comienzo de la Segunda Guerra Mundial (pág. 842)

J

Jainism a religion of India, founded about the same time as Buddhism (c. 500 BC) and in reaction to some Hindu practices; believers renounce worldly things, embrace self-discipline, and practice nonviolence (p. 102)
jainismo religión que promueve la no violencia y cuyos miembros prometen decir sólo la verdad y no robar (pág. 102)

Janissaries highly trained soldiers in the elite guard of the Ottoman Empire (p. 500)
Jenízaros soldados sumamente entrenados de la guardia de élite del Imperio otomano (pág. 500)

Jesuits members of a Catholic religious order, the Society of Jesus, founded by Ignatius Loyola in 1534 (p. 456)
jesuitas miembros de la orden católica de la Compañía de Jesús, fundada por Ignacio de Loyola en 1534 (pág. 456)

jihad "struggle for the faith"; can be thought of as an individual or communal struggle; as the latter, the term embraces notions of defending the Muslim community and holy war (p. 260)
jihad "lucha por la fe"; lucha para obedecer la voluntad divina en la fe musulmana (pág. 260)

joint-stock companies businesses formed by groups of people who jointly make an investment and share in the profits and losses (p. 487)
sociedad por acciones empresas formada por personas que realizan una inversión conjunta y comparten las ganancias y las pérdidas (pág. 487)

joint ventures business partnerships and co-ownership (p. 1032)
empresa conjunta asociación comercial y copropiedad (pág. 1032)

journeyman a skilled worker who was paid wages by the master of a guild (p. 410)
oficial trabajador especializado que recibía su salario del jefe de un gremio (pág. 410)

Judaism a monotheistic religion originating with the Israelites, tracing its origins to Abraham, and having its spiritual and ethical principles embodied chiefly in the Hebrew Scriptures and the Talmud (p. 45)
judaísmo religión monoteísta de los israelitas, cuyos orígenes se remontan a Abraham; sus principios espirituales y éticos se encuentran en las Escrituras Hebreas y el Talmud (pág. 45)

junta a group of leaders who rule jointly (p. 972)
junta grupo de líderes que gobiernan juntos (pág. 972)

K

kabuki a form of Japanese theater dating from the 1600s, featuring a highly stylized blend of singing and dancing; performances can last all day (p. 521)
kabuki forma de teatro japonés que podía durar todo un día y en la cual los actores cantaban, bailaban e interactuaban con el público (pág. 521)

kamikazes in World War II, Japanese pilots who loaded their aircraft with bombs and crashed them into enemy ships (p. 850)
kamikazes en la Segunda Guerra Mundial, pilotos que se estrellaban con su avión cargado de explosivos contra un barco enemigo (pág. 850)

karma in Hinduism, the totality of a person's good and bad deeds and the way in which they affect that individual's fate in the afterlife (p. 99)
karma en el hinduismo, la totalidad de las acciones buenas y malas de una persona y la forma en que afectarán su destino en la otra vida (pág. 99)

khan a Mongol chief or ruler (p. 317)
khan jefe o gobernante mongol (pág. 317)

Khmer Rouge Communists trained by the Vietcong who came to power in Cambodia in 1975 (p. 919)
Khmer Rouge comunistas entrenados por el Vietcong que se hicieron con el poder en Camboya en 1975 (pág. 919)

kivas underground chambers in a Pueblo village, used by the men for religious ceremonies or councils (p. 200)
kivas cámaras subterráneas de los indios Pueblo, usadas por los hombres para celebrar ceremonias religiosas o consejos (pág. 200)

knights in medieval Europe, nobles who were members of a lord's heavily armored cavalry (p. 383)
caballeros en la Europa medieval, nobles que eran miembros de la caballería fuertemente armada de un señor (pág. 383)

Koryu dynasty (835–1392) Korean dynasty founded by the warlord Wang Kon (p. 327)

dinastía Koryu (835–1392) dinastía coreana fundada por el caudillo Wang Kon (pág. 327)

Kristallnacht (1938) "night of broken glass"; an event that occurred on the nights of November 9 and 10 in which Hitler's Nazis encouraged Germans to riot against Jews; nearly 100 Jews died (p. 827)

Kristallnacht (1938) "noche de cristales rotos"; suceso que tuvo lugar en las noches del 9 y 10 de noviembre, en el que ciudadanos alemanes, alentados por los nazis de Hitler, atacaron a los judíos; murieron casi 100 judíos (pág. 827)

labor union an organization representing workers' interests (p. 644)

sindicato organización que representa los intereses de los trabajadores (pág. 644)

laissez-faire a business system where companies are allowed to conduct business without interference by the government (p. 646)

laissez-faire sistema comercial donde las empresas pueden llevar a cabo actividades comerciales sin interferencia del gobierno (pág. 646)

Latin the language of ancient Rome (p. 182)

latín la lengua de Roma (pág. 182)

League of Nations an international body of nations formed after World War I to prevent future wars (p. 797)

Liga de las Naciones cuerpo internacional de naciones formado después de la Primera Guerra Mundial para evitar futuras guerras (pág. 797)

Legalism a Chinese political philosophy that holds that the most effective government is that which rules the people by a harsh set of laws (p. 224)

legalismo filosofía política china que sostiene que el gobierno más eficaz es el que gobierna mediante un conjunto de leyes severas (pág. 224)

Liberation Theology the belief, common in Latin America in the late 1900s, that the Roman Catholic Church should be active in the struggle for economic and political equality (p. 968)

teología de la liberación creencia de que la iglesia cristiana debe participar activamente en la lucha por la igualdad política y económica (pág. 968)

loess fine yellowish soil blown from the desert regions (p. 109)

loess tierra fina y amarillenta de algunas regiones desérticas (pág. 109)

logic the process of making inferences (p. 144)

lógica proceso de hacer inferencias (pág. 144)

Long March (1934) the 6,000-mile journey made by Communist Chinese to escape Nationalist troops (p. 808)

Larga Marcha (1934) viaje de 6,000 millas hecho por los comunistas chinos para escapar de las tropas nacionalistas (pág. 808)

Louisiana Purchase (1803) the purchase of land between the Mississippi River and the Rocky Mountains that nearly doubled the size of the United States (p. 702)

Compra de Luisiana (1803) compra de tierra entre el río Mississippi y las montañas Rocallosas que casi duplicó el tamaño de Estados Unidos (pág. 702)

lyric poetry a type of poetry that gained its name from the lyre, an instrument that played while the poetry was sung (p. 145)

poesía lírica tipo de poesía que debe su nombre a la lira, instrumento que acompañaba la poesía cantada (pág. 145)

Magna Carta (1215) a charter agreed to by King John of England that granted nobles certain rights and restricted the king's powers (p. 389)

Carta Magna (1215) carta de libertades aceptadas por el rey Juan de Inglaterra, que obligaban al rey a obedecer las mismas leyes que los ciudadanos (pág. 389)

Magyars a Hungarian ethnic group (p. 724)

magiares grupo étnico de Hungría (pág. 724)

maize corn (p. 202)

maíz grano (pág. 202)

Manchukuo Japanese puppet state (1932-1945) formed in Manchuria and eastern Inner Mongolia (p. 822)

Manchukuo antiguo estado del este de Asia en Manchuria y el este de Mongolia Interior; fue establecido como estado títere en 1932 después de que los japoneses invadieran Manchuria en 1931 (pág. 822)

Manchurian Incident (1931) using an explosion on a Japanese-controlled Southern Manchurian railroad as an excuse, Japanese military forces conquered Manchuria and set up a puppet government (p. 821)

incidente de Manchuria (1931) plan de los japoneses para incriminar a los chinos en la explosión de una bomba en un ferrocarril controlado por los japoneses en la región china de Manchuria; el gobierno japonés se negó a apoyar la acción con sus tropas, lo que produjo una importante crisis diplomática en Japón (pág. 821)

Mandate of Heaven the Chinese belief that royal authority is the result of divine approval (p. 111)

Mandato del Cielo creencia china de que la autoridad del rey es el efecto de la aprobación divina (pág. 111)

mandates territories once part of the Ottoman Empire that the League of Nations gave to other European powers to rule after World War I (p. 798)
mandatos después de la Primera Guerra Mundial, los territorios del Imperio otomano que serían gobernados por potencias europeas (pág. 798)

manifest destiny a belief shared by many Americans in the mid-1800s that the United States should expand from the Atlantic to the Pacific oceans (p. 703)
destino manifiesto creencia compartida por muchos estadounidenses a mediados del siglo XIX de que Estados Unidos debía expandirse desde el océano Atlántico hasta el Pacífico (pág. 703)

manorial system an economic system in the Middle Ages that was built around large estates called manors (p. 384)
sistema de feudos sistema económico de la Edad Media cuya base eran grandes propiedades llamadas feudos (pág. 384)

maquiladora a large industrial assembly plant located in the border towns of Mexico that produces finished goods for export to the United States (p. 1027)
maquiladora gran planta de montaje industrial ubicada en las ciudades fronterizas de México en la que se fabrican productos elaborados para exportar a Estados Unidos (pág. 1027)

Marshall Plan (1947) plan for the economic reconstruction of Europe after World War II (p. 879)
Plan Marshall (1947) plan para la reconstrucción económica de Europa tras la Segunda Guerra Mundial (pág. 879)

martyrs people put to death for their beliefs (p. 186)
mártires personas ejecutadas por sus creencias (pág. 186)

Marxism-Leninism the political and economic philosophy of the Bolsheviks, expounded by Vladimir Lenin, which looked to an uprising of the proletariat that would abolish private property and enforce social equality (p. 792)
marxismo-leninismo filosofía política y económica de los bolcheviques; se concentraba en el levantamiento contra los burgueses; refutaba el capitalismo y tenía como objetivo final la creación de una sociedad sin clases (pág. 792)

mass production the system of manufacturing large numbers of identical items (p. 645)
producción en masa sistema de fabricación que consiste en producir gran cantidad de artículos idénticos (pág. 645)

Mau Mau a violent movement in Kenya during the 1960s, led by Kikuyu farmers, to rid the country of white settlers (p. 939)
Mau Mau movimiento emprendido por los agricultores kikuyu con el fin de expulsar de Kenia por medios violentos a los agricultores blancos (pág. 939)

medieval the time period in western European history known as the Middle Ages (p. 362)
medieval período de la historia de Europa occidental conocido como la Edad Media (pág. 362)

megacity an urban area with a population of 10 million or more (p. 1027)
megalópolis ciudad con una población de 10 o más millones de habitantes (pág. 1027)

megaliths huge stones used for burial or religious purposes (p. 15)
megalitos grandes piedras usadas en tumbas o para fines religiosos (pág. 15)

mercantilism an economic system used from about the 1500s to the 1700s that held that a nation's power was directly related to its wealth (p. 484)
mercantilismo sistema económico usado desde el siglo XVI hasta el siglo XVIII aproximadamente, que afirmaba que el poder de una nación estaba directamente asociado a su riqueza (pág. 484)

Mesopotamia the area that lies between the Tigris and Euphrates rivers in Southwest Asia (p. 33)
Mesopotamia área ubicada entre los ríos Tigris y Éufrates, en el suroeste de Asia (pág. 33)

Messiah in Judaism, a savior sent by God (p. 184)
Mesías en el judaísmo, un salvador enviado por Dios (pág. 184)

Middle Passage the name for voyages that brought enslaved Africans across the Atlantic Ocean to North America and the West Indies (p. 489)
Paso Central viaje en el que los esclavos africanos atravesaban el océano Atlántico hasta llegar a América del Norte y las Antillas (pág. 489)

Middle Way basic Buddhist teachings of the Eightfold Path; it advises people to live in moderation, avoiding the extremes of either comfort or discomfort in the search for nirvana (p. 105)
Camino Medio enseñanzas básicas del sendero óctuple; aconseja vivir con moderación y evitar los extremos de la comodidad o la incomodidad en la búsqueda del nirvana (pág. 105)

minarets towers attached to the outside of a mosque, from where a crier calls Muslims to worship (p. 274)
minaretes torres adosadas al exterior de una mezquita desde la cual un voceador convoca a los musulmanes a decir sus plegarias (pág. 274)

moksha in Hinduism, the escape from the cycle of rebirth (p. 100)
moksha en el hinduismo, el hecho de liberarse del ciclo de renacimiento (pág. 100)

monasticism voluntary separation from society, usually in monasteries, to dedicate one's life to God; prevalent in the Middle Ages (p. 363)
monacato separación voluntaria de la sociedad para dedicar la vida a Dios (pág. 363)

ENGLISH AND SPANISH GLOSSARY

monotheism the belief in one god (p. 49)
monoteísmo creencia en un solo dios (pág. 49)

Monroe Doctrine (1823) U.S. President James Monroe's statement forbidding further colonization in the Americas and declaring that any attempt by a foreign country to colonize would be considered an act of hostility by the United States (p. 702)
Doctrina Monroe (1823) declaración del presidente Estados Unidos James Monroe en la que se prohibía la colonización del continente americano y se advertía que todo intento de colonización por parte de cualquier país extranjero sería considerado un acto hostil (pág. 702)

monsoons seasonal winds in India (p. 94)
monzóns vientos estacional de la India (pág. 94)

mosaics images created with tiny bits of colored tile fitted together and cemented into place (p. 349)
mosaicos imagens creadas con pequeños trozos de azulejos de colores colocados uno al lado del otro y pegados con cemento (pág. 349)

mosque a building for Muslim prayer (p. 260)
mezquita edificio de oración de los musulmanes (pág. 260)

movable type metal blocks on which symbols were etched (p. 314)
tipo móvil bloque de metal donde se grababan símbolos (pág. 314)

Mughal Empire a Muslim empire in India (1526–1761) founded by Babur (p. 505)
Imperio mughal imperio musulmán en la India (1526–1761) fundado por Babur (pág. 505)

multinational corporations large companies that operate in several different countries and sell their products around the world (p. 992)
corporaciones multinacionales grandes empresas que operan en varios países diferentes y venden sus productos en todo el mundo (pág. 992)

mummification the process of preserving the body with chemicals after death (p. 75)
momificación proceso de preservar el cuerpo mediante sustancias químicas después de la muerte (pág. 75)

Muslim League political group founded in 1906 to protect the rights of Indian Muslims; it later became one of the main forces calling for India independence and a separate nation for Indian Muslims (p. 745)
Liga musulmana grupo político de musulmanes de la India que buscaban proteger sus derechos (pág. 745)

Muslims followers of Islam (p. 258)
musulmanes seguidores del Islam (pág. 258)

Nanjing Massacre (1937) the murder of as many as 300,000 Chinese men, women, and children by Japanese troops (p. 822)
masacre de Nanjing (1937) asesinato de nada menos que 300 mil hombres, mujeres y niños chinos por parte de las tropas japonesas (pág. 822)

nationalism sense of pride and devotion to one's nation (p. 613)
nacionalismo sentido de orgullo y lealtad por la propia nación (pág. 613)

NATO North Atlantic Treaty Organization; a defensive military alliance of twelve Western nations formed in 1949 (p. 880)
OTAN Organización del Tratado del Atlántico Norte; alianza militar defensiva de doce naciones occidentales formada en 1949 (pág. 880)

navigation the guidance of ships from place to place (p. 379)
navegación acto de guiar embaraciones de un lugar a otro (pág. 379)

Nazi Party National Socialist Party; fascist political party of Adolf Hitler governed on totalitarian lines and advocating German racial superiority (p. 826)
Partido Nazi Partido Nacional Socialista de los Trabajadores Alemanes; partido político fascista liderado por Adolf Hitler que se basaba en el totalitarismo, la superioridad racial y el control gubernamental de la industria (pág. 826)

negritude movement African and Afro-Caribbean literary movement founded in Paris in the 1930s that rejected European models and promoted pride in African cultural identity (p. 947)
movimiento de la negritud movimiento literario fundado por un grupo de estudiantes africanos y afrocaribeños que vivían en París en la década de 1930 (pág. 947)

Neolithic Era the New Stone Age; the time period after the Paleolithic Era, marked by the use of tools (p. 13)
Neolítico Nueva Edad de Piedra; periodo posterior al Paleolítico que se destaca por el uso de herramientas (pág. 13)

Neolithic Revolution a period in human history marked by the introduction of agriculture and a shift from food gathering to food production (p. 13)
revolución neolítica período de la historia del hombre marcado por la introducción de la agricultura y el paso de la recolección de alimentos a su producción (pág. 13)

neutral in a war, not aiding either side (p. 781)
neutral en una guerra, que no apoya a ningún bando (pág. 781)

New Deal U.S. President Franklin D. Roosevelt's plan of economic relief, recovery, and reforms for the country during the Great Depression (p. 815)
Nuevo Trato plan del presidente Franklin D. Roosevelt destinado a proporcionar ayuda económica, y a recuperar y reformar económicamente al país después de la Gran Depresión (pág. 815)

New Economic Policy Lenin's plan, started in 1921, to allow limited capitalism, especially among farmers, in order to restore the Soviet economy (p. 793)
Nueva Política Económica Respuesta de Lenin a los campesinos y trabajadores que sufrían después de la Revolución Rusa; autorizó un poco de capitalismo para que estas personas pudieran recuperarse (pág. 793)

NGO a non-governmental organization, or a group not affiliated with any government, formed to provide services or to push for a certain public policy (p. 997)
ONG organización no gubernamental, o grupo no afiliado a ningún gobierno, que se forma para brindar servicios o promover cierta política pública (pág. 997)

nirvana in Buddhism, the release from the world and the achievement of peace and enlightenment (p. 105)
nirvana en el budismo, la liberación del mundo y el logro de la iluminación en una paz espiritual y perfecta (pág. 105)

Nok one of the earliest African peoples to make iron tools (500 BC–AD 200), the Nok lived in what is today Nigeria (p. 287)
nok pueblo que vivió en lo que hoy en día es Nigeria; fue el primero en hacer herramientas agrícolas de hierro (pág. 287)

nomads people who move from place to place in search of food and water (p. 10)
nómadas personas que se trasladan de un lugar a otro en busca de comida y agua (pág. 10)

nonaggression pact an agreement between nations to not attack one another (p. 838)
pacto de no agresión acuerdo entre naciones de no atacarse entre sí (pág. 838)

nonaligned nations nations who refused to ally with either side in the Cold War between the United States and the Soviet Union (p. 886)
naciones no alineadas naciones que se niegan a aliarse con uno de los bandos en un conflicto (pág. 886)

North American Free Trade Agreement (NAFTA) a free trade agreement that eliminated tariffs on trade between Mexico, the United States, and Canada (p. 980)
Tratado de Libre Comercio de América del Norte (NAFTA, por sus siglas en inglés) acuerdo de libre comercio que eliminó las barreras comerciales entre México, Estados Unidos y Canadá (pág. 980)

Nuremberg Laws Nazi laws that eliminated citizenship and many civil and property rights for Jews (p. 827)
Leyes de Nuremberg leyes de los nazis que negaban la ciudadanía y muchos derechos civiles y de propiedad a los judíos (pág. 827)

Nuremberg trials (1945-1949) trials in which an Allied military tribunal tried several dozen top Nazi and military officials; many were executed for war crimes (p. 878)
juicios de Nuremberg (1945-1949) juicios en los que un tribunal militar de los Aliados juzgó a varias decenas de autoridades militares y nazis de alto rango; muchos fueron ejecutados por crímenes de guerra (pág. 878)

obelisks tall, thin pillars with pyramid-shaped tops (p. 73)
obeliscos pilares altos y delgados cuya parte superior tiene forma de pirámide (pág. 73)

offshoring the movement of an entire factory or other business enterprise abroad (p. 1031)
externalización acto de trasladar al extranjero una fábrica o negocio al completo (pág. 1031)

Old Order the political and social system in place in France before the Revolution (p. 593)
Viejo Orden sistema político y social que funcionaba en Francia antes de la Revolución (pág. 593)

one-party system political system in which a single political party controls the government and elections are rarely competitive (p. 945)
sistema de partido único sistema político donde un único partido controla el gobierno y las elecciones no suelen ser competitivas (pág. 945)

Organization of Petroleum Exporting Countries (OPEC) an organization that coordinates petroleum policies of major producing countries (p. 955)
Organización de Países Exportadores de Petróleo (OPEP) organización que coordina las políticas sobre el petróleo de las empresas pais más importantes (pág. 955)

oracle bones inscribed animal bones used to predict the future (p. 110)
huesos oráculos huesos de animales con inscripciones usados para predecir el futuro (pág. 110)

Orthodox Church the church that followed the Eastern traditions of Christianity as opposed to the Western traditions (p. 351)
iglesia ortodoxo iglesia que siguió las tradiciones cristianas orientales, en lugar de las tradiciones occidentales (pág. 351)

Ottomans ruling dynasty of the Ottoman Empire (1293–1922), named for Osman I, the founder; at the Empire's height, the Ottomans ruled a vast area that encompassed southwest Asia, northeast Africa, and southeast Europe (p. 500)
otomanos descendientes de Osmán I, que gobernó el vasto sultanato turco del suroeste de Asia, el noreste de África y el sureste de Europa hasta su disolución tras la Primera Guerra Mundial (pág. 500)

outsourcing the practice of using workers from outside a company to cut costs or increase production (p. 992)
tercerización práctica de las empresas de usar trabajadores externos para reducir los costos o aumentar la producción (pág. 992)

pagoda a multistory Buddhist tower used as a temple or a shrine (p. 313)
pagoda torre budista de varios pisos que se usa como templo o santuario (pág. 313)

Paleolithic Era also known as the Old Stone Age; a prehistoric period that lasted from about 2.5 million years ago to about 8,500 BC (p. 9)
Paleolítico también conocido como la Antigua Edad de Piedra; período prehistórico que duró desde hace aproximadamente 2.5 millones de años hasta aproximadamente 8,500 a.C. (pág. 9)

Pan-Arabism political movement in the 1950s and 1960s promoting Arab unity (p. 953)
panarabismo la unidad de los pueblos de ascendencia árabe (pág. 953)

Papal States territories in central Italy controlled by the pope from 756–1870 (p. 374)
Estados Pontificios región del centro de Italia controlada por el papa (pág. 374)

papyrus a paper-like material made by ancient Egyptians from the stem of the reedy papyrus plant, which grows in the Nile River delta (p. 78)
papiro material semejante al papel que fabricaban los egipcios con los tallos de una planta parecida a la caña llamada papiro, que crece en el delta del Nilo (pág. 78)

Parliament the governing body of England (p. 389)
Parlamento el cuerpo que gobierna Inglaterra (pág. 389)

partition division (p. 910)
partición división (pág. 910)

pasteurization the process of heating liquids to kill bacteria and prevent fermentation (p. 668)
pasteurización proceso de calentar los líquidos para matar las bacterias y evitar la fermentación (pág. 668)

pastoralists nomads who kept herds of livestock on which they depended for most of their food (p. 15)
pastoralistas campesinos nómadas que mantenían ganado, del cual obtenían la mayor parte de su alimento (pág. 15)

paterfamilias the family father (p. 179)
paterfamilias el padre de la familia (pág. 179)

patriarch an ancestral "father" of Judaism (p. 46)
patriarca "padre" ancestral del judaísmo (pág. 46)

patricians a class of powerful landowners in ancient Rome who controlled the government and society (p. 165)
patricios terratenientes romanos poderosos; miembros de la clase alta adinerada que controlaban el gobierno y la sociedad (pág. 165)

patronage the practice of rewarding political loyalty with well-paying government positions (p. 945)
tráfico de influencias dar puestos bien pagados en el gabinete gubernamental a los seguidores leales de un funcionario del gobierno (pág. 945)

Pax Mongolica a period of peace in Mongolia lasting from the mid-1200s until the mid-1300s (p. 318)
Pax Mongolica período de paz en Mongolia que duró desde mediados del siglo XIII hasta mediados del siglo XIV (pág. 318)

Pax Romana a period of peace in Roman Empire lasting from the beginning of Augustus's reign until the death of Marcus Aurelius (27 BC–AD 180) (p. 175)
Pax Romana período de paz en Roma que duró desde el comienzo del gobierno de Augusto hasta la muerte de Marco Aurelio (27 BC–AD 180) (pág. 175)

Peace of Augsburg (1555) an agreement between states in the Holy Roman Empire that gave each German prince the right to decide whether his state would be Catholic or Protestant (p. 536)
Paz de Augsburgo (1555) acuerdo por el cual la religión de cada estado alemán sería decidida por su gobernante (pág. 536)

peacekeeping sending multinational forces into countries to enforce ceasefires or truces among warring countries or warring groups within a single country (p. 1041)
mantenimiento de la paz envío de fuerzas internacionales a otros países para que se respete un cese del fuego o una tregua entre países en guerra o entre grupos en guerra dentro de un mismo país (pág. 1041)

peninsulares colonists in Latin American who were born on the Iberian Peninsula, in Spain or Portugal (p. 696)
peninsulares europeos que nacieron en la península ibérica, es decir, en España o Portugal (pág. 696)

perestroika "restructuring"; restructuring of the corrupt government bureaucracy in the Soviet Union begun by Mikhail Gorbachev (p. 892)

perestroika "reestructuración"; la reestructuración de la burocracia corrupta del gobierno soviético que se realizó bajo la presidencia de Mikhail Gorbachev (pág. 892)

Persian Gulf War (1990–1991) war in which U.S.-led forces liberated Kuwait from Iraq (p. 898)

Guerra del Golfo (1990-1991) guerra en que las fuerzas lideradas por Estados Unidos liberaron Kuwait de Irak (pág. 898)

phalanx a military formation composed of rows of soldiers standing shoulder to shoulder carrying pikes or heavy spears (p. 136)

falange formación militar compuesta por soldados parados hombro contra hombro y portando picas o lanzas pesadas (pág. 136)

pharaoh ruler of ancient Egypt (p. 66)

faraón gobernador de Egipto antigua (pág. 66)

philosophes philosophers of the Enlightenment (p. 576)

philosophes filósofos de la Ilustración (pág. 576)

piety devotion to one's religion (p. 393)

piedad nivel de devoción de una persona a su religión (pág. 393)

plantations large farms that usually specialized in the growing of one type of crop for a profit (p. 488)

plantacións establecimientos agrícolas grande, generalmente especializado en un tipo de cultivo con el fin de obtener una ganancia (pág. 488)

plebeians farmers or workers, who made up a large part of the population in ancient Rome (p. 165)

plebeyos agricultores o trabajadores que formaban gran parte de la población antigua romana (pág. 165)

plebiscite the procedure used to submit the constitution of a new government to the people for a yes-or-no vote (p. 610)

plebiscito procedimiento para someter a votación la aprobación de una nueva constitución o gobierno; los ciudadanos votan a favor o en contra (pág. 610)

pogroms the organized persecutions and massacres of Jews in Russia in the 1880s (p. 730)

pogroms persecucións organizadas y masacres de los judíos en Rusia en la década de 1880 (pág. 730)

polis a city-state of ancient Greece (p. 129)

polis ciudad estado de la antigua Grecia (pág. 129)

polytheism the belief in many gods (p. 34)

politeísmo creencia en muchos dioses (pág. 34)

pontificate papal term in office (p. 394)

pontificado mandato del papa (pág. 394)

popes title given to the heads of the Roman Catholic Church (p. 187)

papas títulos que asumen los jefes de la Iglesia católica romana (pág. 187)

popular culture cultural traits such as food, sports, and music, that are common within a group of people (p. 995)

cultura popular rasgos culturales que son bien conocidos y aceptados (pág. 995)

populist a supporter of the rights of the common people as opposed to the privileged elite (p. 974)

populista defensor de los derechos y el poder del pueblo (pág. 974)

porcelain a type of ceramic made by firing a pure clay at very high temperatures and then glazing it; often called "china" (p. 313)

porcelana tipo de cerámica que se hace al exponer arcilla pura a temperaturas muy altas, y luego vidriarla (pág. 313)

Potsdam Conference (1945) a meeting of Allied leaders in the German city of Potsdam to address issues about the post-World War II Europe (p. 863)

Conferencia de Potsdam (1945) encuentro de los líderes Aliados hacia el final de la Segunda Guerra Mundial (pág. 863)

predestination the belief that at the beginning of time God decided who would gain salvation (p. 452)

predestinación creencia de que al comienzo de los tiempos Dios decidió quién alcanzaría la salvación (pág. 452)

privatization the process of converting businesses or industries from public to private ownership (p. 1032)

privatización el control privado de las industrias, en contraposición al control del gobierno (pág. 1032)

propaganda information such as posters and pamphlets created by governments in order to influence public opinion (p. 785)

propaganda información difundida con la intención de influir en la opinión pública (pág. 785)

Protestant Reformation a religious movement in the 1500s that split the Christian church in western Europe and led to the establishment of a number of new churches (p. 449)

Reforma protestante revolución religiosa del siglo XVI que dividió la iglesia de Europa occidental y llevó al establecimiento de una serie de iglesias nuevas (pág. 449)

pueblo an aboveground structure with many rooms (p. 200)

pueblo estructura de varias habitaciones construida por encima del nivel del suelo (pág. 200)

Puritans English Protestants of the late 1500s and most of the 1600s who wanted to "purify" the Church of England through reforms (p. 547)

puritanos protestantes inglés que quería "purificar" la Iglesia de Inglaterra a través de reformas (pág. 547)

ENGLISH AND SPANISH GLOSSARY

Q

quipu in Incan society, a cord that contained knotted strings of various lengths, weaves, colors, and design, which functioned as a system of record keeping (p. 213)
quipu en la sociedad inca, un sistema de cordeles con nudos de distinta longitud, forma de entrelazarse, color y diseño que servía para llevar registros escritos (pág. 213)

Qur'an the sacred text of Islam (p. 259)
Corán texto sagrado del Islam (pág. 259)

R

radical a person with extreme views (p. 599)
radical persona con opiniones extremas (pág. 599)

radioactivity a process in which certain elements constantly break down and release energy (p. 667)
radioactividad proceso por el cual los átomos de ciertos elementos se desintegran constantemente y liberan energía (pág. 667)

Raj the British rule of India from 1757 until 1947 (p. 743)
Raj gobierno británico en la India desde 1757 hasta 1947 (pág. 743)

rajas leaders of ancient cities in India (p. 96)
rajás líderes de las antiguas ciudades de la India (pág. 96)

reactionary an extremist who not only opposes change but also wants to undo certain changes (p. 618)
reaccionario extremista que no solamente se opone al cambio, sino que también quiere revertir algunos cambios (pág. 618)

realism a mid-1800s movement in art and literature that rejected romanticism and sought to depict the details of everyday life, no matter how unpleasant (p. 676)
realismo movimiento artístico y literario de mediados del siglo XIX que rechazaba el romanticismo y prefería representar el mundo tal cual es (pág. 676)

realpolitik "the politics of reality"; the belief in practical goals instead of theory in political philosophy (p. 719)
realpolitik "la política de la realidad"; la creencia en los objetivos prácticos en lugar de en la teoría de la filosofía política (pág. 719)

reason clear and ordered thinking (p. 144)
razón pensamiento claro y ordenado (pág. 144)

Reconquista the effort of Christian leaders to drive the Muslims out of Spain, occurring between the 1100s and 1492 (p. 391)
Reconquista campaña de los líderes cristianos para expulsar a los musulmanes de España entre el siglo XII y 1492 (pág. 391)

Red Guards a group of young men in China who carried out the work of the Cultural Revolution; they roamed the cities and villages, identifying possible opposition to Mao Zedong's leadership (p. 922)
Guardias Rojos grupo de jóvenes que llevaron a cabo el trabajo de la Revolución cultural; recorrían las ciudades y los pueblos en busca de posibles opositores al liderazgo de Mao Tsé-Tung (pág. 922)

Red Shirts army of volunteer troops led by Giuseppe Garibaldi; in 1860 they attacked the island of Sicily and won it for the Italians (p. 716)
Camisas Rojas ejército de tropas voluntarias dirigidas por Guiseppe Garibaldi; en 1860 atacaron la isla de Sicilia y la conquistaron para los italianos (pág. 716)

refugees people who leave their country to escape danger or persecution (p. 998)
refugiados personas que dejan su país para escapar de un peligro o una persecución (pág. 998)

Reign of Terror a period during the French Revolution in which the Robespierre-led government executed thousands of political figures and ordinary citizens (p. 604)
Reino del Terror período de la Revolución francesa en que el gobierno dirigido por Robespierre ejecutó a miles de figuras políticas y ciudadanos comunes (pág. 604)

reincarnation in Hinduism, the belief that after one dies, the soul is reborn into a different form (p. 99)
reencarnación en el hinduismo, la creencia de que después de la muerte el alma renace bajo una forma diferente (pág. 99)

Renaissance "rebirth"; following the Middle Ages, a movement that centered on the revival of interest in the classical learning of Greece and Rome (p. 439)
Renacimiento movimiento posterior a la Edad Media que se centró en revivir el interés por el legado clásico de Grecia y Roma (pág. 439)

republic a political system in which the citizens of a region elect representatives to run the government (p. 165)
república sistema político en el que los ciudadanos de una región eligen representantes para dirigir el gobierno (pág. 165)

Restoration the period of the reign of Charles II in England when the monarchy was restored after the collapse of Oliver Cromwell's government; there was also a rebirth of English culture during this time (p. 549)
Restauración período de la historia de Inglaterra durante el reinado de Carlos II en el que se restauró la monarquía tras la caída del gobierno de Oliver Cromwell; durante este período, también hubo un renacimiento de la cultura inglesa (pág. 549)

romanticism an artistic and literary movement at the beginning of the 1800s which rejected the rationalism of the Enlightenment in favor of emotion, intuition, and imagination (p. 676)

romanticismo movimiento intelectual de comienzos del siglo XIX que se concentró en el sentimiento y la imaginación, y se ocupó del tema del romance de la vida en contraposición a la razón (pág. 676)

Roosevelt Corollary (1904) a policy proposed by U.S. president Theodore Roosevelt as an addition, or corollary, to the Monroe Doctrine; it pledged to use U.S. military force to prevent European interference in the internal affairs of Latin American nations while reserving for the United States the right to intervene (p. 765)

Corolario de Roosevelt cambio en la Doctrina Monroe en la que se declaraba que Estados Unidos podía intervenir en los asuntos internos de los países latinoamericanos (pág. 765)

Rosetta Stone a granite stone found in 1799 that bears an inscription in hieroglyphics, demotic characters, and Greek; gave the first clue to deciphering Egyptian hieroglyphics (p. 78)

Piedra Roseta piedra de granito hallada en 1799 donde se ve una inscripción en jeroglíficos, en caracteres demóticos y en griego; sirvió como primera pista para descifrar los jeroglíficos egipcios (pág. 78)

Royalists supporters of government by a monarch; used as a name for supporters of England's King Charles I (p. 547)

monárquicos defensors de un gobierno monárquico (pág. 547)

Rus northern European force, probably Vikings, who set up a state centered on Kiev in the mid-800s that grew into Russia (p. 357)

rus nombre que se daba a los europeos del norte a mediados del siglo IX (pág. 357)

Russo-Japanese War (1904–1905) an imperialistic conflict that stemmed from the rival designs of Russia and Japan on Manchuria and Korea, resulting in the defeat of Russia (p. 730)

Guerra ruso-japonesa (1904–1905) conflicto entre imperios que surgió debido a las intenciones rivales de Rusia y Japón respecto a Manchuria y Corea; terminó con la derrota de Rusia (pág. 730)

sagas long stories, written in the early 1200s, about great Icelandic heroes and events (p. 380)

sagas largas historias islandesas acerca de grandes héroes y sucesos (pág. 380)

Sahel a semiarid strip of land across the center of Africa that divides the Sahara from wetter areas (p. 284)

Sahel en África, franja de tierra que separa el desierto de otras zonas más húmedas (pág. 284)

Saint Bartholomew's Day Massacre August 24, 1572; a massacre of 6,000 to 8,000 Huguenots in Paris authorized by King Charles IX and his mother Catherine de Médici (p. 541)

masacre del día de San Bartolomé 24 de agosto de 1572; sangriento episodio que ocurrió durante las guerras religiosas en Francia después del intento de asesinato de un líder militar hugonote, planeado por Catalina de Médici; el resultado fue un extenso combate donde murieron entre 6,000 y 8,000 hugonotes (pág. 541)

salons gatherings in which intellectual and political ideas were exchanged during the Enlightenment (p. 575)

salóns reunión donde se intercambiaban ideas intelectuales y políticas durante la Ilustración (pág. 575)

samurai a professional Japanese warrior hired by wealthy landowners for protection in feudal Japan (p. 517)

samurai guerrero profesional japonés contratado por los terratenientes ricos del Japón feudal para obtener protección (pág. 517)

sanctions economic or political penalties imposed by one country on another to try and force a change in policy (p. 1003)

sanciones penalidades económicas o políticas impuestas por un país a otro para obligarlo a cambiar su política (pág. 1003)

Sandinistas Marxist group who led the revolution against the dictator of Nicaragua and then ruled the country from 1979 to 1990 (p. 972)

sandinistas grupo marxista que dirigió la revolución contra el dictador de Nicaragua (pág. 972)

sansculottes "without breeches"; a radical group of shopkeepers and wage earners during the French Revolution who wanted a larger voice in government and an end to food shortages (p. 595)

sansculottes "sin pantalones"; grupo radical de comerciantes y trabajadores a sueldo que, durante la Revolución francesa, querían tener más participación en el gobierno y poner fin a la escasez de comida (pág. 595)

satraps governors of ancient Persia (p. 53)
  sátrapas gobernadores de Persia antigua (pág. 53)

savanna open grassland (p. 284)
  sabana pradera abierta (pág. 284)

scholar-officials elite, educated members of the government during the Song period in China (p. 312)
  funcionarios eruditos miembros cultos de la élite que gobernaba China durante el período Song (pág. 312)

Scholasticism in the Middle Ages, the theological and philosophical school of thought that attempted to reconcile faith and reason (p. 417)
  escolasticismo escuela de pensamiento teológico y filosófico de la Edad Media que intentaba reconciliar la fe y la razón (pág. 417)

scientific method a method of inquiry that promotes observing, measuring, explaining, and verifying as a way to gain scientific knowledge (p. 568)
  método científico método de investigación basado en la observación, medición, explicación y verificación como la verdadera manera de adquirir el conocimiento científico (pág. 568)

Scientific Revolution a transformation in European thought in the 1500s and 1600s that called for scientific observation, experimentation, and the questioning of traditional opinions (p. 568)
  revolución científica transformación del pensamiento que ocurrió durante los siglos XVI y XVII debida a la observación, experimentación y cuestionamiento científico de las opiniones tradicionales (pág. 568)

secession the act of separating from (p. 703)
  secesión acto de separarse de algo (pág. 703)

Second Estate in pre-Revolution France, the nobles (p. 594)
  Segundo Estado en la Francia anterior a la Revolución, los nobles (pág. 594)

Secretariat body of the United Nations responsible for carrying out the administrative tasks (p. 1041)
  Secretaría de Naciones Unidas; grupo se encarga de las tareas administrativas de NU (pág. 1041)

secular having to do with worldly, as opposed to religious, matters (pp. 439, 1037)
  secular relacionado con cuestiones terrenales, en contraposición a las cuestiones religiosas (pág. 439, 1037)

Security Council body of the United Nations, consisting of 15 members, five of them permanent, charged with being the guardians of world peace (p. 1041)
  Consejo de Seguridad de Naciones Unidas; su función es mantener la paz (pág. 1041)

Senate a body of legislators (p. 166)
  Senado cuerpo de legisladores (pág. 166)

Sepoy Mutiny (1857–1858) a rebellion of Hindu and Muslim soldiers against the British in India (p. 742)
  Motín de Sepoy (1857–1858) rebelión de los soldados hindúes y musulmanes contra los británicos que estaban en la India (pág. 742)

serfs peasants who were legally bound to their lord's land (pp. 384, 729)
  siervos campesinos que estaban legalmente obligados a quedarse en las tierras de su señor (pág. 384, 729)

shah name given to a king of the Safavid Empire (p. 502)
  shah nombre dado al rey del Imperio safavida (pág. 502)

Sharpeville massacre (1960) an incident in which South African police fired on a crowd of apartheid protestors, killing 67 people (p. 944)
  masacre de Sharpeville (1960) incidente en el cual una organización nacionalista africana convocó a una manifestación frente a la estación de policía del municipio de Sharpeville; la policía abrió fuego contra los manifestantes y mató a 67 (pág. 944)

Shia a branch of Islam whose adherents believe that the caliphate must go to a descendent of Muhammad—particularly a member of the family of Ali (p. 264)
  chiita persona que cree que el califato debe ser para un pariente de Mahoma, especialmente un miembro de la familia de Alí (pág. 264)

Shining Path guerrilla group in Peru that terrorized the countryside in the 1980s and 1990s (p. 977)
  Sendero Luminoso grupo guerrillero de Perú que sembró el terror en las áreas rurales en la década de 1990 (pág. 977)

Shinto "Way of the *kami* (spirits)"; an indigenous religion of Japan that holds that everything in nature has a spirit; believers perform ceremonies to ask for the blessings of the spirits; traditionally, Shinto believers venerated the emperor (p. 323)
  shinto "camino de los dioses"; religión indígena de Japón que consiste en rituales y plegarias para apaciguar a los espíritus de la naturaleza y en venerar al emperador (pág. 323)

shogun the hereditary chief of Japan's warrior class who held the real power, while the emperor ruled in name only (p. 519)
  shogun jefe hereditario de la clase guerrera japonesa que poseía el verdadero poder, mientras que el emperador sólo gobernaba nominalmente (pág. 519)

Siege of Leningrad (1941–1942) Nazi army's unsuccessful attempt to capture the city of Leningrad in the Soviet Union during World War II; as many as 1 million civilians perished during the siege (p. 846)
  sitio de Leningrado (1941–1942) toma de Leningrado por parte de Hitler en Rusia; durante este sitio, murieron nada menos que un millón de civiles (pág. 846)

Sikhism an Indian religion founded in the late 1400s whose beliefs blend elements of Hinduism and Islam (p. 506)
  sikhismo religión no violenta cuyas creencias unen las religiones hinduista y musulmana (pág. 506)

ENGLISH AND SPANISH GLOSSARY

Silk Roads trade routes stretching from China to the Mediterranean, which allowed for the exchange of goods and ideas from China to the Roman Empire (p. 231)

Rutas de la Seda rutas comercial que se extendías desde China hasta el Mediterráneo y que permitió el intercambio de bienes e ideas entre China y el Imperio romano (pág. 231)

Sino-Japanese War (1894) war fought between China and Japan for influence over Korea; Japan's victory symbolized its successful modernization (p. 751)

Guerra sinojaponesa (1894) guerra entre China y Japón a causa de una rebelión en Corea; ambas naciones enviaron tropas para someter a los rebeldes coreanos (pág. 751)

Six-Day War (June, 1967) war between Israel and Egypt, Syria, and Jordan; Israel's victory gave it control of areas with large Palestinian populations, including the West Bank and Gaza (p. 956)

Guerra de los Seis Días (junio de 1967) guerra entre Israel y Egipto, Syria, y Jordan; terminó con una victoria aplastante para Israel (pág. 956)

slash-and-burn agriculture a farming method in which fields are cleared for farming by cutting down and burning trees and brush (p. 205)

agricultura de tala y quema método de cultivo en el cual se despeja un campo talando y quemando árboles y arbustos para luego cultivarlo (pág. 205)

smelt to melt or fuse metal in order to separate the metallic components (p. 85)

fundir derretir el metal para separar sus componentes metálicos (pág. 85)

Smoot-Hawley Tariff Act (1930) a U.S. law that set extremely high tariffs on imports in an effort to protect American farmers and manufacturers; the result was a worsening of the Great Depression (p. 815)

Ley arancel Smoot-Hawley (1930) arancel extremadamente alto sobre los productos agrícolas y manufacturados (pág. 815)

social contract an agreement between a people and their government, stating that people would give up some of their freedom and in return, their government would provide them with peace, security, and order (p. 575)

contrato social acuerdo entre un pueblo y su gobierno que establece que el pueblo cederá parte de su libertad a cambio de que el gobierno brinde paz, seguridad y orden (pág. 575)

Social Darwinism an application of Charles Darwin's scientific theories of natural selection and the survival of the fittest to the struggle between nations and races; used in the late 1800s to justify imperialism and racism (p. 757)

darwinismo social visión de la sociedad basada en la teoría científica de la selección natural de Charles Darwin (pág. 757)

socialism a political and economic system in which society, usually in the form of the government, owns the means of production (p. 648)

socialismo sistema económico y político en el cual la sociedad, generalmente en la forma del gobierno, posee los medios de producción (pág. 648)

socialist republic a type of republic in which there is no private property and the state owns and distributes all goods to people (p. 730)

república socialista tipo de república en la cual no hay propiedad privada y el estado posee todos los bienes y los distribuye entre los ciudadanos (pág. 730)

Solidarity an independent labor union founded in Soviet-controlled Poland in 1980 (p. 892)

Solidaridad sindicato independiente fundado en 1980 en la Polonia controlada por los soviéticos (pág. 892)

Soweto Uprising (1976) a major student protest against apartheid that took place in the township of Soweto; the peaceful march turned violent, killing more than 600 people and wounding 4,000 (p. 944)

rebelión de Soweto (1976) importante protesta estudiantil contra el apartheid que ocurrió en el municipio de Soweto; la marcha pacífica se tornó violenta, con más de 600 muertos y 4,000 heridos (pág. 944)

Spanish-American War (1898) war fought between Spain and the United States that began after the sinking of the battleship USS *Maine*; the United States won the war in four months, gaining control of Puerto Rico, Guam, and the Philippines (p. 764)

Guerra hispano-estadounidense (1898) guerra entre España y Estados Unidos que comenzó tras el hundimiento de *Maine*; fue un desastre para España y Estados Unidos ganó la guerra en cuatro meses, tomando el poder de Puerto Rico, Guam y las Filipinas (pág. 764)

Spanish Armada a great fleet (130 ships and 20,000 men) assembled by Spain in 1588 for an invasion of England (p. 538)

Armada española gran flota de barcos; incluía aproximadamente 130 barcos y 20,000 marineros y soldados (pág. 538)

Sputnik (1957) the first artificial satellite; launched by the Soviet Union (p. 884)

Sputnik (1957) primer satélite artificial; lanzado por la Unión soviética (pág. 884)

Stamp Act (1765) a law passed by the British Parliament that raised tax money by requiring the American colonists to pay for an official stamp whenever they bought paper items (p. 581)

Ley del Sello (1765) ley aprobada por el Parlamento británico que aumentaba los impuestos para los colonos estadounidenses, obligándoles a pagar un sello oficial cada vez que compraran artículos de papel (pág. 581)

standard of living a measure of the quality of life (p. 651)
nivel de vida medida de la calidad de vida (pág. 651)

steppes arid grasslands (p. 40)
estepas praderas áridas (pág. 40)

strike a work stoppage (p. 644)
huelga detención del trabajo (pág. 644)

subcontinent a large landmass that is part of a continent but is considered an independent entity either geographically or politically (p. 94)
subcontinente gran masa de tierra que es parte de un continente pero se considera una entidad independiente, ya sea geográfica o políticamente (pág. 94)

subsidies grants of money (p. 485)
subsidios dinero que se otorga (pág. 485)

Suez Canal Egyptian waterway connecting the Mediterranean and Red seas; built in 1869 by Franco-Egyptian company; in 1875 Britain bought Egypt's share in the canal (p. 758)
canal de Suez canal de agua egipcio del que se apoderaron los ingleses en 1882 (pág. 758)

Suez Crisis (1956) Egypt's confrontation with Britain, France, and Israel over control of the Suez Canal (p. 952)
crisis de Suez confrontación entre Egipto por un lado y Gran Bretaña, Francia e Israel por el otro, sobre el control del Canal de Suez (pág. 952)

suffrage the right to vote (p. 688)
sufragio derecho a votar (pág. 688)

Sufis a branch of Islam emphasizing a personal, mystical connection with God (p. 264)
sufís místicos musulmánes que intentaban vivir una vida simple (pág. 264)

sultan title for the ruler of the Ottoman Empire (p. 500)
sultán título del gobernador del Imperio otomano (pág. 500)

Sunnis "people who follow the Sunna (way of the Prophet)"; the largest branch of Islam; believers accepted the first four caliphs as rightful successors of Muhammad (p. 263)
suníes "personas que siguen la Sunna"; rama del Islam que acepta a los cuatro primeros califas como sucesores legítimos de Mahoma (pág. 263)

surplus excess (p. 19)
excedente lo que sobra (pág. 19)

sustainable development economic development that is maintained over a period of time but does not harm the environment (p. 1006)
desarrollo sostenible desarrollo económico que se mantiene durante cierto tiempo, pero que no daña el medio ambiente (pág. 1006)

Swahili an African society that emerged in the late 1100s along the East African coast and combined elements of African, Asian, and Islamic cultures (p. 292)
swahili sociedad africana que surgió a finales del siglo XII a lo largo de la costa africana oriental; combinaba elementos de las culturas africana, asiática e islámica (pág. 292)

Taiping Rebellion (1850–1864) revolt against the Qing dynasty in China led by Hong Xiuquan, a convert to Christianity; over 20 million Chinese died; eventually suppressed with British and French aid (p. 748)
rebelión de Taiping (1850–1864) rebelión en China encabezada por Hong Xiuquan, quien declaró que se establecería una nueva dinastía (pág. 748)

Taj Mahal a mausoleum built by India's Mughal emperor Shah Jahan from 1632–1643 to honor his wife (p. 507)
Taj Mahal maravilla arquitectónica creada por el Shah Jahan (pág. 507)

Taliban Islamist group that took control over much of Afghanistan in the late 1990s; were ousted by the United States invasion of 2001 (p. 899)
talibanes grupo que tomó el control de gran parte de Afganistán después de la ocupación soviética en 1979 (pág. 899)

technology the application of knowledge, skills, and tools to meet people's needs (p. 10)
tecnología aplicación de conocimientos, destrezas y herramientas que usamos para satisfacer nuestras necesidades (pág. 10)

telegraph a machine perfected by Samuel F. B. Morse in 1832; it uses pulses of electric current to send messages across long distances through wires (p. 663)
telégrafo máquina perfeccionada por Samuel F. B. Morse en 1832 que usa pulsaciones de corriente eléctrica para enviar mensajes a larga distancia mediante cables (pág. 663)

terrorism the use of violence by individuals and groups to advance political goals (p. 1000)
terrorismo uso de la violencia, por parte de individuos o grupos, para conseguir objetivos políticos (pág. 1000)

theocracy a government ruled by religious leaders who claim God's authority (pp. 66, 452)
teocracia gobierno de líderes religiosos que afirman tener la autoridad de Dios (pág. 66, 452)

Third Estate in pre-Revolution France, the bourgeoisie, artisans, workers, and peasants (p. 595)
Tercer Estado en la Francia antes de la Revolución, la burguesía, los artesanos, los trabajadores y los campesinos (pág. 595)

Thirty Years' War (1618–1648) a conflict in Europe that began in Prague as a Protestant rebellion against the Holy Roman Empire; fought over religion and power among ruling dynasties (p. 556)
Guerra de los Treinta Años (1618–1648) conflicto europeo que comenzó en Praga como una rebelión protestante contra el Santo Imperio Romano; fue una guerra por motivos religiosos y de poder entre familias dominantes (pág. 556)

Tiananmen Square Massacre violent suppression by the Chinese communist government of a large pro-democracy protest in Beijing's central square in 1989 (p. 923)
masacre de la plaza de Tiananmen gran protesta en favor de la democracia realizada en China en 1989 y que el gobierno reprimió con fuerzas militares; en consecuencia, murieron cientos de personas (pág. 923)

Torah the first five books of the Hebrew Bible; the most sacred texts of the Jewish faith (p. 46)
Torá los primeros cinco libros de la Biblia; los textos más sagrados de la fe judía (pág. 46)

totalitarianism form of government in which the person or party in charge has absolute control over all aspects of life (p. 824)
totalitarismo forma de gobierno en la cual la persona o partido que está en el poder tiene un control absoluto de todos los aspectos de la vida (pág. 824)

total war a war that requires the use of all a society's resources (p. 785)
guerra total guerra que requería el uso de todos los recursos de una sociedad (pág. 785)

traditional economy an economic system in which economic decisions are made based on customs, beliefs, religion, and habits (p. 19)
economía tradicional sistema económico donde las decisiones económicas se toman sobre la base de costumbres, creencias y hábitos (pág. 19)

Trail of Tears (1838–39) an 800-mile march made by the Cherokee from their homeland in Georgia to Indian Territory; resulted in the deaths of almost one-fourth of the Cherokee people (p. 703)
Ruta de las Lágrimas (1838–39) marcha de 800 millas que hizo la tribu cherokee desde su territorio natal en Georgia hasta el Territorio Indígena; tuvo como consecuencia la muerte de casi la cuarta parte del pueblo cherokee (pág. 703)

Trans-Siberian Railroad railroad, begun in 1891, linking western Russia to Siberia in the east (p. 730)
ferrocarril transiberiano ferrocarril que unió Rusia occidental y el este de Siberia (pág. 730)

Treaty of Kanagawa (1854) trade treaty between Japan and the United States opening up two Japanese ports to U.S. trade; signed in response to a show of force by U.S. admiral Matthew Perry (p. 750)
Tratado de Kanagawa (1854) tratado que permitió a los barcos estadounidenses detenerse en dos puertos japoneses (pág. 750)

Treaty of Paris (1783) the agreement that officially ended the American Revolution and established British recognition of the independence of the United States (p. 584)
Tratado de París (1783) acuerdo que puso fin oficialmente a la Guerra de Independencia estadounidense y estableció el reconocimiento británico de la independencia de Estados Unidos (pág. 584)

Treaty of Tordesillas (1494) the agreement between Spain and Portugal that created an imaginary north-south line dividing their territory in the Americas (p. 479)
Tratado de Tordesillas (1494) acuerdo entre España y Portugal que creaba una línea imaginaria de norte a sur que dividía el territorio de las Américas (pág. 479)

Treaty of Utrecht (1713) treaty that ended the War of the Spanish Succession; it gave the throne to Louis XIV's grandson but also stated that France and Spain would never be ruled by the same monarch (p. 544)
Tratado de Utrecht (1713) tratado que supuso el fin de la Guerra de Sucesión Española y dio el trono al nieto de Luis XIV, pero también impuso la condición de que Francia y España nunca serían gobernadas por el mismo rey (pág. 544)

Treaty of Versailles (1919) treaty ending World War I; required Germany to pay huge war reparations and established the League of Nations (p. 797)
Tratado de Versalles (1919) tratado que puso fin a la Primera Guerra Mundial; exigía a Alemania que pagara enormes indemnizaciones de guerra y estableció la Liga de las Naciones (pág. 797)

Treaty of Westphalia (1648) treaty ending the Thirty Years' War; it reduced the power of the Holy Roman Emperor; it extended religious toleration to Protestants and Catholics within most of the empire (p. 556)
Tratado de Westfalia (1648) tratado que puso fin a la Guerra de los Treinta Años; en un sentido general, fue una victoria protestante y extendió la tolerancia religiosa (pág. 556)

trench warfare a form of combat in which soldiers dug trenches, or deep ditches, to seek protection from enemy fire and to defend their positions (p. 784)
guerra de trincheras forma de combate en que los soldados cavaban trincheras, o pozos profundos, para protegerse del fuego enemigo y defender sus posiciones (pág. 784)

ENGLISH AND SPANISH GLOSSARY

triangular trade trading network lasting from the 1600s to the 1800s that carried goods and enslaved people between Europe, the Americas, and Africa (p. 489)
comercio triangular redes de intercambio de bienes y esclavos entre Inglaterra, las colonias norteamericanas y África (pág. 489)

tribute a payment made by conquered peoples to their conquerors in order to obtain security (p. 208)
tributo pago hecho por los pueblos conquistados a sus conquistadores para obtener seguridad (pág. 208)

Triple Alliance an alliance between Germany, Austria-Hungary, and Italy in the late 1800s (p. 780)
Triple Alianza alianza entre Alemania, el Imperio austrohúngaro e Italia (pág. 780)

Triple Entente an alliance between France, Russia, and Great Britain in the late 1800s (p. 780)
Triple Entente alianza entre Francia, Rusia y Gran Bretaña (pág. 780)

triumvirate a ruling body of three members (p. 173)
triunvirato alianza política de tres gobernantes (pág. 173)

troubadours traveling singers who entertained people during the Middle Ages (p. 416)
trovadores cantantes de la Edad Media que viajaban de una ciudad a otra para entretener a las personas (pág. 416)

Truman Doctrine (1947) U.S. president Truman's pledge to provide economic and military aid to countries threatened by communism (p. 879)
Doctrina Truman (1947) compromiso del presidente del Estados Unidos Truman para prestar ayuda económica y militar a los países amenazados por el comunismo (pág. 879)

tyrant a strong man who seized power by force and claimed to rule for the good of the people (p. 135)
tirano hombre poderoso que tomaba el poder por la fuerza y afirmaba gobernar por el bien del pueblo (pág. 135)

U-boats submarines used by Germans in World Wars I and II (p. 795)
U-boats nombre que recibieron los pequeños submarinos que usaron los alemanes en la Primera y la Segunda Guerra Mundial (pág. 795)

Umayyad (661–750) first ruling dynasty over the Muslim Caliphate (p. 263)
Umayyad (661–750) califato de Mu'awiya que marcó un período de enorme crecimiento y cambio para el imperio musulmán (pág. 263)

unequal treaties trade treaties that China signed under pressure of invasion; gave Western powers trade benefits (p. 747)
tratados desiguales tratados comerciales que China firmó bajo amenaza de invasión y que dieron beneficios comerciales a las potencias occidentales (pág. 747)

United Nations international organization formed in 1945 to maintain world peace and encourage cooperation among nations (p. 863)
Naciones Unidas organización internacional que promueve la cooperación entre las naciones (pág. 863)

urbanization the migration of people from rural areas to cities (p. 672)
urbanización migración de las áreas rurales a las ciudades (pág. 672)

varnas the four social classes in Vedic society (p. 97)
varnas las cuatro clases sociales de la sociedad védica (pág. 97)

vassal in medieval Europe, a person granted land from a lord in return for services (p. 383)
vasallo en la Europa medieval, persona que recibía tierras de un señor a cambio de ciertos servicios (pág. 383)

V-E Day (1945) May 8, 1945; a term used by the Allies, it stands for "victory in Europe" during World War II (p. 860)
Día V-E (1945) 8 de mayo de 1945; fecha en que los Aliados celebraron su victoria en Europa en la Segunda Guerra Mundial (pág. 860)

Vedas sacred writings of the Indo-Aryans (p. 96)
Vedas escrituras sagradas de los indoarios (pág. 96)

Velvet Revolution (1989) a quick, peaceful revolution that swept the Communists from power in Czechoslovakia (p. 893)
revolución de terciopelo (1989) revolución rápida y pacífica que expulsó a los comunistas del poder en Checoslovaquia (pág. 893)

veto ban (p. 165)
veto prohibición (pág. 165)

viceroys officials who ruled Spain's American empire (p. 479)
virreyes funcionarios que gobernaban en el imperio español en las Américas (pág. 479)

Victorian Era the era spanning the reign of Queen Victoria of England (1837–1901) (p. 688)
época victoriana reinado de la reina Victoria entre los años 1837 y 1901 (pág. 688)

Vietcong communist guerilla force allied with North Vietnam which fought to overthrow the government of South Vietnam from the 1950s to 1975 (p. 916)
Vietcong fuerzas militares del Frente Nacional de Liberación, grupo que quería derrocar al gobierno de Vietnam (pág. 916)

Vietminh nationalist organization led by Ho Chi Minh that fought for Vietnamese independence from French rule in the 1940s and 1950s (p. 915)
Vietminh fuerza dirigida por Ho Chi Minh que desafió la autoridad de los franceses en Indochina (pág. 915)

villa a home in the country (p. 178)
villa casa de campo (pág. 178)

V-J Day (1945) August 15, 1945; a term used by the Allies, it stands for "victory over Japan" during World War II (p. 862)
Día V-J (1945) 15 de agosto de 1945; fecha en que los Aliados declararon la victoria sobre Japón en la Segunda Guerra Mundial (pág. 862)

Wars of the Roses (1455–1485) civil war for the English crown between the York (white rose) and Lancaster (red rose) families (p. 421)
Guerras de las Rosas (1455–1485) guerra entre las familias inglesas de York y Lancaster (pág. 421)

War of the Spanish Succession (1701–1713) war fought over the Spanish throne; Louis XIV wanted it for his son and fought a war against the Dutch, English, and the Holy Roman Empire to gain the throne for France (p. 544)
Guerra de Sucesión Española (1701–1713) guerra por la sucesión al trono de España; Luis XIV lo quería para su hijo y luchó contra los holandes, los españoles y el Santo Imperio Romano para que el trono quedra en manos francesas (pág. 544)

Warsaw Pact a military alliance of the Soviet-dominated countries of Eastern Europe, established in 1955 (p. 880)
Pacto de Varsovia alianza militar entre los países controlados por los soviéticos de Europa oriental, establecida en 1955 (pág. 880)

weapons of mass destruction (WMD) weapons that kill or injure civilian, as well as military personnel, usually nuclear, chemical, and biological weapons (p. 1002)
armas de destrucción masiva (WMD, por sus siglas en inglés) armas que matan o hieren a los civiles así como a los militares; generalmente, armas nucleares, químicas y biológicas (pág. 1002)

Western Front during World War I, the deadlocked region in northern France where German and Allied armies faced off (p. 782)
frente occidental durante la Primera Guerra Mundial, área del norte de Francia donde los combates habían llegado a un punto en que ninguno de los bandos podía avanzar (pág. 782)

westernization the adoption of the culture and ideas of Western society, namely Europe and America (p. 553)
occidentalización adopción de la cultura e ideas de la sociedad occidental, es decir, de Europa y Estados Unidos (pág. 553)

woodblock printing a type of printing in which text is carved into a block of wood and the block is then coated with ink and pressed on the page (p. 313)
xilografía tipo de impresión que consiste en grabar una página de texto en una plancha de madera, cubrir la plancha de tinta y presionarla sobre un papel (pág. 313)

Xiongnu nomadic raiders from the grasslands north of China during the reign of Han dynasty; emperor Wudi fought against them in the mid-100s BC (p. 226)
xiongnu nómadas que vivían en las praderas del norte de China durante el reino de Wudi; eran una gran amenaza militar para China (pág. 226)

Yalta Conference (February, 1945) a meeting between Franklin Roosevelt, Winston Churchill, and Joseph Stalin to reach an agreement on what to do with Germany after World War II (p. 862)
Conferencia de Yalta (1945) encuentro entre Franklin Roosevelt, Winston Churchill y Joseph Stalin para llegar a un acuerdo sobre qué hacer con Alemania después de la Segunda Guerra Mundial (pág. 862)

yoga a series of physical and mental exercises that teaches people how to focus their bodies and minds (p. 101)
yoga serie de ejercicios físicos y mentales que enseñan a las personas a concentrar la mente y el cuerpo (pág. 101)

ENGLISH AND SPANISH GLOSSARY

Yom Kippur War (1973) war launched by Egypt and Syria against Israel on the Jewish holy day of Yom Kippur; the Israeli counterattack, supported by the United States repulsed the Syrians and Egyptians (p. 956)

Guerra de Yom Kippur (1973) ataque a Israel por parte de Egipto y Siria el día de Yom Kippur; tuvo como consecuencia un contraataque de los israelíes, que expulsaron a los sirios y pasaron a Egipto cruzando el canal de Suez (pág. 956)

Young Turks Turkish reformist and nationalist political party active in the early 20th century (p. 727)

Jóvenes Turcos partido político reformista y nacionalista turco, activo a comienzos del siglo XX (pág. 727)

Zen Buddhism sect of Buddhism that stresses meditation as a means of achieving enlightenment; became popular among Japanese aristocrats and was a part of the samurai's code (p. 517)

budismo zen secta del budismo que enfatiza el valor de la meditación como medio para alcanzar la iluminación; se hizo popular entre los aristócratas japoneses y era parte del código samurai (pág. 517)

ziggurat a Sumerian temple made of sun-dried brick that was dedicated to the chief god or goddess of a particular city-state (p. 34)

zigurat templo sumerio hecho de ladrillos secados al sol, dedicado al dios o diosa principal de una determinada ciudad estado (pág. 34)

Zimmermann Note a telegram sent to a German official in Mexico prior to U.S. entrance into World War I; proposed an alliance between Germany and Mexico (p. 795)

Telegrama Zimmermann telegrama enviado a un funcionario alemán que estaba en México antes de que Estados Unidos entrara en la Primera Guerra Mundial, con la propuesta de una alianza entre Alemania y México (pág. 795)

Zionism nationalist movement, begun in the 1890s, to establish a Jewish state in Palestine (p. 694)

sionismo movimiento nacionalista para establecer un estado judío en Palestina (pág. 694)

Zollverein an economic alliance of most German states in 1834; allowed for free trade among themselves and common tariffs on imports, exports, and transit (p. 719)

Zollverein alianza económica entre la mayor parte de los estados alemanes en 1834, que autorizaba el libre comercio y establecía aranceles comunes para las importaciones, las exportaciones y el tránsito (pág. 719)

Index

D

G

INDEX

INDEX

INDEX

INDEX

INDEX

Credits and Acknowledgments

CREDITS AND ACKNOWLEDGMENTS

For permission to reproduce copyrighted material, grateful acknowledgment is made to the following sources:

From The Settlement of the Americas by Thomas D. Dillehay. Copyright © 2000 by Thomas D. Dillehay. Reproduced by permission of **Basic Books, a member of the Perseus Book Group.**

From *Naser-e Khosraw's Book of Travels (Safarnama)* by Narir-i Khusraw, translated by W. M. Thackston Jr. Copyright © 1986 by **Bibliotheca Persica Press, a division of Persian Heritage Foundation.** Reproduced by permission of the publisher.

From "Biotechnology and the Green Revolution," an interview with Norman Borlaug from *ActionBioscience* Web site, accessed at http://www.actionbioscience.org/biotech/borlllaug.html. Copyright © 2002 by Norman Borlaug. Reproduced by permission of Norman Borlaug and electronic format by permission of ActionBioscience.org.

From "Ending World Hunger. The Promise of Biotechnology and the Threat of Antiscience Zealotry" by Norman Borlaug from *Plant Physiology* Web site, accessed at http://www.plantphysiol.org/misc/about html. Copyright © 2000 by Norman Borlaug. Reproduced by permission of **Norman Borlaug and electronic format by permission of PlantPhysiolorg.**

From *Hanfeitzu*, translated by Lydia Gerber, from *Reading About the World*, Vol. 1, edited by Paul Brians, Mary Gallwey, Douglas Hughes, Azfar Hussain, Richard Law, Michael Myers, Michael Neville, Roger Schlesinger, Alice Spitzer, and Susan Swan. Copyright © 1999 by **Paul Brians.** Originally published by Harcourt Custom Publishing. Reproduced by permission of the copyright holder.

From *History and Description of Africa* by Leo Africanus from *Reading About the World*, Vol., 2, edited by Paul Brians, Mary Gallwey, Douglas Hughes, Azfar Hussain, Richard Law, Michael Myers, Michael Neville, Roger Schlesinger, Alice Spitzer, and Susan Swan. Copyright © 1999 by **Paul Brians**. Originally published by Harcourt Custom Publishing. Reproduced by permission of the copyright holder.

From *The Cambridge Illustrated History of China* by Patricia Buckley Ebrey. Copyright © 1996 by **Cambridge University Press.** Reproduced by permission of the publisher.

From *Prehistory of the Americas* by Stuart J. Fiedel. Copyright © 1987 by **Cambridge University Press.** Reproduced by permission of the publisher.

From *The World of Rome* by Peter Jones and Keith Sidwell. Copyright © 1997 by **Cambridge University Press.** Reproduced by permission of the publisher.

From "Julius Caesar" from *The Twelve Caesars* by Suetonius, translated by Robert Graves, revised with an introduction by Michael Grant. Copyright © 1957 by Robert Graves; copyright © 1979 by Michael Grant Publication Limited. Reproduced by permission of **Carcanet Press Limited and electronic format by permission of A. P. Watt, Ltd. on behalf of the Trustees of the Robert Graves Copyright Trust.** Users must not reproduce, download, store in any medium, distribute, transmit or retransmit, or manipulate any text reproduced on Web site www.apwatt.co.uk.

From "Kilwa in 1331" by Ibn Battatah from *African Civilization Revisited*, translated by G. S. P. Freeman-Grenville. Copyright © 1962 by G. S. P. Freeman-Grenville. Reproduced by permission of **Clarendon Press, a division of Oxford University Press.**

From *The Analects by Confucius* from *Sources of Chinese Tradition*, compiled by Wm. Theodore de Bary, Wing-tsit Chan, Burton Watson, with contribution by Yi-pao Mei, Leon Hurvitz, T'ung-tsu Ch'u, Chester Tan, and John Meskill. Copyright © 1960 by **Columbia University Press, New York.** Reproduced by permission of the publisher.

From *On My Country and the World* by Mikhail Gorbachev, translated from Russian by George Shriver. Copyright © 2000 by **Columbia University Press.** Reproduced by permission of the publisher.

From *The Pillow Book of Sei Shonagon*, translated by Ivan Morris. Copyright © 1967 by Ivan Morris. Reproduced by permission of **Columbia University Press.**

From *Arda Wiraz Namag: The Iranian 'Divina Commedia,'* translated by Fereydun Vahman. Copyright © 1986 by Fereydun Vahman. Reproduced by permission of **Curzon Press Ltd.**

From *Medieval Russia's Epics, Chronicles, and Tales*, edited and translated by Serge A. Zenkovsky. Copyright © 1963, 1974 by Serge A. Zenkovsky. All rights reserved. Reproduced by permission of **Dutton, a division of Penguin Group (USA) Inc.**

From "The Fall of Troy" from *The Aeneid* by Virgil, translated by Robert Fitzgerald. Translation copyright © 1980, 1982, 1983 by Robert Fitzgerald. Reproduced by permission of **Penelope Fitzgerald for the Estate of Robert Fitzgerald.**

From "NAFTA: A Cautionary Tale" by Timothy A. Wise and Kevin P. Gallagher from *Foreign Policy in Focus*, October 24, 2002. Copyright © 2002 by **Foreign Policy in Focus.** Reproduced by permission of the publisher.

From "History" by Herodotus from *Classics of Western Thought: The Ancient World*, edited by Stebelton H. Nulle. Copyright © 1964 by Harcourt, Brace & World, Inc. Reproduced by permission of Harcourt, Inc.

From quote by Pericles from "History of the Peloponnesian War" by Thucydides from *Classics of Western Thought: The Ancient World,* edited by Stebelton H. Nulle. Copyright © 1964 by Harcourt, Brace & World, Inc. Reproduced by permission of **Harcourt, Inc.**

From "Oration on the Dignity of Man" by Giovanni Pico della Mirandola from *Classics of Western Thought: Middle Ages, Renaissance, and Reformation*, Vol. II, edited by Karl F. Thompson. Copyright © 1964, 1973, 1980 by Harcourt Brace Jovanovich, Inc. Reproduced by permission of **Harcourt, Inc.**

From "Hatred" from *Poems: New and Collected, 1957-1997* by Wislawa Szymborska, translated from the Polish by Stanislaw Baranczak and Clare Cavanagh. English translation copyright © 1998 by Harcourt Brace & Company. Reproduced by permission of **Harcourt, Inc.** and electronic format by permission of **Stanislaw Baranczak** and **Clare Cavanagh.**

Adapted from *History of the Indies* (retitled "Bartolomé de las Casas Condemns Spanish Treatment of the Indians") by Bartolomé de las Casas, translated and edited by Andrée Collard. Copyright © 1971 by Andrée Collard. Reproduced by permission of **HarperCollins Publishers, Inc.**

From *China: A New History* by John King Fairbank. Copyright © 1992 by the **President and Fellows of Harvard College, Cambridge, MA.** Reproduced by permission of the publisher.

From *I Speak of Freedom: A Statement of African Ideology* by Kwame Nkrumah. Copyright © 1961 by Kwame Nkrumah. Reproduced by permission of **William Heinemann, Ltd., London.**

From *Travels in Asia and Africa 1325-1354* by Ibn Battuta, translated by H.A.R. Gibb. Copyright 1929 by Broadway House, London. Reproduced by permission of **David Higham Associates Limited.**

From *East Asia: The Great Tradition* by Edwin O. Reischauer and John K. Fairbank. Copyright © 1958, 1960 by Edwin O. Reischauer and John K. Fairbank. All rights reserved. Reproduced by permission of **Houghton Mifflin Company.**

Letter from King Ferdinand and Queen Isabella, adapted from *Readings in Latin American Civilization: 1492 to the Present*, edited by Benjamin Keen. Copyright © 1955 by Benjamin Keen. All rights reserved. Reproduced by permission of **Houghton Mifflin Company.**

Exodus 3:7–14 from *The Holy Scriptures according to the Masoretic Text, A New Translation with The Aid of Previous Versions and with Constant Consultation of Jewish Authorities.* Copyright 1917, © 1955 by **The Jewish Publication Society of America.** Reproduced by permission the publisher.

Exodus 20:2–14 from *The Holy Scriptures according to the Masoretic Text, A New Translation with The Aid of Previous Versions and with Constant Consultation of Jewish Authorities.* Copyright 1917, © 1955 by **The Jewish Publication Society of America.** Reproduced by permission the publisher.

From *The Tale of Genji* by Lady Muraskai Shikibu, translated by Edward G. Seidensticker. Copyright © 1976 by Edward G. Seidensticker. Reproduced by permission of **Alfred A. Knopf, a division of Random House, Inc., www.randomhouse.com.**

From *Ibn Jubayr Voyages*, translated and annotated by Maurice Gaudefroy-Demonbynes. Copyright 1949-1951 by Paul Geuthner, Paris. Reproduced by permission of **Librairie Orientaliste Paul Geuthner.**

From "The Importance of the Hajj" from *The Koran Interpreted*, translated by A. J. Arberry. Copyright © 1955 by A. J. Arberry. Reproduced by permission of **Macmillan Publishing Company.**

From "The Garland of Madurai" from *The Wonder that Was India: A Survey of the Culture of the Indian Sub-continent before the Coming of the Muslims* by A. L. Basham. Copyright © 1954 by **Macmillan Company.** Reproduced by permission of the publisher.

From "Prehistory: The Harappa Culture and the Aryans" from *The Wonder that Was India: A Survey of the Culture of the Indian Sub-continent before the Coming of the Muslims* by A. L. Basham. Copyright © 1954 by **Macmillan Company.** Reproduced by permission of the publisher.

From "Great Zimbabwe (11th–15th Century)" from *Timeline of Art History*. Copyright © 2000 by **The Metropolitan Museum of Art, New York.** Reproduced by permission of the copyright holder.

From "Swahili Coast" by Robert Caputo from *National Geographic* Magazine, vol. 200, no. 4, October 2001. Copyright © 2001 by **National Geographic Society.** Reproduced by permission of the publisher.

"Quiet Night Thoughts" by Li Po from *Li Po and Tu Fu: Poems*, translated by Arthur Cooper. Copyright © 1973 by Arthur Cooper. Reproduced by permission of **Penguin Books, Ltd.**

From "The Merciful" from *The Koran*, translated with notes by N. J. Dawood (Penguin Classics 1956, Fifth revised edition 1990). Copyright © 1956, 1959, 1966, 1968, 1974, 1990, 1993, 1997, 1999, 2003 by N. J. Dawood. Reproduced by permission of **Penguin Books, Ltd.**

From *The Epic of Gilgamesh*, translated by N. K. Sandars (Penguin Classics 1960, Third Edition, 1972). Copyright © 1960, 1964, 1972 by N. K. Sandars. Reproduced by permission of **Penguin Books Ltd.**

From *The Travels of Ibn Jubayr: Being the Chronicle of a Mediaeval Spanish Moor concerning His Journey to the Egypt of Saladin, the Holy Cities of Arabia, Baghdad the City of the Caliphs, the Latin Kingdom of Jerusalem, and the Norman Kingdom of Sicily*, translated by R.J.C. Broadhurst. Copyright 1952 by Jonathan Cape, Ltd., London. Reproduced by permission of **The Random House Archive & Library.**